D0762162

Dear West Customer:

West Academic Publishing has changed the look of its American Casebook Series®.

In keeping with our efforts to promote sustainability, we have replaced our former covers with book covers that are more environmentally friendly. Our casebooks will now be covered in a 100% renewable natural fiber. In addition, we have migrated to an ink supplier that favors vegetable-based materials, such as soy.

Using soy inks and natural fibers to print our textbooks reduces VOC emissions. Moreover, our primary paper supplier is certified by the Forest Stewardship Council, which is testament to our commitment to conservation and responsible business management.

The new cover design has migrated from the long-standing brown cover to a contemporary charcoal fabric cover with silver-stamped lettering and black accents. Please know that inside the cover, our books continue to provide the same trusted content that you've come to expect from West.

We've retained the ample margins that you have told us you appreciate in our texts while moving to a new, larger font, improving readability. We hope that you will find these books a pleasing addition to your bookshelf.

Another visible change is that you will no longer see the brand name Thomson West on our print products. With the recent merger of Thomson and Reuters, I am pleased to announce that books published under the West Academic Publishing imprint will once again display the West brand.

It will likely be several years before all of our casebooks are published with the new cover and interior design. We ask for your patience as the new covers are rolled out on new and revised books knowing that behind both the new and old covers, you will find the finest in legal education materials for teaching and learning.

Thank you for your continued patronage of the West brand, which is both rooted in history and forward looking towards future innovations in legal education. We invite you to be a part of our next evolution.

Best regards,

Louis H. Higgins
Editor in Chief, West Academic Publishing

West's Law School
Advisory Board

JESSE H. CHOPER
Professor of Law,
University of California, Berkeley

JOSHUA DRESSLER
Professor of Law, Michael E. Moritz College of Law,
The Ohio State University

YALE KAMISAR
Professor of Law, University of San Diego
Professor of Law, University of Michigan

MARY KAY KANE
Professor of Law, Chancellor and Dean Emeritus,
University of California,
Hastings College of the Law

LARRY D. KRAMER
Dean and Professor of Law, Stanford Law School

JONATHAN R. MACEY
Professor of Law, Yale Law School

ARTHUR R. MILLER
University Professor, New York University
Professor of Law Emeritus, Harvard University

GRANT S. NELSON
Professor of Law, Pepperdine University
Professor of Law Emeritus, University of California, Los Angeles

A. BENJAMIN SPENCER
Associate Professor of Law,
Washington & Lee University School of Law

JAMES J. WHITE
Professor of Law, University of Michigan

CORPORATIONS AND OTHER BUSINESS ENTERPRISES

CASES AND MATERIALS

Standard Edition
Third Edition

■ ■ ■

By

Thomas Lee Hazen
Cary C. Boshamer Distinguished Professor of Law
University of North Carolina

Jerry W. Markham
Professor of Law
Florida International University School of Law at Miami

AMERICAN CASEBOOK SERIES®

WEST®
A Thomson Reuters business

Mat #40696177

Thomson Reuters created this publication to provide you with accurate and authoritative information concerning the subject matter covered. However, this publication was not necessarily prepared by persons licensed to practice law in a particular jurisdiction. Thomson Reuters does not render legal or other professional advice, and this publication is not a substitute for the advice of an attorney. If you require legal or other expert advice, you should seek the services of a competent attorney or other professional.

American Casebook Series is a trademark registered in the U.S. Patent and Trademark Office.

© West, a Thomson business, 2003, 2006
© 2009 Thomson Reuters

    610 Opperman Drive
    St. Paul, MN 55123
    1–800–313–9378

Printed in the United States of America

ISBN: 978–0–314–18959–2

 TEXT IS PRINTED ON 10% POST CONSUMER RECYCLED PAPER

To Lisa, Elliott, and George
TLH

In memory of my father John Markham
JWM

*

PREFACE

As teachers, we are frequently asked by students whether they will be handicapped in studying corporate law if they are not business majors. The answer is no. The concepts in corporate law are not difficult to grasp, but there are a lot of them. The real trick is to remember those concepts and be able to call on them when a problem is encountered. We assure you that many generations of law students have accomplished that goal successfully.

We have edited the cases to remove extraneous material. Substantive deletions are marked by three asterisks. Headings and subheadings in most of the of the court opinions have been deleted without such an indication, as have citations to the trial records and many of the citations to other sources. Many footnotes have also been deleted. When included, the original footnote numbers are used.

The authors would like to thank the many students who worked on this book and the patience of the students in our classes who worked from these materials while they were still in draft form. We also would like to thank the University of North Carolina for its support of this project.

THOMAS LEE HAZEN

JERRY W. MARKHAM

April 2009

*

INTRODUCTION

Welcome to the world of corporate law. For those aspiring to become "corporate lawyers," this book is only the first step in that journey. This course will, however, lay the groundwork for your securities and corporate finance studies and provide the foundation for your career. For those choosing other paths, we suggest that this course will also be important to you. There are few areas of the law, or indeed life, that do not cross paths with corporations. Family law lawyers will be involved in valuing corporate interests in divorce proceedings, criminal defense lawyers will be defending those involved in corporate crimes, and public interest lawyers will be attacking corporate misdeeds. This course will allow you to understand and deal with the corporation whatever your life role. More than that, we hope that you will enjoy this course as you discover the corporate law is often the result of efforts to govern intimate personal relationships among business owners.

This casebook focuses on the role that corporate lawyers play in advising their clients. That role is unique to most fields of law in that the corporate lawyer is viewed by many as a "gatekeeper" who is responsible for protecting shareholders from management depredations. That obligation may sometimes place the corporate lawyer in an awkward position. These lawyers advise management on a day-to-day basis and quite naturally treat those individual managers as the client. The scandal that followed the collapse of the Enron Corp. in 2001, however, focused attention on the role of the company's lawyers and their perceived failures in protecting shareholders from the abuses of management. legislation was passed in the form of the Sarbanes-Oxley Act that now requires corporate lawyers to police the conduct of management and to report illegal conduct to higher authorities at the corporation. The casebook addresses that requirement and other ethical demands imposed on corprorate lawyers.

*

Summary of Contents

TABLE OF CONTENTS

*

TABLE OF CASES

The principal cases are in bold type. Cases cited or discussed in the text are in roman type. References are to pages. Cases cited in principal cases and within other quoted materials are not included.

*

CORPORATIONS AND OTHER BUSINESS ENTERPRISES

CASES AND MATERIALS

Standard Edition
Third Edition

*

CHAPTER 1

BUSINESS ASSOCIATIONS—BACKGROUND AND HISTORY

■   ■   ■

Corporations and other business associations are the structures through which business is conducted. They are the entities through which business flows and are the means by which business is carried out, profits distributed and losses allocated. Although this course will focus primarily on corporations, there are a number of other forms of business associations, such as sole proprietors, partnerships, limited partnerships, limited liability companies and limited liability partnerships. This proliferation of business entities is due in part to historical reasons, as well as to the peculiar needs of individual businesses for more or less structure in their operations. Liability and tax issues are also important to the selection of the business association best suited to a particular business.

SECTION 1.   A BIT OF HISTORY— INTRODUCTION TO BUSINESS ENTERPRISES

The exact predecessors to the modern corporation and other business associations are difficult to identify precisely. Partnerships were used in ancient Rome, and a corporate body, the *publicani* that divided its ownership into shares, was used by private contractors to the Roman government. In 1000 A.D., an Italian firm, the Maona, was owned in shares and was used to carry out acts of piracy. *Commendas* were operating in Italy in the second century that provided a form of limited liability to their owners in the event of failure. These enterprises were composed of passive investors, as well as active participants that carried out a particular business enterprise. The *commendas* had limited lives. They terminated upon completion of a project, such as transporting a particular cargo. The largest share of any profits was allocated to the passive investors on the ground that "life was cheap and capital scarce."[1] A cargo shipped by sea was often financed by multiple contributors. This was a form of partner-

---

1. Robert W. Hillman, "Limited Liability in Historical Perspective," 54 Wash. & Lee L. Rev. 615 621–26 (1997) (relying on the Cambridge Economic History of Europe).

ship, but it also spread the risk of loss in the event the ship foundered, or was otherwise lost, giving rise to the concept of insurance.

Family enterprises were operating investment banks in the fifteenth century in Italian commercial centers. The government in Florence authorized *societa in accomandite*. These enterprises provided limited liability to passive investors, but investors in another form of enterprise, the *compagnia*, were subject to unlimited liability for the debts of these businesses, which were used in the overland trade. One enterprise operating in Genoa in the fourteenth century allocated its ownership into shares that were transferable. "The world's oldest known stock certificate still in existence is a Swedish document dated June 16, 1288."[2] It represented a share of the ownership of Stora Kopperberg, a company still in existence seven hundred years later. Shares in French textile factories were then being sold, and corporate forms of business were being used by German and Austrian mining enterprises.

The real force behind what is now the American corporation was the sixteenth century "joint-stock" company. These entities had appeared in England as early as 1553, and some seventy such companies would be formed over the next century and a half in Europe as a means to explore the world and bring home its wealth. These joint stock companies included the Dutch East India Company, the English East India Company, the Muscovy Company and the Hudson Bay Company. The successor to the latter company was still in operation four centuries later. Typically, the joint-stock company allowed each investor one vote, regardless of the amount of his or her investment, but the investor's liability for the company's debt was unlimited. The joint-stock company was managed by a committee of directors and employed officers who acted as professional managers. Ownership interests in the joint-stock company were represented by shares that could be transferred.

England sought to exploit and settle America through the use of joint-stock companies. The King sought a system of trade in which the joint-stock companies were to provide "a method of returning to the original investors their capital and interest in the form of dividends on their investment."[3] After Sir Walter Raleigh's initial colonization efforts failed, a charter was granted by the Crown to the London Company (later the Virginia Company) to settle what is now Virginia. The Plymouth Company, which was apparently a water company, was granted the right to settle New England. "Adventurers" in the Virginia Company were stockholders who supplied funds (capital) to the enterprise, while "planters" were those who went to America to found the Jamestown settlement. The planters were given a share of the company's stock plus land in America. Pilgrims sent to America by the Plymouth Company were given a share in the company's stock and double shares if they supplied their own tools.

---

2. Donald T. Regan, *A View From the Street* 99 (1972).

3. Marcus Wilson Jernegan, *The American Colonies 1492–1750* 52–53 (1959).

Business associations colonized other areas of America. New York was settled by the Dutch West India Company, while the Carolinas were settled by a partnership of English nobles called the "Lord Proprietors." Pennsylvania was settled under the sole proprietorship of William Penn. He was given that colony in payment for a debt owed by the king. Penn sold shares in the colony to six hundred investors. Lord Baltimore was given the right to govern Maryland as a "proprietary colony."[4]

The Virginia Company lost its charter in 1625 through a *"quo warranto"* brought by the Crown as a result of abuses by the company. Later, the charters and patents given to the other joint-stock companies and proprietors were revoked or bought back by the Royal government. As late as 1675, however, the colonies were still operating mostly as business enterprises as demonstrated by the following colonial document.

AN ACCOUNT OF HIS MAJESTY'S PLANTATIONS IN AMERICA[5]

His Majesty's Forreign Plantations in America are govern'd either by Proprietors, Corporations, Companies or by Governours immediately appointed by His Majesty.

The Plantations governed by Proprietors are New Yorke belonging to His Royal Highness.
New Jersey belonging to Sir George Cartwright and others.
Maryland belonging to the Lord Baltimore.
Carolina under which is also comprehended the Lucaii and Bahama Islands belonging to the Duke of Albemarle, Earl of Shaftesbury and other Lords and Gentlemen.

The Corporations contained within the bounds of New England are
The Colony of Rhode Island & Providence Plantations.
The Colony of Conecticut.
The Colony of New Plimouth.
The Colony of the Massachusets Bay under which is at present comprehended
The Province of Maine and New Hampshire, and other small Colonies adjoining the first Claimed by Mr. Gorges, the latter by Mr. Mason.

The Plantations governed by Companies residing in England, are
The Colonies and Factories settled in Prince Rupert's Land and Hudsons Bay.
The Bermudos otherwise called the Summer Islands.

The Plantations governed by His Majesty's immediate Commissions, are
Virginia and the Province of Accomack....

America owes much of its early development to these business enterprises, and even after their charters were revoked the colonies in America were administered as business enterprises by a "Board of Trade" in London.

---

4. See generally Alan Taylor, *American Colonies* (2001) (description of American colonization).

5. I Jerry W. Markham, *A Financaial History of the United States, From Christopher Columbus to the Robber Barons (1492–1900)* 29 (2001).

One other legacy of that era is the American flag. The banner used by the East India Company was the model for George Washington's battle flag, and it in turn was the model for the flag that now flies over the nation.

Despite this foundation, the modern commercial corporation was slow to develop in the colonies. Most businesses in America were operated as proprietorships or partnerships until after the Revolution. This was due in part to the South Sea Bubble in England in 1720 that witnessed a speculative mania in a number of enterprises that resulted in large losses to investors. One such venture sought investor's funds "for carrying on an undertaking of great importance, but nobody to know what it is."[6] In the course of that bubble, Parliament passed legislation that required a Royal charter for companies seeking investment funds from the public.[7] That statute was imposed on the American colonies in 1741. A dispute then arose over who could authorize such charters—the Royal governors or the colonial legislatures. As a consequence, few charters were issued and they were mostly granted to charitable societies, libraries, universities (including the College of William & Mary, Dartmouth, Yale and Harvard) and public works.

The Constitution adopted after the Revolution addressed the issue of the power to issue corporate charters by leaving that power to the states.[8] The growth of commercial corporations then proceeded apace. By 1800, over 350 commercial corporations had been chartered in the United States, some of which survive today, including the Revere Copper Company and the Bank of New York. These corporations were soon recognized as juridical entities with rights and responsibilities that very much resemble those available to the modern corporate form.

TRUSTEES OF DARTMOUTH COLLEGE v. WOODWARD

17 U.S. (4 Wheat.) 518, 4 L.Ed. 629 (1819).

STORY, J. concurring,

* * * An aggregate corporation at common law is a collection of individuals united into one collective body, under a special name, and possessing certain immunities, privileges, and capacities in its collective character, which do not belong to the natural persons composing it. Among other things it possesses the capacity of perpetual succession, and of acting by the collected vote or will of its component members, and of suing and being sued in all things touching its corporate rights and duties. It is, in short, an artificial person, existing in contemplation of law, and

---

6. Louis Loss, *Securities Regulation* 4 (1961).

7. The granting of corporate powers was viewed to a prerogative of the government as early as 1612 when Lord Coke asserted that "none but the king alone can create or make a corporation." I Joseph Stancliffe Davis, *Essays in the Earlier History of American Corporations* 6–7 (1965).

8. The Supreme Court later held that Congress could also charter corporations under the necessary and proper clause of the Constitution. M'Culloch v. Maryland, 17 U.S. (4 Wheat.) 316, 4 L.Ed. 579 (1819).

endowed with certain powers and franchises which, though they must be exercised through the medium of its natural members, are yet considered as subsisting in the corporation itself, as distinctly as if it were a real personage. Hence, such a corporation may sue and be sued by its own members; and may contract with them in the same manner as with any strangers. * * *

———

The concept of limited liability for corporate shareholders seemed to have been generally accepted in America by 1784, although some enterprises such as banking sometimes imposed double liability, *i.e.*, liability was limited to double the amount of the shareholders' investment. At first the power to incorporate was granted by special acts of the state legislatures. Some such entities survive to this day, including the Board of Trade of the City of Chicago. The states, however, gradually moved toward laws that freely allowed businesses to be formed as corporations. The following excerpt from a dissent by Justice Brandeis provides some perspective on the development of corporate law in the United States.

LOUIS K. LIGGETT CO. v. LEE

288 U.S. 517, 53 S.Ct. 481, 77 L.Ed. 929 (1933).

BRANDEIS, J. dissenting [from a ruling striking down Florida's anti chain store tax]

* * * The prevalence of the corporation in America has led men of this generation to act, at times, as if the privilege of doing business in corporate form were inherent in the citizen; and has led them to accept the evils attendant upon the free and unrestricted use of the corporate mechanism as if these evils were the inescapable price of civilized life, and, hence, to be borne with resignation. Throughout the greater part of our history a different view prevailed. Although the value of this instrumentality in commerce and industry was fully recognized, incorporation for business was commonly denied long after it had been freely granted for religious, educational, and charitable purposes[2] by corporations. So at first the corporate of encroachment upon the liberties and opportunities of the individual. Fear of the subjection of labor to capital. Fear of monopoly. Fear that the absorption of capital by corporations, and their perpetual life, might bring evils similar to those which attended mortmain.[3] There

---

2. See Joseph S. Davis, Essays in the Earlier History of American Corporations, Vol. II, pp. 16–18, 308–309 New York permitted incorporation under a general law for some business purposes in 1811. By 1850 a general law permitting incorporation for a limited business purpose had become common; and after 1875 extension of the privilege to every lawful business became so.

3. It was doubtless because of this that the earlier statutes limited the life of corporations to fixed terms of 20, 30, or 50 years. See the statutes cited in subsequent notes.

The power of Legislatures to grant special charters was sometimes strictly limited, even before the adoption of constitutional amendments withdrawing that power entirely. Thus the New York Constitution, adopted in convention in November, 1821, and by popular vote in January, 1822,

was a sense of some insidious menace inherent in large aggregations of capital, particularly when held by corporations. So at first the corporate privilege was granted sparingly; and only when the grant seemed necessary in order to procure for the community some specific benefit otherwise unattainable. The later enactment of general incorporation laws does not signify that the apprehension of corporate domination had been overcome. The desire for business expansion created an irresistible demand for more charters; and it was believed that under general laws embodying safeguards of universal application the scandals and favoritism incident to special incorporation could be avoided. The general laws, which long embodied severe restrictions upon size and upon the scope of corporate activity, were, in part, an expression of the desire for equality of opportunity.[4]

Limitation upon the amount of the authorized capital of business corporations was long universal. The maximum limit frequently varied with the kinds of business to be carried on, being dependent apparently upon the supposed requirements of the efficient unit. Although the statutory limits were changed from time to time, this principle of limitation was long retained. Thus in New York the limit was at first $100,000 for some businesses and as little as $50,000 for others. Until 1881 the maximum for business corporations in New York was $2,000,000; and until 1890, $5,000,000. In Massachusetts the limit was at first $200,000 for some businesses and as little as $5,000 for others. Until 1871 the maximum for mechanical and manufacturing corporations was $500,000; and until 1899 $1,000,000. The limit of $1,000,000 was retained for some businesses until 1903.

In many other states, including the leading ones in some industries, the removal of the limitations upon size was more recent. . . .

Limitations upon the scope of a business corporation's powers and activity were also long universal. At first, corporations could be formed under the general laws only for a limited number of purposes—usually those which required a relatively large fixed capital, like transportation, banking, and insurance, and mechanical, mining, and manufacturing enterprises. Permission to incorporate for 'any lawful purpose' was not common until 1875; and until that time the duration of corporate franchises was generally limited to a period of 20, 30, or 50 years. All, or a majority, of the incorporators or directors, or both, were required to be residents of the incorporating state. The powers which the corporation might exercise in carrying out its purposes were sparingly conferred and strictly construed. Severe limitations were imposed on the amount of

---

required the assent of two-thirds of each house for any act 'creating, continuing, altering, or renewing any body politic or corporate' * * *

4. That the desire for equality and the dread of special privilege were largely responsible for the general incorporation laws is indicated by the fact that many states included in their constitutions a prohibition of the grant of special charters. The first constitutional provision requiring incorporation under general laws seems to be that in the New York Constitution of 1846, article 8, § 1 (except where objects of incorporation were not thus attainable). Other states followed in later years.

indebtedness, bonded or otherwise. The power to hold stock in other corporations was not conferred or implied. The holding company was impossible.

The removal by the leading industrial states of the limitations upon the size and powers of business corporations appears to have been due, not to their conviction that maintenance of the restrictions was undesirable in itself, but to the conviction that it was futile to insist upon them; because local restriction would be circumvented by foreign incorporation. Indeed, local restriction seemed worse than futile. Lesser states, eager for the revenue derived from the traffic in charters, had removed safeguards from their own incorporation laws.[34] Companies were early formed to provide charters for corporations in states where the cost was lowest and the laws least restrictive. The states joined in advertising their wares. The race was one not of diligence but of laxity.[37] Incorporation under such

34. The traffic in charters quickly became widespread. In 1894 Cook on Stock and Stockholders (3d Ed.) Vol. 11, pp. 1604, 1605, thus described the situation: 'New Jersey is a favorite state for incorporations. Her laws seem to be framed with a special view to attracting incorporation fees and business fees from her sister states and especially from New York, across the river. She has largely succeeded in doing so, and now runs the state government very largely on revenues derived from New York enterprises. * * * Maine formerly was a resort for incorporators, but a recent decision of its highest court holding stockholders liable on stock which has been issued for property, where the court thought the property was not worth the par value of the stock, makes Maine too dangerous a state to incorporate in, especially where millions of dollars of stock are to be issued for mines, patents and other choice assortments of property. * * * West Virginia for the past ten years has been the Snug Harbor for roaming and piratical corporations. * * * The manufacture of corporations for the purpose of enabling them to do all their business elsewhere seems to be the policy of this young but enterprising state. Its statutes seem to be expressly framed for that purpose. * * *'

In 1906 John S. Parker thus described the practice, in his volume Where and How—A Corporation Handbook (2d Ed.) p. 4: 'Many years ago the corporation laws of New Jersey were so framed as to invite the incorporation of companies by persons residing in other states and countries. The liberality and facility with which corporations could there be formed were extensively advertised, and a great volume of incorporation swept into that state. * * * The policy of New Jersey proved profitable to the state, and soon legislatures of other states began active competition. * * * Delaware and Maine also revised their laws, taking the New Jersey act as a model, but with lower organization fees and annual taxes. Arizona and South Dakota also adopted liberal corporation laws, and contenting themselves with the incorporation fees, require no annual state taxes whatever.

West Virginia for many years has been popular with incorporators, but in 1901, in the face of the growing competition of other states, the legislature increased the rate of annual taxes. And West Virginia thus lost her popularity. See Conyngton and Bennett, Corporation Procedure (Rev. Ed. 1927), p. 712. On the other hand, too drastic price cutting was also unprofitable. The bargain prices in Arizona and South Dakota attracted wildcat corporations. Investors became wary of corporations organized under the laws of Arizona or South Dakota and both states fell in disrepute among them and consequently among incorporators. See Conyngton on Corporate Organizations (1913) c. 5.

37. A change in the policy of New Jersey was urged by Woodrow Wilson in his inaugural address as Governor. 'If I may speak very plainly, we are much too free with grants of charters to corporations in New Jersey. A corporation exists, not of natural right, but only by license of law, and the law, if we look at the matter in good conscience, is responsible for what it creates. * * * I would urge, therefore, the imperative obligation of public policy and of public honesty we are under to effect such changes in the law of the State as will henceforth effectually prevent the abuse of the privilege of incorporation which has in recent years brought so much discredit upon our State. * * * If law is at liberty to adjust the general conditions of society itself, it is at liberty to control these great instrumentalities which nowadays, in so large part, determine the character of society.' Minutes of Assembly of New Jersey, January 17, 1911, pp. 65, 69; reprinted in Public Papers of Woodrow Wilson (Ed. by Baker and Dodd) Vol. II, pp. 273, 274, 275. In 1913 the so-called 'Seven–Sisters' Acts were passed by New Jersey, forbidding, among other things, intercor-

laws was possible; and the great industrial States yielded in order not to lose wholly the prospect of the revenue and the control incident to domestic incorporation.

The history of the changes made by New York is illustrative. The New York revision of 1890, which eliminated the maximum limitation on authorized capital, and permitted intercorporate stockholding in a limited class of cases, was passed after a migration of incorporation from New York, attracted by the more liberal incorporation laws of New Jersey. But the changes made by New York in 1890 were not sufficient to stem the tide. In 1892, the Governor of New York approved a special charter for the General Electric Company, modeled upon the New Jersey act, on the ground that otherwise the enterprise would secure a New Jersey charter.

porate stockholding. Laws 1913, c. 18. These, in turn, were repealed in 1917. Laws 1917, c. 195 (Comp. St. Supp. § 47–176 et seq.). The report recommending the repeal stated: 'Those laws now sought to be repealed are harmful to the State because there is much uncertainty as to their meaning, with the result that those who would have otherwise incorporated here or remained here are going to other States. There is no gain to the people of the country, but this State loses a revenue which is perfectly legitimate. We doubt not that much of the adverse criticism outside of the State which was directed against New Jersey and its corporation laws prior to 1913 was due as much to the desire to divert the organization of corporations to other States as it was to prevent evils which might have arisen, and New Jersey fell for the criticism. To whatever cause may be attributed the loss of revenue to the State, it is plain that it is a condition and not a theory which confronts the State, as the following figures will show: * * * Such losses mean a serious depletion of the revenues of the State, and, unless a different policy is pursued, it will not be long before the corporation business of the State will have been reduced to a minimum. We believe such conditions justify the appointment of the Commission and will also justify the Legislature in adopting the result of our investigation and embodied in the proposed revision.' Report of the Commission to Revise the Corporation Laws of New Jersey, 1917, pp. 7, 8.

For more recent movements, see A. A. Berle and Gardiner C. Means, The Modern Corporation and Private Property (1932) p. 206, n. 18: 'As significant of the trend towards that corporate mechanism with the broad powers to the management, it is interesting to note the steady trend towards the states having a loose incorporation law. Of the 92 holding corporations mentioned above (those whose securities were listed on the New York Stock Exchange and were active in 1928) 44 were organized in Delaware, all of them being formed since 1910. Indeed, of the 44 holding corporations now chartered in that state, 25 were incorporated there between the years 1925 and 1928. In the less liberal New York State 13 of the above holding companies were formed, 6 of them having been chartered between 1910 and 1920, while only 4 were formed since 1920. Ten of the holding companies were chartered in Maryland, one in 1920 and the remaining 9 between 1923 and 1928, presumably in large measure as a result of the looseness of the Maryland corporation law of 1923. New Jersey, a relatively popular state at the turn of the century shows only two of the holding company charters granted there since 1910; while Virginia shows 7 such charters.

'Combined holding and operating corporations likewise show a steady trend towards Delaware. Of the whole list, 148 of the 573 corporations hold Delaware charters, most of them relatively recent; New York is second with 121, most of them relatively old; New Jersey third with 87, most of which grow out of the great merger period from 1898–1910.'

Corporations formed in one state by citizens of another state, to do business in the state of their residence, were frequently subjected to collateral attack. Generally the courts felt bound to uphold the corporate status. See the cases in J. H. Sears, The New Place of the Stockholder (1929) Appendix G. Occasionally, however, states legislated against the practice. Thus California enacted that the statutory liability of stockholders should apply to those in foreign as well as in domestic corporations. In two cases where the foreign corporation was organized specifically to do business in California, this provision was held applicable. Pinney v. Nelson, 183 U.S. 144, 22 S.Ct. 52, 46 L.Ed. 125; Thomas v. Matthiessen, 232 U.S. 221, 34 S.Ct. 312, 58 L.Ed. 577. And more recently this Court has sustained a constitutional provision of Virginia which prohibits foreign public service companies from doing an intrastate business in the state. Railway Express Agency v. Commonwelth of Virginia, 282 U.S. 440, 51 S.Ct. 201, 75 L.Ed. 450. The provision was adopted in the light of widespread incorporation of such companies in West Virginia and New Jersey. See Debates of Constitutional Convention of Virginia, 1901–1902, Vol. II, p. 2811.

Later in the same year the New York corporation law was again revised, allowing the holding of stock in other corporations. But the New Jersey law still continued to be more attractive to incorporators. By specifically providing that corporations might be formed in New Jersey to do all their business elsewhere, the state made its policy unmistakably clear. Of the seven largest trusts existing in 1904, with an aggregate capitalization of over two and a half billion dollars, all were organized under New Jersey law; and three of these were formed in 1899. During the first seven months of that year, 1336 corporations were organized under the laws of New Jersey, with an aggregate authorized capital of over two billion dollars. The Comptroller of New York, in his annual report for 1899, complained that 'our tax list reflects little of the great wave of organization that has swept over the country during the past year and to which this state contributed more capital than any other state in the Union.' 'It is time,' he declared, 'that great corporations having their actual headquarters in this State and a nominal office elsewhere, doing nearly all of their business within our borders, should be brought within the jurisdiction of this State not only as to matters of taxation but in respect to other and equally important affairs.' In 1901 the New York corporation law was again revised.

The history in other states was similar. Thus the Massachusetts revision of 1903 was precipitated by the fact that 'the possibilities of incorporation in other states have become well known, and have been availed of to the detriment of this Commonwealth.'

Able, discerning scholars[50] have pictured for us the economic and social results of thus removing all limitations upon the size and activities of business corporations and of vesting in their managers vast powers once exercised by stockholders—results not designed by the states and long unsuspected. They show that size alone gives to giant corporations a social significance not attached ordinarily to smaller units of private enterprise. Through size, corporations, once merely an efficient tool employed by individuals in the conduct of private business have become an institution—an institution which has brought such concentration of economic power that so-called private corporations are sometimes able to dominate the state. The typical business corporation of the last century, owned by a small group of individuals, managed by their owners, and limited in size by their personal wealth, is being supplanted by huge concerns in which the lives of tens or hundreds of thousands of employees and the property of tens or hundreds of thousands of investors are subjected, through the corporate mechanism, to the control of a few men. Ownership has been separated from control; and this separation has removed many of the checks which formerly operated to curb the misuse of wealth and power. And, as ownership of the shares is becoming continually more dispersed, the power which formerly accompanied ownership is becoming increasingly concentrated in the hands of a few. The changes thereby wrought in the

---

50. Adolf A. Berle, Jr., and Gardiner C. Means, The Modern Corporation and Private Property (1932). Compare William Z. Ripley, Main Street and Wall Street (1927).

lives of the workers, of the owners and of the general public, are so fundamental and far-reaching as to lead these scholars to compare the evolving 'corporate system' with the feudal system; and to lead other men of insight and experience to assert that this 'master institution of civilised life' is committing it to the rule of a plutocracy.[51]

The data submitted in support of these conclusions indicate that in the United States the process of absorption has already advanced so far that perhaps two-thirds of our industrial wealth has passed from individual possession to the ownership of large corporations whose shares are dealt in on the stock exchange; that 200 nonbanking corporations, each with assets in excess of $90,000,000, control directly about one-fourth of all our national wealth, and that their influence extends far beyond the assets under their direct control; that these 200 corporations, while nominally controlled by about 2,000 directors, are actually dominated by a few hundred persons—the negation of industrial democracy. Other writers have shown that, coincident with the growth of these giant corporations, there has occurred a marked concentration of individual wealth; and that the resulting disparity in incomes is a major cause of the existing depression. Such is the Frankenstein monster which states have created by their corporation laws.[57]

Among these 200 corporations, each with assets in excess of $90,000,000, are five of the plaintiffs. These five have, in the aggregate, $820,000,000 of assets; and they operate, in the several states, an aggregate of 19,718 stores. A single one of these giants operates nearly 16,000. Against these plaintiffs, and other owners of multiple stores, the individual retailers of Florida are engaged in a struggle to preserve their independence—perhaps a struggle for existence. The citizens of the state, considering themselves vitally interested in this seemingly unequal struggle, have undertaken to aid the individual retailers by subjecting the owners of multiple stores to the handicap of higher license fees. They may have done so merely in order to preserve competition. But their purpose may have been a broader and deeper one. They may have believed that the chain store, by furthering the concentration of wealth and of power and by promoting absentee ownership, is thwarting American ideals; that it is making impossible equality of opportunity; that it is converting independent tradesmen into clerks; and that it is sapping the resources, the vigor and the hope of the smaller cities and towns. * * *

Before the adoption of the New Jersey legislation described by Justice Brandeis in *Liggett Co. v. Lee*, a corporation could not own the stock of other corporations, precluding the use of "holding" companies that could control vast enterprises. Initially, trusts were used to avoid that restric-

---

51. Thorstein Veblen, Absentee Ownership and Business Enterprise (1923) p. 86; Walther Rathenau, Die Neue Wirstchaft (1918) pp. 78–81.

57. Compare I. Maurice Wormser, Frankenstein, Incorporated (1931).

tion. By placing the stock in the hands of trustees, several enterprises could be centrally controlled. The Standard Oil trust was the most famous use of this device, but numerous other trusts were formed in other industries, including tobacco and sugar. This gave rise to concerns of monopoly and abusive practices, and the trusts came under attack as illegal devices. New Jersey solved that problem by allowing holding companies, a practice that was copied by other states, including Delaware, as its popularity rose. New Jersey was the leading state of incorporation as a result of the lead it gained by being the first, but the state lost that lead when it tightened its chartering practices as a result of the reforms sought by then Governor Woodrow Wilson. Delaware continued its liberal chartering and control policies, and it quickly replaced New Jersey as the place of incorporation for many of the largest corporations. Although New Jersey repealed the Wilson reforms when he became president, Delaware was able to retain its role as the state of incorporation of choice by many large corporations. Soon, some 10,000 corporations were maintaining their technical home on a single floor of a building in Wilmington. Delaware maintains its determination to be the place of incorporation of choice, and it is the stated policy of the state to stand ready to change its laws to meet the requirements of its corporations chartered there. *See* Lucian Bebchuk and Alma Cohen, *Firms' Decisions Where to Incorporate* (2002) (Delaware is the place of incorporation of more than 50 percent of publicly traded corporations). The state maintains a professional staff in the Office of the Secretary of State to assure that incorporation is made easy. The courts of Delaware are also viewed as experts on complex corporate law issues, although their rulings sometimes frustrate the state's goal of making its corporate laws as amenable as possible to the needs of large corporations.

Despite its friendly atmosphere, Delaware is not the only place of incorporation. Local incorporation is often preferred by many start-up companies.[a] Local incorporation is often simple and avoids record keeping and other issues raised by incorporating in another state. This process was aided by the creation of model legislation that is in many ways comparable to Delaware, and sometimes preferable.

COX & HAZEN ON CORPORATIONS,
James D. Cox & Thomas Lee Hazen
§ 2.02 (2d ed. 2003).

The first general corporation chartering laws were cumbersome and unartfully drafted. They were overly restrictive in that they imposed

---

a. Delaware was not without competition:

    At various times, several states—Maine, West Virginia, and later Nevada—have attempted to "out-Delaware Delaware" in an effort to attract incorporation business and, more specifically, tax revenues and fees. These imitators, however, have had little success in displacing Delaware's preeminence in the race for the rechartering business. Still other states have liberalized their statutes to encourage their local businesses to "stay at home" by incorporating locally rather than organizing in Delaware, New Jersey, or some other permissive jurisdiction.

James D. Cox & Thomas Lee Hazen, Corporations § 2.4 (2d ed. 2003).

burdensome conditions precedent to incorporation and unreasonable limitations on the scope of the corporate franchise. This unfortunate state of affairs led to efforts by legislative drafting committees and committees of concerned business lawyers to formulate clear and precise legislation to facilitate legitimate business transactions and eliminate arbitrary, harsh, and unreasonable risks to shareholders and directors without sacrificing appropriate protection to shareholders, corporate creditors, and persons dealing with corporations.

In 1928, after many years of study, the Commissioners on Uniform State Laws recommended a Uniform Business Corporation Act. Notwithstanding its adoption with only minor modifications by three states, the Uniform Business Corporation Act soon began to be regarded more as a source for ideas to use in drafting corporation legislation rather than as an act to be substituted verbatim for existing corporation statutes. A number of states, departing drastically from the Uniform Act, adopted corporation statutes based on the work of state law revision drafting committees. Notable among these departures was the 1933 Illinois Act, which grew out of the drafting efforts of representatives of the Illinois bar. In addition to serving as a model for other state laws, the 1933 Illinois Act was used by the American Bar Association's Committee on Corporate Laws (Section of Corporation, Banking and Business Law) as a guide for the Model Business Corporation Act.

The Model Act first appeared in completed form in 1950. The Model Act continued the liberalizing trend that originated in New Jersey and Delaware and for a long time has been universally viewed as " 'enabling,' 'permissive,' and 'liberal' as distinguished from 'regulatory' and 'paternalistic.' " From time to time, other states have competed for the lead in this type of liberalization (which at times has been referred to as "the race to the bottom" although others view it as a "race to the top"). The Delaware legislature, however, continues to be the leader in originating permissive corporate legislation. Delaware's continued popularity among public corporations is documented by the fact that nearly 90 percent of public corporations that change their corporate domicile choose to reincorporate in Delaware. The Model Act was intended not to become a uniform corporation law but rather to serve as a drafting guide for the states. Eventually the Model Act became the pattern for large parts of the corporation statutes in most states (notable exceptions being California, Delaware, and New York). The Committee on Corporate Laws revises the Model Act from time to time, and typically a number of states amend their corporation statutes to adopt the latest revisions.

The first complete revision of the Model Act appears in the Revised Model Business Corporation Act (1984). The Revised Model Act incorporates many simplifying and innovative provisions that the states had experimented with over the years. In addition, the Revised Model Act has through subsequent revisions continued the liberalizing trend that started in Delaware. * * *

Corporation laws deal with such matters as the following: the content of the articles of incorporation; the rights of shareholders; the powers and liabilities of directors; rules governing shareholders' meetings and directors' meetings; restrictions on corporate finance, such as limitations on the withdrawal of funds by way of dividends and share purchases; the keeping and inspection of corporate records; and authorization of organic changes, such as charter amendments, sale of all corporate assets, merger, and consolidation, and dissolution and winding up. Some of these provisions seek to prevent management and majority shareholders from abusing their power to the detriment of minority shareholders and corporate creditors.

NOTES

1.   Corporate governance was elevated as an area of academic study in 1776 with the publication of Adam Smith's *An Inquiry Into the Nature and Causes of The Wealth of Nations*. He described the business of a joint stock company as being managed by a "court of directors," the equivalent of a modern board of directors. Those directors were subject to "the control of a general court of proprietors," a reference to a meeting of the shareholders. Adam Smith raised some practical concerns with the governance of corporations. He noted that corporate directors "being the managers rather of other people's money than their own, it cannot well be expected, that they should watch over it with the same anxious vigilance with which the partners in a private copartnery frequently watch over their own," and that "negligence and profusion, therefore, must prevail, more or less, in the management of the affairs of such a company." This concern would be echoed by American observers of corporations. In 1833, William Gouge asserted that corporate officers managed the affairs of their company more carelessly and expensively than those of an individual proprietor. Gouge asked, "[W]hat would be the condition of the merchant who should trust everything to his clerks, or the farmer who should trust everything to his laborers?" The law and academics school of thought that developed late in the twentieth century also focused on these "agency costs."

2.   Justice Brandeis elaborated on the views he expressed in *Liggett Co. v. Lee* in his frequently cited book *Other Peoples' Money and How the Bankers Use It* (1932). The utility of corporations has long been an issue of debate, even before Justice Brandeis expressed his concerns. In England at the end of the seventeenth century, John Pollexfen lamented the fact that "companies have bodies, but it is said they have no souls; if no souls, no consciences," noted in Edward Chancellor, *Devil Take the Hindmost: A History of Financial Speculation* 49 (1999). William Gouge raised concern in 1833 that corporations in America could become so powerful that they could challenge the role of the government and gain monopoly power over markets. He also argued that large corporations are inefficient because employees are entrusted with the business owned by shareholders: "[W]hat would be the condition of the merchant who should trust everything to his clerks, or the farmer who should trust everything to his laborers." William M. Gouge, *A Short History of Paper Money and Banking in the United States Including an Account of Provincial*

and Continental Paper Money to Which is Prefixed an Inquiry into the Principles of the System 41 (1833). This defect results in monitoring costs that would not be present, or would at least be diminished, in a business operated by its owners who have a stake in assuring efficiency. Daniel Webster, himself a celebrated corporate lawyer as well as Senator and statesman, defended the corporation. Webster asserted that the corporation was a mechanism for increasing wealth and spreading the value of business ownership to the many, where before it had been limited to the few. He believed that corporations tended "not only to increase property, but to equalize it, to diffuse it, to scatter the advantages among the many, and to give content, cheerfulness, and animation to all classes of the social system." Robert Remini, *Daniel Webster, The Man and his Time* 597 (1997).

COX & HAZEN ON CORPORATIONS,
James D. Cox & Thomas Lee Hazen

§ 2.07   (2d ed. 2003).

In their classic book on the modern corporation, Adolf Berle and Gardiner Means pointed out that the American corporation is no longer merely a private business tool or device; instead, it has evolved into a dominant institution affecting economic, political, and social conditions in modern society. A large amount of the wealth of individuals has shifted from ownership of actual physical property to ownership of shares of stock representing a set of rights and expectations in an enterprise. Professors Berle and Means explained that management, consisting of directors and officers, is responsible for the actual control of a corporation, while owners of shares of stock in a large publicly held corporation are usually passive: "[I]n the corporate system, the 'owner' of industrial wealth is left with a mere symbol of ownership while the power, the responsibility and the substance which have been an integral part of ownership in the past are being transferred to a separate group in whose hands lies control."

Berle's and Mean's view that dispersion of ownership is an inherent characteristic of the public corporation has been seriously questioned by Professor Mark Roe. Professor Roe argues that the present dispersed ownership is the result of a series of political decisions motivated principally out of fear of avoiding the concentration of economic power.[3] Among the most significant regulatory developments that foster dispersed ownership are the various directives that limit, either directly or indirectly, the percentage of stock certain financial institutions can own in a single corporation. His point is that absent such politically motivated directives, ownership may not have fragmented as it has and the problems of the separation of ownership from management would not be what it has become.

The separation of ownership from control gives rise to various conflicts of interest between passive owners and active managers. In the

---

3. Mark J. Roe, Strong Managers, Weak Owners: The Political Roots of American Corporate Finance (1994). For a critical review of this book, see Stephen M. Bainbridge, The Politics of Corporate Governance, 18 Harv. J.L. & Pub. Poly. 671 (1995).

abstract, managers are no different from other individuals when facing an economic choice; so as to maximize their own utility, they can be expected to act like other individuals in exercising discretionary decisions. Utility maximization is an especially interesting problem in the public corporation, where management and ownership are separated. The managers' quest to maximize their utility does not naturally lead to decisions that also maximize the value of the firm.

In a classic article,[5] Ronald Coase developed a powerful model of the firm that explains why firms exist and why they decide to expand. Coase argued that a firm will undertake an activity for itself whenever it is cheaper to do so than to acquire that good or service in the market. A distinct cost of the market is imperfect information about the quality and overall utility of the good or service that others will provide. Further concerns are whether the sellers of goods will be able to produce the desired quantity and make the goods available at competitive prices. Because it is expensive to gather information on these various points and because there may be no economies in relying on the production efforts of others, the firm's managers will decide to provide the good or service itself. The firm thus grows because of its decision to integrate the new activity into the firm's existing operation. * * *

The neoclassical economists (sometimes more generally referred to as "the Chicago School") have prodigiously mined the problems posed by separation of ownership from control. Any examination of the issues flowing from the separation of ownership and management should begin by considering the work of Professors Jensen and Meckling,[6] who theorize that managers have strong market-based incentives to contract with shareholders to reduce the managers' misbehavior. In this context the misbehavior need not rise to the level of constituting practices that are fraudulent or even in breach of the manager's fiduciary duties. They can, however, include a range of relatively benign conduct, such as longer lunch hours and directing the corporation's munificence to the manager's alma mater. * * *

A key point in the neoclassical economic view of the firm is that managers must have an incentive compensation arrangement that substantially ties their fortunes to that of the owners. Such an arrangement accomplishes two objectives. First, the typical stock option plan or bonuses based on firm profitability *bonds* the manager to serve the stockholders' interest. Obviously, the strength of the bond is directly proportional to the extent the managers' total compensation packages depends on the changes in the firm's value or profitability. Second, linking the managers' incentives to those of the firm's owners *signals* to the investors the depth of the firm's managers' resolve to maximize the value of the firm. Signaling addresses the information asymmetry problem, so that investors will not discount the firm's securities by the average risk expected for the indus-

---

5. Ronald H. Coase, The Nature of the Firm, 4 Economica (n.s.) 386 (1937).

6. Michael C. Jensen & William H. Meckling, Theory of the Firm: Managerial Behavior, Agency Costs and Ownership Structure, 3 J. Fin. Econ. 305 (1976).

try. Consistent with agency theorists' view of the firm is the increasing popularity among public corporations of encouraging or requiring their outside directors to acquire a substantial equity investment in the corporation.

A further step to reduce such discounting is the use of *monitoring* devices designed to police management. Conventional examples of monitoring include that of outside boards of directors and independent accountants. However, monitoring is efficient only to the extent its marginal benefits exceed its marginal cost. Because monitoring can be expected to pose diminishing marginal benefits, it generally prevents only the more extreme managerial departures.

The costs of bonding, signaling, and monitoring, as well as the amount of misbehavior that continues in the face of these steps to deter managerial indiscretions, are collectively referred to as *agency costs*. In view of these mechanisms for reducing agency costs, the neoclassical economists who view the corporation as a "nexus of contracts" reason that what binds the firm together as an entity is not the fiction of its separate existence but the numerous contractual intersections among owners, managers, creditors, and workers through which they define their respective roles, risks, and rights. Under this view, the corporation is reduced to the means for efficient contracting among the owners, managers, creditors, and laborers. Corporate statutes are viewed by these economists as off-the-rack contractual provisions the parties would have embodied in their contract if contracting could occur costlessly. And judges in resolving disputes should similarly confine their analysis. * * *

Not surprising, there is abundant criticism of this view of the firm. Certainly, it is correct that firms organize their internal governance and structure to achieve efficient operations, which includes effective monitoring of the performance of all operating units. Even if one accepts the economists' nexus-of-contracts interpretation of the firm, it must be done with a healthy respect for the indeterminacy to its prescription that intramural disputes be resolved by divining the presumed intentions of the parties when the corporation or their relationship was formed. * * *

In the end, the neoclassical view of the corporation is vulnerable to the charges that it is both an empty metaphor and tautological: the neoclassical view allows no room for a higher principle or purpose to resolve corporate law questions; disputes are instead resolved according to the presumed intentions of the contracting parties. Thus law is not an engine for societal change and improvement. The neoclassical view has struck many commentators as antithetical even to the basic premises of corporate law.

The nexus-of-contracts interpretation of the firm provides a free-market approach to the problems posed by the separation of ownership from control. In the meantime, the conflicts of interest inherent in the separation of ownership and control continue to create new concerns, such as the broad public alarm about excessive executive compensation and the competitiveness of American industry. Coupled with these concerns are complaints from public interest and consumer groups about the socially undesirable and scandalous conduct that they attribute to corporations. In combination, they continue to spawn a lively debate and action to improve corporate governance mechanisms.

The so-called "Chicago school of law and economics" has posited that business relationships are governed by contractual agreements, making the corporation simply a "nexus of contracts." Leaders in this school of thought included professors at the University of Chicago law school: Richard A Posner and Frank H. Easterbrook, now federal appellate court judges, and the Dean of that law school, Daniel R. Fischel. These theorists were dubbed "contractarians." The contractual theorists place reliance on the market for discipline instead of fiduciary duties created by jurists with no knowledge or experience in business. They believe that market forces will assure that managers do not overreach in negotiating those contracts, otherwise no one would buy the company's stock. Under the contractual theory, shareholders are assured only of rights they might have under a contract with the corporation. The courts would not be called upon to create rights that the parties themselves did not establish by contract.

The contract theorists did not had an easy time in challenging the conventional wisdom of the importance of a fiduciary model. Corporate law theorists adhering to this contractual view were ridiculed by other law professors inculcated with fiduciary standards for their entire careers. That hostile attitude gradually diminished and contractual theory is now taught in nearly every law school. The contractarians have not been as successful in having the courts consider their views. Delaware and other states have effectively blocked the application of this theory even though in most other business relationships, the parties decide themselves by contract what protections are needed. That is the approach taken by the courts for debts. Bondholders, for example, are not protected by fiduciary duties, except in some rare and extreme instances. The contractarians ask why shareholders should fare any better?

––––––

The scandal involving the bankruptcy of Enron Corp. in 2001, a company that was ranked seventh on the Fortune 500 list of the largest corporations in America, raised renewed concerns with corporate management. In that debacle, managers were operating off-the-book enterprises in which they received large personal profits while keeping debt off Enron's books and inflating its credit rating and analyst's outlooks. These activities pumped up the price of Enron's stock, causing large losses to investors and employee retirement accounts when the company collapsed. *See, e.g.,* Peter C. Fusaro & Ross M. Miller, What Went Wrong at Enron: Everyone's Guide to the Largest Bankruptcy in U.S. History (2002); Report of Investigation by the Special Investigative Committee of the

Board of Directors of Enron Corp. (Feb. 1, 2002) (describing accounting short cuts taken by Enron).

The subprime crisis that occurred between 2007 and 2009 raised further concerns with corporate management. The managers of financial services firms were especially singled out for the large bonuses they were paid from the profits earned from subprime investments before the market broke and destroyed or nearly destroyed their companies, like Bear Stearns, Merrill Lynch, and Lehman Brothers.

NOTES

1. *Race to the Bottom.* Justice Brandeis observed that in his view with respect to the competition among the states to attract corporations was "The race was one not of diligence but of laxity." This became a recurrent theme of critics during the twentieth century. See, e.g., William Cary, A Proposed Federal Minimum Standards Act, 29 Bus. Law. 1101 (1974); William Cary, Federalism and Corporate Law: Reflections upon Delaware, 83 Yale L.J. 663 (1974); Thomas L. Hazen, Corporate Directors' Accountability: The Race to the Bottom—The Second Lap, 66 N.C.L. Rev. 171–182 (1987); Comment, Law for Sale: A Study of the Delaware Corporation Law of 1967, 117 U. Pa. L. Rev. 861 (1969).

2. *Corporate Law as Enabling.* Another way to view the competition for corporate charters is to describe all of this as a laissez faire, free market approach, viewing corporate laws as enabling and thereby giving corporate participants the choice. See, e.g., Elvin R. Latty, Why Are Business Corporation Laws Largely "Enabling"?, 50 Cornell L.Q. 599 (1965); Roberta Romano, The State Competition Debate in Corporate Law, 8 Cardozo L. Rev. 709 (1987). In other words, under a contractarian view, the corporation is a nexus of contracts and the participants should be free to select their governance norms through contractual consent.

3. *Race to the Top.* Following a contractarian perspective, many commentators laud the move towards enabling acts. See, e.g., Daniel R. Fischel, The "Race to the Bottom" Revisited: Reflections on Recent Developments in Delaware's Corporation Law, 76 Nw. U. L. Rev. 913, 921–923 (1982); Ralph K. Winter, Jr., State Law, Shareholder Protection, and the Theory of the Corporation, 6 J. Legal. Stud. 251 (1977). Consequently, these commentators describe the competition as a race to the top. See, e.g., Barry D. Baysinger & Henry N. Butler, Race for the Bottom v. Climb to the Top: The ALI Project and Uniformity in Corporate Law, 10 J. Corp. L. 431 (1985); Lucian Arye Bebchuk & Allen Ferrell, Essay: A New Approach to Takeover Law and Regulatory Competition, 87 Va. L. Rev. 111 (2001); William J. Carney, The Political Economy of Competition for Corporate Charters, 26 J. Legal Stud. 303, 313–17 (1997).

4. One solution suggested for these issues is federal chartering:

Congress, if it so desires, arguably can extend federal chartering power to all corporations engaging in interstate commerce. Over the years, many commentators have advocated federal chartering. Other commentators have suggested a federal uniformity statute or a federal minimum standards act as an alternative to the more comprehensive approach of federal chartering. Proposals for comprehensive or limited federal control of corporations have been stimulated in large part by what their proponents view as blatant over-permissiveness in the state corporation statutes. To date, however, no such federal legislation has been enacted.

James D. Cox & Thomas Lee Hazen, *Corporations* § 2.11 (2d ed. 2003).

SECTION 2. PARTNERSHIPS AND LIMITED LIABILITY ASSOCIATIONS—A FIRST LOOK

Before more fully exploring the role and regulation of corporations, there are some other business organizations to consider. The use of partnerships, large and small, continued in America even with the growth of corporations. Partnerships were subject to state laws that varied in their scope and application. In an effort to achieve uniformity among the states in regulating those enterprises, a Uniform Partnership Act ("UPA") was created in 1914. It was the product of the Conference on Commissioners of Uniform State Laws, which had begun that project in 1902 under the auspices of James Barr Ames, Dean of the Harvard Law School. After Dean Ames' death, William Draper Lewis, Dean of the University of Pennsylvania Law School continued with the UPA. As will be seen in Chapter 2, the differences in the viewpoints of these two deans would touch off a debate over the legal treatment of partnerships that resulted in a revision of the UPA in 1997, the Revised Uniform Partnership Act ("RUPA").

Another form of business enterprise is the limited partnership. New York passed a limited partnership act in 1822 that subjected the "general" partners of such enterprises to unlimited liability, which included the personal assets of the general partners, for the debts of these entities. This legislation, however, limited the liability of "special" or passive partners to the amount of their investment in the enterprise. Several other states adopted similar legislation. A Uniform Limited Partnership Act ("ULPA") was approved by the Conference on Commissioners of Uniform State Laws in 1916. That legislation was subsequently adopted by several states. A revised uniform limited partnership act was approved by the Conference in 1976 and amendments were added in 1985 ("RULPA").

A new form of business enterprise arrived in 1977 when Wyoming created the limited liability company ("LLC"), which is essentially an incorporated partnership that appears to be modeled after the German GmbH that was established in 1892 for small German enterprises.[1] After

---

1. For a description of the German GmbH company see Thomas Stohlmeier & Jan Wrede, "Introduction of "Small" Stock Corporations in Germany, 22 Int'l Bus. Law. 449 (1994).

favorable tax treatment was given to the LLC, other states acted to embrace this enterprise, and a uniform act was approved by the National Conference on Commissioners of Uniform State Laws in 1995.[2] All of the states have now adopted statutes allowing the creation of LLCs. The LLC is said to combine the best features of all other business associations, and it quickly became popular, particularly for start-up businesses.

Professional corporations and professional associations were created in Texas in 1969 to allow lawyers and other professionals who were prohibited from incorporating to obtain certain tax advantages and to create retirement programs that were available only to corporate forms of business.[3] These entities were followed by professional organizations that provided the tax advantages of a corporation and at least some limitation of liability for the conduct of other partners. The limited liability partnership ("LLP") that appeared in Texas in 1991 had spread to the rest of the country by the end of the twentieth century. The amount of limited liability, however, was limited in some instances. Most of these states allow limited liability for conduct in which the partner in an LLP is not involved or which is not due to that partner's negligence. Still another new entrant to the field was the limited liability limited partnerships. Proposals are also being considered for limited liability sole proprietorships.

There are a number of other business associations that corporate lawyers must advise. The not-for-profit corporation is a charitable enterprise that is often regulated separately from commercial (for-profit) corporations under state laws. The not-for-profit corporation raises some unique tax issues. These entities are addressed in other law school courses and will not be dealt with in this casebook. Nevertheless, keep in mind that different or special rules may apply to not-for-profits. Another form of business enterprise is the federally chartered corporation. These may include such things as the Post office, TVA, Comsat, the Government National Mortgage Association and others. National banks also have federal charters and are separately regulated by the federal government, a subject that is covered in banking courses.

NOTE ON BUSINESS TRUSTS

Some states, most notably Massachusetts, permit conducting a business with limited liability in the form of a business trust. The business is organized as a trust so that the trustees manage the business and the beneficiaries (frequently called owners of beneficial interest) share in the profits and appreciation of the assets.

---

2. "The emergence of the LLC improved the menu of business forms by bundling together limited liability, a flexible governance structure, and preferential tax treatment." Joseph A. McCahery, "Comparative Perspectives on the Evolution of the Unincorporated Firm: An Introduction." 26 J. Corp. L. 803 (2001)

3. J. William Callison, "Federalism, Regulatory Competition, and the Limited Liability Movement: The Coyote Howled and the Herd Stampeded," 26 J. Corp. L. 951, 952–953 (2001); Allan Walker Vestal, "... Drawing Near the Fastness?—The Failed United States Experiment in Unincorporated Business Entity Reform", 26 J Corp. L. 1019 (2001).

The business trust is organized through a deed or declaration of trust. The assets to be used in the business are transferred to trustees to be managed under the trust instrument for the benefit and profit of persons holding transferable certificates evidencing the beneficial interests in the trust estate. The trustees have legal title to the property in trust and act as principals for the beneficial owners. As with any trust, the trustees in a business trust have the power to manage the trust's assets.

One major disadvantage of the business trust is its rather shaky legal status in some jurisdictions. Although a number of state statutes expressly declare that the business trust is a permissible form of association for the conduct of business, and although it would probably be sanctioned by courts in most jurisdictions even in the absence of a statute, the courts in a few states have, in the absence of enabling legislation, treated it like a partnership or joint stock company for purposes of shareholder personal liability. Furthermore, even in a jurisdiction that recognizes the business trust, an unskilled attempt to create a business trust may result in the creation of a joint stock company with full partnership liability for its members.

Recently there has been a resurgence of interest in business trusts because they are particularly well-suited for many investor-oriented products such as real estate investment trusts and asset-backed securities. Delaware and Wyoming each have taken the lead in enacting modern business trust statutes authorizing unincorporated business trusts. Both statutes accord the trust's organizers unlimited freedom with respect to the powers, selection, and activities of the trustees.

SECTION 3.   ADVANTAGES AND DISADVANTAGES OF PARTICULAR ENTERPRISES[a]

The following discussion outlines some of the advantages and disadvantages of the various forms of business enterprises.

Proprietorships: These are individually owned businesses that have no separate legal status apart from their owner. This is the typical "mom and pop" grocery or other small business.

Advantages

> **Control**—Unlike the corporation (which separates ownership and control), the owner of a proprietorship controls and operates the business. This allows the proprietor to exercise direct control over the business and safeguard its assets.

> **Simplicity**—The lack of a separate legal structure means that the proprietorship is easy to operate and more flexible than other forms of business associations. There is no need to call sharehold-

---

a. See chapter 2 *infra* for treatment of partnership law and the law of other unincorporated associations.

er or partnership meetings or to provide reports to others or even to register with the state.[11]

Expenses—The proprietorship will encounter less expense in its operations than required for other business enterprises. There is no need to comply with expensive reporting and registration requirements under the federal securities laws, and accounting may be less formal and hence cheaper. Legal issues will be fewer and less complicated than for other forms of business.

Taxes—The proprietorship is not taxed separately. Income and expenses are passed directly through to the owner. In contrast, some corporations are double taxed, i.e., the business is taxed at the corporation level for income and then shareholders of the corporation are taxed again if the remaining income is distributed to them.

Disadvantages

Unlimited liability—The sole proprietor is subject to unlimited liability for any contractual or tort damages caused by the business or its agents. This means that even personal assets, such as the owner's personal bank account, may be seized by creditors of the business.

Management—The proprietorship is usually dependent on the management of the owner. Professional managers are rarely hired. The death or disability of the proprietor often results in the loss of the business because there is no one available to manage and carry on the business, other than family members.

Transferability—Ownership of a proprietorship cannot readily be sold. The entity is usually an integral part of its owner's personal management and control, and there is no separate structure that can be readily transferred.

———

Partnerships: A partnership is an association of two or more persons carrying on a business for profit as co-owners.

Advantages

Control—Like the proprietorship, a partnership does not separate ownership and control. Ownership and control is simply dispersed among the partners by agreement. This allows the owners directly to control the business and safeguard its assets.

---

11. States may require proprietorships to file with county or other officials under fictitious name statutes where the business is being conducted under a name other than the owners. For example, "Ajax Cleaners" could be the name of a proprietorship owned by William Smith. That is considered to be a fictitious name. See e.g., N.C. Stat. 66–68 (fictitious name filing required with office of registrar of deeds in county where business is conducted). Business licenses may also be required by city or other municipal authorities for unincorporated businesses, as well as for corporations.

Simplicity—The partnership has a separate legal structure, but the partners may agree to conduct their business in almost any manner they wish. This allows the partners flexibility in operating their business. This may make the partnership more complicated than a proprietorship, since a partnership agreement should be negotiated. Further, as will be discussed in Chapter 2, the affairs of the partnership must be conducted in accordance with state partnership laws.

Expenses—The operation of a business as a partnership will generally be less expensive than for a corporation, which must report to its shareholders and be subject to numerous state and federal laws that may require additional disclosures and accounting requirements. Winding up the partnership may, however, be expensive and complicated.

Taxes—The partnership is not taxed separately. An information return is required, but income and expenses are passed directly through to the owners.

Disadvantages

Unlimited liability—The partners in a partnership are subject to unlimited liability for any contractual or tort damages incurred by partners or agents in the course of the partnership's business.

Transferability—A partner cannot sell his or her ownership interest in a partnership.

———

Limited Partnerships: This entity has a general partner that operates the business and one or more limited partners that contribute investment capital but do not participate in management.

Advantages

Limited Liability—The liability of the limited partners is limited to the amount of their investment, thereby protecting their other assets. The general partner remains subject to unlimited liability.

Separation of ownership and control—Limited partners may invest capital in an enterprise without becoming involved in management. This allows limited partners to invest in an enterprise they do not have the time or expertise to manage.

Expenses—Simplicity in management is still available since the business may be structured freely under the limited partnership agreement. A filing must be made with the state upon commencement of the business of the limited partnership, and accounting for the limited partners may be more complicated than in a simple partnership. But note that taxes are also complicated because broadly held limited partnerships may be taxed in much the same manner as a corporation.

Disadvantages

Unlimited liability—The general partner in a limited partnership is subject to unlimited liability for any contractual or tort damages incurred in the partnership's business. This may be limited by making the general partner a corporation.

Transferability—A limited partner cannot usually readily sell his or her ownership interest in a partnership unless it is registered under (or exempt from) the federal securities laws with all their attending expenses and liabilities.

Limited liability companies ("LLC's"): The LLC is basically an incorporated partnership that allows members to actively participate in management or to be passive if they wish.

Advantages

Limited Liability—The liability of members of the LLC is limited to the amount of their investment, thereby protecting their other assets.

Separation of ownership and control—LLC members may invest capital in the enterprise without becoming involved in management. Alternatively, they can manage the company, if the LLC's operating agreement so permits, without incurring unlimited liability. This provides the members with maximum flexibility in the management and operation of the businesses.

Expenses—Simplicity in management is still available since the business may be structured freely under the operating agreement. A charter must be obtained from the state upon commencement of the business of the LLC. But note that accounting for the LLC may be more complicated than in a simple partnership.

Taxes—Taxes may be passed through to members, thereby avoiding the double taxation imposed on large corporations.

Disadvantages

Transferability—The ownership interest of a member in an LLC may be transferred, but that transfer may be restricted by the terms of the operating agreement. The sale of ownership interests in an LLC are also subject to state and federal securities laws.

Limited liability partnerships ("LLP's"): The LLP is another form of incorporated partnership. It is particularly popular with law firms.

Advantages

Limited Liability—The liability of members of the LLP is limited to the amount of their investment. In the case of law firms, however, a partner is subject to unlimited liability for his or her own acts. The partner is protected from personal liability for the acts of other partners, but their partnership interest may be seized by creditors of the partnership.

Expenses—LLPs may structure their operations in a manner they deem fit under their partnership agreement.

Taxes—Taxes may be passed through to members, thereby avoiding the double taxation imposed on large corporations.

Disadvantages

Transferability—The ownership interest of a member in an LLP is not easily transferred.

———

Corporations: These are businesses that have a separate legal status apart from their owners.

Advantages

Limited liability—The liability of investors (stockholders) in a corporation is limited to the amount of their investment. This encourages risk taking that is necessary for society to advance.

Separation of management and control—The corporate structure separates ownership and control. Stockholders may invest capital in the enterprise without becoming involved in management. This allows an efficient allocation of capital and professional management of the company's operations.

Transferability—Stock holdings in a corporation may be transferable. Such sales, however may be subject to the requirements of the federal securities laws, and there may not always be a ready market for the stock.

Perpetual life—Unlike the proprietorship or the partnership, the corporation continues in existence until dissolved. The death of the owner does not terminate the life of a corporation.

Disadvantages

Double taxation—The corporation is separately taxed for any profits it may receive. The shareholders of the corporation are then taxed again if the remaining income is distributed to them. This may be avoided in small corporations through so-called subchapter S status that allows a pass-through of profits directly to shareholders in smaller corporations.

Management—Managers of a corporation may manage for their own interests (*e.g.*, higher salaries and perquisites), rather than seeking to maximize shareholder wealth.

Expenses—The corporation will encounter more expense in its operations than required for other business enterprises. A publicly held corporation must comply with expensive reporting and registration requirements under the federal securities laws. Accounting and legal issues involving authorizations and entity structure will be more frequent and more complicated than for other forms of business enterprises.

NOTE

The protection of limited liability for business owners has long been a matter of controversy. Critics charge that the owners of the business set it in motion and should bear any losses from the firm's operations. Proponents contend that limited liability is needed to attract passive investors. Who would invest in a business that could subject the investors to unlimited liability, which could mean the loss of their other personal assets, including their homes and savings? Society, it is claimed, would not be able to advance, industry could not employ large work forces and our economy would fail without such a limitation.

    A.   Do you agree with one side or the other side of these arguments? Is there a middle ground?

    B.   Do you think that lawyers should be given limited liability for the conduct of their partners, employees or themselves?

CHAPTER 2

AGENCY AND PARTNERSHIPS

■ ■ ■

SECTION 1. INTRODUCTION
TO AGENCY PRINCIPLES

Partnership and corporate law are based on a combination of agency and contract law principles. It follows that a basic understanding of agency law is necessary before embarking on an analysis of the law of other business associations. The basic definition of agency is found in section 1(1) of the Restatement of Agency:

> Agency is the fiduciary relation which results from the manifestation of consent by one person [the principal] to another [the agent] that the [agent] shall act on [the principal's] behalf and subject to [the principal's] control, and consent by the [agent] so to act.

This is a very pithy definition. First, it points out that the agency relationship is a *fiduciary* one. Second, it shows that it is based on consent. Agency empowers one person to act on behalf of another provided that is pursuant to the authority created by the relationship. It also permits the agent to cause the principal to incur obligations and liabilities. As a general matter, the principal will be responsible for the acts of the agent where the agent is acting within the scope of the agent's authority.

The materials that follow provide an introduction to these concepts, most of which stay with us throughout the course.

———

A. IDENTIFYING THE AGENCY RELATIONSHIP

A. GAY JENSON FARMS CO. v. CARGILL, INC.

309 N.W.2d 285 (Minn.1981).

PETERSON, JUSTICE.

Plaintiffs, 86 individual, partnership or corporate farmers, brought this action against defendant Cargill, Inc. (Cargill) and defendant Warren Grain & Seed Co. (Warren) to recover losses sustained when Warren defaulted on the contracts made with plaintiffs for the sale of grain. After a trial by jury, judgment was entered in favor of plaintiffs, and Cargill brought this appeal. We affirm.

This case arose out of the financial collapse of defendant Warren Seed & Grain Co., and its failure to satisfy its indebtedness to plaintiffs. Warren, which was located in Warren, Minnesota, was operated by Lloyd Hill and his son, Gary Hill. Warren operated a grain elevator and as a result was involved in the purchase of cash or market grain from local farmers. The cash grain would be resold through the Minneapolis Grain Exchange or to the terminal grain companies directly. Warren also stored grain for farmers and sold chemicals, fertilizer and steel storage bins. In addition, it operated a seed business which involved buying seed grain from farmers, processing it and reselling it for seed to farmers and local elevators.

Lloyd Hill decided in 1964 to apply for financing from Cargill. Cargill's officials from the Moorhead regional office investigated Warren's operations and recommended that Cargill finance Warren.

Warren and Cargill thereafter entered into a security agreement which provided that Cargill would loan money for working capital to Warren on "open account" financing up to a stated limit, which was originally set as $175,000.[2] Under this contract, Warren would receive funds and pay its expenses by issuing drafts drawn on Cargill through Minneapolis banks. The drafts were imprinted with both Warren's and Cargill's names. Proceeds from Warren's sales would be deposited with Cargill and credited to its account. In return for this financing, Warren appointed Cargill as its grain agent for transaction with the Commodity Credit Corporation. Cargill was also given a right of first refusal to purchase market grain sold by Warren to the terminal market.

A new contract was negotiated in 1967, extending Warren's credit line to $300,000 and incorporating the provisions of the original contract. It was also stated in the contract that Warren would provide Cargill with annual financial statements and that either Cargill would keep the books for Warren or an audit would be conducted by an independent firm. Cargill was given the right of access to Warren's books for inspection.

In addition, the agreement provided that Warren was not to make capital improvements or repairs in excess of $5,000 without Cargill's prior consent. Further, it was not to become liable as guarantor on another's indebtedness, or encumber its assets except with Cargill's permission. Consent by Cargill was required before Warren would be allowed to declare a dividend or sell and purchase stock.

Officials from Cargill's regional office made a brief visit to Warren shortly after the agreement was executed. They examined the annual statement and the accounts receivable, expenses, inventory, seed, machinery and other financial matters. Warren was informed that it would be

---

2. Loans were secured by a second mortgage on Warren's real estate and a first chattel mortgage on its inventories of grain and merchandise in the sum of $175,000 with 7% interest. Warren was to use the $175,000 to pay off the debt that it owed to Atwood Larson.

reminded periodically to make the improvements recommended by Cargill.[3] At approximately this time, a memo was given to the Cargill official in charge of the Warren account, Erhart Becker, which stated in part: "This organization (Warren) needs very strong paternal guidance."

In 1970, Cargill contracted with Warren and other elevators to act as its agent to seek growers for a new type of wheat called Bounty 208. Warren, as Cargill's agent for this project, entered into contracts for the growing of the wheat seed, with Cargill named as the contracting party. Farmers were paid directly by Cargill for the seed and all contracts were performed in full. In 1971, pursuant to an agency contract, Warren contracted on Cargill's behalf with various farmers for the growing of sunflower seeds for Cargill. The arrangements were similar to those made in the Bounty 208 contracts, and all those contracts were also completed. Both these agreements were unrelated to the open account financing contract. In addition, Warren, as Cargill's agent in the sunflower seed business, cleaned and packaged the seed in Cargill bags.

During this period, Cargill continued to review Warren's operations and expenses and recommend that certain actions should be taken.[4] Warren purchased from Cargill various business forms printed by Cargill and received sample forms from Cargill which Warren used to develop its own business forms.

Cargill wrote to its regional office in 1970 expressing its concern that the pattern of increased use of funds allowed to develop at Warren was similar to that involved in two other cases in which Cargill experienced severe losses. Cargill did not refuse to honor drafts or call the loan, however. A new security agreement which increased the credit line to $750,000 was executed in 1972, and a subsequent agreement which raised the limit to $1,250,000 was entered into in 1976.

Warren was at that time shipping Cargill 90% of its cash grain. When Cargill's facilities were full, Warren shipped its grain to other companies. Approximately 25% of Warren's total sales was seed grain which was sold directly by Warren to its customers.

As Warren's indebtedness continued to be in excess of its credit line, Cargill began to contact Warren daily regarding its financial affairs. Cargill headquarters informed its regional office in 1973 that, since Cargill money was being used, Warren should realize that Cargill had the right to

---

3. Cargill headquarters suggested that the regional office check Warren monthly. Also, it was requested that Warren be given an explanation for the relatively large withdrawals from undistributed earnings made by the Hills, since Cargill hoped that Warren's profits would be used to decrease its debt balance. Cargill asked for written requests for withdrawals from undistributed earnings in the future.

4. Between 1967 and 1973, Cargill suggested that Warren take a number of steps, including: (1) a reduction of seed grain and cash grain inventories; (2) improved collection of accounts receivable; (3) reduction or elimination of its wholesale seed business and its speciality grain operation; (4) marketing fertilizer and steel bins on consignment; (5) a reduction in withdrawals made by officers; (6) a suggestion that Warren's bookkeeper not issue her own salary checks; and (7) cooperation with Cargill in implementing the recommendations. These ideas were apparently never implemented, however.

make some critical decisions regarding the use of the funds. Cargill headquarters also told Warren that a regional manager would be working with Warren on a day-to-day basis as well as in monthly planning meetings. In 1975, Cargill's regional office began to keep a daily debit position on Warren. A bank account was opened in Warren's name on which Warren could draw checks in 1976. The account was to be funded by drafts drawn on Cargill by the local bank.

In early 1977, it became evident that Warren had serious financial problems. Several farmers, who had heard that Warren's checks were not being paid, inquired or had their agents inquire at Cargill regarding Warren's status and were initially told that there would be no problem with payment. In April 1977, an audit of Warren revealed that Warren was $4 million in debt. After Cargill was informed that Warren's financial statements had been deliberately falsified, Warren's request for additional financing was refused. In the final days of Warren's operation, Cargill sent an official to supervise the elevator, including disbursement of funds and income generated by the elevator.

After Warren ceased operations, it was found to be indebted to Cargill in the amount of $3.6 million. Warren was also determined to be indebted to plaintiffs in the amount of $2 million, and plaintiffs brought this action in 1977 to seek recovery of that sum. Plaintiffs alleged that Cargill was jointly liable for Warren's indebtedness as it had acted as principal for the grain elevator.

The matter was bifurcated for trial in Marshall County District Court. In the first phase, the amount of damages sustained by each farmer was determined by the court. The second phase of the action, dealing with the issue of Cargill's liability for the indebtedness of Warren, was tried before a jury.

The jury found that Cargill's conduct between 1973 and 1977 had made it Warren's principal.[6] Warren was found to be the agent of Cargill with regard to contracts for:

1. The purchase and sale of grain for market.

2. The purchase and sale of seed grain.

3. The storage of grain.

The court determined that Cargill was the disclosed principal of Warren. It was concluded that Cargill was jointly liable with Warren for plaintiffs' losses, and judgment was entered for plaintiffs.

Cargill seeks a reversal of the jury's findings or, if the jury findings are upheld, a reversal of the trial court's determination that Cargill was a disclosed principal. In the alternative, Cargill requests that the court order a new trial based upon the trial court's error in (1) denying Cargill's requested jury instructions; (2) refusing to admit relevant evidence; and

---

6. At trial, plaintiffs sought to establish actual agency by Cargill's course of dealing between 1973 and 1977 rather than "apparent" agency or agency by estoppel, so that the only issue in this case is one of actual agency.

(3) denying Cargill's motion for change of venue. Northwestern County Elevator Association, North Dakota Grain Dealers Association and Northwestern National Bank of Minneapolis have all filed briefs on appeal as amici curiae, seeking to have the jury verdict reversed.

1.   The major issue in this case is whether Cargill, by its course of dealing with Warren, became liable as a principal on contracts made by Warren with plaintiffs. Cargill contends that no agency relationship was established with Warren, notwithstanding its financing of Warren's operation and its purchase of the majority of Warren's grain. However, we conclude that Cargill, by its control and influence over Warren, became a principal with liability for the transactions entered into by its agent Warren.

Agency is the fiduciary relationship that results from the manifestation of consent by one person to another that the other shall act on his behalf and subject to his control, and consent by the other so to act. Restatement (Second) of Agency § 1 (1958). In order to create an agency there must be an agreement, but not necessarily a contract between the parties. Restatement (Second) of Agency § 1, comment b (1958). An agreement may result in the creation of an agency relationship although the parties did not call it an agency and did not intend the legal consequences of the relation to follow. Id. The existence of the agency may be proved by circumstantial evidence which shows a course of dealing between the two parties. When an agency relationship is to be proven by circumstantial evidence, the principal must be shown to have consented to the agency since one cannot be the agent of another except by consent of the latter.

Cargill contends that the prerequisites of an agency relationship did not exist because Cargill never consented to the agency, Warren did not act on behalf of Cargill, and Cargill did not exercise control over Warren. We hold that all three elements of agency could be found in the particular circumstances of this case. By directing Warren to implement its recommendations, Cargill manifested its consent that Warren would be its agent. Warren acted on Cargill's behalf in procuring grain for Cargill as the part of its normal operations which were totally financed by Cargill. Further, an agency relationship was established by Cargill's interference with the internal affairs of Warren, which constituted de facto control of the elevator. * * *

A number of factors indicate Cargill's control over Warren, including the following:

(1) Cargill's constant recommendations to Warren by telephone;

(2) Cargill's right of first refusal on grain;

(3) Warren's inability to enter into mortgages, to purchase stock or to pay dividends without Cargill's approval;

(4) Cargill's right of entry onto Warren's premises to carry on periodic checks and audits;

(5) Cargill's correspondence and criticism regarding Warren's finances, officers salaries and inventory;

(6) Cargill's determination that Warren needed "strong paternal guidance";

(7) Provision of drafts and forms to Warren upon which Cargill's name was imprinted;

(8) Financing of all Warren's purchases of grain and operating expenses; and

(9) Cargill's power to discontinue the financing of Warren's operations.

We recognize that some of these elements, as Cargill contends, are found in an ordinary debtor-creditor relationship. However, these factors cannot be considered in isolation, but, rather, they must be viewed in light of all the circumstances surrounding Cargill's aggressive financing of Warren.

It is also Cargill's position that the relationship between Cargill and Warren was that of buyer-supplier rather than principal-agent. Restatement (Second) of Agency § 14K (1958) compares an agent with a supplier as follows:

One who contracts to acquire property from a third person and convey it to another is the agent of the other only if it is agreed that he is to act primarily for the benefit of the other and not for himself.

Factors indicating that one is a supplier, rather than an agent, are:

(1) That he is to receive a fixed price for the property irrespective of price paid by him. This is the most important. (2) That he acts in his own name and receives the title to the property which he thereafter is to transfer. (3) That he has an independent business in buying and selling similar property.

Restatement (Second) of Agency § 14K, Comment a (1958).

Under the Restatement approach, it must be shown that the supplier has an independent business before it can be concluded that he is not an agent. The record establishes that all portions of Warren's operation were financed by Cargill and that Warren sold almost all of its market grain to Cargill. Thus, the relationship which existed between the parties was not merely that of buyer and supplier.

A case analogous to the present one is Butler v. Bunge Corporation, 329 F.Supp. 47 (N.D.Miss.1971). In *Butler*, the plaintiff brought an action to recover the price of a soybean crop sold to an elevator that was operated by Bayles, a purported agent of the defendant Bunge Corporation. Bayles had agreed to operate a former Bunge elevator pursuant to an agreement in which Bayles was designated as manager. Although Bunge contended that Bayles was an independent contractor, the court determined that the elevator was an agent of Bunge.[8]

In this case, as in *Butler*, Cargill furnished substantially all funds received by the elevator. Cargill did have a right of entry on Warren's premises, and it, like Bunge, required maintenance of insurance against hazards of operation. Warren's activities, like Bayles' operations, formed a substantial part of Cargill's business that was developed in that area. In addition, Cargill did not think of Warren as an operator who was free to become Cargill's competitor, but rather conceded that it believed that Warren owed a duty of loyalty to Cargill. The decisions made by Warren were not independent of Cargill's interest or its control.

Further, we are not persuaded by the fact that Warren was not one of the "line" elevators that Cargill operated in its own name. The Warren operation, like the line elevator, was financially dependent on Cargill's continual infusion of capital. The arrangement with Warren presented a convenient alternative to the establishment of a line elevator. Cargill became, in essence, the owner of the operation without the accompanying legal indicia.

The amici curiae assert that, if the jury verdict is upheld, firms and banks which have provided business loans to county elevators will decline to make further loans. The decision in this case should give no cause for such concern. We deal here with a business enterprise markedly different from an ordinary bank financing, since Cargill was an active participant in Warren's operations rather than simply a financier. Cargill's course of dealing with Warren was, by its own admission, a paternalistic relationship in which Cargill made the key economic decisions and kept Warren in existence.

Although considerable interest was paid by Warren on the loan, the reason for Cargill's financing of Warren was not to make money as a lender but, rather, to establish a source of market grain for its business. As one Cargill manager noted, "We were staying in there because we

---

8. In Butler v. Bunge Corporation, 329 F.Supp. 47 (N.D.Miss.1971), the evidence revealed the following indicia of agency:

(1) Bunge furnished all or practically all of the means and appliances for the work; (2) Bunge furnished substantially all funds received by Bayles; (3) Bunge controlled the destination of all grain handled by Bayles; (4) Bunge controlled the price, weights and grades of all grain handled by Bayles; (5) Bunge, on certain occasions, permitted Bayles to sell a limited quantity of grain to other buyers; (6) Bunge not only had the right to direct details important to grain buying but gave actual direction to Bayles through constant contact, quoting its price to him and consulting with him regarding prices for the farmers; (7) Bunge had a significant degree of control over the operation of the grain elevator at Roundaway in such areas as training Bayles' personnel, inspecting the premises and requiring maintenance of insurance against hazards of operation; (8) Bayles' grain transaction with farmers was the identical type of business activity that was regularly carried on by Bunge, and Bayles' transactions formed a substantial part of Bunge's business that was developed from the area in which Coahoma Grain Elevator operated; and finally (9) although the agreement formally specified a fixed term, the relationship between the parties had no viability apart from grain dealings that were wholly subject to Bunge's will. These findings make clear that Bunge did not consider Bayles an independent operator who was free to become Bunge's competitor in buying grain from the farmers in the region, but rather that he was effectually given authority to buy grain from Bunge.

Id. at 61.

wanted the grain." For this reason, Cargill was willing to extend the credit line far beyond the amount originally allocated to Warren. It is noteworthy that Cargill was receiving significant amounts of grain and that, notwithstanding the risk that was recognized by Cargill, the operation was considered profitable.

On the whole, there was a unique fabric in the relationship between Cargill and Warren which varies from that found in normal debtor-creditor situations. We conclude that, on the facts of this case, there was sufficient evidence from which the jury could find that Cargill was the principal of Warren within the definitions of agency set forth in Restatement (Second) of Agency §§ 1 and 140. * * *

Affirmed.

NOTES

1. The *Cargill* case involved a de facto agency relationship, implied from the parties' conduct. Good planning dictates that such informal arrangements be avoided in favor of tightly drawn agency agreements. Careful planning, however, frequently yields to the exigencies of the situation and the reluctance to consult lawyers. Keep this point in mind when reading the *Martin v. Peyton* case in the partnership section of this chapter. There, lawyers carefully constructed the arrangement, and the outcome was quite different.

2. One theme raised by *Cargill* that continues throughout this course is the issue of the relationship between ownership and control. The court put a good deal of weight on the fact that Cargill exerted significant control over the day to day operations of Warren Grain & Seed. This is an equally important concept in partnership law.

3. Do you think the court's decision in *Cargill* was based on the law or was it simply result oriented? Since Cargill was a big grain company (a deep pocket) and the plaintiffs were small farmers, did that motivate the court to stretch the law to cover this situation? Banks and other creditors frequently lend money to businesses and impose controls that require borrowers to conduct their business in a way that will protect the lender. How do you draw the line between the controls that will subject the lender to unlimited liability for the debts of the borrower and those that do not?

4. Are you surprised that Cargill went as far as it did in lending money and exerting control over Warren? What was motivating Cargill? The answer may owe a bit to history. These events occurred in the midst of the "Great Grain Robbery" that occurred after President Richard Nixon authorized grain sales to the Soviet Union and China. Grain firms like Cargill then sold about 25 percent of America's grain harvest to the Soviet's, pushing up grain prices to unheard of levels ("beans in the teens") and having widespread effects on nearly every area of the economy. "It was one of those economic events ... that ... can truly be said to have changed the world." Dan Morgan, *Merchants of Grain* 121 (1979). Cargill badly needed grain to fulfill the contracts it made with the Soviet Union and other purchasers. It needed Warren's supplies, as well as those of other grain elevators.

B. FIDUCIARY OBLIGATIONS

As the definition of agency makes clear, an agent is a fiduciary. This means that an agent is held to extraordinarily high standards. The ordinary morals of the marketplace are not sufficient: "Not honesty alone, but the punctilio of an honor the most sensitive, is then the standard of behavior." Meinhard v. Salmon, 249 N.Y. 458, 164 N.E. 545, 546 (1928). These fiduciary duties fall into two basic categories: duty of care and duty of loyalty. A large part of this course is devoted to those obligations as they apply in the corporate context. These agency principles provide a brief introduction to these topics.

The duty of care is the counterpart of common law negligence. The duty of loyalty arises in several contexts. Here is a brief overview of some key rules.

    1.   Unless otherwise agreed, an agent is under a duty to act *solely* for the benefit of the principal. Restatement of Agency 2d, § 387. This translates into a duty of undivided loyalty.

    2.   Unless otherwise agreed, an agent may not deal with the principal as an adverse party (conflict of interest). Restatement of Agency 2d, § 389. See also § 390 (acting as adverse party with principal's consent).

    3.   Unless otherwise agreed, an agent who makes a profit while working for a principal is under a duty to give that profit to the principal. Restatement of Agency 2d, § 388. This obligation forms the basis of duties not to compete and duties not to appropriate opportunities belonging to the principal. *See* Meinhard v. Salmon, 249 N.Y. 458, 164 N.E. 545, 547–548 (1928); Guth v. Loft, Inc., 5 A.2d 503, 510–512 (Del.1939). A corollary of this rule forms the basis for the laws against insider trading; as explained below in the official comment in the Restatement of Agency 2d, this is important when considering insider trading:

> *Use of confidential information.* An agent who acquires confidential information in the course of his employment or in violation of his duties has a duty * * * to account for any profits made by the use of such information, although this does not harm the principal. * * * So, if [a corporate officer] has 'inside' information that the corporation is about to purchase or sell securities, or to declare or to pass a dividend, profits made by him in stock transactions undertaken because of his knowledge are held in constructive trust for the principal. * * *

Restatement of Agency 2d, § 388, Comment c. Note that each of the foregoing rules is subject to contractual modification.

As will become evident throughout this course, identifying someone as a fiduciary establishes that special duties exist; it does not give a brightline test as to the scope and breadth of those duties: "to say that a man is a fiduciary only begins analysis; it gives direction to further inquiry. To whom is he a fiduciary? What obligations does he owe as a fiduciary? In what respect has he failed to discharge these obligations? And what are the consequences of his deviation from duty?" Securities and Exchange Commission v. Chenery Corp., 318 U.S. 80, 85–86, 63 S.Ct. 454, 87 L.Ed. 626 (1943).

Notes

1.   An exception to the rule that agents must account to the principal for any profits received in the course of the agency relationship is the receipt of customary gratuities. Restatement of Agency 2d § 388, Comment b. This exception allows bartenders, waiters and other service personnel to retain tips from their customers. Sometimes, fine lines must be drawn, as when an employee receives large payments for activities arising from their agency relationship but not directly related to it. For example, a hostess at a restaurant meets an entrepreneur, and they become friends. The entrepreneur tips the hostess on a business opportunity, and the hostess makes a large profit. Does that profit belong to the restaurant?

2.   Because of the personal nature of the agency relationship and attending liabilities, the principal may terminate the agency relationship at any time, even if to do so would breach an employment contract with the agent. The principal will be liable for damages in such event, but the relationship will, nevertheless, be terminated. See generally Restatement of Agency 2d, ch. 5, Topic 1. Keep this concept in mind when studying corporate proxies in chapters 9 and 12.

3.   Agency is a two-way street. This means that third parties dealing with the agent will be bound to the principal. Restatement of Agency 2d, § 292. The third party may be bound to the principal even where the agency relationship or the identity of the principal is not disclosed. Restatement of Agency 2d, § 321 (partially disclosed principal) and § 322 (undisclosed principal). For the definitions of disclosed and undisclosed principals see Restatement of Agency 2d, § 4. An exception to this rule is that the third party will not be bound where the agent misrepresents that he or she is acting as such, and the third party would not have dealt with the principal if the principal's identity had been disclosed. Restatement of Agency 2d, § 304. The agent will also be liable on a contract where the identity of the principal is not disclosed. Restatement of Agency 2d, §§ 186 & 322. Otherwise, the agent generally is not liable for the principal's obligations. Restatement of Agency 2d, § 320. See e.g., Wishnow v. Kingsway Estates, Inc., 26 A.D.2d 61, 270 N.Y.S.2d 834 (1966) (president of company acting in representative capacity is not personally liable in contract). In contrast, with regard to tort liability, the fact that the principal is liable does not eliminate the agent/tortfeasor's personal liability. Restatement of Agency 2d, § 343. However, indemnification may come into play to hold the principal primarily liable. See e.g., Restatement of Agency 2d, § 216 (principal may be liable for the tortious acts of an agent even though the principal did not authorize the act causing injury).

4. An agent is liable to the principal for liabilities imposed on the principal where the agent acted without actual authority. Restatement of Agency 2d, § 430. Unless otherwise agreed, the principal in turn must indemnify the agent for expenses and other payments made by the agency where the agent is acting within the scope of the agency. Restatement of Agency 2d § 439.

C. AUTHORITY

The concept of authority determines which of an agent's acts fall within the ambit of the agency relationship so as to bind the principal. An agent's acts bind a principal only if the agent acts within the scope of his/her authority.

Actual authority (*express* or *implied*) runs from the principal to the agent. Restatement of Agency 2d, § 7. Actual authority can flow from a contract, title, job description, past course of dealing between principal and agent, etc. Restatement of Agency 2d, § 26. Actual authority may be express or implied. Express authority is a specific authorization of agency, while implied authority flows from an express grant. For example (unless expressly limited in the agency relationship), the title "cashier" at a bank carries with it certain implied authority, such as accepting checks and cash for deposit as agent for the bank.[1]

Apparent authority can exist in the absence of actual authority where the *principal* (not the agent), gives a third party reason to believe that actual authority exists. Restatement of Agency 2d, § 27 (apparent authority). Id. § 26 (actual authority). Apparent authority is analogous to the doctrine of estoppel, but agency by estoppel is not always coincident with apparent authority. Restatement of Agency 2d, § 8 Comment d and § 8B.

Ratification is the principal's after the fact approval of the agent's unauthorized act. Ratification may occur where the principal affirms the acts expressly or acts in a manner showing affirmation or acquiescence. Ratification binds the principal and relates back to the time of the unauthorized acts. Restatement of Agency 2d, § 82.

---

1. The Restatement of Agency 2d also speaks of "inherent" authority. This is a reference to the power of an employee to subject the master to liability for faulty conduct in performing the principal's business. Restatement of Agency 2d, § 8A. The use of this term is somewhat confusing since the Restatement 2d, § 7 comment c and § 8, comment c also use the terms implied and inferred authority that often accompany actual authority, *i.e.*, actual authority may imply some additional powers to carry out that express grant.

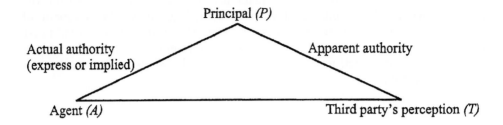

An agent cannot create his or her own apparent authority. The conduct and words of *agent vis a vis* a third party is not relevant unless the *principal* has acquiesced in the conduct, thus creating actual authority. Although an agent cannot create authority and thereby bind the principal, an agent who creates the impression of authority may be held accountable to the third party relying on this on the basis of estoppel or breach of warranty of authority.

In establishing apparent authority, one court observed:

> Apparent authority is essentially a question of fact. It depends not only on the nature of the contract involved, but the officer negotiating it, the corporation's usual manner of conducting business, the size of the corporation and the number of its stockholders, the circumstances that give rise to the contract, the reasonableness of the contract, the amounts involved, and who the contracting third party is, to list a few but not all of the relevant factors. In certain instances a given contract may be so important to the welfare of the corporation that outsiders would naturally suppose that only the board of directors (or even the shareholders) could properly handle it. It is in this light that the 'ordinary course of business' rule should be given its content. Beyond such 'extraordinary' acts, whether or not apparent authority exists is simply a matter of fact.

Lee v. Jenkins Brothers, 268 F.2d 357, 370 (2d Cir.), cert. denied, 361 U.S. 913, 80 S.Ct. 257, 4 L.Ed.2d 183 (1959).

D. VICARIOUS LIABILITY

One consequence of an agency relationship is that the principal is vicariously liable for the acts of the agent. To impose such liability, however, the plaintiff must show that the agent was acting within the scope of his or her agency. Restatement of Agency 2d, § 219. This is a simple rule, but it is often complex to apply. The Restatement of Agency 2d, § 229 provides some guidance, but generally liability must be determined on a case-by-case basis. Further, many businesses are structured so that services are contracted with entities or persons who are acting as "independent contractors," or as vendors or vendees, as was considered in the *Cargill* case. The courts must examine those relationships to determine if agency liability will apply. Restatement of Agency 2d § 2(3).

BUTLER v. McDONALD'S CORPORATION

110 F.Supp.2d 62 (D.R.I.2000).

LAGUEUX, DISTRICT JUDGE.

* * * For eleven years defendant has leased a restaurant building and premises at 6595 Post Road, North Kingstown, Rhode Island ("franchise restaurant") to James Cooper ("Cooper"). Defendant also has a license franchise agreement that allows Cooper to operate the business under the McDonald's name according to a variety of requirements and conditions typically found in franchise arrangements. It is undisputed that the employees working at the franchise restaurant are not employees of defendant but rather are employees of Cooper.

On or about July 25, 1997 plaintiff was a patron at the franchise restaurant. Plaintiff was in the company of other minors (young teens) who frequently visited this particular McDonald's restaurant and other "fast-food" establishments. Plaintiff and his companions were awaiting the arrival of Mr. Groves, father to one of the boys, for a ride back home. Plaintiff saw what he believed to be the Groves car in the parking lot and exited the south side door of the restaurant to inform Mr. Groves that the boys needed more time. After exiting plaintiff realized that he was mistaken—it was not the Groves car. Plaintiff turned to re-enter the restaurant. As plaintiff pushed against the door it shattered, resulting in injury to his right hand which has required two corrective surgeries and physical therapy.

Plaintiff, through his parents, filed this action on September 2, 1998 seeking damages. Plaintiff claims the injury was caused by the negligence of the franchise restaurant operator and/or his employees, but he seeks to hold defendant liable because of the nature of the relationship between defendant and the franchise restaurant.

Specifically, plaintiff alleges there was a "spider crack" in the glass portion of the door for a period of time exceeding two weeks, and that the franchise restaurant operator and/or his employees knew or should have known of this unsafe condition. As a result, plaintiff claims that the alleged unsafe condition should have been repaired, and that the failure to repair the alleged unsafe condition and the resultant structural weakness in the glass was the proximate cause of his injuries. * * *

Agency is " 'the fiduciary relation which results from the manifestation of consent by one person to another that the other shall act on behalf and subject to his control, and consent by the other so to act.' " *Toledo v. Van Waters & Rogers, Inc.,* 92 F.Supp.2d 44, 52 (D.R.I.2000)(citing *Lawrence v. Anheuser–Busch, Inc.,* 523 A.2d 864, 867 (R.I.1987)(quoting Restatement(Second) Agency § 1(1)(1958))). The Rhode Island Supreme Court has outlined three elements that must be shown in order for an agency relationship to exist: (1) the principal must manifest that the agent will act for him, (2) the agent must accept the undertaking, and (3) the parties must agree that the principal will be in control of the undertaking. *See Rosati v. Kuzman,* 660 A.2d 263, 265 (R.I.1995). *See also, Silvestri v. Pawtucket Mem'l Hosp.,* 1991 WL 789928 at *2 (R.I.Super.). "It is essential to the relationship that the principal have the right to control the work of the agent, and that the agent act primarily for the benefit of the principal." *Lawrence,* 523 A.2d at 867 (citing *Narragansett Wire Co. v. Norberg,* 118 R.I. 596, 376 A.2d 1, 5 (1977)). In contrast, an independent contractor relationship exists where one is retained to perform a task independent of and not subject to the control of the employer. *See Toledo,* 92 F.Supp.2d at 53 (citing *Webbier v. Thoroughbred Racing Protective Bureau, Inc.,* 105 R.I. 605, 254 A.2d 285, 289 (1969) and *McAlice v. Safeco Life Ins. Co.,* 1997 WL 839882 at*2 (R.I.Super.), *aff'd,* 741 A.2d 264 (R.I.1999)). Therefore, the key element of an agency relationship is the right of the principal to control the work of the agent. *See Lauro v. Knowles,* 739 A.2d 1183, 1185 (R.I.1999); *Rosati,* 660 A.2d at 265. The critical issue then in determining defendant's liability under an agency theory is whether defendant had the right to control the franchise restaurant operator's activities and operations. * * *

The strongest evidence put forward by defendant that an agency relationship does not exist is the franchise license agreement itself which explicitly states that no agency has been created thereby. However, a party cannot simply rely on statements in an agreement to establish or deny agency. *See Silvestri,* 1991 WL 789928 at *2. Rather, an agency relationship is essentially determined by examining whether there is a right of control of one party over another. *See id.* Further, defendant offers an affidavit from its Senior Corporate Attorney stating on behalf of defendant that defendant does not own, operate, or have a right to control the franchise restaurant.

Plaintiff claims that these representations are hollow since defendant maintains a right to control the operations and management of the franchise restaurant through operational and training manuals, a franchise license agreement, and an operator's lease and license agreement. Additionally, plaintiff claims defendant exercises a right to control through defendant's requirement that the restaurant conform to the McDonald's "comprehensive" system, the frequent and detailed inspections of the premises and its operations, the taking of profits, and the right of defendant to terminate the agreement for material breach.

Other courts have reached different conclusions as to whether these elements of a franchise agreement are sufficient to create an issue of fact regarding the existence of an agency relationship between a franchisor and a franchisee. For example, in *Hoffnagle v. McDonald's Corp.,* 522 N.W.2d 808, 809 (Iowa 1994), on which defendant relies, the Court examined the defendant's right to control the franchisee in the context of determining whether or not the defendant owed a duty of due care to an employee of the franchisee under the employer-independent contractor test contained in the Restatement (Second) of Torts Section 414. The Court, awarding summary judgment to the defendant franchisor, concluded that the defendant's "authority is no more than the authority to insure 'the uniformity and standardization of products and services offered by a [franchisor's] restaurant. [Such] obligations do not affect the control of daily operations.' " *Id.* at 814 (quoting *Little v. Howard Johnson Co.,* 183 Mich.App. 675, 455 N.W.2d 390, 394 (1990)). *See also Folsom v. Burger King,* 135 Wash.2d 658, 958 P.2d 301, 303 (1998).

However, in *Miller v. McDonald's Corp.,* 150 Or.App. 274, 945 P.2d 1107, 1111 (1997), the Court, in examining the existence vel non of an agency relationship between the franchisor and the franchisee, reached the opposite conclusion. The Court noted that the franchise agreement "did not simply set standards that [the franchisee] had to meet. Rather, it required [the franchisee] to use the precise methods that [the franchisor] established.... [The franchisor] enforced the use of those methods by regularly sending inspectors and by its retained power to cancel the [franchise agreement]." *Id.* The Court, denying the defendant franchisor's motion for summary judgment, concluded that such evidence would support a finding that the franchisor had a right to control the franchisee such that an agency relationship existed. *See id.*

The Rhode Island Supreme Court has outlined the indicia for the right to control in an agency relationship. Relevant examples include a principal's beneficial interest in the agent's undertaking, written agreements between the parties, and instructions given to the agent by the principal relating to how to conduct business. *See Baker v. ICA Mortgage Corp.,* 588 A.2d 616, 617 (R.I.1991); *Lawrence,* 523 A.2d at 867.

Because plaintiff has offered the aforesaid evidence to demonstrate defendant's requisite right to control the franchise restaurant, and because the Court finds the reasoning in *Miller* more persuasive than that in *Hoffnagle,* the Court concludes that a reasonable jury could find that an agency relationship exists and that defendant can be held vicariously liable. Therefore, on the issue of whether defendant can be held vicariously liable for the negligence of its franchised restaurant under an agency theory, summary judgment must be denied.

Since defendant's motion for summary judgment must be denied because there are disputed issues of fact as to whether the franchise restaurant operator is an agent of defendant, the Court does not need to address the applicability of the doctrine of apparent agency. However, since plaintiff will undoubtedly rely on that doctrine at trial, this Court should give the parties some guidance in that respect.

In Rhode Island the doctrine of apparent agency, sometimes called agency by estoppel or ostensible agency, was intended to provide recourse to third parties who justifiably contract under the belief that another is an agent of a principal and detrimentally suffer as a result of that reliance. *See Calenda v. Allstate Ins. Co.,* 518 A.2d 624, 628 (R.I.1986); *Petrone v. Davis,* 118 R.I. 261, 373 A.2d 485, 487 (1977). "The doctrine of apparent agency exists in order to allow third parties to depend on agents without investigating their agency before every single transaction." *Schock v. United States,* 56 F.Supp.2d 185, 193 (D.R.I.1999)(citing *Menard & Co. Masonry Bldg. Contractors v. Marshall Bldg. Sys. Inc.,* 539 A.2d 523, 526 (R.I.1988)). The doctrine also serves the purpose of promoting responsible business practices and protecting third party reliance on reasonable perceptions of a party's agency. *See id.* * * *

It is by no means clear that the Rhode Island Supreme Court will apply the doctrine of apparent agency to a franchisor/franchisee situation. But, if it did, clearly it would require the plaintiff to prove: (1) that the franchisor acted in a manner that would lead a reasonable person to conclude that the operator and/or employees of the franchise restaurant were employees or agents of the defendant; (2) that the plaintiff actually believed the operator and/or employees of the franchise restaurant were agents or servants of the franchisor; and (3) that the plaintiff thereby relied to his detriment upon the care and skill of the allegedly negligent operator and/or employees of the franchise restaurant.

Other jurisdictions have used similar criteria in applying the apparent agency doctrine to torts in a franchise situation. *See Crinkley v. Holiday Inns, Inc.,* 844 F.2d 156, 157 (4th Cir.1988)(apparent agency test applied to a hotel franchise relationship); *Gizzi v. Texaco, Inc.,* 437 F.2d 308, 309 (3d Cir.), *cert. denied* 404 U.S. 829, 92 S.Ct. 65, 30 L.Ed.2d 57 (1971) (apparent agency test applied to a gas station franchise relationship); *Miller,* 945 P.2d at 1112 (apparent agency test applied to the instant defendant in a similar franchise relationship); *Orlando Executive Park, Inc. v. P.D.R.,* 402 So.2d 442, 449 (Fla.Dist.Ct.App.1981) (apparent agency test applied to a hotel franchise relationship). These cases are instructive but by no means determinative as to what the Rhode Island Supreme Court would do in this case.

The first requirement, whether defendant acted in manner that would lead a reasonable person to conclude that the operator and/or employees of the franchise restaurant were employees or agents of the defendant, was discussed in *Miller.* In *Miller* the plaintiff sought damages for an injury she sustained when she bit into a sapphire stone contained in a sandwich. *See Miller,* 945 P.2d at 1108. The Court described examples of defendant's behavior that could lead a reasonable person to believe that the franchise restaurant was an agent of the defendant franchisor. These included all means and methods that would maintain an "image of uniformity" among all of defendant's restaurants, including "national advertising, common signs and uniforms, common menus, common appearance, and common standards." *Miller,* 945 P.2d at 1113. *Accord Crinkley,* 844 F.2d at 167; *Gizzi,* 437 F.2d at 310; *Orlando,* 402 So.2d at 449–450.

Plaintiff argues that defendant encourages third persons to think that they are dealing with defendant when they visit one of defendant's franchised restaurants. This belief stems from a customer's difficulty in differentiating between a restaurant that is corporate-owned from one which is franchised. Plaintiff points to defendant's national advertising campaign, highly visible logos throughout the restaurant and on food packaging, a requirement that the employees wear uniforms of designated color, design and other specifications, and volumes of required standards with respect to nearly all aspects of the franchise restaurant's maintenance, appearance, and operation. Seemingly, the purpose of defendant's mandatory procedures and requirements for the appearance and operation of franchised restaurants is to promote uniformity in both product and environment.

Certainly it is arguable that plaintiff, as well as any other customer of defendant's restaurants, would reasonably conclude that the restaurant is owned by defendant and operated by defendant's employees. Because plaintiff has produced enough evidence to support the view that a reasonable person would conclude that the operator and/or employees of the franchise restaurant were employees or agents of defendant, the question must be resolved by the jury.

Second, plaintiff has indicated that he simply went to the franchise restaurant because he and his friends wanted "McDonald's" food, as they had done on numerous occasions. Nowhere does plaintiff indicate that he did or could differentiate a franchised restaurant from a corporate-owned restaurant. Therefore, whether plaintiff actually believed that the franchise restaurant operator and/or his employees were agents of defendant is a question of fact best left for trial and resolution by the jury. * * *

NOTES

1. For other franchise cases finding an issue of fact as to whether there is agency liability on the part of the franchisor for acts of the franchisee see Drexel v. Union Prescription Centers, Inc., 582 F.2d 781 (3d Cir.1978) (applying Pennsylvania law); Singleton v. International Dairy Queen, 332 A.2d 160 (Del.Super.1975).

2. Would the analysis of agency liability be affected if the franchisor printed in its national advertising campaigns, including its Super Bowl commercials, a small trailer at the bottom of its advertisements saying that some restaurant locations are independently owned? Would apparent authority be further negated by a sign on the front door of the restaurant saying that it was an independent operation? Would many people notice such things or understand their import?

3. Would disclaimers of agency in advertisements affect the control analysis for imposing agency liability? As the court noted in the *Butler* case, the degree of control exercised over franchisees varies from franchise to franchise. Some franchisors may exert little control or only sell products to the franchise to be sold as the franchisee sees fit. Other franchisors exert close control over franchisees in order to maintain product or service quality. McDonalds, for example, closely controls almost every aspect of the franchise. Managers in the franchisees are even sent to McDonalds Hamburger University where they receive a Bachelor's degree in "Hamburgerology." Students

there are taught everything from how much ketchup to squirt on a hamburger to how to calibrate a grill in order to assure proper and uniform temperatures.

4. For the classic statement of the highly factual nature of questions relating to apparent authority, *see* the excerpt from *Lee v. Jenkins Brothers* at p. 38, above.

SECTION 2. PARTNERSHIP

There are a number of non-corporate forms of doing business. Aside from the sole proprietorship, the oldest is the partnership, which is recognized at common law and also by statute. As is the case with a sole proprietorship, the general partnership does not provide the owners with a limited liability shield in comparison with the corporate form, which does. The "limited partnership" allows limited liability for passive partners, provided certain conditions are met. In the last part of the twentieth century a legislative revolution occurred that recognized a totally new form of business–the limited liability company—and permitted limited liability partnerships. These limited liability entities are addressed in chapter 3. Because of the allure of limited liability to those who finance start-up businesses, the limited liability company and limited liability partnerships have become the form of choice–to a large extent even competing with the closely held corporation that is discussed in chapter 10 infra.

These developments in limited liability for unincorporated forms of business make the general partnership much less attractive as a choice for doing business. Nevertheless, because of the broad definition of partnership, inadvertent partnerships abound. Furthermore, the well-settled law regarding partnerships is likely to spill over to answer questions regarding limited liability companies and limited liability partnerships. Accordingly, partnership law remains an important part of the law of business organizations.

––––––

A. WHAT IS A PARTNERSHIP?

MARTIN v. PEYTON

246 N.Y. 213, 158 N.E. 77 (1927).

ANDREWS, J.

Much ancient learning as to partnership is obsolete. Today only those who are partners between themselves may be charged for partnership debts by others. There is one exception. Now and then a recovery is allowed where in truth such relationship is absent. This is because the debtor may not deny the claim.

Partnership results from contract, express or implied. If denied, it may be proved by the production of some written instrument, by testimony as to some conversation, by circumstantial evidence. If nothing else appears, the receipt by the defendant of a share of the profits of the business is enough.

Assuming some written contract between the parties, the question may arise whether it creates a partnership. If it be complete, if it expresses in good faith the full understanding and obligation of the parties, then it is for the court to say whether a partnership exists. It may, however, be a mere sham intended to hide the real relationship. Then other results follow. In passing upon it, effect is to be given to each provision. Mere words will not blind us to realities. Statements that no partnership is intended are not conclusive. If as a whole a contract contemplates an association of two or more persons to carry on as co-owners a business for profit, a partnership there is. On the other hand, if it be less than this, no partnership exists. Passing on the contract as a whole, an arrangement for sharing profits is to be considered. It is to be given its due weight. But it is to be weighed in connection with all the rest. It is not decisive. It may be merely the method adopted to pay a debt or wages, as interest on a loan or for other reasons.

An existing contract may be modified later by subsequent agreement, oral or written. A partnership may be so created where there was none before. And again, that the original agreement has been so modified may be proved by circumstantial evidence—by showing the conduct of the parties.

In the case before us the claim that the defendants became partners in the firm of Knauth, Nachod & Kuhne, doing business as bankers and brokers, depends upon the interpretation of certain instruments. There is nothing in their subsequent acts determinative of or indeed material upon this question. And we are relieved of questions that sometimes arise. 'The plaintiff's position is not,' we are told, 'that the agreements of June 4, 1921, were a false expression or incomplete expression of the intention of the parties. We say that they express defendants' intention and that that intention was to create a relationship which as a matter of law constitutes a partnership.' Nor may the claim of the plaintiff be rested on any question of estoppel. 'The plaintiff's claim,' he stipulates, 'is a claim of actual partnership, not of partnership by estoppel. . . .'

Remitted then, as we are, to the documents themselves, we refer to circumstances surrounding their execution only so far as is necessary to make them intelligible. And we are to remember that although the intention of the parties to avoid liability as partners is clear, although in language precise and definite they deny any design to then join the firm of K. N. & K.; although they say their interests in profits should be construed merely as a measure of compensation for loans, not an interest in profits as such; although they provide that they shall not be liable for any losses or treated as partners, the question still remains whether in fact they agree to so associate themselves with the firm as to 'carry on as co-owners a business for profit.'

In the spring of 1921 the firm of K. N. & K. found itself in financial difficulties. John R. Hall was one of the partners. He was a friend of Mr. Peyton. From him he obtained the loan of almost $500,000 of Liberty bonds, which K. N. & K. might use as collateral to secure bank advances. This, however, was not sufficient. The firm and its members had engaged in unwise speculations, and it was deeply involved. Mr. Hall was also intimately acquainted with George W. Perkins, Jr., and with Edward W. Freeman. He also knew Mrs. Peyton and Mrs. Perkins and Mrs. Freeman. All were anxious to help him. He therefore, representing K. N. & K., entered into negotiations with them. While they were pending a proposition was made that Mr. Peyton, Mr. Perkins, and Mr. Freeman, or some of them, should become partners. It met a decided refusal. Finally an agreement was reached. It is expressed in three documents, executed on the same day, all a part of the one transaction. They were drawn with care and are unambiguous. We shall refer to them as 'the agreement,' 'the indenture,' and 'the option.'

We have no doubt as to their general purpose. The respondents were to loan K. N. & K. $2,500,000 worth of liquid securities, which were to be returned to them on or before April 15, 1923. The firm might hypothecate them to secure loans totaling $2,000,000, using the proceeds as its business necessities required. To insure respondents against loss K. N. & K. were to turn over to them a large number of their own securities which may have been valuable, but which were of so speculative a nature that they could not be used as collateral for bank loans. In compensation for the loan the respondents were to receive 40 per cent. of the profits of the firm until the return was made, not exceeding, however, $500,000, and not less than $100,000. Merely because the transaction involved the transfer of securities and not of cash does not prevent its being a loan, within the meaning of [the statute]. The respondents also were given an option to join the firm if they, or any of them, expressed a desire to do so before June 4, 1923.

Many other detailed agreements are contained in the papers. Are they such as may be properly inserted to protect the lenders? Or do they go further? Whatever their purpose, did they in truth associate the respondents with the firm so that they and it together thereafter carried on as co-owners a business for profit? The answer depends upon an analysis of these various provisions.

As representing the lenders, Mr. Peyton and Mr. Freeman are called 'trustees.' The loaned securities when used as collateral are not to be mingled with other securities of K. N. & K., and the trustees at all times are to be kept informed of all transactions affecting them. To them shall be paid all dividends and income accruing therefrom. They may also substitute for any of the securities loaned securities of equal value. With their consent the firm may sell any of its securities held by the respondents, the proceeds to go, however, to the trustees. In other similar ways the trustees may deal with these same securities, but the securities loaned shall always be sufficient in value to permit of their hypothecation for

$2,000,000. If they rise in price, the excess may be withdrawn by the defendants. If they fall, they shall make good the deficiency.

So far, there is no hint that the transaction is not a loan of securities with a provision for compensation. Later a somewhat closer connection with the firm appears. Until the securities are returned, the directing management of the firm is to be in the hands of John R. Hall, and his life is to be insured for $1,000,000, and the policies are to be assigned as further collateral security to the trustees. These requirements are not unnatural. Hall was the one known and trusted by the defendants. Their acquaintance with the other members of the firm was of the slightest. These others had brought an old and established business to the verge of bankruptcy. As the respondents knew, they also had engaged in unsafe speculation. The respondents were about to loan $2,500,000 of good securities. As collateral they were to receive others of problematical value. What they required seems but ordinary caution. Nor does it imply an association in the business.

The trustees are to be kept advised as to the conduct of the business and consulted as to important matters. They may inspect the firm books and are entitled to any information they think important. Finally, they may veto any business they think highly speculative or injurious. Again we hold this but a proper precaution to safeguard the loan. The trustees may not initiate any transaction as a partner may do. They may not bind the firm by any action of their own. Under the circumstances the safety of the loan depended upon the business success of K. N. & K. This success was likely to be compromised by the inclination of its members to engage in speculation. No longer, if the respondents were to be protected, should it be allowed. The trustees therefore might prohibit it, and that their prohibition might be effective, information was to be furnished them. Not dissimilar agreements have been held proper to guard the interests of the lender.

As further security each member of K. N. & K. is to assign to the trustees their interest in the firm. No loan by the firm to any member is permitted and the amount each may draw is fixed. No other distribution of profits is to be made. So that realized profits may be calculated the existing capital is stated to be $700,000, and profits are to be realized as promptly as good business practice will permit. In case the trustees think this is not done, the question is left to them and to Mr. Hall, and if they differ then to an arbitrator. There is no obligation that the firm shall continue the business. It may dissolve at any time. Again we conclude there is nothing here not properly adapted to secure the interest of the respondents as lenders. If their compensation is dependent on a percentage of the profits, still provision must be made to define what these profits shall be.

The 'indenture' is substantially a mortgage of the collateral delivered by K. N. & K. to the trustees to secure the performance of the 'agreement.' It certainly does not strengthen the claim that the respondents were partners.

Finally we have the 'option.' It permits the respondents, or any of them, or their assignees or nominees to enter the firm at a later date if they desire to do so by buying 50 per cent. or less of the interests therein of all or any of the members at a stated price. Or a corporation may, if the respondents and the members agree, be formed in place of the firm. Meanwhile, apparently with the design of protecting the firm business against improper or ill-judged action which might render the option valueless, each member of the firm is to place his resignation in hands of Mr. Hall. If at any time he and the trustees agree that such resignation should be accepted, that member shall then retire, receiving the value of his interest calculated as of the date of such retirement.

This last provision is somewhat unusual, yet it is not enough in itself to show that on June 4, 1921, a present partnership was created, nor taking these various papers as a whole do we reach such a result. It is quite true that even if one or two or three like provisions contained in such a contract do not require this conclusion, yet it is also true that when taken together a point may come where stipulations immaterial separately cover so wide a field that we should hold a partnership exists. As in other branches of the law, a question of degree is often the determining factor. * * *

NOTES

1. Contrast the carefully constructed and documented arrangement in *Martin* with the situation in the *Cargill* case in Section 1 of this chapter. Why do you think liability was found in *Cargill* and not in *Martin*? In *Martin*, the arrangement was carefully structured by the lawyers to avoid the liabilities of Knauth, Nachod & Kuhne ("KNK") and to take advantage of that partnerships' profits, if Hall's efforts to revamp the firm were successful. No thought was given to such concerns in *Cargill*. Compare the results: In *Cargill*, the defendant was exposed to unlimited liability. In *Martin*, not only was no such liability imposed, but the defendants were even able to keep the illiquid securities given as collateral for their loan. At that time, the market was recovering from the downturn that apparently caused KNK and others to fail.[2] Perhaps, that recovery and the ensuing market run up even allowed the defendants in *Martin* to recover all or most of their investment. In any event, they were not personally liable for all of the debts of KNK, while Cargill was the subject of such liability for the debts of Warren Grain & Seed Co.

2. The court in Meinhard v. Salmon, page 52 below, describes the arrangement in that case as a joint venture. A joint venture is an *ad hoc*, one-

---

2. Among the firms bankrupted during that downturn was the haberdashery that future president Harry Truman had started with another partner. His firm operated as a partnership for a time and then incorporated before failing. Truman remained liable on the debts contracted while the firm was a partnership and for other obligations he had signed personally for after incorporation. It took Truman fifteen years to settle those debts. Richard Lawrence Miller, *Truman, The Rise to Power* 162–163 (1986).

shot partnership. It is generally limited to a specific undertaking (rather than to an entire business). Note, however, that a joint venture will meet the definition of partnership under both the statute and common law principles. While there is some scattered dictum in a few cases that suggest some different rules may apply to joint ventures. The overwhelming weight of authority is to the contrary, viewing "joint venture" as merely a description of one variety of partnership.

PEED v. PEED

72 N.C.App. 549, 325 S.E.2d 275 (1985),
cert. denied, 313 N.C. 604, 330 S.E.2d 612 (1985).

ARNOLD, JUDGE.

The plaintiff contends that the trial court erred by granting the defendant's motion for a directed verdict on the issue of whether or not the plaintiff and defendant were partners. * * *

Under the North Carolina Uniform Partnership Act, a "partnership" is defined as "an association of two or more persons to carry on as co-owners a business for profit." G.S. 59–36(a). The statute, G.S. 59–37, sets out factors to be considered in determining whether a partnership exists:

(2) Joint tenancy, tenancy in common, tenancy by the entireties, joint property, common property, or part ownership does not of itself establish a partnership, whether such co-owners do or do not share any profits made by the use of the property.

(3) The sharing of gross returns does not of itself establish a partnership, whether or not the persons sharing them have a joint or common right or interest in any property from which the returns are derived.

(4) The receipt by a person of a share of the profits of a business is prima facie evidence that he is a partner in the business, but no such inference shall be drawn if such profits were received in payment:

    a. As a debt by installments or otherwise,

    b. As wages of an employee or rent to a landlord,

    c. As an annuity to a widow or representative of a deceased partner,

    d. As interest on a loan, though the amount of payment vary with the profits of the business,

    e. As the consideration for the sale of a goodwill of a business or other property by installments or otherwise.

Thus, for example, if a person merely makes repayable advances and loans of money to another, it cannot be inferred from that fact that they are partners. *McGurk v. Moore,* 234 N.C. 248, 253, 67 S.E.2d 53, 56 (1951). Further, if one person is an employee of another, and receives wages, then the two are not partners. *Williams v. Biscuitville, Inc.,* 40

N.C.App. 405, 253 S.E.2d 18 (1979), *disc. rev. denied,* 297 N.C. 457, 256 S.E.2d 810 (1979).

We stress that the determination of whether a partnership exists, and whether the parties are co-owners, involves examining all the circumstances. As the court in *Eggleston v. Eggleston,* 228 N.C. 668, 47 S.E.2d 243 (1948), wrote:

> "Partnership is a legal concept but the determination of the existence or not of a partnership, as in the case of a trust, involves inferences drawn from an analysis of 'all the circumstances attendant on its creation and operation,' " [citations omitted].

> Not only may a partnership be formed orally, but "it may be created by the agreement or conduct of the parties, either express or implied," [citations omitted].... "A voluntary association of partners may be shown without proving an express agreement to form a partnership; and a finding of its existence may be based upon a rational consideration of the acts and declarations of the parties, warranting the inference that the parties understood that they were partners and acted as such." [Citation omitted].

228 N.C. at 674, 47 S.E.2d at 247, *quoted in Reddington v. Thomas,* 45 N.C.App. 236, 240, 262 S.E.2d 841, 843 (1980).

Considering all the evidence in the light most favorable to the plaintiff, we find that the plaintiff did present evidence sufficient to carry the matter of partnership to the jury. The plaintiff testified that she and the defendant conducted the farming operation together. At the time of their marriage, both were employed off the farm, and used their earnings to pay farm expenses. Plaintiff brought her savings of around $3,000 into the marriage, and invested that into the farming operation. The farm was in considerable debt at the time the Peeds were married. Plaintiff testified that she discussed the finances of the farm with her husband, saying that she was not going to continue putting her earnings into the farm and signing notes, when she had no part of it, and received no share of the profits.

Plaintiff testified further that she and defendant reached an agreement that they would become partners in the dairy, that the dairy cows would be registered in both their names, and that the title of the farm would be changed to contain both their names. Defendant quit his public job in 1958 to devote more time to the farm. Plaintiff testified that they discussed from time to time the progress of the farm, and farm purchases, that plaintiff went to the farm almost daily, and that she wrote checks on a joint account kept for the dairy farm. She testified that she and her husband, although separated, discussed the need to sell the dairy cattle, and the price of sale. Plaintiff testified that she did not know whether she and defendant filed a partnership income tax return, and that income tax matters were handled by defendant and accountants.

Defendant testified that he changed the registration of the cows to contain both his and plaintiff's names because the plaintiff had said that if she were the owner, the defendant's family could not take them if something happened to defendant. Defendant also testified that he changed the registration not so much to protect plaintiff, as to stop her from talking to him about it each day. Yet, defendant also testified that the joint registration showed that both he and plaintiff were owners of the cows. He testified that he changed the deeds of the land on which the dairy was operated to add plaintiff's name. Defendant testified that plaintiff did not have much time to work on the farm, with her job at Liggett & Myers; that her earnings from Liggett & Myers were spent on groceries and clothes; and that his wife could have signed notes in the dairy operation back through the years, although he had difficulty remembering. Finally, defendant testified that the money from sale of the cows was his, although he admitted that the cows were bought partly through the sale of milk produced by cows owned by him and plaintiff.

Considering this evidence in the light most favorable to the plaintiff, and therefore believing plaintiff's testimony as true, we find that a jury could infer from the registration of the cattle, the financing of the dairy operation, plaintiff's description of her conversations with defendant, concerning a partnership arrangement, and of her contribution of time and money to the dairy operation that a partnership, an association of two or more persons to carry on as co-owners a business for profit, existed. The evidence was sufficient to produce a question for the jury, and we therefore hold that the trial judge's grant of a directed verdict against plaintiff on the partnership issue was reversible error.

We note that while the registration certificates do not give title, nonetheless, they are evidence of ownership. Indeed, the defendant conceded that by changing the certificates he made himself and his wife co-owners.

Further, we reject defendant's argument that the jury's finding that the parties were not co-owners of the dairy herd made the judge's error on the directed verdict harmless. The partnership statute provides that a partnership is an association of persons as *co-owners of a business.* The fact that one partner owns certain property in the business, or provides the capital, while the other performs certain services, does not mean that they are not co-owners of the *business. Southern Fertilizer Co. v. Reames,* 105 N.C. 283, 11 S.E. 467 (1890). The plaintiff testified that she told her husband that since she contributed her money to the dairy expenses and debts, she wished to have a part in the operation and a share of the profits. He agreed that they would become partners, that the dairy cows would be re-registered in both their names, and that title to the farm would be changed to both their names. The plaintiff contributed considerable money to the operation as well as her time in managing and doing bookkeeping. Even if the defendant were sole owner of the herd, the plaintiff's testimony provides evidence of an agreement which gave her an interest in the operation and a share of the profits, as well as evidence of her contribution in money and effort to the business. This was sufficient as a matter of law to take the issue to the jury. * * *

We remand for retrial upon amended pleadings.

NOTES

1.   See also Tarnavsky v. Tarnavsky, 147 F.3d 674 (8th Cir.1998) (partnership in ranching operation found under North Dakota law among brothers); Cleland v. Thirion, 268 A.D.2d 842, 704 N.Y.S.2d 316 (3d Dept.2000) (live-in-lover of artisan glassblower did not become partner in his business even though she assisted in business and provided loans); Zajac v. Harris, 241 Ark. 737, 410 S.W.2d 593 (1967) (partnership found from course of dealings). Another side to the inadvertent partnership issue is a claim that seeks to hold individuals personally liable for the operations of a business. See Lane v. Spragg, 224 Ga.App. 606, 481 S.E.2d 592 (1997) (father held not to be partner in son's horse farm and, therefore, not responsible for its debts); Hines v. Arnold, 103 N.C.App. 31, 404 S.E.2d 179 (1991) (issue of fact existed as to whether wife was a partner in her husband's commercial fishing business and personally liable on a ship mortgage note that he signed); Bradson Mercantile, Inc. v. Vanderbilt Industrial Contracting Corp., 883 F.Supp. 37 (W.D.N.C. 1995) (issue of fact existed as whether wife of a corporate officer became a partner of his corporations and personally liable where she participated in corporate activities). These cases illustrate the dangers of informal business arrangements. How can the parties protect themselves from such concerns?

2.   Another issue is whether co-tenants in real property should be treated as partners. See generally Johnson v. Wiley, 613 N.E.2d 446 (Ind.App. 1993) (joint tenancy in property does not itself create a partnership but sharing profits from property is *prima facie* evidence of partnership); Bickhardt v. Ratner, 871 F.Supp. 613, 620 (S.D.N.Y.1994) (part ownership of property does not establish a partnership whether such co-owners do or do not share any profits made from use of the property).

B.   FIDUCIARY OBLIGATIONS

MEINHARD v. SALMON

249 N.Y. 458, 164 N.E. 545 (1928).

CARDOZO, C. J.

On April 10, 1902, Louisa M. Gerry leased to the defendant Walter J. Salmon the premises known as the Hotel Bristol at the northwest corner of Forty–Second street and Fifth avenue in the city of New York. The lease was for a term of 20 years, commencing May 1, 1902, and ending April 30, 1922. The lessee undertook to change the hotel building for use as shops and offices at a cost of $200,000. Alterations and additions were to be accretions to the land.

Salmon, while in course of treaty with the lessor as to the execution of the lease, was in course of treaty with Meinhard, the plaintiff, for the necessary funds. The result was a joint venture with terms embodied in a writing. Meinhard was to pay to Salmon half of the moneys requisite to reconstruct, alter, manage, and operate the property. Salmon was to pay to Meinhard 40 per cent. of the net profits for the first five years of the lease and 50 per cent. for the years thereafter. If there were losses, each party was to bear them equally. Salmon, however, was to have sole power to 'manage, lease, underlet and operate' the building. There were to be certain pre-emptive rights for each in the contingency of death.

The two were coadventurers, subject to fiduciary duties akin to those of partners. As to this we are all agreed. The heavier weight of duty rested, however, upon Salmon. He was a coadventurer with Meinhard, but he was manager as well. During the early years of the enterprise, the building, reconstructed, was operated at a loss. If the relation had then ended, Meinhard as well as Salmon would have carried a heavy burden. Later the profits became large with the result that for each of the investors there came a rich return. For each the venture had its phases of fair weather and of foul. The two were in it jointly, for better or for worse.

When the lease was near its end, Elbridge T. Gerry had become the owner of the reversion. He owned much other property in the neighborhood, one lot adjoining the Bristol building on Fifth avenue and four lots on Forty–Second street. He had a plan to lease the entire tract for a long term to some one who would destroy the buildings then existing and put up another in their place. In the latter part of 1921, he submitted such a project to several capitalists and dealers. He was unable to carry it through with any of them. Then, in January, 1922, with less than four months of the lease to run, he approached the defendant Salmon. The result was a new lease to the Midpoint Realty Company, which is owned and controlled by Salmon, a lease covering the whole tract, and involving a huge outlay. The term is to be 20 years, but successive covenants for renewal will extend it to a maximum of 80 years at the will of either party. The existing buildings may remain unchanged for seven years. They are then to be torn down, and a new building to cost $3,000,000 is to be placed upon the site. The rental, which under the Bristol lease was only $55,000, is to be from $350,000 to $475,000 for the properties so combined. Salmon personally guaranteed the performance by the lessee of the covenants of the new lease until such time as the new building had been completed and fully paid for.

The lease between Gerry and the Midpoint Realty Company was signed and delivered on January 25, 1922. Salmon had not told Meinhard anything about it. Whatever his motive may have been, he had kept the negotiations to himself. Meinhard was not informed even of the bare existence of a project. The first that he knew of it was in February, when the lease was an accomplished fact. He then made demand on the defendants that the lease be held in trust as an asset of the venture, making offer upon the trial to share the personal obligations incidental to the guaranty. The demand was followed by refusal, and later by this suit. A referee gave judgment for the plaintiff, limiting the plaintiff's interest in the lease, however, to 25 per cent. The limitation was on the theory that the plaintiff's equity was to be restricted to one-half of so much of the value of the lease as was contributed or represented by the occupation of the Bristol site. Upon cross-appeals to the Appellate Division, the judgment was modified so as to enlarge the equitable interest to one-half of the whole lease. With this enlargement of plaintiff's interest, there went, of course, a corresponding enlargement of his attendant obligations. The case is now here on an appeal by the defendants.

Joint adventurers, like copartners, owe to one another, while the enterprise continues, the duty of the finest loyalty. Many forms of conduct permissible in a workaday world for those acting at arm's length, are forbidden to those bound by fiduciary ties. A trustee is held to something stricter than the morals of the market place. Not honesty alone, but the punctilio of an honor the most sensitive, is then the standard of behavior. As to this there has developed a tradition that is unbending and inveterate. Uncompromising rigidity has been the attitude of courts of equity when petitioned to undermine the rule of undivided loyalty by the 'disintegrating erosion' of particular exceptions. Only thus has the level of conduct for fiduciaries been kept at a level higher than that trodden by the crowd. It will not consciously be lowered by any judgment of this court.

The owner of the reversion, Mr. Gerry, had vainly striven to find a tenant who would favor his ambitious scheme of demolition and construction. Baffled in the search, he turned to the defendant Salmon in possession of the Bristol, the keystone of the project. He figured to himself beyond a doubt that the man in possession would prove a likely customer. To the eye of an observer, Salmon held the lease as owner in his own right, for himself and no one else. In fact he held it as a fiduciary, for himself and another, sharers in a common venture. If this fact had been proclaimed, if the lease by its terms had run in favor of a partnership, Mr. Gerry, we may fairly assume, would have laid before the partners, and not merely before one of them, his plan of reconstruction. The pre-emptive privilege, or, better, the pre-emptive opportunity, that was thus an incident of the enterprise, Salmon appropriate to himself in secrecy and silence. He might have warned Meinhard that the plan had been submitted, and that either would be free to compete for the award. If he had done this, we do not need to say whether he would have been under a duty, if successful in the competition, to hold the lease so acquired for the benefit of a venture then about to end, and thus prolong by indirection its responsibilities and duties. The trouble about his conduct is that he excluded his coadventurer from any chance to compete, from any chance to enjoy the opportunity for benefit that had come to him alone by virtue of his agency. This chance, if nothing more, he was under a duty to concede. The price of its denial is an extension of the trust at the option and for the benefit of the one whom he excluded.

No answer is it to say that the chance would have been of little value even if seasonably offered. Such a calculus of probabilities is beyond the science of the chancery. Salmon, the real estate operator, might have been preferred to Meinhard, the woolen merchant. On the other hand, Meinhard might have offered better terms, or reinforced his offer by alliance with the wealth of others. Perhaps he might even have persuaded the lessor to renew the Bristol lease alone, postponing for a time, in return for higher rentals, the improvement of adjoining lots. We know that even under the lease as made the time for the enlargement of the building was delayed for seven years. All these opportunities were cut away from him through another's intervention. He knew that Salmon was the manager. As the time drew near for the expiration of the lease, he would naturally assume from silence, if from nothing else, that the lessor was willing to extend it for a term of years, or at least to let it stand as a lease from year to year. Not impossibly the lessor would have done so, whatever his protestations of unwillingness, if Salmon had not given assent to a project more attractive. At all events, notice of termination, even if not necessary, might seem, not unreasonably, to be something to be looked for, if the business was over and another tenant was to enter. In the absence of such notice, the matter of an extension was one that would naturally be attended to by the manager of the enterprise, and not neglected altogether. At least, there was nothing in the situation to give warning to any one that while the lease was still in being, there had come to the manager an offer of extension which he had locked within his breast to be utilized by himself alone. The very fact that Salmon was in control with exclusive powers of direction charged him the more obviously with the duty of disclosure, since only through disclosure could opportunity be equalized. If he might cut off renewal by a purchase for his own benefit when four months were to pass before the lease would have an end, he might do so with equal right while there remained as many years. He might steal a march on his comrade under cover of the darkness, and then hold the captured ground. Loyalty and comradeship are not so easily abjured.

Little profit will come from a dissection of the precedents. None precisely similar is cited in the briefs of counsel. What is similar in many, or so it seems to us, is the animating principle. Authority is, of course, abundant that one partner may not appropriate to his own use a renewal of a lease, though its term is to begin at the expiration of the partnership. The lease at hand with its many changes is not strictly a renewal. Even so, the standard of loyalty for those in trust relations is without the fixed divisions of a graduated scale. . . . Equity refuses to confine within the bounds of classified transactions its precept of a loyalty that is undivided and unselfish. Certain at least it is that a 'man obtaining his locus standi, and his opportunity for making such arrangements, by the position he occupies as a partner, is bound by his obligation to his copartners in such dealings not to separate his interest from theirs, but, if he acquires any benefit, to communicate it to them.' Certain it is also that there may be no abuse of special opportunities growing out of a special trust as manager or agent. If conflicting inferences are possible as to abuse or opportunity, the trier of the facts must make the choice between them ... A constructive trust is, then, the remedial device through which preference of self is made subordinate to loyalty to others. * * *

We have no thought to hold that Salmon was guilty of a conscious purpose to defraud. Very likely he assumed in all good faith that with the approaching end of the venture he might ignore his coadventurer and take the extension for himself. He had given to the enterprise time and labor as well as money. He had made it a success. Meinhard, who had given money, but neither time nor labor, had already been richly paid. There might seem to be something grasping in his insistence upon more. Such recriminations are not unusual when coadventurers fall out. They are not without their force if conduct is to be judged by the common standards of competitors. That is not to say that they have pertinency here. Salmon had put himself in a position in which thought of self was to be renounced, however hard the abnegation. He was much more than a coadventurer. He was a managing coadventurer. For him and for those like him the rule of undivided loyalty is relentless and supreme. A different question would be here if there were lacking any nexus of relation between the business conducted by the manager and the opportunity brought to him as an incident of management. For this problem, as for most, there are distinctions of degree. If Salmon had received from Gerry a proposition to lease a building at a location far removed, he might have held for himself the privilege thus acquired, or so we shall assume. Here the subject-matter of the new lease was an extension and enlargement of the subject-matter of the old one. A managing coadventurer appropriating the benefit of such a lease without warning to his partner might fairly expect to be reproached with conduct that was underhand, or lacking, to say the least, in reasonable candor, if the partner were to surprise him in the act of signing the new instrument. Conduct subject to that reproach does not receive from equity a healing benediction. * * *

The judgment should be modified by providing that at the option of the defendant Salmon there may be substituted for a trust attaching to the lease a trust attaching to the shares of stock, with the result that one-half of such shares together with one additional share will in that event be allotted to the defendant Salmon and the other shares to the plaintiff, and as so modified the judgment should be affirmed with costs.

ANDREWS, J., DISSENTED, joined by KELLOGG and O'BRIEN, JJ.

NOTES

1. This classic and frequently cited case is analogous to the corporate opportunity doctrine that is discussed in chapter 8.

2. The decision in *Meinhard* was not without controversy. The court was itself split: 4–3. The modern "contractual" approach to business relations also charges that the imposition of such fiduciary duties is really an effort by

the courts to guess what the parties would have done had they thought to address the problem in a contract before the issue arose. The courts, however, may not be suited to make such guesses. Law and economic scholars view "the corporation as a nexus of contracts, [and] treats common law and state statutory provisions as implied terms of a contract by which both managers and shareholders seek to reduce the agency costs associated with centralized management." This contract model "does not treat fiduciary rules as the primary tool for reducing agency costs because they require costly judicial intervention." Dennis Honabach & Roger Dennis, The Seventh Circuit and the Market for Corporate Control, 65 Chi.-Kent L. Rev. 681, 687 (1989). In Jordan v. Duff and Phelps, Inc., 815 F.2d 429 (7th Cir.1987), cert. dismissed, 485 U.S. 901, 108 S.Ct. 1067, 99 L.Ed.2d 229 (1988), the court noted that:

> Because the fiduciary duty is a standby or off-the-rack guess about what parties would agree to if they dickered about the subject explicitly, parties may contract with greater specificity for other arrangements. It is a violation of duty to steal from the corporate treasury; it is not a violation to write oneself a check that the board has approved as a bonus.

Id. at 436. *Compare* Gotham Partners, L.P. v. Hallwood Realty Partners, L.P., 817 A.2d 160, (Del.2002):

> We refer to one aspect of the Vice Chancellor's discussion of the Delaware Revised Uniform Limited Partnership Act ("DRULPA") in his summary judgment opinion in this case where he stated that section 17–1101(d)(2) "expressly authorizes the *elimination,* modification or enhancement of . . . fiduciary duties in the written agreement governing the limited partnership." It is at least the second time the Court of Chancery has stated in dicta that DRULPA at 6 *Del. C.* § 17–1101(d)(2) permits a limited partnership agreement to *eliminate* fiduciary duties.

> Because the Vice Chancellor's summary judgment order in this matter has not been appealed, his opinion on this point is not before us for review on this appeal. In our view, however, this dictum should not be ignored because it could be misinterpreted in future cases as a correct rule of law. Accordingly, in the interest of avoiding the perpetuation of a questionable statutory interpretation that could be relied upon adversely by courts, commentators and practitioners in the future, we are constrained to draw attention to the statutory language and the underlying general principle in our jurisprudence that scrupulous adherence to fiduciary duties is normally expected.

3. Do you think Meinhard had some responsibility to protect himself? Would a reasonable person in Meinhard's position have assumed that Salmon would extend the joint venture when Meinhard was contributing little to the enterprise? Would not a reasonable person be asking his partner what they were going to do when the partnership terminated in just a few months? After all, this is a business enterprise with a specific term. Meinhard was a business partner, not a ward of Salmon's. What would have happened if Salmon was approached by the new owner one day or one hour after the joint venture with Meinhard ended? Was this still an opportunity of the joint venture? What if the approach was two years later?

4. For those interested in psychology and the law, Benjamin Cardozo, the author of the *Meinhard* opinion, became famous as a jurist for imposing high fiduciary duties in business law cases and was later elevated to the Supreme Court of the United States. His father, however, was removed from the New York bench after assisting the worst of the nineteenth century Robber Barons in looting corporations and manipulating stock and commodity prices. I Jerry W. Markham, *A Financial History of the United States, From Christopher Columbus to the Robber Barons (1492–1900)* 259, 274–275 (2001).

5. Limited partnership interests do not create the same fiduciary duties that exist in a general partnership. However, even in a limited partnership, some fiduciary duties may exist. *See* Red River Wings, Inc. v. Hoot, Inc., 751 N.W.2d 206, 2008 N.D. 117 (2008), page 83, below.

––––––

C. PARTNERS' AUTHORITY AND GOVERNANCE

UPA § 9 and RUPA § 301 both provide that a partner is an agent of the partnership and has the authority to bind the partnership and copartners when acting in the ordinary course of business. Acts not in the ordinary course of business must be specifically authorized by the other partners. Under RUPA § 401(j) a difference arising as to a matter in the ordinary course of business of a partnership may be decided by a majority of the partners. An act outside the ordinary course of business of a partnership and an amendment to the partnership agreement may be taken only with the consent of all of the partners. UPA § 18(h) is to the same effect. Any difference arising as to ordinary matters connected with the partnership business may be decided by a majority of the partners; but no act in contravention of any agreement between the partners may be done rightfully without the consent of all the partners.

SUMMERS v. DOOLEY

94 Idaho 87, 481 P.2d 318 (1971).

DONALDSON, JUSTICE.

This lawsuit, tried in the district court, involves a claim by one partner against the other for $6,000. The complaining partner asserts that he has been required to pay out more than $11,000 in expenses without any reimbursement from either the partnership funds or his partner. The expenditure in question was incurred by the complaining partner (John Summers, plaintiff-appellant) for the purpose of hiring an additional employee. The trial court denied him any relief except for ordering that he be entitled to one half $966.72 which it found to be a legitimate partnership expense.

The pertinent facts leading to this lawsuit are as follows. Summers entered a partnership agreement with Dooley (defendant-respondent) in 1958 for the purpose of operating a trash collection business. The business was operated by the two men and when either was unable to work, the non-working partner provided a replacement at his own expense. In 1962, Dooley became unable to work and, at his own expense, hired an employee to take his place. In July, 1966, Summers approached his partner Dooley regarding the hiring of an additional employee but Dooley refused. Nevertheless, on his own initiative, Summers hired the man and paid him out of his own pocket. Dooley, upon discovering that Summers had hired an additional man, objected, stating that he did not feel additional labor was necessary and refused to pay for the new employee out of the partnership funds. Summers continued to operate the business using the third man and in October of 1967 instituted suit in the district court for $6,000 against his partner, the gravamen of the complaint being that Summers has been required to pay out more than $11,000 in expenses, incurred in the hiring of the additional man, without any reimbursement from either the partnership funds or his partner. After trial before the court, sitting without a jury, Summers was granted only partial relief[1] and he has appealed. He urges in essence that the trial court erred by failing to conclude that he should be reimbursed for expenses and costs connected in the employment of extra help in the partnership business.

The principal thrust of appellant's contention is that in spite of the fact that one of the two partners refused to consent to the hiring of additional help, nonetheless, the non-consenting partner retained profits earned by the labors of the third man and therefore the non-consenting partner should be stopped from denying the need and value of the employee, and has by his behavior ratified the act of the other partner who hired the additional man.

The issue presented for decision by this appeal is whether an equal partner in a two man partnership has the authority to hire a new employee in disregard of the objection of the other partner and then attempt to charge the dissenting partner with the costs incurred as a result of his unilateral decision. * * *

In the instant case the record indicates that although Summers requested his partner Dooley to agree to the hiring of a third man, such requests were not honored. In fact Dooley made it clear that he was 'voting no' with regard to the hiring of an additional employee.

An application of the relevant statutory provisions and pertinent case law to the factual situation presented by the instant case indicates that the trial court was correct in its disposal of the issue since a majority of the partners did not consent to the hiring of the third man. I.C. § 53–318(8) provides:

> 'Any difference arising as to ordinary matters connected with the partnership business may be decided by a majority of the partners * * *.' (emphasis supplied)

* * *

---

1. The trial court did award Summers one half of $966.72 which it found to be a legitimate partnership expense.

The intent of the legislature may be implied from the language used, or inferred on grounds of policy or reasonableness. A careful reading of the statutory provision indicates that subsection 5 bestows equal rights in the management and conduct of the partnership business upon all of the partners.[4] The concept of equality between partners with respect to management of business affairs is a central theme and recurs throughout the Uniform Partnership law, which has been enacted in this jurisdiction. Thus the only reasonable interpretation of I.C. § 53–318(8) is that business differences must be decided by a majority of the partners provided no other agreement between the partners speaks to the issues. * * *

In the case at bar one of the partners continually voiced objection to the hiring of the third man. He did not sit idly by and acquiesce in the actions of his partner. Under these circumstances it is manifestly unjust to permit recovery of an expense which was incurred individually and not for the benefit of the partnership but rather for the benefit of one partner.

Judgment affirmed.[a]

NATIONAL BISCUIT COMPANY, INC. v. STROUD

249 N.C. 467, 106 S.E.2d 692 (1959).

[National Biscuit Company sued C. N. Stroud and Earl Freeman, a partnership trading as Stroud's Food Center, for the nonpayment of $171.04 for goods sold and delivered. Stroud appealed the judgment for plaintiff.]

PARKER, JUSTICE.

C.N. Stroud and Earl Freeman entered into a general partnership to sell groceries under the firm name of Stroud's Food Center. There is nothing in the agreed statement of facts to indicate or suggest that Freeman's power and authority as a general partner were in any way restricted or limited by the articles of partnership in respect to the ordinary and legitimate business of the partnership. Certainly, the purchase and sale of bread were ordinary and legitimate business of Stroud's Food Center during its continuance as a going concern.

Several months prior to February 1956 Stroud advised plaintiff that he personally would not be responsible for any additional bread sold by plaintiff to Stroud's Food Center. After such notice to plaintiff, it from 6 February 1956 to 25 February 1956, at the request of Freeman, sold and delivered bread in the amount of $171.04 to Stroud's Food Center.

In Johnson v. Bernheim, 76 N.C. 139, this Court said: 'A and B are general partners to do some given business; the partnership is, by opera-

---

4. In the absence of an agreement to the contrary. In the case at bar, there is no such agreement....

a. *Accord* Covalt v. High, 675 P.2d 999 (N.M.App.1983).

tion of law, a power to each to bind the partnership in any manner legitimate to the business. If one partner goes to a third person to buy an article on time for the partnership, the other partner cannot prevent it by writing to the third person not to sell to him on time; or, if one party attempts to buy for cash, the other has no right to require that it shall be on time. And what is true in regard to buying is true in regard to selling. What either partner does with a third person is binding on the partnership. It is otherwise where the partnership is not general, but is upon special terms, as that purchases and sales must be with and for cash. There the power to each is special, in regard to all dealings with third persons at least who have notice of the terms.' There is contrary authority. 68 C.J.S. Partnership § 143, pp. 578–579. However, this text of C.J.S. does not mention the effect of the provisions of the Uniform Partnership Act.

The General Assembly of North Carolina in 1941 enacted a Uniform Partnership Act., * * *

Freeman as a general partner with Stroud, with no restrictions on his authority to act within the scope of the partnership business so far as the agreed statement of facts shows, had under the Uniform Partnership Act 'equal rights in the management and conduct of the partnership business.' Under G.S. § 59–48(h) Stroud, his co-partner, could not restrict the power and authority of Freeman to buy bread for the partnership as a going concern, for such a purchase was an 'ordinary matter connected with the partnership business,' for the purpose of its business and within its scope, because in the very nature of things Stroud was not, and could not be, a majority of the partners. Therefore, Freeman's purchases of bread from plaintiff for Stroud's Food Center as a going concern bound the partnership and his co-partner Stroud. * * *

In Crane on Partnership, 2d Ed., p. 277, it is said: 'In cases of an even division of the partners as to whether or not an act within the scope of the business should be done, of which disagreement a third person has knowledge, it seems that logically no restriction can be placed upon the power to act. The partnership being a going concern, activities within the scope of the business should not be limited, save by the expressed will of the majority deciding a disputed question; half of the members are not a majority.' * * *

The judgment of the court below is Affirmed.

Notes

1. The issue in the *Summers* case (page 58, above) was *not* whether there was apparent authority to hire. The employee would have a claim against the partnership and other partner based on apparent authority. The issue was the partner's liability to co-partners for acting beyond his actual authority. In that regard, the decisions in *Dooley* and *National Biscuit* are really two sides of the same coin. A majority vote was required to change the normal course of business, either by expanding or narrowing that business.

2. The partnership agreement can vary the default rules governing partnership governance and a partner's actual authority. The only way to vary the rule *vis a vis* liability to a third party, however, is to provide notice to the third party of limitations on what otherwise would be a partner's apparent authority to bind the partnership (and other partners) to acts within the ordinary course of business. RUPA § 303 provides one mechanism for providing such notice. Is a statement of partnership authority that is duly filed in accordance with RUPA § 303, binding on a third party who does not have actual notice of the limitation on authority?

———

D. ENTITY VERSUS AGGREGATE

An issue that has plagued the bar for years is whether the partnership should be treated as a separate entity from its partners or whether the partnership should be viewed as having no separate existence, making it just an aggregate of its partners. Dean Ames of Harvard who had led the initial effort to create the UPA was a proponent of the entity theory. After his death, however, Dean Lewis at the University of Pennsylvania, an advocate of the aggregate theory, took over the drafting of the uniform partnership act. See generally William Draper Lewis, *The Uniform Partnership Act*, 24 Yale L. J. 43 (1915) (description of this debate from Dean Lewis' view). The result was that, while the UPA has some aspects of the entity theory, it was largely based on the aggregate theory. This raised concerns as to whether the partnership could legally hold property in its own name and whether it could be sued in its own name. Most states have statutes treating partnerships as entities for such purposes. See e.g., N.C. Gen. Stat. § 1–69.1 (partnership may sue and be sued under its own name).

The states usually require partnerships to file under assumed (fictitious) name statutes (although law partnerships are usually excepted), thereby treating them as entities. See e.g., N.Y. Gen Bus § 130 (assumed name statute); N.C. Gen. Stat. § 66–68 (same). For tax purposes, the partnership has to file an "information" return as an entity, but gains and losses are passed through to the individual partners. RUPA retained the aggregate theory for passing through profits and losses for tax purposes.

As described in chapter 3, the LLP (limited liability partnership) has mooted much of the liability concerns raised by the traditional partnership. The LLP creates a structure that has all the attributes and flexibility of a partnership, but treats the partnership as an entity and provides at least some limited liability for conduct outside a particular partner's sphere. The LLP, however, did not solve all the problems of entity vs. aggregate liability, particularly in the area of government regulation. Before the LLP, the aggregate and entity concepts were variously applied in government actions. See generally United States v. A & P Trucking,

358 U.S. 121, 79 S.Ct. 203, 3 L.Ed.2d 165 (1958) (partnership guilty of illegally transporting explosives).The use of the LLP form may cause the government to focus even more on the entity. In one notable case, the federal government indicted Arthur Andersen, LLP, one of the five largest accounting firms in the world, as an entity for obstruction of justice in connection with its auditing of Enron, a Fortune 500 company that went bankrupt in the wake of a scandal over its accounting practices. The indictment was based on the shredding of audit documents by a small number of the 58,000 Arthur Andersen employees. Arthur Andersen argued that only those partners and employees directly involved in the shredding should be indicted and that an indictment of the firm as an entity would destroy its viability, thereby punishing thousands of employees and partners that were not involved. The government was unmoved by those claims. The accounting firm was later convicted, resulting in its destruction as a viable public accounting firm. See generally Ken Brown *et al.*, *Called to Account, Indictment of Andersen says Partners Ordered Enron Files Destroyed*, Wall St. J., March 15, 2002, at A1 (description of indictment).

E.   PARTNERSHIP LIABILITIES AND DUTIES

Partners are jointly and severally liable for the wrongful acts of a partner (or the partnership) (UPA §§ 13 & 14) with a right of contribution against co-partners (UPA § 40(f)). Under the UPA all other liability for partnership obligations is joint (UPA § 15(b)). RUPA, however, changes this by providing for joint and several liability in both instances. RUPA § 306(a). Absent an agreement, an incoming partner is liable for all preexisting partnership debts but this liability can be satisfied only out of specific partnership property. All subsequent obligations result in joint liability.

Procedural issues arise as to the liability of individual partners who are not sued or served when suit is brought against the partnership. See generally e.g., N.Y. CPLR § 1501 (actions against persons jointly liable); N.C. Gen. Stat. § 1–69.1 (a partnership may be sued in the partnership name without naming individual partners, but judgment binds only partnership property); N.C. Gen. Stat. § 1–113 (defendant partners that are served are liable for obligation, as is partnership property, and served partners may seek contribution from non-served partners).

UPA § 11 binds the partnership to admissions made by partners. The partnership is also charged with the knowledge of individual partners. UPA § 12. Partners are agents of the partnership for the purpose of its business and will bind the partnership, unless the third party had knowledge of lack of authority on the part of the partner. UPA § 9. Nevertheless, acts out of the ordinary course of business will not bind the partnership unless it so agrees. Id. UPA § 20 requires partners to render true and full information to other partners. See Meehan v. Shaughnessy, 404 Mass. 419, 535 N.E.2d 1255 (1989) (partner breached duty to other partners in falsely denying that he was planning to leave the firm). UPA § 19 gives partners the right to inspect and copy partnership records.

UPA § 18 defines the rights and duties of partners in the absence of a partnership agreement providing otherwise. This provision of the UPA, among other things, provides that all partners must consent to the admission of new partners, and all partners have equal rights of management. Such terms may be, and often are, varied by the terms of a partnership agreement. Partnership agreements in large law firms have traditionally varied these rights. For example, provision may be made for an executive committee of partners to act on behalf of the partnership, since it would be too awkward and time consuming for all of the partners to manage its business. The executive committee may select new partners, and the partnership agreement may provide for their admission by majority vote, rather than by unanimity, on the theory that it is difficult for lawyers to be unanimous on anything, and that the partnership would die before complete agreement on new partners is reached. Law firms may also appoint a managing partner to conduct the day-to-day business of the firm, and law firms may hire professional managers to carry out at least some of the managerial functions of partners. Law firm partnership agreements contain provisions on allocation of the firm's profits. "Rainmakers" in the firm who bring in the business usually receive a greater portion of the revenues (allocated by "points") than those partners that service the business, with varying levels of compensation for partners supervising lawyers doing the business that others brought in versus those carrying out legal work on their own. Law firm partnership agreements may also provide for capital contributions by partners and specify the amount or computation formula for liquidation of a partner's interest when he or she resigns or otherwise leaves the firm.

Unlike stock ownership in a corporation, partnership interests are not readily transferable. UPA § 24 sets forth a three-tiered approach to this concern. A partnership interest confers:

1) An interest in specific partnership property,

2) an interest in the partnership, and

3) the right to participate in the management of the partnership.

UPA § 25 created the concept of tenancy in partnership. This term defines this right as follows:

1) Possession of partnership property is only for partnership purposes,

2) the partnership property is assignable by all of the partners,

3) the partnership property is *not* subject to the claims of the partners' personal creditors,

4) upon the death of a partner, the partner's interest in the partnership property vests with the partnership for partnership purposes.

RUPA changed the nature and transfer of partnership property by adopting the entity concept rather than applying UPA's confusing tenancy-in-partnership approach. RUPA § 501 states that a "partner is not a co-owner of partnership property and has no interest in partnership property which can be transferred, either voluntarily or involuntarily." Thus RUPA abolishes the concept of tenancy in partnership and substitutes the entity theory. Under RUPA, property held in the partnership name is partnership property (RUPA § 204(a)(1)), and its transfer is pursuant to the individual partners' actual or apparent authority. (RUPA §§ 301 and 302(a)). RUPA's treatment of how the property is held allows third parties to rely on the record of title by placing the risk of wrongful transfer on the partnership and thereby protecting the reasonable expectations of third parties.

A personal creditor of a partner does not have a claim against the partnership itself but can seek satisfaction out of the partner's interest in the partnership. A "charging order" (UPA § 28, RUPA § 504) is the remedy used by personal creditors to attach the ownership interest of the individual partner. The charging order operates like a lien on the partner's interest in the partnership. Courts have the power to order a foreclosure of the partner's partnership interest, but this is a drastic remedy, as it will force dissolution and also may require a sale of the partnership assets. A court is unlikely to order foreclosure unless it is clear that a charging order will not work. Once a charging order is issued, all payments by the partnership to the partner are diverted to the creditor rather than going directly to the partner. A charging order does not affect a partner's rights beyond the partner's interest in withdrawals and distributions from the firm.

F. DISSOLUTION AND DISSOCIATION

The nature of a partnership creates some confusion and complexity when a partner leaves the firm. Unlike the corporation, partnerships do not have perpetual existence. Moreover, partnerships are based on personal relationships that end with the death, bankruptcy or withdrawal of a partner. To accommodate the unique nature of the partnership, the UPA creates a procedure for dissolving, winding up and terminating partnerships.

Dissolution: This is a term of art in the context of partnerships. It does not mean the end of the partnership business; it simply means the end of one form of the partnership. See UPA § 29. Dissolution arises where a partner ceases to be associated from the firm, by reason of death, bankruptcy, voluntary withdrawal or other reasons (UPA § 31)—note that a partner's breach of the partnership agreement does not by itself result in dissolution. Any partner may dissolve at any time even if the partnership is for a specified term and even though dissolution would violate the partnership agreement. Id. Wrongful dissolution, however, will subject the violating partner to damages and will affect that partner's right to partnership property. UPA § 38.

The firm need not be wound up and liquidated upon dissolution. In fact many partnerships are simply reformed and continue on as before when a partner leaves. See generally UPA § 42 (addressing continuation agreements). Unfortunately, this process is not addressed as specifically as it might be in the UPA. This may be attributed to the fact when the UPA was created there were few large partnerships where continuation would be a matter of great concern. The growth of large accounting and law partnerships, however, placed some strains on the dissolution concept because new partners were being added constantly and others were retiring or leaving for other reasons. This problem was addressed by partnership agreements that provided for continuation of the firm upon dissolution. The partnership agreement also contains a mechanism for resolving the claims of withdrawing partners against partnership property. As discussed below, a partner leaving the firm may have a claim against partnership assets. That process is complicated, and the outcome uncertain for the partners. Therefore, partnership agreements are used to specify the amounts owing to departing partners or the method for computing such amounts.

Winding up and Termination: The partnership business is not terminated at the time of dissolution. It may continue if there is a continuation agreement. In the absence of such an agreement, the partnership business continues while its operations are in the process of being terminated. UPA § 30. This process is called "winding up" or liquidation. Termination of the partnership occurs when the partnership's assets are liquidated (turned into cash), partnership debts satisfied and any remaining assets distributed to the partners.

Under UPA § 18(a), subject to any agreement among the partners, in liquidation partners receive back their initial contribution to the partnership and then share equally in the profits and surplus after all liabilities have been paid off (see also RUPA § 401). UPA § 18(a) provides that absent an agreement each partner is liable for the partnership losses to the extent of his share of the profits (RUPA § 401(b)). Note, however, that this addresses the partners' rights inter se and does not affect the joint and several liability of each partner. The only way to limit losses to a third party is through an agreement with the third party.

UPA § 38 provides for the distribution of partnership property (after payment of the partnership's liabilities) where there has been a breach of the partnership agreement. In brief, where the partnership was dissolved in violation of a partnership agreement, the non-breaching partners may seek damages and continue the business. Id. The breaching partner is to be given the value of his or her interest in the partnership property in cash less any damages. Goodwill of the partnership is not considered in determining the value of the breaching partner's interest in partnership property. The breaching partner is then relieved of further partnership liabilities. Id.

PAGE v. PAGE

55 Cal.2d 192, 10 Cal.Rptr. 643, 359 P.2d 41 (1961).

Traynor, Justice.

Plaintiff and defendant are partners in a linen supply business in Santa Maria, California. Plaintiff appeals from a judgment declaring the partnership to be for a term rather than at will.

The partners entered into an oral partnership agreement in 1949. Within the first two years each partner contributed approximately $43,000 for the purchase of land, machinery, and linen needed to begin the business. From 1949 to 1957 the enterprise was unprofitable, losing approximately $62,000. The partnership's major creditor is a corporation, wholly owned by plaintiff, that supplies the linen and machinery necessary for the day-to-day operation of the business. This corporation holds a $47,000 demand note of the partnership. The partnership operations began to improve in 1958. The partnership earned $3,824.41 in that year and $2,282.30 in the first three months of 1959. Despite this improvement plaintiff wishes to terminate the partnership.

The Uniform Partnership Act provides that a partnership may be dissolved 'By the express will of any partner when no definite term or particular undertaking is specified.' Corp.Code, § 15031, subd. (1)(b). The trial court found that the partnership is for a term, namely, 'such reasonable time as is necessary to enable said partnership to repay from partnership profits, indebtedness incurred for the purchase of land, buildings, laundry and delivery equipment and linen for the operation of such business. * * *' Plaintiff correctly contends that this finding is without support in the evidence.

Defendant testified that the terms of the partnership were to be similar to former partnerships of plaintiff and defendant, and that the understanding of these partnerships was that 'we went into partnership to start the business and let the business operation pay for itself, put in so much money, and let the business pay itself out.' There was also testimony that one of the former partnership agreements provided in writing that the profits were to be retained until all obligations were paid.

Upon cross-examination defendant admitted that the former partnership in which the earnings were to be retained until the obligations were repaid was substantially different from the present partnership. The former partnership was a limited partnership and provided for a definite term of five years and a partnership at will thereafter. Defendant insists, however, that the method of operation of the former partnership showed an understanding that all obligations were to be repaid from profits. He nevertheless concedes that there was no understanding as to the term of the present partnership in the event of losses. He was asked: '(W)as there any discussion with reference to the continuation of the business in the event of losses?' He replied, 'Not that I can remember.' He was then asked, 'Did you have any understanding with Mr. Page, your brother, the plaintiff in this action, as to how the obligations were to be paid if there were losses?' He replied, 'Not that I can remember. I can't remember discussing that at all. We never figured on losing, I guess.'

Viewing this evidence most favorably for defendant, it proves only that the partners expected to meet current expenses from current income and to recoup their investment if the business were successful.

Defendant contends that such an expectation is sufficient to create a partnership for a term under the rule of Owen v. Cohen, 19 Cal.2d 147, 150, 119 P.2d 713. In that case we held that when a partner advances a sum of money to a partnership with the understanding that the amount contributed was to be a loan to the partnership and was to be repaid as soon as feasible from the prospective profits of the business, the partnership is for the term reasonably required to repay the loan. It is true that Owen v. Cohen, supra, and other cases hold that partners may impliedly agree to continue in business until a certain sum of money is earned, or one or more partners recoup their investments, or until certain debts are paid, or until certain property could be disposed of on favorable terms. In each of these cases, however, the implied agreement found support in the evidence.

In Owen v. Cohen, supra, the partners borrowed substantial amounts of money to launch the enterprise and there was an understanding that the loans would be repaid from partnership profits. In Vangel v. Vangel, supra, one partner loaned his co-partner money to invest in the partnership with the understanding that the money would be repaid from partnership profits. In Mervyn Investment Co. v. Biber, supra, one partner contributed all the capital, the other contributed his services, and it was understood that upon the repayment of the contributed capital from partnership profits the partner who contributed his services would receive a one-third interest in the partnership assets. In each of these cases the court properly held that the partners impliedly promised to continue the partnership for a term reasonably required to allow the partnership to earn sufficient money to accomplish the understood objective. In Shannon v. Hudson, supra, the parties entered into a joint venture to build and operate a motel until it could be sold upon favorable and mutually satisfactory terms, and the court held that the joint venture was for a reasonable term sufficient to accomplish the purpose of the joint venture.

In the instant case, however, defendant failed to prove any facts from which an agreement to continue the partnership for a term may be implied. The understanding to which defendant testified was no more than a common hope that the partnership earnings would pay for all the necessary expenses. Such a hope does not establish even by implication a 'definite term or particular undertaking' as required by section 15031, subdivision (1)(b) of the Corporations Code. All partnerships are ordinarily entered into with the hope that they will be profitable, but that alone does not make them all partnerships for a term and obligate the partners to continue in the partnerships until all of the losses over a period of many years have been recovered.

Defendant contends that plaintiff is acting in bad faith and is attempting to use his superior financial position to appropriate the now profitable business of the partnership. Defendant has invested $43,000 in the firm, and owing to the long period of losses his interest in the partnership assets is very small. The fact that plaintiff's wholly-owned corporation holds a $47,000 demand note of the partnership may make it difficult to sell the business as a going concern. Defendant fears that upon dissolution he will receive very little and that plaintiff, who is the managing partner and knows how to conduct the operations of the partnership, will receive a business that has become very profitable because of the establishment of Vandenberg Air Force Base in its vicinity. Defendant charges that plaintiff has been content to share the losses but now that the business has become profitable he wishes to keep all the gains.

There is no showing in the record of bad faith or that the improved profit situation is more than temporary. In any event these contentions are irrelevant to the issue whether the partnership is for a term or at will. Since, however, this action is for a declaratory judgment and will be the basis for future action by the parties, it is appropriate to point out that defendant is amply protected by the fiduciary duties of co-partners.

Even though the Uniform Partnership Act provides that a partnership at will may be dissolved by the express will of any partner, this power, like any other power held by a fiduciary, must be exercised in good faith.

We have often stated that 'partners are trustees for each other, and in all proceedings connected with the conduct of the partnership every partner is bound to act in the highest good faith to his copartner, and may not obtain any advantage over him in the partnership affairs by the slightest misrepresentation, concealment, threat, or adverse pressure of any kind.' Although Civil Code § 2411 embodying the foregoing language, was repealed upon the adoption of the Uniform Partnership Act, it was not intended by the adoption of that act to diminish the fiduciary duties between partners.

A partner at will is not bound to remain in a partnership, regardless of whether the business is profitable or unprofitable. A partner may not, however, by use of adverse pressure 'freeze out' a co-partner and appropri-ate the business to his own use. A partner may not dissolve a partnership to gain the benefits of the business for himself, unless he fully compen-sates his co-partner for his share of the prospective business opportunity. In this regard his fiduciary duties are at least as great as those of a shareholder of a corporation.

In the case of In re Security Finance Co., 49 Cal.2d 370, 376–377, 317 P.2d 1, 5 we stated that although shareholders representing 50 per cent of the voting power have a right under Corporations Code, § 4600 to dissolve a corporation, they may not exercise such right in order 'to defraud the other shareholders (citation), to 'freeze out' minority shareholders (cita-tion), or to sell the assets of the dissolved corporation at an inadequate price (citation).'

Likewise in the instant case, plaintiff has the power to dissolve the partnership by express notice to defendant. If, however, it is proved that plaintiff acted in bad faith and violated his fiduciary duties by attempting to appropriate to his own use the new prosperity of the partnership without adequate compensation to his co-partner, the dissolution would be wrongful and the plaintiff would be liable as provided by subdivision (2)(a) of Corporations Code, § 15038 (rights of partners upon wrongful dissolu-tion) for violation of the implied agreement not to exclude defendant wrongfully from the partnership business opportunity.

The judgment is reversed.

G. DISSOCIATION COMPARED

COX & HAZEN ON CORPORATIONS,
James D. Cox & Thomas Lee Hazen

§ 1.07   (2d ed. 2003).

RUPA provides greater stability to partnerships on changes in the partnership membership. Under the UPA, a partner's departure from the partnership "dissolved" the partnership. There is much uncertainty over the meaning of "dissolution" under the UPA, which provides only general guidance as to what dissolution is and what it is not. RUPA clearly delineates the two possible consequences of a partner's departure (referred to as a "dissociation" (RUPA § 601))—either a buyout of the departing partner or a winding up of the partnership. Section 701 of RUPA deals with buyouts of the departing partner and provides default rules for the valuation and payout of that partner's interest. Section 801 of RUPA identifies those instances in which the partnership business must be liquidated and provides default rules for the settlement of partnership accounts.

NOTES

1. *Aggregate versus entity redux.* Recall that RUPA adopts an entity view of the partnership as compared to the aggregate view that prevailed at common law and under UPA. *See* page 62 above. This distinction is highlighted by the provisions of the most recent revisions to the Revised Uniform Limited Partnership Act that follow the pattern of the Model Business Corporation Act by providing that a limited partnership has perpetual existence unless the partnership agreement provides otherwise. Re–RULPA § 104(c).

2. *Dissolution versus dissociation.* Under the aggregate approach, organic changes in the business relation operated as a dissolution since every change in the composition of the partnership resulted in a new aggregate and hence a new partnership. In contrast, recognizing the partnership as an entity means that there is a continuity of existence that previously did not exist. For example, changes in composition of the partnership's members do not affect the entity which continues. Instead of causing a dissolution, the death, withdrawal, bankruptcy, and other enumerated events that caused a dissolution under UPA, result in the partner's dissociation from the partnership while the partnership continues as en entity (unless, of course, the partnership agreement provides to the contrary).

3. *Consequences of dissociation.* A partner's dissociation has several consequences. Dissociation the partner's right to manage or conduct partnership business. Dissociation ends the partner's duty to refrain from competing with the partnership, unless of course the partnership agreement provides otherwise. Dissociation limits the partner's remaining duties of loyalty and care, which continue only as to matters or events that occurred before the partner's dissociation.

As noted above, dissociation does not of itself discharge the partner with respect to a partnership liability incurred *before* the dissociation. However, the partnership agreement may release a dissociated partner from liability for a partnership obligation to the remaining partners. Release from any liability to partnership creditors requires an agreement with those creditors. A dissociated partner will also be released from liability if a creditor of the partnership, with notice of the dissociation but without the partner's consent, agrees to a material alteration in the nature or time of payment of a partnership obligation.

With respect to obligations incurred by a partner *after* his or her dissociation, a partner remains liable as a partner for transactions the partnership enters into within a specified period following the partner's dissociation if at the time of transacting the other party (1) does not have notice of the partner's dissociation, and (2) reasonably believes that the dissociated partner is still a partner. However, once dissociated, a dissociated partner is not liable for obligations of the partnership's ongoing business merely because the business uses the same partnership name or uses the dissociated partner's name.

As pointed out above, a dissociated partner has no *actual* authority to act for the partnership, but there may be lingering *apparent* authority. Thus, in order to protect innocent third parties, for a statutory period following a partner's dissociation, the partnership remains bound for that partner's acts that, before the dissociation would have bound the partnership because of the partner's agency authority. However, the partnership is so bound only if, at the time of the transaction, the other party (1) reasonably believed the dissociated partner was then a partner, and (2) neither had notice of the partner's dissociation nor is deemed to have had knowledge due to filed or recorded limitations on the partner's or dissociated partner's authority.

4. Under RUPA, a partnership may still dissolve and wind-up its business. However, as pointed out above, events that cause a partner's dissociation do not cause a dissolution as is the case under the common law and under UPA. Furthermore, dissociation of a partner is not a condition precedent to dissolution. For example, a RUPA partnership can voluntarily dissolve (as is the case with corporations).

CHAPTER 3

LIMITED PARTNERSHIPS, LIMITED LIABILITY PARTNERSHIPS, AND LIMITED LIABILITY COMPANIES

■ ■ ■

In Chapter 2 we examined the general partnership which for most of our history was the primary alternative to corporate form for conducting a business with multiple owners. Until the latter part of the twentieth century, in most states,[1] the limited partnership was the alternative to the corporation for conducting business and still granting limited liability to its owners. The last part of the century heralded a new form of doing business—the limited liability company (LLC). LLCs and their counterpart the Limited Liability Partnership (LLP) have now become the form of choice for noncorporate businesses and also have replaced the corporation for many companies that previously would have opted for the corporate form. The reason for this sea change is that LLCs and LLPs in essence permit a partnership type organization while letting its owners enjoy limited liability. This chapter begins with a discussion of the limited partnership form of doing business and then looks to LLCs and LLPs.

NOTES

1. *The death of general partnerships?* As you read the materials in this chapter, consider whether there is any reason to consciously select[2] the general partnership form rather than a limited partnership, LLC, or LLP.

2. *The cobbler's son going barefoot?* It is surprising to say the least that even though lawyers are increasingly recommending LLCs and LLPs to their clients, many law firms have remained general partnerships. The naming of law firms as defendants in recent years may have given lawyers a wake-up call. See Anthony Lin, After Enron, Firms Rethink Partnerships, N.Y.L.J. p.1 (April 15, 2002).

---

1. A few states recognize the business trust as a form of doing business, see p. 20 supra.

2. Recall that because of the definition of partnership, partnership remains the default form of doing business with multiple owners where no alternative form has been selected and perfected. See pp. 44–49 supra.

SECTION 1.   LIMITED PARTNERSHIPS

The limited partnership has long been used to provide the flexible advantages of a partnership while allowing passive investors to avoid unlimited liability for the obligations incurred by the operating partners. There are, however, limitations on the activities of the limited partners, and the general partner continues to be subject to unlimited liability.

COX & HAZEN ON CORPORATIONS,
James D. Cox & Thomas Lee Hazen

§ 1.09   (2d ed. 2003).

The limited partnership is a statutorily created method of profit-sharing by passive investors. This form of business organization permits investors to share the profits of a business, with their risk of loss limited to their investment if the investors comply with certain legal formalities. A limited partnership has two classes of partners: (1) one or more general partners, who have complete control, manage the enterprise, and are subject to full liability; and (2) one or more limited partners, who are very similar to firm creditors but are subordinated to creditors if the firm becomes insolvent or is liquidated. The limited partner ordinarily does not take part in the day-to-day control of the business.

The first limited partnership statute in this country was adopted in New York in 1822 and was soon replicated in most other industrial states. These early enactments, however, were filled with pitfalls for the supposed "limited" partner, a malady compounded by the tendency of the courts to construe the statutes strictly because they regarded the privilege of limited liability without incorporation as a special and narrow privilege that should be jealously guarded.

A safer and more satisfactory form of limited partnership arrived in 1916 with the Uniform Limited Partnership Act, which was drafted by the Commissioners on Uniform State Laws. This statute was enacted by every state. In 1976 the Commissioners on Uniform State Laws approved a Revised Uniform Limited Partnership Act (RULPA) as a recommended replacement. Subsequently, the revised act was adopted in most jurisdictions. The National Conference of Commissioners on Uniform State Laws has been considering additional changes to the Revised Act and has proposed a revision of RULPA which is known as Re–RULPA.

Unlike an ordinary partnership, which can be formed by a mere informal agreement among the participants, a limited partnership is formed only by complying with statutory formalities similar to those required for the creation of a corporation. A verified certificate containing provisions similar to those called for in a corporation's articles of incorporation must be filed with the clerk, recorder, or other designated public official of the county in which the limited partnership's principal place of business is located and sometimes must also be filed in other counties in which it has places of business. * * *

Unlike partners in general partnerships, limited partners are not ordinarily agents of the partnership and thus do not have the authority to bind the partnership simply because of their position as limited partners. A corollary issue is the extent to which limited partners owe fiduciary duties to one another. As managers of the business, general partners owe fiduciary obligations to the limited partnership. There is authority that permits limiting those fiduciary duties pursuant to contract in the limited partnership agreement. Limited partners who take an active role in the business will incur the same fiduciary duties as general partners. In contrast, where the limited partner is not exercising managerial control, the fiduciary duties to the other partners will be much lower, if any. Of course, the limited partnership agreement can impose additional fiduciary duties on even passive limited partners. * * *

GATEWAY POTATO SALES v. G.B. INVESTMENT CO.

170 Ariz. 137, 822 P.2d 490 (App.1991).

TAYLOR, JUDGE.

Gateway Potato Sales (Gateway), a creditor of Sunworth Packing Limited Partnership (Sunworth Packing), brought suit to recover payment for goods it had supplied to the limited partnership. Gateway sought recovery from Sunworth Packing, from Sunworth Corporation as general partner, and from G.B. Investment Company (G.B. Investment) as a limited partner, pursuant to Arizona Revised Statutes Annotated (A.R.S.) § 29–319. Under § 29–319, a limited partner may become liable for the obligations of the limited partnership under certain circumstances in which the limited partner has taken part in the control of the business. * * *

Sunworth Corporation and G.B. Investment formed Sunworth Packing in November 1985 for the purpose of engaging in potato farming in Arizona. The limited partnership certificate and agreement of Sunworth Packing, filed with the office of the Arizona Secretary of State, specified Sunworth Corporation as the general partner and G.B. Investment Company as the limited partner. The agreement recited that the limited partner would not participate in the control of the business. The agreement further stated that the limited partner would not become liable to the creditors of the partnership, except to the extent of its initial contribution and any liability it may incur with an Arizona bank as a signatory party or guarantor of a loan and/or line of credit. In late 1985, Robert C. Ellsworth, the president of Sunworth Corporation, called Robert Pribula, the owner of Gateway, located in Minnesota, to see if Gateway would supply Sunworth Packing with seed potatoes. Pribula hesitated to supply the seed potatoes without receiving assurance of payment because Pribula was aware that Ellsworth had previously undergone bankruptcy. Pribula, however, decided to sell the seed potatoes to Sunworth Packing after being assured by Ellsworth that he was in partnership with a large financial institution, G.B. Investment Company, and that G.B. Investment was providing the financing, was actively involved in the operation of the business, and had approved the purchase of the seed potatoes. Thereafter, from February 1986 through April 1986, Gateway sold substantial quantities of seed potatoes to Sunworth Packing.

While supplying the seed potatoes, Pribula believed that he was doing business with a general partnership (i.e., Sunworth Packing Company, formed by Sunworth Corporation and G.B. Investment Company). The sales documents used by the parties specified "Sunworth Packing Company" as the name of the partnership. Pribula was neither aware of the true name of the partnership nor that it was a limited partnership. All of Gateway's dealings were with Ellsworth. Pribula neither contacted G.B. Investment prior to selling the seed potatoes to the limited partnership nor did he otherwise attempt to verify any of the statements Ellsworth had made about G.B. Investment's involvement. The only direct contact between G.B. Investment and Gateway occurred some time after the sale of the seed potatoes. It is, however, disputed whether G.B. Investment ever provided any assurance of payment to Gateway.

G.B. Investment's vice-president, Darl Anderson, testified in his affidavit that G.B. Investment had exerted no control over the daily management and operation of the limited partnership, Sunworth Packing. This testimony was contradicted, however, by the affidavit testimony of Ellsworth which was presented by Gateway in opposing G.B. Investment's motion for summary judgment. According to Ellsworth, G.B. Investment's employees, Darl Anderson and Thomas McHolm, controlled the day-to-day affairs of the limited partnership and made Ellsworth account to them for nearly everything he did. This day-to-day contact included but was not limited to approval of most of the significant operational decisions and expenditures and the use and management of partnership funds without Ellsworth's involvement.

Ellsworth testified further that he had described G.B. Investment's control of the business operation to Pribula. Pribula confirmed that Ellsworth had informed him that G.B. Investment's employees, McHolm and Anderson, were at the partnership's office on a frequent basis, that Ellsworth reported directly to them, that daily operations of the partnership were reviewed by representatives of G.B. Investment, and that Ellsworth had to get their approval before making certain business decisions. * * *

Subsection (a) of A.R.S. § 29–319 sets forth the general rule that a limited partner who is not also a general partner is not liable for the obligations of the limited partnership.

> [A] limited partner is not liable for the obligations of a limited partnership unless he is also a general partner or, in addition to the exercise of his rights and powers as a limited partner, he takes part in the control of the business. However, if the limited partner's partic-

ipation in the control of the business is not substantially the same as the exercise of the powers of a general partner, he is liable only to persons who transact business with the limited partnership with actual knowledge of his participation in control.

Subsection (a) does not discuss the types of activities that might be undertaken by a limited partner which would amount to "control of the business." Subsection (b), however, does contain a listing of activities that are permissible for a limited partner to undertake without being deemed to be taking part in "control of the business."[3]

A limited partner does not participate in the control of the business within the meaning of subsection (a) solely by doing one or more of the following:

(1) Being a contractor for or an agent or employee of the limited partnership or of a general partner;

(2) Consulting with and advising a general partner with respect to the business of the limited partnership;

(3) Acting as surety for the limited partnership;

(4) Approving or disproving an amendment to the partnership agreement; or

(5) Voting on one or more of the following matters:

(i) The dissolution and winding up of the limited partnership;

(ii) The sale, exchange, lease, mortgage, pledge or other transfer of all or substantially all of the assets of the limited partnership other than in the ordinary course of its business;

(iii) The incurrence of indebtedness by the limited partnership other than in the ordinary course of its business;

(iv) A change in the nature of the business; or

(v) The removal of a general partner.

In addition, subsection (c) of A.R.S. § 29–319 provides that "[t]he enumeration in subsection (b) does not mean that the possession or exercise of any other powers by a limited partner constitutes participation by him in the business of the limited partnership."

In responding to the motion for summary judgment, Gateway urged the trial court to find that Gateway had presented a fact question of G.B. Investment's liability to it under A.R.S. § 29–319(a). Gateway argued that the statute imposes liability on a limited partner whose participation in the control of the business is substantially the same as the exercised power of a general partner. Gateway further argued that even if the person transacting business with the limited partnership did not know of

---

3. The drafters of the Revised Uniform Limited Partnership Act (RULPA) from which Arizona's statute is taken, refer to this listing as a "safe harbor." Revised Uniform Limited Partnership Act § 303 cmt., 6 U.L.A. 239 (Supp.1991).

the limited partner's participation in control, there is liability. Alternatively, Gateway argued that the statute imposes liability when the powers exercised in controlling the business might fall short of being "substantially the same as the exercise of powers of a general partner," but the person transacting business with the limited partnership had actual knowledge of the participation in control. Gateway asserted that the evidence it was presenting in response to the motion for summary judgment raised issues of material fact as to whether either of these situations had occurred. If either had occurred, Gateway argued, it would be entitled to recover from the limited partner, G.B. Investment. * * *

To the extent that the trial court's ruling [granting summary judgment in favor of G.B. Investment] may have been based on a belief that a limited partner could never be liable under the statute unless the creditor had contact with the limited partner and learned directly from him of his participation and control of the business, we believe that ruling to be in error.

In A.R.S. § 29–319(a), the legislature stopped short of expressly stating that if the limited partner's participation in the control of the business is substantially the same as the exercise of the powers of a general partner, he is liable to persons who transact business with a limited partnership even though they have no knowledge of his participation and control. It has made this statement by implication, though, by stating to the opposite effect that "if the limited partner's participation in the control of the business is not substantially the same as the exercise of the powers of a general partner, he is liable only to persons who transact business with the limited partnership with actual knowledge of his participation in control." A.R.S. § 29–319(a).

We believe this interpretation is strengthened by an examination of the legislative history of Arizona's limited partnership statute. It is further strengthened by the legislature's refusal to modify this statute to correspond to the Revised Uniform Limited Partnership Act, as amended in 1985. Prior to 1982, Arizona's limited partnership statute was patterned after the Uniform Limited Partnership Act (ULPA), which was drafted in 1916. Section 7 of the ULPA provided that "[a] limited partner shall not become liable as a general partner unless, in addition to the exercise of his rights and powers as a limited partner, he takes part in the control of the business." Uniform Limited Partnership Act § 7, 6 U.L.A. 559 (1969).[4]

The Revised Uniform Limited Partnership Act (RULPA) was drafted in 1976. Revised Uniform Limited Partnership Act, 6 U.L.A. 239, 240 (Supp.1991). In 1982, the Arizona legislature adopted the RULPA after repealing its enactment of the ULPA. *See* 1982 Ariz. Sess. Laws, ch. 192, § 1 (effective July 24, 1982). Presently, A.R.S. § 29–319(a), dealing with a

---

4. The language of Arizona's then § 29–307 was taken verbatim from section 7 of the ULPA. For the text of Arizona's Uniform Limited Partnership Act, since repealed, see Uniform Limited Partnership Act, 1943 Ariz. Sess. Laws 124, *reprinted in* A.R.S. §§ 29–301 to–366 app. (1989) (as amended).

limited partner's liability to third parties, is very similar to the 1976 version of section 303(a) of the RULPA which stated:

> Except as provided in subsection (d), a limited partner is not liable for the obligations of a limited partnership unless he is also a general partner or, and in addition to the exercise of his rights and powers as a limited partner, he takes part in the control of the business. However, if the limited partner's participation in the control of the business is not substantially the same as the exercise of the powers of a general partner, he is liable only to persons who transact business with the limited partnership with actual knowledge of his participation in control.

Revised Uniform Limited Partnership Act § 303(a), 6 U.L.A. 239, 325 (Supp.1991). The drafters' comment to section 303 explained that limited partners exercising all of the powers of a general partner would not escape liability by avoiding direct dealings with third parties. The comment stated:

> Section 303 makes several important changes in Section 7 of the prior uniform law. The first sentence of Section 303(a) carries over the basic test from former Section 7 whether the limited partner "takes part in the control of the business" in order to ensure that judicial decisions under the prior uniform law remain applicable to the extent not expressly changed. The second sentence of Section 303(a) reflects a wholly new concept. Because of the difficulty of determining when the "control" line has been overstepped, it was thought it unfair to impose general partner's liability on a limited partner except to the extent that a third party had knowledge of his participation in control of the business. On the other hand, in order to avoid permitting a limited partner to exercise all of the powers of a general partner while avoiding any direct dealings with third parties, the "is not substantially the same as" test was introduced. . . .

Id. at 326 cmt.

In 1985, the drafters of the RULPA backtracked from the position taken in section 303(a) of the 1976 Act. The new amendments reflect a reluctance to hold a limited partner liable if the limited partner had no direct contact with the creditor. The 1985 revised RULPA section 303(a) was amended to provide as follows:

> Except as provided in Subsection (d), a limited partner is not liable for the obligations of a limited partnership unless he is also a general partner or, in addition to the exercise of his rights and powers as a limited partner, he participates in the control of the business. *However, if the limited partner participates in the control of the business, he is liable only to persons who transact business with the limited partnership reasonably believing, based upon the limited partner's conduct, that the limited partner is a general partner.*

Id. at 325 (emphasis added). The comment to section 303 was also revised to explain the reason for the amendment. The revised comment states:

> Section 303 makes several important changes in Section 7 of the 1916 Act. The first sentence of Section 303(a) differs from the text of Section 7 of the 1916 Act in that it speaks of participating (rather than taking part) in the control of the business; this was done for the sake of consistency with the second sentence of Section 303(a), not to change the meaning of the text. It is intended that judicial decisions interpreting the phrase "takes part in the control of the business" under the prior uniform law will remain applicable to the extent that a different result is not called for by other provisions of Section 303 and other provisions of the Act. The second sentence of Section 303(a) reflects a wholly new concept in the 1976 Act that has been further modified in the 1985 Act. *It was adopted* partly because of the difficulty of determining when the "control" line has been overstepped, but *also (and more importantly) because of a determination that it is not sound public policy to hold a limited partner who is not also a general partner liable for the obligations of the partnership except to persons who have done business with the limited partnership reasonably believing, based on the limited partner's conduct, that he is a general partner. . . .*

Id. at 326 cmt. (emphasis added).

The Arizona legislature, however, has not revised A.R.S. § 29–319(a) to correspond to the section 303 amendments. The Arizona statute continues to impose liability on a limited partner whenever the "substantially the same as" test is met, even though the creditor has no knowledge of the limited partner's control. It follows then that no contact between the creditor and the limited partner is required to impose liability.

Moreover, whereas section 303 of the RULPA states that the creditor's reasonable belief must be "based upon the limited partner's conduct," under A.R.S. § 29–319 the only requirement is that the creditor has had "actual knowledge of [the limited partner's] participation in control." The statute does not state that this knowledge must be based upon the limited partner's conduct. The comments to the original version of section 303 of the RULPA, from which Arizona's statute is taken, make it clear that only when the "substantially the same as" test is met is direct contact not a requirement. Conversely, if the "substantially the same as" test is not met, direct contact is required. Under the facts presented in this case, Gateway had no direct contact with G.B. Investment until after the sales were concluded. We conclude, therefore, that G.B. Investment would be liable only if the "substantially the same as" test was met.

Whether a limited partner has exercised the degree of control that will make him liable to a creditor has always been a factual question. This is so regardless of whether the particular statute involved is patterned after section 7 of the ULPA or after section 303 of the RULPA. *E.g.,*

Alzado v. Blinder, Robinson & Co., Inc., 752 P.2d 544 (Colo.1988); *Gast v. Petsinger,* 228 Pa.Super. 394, 323 A.2d 371 (1974); *Holzman v. De Escamilla,* 86 Cal.App.2d 858, 195 P.2d 833 (1948). Our current Arizona statute lists activities that a limited partner may undertake without participating in controlling the business. It also states that other activities may be excluded from the definition of such control. Where activities do not fall within the "safe harbor" of A.R.S. § 29–319(b), it is necessary for a trier-of-fact to determine whether such activities amount to "control." In the absence of actual knowledge of the limited partner's participation in the control of the partnership business, there must be evidence from which a trier-of-fact might find not only control, but control that is "substantially the same as the exercise of powers of a general partner."

We conclude that the evidence Gateway presented in this case should have allowed it to withstand summary judgment. The affidavit testimony of Ellsworth raises the issue whether he was merely a puppet for the limited partner, G.B. Investment. While a few of the activities Ellsworth listed may have fallen within the protected areas listed in A.R.S. § 29–319(b), others did not. Ellsworth's detailed statement raises substantial issues of material facts. * * *

NOTES

1. There are numerous cases considering whether limited partners engaged in management activities that would subject them to unlimited liability. In Holzman v. De Escamilla, 86 Cal.App.2d 858, 195 P.2d 833 (1948), for example, the court held in a pre-RULPA case that limited partners in a truck crop operation became general partners where they controlled the bank accounts of the business and decided what crops (tomatoes or watermelons) to plant. Later cases, however, suggest a reluctance to impose such liability. See e.g., Trans–Am Builders, Inc. v. Woods Mill, Ltd., 133 Ga.App. 411, 210 S.E.2d 866 (1974) (limited partners who visited construction site and expressed concern with operations did not participate in management and thereby subject themselves to unlimited liability). For similar holdings see Mount Vernon Savings & Loan Association v. Partridge Assocs., 679 F.Supp. 522 (D.Md.1987); First Wis. Nat'l Bank v. Towboat Partners, Ltd., 630 F.Supp. 171 (E.D.Mo.), aff'd, 802 F.2d 1069 (8th Cir.1986); Trans–Am. Builders, Inc. v. Woods Mill, Ltd., 133 Ga.App. 411, 210 S.E.2d 866 (1974). For a case adopting the "creditor-reliance" test discussed in the *Gateway Potato Sales* case see Frigidaire Sales Corp. v. Union Properties, Inc., 14 Wash.App. 634, 544 P.2d 781 (1975), aff'd, 88 Wash.2d 400, 562 P.2d 244 (1977). Contra: Gonzalez v. Chalpin, 77 N.Y.2d 74, 564 N.Y.S.2d 702, 565 N.E.2d 1253 (1990); Delaney v. Fidelity Lease, Ltd., 526 S.W.2d 543 (Tex.1975).

2. As noted in *Gateway Potato Sales,* RULPA § 303(b) establishes "safe harbors" for activities that will not expose a limited partner to unlimited liability for participating in the control of the business. This concept means that such activities are protected, but it does not mean that all other activities will result in liability. Rather, if the activity does not fall within the safe harbor, a court must examine the activity and make an independent decision

on whether liability should attach because the activity constitutes participation in control. Obviously, this exposes the limited partner to the risk of an adverse decision and is not a desirable position for the limited partner.

3. A limited partnership must have at least one general partner. In Frigidaire Sales Corp. v. Union Properties, Inc., 88 Wash.2d 400, 562 P.2d 244 (1977), however, the court held that the general partner could be a corporation and that limited partners would not incur liability as a general partner where they participated in the management of the business of the limited partnership as officers, directors or shareholders of the corporate general partner. RULPA § 303 also provides a safe harbor for limited partners acting as "an officer, director, or shareholder of a general partner that is a corporation." This, of course, effectively establishes limited liability while permitting limited partners to participate in the control of the business of the limited partnership, *albeit* with a different hat. But see Gonzalez v. Chalpin, 77 N.Y.2d 74, 564 N.Y.S.2d 702, 565 N.E.2d 1253 (1990) (burden is on the limited partners to show that their participation in the control of the limited partnership's business was in their capacity as corporate officers rather than as limited partners). Compare Delaney v. Fidelity Lease Ltd., 526 S.W.2d 543 (Tex.1975) (pre-RULPA decision holding personal liability of limited partners acting in the management of the limited partnership could not be evaded by acting through a corporation).

4. RULPA § 201 requires limited partnerships to file a certificate with the Secretary of State in the jurisdiction where it is formed. The certificate must contain certain information concerning the limited partnership. The limited partnership is not considered to be formed until this certificate is filed with the Secretary of State. Id. Courts have held that the failure properly to file the required report will subject the limited partners to unlimited liability as general partners. Direct Mail Specialist, Inc. v. Brown, 673 F.Supp. 1540 (D.Mont.1987); Lowe v. Arizona Power & Light Co., 5 Ariz.App. 385, 427 P.2d 366 (1967). Compare Vulcan Furniture Mfg. Corp. v. Vaughn, 168 So.2d 760 (Fla.App.1964) (limited partnership lost the right to continue to operate as such when it failed to file annual report with Secretary of State but this did not automatically convert it into a general partnership).

5. The role of the limited partner has often been analogized to that of a shareholder in a corporation. See e.g., Lichtyger v. Franchard Corp., 18 N.Y.2d 528, 277 N.Y.S.2d 377, 223 N.E.2d 869, 873 (1966); Energy Investors Fund, L.P. v. Metric Constructors, Inc., 351 N.C. 331, 525 S.E.2d 441, 444 (2000). See also Caley Investments I v. Lowe Family Associates, Ltd., 754 P.2d 793, 795 (Colo.App.1988) (limited partners hold no title or property right in the assets of a limited partnership). Subsequent chapters will deal with the rights of corporate shareholders.

6. Why would you recommend a limited partnership rather than a less restrictive form of doing business such as a limited liability company or a limited liability partnership? One reason for selecting the limited partnership form is to guarantee centralized management and an effective way of limiting the influence of the limited partners. For example, the New York Yankees were formed as a limited partnership with George Steinbrenner at the helm and as one of his limited partners commented, "There is nothing more limited

than a limited partner in the Yankees." See Murray Chass, Steinbrenner Reaches Top of Seniority List, N.Y. Time A23 (Wed. Jan. 19, 2005).

7. Another reason for selected the limited partnership form is that it may prove more suitable for public trading:

> *Master Limited Partnerships.* Limited partnerships are not limited to small business ventures. They may be used for investments sold to the public.

Recall *Mienhard v. Salmon*, page 52, above that addressed the fiduciary duties among partners in a general partnership. As the following case indicates, although limited partners have far less fiduciary obligations, there still are some that apply:

RED RIVER WINGS, INC. v. HOOT, INC.

751 N.W.2d 206, 2008 N.D. 117 (2008).

KAPSNER, JUSTICE.

Thomas M. Lavelle is a Fargo restauranteur who owns and manages restaurants through LTM, Ltd. ("LTM"), a corporation whose only shareholder is Lavelle. Dyan Dockter and Shelly Dockter are employed by the company and they oversee LTM's management duties. In the mid 1990s, Lavelle learned from Arthur Stern, who worked in the restaurant equipment supply business and had a long-standing business relationship with Lavelle, that Hooters of America was looking to expand into Canada and there was the potential to acquire a Hooters franchise there. Hooters of America approved Lavelle as a franchisee, but as a condition for getting a first franchise in Edmonton, Alberta, Lavelle had to purchase options for three additional franchises in Calgary, Alberta; Winnipeg, Manitoba; and Banff, Alberta. The franchise fee for the first restaurant was $75,000, plus a $10,000 nonrefundable fee for each of the additional option locations.

Because of the expenses involved and the business risks, Lavelle decided to find investors and sought advice from a friend and retired securities broker, Louis Emerson. Emerson suggested a limited partnership as the best entity to finance and organize the venture and said he believed he could find a sufficient number of investors in the Fargo area. Emerson also recommended an attorney to draft the necessary legal documents. The attorney prepared a private placement memorandum for Canadian Wings Investment Limited Partnership ("Canadian Wings") and Lavelle formed Red River Wings, Inc. ("Red River Wings"), to serve as the general partner. The private placement memorandum informed potential investors that LTM would provide management services for the restaurants. Ownership units in Canadian Wings were offered for $80,000 per unit, and Emerson sold ten units to various investors. Many of the investors, including Richard Walstad, John Boulger, Hoadley Harris and the Harris Trust, David Butler, and ME Investments, LLP ("ME Investments"), a limited liability partnership formed by Curtis Kesselring and Dennis Leno, invested primarily because of Lavelle's reputation and involvement in the business. For their services, Stern and Emerson received fees and profits-only interests as special limited partners.

Lavelle was required by the West Edmonton Mall and Hooters of America to open the first Canadian restaurant as soon as possible. In order to meet the deadline, Lavelle borrowed money to construct the Edmonton Hooters restaurant. Kesselring and Leno did not make their investment, through ME Investments, until August 1996, one month after the restaurant had opened. The Edmonton restaurant was profitable from the beginning and the limited partners received healthy returns on their investments.

Under the Hooters of America franchise agreement, the option for a second Hooters restaurant in Canada had to be exercised within six months of the opening of the Edmonton restaurant. In December 1996, Lavelle offered to all partners in Canadian Wings the opportunity to invest in Manitoba Wings Investment Limited Partnership ("Manitoba Wings"), a partnership formed to own a Hooters restaurant in Winnipeg. Manitoba Wings was structured in the same manner as Canadian Wings, but the offering price per unit was $56,000 because of lower occupancy costs in Winnipeg. Emerson and Stern undertook their same roles in exchange for profits-only special limited partner interests. Emerson was unable to sell all of the units, however, and Data Enterprises, a partnership consisting of Lavelle and Dyan Dockter, and Wings Unlimited, a partnership consisting of Lavelle, Dyan Dockter, and Shelly Dockter, purchased two of the units to complete the initial offering. ME Investments, David Butler, and Hoadley Harris Trust also purchased units. Lavelle again borrowed money and advanced funds for the construction of the Winnipeg restaurant. Manitoba Wings opened the Winnipeg restaurant in March 1997 shortly before the 1997 Red River flood and in the face of bad pre-opening publicity. Nevertheless, the investors received returns on their investment, but less than the returns from the Edmonton restaurant.

In spring 1998, Stern became disturbed with Lavelle over projects other than the Edmonton and Winnipeg Hooters restaurants. Stern was upset that he was not hired as a consultant for the remodeling of one of Lavelle's restaurants in Billings, Montana, and was unhappy with La-velle's offer regarding his involvement in the development of a Hooters restaurant in Calgary. Stern sent faxes to several of the partners accusing Lavelle of dishonesty. Meanwhile, Lavelle's relationship with Emerson was also becoming strained. Emerson informed Lavelle that he had no investor prospects for the Calgary Hooters restaurant, and Lavelle decided to not use Emerson as the broker. Kesselring and Leno were also pressuring Emerson because the distributions from Manitoba Wings were not meeting his projections.

ME Investments, Emerson, Stern, Jerry Baldwin, Jill Baldwin, Patricia Corwin, and Clinton Emerson held a majority of the interests in the limited partnerships. Because the majority limited partners were dissatisfied with the performance of the Winnipeg restaurant, a meeting was held in May 1998 and their concerns were addressed by an accountant. In summer 1998, the majority limited partners hired a certified public accountant to investigate the financial records of Canadian Wings and Manitoba Wings, but no evidence of wrongdoing was found. The majority limited partners were not satisfied with the report and decided to take over the management of the two partnerships. They consulted with a law firm about removing Red River Wings from the partnerships and installing a new general partner. At the suggestion of Stern, they also contacted Texas Wings, a company that managed many Hooters restaurants in the United States, about taking over the management duties of LTM. The law firm responded that if Red River Wings was removed as the general partner, the limited partnerships would terminate unless a substitute general partner was appointed in accordance with N.D.C.C. § 45–10.1–47.

On October 25, 1998, the majority limited partners, through written action and without notice to minority limited partners, removed Red River Wings as the general partner of the two limited partnerships and appointed Hoot, Inc. ("Hoot"), as the replacement general partner. Hoot was a corporation formed by Kesselring and Leno for the sole purpose of serving as the replacement general partner for the limited partnerships. The majority partners also terminated the management contracts the partnerships had with LTM. Lavelle, who was aware of the majority partners' dissatisfaction, offered to amend the partnership agreements by changing the distribution allocations between the limited partners and the general partner which would have been financially beneficial to the limited partners. Lavelle's offer was not received until the day after the takeover, and the majority partners refused to reverse their decision to oust Red River Wings and LTM from the partnerships and the business ventures. The minority limited partners, which included Walstad, Boulger, Harris, and Butler, protested the takeover.

After executing the written action disposing of Red River Wings as the general partner, Stern and a representative of Texas Wings traveled to Edmonton to physically take control of the Canadian Wings restaurant. At the same time, Emerson and Swede Stelzer, the sole officer, director, and shareholder of Hoot and an employee of Kesselring and Leno, traveled to Winnipeg to take over the Manitoba Wings restaurant. The majority partners had made prior arrangements with the landlords and locksmiths for the physical takeover. Stern's expenses were paid by the partnerships.

Texas Wings performed poorly as the manager of the Edmonton and Winnipeg Hooters restaurants. After Hoot became the general partner, the limited partners did not receive distributions from Canadian Wings for almost two years, and the limited partners received no distributions from Manitoba Wings for almost three years. Within less than one year, Texas Wings voluntarily terminated its services after Stelzer informed Texas Wings of the limited partners' dissatisfaction with its poor performance. The majority partners, without input from the minority partners, hired UD Consulting to manage the Edmonton and Winnipeg restaurants.

The majority partners eventually sued Lavelle, Red River Wings, LTM, Shelly Dockter, Dyan Dockter and others in federal court seeking damages allegedly caused by Lavelle and his group. After the majority partners spent more than two years in litigation and about $350,000 in fees and costs, the federal court in 2002 dismissed the lawsuit without prejudice for lack of standing. On October 3, 2002, the majority partners voted to continue the lawsuit against Lavelle as a partnership claim and for the partnerships to assume the costs of the prior and future litigation. Minority partners objected, but those objections were ignored.

Three cases, which were consolidated for trial, arose from this scenario. The minority limited partners, consisting of Walstad, Harris, Butler, and Boulger, sued the majority limited partners derivatively and individually for breach of the partnership agreements and breach of fiduciary duties, and sought dissolution and an accounting of the partnerships. The majority partners, consisting of Hoot, Emerson, Clinton Emerson, Corwin, Jill Baldwin, Jerry Baldwin, Stern, and ME Investments, refiled their dismissed federal court action against Red River Wings, LTM, Lavelle, and his associates in state court. Lavelle, through Red River Wings, also sued Hoot, the replacement general partner, for damages for wrongfully withholding distributions.

Following a lengthy bench trial, the district court awarded damages to the minority group and Lavelle from the majority group for breach of fiduciary duties and awarded them a partial award of attorney fees. The court dismissed the majority partners' claims against Red River Wings, LTM, Lavelle, and his associates. The court also awarded LTM and Lavelle damages for services provided up to the date of the takeover against the majority partners and Hoot. These appeals followed.

The partnership agreements provide in section 13.1 that 51 percent "in aggregate investment interest" of the partners "may remove and terminate the General Partner for any reason, with or without cause." Section 13.1 does not address replacing a general partner. The majority partners had the authority to remove Red River Wings as the general partner with or without cause under the agreements. Under section 13.3, the "resignation, dissolution or bankruptcy of the General Partner shall dissolve the Partnership unless within 90 days after notice of such event is delivered to the Limited Partners, 51% in aggregate investment interest of the Limited Partners agree in writing to continue the business of the Partnership and appoint a successor General Partner." Red River Wings did not resign, was not dissolved, and was not the subject of a bankruptcy proceeding. Section 13.3 does not address the situation where the general partner is removed by a vote of the limited partners. Under section 13.2(a)(i) of the agreements, the partnerships "shall be dissolved upon . . . an event of withdrawal (as defined under North Dakota law) of the General Partner."

At the pertinent times in this case, limited partnerships were governed by the provisions of former N.D.C.C. ch. 45–10.1, rather than the provisions of N.D.C.C. ch. 45–10.2. Section 45–10.1–26(3), N.D.C.C., provided "a person ceases to be a general partner of a limited partnership upon the happening of any of the following events: . . . The general partner is removed as a general partner in accordance with the partnership agreement." This event occurred when the majority partners voted to remove Red River Wings as the general partner under the terms of the partnership agreements. Section 45–10.1–47(4), N.D.C.C., provided that "[a] limited partnership is dissolved and its affairs must be wound up upon the happening of . . . [a]n event of withdrawal of a general partner unless . . . within ninety days after the withdrawal, all partners agree in writing to continue the business of the limited partnership and to the appointment of one or more additional general partners if necessary or desired." It is undisputed that only the majority partners, not all of the partners, agreed in writing to the appointment of Hoot as the replacement general partner within 90 days after Red River Wings was removed as the general partner.

The terms of the partnership agreements and the relevant statutes are clear and unambiguous. The district court correctly concluded that unanimous written consent of all of the limited partners to appoint a new general partner was required within 90 days of the majority partners' removal of Red River Wings to avoid dissolution of the limited partnerships and that unanimous consent was not acquired. However, we disagree with the district court's conclusion that the limited partnerships were dissolved on October 25, 1998. Under the partnership agreements, the majority partners acted within their rights by removing Red River Wings on October 25, 1998, with or without cause. Under N.D.C.C. § 45–10.1–47(4), the majority partners had 90 days after October 25, 1998, to avoid dissolution by acquiring the written consent of all of the limited partners. Therefore, dissolution of the partnerships occurred not on October 25, 1998, but on January 23, 1999, when the 90–day period expired.

We conclude the district court did not err in granting summary judgment and declaring that Canadian Wings and Manitoba Wings were dissolved as a matter of law because of the majority partners' actions. . . .

The majority partners argue they cannot be held liable under the circumstances of this case because of N.D.C.C. § 45–10.1–22(1), which provided in relevant part:

> [A] limited partner is not liable for the obligations of a limited partnership unless the limited partner is also a general partner or, in addition to the exercise of the limited partner's rights and powers as a limited partner, the limited partner participates in the control of the business. However, if the limited partner participates in the control of the business, the limited partner is liable only to persons who transact business with the limited partnership reasonably believing, based upon the limited partner's conduct, that the limited partner is a general partner.

The majority partners claim that under this statute a limited partner can be liable only if the limited partner participated in control of the business, and that liability is limited to third parties who transacted business with the limited partnership reasonably believing that the limited partner was the general partner.

We reject the majority partners' argument. This Court has said that "in a limited partnership, general partners, with unlimited liability, manage the business; limited partners contribute only investment capital without participating in the business and without liability beyond capital contributed." *Pear v. Grand Forks Motel Assocs.*, 553 N.W.2d 774, 780 n. 2 (N.D.1996). However, N.D.C.C. § 45–10.1–22(1) does not address fiduciary duties owed to a partnership and to limited partners, but addresses only the liability of a limited partner for the "obligations of a limited partnership." Fiduciary duty claims are not obligations owed by the partnership. Section 45–10.1–27, N.D.C.C., retained fiduciary responsibilities by providing "a general partner of a limited partnership has the rights and powers and is subject to the restrictions and liabilities of a partner in a partnership without limited partners." Section 45–16–04, N.D.C.C., sets forth the standards of a partner's conduct:

1. The only fiduciary duties a partner owes to the partnership and the other partners are the duty of loyalty and the duty of care set forth in subsections 2 and 3.

2. A partner's duty of loyalty to the partnership and the other partners is limited to the following:

a. To account to the partnership and hold as trustee for it any property, profit, or benefit derived by the partner in the conduct and winding up of the partnership business or derived from a use by the partner of partnership property, including the appropriation of a partnership opportunity;

b. To refrain from dealing with the partnership in the conduct or winding up of the partnership business as or on behalf of a party having an interest adverse to the partnership; and

c. To refrain from competing with the partnership in the conduct of the partnership business before the dissolution of the partnership.

3. A partner's duty of care to the partnership and the other partners in the conduct and winding up of the partnership business is limited to refraining from engaging in grossly negligent or reckless conduct, intentional misconduct, or a knowing violation of law.

4. A partner shall discharge the duties to the partnership and the other partners under chapters 45–13 through 45–21 or under the partnership agreement and exercise any rights consistently with the obligation of good faith and fair dealing.

5. A partner does not violate a duty or obligation under chapters 45–13 through 45–21 or under the partnership agreement merely because the partner's conduct furthers the partner's own interest.

Other courts have similarly indicated that limited partners who participate in the business of the partnership or act in concert with the general partner are subject to the fiduciary duties of loyalty and care and the obligations of good faith and fair dealing applicable to partners in a general partnership. *See In re Villa West Assocs.,* 193 B.R. 587, 593 (Bkrtcy.D.Kan.1996) (although limited partner is like corporate shareholder who does not, solely by virtue of his interest in partnership, become a fiduciary to other limited partners, fiduciary responsibility develops when one takes a role in management and acts to dominate, interfere with, or mislead others in exercising their rights); *Welch v. Via Christi Health Partners, Inc.,* 281 Kan. 732, 133 P.3d 122, 139–40 (2006) (recognizing majority limited partners owe fiduciary duty to minority limited partners under some circumstances); *Anthony v. Padmar, Inc.,* 320 S.C. 436, 465 S.E.2d 745, 752 (App.1995) ("relationship of [limited] partners is fiduciary and partners are held to high standards of integrity in their dealings with each other," and "[p]arties in a fiduciary relationship must fully disclose to each other all known information that is significant and material").

In *Svihl v. Gress,* 216 N.W.2d 110, 111 Syll. 1 (N.D.1974), this Court stated:

> The conduct of partners during liquidation as well as during any transaction connected with the formation or conduct of the partnership is governed by a fiduciary duty which requires every partner to act with the utmost good faith and integrity in the dealings with one another with respect to partnership affairs. . . .

This Court has further recognized that a partner has a fiduciary duty of loyalty to the partnership and other partners. Fiduciary duties and obligations exist between limited partners and a general partner.

B

The majority limited partners argue the district court erred in ruling they breached their fiduciary duties.

Here, the district court found "[l]imited partners Emerson, Stern, Kesselring and Leno . . . were acting in concert with Hoot,""Emerson and Stern were deeply involved with the takeover and with the restaurant operation after the takeover,""Kesselring and Leno . . . controlled Hoot . . . and acted in concert by way of their controlling actions through the purported general partner," and "[i]nstalling Hoot . . . as general partner for both partnerships and running the partnerships under their own terms was a breach of the [majority] defendants' fiduciary duties to the minority partners." The court found the majority limited partners breached their fiduciary duties based on: 1) their "reckless action" of terminating the management contracts for both partnerships; 2) their knowledge that termination of the management contract with LTM would pose potential liability; 3) their "affirmative action to dominate and interfere with the partnership[s]" by taking them over and installing Hoot, a shell corporation controlled by Kesselring and Leno, as a general partner; 4) their authorizing reimbursement to the majority partners for attorney fees and expenses incurred in the federal litigation against Lavelle and his companies; 5) their causing the loss of the Hooters franchise and thereby significantly reducing the value of the two restaurants; 6) their refusals to cooperate with the court-appointed receiver; and 7) their taking these actions without calling meetings as required by the partnership agreements.

From our review of the record, we cannot say the district court's findings of fact are clearly erroneous. The evidence reflects that the majority group planned a takeover of the limited partnerships and proceeded to do so in a reckless manner. They sought legal advice for the takeover from Kesselring and Leno's attorneys, but failed to secure unanimous consent for a new general partner after having been advised that unanimous consent was necessary. Emerson and Stern attempted to find reasons to remove Lavelle and his companies from the limited partnerships and traveled to the restaurants to accomplish the takeover. The majority disposed of Red River Wings without the required notice or consent of Hooters of America and later sued the franchiser. They hired two replacement management companies, Texas Wings and UD Management, without notice or a vote of all of the limited partners. After the takeover, Kesselring and Leno directly controlled Hoot, and Emerson and Stern were directly involved in controlling the partnerships. Hoot has no assets, no employees, and no separate office, and Stelzer, its sole officer, director, and shareholder, acted on behalf of and at the direction of his employers, Kesselring and Leno. Kesselring and Emerson's control of the partnerships was obvious to Lavelle and the minority limited partners, who dealt directly with Kesselring and Emerson after the takeover in an attempt to resolve the disputes. The majority limited partners authorized reimbursement from the limited partnerships for attorney fees and expenses in the federal lawsuit. Moreover, after the district court appointed a receiver for the limited partnerships, the majority limited partners continued to refuse to surrender control, forcing the receiver to seek a court order to gain control of the partnerships' Canadian bank accounts. The majority limited partners were ultimately held in contempt of court.

The majority partners are incorrect in their assertion that the "limited partnership veil[s]" of Canadian Wings and Manitoba Wings needed to be "pierced" in order to hold Stern, Emerson, and ME Investments individually liable. This Court has held in the context of a close corporation, that minority shareholders are entitled to bring a direct action against majority shareholders for breach of fiduciary duties. *See Schumacher v. Schumacher,*RLINK"http://www.westlaw.com/Find/Default.wl? rs=dfa1.0 & vr=2.0 & DB=595 & FindType=Y & ReferencePositionType=S & SerialNum=1991088032 & ReferencePosition=798" 469

N.W.2d 793, 798–99 (N.D.1991). Likewise, the majority limited partners who controlled or acted in concert with the general partner in this case can be held personally liable to the minority limited partners for damages for breach of fiduciary duties.

We also are not persuaded by the majority partners' argument that Kesselring and Leno cannot be held personally liable because ME Investments was actually the limited partner in the partnerships. ME Investments, a limited liability partnership, was the vehicle used by Kesselring and Leno to invest in Canadian Wings and Manitoba Wings. It is obvious from the district court's decision that the court believed ME Investments to merely be the alter ego of Kesselring and Leno because the court refers to the limited liability partnership and the individuals as being one and the same. Principles for piercing a corporate veil apply to limited liability partnerships. To apply the alter ego doctrine, "there must be such a unity of interest and ownership between the corporation and its equitable owner that the separate personalities of the corporation and the shareholder do not in reality exist," and "there must be an inequitable result if the acts in question are treated as those of the corporation alone." Given the evidence of Kesselring and Leno's participation in the takeover and their direct control and actions in concert with Hoot through their employee, Stelzer, we agree with the district court's implicit finding that it would be inequitable if Kesselring and Leno's acts were treated as those of the limited liability partnership alone. We conclude that the district court did not err in holding Kesselring and Leno individually responsible under these circumstances.

The majority limited partners also argue Kesselring and Leno's actions are protected by the business judgment rule.

Although Kesselring and Leno claim they acted in good faith and exercised honest business judgment, the district court's findings reflect the majority group's actions were reckless, were undertaken in bad faith, and were for the purpose of furthering the group's own perceived interests. Evidence supports the court's finding that the majority partners acted recklessly by installing Hoot as the general partner on a majority vote after being advised that unanimity was required and by terminating LTM's management contracts without cause after being advised that cause was necessary. Bad faith is evidenced by the court's finding that the majority partners' reasons for the removal of Red River Wings and termination of the LTM management contracts were concocted after the fact to justify their actions. The majority partners' refusal to relinquish control of the limited partnerships to the court-appointed receiver and their attempt to use the partnerships' assets to finance the failed federal court action also evidence bad faith. The court specifically found Kesselring, Leno, Emerson, Stern, and Hoot "were acting in what they believed to be their own best interest or for their own reasons when they removed [Red River Wings] and LTM and ran the partnerships through Hoot, Inc., an entity that Kesselring and Leno controlled." We conclude these findings are supported by the evidence in the record and render the majority group's reliance on the business judgment rule unavailing.

———

REGULATING ROLLUPS: GENERAL PARTNERS' FIDUCIARY OBLIGATIONS IN LIGHT OF THE LIMITED PARTNERSHIP ROLLUP REFORM ACT OF 1993

47 Stanford L. Rev. 85.
By
John Geschke

The power to pass partnership losses through to the individual partners made limited partnerships in oil and gas exploration and real estate particularly attractive in the late 1970s and early 1980s. The tax treatment of limited partnerships allowed limited partners to offset the enterprises' large expenses (especially the costs of depreciation and depletion) against their personal incomes. At the same time, oil and gas exploration and real estate promised stable income distributions to limited partners through the lease and eventual sale of the partnership assets. These advantages led to a veritable boom in the offering of limited partnership interests. More than ten million people invested approximately $90 billion in limited partnerships during the 1970s and 1980s. At the time, the average limited partner was an individual between the ages of fifty and sixty who invested approximately $10,000. As these figures illustrate, limited partnership interests attracted individuals who otherwise could not benefit from the economies of scale large pools of capital offer. Institutional investors, which accumulate substantial capital with relative ease, had no need for this advantage and were conspicuously absent from the 1980s market for limited partnership interests.

In the mid–1980s, Congress overhauled the tax code through the Tax Reform Act of 1986. This legislation severely curtailed limited partnerships' greatest advantage, the ability to offset personal income with partnership losses. At the same time, a great many limited partnerships faced a decline in the value of their underlying assets as the markets for real estate and oil nearly collapsed in the late 1980s. As a result, the number of new limited partnership offerings plummeted: Securities and Exchange Commission filings fell from 428 in 1985 to 106 in 1990.

For existing limited partnerships, the market forces and changes in the tax law created a difficult predicament. Although limited partnerships promised stable income distributions, tax advantages, and limited liability, their primary disadvantage was their illiquidity. Investors were essentially "trapped" in the investment until partnership assets were liquidated and the proceeds distributed to the partners. As the value of the underlying assets declined, limited partners lost money with essentially no escape. Although traditional limited partnership interests are freely assignable, the inability to transfer status as a limited partner and the absence of an effective secondary market made transferring limited partnership interests essentially impossible. An informal secondary market exists that brings buyers and sellers of partnership interests together through "matching services." The price for entering this market, however, is steep. Matching services can involve a markup or markdown for executing a trade between 5 and 15 percent.

In an attempt to address this illiquidity, Master Limited Partnerships (MLPs) developed in the mid–1980s. An MLP is a publicly traded limited partnership which lists its interests on either an exchange or the over-the-counter market. These interests are known as "units" in order to circumvent the restrictions on transferability of limited partnership interests. Technically, investors holding these units do not enjoy limited partner status. Instead, they act as assignees of a depository that actually holds the status of limited partner and which assigns the units. Although MLPs carry "limited partnership" as a title, they essentially act as public corporations and may be subject to entity level taxation rather than pure "pass-through" treatment.

Essentially, a rollup transaction is the means to transform illiquid limited partnership interests into more liquid MLP units. In a rollup, several limited partnerships combine into one publicly traded entity. In exchange for their limited partnership interests, investors receive securities (predominantly equity but occasionally debt) in the new entity. Although this entity is often an MLP, limited partnerships have also been "rolled up" into corporations (both new and existing) and Real Estate Investment Trusts (REITs). Between 1985 and 1990, the number of registration statements for limited partnership rollups totaled sixty-five. These rollups involved "1,197 entities, approximately 1.2 million investors and an exchange value of approximately $6.9 billion."

Limited partnership rollups enjoy the clear theoretical advantage of providing liquidity to limited partners who transform into owners of securities in the resulting publicly traded entities. All things equal, the ability to transfer the ownership interest into cash should improve the overall value of the investment. A second perceived advantage of rollups is the diversification they can provide through combining a number of limited partnerships holding varied assets. Finally, rollups should increase returns by consolidating management to achieve economies of scale.

NOTES

1. Limited partnerships sold to the public are securities and are subject to the registration and other requirements of the federal securities laws that are discussed in chapter 12. The Limited Partnership Rollup Reform Act of 1993, Pub. L. No. 103–202, 107 Stat. 2359 (1993) amended the federal securities laws to include further provisions to assure fairness in the rollup of limited partnership interests. See S. Rep. No. 103–121 (1993) and H. R. Rep. No. 103–21 (1993) (description of that legislation and the abuses that led to its enactment).

2. Among the concerns in the public sale of limited partnership interests are fraudulent sales practices such as misleading profit claims or a failure to disclose the risks of the investment. In one case, the Securities and Exchange Commission, the agency responsible for enforcing the federal securities laws, charged that a brokerage firm had used widespread fraudulent sales practices to sell interests in seven hundred limited partnerships valued at $8 billion. Those limited partnership interests were sold to public customers who were often unsophisticated and who could ill afford the losses they sustained from these investments. See generally Kurt Eichenwald, *Serpent on the Rock* (1995) (describing the limited partnership sales practices of Prudential–Bache Securities, Inc. and the effects of losses on investors).

3. Despite the restriction of tax benefits for publicly traded limited partnerships and the creation of alternatives such as limited liability partnerships and limited liability companies, the limited partnership is still a useful business form. Limited partnerships continue to be used as an estate-planning device, especially for family controlled businesses. Because there is no active market for most interests in these limited partnerships, such interests carry discounts (frequently exceeding 25 percent) vis-à-vis the firm's underlying asset value. By establishing a family limited partnership, older family members may reduce their estate taxes substantially by conveying assets to a limited partnership that consists of heirs. D. John Thornton & Gregory A. Bryon, "Valuation of Family Limited Partnership Interests," 32 Idaho L. Rev. 345 (1996).

SECTION 2. LIMITED LIABILITY PARTNERSHIPS

LEWIS v. ROSENFELD

138 F.Supp.2d 466 (S.D.N.Y.2001).

SCHEINDLIN, DISTRICT JUDGE,

Michael P. Lewis brings this action against Eric D. Rosenfeld, Robert Bernstein, Robert B. Tannenhauser (collectively "Individual Defendants") and Rosenfeld, Bernstein & Tannenhauser, L.L.P. ("RBT"), the law firm in which the Individual Defendants were general partners. Lewis asserts state law claims of breach of fiduciary duty, common law fraud, civil conspiracy, and negligent misrepresentation. * * *

This action arises out of a $650,000 loan plaintiff made to Mad Martha's Ice Cream, Inc. ("Mad Martha's") in June 1995—a loan which was never repaid because Mad Martha's filed for bankruptcy on February 27, 1996. Plaintiff agreed to loan Mad Martha's these funds upon the advice of David M. Fresne, a Managing Director and broker at Bear, Stearns & Co., Inc. ("Bear Stearns"), who handled plaintiff's Bear Stearns accounts from April 1992 until April 1996. Neither Fresne nor Bear Stearns are named as defendants in this action.

In 1993, Tom Quinn began negotiating with Robert Young for the purchase from VSL of the Mad Martha's Ice Cream Stores ("Ice Cream Stores") on Martha's Vineyard. Quinn contacted Rosenfeld, seeking both legal assistance and help raising the funds to purchase Mad Martha's. Mad Martha's Management Corp. ("MMMC") was formed for the purpose of soliciting the funds. The Individual Defendants and Fresne also formed a general partnership, Tower Hill Associates ("Tower Hill"), for the purpose of conducting activities relating to the purchase of Mad Martha's.

Although MMMC failed to raise sufficient funds to make the full down payment, it purchased Mad Martha's in late August 1993 by issuing a short-term note for the difference. This left MMMC with little working capital. Nevertheless, in 1994, its first year of operation, MMMC expanded and opened ice cream stores on Nantucket Island and on Block Island. Quinn signed the lease for the Nantucket Store. However, due to the "negligence and incompetence" of Rosenfeld, Bernstein and RBT, the lease to the Nantucket Store was never transferred to MMMC. Because of this, Quinn was able to retain possession of and operate the Nantucket Store as if it were his own, despite being discharged from MMMC and accused of stealing $400,000 from MMMC. As a result, by the end of the 1994 Season, MMMC was absolutely broke. A new corporation, Mad Martha's Ice Cream, Inc. was formed and took over all the assets, activities and operations of MMMC. Mad Martha's stock was issued to Tower Hill, even though Tower Hill contributed no capital to Mad Martha's.

In November 1994, Young caused VSL to repossess the Ice Cream Stores as the first step in foreclosure proceedings. By agreement dated March 9, 1995, Mad Martha's agreed, *inter alia,* to pay VSL substantial funds by June 30, 1995, also known as the "Drop Dead Date." If not paid by then, VSL would be permitted to foreclose without Mad Martha's objection. In early 1995, Fresne, at Rosenfeld's urging, contacted Lewis almost daily for the purpose of soliciting Lewis as an investor in Mad Martha's. Rosenfeld knew that Lewis was Fresne's customer at Bear Stearns and that Fresne owed Lewis fiduciary duties. Lewis received a private offering memorandum for a Mad Martha's equity offering. After reading certain portions of the offering memorandum, Lewis returned it and informed Fresne that he was not interested in investing. Undaunted, Fresne, again at Rosenfeld's urging, continued to press Lewis. Plaintiff alleges that Fresne—who was now acting for Tower Hill, not Bear Stearns—was "acting as a conduit between Rosenfeld and Lewis and was 'parroting' Rosenfeld; i.e., Rosenfeld was telling Fresne what to say to Lewis to induce Lewis to invest the $650,000 into Mad Martha's."

Plaintiff alleges that Fresne and Rosenfeld made numerous oral misrepresentations of material fact during a June 1995 telephone conversation between Fresne, Rosenfeld and Lewis. * * * Plaintiff alleges that Rosenfeld was aware of these misrepresentations and omissions, and that plaintiff relied on them in making the decision to loan Mad Martha's $650,000. * * *

Plaintiff filed this suit on July 20, 2000, asserting four state law claims. Claim I alleges that Rosenfeld and RBT knew of Fresne's fiduciary duties to Lewis and "knowingly participated in, aided and abetted, induced and/or substantially assisted Fresne in committing fraud and breaching [his] fiduciary duties." Plaintiff alleges that Rosenfeld acted for himself, RBT, and Tower Hill. Claim II asserts that Rosenfeld—acting for both RBT and Tower Hill—and RBT committed common law fraud because they knew of Fresne's misrepresentations and omissions and "knowingly committed, participated in, aided and abetted, induced and/or substantially assisted" in Fresne's fraudulent actions. In the alternative, plaintiff asserts in claim III that defendants engaged in a civil conspiracy to divert plaintiff's funds to themselves or their affiliates. Claim IV alleges that the actions of Rosenfeld and RBT constitute negligent misrepresentation. Each claim seeks judgment against all defendants individually, jointly and severally. * * *

Defendants contend that Bernstein and Tannenhauser cannot be liable to plaintiff by reason of their membership in RBT because it was a registered limited liability partnership. Defendants correctly note that under New York law, partners of a limited liability partnership are not liable for the debts or liabilities, arising either in tort or contract, of the partnership solely by reason of their membership in that partnership. *See* N.Y. Partnership Law § 26(b) (McKinney 2001). However, a partner may be liable for "any negligent or wrongful act or misconduct committed by [the partner] or by any person under his or her direct supervision and control while rendering professional services on behalf of" the limited liability partnership. N.Y. Partnership Law § 26(c).

RBT is a limited liability partnership. Moreover, plaintiff has not alleged that any of the tortious acts were committed by Bernstein or Tannenhauser, or any individual under their control. Accordingly, Bernstein and Tannenhauser cannot be held vicariously liable by reason of their membership in RBT. However, because claims I and II assert that Rosenfeld's actions were taken on behalf of RBT and Tower Hill, Bernstein and Tannenhauser can be held vicariously liable for those claims by reason of their alleged membership in Tower Hill, a general partnership, irrespective of their membership in RBT. * * *

NOTES

1. The Limited Liability Partnership ("LLP") first appeared in Texas in 1991 as the result of legislation that sought to protect large law firms from being bankrupted as the result of misconduct by a single partner. That protection was thought necessary after a large Dallas law firm and its partners (including some retired ones) incurred large liabilities from the misconduct of a single partner in connection with his representation of certain savings and loan associations that were at the center of a debacle in that industry during the 1980s. Fearing such liability, more than 1200 Texas law firms became LLPs after the necessary authorizing legislation was enact-

ed. Robert W. Hamilton, "Registered Limited Liability Partnerships: Present at the Birth (Nearly)," 66 U. Colo. L. Rev. 1065 (1995). By 1997, 48 states had adopted legislation to authorize LLPs. James D. Cox & Thomas Lee Hazen, *Corporations* § 1.07[6] (2d ed. 2003).

2. The LLP statutes vary in their terms. Some require a minimum amount of capital or insurance for the firm before limited liability is available. Initially, many of the LLP statutes insulated the partners from tort but not contract liability. Later, many states, and the most recent version of the Revised Uniform Partnership Act, provide that the partners in LLPs are not liable for either the tort or contract obligations of the partnership or of the other partners.

Under Illinois law, limited liability extends to malpractice for the acts of other partners, but not ordinary commercial debt, a distinction that was being pursued in claims being made against a large accounting firm as the result of the bankruptcy of Enron Energy Corp. See Mitchell Pacelle, "Andersen Partners Are Enron Targets," Wall St. J., June 3, 2002, at A3.

The procedures for limited liability registration vary from state to state, but most states permit a general partnership to register as a limited liability partnership upon a majority vote of the partners and upon the filing of a registration form with the Secretary of State. See e.g., Del. Code Ann. § 1544.

3. As suggested in *Lewis v. Rosenfeld*, supra, the courts seem willing to accept the concept of limited liability for LLPs. See generally Dow v. Donovan, 150 F.Supp.2d 249, 268 (D.Mass.2001) (personal liability of individual partner will require proof of some wrongful act or omission on the part of the partner); Kus v. Irving, 46 Conn.Supp. 35, 736 A.2d 946, 947 (1999) (personal liability will be imposed for wrongful conduct of partner or those under the direct supervision or control of the partner). In Middlemist v. BDO Seidman, LLP, 958 P.2d 486, 491 (Colo.App.1997), the court stated that a partner in an LLP could not be held personally liable for the wrongdoing of another partner unless the "veil" created by the LLP is pierced in the same manner as that of a corporation. Veil piercing theories for imposing liability on the shareholders of a corporation are discussed in chapter 5.

SECTION 3.   LIMITED LIABILITY COMPANIES

ELF ATOCHEM NORTH AMERICA, INC. v. JAFFARI

727 A.2d 286 (Del.1999).

Veasey, Chief Justice

This is a case of first impression before this Court involving the Delaware Limited Liability Company Act (the "Act"). The limited liability company ("LLC") is a relatively new entity that has emerged in recent years as an attractive vehicle to facilitate business relationships and transactions. The wording and architecture of the Act is somewhat complicated, but it is designed to achieve what is seemingly a simple concept—to permit persons or entities ("members") to join together in an environment of private ordering to form and operate the enterprise under an LLC agreement with tax benefits akin to a partnership and limited liability akin to the corporate form. * * *

Plaintiff below-appellant Elf Atochem North America, Inc., a Pennsylvania Corporation ("Elf"), manufactures and distributes solvent-based maskants to the aerospace and aviation industries throughout the world. Defendant below-appellee Cyrus A. Jaffari is the president of Malek, Inc., a California Corporation. Jaffari had developed an innovative, environmentally-friendly alternative to the solvent-based maskants that presently dominate the market.

For decades, the aerospace and aviation industries have used solvent-based maskants in the chemical milling process. Recently, however, the Environmental Protection Agency ("EPA") classified solvent-based maskants as hazardous chemicals and air contaminants. To avoid conflict with EPA regulations, Elf considered developing or distributing a maskant less harmful to the environment.

In the mid-nineties, Elf approached Jaffari and proposed investing in his product and assisting in its marketing. Jaffari found the proposal attractive since his company, Malek, Inc., possessed limited resources and little international sales expertise. Elf and Jaffari agreed to undertake a joint venture that was to be carried out using a limited liability company as the vehicle.

On October 29, 1996, Malek, Inc. caused to be filed a Certificate of Formation with the Delaware Secretary of State, thus forming Malek LLC, a Delaware limited liability company under the Act. The certificate of formation is a relatively brief and formal document that is the first statutory step in creating the LLC as a separate legal entity. The certificate does not contain a comprehensive agreement among the parties, and the statute contemplates that the certificate of formation is to be complemented by the terms of the Agreement.

Next, Elf, Jaffari and Malek, Inc. entered into a series of agreements providing for the governance and operation of the joint venture. Of particular importance to this litigation, Elf, Malek, Inc., and Jaffari entered into the Agreement, a comprehensive and integrated document[5] of 38 single-spaced pages setting forth detailed provisions for the governance of Malek LLC, which is not itself a signatory to the Agreement. Elf and Malek LLC entered into an Exclusive Distributorship Agreement in which Elf would be the exclusive, worldwide distributor for Malek LLC. The Agreement provides that Jaffari will be the manager of Malek LLC. Jaffari and Malek LLC entered into an employment agreement providing for Jaffari's employment as chief executive officer of Malek LLC.

---

5. *See* the definition section of the statute, 6 *Del. C.* § 18–101(7), defining the term "limited liability company agreement" as "any agreement ... of the ... members as to the affairs of a limited liability company and the conduct of its business," and setting forth a nonexclusive list of what it may provide.

The Agreement is the operative document for purposes of this Opinion, however. Under the Agreement, Elf contributed $1 million in exchange for a 30 percent interest in Malek LLC. Malek, Inc. contributed its rights to the water-based maskant in exchange for a 70 percent interest in Malek LLC.

The Agreement contains an arbitration clause covering all disputes. * * * The Agreement also contains a forum selection clause, Section 13.7, providing that all members consent to: "exclusive jurisdiction of the state and federal courts sitting in California in any action on a claim arising out of, under or in connection with this Agreement or the transactions contemplated by this Agreement, provided such claim is not required to be arbitrated pursuant to Section 13.8"; and personal jurisdiction in California.

The phenomenon of business arrangements using "alternative entities" has been developing rapidly over the past several years. Long gone are the days when business planners were confined to corporate or partnership structures.

Limited partnerships date back to the 19th Century. They became an important and popular vehicle with the adoption of the Uniform Limited Partnership Act in 1916. Sixty years later, in 1976, the National Conference of Commissioners on Uniform State Laws approved and recommended to the states a Revised Uniform Limited Partnership Act ("RULPA"), many provisions of which were modeled after the innovative 1973 Delaware Limited Partnership (LP) Act. Difficulties with the workability of the 1976 RULPA prompted the Commissioners to amend RULPA in 1985.

To date, 48 states and the District of Columbia have adopted the RULPA in either its 1976 or 1985 form. Delaware adopted the RULPA with innovations designed to improve upon the Commissioners' product. Since 1983, the General Assembly has amended the LP Act eleven times, with a view to continuing Delaware's status as an innovative leader in the field of limited partnerships.

The Delaware Act was adopted in October 1992. The Act is codified in Chapter 18 of Title 6 of the Delaware Code. To date, the Act has been amended six times with a view to modernization. The LLC is an attractive form of business entity because it combines corporate-type limited liability with partnership-type flexibility and tax advantages. The Act can be characterized as a "flexible statute" because it generally permits members to engage in private ordering with substantial freedom of contract to govern their relationship, provided they do not contravene any mandatory provisions of the Act. Indeed, the LLC has been characterized as the "best of both worlds."

The Delaware Act has been modeled on the popular Delaware LP Act. In fact, its architecture and much of its wording is almost identical to that of the Delaware LP Act. Under the Act, a member of an LLC is treated much like a limited partner under the LP Act. The policy of freedom of contract underlies both the Act and the LP Act.

In August 1994, nearly two years after the enactment of the Delaware LLC Act, the Uniform Law Commissioners promulgated the Uniform Limited Liability Company Act (ULLCA).[6] To coordinate with later developments in federal tax guidelines regarding manager-managed LLCS, the Commissioners adopted minor changes in 1995. The Commissioners further amended the ULLCA in 1996. Despite its purpose to promote uniformity and consistency, the ULLCA has not been widely popular. In fact, only seven jurisdictions have adopted the ULLCA since its creation in 1994.[7] A notable commentator on LLCs has argued that legislatures should look to either the Delaware Act or the Prototype Act created by the ABA when drafting state statutes.

The basic approach of the Delaware Act is to provide members with broad discretion in drafting the Agreement and to furnish default provisions when the members' agreement is silent. The Act is replete with fundamental provisions made subject to modification in the Agreement (*e.g.* "unless otherwise provided in a limited liability company agreement....").

Although business planners may find comfort in working with the Act in structuring transactions and relationships, it is a somewhat awkward document for this Court to construe and apply in this case. To understand the overall structure and thrust of the Act, one must wade through provisions that are prolix, sometimes oddly organized, and do not always flow evenly. Be that as it may as a problem in mastering the Act as a whole, one returns to the narrow and discrete issues presented in this case.

Section 18–1101(b) of the Act, like the essentially identical Section 17–1101(c) of the LP Act, provides that "[i]t is the policy of [the Act] to give the maximum effect to the principle of freedom of contract and to the enforceability of limited liability company agreements." Accordingly, the following observation relating to limited partnerships applies as well to limited liability companies:

> The Act's basic approach is to permit partners to have the broadest possible discretion in drafting their partnership agreements and to furnish answers only in situations where the partners have not expressly made provisions in their partnership agreement. Truly, the partnership agreement is the cornerstone of a Delaware limited partnership, and effectively constitutes the entire agreement among

---

6. Jennifer J. Johnson, *Limited Liability for Lawyers: General Partners Need Not Apply,* 51 Bus.Law. 85, n. 69 (1995). In addition to the ULLCA, a Prototype Limited Liability Company Act ("Prototype Act") was drafted by the Subcommittee on Limited Liability Companies of the ABA Section of Business Law. The Prototype Act was released in the Fall of 1993 and has formed the basis for several LLC statutes enacted since that time. *See id.*

7. To date, the seven jurisdictions that have adopted the ULLCA are Alabama, South Dakota, the U.S. Virgin Islands, Hawaii, South Carolina, Vermont, and West Virginia. *See* Uniform Limited Liability Company Act (1995), Table of Jurisdictions Wherein Act Has Been Adopted and additional information provided by the Uniform Law Commissioners (Mar. 17, 1999).

the partners with respect to the admission of partners to, and the creation, operation and termination of, the limited partnership. Once partners exercise their contractual freedom in their partnership agreement, the partners have a great deal of certainty that their partnership agreement will be enforced in accordance with its terms.[8]

In general, the commentators observe that only where the agreement is inconsistent with mandatory statutory provisions will the members' agreement be invalidated. Such statutory provisions are likely to be those intended to protect third parties, not necessarily the contracting members. As a framework for decision, we apply that principle to the issues before us, without expressing any views more broadly.

In vesting the Court of Chancery with jurisdiction, the Act accomplished at least three purposes: (1) it assured that the Court of Chancery has jurisdiction it might not otherwise have because it is a court of limited jurisdiction that requires traditional equitable relief or specific legislation to act;[9] (2) it established the Court of Chancery as the default forum in the event the members did not provide another choice of forum or dispute resolution mechanism; and (3) it tends to center interpretive litigation in Delaware courts with the expectation of uniformity. Nevertheless, the arbitration provision of the Agreement in this case fosters the Delaware policy favoring alternate dispute resolution mechanisms, including arbitration. Such mechanisms are an important goal of Delaware legislation, court rules, and jurisprudence.

Elf argues that because Malek LLC, on whose behalf Elf allegedly brings these claims, is not a party to the Agreement, the derivative claims it brought on behalf of Malek LLC are not governed by the arbitration and forum selection clauses of the Agreement.

Elf argues that Malek LLC came into existence on October 29, 1996, when the parties filed its Certificate of Formation with the Delaware Secretary of State. The parties did not sign the Agreement until November 4, 1996. Elf contends that Malek LLC existed as an LLC as of October 29, 1996, but never agreed to the Agreement because it did not sign it. Because Malek LLC never expressly assented to the arbitration and forum

---

8. Martin I. Lubaroff & Paul Altman, *Delaware Limited Partnerships* § 1.2 (1999) (footnote omitted). In their article on Delaware limited liability companies, Lubaroff and Altman use virtually identical language in describing the basic approach of the LLC Act. Clearly, both the LP Act and the LLC Act are uniform in their commitment to "maximum flexibility."

9. The Court of Chancery has the traditional jurisdiction of equity in England and such additional jurisdiction as shall be conferred by the legislature. *See* Del. Const. art. IV, § 10 ("This court shall have all the jurisdiction and powers vested by the laws of this State in the Court of Chancery."); Del. Const. art. IV, § 17 ("The General Assembly, notwithstanding anything contained in this Article, shall have power to repeal or alter any Act of the General Assembly giving jurisdiction to ... the Court of Chancery, in any matter, or giving any power to either of the said courts. The General Assembly shall also have power to confer upon the ... Court of Chancery jurisdiction and powers in addition to those hereinbefore mentioned."); *Beals v. Washington Int'l, Inc.,* Del.Ch., 386 A.2d 1156, 1159–60 (1978) (holding in the absence of legislative finding and action, Court of Chancery will not alter historical limitation on its jurisdiction and impose punitive damages in stockholder derivative suit); *Box v. Box,* Del. Supr., 697 A.2d 395, 399 n. 12 (1997) (citing *Beals,* 386 A.2d 1156) (same).

selection clauses within the Agreement, Elf argues it can sue derivatively on behalf of Malek LLC pursuant to 6 *Del.C.* § 18–1001.[10]

We are not persuaded by this argument. Section 18–101(7) defines the limited liability company agreement as "any agreement, written or oral, *of the member or members* as to the affairs of a limited liability company and the conduct of its business." Here, Malek, Inc. and Elf, the members of Malek LLC, executed the Agreement to carry out the affairs and business of Malek LLC and to provide for arbitration and forum selection.

Notwithstanding Malek LLC's failure to sign the Agreement, Elf's claims are subject to the arbitration and forum selection clauses of the Agreement. The Act is a statute designed to permit members maximum flexibility in entering into an agreement to govern their relationship. It is the members who are the real parties in interest. The LLC is simply their joint business vehicle. This is the contemplation of the statute in prescribing the outlines of a limited liability company agreement. * * *

We affirm the judgment of the Court of Chancery dismissing Elf Atochem's amended complaint for lack of subject matter jurisdiction.

NOTES

1. Federal income tax advantages spurred the spread of LLC statutes. In 1988, the Internal Revenue Service (IRS) issued Revenue Ruling 88–76, which allowed a Wyoming LLC to be treated as a partnership for federal income tax purposes. This allowed gains and losses to be passed through to the LLC members, avoiding the double taxation experienced in corporations that were taxed as separate entities. Although small corporations could elect "Subchapter S" status under the tax laws (thereby allowing pass-through treatment to shareholders), there were various restrictions that limited the use of that device. The LLC avoided those restrictions. Effective January 1, 1997, however, the Internal Revenue Service adopted a "check-the-box" procedure for entity classification that provided similar flexibility to the Subchapter S entities. Treas. Reg. § 301.7701–3a. This also allowed unincorporated businesses with two or more owners to choose whether to be taxed as a corporation or partnership.

2. The "interests" of the members of an LLC are not represented by stock; the members hold interests much like partners in a partnership. This raises the issue of whether interests in an LLC are securities that are subject to regulation under the federal securities laws. Those regulations are described in Chapters 12, 15, 19, and 22. An ownership interest in an LLC will likely be treated as a security when its members' involvement in the management is akin to that of limited partners or the member is otherwise so dependent on the promoters or active managers as to be essentially a passive investor. However, in a member managed LLC which resembles a general partnership, the active involvement of the members may preclude application

---

10. 6 *Del.C.* § 18–1001 provides: "Right to bring action. A member may . . . bring an action in the Court of Chancery in the right of a limited liability company to recover a judgment in its favor if managers or members with authority to do so have refused to bring the action or if an effort to cause those managers or members to bring the action is not likely to succeed."

of the federal securities laws, which are directed at the regulation of transferable investment interests. James D. Cox & Thomas Lee Hazen, *Corporations* § 1.11 (2d ed. 2003).

3. The court in the *Elf Atochem* case, above, describes the role of Delaware's chancery court in corporate matters. That court has become an important source for much corporate law in America due to the fact that many large corporations are chartered in Delaware in order to take advantage of its liberal corporate laws. Does the availability of arbitration diminish that role? Some ten other states have created specialized courts for corporate and commercial matters, including California, New York, Illinois, Michigan, and Pennsylvania. North Carolina created a Business Court in order to make the state more friendly for businesses. Carrie O'Brien, "The North Carolina Business Court: North Carolina's Special Superior Court for Complex Business Cases," 6 N. C. Banking Instit. 367 (2002). Do you know whether your state has courts specially designated to handle corporate issues?

———

HARBISON v. STRICKLAND

900 So.2d 385 (Ala. 2004).

SEE, JUSTICE.

* * * Harbison argues that the trial court erred in referring only to the four corners of the document in interpreting the operating agreement. Harbison contends that the ALLCA [Alabama Limited Liability Company Act] imposes upon members and managers of limited liability companies fiduciary duties that cannot be eliminated by the adoption of an operating agreement. Thus, Harbison argues, by failing to incorporate the fiduciary duties mandated by the ALLCA into the operating agreement, the trial court has committed reversible error. This is an issue of first impression in this State.

It is well-settled in Alabama that a corporation is a "creature of statute." Baldwin County Elec. Membership Corp. v. Lee, 804 So. 2d 1087, 1090 (Ala. 2001)(quoting 1 Charles Keating & Gail O'Gradney, Fletcher Cyclopedia of the Law of Private Corporations § 3635 at 226 (1990)). A "corporation is ... subject to valid, appropriate measures of control, surveillance, and regulation government may impose...." Fairhope Single Tax Corp. v. Melville, 193 Ala. 289, 305, 69 So. 466, 471 (1915). "The charter of a corporation consists of its articles of incorporation taken in connection with the law under which it was organized...." State ex rel. Carter v. Harris, 273 Ala. 374, 376, 141 So. 2d 175, 176 (1961). "Provisions governing corporate operations include not only a corporation's articles of incorporation and bylaws, but also relevant sections of the statutory scheme under which the corporation exists." Baldwin County Elec. Membership Corp., 804 So. 2d at 1090. Additionally, "where the articles of incorporation or the bylaws conflict with the statute, the statute controls." Id.

The Legislature has imposed on corporations and partnerships fiduciary duties that cannot be waived. In Brooks v. Hill, 717 So. 2d 759, 764 (Ala. 1998), we stated: " 'The statute [§ 10–2A–71, Ala. Code 1975] constitutes a more specific statutory expression of the general fiduciary duty owed by the directors and officers to shareholders under the Alabama Business Corporation Act.' " (Quoting Fulton v. Callahan, 621 So. 2d 1235, 1246–47 (Ala. 1993)(emphasis omitted).) We have similarly held that partners are bound by the fiduciary duties provided by statute. Cox v. F & S, 489 So. 2d 516, 518 (Ala. 1986).

Like corporations and limited partnerships, limited liability companies are creatures of statute. §§ 10–12–1 to 10–12–61, Ala. Code 1975; see also McGee v. Best, 106 S.W.3d 48, 57 (Tenn. Ct. App. 2002)("An LLC is a creature of statute, and any duty which members owe must be set forth in the statute."). Therefore, in interpreting an operating agreement for a limited liability company, the Court must look to the ALLCA.

In 1997 the Legislature added subsections (e) through (*l*) to § 10–12–21, Ala. Code 1975, a part of the ALLCA. Those subsections provide that a member owes a duty of loyalty to the LLC.[1] Section 10–12–21, Ala. Code 1975, imposes these same duties on managers, plus the following additional burdens:

> "(*l*) The articles of organization or operating agreement may modify the duties contained in subsections (e) through (k) but may not provide for the following:
>
> > (1) Unreasonably restrict a right to information or access to records under Section 10–12–16;

---

1. (e) In a limited liability company managed by its members under subsection (a) of Section 10–12–22, the only fiduciary duties a member owes to the company or to its other members are the duty of loyalty and the duty of care imposed by subsections (f) through (g).

(f) A member's duty of loyalty to a member-managed limited liability company and its members is limited to each of the following:

(1) To account to the limited liability company and to hold as trustee for it any property, profit, or benefit derived by the member in the conduct or winding up of the limited liability company's business or derived from a use by the member of the limited liability company's property, including the appropriation of the limited liability company's opportunity.

(2) To refrain from dealing with the limited liability company in the conduct or winding up of the limited liability company's business as or on behalf of a party having an interest adverse to the limited liability company.

(3) To refrain from competing with the limited liability company in the conduct of the limited liability company's business before the dissolution of the limited liability company.

(g) A member's duty of care to a member-managed limited liability company and its other members in the conduct or winding up of the limited liability company's business is limited to refraining from engaging in grossly negligent or reckless conduct, intentional misconduct, or a knowing violation of the law.

(h) A member shall discharge the duties to a member-managed company and its other members under this chapter or under the operating agreement and exercise any rights consistently with the obligation of good faith and fair dealing.

(i) A member of a member-managed company does not violate a duty or obligation under this chapter or under the operating agreement merely because the member's conduct furthers the member's own interest.

(2) Eliminate the duty of loyalty under subsection (f) or subsection (e) of 10–12–36 . . . ;

(3) Unreasonably reduce the duty of care under subsection (g) or subsection (e) of Section 10–12–36;

(4) Eliminate the obligation of good faith and fair dealing under subsection (h), but the operating agreement may determine the standards by which the performance of the obligation is to be measured, if the standards are not manifestly unreasonable.

Thus, the plain language of § 10–12–21(*l*), Ala. Code 1975, does not allow an operating agreement for a limited liability company to unreasonably restrict a member's right to information, to eliminate a manager's duty of loyalty, or to unreasonably reduce the duty of care as defined in § 10–12–36, Ala. Code 1975. We hold that operating agreements of limited liability companies, like those of corporations and limited partnerships, incorporate the provisions of the statutes that allow for the creation of such agreements. Thus, the trial court erred in failing to look past the "four corners" of the document to determine Strickland's fiduciary obligations, if any, to the LLC and its members. On remand the trial court is to determine whether Strickland breached the fiduciary duties imposed on her by the ALLCA.

Harbison also argues that the trial court erroneously concluded that it was within Strickland's authority under the operating agreement to "dispose of the [LLC] property in any way she saw fit," because the LLC is "not for profit." The trial court's interpretation of the operating agreement depends on its finding that the purpose of the LLC was to distribute the Stricklands' assets. The trial court apparently relied on Strickland's testimony that, regardless of what the operating agreement actually provided, her "intent was to give their two children David Strickland . . . and the Plaintiff, Suzy Strickland Harbison, each one-half of what was left of their estate assets."

Operating agreements of limited liability companies serve as contracts that set forth the rights, duties, and relationships of the parties to the agreement. See Love v. Fleetway Air Freight & Delivery Serv., L.L.C., 875 So. 2d 285 (Ala. 2003). "It is elementary that it is the terms of the written contract, not the mental operations of one of the parties, that control its interpretation." Kinmon v. J.P. King Auction Co., 290 Ala. 323, 325, 276 So. 2d 569, 570 (1973)(citing Todd v. Devaney, 265 Ala. 486, 92 So. 2d 24 (1957)). "Stated another way, the law of contracts is premised upon an objective rather than a subjective manifestation of intent approach." Lilley v. Gonzales, 417 So. 2d 161, 163 (Ala. 1982). * * *

Article III of the operating agreement clearly states that "the company is organized to make a profit, increase wealth and provide a means for the Equity Owners to become knowledgeable of, manage and preserve the Company Property."

This language indicates that the trial court's ruling suggesting that the LLC was meant to serve as a "nonprofit" vehicle and that Strickland could therefore dispose of the property as she wished is not supported by the terms of the operating agreement. Indeed, the very provision that the trial court relies upon to support its ruling—Article VI, Section 6.4.1—authorizes the manager of the LLC to make business decisions for the LLC, "based on the best interest of the LLC, [and] the best interests of the Equity Owners." Article VI, Section 6.3.3, further provides:

> Notwithstanding any other provisions of this section 6.3 to the contrary, neither the Managers nor any Member or Members shall have the authority to amend this Operating Agreement or take any action that would have a Material Adverse Effect on a similarly situated group of Equity Owners ... without the consent of Equity Owners....

The trial court's finding that Strickland could dispose of the property of the LLC as she saw fit is irreconcilable with the language of the operating agreement that requires Strickland to consider the best interests of the LLC and the other equity owner, Harbison, before making any business decisions regarding the LLC. Strickland has not produced evidence indicating that she considered the interests of the LLC before she sold the real property. On remand, the trial court is to determine whether Strickland violated her duties as manager of the LLC, under the plain language of the operating agreement.

The summary judgment is reversed and the case remanded for proceedings consistent with this opinion.

REVERSED AND REMANDED.

Nabers, C.J., and Johnstone, Harwood, and Stuart, JJ., concur.

NOTES

1.   The members of an LLC usually enter into an "operating agreement" that functions much like a partnership agreement. Under most LLC statutes, the authority to manage rests with the firm's members, unless the members allocate managerial authority so that some members can be assured of being active while others are passive. In member managed LLCs, each of the members is an agent of the LLC and has the authority to bind it in the ordinary course of business. See generally Taghipour v. Jerez, 26 P.3d 885 (Utah App.2001) (a member-manager could bind an LLC in a real estate transaction even though operating agreement required the approval of all members).

2.   As is the case for participants in other business organizations, the relationship of the members of an LLC may raise issues as to whether they owe each other fiduciary duties and, if so, what are those duties. Many LLC statutes defer to the operating agreement to define the parties' respective

rights and involvement, and some even permit specification of the fiduciary obligations, if any, that will exist among the parties. In one case a court enforced the terms of an LLC's operating agreement that permitted the members to enter into competition with the LLC, which would otherwise breach a duty of loyalty. McConnell v. Hunt Sports Enterprises, 132 Ohio App.3d 657, 725 N.E.2d 1193 (1999). In the absence of such an agreement, the courts may apply fiduciary obligations found in other business enterprises, which usually include the duties of care and loyalty. See Carson v. Lynch Multimedia Corp., 123 F. Supp.2d 1254 (D.Kan.2000) (court rejects claim that there are no fiduciary duties in an LLC unless such duties are specified in the operating agreement). See generally VGS, Inc. v. Castiel, 2000 WL 1277372 (Del.Ch.2000) (merger set aside where, among other things, there was a breach of the duty of loyalty); McConnell v. Hunt Sports Enters., 132 Ohio App.3d 657, 725 N.E.2d 1193, 1214–1216 (1999) (LLC, like partnership, involves fiduciary relationship; members owe one another the duty of utmost trust and loyalty); Flippo v. CSC Associates III, L.L.C., 262 Va. 48, 547 S.E.2d 216 (2001) (breach of fiduciary found and punitive damages of $350,000 awarded). See also Gotham Partners, L.P. v. Hallwood Realty Partners, L.P., 817 A.2d 160 (Del. 2002) (Delaware's version of RULPA does not permit eliminating fiduciary duties in the limited partnership agreement).

3. Voting rights for LLC members may be defined by the operating agreement. In the absence of such an agreement, some states, following the partnership model, grant LLC members an equal voice, while other states set voting rights based on proportional ownership.

LIEBERMAN v. WYOMING.com LLC,

11 P.3d 353 (Wyo.2000).

LEHMAN, CHIEF JUSTICE.

In this case, we review a summary judgment in favor of appellee Wyoming.com LLC, directing it to return only the capital contribution made by a withdrawing member of the LLC, appellant E. Michael Lieberman (Lieberman). Although the district court correctly resolved the return of Lieberman's capital contribution, its order does not resolve the question of what became of the rest of Lieberman's interest in the company. We affirm in part and reverse and remand for full resolution of the parties' dispute. * * *

On September 30, 1994, Steven Mossbrook, Sandra Mossbrook, and Lieberman created Wyoming.com LLC by filing Articles of Organization with the Wyoming Secretary of State. The initial capital contributions to Wyoming.com were valued at $50,000. Lieberman was vested with an initial capital contribution of $20,000, to consist of services rendered and to be rendered. According to the Articles of Organization, Lieberman's contribution represented a 40% ownership interest in the LLC. The Mossbrooks were vested with the remaining $30,000 capital contribution and 60% ownership interest. In August of 1995, the Articles of Organization of Wyoming.com were amended to reflect an increase in capitalization to $100,000. The increase in capitalization was the result of the addition of two members, each of whom was vested with a capital contribution of $25,000, representing a 2.5% ownership interest for each new member. Despite the increase in capitalization, Lieberman's ownership interest, as well as his stated capital contribution, remained the same.

On February 27, 1998, Lieberman was terminated as vice president of Wyoming.com and required to leave the business premises. The other members of Wyoming.com met the same day and approved and ratified the termination. On March 13, 1998, Lieberman served Wyoming.com and its members with a document titled "Notice of Withdrawal of Member Upon Expulsion: Demand for Return of Contributions to Capit[a]l." In addition to giving notice of his withdrawal from the company, Lieberman's notice demanded the immediate return of "his share of the current value of the company," estimating the value of his share at $400,000, "based on a recent offer from the Majority Shareholder."

In response to Lieberman's notice of withdrawal, the members of Wyoming.com held a special meeting on March 17, 1998, and accepted Lieberman's withdrawal. The members also elected to continue, rather than dissolve, Wyoming.com. Additionally, they approved the return of Lieberman's $20,000 capital contribution. However, Lieberman refused to accept the $20,000 when it was offered. * * *

Because this case presents our first opportunity to interpret the Wyoming LLC act, we make a few preliminary observations. Wyoming initiated a national movement in 1977 when it adopted the first limited liability company act in the United States. *See* Carter G. Bishop, *Treatment of Members Upon Their Death and Withdrawal from a Limited Liability Company: The Case for a Uniform Paradigm,* 25 Stetson L.Rev. 255, 256 (1995); 1977 Wyo. Sess. Laws ch. 158. As a business entity, limited liability companies are a conceptual hybrid, sharing some of the characteristics of partnerships and some of corporations. "In general, the purpose of forming a limited liability company is to create an entity that offers investors the protections of limited liability and the flow-through tax status of partnerships." Jonathan R. Macey, *The Limited Liability Company: Lessons for Corporate Law,* 73 Wash.U.L.Q. 433, 434 (1995); Tassma A. Powers & Deby L. Forry, *Partnership Taxation & the Limited Liability Company: Check out the Check-the-Box Entity Classification,* 32 Land & Water L.Rev. 831 (1997).

Little case law exists regarding a member's interest in a LLC. Regardless, the precedential value of cases from other jurisdictions is questionable: "Widely divergent rules on the effects of member dissociation will ultimately create confusion and inhibit the development of uniform case law. As a result, case law will have little precedential value from state to state." *See* Carter G. Bishop, *Treatment of Members Upon Their Death and Withdrawal from a Limited Liability Company: The Case for a*

Uniform Paradigm, 25 Stetson L.Rev. 255, 261–63 (1995). Therefore, we must focus our review on the Wyoming LLC act as well as Wyoming.com's Articles of Organization and Operating Agreement.

Under the Wyoming LLC act, a member's interest in an LLC consists of economic and non-economic interests. One interest is a member's capital contribution, which a member may withdraw under certain conditions. Wyo. Stat. Ann. §§ 17–15–115 and 120. A member also generally has the right to receive profits. Wyo. Stat. Ann. § 17–15–119. A member's interest also usually grants him the ability to participate in management. Wyo. Stat. Ann. § 17–15–116. Overall, a member's interest is transferable, although the management rights of a transferee may be limited. Wyo. Stat. Ann. § 17–15–122. While these statutory provisions provide some guidance regarding a member's interest, we must also look at an LLC's operating agreement and articles of organization.

Turning to the issues presented, we first address whether Lieberman's withdrawal triggered dissolution of Wyoming.com. Wyo. Stat. Ann. § 17–15–123(a)(iii) requires that, upon withdrawal of a member, the LLC must dissolve unless all the remaining members of the company consent to continue under a right to do so stated in the articles of organization. Paragraph 9 of the Articles of Organization of Wyoming.com LLC permits continuation:

> **9.   Continuity.** The remaining members of the LLC, providing they are two or more in number, will have the right to continue the business on the death, retirement, resignation, expulsion, bankruptcy or dissolution of a member or occurrence of any other event which terminates the continued membership of a member in this LLC, in accordance with the voting provisions of the Operating Agreement of the Company.

The minutes of a March 17, 1998, special meeting of Wyoming.com reflect that the remaining members of Wyoming.com elected to continue the LLC after Lieberman's departure. This set of undisputed facts establishes there was no dissolution, and Lieberman is not entitled to distribution of assets under Wyo. Stat. Ann. § 17–15–126, as he claimed.

We next address the propriety of the return of contributions to capital. In his notice of withdrawal, Lieberman invoked Wyo. Stat. Ann. § 17–15–120, which provides in pertinent part:

> § 17–15–120.   Withdrawal or reduction of members' contributions to capital.
>
> (a) A member shall not receive out of limited liability company property any part of his or its contribution to capital until:
>
>> (i) All liabilities of the limited liability company, except liabilities to members on account of their contributions to capital, have been paid or there remains property of the limited liability company sufficient to pay them;

(ii) The consent of all members is had, unless the return of the contribution to capital may be rightfully demanded as provided in this act;

(iii) The articles of organization are cancelled or so amended as to set out the withdrawal or reduction.

(b) Subject to the provisions of subsection (a) of this section, a member may rightfully demand the return of his or its contribution: * * *

(ii) Unless otherwise prohibited or restricted in the operating agreement, after the member has given all other members of the limited liability company prior notice in writing in conformity with the operating agreement. If the operating agreement does not prohibit or restrict the right to demand the return of capital and no notice period is specified, a member making the demand must give six (6) months prior notice in writing.

In applying § 17–15–120(b)(ii), we note that Wyoming.com's Operating Agreement does not prohibit or restrict the right of a member to demand the return of capital contribution. It is undisputed that Lieberman's stated capital contribution was $20,000 when the LLC was formed and that no subsequent amendment to the Articles of Organization changed the stated amount of his contribution. Furthermore, the remaining members of Wyoming.com agreed to return $20,000 to Lieberman, and neither party contends he is not entitled to the return of $20,000. Under these circumstances, Lieberman is entitled to the return of his capital contribution pursuant to Wyo. Stat. Ann. § 17–15–120. However, the question is whether the return is limited to the sum of $20,000.

Lieberman claims the term "contribution to capital" found in Wyo. Stat. Ann. § 17–15–120 should be interpreted to encompass the fair market value of his interest in the LLC and that his return should not be limited to the amount of his initial capital contribution. At this juncture, a distinction must be drawn between withdrawal of a member's capital contribution and the withdrawal from membership in an LLC, often termed dissociation. After a thorough review of § 17–15–120, we conclude nothing in that provision contemplates a member's rights upon dissociation. Besides the fact that § 17–15–120 speaks only to withdrawal of capital contributions, other provisions in the LLC act support our conclusion that § 17–15–120 does not govern dissociation. The following passage from § 17–15–119, which controls division of profits, envisions withdrawal of capital contribution without dissociation: "If the operating agreement does not so provide, distributions shall be made on the basis of the value of the contributions made by each member to the extent they have been received by the limited liability company and have not been returned." This quoted material clearly contemplates a situation where a member has withdrawn some (or even all) of his capital contribution but has not dissociated as a member. We conclude a withdrawal of capital contributions pursuant to § 17–15–120 does not also govern a member's rights upon dissociation.

In addition, we conclude § 17–15–120 permits the return of only the initial or stated capital contribution of a member. First and foremost, nothing in § 17–15–120 indicates that fair market value of a member's interest is to be included in the amount to be paid to a member upon withdrawal of that member's capital contribution. In addition, § 17–15–129(b)(i) requires amendment to an LLC's articles of organization when the amount or character of contributions changes. Thus, the amount of a member's capital contribution is a constant not subject to market fluctuations. Numerous LLC acts from other states do allow a member to receive the fair market value (or fair value) of the member's interest. However, those provisions generally contemplate dissociation, not simply withdrawal of capital contributions.[11]

The foregoing discussion disposes of Lieberman's claim that he is entitled to demand dissolution under Wyo. Stat. Ann. § 17–15–120(d), which provides in pertinent part:

> 17–15–120. Withdrawal or reduction of members' contributions to capital. * * *
>
> (d) A member of a limited liability company may have the limited liability company dissolved and its affairs wound up when:
>
> (i) The member rightfully but unsuccessfully has demanded the return of his or its contribution[.]

To compel dissolution under this provision, Lieberman's demand for the return of his capital contribution must have been unsuccessful.

The record establishes, and Lieberman does not deny, that Wyoming.com offered to return his $20,000 capital contribution. Because Lieberman has been offered all that to which he is entitled, his demand for the return of his capital contribution has not been unsuccessful for purposes of § 17–15–120(d)(i). He, therefore, cannot compel dissolution under § 17–15–120(d)(i). This, however, does not end our discussion.

Having determined that § 17–15–120 does not control a member's rights upon dissociation, we must determine what became of Lieberman's interest, other than his capital contribution, in Wyoming.com. Unfortu-

---

11. *See* Ariz.Rev.Stat. Ann. § 29–707 (West 1998 Supp.); Ark.Code Ann. § 4–32–603 (Michie 1996 Repl.) (Distributions on an event of dissociation); Del.Code Ann. Tit. 6 § 18–604 (1999) (Distribution upon resignation); Fla. Stat. Ann. § 608.427 (West 2000 Supp.) (Withdrawal of member and distribution upon withdrawal); Ga.Code Ann. § 14–11–405 (Harrison 1999 Supp.) (Distributions to disassociated members); Ill.Ann.Stat. ch. 805, para. 180/35–60 (West 2000 Supp.); Ind.Code Ann. § 23–18–5–5.1 (Michie 2000 Supp.) (Rights of dissociating member); Iowa Code Ann. § 490A.805 (West 1999) (Distribution upon withdrawal); Mich. Stat. Ann. § 21.198(4305) (Law. Co-op 2000 Supp.) (Distributions to withdrawing member); Mo. Ann. Stat. § 347.103 (Vernon Supp.2000); N.J. Stat. Ann. 42:2B–39 (West Supp.2000) (Member entitled to receive distribution upon resignation); N.M. Stat. Ann. § 53–19–24 (Michie Supp.1993) (Distribution on event of dissociation); N.Y. Ltd. Liab. Co. Law Vol. 32A § 509 (McKinney Supp.2000) (Distribution upon withdrawal); Wis. Stat. Ann. § 183.0604 (West Supp.1999); Franklin E. Gevurtz, *Squeeze-outs and Freeze-outs in Limited Liability Companies,* 73 Wash.U.L.Q. 497, 514–15 n. 95 (1995).

nately, it is unclear from the district court's decision letter precisely what became of Lieberman's ownership interest. The Articles of Organization of Wyoming.com credited Lieberman with a 40% ownership interest in Wyoming.com, and he now argues he is entitled to payment for this interest at fair market value. In the alternative, he contends he retains that 40% interest because the district court has not resolved that portion of the parties' dispute. Wyoming.com disagrees.

We begin by examining Lieberman's notice of withdrawal. Lieberman strongly disputes any contention that he has simply forfeited his interest, other than his capital contribution, in the LLC. After examining the notice of withdrawal, we cannot say, as a matter of law, that Lieberman forfeited his interest upon his withdrawal because nothing in his withdrawal indicates his intent to do so. Indeed, Lieberman's demand for "his share of the current value of the company," whose value he estimated at $400,000, "based on a recent offer from the Majority Shareholder," indicates he would not easily part with, much less forfeit, his interest. Because we cannot say that, as a matter of law, Lieberman's withdrawal amounted to forfeiture of his interest, and because there is no statutory provision governing dissociation, we look to Wyoming.com's Operating Agreement to determine Lieberman's remedy.

Under the Wyoming.com's Operating Agreement, a member's equity interest was to be represented by a membership certificate. The Operating Agreement provides:

ARTICLE IV

Membership Certificates and their Transfer

4.1 **Certificates.** Membership Certificates representing equity interest in the Company will be in the form determined by the Members. Membership Certificates must be signed by the President and by all other Members. The name and address of the person to whom the Membership Certificate is issued, with the percentage of ownership represented by the certificate, must be entered in the Certificate Register of the Company. In case of a lost, destroyed or mutilated Membership Certificate, a new one may be issued on the terms and indemnity to the Company as the Members may prescribe.

4.2 **Certificate Register.** A Certificate Register will be maintained showing the names and addresses of all members, their total percentage of ownership represented by Membership Certificates, and their respective amount of capital contribution. Any and all changes in Members or their amount of capital contribution may be formalized by filing notice of the same with the Secretary of State by amendment of the Articles of Organization.

4.3 **Transfers of Shares.** Any Member proposing a transfer or assignment of his Certificate must first notify the Company, in writing, of all the details and consideration for the proposed transfer or assignment. The Company, for the benefit of the remaining Members, will have the first right to acquire the equity by cancellation of the Certificate under the same terms and conditions as provided in the formal Articles of Organization as filed with the Wyoming Secretary of State for Members who are deceased, retired, resigned, expelled, or dissolved. If the Company declines to elect this option, the remaining Members who desire to participate may proportionately (or in the proportions as the remaining Members may agree) purchase the interest under the same terms and conditions first proposed by the withdrawing Member. If the transfer or assignment is made as originally proposed and the other Members fail to approve the transfer or assignment by unanimous written consent, the transferee or assignee will have no right to participate in the management of the business and affairs of the Company or to become a Member. The transferee or assignee will only be entitled to receive the share of the profit or other compensation by way of income and the return of contributions to which that Member would otherwise be entitled.

Provision 2.5 provides:

2.5 Quorum. At any meeting of the Members, a majority of the equity interests, as determined from the capital contribution of each Member as reflected by the books of the Company, represented in person or by proxy, will constitute a quorum at a meeting of Members.

Provision 2.7 provides:

2.7 Voting by Certain Members. Membership Certificates standing in the name of a corporation, partnership or Company may be voted by the officer, partner, agent or proxy as the Bylaws of the entity may prescribe or, in the absence of such provision, as the Board of Directors of the entity may determine. Certificates held by a trustee, personal representative, administrator, executor, guardian or conservator may be voted by him, either in person or by proxy, without a transfer of the certificates into his name.

Under these provisions, it is clear that a member's interest in Wyoming.com was to be represented by membership certificates. There is nothing in the record indicating what became of Lieberman's membership certificate; there is no indication it has been canceled or forfeited. * * *

Here, the parties remain uncertain as to their legal relationship because it is unclear what became of Lieberman's ownership or equity interest (as represented by a membership certificate). Therefore, we conclude it appropriate to remand to the district court for a full declaration of the parties' rights.

We affirm the district court's determination that Wyoming.com is not in a state of dissolution and that Lieberman is entitled to the return of his capital contribution, $20,000. However, questions remain regarding Lieberman's equity interest, which was to be represented by his membership certificate. This case is thus remanded for a full resolution of the controversy between the parties.

————

NOTES

1. The remand in the *Lieberman* case resulted in another appeal to the Wyoming Supreme Court. The court stated in that decision that:

> Lieberman has withdrawn as a member of Wyoming.com and all remaining members unanimously accepted his withdrawal as a member. Lieberman thus is no longer a member of Wyoming.com. Lieberman does, however, maintain his equity interest in Wyoming.com. There is no contractual provision for a buy-out of his equity interest. Therefore Lieberman cannot force Wyoming.com to buy his interest, and Wyoming.com cannot force Lieberman to sell his interest. Because the members of Wyoming.com failed to contractually provide for a buy-out, Lieberman remains an equity holder in Wyoming.com. There are no further rights or obligations of the parties for this court to construe with regards to this situation.

Lieberman v. Wyoming.com LLC, 82 P.3d 274 (Wyo. 2004). Two justices dissented, arguing that the LLC should be treated as a partnership and that a forced buyout should be ordered. How does this decision affect the law as announced in the earlier decision in *Lieberman*?

2. As noted in the *Lieberman* case, the operating agreement may provide the terms for dissolution. In the absence of such an agreement, state law default provisions may govern. They are often based on partnership law. See Hurwitz v. Padden, 581 N.W.2d 359 (Minn.App.1998) (Minnesota law incorporates the dissolution concept from the Uniform Partnership Act). In Van Slyke v. Bullock, 1996 WL 937009 (R.I.Super.1996) the court applied the default provisions of the Rhode Island LLC statute and held that an LLC was dissolved when members were wrongfully expelled by locking them out of the business premises and the business was ordered to be wound up. See also World Fuel Services Corp. v. Moorehead, 229 F.Supp.2d 584 (N.D.Tex.2002) (Court refuses to enter charging order against interest in LLC, but that interest was ordered to be turned over to court appointed receiver for liquidation). In Haley v. Talcott, 864 A.2d 86 (Del. Ch. 2004), the judge ordered dissolution of a limited liability company owned in equal parts by two parties. Although there was a buyout provision in the operating agreement that was intended to be an exit mechanism if one of the parties became dissatisfied, the court ruled that the exit mechanism did not provide an adequate remedy.

In In re Silver Leaf, L.L.C., 2005 WL 2045641 (Del. Ch. 2005) (unpublished opinion) a Delaware chancery judge ordered the dissolution of a limited liability company where control in that entity was divided equally between two parties that were deadlocked. The judge also found that the company was being used to defraud other investors by making false claims about a French frying machine that the company was marketing, but which did not work. The judge noted that:

> The judicial dissolution statute for LLCs, 6 *Del. C.* § 18–802, states as follows: "On application by or for a member or manager the Court of Chancery may decree dissolution of a limited liability company whenever it is not reasonably practicable to carry on the business in conformity with a limited liability company agreement." Without much case law applying this statute, the court looks by analogy to the dissolution statute for limited partnerships, 6 *Del. C.* § 17–802, which contains essentially the same wording as the LLC statute.

> "The test of Section 17–802 is whether it is 'reasonably practicable' to carry on the business of a limited partnership, and not whether it is impossible." "In evaluating whether to dissolve a partnership pursuant to § 17–802, courts must determine the business of the partnership and the general partner's ability to achieve that purpose in conformity with the partnership agreement." * * *

> The threshold matter is whether Silver Leaf can, pursuant to its Operating Agreement, take the actions necessary to continue functioning as a business. In this case, Silver Leaf's contending interests are split 50:50. On one side are USIS and Lavi. On the other side are Syndi, Segal, and Romanoff. As two years of litigation and more than three days of trial have shown, the two sides cannot agree on how to run Silver Leaf. Moreover, the Operating Agreement, which mandates an agreement by the majority in interest in order to effectuate important actions for Silver Leaf, provides no mechanism to break the impasse between the parties. * * *

> Silver Leaf was formed for the specific purpose of marketing the vending machines of Tasty Fries. Neither party offered any evidence that Silver Leaf had another business purpose. Thus, at the time the dispute between the parties began, the only asset of Silver Leaf was the SMA, which Tasty Fries executed in consideration for the stock purchase agreement.

> Now, the SMA is no longer an asset of Silver Leaf because Tasty Fries terminated that contract. Although Silver Leaf sought an injunction to prevent the termination of that contract, both the District Court in New Jersey and the Third Circuit found that Section 19.6, the non-suit provision, precluded Silver Leaf's litigation against Tasty Fries. Clearly, the business of marketing Tasty Fries's machines no longer exists for Silver Leaf. * * *

> Given its ownership structure and Operating Agreement, Silver Leaf is no longer able to carry on its business in a reasonably practicable manner. The vote of the members is deadlocked and the Operating Agreement provides no means around the deadlock. Moreover, Silver Leaf has no business to operate. Therefore, upon application of a member, USIS, the court dissolves Silver Leaf.

3. One court has held that, absent a provision in the operating agreement, there is no right to expel an LLC member, even for misconduct. Walker

v. Resource Dev. Co., Ltd., L.L.C., 791 A.2d 799 (Del. Ch. 2000) (member of LLC could not be expelled even though his drinking problem was impairing the performance of his duties). In CCD, L.C. v. Millsap, 116 P.3d 366 (Utah 2005), the court held that a member of a limited liability company could be expelled for misappropriating company funds because the Utah limited liability company act contained provisions allowing expulsion of members for misconduct.

4.   The LLC form of doing business was designed to assure the limited liability of its members. Creditors may try to avoid that limitation by asking a court to ignore or pierce the corporate veil:

> As is the case with corporations, it will be the exceptional case in which a court will be willing to pierce the veil of a limited liability company. Among other things, it would have to be proved that the LLC was in fact a sham and really the alter ego of the members or that it was a mere instrumentality of the owners. Failure to follow proper formalities, such as failing to identify the entity as a limited liability company can result in the personal liability of the owners. Also, the LLC liability shield will not apply to liabilities arising prior to the formation of the LLC.

James D. Cox & Thomas Lee Hazen, *Corporations* § 1.11[4] (2d ed. 2003). Corporate veil piercing theories are further discussed in Chapter 5. See Morris v. Cee Dee, LLC, 90 Conn.App. 403, 877 A.2d 899 (2005) (complaint did not allege facts that would justify piercing the veil of a limited liability company to hold its sole owner liable for an injury to a tenant that resulted in the amputation of the tenant's leg) and Filo America, Inc. v. Olhoss Trading Co., L.L.C., 321 F. Supp.2d 1266 (M.D. Ala. 2004) (the Alabama limited liability act company would permit an action that is based on a veil piercing theory). See also People v. Pacific Landmark, 129 Cal.App.4th 1203, 29 Cal.Rptr.3d 193 (2005) (the manager of a limited liability company was not immune to personal liability where he participated in tortious and criminal conduct while performing his duty as a manager of a limited liability company; in this case operating a massage parlor used for prostitution). *See also, e.g.,* Emily A. Lackey, Comment, Piercing the Veil of Limited Liability in the Non–Corporate Setting, 55 Ark. L. Rev. 553 (2002).

CHAPTER 4

CORPORATIONS—FORMATION AND FINANCES

■ ■ ■

SECTION 1. THE ROLE OF THE CORPORATE LAWYER

Corporations are heavily regulated under both state and federal law. Their management and shareholders must depend on lawyers for advice on issues that range from the formation of the corporation to the liquidation of its assets in the event of failure. The increasingly complicated nature of corporations and their operations, and a corresponding complexity in their regulation, gave rise to the growth of specialized corporate lawyers. Today, most large law firms divide their practices into, at least, corporate and litigation departments (usually with sub-specialties operating within those groups). Corporate lawyers assume the role of counselors to corporate management, while the litigators defend the corporations in court. Even where such a division is not made, as in the case of a small law firm, lawyers must assume different roles when acting either as a litigator or a corporate lawyer.

In deciding whether to be a litigator or a corporate lawyer, remember that the litigator is an advocate while a corporate lawyer is in most instances a counselor. A litigator is faced with a set of historical facts and may, within the bounds of ethical requirements, represent the client by taking aggressive, even extreme, positions in order to prevail in litigation. In contrast, the corporate lawyer will be defining the facts that make the historical record and will be counseling the client on ways to avoid future litigation. The client needs to be advised by the corporate lawyer of the risks of particular courses of action. Often, this advice will be conservative in nature because most clients want to avoid litigation. Of course, clients may wish to pursue an approach that is more aggressive than the most conservative legal position. That is their right, unless the proposed action is clearly illegal, but clients should at least be advised of the legal risks and uncertainties of their actions. That is the role of the corporate lawyer. Unlike the advocate, the corporate lawyer's role is not to win a case, but to avoid exposing the client to unnecessary legal risks and to avoid costly litigation and damages. As a corporate lawyer, therefore, you will usually

117

act as a shield for the client. That being said, there will be times when you will be asked to wield the sword as an advocate, as for example, when you are asked to negotiate contract terms for the client.

In counseling a corporate client, the key is to find out what the officers are seeking to accomplish and to point out any potential legal pitfalls. Corporate lawyers are not supposed to tell the client how to run their business. You will discover that many corporate managers do not like their lawyers expressing opinions on business issues. Those managers simply want advice on whether an activity is legal. A good corporate lawyer knows when to say yes and when to say no when asked such a question. A better corporate lawyer will show the client how to structure the transfer to avoid legal concerns. There will be, of course, instances when a transaction simply cannot be done legally, and the client must be so informed. It is easy to say yes even when there are serious legal problems because that will make the corporate officers happy—they can tell their directors that the lawyers "blessed" the deal. This might bring you further business from the officers receiving that blessing. Some corporate officers have even been known to shop for lawyers who will give them favorable opinions, whatever the legality of the proposed transaction. The risks for lawyers engaging in such activities are enormous. They expose their firms and their clients to large liabilities, they may be personally liable in some instances, and they may even lose their license to practice law.

There will be instances where the law is not clear and the client decides to assume the risk of legal uncertainty. That is perfectly acceptable, if the client is fully aware of the risks and is willing to assume them. As you will discover, many legal issues are unclear and cannot be clarified before the client proceeds. If perfect certainty were required, business would cease. Society cannot advance without incurring risk, and lawyers must recognize that fact. The challenge is to draw the line between illegal conduct and merely uncertain conduct. That is where you must apply your judgment to formulate an opinion as to whether the legal risk is justifiable. Law school will inculcate you with a lot of rules. Those are easily taught, but your professors cannot supply you with judgment and common sense in the gray areas. However, and without being too moralistic, a few simple and practical rules have been handed down through the generations that will help protect you from embarrassment, or worse, in counseling clients.

Rule 1: do not do anything that you would not want to see published on the front page of a national newspaper, or your own local paper for that matter. Do not assume that the attorney-client privilege will shield you from exposure for improper conduct. The privilege has many exceptions and in a corporate context your advice is likely to be leaked by disgruntled employees or otherwise made public. Assume that all "read and burn" memos will be copied and circulated. Your oral advice is also likely to be the subject of depositions. Think about how your advice will look in the harsh light of hindsight if things go wrong.

Rule 2: if you cannot afford to lose a client, you cannot afford to keep the client. In other words, if you cannot render objective advice to a client because you are afraid the client will go elsewhere, you should not be dealing with that client. Remember also that, while you will undoubtedly develop personal friendships with clients, you must still remain objective in your advice. You must maintain some distance. You are not doing friends a favor by supplying favorable advice in order to accommodate them or to boost some short-term goal.

Rule 3: if it is too good to be true, it is too good to be true. We will let you decide how this rule applies in your practice.

The role of the corporate lawyer has developed a certain cachet, but it is not all long lunches and golfing with the client. You can also expect long hours and many time pressures. Although you need not be a rocket scientist to be a corporate lawyer, there are many concepts and legal requirements to be learned. None of those concepts are particularly complex, but there are a lot of them. The trick is to remember and apply all of the various facets of corporate law to particular problems that your clients might encounter. Activities of the corporate lawyer will involve such things as organizing the corporation for its promoters, drafting corporate minutes, advising corporate directors on their fiduciary duties and advising clients on the requirements of the federal securities laws when your client has sold stock to the public. The pervasive nature of the federal securities laws, and the liabilities that lie for violation of their provisions, mandate that you become knowledgeable about the Securities and Exchange Commission and federal restrictions. In some instances, you may need to bring in specialists to aid your client with particular problems outside your expertise. These could include tax, environmental or anti-trust problems.

Finally, as a corporate lawyer, you have a luxury denied most litigators, you have the opportunity to create the historical record. If future litigation arises, the record you create will often determine the outcome. If the record shows that a transaction was carefully vetted, all risks were considered and that decisions were made on bona fide grounds, the job for any future litigator defending that record will be made much easier.

WHERE WERE THE LAWYERS?
BEHIND THE CURTAIN WEARING THEIR MAGIC CAPS

Hearing on Accountability Issues: Lessons Learned From Enron's Fall Testimony
of Susan P. Koniak, Professor of Law, Boston University School of Law
Before the Senate Judiciary Committee February 6, 2002.

Twelve years ago in a court opinion dealing with some aspects of the Lincoln Savings and Loan fraud, Judge Stanley Sporkin wrote: "Where . . . were the . . . accountants and attorneys . . . ? [W]ith all the professional talent involved (both accounting and legal), why [didn't] at least one professional . . . [act] to stop the overreaching that took place in this case?" Now, there is Enron. And we are here asking the same questions, Judge Sporkin and others were asking 12 years ago. To paraphrase Pete Seeger, "When will [we] ever learn?"

No one should have been surprised in the aftermath of the savings and loan crisis to learn that lawyers and accountants had averted their eyes from the fraud being perpetrated by some in the banking industry during the 1980s. . . .

[I]n the 1970s, lawyers and accountants aided and abetted the fraud that brought down National Student Marketing Corporation. And the law firms in most of these instances were not marginal players, they were pillars of the bar: venerable and well respected firms. Firms who settled with the government (and/or with defrauded investors) for their role in assisting Charles Keating, the head of Lincoln Savings and Loan included: Sidley and Austin, Kaye, Scholer and Jones Day. And participating as helpers in the National Student Marketing fraud were the law firms of Lord Bissell and Brook and White & Case. . . . [T]he firms named above did nothing, unfortunately, that most other prestigious law firms haven't done themselves. And now we sit here in 2002 professing to be shocked, shocked that gambling is going on at Rick's saloon and that well respected law firms and accounting firms may have been involved.

Thus far, Enron's accountants have borne the lion's share of the blame for helping the wrongdoers at Enron commit what appears now to have been massive fraud. Let me put this as plainly as possible: To pull the wool over the eyes of the investing public, regulators and the media for any considerable period of time a corporation needs more than malleable accountants, it needs the help of lawyers . . . When all the facts that can be known about what happened here are known, one thing will be clear: everyone in the drama had a lawyer whispering in its ear (Enron, Arthur Andersen, the investment banks, the questionable partnerships that hid Enron's losses and bilked Enron's funds, the investors in those partnerships and on and on). And one more thing will be clear: no lawyer stepped in to stop this calamity.

Tightening the reins on accountants is a good idea, but . . . accountants have lawyers too. Those lawyers are perfectly capable of helping accountants slip loose of whatever reins you devise, just as they apparently helped Enron slip loose the reins of corporate and securities law *unless* Congress, the SEC and state regulators rein in lawyers too. Something needs to be done about the lawyers, if confidence is to be restored in the financial statements issued by companies. What the securities laws demand, is ultimately a legal question, not one for accountants. When documents must be preserved, is not simply a matter of some accounting convention; it depends on law: tax law, statutes prohibiting obstruction of justice, civil rules on spoliation of evidence, state laws on tampering with evidence and other such legal constraints.

All too often lawyers act as if they were wearing magic caps—hats that transport them to some alternative reality, a law free zone, in which they are free to do anything and everything for the person or entity paying the lawyers' fees—hats that transport them to a magic land where lawyers need not fear that law will come crashing down on them. "It may hit the client, but it will never hit me." There are no such magic caps. . . . * * *

To make this as simple as possible a lawyer has done wrong and is likely to be in significant legal trouble when three things are true. One, the client is breaking the law. Two, the lawyer has enough facts in front of her to have been able to figure out, with the exercise of reasonable care, that number one is true. And three, with number one and number two in place, the lawyer either acts to help the client to break the law or does nothing to stop the client from breaking the law in those instances (which are not as few as some would like to think) when the lawyer has a duty to intervene.* * *

NOTES

1. The public's perception of the role lawyers play in financial scandals may be exemplified by the following report:

> But just as a fine, natural football player needs coaching in the fundamentals and schooling in the wiles of the sport, so, too, it takes a corporation lawyer with a heart for the game to organize a great stock swindle or income tax dodge and drill the financiers in all the precise details of their play.

> Otherwise, in their natural enthusiasm to rush in and grab everything that happens not to be nailed down and guarded with shotguns, they would soon be caught offside and penalized, and some of the noted financiers who are now immortalized as all-time all-America larcenists never would have risen beyond the level of the petty thief or short-change man.

Westbrook Pegler, New York World Telegram Jan. 19, 1923 at 19, quoted in William O. Douglas, Directors Who Do Not Direct, 47 Harv. L. Rev. 1305, 1329 n.65 (1934).

2. In SEC v. Frank, 388 F.2d 486, 488–489 (2d Cir.1968), the SEC obtained a district court order enjoining Nylo–Thane, its officers, and its attorney, Martin Frank, from making further misrepresentations concerning the company's business. Frank, who had represented Nylo–Thane in the preparation of a circular offering the corporation's stock, which the SEC had held to be misleading, appealed from the issuance of an injunction against him.

> * * * His position, broadly stated, was that the portion of the offering circular alleged to misrepresent the additive had been prepared by the officers of Nylo–Thane and that his function had been that of a scrivener helping them to place their ideas in proper form. * * *

> A lawyer has no privilege to assist in circulating a statement with regard to securities which he knows to be false simply because his client

has furnished it to him. At the other extreme it would be unreasonable to hold a lawyer who was putting his client's description of a chemical process into understandable English to be guilty of fraud simply because of his failure to detect discrepancies between their description and technical reports available to him in a physical sense but beyond his ability to understand. The instant case lies between these extremes. The SEC's position is that Frank had been furnished with information which even a non-expert would recognize as showing the falsity of many of the representations, notably those implying extensive and satisfactory testing at factories and indicating that all had gone passing well at the test by the Army Laboratories. If this is so, the Commission would be entitled to prevail; a lawyer, no more than others, can escape liability for fraud by closing his eyes to what he saw and could readily understand. Whether the fraud sections of the securities laws go beyond this and require a lawyer passing on an offering circular to run down possible infirmities in his client's story of which he has been put on notice, and if so what efforts are required of him, is a closer question on which it is important that the court be seized of the precise facts, including the extent, as the SEC claimed with respect to Frank, to which his role went beyond a lawyer's normal one.

The court of appeals held that the district court had not made adequate findings of fact, and remanded the case for further proceedings.

3.   The corporate lawyer will face many difficult conflicts that arise in the representation of a corporation. For example, when creating a corporation, the allocation of control among the founders may create conflicting interests that the lawyers must deal with in structuring the corporation. A government investigation may create a conflict between the corporation and the employees involved in the activities being questioned. A matter of some concern arises where a corporate officer or employee engages in some conduct that conflicts with the interests of the corporation's shareholders. Who is the attorney representing? Is it the officer, the corporation, its board of directors or the shareholders?

4.   Many conflicts are resolved by obtaining separate representation. For example, in a government investigation where there are potential conflicts of interest between an involved officer and the corporation, the corporation may arrange for separate representation but pay the fees of both lawyers. What kinds of conduct could give rise to concerns that would require separate representation? Do you think the conflict is resolved where the corporation is paying both lawyers' fees?

5.   A continuing controversy is what the lawyer for a corporation should do when an employee, officer, director or the board itself decides to engage in illegal or questionable conduct. The debate over what is ethically appropriate has been made even more contentious by the role of the lawyers in the failure of the Enron Corporation, the seventh largest on the Fortune 500 list of largest companies in America when it declared bankruptcy in 2001. The American Bar Association has suggested that it may be necessary for a lawyer to appeal to higher authority at the corporation where illegal conduct is proposed by management in dealings with the lawyer, but that such an

approach should be undertaken only where the proposed conduct poses a serious threat to the corporation. See ABA Model Rules of Professional Conduct § 1.13b (and Official Comment). Of course, the lawyer may resign, but that leaves the client in awkward position, and may impair the client's interests. How would you handle such a conflict?

6. In 2002 Congress enacted the Sarbanes–Oxley Act which, among other things, expanded attorney responsibility by calling on attorneys to report serious wrongdoing to high ranking corporate officials. 15 U.S.C.A. § 7245. The Act mandates that the SEC promulgate rules setting forth minimum standards of professional conduct for attorneys appearing and practicing before the SEC in connection with their representation of public companies. The SEC rules must contain a requirement that attorneys report evidence of a material violation of securities laws or breach of fiduciary duty or similar violation by a company, including an agent of the company, to the chief legal counsel or the chief executive officer and, if that officer does not respond appropriately, to the audit committee (or other committee composed entirely of outside directors). The statute makes no distinction between inside and outside counsel advising a reporting company.

SECTION 2.   FORMING THE CORPORATION

The advantages and disadvantages of incorporation versus other forms of business are discussed in Chapter 1. You will be called upon to counsel the clients on what form is best suited for their interests. The choice need not be final, since conversion from one form to another is permitted. Such changes, however, may have tax and other implications and may be expensive. If incorporation is desired, the client must decide where to incorporate. As also discussed in Chapter 1, Delaware strives to be the most liberal state in assuring that its laws are advantageous to business. Nevertheless, corporations at their early stages will not be much affected by the differences in Delaware and local law. Indeed, most states try to assure that their corporate laws are user friendly, lest they lose business to other states. The Revised Model Business Corporation Act adopted by many states has also been carefully crafted to assure that businesses may operate freely.

A.   PROMOTERS' LIABILITY

There are some pre-incorporation concerns that need to be addressed by lawyers in creating a corporation. One is the liability of the promoters or founders of the enterprise for activities they engaged in before incorporation. Businesses often begin as informal affairs. The classic case is the successful business that begins as a hobby in a room over the garage, in the basement or in a nook in the bedroom. The founders of the business might mention their activity to friends or acquaintances, who recognized its economic value. One of those persons begins promoting the ideas to others (often relatives) who invest time or money to expand the business, initially in the home and then through more formal offices. At first, the focus of the promoters in fledgling enterprises is on the product, giving little concern to the legal form of the enterprise. As the business continues to expand, however, someone will suggest consulting a lawyer to make sure that the business is operating properly and that everyone is protected legally. The lawyer might then suggest incorporation or a limited liability company ("LLC") be formed to provide limited liability and to protect the ownership interests of the participants.

Once the corporation is formed, the owners are protected going forward but what about liabilities incurred before incorporation? The owners cannot claim that they were acting simply as the agents for the corporation because there was no corporation in existence, *i.e.*, no agency relationship can exist in the absence of a principal. As a result, those acting on behalf of the preincorporation business will be held personally accountable for their acts. In addition, they are without power to bind the non-existent principal, *i.e.*, the yet-to-be formed corporation, raising the issue of the enforceability of contracts entered on behalf of the yet unformed corporation. As a result of these legal barriers, and the propensity for those forming a corporation to commence business before incorporation, a large body of case law exists that governs pre-incorporation activities. That case law is generally classified under the rubric of "promoters' liability."

Those acting on behalf of a corporation to be formed are generally called promoters. In many instances, the promoters are the organizers of the business. The major issues arising out of their pre-incorporation activities are divided into three categories: (1) personal liability of the promoters for their acts; (2) determining when corporate liability attaches to pre-incorporation activities; and (3) liabilities of the corporation to investors for fraudulent promoters' activities. The principles applicable to promoters' activities shed light on the application of many of the agency principles discussed earlier and also on the nature of the corporate entity. Of course, the entire law relating to promoters can be avoided by incorporating before any organizational activity takes place. The law relating to promoters remains alive, however, because this is not always done.

––––––––

O'RORKE v. GEARY

207 Pa. 240, 56 A. 541 (1903).

The following is the opinion of MCCLUNG, J., in the lower court:

This suit is upon a written agreement, and the main defense is that the defendant did not, in executing the contract, act for himself, but for a corporation to be formed, and that the corporation, and not D. J. Geary, is now liable to the plaintiff for what is due him on said contract. The contract was executed on June 19, 1901. It was between plaintiff, as party of the first part, and 'D. J. Geary for a bridge company to be organized and incorporated,' as party of the second part. It was for the building of a bridge, which it recites the party of the second part 'desires to build across the Allegheny river, and in accordance with specifications and plans * * * heretofore submitted to the party of the first part by the party of the second part.' The work was to be subject to the inspection and approval of P. H. Melvin, his decision to be binding, etc. An estimate was to be made August 1, 1901, and 75 per cent. paid 'by the party of the second part,' and monthly thereafter. Work was to be commenced within 10 days, and completed on or before October 1, 1901. The agreement concludes, 'In witness whereof we have hereunto set our hands and seals,' etc., but is signed simply by plaintiff and defendant without any seal or scroll.

We have examined a great number of authorities which touch more or less closely upon the point involved. We do not propose to review them nor even to cite them, but will simply suggest a few principles which we think are in accord with all of these cases, and which fully warrant the interpretation which we put upon the contract with respect to who is the responsible party of the second part. * * *

We have, then, simply the question as to whether or not Geary bound himself or the company to be incorporated for the building of this bridge. When a party is acting for a proposed corporation, he cannot, of course, bind it by anything he does at the time, but he may (1) take on its behalf an offer from the other, which, being accepted after the formation of the company, becomes a contract; (2) make a contract at the time binding himself, with the stipulation or understanding that if a company is formed it will take his place, and that then he shall be relieved of responsibility; or (3) bind himself personally without more, and look to the proposed company, when formed, for indemnity. It seems to us that Geary in this case comes within No. 3. The writing is not a mere naked offer to be submitted to the corporation not yet either organized or incorporated, because work was certainly to be begun, and probably completed, before it was possible that this corporation should come into existence. Geary certainly intended himself to pay the 75 per cent monthly on the estimates. The affidavit of defense says that the company was incorporated before the bridge was completed, but it does not say that it was incorporated before October 1, 1901, when, by the contract, it was to be completed. It is just as clear that there is no provision for a substitution of responsibility. The corporation might be accepted by O'Rorke and by novation become the party of the second part, or it might, under certain circumstances, become liable to plaintiff without releasing Geary; but there is nothing in the writing which authorizes Geary to substitute at any time another for himself as the responsible party. The bridge company is not mentioned in the contract save when the party of the second part is described as 'D. J. Geary for the bridge company to be formed,' etc.

In his opinion in Hopkins v. Mehaffy, 11 Serg. & R. 126, Judge Gibson calls attention to the difference between the covenant of an agent who describes himself as contracting for his principal, and the covenant of a principal through the means and by the instrumentality of an agent. We have here no covenant of a principal through an agent, as is shown by the language used, and for the further reason that the alleged principal was not then in existence.

In many of the discussions of this subject, 'ratification of the act of an unauthorized agent' and 'the responsibility of an undisclosed principal' are spoken of. These references serve in some cases as illustrations of the nature of the responsibility incurred, but, when applied loosely, confuse rather than enlighten. We have no question of ratification, because that implies the existence at the time of a principal who might have given the agent authority. Nor do we have any such thing as an undisclosed principal. There was nothing undisclosed. We have a case that is *sui generis*. The bridge was for a company that did not then exist, but was to be afterwards organized and incorporated. O'Rorke might have built the bridge and taken the chances of the company paying him, or he might have made a contract by which Geary was to be liable until the company was formed, and then the company was to step into his shoes and relieve him. Neither of these things was done. A third course was adopted whereby Geary became liable personally on the contract, he taking the chances of the incorporation of the company and of its indemnifying him. He is liable to the plaintiff in the present action.

There are some special defenses as to various items, many of which, it must be admitted, are set out with little definiteness. Under the circumstances of the case, however, we have concluded that we should treat these averments as sufficient to prevent judgment, and enter it only for the sum as to which the only defense is the allegation that the bridge company and not the present defendant is the party of the second part to the written contract. This judgment will be entered, with leave to proceed as to the disputed items. An order should be drawn showing just what is covered by the judgment now entered. The statement of the matter in plaintiff's brief seems to be correct, except that the amount should be further reduced by $218.25 for labor, which the affidavit of defense avers plaintiff agreed to credit on the amount due under the written contract.

PER CURIAM.

On a rule for judgment for want of a sufficient affidavit of defense the court below entered judgment for plaintiff for the larger part of his claim. That opinion sufficiently vindicates the judgment.

The assignments of error are overruled, and the judgment affirmed, for the reasons given in the opinion of the court below.

NOTES

1. The rules enunciated in *O'Rorke* are the necessary consequence of applying traditional agency principles. To what extent can the third party's knowledge of the situation and the intent to bind the corporation operate as a release of the promoter's liability?

2. In Goodman v. Darden, Doman & Stafford Associates, 100 Wash.2d 476, 670 P.2d 648, 652 (1983), the court reasoned: "The fact that a contracting party knows that the corporation is nonexistent does not indicate any agreement to release the promoter. To the contrary, such knowledge alone would seem to indicate that the [third party] members of DDS intended to make [the promoter] a party to the contract."

3. Some courts have reached the contrary conclusion. In Company Stores Development Corp. v. Pottery Warehouse, Inc., 733 S.W.2d 886 (Tenn. App.1987), the court explained: "At the time the lease was signed, plaintiff was aware of the nonexistence of the corporate entity and did not require [the promoter] to sign the agreement in an individual capacity but as a president of a future corporate entity. The lease imputes no intention on the part of [the promoter] to be bound personally."

4. Even aside from contract principles, could estoppel be used to preclude a third party from seeking recovery from the promoter individually?

COX & HAZEN ON CORPORATIONS,
James D. Cox & Thomas Lee Hazen

§ 5.04   (2d ed. 2003).

American courts have professed difficulty in finding a rational explanation of how a corporation can make itself a party to its promoters' pre-incorporation contracts. A corporation may assume the burdens of a contract by agreement with a promoter on sufficient consideration. But such an assumption of the promoter's obligations under the contract does not give the corporation a right to sue on the contract, a right that it could acquire only by assignment from the promoter or as a third-party beneficiary of the contract. It follows that the mere existence of a promotional relationship is not sufficient to establish the liability of a corporation subsequently formed for pre-incorporation promoters' contracts. Five theories have been advanced as to how the liability of the corporation on the promoters' contracts can arise: (1) ratification; (2) adoption; (3) acceptance of a continuing offer; (4) formation of a new contract; and (5) novation.

Adoption. Adoption is a corporation's assent to a contract that was made in contemplation of the corporation's assuming it after organization. In other words, adoption occurs when a corporation takes the contract rights and obligations of the promoter and make them its own.

Ratification. Ratification is the corporation's acceptance of an act purportedly made on its behalf by an agent. Strictly speaking, a purported principal must have been in existence at the time of a contract in order to have the capacity to ratify it; therefore ratification is only properly applicable to post-incorporation contracts.

Adoption and ratification compared. Courts, however, often use the term "ratification" loosely to refer to a corporation's acceptance or adoption of a promoter's contract. Adoption and ratification may be shown by any words or acts of responsible corporate officers showing assent or approval, such as by their knowingly accepting benefits of the contract or proceeding to perform obligations imposed on it.

Some courts have drawn a distinction between the effect of ratification and adoption; a ratified contract relates back to the date the promoter made it, whereas an adopted contract becomes binding on the corporation on the date of adoption. However, nothing seems to prevent a corporation from adopting a promoter's contract as of the date it was originally made if the corporation expressly or impliedly agrees to do so.

Acceptance of a continuing offer. On what theory does a person who is not a party to a contract become a party by adoption? One theory is that the original promoter's contract is in the nature of a continuing proposal, which the corporation may accept when it comes into existence.

Formation of a new contract. Another theory is that a corporation's adoption of a promoter's contract is nothing more than the making of a new contract for new consideration.

Novation. Still another theory is that whenever the parties to a promoter's contract anticipate that the corporation when formed will accept the contract and take over its performance, the contract is to be viewed as contemplating a novation, by which the corporation, when it assents after organization, is substituted for the promoter. Courts in the past have shown some readiness to take this novation view of a promoter's contract, but more recent decisions have relied on an adoption/ratification theory and have been reluctant to find that such a contract contemplated a novation.

––––––––

To what extent can the shareholders of a corporation complain of promoter's fraud in the reincorporating stage? Today, this question is largely handled by state and federal securities laws that are designed to promote investor protection against unscrupulous promoters. The cases decided outside the context of these special investor protection statutes raise pointed questions as to the nature of the corporate entity.

OLD DOMINION COPPER MINING & SMELTING CO. v. LEWISOHN

210 U.S. 206, 28 S.Ct. 634, 52 L.Ed. 1025 (1908).

MR. JUSTICE HOLMES delivered the opinion of the court:

This is a bill in equity brought by the petitioner to rescind a sale to it of certain mining rights and land by the defendants' testator, or, in the alternative, to recover damages for the sale. The bill was demurred to and the demurrer was sustained. Then the bill was amended and again demurred to, and again the demurrer was sustained, and the bill was dismissed. This decree was affirmed by the circuit court of appeals. The ground of the petitioner's case is that Lewisohn, the deceased, and one Bigelow, as promoters, formed the petitioner that they might sell certain properties to it at a profit, that they made their sale while they owned all the stock issued, but in contemplation of a large further issue to the public without disclosure of their profit, and that such an issue in fact was made. The supreme judicial court of Massachusetts has held the plaintiff entitled to recover from Bigelow upon a substantially similar bill.

The facts alleged are as follows: The property embraced in the plan was the mining property of the Old Dominion Copper Company of Baltimore, and also the mining rights and land now in question, the latter being held by one Keyser, for the benefit of himself and of the executors of one Simpson, who, with Keyser, owned the stock of the Baltimore company. Bigelow and Lewisohn, in May and June, 1895, obtained options from Simpson's executors and Keyser for the purchase of the stock and the property now in question. They also formed a syndicate to carry out their plan, with the agreement that the money subscribed by the members should be used for the purchase and the sale to a new corporation, at a large advance, and that the members, in the proportion of their subscriptions, should receive in cash or in stock of the new corporation the profit made by the sale. On May 28, 1895, Bigelow paid Simpson's executors for their stock on behalf of the syndicate, in cash and notes of himself and Lewisohn, and in June Keyser was paid in the same way.

On July 8, 1895, Bigelow and Lewisohn started the plaintiff corporation, the seven members being their nominees and tools. The next day the stock of the company was increased to 150,000 shares of twenty-five dollars each, officers were elected, and the corporation became duly organized. July 11, pursuant to instructions, some of the officers resigned, and Bigelow and Lewisohn and three other absent members of the syndicate came in. Thereupon an offer was received from the Baltimore company, the stock of which had been bought, as stated, by Bigelow and Lewisohn, to sell substantially all its property for 100,000 shares of the plaintiff company. The offer was accepted, and then Lewisohn offered to sell the real estate now in question, obtained from Keyser, for 30,000 shares, to be issued to Bigelow and himself. This also was accepted and possession of all the mining property was delivered the next day. The sales "were consummated" by delivery of deeds, and afterwards, on July 18, to raise working capital, it was voted to offer the remaining 20,000 shares to the public at par, and they were taken by subscribers who did not know of the profit made by Bigelow and Lewisohn and the syndicate. On September 18 the 100,000 and 30,000 shares were issued, and it was voted to issue the 20,000 when paid for. The bill alleges that the property of the Baltimore company was not worth more than $1,000,000, the sum paid for its stock, and the property here concerned not over $5,000, as Bigelow and Lewisohn knew. The market value of the petitioner's stock was less than par, so that the price paid was $2,500,000, it is said, for the Baltimore company's property and $750,000 for that here concerned. Whether this view of the price paid is correct, it is unnecessary to decide.

Of the stock in the petitioner, received by Bigelow and Lewisohn or their Baltimore corporation, 40,000 shares went to the syndicate as profit, and the members had their choice of receiving a like additional number of shares or the repayment of their original subscription. As pretty nearly all took the stock, the syndicate received about 80,000 shares. The remaining 20,000 of the stock paid to the Baltimore company, Bigelow and Lewisohn divided, the plaintiff believes, without the knowledge of the syndicate. The 30,000 shares received for the property now in question they also divided. Thus the plans of Bigelow and Lewisohn were carried out.

The argument for the petitioner is that all would admit that the promoters (assuming the English phrase to be well applied) stood in a fiduciary relation to it, if, when the transaction took place, there were members who were not informed of the profits made and who did not acquiesce, and that the same obligation of good faith extends down to the time of the later subscriptions, which it was the promoters' plan to obtain. It is an argument that has commanded the assent of at least one court, and is stated at length in the decision. But the courts do not agree. There is no authority binding upon us and in point. Without spending time upon the many *dicta* that were quoted to us, we shall endeavor to weigh the considerations on one side and the other afresh.

The difficulty that meets the petitioner at the outset is that it has assented to the transaction with the full knowledge of the facts. It is said, to be sure, that on September 18, when the shares were issued to the sellers, there were already subscribers to the 20,000 shares that the public took. But this does not appear from the bill, unless it should be inferred from the ambiguous statement that on that day it was voted to issue those shares "to persons who had subscribed therefor," upon receiving payment, and that the shares 'were thereafter duly issued to said persons,' etc. The words "had subscribed" may refer to the time of issue and be equivalent to "should have subscribed," or may refer to an already past event. But that hardly matters. The contract had been made and the property delivered on July 11 and 12, when Bigelow, Lewisohn, and some other members of the syndicate held all the outstanding stock, and it is alleged in terms that the sales were consummated before the vote of July 18 to offer stock to the public had been passed.

At the time of the sale to the plaintiff, then, there was no wrong done to anyone. Bigelow, Lewisohn, and their syndicate were on both sides of the bargain, and they might issue to themselves as much stock in their corporation as they liked in exchange for their conveyance of their land. If there was a wrong it was when the innocent public subscribed. But what one would expect to find, if a wrong happened then, would not be that the sale became a breach of duty to the corporation *nunc pro tunc*, but that the invitation to the public without disclosure, when acted upon, became a fraud upon the subscribers from an equitable point of view, accompanied by what they might treat as damage. For it is only by virtue of the innocent subscribers' position and the promoter's invitation that the corporation has any pretense for a standing in court. If the promoters, after starting their scheme, had sold their stock before any subscriptions were taken, and then the purchasers of their stock, with notice, had invited the public to come in, and it did, we do not see how the company could maintain this suit. If it could not then, we do not see how it can now.

But it is said that, from a business point of view, the agreement was not made merely to bind the corporation as it then was, with only 40 shares issued, but to bind the corporation when it should have a capital of $3,750,000; and the implication is that practically this was a new and different corporation. Of course, legally speaking, a corporation does not change its identity by adding a cubit to its stature. The nominal capital of the corporation was the same when the contract was made and after the public had subscribed. Therefore, what must be meant is, as we have said, that the corporation got a new right from the fact that new men, who did not know what it had done, had put in their money and had become members. It is assumed in argument that the new members had no ground for a suit in their own names, but it is assumed also that their position changed that of the corporation, and thus that the indirect effect of their acts was greater than the direct; that facts that gave them no claim gave one to the corporation because of them, notwithstanding its assent. We shall not consider whether the new members had a personal claim of any kind, and therefore we deal with the case without prejudice to that question, and without taking advantage of what we understand the petitioner to concede.

But, if we are to leave technical law on one side, and approach the case from what is supposed to be a business point of view, there are new matters to be taken into account. If the corporation recovers, all the stockholders, guilty as well as innocent, get the benefit. It is answered that the corporation is not precluded from recovering for a fraud upon it, because the party committing the fraud is a stockholder. *Old Dominion Copper Mining & Smelting Co. v. Bigelow.* If there had been innocent members at the time of the sale, the fact that there were also guilty ones would not prevent a recovery, and even might not be a sufficient reason for requiring all the guilty members to be joined as defendants in order to avoid a manifest injustice. The same principle is thought to apply when innocent members are brought in later under a scheme. But it is obvious that this answer falls back upon the technical diversity between the corporation and its members, which the business point of view is supposed to transcend, as it must, in order to avoid the objection that the corporation has assented to the sale with full notice of the facts. It is mainly on this diversity that the answer to the objection of injustice is based.

Let us look at the business aspect alone. The syndicate was a party to the scheme to make a profit out of the corporation. Whether or not there was a subordinate fraud committed by Bigelow and Lewisohn on the agreement with them, as the petitioner believes, is immaterial to the corporation. The issue of the stock was apparent, we presume, on the books, so that it is difficult to suppose that at least some members of the syndicate, representing an adverse interest, did not know what was done. But all the members were engaged in the plan of buying for less and selling to the corporation for more, and were subject to whatever equity the corporation has against Bigelow and the estate of Lewisohn. There was some argument to the contrary, but this seems to us the fair meaning of the bill. Bigelow and Lewisohn, it is true, divided the stock received for the real estate now in question. But that was a matter between them and the syndicate. The real estate was bought from Keyser by the syndicate, along with his stock in the Baltimore company, and was sold by the syndicate to the petitioner, along with the Baltimore company's property, as part of the scheme. The syndicate was paid for it, whoever received the stock. And this means that two-fifteenths of the stock of the corporation, the 20,000 shares sold to the public, are to be allowed to use the name of the corporation to assert rights against Lewisohn's estate that will enure to the benefit of thirteen-fifteenths of the stock that are totally without claim. It seems to us that the practical objection is as strong as that arising if we adhere to the law.

Let us take the business point of view for a moment longer. To the lay mind it would make little or no difference whether the 20,000 shares sold to the public were sold on an original subscription to the articles of incorporation or were issued under the scheme to some of the syndicate and sold by them. Yet it is admitted, in accordance with the decisions, that, in the latter case, the innocent purchasers would have no claim against anyone. If we are to seek what is called substantial justice, in disregard of even peremptory rules of law, it would seem desirable to get a rule that would cover both of the almost equally possible cases of what is deemed a wrong. It might be said that if the stock really was taken as a preliminary to selling to the public, the subscribers would show a certain confidence in the enterprise, and give at least that security for good faith. But the syndicate believed in the enterprise, notwithstanding all the profits that they made it pay. They preferred to take stock at par rather than cash. Moreover, it would have been possible to issue the whole stock in payment for the property purchased, with an understanding as to 20,000 shares.

Of course, it is competent for legislators, but not, we think, for judges, except by a quasi-legislative declaration, to establish that a corporation shall not be bound by its assent in a transaction of this kind, when the parties contemplate an invitation to the public to come in and join as original subscribers for any portion of the shares. It may be said that the corporation cannot be bound until the contemplated adverse interest is represented, or it may be said that promoters cannot strip themselves of the character of trustees until that moment. But it seems to us a strictly legislative determination. It is difficult, without inventing new and quali-fying established doctrines, to go behind the fact that the corporation remains one and the same after once it really exists. When, as here, after it really exists, it consents, we at least shall require stronger equities than are shown by this bill to allow it to renew its claim at a later date because its internal constitution has changed.

To sum up: In our opinion, on the one hand, the plaintiff cannot recover without departing from the fundamental conception embodied in the law that created it, the conception that a corporation remains unchanged and unaffected in its identity by changes in its members. On the other hand, if we should undertake to look through fiction to facts, it appears to us that substantial justice would not be accomplished, but rather a great injustice done, if the corporation were allowed to disregard its previous assent in order to charge a single member with the whole results of a transaction to which thirteen-fifteenths of its stock were parties, for the benefit of the guilty, if there was guilt in anyone, and the innocent alike. We decide only what is necessary. We express no opinion as to whether the defendant properly is called a promoter, or whether the plaintiff has not been guilty of laches, or whether a remedy can be had for a part of a single transaction in the form in which it is sought, or whether there was any personal claim on the part of the innocent subscribers, or as to any other question than that which we have discussed.

The English case chiefly relied upon, Erlanger v. New Sombrero Phosphate Co., 3 App. Cas. 1218, affirming 5 Ch. D. 73, seems to us far from establishing a different doctrine for that jurisdiction. There, to be sure, a syndicate had made an agreement to sell, at a profit, to a company to be got up by the sellers. But the company, at the first stage, was made up mainly of outsiders, some of them instruments of the sellers, but innocent instruments, and, according to Lord Cairns, the contract was provisional on the shares being taken and the company formed. There never was a moment when the company had assented with knowledge of the facts. The shares, with perhaps one exception, all were taken by subscribers ignorant of the facts, and the contract seems to have reached forward to the moment when they subscribed. As it is put in 2 Morawetz, Corp. (2d ed.) § 292, there was really no company till the shares were issued. Here, thirteen-fifteenths of the stock had been taken by the syndicate, the corporation was in full life and had assented to the sale with knowledge of the facts before an outsider joined. There most of the syndicate were strangers to the corporation, yet all were joined as defendants. Here the members of the syndicate, although members of the corporation, are not joined, and it is sought to throw the burden of their act upon a single one. * * *

Decree affirmed.

NOTES

1. The harsh rule adopted by Justice Holmes in the *Lewisohn* case stems from the fact that a corporation has a personality separate and apart from its shareholders. The resulting conclusion is that ratification by a corporation upon full disclosure will preclude corporate complaints when the shares change hands.

2. Clearly, Justice Holmes is correct that, unlike a partnership at common law, a change in ownership of a corporation does not alter the corporate personality.

3. Is there no way to fashion a fiduciary duty to future shareholders? In OLD DOMINION COPPER MINING & SMELTING CO. v. BIGELOW, 203 Mass. 159, 89 N.E. 193 (1909), *aff'd*, 225 U.S. 111, 32 S.Ct. 641, 56 L.Ed. 1009 (1912), a Massachusetts court held on essentially the same facts that a fiduciary duty was owed by the promoters of the corporation to the corporation itself as a separate legal entity. Disagreeing with the earlier decision by the U.S. Supreme Court, the Supreme Judicial Court of Massachusetts found that, at least where there is a preplanned transaction contemplating future shareholders, the promoters' duty to the corporation encompasses those future shareholders.

4. Other courts have recognized a corporate right of action against promoters selling property to the corporation at inflated values. See, e.g., San Juan Uranium Corp. v. Wolfe, 241 F.2d 121 (10th Cir.1957); Topanga Corp. v. Gentile, 249 Cal.App.2d 681, 58 Cal.Rptr. 713 (1967).

5. A common scheme employed by unscrupulous stock promoters was the use of "watered" stock. This practice was said to have been the product of Daniel Drew, an infamous robber baron in the nineteenth century. Early in his career, Drew had been a cattle driver. Taking advantage of the fact that cattle were sold by the pound while still on the hoof, Drew would supply his cattle with large amounts of salt just before their sale so that they would drink large quantities of water, thereby increasing their weight and sale price. Drew later applied this practice to the stock market by selling assets to corporations at inflated prices in exchange for stock with a par value that was set at the inflated price. The stock was then sold to unsuspecting investors who thought the corporation's assets were properly valued. 1 Jerry W. Markham, *A Financial History of the United States, From Christopher Columbus to the Robber Barons (1492–1900)* 255 (2002).

———

B. MECHANICS OF INCORPORATION

The mechanics of incorporation, as will be described below, are fairly simple. There are some preparatory steps, however, that are a bit more complex. The client should have developed a business plan that will include, at a minimum, a description of the capitalization of the business, i.e., how much of the money needed to start up the business will be borrowed and how much will be invested by the owners? Another concern will be allocation of the ownership interests in the business. If there is more than one owner, what percentage of the company will be owned by each? If there is more than one owner, how will voting control be allocated. Should each owner have a veto over company operations? Should the majority rule? What is to be done in the event of a deadlock in voting by the owners? Another concern is how will the company be managed, i.e., by the owners or by professional managers? How will they be hired, fired and compensated? What happens if one of the owners dies? Should the remaining owners be allowed to buyout the deceased owner's interest and at what price? These ostensible business issues are best handled in a pre-incorporation shareholder agreement that will be available in the event of a dispute. Shareholder agreements are further discussed in Chapter 10.

Once these and other start-up issues are addressed, the client should select a corporate name. That name must be cleared with the Secretary of State in the state of incorporation to assure that it does not conflict with the name of an existing corporation. For an example of such a requirement see Model Bus. Corp. Act § 4.03. Most states allow the client, for a fee (Model Bus. Corp. Act § 1.22(3)), to reserve a name until the company is incorporated or for some maximum period (up to four months under Model Bus. Corp. Act § 4.02). The lawyer should also make a copyright check to make sure that the corporate name does not conflict with the copyrighted names or logos of corporations in other states. There are services that allow you to check such copyrights for possible conflicts.

The new corporation must maintain an office in the state of incorporation. Model Bus. Corp. Act § 5.01(1) and Del. § 131(1). For out-of-state companies incorporating in Delaware, there are services available that will supply a technical office for a nominal fee. The company must also have a registered agent in the state that is authorized to accept service for the corporation. Model Bus. Corp. Act § 5.01 and Del. 132. In Delaware, the service supplying the technical office may also act as the company's registered agent. Del. § 132.

The next step in the formation process is the preparation and filing of the corporate charter with the Secretary of State. Model Bus. Corp. Act § 2.03 and Del. § 101. This document may also be referred to as the articles of incorporation or certificate of incorporation. The company does not become a corporation that is entitled to limited liability until this document is filed with the Secretary of State. Model Bus. Corp. Act § 2.03 and Del. § 106. As a corporate lawyer, it may be your responsibility to file the articles of incorporation. You should, therefore, confirm with the Secretary of State that the charter was received and filed properly. Franchise taxes and filing fees must also be paid to the Secretary of State.

The modern certificate of incorporation is a very simple form. Under the Model Business Corporation Act, it is usually a one page document that sets forth the name of the business, its address, the number of shares of stock authorized to be issued and the name and addresses of its incorporators. Model Bus. Corp. Act § 2.02(a). The corporation may set forth other provisions in the charter concerning the governance of the corporation and other matters. Model Bus. Corp. Act § 2.02(b). Corporate lawyers should be cautious in adding additional provisions because they could curb the scope of the company's business and affect the rights of shareholders in unexpected ways. Under Model Bus. Corp. Act § 3.01(a), the newly formed corporation will be authorized to engage in any lawful business, unless otherwise specified.

Delaware chartering requirements are a bit more complex. The incorporators must specify the nature of the corporation's business, but may state that it is any lawful activity. Del. § 102(a)(3). Incorporators would normally be well advised to specify that the company's business is any lawful activity. This will avoid unintended restrictions on future activities.

The power to adopt and amend by-laws may be a subject addressed in the corporate charter. The by-laws are simply rules of order that govern the operations of the corporation. They may address such things as who may call a special meeting of shareholders or the board of directors, notice and quorum requirements for meetings and other matters. In the absence of such by-law provisions, state corporate statutes may have default provisions that govern those and other matters.

Under Delaware law, the power to adopt or amend the by-laws lies solely with the corporation's shareholders, unless the certificate of incorporation allows the board of directors to share that power with the shareholders. Del. § 109(a). This decision is something to be attended to by the lawyers, if the incorporators want that power to vest in the board. In contrast, the Model Bus. Corp. Act provides that the board of directors shares with shareholders the power to adopt or amend the corporation's by-laws, unless the articles of incorporation provide otherwise. Model Bus. Corp. Act § 10.20. The decision where to vest such power is an important one, since the procedures required by the by-laws may provide an advantage to one side or the other in a battle for corporate control and may restrict the flexibility of the board in responding to business situations. See Chapter 6. There are any number of form by-laws that may be followed in creating a corporation, but remember that they are only forms and should be carefully reviewed to assure they comport with your client's needs.

If the new corporation plans to have operations in other states, it may qualify for doing business by filing with the Secretary of State in that state. Model Bus. Corp. Act §§ 5.01 and 5.02 and Del. §§ 131–132. The corporation must also obtain a tax identification number from the Internal Revenue Service and any required business licenses from the local government where it has offices.

The newly formed corporation should conduct an organizational meeting. Model Bus. Corp. Act § 2.05 and Del. § 108. This meeting is often conducted in writing with the unanimous approval of the incorporators or newly appointed directors. Id. The meeting will be used to issue stock to the owners of the corporation and to appoint the corporation's initial directors (if this has not already been done) so that they may appoint officers. Some states require certain officers. Model Bus. Corp. Act § 8.40 requires that an officer be appointed to prepare minutes, a role usually filled by the corporate secretary. See also Del. § 142. State statutes usually provide that one person may hold more than one office. Id. The compensation of officers and directors should also be decided at this meeting. The organizational meeting should ratify any contracts and other obligations incurred on behalf of the corporation by the incorporators before its existence was formalized. As described above, this may not relieve the incorporators of all liability, but the corporation will have to pay the debts, at least to the extent of any assets that it may have. The organizational meeting should also approve necessary resolutions for opening bank accounts, and entering into leases and other contracts needed by the corporation to commence operations.

Minutes of the organizational meeting and of any board or shareholder meeting must be created and maintained. Model Bus. Corp. Act §§ 8.40(c) and 16.01 and Del. § 142(a). The minutes should contain the date, time and place of the meeting and whether the meeting was held after the required notice, if any, or whether notice was waived. The minutes should specify whether the meeting was a special meeting or a regularly scheduled one and whether a quorum was present. They should indicate any departures by board members from the meeting and any members returning to the meeting. The minutes should further identify any actions taken and reference any discussion or reports. The person preparing the minutes should remember that the minutes form the historical record for the action taken. Therefore, caution is in order. Generally, minutes should be only summary in form. Remember that characterizing particular discussion or reports is dangerous and often misleading. Usually, the best approach is to just reference that there was discussion and attach or reference any written reports. The person preparing the minutes may find that the discussion is fast moving, and it is sometimes difficult to determine exactly what happened. In such a case, clarification should be sought. The minutes are usually brought to the next meeting for approval, and any remaining ambiguities may be resolved at that time.

To aid the incorporation process, many stationery stores supply kits that contain blank stock certificates, stock registers to record ownership and transfers of the stock and blank forms for minutes that may be in the kit as a minute book. These kits also usually contain a corporate seal that you may order. It will have the company's name engraved on the seal and will be used by the corporate secretary to authenticate corporate documents and signatures.

———

SECTION 3.   DEFECTIVE INCORPORATION

POCAHONTAS FUEL CO. v. TARBORO COTTON FACTORY

174 N.C. 245, 93 S.E. 790 (1917).

HOKE, J.

[In considering the personal liability of individual shareholders of a company claimed to be operating under a defective charter, the Court notes that]: In Board of Education v. Berry, it was held, among other things:

> If there has been a bona fide effort to comply with the law to effectuate an incorporation and the persons affected thereby have acquiesced therein, and have exercised the functions pertaining to the corporation, it becomes a de facto corporation whose corporate existence cannot be litigated in actions between private individuals nor between private individuals and the assumed corporation. And, again, if a corporation de facto exists, it may exercise the powers assumed, and the question of its having a right to exercise them will be deemed one that can be raised only by the state.

> If it be conceded therefore that, in this instance, there has not been substantial compliance with the law as to organization, constituting a corporation de jure, we are of opinion on this record that these purchasers, holding a charter which gave them the authority, have met all the requirements as to a corporation de facto, and have been properly protected from individual liability.

We have purposely refrained from resting our opinion on the position of incorporation by estoppel, which was also suggested for defendants. That doctrine is recognized in proper instances, but it usually arises in cases where one, having received value from an assumed corporation and under obligations for it, is seeking to resist recovery, on the ground solely that the alleged corporation had no existence. It is an equitable doctrine resting in part on the ground of value having passed and under circumstances which render it unjust that the suggested defense be upheld. It is very rarely, if ever, allowed where the claimant, having extended credit or value towards the alleged corporation, is seeking to recover his debt. In such case, no estoppel arises from the mere fact that a creditor or claimant has dealt with defendant as a corporation, and unless there is one either de jure or de facto, the members can, ordinarily, be held liable as partners.

We find no error in the record, and the judgment of the court is affirmed.

———

CRANSON v. INTERNATIONAL BUSINESS MACHINES CORP.

234 Md. 477, 200 A.2d 33 (1964).

HORNEY, JUDGE.

On the theory that the Real Estate Service Bureau was neither a *de jure* nor a *de facto* corporation and that Albion C. Cranson, Jr., was a partner in the business conducted by the Bureau and as such was personally liable for its debts, the International Business Machines Corporation brought this action against Cranson for the balance due on electric typewriters purchased by the Bureau. At the same time it moved for summary judgment and supported the motion by affidavit. In due course, Cranson filed a general issue plea and an affidavit in opposition to summary judgment in which he asserted in effect that the Bureau was a *de facto* corporation and that he was not personally liable for its debts.

The agreed statement of facts shows that in April 1961, Cranson was asked to invest in a new business corporation which was about to be created. Towards this purpose he met with other interested individuals and an attorney and agreed to purchase stock and become an officer and director. Thereafter, upon being advised by the attorney that the corporation had been formed under the laws of Maryland, he paid for and received a stock certificate evidencing ownership of shares in the corporation, and was shown the corporate seal and minute book. The business of the new venture was conducted as if it were a corporation, through corporate bank accounts, with auditors maintaining corporate books and records, and under a lease entered into by the corporation for the office from which it operated its business. Cranson was elected president and all transactions conducted by him for the corporation, including the dealings with I.B.M., were made as an officer of the corporation. At no time did he assume any personal obligation or pledge his individual credit to I.B.M. Due to an oversight on the part of the attorney, of which Cranson was not aware, the certificate of incorporation, which had been signed and acknowledged prior to May 1, 1961, was not filed until November 24, 1961. Between May 17 and November 8, the Bureau purchased eight typewriters from I.B.M., on account of which partial payments were made, leaving a balance due of $4,333.40, for which this suit was brought. * * *

The fundamental question presented by the appeal is whether an officer of a defectively incorporated association may be subjected to personal liability under the circumstances of this case. We think not.

Traditionally, two doctrines have been used by the courts to clothe an officer of a defectively incorporated association with the corporate attribute of limited liability. The first, often referred to as the doctrine of *de facto* corporations, has been applied in those cases where there are elements showing: (1) the existence of law authorizing incorporation; (2) an effort in good faith to incorporate under the existing law; and (3) actual user or exercise of corporate powers. . . . The second, the doctrine of estoppel to deny the corporate existence, is generally employed where the person seeking to hold the officer personally liable has contracted or otherwise dealt with the association in such a manner as to recognize and in effect admit its existence as a corporate body. * * *

It is not at all clear what Maryland has done with respect to the two doctrines. There have been no recent cases in this State on the subject and some of the seemingly irreconcilable earlier cases offer little to clarify the problem. * * *

I.B.M. contends that the failure of the Bureau to file its certificate of incorporation debarred *all* corporate existence. But, in spite of the fact that the omission might have prevented the Bureau from being either a corporation *de jure* or *de facto*,[1] we think that I.B.M. having dealt with the Bureau as if it were a corporation and relied on its credit rather than that of Cranson, is estopped to assert that the Bureau was not incorporated at the time the typewriters were purchased. In 1 Clark and Marshall, Private Corporations, § 89, it is stated:

> The doctrine in relation to estoppel is based upon the ground that it would generally be inequitable to permit the corporate existence of an association to be denied by persons who have represented it to be a corporation, or held it out as a corporation, or by any persons who have recognized it as a corporation by dealing with it as such; and by the overwhelming weight of authority, therefore, a person may be estopped to deny the legal incorporation of an association which is not even a corporation *de facto*.

In cases similar to the one at bar, involving a failure to file articles of incorporation, the courts of other jurisdictions have held that where one has recognized the corporate existence of an association, he is estopped to assert the contrary with respect to a claim arising out of such dealings. See, for example, Tarbell v. Page, 24 Ill. 46 (1860); Magnolia Shingle Co. v. J. Zimmern's Co., 3 Ala.App. 578, 58 So. 90 (1912); Lockwood v. Wynkoop, 178 Mich. 388, 144 N.W. 846 (1914) John Lucas & Co. v. Bernhardt's Estate, 156 La. 207, 100 So. 399 (1924).

Since I.B.M. is estopped to deny the corporate existence of the Bureau, we hold that Cranson was not liable for the balance due on account of the typewriters.

Judgment reversed; the appellee to pay the costs.

---

1. Those states which recognize the *de facto* doctrine are not in accord as to whether a corporation *de facto* may be created in spite of the failure to file the necessary papers. Some courts, without making clear in every instance whether a *de facto* corporation was meant or not, have stated that failure to file the required papers prevented the organizations from becoming a corporation and have held in effect that the persons acting as a corporation are a mere association or partnership Other courts, without expressly deciding whether a *de facto* corporation was created, hold that the statutes of the state imply corporate existence prior to the filing of articles of incorporation. Still other courts hold that a *de facto* existence is not precluded by failure to file the articles of incorporation.

NOTES

1. The official comment to Model Bus. Corp. Act § 2.04 notes there are five classes of cases where the issue of a *de facto* corporation may arise: where (1) the participant honestly and reasonably believes the certificate of incorporation has been filed by an attorney when, in fact, it has not been; (2) the articles of incorporation are mailed to the Secretary of State but are delayed or returned by the Secretary due to some error; (3) a third party agrees to enter into a contract with a company in its corporate name even though the third party knows that the company has not filed its charter with the Secretary of State; (4) a defendant enters into a contract on behalf of a company even though its charter has not been filed. The opposite party, however, dealt with the defective corporation and not with the defendant as an individual; (5) a passive investor provides funds with the instruction not to engage in business until the articles of incorporation are filed, but business is commenced anyway before incorporation. The Model Business Corporation Act comment notes there are varying policy issues as to whether liability should be imposed in each of these instances. Under what circumstances do you think liability should be imposed on persons acting on behalf of a defective corporation?

2. The former Model Business Corporation Act, before its revision, provided that the corporate existence began on filing of the articles of incorporation with the Secretary of State. Anything short of filing was not compliance, and personal liability would result for those acting on behalf of the company. This was an attempt to eliminate the *de facto* corporation doctrine. Thereafter, in Timberline Equipment Co., Inc. v. Davenport, 267 Or. 64, 514 P.2d 1109 (1973), the court held that, because Oregon had adopted the model act requirement, it would not apply the *de facto* corporation doctrine to a company that had been defectively incorporated. The court ruled that shareholders of the company actively participating in its business were jointly and severally liable for the company's debts. The court held, however, that merely passive shareholders would not be personally liable, thereby creating a sort of *de facto* limited partnership. There was much criticism of the *Timberline* decision, and the revisions to Model Business Corporation Act took a different approach when it was adopted. Model Bus. Corp. Act § 2.04 now provides that liability will be imposed only on persons who act on behalf of a corporation "knowing" that the corporation does not yet exist. This provision protects persons who "erroneously but in good faith" believe a charter has been filed properly. Official Comment, Model Bus. Corp. Act § 2.04. The drafters of the Model Business Corporation Act also noted that the doctrine of estoppel might apply to a third party who urged a defendant to enter into a contract in the corporation's name even though the third party knew there was no corporation. Estoppel would not apply where the plaintiff did not know that the corporation was defective. In such cases, the defendant would be liable if he or she knew that the corporate charter had not been filed. Id. Compare the *Timberline* decision with Robertson v. Levy, 197 A.2d 443 (D.C.App.1964) which held that the Model Act abrogated both the de facto doctrine and corporation by estoppel.

3. Some states that adopted the Model Act consciously decided not to include § 2.04. What is the effect of such a decision? For example, North Carolina did not adopt the "knowing" provision in Model Bus. Corp. Act § 2.04, even though it adopted most of the other provisions in the revised act. The North Carolina drafting committee was split as to whether Model Bus. Corp. Act § 2.04 expanded or contracted common law standards for *de facto* corporations and estoppel doctrines.[a] What do you think? What case law will the North Carolina courts apply when the issue arises—the traditional common law standards in the *Pocahontas Fuel Co.* decision or the more modern decision in the *Cranson* case?

4. The Delaware Act in § 329 provides that the want of legal organization may not be used as a defense to any claim. What effect does this provision have on the liability of a person acting on behalf of a defective corporation that deals with a third party when both have knowledge that the corporation is defective?

SECTION 4. CAPITAL FORMATION— A FIRST LOOK

A corporation needs money to commence and carry out its operations. Those funds will initially be borrowed, contributed by the owners of the company or acquired from the company's profits. The company will use these funds to pay its bills or acquire assets. The corporation may also distribute its profits to shareholders in the form of dividends. Accounting for these funds and their expenditure play an important role in corporate finance. Corporate lawyers, therefore, must be familiar with some basic accounting concepts.

A. WHAT IS A BOND?

The corporation may borrow funds to commence and carry out its operations. The funds will be loaned for a specified period of time at a fixed or variable rate of interest. The borrowing may be a "non-recourse" loan, if the corporation has sufficient funds or assets to assure repayment. Otherwise, the individual owners of the corporation may be required to guarantee the loan. The owners of the company may also loan funds to the corporation, as well as contribute funds as shareholders by buying stock. Third parties may make loans on such terms as may be negotiated. When the corporation is larger, it may seek to borrow funds from the public by selling bonds. A bond or debenture, as it is sometimes called, is simply a certificate that contains a promise from the corporation to repay the lender the principal (plus interest) at some future date. The terms of the loan are set forth in a separate document called a trust indenture agreement. The trust indenture is administered by a trustee that makes transfers of interest and principal payment to the lenders.

---

a. One of the authors (Thomas Hazen) was a member of that drafting committee.

B. WHAT IS STOCK?

Stocks are simply certificates that reflect an ownership interest in a corporation. Stocks may take many forms, depending on the nature of the ownership interests conferred. For example, ownership shares in the corporation may be common or preferred stocks.

Common stocks usually represent an aliquot ownership position in the corporation. For example, if a corporation has issued 10,000 shares of its common stock, and if you own 1,000 of those shares, you will own ten percent of the corporation. In the event the corporation is liquidated, you will receive ten percent of any assets left over after payment of the company's debts, including any amounts owed to bondholders. This means that debtors have priority over stockowners in bankruptcy. The shareholders will share only in assets left over after all of the debts of the corporation have been paid.

Common stocks usually confer the right to vote to elect the board of directors and to vote on other issues submitted to the shareholders. Common stocks usually provide a right to a proportional amount of any dividends "declared" by the board of directors. Dividends represent a claim by the shareholder on the earnings of the corporation on a *pro rata* basis. The shareholders, however, are not entitled to any dividends until the board of directors declare them.

Remember that the corporate charter may vary the rights of common stockholders in any number of ways. This means that common stocks may be divided into separate classes that have differing ownership rights. In some corporations, for example, one class of common stock may not have the right to vote, but may be entitled to dividends, when declared. Another class of common stock in this same corporation may have the right to vote but be excluded from dividends, or there may be some combination of such rights and exclusions. *See* Model Bus. Corp. Act § 6.01 and Del. § 151.

Preferred stocks give their holders a preference over common stockholders in the receipt of dividends and in liquidation. This means that the preferred shareholders are given a specified dividend, usually a percentage of the preferred stock's liquidation value, before the common shareholders receive dividend payments. The preferred stock also usually has a liquidation value that must be paid before the common stockholders receive anything in liquidation. To illustrate, assume the owner of a six percent preferred stock with a liquidation value of $100 will receive a dividend each year of $6, provided that funds are available for such a payment. Although the preferred shareholders have no right to require the board of directors to declare a dividend, there is an incentive for the board to do so, *i.e.*, the common stockholders cannot receive a dividend until the preferred stockholders receive their $6 in the above example. In liquidation, after payment of all liabilities, the preferred shareholder will be paid $100, if available. The common shareholders will share proportionally with each other in whatever is left.

Preferred stock usually is not entitled to vote unless dividends are missed for some specified period of time. In such event, the preferred stockholders may be authorized to elect a specified number of directors. Preferred stock may be cumulative or non-cumulative. Cumulative means that, if a preferred dividend is missed in any year or years, the common stockholders cannot receive a dividend until any dividends in arrears are paid to the preferred. Non-cumulative preferred simply forfeits any right to dividends if the board of directors does not declare them in any given year. The non-cumulative preferred shareholders will be the first to receive any dividends declared in subsequent years but have no claims for dividends missed in prior years.

C. THE BALANCE SHEET

A useful tool for understanding the finances of a corporation is the balance sheet. An example of a balance sheet is set forth below. The balance sheet identifies the assets of the corporation and sets forth the source of funds for those assets. The balance sheet must balance. This means the amount of the assets on the left side of the balance sheet must equal the liabilities, equity investments and retained earnings (profits not paid out as dividends) on the right side of the balance sheet.

BALANCE SHEET

Assets		Liabilities	
Current Assets		Current Liabilities	
Cash	$250,000	Accounts payable	$100,000
Acct. Receivable	$500,000	Notes payable	$100,000
Inventory	$250,000	Income taxes payable	$20,000
(FIFO)			
Fixed Assets		Long Term Liabilities	
Land	$500,000	5 yr notes payable	$780,000
Building	$300,000		
Equip.	$200,000	Total Liabilities	$1,000,000
Total	$1,000,000		
Less Depr.	−$100,000)	Shareholder Equity	
	$900,000		
		Preferred Stock	
		2500@ $100 Liquidating value	
		preference = $250,000	
		Common Stock	
		250,000 common stock @ $1 par	
Intangibles	$100,000	Stated Capital =	$250,000
		Capital Surplus =	$250,000

Assets	Liabilities
	Retained Earnings = $250,000
	Total Shareholders Equity = $1,000,000
	TOTAL EQUITY AND
TOTAL ASSETS = $2,000,000	LIAB. = $2,000,000

Assets on the balance sheet may be short or long term. A short-term asset is cash or an asset that is readily convertible into cash. This could include such things as accounts receivable or tax refunds due to the corporation. A long-term asset is one that will not be converted into cash within a year. Long-term assets include such things as real property, buildings and equipment. The corporation's assets need to be valued before their inclusion on the balance sheet. Usually, the value of the asset will be its purchase price, but that valuation is not always easy to arrive at, particularly in the case of inventory. To illustrate: a shoe store's inventory of goods must be valued. Assume that the company has sold some shoes it ordered, but not all of them. A new shipment arrives subsequently, but the prices for the shoes are different. The corporation could possibly count the old shoes left, value them individually and then use the new price for the new shoes, but over time the shoes became intermingled. Some of the new shoes were sold, and some of the old ones remain. Rather than trying to sort them out, we can simply use one of several common inventory valuation techniques such as FIFO (first-in-first-out) or LIFO (last-in-first-out). Under FIFO, we simply assume that the first goods purchased were the first ones sold. Under LIFO, we assume that the last shoes purchased were the first ones sold on the theory that the new shoes were put on the front of the shelf and sold first before the older shoes on the back of the shelf. These assumptions may not be completely accurate, but they provide a convenient way to value inventory.

Valuing assets on the balance sheet raises additional issues. For example, assets are usually carried on the balance sheet at their purchase price ("book value"), but that may not accurately reflect their current market value. In some instances, accounting principles will require "mark-to-market" accounting for assets, requiring them to be valued at their current market value. Even where assets are not required to be marked-to-the-market, however, their value needs to be adjusted to reflect the decline in their value as they wear out from use. To deal with that concern, these assets are depreciated each year on the balance sheet using any number of depreciation methods that range from the simple (*e.g.*, dividing the cost of the asset by the number of years of its expected life and deducting the resulting amount each year) to the complex (*e.g.*, accelerating depreciation in early years to reduce taxes or deferring depreciation to later years in order to increase earnings). Land is not depreciated.

Still another asset valuation concern is the collection of accounts receivable, which are carried as assets on the balance sheet. Say that the corporation sells some of its goods on credit, allowing purchasers 90 days to pay. Some purchasers will fail to pay and their accounts become uncollectable. The corporation needs to reserve an amount on its balance sheet to reflect its loss experience from such bad accounts. That reserve amount is deducted from its account receivable on the balance sheet to provide a more realistic valuation of the corporation's assets.

More complex valuation issues are raised by intangible assets, such as patents and goodwill. A patent has a limited life and its value is intangible, but may be valued in a reasonable manner on the balance sheet. This means that its value may be amortized over the expected life of the patent so that a huge write-off will not be required when it expires. Another intangible asset is goodwill. This asset will arise where a corporation purchases another business and pays more for that business than its tangible assets will justify. The excess of the price over the value of those tangible assets is treated as goodwill. Why would a corporation pay more for another business than the value of that business's assets? Assume that ABC, LLC is a shoe store. Its only significant asset is an inventory of shoes valued (by LIFO) at $90,000. The only other assets are a cash register, some computers, lamps and other equipment at the store it rents valued at $10,000. XYZ, Inc has agreed to pay $1 million for ABC's business. Why would XYZ make such an offer? The answer is that ABC sells a lot of shoes, turning its inventory over rapidly and making nice profits. XYZ wants that revenue flow and its profits. The tangible assets acquired from ABC will be carried on XYZ's balance sheet at a value of $100,000. The remainder of the purchase price ($900,000) will be carried as goodwill on XYZ's balance sheet. Under current accounting rules, goodwill must be written off if the acquired business declines in value.

The right side of the balance sheet must also be analyzed. It is divided into liabilities and equity capital. The liabilities section sets forth the funds borrowed by the corporation. Liabilities are divided into long and short-term. Liabilities that must be repaid within a year are short-term, while those with a maturity of more than one year are long-term. Short-term liabilities include bank loans with maturities less than one year. These could be a revolving credit line used by the corporation for working capital needs or simply a short-term loan such as commercial paper, which is simply a promissory note sold to institutional investors. Long-term debt includes bank loans of longer duration, secured loans that are collateralized by particular assets of the corporation and debentures (general obligation bonds) that are usually unsecured. Debt on the balance sheet may be senior or junior. Senior debt will have priority over payment in bankruptcy over more junior debt. Remember that all debt must be paid in full before stockholders receive anything in bankruptcy.

Below the liabilities on the right side of the balance sheet is equity capital, which may include preferred stock. Where preferred stock has been issued, its liquidation value is listed. This is the preference for the preferred shareholder in the event of liquidation or insolvency. Model Bus. Corp. Act § 6.40(c) restricts a corporation from paying dividends to common shareholders where the dividend would impair the corporation's ability to pay liquidation preferences.

As you can see from the balance sheet, there may be two accounts on the right side of the balance sheet that describe the contribution to the corporation's assets by the common stockholders—a "stated" capital account and a capital "surplus" account. The stated capital account is used to reflect the "par" value of the common stock. This confusing concept is the result of history and not economics. In earlier years, par value was what the stock was sold for and was used to value the stock when sold. Common stock is no longer traded on the basis of par value, but the concept still lingers. Some states prohibit payment of dividends out of stated capital, and some states restrict dividends from capital surplus, which is the amount the corporation received for the stock in excess of its par value. Therefore, distinction must be made between the two. Corporations usually set a low par value for their stock to avoid such restrictions. To add further confusion, the Model Business Corporation Act does not require par value for common stock. This is because the Model Business Corporation Act ties dividend restrictions to solvency tests, rather than to capital accounts. Model Bus. Corp. Act § 6.40(c).[2] Delaware also authorizes no-par stock (Del. § 151) but then provides for the corporation to designate an amount that acts as stated capital or provides a formula for such a computation in the absence of such a determination. Del. § 154. The latter requirement is tied to Delaware's limitations on dividends from a corporation's capital. Del. § 170. For a further description of dividend limitations see Chapter 22. For present purposes, you need only remember that stated capital and surplus, when added together, tell you what the corporation sold its stock for to the original purchaser.

Still another capital account is for retained earnings or earned surplus. This account simply reflects profits of the corporation that have not been paid out in dividends. The retained earnings account may be in deficit if the company has lost money in excess of any retained earnings. Retained earnings are the usual source for dividends. See Randall v. Bailey, 288 N.Y. 280, 43 N.E.2d 43 (1942), page 1362 below.

----

2. Under the Model Business Corporation Act the concept of "par" may be relegated to the golf course where it properly belongs and where the definition is a bit more straightforward:

"Regulation" is a term used to indicate the number of strokes it takes a golfer to reach the green on a particular hole. Regulation for each hole in golf is based on "par" for that hole. Par is the score expected of an expert golfer on a given hole and allows for two strokes on the putting green. Regulation is the number of strokes left after subtracting the two strokes on the putting green from par. For example, regulation on a par three hole is one. On a par five hole, regulation is three.

Gilder v. PGA Tour, Inc., 936 F.2d 417, 420, n. 4 (9th Cir.1991).

D. THE INCOME STATEMENT

Another useful tool for corporate finance is the income statement (or profit and loss statement as it is sometimes called):

Income Statement

Net Sales	$10,000
Cost of Goods Sold and Operating Expenses	$7,000
Depreciation	$1,000
Selling & Administrative Expenses	$1,000
Operating Income	$1,000
Less Interest on Long Term Notes	$100
Income Before Taxes	$900
Income Taxes	$500
Net Income	$400
Net Income Per Share (1000 shares)	$00.40

The income statement is useful in showing revenue, expenses and income. This information allows planning by the corporation (*e.g.*, the officers of the corporation may perceive the need to cut certain expenses or add resources in an effort to increase revenues). Managers and stockholders are also provided a picture of whether, and to what extent, the corporation is profitable. In evaluating a corporation's performance, various financial ratios are helpful and may be used to compare its performance with other corporations. For example "ROE" (return on equity) may be computed by dividing the dollar amount of the corporation's earnings by the dollar amount of equity capital obtained from the balance sheet. Another useful measure is a corporation's PE ratio. This is the market price of a share of stock divided by the corporation's earnings per share. A high ratio may suggest a belief that the company's prospects for future growth is high, while a lower ratio could suggest that a lot of growth is not expected. Of course, other market factors can also affect this ratio.

A statement of cash flows is similar to the income statement except that depreciation is added back to the income figure along with any other non-cash charges, including amortization. This statement allows managers to manage cash flows and determine if there is excess cash that may be used for productive purposes and to determine whether they should borrow additional funds or raise additional capital by selling ("issuing") stock. A useful computation derived from the statement of cash flows is "EBITDA" (earnings before interest, taxes, depreciation and amortization). EBITDA, as will be seen in later chapters, may be used to finance the acquisition of other businesses.

A NOTE ON LEVERAGE

A corporation must determine what amount of the funds it needs should be borrowed and what amount should be obtained through sales of stock. Borrowing the funds will require payments of interest (which are tax deductible) and repayment of the principal. A sale of stock will raise funds, without interest charges, and the funds are contributed permanently, which means that they need not be repaid. However, the number of owners is increased and existing shareholders will have to share future profits and control with the new stockholders, thereby diluting the ownership interest of the existing shareholders. For that reason, borrowing may be preferred, i.e., borrowing provides existing shareholders with "leverage" and avoids dilution.

To understand the concept of leveraging, think about the purchase of a single family residence. The family buying the home will probably make a down payment to the bank of, say, 20% ($80,000) in order to borrow the balance on a $400,000 home. The family will then make fixed monthly payments that will reflect annual interest payments of, say, 7% on the balance plus a remaining amount that will repay a portion of the principal each month over the life of the loan. The leverage gained from borrowing will allow this family to live in a $400,000 house even though they only had $80,000 available for such an investment. Leverage has another effect. Assume that the value of this real estate increased to $500,000 in a single year. Assume that the family has a pre-tax profit of $50,000, after real estate commissions, closing costs and adjustment for interest on the loan. This is a return of 62.5% on the family's investment of $80,000. Now consider what the return on this property would be if the family had paid the entire $400,000 purchase price and paid cash for the house. The return on their investment of $400,000 with a profit from the sale of the house of $50,000 would only be a relatively paltry 12.5%, rather than the rather robust 62.5 percent obtained by the leverage from a mortgage. Remember, however, that leverage works both ways. If the value of the real estate had gone down, the loss in percentage terms would be far greater for the leveraged purchase than for full payment.

Careful financial officers seek to prevent their corporations from being over-leveraged, while at the same time seeking to use the advantages of at least some leverage. Banks are also careful in extending loans to make sure that a corporate borrower is not over-leveraged.

CHAPTER 5

LIMITED LIABILITY AND ULTRA VIRES

■ ■ ■

SECTION 1. PIERCING THE CORPORATE VEIL

MINTON v. CAVANEY

56 Cal.2d 576, 15 Cal.Rptr. 641, 364 P.2d 473 (1961).

TRAYNOR, JUSTICE.

The Seminole Hot Springs Corporation, hereinafter referred to as Seminole, was duly incorporated in California on March 8, 1954. It conducted a public swimming pool that it leased from its owner. On June 24, 1954 plaintiffs' daughter drowned in the pool, and plaintiffs recovered a judgment for $10,000 against Seminole for her wrongful death. The judgment remains unsatisfied.

On January 30, 1957, plaintiffs brought the present action to hold defendant Cavaney personally liable for the judgment against Seminole. Cavaney died on May 28, 1958 and his widow, the executrix of his estate, was substituted as defendant. The trial court entered judgment for plaintiffs for $10,000. Defendant appeals.

Plaintiffs introduced evidence that Cavaney was a director and secretary and treasurer of Seminole and that on November 15, 1954, about five months after the drowning, Cavaney as secretary of Seminole and Edwin A. Kraft as president of Seminole applied for permission to issue three shares of Seminole stock, one share to be issued to Kraft, another to F. J. Wettrick and the third to Cavaney. The commissioner of corporations refused permission to issue these shares unless additional information was furnished. The application was then abandoned and no shares were ever issued. There was also evidence that for a time Seminole used Cavaney's office to keep records and to receive mail. Before his death Cavaney answered certain interrogatories. He was asked if Seminole 'ever had any assets?' He stated that 'insofar as my own personal knowledge and belief is concerned said corporation did not have any assets.' Cavaney also stated in the return to an attempted execution that '(I)nsofar as I know, this corporation had no assets of any kind or character. The corporation was duly organized but never functioned as a corporation.'

150

Defendant introduced evidence that Cavaney was an attorney at law, that he was approached by Kraft and Wettrick to form Seminole, and that he was the attorney for Seminole. Plaintiffs introduced Cavaney's answer to several interrogatories that he held the post of secretary and treasurer and director in a temporary capacity and as an accommodation to his client.

Defendant contends that the evidence does not support the court's determination that Cavaney is personally liable for Seminole's debts and that the "alter ego" doctrine is inapplicable because plaintiffs failed to show that there was " '(1) * * * such unity of interest and ownership that the separate personalities of the corporation and the individual no longer exist and (2) that, if the acts are treated as those of the corporation alone, an inequitable result will follow.' " Riddle v. Leuschner, 51 Cal.2d 574, 580, 335 P.2d 107, 110.

The figurative terminology "alter ego" and "disregard of the corporate entity" is generally used to refer to the various situations that are an abuse of the corporate privilege. Ballantine, Corporations (rev. ed. 1946) § 122, pp. 292–293; Lattin, Corporations, p. 66; Latty, The Corporate Entity as a Solvent of Legal Problems, 34 Mich.L.Rev. 597 (1936). The equitable owners of a corporation, for example, are personally liable when they treat the assets of the corporation as their own and add or withdraw capital from the corporation at will when they hold themselves out as being personally liable for the debts of the corporation or when they provide inadequate capitalization and actively participate in the conduct of corporate affairs.

In the instant case the evidence is undisputed that there was no attempt to provide adequate capitalization. Seminole never had any substantial assets. It leased the pool that it operated, and the lease was forfeited for failure to pay the rent. Its capital was "trifling compared with the business to be done and the risks of loss * * *." Automotriz Del Golfo De California S. A. De C. V. v. Resnick, supra, 47 Cal.2d 792, 797, 306 P.2d 1, 4. The evidence is also undisputed that Cavaney was not only the secretary and treasurer of the corporation but was also a director. The evidence that Cavaney was to receive one third of the shares to be issued supports an inference that he was an equitable owner and the evidence that for a time the records of the corporation were kept in Cavaney's office supports an inference that he actively participated in the conduct of the business. The trial court was not required to believe his statement that he was only a 'temporary' director and officer 'for accommodation.' In any event it merely raised a conflict in the evidence that was resolved adversely to defendant. Moreover, section 800 of the Corporations Code provides that ' * * * the business and affairs of every corporation shall be controlled by, a board of not less than three directors.' Defendant does not claim that Cavaney was a director with specialized duties (see 5 U.Chi. L.Rev. 668). It is immaterial whether or not he accepted the office of director as an 'accommodation' with the understanding that he would not exercise any of the duties of a director. A person may not in this manner divorce the responsibilities of a director from the statutory duties and powers of that office.

In this action to hold defendant personally liable upon the judgment against Seminole plaintiffs did not allege or present any evidence on the issue of Seminole's negligence or on the amount of damages sustained by plaintiffs. They relied solely on the judgment against Seminole. Defendant correctly contends that Cavaney or his estate cannot be held liable for the debts of Seminole without an opportunity to relitigate these issues. Cavaney was not a party to the action against the corporation, and the judgment in that action is therefore not binding upon him unless he controlled the litigation leading to the judgment. Although Cavaney filed an answer to the complaint against Seminole as its attorney, he withdrew before the trial and did not thereafter participate therein. The filing of an answer without any other participation is not sufficient to bind Cavaney. "In order that the rule stated in this section (that a person in control of the litigation is bound by the judgment) should apply it is necessary that the one in whose favor or against whom the rules of res judicata operate participate in the control of the action and if judgment is adverse, be able to determine whether or not an appeal should be taken. It is not sufficient that he supplies the funds for the prosecution or defense, that he appears as a witness or cooperates without having control."

SCHAUER, JUSTICE (CONCURRING AND DISSENTING).

I dissent from any implication that *mere professional activity by an attorney at law, as such,* in the organization of a corporation, can constitute any basis for a finding that the corporation is the attorney's alter ego or that he is otherwise personally liable for its debts, whether based on contract or tort. That in such circumstances an attorney does not incur any personal liability for debts of the corporation remains true whether or not the attorney's professional services include the issuance to him of a qualifying share of stock, the attendance at and participation in an organization meeting or meetings, the holding and exercise for such preliminary purposes, in the course of his professional services, of an office of offices, whether secretary or treasurer or presiding officer or any combination of offices in the corporation.

The acts and services performed in *organizing* a corporation do not constitute the carrying on of business *by a corporation.* In this respect a corporation cannot properly be regarded as organized and ready to even begin carrying on business until at least qualifying shares of stock have been issued, a stockholders' meeting held, by-laws adopted and directors and officers elected. Furthermore, a permit from the Commissioner of Corporations must have been secured and minimum requirements of that agency met before the corporation can secure assets for which its stock may issue (possibly to be impounded on conditions) and without which it cannot (at least normally) commence business. The scope of a lawyer's services in corporate organization may often include advice and direction as to the legal architecture of financial structures but does not, as such, encompass responsibility for securing assets.

In the process of developing an idea of a person or persons into an embryonic corporation and finally to full legal entity status with a permit issued, directors and officers elected, and assets in hand ready to begin business, there may often be delays. In such event a qualifying share of stock may stand in the name of the organizing attorney for substantial periods of time. In none of the activities indicated is the corporation actually engaging in business. And the lawyer who handles the task of determining and directing and participating in the steps appropriate to transforming the idea into a competent legal entity *ready to engage in business* is not an alter ego of the corporation. By his professional acts he has not been engaging in business in the name of the corporation; he has been merely practicing law.

NOTES

1. *Thin capitalization.* How can you reconcile *Minton* with the following observation?

> Evidence of inadequate capitalization is, at best, merely a factor to be considered by the trial court in deciding whether to pierce the corporate veil. To be sure, it is an important factor, but no case has been cited, nor have any been found, where it has been held that this factor alone *requires* invoking the equitable doctrine....

Arnold v. Browne, 27 Cal.App.3d 386, 396, 103 Cal.Rptr. 775, 783 (1972) (citation omitted). This suggests that you will need under-capitalization plus some other factor before the veil will be pierced. To date, no publicly owned corporation has had its veil pierced for lack of capitalization. Robert B. Thompson, "Piercing the Corporate Veil: An Empirical Study," 76 Cornell L. Rev. 1036 (1991).

2. In earlier years, many states had minimum capital requirements, often $500 or $1000. That amount of money had to be contributed by the shareholders before the company could commence business. See Tri–State Developers, Inc. v. Moore, 343 S.W.2d 812, 816 (Ky.1961) ("One may start business on a shoestring in Kentucky, but if it is a corporate business the shoestring must be worth $1,000."). Most states abandoned such requirements because they were arbitrary. The sum of $500 might be sufficient to start a watermelon growing business on a leased plot, but $1 million might not be enough for a highly hazardous operation such as handling some forms of particularly toxic waste. What happens where a corporation's capital was adequate when the operation began but is now inadequate because of losses or growth in the business? See Truckweld Equip. Co., Inc. v. Olson, 26 Wash. App. 638, 618 P.2d 1017 (1980) (controlling shareholder was not obligated to contribute additional capital to faltering corporation). Generally, such changes will not result in liability unless the owners removed capital from the business that undermined its ability to continue. See generally, Costello v. Fazio, 256 F.2d 903 (9th Cir.1958), discussed below.

3.   Who is being protected by requiring adequate capital? Is it voluntary or involuntary creditors, or both? Is there any policy factor that would support seeking to protect voluntary creditors by requiring adequate capital? Remember that limited liability in a small corporation has other limitations. Creditors often require personal guarantees from the individual owners and may require specific security, including a first or second mortgage on their homes.

4.   The more traditional approach to piercing the veil is found in the following leading case. Note the dissent's reliance on *Minton v. Cavaney*.

WALKOVSZKY v. CARLTON

18 N.Y.2d 414, 276 N.Y.S.2d 585, 223 N.E.2d 6 (1966).

FULD, JUDGE.

This case involves what appears to be a rather common practice in the taxicab industry of vesting the ownership of a taxi fleet in many corporations, each owning only one or two cabs.

The complaint alleges that the plaintiff was severely injured four years ago in New York City when he was run down by a taxicab owned by the defendant Seon Cab Corporation and negligently operated at the time by the defendant Marchese. The individual defendant, Carlton, is claimed to be a stockholder of 10 corporations, including Seon, each of which has but two cabs registered in its name, and it is implied that only the minimum automobile liability insurance required by law (in the amount of $10,000) is carried on any one cab. Although seemingly independent of one another, these corporations are alleged to be "operated * * * as a single entity, unit and enterprise" with regard to financing, supplies, repairs, employees and garaging, and all are named as defendants. The plaintiff asserts that he is also entitled to hold their stockholders personally liable for the damages sought because the multiple corporate structure constitutes an unlawful attempt "to defraud members of the general public" who might be injured by the cabs.

The defendant Carlton has moved to dismiss the complaint on the ground that as to him it "fails to state a cause of action". The court at Special Term granted the motion but the Appellate Division, by a divided vote, reversed, holding that a valid cause of action was sufficiently stated. The defendant Carlton appeals to us, from the nonfinal order, by leave of the Appellate Division on a certified question.

The law permits the incorporation of a business for the very purpose of enabling its proprietors to escape personal liability but, manifestly, the privilege is not without its limits. Broadly speaking, the courts will disregard the corporate form, or, to use accepted terminology, "pierce the corporate veil", whenever necessary "to prevent fraud or to achieve equity". In determining whether liability should be extended to reach assets beyond those belonging to the corporation, we are guided, as Judge Cardozo noted, by "general rules of agency". (Berkey v. Third Ave. Ry.

Co., 244 N.Y. 84, 95, 155 N.E. 58, 61, 50 A.L.R. 599.) In other words, whenever anyone uses control of the corporation to further his own rather than the corporation's business, he will be liable for the corporation's acts 'upon the principle of *respondeat superior* applicable even where the agent is a natural person'. Such liability, moreover, extends not only to the corporation's commercial dealings but to its negligent acts as well.

In the Mangan case (247 App.Div. 853, 286 N.Y.S. 666), the plaintiff was injured as a result of the negligent operation of a cab owned and operated by one of four corporations affiliated with the defendant Terminal. Although the defendant was not a stockholder of any of the operating companies, both the defendant and the operating companies were owned, for the most part, by the same parties. The defendant's name (Terminal) was conspicuously displayed on the sides of all of the taxis used in the enterprise and, in point of fact, the defendant actually serviced, inspected, repaired and dispatched them. These facts were deemed to provide sufficient cause for piercing the corporate veil of the operating company—the nominal owner of the cab which injured the plaintiff—and holding the defendant liable. The operating companies were simply instrumentalities for carrying on the business of the defendant without imposing upon it financial and other liabilities incident to the actual ownership and operation of the cabs.

In the case before us, the plaintiff has explicitly alleged that none of the corporations "had a separate existence of their own" and, as indicated above, all are named as defendants. However, it is one thing to assert that a corporation is a fragment of a larger corporate combine which actually conducts the business. (See Berle, The Theory of Enterprise Entity, 47 Col.L.Rev. 343, 348—350.) It is quite another to claim that the corporation is a "dummy" for its individual stockholders who are in reality carrying on the business in their personal capacities for purely personal rather than corporate ends. Either circumstance would justify treating the corporation as an agent and piercing the corporate veil to reach the principal but a different result would follow in each case. In the first, only a larger *corporate* entity would be held financially responsible while, in the other, the stockholder would be personally liable. Either the stockholder is conducting the business in his individual capacity or he is not. If he is, he will be liable; if he is not, then it does not matter—insofar as his personal liability is concerned—that the enterprise is actually being carried on by a larger "enterprise entity".

. . . . Reading the complaint in this case most favorably and liberally, we do not believe that there can be gathered from its averments the allegations required to spell out a valid cause of action against the defendant Carlton.

The individual defendant is charged with having "organized, managed, dominated and controlled" a fragmented corporate entity but there are no allegations that he was conducting business in his individual capacity. Had the taxicab fleet been owned by a single corporation, it would be readily apparent that the plaintiff would face formidable barriers in attempting to establish personal liability on the part of the corporation's stockholders. The fact that the fleet ownership has been deliberately split up among many corporations does not ease the plaintiff's burden in that respect. The corporate form may not be disregarded merely because the assets of the corporation, together with the mandatory insurance coverage of the vehicle which struck the plaintiff, are insufficient to assure him the recovery sought. If Carlton were to be held individually liable on those facts alone, the decision would apply equally to the thousands of cabs which are owned by their individual drivers who conduct their businesses through corporations organized pursuant to section 401 of the Business Corporation Law, Consol.Laws, c. 4 and carry the minimum insurance required by subdivision 1 (par. (a)) of section 370 of the Vehicle and Traffic Law, Consol.Laws, c. 71. These taxi owner-operators are entitled to form such corporations and we agree with the court at Special Term that, if the insurance coverage required by statute 'is inadequate for the protection of the public, the remedy lies not with the courts but with the Legislature.' It may very well be sound policy to require that certain corporations must take out liability insurance which will afford adequate compensation to their potential tort victims. However, the responsibility for imposing conditions on the privilege of incorporation has been committed by the Constitution to the Legislature (N.Y. Const., art. X, § 1) and it may not be fairly implied, from any statute, that the Legislature intended, without the slightest discussion or debate, to require of taxi corporations that they carry automobile liability insurance over and above that mandated by the Vehicle and Traffic Law.

This is not to say that it is impossible for the plaintiff to state a valid cause of action against the defendant Carlton. However, the simple fact is that the plaintiff has just not done so here. While the complaint alleges that the separate corporations were undercapitalized and that their assets have been intermingled, it is barren of any 'sufficiently particular(ized) statements' that the defendant Carlton and his associates are actually doing business in their individual capacities, shuttling their personal funds in and out of the corporations 'without regard to formality and to suit their immediate convenience.' Such a 'perversion of the privilege to do business in a corporate form' (Berkey v. Third Ave. Ry. Co., 244 N.Y. 84, 95, 155 N.E. 58, 61, 50 A.L.R. 599, supra) would justify imposing personal liability on the individual stockholders. Nothing of the sort has in fact been charged, and it cannot reasonably or logically be inferred from the happenstance that the business of Seon Cab Corporation may actually be carried on by a larger corporate entity composed of many corporations which, under general principles of agency, would be liable to each other's creditors in contract and in tort.[3]

---

3. In his affidavit in opposition to the motion to dismiss, the plaintiff's counsel claimed that corporate assets had been 'milked out' of, and 'siphoned off' from the enterprise. Quite apart from the fact that these allegations are far too vague and conclusory, the charge is premature. If the plaintiff succeeds in his action and becomes a judgment creditor of the corporation, he may

In point of fact, the principle relied upon in the complaint to sustain the imposition of personal liability is not agency but fraud. Such a cause of action cannot withstand analysis. If it is not fraudulent for the owner-operator of a single cab corporation to take out only the minimum required liability insurance, the enterprise does not become either illicit or fraudulent merely because it consists of many such corporations. The plaintiff's injuries are the same regardless of whether the cab which strikes him is owned by a single corporation or part of a fleet with ownership fragmented among many corporations. Whatever rights he may be able to assert against parties other than the registered owner of the vehicle come into being not because he has been defrauded but because, under the principle of Respondeat superior, he is entitled to hold the whole enterprise responsible for the acts of its agents.

In sum, then, the complaint falls short of adequately stating a cause of action against the defendant Carlton in his individual capacity.

The order of the Appellate Division should be reversed, with costs in this court and in the Appellate Division, the certified question answered in the negative and the order of the Supreme Court, Richmond County, reinstated, with leave to serve an amended complaint.

KEATING, JUDGE (DISSENTING).

The defendant Carlton, the shareholder here sought to be held for the negligence of the driver of a taxicab, was a principal shareholder and organizer of the defendant corporation which owned the taxicab. The corporation was one of 10 organized by the defendant, each containing two cabs and each cab having the 'minimum liability' insurance coverage mandated by section 370 of the Vehicle and Traffic Law. The sole assets of these operating corporations are the vehicles themselves and they are apparently subject to mortgages.*

From their inception these corporations were intentionally undercapitalized for the purpose of avoiding responsibility for acts which were bound to arise as a result of the operation of a large taxi fleet having cars out on the street 24 hours a day and engaged in public transportation. And during the course of the corporations' existence all income was continually drained out of the corporations for the same purpose.

The issue presented by this action is whether the policy of this State, which affords those desiring to engage in a business enterprise the privilege of limited liability through the use of the corporate device, is so strong that it will permit that privilege to continue no matter how much it is abused, no matter how irresponsibly the corporation is operated, no matter what the cost to the public. I do not believe that it is. * * *

In Minton v. Cavaney, 56 Cal.2d 576, 15 Cal.Rptr. 641, 364 P.2d 473, the Supreme Court of California had occasion to discuss this problem in a

---

then sue and attempt to hold the individual defendants accountable for any dividends and property that were wrongfully distributed.

　* It appears that the medallions, which are of considerable value, are judgment proof.

negligence case. The corporation of which the defendant was an organizer, director and officer operated a public swimming pool. One afternoon the plaintiffs' daughter drowned in the pool as a result of the alleged negligence of the corporation.

Justice Roger Traynor, speaking for the court, outlined the applicable law in this area. "The figurative terminology 'alter ego' and 'disregard of the corporate entity' ", he wrote, "is generally used to refer to the various situations that are an abuse of the corporate privilege. * * * The equitable owners of a corporation, for example, are personally liable when they treat the assets of the corporation as their own and add or withdraw capital from the corporation at will * * *; when they hold themselves out as being personally liable for the debts of the corporation * * *; *or when they provide inadequate capitalization and actively participate in the conduct of corporate affairs*".

Examining the facts of the case in light of the legal principles just enumerated, he found that "(it was) undisputed that there was no attempt to provide adequate capitalization. (The corporation) never had any substantial assets. It leased the pool that it operated, and the lease was forfeited for failure to pay the rent. Its capital was 'trifling compared with the business to be done and the risks of loss' ". (56 Cal.2d, p. 580, 15 Cal.Rptr., p. 643, 364 P.2d p. 475)

It seems obvious that one of 'the risks of loss' referred to was the possibility of drownings due to the negligence of the corporation. And the defendant's failure to provide such assets or any fund for recovery resulted in his being held personally liable. * * *

The court [in Anderson v. Abbott, 321 U.S. 349, 64 S.Ct. 531, 88 L.Ed. 793 (1944)] had found that ... transfers were made in good faith, that other defendant shareholders who had purchased shares in the holding company had done so in good faith and that the organization of such a holding company was entirely legal. Despite this finding, the Supreme Court, speaking through Mr. Justice Douglas, pierced the corporate veil of the holding company and held all the shareholders, even those who had no part in the organization of the corporation, individually responsible for the corporate obligations as mandated by the statute.

"Limited liability", he wrote, "is the rule, not the exception; and on that assumption large undertakings are rested, vast enterprises are launched, and huge sums of capital attracted. But there are occasions when the limited liability sought to be obtained through the corporation will be qualified or denied. Mr. Chief Judge Cardozo stated that a surrender of that principle of limited liability would be made 'when the sacrifice is so essential to the end that some accepted public policy may be defended or upheld.' * * * The cases of fraud make up part of that exception * * * But they do not exhaust it. *An obvious inadequacy of capital, measured by the nature and magnitude of the corporate undertaking, has frequently been an important factor in cases denying stockholders their defense of limited liability. * * * That rule has been invoked even in* *absence of a legislative policy which undercapitalization would defeat.* It becomes more important in a situation such as the present one where the statutory policy of double liability will be defeated if impecunious bank-stock holding companies are allowed to be interposed as non-conductors of liability. It has often been held that the interposition of a corporation will not be allowed to defeat a legislative policy, whether that was the aim or only the result of the arrangement. * * * 'the courts will not permit themselves to be blinded or deceived by mere forms of law but 'will deal' with the substance of the transaction involved as if the corporate agency did not exist and as the justice of the case may require.' " (321 U.S., pp. 362—363, 64 S.Ct., p. 537; emphasis added.) * * *

The defendant Carlton claims that, because the minimum amount of insurance required by the statute was obtained, the corporate veil cannot and should not be pierced despite the fact that the assets of the corporation which owned the cab were 'trifling compared with the business to be done and the risks of loss' which were certain to be encountered. I do not agree.

The Legislature in requiring minimum liability insurance of $10,000, no doubt, intended to provide at least some small fund for recovery against those individuals and corporations who just did not have and were not able to raise or accumulate assets sufficient to satisfy the claims of those who were injured as a result of their negligence. It certainly could not have intended to shield those individuals who organized corporations, with the specific intent of avoiding responsibility to the public, where the operation of the corporate enterprise yielded profits sufficient to purchase additional insurance. Moreover, it is reasonable to assume that the Legislature believed that those individuals and corporations having substantial assets would take out insurance far in excess of the minimum in order to protect those assets from depletion. Given the costs of hospital care and treatment and the nature of injuries sustained in auto collisions, it would be unreasonable to assume that the Legislature believed that the minimum provided in the statute would in and of itself be sufficient to recompense "innocent victims of motor vehicle accidents * * * for the injury and financial loss inflicted upon them".

The defendant, however, argues that the failure of the Legislature to increase the minimum insurance requirements indicates legislative acquiescence in this scheme to avoid liability and responsibility to the public. In the absence of a clear legislative statement, approval of a scheme having such serious consequences is not to be so lightly inferred.

The defendant contends that the court will be encroaching upon the legislative domain by ignoring the corporate veil and holding the individual shareholder. This argument was answered by Mr. Justice DOUGLAS in Anderson v. Abbott, supra, pp. _____—_____, 64 S.Ct. p. 540, where he wrote that: "In the field in which we are presently concerned, judicial power hardly oversteps the bounds when it refuses to lend its aid to a promotional project which would circumvent or undermine a legislative policy. To deny it that function would be to make it impotent in situations where historically it has made some of its most notable contributions. If the judicial power is helpless to protect a legislative program from schemes for easy avoidance, then indeed it has become a handy implement of high finance. *Judicial interference to cripple or defeat a legislative policy is one thing; judicial interference with the plans of those whose corporate or other devices would circumvent that policy is quite another.* Once the purpose or effect of the scheme is clear, once the legislative policy is plain, we would indeed forsake a great tradition to say we were helpless to fashion the instruments for appropriate relief." (Emphasis added.)

The defendant contends that a decision holding him personally liable would discourage people from engaging in corporate enterprise.

What I would merely hold is that a participating shareholder of a corporation vested with a public interest, organized with capital insufficient to meet liabilities which are certain to arise in the ordinary course of the corporation's business, may be held personally responsible for such liabilities. Where corporate income is not sufficient to cover the cost of insurance premiums above the statutory minimum or where initially adequate finances dwindle under the pressure of competition, bad times or extraordinary and unexpected liability, obviously the shareholder will not be held liable (Henn, Corporations, p. 208, n. 7).

The only types of corporate enterprises that will be discouraged as a result of a decision allowing the individual shareholder to be sued will be those such as the one in question, designed solely to abuse the corporate privilege at the expense of the public interest.

For these reasons I would vote to affirm the order of the Appellate Division.

NOTES

1. The complaint in *Walkovszky* was later successfully amended to comport with Judge Fuld's suggested theory. Walkovszky v. Carlton, 29 A.D.2d 763, 287 N.Y.S.2d 546 (2d Dept.), aff'd, 23 N.Y.2d 714, 296 N.Y.S.2d 362, 244 N.E.2d 55 (1968).

2. The Court in *Walkovszky* relied in part on the opinion by Judge Cardozo in In Berkey v. Third Ave. Ry. Co., 244 N.Y. 84, 155 N.E. 58 (1926), which considered the applicability of piercing to a parent/subsidiary relationship:

The plaintiff boarded a street car at Fort Lee Ferry and One Hundred and Twenty–Fifth street on October 4, 1916, in order to go east on One Hundred and Twenty–Fifth street to Broadway, and thence south on Broadway to Columbia University at One Hundred and Seventeenth street. She was hurt in getting out of the car through the negligence of the motorman in charge of it. The franchise to operate a street railroad along the route traveled by the plaintiff belongs to the Forty–Second Street, Manhattanville & Saint Nicholas Avenue Railway Company (described for convenience as the Forty–Second Street Company), and no one else. Substantially all the stock of that company is owned by the Third Avenue Railway Company, the defendant, which has its own franchise along other streets and avenues. Stock ownership alone would be insufficient to charge the dominant company with liability for the torts of the subsidiary.

The theory of the action is that under the screen of this subsidiary and others, the defendant does in truth operate for itself the entire system of connected roads, and is thus liable for the torts of the consolidated enterprise. * * *

One other circumstance or group of circumstances is the subject of much emphasis in the arguments of counsel. The defendant was the dominant stockholder, not only in this subsidiary, but also in many others. The routes, when connected, cover an area from the lower part of Manhattan at the south to Yonkers and other points in Westchester at the north. All the cars, wherever used, are marked 'Third Avenue System.' On the other hand, the transfer slips bear the name in each instance of the company that issues them. The cars, when new ones become necessary, are bought by the defendant, and then leased to the subsidiaries, including, of course, the Forty–Second Street Company, for a daily rental which is paid. The cars leased to one road do not continue along the routes of others. The motormen and conductors do not travel beyond their respective lines. With the approval of the Public Service Commission, transfer slips are issued between one route and another, but transfers could have been required by the commission if not voluntarily allowed. * * *

The whole problem of the relation between parent and subsidiary corporations is one that is still enveloped in the mists of metaphor. Metaphors in law are to be narrowly watched, for starting as devices to liberate thought, they end often by enslaving it. We say at times that the corporate entity will be ignored when the parent corporation operates a business through a subsidiary which is characterized as an 'alias' or a 'dummy.' All this is well enough if the picturesqueness of the epithets does not lead us to forget that the essential term to be defined is the act of operation. Dominion may be so complete, interference so obtrusive, that by the general rules of agency the parent will be a principal and the subsidiary an agent. Where control is less than this, we are remitted to the tests of honesty and justice. Ballantine, Parent and Subsidiary Corporations, 14 Cal. Law Review, 12, 18, 19, 20. The logical consistency of a juridical conception will indeed be sacrificed at times, when the sacrifice is essential to the end that some accepted public policy may be defended or upheld. This is so, for illustration, though agency in any proper sense is lacking, where the attempted separation between parent and subsidiary will work a fraud upon the law. At such times unity is ascribed to parts which, at least for many purposes, retain an independent life, for the reason that only thus can we overcome a perversion of the privilege to do business in a corporate form. We find in the case at hand neither agency on the one hand, nor, on the other, abuse to be corrected by the implication of a merger. On the contrary, merger might beget more abuses than it stifled. Statutes carefully framed for the protection, not merely of creditors, but of all who travel upon railroads, forbid the confusion of liabilities by extending operation over one route to operation on another. In such circumstances, we thwart the public policy of the state instead of defending or upholding it, when we ignore the separation between subsidiary and parent and treat the two as one.

3.   Do you think the capital in the corporations attacked in *Walkovszky* was inadequate for their actual operation? After all, each company had a taxi and a medallion worth thousands of dollars, as well as the minimum amount of insurance. The fact that the medallion was judgment proof was a legislative decision that shielded the assets of those companies as much or more than the corporate veil.

4.   The courts tend to scrutinize small corporations more closely than larger ones in applying veil piercing theories. See Laya v. Erin Homes, Inc., 177 W.Va. 343, 352 S.E.2d 93, 100–101 (1986). That same pattern will probably be applied to limited liability companies. See generally Litchfield Asset Management v. Howell, 2000 WL 1785122 (Conn.Super.2000) (LLCs were held to be alter egos of a wife that were used to avoid a debt). Compare Jordan v. Commonwealth, 36 Va.App. 270, 549 S.E.2d 621 (2001) (individual members could not be prosecuted for maintaining a nuisance on property owned by their LLC); Rafferty v. Noto Bros. Construct., 2001 WL 459073 (Conn.Super.2001) (corporate veil piercing theories applied to LLC); Ditty v. CheckRite 973 F.Supp. 1320 (D.Utah 1997) (most commentators assert that same standards will be used to pierce the veil of an LLC as are applied to corporations). Compare Hollowell v. Orleans Reg'l Hosp., 1998 WL 283298 (D.La.1998) (notes that one commentator has asserted that, since state LLC statute requires less formalities than corporations, failure to follow formalities such as holding meetings and keeping minutes should not be a basis for piercing an LLC); Harold Cohn & Co. v. Harco Int'l, LLC, 2001 WL 523540 (2001) (LLC officer may be held liable without piercing veil where complaint alleged that he committed a tort). There are several reasons for this closer scrutiny. Most small corporations start on a shoestring, and the owners are likely to be unsophisticated in legal matters and, therefore, fail to follow corporate formalities. These owners tend to treat the business as their own candy store—taking money from the till when they need it for personal expenses and throwing in cash to meet pressing bills without any proper accounting. In contrast, the larger corporation usually has a more formal structure, the resources to employ lawyers, following at least some of their advice, and accountants who assure proper separation between the corporate owners and the corporation. In a publicly held corporation, the federal securities laws require even more formalization in accounting and corporate structure.

5.   The Comprehensive Environmental Response Compensation and Liability Act ("CERCLA") seeks to impose liability for cleaning up hazardous wastes on those responsible for improperly dumping those wastes. 42 U.S.C. §§ 9601–75. In United States v. Bestfoods, 524 U.S. 51, 118 S.Ct. 1876, 141 L.Ed.2d 43 (1998) the Supreme Court held that a parent corporation would incur derivative liability under Section 107(a)(2) of CERCLA for the activities of a subsidiary if requirements for piercing the corporate veil are met, or if

the parent company was itself acting as an operator of the facility because it has taken an active role and exercised control over the facility that produced the pollution. Under amendments added to CERCLA in 1996, the mere ability to influence management would not result in liability. 42 U.S.C. § 9601(F)(i)(II) (Supp. 2001).

COX & HAZEN ON CORPORATIONS,
James D. Cox & Thomas Lee Hazen

§ 7.08   (2d ed. 2003).

* * *There are three primary variants within the "piercing the corporate veil" jurisprudence—(1) the "instrumentality" doctrine, (2) the "alter ego" doctrine, and (3) the "identity" doctrine. The instrumentality doctrine's overall approach focuses on the presence of three factors, as reflected in the frequently cited language of its leading case, *Lowendahl v. Baltimore & Ohio Railroad*, 287 N.Y.S. 62 (App. Div.), *aff'd*, 6 N.E.2d 56 (N.Y.1936):

(1) Control, not merely majority or complete stock control, but complete domination, not only of finances, but of policy and business practices in respect to the transaction attacked so that the corporate entity had at the time no separate mind, will, or existence of its own; and

(2) Such control must have been used by the defendant to commit fraud or wrong, to perpetuate the violation of a statutory or other positive legal duty, or a dishonest and unjust act in contravention of the plaintiff's legal rights; and

(3) The aforesaid control and breach of duty must proximately cause the injury or unjust loss complained of.

The "alter ego" doctrine is stated with a far greater economy of words but with much less precision than the statement of instrumentality doctrine. The alter ego doctrine holds that it is appropriate to pierce the veil when (1) a unity of ownership and interests exists between the corporation and its controlling stockholder such that the corporation has ceased to exist as a separate entity and the corporation has been relegated to the status of the controlling stockholder's alter ego and (2) to recognize the corporation and its controlling stockholder as separate entities would be sanctioning fraud or would lead to an inequitable result.

The leading case for the "identity" doctrine is *Zaist v. Olson*, 227 A.2d 552, 558 (1967) where the court states:

If plaintiff can show that there was such a unity of interest and ownership that the independence of the corporations had in effect ceased or had never begun, an adherence to the fiction of separate identity would serve only to defeat justice and equity by permitting the economic entity to escape liability arising out of an operation of one corporation for the benefit of the whole enterprise.

On close scrutiny, none of the three above variants of "piercing the veil" offers precision or a characteristic that distinguishes it from the other two variants. In practice, they are virtually indistinguishable from one another, and the outcome of the cases does not appear to depend on which standard is applied. As commentators have frequently noted, the results in cases appear guided not so much by the doctrine invoked as by the "mist of metaphors."

Courts sometimes attempt to overcome the lack of precision with doctrine by articulating a lengthy list of factors considered important in deciding whether to "pierce the corporate veil":

> gross undercapitalization ... nonobservance of corporate formalities, nonpayment of dividends, insolvency of the corporation at the time of the litigated transaction, siphoning of corporate funds by the dominant shareholders, nonfunctioning of officers and directors other than the [dominant] shareholders, absence of corporate record, use of corporation as a facade for the conduct of the shareholders' business.
> * * *

DeWitt Truck Brokers, Inc. v. W. Ray Flemming Fruit Co. The cases looking to pierce a corporate veil look to various factors. The ultimate decision to pierce through the veil and set aside the limited liability that otherwise would attach is highly factual depending upon the facts of each case. It is not possible to identify each and every factor that a court may look to but a number of factors can be identified. Those factors include:

(1) commingling of funds and other assets of the corporation with those of the individual shareholders;

(2) diversion of the corporation's funds or assets to noncorporate uses (to the personal uses of the corporation's shareholders);

(3) failure to maintain the corporate formalities necessary for the issuance of or subscription to the corporation's stock, such as formal approval of the stock issue by the board of directors;

(4) an individual shareholder representing to persons outside the corporation that he or she is personally liable for the debts or other obligations of the corporation;

(5) failure to maintain corporate minutes or adequate corporate records;

(6) identical equitable ownership in two entities;

(7) identity of the directors and officers of two entities who are responsible for supervision and management (a partnership or sole proprietorship and a corporation owned and managed by the same parties);

(8) failure to adequately capitalize a corporation for the reasonable risks of the corporate undertaking;

(9) absence of separately held corporate assets;

(10) use of a corporation as a mere shell or conduit to operate a single venture or some particular aspect of the business of an individual or another corporation;

(11) sole ownership of all the stock by one individual or members of a single family;

(12) use of the same office or business location by the corporation and its individual shareholder(s);

(13) employment of the same employees or attorney by the corporation and its shareholder(s);

(14) concealment or misrepresentation of the identity of the ownership, management or financial interests in the corporation, and concealment of personal business activities of the shareholders (sole shareholders do not reveal the association with a corporation, which makes loans to them without adequate security);

(15) disregard of legal formalities and failure to maintain proper arm's length relationships among related entities;

(16) use of a corporate entity as a conduit to procure labor, services or merchandise for another person or entity;

(17) diversion of corporate assets from the corporation by or to a stockholder or other person or entity to the detriment of creditors, or the manipulation of assets and liabilities between entities to concentrate the assets in one and the liabilities in another;

(18) contracting by the corporation with another person with the intent to avoid the risk of nonperformance by use of the corporate entity; or the use of a corporation as a subterfuge for illegal transactions;

(19) the formation and use of the corporation to assume the existing liabilities of another person or entity.

Not every factor will be present in each case. Nevertheless, the more factors that are present, the more likely it is that a court will disregard the veil of limited liability.

NOTE

Could you incorporate yourself to avoid any personal liability? Could a corporation that has numerous employees and operations incorporate each employee, desk, chair and even pencil to limit its liability? Would *Walkovszky* be available to impose liability, if corporate formalities are observed? In Luckenbach S.S. Co. v. W.R. Grace & Co., 267 F. 676, 681 (4th Cir.1920) the court considered the following set of circumstances:

From the statements and admissions in their respective answers these facts appear: The Luckenbach Steamship Company has a capital of only $10,000. The Luckenbach Company, also a Delaware corporation, is capitalized at $800,000. They have the same directors and the same officers, and Edgar F. Luckenbach, who was president of and personally managed both companies, owns 94 per cent. of the stock of the Luckenbach Steamship Company, and almost 90 per cent. of the stock of the Luckenbach Company. The latter company owns all or most of the steamers referred to in the record, some eight or nine in number. By contracts of May 1, July 1, and October 1, 1915, these steamers were leased to the steamship company for terms running into the year 1926, and upon terms which, though something more than nominal, are obviously far below their rental value.

Putting aside any inquiry into the motive for this arrangement, we think it too plain for serious question that the facts here considered show such identity of the two corporations, or at least give rise to such a strong presumption of their identity, as warrants the conclusion that the Luckenbach Company is equally responsible with the steamship company for the breach by the latter of its contract with the appellee. For all practical purposes the two concerns are one, and it would be unconscionable to allow the owner of this fleet of steamers, worth millions of dollars, to escape liability because it had turned them over a year before to a $10,000 corporation, which is simply itself in another form.

EQUITABLE SUBORDINATION

COSTELLO v. FAZIO

256 F.2d 903 (9th Cir.1958).

HAMLEY, CIRCUIT JUDGE.

* * * A partnership known as 'Leonard Plumbing and Heating Supply Co.' was organized in October, 1948. The three partners, Fazio, Ambrose, and B. T. Leonard, made initial capital contributions to the business aggregating $44,806.40. The capital contributions of the three partners, as they were recorded on the company books in September 1952, totaled $51,620.78, distributed as follows: Fazio, $43,169.61; Ambrose, $6,451.17; and Leonard, $2,000.

In the fall of that year, it was decided to incorporate the business. In contemplation of this step, Fazio and Ambrose, on September 15, 1952, withdrew all but $2,000 apiece of their capital contributions to the business. This was accomplished by the issuance to them, on that date, of partnership promissory notes in the sum of $41,169.61 and $4,451.17, respectively. These were demand notes, no interest being specified. The capital contribution to the partnership business then stood at $6,000—$2,000 for each partner.

The closing balance sheet of the partnership showed current assets to be $160,791.87, and current liabilities at $162,162.22. There were also fixed assets in the sum of $6,482.90, and other assets in the sum of

$887.45. The partnership had cash on hand in the sum of $66.66, and an overdraft at the bank in the amount of $3,422.78.

Of the current assets, $41,357.76, representing 'Accounts receivable—Trade,' was assigned to American Trust Co., to secure $50,000 of its $59,000 in notes payable. Both before and after the incorporation, the business had a $75,000 line of credit with American Trust Co., secured by accounts receivable and the personal guaranty of the three partners and stockholders, and their marital communities.

The net sales of the partnership during its last year of operations were $389,543.72, as compared to net sales of $665,747.55 in the preceding year. A net loss of $22,521.34 was experienced during this last year, as compared to a net profit of $40,935.12 in the year ending September 30, 1951.

Based on the reduced capitalization of the partnership, the corporation was capitalized for six hundred shares of no par value common stock valued at ten dollars per share. Two hundred shares were issued to each of the three partners in consideration of the transfer to the corporation of their interests in the partnership. Fazio became president, and Ambrose, secretary-treasurer of the new corporation. Both were directors. The corporation assumed all liabilities of the partnership, including the notes to Fazio and Ambrose.

In June 1954, after suffering continued losses, the corporation made an assignment to the San Francisco Board of Trade for the benefit of creditors. On October 8, 1954, it filed a voluntary petition in bankruptcy. At this time, the corporation was not indebted to any creditors whose obligations were incurred by the pre-existing partnership, saving the promissory notes issued to Fazio and Ambrose.

Fazio filed a claim against the estate in the sum of $34,147.55, based on the promissory note given to him when the capital of the partnership was reduced. Ambrose filed a similar claim in the sum of $7,871.17. The discrepancy between these amounts and the amounts of the promissory notes is due to certain setoffs and transfers not here in issue.

In asking that these claims be subordinated to the claims of general unsecured creditors, the trustee averred that the amounts in question represent a portion of the capital investment in the partnership. It was alleged that the transfer of this sum from the partnership capital account to an account entitled 'Loans from Copartners,' effectuated a scheme and plan to place copartners in the same class as unsecured creditors. The trustee further alleged, with respect to each claimant:

> '* * * If said claimant is permitted to share in the assets of said bankrupt now in the hands of the trustee, in the same parity with general unsecured creditors, he will receive a portion of the capital invested which should be used to satisfy the claims of creditors before any capital investment can be returned to the owners and stockholders of said bankrupt.'

William B. Logan, a business analyst and consultant called by the trustee, expressed the view that $6,000 was inadequate capitalization for this company. John S. Curran, a business analyst, also called by the trustee, expressed the view that the corporation needed at least as much capital as the partnership required prior to the reduction of capital.

Robert H. Laborde, Jr., a certified public accountant, has handled the accounting problems of the partnership and corporation. He was called by the trustee as an adverse witness. Laborde readily conceded that the transaction whereby Fazio and Ambrose obtained promissory notes from the partnership was for the purpose of transferring a capital account into a loan or debt account. He stated that this was done in contemplation of the formation of the corporation, and with knowledge that the partnership was losing money.

The prime reason for incorporating the business, according to Laborde, was to protect the personal interest of Fazio, who had made the greatest capital contribution to the business. In this connection, it was pointed out that the 'liabilities on the business as a partnership were pretty heavy.' There was apparently also a tax angle. Laborde testified that it was contemplated that the notes would be paid out of the profits of the business. He agreed that, if promissory notes had not been issued, the profits would have been distributed only as dividends, and that as such they would have been taxable. * * *

In any event, when we speak of inadequacy of capital in regard to whether loans to shareholders shall be subordinated to claims of general creditors, we are not referring to working capital. We are referring to the amount of the investment of the shareholders in the corporation. This capital is usually referred to as legal capital, or stated capital in reference to restrictions on the declaration of dividends to stockholders. As before stated, Laborde expressed no opinion as to the adequacy of proprietary capital put at the risk of the business. On the other hand, the corporate accounts and the undisputed testimony of three accounting experts demonstrate that stated capital was wholly inadequate.

On the evidence produced at this hearing, as summarized above, the referee found that the paid-in stated capital of the corporation at the time of its incorporation was adequate for the continued operation of the business. He found that while Fazio and Ambrose controlled and dominated the corporation and its affairs they did not mismanage the business. He further found that claimants did not practice any fraud or deception, and did not act for their own personal or private benefit and to the detriment of the corporation or its stockholders and creditors. The referee also found that the transaction which had been described was not a part of any scheme or plan to place the claimants in the same class as unsecured creditors of the partnership.

On the basis of these findings, the referee concluded that, in procuring the promissory notes, the claimants acted in all respects in good faith and took no unfair advantage of the corporation, or of its stockholders or creditors. * * *

The factual conclusion of the referee, that the paid-in capital of the corporation at the time of its incorporation was adequate for the continued operation of the business, was based upon certain accounting data and the expert testimony of four witnesses. The accounting data, summarized above, is contained in the opening balance sheet and the comparative profit and loss statements of the corporation, and is not in dispute.

It does not require the confirmatory opinion of experts to determine from this data that the corporation was grossly undercapitalized. In the year immediately preceding incorporation, net sales aggregated $390,000. In order to handle such a turnover, the partners apparently found that capital in excess of $50,000 was necessary. They actually had $51,620.78 in the business at that time. Even then, the business was only 'two jumps ahead of the wolf.' A net loss of $22,000 was sustained in that year; there was only $66.66 in the bank; and there was an overdraft of $3,422.78.

Yet, despite this precarious financial condition, Fazio and Ambrose withdrew $45,620.78 of the partnership capital—more than eighty-eight per cent of the total capital. The $6,000 capital left in the business was only one-sixty-fifth of the last annual net sales. All this is revealed by the books of the company.

But if there is need to confirm this conclusion that the corporation was gross undercapitalized, such confirmation is provided by three of the four experts who testified. The fourth expert, called by appellees, did not express an opinion to the contrary.

We therefore hold that the factual conclusion of the referee, that the corporation was adequately capitalized at the time of its organization, is clearly erroneous.

The factual conclusion of the trial court, that the claimants, in withdrawing capital from the partnership in contemplation of incorporation, did not act for their own personal or private benefit and to the detriment of the corporation or of its stockholders and creditors, is based upon the same accounting data and expert testimony.

Laborde, testifying for the claimants, made it perfectly clear that the depletion of the capital account in favor of a debt account was for the purpose of equalizing the capital investments of the partners and to reduce tax liability when there were profits to distribute. It is therefore certain, contrary to the finding just noted, that, in withdrawing this capital, Fazio and Ambrose did act for their own personal and private benefit.

It is equally certain, from the undisputed facts, that in so doing they acted to the detriment of the corporation and its creditors. The best evidence of this is what happened to the business after incorporation, and what will happen to its creditors if the reduction in capital is allowed to stand. The likelihood that business failure would result from such undercapitalization should have been apparent to anyone who knew the company's financial and business history and who had access to its balance sheet and profit and loss statements. Three expert witnesses confirmed this view, and none expressed a contrary opinion.

Accordingly, we hold that the factual conclusion, that the claimants, in withdrawing capital, did not act for their own personal or private benefit and to the detriment of the corporation and creditors, is clearly erroneous.

Recasting the facts in the light of what is said above, the question which appellant presents is this:

Where, in connection with the incorporation of a partnership, and for their own personal and private benefit, two partners who are to become officers, directors, and controlling stockholders of the corporation, convert the bulk of their capital contributions into loans, taking promissory notes, thereby leaving the partnership and succeeding corporation grossly undercapitalized, to the detriment of the corporation and its creditors, should their claims against the estate of the subsequently bankrupted corporation be subordinated to the claims of the general unsecured creditors? The question almost answers itself.

In allowing and disallowing claims, courts of bankruptcy apply the rules and principles of equity jurisprudence. Pepper v. Litton, 308 U.S. 295, 304. Where the claim is found to be inequitable, it may be set aside (Pepper v. Litton, supra), or subordinated to the claims of other creditors. As stated in Taylor v. Standard Gas Co., supra, 306, U.S. at page 315, the question to be determined when the plan or transaction which gives rise to a claim is challenged as inequitable is 'whether, within the bounds of reason and fairness, such a plan can be justified.'

Where, as here, the claims are filed by persons standing in a fiduciary relationship to the corporation, another test which equity will apply is 'whether or not under all the circumstances the transaction carries the earmarks of an arm's length bargain.' Pepper v. Litton, supra, 308 U.S. at page 306.

Under either of these tests, the transaction here in question stands condemned.

Appellees argue that more must be shown than mere undercapitalization if the claims are to be subordinated. Much more than mere undercapitalization was shown here. Persons serving in a fiduciary relationship to the corporation actually withdrew capital already committed to the business, in the face of recent adverse financial experience. They stripped the business of eighty-eight per cent of its stated capital at a time when it had a minus working capital and had suffered substantial business losses. This was done for personal gain, under circumstances which charge them with knowledge that the corporation and its creditors would be endangered. Taking advantage of their fiduciary position, they thus sought to gain equality of treatment with general creditors.

In Taylor v. Standard Gas & Electric Co., 306 U.S. 307, 59 S.Ct. 543, 83 L.Ed. 669, and some other cases, there was fraud and mismanagement present in addition to undercapitalization. Appellees argue from this that fraud and mismanagement must always be present if claims are to be subordinated in a situation involving undercapitalization.

This is not the rule. The test to be applied, as announced in the Taylor case and quoted above, is whether the transaction can be justified 'within the bounds of reason and fairness.' In the more recent Heiser case, 327 U.S. pages 732–733, the Supreme Court made clear, in these words, that fraud is not an essential ingredient:

'* * * In appropriate cases, acting upon equitable principles, it (bankruptcy court) may also subordinate the claim of one creditor to those of others in order to prevent the consummation of a course of conduct by the claimant, which, as to them, would be fraudulent *or otherwise inequitable.* * * *' (Emphasis supplied.)

The fact that the withdrawal of capital occurred prior to incorporation is immaterial. This transaction occurred in contemplation of incorporation. The participants then occupied a fiduciary relationship to the partnership; and expected to become controlling stockholders, directors, and officers of the corporation. This plan was effectuated, and they were serving in those fiduciary capacities when the corporation assumed the liabilities of the partnership, including the notes here in question.

Nor is the fact that the business, after being stripped of necessary capital, was able to survive long enough to have a turnover of creditors a mitigating circumstance. The inequitable conduct of appellees consisted not in acting to the detriment of creditors then known, but in acting to the detriment of present or future creditors, whoever they may be.

In our opinion, it was error to affirm the order of the referee denying the motion to subordinate the claims in question. We do not reach appellant's other major contention, that the notes are not provable in bankruptcy because they were to be paid only out of profits, and there were no profits. * * *

NOTES

1. *"Deep Rock" Doctrine.* In Taylor v. Standard Gas & Electric Co., 306 U.S. 307, 59 S.Ct. 543, 83 L.Ed. 669 (1939), the Supreme Court applied the equitable subordination doctrine to a parent corporation's claim against its subsidiary (Deep Rock). The Court found that the subsidiary was not adequately capitalized. Justice Douglas later stated in Pepper v. Litton, 308 U.S. 295, 308–10, 60 S.Ct. 238, 84 L.Ed. 281 (1939), that the Deep Rock doctrine is based on equitable principles, a sense of fairness and fiduciary standards. See also Gannett Co. v. Larry, 221 F.2d 269 (2d Cir.1955) (parent company that used its subsidiary as a source of newsprint, rather than as an ongoing business operation, was subordinated in its loans claims against the subsidiary to the claims of the other debtor). In Arnold v. Phillips, 117 F.2d 497 (5th

Cir.1941), the court held that a controlling shareholder would be subordinated to other creditors for an initial loan he made to the corporation where its capital was inadequate. The court further held, however, that subsequent advances made by this shareholder would not be subordinated where the company had prospered for a time before failing as a result of unexpected problems. The company needed the loans, and the controlling shareholder should not be punished for making those loans, which would otherwise have been sought from a third party who would not be subject to equitable subordination claims.

2. It has been suggested that equitable subordination is "much less drastic" than piercing the corporate veil. William P. Hackney & Tracey G. Benson, Shareholder Liability for Inadequate Capital, 43 U. Pitt. L. Rev. 837, 882 (1982). What is less drastic about it? It is suggested that among other things unlike piercing the veil, equitable subordination does not involve affirmatively imposing liability. Id.

3. *Fraudulent conveyance law.* The federal bankruptcy laws may require preferential transfers to shareholders or others to be set aside. 11 U.S.C. § 548 (1995 & Supp. 2002). See generally 4 *Collier on Bankruptcy* § 548.01 (15th ed. 1996 & Supp. 1996) (description and application of bankruptcy provision for preferential transfers). Several states have also adopted "fraudulent conveyance statutes that are designed to avoid corporate assets from being removed to the disadvantage of creditors. Those statutes are descendants of prohibitions in Roman law and an English statute that was passed in 1570. David G. Epstein, Steve Nickles & James J. White, *Bankruptcy* § 6–46 (1993). Approximately one half of the states adopted the Uniform Fraudulent Conveyance Act before it was withdrawn in 1984 in favor of a new uniform act–the Uniform Fraudulent Transfer Act that was adopted by twenty states. Id. These statutes vary in their terms but generally prohibit the assets of corporations to be sold or exchanged for an amount less than their fair value. This is an objective test, actual fraud is not required. An example of the type of transactions that you are likely to encounter that would be subject to such a statute would be as follows: The client is a controlling shareholder of a corporation that is in serious financial trouble. She wants to sell the remaining assets of the corporation at a bargain price to a new corporation that she has formed. She believes that, if she can start with a new business, she will be able to avoid prior mistakes and be successful. This plan, however, leaves little for the creditors. They may sue under a fraudulent conveyance statute and recover the assets that were transferred or their full value. In bankruptcy, the court may invoke state fraudulent conveyance laws to avoid a preferential transfer made for less than fair value. 11 U.S.C. § 544(b).

COX & HAZEN ON CORPORATIONS,
James D. Cox & Thomas Lee Hazen
§ 7.20   (2d ed. 2003).

One method of evading debts and liabilities practiced both by individuals and by corporations is the use of a fraudulent conveyance to some friendly or related transferee in order to put the property beyond the creditors' reach. If insolvent debtors organize a family corporation through which they conduct business for their own benefit with assets formerly used in their individual businesses and the corporation's affairs so closely resemble the affairs of the dominant shareholder "that in substance it is little more than his corporate pocket," or if the corporation is organized to continue the debtors' businesses free from debts incurred by them personally while the insolvent debtor remains in control, such a corporation may not assert that it is sufficiently separate and insulated from the debtors' other affairs as to stand in an independent position free from their personal liabilities.

A fraudulent conveyance is voidable at the insistence of creditors who are in a position to attack it; the transferred assets may be pursued into the hands of the corporate transferee without disregarding the separate corporate entity. The transferee, however, may be held personally liable for the fraudulent transferor's debts in certain exceptional cases, such as where it is a successor corporation in which the shareholders are the same and it may be regarded merely as a continuation of the corporation in a new guise. Thus, when a gas company conveyed all its property to a new corporation after an explosion resulting in tort liability, injured persons could recover against either or both corporations, as the circumstances indicated that the new company was merely a continuation or reorganization of the old. The successor corporation may be held liable on a theory of either fraudulent conveyance or "continuation." Liability on the latter theory is not restricted to the value of the assets received. The liability of successor corporations is a frequent issue in product liability litigation.

SECTION 2. ULTRA VIRES

WISWALL v. THE GREENVILLE AND RALEIGH PLANK ROAD COMPANY

56 N.C. 183 (1857).

The bill in this case set forth that the plaintiffs are stockholders in the Greenville and Raleigh Plank–Road Company, which was chartered by the General Assembly at its session of 1850, and was duly organized by complying with the terms of the said Act; that the said company was incorporated for "the purpose of effecting a communication by means of a plank road from within the limits of the town of Greenville in Pitt County, to the city of Raleigh," that in accordance with the said charter a plank road has been built from the said town of Greenville to the town of Wilson in Wilson County, which is in the most direct and practical line towards the city of Raleigh, but that the same has not been extended further, for the want of the necessary funds. The bill goes on to recite the various clauses of the act of incorporation, prescribing the nature and extent of the duties of the company, the extent of its powers and privileges, and the object of its incorporation, which clauses are fully set forth in the opinion of the Court, and therefore need not be stated here. It further sets forth that the said company has been for several years in operation, and has, from the tolls received, accumulated a fund of about $4000; that the individuals named in the bill are the president and directors of the said road for the time being, and as such have the control and management of the affairs of the said company; that the said president and directors, or a majority of them, with the sanction and approbation of a majority of the stockholders, have adopted a resolution to purchase with the said funds a line of stages with the necessary appurtenances, to be run as their property upon the said road, and further, to procure a contract from the United States Government for carrying the public mail by such stage line upon the said road; and that they have appointed one of their number, the defendant Johnston, an agent to effectuate these purposes, and that the said president and directors, through their agent, the said Johnston, are taking measures to accomplish both these purposes. They insist in their bill that this would be a misapplication of the funds, which are needed for the repair of the road, which is in a worn and dilapidated condition, or should be divided amongst the stockholders; that such enterprises are foreign to the purpose for which the company was instituted, and not authorized by their charter; that besides exposing the company to the risk of loss from the undertaking, these measures will expose them to the danger of a forfeiture of their corporate privileges; they, therefore, pray for an injunction.

To this bill the defendants demurred. There was a joinder in demurrer; and the cause being set down for argument, was sent to this Court.

PEARSON, J.

It was conceded in the argument that a corporation has a right to restrain by injunction the corporators from doing any act which is not embraced within the scope and purpose for which the corporate body was created, and which would be a violation of the charter; not only on the ground that such act would operate injuriously upon the rights and interests of the corporators, but on the further ground that a forfeiture of the charter would be thereby incurred.

So the only question made by the demurrer is this: Has the company power to purchase stages and horses to be run upon the said road?—and has it likewise power to enter into a contract to carry the United States mail on the road by means of such stages?

This question must be decided by a construction of the charter. We have examined it, and declare our opinion to be that no such power is given to the company.

The first section sets out the object of the incorporation, to wit, "for the purpose of effecting a communication by means of a plank road from Greenville to Raleigh."

The third section grants the franchise of incorporation, and gives all the powers, rights and privileges necessary "for the purposes mentioned in this act."

The ninth section invests the president and directors of the company "with all the rights and powers necessary for the *construction, repairs and maintaining* of a plank road to be located as aforesaid."

The fourteenth section provides for the erection of *toll-houses and gates.*

The fifteenth section provides for the collection of toll to be *"demanded and received from all persons using the said plank road,"* with a proviso that the tolls shall be so regulated that the profits shall not exceed twenty-five per cent on the capital in any one year.

These sections contain the substantive provisions; the others merely embrace the details necessary for the formation of the company, etc.

The mere statement makes the question too plain for observation. If, under the power to construct, repair and maintain a plank road, a power can be implied to buy stages and horses and become a mail contractor, the company, by a parity of reasoning, has an implied power to set up establishments at convenient points along the road for the purchase of produce to be carried over its road. Besides, how are tolls to be demanded and received, and how are the profits of this enlarged operation to be regulated? How are losses from such speculations to be guarded against?

It may as well be contended that a turnpike company, from its power to construct, repair and maintain the road, has, by implication, power to embark in the business of mail contractor, or in buying and selling horses, cattle, or produce, under the suggestion that the road would be subservient to these purposes.

Let the demurrer be overruled.

PER CURIAM, Decree accordingly.

NOTES

1. The boom in plank road companies that occurred at the time of the *Wiswall* decision has been likened to the bubble in Internet companies that arose at the end of the last century:

> [An] economist pointed out how during the middle of the nineteenth century, herd behavior led to the construction of more than 10,000 miles of plank roads. The first wooden road was built in Salina, a small town in upstate New York, where an entrepreneur named George Geddes had persuaded people that the planks would last about eight years. Word of the exciting innovation quickly spread, and almost three hundred plank road companies incorporated, many of them claiming that the planks would last between ten and fifteen years. After just four years, however, the wooden road in Salina had decayed to such an extent that the entire idea was discredited. Construction elsewhere came to a rapid halt.

John Cassidy, *dot.con, The Greatest Story Ever Told* 124–125 (2002).

2. As seen from the decision in *Wiswall*, the courts at common law required corporations to confine their business to those activities specified in

their charter. Corporate purposes had to be stated with specificity. Namely, each purpose had to be spelled out or the corporation risked being held to be acting illegally. Within the context of most corporations, the organizers desired a broad purpose clause so as not to limit the directors' discretion. The requirement of specificity leads to extremely long and cumbersome drafting, we might say to the point of being ridiculous, as demonstrated by just a small excerpt from the corporate charter of the Uniroyal Corporation:

> The objects for which said company is formed are:
>
> 1. To manufacture, formulate, construct, grow, raise, produce, mine, develop, purchase, lease, buy or acquire in any other manner, import, export, convert, combine, compound, spin, twist, knit, weave, dye, grind, mix, process, introduce, improve, exploit, repair, design, treat or use in any other manner, to lease, sell, assign, exchange, transfer or dispose of in any other manner, and generally to deal and trade in and with any or all of the following:
>
> > (a) rubber, balata, gutta percha, all other related or unrelated natural gums, artificially prepared rubber, reclaims of such rubbers and other gums; raw or processed natural latex, artificially prepared aqueous dispersions of crude or reclaimed rubber, aqueous dispersions of synthetic rubber or of rubber-like or other materials, and equivalents, derivatives and substitutes of any of the foregoing, whether now or hereafter known or used in industry, and all other commodities and materials competent to be put to any use similar to any of the uses of any of them, and articles, goods or commodities produced in whole or in part from any thereof or from the use of any thereof. . . .

Uniroyal, Inc., Amended Certificate of Organization (as amended April 18, 1969). The purpose clause in the Uniroyal charter actually continues for twenty additional similar paragraphs and subparagraphs.

3. *Implied power*. If the conduct in question was neither specifically nor generally authorized by the statement of purpose in the articles of incorporation, courts sometimes *implied* the power to engage in conduct that furthers the stated purpose. For example, in Jacksonville M., P. Ry. & Nav. Co. v. Hooper, 160 U.S. 514, 16 S.Ct. 379, 40 L.Ed. 515 (1896), the Court held that a railway company had the implied power to lease and operate a hotel along the tracks as incidental to its railway business. See also, e.g., Union Pac. R. Co. v. Trustees, Inc., 8 Utah 2d 101, 329 P.2d 398 (1958) (recognizing implied power to make charitable donations); Sutton's Hospital Case, 10 Coke 23a (1613).

––––––––

COX & HAZEN ON CORPORATIONS,
James D. Cox & Thomas Lee Hazen
§ 4.01   (2d ed. 2003).

At common law, a corporation had the powers enumerated in its purpose clause as well as the implied powers necessary to the accomplishment of its purpose. If a corporation engaged in conduct not authorized by its express or implied powers, the conduct was deemed *ultra vires* and void. With the decline in the concession theory of corporations and the universal recognition of the serious inequities that accompanied sanctioning *ultra vires* acts, courts over time interpreted corporate powers broadly. Legislatures also addressed these concerns by authorizing a corporation's articles to broadly enable the corporation to engage in "any lawful purpose" and by limiting the relief and sanctions available for *ultra vires* acts.

Corporate purposes and corporate powers, although often confused, are fundamentally different. A purpose clause properly refers to a statement describing the business the corporation is to conduct. The stated purpose or object of a corporation, for instance, may be "to manufacture textiles" or "to conduct a retail shoe business and to buy, sell, and deal in all kinds of shoes." The term "corporate powers," on the other hand, refers to methods the corporation may use to achieve its purpose. The retail shoe company, for instance, must have the power to contract and the power to borrow money.

Formerly, corporations were usually created by special act of the legislature. It was then natural to regard a corporation as a legal person deriving its existence and powers from a grant from the state. Today, because corporations are created under general corporation laws by filing articles of incorporation, which typically include broad language authorizing them to engage in "any lawful purpose or business," it is more realistic to translate the traditional terminology referring to corporate "powers" into terms of the authority and limitations that the articles impose on those who act for the corporation.

At an earlier time, purpose clauses were so multifarious, drafted with such absurd particularity of enumeration, that it has been well said that they aimed "not to specify, not to disclose, but to bury beneath a mass of words, the real object or objects of the company with the intent that every conceivable form of activity shall be found included somewhere within its terms."

An English judge commented with reference to a broadly stated clause: "Therefore, we have here the enumeration of things so large that when I put it to Mr. Cozens–Hardy whether he could say that it would not extend to authorize the company to establish and work a line of balloons passing backwards and forwards between the earth and the moon, he admitted that he could not say that it would not." Even though many corporate statutes still require that a "purpose clause" (or, as it is sometimes called, "specific object clause") be included in a corporation's charter, modern corporate statutes introduce a good deal of economy here by permitting the articles of incorporation simply to authorize the corporation to engage "in any lawful purpose." And states following the Revised Model Business Corporation Act do not even require a statement of the corporation's purpose or object.

A statement in a corporation's charter of its objects or purposes or powers has the practical effect of defining the scope of the authorized corporate enterprise or undertaking. Second, the statement both confers and limits the officers' and directors' authority by impliedly excluding activities that are not in furtherance of the stated purposes.

————

NOTES

1.   Model Business Corporation Act § 3.01(a) states that, unless otherwise provided, a corporation has the power to conduct all lawful business. In other words, in states adopting this provision, there is no requirement that there be a purpose clause, and the default is a so-called all-purpose clause. The availability of an all-purpose clause does not mean it is always the right way to go. The organizers of a company may want to restrict directors' discretion, thus giving tighter reign to the shareholders. One of the ways to accomplish this is through a limited purpose clause. Also, there no doubt are a number of older corporations that still have limited purpose clauses that have not been amended. Such restrictions, may, however, have unintended effects that could hamper the company's business as it evolves over the years.

In contrast to the Model Business Corporation Act, Delaware still adheres to the more traditional approach of requiring a stated purpose but permitting the use of an all-purpose clause. Del. Gen. Stat. Ann. tit. 8 § 102(a)(3).

2.   In addition to the broadening of purpose clauses, many states adopted statutes which restricted the defense of ultra vires. Under Model Bus. Corp. Act § 3.04, a claim that an act is contrary to the corporate purposes (and hence *ultra vires*) could be brought only in three contexts:

  A.   In an action by the shareholders challenging the act (seeking an injunction or damages),

  B.   In an action by the corporation against officers directors or employees, and

  C.   In an action by the state (*quo warranto*).[1]

Delaware takes a similar approach. Del. § 124.

3.   *Ultra vires and Lack of Authority Compared.* Another way to challenge a corporate act is to establish that the agent executing the act on the corporation's behalf lacked authority to do so. In those cases, if a third party can establish the absence of authority, then the corporation will not be bound by the agent's act, and the contract may be avoided. See e.g., Lee v. Jenkins Brothers, 268 F.2d 357 (2d Cir.1959), cert. denied, 361 U.S. 913, 80 S.Ct. 257, 4 L.Ed.2d 183 (1959).

4.   The doctrine of *ultra vires* has been replaced to some extent with laws regulating corporate conduct, including the federal securities laws, environ-

———

1.   A state may test a corporation's status or seek to revoke its charter through a *quo warranto* proceeding. This is an ancient concept. As noted in Chapter 1, it was used to revoke the charters of the original settlements in America.

mental laws and antitrust proscriptions. Nevertheless, the *ultra vires* doctrine is not dead and has been used imaginatively as in the following case.

CROSS v. MIDTOWN CLUB, INC.

33 Conn.Supp. 150, 365 A.2d 1227 (Super.1976).

STAPLETON, JUDGE.

* * * The following facts are admitted or undisputed: The plaintiff is a member in good standing of the defendant nonstock Connecticut corporation. Each of the individual defendants is a director of the corporation, and together the individual defendants constitute the entire board of directors. The certificate of incorporation sets forth that the sole purpose of the corporation is 'to provide facilities for the serving of luncheon or other meals to members.' Neither the certificate of incorporation nor the bylaws of the corporation contain any qualifications for membership, nor does either contain any restrictions on the luncheon guests members may bring to the club. The plaintiff sought to bring a female to lunch with him, and both he and his guest were refused seating at the luncheon facility. . . .

[T]he court finds: that the corporation had a policy of not accepting women as members or as guests for lunch; that the application of the plaintiff's proposed female candidate for membership was denied because of her sex; and, that the plaintiff has exhausted his effective remedies within the corporation.

The plaintiff's complaint is that the corporation's board of directors has refused to admit the plaintiff's proposed candidate as a member solely because she is a female, and, likewise, that the board has refused to allow the plaintiff to bring female guests to the corporation's luncheon facility. The plaintiff claims that the corporation and its directors, in establishing those policies, have acted ultra vires in that they have exceeded the powers conferred upon them by the certificate of incorporation, the bylaws, and the state statutes regulating corporate powers, and that, in so doing, they have breached the plaintiff's rights as a member of the corporation. * * *

We come, thus, to the nub of this controversy and the basic legal question raised by the facts in this case: is it necessary or convenient to the purpose for which this corporation was organized for it to exclude women members? This court concludes that it is not. While a corporation might be organized for the narrower purpose of providing a luncheon club for men only, this one was not so organized. Its stated purpose is broader and this court cannot find that it is either necessary or convenient to that purpose for its membership to be restricted to men. It should be borne in mind that this club is one of the principal luncheon clubs for business and professional people in Stamford. It is a gathering place where a great many of the civic, business, and professional affairs of the Stamford community are discussed in an atmosphere of social intercourse. Given the scope of the entry of women today into the business and professional life of the community and the changing status of women before the law and in society, it would be anomalous indeed for this court to conclude that it is either necessary or convenient to the stated purpose for which it was organized for this club to exclude women as members or guests.

While the bylaws recognize the right of a member to bring guests to the club, the exclusion of women guests is nowhere authorized and would not appear to be any more necessary and convenient to the purpose of the club than the exclusion of women members. The bylaws at present contain no restrictions against female members or guests and even if they could be interpreted as authorizing those restrictions, they would be of no validity in light of the requirement of § 33–459(a) of the General Statutes that the bylaws must be "reasonable (and) germane to the purposes of the corporation...."

The court therefore concludes that the actions and policies of the defendants in excluding women as members and guests solely on the basis of sex is ultra vires and beyond the power of the corporation and its management under its certificate of incorporation and the Nonstock Corporation Act, and in derogation of the rights of the plaintiff as a member thereof. The plaintiff is entitled to a declaratory judgment to that effect and one may enter accordingly.

NOTE

For another innovative use of the *ultra vires* doctrine, see, Kent Greenfield, Ultra Vires Lives! A Stakeholder Analysis of Corporate Illegality (with Notes on How Corporate Law Could Reinforce International Law Norms), 87 Va. L. Rev. 1279 (2001).

––––––––

SECTION 3. CORPORATE RESPONSIBILITY

A. P. SMITH MFG. CO. v. BARLOW

13 N.J. 145, 98 A.2d 581 (1953), cert. denied, 346
U.S. 861, 74 S.Ct. 107, 98 L.Ed. 373 (1953).

JACOBS, J.

* * * The company was incorporated in 1896 and is engaged in the manufacture and sale of valves, fire hydrants and special equipment, mainly for water and gas industries. Its plant is located in East Orange and Bloomfield and it has approximately 300 employees. Over the years the company has contributed regularly to the local community chest and on occasions to Upsala College in East Orange and Newark University, now part of Rutgers, the State University. On July 24, 1951 the board of directors adopted a resolution which set forth that it was in the corporation's best interests to join with others in the 1951 Annual Giving to

Princeton University, and appropriated the sum of $1,500 to be transferred by the corporation's treasurer to the university as a contribution towards its maintenance. When this action was questioned by stockholders the corporation instituted a declaratory judgment action in the Chancery Division and trial was had in due course.

Mr. Hubert F. O'Brien, the president of the company, testified that he considered the contribution to be a sound investment, that the public expects corporations to aid philanthropic and benevolent institutions, that they obtain good will in the community by so doing, and that their charitable donations create favorable environment for their business operations. In addition, he expressed the thought that in contributing to liberal arts institutions, corporations were furthering their self-interest in assuring the free flow of properly trained personnel for administrative and other corporate employment. Mr. Frank W. Abrams, chairman of the board of the Standard Oil Company of New Jersey, testified that corporations are expected to acknowledge their public responsibilities in support of the essential elements of our free enterprise system. He indicated that it was not 'good business' to disappoint "this reasonable and justified public expectation," nor was it good business for corporations "to take substantial benefits from their membership in the economic community while avoiding the normally accepted obligations of citizenship in the social community." Mr. Irving S. Olds, former chairman of the board of the United States Steel Corporation, pointed out that corporations have a self-interest in the maintenance of liberal education as the bulwark of good government. He stated that "Capitalism and free enterprise owe their survival in no small degree to the existence of our private, independent universities" and that if American business does not aid in their maintenance it is not "properly protecting the long-range interest of its stockholders, its employees and its customers." Similarly, Dr. Harold W. Dodds, President of Princeton University, suggested that if private institutions of higher learning were replaced by governmental institutions our society would be vastly different and private enterprise in other fields would fade out rather promptly. Further on he stated that "democratic society will not long endure if it does not nourish within itself strong centers of non-governmental fountains of knowledge, opinions of all sorts not governmentally or politically originated. If the time comes when all these centers are absorbed into government, then freedom as we know it, I submit, is at an end."

The objecting stockholders have not disputed any of the foregoing testimony nor the showing of great need by Princeton and other private institutions of higher learning and the important public service being rendered by them for democratic government and industry alike. Similarly, they have acknowledged that for over two decades there has been state legislation on our books which expresses a strong public policy in favor of corporate contributions such as that being questioned by them. Nevertheless, they have taken the position that (1) the plaintiff's certificate of incorporation does not expressly authorize the contribution and under common-law principles the company does not possess any implied or incidental power to make it, and (2) the New Jersey statutes which expressly authorize the contribution may not constitutionally be applied to the plaintiff, a corporation created long before their enactment. See R.S. 14:3—13, N.J.S.A.; R.S. 14:3—13.1 et seq., N.J.S.A.

In his discussion of the early history of business corporations Professor Williston refers to a 1702 publication where the author stated flatly that "The general intent and end of all civil incorporations is for better government." And he points out that the early corporate charters, particularly their recitals, furnish additional support for the notion that the corporate object was the public one of managing and ordering the trade as well as the private one of profit for the members. See 3 Select Essays on Anglo–American Legal History 201 (1909); 1 Fletcher, Corporations (rev. ed. 1931), 6. See also Currie's Administrators v. Mutual Assurance Society, 4 Hen. & M. 315, 347 (Va.Sup.Ct.App.1809), where Judge Roane referred to the English corporate charters and expressed the view that acts of incorporation ought never to be passed 'but in consideration of services to be rendered to the public.' However, with later economic and social developments and the free availability of the corporate device for all trades, the end of private profit became generally accepted as the controlling one in all businesses other than those classed broadly as public utilities. Cf. Dodd, For Whom Are Corporate Managers Trustees?, 45 Harv.L.Rev. 1145, 1148 (1932). As a concomitant the common-law rule developed that those who managed the corporation could not disburse any corporate funds for philanthropic or other worthy public cause unless the expenditure would benefit the corporation. Hutton v. West Cork Railway Company, 23 Ch.D. 654 (1883); Dodge v. Ford Motor Co., 204 Mich. 459, 170 N.W. 668, 3 A.L.R. 413 (Sup.Ct.1919). Ballantine, Corporations, (rev. ed. 1946), 228; 6A Fletcher, supra, 667, 170 N.W. 668. During the 19th Century when corporations were relatively few and small and did not dominate the country's wealth, the common-law rule did not significantly interfere with the public interest. But the 20th Century has presented a different climate. Berle and Means, The Modern Corporation and Private Property (1948). Control of economic wealth has passed largely from individual entrepreneurs to dominating corporations, and calls upon the corporations for reasonable philanthropic donations have come to be made with increased public support. In many instances such contributions have been sustained by the courts within the common-law doctrine upon liberal findings that the donations tended reasonably to promote the corporate objectives. See Cousens, How Far Corporations May Contribute to Charity, 35 Va.L.Rev. 401 (1949).

Thus, in the leading case of Evans v. Brunner, Mond & Company, Ltd. (1921) 1 Ch. 359, the court held that it was within the incidental power of a chemical company to grant £ 100,000 to universities or other scientific institutions selected by the directors 'for the furtherance of scientific education and research.' The testimony indicated that the company desired to encourage and assist men who would devote their time and abilities to scientific study and research generally, a class of men for whom the company was constantly on the lookout. This benefit was not considered by the court to be so remote as to bring it outside the common-law rule. Similarly, in Armstrong Cork Co. v. H. A. Meldrum Co., 285 F. 58 (W.D.N.Y.1922), the court sustained contributions made by the corporation to the University of Buffalo and Canisius College. In the course of its opinion the court quoted the familiar comment from Steinway v. Steinway & Sons, 17 Misc. 43, 40 N.Y.S. 718 (Sup.Ct.1896), to the effect that as industrial conditions change business methods must change with them and acts become permissible which theretofore were considered beyond the corporate powers; and on the issue as to whether the corporation had received any corporate benefit it said:

> It was also considered, in making the subscriptions or donations, that the company would receive advertisement of substantial value, including the good will of many influential citizens and of its patrons, who were interested in the success of the development of these branches of education, and, on the other hand, suffer a loss of prestige if the contributions were not made, in view of the fact that business competitors had donated and shown a commendable public spirit in that relation. In the circumstances the rule of law that may fairly be applied is that the action of the officers of the company was not ultra vires, but was in fact within their corporate powers, since it tended to promote the welfare of the business in which the corporation was engaged.

In American Rolling Mill Co. v. Commissioner of Internal Revenue, 41 F.2d 314 (C.C.A.6, 1930), the corporation had joined with other local industries in the creation of a civic improvement fund to be distributed amongst community enterprises including the Boy Scouts and Girl Scouts, the Y.M.C.A., the Hospital, etc. The court readily sustained the contribution as an ordinary and necessary expense of the business within the Revenue Act. And in Greene County Nat. Farm Loan Ass'n v. Federal Land Bank of Louisville, 57 F.Supp. 783, 789 (D.C.W.D.Ky.1944), affirmed 152 F.2d 215 (6th Cir.1945), certiorari denied 328 U.S. 834 (1946) the court in dealing with a comparable problem said:

> But it is equally well established that corporations are permitted to make substantial contributions to have the outward form of gifts where the activity being promoted by the so-called gift tends reasonably to promote the good-will of the business of the contributing corporation. Courts recognize in such cases that although there is no dollar and cent supporting consideration, yet there is often substantial indirect benefit accruing to the corporation which supports such action. So-called contributions by corporations to churches, schools, hospitals, and civic improvement funds, and the establishment of bonus and pension plans with the payment of large sums flowing therefrom have been upheld many times as reasonable business expenditures rather than being classified as charitable gifts.

The foregoing authorities illustrate how courts, while adhering to the terms of the common-law rule, have applied it very broadly to enable worthy corporate donations with indirect benefits to the corporations. In State ex rel. Sorensen v. Chicago B. & Q.R.Co., 112 Neb. 248, 199 N.W. 534, 537 (1924), the Supreme Court of Nebraska, through Justice Letton, went even further and without referring to any limitation based on economic benefits to the corporation said that it saw 'no reason why if a railroad company desires to foster, encourage and contribute to a charitable enterprise, or to one designed for the public weal and welfare, it may not do so'; later in its opinion it repeated this view with the expression that it saw 'no reason why a railroad corporation may not, to a reasonable extent, donate funds or services to aid in good works.' Similarly, the court in Carey v. Corporation Commission of Oklahoma, 168 Okl. 487, 33 P.2d 788, 794 (Sup.Ct.1934), while holding that a public service company was not entitled to an increase in its rates because of its reasonable charitable donations, broadly recognized that corporations, like individuals, have power to make them. In the course of his opinion for the court in the Carey case Justice Bayless said:

> Next is the question of dues, donations, and philanthropies of the Company. It is a matter for the discretion of corporate management in making donations and paying dues. In that respect a corporation does not occupy a status far different from an individual. An individual determines the propriety of joining organizations, and contributing to their support by paying dues, and all contribution to public charities, etc., according to his means. He does not make such contributions above his means with the hope that his employer will increase his compensation accordingly. A corporation likewise should not do so. Its ultimate purpose, from its own standpoint, is to earn and pay dividends. If, as a matter of judgment, it desires to take part of its earnings, just as would an individual, and contribute them to a worthy public cause, it may do so; but we do not feel that it should be allowed to increase its earnings to take care thereof. * * *

* * *

When the wealth of the nation was primarily in the hands of individuals they discharged their responsibilities as citizens by donating freely for charitable purposes. With the transfer of most of the wealth to corporate hands and the imposition of heavy burdens of individual taxation, they have been unable to keep pace with increased philanthropic needs. They have therefore, with justification, turned to corporations to assume the modern obligations of good citizenship in the same manner as humans do. Congress and state legislatures have enacted laws which encourage corporate contributions, and much has recently been written to indicate the crying need and adequate legal basis therefor. In actual practice corporate giving has correspondingly increased. Thus, it is estimated that annual corporate contributions throughout the nation aggregate over 300 million dollars, with over 60 million dollars thereof going to universities and other educational institutions. Similarly, it is estimated that local community chests receive well over 40% of their contributions from corporations; these contributions and those made by corporations to the American Red Cross, to Boy Scouts and Girl Scouts, to 4–H Clubs and similar organizations have almost invariably been unquestioned.

During the first world war corporations loaned their personnel and contributed substantial corporate funds in order to insure survival; during the depression of the '30s they made contributions to alleviate the desperate hardships of the millions of unemployed; and during the second world war they again contributed to insure survival. They now recognize that we are faced with other, though nonetheless vicious, threats from abroad which must be withstood without impairing the vigor of our democratic institutions at home and that otherwise victory will be pyrrhic indeed. More and more they have come to recognize that their salvation rests upon sound economic and social environment which in turn rests in no insignificant part upon free and vigorous nongovernmental institutions of learning. It seems to us that just as the conditions prevailing when corporations were originally created required that they serve public as well as private interests, modern conditions require that corporations acknowledge and discharge social as well as private responsibilities as members of the communities within which they operate. Within this broad concept there is no difficulty in sustaining, as incidental to their proper objects and in aid of the public welfare, the power of corporations to contribute corporate funds within reasonable limits in support of academic institutions. But even if we confine ourselves to the terms of the common-law rule in its application to current conditions, such expenditures may likewise readily be justified as being for the benefit of the corporation; indeed, if need be the matter may be viewed strictly in terms of actual survival of the corporation in a free enterprise system. The genius of our common law has been its capacity for growth and its adaptability to the needs of the times. Generally courts have accomplished the desired result indirectly through the molding of old forms. Occasionally they have done it directly through frank rejection of the old and recognition of the new. But whichever path the common law has taken it has not been found wanting as the proper tool for the advancement of the general good.

In 1930 a statute was enacted in our State which expressly provided that any corporation could cooperate with other corporations and natural persons in the creation and maintenance of community funds and charitable, philanthropic or benevolent instrumentalities conducive to public welfare, and could for such purposes expend such corporate sums as the directors "deem expedient and as in their judgment will contribute to the protection of the corporate interests." Under the terms of the statute donations in excess of 1% of the capital stock required 10 days' notice to stockholders and approval at a stockholders' meeting if written objections were made by the holders of more than 25% of the stock; in 1949 the statute was amended to increase the limitation to 1% of capital and surplus. In 1950 a more comprehensive statute was enacted. In this enactment the Legislature declared that it shall be the public policy of our State and in furtherance of the public interest and welfare that encouragement be given to the creation and maintenance of institutions engaged in community fund, hospital, charitable, philanthropic, educational, scientific or benevolent activities or patriotic or civic activities conducive to the betterment of social and economic conditions; and it expressly empowered corporations acting singly or with others to contribute reasonable sums to such institutions, provided, however, that the contribution shall not be permissible if the donee institution owns more than 10% of the voting stock of the donor and provided, further, that the contribution shall not exceed 1% of capital and surplus unless the excess is authorized by the stockholders at a regular or special meeting. To insure that the grant of express power in the 1950 statute would not displace pre-existing power at common law or otherwise, the Legislature provided that the 'act shall not be construed as directly or indirectly minimizing or interpreting the rights and powers of corporations, as heretofore existing, with reference to appropriations, expenditures or contributions of the nature above specified.' It may be noted that statutes relating to charitable contributions by corporations have now been passed in 29 states. See Andrews, supra, 235, 33 P.2d 788. * * * [The court went on to hold that the statute applied even though it was enacted after the A.P.Smith company had been incorporated—see discussion below].

Affirmed.

___

NOTES

1.   The ability to make charitable contributions is now embodied in state corporate statutes. Model Bus. Corp. Act § 3.02(13) (1994) states that, unless the articles of incorporation provide otherwise, a corporation may "make donations for the public welfare or for charitable, scientific, or educational purposes." See also Del. Code Ann. tit. 8, § 122(9) (2001) (similar provisions). Model Bus. Corp. Act § 3.02(15) (1994) also authorizes payments or donations that further the corporation's business, if not inconsistent with law. The comments to Model Bus. Corp. Act § 3.02 state that these provisions allow corporations to make payments for political purposes and to influence elections. Why should corporations make such contributions, since they do not vote? The Tillman Act that was passed by Congress in 1907 prohibited contributions by corporations to candidates in federal elections. 34 Stat. 864, 2 U.S.C. § 441(b). Subsequent legislation sought to further restrict campaign contributions. See generally Eric L. Richards, The Emergence of Covert Speech and its Implications for First Amendment Jurisprudence, 38 Am. Bus. L. J. 559 (2001). There were, however, several loopholes in that legislation, including "soft money" and the use of political action committees ("PACs") that provided a means to channel corporate funds indirectly to political campaigns. That gap was sought to be filled in 2002, after concern arose with

campaign contributions by the Enron Corp., which had made millions of dollars of campaign contributions before its bankruptcy. Still, loopholes remain by which corporations may use "stealth" PACs to support candidates. These are supposedly independent political groups, but at least some of the stealth PACs were identifying directly with candidates. Thomas B. Edsall, Lawmakers Embracing 'Stealth PAC' Advantage; Committees Allow Relatively Unregulated Fundraising, Wash. Post, April 11, 2002, at A4.

2. In Ella M. Kelly & Wyndham, Inc. v. Bell, 266 A.2d 878 (Del.1970), a corporation agreed to continue making property tax payments to the county, if legislation were passed exempting from taxation all acquisitions of machinery after a specified date. The corporation believed that opposition to the legislation stemmed largely from concerns about the county losing much needed revenues and that its commitment to continue making tax payments would make passage of the exempting legislation more likely. Legislation was enacted that exempted *all* property taxes on machinery, and the corporation continued to make the payments to the county in the amount of its former tax assessments. The court characterized the tax payments as corporate donations. The court did not confine its inquiry to the *ultra vires* doctrine but examined the question within the more flexible standards of the business judgment rule. The court upheld the payments because the board of directors had reasonably arrived at a business rationale for continuing to make the payments for a purpose that advanced the corporation's interest:

> The Chancellor was of the opinion that the payments were in effect donations and were justified as coming within the 'sound business judgment' rule. We have doubts about describing the payments as gifts. They were not so treated by Steel; moreover, in making the agreement, the officers believed with good reason that Steel would derive substantial financial benefit therefrom—a belief which has apparently proven justified. We do not decide, however, into what category the payments properly fall. Nor do we decide whether the promise and the payments thereunder are contrary to any public policy of Pennsylvania; even if they did in fact violate some such public policy, the directors or officers were not necessarily liable to the corporation because they honored the commitment, provided they exercised honest business judgment in doing so. * * *

> The record before us contains no suggestion of fraud. There is no evidence that any director or officer was motivated by expectation of personal gain, by bad faith or by any consideration other than that of doing what was best for Steel. For the reasons set forth in the Chancellor's opinion, we agree with his decision that these acts are governed by the 'business judgment' rule, and were in fact the result for the exercise by them of honest business judgment.

Cf. Finley v. Superior Court, 80 Cal.App.4th 1152, 96 Cal.Rptr.2d 128, 135 (2000) (assuming, without deciding, that business judgment rule would not apply to decision of directors of homeowners association to make contributions to political action committee if such contributions were *ultra vires*). Note that the court's approach in *Kelly v. Bell* is to judge the contribution in terms of whether the board of directors acted reasonably in what they believed advanced the corporation's interest. Accord, e.g., Kahn v. Sullivan, 594 A.2d 48, 58 (Del.1991). See also, e.g., Nell Minow, Corporate Charity: An Oxymoron?, 54 Bus. Law. 997 (1999).

3.   How would you judge a corporate board that decides to make contributions to a pro-choice for abortions or pro-life anti-abortions group that will result in a boycott of the corporation's products? When answering this question, assume that the contribution is being made to whatever group you oppose. What if the donation is made individually by a corporate officer, but protestors still threaten a boycott? These questions are not entirely hypothetical. The founder of Dominos pizza, himself an adopted child, supported those opposing abortions through large contributions. This resulted in a boycott off Dominos by the National Organization of Women. Jim Suhr, *Pizza Magnate Puts His Fortune Where His Faith Is*, Chicago Tribune, Nov. 10, 2000, at 8. How do we monitor donations to assure that they are not given to a pet charity of a corporate officer that will not have any benefit to the corporation?

4.   In Theodora Holding Corp. v. Henderson, 257 A.2d 398 (Del.Ch.1969), a shareholder challenged a corporate charitable contribution in excess of $525,000. The Delaware Court of Chancery upheld the validity of the contribution, relying on both the state corporation statute and the parameters of permissible charitable deductions as established by the federal tax code. In Kahn v. Sullivan, 594 A.2d 48, 58 (Del.1991), the Delaware Supreme Court reaffirmed its view that reasonable charitable gifts are proper and that the tax code provides the guide of reasonableness. See also, e.g., Union Pac. R. Co. v. Trustees, Inc., 8 Utah 2d 101, 329 P.2d 398 (1958) (although corporate charter did not authorize charitable donations, corporation had the implied power to make a $5,000 donation to a related foundation; the court also noted the corporation had made previous large donations to earthquake victims in San Francisco). Critics of corporations sometimes charge that Congress provides "corporate welfare" through tax deductions and credits that reduce corporate taxes. The Internal Revenue Code allows corporations to deduct donations to charitable enterprises, thereby decreasing their taxes. IRC § 170. Does this constitute corporate welfare?

5.   One aspect of the decision in A.P. Smith Mfg. Co. v. Barlow, 13 N.J. 145, 98 A.2d 581 (1953) was a reserved powers provision in Delaware law. Such statutes were passed after the decision of the Supreme Court in Trustees of Dartmouth College v. Woodward, 17 U.S. (4 Wheat.) 518, 4 L.Ed. 629 (1819), which held that the constitution prohibited the states from passing statutes that would impair the obligations of contracts. A corporate charter was held to be such a contract. This would sharply curtail the ability of a state to regulate those corporations already holding charters. Justice Story, however, in a concurring opinion in the *Woodward* case suggested a way around this limitation:

> In my judgment, it is perfectly clear, that any act of a legislature which takes away any powers or franchises vested by its charter in a private corporation, or its corporate officers, or which restrains or controls the legitimate exercise of them, or transfers them to other persons, without its assent, is a violation of the obligations of that charter. If the legislature mean to claim such an authority, it must be reserved in the grant.

> The charter of Dartmouth College contains no such reservation; and I am, therefore, bound to declare, that the acts of the legislature of New Hampshire, now in question, do impair the obligations of that charter, and are, consequently, unconstitutional and void.

17 U.S. at 712. The court in *A. P. Smith Mfg. Co. v. Barlow* upheld the application of a post incorporation amendment to the Delaware corporation statute:

> The appellants contend that the foregoing New Jersey statutes may not be applied to corporations created before their passage. Fifty years before the incorporation of The A. P. Smith Manufacturing Company our Legislature provided that every corporate charter thereafter granted 'shall be subject to alteration, suspension and repeal, in the discretion of the legislature.' A similar reserved power was placed into our State Constitution in 1875, and is found in our present Constitution. * * *

> State legislation adopted in the public interest and applied to pre-existing corporations under the reserved power has repeatedly been sustained by the United States Supreme Court above the contention that it impairs the rights of stockholders and violates constitutional guarantees under the Federal Constitution. * * *

98 A.2d at 587–590. Contrary to the view of most commentators, the issue raised in the *Dartmouth College* case remains in various forms despite the use of reserved powers clauses by the legislatures. *See* Nelson Ferebee Taylor, Evolution of Corporate Combination Law: Policy Issues and Constitutional Questions, 76 N.C.L. Rev. 687 (1998) (impairment of contract issues arising in the context of corporate reorganizations).

ADAMS v. SMITH

275 Ala. 142, 153 So.2d 221 (1963).

COLEMAN, JUSTICE.

* * * The averments of the bill are to effect that the directors have adopted resolutions to pay certain sums of the moneys of the corporation to the widow of the president and to the widow of the comptroller of the corporation; that the payments constitute unauthorized gifts of property of the corporation, made without consideration; that complainant has made demand on the directors and stockholders to take the necessary steps to restore to the corporation the funds alleged to have been thus misappropriated; but the directors and stockholders have refused to take said steps.

The complainant does not charge the directors with intentional wrongdoing or that they have received any personal benefit from the payments to the widows.

The respondents are the directors, the corporation, and the widows. The prayer is for personal judgment against the directors and the widows for the full amount of the sums paid to the widows; for injunction against further payments; and for general relief. * * *

In the briefs on behalf of directors and corporation, two propositions are argued: first, that the allegation, that the payments to the widows are "ultra vires the powers of the corporation," is a mere conclusion of the pleader.

Complainant's right to relief is founded on the proposition that the payment of the corporation's money to the widows, without consideration, is illegal and not within the power of a mere majority of the stockholders over the objection of a single stockholder. As we hereinafter undertake to show, we are of opinion that complainant's contention is correct, unless there is in the charter of the corporation a provision which confers on the majority the power to give away the corporation's money without consideration. * * *

So far as we are advised, a provision in the charter of a business corporation permitting a majority to give away corporate property, without consideration, would be unusual if not unique. In the logic of the strict rule construing a pleading against the pleader on demurrer, however, it appears to us that it must be admitted that a corporation's charter could contain a provision permitting such a gift.

Complainant undertakes to aver that the alleged payment is illegal because it is not authorized by the charter. For the complainant to aver merely that such provision is not in the charter, or that such a payment by the majority is ultra vires, is to aver a conclusion merely.

The instant bill does not contain a copy of the certificate of incorporation nor are the charter powers otherwise stated in the bill. It follows, therefore, that the averment that the alleged payments are ultra vires is not a proper pleading of facts and the grounds of demurrer taking that point were due to be sustained. For that error, the decree must be reversed.

The second proposition argued by the directors is that the bill is without equity.

If, in fact, there is no provision in the charter which authorizes the majority stockholders to pay out corporate funds without consideration, then we are of opinion that the bill does have equity. Appellants have devoted many pages of brief and citation of more than fifty cases to establish the propositions that the alleged payments to the widows are authorized under the so-called 'Business Judgment Rule,' and that the alleged payments may be made lawfully by the directors under their power to manage the internal affairs of the corporation without interference by the courts, or, that if the directors could not do so, then the majority of the stockholders could ratify the alleged acts of the directors, who would not be liable after such ratification. We will respond to these contentions.

The directors say in brief that they "do not question the existence or validity of this rule" that "neither the Board of Directors nor the majority stockholders can give away corporate property," and that the rule "is and must be the law of the land."

"It is a universal rule that neither the board of directors nor the majority stockholders can, over the protest of a minority stockholder, give away corporate property."

The appellants argue, however, that directors or majority stockholders have power to make bonus or retirement payments to officers and employees of the corporation, and their widows or dependents, because such payments can be and are for the benefit and furtherance of the business of the corporation. We are not disposed to contest the proposition that, in a proper case and under proper procedure, corporations can make bonus and pension payments. That, however, is not the case averred in the bill. The averment is that the payment to the widow was without valid consideration and that the corporation had no contract for the payment of the alleged sums.

DODGE v. FORD MOTOR CO.

204 Mich. 459, 170 N.W. 668 (1919).

GEORGE S. HOSMAN, JUDGE

* * * The surplus above capital stock was, September 30, 1912, $14,745,095.67, and was increased year by year to $28,124,173.68, $48,827,032.07, $59,135,770.66. July 31, 1916, it was $111,960,907.53. Originally, the car made by the Ford Motor Company sold for more than $900. From time to time, the selling price was lowered and the car itself improved until in the year ending July 31, 1916, it sold for $440. Up to July 31, 1916, it had sold 1,272,986 cars at a profit of $173,895,416.06. As the cars in use multiplied, sales of parts and or repairs increased, so that, in the year ending July 31, 1916, the gross profits from repairs and parts was $3,915,778.94; sales being more than $600,000 for each of the months of May, June, and July. For the year beginning August 1, 1916, the price of the car was reduced $80 to $360.

The following is admitted to be a substantially correct statement of the financial affairs of the company on July 31, 1916:

```
       Assets.
   Working—
Cash on hand and in bank ...........................$52,550,771.92
Michigan municipal bonds ............................. 1,259,029.01
Accounts Receivable................................... 8,292,778.41
Merchandise and supplies ............................ 31,895,434.69
Investments—outside...................................... 9,200.00
Expense inventories ................................... 434,055.19
   Plant—
Land................................................. 5,232,156.10
```

Buildings and fixtures 17,293,293.40
Machinery and power plant 8,896,342.31
Factory Equipment..................................... 3,868,261.02
Tools.. 1,690,688.54
Patterns... 170,619.77
Patents 64,339.85
Office Equipment 431,249.37
  Total assets..................................... $132,088,219.58

   Liabilities.
  Working—
Accounts payable...................................... $7,680,866.17
Contract deposits 1,519,296.40
Accrued pay rolls..................................... 847,953.68
Accrued salaries...................................... 338,268.80
Accrued expenses 1,175,070.72
Contract rebates 2,199,988.00
Buyers' P. S. rebate 48,099.00
  Reserves—
For fire insurance 57,493.89
For depreciation of plant............................. 4,260,275.53
  Total liabilities................................. $18,127,312.05
Surplus 111,960,907.53
Capital stock.. 2,000,000.00
  Total.. $132,088,219.58

The following statement gives details of the business of the Ford Motor Company for the fiscal year July 31, 1915, to July 31, 1916:

Number of cars made in year 508,000.00
Total business done.................................. $206,867,347.46
Profit for the year 59,994,118.01
Cash in hand and in banks 52,550,771.92
Materials on hand 31,895,434.69
Cars in transit and at branch assembling plants (about
 2 1/2 weeks' output) 35,650.00
Cars sold during year 472,350.00
Employed at home plant 34,489.00
Employed at home offices 1,028.00
Total employes in Detroit plant getting $5 a day or
 more 27,002.00
Employed at 84 branch plants 14,355.00
Total employes (all plants) 49,872.00
Total employes getting $5 a day or more 36,626.00

From a mere assembling plant, the plant of the Ford Motor Company came to be a manufacturing plant, in which it made many of the parts of the car which in the beginning it had purchased from others. At no time has it been able to meet the demand for its cars or in a large way to enter upon the manufacture of motor trucks.

No special dividend having been paid after October, 1915 (a special dividend of $2,000,000 was declared in November, 1916, before the filing of the answers), the plaintiffs, who together own 2,000 shares, or one-tenth of the entire capital stock of the Ford Motor Company, on the 2d of November, 1916, filed in the circuit court for the county of Wayne, in chancery, their bill of complaint, which bill was later, upon leave granted, on April 26, 1917, amended, in which bill they charge that since 1914 they have not been represented on the board of directors of the Ford Motor Company, and that since that time the policy of the board of directors has been dominated and controlled absolutely by Henry Ford, the president of the company, who owns and for several years has owned 58 per cent. of the entire capital stock of the company; that the directors of the company are Henry Ford, David H. Gray, Horace H. Rackham, F. L. Klingensmith, and James Couzens, and the executive officers Henry Ford, president, F. L. Klingensmith, treasurer, and Edsel B. Ford, son of Henry Ford, secretary; that after the filing of the original, and before the filing of the amended, bill, at the annual meeting of the stockholders, David H. Gray retired from the board of directors and Edsel B. Ford was elected and is acting as a director. Setting up that on the 31st of July, 1916, the end of its last fiscal year, the said Henry Ford gave out for publication a statement of the financial condition of the company (the same as herein-above set out), that for a number of years a regular dividend, payable quarterly, equal to 5 per cent. monthly upon the authorized capital stock, and the special dividends hereinbefore referred to, had been paid, it is charged that notwithstanding the earnings for the fiscal year ending July 31, 1916, the Ford Motor Company has not since that date declared any special dividends:

> And the said Henry Ford, president of the company, has declared it to be the settled policy of the company not to pay in the future any special dividends, but to put back into the business for the future all of the earnings of the company, other than the regular dividend of five per cent. (5%) monthly upon the authorized capital stock of the company—two million dollars ($2,000,000).

This declaration of the future policy, it is charged in the bill, was published in the public press in the city of Detroit and throughout the United States in substantially the following language:

> 'My ambition,' declared Mr. Ford, 'is to employ still more men; to spread the benefits of this industrial system to the greatest possible number, to help them build up their lives and their homes. To do this, we are putting the greatest share of our profits back into the business.'

It is charged that——

> The said Henry Ford, "dominating and controlling the policy of said company, has declared it to be his purpose—and he has actually engaged in negotiations looking to carrying such purposes into effect—to invest millions of dollars of the company's money in the purchase of iron ore mines in the Northern Peninsula of Michigan or state of Minnesota; to acquire by purchase or have built ships for the

purpose of transporting such ore to smelters to be erected on the River Rouge adjacent to Detroit in the county of Wayne and state of Michigan; and to construct and install steel manufacturing plants to produce steel products to be used in the manufacture of cars at the factory of said company; and by this means to deprive the stockholders of the company of the fair and reasonable returns upon their investment by way of dividends to be declared upon their stockholding interest in said company."

* * * Plaintiffs ask for an injunction to restrain the carrying out of the alleged declared policy of Mr. Ford and the company, for a decree requiring the distribution to stockholders of at least 75 per cent. of the accumulated cash surplus, and for the future that they be required to distribute all of the earnings of the company except such as may be reasonably required for emergency purposes in the conduct of the business. * * *

OSTRANDER, C. J. (after stating the facts excerpted above).

* * * The plan, as affecting the profits of the business for the year beginning August 1, 1916, and thereafter, calls for a reduction in the selling price of the cars. It is true that this price might be at any time increased, but the plan called for the reduction in price of $80 a car. The capacity of the plant, without the additions thereto voted to be made (without a part of them at least), would produce more than 600,000 cars annually. This number, and more, could have been sold for $440 instead of $360, a difference in the return for capital, labor, and materials employed of at least $48,000,000. In short, the plan does not call for and is not intended to produce immediately a more profitable business, but a less profitable one; not only less profitable than formerly, but less profitable than it is admitted it might be made. The apparent immediate effect will be to diminish the value of shares and the returns to shareholders.

It is the contention of plaintiffs that the apparent effect of the plan is intended to be the continued and continuing effect of it, and that it is deliberately proposed, not of record and not by official corporate declaration, but nevertheless proposed, to continue the corporation henceforth as a semi-eleemosynary institution and not as a business institution. In support of this contention, they point to the attitude and to the expressions of Mr. Henry Ford.

Mr. Henry Ford is the dominant force in the business of the Ford Motor Company. No plan of operations could be adopted unless he consented, and no board of directors can be elected whom he does not favor. One of the directors of the company has no stock. One share was assigned to him to qualify him for the position, but it is not claimed that he owns it. A business, one of the largest in the world, and one of the most profitable, has been built up. It employs many men, at good pay.

"My ambition," said Mr. Ford, "is to employ still more men, to spread the benefits of this industrial system to the greatest possible number, to help them build up their lives and their homes. To do this we are putting the greatest share of our profits back in the business."

"With regard to dividends, the company paid sixty per cent. on its capitalization of two million dollars, or $1,200,000, leaving $58,000,000 to reinvest for the growth of the company. This is Mr. Ford's policy at present, and it is understood that the other stockholders cheerfully accede to this plan."

He had made up his mind in the summer of 1916 that no dividends other than the regular dividends should be paid, "for the present."

The record, and especially the testimony of Mr. Ford, convinces that he has to some extent the attitude towards shareholders of one who has dispensed and distributed to them large gains and that they should be content to take what he chooses to give. His testimony creates the impression, also, that he thinks the Ford Motor Company has made too much money, has had too large profits, and that, although large profits might be still earned, a sharing of them with the public, by reducing the price of the output of the company, ought to be undertaken. We have no doubt that certain sentiments, philanthropic and altruistic, creditable to Mr. Ford, had large influence in determining the policy to be pursued by the Ford Motor Company—the policy which has been herein referred to.

It is said by his counsel that—"Although a manufacturing corporation cannot engage in humanitarian works as its principal business, the fact that it is organized for profit does not prevent the existence of implied powers to carry on with humanitarian motives such charitable works as are incidental to the main business of the corporation." And again: "As the expenditures complained of are being made in an expansion of the business which the company is organized to carry on, and for purposes within the powers of the corporation as hereinbefore shown, the question is as to whether such expenditures are rendered illegal because influenced to some extent by humanitarian motives and purposes on the part of the members of the board of directors." * * *

There is committed to the discretion of directors, a discretion to be exercised in good faith, the infinite details of business, including the wages which shall be paid to employees, the number of hours they shall work, the conditions under which labor shall be carried on, and the price for which products shall be offered to the public.

It is said by appellants that the motives of the board members are not material and will not be inquired into by the court so long as their acts are within their lawful powers. As we have pointed out, and the proposition does not require argument to sustain it, it is not within the lawful powers of a board of directors to shape and conduct the affairs of a corporation for the merely incidental benefit of shareholders and for the primary purpose of benefiting others, and no one will contend that, if the avowed purpose of the defendant directors was to sacrifice the interests of shareholders, it would not be the duty of the courts to interfere. * * *

Assuming the general plan and policy of expansion and the details of it to have been sufficiently, formally, approved at the October and November, 1917, meetings of directors, and assuming further that the plan and policy and the details agreed upon were for the best ultimate interest of the company and therefore of its shareholders, what does it amount to in justification of a refusal to declare and pay a special dividend or dividends? The Ford Motor Company was able to estimate with nicety its income and profit. It could sell more cars than it could make. Having ascertained what it would cost to produce a car and to sell it, the profit upon each car depended upon the selling price. That being fixed, the yearly income and profit was determinable, and, within slight variations, was certain. * * *

Defendants say, and it is true, that a considerable cash balance must be at all times carried by such a concern. But, as has been stated, there was a large daily, weekly, monthly, receipt of cash. The output was practically continuous and was continuously, and within a few days, turned into cash. Moreover, the contemplated expenditures were not to be immediately made. The large sum appropriated for the smelter plant was payable over a considerable period of time. So that, without going further, it would appear that, accepting and approving the plan of the directors, it was their duty to distribute on or near the 1st of August, 1916, a very large sum of money to stockholders. * * *

The decree of the court below fixing and determining the specific amount to be distributed to stockholders is affirmed. In other respects, except as to the allowance of costs, the said decree is reversed. * * *

NOTES

1. The issue of whether corporate managers could manage in the name of "corporate responsibility" continued to be debated by scholars following the decision of the court in *Dodge v. Ford Motor Co.*:

> The determination of the proper role of the shareholder in the development of corporate policy and the management of corporate affairs usually presupposes at least a minimal understanding of the corporate mission and its role in contemporary society. Since the inception of the private corporation and the advent of the general chartering statutes, there has been a great debate among the scholars whether the regulation of corporations is, and should be, a matter of public law or private law. Certainly, to the extent that a corporation is to be made a responsible citizen of society, the use of corporate law is reaching beyond the traditional scope of the chartering statutes. However, that need not necessarily bar the creation of an increased corporate conscience so long as the courts and legislatures proceed cautiously. While independent statutory schemes regulating corporate conduct may be necessary to assure that the corporate citizen fulfills the societal functions, too great of an invasion of the state corporate laws or the federal and state securities laws into these areas is not only beyond their intended scope, but it is also unwise.

The general question of the corporate mission requires resolution of the narrower issue of whether corporate concerns validly extend beyond the question of the profit motive. In its most recent litigational settings and scrutiny by corporate commentators the issue usually raises its head with the shareholders, or their champion, clamoring for social consciousness, while management is placed in the posture of arguing in favor of the profit motive and corporate selfishness. Interestingly, the same issues surfaced long ago but with the conceptual battle lines being drawn in the opposite camps. Specifically, the question was framed and was litigated within the context of the propriety of beneficent corporate generosity. The question of the legitimacy of such charitable gifts arises in terms of whether the act of authorization by management is ultra vires, or beyond the corporate purposes and powers.

Thomas L. Hazen, Corporate Chartering and the Securities Markets: Shareholder Sufferage, Corporate Responsibility and Managerial Accountability, 1978 Wisc. L. Rev. 391, 397–98.

2. *Other Constituency Statutes.* Seeking to avoid ultra vires issues and concerns that board members would violate their fiduciary duties to stockholders, twenty-eight states enacted "stakeholder" or "other constituency" statutes. This legislation specifically enables the board of directors to consider interests other than shareholder wealth maximization in making corporate decisions. Only one of those statutes, however, requires the board to consider such interests, and only a few state that non-shareholder interests may be given equal weight with those of shareholders. Steven Wallman, The Proper Interpretation of Corporate Constituency Statutes and Formulation off Director Duties, 21 Stetson L. Rev. 163 (1991). See also Charles Hansen, "Other Constituency Statutes, A Search for Perspective, 46 Bus. Law. 1355 (1991) (describing application and limitations of these statutes); Jonathan R. Macey, An Economic Analysis of the Various Rationales for Making Shareholders the Exclusive Beneficiaries of Corporate Duties," 21 Stetson L. Rev. 23 (1991) (same); Lawrence E. Mitchell, A Theoretical and Practical Framework for Enforcing Corporate Constituency Statutes, 70 Texas. L. Rev. 579 (1992) (same). Does *Dodge v. Ford* have any continuing vitality in states adopting such legislation?

3. Milton Friedman, a Nobel prize winning economist from the University of Chicago, has asserted that corporate managers should have as their exclusive goal to make as much money as possible for shareholders while conforming to legal and ethical standards of society. Milton Friedman, "The Social Responsibility of Business to Increase Its Profits," N.Y. Times, (Magazine) at 32, Sept. 13, 1970. Do you agree? Do you think that an efficient, profitable corporation will supply more jobs and benefits to society than a corporation that seeks other goals? In answering that question, consider the effects from short-term corporate goals that seek immediate profit at the expense of long-term societal effects, such as the depletion of scarce non-renewable resources. Should the corporate managers assume that alternatives will be available or invented when those resources are depleted? If such an assumption is not made, conservation will be needed. Will this require rationing? Will rationing be on the basis of price? Would that be fair? Do governmental attempts at rationing always end in evasion? Is there another

alternative? How do we dictate that corporations plan for the long run? Of course, we should remember the famous *bon mot* of Lord John Maynard Keynes, the English economist: "In the long run, we are all dead."

4.   As will be seen in Chapter 6, there are limitations on the ability of individual shareholders to demand that their board of directors manage the business in any particular manner. The shareholder *may* be able to have the other shareholders vote on resolutions that request the board of directors to take particular actions that the shareholders believe are socially responsible. The shareholders may also remove the board of directors and appoint individuals that will manage the business in the desired manner. Such actions, however, are rarely successful. For that reason, many shareholders, at least those in a widely traded public company, vote with their feet, i.e., they sell their stock and invest in another company they believe is better managed. There are now numerous mutual funds that will invest your money for you in the stocks of companies pursuing socially responsible goals that you select. Danny Hakim, On Wall St., More Investors Push Social Goals, N.Y. Times, Feb. 11, 2001, at 1 (social goals include religious groups that want to avoid investing in companies that are involved with abortions, alcohol, gambling or pornography, and animal rights groups that want to avoid stocks in companies that are involved in the meat business, hunting equipment or testing of products using animals).

5.   The Social Security system in America will be bankrupt in the next several years, unless benefits are drastically reduced or payroll contributions dramatically increased. Debate is now raging over whether Social Security should be privatized by investing in the stocks of private companies. Concern has been raised that, if the government is assigned the duty of managing such investments, it will seek to engage in socially responsible or "politically correct" investing, as is already the case for some state pension plans. This raises some troubling concerns:

> In America, there is a sharp divergence on what are appropriate social goals. Even where there is general agreement, a sharp division often exists on how to accomplish a particular goal. Tobacco stocks are repulsive to many non-smokers, but tobacco farmers, tobacco company employees and suppliers for the tobacco companies, as well a members of their families, might be expected to support such investments. Those opposing the use of contraceptive devices might seek to block investments in pharmaceutical companies that produce a morning after pill, while others might support such investments. Right-to-life proponents may not want to invest in hospitals or clinics that provide abortion services, while pro-choice advocates might support such investments. Some individuals may oppose investments in fossil fuel companies and demand that, instead, investments be made in alternative energy sources. Others might want investments in gas and oil exploration in remote wilderness areas in order to increase existing fuel supplies, an investment strategy that many oppose. Some might not want to invest in companies involved in defense work, while many support those enterprises. Others might not want to invest in meat packing companies that slaughter animals, while still others might not want to invest in entertainment companies that do not reflect their moral values in programming content. Surely, investment

programs will be needed for the Luddites who oppose advances in technology, for the anti-globalization crowd and for militia members who may want to invest in companies making advances in private weaponry or night scopes. Hunters might want to invest in gun manufacturers, while others object to such activity. The list is endless and would exclude many businesses in America as an investment, if everyone's social goals were to be satisfied.[329]

Jerry W. Markham, "Privatizing Social Security," 38 San Diego L. Rev. 747, 810 (2001). What do you think?

---

329. Many industries in America could be objectionable to at least some investors. Nuclear energy, hydroelectric construction, products requiring animal testing, genetic engineering and cloning, automobile manufactures (polluting engines), gambling, and the construction of single family dwellings have all raised objections. It is foreseeable that some shareholders will demand that companies should affirmatively direct their activities into particular areas such as mass transit, even if it is not economically viable. * * *

CHAPTER 6

MANAGEMENT OF CORPORATIONS

■ ■ ■

SECTION 1.   CORPORATE STRUCTURE

As illustrated in the following Diagram, the business of a modern corporation is composed of several units that include shareholders, officers, directors and employees. There are also others involved in the flow of the corporation's business, including lawyers, accountants and consultants. This section focuses on the authority of directors and officers in this matrix and how statutes affect their decision making. Section 2 introduces some limitations imposed on shareholders in their decision making process.

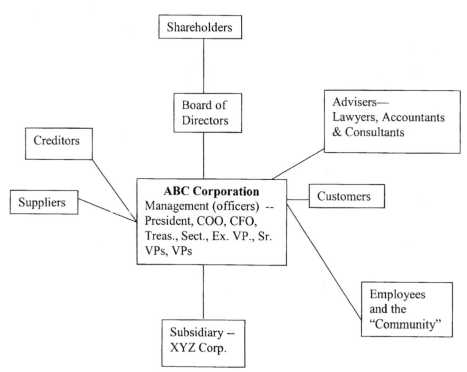

The following diagram illustrates the hierarchy of control in the governance structure of a corporation:

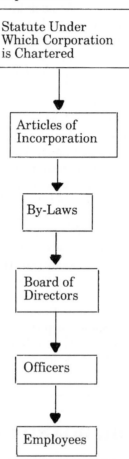

NOTES

1.　The ABC Corp. depicted in in the foregoing diagram owns a subsidiary. This means that it controls another corporation (XYZ Corp.) through stock ownership. ABC Corp. is referred to as the "parent" company, and XYZ is the "sub." Like an individual, ABC Corp. will have all the rights and responsibilities of a shareholder with respect to the sub. Large corporations may own or control several subs. Why do you think one corporation would want to own another corporation?

2.　As suggested by the diagram, creditors, suppliers and employees are among those having a role in the corporation. The duties owed to them by the corporation and its board of directors are largely contractual. As you progress through this casebook, contrast such contractual obligations with the fiduciary duties owed by the board of directors to shareholders.

3.　What duties are owed to the community and the employees where the corporation conducts its business operations? Imagine the effect on your community, if the largest employers were to shut down or move their operations. Such concerns gave rise to the "other constituency" or stakeholder statutes that permit directors to consider interests other than maximization of shareholder value. Are there other solutions? In Germany labor representatives are included on the managing boards and committees of large publicly owned companies. Control of such companies is shared between management and labor representatives. Although the shareholder representative essentially has a tie-breaking vote in the event of deadlock, its use is rare. Rather, labor and management work together to adopt policies acceptable to both shareholders and employees. Herbert Wiedemann, "Codetermination by Workers in German Enterprises," 28 Am. J. Comp. L. 79 (1980). This practice ("codetermination") was not readily adaptable to the United States where management and labor relations are more adversarial and where separation of management from labor unions is mandated to avoid "company" unions that do not place employee interests first. Jerry W. Markham, "Restrictions On Shared Decision—Making Authority In American Business," 11 Cal. West. L. Rev. 217 (1975). Some American corporations with labor intensive operations did allow the election of a few labor representatives to their boards, but this practice did not become popular or widespread. Henry Hansmann and Reinier Kraakman, "Essay: The End of History For Corporate Law," 89 Geo. L. J. 439, 445–446 (2001); Clyde Summers, "Worker Participation in the U.S. and West Germany: A Comparative Study From an American Perspective," 28 Am. J. Comp. L. 367 (1980). Some corporations in the United States are largely owned by employees, which raises additional issues as to whether they should manage for profit or employee welfare.

SECTION 2. THE BOARD OF DIRECTORS

CHARLESTOWN BOOT & SHOE CO. v. DUNSMORE

60 N.H. 85 (1880).

Demurrer to the declaration in which the following facts were alleged:— The plaintiffs are a manufacturing corporation having for its object a dividend of profits, and commenced business in 1871. Dunsmore was elected director in 1871 and Willard in 1873, and entered upon the discharge of their duties, and have continued so to act by virtue of successive elections until the present time. December 10, 1874, the corporation voted to choose a committee to act with the directors to close up its affairs, and chose one Osgood for such committee. Osgood tendered his services, but the defendants refused to act with him, and contracted new debts to a larger extent than allowed by law. By their negligence, debts due to the corporation to the amount of $2,161.23 have been wholly lost. By their negligence in disposing of the goods of the corporation, a loss has accrued of $3,300.40. By their neglect to sell the buildings and machinery of the corporation when they might and ought, and were urged by Osgood to sell, the same depreciated in value to the extent of $20,000. * * *

Smith, J.

The provision of the statute is, that the business of a dividend paying corporation shall be managed by the directors. The statute reads, "The business of every such corporation shall be managed by the directors thereof, subject to the by-laws and votes of the corporation, and under their direction by such officers and agents as shall be duly appointed by the directors or by the corporation." G. L., *c.* 148, *s.* 3; Gen. Stats., *c.* 134, *s.* 3. The only limitation upon the judgment or discretion of the directors is such as the corporation by its by-laws and votes shall impose. It may define its business, its nature and extent, prescribe rules and regulations for the government of its officers and members, and determine whether its business shall be wound up or continued; but when it has thus acted, the business as thus defined and limited is to be managed by its directors, and by such officers and agents under their direction as the directors or the corporation shall appoint. The statute does not authorize a corporation to join another officer with the directors, nor compel the directors to act with one who is not a director. They are bound to use ordinary care and diligence in the care and management of the business of the corporation, and are answerable for ordinary negligence. *March v. Railroad,* 43 N. H. 515, 529; *Scott v. Depeyster,* 1 Edw. Ch. 513, 543; Ang. & Ames Corp., *s.* 314. There is no difference in this respect between the agents of corporations and those of natural persons, unless expressly made by the charter or by-laws. It would be unreasonable to hold them responsible for the management of the affairs of the corporation if compelled to act with one who to a greater or less extent could control their acts. The statute not only entrusts the management of the business of the corporation to the directors, but places its other officers and agents under their direction. When a statute provides that powers granted to a corporation shall be exercised by any set of officers or any particular agents, such powers can be exercised only by such officers or agents, although they are required to be chosen by the whole corporation; and if the whole corporation attempts to exercise powers which by the charter are lodged elsewhere, its action upon the subject is void. *Insurance Co. v. Keyser,* 32 N. H. 313, 315. The vote choosing Osgood a committee to act with the directors in closing up the affairs of the plaintiff corporation was inoperative and void. * * *

Demurrer sustained.

Stanley, J., did not sit: the others concurred.

Notes

1.   In People ex rel. Manice v. Powell, 201 N.Y. 194, 94 N.E. 634 (1911), the New York court of appeals further delineated the role of directors *vis a vis* the stockholders. The court stated that directors are not agents of the shareholders, and the board's powers are original and undelegated. "As a general rule the shareholders cannot act in relation to the ordinary business of the corporation, nor can they control the exercise of the judgement vested in them by virtue of their office." 94 N.E. at 637. Rather, board members essentially act as trustees and the shareholders are the *cestui que trust.*

2. A corporation operates for the benefit of its shareholders, but they do not manage the corporation. Rather, that responsibility is vested in the board of directors, which hires managers to conduct the day-to-day business operations of the company. Formerly, it was said that the board of directors managed the business of a corporation. The current statutory formulation is that the business is managed "by or *under the direction of*" the board. Model Bus. Corp. Act § 8.01. The explanation for this change is the desire to point out that, in the modern larger corporation, directors tend to be overseers rather than day-to-day managers. Of course, top management officials (i.e. executive officers such as the president or chief executive officer) who do serve as the day-to-day managers will also be directors.

3. Model Bus. Corp. Act § 8.01 requires corporations to have a board of directors, unless provided otherwise in a shareholder agreement authorized under Model Bus. Corp. Act § 7.32. The latter provision allows the shareholders to eliminate the board of directors or restrict their discretion. Why would the shareholders eliminate the board? What management structure would replace the board in such a case?

4. Under the doctrine announced in *Charlestown Boot & Shoe Co.*, absent a shareholder agreement, the only recourse for shareholders dissatisfied with the managers and directors would seem to be to elect directors to appoint managers that will carry out the shareholders' wishes. The following two cases, however, point out that the shareholders may, nevertheless, have their voice heard.

AUER v. DRESSEL

306 N.Y. 427, 118 N.E.2d 590 (1954).

DESMOND, JUDGE.

This article 78 of the Civil Practice Act proceeding was brought by class A stockholders of appellant R. Hoe & Co., Inc., for an order in the nature of mandamus to compel the president of Hoe to comply with a positive duty imposed on him by the corporation's by-laws. Section 2 of article I of those by-laws says that 'It shall be the duty of President to call a special meeting whenever requested in writing so to do, by stockholders owning a majority of the capital stock entitled to vote at such meeting'. On October 16, 1953, petitioners submitted to the president written requests for a special meeting of class A stockholders, which writings were signed in the names of the holders of record of slightly more than 55% of the class A stock. The president failed to call the meeting and, after waiting a week, the petitioners brought the present proceeding. The answer of the corporation and its president was not forthcoming until October 28, 1953, and it contained, in response to the petition's allegation that the demand was by more than a majority of class A stockholders, only a denial that the corporation and the president had any knowledge or information sufficient to form a belief as to the stockholding of those who has signed the requests. Since the president, when he filed that answer has had before him for at least ten days the signed requests themselves, his denial that he had any information sufficient for a belief as to the adequacy of the number of signatures was obviously perfunctory and raised no issue whatever. There was no discretion in this corporate officer as to whether or not to call a meeting when a demand therefor was put before him by owners of the required number of shares. The important right of stockholders to have such meetings called will be of little practical value if corporate management can ignore the requests, force the stockholders to commence legal proceedings, and then, by purely formal denials, put the stockholders to lengthy and expensive litigation, to establish facts as to stockholdings which are peculiarly within the knowledge of the corporate officers. In such a situation, Special Term did the correct thing in disposing of the matter summarily, as commanded by section 1295 of the Civil Practice Act....

The petition was opposed on the further alleged ground that none of the four purposes for which petitioners wished the meeting called was a proper one for such a class A stockholders' meeting. Those four stated purposes were these: (A) to vote, upon a resolution indorsing the administration of petitioner Joseph L. Auer, who had been removed as president by the directors, and demanding that he be reinstated as such president; (B) voting upon a proposal to amend the charter and by-laws to provide that vacancies on the board of directors, arising from the removal of a director by stockholders or by resignation of a director against whom charges have been preferred, may be filled, for the unexpired term, by the stockholders only of the class theretofore represented by the director so removed or so resigned; (C) voting upon a proposal that the stockholders hear certain charges preferred, in the requests, against four of the directors, determine whether the conduct of such directors or any of them was inimical to the corporation and, if so, to vote upon their removal and vote for the election of their successors; and (D) voting upon a proposal to amend the by-laws so as to provide that half of the total number of directors in office and, in any event, not less than one third of the whole authorized number of directors constitute a quorum of the directors.

The Hoe certificate of incorporation provides for eleven directors, of whom the class A stockholders, more than a majority of whom join in this petition, elect nine and the common stockholders elect two. The obvious purpose of the meeting here sought to be called (aside from the indorsement and reinstatement of former president Auer) is to hear charges against four of the class A directors, to remove them if the charges be proven, to amend the by-laws so that the successor directors be elected by the class A stockholders, and further to amend the by-laws so that an effective quorum of directors will be made up of no fewer than half of the directors in office and no fewer than one third of the whole authorized number of directors. No reason appears why the class A stockholders should not be allowed to vote on any or all of those proposals.

The stockholders, by expressing their approval of Mr. Auer's conduct as president and their demand that he be put back in that office, will not be able, directly, to effect that change in officers, but there is nothing invalid in their so expressing themselves and thus putting on notice the directors who will stand for election at the annual meeting. As to purpose (B), that is, amending the charter and by-laws to authorize the stockholders to fill vacancies as to class A directors who have been removed on charges or who have resigned, it seems to be settled law that the stockholders who are empowered to elect directors have the inherent power to remove them for cause, In re Koch, 178 N.E. 545, 546. Of course, as the Koch case points out, there must be the service of specific charges, adequate notice and full opportunity of meeting the accusations, but there is no present showing of any lack of any of those in this instance. Since these particular stockholders have the right to elect nine directors and to remove them on proven charges, it is not inappropriate that they should use their further power to amend the by-laws to elect the successors of such directors as shall be removed after hearing, or who shall resign pending hearing. Quite pertinent at this point is Rogers v. Hill, 289 U.S. 582, 589, which made light of an argument that stockholders, by giving power to the directors to make by-laws, had lost their own power to make them; quoting a New Jersey case, In re Griffing Iron Co., 63 N.J.L. 168, 41 A. 931, the United States Supreme Court said: "It would be preposterous to leave the real owners of the corporate property at the mercy of their agents, and the law has not done so". Such a change in the by-laws, dealing with class A directors only, has no effect on the voting rights of the common stockholders, which rights have to do with the selection of the remaining two directors only. True, the certificate of incorporation authorizes the board of directors to remove any director on charges, but we do not consider that provision as an abdication by the stockholders of their own traditional, inherent power to remove their own directors. Rather, it provides an additional method. Were that not so, the stockholders might find themselves without effective remedy in a case where a majority of the directors were accused of wrongdoing and, obviously, would be unwilling to remove themselves from office.

We fail to see, in the proposal to allow class A stockholders to fill vacancies as to class A directors, any impairment or any violation of paragraph (h) of article Third of the certificate of incorporation, which says that class A stock has exclusive voting rights with respect to all matters 'other than the election of directors'. That negative language should not be taken to mean that class A stockholders, who have an absolute right to elect nine of these eleven directors, cannot amend their by-laws to guarantee a similar right, in the class A stockholders and to the exclusion of common stockholders, to fill vacancies in the class A group of directors.

There is urged upon us the impracticability and unfairness of constituting the numerous stockholders a tribunal to hear charges made by themselves, and the incongruity of letting the stockholders hear and pass on those charges by proxy. Such questions are really not before us at all on this appeal. The charges here are not, on their face, frivolous or inconsequential, and all that we are holding as to the charges is that a meeting may be held to deal with them. Any director illegally removed can have his remedy in the courts.

The order should be affirmed, with costs, and the Special Term directed forthwith to make an order in the same form as the Appellate Division order with appropriate changes of dates.

VAN VOORHIS, J., DISSENTS IN OPINION IN WHICH CONWAY, J., CONCURS.

* * * It is not for the courts to determine which of these warring factions is pursuing the wiser policy for the corporation. If these petitioners consider that the stockholders made a mistake in the election of the present directors, they should not be permitted to correct it by recalling them before the expiration of their terms on charges of fraud or breach of fiduciary duty without a full and fair trial ... * * * In ancient Athens evidence is said to have been heard and judgment pronounced in court by as many as 500 jurors known as dicasts, but in this instance, if petitioners be correct in their figures, there are 1200 class A stockholders who have signed requests or proxies, and these are alleged to hold only somewhat more than half of the outstanding shares. Since it would be impossible for so large a number to conduct a trial in person, they could only do so by proxy. Voting by proxy is the accepted procedure to express the will of large numbers of stockholders on questions of corporate policy within their province to determine, and it would be suitable in this instance if the certificate of incorporation had reserved to stockholders the power to recall directors without cause before expiration of term, as in Abberger v. Kulp, 156 Misc. 210, 281 N.Y.S. 373, but it is altogether unsuited to the performance of duties which partake of the nature of the judicial function, involving, as this would need to do if the accused directors are to be removed before the expiration of their terms, a decision after trial that they have been guilty of faithlessness or fraud. * * *

LEWIS, C. J., and DYE, FULD and FROESSEL, JJ., concur with DESMOND, J.

NOTES

1. In *Auer v. Dressel*, there were two classes of common stock with differing voting rights. The intent of the organizers was to keep voting control with the Class A shareholders, while at the same time providing a voice in management to the class B shareholders. The defection of the four class A board members frustrated that purpose. Do you think those defectors were receiving their just deserts after they tried to turn control of the board over to the class B shareholders? How would the proposed by-law changes protect the class A shareholders in the future?

2. The dissent in *Auer* considered the use of proxies as the means for casting shareholder votes. A proxy may be likened to an absentee ballot in a political election, but there are some critical differences. A proxy is an

appointment by the shareholder of a third person (often the secretary of the corporation) to act as the shareholder's agent in casting the vote in a designated manner. This is an agency relationship, and agency law will control the actions of the proxy holder.

3. Do you agree with the dissenting judge in *Auer* that a fair trial will be impossible. The absence of cross-examination and other trial procedures will make this more like a political contest than an adjudication. Is that appropriate or is this really just a political contest over who will represent the shareholders?

CAMPBELL v. LOEW'S INCORPORATED

134 A.2d 852 (Del.Ch.1957).

Seitz, Chancellor: This is the decision on plaintiff's request for a preliminary injunction to restrain the holding of a stockholders' meeting or alternatively to prevent the meeting from considering certain matters or to prevent the voting of certain proxies. Certain other relief is also requested.

Some background[a] is in order if the many difficult and novel issues are to be understood. Two factions have been fighting for control of Loew's. One faction is headed by Joseph Tomlinson (hereafter "Tomlinson faction") while the other is headed by the President of Loew's, Joseph Vogel (hereafter "Vogel faction"). At the annual meeting of stockholders last February a compromise was reached by which each nominated six directors and they in turn nominated a thirteenth or neutral director. But the battle had only begun. Passing by much of the controversy, we come to the July 17–18 period of this year when two of the six Vogel directors and the thirteenth or neutral director resigned. A quorum is seven.

On the 19th of July the Tomlinson faction asked that a directors' meeting be called for July 30 to consider, *inter alia*, the problem of filling director vacancies. On the eve of this meeting one of the Tomlinson directors resigned. This left five Tomlinson directors and four Vogel directors in office. Only the five Tomlinson directors attended the July 30 meeting. They purported to fill two of the director vacancies and to take other action. This Court has now ruled that for want of a quorum the two

---

[a]. This case was one chapter in a bitter proxy battle. Louis B. Mayer controlled MGM for nearly 30 years. In the late 1940s, however, Mayer's interests turned to horse racing, and MGM lost millions of dollars. Mayer was then ousted from control of MGM and was replaced in 1956 by Vogel who was the head of Loew's theaters. Mayer wanted to regain control and formed an alliance with Tomlinson who was Loew's largest shareholder and was on the board of directors. In order to avoid a proxy fight, Vogel agreed to a compromise that created a thirteen member board of directors—6 chosen by Vogel, 6 chosen by the Mayer/Tomlinson faction and a 13th director agreed upon by both camps. Following this compromise, Tomlinson started his campaign for control and attempted to remove Vogel as president but this failed because of a by-law requiring special notice that had not been given. Vogel then called a special shareholder meeting to expand the board from 13 to 19 directors and to elect new directors. Two Vogel directors and the neutral director resigned leaving 6 Tomlinson directors and 4 Vogel directors. Tomlinson attempted to take advantage of this by calling a directors meeting but this was boycotted by the Vogel directors and thus there was no quorum. Additional background on the case is found in Louis Nizer, *My Life in Court* (1961) [eds.].

directors were not validly elected and the subsequent action taken at that meeting was invalid. See *Tomlinson v. Loew's, Inc., supra p.* 516, 134 A.2d 518.

On July 29, the day before the noticed directors' meeting, Vogel, as president, sent out a notice calling a stockholders' meeting for September 12 for the following purposes:

1. to fill director vacancies.

2. to amend the by-laws to increase the number of the board from 13 to 19; to increase the quorum from 7 to 10 and to elect six additional directors.

3. to remove Stanley Meyer and Joseph Tomlinson as directors and to fill such vacancies.

Still later, another notice for a September 12 stockholders' meeting as well as a proxy statement went out over the signature of Joseph R. Vogel, as president. It was accompanied by a letter from Mr. Vogel dated August 9, 1957, soliciting stockholder support for the matters noticed in the call of the meeting, and particularly seeking to fill the vacancies and newly created directorships with "his" nominees. Promptly thereafter, plaintiff began this action. An order was entered requiring that the stockholders' meeting be adjourned until October 15, to give the Court more time to decide the serious and novel issues raised. See *Campbell v. Loew's, Inc., supra p.* 533, 134 A.2d 565.

I believe it is appropriate first to consider those contentions made by plaintiff which concern the legality of the call of the stockholders' meeting for the purposes stated.

Plaintiff contends that the president had no authority in fact to call a special meeting of stockholders to act upon policy matters which have not been defined by the board of directors. Defendant says that the by-laws specifically authorize the action taken.

It is helpful to have in mind the pertinent by-law provisions:

Section 7 of *Article* I provides:

> "Special meetings of the stockholders for any purpose or purposes, other than those regulated by statute, may be called by the President * * * "

Section 2 of *Article* IV reads:

> "The President * * * shall have power to call special meetings of the stockholders * * * for any purpose or purposes * * * "

It is true that *Section* 8(11) of *Article* II also provides that the board of directors may call a special meeting of stockholders for any purpose. But, in view of the explicit language of the by-laws above quoted, can this Court say that the president was without authority to call this meeting for the purposes stated? I think not. I agree that the purposes for which the president called the meeting were not in furtherance of the routine business of the corporation. Nevertheless, I think the stockholders, by permitting the quoted by-laws to stand, have given the president the power to state these broad purposes in his call. Moreover, it may be noted that at least one other by-law (*Article* V, § 2) makes certain action of the president subject to board approval. The absence of such language in connection with the call provision, while not conclusive, is some evidence that it was intended that the call provision should not be so circumscribed.

The plaintiff argues that if this by-law purports to give the president the power to call special stockholders' meetings for the purposes here stated, then it is contrary to 8 *Del.C.* § 141(a), which provides:

> "The business of every corporation organized under the provisions of this chapter shall be managed by a board of directors, except as hereinafter or in its certificate of incorporation otherwise provided."

I do not believe the call of a stockholders' meeting for the purposes mentioned is action of the character which would impinge upon the power given the directors by the statute. I say this because I believe a by-law giving the president the power to submit matters for stockholder action presumably only embraces matters which are appropriate for stockholder action. So construed the by-laws do not impinge upon the statutory right and duty of the board to manage the business of the corporation. Plaintiff does not suggest that the matters noticed are inappropriate for stockholder consideration. And, of course, the Court is not concerned with the wisdom of the grant of such power to the president.

Plaintiff's next argument is that the president has no authority, without board approval, to propose an amendment of the by-laws to enlarge the board of directors. Admittedly this would be a most radical change in this corporate management. Indeed, it may well involve the determination of control. However, as I have already indicated, I believe the wording of the by-laws authorizes such action.

Plaintiff next argues that the president had no power to call a stockholders' meeting to fill vacancies on the board. As I understand plaintiff's argument it is that the existence of *Article* V, § 2 of the by-laws, which provides that the stockholders or the remaining directors may fill vacancies, by implication, precludes the president from calling a stockholders' meeting for that purpose, that provision being intended for stockholder use only at the initiative of the stockholders. First of all, the by-laws permit the president to call a meeting for any purpose. This is broad and all-embracing language and I think it must include the power to call a meeting to fill vacancies. The fact that the stockholders may on their initiative have the right to call a meeting for that purpose does not seem to be a sufficient reason for implying that the president is thereby deprived of such power.

Plaintiff points to the "extraordinary state of affairs" which the recognition of such power in the president would create. Obviously it gives the president power which may place him in conflict with the members of the board. But such consequences inhere in a situation where those adopting the by-laws grant such broad and concurrent power to the board and to the president. The validity but not the wisdom of the grant of power is before the Court. I conclude that under the by-laws the president has the power to call a meeting to fill vacancies on the board.

Plaintiff next argues that the president's action in calling a stockholders' meeting to fill vacancies was unlawful because it was in conflict with the previously scheduled action by the board on the same subject. It should be noted that the proxy statement sent out by the president states that the stockholders would only fill the two vacancies purportedly filled by the board, if their election by the board was held to be invalid. To this extent then the call was not in conflict with this aspect of the board's action. But in any event I have now ruled that the board did not legally fill the vacancies and so the matter would seem to be moot. Moreover, the record is so cloudy as to some of the facts involved on this point that it would not warrant the granting of relief at this time.

The next point made in plaintiff's brief is that the president had no power to fix the record date for voting purposes. However, it turned out that the executive committee fixed the record date and plaintiff's counsel, although given the opportunity at oral argument, did not attack the action of the executive committee. I assume that plaintiff has in effect abandoned this contention.

I therefore conclude that the president had the power to call the meeting for the purposes noticed. I need not consider the effect of the fact that the executive committee recommended that a special stockholders' meeting be called.

Plaintiff next argues that the stockholders have no power between annual meetings to elect directors to fill newly created directorships.

Plaintiff argues in effect that since the Loew's by-laws provide that the stockholders may fill "vacancies", and since our Courts have construed "vacancy" not to embrace "newly created directorships" (*Automatic Steel Products v. Johnston*, 31 Del. Ch. 469, 64 A.2d 416, 6 A.L.R.2d 170), the attempted call by the president for the purpose of filling newly created directorships was invalid.

Conceding that "vacancy" as used in the by-laws does not embrace "newly created directorships", that does not resolve this problem. I say this because in *Moon v. Moon Motor Car Co.*, 17 Del. Ch. 176, 151 A. 298, it was held that the stockholders had the inherent right between annual meetings to fill newly created directorships. There is no basis to distinguish the *Moon* case unless it be because the statute has since been amended to provide that not only vacancies but newly created directorships "may be filled by a majority of the directors then in office * * * unless it is otherwise provided in the certificate of incorporation or the by-laws * * * ". 8 *Del.C.* § 223. Obviously, the amendment to include new directors is not worded so as to make the statute exclusive. It does not prevent the stockholders from filling the new directorships.

Is there any reason to consider the absence of a reference in the by-laws to new directorships to be significant? I think not. The by-law relied upon by plaintiff was adopted long before the statutory amendment and it does not purport to be exclusive in its operation. It would take a strong by-law language to warrant the conclusion that those adopting the by-laws intended to prohibit the stockholders from filling new directorships between annual meetings. No such strong language appears here and I do not think the implication is warranted in view of the subject matter.

I therefore conclude that the stockholders of Loew's do have the right between annual meetings to elect directors to fill newly created directorships.

Plaintiff next argues that the shareholders of a Delaware corporation have no power to remove directors from office even for cause and thus the call for that purpose is invalid. The defendant naturally takes a contrary position.

While there are some cases suggesting the contrary, I believe that the stockholders have the power to remove a director for cause. See *Auer v. Dressel*, 306 *N.Y.* 427, 118 N.E.2d 590, 48 A.L.R.2d 604; compare *Bruch v. National Guarantee Credit Corp.*, 13 Del. Ch. 180, 116 A. 738. This power must be implied when we consider that otherwise a director who is guilty of the worst sort of violation of his duty could nevertheless remain on the board. It is hardly to be believed that a director who is disclosing the corporation's trade secrets to a competitor would be immune from removal by the stockholders. Other examples, such as embezzlement of corporate funds, etc., come readily to mind.

But plaintiff correctly states that there is no provision in our statutory law providing for the removal of directors by stockholder action. In contrast he calls attention to § 142 of 8 *Del.C.*, dealing with officers, which specifically refers to the possibility of a vacancy in an office by removal. He also notes that the Loew's by-laws provide for the removal of officers and employees but not directors. From these facts he argues that it was intended that directors not be removed even for cause. I believe the statute and by-law are of course some evidence to support plaintiff's contention. But when we seek to exclude the existence of a power by implication, I think it is pertinent to consider whether the absence of the power can be said to subject the corporation to the possibility of real damage. I say this because we seek intention and such a factor would be relevant to that issue. Considering the damage a director might be able to inflict upon his corporation, I believe the doubt must be resolved by construing the statutes and by-laws as leaving untouched the question of director removal for cause. This being so, the Court is free to conclude on reason that the stockholders have such inherent power.

I therefore conclude that as a matter of Delaware corporation law the stockholders do have the power to remove directors for cause. I need not and do not decide whether the stockholders can by appropriate charter or by-law provision deprive themselves of this right.

Plaintiff next argues that the removal of Tomlinson and Meyer as directors would violate the right of minority shareholders to representation on the board and would be contrary to the policy of the Delaware law regarding cumulative voting. Plaintiff contends that where there is cumulative voting, as provided by the Loew's certificate, a director cannot be removed by the stockholders even for cause.

It is true that the Chancellor noted in the *Bruch* case that the provision for cumulative voting in the Delaware law was one reason why directors should not be considered to have the power to remove a fellow director even for cause. And it is certainly evident that if not carefully supervised the existence of a power in the stockholders to remove a director even for cause could be abused and used to defeat cumulative voting. See 66 *Harvard* L.R. 531.

Does this mean that there can be no removal of a director by the stockholders for cause in any case where cumulative voting exists? The conflicting considerations involved make the answer to this question far from easy. Some states have passed statutes dealing with this problem but Delaware has not. The possibility of stockholder removal action designed to circumvent the effect of cumulative voting is evident. This is particularly true where the removal vote is, as here, by mere majority vote. On the other hand, if we assume a case where a director's presence or action is clearly damaging the corporation and its stockholders in a substantial way, it is difficult to see why that director should be free to continue such damage merely because he was elected under a cumulative voting provision.

On balance, I conclude that the stockholders have the power to remove a director for cause even where there is a provision for cumulative voting. I think adequate protection is afforded not only by the legal safeguards announced in this opinion but by the existence of a remedy to test the validity of any such action, if taken.

The foregoing points constitute all of the arguments advanced by plaintiff which go to the validity of the call of the meeting for the purposes stated. It follows from my various conclusions that the meeting was validly called by the president to consider the matters noticed.

I turn next to plaintiff's charges relating to procedural defects and to irregularities in proxy solicitation by the Vogel group.

Plaintiff's first point is that the stockholders can vote to remove a director for cause only after such director has been given adequate notice of charges of grave impropriety and afforded an opportunity to be heard.
* * *

I am inclined to agree that if the proceedings preliminary to submitting the matter of removal for cause to the stockholders appear to be legal and if the charges are legally sufficient on their face, the Court should ordinarily not intervene. The sufficiency of the evidence would be a matter for evaluation in later proceedings. But where the procedure adopted to remove a director for cause is invalid on its face, a stockholder can attack such matters before the meeting. This conclusion is dictated both by the desirability of avoiding unnecessary and expensive action and by the importance of settling internal disputes, where reasonably possible, at the earliest moment. Otherwise a director could be removed and his successor could be appointed and participate in important board action before the illegality of the removal was judicially established. This seems undesirable where the illegality is clear on the face of the proceedings. * * *

Turning now to plaintiff's contentions, it is certainly true that when the shareholders attempt to remove a director for cause, " * * * there must be the service of specific charges, adequate notice and full opportunity of meeting the accusation * * * ". See *Auer v. Dressel* [306 *N.Y.* 427, 118 N.E.2d 590], above. While it involved an invalid attempt by directors to remove a fellow director for cause, nevertheless, this same general standard was recognized in *Bruch v. National Guarantee Credit Corp.* [13 Del. Ch. 180, 116 A. 738], above. The Chancellor said that the power of removal could not "be exercised in an arbitrary manner. The accused director would be entitled to be heard in his own defense".

Plaintiff asserts that no specific charges have been served upon the two directors sought to be ousted; that the notice of the special meeting fails to contain a specific statement of the charges; that the proxy statement which accompanied the notice also failed to notify the stockholders of the specific charges; and that it does not inform the stockholders that the accused must be afforded an opportunity to meet the accusations before a vote is taken.

Matters for stockholder consideration need not be conducted with the same formality as judicial proceedings. The proxy statement specifically recites that the two directors are sought to be removed for the reasons stated in the president's accompanying letter. Both directors involved received copies of the letter. Under the circumstances I think it must be said that the two directors involved were served with notice of the charges against them. It is true, as plaintiff says, that the notice and the proxy statement failed to contain a specific statement of charges. But as indicated, I believe the accompanying letter was sufficient compliance with the notice requirement.

Contrary to plaintiff's contention, I do not believe the material sent out had to advise the stockholders that the accused must be afforded an opportunity to defend the charges before the stockholders voted. Such an opportunity had to be afforded as a matter of law and the failure to so advise them did not affect the necessity for compliance with the law. Thus, no prejudice is shown.

I next consider plaintiff's contention that the charges against the two directors do not constitute "cause" as a matter of law. It would take too much space to narrate in detail the contents of the president's letter. I must therefore give my summary of its charges. First of all, it charges that the two directors (Tomlinson and Meyer) failed to cooperate with Vogel in his announced program for rebuilding the company; that their purpose has been to put themselves in control; that they made baseless accusations against him and other management personnel and attempted to divert him from his normal duties as president by bombarding him with correspondence containing unfounded charges and other similar acts; that they moved into the company's building, accompanied by lawyers and accountants, and immediately proceeded upon a planned scheme of harassment. They called for many records, some going back twenty years, and were rude to the personnel. Tomlinson sent daily letters to the directors making serious charges directly and by means of innuendoes and misinterpretations.

Are the foregoing charges, if proved, legally sufficient to justify the ouster of the two directors by the stockholders? I am satisfied that a charge that the directors desired to take over control of the corporation is not a reason for their ouster. Standing alone, it is a perfectly legitimate objective which is a part of the very fabric of corporate existence. Nor is a charge of lack of cooperation a legally sufficient basis for removal for cause.

The next charge is that these directors, in effect, engaged in a calculated plan of harassment to the detriment of the corporation. Certainly a director may examine books, ask questions, etc., in the discharge of his duty, but a point can be reached when his actions exceed the call of duty and become deliberately obstructive. In such a situation, if his actions constitute a real burden on the corporation then the stockholders are entitled to relief. The charges in this area made by the Vogel letter are legally sufficient to justify the stockholders in voting to remove such directors. In so concluding I of course express no opinion as to the truth of the charges.

I therefore conclude that the charge of "a planned scheme of harassment" as detailed in the letter constitutes a justifiable legal basis for removing a director.

I next consider whether the directors sought to be removed have been given a reasonable opportunity to be heard by the stockholders on the charges made.

The corporate defendant freely admits that it has flatly refused to give the five Tomlinson directors or the plaintiff a stockholders' list. Any doubt about the matter was removed by the statement of defendant's counsel in open court at the argument that no such list would be supplied. The Vogel faction has physical control of the corporate offices and facilities. By this action the corporation through the Vogel group has deliberately refused to afford the directors in question an adequate opportunity to be heard by the stockholders on the charges made. This is contrary to the legal requirements which must be met before a director can be removed for cause.

At the oral argument the defendant's attorney offered to mail any material which might be presented by the Tomlinson faction. This falls far short of meeting the requirements of the law when directors are sought to be ousted for cause. Nor does the granting of the statutory right to inspect and copy some 26,000 names fulfill the requirement that a director sought to be removed for cause must be afforded an opportunity to present his case to the stockholders before they vote.

When Vogel as president caused the notice of meeting to be sent, he accompanied it with a letter requesting proxies granting authority to vote for the removal of the two named directors. It is true that the proxy form also provided a space for the stockholder to vote against such removal. However, only the Vogel accusations accompanied the request for a proxy. Thus, while the stockholder could vote for or against removal, he would be voting with only one view-point presented. This violates every sense of equity and fair play in a removal for cause situation.

While the directors involved or some other group could mail a letter to the stockholders and ask for a proxy which would revoke the earlier proxy, this procedure does not comport with the legal requirement that the directors in question must be afforded an opportunity to be heard before the shareholders vote. This is not an ordinary proxy contest case and a much more stringent standard must be invoked, at least at the initial stage, where it is sought to remove a director for cause. This is so for several reasons. Under our statute the directors manage the corporation and each has a somewhat independent status during his term of office. This right could be greatly impaired if substantial safeguards were not afforded a director whose removal for cause is sought. The possibility of abuse is evident. Also, as the Chancellor pointed out in the *Bruch* case, the power of removal can be a threat to cumulative voting rights. This is particularly true where, as here, the removal is by mere majority vote.

There seems to be an absence of cases detailing the appropriate procedure for submitting a question of director removal for cause for stockholder consideration. I am satisfied, however, that to the extent the matter is to be voted upon by the use of proxies, such proxies may be solicited only after the accused directors are afforded an opportunity to present their case to the stockholders. This means, in my opinion, that an opportunity must be provided such directors to present their defense to the stockholders by a statement which must accompany or precede the initial solicitation of proxies seeking authority to vote for the removal of such director for cause. If not provided then such proxies may not be voted for removal. And the corporation has a duty to see that this opportunity is given the directors at its expense. Admittedly, no such opportunity was given the two directors involved. Indeed, the corporation admittedly refused to supply them with a stockholders' list.

To require anything less than the foregoing is to deprive the stock-holders of the opportunity to consider the case made by both sides before voting and would make a mockery of the requirement that a director sought to be removed for cause is entitled to an opportunity to be heard before the stockholders vote. See the persuasive language of the dissent in

Auer v. Dressel, above. But in referring to the language of the dissent I do not thereby suggest that my conclusion here is necessarily contrary to the majority decision on this point.

I therefore conclude that the procedural sequence here adopted for soliciting proxies seeking authority to vote on the removal of the two directors is contrary to law. The result is that the proxy solicited by the Vogel group, which is based upon unilateral presentation of the facts by those in control of the corporate facilities, must be declared invalid insofar as they purport to give authority to vote for the removal of the directors for cause.

A preliminary injunction will issue restraining the corporation from recognizing or counting any proxies held by the Vogel group and others insofar as such proxies purport to grant authority to vote for the removal of Tomlinson and Meyer as directors of the corporation.

The Court emphasizes that it is considering only the proxy solicitation and use aspect of this problem and is considering those only where advance authority is given to vote in a particular way. I am not called upon to consider what procedural and substantive requirements must be met if the matter is raised for consideration by stockholders present in person at the meeting.

NOTES

1. For later developments in the saga of the fight for control of MGM, see e.g., Levin v. Metro–Goldwyn–Mayer, Inc., 264 F.Supp. 797 (S.D.N.Y. 1967).[b]

2. Some state statutes now provide for the removal of directors by the shareholders with or without cause, although some states may require the right to remove without cause to be stated in the articles of incorporation. Model Bus. Corp. Act § 8.08, for example, provides for removal of directors with or without cause, unless the articles of incorporation provide otherwise. Removal is allowed only after a special meeting is called with notice of its purpose. Id. Most state statutes protect the rights of stock classes that are

---

[b]. Vogel retained control as a result of his victory at the 1957 shareholder meeting. The board was enlarged to 19 and all but one of the new directors were in Vogel's camp. Tomlinson could not be removed from the board because of cumulative voting (a topic discussed in Chapter 9). After another Tomlinson attempt to gain more representation on the board, Vogel led the elimination of cumulative voting and as a result was able to secure unanimous support from the board. The *Levin* case involved a control battle initiated by Philip J. Levin, a real estate developer, against Robert H. O'Brien who was Vogel's successor. Levin won, and in late 1967 and 1968, another contest for control was initiated by Time, Inc. and Edgar Bronfman (who later headed Seagram Co., which owns large entertainment businesses). Levin sold his interest in MGM to those parties, and MGM was subsequently sold to Kirk Kerkorian, a well-known corporate raider. Leslie Eaton, Robert H. O'Brien (obituary), N.Y. Times, Oct. 11, 1997, at B7. Kerkorian, thereafter, bought and sold MGM more than once. In one of those sales, MGM was acquired by Giancarlo Parretti and Florio Fiorini, two Italian businessmen. They were later accused by federal authorities of engaging in massive fraud in acquiring control of American companies. Fiorini was sentenced to 41 months in federal prison and Parretti was fighting extradition from Sicily where he had been jailed for tax evasion. David Rosenzweig, "Financier Gets Prison Term in MGM Deal," Los Angeles Times, Nov. 20, 2001, pt. 2, at 3. [eds.].

entitled to elect a certain number of directors. These statutes prohibit the removal of those directors by other shareholders. Cumulative voting rights are also protected. Delaware has a similar provision, but allows one class of stock to vote to remove a director of another class for cause. Del. § 141(k).

3.   Model Bus. Corp. Act § 8.09 allows directors to be removed in a judicial proceeding where they have engaged in fraudulent or other improper conduct upon petition by the corporation or ten percent of the shareholders. The comments to this section state that its provisions do no allow judicial resolution of internal corporate fights for control.

4.   The number of directors on the board is set by the by-laws or certificate of incorporation. Model Bus. Corp. Act § 803(a); Del. § 141(b). Directors are normally elected each year at the annual meeting of shareholders. Model Bus. Corp. Act § 8.03(c). Some corporations, however, elect a "staggered" or "classified" board of directors. This means that only a portion of the board members are elected each year. Model Bus. Corp. Act § 8.06. For example, a classified board might have twelve members, but only four are elected each year. Delaware law § 141 (k) allows the removal of directors on a staggered board only for cause, unless the certificate of incorporation provides otherwise. The purpose of such arrangements is to assure the continuity of management and make it harder to take over control of the board. Thus, in the above example, it would take two elections and two years to assume control of the board. That is a considerable period of time and would require an extended and costly effort to remove the board through normal voting procedures. Do you think such an arrangement is sound policy? Consider the following from the comments to Model Bus. Corp. Act § 8.06:

> The traditional purpose of a staggered board has been to assure the continuity and stability of the corporation's business strategies and policies as determined by the board. In recent years the practice has been employed with increasing frequency to ensure that a majority of the board of directors remains in place following a sudden change in shareholdings or a proxy contest.... A staggered board of directors also can have the effect of making unwanted takeover attempts more difficult....

Do you think that a staggered board should be used for such purposes?

5.   In Scott County Tobacco Warehouses, Inc. v. Harris, 214 Va. 508, 201 S.E.2d 780 (1974) the court held that the statutory right of shareholders to remove the directors with or without cause, included the right to remove all directors (16 of them) and replace them with a lesser number (3). The court rejected the claim that only the directors could decrease the number of directors through a bylaw amendment. The court also was not impressed with the argument that the shareholders were being allowed to shorten the terms of existing directors through the device of decreasing the number of directors.

6.   In the course of his opinion in the *Campbell* case, Chancellor Seitz stated: "While a concerted plan to abstain from attending directors' meetings may be improper under some circumstances, I cannot find that the fact that the so-called Vogel directors did not attend directors meetings called to take action which would give an opposing faction an absolute majority of the board—solely because of director resignations—is such a breach of their fiduciary duty that they should be judicially compelled to attend board

meetings. This is particularly so where stockholder action is in the offing to fill the board." In some contexts, intentionally absenting oneself from a directors meeting will be a breach of duty. See e.g., Gearing v. Kelly, 11 N.Y.2d 201, 227 N.Y.S.2d 897, 182 N.E.2d 391 (1962), page 515 below, (board member who sought to paralyze board of directors by refusing to attend a board meeting, thereby preventing a quorum, would not be allowed to contest board actions taken at those meetings).

SECTION 3. BOARD FUNCTIONS AND COMPENSATION

A. BOARD FUNCTIONS

State statutes are generally permissive in defining board functions. There are, however, five groups of functions normally associated with directors:

1.   Select, evaluate and, when appropriate, replace the chief executive officer (monitoring the management). Determining management compensation. Review planning for the future.

2.   Review and, when appropriate, approve financial objectives, strategies, and plans. Provide advice to shareholders on votes concerning strategic issues facing the corporation such as a merger with another corporation.

3.   Provide advice and counsel to top management (generally the executive officers).

4.   Select and recommend to shareholders for election the slate of directors (this permits self-perpetuation unless there is an actively supported competing slate).

5.   Review adequacy of internal controls and other systems to assure compliance with applicable laws and regulations. Also, internal controls are useful for monitoring management and the use of assets.

B. DIRECTORS' COMPENSATION

At one time there was some question as to whether directors who were not also officers or employees could receive compensation for their services as directors. See generally e.g., Alexander v. Lindsay, 152 So.2d 261 (La.App.1963) (directors are presumed to serve without compensation unless their compensation is fixed before they render their service as director). Today, many statutes expressly recognize the power of the board of directors to fix directors' compensation. Model Bus. Corp. Act § 8.11 and Del. § 141(h). In large, publicly owned corporations, directors generally receive annual stipends in addition to fees for each meeting attended. See Marx v. Akers, 88 N.Y.2d 189, 644 N.Y.S.2d 121, 666 N.E.2d 1034 (1996).

———

SECTION 4. HOUSEKEEPING REQUIREMENTS

State corporate statutes contain, for want of a better term, what we refer to as housekeeping requirements for boards of directors. These include such things as a mandate that board members meet as a group, notice requirements for such meetings, quorum provisions, and rules setting the number of directors needed to approve corporate action. Such statutes cannot be dismissed as merely administrative technicalities because their breach may invalidate the corporate action taken at an improperly conducted meeting. Lawyers, therefore, are well advised to pay close attention to these requirements. You should also remember that housekeeping requirements for shareholder actions often vary from those required for meetings of the board of directors. See Chapter 9 for the rules applicable to shareholder meetings.

A. DIRECTORS' MEETINGS

State corporate statutes require that board action be taken at a duly convened meeting. This requirement lies at the very heart of the corporate decision making model. These statutes seek collegial decision making. It is generally believed that directors should act only after a complete airing of all views. This better assures informed decisions. For that reason, directors cannot vote by proxy, but many statutes do permit directors to be present by telephone or other electronic communications. Model Bus. Corp. Act § 8.20(b) and Del. § 141(i) provide that, unless the articles of incorporation or by-laws state otherwise, a meeting can be held by means of a communication which can be *heard* by all directors with two way communication. This assures that conflicting views of all directors present at the meeting are heard. Thus, it would appear that a computer hook-up without sound will not constitute presence at the meeting for a director using that form of communication. Modern telecommunications have extended the means by which directors can be present. Previously, board meetings were often conducted with a speakerphone placed in the middle of the table in the board room so that directors unable to appear could be present and listen and speak. Today, such presence is often accomplished by televised video conferences that allow two way communications. Such devices are becoming increasingly important to corporations with global operations and directors located around the world. Delaware has eliminated a requirement that "other" communications equipment be "similar" to a conference telephone, as long as all the directors can hear each other.

Del. § 141(i). Some states have broadened their statutes to specifically permit not only video conference meetings but also electronic board meetings (via computer modems). See e.g., Cal. Corp. Code § 307(a)(6) (1999). Two way communication may still be required for all participants.

State statutes usually allow corporate action to be taken without a meeting where there is unanimous approval by all members of the board of directors. Model Bus. Corp. Act § 8.21 and Del. § 141(f). The theory in allowing such actions is that a meeting is not required if everyone is in agreement, i.e., there are no differing views to be considered. The certificate of incorporation or by-laws may restrict the use of such meetings. Id. Further, action taken by unanimous consent must be memorialized by the directors in writing, and those consents must be kept with other minutes of the board. Id.

B. NOTICE OF DIRECTOR MEETINGS

Under Model Bus. Corp. Act § 8.22(a), regular meetings of the board of directors may be held without notice to the directors of the date, time, place or purpose of the meeting. The theory here is that, since the meeting is a regularly scheduled one, no further notice is deemed necessary. Model Bus. Corp. Act § 8.22(a). Unless the by-laws or articles of incorporation provide otherwise, however, two days notice to board members of special board meetings is required. The notice need not describe the purpose of the special meeting. Model Bus. Corp. Act § 8.22(b). See Smith v. Van Gorkom, 488 A.2d 858 (Del.1985)0059795;0028;85114193#P##(directors met and approved a merger of the company without advance notice of the meeting's purpose).

Notice of a meeting may be waived by a director in writing. Model Bus. Corp. Act § 8.23(a). Notice is also waived by the director's attendance at the meeting, unless the appearance is made only to protest the lack of notice, and the director does not vote for or assent to action taken at the meeting. Model Bus. Corp. Act § 823(b). See also Del. § 229 (similar provisions).

C. QUORUM AND VOTING REQUIREMENTS

Ordinarily, a quorum for directors' meetings consists of a majority of the total number of directors on the board (not just those present). Model Bus. Corp. Act § 8.24(a); Del. § 141(b). A super majority quorum provision, including a requirement of unanimity, can be established by the articles or bylaws. Id. In contrast, special quorum requirements for shareholder meetings must be stated in the articles of incorporation. The articles of incorporation or bylaws may fix a directors' quorum of less than a majority but not lower than one third. Model Bus. Corp. Act § 8.24(a) and Del. § 141(b). The theory here is that there is no harm in requiring more than majority approval, even unanimity. Adherence to the doctrine of collegial decision making by boards, however, requires at least the presence of a third of the directors.

If a quorum is present, the affirmative vote of the majority of directors present (not just those voting) will constitute an act of the board. Model Bus. Corp. Act § 8.24(c) and Del. § 141(b). See e.g., Peoples Bank v. Banking Board, 164 Colo. 564, 436 P.2d 681 (1968) (five of seven board members were available, a three to two vote was sufficient to constitute an act of the board); Compare the rule for shareholders in Model Bus. Corp. Act § 7.25, discussed in Chapter 9. The articles of incorporation or bylaws may provide for a greater than majority voting requirement. Model Bus. Corp. Act § 8.24(c). There is no express statutory authority for a less than majority vote requirement, although as noted above, there can be a lower than majority quorum provision, but not less than one third.

A director will be deemed to have assented to the action taken by the board unless the director records a dissent or abstention. Model Bus. Corp. Act § 8.24(d). An abstention will act as a no vote because of the requirement of affirmative vote by the majority. Model Bus. Corp. Act § 8.24(c).

The house keeping rules described above generally permit higher quorum and voting requirements if in the articles of incorporation or in the bylaws.

NOTES

1. What is the relative hierarchy between the articles of incorporation and the bylaws? Note the different procedures for amendment (compare, e.g., Model Bus. Corp. Act § 10.03 and Del. § 242(b) (amendment of articles) with Model Bus. Corp. Act § 10.20 and Del. § 109 (amendment of bylaws)). Why are there these differing procedures for the articles and bylaws?

2. A review of the corporation statutes reveals differences in whether matters are to be addressed in a corporation's articles of incorporation or in its bylaws.

    a. Some provisions of the statute permit variations in the articles of incorporation. Consider, for example, Model Bus. Corp. Act § 3.02 which permits the articles to limit the corporation's general powers (accord Del. § 122). What would be the effect of a bylaw provision purporting to limit the corporation's powers?

    b. Some provisions permit variation in either the articles of incorporation or the bylaws. Consider, for example, Model Bus. Corp. Act § 8.24, which permits a corporation to set the directors' quorum requirement.

    c. Still other provisions permit variation in the bylaws. Consider, for example, Model Bus. Corp. Act §§ 8.40, 8.41 which states that officers are defined in the bylaws or by the directors in accordance with the bylaws. Could a corporation validly describe the officers in the articles of incorporation?

————

COX & HAZEN ON CORPORATIONS,
James D. Cox & Thomas Lee Hazen
§ 9.07   (2d ed. 2003).

The authority to manage the affairs of the corporation is vested in the directors not individually but as a board. The traditional rule, as usually stated, is that directors cannot act individually to bind the corporation but must act as a board at a legally convened meeting.... [S]tatutes frequently authorize important exceptions to this rule, and courts have upheld informal director approval where it is equitable to bend the requirements that the board act as a deliberative body.

Many cases have held that if directors act or give their consent separately or if they act at other than a legal meeting, their action is not that of the corporation, even though all may consent, and, in the absence of statute, ratification, or estoppel, the corporation is not bound. These holdings proceed on the theory that the directors must meet and counsel with each other, and that any determination affecting the corporation shall only be arrived at after a consultation at a meeting of the board on notice to all and attended by at least a quorum of its members. The shareholders are entitled to the directors' combined wisdom, knowledge, and business foresight, which give efficiency and safety to corporate management. It has been said:

> The general rule seems to rest upon two reasons: First, that collective action is necessary, in order that the act may be deliberately adopted, after opportunity for discussion and an interchange of views; and second, that the directors are, for the purpose of managing the affairs of the corporation, the agents of the stockholders, and given no power to act otherwise than as a board.

The strict rule requiring formal board action at a duly assembled meeting has been recognized as impractical in close (small) corporations, where informal internal decisions are common practice. Where it is customary in a close corporation for the board of directors to convene without notice of the meeting, courts are reluctant to allow the absence of notice to be raised to invalidate the board action. Furthermore, even if the strict rule is applied, a gathering of the directors may be held to be a valid meeting, even though no special formalities have been observed. The presence and participation of all directors is all that is necessary to constitute a valid meeting. The fact that minutes are not kept nor recorded does not invalidate acts done or authorized at the meeting. Proof of directors' actions need not be confined to the formal minutes of directors' meetings; they may be established by other means. * * *

Courts in many instances have upheld the directors' approval, even though the directors' approval was not the product of a meeting convened in accordance with the statutes or bylaws. For example:

(1) Considerable judicial support exists for the proposition that even in the absence of a statute, the separate consent of all the directors is sufficient to bind the corporation without a formal meeting as a board, and some support exists for the proposition that consent of a majority of the board, although acting separately, will suffice.

(2) Courts tend not to apply the strict rule requiring a formal meeting where the shareholders have acquiesced in the directors' custom and usage of acting separately and not as a board.

(3) If the directors own all of a corporation's shares, a conveyance, mortgage, or contract authorized by them, although not assembled at a meeting, is valid. Courts have repeatedly departed from the traditional rule in order to sustain action taken by owner-directors in family and close corporations.

(4) The shareholders may waive the necessity of a board meeting and thereby authorize acts to be done by agents of the corporation or ratify acts already done and thus bind the corporation. The shareholders are the residuary owners, and the rule requiring directors' meetings be held to authorize acts is for the shareholders' benefit. Where, by acquiescence, the shareholders vest the executive officers with the powers of the directors as the usual method of doing business and the board is inactive, the acts of such officers, although not authorized by a vote of either shareholders or directors, generally will bind the corporation.

(5) A corporation may be estopped, as against an innocent third person, to deny the validity of a mortgage or other act done or authorized by the directors separately, or otherwise than at a legal meeting, by long acquiescence or voluntary receipt or retention of benefits with either actual or presumed knowledge.

(6) Many cases hold that where a single shareholder owns substantially all the shares of stock, she may bind the corporation by her acts without a resolution of the board of directors. This is usually based on the ground of disregarding the separate corporate entity but may better be explained as a liberalized agency doctrine and a dispensing with the formalities of usual corporate procedure where they can serve no useful purpose.

(7) Ratification by vote or acquiescence of the shareholders, on full disclosure of the circumstances, is generally held effective to validate irregular or voidable acts of the directors. A few cases, however, go to the extent of holding that the shareholders cannot ratify any irregular or invalid act of the board that they, as shareholders, could not authorize. But even when an effective ratification does

not take place, the corporation may be "estopped" by the receipt or retention of benefits to deny its liability.

NOTES

1. In the absence of a special provision in the articles of incorporation or the by-laws, how many directors are needed for a quorum on a ten member board where there are only eight members in office? What is the quorum requirement if three additional directors resign, i.e., is there a quorum? Can the remaining directors fill the vacancies? Model Bus. Corp. Act § 8.10(a)(3) says yes, even if there is no quorum, provided that the action is taken by a majority of the remaining directors. The directors cannot fill the vacancy, however, if the vacating director was elected by a voting group. Model Bus. Corp. Act § 8.10(b). See also Del. § 223. Special quorum and voting requirements are also imposed in director conflict-of-interest transactions. Those requirements are discussed in Chapter 8.

2. The fact that directors are not agents and can act only as a board means there must be a meeting—formal or as otherwise—authorized by statute. What happens in the case where all board members agree or acquiesce to corporate action but there is no formal meeting by consent or otherwise? This is a common practice in many small corporations. The traditional older view is that directors cannot act informally even if the action is unanimous. Baldwin v. Canfield, 26 Minn. 43, 1 N.W. 261, 270 (1879). The more modern view is to recognize informal but unanimous board action, at least in cases where the corporation is trying to avoid liability from a contract with a third party. Gerard v. Empire Square Realty Co., 195 A.D. 244, 187 N.Y.S. 306 (App.Div.1921). See also Remillong v. Schneider, 185 N.W.2d 493 (N.D.1971) (ordinary rule that corporate action may only be taken at meeting of the board of directors may not apply to closely held corporations) This is to be compared to the process of ratification, which is discussed below. Compare also the process for shareholder consent without a meeting which in many states can be by a majority. See Chapter 9. Although corporate formalities may not be as rigidly enforced in small corporations, there still exists a danger of lack of authority for particular contracts and may require the court to examine the practices of the corporation before determining that the officers acting for the corporation had the requisite authority. This is to be avoided because the result may not always be favorable, and it may be your job as a corporate lawyer to advise clients of the danger of informal actions.

SECTION 5. BOARD COMMITTEES

State statutes authorize the board of directors to divide into committees that have the powers of the full board, at least with respect to certain types of director action. Del. § 141(c). Under Model Bus. Corp. Act § 8.25(e), certain board actions cannot be delegated to committee (although advisory committees may be used). Among other things, a committee may not fill vacancies on the board of directors or adopt, amend or repeal by-laws. The committee system represents a movement towards specialization of the board with a view towards increasing accountability. Delegation to a committee does not absolve the board (or individual board members) of liability, although it will affect their standard of care.

Can the board appoint non-directors to committees? Apparently not under Model Bus. Corp. Act § 8.25(a) and Del. § 141(c). But the board may appoint advisory committees with non-directors. Even without statutory or judicial authority, a board is free to appoint as many advisory committees as it pleases. The committee so chosen can be made up of anyone, but it is only advisory in nature—the action must come from the board; this is not a type of delegation, the committee is purely advisory.

Some courts have limited the delegation of authority to officers acting as committees of the board of directors. For example, the board cannot delegate to the president the authority to select assets for sale and fix the terms thereof. Clarke Memorial College v. Monaghan Land Co., 1968 WL 2173 (Del.Ch.1968). Compare Ella M. Kelly & Wyndham, Inc. v. Bell, 266 A.2d 878 (Del.1970) (court allowed board delegation to officers of decision to pay $29 million to county in lieu of a recently repealed tax).

Most small corporations need not employ the formalities of a committee system. These "close" corporations tend not to have large boards or committees in order to keep things simple and also in order to facilitate shareholder control. The use of committees is, however, now firmly ingrained in large publicly owned corporations:

> The Committee system permits a board to operate more effectively and expeditiously. Committees can study assigned problems in much greater depth than is possible for a full board; they can develop and utilize specialized knowledge and experience; and they can provide a sharper and more intensive focus on particular business issues and activities. Indeed, the boards of large, publicly held corporations could not function effectively without committees. Most large corporations, it has been said, "are in fact run by committees of the board of directors, not by the boards themselves."

James D. Cox & Thomas Lee Hazen & F. Hodge O'Neal, Corporations § 9.16 (2d ed. 2003).

The most common committees used by large corporations include:

1. Executive committee
2. Compensation committee
3. Audit committee
4. Special litigation committee
5. Nominating committee.

The executive committee is often empowered to act for the board in reviewing and approving much of the business of the corporation. The executive committee will provide information to the board on its activities, but it will usually bring only the most important matters to the board for further approval.

The compensation committee will be assigned the task of passing on salaries and bonuses of officers. Some corporations have stock option committees to administer such bonuses. These options entitle the recipient to purchase the company's stock at a specific price. If the market price of the stock exceeds that price, the employee may buy the stock at the option price and sell it at the market price. This operates as a bonus and gives the officer an incentive to increase the value of the stock, thereby benefiting shareholders as well, at least in the short term.

The audit committee is responsible for assuring that the company's books and records are accurate. A corporation may also use a finance committee to manage the company's finances, e.g., managing credit lines, cash flows and related matters. The role of the audit committee has increased in importance over the years. Financial scandals involving the "cooking" of corporation books in order to increase the stock price by covering up losses and falsifying profits has led to the destruction of more than one business. The failure of the Enron Corp. in 2001 increased those concerns. The audit committee is supposed to act as a check on officers who may want to conceal the true condition of the company in order to protect their bonuses or other compensation. The audit committee seeks to assure that the corporation's accounting controls and procedures are functioning properly and are adequate.

The special litigation committee will be used to review issues related to "derivative" suits sought by shareholders of the corporation. Under certain conditions, shareholders may bring a derivative suit in the name of the corporation to pursue a cause of action that the corporation failed to pursue. These derivative suits, and the role played by the special litigation committee, is discussed in Chapter 21. The special litigation committee may also be asked to investigate internal corporate misconduct. Such investigations are often used by corporations to convince governmental authorities that the corporation is cleaning its own house and that prosecution, at least against the corporation, is not needed.

The nominating committee is used to select candidates for the board of directors. This committee will review the performance of existing board members to determine whether they should be reelected. Corporate boards are often criticized as being self-perpetuating by nominating themselves each year. Nominating committees are being made more independent in response to such criticism.

The Securities and Exchange Commission ("SEC"), the agency charged with enforcing the federal securities laws, requires publicly traded corporations to disclose to the public whether the company has an audit or other committees and their membership. Securities Exchange Act Release No. 15384 (July 18, 1978). This placed increased pressure on publicly traded corporations to form such committees. Some of those committees are staffed entirely by "outside" directors.

A. INSIDE AND "OUTSIDE" DIRECTORS

The boards of directors of most corporations are heavily weighted with, or at least contain several of, its own officers. Those individuals wear two hats: they are both officers and directors and will have separate obligations and responsibilities in those roles. A director holding a management position with the company may function as an agent when wearing that hat, but not when acting as a director. These roles also, as will be seen in later chapters, sometimes conflict. These "inside" directors may be supplemented with directors representing the interests of large shareholders, but who are not employed as officers. These shareholders own enough stock to elect one or more directors but may not want, or not have enough voting control, to be appointed as officers of the company. The board members they elect are there for the primary purpose of protecting the interests of the large shareholder, but those directors still owe duties to all shareholders when acting in their capacity as a board member.

Many corporations, particularly publicly held companies, also elect "outside" directors to their boards. These outside directors are individuals who are not employees, representatives of large shareholders or otherwise affiliated with the corporation (although they typically own small amounts of the corporation's stock). Outside directors are often former government officials, successful business people, or even law professors. Current thinking is that such individuals bring independence, broadened experience and perspective to the corporate decision making process even though they have no day-to-day involvement in the corporation's affairs. These outside directors may supply strategic vision without being conflicted by a desire for personal gain from the corporation. In prior years, these positions tended to be titular in nature but increased concerns with conflicts has moved these directors into the frontlines.

Boards now often delegate much of their authority to committees on which outside directors serve in order to reduce potential conflict of interest concerns raised by inside director/managers that have a personal interest in corporation actions such as compensation and auditing. Auditing committees are often composed entirely of outside directors. Compensation committee membership is frequently limited to outside directors, or at least control of the committee is vested in those directors. For discussion of corporate governance issues and the role of outside directors see "Symposium: Corporate Law and Social Norms," 99 Colum. L. Rev. 1253 (1999); Henry Hansmann and Reinier Kraakman, "Essay: The End of History For Corporate Law," 89 Geo. L. J. 439 (2001); Mark J. Loewenstein, "The SEC and The Future of Corporate Governance," 45 Ala. L.

Rev. 783 (1994); Arthur W. Hahn and Carol B. Manzoni, The Monitoring Committee and Outside Directors' Evolving Duty of Care, 9 Loy. U. Chi. 587 (1978).

The New York Stock exchange adopted rules in the wake of the Enron scandal requiring a majority of the board of directors of exchange-listed companies to be outside directors. The nominating, compensation, and audit committees of these companies must also be entirely outside directors. The Sarbanes–Oxley Act of 2002 which was also passed in the wake of the Enron fiasco requires the audit committees of publicly owned corporations to be composed of "independent" outside directors who are neither employees of nor consultants to the corporation. Pub.Law 107–204 (July 30, 2002).

There are various types of relationships that can result in a director lacking the independence necessary to receive the presumption of the business judgment rule. Consider, for example, In re Oracle Corp. Derivative Litigation, 824 A.2d 917 (Del. Ch. 2003), where the court disqualified two Stanford University professors from serving on a committee investigating whether to continue a derivative suit against various defendants, including one who was also a Stanford professor and had been a major donor to the university.

———

Academic studies have found that companies with boards of directors staffed by at least a majority of outside directors did not perform better than firms having a majority of inside directors. In that regard, the Enron Corp., which is now viewed to be the epitome of bad management, had an audit committee staffed with outside directors. Eleven of the fourteen directors on Enron's board were independent outside directors at the time of its collapse. They included some experienced and notable executives, academics and former government officials. Among those Enron board members were Robert Jaedicke, professor of accounting and former dean of the Stanford University graduate school of business, Charls Walker, former deputy secretary of the Treasury, John Mendelsohn, president of the University of Texas, John Wakeham, former secretary of state for energy in the United Kingdom and leader of the Houses of Lords and Commons, Norman Blake, Jr., secretary general of the U.S. Olympic Committee and Dr. Wendy Gramm, an economics professor at George Mason University in Virginia and former chairman of the Commodity Futures Trading Commission. The board also included present or former senior executives at General Electric, Penn Central Corp., Gulf & Western Industries, Inc., Alliance Capital Management, and the State Bank of Rio de Janerio. Another firm with a massive accounting failure was Xerox. Its board of directors had a majority of outside directors, including several prominent individuals such as Vernon Jordan and former Senator George Mitchell. Global Crossing, another colossal scandal, had a board laden with prominent outside directors, including Maria Elena Lagomasino, co-head of J.P. Morgan Private Bank, Pieter Knook a senior Microsoft executive, William E. Conway, Jr., a managing director of the Carlyle Group, and Steven J. Green, former ambassador to Singapore. The outside director chairing the audit committee at Waste Management, where massive accounting fraud occurred, was Roderick M. Hills, a former SEC chairman. His wife, Carla Hills, the former U.S. Trade Representative, served on the boards of Lucent Technologies and AOL Time Warner, two more companies with massive accounting problems.

Politically correct corporate governance also does not assure business success. The Eastman Kodak Co. is possibly the worst managed company in America but was among the one percent of companies receiving a perfect score for corporate governance in a survey of public corporations by an international governance rating body. In contrast, Berkshire Hathaway, one of the most successful companies in the country in recent years, had one of the most politically incorrect board of directors until it was required to add more outside directors after the Enron scandal. The members of the Berkshire Hathaway board included investment guru Warren Buffett, his wife (before her death), his son, his longtime business partner and an insider who was a co-investor.

This gives rise to the question of what value do outside directors provide? The answer is considerable. Outside directors are useful in providing wisdom, differing perspectives and, yes, contacts that can be used to further business, but their usefulness is limited in preventing management abuses. Outside directors, by definition, are not involved in the day-to-day management of the company, and they are controlled by information flows from management. As the American Law institute has noted: "As a practical matter, the initiation and formulation of major corporate plans and actions must depend in large part on an intimate knowledge of the business of the corporation, and this knowledge is more likely to be possessed by the senior executives than by the board." American Law Institute, *Principles of Corporate Governance* § 301, comments. See Jerry W. Markham, A Financial History of Modern U.S. Corporate Scandals: From Enron to Reform (2005).

A current reformist proposal is to split the role of the chairman of the board of directors and the chief executive officer ("CEO"). The CEO usually wants to assume both roles to assure control of the board of directors, the only real threat to control over the corporation. Reformists believe that separating the positions will assure better monitoring of the CEO. This debate came to a head over a rule adopted by the United States Securities and Exchange Commission ("SEC") to require mutual funds to separate those roles. That rule was adopted after a massive scandal over the trading practices allowed by several mutual funds. The U.S. Chamber of Commerce sued the SEC to block implementation of that rule, which was approved by a split 3–2 vote of the Commission. The SEC rule was approved despite a study showing that mutual funds with non-independent chairman charged expenses that were on average lower than those with an independent chairman. Further, boards with management chairman performed better on average. Congress then enacted legislation to require the SEC to conduct a study of whether companies with independent chairman actually perform better. This was an effort to shame the SEC into reversing its rule, but the SEC was undeterred. The United States Court of Appeals for the District of Columbia Circuit then granted the Chamber of Commerce's request that the rule be set aside. The court concluded that the SEC had not adequately considered the proposal before adopting it. Chamber of Commerce of the United States v. Securities and Exchange Commission, 412 F.3d 133 (D.C. Cir. 2005). The SEC then readopted the rule after only a few days consideration, essentially thumbing its nose at the court. The new rule was challenged and was set aside once again by the Court of Appeals. The Court held that the SEC should have sought public comment before adopting the rule so quickly after the Court's prior ruling. Chamber of Commerce of the United States v. SEC, 443 F.3d 890 (D.C. Cir. 2006).

Another reformist effort to increase the power of outside directors is to have them meet separately from management directors periodically and to have their own lawyers paid for by the company. Outside directors are being placed in charge of internal corporate investigations of possible misconduct by officers. Traditionally such internal investigations have been used to white wash problems or to place the blame on lower level employees. That role changed with Enron. That scandal led to an internal investigation that was conducted by a former head of the Enforcement Division of the SEC. His report, which was prepared for a committee of independent directors, was a devastating indictment of senior management.

B. DIRECTORS' INFORMATIONAL RIGHTS

Members of a board of directors must be able to inform themselves on the corporation's operations in order to properly carry out their duties. Directors are, therefore, given broad rights to inspect corporate books and records. Should such rights be unlimited? For example, what if the director wants to examine books and records in order to further his or her personal interests, such as taking advantage of a corporate opportunity or aiding the competition? Despite such concerns, many cases say that directors' inspection rights are absolute. Some allow inspection even where the director is acting on behalf of a competitor. See generally e.g., Cohen v. Cocoline Products, Inc., 309 N.Y. 119, 127 N.E.2d 906 (1955); Wilkins v. M Ascher Silk Corp., 207 A.D. 168, 201 N.Y.S. 739 (App.Div. 1923), aff'd, 237 N.Y. 574, 143 N.E. 748 (1924). This unqualified approach is thought necessary in order to assure that the corporation's officers do not block or delay access by the director to information by claims that the director is acting improperly. The courts adopting this approach believe that there are adequate remedies available that may be employed to hold directors acting improperly accountable, including personal liability for breaches of fiduciary duties owed to the corporation, without restricting access to documents. Other courts may allow some restrictions on director access when the director's purpose is hostile to or threatens a corporate interest. Such decisions usually state that the inspecting director must be acting in good faith and cannot use the inspection right for purposes that are in conflict with the director's fiduciary relationship with shareholders. See e.g. Strassburger v. Philadelphia Record Co., 335 Pa. 485, 6 A.2d 922, 924 (1939).

In State ex rel. Farber v. Seiberling Rubber Co., 53 Del. 295, 168 A.2d 310 (Del.Super.1961) the court held that the right of a director to inspect corporate books and records ceases when the director's motive for seeking inspection is improper. In Henshaw v. American Cement Corp., 252 A.2d 125 (Del.Ch.1969), however, the Delaware Chancery court allowed inspection even though the director was hostile to management and could have disclosed confidential information to parties whose interests were adverse to the corporation. The court noted the director would be personally liable to the corporation for improper use of the information. Delaware § 220(d), which was enacted subsequent to those decisions, now provides that the director's right to inspect must be reasonably related to his position as a director. The Chancery court is given the authority to determine whether such inspection is for a proper purpose and may impose restrictions on the access to documents.

As will be seen in Chapter 9, shareholders have more limited inspection rights than do directors.

SECTION 6. OFFICERS AND THEIR SOURCES OF POWER

Corporations are managed by their officers who act under the direction of the board of directors.[1] The older corporate statutes typically mentioned four officer positions: the president, vice president, treasurer, and secretary which were the traditional officers of the corporation. The modern trend is not to list specific officers in the corporate statute but rather to simply authorizes the officers that are provided for in the by-laws. Model Bus. Corp. Act § 8.40.

While most officer functions have remained constant over time, roles, duties, and titles have changed considerably. Today, many corporations, especially the large publicly held corporations, have numerous executives and agents who are denominated "officers." For example, the title of "president" was once reserved for the head corporate officer but today many corporations use the title of "chief executive officer" (CEO). Under

---

1. The following discussion is adapted from James D. Cox, Thomas Lee Hazen & F. Hodge O'Neal, Corporations § 8.2 (2d ed 2002).

this structure, there often is a president who is subordinate to the CEO. When corporations have both a CEO and president, the CEO's power is superior and broader than that of the president. There may be a chief operating officer (COO); this resembles the position of general manager that may exist in a small business or within corporate divisions.

Large corporations may have many vice presidents, assistant vice presidents, assistant secretaries, assistant treasurers, and so on. As the number of vice presidents in corporations has proliferated, super vice presidencies under such titles as "executive vice president" or "senior vice president" have been created in an effort to retain distinctive titles. Most large corporations have a chairman of the board of the board of directors who also may hold one of the higher officer positions. In many instances the chief executive officer also serves as chairman of the board.

As agents of the corporation, officers' authority derives from agency law. An officer's authority to act may be found in the corporation's bylaws, a resolution of the board of directors, or a job description of that particular officer's or agent's duties approved by the board or some superior corporate agent. In larger businesses, much of a corporation's activities are conducted by agents who are selected and given authority by other corporate agents. These "sub agents" may be a number of levels removed from the board of directors.

A. APPARENT AUTHORITY OF CORPORATE OFFICERS

Apparent authority is essentially a question of fact. Lee v. Jenkins Brothers, 268 F.2d 357 (2d Cir.), cert. denied, 361 U.S. 913, 80 S.Ct. 257, 4 L.Ed.2d 183 (1959). Certain maxims exist, however, with respect to the authority of corporate officials. ". . . [A]s a general rule, the business of the corporation is to be managed by its board of directors." TJI Realty, Inc. v. Harris, 250 A.D.2d 596, 672 N.Y.S.2d 386, 388 (App.Div. 2d Dept. 1998). Ordinarily, this means that express authorization for officers and agents to act requires a duly enacted resolution of the board of directors. As a practical matter, however, it may be difficult to obtain a resolution because boards of directors meet only infrequently. Corporations, therefore, act through officers and employees who often operate with delegated actual authority or apparent or implied authority.[1] That authority is necessary as a practical matter for most businesses to operate. For example, assume your client is a computer store, and an employee of ABC Corp., a local corporation, visits the store and signs a contract for a $1,000 computer to be delivered to ABC's office, payments within 30 days. Your

---

1. This is illustrated by the following quote:

> . . . a corporation is an artificial, not a natural person. As an artificial person, a corporation 'can act, and does act, alone through agents. It deals with other corporations and with natural persons by its agents; it can deal with the world in no other way.'

Eckles v. Atlanta Technology Group, Inc., 267 Ga. 801, 485 S.E.2d 22, 24 (1997) (citation omitted).

client could demand a certified board resolution from the ABC Corp. to assure proper authorization, but it will probably lose the sale. Depending on the circumstances, many businesses would simply make the sale and rely on the apparent authority of the purchasing agent. As the Supreme Court has noted:

> ... principles of corporate law provide a ready-made set of rules for determining, in whatever context, who has authority to make decisions on behalf of a company. Consider, for example, an ordinary sales contract between "Company X" and a third party. We would not think of regarding the contract as meaningless, and thus unenforceable, simply because it does not specify on its face exactly who within "Company X" has the power to enter into such an agreement or carry out its terms. Rather, we would look to corporate law principles to give "Company X" content. See 2 W. Fletcher, Cyclopedia of Law of Private Corporations § 466, p. 505 (rev. ed. 1990) ("[A] corporation is bound by contracts entered into by its officers and agents acting on behalf of the corporation and for its benefit, provided they act within the scope of their express or implied powers").

Curtiss–Wright Corp. v. Schoonejongen, 514 U.S. 73, 80–81, 115 S.Ct. 1223, 131 L.Ed.2d 94 (1995). Even where there is express authority from the board of directors, however, the issue may arise as to what is the scope of that authority.

EVANSTON BANK v. CONTICOMMODITY SERVICES, INC.

623 F.Supp. 1014 (N.D.Ill.1985).

MORAN, DISTRICT JUDGE.

In late May of 1982 the board of directors of the Evanston Bank discovered that the bank had lost over $1,200,000 in about one year of trading in commodities, while paying over $270,000 in commissions. The bank now brings this action for commodities fraud against ContiCommodity Services, Inc. (Conti), the futures commission merchant through which it traded in commodity futures, and Ted Thomas, the broker who handled its account.

The bank's version of how the loss occurred appears in the six counts of its complaint. Counts I and II allege violations of the Commodity Exchange Act (CEA), 7 U.S.C. § 1 et seq., specifically that Conti and Thomas used the bank's account for unauthorized trading and "churned" it (traded it excessively) to generate unnecessary commissions. The bank maintains that it intended only to hedge in commodities as a protection against rising interest rates, a conservative investment strategy. It says that it got speculative trading instead. Since Conti and Thomas used the mails and the telephone in connection with the trading, count IV alleges mail and wire fraud in violation of 18 U.S.C. § 1961 et seq., the Racketeer Influenced and Corrupt Organization Act (RICO). The remaining counts are pendent claims under Illinois law. Count III, for common law fraudulent misrepresentation and concealment, and count V, for fraudulent or deceptive business practices under Ill.Rev.Stat. ch. 1211/2 ¶ 262, rest on Thomas' alleged assurances that the bank's account would be traded in accordance with appropriate banking regulations and Federal Deposit Insurance Corporation (FDIC) policies, and that the bank would be charged commissions at the same rate as other banks. Since an FDIC policy statement in effect then and now allows hedging in commodities but strongly discourages banks from speculative trading, and the bank was charged $94 per "round turn" (per transaction) while other Conti customers with similar account activity were charged $30 to $35 (and apparently some banks with other firms had a rate of only $11 to $20), the bank claims fraud and deception. Finally, count VI, apparently in the alternative, alleges negligence in the handling of the bank's account.

Conti, however, presents a different version of how the loss occurred and moves for summary judgment in its favor. The board of directors of the bank fully authorized Richard Christiansen, at that time both the chairman of the bank's board of directors and the bank's chief executive officer, to handle commodities trading for the bank. Conti maintains that all of the trades followed Christiansen's instructions on the bank's objectives and the overwhelming majority of them were either specifically approved or later ratified by him. Christiansen also executed a power of attorney to Thomas to make trades on behalf of the bank. The bank may now regret its choice of Christiansen as its agent (he was fired in June 1982, after the rest of the board discovered the extent of his trading), but nevertheless it chose him and so must bear the loss from his acts. And, if any further authority is needed, Conti points out that it strictly complied with the bank's instructions to send daily written confirmation of each trade to the cashier of the bank, Hindrek Ott. Neither Ott nor any other representative of the bank disavowed any trade until May 28, 1982. Since the bank was fully informed, both through its agent Christiansen and through the notice to the cashier, Conti argues, its silence ratified the trades. Therefore, Conti is not liable for the bank's losses as a matter of law. Defendant Thomas has moved to adopt Conti's motion. * * *

To find that the bank authorized Thomas' acts, his authority must be legally traceable, directly or indirectly, to the bank's board of directors. The authority of an agent, whether express or implied, must stem from the words or actions of his principal. *Chase v. Consolidated Foods Corp.*, 744 F.2d 566 (7th Cir.1984). The principal in question here is not a natural person, but a corporation—the bank. The board of directors of a corporation functions more or less as its collective legal guardian, and formal actions of the board are the actions of the corporation. Since a corporation can act only through its agents, some individual agents will have authority to act for the corporation in a variety of situations. But their authority is only effective insofar as it can be traced back to a board of directors' action (or, in a few cases not relevant here, to the action of stockholders): either through an express grant of authority from the board, or impliedly, for example through the board's having placed the individual in a corporate office or position which carries the inherent authority to act for the corporation in certain transactions.[8] *See generally Chase,* 744 F.2d at 568–569; 2 Fletcher, *Cyclopedia of the Law of Private Corporations,* §§ 434, 444, 483.1 (1982). If the authority is based on ratification, again that ratification must be traceable ultimately to the board of directors, either because the board expressly adopted a transaction, or because it knew or should have known all the material facts and behaved in a way that implied ratification.

With these basic principles in mind, our analysis turns first to the evidence for express actual authority. Thomas held a power of attorney ostensibly executed on behalf of the bank, which made the account discretionary. However, that document was signed by Christiansen alone and the board denies all knowledge of it. For purposes of summary judgment, then, it can function as a binding grant of authority from the bank only if Christiansen indisputably already held authority from the board to give Thomas such power. For Christiansen to have such authority, it would have to stem either from the board's express grant of authority to him for commodities transactions, or from his inherent authority as chief executive officer of the bank.

Neither line is without dispute. If the ostensible source was Christiansen's own power to buy and sell, then the power of attorney is presumptively void as a matter of law. As a general rule an agent can delegate to someone else the ministerial tasks which his principal has assigned to him, but not those which require the exercise of judgment or discretion. 1 *Restatement of the Law of Agency 2d,* §§ 18, 78 (1958). The rule is less strictly applied when the principal is a corporation. But, nevertheless, a corporate officer normally "has no authority to delegate special powers conferred on him, and which involve the exercise of judgment or discretion, unless he is expressly authorized to do so, or unless the circumstances are such that the authority is necessarily implied." 2 Fletcher, *Cyclopedia,* § 503. Since buying and selling commodities involves the exercise of judgment and discretion, and the bank selected Christiansen and McGreal to do it, the law presumes that neither of them has the authority to delegate that trust to another. Conti offers no proof to the contrary.

---

8. "Inherent authority" is a term adopted from 1 Restatement of the Law of Agency 2d, § § 8A. 161(b) (1958). It is used for the authority which arises when a principal designates an agent of a kind who ordinarily possesses certain powers. For example, a corporate president would be expected to have a range of inherent authority which more or less "goes with the office." *See, e.g., Lind v. Schenley Industries, Inc.,* 278 F.2d 79, 85 (3d Cir.1960). Illinois case law usually places this type of authority under the umbrella label of apparent authority, since the agent appears to a third party to have the authority which similarly situated agents customarily possess. *See, e.g., Corn Belt Bank v. Lincoln Savings and Loan Ass'n,* 119 Ill.App.3d 238, 456 N.E.2d 150, 74 Ill.Dec. 648 (4th Dist.1983). But it could just as well be considered a species of implied authority. When a principal gives an agent tasks to perform, the law will imply the authority reasonably necessary to carry them out. *See* the discussion in *Lind,* 278 F.2d at 84–85. Since the term "inherent authority" avoids this problem and has more precision than either "apparent" or "implied," it is used here.

Neither is it clear that Christiansen, as the bank's chief executive officer, had the inherent authority to execute such a power of attorney on behalf of the bank. Unquestionably, the president or chief executive officer of a corporation has very broad powers to bind the corporation by virtue of the office he holds. However, those powers extend only to transactions within the usual and ordinary business of the corporation. Persons doing business with a corporation are entitled to assume that a chief executive is authorized to act for it, as long as the transaction falls within ordinary bounds. Those seeking unusual or extraordinary arrangements, however, are not entitled to simply rely on the officer's own assertions of authority.

The question of what is unusual or extraordinary is normally one for the trier of fact, since it depends on the facts and circumstances of the business, the officer's position and the specific transaction. For example, in *Sacks v. Helene Curtis Industries, Inc.,* 340 Ill.App. 76, 91 N.E.2d 127 (1st Dist.1950), a corporate president had inherent authority to hire, but not to give a percentage of profits as compensation. Similarly, in *Melish v. Vogel,* 35 Ill.App.3d 125, 343 N.E.2d 17 (1st Dist.1975), the president had inherent authority to retain an attorney, but not for fifteen years. Both decisions found that a board would not normally allow a single officer to commit that great a proportion of corporate assets to another, without at least consulting the board. Here the power of attorney involved entrusting ultimately a far greater proportion of the bank's assets to Thomas. A trier of fact could reasonably infer that the grant was extraordinary and beyond Christiansen's inherent power. With Christiansen's authority to issue the power of attorney in dispute, it cannot serve as a basis for finding that Conti and Thomas are not liable as a matter of law.

Thomas, however, also maintains that Christiansen personally either authorized or ratified all the trades. Christiansen's silence of course does not refute the claim. Ordinarily, proof of Christiansen's approval would settle the issue. The board had expressly authorized Christiansen to buy and sell commodities. Third parties can normally rely on express grants of authority. However, if a third party knows or has reason to know that the agent with whom he is dealing is in fact exceeding his authority, the right to rely is extinguished. *Chase,* 744 F.2d at 569. For example, a third party who knows that an agent is faithless and engaged in a fraud on his principal, cannot join in the fraud and then claim innocent reliance on the agent's authority. *Fustok v. Conticommodity Services, Inc.,* 577 F.Supp. 852 (S.D.N.Y.1984), *complaint dismissed on other grounds,* 610 F.Supp. 986 (S.D.N.Y.1985); Restatement, § 166 and comment a.

A trier of fact could reasonably infer that Thomas knew, or should have been on notice, that Christiansen was exceeding his authority from the bank. Even an agent with an express grant of authority has no authority to act contrary to the known wishes and instructions of his principal. *Old Security Life Insurance Co. v. Continental Illinois National Bank,* 740 F.2d 1384, 1391 (7th Cir.1984). For example, when the agent's acts or assertions conflict with the reasonable inferences that can be drawn from a corporate resolution, a third party may be found on notice of limits to that agent's authority. *Old Security,* 740 F.2d at 1391. Here the bank had authorized Christiansen and McGreal to trade, but Christiansen alone purported to grant discretionary power over the bank's account to Thomas. The contradiction might have spurred a prudent person to make further inquiry. * * *[a]

NOTES

1. The *Evanston Bank* decision raises the question of what authority may result from a particular officer position. See also, e.g., Lee v. Jenkins Brothers, 268 F.2d 357 (2d Cir.), cert. denied, 361 U.S. 913, 80 S.Ct. 257, 4 L.Ed.2d 183 (1959). Courts frequently associate certain powers with traditional officer positions.

2. *President.* The president is usually viewed as having broad implied and apparent authority. In Schmidt v. Farm Credit Services, 977 F.2d 511 (10th Cir.1992) the court held that although the corporate president lacked actual authority to mortgage certain assets, apparent authority was a question of fact. Compare e.g., Indian Acres Club of Thornburg v. Estate of Glover, 37 Va. Cir. 478, 1996 WL 1065481 (1996) (president lacked actual authority to execute lease assignment; third party's knowledge precluded a finding of actual authority). In Wishnow v. Kingsway Estates, Inc., 26 A.D.2d 61, 270 N.Y.S.2d 834 (1966), the court found that the president had the authority to engage a broker to sell real estate on behalf of the corporation. The court pointed out that this authority was not dependant on the president's having the authority to dispose of the real estate in question. The court further held that, since the broker was dealing with the President as agent, the president was not personally liable on the contract. For other cases involving the authority of corporate presidents see e.g., Bell Atlantic Tricon Leasing Corp. v. DRR, Inc., 114 N.C.App. 771, 443 S.E.2d 374, 376 (1994) (apparent authority of president); Lee v. Jenkins Brothers, 268 F.2d 357 (2d Cir.), cert. denied, 361 U.S. 913, 80 S.Ct. 257, 4 L.Ed.2d 183 (1959) (president had power to enter into ordinary but not extraordinary employment contracts); Ennis Business Forms, Inc. v. Todd, 523 S.W.2d 83 (Tex.Civ.App.1975)(discussion of ordinary versus extraordinary employment contracts); Goldenberg v. Bartell Broadcasting Corp., 47 Misc.2d 105, 262 N.Y.S.2d 274 (1965) (employment contract calling for payment of corporate stock not enforceable on basis of apparent authority); Schwartz v. United Merchants & Manufacturers, Inc., 72 F.2d 256 (2d Cir.1934) (president did not have apparent authority to enter into unusual exclusive selling agent arrangement); Hessler, Inc. v. Farrell, 226 A.2d 708 (Del.1967) (president had authority to obligate the corporation for retirement benefits. The court further held that the statute of frauds did not

---

[a]. For a similar result involving an employee who was not the customer's president, *see* Drexel Burnham Lambert Inc. v. CFTC, 850 F.2d 742 (D.C.Cir.1988), where a corporation claimed it had been injured by its broker through a series commodities orders placed by an employee of the customer with the defendant broker. The customer's employee who dealt with the broker was a compulsive gambler and convicted felon. The court upheld the customer's claim that the employee was not authorized to enter the trades at issue and that liability should therefore rest with the broker who accepted the unauthorized orders. The court upheld finding that the broker acted with "willful disregard" of whether the customer's employee had authority to trade on behalf of customer. [eds.]

bar enforcement of the president's oral promise of retirement benefits). The role of the president has largely been superseded by the chief executive officer in many large corporations, leaving the apparent authority of the president as uncertain.

3. *Chairman and Chief Executive Officer.* The apparent authority of the chairman of the board and chief executive officer is uncertain. In many instances the chief executive officer has replaced the president as the dominant official in large corporations. The chief executive officer may also hold the dual title of chairman of the board of directors. The chairman position may in some instances be simply titular for an older executive who has been "kicked upstairs." In other instances, the chairman is the senior management executive and may carry apparent authority in that role. See generally Management Technologies, Inc. v. Morris, 961 F.Supp. 640, 646–647 (S.D.N.Y. 1997) (discussion concerning the apparent authority of a chief executive officer); Wojcik v. Lewis, 204 Ga.App. 301, 419 S.E.2d 135 (1992) (issue of fact raised as to whether chairman of board was acting in personal rather than corporate capacity in granting an employment contract).

4. *Vice Presidents.* There is no inherent power in the vice president title, but the functions generally performed by someone with a vice president title can create apparent authority. See e.g., Townsend v. Daniel, Mann, Johnson & Mendenhall, 196 F.3d 1140 (10th Cir.1999) (discussion concerning the apparent authority of a corporate vice president); Kanavos v. Hancock Bank & Trust Co., 14 Mass.App.Ct. 326, 439 N.E.2d 311 (1982) (sufficient evidence to support apparent authority); C.E. Towers Co. v. Trinidad and Tobago (BWIA International Airways Corp., 903 F.Supp. 515, 522–525 (S.D.N.Y.1995) (senior vice president had apparent authority to enter into a lease); Thomas Register of American Manufacturers, Inc. v. Proto Systems Electronic Packaging, Inc., 221 Ga.App. 779, 471 S.E.2d 235 (1996) (issue of fact existed as to whether sales vice president had apparent or actual authority to order advertisement, but corporation ratified the contract). Frequently, the vice president's title will carry with it a description of functions of the office. For example, the First Vice President may succeed to the president and otherwise preside in the president's absence.

5. *Treasurer.* The position of treasurer is generally ministerial—to sign checks and otherwise deal with financial matters. See e.g., Ideal Foods, Inc. v. Action Leasing Corp., 413 So.2d 416 (Fla.App.1982); John and Mary Markle Foundation v. Manufacturers Hanover Trust Company, 209 A.D.2d 587, 619 N.Y.S.2d 109, 111 (1994) (corporate treasurer did not have apparent authority to circumvent corporate resolution requiring two signatures on checks); Varney Bros. Sand & Gravel, Inc. v. Champagne, 46 Mass.App.Ct. 54, 703 N.E.2d 721, 725 (1998) (corporate treasurer did not have apparent authority to bind corporation to a lifetime stipend and a life interest in corporate assets for the benefit of the treasurer's nursing aide).

6. *Chief Financial Officer.* In contrast to the ministerial position of treasurer, many companies have a policy-making financial officer—the Chief Financial Officer. Unlike someone functioning merely as a treasurer, the CFO has discretionary decision-making authority. This could include borrowing large sums from banks or other sources, investing excess funds on behalf of

the corporation and even restructuring operations in order to improve profits. In some corporations, the treasurer and chief financial officer are the same person, while in others the two functions are separated. Many corporations (especially closely held ones) do not have a policy-making financial officer.

The role of CFOs have come under close scrutiny as a result of the Enron and other financial scandals. The CFOs of the firms involved in those accounting manipulations were often found to be the architects of the fraud. Andrew Fastow at Enron and Scott Sullivan at WorldCom were particularly innovative in their accounting manipulations. HealthSouth Corp. in Birmingham, Alabama was one of the largest provider's of out patient health services, reporting revenues of $4 billion. That company's management improperly accounted for some $2.7 billion of assets and earnings. All five of the company's chief financial officers over a fifteen year period were among those pleading guilty to fraud charges.

7. *Corporate Secretary.* The corporate secretary's power is purely ministerial. The secretary's function is to certify corporate action and ensure that corporate acts have been duly authorized. See e.g., Contel Credit Corp. v. Central Chevrolet, Inc., 29 Mass.App.Ct. 83, 557 N.E.2d 77 (1990). The certification by the secretary will bind the corporation. As such, the secretary is the keeper of the corporate seal. The secretary does not possess any discretionary authority. See e.g., Ideal Foods, Inc. v. Action Leasing Corp. 413 So.2d 416 (Fla.App.1982) (corporate secretary-treasurer did not have apparent authority to bind corporation on a lease); Gaar v. Gaar's Inc., 994 S.W.2d 612 (Mo.App.1999) (corporate secretary had no inherent power to obligate corporation to pay money). Although purely ministerial, the corporate secretary's authority is still significant. A third party seeking reassurance that a transaction is authorized may rely with impunity on the secretary's certification. The secretary's certification trumps the absence of actual authority with respect to the act in question.

8. *Others.* Other corporate officials may be clothed with apparent authority by their offices. See e.g., Rodowicz v. Massachusetts Mutual Life Ins. Co., 192 F.3d 162 (1st Cir.1999) (human resources personnel clothed with at least apparent authority to speak on behalf of company on retirement issues but not other officers, even more senior executives, working elsewhere in the corporation).

9. *Belt and Suspenders.* The above cases and discussion illustrate the dangers of dealing with a corporate agent. Such agents may be acting outside the scope of their authority and a trial may be necessary to determine whether they had apparent authority to bind the corporation. The risk of lack of authority may reasonably be assumed in transactions that involve small sums. In larger transactions, however, your client may want both a belt and suspenders to assure that the transaction has been fully and properly authorized by a corporate counter party. Your job as a corporate lawyer may be to assure that the corporate officers representing a corporation have actual authority. This will involve examination of the relevant state law governing the corporation, the company's charter, by-laws and corporate minutes, etc. You may even be asked to give an opinion that your client has expressly authorized the transactions and that the officers signing have the requisite authority. The flow chart set forth on page 201 traces the sources of authority through this process.

CHAPTER 7

THE DUTY OF CARE

■ ■ ■

SECTION 1. THE STANDARD OF CARE

BATES v. DRESSER

251 U.S. 524, 40 S.Ct. 247, 64 L.Ed. 388 (1920).

MR. JUSTICE HOLMES DELIVERED THE OPINION OF THE COURT.

This is a bill in equity brought by the receiver of a national bank to charge its former president and directors with the loss of a great part of its assets through the thefts of an employee of the bank while they were in power. The case was sent to a master who found for the defendants; but the District Court entered a decree against all of them. The Circuit Court of Appeals reversed this decree, dismissed the bill as against all except the administrator of Edwin Dresser, the president, cut down the amount with which he was charged and refused to add interest from the date of the decree of the District Court. Dresser's administrator and the receiver both appeal, the latter contending that the decree of the District Court should be affirmed with interest and costs.

The bank was a little bank at Cambridge with a capital of $100,000 and average deposits of somewhere about $300,000. It had a cashier, a bookkeeper, a teller and a messenger. Before and during the time of the losses Dresser was its president and executive officer, a large stockholder, with an inactive deposit of from $35,000 to $50,000. From July, 1903, to the end, Frank L. Earl was cashier. Coleman, who made the trouble, entered the service of the bank as messenger in September, 1903. In January, 1904, he was promoted to be bookkeeper, being then not quite eighteen but having studied bookkeeping. In the previous August an auditor employed on the retirement of a cashier had reported that the daily balance book was very much behind, that it was impossible to prove the deposits, and that a competent bookkeeper should be employed upon the work immediately. Coleman kept the deposit ledger and this was the work that fell into his hands. There was no cage in the bank, and in 1904 and 1905 there were some small shortages in the accounts of three successive tellers that were not accounted for, and the last of them, Cutting, was asked by Dresser to resign on that ground. Before doing so he told Dresser that someone had taken the money and that if he might be

241

allowed to stay he would set a trap and catch the man, but Dresser did not care to do that and thought that there was nothing wrong. From Cutting's resignation on October 7, 1905, Coleman acted as paying and receiving teller, in addition to his other duty, until November, 1907. During this time there were no shortages disclosed in the teller's accounts. In May, 1906, Coleman took $2,000 cash from the vaults of the bank, but restored it the next morning. In November of the same year he began the thefts that come into question here. Perhaps in the beginning he took the money directly. But as he ceased to have charge of the cash in November, 1907, he invented another way. Having a small account at the bank, he would draw checks for the amount he wanted, exchange checks with a Boston broker, get cash for the broker's check, and, when his own check came to the bank through the clearing house, would abstract it from the envelope, enter the others on his book and conceal the difference by a charge to some other account or a false addition in the column of drafts or deposits in the depositors' ledger. He handed to the cashier only the slip from the clearing house that showed the totals. The cashier paid whatever appeared to be due and thus Coleman's checks were honored. So far as Coleman thought it necessary, in view of the absolute trust in him on the part of all concerned, he took care that his balances should agree with those in the cashier's book.

By May 1, 1907, Coleman had abstracted $17,000, concealing the fact by false additions in the column of total checks, and false balances in the deposit ledger. Then for the moment a safer concealment was effected by charging the whole to Dresser's account. Coleman adopted this method when a bank examiner was expected. Of course when the fraud was disguised by overcharging a depositor it could not be discovered except by calling in the passbooks, or taking all the deposit slips and comparing them with the depositors's ledger in detail. By November, 1907, the amount taken by Coleman was $30,100, and the charge on Dresser's account was $20,000. In 1908 the sum was raised from $33,000 to $49,671. In 1909 Coleman's activity began to increase. In January he took $6,829.26; in March, $10,833.73; in June, his previous stealings amounting to $83,390.94, he took $5,152.06; in July, $18,050; in August, $6,250; in September, $17,350; in October, $47,277.08; in November, $51,847; in December, $46,956.44; in January, 1910, $27,395.53; in February, $6,473.97; making a total of $310,143.02, when the bank closed on February 21, 1910. As a result of this the amount of the monthly deposits seemed to decline noticeably and the directors considered the matter in September, but concluded that the falling off was due in part to the springing up of rivals, whose deposits were increasing, but was parallel to a similar decrease in New York. An examination by a bank examiner in December, 1909, disclosed nothing wrong to him.

In this connection it should be mentioned that in the previous semi-annual examinations by national bank examiners nothing was discovered pointing to malfeasance. The cashier was honest and everybody believed that they could rely upon him, although in fact he relied too much upon

Coleman, who also was unsuspected by all. If Earl had opened the envelopes from the clearing house, and had seen the checks, or had examined the deposit ledger with any care he would have found out what was going on. The scrutiny of anyone accustomed to such details would have discovered the false additions and other indicia of fraud that were on the face of the book. But it may be doubted whether anything less than a continuous pursuit of the figures through pages would have done so except by a lucky chance.

The question of the liability of the directors in this case is the question whether they neglected their duty by accepting the cashier's statement of liabilities and failing to inspect the depositors' ledger. The statements of assets always were correct. A bylaw that had been allowed to become obsolete or nearly so is invoked as establishing their own standard of conduct. By that a committee was to be appointed every six months 'to examine into the affairs of the bank, to count its cash, and compare its assets and liabilities with the balances on the general ledger, for the purpose of ascertaining whether or not the books are correctly kept, and the condition of the bank in a sound and solvent condition.' Of course liabilities as well as assets must be known to know the condition and, as this case shows, peculations may be concealed as well by a false understatement of liabilities as by a false show of assets. But the former is not the direction in which fraud would have been looked for, especially on the part of one who at the time of his principal abstractions was not in contact with the funds. A debtor hardly expects to have his liability understated. Some animals must have given at least one exhibition of dangerous propensities before the owner can be held. This fraud was a novelty in the way of swindling a bank so far as the knowledge of any experience had reached Cambridge before 1910. We are not prepared to reverse the finding of the master and the Circuit Court of Appeals that the directors should not be held answerable for taking the cashier's statement of liabilities to be as correct as the statement of assets always was. If he had not been negligent without their knowledge it would have been. Their confidence seemed warranted by the semiannual examinations by the Government examiner and they were encouraged in their belief that all was well by the president, whose responsibility, as executive officer; interest, as large stockholder and depositor; and knowledge, from long daily presence in the bank, were greater than theirs. They were not bound by virtue of the office gratuitously assumed by them to call in the pass books and compare them with the ledger, and until the event showed the possibility they hardly could have seen that their failure to look at the ledger opened a way to fraud. We are not laying down general principles, however, but confine our decision to the circumstances of the particular case.

The position of the president is different. Practically he was the master of the situation. He was daily at the bank for hours, he had the deposit ledger in his hands at times and might have had it at any time. He had had hints and warnings in addition to those that we have mentioned, warnings that should not be magnified unduly, but still that taken with the auditor's report of 1903, the unexplained shortages, the suggestion of the teller, Cutting, in 1905, and the final seeming rapid decline in deposits, would have induced scrutiny but for an invincible repose upon the status quo. In 1908 one Fillmore learned that a package containing $150 left with the bank for safe keeping was not to be found, told Dresser of the loss, wrote to him that he could not conclude that the package had been destroyed or removed by someone connected with the bank, and in later conversation said that it was evident that there was a thief in the bank. He added that he would advise the president to look after Coleman, that he believed he was living at a pretty fast pace, and that he had pretty good authority for thinking that he was supporting a woman. In the same year or the year before, Coleman, whose pay was never more than twelve dollars a week, set up an automobile, as was known to Dresser and commented on unfavorably, to him. There was also some evidence of notice to Dresser that Coleman was dealing in copper stocks. In 1909 came the great and inadequately explained seeming shrinkage in the deposits. No doubt plausible explanations of his conduct came from Coleman and the notice as to speculations may have been slight, but taking the whole story of the relations of the parties, we are not ready to say that the two courts below erred in finding that Dresser had been put upon his guard. However little the warnings may have pointed to the specific facts, had they been accepted they would have led to an examination of the depositors' ledger, a discovery of past and a prevention of future thefts.

* * * In accepting the presidency Dresser must be taken to have contemplated responsibility for losses to the bank, whatever they were, if chargeable to his fault. Those that happened were chargeable to his fault, after he had warnings that should have led to steps that would have made fraud impossible, even though the precise form that the fraud would take hardly could have been foreseen. We accept with hesitation the date of December 1, 1908, as the beginning of Dresser's liability, but think it reasonable that interest should be charged against his estate upon the sum found by the Circuit Court of Appeals to be due.

MR. JUSTICE MCKENNA and MR. JUSTICE PITNEY dissent, upon the ground that not only the administrator of the president of the bank but the other directors ought to be held liable to the extent to which they were held by the District Court.

MR. JUSTICE VAN DEVANTER and MR. JUSTICE BRANDEIS took no part in the decision.

NOTES

1. Model Bus. Corp. Act § 8.30 allows directors in carrying out their duties to rely on corporate records and on the reports of officers, employees and third parties such as lawyers and accountants. Del. § 141(e) provides similar relief, stating that directors shall be "fully protected in relying in good faith" upon such reports. Would these statutes now absolve Mr. Dresser of personal liability for Coleman's defalcations?

2. Will imposing liability on persons in Mr. Dresser's position encourage excess caution? Is that good for business? How far should officers and directors go in imposing monitoring costs, which at the end of the day the shareholders will have to bear? Do you agree with the dissent in *Bates v. Dresser* that the other directors should also have been held liable?

3. Was Justice Holmes being entirely fair to the president? Hindsight is twenty-twenty. All fraud would be stopped in its tracks with its piercing light. Indeed, with its benefit, no one would ever lose money in the stock market and no battle in any war would be lost. Government investigations of financial fraud often take months or years of intensive work by professional investigators, accountants and lawyers, who armed with subpoenas, access to phone and other records and often using informants' make the case. Even then, their charges do not always stand up in court. Dresser appeared to be a trusting and well-meaning man, but he is certainly no trained investigator, and other corporate officers are unlikely to have such qualifications. Is it, therefore, really fair to impose personal liability on an officer for a fraud he did not commit, indeed, was even a victim of that fraud? Nevertheless, we must impose some duties on officers to protect the assets of the corporation. How do we draw that line? Did Justice Holmes get it right?

4. To what extent can a company's management insulate themselves from liability by creating a corporate structure that permits deniability? Graham v. Allis–Chalmers Manufacturing Co., 188 A.2d 125 (Del.1963) involved a derivative suit against a company's directors for failing to have prevented illegal price fixing that led to substantial judgments against the company. In refusing to hold the directors accountable, the court pointed to the corporate structure:

> The precise charge made against these director defendants is that, even though they had no knowledge of any suspicion of wrongdoing on the part of the company's employees, they still should have put into effect a system of watchfulness which would have brought such misconduct to their attention in ample time to have brought it to an end. However, the Briggs case expressly rejects such an idea. On the contrary, it appears that directors are entitled to rely on the honesty and integrity of their subordinates until something occurs to put them on suspicion that something is wrong. If such occurs and goes unheeded, then liability of the directors might well follow, but absent cause for suspicion there is no duty upon the directors to install and operate a corporate system of espionage to ferret out wrongdoing which they have no reason to suspect exists.

> The duties of the Allis–Chalmers Directors were fixed by the nature of the enterprise which employed in excess of 30,000 persons, and extended over a large geographical area. By force of necessity, the company's Directors could not know personally all the company's employees. The very magnitude of the enterprise required them to confine their control to the broad policy decisions. That they did this is clear from the record. At the meetings of the Board in which all Directors participated, these questions were considered and decided on the basis of summaries, reports and corporate records. These they were entitled to rely on, not

only, we think, under general principles of the common law, but by reason of 8 Del.C. § 141(e) as well, which in terms fully protects a director who relies on such in the performance of his duties.

In the last analysis, the question of whether a corporate director has become liable for losses to the corporation through neglect of duty is determined by the circumstances. If he has recklessly reposed confidence in an obviously untrustworthy employee, has refused or neglected cavalierly to perform his duty as a director, or has ignored either willfully or through inattention obvious danger signs of employee wrongdoing, the law will cast the burden of liability upon him. This is not the case at bar, however, for as soon as it became evident that there were grounds for suspicion, the Board acted promptly to end it and prevent its recurrence.

Plaintiffs say these steps should have been taken long before, even in the absence of suspicion, but we think not, for we know of no rule of law which requires a corporate director to assume, with no justification whatsoever, that all corporate employees are incipient law violators who, but for a tight checkrein, will give free vent to their unlawful propensities.

We therefore affirm the Vice Chancellor's ruling that the individual director defendants are not liable as a matter of law merely because, unknown to them, some employees of Allis–Chalmers violated the antitrust laws thus subjecting the corporation to loss.

5. The *Graham* decision was criticized by the American Law Institute in its Principles of Corporate Governance: Analysis and recommendations 165–166 (1994):

The *Allis-Chalmers* case was decided nearly 30 years ago.... Today, an ordinarily prudent person serving as the director of a corporation of any significant scale should recognize the need to be reasonably concerned with the existence and effectiveness of procedures, programs, and other techniques to assist the board in its oversight role.

It has also been suggested that:

The corporate director should be concerned that the corporation has programs looking toward compliance with applicable laws and regulations, both foreign and domestic, that it circulates (as appropriate) policy statements to this effect to its employees and that it maintains procedures for monitoring such compliance.

ABA, Corporate Director's Guidebook, 33 Bus. Law. 1591, 1610 (1978). See also, e.g., Business Roundtable Statement of Position Concerning the Role of Corporate Directors, 33 Bus. Law. 2083, 2101 (1978).

6. Section 13(b) of the Securities Exchange Act of 1934, 15 U.S.C. § 78m(b), requires public companies to report on the adequacy of their systems of internal controls that are designed to detect misuse of corporate assets and other forms of mismanagement. Their accountants are also required by Section 10A of the Securities Exchange Act, 15 U.S.C. § 78j–1, to utilize procedures in their audits that are designed to detect illegal acts. The accountants must report illegal acts they uncover to management and, if not remedied, to the board of directors. The company must then report that

information to the Securities and Exchange Commission. Should accountants be required to be policemen? Should companies have to inform on themselves?

7. The internal controls described in note 6 above are supplemented by the provisions of the Sarbanes–Oxley Act of 2002. For example, section 404 of the Sarbanes–Oxley Act mandates SEC rulemaking requiring a company's annual report to address (1) management's responsibility for establishing and maintaining an adequate system of internal controls for financial reporting and (2) management's year-end assessment of the internal control system's effectiveness. The company's auditors must attest to, and report on management's assessment of the internal controls' effectiveness in accordance with standards established by the Public Company Accounting Oversight Board. The SEC rules as adopted specify the details of the required statement and auditor certification. The internal controls are furthered strengthened by the Sarbanes–Oxley Act's requirements that the Chief Executive Officer and Chief Financial Officer each personally certify the accuracy of disclosures in SEC filings.

BARNES v. ANDREWS

298 F. 614 (S.D.N.Y.1924).

LEARNED HAND, DISTRICT JUDGE

This cause may be divided into three parts: First, the defendant's general liability for the collapse of the enterprise; second, his specific liability for overpayments made to Delano; third, his specific liability for the expenses of printing pamphlets and circulars used in selling the corporate shares.

The first liability must rest upon the defendant's general inattention to his duties as a director. He cannot be charged with neglect in attending directors' meetings, because there were only two during his incumbency, and of these he was present at one and had an adequate excuse for his absence from the other. His liability must therefore depend upon his failure in general to keep advised of the conduct of the corporate affairs. The measure of a director's duties in this regard is uncertain; the courts contenting themselves with vague declarations, such as that a director must give reasonable attention to the corporate business. While directors are collectively the managers of the company, they are not expected to interfere individually in the actual conduct of its affairs. To do so would disturb the authority of the officers and destroy their individual responsibility, without which no proper discipline is possible. To them must be left the initiative and the immediate direction of the business; the directors can act individually only by counsel and advice to them. Yet they have an individual duty to keep themselves informed in some detail, and it is this duty which the defendant in my judgment failed adequately to perform.

All he did was to talk with Maynard as they met, while commuting from Flushing, or at their homes. That, indeed, might be enough, because Andrews had no reason to suspect Maynard's candor, nor has any reason to question it been yet disclosed. But it is plain that he did not press him for details, as he should. It is not enough to content oneself with general answers that the business looks promising and that all seems prosperous. Andrews was bound, certainly as the months wore on, to inform himself of what was going on with some particularity, and, if he had done so, he would have learned that there were delays in getting into production which were putting the enterprise in most serious peril. It is entirely clear from his letters of April 14, 1920, and June 21, 1920, that he had made no effort to keep advised of the actual conduct of the corporate affairs, but had allowed himself to be carried along as a figurehead, in complete reliance upon Maynard. In spite of his own substantial investment in the company, which I must assume was as dear to him as it would be to other men, his position required of him more than this. Having accepted a post of confidence, he was charged with an active duty to learn whether the company was moving to production, and why it was not, and to consider, as best he might, what could be done to avoid the conflicts among the personnel, or their incompetence, which was slowly bleeding it to death.

Therefore I cannot acquit Andrews of misprision in his office, though his integrity is unquestioned. The plaintiff must, however, go further than to show that he should have been more active in his duties. This cause of action rests upon a tort, as much though it be a tort of omission as though it had rested upon a positive act. The plaintiff must accept the burden of showing that the performance of the defendant's duties would have avoided loss, and what loss it would have avoided. I pressed Mr. Alger to show me a case in which the courts have held that a director could be charged generally with the collapse of a business in respect of which he had been inattentive, and I am not aware that he has found one. * * *

* * * When the corporate funds have been illegally lent, it is a fair inference that a protest would have stopped the loan, and that the director's neglect caused the loss. But when a business fails from general mismanagement, business incapacity, or bad judgment, how is it possible to say that a single director could have made the company successful, or how much in dollars he could have saved? Before this cause can go to a master, the plaintiff must show that, had Andrews done his full duty, he could have made the company prosper, or at least could have broken its fall. He must show what sum he could have saved the company. Neither of these has he made any effort to do.

The defendant is not subject to the burden of proving that the loss would have happened, whether he had done his duty or not. If he were, it would come to this: That, if a director were once shown slack in his duties, he would stand charged prima facie with the difference between the corporate treasury as it was, and as it would be, judged by a hypothetical standard of success. How could such a standard be determined? How could any one guess how far a director's skill and judgment would have prevailed upon his fellows, and what would have been the ultimate fate of the business, if they had? How is it possible to set any measure of liability, or to tell what he would have contributed to the event? Men's fortunes may not be subjected to such uncertain and speculative conjectures. It is hard to see how there can be any remedy, except one can put one's finger on a definite loss and say with reasonable assurance that protest would have deterred, or counsel persuaded, the managers who caused it. No men of sense would take the office, if the law imposed upon them a guaranty of the general success of their companies as a penalty for any negligence.

It is, indeed, hard to determine just what went wrong in the management of this company. Any conclusion is little better than a guess. Still some discussion of the facts is necessary, and I shall discuss them. The claim that there were too many general employees turned out to be true, but, so far as I can see, only because of the delay in turning out the finished product. Had the factory gone into production in the spring of 1920, I cannot say, and the plaintiff cannot prove, that the selling department would have been prematurely or extravagantly organized. The expense of the stock sales was apparently not undue, and in any event Andrews was helpless to prevent it, because he found the contract an existing obligation of the company. So far as I can judge, the company had a fair chance of life, if the factory could have begun to turn out starters at the time expected. Whether this was the fault of Delano, as I suspect, is now too uncertain to say. It seems to me to make no difference in the result whether Delano, through inattention, or through sickness, or through contempt for Taylor, or for all these reasons, did not send along 'Van Dycks,' or whether Taylor should have got along without them, or should have shown more initiative and competence than he did. Between them the production lagged, until it was too late to resuscitate the dying company; its funds had oozed out in fixed payments, till there was nothing left with which to continue the business.

Suppose I charge Andrews with a complete knowledge of all that we have now learned. What action should he have taken, and how can I say that it would have stopped the losses? The plaintiff gives no definite answer to that question. Certainly he had no right to interject himself personally into the tangle; that was for Maynard to unravel. He would scarcely have helped to a solution by adding another cook to the broth. What suggestion could he have made to Maynard, or to his colleagues? The trouble arose either from an indifferent engineer, on whom the company was entirely dependent, or from an incompetent factory manager, who should have been discharged, or because the executives were themselves inefficient. Is Andrews to be charged for not insisting upon Taylor's discharge, or for not suggesting it? Suppose he did suggest it; have I the slightest reason for saying that the directors would have discharged him? Or, had they discharged him, is it certain that a substitute employed in medias res would have speeded up production? Was there not as fair a chance that Delano and Taylor might be brought to an accommodation as there was in putting in a green man at that juncture? How can I, sitting here, lay it down that Andrews' intervention would have brought order out of this chaos, or how can I measure in dollars the losses he would have saved? Or am I to hold Andrews because he did not move to discharge Maynard? How can I know that a better man was available? It is easy to say that he should have done something, but that will not serve to harness upon him the whole loss, nor is it the equivalent of saying that, had he acted, the company would now flourish.

True, he was not very well-suited by experience for the job he had undertaken, but I cannot hold him on that account. After all, it is the same corporation that chose him which now seeks to charge him. I cannot agree with the language of Hun v. Cary, supra, that in effect he gave an implied warranty of any special fitness. Directors are not specialists, like lawyers or doctors. They must have good sense, perhaps they must have acquaintance with affairs; but they need not—indeed, perhaps they should not—have any technical talent. They are the general advisers of the business, and if they faithfully give such ability as they have to their charge, it would not be lawful to hold them liable. Must a director guarantee that his judgment is good? Can shareholders call him to account for deficiencies which their votes assured him did not disqualify him for his office? While he may not have been the Cromwell for that Civil War, Andrews did not engage to play any such role.

I conclude, therefore, as to this first claim that there is no evidence that the defendant's neglect caused any losses to the company, and that, if there were, that loss cannot be ascertained.

NOTE

Putting a strict burden of causation on the plaintiff means that, even if a breach of reasonable care is established, many damage actions like the one in *Barnes v. Andrews* will, nevertheless, fail. In Cede & Co. v. Technicolor, Inc., 634 A.2d 345, 371 (Del.1993), the Delaware Supreme Court concluded that the *Barnes* case was a tort case (negligence) and would not control liability in cases involving breaches of an officer's or director's fiduciary duties. The Court in *Cede* stated that:

> This Court has consistently held that the breach of the duty of care, without any requirement of proof of injury.... rebuts the presumption that the directors have acted in the best interests of the shareholders, and requires the directors to prove that the transaction was entirely fair.

SECTION 2. THE BUSINESS JUDGMENT RULE

SHLENSKY v. WRIGLEY

95 Ill.App.2d 173, 237 N.E.2d 776 (1968).

SULLIVAN, JUSTICE.

This is an appeal from a dismissal of plaintiff's amended complaint on motion of the defendants. The action was a stockholders' derivative suit against the directors for negligence and mismanagement. The corporation was also made a defendant. Plaintiff sought damages and an order that defendants cause the installation of lights in Wrigley Field and the scheduling of night baseball games.

Plaintiff is a minority stockholder of defendant corporation, Chicago National League Ball Club (Inc.), a Delaware corporation with its principal place of business in Chicago, Illinois. Defendant corporation owns and operates the major league professional baseball team known as the Chicago Cubs. The corporation also engages in the operation of Wrigley Field, the Cubs' home park, the concessionaire sales during Cubs' home games, television and radio broadcasts of Cubs' home games, the leasing of the field for football games and other events and receives its share, as visiting team, of admission moneys from games played in other National League stadia. The individual defendants are directors of the Cubs and have served for varying periods of years. Defendant Philip K. Wrigley is also president of the corporation and owner of approximately 80% of the stock therein.

Plaintiff alleges that since night baseball was first played in 1935 nineteen of the twenty major league teams have scheduled night games. In 1966, out of a total of 1620 games in the major leagues, 932 were played at night. Plaintiff alleges that every member of the major leagues, other than the Cubs, scheduled substantially all of its home games in 1966 at night, exclusive of opening days, Saturdays, Sundays, holidays and days prohibited by league rules. Allegedly this has been done for the specific purpose of maximizing attendance and thereby maximizing revenue and income.

The Cubs, in the years 1961–65, sustained operating losses from its direct baseball operations. Plaintiff attributes those losses to inadequate attendance at Cubs' home games. He concludes that if the directors continue to refuse to install lights at Wrigley Field and schedule night baseball games, the Cubs will continue to sustain comparable losses and its financial condition will continue to deteriorate.

Plaintiff alleges that, except for the year 1963, attendance at Cubs' home games has been substantially below that at their road games, many of which were played at night.

Plaintiff compares attendance at Cubs' games with that of the Chicago White Sox, an American League club, whose weekday games were generally played at night. The weekend attendance figures for the two teams was similar; however, the White Sox week-night games drew many more patrons than did the Cubs' weekday games.

Plaintiff alleges that the funds for the installation of lights can be readily obtained through financing and the cost of installation would be far more than offset and recaptured by increased revenues and incomes resulting from the increased attendance.

Plaintiff further alleges that defendant Wrigley has refused to install lights, not because of interest in the welfare of the corporation but because of his personal opinions 'that baseball is a 'daytime sport' and that the installation of lights and night baseball games will have a deteriorating effect upon the surrounding neighborhood.' It is alleged that he has admitted that he is not interested in whether the Cubs would benefit financially from such action because of his concern for the neighborhood, and that he would be willing for the team to play night games if a new stadium were built in Chicago.

Plaintiff alleges that the other defendant directors, with full knowledge of the foregoing matters, have acquiesced in the policy laid down by Wrigley and have permitted him to dominate the board of directors in matters involving the installation of lights and scheduling of night games, even though they knew he was not motivated by a good faith concern as to the best interests of defendant corporation, but solely by his personal views set forth above. It is charged that the directors are acting for a reason or reasons contrary and wholly unrelated to the business interests of the corporation; that such arbitrary and capricious acts constitute mismanagement and waste of corporate assets, and that the directors have been negligent in failing to exercise reasonable care and prudence in the management of the corporate affairs.

The question on appeal is whether plaintiff's amended complaint states a cause of action. It is plaintiff's position that fraud, illegality and conflict of interest are not the only bases for a stockholder's derivative action against the directors. Contrariwise, defendants argue that the courts will not step in and interfere with honest business judgment of the directors unless there is a showing of fraud, illegality or conflict of interest.

The cases in this area are numerous and each differs from the others on a factual basis. However, the courts have pronounced certain ground rules which appear in all cases and which are then applied to the given factual situation. The court in Wheeler v. Pullman Iron and Steel Company, 143 Ill. 197, 207, 32 N.E. 420, 423, said:

> It is, however, fundamental in the law of corporations, that the majority of its stockholders shall control the policy of the corporation, and regulate and govern the lawful exercise of its franchise and business. * * * Every one purchasing or subscribing for stock in a corporation impliedly agrees that he will be bound by the acts and proceedings done or sanctioned by a majority of the shareholders, or by the agents of the corporation duly chosen by such majority, within the scope of the powers conferred by the charter, and courts of equity will not undertake to control the policy or business methods of a corporation, although it may be seen that a wiser policy might be adopted and the business more successful if other methods were pursued. The majority of shares of its stock, or the agents by the holders thereof lawfully chosen, must be permitted to control the business of the corporation in their discretion, when not in violation of its charter or some public law, or corruptly and fraudulently

subversive of the rights and interests of the corporation or of a shareholder.

The standards set in Delaware are also clearly stated in the cases. In Davis v. Louisville Gas & Electric Co., 16 Del.Ch. 157, 142 A. 654, a minority shareholder sought to have the directors enjoined from amending the certificate of incorporation. The court said:

> We have then a conflict in view between the responsible managers of a corporation and an overwhelming majority of its stockholders on the one hand and a dissenting minority on the other—a conflict touching matters of business policy, such as has occasioned innumerable applications to courts to intervene and determine which of the two conflicting views should prevail. The response which courts make to such applications is that it is not their function to resolve for corporations questions of policy and business management. The directors are chosen to pass upon such questions and their judgment unless shown to be tainted with fraud is accepted as final. The judgment of the directors of corporations enjoys the benefit of a presumption that it was formed in good faith and was designed to promote the best interests of the corporation they serve.

* * * Plaintiff argues that the allegations of his amended complaint are sufficient to set forth a cause of action under the principles set out in Dodge v. Ford Motor Co., 204 Mich. 459, 170 N.W. 668. In that case plaintiff, owner of about 10% of the outstanding stock, brought suit against the directors seeking payment of additional dividends and the enjoining of further business expansion. In ruling on the request for dividends the court indicated that the motives of Ford in keeping so much money in the corporation for expansion and security were to benefit the public generally and spread the profits out by means of more jobs, etc. The court felt that these were not only far from related to the good of the stockholders, but amounted to a change in the ends of the corporation and that this was not a purpose contemplated or allowed by the corporate charter. * * *

From the authority relied upon in that case it is clear that the court felt that there must be fraud or a breach of that good faith which directors are bound to exercise toward the stockholders in order to justify the courts entering into the internal affairs of corporations. This is made clear when the court refused to interfere with the directors' decision to expand the business. The following appears on page 684 of 170 N.W.:

> We are not, however, persuaded that we should interfere with the proposed expansion of the business of the Ford Motor Company. In view of the fact that the selling price of products may be increased at any time, the ultimate results of the larger business cannot be certainly estimated. The judges are not business experts. It is recognized that plans must often be made for a long future, for expected competition, for a continuing as well as an immediately profitable venture. * * * We are not satisfied that the alleged motives of the

directors, in so far as they are reflected in the conduct of business, menace the interests of the shareholders.

Plaintiff in the instant case argues that the directors are acting for reasons unrelated to the financial interest and welfare of the Cubs. However, we are not satisfied that the motives assigned to Philip K. Wrigley, and through him to the other directors, are contrary to the best interests of the corporation and the stockholders. For example, it appears to us that the effect on the surrounding neighborhood might well be considered by a director who was considering the patrons who would or would not attend the games if the park were in a poor neighborhood. Furthermore, the long run interest of the corporation in its property value at Wrigley Field might demand all efforts to keep the neighborhood from deteriorating. By these thoughts we do not mean to say that we have decided that the decision of the directors was a correct one. That is beyond our jurisdiction and ability. We are merely saying that the decision is one properly before directors and the motives alleged in the amended complaint showed no fraud, illegality or conflict of interest in their making of that decision. * * *

There is no allegation that the night games played by the other nineteen teams enhanced their financial position or that the profits, if any, of those teams were directly related to the number of night games scheduled. There is an allegation that the installation of lights and scheduling of night games in Wrigley Field would have resulted in large amounts of additional revenues and incomes from increased attendance and related sources of income. Further, the cost of installation of lights, funds for which are allegedly readily available by financing, would be more than offset and recaptured by increased revenues. However, no allegation is made that there will be a net benefit to the corporation from such action, considering all increased costs.

Plaintiff claims that the losses of defendant corporation are due to poor attendance at home games. However, it appears from the amended complaint, taken as a whole, that factors other than attendance affect the net earnings or losses. For example, in 1962, attendance at home and road games decreased appreciably as compared with 1961, and yet the loss from direct baseball operation and of the whole corporation was considerably less.

The record shows that plaintiff did not feel he could allege that the increased revenues would be sufficient to cure the corporate deficit. The only cost plaintiff was at all concerned with was that of installation of lights. No mention was made of operation and maintenance of the lights or other possible increases in operating costs of night games and we cannot speculate as to what other factors might influence the increase or decrease of profits if the Cubs were to play night home games. * * *

Finally, we do not agree with plaintiff's contention that failure to follow the example of the other major league clubs in scheduling night games constituted negligence. Plaintiff made no allegation that these teams' night schedules were profitable or that the purpose for which night baseball had been undertaken was fulfilled. Furthermore, it cannot be said that directors, even those of corporations that are losing money, must follow the lead of the other corporations in the field. Directors are elected for their business capabilities and judgment and the courts cannot require them to forego their judgment because of the decisions of directors of other companies. Courts may not decide these questions in the absence of a clear showing of dereliction of duty on the part of the specific directors and mere failure to 'follow the crowd' is not such a dereliction.

NOTES

1. The Chicago Cubs management tried to add lights to Wrigley Field in 1982, but neighborhood opposition led to legislation banning them. In 1988, a compromise was reached under which the Cubs were allowed to light the field, but they were limited to only eighteen night games per season. Phil Vettel, "August 8, 1988; Button Brings Light to the Last Bastion of Daytime Baseball," Chicago Tribune, Nov. 23, 1997, Metro at 2. The lights did not bring the Cubs a World Series title; their last title was in 1908, and Wrigley field remains the smallest park in the major leagues.

2. Consider the following description of the business judgment rule:

> What should be understood, but may not widely be understood by courts or commentators who are not often required to face such questions, is that compliance with a director's duty of care can never appropriately be judicially determined by reference to *the content of the board decision* that leads to a corporate loss, apart from consideration of the good faith *or* rationality of the process employed. That is, whether a judge or jury considering the matter after the fact, believes a decision substantively wrong, or degrees of wrong extending through "stupid" to "egregious" or "irrational", provides no ground for director liability, so long as the court determines that the process employed was either rational or employed in *a good faith* effort to advance corporate interests. To employ a different rule—one that permitted an "objective" evaluation of the decision— would expose directors to substantive second guessing by ill-equipped judges or juries, which would, in the long-run, be injurious to investor interests. Thus, the business judgment rule is process oriented and informed by a deep respect for all *good faith* board decisions.

In re Caremark International, Inc. Derivative Litigation, 698 A.2d 959, 967– 968 (Del.Ch.1996). The Delaware Supreme Court had earlier explicated the business judgement rule in Cede & Co. v. Technicolor, Inc., 634 A.2d 345, 360–361 (Del.1993) as follows:

> Our starting point is the fundamental principle of Delaware law that the business and affairs of a corporation are managed by or under the direction of its board of directors. 8 *Del.C.* § 141(a). In exercising these powers, directors are charged with an unyielding fiduciary duty to protect the interests of the corporation and to act in the best interests of its shareholders.

The business judgment rule is an extension of these basic principles. The rule operates to preclude a court from imposing itself unreasonably on the business and affairs of a corporation. The rule, though formulated many years ago, was most recently restated by this Court as follows:

> The rule operates as both a procedural guide for litigants and a substantive rule of law. As a rule of evidence, it creates a "presumption that in making a business decision, the directors of a corporation acted on an informed basis [i.e., with due care], in good faith and in the honest belief that the action taken was in the best interest of the company."

Aronson v. Lewis, Del.Supr., 473 A.2d 805, 812 (1984). The presumption initially attaches to a director-approved transaction within a board's conferred or apparent authority in the absence of any evidence of "fraud, bad faith, or self-dealing in the usual sense of personal profit or betterment."

The rule posits a powerful presumption in favor of actions taken by the directors in that a decision made by a loyal and informed board will not be overturned by the courts unless it cannot be "attributed to any rational business purpose." Thus, a shareholder plaintiff challenging a board decision has the burden at the outset to rebut the rule's presumption. To rebut the rule, a shareholder plaintiff assumes the burden of providing evidence that directors, in reaching their challenged decision, breached any one of the *triads* of their fiduciary duty—good faith, loyalty or due care. If a shareholder plaintiff fails to meet this evidentiary burden, the business judgment rule attaches to protect corporate officers and directors and the decisions they make, and our courts will not second-guess these business judgments. If the rule is rebutted, the burden shifts to the defendant directors, the proponents of the challenged transaction, to prove to the trier of fact the "entire fairness" of the transaction to the shareholder plaintiff.

Delaware's process oriented approach to the directors' duty of care was further explored in the following landmark case.

SMITH v. VAN GORKOM

488 A.2d 858 (Del.1985).

HORSEY, JUSTICE (for the majority): * * *

The nature of this case requires a detailed factual statement. The following facts are essentially uncontradicted:

Trans Union was a publicly-traded, diversified holding company, the principal earnings of which were generated by its railcar leasing business. During the period here involved, the Company had a cash flow of hundreds of millions of dollars annually. However, the Company had difficulty in generating sufficient taxable income to offset increasingly large investment tax credits (ITCs). Accelerated depreciation deductions had decreased available taxable income against which to offset accumulating ITCs. The Company took these deductions, despite their effect on usable

ITCs, because the rental price in the railcar leasing market had already impounded the purported tax savings.

In the late 1970's, together with other capital-intensive firms, Trans Union lobbied in Congress to have ITCs refundable in cash to firms which could not fully utilize the credit. During the summer of 1980, defendant Jerome W. Van Gorkom, Trans Union's Chairman and Chief Executive Officer, testified and lobbied in Congress for refundability of ITCs and against further accelerated depreciation. By the end of August, Van Gorkom was convinced that Congress would neither accept the refundability concept nor curtail further accelerated depreciation.

Beginning in the late 1960's, and continuing through the 1970's, Trans Union pursued a program of acquiring small companies in order to increase available taxable income. In July 1980, Trans Union Management prepared the annual revision of the Company's Five Year Forecast. This report was presented to the Board of Directors at its July, 1980 meeting. The report projected an annual income growth of about 20%. The report also concluded that Trans Union would have about $195 million in spare cash between 1980 and 1985, "with the surplus growing rapidly from 1982 onward." The report referred to the ITC situation as a "nagging problem" and, given that problem, the leasing company "would still appear to be constrained to a tax breakeven." The report then listed four alternative uses of the projected 1982–1985 equity surplus: (1) stock repurchase; (2) dividend increases; (3) a major acquisition program; and (4) combinations of the above. The sale of Trans Union was not among the alternatives. The report emphasized that, despite the overall surplus, the operation of the Company would consume all available equity for the next several years, and concluded: "As a result, we have sufficient time to fully develop our course of action."

On August 27, 1980, Van Gorkom met with Senior Management of Trans Union. Van Gorkom reported on his lobbying efforts in Washington and his desire to find a solution to the tax credit problem more permanent than a continued program of acquisitions. Various alternatives were suggested and discussed preliminarily, including the sale of Trans Union to a company with a large amount of taxable income.

Donald Romans, Chief Financial Officer of Trans Union, stated that his department had done a "very brief bit of work on the possibility of a leveraged buy-out." This work had been prompted by a media article which Romans had seen regarding a leveraged buy-out by management. The work consisted of a "preliminary study" of the cash which could be generated by the Company if it participated in a leveraged buy-out. As Romans stated, this analysis "was very first and rough cut at seeing whether a cash flow would support what might be considered a high price for this type of transaction."

On September 5, at another Senior Management meeting which Van Gorkom attended, Romans again brought up the idea of a leveraged buy-out as a "possible strategic alternative" to the Company's acquisition program. Romans and Bruce S. Chelberg, President and Chief Operating Officer of Trans Union, had been working on the matter in preparation for the meeting. According to Romans: They did not "come up" with a price for the Company. They merely "ran the numbers" at $50 a share and at $60 a share with the "rough form" of their cash figures at the time. Their "figures indicated that $50 would be very easy to do but $60 would be very difficult to do under those figures." This work did not purport to establish a fair price for either the Company or 100% of the stock. It was intended to determine the cash flow needed to service the debt that would "probably" be incurred in a leveraged buy-out, based on "rough calculations" without "any benefit of experts to identify what the limits were to that, and so forth." These computations were not considered extensive and no conclusion was reached.

At this meeting, Van Gorkom stated that he would be willing to take $55 per share for his own 75,000 shares. He vetoed the suggestion of a leveraged buy-out by Management, however, as involving a potential conflict of interest for Management. Van Gorkom, a certified public accountant and lawyer, had been an officer of Trans Union for 24 years, its Chief Executive Officer for more than 17 years, and Chairman of its Board for 2 years. It is noteworthy in this connection that he was then approaching 65 years of age and mandatory retirement.

For several days following the September 5 meeting, Van Gorkom pondered the idea of a sale. He had participated in many acquisitions as a manager and director of Trans Union and as a director of other companies. He was familiar with acquisition procedures, valuation methods, and negotiations; and he privately considered the pros and cons of whether Trans Union should seek a privately or publicly-held purchaser.

Van Gorkom decided to meet with Jay A. Pritzker, a well-known corporate takeover specialist and a social acquaintance. However, rather than approaching Pritzker simply to determine his interest in acquiring Trans Union, Van Gorkom assembled a proposed per share price for sale of the Company and a financing structure by which to accomplish the sale. Van Gorkom did so without consulting either his Board or any members of Senior Management except one: Carl Peterson, Trans Union's Controller. Telling Peterson that he wanted no other person on his staff to know what he was doing, but without telling him why, Van Gorkom directed Peterson to calculate the feasibility of a leveraged buy-out at an assumed price per share of $55. Apart from the Company's historic stock market price,[5] and Van Gorkom's long association with Trans Union, the record is devoid of any competent evidence that $55 represented the per share intrinsic value of the Company.

Having thus chosen the $55 figure, based solely on the availability of a leveraged buy-out, Van Gorkom multiplied the price per share by the

---

5. The common stock of Trans Union was traded on the New York Stock Exchange. Over the five year period from 1975 through 1979, Trans Union's stock had traded within a range of a high of $39 1/2 and a low of $24 1/4 . Its high and low range for 1980 through September 19 (the last trading day before announcement of the merger) was $38 1/4-$29 1/2 .

number of shares outstanding to reach a total value of the Company of $690 million. Van Gorkom told Peterson to use this $690 million figure and to assume a $200 million equity contribution by the buyer. Based on these assumptions, Van Gorkom directed Peterson to determine whether the debt portion of the purchase price could be paid off in five years or less if financed by Trans Union's cash flow as projected in the Five Year Forecast, and by the sale of certain weaker divisions identified in a study done for Trans Union by the Boston Consulting Group ("BCG study"). Peterson reported that, of the purchase price, approximately $50–80 million would remain outstanding after five years. Van Gorkom was disappointed, but decided to meet with Pritzker nevertheless.

Van Gorkom arranged a meeting with Pritzker at the latter's home on Saturday, September 13, 1980. Van Gorkom prefaced his presentation by stating to Pritzker: "Now as far as you are concerned, I can, I think, show how you can pay a substantial premium over the present stock price and pay off most of the loan in the first five years. * * * If you could pay $55 for this Company, here is a way in which I think it can be financed."

Van Gorkom then reviewed with Pritzker his calculations based upon his proposed price of $55 per share. Although Pritzker mentioned $50 as a more attractive figure, no other price was mentioned. However, Van Gorkom stated that to be sure that $55 was the best price obtainable, Trans Union should be free to accept any better offer. Pritzker demurred, stating that his organization would serve as a "stalking horse" for an "auction contest" only if Trans Union would permit Pritzker to buy 1,750,000 shares of Trans Union stock at market price which Pritzker could then sell to any higher bidder. After further discussion on this point, Pritzker told Van Gorkom that he would give him a more definite reaction soon.

On Monday, September 15, Pritzker advised Van Gorkom that he was interested in the $55 cash-out merger proposal and requested more information on Trans Union. Van Gorkom agreed to meet privately with Pritzker, accompanied by Peterson, Chelberg, and Michael Carpenter, Trans Union's consultant from the Boston Consulting Group. The meetings took place on September 16 and 17. Van Gorkom was "astounded that events were moving with such amazing rapidity."

On Thursday, September 18, Van Gorkom met again with Pritzker. At that time, Van Gorkom knew that Pritzker intended to make a cash-out merger offer at Van Gorkom's proposed $55 per share. Pritzker instructed his attorney, a merger and acquisition specialist, to begin drafting merger documents. There was no further discussion of the $55 price. However, the number of shares of Trans Union's treasury stock to be offered to Pritzker was negotiated down to one million shares; the price was set at $38—75 cents above the per share price at the close of the market on September 19. At this point, Pritzker insisted that the Trans Union Board act on his merger proposal within the next three days, stating to Van Gorkom: "We have to have a decision by no later than

Sunday [evening, September 21] before the opening of the English stock exchange on Monday morning." Pritzker's lawyer was then instructed to draft the merger documents, to be reviewed by Van Gorkom's lawyer, "sometimes with discussion and sometimes not, in the haste to get it finished."

On Friday, September 19, Van Gorkom, Chelberg, and Pritzker consulted with Trans Union's lead bank regarding the financing of Pritzker's purchase of Trans Union. The bank indicated that it could form a syndicate of banks that would finance the transaction. On the same day, Van Gorkom retained James Brennan, Esquire, to advise Trans Union on the legal aspects of the merger. Van Gorkom did not consult with William Browder, a Vice–President and director of Trans Union and former head of its legal department, or with William Moore, then the head of Trans Union's legal staff.

On Friday, September 19, Van Gorkom called a special meeting of the Trans Union Board for noon the following day. He also called a meeting of the Company's Senior Management to convene at 11:00 a.m., prior to the meeting of the Board. No one, except Chelberg and Peterson, was told the purpose of the meetings. Van Gorkom did not invite Trans Union's investment banker, Salomon Brothers or its Chicago-based partner, to attend.

Of those present at the Senior Management meeting on September 20, only Chelberg and Peterson had prior knowledge of Pritzker's offer. Van Gorkom disclosed the offer and described its terms, but he furnished no copies of the proposed Merger Agreement. Romans announced that his department had done a second study which showed that, for a leveraged buy-out, the price range for Trans Union stock was between $55 and $65 per share. Van Gorkom neither saw the study nor asked Romans to make it available for the Board meeting.

Senior Management's reaction to the Pritzker proposal was completely negative. No member of Management, except Chelberg and Peterson, supported the proposal. Romans objected to the price as being too low;[6] he was critical of the timing and suggested that consideration should be given to the adverse tax consequences of an all-cash deal for low-basis shareholders; and he took the position that the agreement to sell Pritzker one million newly-issued shares at market price would inhibit other offers, as would the prohibitions against soliciting bids and furnishing inside information to other bidders. Romans argued that the Pritzker proposal was a "lock up" and amounted to "an agreed merger as opposed to an offer." Nevertheless, Van Gorkom proceeded to the Board meeting as scheduled without further delay.

---

6. Van Gorkom asked Romans to express his opinion as to the $55 price. Romans stated that he "thought the price was too low in relation to what he could derive for the company in a cash sale, particularly one which enabled us to realize the values of certain subsidiaries and independent entities."

Ten directors served on the Trans Union Board, five inside (defendants Bonser, O'Boyle, Browder, Chelberg, and Van Gorkom) and five outside (defendants Wallis, Johnson, Lanterman, Morgan and Reneker). All directors were present at the meeting, except O'Boyle who was ill. Of the outside directors, four were corporate chief executive officers and one was the former Dean of the University of Chicago Business School. None was an investment banker or trained financial analyst. All members of the Board were well informed about the Company and its operations as a going concern. They were familiar with the current financial condition of the Company, as well as operating and earnings projections reported in the recent Five Year Forecast. The Board generally received regular and detailed reports and was kept abreast of the accumulated investment tax credit and accelerated depreciation problem.

Van Gorkom began the Special Meeting of the Board with a twenty-minute oral presentation. Copies of the proposed Merger Agreement were delivered too late for study before or during the meeting.[7] He reviewed the Company's ITC and depreciation problems and the efforts theretofore made to solve them. He discussed his initial meeting with Pritzker and his motivation in arranging that meeting. Van Gorkom did not disclose to the Board, however, the methodology by which he alone had arrived at the $55 figure, or the fact that he first proposed the $55 price in his negotiations with Pritzker.

Van Gorkom outlined the terms of the Pritzker offer as follows: Pritzker would pay $55 in cash for all outstanding shares of Trans Union stock upon completion of which Trans Union would be merged into New T Company, a subsidiary wholly-owned by Pritzker and formed to implement the merger; for a period of 90 days, Trans Union could receive, but could not actively solicit, competing offers; the offer had to be acted on by the next evening, Sunday, September 21; Trans Union could only furnish to competing bidders published information, and not proprietary information; the offer was subject to Pritzker obtaining the necessary financing by October 10, 1980; if the financing contingency were met or waived by Pritzker, Trans Union was required to sell to Pritzker one million newly-issued shares of Trans Union at $38 per share.

Van Gorkom took the position that putting Trans Union "up for auction" through a 90-day market test would validate a decision by the Board that $55 was a fair price. He told the Board that the "free market will have an opportunity to judge whether $55 is a fair price." Van Gorkom framed the decision before the Board not as whether $55 per share was the highest price that could be obtained, but as whether the $55 price was a fair price that the stockholders should be given the opportuni-

---

7. The record is not clear as to the terms of the Merger Agreement. The Agreement, as originally presented to the Board on September 20, was never produced by defendants despite demands by the plaintiffs. Nor is it clear that the directors were given an opportunity to study the Merger Agreement before voting on it. All that can be said is that Brennan had the Agreement before him during the meeting.

ty to accept or reject.[8]

Attorney Brennan advised the members of the Board that they might be sued if they failed to accept the offer and that a fairness opinion was not required as a matter of law.

Romans attended the meeting as chief financial officer of the Company. He told the Board that he had not been involved in the negotiations with Pritzker and knew nothing about the merger proposal until the morning of the meeting; that his studies did not indicate either a fair price for the stock or a valuation of the Company; that he did not see his role as directly addressing the fairness issue; and that he and his people "were trying to search for ways to justify a price in connection with such a [leveraged buy-out] transaction, rather than to say what the shares are worth." Romans testified:

> I told the Board that the study ran the numbers at 50 and 60, and then the subsequent study at 55 and 65, and that was not the same thing as saying that I have a valuation of the company at X dollars. But it was a way—a first step towards reaching that conclusion.

Romans told the Board that, in his opinion, $55 was "in the range of a fair price," but "at the beginning of the range."

Chelberg, Trans Union's President, supported Van Gorkom's presentation and representations. He testified that he "participated to make sure that the Board members collectively were clear on the details of the agreement or offer from Pritzker;" that he "participated in the discussion with Mr. Brennan, inquiring of him about the necessity for valuation opinions in spite of the way in which this particular offer was couched;" and that he was otherwise actively involved in supporting the positions being taken by Van Gorkom before the Board about "the necessity to act immediately on this offer," and about "the adequacy of the $55 and the question of how that would be tested."

The Board meeting of September 20 lasted about two hours. Based solely upon Van Gorkom's oral presentation, Chelberg's supporting representations, Romans' oral statement, Brennan's legal advice, and their knowledge of the market history of the Company's stock,[9] the directors approved the proposed Merger Agreement. However, the Board later claimed to have attached two conditions to its acceptance: (1) that Trans Union reserved the right to accept any better offer that was made during the market test period; and (2) that Trans Union could share its proprietary information with any other potential bidders. While the Board now claims to have reserved the right to accept any better offer received after

---

8. In Van Gorkom's words: The "real decision" is whether to "let the stockholders decide it" which is "all you are being asked to decide today."

9. The Trial Court stated the premium relationship of the $55 price to the market history of the Company's stock as follows:

> * * * the merger price offered to the stockholders of Trans Union represented a premium of 62% over the average of the high and low prices at which Trans Union stock had traded in 1980, a premium of 48% over the last closing price, and a premium of 39% over the highest price at which the stock of Trans Union had traded any time during the prior six years.

the announcement of the Pritzker agreement (even though the minutes of the meeting do not reflect this), it is undisputed that the Board did not reserve the right to actively solicit alternate offers.

The Merger Agreement was executed by Van Gorkom during the evening of September 20 at a formal social event that he hosted for the opening of the Chicago Lyric Opera. Neither he nor any other director read the agreement prior to its signing and delivery to Pritzker. * * *

On Monday, September 22, the Company issued a press release announcing that Trans Union had entered into a "definitive" Merger Agreement with an affiliate of the Marmon Group, Inc., a Pritzker holding company. Within 10 days of the public announcement, dissent among Senior Management over the merger had become widespread. Faced with threatened resignations of key officers, Van Gorkom met with Pritzker who agreed to several modifications of the Agreement. Pritzker was willing to do so provided that Van Gorkom could persuade the dissidents to remain on the Company payroll for at least six months after consummation of the merger.

Van Gorkom reconvened the Board on October 8 and secured the directors' approval of the proposed amendments—sight unseen. The Board also authorized the employment of Salomon Brothers, its investment banker, to solicit other offers for Trans Union during the proposed "market test" period.

The next day, October 9, Trans Union issued a press release announcing: (1) that Pritzker had obtained "the financing commitments necessary to consummate" the merger with Trans Union; (2) that Pritzker had acquired one million shares of Trans Union common stock at $38 per share; (3) that Trans Union was now permitted to actively seek other offers and had retained Salomon Brothers for that purpose; and (4) that if a more favorable offer were not received before February 1, 1981, Trans Union's shareholders would thereafter meet to vote on the Pritzker proposal.

It was not until the following day, October 10, that the actual amendments to the Merger Agreement were prepared by Pritzker and delivered to Van Gorkom for execution. As will be seen, the amendments were considerably at variance with Van Gorkom's representations of the amendments to the Board on October 8; and the amendments placed serious constraints on Trans Union's ability to negotiate a better deal and withdraw from the Pritzker agreement. Nevertheless, Van Gorkom proceeded to execute what became the October 10 amendments to the Merger Agreement without conferring further with the Board members and apparently without comprehending the actual implications of the amendments.

Salomon Brothers' efforts over a three-month period from October 21 to January 21 produced only one serious suitor for Trans Union—General Electric Credit Corporation ("GE Credit"), a subsidiary of the General Electric Company. However, GE Credit was unwilling to make an offer for

Trans Union unless Trans Union first rescinded its Merger Agreement with Pritzker. When Pritzker refused, GE Credit terminated further discussions with Trans Union in early January.

In the meantime, in early December, the investment firm of Kohlberg, Kravis, Roberts & Co. ("KKR"), the only other concern to make a firm offer for Trans Union, withdrew its offer under circumstances hereinafter detailed.

On December 19, this litigation was commenced and, within four weeks, the plaintiffs had deposed eight of the ten directors of Trans Union, including Van Gorkom, Chelberg and Romans, its Chief Financial Officer. On January 21, Management's Proxy Statement for the February 10 shareholder meeting was mailed to Trans Union's stockholders. On January 26, Trans Union's Board met and, after a lengthy meeting, voted to proceed with the Pritzker merger. The Board also approved for mailing, "on or about January 27," a Supplement to its Proxy Statement. The Supplement purportedly set forth all information relevant to the Pritzker Merger Agreement, which had not been divulged in the first Proxy Statement.

On February 10, the stockholders of Trans Union approved the Pritzker merger proposal. Of the outstanding shares, 69.9% were voted in favor of the merger; 7.25% were voted against the merger; and 22.85% were not voted.

We turn to the issue of the application of the business judgment rule to the September 20 meeting of the Board.

The Court of Chancery concluded from the evidence that the Board of Directors' approval of the Pritzker merger proposal fell within the protection of the business judgment rule. The Court found that the Board had given sufficient time and attention to the transaction, since the directors had considered the Pritzker proposal on three different occasions, on September 20, and on October 8, 1980 and finally on January 26, 1981. On that basis, the Court reasoned that the Board had acquired, over the four-month period, sufficient information to reach an informed business judgment on the cash-out merger proposal. The Court ruled:

> ... that given the market value of Trans Union's stock, the business acumen of the members of the board of Trans Union, the substantial premium over market offered by the Pritzkers and the ultimate effect on the merger price provided by the prospect of other bids for the stock in question, that the board of directors of Trans Union did not act recklessly or improvidently in determining on a course of action which they believed to be in the best interest of the stockholders of Trans Union.

The Court of Chancery made but one finding; i.e., that the Board's conduct over the entire period from September 20 through January 26, 1981 was not reckless or improvident, but informed. This ultimate conclusion was premised upon three subordinate findings, one explicit and two implied. The Court's explicit finding was that Trans Union's Board was "free to turn down the Pritzker proposal" not only on September 20 but also on October 8, 1980 and on January 26, 1981. The Court's implied, subordinate findings were: (1) that no legally binding agreement was reached by the parties until January 26; and (2) that if a higher offer were to be forthcoming, the market test would have produced it, and Trans Union would have been contractually free to accept such higher offer. However, the Court offered no factual basis or legal support for any of these findings; and the record compels contrary conclusions. * * *

Applying ... governing principles of law to the record and the decision of the Trial Court, we conclude that the Court's ultimate finding that the Board's conduct was not "reckless or imprudent" is contrary to the record and not the product of a logical and deductive reasoning process.

The plaintiffs contend that the Court of Chancery erred as a matter of law by exonerating the defendant directors under the business judgment rule without first determining whether the rule's threshold condition of "due care and prudence" was satisfied. The plaintiffs assert that the Trial Court found the defendant directors to have reached an informed business judgment on the basis of "extraneous considerations and events that occurred after September 20, 1980." The defendants deny that the Trial Court committed legal error in relying upon post-September 20, 1980 events and the directors' later acquired knowledge. The defendants further submit that their decision to accept $55 per share was informed because: (1) they were "highly qualified;" (2) they were "well-informed;" and (3) they deliberated over the "proposal" not once but three times. On essentially this evidence and under our standard of review, the defendants assert that affirmance is required. We must disagree.

Under Delaware law, the business judgment rule is the offspring of the fundamental principle, codified in 8 *Del.C.* § 141(a), that the business and affairs of a Delaware corporation are managed by or under its board of directors. In carrying out their managerial roles, directors are charged with an unyielding fiduciary duty to the corporation and its shareholders. *Loft, Inc. v. Guth,* Del.Ch., 2 A.2d 225 (1938), *aff'd,* Del.Supr., 5 A.2d 503 (1939). The business judgment rule exists to protect and promote the full and free exercise of the managerial power granted to Delaware directors. The rule itself "is a presumption that in making a business decision, the directors of a corporation acted on an informed basis, in good faith and in the honest belief that the action taken was in the best interests of the company." Thus, the party attacking a board decision as uninformed must rebut the presumption that its business judgment was an informed one.

The determination of whether a business judgment is an informed one turns on whether the directors have informed themselves "prior to making a business decision, of all material information reasonably available to them."

Under the business judgment rule there is no protection for directors who have made "an unintelligent or unadvised judgment." A director's duty to inform himself in preparation for a decision derives from the fiduciary capacity in which he serves the corporation and its stockholders. Since a director is vested with the responsibility for the management of the affairs of the corporation, he must execute that duty with the recognition that he acts on behalf of others. Such obligation does not tolerate faithlessness or self-dealing. But fulfillment of the fiduciary function requires more than the mere absence of bad faith or fraud. Representation of the financial interests of others imposes on a director an affirmative duty to protect those interests and to proceed with a critical eye in assessing information of the type and under the circumstances present here.

Thus, a director's duty to exercise an informed business judgment is in the nature of a duty of care, as distinguished from a duty of loyalty. Here, there were no allegations of fraud, bad faith, or self-dealing, or proof thereof. Hence, it is presumed that the directors reached their business judgment in good faith, and considerations of motive are irrelevant to the issue before us.

The standard of care applicable to a director's duty of care has also been recently restated by this Court. In *Aronson, supra,* we stated:

> While the Delaware cases use a variety of terms to describe the applicable standard of care, our analysis satisfies us that under the business judgment rule director liability is predicated upon concepts of gross negligence. (footnote omitted)

473 A.2d at 812.

We again confirm that view. We think the concept of gross negligence is also the proper standard for determining whether a business judgment reached by a board of directors was an informed one.

In the specific context of a proposed merger of domestic corporations, a director has a duty under 8 *Del.C.* § 251(b) along with his fellow directors, to act in an informed and deliberate manner in determining whether to approve an agreement of merger before submitting the proposal to the stockholders. Certainly in the merger context, a director may not abdicate that duty by leaving to the shareholders alone the decision to approve or disapprove the agreement. Only an agreement of merger satisfying the requirements of 8 *Del.C.* § 251(b) may be submitted to the shareholders under § 251(c).

It is against those standards that the conduct of the directors of Trans Union must be tested, as a matter of law and as a matter of fact, regarding their exercise of an informed business judgment in voting to approve the Pritzker merger proposal.

The defendants argue that the determination of whether their decision to accept $55 per share for Trans Union represented an informed business judgment requires consideration, not only of that which they knew and learned on September 20, but also of that which they subsequently learned and did over the following four-month period before the shareholders met to vote on the proposal in February, 1981. The defendants thereby seek to reduce the significance of their action on September 20 and to widen the time frame for determining whether their decision to accept the Pritzker proposal was an informed one. Thus, the defendants contend that what the directors did and learned subsequent to September 20 and through January 26, 1981, was properly taken into account by the Trial Court in determining whether the Board's judgment was an informed one. We disagree with this *post hoc* approach.

The issue of whether the directors reached an informed decision to "sell" the Company on September 20, 1980 must be determined only upon the basis of the information then reasonably available to the directors and relevant to their decision to accept the Pritzker merger proposal. This is not to say that the directors were precluded from altering their original plan of action, had they done so in an informed manner. What we do say is that the question of whether the directors reached an informed business judgment in agreeing to sell the Company, pursuant to the terms of the September 20 Agreement presents, in reality, two questions: (A) whether the directors reached an informed business judgment on September 20, 1980; and (B) if they did not, whether the directors' actions taken subsequent to September 20 were adequate to cure any infirmity in their action taken on September 20. We first consider the directors' September 20 action in terms of their reaching an informed business judgment.

On the record before us, we must conclude that the Board of Directors did not reach an informed business judgment on September 20, 1980 in voting to "sell" the Company for $55 per share pursuant to the Pritzker cash-out merger proposal. Our reasons, in summary, are as follows:

The directors (1) did not adequately inform themselves as to Van Gorkom's role in forcing the "sale" of the Company and in establishing the per share purchase price; (2) were uninformed as to the intrinsic value of the Company; and (3) given these circumstances, at a minimum, were grossly negligent in approving the "sale" of the Company upon two hours' consideration, without prior notice, and without the exigency of a crisis or emergency.

As has been noted, the Board based its September 20 decision to approve the cash-out merger primarily on Van Gorkom's representations. None of the directors, other than Van Gorkom and Chelberg, had any prior knowledge that the purpose of the meeting was to propose a cash-out merger of Trans Union. No members of Senior Management were present, other than Chelberg, Romans and Peterson; and the latter two had only learned of the proposed sale an hour earlier. Both general counsel Moore and former general counsel Browder attended the meeting, but were equally uninformed as to the purpose of the meeting and the documents to be acted upon.

Without any documents before them concerning the proposed transaction, the members of the Board were required to rely entirely upon Van Gorkom's 20–minute oral presentation of the proposal. No written summary of the terms of the merger was presented; the directors were given no documentation to support the adequacy of $55 price per share for sale of the Company; and the Board had before it nothing more than Van Gorkom's statement of his understanding of the substance of an agreement which he admittedly had never read, nor which any member of the Board had ever seen.

Under 8 *Del.C.* § 141(e), "directors are fully protected in relying in good faith on reports made by officers." The term "report" has been liberally construed to include reports of informal personal investigations by corporate officers. However, there is no evidence that any "report," as defined under § 141(e), concerning the Pritzker proposal, was presented to the Board on September 20.[16] Van Gorkom's oral presentation of his understanding of the terms of the proposed Merger Agreement, which he had not seen, and Romans' brief oral statement of his preliminary study regarding the feasibility of a leveraged buy-out of Trans Union do not qualify as § 141(e) "reports" for these reasons: The former lacked substance because Van Gorkom was basically uninformed as to the essential provisions of the very document about which he was talking. Romans' statement was irrelevant to the issues before the Board since it did not purport to be a valuation study. At a minimum for a report to enjoy the status conferred by § 141(e), it must be pertinent to the subject matter upon which a board is called to act, and otherwise be entitled to good faith, not blind, reliance. Considering all of the surrounding circumstances—hastily calling the meeting without prior notice of its subject matter, the proposed sale of the Company without any prior consideration of the issue or necessity therefor, the urgent time constraints imposed by Pritzker, and the total absence of any documentation whatsoever—the directors were duty bound to make reasonable inquiry of Van Gorkom and Romans, and if they had done so, the inadequacy of that upon which they now claim to have relied would have been apparent.

The defendants rely on the following factors to sustain the Trial Court's finding that the Board's decision was an informed one: (1) the magnitude of the premium or spread between the $55 Pritzker offering price and Trans Union's current market price of $38 per share; (2) the amendment of the Agreement as submitted on September 20 to permit the Board to accept any better offer during the "market test" period; (3) the collective experience and expertise of the Board's "inside" and "outside" directors; and (4) their reliance on Brennan's legal advice that the

---

16. In support of the defendants' argument that their judgment as to the adequacy of $55 per share was an informed one, the directors rely on the BCG study and the Five Year Forecast. However, no one even referred to either of these studies at the September 20 meeting; and it is conceded that these materials do not represent valuation studies. Hence, these documents do not constitute evidence as to whether the directors reached an informed judgment on September 20 that $55 per share was a fair value for sale of the Company.

directors might be sued if they rejected the Pritzker proposal. We discuss each of these grounds *seriatim:*

A substantial premium may provide one reason to recommend a merger, but in the absence of other sound valuation information, the fact of a premium alone does not provide an adequate basis upon which to assess the fairness of an offering price. Here, the judgment reached as to the adequacy of the premium was based on a comparison between the historically depressed Trans Union market price and the amount of the Pritzker offer. Using market price as a basis for concluding that the premium adequately reflected the true value of the Company was a clearly faulty, indeed fallacious, premise, as the defendants' own evidence demonstrates.

The record is clear that before September 20, Van Gorkom and other members of Trans Union's Board knew that the market had consistently undervalued the worth of Trans Union's stock, despite steady increases in the Company's operating income in the seven years preceding the merger. The Board related this occurrence in large part to Trans Union's inability to use its ITCs as previously noted. Van Gorkom testified that he did not believe the market price accurately reflected Trans Union's true worth; and several of the directors testified that, as a general rule, most chief executives think that the market undervalues their companies' stock. Yet, on September 20, Trans Union's Board apparently believed that the market stock price accurately reflected the value of the Company for the purpose of determining the adequacy of the premium for its sale.

In the Proxy Statement, however, the directors reversed their position. There, they stated that, although the earnings prospects for Trans Union were "excellent," they found no basis for believing that this would be reflected in future stock prices. With regard to past trading, the Board stated that the prices at which the Company's common stock had traded in recent years did not reflect the "inherent" value of the Company. But having referred to the "inherent" value of Trans Union, the directors ascribed no number to it. Moreover, nowhere did they disclose that they had no basis on which to fix "inherent" worth beyond an impressionistic reaction to the premium over market and an unsubstantiated belief that the value of the assets was "significantly greater" than book value. By their own admission they could not rely on the stock price as an accurate measure of value. Yet, also by their own admission, the Board members assumed that Trans Union's market price was adequate to serve as a basis upon which to assess the adequacy of the premium for purposes of the September 20 meeting.

The parties do not dispute that a publicly-traded stock price is solely a measure of the value of a minority position and, thus, market price represents only the value of a single share. Nevertheless, on September 20, the Board assessed the adequacy of the premium over market, offered by Pritzker, solely by comparing it with Trans Union's current and historical stock price.

Indeed, as of September 20, the Board had no other information on which to base a determination of the intrinsic value of Trans Union as a going concern. As of September 20, the Board had made no evaluation of the Company designed to value the entire enterprise, nor had the Board ever previously considered selling the Company or consenting to a buy-out merger. Thus, the adequacy of a premium is indeterminate unless it is assessed in terms of other competent and sound valuation information that reflects the value of the particular business.

Despite the foregoing facts and circumstances, there was no call by the Board, either on September 20 or thereafter, for any valuation study or documentation of the $55 price per share as a measure of the fair value of the Company in a cash-out context. It is undisputed that the major asset of Trans Union was its cash flow. Yet, at no time did the Board call for a valuation study taking into account that highly significant element of the Company's assets.

We do not imply that an outside valuation study is essential to support an informed business judgment; nor do we state that fairness opinions by independent investment bankers are required as a matter of law. Often insiders familiar with the business of a going concern are in a better position than are outsiders to gather relevant information; and under appropriate circumstances, such directors may be fully protected in relying in good faith upon the valuation reports of their management. *See* 8 *Del.C.* § 141(e).

Here, the record establishes that the Board did not request its Chief Financial Officer, Romans, to make any valuation study or review of the proposal to determine the adequacy of $55 per share for sale of the Company. On the record before us: The Board rested on Romans' elicited response that the $55 figure was within a "fair price range" within the context of a leveraged buy-out. No director sought any further information from Romans. No director asked him why he put $55 at the bottom of his range. No director asked Romans for any details as to his study, the reason why it had been undertaken or its depth. No director asked to see the study; and no director asked Romans whether Trans Union's finance department could do a fairness study within the remaining 36–hour[18] period available under the Pritzker offer.

Had the Board, or any member, made an inquiry of Romans, he presumably would have responded as he testified: that his calculations were rough and preliminary; and, that the study was not designed to determine the fair value of the Company, but rather to assess the feasibility of a leveraged buy-out financed by the Company's projected cash flow, making certain assumptions as to the purchaser's borrowing needs. Romans would have presumably also informed the Board of his

---

18. Romans' department study was not made available to the Board until circulation of Trans Union's Supplementary Proxy Statement and the Board's meeting of January 26, 1981, on the eve of the shareholder meeting; and, as has been noted, the study has never been produced for inclusion in the record in this case.

view, and the widespread view of Senior Management, that the timing of the offer was wrong and the offer inadequate.

The record also establishes that the Board accepted without scrutiny Van Gorkom's representation as to the fairness of the $55 price per share for sale of the Company—a subject that the Board had never previously considered. The Board thereby failed to discover that Van Gorkom had suggested the $55 price to Pritzker and, most crucially, that Van Gorkom had arrived at the $55 figure based on calculations designed solely to determine the feasibility of a leveraged buy-out.[19] No questions were raised either as to the tax implications of a cash-out merger or how the price for the one million share option granted Pritzker was calculated.

We do not say that the Board of Directors was not entitled to give some credence to Van Gorkom's representation that $55 was an adequate or fair price. Under § 141(e), the directors were entitled to rely upon their chairman's opinion of value and adequacy, provided that such opinion was reached on a sound basis. Here, the issue is whether the directors informed themselves as to all information that was reasonably available to them. Had they done so, they would have learned of the source and derivation of the $55 price and could not reasonably have relied thereupon in good faith.

None of the directors, Management or outside, were investment bankers or financial analysts. Yet the Board did not consider recessing the meeting until a later hour that day (or requesting an extension of Pritzker's Sunday evening deadline) to give it time to elicit more information as to the sufficiency of the offer, either from inside Management (in particular Romans) or from Trans Union's own investment banker, Salomon Brothers, whose Chicago specialist in merger and acquisitions was known to the Board and familiar with Trans Union's affairs.

Thus, the record compels the conclusion that on September 20 the Board lacked valuation information adequate to reach an informed business judgment as to the fairness of $55 per share for sale of the Company.

This brings us to the post-September 20 "market test" upon which the defendants ultimately rely to confirm the reasonableness of their September 20 decision to accept the Pritzker proposal. In this connection, the directors present a two-part argument: (a) that by making a "market test" of Pritzker's $55 per share offer a condition of their September 20 decision to accept his offer, they cannot be found to have acted impulsively or in an uninformed manner on September 20; and (b) that the adequacy of the $17 premium for sale of the Company was conclusively established

---

19. As of September 20 the directors did not know: that Van Gorkom had arrived at the $55 figure alone, and subjectively, as the figure to be used by Controller Peterson in creating a feasible structure for a leveraged buy-out by a prospective purchaser; that Van Gorkom had not sought advice, information or assistance from either inside or outside Trans Union directors as to the value of the Company as an entity or the fair price per share for 100% of its stock; that Van Gorkom had not consulted with the Company's investment bankers or other financial analysts; that Van Gorkom had not consulted with or confided in any officer or director of the Company except Chelberg; and that Van Gorkom had deliberately chosen to ignore the advice and opinion of the members of his Senior Management group regarding the adequacy of the $55 price.

over the following 90 to 120 days by the most reliable evidence available—the marketplace. Thus, the defendants impliedly contend that the "market test" eliminated the need for the Board to perform any other form of fairness test either on September 20, or thereafter.

Again, the facts of record do not support the defendants' argument. There is no evidence: (a) that the Merger Agreement was effectively amended to give the Board freedom to put Trans Union up for auction sale to the highest bidder; or (b) that a public auction was in fact permitted to occur. The minutes of the Board meeting make no reference to any of this. Indeed, the record compels the conclusion that the directors had no rational basis for expecting that a market test was attainable, given the terms of the Agreement as executed during the evening of September 20. We rely upon the following facts which are essentially uncontradicted:

The Merger Agreement, specifically identified as that originally presented to the Board on September 20, has never been produced by the defendants, notwithstanding the plaintiffs' several demands for production before as well as during trial. No acceptable explanation of this failure to produce documents has been given to either the Trial Court or this Court. Significantly, neither the defendants nor their counsel have made the affirmative representation that this critical document has been produced. Thus, the Court is deprived of the best evidence on which to judge the merits of the defendants' position as to the care and attention which they gave to the terms of the Agreement on September 20.

Van Gorkom states that the Agreement as submitted incorporated the ingredients for a market test by authorizing Trans Union to receive competing offers over the next 90-day period. However, he concedes that the Agreement barred Trans Union from actively soliciting such offers and from furnishing to interested parties any information about the Company other than that already in the public domain. Whether the original Agreement of September 20 went so far as to authorize Trans Union to receive competitive proposals is arguable. The defendants' unexplained failure to produce and identify the original Merger Agreement permits the logical inference that the instrument would not support their assertions in this regard. It is a well established principle that the production of weak evidence when strong is, or should have been, available can lead only to the conclusion that the strong would have been adverse. Van Gorkom, conceding that he never read the Agreement, stated that he was relying upon his understanding that, under corporate law, directors always have an inherent right, as well as a fiduciary duty, to accept a better offer notwithstanding an existing contractual commitment by the Board.

The defendant directors assert that they "insisted" upon including two amendments to the Agreement, thereby permitting a market test: (1) to give Trans Union the right to accept a better offer; and (2) to reserve to Trans Union the right to distribute proprietary information on the Company to alternative bidders. Yet, the defendants concede that they did not seek to amend the Agreement to permit Trans Union to solicit competing offers.

Several of Trans Union's outside directors resolutely maintained that the Agreement as submitted was approved on the understanding that, "if we got a better deal, we had a right to take it." Director Johnson so testified; but he then added, "And if they didn't put that in the agreement, then the management did not carry out the conclusion of the Board. And I just don't know whether they did or not." The only clause in the Agreement as finally executed to which the defendants can point as "keeping the door open" is the following underlined statement found in subparagraph (a) of section 2.03 of the Merger Agreement as executed:

> The Board of Directors shall recommend to the stockholders of Trans Union that they approve and adopt the Merger Agreement ('the stockholders' approval') and to use its best efforts to obtain the requisite votes therefor. *GL acknowledges that Trans Union directors may have a competing fiduciary obligation to the shareholders under certain circumstances.*

Clearly, this language on its face cannot be construed as incorporating either of the two "conditions" described above: either the right to accept a better offer or the right to distribute proprietary information to third parties. The logical witness for the defendants to call to confirm their construction of this clause of the Agreement would have been Trans Union's outside attorney, James Brennan. The defendants' failure, without explanation, to call this witness again permits the logical inference that his testimony would not have been helpful to them. The further fact that the directors adjourned, rather than recessed, the meeting without incorporating in the Agreement these important "conditions" further weakens the defendants' position. As has been noted, nothing in the Board's Minutes supports these claims. No reference to either of the so-called "conditions" or of Trans Union's reserved right to test the market appears in any notes of the Board meeting or in the Board Resolution accepting the Pritzker offer or in the Minutes of the meeting itself. That evening, in the midst of a formal party which he hosted for the opening of the Chicago Lyric Opera, Van Gorkom executed the Merger Agreement without he or any other member of the Board having read the instruments.

The defendants attempt to downplay the significance of the prohibition against Trans Union's actively soliciting competing offers by arguing that the directors "understood that the entire financial community would know that Trans Union was for sale upon the announcement of the Pritzker offer, and anyone desiring to make a better offer was free to do so." Yet, the press release issued on September 22, with the authorization of the Board, stated that Trans Union had entered into "definitive agreements" with the Pritzkers; and the press release did not even disclose Trans Union's limited right to receive and accept higher offers. Accompanying this press release was a further public announcement that

Pritzker had been granted an option to purchase at any time one million shares of Trans Union's capital stock at 75 cents above the then-current price per share.

Thus, notwithstanding what several of the outside directors later claimed to have "thought" occurred at the meeting, the record compels the conclusion that Trans Union's Board had no rational basis to conclude on September 20 or in the days immediately following, that the Board's acceptance of Pritzker's offer was conditioned on (1) a "market test" of the offer; and (2) the Board's right to withdraw from the Pritzker Agreement and accept any higher offer received before the shareholder meeting.

The directors' unfounded reliance on both the premium and the market test as the basis for accepting the Pritzker proposal undermines the defendants' remaining contention that the Board's collective experience and sophistication was a sufficient basis for finding that it reached its September 20 decision with informed, reasonable deliberation.[21] *Compare Gimbel v. Signal Companies, Inc.,* Del. Ch., 316 A.2d 599 (1974), *aff'd per curiam,* Del.Supr., 316 A.2d 619 (1974). There, the Court of Chancery preliminary enjoined a board's sale of stock of its wholly-owned subsidiary for an alleged grossly inadequate price. It did so based on a finding that the business judgment rule had been pierced for failure of management to give its board "the opportunity to make a reasonable and reasoned decision." The Court there reached this result notwithstanding the board's sophistication and experience; the company's need of immediate cash; and the board's need to act promptly due to the impact of an energy crisis on the value of the underlying assets being sold—all of its subsidiary's oil and gas interests. The Court found those factors denoting competence to be outweighed by evidence of gross negligence; that management in effect sprang the deal on the board by negotiating the asset sale without informing the board; that the buyer intended to "force a quick decision" by the board; that the board meeting was called on only one-and-a-half days' notice; that its outside directors were not notified of the meeting's purpose; that during a meeting spanning "a couple of hours" a sale of assets worth $480 million was approved; and that the Board failed to obtain a *current* appraisal of its oil and gas interests. The analogy of *Signal* to the case at bar is significant.

Part of the defense is based on a claim that the directors relied on legal advice rendered at the September 20 meeting by James Brennan, Esquire, who was present at Van Gorkom's request. Unfortunately, Bren-

---

21. Trans Union's five "inside" directors had backgrounds in law and accounting, 116 years of collective employment by the Company and 68 years of combined experience on its Board. Trans Union's five "outside" directors included four chief executives of major corporations and an economist who was a former dean of a major school of business and chancellor of a university. The "outside" directors had 78 years of combined experience as chief executive officers of major corporations and 50 years of cumulative experience as directors of Trans Union. Thus, defendants argue that the Board was eminently qualified to reach an informed judgment on the proposed "sale" of Trans Union notwithstanding their lack of any advance notice of the proposal, the shortness of their deliberation, and their determination not to consult with their investment banker or to obtain a fairness opinion.

nan did not appear and testify at trial even though his firm participated in the defense of this action. There is no contemporaneous evidence of the advice given by Brennan on September 20, only the later deposition and trial testimony of certain directors as to their recollections or understanding of what was said at the meeting. Since counsel did not testify, and the advice attributed to Brennan is hearsay received by the Trial Court over the plaintiffs' objections, we consider it only in the context of the directors' present claims. In fairness to counsel, we make no findings that the advice attributed to him was in fact given. We focus solely on the efficacy of the defendants' claims, made months and years later, in an effort to extricate themselves from liability.

Several defendants testified that Brennan advised them that Delaware law did not require a fairness opinion or an outside valuation of the Company before the Board could act on the Pritzker proposal. If given, the advice was correct. However, that did not end the matter. Unless the directors had before them adequate information regarding the intrinsic value of the Company, upon which a proper exercise of business judgment could be made, mere advice of this type is meaningless; and, given this record of the defendants' failures, it constitutes no defense here.[22]

We conclude that Trans Union's Board was grossly negligent in that it failed to act with informed reasonable deliberation in agreeing to the Pritzker merger proposal on September 20; and we further conclude that the Trial Court erred as a matter of law in failing to address that question before determining whether the directors' later conduct was sufficient to cure its initial error.

A second claim is that counsel advised the Board it would be subject to lawsuits if it rejected the $55 per share offer. It is, of course, a fact of corporate life that today when faced with difficult or sensitive issues, directors often are subject to suit, irrespective of the decisions they make. However, counsel's mere acknowledgement of this circumstance cannot be rationally translated into a justification for a board permitting itself to be stampeded into a patently unadvised act. While suit might result from the rejection of a merger or tender offer, Delaware law makes clear that a board acting within the ambit of the business judgment rule faces no ultimate liability. Thus, we cannot conclude that the mere threat of litigation, acknowledged by counsel, constitutes either legal advice or any valid basis upon which to pursue an uninformed course.

Since we conclude that Brennan's purported advice is of no consequence to the defense of this case, it is unnecessary for us to invoke the adverse inferences which may be attributable to one failing to appear at trial and testify.

---

22. Nonetheless, we are satisfied that in an appropriate factual context a proper exercise of business judgment may include, as one of its aspects, reasonable reliance upon the advice of counsel. This is wholly outside the statutory protections of 8 *Del.C.* § 141(e) involving reliance upon reports of officers, certain experts and books and records of the company.

We now examine the Board's post-September 20 conduct for the purpose of determining first, whether it was informed and not grossly negligent; and second, if informed, whether it was sufficient to legally rectify and cure the Board's derelictions of September 20.[23]

First, as to the Board meeting of October 8: Its purpose arose in the aftermath of the September 20 meeting: (1) the September 22 press release announcing that Trans Union "had entered into definitive agreements to merge with an affiliate of Marmon Group, Inc.;" and (2) Senior Management's ensuing revolt.

Trans Union's press release stated:

FOR IMMEDIATE RELEASE:

CHICAGO, IL—Trans Union Corporation announced today that it had entered into definitive agreements to merge with an affiliate of The Marmon Group, Inc. in a transaction whereby Trans Union stockholders would receive $55 per share in cash for each Trans Union share held. The Marmon Group, Inc. is controlled by the Pritzker family of Chicago.

The merger is subject to approval by the stockholders of Trans Union at a special meeting expected to be held sometime during December or early January.

Until October 10, 1980, the purchaser has the right to terminate the merger if financing that is satisfactory to the purchaser has not been obtained, but after that date there is no such right.

In a related transaction, Trans Union has agreed to sell to a designee of the purchaser one million newly-issued shares of Trans Union common stock at a cash price of $38 per share. Such shares will be issued only if the merger financing has been committed for no later than October 10, 1980, or if the purchaser elects to waive the merger financing condition. In addition, the New York Stock Exchange will be asked to approve the listing of the new shares pursuant to a listing application which Trans Union intends to file shortly.

Completing of the transaction is also subject to the preparation of a definitive proxy statement and making various filings and obtaining the approvals or consents of government agencies.

The press release made no reference to provisions allegedly reserving to the Board the rights to perform a "market test" and to withdraw from the Pritzker Agreement if Trans Union received a better offer before the shareholder meeting. The defendants also concede that Trans Union never made a subsequent public announcement stating that it had in fact reserved the right to accept alternate offers, the Agreement notwithstanding.

---

23. As will be seen, we do not reach the second question.

The public announcement of the Pritzker merger resulted in an "en masse" revolt of Trans Union's Senior Management. The head of Trans Union's tank car operations (its most profitable division) informed Van Gorkom that unless the merger were called off, fifteen key personnel would resign.

Instead of reconvening the Board, Van Gorkom again privately met with Pritzker, informed him of the developments, and sought his advice. Pritzker then made the following suggestions for overcoming Management's dissatisfaction: (1) that the Agreement be amended to permit Trans Union to solicit, as well as receive, higher offers; and (2) that the shareholder meeting be postponed from early January to February 10, 1981. In return, Pritzker asked Van Gorkom to obtain a commitment from Senior Management to remain at Trans Union for at least six months after the merger was consummated.

Van Gorkom then advised Senior Management that the Agreement would be amended to give Trans Union the right to solicit competing offers through January, 1981, if they would agree to remain with Trans Union. Senior Management was temporarily mollified; and Van Gorkom then called a special meeting of Trans Union's Board for October 8.

Thus, the primary purpose of the October 8 Board meeting was to amend the Merger Agreement, in a manner agreeable to Pritzker, to permit Trans Union to conduct a "market test."[24] Van Gorkom understood that the proposed amendments were intended to give the Company an unfettered "right to openly solicit offers down through January 31." Van Gorkom presumably so represented the amendments to Trans Union's Board members on October 8. In a brief session, the directors approved Van Gorkom's oral presentation of the substance of the proposed amendments, the terms of which were not reduced to writing until October 10. But rather than waiting to review the amendments, the Board again approved them sight unseen and adjourned, giving Van Gorkom authority to execute the papers when he received them.[25]

Thus, the Court of Chancery's finding that the October 8 Board meeting was convened to *reconsider* the Pritzker "proposal" is clearly erroneous. Further, the consequence of the Board's faulty conduct on October 8, in approving amendments to the Agreement which had not

---

24. As previously noted, the Board mistakenly thought that it had amended the September 20 draft agreement to include a market test. A secondary purpose of the October 8 meeting was to obtain the Board's approval for Trans Union to employ its investment advisor, Salomon Brothers, for the limited purpose of assisting Management in the solicitation of other offers. Neither Management nor the Board then or thereafter requested Salomon Brothers to submit its opinion as to the fairness of Pritzker's $55 cash-out merger proposal or to value Trans Union as an entity.

There is no evidence of record that the October 8 meeting had any other purpose; and we also note that the Minutes of the October 8 Board meeting, including any notice of the meeting, are not part of the voluminous records of this case.

25. We do not suggest that a board must read *in haec verba* every contract or legal document which it approves, but if it is to successfully absolve itself from charges of the type made here, there must be some credible contemporary evidence demonstrating that the directors knew what they were doing, and ensured that their purported action was given effect. That is the consistent failure which cast this Board upon its unredeemable course.

even been drafted, will become apparent when the actual amendments to the Agreement are hereafter examined.

The next day, October 9, and before the Agreement was amended, Pritzker moved swiftly to off-set the proposed market test amendment. First, Pritzker informed Trans Union that he had completed arrangements for financing its acquisition and that the parties were thereby mutually bound to a firm purchase and sale arrangement. Second, Pritzker announced the exercise of his option to purchase one million shares of Trans Union's treasury stock at $38 per share—75 cents above the current market price. Trans Union's Management responded the same day by issuing a press release announcing: (1) that all financing arrangements for Pritzker's acquisition of Trans Union had been completed; and (2) Pritzker's purchase of one million shares of Trans Union's treasury stock at $38 per share.

The next day, October 10, Pritzker delivered to Trans Union the proposed amendments to the September 20 Merger Agreement. Van Gorkom promptly proceeded to countersign all the instruments on behalf of Trans Union without reviewing the instruments to determine if they were consistent with the authority previously granted him by the Board. The amending documents were apparently not approved by Trans Union's Board until a much later date, December 2. The record does not affirmatively establish that Trans Union's directors ever read the October 10 amendments.[26]

The October 10 amendments to the Merger Agreement did authorize Trans Union to solicit competing offers, but the amendments had more far-reaching effects. The most significant change was in the definition of the third-party "offer" available to Trans Union as a possible basis for withdrawal from its Merger Agreement with Pritzker. Under the October 10 amendments, a better *offer* was no longer sufficient to permit Trans Union's withdrawal. Trans Union was now permitted to terminate the Pritzker Agreement and abandon the merger only if, prior to February 10, 1981, Trans Union had either consummated a merger (or sale of assets) with a third party or had entered into a "definitive" merger agreement more favorable than Pritzker's and for a greater consideration—subject only to stockholder approval. Further, the "extension" of the market test period to February 10, 1981 was circumscribed by other amendments which required Trans Union to file its preliminary proxy statement on the Pritzker merger proposal by December 5, 1980 and use its best efforts to mail the statement to its shareholders by January 5, 1981. Thus, the market test period was effectively reduced, not extended.

In our view, the record compels the conclusion that the directors' conduct on October 8 exhibited the same deficiencies as did their conduct on September 20. The Board permitted its Merger Agreement with Pritz-

---

26. There is no evidence of record that Trans Union's directors ever raised any objections, procedural or substantive, to the October 10 amendments or that any of them, including Van Gorkom, understood the opposite result of their intended effect—until it was too late.

ker to be amended in a manner it had neither authorized nor intended. The Court of Chancery, in its decision, overlooked the significance of the October 8–10 events and their relevance to the sufficiency of the directors' conduct. The Trial Court's letter opinion ignores: the October 10 amendments; the manner of their adoption; the effect of the October 9 press release and the October 10 amendments on the feasibility of a market test; and the ultimate question as to the reasonableness of the directors' reliance on a market test in recommending that the shareholders approve the Pritzker merger.

We conclude that the Board acted in a grossly negligent manner on October 8; and that Van Gorkom's representations on which the Board based its actions do not constitute "reports" under § 141(e) on which the directors could reasonably have relied. Further, the amended Merger Agreement imposed on Trans Union's acceptance of a third party offer conditions more onerous than those imposed on Trans Union's acceptance of Pritzker's offer on September 20. After October 10, Trans Union could accept from a third party a better offer only if it were incorporated in a definitive agreement between the parties, and not conditioned on financing or on any other contingency.

The October 9 press release, coupled with the October 10 amendments, had the clear effect of locking Trans Union's Board into the Pritzker Agreement. Pritzker had thereby foreclosed Trans Union's Board from negotiating any better "definitive" agreement over the remaining eight weeks before Trans Union was required to clear the Proxy Statement submitting the Pritzker proposal to its shareholders.

Next, as to the "curative" effects of the Board's post-September 20 conduct, we review in more detail the reaction of Van Gorkom to the KKR proposal and the results of the Board-sponsored "market test."

The KKR proposal was the first and only offer received subsequent to the Pritzker Merger Agreement. The offer resulted primarily from the efforts of Romans and other senior officers to propose an alternative to Pritzker's acquisition of Trans Union. In late September, Romans' group contacted KKR about the possibility of a leveraged buy-out by all members of Management, except Van Gorkom. By early October, Henry R. Kravis of KKR gave Romans written notice of KKR's "interest in making an offer to purchase 100%" of Trans Union's common stock.

Thereafter, and until early December, Romans' group worked with KKR to develop a proposal. It did so with Van Gorkom's knowledge and apparently grudging consent. On December 2, Kravis and Romans hand-delivered to Van Gorkom a formal letter-offer to purchase all of Trans Union's assets and to assume all of its liabilities for an aggregate cash consideration equivalent to $60 per share. The offer was contingent upon completing equity and bank financing of $650 million, which Kravis represented as 80% complete. The KKR letter made reference to discussions with major banks regarding the loan portion of the buy-out cost and stated that KKR was "confident that commitments for the bank financing

* * * can be obtained within two or three weeks." The purchasing group was to include certain named key members of Trans Union's Senior Management, excluding Van Gorkom, and a major Canadian company. Kravis stated that they were willing to enter into a "definitive agreement" under terms and conditions "substantially the same" as those contained in Trans Union's agreement with Pritzker. The offer was addressed to Trans Union's Board of Directors and a meeting with the Board, scheduled for that afternoon, was requested.

Van Gorkom's reaction to the KKR proposal was completely negative; he did not view the offer as being firm because of its financing condition. It was pointed out, to no avail, that Pritzker's offer had not only been similarly conditioned, but accepted on an expedited basis. Van Gorkom refused Kravis' request that Trans Union issue a press release announcing KKR's offer, on the ground that it might "chill" any other offer.[27] Romans and Kravis left with the understanding that their proposal would be presented to Trans Union's Board that afternoon.

Within a matter of hours and shortly before the scheduled Board meeting, Kravis withdrew his letter-offer. He gave as his reason a sudden decision by the Chief Officer of Trans Union's rail car leasing operation to withdraw from the KKR purchasing group. Van Gorkom had spoken to that officer about his participation in the KKR proposal immediately after his meeting with Romans and Kravis. However, Van Gorkom denied any responsibility for the officer's change of mind.

At the Board meeting later that afternoon, Van Gorkom did not inform the directors of the KKR proposal because he considered it "dead." Van Gorkom did not contact KKR again until January 20, when faced with the realities of this lawsuit, he then attempted to reopen negotiations. KKR declined due to the imminence of the February 10 stockholder meeting.

GE Credit Corporation's interest in Trans Union did not develop until November; and it made no written proposal until mid-January. Even then, its proposal was not in the form of an offer. Had there been time to do so, GE Credit was prepared to offer between $2 and $5 per share above the $55 per share price which Pritzker offered. But GE Credit needed an additional 60 to 90 days; and it was unwilling to make a formal offer without a concession from Pritzker extending the February 10 "deadline" for Trans Union's stockholder meeting. As previously stated, Pritzker refused to grant such extension; and on January 21, GE Credit terminated further negotiations with Trans Union. Its stated reasons, among others, were its "unwillingness to become involved in a bidding contest with Pritzker in the absence of the willingness of [the Pritzker interests] to terminate the proposed $55 cash merger."

---

27. This was inconsistent with Van Gorkom's espousal of the September 22 press release following Trans Union's acceptance of Pritzker's proposal. Van Gorkom had then justified a press release as encouraging rather than chilling later offers.

In the absence of any explicit finding by the Trial Court as to the reasonableness of Trans Union's directors' reliance on a market test and its feasibility, we may make our own findings based on the record. Our review of the record compels a finding that confirmation of the appropriateness of the Pritzker offer by an unfettered or free market test was virtually meaningless in the face of the terms and time limitations of Trans Union's Merger Agreement with Pritzker as amended October 10, 1980.

Finally, we turn to the Board's meeting of January 26, 1981. The defendant directors rely upon the action there taken to refute the contention that they did not reach an informed business judgment in approving the Pritzker merger. The defendants contend that the Trial Court correctly concluded that Trans Union's directors were, in effect, as "free to turn down the Pritzker proposal" on January 26, as they were on September 20.

Applying the appropriate standard of review set forth in *Levitt v. Bouvier, supra,* we conclude that the Trial Court's finding in this regard is neither supported by the record nor the product of an orderly and logical deductive process. Without disagreeing with the principle that a business decision by an originally uninformed board of directors may, under appropriate circumstances, be timely cured so as to become informed and deliberate, we find that the record does not permit the defendants to invoke that principle in this case.

The Board's January 26 meeting was the first meeting following the filing of the plaintiffs' suit in mid-December and the last meeting before the previously-noticed shareholder meeting of February 10. All ten members of the Board and three outside attorneys attended the meeting. At that meeting the following facts, among other aspects of the Merger Agreement, were discussed:

(a) The fact that prior to September 20, 1980, no Board member or member of Senior Management, except Chelberg and Peterson, knew that Van Gorkom had discussed a possible merger with Pritzker;

(b) The fact that the price of $55 per share had been suggested initially to Pritzker by Van Gorkom;

(c) The fact that the Board had not sought an independent fairness opinion;

(d) The fact that, at the September 20 Senior Management meeting, Romans and several members of Senior Management indicated both concern that the $55 per share price was inadequate and a belief that a higher price should and could be obtained;

(e) The fact that Romans had advised the Board at its meeting on September 20, that he and his department had prepared a study which indicated that the Company had a value in the range of $55 to

$65 per share, and that he could not advise the Board that the $55 per share offer made by Pritzker was unfair.

The defendants characterize the Board's Minutes of the January 26 meeting as a "review" of the "entire sequence of events" from Van Gorkom's initiation of the negotiations on September 13 forward. The defendants also rely on the testimony of several of the Board members at trial as confirming the Minutes. On the basis of this evidence, the defendants argue that whatever information the Board lacked to make a deliberate and informed judgment on September 20, or on October 8, was fully divulged to the entire Board on January 26. Hence, the argument goes, the Board's vote on January 26 to again "approve" the Pritzker merger must be found to have been an informed and deliberate judgment.

On the basis of this evidence, the defendants assert: (1) that the Trial Court was legally correct in widening the time frame for determining whether the defendants' approval of the Pritzker merger represented an informed business judgment to include the entire four-month period during which the Board considered the matter from September 20 through January 26; and (2) that, given this extensive evidence of the Board's further review and deliberations on January 26, this Court must affirm the Trial Court's conclusion that the Board's action was not reckless or improvident.

We cannot agree. We find the Trial Court to have erred, both as a matter of fact and as a matter of law, in relying on the action on January 26 to bring the defendants' conduct within the protection of the business judgment rule.

Johnson's testimony and the Board Minutes of January 26 are remarkably consistent. Both clearly indicate recognition that the question of the alternative courses of action, available to the Board on January 26 with respect to the Pritzker merger, was a legal question, presenting to the Board (*after* its review of the full record developed through pre-trial discovery) *three* options: (1) to "continue to recommend" the Pritzker merger; (2) to "recommend that the stockholders vote against" the Pritzker merger; or (3) to take a noncommittal position on the merger and "simply leave the decision to [the] shareholders."

We must conclude from the foregoing that the Board was mistaken as a matter of law regarding its available courses of action on January 26, 1981. Options (2) and (3) were not viable or legally available to the Board under 8 *Del.C.* § 251(b). The Board could not remain committed to the Pritzker merger and yet recommend that its stockholders vote it down; nor could it take a neutral position and delegate to the stockholders the unadvised decision as to whether to accept or reject the merger. Under § 251(b), the Board had but two options: (1) to proceed with the merger and the stockholder meeting, with the Board's recommendation of approval; *or* (2) to rescind its agreement with Pritzker, withdraw its approval of the merger, and notify its stockholders that the proposed shareholder meeting was cancelled. There is no evidence that the Board gave any consideration to these, its only legally viable alternative courses of action.

But the second course of action would have clearly involved a substantial risk—that the Board would be faced with suit by Pritzker for breach of contract based on its September 20 agreement as amended October 10. As previously noted, under the terms of the October 10 amendment, the Board's only ground for release from its agreement with Pritzker was its entry into a more favorable definitive agreement to sell the Company to a third party. Thus, in reality, the Board was not "free to turn down the Pritzker proposal" as the Trial Court found. Indeed, short of negotiating a better agreement with a third party, the Board's only basis for release from the Pritzker Agreement without liability would have been to establish fundamental wrongdoing by Pritzker. Clearly, the Board was not "free" to withdraw from its agreement with Pritzker on January 26 by simply relying on its self-induced failure to have reached an informed business judgment at the time of its original agreement.

Therefore, the Trial Court's conclusion that the Board reached an informed business judgment on January 26 in determining whether to turn down the Pritzker "proposal" on that day cannot be sustained. The Court's conclusion is not supported by the record; it is contrary to the provisions of § 251(b) and basic principles of contract law; and it is not the product of a logical and deductive reasoning process.

Upon the basis of the foregoing, we hold that the defendants' post-September conduct did not cure the deficiencies of their September 20 conduct; and that, accordingly, the Trial Court erred in according to the defendants the benefits of the business judgment rule.

Whether the directors of Trans Union should be treated as one or individually in terms of invoking the protection of the business judgment rule and the applicability of 8 *Del.C.* § 141(c) are questions which were not originally addressed by the parties in their briefing of this case. This resulted in a supplemental briefing and a second rehearing en banc on two basic questions: (a) whether one or more of the directors were deprived of the protection of the business judgment rule by evidence of an absence of good faith; and (b) whether one or more of the outside directors were entitled to invoke the protection of 8 *Del.C.* § 141(e) by evidence of a reasonable, good faith reliance on "reports," including legal advice, rendered the Board by certain inside directors and the Board's special counsel, Brennan.

The parties' response, including reargument, has led the majority of the Court to conclude: (1) that since all of the defendant directors, outside as well as inside, take a unified position, we are required to treat all of the directors as one as to whether they are entitled to the protection of the business judgment rule; and (2) that considerations of good faith, including the presumption that the directors acted in good faith, are irrelevant in determining the threshold issue of whether the directors as a Board exercised an informed business judgment. For the same reason, we must reject defense counsel's *ad hominem* argument for affirmance: that reversal may result in a multi-million dollar class award against the defendants for having made an allegedly uninformed business judgment in a transaction not involving any personal gain, self-dealing or claim of bad faith.

In their brief, the defendants similarly mistake the business judgment rule's application to this case by erroneously invoking presumptions of good faith and "wide discretion":

> This is a case in which plaintiff challenged the exercise of business judgment by an independent Board of Directors. There were no allegations and no proof of fraud, bad faith, or self-dealing by the directors....

The business judgment rule, which was properly applied by the Chancellor, allows directors wide discretion in the matter of valuation and affords room for honest differences of opinion. In order to prevail, plaintiffs had the heavy burden of proving that the merger price was so grossly inadequate as to display itself as a badge of fraud. That is a burden which plaintiffs have not met.

However, plaintiffs have not claimed, nor did the Trial Court decide, that $55 was a grossly inadequate price per share for sale of the Company. That being so, the presumption that a board's judgment as to adequacy of price represents an honest exercise of business judgment (absent proof that the sale price was grossly inadequate) is irrelevant to the threshold question of whether an informed judgment was reached.

The defendants ultimately rely on the stockholder vote of February 10 for exoneration. The defendants contend that the stockholders' "overwhelming" vote approving the Pritzker Merger Agreement had the legal effect of curing any failure of the Board to reach an informed business judgment in its approval of the merger.

The parties tacitly agree that a discovered failure of the Board to reach an informed business judgment in approving the merger constitutes a voidable, rather than a void, act. Hence, the merger can be sustained, notwithstanding the infirmity of the Board's action, if its approval by majority vote of the shareholders is found to have been based on an informed electorate. The disagreement between the parties arises over: (1) the Board's burden of disclosing to the shareholders all relevant and material information; and (2) the sufficiency of the evidence as to whether the Board satisfied that burden.

On this issue the Trial Court summarily concluded "that the stockholders of Trans Union were fairly informed as to the pending merger...." The Court provided no supportive reasoning nor did the Court make any reference to the evidence of record.

The plaintiffs contend that the Court committed error by applying an erroneous disclosure standard of "adequacy" rather than "completeness" in determining the sufficiency of the Company's merger proxy materials. The plaintiffs also argue that the Board's proxy statements, both its original statement dated January 19 and its supplemental statement dated January 26, were incomplete in various material respects. Finally, the plaintiffs assert that Management's supplemental statement (mailed "on or about" January 27) was untimely either as a matter of law under 8 *Del.C.* § 251(c), or untimely as a matter of equity and the requirements of complete candor and fair disclosure.

The defendants deny that the Court committed legal or equitable error. On the question of the Board's burden of disclosure, the defendants state that there was no dispute at trial over the standard of disclosure required of the Board; but the defendants concede that the Board was required to disclose "all germane facts" which a reasonable shareholder would have considered important in deciding whether to approve the merger. Thus, the defendants argue that when the Trial Court speaks of finding the Company's shareholders to have been "fairly informed" by Management's proxy materials, the Court is speaking in terms of "complete candor" as required under *Lynch v. Vickers Energy Corp.,* Del.Supr., 383 A.2d 278 (1977).

The settled rule in Delaware is that "where a majority of fully informed stockholders ratify action of even interested directors, an attack on the ratified transaction normally must fail." The question of whether shareholders have been fully informed such that their vote can be said to ratify director action, "turns on the fairness and completeness of the proxy materials submitted by the management to the . . . shareholders." As this Court stated:

> [T]he entire atmosphere is freshened and a new set of rules invoked where a formal approval has been given by a majority of independent, fully informed stockholders. . . .

In *Lynch v. Vickers Energy Corp., supra,* this Court held that corporate directors owe to their stockholders a fiduciary duty to disclose all facts germane to the transaction at issue in an atmosphere of complete candor. We defined "germane" in the tender offer context as all "information such as a reasonable stockholder would consider important in deciding whether to sell or retain stock." In reality, "germane" means material facts.

Applying this standard to the record before us, we find that Trans Union's stockholders were not fully informed of all facts material to their vote on the Pritzker Merger and that the Trial Court's ruling to the contrary is clearly erroneous. We list the material deficiencies in the proxy materials:

(1) The fact that the Board had no reasonably adequate information indicative of the intrinsic value of the Company, other than a concededly depressed market price, was without question material to the shareholders voting on the merger. . . . Accordingly, the Board's lack of valuation information should have been disclosed. Instead, the directors cloaked the absence of such information in both the Proxy Statement and the Supplemental Proxy Statement. Through artful drafting, noticeably absent at the

September 20 meeting, both documents create the impression that the Board knew the intrinsic worth of the Company. . . .

(2) We find false and misleading the Board's characterization of the Romans report in the Supplemental Proxy Statement. . . . Nowhere does the Board disclose that Romans stated to the Board that his calculations were made in a "search for ways to justify a price in connection with" a leveraged buy-out transaction, "rather than to say what the shares are worth," and that he stated to the Board that his conclusion thus arrived at "was not the same thing as saying that I have a valuation of the Company at X dollars." Such information would have been material to a reasonable shareholder because it tended to invalidate the fairness of the merger price of $55. Furthermore, defendants again failed to disclose the absence of valuation information, but still made repeated reference to the "substantial premium."

(3) We find misleading the Board's references to the "substantial" premium offered. The Board gave as their primary reason in support of the merger the "substantial premium" shareholders would receive. But the Board did not disclose its failure to assess the premium offered in terms of other relevant valuation techniques, thereby rendering questionable its determination as to the substantiality of the premium over an admittedly depressed stock market price.

(4) We find the Board's recital in the Supplemental Proxy of certain events preceding the September 20 meeting to be incomplete and misleading. It is beyond dispute that a reasonable stockholder would have considered material the fact that Van Gorkom not only suggested the $55 price to Pritzker, but also that he chose the figure because it made feasible a leveraged buy-out. The directors disclosed that Van Gorkom suggested the $55 price to Pritzker. But the Board misled the shareholders when they described the basis of Van Gorkom's suggestion. . . .

(5) The Board's Supplemental Proxy Statement, mailed on or after January 27, added significant new matter, material to the proposal to be voted on February 10, which was not contained in the Original Proxy Statement. Some of this new matter was information which had only been disclosed to the Board on January 26; much was information known or reasonably available before January 21 but not revealed in the Original Proxy Statement. Yet, the stockholders were not informed of these facts.
* * *

Since we have concluded that Management's Supplemental Proxy Statement does not meet the Delaware disclosure standard of "complete candor" under *Lynch v. Vickers, supra,* it is unnecessary for us to address the plaintiffs' legal argument as to the proper construction of § 251(c). However, we do find it advisable to express the view that, in an appropriate case, an otherwise candid proxy statement may be so untimely as to defeat its purpose of meeting the needs of a fully informed electorate.

In this case, the Board's ultimate disclosure as contained in the Supplemental Proxy Statement related either to information readily accessible to all of the directors if they had asked the right questions, or was information already at their disposal. In short, the information disclosed by the Supplemental Proxy Statement was information which the defendant directors knew or should have known at the time the first Proxy Statement was issued. The defendants simply failed in their original duty of knowing, sharing, and disclosing information that was material and reasonably available for their discovery. They compounded that failure by their continued lack of candor in the Supplemental Proxy Statement. While we need not decide the issue here, we are satisfied that, in an appropriate case, a completely candid but belated disclosure of information long known or readily available to a board could raise serious issues of inequitable conduct. *Schnell v. Chris–Craft Industries, Inc.*, Del.Supr., 285 A.2d 437, 439 (1971).

The burden must fall on defendants who claim ratification based on shareholder vote to establish that the shareholder approval resulted from a fully informed electorate. On the record before us, it is clear that the Board failed to meet that burden. *Weinberger v. UOP, Inc., supra* at 703; *Michelson v. Duncan, supra.*

For the foregoing reasons, we conclude that the director defendants breached their fiduciary duty of candor by their failure to make true and correct disclosures of all information they had, or should have had, material to the transaction submitted for stockholder approval.

To summarize: we hold that the directors of Trans Union breached their fiduciary duty to their stockholders (1) by their failure to inform themselves of all information reasonably available to them and relevant to their decision to recommend the Pritzker merger; and (2) by their failure to disclose all material information such as a reasonable stockholder would consider important in deciding whether to approve the Pritzker offer.

We hold, therefore, that the Trial Court committed reversible error in applying the business judgment rule in favor of the director defendants in this case.

On remand, the Court of Chancery shall conduct an evidentiary hearing to determine the fair value of the shares represented by the plaintiffs' class, based on the intrinsic value of Trans Union on September 20, 1980. Such valuation shall be made in accordance with *Weinberger v. UOP, Inc., supra* at 712–715. Thereafter, an award of damages may be entered to the extent that the fair value of Trans Union exceeds $55 per share.

McNEILLY, JUSTICE, dissenting:

The majority opinion reads like an advocate's closing address to a hostile jury. And I say that not lightly. Throughout the opinion great emphasis is directed only to the negative, with nothing more than lip service granted the positive aspects of this case. In my opinion Chancellor Marvel (retired) should have been affirmed. The Chancellor's opinion was the product of well reasoned conclusions, based upon a sound deductive process, clearly supported by the evidence and entitled to deference in this appeal. Because of my diametrical opposition to all evidentiary conclusions of the majority, I respectfully dissent.

It would serve no useful purpose, particularly at this late date, for me to dissent at great length. I restrain myself from doing so, but feel compelled to at least point out what I consider to be the most glaring deficiencies in the majority opinion. The majority has spoken and has effectively said that Trans Union's Directors have been the victims of a "fast shuffle" by Van Gorkom and Pritzker. That is the beginning of the majority's comedy of errors. The first and most important error made is the majority's assessment of the directors' knowledge of the affairs of Trans Union and their combined ability to act in this situation under the protection of the business judgment rule. Trans Union's Board of Directors consisted of ten men, five of whom were "inside" directors and five of whom were "outside" directors. The "inside" directors were Van Gorkom, Chelberg, Bonser, William B. Browder, Senior Vice-President–Law, and Thomas P. O'Boyle, Senior Vice–President–Administration. At the time the merger was proposed the inside five directors had collectively been employed by the Company for 116 years and had 68 years of combined experience as directors. The "outside" directors were A.W. Wallis, William B. Johnson, Joseph B. Lanterman, Graham J. Morgan and Robert W. Reneker. With the exception of Wallis, these were all chief executive officers of Chicago based corporations that were at least as large as Trans Union. The five "outside" directors had 78 years of combined experience as chief executive officers, and 53 years cumulative service as Trans Union directors.

The inside directors wear their badge of expertise in the corporate affairs of Trans Union on their sleeves. But what about the outsiders? Dr. Wallis is or was an economist and math statistician, a professor of economics at Yale University, dean of the graduate school of business at the University of Chicago, and Chancellor of the University of Rochester. Dr. Wallis had been on the Board of Trans Union since 1962. He also was on the Board of Bausch & Lomb, Kodak, Metropolitan Life Insurance Company, Standard Oil and others. William B. Johnson is a University of Pennsylvania law graduate, President of Railway Express until 1966, Chairman and Chief Executive of I.C. Industries Holding Company, and member of Trans Union's Board since 1968.

Joseph Lanterman, a Certified Public Accountant, is or was President and Chief Executive of American Steel, on the Board of International Harvester, Peoples Energy, Illinois Bell Telephone, Harris Bank and Trust Company, Kemper Insurance Company and a director of Trans Union for four years.

Graham Morgan is a chemist, was Chairman and Chief Executive Officer of U.S. Gypsum, and in the 17 and 18 years prior to the Trans Union transaction had been involved in 31 or 32 corporate takeovers.

Robert Reneker attended University of Chicago and Harvard Business Schools. He was President and Chief Executive of Swift and Company, director of Trans Union since 1971, and member of the Boards of seven other corporations including U.S. Gypsum and the Chicago Tribune.

Directors of this caliber are not ordinarily taken in by a "fast shuffle". I submit they were not taken into this multi-million dollar corporate transaction without being fully informed and aware of the state of the art as it pertained to the entire corporate panorama of Trans Union. True, even directors such as these, with their business acumen, interest and expertise, can go astray. I do not believe that to be the case here. These men knew Trans Union like the back of their hands and were more than well qualified to make on the spot informed business judgments concerning the affairs of Trans Union including a 100% sale of the corporation. Lest we forget, the corporate world of then and now operates on what is so aptly referred to as "the fast track". These men were at the time an integral part of that world, all professional business men, not intellectual figureheads.

The majority of this Court holds that the Board's decision, reached on September 20, 1980, to approve the merger was not the product of an *informed* business judgment, that the Board's subsequent efforts to amend the Merger Agreement and take other curative action were *legally and factually* ineffectual, and that the Board did *not deal with complete candor* with the stockholders by failing to disclose all material facts, which they knew or should have known, before securing the stockholders' approval of the merger. I disagree.

At the time of the September 20, 1980 meeting the Board was acutely aware of Trans Union and its prospects. The problems created by accumulated investment tax credits and accelerated depreciation were discussed repeatedly at Board meetings, and all of the directors understood the problem thoroughly. Moreover, at the July, 1980 Board meeting the directors had reviewed Trans Union's newly prepared five-year forecast, and at the August, 1980 meeting Van Gorkom presented the results of a comprehensive study of Trans Union made by The Boston Consulting Group. This study was prepared over an 18 month period and consisted of a detailed analysis of all Trans Union subsidiaries, including competitiveness, profitability, cash throw-off, cash consumption, technical competence and future prospects for contribution to Trans Union's combined net income.

At the September 20 meeting Van Gorkom reviewed all aspects of the proposed transaction and repeated the explanation of the Pritzker offer he had earlier given to senior management. Having heard Van Gorkom's explanation of the Pritzker's offer, and Brennan's explanation of the merger documents the directors discussed the matter. Out of this discussion arose an insistence on the part of the directors that two modifications to the offer be made. First, they required that any potential competing bidder be given access to the same information concerning Trans Union that had been provided to the Pritzkers. Second, the merger documents were to be modified to reflect the fact that the directors could accept a better offer and would not be required to recommend the Pritzker offer if a better offer was made. The following language was inserted into the agreement:

"Within 30 days after the execution of this Agreement, TU shall call a meeting of its stockholders (the 'Stockholder's Meeting') for the purpose of approving and adopting the Merger Agreement. The Board of Directors shall recommend to the stockholders of TU that they approve and adopt the Merger Agreement (the 'Stockholders' Approval') and shall use its best efforts to obtain the requisite vote therefor; *provided, however, that GL and NTC acknowledge that the Board of Directors of TU may have a competing fiduciary obligation to the Stockholders under certain* circumstances." (Emphasis added)

While the language is not artfully drawn, the evidence is clear that the intention underlying that language was to make specific the right that the directors assumed they had, that is, to accept any offer that they thought was better, and not to recommend the Pritzker offer in the face of a better one. At the conclusion of the meeting, the proposed merger was approved.

At a subsequent meeting on October 8, 1981 the directors, with the consent of the Pritzkers, amended the Merger Agreement so as to establish the right of Trans Union to *solicit* as well as to receive higher bids, although the Pritzkers insisted that their merger proposal be presented to the stockholders at the same time that the proposal of any third party was presented. A second amendment, which became effective on October 10, 1981, further provided that Trans Union might unilaterally terminate the proposed merger with the Pritzker company in the event that prior to February 10, 1981 there existed a definitive agreement with a third party for a merger, consolidation, sale of assets, or purchase or exchange of Trans Union stock which was more favorable for the stockholders of Trans Union than the Pritzker offer and which was conditioned upon receipt of stockholder approval and the absence of an injunction against its consummation.

Following the October 8 board meeting of Trans Union, the investment banking firm of Salomon Brothers was retained by the corporation to search for better offers than that of the Pritzkers, Salomon Brothers being charged with the responsibility of doing "whatever possible to see if there is a superior bid in the marketplace over a bid that is on the table for Trans Union". In undertaking such project, it was agreed that Salomon Brothers would be paid the amount of $500,000 to cover its expenses as well as a fee equal to 3/8 ths of 1% of the aggregate fair market value of the consideration to be received by the company in the case of a merger or the like, which meant that in the event Salomon Brothers should find a buyer willing to pay a price of $56.00 a share instead of $55.00, such firm would receive a fee of roughly $2,650,000 plus disbursements.

As the first step in proceeding to carry out its commitment, Salomon Brothers had a brochure prepared, which set forth Trans Union's financial history, described the company's business in detail and set forth Trans Union's operating and financial projections. Salomon Brothers also prepared a list of over 150 companies which it believed might be suitable merger partners, and while four of such companies, namely, General Electric, Borg–Warner, Bendix, and Genstar, Ltd. showed some interest in such a merger, none made a firm proposal to Trans Union and only General Electric showed a sustained interest.[1] As matters transpired, no firm offer which bettered the Pritzker offer of $55 per share was ever made.

On January 21, 1981 a proxy statement was sent to the shareholders of Trans Union advising them of a February 10, 1981 meeting in which the merger would be voted. On January 26, 1981 the directors held their regular meeting. At this meeting the Board discussed the instant merger as well as all events, including this litigation, surrounding it. At the conclusion of the meeting the Board unanimously voted to recommend to the stockholders that they approve the merger. Additionally, the directors reviewed and approved a Supplemental Proxy Statement which, among other things, advised the stockholders of what had occurred at the instant meeting and of the fact that General Electric had decided not to make an offer. On February 10, 1981 the stockholders of Trans Union met pursuant to notice and voted overwhelmingly in favor of the Pritzker merger, 89% of the votes cast being in favor of it.

I have no quarrel with the majority's analysis of the business judgment rule. It is the application of that rule to these facts which is wrong. An overview of the entire record, rather than the limited view of bits and pieces which the majority has exploded like popcorn, convinces me that the directors made an informed business judgment which was buttressed by their test of the market.

At the time of the September 20 meeting the 10 members of Trans Union's Board of Directors were highly qualified and well informed about the affairs and prospects of Trans Union. These directors were acutely aware of the historical problems facing Trans Union which were caused by the tax laws. They had discussed these problems *ad nauseam*. In fact,

---

1. Shortly after the announcement of the proposed merger in September senior members of Trans Union's management got in touch with KKR to discuss their possible participation in a leverage buyout scheme. On December 2, 1980 KKR through Henry Kravis actually made a bid of $60.00 per share for Trans Union stock on December 2, 1980 but the offer was withdrawn three hours after it was made because of complications arising out of negotiations with the Reichman family, extremely wealthy Canadians and a change of attitude toward the leveraged buyout scheme, by Jack Kruzenga, the member of senior management of Trans Union who most likely would have been President and Chief Operating Officer of the new company. Kruzenga was the President and Chief Operating Officer of the seven subsidiaries of Trans Union which constituted the backbone of Trans Union as shown through exhaustive studies and analysis of Trans Union's intrinsic value on the market place by the respected investment banking firm of Morgan Stanley. It is interesting to note that at no time during the market test period did any of the 150 corporations contacted by Salomon Brothers complain of the time frame or availability of corporate records in order to make an independent judgment of market value of 100% of Trans Union.

within two months of the September 20 meeting the board had reviewed and discussed an outside study of the company done by The Boston Consulting Group and an internal five year forecast prepared by management. At the September 20 meeting Van Gorkom presented the Pritzker offer, and the board then heard from James Brennan, the company's counsel in this matter, who discussed the legal documents. Following this, the Board directed that certain changes be made in the merger documents. These changes made it clear that the Board was free to accept a better offer than Pritzker's if one was made. The above facts reveal that the Board did not act in a grossly negligent manner in informing themselves of the relevant and available facts before passing on the merger. To the contrary, this record reveals that the directors acted with the utmost care in informing themselves of the relevant and available facts before passing on the merger.

The majority finds that Trans Union stockholders were not fully informed and that the directors breached their fiduciary duty of complete candor to the stockholders required by *Lynch v. Vickers Energy Corp.*, Del.Supr. 383 A.2d 278 (1977) [Lynch I], in that the proxy materials were deficient in five areas.

Here again is exploitation of the negative by the majority without giving credit to the positive. To respond to the conclusions of the majority would merely be unnecessary prolonged argument. But briefly what did the proxy materials disclose? The proxy material informed the shareholders that projections were furnished to potential purchasers and such projections indicated that Trans Union's net income might increase to approximately $153 million in 1985. That projection, what is almost three times the net income of $58,248,000 reported by Trans Union as its net income for December 31, 1979 confirmed the statement in the proxy materials that the "Board of Directors believes that, assuming reasonably favorable economic and financial conditions, the Company's prospects for future earnings growth are excellent." This material was certainly sufficient to place the Company's stockholders on notice that there was a reasonable basis to believe that the prospects for future earnings growth were excellent, and that the value of their stock was more than the stock market value of their shares reflected.

Overall, my review of the record leads me to conclude that the proxy materials adequately complied with Delaware law in informing the shareholders about the proposed transaction and the events surrounding it.

The majority suggests that the Supplemental Proxy Statement did not comply with the notice requirement of 8 *Del.C.* § 251(c) that notice of the time, place and purpose of a meeting to consider a merger must be sent to each shareholder of record at least 20 days prior to the date of the meeting. In the instant case an original proxy statement was mailed on January 18, 1981 giving notice of the time, place and purpose of the meeting. A Supplemental Proxy Statement was mailed January 26, 1981 in an effort to advise Trans Union's shareholders as to what had occurred at the January 26, 1981 meeting, and that General Electric had decided not to make an offer. The shareholder meeting was held February 10, 1981 fifteen days after the Supplemental Proxy Statement had been sent. All § 251(c) requires is that notice of the time, place and purpose of the meeting be given at least 20 days prior to the meeting. This was accomplished by the proxy statement mailed January 19, 1981. Nothing in § 251(c) prevents the supplementation of proxy materials within 20 days of the meeting. Indeed when additional information, which a reasonable shareholder would consider important in deciding how to vote, comes to light that information must be disclosed to stockholders in sufficient time for the stockholders to consider it. But nothing in § 251(c) requires this additional information to be disclosed at least 20 days prior to the meeting. To reach a contrary result would ignore the current practice and would discourage the supplementation of proxy materials in order to disclose the occurrence of intervening events. In my opinion, fifteen days in the instant case was a sufficient amount of time for the stockholders to receive and consider the information in the supplemental proxy statement.

CHRISTIE, JUSTICE, DISSENTING: I respectfully dissent.

Considering the standard and scope of our review under *Levitt v. Bouvier,* Del.Supr., 287 A.2d 671, 673 (1972), I believe that the record taken as a whole supports a conclusion that the actions of the defendants are protected by the business judgment rule. *Aronson v. Lewis,* Del.Supr., 473 A.2d 805, 812 (1984); *Pogostin v. Rice,* Del.Supr., 480 A.2d 619, 627 (1984). I also am satisfied that the record supports a conclusion that the defendants acted with the complete candor required by *Lynch v. Vickers Energy Corp.,* Del.Supr., 383 A.2d 278 (1977). Under the circumstances I would affirm the judgment of the Court of Chancery.

NOTES

1. *Aftermath.* The *Smith v. Van Gorkom* litigation was later settled for a reported $23.5 million that was paid in part by the directors' liability insurance and in part by the Pritzker group. Absent that insurance and settlement the inside and outside directors would have been personally liable for any damages. Bayless Manning, "Reflections and Practical Tips on Life in the Boardroom After Van Gorkom," 41 Bus. Law. 1, n.a1 (1985). As a result of Van Gorkom and similar cases, director and officer liability insurance costs rose 360 percent in a single year and became almost impossible to obtain by many corporations. James J. Hanks, Jr., "Recent State Legislation on Director and Officer Liability Limitation and Indemnification," 43 Bus. Law. 1207, 1209 (1988). Criticism of the court's decision in *Smith v. Van Gorkom* was widespread (described as "ludicrous" in one report). Delaware and some other thirty states also enacted legislation that allowed corporations to remove directors from the duty of care. Hanks, supra, 43 Bus. Law. at 1210. See e.g., Del. § 102(b)(7). A survey found that some ninety percent of Delaware corporations opted out of imposing that duty on their directors. Roberta Romano, "Corporate Governance in the Aftermath of the Insurance Crisis," 39 Emory L. J. 1155, 1160–1161 (1990). Those proposals were

approved by large majorities of the shareholders. Hanks, supra, 43 Bus. Law. at 1211. The court's decision in *Van Gorkom* thus had the two-sided effect of providing shareholder protection that shareholders did not want and removing shareholder protection that may have been desirable under a reasonably applied standard.

2.   Jerome Van Gorkom, the Chairman and Chief Executive Officer at Trans Union, did not quietly fade away into retirement. He continued to act as Chairman of the Chicago Lyric Opera Society and became Under Secretary of State in the United States State Department. He also served as the deputy director of a Catholic relief organization where he acted as a volunteer personally distributing food to the needy. He was given credit for bailing the Chicago school system out of a dire crisis and served (less successfully) as the head of the Chicago Housing Authority. While at Trans Union, Van Gorkom also served on the boards of thirteen companies, nine universities and various hospitals and charities. He was appointed to serve on two Social Security advisory commissions that sought reform of the nation's Social Security System. Trained as both a lawyer and an accountant, Van Gorkom died at age 80 in 1998. Marney Keenan, "A Man for All Challenges Corporations, Embassies, Charities, Civic Institutions–Jerome Van Gorkom Has Managed Them All," Chicago Tribune, Oct. 2, 1988 (Sunday Magazine), at 12; Bryan Smith, "Jerome Van Gorkom, Aided Schools," Chicago Sun–Times, March 20, 1998, at 69. Jay Pritzker, also a lawyer and accountant, died about a year later. He and his brother Robert owned the Hyatt hotel chain and other businesses. They were considered to be among the richest people in the world at one point, with an estimated net worth of $13.5 billion. Anthony Romirez, "Jay Pritzker, Who Built Hyatt Chain, is Dead at 76," N.Y. Times, Jan. 25, 1999, at 21.

3.   Why should the board in *Van Gorkom* be any less entitled to rely on its president than the bank directors in *Bates v. Dresser*? The court in *Van Gorkom* apparently wants decision making by a board of directors to be conducted in a very formal and ritualistic way, something akin to the way the court renders its own decisions. Does this overlook the way businesses operate? As the dissent notes, business decisions often have to be made quickly or an opportunity will be lost. In the case of Trans Union, there was a downturn in the industry after its sale, and it became clear that the shareholders had received a bargain from its sale to the Pritzkers. See Keenan, supra. The court's demand for top price for shareholders is also a very dangerous business approach. Any investor that seeks to hold out only for the top of the market will die poor because no one is able to predict that event, a fact you may want to keep in mind in managing your own investments. "As the Rothschilds used to say, only fools set out to make the highest returns."[2] A reasonable profit should satisfy all but the greediest, or those uniformed on the vagaries of the market. Some business people also like to "leave money on the table" by not demanding the dearest bargain. This helps prevent deals from breaking up, generates good feelings that may be needed if problems develop and discourages disappointed investors from seeking to better their price through litigation or other tactics.

---

2.   Derek Leebaert, *The Fifty–Year Wound, The True Price of America's Cold War Victory* 642 (2002).

4. The *Van Gorkom* court indicates that a fairness opinion from an independent investment banker would have gone a long way to help the defendants' case. But see *Weinberger v. UOP*, set forth at page 1071.

5. If serious people indulge in such acts, the Trans Union directors probably would have liked to have exchanged corporate "high-fives" with Van Gorkom over the deal with the Pritzkers. After all, the stock had been trading at less than $40 in the public markets, the company had run out of solutions for solving its problems, and the sale to the Pritzkers was a clean deal that would give the shareholders a premium of at least $15 per share over the market high, an increase of over one-third. Yet, the board members found themselves facing personal liability and charges that they breached their fiduciary duties. In that regard, the *Van Gorkom* majority charges that the Trans Union board was indifferent to, and uninformed of, the possibility that the company could be sold at a higher price to others or even to existing management. As the dissent points out, however, the likelihood of success of such a deal was remote, the KKR proposal fell through and the intensive efforts of Salomon Brothers failed to unearth a serious offer. As will be seen in later chapters, the announcement of the sale of a company that others view to be undervalued often results in fierce competitive battles with bidding wars furiously fought.

6. Why do you think the Trans Union board members took so little interest in the actual merger agreement? The court spends much time addressing that omission and seems outraged by the failure of the board members even to read it. The answer might be a simple one. They were directors being asked to make a policy decision. The issue before them was the sale of the company at $55. They wanted that deal, the essential term of the deal was its price, and the directors had little or no interest in the details. The details would be for the lawyers handle. Do you think such an approach is irresponsible?

7. As noted, following the *Van Gorkom* decision, the Delaware legislature enacted Del. § 102(b)(7), which permits the articles of incorporation to eliminate director liability for duty of care violations. The opinion in *Emerald Partners v. Berlin*, p. 327 infra, examines the scope of that section.

BREHM v. EISNER

746 A.2d 244 (Del.2000).

VEASEY CHIEF JUSTICE:

* * * By an agreement dated October 1, 1995, Disney hired Ovitz as its president. He was a long-time friend of Disney Chairman and CEO Michael Eisner. At the time, Ovitz was an important talent broker in Hollywood. Although he lacked experience managing a diversified public company, other companies with entertainment operations had been interested in hiring him for high-level executive positions. The Employment Agreement was unilaterally negotiated by Eisner and approved by the Old

Board. Their judgment was that Ovitz was a valuable person to hire as president of Disney, and they agreed ultimately with Eisner's recommendation in awarding him an extraordinarily lucrative contract.

Ovitz' Employment Agreement had an initial term of five years and required that Ovitz "devote his full time and best efforts exclusively to the Company," with exceptions for volunteer work, service on the board of another company, and managing his passive investments. In return, Disney agreed to give Ovitz a base salary of $1 million per year, a discretionary bonus, and two sets of stock options (the "A" options and the "B" options) that collectively would enable Ovitz to purchase 5 million shares of Disney common stock.

The "A" options were scheduled to vest in three annual increments of 1 million shares each, beginning on September 30, 1998 (*i.e.,* at the end of the third full year of employment) and continuing for the following two years (through September 2000). The agreement specifically provided that the "A" options would vest immediately if Disney granted Ovitz a non-fault termination of the Employment Agreement. The "B" options, consisting of 2 million shares, differed in two important respects. Although scheduled to vest annually starting in September 2001 (*i.e.,* the year *after* the last "A" option would vest), the "B" options were conditioned on Ovitz and Disney first having agreed to extend his employment beyond the five-year term of the Employment Agreement. Furthermore, Ovitz would forfeit the right to qualify for the "B" options if his initial employment term of five years ended prematurely for any reason, even if from a non-fault termination.

The Employment Agreement provided for three ways by which Ovitz' employment might end. He might serve his five years and Disney might decide against offering him a new contract. If so, Disney would owe Ovitz a $10 million termination payment.[6] Before the end of the initial term, Disney could terminate Ovitz for "good cause" only if Ovitz committed gross negligence or malfeasance, or if Ovitz resigned voluntarily. Disney would owe Ovitz no additional compensation if it terminated him for "good cause." Termination without cause (non-fault termination) would entitle Ovitz to the present value of his remaining salary payments through September 30, 2000, a $10 million severance payment, an additional $7.5 million for each fiscal year remaining under the agreement, and the immediate vesting of the first 3 million stock options (the "A" Options).

Plaintiffs allege that the Old Board knew that Disney needed a strong second-in-command. Disney had recently made several acquisitions, and questions lingered about Eisner's health due to major heart surgery. The Complaint further alleges that "Eisner had demonstrated little or no capacity to work with important or well-known subordinate executives who wanted to position themselves to succeed him," citing the departures of Disney executives Jeffrey Katzenberg, Richard Frank, and Stephen

---

6.   All the "A" options would have vested, but he would not receive the "B" options.

Bollenbach as examples. Thus, the Board knew that, to increase the chance for long-term success, it had to take extra care in reviewing a decision to hire Disney's new president.

But Eisner's decision that Disney should hire Ovitz as its president was not entirely well-received. When Eisner told three members of the Old Board in mid-August 1995 that he had decided to hire Ovitz, all three "denounced the decision." Although not entirely clear from the Complaint, the vote of the Old Board approving the Ovitz Employment Agreement two months later appears to have been unanimous. Aside from a conclusory attack that the Old Board followed Eisner's bidding, the Complaint fails to allege any particularized facts that the three directors changed their initial reactions through anything other than the typical process of further discussion and individual contemplation.

The Complaint then alleges that the Old Board failed properly to inform itself about the total costs and incentives of the Ovitz Employment Agreement, especially the severance package. This is the key allegation related to this issue on appeal. Specifically, plaintiffs allege that the Board failed to realize that the contract gave Ovitz an incentive to find a way to exit the Company via a non-fault termination as soon as possible because doing so would permit him to earn more than he could by fulfilling his contract. The Complaint alleges, however, that the Old Board had been advised by a corporate compensation expert, Graef Crystal, in connection with its decision to approve the Ovitz Employment Agreement. Two public statements by Crystal form the basis of the allegation that the Old Board failed to consider the incentives and the total cost of the severance provisions, but these statements by Crystal were not made until after Ovitz left Disney in December 1996, approximately 14 1/2 months after being hired.

The first statement, published in a December 23, 1996 article in the web-based magazine *Slate,* quoted Crystal as saying, in part, "Of course, the overall costs of the package would go up sharply in the event of Ovitz's termination (*and I wish now that I'd made a spreadsheet showing just what the deal would total if Ovitz had been fired at any time*)." The second published statement appeared in an article about three weeks later in the January 13, 1997 edition of *California Law Business.* The article appears first to paraphrase Crystal: "With no one expecting failure, the sleeper clauses in Ovitz's contract seemed innocuous, Crystal says, explaining that no one added up the total cost of the severance package." The article then quotes Crystal as saying that the amount of Ovitz' severance was "shocking" and that "*[n]obody quantified this and I wish we had.*" One of the charging paragraphs of the Complaint concludes:

57. As has been conceded by Graef Crystal, the executive compensation consultant who advised the Old Board with respect to the Ovitz Employment Agreement, the Old Board *never* considered the costs that would be incurred by Disney in the event Ovitz was terminated

from the Company for a reason other than cause prior to the natural expiration of the Ovtiz Employment Agreement.

Although repeated in various forms in the Complaint, these quoted admissions by Crystal constitute the extent of the factual support for the allegation that the Old Board failed properly to consider the severance elements of the agreement. This Court, however, must juxtapose these allegations with the legal presumption that the Old Board's conduct was a proper exercise of business judgment. That presumption includes the statutory protection for a board that relies in good faith on an expert advising the Board. We must decide whether plaintiffs' factual allegations, if proven, would rebut that presumption.

Soon after Ovitz began work, problems surfaced and the situation continued to deteriorate during the first year of his employment. To support this allegation, the plaintiffs cite various media reports detailing internal complaints and providing external examples of alleged business mistakes. The Complaint uses these reports to suggest that the New Board had reason to believe that Ovitz' performance and lack of commitment met the gross negligence or malfeasance standards of the termination-for-cause provisions of the contract.

The deteriorating situation, according to the Complaint, led Ovitz to begin seeking alternative employment and to send Eisner a letter in September 1996 that the Complaint paraphrases as stating his dissatisfaction with his role and expressing his desire to leave the Company. The Complaint also admits that Ovitz would not actually resign before negotiating a non-fault severance agreement because he did not want to jeopardize his rights to a lucrative severance in the form of a "non-fault termination" under the terms of the 1995 Employment Agreement.

On December 11, 1996, Eisner and Ovitz agreed to arrange for Ovitz to leave Disney on the non-fault basis provided for in the 1995 Employment Agreement. Eisner then "caused" the New Board "to rubber-stamp his decision (by 'mutual consent')." This decision was implemented by a December 27, 1996 letter to Ovitz from defendant Sanford M. Litvack, an officer and director of Disney. That letter stated:

This will confirm the terms of your agreement with the Company as follows:

1. The Term of your employment under your existing Employment Agreement with The Walt Disney Company will end at the close of business today. Consequently, your signature confirms the end of your service as an officer, and your resignation as a director, of the Company and its affiliates.

2. This letter will for all purposes of the Employment Agreement be treated as a "Non–Fault Termination." By our mutual agreement, the total amount payable to you under your Employment Agreement, including the amount payable under Section 11(c) in the event of a "Non–Fault Termination," is $38,888,230.77, net of with-

holding required by law or authorized by you. By your signature on this letter, you acknowledge receipt of all but $1,000,000 of such amount. Pursuant to our mutual agreement, this will confirm that payment of the $1,000,000 balance has been deferred until February 5, 1997, pending final settlement of accounts.

    3.   This letter will further confirm that the option to purchase 3,000,000 shares of the Company's Common Stock granted to you pursuant to Option A described in your Employment Agreement will vest as of today and will expire in accordance with its terms on September 30, 2002.

Although the non-fault termination left Ovitz with what essentially was a very lucrative severance agreement, it is important to note that Ovitz and Disney had negotiated for that severance payment at the time they initially contracted in 1995, and in the end the payout to Ovitz did not exceed the 1995 contractual benefits. Consequently, Ovitz received the $10 million termination payment, $7.5 million for part of the fiscal year remaining under the agreement and the immediate vesting of the 3 million stock options (the "A" options). As a result of his termination Ovitz would not receive the 2 million "B" options that he would have been entitled to if he had completed the full term of the Employment Agreement and if his contract were renewed.[12]

    * * * This is a case about whether there should be personal liability of the directors of a Delaware corporation to the corporation for lack of due care in the decisionmaking process and for waste of corporate assets. This case is not about the failure of the directors to establish and carry out ideal corporate governance practices.

    All good corporate governance practices include compliance with statutory law and case law establishing fiduciary duties. But the law of corporate fiduciary duties and remedies for violation of those duties are distinct from the aspirational goals of ideal corporate governance practices. Aspirational ideals of good corporate governance practices for boards of directors that go beyond the minimal legal requirements of the corporation law are highly desirable, often tend to benefit stockholders, sometimes reduce litigation and can usually help directors avoid liability. But they are not required by the corporation law and do not define standards of liability.[29]

---

    12. Under the 1995 Employment Agreement, Ovitz' "B" options to purchase 2,000,000 shares were scheduled to vest "in increments of 1,000,000 shares on each of September 30, 2001 and September 30, 2002." But they would not vest if Ovitz' employment "shall have terminated for any reason whatsoever more than three months prior to such scheduling date." If Ovitz' employment should terminate before October 1, 2000 (the expiration of the 1995 agreement), the "B" options "shall thereupon irrevocably terminate."

    29. *See id.* at 332; *see also* E. Norman Veasey, *An Economic Rationale for Judicial Decisionmaking in Corporate Law,* 53 Bus.Law. 681, 699–700 (1998) (listing seven suggestions of aspirational norms for good corporate practice that are "purely precatory" and do "not foreshadow how any case should be decided," but "may be in the nature of safe harbors in certain circumstances"). For example, the Complaint quotes a *Wall Street Journal* article critical of the Board's functioning: the directors own little stock; they do not "hold a regular retreat"; they "don't meet regularly in the absence of company executives such as Mr. Eisner"; and they do not

The inquiry here is not whether we would disdain the composition, behavior and decisions of Disney's Old Board or New Board as alleged in the Complaint if we were Disney stockholders. In the absence of a legislative mandate, that determination is not for the courts. That decision is for the stockholders to make in voting for directors, urging other stockholders to reform or oust the board, or in making individual buy-sell decisions involving Disney securities. The sole issue that this Court must determine is whether the particularized facts alleged in this Complaint provide a reason to believe that the conduct of the Old Board in 1995 and the New Board in 1996 constituted a violation of their fiduciary duties. * * *

Plaintiffs claim that the Court of Chancery erred when it concluded that a board of directors is "not required to be informed of every fact, but rather is required to be reasonably informed." Applying that conclusion, the Court of Chancery held that the Complaint did not create a reasonable doubt that the Old Board had satisfied the requisite informational component when it approved the Ovitz contract in 1995. In effect, Plaintiffs argue that being "reasonably informed" is too lax a standard to satisfy Delaware's legal test for the informational component of board decisions. They contend that the Disney directors on the Old Board did not avail themselves of all material information reasonably available in approving Ovitz' 1995 contract, and thereby violated their fiduciary duty of care.

The "reasonably informed" language used by the Court of Chancery here may have been a short-hand attempt to paraphrase the Delaware jurisprudence that, in making business decisions, directors must consider all material information reasonably available, and that the directors' process is actionable only if grossly negligent. The question is whether the trial court's formulation is consistent with our objective test of reasonableness, the test of materiality and concepts of gross negligence. We agree with the Court of Chancery that the standard for judging the informational component of the directors' decisionmaking does not mean that the Board must be informed of *every* fact. The Board is responsible for considering only *material* facts that are *reasonably available,* not those that are immaterial or out of the Board's reasonable reach.[47] * * *

Certainly in this case the economic exposure of the corporation to the payout scenarios of the Ovitz contract was material, particularly given its large size, for purposes of the directors' decisionmaking process. And those dollar exposure numbers were reasonably available because the logical

"give Mr. Eisner a written assessment of his performance" as do "89% of the nation's biggest industrial corporations." These are very desirable practices to be sure, but they are not required by the corporation law.

47. Compare the American Law Institute test, which requires that a director must be "informed ... to the extent the director reasonably believes to be appropriate under the circumstances." *Principles of Corporate Governance, supra* note 30, at § 4.01(c)(2). Because this test also is based on the objective test of reasonableness, it could be argued that it is essentially synonymous with the Delaware test. But there is room to argue that the Delaware test is stricter. *See* Roswell Perkins, *ALI Corporate Governance Project in Midstream,* 41 Bus.Law. 1195, 1210–11 (1986). In the end, the debate may be mostly semantic.

inference from plaintiffs' allegations is that Crystal or the New Board could have calculated the numbers. Thus, the objective tests of reasonable availability and materiality were satisfied by this Complaint. But that is not the end of the inquiry for liability purposes. * * *

The Complaint, fairly construed, admits that the directors were advised by Crystal as an expert and that they relied on his expertise. Accordingly, the question here is whether the directors are to be "fully protected" (*i.e.,* not held liable) on the basis that they relied in good faith on a qualified expert under Section 141(e) of the Delaware General Corporation Law. The Old Board is entitled to the presumption that it exercised proper business judgment, including proper reliance on the expert. In fact, the Court of Chancery refers to the "Board's reliance on Crystal and his decision not to fully calculate the amount of severance." The Court's invocation here of the concept of the protection accorded directors who rely on experts, even though no reference is made to the statute itself, is on the right track, but the Court's analysis is unclear and incomplete.

Although the Court of Chancery did not expressly predicate its decision on Section 141(e), Crystal is presumed to be an expert on whom the Board was entitled to rely in good faith under Section 141(e) in order to be "fully protected." Plaintiffs must rebut the presumption that the directors properly exercised their business judgment, including their good faith reliance on Crystal's expertise. What Crystal *now* believes *in hindsight* that he and the Board *should have done* in 1995 does not provide that rebuttal. That is not to say, however, that a rebuttal of the presumption of proper reliance on the expert under Section 141(e) cannot be pleaded ... in a properly framed complaint setting forth particularized facts creating reason to believe that the Old Board's conduct was grossly negligent.

To survive a ... motion to dismiss in a due care case where an expert has advised the board in its decisionmaking process, the complaint must allege particularized facts (not conclusions) that, if proved, would show, for example, that: (a) the directors did not in fact rely on the expert; (b) their reliance was not in good faith; (c) they did not reasonably believe that the expert's advice was within the expert's professional competence; (d) the expert was not selected with reasonable care by or on behalf of the corporation, and the faulty selection process was attributable to the directors; (e) the subject matter (in this case the cost calculation) that was material and reasonably available was so obvious that the board's failure to consider it was grossly negligent regardless of the expert's advice or lack of advice; or (f) that the decision of the Board was so unconscionable as to constitute waste or fraud. This Complaint includes no particular allegations of this nature, and therefore it was subject to dismissal as drafted. * * *

NOTES

1.   Do you think the board acted with proper concern for the shareholders' interests? The court in *Brehm v. Eisner* intensively analyzes the board's decision making process but professes to have no interest in whether the decision was a correct one? If that is the case, what does all of this analysis really accomplish? Can you think of a better analytical framework to assure that corporate directors are giving adequate thought to their decisions?

2.   Following the decision in *Brehm v. Eisner*, the complaint was amended to include more specific factual allegations that tended to undermine application of the business judgment rule. A Delaware Chancery Judge then ruled that the complaint created a cause of action and ordered a trial. The Court stated that "plaintiffs must plead particularized facts sufficient to raise (1) a reason to doubt that the action was taken honestly and in good faith or (2) a reason to doubt that the board was adequately informed in making the decision." After reviewing the factual allegations in the amended complaint, The Chancery Judge found that the plaintiffs' claims were "based on an alleged knowing and deliberate indifference to a potential risk of harm to the corporation. Where a director consciously ignores his or her duties to the corporation, thereby causing economic injury to its stockholders, the director's actions are either 'not in good faith' or 'involve intentional misconduct.' Thus, plaintiffs' allegations support claims that fall *outside* the liability waiver provided under Disney's certificate of incorporation." In re Walt Disney Company Derivative Litigation, 825 A.2d 275 (Del Ch. 2003). The subsequent trial over the Ovitz contract lasted thirty-seven days and generated almost 10,000 pages of testimony. In a 175 page opinion, the Delaware chancery judge ruled that, while the actions of the Disney board did not meet ideal corporate practices, they did not rise to the level of a breach of fiduciary duties. The court also tried to explain the complex approach taken by the Delaware courts to Delaware Section 107(b)(7).

IN RE WALT DISNEY COMPANY DERIVATIVE LITIGATION

907 A.2d 693, (Del. Ch. 2005).

CHANDLER, J.

Unlike ideals of corporate governance, a fiduciary's duties do not change over time. How we understand those duties may evolve and become refined, but the duties themselves have not changed, except to the extent that fulfilling a fiduciary duty requires obedience to other positive law. This Court strongly encourages directors and officers to employ best practices, as those practices are understood at the time a corporate decision is taken. But Delaware law does not—indeed, the common law cannot—hold fiduciaries liable for a failure to comply with the aspirational ideal of best practices, any more than a common-law court deciding a medical malpractice dispute can impose a standard of liability based on ideal—rather than competent or standard—medical treatment practices, lest the average medical practitioner be found inevitably derelict.

Fiduciaries are held by the common law to a high standard in fulfilling their stewardship over the assets of others, a standard that (depending on the circumstances) may not be the same as that contemplated by ideal corporate governance. Yet therein lies perhaps the greatest strength of Delaware's corporation law. Fiduciaries who act faithfully and honestly on behalf of those whose interests they represent are indeed granted wide latitude in their efforts to maximize shareholders' investment. Times may change, but fiduciary duties do not. Indeed, other institutions may develop, pronounce and urge adherence to ideals of corporate best practices. But the development of aspirational ideals, however worthy as goals for human behavior, should not work to distort the legal requirements by which human behavior is actually measured. Nor should the common law of fiduciary duties become a prisoner of narrow definitions or formulaic expressions. It is thus both the province and special duty of this Court to measure, in light of all the facts and circumstances of a particular case, whether an individual who has accepted a position of responsibility over the assets of another has been unremittingly faithful to his or her charge.

Because this matter, by its very nature, has become something of a public spectacle—commencing as it did with the spectacular hiring of one of the entertainment industry's best-known personalities to help run one of its iconic businesses, and ending with a spectacular failure of that union, with breathtaking amounts of severance pay the consequence—it is, I think, worth noting what the role of this Court must be in evaluating decision-makers' performance with respect to decisions gone awry, spectacularly or otherwise. It is easy, of course, to fault a decision that ends in a failure, once hindsight makes the result of that decision plain to see. But the essence of business is risk—the application of informed belief to contingencies whose outcomes can sometimes be predicted, but never known. The decision-makers entrusted by shareholders must act out of loyalty to those shareholders. They must in good faith act to make informed decisions on behalf of the shareholders, untainted by self-interest. Where they fail to do so, this Court stands ready to remedy breaches of fiduciary duty.

Even where decision-makers act as faithful servants, however, their ability and the wisdom of their judgments will vary. The redress for failures that arise from faithful management must come from the markets, through the action of shareholders and the free flow of capital, and not from this Court. Should the Court apportion liability based on the ultimate outcome of decisions taken in good faith by faithful directors or officers, those decision-makers would necessarily take decisions that minimize risk, not maximize value. The entire advantage of the risk-taking, innovative, wealth-creating engine that is the Delaware corporation would cease to exist, with disastrous results for shareholders and society alike. That is why, under our corporate law, corporate decision-makers are held strictly to their fiduciary duties, but within the boundaries of those duties are free to act as their judgment and abilities dictate, free of *post hoc* penalties from a reviewing court using perfect hindsight. Corporate decisions are made, risks are taken, the results become apparent, capital flows accordingly, and shareholder value is increased.

* * *

A. The Business Judgment Rule

Delaware law is clear that the business and affairs of a corporation are managed by or under the direction of its board of directors. The business judgment rule serves to protect and promote the role of the board as the ultimate manager of the corporation. Because courts are ill equipped to engage in *post hoc* substantive review of business decisions, the business judgment rule "operates to preclude a court from imposing itself unreasonably on the business and affairs of a corporation."

The business judgment rule is not actually a substantive rule of law, but instead it is a presumption that "in making a business decision the directors of a corporation acted on an informed basis, ... and in the honest belief that the action taken was in the best interests of the company [and its shareholders]. This presumption applies when there is no evidence of fraud, bad faith, or self-dealing in the usual sense of personal profit or betterment" on the part of the directors. In the absence of this evidence, the board's decision will be upheld unless it cannot be "attributed to any rational business purpose." When a plaintiff fails to rebut the presumption of the business judgment rule, she is not entitled to any remedy, be it legal or equitable, unless the transaction constitutes waste.

B. Waste

Corporate waste is very rarely found in Delaware courts because the applicable test imposes such an onerous burden upon a plaintiff—proving "an exchange that is so one sided that no business person of ordinary, sound judgment could conclude that the corporation has received adequate consideration." In other words, waste is a rare, "unconscionable case" where directors irrationally squander or give away corporate assets.

The Delaware Supreme Court has implicitly held that committing waste is an act of bad faith. It is not necessarily true, however, that every act of bad faith by a director constitutes waste. For example, if a director acts in bad faith (for whatever reason), but the transaction is one in which a businessperson of ordinary, sound judgment concludes that the corporation received adequate consideration, the transaction would not constitute waste.

C. The Fiduciary Duty of Due Care

The fiduciary duty of due care requires that directors of a Delaware corporation "use that amount of care which ordinarily careful and prudent men would use in similar circumstances," and—"consider all material information reasonably available" in making business decisions, and that deficiencies in the directors' process are actionable only if the directors' actions are grossly negligent. * * *

In the duty of care context with respect to corporate fiduciaries, gross negligence has been defined as a "reckless indifference to or a deliberate disregard of the whole body of stockholders' or actions which are without the bounds of reason.'" Because duty of care violations are actionable only if the directors acted with gross negligence, and because in most instances money damages are unavailable to a plaintiff who could theoretically prove a duty of care violation, duty of care violations are rarely found. * * *

D. Section 102(b)(7)

Following the Delaware Supreme Court's landmark decision in *Van Gorkom*, n438 the Delaware General Assembly acted swiftly to enact 8 *Del. C.* § 102(b)(7). Section 102(b)(7) states that a corporation may include in its certificate of incorporation:

> (7) A provision eliminating or limiting the personal liability of a director to the corporation or its stockholders for monetary damages for breach of fiduciary duty as a director, provided that such provision shall not eliminate or limit the liability of a director: (i) For any breach of the director's duty of loyalty to the corporation or its stockholders; (ii) for acts or omissions not in good faith or which involve intentional misconduct or a knowing violation of law; (iii) under § 174 of this title; or (iv) for any transaction from which the director derived an improper personal benefit. No such provision shall eliminate or limit the liability of a director for any act or omission occurring prior to the date when such provision becomes effective. All references in this paragraph to a director shall also be deemed to refer (x) to a member of the governing body of a corporation which is not authorized to issue capital stock, and (y) to such other person or persons, if any, who, pursuant to a provision of the certificate of incorporation in accordance with § 141(a) of this title, exercise or perform any of the powers or duties otherwise conferred or imposed upon the board of directors by this title.

Recently, Vice Chancellor Strine wrote that, "one of the primary purposes of § 102(b)(7) is to encourage directors to undertake risky, but potentially value-maximizing, business strategies, so long as they do so in good faith." Or in other words, § 102(b)(7) is most useful "when, despite the directors' good intentions, [the challenged transaction] did not generate financial success and ... the possibility of hindsight bias about the directors' prior ability to foresee that their business plans would not pan out" could improperly influence a *post hoc* judicial evaluation of the directors' actions.

The vast majority of Delaware corporations have a provision in their certificate of incorporation that permits exculpation to the extent provided for by § 102(b)(7). This provision prohibits recovery of monetary damages from directors for a successful shareholder claim, either direct or derivative, that is exclusively based upon establishing a violation of the duty of due care. The existence of an exculpation provision authorized by

§ 102(b)(7) does not, however, eliminate a director's fiduciary duty of care, because a court may still grant injunctive relief for violations of that duty.

An exculpation provision such as that authorized by § 102(b)(7) is in the nature of an affirmative defense. As a result, it is the burden of the director defendants to demonstrate that they are entitled to the protections of the relevant charter provision.

E.   Acting in Good Faith

Decisions from the Delaware Supreme Court and the Court of Chancery are far from clear with respect to whether there is a separate fiduciary duty of good faith. Good faith has been said to require an "honesty of purpose," and a genuine care for the fiduciary's constituents, but, at least in the corporate fiduciary context, it is probably easier to define bad faith rather than good faith. This may be so because Delaware law presumes that directors act in good faith when making business judgments. Bad faith has been defined as authorizing a transaction "for some purpose *other than* a genuine attempt to advance corporate welfare or [when the transaction] is *known to constitute* a violation of applicable positive law." In other words, an action taken with the intent to harm the corporation is a disloyal act in bad faith. A similar definition was used seven years earlier, when Chancellor Allen wrote that bad faith (or lack of good faith) is when a director acts in a manner "unrelated to a pursuit of the corporation's best interests. It makes no difference the reason why the director intentionally fails to pursue the best interests of the corporation.

Bad faith can be the result of "any emotion [that] may cause a director to [intentionally] place his own interests, preferences or appetites before the welfare of the corporation," including greed, "hatred, lust, envy, revenge, . . . shame or pride." Sloth could certainly be an appropriate addition to that incomplete list if it constitutes a systematic or sustained shirking of duty. Ignorance, in and of itself, probably does not belong on the list, but ignorance attributable to any of the moral failings previously listed could constitute bad faith. It is unclear, based upon existing jurisprudence, whether motive is a necessary element for a successful claim that a director has acted in bad faith, n456 and, if so, whether that motive must be shown explicitly or whether it can be inferred from the directors' conduct.

Shrouded in the fog of this hazy jurisprudence, the defendants' motion to dismiss this action was denied because I concluded that the complaint, together with all reasonable inferences drawn from the well-plead allegations contained therein, could be held to state a non-exculpated breach of fiduciary duty claim, insofar as it alleged that Disney's directors "*consciously and intentionally disregarded their responsibilities*, adopting a we don't care about the risks' attitude concerning a material corporate decision."

Upon long and careful consideration, I am of the opinion that the concept of *intentional dereliction of duty*, a *conscious disregard for one's responsibilities*, is an appropriate (although not the only) standard for determining whether fiduciaries have acted in good faith. Deliberate indifference and inaction *in the face of a duty to act* is, in my mind, conduct that is clearly disloyal to the corporation. It is the epitome of faithless conduct.

To act in good faith, a director must act at all times with an honesty of purpose and in the best interests and welfare of the corporation. The presumption of the business judgment rule creates a presumption that a director acted in good faith. In order to overcome that presumption, a plaintiff must prove an act of bad faith by a preponderance of the evidence. To create a definitive and categorical definition of the universe of acts that would constitute bad faith would be difficult, if not impossible. And it would misconceive how, in my judgment, the concept of good faith operates in our common law of corporations. Fundamentally, the duties traditionally analyzed as belonging to corporate fiduciaries, loyalty and care, are but constituent elements of the overarching concepts of allegiance, devotion and faithfulness that must guide the conduct of every fiduciary. The good faith required of a corporate fiduciary includes not simply the duties of care and loyalty, in the narrow sense that I have discussed them above, but all actions required by a true faithfulness and devotion to the interests of the corporation and its shareholders. A failure to act in good faith may be shown, for instance, where the fiduciary intentionally acts with a purpose other than that of advancing the best interests of the corporation, where the fiduciary acts with the intent to violate applicable positive law, or where the fiduciary intentionally fails to act in the face of a known duty to act, demonstrating a conscious disregard for his duties. There may be other examples of bad faith yet to be proven or alleged, but these three are the most salient. As evidenced by previous rulings in this case both from this Court and the Delaware Supreme Court, issues of the Disney directors' good faith (or lack thereof) are central to the outcome of this action.

NOTE

The Ovitz contract was not the biggest such disaster at Disney. Another executive, Jeffrey Katzenberg, was forced out by Eisner before Ovitz's arrival. After his hiring, Ovitz negotiated a settlement of Katzenberg's severance claims for $90 million, but Eisner refused to pay. Disney did not fare well in the subsequent litigation, but Eisner turned down several settlement proposals that would have resolved the matter for considerably less than the $285 million Disney ultimately had to pay Katzenberg. James B. Stewart, "Disney War" (2005).

The Delaware Supreme court's decision in the *Disney* case provides a basis for comparing the relationship between the business judgment rule, "good faith," and Del. § 1029b)(7):

IN RE THE WALT DISNEY CO.
DERIVATIVE LITIGATION

906 A.2d 27, (Del. 2006).

JACOBS, JUSTICE:

In August 1995, Michael Ovitz ("Ovitz") and The Walt Disney Company ("Disney" or the "Company") entered into an employment agreement under which Ovitz would serve as President of Disney for five years. In December 1996, only fourteen months after he commenced employment, Ovitz was terminated without cause, resulting in a severance payout to Ovitz valued at approximately $ 130 million.

In January 1997, several Disney shareholders brought derivative actions in the Court of Chancery, on behalf of Disney, against Ovitz and the directors of Disney who served at the time of the events complained of (the "Disney defendants"). The plaintiffs claimed that the $ 130 million severance payout was the product of fiduciary duty and contractual breaches by Ovitz, and breaches of fiduciary duty by the Disney defendants, and a waste of assets. after the disposition of several pretrial motions and an appeal to this Court, the case was tried before the Chancellor over 37 days between October 20, 2004 and January 19, 2005. In August 2005, the Chancellor handed down a well-crafted 174 page Opinion and Order, determining that "the director defendants did not breach their fiduciary duties or commit waste." The Court entered judgment in favor of all defendants on all claims alleged in the amended complaint.

The plaintiffs have appealed from that judgment, claiming that the Court of Chancery committed multitudinous errors. We conclude, for the reasons that follow, that the Chancellor's factual findings and legal rulings were correct and not erroneous in any respect. Accordingly, the judgment entered by the Court of Chancery will be affirmed.

I. *THE FACTS*

We next summarize the facts as found by the Court of Chancery that are material to the issues presented on this appeal. The critical events flow from what turned out to be an unfortunate hiring decision at Disney, a company that for over half a century has been one of America's leading film and entertainment enterprises.

In 1994 Disney lost in a tragic helicopter crash its President and Chief Operating Officer, Frank Wells, who together with Michael Eisner, Disney's Chairman and Chief Executive Officer, had enjoyed remarkable success at the Company's helm. Eisner temporarily assumed Disney's presidency, but only three months later, heart disease required Eisner to undergo quadruple bypass surgery. Those two events persuaded Eisner and Disney's board of directors that the time had come to identify a successor to Eisner.

Eisner's prime candidate for the position was Michael Ovitz, who was the leading partner and one of the founders of Creative Artists Agency ("CAA"), the premier talent agency whose business model had reshaped the entire industry. By 1995, CAA had 550 employees and a roster of about 1400 of Hollywood's top actors, directors, writers, and musicians. That roster generated about $ 150 million in annual revenues and an annual income of over $ 20 million for Ovitz, who was regarded as one of the most powerful figures in Hollywood.

Eisner and Ovitz had enjoyed a social and professional relationship that spanned nearly 25 years. Although in the past the two men had casually discussed possibly working together, in 1995, when Ovitz began negotiations to leave CAA and join Music Corporation of America ("MCA"), Eisner became seriously interested in recruiting Ovitz to join Disney. Eisner shared that desire with Disney's board members on an individual basis.[4]

A. Negotiation of The Ovitz Employment Agreement

Eisner and Irwin Russell, who was a Disney director and chairman of the compensation committee, first approached Ovitz about joining Disney. Their initial negotiations were unproductive, however, because at that time MCA had made Ovitz an offer that Disney could not match. The MCA-Ovitz negotiations eventually fell apart, and Ovitz returned to CAA in mid-1995. Business continued as usual, until Ovitz discovered that Ron Meyer, his close friend and the number two executive at CAA, was leaving CAA to join MCA. That news devastated Ovitz, who concluded that to remain with the company he and Meyer had built together was no longer palatable. At that point Ovitz became receptive to the idea of joining Disney. Eisner learned of these developments and re-commenced negotiations with Ovitz in earnest. By mid-July 1995, those negotiations were in full swing.

Both Russell and Eisner negotiated with Ovitz, over separate issues and concerns. From his talks with Eisner, Ovitz gathered that Disney needed his skills and experience to remedy Disney's current weaknesses, which Ovitz identified as poor talent relationships and stagnant foreign growth. Seeking assurances from Eisner that Ovitz's vision for Disney was shared, at some point during the negotiations Ovitz came to believe that he and Eisner would run Disney, and would work together in a relation akin to that of junior and senior partner. Unfortunately, Ovitz's belief was mistaken, as Eisner had a radically different view of what their respective roles at Disney should be.

---

4. The Disney board of directors at that time and at the time the Ovitz Employment Agreement was approved (the "old board") consisted of Eisner, Roy E. Disney, Stanley P. Gold, Sanford M. Litvack, Richard A. Nunis, Sidney Poitier, Irwin E. Russell, Robert A.M. Stern, E. Cardon Walker, Raymond L. Watson, Gary L. Wilson, Reveta F. Bowers, Ignacio E. Lozano, Jr., George J. Mitchell, and Stephen F. Bollenbach. The board of directors at the time 4 T Ovitz was terminated as President of Disney (the "new board") consisted of the persons listed above (other than Bollenbach), plus Leo J. O'Donovan and Thomas S. Murphy. Neither O'Donovan nor Murphy served on the old board.

Russell assumed the lead in negotiating the financial terms of the Ovitz employment contract. In the course of negotiations, Russell learned from Ovitz's attorney, Bob Goldman, that Ovitz owned 55% of CAA and earned approximately $ 20 to $ 25 million a year from that company. From the beginning Ovitz made it clear that he would not give up his 55% interest in CAA without "downside protection." Considerable negotiation then ensued over downside protection issues. During the summer of 1995, the parties agreed to a draft version of Ovitz's employment agreement (the 'OEA') modeled after Eisner's and the late Mr. Wells' employment contracts. As described by the Chancellor, the draft agreement included the following terms:

> Under the proposed OEA, Ovitz would receive a five-year contract with two tranches of options. The first tranche consisted of three million options vesting in equal parts in the third, fourth, and fifth years, and if the value of those options at the end of the five years had not appreciated to $ 50 million, Disney would make up the difference. The second tranche consisted of two million options that would vest immediately if Disney and Ovitz opted to renew the contract.

The proposed OEA sought to protect both parties in the event that Ovitz's employment ended prematurely, and provided that absent defined causes, neither party could terminate the agreement without penalty. If Ovitz, for example, walked away, for any reason other than those permitted under the OEA, he would forfeit any benefits remaining under the OEA and could be enjoined from working for a competitor. Likewise, if Disney fired Ovitz for any reason other than gross negligence or malfeasance, Ovitz would be entitled to a non-fault payment (Non-Fault Termination or "NFT"), which consisted of his remaining salary, $ 7.5 million a year for unaccrued bonuses, the immediate vesting of his first tranche of options and a $ 10 million cash out payment for the second tranche of options.

As the basic terms of the OEA were crystallizing, Russell prepared and gave Ovitz and Eisner a "case study" to explain those terms. In that study, Russell also expressed his concern that the negotiated terms represented an extraordinary level of executive compensation. Russell acknowledged, however, that Ovitz was an "exceptional corporate executive" and "highly successful and unique entrepreneur" who merited "downside protection and upside opportunity." Both would be required to enable Ovitz to adjust to the reduced cash compensation he would receive from a public company, in contrast to the greater cash distributions and other perquisites more typically available from a privately held business. But, Russell did caution that Ovitz's salary would be at the top level for any corporate officer and significantly above that of the Disney CEO. Moreover, the stock options granted under the OEA would exceed the standards applied within Disney and corporate America and would "raise very strong criticism." Russell shared this original case study only with Eisner and Ovitz. He also recommended another, additional study of this issue.

To assist in evaluating the financial terms of the OEA, Russell recruited Graef Crystal, an executive compensation consultant, and Raymond Watson, a member of Disney's compensation committee and a past Disney board chairman who had helped structure Wells' and Eisner's compensation packages. Before the three met, Crystal prepared a comprehensive executive compensation database to accept various inputs and to conduct Black-Scholes analyses to output a range of values for the options.[8]Watson also prepared similar computations on spreadsheets, but without using the Black-Scholes method.

On August 10, Russell, Watson and Crystal met. They discussed and generated a set of values using different and various inputs and assumptions, accounting for different numbers of options, vesting periods, and potential proceeds of option exercises at various times and prices. After discussing their conclusions, they agreed that Crystal would memorialize his findings and fax them to Russell. Two days later, Crystal faxed to Russell a memorandum concluding that the OEA would provide Ovitz with approximately $ 23.6 million per year for the first five years, or $ 23.9 million a year over seven years if Ovitz exercised a two year renewal option. Those sums, Crystal opined, would approximate Ovitz's current annual compensation at CAA.

During a telephone conference that same evening, Russell, Watson and Crystal discussed Crystal's memorandum and its assumptions. Their discussion generated additional questions that prompted Russell to ask Crystal to revise his memorandum to resolve certain ambiguities in the current draft of the employment agreement. But, rather than address the points Russell highlighted, Crystal faxed to Russell a new letter that expressed Crystal's concern about the OEA's $ 50 million option appreciation guarantee. Crystal's concern, based on his understanding of the current draft of the OEA, was that Ovitz could hold the first tranche of options, wait out the five-year term, collect the $ 50 million guarantee, and then exercise the in-the-money options and receive an additional windfall. Crystal was philosophically opposed to a pay package that would give Ovitz the best of both worlds—low risk and high return.

Addressing Crystal's concerns, Russell made clear that the guarantee would not function as Crystal believed it might. Crystal then revised his original letter, adjusting the value of the OEA (assuming a two year renewal) to $ 24.1 million per year. Up to that point, only three Disney directors—Eisner, Russell and Watson—knew the status of the negotiations with Ovitz and the terms of the draft OEA.

While Russell, Watson and Crystal were finalizing their analysis of the OEA, Eisner and Ovitz reached a separate agreement. Eisner told Ovitz that: (1) the number of options would be reduced from a single grant of five million to two separate grants, the first being three million options for the first five years and the second consisting of two million

---

8. The Black-Scholes method is a formula for option valuation that is widely used and accepted in the industry and by regulators.

more options if the contract was renewed; and (2) Ovitz would join Disney only as President, not as a co-CEO with Eisner. After deliberating, Ovitz accepted those terms, and that evening Ovitz, Eisner, Sid Bass[10] and their families celebrated Ovitz's decision to join Disney.

Unfortunately, the celebratory mood was premature. The next day, August 13, Eisner met with Ovitz, Russell, Sanford Litvack (an Executive Vice President and Disney's General Counsel), and Stephen Bollenbach (Disney's Chief Financial Officer) to discuss the decision to hire Ovitz. Litvack and Bollenbach were unhappy with that decision, and voiced concerns that Ovitz would disrupt the cohesion that existed between Eisner, Litvack and Bollenbach. Litvack and Bollenbach were emphatic that they would not report to Ovitz, but would continue to report to Eisner. Despite Ovitz's concern about his "shrinking authority" as Disney's future President, Eisner was able to provide sufficient reassurance so that ultimately Ovitz acceded to Litvack's and Bollenbach's terms.

On August 14, Eisner and Ovitz signed a letter agreement (the "OLA"), which outlined the basic terms of Ovitz's employment, and stated that the agreement (which would ultimately be embodied in a formal contract) was subject to approval by Disney's compensation committee and board of directors. Russell called Sidney Poitier, a Disney director and compensation committee member, to inform Poitier of the OLA and its terms. Poitier believed that hiring Ovitz was a good idea because of Ovitz's reputation and experience. Watson called Ignacio Lozano, another Disney director and compensation committee member, who felt that Ovitz would successfully adapt from a private company environment to Disney's public company culture. Eisner also contacted each of the other board members by phone to inform them of the impending new hire, and to explain his friendship with Ovitz and Ovitz's qualifications.

That same day, a press release made the news of Ovitz's hiring public. The reaction was extremely positive: Disney was applauded for the decision, and Disney's stock price rose 4.4 % in a single day, thereby increasing Disney's market capitalization by over $ 1 billion. * * *

On September 26, 1995, the Disney compensation committee (which consisted of Messrs. Russell, Watson, Poitier and Lozano) met for one hour to consider, among other agenda items, the proposed terms of the OEA. A term sheet was distributed at the meeting, although a draft of the OEA was not. The topics discussed were historical comparables, such as Eisner's and Wells' option grants, and also the factors that Russell, Watson and Crystal had considered in setting the size of the option grants and the termination provisions of the contract. Watson testified that he provided the compensation committee with the spreadsheet analysis that he had performed in August, and discussed his findings with the committee. Crystal did not attend the meeting, although he was available by telephone to respond to questions if needed, but no one from the committee called. After Russell's and Watson's presentations, Litvack also re-

---

10. Sid Bass was one of Disney's largest individual shareholders.

sponded to substantive questions. At trial Poitier and Lozano testified that they believed they had received sufficient information from Russell's and Watson's presentations to exercise their judgment in the best interests of the Company. The committee voted unanimously to approve the OEA terms, subject to "reasonable further negotiations within the framework of the terms and conditions" described in the OEA.

Immediately after the compensation committee meeting, the Disney board met in executive session. The board was told about the reporting structure to which Ovitz had agreed, but the initial negative reaction of Litvack and Bollenbach to the hiring was not recounted. Eisner led the discussion relating to Ovitz, and Watson then explained his analysis, and both Watson and Russell responded to questions from the board. After further deliberation, the board voted unanimously to elect Ovitz as President.

B.   Ovitz's Performance As President of Disney

Ovitz's tenure as President of the Walt Disney Company officially began on October 1, 1995, the date that the OEA was executed. When Ovitz took office, the initial reaction was optimistic, and Ovitz did make some positive contributions while serving as President of the Company. By the fall of 1996, however, it had become clear that Ovitz was "a poor fit with his fellow executives." By then the Disney directors were discussing that the disconnect between Ovitz and the Company was likely irreparable and that Ovitz would have to be terminated. * * *

On September 30, 1996, the Disney board met. During an executive session of that meeting, and in small group discussions where Ovitz was not present, Eisner told the other board members of the continuing problems with Ovitz's performance. On October 1, Eisner wrote a letter to Russell and Watson detailing Eisner's mounting difficulties with Ovitz, including Eisner's lack of trust of Ovitz and Ovitz's failures to adapt to Disney's culture and to alleviate Eisner's workload. Eisner's goal in writing this letter was to prevent Ovitz from succeeding him at Disney. Because of that purpose, the Chancellor found that the letter contained "a good deal of hyperbole to help Eisner unsell' Ovitz as his successor." Neither that letter nor its contents were shared with other members of the board.

Those interchanges set the stage for Ovitz's eventual termination as Disney's President.

C.   Ovitz's Termination At Disney

* * * During this period Eisner was also working with Litvack to explore whether they could terminate Ovitz under the OEA for cause. If so, Disney would not owe Ovitz the NFT payment. From the very beginning, Litvack advised Eisner that he did not believe there was cause to terminate Ovitz under the OEA. Litvack's advice never changed.

At the end of November 1996, Eisner again asked Litvack if Disney had cause to fire Ovitz and thereby avoid the costly NFT payment. Litvack proceeded to examine that issue more carefully. He studied the OEA, refreshed himself on the meaning of "gross negligence" and "malfeasance," and reviewed all the facts concerning Ovitz's performance of which he was aware. Litvack also consulted Val Cohen, co-head of Disney's litigation department and Joseph Santaniello, in Disney's legal department. Cohen and Santaniello both concurred in Litvack's conclusion that no basis existed to terminate Ovitz for cause. Litvack did not personally conduct any legal research or request an outside opinion on the issue, because he believed that it "was not a close question, and in fact, Litvack described it as a no brainer." Eisner testified that after Litvack notified Eisner that he did not believe cause existed, Eisner "checked with almost anybody that [he] could find that had a legal degree, and there was just no light in that possibility. It was a total dead end from day one." Although the Chancellor was critical of Litvack and Eisner for lacking sufficient documentation to support his conclusion and the work they did to arrive at that conclusion, the Court found that Eisner and Litvack "did in fact make a concerted effort to determine if Ovitz could be terminated for cause, and that despite these efforts, they were unable to manufacture the desired result."

Litvack also believed that it would be inappropriate, unethical and a bad idea to attempt to coerce Ovitz (by threatening a for-cause termination) into negotiating for a smaller NFT package than the OEA provided. The reason was that when pressed by Ovitz's attorneys, Disney would have to admit that in fact there was no cause, which could subject Disney to a wrongful termination lawsuit. Litvack believed that attempting to avoid legitimate contractual obligations would harm Disney's reputation as an honest business partner and would affect its future business dealings.

* * * On December 11, Eisner met with Ovitz to agree on the wording of a press release to announce the termination, and to inform Ovitz that he would not receive any of the additional items that he requested. By that time it had already been decided that Ovitz would be terminated without cause and that he would receive his contractual NFT payment, but nothing more. Eisner and Ovitz agreed that neither Ovitz nor Disney would disparage each other in the press, and that the separation was to be undertaken with dignity and respect for both sides. After his December 11 meeting with Eisner, Ovitz never returned to Disney. * * *

1. *The Due Care Determinations*

The plaintiff-appellants advance five contentions to support their claim that the Chancellor reversibly erred by concluding that the plaintiffs had failed to establish a violation of the Disney defendants' duty of care. The appellants claim that the Chancellor erred by: (1) treating as distinct questions whether the plaintiffs had established by a preponderance of the evidence either gross negligence or a lack of good faith; (2) ruling that the old board was not required to approve the OEA; (3) determining whether the old board had breached its duty of care on a director-by-director basis rather than collectively; (4) concluding that the compensation committee members did not breach their duty of care in approving the NFT provisions of the OEA; and (5) holding that the remaining members of the old board (*i.e.*, the directors who were not members of the compensation committee) had not breached their duty of care in electing Ovitz as Disney's President. * * *

(a) TREATING DUE CARE AND BAD FAITH AS SEPARATE GROUNDS FOR DENYING BUSINESS JUDGMENT RULE REVIEW

This argument is best understood against the backdrop of the presumptions that cloak director action being reviewed under the business judgment standard. Our law presumes that "in making a business decision the directors of a corporation acted on an informed basis, in good faith, and in the honest belief that the action taken was in the best interests of the company." Those presumptions can be rebutted if the plaintiff shows that the directors breached their fiduciary duty of care or of loyalty or acted in bad faith. If that is shown, the burden then shifts to the director defendants to demonstrate that the challenged act or transaction was entirely fair to the corporation and its shareholders.

Because no duty of loyalty claim was asserted against the Disney defendants, the only way to rebut the business judgment rule presumptions would be to show that the Disney defendants had either breached their duty of care or had not acted in good faith. At trial, the plaintiff-appellants attempted to establish both grounds, but the Chancellor determined that the plaintiffs had failed to prove either.

The appellants' first claim is that the Chancellor erroneously (i) failed to make a "threshold determination" of gross negligence, and (ii) "conflated" the appellants' burden to rebut the business judgment presumptions, with an analysis of whether the directors' conduct fell within the 8 Del. C. § 102(b)(7) provision that precludes exculpation of directors from monetary liability "for acts or omissions not in good faith." The argument runs as follows: *Emerald Partners v. Berlin*[63] required the Chancellor first to determine whether the business judgment rule presumptions were rebutted based upon a showing that the board violated its duty of care, *i.e.*, acted with gross negligence. If gross negligence were established, the burden would shift to the directors to establish that the OEA was entirely fair. Only if the directors failed to meet that burden could the trial court then address the directors' Section 102(b)(7) exculpation defense, including the statutory exception for acts not in good faith.

This argument lacks merit. To make the argument the appellants must ignore the distinction between (i) a determination of bad faith for the threshold purpose of rebutting the business judgment rule presumptions, and (ii) a bad faith determination for purposes of evaluating the

---

63. 787 A.2d 85 (Del.2001).

availability of charter-authorized exculpation from monetary damage liability after liability has been established. Our law clearly permits a judicial assessment of director good faith for that former purpose. Nothing in Emerald Partners requires the Court of Chancery to consider only evidence of lack of due care (i.e. gross negligence) in determining whether the business judgment rule presumptions have been rebutted.

Even if the trial court's analytical approach were improper, the appellants have failed to demonstrate any prejudice. The Chancellor's determinations of due care and good faith were analytically distinct and were separately conducted, even though both were done for the purpose of deciding whether to apply the business judgment standard of review. Nowhere have the appellants shown that the result would have been any different had the Chancellor proceeded in the manner that they now advocate. * * *

(d) HOLDING THAT THE COMPENSATION COMMITTEE MEMBERS DID NOT FAIL TO EXERCISE DUE CARE IN APPROVING THE OEA

The appellants next challenge the Chancellor's determination that although the compensation committee's decision-making process fell far short of corporate governance "best practices," the committee members breached no duty of care in considering and approving the NFT terms of the OEA. That conclusion is reversible error, the appellants claim, because the record establishes that the compensation committee members did not properly inform themselves of the material facts and, hence, were grossly negligent in approving the NFT provisions of the OEA.

The appellants advance five reasons why a reversal is compelled: (i) not all committee members reviewed a draft of the OEA; (ii) the minutes of the September 26, 1995 compensation committee meeting do not recite any discussion of the grounds for which Ovitz could receive a non-fault termination; (iii) the committee members did not consider any comparable employment agreements or the economic impact of extending the exercisability of the options being granted to Ovitz; (iv) Crystal did not attend the September 26, 1995 committee meeting, nor was his letter distributed to or discussed with Poitier and Lozano; and (v) Poitier and Lozano did not review the spreadsheets generated by Watson. These contentions amount essentially to an attack upon underlying factual findings that will be upheld where they result from the Chancellor's assessment of live testimony.

Although the appellants have balkanized their due care claim into several fragmented parts, the overall thrust of that claim is that the compensation committee approved the OEA with NFT provisions that could potentially result in an enormous payout, without informing themselves of what the full magnitude of that payout could be. Rejecting that claim, the Court of Chancery found that the compensation committee members were adequately informed. The issue thus becomes whether that finding is supported by the evidence of record. We conclude that it is.

In our view, a helpful approach is to compare what actually happened here to what would have occurred had the committee followed a "best practices" (or "best case") scenario, from a process standpoint. In a 'best case' scenario, all committee members would have received, before or at the committee's first meeting on September 26, 1995, a spreadsheet or similar document prepared by (or with the assistance of) a compensation expert (in this case, Graef Crystal). Making different, alternative assumptions, the spreadsheet would disclose the amounts that Ovitz could receive under the OEA in each circumstance that might foreseeably arise. One variable in that matrix of possibilities would be the cost to Disney of a non-fault termination for each of the five years of the initial term of the OEA. The contents of the spreadsheet would be explained to the committee members, either by the expert who prepared it or by a fellow committee member similarly knowledgeable about the subject. That spreadsheet, which ultimately would become an exhibit to the minutes of the compensation committee meeting, would form the basis of the committee's deliberations and decision.

Had that scenario been followed, there would be no dispute (and no basis for litigation) over what information was furnished to the committee members or when it was furnished. Regrettably, the committee's informational and decisionmaking process used here was not so tidy. That is one reason why the Chancellor found that although the committee's process did not fall below the level required for a proper exercise of due care, it did fall short of what best practices would have counseled.

The Disney compensation committee met twice: on September 26 and October 16, 1995. The minutes of the September 26 meeting reflect that the committee approved the terms of the OEA (at that time embodied in the form of a letter agreement), except for the option grants, which were not approved until October 16-after the Disney stock incentive plan had been amended to provide for those options. At the September 26 meeting, the compensation committee considered a "term sheet" which, in summarizing the material terms of the OEA, relevantly disclosed that in the event of a non-fault termination, Ovitz would receive: (i) the present value of his salary ($ 1 million per year) for the balance of the contract term, (ii) the present value of his annual bonus payments (computed at $ 7.5 million) for the balance of the contract term, (iii) a $ 10 million termination fee, and (iv) the acceleration of his options for 3 million shares, which would become immediately exercisable at market price.

Thus, the compensation committee knew that in the event of an NFT, Ovitz's severance payment alone could be in the range of $ 40 million cash, plus the value of the accelerated options. Because the actual payout to Ovitz was approximately $ 130 million, of which roughly $ 38.5 million was cash, the value of the options at the time of the NFT payout would have been about $ 91.5 million. Thus, the issue may be framed as whether the compensation committee members knew, at the time they approved the OEA, that the value of the option component of the severance package could reach the $ 92 million order of magnitude if they terminated Ovitz without cause after one year. The evidentiary record shows that the committee members were so informed.

On this question the documentation is far less than what best practices would have dictated. There is no exhibit to the minutes that discloses, in a single document, the estimated value of the accelerated options in the event of an NFT termination after one year. The information imparted to the committee members on that subject is, however, supported by other evidence, most notably the trial testimony of various witnesses about spreadsheets that were prepared for the compensation committee meetings.

The compensation committee members derived their information about the potential magnitude of an NFT payout from two sources. The first was the value of the "benchmark" options previously granted to Eisner and Wells and the valuations by Watson of the proposed Ovitz options. Ovitz's options were set at 75% of parity with the options previously granted to Eisner and to Frank Wells. Because the compensation committee had established those earlier benchmark option grants to Eisner and Wells and were aware of their value, a simple mathematical calculation would have informed them of the potential value range of Ovitz's options. Also, in August and September 1995, Watson and Russell met with Graef Crystal to determine (among other things) the value of the potential Ovitz options, assuming different scenarios. Crystal valued the options under the Black-Scholes method, while Watson used a different valuation metric. Watson recorded his calculations and the resulting values on a set of spreadsheets that reflected what option profits Ovitz might receive, based upon a range of different assumptions about stock market price increases. Those spreadsheets were shared with, and explained to, the committee members at the September meeting.

The committee's second source of information was the amount of "downside protection" that Ovitz was demanding. Ovitz required financial protection from the risk of leaving a very lucrative and secure position at CAA, of which he was a controlling partner, to join a publicly held corporation to which Ovitz was a stranger, and that had a very different culture and an environment which prevented him from completely controlling his destiny. The committee members knew that by leaving CAA and coming to Disney, Ovitz would be sacrificing "booked" CAA commissions of $ 150 to $ 200 million-an amount that Ovitz demanded as protection against the risk that his employment relationship with Disney might not work out. Ovitz wanted at least $ 50 million of that compensation to take the form of an "up-front" signing bonus. Had the $ 50 million bonus been paid, the size of the option grant would have been lower. Because it was contrary to Disney policy, the compensation committee rejected the up-front signing bonus demand, and elected instead to compensate Ovitz at the "back end," by awarding him options that would be phased in over the five-year term of the OEA.

It is on this record that the Chancellor found that the compensation committee was informed of the material facts relating to an NFT payout. If measured in terms of the documentation that would have been generated if "best practices" had been followed, that record leaves much to be desired. The Chancellor acknowledged that, and so do we. But, the Chancellor also found that despite its imperfections, the evidentiary record was sufficient to support the conclusion that the compensation committee had adequately informed itself of the potential magnitude of the entire severance package, including the options, that Ovitz would receive in the event of an early NFT.

The OEA was specifically structured to compensate Ovitz for walking away from $ 150 million to $ 200 million of anticipated commissions from CAA over the five-year OEA contract term. This meant that if Ovitz was terminated without cause, the earlier in the contract term the termination occurred the larger the severance amount would be to replace the lost commissions. Indeed, because Ovitz was terminated after only one year, the total amount of his severance payment (about $ 130 million) closely approximated the lower end of the range of Ovitz's forfeited commissions ($ 150 million), less the compensation Ovitz received during his first and only year as Disney's President. Accordingly, the Court of Chancery had a sufficient evidentiary basis in the record from which to find that, at the time they approved the OEA, the compensation committee members were adequately informed of the potential magnitude of an early NFT severance payout. * * *

(e) HOLDING THAT THE REMAINING DISNEY DIRECTORS DID NOT FAIL TO EXERCISE DUE CARE IN APPROVING THE HIRING OF OVITZ AS THE PRESIDENT OF DISNEY

The appellants' final claim in this category is that the Court of Chancery erroneously held that the remaining members of the old Disney board n85 had not breached their duty of care in electing Ovitz as President of Disney. This claim lacks merit, because the arguments appellants advance in this context relate to a different subject-the approval of the OEA, which was the responsibility delegated to the compensation committee, not the full board.

The appellants argue that the Disney directors breached their duty of care by failing to inform themselves of all material information reasonably available with respect to Ovitz's employment agreement. We need not dwell on the specifics of this argument, because in substance they repeat the gross negligence claims previously leveled at the compensation committee-claims that were rejected by the Chancellor and now also by this Court. The only properly reviewable action of the entire board was its decision to elect Ovitz as Disney's President. In that context the sole issue, as the Chancellor properly held, is "whether [the remaining members of the old board] properly exercised their business judgment and acted in accordance with their fiduciary duties when they elected Ovitz to the Company's presidency." The Chancellor determined that in electing Ovitz, the directors were informed of all information reasonably available and, thus, were not grossly negligent. We agree.

The Chancellor found and the record shows the following: well in advance of the September 26, 1995 board meeting the directors were fully aware that the Company needed—especially in light of Wells' death and Eisner's medical problems—to hire a 'number two" executive and potential successor to Eisner. There had been many discussions about that need and about potential candidates who could fill that role even before Eisner decided to try to recruit Ovitz. Before the September 26 board meeting Eisner had individually discussed with each director the possibility of hiring Ovitz, and Ovitz's background and qualifications. The directors thus knew of Ovitz's skills, reputation and experience, all of which they believed would be highly valuable to the Company. The directors also knew that to accept a position at Disney, Ovitz would have to walk away from a very successful business—a reality that would lead a reasonable person to believe that Ovitz would likely succeed in similar pursuits elsewhere in the industry. The directors also knew of the public's highly positive reaction to the Ovitz announcement, and that Eisner and senior management had supported the Ovitz hiring. Indeed, Eisner, who had long desired to bring Ovitz within the Disney fold, consistently vouched for Ovitz's qualifications and told the directors that he could work well with Ovitz.

The board was also informed of the key terms of the OEA (including Ovitz's salary, bonus and options). Russell reported this information to them at the September 26, 1995 executive session, which was attended by Eisner and all non-executive directors. Russell also reported on the compensation committee meeting that had immediately preceded the executive session. And, both Russell and Watson responded to questions from the board. Relying upon the compensation committee's approval of the OEA and the other information furnished to them, the Disney directors, after further deliberating, unanimously elected Ovitz as President.

Based upon this record, we uphold the Chancellor's conclusion that, when electing Ovitz to the Disney presidency the remaining Disney directors were fully informed of all material facts, and that the appellants failed to establish any lack of due care on the directors' part.

2. *The Good Faith Determinations*

The Court of Chancery held that the business judgment rule presumptions protected the decisions of the compensation committee and the remaining Disney directors, not only because they had acted with due care but also because they had not acted in bad faith. That latter ruling, the appellants claim, was reversible error because the Chancellor formulated and then applied an incorrect definition of bad faith.

In its Opinion the Court of Chancery defined bad faith as follows:

Upon long and careful consideration, I am of the opinion that the concept of *intentional dereliction of duty, a conscious disregard for one's responsibilities*, is an appropriate (although not the only) standard for determining whether fiduciaries have acted in good faith. Deliberate indifference and inaction in the face of a duty to act is, in my mind, conduct that is clearly disloyal to the corporation. It is the epitome of faithless conduct.

The appellants contend that definition is erroneous for two reasons. First they claim that the trial court had adopted a different definition in its 2003 decision denying the motion to dismiss the complaint, and the Court's post-trial (2005) definition materially altered the 2003 definition to appellants' prejudice. Their argument runs as follows: under the Chancellor's 2003 definition of bad faith, the directors must have "*consciously and intentionally disregarded their responsibilities*, adopting a we don't care about the risks' attitude concerning a material corporate decision." Under the 2003 formulation, appellants say, "directors violate their duty of good faith if they are making material decisions without adequate information and without adequate deliberation[,]" but under the 2005 post-trial definition, bad faith requires proof of a subjective bad motive or intent. This definitional change, it is claimed, was procedurally prejudicial because appellants relied on the 2003 definition in presenting their evidence of bad faith at the trial. Without any intervening change in the law, the Court of Chancery could not unilaterally alter its definition and then hold the appellants to a higher, more stringent standard.

Second, the appellants claim that the Chancellor's post-trial definition of bad faith is erroneous substantively. They argue that the 2003 formulation was (and is) the correct definition, because it is "logically tied to board decision-making under the duty of care." The post-trial formulation, on the other hand, "wrongly incorporated substantive elements regarding the rationality of the decisions under review rather than being constrained, as in a due care analysis, to strictly procedural criteria." We conclude that both arguments must fail.

The appellants' first argument-that there is a real, significant difference between the Chancellor's pre-trial and post-trial definitions of bad faith-is plainly wrong. We perceive no substantive difference between the Court of Chancery's 2003 definition of bad faith-a "conscious and intentional disregard [of] responsibilities, adopting a we don't care about the risks' attitude ...—and its 2005 post-trial definition—an "intentional dereliction of duty, a conscious disregard for one's responsibilities." Both formulations express the same concept, although in slightly different language.

The most telling evidence that there is no substantive difference between the two formulations is that the appellants are forced to contrive a difference. Appellants assert that under the 2003 formulation, "directors violate their duty of good faith if they are making material decisions without adequate information and without adequate deliberation." For that *ipse dixit* they cite no legal authority. That comes as no surprise because their verbal effort to collapse the duty to act in good faith into the duty to act with due care, is not unlike putting a rabbit into the proverbial hat and then blaming the trial judge for making the insertion.

The appellants essentially concede that their proof of bad faith is insufficient to satisfy the standard articulated by the Court of Chancery. That is why they ask this Court to treat a failure to exercise due care as a failure to act in good faith. Unfortunately for appellants, that "rule," even if it were accepted, would not help their case. If we were to conflate these two duties and declare that a breach of the duty to be properly informed violates the duty to act in good faith, the outcome would be no different, because, as the Chancellor and we now have held, the appellants failed to establish any breach of the duty of care. To say it differently, even if the Chancellor's definition of bad faith were erroneous, the error would not be reversible because the appellants cannot satisfy the very test they urge us to adopt.

For that reason, our analysis of the appellants' bad faith claim could end at this point. In other circumstances it would. This case, however, is one in which the duty to act in good faith has played a prominent role, yet to date is not a well-developed area of our corporate fiduciary law. Although the good faith concept has recently been the subject of considerable scholarly writing, which includes articles focused on this specific case, the duty to act in good faith is, up to this point relatively uncharted. Because of the increased recognition of the importance of good faith, some conceptual guidance to the corporate community may be helpful. For that reason we proceed to address the merits of the appellants' second argument.

The precise question is whether the Chancellor's articulated standard for bad faith corporate fiduciary conduct—intentional dereliction of duty, a conscious disregard for one's responsibilities—is legally correct. In approaching that question, we note that the Chancellor characterized that definition as "*an* appropriate (*although not the only*) standard for determining whether fiduciaries have acted in good faith." That observation is accurate and helpful, because as a matter of simple logic, at least three different categories of fiduciary behavior are candidates for the "bad faith" pejorative label.

The first category involves so-called "subjective bad faith," that is, fiduciary conduct motivated by an actual intent to do harm. That such conduct constitutes classic, quintessential bad faith is a proposition so well accepted in the liturgy of fiduciary law that it borders on axiomatic. We need not dwell further on this category, because no such conduct is claimed to have occurred, or did occur, in this case.

The second category of conduct, which is at the opposite end of the spectrum, involves lack of due care-that is, fiduciary action taken solely by reason of gross negligence and without any malevolent intent. In this case, appellants assert claims of gross negligence to establish breaches not only of director due care but also of the directors' duty to act in good faith. Although the Chancellor found, and we agree, that the appellants failed to establish gross negligence, to afford guidance we address the issue of whether gross negligence (including a failure to inform one's self of available material facts), without more, can also constitute bad faith. The answer is clearly no.

From a broad philosophical standpoint, that question is more complex than would appear, if only because (as the Chancellor and others have observed) 'issues of good faith are (to a certain degree) inseparably and necessarily intertwined with the duties of care and loyalty....'' But, in the pragmatic, conduct-regulating legal realm which calls for more precise conceptual line drawing, the answer is that grossly negligent conduct, without more, does not and cannot constitute a breach of the fiduciary duty to act in good faith. The conduct that is the subject of due care may overlap with the conduct that comes within the rubric of good faith in a psychological sense,[104] but from a legal standpoint those duties are and must remain quite distinct. Both our legislative history and our common law jurisprudence distinguish sharply between the duties to exercise due care and to act in good faith, and highly significant consequences flow from that distinction.

The Delaware General Assembly has addressed the distinction between bad faith and a failure to exercise due care (i.e., gross negligence) in two separate contexts. The first is Section 102(b)(7) of the DGCL, which authorizes Delaware corporations, by a provision in the certificate of incorporation, to exculpate their directors from monetary damage liability for a breach of the duty of care. That exculpatory provision affords significant protection to directors of Delaware corporations. The statute carves out several exceptions, however, including most relevantly, "for acts or omissions not in good faith...." Thus, a corporation can exculpate its directors from monetary liability for a breach of the duty of care, but not for conduct that is not in good faith. To adopt a definition of bad faith that would cause a violation of the duty of care automatically to become an act or omission "not in good faith," would eviscerate the protections accorded to directors by the General Assembly's adoption of Section 102(b)(7).

A second legislative recognition of the distinction between fiduciary conduct that is grossly negligent and conduct that is not in good faith, is Delaware's indemnification statute, found at 8 Del. C. § 145. To oversimplify, subsections (a) and (b) of that statute permit a corporation to indemnify (inter alia) any person who is or was a director, officer, employee or agent of the corporation against expenses (including attorneys' fees), judgments, fines and amounts paid in settlement of specified

---

104. An example of such overlap might be the hypothetical case where a director, because of subjective hostility to the corporation on whose board he serves, fails to inform himself of, or to devote sufficient attention to, the matters on which he is making decisions as a fiduciary. In such a case, two states of mind coexist in the same person: subjective bad intent (which would lead to a finding of bad faith) and gross negligence (which would lead to a finding of a breach of the duty of care). Although the coexistence of both states of mind may make them indistinguishable from a psychological standpoint, the fiduciary duties that they cause the director to violate-care and good faith-are legally separate and distinct.

actions, suits or proceedings, where (among other things): (i) that person is, was, or is threatened to be made a party to that action, suit or proceeding, and (ii) that person "acted in good faith and in a manner the person reasonably believed to be in or not opposed to the best interests of the corporation. . . ." Thus, under Delaware statutory law a director or officer of a corporation can be indemnified for liability (and litigation expenses) incurred by reason of a violation of the duty of care, but not for a violation of the duty to act in good faith.

Section 145, like Section 102(b)(7), evidences the intent of the Delaware General Assembly to afford significant protections to directors (and, in the case of Section 145, other fiduciaries) of Delaware corporations. To adopt a definition that conflates the duty of care with the duty to act in good faith by making a violation of the former an automatic violation of the latter, would nullify those legislative protections and defeat the General Assembly's intent. There is no basis in policy, precedent or common sense that would justify dismantling the distinction between gross negligence and bad faith.

That leaves the third category of fiduciary conduct, which falls in between the first two categories of (1) conduct motivated by subjective bad intent and (2) conduct resulting from gross negligence. This third category is what the Chancellor's definition of bad faith-intentional dereliction of duty, a conscious disregard for one's responsibilities—is intended to capture. The question is whether such misconduct is properly treated as a non-exculpable, non-indemnifiable violation of the fiduciary duty to act in good faith. In our view it must be, for at least two reasons.

First, the universe of fiduciary misconduct is not limited to either disloyalty in the classic sense (*i.e.*, preferring the adverse self-interest of the fiduciary or of a related person to the interest of the corporation) or gross negligence. Cases have arisen where corporate directors have no conflicting self-interest in a decision, yet engage in misconduct that is more culpable than simple inattention or failure to be informed of all facts material to the decision. To protect the interests of the corporation and its shareholders, fiduciary conduct of this kind, which does not involve disloyalty (as traditionally defined) but is qualitatively more culpable than gross negligence, should be proscribed. A vehicle is needed to address such violations doctrinally, and that doctrinal vehicle is the duty to act in good faith. The Chancellor implicitly so recognized in his Opinion, where he identified different examples of bad faith as follows:

The good faith required of a corporate fiduciary includes not simply the duties of care and loyalty, in the narrow sense that I have discussed them above, but all actions required by a true faithfulness and devotion to the interests of the corporation and its shareholders. A failure to act in good faith may be shown, for instance, where the fiduciary intentionally acts with a purpose other than that of advancing the best interests of the corporation, where the fiduciary acts with the intent to violate applicable positive law, or where the fiduciary intentionally fails to act in the face of a known duty to act, demonstrating a conscious disregard for his duties. There may be other examples of bad faith yet to be proven or alleged, but these three are the most salient.

Those articulated examples of bad faith are not new to our jurisprudence. Indeed, they echo pronouncements our courts have made throughout the decades.

Second, the legislature has also recognized this intermediate category of fiduciary misconduct, which ranks between conduct involving subjective bad faith and gross negligence. Section 102(b)(7)(ii) of the DGCL expressly denies money damage exculpation for "acts or omissions not in good faith or which involve intentional misconduct or a knowing violation of law." By its very terms that provision distinguishes between "intentional misconduct" and a "knowing violation of law" (both examples of subjective bad faith) on the one hand, and "acts ... not in good faith," on the other. Because the statute exculpates directors only for conduct amounting to gross negligence, the statutory denial of exculpation for "acts ... not in good faith" must encompass the intermediate category of misconduct captured by the Chancellor's definition of bad faith.

For these reasons, we uphold the Court of Chancery's definition as a legally appropriate, although not the exclusive, definition of fiduciary bad faith. We need go no further. To engage in an effort to craft (in the Court's words) "a definitive and categorical definition of the universe of acts that would constitute bad faith"[112] would be unwise and is unnecessary to dispose of the issues presented on this appeal.

Having sustained the Chancellor's finding that the Disney directors acted in good faith when approving the OEA and electing Ovitz as President, we next address the claims arising out of the decision to pay Ovitz the amount called for by the NFT provisions of the OEA. * * *

V. *THE WASTE CLAIM*

The appellants' final claim is that even if the approval of the OEA was protected by the business judgment rule presumptions, the payment of the severance amount to Ovitz constituted waste. This claim is rooted in the doctrine that a plaintiff who fails to rebut the business judgment rule presumptions is not entitled to any remedy unless the transaction constitutes waste. The Court of Chancery rejected the appellants' waste claim, and the appellants claim that in so doing the Court committed error.

To recover on a claim of corporate waste, the plaintiffs must shoulder the burden of proving that the exchange was "so one sided that no business person of ordinary, sound judgment could conclude that the corporation has received adequate consideration." A claim of waste will

---

112. For the same reason, we do not reach or otherwise address the issue of whether the fiduciary duty to act in good faith is a duty that, like the duties of care and loyalty, can serve as an independent basis for imposing liability upon corporate officers and directors. That issue is not before us on this appeal.

arise only in the rare, "unconscionable case where directors irrationally squander or give away corporate assets." This onerous standard for waste is a corollary of the proposition that where business judgment presumptions are applicable, the board's decision will be upheld unless it cannot be "attributed to any rational business purpose."

The claim that the payment of the NFT amount to Ovitz, without more, constituted waste is meritless on its face, because at the time the NFT amounts were paid, Disney was contractually obligated to pay them. The payment of a contractually obligated amount cannot constitute waste, unless the contractual obligation is itself wasteful. Accordingly, the proper focus of a waste analysis must be whether the amounts required to be paid in the event of an NFT were wasteful *ex ante*.

Appellants claim that the NFT provisions of the OEA were wasteful because they incentivized Ovitz to perform poorly in order to obtain payment of the NFT provisions. The Chancellor found that the record did not support that contention:

> Terminating Ovitz and paying the NFT did not constitute waste because he could not be terminated for cause and because many of the defendants gave credible testimony that the Company would be better off without Ovitz, meaning that would be impossible for me to conclude that the termination and receipt of NFT benefits result in "an exchange that is so one sided that no business person of ordinary, sound judgment could conclude that the corporation has received adequate consideration," or a situation where the defendants have "irrationally squandered or given away corporate assets." In other words, defendants did not commit waste.

That ruling is erroneous, the appellants argue, because the NFT provisions of the OEA were wasteful in their very design. Specifically, the OEA gave Ovitz every incentive to leave the Company before serving out the full term of his contract. The appellants urge that although the OEA may have induced Ovitz to join Disney as President, no contractual safeguards were in place to retain him in that position. In essence, appellants claim that the NFT provisions of the OEA created an irrational incentive for Ovitz to get himself fired.

That claim does not come close to satisfying the high hurdle required to establish waste. The approval of the NFT provisions in the OEA had a rational business purpose: to induce Ovitz to leave CAA, at what would otherwise be a considerable cost to him, in order to join Disney. The Chancellor found that the evidence does not support any notion that the OEA irrationally incentivized Ovitz to get himself fired. Ovitz had no control over whether or not he would be fired, either with or without cause. To suggest that at the time he entered into the OEA Ovitz would engineer an early departure at the cost of his extraordinary reputation in the entertainment industry and his historical friendship with Eisner, is not only fanciful but also without proof in the record. Indeed, the Chancellor found that it was "patently unreasonable to assume that Ovitz intended to perform just poorly enough to be fired quickly, but not so poorly that he could be terminated for cause."

We agree. Because the appellants have failed to show that the approval of the NFT terms of the OEA was not a rational business decision, their waste claim must fail.

VI. *CONCLUSION*

For the reasons stated above, the judgment of the Court of Chancery is affirmed.

EMERALD PARTNERS v. BERLIN

787 A.2d 85 (Del.2001).

[This case involved a shareholder derivative suit challenging a merger in which the controlling stockholder had an interest in both corporate parties to the merger. As a conflict of interest situation, the court placed the burden on the defendant to show the fairness of the challenged transaction.[a] The excerpt of the decision that follows explores how Del § 102(b)(7) applies to divided loyalty cases.]

HOLLAND, JUSTICE.

* * * The appellant, Emerald Partners, a New Jersey limited partnership, filed this action on March 1, 1988, to enjoin the consummation of a merger between May Petroleum, Inc. ("May"), a Delaware corporation and thirteen corporations owned by Craig Hall ("Hall"), the Chairman and Chief Executive Officer of May. Also joined as defendants were May's directors, Ronald P. Berlin, David L. Florence, Rex A. Sebastian, and Theodore H. Strauss (collectively the "'director defendants"). Added later as a defendant was Hall Financial, the successor in interest to Hall Financial Group, Inc., the corporate defendant produced by the merger of May and the Hall corporations.

In October 1987, Hall, at that time a holder of 52.4% of May's common stock, proposed a merger of May and thirteen sub-chapter S corporations owned by Hall that were primarily engaged in the real estate service business. The board of directors of May consisted of Hall and Berlin, the inside directors, and Florence, Sebastian and Strauss, the outside directors.

The outside directors authorized the engagement of Bear Stearns & Company ("Bear Stearns") to act as investment advisor and render a fairness opinion to the board and the May stockholders. On the basis of company valuations and the Bear Stearns fairness letter, the transaction, as eventually crafted, contemplated that Hall would receive twenty-seven

---

a. The entire fairness requirement in conflict of interest transactions is explored in Sinclair v. Levien, p. 544, *infra. See also* Weinberger v. UOP (p. 1071 *infra*) dealing with interested-party mergers.

million May common shares in exchange for the merger of the Hall corporations with May, increasing Hall's shareholding to 73.5% of May's outstanding common stock as reflected in the post-merger entity. * * *

The directors of Delaware corporations have a triad of primary fiduciary duties: due care, loyalty, and good faith. Those fiduciary responsibilities do not operate intermittently. Accordingly, the shareholders of a Delaware corporation are entitled to rely upon their board of directors to discharge each of their three primary fiduciary duties at all times.

In 1986, Section 102(b)(7) was enacted by the Delaware General Assembly, following a "'directors and officers insurance liability crisis and the 1985 ... decision [of this Court] in *Smith v. Van Gorkom.*"[23] In *Van Gorkom,* we held that directors were personally liable in monetary damages for gross negligence in the process of decisionmaking. The purpose of Section 102(b)(7) was to *permit shareholders*—who are entitled to rely upon directors to discharge their fiduciary duties at all times—to adopt a provision in the certificate of incorporation to exculpate directors from any personal liability for the payment of monetary damages for breaches of their duty of care, but not for duty of loyalty violations, good faith violations and certain other conduct.[25] Following the enactment of Section 102(b)(7), the shareholders of many Delaware corporations approved charter amendments containing these exculpatory provisions with full knowledge of their import. * * *

The statutory enactment of Section 102(b)(7) was a logical corollary to the common law principles of the business judgment rule. Since its enactment, Delaware courts have consistently held that the adoption of a charter provision, in accordance with Section 102(b)(7), bars the recovery of monetary damages from directors for a successful shareholder claim that is based exclusively upon establishing a violation of the duty of care. Accordingly, in *Malpiede,* [780 A.2d 1075, 1095 (2001)] this Court held that if a shareholder complaint unambiguously asserts *only* a due care claim, the complaint is dismissible once the corporation's Section 102(b)(7) provision is properly invoked. * * *

When the General Assembly enacted Section 102(b)(7), three years after this Court's landmark decision in *Weinberger v. UOP, Inc.*[70] it not only recognized but reinforced *Weinberger's* restatement of a venerable and fundamental principle of our common law corporate fiduciary jurisprudence: "there is no "safe harbor' for ... divided loyalties in Delaware." The fact that Section 102(b)(7) does not permit shareholders to exculpate directors for violations of loyalty or good faith reflects that the provision was a thoughtfully crafted legislative response to our holding in

---

23. Malpiede v. Townson, 780 A.2d 1075, 1095 (2001) (citing *Smith v. Van Gorkom*, Del.Supr., 488 A.2d 858 (1985).

25. *Malpiede v. Townson,* 780 A.2d at 1095. Such a charter provision does not affect injunctive proceedings based on gross negligence. *Id.; see also* E. Norman Veasey et al., Delaware Supports Directors with a Three–Legged Stool of Limited Liability, Indemnification and Insurance, 42 BUS. LAW. 399, 401–04 (1987).

70. *Weinberger v. UOP, Inc.,* Del.Supr., 457 A.2d 701 (1983).

Van Gorkom and, simultaneously, reflected the General Assembly's own expression of support for our assertion in *Weinberger* that when the standard of review is entire fairness "'the requirement of fairness is unflinching in its demand....'" * * *

To demonstrate entire fairness, the board must present evidence of the cumulative manner by which it discharged *all* of its fiduciary duties. An entire fairness analysis then requires the Court of Chancery "'to consider carefully how the board of directors discharged all of its fiduciary duties with regard to each aspect of the non-bifurcated components of entire fairness: fair dealing and fair price.'"

... the Court of Chancery's consideration of the Section 102(b)(7) charter provision was premature. The same policy rationale that subjects a transaction to judicial review for entire fairness, even if the burden of persuasion shifts, requires a finding of unfairness and the basis of liability for monetary damages, before the exculpatory nature of a Section 102(b)(7) provision is examined. * * *

NOTES

1. The *Emerald Partners* case, which was affirmed in Emerald Partners v. Berlin, 840 A.2d 641 (Del. 2003), shows that plaintiffs' lawyers are well-advised to add a divided loyalty claim whenever the facts permit.

2. Does the business judgment rule have any role to play in divided loyalty cases?

CHAPTER 8

THE DUTY OF LOYALTY

■ ■ ■

The fiduciary duty concept was imported into corporate law from a body of existing law dealing with trusts. However, these two areas of the law are not completely coincident. For example, a trustee must not take unnecessary risks in investing trust assets. The trustee is expected to protect the corpus of the trust, even if this means forgoing profits that could otherwise be earned. In contrast, a business manager is expected to incur risk, even great risk, in order to maximize profits. Business managers are also expected to profit from the business operation for which they act as a fiduciary, while a trustee is normally only paid a fee for services. Nevertheless, a business manager with fiduciary duties is not permitted to self deal at the expense of the company for which he acts as a fiduciary. As a corporate lawyer, you will spend a lot of time examining various business relationships to determine if there is a conflict of interest that would breach the fiduciary duty of loyalty. The following cases show how such conflicts may arise.

SECTION 1.   SELF–DEALING TRANSACTIONS

GLOBE WOOLEN CO. v. UTICA GAS & ELECTRIC CO.

224 N.Y. 483, 121 N.E. 378 (1918).

CARDOZO, J.

The plaintiff, a corporation, sues to compel the specific performance of contracts to supply electric current to its mills. The defendant, also a corporation, answers that the contracts were made under the dominating influence of a common director; that their terms are unfair, and their consequences oppressive; and that hence they may not stand. A referee has sustained the defense; and the Appellate Division, with some modification, has affirmed his judgment.

The plaintiff is the owner of two mills in the city of Utica. One is for the manufacture of worsteds, and the other for that of woolens. The defendant generates and sells electricity for light and power. For many years John F. Maynard has been the plaintiff's chief stockholder, its president, and a member of its board of directors. He has also been a director of the defendant, and chairman of its executive committee. He received a single share of the defendant's stock to qualify him for office. He returned the share at once, and he has never held another. His property interest in the plaintiff is large. In the defendant he has none.

The history of the transaction may be briefly stated. At the beginning the mills were run by steam, and the plant was antiquated and inadequate. As early as 1903 one Greenidge, then the superintendent and later the general manager of the defendant's electrical department, suggested to Mr. Maynard the substitution of electric power. Nothing came of the suggestion then. Mr. Maynard was fearful that the cost of equipment would be too great unless the defendant would guarantee a saving in the cost of operation. None the less a change was felt to be important, and from time to time the subject was taken up anew. In 1904 there was an investigation of the power plant by Greenidge and a written report of its condition. For this service, though he was still in the defendant's employ, he was paid by Mr. Maynard. In 1905 the substitution of electricity was again considered, but dismissed as impracticable because of the plaintiff's continued insistence upon a guaranty of saving. In the fall of 1906 the project was renewed. It was renewed by Maynard and Greenidge, who debated it between themselves. There were other officers of the defendant who knew that the project was afoot, but they took no part in formulating it. Maynard still insisted on a guaranty of saving. The plaintiff's books were thrown open to Greenidge, who calculated for himself the cost of operation with steam and the probable cost with electricity. When the investigation was over, a contract was closed. It took the form of letters exchanged between Greenidge and Maynard. In the letter signed by Greenidge, the defendant proposed to supply the plaintiff's worsted mill with electricity at a maximum rate of $.0104 per kilowatt hour, and to guarantee that the cost for heat and light and power would show a saving each month of $300 as compared with the cost for the corresponding month in the year previous to the change. There was to be a trial period ending July 1, 1907. Then, at the plaintiff's option, the contract was to run for five years, with a privilege of renewal for a like term. In a letter signed by Maynard on October 22, 1906, the plaintiff accepted the proposal. At once the defendant made preparations to install the new equipment. Six weeks, later, on December 1, 1906, Mr. Maynard laid the contract before the defendant's executive committee. He went to the meeting with Mr. Greenidge. The contract was read. Mr. Lewis, the vice president, asked Mr. Greenidge what the rate would be, and was told about $.0104 per kilowatt hour. Mr. Beardsley, another director, asked whether the contract was a profitable one for the company, and was told by Mr. Greenidge that it was. Mr. Maynard kept silent. A resolution was moved and carried that the contract be ratified. Mr. Maynard presided at the meeting, and put the resolution, but was excused from voting.

This settled the problem of power for the worsted mill. Attention was next directed to the woolen mill. Again Mr. Maynard and Mr. Greenidge put the project through unaided. In February, 1907, letters, similar in most things to the earlier ones, were exchanged. The guaranty of saving for this mill as for the other was to be $300 a month. There were, however, new provisions to the effect that the contract should apply to 'current used for any purposes in any extensions or additions to the mills,' and that in case of shortage of electricity the plaintiff should be preferred in service over all other customers except the city of Utica. At a meeting of the executive committee held February 11, 1907, this contract was ratified. The statement was made by Mr. Greenidge, in the presence of Mr. Maynard, that it was practically a duplicate of the first contract, except that it related to another mill. Nothing was said about the new provisions. Mr. Maynard presided and put the resolution, but did not vote.

At a cost to the plaintiff of more than $21,000 the requisite changes in the mills were made, and the new power was supplied. It quickly appeared that the defendant had made a losing contract; but only gradually did the extent of the loss, its permanence, and its causes unfold themselves. Greenidge had miscalculated the amount of steam that would be required to heat the dye houses. The expenditure for coal mounted by leaps and bounds. The plaintiff dyed more yarn and less slubbing than before. But the dyeing of yarn takes twice as much heat as that of slubbing, and thus doubles the cost of fuel. These and like changes in the output of the mills had not been foreseen by Greenidge, and Maynard had not warned of them. In 1909 the defendant became alarmed at the mounting loss. Various tests and palliatives were suggested and adopted, but there was no change in the result. Finally, in February, 1911, the defendant gave notice of rescission. At that time it had supplied the plaintiff with electricity worth $69,500.75 if paid for at the maximum rate fixed by the contract, and $60,000 if paid for at the lowest rate charged to any customer in Utica. Yet not only had it received nothing, but it owed the plaintiff under its guaranty $11,721.41. The finding is that a like loss prolonged to the end of the term would amount to $300,000.

These are the contracts which the courts below have annulled. The referee annulled them absolutely. The Appellate Division imposed the condition that the defendant reimburse the plaintiff for the cost of installation. The defendant makes no complaint of the condition. The plaintiff, appealing, stands upon its bargain.

We think the evidence supports the conclusion that the contracts are voidable at the election of the defendant. The plaintiff does not deny that this would be true if the dual director had voted for their adoption. But the argument is that by refusing to vote he shifted the responsibility to his associates, and may reap a profit from their errors. One does not divest oneself so readily of one's duties as trustee. The refusal to vote has, indeed, this importance: It gives to the transaction the form and presumption of propriety, and requires one who would invalidate it to probe beneath the surface. But 'the great rule of law' which holds a trustee to the duty of constant and unqualified fidelity is not a thing of forms and phrases. A dominating influence may be exerted in other ways than by a vote. A beneficiary, about to plunge into a ruinous course of dealing, may be betrayed by silence as well as by the spoken word.

The trustee is free to stand aloof, while others act, if all is equitable and fair. He cannot rid himself of the duty to warn and to denounce, if there is improvidence or oppression, either apparent on the surface, or lurking beneath the surface, but visible to his practiced eye.

There was an influence here, dominating, perhaps, and surely potent and persuasive, which was exerted by Mr. Maynard from the beginning to the end. In all the stages of preliminary treaty he dealt with a subordinate, who looked up to him as to a superior, and was alert to serve his pleasure. There was no clean-cut cleavage in those stages between his conflicting offices and agencies. No label identified the request of Mr. Maynard, the plaintiff's president, as something separate from the advice of Mr. Maynard, the defendant's chairman. Superior and subordinate together framed a contract, and together closed it. It came before the executive committee as an accomplished fact. The letters had been signed and delivered. Work had been begun. All that remained was a ratification, which may have been needless, and which, even if needful, took the aspect of a mere formality. There was some attempt to show that Mr. Lewis, the vice president, had seen the letters before. The testimony of Mr. Greenidge indicates the contrary. In support of the judgment, we accept his testimony as true. That the letters had been seen by others, there is not even a pretense. The members of the committee, hearing the contract for the first time, knew that it had been framed by the chairman of the meeting. They were assured in his presence that it was just and equitable. Faith in his loyalty disarmed suspicion.

There was, then, a relation of trust reposed, of influence exerted, of superior knowledge on the one side and legitimate dependence on the other. At least, a finding that there was this relation has evidence to sustain it. A trustee may not cling to contracts thus won, unless their terms are fair and just. Crocker v. Cumberland Mining & Milling Co., supra, and cases there cited; Dongan v. MacPherson, 1902 A. C. 197, 200; Thompson on Corp. 1228, 1231. His dealings with his beneficiary are 'viewed with jealousy by the courts, and may be set aside on slight grounds.' Twin–Lick Oil Co. v. Marbury, 91 U. S. 587, 588. He takes the risk of an enforced surrender of his bargain if it turns out to be improvident. There must be candor and equity in the transaction, and some reasonable proportion between benefits and burdens.

The contracts before us do not survive these tests. The unfairness is startling, and the consequences have been disastrous. The mischief consists in this: That the guaranty has not been limited by a statement of the conditions under which the mills are to be run. No matter how large the business, no matter how great the increase in the price of labor or of fuel, no matter what the changes in the nature or the proportion of the products, no matter even though there be extensions of the plant, the defendant has pledged its word that for ten years there will be a saving of

$600 a month, $300 for each mill, $7,200 a year. As a result of that pledge it has supplied the plaintiff with electric current for nothing, and owes, if the contract stands, about $11,000 for the privilege. These elements of unfairness Mr. Maynard must have known, if indeed his knowledge be material. He may not have known how great the loss would be. He may have trusted to the superior technical skill of Mr. Greenidge to compute with approximate accuracy the comparative cost of steam and electricity. But he cannot have failed to know that he held a one-sided contract which left the defendant at his mercy. He was not blind to the likelihood that in a term of ten years there would be changes in the business. The swiftness with which some of the changes followed permits the inference that they were premeditated. There was a prompt increase in the proportion of yarns as compared with slubbing when the guaranty of saving charged the defendant with the greater cost of fuel. But, whether these and other changes were premeditated or not, at least they were recognized as possible. With that recognition, no word of warning was uttered to Greenidge or to any of the defendant's officers. There slumbered within these contracts a potency of profit which the plaintiff neither ignored in their making nor forgot in their enforcement.

It is no answer to say that this potency, if obvious to Maynard, ought also to have been obvious to other members of the committee. They did not know, as he did, the likelihood or the significance of changes in the business. There was need, too, of reflection and analysis before the dangers stood revealed. For the man who framed the contracts, there was opportunity to consider and to judge. His fellow members, hearing them for the first time, and trustful of his loyalty, would have no thought of latent peril. That they had none is sufficiently attested by the fact that the contracts were approved. There was inequality, therefore, both in knowledge and in the opportunity for knowledge. It is not important in such circumstances whether the trustee foresaw the precise evils that developed. The inference that he did might not be unsupported by the evidence. But the indefinite possibilities of hardship, the opportunity in changing circumstances to wrest unlooked-for profits and impose unlooked-for losses, these must have been foreseen. Foreseen or not, they were there, and their presence permeates the contracts with oppression and inequity.

We hold, therefore, that the refusal to vote does not nullify as of course an influence and predominance exerted without a vote. We hold that the constant duty rests on a trustee to seek no harsh advantage to the detriment of his trust, but rather to protest and renounce if through the blindness of those who treat with him he gains what is unfair. And, because there is evidence that in the making of these contracts that duty was ignored, the power of equity was fittingly exercised to bring them to an end.

The judgment should be affirmed, with costs.

COX & HAZEN ON CORPORATIONS,
James D. Cox & Thomas Lee Hazen
§ 10.14   (2d ed. 2003).

A provision of the California general corporation law, adopted in 1931, changed the former rule as to the disqualification of directors to represent their corporation. Under that statute, if financially interested directors have to be counted to make up a quorum or majority to authorize a transaction, such transactions are no longer voidable at the option of the corporation merely by reason of the fact of such participation, provided one of three alternative safeguards or conditions is met: (1) ratification by an independent majority of directors, (2) approval or ratification by the shareholders, or (3) a showing that the contract is just and reasonable as to the corporation. The statute thus permits contracts between a corporation and a majority of its directors as well as contracts between two corporations having a majority of their directors in common.

Following the lead of the California statute, the Model Business Corporation Act establishes the same three alternative safeguards. Under the Model Act, an interested director may be counted in the quorum, and a particular contract or transaction is not void or voidable "because of such relationship or interest." The statute does not provide per se validation of all contracts where the statutory procedure has been followed and thus does not preclude further scrutiny. The Model Act deals only with director conflict-of-interest transactions. Conflict-of-interest transactions involving non-director officers or employees are dealt with under the general principles of fiduciary obligations and the law of agency.

In 1984, Revised Model Business Corporation Act section 8.31 carried forward the overall structure of the predecessor Model Act's conflict-of-interest provision. While section 8.31 provided somewhat detailed descriptions of what constituted an "indirect" conflict of interest as well as the voting requirements for *impartial* director or shareholder approval, this section, like its Model Act predecessor, remained general and sometimes vague in its requirements and scope. Because generality and vagueness necessarily robs transactions of predictability, the 1988 revision of the Revised Model Business Corporations Act substituted new sections 8.60–8.62. The overall philosophy of the 1988 amendments is to adopt a "brightline test" and to make the provisions' proscription exclusive (circumstances falling outside the statutory definition of conflicting interests cannot be the grounds to attack a transaction). The most distinguishing characteristics of the 1988 amendments are the level of detail with which they define "conflicting interests" and specify when judicial intervention is appropriate. The 1988 amendments have met with little success in the state legislatures; most states have patterned their conflict-of-interest provisions on the 1984 versions of the Revised Model Business Corporations Act. * * *

Methods of Satisfying the Statute. . . . [A] practical question posed by state conflict-of-interest statutes is how to comply with the statute's requirements. The typical conflict-of-interest statute sets forth three *alternative* mechanisms for validating a conflict-of-interest transaction: impartial director approval, impartial shareholder approval, or proof of the transaction's fairness. From the view of counseling a client, the least attractive of the three options is relying on proof of the transaction's fairness or reasonableness to the corporation. Courts uniformly place the burden of establishing fairness on the interested director or officer. Fairness typically requires that the transaction reflect terms one would expect in an arm's length transaction, which means generally that a self-dealing fiduciary must treat his corporation's interest as his own. The fiduciary should neither take any advantage from his position on both sides of the transaction nor act in conflict with the corporation's interest to even the slightest extent. Moreover, fairness is more encompassing than the adequacy of consideration; it includes the entirety of the transaction. An important factor in any such fairness inquiry is the actual consideration paid compared with an independent appraisal of the property's fair market value. Thus, the fairness of a lease transaction was considered in light of evidence of the market price of similar leases, the corporation's need for the property, the absence of any evidence that a better deal was possible with a noninterested party, the possibility that the interested party was diverting gain to himself, and whether full disclosure to the disinterested directors and shareholders was made.

As between the two other validating mechanisms—impartial approval by the shareholders and impartial approval by the directors—the latter is certainly the more efficient. One needs to take care when seeking ratification of a completed conflict-of-interest transaction as to whether the applicable statute permits the disinterested directors to *ratify* a consummated conflict-of-interest transaction or merely to *approve* a yet to be consummated conflict-of-interest transaction. It is generally recognized and so expressed in most conflict-of-interest statutes that the shareholders have the inherent power to both approve and ratify conflict-of-interest transactions. Central to the power of the disinterested directors or stockholders to approve or ratify a conflict-of-interest transaction is that their approval be impartial, in good faith, and following full disclosure of the material facts as to the director's or officer's interest as well as to the transaction itself. Each of these requirements is examined in the following paragraphs.

Many state statutes adhere to the 1984 Revised Model Business Corporation Act's scheme of providing detailed rules for ascertaining whether the approving or ratifying body, whether stockholders or directors, is impartial—that is, disinterested. For example, the Model Business Corporation Act requires that approval be by a majority of the voting shares not owned or under the control of the interested party. In states whose statutes do not so limit the shares that can approve or ratify a conflict-of-interest transaction, the result similar to that achieved in the Model Business Corporation Act can be achieved by a reasonable construction of the "good faith" approval requirement so that "good faith" minimally requires impartiality on the part of the decisionmaker.

Special care must be taken with respect to the type of vote required to satisfy a state's conflict-of-interest statute via impartial director approval. Different patterns exist among the states. Delaware, for example, requires that the approval be "by a majority of the disinterested directors." Del. § 144. On the other hand, some states merely condition approval being by votes normally sufficient after disregarding the votes of the interested directors. Thus, consider the vote necessary at a meeting attended by a corporation's seven authorized directors and approval is sought for a transaction in which four of the directors are interested. The Delaware conflict-of-interest provision would be satisfied if at least two of the disinterested directors vote favorably. But in a state that merely disregards the votes but not the physical presence of the interested directors, the transaction would not be approved. A common mechanism for overcoming any problems in securing a proper vote at the board of directors is for the board to exercise its powers under the charter or bylaws to create a committee of disinterested directors and to assign to that committee the responsibility to approve or ratify the conflict-of-interest transaction.

Whether authorization or ratification is by the board of directors or by the stockholders, it is subject to a requirement of good faith. Good faith implicates the motives or intentions of the approving or ratifying body. As is true in any area of the law that turns on a person's intentions or motives, good faith is established circumstantially. In this regard, impartiality in terms of the voting directors or shareholders not having a financial interest served by the contract or transaction (except to the extent it is beneficial to the corporation itself) is the best measure of whether their approval or ratification is in good faith. Minimally, therefore, good faith requires impartiality. * * *

Disclosure can well be viewed as the sine qua non of conflict-of-interest statutes. Not only have courts equated the absence of disclosure with inherent unfairness, but also the efficacy of impartial director or shareholder approval is necessarily dependent on the reviewing body's knowledge of all material facts. It is that body's independent and thoughtful approval after deliberating on all the facts that is intended by the conflict-of-interest statute to protect the corporation from the director's or officer's conflict of interest. Disclosure requires that the interested director or officer bring to the approving or ratifying body of directors or shareholders all facts material to the transaction, not merely that the transaction involves self-dealing by the director or officer.

The final question posed by conflict-of-interest statutes is the effect of complying with one of its alternative validation provisions. The preamble to most conflict-of-interest statutes provides that the contract or transaction will not be voidable solely because of the director's or officer's interest if one of the three validating alternatives is satisfied. Some courts interpret this language literally so that the effect of, for example, good faith independent stockholder approval is that such approval shields the transaction from being rescinded *solely* because it involves a conflict of interest. Thus, under this approach, the effect of a transaction having satisfied one of the conflict-of-interest statute's three authorizing provisions is that such satisfaction removes any adverse inference that otherwise would be drawn because of the director's interest. As a correlative proposition, satisfaction of the statute's authorizing provisions shifts the burden of proof back to the objecting stockholder. * * *

A different and more sweeping view of satisfying any of the conflict-of-interest statute's validating mechanisms is that it removes the transaction from any further scrutiny. That is, the requirements within the validating mechanisms of the statute that are relied on become the exclusive focus of any judicial attack. Thus, once the court is satisfied that the shareholders have independently and in good faith approved a self-dealing transaction after full disclosure of all material facts, the inquiry is closed. Under this view, proof of the transaction's overall unfairness is pushed aside by deference to the will of the independent approving body acting in good faith. Such a perspective appears to comport with a sound view of the role of the reviewing court. A court should avoid second-guessing the diligent and fair deliberations of the independent stockholders or directors. However, there is ample authority to the contrary. Courts have been much influenced in this area by a leading conflict-of-interest case, *Remillard Brick Co. v. Remillard–Dandini Company,* 241 P.2d 66 (Cal.1952), which held that bare technical compliance with the validating provisions of the California conflict-of-interest statute did not remove the transaction from having to be inherently fair to the corporation. *Remillard Brick Co.* has been consistently relied on as standing for the proposition that good faith impartial approval after full disclosure does not obviate the need for the transaction to also be fair to the corporation. While this view is consistent with the *language* used by *Remillard Brick Co.,* the facts of the case are considerably narrower: the defendants held proxies for most of the voting shares of the company and voted those shares in approval of an arrangement that would allow the defendants to divert much of the company's sales to themselves. The court could easily have found that the approval expressed by the defendants was not granted in "good faith," the operative term in the statute. Instead, the court assumed the statute was complied with and added its own veneer by requiring that the transaction be fair. Ever since *Remillard Brick Co.,* there has been a good deal of confusion as to the substantive effects of satisfying a conflict-of-interest statute's provisions pertaining to impartial director or shareholder approval.

NOTES

1. The Model Bus. Corp. Act § 8.30(a) defines standards of conduct to be adhered to by board members in carrying out their duties. It requires a board member to act "in good faith" and "in a manner the director reasonably

believes to be in the best interests of the corporation." Is this a duty of loyalty, care or both? Rev. Model Bus. Corp. Act § 8.31 provides standards for imposing liability on directors who fail to properly discharge their duties. Among the grounds for liability are acts taken "not in good faith" and, under certain circumstances, where there is a "lack of objectivity" because the director has a financial, business or other relationship with a person having an interest in the conduct at issue. Do these provisions create standards different than those in cases decided by the Delaware courts? Where do the Delaware courts find their source of authority for the fiduciary duties they formulate in their decisions?

2.   Model Bus. Corp. Act § 2.02(b)(4) allows corporations to include in their articles of incorporation a provision that eliminates the liability of a director except for certain acts, i.e., improper financial benefits, intentional infliction of harm on the corporation or its shareholders, declaring improper dividends or intentional violation of criminal law. Does this otherwise allow a waiver of the directors' duties of loyalty and care? Compare Del. § 102 (b)(7).

SECTION 2.   CONFLICTS OF INTEREST

GILDER v. PGA TOUR, INC.

936 F.2d 417 (9th Cir.1991).

TANG, CIRCUIT JUDGE:

Karsten Manufacturing Corporation and eight professional golf players challenge the implementation of a new rule by the PGA Tour (PGA) banning clubs with U-shaped grooves. Karsten and the professional player plaintiffs challenge the actions of the PGA on antitrust and state law grounds. After a three day hearing, the district court granted a preliminary injunction enjoining the PGA from implementing the rule. The PGA appeals. We affirm.

This action concerns a rule change implemented by the PGA that bans all clubs on which the cross-section of the grooves on the face of the club is in the shape of a square or "U" as opposed to a "V" * * *

Karsten Manufacturing Corporation (Karsten) designs, manufactures, and sells a variety of golf equipment including: putters, woods, golf bags and "Ping Eye 2" golf clubs. All of Karsten's Ping Eye 2 golf clubs have U-shaped grooves. Karsten's Ping Eye 2 golf clubs are top selling clubs in the United States for both professional and amateur players. Karsten's marketing strategy is that it supplies the same equipment to the amateur as to the professional. Karsten maintains that the U-groove rule will harm its reputation if it is forced to make what the company feels is an inferior product with V-grooves.

Bob Gilder and the seven other plaintiffs in this action are eight professional golfers who are members of the PGA. Each of the eight professionals players uses Karsten's Ping Eye 2 clubs on the Tour. Karsten is paying the attorney's fees for these players.

The defendants in this action are the PGA; Dean A. Beman, the Commissioner and Chief Executive Officer of the PGA; and E. Mandell deWindt, Roger E. Birk, and Hugh E. Culverhouse, members of the PGA Tour Tournament Policy Board. The PGA is the organization which administers professional golf tournaments for the regular Tour and the Senior Tour.

The PGA Policy Board is composed of ten directors. Four of the directors are players elected from the membership of the PGA. The board also includes three officers of the PGA of America and three independent directors with no ties to golf. The independent directors volunteer their time.

In 1984, the United States Golf Association (USGA) changed the rules of golf to allow grooves in the shape of a U. Karsten developed its U-groove club. In 1985, players on the Tour began to complain that the U-groove golf clubs were detracting from the skill level of the game. These players complained that the U-grooves imparted more spin on the golf ball and thus provided greater control for shots from grassy lies of the rough. This characteristic offsets the advantage of players with the skill necessary to keep the golf shot in the fairways.[1]

In January 1987, the USGA conducted tests and concluded that the U-grooves impart more spin on the ball than V-grooves. However, in June 1987, the USGA concluded that there was not enough information to bar clubs with the U-grooves.[2]

On August 10, 1987, the PGA released the results of an equipment survey. One hundred seventy-one of the two hundred golfers on the tour had responded. Of those, seventy-three percent responded that they used U-groove clubs. When asked the advantages of the club, seventy-four percent indicated that the grooves provide for greater control from the wet grass and rough. When asked if the PGA should ban the U-groove, sixty percent responded in the affirmative.

In September 1987, Commissioner Beman wrote to all the golf club manufacturers advising them that the PGA had engaged two technical experts to study the issue of the U-groove. The letter asked the manufacturers to provide pertinent information and relevant data. Karsten did not respond to this request.

In November of 1987, the independent testing expert conducted elaborate field tests trying to localize the effect of the groove. The PGA

---

1. The grass on the fairways is kept short enough to provide a good lie for the golf ball. The areas of the "rough" have taller grass which provides for a bad lie for the golf ball. A golfer in the fairway has an advantage over a golfer whose ball lands in the grassy area of the "rough."

2. The USGA did however adopt a new method for measuring the groove-to-land (space between the grooves) ratio which had the effect of banning the Ping Eye 2 clubs. Karsten and the USGA have settled their differences and Ping Eye 2 clubs are considered a conforming club for purposes of the USGA.

gave the resulting data to two separate consulting groups, one at the University of Texas and one at the University of Delaware. Each of the Universities devised its own methodology to interpret the data. Both studies concluded that the U-grooves impart more spin to the golf ball than the V-grooves. Commissioner Beman testified that in the lesser lofted clubs,[3] the spin of the golf ball was affected to a much lesser extent, if at all.

On May 12, 1988, Commissioner Beman recommended to the board that a proposed rule change banning U-grooves be circulated for public comment. On May 24, 1988, the board accepted Beman's recommendation. The PGA received comments from some manufacturers and the PGA made some changes in the rule.

On August 16, 1988, the PGA deferred action on the proposed rule until the USGA conducted further player study. The USGA tests confirmed that balls hit from the rough with U-grooves have a different spin rate than those hit with V-grooves. The USGA determined, however, that the tests did not show a significant enough difference to ban the clubs with U-grooves.

Beman recommended that the PGA Policy Board adopt the U-groove ban. The PGA's bylaws at that time required a majority of the directors present and three of the player directors to vote on any rule change. At its February 28, 1989 meeting, the four player directors and the PGA officer directors abstained from voting because of conflicts of interest. Each of the abstaining directors had ties to golf club manufacturers. The three independent directors unanimously voted for the rule. The effective date of the rule was January 1, 1990.

Karsten contacted the PGA on June 23, 1989. Karsten met with the PGA to express its concerns on August 14, 1989. At that meeting, Karsten argued, based on its own testing, that the U-grooves do not affect the spin of the ball.

On August 11, 1989, Karsten sued the USGA challenging its June 1987 decision relating to the groove-to-land ratio which had effectively banned Karsten's U-groove clubs. The USGA rule applied to USGA tournaments effective in 1990 and in all amateur tournaments in 1996. Karsten and the USGA have settled this law suit. Karsten filed the instant lawsuit against the PGA on December 1, 1989. The complaint sought injunctive relief and alleged that the actions of the PGA and its directors (1) violated.... the Sherman Anti–Trust Act; (2) violated the Arizona antitrust laws, and (3) interfered with the Karsten's and the professionals' business relationships. The complaint also charged the PGA directors with breaching their fiduciary duties and sought to hold them liable for their allegedly tortious conduct.

On December 5, 1989, all ten members of the PGA board met in a special session. At that meeting, all ten directors voted to change the by

---

3. The five iron through the one iron.

laws of the PGA so that the disinterested members could take binding action on behalf of the PGA policy board when the majority of the directors could not vote because of a conflict. The three disinterested directors then unanimously voted to readopt the groove rule.

Karsten's suit came on for an evidentiary hearing on December 15, 19, and 20, 1989. At the hearing, John Solheim, Karsten's Vice–President, testified that he believes that the U-grooves do not improve player performance.

At the hearing, Karsten presented an economist from Arizona State University, Dr. Richard Smith, who testified that the grooves have not had a negative effect on the PGA. Smith testified that the percentage of prize money that Ping Eye 2 players won is less than the percentage of players who used the Ping Eye 2 clubs. Thus, the Ping Eye 2 clubs do not give the players who use them an advantage. Smith also concluded that the Ping golf clubs do not help the players get their ball to the greens in less than regulation.

The expert testified that there is a correlation between a consumer's choice of golf clubs and the professional's choice of clubs.[4] Smith testified that Karsten had experienced a drop in its market share in its sales of golf clubs and other products because of the PGA ban of U-groove clubs. The PGA's expert challenged these last two assertions in his declaration. Smith testified that Karsten would experience harm to its reputation if forced to manufacture a club conforming to the PGA rule. Smith testified that the professional players would lose endorsements to the extent that the change in clubs adversely affects their performance on the Tour.

Two of the plaintiff players testified at the hearing. Bob Gilder testified that switching clubs would hurt his game, which in turn would affect his endorsement income. Gilder has been using Ping clubs since 1970. He likes the design and dynamics of the club. He cannot identify a difference in the club based on the shape of the grooves. He had switched to the Ping Eye 2 clubs in October of 1989. Gilder testified that he would probably use the Ping Eye 2 clubs with V-grooves if Karsten manufactured them.

George Lanning testified that he is a left-handed golfer. Lanning testified to his belief that Karsten makes the only quality left-handed clubs on the market. He further testified that he might lose his exemption card, which allows him to play on the Tour, if he is forced to change clubs.

Tom Kite, the all-time leading money winner on the Tour, testified that U-grooves diminished the skill factor of the game because the clubs

---

4. On cross-examination, the PGA brought out the fact that the professionals use a different ball than the average consumer. When asked why this does not affect the golf ball market, John Solheim responded that the professional's ball has a much shorter life span and thus is not economical for the average golfer. Additionally, John Solheim responded, the golf ball manufacturers do not advertise this distinction but concentrate on the name of the ball, not the actual type. By contrast, the U-groove has been extensively identified with Karsten and its Ping Eye 2 clubs.

offset the traditional advantage of being able to hit the ball in the fairway of the golf course.

Commissioner Beman testified that the issuance of the preliminary injunction would have dire consequences for the PGA. He testified that the PGA would not be able to propagate any rules for the professional tournaments that it oversees.

After this lengthy evidentiary hearing, the district court held that Karsten and the professional player plaintiffs had demonstrated that (1) they had a reasonable chance of success on the merits, (2) they would suffer irreparable injury if the injunction were not imposed, (3) the balance of hardships tips sharply in favor of the plaintiffs, and (4) there are serious questions for litigation. The PGA appeals. * * *

The district court held that there were substantial questions raised about the propriety of the manner in which the board passed the U-groove ban. The individual professional player plaintiffs have alleged that the PGA directors breached their fiduciary duties by breaching the by-laws, directly and indirectly, and by voting on an issue in which they had conflicting financial interests.

To the extent that the individual plaintiffs are members of the PGA organization, the individual plaintiffs argue that the members of the board of directors owe them a fiduciary duty. *See Levin v. Levin*, 43 Md.App. 380, 390, 405 A.2d 770, 777 (1979) (board of directors member owes the corporation a fiduciary duty). The professional player plaintiffs argue that the player directors and the officer directors have a duty to act "in the best interests of the corporation and [they are] prohibited from using [their] position ... for [their] private gain." *Id.* The PGA argues that Maryland law allows interested directors to act after full disclosure to the board and approval by the non-interested directors. *See* Md.Corps. & Ass'ns Ann.Code § 2–419. However, that statute only states that a contract or transaction is not void or voidable solely on the basis that an interested director voted on it. That section does not address whether there is a violation of the director's fiduciary duties when the interested director votes. The district court did not misapprehend Maryland law in the present case. *See Caribbean Marine Servs. Co.*, 844 F.2d at 673 (preliminary injunction will be reversed if the district court misapprehends the substantive law in assessing the merits).

The district court held that the first vote of the PGA Policy Board violated the by-laws of the PGA. The by-laws required the player directors to vote on rule changes. However, the district court found that none of the player directors voted to adopt the U-groove ban in violation of those by-laws because each of the player directors had a financial conflict. This conflict was due to ties to competing manufacturers of golf clubs. Subsequently, each of the directors voted to change the by-laws to allow the noninterested directors to vote, in the very same meeting and possibly with the intention of allowing the other directors to pass the regulation. Voting on a matter on which a director has a conflict of interest may violate that director's fiduciary duty. A court "may intervene to prevent (or annul) conduct on the part of directors that is fraudulent or represents a breach of their fiduciary obligations." *Mountain Manor Realty, Inc. v. Buccheri,* 55 Md.App. 185, 194, 461 A.2d 45, 51 (1983).

We are not prepared to rule on the merits of these questions at this stage of the litigation and on this undeveloped record. We hold only that the district court did not abuse its discretion in determining that this case raises serious questions that must be resolved at trial. * * *

NOTE

The PGA Tour later settled by agreeing among other things to grandfather existing U-groove clubs. New clubs were to be manufactured in accordance with the rules of the United States Golf Association (USGA), which had also grandfathered the existing U-groove clubs. Square Deal: The PGA Tour And Karsten Manufacturing Solved Their Dispute Over Square Grooves, Gol Magazine 142 (June 1993). The USGA later authorized the production of new U-groove clubs but limited the width and depth of the grooves. Other Equipment Battles, Palm Beach Post, Feb. 14, 2001, at 7C.

MARCIANO v. NAKASH

535 A.2d 400 (Del.1987).

WALSH, JUSTICE.

This is an appeal from a decision of the Court of Chancery which validated a claim in liquidation of Gasoline, Ltd. ("Gasoline"), a Delaware corporation, placed in custodial status pursuant to 8 *Del.C.* § 226 by reason of a deadlock among its board of directors. Fifty percent of Gasoline is owned by Ari, Joe, and Ralph Nakash (the "Nakashes") and fifty percent by Georges, Maurice, Armand and Paul Marciano (the "Marcianos"). The Vice Chancellor ruled that $2.5 million in loans made by the Nakashes faction to Gasoline were valid and enforceable debts of the corporation, notwithstanding their origin in self-dealing transactions. The Marcianos argue that the disputed debt is voidable as a matter of law but, in any event, the Nakashes failed to meet their burden of establishing full fairness. We conclude that the Vice Chancellor applied the proper standard for review of self-dealing transactions and the finding of full fairness is supported by the record. Accordingly, we affirm.

The factual basis underlying the contested loans was fully developed in the Court of Chancery. The liquidation proceeding marked the end of a joint venture launched in 1984 by the Marcianos and the Nakashes to market designer jeans and sportswear. Through a solely owned corporation called Guess? Inc. ("Guess"), the California based Marcianos had been engaged in the design and distribution of stylized jeans for several years. In 1983 they decided to form a separate division to market copies of

Guess creations in a broader retail market. In order to secure financing and broaden market exposure the Marcianos entered into negotiations with the New York based Nakash brothers, the owners of Jordache Enterprises, Inc. a leading manufacturer of jeans. Ultimately, it was agreed that the Nakashes would receive fifty percent of the stock of Guess for a consideration of $4.7 million. As a result, the three Nakash brothers joined three of the Marcianos on the Guess board of directors.

Similarly, when Gasoline was formed, stock ownership and board composition was shared equally by the two families. Although corporate control and direction were equally divided, from an operational standpoint Gasoline functioned in New York under the Nakashes' operational guidance while the parent, Guess, continued under the primary attention of the Marcianos. Differences between the two factions quickly surfaced with resulting deadlocks at the director level of both Guess and Gasoline. The Marcianos filed an action, partly derivative, against Guess and the Nakashes in California followed by the Delaware proceeding in which the Marcianos sought the appointment of a custodian for Gasoline in addition to asserting derivative claims for diversion of corporate opportunities and assets arising out of the Nakashes' operation of Gasoline. Ultimately, the derivative aspect of the Delaware action was stayed in favor of the California proceedings and the Court of Chancery, after a court-ordered shareholder's meeting failed to resolve the director deadlock, appointed a custodian whose power was limited to resolving deadlocks on the Gasoline board.

The custodial arrangement failed to resolve the underlying policy differences between the two factions and neither group appeared willing to invest additional funds or provide guarantees to permit Gasoline to function as a viable commercial enterprise. In early 1987 the custodian advised the Court of Chancery that because of a lack of financing Gasoline had no prospects of continuation and recommended liquidation. A court-approved plan of liquidation authorized the custodian to sell the assets of Gasoline (with both the Marcianos and the Nakashes permitted to bid), pay all valid debts of the corporation and distribute the net proceeds to the shareholders. The determination of those debts, in particular the loan claims asserted by the Nakashes, was sharply disputed in the Court of Chancery and is the focus of this appeal.

The circumstances underlying the Nakashes' claim were determined by the Vice Chancellor following an evidentiary hearing. Prior to March, 1986, Gasoline had secured the necessary financing to support its inventory purchases from the Israel Discount Bank in New York. The bank advanced funds at one percent above prime rate secured by Gasoline's accounts receivable and the Nakashes' personal guarantee. Although requested to do so, the Marcianos were unwilling to participate in loan guarantees because of their dissatisfaction with the Nakashes' management. In response, the Nakashes withdrew their guarantees causing the Israel Discount Bank to terminate its outstanding loan of $1.6 million.

Without consulting the Marcianos, the Nakashes advanced approximately $2.3 million of their personal funds to Gasoline to enable the corporation to pay outstanding bills and acquire inventory. In June, 1986, the Nakashes arranged for U.F. Factors, an entity owned by them, to assume their personal loans and become Gasoline's lender. U.F. Factors charged interest at one percent over prime to which the Nakashes added one percent for their personal guarantees of the U.F. Factors loan. As of April 24, 1987, Gasoline's debt to U.F. Factors amounted to $2,575,000 of which $25,000 represented the Nakashes' guarantee fee. Another Nakash entity, Jordach Enterprises, also sought payment from Gasoline of two percent of the company's gross sales, or $30,000 for warehousing and invoicing services.

In November, 1986, the Nakashes had replaced the U.F. Factors loan, secured by a series of promissory notes executed by Gasoline, with a line of credit collateralized by Gasoline's assets including trademarks and copyrights. This action took place without the knowledge or consent of the custodian and was subsequently rescinded by the Nakashes. At the time of the court-ordered sale of assets, the Nakashes and their entities were general creditors of Gasoline. If allowed in full the Nakashes' claim will exhaust Gasoline's assets, leaving nothing for its shareholders.

The parties agree that the loans made by the Nakashes to Gasoline were interested transactions. The Nakashes as officers of Gasoline executed the various documents which supported the loans and at the same time guaranteed those loans extended through their wholly owned entities. It is also not disputed that, given the control deadlock, the questioned transactions did not receive majority approval of Gasoline's directors or shareholders. The Marcianos argue that the loan transaction is voidable at the option of the corporation notwithstanding its fairness or the good faith of its participants. A review of this contention, rejected by the Court of Chancery, requires analysis of the concept of director self-dealing under Delaware law.

It is a long-established principle of Delaware corporate law that the fiduciary relationship between directors and the corporation imposes fundamental limitations on the extent to which a director may benefit from dealings with the corporation he serves. *Guth v. Loft, Inc.*, Del. Supr., 5 A.2d 503 (1939). Thus, the "voting [for] and taking" of compensation may be deemed "constructively fraudulent" in the absence of shareholder ratification, or statutory or bylaw authorization. *Cahall v. Lofland*, Del. Ch., 114 A. 224, 232 (1921). Perhaps the strongest condemnation of interested director conduct appears in *Potter v. Sanitary Co. of America* Del.Ch., 194 A. 87 (1937), a decision which the Marcianos advance as definitive of the rule of per se voidability. In *Potter* the Court of Chancery characterized transactions between corporations having common directors and officers "constructively fraudulent," absent shareholder ratification.

Support can also be found for the per se rule of voidability in this Court's decision in *Kerbs v. California Eastern Airways Inc.*, Del. Supr., 90

A.2d 652 (1952). The *Kerbs* court, in considering the validity of a profit sharing plan, ruled that the self-interest of the directors who voted on the plan caused the transaction to be voidable. The court concluded that the profit sharing plan was voidable based on the common law rule that the vote of an interested director will not be counted in determining whether the challenged action received the affirmative vote of a majority of the board of directors. *Id.* at 658 (*citing Bovay v. H.M. Byllesby & Co.*, Del. Supr., 38 A.2d 808 (1944)).

The principle of per se voidability for interested transactions, which is sometimes characterized as the common law rule, was significantly ameliorated by the 1967 enactment of Section 144 of the Delaware General Corporation Law.[2] The Marcianos argue that section 144(a) provides the only basis for immunizing self-interested transactions and since none of the statute's component tests are satisfied the stricture of the common law per se rule applies. The Vice Chancellor agreed that the disputed loans did not withstand a section 144(a) analysis but ruled that the common law rule did not invalidate transactions determined to be intrinsically fair. We agree that section 144(a) does not provide the only validation standard for interested transactions.

It overstates the common law rule to conclude that relationship, alone, is the controlling factor in interested transactions. Although the application of the per se voidability rule in early Delaware cases resulted in the invalidation of interested transactions, the result was not dictated simply by a tainted relationship. Thus in *Potter,* the Court, while adopting the rule of voidability, emphasized that interested transactions should be subject to close scrutiny. Where the undisputed evidence tended to show that the transaction would advance the personal interests of the directors at the expense of stockholders, the stockholders, upon discovery, are entitled to disavow the transaction. *Potter,* 194 A. at 91. Further, the court

---

2. Section 144 of Title 8 *Del.C.* now provides:

(a) No contract or transaction between a corporation and 1 or more of its directors or officers, or between a corporation and any other corporation, partnership, association, or other organization in which 1 or more of its directors or officers, are directors or officers, or have a financial interest, shall be void or voidable solely for this reason, or solely because the director or officer is present at or participates in the meeting of the board or committee which authorizes the contract or transaction, or solely because his or their votes are counted for such purpose, if:

(1) The material facts as to his relationship or interest and as to the contract or transaction are disclosed or are known to the board of directors or the committee, and the board or committee in good faith authorizes the contract or transaction by the affirmative votes of a majority of the disinterested directors, even though the disinterested directors be less than a quorum; or

(2) The material facts as to his relationship or interest and as to the contract or transaction are disclosed or are known to the shareholders entitled to vote thereon, and the contract or transaction is specifically approved in good faith by vote of the shareholders; or

(3) The contract or transaction is fair as to the corporation as of the time it is authorized, approved or ratified, by the board of directors, a committee or the shareholders.

(b) Common or interested directors may be counted in determining the presence of a quorum at a meeting of the board of directors or of a committee which authorizes the contract or transaction.

examined the motives of the defendant directors and the effect the transaction had on the corporation and its shareholders. *Id.*

In other Delaware cases, decided before the enactment of section 144, interested director transactions were deemed voidable only after an examination of the fairness of a particular transaction *vis-a-vis* the nonparticipating shareholders and a determination of whether the disputed conduct received the approval of a noninterested majority of directors or shareholders. *Keenan v. Eshleman,* Del. Supr., 2 A.2d 904, 908 (1938); *Blish v. Thompson Automatic Arms Corp.,* Del. Supr., 64 A.2d 581, 602 (1948); *Kerbs,* 90 A.2d at 658. The latter test is now crystallized in the ratification criteria of section 144(a), although the non-quorum restriction of *Kerbs* has been superceded by the language of subparagraph (b) of section 144.

The Marcianos view compliance with section 144 as the sole basis for avoiding the per se rule of voidability. The Court of Chancery rejected this contention and we agree that it is not consonant with Delaware corporate law. This Court in *Fliegler v. Lawrence,* Del.Supr., 361 A.2d 218 (1976), a post-section 144 decision, refused to view section 144 as either completely preemptive of the common law duty of director fidelity or as constituting a grant of broad immunity. As we stated in *Fliegler:* "It merely removes an 'interested director' cloud when its terms are met and provides against invalidation of an agreement 'solely' because such a director or officer is involved." *Id. at 222. In* Fliegler this Court applied a two-tiered analysis: application of section 144 coupled with an intrinsic fairness test.

If section 144 validation of interested director transactions is not deemed exclusive, as *Fliegler* clearly holds, the continued viability of the intrinsic fairness test is mandated not only by fact situations, such as here present, where shareholder deadlock prevents ratification but also where shareholder control by interested directors precludes independent review. Indeed, if an independent committee of the board, contemplated by section 144(a)(1) is unavailable, the sole forum for demonstrating intrinsic fairness may be a judicial one. *See Merritt v. Colonial Foods, Inc.,* Del.Ch., 505 A.2d 757, 764 (1986). In such situations the intrinsic fairness test furnishes the substantive standard against which the evidential burden of the interested directors is applied. It is this burden which was addressed by this Court in *Weinberger v. UOP, Inc.,* Del. Supr., 457 A.2d 701 (1983):

> When directors of a Delaware corporation are on both sides of a transaction, they are required to demonstrate their utmost good faith and the most scrupulous inherent fairness of the bargain.* * *The requirement of fairness is unflinching in its demand that where one stands on both sides of a transaction, he has the burden of establishing its entire fairness, sufficient to pass the test of careful scrutiny by the courts.

Id. at 710.

This case illustrates the limitation inherent in viewing section 144 as the touchstone for testing interested director transactions. Because of the shareholder deadlock, even if the Nakashes had attempted to invoke section 144, it was realistically unavailable. The ratification process contemplated by section 144 presupposes the functioning of corporate constituencies capable of providing assents. Just as the statute cannot "sanction unfairness" neither can it invalidate fairness if, upon judicial review, the transaction withstands close scrutiny of its intrinsic elements.[3]

On the issue of intrinsic fairness, the Court of Chancery concluded that the "U.F. Factors loans compared favorably with the terms available from unrelated lenders" and that the need for external financing had been clearly demonstrated. The Marcianos attack this ruling as factually and legally erroneous. Since the Vice Chancellor's factual findings were arrived at after an evidentiary hearing we are not free to reject them unless they are without record support or not the product of a logical deductive process. *Levitt v. Bouvier,* Del. Supr., 287 A.2d 671, 673 (1972). We find this standard to have been fully satisfied here. * * *

A finding of fairness is particularly appropriate in this case because the evidence indicates that the loans were made by the Nakashes with the *bona fide* intention of assisting Gasoline's efforts to remain in business. Directors who advance funds to a corporation in such circumstances do not forefeit their claims as creditors merely because of relationship. *New York Stock Exchange v. Pickard & Co., Inc.,* Del. Ch., 296 A.2d 143, 149 (1972). Further, in arranging for the loan, the interested directors were not depriving the corporation of a business opportunity but were instead providing a benefit for the corporation which was unavailable elsewhere. * * *

We hold, therefore, that the Court of Chancery properly applied the intrinsic fairness test in determining the validity of the interested director transactions and its finding of full fairness is clearly supported by the record. Accordingly, the decision is AFFIRMED.

NOTE

Do the safe harbor statutes add anything to the analysis, if an overriding fairness standard is imposed? Why do you think that the state legislatures broadened the circumstances under which interested director transactions may occur?

---

3. Although in this case none of the curative steps afforded under section 144(a) were available because of the director-shareholder deadlock, a non-disclosing director seeking to remove the cloud of interestedness would appear to have the same burden under section 144(a)(3), as under prior case law, of proving the intrinsic fairness of a questioned transaction which had been approved or ratified by the directors or shareholders. Folk, *The Delaware General Corp. Law: A Commentary and Analysis,* 86 (1972). On the other hand, approval by fully-informed disinterested directors under section 144(a)(1), or disinterested stockholders under section 144(a)(2), permits invocation of the business judgment rule and limits judicial review to issues of gift or waste with the burden of proof upon the party attacking the transaction.

SECTION 3. CORPORATE OPPORTUNITIES

GUTH v. LOFT, INC.

5 A.2d 503 (Del.1939).

[Charles G. Guth, the president of Loft, Inc. personally acquired the Pepsi–Cola name and formula. That purchase was challenged as an improper taking of a corporate opportunity that rightfully belonged to Loft. The relevant facts are set forth in the parts of the opinion that are excerpted below]

LAYTON, CHIEF JUSTICE, DELIVERING THE OPINION OF THE COURT:

Corporate officers and directors are not permitted to use their position of trust and confidence to further their private interests. While technically not trustees, they stand in a fiduciary relation to the corporation and its stockholders. A public policy, existing through the years, and derived from a profound knowledge of human characteristics and motives, has established a rule that demands of a corporate officer or director, peremptorily and inexorably, the most scrupulous observance of his duty, not only affirmatively to protect the interests of the corporation committed to his charge, but also to refrain from doing anything that would work injury to the corporation, or to deprive it of profit or advantage which his skill and ability might properly bring to it, or to enable it to make in the reasonable and lawful exercise of its powers. The rule that requires an undivided and unselfish loyalty to the corporation demands that there shall be no conflict between duty and self-interest. The occasions for the determination of honesty, good faith and loyal conduct are many and varied, and no hard and fast rule can be formulated. The standard of loyalty is measured by no fixed scale.

If an officer or director of a corporation, in violation of his duty as such, acquires gain or advantage for himself, the law charges the interest so acquired with a trust for the benefit of the corporation, at its election, while it denies to the betrayer all benefit and profit. The rule, inveterate and uncompromising in its rigidity, does not rest upon the narrow ground of injury or damage to the corporation resulting from a betrayal of confidence, but upon a broader foundation of a wise public policy that, for the purpose of removing all temptation, extinguishes all possibility of profit flowing from a breach of the confidence imposed by the fiduciary relation. Given the relation between the parties, a certain result follows; and a constructive trust is the remedial device through which precedence of self is compelled to give way to the stern demands of loyalty.

The rule, referred to briefly as the rule of corporate opportunity, is merely one of the manifestations of the general rule that demands of an officer or director the utmost good faith in his relation to the corporation which he represents.

It is true that when a business opportunity comes to a corporate officer or director in his individual capacity rather than in his official capacity, and the opportunity is one which, because of the nature of the enterprise, is not essential to his corporation, and is one in which it has no interest or expectancy, the officer or director is entitled to treat the opportunity as his own, and the corporation has no interest in it, if, of course, the officer or director has not wrongfully embarked the corporation's resources therein. [citing cases] But, in all of these cases, except, perhaps, in one, there was no infidelity on the part of the corporate officer sought to be charged. . . .

Duty and loyalty are inseparably connected. Duty is that which is required by one's station or occupation; is that which one is bound by legal or moral obligation to do or refrain from doing; and it is with this conception of duty as the underlying basis of the principle applicable to the situation disclosed, that the conduct and acts of Guth with respect to his acquisition of the Pepsi–Cola enterprise will be scrutinized. Guth was not merely a director and the president of Loft. He was its master. It is admitted that Guth manifested some of the qualities of a dictator. The directors were selected by him. Some of them held salaried positions in the company. All of them held their positions at his favor. Whether they were supine merely, or for sufficient reasons entirely subservient to Guth, it is not profitable to inquire. It is sufficient to say that they either wilfully or negligently allowed Guth absolute freedom of action in the management of Loft's activities, and theirs is an unenviable position whether testifying for or against the appellants.

Prior to May, 1931, Guth became convinced that Loft was being unfairly discriminated against by the Coca–Cola Company of whose syrup it was a large purchaser, in that Loft had been refused a jobber's discount on the syrup, although others, whose purchases were of far less importance, had been given such discount. He determined to replace Coca–Cola as a beverage at the Loft stores with some other cola drink, if that could be accomplished. So, on May 19, 1931, he suggested an inquiry with respect to desirability of discontinuing the use of Coca–Cola, and replacing it with Pepsi–Cola at a greatly reduced price. Pepsi–Cola was the syrup produced by National Pepsi–Cola Company. As a beverage it had been on the market for over twenty-five years, and while it was not known to consumers in the area of the Loft stores, its formula and trademark were well established. Guth's purpose was to deliver Loft from the thraldom of the Coca–Cola Company, which practically dominated the field of cola beverages, and, at the same time, to gain for Loft a greater margin of profit on its sales of cola beverages. Certainly, the choice of an acceptable substitute for Coca–Cola was not a wide one, and, doubtless, his experience in the field of bottled beverages convinced him that it was necessary for him to obtain a cola syrup whose formula and trademark were secure against attack. Although the difficulties and dangers were great, he concluded to make the change. Almost simultaneously, National Pepsi–Cola Company, in which Megargel was predominant and whom Guth knew, went into bankruptcy; and Guth was informed that the long established Pepsi–Cola formula and trademark could be had at a small price. Guth, of course, was Loft; and Loft's determination to replace Coca–Cola with some other cola beverage in its many stores was practically coincidental with the opportunity to acquire the Pepsi–Cola formula and trademark. This was the condition of affairs when Megargel approached Guth. Guth contended that his negotiation with Megargel in 1931 was but a continuation of a negotiation begun in 1928, when he had no connection with Loft; but the Chancellor found to the contrary, and his finding is accepted.

It is urged by the appellants that Megargel offered the Pepsi–Cola opportunity to Guth personally, and not to him as president of Loft. The Chancellor said that there was no way of knowing the fact, as Megargel was dead, and the benefit of his testimony could not be had; but that it was not important, for the matter of consequence was how Guth received the proposition.

It was incumbent upon Guth to show that his every act in dealing with the opportunity presented was in the exercise of the utmost good faith to Loft; and the burden was cast upon him satisfactorily to prove that the offer was made to him individually. Reasonable inferences, drawn from acknowledged facts and circumstances, are powerful factors in arriving at the truth of a disputed matter, and such inferences are not to be ignored in considering the acts and conduct of Megargel. He had been for years engaged in the manufacture and sale of a cola syrup in competition with Coca–Cola. He knew of the difficulties of competition with such a powerful opponent in general, and in particular in the securing of a necessary foothold in a new territory where Coca–Cola was supreme. He could not hope to establish the popularity and use of his syrup in a strange field, and in competition with the assured position of Coca–Cola, by the usual advertising means, for he, himself, had no money or resources, and it is entirely unbelievable that he expected Guth to have command of the vast amount of money necessary to popularize Pepsi-Cola by the ordinary methods. He knew of the difficulty, not to say impossibility, of inducing proprietors of soft drink establishments to use a cola drink utterly unknown to their patrons. It would seem clear, from any reasonable point of view, that Megargel sought to interest someone who controlled an existing opportunity to popularize his product by an actual presentation of it to the consuming public. Such person was Guth, the president of Loft. It is entirely reasonable to infer that Megargel approached Guth as president of Loft, operating, as it did, many soft drink fountains in a most necessary and desirable territory where Pepsi–Cola was little known, he well knowing that if the drink could be established in New York and circumjacent territory, its success would be assured. Every reasonable inference points to this conclusion. What was finally agreed upon between Megargel and Guth, and what outward appearance their agreement assumed, is of small importance. It was a matter of indifference to Megargel whether his co-adventurer was Guth personally, or Loft, so long as his terms were met and his object attained.

Leaving aside the manner of the offer of the opportunity, certain other matters are to be considered in determining whether the opportunity, in the circumstances, belonged to Loft; and in this we agree that

Guth's right to appropriate the Pepsi–Cola opportunity to himself depends upon the circumstances existing at the time it presented itself to him without regard to subsequent events, and that due weight should be given to character of the opportunity which Megargel envisioned and brought to Guth's door.

The real issue is whether the opportunity to secure a very substantial stock interest in a corporation to be formed for the purpose of exploiting a cola beverage on a wholesale scale was so closely associated with the existing business activities of Loft, and so essential thereto, as to bring the transaction within that class of cases where the acquisition of the property would throw the corporate officer purchasing it into competition with his company. This is a factual question to be decided by reasonable inferences from objective facts.

It is asserted that, no matter how diversified the scope of Loft's activities, its primary business was the manufacturing and selling of candy in its own chain of retail stores, and that it never had the idea of turning a subsidiary product into a highly advertised, nation-wide specialty. Therefore, it had never initiated any investigation into the possibility of acquiring a stock interest in a corporation to be formed to exploit Pepsi–Cola on the scale envisioned by Megargel, necessitating sales of at least 1,000,000 gallons a year. It is said that the most effective argument against the proposition that Guth was obligated to take the opportunity for Loft is to be found in the complainant's own assertion that Guth was guilty of an improper exercise of business judgment when he replaced Coca–Cola with Pepsi–Cola at the Loft Stores. Assuming that the complainant's argument in this respect is incompatible with its contention that the Pepsi–Cola opportunity belonged to Loft, it is no more inconsistent than is the position of the appellants on the question. In the Court below, the defendants strove strenuously to show, and to have it believed, that the Pepsi–Cola opportunity was presented to Loft by Guth, with a full disclosure by him that if the company did not embrace it, he would. This, manifestly, was a recognition of the necessity for his showing complete good faith on his part as a corporate officer of Loft. In this Court, the Chancellor having found as a fact that Guth did not offer the opportunity to his corporation, it is asserted that no question of good faith is involved for the reason that the opportunity was of such character that Guth, although Loft's president, was entirely free to embrace it for himself. The issue is not to be enmeshed in the cobwebs of sophistry. It rises far above inconsistencies in argument.

The appellants suggest a doubt whether Loft would have been able to finance the project along the lines contemplated by Megargel, viewing the situation as of 1931. The answer to this suggestion is two-fold. The Chancellor found that Loft's net asset position at that time was amply sufficient to finance the enterprise, and that its plant, equipment, executives, personnel and facilities, supplemented by such expansion for the necessary development of the business as it was well able to provide, were in all respects adequate. The second answer is that Loft's resources were found to be sufficient, for Guth made use of no other to any important extent.

Next it is contended that the Pepsi–Cola opportunity was not in the line of Loft's activities which essentially were of a retail nature. It is pointed out that, in 1931, the retail stores operated by Loft were largely located in the congested areas along the Middle Atlantic Seaboard, that its manufacturing operations were centered in its New York factory, and that it was a definitely localized business, and not operated on a national scale; whereas, the Megargel proposition envisaged annual sales of syrup at least a million gallons, which could be accomplished only by a wholesale distribution. Loft, however, had many wholesale activities. Its wholesale business in 1931 amounted to over $800,000. It was a large company by any standard. It had an enormous plant. It paid enormous rentals. Guth, himself, said that Loft's success depended upon the fullest utilization of its large plant facilities. Moreover, it was a manufacturer of syrups and, with the exception of cola syrup, it supplied its own extensive needs. The appellants admit that wholsesale distribution of bottled beverages can best be accomplished by license agreements with bottlers. Guth, president of Loft, was an able and experienced man in that field. Loft, then, through its own personnel, possessed the technical knowledge, the practical business experience, and the resources necessary for the development of the Pepsi–Cola enterprise.

But, the appellants say that the expression, 'in the line' of a business, is a phrase so elastic as to furnish no basis for a useful inference. The phrase is not within the field of precise definition, nor is it one that can be bounded by a set formula. It has a flexible meaning, which is to be applied reasonably and sensibly to the facts and circumstances of the particular case. Where a corporation is engaged in a certain business, and an opportunity is presented to it embracing an activity as to which it has fundamental knowledge, practical experience and ability to pursue, which, logically and naturally, is adaptable to its business having regard for its financial position, and is one that is consonant with its reasonable needs and aspirations for expansion, it may be properly said that the opportunity is in the line of the corporation's business.

The manufacture of syrup was the core of the Pepsi–Cola opportunity. The manufacture of syrups was one of Loft's not unimportant activities. It had the necessary resources, facilities, equipment, technical and practical knowledge and experience. The tie was close between the business of Loft and the Pepsi-Cola enterprise. Conceding that the essential of an opportunity is reasonably within the scope of a corporation's activities, latitude should be allowed for development and expansion. To deny this would be to deny the history of industrial development.

It is urged that Loft had no interest or expectancy in the Pepsi–Cola opportunity. That it had no existing property right therein is manifest; but we cannot agree that it had no concern or expectancy in the opportunity within the protection of remedial equity. Loft had a practical and essential concern with respect to some cola syrup with an established formula and trademark. A cola beverage has come to be a business necessity for soft drink establishments; and it was essential to the success of Loft to serve at its soda fountains an acceptable five cent cola drink in order to attract into its stores the great multitude of people who have formed the habit of drinking cola beverages. When Guth determined to discontinue the sale of Coca–Cola in the Loft stores, it became, by his own act, a matter of urgent necessity for Loft to acquire a constant supply of some satisfactory cola syrup, secure against probable attack, as a replacement; and when the Pepsi–Cola opportunity presented itself, Guth having already considered the availability of the syrup, it became impressed with a Loft interest and expectancy arising out of the circumstances and the urgent and practical need created by him as the directing head of Loft.

As a general proposition it may be said that a corporate officer or director is entirely free to engage in an independent, competitive business, so long as he violates no legal or moral duty with respect to the fiduciary relation that exists between the corporation and himself. The appellants contend that no conflict of interest between Guth and Loft resulted from his acquirement and exploitation of the Pepsi–Cola opportunity. They maintain that the acquisition did not place Guth in competition with Loft any more than a manufacturer can be said to compete with a retail merchant whom the manufacturer supplies with goods to be sold. However true the statement, applied generally, may be, we emphatically dissent from the application of the analogy to the situation of the parties here. There is no unity between the ordinary manufacturer and the retailer of his goods. Generally, the retailer, if he becomes dissatisfied with one supplier of merchandise, can turn to another. He is under no compulsion and no restraint. In the instant case Guth was Loft, and Guth was Pepsi. He absolutely controlled Loft. His authority over Pepsi was supreme. As Pepsi, he created and controlled the supply of Pepsi–Cola syrup, and he determined the price and the terms. What he offered, as Pepsi, he had the power, as Loft, to accept. Upon any consideration of human characteristics and motives, he created a conflict between self-interest and duty. He made himself the judge in his own cause. This was the inevitable result of the dual personality which Guth assumed, and his position was one which, upon the least austere view of corporate duty, he had no right to assume. Moreover, a reasonable probability of injury to Loft resulted from the situation forced upon it. Guth was in the same position to impose his terms upon Loft as had been the Coca–Cola Company. If Loft had been in servitude to that company with respect to its need for a cola syrup, its condition did not change when its supply came to depend upon Pepsi, for, it was found by the Chancellor, against Guth's contention, that he had not given Loft the protection of a contract which secured to it a constant supply of Pepsi-Cola syrup at any definite price or for any definite time.

It is useless to pursue the argument. The facts and circumstances demonstrate that Guth's appropriation of the Pepsi–Cola opportunity to himself placed him in a competitive position with Loft with respect to a commodity essential to it, thereby rendering his personal interests incompatible with the superior interests of his corporation; and this situation was accomplished, not openly and with his own resources, but secretly and with the money and facilities of the corporation which was committed to his protection.

Although the facts and circumstances disclosed by the voluminous record clearly show gross violations of legal and moral duties by Guth in his dealings with Loft, the appellants make bold to say that no duty was cast upon Guth, hence he was guilty of no disloyalty. The fiduciary relation demands something more than the morals of the market place. Meinhard v. Salmon, supra. Guth's abstractions of Loft's money and materials are complacently referred to as borrowings. Whether his acts are to be deemed properly cognizable in a civil court at all, we need not inquire, but certain it is that borrowing is not descriptive of them. A borrower presumes a lender acting freely. Guth took without limit or stint from a helpless corporation, in violation of a statute enacted for the protection of corporations against such abuses, and without the knowledge or authority of the corporation's Board of Directors. Cunning and craft supplanted sincerity. Frankness gave way to concealment. He did not offer the Pepsi–Cola opportunity to Loft, but captured it for himself. He invested little or no money of his own in the venture, but commandeered for his own benefit and advantage the money, resources and facilities of his corporation and the services of its officials. He thrust upon Loft the hazard, while he reaped the benefit. His time was paid for by Loft. The use of the Grace plant was not essential to the enterprise. In such manner he acquired for himself and Grace ninety one percent of the capital stock of Pepsi, now worth many millions. A genius in his line he may be, but the law makes no distinction between the wrong doing genius and the one less endowed.

Upon a consideration of all the facts and circumstances as disclosed we are convinced that the opportunity to acquire the Pepsi–Cola trademark and formula, goodwill and business belonged to the complainant, and that Guth, as its President, had no right to appropriate the opportunity to himself.

The Chancellor's opinion may be said to leave in some doubt whether he found as a fact that the Pepsi–Cola opportunity belonged to Loft. Certain it is that he found all of the elements of a business opportunity to exist. Whether he made use of the word 'estopped' as meaning that he found in the facts and circumstances all of the elements of an equitable estoppel, or whether the word was used loosely in the sense that the facts and circumstances were so overwhelming as to render it impossible for Guth to rebut the conclusion that the opportunity belonged to Loft, it is needless to argue. It may be said, however, that we are not at all convinced that the elements of an equitable estoppel may not be found having regard for the dual personality which Guth assumed.

The decree of the Chancellor is sustained.

NOTES

1. Compare the corporate opportunity doctrine to the parallel partnership issues raised in *Meinhard v. Salmon,* in Chapter 2.

Was Guth really guilty of misconduct? Loft, Inc. had been purchasing Coca Cola syrup for its stores in large amounts, but Guft became dissatisfied with Coca Cola because it would not give him a discount for volume purchases; such discounts were against company policy at Coca Cola. Pepsi was in bankruptcy after suffering large losses from speculations in sugar futures; it had guessed wrong on the effect of World War I on sugar prices. Guth began negotiating with Pepsi and was able to purchase its trademark and formula for a small amount and began selling it through Guth, thereby breaking the Coca–Cola monopoly that was hurting Loft. Loft's only expectation was cheaper syrup, not a new business distributing that syrup to others.

2. A key issue in corporate opportunity cases is whether the opportunity really belonged to the corporation. For example, assume that a director of a dairy company is told of an opportunity for a bicycle business. Is that a corporate opportunity for a dairy? What if the opportunity was a milk machine business, but the dairy could not afford it? What if the opportunity came to the director in his personal capacity, rather than as director of the dairy company? *Guth v. Loft, Inc.* related the corporation's line of business to protectable expectancies under the corporate opportunity doctrine. In Lagarde v. Anniston Lime & Stone Co., 126 Ala. 496, 28 So. 199, 201 (1900), the court talked in terms of a corporate expectancy arising out of an existing right. How do those two tests differ? Rather than link the corporate opportunity doctrine to specific lines of business or specific rights, some courts look to general fairness:

> We do not concur in the argument of counsel for the defendant to the effect that the test is whether the corporation has an existing interest or an expectancy thereof in the property involved, being of the opinion that the true basis of the governing doctrine rests fundamentally on the unfairness in the particular circumstances of a director, whose relation to the corporation is fiduciary, 'taking advantage of an opportunity [for his personal profit] when the interest of the corporation justly call for protection. This calls for the application of ethical standards of what is fair and equitable * * * [in] particular sets of facts.'

Durfee v. Durfee & Canning, Inc., 323 Mass. 187, 80 N.E.2d 522, 529 (1948), quoting Henry W. Ballantine on Corporations 204–205 (Rev.Ed.1946). Another approach is to apply a two-step test. First, whether the line of business test is satisfied and second, looking at the equitable considerations surrounding the defendant's acquisition of the opportunity:

> The threshold question to be answered is whether a business opportunity presented is also a 'corporate' opportunity, i.e., whether the business opportunity is of sufficient importance and is so closely related to the existing or prospective activity of the corporation as to warrant judicial sanctions against its personal acquisition by a managing officer or director of the corporation.... [T]he second step in the two-step process

leading to the determination of the ultimate question of liability involves close scrutiny of the equitable considerations existing prior to, at the time of, and following the officer's acquisition. Resolution will necessarily depend upon a consideration of all the facts and circumstances of each case considered in the light of those factors which control the decision that the opportunity was in fact a corporate opportunity. Significant factors which should be considered are the nature of the officer's relationship of the management and control of the corporation; whether the opportunity was presented to him in his official or individual capacity; his prior disclosure of the opportunity to the board of directors or shareholders and their response; whether or not he used or exploited corporate facilities, assets, or personnel in acquiring the opportunity; whether his acquisition harmed or benefited the corporation; and all other facts and circumstances bearing on the officer's good faith and whether he exercised the diligence, devotion, care, and fairness toward the corporation which ordinarily prudent men would exercise under similar circumstances in like positions.

Miller v. Miller, 301 Minn. 207, 222 N.W.2d 71, 81–82 (1974). It has been suggested that "the test adopted in *Miller* merely piles the uncertainty and vagueness of the fairness test on top of the weaknesses in the line of business test." Northeast Harbor Golf Club, Inc. v. Harris, 661 A.2d 1146, 1150 (Me.1995).

3. *Another variation.* In Meiselman v. Meiselman, 309 N.C. 279, 307 S.E.2d 551 (1983), the North Carolina Supreme Court articulated the test a bit differently. Michael and Ira Meiselman were co-owners of Eastern Federal Corporation, a chain of movie theaters. Ira was the majority owner and Michael had a minority interest. Michael, became sole owner of Republic, Inc. Republic's sole business was managing Eastern Federal and other interests co-owned by the two brothers. The details are set forth in Chapter 10. On the corporate opportunity issue, the court explained:

> In essence, then, Michael is claiming that Ira breached his fiduciary duty to the corporate defendants by usurping a corporate opportunity which belonged to them—the opportunity to buy the stock of Republic. Having thus framed Michael's claim that Ira breached his fiduciary duty to the corporate defendants as one involving a usurpation of a corporate opportunity, we will first set out the rules governing this area of the law before examining the trial court's finding of fact to determine if it adequately addressed this issue.

> In order for plaintiff to succeed in this claim, he must prove that (a) he has standing as a shareholder in the corporate defendants to bring suit on this claim against Ira as a director and officer of the defendant corporations, and (b) Ira in his role as a corporate director and officer breached a fiduciary duty owed to the corporate defendants not to usurp a corporate opportunity of the corporate defendants. * * *

> The doctrine of corporate opportunity is "a species of the duty of a fiduciary to act with undivided loyalty; it is one of the manifestations of the general rule that demands of an officer or director the utmost good faith in his relations with the corporation that he represents; in general,

a corporate officer or director is under a fiduciary obligation not to divert a corporate business opportunity for his own personal gain." Annot., 77 A.L.R.3d 961, 965 (1977). Stated more simply, the "corporate opportunity doctrine provides that a corporate fiduciary may not appropriate to himself an opportunity that rightfully belongs to his corporation." Note, *Corporate Opportunity and Corporate Competition: A Double–Barreled Theory of Fiduciary Liability,* 10 Hofstra L.Rev. 1193 (1982) [hereinafter cited as Note, *Corporate Opportunity*], citing Guth v. Loft, Inc., 23 Del.Ch. 255, 271–73, 5 A.2d 503, 510–11 (1939). * * *

Generally speaking, there are three types of business opportunities a corporate fiduciary can attempt to take advantage of: "those entirely extraneous to the corporation's business, those in the same or a direct line with it, and finally, those complementary to it." Note, *Liability of Directors for Taking Corporate Opportunities, Using Corporate Facilities, or Engaging in a Competing Business,* 39 Colum.L.Rev. 219, 220 (1939). The courts have formulated three tests to differentiate between an extraneous opportunity and those upon which a corporation would wish to act. The first test focuses on whether the corporation had an "interest or expectancy" in the opportunity. The second test considers whether the opportunity was within the corporation's "line of business". The third test asks whether considerations of "fairness" indicate that the opportunity is one which belonged to the corporation. Id. We find it unnecessary to label the North Carolina test because the General Assembly, in its wisdom, has enacted a statutory standard, N.C.G.S. § 55–30(b). The specific part of that statute applicable to this case, N.C.G.S. § 55–30(b)(3) provides as follows:

> (b) No corporate transaction in which a director has an adverse interest is either void or voidable, if: * * * (3) The adversely interested party proves that the transaction was just and reasonable to the corporation at the time when entered into or approved. In the case of compensation paid or voted for services of a director as director or as officer or employee the standard of what is "just and reasonable" is what would be paid for such services at arm's length under competitive conditions.

This presents the question as to whether the common law rule stated in *Highland Cotton Mills* is a rule substantially different from that set out in N.C.G.S. § 55–30(b)(3). We hold that the two standards are the same. Under both N.C.G.S. § 55–30(b)(3) and this Court's holding in *Highland Cotton Mills* the adversely interested party must demonstrate that the transaction at issue was "just and reasonable". Thus, once an adversely interested party proves that the transaction at issue was "just and reasonable to the corporation at the time when entered into or approved", N.C.G.S. § 55–30(b)(3), it follows that the interested party has satisfied its burden under this Court's decision in *Highland Cotton Mills.*

In essence, then, when an officer or director is charged with having usurped a corporate opportunity, he or she must establish that the "corporate transaction" in which he or she has engaged is "just and reasonable" to the corporation because it was not an opportunity or "corporate transaction" which the corporation itself would have wanted. A determination of what is "just and reasonable" and, thus, whether a corporate opportunity has indeed been usurped, is, of course, one in which "no hard and fast rule can be formulated." See Guth v. Loft, Inc., supra, 23 Del.Ch. at 270, 5 A.2d at 510.

As one commentator noted, the courts determine whether a corporate opportunity has been usurped by examining the facts of each particular case. Comment, *The Corporate Opportunity Doctrine,* 18 Sw.L.J. 96, 100 (1964). However, some of the "recurring circumstances" which courts continually find relevant in determining whether a corporate opportunity has been usurped include the following: 1) the ability, financial or otherwise, of the corporation to take advantage of the opportunity; 2) whether the corporation engaged in prior negotiations for the opportunity; 3) whether the corporate director or officer was made aware of the opportunity by virtue of his or her fiduciary position; 4) whether the existence of the opportunity was disclosed to the corporation; 5) whether the corporation rejected the opportunity; and 6) whether the corporate facilities were used to acquire the opportunity. Id. at 100–107. * * *

In taking into account the fact that a corporate opportunity may arise not only in the same or direct line with a corporation's business, but also in a line complementary to it, we hold that in determining whether a corporate fiduciary has usurped a corporate opportunity—and thus that the "corporate transaction" in which he or she has entered is not "just and reasonable" to the corporation—a trial court is to approach the problem from two perspectives. It is to examine not only whether the disputed opportunity is functionally related to the corporation's business, but also whether the corporation has an interest or expectancy in the opportunity. In so doing, the trial court is to examine all of the facts in the particular case, including the "recurring circumstances" other courts have found relevant, in determining whether a corporate opportunity has indeed been usurped.

The court in *Meiselman* remanded the matter to the lower court to make findings consistent with this analysis.

4. *The American Law Institute's approach.* The American Law Institute has taken a disclosure approach that seeks to assure that the issue is surfaced and addressed before the officer or director takes the opportunity. In Northeast Harbor Golf Club, Inc. v. Harris, 661 A.2d 1146 (Me.1995), the court adopted the test suggested by the ALI's Principles of Corporate Governance:

In an attempt to protect the duty of loyalty while at the same time providing long-needed clarity and guidance for corporate decisionmakers, the American Law Institute has offered the most recently developed version of the corporate opportunity doctrine. Principles of Corporate Governance § 5.05 (May 13, 1992), provides as follows:

§ 505 Taking of Corporate Opportunities by Directors or Senior Executives

(a) *General Rule.* A director or senior executive may not take advantage of a corporate opportunity unless:

(1) The director or senior executive first offers the corporate opportunity to the corporation and makes disclosure concerning the conflict of interest and the corporate opportunity;

(2) The corporate opportunity is rejected by the corporation; and

(3) Either:

(A) The rejection of the opportunity is fair to the corporation;

(B) The opportunity is rejected in advance, following such disclosure, by disinterested directors, or, in the case of a senior executive who is not a director, by a disinterested superior, in a manner that satisfies the standards of the business judgment rule; or

(C) The rejection is authorized in advance or ratified, following such disclosure, by disinterested shareholders, and the rejection is not equivalent to a waste of corporate assets.

(b) *Definition of a Corporate Opportunity.* For purposes of this Section, a corporate opportunity means:

(1) Any opportunity to engage in a business activity of which a director or senior executive becomes aware, either:

(A) In connection with the performance of functions as a director or senior executive, or under circumstances that should reasonably lead the director or senior executive to believe that the person offering the opportunity expects it to be offered to the corporation; or

(B) Through the use of corporate information or property, if the resulting opportunity is one that the director or senior executive should reasonably be expected to believe would be of interest to the corporation; or

(2) Any opportunity to engage in a business activity of which a senior executive becomes aware and knows is closely related to a business in which the corporation is engaged or expects to engage. * * *

661 A.2d at 1150–51 The court in *Northeast Harbor Golf Club* further stated that "the central feature of the ALI test is the strict requirement of full disclosure prior to taking advantage of any corporate opportunity. 'If the opportunity is not offered to the corporation, the director or senior executive will not have satisfied § 5.05(a).' ... '[F]ull disclosure to the appropriate corporate body is ... an absolute condition precedent to the validity of any forthcoming rejection as well as to the availability to the director or principal senior executive of the defense of fairness.' " (citation omitted). Id.

5. *Old wine in new bottles?* How different are each of the foregoing formulations? Is this not merely an example of courts trying to articulate some guidelines for an "I know it when I see it" analysis. The various courts do seem to have a different attitude in how broadly to define a protectable opportunity but, in the last analysis, there are a number of variables to be

considered and the cases are highly fact specific. For a discussion of the competing interests involved in duty of loyalty situations, see, e.g., Pat K. Chew, "Competing Interests in the Corporate Opportunity Doctrine," 67 N.C. L. Rev. 435 (1989).

6. How should the corporation's financial condition affect the corporate opportunity doctrine? *See* Irving Trust Co. v. Deutsch, 73 F.2d 121 (2d Cir. 1934).

7. If disclosure is made, and the corporation demands the opportunity even though it does not have the finances to take advantage of it, should the director be allowed to proceed? In Klinicki v. Lundgren, 67 Or.App. 160, 678 P.2d 1250 (1984), the court adopted the approach of the ALI Corporate Governance Standards for application to a corporate opportunity case. There, the issue was whether the defendant had to disclose an opportunity to the corporation where the corporation's finances would not have permitted it to take the opportunity:

> We hold that a corporation's financial ability to undertake a business opportunity is not a factor in determining the existence of a corporate opportunity unless the defendant demonstrates that the corporation is technically or de facto insolvent. * * * To allow a corporate fiduciary to take advantage of a business opportunity when the fiduciary determines the corporation to be unable to avail itself of it would create the worst sort of temptation for the fiduciary to rationalize an inaccurate and self-serving assessment of the corporation's financial ability and thereby compromise the duty of loyalty to the corporation. If a corporate fiduciary's duty of loyalty conflicts with his personal interest, the latter must give way. Unless a corporation is technically or de facto insolvent, a determination whether a business opportunity is corporate or personal does not depend on the corporation's relative financial ability to undertake the opportunity. To avoid liability for usurping a corporate opportunity on the basis that the corporation was insolvent, the fiduciary must prove insolvency.

> The appropriate method to determine whether or not a corporate opportunity exists is to let the corporation decide at the time the opportunity is presented. If a fiduciary is uncertain whether a given opportunity is corporate or not, or whether the corporation has the financial ability to pursue it, he needs merely to disclose the existence of the opportunity to the directors and let them decide. Disclosure is a fundamental fiduciary duty. It cannot be burdensome, and it resolves the issue for all parties concerned and eliminates the necessity for a judicial determination after the fact.

> In the present case, defendants do not contend that Berlinair was technically or de facto insolvent. Although the company has run a deficit since commencing operations in 1977 and periodic infusions of capital have been required, that state of affairs does not constitute technical or de facto insolvency unless there is an imminent threat to the business' continued vitality. Plaintiff offered expert testimony that Berlinair could have obtained adequate financing to secure the BFR contract. Defendants' expert witness, Beyer, an airline management expert, expressed

the opposite opinion. However, there is nothing in his testimony or otherwise in the record to suggest that Berlinair was insolvent or was no longer a viable corporate entity. We conclude that ABC usurped a corporate opportunity belonging to Berlinair when, acting through Lundgren, the BFR contract was diverted. Accordingly, the constructive trust, injunction, duty to account and other relief granted by the trial court are appropriate remedies.

8.   What happens where the opportunity came to the director or officer in another capacity? In Johnston v. Greene, 121 A.2d 919 (Del.1956), the court held that an opportunity that came to a director of several corporations in his individual capacity was not a corporate opportunity of any one of the corporations he directed. This was the case even though at least one corporation had a large amount of liquidity that would have allowed it to take the opportunity. The court stated that the opportunity was a personal one and the individual could keep the opportunity or offer it to any of the corporations he directed:

> At the time when the Nutt–Shel business was offered to Odlum, his position was this: He was the part-time president of Airfleets. He was also president of Atlas—an investment company. He was a director of other corporations and a trustee of foundations interested in making investments. If it was his fiduciary duty, upon being offered any investment opportunity, to submit it to a corporation of which he was a director, the question arises, Which corporation? Why Airfleets instead of Atlas? Why Airfleets instead of one of the foundations? So far as appears, there was no specific tie between the Nutt–Shel business and any of these corporations or foundations. Odlum testified that many of his companies had money to invest, and this appears entirely reasonable. How, then, can it be said that Odlum was under any obligation to offer the opportunity to one particular corporation? And if he was not under such an obligation, why could he not keep it for himself?

> Plaintiff suggests that if Odlum elects to assume fiduciary relationships to competing corporations he must assume the obligations that are entailed by such relationships. So he must, but what are the obligations? The mere fact of having funds to invest does not ordinarily put the corporations 'in competition' with each other, as that phrase is used in the law of corporate opportunity. There is nothing inherently wrong in a man of large business and financial interests serving as a director of two or more investment companies, and both Airfleets and Atlas (to mention only two companies) must reasonably have expected that Odlum would be free either to offer to any of his companies any business opportunity that came to him personally, or to retain it for himself—provided always that there was no tie between any of such companies and the new venture or any specific duty resting upon him with respect to it.

121 A.2d at 924. Compare David J. Greene & Co. v. Dunhill International, 249 A.2d 427, 435 (Del.Ch.1968) (the parent company of a majority owned subsidiary was found to have taken a corporate opportunity of a subsidiary that was available to both companies). In another case, Burg v. Horn, 380 F.2d 897 (2d Cir.1967) the court held that, since the defendant directors of a

corporation operating low rent housing buildings spent most of their time in unrelated enterprises and already owned other corporations holding similar properties when the corporation in which plaintiff was a stockholder was formed, no duty to offer the corporation all such low rent buildings coming to their attention could be implied absent further evidence of an agreement or understanding to that effect.

SECTION 4. COMPETITION AND THE DUTY OF LOYALTY

LINCOLN STORES, INC. v. GRANT

309 Mass. 417, 34 N.E.2d 704 (1941).

COX, JUSTICE.

This bill in equity, filed August 1, 1939, originally sought to enjoin the defendants Grant, Martin and Haley from operating a store similar to those of the plaintiff, and from making use of information acquired by them while they were officers and employees of it. An accounting also was sought for the purpose of determining what damage the plaintiff had sustained by reason of the alleged unfaithful acts of said three defendants. Thereafter, by amendment, the bill sought to have a constructive trust declared of the shares owned by Grant, Martin and Haley of the capital stock of the Connecticut corporation that was operating a store in alleged competition with one owned and operated by the plaintiff. Subsequently, the wife of the defendant Martin was joined as a defendant. The suit was referred to a master, whose report was confirmed by interlocutory decree, and a final decree was entered which, among other things, ordered Grant, Martin and Haley to pay the plaintiff damages and dismissed the bill as against Mrs. Martin. The plaintiff appealed from these decrees. The vital question for determination is whether, upon the facts found, it should have been decreed, as it was not, that a constructive trust be established.

The plaintiff, hereinafter called the company, for several years had operated stores in fourteen cities, including one in Norwich, Connecticut. Grant was a director of the company, and for some time prior to June 7, 1937, was manager of its store in Rochester, New York, and supervisor of two other stores in that State. Martin also was a director, and, until June 7, 1937, was the general manager of all the company's stores. Haley entered the employ of the company about 1927. From 1932 he was a buyer, and on May 19, 1937, he resigned this position. The company store in Norwich was opened in 1927. It was in 'a 100% location, right in the center of the city,' was conspicuously successful, and, as early as 1927, the company's officers felt that it was handicapped by lack of selling space. The possibility of getting more space was frequently discussed. The company had a lease that expired in 1943. It contained an option, expiring April 1, 1933, to lease two other stores in the same building. In 1932, four of the officers, including Grant and Martin, discussed the advisability of exercising the option by leasing one of the two stores, but it was concluded that to do so would involve more expense than the return in sales would warrant, and the option was not exercised. Thereafter, the company's officers did not again consider the acquisition of more space in Norwich until 1938.

There was an 'old-time' department store in Norwich that had been operated since about 1880 by the Reid & Hughes Company, a Connecticut corporation. It was on the same side of the street as the company's store, but afforded little competition to it.

In April, 1937, a real estate broker in New York informed Grant that the capital stock of the Reid & Hughes store in Norwich was for sale. Grant immediately sent this information with the proposed terms of sale to Martin. Within a few days the broker telephoned Haley, describing the offer. It is unnecessary to recite in detail the conduct of Grant, Martin and Haley up to May 22, 1937, when the purchase of the Reid & Hughes stock was completed. It is enough to say that on April 27 Grant, Martin and Haley agreed to go forward with its purchase. Haley was to resign from the plaintiff's employ and go to Norwich to take charge of the Reid & Hughes store. Grant and Martin desired to continue in the company's employ and planned to conceal their interests in the Reid & Hughes store, to continue in the company's employ for an indefinite period, and to give such assistance and direction in the management of the Reid & Hughes store as they could without letting their interests become known to the company. The three had various conferences in New York, Massachusetts and Connecticut directly relating to their proposed purchase, and charged their traveling expenses to the company. In the meantime, Grant availed himself of certain information that he obtained from confidential records of the company, which he used in determining the amount of inventory and capital that would be required in similar departments in the Reid & Hughes store if it was purchased. The three intended to utilize the knowledge and experience they had acquired in the company's employ in merchandising goods similar to those sold in the company's store in Norwich.

On June 7, Grant and Martin attended a meeting of the company's directors at which they were both discharged from their positions. Grant denied that he was connected with the Reid & Hughes store, and Martin said that he would not deny that he was. About June 19, 1937, their resignations as directors were requested, but they refused to resign and continued as directors until March, 1938, although after June 7, they attended no meetings and received no information as directors other than notices of meetings.

On April 3, 1939, two hundred shares of the stock of the Reid & Hughes Company stood in the name of Haley and Grace A. Haley, two hundred shares in the name of Grant's wife, two hundred shares in the name of Martin's wife, and five shares each in the names of Grant, Martin and Haley. No certificates have since been issued. The Reid & Hughes Company, a Connecticut corporation, is not a party, nor is Grace A. Haley or Mrs. Grant, and the certificates of stock are not in the custody of the court.

The master found that Grant and Martin, as directors of the company, were under a duty not to engage in competition with the company and not to acquire interests which conflicted with its interests; that in the purchase of the Reid & Hughes stock and the conduct of the store in competition with the company's store, they violated their duty, and that Haley, who participated in their acts, also violated his duty as an employee. He found that the company had sustained damages in the loss of profits that it otherwise would have earned had it not been for this competition, and also that it should be reimbursed for the compensation paid Grant, Martin and Haley from April 27 until they left the company's employ, together with the travel expenses that they had charged to the company while they were forming and executing their plan to acquire the Reid & Hughes stock.

If we assume, without deciding, that all necessary parties are before the court, nevertheless, we are of opinion, on the facts found, that the establishment of a constructive trust, by the terms of which Grant, Martin and Haley would be declared trustees of the stock of the Reid & Hughes Company that was acquired, is not warranted. All these defendants were employees of the company, and two were directors. In the circumstances disclosed, the finding of the master that Haley, who was not a director, participated in the acts of the other two and also violated his own duty as an employee was warranted. Directors of corporations have often been said to be trustees. In any event, they occupy a fiduciary relation toward the corporation, and have a duty of reasonably protecting and conserving its interests. It does not appear that any duty whatever rested upon any of these defendants to acquire the Reid & Hughes stock directly for the company so that there was any breach of a specific, as distinguished from a general, duty in acquiring it for themselves. In this connection it has been said that the duty is only co-extensive with the trust so that, in general, the legal restrictions that rest upon officers in their acquisitions are generally limited to property in which the corporation has an interest already existing, or in which it has an expectancy growing out of an existing right, or to cases where the officers' interference will, in some degree, prevent or hinder the corporation in effecting the purposes of its creation. It has been said that a director cannot be allowed to profit personally by acquiring property that he knows the corporation will need or intends to acquire, and that this interest, actual or in expectancy, must have existed while the person involved was a director or officer.

From an examination of the facts in the case at bar, we think it follows that the Reid & Hughes store was not essential to the company, and that it was something in which the company had no interest or expectancy. For that matter, it appears that it was being operated many years before the plaintiff company opened its store in Norwich. Its acquisition by the company had never been considered. It would seem obvious that practical business considerations would be against its acquisition. The company had no interest in or thought of acquiring it when the opportunity came to these defendants to purchase the stock.

Was there a connection between the general scope of the duties of the defendants, considered collectively, and the purchase of the stock, so that it was improper for them to purchase it themselves? We are of opinion, on the facts found, that there was not. Not only had the company declined to exercise its option and acquire additional floor space for its store before that option expired in 1933, but at no time thereafter did its officers even consider the acquisition of more space in Norwich until 1938, which was some time after the three defendants acquired the Reid & Hughes stock. If we put to one side for the moment the facts surrounding the operation of the store by the three defendants after its purchase, we have, in effect, the case of the acquisition of a store that was ninety feet away from the company's store in which a going business was being conducted. The absence of any interest, express or implied, on the part of the company in the acquisition of this store, or for that matter, of any other space, is significant. In the acquisition of a store, as distinguished from its operation, we are of opinion that the three defendants violated no duty. The case at bar is not one in which the Reid & Hughes stock was acquired because the three defendants had in mind that it was desirable, if not necessary, for the plaintiff's business. No purpose is disclosed to attempt to dispose of the stock to the company at a profit. On the contrary, it would seem that the three defendants conceived the idea of going into business on their own account by the purchase of stock which would give them control of a going concern. They availed themselves of no information to the effect that the business was desired or needed by the company. It does not appear that the officers of the company had ever entertained any thought that it was. The defendants did, however, avail themselves of information as to methods of conducting the business that was to be acquired. They made use of this information, and, as the master found, to the damage of the company.

Directors or officers of a corporation are not, by reason of the fiduciary relationship they bear toward the corporation necessarily precluded from entering into an independent business in competition with it, but, in doing so, they must act in good faith.

The case at bar is distinguishable from Essex Trust Co. v. Enwright, 102 N.E. 441. It is true that in that case the defendant contended that he was not within the rule as to fiduciaries because the duty of securing the lease that he obtained was not entrusted by his employer to him. But, it was pointed out, that in obtaining the lease, he had made use of information that came to him in his employment to the detriment of his employer. It is true that in the case at bar the defendants made use of information that they had obtained while in the employ of the company. But it seems that that information was used not for the purpose of acquiring the Reid & Hughes stock as something that would be valuable to the company, but rather for the purpose of operating the store after it had been acquired. And for the wrongful use of this information, and for the wrongful conduct of the defendants, in so far as it related to competition with the company, the latter has been compensated in damages.

It is true that the company, by its amended bill, evinces a desire, in effect, to take the Reid & Hughes stock, and it is assumed that it would expect to reimburse the three defendants to the extent to which they would be entitled. But we think it follows from what has been said that the facts found do not warrant the establishment of a constructive trust as to the capital stock of the Reid & Hughes Company. The conduct of the three defendants in acquiring the stock was, in a sense, to the end that the company was damaged as a result of the wrongful use of information obtained by them, while in the service of the company, whereby they transformed a noncompetitive store into one that was in active competition. But we think the wrong arose, not out of the acquisition of the store, but in the operation of the business.

The company's contention in this court is that 'in addition to the relief already afforded by the final decree,' it is entitled to the imposition of a constructive trust in its favor on the shares of the Reid & Hughes Company stock. In the circumstances, it is unnecessary to consider whether, apart from the question of the imposition of a constructive trust, the plaintiff is entitled to anything more than it obtained by the final decree.

DUANE JONES CO., INC. v. BURKE

306 N.Y. 172, 117 N.E.2d 237 (1954).

LEWIS, CHIEF JUDGE.

The plaintiff corporation, by this action, seeks damages from the ten individual and two corporate defendants alleged to have been sustained as a result of a conspiracy by defendants to deprive plaintiff of its principal customers and its key employees. * * *

In 1942, Duane Jones, a man of experience in the field of advertising, organized the plaintiff corporation. From the date of its formation, Jones has continued to be the dominating personality and the policy maker of plaintiff corporation, which by 1951 had acquired accounts in such number and quality as produced a gross billing of $9,000,000. Plaintiff's income was derived from commissions paid to it in the amount of 15% of the sum spent by plaintiff's customers with advertising media. Plaintiff's service consisted of originating advertising ideas and campaigns satisfactory to its customers, and of arranging for the execution of such campaigns through various media. To effect that service, plaintiff referred each of its principal customers to one or more 'account executives' in its employ who worked in close co-operation with the customer and were directly responsible for the handling of the account thus serviced. Although an advertiser might commit itself to noncancelable contracts with advertising media, it was generally not bound by any agreement with the advertising agency through which it carried on its advertising. In other words, in the case at hand plaintiff's customers were free at any time to discharge plaintiff as its agency; and similarly, plaintiff had the right at will to resign any of its accounts. Likewise plaintiff's employees were not under formal contract to it.

We come then to a consideration of evidence of the alleged conspiracy by the defendants wrongfully to deprive plaintiff of its customers and key employees. In July, 1951, plaintiff serviced approximately twenty-five customers or accounts, including the following which the amended complaint alleges were diverted to the defendant Scheideler, Beck & Werner, Inc.: Manhattan Soap Co., Inc., G. F. Heublein & Bro., Inc., International Salt Co., Inc., Wesson Oil & Snowdrift Sales Co., C. F. Mueller Co., The Borden Company, The Marlin Fire Arms Co. and McIlhenny Corp. At that time the number of plaintiff's employees was one hundred thirty-two, of whom fifteen were described by plaintiff's president as 'key men.'

During the preceding six months plaintiff had lost three of its accounts total gross billings of which approximated $6,500,000 and had received resignations from three executives as well as from certain staff members of the organization. It also appears that Duane Jones, the president of plaintiff corporation, had been guilty of certain behavior lapses at his office, at business functions and during interviews with actual and prospective customers. As a result of those occasions of misbehavior, several of plaintiff's officers and directors expressed dissatisfaction with conditions described as 'intolerable' which existed at the plaintiff agency in the spring and summer of 1951.

On June 28, 1951, a meeting took place at the Park Lane Hotel in Manhattan, which was attended by a number of the plaintiff's officers, directors and employees, including all the individual defendants named in this action except the defendant Burke. Witnesses called by the plaintiff and the defendants gave accounts which varied in minor particulars as to what transpired at that meeting of June 28, 1951. However, the choice as to which version was accurate, and as to which version if any, could be drawn therefrom, was for the jury, if there was substantial evidence to support that choice. There was substantial evidence of record that at the meeting of June 28th, the defendant Scheideler informed the group that he had spoken to several of plaintiff's customers whose accounts he serviced from whom he gained favorable reaction to a proposal that the group either buy out Duane Jones' interest in the plaintiff corporation or that they form a new corporation. It also appears that Scheideler suggested to the others present that they inquire whether the accounts being serviced by them for the plaintiff would favor such a project. Defendants Scheideler and Hayes each admitted that at the June 28th meeting it was decided that Hayes should speak to Duane Jones concerning a possible purchase by the defendants of Jones' interest in the plaintiff corporation. According to Hayes, he informed Duane Jones on July 3, 1951, that the nine defendants associated with plaintiff were interested in purchasing Jones' stock in the plaintiff agency. Mr. Jones' recital of that conversation was that Hayes told him of the group's intention either to buy him out or to start their own agency, and that if he did not agree to a sale they would resign en masse within forty-eight hours. Duane Jones further testified that Hayes indicated to him that the agency's customers had been 'already presold' on the alternative plan and that the group would notify him on July 5th of the price they would pay for the business. According to Jones he said to Hayes: 'In other words, you are standing there with a Colt .45, holding it at my forehead, and there is not much I can do except to give up?', to which Hayes replied: 'Well, you can call it anything you want, but that is what we are going to do.'

Witnesses called by both sides testified that a meeting was held on July 5, 1951, attended by Duane Jones and the defendants who are ex-employees of plaintiff. Again, the record contains conflicting versions of what occurred. The defendants Scheideler and Hayes stated that the defendant employees made an offer to purchase Jones' stock which was accepted by Jones. Jones testified however that, after hearing the proposal submitted by Hayes as their spokesman, he 'told them there was nothing I could do but accept if they had the clients all presold' and agreed to accept the proposal if it could be worked out along the lines of a plan advantageous to him tax-wise. On the following day, Duane Jones issued a statement to plaintiff's employees that he was retiring from the agency and expressing his appreciation for their past co-operation.

However, despite frequent meetings between representatives of Duane Jones and the individual defendants the proposed sale was never consummated. Negotiations terminated on or about August 6, 1951, the claim of both Duane Jones and the defendants being that the failure to agree was the result of the other's increased demands and refusal to abide by the terms allegedly decided upon at the meeting of July 5th. On August 7, 1951, there was held a special meeting of the board of directors of plaintiff corporation, at which there were presented and accepted written resignations by the defendants Scheideler, Werner, Hayes, Gill, Hubbard and Hughes as officers and as directors of plaintiff. The resignations were substantially identical in form; each was a resignation effective only insofar as the writer was a director or officer, or both, of plaintiff; each contained a statement that the writer would continue his duties as an employee of the plaintiff agency, and stated 'As an employee, I will continue to service those accounts now assigned to me, to the best of my ability.'

Defendant Hulshizer testified that he submitted an oral resignation as officer, director and employee of plaintiff corporation at the meeting held August 7, 1951, but that, at the request of Jones, he agreed to stay on 'in a nominal capacity' because if he resigned there would not be a quorum of the board of directors. The witness stated that he acted as secretary of the corporation and retained possession of the corporate records until September 26, 1951; that he continued as an employee of plaintiff until September 30, 1951, having been told by Jones that his services would not be required after that date. Also on August 7th, defendant Manhattan Soap Co. wrote a letter to Scheideler informing him that 'With reference to the various conversations and meetings which we have held in regard to the make-up of the Duane Jones Company, we now wish to tell you that, as the agency is now constituted, we will move our account from the Duane Jones Company not later than September 30, 1951.' On August 10, 1951, defendant Scheideler addressed a letter to Duane Jones stating that he was resigning as of September 30, 1951.

A special meeting of the board of directors of plaintiff was held August 17, 1951, at which the resignation of defendant Scheideler as an employee was read and in view of his status as a member of the plaintiff's pension trust plan it was 'Resolved, that action upon the resignation of Mr. Scheideler as employee of this Company be suspended pending an investigation of his conduct to determine if he should be discharged for cause.' At that meeting the board also voted to discharge immediately and for cause (with two weeks severance pay) the defendants Hayes, Hughes, Hubbard, Beck and Brooks. On the same date, the defendant Werner submitted his resignation as an employee, effective September 15th, and thereafter on August 23d he submitted a second resignation effective immediately.

Despite their resignations as employees of plaintiff, defendants Scheideler, Werner and Hulshizer testified that they continued to receive payments from, and to perform services for, plaintiff for varying periods of time extending to September 30, 1951. Scheideler stated that he rendered services to plaintiff during August and September, 1951, and that he received salary payment through September 14, 1951. Werner testified that he serviced accounts for plaintiff in the period from August 15 to September 15, 1951 during which time he signed and received payment on petty cash slips drawn upon plaintiff and that he received a salary up to September 15, 1951. Defendant Hulshizer worked at plaintiff's office until September 30, 1951, and received his last salary check from plaintiff on September 28, 1951. With regard to the defendants discharged for cause on August 17th, Duane Jones testified that he asked the men 'as a matter of courtesy' to stay on until they could be replaced and that the severance pay was intended to cover their services during that holdover period.

On August 22, 1951, the defendants Scheideler, Werner and Beck signed a certificate of incorporation of the defendant Shceideler, Beck & Werner, Inc., which certificate was filed with the Secretary of State on August 23, 1951. A few days later, on August 30th, the corporate defendant executed a lease of office space at 487 Park Avenue, where it opened for business as an advertising agency on September 10, 1951. Within six weeks after its formal opening, the defendant Scheideler, Beck & Werner, Inc., had in its employ seventy one of the one hundred thirty-two persons formerly employed by plaintiff, including the defendants Scheideler, Werner, Beck, Hughes, Brooks, Hubbard and Hulshizer * * *

The foregoing evidence has led us to conclude that the conduct of the individual defendants-appellants as officers, directors or employees of the plaintiff corporation ' * * * fell below the standard required by the law of one acting as an agent or employee of another.' Lamdin v. Broadway Surface Adv. Corp., 272 N.Y. 133, 138, 5 N.E.2d 66, 67. Each of these defendants was * * * prohibited from acting in any manner inconsistent with his agency or trust and (was) at all times bound to exercise the utmost good faith and loyalty in the performance of his duties.' 272 N.Y. at page 138, 5 N.E.2d at page 67. Plaintiff's evidence which the jury apparently believed established that on June 28, 1951, the individual defendants-appellants met and agreed to take over the business of the plaintiff agency, either by purchase of the controlling interest in the corporation or by resignation en masse and the formation of a new agency; that at that meeting it was proposed that the defendants contact plaintiff's customers whose advertising accounts were then being serviced by the defendants as account executives of plaintiff, with reference to prospective control of plaintiff's business by the individual defendants; that on July 3d the employees-defendants offered to purchase, at a fixed price, the controlling interest in plaintiff agency and stated that, if the offer were not accepted, they would resign and that plaintiff's customers had been 'presold' on the proposed action; that a day or two after termination of unsuccessful negotiations for their purchase of the stock, the defendants who were officers and directors submitted to plaintiff their resignations from those positions, all (save one) of which resignations were received by plaintiff on the same day and were in substantially identical form; that three of the individual defendants immediately commenced negotiations leading to the incorporation on August 23d of a rival advertising agency which agency commenced operations on September 10th; that, at or about the time it commenced business, the defendant agency had as its customers nine accounts formerly serviced by plaintiff and employed more than 50% of plaintiff's personnel; that the accounts and personnel were acquired through solicitation by, or at the direction of, the individual defendants prior to or during the period when they were completing their duties as employees of plaintiff; and finally, that the rival agency was formed and the accounts and personnel were solicited without disclosure of such activities to plaintiff.

The inferences reasonably to be drawn from the record justify the conclusion reached by the jury and by a majority of the Appellate Division that the individual defendants-appellants, while employees of plaintiff corporation, determined upon a course of conduct which, when subsequently carried out, resulted in benefit to themselves through destruction of plaintiff's business, in violation of the fiduciary duties of good faith and fair dealing imposed on defendants by their close relationship with plaintiff corporation. The jury's determination of those questions of fact affirmed by the Appellate Division is beyond our power to disturb. 'If conflicting inferences are possible as to abuse or opportunity, the trier of the facts must make the choice between them. There can be no revision in this court unless the choice is clearly wrong.' Meinhard v. Salmon, 249 N.Y. 458, 467, 164 N.E. 545, 548, 62 A.L.R. 1.

Nor is it a defense to say that the defendants-appellants did not avail themselves of the benefit of the customers and personnel diverted from plaintiff until after defendants had received notice of discharge or had informed plaintiff of their intention to leave Duane Jones Company. Upon this record the jury might have found that the conspiracy originated in June or July while a fiduciary duty existed, and that the benefits realized when defendant Scheideler, Beck & Werner, Inc., commenced operation in September were merely the results of a predetermined course of action. In view of that circumstance, the individual defendants would not be relieved of liability for advantages secured by them, after termination of their employment, as a result of opportunities gained by reason of their employment relationship.* * *

CONWAY, DESMOND, DYE, FULD AND FROESSEL, JJ., CONCUR.

VAN VOORHIS, J., TAKING NO PART.[5]

DALTON v. CAMP

353 N.C. 647, 548 S.E.2d 704 (2001).

ORR, JUSTICE.

This case arises out of an employer's allegations of unfair competitive activity by former employees and a new corporation formed by them. Plaintiff Robert Earl Dalton d/b/a B. Dalton & Company ("Dalton") produced, under a thirty-six month contract, an employee newspaper for Klaussner Furniture Industries ("KFI"). Dalton hired defendant David Camp ("Camp") to produce the publication and subsequently hired Nancy Menius ("Menius") to assist in the production of the employee newspaper. Near the conclusion of the contract period, Dalton began negotiations with KFI to continue publication. After the contract had expired, Dalton continued to publish the employee newspaper without benefit of a contract while talks between the parties continued. During this period, Camp, who was contemplating leaving Dalton's employ, established a competing publications entity, Millennium Communication Concepts, Inc. ("MCC"), and discussed with KFI officials the possibility of replacing Dalton as publisher of KFI's employee newspaper. Soon thereafter, Camp entered into a contract with KFI to produce the newspaper. He resigned from Dalton's employment approximately two weeks later. * * *

We begin our analysis with an examination of Dalton's first claim against Camp which, as described in Dalton's complaint, constituted a breach of fiduciary duty, including a duty of loyalty. From the outset, we

---

5. It was reported that plaintiff donated the $300,000 he was awarded in this suit to establish a chaired professorship in business ethics at the University of Pennsylvania. *See* Harry G. Henn, *Corporations, Partnerships—Agency Teaching Materials* 443 (2d ed. 1986).

note that Dalton argues this claim from two distinct vantage points. First, he alleges that Camp breached his fiduciary duty by being disloyal. *See Long v. Vertical Techs., Inc.*, 113 N.C.App. 598, 604, 439 S.E.2d 797, 802 (1994) (defining fiduciary duty as one requiring good faith, fair dealing, and loyalty). Second, he argues that a separate and distinct action for breach of duty of loyalty exists and that Camp's conduct constituted a breach of that duty. We disagree with both contentions, holding that Dalton has failed to establish: (1) facts supporting a breach of fiduciary duty, and (2) that any independent tort for breach of duty of loyalty exists under state law. * * *

For a breach of fiduciary duty to exist, there must first be a fiduciary relationship between the parties. Such a relationship has been broadly defined by this Court as one in which "there has been a special confidence reposed in one who in equity and good conscience is bound to act in good faith and with due regard to the interests of the one reposing confidence . . . , [and] 'it extends to any possible case in which a fiduciary relationship exists in fact, and in which there is confidence reposed on one side, and *resulting domination and influence on the other.*' " *Abbitt v. Gregory*, 201 N.C. 577, 598, 160 S.E. 896, 906 (1931) (quoting 25 C.J. *Fiduciary* § 9, at 1119 (1921)) (emphasis added), *quoted in Patterson v. Strickland*, 133 N.C.App. 510, 516, 515 S.E.2d 915, 919 (1999). However, the broad parameters accorded the term have been specifically limited in the context of employment situations. Under the general rule, "the relation of employer and employee is not one of those regarded as confidential."

In applying this Court's definition of fiduciary relationship to the facts and circumstances of the instant case—in which employee Camp served as production manager for a division of employer Dalton's publishing business—we note the following: (1) the managerial duties of Camp were such that a certain level of confidence was reposed in him by Dalton; and (2) as a confidant of his employer, Camp was therefore bound to act in good faith and with due regard to the interests of Dalton. In our view, such circumstances, as shown here, merely serve to define the nature of virtually all employer-employee relationships; without more, they are inadequate to establish Camp's obligations as fiduciary in nature. No evidence suggests that his position in the workplace resulted in "domination and influence on the other [Dalton]," an essential component of any fiduciary relationship. *See Abbitt*, 201 N.C. at 598, 160 S.E. at 906. Camp was hired as an at-will employee to manage the production of a publication. His duties were those delegated to him by his employer, such as overseeing the business's day-to-day operations by ordering parts and supplies, operating within budgetary constraints, and meeting production deadlines. In sum, his responsibilities were not unlike those of employees in other businesses and can hardly be construed as uniquely positioning him to exercise dominion over Dalton. Thus, absent a finding that the employer in the instant case was somehow subjugated to the improper influences or domination of his employee—an unlikely scenario as a general proposition and one not evidenced by these facts in particular—we cannot conclude that a fiduciary relationship existed between the two. As a result, we hold that the trial court properly granted defendant Camp's motion for summary judgment as to Dalton's claim alleging a breach of fiduciary duty and reverse the Court of Appeals on this issue.

As for any claim asserted by Dalton for breach of a duty of loyalty (in an employment-related circumstance) outside the purview of a fiduciary relationship, we note from the outset that: (1) no case cited by plaintiff recognizes or supports the existence of such an independent claim, and (2) no pattern jury instruction exists for any such separate action. We additionally note that Dalton relies on cases he views as defining an independent duty of loyalty, *see McKnight v. Simpson's Beauty Supply*, Inc., 86 N.C.App. 451, 358 S.E.2d 107 (1987); *In re Burris*, 263 N.C. 793, 140 S.E.2d 408 (1965) (per curiam), even though those cases were devoid of claims or counterclaims alleging a breach of such duty. In *McKnight*, the Court of Appeals held that every employee was obliged to "serve his employer faithfully and discharge his duties with reasonable diligence, care and attention." 86 N.C.App. at 453, 358 S.E.2d at 109. However, the rule's role in deciding the case was limited; it was but a factor in determining whether an employer was justified in terminating an employee. The circumstance and conclusion reached in *Burris* are strikingly similar. At issue in that case was whether a civil service employee was properly discharged after he "knowingly ... brought about a conflict of interest between himself and his employer." *Burris*, 263 N.C. at 795, 140 S.E.2d at 410. In deciding the case, this Court wrote "[w]here an employee deliberately acquires an interest adverse to his employer, he is disloyal, *and his discharge is justified.*" *Id.* (emphasis added). Conspicuously absent from the *Burris* Court's consideration was any claim or counterclaim seeking damages resulting from an alleged breach of a duty of loyalty.

In our view, if *McKnight and* Burris indeed serve to define an employee's duty of loyalty to his employer, the net effect of their respective holdings is limited to providing an employer with a defense to a claim of wrongful termination. No such circumstance is at issue in the instant case, in which Camp resigned from Dalton's employ. Thus, we hold that: (1) there is no basis for recognizing an independent tort claim for a breach of duty of loyalty; and (2) since there was no genuine issue as to any material fact surrounding the claim as stated in the complaint (breach of fiduciary duty, including a duty of loyalty), the trial court properly concluded as a matter of law that summary judgment was appropriate for Camp.

To the extent that the holding in *Food Lion, Inc. v. Capital Cities/ABC, Inc.*, 951 F.Supp. 1224 (M.D.N.C.1996), can be read to sanction an independent action for breach of duty of loyalty, *see id.* at 1229 ("There is a cause of action for violation of the duty of loyalty."), we conclude that the federal district court incorrectly interpreted our state case law by assuming that: (1) "[s]ince the [state's] courts recognize the existence of the duty of loyalty, it follows that they *would* recognize a claim for breach of that duty," *id.* (emphasis added); and (2) the "North Carolina ...

Supreme Court [ ] *likely would* recognize a broader claim" for a breach of fiduciary duty, *id.* (emphasis added). As previously explained, although our state courts recognize the existence of an employee's duty of loyalty, we do not recognize its breach as an independent claim. Evidence of such a breach serves only as a justification for a defendant-employer in a wrongful termination action by an employee. Moreover, an examination of our state's case law fails to reveal support for the federal district court's contention that this Court would broaden the scope of fiduciary duty to include food-counter clerks employed by a grocery store chain. As for the holding in *Long*, we note that the corporate employer in that case was awarded damages for "a material breach of fiduciary duty of good faith, fair dealing and loyalty" by its employees. 113 N.C.App. at 604, 439 S.E.2d at 802. Essentially, the *Long* court determined that the employees, who originally founded the company in question and served respectively as its president and senior vice president, owed a fiduciary duty to the parent firm and that they breached that duty by taking actions contrary to the parent firm's best interests. Thus, the claim and damages awarded in Long resulted from: (1) a showing of a fiduciary relationship, (2) thereby establishing a fiduciary duty, and (3) a breach of that duty. No such fiduciary relationship or duty is evidenced by the circumstances of the instant case.

NOTES

1. As the *Lincoln Stores* and *Duane Jones* cases point out, agents have a duty not to compete while employed that is independent of their duty not to take a corporate opportunity. Does the decision in *Dalton v. Camp* mean that employees in North Carolina may use the employer's confidential information for the employee's own benefit? Would such conduct constitute theft or misappropriation that could be prosecuted? The role of officers, directors and employees as fiduciaries in handling confidential information will be revisited in Chapter 14, which deals with prohibitions on using "inside" information to trade stocks.

2. *Lawyers and law firms.* In Meehan v. Shaughnessy, 404 Mass. 419, 535 N.E.2d 1255 (1989), the court held that the defendant partners and associates breached their fiduciary duties in soliciting clients to move their business to a new firm being created by the defendants. The defendant partners had falsely denied they had plans to leave when asked by other partners, and clients were solicited through a one-sided announcement the defendants sent on their old firm's stationery. In Johnson v. Brewer & Pritchard, P.C., 73 S.W.3d 193 (Tex.2002), the Supreme Court of Texas held that an associate in a law firm could refer clients to other law firms without breaching any fiduciary duty to his own firm. Such a breach would occur, however, if the associate were given compensation or anything of value for such a referral. *See also* Arthur J. Ciampi, Partners in Change: Neither 'Fish Nor Fowl' Notice Terms, N.Y.L.J. p.3 col. 1 (July 25, 2008).

3. *Duty not to compete.* As long as they do not breach a fiduciary duty while employed (e.g., by using firm information or facilities of the employer),

employees are free to compete with their employer once their employment is terminated. Employers, however, may limit such post-employment competition through employment contracts. These "non-compete" clauses must, however, be reasonable in scope and duration. For a discussion concerning whether a non-compete clause will be enforced see A.N. Deringer, Inc. v. Strough, 103 F.3d 243 (2d Cir.), reversing 918 F.Supp. 129 (D.Vt.1996). Does the availability of such clauses alleviate the concern that the decision in *Dalton v. Camp* will leave corporations in North Carolina unfairly exposed to improper employee actions?

———

SECTION 5. EXECUTIVE COMPENSATION

Compensation programs for corporate officers raise further concerns that shareholders' interests may be disregarded in favor of those of the managers. At what point does an executive's compensation reach such a level that it constitutes looting, waste or spoilage? In addressing these concerns, consideration must be given to the fact that there is wide variety in executive compensation. Corporate managers are extremely imaginative with various forms of non-cash compensation, ranging from corporate "perks" to stock ownership or option plans and other profit sharing formulas. The federal tax laws provide an incentive to defer compensation or provide it in forms other than cash in order to limit or defer taxation of the benefits. Pension plans, health plans and the like are important parts of any compensation package, but frequently these benefits are dwarfed by other forms of compensation to corporate executives. As explained in *James D. Cox & Thomas Lee Hazen, Corporations* § 11.02 (2d ed. 2003):

> Traditionally, there have been three basic ways of compensating the corporate executive: (1) salary, (2) bonuses, and (3) a pension or other deferred compensation. As a result of increased sophistication in planning, the variations of the three basic forms of compensation defy exhaustive categorization. The growing use of compensation "packages" arises out of a desire to attract and hold top-flight personnel, provide them with incentives for greater effort and dedication, and fully utilize tax advantages offered by some forms of compensation. Tailoring the most advantageous compensation plan requires careful consideration of the securities law, tax consequences, and the Federal Employment Retirement Income Security Act (ERISA). There is a widespread use in publicly held corporations, and in the large close corporations for that matter, of various kinds of contingent or deferred compensation—cash bonuses, stock bonuses, stock options, stock purchase plans, profit-sharing plans, pension programs, allowances to surviving spouses and dependents, medical and dental payment plans, and other kinds of employee benefits.

> Stock options are a highly popular form of executive compensation. The granting of stock options does not require a present expen-

diture of corporate funds, which may be badly needed for business operations or for expansion. Executives find stock options attractive because of their speculative appeal in offering a chance for really large financial gain. Further, under some circumstances, stock options carry substantial tax advantages for executives. When the options are exercised, the proportionate interests of existing shareholders in the company will be diluted, but presumably by that time the employees exercising the options will have proved their worth and have benefited the shareholders by contributing to an increase in the value of the corporation's shares.

A deferred compensation unit plan ("phantom stock" plan) is sometimes used as an alternative to or in addition to traditional pension arrangements for executive employees. Under a phantom stock plan, the company, instead of requiring the employee to buy stock or giving the employee stock in the company, pays the employee additional annual compensation or gives credit toward retirement benefits equal to dividends paid on a share of the company's stock multiplied by the number of units the employee holds in the plan, and on retirement the employee gets deferred compensation based on the increase, if any, in the market value of the company's stock during the time the employee has held units in the plan. Although the decisions are in conflict on whether a phantom stock plan of this kind is valid, the general view is that such a plan will be sustained in the future if challenged.

To use bonuses, stock options, profit sharing, and other compensation arrangements to best advantage, those arrangements must be tailored to the needs of the particular business and the needs and desires of the employees. Compensation arrangements may be used in almost infinite variation and combination. What is appropriate for one business may not be suitable for another.

NOTES

1. Stock appreciation rights ("SARs") are similar to phantom stock but do not provide dividends. SARs may be used to provide cash to allow the exercise of options also granted to employees, *i.e.*, the employee must come up with cash to pay for that stock when the option is exercised, even if that price is below the existing market price of the stock. The employee may then sell the shares and regain the cash and possibly a profit, but cash was needed before that sale in order to exercise the option.

2. Options have come under increased attack as a result of the failure of the Enron Corp. Much criticism was directed at the fact that companies such as Enron were not required to treat options granted to executives and employees as an expense for accounting purposes. Floyd Norris, "Promises of a Nimbler Accounting Board," N.Y. Times April 25, 2002, at C5. There was also concern that Enron executives were engaging in improper activities in order to support the price of the company's stock so that the executives could

profit from options granted as compensation. The Chairman of the SEC addressed those problems as follows:

> Our primary concern is to ensure that management's interests are aligned with shareholders' interests. This is tougher than it sounds. For example, for years, conventional wisdom was that granting corporate managers stock options would align their interests with those of their shareholders. We now know that that is not necessarily so. Options can align those interests, but if managers can reap profits from their options while shareholders are losing some or all of their equity stake, the options create conflicting, not aligned, interests.

> The key, in my view, is to ensure that, if a company chooses to grant options to corporate managers to create incentives to build value in the company, the options actually work as intended, rather than create an unearned windfall for those managers. There are, in my view, several components to this.

> First, I believe that stock option plans (and other equity compensation plans) for officers and directors should be approved by shareholders. Making equity incentive compensation available to management is in the interest of shareholders, but because it is (or is supposed to be), companies should be required to make full disclosure and submit such plans to a shareholder vote as a fundamental first step.

> Second, the decision to grant options to senior management, and the terms of those grants, should be entrusted to a committee of independent directors. The decision to grant options should, in most cases, be entrusted to a formal compensation committee, which would have the same authority over compensation matters that audit committees today have over financial matters and reporting. The core function, and key benefit, of the independent directors is to help prevent management practices that may deliberately, or inadvertently, misalign shareholder and management interests. Overall, the role of all independent directors is critical to good corporate governance, and should be strengthened.

> Third, it seems to me that options are potentially troublesome if they are structured to reward, or are capable of rewarding, short-term performance. Corporate boards would do well to consider whether officers should be required to demonstrate sustained, long-term growth and success before they can actually exercise any of their options. This would help abolish perverse incentives to manage earnings, distort accounting or emphasize short-term stock performance. The award of options would seem to be most compatible with shareholder interests if they are tied in the main to the long-term performance of companies. * * *

Remarks of SEC Chairman Harvey L. Pitt at the Inaugural Lecture of the JD/MBA Lecture Series at the Kellogg Graduate School of Management and Northwestern Law School, Chicago, Ill., April 4, 2002.

Interestingly, "[t]he use of stock options as a form of compensation grew out of the 'shareholder value' movement of the 1980s. Options, it was said, made the interests of managers and the interests of shareholders the same. It was a seductive argument, but, as events proved, a deeply flawed one" Joseph

E. Stiglitz, *The Roaring Nineties*, 122 (2003). Reformers argued that an executive given only a salary had no incentive to raise the price of the company's stock, which is what shareholders most desire. If options formed the greater part of the executive's compensation, it was argued, the executive would have a powerful incentive to work hard to boost the stock price, which is in the interests of the shareholders. Reformers recognized that executives in large companies might not want to give up multi-million dollar salaries in an exchange for a gamble in their company's stock. So, those executives had to be given a push in the form of the Omnibus Revenue Reconciliation Bill of 1993. It prohibited corporations from deducting more than $1 million for an executive's salary or other non-incentive based compensation without obtaining shareholder approval. This made stock options attractive to high roller executives because there was no cap on such incentive based compensation. The Financial Economists Round Table concluded that this change in the tax laws encouraged the use of options and other "performance based" provisions not subject to the $1 million cap.

Executives soon discovered that by pushing up their company's stock price they could reap millions of dollars in compensation. Some eighty percent of executive compensation was paid in stock options at the end of the last century. Options presented another advantage to management because that compensation did not have to be treated as an expense on the company's income statement. This meant that such compensation did not reduce earnings, allowing management to report higher earnings than would be the case for a large salary that would have to be expensed. Those higher earnings pushed the price of the stock higher and further boosted the value of the executive's options. By way of illustration, Cisco Systems, a high-flying Internet company, claimed a profit of $4.6 billion in one year but would have had a $2.7 billion loss if options had been expensed. Yahoo Inc., another Internet firm, announced profits of $71 million in one year, but would have had a loss of $1.3 billion if stock options had been expensed.

Before the Enron scandal, the Financial Accounting Standards Board ("FASB"), the accounting industry's body for setting financial standards, had tried to require that options be expensed when granted as compensation. That effort was thwarted in Congress because of concerns that small startup companies, especially those involved in exploiting the then new Internet, would be hurt because they needed options to attract management talent. Expensing those options would bankrupt many of those startups. After Enron, the FASB again ruled that options should be expensed, but the SEC delayed implementation of that requirement.

3. Restricted stock is another popular form of compensation. The executive receiving this benefit must hold the stock for some period of time before selling. This is designed to provide an incentive for the executive to stay with the company and to seek to increase its value. The federal securities laws also impose restrictions on the ability of executives to sell stock they receive from the company. *Thomas Lee Hazen, Treatise on the Law of Securities Regulation* § 4.29 (6th ed. 2009).

4. Many companies use complex arrangements for compensation that will contain elements of personal performance, unit performance and company earnings. All of these arrangements may be abused.

5. *Loans to Officers and Directors.* In response to widespread abuses, the Sarbanes–Oxley Act prohibited public corporations from making personal loans to officers or directors. Pub. L. No.107–204, § 402(a), codified at 15 U.S.C. § 78m(k)(1). This prohibits loans to directors and executive officers of publicly traded companies. The loan prohibitions outlaw transactions such as relocation loans to induce new hires. There is a narrow exception for companies which make loans in the ordinary course of business, such as a bank. As such, a bank would not be prohibited from extending a mortgage or other loan in the regular course of business.

Numerous questions have arisen regarding the scope of the loan prohibitions in Sarbanes–Oxley. For example, prior to this legislation, companies routinely permitted "cashless exercise" of stock options that was facilitated through a short-term loan to enable the executive to pay for the exercise of stock options and then repay the loan with the proceeds from sale of the underlying stock. Most state statutes permit companies to provide an advance to executives of litigation expenses that might be covered by indemnification agreements. To the extent that these advances may have to be returned depending on the outcome of the litigation, they could arguably be categorized as loans subject to the Sarbanes–Oxley prohibition.

6. Section 304 of the Sarbanes-Oxley Act provides that, where a public company is required to restate its financial results as a result of misconduct, the chief executive officer and chief financial officer must reimburse the company for any bonus or other incentive-based compensation received by those officers during the 12 month period following the filing of the inaccurate financial statements. In addition, any profits realized from the sale of securities of the company by those officers during a 12 month period must be forfeited.

————

In Rogers v. Hill, 289 U.S. 582, 53 S.Ct. 731, 77 L.Ed. 1385 (1933), the Supreme Court permitted an equitable review of the compensation:

> While the amounts produced by the application of the prescribed percentages give rise to no inference of actual or constructive fraud, the payments under the by-law have by reason of increase of profits become so large as to warrant investigation in equity in the interest of the company. Much weight is to be given to the action of the stockholders, and the by-law is supported by the presumption of regularity and continuity. But the rule prescribed by it cannot, against the protest of a shareholder, be used to justify payments of sums as salaries so large as in substance and effect to amount to spoliation or waste of corporate property. The dissenting opinion of Judge Swan indicates the applicable rule: 'If a bonus payment has no relation to the value of services for which it is given, it is in reality a gift in part, and the majority stockholders have no power to give away corporate property against the protest of the minority.' 60 F.2d 109, 113.The facts alleged by plaintiff are sufficient to require that the District Court, upon a consideration of all the relevant facts brought

forward by the parties, determine whether and to what extent payments to the individual defendants under the by-laws constitute misuse and waste of the money of the corporation.

For the aftermath of the Supreme Court's decision, see, e.g., Heller v. Boylan, 29 N.Y.S.2d 653, aff'd without opinion 263 A.D. 815, 32 N.Y.S.2d 131 (1941).

NOTES

1. The concern with excessive compensation did not end with the *Rogers v. Hill* litigation. Over the years, the Securities and Exchange Commission has shown considerable concern over the disclosure of executive compensation. Senior executives and directors of public companies must disclose all compensation—both cash and non-cash, including perks. *See* Regulation S–K item 402 and Schedule 14A, Item 8. This was an apparent effort to shame executive officers from overreaching and to alert the shareholders when that was the case. The shame factor did not seem to have much effect. The following is a description of some contemporary counterparts to the American Tobacco compensation program:

> IBM announced that it was paying its chief executive officer, Louis Gerstner, a salary and bonus of over $9 million in 1997. In 1998, Michael Eisner of Walt Disney Co. was paid $575.6 million (after a bad year in 1999, he got nothing in the way of a bonus), Sanford Weill at Citigroup Inc. was paid $166.9 million, Stephen M. Case at America Online was paid $159.2 million, while John F. Welch, Jr. at the General Electric Company received a relatively paltry $83.6 million. The compensation being received by executives in 1999 included large amounts of stock options. Some executives were given "reload options," in which they were granted additional options when the old ones were exercised.

III *Jerry W. Markham, A Financial History of the United States, From the Age of Derivatives to the New Millennium (1970–2001)* 313 (2001). Reset options also became popular. These options allowed their terms to be reset (*i.e.*, lowered). This allowed executives to profit even though the stock did not perform as hoped when the original option was granted. In other words, the companies allowing the reset were lowering rather than raising the bar for their executives.

2. Lest you be concerned with the failure of Mr. Eisner to receive a bonus in 1999, as noted in the above quote, consider the following information appearing in a Walt Disney Co. filing with the Securities & Exchange Commission concerning his compensation:

Salary	Bonus	Stock Options Granted	Other Compensation
$813,462	$8,500,000	$37,740,000 (hypothetical value when granted)	$3,004,020

The same filing reveals the following aggregated option exercises during fiscal 2000 and option values on September 29, 2000:

Number of shares acquired upon exercise of option	Value realized upon exercise
3,000,000	$60,531,000
Number of Unexercised options 9/30/99 (unexercisable)	value of unexercised in-the-money options 9/29/00 (unexercisable)
21,000,000	$266,765,100

3. The $187.5 million retirement package given to the head of the New York Stock Exchange ("NYSE") in 2003 created a storm of controversy when revealed in the press. New York attorney general Eliot Spitzer then sued Grasso claiming that the payments to Grasso violated the New York not-for-profit corporate law because the NYSE is a not-for-profit corporation and compensation to executives of such institutions must be reasonable. Spitzer further claimed that Grasso misled the highly sophisticated NYSE board of directors on the amount of Grasso's compensation. Some Wall Streeters claimed that Grasso deserved the compensation. Grasso was a long time employee of the NYSE who had worked his way through the ranks without even the benefit of a college education. Grasso was a successful executive, keeping the NYSE competitive in the face of severe threats from Nasdaq, electronic communications networks and international trading. Despite that competition, NYSE market share in the stocks it listed for trading was eighty-five percent in 2001 and NYSE made profits of $2.12 billion between 1995 and 2000. The price of NYSE memberships nearly doubled during Grasso's tenure and trading volume was at a level scarcely believable when he assumed command. Average daily trading volume on that exchange increased from 179 million shares in 1991 to about 1.4 billion shares in 2000. Grasso had also acted heroically in reopening the NYSE after the September 11 attacks, sending an important message to the world that American markets were robust and undeterred by that wanton destruction. The New York Court of Appeals later held at Spitzer had exceeded his authority in bringing the action against Grasso and all further proceedings in the matter were dropped. People ex rel. v. Grasso, 11 N.Y.3d 64, 862 N.Y.S.2d 828, 893 N.E.2d 105 N.Y. 2008).

For a discussion of the public outrage raised by bonuses given to executives at financial services firms receiving government bailout funds during the subprime crisis in 2008 and 2009 see Chapter 12, Section 9.

4. In Brehm v. Eisner, 746 A.2d 244 (Del.2000), set forth in part in Chapter 7, the court considered a challenge to a $10 million termination payment from Walt Disney. The court stated that:

> To be sure, directors have the power, authority and wide discretion to make decisions on executive compensation. See 8 Del.C. § 122(5). As the often-cited Court of Chancery decision by Chancellor Seitz in Saxe v. Brady warns, there is an outer limit to that discretion, at which point a decision of the directors on executive compensation is so disproportionately large as to be unconscionable and constitute waste. Del.Ch., 184 A.2d 602, 610 (1962); see Grimes, 673 A.2d at 1215 (noting that compensation decisions by an independent board are protected by the business judgment rule "unless the facts show that such amounts, compared with the

services to be received in exchange, constitute waste or could not otherwise be the product of a valid exercise of business judgment").

746 A.2d at 262, n. 56. Both *Brehm v. Eisner* and *Marx v. Akers*, and the SEC's Chairman as described above, advocate the use of committees of outside directors to make compensation decisions. Who selects those directors and how much of a check are they on the avarice of management?

5.   The courts have recognized that, although gifts of corporate funds to private parties ordinarily are ultra vires, the rule is otherwise with respect to bonuses to employees and their survivors. As explained in Adams v. Smith, 275 Ala. 142, 153 So.2d 221 (1963) where the directors paid bonuses to widows of two executives:

> Of the cases cited by appellants, the only ones bearing on payments to widows appear to be cases affecting tax liability for payments to widows of corporate officers. Among these are Simpson v. United States, 7 Cir., 261 F.2d 497, and Fifth Avenue Coach Lines, Inc. v. Commissioner, 31 T.C. 1080, 1959 WL 1252.

> In Simpson, the court held that payment to widow by corporation was not a gift but was taxable income to the widow. In Fifth Avenue, the tax court held that payments to the widow were deductible by the corporation as business expense.

> In Simpson, for aught that appears, the stockholders unanimously approved, and in Fifth Avenue, 'a great majority' (31 T.C. 1084,), of the stockholders approved. It does not appear in either case that a minority was contesting the power of the majority to make the payment to the widow. The issue in those cases was not the issue in the instant case and they are not persuasive here.

> On the other hand, in Moore v. Keystone Macaroni Mfg. Co., 370 Pa. 172, 87 A.2d 295, a minority stockholder sought to enjoin payments by corporation to the widow of a former officer of the corporation and for restitution of payments theretofore made.

> The trial court, * * * after hearing, held that the action of the corporation was ultra vires and illegal, and directed Mrs. Guerrisi to repay to the corporation the sum of $23,958.32 which she received pursuant to a resolution of the board of directors; ordered the directors to pay to the corporation any balance which Mrs. Guerrisi failed to pay; and enjoined the corporation from paying any additional sums of money to Mrs. Guerrisi. From the court's decree this appeal was taken.' (87 A.2d, at page 296).

> The Supreme Court of Pennsylvania, in affirming the decree appealed from, said:

>> 'To further support their argument, appellants point to the modern trend in favor of pensions and of permitting corporations to make charitable gifts, and to take other actions which the board of directors are convinced will be for the best interests of the corporation even though no immediate or direct quid pro quo results therefrom. It will be noted, of course, that the payments to Mrs. Guerrisi were not and did not purport to be a pension,

nor did they constitute a gift or contribution to a charity or to a community chest as specifically authorized by the amendment to the Pennsylvania Business Corporation Law, Section 1, Act of 1945, as amended 1947. Osborne v. United Gas Improvement Co., 354 Pa. 57, 46 A.2d 208, relied on by appellants is clearly inapplicable to the facts in this case.

Moreover, we cannot overlook the fact that to approve the action of this board of directors would result in opening wide the door to a dissipation of the assets of a corporation and to fraud; and it is still the law of Pennsylvania that it is ultra vires and illegal for a corporation (unless authorized by statute) to give away, dissipate, waste or divert the corporate assets even though the objective be worthy. This general principle is widely recognized. In Fletcher Cyclopedia of Corporations, Permanent Edition, Vol. 6–a, paragraph 2939, pages 667, 668, the law is thus stated: 'It is the general rule that a gift of its property by a corporation not created for charitable purposes is in violation of the rights of its stockholders and is ultra vires, however worthy of encouragement or aid the object of the gift may be. It seems to be the rule that a private corporation has no power voluntarily to pay to a former officer or employee a sum of money for past services, which it is under no legal duty to pay, and which would not constitute a legal consideration for a promise to pay.' In Rogers v. Hill, 289 U.S. 582, 591, 53 S.Ct. 731, 77 L.Ed. 1385, the Court, after upholding the legality of reasonable bonus payments, said: "If a bonus payment has no relation to the value of services for which it is given, it is in reality a gift in part, and the majority stockholders have no power to give away corporate property against the protest of the minority." Compare also Hornsby v. Lohmeyer, 364 Pa. 271, 275, 72 A.2d 294, 298, where this Court after sustaining the payment of reasonable bonuses and pointing out that a court is not ordinarily warranted in substituting its own judgment as to the proper compensation of officers for the judgment of the directors, said: ' * * * It is also true that directors may not vote to themselves or to the officers of the corporation compensation which is excessive, unreasonable and out of proportion to the value of the services rendered, and, if any such payments are made, the court, upon protest of a minority shareholder, may examine into their propriety and reduce them if found to be exorbitant. * * * '

'We therefore hold that where the action of a board of directors or of stockholders is an abuse of discretion, or is forbidden by statute or is against public policy, or is ultra vires, or is a fraud upon minority stockholders or creditors, or will result in waste, dissipation or misapplication of the corporate assets, a court of equity has the power to grant appropriate relief.' (87 A.2d, at pages 297, 298)

We do not agree with appellant that Chambers v. Beaver–Advance Corporation, 392 Pa. 481, 140 A.2d 808, modified or overruled Moore.

In Chambers, the court approved the payment of fair and *reasonable* bonuses for the current or prior calendar or fiscal year if such bonuses were approved by the majority stockholders. That was not the Moore case and is not the instant case.

6. Another issue pertaining to bonus plans is the question of enforceability as a matter of contract law. It is elementary contract law that a promise to make a future gift is not enforceable. For this reason, a promise to pay a bonus not given in exchange for consideration is not binding on the corporation. See Feinberg v. Pfeiffer Co., 322 S.W.2d 163 (Mo.App.1959). Good drafting, therefore, dictates that plans be drafted in terms of an exchange of compensation for services rather than a promised bonus as an unenforceable gratuitous promise. Where there has been substantial reliance on a promised bonus, promissory estoppel may provide an alternative basis for enforcement. Id.

Required Disclosures for Publicly Held Companies—Compensation Discussion and Analysis

As a result of the changes adopted in 2006, the executive compensation disclosure requirements now have a component analogous the SEC's Management's Discussion and Analysis (MD & A) disclosures. Executive Compensation and Related Person Disclosure, Sec. Act Rel. No. 33–8732, Sec. Exch. Act Rel. No. 34–54302, Inv. Co. Act Rel. No. IC–27444, 2006 WL 2335558 (SEC Aug. 11, 2006). This is known as compensation discussion and analysis (CD & A). As explained by the SEC, "the new Compensation Discussion and Analysis calls for a discussion and analysis of the material factors underlying compensation policies and decisions reflected in the data presented in the tables. This overview addresses in one place these factors with respect to both the separate elements of executive compensation and executive compensation as a whole." CD & A is designed to provide a narrative description and analysis of a company's compensation for named executive officers. In particular, the CD & A disclosure requires answers to the following questions:

What are the objectives of the company's compensation programs?

What is the compensation program designed to reward?

What is each element of compensation?

Why does the company choose to pay each element?

How does the company determine the amount (and, where applicable, the formula) for each element?

How do each element and the company's decisions regarding that element fit into the company's overall compensation objectives and affect decisions regarding other elements?

Compensation of Directors

MARX v. AKERS

88 N.Y.2d 189, 644 N.Y.S.2d 121, 666 N.E.2d 1034 (1996).

SMITH, JUDGE.

* * * We must ... determine whether plaintiff has stated a cause of action regarding [IBM corporation] director compensation, i.e., some wrong to the corporation. We conclude that plaintiff has not, and thus dismiss the complaint in its entirety.

Historically, directors did not receive any compensation for their work as directors (*see*, 5A [1995 rev vol] Fletcher, Cyclopedia of Private Corporations § 2109 [perm ed]). Thus, a bare allegation that corporate directors voted themselves excessive compensation was sufficient to state a cause of action (*e.g., Walsh v. Van Ameringen–Haebler, Inc.*, 257 N.Y. 478, 480, 178 N.E. 764; *Jacobson v. Brooklyn Lbr. Co.*, 184 N.Y. 152, 162, 76 N.E. 1075). Many jurisdictions, including New York, have since changed the common-law rule by statute providing that a corporation's board of directors has the authority to fix director compensation unless the corporation's charter or bylaws provides otherwise. Thus, the allegation that directors have voted themselves compensation is clearly no longer an allegation which gives rise to a cause of action, as the directors are statutorily entitled to set those levels. Nor does a conclusory allegation that the compensation directors have set for themselves is excessive give rise to a cause of action.

"The courts will not undertake to review the fairness of official salaries, at the suit of a shareholder attacking them as excessive, unless wrongdoing and oppression or possible abuse of a fiduciary position are shown. However, the courts will take a hand in the matter at the instance of the corporation or of shareholders in extreme cases. A case of fraud is presented where directors increase their collective salaries so as to use up nearly the entire earnings of a company; where directors or officers appropriate the income so as to deprive shareholders of reasonable dividends, or perhaps so reduce the assets as to threaten the corporation with insolvency" (5A [1995 rev vol] Fletcher, Cyclopedia of Private Corporations § 2122, at 46–47 [perm ed]).

Thus, a complaint challenging the excessiveness of director compensation must—to survive a dismissal motion—allege compensation rates excessive on their face or other facts which call into question whether the compensation was fair to the corporation when approved, the good faith of the directors setting those rates, or that the decision to set the compensation could not have been a product of valid business judgment.[6]

---

6. There is general agreement that the allocation of the burden of proof differs depending on whether the compensation was approved by disinterested directors or shareholders, or by interested directors. Plaintiffs must prove wrongdoing or waste as to compensation arrangements regarding disinterested directors or shareholders, but directors who approve their own compensation bear the burden of proving that the transaction was fair to the corporation (*see*, Block, Barton and Radin, Business Judgment Rule, at 149 [4th ed]; 2 [1990 rev vol] Fletcher, *op. cit.*,

Applying the foregoing principles to plaintiff's complaint, it is clear that it must be dismissed. The complaint alleges that the directors increased their compensation rates from a base of $20,000 plus $500 for each meeting attended to a retainer of $55,000 plus 100 shares of IBM stock over a five-year period. The complaint also alleges that "[t]his compensation bears little relation to the part-time services rendered by the Non–Employee Directors or to the profitability of IBM. The board's responsibilities have not increased, its performance, measured by the company's earnings and stock price, has been poor yet its compensation has increased far in excess of the cost of living."

These conclusory allegations do not state a cause of action. There are no factually based allegations of wrongdoing or waste which would, if true, sustain a verdict in plaintiff's favor. Plaintiff's bare allegations that the compensation set lacked a relationship to duties performed or to the cost of living are insufficient as a matter of law to state a cause of action.

NOTE

Time and inflation have rendered the actual compensation in Akers small in comparison with today's going rate. For example, "[in 2002, director compensation averaged $152,000 in the largest 200 companies and $116,000 in the largest 1,000 companies." Lucian Bebchuk & Jesse Fried, Pay Without Performance—The Unfulfilled Promise of Executive Compensation 25 (2004). As Professors Bebchuck and Freed point out, the benefits of being a director transcend these cash payments: "There are often additional perks and indirect benefits; for example, directors of UAL Corp. (which owns United Airlines) can fly United free of charge, and directors of Starwood Hotels get complimentary nights in company hotels." *Id.*

---

§ 514.1, at 632; 1 ALI, *op. cit.,* § 5.03). However, at the pleading stage we are not concerned with burdens of proof.

CHAPTER 9

CORPORATE DEMOCRACY—STATE LAW

■ ■ ■

SECTION 1. SHAREHOLDER SUFFRAGE— AN INTRODUCTION

An essential part of state corporate statutes is the protection they extend to shareholders in electing directors and voting on matters affecting the company, such as merging with another corporation. As will be seen in Chapter 12, the federal securities laws extend further protections to assure informed votes by shareholders in publicly traded corporations when they vote by proxy. As a practical matter, however, voting is not a right highly valued or used much by most shareholders in publicly traded corporations. Instead shareholders in public corporations often vote with their feet by selling their stock. When they do vote, shareholders in publicly traded securities generally vote in favor of management nominated directors and in accordance with management recommendations on other issues. Some have argued that, for this reason, it does not make economic sense to give voting rights to shareholders of publicly held corporations. The basis of the argument is that a lot of time and expense is wasted on meetings and proxies. Since there is a market for the stock, the market can keep management in place, i.e., if there is bad management, the company's stock price will drop as disaffected shareholders sell their stock.

Today, the shareholder populations of most large corporations are heavily weighted with so-called institutional investors. They include pension funds, insurance companies, mutual funds and bank trust departments. These institutions are also usually "passive" investors that do not involve themselves in matters affecting the internal affairs of the company. They, therefore, usually vote in favor of the management of the company on issues submitted to shareholders. There are exceptions. "Calpers", the California state pension fund, has frequently taken an activist approach in its role as a shareholder and opposed management. Other state pension funds have also acted to seek to sway management views through their role as shareholders. The New York City retirement system, for example, uses its shareholder status as a "bully pulpit" for pursuing social goals it deems desirable. New York City Employees' Retirement System v. S.E.C., 45 F.3d 7, 9 (2d Cir.1995). See also David J.

Friedman, SEC No–Action Letter (Dec. 19, 2000) (Minnesota Investment Board seeking proxy vote that would require company to study the effect of its advertising on children). See generally "Symposium: Socio–Economics and Corporate Law—The New Corporate Responsibility," 76 Tulane L. Rev. 1187 (2002) (discussion concerning the social responsibility of corporations). Some public companies also have large shareholders that occasionally oppose management on particular issues. These shareholders use their holdings as a base for that opposition but also seek to sway other shareholders through hard fought campaigns for their proxies. Those fights are a rarity, and even with social investing pension funds, almost all proxies are voted in favor of management proposals.

The lack of active shareholder participation in proxy contests has been of concern for many years. Professors Adolf A. Berle and Gardiner C. Means studied the use of the shareholder franchise in their 1932 book entitled *The Modern Corporation and Private Property*. Berle and Means concluded that most large corporations were being run by management for its own advantage, rather than for the benefit of shareholders—the owners of the company. They found, however, varying degrees of control being exercised by management, which Berle and Means separated into three categories:

1. *Majority Control*—One shareholder or group owns or controls 35 percent or more of the company's stock. Even where a majority vote is required for shareholder action, the holder of at least 35 percent of the stock will likely be able to obtain the support of the small percentage of shareholders needed for victory.

2. *Management Control*—the largest block of stock owned in these companies does not exceed five to ten percent of the outstanding shares of the company. Because management controls the proxy machinery, and most shareholders are passive, management will have almost complete control of the company. Management of publicly held corporations rarely lose proxy battles. Even with regard to election of directors, management controls the process, i.e., management sponsored proxy materials set forth the management slate of directors in these corporations.

3. *Minority Control*—In these companies, a single shareholder or group control somewhere between ten and thirty-five percent of the company's shares. If the holder of this block of stock is not participating in management, then control is shared between that shareholder and management. They will usually work together, since each is in a position to win a contested proxy fight, i.e., on the one hand, management has control of the proxy machinery, but on the other hand, the large stockholder controls a large amount of stock and will likely have the resources to wage a campaign to convince other shareholders to vote actively against management.

Note

Some states have "control share" statutes that are designed as a protection against unwanted takeovers by disenfranchising shares owned by a new controlling shareholder, unless that shareholder is given the vote by a majority of the disinterested shares. Those statutes are described in Chapter 20. Such statutes define a controlling stock position to be as low as twenty percent. See CTS Corp. v. Dynamics Corp. of America, 481 U.S. 69, 107 S.Ct. 1637, 95 L.Ed.2d 67 (1987) (describing Indiana control share statute).

SECTION 2. CUMULATIVE VOTING

Model Bus. Corp. Act § 7.28 provides that, unless the articles of incorporation provide otherwise, directors are elected by a plurality of the votes cast by shareholders. For example, if there are ten individuals seeking election to eight available positions on the board, the eight individuals receiving the highest number of votes will be elected. Most corporations use so-called straight voting systems that limit a shareholder to one vote per share for each director position that is open for election in a given year. This means that a majority shareholder may elect all of the board members by voting that majority for each director. One way to allow a greater opportunity for representation of minority interests on a board of directors is through "cumulative" voting. Cumulative voting permits a shareholder to combine (or accumulate) all their votes and cast them for one or more candidates. See Model Bus. Corp. Act § 7.28 (defining cumulative voting and requiring cumulative voting to be specified in articles of incorporation if used for elections). Thus, under cumulative voting, the shareholder's voting power consists of a number arrived at by multiplying the number of voting shares owned by the shareholder times the number of directors to be elected in that year (votes = shares owned x number of directors to be elected).

The effect of cumulative voting can be seen from the following example. Assume that Jack and Jill are the sole shareholders of a company. Jack owns 49 shares and Jill owns 51 shares. Assume further that the corporation has 3 directors who are elected annually. With straight voting, Jill can elect all three directors since she has a majority of 51 as opposed to Jack's 49 votes per director. This leaves Jack with no representation on the board. In contrast, if the corporation has cumulative voting, each has the following number of votes to be cast:

Jack has 49 (shares) x 3 (directors) = 147 votes to be cast as Jack pleases

Jill has 51 (shares) x 3 (directors) = 153 votes to cast as she pleases.

If Jack casts 74 votes for his first choice as director and 73 shares for his second choice, he will guarantee that his first choice will be elected.

This is because Jill would have to cast at least 74 votes each for her top choices in order for her to elect two directors, this would leave her with only 5 remaining votes (153–148).

The following formula can be used to determine how many votes of those present is sufficient to elect a specified number of directors using cumulative voting; for example how many votes are needed to elect 3 directors where there are nine directors in total standing for election:

$$X = \frac{a \times b}{c + 1} + 1$$

In this formula, "a" is the number of directors the shareholder seeks to elect (in this case three), "b" is the number of shares present and voting, while "c" is the number of directors being elected (in this case nine). X is the number of shares needed to elect three directors. Another formula allows you to determine how many directors you can elect with a given number of shares:

$$X = \frac{(n-1)(d+1)}{s}$$

In this formula, "n" is the number of shares to be voted by the shareholder, "D" is the number of directors to be elected and "s" is the total number of shares to be voted by all shareholders. "X" is the number of directors that can be elected by n shares. Look what could happen if this calculation is not made. Assume there are two shareholders in a corporation, one owns 550 shares, the other owns 450 shares, and three directors are to be elected. Assume that the shareholder with 550 shares votes equally for each director (straight voting), while the other cumulates her shares.

	Director 1	Director 2	Director 3
Shareholder with 550 shares	550	550	550
Shareholder with 450 shares	551	551	248

The shareholder voting cumulatively was able to elect two directors because the majority shareholder did not cumulate her shares. The majority shareholder may change her vote before the presiding officer announces the result of the voting but may be precluded from doing so afterwards. See e.g., Zachary v. Milin, 294 Mich. 622, 293 N.W. 770, 772 (1940) (allowing change before vote was final). In Stancil v. Bruce Stancil Refrigeration, Inc., 81 N.C.App. 567, 344 S.E.2d 789 (1986) two equal shareholders (brothers) in a corporation with cumulative voting were electing three directors. One brother (Bruce Stancil) controlled the board with his wife. He split his votes equally among his three candidates (his wife and himself and a third person). His brother, Howard, split his votes equally between two other candidates (himself and his wife). The court ruled that Howard, the shareholder splitting his votes on just two directors, elected those directors, giving him control of the company. Bruce was found not to have elected anyone because none of his candidates received a plurality of votes, i.e., because all received an equal number of votes, none had a plurality. Could Howard fill that vacancy? What will happen at the next election? Rev. Model Bus. Corp. Act § 8.05(e) states that a director will continue to serve as such until his successor is elected even though his term has expired. What effect will this have if each brother voting an equal amount of shares votes cumulatively for themselves and their wives? Bruce could vote all his shares cumulatively on himself, but he has still lost control of the corporation.

NOTES

1. The desirability of mandatory cumulative voting is a frequently debated proposition. See Hans A. Mattes, "The Burden of the Corporate Director Elected Noncumulatively," 63 Cal. L. Rev. 463, 465 (1975); John G. Sobeiski, "In Support of Cumulative Voting," 15 Bus. Law. 316 (1960); Charles W. Steadman & George D. Gibson, "Should Cumulative Voting for Directors be Mandatory? A Debate," 11 Bus. Law. 9 (1955); Herbert F. Sturdy, Mandatory Cumulative Voting: An Anachronism, 16 Bus. Law. 550 (1961). A few states mandate cumulative voting for directors. See *Richard W. Jennings & Richard M. Buxbaum, Corporations: Cases and Materials* 283 (5th ed. 1979). Some states have repealed constitutional provisions for mandatory cumulative voting and replaced them with statutes permitting limitation or elimination of cumulative voting, e.g., Ill. Ann. Stat. ch. 805, § 5/7.40 (Smith–Hurd 1993). See also Roanoke Agency, Inc. v. Edgar, 101 Ill.2d 315, 78 Ill.Dec. 258, 461 N.E.2d 1365 (1984). Today, in most states, cumulative voting is only permissive and thus does not exist unless specifically authorized by a provision in the articles of incorporation. See e.g., Del. § 141(d).

2. The use of classified (staggered) boards can undermine the effectiveness of cumulative voting. As one court noted:

> It is not disputed that in an election of only three members of a nine-member board, approximately 250 per cent as many votes are required to elect a single director as would be necessary if all nine were to be elected at the same time. In an election of the full board of nine directors, the owners of 10 percent of the stock voted, plus one share, could elect one out of the nine directors to be elected. On the other hand, if the board of directors is classified so that only three members are elected each year, it would require 25 per cent of the stock voted, plus one share, to gain a single seat on the board.

Wolfson v. Avery, 6 Ill.2d 78, 126 N.E.2d 701, 704 (1955). The question of the validity of staggered elections where cumulative voting is mandatory has led to conflicting answers. A Pennsylvania case held that a *constitutional* cumulative voting requirement did not prohibit the classification of directors and the staggering of elections. Janney v. Philadelphia Transp. Co., 387 Pa. 282, 128 A.2d 76 (1956). See Stockholders Comm. for Better Management v. Erie Tech.

Prods., Inc., 248 F.Supp. 380 (W.D.Pa.1965) the Pennsylvania constitutional provision has since been repealed and replaced by statutory discretionary cumulative voting). See also Humphrys v. Winous Co., 165 Ohio St. 45, 133 N.E.2d 780 (1956) (upholding classification in face of statutorily mandated cumulative voting). Cf. McDonough v. Copeland Refrigeration Corp., 277 F.Supp. 6 (E.D.Mich.1967); Bohannan v. Corporation Comm'n, 82 Ariz. 299, 313 P.2d 379 (1957). In Illinois the staggered election was held unconstitutional, Wolfson v. Avery, 6 Ill.2d 78, 126 N.E.2d 701 (1955), but as noted above, Illinois' mandatory cumulative voting requirement was subsequently repealed. See generally W. Edward Sell & Lloyd H. Fuge, "Impact of Classified Corporate Directors and the Constitutional Right of Cumulative Voting," 17 U. Pitt. L. Rev. 151 (1956).

3.   Where cumulative voting rights are granted, there are certain statutory protections. For example, Model Bus. Corp. Act § 8.08(c) requires "reverse cumulative voting" to remove directors. This means the shareholders cannot vote to remove a director elected by cumulative voting unless the number of votes cast against removal are less than the amount that was sufficient to have elected him originally. Delaware has a similar provision. Del. § 141(k).

SECTION 3.   VARYING SHAREHOLDER RIGHTS

State statutes grant corporations wide latitude in varying the voting and other rights among classes. Rev. Model Bus. Corp. Act § 6.01 provides that the articles of incorporation may authorize one or more classes of stock that have special or even no voting rights and varying dividend and other rights, as say between preferred and common stockholders. Del. § 151 contains similar authority. The following is a description of some variations among classes of stock.

Weighted Voting. Corporations may use weighted voting schemes. For example, one class of shares may be given a multiple number of votes for each share held. This allows that class to cast a disproportionate number of votes and allows acquisition of control with fewer shares than would otherwise be required.

Class Voting. The articles of incorporation may create different classes of shares or subclasses with varying voting rights. The Model Act refers to this type of class voting as voting by voting groups. See Model Bus. Corp. Act §§ 7.25, 7.26. Class voting may be used in several ways. For example, one class of shares (*e.g.* common stockholders) may be allowed to vote as a class on matters before the shareholders such as the election of directors, while another class.(*e.g.* preferred stockholders) is denied that right. Class voting can be used to guarantee representation on the board by dividing the directors into classes with certain director positions to be elected by specified groups of shareholders. Model Bus.

Corp. Act § 7.25 creates quorum and voting rights for voting groups. Where a director is elected by a specified class of stock, state statutes will limit the ability of other shareholders to remove that director without the approval of the electing group. See Chapter 6.

Contingent Voting. Corporations may want to provide contingent voting rights to certain classes of shares or even to debt securities. For example, preferred shareholders might have contingent voting rights in the event that the directors do not declare dividends. This may include allowing the election of a specified number, or all, of directors to the board.

Disparate Voting. At common law, all stock had to be voting stock. Today, most corporate laws permit nonvoting common stock—thereby deviating from the customary one-share one-vote regime. See e.g., Rev. Model Bus. Corp. Act § 6.01(c)(1). Unless the articles so state, stock is voting stock. Even nonvoting shares are entitled to vote on matters that affect them as a class. See, e.g., Model Bus. Corp. Act §§ 10.03(e), 10.04, 13.02(a)(4). An example of disparate voting rights is to grant one class of shares several votes for each share held, say ten votes for each share held, while another class has only one vote per share.

LACOS LAND CO. v. ARDEN GROUP, INC.

517 A.2d 271 (Del.Ch.1986).

ALLEN, CHANCELLOR

This action constitutes a multi-pronged attack upon a proposed recapitalization of defendant Arden Group, Inc., authorized by a vote of Arden's shareholders at their June 10, 1986 annual meeting. The recapitalization, if effectuated, will create a new Class B Common Stock possessing ten votes per share and entitled, as a class, to elect seventy-five percent of the members of Arden's board of directors. This new stock is, pursuant to the terms of a presently pending exchange offer, available on a share-for-share basis to all holders of Arden's Class A Common Stock. It is, however, acknowledged by defendants that the new Class B Common Stock has been deliberately fashioned to be attractive mainly to defendant Briskin—Arden's principal shareholder and chief executive officer. Thus, the recapitalization is not itself a device to raise capital but rather is a technique to transfer stockholder control of the enterprise to Mr. Briskin.

Plaintiff is an Arden stockholder owning approximately 4.5% of Arden's Class A Common Stock; an additional stockholder owning approximately 4.6% of that stock has moved to intervene in this action as a plaintiff. Defendants are the members of Arden's board of directors. Pending is an application to preliminarily enjoin the issuance of Class B Common Stock which was originally scheduled to occur on July 18, 1986, but which has been voluntarily delayed by defendants. * * *

The new supervoting common stock whose issuance is sought to be enjoined will differ from Arden's other authorized class of common stock, Class A Common Stock, most importantly, in its enhanced voting power, its diminished dividend rights and in restrictions upon its transfer.

Specifically, with respect to voting rights, the recent charter amendment provides that "on every matter submitted to a vote or consent of the stockholder, every holder of Class A Common Stock shall be entitled to one vote . . . for each share . . . and every holder of Class B Common Stock shall be entitled to 10 votes . . . for each share. . . .".

As to the election of directors, the restated certificate provides that Class A shares, together with the Company's preferred stock, voting as a class shall "be entitled to elect 25% of the total number of directors to be elected" rounded up to the nearest whole number. The Class B shares are entitled to vote as a separate class and to elect the remaining 75% of directors to be elected.[1]

With respect to dividend rights, Class A Common Stock will, following the initial issuance of Class B shares, have the right to receive a one-time dividend of $.30 per share; Class B shares are to have no right to participate to any extent in that cash dividend. Excepting this one-time $.30 dividend, each share of Class B stock is to be entitled to participate in all dividends declared and paid with respect to a share of Class A stock but only to the extent of 90% of such dividend.

Class B shares may be transferred only to a Permitted Transferee, but under certain circumstances may be converted on a share-for-share basis into Class A stock. A transfer of Class B to a person other than a Permitted Transferee at a time when conversion to Class A would be permitted would convert the transferred stock into Class A stock. Generally, Class B stock may, at the option of the holder, be converted to Class A stock on a share-for-share basis at the earlier of (i) the third anniversary of its issuance or (ii) the death of the holder.[2]

Defendant Briskin owns or controls 16.9% of Arden's Class A Common Stock (21.1% were he to exercise certain presently exercisable stock options). The proxy statement states:

> Based on Mr. Briskin's expressed intention to exchange all of the Briskin Shares for Class B Common Stock, the Briskin Shares would represent approximately 67.7% of the combined voting power of the capital stock of the Company if no shares of Class A Common Stock

---

1. If, on the record date for the meeting to elect directors, the Class B shares equal less than 12 1/2% of the total of Class A and Class B shares together, then Class A will continue to vote as a class in the filling of 25% of the positions to be filled but will have the right to vote in the Class B election as well, with Class B shares continuing to be entitled to ten votes per share.

2. For a natural person Permitted Transferees include (1) the holder's spouse or any lineal descendant of a grandparent of the holder or the holder's spouse, (2) the trustee of any trust for the benefit of the holder or a Permitted Transferee, (3) charitable organizations, (4) a corporation or partnership under majority control of the holder or a Permitted Transferee and (5) the holder's estate.

other than the Briskin Shares were exchanged for Class B Common Stock.* * *

In view of the lack of transferability and reduced dividend rights of the Class B Common Stock, the Board of Directors does not anticipate that any significant number of holders of Class A Common Stock other than Mr. Briskin will accept the Exchange Offer.

The creation of a dual common stock structure with one class exercising effective control of the company is, of course, not a novel idea, although it is one that, thanks to its potential as an anti-takeover device, has recently emerged from the reaches of the corporation law chorus to strut its moment upon center stage where corporate drama is acted out. In this instance, the notion of employing this dual common stock structure apparently originated with defendant Briskin.

Mr. Briskin became Arden chief executive officer in 1976 at a time when the Company was apparently in a desperate condition. Its stock was then trading between $1 and $2 per share. Briskin's stewardship has apparently been active and effective. While Arden has paid no dividends since 1970, during Briskin's tenure Arden's stock price has risen steadily; currently Arden common stock is publicly trading at around $25 per share, a price somewhat higher than the range of prices at which its stock traded in the weeks prior to the announcement of the plan that is the subject matter of this litigation.

In instigating the dual common stock voting structure, Mr. Briskin was apparently not responding to any specific threat to existing policies or practices of Arden posed by a specific takeover threat. Rather, he apparently was motivated to protect his power to control Arden's business future. Such a motivation, while it may be suspect—since it may reflect not a desire to protect business policies and capabilities for the benefit of the corporation and its shareholders but rather a wish simply to retain the benefits of office—does not itself constitute a wrong.

In this instance, Briskin initially took his idea to the board of directors at its November 22, 1985 meeting. The Board established a three member committee of non-officer directors to consider the matter. Prior to the committee's first meeting, its chairman sent the other two committee members the proxy statement of another company that had adopted a dual class common stock structure, together with materials on other companies that had adopted supervoting plans and some materials relating to a report written by Professor Fischel on "Organized Exchanges and the Regulation of Dual Class Common Stock." The special committee retained neither independent counsel nor an independent financial advisor. At its first meeting, held on April 7, 1986, the chairman of this group distributed to the committee a draft report that he had previously prepared which gave approval to a supervoting stock plan. The committee reviewed this draft and suggested changes. The chairman noted the suggested changes and prepared a final three page report which was signed four days later at the committee's second, and final, meeting.

The committee's report was presented to the board at its April 22 meeting at which time the board approved the supervoting stock plan. At that meeting the board fixed the date of the Company's annual meeting for June 10, 1986. Management of the Company prepared a proxy statement describing the proposed charter amendments authorizing the new supervoting Class B Common Stock, describing the Exchange Offer by which it was proposed that such new stock be distributed and setting out the background of, and the reasons for, this proposal.

At the June 10 annual meeting the Arden stockholders approved the proposed certificate amendments. Of 2,303,170 shares outstanding, 1,463,-155 voted in favor (64%) and 325,004 (14%) voted to reject the proposal. Of the affirmative votes, 427,347 were voted by Briskin or his family and 388,493 were voted by a trustee as directed by Arden's management. As to the preferred stock, 74.4% of the 136,359 shares outstanding voted in favor of the proposal, more than half of which were voted by a trustee as directed by Arden's management.

As a consequence of the stockholders' approval of the proposal, the Company, on June 18, 1986, distributed to all holders of its Class A Common Stock an Offering Circular offering to exchange for each share of such common stock one share of Class B Common Stock with the rights, preferences, etc. described above.

Our corporation law provides great flexibility to shareholders in creating the capital structure of their firm. *See, e.g., Providence and Worcester Co. v. Baker,* Del.Supr., 378 A.2d 121 (1977). Differing classes of stock with differing voting rights are permissible under our law, 8 *Del.C.* § 151(a); *Topkis v. Delaware Hardware Co.,* Del.Ch., 2 A.2d 114 (1938); restriction on transfers are possible, 8 *Del.C.* § 202, and charter provisions requiring the filling of certain directorates by a class of stock are, if otherwise properly adopted, valid. *Lehrman v. Cohen,* Del.Supr., 222 A.2d 800 (1966). Thus, each of the significant characteristics of the Class B Common Stock is in principle a valid power or limitation of common stock. The primary inquiry therefore is whether the Arden shareholders have effectively exercised their will to amend the Company's restated certificate of incorporation so as to authorize the implementation of the dual class common stock structure. The charge is that they have not done so— despite the report of the judge of elections that the proposed amendments carried—in part because the proxy statement upon which the vote was solicited was materially misleading and in part because the entire plan to put in place the Class B stock constitutes a breach of duty on the part of a dominated board.

For the reasons that follow I conclude that plaintiff has demonstrated a reasonable probability that on final hearing it will be demonstrated that the June 10, 1986 vote of the Arden shareholders has been fundamentally and fatally flawed and that, therefore, the amendments to Arden's restated certificate of incorporation purportedly authorized by that vote are voidable. In summary, the basis for this conclusion is two-fold. First, I conclude provisionally on the basis of the record now available, that the June 10 vote was inappropriately affected by an explicit threat of Mr. Briskin that unless the proposed amendments were approved, he would use his power (and not simply his power *qua* shareholder) to block transactions that may be in the best interests of the Company, if those transactions would dilute his ownership interest in Arden. I use the word threat because such a position entails, in my opinion, the potential for a breach of Mr. Briskin's duty, as the principal officer of Arden and as a member of its board of directors, to exercise corporate power unselfishly, with a view to fostering the interests of the corporation and all of its shareholders. Second, I conclude provisionally, that the proxy statement presents a substantial risk of misleading shareholders on a material point concerning Mr. Briskin's status as a "Restricted Person" under Article Twelfth of the Company's certificate of incorporation.

Judging from what is stated in the proxy materials, Arden's board in recommending the charter amendments and Arden's shareholders in approving them were both placed, inappropriately, in a position that made it significantly less likely than it might otherwise have been that approval of the plan to effectively transfer all shareholder power to Mr. Briskin would have been given.

To a shareholder who wondered why his board of directors was recommending a plan expected to place all effective shareholder power in a single shareholder, the proxy statement gives a clear answer: Mr. Briskin is demanding it; it's not such a big deal anyway since, as a practical matter, he has great power already; and if he doesn't get these amendments, he may exercise his power to thwart corporate transactions that may be in the Company's best interests. * * *

Thus, Arden shareholders were unmistakably told that should they fail to approve the proposed amendments, Mr. Briskin "would not give his support to any transaction [that might make the Company vulnerable to an unsolicited or hostile takeover attempt] for which his approval might be required . . .". Using the term in the vague way which we ordinarily do, a vote in such circumstances as these could be said to be "coerced". But that label itself supplies no basis to conclude that the legal effect of the vote is impaired in any way. * * *

The determination of whether it was inappropriate for Mr. Briskin to structure the choice of Arden's shareholders (and its directors), as was done here, requires, first, a determination of which of his hats—shareholder, officer or director—Mr. Briskin was wearing when he stated his position concerning the possible withholding of his "support" for future transactions unless steps were taken "to secure his voting position". If he spoke only as a shareholder, and should have been so understood, an evaluation of the propriety of his position might be markedly different than if the "support" referred to could be or should be interpreted as involving the exercise of his power as either an officer or director of Arden.

On this point defendants' position at oral argument confirms that which the proxy language itself indicates—that, in taking this position, Mr. Briskin did not limit, and could not be understood to have limited, himself to exercising only stockholder power. Defendants have emphasized that Briskin's "practical" power derives in part from his notable success as a chief executive officer; his history of success, I was reminded, creates influence and his position confers power to initiate board consideration of important matters. Moreover, the proxy statement made clear that the approval that Briskin threatened to withhold included approval of transactions that did not require a vote of stockholders. Accordingly, the conclusion seems inescapable that, in announcing an intent to withhold support for corporate action that might entail, for instance, the issuance of stock, even if that act might be in the best interests of the corporation, unless "steps were taken to preserve his voting position", Mr. Briskin could not be understood to have been acting only as a shareholder.

As a director and as an officer, of course, Mr. Briskin has a duty to act with complete loyalty to the interests of the corporation and its shareholders. *Weinberger v. UOP, Inc.,* Del.Supr., 457 A.2d 701 (1983); *Guth v. Loft,* Del.Supr., 5 A.2d 503 (1939). His position as stated to the shareholders in the Company proxy statement seems inconsistent with that obligation. In form at least, the statement by a director and officer that he will not give his support to a corporate transaction unless steps are taken to confer a personal power or benefit, suggests an evident disregard of duty. However, the nature of the *quid pro quo* sought by Mr. Briskin in this case is at least consistent with a benign or selfless motive. The Class B stock he sought to have the board recommend and the stockholders approve would transfer complete control of the enterprise to him for an indefinite period, but it is a control that may not be transferred generally and so it is unlikely that Mr. Briskin was motivated to gain access to a control premium for his stock by insisting on a device of this kind as a price of his supporting certain types of future action.

Two alternative motivations suggest themselves. Mr. Briskin may have been motivated, as plaintiff warmly contends is the fact, by a selfish desire to protect his salary and the perquisites of his office from the threat to them that a hostile takeover of Arden would represent. The issuance of the Class B stock, in the totality of the circumstances present, will assuredly place Mr. Briskin in a position (1) to protect his tenure for as long as he wants to do so and (2) to negotiate and assure stockholder acceptance of the full terms of any change in control, including employment contracts or severance agreements.

On the other hand, Briskin may have been motivated selflessly to put in place the most powerful of anti-takeover devices so that he could be assured the opportunity to reject (for all the shareholders) any offer for Arden that he—who presumably knows more about the Company than anyone else—regards as less than optimum achievable value. Accordingly, while I regard the form of the Briskin position ("I, as fiduciary will not support ... unless a personal benefit is conferred") as superficially shocking, I recognize that Mr. Briskin's position as stated in the proxy statement is logically consistent with and may indeed in fact be driven by a benevolent motivation.

Mr. Briskin's motivation in fact, however, need not be determined in order to conclude that the stockholder vote of June 10, 1986 was fatally flawed by the implied (indeed, the expressed) threats that unless the proposed amendments were authorized, he would oppose transactions "which could be determined by the Board of Directors to be in the best interests of all of the stockholders." As a corporate fiduciary, Mr. Briskin has no right to take such a position, even if benevolently motivated in doing so. Shareholders who respect Mr. Briskin's ability and performance—and who are legally entitled to his undivided loyalty—were inappropriately placed in a position in which they were told that if they refused to vote affirmatively, Mr. Briskin would not support future possible transactions that might be beneficial to the corporation. A vote of shareholders under such circumstances cannot, in the face of a timely challenge by one of the corporation's shareholders, be said, in my opinion, to satisfy the mandate of Section 242(b) of our corporation law requiring shareholder consent to charter amendments. * * *

For the foregoing reasons, plaintiff's motion shall be granted. Plaintiff shall submit a form of implementing order on notice.

Notes

1. Do you think the court was being entirely fair to Mr. Briskin? After all, he was simply stating his rights as a shareholder that he could exercise through his election of directors. He also seems to be an effective manager, pushing the stock price up to $25 from its prior range of $1 to $2. Do you think the court's ruling actually provided protection to the shareholders? Only 14 percent of the shareholders voted against this proposal, and look at what this litigation cost the large number of shareholders approving it. They lost a 30 cent per share one-time dividend, plus they will have to share dividends equally with Briskin instead of him having only 90 percent of their dividends. Since most shareholders vote for management anyway, the loss of their voting power in electing directors must have seemed like a small price to pay for those benefits. Nevertheless, in the event of a takeover any premium paid for control of the corporation would go to Mr. Briskin. Shareholders would be giving up that benefit, which could be large, for the improved dividend payments.

2. A variation of the disparate voting arrangement in *Lacos Land Co.* that became popular for a time was to have one class of common stock, say Class A stock, with no voting rights but with a superior right to dividends when declared. These corporations would have another class, say Class B stock, that held all voting rights but had no or reduced rights to dividends when declared by the board of directors. These arrangements were usually put in place through an exchange offer to shareholders in an existing corporation with a single class of common stock having equal voting and dividend rights. The shareholders were invited to exchange their common

stock for one or the other classes of A or B stock. Why do you think a shareholder would accept the Class B stock versus the Class A? The answer is that the Class B stock will give its holder control of the corporation. That individual is willing to give up dividends in exchange for control. That control will provide access to all the resources of the corporation, including possibly a large salary for the Class B shareholder as a manager of the firm and a premium for the stock if the company is sold to a third party. That control will also prevent an unfriendly party from taking control away from the Class B holder. Such a party will have to deal with the Class B shareholder and no others. The Class A shareholders, in contrast are looking for a return on their investment from dividends. They are in effect being induced ("bribed"?) to give up their voting rights in exchange for cash payments in the form of increased access to dividends. The use of such disparate voting arrangements was criticized as a disenfranchisement of shareholders. Critics also contended that such arrangements placed the voting shareholder (Class B) in a position to abuse control without any check from the other shareholders. The Securities and Exchange Commission's effort to mandate such a regime was held to be beyond the scope of the federal securities laws, which focus on disclosure rather than substantive voting rights. Business Roundtable v. S.E.C., 905 F.2d 406 (D.C.Cir.1990). The New York Stock Exchange has acted to preclude the use of nonvoting stock on its trading floor. It will not list nonvoting stock, common or preferred. The National Association of Securities Dealers, Inc. ("NASD"), a self-regulatory body for broker-dealers selling securities not listed on the exchanges (i.e., "over-the-counter stocks), adopted a parallel rule for its over-the-counter markets. That action was taken by the NASD in the wake of the *Business Roundtable* decision, thus barring the future use of Class A and Class B arrangements for publicly traded stock. For a discussion of the merits of disparate voting in public corporations see, e.g., Ronald J. Gilson, "Evaluating Dual Class Common Stock: The Relevance of Substitutes," 73 Va. L. Rev. 807 (1987).

3. Although not related directly to the allocation of voting rights, corporations frequently use other varieties of share classifications. These can include convertible securities, warrants, redemption rights and tracking stock. These are discussed in the notes following Zahn v. Transamerica Corp. at page 550 below.

4. *Treasury Shares.* Treasury shares is a reference to shares repurchased by the corporation that issued them. A corporation cannot vote or receive dividends from treasury shares. See Del. § 161(c). Some states allow corporations to treat such stock as authorized but unissued shares. This means that the shares have been authorized by the articles of incorporation but their distribution has not been approved by the corporation's board of directors. The capital accounts of the corporation must be reduced in such instances to reflect the reduction in the number of shares outstanding. Alternatively, some states allow corporations to treat repurchased shares as treasury shares that are still issued and subject to resale. *James D. Cox & Thomas Lee Hazen, Corporations* § 21.04 (2d ed. 2003). The Model Business Corporation Act has eliminated the concept of treasury shares as being issued and subject to resale. Instead, when a corporation reacquires its own shares they become "authorized but unissued shares." Model Bus. Corp. Act § 6.31.

5. *Cross Ownership.* Although dispensing with the concept of treasury shares, Model Bus. Corp. Act § 7.21(b) provides that there are no voting rights to shares owned by a second corporation whose shares are owned by the corporation whose shares are to be voted. This section is designed to preclude management from establishing a subsidiary, funding the subsidiary with shares in the parent and then voting the parent shares owned by the subsidiary to perpetuate the parent's management.

6. *A Corporation Cannot Own Itself.* Similarly, Model Bus. Corp Act § 6.01(b) requires the articles of incorporation to authorize one or more classes of shares that together have unlimited voting rights and are entitled to receive the net assets of the company on dissolution. This prevents a corporation from owning itself and avoiding shareholder control of any kind.

SADLER v. NCR CORP.

928 F.2d 48 (2d Cir.1991).

Jon O. Newman, Circuit Judge:

* * * NCR, a large computer company, is incorporated in Maryland and has its principal place of business in Dayton, Ohio. It is undisputed that NCR maintains at least eight offices in New York and conducts substantial business there. NCR has 75,000 shareholders. AT&T, the well-known telecommunications company, is a New York corporation with its principal executive offices in New York City. AT&T became a beneficial owner of 100 shares of NCR stock on November 21, 1990. The Sadlers are New York residents who own more than 6,000 shares of NCR stock and have been record holders of NCR stock for more than six months prior to this lawsuit.

On December 6, 1990, AT&T began a tender offer for the shares of NCR, offering to purchase all of the common stock of NCR for $90 a share. In compliance with Rule 14d–5 of the Securities and Exchange Commission, 17 C.F.R. § 240.14d–5 (1990), NCR mailed the offer to purchase to all NCR stockholders. The NCR board rejected the tender offer and declined to redeem a "poison pill" shareholders' rights plan, which presented and continues to present an obstacle to a hostile tender offer. AT&T responded to this opposition by soliciting NCR shareholders to convene a special meeting of stockholders to replace a majority of the NCR directors so that the barriers to the tender offer could be removed. Maryland law permits a special meeting of stockholders to be called upon the request of stockholders entitled to cast 25 percent of the votes at the meeting. Md. Corps. & Ass'ns Code Ann. § 2–502 (1985 & Supp.1990). NCR's corporate charter permits directors to be replaced at a special meeting of stockholders upon the affirmative vote of 80 percent of all outstanding shares. Soon after soliciting calls for a special meeting, AT&T submitted to NCR requests for a special meeting from holders of more than half of NCR stock. NCR subsequently scheduled a special meeting for March 28, 1991, the date selected for its annual meeting.

Beginning in early January 1991, AT&T and the Sadlers, acting at AT&T's request, sought from NCR its stockholder list and related materials to facilitate communication with owners of NCR shares. In addition to the list of record owners, AT&T sought a magnetic computer tape of the list and daily transfer sheets showing changes in shareholders from the date of demand to the date of the annual meeting. AT&T also sought two other lists, a "CEDE list" and a "NOBO list." A "CEDE list" identifies the brokerage firms and other record owners who bought shares in a street name for their customers and who have placed those shares in the custody of depository firms such as Depository Trust Co.; these shares are reflected in the corporation's records only under the names of nominees used by such depository firms. Depository Trust Co. uses "CEDE & Co." as the name of the nominee for shares it holds for brokerage firms, and such lists, regardless of the nominee names adopted by other depository firms, are known as "CEDE lists." *See Hatleigh Corp. v. Lane Bryant, Inc.*, 428 A.2d 350, 353–54 (Del.Ch.1981) (quoting description in *Giovanini v. Horizon Corp.*, C.A. #5961–NC (Del.Ch. Sept. 12, 1979)). A "NOBO list" (non-objecting beneficial owners) contains the names of those owning beneficial interests in shares of a corporation who have given consent to the disclosure of their identities. The Securities and Exchange Commission requires brokers and other record holders of stock in street name to compile a NOBO list at a corporation's request. *See* SEC Rule 14b–1(c), 17 C.F.R. § 240.14b–1(c) (1990).

Upon NCR's refusal to produce the requested materials, the Sadlers and AT&T brought this suit in the Southern District, relying on section 1315 of the New York Business Corporation Law, N.Y.Bus.Corp.Law § 1315 (McKinney 1986). Section 1315, which we consider in detail below, enables New York residents owning shares of a foreign corporation to obtain a list of the corporation's shareholders. On January 28, 1991, the District Court ruled that the Sadlers qualified under section 1315 to obtain NCR's stockholder list and that the statute could constitutionally be applied to require NCR to comply with their request, notwithstanding NCR's Commerce Clause objections. Later that day, Judge Stanton issued a supplemental ruling rejecting NCR's contention that the NOBO list was not producible under section 1315 because it was not then in existence but required compilation. He entered an order requiring NCR to produce all the materials sought by the Sadlers and AT&T.

This Court stayed the District Court's order and heard the appeal on an expedited basis on February 8. On February 11, we vacated all aspects of the stay except those relating to the NOBO list, on condition that NCR would promptly request compilation of a NOBO list, without prejudice to its rights. On February 20, we vacated the stay in its entirety, thereby permitting the District Court's order to go into effect.

Section 1315 permits any New York resident who for six months has been a stockholder of record of a foreign corporation doing business in New York, or who holds or acts for those who hold five percent of any class of outstanding shares to require the corporation, on five days' written notice, to produce "a record of its shareholders setting forth the names and addresses of all shareholders, the number and class of shares held by each and the dates when they respectively became the owners of record." N.Y. Bus. Corp. Law (McKinney 1986). Such a resident is also entitled "to examine in person or by agent ... the record of shareholders" at specified locations. *Id.* The corporation may require the requesting shareholder to furnish an affidavit assuring that "inspection is not desired for a purpose ... other than the business of" the corporation and that the shareholder has not engaged in the sale of stockholder lists within the past five years. *Id.* § 1315(b). A substantially similar provision of New York law applies to stockholder lists of New York corporations. N.Y. Bus. Corp. Law § 624 (McKinney 1986). *See Crane Co. v. Anaconda Co.,* 39 N.Y.2d 14, 18–20, 346 N.E.2d 507, 510–11, 382 N.Y.S.2d 707, 710–11 (1976) (outlining origin of the New York statutory right to inspect stockholder lists).

The Sadlers qualify under section 1315 as persons entitled to obtain a "record" of NCR's shareholders. The Sadlers are residents of New York and have owned NCR stock for six months prior to their demand. The corporation whose stockholder list they seek does business in New York.

Nevertheless, NCR challenges the Sadlers' right to invoke section 1315 because of the arrangement between the Sadlers and AT&T under which the Sadlers initiated their request. Since AT&T had not held its NCR stock for more than six months, it sought out a New York resident who qualified under section 1315. AT&T's agreement with the Sadlers provides that the Sadlers will demand the NCR stockholder list, that AT&T will reimburse the Sadlers for any expenses and indemnify them for any losses arising out of the demand, and that the Sadlers will not settle any claim or lawsuit concerning the demand without the consent of AT&T, which will not be unreasonably withheld. Pursuant to this agreement, the Sadlers requested that NCR produce the stockholder records to AT&T, which it characterized as "our agent," and informed NCR that AT&T would reimburse NCR for any expenses incurred in complying with the demand. NCR contends that AT&T is not the agent of the Sadlers, but in reality is the principal, using the Sadlers as its agent for a demand that AT&T itself is not entitled to make.

We agree with Judge Stanton that the agreement between the Sadlers and AT&T does not disqualify the Sadlers from invoking section 1315. Though section 1315 permits an "agent" to act for the qualifying New York resident in inspecting the shareholder record, it does not inevitably apply all the technical aspects of the law of agency to the permissible relationship between the requesting shareholder and another entity with whom the shareholder chooses to act. Section 1315 "should be liberally construed in favor of the stockholder," *Crane Co.,* 39 N.Y.2d at 20–21, 346 N.E.2d at 512, 382 N.Y.S.2d at 712. Once the resident shareholder alleges compliance with the statute, "the *bona fides* of the shareholder will be assumed ... and it becomes incumbent on the corporation to justify its refusal by showing an improper purpose or bad faith." *Id.* at 20, 346 N.E.2d at 511, 382 N.Y.S.2d at 711 (citations omitted).

We see no reason to believe that New York would deny the Sadlers the right to invoke section 1315 because of the arrangement they have made with AT&T. Though that arrangement gives AT&T considerable control of the demand, particularly the right reasonably to refuse settlement of the demand or litigation arising from it, that control was agreed to by the Sadlers in exchange for AT&T's assurance that they would incur no financial exposure. Since New York wishes to accord its residents the rights specified in section 1315, it is not likely to impose any restrictions upon their exercise of that right, other than those specified in the statute, unless necessary to prevent the statute from being used in bad faith. Nothing in the arrangement between the Sadlers and AT&T creates a risk of using the statute for an improper purpose or in bad faith. The demanding stockholder is entitled to turn the list over to others involved in a proxy contest, *see In re Lopez,* 71 A.D.2d 976, 420 N.Y.S.2d 225 (1st Dep't 1979), and we see no reason why he may not make reasonable arrangements to avoid his own financial exposure.

Whether New York law entitles the Sadlers to require NCR to assemble a NOBO list presents a more substantial question. The parties agree that section 1315 applies to NOBO lists in a corporation's possession, but it is undisputed that at the time of the demand, NCR did not have a NOBO list in its possession. It is also undisputed that a corporation can obtain a NOBO list, normally within ten days, by requesting compilation of the list by firms that offer data processing services for this task. NCR reads *section 1315* as limited to production of lists in existence, as distinguished from those readily capable of being compiled. NCR contends that no court has ever required a corporation to compile a NOBO list, and relies on a New York decision, *Bohrer v. International Banknote Co.,* 150 A.D.2d 196, 540 N.Y.S.2d 445 (1st Dep't 1989), and a Delaware decision, *R.B. Associates v. The Gillette Co.,* C.A. No. 9711, 1988 WL 27731 (Del.Ch. Mar.22, 1988), for the proposition that stockholders are not entitled to have such lists compiled. AT&T reads these decisions more narrowly and finds them distinguishable, and argues that New York would require compilation of a NOBO list in this case in view of the NCR requirement that directors may be replaced at a special meeting only upon the affirmative vote of 80 percent of the stockholders. Judge Stanton concluded that the case law did not provide an answer and ruled that it would not be "equitable" to deny AT&T an opportunity to communicate with the NOBOs in view of NCR's 80 percent rule.

The text of section 1315 does not resolve the dispute, although a narrow reading of its terms might favor NCR. The statute could be read to be limited to production or examination of lists already in existence and could also be limited to lists reflecting the names and addresses of owners of record. But New York courts have made clear that the statute is to be "liberally construed," *Crane Co.,* 39 N.Y.2d at 20–21, 346 N.E.2d at 512, 382 N.Y.S.2d at 712, to "facilitate communication among shareholders on issues respecting corporate affairs," *Bohrer,* 150 A.D.2d at 196, 540 N.Y.S.2d at 446. A narrow reading of section 1315 would therefore not accord with New York law.

The precise issue of whether New York requires a corporation to obtain a NOBO list at the request of a shareholder qualified to demand stockholder records under section 1315 has not previously been decided. *Bohrer* implicates the issue but does not resolve it. The demand in that case, as presented to the trial court, included the following:

> The Record containing all information in or which comes into the Corporation's possession or control, *or which can reasonably be obtained from* brokers, dealers, banks, clearing agencies or voting trustees relating to the names of the beneficial owners of the Corporation's common stock and preferred stock (commonly known as "NOBO's")....

This portion of the applicant's proposed order was entirely deleted by the trial judge. On appeal, the applicant complained that the corporation had refused to make available "shareholder identification records *in its possession,*" (emphasis added), and contended that "if [the corporation] *has or intends to obtain* a NOBO list, it must be promptly produced....,'" (emphasis added). The Appellate Division was not asked to order the corporation to compile a NOBO list, and its ruling granting the applicant access to "any 'NOBO' list currently in the possession of the corporation," or that "comes into the possession of" the corporation, *Bohrer,* 150 A.D.2d at 196, 540 N.Y.S.2d at 446, cannot be taken as a rejection of such a request.

Other courts, however, construing statutes similar to section 1315, have expressly declined to order compilation of NOBO lists. *RB Associates, supra; Cenergy Corp. v. Bryson Oil & Gas P.L.C.,* 662 F.Supp. 1144, 1148 (D.Nev.1987). The matter was given extended consideration by Chancellor Allen in *RB Associates.* In declining to order compilation of a NOBO list, he distinguished it in two respects from CEDE lists, which Delaware and New York require a corporation to compile upon request of a qualified shareholder. *RB Associates, supra; Hatleigh Corp.,* 428 A.2d at 353–54; *Bohrer,* 150 A.D.2d at 196, 540 N.Y.S.2d at 446. CEDE lists, he pointed out, can be generated rapidly by a computer, whereas a NOBO list takes up to ten days to compile. Second, he expressed the view that it would be extremely inefficient without a CEDE list to attempt to distribute proxy materials to persons for whom a depository company holds shares, whereas a NOBO list "plays no central role in a proxy contest." *RB Associates, supra.*

We do not find either distinction compelling. Since compilation of a NOBO list is a relatively simple mechanical task, the fact that compilation takes longer than for a CEDE list is an insubstantial basis for distinction. As to both sets of information, the underlying data exist in discrete records readily available to be compiled into an aggregate list. Nor are the functions of the lists significantly dissimilar. Both facilitate direct communication with stockholders, in the case of a NOBO list, at least with those beneficial owners who have indicated no objection to disclosure of their names and addresses.

Though Delaware chooses to construe the reach of its requirements on stockholder list disclosure narrowly in this respect, we think New York would construe section 1315 more generously. Once the Securities and Exchange Commission has acted to enable a corporation to obtain from brokers and other record owners a list of beneficial owners of its shares who do not object to such disclosure, we think New York would apply section 1315 to permit a qualifying shareholder to require the compilation and production of such a list.

Even if the statute might not require compilation of NOBO lists routinely, we agree with Judge Stanton that compilation was properly ordered in this case. The effect of NCR's 80 percent rule is to count as a "no" vote on the replacement of directors every share that is not voted at the special meeting. Thus, the shares of non-voting beneficial owners who might oppose management if solicited by management opponents armed with a NOBO list are counted in favor of management. Denying such opponents an opportunity to contact the NOBOs is inconsistent with the statute's objective of seeking "to the extent possible, to place shareholders on an equal footing with management in obtaining access to sharehold-ers." *Bohrer,* 150 A.D.2d at 196–97, 540 N.Y.S.2d at 446. In effect, NCR already has the votes of those NOBOs who, for lack of solicitation, decline to vote. As to them, NCR has all the access it needs. * * *

The order of the District Court is affirmed.

NOTES

1.   See also Parsons v. Jefferson–Pilot Corp., 106 N.C.App. 307, 416 S.E.2d 914, 919, nn. 1 & 2 (1992) (describing CEDE and NOBO lists). The official Comments to Model Bus. Act § 16.03 (governing the scope of share-holder inspection rights) state that:

> Under applicable law, a list of shareholders will generally include under-lying information in the corporation's possession relating to stock owner-ship, including, where applicable, breakdowns of stock holdings by nomi-nees and nonobjecting beneficial ownership (NOBO) lists. However, a corporation generally is not required to generate this information for the requesting shareholder and is only required to provide NOBO and other similar lists to the extent such information is in the corporation's possession.

2.   The use of CEDE and NOBOS list was necessitated by a crisis in the securities industry. In the late 1960s, increased volume on the New York Stock Exchange resulted in a paperwork snarl that caused several large broker-dealers to fail and endangered many others because those firms could not keep track of their customers' transactions. This caused many errors that resulted in losses to customers that the broker-dealers had to cover. The single most important contributing factor in those problems was the need to

transfer stock certificates from one customer to another. This required a massive amount of paperwork and caused many errors in fast moving markets that were encountering exploding volumes that the broker-dealers systems simply could not handle. Because of state laws, it was thought that eliminating stock certificates in favor of book entries was not possible. See generally II *Jerry W. Markham, A Financial History of the United States, From J.P. Morgan to the Institutional Investor (1900–1970)* 362–364 (2002) (describing paper work crisis in the securities industry). To rectify this problem, central depositories were created where stock certificates could be held in a secure location, obviating the prior practice of physically moving the certificates from one broker-dealer to another upon settlement as the stock was bought and sold. Further, stock certificates were, to the extent possible, held in "street name," i.e., the certificates were registered in the name of the broker-dealer instead of the customer. This allowed the firms to avoid a physical transfer and separate record keeping at the depository level for each customer. The certificates were essentially frozen at the depository level and positions were transferred by the depository among broker-dealers as their customers bought and sold. This reduced the paperwork problem, but now the stockholder of record was the Depository Trust Company in most instances. The SEC was concerned that this would interfere with the right of the ultimate beneficial owners to vote their stock. To avoid that concern, the CEDE and NOBOS lists were required in order to assure that the actual beneficial owners received the proxy materials sent out by the issuing company.

3. The paperwork crisis had other effects. Since some eighty percent of all stock was held in street name, customers faced a loss of their stock in the event of the insolvency of their broker-dealer Congress enacted the Securities Investor Protection Act of 1970 (15 U.S.C. §§ 78aaa–78lll) to insure the accounts of customers from losses caused by the bankruptcy of their broker-dealer. The amount of that insurance is now $500,000 per customer. This insurance does not protect customers from investment losses. It only covers losses caused by a shortage of assets at a bankrupt broker-dealer. The SEC also strengthened the regulation of broker-dealers by requiring them to segregate customer funds and fully paid securities from those of the broker-dealer. 17 C.F.R. § 240.15c3–3. Net capital requirements were imposed to better assure that broker-dealers had sufficient liquid assets on hand to meet customer obligations. 17 C.F.R. § 240.15c3–1. The federal securities laws were also amended to provide the SEC with regulatory authority over transfer agents, i.e., firms that record changes of stock ownership for corporations. 15 U.S.C. § 78q–1 These firms were required to register with the SEC, complete transfers promptly and to respond to investor inquiries concerning possible transfer errors. 17 C.F.R. § 240.17Ad–1 *et seq.* Clearing agencies that provide for the transfer of funds and securities as a part of the settlement of buy and sell transactions were also subject to regulation. 15 U.S.C. § 78q–1. Another more recent innovation was a requirement that securities transactions be cleared and settled within three days ("T+3"). This reduced the time in which errors may be discovered and lessened the chance that errors would be compounded or losses increased where a firm defaults on settlement. 17 C.F.R. § 240.15c6–1. As a result of these improvements and the wide spread use of computers, the securities industry is able to handle volumes of two

billion shares or more a day. It had nearly choked on volume of 16 million shares a day during the paperwork crisis. In addition, effective August 1, 2005, Del. Gen. Cor. L. § 158 was amended to eliminate any statutory obstacles that previously preventedpublicly held corporations from using book entries instead of share certificates.Such corporations may now be "certificateless."

4. The SEC's NOBO rules (as well as the rules of the NYSE and the NASD) require broker-dealers holding stock in street name to deliver proxy materials from the issuer to the beneficial owners of the stock. 17 C.F.R. § 240.14b–1. The Shareholders Communication Act of 1985 (99 Stat. 1737) extended this requirement to banks that were holding stock in street name for trust and other accounts. The SEC allows broker-dealers to vote for the stock held in street name on certain routine matters, if the beneficial owners do not respond to the broker-dealer's request for their proxy. Under NYSE rules, the broker-dealer may not vote on more significant issues where the beneficial owner does not respond, such as approving a merger of the issuer with another company or in contested proxy solicitations. NYSE Rules 451 and 452. A NYSE committee proposed to change the rule to remove compensation matters involving equity compensation plans (stock option plans) from routine voting of NOBO shares. Phyllis Plitch, NYSE Change Seen as Boon For Holders, Wall St. J., June 19, 2002, at B11A. The proposal was not adopted.

5. Most broker-dealers and other street name holders of securities have out sourced their proxy delivery obligations to a firm that specializes in that function. Issuers and persons engaged in contested proxy issues also employ specialized proxy solicitation firms. These firms assist in the development of strategies that will convince shareholders to vote one way or the other. They identify large beneficial owners who may be approached directly for their vote and keep track of the shareholder vote that can be expected to support their principal's position. The proxy solicitation firms also monitor the voting process and challenge proxies that are not properly voted or filled out by the beneficial owner. The solicitation process in a contested vote often resembles a political campaign with polls, campaign speeches and arm twisting to obtain votes. Large investors are wined and dined and otherwise vigorously pursued for their vote. Solicitations can sometimes become overly aggressive. See Michael Siconolfi, "Trading Secrets: Bear Stearns is Aghast to Find Data Leaking to a Proxy Solicitor," Wall St. J., Dec. 19, 1996, at A1 (claim that clerk at broker-dealer was plied with gifts by proxy solicitor in order to obtain confidential information disclosing the names of large beneficial shareholders whose stock was held in street name). More bizarrely, a large international corporation using electronic proxy voting through remote hand held devices had the process disrupted by a hacker. A vote on executive compensation that management was losing had to be conducted again at a subsequent time. James Harding & Jo Johnson, "Key Vivendi Votes Hit by Hackers," Financial Times (London), April 27–28, 2002.

SECTION 4. FORMALITIES FOR SHAREHOLDER MEETINGS

Corporate statutes generally require an annual meeting of shareholders. Model Bus. Corp. Act § 7.01(a), Del. § 211(b). These statutes also provide that failure to hold the annual meeting in accordance with the bylaws does not affect the validity of corporate action. Model Bus. Corp. § 7.01(c), Del. § 211(c). Cf. In re Unexcelled, Inc., 28 A.D.2d 44, 281 N.Y.S.2d 173 (1967) (upholding annual meeting held less than 12 months since the last one even though it had the effect of shortening directors' terms).

In addition to the annual meeting that is fixed in the bylaws, there can be special meetings of the shareholders. Special meetings can be called by the board of directors or persons so authorized in the articles of incorporation or the bylaws. Model Bus. Corp. Act § 7.02(a)(1). See also Del. § 211(a)(1). A number of states also empower a stated percentage of voting shares to mandate a special meeting. Model Bus. Corp. Act § 7.02(a)(2) (10% of the shares entitled to vote on the issue proposed for the special meeting). See also e.g., Auer v. Dressel, 306 N.Y. 427, 118 N.E.2d 590 (1954) (interpreting a bylaw which provided a similar right).

The annual shareholder meeting is to be held at the time and place as fixed in the bylaws. (Model Bus. Corp. Act § 7.01(a); Del. § 211(b). Under Model Bus. Corp. Act § 7.05, notice is required for annual meetings held according to the bylaws. Special shareholder meetings require more specific notice. That statute requires that notice for special (i.e., other than annual) shareholder meetings must be at least ten and no more than 60 days in advance of the meeting date. For the annual meeting of shareholders, the notice must state the date, time, and place. Model Bus. Corp. Act § 7.05. For a special meeting the notice must contain a description of purpose(s) and the matters to be voted upon. *Id*. Notice requirements vary among the states. Thus, for example under § 813 of the California corporate statute, there must be at least 7 days notice of all meetings, except that no notice is required for annual meetings if notice is dispensed with in the bylaws. Some states require different notice requirements for mergers and other organic changes such as amendments to the articles of incorporation. See e.g., Model Bus. Corp. Act § 10.03(d) (special notice for articles amendments) and § 11.04 (shareholder notice of merger and share exchange proposals).

Notice of meetings is to be given to shareholders of record. This is an important concept for voting rights and dividends. Stocks, particularly in publicly traded companies, are often being bought and sold constantly. Consequently, there may be a new owner between the time the meeting is announced and the date of the meeting or, in the case of dividends between the time the dividend is declared and its actual payment. To avoid this problem the corporation will set a "record date" for those entitled to vote, *i.e.*, only those shareholders listed as owners on that date will be entitled to vote or receive a dividend. Model Bus. Corp. Act § 7.07 provides that for votes the record date may be set by the by-laws or the board of directors if the by-laws fail to do so. A record date under this provision may not be more than 70 days before the meeting. See also Del. § 213 (board of directors may set record date for notice of shareholder meetings, which shall not be less than ten days or more than sixty).

State statutes also address quorum requirements. Model Bus. Corp. Act § 7.27 permits a greater than majority quorum and says nothing about a lower than majority quorum. It would seem to follow that lower than majority quorums are not permissible under this statute. Compare Model Bus. Corp. Act 8.24(a) which does not permit a director quorum to be less than 1/3 with Del. § 216 (stockholder meeting quorum requirement may be set as low as one-third). Can a quorum at a shareholder meeting be destroyed by a shareholder leaving the meeting? The general rule is that it cannot since once there is a quorum, the meeting is valid and a shareholder is deemed to be present for all purposes. Model Bus. Corp. Act § 7.25(b). There is, however, a different rule for director meetings since a quorum consists of those present at the time a vote is taken. Model Bus. Corp. Act § 8.24(c).

Model Bus. Corp. Act § 7.25(c) states that, unless otherwise provided in the articles of incorporation, once there is a quorum, action is taken at a shareholder meeting when a plurality of those voting approve, i.e., more vote for the proposal than against. This means that an abstention disenfranchises the abstaining shareholder. In contrast, under Delaware § 216(2), for amendments to the articles of incorporation and for mergers and share exchanges, the vote must be by a majority of the shares *entitled to vote* of each voting group allowed to vote as a group. Model Bus. Corp. Act § 11.04 also requires a majority of votes to be cast to be voted in order to approve a merger. This means that in such a vote, an abstention will act as a no vote.

State statutes contain provisions establishing quorum and voting requirements where a corporation has classes of stock that vote in different groups. Essentially, those statutes will require a quorum composed of the group or groups of stockholders entitled to vote and will impose voting requirements for each group in order to approve action. See Model Bus. Corp. Act. §§ 7.25; 7.26 and 11.04; Del. § 216(4).

Traditionally, all shareholder action had to take place at a meeting that was duly convened according to the foregoing formalities. Many states adopted an exception for action by unanimous written consent. For example, Model Bus. Corp. Act § 7.04(a) permits action without a meeting by unanimous written consent. As a practical matter, this is useful only in a closely held corporation with few shareholders. The unanimous written consent requirement which is applicable to directors meetings as well was for a long time the norm for shareholder meetings but statutes have become more permissive for shareholder meetings. For example, Del.

§ 228 permits consent by a majority of shares entitled to vote. The Model Act in § 7.04(b) and an increasing number of states now allow such action if authorized by the articles of incorporation. See e.g., Cal Corp Code § 603 (2001); Ark C.A. § 4–27–704 (2001); Conn. Gen. Stat. § 33–698 (2001); Fla. Stat. § 617.0701 (2000); § 805 Ill. LCS 5/7.10. (2001); N.J. Stat. § 14A:5–6 (2001); O.C.G.A. § 14–2–704 (2000); Tex. Bus. Corp. Act art. 9.10 (2000). See also, e.g., N.C. Gen. Stat. § 55–7–04 (permits such a provision only if adopted by a corporation that is not a public corporation).

———

SCHNELL v. CHRIS–CRAFT INDUSTRIES, INC.

285 A.2d 437 (Del.1971).

HERRMANN, JUSTICE (FOR THE MAJORITY OF THE COURT):

This is an appeal from the denial by the Court of Chancery of the petition of dissident stockholders for injunctive relief to prevent management from advancing the date of the annual stockholders' meeting from January 11, 1972, as previously set by the by-laws, to December 8, 1971. * * *

It will be seen that the Chancery Court considered all of the reasons stated by management as business reasons for changing the date of the meeting; but that those reasons were rejected by the Court below in making the following findings:

> I am satisfied, however, in a situation in which present management has disingenuously resisted the production of a list of its stockholders to plaintiffs or their confederates and has otherwise turned a deaf ear to plaintiffs' demands about a change in management designed to lift defendant from its present business doldrums, management has seized on a relatively new section of the Delaware Corporation Law for the purpose of cutting down on the amount of time which would otherwise have been available to plaintiffs and others for the waging of a proxy battle. Management thus enlarged the scope of its scheduled October 18 directors' meeting to include the by-law amendment in controversy after the stockholders committee had filed with the S.E.C. its intention to wage a proxy fight on October 16.

> Thus plaintiffs reasonably contend that because of the tactics employed by management (which involve the hiring of two established proxy solicitors as well as a refusal to produce a list of its stockholders, coupled with its use of an amendment to the Delaware Corporation Law to limit the time for contest), they are given little chance, because of the exigencies of time, including that required to clear material at the S.E.C., to wage a successful proxy fight between now and December 8. * * *.

In our view, those conclusions amount to a finding that management has attempted to utilize the corporate machinery and the Delaware Law for the purpose of perpetuating itself in office; and, to that end, for the purpose of obstructing the legitimate efforts of dissident stockholders in the exercise of their rights to undertake a proxy contest against management. These are inequitable purposes, contrary to established principles of corporate democracy. The advancement by directors of the by-law date of a stockholders' meeting, for such purposes, may not be permitted to stand.

When the by-laws of a corporation designate the date of the annual meeting of stockholders, it is to be expected that those who intend to contest the reelection of incumbent management will gear their campaign to the by-law date. It is not to be expected that management will attempt to advance the date in order to obtain an inequitable advantage in the contest.

Management contends that it has complied strictly with the provisions of the new Delaware Corporation Law in changing the by-law date. The answer to that contention, of course, is that inequitable action does not become permissible simply because it is legally possible.

Management relies upon American Hardware Corp. v. Savage Arms Corp., 37 Del.Ch. 10, 135 A.2d 725, aff'd 37 Del.Ch. 59,136 A.2d 690 (1957). The case is inapposite for two reasons: It involved an effort by stockholders, engaged in a proxy contest, to have the stockholders' meeting adjourned and the period for the proxy contest enlarged; and there was no finding there of inequitable action on the part of management. We agree with the rule of *American Hardware* that, in the absence of fraud or inequitable conduct, the date for a stockholders' meeting and notice thereof, duly established under the by-laws, will not be enlarged by judicial interference at the request of dissident stockholders solely because of the circumstance of a proxy contest. That, of course, is not the case before us.

We are unable to agree with the conclusion of the Chancery court that the stockholders' application for injunctive relief here was tardy and came too late. The stockholders' learned of the action of management unofficially on Wednesday, October 27, 1971; they filed this action on Monday, November 1, 1971. Until management changed the date of the meeting, the stockholders had no need of judicial assistance in that connection. There is no indication of any prior warning of management's intent to take such action; indeed, it appears that an attempt was made by management to conceal its action as long as possible. Moreover, stockholders may not be charged with the duty of anticipating inequitable action by management, and of seeking anticipatory injunctive relief to foreclose such action, simply because the new Delaware Corporation Law makes such inequitable action legally possible.

Accordingly, the judgment below must be reversed and the cause remanded, with instruction to nullify the December 8 date as a meeting date for stockholders; to reinstate January 11, 1972 as the sole date of the next annual meeting of the stockholders of the corporation; and to take such other proceedings and action as may be consistent herewith regarding the stock record closing date and any other related matters.

NOTE

Once notice is given for a meeting, what other action can take place? In one case it was held that, where the stated purpose of special meeting was to amend the articles of incorporation to increase the number of directors, the directors could be elected but it was not proper to amend the bylaws to change a quorum requirement. Blum v. Latter, 163 So.2d 189 (La.App.1964).

SECTION 5. SHAREHOLDER INSPECTION RIGHTS

Shareholders are the owners of the corporation and should have the right to inspect its books and records in order to determine the condition of their investment. Such access should not, however, be used to harm the company or expose its confidential information. For example, should a shareholder owning a single share of stock be allowed access to the source code for Microsoft's Windows program or the formula for Coca Cola? Should a Lockheed shareholder have access to the stealth technology it developed for the Air Force?

HAYWOOD v. AMBASE CORP.

2005 WL 2130614 (Del.Ch. 2005).

PARSONS, Vice Chancellor.

Plaintiffs, George Haywood and Denis Cronin, are beneficial owners of Defendant AmBase Corporation's ("AmBase" or the "Company") common stock. AmBase is a publicly held Delaware corporation whose primary business purpose, at this point in time, is to pursue pending litigation against the United States government based on the impact of the Financial Institutions Reform, Recovery and Enforcement Act of 1989 ("FIRREA") on its business. Richard Bianco is the chairman, president and chief executive officer of AmBase.

In 2003, Haywood and Cronin became alarmed by the payment of compensation and benefits to Bianco that, in their view, seemed patently excessive. After confronting Bianco and receiving no satisfactory explanation for what they considered his lavish compensation, Haywood and Cronin made written demands to inspect AmBase's books and records. AmBase refused to permit inspection of the documents requested. Consequently, Haywood and Cronin brought this suit to compel inspection of certain of AmBase's books and records pursuant to 8 *Del. C.* § 220.

AmBase was incorporated in 1975. In August 1988, AmBase acquired Carteret Bancorp, Inc., which wholly owned Carteret Savings Bank, F.A. ("Carteret"), a savings and loan institution. On December 4, 1992, the Office of Thrift Supervision placed Carteret into receivership under the management of the Resolution Trust Company. Shortly thereafter, AmBase commenced litigation against the Office of Thrift Supervision (the "Supervisory Goodwill Litigation"), seeking damages based on FIRREA's elimination of AmBase's "supervisory goodwill" in Carteret.

Since 1993, AmBase's principal business operation has been to manage its assets and liabilities remaining after the loss of Carteret, including resolution of IRS claims against AmBase for alleged tax withholding liabilities, and prosecution of the Supervisory Goodwill Litigation. AmBase presently employs only Bianco and two other individuals. In addition to serving as AmBase's CEO, president and chairman, Bianco served as the CEO, president and chairman of Carteret between 1991 and 1992.

Bianco receives a base salary, bonuses, stock options and retirement benefits from various compensation plans instituted by AmBase. In 1989, the board adopted the Supplemental Retirement Plan ("SERP"), a continuation of an existing retirement plan that AmBase used when it ran Carteret. Presently, Bianco is the only executive who participates in SERP. In 1994, the personnel committee of AmBase's board of directors (the "Personnel Committee") adopted, subject to stockholder approval, a Senior Management Incentive Compensation Plan (the "SMIC Plan"). The purpose of the SMIC Plan was to "attract and retain the best available personnel" and "stimulate efforts of executive officers by giving them a direct economic interest in the performance of [AmBase]." Though the SMIC Plan tied the award of bonuses to AmBase's performance, it also allowed the Personnel Committee to grant additional awards of cash or other incentive compensation at their discretion. In fact, though AmBase failed to meet its target performance under the SMIC Plan in 2002 and 2003, Bianco was awarded discretionary bonuses of $800,000 and $1,000,000, respectively, for those years.

Both Haywood and Cronin felt that Bianco's compensation was patently excessive. Bianco's annual compensation between 2001 and 2003 amounted to approximately 10% of the market capitalization of the Company. Haywood, who looks at "hundreds of companies" a year as a private investor, testified that he has "[n]ever seen anything like it"; "[it] just sticks out like a sore thumb. It's extraordinary." Cronin, who has come across many pension plans in the course of his work, commented that "in my career of 32 years, I don't think that I've seen on a comparable basis a pension plan that is as excessive as this plan is." In late 2003, Haywood called Bianco and expressed concern that he was "getting paid way, way, way too much." Bianco, however, disagreed and asserted that, if anything, he was being under-compensated.

In January 2004, Haywood and Cronin's unabated concerns regarding Bianco's compensation lead them to make written demands to inspect certain categories of AmBase's documents. * * *

Section 220 of the DGCL requires that a stockholder state a proper purpose for their requested inspection of books and records. A "proper purpose" is defined by § 220(b) as one "reasonably related to such person's interest as a stockholder." It is well settled that investigation of mismanagement is a proper purpose to inspect books and records. While "actual wrongdoing itself need not be proved in a Section 220 proceeding," a plaintiff must demonstrate a "credible basis to find probable wrongdoing" by a preponderance of the evidence.

The Demand Letters assert that the purpose of their requests to inspect AmBase's books and records is to "investigate possible mismanagement, breaches of fiduciary duty, waste of corporate assets and fraud at [AmBase], to assess the independence or lack thereof of the non-management members of the board of directors of [AmBase], and to communicate with other stockholders about the results of such investigation.".

I find that Haywood and Cronin have demonstrated, by a preponderance of the evidence, a credible basis to find probable wrongdoing. Bianco's annual compensation between 2001 and 2003 amounted to approximately 10% of the market capitalization of AmBase. The lavish compensation that Bianco received for performing what appears to be an unremarkable amount of work, itself, raises some concern. Nevertheless, stockholders generally cannot satisfy their burden in a § 220 action "merely by expressing disagreement with a business decision." Haywood and Cronin, however, have plead facts that reflect more than a mere disagreement with a business decision.

Delaware follows the "American Rule," under which a prevailing party generally is expected to pay its own attorney's fees and costs . * * * Having presided over all aspects of this litigation, I conclude that Plaintiffs have not shown that Ambase's conduct was in bad faith or otherwise sufficiently egregious to justify an award of attorneys' fees. There was no evidence of any intentional misconduct by Ambase. Though AmBase resisted Haywood and Cronin's demands every step of the way, they did appear to have a legitimate basis for their first motion to dismiss, which resulted in Plaintiffs voluntarily amending their complaint, and valid concerns regarding the scope of the documents requested. Ambase also made a colorable, albeit strained, argument that Bianco's compensation was merely a business decision and that Plaintiffs' disagreement with it could not support a § 220 demand. In the latter regard, I further note that the publicly available information suggested that Ambase's directors, other than Bianco, were disinterested in the challenged actions and at least arguably capable of acting independently from Bianco.

For the reasons stated above, the Court finds that Haywood and Cronin have met the technical requirements of, and stated a proper purpose under, 8 *Del. C.* § 220, including the investigation of possible wrongdoing.

———

The foregoing case shows that even in the case of publicly held corporations subject to the SEC reporting requirements, there may be additional relevant information in books and records that are not publicly available.

The following case explores whether a shareholder's inspection right is limited to matters of economic concern:

STATE EX REL PILLSBURY v. HONEYWELL, INC.

291 Minn. 322, 191 N.W.2d 406 (1971).

KELLY, JUSTICE.

Petitioner appeals from an order and judgment of the district court denying all relief prayed for in a petition for writs of mandamus to compel respondent, Honeywell, Inc., (Honeywell) to produce its original shareholder ledger, current shareholder ledger, and all corporate records dealing with weapons and munitions manufacture. We must affirm. * * *

Petitioner attended a meeting on July 3, 1969, of a group involved in what was known as the 'Honeywell Project.' Participants in the project believed that American involvement in Vietnam was wrong, that a substantial portion of Honeywell's production consisted of munitions used in that war, and that Honeywell should stop this production of munitions. Petitioner had long opposed the Vietnam war, but it was at the July 3rd meeting that he first learned of Honeywell's involvement. He was shocked at the knowledge that Honeywell had a large government contract to produce anti-personnel fragmentation bombs. Upset because of knowledge that such bombs were produced in his own community by a company which he had known and respected, petitioner determined to stop Honeywell's munitions production.

On July 14, 1969, petitioner ordered his fiscal agent to purchase 100 shares of Honeywell. He admits that the sole purpose of the purchase was to give himself a voice in Honeywell's affairs so he could persuade Honeywell to cease producing munitions. Apparently not aware of that purpose, petitioner's agent registered the stock in the name of a Pillsbury family nominee—Quad & Co. Upon discovering the nature of the registration, petitioner bought one share of Honeywell in his own name on August 11, 1969. In his deposition testimony petitioner made clear the reason for his purchase of Honeywell's shares: * * * (D)o I understand that you requested Mr. Lacey to buy these 100 shares of Honeywell in order to follow up on the desire you had to bring to Honeywell management and to stockholders these theses that you have told us about here today? 'A. Yes. That was my motivation.' The 'theses' referred to are petitioner's beliefs concerning the propriety of producing munitions for the Vietnam war.

During July 1969, Subsequent to the July 3, 1969, meeting and after he had ordered his agent to purchase the 100 shares of Honeywell stock, petitioner inquired into a trust which had been formed for his benefit by his grandmother. The purpose of the inquiry was to discover whether shares of Honeywell were included in the trust. It was then, for the first time, that petitioner discovered that he had a contingent beneficial interest under the terms of the trust in 242 shares of Honeywell.

Prior to the instigation of this suit, petitioner submitted two formal demands to Honeywell requesting that it produce its original shareholder ledger, current shareholder ledger, and all corporate records dealing with weapons and munitions manufacture. Honeywell refused.

On November 24, 1969, a petition was filed for writs of mandamus ordering Honeywell to produce the above mentioned records. In response, Honeywell answered the petition and served a notice of deposition on petitioner, who moved that the answer be stricken as procedurally premature and that an order be issued to limit the deposition. After a hearing, the trial court denied the motion, and the deposition was taken on December 15, 1969.

In the deposition petitioner outlined his beliefs concerning the Vietnam war and his purpose for his involvement with Honeywell. He expressed his desire to communicate with other shareholders in the hope of altering Honeywell's board of directors and thereby changing its policy. To this end, he testified, business records are necessary to insure accuracy.

A hearing was held on January 8, 1970, during which Honeywell introduced the deposition, conceded all material facts stated therein, and argued that petitioner was not entitled to any relief as a matter of law. Petitioner asked that alternative writs of mandamus issue for all the relief requested in his petition. On April 8, 1970, the trial court dismissed the petition, holding that the relief requested was for an improper and indefinite purpose. Petitioner contends in this appeal that the dismissal was in error.

Honeywell is a Delaware corporation doing business in Minnesota. Both petitioner and Honeywell spent considerable effort in arguing whether Delaware or Minnesota law applies. The trial court, applying Delaware law, determined that the outcome of the case rested upon whether or not petitioner has a proper purpose germane to his interest as a shareholder. Del.Code Ann. tit. 8, s 220 (Supp. 1968). This test is derived from the common law and is applicable in Minnesota. * * *

Under the Delaware statute the shareholder must prove a proper purpose to inspect corporate records other than shareholder lists. Del. Code Ann. tit. 8, s 220(c) (Supp.1968). This facet of the law did not affect the trial court's findings of fact. The case was decided solely on the pleadings and the deposition of petitioner, the court determining from them that petitioner was not entitled to relief as a matter of law. Thus, problems of burden of proof did not confront the trial court and this issue was not even raised in this court.

The trial court ordered judgment for Honeywell, ruling that petitioner had not demonstrated a proper purpose germane to his interest as a stockholder. Petitioner contends that a stockholder who disagrees with management has an absolute right to inspect corporate records for purposes of soliciting proxies. He would have this court rule that such solicitation is per se a 'proper purpose.' Honeywell argues that a 'proper purpose' contemplates concern with investment return. We agree with Honeywell.

This court has had several occasions to rule on the propriety of shareholders' demands for inspection of corporate books and records. Minn.St. 300.32, not applicable here, has been held to be declaratory of the common-law principle that a stockholder is entitled to inspection for a proper purpose germane to his business interests. While inspection will not be permitted for purposes of curiosity, speculation, or vexation, adverseness to management and a desire to gain control of the corporation for economic benefit does not indicate an improper purpose.

Several courts agree with petitioner's contention that a mere desire to communicate with other shareholders is, per se, a proper purpose. Lake v. Buckeye Steel Castings Co., 2 Ohio St.2d 101, 206 N.E.2d 566 (1965). This would seem to confer an almost absolute right to inspection. We believe that a better rule would allow inspections only if the shareholder has a proper purpose for such communication. This rule was applied in McMahon v. Dispatch Printing Co., 101 N.J.L. 470, 129 A. 425 (1925), where inspection was denied because the shareholder's objective was to discredit politically the president of the company, who was also the New Jersey secretary of state.

The act of inspecting a corporation's shareholder ledger and business records must be viewed in its proper perspective. In terms of the corporate norm, inspection is merely the act of the concerned owner checking on what is in part his property. In the context of the large firm, inspection can be more akin to a weapon in corporate warfare. The effectiveness of the weapon is considerable:

> 'Considering the huge size of many modern corporations and the necessarily complicated nature of their bookkeeping, it is plain that to permit their thousands of stockholders to roam at will through their records would render impossible not only any attempt to keep their records efficiently, but the proper carrying on of their businesses.' Cooke v. Outland, 265 N.C. 601, 611, 144 S.E.2d 835, 842 (1965). Because the power to inspect may be the power to destroy, it is important that only those with a bona fide interest in the corporation enjoy that power.

That one must have proper standing to demand inspection has been recognized by statutes in several jurisdictions. Courts have also balked at compelling inspection by a shareholder holding an insignificant amount of stock in the corporation.

Petitioner's standing as a shareholder is quite tenuous. He only owns one share in his own name, bought for the purposes of this suit. He had previously ordered his agent to buy 100 shares, but there is no showing of investment intent. While his agent had a cash balance in the $400,000 portfolio, petitioner made no attempt to determine whether Honeywell was a good investment or whether more profitable shares would have to be sold to finance the Honeywell purchase. Furthermore, petitioner's agent had the power to sell the Honeywell shares without his consent. Petitioner also had a contingent beneficial interest in 242 shares. Courts are split on the question of whether an equitable interest entitles one to inspection. See 5 Fletcher, Private Corporations, s 2230 at 862 (Perm. ed. rev. vol. 1967). Indicative of petitioner's concern regarding his equitable holdings is the fact that he was unaware of them until he had decided to bring this suit.

Petitioner had utterly no interest in the affairs of Honeywell before he learned of Honeywell's production of fragmentation bombs. Immediately after obtaining this knowledge, he purchased stock in Honeywell for the sole purpose of asserting ownership privileges in an effort to force Honeywell to cease such production. We agree with the court in Chas. A. Day & Co. v. Booth, 123 Maine 443, 447, 123 A. 557, 558 (1924) that 'where it is shown that such stockholding is only colorable, or solely for the purpose of maintaining proceedings of this kind, (we) fail to see how the petitioner can be said to be a 'person interested,' entitled as of right to inspect * * *.' But for his opposition to Honeywell's policy, petitioner probably would not have bought Honeywell stock, would not be interested in Honeywell's profits and would not desire to communicate with Honeywell's shareholders. His avowed purpose in buying Honeywell stock was to place himself in a position to try to impress his opinions favoring a reordering of priorities upon Honeywell management and its other shareholders. Such a motivation can hardly be deemed a proper purpose germane to his economic interest as a shareholder.[5]

The fact that petitioner alleged a proper purpose in his petition will not necessarily compel a right to inspection. 'A mere statement in a petition alleging a proper purpose is not sufficient. The facts in each case may be examined.' Sawers v. American Phenolic Corp., 404 Ill. 440, 449, 89 N.E.2d 374, 379 (1949). Neither is inspection mandated by the recitation of proper purpose in petitioner's testimony. Conversely, a company cannot defeat inspection by merely alleging an improper purpose. From the deposition, the trial court concluded that petitioner had already formed strong opinions on the immorality and the social and economic wastefulness of war long before he bought stock in Honeywell. His sole motivation was to change Honeywell's course of business because that

---

5. We do not question petitioner's good faith incident to his political and social philosophy; nor did the trial court. In a well-prepared memorandum, the lower court stated: 'By enumerating the foregoing this Court does not mean to belittle or to be derisive of Petitioner's motivations and intentions because this Court cannot but draw the conclusion that the Petitioner is sincere in his political and social philosophy, but this Court does not feel that this is a proper forum for the advancement of these political-social views by way of direct contact with the stockholders of Honeywell Company or any other company. If the courts were to grant these rights on the basis of the foregoing, anyone who has a political-social philosophy which differs with that of a company in which he becomes a shareholder can secure a writ and any company can be faced with a rash and multitude of these types of actions which are not bona fide efforts to engage in a proxy fight for the purpose of taking over the company or electing directors, which the courts have recognized as being perfectly legitimate and acceptable.'

course was incompatible with his political views. If unsuccessful, petitioner indicated that he would sell the Honeywell stock.

We do not mean to imply that a shareholder with a bona fide investment interest could not bring this suit if motivated by concern with the long-or short-term economic effects on Honeywell resulting from the production of war munitions. Similarly, this suit might be appropriate when a shareholder has a bona fide concern about the adverse effects of abstention from profitable war contracts on his investment in Honeywell. In the instant case, however, the trial court, in effect, has found from all the facts that petitioner was not interested in even the long-term well-being of Honeywell or the enhancement of the value of his shares. His sole purpose was to persuade the company to adopt his social and political concerns, irrespective of any economic benefit to himself or Honeywell. This purpose on the part of one buying into the corporation does not entitle the petitioner to inspect Honeywell's books and records.[7]

Petitioner argues that he wishes to inspect the stockholder ledger in order that he may correspond with other shareholders with the hope of electing to the board one or more directors who represent his particular viewpoint. [H]e states that this purpose alone compels inspection: ' * * * (T)his Court has said that a stockholder's motives or 'good faith' are not a test of his right of inspection, except as 'bad faith' actually manifests some recognized 'improper purpose'—such as vexation of the corporation, or purely destructive plans, or nothing specific, just pure idle curiosity, or necessarily illegal ends, or nothing germane to his interests. State ex rel. G. M. Gustafson Co. v. Crookston Trust Co. (222 Minn. 17, 22 N.W.2d 911 (1946)) * * *.'

While a plan to elect one or more directors is specific and the election of directors normally would be a proper purpose, here the purpose was not germane to petitioner's or Honeywell's economic interest. Instead, the plan was designed to further petitioner's political and social beliefs. Since the requisite propriety of purpose germane to his or Honeywell's economic interest is not present, the allegation that petitioner seeks to elect a new board of directors is insufficient to compel inspection.* * *

The order of the trial court denying the writ of mandamus is affirmed.

---

7. Petitioner cites Medical Committee for Human Rights v. S.E.C., 432 F.2d 659 (D.C. Cir.1970), for the proposition that economic benefit and community service may, in the motives of a shareholder, blend together. We have ruled that petitioner does not meet this test because he had no investment motivation for his inspection demands. The Medical Committee case did not reach the merits, the court ruling only that S.E.C. actions concerning the inclusion of proxy statements are reviewable. It is interesting to note, however, that the case presents an analogous factual situation. Shareholders sought to solicit proxies to stop the Dow Chemical Company's manufacture of napalm on grounds that management had 'decided to pursue a course of activity which generated little profit * * * and actively impaired the company's public relations and recruitment activities because Management considered this action morally and politically desirable.' 139 App.D.C. 249, 432 F.2d 681. The court, in dictum, expressed its disapproval of Dow's claim that it could use its power to impose management's personal political and moral prejudices. It would be even more anomalous if an outsider with no economic concern for the corporation could attempt to adapt Honeywell's policies to his own social convictions.

NOTES

1. What if the petitioner had couched his beliefs in economic terms, e.g., he wanted to see if the company was losing money on napalm and whether those resources could more profitably be employed elsewhere? The court in *Honeywell* suggests that access would be given under such circumstances. Today social responsibility investment strategies are popular. Should those investors be excluded from examining the corporation's books and records? The Delaware courts have not followed the *Honeywell* decision. In Credit Bureau of St. Paul, Inc. v. Credit Bureau Reports, Inc., 290 A.2d 689, aff'd, 290 A.2d 691 (Del.1972), the court stated that a request stating that the purpose of inspection was to aid in opposition to management nominated directors was sufficient and refused to follow the *Honeywell* analysis. Similarly, *Honeywell* was distinguished and rejected by the court in Conservative Caucus Research Analysis & Ed. Foundation, Inc. v. Chevron Corp., 525 A.2d 569 (Del.Ch.1987). In the *Conservative Caucus* case the shareholder's request was justified as follows:

> Plaintiff has testified that it seeks the stocklist to warn the stockholders about the allegedly dire economic consequences which will fall upon Chevron if it continues to do business in Angola. Some of these possible economic consequences, according to plaintiff, are: sanctions by the U.S. Government; adverse consequences imposed by the Export–Import Bank; an embargo by the U.S. Defense Department on purchases of oil which has its source in Angola; a denial of certain federal tax credits; the risk to personnel and facilities of an unstable government; and, the risk of war in Angola. These are surely matters which might have an adverse affect on the value of the stock of Chevron.

525 A.2d at 572.

2. Del. § 220(c) places the burden on the corporation to show an improper purpose for a shareholder seeking a list of shareholders. The burden is on the shareholder, however, to show a proper purpose when seeking other records. Compare the rights of directors in seeking access to corporate records. See Chapter 6.

3. At common law, a shareholder, regardless of the amount of stock owned, had the right to inspect the records of the corporation upon a showing of proper purpose. *Honeywell* notes the common law rule for shareholder inspection rights, but statutes now may affect that common law right. Generally, these statutes are thought to supplement the common law right of inspection, but in some instances statutes may limit the common law. Some state statutes, for example, may require that the shareholder own at least a specified per cent of the corporation's stock or to have held at least some stock for a minimum amount of time. This requirement is designed to assure that the shareholder has an investment interest and discourages minimal short-term purchases simply to gain access to the company's records. See generally Caspary v. Louisiana Land & Exploration Co., 707 F.2d 785 (4th Cir.1983) (describing Maryland inspection statute requiring five percent stock ownership and ownership for at least six months). See also N.C. Gen. Stat. 55–16–02

(inspection limited to a "qualified" shareholder owning stock for at least six months or holding at least five percent of the corporation's stock, but accounting records need not be disclosed even to a qualified shareholder if disclosure would harm corporation or disclose material nonpublic information).

4. Model Bus. Corp. Act § 16.01 specifies the records to be kept by the corporations it governs. Model Bus. Corp. Act § 16.02 then sets forth the requirements that must be met to inspect corporation documents. No showing of purpose is required for seeking certain quasi-public documents such as the articles of incorporation, by-laws, and minutes of shareholder meetings. Access to other records requires that the shareholder's inspection demand be in "good faith and for a proper purpose." Further, when these records are sought, they must be "directly connected" with the shareholder's stated purpose for the inspection. Id. Even then, the inspection right is also limited to minutes of meetings of the board of directors and shareholders, a list of shareholders and accounting records of the corporation. Id. Would this entitle the shareholder to obtain copies of internal memorandum between managers discussing company finances? An additional right of inspection of the shareholder list is set forth in Model Bus. Corp. Act § 7.20 for shareholders in advance of the corporation's annual meeting.

5. May a shareholder who has not held the shares long enough to qualify under the applicable state statute use an existing shareholder as an agent to obtain a list of the shareholders? Sadler v. NCR Corp., 928 F.2d 48 (2d Cir.1991), page 403 above, answers this question.

SECTION 6. PROXY CONTESTS

CAMPBELL v. LOEW'S INCORPORATED

134 A.2d 852 (Del.Ch.1957).

[The remainder of this opinion is excerpted in Chapter 6]

* * * Plaintiff seeks a preliminary injunction restraining the defendant from using the corporate funds, employees and facilities for the solicitation of proxies for the Vogel group and from voting proxies so solicited. Plaintiff bases this request upon the contention that Vogel and his group, by calling the meeting and by using corporate funds and facilities, are usurping the authority of the board of directors. Plaintiff says that the president in effect is using his corporate authority and the corporate resources to deny the will of the board of directors and to maintain himself in office.

This brings the Court to an analysis of this most unusual aspect of this most unusual case. The by-laws provide for thirteen directors. Seven is a quorum. Due to four resignations there are now nine directors in office. Five of the nine are of the Tomlinson faction while the remaining four are of the Vogel faction. Since the Vogel faction will not attend directors' meetings, or at least will not attend directors meetings at which matters may possibly be considered which they do not desire to have considered, it follows that the Tomlinson faction is unable to muster a quorum of the board and thus is unable to take action on behalf of the board. See *Tomlinson v. Loew's, Inc., supra p.* 516, 134 A.2d 518. In this setting, where a special stockholders' meeting for the election of directors is pending, it becomes necessary to determine the status of each faction in order to resolve the issues posed. And it must be kept in mind that this election can determine which faction will control the corporation.

We start with the basic proposition that the board of directors acting as a board must be recognized as the only group authorized to speak for "management" in the sense that under the statute they are responsible for the management of the corporation. 8 *Del.C.* § 141(a). In substance that was the holding of the Court in *Empire Southern Gas Co. v. Gray*, 29 Del. Ch. 95, 46 A.2d 741. However, we are not here confronted with the situation in the *Gray* case because Loew's board as such cannot act for want of a quorum. Thus, there is no board policy as such with respect to the matters noticed for stockholder consideration. I am nevertheless persuaded that at least where a quorum of directors is in office the majority thereof are not "outsiders" merely because they cannot procure the attendance of a quorum at a meeting. By this I mean that they are not like the customary opposition which is seeking to take control of corporate management. To hold otherwise would be to set a most undesirable legal precedent in connection with the allocation of corporate powers.

Since the Vogel group, being in physical possession of the records and facilities of the corporation, treated the request of the directors for a stockholders' list as though it were to be judged by standards applicable to a mere stockholder's request, I think they violated the duty owed such directors as directors. I need not decide how far the rights of such directors go but I am satisfied that they are not less than the rights of the four "in" directors insofar as the right to have a stockholders' list is concerned. The fact that Vogel, as president, had the power to call a stockholders' meeting to elect directors, and is, so to speak, in physical control of the corporation, cannot obscure the fact that the possible proxy fight is between two sets of directors. Vogel, as president, has no legal standing to make "his" faction the exclusive voice of Loew's in the forthcoming election.

On balance, I believe the conclusion on this point should not result in the absolute nullification of all proxies submitted by the Vogel group. However, I believe it does require that their use be made subject to terms. I say this because they should not be permitted to benefit merely because they have physical control of the corporate facilities when they represent less than a majority of the directors in office.

I conclude that the Vogel group should be enjoined from voting any proxies unless and until the Tomlinson board members are given a reasonable period to solicit proxies after a stockholders' list is made available to them without expense by the corporation. * * *

I next consider how these two groups should be classified for purposes of determining the rights of the Vogel group in connection with the use of corporate money and facilities for proxy solicitation at a stockholders' meeting duly called by the president. Basically, the stockholders are being asked whether they approve of a record made by one group and perhaps opposed by another. While the Tomlinson faction has five of the nine directors, it would be most misleading to have them represent to the stockholders that they are "management" in the sense that they have been responsible for the corporate policy and administration up to this stage. Resignations of directors have created the unusual situation now presented.

Viewing the situation in the light of what has just been said, it is apparent that the Vogel group is entitled to solicit proxies, not as representing a majority of the board, but as representing those who have been and are now responsible for corporate policy and administration. Whereas, the Tomlinson group, while not management in the sense that it is able on its own to take effective director action, is representative of the majority of the incumbent directors and is entitled to so represent to the stockholders if it decides to solicit proxies.

Since the stockholders will, in the event of a proxy fight, be asked to determine which group should run the corporation in the future, the Vogel faction, because it symbolizes existing policy, has sufficient status to justify the reasonable use of corporate funds to present its position to the stockholders. I am not called upon to decide whether the Tomlinson board members would also be entitled to have the corporation pay its reasonable charges for proxy solicitation.

Since I have concluded that the Vogel faction is entitled to expend reasonable sums of corporate funds in the solicitation of proxies, it follows that the request for a preliminary injunction against such use will be denied. The restraining order heretofore entered will be vacated to the extent that it prevents such expenditures.

I next consider whether the Vogel faction is entitled to use corporate facilities and employees in connection with its solicitation. Because such action would carry the intra-corporate strife even deeper within the corporation and because there is no practical way, if there is a proxy contest, to assure equal treatment for both factions in this area when only one is in physical control of such facilities and personnel, I conclude that the defendant should be preliminarily enjoined from using corporate facilities and personnel in soliciting proxies. I emphasize that this conclusion is based upon the corporate status of the two factions herein involved.

Plaintiff next claims that the Vogel group should be enjoined from voting any proxies obtained as a result of the material sent out by Vogel. He argues that Vogel's letter to the stockholders, the proxy statement and the form of proxy deceived and misled the stockholders into believing that the matters noticed for consideration by the stockholders were proposed by the company or its management, whereas the Vogel group is not authorized to speak as "management".

I should say preliminarily that I believe the proxy statement would have been more accurately informative had it contained a concise statement showing the factual situation which created the present status of the two groups. The proxy statement did receive S.E.C. clearance. However, that agency labored under a difficult burden since it did not know the legal rights and status of the Vogel group. * * * [The court went on to analyze whether the proxy solicitation was materially misleading under Delaware law. See also Hewlett v. Hewlett–Packard, page 432 below]

ROSENFELD v. FAIRCHILD ENGINE & AIRPLANE CORP.

309 N.Y. 168, 128 N.E.2d 291 (1955).

FROESSEL, JUDGE.

In a stockholder's derivative action brought by plaintiff, an attorney, who owns 25 out of the company's over 2,300,000 shares, he seeks to compel the return of $261,522, paid out of the corporate treasury to reimburse both sides in a proxy contest for their expenses. The Appellate Division has unanimously affirmed a judgment of an Official Referee, dismissing plaintiff's complaint on the merits, and we agree.

Of the amount in controversy $106,000 were spent out of corporate funds by the old board of directors while still in office in defense of their position in said contest; $28,000 were paid to the old board by the new board after the change of management following the proxy contest, to compensate the former directors for such of the remaining expenses of their unsuccessful defense as the new board found was fair and reasonable; payment of $127,000, representing reimbursement of expenses to members of the prevailing group, was expressly ratified by a 16 to 1 majority vote of the stockholders.

The essential facts are not in dispute, and, since the determinations below are amply supported by the evidence, we are bound by the findings affirmed by the Appellate Division. The Appellate Division found that the difference between plaintiff's group and the old board 'went deep into the policies of the company', and that among these Ward's contract was one of the 'main points of contention'. The Official Referee found that the controversy 'was based on an understandable difference in policy between the two groups, at the very bottom of which was the Ward employment contract.'

By way of contrast with the findings here, in Lawyers' Advertising Co. v. Consolidated Ry., Lighting & Refrigerating Co., 80 N.E. 199, at page 200, which was an action to recover for the cost of publishing newspaper notices not authorized by the board of directors, it was expressly found that the proxy contest there involved was 'by one faction in its contest with another for the control of the corporation * * * a contest for the perpetuation of their offices and control.' We there said by way of dicta that under such circumstances the publication of certain notices on behalf of the management faction was not a corporate expenditure which the directors had the power to authorize.

Other jurisdictions and our own lower courts have held that management may look to the corporate treasury for the reasonable expenses of soliciting proxies to defend its position in a bona fide policy contest.

It should be noted that plaintiff does not argue that the aforementioned sums were fraudulently extracted from the corporation; indeed, his counsel conceded that 'the charges were fair and reasonable', but denied 'they were legal charges which may be reimbursed for'. This is therefore not a case where a stockholder challenges specific items, which, on examination, the trial court may find unwarranted, excessive or otherwise improper. Had plaintiff made such objections here, the trial court would have been required to examine the items challenged.

If directors of a corporation may not in good faith incur reasonable and proper expenses in soliciting proxies in these days of giant corporations with vast numbers of stockholders, the corporate business might be seriously interfered with because of stockholder indifference and the difficulty of procuring a quorum, where there is no contest. In the event of a proxy contest, if the directors may not freely answer the challenges of outside groups and in good faith defend their actions with respect to corporate policy for the information of the stockholders, they and the corporation may be at the mercy of persons seeking to wrest control for their own purposes, so long as such persons have ample funds to conduct a proxy contest. The test is clear. When the directors act in good faith in a contest over policy, they have the right to incur reasonable and proper expenses for solicitation of proxies and in defense of their corporate policies, and are not obliged to sit idly by. The courts are entirely competent to pass upon their bona fides in any given case, as well as the nature of their expenditures when duly challenged.

It is also our view that the members of the so-called new group could be reimbursed by the corporation for their expenditures in this contest by affirmative vote of the stockholders. With regard to these ultimately successful contestants, as the Appellate Division below has noted, there was, of course, 'no duty * * * to set forth the facts, with corresponding obligation of the corporation to pay for such expense'. However, where a majority of the stockholders chose in this case by a vote of 16 to 1 to reimburse the successful contestants for achieving the very end sought and voted for by them as owners of the corporation, we see no reason to deny the effect of their ratification nor to hold the corporate body powerless to determine how its own moneys shall be spent.

The rule then which we adopt is simply this: In a contest over policy, as compared to a purely personal power contest, corporate directors have the right to make reasonable and proper expenditures, subject to the scrutiny of the courts when duly challenged, from the corporate treasury for the purpose of persuading the stockholders of the correctness of their position and soliciting their support for policies which the directors believe, in all good faith, are in the best interests of the corporation. The stockholders, moreover, have the right to reimburse successful contestants for the reasonable and bona fide expenses incurred by them in any such policy contest, subject to like court scrutiny. That is not to say, however, that corporate directors can, under any circumstances, disport themselves in a proxy contest with the corporation's moneys to an unlimited extent. Where it is established that such moneys have been spent for personal power, individual gain or private advantage, and not in the belief that such expenditures are in the best interests of the stockholders and the corporation, or where the fairness and reasonableness of the amounts allegedly expended are duly and successfully challenged, the courts will not hesitate to disallow them.

The judgment of the Appellate Division should be affirmed, without costs.

Van Voorhis, Judge (dissenting).

The decision of this appeal is of far reaching importance insofar as concerns payment by corporations of campaign expenses by stockholders in proxy contests for control. This is a stockholder's derivative action to require directors to restore to a corporation moneys paid to defray expenses of this nature, incurred both by an incumbent faction and by an insurgent faction of stockholders. The insurgents prevailed at the annual meeting, and payments of their own campaign expenses were attempted to be ratified by majority vote. It was a large majority, but the stockholders were not unanimous. Regardless of the merits of this contest, we are called upon to decide whether it was a corporate purpose (1) to make the expenditures which were disbursed by the incumbent or management group in defense of their acts and to remain in control of the corporation, and (2) to defray expenditures made by the insurgent group, which succeeded in convincing a majority of the stockholders. The Appellate Division held that stockholder authorization or ratification was not necessary to reasonable expenditures by the management group, the purpose of which was to inform the stockholders concerning the affairs of the corporation, and that, although these incumbents spent or incurred obligations of $133,966 (the previous expenses of annual meetings of this corporation ranging between $7,000 and $28,000), plaintiff must fail for having omitted to distinguish item by item between which of these expenditures were warranted and which ones were not; and the Appellate Division held that the insurgents also should be reimbursed, but subject to the qualification that 'The expenses of those who were seeking to displace the management should not be reimbursed by the corporation except upon approval by the stockholders.' It was held that the stockholders had approved.

No resolution was passed by the stockholders approving payment to the management group. It has been recognized that not all of the $133,966 in obligations paid or incurred by the management group was designed merely for information of stockholders. This outlay included payment for all of the activities of a strenuous campaign to persuade and cajole in a hard-fought contest for control of this corporation. It included, for example, expenses for entertainment, chartered airplanes and limousines, public relations counsel and proxy solicitors. However legitimate such measures may be on behalf of stockholders themselves in such a controversy, most of them do not pertain to a corporate function but are part of the familiar apparatus of aggressive factions in corporate contests. * * *

The Appellate Division acknowledged in the instant case that 'It is obvious that the management group here incurred a substantial amount of needless expense which was charged to the corporation,' but this conclusion should have led to a direction that those defendants who were incumbent directors should be required to come forward with an explanation of their expenditures under the familiar rule that where it has been established that directors have expended corporate money for their own purposes, the burden of going forward with evidence of the propriety and reasonableness of specific items rests upon the directors. The complaint should not have been dismissed as against incumbent directors due to failure of plaintiff to segregate the specific expenditures which are ultra vires, but, once plaintiff had proved facts from which an inference of impropriety might be drawn, the duty of making an explanation was laid upon the directors to explain and justify their conduct.

The second ground assigned by the Appellate Division for dismissing the complaint against incumbent directors is stockholder ratification of reimbursement to the insurgent group. Whatever effect or lack of it this resolution had upon expenditures by the insurgent group, clearly the stockholders who voted to pay the insurgents entertained no intention of reimbursing the management group for their expenditures. The insurgent group succeeded as a result of arousing the indignation of these very stockholders against the management group; nothing in the resolution to pay the expenses of the insurgent group purported to authorize or ratify payment of the campaign expenses of their adversaries, and certainly no inference should be drawn that the stockholders who voted to pay the insurgents intended that the incumbent group should also be paid. Upon the contrary, they were removing the incumbents from control mainly for the reason that they were charged with having mulcted the corporation by a long-term salary and pension contract to one of their number, J. Carlton Ward, Jr. If these stockholders had been presented with a resolution to pay the expenses of that group, it would almost certainly have been voted down. The stockholders should not be deemed to have authorized or ratified reimbursement of the incumbents.

There is no doubt that the management was entitled and under a duty to take reasonable steps to acquaint the stockholders with essential facts concerning the management of the corporation, and it may well be that the existence of a contest warranted them in circularizing the stockholders with more than ordinarily detailed information. * * *

What expenses of the incumbent group should be allowed and what should be disallowed should be remitted to the trial court to ascertain, after taking evidence, in accordance with the rule that the incumbent directors were required to assume the burden of going forward in the first instance with evidence explaining and justifying their expenditures. Only such as were reasonably related to informing the stockholders fully and fairly concerning the corporate affairs should be allowed. The concession by plaintiff that such expenditures as were made were reasonable in amount does not decide this question. By way of illustration, the costs of entertainment for stockholders may have been, and it is stipulated that they were, at the going rates for providing similar entertainment. That does not signify that entertaining stockholders is reasonably related to the purposes of the corporation. The Appellate Division, as above stated, found that the management group incurred a substantial amount of needless expense. That fact being established, it became the duty of the incumbent directors to unravel and explain these payments.

Regarding the $127,556 paid by the new management to the insurgent group for their campaign expenditures, the question immediately arises whether that was for a corporate purpose. The Appellate Division has recognized that upon no theory could such expenditures be reimbursed except by approval of the stockholders and, as has been said, it is the insurgents' expenditures alone to which the stockholders' resolution of ratification was addressed. If unanimous stockholder approval had been obtained and no rights of creditors or of the public intervened, it would make no practical difference whether the purpose were ultra vires i.e., not a corporate purpose. * * *

The questions involved in this case assume mounting importance as the capital stock of corporations becomes more widely distributed. To an enlarged extent the campaign methods consequently come more to resemble those of political campaigns, but, as in the latter, campaign expenses should be borne by those who are waging the campaign and their followers, instead of being met out of the corporate or the public treasury. Especially is this true when campaign promises have been made that the expenses would not be charged to the corporation. Nothing which is said in this opinion is intended as any reflection upon the motives of the insurgent group in instigating this corporate contest, nor upon the management group. * * *

Conway, C. J., and Burke, J., concur with Froessel, J.; Desmond, J., concurs in part in a separate opinion [omitted]; Van Voorhis, J., dissents in an opinion in which Dye and Fuld, JJ., concur.

NOTES

1. Is the majority of the court in *Fairchild* being a bit disingenous? Would any candidate for the board of directors or proponent of corporate action run on a platform of personal power in a proxy contest? Who would vote for him? How do you determine whether the candidate is acting for personal power or for policy reasons?

2. Do you think the limousine and chartered airplanes described in the dissent in *Fairchild* were reasonable expenses that shareholders should reimburse? Proxy contests are, in any event, quite expensive. Large investors must be visited and wined and dined. Professional proxy solicitors must be hired to conduct polls, provide advice on what proposals are likely to succeed, to assist in advertising campaigns, prepare speeches etc. They act very much like campaign advisers in a political contest.

3. A high profile proxy fight arose in 2001 over a planned merger between First Union Corp. and Wachovia Corp., two of North Carolina's largest banks. SunTrust Banks, Inc. interceded and sought Wachovia for itself. That fight for control was waged by a proxy fight over shareholder approval of the merger with First Union. SunTrust spent $30 million in the course of its proxy campaign, about one-half of that amount went for advertisements appealing to Wachovia shareholders. The North Carolina legislature even became involved, passing a law that blocked SunTrust's ability to call a special meeting of Wachovia's shareholders to approve by-law changes that would allow SunTrust to gain control of the Wachovia board. The battle moved to the North Carolina court's, and the North Carolina Business Court rejected SunTrust's effort to stop the merger by litigation. First Union also prevailed in the shareholder vote (the merged bank became Wachovia Corp.), creating the fourth largest bank in the United States. First Union Corp. v. SunTrust Banks, Inc., 2001 WL 1885686 (N.C.Bus.Ct. 2001), page 1216 below; Lijun K. Yang, "First Union v. SunTrust Banks: The Fight for Wachovia and Its Impact on North Carolina Corporate Law," 6 N.C. Bank. Inst. 335 (2002). The following case describes another hard fought proxy contest.

HEWLETT v. HEWLETT–PACKARD COMPANY

2002 WL 818091 (Del.Ch.2002).

CHANDLER, CHANCELLOR

This lawsuit challenges the shareholder vote in connection with the proposed merger of defendant Hewlett–Packard Company ("HP") and Compaq Computer Corporation ("Compaq"). HP is a publicly traded Delaware corporation with its principal place of business in Palo Alto, California. Compaq is a publicly traded Delaware corporation with its principal place of business in Houston, Texas. Both companies are global providers of computers and computer-related products and services. Plaintiff Walter B. Hewlett ("Hewlett") has been a director of HP for approximately 15 years. He is the son of the late William R. Hewlett, one of HP's founders. Hewlett and plaintiff Edwin E. van Bronkhorst serve as co-trustees of the William R. Hewlett Revocable Trust (together with Hewlett and van Bronkhorst, the "Hewlett Parties").

After a hotly contested proxy battle between Hewlett and HP, HP's shareholders approved the issuance of shares in connection with the merger at a special meeting on March 19, 2002, by a very slim margin. On March 28, the Hewlett Parties filed this action pursuant to 8 *Del. C.* § 225(b) challenging the validity of that vote. * * *

The merger between HP and Compaq was first rumored in the market in late summer of the year 2000. In the spring of 2001, HP began to consider seriously the prospect of acquiring and merging with Compaq. The merger was first discussed by HP's board as a whole at a board dinner in May, 2001. From that point forward, the HP board met thirteen times to discuss the proposed merger before it finally voted unanimously in favor of the merger on September 3, 2001.

In connection with the proposed merger, HP engaged McKinsey & Company ("McKinsey") to assess its strategic alternatives. At a board meeting on July 17, 2001, McKinsey made a presentation to HP's board. One portion of this presentation addressed the long-term strategic options available to HP, a subject on which the board conducted a "pretty rich dialogue." Another portion of the presentation addressed the projected effects of a merger with Compaq and identified five main areas of synergy and risk that would aggregate to create the overall financial impact of the merger. HP decided to focus specifically on two of these five items, hard cost synergy and revenue risk, in its external models. The other three items, all of which would have positive financial effects, were purposely omitted from external models in order to allow HP to "under-promise and over-deliver" on its targets.

HP management, including CEO and Chairwoman Carleton S. Fiorina, CFO Robert Wayman, and others, believed that the integration of the two companies would be vital to the ultimate success of the merger. Accordingly, HP began planning the integration process very early on. Fiorina asked McKinsey to present a report about integration to HP's board at a meeting on July 30, 2001, because she wanted to ensure that HP "had thought early and thoroughly about integration." In this report, McKinsey outlined the integration process that ultimately was followed by HP and Compaq in the months following the announcement of the deal.

On September 3, 2001, HP and Compaq entered into a merger agreement, effective September 4, 2001. The merger was announced publicly on September 4. * * *

Shortly after the merger was announced, Fiorina and Wayman attended a meeting in New York with several people from Deutsche Bank, including George Elling, a senior research analyst at Deutsche Bank who was an early and enthusiastic supporter of the merger. At the meeting, HP and Deutsche Bank discussed the merger and their commercial relationship. Deutsche Bank had a prior business relationship with HP, and since August 2001 Deutsche Bank's investment bankers had been working to expand that relationship. At this meeting, Deutsche Bank attempted to convince HP that Deutsche Bank should be a co-lead bank on the merger along with Goldman Sachs, echoing the requests of "virtually every other bank" at the time. HP indicated that it would be happy to continue its dialogue with Deutsche Bank about expanding their commercial relationship but informed Deutsche Bank that it did not want to have multiple co-lead banks for the merger.

On September 19, 2001, Deutsche Bank sent a letter to Wayman urging HP to engage Deutsche Bank as an advisor in support of the merger. Wayman initially was not sure he wanted to hire Deutsche Bank at that time. Then, on November 6, 2001, Hewlett publicly announced his opposition to the merger. Wayman testified that "it wasn't really until the proxy battle was announced" that he decided to consider Deutsche Bank's offer. At that point, Wayman arranged to meet with Robert Thornton (a managing director of Deutsche Bank) and other Deutsche Bank representatives to discuss what Deutsche Bank proposed to do for HP. This face-to-face meeting did not take place until early January, although Wayman had decided in November, based on phone conversations and e-mails, to retain Deutsche Bank. On February 22, 2002, after negotiations about the fee and the scope of the engagement, the parties entered into an engagement letter according to which HP paid Deutsche Bank $1 million, with an additional $1 million to be paid in the event the merger was consummated.

At or around the same time that HP and Deutsche Bank were negotiating the engagement with respect to the proxy contest, negotiations for HP's new revolving credit facility were also ongoing. The credit facility negotiations appear to have been entirely separate from and unrelated to any negotiations pertaining to the merger. Deutsche Bank signed a commitment letter to participate in the facility in December 2001, ultimately committing several hundred million dollars as a co-arranger of the multi-billion dollar facility. Each of the many banks participating in the new credit facility is compensated on a pro-rata basis. Due to protracted negotiations between HP and the two lead investment arrangers (JP Morgan Chase & Co. and Solomon Smith Barney) over terms of the credit facility, the final contract was not signed until March 15, 2002, just four days before HP's special meeting for shareholders to vote on the merger. * * *

On January 17, 2002, HP announced that it had established January 28, 2002, as the record date for a special meeting of its shareholders to consider and vote upon the issuance of shares required for the proposed merger. The meeting date was set for March 19, 2002, and management's final joint proxy statement/prospectus (the "S–4") was mailed to shareholders on or about February 6, 2002. * * *

The plaintiffs ... allege that HP improperly enticed or coerced Deutsche Bank to vote in favor of the merger by using the "carrot" of potential future business. Deutsche Bank is a global banking company comprised of three separate groups: Corporate and Investment Bank ("CIB"), Corporate Investments ("CI"), and Private Clients and Asset

Management ("PCAM"). Deutsche Bank Asset Management ("DBAM"), which is part of PCAM, is a very large asset fund manager that operates a number of funds that invest money on behalf of individuals and institutions worldwide. DBAM had voting authority over approximately 17 million shares of HP stock as of the record date for the special meeting.[1] Most of those shares were held in United States funds, with the remainder held in funds in Germany.

Voting decisions for shares held by DBAM are made by a five-member committee known as the Proxy Working Group (the "PWG"). For much of the proxy contest, both HP management and Spencer Fleischer, one of Hewlett's advisors, believed that DBAM would follow its common practice and vote its shares in accordance with ISS's recommendation. Thornton and Griswold, the Deutsche Bank commercial bankers advising HP, were told by Margaret Preston of DBAM that this was the case, and they informed Wayman accordingly. Deutsche Bank had also told both Hewlett and HP that it did not meet with participants in proxy fights. Consequently, HP never arranged a meeting with DBAM or the PWG to present on the merits of the merger.

The PWG first met to discuss the merger on March 11, 2002. At that point, the PWG had not met with representatives for either side; the PWG members had merely reviewed the ISS report and certain public information about the merger. The PWG made no decision on the merger at this meeting, but instead arranged another meeting on Friday, March 15, in order to allow additional time for research and deliberation. At the March 15 meeting, the PWG decided to vote its Compaq shares in favor of the merger, but its HP shares against the merger. Dean Barr, Global Chief Investment Officer of PCAM, informed Fleischer later that day of this result and of the similar independent determination by Deutsche Bank's European Proxy Committee.

On Friday, March 15, and Sunday, March 17, Alan Miller, HP's proxy solicitor, contacted Fiorina to tell her he had heard rumors that DBAM was voting against the merger. Miller told Fiorina that she might need to arrange a meeting with Deutsche Bank to argue the merits of the merger. On Sunday night, Fiorina called Wayman and left him the now-famous voicemail that was leaked to the San Jose Mercury News informing Wayman of Miller's concern. Fiorina asked Wayman to contact Deutsche Bank and told him that HP might have to do "something extraordinary" to try to secure DBAM's vote.

On Monday, March 18, the day before the special meeting, Wayman called Deutsche Bank to try to arrange a meeting with DBAM to discuss the merger. Thornton and Griswold, "embarrassed" that they had earlier given Wayman incorrect information about DBAM's voting procedures, offered to arrange a meeting between HP and the PWG. They called Barr,

---

1. Most of these were "passive" shares held in funds—primarily index funds—administered by DBAM. Consequently, DBAM was not the beneficial owner of these shares, and in voting them, it owed a fiduciary duty to its clients, who were the beneficial owners of the HP shares.

who agreed to set up the meeting, but only if, as before, there would be an opportunity for both sides to present. Accordingly, Barr's assistant attempted to reach Hewlett and his advisors on Monday night and eventually reached him early Tuesday. It was decided that the PWG would meet telephonically with Hewlett and Fleischer at 6:30 a.m. Pacific Time and then with Fiorina and Wayman at 7:00 a.m.

The discussion at the March 19 meeting is recorded on tape and reflected in various contemporaneous notes and minutes. On Deutsche Bank's side, the PWG, several other DBAM representatives, and Thornton, the commercial banker, participated in the call. Hewlett and Fleischer made a presentation and then answered several questions about the merger. After they left the call, Fiorina and Wayman joined the call, presented their views, and then also answered a series of questions from the bankers. After Fiorina and Wayman left the call, the PWG deliberated about the merits of the merger and re-voted, this time deciding to vote DBAM's HP shares in favor of the merger. During the conference call, no one from HP used any threats or inducements regarding future business relationships in an attempt to persuade the PWG to support the merger. Instead, Fiorina and Wayman argued HP's case entirely on the merits.

While the PWG was debating about the merger, Fiorina was beginning to conduct the special meeting of HP shareholders. The meeting, which was scheduled to begin at 8:00 a.m., actually began around 8:30 a.m. because of long lines and heightened security. Fiorina conducted the meeting, closing the polls "when I ascertained that we had no more lines, the cards had been collected and I could see no further hands in the audience indicating they had cards that they wanted to be collected," and ending the meeting shortly after 10:00 a.m. Following the special meeting, HP management publicly claimed that the HP shareholders had approved the proposed merger by a "slim but sufficient" margin, which currently appears to be approximately 45.2 million votes (subject to successful challenges to individual votes in the "snake pit" process) out of 1,644,-781,070 shares present at the special meeting. This lawsuit was then filed on March 28, 2002. * * *

IV. The Vote–Buying Claim[92]

The Hewlett Parties' vote-buying claim centers on the March 19, 2002 telephone conference at which members of Deutsche Bank's PWG enter-

---

92. I note initially, although the matter is disputed, that it appears at this point that the number of votes switched by Deutsche Bank likely will not be enough to change the ultimate outcome in this case. Hewlett's vote-buying claim, therefore, may be of greater academic than practical interest. At the special meeting on March 19, HP's shareholders approved the transaction by a preliminary margin of 45,240,287 votes. The defendants, relying on discovery documents, an April 27 letter from Deutsche Bank's counsel, and voting results provided by IVS Associates, Inc., contend that the participants in the March 19 conference call voted 17,015,988 HP shares in favor of the merger on March 19. Even assuming that all of these shares initially were voted against the merger (a matter that is also in dispute), HP's margin of victory would still be more than 11 million votes, probably enough to withstand the remaining "snake pit" challenges. The plaintiffs, however, also relying on record evidence, contend that the number of shares voted by Deutsche Bank (as a whole, apparently, and not just by the participants in the

tained competing presentations on the merits of the proposed merger from Walter Hewlett and HP management. The plaintiffs contend that during the telephone conference, Deutsche Bank was coerced by threats, either implied or explicit, from HP management that Deutsche Bank's future business relationship with HP would suffer if the shares of HP held by Deutsche Bank were voted against the merger. Accordingly, they ask this Court to set aside the resulting vote of a portion of the HP shares held by Deutsche Bank in favor of the merger.

As stated in the opinion denying HP's motion to dismiss, the Hewlett Parties bear the following burden with respect to the vote-buying claim:

> At trial, the plaintiffs will have the significant burden of presenting sufficient evidence for me to find that Deutsche Bank was coerced by HP management during their March 19, 2002 telephone conference into voting 17 million shares in favor of the proposed merger and that the switch of those votes was not made by Deutsche Bank for independent business reasons.

Therefore, the plaintiffs must prove that HP management used the business relationship between HP and Deutsche Bank as a weapon to coerce Deutsche Bank into voting for the merger. That is, they must establish that it was HP management's improper influence that caused Deutsche Bank to switch some of the proxies it had voted against the merger on March 15 to favor the merger on March 19.

The vote-buying claim turns entirely on circumstantial evidence. The Hewlett Parties point to circumstances surrounding the arranging of the March 19 telephone conference and to one statement by Fiorina at the end of HP's presentation during that call to support their claim of illegal vote-buying. Having considered all of the testimony and exhibits offered at trial, I conclude that plaintiffs have failed to meet their burden of proving the existence of such a vote-buying arrangement.

The plaintiffs first rely upon a voicemail message left by Fiorina for Wayman on March 17 after HP management became aware that Deutsche Bank might have voted against the merger. In that message, Fiorina told Wayman:

> Talking to Alan Miller again today. He remains very nervous about Deutsche ... And so the suggestion is that you call the guy at Deutsche again first thing Monday morning. And if you don't get the right answer from him, then you and I need to demand a conference call, an audience, etc. to make sure that we get them in the right place.... So if you take Deutsche ... get on the phone and see what we can get, but we may have to do something extraordinary for those two to bring 'em over the line here.

March 19 call) may be as high as 24 million. If this number is in fact correct, and if all of these shares were initially voted against the merger and then later voted in favor of the merger as a result of improper influence by HP management, then the resulting swing—48 million votes— would appear to be outcome-determinative.

The plaintiffs contend that Fiorina's comment that HP "demand a conference call" and her reference to "do[ing] something extraordinary" support their allegation that HP management was willing to, and did, improperly pressure Deutsche Bank to switch its vote.

The plaintiffs next question the motive behind the scheduling of the March 19, 2002, conference call. The parties acknowledge that Deutsche Bank had existing commercial relationships with HP. Deutsche Bank was also providing services to HP in connection with the merger. It is undisputed that Deutsche Bank desired to continue and expand its business relationships with HP. Because of this desire, the plaintiffs contend, Deutsche Bank was susceptible to the threat that business opportunities would be withheld if Deutsche Bank voted against the merger.

Based on these statements and inferences, the plaintiffs allege that HP management coerced Deutsche Bank by using the threat of lost future business opportunities to compel the CIB group, through Griswold and Thornton, in turn to force PCAM, of which the PWG was a part, to reconsider its vote against the merger. In the face of this threat, the plaintiffs insist, the PWG ignored its fiduciary duty to the beneficial owners of HP shares controlled by PCAM and voted in favor of the merger so that Deutsche Bank's CIB group might avoid the loss of some unspecified future business. Based on the evidence before me, however, I cannot agree that these circumstances are sufficient to demonstrate a vote-buying scheme.

First, I do not believe that Fiorina's voicemail evidences an intent to employ improper means to persuade Deutsche Bank to vote in favor of the merger. Fiorina testified credibly at trial that by "do[ing] something extraordinary," she meant that HP management needed to take the steps necessary to gain an audience at Deutsche Bank for HP's presentation in favor of the merger. These steps included flying to New York for a personal presentation to Deutsche Bank, making independent HP board members available to speak to Deutsche Bank, or having someone from Compaq speak to Deutsche Bank.[96] Under the circumstances, with the hotly contested shareholder vote less than 48 hours away, such actions would be somewhat extraordinary. In light of the proximity of the shareholder vote and the perceived narrow margin separating votes for or against the merger, I believe the contents of Fiorina's message are not sufficient to support an inference that HP management intended to coerce Deutsche Bank. Rather, Fiorina's message reflects reasonable actions taken by an executive faced with unexpected adverse information.

Second, although members of Deutsche Bank's CIB group were contacted by HP management and attempted to arrange a meeting with the PWG, the evidence does not show that the intervention of the commercial bankers resulted from a threat by HP to withdraw future business from

---

96. HP had made presentations to many investors whose vote on the merger was uncertain, but had not previously requested the opportunity to make its case to Deutsche Bank because of its long-held belief that Deutsche Bank would vote in favor of the merger.

Deutsche Bank. Other than introducing the participants in the March 19 conference call, the CIB individuals (Griswold and Thornton) neither contributed to the substantive discussions of the proposed merger nor offered any input during the PWG's consideration of how to vote the HP shares controlled by Deutsche Bank. Moreover, it appears that Griswold and Thornton helped arrange the hastily convened conference call because they were distressed that they had misled their client, HP, about the process DBAM would follow in voting shares on the merger. Both Griswold and Thornton testified, without exception, that they had erroneously advised HP that shares held by DBAM as index, or passive, shares would be voted according to the ISS recommendation. Feeling "stupid," "shocked," and "embarrassed" about having misstated the facts regarding the voting process, both Griswold and Thornton believed that it was only appropriate to create an opportunity, albeit at the last minute and with no assurance as to its outcome, for the proxy contestants (and particularly their client) to present their positions on the merits of the merger to the PWG. This was the good news that Griswold and Thornton could offer HP in conjunction with the bad news that the vote was against the merger. From these circumstances, the plaintiffs contend that the only reasonable inference is that Griswold and Thornton, responding to HP's threat to withhold future business, coerced and pressured the PWG to switch its vote.

The circumstances surrounding the March 19 conference call give rise to reasonably conflicting inferences, not all of which are benevolent. It is troubling, for example, that the March 19 telephone conference was initiated at the urging of individuals from the CIB group of Deutsche Bank and that those individuals also attended the telephone conference. This fact raises clear questions about the integrity of the internal ethical wall that purportedly separates Deutsche Bank's asset management division from its commercial division. Nevertheless, no evidence credibly demonstrates that Griswold and Thornton arranged the conference call in response to a threat from HP management to withhold future business.

Ultimately, the recording of the March 19 conference call, as well as the testimonies of Fiorina, Wayman, and the individuals at Deutsche Bank participating in the call, fail to support the plaintiffs' vote-buying contention. This testimony, which I find credible, disproves the assertion that HP management improperly coerced or influenced the PWG in the ultimate deliberations about the vote. The recording reveals that the presentation made by Fiorina and Wayman on behalf of HP, the questions posed by Deutsche Bank, and the responses by Fiorina and Wayman all concerned the merits of the proposed merger and not the effect of Deutsche Bank's vote on its future business relationship with HP.[98]

---

98. The call was recorded in Germany by Klaus Kaldermorgen (a representative Deutsche Bank's European Proxy Committee) and produced for the first time during trial. The fact that the call was being recorded apparently without the knowledge of either the Hewlett Parties, the HP representatives, or Deutsche Bank's American participants reinforces my conclusion about the innocuous nature of the call. This lack of knowledge makes it less likely that discussions during the call were merely scripted as a smoke screen for an improper voting agreement.

Following HP management's presentation on the merits, the PWG debated about the merger without reference to how its decision would affect business between HP and Deutsche Bank. The PWG focused instead on the harm the companies and their shareholders would suffer if the merger was not approved, as well as other substantive issues relating to the merits of the merger, such as the revenue synergy from printer pull-through. After this substantive discussion, the PWG voted 4–1, by secret ballot, in favor of the merger.

The committee then spoke to Klaus Kaldermorgen, Deutsche Bank's European Proxy Committee representative, about how he would vote the shares he controlled. Again, the discussion concerned the substantive merits of the merger and no mention was made of any threat to Deutsche Bank from a business relationship standpoint. All of this evidence indicates that the ultimate decision of the PWG to vote the shares of HP it controlled in favor of the merger was made with regard to what the PWG believed to be in the best interests of the beneficial owners of those shares. On its face, none of the evidence suggests an effort was made to coerce or manipulate the PWG's vote.

The final circumstance offered by the plaintiffs to prove that the PWG's vote was the result of improper influence from HP management is Fiorina's closing remarks during the conference call. Fiorina ended her presentation by stating:

> Gentlemen, we appreciate your time. I need to go try and get ready for a shareowner meeting. We very, very much appreciate your willingness to listen to us this morning. This is obviously of great importance to us as a company. *It is of great importance to our ongoing relationship.* We very much would like to have your support here. We think this is a crucially important decision for this company.

This is the only statement from HP management that plaintiffs point to as evidence that Deutsche Bank was coerced during the March 19, 2002, telephone conference. That statement does not, in my opinion, demonstrate that Fiorina was attempting to coerce Deutsche Bank. Fiorina testified that the statement was the typical way she ended similar calls after making HP's standard presentation to investors. For thirty minutes prior to that closing statement, Fiorina and Wayman presented management's case for the merger and responded to concerns specifically raised by members of the PWG. The plaintiffs can point to nothing in those exchanges that indicates a threat from management that future business would be withheld by HP from Deutsche Bank and there is no indication that the PWG believed its discretion had been limited because of such a threat. Instead, the record establishes that all of the questions posed by the proxy committee—some of which were prompted by concerns raised just minutes before by Walter Hewlett's presentation in opposition to the merger—went to the merits of the transaction. Accordingly, I must find in favor of HP on the vote-buying claim. * * *

NOTES

1. The fight between Walter Hewlett and Hewlett–Packard management, led by chairwoman, Carelton ("Carly") Fiorina, was carried in full-page advertisements in the *Wall Street Journal* and other publications and through direct appeals to large shareholders. The vote was extremely close, with 51.4 percent approving versus 48.6 percent opposed. Immediately following the vote, Walter Hewlett filed suit in Delaware claiming that the Hewlett–Packard management had misled shareholders on the value of the merger and placed improper pressure on an institutional investor to vote in favor of the merger. Management responded by refusing to re-nominate him for a position on the Hewlett–Packard board of directors. See generally Aaron Lucchetti *et al.*, "Deutsche Deals Way Into Proxy Battle," Wall St. J., April 23, 2002, at C1 (describing aspects of this fight).

The U.S. Securities and Exchange Commission sanctioned the assets managers at Deutsche Asset Management, Inc. ("DeAM") for failing to disclose to clients that they had a material conflict of interest in casting the client's proxies. "Specifically, Deutsche Bank, through its investment banking division, had been retained to advise HP (Hewlett–Packard) on the proposed merger and senior Deutsche Bank investment bankers had intervened in DeAM's voting process by requesting that HP have an opportunity to present its strategy to the DeAM Proxy Working Group." In the Matter of Deutsche Asset Management, Inc., Investment Advisors Act of 1940 Release No. 2160 (August 19, 2003).

Carly Fiorina had a few years to savor her victory, but the merger at first appeared to be a failure. Fiorina was ousted in February 2005 in a boardroom coup that occurred after she resisted efforts by the board to limit her operational role. Her pain was eased somewhat by a $42 million severance and retirement package. The company announced higher than expected results one week after Fiorina was fired. She was replaced by Mark Hurd from NCR Corp. *See, e.g.,* Peter Burrows, HP Says Goodbye to Drama, Business Week Online, http://yahoo.businessweek.com/technology/content/sep2005/tc 2005091_4868_tc119.htm (Sept. 1, 2005).

2. In Schreiber v. Carney, 447 A.2d 17 (Del.Ch.1982), the court noted that vote buying was considered at common law to be illegal *per se* on the policy ground that each shareholder should be able to rely on the independent judgement of fellow shareholders. The court in *Schreiber*, however, concluded that such a policy is "outmoded" and allowed a large loan to be made to a shareholder in exchange for his support in a vote on a merger. Do you think vote buying is bad? Is this just a financial transaction and, therefore, saleable, or is it a part of corporate democracy that should be protected in the same way as votes in a political campaign? Is it proper to coerce votes from shareholders by threatening them with loss of business or other action. That was the charge that was not proved in the HP fight, but see Lacos Land Co. v. Arden Group, Inc., 517 A.2d 271 (Del.Ch.1986), set forth at page 395 above.

CHAPTER 10

CLOSELY HELD CORPORATIONS AND OTHER CLOSELY HELD ENTITIES

■ ■ ■

SECTION 1. HEIGHTENED FIDUCIARY DUTIES IN CLOSELY HELD CORPORATIONS

DONAHUE v. RODD ELECTROTYPE COMPANY OF NEW ENGLAND, INC.

367 Mass. 578, 328 N.E.2d 505 (1975).

TAURO, CHIEF JUSTICE.

The plaintiff, Euphemia Donahue, a minority stockholder in the Rodd Electrotype Company of New England, Inc. (Rodd Electrotype), a Massachusetts corporation, brings this suit against the directors of Rodd Electrotype, Charles H. Rodd, Frederick I. Rodd and Mr. Harold E. Magnuson, against Harry C. Rodd, a former director, officer, and controlling stockholder of Rodd Electrotype and against Rodd Electrotype (hereinafter called defendants). The plaintiff seeks to rescind Rodd Electrotype's purchase of Harry Rodd's shares in Rodd Electrotype and to compel Harry Rodd 'to repay to the corporation the purchase price of said shares, $36,000, together with interest from the date of purchase.' The plaintiff alleges that the defendants caused the corporation to purchase the shares in violation of their fiduciary duty to her, a minority stockholder of Rodd Electrotype.

The trial judge, after hearing oral testimony, dismissed the plaintiff's bill on the merits. He found that the purchase was without prejudice to the plaintiff and implicitly found that the transaction had been carried out in good faith and with inherent fairness. The Appeals Court affirmed with costs. * * *

The evidence may be summarized as follows: In 1935, the defendant, Harry C. Rodd, began his employment with Rodd Electrotype, then styled the Royal Electrotype Company of New England, Inc. (Royal of New England). At that time, the company was a wholly-owned subsidiary of a

442

Pennsylvania corporation, the Royal Electrotype Company (Royal Electrotype). Mr. Rodd's advancement within the company was rapid. The following year he was elected a director, and, in 1946, he succeded to the position of general manager and treasurer.

In 1936, the plaintiff's husband, Joseph Donahue (now deceased), was hired by Royal of New England as a 'finisher' of electrotype plates. His duties were confined to operational matters within the plant. Although he ultimately achieved the positions of plant superintendent (1946) and corporate vice president (1955), Donahue never participated in the 'management' aspect of the business.

In the years preceding 1955, the parent company, Royal Electrotype, made available to Harry Rodd and Joseph Donahue shares of the common stock in its subsidiary, Royal of New England. Harry Rodd took advantage of the opportunities offered to him and acquired 200 shares for $20 a share. Joseph Donahue, at the suggestion of Harry Rodd, who hoped to interest Donahue in the business, eventually obtained fifty shares in two twenty-five share lots priced at $20 a share. The parent company at all times retained 725 of the 1,000 outstanding shares. One Lawrence W. Kelley owned the remaining twenty-five shares.

In June of 1955, Royal of New England purchased all 725 of its shares owned by its parent company. The total price amounted to $135,000. Royal of New England remitted $75,000 of this total in cash and executed five promissory notes of $12,000 each, due in each of the succeeding five years. Lawrence W. Kelley's twenty-five shares were also purchased at this time for $1,000. A substantial portion of Royal of New England's cash expenditures was loaned to the company by Harry Rodd, who mortgaged his house to obtain some of the necessary funds.

The stock purchases left Harry Rodd in control of Royal of New England. Early in 1955, before the purchases, he had assumed the presidency of the company. His 200 shares gave him a dominant eighty per cent interest. Joseph Donahue, at this time, was the only minority stockholder.

Subsequent events reflected Harry Rodd's dominant influence. In June, 1960, more than a year after the last obligation to Royal Electrotype had been discharged, the company was renamed the Rodd Electrotype Company of New England, Inc. In 1962, Charles H. Rodd, Harry Rodd's son (a defendant here), who had long been a company employee working in the plant, became corporate vice president. In 1963, he joined his father on the board of directors. In 1964, another son, Frederick I. Rodd (also a defendant), replaced Joseph Donahue as plant superintendent. By 1965, Harry Rodd had evidently decided to reduce his participation in corporate management. That year Charles Rodd succeeded him as president and general manager of Rodd Electrotype.

From 1959 to 1967, Harry Rodd pursued what may fairly be termed a gift program by which he distributed the majority of his shares equally among his two sons and his daughter, Phyllis E. Mason. Each child received thirty-nine shares. Two shares were returned to the corporate treasury in 1966.

We come now to the events of 1970 which form the grounds for the plaintiff's complaint. In May of 1970, Harry Rodd was seventy-seven years old. The record indicates that for some time he had not enjoyed the best of health and that he had undergone a number of operations. His sons wished him to retire. Mr. Rodd was not averse to this suggestion. However, he insisted that some financial arrangements be made with respect to his remaining eighty-one shares of stock. A number of conferences ensued. Harry Rodd and Charles Rodd (representing the company) negotiated terms of purchase for forty-five shares which, Charles Rodd testified, would reflect the book value and liquidating value of the shares.

A special board meeting convened on July 13, 1970. As the first order of business, Harry Rodd resigned his directorship of Rodd Electrotype. The remaining incumbent directors, Charles Rodd and Mr. Harold E. Magnuson (clerk of the company and a defendant and defense attorney in the instant suit), elected Frederick Rodd to replace his father. The three directors then authorized Rodd Electrotype's president (Charles Rodd) to execute an agreement between Harry Rodd and the company in which the company would purchase forty-five shares for $800 a share ($36,000).

The stock purchase agreement was formalized between the parties on July 13, 1970. Two days later, a sale pursuant to the July 13 agreement was consummated. At approximately the same time, Harry Rodd resigned his last corporate office, that of treasurer.

Harry Rodd completed divestiture of his Rodd Electrotype stock in the following year. As was true of his previous gifts, his later divestments gave equal representation to his children. Two shares were sold to each child on July 15, 1970, for $800 a share. Each was given ten shares in March, 1971. Thus, in March, 1971, the shareholdings in Rodd Electrotype were apportioned as follows: Charles Rodd, Frederick Rodd and Phyllis Mason each held fifty-one shares; the Donahues[8] held fifty shares.

A special meeting of the stockholders of the company was held on March 30, 1971. At the meeting, Charles Rodd, company president and general manager, reported the tentative results of an audit conducted by the company auditors and reported generally on the company events of the year. For the first time, the Donahues learned that the corporation had purchased Harry Rodd's shares. According to the minutes of the meeting, following Charles Rodd's report, the Donahues raised questions about the purchase. They then voted against a resolution, ultimately adopted by the remaining stockholders, to approve Charles Rodd's report. Although the minutes of the meeting show that the stockholders unanimously voted to accept a second resolution ratifying all acts of the

---

8. Joseph Donahue gave his wife, the plaintiff, joint ownership of his fifty shares in 1962. In 1968, they transferred five shares to their son, Dr. Robert Donahue. On Joseph Donahue's death, the plaintiff became outright owner of the forty-five share block. This was the ownership pattern which obtained in March, 1971.

company president (he executed the stock purchase agreement) in the preceding year, the trial judge found, and there was evidence to support his finding, that the Donahues did not ratify the purchase of Harry Rodd's shares.

A few weeks after the meeting, the Donahues, acting through their attorney, offered their shares to the corporation on the same terms given to Harry Rodd. Mr. Harold E. Magnuson replied by letter that the corporation would not purchase the shares and was not in a financial position to do so.[10] This suit followed.

In her argument before this court, the plaintiff has characterized the corporate purchase of Harry Rodd's shares as an unlawful distribution of corporate assets to controlling stockholders. She urges that the distribution constitutes a breach of the fiduciary duty owed by the Rodds, as controlling stockholders, to her, a minority stockholder in the enterprise, because the Rodds failed to accord her an equal opportunity to sell her shares to the corporation. The defendants reply that the stock purchase was within the powers of the corporation and met the requirements of good faith and inherent fairness imposed on a fiduciary in his dealings with the corporation. They assert that there is no right to equal opportunity in corporate stock purchases for the corporate treasury. For the reasons hereinafter noted, we agree with the plaintiff and reverse the decree of the Superior Court. However, we limit the applicability of our holding to 'close corporations,' as hereinafter defined. Whether the holding should apply to other corporations is left for decision in another case, on a proper record.

A. *Close Corporations.* In previous opinions, we have alluded to the distinctive nature of the close corporation, but have never defined precisely what is meant by a close corporation. There is no single, generally accepted definition. Some commentators emphasize an 'integration of ownership and management' (Note, Statutory Assistance for Closely Held Corporations, 71 Harv.L.Rev. 1498 (1958)), in which the stockholders occupy most management positions. Others focus on the number of stockholders and the nature of the market for the stock. In this view, close corporations have few stockholders; there is little market for corporate stock. The Supreme Court of Illinois adopted this latter view in Galler v. Galler, 32 Ill.2d 16, 203 N.E.2d 577 (1964): 'For our purposes, a close corporation is one in which the stock is held in a few hands, or in a few families, and wherein it is not at all, or only rarely, dealt in by buying or selling.' See, generally, F. H. O'Neal, Close Corporations: Law and Practice, § 1.02 (1971).[11] We accept aspects of both definitions. We deem a close corporation to the typified by: (1) a small number of stockholders; (2) no ready market for the corporate stock; and (3) substantial majority

---

10. Between 1965 and 1969, the company offered to purchase the Donahue shares for amounts between $2,000 and $10,000 ($40 to $200 a share). The Donahues rejected these offers.

11. O'Neal restricts his definition of the close corporation to those corporations whose shares are not generally traded in securities markets. F. H. O'Neal, Close Corporations: Law and Practice, § 1.02 (1971).

stockholder participation in the management, direction and operations of the corporation.

As thus defined, the close corporation bears striking resemblance to a partnership. Commentators and courts have noted that the close corporation is often little more than an 'incorporated' or 'chartered' partnership. Ripin v. United States Woven Label Co., 205 N.Y. 442, 447, 98 N.E. 855, 856 (1912) ('little more (though not quite the same as) than chartered partnerships'). Clark v. Dodge, 269 N.Y. 410, 416, 199 N.E. 641 (1936). Hornstein, Stockholders' Agreements in the Closely Held Corporation, 59 Yale L.J. 1040 (1950). Hornstein, Judicial Tolerance of the Incorporated Partnership, 18 Law & Contemp.Prob. 435, 436 (1953). The stockholders 'clothe' their partnership 'with the benefits peculiar to a corporation, limited liability, perpetuity and the like.' In essence, though, the enterprise remains one in which ownership is limited to the original parties or transferees of their stock to whom the other stockholders have agreed,[13] in which ownership and management are in the same hands, and in which the owners are quite dependent on one another for the success of the enterprise. Many close corporations are 'really partnerships, between two or three people who contribute their capital, skills, experience and labor.' Kruger v. Gerth, 16 N.Y.2d 802, 805, 263 N.Y.S.2d 1, 3, 210 N.E.2d 355, 356 (1965) (Desmond, C.J., dissenting). Just as in a partnership, the relationship among the stockholders must be one of trust, confidence and absolute loyalty if the enterprise is to succeed. Close corporations with substantial assets and with more numerous stockholders are no different from smaller close corporations in this regard. All participants rely on the fidelity and abilities of those stockholders who hold office. Disloyalty and self-seeking conduct on the part of any stockholder will engender bickering, corporate stalemates, and, perhaps, efforts to achieve dissolution.

In Helms v. Duckworth, 101 U.S.App.D.C. 390, 249 F.2d 482 (1957), the United States Court of Appeals for the District of Columbia Circuit had before it a stockholders' agreement providing for the purchase of the shares of a deceased stockholder by the surviving stockholder in a small 'two-man' close corporation. The court held the surviving stockholder to a duty 'to deal fairly, honestly, and openly with . . . (his) fellow stockholders.' Judge Burger, now Chief Justice Burger, writing for the court, emphasized the resemblance of the two-man close corporation to a partnership: 'In an intimate business venture such as this, stockholders of a close corporation occupy a position similar to that of joint adventurers and partners. While courts have sometimes declared stockholders 'do not bear

---

13. The original owners commonly impose restrictions on transfers to stock designed to prevent outsiders who are unacceptable to the other stockholders from acquiring an interest in the close corporation. These restrictions often take the form of agreements among the stockholders and the corporation or by-laws which give the corporation or the other stockholders a right of 'first refusal' when any stockholder desires to sell his shares. See Albert E. Touchet, Inc. v. Touchet, 264 Mass. 499, 502, 163 N.E. 184 (1928); Hornstein, Stockholders' Agreements in the Closely Held Corporation, 59 Yale L.J. 1040, 1048—1049 (1950). In a partnership, of course, a partner cannot transfer his interest in the partnership so as to give his assignee a right to participate in the management or business affairs of the continuing partnership without the agreement of the other partners.

toward each other that same relation of trust and confidence which prevails in partnerships,' this view ignores the practical realities of the organization and functioning of a small 'two-man' corporation organized to carry on a small business enterprise in which the stockholders, directors, and managers are the same persons' (footnotes omitted).

Although the corporate form provides the above-mentioned advantages for the stockholders (limited liability, perpetuity, and so forth), it also supplies an opportunity for the majority stockholders to oppress or disadvantage minority stockholders. The minority is vulnerable to a variety of oppressive devices, termed 'freezeouts,' which the majority may employ. See, generally, Note, Freezing Out Minority Shareholders, 74 Harv.L.Rev. 1630 (1961). An authoritative study of such 'freeze-outs' enumerates some of the possibilities: 'The squeezers (those who employ the freeze-out techniques) may refuse to declare dividends; they may drain off the corporation's earnings in the form of exorbitant salaries and bonuses to the majority shareholder-officers and perhaps to their relatives, or in the form of high rent by the corporation for property leased from majority shareholders ... ; they may deprive minority shareholders of corporate offices and of employment by the company; they may cause the corporation to sell its assets at an inadequate price to the majority shareholders....' F.H. O'Neal and J. Derwin, Expulsion or Oppression of Business Associates, 42 (1961). In particular, the power of the board of directors, controlled by the majority, to declare or withhold dividends and to deny the minority employment is easily converted to a device to disadvantage minority stockholders.

The minority can, of course, initiate suit against the majority and their directors. Self-serving conduct by directors is proscribed by the director's fiduciary obligation to the corporation. However, in practice, the plaintiff will find difficulty in challenging dividend or employment policies.[14] Such policies are considered to be within the judgment of the directors. This court has said: 'The courts prefer not to interfere ... with the sound financial management of the corporation by its directors, but declare as general rule that the declaration of dividends rests within the sound discretion of the directors, refusing to interfere with their determination unless a plain abuse of discretion is made to appear.' Judicial reluctance to interfere combines with the difficulty of proof when the standard is 'plain abuse of discretion' or bad faith, to limit the possibilities for relief. Although contractual provisions in an 'agreement of association and articles of organization' or in by-laws, have justified decrees in this jurisdiction ordering dividend declarations, generally, plaintiffs who seek judicial assistance against corporate dividend or employment policies[15] do

---

14. It would be difficult for the plaintiff in the instant case to establish breach of a fiduciary duty owed to the corporation, as indicated by the finding of the trial judge.

15. Attacks on allegedly excessive salaries voted for officers and directors fare better in the courts. See Stratis v. Andreson, 254 Mass. 536, 150 N.E. 832 (1926); Sagalyn v. Meekins, Packard & Wheat, Inc., 290 Mass. 434, 195 N.E. 769 (1935). What is 'reasonable compensation' is a question of fact. Black v. Parker Mfg. Co., 329 Mass. 105, 116, 106 N.E.2d 544 (1952). The proof

not prevail. Note, Minority Shareholders' Power to Compel Declaration of Dividends in Close Corporations—A New Approach, 10 Rutgers L.Rev. 723, 724 (1956). But see Dodge v. Ford Motor Co., 204 Mich. 459, 170 N.W. 668 (1919); Patton v. Nicholas, 154 Tex. 385, 279 S.W.2d 848 (1955).

Thus, when these types of 'freeze-outs' are attempted by the majority stockholders, the minority stockholders, cut off from all corporation-related revenues, must either suffer their losses or seek a buyer for their shares. Many minority stockholders will be unwilling or unable to wait for an alteration in majority policy. Typically, the minority stockholder in a close corporation has a substantial percentage of his personal assets invested in the corporation. Galler v. Galler, 32 Ill.2d 16, 27, 203 N.E.2d 577 (1964). The stockholder may have anticipated that his salary from his position with the corporation would be his livelihood. Thus, he cannot afford to wait passively. He must liquidate his investment in the close corporation in order to reinvest the funds in income-producing enterprises.

At this point, the true plight of the minority stockholder in a close corporation becomes manifest. He cannot easily reclaim his capital. In a large public corporation, the oppressed or dissident minority stockholder could sell his stock in order to extricate some of his invested capital. By definition, this market is not available for shares in the close corporation. In a partnership, a partner who feels abused by his fellow partners may cause dissolution by his 'express will ... at any time' and recover his share of partnership assets and accumulated profits. If dissolution results in a breach of the partnership articles, the culpable partner will be liable in damages. By contrast, the stockholder in the close corporation or 'incorporated partnership' may achieve dissolution and recovery of his share of the enterprise assets only by compliance with the rigorous terms of the applicable chapter of the General Laws. 'The dissolution of a corporation which is a creature of the Legislature is primarily a legislative function, and the only authority courts have to deal with this subject is the power conferred upon them by the Legislature.' Leventhal v. Atlantic Fin. Corp., 316 Mass. 194, 205, 55 N.E.2d 20, 26 (1944). To secure dissolution of the ordinary close corporation subject to G.L. c. 156B, the stockholder, in the absence of corporate deadlock, must own at least fifty per cent of the shares or have the advantage of a favorable provision in the articles of organization. The minority stockholder, by definition lacking fifty per cent of the corporate shares, can never 'authorize' the corporation to file a petition for dissolution under G.L. c. 156B, § 99(a), by his own vote. He will seldom have at his disposal the requisite favorable provision in the articles of organization.

Thus, in a close corporation, the minority stockholders may be trapped in a disadvantageous situation. No outsider would knowingly assume the position of the disadvantaged minority. The outsider would

---

which establishes an excess over such 'reasonable compensation' appears easier than the proof which would establish bad faith or plain abuse of discretion.

have the same difficulties. To cut losses, the minority stockholder may be compelled to deal with the majority. This is the capstone of the majority plan. Majority 'freeze-out' schemes which withhold dividends are designed to compel the minority to relinquish stock at inadequate prices. When the minority stockholder agrees to sell out at less than fair value, the majority has won.

Because of the fundamental resemblance of the close corporation to the partnership, the trust and confidence which are essential to this scale and manner of enterprise, and the inherent danger to minority interests in the close corporation, we hold that stockholders[17] in the close corporation owe one another substantially the same fiduciary duty in the operation of the enterprise[18] that partners owe to one another. In our previous decisions, we have defined the standard of duty owed by partners to one another as the 'utmost good faith and loyalty.' Stockholders in close corporations must discharge their management and stockholder responsibilities in conformity with this strict good faith standard. They may not act out of avarice, expediency or self-interest in derogation of their duty of loyalty to the other stockholders and to the corporation.

We contrast[19] this strict good faith standard with the somewhat less stringent standard of fiduciary duty to which directors and stockholders[20] of all corporations must adhere in the discharge of their corporate responsibilities. Corporate directors are held to a good faith and inherent fairness standard of conduct and are not 'permitted to serve two masters whose interests are antagonistic.' 'Their paramount duty is to the corporation, and their personal pecuniary interests are subordinate to that duty.'

The more rigorous duty of partners and participants in a joint adventure, here extended to stockholders in a close corporation, was described by then Chief Judge Cardozo of the New York Court of Appeals

---

17. We do not limit our holding to majority stockholders. In the close corporation, the minority may do equal damage through unscrupulous and improper 'sharp dealings' with an unsuspecting majority. See Helms v. Duckworth, 101 U.S.App.D.C. 390, 249 F.2d 482 (1957).

18. We stress that the strict fiduciary duty which we apply to stockholders in a close corporation in this opinion governs only their actions relative to the operations of the enterprise and the effects of that operation on the rights and investments of other stockholders. We express no opinion as to the standard of duty applicable to transactions in the shares of the close corporation when the corporation is not a party to the transaction. Cf. Andrews, The Stockholder's Right to Equal Opportunity in the Sale of Shares, 78 Harv.L.Rev. 505 (1965). Compare Perlman v. Feldmann, 219 F.2d 173 (2d Cir.), cert. den. 349 U.S. 952 (1955) with Zahn v. Transamerica Corp., 162 F.2d 36 (3d Cir.1947).

19. Several scholarly articles have suggested that the standard of duty of stockholding officers in close corporations may be more demanding than the standard applicable to their counterparts in publicly-held corporations. See Brudney and Chirelstein, Fair Shares in Corporate Mergers and Takeovers, 88 Harv.L.Rev. 297, 325 n. 60 (1974); Note, Corporate Opportunity in the Close Corporation—A Different Result? 56 Geo.L.J. 381 (1967).

20. The rule set out in many jurisdictions is: 'The majority has the right to control; but when it does so, it occupies a fiduciary relation toward the minority, as much so as the corporation itself or its officers and directors.' Southern Pac. Co. v. Bogert, 250 U.S. 483, 487—488 (1919). Accord, e.g., Jones v. H. F. Ahmanson & Co., 1 Cal.3d 93, 108, 81 Cal.Rptr. 592, 460 P.2d 464 (1969); Allied Chem. & Dye Corp. v. Steel & Tube Co. of America, 14 Del.Ch. 1, 12, 120 A. 486 (Ch.1923); Kavanaugh v. Kavanaugh Knitting Co., 226 N.Y. 185, 195, 123 N.E. 148 (1919); Zahn v. Transamerica Corp., 162 F.2d 36, 42 (3d Cir.1947). See generally Berle, 'Control' in Corporate Law, 58 Col.L.Rev. 1212, 1222 (1958).

in Meinhard v. Salmon, 249 N.Y. 458, 164 N.E. 545 (1928): 'Joint adventurers, like copartners, owe to one another, while the enterprise continues, the duty of the finest loyalty. Many forms of conduct permissible in a workaday world for those acting at arm's length, are forbidden to those bound by fiduciary ties. . . . Not honesty alone, but the punctilio of an honor the most sensitive, is then the standard of behavior.'

Application of this strict standard of duty to stockholders in close corporations is a natural outgrowth of the prior case law. In a number of cases involving close corporations, we have held stockholders participating in management to a standard of fiduciary duty more exacting than the traditional good faith and inherent fairness standard because of the trust and confidence reposed in them by the other stockholders. . . . In these and other cases, we have imposed a duty of loyalty more exacting than that duty owed by a director to his corporation or by a majority stockholder to the minority in a public corporation because of facts particular to the close corporation in the cases. In the instant case, we extend this strict duty of loyalty to all stockholders in close corporations. The circumstances which justified findings of relationships of trust and confidence in these particular cases exist universally in modified form in all close corporations. Statements in other cases which suggest that stockholders of a corporation do not stand in a relationship of trust and confidence to one another will not be followed in the close corporation context.

B. Equal Opportunity in a Close Corporation. Under settled Massachusetts law, a domestic corporation, unless forbidden by statute, has the power to purchase its own shares. An agreement to reacquire stock '(is) enforceable, subject, at least, to the limitations that the purchase must be made in good faith and without prejudice to creditors and stockholders.' When the corporation reacquiring its own stock is a close corporation, the purchase is subject to the additional requirement, in the light of our holding in this opinion, that the stockholders, who, as directors or controlling stockholders, caused the corporation to enter into the stock purchase agreement, must have acted with the utmost good faith and loyalty to the other stockholders.

To meet this test, if the stockholder whose shares were purchased was a member of the controlling group, the controlling stockholders must cause the corporation to offer each stockholder an equal opportunity to sell a ratable number of his shares to the corporation at an identical price.[24] Purchase by the corporation confers substantial benefits on the members of the controlling group whose shares were purchased. These benefits are not available to the minority stockholders if the corporation does not also offer them an opportunity to sell their shares. The controlling group may not, consistent with its strict duty to the minority, utilize

---

24. Of course, a close corporation may purchase shares from one stockholder without offering the others an equal opportunity if all other stockholders give advance consent to the stock purchase arrangements through acceptance of an appropriate provision in the articles of organization, the corporate by-laws, or a stockholder's agreement. Similarly, all other stockholders may ratify the purchase.

its control of the corporation to obtain special advantages and disproportionate benefit from its share ownership. See Jones v. H. F. Ahmanson & Co., 1 Cal.3d 93, 108, 81 Cal.Rptr. 592, 460 P.2d 464 (1969).

The benefits conferred by the purchase are twofold: (1) provision of a market for shares; (2) access to corporate assets for personal use. By definition, there is no ready market for shares of a close corporation. The purchase creates a market for shares which previously had been unmarketable. It transforms a previously illiquid investment into a liquid one. If the close corporation purchases shares only from a member of the controlling group, the controlling stockholder can convert his shares into cash at a time when none of the other stockholders can. Consistent with its strict fiduciary duty, the controlling group may not utilize its control of the corporation to establish an exclusive market in previously unmarketable shares from which the minority stockholders are excluded.

The purchase also distributes corporate assets to the stockholder whose shares were purchased. Unless an equal opportunity is given to all stockholders, the purchase of shares from a member of the controlling group operates as a preferential distribution of assets. In exchange for his shares, he receives a percentage of the contributed capital and accumulated profits of the enterprise. The funds he so receives are available for his personal use. The other stockholders benefit from no such access to corporate property and cannot withdraw their shares of the corporate profits and capital in this manner unless the controlling group acquiesces. Although the purchase price for the controlling stockholder's shares may seem fair to the corporation and other stockholders under the tests established in the prior case law, the controlling stockholder whose stock has been purchased has still received a relative advantage over his fellow stockholders, inconsistent with his strict fiduciary duty—an opportunity to turn corporate funds to personal use.

The rule of equal opportunity in stock purchases by close corporations provides equal access to these benefits for all stockholders. We hold that, in any case in which the controlling stockholders have exercised their power over the corporation to deny the minority such equal opportunity, the minority shall be entitled to appropriate relief.

C. Application of the Law to this Case. We turn now to the application of the learning set forth above to the facts of the instant case.

The strict standard of duty is plainly applicable to the stockholders in Rodd Electrotype. Rodd Electrotype is a close corporation. Members of the Rodd and Donahue families are the sole owners of the corporation's stock. In actual numbers, the corporation, immediately prior to the corporate purchase of Harry Rodd's shares, had six stockholders. The shares have not been traded, and no market for them seems to exist. Harry Rodd, Charles Rodd, Frederick Rodd, William G. Mason (Phyllis Mason's husband), and the plaintiff's husband all worked for the corporation. The Rodds have retained the paramount management positions.

Through their control of these management positions and of the majority of the Rodd Electrotype stock, the Rodds effectively controlled the corporation. In testing the stock purchase from Harry Rodd against the applicable strict fiduciary standard, we treat the Rodd family as a single controlling group. We reject the defendants' contention that the Rodd family cannot be treated as a unit for this purpose. From the evidence, it is clear that the Rodd family was a close-knit one with strong community of interest. Harry Rodd had hired his sons to work in the family business, Rodd Electrotype. As he aged, he transferred portions of his stock holdings to his children. Charles Rodd and Frederick Rodd were given positions of responsibility in the business as he withdrew from active management. In these circumstances, it is realistic to assume that appreciation, gratitude, and filial devotion would prevent the younger Rodds from opposing a plan which would provide funds for their father's retirement.

Moreover, a strong motive of interest requires that the Rodds be considered a controlling group. When Charles Rodd and Frederick Rodd were called on to represent the corporation in its dealings with their father, they must have known that further advancement within the corporation and benefits would follow their father's retirement and the purchase of his stock. The corporate purchase would take only forty-five of Harry Rodd's eighty-one shares. The remaining thirty-six shares[27] were to be divided among Harry Rodd's children in equal amounts by gift and sale.[28] Receipt of their portion of the thirty-six shares and purchase by the corporation of forty-five shares would effectively transfer full control of the corporation to Federick Rodd and Charles Rodd, if they chose to act in concert with each other or if one of them chose to ally with his sister. Moreover, Frederick Rodd was the obvious successor to his father as director and corporate treasurer when those posts became vacant after his father's retirement. Failure to complete the corporate purchase (in other words, impeding their father's retirement plan) would have delayed, and perhaps have suspended indefinitely, the transfer of these benefits to the younger Rodds. They could not be expected to oppose their father's wishes in this matter. Although the defendants are correct when they assert that no express agreement involving a quid pro quo—subsequent stock gifts for votes from the directors—was proved, no express agreement is necessary to demonstrate the identity of interest which disciplines a controlling group acting in unison.

On its face, then, the purchase of Harry Rodd's shares by the corporation is a breach of the duty which the controlling stockholders, the Rodds, owed to the minority stockholders, the plaintiff and her son. The

---

27. The mistaken finding of the trial judge that Harry Rodd had only fifty-one shares prior to the corporate purchase becomes significant in assessing motive and interest in this context.

28. Charles Rodd admitted in his trial testimony that the parties to the negotiations which led to the stock purchase agreement structured subsequent transactions so that each of the Rodd children would eventually own fifty-one shares of corporate stock. The plaintiff points out that this was precisely the number of shares which would permit any two of Harry Rodd's children to outvote the third child and the remaining stockholders.

purchase distributed a portion of the corporate assets to Harry Rodd, a member of the controlling group, in exchange for his shares. The plaintiff and her son were not offered an equal opportunity to sell their shares to the corporation. In fact, their efforts to obtain an equal opportunity were rebuffed by the corporate representative. As the trial judge found, they did not, in any manner, ratify the transaction with Harry Rodd.

Because of the foregoing, we hold that the plaintiff is entitled to relief. Two forms of suitable relief are set out hereinafter. The judge below is to enter an appropriate judgment. The judgment may require Harry Rodd to remit $36,000 with interest at the legal rate from July 15, 1970, to Rodd Electrotype in exchange for forty-five shares of Rodd Electrotype treasury stock. This, in substance, is the specific relief requested in the plaintiff's bill of complaint. Interest is manifestly appropriate. A stockholder, who, in violation of his fiduciary duty to the other stockholders, has obtained assets from his corporation and has had those assets available for his own use, must pay for that use. In the alternative, the judgment may require Rodd Electrotype to purchase all of the plaintiff's shares for $36,000 without interest. In the circumstances of this case, we view this as the equal opportunity which the plaintiff should have received. Harry Rodd's retention of thirty-six shares, which were to be sold and given to his children within a year of the Rodd Electrotype purchase, cannot disguise the fact that the corporation acquired one hundred per cent of that portion of his holdings (forty-five shares) which he did not intend his children to own. The plaintiff is entitled to have one hundred per cent of her forty-five shares similarly purchased.

The case is remanded to the Superior Court for entry of judgment in conformity with this opinion. So ordered.

WILKINS, JUSTICE (CONCURRING).

I agree with much of what the Chief Justice says in support of granting relief to the plaintiff. However, I do not join in any implication that the rule concerning a close corporation's purchase of a controlling stockholder's shares applies to all operations of the corporation as they affect minority stockholders. That broader issue, which is apt to arise in connection with salaries and dividend policy, is not involved in this case. The analogy to partnerships may not be a complete one.

NOTES

1. The allocation of shares to his family by Harry Rodd was a carefully crafted estate plan that allocated control among his children. The shares were dispersed as follows:

Charles Rodd	Fred Rodd	Phyllis Mason (daughter)	Donahues
51 shares	51 shares	51 shares	50 shares

As the court noted, this allocation precluded any one Rodd sibling from joining with the Donahues to take over control of the company. In the event of a deadlock between the two Rodd sons that were active in the business, a tie-breaker was created by the shares of the third child, held by Rodd's daughter, Phyllis Mason. At the same time, ownership of the principal asset in Harry Rodd's estate was distributed in an equitable manner to the children, after providing for his retirement.

2. Was the purchase of Harry Rodd's shares really unfair to the Donahues? It appears from the court's decision, that Joseph Donahue did little to build the business. Did Harry Rodd not deserve some reward for building up the business? Moreover, were the Donahues really being short-changed by the purchase of the treasury shares? Before the purchase of the treasury shares and redistribution of the stock to Harry Rodd's children, Joseph Donahue owned only twenty per cent of Rodd Electrotype. After the purchase of the treasury shares from Harry Rodd, the Donahue's ownership percentage increased to almost twenty-five percent.

3. Could the Rodd family have avoided this problem by increasing the salaries of the Rodd children so that they could support their father without having the corporation make a payment to him? There would be, of course, tax implications from such an arrangement.

4. The *Donahue* case focused on the liquidity problem in closely held concerns. Namely, that, since there is no ready market, minority shareholders are locked in. Is the *Donahue* decision limited to cases involving a right to exit from the company? In Wilkes v. Springside Nursing Home, Inc., 370 Mass. 842, 353 N.E.2d 657 (1976), the same court pointed out that access to funds such as through employment can be equally important:

In *Donahue*, we held that 'stockholders in the close corporation owe one another substantially the same fiduciary duty in the operation of the enterprise that partners owe to one another.' As determined in previous decisions of this court, the standard of duty owed by partners to one another is one of 'utmost good faith and loyalty.' Thus, we concluded in Donahue, with regard to 'their actions relative to the operations of the enterprise and the effects of that operation on the rights and investments of other stockholders,' (s)tockholders in close corporations must discharge their management and stockholder responsibilities in conformity with this strict good faith standard. They may not act out of avarice, expediency or self-interest in derogation of their duty of loyalty to the other stockholders and to the corporation.

In the *Donahue* case we recognized that one peculiar aspect of close corporations was the opportunity afforded to majority stockholders to oppress, disadvantage or 'freeze out' minority stockholders. In Donahue itself, for example, the majority refused the minority an equal opportunity to sell a ratable number of shares to the corporation at the same price available to the majority. The net result of this refusal, we said, was that the minority could be forced to 'sell out at less than fair value,' since there is by definition no ready market for minority stock in a close corporation.

Freeze outs, however, may be accomplished by the use of other devices. One such device which has proved to be particularly effective in accomplishing the purpose of the majority is to deprive minority stockholders of corporate offices and of employment with the corporation. F. H. O'Neal, 'Squeeze–Outs' of Minority Shareholders 59, 78—79 (1975). This 'freeze-out' technique has been successful because courts fairly consistently have been disinclined to interfere in those facets of internal corporate operations, such as the selection and retention or dismissal of officers, directors and employees, which essentially involve management decisions subject to the principle of majority control. See Note, 35 N.C.L.Rev. 271, 277 (1957). As one authoritative source has said, '(M)any courts apparently feel that there is a legitimate sphere in which the controlling (directors or) shareholders can act in their own interest even if the minority suffers.' F. H. O'Neal, supra at 59 (footnote omitted). Comment, 1959 Duke L.J. 436, 437.

The denial of employment to the minority at the hands of the majority is especially pernicious in some instances. A guaranty of employment with the corporation may have been one of the 'basic reason(s) why a minority owner has invested capital in the firm.' The minority stockholder typically depends on his salary as the principal return on his investment, since the 'earnings of a close corporation ... are distributed in major part in salaries, bonuses and retirement benefits.' 1 F. H. O'Neal, Close Corporations § 1.07 (1971). Other noneconomic interests of the minority stockholder are likewise injuriously affected by barring him from corporate office. See F. H. O'Neal, 'Squeeze–Outs' of Minority Shareholders 79 (1975). Such action severely restricts his participation in the management of the enterprise, and he is relegated to enjoying those benefits incident to his status as a stockholder. See Symposium—The Close Corporation, 52 Nw.U.L.Rev. 345, 386 (1957). In sum, by terminating a minority stockholder's employment or by severing him from a position as an officer or director, the majority effectively frustrate the minority stockholder's purposes in entering on the corporate venture and also deny him an equal return on his investment.

The Donahue decision acknowledged, as a 'natural outgrowth' of the case law of this Commonwealth, a strict obligation on the part of majority stockholders in a close corporation to deal with the minority with the utmost good faith and loyalty. On its face, this strict standard is applicable in the instant case. The distinction between the majority action in Donahue and the majority action in this case is more one of form than of substance. Nevertheless, we are concerned that untempered application of the strict good faith standard enunciated in Donahue to cases such as the one before us will result in the imposition of limitations on legitimate action by the controlling group in a close corporation which will unduly hamper its effectiveness in managing the corporation in the best interests of all concerned. The majority, concededly, have certain rights to what has been termed 'selfish ownership' in the corporation which should be balanced against the concept of their fiduciary obligation to the minority.

Therefore, when minority stockholders in a close corporation bring suit against the majority alleging a breach of the strict good faith duty owed to them by the majority, we must carefully analyze the action taken by the controlling stockholders in the individual case. It must be asked whether the controlling group can demonstrate a legitimate business purpose for its action. In asking this question, we acknowledge the fact that the controlling group in a close corporation must have some room to maneuver in establishing the business policy of the corporation. It must have a large measure of discretion, for example, in declaring or withholding dividends, deciding whether to merge or consolidate, establishing the salaries of corporate officers, dismissing directors with or without cause, and hiring and firing corporate employees.

Applying this approach to the instant case it is apparent that the majority stockholders in Springside have not shown a legitimate business purpose for severing Wilkes from the payroll of the corporation or for refusing to reelect him as a salaried officer and director. The master's subsidiary findings relating to the purpose of the meetings of the directors and stockholders in February and March, 1967, are supported by the evidence. There was no showing of misconduct on Wilkes's part as a director, officer or employee of the corporation which would lead us to approve the majority action as a legitimate response to the disruptive nature of an undesirable individual bent on injuring or destroying the corporation. On the contrary, it appears that Wilkes had always accomplished his assigned share of the duties competently, and that he had never indicated an unwillingness to continue to do so.

It is an inescapable conclusion from all the evidence that the action of the majority stockholders here was a designed 'freeze out' for which no legitimate business purpose has been suggested. Furthermore, we may infer that a design to pressure Wilkes into selling his shares to the corporation at a price below their value well may have been at the heart of the majority's plan.

In the context of this case, several factors bear directly on the duty owed to Wilkes by his associates. At a minimum, the duty of utmost good faith and loyalty would demand that the majority consider that their action was in disregard of a long-standing policy of the stockholders that each would be a director of the corporation and that employment with the corporation would go hand in hand with stock ownership; that Wilkes was one of the four originators of the nursing home venture; and that Wilkes, like the others, had invested his capital and time for more than fifteen years with the expectation that he would continue to participate in corporate decisions. Most important is the plain fact that the cutting off of Wilkes's salary, together with the fact that the corporation never declared a dividend, assured that Wilkes would receive no return at all from the corporation.

The excerpt from *Wilkes* refers to freeze-out transactions whereby the minority shareholders are eliminated from further participation in the business. We have seen this in the partnership context. See Page v. Page, 55 Cal.2d 192, 10 Cal.Rptr. 643, 359 P.2d 41 (1961) set forth at page 67 above and Meinhard v. Salmon, 249 N.Y. 458, 164 N.E. 545 (1928), set forth at page 52 below.

5. The following case also involved termination of employment. It has become one of the leading cases defining the scope of the majority's duty to the minority. The facts read like a script to a soap opera. This is quite common since many closely held concerns are family-run businesses. As a

result, the corporate disputes that arise are merely another venue for airing family discord.[a] It is thus not at all uncommon for the parties' emotions to prevail over rationality.

MEISELMAN v. MEISELMAN

309 N.C. 279, 307 S.E.2d 551 (1983).

FRYE, JUSTICE.

In this appeal, we must determine whether Michael Meiselman, a minority shareholder with a substantial percentage of the outstanding stock in a group of family-owned close corporations, is entitled to relief under N.C.G.S. § 55–125(a)(4) and N.C.G.S. § 55–125.1, the statutes granting trial courts the authority to order dissolution or another more appropriate remedy when "reasonably necessary" for the protection of the "rights or interests" of the complaining shareholder. In so doing, we will articulate for the first time the analysis a trial court is to apply in resolving suits brought under these two statutes. We must also determine whether the trial court erred in concluding that Ira Meiselman, Michael's brother, committed "no actionable breach of fiduciary responsibility" as an officer or director of the defendant corporations through his sole ownership of the stock in a corporation holding a management contract with one of the family corporations.

Michael Meiselman, the plaintiff and complaining minority shareholder in this action, and Ira Meiselman, one of the defendants in this action, are brothers. Michael, the older of the two, was born in 1932 and has never married. Ira was born ten years later. He is married and has two children. The two men are the only surviving children of Mr. H.B. Meiselman, who immigrated to the United States from Austria in 1913. Over the years, Mr. Meiselman accumulated substantial wealth through his development of several family business enterprises. Specifically, Mr. Meiselman invested in and developed movie theaters and real estate. Several of the enterprises were merged into Eastern Federal Corporation [hereinafter referred to as Eastern Federal], a close corporation, most of the stock of which is owned by Ira and Michael. In addition, there are seven other corporations which, together with Eastern Federal, comprise the Meiselman family business and are the corporate defendants in this case.

Beginning in 1951, Mr. Meiselman started a series of *inter vivos* transfers of corporate stock in the various corporations which, generally speaking, he divided equally between his two sons. However, in March 1971 Mr. Meiselman transferred 83,072 shares of stock in Eastern Federal to Ira, while Michael received only 1,966 shares in the corporation. The next month Michael transferred the control of his stock in the family

---

a. It is not surprising that the plaintiffs and defendants in so many of the cases share the same family name (e.g., Galler v. Galler, Ringling v. Ringling, Meiselman v. Meiselman), thus making the table of cases resemble a book on family law.

corporations to his father in trust, a trust Michael could revoke without his father's consent only if he married a Jewish woman.[2]

The effect, then, of these transfers of stock from Mr. Meiselman to his two sons was to give Ira, the younger son, majority shareholder status in Eastern Federal while relegating Michael, the older son, to the position of minority shareholder. In addition, Ira owns a controlling interest in all of the other family corporations except General Shopping Centers, Inc., the corporation in which he and Michael hold an equal number of shares.

Michael owns 29.82 percent of the total shares in the family corporations, although he contends that once the shares attributed to intercorporate ownership (shares the various corporations own in each other) are distributed between himself and Ira, his ownership would amount to about 43 percent of the family business. The book value of all of the corporations was $11,168,778 as of 31 December 1978. The book value of Michael's shares in all of the corporations using the 29.82 percent figure, was $3,330,303 as of that date.

As is true of many close corporations, the two shareholders—Michael and Ira—were employed by the family corporations. Michael began working for the family business in 1956 and Ira began nine years later in 1965. The extent of Michael's participation in the family corporations from 1961 until 1973 is not clear. Michael contends that he has worked continuously for the family business except for an interim of about one and one-half years. Ira would characterize Michael's participation differently. At any rate, both sides agree that from 1973 until 1979 Michael was employed by the family business. It is also clear that Ira fired Michael in September 1979, less than one month after Michael filed suit against Ira in connection with Ira's sole ownership of the stock in a corporation which held a management contract with Eastern Federal.

In the certified letter Ira sent to Michael informing Michael that he was being fired, Ira also notified his brother that his car insurance, his hospital insurance and his life insurance policies were all being terminated. In addition, Ira asked his brother in that same letter to return his "Air Travel credit card" and "any other corporate cards you might have as any further use of them is not authorized." Ira then sent his brother a second certified letter demanding payment within ten days to Eastern Federal of Michael's note of $61,500 plus interest of $2,028.66 and the balance of Michael's open account, $19,000. Furthermore, Lawrence A. Poston, Vice President and Treasurer of Eastern Federal stated that the effect of the letter terminating Michael's employment "also was to terminate Michael's participation in the profit-sharing trust."

In his deposition, Ira essentially admitted that he fired his brother in response to the lawsuit Michael had brought challenging Ira's sole ownership of Republic Management Corporation [hereinafter referred to as Republic], the corporation with which Eastern Federal had contracted to provide management services. However, Ira indicated that Michael's loss

---

2. Michael and his father revoked the trust by agreement in February 1976.

of employment was only an incidental effect of his termination of the employment contract between the two corporations, a corporate decision he felt was justified in light of the threat of continuing litigation on this matter. Ira stated that "[t]he purpose and the effect of the letter [terminating Michael's employment] were principally to advise [Michael] that we were terminating the arrangement between Eastern Federal and Republic and, correspondingly, that it would alter, affect, or eliminate his source of compensation as applied to Republic."

Republic was formed in 1973. As Ira stated, Republic was a "successor to two, or possibly three, previous companies of the same genre that had operated within the family framework back to 1951." Ira also stated that he did not own all of the stock in those predecessor corporations, that "there were some that I remember in the early years that Michael might have owned 100% of that I didn't." The record indicates that Michael was one of the initial shareholders in 1951 of Fran–Mack Management, Inc., one of those predecessor corporations and that Ira did not become a shareholder in that particular corporation until 31 December 1963.

According to Ira, the function of Republic "was to provide a means whereby, primarily now, administrative and primarily home office expenses utilized on behalf of all the companies, or all the individual operating units, were apportioned back to those individual operating units or operating companies." In short, Republic was "nothing more than a tool" through which the administrative costs incurred in operating the various Meiselman business units—including over 30 theaters—were apportioned.

As noted above, Republic agreed to perform these management services as a result of a contract entered into between it and Eastern Federal. Specifically, Republic agreed to perform the management services in exchange for 5.5 percent of Eastern Federal's theater admissions and concession sales. Although Republic paid Michael an annual salary from 1973 until he was fired in 1979, Michael did not own any of the stock in the management corporation; Ira owned all of it. Although Republic earned profits some years while losing money in others, the net result was that it had retained earnings of over $65,000, earnings which only Ira as sole shareholder in Republic would enjoy and in which Michael claims he is entitled to share. It is this ownership to which Michael objects and upon which he bases his shareholder's derivative claim that Ira has breached the fiduciary duty he owes to the corporate defendants.

We turn now to an examination of the tenor of the relationship existing between Michael and Ira. In his brief, Ira contends "[t]he Record on Appeal reflects no bitterness and hostility between Michael and Ira, other than that which Michael generated after Mr. Meiselman's death in an effort to secure a redistribution of his father's patrimony." Further, he contends that "Michael was never denied participation in the management of the corporate defendants," that, on the contrary, Michael "voluntarily limited his participation in their affairs."

On the other hand, Michael vehemently denies Ira's characterization of their relationship and of his participation in the management of the corporations. In his deposition, Michael stated that his job has been "out in the field", and that when he had a recommendation to make he was, for the most part, to report it to his brother. Michael indicated that he was allowed to participate in the management of Eastern Federal in this manner apparently until the corporation entered into the management contract with Republic at issue here. Michael characterized this alleged change in his participation of the management of Eastern Federal as follows:

> My brother had the majority of stock in Eastern Federal Corporation before this management contract. As to whether he had the final say in the control of Eastern Federal Corporation, that is the point. He might have been the final say, but when Republic Management started, I lost all say-so because he wouldn't listen to anybody.

In addition, Michael contends that, among other things, he has not been "allowed to even come up to the office and have [sic] been discouraged in getting the full details as to what they [the companies] borrow"; that Ira "will not let me walk in the office where the film buyer is and talk to him, not even [to] help"; that "theaters are being sold without my knowledge and theaters are being built without my knowledge"; and that "my brother solely and without my consent, not only develops but closes, sells, does anything he wants with all of the properties." Finally, Michael claims that although he previously worked 60 to 70 hours a week, he has been "discouraged systematically over a number of years to where I cannot exert the time and effort that I want to."

In examining the record we are struck by the tone of Ira's comments when referring to his dealings with his brother. Indeed, many of his statements indicate that although Michael may not have been actively prevented from entering the corporate offices, his participation in the decision-making carried on within those offices was less than welcome. For example, in testifying that Michael has never been barred from the home offices of the company, Ira stated that Michael "has exercised the privilege of going there on frequent occasions, *unannounced,* whenever he felt like it." (Emphasis added). He also stated that "[w]e have never failed, *when he is entitled to notice,* to give him adequate notice of stockholders' meetings." (Emphasis added). Furthermore, in a letter to Michael's lawyer concerning, among other things, the possibility of Michael's serving on the boards of directors of the family enterprises, Ira's lawyer stated that, "[w]e have no desire to see the productive efforts of the boards be affected by possibly allowing them to function as a forum for airing personal hurts and slights; and we all recognize that the course of business activity for the companies is not going to be altered by Michael's representation."

Apparently in an attempt to further support his contention that Michael has never been excluded from participating in the management of the corporations, Ira testified that two corporate decisions were made or changed on the basis of objections Michael had lodged. In describing the abandonment of a proposed merger to which Michael had objected, Ira testified as follows:

I don't mean to belittle him. In one of those instances, as a sign we were not completely ignoring him, we made some changes. Specifically, I know of one single complaint and that was a proposed merger of some of these defendants [in] 1976, regarding a real estate company similar to our previous merger with Eastern Federal. Unfortunately, my timing was very poor because he was taking his first what he called his pre-test, I'm not sure, I guess it's preparation for the bar exam. He did very poorly with it and it came at the same time, and he just raised cain with me.

The second corporate action to which Michael objected was Ira's sole ownership of the stock in Republic. Ira contends that he terminated the management contract between Republic and Eastern Federal (and in so doing fired Michael) in response to Michael's objections to Ira's sole ownership of Republic. We note, however, that in responding to Michael's objections, Ira terminated the employment contract between the two corporations, and, thus, Michael's employment, even though it was Ira's sole ownership of the stock in Republic and not the contract between Republic and Eastern Federal which was the source of their disagreement.

Perhaps most indicative of the tenor of the relationship between the two brothers is Ira's comment that "[y]es, it is my position in this case that my brother, Michael, suffers as stated there [in defendant's brief] from crippling mental disorders and that was a reason that my father put me in control of the family corporations." Apparently in support of his allegations that his brother suffers from "crippling mental disorders", Ira presented evidence of an argument Michael had with his father which took place about 20 years ago during which Mr. Meiselman castigated Michael for having a non-Jewish woman at a family function. In addition, Ira testified to another fight which occurred between himself and Michael after he had failed to invite Michael to a football game to which all of the males in the family traditionally had been invited.

Finally, it appears the history of this litigation itself indicates a breakdown of the personal relationship between Michael and Ira. In June 1978, about two months after their father's death, Michael and Ira began negotiations in an effort to work out their differences. Over one year later, in August 1979, Michael filed suit. He was fired the next month. In short, this litigation and the tensions inherent in such activity have been going on for over four years now. * * *

The trial court denied both of Michael's claims. Michael then appealed to the Court of Appeals. In its well written majority opinion, the Court of Appeals interpreted N.C.G.S. § 55–125(a)(4) as authorizing liquidation in cases where the complaining shareholder has shown that "basic 'fairness' compels dissolution." The Court of Appeals concluded that the complaining shareholder is not required to show "bad faith, mismanagement or wrongful conduct, but only real harm." *Id.* In finding "a plethora of evidence to suggest that Ira's actions have irreparably harmed Michael," the Court of Appeals further concluded that the trial court "misapplied the applicable law *and* abused its discretion by concluding that relief, other than dissolution, under G.S. 55–125.1 was not reasonably necessary for Michael's protection." In so doing it reversed the trial court judgment and remanded the case to the trial court "for the determination of an appropriate remedy under G.S. 55–125.1 that is reasonably necessary to protect Michael's rights and interests."

In addition, the Court of Appeals also determined that the trial court erred in concluding that Ira had not breached the fiduciary duty he owes to the corporate defendants through his sole ownership of Republic. It reversed the judgment of the trial court on this derivative claim and remanded the case to the trial court "for entry of judgment on behalf of the defendant corporation against Ira, as sole owner of Republic, in the total amount of the profits accumulated to date in Republic plus interest and cost of this action." *Id.* * * *

We note at the outset that the enterprises with which we are dealing are close corporations, not publicly held corporations. This distinction is crucial because the two types of corporations are functionally quite different. Indeed, the commentators all appear to agree that "[c]lose corporations are often little more than incorporated partnerships." Comment, *Oppression as a Statutory Ground for Corporate Dissolution,* 1965 Duke L.J. 128, 138 (1965) [hereinafter cited as Comment, *Oppression*]. *See also* 2 F. O'Neal, *Close Corporations* § 9.02 (2d ed. 1971); Hetherington and Dooley, *Illiquidity and Exploitation: A Proposed Statutory Solution to the Remaining Close Corporation Problem,* 63 Va.L.Rev. 1, 2 (1977); Israels, *The Sacred Cow of Corporate Existence: Problems of Deadlock and Dissolution,* 19 U.Chi.L.Rev. 778, 778–79 (1952); Comment, *Deadlock and Dissolution in the Close Corporation: Has the Sacred Cow Been Butchered?,* 58 Neb.L.Rev. 791, 796 (1979) [hereinafter cited as Comment, *Deadlock and Dissolution*].

Israels, a recognized expert in this area, succinctly defines a close corporation as a "corporate entity typically organized by an individual, or a group of individuals, seeking the recognized advantages of incorporation, limited liability, perpetual existence and easy transferability of interests— but regarding themselves basically as partners and seeking veto powers as among themselves much more akin to the partnership relation than to the statutory scheme of representative corporate government." Israels, *supra,* at 778–79.

This characterization of close corporations as little more than "incorporated partnerships" rests primarily on the fact that the "relationship between the participants [in a close corporation], like that among partners, is one which requires close cooperation and a high degree of good faith and mutual respect. . . ." 2 F. O'Neal, *Close Corporations* § 9.02. Indeed, one commentator noted that "[a]n organizational structure of this nature—in which the investment interests are interwoven with continuous, often daily, interaction among the principals—necessarily requires substantial trust among the individuals." Comment, *Deadlock and Dissolution, supra,* at 795.

Professor O'Neal, perhaps the foremost authority on close corporations, points out that many close corporations are companies based on personal relationships that give rise to certain "reasonable expectations" on the part of those acquiring an interest in the close corporation. Those "reasonable expectations" include, for example, the parties' expectation that they will participate in the management of the business or be employed by the company. O'Neal, *Close Corporations: Existing Legislation and Recommended Reform,* 33 Bus.Law 873, 885 (1978). Other commentators have also noted that those investing in close corporations have some of these same "reasonable expectations." ... Comment, *Dissolution Under the California Corporations Code: A Remedy for Minority Shareholders,* 22 U.C.L.A.L.Rev. 595, 616 (1975) [hereinafter cited as Comment, *Dissolution Under the California Corporations Code*].

Thus, when personal relations among the participants in a close corporation break down, the "reasonable expectations" the participants had, for example, an expectation that their employment would be secure, or that they would enjoy meaningful participation in the management of the business—become difficult if not impossible to fulfill. In other words, when the personal relationships among the participants break down, the majority shareholder, because of his greater voting power, is in a position to terminate the minority shareholder's employment and to exclude him from participation in management decisions.

Some may argue that the minority shareholder should have bargained for greater protection before agreeing to accept his minority shareholder position in a close corporation. However, the practical realities of this particular business situation oftentimes do not allow for such negotiations. In his article, *Special Characteristics, Problems, and Needs of the Close Corporation,* 1969 U.Ill.L.F. 1 (1969), Professor Hetherington, another recognized authority in this field, explains the situation as follows:

> ... the circumstances under which a party takes a minority stock position in a close corporation vary widely. Many involve situations where the minority party, because of lack of awareness of the risks, or because of the weakness of his bargaining position, fails to negotiate for protection. Probably a common instance of this kind occurs where an employee or an outsider is given an opportunity to buy stock in a close corporation wholly or substantially owned by a single stockholder or a small group of associates, often a family. Typically, the controlling individual or group retains a substantial majority position. The opportunity to buy into the business is highly valued by the recipient; his enthusiasm and weak bargaining position make it unlikely almost to a certainty that he will ask for—let alone insist upon—protection for his position as a minority stockholder. Pur-

chases of stock in such situations are likely to be arranged without either party consulting a lawyer. The result is the assumption of a minority stock position without, or with only limited, appreciation of the risks involved.

In short, then, the "minority shareholder who acquired his shares to secure his position with the firm may have lacked sufficient bargaining power to force the majority to agree to terms which would enable him to protect his interests." Comment, *Dissolution Under the California Corporations Code, supra,* at 603–04. Indeed, as one commentator notes, "close corporations are often formed by friends or family members who simply may not believe that disagreements could ever arise." *Id.* Furthermore, when a minority shareholder receives his shares in a close corporation from another in the form of a gift or inheritance, as did plaintiff here, the minority shareholder never had the opportunity to negotiate for any sort of protection with respect to the "reasonable expectations" he had or hoped to enjoy in the close corporation.

Unfortunately, when dissension develops in such a situation, as Professor O'Neal notes, "American courts traditionally have been reluctant to interfere in the internal affairs of corporations...." F. O'Neal, *Oppression of Minority Shareholders* § 9.04, at 582 (1975). This reluctance, as applied to a minority shareholder holding an interest in a close corporation, places the minority shareholder in a remediless situation. As Professor O'Neal points out, when the personal relationship among the participants in a close corporation breaks down, the minority shareholder has neither the power to dissolve the business unit at will, as does a partner in a partnership, nor does he have the "way out" which is open to a shareholder in a publicly held corporation, the opportunity to sell his shares on the open market. 2 F. O'Neal, *Close Corporations* § 9.02. Thus, the illiquidity of a minority shareholder's interest in a close corporation renders him vulnerable to exploitation by the majority shareholders. *E.g.,* Hetherington and Dooley, *supra,* at 3–6. Professor Hetherington, succinctly outlines in one of his articles the uniquely vulnerable position a minority shareholder occupies in a close corporation:

> The right of the majority to control the enterprise achieves a meaning and has an impact in close corporations that it has in no other major form of business organization under our law. Only in the close corporation does the power to manage carry with it the de facto power to allocate the benefits of ownership arbitrarily among the shareholders and to discriminate against a minority whose investment is imprisoned in the enterprise. The essential basis of this power in the close corporation is the inability of those so excluded from the benefits of proprietorship to withdraw their investment at will. The power to withdraw one's capital from a publicly held corporation or from a partnership is unqualified in the sense that the participant's right is not dependent upon misconduct by the management or upon the occurrence of any other event. The shareholder or partner can withdraw his capital for any or no reason.

Hetherington, *supra,* at 21.

According to Professor O'Neal, the "two principal conceptualistic barriers to the courts' granting relief to aggrieved shareholders" in such a situation are: "(1) the principle of majority rule in corporate management and (2) the business judgment rule." F. O'Neal, *Oppression of Minority Shareholders* § 9.04 at 582. In explaining the inapplicability of the legal construct firmly established in corporate law that when out voted the minority must submit to the will of the majority, he writes as follows:

> Apparently without close examination, courts accord the principle of majority rule the same sanctity in corporate enterprises, including small businesses, that it enjoys in the political world. The principle of majority rule is in traditional legal thought a firmly established attribute of the corporate form. Yet not uncommonly a person, unsophisticated in business and financial matters, invests all his assets in a closely held enterprise with an expectation, often reasonable under the circumstances even in the absence of express contract, that he will be a key employee in the company and will have a voice in business decisions. Thus, when courts apply the principle of majority rule in close corporations, they often disappoint the reasonable expectations of the participants.

Id. at 582–83.

In short, then, when the courts fail to provide a remedy for a minority shareholder whose "reasonable expectations" have been disappointed in the close corporation situation, the court, in effect, "compels a continuation of the association by legal constraint—what was once called 'togetherness by injunction'—a prospect which scarcely seems a desirable policy goal." Hetherington, *supra,* at 29. In other words, an "insistence that the antagonistic parties resolve their differences within the corporate framework" would seem "inconsistent with the traditional hesitance of courts of equity to enforce unwelcome personal relationships." Note, *Corporations—Dissolution, supra,* at 1463.

Apparently in response to these commentators' uniform calls for reform in this area of corporate law, many state legislatures have enacted statutes giving the tribunals in their states the power to grant relief to minority shareholders under more liberal circumstances. For example, at least seven states have given their courts the authority to grant dissolution of a corporation when the acts of the directors or those in control of the corporation are "oppressive" to the shareholders.

In interpreting the term "oppressive" as used in its dissolution statute, a New York Trial Court recently held in a case of first impression that where two controlling shareholders discharged the minority shareholder as an employee and officer of the two corporations in which he had an interest, thus severely damaging the minority shareholder's "reasonable expectations", their actions were deemed to be "oppressive" under New York Law.

Furthermore, the Supreme Court of Illinois affirmed a Superior Court decree of dissolution where one shareholder was deemed to have engaged in "oppressive" conduct within the meaning of its dissolution statute in depriving the other shareholders of participation in the management of the corporation. *Gidwitz v. Lanzit Corrugated Box Co.,* 20 Ill.2d 208, 220, 170 N.E.2d 131, 138 (1960). In defining the term "oppressive" in *Gidwitz,* the Supreme Court of Illinois wrote that the "word does not necessarily savor of fraud, and the absence of 'mismanagement, or misapplication of assets,' does not prevent a finding that the conduct of the dominant directors or officers has been oppressive." The court also stated that the term is "not synonymous with 'illegal' and 'fraudulent' ".

Similarly, at least three states have statutes authorizing a court to grant dissolution when those in control of the corporation are guilty of treating the corporate shareholders "unfairly".

In helping to establish this growing trend toward enactment of more liberal grounds under which dissolution will be granted to a complaining shareholder, the legislature in this State enacted in 1955 N.C.G.S. § 55–125(a)(4), the statute granting superior court judges the "power to liquidate the assets and business of a corporation in an action by a shareholder when it is established" that "[l]iquidation is reasonably necessary for the protection of the rights or interests of the complaining shareholder". Two other states have similar statutes—California and New York. Cal.Corp. Code § 1800(b)(5) (West 1977) (formerly § 4651(f)); N.Y.Bus.Corp.Law § 1104–a(b)(2) (McKinney Cum.Supp.1983). Indeed, one of the members of the drafting committee of the new Business Corporation Act, the Act which included N.C.G.S. § 55–125(a)(4), stated that in drafting the Act the committee "drew heavily on the Model Act of the American Bar Association and on the corporation laws of other states, particularly California and Ohio." Latty, *The History, Purpose, Spirit and Philosophy of the New Act, North Carolina Corporation Manual* (1960) (emphasis added). Furthermore, in commenting upon the new Act, Professor Latty stated that "[t]here would seem, then, to be no reason under the new Act for a court to approach the problem of liquidation of the business of a close corporation with substantially more conservatism than it would show in dissolving a partnership, free from any carry-over of the 'sacred cow' tradition of corporate existence." Latty, *The Close Corporation and the New North Carolina Business Corporation Act,* 34 N.C.L.Rev. 432, 449–50 (1956).

In interpreting the provision of its corporate dissolution statute which provides that such relief will be ordered where "liquidation is reasonably necessary for the protection of the rights or interests" of the shareholders, a California Appellate Court affirmed in *Stumpf v. C.E. Stumpf & Sons, Inc.,* 47 Cal.App.3d 230, 120 Cal.Rptr. 671 (1975), a trial court's conclusion that relief was appropriate when supported by the following evidence: "The hostility between the two brothers had grown so extreme that respondent severed contact with his family and was allowed no say in the operation of the business. After respondent's withdrawal from the business, he received no salary, dividends, or other revenue from his investment in the corporation." *See also In re the Application of Topper*, 433 N.Y.S.2d at 366 ("rights and interests" of a minority shareholder in a close corporation "derive from the expectations of the parties and special circumstances that underlie the formation of close corporations").

In short, then, it appears that these new statutory schemes which permit involuntary dissolution of corporations pursuant to actions brought by minority shareholders—and which "virtually every state has"—"represent a concerted effort and recognition by the states that the perpetual existence of the corporate structure at common law is ill suited to the functional realities of the closely held corporation." Comment, *Deadlock and Dissolution, supra* at 793. However, it is important to recognize that the statutes in question apply to *all* corporations, not just "close" corporations. Of course, "the rights or interests of the complaining shareholder" will vary according to the circumstances, including the circumstance of the nature of the corporation, whether public or a close corporation. Likewise, whether liquidation (or some alternate form of relief) "is reasonably necessary for the protection of" those "rights or interests" will also depend, to a great extent, on whether the corporation is a public corporation or a close corporation. * * *

The basic question at issue is what standard we should adopt to determine whether a minority shareholder is entitled to dissolution or other relief. The statutes require a standard in which all of the circumstances surrounding the parties are considered in deciding whether relief should be granted and, if so, the nature and method of such relief.

When a shareholder brings suit seeking relief under N.C.G.S. § 55–125(a)(4) and N.C.G.S. § 55–125.1, he has the burden of proving that his "rights or interests" as a shareholder are being contravened. However, once the shareholder has established this, the trial court, in deciding whether to grant relief, "must exercise its equitable discretion, and consider the actual benefit and injury to [all of] the shareholders resulting from dissolution" or other possible relief. *Henry George & Sons, Inc. v. Cooper–George, Inc.,* 95 Wash.2d 944, 632 P.2d 512, 516 (1981). "The question is essentially one for resolution through the familiar balancing process and flexible remedial resources of courts of equity." *Id.* To hold otherwise would allow a plaintiff to demand at will dissolution of a corporation or a forced buy out of his shares or other relief at the expense of the corporation and without regard to the rights and interests of the other shareholders.

Michael, as the complaining shareholder in this case, brought an action under N.C.G.S. § 55–125(a), the statutory provision which articulates four situations, one of which must be "established" before a Superior Court Judge has the power to liquidate a corporation in an action brought by a shareholder. Specifically, N.C.G.S. § 55–125(a) provides as follows:

The superior court shall have power to liquidate the assets and business of a corporation in an action by a shareholder when it is established that:

(1) The directors are deadlocked in the management of the corporate affairs and the shareholders are unable to break the deadlock, so that the business can no longer be conducted to the advantage of all the shareholders; or

(2) The shareholders are deadlocked in voting power, otherwise than by virtue of special provisions or arrangements designed to create veto power among the shareholders, and for that reason have been unable at two consecutive annual meetings to elect successors to directors whose terms had expired; or

(3) All of the present shareholders are parties to, or are transferees or subscribers of shares with actual notice of a written agreement, whether embodied in the charter or separate therefrom, entitling the complaining shareholder to liquidation or dissolution of the corporation at will or upon the occurrence of some event which has subsequently occurred; or

(4) Liquidation is reasonably necessary for the protection of the rights or interests of the complaining shareholder.

Michael alleged that he was entitled to relief under subsection (4); in effect, he is claiming that liquidation is "reasonably necessary" for the protection of his "rights or interests." However, before it can be determined whether, in any given case, it has been "established" that liquidation is "reasonably necessary" to protect the complaining shareholder's "rights or interests," the particular "rights or interests" of the complaining shareholder must be articulated. This is so because N.C.G.S. § 55–125(a)(4) refers to the "rights or interests" of "*the complaining shareholder*;" the statute does not refer to the "rights or interests" of shareholders generally. Therefore, the "rights or interests" which Michael has in these family-run, close corporations must be determined with reference to the specific facts in this case. In so doing, we hold that a complaining shareholder's "rights or interests" in a close corporation include the "reasonable expectations" the complaining shareholder has in the corporation. These "reasonable expectations" are to be ascertained by examining the entire history of the participants' relationship. That history will include the "reasonable expectations" created at the inception of the participants' relationship; those "reasonable expectations" as altered over time; and the "reasonable expectations" which develop as the participants engage in a course of dealing in conducting the affairs of the corporation. The interests and views of the other participants must be considered in determining "reasonable expectations." The key is "*reasonable*." In order for plaintiff's expectations to be reasonable, they must be known to or assumed by the other shareholders and concurred in by them. Privately held expectations which are not made known to the other participants are not "reasonable." Only expectations embodied in understandings, express or implied, among the participants should be recognized by the court. Hillman, *The Dissatisfied Participant in the Solvent Business Venture: A Consideration of the Relative Permanence of Partnerships and Close Corporations,* 67 Minn.L.Rev. 1, 77–81 (1983). Also, only substantial expectations should be considered and this must be determined on a case-by-case basis. These requirements provide needed protection to potential defendants in this type case.

In short, then, the "rights or interests" of a shareholder in any given case will not necessarily be the same "rights or interests" of any other shareholder. An articulation of those "rights or interests" will necessarily require a case-by-case determination based on an examination of the entire history of the participants' relationship—an examination not only of the "expectations generated by the participants' original business bargain," but also of the "history of the participants' relationship as expectations alter and new expectations develop over the course of the participants' cooperative efforts in operating the business." O'Neal, *supra,* at 888. In so holding, we recognize the rule that Professor O'Neal suggests should be applied in a corporation based on a "personal relationship":

> [A] court should give relief, dissolution or some other remedy to a minority shareholder whenever corporate managers or controlling shareholders act in a way that disappoints the minority shareholder's reasonable expectations, even though the acts of the managers or controlling shareholders fall within the literal scope of powers or rights granted them by the corporation act or the corporation's charter or bylaws.
>
> The reasonable expectations of the shareholders, as they exist at the inception of the enterprise, and as they develop thereafter through a course of dealing concurred in by all of them, is perhaps the most reliable guide to a just solution of a dispute among shareholders, at least a dispute among shareholders in the typical close corporation. In a close corporation, the corporation's charter and bylaws almost never reflect the full business bargain of the participants.

O'Neal, *supra,* at 886.

After articulating the "rights or interests" of the complaining shareholder, the trial court is then to determine if liquidation is "reasonably necessary" for the protection of those "rights or interests". * * *

In sum, therefore, we hold that under N.C.G.S. § 55–125(a)(4) a trial court is: (1) to define the "rights or interests" the complaining shareholder has in the corporation; and (2) to determine whether some form of relief is "reasonably necessary" for the protection of those "rights or interests". For plaintiff to obtain relief under the expectations analysis, he must prove that (1) he had one or more substantial reasonable expectations known or assumed by the other participants; (2) the expectation has been frustrated; (3) the frustration was without fault of plaintiff and was in large part beyond his control; and (4) under all of the circumstances of the case plaintiff is entitled to some form of equitable relief.

We will now review the "rights or interests" each party contends Michael has in the family corporations. Michael suggests in his brief that the "rights or interests" he has as a shareholder in these close corporations include "rights or interests" in secure employment, fringe benefits which flow from his association with the corporations, and meaningful participation in the management of the family business. As noted above, several commentators have suggested that the "reasonable expectations" of shareholders in close corporations often include some of these same "rights or interests". Further, Michael indicates that these "rights or interests" are in need of protection: Michael was fired from his job after suing his brother; his fringe benefits were terminated at that time as well; he has been "systematically" excluded from any meaningful participation in management decisions apparently since the inception of the management contract between Eastern Federal and Republic.

Defendants argue, however, that Michael, as a shareholder, is only entitled to relief if his traditional shareholder rights have been infringed. They contend that those traditional shareholder rights include the right to notice of stockholders' meetings, the right to vote cumulatively, the right of access to the corporate offices and to corporate financial information, and the right to compel the payment of dividends. Because these rights have not been violated, they argue, Michael is not entitled to relief. Indeed, defendants contend that the dividends distributed to Michael have been generous.

While it may be true that a shareholder in, for example, a publicly held corporation may have "rights or interests" defined as defendants argue, a shareholder's rights in a closely held corporation may not necessarily be so narrowly defined. In short, we hold that the shareholder in this case—one who owns stock worth well over $3,000,000 and which accounts for a 30 to 40 percent ownership in these closely held, family-run corporations worth well over $11,000,000 and who also has been employed by the corporations, provided with fringe benefits, and, to some extent, allowed to participate in management decisions—has "rights or interests" more broadly defined than defendants contend. Put another way, Michael's "reasonable expectations" are not as limited as defendants contend.

Again, we note that N.C.G.S. § 55–125(a)(4) speaks in terms of the "rights or interests" of *"the complaining shareholder."* Thus, those "rights or interests" must be defined with reference to the "rights or interests" the complaining shareholder has under the facts of the particular case—the "reasonable expectations" the participants' relationship has generated. Indeed, the legislature would not have had reason to enact N.C.G.S. § 55–125(a)(4) if "rights or interests" were to always comprise only the traditional shareholder rights: other statutes already address the traditional rights and remedies to which shareholders have been entitled. *See e.g.,* N.C.G.S. § 55–62(a) (notice of shareholder's meetings); N.C.G.S. § 55–67(c) (right to cumulative voting); N.C.G.S. § 55–37(a)(4) and

N.C.G.S. § 55–38(b) (right to examine books and records); and N.C.G.S. § 55–50(*l*) and (m) (right to compel payment of dividends). * * *

Because the trial court's findings of fact failed to address the "rights or interests" Michael has in these family corporations, we must remand the case to the trial court for an evidentiary hearing to resolve this issue. On remand, after hearing the evidence, the trial court is to: (1) articulate specifically Michael's "rights or interests"—his "reasonable expectations"—in the corporate defendants; and (2) determine if these "rights or interests" are in need of protection, and, thus, that relief of some sort should be granted. In addition, the trial court is to prescribe the form of relief which the evidence indicates is most appropriate, should it find that relief is warranted. In remanding this case for an evidentiary hearing and new findings, we need not address the issue of whether the trial court abused its discretion in refusing to grant relief to Michael. * * *

[The breach of fiduciary duty claim is discussed in Chapter 8]

MARTIN, JUSTICE, concurring in the result.

Except as herein set forth, I concur in the majority opinion. There are, however, certain aspects of the case that should be discussed that the majority does not address. In determining whether plaintiff's expectations have been frustrated, the actions of all the participants, including plaintiff, must be considered. The majority fails to address this aspect of the case. * * *

In determining whether to grant equitable relief under N.C.G.S. 55–125.1, the trial court must consider all the circumstances of the case. If it is determined that plaintiff's rights or interests require protection because of plaintiff's own conduct, it would be improper to grant equitable relief. He who seeks equity must do equity. The reasons *why* the complaining shareholder's interests require protection is highly relevant in the resolution of the case.

The court should also consider what effect the granting of relief will have upon the corporation and other shareholders. Will it interfere with the corporation's ability to attract financing for its business? Will it interfere with its ability to attract additional capital? Will it require burdensome financing upon the corporation or the shareholders? Will it interfere with the rights of creditors? If a buy-out of plaintiff's shares is forced upon the company, it may be far from painless. If it is determined that the granting of relief will be unduly burdensome to the corporation or other shareholders, the trial court should consider this in determining whether to grant relief and, if so, whether this should affect the purchase price or value attached to plaintiff's shares or the method of payment. It is an equitable proceeding.

Another circumstance to be considered is whether plaintiff's condition is a result of oppression or bad conduct by the other shareholders. Oppression for these purposes may be defined as: burdensome, harsh and wrongful conduct; a lack of fair dealing in the affairs of the company to the detriment of other shareholders; a violation of fair play on which every shareholder is entitled to rely. In making this determination, the court will consider the substance of the conduct rather than its form.

Oppression in this context is close to a breach of fiduciary duty. The West Virginia Supreme Court, in a "reasonable expectations" case, analyzed oppression from the point of view of breach of a fiduciary duty. It held in substance that oppressive conduct in a close corporation is closely related to the fiduciary duty of good faith and fair dealing owed by majority stockholders to minority stockholders.

In this connection, I cannot agree that merely because plaintiff's expectations were not fulfilled it necessarily follows that the majority stockholders were guilty of oppression.

Another circumstance to be considered is the fact that most, if not all, of plaintiff's stock was given to him by his father. He did not contribute his own hard-earned cash to the enterprise. This could indicate that he did not assume the risk of having his investment held hostage by the majority, or it could be that one has to accept what one gets by gift—in this case, a locked-in minority interest in a family corporation. * * *

Branch, C.J., and Copeland, J., join in this concurring opinion.

Notes

1. In Baker v. Commercial Body Builders, Inc. 264 Or. 614, 507 P.2d 387 (1973), the court took a more narrow view of what constitutes oppression of a minority shareholder in a close corporation. There, the court held that oppression would require a serious breach of good faith and fair dealing such as plundering the corporation. A single act would not constitute oppression unless it caused serious damage to the minority. The focus of the court in *Baker* was on the conduct of those in control and not the expectation of the minority. Most states, including the Model Business Corporation Act, provide that "oppression" by the majority may be grounds for dissolution. Does the *Meiselman* "reasonable expectations" analysis have equal effect under these oppression statutes? For an affirmative answer to this question, see, e.g., Matter of Kemp & Beatley, Inc., 64 N.Y.2d 63, 484 N.Y.S.2d 799, 473 N.E.2d 1173 (1984); Bonvavita v. Corbo, 300 N.J.Super. 179, 692 A.2d 119 (1996).

2. *Which expectations are reasonable?* Do you agree with the suggestion of the concurring opinion in Meiselmann that Michael had no expectation of anything beyond a minority interest in a corporation that was a gift from a father who wanted Ira to control the company? Assume a minority stockholder in a corporation is working and receiving compensation but decides to retire. The company replaces her at the same level of compensation with an employee that is not a stockholder. What is the retiring stockholder entitled to thereafter? Not every employment relationship in the closely held corporation will create reasonable expectations of continued employment. Consider the reasoning of the Massachusetts court in Merola v. Exergen Corp., 423 Mass. 461, 668 N.E.2d 351 (1996):

Principles of employment law permit the termination of employees at will, with or without cause excepting situations within a narrow public policy exception. However, the termination of a minority shareholder's employment may present a situation where the majority interest has breached its fiduciary duty to the minority interest . . . . .

Here, although the plaintiff invested in the stock of Exergen with the reasonable expectation of continued employment, there was no general policy regarding stock ownership and employment, and there was no evidence that any other stockholders had expectations of continuing employment because they purchased stock. The investment in the stock was an investment in the equity of the corporation which was not tied to employment in any formal way. The plaintiff acknowledged that he could have purchased 5,000 shares of stock while he was working part time before resigning from his position at Analogic Corporation and accepting full-time employment at Exergen. He testified that he was induced to work for Exergen with the promise that he could become a major stockholder. There was no testimony that he was ever required to buy stock as a condition of employment.

Unlike the *Wilkes* case, there was no evidence that the corporation distributed all profits to shareholders in the form of salaries. On the contrary, the perceived value of the stock increased during the time that the plaintiff was employed. The plaintiff first purchased his stock at $2.25 per share and, one year later, he purchased more for $5 per share. This indicated that there was some increase in value to the investment independent of the employment expectation. Neither was the plaintiff a founder of the business, his stock purchases were made after the business was established, and there was no suggestion that he had to purchase stock to keep his job.

The plaintiff testified that, when he sold his stock back to the corporation in 1991, he was paid $17 per share. This was a price that had been paid to other shareholders who sold their shares to the corporation at a previous date, and it is a price which, after consulting with his attorney, he concluded was a fair price. With this payment, the plaintiff realized a significant return on his capital investment independent of the salary he received as an employee.

We conclude that this is not a situation where the majority shareholder breached his fiduciary duty to a minority shareholder. "[T]he controlling group in a close corporation must have some room to maneuver in establishing the business policy of the corporation." Wilkes v. Springside Nursing Home, Inc., 370 Mass. 842, 353 N.E.2d 657. Although there was no legitimate business purpose for the termination of the plaintiff, neither was the termination for the financial gain of Pompei or contrary to established public policy. Not every discharge of an at-will employee of a close corporation who happens to own stock in the corporation gives rise to a successful breach of fiduciary duty claim. The plaintiff was terminated in accordance with his employment contract and fairly compensated for his stock. He failed to establish a sufficient basis for a breach of fiduciary duty claim under the principles of *Donahue v. Rodd Electrotype Co.*

3. *Differing objectives.* Even if we put aside the family strife in *Meiselman,* there are significant differences in the expectations of the shareholders that point out some poignant problems applicable to any business enterprise. Because of their family situations and life-styles, Michael and Ira had different investment objectives. Ira, with a family, wanted to build the value of the business in order to maximize what he could pass on to his children. Michael, on the other hand was a bachelor with no desire to amass wealth beyond his life. Instead, it was in his interest to maximize payouts from the business to the shareholders. Both are equally valid albeit mutually exclusive investment objectives—capital appreciation and maximizing cash outflow to the owners. Either choice would ordinarily lie within the sound discretion of the board of directors. Similar divergence in investment objectives are commonplace when forming closely held concerns—whether they be LLCs or closely-held corporations. The *Meiselman* case demonstrates the desirability of confronting these issues at the outset when organizing the enterprise and assuring that the reasonable expectations of the parties are contained in well drawn agreements and/or bylaws.

4. *Applicability to Limited Liability Companies.* The fiduciary obligations in *Donahue* and *Meiselman* are based on analogy to partnership law. What basis, if any, is there for finding a different standard of conduct applicable to dealings between members in limited liability companies? *See, e.g., Robert W. Hillman,* Law, Culture, and The Lore of Partnership: of Entrepreneurs, Accountability, and The Evolving Status of Partners, 40 Wake Forest L. Rev. 793 (2005); Douglas K. Moll, Minority Oppression & the Limited Liability Company: Learning (or Not) From Close Corporation History, 40 Wake Forest L. Rev. 883 (2005).

5. *Contracting out of fiduciary duties.* To what extent may a majority shareholder contract out of her fiduciary duties to the minority? *Cf., e.g.,* Neubauer v. Goldfarb, 108 Cal.App.4th 47, 133 Cal.Rptr.2d 218 (2003) (purported waiver of majority shareholders' fiduciary duties was void as against public policy).

6. In Nixon v. Blackwell, 626 A.2d 1366 (Del. 1993), *see also* note 1, page 534 below, the Delaware Supreme Court held that if a Delaware corporation wants the special judicial treatment given to closely held concerns, the corporation must elect to be treated as a close corporation under section 344 of the Delaware Corporation Act. Should this ruling be extended to preclude recognition of the heightened fiduciary duties described in the *Donahue* and *Meiselman* decisions?

SECTION 2. VOTING AGREEMENTS

RINGLING v. RINGLING BROS.–BARNUM & BAILEY COMBINED SHOWS, INC.

49 A.2d 603 (Del.Ch.1946), modified 53 A.2d 441 (Del.1947).

SEITZ, VICE-CHANCELLOR.

Petitioner in this proceeding contests the validity of the election of directors and officers of the defendant corporation which took place at its annual stockholders' and directors' meetings held this year.[a]

At all times here involved, the 1000 shares of authorized and issued common stock of the defendant corporation, Ringling Bros.-Barnum & Bailey Combined Shows, Inc. (hereafter called the 'defendant corporation' or the 'corporation'), were owned or controlled as follows:

Edith Conway Ringling—petitioner—315 shares

Aubrey B. Haley—a defendant—315 shares

John Ringling North—a defendant—370 shares.

These shares of stock which possessed cumulative voting rights were all registered in the individual names of the parties set forth above, or in their names in a representative capacity. It is undisputed, however, that these parties were the beneficial owners of the number of shares recited.

The other individual defendants are named because they constitute the remaining persons whose title to office is brought into question by this proceeding. Since certain of the named defendants are obviously sympathetic to petitioner's case, I shall when referring to 'defendants', intend to encompass only those whose position is truly antagonistic.

The defendant corporation's certificate of incorporation provides for a board of seven directors and its by-laws require the holding of the annual stockholders' meeting at the corporation's offices in New York City, or such other place as should be designated in the notice of meeting. The Circus business operated by the defendant corporation forms a well-known feature of the American scene. All the stockholders and all the other persons involved in this litigation are intimately connected with the affairs of the corporate defendant.

On or about September 15, 1941, the petitioner, Edith Conway Ringling, and the defendant Aubrey B. Haley (then Aubrey B. Ringling) admittedly executed in Evanston, Illinois, a writing entitled 'Memorandum of Agreement', dated September 15, 1941. Since the entire controver-

---

[a]. The dispute that arose with the Haleys was a result of a fire that broke out on July 6, 1944 during a circus performance at Hartford Connecticut. The fire claimed the lives of 168 individuals present at the performance. James Haley, the circus's vice president, was jailed after he pleaded no contest to charges of involuntary manslaughter in connection with that disaster. Haley thought he had been treated unfairly by other family members during that crisis, and the Haleys decided to join forces with John Ringling North. Ernest J. Albrecht, A Ringling By Any Other Name, The Story of John Ringling North and His Circus 150–159 (1989). [eds.]

sy before the court revolves around the legal efficacy, if any, of the Memorandum of Agreement (hereafter called 'Agreement'), it is necessary to narrate the substance of the provisions of this Agreement somewhat at the expense of brevity.

The Agreement recites that each of the two parties owned 300 shares of the defendant corporation's stock and 300 shares of stock of Circus City Zoological Gardens, Incorporated (hereafter called 'Circus City'); that certificates therefor were on deposit under a voting trust agreement dated June 24, 1938, and that the parties held voting trust certificates therefor. It is further recited that the certificates representing the 600 shares of Circus City stock were on deposit as collateral security with the John Ringling Estate to secure the payment of a note executed by the two corporations, and held by that Estate, and that upon its payment, the parties would each be entitled to voting trust certificates representing 300 shares of stock. Further, it is set forth that each party also owned individually 15 shares of stock in each of the named corporations.

The Agreement then says that the voting trust agreements will terminate October 22, 1947, or earlier, should the corporation pay the promissory note heretofore mentioned, and should the corporate defendant pay a certain designated indebtedness which it had incurred. Finally, it is recited that the parties in April 1934 entered into an agreement providing for joint action in matters affecting their ownership of stock and interest in the corporate defendant, and that the parties desired to continue to act jointly in all matters relating to their stock ownership or interest in both the corporate defendant and Circus City.

After setting forth the recitals mentioned, the Agreement then provides:

'NOW, THEREFORE, in consideration of the mutual covenants and agreements hereinafter contained the parties hereto agree as follows:

'1. Neither party will sell any shares of stock or any voting trust certificates in either of said corporations to any other person whomsoever, without first making a written offer to the other party hereto of all of the shares or voting trust certificates proposed to be sold, for the same price and upon the same terms and conditions as in such proposed sale, and allowing such other party a time of not less than 180 days from the date of such written offer within which to accept same.

'2. In exercising any voting rights to which either party may be entitled by virtue of ownership of stock or voting trust certificates held by them in either of said corporations each party will consult and confer with the other and the parties will act jointly in exercising such voting rights in accordance with such agreement as they may reach with respect to any matter calling for the exercise of such voting rights.

'3. In the event the parties fail to agree with respect to any matter covered by paragraph 2 above, the question in disagreement shall be submitted for arbitration to Karl D. Loos, of Washington, D. C., as arbitrator and his decision thereon shall be binding upon the parties hereto. Such arbitration shall be exercised to the end of assuring for the respective corporations good management and such participation therein by the members of the Ringling family as the experience, capacity and ability of each may warrant. The parties may at any time by written agreement designate any other individual to act as arbitrator in lieu of said Loos.

'4. Each of the parties hereto will enter into and execute such voting trust agreement or agreements and such other instruments as, from time to time they may deem advisable and as they may be advised by counsel are appropriate to effectuate the purposes and objects of this agreement.

'5. This agreement shall be in effect from the date hereof and shall continue in effect for a period of ten years unless sooner terminated by mutual agreement in writing by the parties hereto.

'6. The agreement of April 1934 is hereby terminated.

'7. This agreement shall be binding upon and inure to the benefit of the heirs, executors, administrators and assigns of the parties hereto respectively.'

By the time the annual stockholders' meeting took place in 1943 the corporate indebtedness mentioned had been paid in full and the real owners of the shares had regained complete control of the election of directors. At the 1943, 1944, and 1945 stockholders' meetings the parties to the Agreement voted together and by virtue of their ownership of a majority of the stock and the cumulative voting provisions thereof, they elected five out of the seven directors on each occasion.

While the parties to the Agreement had their troubles, at no time prior to the stockholders' meeting here involved was it necessary to invoke what I may denominate as the 'coercive' terms of the Agreement whereby the arbitrator directed how the stock should be voted. It is undisputed that for some time prior to the 1946 stockholders' meeting, which is here being reviewed, numerous efforts had been made to arrive at an understanding as to how the parties to the Agreement would vote their shares at the 1946 meeting. Just who was the moving spirit in these negotiations is unimportant. The fact is that no agreement on this point was reached although the negotiations continued up until almost midnight of the night before the annual meeting. The so-called 'arbitrator' named in the Agreement, one Karl D. Loos, of Washington, D. C., was very active in these negotiations in an attempt to procure a satisfactory solution, or at least to procure a postponement of the meeting until some solution could be evolved.

Defendants seek to make the point that Mr. Loos was not truly impartial in these negotiations, but, if it be important, I find such a contention unsupported by the record. A person desirous of reconciling parties on a substantial issue cannot be expected to convey to each one all the statements and actions of the other. In such a situation frankness has its place, but so does tact. On the other side, petitioner contends that Mr. Haley as proxy for his wife agreed to a postponement of the meeting and that such agreement was acted upon by the petitioner to her detriment, in that attempts to reach an agreement were broken off. In view of my conclusion, I think it is unnecessary to make a finding of fact on this point.

I shall not narrate the specific facts in connection with the holding of the annual stockholders' meeting here reviewed, as well as the election of directors and officers and the election of an executive committee and the fixing of salaries. The facts are not in dispute. In each instance Loos, acting as arbitrator pursuant to the Agreement, upon the request of petitioner's representative and upon a showing that the parties were unable to agree as to how their shares should be voted, directed that the shares held by the parties to the Agreement should be voted by their holders in a particular manner. When Haley, as proxy for Mrs. Haley, the other party to the Agreement, refused to follow the instructions given by Loos that the stock be voted for an adjournment and the meeting continued, the arbitrator Loos then directed that the stock of the two parties should be voted for five named nominees for directors (Edith Conway Ringling, Robert Ringling, William P. Dunn, Jr., Aubrey B. Haley and James A. Haley). Mr. Haley as proxy for his wife, contrary to the instructions of Loos, voted all his wife's shares for the election of Aubrey B. Haley and James A. Haley.

Petitioner preserved her rights before participating in each of the several matters which came before the stockholders' and directors' meeting so that this case must be decided on its merits.

It is at once apparent that the right of Loos to direct the voting of the stock of the parties to the Agreement is the crucial point for decision. The determination of this point depends upon the answer to the broader question of the legality of the Memorandum of Agreement dated September 15, 1941, under which he purported to operate.

Is the September 15, 1941 Agreement enforceable under the facts presented? * * *

It is fair ... to characterize the Agreement as one dealing with the voting rights of stockholders of a Delaware corporation. It appears to be settled, and is an almost necessary rule of convenience, that in such a situation the validity of an agreement affecting such voting rights is tested by the law of the state of incorporation, in this case Delaware. Thus, the nature of the subject matter of the Agreement renders the usual rule governing the validity of contracts inapplicable and as a consequence, neither the Illinois nor the New York law is controlling here.

Having concluded that the Delaware law must be applied to test the validity of this Agreement, it is next pertinent to examine defendants' contentions that the Agreement is unenforceable under Delaware law because it is only 'an agreement to agree', or because it involves an attempted delegation of irrevocable control over voting rights in a manner which is against the public policy of this state.

Do we have here only 'an agreement to agree', by which defendants mean that there exists no legally enforceable obligation?

Preliminarily, I think it clear that the mutual promises contained in the Agreement constitute sufficient consideration to support it. The mutual restraints on the actions of the parties with respect to the sale and voting of their stock comply with the consideration requirements of contract law.

Did the parties only agree to agree? Certainly the parties agreed to agree as to how they would vote their stock, but they also provided that they would be bound by the decision of a named person in the event they were unable to agree. Thus, an explicitly stated consequence follows their inability to agree. This consequence is conditioned upon the existence of a fact which is objectively ascertainable by the so-called arbitrator as well as a court of equity, namely, that the parties are in disagreement as to how their stock should be voted. The Agreement to agree has, therefore, provisions which are capable of being enforced with respect to particular facts. Moreover, the very nature and object of the Agreement render it impossible for the parties to do more than agree to agree, and to provide an enforceable alternative in the event no agreement is reached.

Defendants urge that no standard is provided in the Agreement for the guidance of the parties in reaching an agreement and that the purposes and policies which should guide them are not set forth and cannot be foretold. The Agreement does perhaps leave something to be desired in the way of explicitly setting forth the function and purpose of the Agreement for the guidance of the parties. However, I think it clear that the same language which is expressed as the standard by which the arbitrator should act must necessarily be read as the governing standard for the parties. This language provides: ' * * * Such arbitration shall be exercised to the end of assuring for the respective corporations good management and such participation therein by the members of the Ringling family as the experience, capacity and ability of each may warrant. The parties may at any time by written agreement designate any other individual to act as arbitrator in lieu of said Loos.'

It is quite evident that no agreement could set forth explicit guides to govern the parties because it is impossible in the nature of things to anticipate all the various subjects on which the vote of the stockholders might be required. Moreover, there is no reason to believe that the arbitrator would be expected to apply a different guiding principle in arriving at a decision than that which would guide the stockholders who agreed to submit to such arbitration.

I conclude that the Agreement is sufficiently definite in terms of the duties and obligations imposed on the parties to be legally enforceable on the state of facts here presented.

Turning to defendants' second objection, is the Agreement invalid as an attempted delegation of irrevocable control and voting rights in a manner which is against the public policy of this state? The answer to the question must depend upon the answer to two questions of a more explicit character, namely:

(1) Is the Agreement a voting trust agreement in which event it would admittedly be invalid for failure to comply with the statutory requirements of this state governing voting trusts?

(2) If not a voting trust agreement, is it, nevertheless, invalid as being against public policy because of the provision that the parties shall be bound by the instructions of the arbitrator as to how they shall vote in the event of a disagreement?

Section 18 of our General Corporation Law, Rev.Code 1935, § 2050, provides the exclusive method for creating voting trusts of stock of a Delaware corporation. Does the present Agreement create a voting trust as that term is employed in Section 18? This court in Peyton v. William C. Peyton Corporation et al., 22 Del.Ch. 187, 199, 194 A. 106, 111, reversed on other grounds 23 Del.Ch. 321 7 A.2d 737, has thus described a voting trust: 'A voting trust as commonly understood is a device whereby two or more persons owning stock with voting powers, divorce the voting rights thereof from the ownership, retaining to all intents and purposes the latter in themselves and transferring the former to trustees in whom the voting rights of all the depositors in the trust are pooled.'

Does the present Agreement fall within the limitations of the quoted definition? I think not. The stockholders under the present Agreement vote their own stock at all times which is the antithesis of a voting trust because the latter has for its chief characteristic the severance of the voting rights from the other attributes of ownership. See in re Chilson, 19 Del.Ch. 398, 168 A. 82. In the cases where the parties to the present Agreement cannot reach an accord as to how they will vote, and are directed by the arbitrator as to how they shall vote their shares, the substance of the matter may be said not to differ in effect from a voting trust situation. However, considering the whole Agreement, there is this substantial distinction. Voting trustees have continuous voting control for the period of time stipulated in the agreement of trust. While here, the right of the arbitrator to direct the vote is limited to those particular cases where a stockholder's vote is called for and the parties cannot agree. True, the arbitration provision gives teeth to the Agreement but the parties desired that they should have the initial choice to determine policy in so far as it was determined by the vote of their shares and that a third party identified as an arbitrator should only resolve a conflict. In a voting trust as generally understood, the trustees in the very first instance determine policy and implement it by their votes.

This Agreement is actually a variation of the well-known stock pooling agreement and as such is to be distinguished from a voting trust. As is stated in 5 Fletcher Cyc. Corp. (Perm.Ed.) § 2064, 'Such agreements are distinct from voting trusts, and are not controlled by the same principles.' It is my conclusion that the present Agreement is not a voting trust within the meaning of that term as used in Section 18 of our General Corporation Law and as a consequence, is not invalid for failure to comply with the provisions thereof.

Does the provision for arbitration constitute such a severance of voting control from ownership as to violate some public policy of this state with respect thereto?

The law with respect to agreements of the general type with which we are here concerned is fairly stated as follows in 5 Fletcher Cyc. Corp. (Perm.Ed.) § 2064: 'Generally, agreements and combinations to vote stock or control corporate action and policy are valid, if they seek without fraud to accomplish only what the parties might do as stockholders and do not attempt it by illegal proxies, trusts, or other means in contravention of statutes or law.'

The principle of law stated seems to be sound and I think it is applicable here with respect to the legality of the Agreement under consideration. In the first place, there is no constitutional or statutory objection to the Agreement and defendants do not seriously challenge the legality of its objects. Indeed, in my opinion the objects and purposes of the Agreement as they are recited in the Agreement are lawful in principle and no evidence was introduced which tended to show that they were unlawful in operation.

The only serious question presented under this point arises from the defendants' contention that the arbitration provision has the effect of providing for an irrevocable separation of voting power from stock owner-ship and that such a provision is contrary to the public policy of this state. Perhaps in no field of the law are the precedents more varied and irreconcilable than those dealing with this phase of the case.

By adhering to strict literalism, it can be said that the present Agreement does not separate voting rights from ownership because the arbitrator only directs the parties as to how they shall vote in case of disagreement. However, recognizing substance rather than form, it is apparent that the arbitrator has voting control of the shares in the instances when he directs the parties as to how they shall vote since, if the Agreement is to be binding, they are also bound by his direction. When so considered, it is perhaps at variance with many, but not all of the precedents in other jurisdictions dealing with agreements of this general nature.

To the extent that the precedents elsewhere are based on questions other than public policy, they are inapplicable here. As to those cases which strike down agreements containing provisions which have the effect of severing voting control from ownership because of some judicially constructed public policy, I am not satisfied that the invocation of such a sanction is justified.

No controlling Delaware precedent has been cited. The case of Aldridge v. Franco–Wyoming Oil Co., supra, relied upon by defendants, dealt only with the question of whether or not the particular Agreement before the court was or was not a voting trust agreement. The court was not called upon, as I am here, to determine whether or not the public policy of Delaware invalidates an agreement of the general type here involved (not being a voting trust), without regard to statutory law. In re Chilson, supra, actually turned on the question of the existence of an irrevocable proxy in the absence of a property interest in the holder. In view of the sweeping assumptions made in the case, it is not clear that it can be considered as having to do with anything more than a simple proxy situation—a very different situation from the contractual arrangement here involved.

Directing attention to the present Agreement, what vice exists in having an arbitrator agreed upon by the parties decide how their stock shall be voted in the event they are unable to agree? The parties obviously decided to contract with respect to this very situation and to appoint as arbitrator one in whom both had confidence. The cases which strike down agreements on the ground that some public policy prohibits the severance of ownership and voting control argue that there is something very wrong about a person 'who has no beneficial interest or title in or to the stock' directing how it shall be voted. Such a person, according to these cases, has 'no interest in the general prosperity of the corporation' and moreover, the stockholder himself has a duty to vote. Such reasons ignore the realities because obviously the person designated to determine how the shares shall be voted has the confidence of such shareholders. Quite naturally they would not want to place such power over their investment in the hands of one whom they felt would not be concerned with the welfare of the corporation. The objection based on the so-called duty of the stockholders to vote, presumably in person, is ludicrous when considered in the light of present day corporate practice. Thus, precedents from other jurisdictions which are based on reasons which have, in my opinion, lost their substance under present day conditions cannot be accorded favorable recognition. No public policy of this state requires a different conclusion. * * *

Defendants say that even if the Agreement is valid under the statutes and public policy of this state, it is, nevertheless, to be governed by 'principles applicable to proxy delegations and, hence, would be revocable.' Defendants go on to show how, in their opinion, the alleged proxy was revoked and conclude therefrom that the Agreement was not violated. It is perfectly obvious that the construction of the Agreement contended for by defendants, if accepted, would in effect render it meaningless. The answer to this contention of the defendants must be that we are not here concerned with a proxy situation as between the parties to the Agreement on one hand, and the arbitrator Loos on the other. The Agreement does not contemplate such a proxy either in form or in substance.

Defendants make several contentions based on the theory that we are here dealing with an Agreement containing an arbitration provision and that such a provision will not be specifically enforced in this state. Although Loos is referred to in the Agreement as an arbitrator, it is evident that this Agreement does not possess the characteristics which go to make up an arbitration Agreement. Here the action by the arbitrator, so-called, constitutes one of the principal, if not the principal feature of the Agreement. Obviously no Agreement was needed as to the action to be taken by the parties so long as they agreed. Under this Agreement, the arbitrator is *not* given both sides of a conflict and required to resolve the issue. The *fact* of the conflict gives to him the power to direct how the stock shall be voted without necessarily being bound by the facts which controlled the decisions of the parties, although both operate pursuant to the same general standard. Moreover, the so-called arbitrator is not called upon to resolve a conflict which would otherwise be decided by a court. The parties agreed to a specific procedure and made it an integral part of the contract itself—not something over and above the contract—which is the only way they could secure the objective they obviously sought in making the Agreement, namely, that the stock would be voted jointly.
* * *

Other contentions made with respect to the invalidity of the Agreement based on the premise that it constituted an arbitration agreement must fall in the light of my conclusion that it was not such an arbitration agreement as is governed by the principles of law relied upon by defendants. Moreover, I cannot agree with the defendants that the validity of this Agreement must in some way be adversely affected by the fact that it provides for a possible further agreement by way of a voting trust.

I conclude that the stock held under the Agreement should have been voted pursuant to the direction of the arbitrator Loos to the parties or their representatives. When a party or her representative refuses to comply with the direction of the arbitrator, while he is properly acting under its provisions (as did Aubrey B. Haley's proxy here), then I believe the Agreement constitutes the willing party to the Agreement an implied agent possessing the irrevocable proxy of the recalcitrant party for the purpose of casting the particular vote. Here an implied agency based on an irrevocable proxy is fully justified to implement the Agreement without doing violence to its terms. Moreover, the provisions of the Agreement make it clear that the proxy may be treated as one coupled with an interest so as to render it irrevocable under the circumstances. In re Chilson, supra.

It is the opinion of the court that the nature of the Agreement does not preclude the granting of specific performance, e.g., see Clark v. Dodge, 269 N.Y. 410, 199 N.E. 641. Indeed, the granting of such relief here is well within the spirit of certain principles laid down by our courts in cases granting specific performance of contracts to sell stock which would give the vendee voting control. Obviously, to deny specific performance here would be tantamount to declaring the Agreement invalid. Since petitioner's rights in this respect were properly preserved at the stockholders' meeting, the meeting was a nullity to the extent that it failed to give effect to the provisions of the Agreement here involved. However, I believe it preferable to hold a new election rather than attempt to reconstruct the contested meeting. In this way the parties will be acting with explicit knowledge of their rights.

A meeting of the stockholders should be held before a master to be appointed by this court pursuant to the provisions of Section 31 of the General Corporation Law, Rev. Code 1935, § 2063. It is conceivable that prior to such meeting the parties to the Agreement will be able to agree as to how they will vote their stock, since such a possibility was lost prior to the meeting here reviewed through certain unfortunate happenings having nothing to do with the merits of the policy disagreement. It is obviously to the advantage of both parties to avoid the necessity for calling upon the arbitrator to act, and he will only act if the parties are unable to agree and action by him is requested. It must and should be assumed that the so-called arbitrator, if called upon to act, will bring to bear that sense of duty and impartiality which doubtless motivated the parties in selecting him for such an important role. In any event, the master in conducting the election will be bound to recognize and to give effect to the Agreement here involved, if its terms are properly invoked.

A decree accordingly will be advised.

RINGLING BROS.—BARNUM & BAILEY COMBINED SHOWS, INC. v. RINGLING

53 A.2d 441 (Del.1947).

PEARSON, JUDGE.

The Court of Chancery was called upon to review an attempted election of directors at the 1946 annual stockholders meeting of the corporate defendant. The pivotal questions concern an agreement between two of the three present stockholders, and particularly the effect of this agreement with relation to the exercise of voting rights by these two stockholders. At the time of the meeting, the corporation had outstanding 1000 shares of capital stock held as follows: 315 by petitioner Edith Conway Ringling; 315 by defendant Aubrey B. Ringling Haley (individually or as executrix and legatee of a deceased husband); and 370 by defendant John Ringling North. The purpose of the meeting was to elect the entire board of seven directors. The shares could be voted cumulatively. Mrs. Ringling asserts that by virtue of the operation of an agreement between her and Mrs. Haley, the latter was bound to vote her shares for an adjournment of the meeting, or in the alternative, for a certain slate of directors. Mrs. Haley contends that she was not so bound for reason that the agreement was invalid, or at least revocable. * * *

At the annual meetings in 1943 and the two following years, the parties voted their shares in accordance with mutual understandings arrived at as a result of discussions. In each of these years, they elected five of the seven directors. Mrs. Ringling and Mrs. Haley each had sufficient votes, independently of the other, to elect two of the seven directors. By both voting for an additional candidate, they could be sure of his election regardless of how Mr. North, the remaining stockholder, might vote.[1]

Some weeks before the 1946 meeting, they discussed with Mr. Loos the matter of voting for directors. They were in accord that Mrs. Ringling should cast sufficient votes to elect herself and her son; and that Mrs. Haley should elect herself and her husband; but they did not agree upon a fifth director. The day before the meeting, the discussions were continued, Mrs. Haley being represented by her husband since she could not be present because of illness. In a conversation with Mr. Loos, Mr. Haley indicated that he would make a motion for an adjournment of the meeting for sixty days, in order to give the ladies additional time to come to an agreement about their voting. On the morning of the meeting, however, he stated that because of something Mrs. Ringling had done, he would not consent to a postponement. Mrs. Ringling then made a demand upon Mr. Loos to act under the third paragraph of the agreement 'to arbitrate the disagreement' between her and Mrs. Haley in connection with the manner in which the stock of the two ladies should be voted. At the opening of the meeting, Mr. Loos read the written demand and stated that he determined and directed that the stock of both ladies be voted for an adjournment of sixty days. Mrs. Ringling then made a motion for adjournment and voted for it. Mr. Haley, as proxy for his wife, and Mr. North voted against the motion. Mrs. Ringling (herself or through her attorney, it is immaterial which,) objected to the voting of Mrs. Haley's stock in any manner other than in accordance with Mr. Loos' direction. The chairman ruled that the stock could not be voted contrary to such direction, and declared the motion for adjournment had carried. Nevertheless, the meeting proceeded to the election of directors. Mrs. Ringling stated that she would continue in the meeting 'but without prejudice to her position with respect to the voting of the stock and the fact that adjournment had not been taken.' Mr. Loos directed Mrs. Ringling to cast her votes 882 for Mrs. Ringling, 882 for her son, Robert, and 441 for a Mr. Dunn, who had been a member of the board for several years. She complied. Mr. Loos directed that Mrs. Haley's votes be cast 882 for Mrs. Haley, 882 for Mr. Haley, and 441 for Mr. Dunn. Instead of complying, Mr. Haley attempted to vote his wife's

---

1. Each lady was entitled to cast 2205 votes (since each had the cumulative voting rights of 315 shares, and there were 7 vacancies in the directorate). The sum of the votes of both is 4410, which is sufficient to allow 882 votes for each of 5 persons. Mr. North, holding 370 shares, was entitled to cast 2590 votes, which obviously cannot be divided so as to give to more than two candidates as many as 882 votes each. It will be observed that in order for Mrs. Ringling and Mrs. Haley to be sure to elect five directors (regardless of how Mr. North might vote) they must act together in the sense that their combined votes must be divided among five different candidates and at least one of the five must be voted for by both Mrs. Ringling and Mrs. Haley.

shares 1103 for Mrs. Haley, and 1102 for Mr. Haley. Mr. North voted his shares 864 for a Mr. Woods, 863 for a Mr. Griffin, and 863 for Mr. North.

The chairman ruled that the five candidates proposed by Mr. Loos, together with Messrs. Woods and North, were elected. The Haley–North group disputed this ruling insofar as it declared the election of Mr. Dunn; and insisted that Mr. Griffin, instead, had been elected. A director's meeting followed in which Mrs. Ringling participated after stating that she would do so 'without prejudice to her position that the stockholders' meeting had been adjourned and that the directors' meeting was not properly held.' Mr. Dunn and Mr. Griffin, although each was challenged by an opposing faction, attempted to join in voting as directors for different slates of officers. Soon after the meeting, Mrs. Ringling instituted this proceeding.

Having examined what the parties sought to provide by the agreement, we come now to defendants' contention that the voting provisions are illegal and revocable. They say that the courts of this state have definitely established the doctrine 'that there can be no agreement, or any device whatsoever, by which the voting power of stock of a Delaware corporation may be irrevocably separated from the ownership of the stock, except by an agreement which complies with Section 18' of the Corporation Law, Rev.Code 1935, § 2050, and except by a proxy coupled with an interest. * * *

In our view, neither the cases nor the statute sustain the rule for which the defendants contend. Their sweeping formulation would impugn well-recognized means by which a shareholder may effectively confer his voting rights upon others while retaining various other rights. For example, defendants' rule would apparently not permit holders of voting stock to confer upon stockholders of another class, by the device of an amendment of the certificate of incorporation, the exclusive right to vote during periods when dividends are not paid on stock of the latter class. The broad prohibitory meaning which defendants find in Section 18 seems inconsistent with their concession that proxies coupled with an interest may be irrevocable, for the statute contains nothing about such proxies. The statute authorizes, among other things, the deposit or transfer of stock in trust for a specified purpose, namely, 'vesting' in the transferee 'the right to vote thereon' for a limited period; and prescribes numerous requirements in this connection. Accordingly, it seems reasonable to infer that to establish the relationship and accomplish the purpose which the statute authorizes, its requirements must be complied with. But the statute does not purport to deal with agreements whereby shareholders attempt to bind each other as to how they shall vote their shares. Various forms of such pooling agreements, as they are sometimes called, have been held valid and have been distinguished from voting trusts. We think the particular agreement before us does not violate Section 18 or constitute an attempted evasion of its requirements, and is not illegal for any other reason. Generally speaking, a shareholder may exercise wide liberality of judgment in the matter of voting, and it is not objectionable that his motives may be for personal profit, or determined by whims or caprice, so long as he violates no duty owed his fellow shareholders. The ownership of voting stock imposes no legal duty to vote at all. A group of shareholders may, without impropriety, vote their respective shares so as to obtain advantages of concerted action. They may lawfully contract with each other to vote in the future in such way as they, or a majority of their group, from time to time determine. (See authorities listed above.) Reasonable provisions for cases of failure of the group to reach a determination because of an even division in their ranks seem unobjectionable. The provision here for submission to the arbitrator is plainly designed as a deadlock-breaking measure, and the arbitrator's decision cannot be enforced unless at least one of the parties (entitled to cast one-half of their combined votes) is willing that it be enforced. We find the provision reasonable. It does not appear that the agreement enables the parties to take any unlawful advantage of the outside shareholder, or of any other person. It offends no rule of law or public policy of this state of which we are aware.

Legal consideration for the promises of each party is supplied by the mutual promises of the other party. The undertaking to vote in accordance with the arbitrator's decision is a valid contract. The good faith of the arbitrator's action has not been challenged and, indeed, the record indicates that no such challenge could be supported. Accordingly, the failure of Mrs. Haley to exercise her voting rights in accordance with his decision was a breach of her contract. It is no extenuation of the breach that her votes were cast for two of the three candidates directed by the arbitrator. His directions to her were part of a single plan or course of action for the voting of the shares of both parties to the agreement, calculated to utilize an advantage of joint action by them which would bring about the election of an additional director. The actual voting of Mrs. Haley's shares frustrates that plan to such an extent that it should not be treated as a partial performance of her contract.

Throughout their argument, defendants make much of the fact that all votes cast at the meeting were by the registered shareholders. The Court of Chancery may, in a review of an election, reject votes of a registered shareholder where his voting of them is found to be in violation of rights of another person. It seems to us that upon the application of Mrs. Ringling, the injured party, the votes representing Mrs. Haley's shares should not be counted. Since no infirmity in Mr. North's voting has been demonstrated, his right to recognition of what he did at the meeting should be considered in granting any relief to Mrs. Ringling; for her rights arose under a contract to which Mr. North was not a party. With this in mind, we have concluded that the election should not be declared invalid, but that effect should be given to a rejection of the votes representing Mrs. Haley's shares. No other relief seems appropriate in this proceeding. Mr. North's vote against the motion for adjournment was sufficient to defeat it. With respect to the election of directors, the return of the inspectors should be corrected to show a rejection of Mrs. Haley's votes, and to declare the election of the six persons for whom Mr. North and Mrs. Ringling voted.

This leaves one vacancy in the directorate. The question of what to do about such a vacancy was not considered by the court below and has not been argued here. For this reason, and because an election of directors at the 1947 annual meeting (which presumably will be held in the near future) may make a determination of the question unimportant, we shall not decide it on this appeal. If a decision of the point appears important to the parties, any of them may apply to raise it in the Court of Chancery, after the mandate of this court is received there.

An order should be entered directing a modification of the order of the Court of Chancery in accordance with this opinion.

NOTES

1. The court's opinion in *Ringling* is instructive on the operation of cumulative voting, which is considered further in Chapter 9. The result here was to allow John Ringling North to elect three of the seven directors, giving him control as long as the two other shareholders were split. North did eventually gain control of the company, but it was placed into bankruptcy in 1956. The company was then reorganized and North sold his remaining interest in the circus in 1967 for $8 million.

2. Mrs. Ringling could not obtain specific performance for breach of the voting agreement, but could she obtain damages? What would those damages be and how would they be valued? How would you structure this arrangement to make the agreement specifically enforceable? Why do you think the courts are concerned with separating voting control from beneficial ownership?

3. Del. § 218(b) and (c) now provide that voting agreements, as well as voting trusts, are valid, but Delaware law continues to draw a distinction between irrevocable proxies and other voting arrangements. Del. § 212(e) states that:

> A duly executed proxy shall be irrevocable if it states that it is irrevocable and if, and only as long as, it is coupled with an interest sufficient in law to support an irrevocable power. A proxy may be made irrevocable regardless of whether the interest with which it is coupled is an interest in the stock itself or an interest in the corporation generally.

Model Bus. Corp. Act § 7.22(d) lists five examples of a proxy coupled with an interest. Many states have enacted similar provisions. See e.g., Ga. Code Ann. § 14–2–722(d) (a proxy coupled with an interest includes a pledgee, a person purchasing or agreeing to purchase the shares, an employee whose employment contract requires the appointment and a party to a voting agreement) and N.Y. Bus. Corp. L. § 608(f) (similar to Ga. Statute but also includes creditors of the corporation). For cases considering what constitutes a proxy coupled with an interest see Auto West, Inc. v. Baggs, 678 P.2d 286 (Utah 1984) (proxy coupled with an interest when given to protect a Volkswagon franchise); Williams v. Williams, 427 N.E.2d 727 (Ind.App.1981)(discussion concerning whether buy-sell agreement for business created a proxy coupled with an interest); Mobile & O.R. Co. v. Nicholas, 98 Ala. 92, 12 So. 723 (1893) (proxy coupled with an interest when given as security for creditors of corporation).

ABERCROMBIE v. DAVIES

130 A.2d 338 (Del.1957).

SOUTHERLAND, CHIEF JUSTICE.

The pertinent facts are as follows:

American Independent Oil Company ('American') is a Delaware corporation. It was formed to develop an oil concession in the Kuwait–Saudi Arabian neutral zone. The organizers were James S. Abercrombie, Sunray Oil Corporation ('Sunray'), Phillips Petroleum Company ('Phillips'), Ralph K. Davies, Signal Oil and Gas Company ('Signal'), The Hancock Oil Company ('Hancock'), The Globe Oil and Refining Company ('Globe'), Lario Oil and Gas Company ('Lario'), Ashland Oil & Refining Company ('Ashland'), Deep Rock Oil Corporation ('Deep Rock'), and Allied Oil Company (later acquired by Ashland). The organizers subscribed in varying proportions to American's original issue of stock. Additional stock was later issued, and there are now outstanding 150,000 shares.

The organization agreement provided that the Board of Directors of American should consist of one director for each 5,000 shares held, and that the directors should be elected by cumulative voting. In effect, each stockholder has been permitted to name the director or directors to represent on the board his or its interests. Davies represents his own interest and is president of the corporation. At all times the number of directors has been fifteen. No one stockholder holds a majority of stock, and no one stockholder is represented by more than four directors. Obviously, smooth functioning of such a board was dependent either upon substantial harmony among the interests represented on it or upon an effective coalition of the interests of a majority. On March 30, 1950, six of the stockholders took steps to form such a coalition. On that date an agreement was executed between eight individuals designated 'Agents', and the six stockholders—Davies, Ashland, Globe, Lario, Hancock and Signal. These stockholders hold about 54 1/2% of the shares. They are represented on the board by eight of the fifteen directors. The Agents named in the agreement were at the time the eight directors representing these six stockholders.

The obvious purpose of the agreement was to achieve effective control of the board and thus control of corporate policy. The motive for the agreement, according to the defendants, was to prevent acquisition of control by Phillips, which was the largest single stockholder, holding about one-third of the stock. In the view we take of the case, only the purpose is material.

The Agents' Agreement is an unusual one. In effect, it transfers voting control of the stock of the six stockholders to the eight Agents for a period of ten years (subject to termination by seven of the Agents). The Agents are to be, as far as possible, identical with the directors. The agreement of seven of the eight is required to vote the stock and elaborate provisions are added for the choice of an arbitrator to resolve disagreements. Somewhat similar provisions attempt to control the action of the directors. A more detailed examination of the agreement will later be made. At the moment we note that the majority of the board secured by this agreement (eight of the fifteen) comprised Davies, the two Signal directors, the two Hancock directors, the director representing Globe and Lario, and the two Ashland directors.

The effective control thus sought to be achieved apparently lasted until December 9, 1954. On that date a meeting of the Board of Directors was held in Chicago. A resolution was adopted calling a special meeting of the board for December 16, to consider and take action upon certain amendments to the by-laws and other matters. This resolution was adopted by a vote of nine to six. This majority consisted of Abercrombie, the four Phillips directors, the Sunray director, the Deep Rock director, and the two Ashland directors. The minority consisted of Davies and the Globe, Lario, Hancock and Signal directors. The nature of the action to be considered at the proposed meeting was such as to indicate to the minority that the control of the board set up by the Agents' Agreement was seriously threatened. The Ashland directors, it was charged, had violated the Agents' Agreement. Counter moves were made by Davies. Litigation was instituted in California by Davies, Signal, Hancock, Globe and Lario against Ashland and its two directors. American, named as a defendant, was preliminarily enjoined from recognizing any action taken at a board meeting of December 16, and Ashland was enjoined from violating the Agents' Agreement.

In the meantime, the suit below was filed by Abercrombie, Phillips and Sunray against the other shareholders and the Agents. Davies, Signal, Hancock, Lario, Globe and six of the Agents appeared and answered. Plaintiffs filed a motion for summary judgment. Several contentions arose out of the hearings on this motion. The Chancellor made the following rulings of law: (1) Certain provisions of the Agents' Agreement attempting to control directorate action are invalid on their face; (2) The agreement is not a voting trust; (3) The provisions respecting stockholder action are severable from the illegal provisions, and constitute a valid stockholders' pooling agreement. Both sides appeal. All of the issues argued below have been presented here. We turn to an analysis of the Agents' Agreement.

Paragraph 1 provides in part:

> Upon the signing of this Agreement, or as soon thereafter as it may be possible for them to do so, by those whose certificates may be pledged or deposited, as hereinafter referred to, the Shareholders will deliver to the Agents the certificate or certifi-

cates representing all the shares of American Independent Oil Company now owned or controlled by them, said certificates to be endorsed in blank or attached to a stock power endorsed in blank. Said Agents will give to each depositing Shareholder a proper receipt for all certificates so delivered.

The certificates and stock powers are to be deposited in escrow in a bank or trust company, subject to withdrawal at any time by any seven of the agents.

Paragraph 2 sets forth a method of dealing with a possible increase in the number of Agents '(or in case a Voting Trust shall have been created, the number of Trustees)'.

Paragraph 3 provides in part:

> During the term of this Agreement the Agents or their successors shall have the sole and exclusive voting power of the stock subject to this Agreement. The Shareholders shall deliver to the Agents and shall keep in effect during the life of this Agreement proxies giving said Agents or their successors jointly and each of them severally, with full power of substitution to any or all of them, the power to vote the stock at all regular and special meetings of the stockholders and to vote for, do or assent or consent to any act or proceeding which the Shareholders of said corporation might or could vote for, do or assent or consent to.

Paragraph 3 also provides:

> The vote of the Agents shall always be exercised as a unit, on any matter on which a vote of the stockholders is called for, as any seven of said Agents shall direct and determine. If any seven Agents fail to agree on any such matter, then the question in disagreement shall be submitted for arbitration to some disinterested person (i.e., one having no financial interest in American Independent Oil Company), chosen by the affirmative vote of seven of the Agents, as sole arbitrator.

Then follow provisions for the choice of an arbitrator if seven Agents fail to agree upon the matter, and for the enforcement of his decision. Then follow two paragraphs dealing with control of directorate action. These are the provisions held invalid by the Chancellor as an unlawful attempt to strip the directors of their statutory right and duty to manage the corporate affairs.

Paragraph 3 then concludes:

> In the event a Voting Trust is established as provided in Paragraph 7 hereof, the provisions of the two preceding subparagraphs shall remain in effect, substituting the words 'Trustee' or 'Trustees' for the words 'Agent' or 'Agents' wherever those words occur in said two subparagraphs.

Paragraph 4 provides for filling a vacancy in the position of Agent. As to the corporate shareholders, the successor is to be named by the shareholder that the Agent was representing. As to Davies, his successor is to be named by the majority of the remaining Agents. Each corporate shareholder has the right to remove its Agent or Agents at any time without cause.

Paragraphs 6 and 7 provide:

> 6.   Except as herein otherwise provided, the proxies to be given hereunder shall not be revoked and the powers herein delegated to said Agents shall be irrevocable during a period of ten years from and after the date of said Agreement. This Agreement, however, shall terminate if any seven of the Agents hereunder declare in writing that the Agreement is terminated. Unless the Agents by unanimous vote otherwise determine, this Agreement shall also terminate if and when less than 50% of the outstanding shares of American Independent Oil Company remain subject to this Agreement. Upon the termination of said Agreement the certificates representing all of the shares so held under this Agreement and then remaining in escrow or in the hands of said Agents or their successors shall be returned or assigned to the parties then entitled thereto, upon surrender to said Agents of the receipts given for said certificates.

> 7.   Any seven of said Agents may at any time withdraw said stock certificates from escrow and transfer said stock to the persons then acting as Agents, as trustees to be held under a voting trust. The parties agree, upon the written request of seven of said Agents to execute a voting trust agreement substantially in the form attached hereto marked Exhibit 'A', the persons then acting as Agents to be Trustees, and the Shareholders parties hereto to be Beneficiaries thereunder. The parties do hereby constitute any one of said Agents their attorney in fact to execute said voting trust agreement for them and in their names, in the event any of them should be unable, or should fail or refuse to sign said voting trust agreement upon the written request of seven of said Agents. Upon the execution of said voting trust agreement the Shareholders will surrender to said Agents the receipts given for said certificates.

This agreement, plaintiffs assert, is invalid on its face. Among other contentions they say that in substance, though not in form, it is a voting trust, and that it is void because it does not comply with the provisions of our voting trust statute. Defendants reply that it is not, and was not intended to be, a voting trust, and is a mere pooling agreement of the kind recognized as legal in Delaware by the decision in Ringling Bros.-Barnum & Bailey Combined Shows v. Ringling, 29 Del.Ch. 610, 53 A.2d 441. The General Corporation Law, 8 Del.C. § 218, provides in part:

(a) One or more stockholders may by agreement in writing deposit capital stock of an original issue with or transfer capital stock to any person or persons, or corporation or corporations authorized to act as trustee, for the purpose of vesting in such person or persons, corporation or corporations, who may be designated voting trustee or voting trustees, the right to vote thereon for any period of time determined by such agreement, not exceeding ten years, upon the terms and conditions stated in such agreement. Such agreement may contain any other lawful provisions not inconsistent with said purpose. After the filing of a copy of such agreement in the principal office of the corporation in the State of Delaware, which copy shall be open to the inspection of any stockholder of the corporation or any beneficiary of the trust under said agreement daily during business hours, certificates of stock shall be issued to the voting trustees to represent any stock of an original issue so deposited with them, and any certificates of stock so transferred to the voting trustees shall be surrendered and cancelled and new certificates therefor shall be issued to the voting trustees, and in the certificates so issued it shall appear that they are issued pursuant to such agreement, and in the entry of such voting trustees as owners of such stock in the proper books of the issuing corporation that fact shall also be noted. The voting trustees may vote upon the stock so issued or transferred during the period in such agreement specified.

This statute was enacted in 1925. 34 Del.L. c. 112, § 6. Prior to its passage there was no Delaware decision declaring that voting trusts were lawful at common law—a question upon which the decisions in other states were in disagreement. See 5 Fletcher, Cyclopedia Corporations, § 2078. In Perry v. Missouri–Kansas Pipe Line Co., 22 Del.Ch. 33, 191 A. 823, it was determined that in Delaware, as in New York, voting trusts derive their validity solely from the statute. *'The test of validity is the rule of the statute. When the field was entered by the Legislature it was fully occupied and no place was left for other voting trusts.'* Quoted by the Chancellor with approval from Matter of Morse, 247 N.Y. 290, 160 N.E. 374, 376. The statute lays down for voting trusts 'the law of their life'; compliance with its provisions is mandatory. Voting trusts not so complying are illegal. Perry v. Missouri-Kansas Pipe Line Co., supra; In re Chilson, 19 Del.Ch. 398, 168 A. 82; Smith v. Biggs Boiler Works Co., 32 Del.Ch. 147, 82 A.2d 372.

The correctness of the holding in the Missouri–Kansas case has never been questioned in Delaware, so far as we know. It has a direct bearing upon the instant case. If any stockholders' agreement provided for joint or concerted voting is so drawn as in effect to occupy the field reserved for the statutory voting trust, it is illegal, whatever mechanics may be devised to attain the result. The provisions of the instrument determine its legal effect, and if they clearly create a voting trust, any intention of the parties to the contrary is immaterial.

A review of the Delaware decisions upon the subject of voting trusts shows that our courts have indicated that one essential feature that characterizes a voting trust is the separation of the voting rights of the stock from the other attributes of ownership. In Peyton v. William C. Peyton Corporation, 22 Del.Ch. 187, 199, 194 A. 106, 111, Chancellor Wolcott said: 'A voting trust as commonly understood is a device whereby two or more persons owning stock with voting powers, divorce the voting rights thereof from the ownership, retaining to all intents and purposes the latter in themselves and transferring the former to trustees in whom the voting rights of all the depositors in the trust are pooled.'

This definition was followed in Aldridge v. Franco–Wyoming Oil Co., supra, with an additional element—'that the voting rights given are intended to be irrevocable for a definite period'. 24 Del.Ch. 148, 7 A.2d 764. And in Tracey v. Franklin, 30 Del.Ch. 407, 411, 61 A.2d 780, 782, affirmed 31 Del.Ch. 477, 67 A.2d 56, 11 A.L.R.2d 990, the Vice Chancellor spoke of the primary purpose of the statute as 'the separation of voting rights from the other attributes of ownership for a protracted period.' To all these elements should be added that of the principal object of such a trust, which is voting control. Note the language of § 218, and see 5 Fletcher, Cyclopedia Corporations, § 2075.

When we apply these tests to the Agents' Agreement we find: (1) that the voting rights of the pooled stock have been divorced from the beneficial ownership, which is retained by the stockholders; (2) that the voting rights have been transferred to fiduciaries denominated Agents; (3) that the transfer of such rights is, through the medium of irrevocable proxies, effective for a period of ten years; (4) that all voting rights in respect of all the stock are pooled in the Agents as a group, through the device of proxies running to the agents jointly and severally, and no stockholder retains the right to vote his or its shares; and (5) that on its face the agreement has for its principal object voting control of American.

These elements, under our decisions, are the elements of a voting trust. We find one other significant circumstance.

Paragraph 7 of the Agents' Agreement gives any seven of the eight agents the power to withdraw the stock from escrow and to transform the Agreement into a formal voting trust. Any one of the agents is authorized to sign the voting trust agreement for any shareholder who fails to do so upon the request of any seven of the agents. A form of a voting trust agreement is attached as an exhibit to the Agents' Agreement. A comparison of this form with the provisions of the Agents' Agreement shows that upon the execution of the Voting Trust Agreement the scheme of control functions just as it functions under the Agents' Agreement. Without pausing for a detailed analysis, we note that Paragraphs 2, 4, 5 and 6 of the Agents' Agreement are paralleled (in some cases almost verbatim) by Paragraphs 2, 5, 8 and 10, respectively, of the Voting Trust Agreement. Paragraph 3 of the Agents' Agreement is paralleled in part by Paragraph 3 of the Voting Trust Agreement. The provisions of Paragraph 3 of the

Agents' Agreement controlling directorate action remain in effect as part of the Voting Trust Agreement.

Thus the only significant changes made in transforming the Agents' Agreement into a Voting Trust Agreement are the provisions formalizing the trust, viz.: (1) the Agents become Trustees—a change of name and nothing more; (2) the stock with irrevocable stock powers running to the Agents becomes stock registered in their names as Trustees; and (3) voting trust certificates instead of receipts are issued to the stockholders.

To sum up: the substance of the voting trust already existed; the transformation added only the special mechanics that the statute requires. Now, the provisions of the statute that were not complied with are the requirement that the shares be transferred on the books and the requirement that a copy of the agreement shall be filed in the corporation's principal office in Delaware. The effect was to create a secret voting trust. The provision respecting the filing of a copy in the principal office in Delaware 'open to the inspection of any stockholder * * * or any beneficiary of the trust' is a provision obviously for the benefit of all stockholders and of all beneficiaries of the trust, who are entitled to know where voting control of a corporation resides. And the provision for transfer of the stock on the corporate books necessarily serves, though perhaps only incidentally, a similar purpose with respect to the officers and directors. If the validity of a stockholders' pooling agreement of the kind here presented were to be sustained, the way is clear for the creation of secret voting trusts. The statute clearly forbids them. The Chancellor took the contrary view. He held the Agents' Agreement not to be a voting trust because (1) title to the stock did not pass to the Agents, and (2) because the Agents are in fact the agents and are subject to the directions of their principals.

The failure to transfer the stock on the books is not a sufficient reason in this case for holding the Agents' Agreement not a voting trust. It is an indication that the parties did not intend to create a voting trust; but that subjective intention is unimportant. The stock here was endorsed in blank and delivered to the agents for deposit in escrow with irrevocable proxies. Transfer of the stock on the books is not essential to effect an irrevocable transfer of voting rights to fiduciaries, divorced from the other attributes of the stock, in order to secure voting control, as the Agents' Agreement demonstrates. It is such a transfer that is the characteristic feature of a voting trust.[1]

The fact that the Agents are subject to control by their respective principals does not prevent the agreement from constituting a voting trust. The stock is voted by the Agents as a group. No one stockholder retains complete control over the voting of its stock. It cannot vote its own stock directly; all it can do is to direct its Agent how to vote on a decision to be made by the Agents as a group. The stock of any corporate

---

1. The relationship between the 'irrevocable proxy' to fiduciaries and the voting trust is so close that one writer has said: 'To achieve irrevocable proxies the voting trust was developed.' Rohrlich, Law and Practice in Corporate Control; quoted in Ballantine on Corporations, § 184.

stockholder may at any time be voted against its will by the vote of the seven other agents. The control of the agents rests upon the provisions that they are severally chosen by the respective stockholders and each may be removed and replaced by the stockholder he represents. In effect, these provisions come to this: that each corporate stockholder participating in the agreement reserves the right to name and remove the fiduciary or fiduciaries representing him. Such a provision is not inconsistent with a voting trust. In fact, the scheme is carried forward to the voting trust set out as 'Exhibit A' to the Agents' Agreement. See Paragraphs 3 and 5, paralleling Paragraphs 3 and 4 of the Agents' Agreement. And the alleged continuing control of the Agent by the stockholder clearly would not exist in the event of the death, removal or resignation of Davies in his capacity of Agent. In that case his successor, whether Agent or Trustee, is named by a majority of the remaining Agents or Trustees, as the case may be, and his estate has no control whatever over the Agent so named.

Defendants stress the contention that the parties to the Agents' Agreement did not intend to create a voting trust. As above noted, the intent that governs is the intent derived from the instrument itself. A desire to avoid the legal consequences of the language used is immaterial. Additional arguments (1) that the fiduciaries vested with voting rights are called agents instead of trustees, and (2) that title to the stock did not pass to the agents, have already been noticed.

In support of their argument that the Agents' Agreement creates only a stockholders' pooling agreement and not a voting trust, defendants lean heavily on the decision of this Court in Ringling Bros.-Barnum & Bailey Combined Shows v. Ringling, 29 Del.Ch. 610, 53 A.2d 441. That case involved a true pooling agreement, far short of a voting trust. Two stockholders agreed to act jointly in exercising their voting rights. There was no deposit of the stock with irrevocable stock powers conferring upon a group of fiduciaries exclusive voting powers over the pooled stock. Indeed, the Supreme Court (modifying the decision below) held that the agreement did not provide, either expressly or impliedly, for a proxy to either stockholder to vote the other's shares. The Ringling case is clearly distinguishable on the facts. And although the case recognizes the validity of various forms of pooling agreements, it does not announce, as defendants appear to think, an unrestricted and uncritical approval of all agreements between stockholders relating to the voting of their stock. Not all pooling agreements are lawful. Defendants would push the general statements of the Ringling case to unwarranted lengths. They quote extensively from that part of the opinion which deals with the scope of the voting trust statute. Among other things, the Court: 'But the statute does not purport to deal with agreements whereby stockholders attempt to bind each other as to how they shall vote their shares.'

We gather that defendants go so far as to say that a pooling agreement may assume any form whatever without running afoul of the voting trust statute. Thus, if we understand defendants' argument, a pooling agreement may, through the medium of fiduciaries with exclusive voting powers, lawfully accomplish substantially the same purposes as a voting trust and thus avoid compliance with § 218. We disagree. Obviously, as a pooling agreement in substance and purpose approaches more and more nearly the substance and purpose of the statute, there comes a point at which, if the statute is not complied with, the agreement is illegal. A pooling agreement may not escape the statutory controls by calling the trustees agents and giving to the stockholders receipts instead of voting trust certificates. If this were not so, stockholders could, through the device of an agreement such as the one before us, accept for themselves the chief benefits of the statute: unified voting control through fiduciaries for an appreciable period of time; and escape its burdens: the requirements for making an open record of the matter, and the limitations in respect of time. If the agreement before us is upheld, what is there to prevent a similar agreement for 15 years—or 25 years?

Although the general language of the Ringling case, if read literally, may seem to lend some support to the position of the defendants, we do not think that it should be carried so far as to permit the result urged by them in this case. Defendants also rely on the decision of the Chancellor in Aldridge v. Franco–Wyoming Oil Co., supra. In that case an agreement provided for the desposit of shares with a trustee and the issuance of 'bearer certificates' to the depositing stockholder. It was held not to be a voting trust, because under the agreement each stockholder retained full control of his stock. He could withdraw the stock from the trust at any time, or, as long as it remained in the trust, he could obtain a proxy to vote it at any time. The Aldridge case is not in point.

For the foregoing reasons, we are compelled to disagree with the holding of the Chancellor upon the question discussed. We are of opinion that the Agents' Agreement is void as an illegal voting trust.

NOTES

1.   Voting trusts may be used for several purposes beyond just preventing other shareholders to acquire control. Creditors might want voting control placed with trustees to protect the company's assets from waste. A family corporation might need trustees where the founder has no successor in the family that can take control and operate the business. The trustees can appoint professional managers and oversee the company's business for the benefit of the family. Voting trusts have also been used to divest control for antitrust or other purposes.

2.   As seen from these cases, voting trusts have their limitations. The Delaware statute no longer has a time limitation on voting trusts, but other state statutes may have such provisions. Compare Del. § 218, with, Model Bus. Corp. Act § 7.30 (10 year limitation that may be renewed).

LEHRMAN v. COHEN

222 A.2d 800 (Del.1966).

HERRMANN, JUSTICE.

The primary problem presented on this appeal involves the applicability of the Delaware Voting Trust Statute. Other questions involve the legality of stock having voting power but no dividend or liquidation rights except repayment of par value, and an alleged unlawful delegation of directorial duties and powers.

These are the material facts:

Giant Food Inc. (hereinafter the 'Company') was incorporated in Delaware in 1935 by the defendant N. M. Cohen and Samuel Lehrman, deceased father of the plaintiff Jacob Lehrman. From its inception, the Company was controlled by the Cohen and Lehrman families, each of which owned equal quantities of the voting stock, designated Class AC (held by the Cohen family) and Class AL (held by the Lehrman family) common stock. The two classes of stock have cumulative voting rights and each is entitled to elect two members of the Company's four-member board of directors.

Over the years, as may have been expected, there were differences of opinion between the Cohen and Lehrman families as to operating policies of the Company. Samuel Lehrman died in 1949; each of his children inherited part of his stock in the Company; but a dispute arose among the children regarding an Inter vivos gift of certain shares made to the plaintiff by his father shortly before his death. To eliminate the Lerhman family dispute and its possible disruption of the affairs of the Company, an arrangement was made which settled the dispute and permitted the plaintiff to acquire all of the outstanding Class AL stock, thereby vesting in him voting power equal to that held by the Cohen family. The arrangement involved repurchase by the Company of the stock held by the plaintiff's brothers and sister, their relinquishment of any claim to the stock gift, and an equalizing surrender of certain stock by the Cohens to the Company for retirement. An essential part of the arrangement, upon the insistence of the Cohens, was the establishment of a fifth directorship to obviate the risk of deadlock which would have continued if the equal division of voting power between AL and AC stock were continued.

To implement the arrangement, on December 31, 1949, the Company's certificate of incorporation was amended, inter alia, to create a third class of voting stock, designated Class AD common stock, entitled to elect the fifth director. Article Fourth of the amendment to the certificate of incorporation provided for the issuance of one share of Class AD stock, having a par value of $10 and the following rights and powers:

> The holder of Class AD common stock shall be entitled to all of the rights and privileges pertaining to common stock without any limitations, prohibitions, restrictions, or qualifications except that the

holder of said Class AD stock shall not be entitled to receive any dividends declared and paid by the corporation, shall not be entitled to share in the distribution of assets of the corporation upon liquidation or dissolution either partial or final, except to the extent of the par value of said Class AD common stock, and in the election of Directors shall have the right to vote for and elect one of the five Directors hereinafter provided for.

The corporation shall have the right, at any time, to redeem and call in the Class AD stock by paying to the holder thereof the par value of said stock, provided however, that such redemption or call shall be authorized and directed by the affirmative vote of four of the five Directors hereinafter provided for.[2]

By resolution of the board of directors, the share of Class AD stock was issued forthwith to the defendant Joseph B. Danzansky, who had served as counsel to the Company since 1944. All corporate action regarding the creation and the issuance of the Class AD stock was accomplished by the unanimous vote of the AC and AL stockholders and of the board of directors. In April 1950, pursuant to the arrangement, Danzansky voted his share of AD stock to elect himself as the Company's fifth director; and he served as such until the institution of this action in 1964. During that entire period, the AC and AL stock have been voted to elect two directors each. From 1950 through 1964, Danzansky regularly attended board meetings, raised and discussed general items of business, and voted on all issues as they came before the board. He was not obliged to break any deadlock among the directors prior to October 1, 1964 because no such deadlock arose before that date.

Beginning in December 1959, 200,000 shares of non-voting common stock of the Company were sold in a public issue for over $3,000,000. Each prospectus published in connection with the public issue contained the following statement:

Common Stock AD is not a participating stock, and the only purpose for the provision and issuance of such stock is to prevent a deadlock in case the Directors elected by the Common Stock AC and the Directors elected by the Common Stock AL cannot teach an agreement.

Similarly, a letter on behalf of the Company to the Commissioner of Internal Revenue, dated July 15, 1959, contained the following statement:

---

2. Article Fourth of the amendment also co-related the Class AL and the Class AC stock as follows:

The holders of Class AL common stock shall be entitled to all of the right and privileges pertaining to common stock without any limitations, prohibitions, restrictions, or qualifications except that the holder or holders of said Class AL common stock, in the election of Directors, shall have the right to vote for and elect two of the five Directors hereinafter provided for.

The holders of Class AC common stock shall be entitled to all of the rights and privileges pertaining to common stock without any limitations, prohibitions, restrictions, or qualifications except that the holder or holders of said Class AC common stock, in the election of Directors, shall have the right to vote for and elect two of the five Directors hereinafter provided for.

As can be seen from the enclosed certified copy of the stock provisions of the certificate of Incorporation, as amended, the Class AD common stock is not a participating stock, the only purpose for the provision and issuance of such a stock being to prevent a deadlock in case the AC and AL Directors cannot reach an agreement.

From the outset and until October 1, 1964, the defendant N. M. Cohen was president of the Company. On that date, a resolution was adopted at the Company's annual stockholders' meeting to give Danzansky a fifteen year executive employment contract at an annual salary of $67,600., and options for 25,000 shares of the non-voting common stock of the Company. The AC and AD stock were voted in favor and the AL stock was voted against the resolution. At a directors meeting held the same day, Danzansky was elected president of the Company by a 3—2 vote, the two AL directors voting in opposition. On December 11, 1964, Danzansky resigned as director and voted his share of AD stock to elect as the fifth director Millard F. West, Jr., a former AL director and investment banker whose firm was one of the underwriters of the public issue of the Company's stock. The newly constituted board ratified the election of Danzansky as president; and, on January 27, 1965, after the commencement of this action and after a review and report by a committee consisting of the new AD director and one AL director, Danzansky's employment contract was approved and adopted with certain modifications.

The plaintiff brought this action on December 11, 1964, basing it upon two claims: The First Claim charges that the creation, issuance, and voting of the one share of Class AD stock resulted in an arrangement illegal under the law of this State for the reasons hereinafter set forth. The Second Claim, addressed to the events of October 1, 1964, charges that the election of Danzansky as president of the Company and his employment contract violated the terms of the 1959 deadlock-breaking arrangement, as made between the holders of the AC and AL stock, and constituted breaches of contract and fiduciary duty. The plaintiff and the defendants filed cross-motions for summary judgment as to the First Claim. The Court of Chancery, after considering the contentions now before us and discussed infra, granted summary judgment in favor of the defendants and denied the plaintiff's motion for summary judgment. The plaintiff appeals.

The plaintiff's primary contention is that the Class AD stock arrangement is, in substance and effect, a voting trust; that, as such, it is illegal because it is not limited to a ten year period as required by the Voting Trust Statute. The defendants deny that the AD stock arrangement constitutes a disguised voting trust; but they concede that if it is, the arrangement is illegal for violation of the Statute. Thus, issue is clearly joined on the point.

The criteria of a voting trust under our decisions have been summarized by this Court in Abercrombie v. Davies, 36 Del.Ch. 371, 130 A.2d 338

(1957). The tests there set forth, accepted by both sides of this cause as being applicable, are as follows: (1) the voting rights of the stock are separated from the other attributes of ownership; (2) the voting rights granted are intended to be irrevocable for a definite period of time; and (3) the principal purpose of the grant of voting rights is to acquire voting control of the corporation.

Adopting and applying these tests, the plaintiff says, as to the first element, that the AD arrangement provides for a divorcement of voting rights from beneficial ownership of the AC and AL stock; that the creation and issuance of the share of AD stock is tantamount to a pooling by the AC and AL stockholders of a portion of their voting stock and giving it to a trustee, in the person of the AD stockholder, to vote for the election of the fifth director; that after the creation of the AD stock, the AC and AL stockholders each hold but 40% of the voting power, and the AD stockholder holds the controlling balance of 20%; that the AD stock has no property rights except the right to a return of the $10 paid as the par value; and that, therefore, there has been a transfer of the voting rights devoid of any participating property rights. So runs the argument of the plaintiff in support of his contention that the first of the Abercrombie criteria for a voting trust is met.

The contention is unacceptable. The AD arrangement did not separate the voting rights of the AC or the AL stock from the other attributes of ownership of those classes of stock. Each AC and AL stockholder retains complete control over the voting of his stock; each can vote his stock directly; no AL or AC stockholder is divested of his right to vote his stock as he sees fit; no AL or AC stock can be voted against the shareholder's wishes; and the AL and AC stock continue to elect two directors each.

The AD stock arrangement, as we view it, became a part of the capitalization of the Company. The fact that there is but a single share, or that the par value is nominal, is of no legal significance; the one share and the $10. par value might have been multiplied many times over, with the same consequence. It is true that the creation of the separate class of AD stock may have diluted the voting Power which had previously existed in the AC and AL stock—the usual consequence when additional voting stock is created—but the creation of the new class did not divest and separate the voting Rights which remain vested in each AC and AL shareholder, together with the other attributes of the ownership of that stock. The fallacy of the plaintiff's position lies in his premise that since the voting power of the AC and AL stock was reduced by the creation of the AD stock, the percentage of reduction became the res of a voting trust. In any recapitalization involving the creation of additional voting stock, the voting power of the previously existing stock is diminished; but a voting trust is not necessarily the result.

Since the holders of the Class AC and Class AL stock of the Company did not separate the voting rights from the other attributes of ownership of those classes when they created the Class AD stock, the first Abercrombie test of a voting trust is not met.

This conclusion disposes of the second and third Abercrombie tests, i.e., that the voting rights granted are irrevocable for a definite period of time, and that the principal object of the grant of voting rights is voting control of the corporation. Having held that the AC and AL stockholders have not divested themselves of their voting rights, although they may have diluted their voting powers, we do not reach the remaining Abercrombie tests, both of which assume the divestiture of voting rights.

In the final analysis, the essence of the question raised by the plaintiff in this connection is this: Is the substance and purpose of the AD stock arrangement sufficiently close to the substance and purpose of § 218 to warrant its being subjected to the restrictions and conditions imposed by that Statute? The answer is negative not only for the reasons above stated, but also because § 218 regulates trusts and pooling agreements amounting to trusts, not other and different types of arrangements and undertakings possible among stockholders. Compare Ringling Bros.—Barnum & Bailey Combined Shows, Inc. v. Ringling, 29 Del.Ch. 610, 53 A.2d 441 (1947); Abercrombie v. Davies, supra. The AD Stock arrangement is neither a trust nor a pooling agreement. See 5 Fletcher Cyclopedia Corporations (Perm.Ed.) § 2077.

We hold, therefore, that the Class AD stock arrangement is not controlled by the Voting Trust Statute.

The plaintiff's second point is that even if the Class AD stock arrangement is not a voting trust in substance and effect, the AD stock is illegal, nevertheless, because the creation of a class of stock having voting rights only, and lacking any substantial participating proprietary interest in the corporation, violates the public policy of this State as declared in § 218.

The fallacy of this argument is twofold: First, it is more accurate to say that what the law has disfavored, and what the public policy underlying the Voting Trust Statute means to control, is the separation of the vote from the stock—not from the stock ownership. Clearly, the AD stock arrangement is not violative of that public policy. Secondly, there is nothing in § 218, either expressed or implied, which requires that all stock of a Delaware corporation must have both voting rights and proprietary interests. Indeed, public policy to the contrary seems clearly expressed by 8 Del.C. § 151(a) which authorizes, in very broad terms, such voting powers and participating rights as may be stated in the certificate of incorporation. Non-voting stock is specifically authorized by § 151(a); and in the light thereof, consistency does not permit the conclusion, urged by the plaintiff, that the present public policy of this State condemns the separation of voting rights from beneficial stock ownership.

We conclude that the plaintiff's contention in this regard cannot withstand the force and effect of § 151(a). In our view, that Statute permits the creation of stock having voting rights only, as well as stock having property rights only. The voting powers and the participating rights of the Class AD stock being specified in the Company's certificate of incorporation, we are of the opinion that the Class AD stock is legal by virtue of § 151(a).

We are told that if the AD stock arrangement is allowed thus to stand, our Voting Trust Statute will become a 'dead letter' because it will be possible to evade and circumvent its purpose simply by issuing a class of non-participating voting stock, as was done here. We have three negative reactions to this argument:

First, it presupposes a divestiture of the voting rights of the AC and AL stock—an untenable supposition as has been stated. Secondly, it fails to take into account the main purpose of a Voting Trust Statute: to avoid secret, uncontrolled combinations of stockholders formed to acquire voting control of the corporation to the possible detriment of non-participating shareholders. It may not be said that the AD stock arrangement contravenes that purpose. Finally on this point, if we misconceive the legislative intent, and if the AD stock arrangement in this case reveals a loophole in § 218 which should be plugged, it is for the General Assembly to accomplish—not for us to attempt by interstitial judicial legislation.

The plaintiff advances yet another reason for invalidating the AD stock. The essence of this argument is that the only function of that class of stock is to break directorial deadlocks; that the issuance of the AD stock is merely a technical device to permit that result; that, as such, it is illegal because it permits the AC and AL directors of the Company to delegate their statutory duties to the AD director as an arbitrator.

We see nothing inherently wrong or contrary to the public policy of this State, as plaintiff seems to suggest, about a device, otherwise lawful, designed by the stockholders of a corporation to break deadlocks of directors. The plaintiff says in this connection, that if public policy sanctioned such device, our General Corporation Law would provide for it. The fallacy of this argument lies in the assumption that legislative silence is a dependable indicator of public policy. We know of no reason, either under our statutes or our decisions, which would prevent the stockholders of a Delaware corporation from protecting themselves and their corporation, by a plan otherwise lawful, against the paralyzing and often fatal consequences of a stalemate in the directorate of the corporation. We hold, therefore, that the AD stock arrangement had a proper purpose.

As to the means adopted for the accomplishment of that purpose, we find the AD stock arrangement valid by virtue of § 141(a) of the Delaware Corporation Law which provides:

> The business of every corporation organized under the provisions of this chapter shall be managed by a board of directors, except as hereinafter or in its certificate of incorporation otherwise provided.

The AD stock arrangement was created by the unanimous action of the stockholders of the Company by amendment to the certificate of incorporation. The stockholders thereby provided how the business of the corporation is to be managed, as is their privilege and right under § 141(a). It was this stockholder action which delegated to the AD director whatever powers and duties he possesses; they were not delegated to him by his fellow directors, either out of their own powers and duties, or otherwise.

It is settled, of course, as a general principle, that directors may not delegate their duty to manage the corporate enterprise. But there is no conflict with that principle where, as here, the delegation of duty, if any, is made not by the directors but by stockholder action under § 141(a), via the certificate of incorporation.

In our judgment, therefore, the AD stock arrangement is not invalid on the ground that it permits the AC and AL directors of the Company to delegate their statutory duties to the AD director.

On this point, the plaintiff relies mainly upon the Chancery Court decision in Abercrombie v. Davies, 35 Del.Ch. 599, 611, 123 A.2d 893 (1956). There, in considering an agreement requiring all eight directors to submit a disputed question to an arbitrator if seven were unable to agree, the Chancery Court stated that legal sanction may not be accorded to an agreement, at least when made by less than all the stockholders, which takes from the board of directors the power of determining substantial management policy. The plaintiff's reliance is misplaced, because, Inter alia, the Abercrombie arrangement was not created by the certificate of incorporation, within the authority of § 141(a). * * * Finally, the plaintiff relies upon Sterling Industries, Inc. v. Ball Bearing Pen Corp., 298 N.Y. 483, 84 N.E.2d 790 (1949) and 7 White, New York Corporations, 8.18 (1953). The New York authorities, uncontrolled by § 141(a), are inapposite.

Our conclusions upon these questions make it unnecessary to discuss the defendants' contentions that the plaintiff's action is barred by the principles of estoppel, laches, acquiescence and ratification.

Finding no error in the judgment below, it is affirmed.

NOTES

1. The stakes (not steaks) at Giant Food were high. The company was, indeed, a giant that became a Fortune 500 company. Although considered nominal in value when issued, the AD share allowed its holder to allocate control in this massive enterprise with a class of publicly owned stock that was nonvoting. This was a right of considerable value!

2. Of similar effect to the *Lehrman* case is Stroh v. Blackhawk Holding Corp., 48 Ill.2d 471, 272 N.E.2d 1 (1971). However, not everyone has agreed with the validity of voting only shares. Op. N.C. Atty. Gen., Feb. 12, 1960 (ruling that public policy precluded a corporate structure including a class of shares with voting rights but no right to share in dividends nor to participate in distributions of assets).

3. Do you have any ideas on how to achieve a more perfect arrangement where voting is equally split? The lawyers in the preceding cases were all trying to deal with the various decisions of the Delaware court in this area, but they were not always successful in anticipating how the court would rule, even when the lawyers thought they were complying with earlier holdings.

OCEANIC EXPLORATION CO. v. GRYNBERG

428 A.2d 1 (Del.1981).

QUILLEN, JUSTICE:

* * * Plaintiffs, individually and as trustees, are the owners of 76 per cent of the outstanding stock of the defendant Oceanic Exploration Company (Oceanic). In particular, the beneficial ownership of the stock interest is with Jack J. Grynberg and members of his family, the majority shareholder group. On February 10, 1976, plaintiffs entered into a written agreement whereby 51 per cent of the company's stock was placed into a "voting trust agreement" which gave their voting rights in the stock to others. The "voting trust agreement" was to expire four years later on February 9, 1980.

On June 2, 1976 this "voting trust agreement" was "amended", again by written instrument, as a result of which all of plaintiffs' stock, 76 per cent of the company's stock, totaling some 5,222,558 shares, was placed in this trust. The "Amendment to Voting Trust Agreement and Purchase Option Agreement" took the form of an agreement between the depositing shareholders and the corporation. It was not signed by the voting trustees. The June 2 instrument also added to the "voting trust agreement" an option in favor of the corporation which gave it the right for a period of 5 years to purchase "all or any part" of plaintiffs' stock. The term of the trust was amended to correspond with the option period ending 5 years from June 2, 1976. The purchase price under the option was fixed at $2.87 per share (or one-half of the then current market price of the stock) for the first year, with this price increasing by 10 per cent on each anniversary date thereafter for the term of the option. The agreement further provides that during the term of the option plaintiffs may not " 'sell, hypothecate, pledge or otherwise encumber said shares of their interests therein'." The "amendment" also required Grynberg to resign as a Director and Chairman of the Board and from positions with subsidiaries, to release the company from an employment contract, and to agree not to compete with the company to a substantial extent. It further recited a general plan for the internal management of the company including a proposal to enlarge the Board of Directors. The voting trustees were to possess and be entitled "to exercise all stockholders' rights of every kind." It is fair to say that the "amendment" radically changed the nature of the agreement. Indeed, in substance it was not the same agreement.

Basically this lawsuit, filed on October 26, 1976, involves plaintiffs' attempt to have the "voting trust agreement and purchase option agreement" declared void so as to regain control of the corporation.* * *

The Vice Chancellor found the "voting trust" portion of the agreement was governed by 8 Del.C. § 218 and that the June 2 "extension" agreement was invalid in that it was executed in violation of extension restrictions of § 218(b) . . . . .

The Vice Chancellor went on to hold that, since the June 2 agreement on its face showed the majority of the covered shares were pledged and thus incapable of being deposited in the trust, the terms of the agreement violated the mandatory certificate deposit provisions of 8 Del.C. § 218. . . .

Some financial background is necessary to understand the appeal. "By February 1976, Oceanic was in deep financial trouble, several large loans were overdue, and, as to one such loan, Morgan Guaranty Trust Company of New York had filed suit for recovery. It was at this point that the original voting trust concept was suggested and put into effect. Without going into the contested details at this point, it is sufficient to note that with the surrender of voting control of the corporation to three outside directors by means of the voting trust, Morgan Guaranty Trust Company withdrew its lawsuit and extended the loan."

While the Vice Chancellor found it unnecessary to go into the facts surrounding the execution of the June 2 document, it should be noted generally that the background facts and the reasons for the execution of that document are hotly contested and indeed constitute the heart of the dispute between the opposing sides, at least factually. The company says that, despite the February agreement, Grynberg remained in control and the financial situation worsened. As summarized in the appellants' brief, the company was on the brink of bankruptcy, was failing to meet its obligations, was facing a renewal of the Morgan suit, and was threatened by a minority shareholder suit. It was in this atmosphere, the company says, that Grynberg and his family, fully advised, entered the June 2 agreement relinquishing control and granting the option in exchange for valuable benefits including indemnity for large liabilities. Having reaped the benefit of the contract debt elimination and stock resurrection, the company says Grynberg now seeks to escape his legitimate burden under the contract.

Plaintiffs' view is different. They say they were given 24 hours notice to agree to changes in the February agreement on the fraudulent representations that a partner in a Greek venture was willing to purchase a certain interest in a Greek concession, sufficient to solve the company's financial crisis, if the amendments were made. This fraudulent inducement appears to be the major contention of the original complaint.

The Vice Chancellor, with customary precision, isolated a threshold question, namely: Is the "voting trust agreement" here governed by Delaware § 218. He concluded that it was and, in so doing, as a matter of law, voided the trust for the reasons noted above, thereby eliminating the conflicting factual equities argued by the parties as to the voting trust. He did not disturb at this stage the option in the June 2 agreement. We are unable to agree to that disposition and therefore we are compelled to reverse. But we do not do so with ease and we candidly find our position difficult to express and regretfully perhaps less clear than the view so positively expressed below. Stated as directly and simply as possible, there are prominent facts which weigh against our conclusion. The February and June agreements were expressly labeled "VOTING TRUST AGREE-MENT" and "AMENDMENT TO VOTING TRUST AGREEMENT AND PURCHASE OPTION AGREEMENT" and both were filed in the registered office of the corporation in Delaware as required by § 218(a). The description used and action taken by the parties thus brings the role of statute directly into play.

While the statute, § 218(a) and (b) does not expressly state it is exclusive, the case law rather pointedly supports the view that § 218 of the Delaware General Corporation Law provides the exclusive method for creating voting trusts of stock of a Delaware corporation. But our decision can neither rest blindly on the form elected by the parties to the June agreement without regard to the substance of the whole contract nor on the exclusivity of the statute without regard to its scope or intended purpose. Deciding the case on such bases would constitute an abstraction divorced from the facts of the case and the intent of the law. The term voting trust as used in our law is a concept which flows from our statute and is specifically defined by our statute and case law. Case comment as to statutory exclusivity has to be related to that definition. In determining the applicability of § 218(a) and (b), the test is whether the substance and purpose of the stock arrangement is "sufficiently close to the substance and the purpose of (the statute) to warrant its being subject to the restrictions and conditions imposed by that statute". Lehrman v. Cohen, Del.Supr., 222 A.2d 800, 806 (1966). As did the Vice Chancellor, we take a frontal tack and direct our attention to the same threshold question. Is the voting trust arrangement here governed by § 218(a) and (b)?

Without attempting to resolve factual disputes, we note the defendant alleges, with some record support, evidence of the following factors:

(1) The final overall contract is one of internal corporate reorganization with integrated portions of which the voting trust is merely one.

(2) The final contract here, including the voting trust feature, is an agreement between the majority shareholder group and the corporation.

(3) While the voting trust portion of the contract is important, it is basically an enforcement provision to a purchase option agreement involving the sale of the majority interest and incidents connected with such sale such as change in management and an agreement not to compete.

(4) The contract is open and notorious within the corporation. Not only was the contract with the corporation itself and not only did it occasion fundamental changes in corporate management but it was prominently featured and positively represented in the proxy statement dated October 14, 1976 and in the 1975 annual report. The operations of the company and the involvement of minority shareholders, officers and employees proceeded in reliance on the contract.

(5) The contract serves a valid corporate purpose, being designed to end financial hardship, and perhaps to end financial ruin.

(6) The contract has been significantly performed by the corporation, its officers and employees.

(7) A substantial benefit has been conferred on the depositing majority shareholder group.

(8) The contemplated benefit to the corporation and the minority shareholders remains largely executory.

(9) The party seeking a declaration that the agreement is void is the depositing majority shareholder group itself.

In such a factual setting, if established or substantially established at trial, we do not find that the Vice Chancellor should be legally prohibited from specifically enforcing the "voting trust agreement" in issue here as a consequence of the statutory provisions contained in § 218. Our reasons are simple: statutory language, statutory purpose and public policy.

First, even viewed historically, § 218, from its original enactment in 1925, was designed to regulate agreements by "(o)ne or more stockholders". 34 Del.Laws Ch. 112, § 6 (1925). Not all trusts of corporate stock which, either expressly or by implication, give voting rights to a trustee are voting trusts. As was noted in Fixman v. Diversified Industries, Inc., Del.Ch., 1 Del.J.Corp.Law 171, 178–79 (1975), the statutory language contemplates an association of stockholders whether it be created by way of individual agreements or joint agreements. The Court of Chancery defined a voting trust in Peyton v. William C. Peyton Corp., Del.Ch., 194 A. 106, 111 (1937), rev'd on other grounds, Del.Supr., 7 A.2d 737 (1939) in the following manner:

> A voting trust as commonly understood is a device whereby two or more persons owning stock with voting powers, divorce the voting rights thereof from the ownership, retaining to all intents and purposes the latter in themselves and transferring the former to trustees in whom the voting rights of all the depositors in the trust are pooled. "This definition has been adopted in several cases. Regulation of voting trusts is directed to a class of trusts created to unify voting. See 5 W. Fletcher, Cyclopedia of the Law of Private Corporations, § 2075 at 333 n. 2 (rev. perm. ed. 1976). Fletcher goes on to note in § 2077 at 336 that:" At the bottom of a voting trust is an agreement among stockholders. . . .

Thus, the voting trust statute was not intended to be all inclusive in the sense that it was designed to apply to every set of facts in which voting rights are transferred to trustees incident to or as part of the assignment of other stockholder rights. Rather, a voting trust is a stockholder pooling arrangement with the criteria that voting rights are separated out and irrevocably assigned for a definite period of time to voting trustees for control purposes while other attributes of ownership are retained by the depositing stockholders. While we do not suggest that the mere fact that the corporation is a party removes a trust from the statute, we do find that the final contract in issue here, with its multi-faceted aspects including a stock purchase option agreement running from an already unified majority shareholder group to the corporation may be so foreign to the stockholder voting trust agreement to which the language used by the General Assembly was directed that it is beyond the contemplated scope of the statute. Given the scope of this agreement it may be that the voting rights are not separated from the other retained attributes of ownership. In short, the agreement here may not be a voting trust as that term is used in our law.

Second, our case law makes it clear that the main purpose of a voting trust statute is "to avoid secret, uncontrolled combinations of stockholders formed to acquire control of the corporation to the possible detriment of non-participating shareholders." The contract involved in this case, given the factual contentions of the defendants, may be so far divorced from that purpose that it makes the contemplated regulation unnecessary and irrelevant.

Third, it is important to recognize there has been a significant change from the days of our original 1925 statute. Voting trusts were viewed with "disfavor" or "looked upon ... with indulgence" by the courts. Other contractual arrangements interfering with stock ownership, such as irrevocable proxies, were viewed with suspicion. The desire for flexibility in modern society has altered such restrictive thinking. The trend of liberalization was markedly apparent in the 1967 changes to our own § 218. Voting or other agreements and irrevocable proxies were given favorable treatment and restrictive judicial interpretations as to the absolute voiding of voting trusts for terms beyond the statutory limit were changed by statute. The trend was not to extend the voting trust restrictions beyond the class of trust being regulated and beyond the reasons for statutory regulation. That public policy cannot be ignored here.

Thus we are faced with a "voting trust agreement" which: (1) may not fit into the situation contemplated by the language of the restrictive statute, (2) may have little, if any, connection with the purpose for which the statute was enacted, and (3) may have no evil or improper aspects under any current ascertainable public policy. Given such circumstances, we are hard pressed to see why § 218 should be a legal bar to a factual inquiry and a discretionary consideration by the Court of Chancery of full enforcement of the contract in this case. We conclude the Vice Chancellor erred in holding the voting trust aspect of the contract in this case to be, as a matter of law, a § 218(a) and (b) voting trust.

The interlocutory order of the Court of Chancery is reversed and the case is remanded.

SECTION 3. VOTING AND QUORUM REQUIREMENTS FOR CONTROL

One way to provide for a minority voice in corporate operations is to have high quorum and voting requirements thus giving the minority an effective veto power. One problem with such an arrangement is that it increases the chance of deadlock. In Benintendi v. Kenton Hotel, Inc., 294 N.Y. 112, 60 N.E.2d 829 (1945), the bylaws provided for across-the board unanimity requirements, including for election of directors and all director action. The majority shareholder successfully challenged the unanimous quorum and voting requirements. The court found the unanimity requirements to be "utterly inconsistent" with New York law. Shortly after the *Benintendi* decision, the New York legislature amended its corporate statute to make it clear that high vote and quorum requirements are not *per se* invalid. See N.Y. Bus. Corp. L. § 614. Courts have been much more receptive to unanimity requirements when embodied in shareholder agreements, rather than corporate bylaws or charter provisions. Many courts have also been willing to view unanimously adopted bylaws or charter provisions as contracts and thus enforce them much as they would shareholder agreements. Even though the precise holding of *Benintendi* has been legislatively rejected in most states, the courts' distaste for unanimity lingers. Consider the following case where the court interpreted a unanimously adopted bylaw as a shareholder agreement.

BLOUNT v. TAFT
295 N.C. 472, 246 S.E.2d 763 (1978).

SHARP, CHIEF JUSTICE.

This appeal presents a two-part question: Was Section 7 of Eastern's bylaws, adopted 20 August 1971, a valid shareholders' agreement; and, if so, was it subject to amendment under Section 4, which authorized amendment, repeal, or re-write of the bylaws by the affirmative vote of a majority of the stockholders?

The trial judge found as a fact that on 20 August 1971 all the shareholders of Eastern, by unanimous vote, adopted a set of bylaws. Among these was Section 7, which authorized the board of directors, by a majority vote, to designate an executive committee composed of three of its members one from each of the three families who owned the stock of Eastern. This committee was given exclusive authority to select the company's employees but the unanimous consent of its members was required for the employment of any individual. * * *

Defendants do not seriously question any of the trial judge's findings of fact. They do, however, dispute his conclusions of law (1) that Section 7, albeit incorporated in the bylaws of 20 August 1971 by unanimous consent of the stockholders, was a shareholders' agreement within the intent and meaning of G.S. 55–73(b); and (2) that Section 7 is binding upon the shareholders for a period not to exceed ten years from 20 August 1971 unless repealed or amended by the unanimous consent of all Eastern's shareholders . . . . .

We shall here attempt no precise definition of a "shareholders' agreement." In a broad sense the term refers to any agreement among two or more shareholders regarding their conduct in relation to the corporation whose shares they own. See N.C.Gen.Stats. § 55–73 (1975). The form and substance of such an agreement will vary with the nature of the business and the objectives of the parties. It may be an agreement between stockholders in a corporation the shares of which are publicly traded or one whose shares are closely held. However, "(a)greements among shareholders are primarily a feature of close corporations." 6 Cavitch, Business Organizations § 114.01 (1978). In the context of this case the term refers to an arrangement whereby all the shareholders in a close corporation, the stock of which is not traded in markets maintained by securities dealers or brokers, seek to conduct their business as if they were partners operating under a partnership agreement. G.S. 55–73(b).

By means of a shareholders' agreement a small group of investors who seek gain from direct participation in their business and not from trading its stock or securities in the open market can adopt the decision-making procedures of a partnership, avoid the consequences of majority rule (the standard operating procedure for corporations), and still enjoy the tax advantages and limited liability of a corporation. Such businesses are, with reason, often called "incorporated partnerships." Cary, How Close Corporations May Enjoy Partnership Advantages: Planning for the Closely Held Firm. See 48 N.W.U.L.Rev. 427 (1953); 6 Cavitch, Business Corporations § 114.01 (1978).

In earlier years, when statutes and principles governing the law of corporations were principally concerned with corporations having publicly traded stocks, agreements among shareholders whether taking the form of voting trusts, pooling agreements, or extrinsic contracts confronted considerable judicial antipathy. Courts would invalidate such consensual arrangements on the grounds that they severed from the stock incidents of ownership, such as the rights of voting and alienation, or prevented stockholders from voting "in the best interests of the corporation," or were inconsistent with the principle of majority rule embedded in the statutory norms. 1 O'Neal, Close Corporations, ss 5.04, 5.06 (2nd Ed. 1971). In connection with close corporations, agreements were also stricken if they violated the judicial doctrine, succinctly enunciated in Jackson

v. Hooper, 75 A. 568, 571 (N. J. Ct. Err. & App.1910), that shareholders "cannot be partners inter sese and a corporation as to the rest of the world." See Benintendi v. Kenton Hotel, 294 N.Y. 112, 60 N.E.2d 829 (1945).

Over the years, however, both courts and legislatures gradually changed their thinking about the relationship which incorporation created between the state and businessman and their attitude toward shareholders' agreements. 1 O'Neal, supra, § 3.52. For example, subject to certain specified limitations, voting trusts were expressly authorized by statutes, and shareholders were also given wider authority to agree upon arrangements deviating from certain corporate norms. As the number of closely held corporations increased, experience revealed that the problems of a corporation whose stock is not generally publicly traded are different from those of a publicly held corporation. The authorization of shareholders' agreements was a recognition of the needs of stockholders in a close corporation to be able to protect themselves from each other and from hostile invaders.

In such a business, if the internal "government" of the corporations were conducted strictly by the vote of the majority of the outstanding shares, the largest shareholder(s) could dominate the policies of the corporation over the objections of other shareholders. "In a nutshell, Family A with 51% Ownership of a close corporation can live in luxury off a profitable business while Family B starves with 49%." Undoubtedly, "Family B" would not have invested their money in a rarely traded stock if they had thought that they would be excluded from the decision making process and thereby the benefits of the business. See, Latty, Close Corporations and the New North Carolina Business Corporation Act, 34 N.C.L.Rev. 432, 435 (1956) (hereinafter cited as Latty); O'Neal, "Squeeze–Outs" of Minority Shareholders, § 2.10 (1975).

To protect their investment minority shareholders frequently resort to agreements (usually, and wisely, made at the time of incorporation) between themselves and the other shareholders which guarantee to the minority such things as restrictions on the transfer of stock; a veto power over hiring and decisions concerning salaries, corporate policies or distribution of earnings; or procedures for resolving disputes or making fundamental changes in the corporate charter. See 6 Cavitch, supra, §§ 114.02, 114.03(3); Robinson, North Carolina Corporation Law and Practice § 7–7 (1974). See generally 1 O'Neal, Close Corporations § 4.10 (2d Ed. 1971). The agreements may also require certain affirmative actions, such as the payment of dividends. Galler v. Galler, 32 Ill.2d 16, 203 N.E.2d 577 (1964); Arizona Ins. Co. v. L. L. Constantin & Co., 247 F.2d 388 (3d Cir.), Cert. denied, 355 U.S. 905, 78 S.Ct. 332, 2 L.Ed.2d 260 (1957). See generally, O'Neal, "Squeeze Outs" of Minority Shareholders §§ 8.05–12 (1975). It has been said that "a well-drawn stockholders' agreement entered into contemporaneously with the formation of a corporation is the most effective means of protecting the minority shareholder." Elson, Shareholders Agreements, a Shield for Minority Shareholders of Close Corporations, 22 Bus. Lawyer 449, 457 (1967) * * *

Counsel have debated at length the question whether Section 7 of Eastern's bylaws is a bylaw or a shareholders' agreement within the meaning of G.S. 55–73(b). In our view this debate is sterile, for these terms are not mutually exclusive. Bylaws which are unanimously enacted by all the shareholders of a corporation are also shareholders' agreements. Consensual agreements coming within G.S. 55–73(b) are shareholders' agreements whether they are embodied in the bylaws or in a duly executed side agreement. No particular title, phrasing or content is necessary for a consensual arrangement among all shareholders to constitute a "shareholders' agreement." Consequently, we hold that Section 7 of the bylaws adopted on 20 August 1971 is a shareholders' agreement within the meaning of G.S. 55–73(b). The decision of the Court of Appeals to the contrary is disapproved.

However, contrary to the arguments of counsel, this holding does not determine this case. Since consensual arrangements among shareholders are Agreements—the products of negotiation—they should be construed and enforced like any other contract so as to give effect to the intent of the parties as expressed in their agreements, unless they "violate the express charter or statutory provision, contemplate an illegal object, involve ... fraud, oppression or wrong against other stockholders, or are made in consideration of a private benefit to the promisor...." Wilson v. McClenny, 262 N.C. 121, 129, 136 S.E.2d 569, 575 (1964) * * *

"All contemporaneously executed written instruments between the parties, relating to the subject matter of the contract, are to be construed together in determining what was undertaken." Yates v. Brown, 275 N.C. 634, 640, 170 S.E.2d 477, 482 (1969). Here Section 7 and Section 4 were unanimously incorporated into the bylaws at the same time. There being no internal provision in Section 7 or elsewhere in the bylaws prohibiting its amendment except by unanimous consent of the shareholders, we conclude that the parties intended Section 7 to be subject to amendment by the directors or shareholders according to the procedures applicable to the other bylaws. In any event, that is the agreement they made. We hold, therefore, that if a shareholders' agreement is made a part of the charter of bylaws it will be subject to amendment as provided therein or, in the absence of an internal provision governing amendments, as provided by the statutory norms.

Ordinarily the function of a shareholders' agreement is to avoid the consequences of majority rule or other statutory norms imposed by the corporate form. Since the purpose of these arrangements is to deviate from the structures which are generally regarded as the incidents of a corporation, it is not unreasonable to require that the degree of deviation intended be explicitly set out. Most commentators advise the draftsman of a shareholders' agreement to include a specific provision governing amendments * * *

This decision, of course, will expose plaintiffs as minority shareholders in a close corporation to a risk from which Section 7 for a while protected them. However, minority shareholders who would have protection greater than that afforded by Chapter 55 of the General Statutes and the judicial doctrines prohibiting breach of a fiduciary relationship must secure it themselves in the form of "a well drawn" shareholders' agreement.

For the reasons stated in this opinion the action of the Court of Appeals in reversing the judgment of the trial court is affirmed.

NOTES

1.   The court in *Blount* stated that the only way to achieve protections beyond that afforded by the statute is through a " 'well-drawn' shareholders' agreement." This explained the court's unwillingness to enforce the bylaw as one involving across-the-board unanimity even though that clearly appeared to be the parties' intent when it was unanimously adopted. The court suggests that it will not search to find implied rights in a shareholders' agreements; such rights must be express. How can this case be reconciled with Meiselman v. Meiselman, 309 N.C. 279, 307 S.E.2d 551 (1983) where the court indicated that it would uphold a minority shareholder's reasonable expectations even in the absence of a contractual right. Curiously, the court in *Meiselman* did not even cite the *Blount* decision.

2.   Note the interplay between corporate law and contract principles as evidenced by the North Carolina court's opinion in Penley v. Penley, 314 N.C. 1, 332 S.E.2d 51 (1985):

> Plaintiff further alleged that in late 1977 a corporation was formed pursuant to an earlier oral agreement with defendant, whereby each of the parties was to own forty-eight percent of the shares of stock in the corporation and the parties' son would own four percent of the shares. From late 1977 through 9 April 1979, plaintiff and defendant-wife served as officers and directors of the corporate defendant, both parties devoting substantially all of their efforts to the operation of the corporation's business, receiving equal salaries and benefits as employees and shareholders of the corporation.
>
> The complaint further alleged that defendant-wife abandoned the plaintiff-husband on 9 April 1979 and filed a civil action which she voluntarily dismissed on 2 July 1979 at which time she acknowledged the plaintiff-husband's ownership interest in the corporation and property which had been purchased with the proceeds of the defendant corporation and that the parties would continue to operate the business as in the past. Subsequently, on 31 December 1979, defendant-wife again abandoned the plaintiff and since that time "has wrongfully and intentionally denied the plaintiff any rights" in the corporate defendant, "either as an officer, employee, shareholder, or otherwise" and has "wilfully and wrongfully converted to her own use and benefit" proceeds from the operation of the corporate defendant and has otherwise "so conducted the business and affairs of the [corporate defendant] as to dissipate its assets

and render the interest of [plaintiff] in that corporation essentially worthless." * * *

[P]laintiff contends that the majority incorrectly concluded that the Business Corporation Act defeats his claim. We agree with plaintiff.

The Court of Appeals determined that the agreement between plaintiff and defendant was essentially a stock subscription pursuant to G.S. 55–43. Since G.S. 55–43(b) requires such agreements to be in writing, that court concluded that this agreement was unenforceable. We do not agree with the court below that G.S. 55–43 is applicable to the present case.... This is not an action in which defendant is trying to enforce plaintiff's *promise to take* shares. Rather, we view plaintiff's present action as an attempt to enforce defendant's *promise or contract to issue* shares to plaintiff, the number of shares to represent a certain percentage of ownership within a corporation to be formed.

The majority in the Court of Appeals also considered the oral agreement between the parties to be a shareholder's agreement, unenforceable because not in writing as required by G.S. 55–73(b). Pigeonholing plaintiff's theory of recovery in such a narrow and inflexible fashion is incorrect in these circumstances. G.S. 55–73(b) provides, *inter alia,* that

> [N]o written agreement to which all of the shareholders have actually assented ... which relates to any phase of the affairs of the corporation, ... shall be invalid ... on the ground that it is an attempt by the parties thereto to treat the corporation as if it were a partnership or to arrange their relationships in a manner that would be appropriate only between partners.

Subsection (b), like the other two subsections of G.S. 55–73, simply abrogates, as to agreements within its purview, certain judicial doctrines which had formerly invalidated particular shareholders' agreements on those grounds which this section now disallows. Blount v. Taft, 295 N.C. 472, 246 S.E.2d 763 (1978) While G.S. 55–73 has been referred to as the "heart" of the North Carolina Business Corporation Act with respect to close corporations, see Latty, *Close Corporations and the New North Carolina Business Corporation Act,* 34 N.C.L.Rev. 432, at 438–440 (1956), we do not view this statute as plaintiff's exclusive legal remedy. Plaintiff has properly chosen an alternate legal theory, premised primarily on defendant's oral agreement to convey an interest in the corporation—a question of simple contract law. Accordingly, we do not view the parties' agreement as an unenforceable shareholders' agreement.

GEARING v. KELLY

11 N.Y.2d 201, 227 N.Y.S.2d 897, 182 N.E.2d 391 (1962).

PER CURIAM.

Appellants, who own 50% of the stock of the Radium Chemical Company, Inc., seek ... to set aside the election of a director.... [T]he court sits as a court of equity which may order a new election 'as justice may require'. We have concluded, as did the majority of the Appellate Division, that appellants had failed to show that justice requires a new election, in that they may not now complain of a irregularity which they themselves have caused.

Mrs. Meacham stayed away from the meeting of March 6, 1961 for the sole purpose of preventing a quorum from assembling, and intended, in that manner, to paralyze the board. There can be no doubt, and indeed it is not even suggested, that she lacked notice or in any manner found it temporarily inconvenient to present herself at that particular time and place. It is certain, then, that Mrs. Meacham's absence from the noticed meeting of the board was intentional and deliberate. Much is said by appellants about a desire to protect their equal ownership of stock through equal representation on the board. It is, however, clear that such balance was voluntarily surrendered in 1955. Whether this was done in reliance on representations of Kelly, Sr., as alleged in the plenary suit, is properly a matter for that litigation, rather than the summary type of action here.

The relief sought by appellants, the ordering of a new election, would, furthermore, be of no avail to them, for Mrs. Meacham would then be required, as evidence of her good faith, to attend. Such a futile act will not be ordered.

The identity of interests of the appellants is readily apparent. Mrs. Gearing has fully indorsed and supported all of the demands and actions of her daughter, and has associated herself with the refusal to attend the directors' meeting. A court of equity need not permit Mrs. Gearing to attack actions of the board of directors which were marred through conduct of the director whom she has actively encouraged. To do so would allow a director to refuse to attend meetings, knowing that thereafter an associated stockholder could frustrate corporate action until all of their joint demands were met.

The failure of Mrs. Meacham to attend the directors' meeting, under the present circumstances, bars appellants from invoking an exercise of the equitable powers lodged in the courts under the statute.

The order appealed from should be affirmed, with costs.

FROESSEL, JUDGE (DISSENTING).

The by-laws of Radium Chemical Company, Inc., provided for a board of four directors, a majority of whom 'shall constitute a quorum for the transaction of business'. Prior to 1955 the board consisted of appellant Meacham, who had succeeded her father (appellant Gearing's late husband), respondent Kelly, Sr., and Margaret E. Lee. In 1955 Kelly, Jr., was elected to the then vacant directorship. The board continued thus until Margaret Lee offered her resignation in 1961 and, on March 6 of that year, at a meeting of the board of directors at which she and the two Kellys were present, her resignation was accepted. Thereupon the two

Kellys elected Julian Hemphill, a son-in-law of Kelly, Sr., to replace Margaret Lee.

I agree with Justice Eager, who dissented in the Appellate Division, that two members of the board were insufficient to constitute a quorum in this case for the purpose of electing the new director. It necessarily follows that the election of Julian Hemphill is not merely irregular, as the majority hold, but is wholly void and must be set aside.

Section 25 of the General Corporation Law grants to the court two alternatives in a case such as this: (1) to confirm the election, or (2) to order a new election as justice may require. [T]he clause 'as justice may require' does not enlarge the court's power nor authorize it to grant different relief from that specified in the statute. There is no basis whatever here for the application of the doctrine of estoppel, and in no event could it reasonably be applied to the non-director, appellant Gearing, a substantial stockholder in this corporation. The purported election is, therefore, a nullity.

This is a mere contest for control, and the court should not assist either side, each of which holds an equal interest in the corporation, particularly where, as here, petitioners were willing that director Meacham attend meetings for the purpose of transacting all the necessary business of the board, but were unwilling that she attend a meeting, the purpose of which was to strip them of every vestige of control. Appellant Meacham had surrendered nothing in 1955 when she permitted Kelly, Jr., to become a director as well as his father, Margaret Lee was then a third director.

The statute mandates a new election and that should be ordered. It is no answer to say that the results will probably be the same. If the parties are deadlocked, whether as directors or stockholders, and choose to remain that way, they have other remedies, and I see no reason why we should help one side or the other by disregarding a by-law that follows the statute, particularly when it results in giving the Kellys complete control of the corporation.

NOTES

1. Compare, *Campbell v. Loew's,* set forth in Chapter 6 where the court did not complain about directors' intentionally absenting themselves from a meeting in order to prevent a forum and therefore leave the matter to the shareholders.[a]

2. New York subsequently changed its laws to allow directors to fill a vacancy even though there is less than a quorum of directors in office,

---

a. The court there noted (134 A.2d at 853):

While a concerted plan to abstain from attending directors' meetings may be improper under some circumstances, I cannot find that the fact that the so-called Vogel directors did not attend directors meetings called to take action which would give an opposing faction an absolute majority of the board—solely because of director resignations—is such a breach of their fiduciary duty that they should be judicially compelled to attend board meetings. This is particularly so where stockholder action is in the offing to fill the board.

provided a majority of those in office approve the selection. The director so appointed will serve until his successor is elected and qualified. See N.Y. Bus. Corp. L. § 705. Delaware and the Model Act have similar provisions Model Bus. Corp. Act § 8.10(a); Del. § 223(a)(1).

Under these statutes, what happens if the shareholders are deadlocked at the next meeting and no successor can be elected? Would this provision have made a difference in the *Gearing* case?

———

SECTION 4. SHAREHOLDER AGREEMENTS AND DIRECTOR DISCRETION

McQUADE v. STONEHAM

263 N.Y. 323, 189 N.E. 234 (1934).

POUND, CHIEF JUDGE.

The action is brought to compel specific performance of an agreement between the parties, entered into to secure the control of National Exhibition Company, also called the Baseball Club (New York Nationals or 'Giants'). This was one of Stoneham's enterprises which used the New York polo grounds for its home games. McGraw was manager of the Giants. McQuade was at the time the contract was entered into a city magistrate. He resigned December 8, 1930.

Defendant Stoneham became the owner of 1,306 shares, or a majority of the stock of National Exhibition Company. Plaintiff and defendant McGraw each purchased 70 shares of his stock. Plaintiff paid Stoneham $50,338.10 for the stock he purchased. As a part of the transaction, the agreement in question was entered into. It was dated May 21, 1919. Some of its pertinent provisions are

'VIII.   The parties hereto will use their best endeavors for the purpose of continuing as directors of said Company and as officers thereof the following:

'Directors:

'Charles A. Stoneham,

'John J. McGraw,

'Francis X. McQuade

'—with the right to the party of the first part [Stoneham] to name all additional directors as he sees fit:

'Officers:

'Charles A. Stoneham, President,

'John J. McGraw, Vice–President,

'Francis X. McQuade, Treasurer.

'IX.　No salaries are to be paid to any of the above officers or directors, except as follows:

'President $45,000
'Vice–President 7,500
'Treasurer 7,500

'X.　There shall be no change in said salaries, no change in the amount of capital, or the number of shares, no change or amendment of the by-laws of the corporation or any matters regarding the policy of the business of the corporation or any matters which may in anywise affect, endanger or interfere with the rights of minority stockholders, excepting upon the mutual and unanimous consent of all of the parties hereto. * * *

'XIV.　This agreement shall continue and remain in force so long as the parties or any of them or the representative of any, own the stock referred to in this agreement, to wit, the party of the first part, 1,166 shares, the party of the second part 70 shares and the party of the third part 70 shares, except as may otherwise appear by this agreement. * * * '

In pursuance of this contract Stoneham became president and McGraw vice president of the corporation. McQuade became treasurer. In June, 1925, his salary was increased to $10,000 a year. He continued to act until May 2, 1928, when Leo J. Bondy was elected to succeed him. The board of directors consisted of seven men. The four outside of the parties hereto were selected by Stoneham and he had complete control over them. At the meeting of May 2, 1928, Stoneham and McGraw refrained from voting, McQuade voted for himself, and the other four voted for Bondy. Defendants did not keep their agreement with McQuade to use their best efforts to continue him as treasurer. On the contrary, he was dropped with their entire acquiescence. At the next stockholders' meeting he was dropped as a director although they might have elected him.

The courts below have refused to order the reinstatement of McQuade, but have given him damages for wrongful discharge, with a right to sue for future damages.

The cause for dropping McQuade was due to the falling out of friends. McQuade and Stoneham had disagreed. The trial court has found in substance that their numerous quarrels and disputes did not affect the orderly and efficient administration of the business of the corporation; that plaintiff was removed because he had antagonized the dominant Stoneham by persisting in challenging his power over the corporate treasury and for no misconduct on his part. The court also finds that plaintiff was removed by Stoneham for protecting the corporation and its minority stockholders. We will assume that Stoneham put him out when he might have retained him, merely in order to get rid of him.

Defendants say that the contract in suit was void because the directors held their office charged with the duty to act for the corporation according to their best judgment and that any contract which compels a director to vote to keep any particular person in office and at a stated salary is illegal. Directors are the exclusive executive representatives of the corporation, charged with administration of its internal affairs and the management and use of its assets. They manage the business of the corporation. (General Corporation Law, Consol. Laws, c. 23, § 27.) 'An agreement to continue a man as president is dependent upon his continued loyalty to the interests of the corporation.' Fells v. Katz, 256 N. Y. 67, 72, 175 N. E. 516, 517. So much is undisputed.

Plaintiff contends that the converse of this proposition is true and that an agreement among directors to continue a man as an officer of a corporation is not to be broken so long as such officer is loyal to the interests of the corporation and that, as plaintiff has been found loyal to the corporation, the agreement of defendants is enforceable.

Although it has been held that an agreement among stockholders whereby it is attempted to divest the directors of their power to discharge an unfaithful employee of the corporation is illegal as against public policy (Fells v. Katz, supra), it must be equally true that the stockholders may not, by agreement among themselves, control the directors in the exercise of the judgment vested in them by virtue of their office to elect officers and fix salaries. Their motives may not be questioned so long as their acts are legal. The bad faith or the improper motives of the parties does not change the rule. Manson v. Curtis, 119 N. E. 559. Directors may not by agreements entered into as stockholders abrogate their independent judgment.

Stockholders may, of course, combine to elect directors. That rule is well settled. As Holmes, C. J., pointedly said (Brightman v. Bates, 175 Mass. 105, 111, 55 N. E. 809, 811): 'If stockholders want to make their power felt, they must unite. There is no reason why a majority should not agree to keep together.' The power to unite is, however, limited to the election of directors and is not extended to contracts whereby limitations are placed on the power of directors to manage the business of the corporation by the selection of agents at defined salaries.

The minority shareholders whose interests McQuade says he has been punished for protecting, are not, aside from himself, complaining about his discharge. He is not acting for the corporation or for them in this action. It is impossible to see how the corporation has been injured by the substitution of Bondy as treasurer in place of McQuade. As McQuade represents himself in this action and seeks redress for his own wrongs, 'we prefer to listen to [the corporation and the minority stockholders] before any decision as to their wrongs.' Faulds v. Yates, 57 Ill. 416, 417, 11 Am. Rep. 24.

It is urged that we should pay heed to the morals and manners of the market place to sustain this agreement and that we should hold that its violation gives rise to a cause of action for damages rather than base our decision on any outworn notions of public policy. Public policy is a dangerous guide in determining the validity of a contract and courts should not interfere lightly with the freedom of competent parties to make their own contracts. We do not close our eyes to the fact that such agreements, tacitly or openly arrived at, are not uncommon, especially in close corporations where the stockholders are doing business for convenience under a corporate organization. We know that majority stockholders, united in voting trusts, effectively manage the business of a corporation by choosing trustworthy directors to reflect their policies in the corporate management. Nor are we unmindful that McQuade has, so the court has found, been shabbily treated as a purchaser of stock from Stoneham. We have said: 'A trustee is held to something stricter than the morals of the market place' (Meinhard v. Salmon, 164 N. E. 545, 546), but Stoneham and McGraw were not trustees for McQuade as an individual. Their duty was to the corporation and its stockholders, to be exercised according to their unrestricted lawful judgment. They were under no legal obligation to deal righteously with McQuade if it was against public policy to do so.

The courts do not enforce mere moral obligations, nor legal ones either, unless some one seeks to establish rights which may be waived by custom and for convenience. We are constrained by authority to hold that a contract is illegal and void so far as it precludes the board of directors, at the risk of incurring legal liability, from changing officers, salaries, or policies or retaining individuals in office, except by consent of the contracting parties. On the whole, such a holding is probably preferable to one which would open the courts to pass on the motives of directors in the lawful exercise of their trust.

A further reason for reversal exists. At the time the contract was made the plaintiff was a city magistrate. He complains that the defendant Stoneham breached the contract by failure 'to use his best endeavors' for the purpose of continuing him as a director and treasurer of the corporation which Stoneham controlled. The plaintiff resigned as city magistrate after the commencement of this action. He has recovered a judgment for 'the amount of the salary of the treasurer of the National Exhibition Company at the rate of $10,000 per year from the second day of May, 1928, to the date of the entry of this decree.' * * * *

Judgments reversed, etc.

CLARK v. DODGE
269 N.Y. 410, 199 N.E. 641 (1936).

CROUCH, JUDGE.

The action is for the specific performance of a contract between the plaintiff, Clark, and the defendant Dodge, relating to the affairs of the two defendant corporations.

Those facts, briefly stated, are as follows: The two corporate defendants are New Jersey corporations manufacturing medicinal preparations by secret formulae. The main office, factory, and assets of both corporations are located in the state of New York. In 1921, and at all times since, Clark owned 25 per cent and Dodge 75 per cent of the stock of each corporation. Dodge took no active part in the business, although he was a director, and through ownership of their qualifying shares, controlled the other directors of both corporations. He was the president of Bell & Co., Inc., and nominally general manager of Hollings–Smith Company, Inc. The plaintiff, Clark, was a director and held the offices of treasurer and general manager of Bell & Co., Inc., and also had charge of the major portion of the business of Hollings–Smith Company, Inc. The formulae and methods of manufacture of the medicinal preparations were known to him alone. Under date of February 15, 1921, Dodge and Clark, the sole owners of the stock of both corporations, entered into a written agreement under seal, which after reciting the stock ownership of both parties, the desire of Dodge that Clark should continue in the efficient management and control of the business of Bell & Co., Inc., so long as he should 'remain faithful, efficient and competent to so manage and control the said business'; and his further desire that Clark should not be the sole custodian of a specified formula, but should share his knowledge thereof and of the method of manufacture with a son of Dodge, provided, in substance, as follows: That Dodge during his lifetime and, after his death, a trustee to be appointed by his will, would so vote his stock and so vote as a director that the plaintiff (a) should continue to be a director of Bell & Co., Inc.; and (b) should continue as its general manager so long as he should be 'faithful, efficient and competent'; (c) should during his life receive one-fourth of the net income of the corporations either by way of salary or dividends; and (d) that no unreasonable or incommensurate salaries should be paid to other officers or agents which would so reduce the net income as materially to affect Clark's profits. Clark on his part agreed to disclose the specified formula to the son and to instruct him in the details and methods of manufacture; and, further, at the end of his life to bequeath his stock—if no issue survived him—to the wife and children of Dodge.

It was further provided that the provisions in regard to the division of net profits and the regulation of salaries should also apply to the Hollings–Smith Company.

The complaint alleges due performance of the contract by Clark and breach thereof by Dodge in that he has failed to use his stock control to continue Clark as a director and as general manager, and has prevented Clark from receiving his proportion of the income, while taking his own, by causing the employment of incompetent persons at excessive salaries, and otherwise.

The relief sought is reinstatement as director and general manager and an accounting by Dodge and by the corporations for waste and for the proportion of net income due plaintiff, with an injunction against further violations.

The only question which need be discussed is whether the contract is illegal as against public policy within the decision in McQuade v. Stoneham, 189 N.E. 234, upon the authority of which the complaint was dismissed by the Appellate Division.

'The business of a corporation shall be managed by its board of directors.' General Corporation Law (Consol.Laws, c. 23) § 27. That is the statutory norm. Are we committed by the McQuade Case to the doctrine that there may be no variation, however slight or innocuous, from that norm, where salaries or policies or the retention of individuals in office are concerned? There is ample authority supporting that doctrine … and something may be said for it, since it furnishes a simple, if arbitrary, test. Apart from its practical administrative convenience, the reasons upon which it is said to rest are more or less nebulous. Public policy, the intention of the Legislature, detriment to the corporation, are phrases which in this connection mean little. Possible harm to bona fide purchasers of stock or to creditors or to stockholding minorities have more substance; but such harms are absent in many instances. If the enforcement of a particular contract damages nobody—not even, in any perceptible degree, the public—one sees no reason for holding it illegal, even though it impinges slightly upon the broad provision of section 27. Damage suffered or threatened is a logical and practical test, and has come to be the one generally adopted by the courts. See 28 Columbia Law Review 366, 372. Where the directors are the sole stockholders, there seems to be no objection to enforcing an agreement among them to vote for certain people as officers. There is no direct decision to that effect in this court, yet there are strong indications that such a rule has long been recognized. The opinion in Manson v. Curtis, 119 N.E. 559, 562, closed its discussion by saying: 'The rule that all the stockholders by their universal consent may do as they choose with the corporate concerns and assets, provided the interests of creditors are not affected, because they are the complete owners of the corporation, cannot be invoked here.' That was because all the stockholders were not parties to the agreement there in question. So, where the public was not affected, 'the parties in interest, might, by their original agreement of incorporation, limit their respective rights and powers,' even where there was a conflicting statutory standard. Ripin v. United States Woven Label Co., 98 N.E. 855, 857. 'Such corporations were little more (though not quite the same as) than chartered partnerships.' (Id. at 856). In Lorillard v. Clyde, 86 N.Y. 384, and again in Drucklieb v. Sam H. Harris, 102 N.E. 599, where the questioned agreements were entered into by all the stockholders of small corporations about to be organized, the fact that the agreements conflicted to some extent with the statutory duty of the directors to manage the corporate affairs was thought not to render the agreements illegal as against public policy, though it was said they might not be binding upon the directors of the corporation when organized. Cf. Lehman, J., dissenting opinion in the McQuade Case. The rule recognized in Manson v. Curtis, and quoted above, was thus stated by Blackmar, J., in Kassel v. Empire Tinware Co.,

178 App.Div. 176, 180, 164 N.Y.S. 1033, 1035: 'As the parties to the action are the complete owners of the corporation, there is no reason why the exercise of the power and discretion of the directors cannot be controlled by valid agreement between themselves, provided that the interests of creditors are not affected.'

Fells v. Katz, 175 N.E. 516, where all the stockholders were parties to the agreement, is no authority to the contrary. The decision there merely construed the agreement and found that plaintiff had breached it, thereby justifying his removal. 'The agreement of the stockholders to continue a man in the directorate must be construed as an obligation to retain him only so long as he keeps the agreement on his part faithfully to act as a trustee for the stockholders.' 175 N.E. 516, 517. Indeed, the case may be regarded as applying the test of damage above referred to. Any other construction would have caused damage to the corporation and its stockholders and would have been illegal.

Except for the broad dicta in the McQuade opinion, we think there can be no doubt that the agreement here in question was legal and that the complaint states a cause of action. There was no attempt to sterilize the board of directors, as in the Manson and McQuade Cases. The only restrictions on Dodge were (a) that as a stockholder he should vote for Clark as a director—a perfectly legal contract; (b) that as director he should continue Clark as general manager, so long as he proved faithful, efficient, and competent—an agreement which could harm nobody; (c) that Clark should always receive as salary or dividends one-fourth of the 'net income.' For the purposes of this motion, it is only just to construe that phrase as meaning whatever was left for distribution after the directors had in good faith set aside whatever they deemed wise; (d) that no salaries to other officers should be paid, unreasonable in amount or incommensurate with services rendered—a beneficial and not a harmful agreement.

If there was any invasion of the powers of the directorate under that agreement, it is so slight as to be negligible; and certainly there is no damage suffered by or threatened to anybody. The broad statements in the McQuade opinion, applicable to the facts there, should be confined to those facts.

The judgment of the Appellate Division should be reversed and the order of the Special Term affirmed, with costs in this court and in the Appellate Division.

NOTES

1. Why is the agreement in *Clark v. Dodge* valid, while the one in *McQuade* was not?

2. *Statutory Responses.* For a statute that draws similar distinctions, compare N.C. Gen. Stats. § 55–7–31(b) ("Except in the case of a public corporation, no written agreement to which all of the shareholders have

actually assented, whether embodied in the articles of incorporation or bylaws or in any side agreement in writing and signed by all the parties thereto, and which relates to any phase of the affairs of the corporation, whether to the management of its business or division of its profits or otherwise, shall be invalid as between the parties thereto, on the ground that it is an attempt by the parties thereto to treat the corporation as if it were a partnership or to arrange their relationships in a manner that would be appropriate between partners. A transferee of shares covered by such agreement who acquires them with knowledge thereof is bound by its provisions.") with Id. § 55–7–31(c) ("A written agreement between all or less than all of the shareholders, whether solely between themselves or between one or more of them and a party who is not a shareholder, is not invalid as between the parties thereto on the ground that it so relates to the conduct of the affairs of the corporation as to interfere with the discretion of the board of directors. The effect of any such agreement shall be to relieve the directors and impose upon the shareholders who are parties to the agreement the liability for managerial acts or omissions which is imposed on directors to the extent and so long as the discretion or powers of the board in its management of corporate affairs is controlled by such agreement"). Under the leadership of Dean Latty, a professor at Duke University Law School, North Carolina adopted this forward looking legislation that has since been followed in many other jurisdictions.

GALLER v. GALLER

32 Ill.2d 16, 203 N.E.2d 577 (1964).

UNDERWOOD, JUSTICE.

Plaintiff, Emma Galler, sued in equity for an accounting for specific performance of an agreement made in July, 1955, between plaintiff and her husband, of one part, and defendants, Isadore A. Galler and his wife, Rose, of the other. Defendants appealed from a decree of the superior court of Cook County granting the relief prayed. The First District Appellate Court reversed the decree and denied specific performance, affirming in part the order for an accounting, and modifying the order awarding master's fees. That decision is appealed here on a certificate of importance.

There is no substantial dispute as to the facts in this case. From 1919 to 1924, Benjamin and Isadore Galler, brothers, were equal partners in the Galler Drug Company, a wholesale drug concern. In 1924 the business was incorporated under the Illinois Business Corporation Act, each owning one half of the outstanding 220 shares of stock. In 1945 each contracted to sell 6 shares to an employee, Rosenberg, at a price of $10,500 for each block of 6 shares, payable within 10 years. They guaranteed to repurchase the shares if Rosenberg's employment were terminated, and further agreed that if they sold their shares, Rosenberg would receive the same price per share as that paid for the brothers' shares.

Rosenberg was still indebted for the 12 shares in July, 1955, and continued to make payments on account even after Benjamin Galler died in 1957 and after the institution of this action by Emma Galler in 1959. Rosenberg was not involved in this litigation either as a party or as a witness, and in July of 1961, prior to the time that the master in chancery hearings were concluded, defendants Isadore and Rose Galler purchased the 12 shares from Rosenberg. A supplemental complaint was filed by the plaintiff, Emma Galler, asserting an equitable right to have 6 of the 12 shares transferred to her and offering to pay the defendants one half of the amount that the defendants paid Rosenberg. The parties have stipulated that pending disposition of the instant case, these shares will not be voted or transferred. For approximately one year prior to the entry of the decree by the chancellor in July of 1962, there were no outstanding minority shareholder interests.

In March, 1954, Benjamin and Isadore, on the advice of their accountant, decided to enter into an agreement for the financial protection of their immediate families and to assure their families, after death of either brother, equal control of the corporation. In June, 1954, while the agreement was in the process of preparation by an attorney-associate of the accountant, Benjamin suffered a heart attack. Although he resumed his business duties some months later, he was again stricken in February, 1955, and thereafter was unable to return to work. During his brother's illness, Isadore asked the accountant to have the shareholders' agreement put in final form in order to protect Benjamin's wife, and this was done by another attorney employed in the accountant's office.[a] On a Saturday

[a]. As described by the court: "The July, 1955, agreement in question here, entered into between Benjamin, Emma, Isadore and Rose, recites that Benjamin and Isadore each own 47 1/2% of the issued and outstanding shares of the Galler Drug Company, an Illinois corporation, and that Benjamin and Isadore desired to provide income for the support and maintenance of their immediate families. No reference is made to the shares then being purchased by Rosenberg. The essential features of the contested portions of the agreement are substantially as set forth in the opinion of the Appellate Court: that the bylaws of the corporation will be amended to provide for a board of four directors; that the necessary quorum shall be three directors; and that no directors' meeting shall be held without giving ten days notice to all directors. The shareholders will cast their votes for the above named persons (Isadore, Rose, Benjamin and Emma) as directors at said special meeting and at any other meeting held for the purpose of electing directors. In the event of the death of either brother his wife shall have the right to nominate a director in place of the decedent. Certain annual dividends will be declared by the corporation. The dividend shall be $50,000 payable out of the accumulated earned surplus in excess of $500,000. If 50% of the annual net profits after taxes exceeds the minimum $50,000, then the directors shall have discretion to declare a dividend up to 50% of the annual net profits. If the net profits are less than $50,000, nevertheless the minimum $50,000 annual dividend shall be declared, providing the $500,000 surplus is maintained. Earned surplus is defined. The certificates evidencing the said shares of Benjamin Galler and Isadore Galler shall be a legend that the shares are subject to the terms of this agreement. (10) A salary continuation agreement shall be entered into by the corporation which shall authorize the corporation upon the death of Benjamin Galler or Isadore Galler, or both, to pay a sum equal to twice the salary of such officer, payable monthly over a five-year period. Said sum shall be paid to the widow during her widowhood, but should be paid to such widow's children if the widow remarries within the five-year period. The parties to this agreement further agree and hereby grant to the corporation the authority to purchase, in the event of the death of either Benjamin or Isadore, so much of the stock of Galler Drug Company held by the estate as is necessary to provide sufficient funds to pay the federal estate tax, the Illinois inheritance tax and other administrative expenses of the estate. If as a result of such purchase from the estate of the decedent the amount of dividends to be received by the heirs is reduced, the parties shall nevertheless vote for directors so as to give the estate and

night in July, 1955, the accountant brought the agreement to Benjamin's home, and 6 copies of it were executed there by the two brothers and their wives. The accountant then collected all signed copies of the agreement and informed the parties that he was taking them for safe keeping. Between the execution of the agreement in July, 1955, and Benjamin's death in December, 1957, the agreement was not modified. Benjamin suffered a stroke late in July, 1955, and on August 2, 1955, Isadore and the accountant and a notary public brought to Benjamin for signature two powers of attorney which were retained by the accountant after Benjamin executed them with Isadore as a witness. The plaintiff did not read the powers and she never had them. One of the powers authorized the transfer of Benjamin's bank account to Emma and the other power enabled Emma to vote Benjamin's 104 shares. Because of the state of Benjamin's health, nothing further was said to him by any of the parties concerning the agreement. It appears from the evidence that some months after the agreement was signed, the defendants Isadore and Rose Galler and their son, the defendant, Aaron Galler sought to have the agreements destroyed. The evidence is undisputed that defendants had decided prior to Benjamin's death they would not honor the agreement, but never disclosed their intention to plaintiff or her husband.

On July 21, 1956, Benjamin executed an instrument creating a trust naming his wife as trustee. The trust covered, among other things, the 104 shares of Galler Drug Company stock and the stock certificates were endorsed by Benjamin and delivered to Emma. When Emma presented the certificates to defendants for transfer into her name as trustee, they sought to have Emma abandon the 1955 agreement or enter into some kind of a noninterference agreement as a price for the transfer of the shares. Finally, in September, 1956, after Emma had refused to abandon the shareholders' agreement, she did agree to permit defendant Aaron to become president for one year and agreed that she would not interfere with the business during that year. The stock was then reissued in her name as trustee. During the year 1957 while Benjamin was still alive, Emma tried many times to arrange a meeting with Isadore to discuss business matters but he refused to see her.

Shortly after Benjamin's death, Emma went to the office and demanded the terms of the 1955 agreement be carried out. Isadore told her that anything she had to say could be said to Aaron, who then told her that his father would not abide by the agreement. He offered a modification of the agreement by proposing the salary continuation payment but without her becoming a director. When Emma refused to modify the agreement and sought enforcement of its terms, defendants refused and this suit followed.

heirs the same representation as before (2 directors out of 4, even though they own less stock), and also that the corporation pay an additional benefit payment equal to the diminution of the dividends. In the event either Benjamin or Isadore decides to sell his shares he is required to offer them first to the remaining shareholders and then to the corporation at book value, according each six months to accept the offer.''

During the last few years of Benjamin's life both brothers drew an annual salary of $42,000. Aaron, whose salary was $15,000 as manager of the warehouse prior to September, 1956, has since the time that Emma agreed to his acting as president drawn an annual salary of $20,000. In 1957, 1958, and 1959 a $40,000 annual dividend was paid. Plaintiff has received her proportionate share of the dividend. * * *

The Appellate Court found the 1955 agreement void because 'the undue duration, stated purpose and substantial disregard of the provisions of the Corporation Act outweigh any considerations which might call for divisibility' and held that 'the public policy of this state demands voiding this entire agreement'.

While the conduct of defendant towards plaintiff was clearly inequitable, the basically controlling factor is the absence of an objecting minority interest, together with the absence of public detriment. Since the issues here presented must be resolved in accordance with the public policy of this State as exemplified in prior decisions or pertinent statutes, it will be helpful to review the applicable case law.

Faulds v. Yates, 57 Ill. 416, decided by this court in 1870, established the general rule that the owners of the majority of the stock of a corporation have the right to select the agents for the management of the corporation. This court observed: 'It is strange that a man can not, for honest purposes, unite with others in the protection and security of his property and rights without liability to the charge of fraud and inequity'. * * *

Again, in 1913, this court in Venner v. Chicago City Railway Co., 258 Ill. 523, 539, 101 N.E. 949, 953, followed the Faulds case and said: 'There is no statute of this state which prohibits a trust of the stock of a corporation for the purpose of controlling its management. There is no rule of public policy in this state which prohibits a combination of the owners of the majority of the stock of a corporation for the purpose of controlling the corporation. On the contrary, it has been expressly held that a contract by the owners of more than one-half of the shares of stock of a corporation to elect the directors of the corporation so as to secure the management of its property, to ballot among themselves for directors and officers if they could not agree, to cast their vote as a unit as the majority should decide so as to control the election, and not to buy or sell stock except for their joint benefit, is not dishonest, violative of the rights of others, or in contravention of public policy. This case has been sustained by later decision of this court [citing cases], has been approved by the decisions of the courts of other states (citing cases,) has been cited by text-writers announcing the law as therein stated (citation,) and we regard the decision as sound in principle.' * * *

The power to invalidate the agreements on the grounds of public policy is so far reaching and so easily abused that it should be called into action to set aside or annul the solemn engagement of parties dealing on equal terms only in cases where the corrupt or dangerous tendency clearly and unequivocally appears upon the face of the agreement itself or is the necessary inference from the matters which are expressed, and the only apparent exception to this general rule is to be found in those cases where the agreement, though fair and unobjectionable on its face, is a part of a corrupt scheme and is made to disguise the real nature of the transaction. 12 Am.Jur. 671.

Defendants have referred us to cases in other jurisdictions and the Appellate Courts of this State. Neither is persuasive, for Odman exemplifies the public policy of Massachusetts whose courts, while not holding agreements such as we have here invalid per se, have not relaxed their requirements of strict statutory compliance when dealing with close corporations, at least where all the stockholders have not signed the agreement in question. Anno: Validity and Effect of Agreement Controlling the Vote of Corporate Stock, 45 A.L.R.2d 799, 815. In any event, decisions setting forth the public policies of other jurisdictions will not be followed if not harmonious with the judicially declared public policy of Illinois.

At this juncture it should be emphasized that we deal here with a so-called close corporation. Various attempts at definition of the close corporation have been made. For a collection of those most frequently proffered, see O'Neal, Close Corporations, § 1.02 (1958). For our purposes, a close corporation is one in which the stock is held in a few hands, or in a few families, and wherein it is not at all, or only rarely, dealt in by buying or selling. Moreover, it should be recognized that shareholder agreements similar to that in question here are often, as a practical consideration, quite necessary for the protection of those financially interested in the close corporation. While the shareholder of a public-issue corporation may readily sell his shares on the open market should management fail to use, in his opinion, sound business judgment, his counterpart of the close corporation often has a large total of his entire capital invested in the business and has no ready market for his shares should he desire to sell. He feels, understandably, that he is more than a mere investor and that his voice should be heard concerning all corporate activity. Without a shareholder agreement, specifically enforceable by the courts, insuring him a modicum of control, a large minority shareholder might find himself at the mercy of an oppressive or unknowledgeable majority. Moreover, as in the case at bar, the shareholders of a close corporation are often also the directors and officers thereof. With substantial shareholding interests abiding in each member of the board of directors, it is often quite impossible to secure, as in the large public-issue corporation, independent board judgment free from personal motivations concerning corporate policy. For these and other reasons too voluminous to enumerate here, often the only sound basis for protection is afforded by a lengthy, detailed shareholder agreement securing the rights and obligations of all concerned.

As the preceding review of the applicable decisions of this court points out, there has been a definite, albeit inarticulate, trend toward eventual judicial treatment of the close corporation as sui generis. Several share-holder-director agreements that have technically 'violated' the letter of the Business Corporation Act have nevertheless been upheld in the light of the existing practical circumstances, i. e., no apparent public injury, the absence of a complaining minority interest, and no apparent prejudice to creditors. However, we have thus far not attempted to limit these decisions as applicable only to close corporations and have seemingly implied that general considerations regarding judicial supervision of all corporate behavior apply.

The practical result of this series of cases, while liberally giving legal efficacy to particular agreements in special circumstances notwithstanding literal 'violations' of statutory corporate law, has been to inject much doubt and uncertainty into the thinking of the bench and corporate bar of Illinois concerning shareholder agreements.

It is therefore necessary, we feel, to discuss the instant case with the problems peculiar to the close corporation particularly in mind.

It would admittedly facilitate judicial supervision of corporate behavior if a strict adherence to the provisions of the Business Corporation Act were required in all cases without regard to the practical exigencies peculiar to the close corporation. However, courts have long ago quite realistically, we feel, relaxed their attitudes concerning statutory compliance when dealing with close corporate behavior, permitting 'slight deviations' from corporate 'norms' in order to give legal efficacy to common business practice. See e. g., Clark v. Dodge, 269 N.Y. 410, 199 N.E. 641; Benintendi v. Kenton Hotel, 294 N.Y. 112, 60 N.E.2d 829 (dissenting opinion subsequently legislatively approved.). This attitude is illustrated by the following language in Clark v. Dodge: 'Public policy, the intention of the Legislature, detriment to the corporation, are phrases which in this connection (the court was discussing a shareholder-director agreement whereby the directors pledged themselves to vote for certain people as officers of the corporation) mean little. Possible harm to bona fide purchasers of stock or to creditors or to stockholding minorities have more substance; but such harms are absent in many instances. If the enforcement of a particular contract damages nobody—not even, in any perceptible degree, the public—one sees no reason for holding it illegal, even though it impinges slightly upon the broad provisions of (the relevant statute providing that the business of a corporation shall be managed by its board of directors.). Damage suffered or threatened is a logical and practical test, and has come to be the one generally adopted by the courts.'

Again, 'As the parties to the action are the complete owners of the corporation, there is no reason why the exercise of the power and discretion of the directors cannot be controlled by valid agreement between themselves, provided that the interests of creditors are not affected.' Clark v. Dodge, 199 N.E. 641, 643.

Numerous helpful textual statements and law review articles dealing with the judicial treatment of the close corporation have been pointed out by counsel. One article concludes with the following: 'New needs compel fresh formulation of corporate 'norms'. There is no reason why mature men should not be able to adapt the statutory form to the structure they want, so long as they do not endanger other stockholders, holders, creditors, or the public, or violate a clearly mandatory provision of the corporation laws. In a typical close corporation the stockholders' agreement is usually the result of careful deliberation among all initial investors. In the large public-issue corporation, on the other hand, the 'agreement' represented by the corporate charter is not consciously agreed to by the investors; they have no voice in its formulation, and very few ever read the certificate of incorporation. Preservation of the corporate norms may there be necessary for the protection of the public investors.' Hornstein, 'Stockholders' Agreements in the Closely Held Corporation', 59 Yale L. Journal, 1040, 1056.

This court has recognized, albeit sub silentio, the significant conceptual differences between the close corporation and its public-issue counterpart in, among other cases, Kantzler v. Benzinger, 214 Ill. 589, 73 N.E. 874, where an agreement quite similar to the one under attack here was upheld. Where, as in Kantzler and here, no complaining minority interest appears, no fraud or apparent injury to the public or creditors is present, and no clearly prohibitory statutory language is violated, we can see no valid reason for precluding the parties from reaching any arrangements concerning the management of the corporation which are agreeable to all.

Perhaps, as has been vociferously advanced, a separate comprehensive statutory scheme governing the close corporation would best serve here. See Note 'A Plea for Separate Statutory Treatment of the Close Corporation', 33 N.Y.U.L.Rev. 700. Some states have enacted legislation dealing specifically with the close corporation. See Fla.Stats. § 608.0100 et seq., F.S.A.; N.C.Gen.Stats. Gen.Stats. § 55–73(b), (c); N.Y.Bus.Corp. Law, McKinney's Consol. Laws, c. 4, § 620.

At any rate, however, the courts can no longer fail to expressly distinguish between the close and public-issue corporation when confronted with problems relating to either. What we do here is to illuminate this problem-before the bench, corporate bar, and the legislature, in the context of a particular fact situation. To do less would be to shirk our responsibility, to do more would, perhaps be to invade the province of the legislative branch.

We now, in the light of the foregoing, turn to specific provisions of the 1955 agreement.

The Appellate Court correctly found many of the contractual provisions free from serious objection, and we need not prolong this opinion with a discussion of them here. That court did, however, find difficulties in the stated purpose of the agreement as it relates to its duration, the election of certain persons to specific offices for a number of years, the requirement for the mandatory declaration of stated dividends (which the Appellate Court held invalid), and the salary continuation agreement.

Since the question as to the duration of the agreement is a principal source of controversy, we shall consider it first. The parties provided no specific termination date, and while the agreement concludes with a paragraph that its terms 'shall be binding upon and shall inure to the benefits of' the legal representatives, heirs and assigns of the parties, this clause is, we believe, intended to be operative only as long as one of the parties is living. It further provides that it shall be so construed as to carry out its purposes, and we believe these must be determined from a consideration of the agreement as a whole. Thus viewed, a fair construction is that its purposes were accomplished at the death of the survivor of the parties. While these life spans are not precisely ascertainable, and the Appellate Court noted Emma Galler's life expectancy at her husband's death was 26.9 years, we are aware of no statutory or public policy provision against stockholder's agreements which would invalidate this agreement on that ground. (Thompson v. J. D. Thompson Carnation Co., 279 Ill. 54, 116 N.E. 648.) Vogal v. Melish, Ill., 203 N.E.2d 411, also involved a construction of a contract in a close corporation, but not the validity of the contract. While defendants argue that the public policy evinced by the legislative restrictions upon the duration of voting trust agreements (Ill.Rev.Stat.1963, chap. 32, par. 157.30a) should be applied here, this agreement is not a voting trust, but as pointed out by the dissenting justice in the Appellate Court, is a straight contractual voting control agreement which does not divorce voting rights from stock ownership. That the policy against agreements in which stock ownership and voting rights are separated, indicated in Luthy v. Ream, 270 Ill. 170, 110 N.E. 373, is inapplicable to voting control agreements was emphasized in Thompson wherein a control agreement was upheld as not attempting to separate ownership and voting power. While limiting voting trusts in 1947 to a maximum duration of 10 years, the legislature has indicated no similar policy regarding straight voting agreements although these have been common since prior to 1870. In view of the history of decisions of this court generally upholding, in the absence of fraud or prejudice to minority interests or public policy, the right of stockholders to agree among themselves as to the manner in which their stock will be voted, we do not regard the period of time within which this agreement may remain effective as rendering the agreement unenforceable.

The clause that provides for the election of certain persons to specified offices for a period of years likewise does not require invalidation. In Kantzler v. Benzinger, 214 Ill. 589, 73 N.E. 874, this court upheld an agreement entered into by all the stockholders providing that certain parties would be elected to the offices of the corporation for a fixed period. In Faulds v. Yates, 57 Ill. 416, we upheld a similar agreement among the majority stockholders of a corporation, notwithstanding the existence of a minority which was not before the court complaining thereof. See also Hornstein, 'Judicial Tolerance of the Incorporated Partnership,' 18 Law and Contemporary Problems 435 at 444.

We turn next to a consideration of the effect of the stated purpose of the agreement upon its validity. The pertinent provision is: 'The said Benjamin A. Galler and Isadore A. Galler desire to provide income for the support and maintenance of their immediate families.' Obviously, there is no evil inherent in a contract entered into for the reason that the persons originating the terms desired to so arrange their property as to provide post-death support for those dependent upon them. Nor does the fact that the subject property is corporate stock alter the situation so long as there exists no detriment to minority stock interests, creditors or other public injury. It is however, contended by defendants that the methods provided by the agreement for implementation of the stated purpose are, as a whole, violative of the Business Corporation Act (Ill.Rev.Stat.1963, chap. 32, pars. 157.28, 157.30a, 157.33, 157.34, 157.41) to such an extent as to render it void in toto.

The terms of the dividend agreement require a minimum annual dividend of $50,000, but this duty is limited by the subsequent provision that it shall be operative only so long as an earned surplus of $500,000 is maintained. It may be noted that in 1958, the year prior to commencement of this litigation, the corporation's net earnings after taxes amounted to $202,759 while its earned surplus was $1,543,270, and this was increased in 1958 to $1,680,079 while earnings were $172,964. The minimum earned surplus requirement is designed for the protection of the corporation and its creditors, and we take no exception to the contractual dividend requirements as thus restricted. Kantzler v. Benzinger, 214 Ill. 589, 73 N.E. 874.

The salary continuation agreement is a common feature, in one form or another, of corporate executive employment. It requires that the widow should receive a total benefit, payable monthly over a five-year period, aggregating twice the amount paid her deceased husband in one year. This requirement was likewise limited for the protection of the corporation by being contingent upon the payments being income tax-deductible by the corporation. The charge made in those cases which have considered the validity of payments to the widow of an officer and shareholder in a corporation is that a gift of its property by a noncharitable corporation is in violation of the rights of its shareholders and ultra vires. Since there are no shareholders here other than the parties to the contract, this objection is not here applicable, and its effect, as limited, upon the corporation is not so prejudicial as to require its invalidation.

Having concluded that the agreement, under the circumstances here present, is not vulnerable to the attack made on it, we must consider the accounting feature of this action. The trial court allowed the relief prayed, an action we deem proper except as to the master's fees which were modified by the Appellate Court. Since no question is here raised regarding them, we affirm the action of that court in this respect. The questions as to salary which the Appellate Court correctly held were improperly increased became ones of fact to be determined by the trial court.

We hold defendants must account for all monies received by them from the corporation since September 25, 1956, in excess of that theretofore authorized.

Accordingly, the judgment of the Appellate Court is reversed except insofar as it relates to fees, and is, as to them affirmed. The cause is remanded to the circuit court of Cook County with directions to proceed in accordance herewith.

Affirmed in part and reversed in part, and remanded with directions.

NOTES

1. *Special Statutes.* As the *Galler* case points out, many states have enacted special statutes for closely held corporations. This special statutory regulation typically requires that a close corporation's charter provide that (1) its stock shall be held by not more than a specified number of persons; (2) its stock is subject to transfer restrictions; and (3) it shall not engage in public offerings of its stock. Del. Code Ann. tit. 8, § 342(a)(1)-(3) (1991) (30 nominal shareholders); Ill. Ann. Stat. ch. 805, § 5/2A.10 (Smith–Hurd 1993); 15 Pa. Cons. Stat. Ann. § 2304(a) (Supp. 1994). In Maryland, any corporation's shareholders may agree that the corporation will act as a close corporation. Md. Code Ann., Corps. & Assns. § 4–201 (1993). See Edwin J. Bradley, A Comparative Evaluation of the Delaware and Maryland Close Corporation Statutes, 1968 Duke L.J. 525.[2] It had generally been assumed in most states that while this might provide additional certainty, compliance with these statutes was not mandatory to qualify for the special treatment granted by courts like *Galler*. However, there has been a line of cases in Delaware holding that special close corporation considerations will not be considered if corporations have not elected to qualify under the Delaware statute's close corporation provisions. Nixon v. Blackwell, 626 A.2d 1366 (Del.1993).

2. On remand in *Galler*, the lower court entered an order directing who the officers of the company would be and their salaries. Galler v. Galler, 69 Ill.App.2d 397, 217 N.E.2d 111 (1966). This did not settle the issue. The representatives from the Isadore Galler faction sought to discontinue salary payments until such time as the opposing faction dropped their demand for an accounting for the prior payments found to have been improperly made. That action was also found to be improper by the Illinois courts. Galler v. Galler, 95 Ill.App.2d 340, 238 N.E.2d 274 (1968). An accounting was finally rendered in 1975. The Isadore Galler estate was required to repay the company $266,666 plus interest, and Aaron Galler was required to repay $41,666 plus interest. Galler v. Galler, 61 Ill.2d 464, 336 N.E.2d 886 (1975).

3. The *Galler* opinion stresses the courts' willingness to allow informality in the closely held corporation that would not be permitted in other

---

2. In 1982, the Committee on Corporate Laws of the Section of Corporation, Banking and Business Law of the American Bar Association adopted a close corporation supplement to the Model Business Corporation Act. See Edwin J. Bradley, An Analysis of the Model Close Corporation Act and a Proposed Legislative Strategy, 10 J. Corp. L. 817 (1985); ABA Committee on Corporate Law, Proposed Statutory Close Corporation Supplement to the Model Business Corporation Act, 37 Bus. Law. 269 (1981); Statutory Close Corporation Supplement to the Model Business Corporation Act, 38 Bus. Law. 1031 (1983).

contexts. This is due to the now familiar recognition that a closely held corporation will be treated much like an incorporated partnership. In the case that follows, the court was not so tolerant.

SOMERS v. AAA TEMPORARY SERVICES, INC.

5 Ill.App.3d 931, 284 N.E.2d 462 (1972).

Lorenz, Presiding Justice.

This case involves an action brought to declare invalid the action by the two sole shareholders of a corporation amending the corporate by-laws to reduce the number of directors from three to two. The plaintiff, Wesley Somers, was not a shareholder but was the third director whose position was eliminated by the change in the by-laws. The trial court entered judgment on the pleadings in favor of plaintiff. From that judgment the defendant corporation and Lillian Raimer, one of the Shareholders, now appeal. Defendant Michaelene Kay, the other shareholder, did not file an appearance in the trial court nor is she prosecuting this appeal.

Defendant corporation, AAA Temporary Services, Inc., (hereinafter referred to as the 'corporation') was incorporated under the laws of the State of Illinois on April 29, 1967, for the purpose of furnishing and supplying temporary stenographers, clerical, industrial and other forms of male and female help and assistance. Its issued and outstanding capital stock at the time plaintiff filed his action consisted of 50 shares of common stock. Twenty-five of these shares were owned by defendant Lillian Raimer, who was the president of the corporation; the remaining twenty-five shares were owned by defendant Michaelene Kay, who was the secretary and treasurer of the corporation. Plaintiff did not own any shares at the time he filed his action, nor had he ever owned any of the capital stock of the corporation.

The corporation's articles of incorporation provided that 'The number of directors to be elected at the first meeting of the shareholders is three.' It is undisputed that the first meeting of shareholders was held on May 2, 1967. The three directors elected at that meeting were Lillian Raimer, Michaelene Kay and Wesley Somers. The by-laws were adopted shortly after incorporation and provided in pertinent part that 'Each director shall hold office until the annual meeting of shareholders, or until his successor shall have been elected and qualified.' The by-laws also called for an annual meeting of the shareholders to be held on the second Monday of each year. The by-laws further provided that a regular meeting of the board of directors would be held ' . . . immediately after, and at the same place as the annual meeting of shareholders.'

No annual meeting was held on the second Monday in 1968 nor at any time during 1968. The second Monday in 1969 was on January 13, 1969. On that date, defendant Lillian Raimer contends that she and Michaelene Kay, the sole shareholders of the corporation, signed a waiver of notice of the annual shareholders meeting. The meeting was then allegedly conducted for the purpose of, among other things, amending the by-laws of the corporation to reduce the number of directors from three to two. Thereupon, the by-laws were purportedly amended to provide that the 'number of directors shall be two.' The two shareholders then elected themselves as the two directors, signed a waiver of notice for the annual directors' meeting and conducted the directors' meeting.

Plaintiff denies that the annual shareholders' and directors' meetings for 1969 were actually convened or held on January 13, 1969. He further contends that the actions allegedly taken at the meetings by the two shareholders were not discussed until the last several days of January, 1969. Even if it is conceded that such meetings were held, it is appellee's contention that the resolutions adopted by the shareholders were unlawful and not within the power and authority of the shareholders. Accordingly, plaintiff brought an action to declare invalid the action by the shareholders reducing the number of directors from three to two. Upon his motion for judgment on the pleadings, the trial court declared the reduction of directors by the two shareholders to be illegal and void, found the correct number of directors of the corporation to be three not two and held that Wesley Somers is still a director of the corporation. Defendants Lillian Raimer and the corporation appeal from the trial court's judgment on the pleadings.

Appellants urge that the principal question presented on appeal is simply whether the two sole shareholders of a close corporation may validly agree that the by-laws of the corporation be amended to reduce the number of directors from three to two and thereupon elect themselves as the two sole directors. We feel that this statement of the issue is somewhat misleading in view of the facts in this case. The question is not whether such an agreement can be made. At issue is whether the shareholders have the power to amend the by-laws where, as here, such power has not been reserved to the shareholders by the Articles of Incorporation.

The Illinois Business Corporation Act provides that the number of directors may be increased or decreased by amendment to the by-laws. Ill.Rev.Stat.1969, ch. 32, par. 157.34. The Act further states that the power to amend the by-laws is 'vested in the board of directors, unless reserved to the shareholders by the articles of incorporation.' Ill.Rev.Stat. 1969, ch. 32, par. 157.25. The power to amend the by-laws of AAA Temporary Services, Inc. was not reserved to the shareholders by its Articles of Incorporation. Therefore, this power would rest with the directors. It is clear that the action of the shareholders, amending the by-laws to provide for two instead of three directors, was not in compliance with Section 25 of the Illinois Business Corporation Act. Since only the directors of a corporation have the statutory right to amend the by-laws, where such power has not been reserved to the shareholders, we sustain the trial court's holding that the amendment to the by-laws of the corporation at the January 13, 1969, meeting was a nullity. (In this regard, note that we accept the trial court's ruling to the effect that a meeting of shareholders was in fact convened and held on January 13, 1969.)

In spite of the language of Section 25 of the Illinois Business Corporation Act, appellants strongly urge that the action by the shareholders of the corporation should be allowed to stand because the corporation is a close one. As a matter of fact, appellants have constructed almost their entire argument around the framework of the Illinois Supreme Court's decision in the case of Galler v. Galler, (1964), 32 Ill.2d 16, 203 N.E.2d 577. The principal thrust of the Galler decision is that, in the context of a particular fact situation, there is no reason for preventing those in control of a close corporation from reaching any agreements concerning the management of the corporation which are agreeable to all, though such agreements are not within the letter of the Business Corporation Act.

It is important to note, however, that the Supreme Court in Galler imposed limitations on the operation and use of this general rule for close corporations. First, the Court indicated that such agreements should be permitted only where no fraud or apparent injury would be worked upon the public, minority interests or creditors. Then, more directly in point to the instant case, the Court went on to caution that shareholder agreements which violate statutory language are not permitted. The Court said in its opinion:

> There is no reason why mature men should not be able to adapt the statutory form to the structure they want, so long as they do not endanger other stockholders, creditors, or the public, Or violate a clearly mandatory provision of the corporation laws. (Emphasis added.)

The Galler Court did not say that the Illinois Business Corporation Act may be disregarded in the case of a close corporation. Slight deviations from corporate norms may be permitted. However, action by the shareholders which is in direct contravention of the statute cannot be allowed. Appellant's contention that there is no conceivable way in which Galler can be distinguished from the instant case must, therefore, be rejected. The language of Section 25 of the Business Corporation Act is clearly mandatory regarding the amendment of the corporate by-laws. Accordingly, it is obvious to us that the holding in the Galler case gives no sanction to appellants to disregard the clear and unambiguous language of that section of the Act.

Finally, defendant Raimer in her answer questions the motives of plaintiff in bringing this action by alleging a conspiracy between Somers and defendant Kay. Raimer alleges that plaintiff is a close friend and business adviser of Kay. It is Raimer's contention that, in this capacity, Somers conspired with Kay to oust Raimer from her office as president and a director of the corporation by filing the instant complaint. Although plaintiff in his reply admitted that he was a close friend and adviser of Kay and worked part-time for her in a separate business venture, he denied any bad motives in instituting this suit. An examination of Illinois law on the question as to whether an alleged bad motive constitutes a valid legal defense reveals that our courts have consistently held that it does not. It is generally accepted that where the plaintiff asserts a valid cause of action, his motive in bringing the action is immaterial. A plaintiff's right of recovery is in no way barred by the motive which prompts him to bring the action. Since plaintiff had a valid cause of action in this case, we find his motives in bringing the action to be immaterial.

The judgment of the trial court is affirmed.

NOTES

1. Why did the Illinois court in *Somers* abandon the tolerance for informality typically found in closely held corporations?

2. Compare e.g., White v. Thatcher Financial Group, Inc., 940 P.2d 1034 (Colo.App.1996) where the statute called for a minimum of 3 directors and the corporation only had 2:

> Here, the record reflects that TFG had approximately ten minority shareholders and a small board of directors, members of which actually, directly, and personally conducted the business of the corporation. Clearly, the custom and practice of the corporation was to operate with fewer than the required number of directors, but still with a quorum of the board, and the jury here apparently so found. Therefore, we conclude that any actions taken by TFG's board of directors when it consisted of only two directors were binding on TFG.

SECTION 5. RESTRICTIONS ON TRANSFERS

ST. LOUIS UNION TRUST CO. v. MERRILL LYNCH, PIERCE, FENNER & SMITH INC.

562 F.2d 1040 (8th Cir.1977).

Ross, Circuit Judge.

This appeal raises substantial questions concerning the validity of an option held by Merrill Lynch, Pierce, Fenner & Smith, Inc. (hereinafter Merrill Lynch) to repurchase its own stock from a deceased shareholder's executors. * * *

The plaintiffs are the executors of the Estate of Kenneth H. Bitting, a former officer, employee and stockholder of Merrill Lynch. The defendants are Merrill Lynch and three of its senior executives, Donald T. Regan, Ned B. Ball and George L. Shinn.

In 1947, Kenneth Bitting operated a stock brokerage partnership known as Bitting, Jones & Company in St. Louis, Missouri. In that year, the Bitting partnership merged into Merrill Lynch, which was then a national stock brokerage partnership, and became the St. Louis office of Merrill Lynch. Between 1947 and 1951, Bitting was an employee of the Merrill Lynch partnership. In 1951, he became a general partner of the firm.

In 1959, the Merrill Lynch partnership was dissolved and the business was incorporated. In return for their interests in the partnership, each partner, including Kenneth Bitting, received shares of common stock in Merrill Lynch. Bitting received 9,100 shares of voting stock and a $58,000 debenture in exchange for his partnership capital. In October 1959, Merrill Lynch split its stock on a three for one basis and Bitting became the owner of 27,300 shares of voting stock. Bitting had acquired all of his stock at a cost based on book value.

Under Merrill Lynch's original Certificate of Incorporation, all common stock, including that issued to Kenneth Bitting, was restricted against transfer. Under the terms of the Charter, Merrill Lynch was granted an option to purchase the holder's stock at an adjusted net book value price upon the occurrence of several specified contingencies, including the death of the holder. This transfer restriction was conspicuously noted on each stock certificate. Likewise the stockholder or his executors were given a right to "put" the stock to Merrill Lynch and it was then required to purchase that stock at book value.

In 1962, Bitting retired from the company. At that time, in accordance with company policy, he exchanged his 27,300 shares of voting stock for over $400,000 in cash and 10,000 shares of nonvoting stock. Between 1962 and 1970, Bitting became the owner of 40,000 shares of nonvoting stock as a result of two additional stock splits.

On October 8, 1970, Kenneth Bitting died. Pursuant to its Charter, Merrill Lynch exercised its option to purchase the 40,000 shares at a price of $26.597 per share, the net book value as of October 30, 1970. The option was exercised by the company on November 18, 1970. The total price was $1,063,880. Thereafter the corporation offered Bitting's widow an opportunity to purchase 10,000 shares of nonvoting stock at the same price, which she accepted. Some other widows had been given similar options.

Between 1959 and 1971, Merrill Lynch was a privately held company. On April 12, 1971, the company publicly announced that it was "going public" that it was going to make its shares available to the public. On June 23, 1971, following registration with the SEC and a three for one stock split, four million shares of the company's stock were offered to the public at a price of $28 per share. The offering price per share was approximately three times the price which was paid to the Bitting executors in accordance with the terms of the stock restriction contained in Merrill Lynch's Certificate of Incorporation. * * *

We ... address the issue of whether the stock restriction was enforceable under Delaware law when the stock option was exercised in November 1970. The district court held that the option was not enforceable at that time. We disagree and hold that the restriction was enforceable under § 202(c)(1) of the Delaware General Corporation Law.

Article VI, Section 1(a) of the Merrill Lynch Certificate of Incorporation, the provision under which Kenneth Bitting's stock was called, provides in pertinent part as follows:

> * * * (I)n the event of the death * * * of any holder of common stock of the Corporation * * *, the Corporation shall have the right and option which shall be prior to any other right and option, to purchase the shares of common stock of the Corporation held by the deceased * * * for a period of ninety (90) days from the earlier of: (i) the date the Corporation receives from the legal representative of such holder written notice * * * of the death * * * of such holder, or (ii) the date the Corporation mails written notice * * * that the Corporation is on notice of such death * * *. This restriction was noted conspicuously on each Merrill Lynch stock certificate and was indisputably assented to by Bitting when the stock was issued to him. There has been no contention, nor could there be on this record, that Bitting's assent was induced by fraud, deceit or any other improper motive.

The enforceability of the restriction rests on our construction of Section 202 of the Delaware General Corporation Law, which was in existence in November 1970 when the restriction was enforced. Section 202(a) carries the label "Restriction on transfer of securities" and reads as follows:

> A written restriction on the transfer or registration of transfer of a security of a corporation, if permitted by this section and noted conspicuously on the security, may be enforced against the holder of the restricted security or any successor or transferee of the holder including an executor, administrator, trustee, guardian or other fiduciary entrusted with like responsibility for the person or estate of the holder.

Section 202(c) declares four types of restrictions valid without inquiry into the existence vel non of a lawful or reasonable purpose. Section 202(c)(1), the pertinent provision for our purposes, provides as follows:

> (b) A restriction on the transfer of securities of a corporation is permitted by this section if it:
>
> > (1) Obligates the holder of the restricted securities to offer to the corporation or to any other holders of securities of the corporation or to any other person or to any combination of the foregoing, a prior opportunity, to be exercised within a reasonable time, to acquire the restricted securities; * * *.

This statute on its face validates the stock restriction at issue. The statute declares the enforceability of any restriction which "(o)bligates the holder of the restricted securities to offer to the corporation * * * a prior opportunity * * * to acquire the restricted securities * * *." That is precisely what Merrill Lynch's Charter required of Kenneth Bitting's estate in this case.

We have not found, and the parties have not cited to us, any reported Delaware decision construing § 202(c)(1). However, in DeVries v. Westgren, 119 Pittsburgh L.J. 61 and 109 (C.P. Allegheny County 1970), aff'd as modified, 446 Pa. 205, 287 A.2d 437 (1971), the court enforced a stock restriction requiring a shareholder to offer all of his common stock to the corporation upon the voluntary or involuntary termination of his employment under a Pennsylvania statute identical to § 202(c)(1). The defendant shareholder was involuntarily terminated by the company and was sued by the other shareholders when he refused to surrender his shares pursuant to the stock restriction. The court enforced the stock restriction, holding that the option was a legal and enforceable agreement "clearly" within the permissive language of the statute. In affirming, the Pennsylvania Supreme Court held:

> (U)nlike a right of first refusal whereby the appellant could elect to retain his shares and never sell to anyone, the stock purchase agreement requires the appellant to offer his shares to the remaining shareholders upon the termination of his employment. In our view, the requirement that appellant offer his shares, whether or not he wished to retain them, lends a quality of irrevocability to the stock purchase agreement and justifies our treatment of this agreement as an option contract.

Id., 287 A.2d at 438.

The plaintiffs advance the argument, embraced by the district court, that § 202(c)(1) was intended to permit only the exercise of a right of first refusal and not the exercise of an automatic option to purchase triggered by the contingency of death or other circumstance. In accepting this argument, the district court couched the distinction in terms of voluntary transfers, permitted by, and transfers by operation of law, not permitted by, § 202(c)(1). The construction urged by the plaintiffs would amount to nothing less than a judicial rewriting of the statute, and we reject it. Section 202(a), which modifies each subsection of the statute including § 202(c)(1), provides that a transfer restriction permitted by the section is enforceable against " * * * any successor or transferee of the holder including an executor, administrator, trustee, guardian or other fiduciary entrusted with like responsibility for the person or estate of the holder." We perceive this to be at least implicit recognition that repurchase options which become operable on the happening of a specified contingency including an "involuntary" contingency such as death or incompetency are permitted under § 202(c)(1). Furthermore, Professor Folk, the Reporter for the Delaware revision commission which prepared the law for adoption, has stated that § 202(c)(1) was intended to validate options to purchase as well as mere rights of first refusal:

> A restriction is valid if it requires the holder of restricted securities to tender them to designated persons who must act within a reasonable period of time thereafter. Such a restriction could take the form of a mere first refusal or of an option to acquire the securities.

Folk, The Delaware General Corporation Law, 198 (1972) (emphasis added); cf. Ketchum v. Green, 415 F.Supp. 1367, 1372 (W.D.Pa.1976); DeVries v. Westgren, supra, 446 Pa. 205, 287 A.2d at 438. Had the Delaware legislature intended to exclude commonly used and accepted repurchase options such as the transfer restriction before us,[9] it could easily have done so.

The plaintiffs' construction would also violate the purpose of § 202(c)(1). That purpose was to broaden, not limit, the circumstances in which such restrictions would be enforced in order to clear up the preexisting uncertain contours of the common law. See Arsht & Stapleton, Analysis of the 1967 Delaware Corporation Law, 2 P–H Corp. Delaware 311, 333 (1967); Folk, The Delaware General Corporation Law, 197–199 (1972). Before § 202(c)(1) was adopted in 1967, the Delaware courts required that a stock restriction be supported by specific justification, e. g., a reasonable or lawful purpose, to be enforceable. See, e. g., Greene v. E. H. Rollins & Sons, Inc., 22 Del.Ch. 394, 2 A.2d 249 (1938). What specific justification was sufficient to sustain a restriction under the common law was the subject of much uncertainty. See Folk, The Delaware General Corporation Law, 198 (1972). It was the purpose of § 202(c) to eliminate this uncertainty by substantively validating a wide variety of commonly accepted stock restrictions such as the provision before us. Id. at 198–199, 2 A.2d 249. * * *

Accordingly, we hold that the stock restriction was enforceable under Delaware law.

NOTES

1. A factor common to the closely held corporation is the use of restrictions on the transfer of stock. The reasons for such restrictions are numerous, but frequently reflect the fact that the close corporation is really just an incorporated partnership, and the shareholders want to control entry just as is the case for partnerships. The difference is that stock, unlike a partnership interest, is personal property. The courts have traditionally viewed with disfavor restrictions on the alienation of personal property. Such restrictions must be reasonable in nature.

2. Transfer restrictions on stock that are common include:

> *Right of First Refusal.* For example, the shareholders in a close corporation may agree that, if anyone wants to sell their stock, that person must first offer it to the other shareholders before selling it to a third party. These arrangements are generally upheld by the courts as being reasonable restraints on the alienation of stock.

> *Options.* Each shareholder has the option to purchase the other shareholders' stock at a specified price before it may be sold to a

---

9. We observe that repurchase options such as the stock restriction in this case have been recognized as serving a number of legitimate business purposes, including restrictive ownership of corporate stock, and have been generally upheld by the courts. See, e. g., Palmer v. Chamberlin, 191 F.2d 532, 537–538 (5th Cir.1951); cf. DeVries v. Westgren, 446 Pa. 205, 287 A.2d 437, 438 (1971). See generally, 6 Cavitch, Business Organizations, § 113.02(2) at 19–20 (1977).

third party or upon the occurrence of some event such as death or leaving the employment of the company. This assures that the other shareholders will not become involved in a bidding war with third parties for the stock. The problem with these arrangements is setting a price at which the option may be exercised. Option arrangements are usually upheld as reasonable, even if the purchase price is much less than the actual market value of the stock.

Consent Restraints. A more restrictive provision, and the one most disfavored by the courts, requires the approval of other shareholders before the stock may be sold. The concern is that the consent will be unreasonably withheld, trapping the shareholder in the corporation.

3.　Rev. Model Bus. Corp. Act § 6.27 makes a restriction on transfer of stock valid and enforceable, if its existence is noted conspicuously on the certificate, and provided the restriction is reasonable. Section 6.27(c) specifies certain reasonable restrictions, including a right of first refusal. The statute further states that a consent restriction is permitted, "if the restriction is not manifestly unreasonable." Del. § 202 also addresses restrictions on transfer in a similar fashion but does not specifically state that a consent restriction must not be manifestly unreasonable. Uniform Commercial Code § 8–204 also requires the issuer to provide notice of transfer restrictions imposed by the corporation on the shares it issues. It is unclear whether restrictions imposed only by shareholder agreements need to be noted.

4.　Related to the issue of transfer restrictions are buy-sell agreements among shareholders in a close corporation. These are often used as a planning tool for the contingency of the death of a large shareholder. Absent a buy-sell agreement, the estate of the decedent will become the owner of the stock, which may not be wanted by either party. Since there is no market for the stock, the estate may not be able to sell it, and the surviving shareholders might not want a new owner, even if there were a market. The buy-sell agreement meets both of those concerns. There are, however, at least two concerns with such agreements. In the first instance, funds must be available to pay for the stock by the survivors or by the corporation. Usually, there are no such excess funds in hand, but the purchase may be effected by life insurance carried on the life of the corporate shareholders, often at reasonable rates where term insurance is used. There are, however, complicated issues as to whether the proceeds of the policy and premium payments are taxable. The second concern is how to price the shares for purposes of a buyout. A set price may be quickly out-dated as the company grows, and resetting the price may be difficult or forgotten. Appraisals at the time of death may be used, but they are not scientific and a broad range of values may be reached under different appraisal methods. Chapter 18 addresses those issues.

5.　Restrictions on transfers may be interpreted narrowly by the courts. This could mean that a transfer by operation of law (e.g., testamentary transfer or through a divorce decree) might be construed to fall outside a transfer restriction unless the restriction specifically states that such a transfer is subject to its terms.

CHAPTER 11

DUTIES OF CONTROLLING SHAREHOLDERS

■ ■ ■

In prior chapters, we have examined the application of fiduciary duties to officers, directors and partners or persons in a partner like relationship. This leaves the issue of whether shareholders owe any fiduciary duties to their fellow shareholders? Should they be viewed to be partners in the enterprise with each other or are they simply owners that can exercise their ownership rights without regard to the effect of their actions on fellow shareholders? Without giving too much away, the courts have generally focused their inquiries in this area on charges of over-reaching by controlling shareholders.

SECTION 1. FIDUCIARY DUTIES OF CONTROLLING SHAREHOLDERS

SINCLAIR OIL CORP. v. LEVIEN

280 A.2d 717 (Del.1971).

WOLCOTT, CHIEF JUSTICE.

This is an appeal by the defendant, Sinclair Oil Corporation (hereafter Sinclair), from an order of the Court of Chancery, in a derivative action requiring Sinclair to account for damages sustained by its subsidiary, Sinclair Venezuelan Oil Company (hereafter Sinven), organized by Sinclair for the purpose of operating in Venezuela, as a result of dividends paid by Sinven, the denial to Sinven of industrial development, and a breach of contract between Sinclair's wholly-owned subsidiary, Sinclair International Oil Company, and Sinven.

Sinclair, operating primarily as a holding company, is in the business of exploring for oil and of producing and marketing crude oil and oil products. At all times relevant to this litigation, it owned about 97% of Sinven's stock. The plaintiff owns about 3000 of 120,000 publicly held shares of Sinven. Sinven, incorporated in 1922, has been engaged in petroleum operations primarily in Venezuela and since 1959 has operated exclusively in Venezuela.

Sinclair nominates all members of Sinven's board of directors. The Chancellor found as a fact that the directors were not independent of

Sinclair. Almost without exception, they were officers, directors, or employees of corporations in the Sinclair complex. By reason of Sinclair's domination, it is clear that Sinclair owed Sinven a fiduciary duty. Getty Oil Company v. Skelly Oil Co., 267 A.2d 883 (Del.1970); Cottrell v. Pawcatuck Co., 116 A.2d 787 (Del.Ch. 1955). Sinclair concedes this.

The Chancellor held that because of Sinclair's fiduciary duty and its control over Sinven, its relationship with Sinven must meet the test of intrinsic fairness. The standard of intrinsic fairness involves both a high degree of fairness and a shift in the burden of proof. Under this standard the burden is on Sinclair to prove, subject to careful judicial scrutiny, that its transactions with Sinven were objectively fair. Guth v. Loft, Inc., 5 A.2d 503 (Del.1939); Sterling v. Mayflower Hotel Corp., 93 A.2d 107 (Del.1952); Getty Oil Co. v. Skelly Oil Co., supra.

Sinclair argues that the transactions between it and Sinven should be tested, not by the test of intrinsic fairness with the accompanying shift of the burden of proof, but by the business judgment rule under which a court will not interfere with the judgment of a board of directors unless there is a showing of gross and palpable overreaching. A board of directors enjoys a presumption of sound business judgment, and its decisions will not be disturbed if they can be attributed to any rational business purpose. A court under such circumstances will not substitute its own notions of what is or is not sound business judgment.

We think, however, that Sinclair's argument in this respect is misconceived. When the situation involves a parent and a subsidiary, with the parent controlling the transaction and fixing the terms, the test of intrinsic fairness, with its resulting shifting of the burden of proof, is applied. Sterling v. Mayflower Hotel Corp., supra. The basic situation for the application of the rule is the one in which the parent has received a benefit to the exclusion and at the expense of the subsidiary.

Recently, this court dealt with the question of fairness in parent-subsidiary dealings in Getty Oil Co. v. Skelly Oil Co., supra. In that case, both parent and subsidiary were in the business of refining and marketing crude oil and crude oil products. The Oil Import Board ruled that the subsidiary, because it was controlled by the parent, was no longer entitled to a separate allocation of imported crude oil. The subsidiary then contended that it had a right to share the quota of crude oil allotted to the parent. We ruled that the business judgment standard should be applied to determine this contention. Although the subsidiary suffered a loss through the administration of the oil import quotas, the parent gained nothing. The parent's quota was derived solely from its own past use. The past use of the subsidiary did not cause an increase in the parent's quota. Nor did the parent usurp a quota of the subsidiary. Since the parent received nothing from the subsidiary to the exclusion of the minority stockholders of the subsidiary, there was no self-dealing. Therefore, the business judgment standard was properly applied.

A parent does indeed owe a fiduciary duty to its subsidiary when there are parent-subsidiary dealings. However, this alone will not evoke the intrinsic fairness standard. This standard will be applied only when the fiduciary duty is accompanied by self-dealing—the situation when a parent is on both sides of a transaction with its subsidiary. Self-dealing occurs when the parent, by virtue of its domination of the subsidiary, causes the subsidiary to act in such a way that the parent receives something from the subsidiary to the exclusion of, and detriment to, the minority stockholders of the subsidiary.

We turn now to the facts. The plaintiff argues that, from 1960 through 1966, Sinclair caused Sinven to pay out such excessive dividends that the industrial development of Sinven was effectively prevented, and it became in reality a corporation in dissolution.

From 1960 through 1966, Sinven paid out $108,000,000 in dividends ($38,000,000 in excess of Sinven's earnings during the same period). The Chancellor held that Sinclair caused these dividends to be paid during a period when it had a need for large amounts of cash. Although the dividends paid exceeded earnings, the plaintiff concedes that the payments were made in compliance with 8 Del.C. § 170, authorizing payment of dividends out of surplus or net profits. However, the plaintiff attacks these dividends on the ground that they resulted from an improper motive—Sinclair's need for cash. The Chancellor, applying the intrinsic fairness standard, held that Sinclair did not sustain its burden of proving that these dividends were intrinsically fair to the minority stockholders of Sinven.

Since it is admitted that the dividends were paid in strict compliance with 8 Del.C. § 170, the alleged excessiveness of the payments alone would not state a cause of action. Nevertheless, compliance with the applicable statute may not, under all circumstances, justify all dividend payments. If a plaintiff can meet his burden of proving that a dividend cannot be grounded on any reasonable business objective, then the courts can and will interfere with the board's decision to pay the dividend.

Sinclair contends that it is improper to apply the intrinsic fairness standard to dividend payments even when the board which voted for the dividends is completely dominated. In support of this contention, Sinclair relies heavily on American District Telegraph Co. (ADT) v. Grinnell Corp., (N.Y.Sup.Ct.1969) aff'd. 33 A.D.2d 769, 306 N.Y.S.2d 209 (1969). Plaintiffs were minority stockholders of ADT, a subsidiary of Grinnell. The plaintiffs alleged that Grinnell, realizing that it would soon have to sell its ADT stock because of a pending anti-trust action, caused ADT to pay excessive dividends. Because the dividend payments conformed with applicable statutory law, and the plaintiffs could not prove an abuse of discretion, the court ruled that the complaint did not state a cause of action. Other decisions seem to support Sinclair's contention. In Metropolitan Casualty Ins. Co. v. First State Bank of Temple, 54 S.W.2d 358 (Tex.Civ.App.1932) rev'd. on other grounds, 79 S.W.2d 835 (Sup.Ct.1935), the court held that a majority of interested directors does not void a declaration of dividends because all directors, by necessity, are interested in and benefited by a dividend declaration.

We do not accept the argument that the intrinsic fairness test can never be applied to a dividend declaration by a dominated board, although a dividend declaration by a dominated board will not inevitably demand the application of the intrinsic fairness standard. Moskowitz v. Bantrell, 190 A.2d 749 (Del.1963). If such a dividend is in essence self-dealing by the parent, then the intrinsic fairness standard is the proper standard. For example, suppose a parent dominates a subsidiary and its board of directors. The subsidiary has outstanding two classes of stock, X and Y. Class X is owned by the parent and Class Y is owned by minority stockholders of the subsidiary. If the subsidiary, at the direction of the parent, declares a dividend on its Class X stock only, this might well be self-dealing by the parent. It would be receiving something from the subsidiary to the exclusion of and detrimental to its minority stockholders. This self-dealing, coupled with the parent's fiduciary duty, would make intrinsic fairness the proper standard by which to evaluate the dividend payments.

Consequently it must be determined whether the dividend payments by Sinven were, in essence, self-dealing by Sinclair. The dividends resulted in great sums of money being transferred from Sinven to Sinclair. However, a proportionate share of this money was received by the minority shareholders of Sinven. Sinclair received nothing from Sinven to the exclusion of its minority stockholders. As such, these dividends were not self-dealing. We hold therefore that the Chancellor erred in applying the intrinsic fairness test as to these dividend payments. The business judgment standard should have been applied.

We conclude that the facts demonstrate that the dividend payments complied with the business judgment standard and with 8 Del.C. § 170. The motives for causing the declaration of dividends are immaterial unless the plaintiff can show that the dividend payments resulted from improper motives and amounted to waste. The plaintiff contends only that the dividend payments drained Sinven of cash to such an extent that it was prevented from expanding.

The plaintiff proved no business opportunities which came to Sinven independently and which Sinclair either took to itself or denied to Sinven. As a matter of fact, with two minor exceptions which resulted in losses, all of Sinven's operations have been conducted in Venezuela, and Sinclair had a policy of exploiting its oil properties located in different countries by subsidiaries located in the particular countries.

From 1960 to 1966 Sinclair purchased or developed oil fields in Alaska, Canada, Paraguay, and other places around the world. The plaintiff contends that these were all opportunities which could have been taken by Sinven. The Chancellor concluded that Sinclair had not proved that its denial of expansion opportunities to Sinven was intrinsically fair.

He based this conclusion on the following findings of fact. Sinclair made no real effort to expand Sinven. The excessive dividends paid by Sinven resulted in so great a cash drain as to effectively deny to Sinven any ability to expand. During this same period Sinclair actively pursued a company-wide policy of developing through its subsidiaries new sources of revenue, but Sinven was not permitted to participate and was confined in its activities to Venezuela.

However, the plaintiff could point to no opportunities which came to Sinven. Therefore, Sinclair usurped no business opportunity belonging to Sinven. Since Sinclair received nothing from Sinven to the exclusion of and detriment to Sinven's minority stockholders, there was no self-dealing. Therefore, business judgment is the proper standard by which to evaluate Sinclair's expansion policies.

Since there is no proof of self-dealing on the part of Sinclair, it follows that the expansion policy of Sinclair and the methods used to achieve the desired result must, as far as Sinclair's treatment of Sinven is concerned, be tested by the standards of the business judgment rule. Accordingly, Sinclair's decision, absent fraud or gross overreaching, to achieve expansion through the medium of its subsidiaries, other than Sinven, must be upheld.

Even if Sinclair was wrong in developing these opportunities as it did, the question arises, with which subsidiaries should these opportunities have been shared? No evidence indicates a unique need or ability of Sinven to develop these opportunities. The decision of which subsidiaries would be used to implement Sinclair's expansion policy was one of business judgment with which a court will not interfere absent a showing of gross and palpable overreaching. Meyerson v. El Paso Natural Gas Co., 246 A.2d 789 (Del.Ch.1967). No such showing has been made here.

Next, Sinclair argues that the Chancellor committed error when he held it liable to Sinven for breach of contract.

In 1961 Sinclair created Sinclair International Oil Company (hereafter International), a wholly owned subsidiary used for the purpose of coordinating all of Sinclair's foreign operations. All crude purchases by Sinclair were made thereafter through International.

On September 28, 1961, Sinclair caused Sinven to contract with International whereby Sinven agreed to sell all of its crude oil and refined products to International at specified prices. The contract provided for minimum and maximum quantities and prices. The plaintiff contends that Sinclair caused this contract to be breached in two respects. Although the contract called for payment on receipt, International's payments lagged as much as 30 days after receipt. Also, the contract required International to purchase at least a fixed minimum amount of crude and refined products from Sinven. International did not comply with this requirement.

Clearly, Sinclair's act of contracting with its dominated subsidiary was self-dealing. Under the contract Sinclair received the products produced by Sinven, and of course the minority shareholders of Sinven were not able to share in the receipt of these products. If the contract was breached, then Sinclair received these products to the detriment of Sinven's minority shareholders. We agree with the Chancellor's finding that the contract was breached by Sinclair, both as to the time of payments and the amounts purchased.

Although a parent need not bind itself by a contract with its dominated subsidiary, Sinclair chose to operate in this manner. As Sinclair has received the benefits of this contract, so must it comply with the contractual duties.

Under the intrinsic fairness standard, Sinclair must prove that its causing Sinven not to enforce the contract was intrinsically fair to the minority shareholders of Sinven. Sinclair has failed to meet this burden. Late payments were clearly breaches for which Sinven should have sought and received adequate damages. As to the quantities purchased, Sinclair argues that it purchased all the products produced by Sinven. This, however, does not satisfy the standard of intrinsic fairness. Sinclair has failed to prove that Sinven could not possibly have produced or someway have obtained the contract minimums. As such, Sinclair must account on this claim.

Finally, Sinclair argues that the Chancellor committed error in refusing to allow it a credit or setoff of all benefits provided by it to Sinven with respect to all the alleged damages. The Chancellor held that setoff should be allowed on specific transactions, e.g., benefits to Sinven under the contract with International, but denied an over all setoff against all damages claimed. We agree with the Chancellor, although the point may well be moot in view of our holding that Sinclair is not required to account for the alleged excessiveness of the dividend payments.

We will therefore reverse that part of the Chancellor's order that requires Sinclair to account to Sinven for damages sustained as a result of dividends paid between 1960 and 1966, and by reason of the denial to Sinven of expansion during that period. We will affirm the remaining portion of that order and remand the cause for further proceedings.

NOTES

1. The holding in *Sinclair* that the burden is on the defendants to prove the fairness of a self-dealing transaction is not a controversial one and generally represents the law elsewhere. Does the *Sinclair* case, however, take a narrow definition of self-dealing? The dividend was clearly worth more to Sinclair that the other Sinven shareholders when viewed pragmatically in terms of after-tax dollars. Since affiliated corporations may qualify to pay consolidated federal tax returns, the dividend payment to Sinclair was not taxable. As a result, Sinclair received the entire benefit of the dividend whereas the other shareholders had to pay a significant percentage in taxes. As a consequence, the after-tax benefits of the dividend were far greater to

Sinclair than to the other shareholders. Should the court have considered this in deciding on the fairness of the dividend?

2. *Self dealing and tax consequences.* In Smith v. Tele–Communication, Inc., 134 Cal.App.3d 338, 184 Cal.Rptr. 571 (1982), a parent corporation elected to file a consolidated tax return and thereby take advantage of the subsidiary's losses to offset some of the parent's taxable income. The court held that, since both the parent and subsidiary contributed to the tax loss, fairness required that the tax savings to the parent resulting from the consolidated filing should be shared proportionately with the subsidiary. The court rejected the defendant's reliance on the *Sinclar* holding since the defendant "overlooked the basis of the court's conclusion in *Sinclair*, namely, that there was no "overreaching" by the parent because the outside share-holders received the disputed dividends in proportion to their shareholdings." Id. at 344, 184 Cal.Rptr. 571. See also e.g., Case v. New York Central R.R., 15 N.Y.2d 150, 256 N.Y.S.2d 607, 204 N.E.2d 643, 647 (1965), rev'g, 19 A.D.2d 383, 243 N.Y.S.2d 620, rev'g 232 N.Y.S.2d 702 (1962) (applying the intrinsic fairness test but finding no unfairness in agreement resulting in $3,556,992 in tax savings to the parent and giving the subsidiary $268,725 in tax savings: "No such faithlessness of the majority of [the] directors to its corporate interests has been demonstrated as to warrant judicial interference with the challenged corporate decision").

3. For a case involving abuse of a subsidiary by the reclusive and eccentric billionaire Howard Hughes who controlled the parent company see Summa Corp. v. Trans World Airlines, Inc., 540 A.2d 403 (Del.1988).

ZAHN v. TRANSAMERICA CORP.

162 F.2d 36 (3d Cir.1947).

BIGGS, CIRCUIT JUDGE.

Zahn, a holder of Class A common stock of Axton–Fisher Tobacco Company, a corporation of Kentucky, sued Transamerica Corporation, a Delaware company, on his own behalf and on behalf of all stockholders similarly situated, in the District Court of the United States for the District of Delaware. His complaint as amended asserts that Transamerica caused Axton–Fisher to redeem its Class A stock at $80.80 per share on July 1, 1943, instead of permitting the Class A stockholders to participate in the assets on the liquidation of their company in June, 1944. He alleges in brief that if the Class A stockholders had been allowed to participate in the assets on liquidation of Axton–Fisher and had received their respective shares of the assets, he and the other Class A stockholders would have received $240 per share instead of $80.80. Zahn ..... prayed the court below to direct Transamerica to pay over to the shareholders who had not surrendered their stock the liquidation value and to pay over to those shareholders who had surrendered their stock the liquidation value less $80.80. Transamerica filed a motion to dismiss. The court below granted the motion holding that Zahn had failed to state a cause of action. He appealed.

The facts follow as appear from the pleadings, which recite provisions of Axton–Fisher's charter. Prior to April 30, 1943, Axton–Fisher had authorized and outstanding three classes of stock, designated respectively as preferred stock, Class A stock and Class B stock. Each share of preferred stock had a par value of $100 and was entitled to cumulative dividends at the rate of $6 per annum and possessed a liquidation value of $105 plus accrued dividends. The Class A stock, specifically described in the charter as a 'common' stock, was entitled to an annual cumulative dividend of $3.20 per share. If further funds were made available by action of the board of directors by way of dividends, the Class A stock and the Class B stock were entitled to share equally therein. Upon liquidation of the company and the payment of the sums required by the preferred stock, the Class A stock was entitled to share with the Class B stock in the distribution of the remaining assets, but the Class A stock was entitled to receive twice as much per share as the Class B stock.[2]

Each share of Class A stock was convertible at the option of the shareholder into one share of Class B stock. All or any of the shares of Class A stock were callable by the corporation at any quarterly dividend date upon sixty days' notice to the shareholders, at $60 per share with accrued dividends.[3] The voting rights were vested in the Class B stock but if there were four successive defaults in the payment of quarterly dividends, the class or classes of stock as to which such defaults occurred gained voting rights equal share for share with the Class B stock. By reason of this provision the Class A stock had possessed equal voting rights with the Class B stock since on or about January 1, 1937.

On or about May 16, 1941, Transamerica purchased 80,160 shares of Axton-Fisher's Class B common stock. This was about 71.5% of the

---

2. The charter provides as follows:

In the event of the dissolution, liquidation, merger or consolidation of the corporation, or sale of substantially all its assets, whether voluntary or involuntary, there shall be paid to the holders of the preferred stock then outstanding $105 per share, together with all unpaid accrued dividends thereon, before any sum shall be paid to or any assets distributed among the holders of the Class A common stock and/or the holders of the Class B common stock. After such payment to the holders of the preferred stock, and all unpaid accrued dividends on the Class A common stock shall have been paid, then all remaining assets and funds of the corporation shall be divided among and paid to the holders of the Class A common stock and to the holders of the Class B common stock in the ratio of 2 to 1; that is to say, there shall be paid upon each share of Class A common stock twice the amount paid upon each share of Class B common stock, in any such event.

3. The charter provides as follows:

The whole or any part of the Class A common stock of the corporation at the option of the Board of Directors, may be redeemed on any quarterly dividend payment date by paying therefor in cash Sixty dollars ($60.00) per share and all unpaid and accrued dividends thereon at the date fixed for such redemption, upon sending by mail to the registered holders of the Class A common stock at least sixty (60) days' notice of the exercise of such option. If at any time the Board of Directors shall determine to redeem less than the whole amount of Class A common stock then outstanding, the particular stock to be so redeemed shall be determined in such manner as the Board of Directors shall prescribe; provided, however, that no holder of Class A common stock shall be preferred over any other holder of such stock.

outstanding Class B stock and about 46.7% of the total voting stocks of Axton–Fisher. By August 15, 1942, Transamerica owned 5,332 shares of Class A stock and 82,610 shares of Class B stock. By March 31, 1943, the amount of Class A stock of Axton–Fisher owned by Transamerica had grown to 30,168 shares or about 66 2/3% of the total amount of this stock outstanding, and the amount of Class B stock owned by Transamerica had increased to 90,768 shares or about 80% of the total outstanding. Additional shares of Class B stock were acquired by Transamerica after April 30, 1943, and Transamerica converted the Class A stock owned by it into Class B stock so that on or about the end of May, 1944 Transamerica owned virtually all of the outstanding Class B stock of Axton–Fisher. Since May 16, 1941, Transamerica had control of and had dominated the management, directorate, financial policies, business and affairs of Axton–Fisher. Since the date last stated Transamerica had elected a majority of the board of directors of Axton–Fisher. These individuals are in large part officers or agents of Transamerica.

In the fall of 1942 and in the spring of 1943 Axton–Fisher possessed as its principal asset leaf tobacco which had cost it about $6,361,981. This asset was carried on Axton–Fisher's books in that amount. The value of leaf tobacco had risen sharply and, to quote the words of the complaint, 'unbeknown to the public holders of * * * Class A common stock of Axton–Fisher, but known to Transamerica, the market value of * * * (the) tobacco had, in March and April of 1943, attained the huge sum of about $20,000,000.'

The complaint then alleges the gist of the plaintiff's grievance, viz., that Transamerica, knowing of the great value of the tobacco which Axton–Fisher possessed, conceived a plan to appropriate the value of the tobacco to itself by redeeming the Class A stock at the price of $60 a share plus accrued dividends, the redemption being made to appear as if 'incident to the continuance of the business of Axton–Fisher as a going concern,' and thereafter, the redemption of the Class A stock being completed, to liquidate Axton–Fisher; that this would result, after the disbursal of the sum required to be paid to the preferred stock, in Transamerica gaining for itself most of the value of the warehouse tobacco. The complaint further alleges that in pursuit of this plan Transamerica, by a resolution of the Board of Directors of Axton–Fisher on April 30, 1943, called the Class A stock at $60 and, selling a large part of the tobacco to Phillip–Morris Company, Ltd., Inc., together with substantially all of the other assets of Axton–Fisher, thereafter liquidated Axton–Fisher, paid off the preferred stock and pocketed the balance of the proceeds of the sale. Warehouse receipts representing the remainder of the tobacco were distributed to the Class B stockholders. * * *

The decision of the Court of Appeals of Kentucky in the Taylor case requires careful analysis. The following appears. Charlotte Taylor, a citizen of Jefferson County, Kentucky, sued Axton–Fisher in the Jefferson Circuit Court, Chancery Branch, First Division, stating that she was the holder of nine shares of its Class B stock and, setting up in her complaint the provisions of Axton–Fisher's charter hereinbefore referred to, alleged that Axton–Fisher's board of directors by a resolution of June 16, 1943 had provided that the Class A stock not presented for redemption on or before July 1, 1943, should 'continue in full force and effect with all the rights and privileges thereunto appertaining, as fully as if the call for redemption (pursuant to the resolution of April 30, 1943) had never been issued * * * ' and that those Class A stockholders who had surrendered their stock for redemption might change their positions and remain as Class A stockholders of their corporation provided recissions of surrenders of their stock were filed with the corporation's agent on or before July 1, 1943. Taylor alleged, in short, that by the resolution of June 16, 1943 the board of directors attempted to change the call for the redemption of the Class A stock from a mandatory to an optional one, leaving it to the choice of the stockholders whether they would surrender their stock or not. Taylor asked the court to declare that the resolution of the board of April 30, 1943 was a final and irrevocable act of the board of directors, binding upon Axton–Fisher and on all Class A stockholders; that the attempted modification of the terms of the resolution of April 30, 1943 by the resolution of June 16, 1943 was void and that Axton–Fisher was required to carry out the redemption of the Class A stock as provided by the resolution of April 30, 1943.

A demurrer was filed and the cause proceeded to judgment. The Circuit Court of Jefferson County held that the board of directors had the right to modify the call embodied in the resolution of April 30 by the resolution of June 16. A brief opinion was filed. The case was appealed to the Court of Appeals of Kentucky. See 295 Ky. 226, 173 S.W.2d 377, 379, 148 A.L.R. 834. That Court, speaking through Commissioner Stanley, one Judge dissenting, stated inter alia: 'The rights of the holders of Class A stock and of the corporation as to its redemption rested on an express contract, namely, the provision of the articles of incorporation which made them junior preferred stockholders and subject at all times to have their stock retired.' * * * Commissioner Stanley went on to say: 'Manifestly, it was very much to the interest of the holders of Class B stock to have all these priorities, obligations and restrictions on and conditional joint control of the management eliminated. A substantial advantage was given to and acquired by the Class B stockholders by the resolution definitely and unqualifiedly calling Class A stock for redemption. That being true, it was vested and fixed, so that the directors could not withdraw or cancel or modify their action to the prejudice or detriment of Class B stockholders.

'The first action of the directors may not be regarded as but an offer or proffer, or in the nature of such, capable of being withdrawn before acceptance or consummation. Rather it is the converse. The charter provision constituted a continuing contractual power and corresponding right which only waited action by the directors for use and consummation. It was a continuing option.' Commissioner Stanley said that while the acts of boards of directors, exercised in good faith and not in fraud of the rights of the stockholders, should not be interfered with by the courts, if the prior action of the board of directors had vested rights in others the board could 'not (subsequently) alter or affect those rights * * * '. Discussing Axton–Fisher's charter provisions at some length, Commissioner Stanley stated, ' * * * we (cannot) agree with the appellee (Axton-Fisher) that the result of this action of the directors is to be regarded only as an incidental benefit flowing to the Class B stockholders since they were not promises of the (redemption) contract nor parties to whom performance was to be rendered. * * * The provision of the articles of incorporation and the effect of the action of the directors are too substantial and too great to be so regarded. We think the provision for redemption of Class A stock was made as much for the one as for the other class. If it was not, then it was very delusive. * * *

The tenor of the federal decisions in respect to the general fiduciary duty of those in control of a corporation is unmistakable. The Supreme Court in Southern Pacific Co. v. Bogert, 250 U.S. 483, 487, 488 said: 'The rule of corporation law and of equity invoked is well settled and has been often applied. The majority has the right to control; but when it does so, it occupies a fiduciary relation toward the minority, as much so as the corporation itself or its officers and directors.' In Pepper v. Litton, 308 U.S. 295, 306, the Supreme Court stated: 'A director is a fiduciary. * * * So is a dominant or controlling stockholder or group of stockholders. * * * Their powers are powers in trust. * * * Their dealings with the corporation are subjected to rigorous scrutiny and where any of their contracts or engagements with the corporation is challenged the burden is on the director or stockholder not only to prove the good faith of the transaction but also to show its inherent fairness from the viewpoint of the corporation and those interested therein.' Hyams v. Calumet & Hecla Mining Co., 6 Cir., 221 F. 529, 537, ' * * * the rule, independently of state or national anti-trust statutes, is fundamental that one in control of a majority of the stock and of the board of directors of a corporation occupies a fiduciary relation towards the minority stockholders, and is charged with the duty of exercising a high degree of good faith, care, and diligence for the protection of such minority interests. Every act in its own interest to the detriment of the holders of minority stock becomes a breach of duty and of trust, and entitles to plenary relief from a court of equity. * * *'

It is appropriate to emphasize at this point that the right to call the Class A stock for redemption was confided by the charter of Axton–Fisher to the directors and not to the stockholders of that corporation. We must also re-emphasize ... that there is a radical difference when a stockholder is voting strictly as a stockholder and when voting as a director; that when voting as a stockholder he may have the legal right to vote with a view of his own benefits and to represent himself only; but that when he votes as a director he represents all the stockholders in the capacity of a trustee for them and cannot use his office as a director for his personal benefit at the expense of the stockholders.

Two theories are presented on one of which the case at bar must be decided: One, vigorously asserted by Transamerica and based on its interpretation of the decision in the Taylor case, is that the board of directors of Axton–Fisher, whether or not dominated by Transamerica, the principal Class B stockholder, at any time and for any purpose, might call the Class A stock for redemption; the other, asserted with equal vigor by Zahn, is that the board of directors of Axton–Fisher as fiduciaries were not entitled to favor Transamerica, the Class B stockholder, by employing the redemption provisions of the charter for its benefit.

We must of course treat the decision of the Court of Appeals of Kentucky in the Taylor case as evidence of what is the law of Kentucky. The Court took the position on that record that the directors at any time might call the Class A stock for redemption and that the redemption provision of the charter was written as much for the benefit of the Class B as for the Class A stock. It is argued by Transamerica very persuasively that what the Court of Appeals of Kentucky held was that when the Class A stock received its allocation of $60 a share plus accrued dividends it received its full due and that the directors had the right at any time to eliminate Class A stock from the corporate setup for the benefit of the Class B stock. It does not appear from the opinion of the Court of Appeals of Kentucky whether or not the subsequent liquidation of Axton–Fisher was brought to the attention of the Court. But it is clear from the pleading that the subsequent liquidation was not an issue in the case and from the language of the Court there is some indication that it believed that Axton–Fisher was to continue in existence because Commissioner Stanley spoke of the elimination of the Class A stock, which possessed voting rights, from the management and control of Axton-Fisher. Such surmises are hazardous, however, and are not really apposite since it is our duty to determine the law of Kentucky and not to delve into subjective mental processes. It should be noted that Commissioner Stanley stated the justiciable controversy before the Court of Appeals of Kentucky as follows: 'The case presents a novel question of power of the board of directors of a corporation to rescind or modify its action in calling certain stock for redemption or retirement.' This, and only this, was the question before the Court. It is notable that Commissioner Stanley said also that the acts of boards of directors 'exercised in good faith and not in fraud of the rights of the stockholders' should not be interfered with by the courts and that he spoke as well of the 'fair discretion' of directors to be exercised in the same manner as would be the case in the declaration of dividends, citing Smith v. Southern Foundry Co., referred to in the body of this opinion. . . . We think that it is the settled law of Kentucky that directors may not declare or withhold the declaration of dividends for the purpose of personal profit or, by analogy, take any corporate action for such a purpose.

The difficulty in accepting Transamerica's contentions in the case at bar is that the directors of Axton–Fisher, if the allegations of the complaint be accepted as true, were the instruments of Transamerica, were directors voting in favor of their special interest, that of Transamerica, could not and did not exercise an independent judgment in calling the Class A stock, but made the call for the purpose of profiting their true principal, Transamerica. In short a puppet-puppeteer relationship existed between the directors of Axton-Fisher and Transamerica.

The act of the board of directors in calling the Class A stock, an act which could have been legally consummated by a disinterested board of directors, was here effected at the direction of the principal Class B stockholder in order to profit it. Such a call is voidable in equity at the instance of a stockholder injured thereby. It must be pointed out that under the allegations of the complaint there was no reason for the redemption of the Class A stock to be followed by the liquidation of Axton–Fisher except to enable the Class B stock to profit at the expense of the Class A stock. As has been hereinbefore stated the function of the call was confided to the board of directors by the charter and was not vested by the charter in the stockholders of any class. It was the intention of the framers of Axton–Fisher's charter to require the board of directors to act disinterestedly if that body called the Class A stock, and to make the call with a due regard for its fiduciary obligations. If the allegations of the complaint be proved, it follows that the directors of Axton-Fisher, the instruments of Transamerica, have been derelict in that duty. Liability which flows from the dereliction must be imposed upon Transamerica which, under the allegations of the complaint, constituted the board of Axton-Fisher and controlled it. * * *

In our opinion, if the allegations of the complaint be proved, Zahn may maintain his cause of action to recover from Transamerica the value of the stock retained by him as that shall be represented by its aliquot share of the proceeds of Axton–Fisher on dissolution. It is also our opinion that he may maintain a cause of action to recover the difference between the amount received by him for the shares already surrendered and the amount which he would have received on liquidation of Axton–Fisher if he had not surrendered his stock. * * *

The judgment will be reversed.

NOTES

1.   The following chart may better assist you in understanding the rights of the various classes of securities at Axton–Fisher:

	Class A	Class B	Preferred Stock
Dividends	Cumulative Dividend of $3.20, & share any additional amounts with Class B	$1.60 Dividend, & share any additional amounts with Class A	$6 cumulative dividend
Liquidation Preferences	Twice amount received by Class B after payment of creditors & Preferred Stock liquidation	One-half amount received by A	Liquidation of $105 plus accrued dividends

Conversion and Call Features		
Convertible to B and callable at $60 plus accumulated dividends	None	None

Voting		
No votes unless 4 dividends missed	Sole voting rights	Same as Class A unless 4 dividends missed

What are the advantages and disadvantages accorded to each class? Why would an investor choose one class over another? Were the Class A shareholders being deprived of any right? The Class A shareholders had a contractual right to redeem if they desired, but did this require the corporation to notify those shareholders when it would be advantageous to do so? In subsequent proceedings, the Class A shareholders were held not to be entitled to the liquidation preference of twice the amount received by the Class B shareholders. The court held that a disinterested board of directors would have informed the Class A shareholders of the planned liquidation and its effects and would then have afforded the Class A shareholders the opportunity to convert to Class B before calling the Class A shares. This would have effectively required the Class A shares to convert into Class B shares and, therefore, they would be treated as such. Speed v. Transamerica Corp., 135 F.Supp. 176, 180 (D.Del.1955).

2. *Convertible Securities.* Some classes of stocks may be provided conversion privileges. See Model Bus. Corp. Act § 6.01(c)(2). For example, a bondholder may be entitled to convert the bond into a specified number of common shares of the company. Preferred stock might also have conversion privileges. The conversion period may be limited in length. The conversion price is usually computed at a price above the existing market price of the stock so that conversion will occur only if there is a substantial increase in share price of the security into which conversion is made. The owner of the convertible security does not become the owner of the securities subject to conversion until the conversion occurs. Nerken v. Standard Oil Co., 810 F.2d 1230 (D.C.Cir.1987). The conversion feature makes convertible securities more popular with investors, therefore, those securities will be more valuable. For example, a holder of a non-convertible bond will not have the ability to share in the capital appreciation of the company. If the conversion feature is added, however, the bondholder will be able to profit from the capital appreciation, receive interest until conversion or, if no capital appreciation, continue to receive interest payments and return of principal when the bond matures. The bondholder will pay for this right by agreeing to receive a lower interest rate than he or she would accept on a comparable bond without such a conversion feature. The conversion feature is liked by many corporations because it reduces borrowing costs and, when conversion occurs, the company can simply print the necessary shares into which conversion is made. This, of course, dilutes the ownership of other shareholders holding the class of stock into which conversion is made.

3. *Warrants.* Some securities may be sold with warrants. This is simply an option of a specified time duration that entitles the holder to purchase a security of the corporation at a specified price, which is usually above the existing market price. The warrants may be attached or detached. If detached

the warrants may be traded separately from the security with which the warrants were issued. If detachable, the warrant may have a market value that will be based, among other things, on the price of the shares subject to the warrant, the prospects of the company and the remaining time left before the warrant expires.

4. *Redemption and Call Rights.* A corporation may offer securities that are callable or redeemable. A security that is callable means the corporation may purchase or redeem the security from the holder at the corporation's option for a specified price. A redeemable security may limit the owner's future prospects. For example, the holder of a cumulative preferred stock that is paying dividends of a specified amount, say 7 percent of its liquidation value of $100 (or a bond paying interest in that amount), might have their securities redeemed by the corporation when interest rates fall. The corporation will call the security because the corporation can refinance by issuing new preferred stocks or bonds that pay a lower rate and thereby reducing the corporation's financing costs. Usually, the call price is above the principal or original issue price of the security being redeemed. This provides the holder with some protection against being called since interest rates will have to fluctuate somewhat to make it worthwhile for the corporation to make the call.

5. *Tracking Stock.* Another method for allocating differing shareholder rights is through the use of so-called "tracking stock." This stock grants the holder rights to only a portion of the business of a corporation. Say a large corporation has a profitable division and several not-so-profitable ones. You would like to invest in the profitable line of business but not the others. Tracking stock permits such an arrangement. In Sedighim v. Donaldson, Lufkin & Jenrette, Inc., 167 F. Supp.2d 639 (S.D.N.Y.2001), the district court in dismissing a lawsuit described one tracking stock arrangement:

> Plaintiffs assert claims that raise questions of first impression with respect to the rights of holders of "tracking stock." This is a purported class action on behalf of all holders of DLJdirect stock, a type of common stock designed to "track" the performance of the online brokerage business of Donaldson, Lufkin & Jenrette, Inc. ("DLJ"). * * * In late May, 1999, DLJ issued 16 million shares of DLJdirect stock for $20 per share in an initial public offering ["IPO"]. It retained 84.3 million DLJdirect shares. The DLJdirect stock was intended to "track" the DLJdirect online brokerage business. In other words, the value of DLJdirect shares would vary with the performance of the online brokerage business. The DLJdirect business was separated from the rest of DLJ's business for accounting purposes. A wholly-owned subsidiary of DLJ, DLJdirect Holdings ("Holdings"), held title to a majority of DLJdirect assets, but DLJdirect, itself, was a division of DLJ and not a separate corporate entity.

> In connection with the IPO, DLJ filed a Registration Statement and Prospectus (the "Prospectus") with the SEC. The Prospectus stated the following:

> > Holders of DLJdirect common stock will not have any claims on the assets of DLJdirect. Even though from a financial reporting standpoint we have allocated our consolidated assets, liabilities, revenue,

expenses and cash flow between DLJdirect and DLJ, that allocation will not change the legal title to any assets or responsibility for any liabilities ... Further, in any liquidation, holders of DLJdirect common stock will receive a share of the net assets of [DLJ] based on the relative trading prices of DLJdirect common stock and DLJ common stock rather than on any assessment of the actual value of DLJdirect or DLJ.

It also said that holders of DLJdirect stock will have no voting rights, except in limited circumstances where a separate class vote is required by Delaware law.

In the section on risk factors, the Prospectus stated that DLJ could not guarantee that the price of the stock would track the performance of the DLJdirect business as intended, and that DLJdirect shareholders would be common shareholders of DLJ, subject to all of the risks of investment in DLJ and all its businesses. It also said that material financial events which occur at DLJ may affect DLJdirect's financial position.

Contrary to plaintiffs' allegations, the Prospectus did not represent that DLJdirect shareholders would be entitled to all the benefits of ownership of DLJ common stock. The Prospectus said that DLJdirect shareholders would be "common shareholders of Donaldson, Lufkin and Jenrette, Inc.," but it made clear that DLJdirect common stock was not the same as DLJ common stock. For example, the Prospectus Summary stated that "[w]e are offering you shares of DLJdirect common stock, but we are not offering you any shares of DLJ common stock."

The Prospectus further disclosed that there would be conflicts of interest between DLJ shareholders and DLJdirect shareholders, and that the DLJ board might make decisions favoring DLJ shareholders. As an example of the type of decisions in which a conflict might arise, the Prospectus mentioned "decisions on how to allocate consideration received from a merger involving [DLJ] between holders of DLJ common stock and DLJdirect common stock."

The Prospectus also stated that in the event of a sale of more than 80% of the assets of DLJdirect, DLJdirect shareholders would be entitled to one of the following: (1) a dividend in an amount equal to the proportionate interest in the net proceeds of the sale, (2) redemption of DLJdirect shares for an amount equal to the proportionate interest in the net proceeds of the sale, or (3) issuance of DLJ stock at a 10% premium over the value of DLJdirect shares.

Finally, in a paragraph captioned "Relationship with DLJ," in which the Prospectus discussed potential conflicts between DLJdirect and DLJ with respect to cash management and allocation policies, the Prospectus stated that

DLJ intends to reconstitute the board of [Holdings].... Shortly after the consummation of the offering, DLJ intends to add two outside directors to the board of directors of [Holdings]. DLJ's current intent is to submit all significant transactions including significant 'intercompany' transactions between DLJ and DLJdirect, for approval by the board of directors of [Holdings]. The decisions of the board of DLJ and Holdings would be subject to the board of directors general fiduciary duty. However, there can be no assurance that transactions between DLJdirect and DLJ could not be effected on more favorable terms with unaffiliated, third parties. * * *

See also In re General Motors Class H Shareholders Litigation, 734 A.2d 611 (Del.Ch.1999) (rejecting breach of fiduciary duty claims in connection with tracking stock). The Loews Corp. created a tracking stock for its profitable, but threatened, tobacco subsidiary, Lorillard, Inc. These tracking stock shares, called the "Carolina Group," were created as a class of common stock of Loews, rather than Lorillard. The Carolina Group shareholders were given one tenth of a vote for each share of tracking stock. Dean Foust, 'This Stock May Harm Your Portfolio's Health," Business Week, Feb. 4, 2002, at 80.

JONES v. H. F. AHMANSON & COMPANY

1 Cal.3d 93, 81 Cal.Rptr. 592, 460 P.2d 464 (1969).

TRAYNOR, CHIEF JUSTICE.

June K. Jones, the owner of 25 shares of the capital stock of United Savings and Loan Association of California brings this action on behalf of herself individually and of all similarly situated minority stockholders of the Association. The defendants are United Financial Corporation of California, fifteen individuals, and four corporations, all of whom are present or former stockholders or officers of the Association. Plaintiff seeks damages and other relief for losses allegedly suffered by the minority stockholders of the Association because of claimed breaches of fiduciary responsibility by defendants in the creation and operation of United Financial, a Delaware holding company that owns 87 percent of the outstanding Association stock.

Plaintiff appeals from the judgment entered for defendants after an order sustaining defendants' general and special demurrers to her third amended complaint without leave to amend. Defendants have filed a protective cross-appeal. We have concluded that the allegations of the complaint and certain stipulated facts sufficiently state a cause of action and that the judgment must therefore be reversed.

The following facts appear from the allegations of the complaint and stipulation.

United Savings and Loan Association of California is a California chartered savings and loan association that first issued stock on April 5, 1956. Theretofore it had been owned by its depositors, who, with borrowing members, elected the board of directors. No one depositor had sufficient voting power to control the Association.

The Association issued 6,568 shares of stock on April 5, 1956. No additional stock has been issued. Of these shares, 987 (14.8 percent) were purchased by depositors pursuant to warrants issued in proportion to the amount of their deposits. Plaintiff was among these purchasers. The shares allocated to unexercised warrants were sold to the then chairman of the board of directors who later resold them to defendants and others. The stockholders have the right to elect a majority of the directors of the Association.

The Association has retained the major part of its earnings in tax-free reserves with the result that the book value of the outstanding shares has increased substantially.[2] The shares were not actively traded. This inactivity is attributed to the high book value, the closely held nature of the Association,[3] and the failure of the management to provide investment information and assistance to shareholders, brokers, or the public. Transactions in the stock that did occur were primarily among existing stockholders. Fourteen of the nineteen defendants comprised 95 percent of the market for Association shares prior to 1959.

In 1958 investor interest in shares of savings and loan associations and holding companies increased. Savings and loan stocks that were publicly marketed enjoyed a steady increase in market price thereafter until June 1962, but the stock of United Savings and Loan Association was not among them. Defendants determined to create a mechanism by which they could participate in the profit taking by attracting investor interest in the Association. They did not, however, undertake to render the Association shares more readily marketable. Instead, the United Financial Corporation of California was incorporated in Delaware by all of the other defendants except defendant Thatcher on May 8, 1959. On May 14, 1959, pursuant to a prior agreement, certain Association stockholders who among them owned a majority of the Association stock exchanged their shares for those of United Financial, receiving a 'derived block' of 250 United Financial shares for each Association share.[4]

After the exchange, United Financial held 85 percent of the outstanding Association stock. More than 85 percent of United Financial's consolidated earnings and book value of its shares reflected its ownership of this Association stock. The former majority stockholders of the Association had become the majority shareholders of United Financial and continued to control the Association through the holding company. They did not offer the minority stockholders of the Association an opportunity to exchange their shares.

The first public offering of United Financial stock was made in June 1960. To attract investor interest, 60,000 units were offered, each of which comprised two shares of United Financial stock and one $100, 5 percent

---

2. Between 1959 and 1966 the book value of each share increased from $1,131 to $4,143.70.

3. H. F. Ahmanson & Co. acquired a majority of the shares in May 1958. On May 14, 1959, the company owned 4,171 of the outstanding shares.

4. The number of shares in these derived blocks of United Financial stock was later modified by pro-rata surrenders and stock dividends in a series of transactions not pertinent here.

interest-bearing, subordinated, convertible debenture bond. The offering provided that of the $7,200,000 return from the sale of these units, $6,200,000 would be distributed immediately as a return of capital to the original shareholders of United Financial, i.e., the former majority stockholders of the Association.[6] * * *

In the Securities and Exchange Commission prospectus accompanying this first public offering, United Financial acknowledged that its prior earnings were not sufficient to service the debentures and noted that United Financial's direct earnings would have to be augmented by dividends from the Association.

A public offering of 50,000 additional shares by United Financial with a secondary offering of 600,000 shares of the derived stock by the original investors was made in February 1961 for a total price of $15,275,000. The defendants sold 568,190 shares of derived stock in this secondary offering. An underwriting syndicate of 70 brokerage firms participated. The resulting nationwide publicity stimulated trading in the stock until, in mid–1961, an average of 708.5 derived blocks were traded each month. Sales of Association shares decreased during this period from a rate of 170 shares per year before the formation of United Financial to half that number. United Financial acquired 90 percent of the Association shares that were sold.

Shortly after the first public offering of United Financial shares, defendants caused United Financial to offer to purchase up to 350 shares of Association stock for $1,100 per share. The book value of each of these shares was $1,411.57, and earnings were $301.15 per share. The derived blocks of United Financial shares then commanded an aggregate price of $3,700 per block exclusive of the $927.50 return of capital. United Financial acquired an additional 130 shares of Association stock as a result of this offer.

In 1959 and 1960 extra dividends of $75 and $57 per share had been paid by the Association, but in December 1960, after the foregoing offer had been made, defendants caused the Association's president to notify each minority stockholder by letter that no dividends other than the regular $4.00 per share annual dividend would be paid in the near future. The Association president, defendant M.D. Jameson, was then a director of both the Association and United Financial.

Defendants then proposed an exchange of United Financial shares for Association stock. Under this proposal each minority stockholder would have received approximately 51 United Financial shares of a total value of $2,400 for each Association share. When the application for a permit was filed with the California Corporations Commissioner on August 28, 1961, the value of the derived blocks of United Financial shares received by defendants in the initial exchange had risen to approximately $8,800.[9] The

---

6.   This distribution was equivalent to a $927.50 return of capital on each derived block of shares.

9.   The derived block sold for as much as $13,127.41 during 1960—1961. On January 30, 1962, the date upon which plaintiff commenced this action, the mean value was $9,116.08.

book value of the Association stock was in excess of $1,700 per share, and the shares were earning at an annual rate of $615 per share. Each block of 51 United Financial shares had a book value of only $210 and earnings of $134 per year, 85 percent of which reflected Association earnings. At the hearings held on the application by the Commissioner, representatives of United Financial justified the higher valuation of United Financial shares on the ground that they were highly marketable, whereas Association stock was unmarketable and poor collateral for loans. Plaintiff and other minority stockholders objected to the proposed exchange, contending that the plan was not fair, just, and equitable. Defendants then asked the Commissioner to abandon the application without ruling on it.

Plaintiff contends that in following this course of conduct defendants breached the fiduciary duty owed by majority or controlling shareholders to minority shareholders. She alleges that they used their control of the Association for their own advantage to the detriment of the minority when they created United Financial, made a public market for its shares that rendered Association stock unmarketable except to United Financial, and then refused either to purchase plaintiff's Association stock at a fair price or exchange the stock on the same basis afforded to the majority. She further alleges that they also created a conflict of interest that might have been avoided had they offered all Association stockholders the opportunity to participate in the initial exchange of shares. Finally, plaintiff contends that the defendants' acts constituted a restraint of trade in violation of common law and statutory antitrust laws. * * *

Defendants take the position that as shareholders they owe no fiduciary obligation to other shareholders, absent reliance on inside information, use of corporate assets, or fraud. This view has long been repudiated in California. The Courts of Appeal have often recognized that majority shareholders, either singly or acting in concert to accomplish a joint purpose, have a fiduciary responsibility to the minority and to the corporation to use their ability to control the corporation in a fair, just, and equitable manner. Majority shareholders may not use their power to control corporate activities to benefit themselves alone or in a manner detrimental to the minority. Any use to which they put the corporation or their power to control the corporation must benefit all shareholders proportionately and must not conflict with the proper conduct of the corporation's business.

The extensive reach of the duty of controlling shareholders and directors to the corporation and its other shareholders was described by the Court of Appeal in Remillard Brick Co. v. Remillard–Dandini, Supra, 109 Cal.App.2d 405, 241 P.2d 66, where, quoting from the opinion of the United States Supreme Court in Pepper v. Litton, 308 U.S. 295, the court held: "A director is a fiduciary. * * * So is a dominant or controlling stockholder or group of stockholders. * * * Their powers are powers in trust. * * * Their dealings with the corporation are subjected to rigorous scrutiny and where any of their contracts or engagements with the corporation is challenged the burden is on the director or stockholder not only to prove the good faith of the transaction but also to show its inherent fairness from the viewpoint of the corporation and those interested therein. '* * * The essence of the test is whether or not under all the circumstances the transaction carries the earmarks of an arm's length bargain. If it does not, equity will set it aside.' Referring directly to the duties of a director the court stated * * *: 'He who is in such a fiduciary position cannot serve himself first and his Cestuis second. He cannot manipulate the affairs of his corporation to their detriment and in disregard of the standards of common decency and honesty. He cannot by the intervention of a corporate entity violate the ancient precept against serving two masters. He cannot by the use of the corporate device avail himself of privileges normally permitted outsiders in a race of creditors. He cannot utilize his inside information and his strategic position for his own preferment. He cannot violate rules of fair play by doing indirectly through the corporation what he could not do directly. He cannot use his power for his personal advantage and to the detriment of the stockholders and creditors no matter how absolute in terms that power may be and no matter how meticulous he is to satisfy technical requirements. For that power is at all times subject to the equitable limitation that it may not be exercised for the aggrandizement, preference, or advantage of the fiduciary to the exclusion or detriment of the Cestuis. Where there is a violation of these principles, equity will undo the wrong or intervene to prevent its consummation.' [T]he fiduciary obligations of directors and shareholders are neither limited to specific statutory duties and avoidance of fraudulent practices nor are they owed solely to the corporation to the exclusion of other shareholders.

Defendants assert, however, that in the use of their own shares they owed no fiduciary duty to the minority stockholders of the Association. They maintain that they made full disclosure of the circumstances surrounding the formation of United Financial, that the creation of United Financial and its share offers in no way affected the control of the Association, that plaintiff's proportionate interest in the Association was not affected, that the Association was not harmed, and that the market for Association stock was not affected. Therefore, they conclude, they have breached no fiduciary duty to plaintiff and the other minority stockholders.

Defendants would have us retreat from a position demanding equitable treatment of all shareholders by those exercising control over a corporation to a philosophy much criticized by commentators and modified by courts in other jurisdictions as well as our own. In essence defendants suggest that we reaffirm the so-called 'majority' rule reflected in our early decisions. This rule, exemplified by the decision in Ryder v. Bamberger, 172 Cal. 791, 158 P. 753 but since severely limited, recognized the 'perfect right (of majority shareholders) to dispose of their stock * * * without the slightest regard to the wishes and desires or knowledge of the minority stockholders; * * *' and held that such fiduciary duty as did exist in officers and directors was to the corporation only. The duty of shareholders as such was not recognized unless they, like officers and directors, by virtue of their position were possessed of information relative to the value of the corporation's shares that was not available to outside shareholders. In such case the existence of special facts permitted a finding that a fiduciary relationship to the corporation and other shareholders existed. (Hobart v. Hobart Estate Co., 26 Cal.2d 412, 159 P.2d 958.)

We had occasion to review these theories as well as the 'minority rule' that directors and officers have an obligation to shareholders individually not to profit from their official position at the shareholders' expense ... The rule that has developed in California is a comprehensive rule of 'inherent fairness from the viewpoint of the corporation and those interested therein.' The rule applies alike to officers, directors, and controlling shareholders in the exercise of powers that are theirs by virtue of their position and to transactions wherein controlling shareholders seek to gain an advantage in the sale or transfer or use of their controlling block of shares. * * *

The extension of fiduciary obligations to controlling shareholders in their exercise of corporate powers and dealings with their shares is not a recent development. The Circuit Court for the Southern District of New York said in 1886 that 'when a number of stockholders combine to constitute themselves a majority in order to control the corporation as they see fit, they become for all practical purposes the corporation itself, and assume the trust relation occupied by the corporation towards its stockholders.' (Ervin v. Oregon Ry. & Nav. Co. (C.C.S.D.N.Y.1886) 27 F. 625, 631.) Professor Lattin has suggested that 'the power to control, or rather its use, should be considered in no lesser light than that of a trustee to deal with the trust estate and with the beneficiary. Self-dealing in whatever form it occurs should be handled with rough hands for what it is—dishonest dealing. And while it is often difficult to discover self-dealing in mergers, consolidations, sale of all the assets or dissolution and liquidation, the difficulty makes it even more imperative that the search be thorough and relentless.' Lattin, Corporations (1959) 565.)

The increasingly complex transactions of the business and financial communities demonstrate the inadequacy of the traditional theories of fiduciary obligation as tests of majority shareholder responsibility to the minority. These theories have failed to afford adequate protection to minority shareholders and particularly to those in closely held corporations whose disadvantageous and often precarious position renders them particularly vulnerable to the vagaries of the majority. Although courts have recognized the potential for abuse or unfair advantage when a controlling shareholder sells his shares at a premium over investment value (Perlman v. Feldmann, [page 586 below] (premium paid for control over allocation of production in time of shortage); Gerdes v. Reynolds, [page 572 below](sale of control to looters or incompetents); Brown v. Halbert, supra, 271 A.C.A. 307, 76 Cal.Rptr. 781 (sale of only controlling shareholder's shares to purchaser offering to buy assets of corporation or all shares)) or in a controlling shareholder's use of control to avoid equitable distribution of corporate assets (Zahn v. Transamerica Corporation (3rd Cir. 1946) (use of control to cause subsidiary to redeem stock prior to liquidation and distribution of assets)), no comprehensive rule has emerged in other jurisdictions. Nor have most commentators approached the problem from a perspective other than that of the advantage gained in the sale of control. Some have suggested that the price paid for control shares over their investment value be treated as an asset belonging to the corporation itself (Berle and Means, The Modern Corporation and Private Property (1932) p. 243), or as an asset that should be shared proportionately with all shareholders through a general offer (Jennings, Trading in Corporate Control (1956) 44 Cal.L.Rev. 1, 39), and another contends that the sale of control at a premium is always evil (Bayne, The Sale-of-Control Premium: the Intrinsic Illegitimacy (1969) 47 Tex.L.Rev. 215).

The additional potential for injury to minority shareholders from majority dealings in its control power apart from sale has not gone unrecognized, however. The ramifications of defendants' actions here are not unlike those described by Professor Gower as occurring when control of one corporation is acquired by another through purchase of less than all of the shares of the latter: 'The (acquired) company's existence is not affected, nor need its constitution be altered; all that occurs is that its shareholders change. From the legal viewpoint this methodological distinction is formidable, but commercially the two things may be almost identical. If * * * a controlling interest is acquired, the (acquired) company * * * will become a subsidiary of the acquiring company * * * and cease, in fact though not in law, to be an independent entity.

'This may produce the situation in which a small number of dissentient members are left as a minority in a company intended to be operated as a member of a group. As such, their position is likely to be unhappy, for the parent company will wish to operate the subsidiary for the benefit of the group as a whole and not necessarily for the benefit of that particular subsidiary.' (Gower, The Principles of Modern Company Law (2d ed. 1957 p. 561).) Professor Eisenberg notes that as the purchasing corporation's proportionate interest in the acquired corporation approaches 100 percent, the market for the latter's stock disappears, a problem that is aggravated if the acquiring corporation for its own business purposes reduces or eliminates dividends. (Eisenberg, The Legal Role of Shareholders and Management in Modern Corporate Decision-making (1969) 57 Cal.L.Rev. 1, 132. See also, O'Neal and Derwin, Expulsion or Oppression of Business Associates (1961) Passim; Leech, Transactions in Corporate Control (1956) 104 U.Pa.L.Rev. 725, 728; Comment, The Fiduciary Relation of the Dominant Shareholder to the Minority Shareholders (1958) 9 Hastings L.J. 306, 314.) The case before us, in which no sale or transfer of actual control is directly involved, demonstrates that the injury anticipated by these authors can be inflicted with impunity under the traditional rules and supports our conclusion that the comprehensive rule of good faith and inherent fairness to the minority in any transaction where control of the corporation is material properly governs controlling shareholders in this state.

We turn now to defendants' conduct to ascertain whether this test is met.

Defendants created United Financial during a period of unusual investor interest in the stock of savings and loan associations. They then owned a majority of the outstanding stock of the Association. This stock was not readily marketable owing to a high book value, lack of investor information and facilities, and the closely held nature of the Association. The management of the Association had made no effort to create a market for the stock or to split the shares and reduce their market price to a more attractive level. Two courses were available to defendants in their effort to exploit the bull market in savings and loan stock. Both were made possible by defendants' status as controlling stockholders. The first was either to cause the Association to effect a stock split and create a market for the Association stock or to create a holding company for Association shares and permit all stockholders to exchange their shares before offering holding company shares to the public. All stockholders would have benefited alike had this been done, but in realizing their gain on the sale of their stock the majority stockholders would of necessity have had to relinquish some of their control shares. Because a public market would have been created, however, the minority stockholders would have been able to extricate themselves without sacrificing their investment had they elected not to remain with the new management.

The second course was that taken by defendants. A new corporation was formed whose major asset was to be the control block of Association stock owned by defendants, but from which minority shareholders were to be excluded. The unmarketable Association stock held by the majority was transferred to the newly formed corporation at an exchange rate equivalent to a 250 for 1 stock split. The new corporation thereupon set out to create a market for its own shares. Association stock constituted 85 percent of the holding company's assets and produced an equivalent proportion of its income. The same individuals controlled both corporations. It appears therefrom that the market created by defendants for United Financial shares was a market that would have been available for Association stock had defendants taken the first course of action.[13]

---

13. The situation of minority stockholders and the difficulties they faced in attempting to market their savings and loan stock were described in The Savings and Loan Industry in California, a report prepared by the Stanford Research Institute for the California Savings and Loan Commissioner, and published by the Commissioner in 1960. The attractiveness of the holding company as a device to enhance liquidity was recognized: 'The majority and minority stockholders in the original associations often found that they had difficulties in selling their shares at a price approximating their book value. Their main difficulties arose from the fact that book values and prices of shares often ran into many thousands of dollars, a price not generally suitable for wide public sale. These shares were usually owned by a relatively small number of stockholders. When one of them, or his heirs, wished to sell his shares, he had to negotiate with a buyer in this small group or attempt to find an outside purchaser. Minority stockholders had a special problem, because they could not sell control with their stock.

After United Financial shares became available to the public it became a virtual certainty that no equivalent market could or would be created for Association stock. United Financial had become the controlling stockholder and neither it nor the other defendants would benefit from public trading in Association stock in competition with United Financial shares. Investors afforded an opportunity to acquire United Financial shares would not be likely to choose the less marketable and expensive Association stock in preference. Thus defendants chose a course of action in which they used their control of the Association to obtain an advantage not made available to all stockholders. They did so without regard to the resulting detriment to the minority stockholders and in the absence of any compelling business purpose. Such conduct is not consistent with their duty of good faith and inherent fairness to the minority stockholders. Had defendants afforded the minority an opportunity to exchange their stock on the same basis or offered to purchase them at a price arrived at by independent appraisal, their burden of establishing good faith and inherent fairness would have been much less. At the trial they may present evidence tending to show such good faith or compelling business purpose that would render their action fair under the circumstances. On appeal from the judgment of dismissal after the defendants' demurrer was sustained we decide only that the complaint states a cause of action entitling plaintiff to relief.

Defendants gained an additional advantage for themselves through their use of control of the Association when they pledged that control over the Association's assets and earnings to secure the holding company's debt, a debt that had been incurred for their own benefit.[14] In so doing the

'The holding company was regarded by many stockholders as an attractive device to solve the problem of the marketability of their shares. Through this method, the control of one, two, or several associations could be consolidated and offered to the investing public in a single large stock issue at relatively low prices, either over the counter or through a stock exchange. The wide public ownership of holding company shares would thus provide a more active market and more protection against large capital losses in the event the original owners or their heirs wished to sell their holding company stock. * * *

'Large capital gains on the sale of holding company stock to the public have been an important incentive and consequence of this form of organization. The issuance of holding company stock to the general public usually found an enthusiastic demand which made it possible to sell the stock for as much as two to three times book value. In many but not all cases, the majority stockholders in the original associations have offered less than 50 percent of the holding company's stock to the public, thus retaining control of the association and the holding companies.' (The Savings and Loan Industry in California (1960) pp. VI—6—VI—7.) Although defendants suggest that their transfer of the insurance businesses and the later acquisition of another savings and loan association by United Financial were necessary to the creation of a market for United Financial shares and that no market could be created for the shares of a single savings and loan association, the study does not support their claim. Whether defendants could have created a market for a holding company that controlled a single association or reasonably believed that they could not, goes to their good faith and to the existence of a proper business purpose for electing the course that they chose to follow. At the trial of the cause defendants can introduce evidence relevant to the necessity for inclusion of other businesses.

14. Should it become necessary to encumber or liquidate Association assets to service this debt or to depart from a dividend policy consistent with the business needs of the Association, damage to the Association itself may occur. We need not resolve here, but note with some concern, the problem facing United Financial, which owes the same fiduciary duty to its own shareholders as to those of the Association. Any decision regarding use of Association assets and earnings to service the holding company debt must be made in the context of these potentially conflicting interests.

defendants breached their fiduciary obligation to the minority once again and caused United Financial and its controlling shareholders to become inextricably wedded to a conflict of interest between the minority stockholders of each corporation. Alternatives were available to them that would have benefited all stockholders proportionately. The course they chose affected the minority stockholders with no less finality than does dissolution and demands no less concern for minority interests.

In so holding we do not suggest that the duties of corporate fiduciaries include in all cases an obligation to make a market for and to facilitate public trading in the stock of the corporation. But when, as here, no market exists, the controlling shareholders may not use their power to control the corporation for the purpose of promoting a marketing scheme that benefits themselves alone to the detriment of the minority. Nor do we suggest that a control block of shares may not be sold or transferred to a holding company. We decide only that the circumstances of any transfer of controlling shares will be subject to judicial scrutiny when it appears that the controlling shareholders may have breached their fiduciary obligation to the corporation or the remaining shareholders.

Plaintiff contends that she should have been afforded the opportunity to exchange her stock for United Financial shares at the time of and on the same basis as the majority exchange. She therefore proposes that upon tender of her Association stock to the defendants she be awarded the fair market value of a derived block of United Financial shares during 1960—1962 plus interest from the date of her action as well as a return of capital of $927.50 plus interest from the date the same was made to the former majority shareholders. In addition she seeks exemplary damages and other relief.

Defendants, on the other hand, claim that plaintiff seeks a 'free ride' after they have taken all of the risks in creating United Financial and marketing its stock. They maintain that plaintiff has not been damaged by their conduct and that they have breached no duty owed to plaintiff and the other minority stockholders. We are thus without guidance from defendants as to the remedy that a court of equity might appropriately fashion in these circumstances.

From the perspective of the minority stockholders of the Association, the transfer of control under these circumstances to another corporation and the resulting impact on their position as minority stockholders accomplished a fundamental corporate change as to them. Control of a closely held savings and loan association, the major portion of whose earnings had been retained over a long period while its stockholders remained stable, became an asset of a publicly held holding company. The position of the minority shareholder was drastically changed thereby. His practical ability to influence corporate decision making was diminished substantially when control was transferred to a publicly held corporation that was in turn controlled by the owners of more than 750,000 shares. The future business goals of the Association could reasonably be expected to reflect the needs and interest of the holding company rather than the aims of the Association stockholders thereafter. In short, the enterprise into which the minority stockholders were now locked was not that in which they had invested. * * *

If, after trial of the cause, plaintiff has established facts in conformity with the allegations of the complaint and stipulation, then upon tender of her Association stock to defendants she will be entitled to receive at her election either the appraised value of her shares on the date of the exchange, May 14, 1959, with interest at 7 percent a year from the date of this action or a sum equivalent to the fair market value of a 'derived block' of United Financial stock on the date of this action with interest thereon from that date, and the sum of $927.50 (the return of capital paid to the original United Financial shareholders) with interest thereon from the date United Financial first made such payments to its original shareholders, for each share tendered. The appraised or fair market value shall be reduced, however, by the amount by which dividends paid on Association shares during the period from May 14, 1959 to the present exceeds the dividends paid on a corresponding block of United Financial shares during the same period.

PETERS, TOBRINER, BURKE, AND SULLIVAN, JJ., AND COUGHLIN, J. PRO TEM., CONCUR. McCOMB, JUSTICE (DISSENTED).

NOTES

1. Is the court in *Jones v. Ahmanson* finding an injury where none really existed?

2. What would have prevented the plaintiff class from setting up its own holding company ("Divided Financial") as a vehicle for a public offering? In the course of the *Jones v. Ahmanson* opinion, the court considered the various theories for placing limits on the sale of corporate control. The receptivity by the courts to those theories is discussed in the section that follows.

SECTION 2.   SALE OF CONTROL TRANSACTIONS

TRANSFERS OF CORPORATE CONTROL AND DUTIES OF CONTROLLING SHAREHOLDERS—COMMON LAW, TENDER OFFERS, INVESTMENT COMPANIES— AND A PROPOSAL FOR REFORM

Thomas L. Hazen.
125 U. Pa. L. Rev. 1023–1067 (1977).

Much scholarly energy has been devoted to the sale of corporate control and the appropriate treatment of the resulting premium, with the common goal of providing the courts with unifying principles to aid in their analysis of control transfers. The various theories that would prohibit the receipt of control premiums can be divided into three basic approaches. None of these theories has achieved more than partial and sporadic judicial acceptance. Nevertheless, they have provided the courts with insight and a basic framework for analyzing control transfer issues. Accordingly, a brief description of the leading theories is a prerequisite to understanding current state of the law.

In 1932, Professor Berle developed what is now called the "corporate asset" theory of control. The basis of Berle's theory is that the premium above the per share market price that the seller realizes in return for a controlling block of stock is a corporate asset because it "arises out of the ability which the holder has to dominate property which in equity belongs to others." The corollary of this theory is that the entire premium "if it goes anywhere, must go into the corporate treasury." A major objection to Professor Berle's approach is that the price paid for a controlling block will necessarily be higher than the previously prevailing per share price because the control purchaser creates an increased demand that, combined with a constant supply, results in an upward pressure on the price. Another reason for rejecting Professor Berle's per se prohibition of control premiums is that the ability to exercise control as a vehicle for making the enterprise more valuable is a cognizable property right attaching to a controlling interest rather than representing a corporate asset. The courts have been persuaded by these and similar objections to a per se attack. * * *

Notwithstanding the varying scholarly approaches to invalidating a control premium, the courts agree that, absent special circumstances, a shareholder is not precluded from receiving a premium above the market price for selling a controlling block of stock.

———

Some commentators believe that, since voting control is tied to a controlling interest in the shares, it is an asset that can readily be transferred with the shares. See e.g., Frank Easterbrook & Danile Fischel, The Economic Structure of Corporate Law 119–127 (1991); Javaras, Equal Opportunity in the Sale of Controlling Shares: A Reply to Professor Andrews, 32 U. Chi. L. Rev. 420 (1965). The majority rule clearly sides with this view. The following case is typical.

ZETLIN v. HANSON HOLDINGS, INC.

48 N.Y.2d 684, 421 N.Y.S.2d 877, 397 N.E.2d 387 (1979).

MEMORANDUM.

Plaintiff Zetlin owned approximately 2% of the outstanding shares of Gable Industries, Inc., with defendants Hanson Holdings, Inc., and Sylvestri together with members of the Sylvestri family, owning 44.4% Of

Gable's shares. The defendants sold their interests to Flintkote Co. for a premium price of $15 per share, at a time when Gable was selling on the open market for $7.38 per share. It is undisputed that the 44.4% Acquired by Flintkote represented effective control of Gable.

Recognizing that those who invest the capital necessary to acquire a dominant position in the ownership of a corporation have the right of controlling that corporation, it has long been settled law that, absent looting of corporate assets, conversion of a corporate opportunity, fraud or other acts of bad faith, a controlling stockholder is free to sell, and a purchaser is free to buy, that controlling interest at a premium price (see Barnes v. Brown, 80 N.Y. 527; Levy v. American Beverage Corp., 265 App.Div. 208, 38 N.Y.S.2d 517; Essex Universal Corp. v. Yates, 2nd Cir., 305 F.2d 572).

Certainly, minority shareholders are entitled to protection against such abuse by controlling shareholders. They are not entitled, however, to inhibit the legitimate interests of the other stockholders. It is for this reason that control shares usually command a premium price. The premium is the added amount an investor is willing to pay for the privilege of directly influencing the corporation's affairs.

In this action plaintiff Zetlin contends that minority stockholders are entitled to an opportunity to share equally in any premium paid for a controlling interest in the corporation. This rule would profoundly affect the manner in which controlling stock interests are now transferred. It would require, essentially, that a controlling interest be transferred only by means of an offer to all stockholders, i.e., a tender offer. This would be contrary to existing law and if so radical a change is to be effected it would best be done by the Legislature.

Order affirmed.

NOTE

Although *Zetlin* reflects the general rule, there are three important exceptions to the rule that a majority shareholder may retain a premium received in the sale of control shares. Those exceptions involve (1) sales to a looter, (2) sales of a corporate office, and (3) sales of corporate assets.

GERDES v. REYNOLDS
28 N.Y.S.2d 622 (Sup.Ct.1941).

[Defendants who controlled Reynolds securities sold their controlling interest at a price in excess of the market price. The purchasers of control proceeded to liquidate the corporation to the detriment of the remaining shareholders].

WALTER, JUSTICE

There remains for consideration the liability of the so-called 'Reynolds group' of defendants, consisting of (a) those who sold their stock and resigned as officers and directors, and (b) the members of the firm of Granberry & Co. who, for a substantial consideration, guaranteed performance of the contract of sale by the sellers and received and disbursed the proceeds of sale. As already noted, no adjudication can be made with respect to R. S. Reynolds and R. S. Reynolds, Jr., because they were not served with process; but the liability of C. K. Reynolds and Wood-ward must be determined on the basis of the four together being sellers of stock and the officers and directors who resigned.

There is not a scintilla of evidence that any of the defendants in this group in any way participated in or knew of any of the transactions respecting First Income, Continental, Hanseatic, Corporate Administration or American International Corporation, or that they ever heard of any of the persons connected with any of those transactions. Neither is there a scintilla of evidence that any of such defendants in any way participated in or knew of the use made of the assets of Reynolds Investing Company after December 31, 1937. Liability is asserted against them upon the grounds (a) that the sale of the stock, accompanied by their resignations and the election of successors nominated by the purchaser, was itself an illegal transaction because in violation of fiduciary duties owed to the corporation and the holders of its debentures and preferred stock and its minority common stockholders; and (b) that even if the transaction were not illegal in itself, it is made so because the selling defendants negligently or in bad faith failed to make proper investigation of the purchaser or to give advance notice to the other stockholders of an impending change of management, especially so inasmuch as what is claimed to be the excessive price paid was itself sufficient to put those defendants upon notice that some wrongful act was intended. Those contentions present interesting and important and difficult questions of law.

Inherent in the very nature of stock corporations as constituted by our law are the settled principles that the shares of stock are the property of the stockholders, that the stockholders may sell their shares when and to whom they please and for such price as they can get, that they may sell to buyers of whose identity and integrity and responsibility they are unaware (as is the common practice in the multitudinous sales through brokers on and off exchanges), that the purchase price paid upon such sales belongs to the sellers, and that these same rights exist even where the stockholders hold a majority of the stock and where the sellers are a group who together own and sell such a majority. Equally inherent is the further principle that the holders of a majority (or other statutorally fixed percentage) of the voting shares elect the directors who are to manage the business affairs of the corporation, and in that sense and to that extent control the corporation and its assets. Equally inherent is the further principle that, in the absence of some statutory restriction, officers and directors may resign when they please; and in the case of this particular corporation, as in many others, the remaining directors were specifically authorized to fill vacancies. Over against these principles and rules there is the principle that officers and directors of a corporation, and under certain circumstances and for some purposes the majority stockholders, whether one or many, stand in a fiduciary relation to the corporation and to the minority stockholders, and must observe the high standards of diligence, good faith and loyalty required of all fiduciaries. These principles are not destructive one of the other. They are complementary to each other, and are merely misinterpreted when thought to be otherwise.

The cases in which majority stockholders have been said to stand in a fiduciary relation to the minority have been cases in which the court was speaking of a matter of corporate management committed by statute directly to the stockholders rather than to the directors or cases in which the majority have in fact assumed the management of the corporation's property or business or cases in which the majority have undertaken to act for the minority. Such cases may not exhaust the entire list of situations in which the majority may be held to be fiduciaries, but certainly as to matters not relating to management of the corporation's business or property, and in the absence of any express undertaking, the stockholders do not stand in a fiduciary relation to each other. Clearly, therefore, in the matter of selling their stock the holders of a majority thereof, whether one or a group, act for themselves alone and not as trustees, either technically or substantially, for the other stockholders, and no fiduciary duty is violated by such a sale, even though such sale ultimately bring about a change in the directorate. As long ago as 1896 the Court of Appeals, in speaking of a railroad corporation, said that 'it is a matter of common knowledge that, where the ownership of a majority of the stock of such a corporation changes, the board usually changes, unless its members are already in harmony with the policy of the purchasers' and that it is true today and is equally true of other kinds of corporations. No illegality can be found, therefore, in the mere fact of a sale of a majority of the voting stock with the necessarily accompanying incident of a change in the personality of those who by reason of stock ownership have the right to choose the directorate.

In this case, however, it indisputably was a condition of the sale that all the officers and directors then in office should forthwith resign and that under their power to fill vacancies they should forthwith elect an entirely new directorate chosen wholly by the purchaser of the stock, and all the officers and directors then in office did so resign and did so elect as directors persons designated by the purchaser. Furthermore, the brief submitted on behalf of this group of defendants accurately portrays the situation where it specifically states that the purchaser 'insisted that on the closing date sufficient stock to constitute a majority should be actually delivered or placed in escrow beyond the control of the sellers,' and 'made certain that the purchaser was bound to get delivery of enough shares to constitute a clear majority contemporaneously with the closing on December 31st,' and the contract was so arranged as to insure the purchaser that 'the majority block was irrevocably within his control the minute the deal closed on the 31st of December.' Immediate and complete control in advance of payment of the entire purchase price was thus specifically bargained for and accorded. The officers and directors were made specifically aware of the fact that what the purchaser or purchasers wanted was immediate and actual control, and not merely the right to elect directors which incidentally follows from a sale of a majority of voting stock.

Officers and directors always and necessarily stand in a fiduciary relation to the corporation and to its stockholders and creditors. They undoubtedly may free themselves of that fiduciary relationship by ceasing to be officers and directors, but their right to resign, although sometimes stated with seeming absoluteness is qualified by their fiduciary obligations to others. 'Rights are never absolute and independent of those of others.' Officers and directors thus 'cannot terminate their agency or accept the resignation of others if the immediate consequence would be to leave the interests of the company without proper care and protection.' Neither can they accept pay in any form or guise, direct or devious, for their own resignation or for the election of others in their place.

The statement in 3 Cook on Corporations, 8th Ed., section 622a, that 'a contract by which the directors who own a majority of the stock sell such stock and agree to substitute the vendees as directors of the company is legal,' may be literally correct, but it must be read subject to many limitations, many of which are plainly stated in other sentences of the same section and in the accompanying footnotes and cited cases, and all which perhaps can be summed up by saying that such a contract cannot be made a vehicle for a violation of any fiduciary duty. As stated on the next page of the text, 'All such transactions are closely scrutinized by the courts, and if fraudulent, as a matter of fact, the retiring directors are personally responsible for any losses.' Needless to say, constructive fraud or breach of fiduciary duty would have the same result. Barnes v. Brown, 80 N.Y. 527, likewise merely recognizes what I already have stated as inherent in the nature of stock corporations, namely, that majority stockholders may dispose of their stock, and that when they do so such right of control as the law vests in the majority necessarily passes to the buyer as a legal incident of the sale. It gives no countenance to any idea that either the ownership of stock or the right to sell it carries with it any license to breach any sort of duty owed to anyone.

It is obvious, of course that it would be illegal for officers and directors to resign and elect as their successors persons who they knew intended to loot the corporation's treasury. Even stockholders, despite their right to sell their stock to whom they please, could not legally do that. Liability for such an act would not have to be predicated upon breach of a fiduciary relation, for the act would amount to a wilful and malicious injury to property, tortious in its very nature. I here find as a fact that none of the sellers of the stock of Reynolds Investing Company had any knowledge that the purchasers thereof, or any one acting for them, had any intention to loot the corporation or to pay any part of the purchase price out of the corporation's own assets. Whether or not the resigning officers and directors nevertheless are chargeable with notice of such an intention—whether or not it was, under all the circumstances, a risk reasonably to be perceived—is, of course, another question.

The questions determinative of the liability of corporate officers and directors in such a situation as is here disclosed thus appear to me to be these: (1) Are the circumstances such that, despite actual ignorance of unlawful plans and designs on the part of the purchasers, they are chargeable with notice of such plans and designs, or, perhaps more accurately, with notice that unlawful plans and designs are a risk reasonably to be perceived? 'The risk reasonably to be perceived defines the duty to be obeyed.' Palsgraf v. Long Island R. R. Co., 248 N.Y. 339, 344, 162 N.E. 99, 100, 59 A.L.R. 1253. (2) Is the price paid in reality a price paid for the stock, or is it, in part at least, a price paid for the resignations of the existing officers and directors and the election of the buyer's nominees? And the principal factors which must supply the answers to these questions are the nature of the assets which are to pass into the possession and control of the purchasers by reason of the transaction, the method by which the transaction is to be consummated, and the relation of the price paid to the value of the stock.

The immediate consequence of the resignation of the entire body of officers and directors of a corporation obviously is at least potentially different where the corporation's assets are land and buildings and where they are securities which to all intents and purposes are practically negotiable, and such potential difference must be taken into account, both by the officers and directors and by a court judging their conduct, in considering whether their en masse resignations would leave the assets without proper care and protection, because the risk of dissipation or speedy misapplication obviously is greater. Such difference in the nature of the assets must be considered, also, in gauging the significance of the purchaser's conceded requirement that custody and possession of the assets be accorded before payment of a substantial part of the purchase price. An assumption that the officers and directors of Reynolds Investing Company fully performed the fiduciary duty resting upon them thus requires an assumption that they realized that by doing what they did they were placing in the hands of those whom they elected as their successors the custody and possession of practically negotiable securities of a value of more than double the amount of the agreed purchase price, and were so placing such custody and possession at a time when a large part of the purchase price (over $600,000) still remained unpaid. For fiduciaries confronted with such a realization, I gravely doubt whether it is sufficient that they truthfully can say that they actually knew nothing against the character of the purchasers or of their nominees, or even that they had affirmative evidence that the purchasers were of good reputation. A man dealing with his own affairs may be as confiding and trusting as he pleases, and may be grossly negligent without being guilty of bad faith; but a fiduciary charged with the care of the property of others must be reasonably vigilant, and will not be heard to say that he did not know what the circumstances plainly indicated or that his faith in people was such that obvious opportunities for wrongdoing gave him no inkling that wrongdoing might be done, and schemes to acquire the stock of corporations by using assets of the corporation to pay the purchase price did not originate in the year 1937.

Precisely what would be the situation of directors who, by resignation and election, turned practically negotiable securities over to strangers who had not completed payment, need not be here determined, however, because here there is the added element that in connection with the same transaction a price was paid which is claimed to be grossly in excess of the value of the stock, and the situation of these directors must be considered in connection with that additional element.

Gross inadequacy of price long and frequently has been regarded as important evidence upon the question of good faith, and sometimes is sufficient in itself to charge a buyer with notice of fraudulent intent on the part of a seller. For the same reasons, gross excessiveness of price may be equally significant in determining for what it really was paid, and may be sufficient to charge a seller with notice of a fraudulent intent on the part of a buyer. * * *

I return now to the question of excessiveness of price. On December 31, 1937, Reynolds Investing Company had outstanding $3,446,900 face amount of 5 per cent debentures, $991,500 stated value of preferred stock upon which there were $327,195 of accrued and unpaid dividends, a bank loan of $484,623, and accrued interest and taxes of $62,629. The total of those items is $5,312,847. It had cash and receivables of $149,218, a diversified portfolio of marketable securities of the market value of $2,814,222, and 400 shares of Reynolds Research Corporation worth $4,000. The total of those items is $2,967,440. Its other assets consisted of substantial blocks of stocks of a few companies, which are referred to as 'special situations' and the values of which are in dispute. * * *

I conclude on the whole, therefore, that on December 31, 1937, any price of more than six cents per share for the common stock of Reynolds Investing Company necessarily was not a payment for any actual value then existing therein. At best, it could be nothing more than an expression of belief that the course of events in the future would be such as to produce a value of more than six cents. The next question for consideration, therefore, is whether or not and to what extent such belief then was and honestly and reasonably could be entertained. * * *

Viewing all the elements which the fiduciary obligations of the officers and directors of Reynolds Investing Company required them to view I am convinced that $2,110,000 was so grossly in excess of the value of the stock that it carried upon its face a plain indication that it was not for the stock alone but partly for immediate en masse resignations and immediate election of the purchasers' nominees as successors. The transaction was not one in which there was merely a sale of stock, with the right to elect directors passing to the purchasers as a legal incident of the sale, and I think it proper to add that these officers and directors did not submit to the lawyers whom they retained in the matter the question of the price paid or its significance. They had their eyes and minds so centered upon the personal interests of themselves and their families and associates as stockholders and upon a desire to get what they could for what they regarded as theirs, that they failed to consider their position as officers and directors, and the consequent duty they owed as such to the corporation itself and its creditors and other stockholders. * * *

NOTES

1.   Other courts have agreed that a high premium in the sale of control, followed by looting of the corporation by the control purchasers will result in an obligation of the selling shareholders to disgorge the improper control premium. See e.g., Insuranshares Corp. of Delaware v. Northern Fiscal Corp., 35 F.Supp. 22 (E.D.Pa.1940); DeBaun v. First Western Bank & Trust Co., 46 Cal.App.3d 686, 120 Cal.Rptr. 354 (1975).

2.   In Swinney v. Keebler Co., 480 F.2d 573, 577–578 (4th Cir.1973), the court held that recovery in a looting case requires that the controlling shareholder be shown to have had knowledge of the likelihood of fraud on the part of the purchaser, which would then give rise to the duty to investigate.

———

ESSEX UNIVERSAL CORPORATION v. YATES
305 F.2d 572 (2d Cir.1962).

LUMBARD, CHIEF JUDGE.

The defendant Herbert J. Yates, a resident of California, was president and chairman of the board of directors of Republic Pictures Corporation, a New York corporation which at the time relevant to this suit had 2,004,190 shares of common stock outstanding. Republic's stock was listed and traded on the New York Stock Exchange. In August 1957, Essex Universal Corporation, a Delaware corporation owning stock in various diversified businesses, learned of the possibility of purchasing from Yates an interest in Republic. Negotiations proceeded rapidly, and on August 28 Yates and Joseph Harris, the president of Essex, signed a contract in which Essex agreed to buy, and Yates agreed 'to sell or cause to be sold' at least 500,000 and not more than 600,000 shares of Republic stock. The price was set at eight dollars a share, roughly two dollars above the then market price on the Exchange. Three dollars per share was to be paid at the closing on September 18, 1957 and the remainder in twenty-four equal monthly payments beginning January 31, 1958. The shares were to be transferred on the closing date, but Yates was to retain the certificates, endorsed in blank by Essex, as security for full payment. In addition to other provisions not relevant to the present motion, the contract contained the following paragraph:

'6.　Resignations.

Upon and as a condition to the closing of this transaction if requested by Buyer at least ten (10) days prior to the date of the closing:

> (a) Seller will deliver to Buyer the resignations of the majority of the directors of Republic.

> (b) Seller will cause a special meeting of the board of directors of Republic to be held, legally convened pursuant to law and the by-laws of Republic, and simultaneously with the acceptance of the directors' resignations set forth in paragraph 6(a) immediately preceding will cause nominees of Buyer to be elected directors of Republic in place of the resigned directors.'

Before the date of the closing, as provided in the contract, Yates notified Essex that he would deliver 566,223 shares, or 28.3 per cent of the Republic stock then outstanding, and Essex formally requested Yates to arrange for the replacement of a majority of Republic's directors with Essex nominees pursuant to paragraph 6 of the contract. This was to be accomplished by having eight of the fourteen directors resign seriatim, each in turn being replaced by an Essex nominee elected by the others; such a procedure was in form permissible under the charter and by-laws of Republic, which empowered the board to choose the successor of any of its members who might resign.

On September 18, the parties met as arranged for the closing at Republic's office in New York City. Essex tendered bank drafts and cashier's checks totaling $1,698,690, which was the 37 1/2 per cent of the total price of $4,529,784 due at this time. The drafts and checks were payable to one Benjamin C. Cohen, who was Essex' banker and had arranged for the borrowing of the necessary funds. Although Cohen was prepared to endorse these to Yates, Yates upon advice of his lawyer rejected the tender as 'unsatisfactory' and said, according to his deposition testimony, 'Well, there can be no deal. We can't close it.'

Essex began this action in the New York Supreme Court, and it was removed to the district court on account of diversity of citizenship. Essex seeks damages of $2,700,000, claiming that at the time of the aborted closing the stock was in actuality worth more than $12.75 a share. Yates' answer raised a number of defenses, but the motion for summary judgment now before us was made and decided only on the theory that the provision in the contract for immediate transfer of control of the board of directors was illegal per se and tainted the entire contract. We have no doubt, and the parties agree, that New York law governs. * * *

Our examination of the New York cases discussed thus far gives us no reason to regard as impaired the holding of the early case of Barnes v. Brown, 80 N.Y. 527 (1880), that a bargain for the sale of a majority stock interest is not made illegal by a plan for immediate transfer of management control by a program like that provided for in the Essex–Yates contract. Judge Earl wrote:

'(The seller) had the right to sell out all his stock and interest in the corporation, * * * and when he ceased to have any interest in the corporation, it was certainly legitimate and right that he should cease to control it * * * It was simply the mode of transferring the control of the corporation to those who by the policy of the law ought to have it, and I am unable to see how any policy of the law was violated, or in what way, upon the evidence, any wrong was thereby done to anyone.' 80 N.Y. at 537. * * *

Given this principle that it is permissible for a seller thus to choose to facilitate immediate transfer of management control, I can see no objection to a contractual provision requiring him to do so as a condition of the sale. Indeed, a New York court has upheld an analogous contractual term requiring the board of directors to elect the nominees of the purchasers of a majority stock interest to officerships. San Remo Copper Mining Co. v. Moneuse, 149 App.Div. 26, 133 N.Y.S. 509 (1st Dept.1912). The court said that since the purchaser was about to acquire 'absolute control' of the corporation, 'it certainly did not destroy the validity of the contract that by one of its terms defendant was to be invested with this power of control at once, upon acquiring the stock, instead of waiting for the next annual meeting.' * * *

The easy and immediate transfer of corporate control to new interests is ordinarily beneficial to the economy and it seems inevitable that such transactions would be discouraged if the purchaser of a majority stock interest were required to wait some period before his purchase of control could become effective. Conversely it would greatly hamper the efforts of any existing majority group to dispose of its interest if it could not assure the purchaser of immediate control over corporation operations. I can see no reason why a purchaser of majority control should not ordinarily be permitted to make his control effective from the moment of the transfer of stock.

Thus if Essex had been contracting to purchase a majority of the stock of Republic, it would have been entirely proper for the contract to contain the provision for immediate replacement of directors. Although in the case at bar only 28.3 per cent of the stock was involved, it is commonly known that a person or group owning so large a percentage of the voting stock of a corporation which, like Republic, has at least the 1,500 shareholders normally requisite to listing on the New York Stock Exchange, is almost certain to have share control as a practical matter. If Essex was contracting to acquire what in reality would be equivalent to ownership of a majority of stock, i.e., if it would as a practical certainty have been guaranteed of the stock voting power to choose a majority of the directors of Republic in due course, there is no reason why the contract should not similarly be legal. Whether Essex was thus to acquire the equivalent of majority stock control would, if the issue is properly raised by the defendants, be a factual issue to be determined by the district court on remand.

Because 28.3 per cent of the voting stock of a publicly owned corporation is usually tantamount to majority control, I would place the burden of proof on this issue on Yates as the party attacking the legality of the transaction. Thus, unless on remand Yates chooses to raise the question whether the block of stock in question carried the equivalent of majority control, it is my view that the trial court should regard the contract as legal and proceed to consider the other issues raised by the pleadings. If Yates chooses to raise the issue, it will, on my view, be necessary for him to prove the existence of circumstances which would have prevented Essex from electing a majority of the Republic board of directors in due course. It will not be enough for Yates to raise merely hypothetical possibilities of opposition by the other Republic shareholders to Essex' assumption of management control. Rather, it will be necessary for him to show that, assuming neutrality on the part of the retiring management, there was at the time some concretely foreseeable reason why Essex' wishes would not have prevailed in shareholder voting held in due course. In other words, I would require him to show that there was at the time of the contract some other organized block of stock of sufficient size to outvote the block Essex was buying, or else some circumstance making it likely that enough of the holders of the remaining Republic stock would band together to keep Essex from control.

Reversed and remanded for further proceedings not inconsistent with the judgment of this court.

CLARK, CIRCUIT JUDGE (concurring in the result).

Since Barnes v. Brown, 80 N.Y. 527, teaches us that not all contracts like the one before us are necessarily illegal, summary judgment seems definitely improper and the action should be remanded for trial. But particularly in view of our lack of knowledge of corporate realities and the current standards of business morality, I should prefer to avoid too precise instructions to the district court in the hope that if the action again comes before us the record will be generally more instructive on this important issue than it now is. I share all the doubts and questions stated by my brothers in their opinions and perhaps have some additional ones of my own. My concern is lest we may be announcing abstract moral principles which have little validity in daily business practice other than to excuse a defaulting vendor from performance of his contract of sale. Thus for fear of a possible occasional contract inimical to general stockholder interest we may be condemning out of hand what are more often normal and even desirable business relationships. As at present advised I would think that the best we can do is to consider each case on its own facts and with the normal presumption that he who asserts illegality must prove it.

I add that while New York law may render unlawful an agreement for the naked transfer of corporate office, see McClure v. Law, 161 N.Y. 78, 55 N.E. 388, the record before us does not present such a situation and there is no ground for declaring the present agreement void on its face. Surely an otherwise unlawful sale of office should not become lawful simply on the simultaneous transfer of a few shares of stock. But such formalistic niceties are not involved here, and in any event such an approach would raise factual questions to be resolved only by trial. Further I am constrained to point out that I do not believe a district court determination as to whether or not 'working control' was transferred to the vendee can or should affect the outcome of this case. The contract provides for transfer of 28.3 per cent of the outstanding stock and effective control of the board of directors, and there is no evidence at this stage that the vendor's power to transfer control of the board was to be secured unlawfully, as for example, by bribe or duress. Surely in the normal course of events a management which has behind it 28.3 per cent of the stock has working control, absent perhaps a pitched proxy battle which might unseat it. But the court cannot foresee such an unlikely event or predict its outcome; thus it is difficult to see what further evidence on the question of control could be adduced. My conclusion that there is no reason to declare this contract illegal on its face would remain unaffected by any hypothetical findings on 'control.' It seems that we are all agreed on the need of a remand for trial, though we disagree as to the scope of such remand. Since our decision returns the case to the jurisdiction of the trial court, with nothing settled beyond that, the trial judge will have to decide initially at least how extensive that trial is to be. For my part I believe it incumbent on the judge to explore all issues which the pleadings may eventually raise.

FRIENDLY, CIRCUIT JUDGE (CONCURRING).

Chief Judge Lumbard's thoughtful opinion illustrates a difficulty, inherent in our dual judicial system, which has led at least one state to authorize its courts to answer questions about its law that a Federal court may ask. Here we are forced to decide a question of New York law, of enormous importance to all New York corporations and their stockholders, on which there is hardly enough New York authority for a really informed prediction what the New York Court of Appeals would decide on the facts here presented. * * *

I have no doubt that many contracts, drawn by competent and responsible counsel, for the purchase of blocks of stock from interests thought to 'control' a corporation although owning less than a majority, have contained provisions like paragraph 6 of the contract sub judice. However, developments over the past decades seem to me to show that such a clause violates basic principles of corporate democracy. To be sure, stockholders who have allowed a set of directors to be placed in office, whether by their vote or their failure to vote, must recognize that death, incapacity or other hazard may prevent a director from serving a full term, and that they will have no voice as to his immediate successor. But the stockholders are entitled to expect that, in that event, the remaining directors will fill the vacancy in the exercise of their fiduciary responsibility. A mass seriatim resignation directed by a selling stockholder, and the filling of vacancies by his henchmen at the dictation of a purchaser and without any consideration of the character of the latter's nominees, are beyond what the stockholders contemplated or should have been expected to contemplate. This seems to me a wrong to the corporation and the other stockholders which the law ought not countenance, whether the selling stockholder has received a premium or not. Right in this Court we have seen many cases where sudden shifts of corporate control have caused serious injury. To hold the seller for delinquencies of the new directors only if he knew the purchaser was an intending looter is not a sufficient sanction. The difficulties of proof are formidable even if receipt of too high a premium creates a presumption of such knowledge, and, all too often, the doors are locked only after the horses have been stolen. Stronger medicines are needed—refusal to enforce a contract with such a clause, even though this confers an unwarranted benefit on a defaulter, and continuing responsibility of the former directors for negligence of the new ones until an election has been held. Such prophylactics are not contraindicated, as Judge Lumbard suggests, by the conceded desirability of preventing the dead hand of a former 'controlling' group from continuing to dominate the board after a sale, or of protecting a would-be purchaser from finding himself without a majority of the board after he has spent his money. A special meeting of stockholders to replace a board may always be called, and there could be no objection to making the closing of a purchase contingent on the results of such an election. I perceive some of the difficulties of mechanics such a procedure presents, but I have enough confidence in the ingenuity of the corporate bar to believe these would be surmounted.

Hence, I am inclined to think that if I were sitting on the New York Court of Appeals, I would hold a provision like Paragraph 6 violative of public policy save when it was entirely plain that a new election would be a mere formality—i.e., when the seller owned more than 50% of the stock. I put it thus tentatively because, before making such a decision, I would want the help of briefs, including those of amici curiae, dealing with the serious problems of corporate policy and practice more fully than did those here, which were primarily devoted to argument as to what the New York law has been rather than what it ought to be. Moreover, in view of the perhaps unexpected character of such a holding, I doubt that I would give it retrospective effect. * * *

Chief Judge Lumbard's proposal goes part of the way toward meeting the policy problem I have suggested. Doubtless proceeding from what, as it seems to me, is the only justification in principle for permitting even a majority stockholder to condition a sale on delivery of control of the board—namely that in such a case a vote of the stockholders would be a useless formality, he sets the allowable bounds at the line where there is 'a practical certainty' that the buyer would be able to elect his nominees and, in this case, puts the burden of disproving that on the person claiming illegality.

Attractive as the proposal is in some respects, I find difficulties with it. One is that I discern no sufficient intimation of the distinction in the New York cases, or even in the writers, who either would go further in voiding such a clause, see Berle, 'Control' in Corporate Law, 58 Co-lum.L.Rev. 1212, 1224 (1958); Leech, Transactions in Corporate Control, 104 U.Pa.l.Rev. 725, 809 (1956) (proposing legislation), or believe the courts have not yet gone that far, see Baker & Cary, Corporations: Cases and Materials (3d ed. unabr. 1959) 590. To strike down such a condition only in cases falling short of the suggested line accomplishes little to prevent what I consider the evil; in most instances a seller will not enter into a contract conditioned on his 'delivering' a majority of the directors unless he has good reason to think he can do that. When an issue does arise, the 'practical certainty' test is difficult to apply. The existence of such certainty will depend not merely on the proportion of the stock held by the seller but on many other factors—whether the other stock is widely or closely held, how much of it is in 'street names,' what success the corporation has experienced, how far its dividend policies have satisfied its stockholders, the identity of the purchasers, the presence or absence of cumulative voting, and many others. Often, unless the seller has nearly 50% of the stock, whether he has 'working control' can be determined only by an election; groups who thought they had such control have experienced unpleasant surprises in recent years. Judge Lumbard correctly recognizes that, from a policy standpoint, the pertinent question must be the buyer's prospects of election, not the seller's—yet this inevitably requires the court to canvass the likely reaction of stockholders to a group of whom they know nothing and seems rather hard to reconcile with a position that it is 'right' to insert such a condition if a seller has a larger proportion of the stock and 'wrong' if he has a smaller. At the very least the problems and uncertainties arising from the proposed line of demarca-tion are great enough, and its advantages small enough, that in my view a Federal court would do better simply to overrule the defense here, thereby accomplishing what is obviously the 'just' result in this particular case, and leave the development of doctrine in this area to the State, which has primary concern for it.

I would reverse the grant of summary judgment and remand for consideration of defenses other than a claim that the inclusion of para-graph 6 ex mero motu renders the contract void.

NOTES

1. Consider the effect, if any, on the *Essex* rationale if there had been staggered elections so that it would have taken a number of years for a new controlling shareholder to take control of the board. In such a case the directors' agreements to resign would be a significant benefit to the share-holder acquiring a controlling interest.

2. In Honigman v. Green Giant Co., 309 F.2d 667 (8th Cir.1962), cert. denied, 372 U.S. 941, 83 S.Ct. 934, 9 L.Ed.2d 967 (1963), the Eighth Circuit refused to disturb an internal recapitalization under which the defendants, as owners of all the voting stock, received a premium as compared to the exchange rate for the complaining nonvoting shareholders. Notwithstanding

approval of the plan by over ninety percent of the nonvoting shares, the plaintiff attacked the unfairness of the reorganization on the grounds that the defendants' compensation for relinquishing their voting control constituted payment for a corporate asset. The court first held that the plaintiff failed to demonstrate that Minnesota had adopted Professor Berle's approach to control premiums; second, it relied upon the subsequent ratification by the holders of nonvoting stock.

3.   In Caplan v. Lionel Corp., 20 A.D.2d 301, 246 N.Y.S.2d 913 (1964), aff'd 14 N.Y.2d 679, 249 N.Y.S.2d 877, 198 N.E.2d 908 (1964) the court found that Roy Cohn, a rather infamous lawyer who rose to fame during the McCarthy era as that Senator's assistant, somehow controlled seven of the ten director positions on the Lionel board even though he owned only three percent of the company's stock. Cohn agreed to sell his stock and to cause the sitting directors to resign and replace them with the purchaser's nominees. The court set aside the election of the new directors on the ground that the agreement was an attempt to make an illegal sale of a corporate office:

> The underlying principle is that the management of a corporation is not the subject of trade and cannot be bought apart from actual stock control (McClure v. Law, 161 N.Y. 78, 55 N.E. 388). Where there has been a transfer of the majority of the stock, or even such a percentage as gives working control, a change of directors by resignation and filling of vacancies is proper. Here no claim was made that the stock interest which changed hands even approximated the percentage necessary to validate the substitution.

See also Brecher v. Gregg, 89 Misc.2d 457, 392 N.Y.S.2d 776 (Sup. Ct.1975):

> The Court concludes as a matter of law that the agreement insofar as it provided for a premium in exchange for a promise of control, with only 4% Of the outstanding shares actually being transferred, was contrary to public policy and illegal. . . .
>
> In summary, an officer's transfer of fewer than a majority of his corporation's shares, at a price in excess of that prevailing in the market, accompanied by his promise to effect the transfer of offices and control in the corporation to the vendee, is a transaction which breaches the fiduciary duty owed the corporation and upon application to a court of equity: the officer will be made to forfeit that portion of his profit ascribable to the unlawful promise as he has been unjustly enriched; and an accounting made on behalf of the corporation, since it is, of the two, the party more entitled to the proceeds.

4.   Similarly, in Harris v. Carter, 582 A.2d 222 (Del.Ch.1990), it was noted:

> Several principles deducible from that law are pertinent. First, is the principle that a shareholder has a right to sell his or her stock and in the ordinary case owes no duty in that connection to other shareholders when acting in good faith . . . . . Equally well established is the principle that when a shareholder presumes to exercise control over a corporation, to direct its actions, that shareholder assumes a fiduciary duty of the same kind as that owed by a director to the corporation. Sterling v. Mayflower

Hotel Corp., Del.Supr., 93 A.2d 107, 109–10 (1952). A sale of controlling interest in a corporation, at least where, as is alleged here, that sale is coupled with an agreement for the sellers to resign from the board of directors in such a way as to assure that the buyer's designees assume that corporate office, does, in my opinion, involve or implicate the corporate mechanisms so as to call this principle into operation.

5.   What is wrong with selling a corporate office? Is it not just another property right? What is being sold when a premium is paid for a controlling block of stock? Why is the purchaser willing to pay that premium?

6.   Professor Berle's corporate asset theory had better reception in the following decision.

PERLMAN v. FELDMANN

219 F.2d 173 (2d Cir.1955), cert. denied 349 U.S. 952,
75 S.Ct. 880, 99 L.Ed. 1277 (1955)..

CLARK, CHIEF JUDGE.

This is a derivative action brought by minority stockholders of Newport Steel Corporation to compel accounting for, and restitution of, allegedly illegal gains which accrued to defendants as a result of the sale in August, 1950, of their controlling interest in the corporation. The principal defendant, C. Russell Feldmann, who represented and acted for the others, members of his family,[1] was at that time not only the dominant stockholder, but also the chairman of the board of directors and the president of the corporation. Newport, an Indiana corporation, operated mills for the production of steel sheets for sale to manufacturers of steel products, first at Newport, Kentucky, and later also at other places in Kentucky and Ohio. The buyers, a syndicate organized as Wilport Company, a Delaware corporation, consisted of end-users of steel who were interested in securing a source of supply in a market becoming ever tighter in the Korean War. Plaintiffs contend that the consideration paid for the stock included compensation for the sale of a corporate asset, a power held in trust for the corporation by Feldmann as its fiduciary. This power was the ability to control the allocation of the corporate product in a time of short supply, through control of the board of directors; and it was effectively transferred in this sale by having Feldmann procure the resignation of his own board and the election of Wilport's nominees immediately upon consummation of the sale.

The present action represents the consolidation of three pending stockholders' actions in which yet another stockholder has been permitted to intervene. Jurisdiction below was based upon the diverse citizenship of the parties. Plaintiffs argue here, as they did in the court below, that in the situation here disclosed the vendors must account to the non-partici-

---

1. The stock was not held personally by Feldmann in his own name, but was held by the members of his family and by personal corporations. The aggregate of stock thus had amounted to 33% of the outstanding Newport stock and gave working control to the holder. The actual sale included 55,552 additional shares held by friends and associates of Feldmann, so that a total of 37% of the Newport stock was transferred.

pating minority stockholders for that share of their profit which is attributable to the sale of the corporate power. Judge Hincks denied the validity of the premise, holding that the rights involved in the sale were only those normally incident to the possession of a controlling block of shares, with which a dominant stockholder, in the absence of fraud or foreseeable looting, was entitled to deal according to his own best interests. Furthermore, he held that plaintiffs had failed to satisfy their burden of proving that the sales price was not a fair price for the stock per se. Plaintiffs appeal from these rulings of law which resulted in the dismissal of their complaint.

The essential facts found by the trial judge are not in dispute. Newport was a relative newcomer in the steel industry with predominantly old installations which were in the process of being supplemented by more modern facilities. Except in times of extreme shortage Newport was not in a position to compete profitably with other steel mills for customers not in its immediate geographical area. Wilport, the purchasing syndicate, consisted of geographically remote end-users of steel who were interested in buying more steel from Newport than they had been able to obtain during recent periods of tight supply. The price of $20 per share was found by Judge Hincks to be a fair one for a control block of stock, although the over-the-counter market price had not exceeded $12 and the book value per share was $17.03. But this finding was limited by Judge Hincks' statement that 'what value the block would have had if shorn of its appurtenant power to control distribution of the corporate product, the evidence does not show.' It was also conditioned by his earlier ruling that the burden was on plaintiffs to prove a lesser value for the stock.

Both as director and as dominant stockholder, Feldmann stood in a fiduciary relationship to the corporation and to the minority stockholders as beneficiaries thereof. Pepper v. Litton, 308 U.S. 295, 60 S.Ct. 238, 84 L.Ed. 281; Southern Pac. Co. v. Bogert, 250 U.S. 483, 39 S.Ct. 533, 63 L.Ed. 1099. His fiduciary obligation must in the first instance be measured by the law of Indiana, the state of incorporation of Newport. Although there is no Indiana case directly in point, the most closely analogous one emphasizes the close scrutiny to which Indiana subjects the conduct of fiduciaries when personal benefit may stand in the way of fulfillment of trust obligations. 'Directors of a business corporation act in a strictly fiduciary capacity. Their office is a trust. When a director deals with his corporation, his acts will be closely scrutinized. Directors of a corporation are its agents, and they are governed by the rules of law applicable to other agents, and, as between themselves and their principal, the rules relating to honesty and fair dealing in the management of the affairs of their principal are applicable. They must not, in any degree, allow their official conduct to be swayed by their private interest, which must yield to official duty. In a transaction between a director and his corporation, where he acts for himself and his principal at the same time in a matter connected with the relation between them, it is presumed, where he is thus potential on both sides of the contract, that self-interest will overcome his fidelity to his principal, to his own benefit and to his principal's hurt.' And the judge added: 'Absolute and most scrupulous good faith is the very essence of a director's obligation to his corporation. The first principal duty arising from his official relation is to act in all things of trust wholly for the benefit of his corporation.'

In Indiana, then, as elsewhere, the responsibility of the fiduciary is not limited to a proper regard for the tangible balance sheet assets of the corporation, but includes the dedication of his uncorrupted business judgment for the sole benefit of the corporation, in any dealings which may adversely affect it. Although the Indiana case is particularly relevant to Feldmann as a director, the same rule should apply to his fiduciary duties as majority stockholder, for in that capacity he chooses and controls the directors, and thus is held to have assumed their liability. Pepper v. Litton, supra, 308 U.S. 295, 60 S.Ct. 238. This, therefore, is the standard to which Feldmann was by law required to conform in his activities here under scrutiny.

It is true, as defendants have been at pains to point out, that this is not the ordinary case of breach of fiduciary duty. We have here no fraud, no misuse of confidential information, no outright looting of a helpless corporation. But on the other hand, we do not find compliance with that high standard which we have just stated and which we and other courts have come to expect and demand of corporate fiduciaries. In the often-quoted words of Judge Cardozo: 'Many forms of conduct permissible in a workaday world for those acting at arm's length, are forbidden to those bound by fiduciary ties. A trustee is held to something stricter than the morals of the market place. Not honesty alone, but the punctilio of an honor the most sensitive, is then the standard of behavior. As to this there has developed a tradition that is unbending and inveterate. Uncompromising rigidity has been the attitude of courts of equity when petitioned to undermine the rule of undivided loyalty by the 'disintegrating erosion' of particular exceptions.' Meinhard v. Salmon, supra, 249 N.Y. 458, 464, 164 N.E. 545, 546. The actions of defendants in siphoning off for personal gain corporate advantages to be derived from a favorable market situation do not betoken the necessary undivided loyalty owed by the fiduciary to his principal.

The corporate opportunities of whose misappropriation the minority stockholders complain need not have been an absolute certainty in order to support this action against Feldmann. If there was possibility of corporate gain, they are entitled to recover. In Young v. Higbee Co., supra, 324 U.S. 204, two stockholders appealing the confirmation of a plan of bankruptcy reorganization were held liable for profits received for the sale of their stock pending determination of the validity of the appeal. They were held accountable for the excess of the price of their stock over its normal price, even though there was no indication that the appeal could have succeeded on substantive grounds. And in Irving Trust Co. v. Deutsch, supra, 2 Cir., 73 F.2d 121, 124, an accounting was required of corporate directors who bought stock for themselves for corporate use, even though there was an affirmative showing that the corporation did not have the finances itself to acquire the stock. Judge Swan speaking for the court pointed out that 'The defendants' argument, contrary to Wing v. Dillingham (5 Cir., 239 F. 54), that the equitable rule that fiduciaries should not be permitted to assume a position in which their individual interests might be in conflict with those of the corporation can have no application where the corporation is unable to undertake the venture, is not convincing. If directors are permitted to justify their conduct on such a theory, there will be a temptation to refrain from exerting their strongest efforts on behalf of the corporation since, if it does not meet the obligations, an opportunity of profit will be open to them personally.'

This rationale is equally appropriate to a consideration of the benefits which Newport might have derived from the steel shortage. In the past Newport had used and profited by its market leverage by operation of what the industry had come to call the 'Feldmann Plan.' This consisted of securing interest-free advances from prospective purchasers of steel in return for firm commitments to them from future production. The funds thus acquired were used to finance improvements in existing plants and to acquire new installations. In the summer of 1950 Newport had been negotiating for cold-rolling facilities which it needed for a more fully integrated operation and a more marketable product, and Feldmann plan funds might well have been used toward this end.

Further, as plaintiffs alternatively suggest, Newport might have used the period of short supply to build up patronage in the geographical area in which it could compete profitably even when steel was more abundant. Either of these opportunities was Newport's, to be used to its advantage only. Only if defendants had been able to negate completely any possibility of gain by Newport could they have prevailed. It is true that a trial court finding states: 'Whether or not, in August, 1950, Newport's position was such that it could have entered into 'Feldmann Plan' type transactions to procure funds and financing for the further expansion and integration of its steel facilities and whether such expansion would have been desirable for Newport, the evidence does not show.' This, however, cannot avail the defendants, who—contrary to the ruling below—had the burden of proof on this issue, since fiduciaries always have the burden of proof in establishing the fairness of their dealings with trust property. Pepper v. Litton, supra, 308 U.S. 295.

Defendants seek to categorize the corporate opportunities which might have accrued to Newport as too unethical to warrant further consideration. It is true that reputable steel producers were not participating in the gray market brought about by the Korean War and were refraining from advancing their prices, although to do so would not have been illegal. But Feldmann plan transactions were not considered within this self-imposed interdiction; the trial court found that around the time of the Feldmann sale Jones & Laughlin Steel Corporation, Republic Steel Company, and Pittsburgh Steel Corporation were all participating in such arrangements. In any event, it ill becomes the defendants to disparage as unethical the market advantages from which they themselves reaped rich benefits.

We do not mean to suggest that a majority stockholder cannot dispose of his controlling block of stock to outsiders without having to account to his corporation for profits or even never do this with impunity when the buyer is an interested customer, actual or potential, for the corporation's product. But when the sale necessarily results in a sacrifice of this element of corporate good will and consequent unusual profit to the fiduciary who has caused the sacrifice, he should account for his gains. So in a time of market shortage, where a call on a corporation's product commands an unusually large premium, in one form or another, we think it sound law that a fiduciary may not appropriate to himself the value of this premium. Such personal gain at the expense of his coventurers seems particularly reprehensible when made by the trusted president and director of his company. In this case the violation of duty seems to be all the clearer because of this triple role in which Feldmann appears, though we are unwilling to say, and are not to be understood as saying, that we should accept a lesser obligation for any one of his roles alone.

Hence to the extent that the price received by Feldmann and his codefendants included such a bonus, he is accountable to the minority stockholders who sue here. Restatement, Restitution §§ 190, 197 (1937); Seagrave Corp. v. Mount, supra, 6 Cir., 212 F.2d 389. And plaintiffs, as they contend, are entitled to a recovery in their own right, instead of in right of the corporation (as in the usual derivative actions), since neither Wilport nor their successors in interest should share in any judgment which may be rendered. See Southern Pacific Co. v. Bogert, 250 U.S. 483. Defendants cannot well object to this form of recovery, since the only alternative, recovery for the corporation as a whole, would subject them to a greater total liability.

The case will therefore be remanded to the district court for a determination of the question expressly left open below, namely, the value of defendants' stock without the appurtenant control over the corporation's output of steel. We reiterate that on this issue, as on all others relating to a breach of fiduciary duty, the burden of proof must rest on the defendants. Judgment should go to these plaintiffs and those whom they represent for any premium value so shown to the extent of their respective stock interests.

The judgment is therefore reversed and the action remanded for further proceedings pursuant to this opinion.

Swan, Circuit Judge (dissenting).

With the general principles enunciated in the majority opinion as to the duties of fiduciaries I am, of course, in thorough accord. But, as Mr. Justice Frankfurter stated in Securities and Exchange Comm. v. Chenery Corp., 318 U.S. 80, 85, 'to say that a man is a fiduciary only begins analysis; it gives direction to further inquiry. To whom is he a fiduciary? What obligations does he owe as a fiduciary? In what respect has he failed to discharge these obligations?' My brothers' opinion does not specify precisely what fiduciary duty Feldmann is held to have violated or whether it was a duty imposed upon him as the dominant stockholder or as a director of Newport. Without such specification I think that both the legal profession and the business world will find the decision confusing and will be unable to foretell the extent of its impact upon customary practices in the sale of stock.

The power to control the management of a corporation, that is, to elect directors to manage its affairs, is an inseparable incident to the ownership of a majority of its stock, or sometimes, as in the present instance, to the ownership of enough shares, less than a majority, to control an election. Concededly a majority or dominant shareholder is ordinarily privileged to sell his stock at the best price obtainable from the purchaser. In so doing he acts on his own behalf, not as an agent of the corporation. If he knows or has reason to believe that the purchaser intends to exercise to the detriment of the corporation the power of management acquired by the purchase, such knowledge or reasonable suspicion will terminate the dominant shareholder's privilege to sell and will create a duty not to transfer the power of management to such purchaser. The duty seems to me to resemble the obligation which everyone is under not to assist another to commit a tort rather than the obligation of a fiduciary. But whatever the nature of the duty, a violation of it will subject the violator to liability for damages sustained by the corporation. Judge Hincks found that Feldmann had no reason to think that Wilport would use the power of management it would acquire by the purchase to injure Newport, and that there was no proof that it ever was so used. Feldmann did know, it is true, that the reason Wilport wanted the stock was to put in a board of directors who would be likely to permit Wilport's members to purchase more of Newport's steel than they might otherwise be able to get. But there is nothing illegal in a dominant shareholder purchasing from his own corporation at the same prices it offers to other customers. That is what the members of Wilport did, and there is no proof that Newport suffered any detriment therefrom.

My brothers say that 'the consideration paid for the stock included compensation for the sale of a corporate asset', which they describe as 'the ability to control the allocation of the corporate product in a time of short supply, through control of the board of directors; and it was effectively transferred in this sale by having Feldmann procure the resignation of his own board and the election of Wilport's nominees immediately upon consummation of the sale.' The implications of this are not clear to me. If it means that when market of a corporation's product to wish to buy a controlling block of stock in order to be able to purchase part of the corporation's output at the same mill list prices as are offered to other customers, the dominant stockholder is under a fiduciary duty not to sell his stock, I cannot agree. For reasons already stated, in my opinion Feldmann was not proved to be under any fiduciary duty as a stockholder not to sell the stock he controlled.

Feldmann was also a director of Newport. Perhaps the quoted statement means that as a director he violated his fiduciary duty in voting to elect Wilport's nominees to fill the vacancies created by the resignations of the former directors of Newport. As a director Feldmann was under a fiduciary duty to use an honest judgment in acting on the corporation's behalf. A director is privileged to resign, but so long as he remains a director he must be faithful to his fiduciary duties and must not make a personal gain from performing them. Consequently, if the price paid for Feldmann's stock included a payment for voting to elect the new directors, he must account to the corporation for such payment, even though he honestly believed that the men he voted to elect were well qualified to serve as directors. He can not take pay for performing his fiduciary duty. There is no suggestion that he did do so, unless the price paid for his stock was more than its value. * * *

The final conclusion of my brothers is that the plaintiffs are entitled to recover in their own right instead of in the right of the corporation. This appears to be completely inconsistent with the theory advanced at the outset of the opinion, namely, that the price of the stock 'included compensation for the sale of a corporate asset.' If a corporate asset was sold, surely the corporation should recover the compensation received for it by the defendants. Moreover, if the plaintiffs were suing in their own right, Newport was not a proper party. The case of Southern Pacific Co. v. Bogert, 250 U.S. 483, relied upon as authority for the conclusion that the plaintiffs are entitled to recover in their own right, relates to a situation so different that the decision appears to me to be inapposite.

I would affirm the judgment on appeal.

NOTES

1.   The court in *Perlman* limited recovery to the amount of the control premium that was unreasonable. The court thus seemed to recognize that at least a portion of the premium could be retained by the selling shareholder. The difficulty of computing the premium based on the enterprise value is evident from the decision on remand in Perlman v. Feldmann, 154 F.Supp. 436 (D.Conn.1957). The court looked to Newport Steel's book value and earnings potential of the company to determine a per share value of $14.67 for an aggregate value of $15,825,777. This resulted in a finding of a premium of $2,126,280 ($5.33 per share of Newport stock). The plaintiffs owned 63% of Newport Steel and the court thus awarded plaintiffs their pro rata share—a judgment for $1,339,769.

2.   The facts of the *Perlman* transaction also formed the basis for an unsuccessful challenge to the transaction under federal securities law. Birnbaum v. Newport Steel Corp., 193 F.2d 461 (2d Cir.), cert. denied, 343 U.S. 956, 72 S.Ct. 1051, 96 L.Ed. 1356 (1952) discussed in Chapter 13.

3.   As seen in the next case, sale of control may also raise issues of duty of loyalty on the part of directors that may conflict with their rights as

shareholders. The Supreme Court of Delaware found itself having to resolve the interplay of those rights and duties.

THORPE v. CERBCO, INC.

676 A.2d 436 (Del.1996).

WALSH, JUSTICE.

In this appeal from the Court of Chancery we address the duties owed to a corporation by controlling shareholders who are also directors. The shareholder-plaintiff in this derivative suit, Merle Thorpe ("Thorpe") alleged that the controlling shareholders of CERBCO, Inc. had usurped an opportunity which belonged to the corporation. That opportunity was the potential sale of control of one of CERBCO's subsidiaries. The Chancellor held that the defendants, George and Robert Erikson ("the Eriksons"), who were directors, officers and controlling shareholders of CERBCO, breached their duty of loyalty by failing to make complete disclosure to CERBCO of this corporate opportunity and by not removing themselves from consideration of the matter. The court concluded however that, as controlling shareholders, the Eriksons had the right under 8 *Del.C.* § 271[a] to veto any transaction which CERBCO would have entered into which constituted the sale of all or substantially all of the assets of the corporation. Thus, according to the Chancellor, the Eriksons' conduct caused no injury to CERBCO.

We agree with the Court of Chancery that the Eriksons breached their duty of loyalty, and we acknowledge their entitlement as shareholders to act in their self-interest under section 271. Since the exercise of this self-interest meant, as a practical matter, that they would not allow CERBCO to take advantage of the opportunity itself, damages based on the noncompletion of an INA–CERBCO transaction are not cognizable. We conclude, however, that the Eriksons' conceded breach of their fiduciary duty renders them liable to disgorge any benefits emanating from, and providing compensation for any damages attributable to, that breach. Accordingly, the decision of the Court of Chancery is reversed in part and remanded. * * *

CERBCO is a holding company with voting control of three subsidiaries. At the relevant time, 1990, only one of these subsidiaries, Insituform East, Inc. ("East"), was profitable. The continued profitability of East was in doubt, however, because its regional license to conduct its primary business was about to expire. This license to exploit a process used in the in-place repair of pipes was obtained from Insituform of North America, Inc. ("INA").

CERBCO's capital structure consisted of two classes of stock. Class A was entitled to one vote per share, and Class B was entitled to 10 votes per share. In addition, the Class B shares were empowered to elect 75% of

---

[a]. 8 *Del.C.* § 271 provides that "[e]very corporation may ... sell ... all or substantially all of its property and assets ... as authorized by a resolution adopted by the holders of a majority of the outstanding stock of the corporation entitled to vote thereon...."

the board of directors. The Erikson brothers constituted CERBCO's controlling group of shareholders, owning 247,564 or 78% of the outstanding Class B shares, and 111,000 or 7.6% of the outstanding shares of Class A. Thus, while the Eriksons owned 24.6% of CERBCO's total equity, they exercised effective voting control with approximately 56% of the total votes. The Eriksons also constituted two of the four members of CERBCO's board of directors.

East's capital structure and that of the other two subsidiaries is similar to that of CERBCO. East's certificate of incorporation provides for each of the 318,000 Class B shares to have ten votes, while the 4.3 million Class A shares have one vote each. In addition, the Class B shares elect 75% of the board of directors. CERBCO owned 1.1 million shares of Class A (26% of the outstanding Class A shares) and 93% of the Class B shares.

In the fall of 1989, INA explored the possibility of acquiring one of its sublicensees. East, because of its location and profitability, seemed a likely prospect. James D. Krugman ("Krugman"), INA's Chairman, retained Drexel, Burnham, Lambert & Company ("Drexel") to advise him. Based on public information, Drexel performed financial analyses and devised hypothetical plans for acquisition of control of East. These financial analyses, however, incorrectly assumed that East had a single class of shares and that the market capitalization of its Class A common stock represented the market capitalization of the whole firm. In January 1990, Krugman met with the Eriksons to discuss the possibility of INA's acquiring East. At this first meeting Krugman was unaware of CERBCO's capital structure, which conferred control on the Eriksons, and presumably approached the Eriksons in their representative capacities as officers and directors. Although the factual record is disputed as to what occurred at this meeting, the Chancellor found that the Eriksons made a counterproposal to Krugman after he expressed interest in purchasing East from CERBCO.[2] This counterproposal involved the Eriksons' selling their controlling interest in CERBCO to INA. It is unclear whether or not the Eriksons explicitly stated that they would block an attempt by INA to buy East from CERBCO. Nevertheless, the Chancellor found that Krugman was led to believe that the Eriksons would permit only the transaction involving their sale of CERBCO stock to INA.

After the first meeting with the Eriksons, Krugman believed it necessary to consider seriously the Eriksons' proposal. Thereafter, INA had Drexel perform comparative financial projections of transactions by which it could gain control of East. In one of these studies, Drexel analyzed three potential transactions: (1) acquiring all of CERBCO's common stock and Class B stock in East (1.1 million common and 297,000 Class B or 30.2% of East) for a total price of $10.5 million; (2) acquiring 247,550 CERBCO Class B shares from the Eriksons for $6.0 million; and (3) acquiring all of CERBCO's Class A shares (1.14 million) via a cash

---

2.   The Chancellor noted "that Krugman, himself, repeatedly stated in his deposition that once the Eriksons knew that INA was interested in controlling East, it was the Eriksons who proposed that INA purchase their stock, rather than the East stock from CERBCO."

tender offer of $3.8 million and all of CERBCO's Class B shares (318,000 shares) for $7.7 million in cash, for a total acquisition cost of $11.5 million. These scenarios suggested that, while a direct purchase of CERB-CO's East stock had a higher initial cost than a purchase of the Eriksons' holdings, in certain respects it would be preferable since the indebtedness of Capital Copy, one of CERBCO's subsidiaries, would not be assumed in the latter transaction.

The Eriksons did not inform CERBCO's outside directors, George Davies and Robert Long, that INA had approached the Eriksons with the intention of buying East from CERBCO, but did inform them of INA's interest in buying the Eriksons' stock. Upon learning this, Davies suggested to Robert Erikson that CERBCO sell East to INA, but Robert Erikson rejected this idea.

At the February 22, 1990 CERBCO board meeting, Davies asked whether INA had ever been interested in buying East. The Eriksons denied that INA had ever made such an offer, and had INA done so, the Eriksons indicated that they would likely vote their shares to reject it.

According to draft minutes of the February 22, 1990 meeting, Rogers & Wells, who regularly served as counsel to CERBCO, advised the members of the Board that, as part of a proposed letter of intent that was being negotiated between the parties, INA would be given access to CERBCO's books and records for its due diligence review prior to the execution of a final agreement. The outside directors agreed.

In addition to securing the cooperation of CERBCO officials in making CERBCO's records available in INA's due diligence examination, the Eriksons also sought board approval of their use of Rogers & Wells as their personal counsel in their negotiations with INA. Rogers & Wells gave CERBCO its written statement that, in its opinion, there was no conflict of interest between the Eriksons and CERBCO because the proposed transaction was a private deal by the Eriksons that did not implicate CERBCO's interests. The board thereafter consented to the representation.

On March 12, 1990, the Eriksons and INA signed a letter of intent ("LOI") for the sale of the Eriksons' controlling interest in CERBCO for $6 million. The letter of intent required the Eriksons to give INA access to CERBCO's books and records, subject to INA's agreement to keep the information confidential, and required INA to indemnify the Eriksons for any costs associated with litigation arising from the consummation of the proposed transaction. It also restricted the Eriksons' activities with respect to other potential buyers:

> The Sellers (or either of them) shall not for a period from the date hereof to the first to occur of (a) April 23, 1990, (b) the Closing or (c) the date of abandonment by INA of negotiations regarding the Stock Purchase Agreement, elicit, enter into, entertain or pursue any discussions or negotiations with any other person or entity with respect

to the sale of any of the Shares or any other transaction the effect of which if completed, would frustrate the purposes of this letter.

The LOI required that the parties not disclose its terms unless such disclosure was required by law. The outside directors reviewed the letter at a March 1990 INA sublicensees convention in Hawaii.

On May 11, 1990, Thorpe lodged a demand with the CERBCO board that the proposed transaction be rejected or that the Eriksons provide an accounting for the control premium associated with the sale of their Class B shares. In July, the two outside directors formed a special committee, which terminated representation by Rogers & Wells and hired Morgan, Lewis & Bockius to represent CERBCO.

While negotiations between the Eriksons and INA continued, the LOI expired and on May 30 INA paid the Eriksons $75,000 to extend the terms through August 1, 1990. At the September 14, 1990 CERBCO board meeting, the board considered an alternative transaction involving the issuance of authorized CERBCO Class B stock to INA so that it could have a measure of control over East. The Eriksons objected to this proposal, which would destroy not only the Eriksons' control value, but that of the other CERBCO shareholders.

On September 18, 1990, the letter of intent between the Eriksons and INA expired without consummation of the sale. Evidently, the Eriksons and INA were unable to agree on such issues as indemnification for liabilities that might arise out of an SEC suit pending at the time, and the payment of litigation costs related to the transaction which the Eriksons had already incurred.

Thorpe filed suit on August 24, 1990, contending that the Eriksons had diverted from CERBCO the opportunity to sell East to INA so that the Eriksons could instead sell their control over CERBCO.* * *

The August 9, 1995 opinion of the Court of Chancery, after trial, is the subject of this appeal and can be summarized as follows. The Chancellor found that the Eriksons did not act appropriately when Krugman informed them of INA's interest in gaining control of East. The Eriksons' lack of candor and negotiations with INA on their own behalf constituted a breach of the duty of loyalty which the Eriksons owed as directors to the corporation * * *

As the Chancellor acknowledged at the threshold of his opinion, this "action raises issues falling within the gravitational pull of two basic precepts of corporate law: (1) that controlling shareholders have a right to sell their shares, and in doing so capture and retain a control premium; and (2) that corporate officers or directors may not usurp a corporate opportunity." Forced to reconcile these two imperatives, the trial court, in essence, concluded that the former trumped the latter. Thus, the Eriksons' right to pursue a control premium relieved them from any liability for the breach of fiduciary duty in the process.

We agree that in a particular setting these two precepts of corporate law may tend to pull in opposite directions, but the statutorily granted rights under § 271 cannot be interpreted to completely vitiate the obligation of loyalty. The shareholder vote provided by § 271 does not supersede the duty of loyalty owed by control persons, just as the statutory power to merge does not allow oppressive conduct in the effectuation of a merger. Rather, this statutorily conferred power must be exercised within the constraints of the duty of loyalty. *Bershad v. Curtiss–Wright Corp.*, Del.Supr., 535 A.2d 840, 845 (1987); *Ringling Bros.-Barnum & Bailey Combined Shows v. Ringling*, Del.Supr., 53 A.2d 441, 447 (1947). In practice, the reconciliation of these two precepts of corporate law means that the duty of a controlling shareholder/director will vary according to the role being played by that person and the stage of the transaction at which the power is employed.

The fundamental proposition that directors may not compete with the corporation mandates the finding that the Eriksons breached the duty of loyalty. *Guth v. Loft, Inc.*, Del.Supr., 5 A.2d 503, 510 (1939); *see also Broz v. Cellular Information Systems, Inc.*, Del.Supr., 673 A.2d 148, 154–55, (1996). When INA's president, Krugman, approached the Eriksons, he did so to inquire about INA's purchase of CERBCO's shares in East, not the purchase of the Eriksons' shares in CERBCO. Since the Eriksons were approached in their capacities as directors, their loyalty should have been to the corporation. The Chancellor correctly found that the Eriksons had breached that duty of loyalty through self-interest in subsequent actions. The Eriksons should have informed the CERBCO board of INA's interest in gaining control of East since INA originally wanted to deal with CERBCO.[7] *See Restatement (Second) of Agency* § 381.

Once INA had expressed an interest in acquiring East, CERBCO should have been able to negotiate with INA unhindered by the dominating hand of the Eriksons. *Cf. Weinberger v. UOP, Inc.*, Del.Supr., 457 A.2d 701, 710–11 (1983) (director should not participate in negotiations if conflict of interest would result); *Bershad*, 535 A.2d at 845. The Eriksons were entitled to profit from their control premium and to that end compete with CERBCO but only after informing CERBCO of the opportunity. Thereafter, they should have removed themselves from the negotiations and allowed the disinterested directors to act on behalf of CERBCO.

After finding a breach of the duty of loyalty, the Chancellor tested the defendants' actions for entire fairness, but this test is an unwieldy instrument to use in circumstances such as the breach of duty that occurred here. The test of entire fairness comprises price and procedure.

---

7. Because of CERBCO's clear interest in the opportunity in this case, disclosure to the board of directors was required. *See Restatement (Second) of Agency* § 381. Disclosure to and informed approval by the board may insulate a director from liability where the corporate opportunity doctrine otherwise applies. *See Fliegler v. Lawrence*, Del.Supr., 361 A.2d 218, 220 (1976). A director who opts not to inform the board of the opportunity acts at his peril, unless he is ultimately able to demonstrate *post hoc* that the corporation was not deprived of an opportunity in which it had an interest in or capability of engaging. *Broz v. Cellular Information Systems, Inc.*, Del.Supr., 673 A.2d 148, 157, (1996).

Weinberger, 457 A.2d at 711. Because no price was ever received and the procedure amounted to a breach of the duty of loyalty, the Chancellor's finding of entire fairness here is enigmatic. We find the corporate opportunity doctrine to be a better framework than entire fairness analysis for addressing the Eriksons' duties as directors.[9]

In applying the corporate opportunity doctrine, *Guth v. Loft* requires the Court to examine several elements: [I]f there is presented to a corporate officer or director a business opportunity which the corporation is financially able to undertake, is, from its nature, in the line of the corporation's business and is of practical advantage to it, is one in which the corporation has an interest or a reasonable expectancy, and, by embracing the opportunity, the self-interest of the officer or director will be brought into conflict with that of his corporation, the law will not permit him to seize the opportunity for himself. In this case, it is clear that the opportunity was one in which the corporation had an interest. Despite this fact, CERBCO would never be able to undertake the opportunity to sell its East shares. Every economically viable CERBCO sale of stock could have been blocked by the Eriksons under § 271. Since the corporation was not able to take advantage of the opportunity, the transaction was not one which, considering all of the relevant facts, fairly belonged to the corporation. *See Fliegler v. Lawrence,* Del.Supr., 361 A.2d 218, 220 (1976) (finding no liability since corporation was not financially or legally able to take advantage of opportunity).

Generally, the corporate opportunity doctrine is applied in circumstances where the director and the corporation compete against each other to buy something, whether it be a patent, license, or an entire business. This case differs in that both the Eriksons and CERBCO wanted to sell stock, and the objects of the dispute, their respective blocks of stock to be sold, were not perfectly fungible. In order for the Eriksons and CERBCO to compete against one another, their stock must have been rough substitutes in the eyes of INA. If INA considered none of the CERBCO transactions to be an acceptable substitute to the INA–Erikson transaction, then the opportunity was never really available to CERBCO. Thus, those transactions which were not economically rational alternatives need not be considered by a court evaluating a corporate opportunity scenario.

---

9. The facts here resemble the paradigm usurpation of a corporate opportunity. See, e.g., *Guth v. Loft, Inc.,* Del.Supr., 5 A.2d 503 (1939) (officer may not compete with corporation). In contrast, the entire fairness test is usually applied in a situation where minority shareholders have actually received some value in return for their shares, but the value was determined as a result of a bargaining process in which the controlling shareholder was in a position to influence both bargaining parties. See, e.g., *Kahn v. Lynch Communication Systems, Inc.,* Del.Supr., 638 A.2d 1110, 1115 (1994) (entire fairness test applied in buy-out of minority shareholders by controlling shareholder).

Not only were the Eriksons without power to force INA to offer a potentially unfair price, the Eriksons had no financial incentive to do so. The premise of the entire fairness test is that the business judgment rule is inapplicable where self-interest may have colored directors' actions. *Weinberger,* 457 A.2d at 710. Since the Eriksons could not further their own interests by depressing the price paid by INA, the purpose for applying the entire fairness test is absent in this case.

The Chancellor thoroughly examined the evidence presented by the parties to determine that only one transaction presented a serious alternative to an Erikson–INA deal. This one viable alternative involved the sale of all of CERBCO's East stock for a price of $12.8 million. This finding was logically derived from the record below and will not be disturbed on appeal. *Levitt v. Bouvier,* Del.Supr., 287 A.2d 671, 673 (1972). * * *

[Nevertheless], the Eriksons had the statutory right as shareholders to veto this transaction. Given their power, the Eriksons would obviously never allow CERBCO to enter a transaction against their economic interests. Damages cannot be awarded on the basis of a transaction that has a zero probability of occurring due to the lawful exercise of statutory rights.

It is true that the Eriksons breached their fiduciary duties and that damages flowing from that breach are to be liberally calculated. *See Milbank, Tweed, Hadley & McCloy v. Boon,* 2d Cir., 13 F.3d 537, 543 (1994). Section 271 must, however, be given independent legal significance apart from the duty of loyalty. *Cf. Orzeck v. Englehart,* Del.Supr., 195 A.2d 375, 377 (1963) (compliance with one provision of the General Corporation Law protects actions from invalidation). While the failure of CERBCO to sell East to INA is certainly related to the Eriksons' faithlessness, that failure did not proximately result from the breach. Instead the Eriksons' § 271 rights are ultimately responsible for the nonconsummation of the transaction. Even if the Eriksons had behaved faithfully to their duties to CERBCO, they still could have rightfully vetoed a sale of substantially all of CERBCO's assets under § 271. Thus, the § 271 rights, not the breach, were the proximate cause of the nonconsummation of the transaction. Accordingly, transactional damages are inappropriate.

While this denial of transactional damages may seem incompatible with our decision to award damages for the breach of fiduciary duty, the two holdings are reconcilable. At the time that Krugman approached the Eriksons, they had the duty to present that opportunity to CERBCO. Instead the Eriksons negotiated with INA for their own benefit and are therefore liable for value received in the course of this negotiation and expenditures made by CERBCO to aid the Eriksons in their negotiations. While the Eriksons did have a duty to present that opportunity to CERBCO, they had no responsibility to ensure that a transaction was consummated. Any INA–CERBCO transaction would have required a shareholder vote and the Eriksons were entitled to pursue their own interests in voting their shares. The failure of INA and CERBCO to reach an agreement was proximately caused by the Eriksons' ability to block the transaction, not by the Eriksons' breach of the duty of loyalty. Consequently, no liability arises from the breach for the inability of CERBCO to take advantage of the opportunity to sell its control of East to INA. * * *

Even though the corporation may not have been able to effectuate the transaction because of the Eriksons' rights under § 271, some recovery is warranted because of the breach of fiduciary duty. Delaware law dictates that the scope of recovery for a breach of the duty of loyalty is not to be determined narrowly. Although this Court in *In re Tri–Star Pictures, Inc., Litig.,* Del.Supr., 634 A.2d 319 (1993), was addressing disclosure violations, we reasoned from a more general standard concerning the duty of loyalty: "[T]he absence of specific damage to a beneficiary is not the sole test for determining disloyalty by one occupying a fiduciary position. It is an act of disloyalty for a fiduciary to profit personally from the use of information secured in a confidential relationship, even if such profit or advantage is not gained at the expense of the fiduciary. The result is nonetheless one of unjust enrichment which will not be countenanced by a Court of Equity." *Oberly v. Kirby,* Del.Supr., 592 A.2d 445, 463 (1991). The distinction we noted in *Oberly* explains why no Delaware court has extended the damage rule to actions for breach of the duty of loyalty.... *In re Tri–Star Pictures,* 634 A.2d at 334 (footnote omitted); *accord Milbank,* 13 F.3d at 543 ("breaches of a fiduciary relationship in any context comprise a special breed of cases that often loosen normally stringent requirements of causation and damages"). The strict imposition of penalties under Delaware law are designed to discourage disloyalty.

The rule, inveterate and uncompromising in its rigidity, does not rest upon the narrow ground of injury or damage to the corporation resulting from a betrayal of confidence, but upon a broader foundation of a wise public policy that, for the purpose of removing all temptation, extinguishes all possibility of profit flowing from a breach of the confidence imposed by the fiduciary relation. *Guth v. Loft, Inc.,* Del.Supr., 5 A.2d 503, 510 (1939). Once disloyalty has been established, the standards evolved in *Oberly v. Kirby* and *Tri-Star* require that a fiduciary not profit personally from his conduct, and that the beneficiary not be harmed by such conduct. While there are no transactional damages in this case, we find the Eriksons liable for damages incidental to their breach of duty. Specifically the Eriksons are liable to CERBCO for the amount of $75,000 received from INA in connection with the letter of intent. *See J. Leo Johnson, Inc. v. Carmer,* Del.Supr., 156 A.2d 499, 503 (1959); *see also Restatement (Second) of Agency* § 388 (agent must account for value received from third parties in connection with services on behalf of principal). In addition, the Eriksons must reimburse CERBCO for any expenses, including legal and due diligence costs, that the corporation incurred to accommodate the Eriksons' pursuit of their own interests prior to the deal being abandoned by the Eriksons and INA.

The opinion below is AFFIRMED IN PART and REVERSED IN PART, and this matter is REMANDED to the Court of Chancery for a further determination of damages. Once those damages are fixed, the court should proceed to examine anew any petition for counsel fees on behalf of the plaintiffs.

NOTES

1.　Should controlling shareholders be allowed to block a corporate opportunity in order to take that opportunity for themselves?

2.　Do you agree with the court in *Thorpe* that the opportunity must be presented to the corporation even though the majority shareholders will block the corporation from taking the opportunity and can do so by consent without holding a meeting under the terms of Del. § 228? Del. § 228 allows shareholder action by consent in lieu of a meeting. Del § 271(a) contemplates a shareholder meeting to approve a sale of substantially all of the assets. How do you provide equal dignity to these two provisions? Can a majority consent be used to bypass the meeting contemplated by Del, § 271(a)? Is this form over substance?

3.　On remand in *Thorpe*, damages to Cerbco were assessed as $435,491.81, and attorney fees to be paid to the minority shareholders were set at $143,364.23. Thorpe v. Cerbco, Inc., 703 A.2d 645 (Del.1997).

CHAPTER 12

PUBLICLY TRADED STOCKS— SEC REGULATION

■ ■ ■

SECTION 1. OVERVIEW OF THE FEDERAL SECURITIES LAWS

The core of the federal securities laws are six statutes enacted between 1933 and 1940. They are:

Securities Act of 1933. This statute regulates public offerings of securities and prohibits offers and sales of securities which are not registered with the Securities and Exchange Commission. Certain securities, such as municipal bonds, are exempted from those registration requirements. The statute and SEC regulations specify the contents of the registration statement and prospectus. This legislation requires the disclosure of material information about companies that sell their stock to the public. This legislation was based on the theory propounded by Justice Louis Brandeis. He stated that "publicity is justly commended as a remedy for social and industrial diseases. Sun light is said to be the best of disinfectants; electric light the most efficient policeman." *Louis Brandeis, Other People's Money and How the Brokers Use It* 4 (1932). The Securities Act of 1933 sought to bring full disclosure to securities sales as a way of exposing and deterring abuses. It added "to the ancient rule of caveat emptor, the further doctrine 'let the seller also beware.'" H.R .. Rep. No. 85, 73d Cong., 1st Sess. 2 (1934). The Securities Act did not seek to "guarantee the present soundness or the future value of any security. The investor must still, in the final analysis, select the security which he deems appropriate for investment." S. Rep. No. 1455, 73d Cong., 2d Sess. 153 (1934). Rather, the act sought to assure that the investor has "complete and truthful information from which he may intelligently appraise the value of a security...." Id. The Securities Act of 1933 required a twenty-day waiting period between the filing of the registration statement with the SEC and the offer of the stock to the public. This allowed investors time to assess the information being disclosed and to make an informed, unhurried investment decision.

Securities Exchange Act of 1934. This act extended federal regulation to trading in securities which are already issued to the public. Section 13 of the Securities Exchange Act of 1934 requires public companies to report periodically on their financial condition. Another section of the Securities Exchange Act, Section 14, regulates the solicitation of proxies from holders of such securities. Still another provision regulates take-over bids, tender offers and purchases by companies of their own shares. Section 16 of the Securities Exchange Act restricts the ability of insiders to make short-term profits by trading in their company's stock, and Section 10 prohibited manipulation of securities prices and imposes a broad antifraud prohibition in connection with the purchase and sale of stocks and other securities.

Public Utility Holding Company Act of 1935. This act was designed to correct abuses in the financing and operation of electric and gas public utility holding company systems, and to achieve physical integration and corporate simplification of those systems. This legislation was repealed in August 2005. Another part of the New Deal securities legislation was the Chandler Act that gave the SEC supervisory authority over corporate reorganizations in bankruptcy. That act was repealed by the Bankruptcy Reform Act in 1978.

Trust Indenture Act of 1939. This act applies generally to public issues of debt securities in excess of $1,000,000. Trust indentures are master agreements that govern the terms and conditions of general obligation corporate bonds (debentures) that are offered to the public under the Securities Act of 1933. The trust indenture covering the securities is also subject to the Trust Indenture Act of 1939, which defines standards of independence and responsibility on the indenture trustee and requires other provisions for the protection of the debenture holders in the event of a default.

Investment Company Act of 1940. This statute resulted from an SEC study directed by Congress in the Public Utility Holding Company Act. This legislation granted the SEC regulatory authority over investment companies, which include the mutual funds that are so popular today. The mutual fund is simply a pool of money collected from investors and then invested by an advisor to the fund in various securities. The investor may have his or her interest in the mutual fund liquidated at any time by the mutual fund at the net asset value of the investor's share of the fund. The mutual fund is continuously offering its shares to the public.

The Investment Company Act of 1940 is said to be "the most intrusive financial legislation known to man or beast." *Clifford E. Kirsch, The Financial Services Revolution: Understanding the Changing Role of Banks, Mutual Funds, and Insurance Companies* 382 (1997). Among other things, this legislation regulates the composition of the management of investment companies, their capital structure, approval of their advisory contracts and changes in investment policy.

Investment Advisers Act of 1940. This statute requires the registration and regulation of investment advisers after an SEC study of their operations found abuses. This act prohibits fraud by investment advisers.

Traditionally, investment advisers were regulated more lightly than broker-dealers. However, the uncovering in 2008 of a reported $50 billion Ponzi that was being run by Bernard L. Madoff, a registered investment adviser and industry leader, has placed pressure on the SEC to heighten its regulation of these registrants.

The Securities and Exchange Commission (SEC) is an independent federal agency that is charged with responsibility for the enforcement and administration of the federal securities laws. The SEC is composed of five members appointed by the President, with the advice and consent of the Senate, for five-year terms (the term of one Commissioner expires each year), not more than three of whom shall be members of the same political party. Much of the SEC's work is carried out through its staff, most of whom are housed at the SEC's headquarters in Washington, D.C. The SEC, however, also maintains several regional offices across the country, the largest of which is located in New York City.

The SEC's headquarters staff is divided into four "divisions" and a number of separate "offices." The Division of Corporation Finance reviews the various disclosure documents filed by corporations and other issuers to assure full disclosure and compliance with SEC requirements. The Division of Enforcement is responsible for investigations of violations and prosecutes administrative and court proceedings against alleged violators. The Division of Trading and Markets is responsible for developing regulatory policy over the markets and broker-dealers. The Division of Investment Management is responsible for administering the regulation of investment companies (including mutual funds) and investment advisers. The Office of General Counsel advises the SEC and its Divisions on questions of law, and represents the SEC in appellate court proceedings. The Office of Chief Accountant develops policy on accounting questions and presents the SEC's positions on accounting issues to the standard-setting bodies in the accounting profession. Diagram—describes the SEC structure:

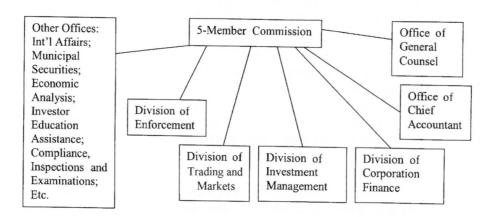

SECTION 2. UNDERWRITING—THE IPO

A key aspect of an investment in stock is liquidity. As seen from the cases in Chapters 10, stock in a closely held corporation is illiquid, thereby trapping its investors in the corporation. How does stock become liquid? The first step is to sell some percentage of the company to the public through an initial public offering, or "IPO" in Wall Street terms. This will require the services of an underwriter.

UNITED STATES v. MORGAN

118 F.Supp. 621 (S.D.N.Y.1953).

Medina, Circuit Judge.

[In dismissing antitrust claims against several investment banking firms, the court provided the following description of the growth and operation of underwriting syndicates in America].

It would be difficult to exaggerate the importance of investment banking to the national economy. The vast industrial growth of the past fifty years has covered the United States with a network of manufacturing, processing, sales and distributing plants, the smooth functioning of which is vital to our welfare as a nation. They vary from huge corporate structures such as the great steel and automobile companies, railroads and airlines, producers of commodities and merchandise of all kinds, oil companies and public utilities, down to comparatively small manufacturing plants and stores. The variety and usefulness of these myriad enterprises defy description. They are the result of American ingenuity and the will to work unceasingly and to improve our standard of living. But adequate financing for their needs is the life blood without which many if not most of these parts of the great machine of business would cease to function in a healthy, normal fashion. * * *

The present method for issuing and distributing new security issues thus has its roots in the latter part of the nineteenth century. It is the product of a gradual evolution to meet specific economic problems created by demands for capital, which arose as the result of the increasing industrialization of the country and the growth of a widely dispersed investor class. It was born in large part because of, and gradually adapted itself to, conditions and needs which are peculiar to the business of raising capital. * * *

The evolution of the investment banking industry in the United States is illustrated by the early phases of the development of two of the defendant investment banking firms, Goldman, Sachs & Co. and Lehman Brothers.

Goldman, Sachs & Co. traces its origin back to the year 1869, when Marcus Goldman started a small business buying and selling commercial paper. In the year 1882, he was joined in that business by Samuel Sachs, and at that time the firm, which had been known as Marcus Goldman, became M. Goldman & Sachs. In the year 1885, when additional partners joined the firm, the firm became Goldman, Sachs & Co., and has continued as such from then on to today. At that time, it was very difficult for small manufacturers and merchants to get capital with which to operate, so Goldman, Sachs & Co. developed the business of buying their short-term promissory notes, thus furnishing them with needed capital, and selling these notes to banks or other investors. * * *

After the beginning of this century, as family corporations grew larger and needed more capital for expansion, or when the head of a family died and money was needed to pay inheritance taxes, it became increasingly apparent that commercial paper, which was short-term money, was insufficient to meet the capital requirements of those small enterprises. At about this time, Goldman, Sachs & Co., desirous of entering the business of underwriting securities, conceived the idea of inducing privately owned business enterprises to incorporate and to launch public offerings of securities. In the early 1900's it was considered undignified to peddle retail store securities, but Goldman, Sachs & Co. believed that, with the growth in size of family corporations and other privately owned business enterprises, there would be a market on a national basis for their security issues. The problems involved in offering securities to the public, where no securities were previously outstanding in the hands of the public, were new and difficult of solution, and different from the problems involved in the underwriting of bonds of a well known railroad. The sale of retail or department store securities required a different market. When the opportunity arose in the year 1906 for Goldman, Sachs & Co. to underwrite the financing of United Cigar Manufacturers, it was unable to undertake the entire commitment alone, and could not get the additional funds which it needed to underwrite from commercial banks or other underwriters, as they would not at that time underwrite this type of security. Henry Goldman prevailed upon his friend Philip Lehman of Lehman Brothers to divert some of his capital from the commodity business and to take a share in the underwriting. The result was that the two firms, Goldman, Sachs & Co. and Lehman Brothers, became partners in the underwriting of the financing of United Cigar Manufacturers. When the opportunity arose in that same year for Goldman, Sachs & Co. to underwrite the financing of Sears, Roebuck & Co., it was perfectly natural for it again to turn to Lehman Brothers for assistance, and the two firms became partners in that enterprise. * * *

In the period from the year 1906 to the year 1917, Goldman, Sachs & Co. and Lehman Brothers together underwrote the financings of many enterprises which had a small and humble beginning, but which later grew to very great size, among them being United Cigar Manufacturers, Sears, Roebuck & Co., B. F. Goodrich Company, May Department Stores Company and F. W. Woolworth Company. Many of the business concerns whose securities were underwritten by Goldman, Sachs & Co. and Lehman Brothers during this period were houses with which Goldman, Sachs & Co. had previously had commercial paper transactions. As Goldman, Sachs & Co. and Lehman Brothers were better known at the time than many of the business enterprises whose securities they underwrote, investors bought the securities to some extent in reliance on their reputation. * * *

There was then no network of securities dealers throughout the country, such as there is at the present time. In or about the year 1905 or 1906, there were only about five investment banking houses which had a national distribution system for securities: Lee Higginson & Co.; N. W. Harris & Co.; N. W. Halsey & Co.; Kidder, Peabody & Co.; and William Salomon & Co. Investment banking houses such as J. P. Morgan & Co., Kuhn, Loeb & Co., and William A. Read & Co. were underwriters of securities primarily in the New York market. Up to about the year 1912 or 1915, there were approximately only two hundred and fifty securities dealers in the entire United States, most of whom were concentrated in the eastern and middle eastern parts of the country. It was not until the time of the launching of the Liberty Loan in the year 1917 that we find a large number of independent dealers engaged in the business of distributing securities throughout the country. * * *

In the period under discussion, it was common for an investment banker to purchase an entire issue directly from the issuer at stated price, and that banker alone would sign the purchase contract with the issuer. Generally, the investment banker's agreement to purchase represented a firm obligation. This investment banker would then immediately organize a larger group, composed of a limited number of investment banking firms, which was sometimes called a 'purchase syndicate,' whereby he would, in effect, sub-underwrite his risk by selling the securities which he had purchased alone from the issuer to this larger group, at an increase or 'step-up' in price. The investment banker who purchased the entire issue directly from the issuer was known as the 'originating banker' or 'house of issue.' The originating banker became a member and the manager of the 'purchase syndicate.' Goldman, Sachs & Co. is said to be one of the first investment banking firms to develop this method of underwriting securities; and, although this method may have been developed to underwrite the securities of the smaller, less well-known industrial enterprises and of the family concerns which were for the first time launching securities for sale to the public, other investment bankers used the same method to underwrite the securities of large industrial enterprises, railroads and utilities. As business enterprises in this country grew in size, and as the amounts of capital required by these enterprises became larger, sometimes a second group, more numerous than the 'purchase syndicate,' would be formed in order to spread still wider the risk involved in the purchase and sale of the securities. The 'purchase syndicate' would then sell the securities which it had purchased at an increase in price from the originating banker to this second larger group, which was sometimes called a 'banking syndicate,' at another increase or 'step-up' in price. The originating banker and the other investment banking firms, which were members of the 'purchase syndicate,' usually became members of the 'banking syndicate' and the originating banker became its manager. The transfer of the securities to the 'purchase syndicate' and then to the 'banking syndicate' was practically simultaneous with the original purchase of the securities from the issuer by the originating banker. * * *

From all the above it is evident that the various steps which were taken, including use of the purchase and banking groups above described, were all part of the development of a single effective method of security underwriting and distribution, with such features as maintenance of a fixed price during distribution, stabilization and direction by a manager of the entire coordinated operation of originating, underwriting and distributing the entire issue. This evolution of the syndicate system was in no sense a plan or scheme invented by anyone. Its form and development were due entirely to the economic conditions in the midst of which investment bankers functioned. No single underwriter could have borne alone the underwriting risk involved in the purchase and sale of a large security issue. No single underwriter could have effected a successful public distribution of the issue. The various investment bankers combined and formed groups, and pooled their underwriting resources in order to compete for business. * * *

The number of underwriters in the syndicates increased [after World War I], in order both to spread the risk and to effect a widespread and rapid distribution of the securities to the public. Even so the problems of distribution became so complicated that it became customary to form an additional group called a 'selling syndicate' or 'selling group.' The new 'selling syndicate' was much larger and more widely dispersed than the purchase and banking groups had been. There were three types of these selling syndicates throughout this period. While they represented successive steps in the development of investment banking, and while there were shifts in the type that was most extensively used, all three were used throughout the 1920's. The first type was known as the 'unlimited liability selling syndicate.' In this group, each member agreed to take a pro rata share in the purchase of the security issue by the selling syndicate from the previous group, at a stated price, and to take up his share of any unsold securities, which remained in the syndicate at the time of its expiration. The syndicate agreement stated the terms upon which the offering to the public was to be made. Each member was given the right to offer securities to the public, and he received a stated commission on all confirmed sales. However, regardless of the amount of securities which he sold, he still retained his liability to take up his proportionate share of unsold securities. The undivided syndicate combined selling with the assumption of risk; therefore, both houses with distributing ability and houses with financial capacity, but without distributing ability, were included in the syndicate. Usually, a banking group was not organized where this type of selling syndicate was to be used. The purchase group sold the security issue directly to the selling syndicate.

The dealers who did the actual selling of the securities objected to the 'unlimited liability selling syndicate,' as they were compelled to take up in their proportionate shares the securities, which the other dealers, who were members of the selling syndicate, were unable to sell. Consequently, the second type of selling syndicate, which was known as the 'limited liability selling syndicate,' subsequently was developed. This syndicate operated in much the same manner as the undivided syndicate, except that the obligation of each member was limited to the amount of his commitment, and, when he distributed that amount, he was relieved of further liability. Each member retained his proportionate liability for the costs of carrying the securities, shared in the profits or losses of the trading account, and was liable for such other expenses as occurred after the purchase from the purchase or banking group. A banking group was usually organized where the 'limited liability selling syndicate' was to be used.

The 'limited liability selling syndicate' gradually evolved into the third type of selling syndicate, which was simply known as the 'selling group.' The 'selling group' differed from the 'limited liability selling syndicate' in that its members relieved themselves of all liability for carrying costs, the trading account and other expenses. Each member of the 'selling group' was concerned only with expenses connected with the actual retail distribution of securities. The financial liability of the member was restricted to selling or taking up the amount of securities for which he subscribed. Usually, a large banking group was organized where the 'selling group' was to be used. The banking group took over the liability for carrying costs, the trading account and other expenses.

The size and makeup of the selling syndicates varied with the circumstances of the particular security issue. Among the important factors, which were considered in the selection of dealers, were the size of the security issue, the type and quality of the security, the size and nature of the class of investors to whom the distribution was to be made, and the ability of a dealer to distribute securities of a particular type. All of these factors were considered in the selection of underwriters and dealers for the formation of the underwriting syndicates and selling groups.

In all of these types of selling syndicates, the members acted as principals, and not as agents of the manager, in distributing securities to the public. The syndicate agreement specified the price at which the securities were to be sold, and it was a violation of the agreement for a member to sell at any other price. The manager traded in the open market during the period of distribution in order to maintain the public offering price. Through such stabilizing operations, the manager sought to prevent any securities, which had been sold by dealers, from coming back into the market in such a manner as to depress the public offering price. It was felt that with respect to the securities which appeared in the market, the members of the selling syndicate had not performed their function of 'placing' with investors, for which they were paid a selling commission; and, consequently, 'repurchase penalties' were provided for, whereby the manager had the right to cancel the selling commission on the sale of those securities which he purchased in the market at or below the public offering price. Under most agreements, the manager had the option of either cancelling the selling commission on the sale of the securities, or of requiring the member who sold the securities to take them up at their cost to the trading account. Records of the serial numbers of securities were kept, and the securities which appeared in the market were thus traced to the dealers who sold them. Stabilizing operations and the repurchase penalty were used in all of the three types of selling syndicates which prevailed throughout this period. However, where a 'selling group' was used, it became more and more common practice to restrict the repurchase penalty to the cancellation of commissions.

The operations of the 'selling syndicate' like those of the pre-war withdrawing subscribers, dealers and selling agents, were directed by the manager whose general supervisory function over the whole machinery of purchase and distribution was continued. Even in the earlier period provisions for maintenance of the public offering price by persons to whom title had passed had been included in some agreements. * * *

As the amounts of capital required by business enterprises became larger, and the number and size of securities issues greatly increased, the problems with which investment bankers were confronted, in connection with the underwriting of security issues, multiplied. Extensive investigations had to be conducted into the affairs of a business enterprise, and studies made of its financial structure and capital needs, at considerable expense to the investment banker, before that banker would undertake the risk and underwrite the securities of that enterprise. In this connection, investment banking firms were compelled to bring into their organizations individuals who had new types of specialized knowledge and experience; so that they gradually built up teams of specialists, who were experts in the different fields in which their respective investment banking firms underwrote securities. * * *

More important than any of the other developments between World War I and the passage of the Securities Act of 1933 was the effect of the unprecedented era of expansion upon the participation of the great banking institutions and their affiliates. As the need for vast amounts of new capital for expansion, plant construction and the establishment of thousands of new enterprises made increasing demands for new money, the banks and their affiliates became increasingly interested in managing and participating in the various underwritings. While the evidence in this case relative to the pre-Securities Act period is far from complete, there is ample documentary evidence to show that many of the banks became directly interested through their bond departments and many others formed affiliates, as above stated. J. P. Morgan & Co., the First National Bank and the Bankers Trust Company and many others in New York City, as well as large banking institutions in Chicago, Cleveland and other cities did a large investment banking business. The National City Company, the Guaranty Company and Chase Securities Corporation, affiliates of the National City Bank, the Guaranty Trust Company of New York and the Chase National Bank were in the investment banking business in a big way. The National City Company as of December 31, 1929, had a capital of $110,000,000. On the same date the capital of the Chase Securities Corporation was over $101,000,000. The economic power of these huge aggregations of capital vis-a-vis the relatively small capital of issuers was a factor of no mean significance in the period just before the great depression. There was an additional leverage in the multiplicity of banking functions which could be placed at the disposal of issuers. Added to this was the vast influence and prestige which must have made itself felt in a variety of ways. Issuers were dependent upon these great banking institutions in a way which finds no parallel in the relations between issuers and investment bankers in the period subsequent to the passage of the Banking and Securities Acts.

Before it became necessary by law to choose between commercial banking on the one hand and investment banking on the other, many of these great banking institutions were private banking houses under no statutory duty to make the disclosures required of national banks and others and this, coupled with the lack of legal requirements for disclosure of relevant facts connected with security issues, helped to make the period under discussion what has been described in the trial as an era of 'dignity and mystery.' * * *

Following the Armstrong Insurance investigation in 1905 and Governor Hughes' Committee Report in 1909 there had been other investigations which covered activities of investment bankers. The Pujo investigation was conducted in 1912 and 1913, the Utility Corporation inquiry by the Federal Trade Commission started in 1928; and these were followed by a long series of hearings, under the auspices of various committees of the Congress, which resulted in the Banking Act of 1933 (known also as the Glass–Steagall Act), the Securities Act of 1933 and the Securities Exchange Act of 1934. From December 10, 1931 through February 1932 the Senate Committee on Finance pursuant to the Johnson Resolution undertook to investigate the flotation of foreign bonds and other securities in the United States. Perhaps the most important of these investigations was the Gray–Pecora investigation of the Senate Committee on Banking and Currency which began on April 11, 1932 and continued through May 4, 1934.

In this chronological survey of the history and development of the investment banking business it will suffice to say that these statutes, together with the Public Utility Holding Company Act of 1935 and the Maloney Act, effective June 25, 1938, which added Section 15A to the Securities Exchange Act of 1934, and authorized the organization of the National Association of Securities Dealers, Inc. (NASD), under the supervision of the SEC, which followed, effected changes of the most radical and pervasive character; and these changes were made with a complete and comprehensive understanding by the Congress of current methods of operation in common use in the securities issue business, such information having been made available in the course of the investigations to which reference has just been made. Institutions which had previously engaged both in commercial and deposit banking on the one hand and investment banking on the other were required to elect prior to June 16, 1934, which of the two functions they would pursue to the exclusion of the other. This resulted in the complete elimination of the commercial banks and trust companies from the investment banking business; and the various bank affiliates were dissolved and liquidated.

The elaborate procedures which now became necessary in connection with the sale of new issues of securities were at first implemented by the Federal Trade Commission and then, upon the creation of the Securities and Exchange Commission, transferred to it. The regulation of the securities business which followed with such salutary and beneficial results has been one of the significant developments of our time. The era of 'dignity and mystery' was over. When we come to discuss the syndicate system and its operation, it will be appropriate to treat in some detail the various applicable provisions of the Securities Act of 1933 and the Securities Exchange Act of 1934, with their respective amendments, and also the numerous regulations, interpretations and releases of the SEC relative thereto. For the sake of continuity and clarity, however, this brief recital of the development of the investment banking business will be continued in order to furnish general background. * * *

Due largely to the impact of the income and inheritance tax laws, the importance of the individual as an investor diminished and there was an extraordinary and continued growth in the size and investment needs of large institutional investors such as life and casualty companies, savings banks, investment trusts, pension funds, universities, hospitals and fraternal orders. Perhaps the most significant change of all was caused by the withdrawal from the field of investment banking of the capital funds of the commercial banks and their affiliates, which had previously been among the foremost managers and underwriters of security issues. * * *

The form in which underwriting transactions commonly took place from the passage of the Banking and Securities legislation up to the present time is that of a purchase or 'underwriting agreement' between the issuer and the underwriters represented by the manager, and an 'agreement among underwriters.'

The substance of the entire transaction is substantially what it was before. The manager, like the originating banker or manager in the previous periods, handles the negotiations with the issuer and supervises the whole process of underwriting and distribution. The management for of today is not a new development either in form or in purpose after the Securities Act of 1933, but is the direct equivalent of the management fee paid by the members of the syndicate to the manager for his services in pre–1933 financings, where the syndicate either purchased directly from the issuer or from a prior 'original purchaser.'

Dealer and group sales are still made, under the authority of the manager who directs the entire process of distribution. But the change in the character of the investing public and especially the development of institutional investors on such a large scale and the impact of regulation by the SEC and of the Securities Act of 1933, the Securities Exchange Act of 1934 and the organization and functioning of the NASD, brought about a gradual decrease in the use of selling group agreements, especially in issues of the higher grades of debt financing and preferred stock. It is worthy of note that in performing his function of making sales for the accounts of the underwriters both to dealers and to institutions the manager sells 'out of the pot.' In other words, he does not allocate particular bonds to particular underwriters but simply sells 'bonds' and does not allocate numbers to any participant until the time comes for delivery of securities to the purchasers.

In accordance with the trend of the previous period spreads are gradually becoming smaller and smaller; and the maximum life of the syndicates is now 15, 20 or 30 days, although in some cases the maximum period may be longer, and it is not unusual to find clauses authorizing the manager to extend the period with or without the consent of a certain proportion of the underwriters. Price restrictions may, however, be removed earlier than the actual termination date of the syndicate, and as a practical matter they are generally terminated within a few days after the offering.

Stabilization provisions have become commonplace pursuant to statutory provisions and administrative regulations and interpretations relating to their use. While the authority to stabilize is generally given, it is only in relatively few cases that the authority has been exercised. The use of 'penalty clauses' has varied and the same is true of the use of price maintenance clauses.... But it is well to bear in mind throughout that the entire pattern of the statutory scheme above referred to, as implemented by the various rules and regulations of the SEC and the rules of Fair Practice of the National Association of Securities Dealers, Inc., approved by the SEC pursuant to legislative authority, contemplates the sale of each security issue at the public offering price proposed in the prospectus and set forth in the registration statement as finally made effective by the SEC. Having proposed and tendered a security issue to the public at the public offering price, it is not strange that those who propose to sell the entire issue at this public offering price should be required to make a bona fide attempt to do so. Otherwise, the elaborate statutory provisions relative to 'the public offering price' would be meaningless. Nor, under these circumstances, should one wonder that some investment banking houses continued to use price maintenance clauses while others did not. * * *

Due in part to the registration provisions of the Securities Act of 1933, but also in large measure to the increase in the number of institutional investors and their particular requirements, private placements grew by leaps and bounds. * * * Where the services of an investment banker are used, the typical transactions are even more varied. The principal ones are:

1. A negotiated underwritten public offering.

2. An underwritten public offering awarded on the basis of publicly invited sealed bids, an investment banker having been retained on a fee basis to shape up the issue.

3. A negotiated underwritten offering to existing security-holders. Here the investment banker enters into a commitment to 'stand by' until the subscription or exchange period has expired, at which time the investment banker must take up the securities not subscribed or exchanged.

4. An underwritten offering to existing security-holders awarded on the basis of publicly invited sealed bids, an investment banker having been retained on a fee basis to render the necessary assistance.

5. A non-underwritten offering to existing security-holders, with an investment banker acting as agent of the seller on a negotiated basis.

6. A private placement with an investment banker acting as agent of the seller on a negotiated basis.

There are many and sundry variations of the types of transactions just described, depending on the designing of the plan, the amount of risk-taking involved and the problems of distribution; and these variations are reflected in the amount of compensation to be paid to the investment banker, which is always subject to negotiation. * * *

The actual design of the issue involves preparation of the prospectus and registration statement, with supporting documents and reports, compliance with the numerous rules and regulations of the SEC or ICC or FPC and the various Blue Sky Laws passed by the several States. In view of the staggering potential liabilities under the Securities Act of 1933 this is no child's play, as is known only too well by the management of issuers.

This hasty and far from complete recital of available alternatives will suffice to indicate the milieu in which the investment banker demonstrates his skill, ingenuity and resourcefulness, to the extent and to the extent only that an issuer wishes to avail itself of his services. It is always the hope of the investment banker that the issuer will use the full range of the services of the investment banker, including the design and setting up of the issue, the organization of the group to underwrite the risk and the planning of the distribution. If he cannot wholly succeed, the investment banker will try to get as much of the business as he can. Thus he may wind up as the manager or co-manager, or as a participant in the group of underwriters with or without an additional selling position; or he may earn a fee as agent for a private placement or other transaction without any risk-bearing feature. Or someone else may get the business away from him.

Thus we find that in the beginning there is no 'it.' The security issue which eventuates is a nebulous thing, still in future. Consequently the competition for business by investment bankers must start with an effort to establish or continue a relationship with the issuer. That is why we hear so much in this case about ingenious ways to prevail upon the issuers in particular instances to select this or that investment banking house to work on the general problem of shaping up the issue and handling the financing. This is the initial step; and it is generally taken many months prior to the time when it is expected that the money will be needed. It is clear beyond any reasonable doubt that this procedure is due primarily to the wishes of the issuers; and one of the reasons why issuers like this form of competition is that they are under no legal obligation whatever to the investment banker until some document such as an underwriting agreement or agency contract with the investment banker has actually been signed.

Sometimes an investment banking house will go it alone at this initial stage. At times two or three houses or even more will work together in seeking the business, with various understandings relative to the managership or co-managership and the amount of their underwriting participations. These are called nucleus groups. Occasionally one comes across documents pertaining to such nucleus groups which seem to contemplate the continuance of the group for future business, only to find that in a few weeks or less the whole picture has changed and some realignment of forces has taken place.

The tentative selection of an investment banker to shape up the issue and handle the financing has now been made; and there ensues a more or less prolonged period during which the skilled technicians of the investment banker are working with the executive and financial advisers of the issuer, studying the business from every angle, becoming familiar with the industry in which it functions, its future prospects, the character and efficiency of its operating policies and similar matters. Much of this information will eventually find its way in one form or another into the prospectus and registration statement. Sometimes engineers will be employed to make a survey of the business. The investment banker will submit a plan of the financing, often in writing; and this plan and perhaps others will be the subject of discussions. Gradually the definitive plan will be agreed upon, or perhaps the entire matter will be dropped in favor of a private placement, without the services of an investment banker. Often, and after many months of effort on the part of the investment banker, the issuer will decide to postpone the raising of the money for a year or two.

In the interval between the time when the investment banker is put on the job and the time when the definitive product begins to take form, a variety of other problems of great importance require consideration. The most vital of these, in terms of money and otherwise, is the timing of the issue. It is here, with his feel and judgment of the market, that the top-notch investment banker renders what is perhaps his most important service. The probable state of the general security market at any given future time is a most difficult thing to forecast. Only those with ripe trading experience and the finest kind of general background in financial affairs and practical economics can effectively render service of this character.

At last the issue has been cast in more or less final form, the prospectus and registration statement have been drafted and decisions relative to matters bearing a direct relation to the effective cost of the money, such as the coupon or dividend rate, sinking fund, conversion and redemption provisions and serial dates, if any, are shaped up subject to further consideration at the last moment. The work of organizing the syndicate, determining the participation positions of those selected as underwriters and the making up of a list of dealers for the selling group or, if no selling group is to be used, the formulation of plans for distribution by some other means, have been gradually proceeding, practically always in consultation with the issuer, who has the final say as to who the participating underwriters are to be. The general plans for distribution of the issue require the most careful and expert consideration, as the credit of the issuer may be seriously affected should the issue not be successful. Occasionally an elaborate campaign of education of dealers and investors is conducted.

Thus, if the negotiated underwritten public offering route is to be followed, we come at last to what may be the parting of the ways between the issuer and the investment banker—negotiation relative to the public offering price, the spread and the price to be paid to the issuer for the securities. These three are inextricably interrelated. The stating point is and must be the determination of the price at which the issue is to be offered to the public. This must in the very nature of things be the price at which the issuer and the investment banker jointly think the security can be put on the market with reasonable assurance of success; and at times the issuer, as already indicated in this brief recital of the way the investment banker functions, will for good and sufficient reasons not desire the public offering price to be placed at the highest figure attainable.

Once agreement has been tentatively reached on the public offering price, the negotiation shifts to the amount of the contemplated gross spread. This figure must include the gross compensation of all those who participate in the distribution of the issue: the manager, the underwriting participants and the dealers who are to receive concessions and re-allowances. Naturally, the amount of the spread will be governed largely by the nature of the problems of distribution and the amount of work involved. The statistical charts and static data indicate that the amount of the contemplated gross spreads is smallest with the highest class of bonds and largest with common stock issues, where the actual work of selling is at its maximum. While no two security issues are precisely alike and they vary as the leaves on the trees, it is apparent that the executive and financial officers of issuers may sit down on the other side of the bargaining table confidently, and without apprehension of being imposed upon, as data relating to public offering prices, spreads, and net proceeds to issuers from new security issues registered under the Securities Act of 1933 are all public information which are publicized among other means by the wide distribution of the prospectuses for each issue.

And so in the end the 'pricing' of the issue is arrived at as a single, unitary determination of the public offering price, spread and price to the issuer. * * *

NOTES

1. As Judge Medina pointed out in the *Morgan* case, IPOs are subject to the provisions of the federal securities laws. The following is a description of the background that led to the creation of the SEC:

The SEC's foundation was laid in an era that was ripe for reform. Before the Great Crash of 1929, there was little support for federal regulation of the securities markets. This was particularly true during the post-World War I surge of securities activity. Proposals that the federal government require financial disclosure and prevent the fraudulent sale of stock were never seriously pursued.

Tempted by promises of "rags to riches" transformations and easy credit, most investors gave little thought to the dangers inherent in uncontrolled market operation. During the 1920s, approximately 20 million large and small shareholders took advantage of post-war prosperity and set out to make their fortunes in the stock market. It is estimated that of the $50 billion in new securities offered during this period, half became worthless.

When the stock market crashed in October 1929, the fortunes of countless investors were lost. Banks also lost great sums of money in the Crash because they had invested heavily in the markets. When people feared their banks might not be able to pay back the money that depositors had in their accounts, a "run" on the banking system caused many bank failures.

With the Crash and ensuing depression, public confidence in the markets plummeted. There was a consensus that for the economy to recover, the public's faith in the capital markets needed to be restored. Congress held hearings to identify the problems and search for solutions.

Based on the findings in these hearings, Congress passed the Securities Act of 1933 and the Securities Exchange Act of 1934. These laws were designed to restore investor confidence in our capital markets by providing more structure and government oversight. The main purposes of these laws can be reduced to two common-sense notions:

- Companies publicly offering securities for investment dollars must tell the public the truth about their businesses, the securities they are selling, and the risks involved in investing.

- People who sell and trade securities—brokers, dealers, and exchanges—must treat investors fairly and honestly, putting investors' interests first.

Monitoring the securities industry requires a highly coordinated effort. Congress established the Securities and Exchange Commission in 1934 to enforce the newly-passed securities laws, to promote stability in the markets and, most importantly, to protect investors. President Franklin Delano Roosevelt appointed Joseph P. Kennedy, President John F. Kennedy's father, to serve as the first Chairman of the SEC.

SEC Website visited on May 26, 2002: www.sec.gov/about/whatwedo.shtml

2.   Underwriters play a major role in pricing securities during an offering. To what extent do the underwriters' interest diverge from that of the issuer? *See* EBC I, Inc. v. Goldman Sachs & Co., 5 N.Y.3d 11, 799 N.Y.S.2d 170, 832 N.E.2d 26 (N.Y. Ct. App. 2005) (in a in a firm commitment underwriting, the underwriter owes a fiduciary duty to the issuer to disclose conflicts of interest in connection with the pricing of securities; complaint alleged intentional underpricing by the underwriter). The court held that a fiduciary duty may exist even if not spelled out in the underwriting agreement if the underwriter stood in an advisory relationship to the issuer.

The Second Circuit gave the following overview of IPO practices in the following case that eventually wound up in the Supreme Court.

———

BILLING v. CREDIT SUISSE FIRST BOSTON LTD.

426 F.3d 130 (2d Cir. 2005), reversed 551 U.S. 264 (2007).

WESLEY, CIRCUIT JUDGE:

Plaintiffs allege an epic Wall Street conspiracy. They charge that the nation's leading underwriting firms entered into illegal contracts with purchasers of securities distributed in initial public offerings ("IPOs"). Through these contracts and by other illegal means, the underwriting firms allegedly executed a series of manipulations that grossly inflated the price of the securities after the IPOs in the so-called aftermarket. Plaintiffs contend that the firms capitalized on this artificial inflation, profiting at the expense of the investing public.

Plaintiffs tell a compelling story and are not the first to tell it. Similar allegations have appeared in a separate class action, *see In re Initial Pub. Offering Sec. Litig.*, 241 F. Supp. 2d 281, 293–94 (S.D.N.Y. 2003), in a report of the New York Stock Exchange ("NYSE") and the National Association of Securities Dealers ("NASD"), *see* NYSE/NASD IPO Advisory Committee, NYSE/NASD, Report and Recommendations 1–2 (May 2003), *available at* http://www.nasd.com/web/groups/rules_regs/documents/rules_regs/nasdw_010373.pdf, and in complaints filed by the Securities and Exchange Commission (the "SEC" or "Commission"). What most immediately distinguishes the present charges from prior ones is that the earlier allegations were made in the context of the laws governing securities—laws and regulations arising primarily from the Securities Act of 1933, Pub. L. No. 73–22, 48 Stat. 74 ("the Securities Act" or "the 1933 Act"), and the Securities Exchange Act of 1934, Pub. L. No. 73–290, 48

Stat. 881 ("the Securities Exchange Act," "the Exchange Act," or "the 1934 Act"). By contrast, the present actions arise under the antitrust laws—specifically, section 1 of the Sherman Act, section 2(c) of the Robinson–Patman Act, and various state antitrust provisions.

The question on appeal is whether these antitrust claims can stand. * * * The heart of the alleged anticompetitive behavior finds no shelter in the securities laws. Accordingly, we vacate and remand for further proceedings.

Essential to this appeal is a basic understanding of the securities underwriting process and certain manipulations of the process, most particularly the practice of tying excess consideration to an IPO securities allocation.

An underwriting firm provides underwriting services to issuers of securities. The most common delivery of those services is by firm-commitment agreements. 1 Thomas Lee Hazen, The Law of Securities Regulation § 2.1[2][B], at 156 (5th ed. 2005). The appeal of this type of agreement is certainty for the issuer: "The underwriting investment banker agrees that on a fixed date the corporation will receive a fixed sum for a fixed amount of its securities." Statement of the Commission on the Problem of Regulating the "Pegging, Fixing and Stabilizing" of Security Prices Under Sections 9(a)(2), 9(a)(6), and 15(c)(1) of the Securities Exchange Act, Exchange Act Release No. 2446 (March 18, 1940), 11 Fed. Reg. 10,971, 10,972 (Sept. 27, 1946) ("1940 Statement"). The underwriting agreement thus removes "factors of uncertainty" for the issuer, *see id.*, and transfers to the underwriter the risk of any inability to sell an issue, *see* Going Public and Listing on the U.S. Securities Markets, NASD 167.

Syndicates emerged in the first half of the nineteenth century as an essential means by which underwriters could manage the risks inherent in underwriting. *See generally United States v. Morgan*, 118 F. Supp. 621, 635–55 (S.D.N.Y. 1953). At that time, "no single underwriter could have borne alone the underwriting risk involved in the purchase and sale of a large security issue," and "no single underwriter could have effected a successful public distribution of the issue."[3] *Id.* at 640. The syndicate was a group typically "consisting of from a few to well over one hundred underwritten houses, [that bought] the entire new issue of securities from the issuing corporation at a predetermined fixed price"—the "purchase" price—"and immediately reoffered it to the public at a slightly higher price which is also a predetermined fixed price (the 'offering' or 'issue' price)." 1940 Statement, 11 Fed. Reg. at 10,972. "The issue was typically resold to the public both by the underwriters and by a so-called 'selling group' . . . who acted as retailers for the underwriting syndicate." *Id.* The

---

3. Thus in 1906, when Goldman, Sachs & Co. desired to enter the underwriting business and was unable to raise enough capital to do so, Henry Goldman convinced Philip Lehman to share the risk, and together Goldman, Sachs & Co. and Lehman Brothers obtained sufficient capital to finance United Cigar Manufacturers (later named the General Cigar Co.). *See Morgan*, 118 F. Supp. at 637. This partnership, which involved jointly purchasing security issues directly from issuers and equally dividing what profits they realized from the sale, allowed the two firms to finance other enterprises like Sears, Roebuck & Co. and B.F. Goodrich Co. *See id.* at 637–38.

syndicate system remains a prominent feature of the modern underwriting industry. *See IPO Antitrust Litig.*, 287 F. Supp. at 507.[4]

A lead underwriter in a syndicate must assess the appropriate issue quantity and pricing for the IPO. *See* Commission Guidance Regarding Prohibited Conduct in Connection with IPO Allocations; Final Rule, Securities Act Release No. 8565, Exchange Act Release No. 51,500 (Apr. 7, 2005), 70 Fed. Reg. 19,672, 19,674 & n.30 (Apr. 13, 2005) ("2005 Guidance Statement"). This is a difficult task, *see* 2 Hazen, *supra* § 6.3[1], at 23–24, in which the lead underwriter is aided in part by "book-building":

> When used, the IPO book-building process begins with the filing of a registration statement with an initial estimated price range. Underwriters and the issuer then conduct "road shows" to market the offering to potential investors, generally institutions. The road shows provide investors, the issuer, and underwriters the opportunity to gather important information from each other. Investors seek information about a company, its management and its prospects, and underwriters seek information from investors that will assist them in determining particular investors' interest in the company, assessing demand for the offering, and improving pricing accuracy for the offering. Investors' demand for an offering necessarily depends on the value they place, and the value they expect the market to place, on the stock, both initially and in the future. In conjunction with the road shows, there are discussions between the underwriter's sales representatives and prospective investors to obtain investors' views about the issuer and the offered securities, and to obtain indications of the investors' interest in purchasing quantities of the underwritten securities in the offering at particular prices ... By aggregating information obtained during this period from investors with other information, the underwriters and the issuer will agree on the size and pricing of the offering, and the underwriters will decide how to allocate the IPO shares to purchasers.

2005 Guidance Statement, 70 Fed. Reg. at 19,674–75 (footnote omitted). Underwriters thus use this process to collect indications of interest regarding the IPO, as well as potential investors' views on the value of the proposed security. *See id.* at 19,675.

The SEC has noted that the book-building process can become a locus of IPO and IPO-aftermarket manipulation by syndicate members. *See*

---

4. Typically, the principal underwriters will sign the firm-commitment underwriting agreement. These managers or principal underwriters in turn contact other broker-dealers to become members of the underwriting group who are to act as wholesalers of the securities to be offered. In many instances the securities distribution network will include the use of a selling group of other investment bankers or brokerage houses. Members of the selling group generally do not share the underwriters' risk and are thus retailers who are compensated with agents' or brokers' commission rather than by sharing in the underwriting fee.

Hazen, *supra* § 2.1[2][B], at 156; *cf.* Review of Antimanipulation Regulation of Securities Offerings, Securities Act Release No. 7057, Securities Exchange Act Release No. 33,924 (Apr. 25, 1994), 59 Fed. Reg. 21,681, 21,686 (Apr. 26, 1994) ("A firm commitment underwriting typically involves a group of underwriters, represented by one or more managing underwriters, an underwriting group, and a number of 'selling group' members.").

2005 Guidance Statement, 70 Fed. Reg. at 19,675. Underwriters have strong incentives to manipulate the IPO process to facilitate the complete distribution and sale of an issue. Underwriting is a business; competitive forces dictate that underwriters associated with successful IPOs will attract future issuers. Moreover, because underwriters assume a large measure of risk in the event an IPO fails, they have a direct interest in the IPO's success. *See* Amendments to Regulation M: Anti–Manipulation Rules Concerning Securities Offerings, Securities Act Release No. 8511, Exchange Act Release No. 50,831 (Dec. 9, 2004), 69 Fed. Reg. 75,774, 75,783–84 (Dec. 17, 2004) ("2004 Proposed Amendments").

Underwriters also have incentives to manipulate the price of securities in the aftermarket. Again, competition is one force at play: "Underwriters have an incentive to artificially influence aftermarket activity because they have underwritten the risk of the offering, and a poor aftermarket performance could result in reputational and subsequent financial loss." Staff Legal Bulletin No. 10: Prohibited Solicitation and "Tie-in" Agreements for Aftermarket Purchases, Division of Market Regulation (Aug. 25, 2000), *available at* http://www.sec.gov/interps/legal/slbmr10.htm ("Staff Legal Bulletin No. 10"). Another incentive arises from underwriters' control over the allocation of securities. Persons or entities receiving allocations can make quick profits from an artificial rise in the immediate aftermarket during a "hot issue,"[7] and underwriters might "desire to allocate at least some shares to their best customers in order to maintain client relationships." IPO Advisory Committee Report 10.

Not all underwriter manipulations are prohibited: the securities regime tolerates "a little price manipulation" in order to further other goals. *Strobl v. New York Mercantile Exch.*, 768 F.2d 22, 28 (2d. Cir. 1985). The SEC has traditionally recognized certain types of manipulations, deemed "stabilizing" activities, as legitimate and permissible under section 9(a)(6) of the Exchange Act, 48 Stat. at 890 (codified at 15 U.S.C. § 78i(a)(6)), and SEC Rule 10b–1, 17 C.F.R. § 240.10b–1. Section 9(a)(6) makes it unlawful

> to effect either alone or with one or more other persons any series of transactions for the purchase and/or sale of any security registered on a national securities exchange for the purpose of pegging, fixing, or stabilizing the price of such security in contravention of such rules and regulations as the Commission may prescribe as necessary or appropriate in the public interest or for the protection of investors.

48 Stat. at 890 (codified at 15 U.S.C. § 78i(a)(6)). In 1948, the SEC incorporated the prohibitions arising under section 9 and the rules and regulations thereunder into the definition of "manipulation" of section 10(b) of the Exchange Act, 48 Stat. at 891 (codified as amended at 15

---

7. "Hot issues" are securities "that generate a good deal of buying interest." 2 Hazen, *supra* § 6.0, at 1–2. "In 'hot' IPOs, investor demand significantly exceeds the supply of securities in the offering and the stock trades at a premium in the immediate aftermarket." 2005 Guidance Statement, 70 Fed. Reg. at 19,672 n.5.

U.S.C. § 78j(b)), thereby extending section 9's "stabilization" rules to securities not traded on exchanges. *See* Manipulative and Deceptive Devices and Contrivances, 13 Fed. Reg. 8183 (Dec. 22, 1948); 17 C.F.R. § 240.10b–1. Stabilization in the context of exchange trading and non-exchange trading has been continuously regulated and, to some extent, recognized as legitimate and permissible.[8]

Significantly, from its earliest statements on stabilization, the SEC has recognized that permissible forms of stabilization are limited to those attempts to maintain price levels of a security or to retard a decline in a security's price. In 1954, for instance, the Commission proposed new stabilization regulations that it viewed as "a formulation of principles which historically have been applied in considering questions relating to manipulative activity and stabilization in connection with a distribution." Manipulative and Deceptive Devices and Contrivances, 19 Fed. Reg. 2986, 2986 (May 22, 1954) ("1954 Proposed Rules"). These regulations limited permissible stabilizing bids to those with "the purpose of preventing or retarding a decline in the open market price of [a] security." *Id*.; *see* Manipulative and Deceptive Devices and Contrivances, 20 Fed. Reg. 5075 (July 15, 1955) (adopting the 1954 Proposed Rules as 17 C.F.R. § § 240.10b–6, 240.10b–7, and 240.10b–8). Likewise, in 1959, while issuing proposed amendments, the Commission commented, "The term 'stabilizing' has generally been accepted to mean the placing of any bid or the effecting of any purchase . . . for the purpose of preventing or retarding a decline in the open market price of a security." Manipulative and Deceptive Devices and Contrivances, Notice of Proposed Rule Making, 24 Fed. Reg. 9946, 9947 (Dec. 9, 1959) ("1959 Proposed Rules"). And, alongside a 1991 proposed rule, the Commission cautioned that "stabilization does not contemplate transactions in excess of those required to prevent or retard a decline in the market price, or those which raise the market price of a security. . . ." Stabilizing to Facilitate a Distribution, Securities Act Release No. 6880, Exchange Act Release No. 28,732 (Jan. 3, 1991), 56 Fed. Reg. 815 (Jan. 9, 1991) ("1991 Proposed Rules").

Permissible stabilization activities are often contrasted with activities raising prices, which are prohibited under section 9(a)(2) of the Exchange Act, 48 Stat. at 889 (codified as amended at 15 U.S.C. § 78i(a)(2)). For instance, in 1994, the SEC engaged in a comprehensive review of its rules governing manipulation in securities offerings. *See* Review of Antimanipulation Regulation of Securities Offerings, Securities Act Release No. 7057,

---

8.   8 *See, e.g.,* 1940 Statement, 11 Fed. Reg. at 10,974 ("Stabilization, it must be recognized, is now an integral part of the American system of fixed price security distribution."); Reports on Stabilizing Activities, 21 Fed. Reg. 501 (Jan. 21, 1956); Reports on Stabilizing Activities, 21 Fed. Reg. 2787 (Apr. 28, 1956); Manipulative and Deceptive Devices and Contrivances, Notice of Proposed Rule Making, 21 Fed. Reg. 9983 (Dec. 14, 1956); Reports on Stabilizing Activities, Notice of Proposed Rule Making, Exchange Act Release No. 9605, 37 Fed. Reg. 10,960 (June 1, 1972); Presentation of Records, Reports, and Forms for Reports on Stabilizing Activities, Exchange Act Release No. 9717 (Aug. 15, 1972), 37 Fed. Reg. 17,383 (Aug. 26, 1972); Amendments Relating to Reports of Stabilizing Transactions, Exchange Act Release No. 18,983 (Aug. 19, 1982), 47 Fed. Reg. 37,560 (Aug. 26, 1982); Trading Practices Rules Concerning Securities Offerings, 61 Fed. Reg. at 17,123–25.

Securities Exchange Act Release No. 33,924 (Apr. 25, 1994), 59 Fed. Reg. 21,681, 21,681 (Apr. 26, 1994) ("1994 Review"). One section of the review dealt with stabilization and expressed the Commission's "concept" that "stabilization of offerings should be restricted in order to minimize its manipulative impact." *Id.* at 21,689. The 1994 Review explained that underwriters engage in various activities in the aftermarket—although the particular activities are not defined—and that some of those activities "may support, or even raise, the market price of the security." *Id.* The 1994 Review also recounted in its appendix that "Congress enacted the Exchange Act to put an end to the practices that it found had contributed to the economic problems facing the Nation." *Id.* at 21,694. "One of the 'chief evils,'" prohibited by section 9(a)(2), "was the operation of 'pools,' which were agreements among several persons to trade actively in a security, generally to raise the price of a security by concerted activity, in order to sell their holdings at a profit to the public, which is attracted by the activity or by information disseminated about the stock." *Id.* at 21,694 n.3. The Commission expressly distinguished between section 9(a)(2), which covered absolutely prohibited manipulations, and section 9(a)(6), which covered manipulations that the SEC could choose to permit. *Id.* at 21,694–95 & nn.3, 14. The Commission noted that the prohibitions in section 9(a)(2) represented the "heart" of the Act. *Id.* at 21,694. The SEC currently regulates stabilization practices with SEC Rule 104, which is part of Regulation M. *See* 17 C.F.R. § 242.104. That rule, consistent with historic SEC regulations, prohibits stabilization "except for the purpose of preventing or retarding a decline in the market price of a security." *Id.* § 242.104(b).

Among the impermissible manipulative practices regulated by the SEC is a general category of relationships between underwriters and prospective purchasers termed "tie-ins." "A 'tie-in agreement' in the securities offering context generally refers to requiring either implicitly or explicitly that customers give consideration in addition to the stated offering price of any security in order to obtain an allocation of the offered shares." 2004 Proposed Amendments, 69 Fed. Reg. at 75,783 n.95. Thus, the broadest category of tie-in arrangements includes all agreements requiring consideration from purchasers above the offering price. These have been termed *quid pro quo* arrangements. *See, e.g.*, Self–Regulatory Organizations, Notice of Filing of Proposed Rule Changes, Exchange Act Release No. 50,896 (Dec. 20, 2004), 69 Fed. Reg. 77,804, 77,805–06, 77,807, 77,810 (Dec. 28, 2004) ("2004 SRO Notice"). The *quid pro quo* consideration could, for instance, require customers to participate in another offering, including an offering in which supply exceeds demand, a "cold" offering.[10] *See* 2004 Proposed Amendments, 69 Fed. Reg. at 75,783.

---

10. In 1974, the SEC proposed a rule that would expressly prohibit these aftermarket tie-in arrangements. *See* Certain Short Selling Of Securities and Securities Offerings, Exchange Act Release No. 10,636 (Feb. 11, 1974), 39 Fed. Reg. 7806, 7806–07 (Feb. 28, 1974) ("1974 Rule Proposal"); Certain Manipulative Practices in Public Offerings, Supplemental Notice of Proposed Rulemaking, Exchange Act Release No. 11,328 (Feb. 11, 1975), 40 Fed. Reg. 16,090, 16,090 (Apr. 9, 1975) ("Supplemental 1974 Proposed Rule"). The SEC withdrew the rule, however, because

"The Commission has long considered tying the award of allocations of offered shares to additional consideration to be fraudulent and manipulative, and such practices have always been actionable under Section 17(a) of the Securities Act and Section 10(b) and Rule 10b–5 of the Exchange Act." *Id*. at 75,784; *see also id*. at 75,785 n.104.

In exchange for receiving an IPO allocation, certain tie-in arrangements require customers to place orders for aftermarket shares of the same security offered in the IPO. *See* 2005 Guidance Statement, 70 Fed. Reg. at 19,672–73. These sorts of arrangements—sometimes described as arrangements to "pre-sell the aftermarket"[11]—can create artificial demand. They "generate additional aftermarket buying activity that is manipulative, in that it is designed to push the price higher once the security comes to the market." 2 Hazen, *supra* § 6.3[2][A], at 1. Buying pressure created by pre-selling the aftermarket spills over into the IPO. *See* Staff Legal Bulletin No. 10. For some time, the SEC has specifically recognized these arrangements as prohibited. *See, e.g.*, 2005 Guidance Statement, 70 Fed. Reg. at 19,674.

A variation on tie-in agreements effectuating a pre-sale of the aftermarket are arrangements called "laddering." *See, e.g.*, 2005 Guidance Statement, 70 Fed. Reg. at 19,674 & n.29; "NASD Board Approves Proposed Conduct Rules for IPO Activities," NASD Press Room (NASD July 25, 2002), *available at* http://www.nasd.com/web/idcplg?IdcService= SS_GET_ PAGE & ssDocName=NASDW_002921. Laddering has been defined "as inducing investors to give orders to purchase shares in the aftermarket at pre-arranged, *escalating prices* in exchange for receiving IPO allocations...." 2005 Guidance Statement, 70 Fed. Reg. at 19,674 n.29 (emphasis added). Even more than pre-sales of the aftermarket, laddering agreements "stimulate[] demand for a hot issue in the aftermarket, thereby facilitating the process by which stock prices rise to a premium." Report of the SEC Concerning the Hot Issues Markets 37–38 (Aug. 1984) ("Hot Issues Markets"); *see also* 2 Hazen, *supra* § 6.0, 2005 supp. at 31. "This conduct distorts the offering and the aftermarket." 2005 Guidance Statement, 70 Fed. Reg. at 19,674 n.29 (quotation marks, alterations, and citations omitted). The SEC has identified laddering agreements as a serious and harmful means of manipulation that "violates the antifraud and antimanipulation provisions of the federal securities laws." Hot Issues Markets 37–38; *see also* 2005 Guidance Statement, 70 Fed. Reg. at 19,674.

---

the tie-in arrangements prohibited by it were already prohibited by "existing antifraud and anti-manipulation provisions of the federal securities laws." Withdrawal of Proposed Rules Under the Securities Exchange Act of 1934, Exchange Act Release No. 26,182 (Oct. 14, 1988), 53 Fed. Reg. 41,206, 41,207 (Oct. 20, 1988) ("1988 Withdrawal"); *see also* 2004 Proposed Amendments, 69 Fed. Reg. at 75,784.

11. *See* 2 Hazen, *supra* § 6.3[2][A], at 30–31 ("Under this manipulation, registered representatives ... require or encourage customers to commit to purchasing shares in the after market in order to get part of the allotment out of the original issue."); *id*. § 6.3[2][A], at 34–35 & n.68; NASDR, Disciplinary Actions Reported for April, 1999 WL 33176514, at *16 (NASDR Apr. 1999) ("The preselling of the aftermarket" occurred where respondents "solicited customers to purchase securities in aftermarket trading as a requirement to purchase in the IPO ....").

* * *

There may be reasons why Congress might choose to immunize such conduct. The SEC and defendants have vigilantly reminded us that the securities markets *in toto* might be better entrusted to an expert agency than to the federal courts. While we might agree, we do not have the responsibility for making national policy. Congress knows how to immunize regulated conduct from the antitrust laws. To date, it has not done so here either expressly or impliedly. Construing the statutes as written, we find no repeal.

For the reasons stated above, the district court's judgment of November 6, 2003 is vacated, and the case is remanded for further proceedings consistent with this opinion.

SECTION 3.   AFTER THE IPO—THE OVER–THE–COUNTER MARKET

IN THE MATTER OF CERTAIN MARKET MAKING ACTIVITIES ON NASDAQ

1998 WL 919673 (S.E.C. 1998).

* * *The Respondents are entities registered with the Commission as broker-dealers pursuant to Section 15(b) of the Exchange Act and individuals who, at relevant times, were associated with such entities or their predecessors. During the relevant time period, all of the entity Respondents or their predecessors were market makers in Nasdaq securities. All of the individual Respondents were at relevant times employed at Nasdaq market-making firms as traders or assistant traders making markets in Nasdaq stocks, institutional or retail salespeople dealing in Nasdaq stocks, or supervisors of Nasdaq trading and sales.

The Nasdaq Stock Market, Inc. ("Nasdaq") is an electronic interdealer quotation system owned and operated by the National Association of Securities Dealers, Inc. ("NASD"), a national securities association registered with the Commission under Section 15A of the Exchange Act. The Nasdaq market is a dealer market, in which a number of broker-dealers make markets in the same security and execute trades. Making a market consists of standing ready to buy and sell a security at prices and quantities displayed on Nasdaq's computerized quotation system which links the market makers. The market makers in Nasdaq are required simultaneously to quote two prices: a "bid" price, at which they are willing to buy the security, and an "ask" price, at which they are willing to sell the security. The "inside bid" is the highest prevailing bid price in a stock at any given time, while the "inside ask" is the lowest prevailing asked price. Together, the inside bid and inside ask represent the "inside market." The difference between the inside bid and the inside ask is commonly referred to as the "spread" or "inside spread." As noted in the Commission's Report Pursuant to Section 21(a) of the Securities Exchange Act of 1934 Regarding the NASD and Nasdaq Market, Exchange Act

Release 37542 (hereinafter referred to as the "21(a) Report"), most customer orders during the time period in question were executed by market makers at the inside bid or ask. Trades in the Nasdaq market can be executed in a variety of ways, including, without limitation, through telephone calls to other dealers, the Instinet trading system, and certain electronic order delivery and execution systems owned and operated by Nasdaq (such as SOES, SelectNet and ACES). The time, price and volume of most transactions must be reported to Nasdaq, which in turn disseminates this information publicly through its electronic network.

On August 8, 1996, the Commission issued the 21(a) Report, which described, among other things, coordination among market makers of quotations and trades that may have advanced or protected their proprietary interests, in a manner that may have been contrary to the best interests of their customers, and that may have created a false or misleading appearance of trading activity in the Nasdaq market. After the issuance of the 21(a) Report, the Commission's investigation of market making activities in the Nasdaq market continued, and these proceedings result from the continuation of the investigation.

The investigation uncovered a number of anticompetitive and improper practices by Nasdaq market makers during 1994 which violated certain provisions of the federal securities laws. Nasdaq market making firms and their traders coordinated their trading and other activities with other market makers to create false or misleading appearances in, or otherwise artificially influence, the market for various Nasdaq stocks. This coordination was primarily accomplished by market maker asking another to move its quoted prices in order to create a different appearance to the market from which the requesting market maker could benefit, and violated the antifraud provisions of Section 15(c)(1) of the Exchange Act and Rule 15c1–2 thereunder, and the prohibition against fictitious quotations provided in Section 15(c)(2) of the Exchange Act and Rule 15c2–7 thereunder. Nasdaq market makers also engaged in other violations related to their trading of Nasdaq stocks, including failing to provide the best execution of customer orders, intentionally delaying trade reports, failing to honor their quoted prices on Nasdaq, failing to create or maintain required books and records and failing reasonably to establish and enforce policies and procedures to supervise Nasdaq trading personnel with a view to preventing violations of law. Market maker misconduct was typically, but not always, limited in duration and scope to intraday violations relating to particular stocks, but cumulatively had a detrimental impact on the fairness and efficient functioning of the Nasdaq market. Most of the conduct described herein was intended to increase the market makers' trading profits or otherwise advance their proprietary interests, often at the expense of their customers and other market participants. The following section summarizes the violative practices uncovered and discusses the manner in which the conduct violated the federal securities laws.

The most common form of violative activity uncovered by the staff's investigation was the coordinated entry of bid and/or ask quotations by market makers into the Nasdaq system for the purpose of artificially affecting the price of subsequent transactions. This behavior typically consisted of one market maker soliciting the agreement of a second market maker to change the Nasdaq quotations disseminated by one or both market makers. Although the specific reasons for the coordination of quote movement requests varied from transaction to transaction, all involved obtaining an unfair trading advantage for the participating market makers. These arrangements, which changed the inside spread or harmed customers or other market participants, were not disclosed by the market makers involved in the scheme to other market participants or the Nasdaq market. Such coordinated activity constituted market manipulation in violation of the antifraud provisions of Section 15(c)(1) of the Exchange Act and Rule 15c1–2 thereunder, and the prohibition on the entry of fictitious quotations provided in Section 15(c)(2) of the Exchange Act and Rule 15c2–7 thereunder.

Market makers coordinated quote movements in order to create a false or misleading appearance of change in the supply or demand for a particular Nasdaq stock. The coordinated quote movements often involved one market maker moving one of its quotations to or from the inside quotes in order to change the number of market makers at the inside quote, which other market participants could reasonably perceive as an apparent change in the level of buying or selling interest. For example, a market maker needing to buy stock because of a customer order to purchase stock, or a short inventory position, would ask another market maker to move his quote downwards to join the inside ask. The purpose of the requested quote movement was to signal a downward price trend and the apparent addition of supply at the inside ask, thus misleading potential sellers on Nasdaq or Instinet into reducing their price expectations. After the quote movement, the requesting market maker would purchase stock on Nasdaq or Instinet at a reduced price, at the expense of the seller. The same strategy was also employed when the requesting market maker held a customer sell order, or had a long position in its inventory account. In such instances, the request was usually for the other market maker to join the inside bid, in order to signal an upward movement in price. In some instances, market makers entered large orders to buy stock on Instinet that created the appearance of rising demand for the stock, in connection with requesting a quote move from another market maker, in order to induce other market participants to buy the stock on the Nasdaq market (or vice versa to induce other market participants to sell).

At times, market makers also asked other market makers to move their quotes in a manner designed to create a new inside bid or ask price for a particular security in order to allow the requesting market maker to execute existing or anticipated customer orders at the new price levels, which benefitted the requesting market maker and disadvantaged its customer(s). In some instances where a customer had submitted a market order to buy stock, a trader would ask a lone market maker on the inside ask to move its ask quotation upwards. This quote movement created a higher inside ask, and the requesting market maker would then sell stock to its customer at the new, higher price. Additionally, institutional investors frequently transacted at prices between the inside bid and ask by a process of negotiation with market makers. Both institutional investors and market makers viewed the prices quoted at the inside spread as benchmarks for these negotiations, and the movement of the inside quotes upwards or downwards tended to move the ultimate transaction price in the direction of the quote move. Thus, changes in the inside quotes allowed market makers in some instances to influence the price even with respect to negotiated trades that were executed between the inside spread.

The undisclosed collaboration among market makers was detrimental to the interests of investors. By coordinating quote movements to move the quoted price of a stock up or down, traders facilitated trades at prices that were more favorable for the market makers, often at the expense of their customers or other market participants. Where customer orders were executed at prices detrimental to the customers, the coordinated misconduct also breached market makers' obligation to provide best execution and deal fairly with their customers. The undisclosed arrangements to move quotations also distorted the appearance of supply and demand in the Nasdaq market, potentially undermining investor confidence and the integrity of widely disseminated trading and market data. * * *

The coordinated entry of Nasdaq quotes for the purpose of altering the inside market, painting a deceptive picture of market conditions, or inducing another market participant into buying or selling at an artificial price constitutes an "arrangement" as that term is used in Rule 15c2–7. Since there was no disclosure of such arrangements to Nasdaq or other market participants, such quotations violated Section 15(c)(2) of the Exchange Act and Rule 15c2–7 thereunder. * * *

The investigation uncovered instances in which certain market makers entered into explicit agreements to delay reporting significant trades, and other scenarios where market makers unilaterally failed to report significant trades. This practice of intentionally delaying trade reports typically occurred when a timely report of a significant trade could have moved prices in a direction adverse to the market maker's interests. For example, a market maker that purchased a large amount from a customer selling stock would, either singly or in concert with other market makers, deliberately delay reporting the trade. The purpose of holding the trade report was to avoid the natural downward price movement that would reasonably be expected to result from the report of a large sale of stock by a customer. In order to reduce the long position resulting from its purchase from the customer, the relevant market maker would then sell stock in the open market at a price unaffected by the information contained in the withheld trade report. These market sales were typically executed at higher prices than would have been available if the customer's trade had been properly reported, to the detriment of the market as a whole, as well as the parties who purchased stock from the market maker. The delay of trade reports under such circumstances was manipulative and resulted in market makers obtaining an unfair and unlawful informational advantage in the market. * * *

The investigation uncovered a number of instances in which Nasdaq market makers failed to provide best execution for their customers' orders. The duty of best execution has generally been defined as the obligation of the broker-dealer to seek to obtain the most favorable terms reasonably available under the circumstances for a customer's order. When a broker-dealer acting with scienter fails to seek the most favorable price reasonably available under the circumstances for a customer order, the broker has failed to meet its obligation of best execution in violation of the antifraud provisions of Section 15(c) of the Exchange Act and Rule 15c1–2 thereunder.

During the relevant time period, best execution violations occurred in a number of different situations. A common denominator in such scenarios was the favoring by the market maker of its own interests, or those of a cooperating market maker, over the interests of its customers. First, in many instances, market makers' coordination of quotations allowed them to execute customer orders at artificial prices unfavorable to the customer. In other instances, market makers in the process of executing customer orders sometimes suggested to cooperating market makers on the inside bid or ask that they move away from the inside quote without executing a trade, thereby depriving the customer of a more favorable execution. On occasion, market makers did not execute or cancelled customer trades at advantageous prices in order to maintain good relations with other market makers. Market makers also sometimes entered into "print-splitting" arrangements with other market makers, by which they agreed to share any executions. If a market maker was holding a customer order at the time which was left unfilled as a result of the print-splitting arrangement, the failure to fill the order as promptly as possible violated its best execution obligations. Other violations occurred when market makers sometimes traded with customers at prices outside of the inside spread, with no apparent justification. In certain instances, market makers delayed the execution of large customer orders in order to trade first for their own account at more favorable prices, e.g., by selling stock for their own account first, while delaying the execution of a customer sell order, and later purchasing the customer's stock at market prices that had been depressed by the market maker's earlier sales for its own account. Finally, market makers sometimes traded with cooperating market makers at a particular price without filling customer limit orders at the same price, and without advance disclosure of and consent by their customers to their limit order policies.

Under the Commission's "firm quote" rule, a market maker is required to execute any order presented to it to buy or sell a security at a price at least as favorable to the buyer or seller as the market maker's published bid or offer and up to its published quotation size. On certain occasions, Nasdaq traders failed to honor the quotations that they disseminated. Market makers backed away from orders presented to them by firms whose trading practices they disliked or for other improper reasons. The failure of Nasdaq market makers to honor their quotations prevented investors from accessing the best advertised price, and reduced liquidity in the market. * * *

Under Section 15(b)(4) of the Exchange Act, the Commission may sanction a broker-dealer for failing reasonably to supervise a person under its supervision. Supervision is an essential function of broker-dealers. The Commission has made it clear that it is critical for investor protection that a broker-dealer establish and enforce procedures reasonably designed to supervise its employees. In large organizations in particular, it is imperative that the system of internal control be adequate and effective. A firm's failure to establish such procedures is symptomatic of a failure to supervise reasonably.

The frequency of the violations described herein raised serious questions concerning the adequacy of supervision by the respondent firms of their Nasdaq traders, and the investigation uncovered supervisory deficiencies at numerous of the respondent firms. Most of the respondent firms failed reasonably to supervise with a view to preventing or detecting these violations, in that they did not have adequate policies or procedures. . . . In addition, some respondent firms' policies and procedures were inadequately documented, promulgated and enforced. * * *

Each Respondent has submitted an Offer of Settlement which, as set forth in the accompanying Orders Making Findings and Imposing Sanctions, the Commission has determined to accept.

By the Commission.

Jonathan G. Katz, Secretary

NOTES

1. *Nasdaq.* The Nasdaq market is what we traditionally called the "over-the-counter" market where brokers simply trade among themselves. At an earlier date, these brokers would learn of each other's interest in a particular stock through trading in the streets (the "curb" market) and later through something called the "pink sheets." These were simply reports of trading interest that were printed on pink colored paper by the publisher of those quotations. A broker wanting to purchase a stock quoted in the pink sheets for himself or a customer would call the dealer making the quote and negotiate a purchase and sale. Nasdaq automated that process. As described in the SEC's decision above, this is an electronic network in which broker-dealers post their stock quotations in a central computer so that other brokers may see them on computer screens located in their offices. This allows broker-dealers to post competing quotations or to call the broker-dealer posting the quotation and negotiate a purchase or sale of the stock. A key element in the Nasdaq market is the "market-maker," actually there are several market-makers for many of the more actively traded stocks. These are simply dealers who stand ready to buy and sell particular stocks for their own account as principal. They include many of the large brokerage firms. Their "bids" and

"offers" will be listed on the Nasdaq computer screen for particular stocks. They are required to make a continuous two sided market in that security by both bidding to buy the stocks in which they make a market and offering to sell it. The concept of a continuous two sided market is critical to the liquidity of your investment in a stock. Market-makers must both buy and sell the stock at any time during trading hours in a minimum quantity at the price posted on the Nasdaq computer screen. This means that, if you want to buy the stock, the market-maker stands ready to sell it to you. Conversely, if you want to sell that same stock, the market-maker will buy it back from you. This provides liquidity. It allows you to buy and sell easily at the best available price for that stock, as determined by competing market-makers and other investors interested in that stock.

2.   There are limitations on liquidity. Quotations by market-makers on Nasdaq are good only up to a limited number of shares. Small orders up to that minimum are executed automatically at the best quoted prices through Nasdaq's Small Order Execution System ("SOES"), which was later replaced by SuperMontage. Larger orders must be negotiated and executed with the market-makers by your broker-dealer over the telephone. For amounts greater than that minimum, the price will have to be negotiated directly with the market-maker. Market-makers may also change their quotations at any time before receiving an order even for the minimum amount they are required to trade, possibly resulting in a less favorable price. One rule that every investor must know is that there is no free lunch on Wall Street. This liquidity is being made available to you at a price. The market-makers are not providing this service *gratis*. They may profit in several ways. First, they may profit from the "spread." This means that the market-makers quotes for the prices at which they will buy and sell your stock will not be the same. The price at which they will buy the stock from you will be lower than the price at which they will sell it to you. The market-makers seek to profit from that spread. As a hypothetical example, assume that Dot.Com. Inc. stock is being quoted by market-makers at $9.25 and $9.50. This means that the market-makers will buy the stock from you at $9.25 and sell it to you for $9.50. All things being equal, they stand to make $.25 on each share of stock they buy and sell. So if you bought and sold the stock immediately, and there was nothing that would otherwise affect its price, you would lose $.25 per share. The width or amount of the spread will depend on a number of factors. To over simplify a bit, the more competition, the narrower the spread. A sign of an illiquid security is a wide spread between the bid and offer price.

Further consideration of a hypothetical trade for Dot.com, Inc. may simplify this whole process for you. Let us suppose that you were not an original investor in that company. But you have been reading about its product and think that it will increase in value. You call your broker at Morgan Stanley (a large broker-dealer) and ask for its current price. She tells you that it is a NASDAQ stock and that the best current quote bid for the stock is $9.25 and the offer is $9.50. You enter an order to buy 10 shares, and the order is executed at the quoted price. This means that you will pay $95.00 for the ten shares. You will also have to pay a commission on the shares if your broker was acting as agent on the transaction. That amount could vary widely from broker to broker. If the stock is owned by Smith Barney and it is being sold from its own account to you, you will be charged a markup. Under Nasdaq rules this amount is limited to less than 5% of the transaction price. Now what would happen if you immediately resold your stock and no changes have occurred in its price? You would be paid $92.50 by the market-makers, a loss of $2.50, plus another commission or markup. Assuming that the total markups on the round-turn buy and sell transactions were 10 percent, your loss on the transaction would be $21.25. That is a pretty hefty loss on a $95 investment. But that is the cost of liquidity. You hope to offset those costs through an increase in the value of the stock if the company becomes successful.

3. *More on NASDAQ*. The NASD was reorganized following the SEC's finding that the NASD failed to police its market-makers. A separate subsidiary called NASD Regulation, Inc. was created to regulate the activities of NASD members. Another subsidiary, NASD Dispute Resolution, Inc. was created to conduct arbitrations, including those involving customer claims brought against broker-dealers. The Nasdaq market operates as a separate entity that is divided into three basic tiers. The National Market System ("NMS") is a grouping of the most heavily capitalized and actively traded stocks listed on NASDAQ. NMS stocks have several market-makers that compete with each, which usually means that these stocks are highly liquid, have narrow spreads and are efficiently priced. NMS stocks include such established corporate giants as Microsoft and Budweiser. A second tier of NASD securities are the so-called "small-cap" securities. These are generally stocks issued by small start up companies. They are often thinly capitalized and sometimes speculative in nature. The number of market-makers for each stock will vary from several to a few. Some of these stocks may not be highly liquid, may have wider spreads and be less efficiently priced than the NMS stocks. Some of the companies issuing these securities will become successful and join the NMS system. Traders are always looking to invest in the small-cap stocks they believe will be successful. A third tier is the "Bulletin Board." This is a group of stocks that are not actively traded. Market-makers will post indications of interest in these securities. Your broker-dealer will have to contact the market-makers in these securities and negotiate a price to execute an order. These stocks are usually illiquid and may be speculative in nature.

4. The NASD Regulation and NASD Resolution entities were merged with the New York Stock Exchange's self-regulatory and arbitration divisions in 2007. The merged entity was called the Financial Industry Regulatory Authority ("FINRA"). FINRA then had some 3,000 employees to carry out its duties. That compared favorably with the 3,500 employees at the SEC.

5. What is a broker-dealer? It is simply the technical name for a stockbroker that may execute trades for customers and for its own account. The broker-dealer may buy or sell stock for you as your agent by purchasing or selling it to some third party. In that agency role, the firm is acting as a "broker," and you will be charged a commission for that service. The broker-dealer may also buy and sell stock to you that it has purchased for its own account. In that role, the broker-dealer is acting as a "principal," or in Wall Street terms as a "dealer." Instead of a commission, you will be charged a mark-up for the stock purchased from a dealer. This is an amount (usually less than 5 percent) of the price paid by the dealer for the stock. Broker-

dealers are subject to extensive regulation by the SEC which not only regulates the industry directly but also oversees the pervasive self-regulatory system. *See, e.g.,* see Jerry W. Markham & Thomas L. Hazen, Broker–Dealer Operations Under Securities and Commodities Law: Financial Responsibilities, Credit Regulation, and Customer Protection (2d ed. 2002).

SECTION 4. THE NEW YORK STOCK EXCHANGE

SILVER v. NEW YORK STOCK EXCHANGE

373 U.S. 341, 83 S.Ct. 1246, 10 L.Ed.2d 389 (1963).

MR. JUSTICE GOLDBERG DELIVERED THE OPINION OF THE COURT.

We deal here today with the question, of great importance to the public and the financial community, of whether and to what extent the federal antitrust laws apply to securities exchanges regulated by the Securities Exchange Act of 1934. More particularly, the question is whether the New York Stock Exchange is to be held liable to a nonmember broker-dealer under the antitrust laws or regarded as impliedly immune therefrom when, pursuant to rules the Exchange has adopted under the Securities Exchange Act of 1934, it orders a number of its members to remove private direct telephone wire connections previously in operation between their offices and those of the nonmember, without giving the nonmember notice, assigning him any reason for the action, or affording him an opportunity to be heard. * * *

The facts material to resolution of this question are not in dispute. Harold J. Silver, who died during the pendency of this action, entered the securities business in Dallas, Texas, in 1955, by establishing the predecessor of petitioner Municipal Securities (Municipal) to deal primarily in municipal bonds. The business of Municipal having increased steadily, Silver, in June 1958, established petitioner Municipal Securities, Inc. (Municipal,**1250 Inc.), to trade in corporate over-the-counter securities. Both firms are registered broker-dealers and members of the National Association of Securities Dealers, Inc. (NASD); neither is a member of the respondent Exchange.

The difficult problem here arises from the need to reconcile pursuit of the antitrust aim of eliminating restraints on competition with the effective operation of a public policy contemplating that securities exchanges will engage in self-regulation which may well have anti-competitive effects in general and in specific applications.

The need for statutory regulation of securities exchanges and the nature of the duty of self-regulation imposed by the Securities Exchange Act are properly understood in the context of a consideration of both the economic role played by exchanges and the historical setting of the Act.

Stock exchanges perform an important function in the economic life of this country. They serve, first of all, as an indispensable mechanism through which corporate securities can be bought and sold. To corporate enterprise such a market mechanism is a fundamental element in facilitating the successful marshaling of large aggregations of funds that would otherwise be extremely difficult to access. To the public the exchanges are an investment channel which promises ready convertibility of stock holdings into cash. The importance of these functions in dollar terms is vast— in 1962 the New York Stock Exchange, by far the largest of the 14 exchanges which are registered with the Securities and Exchange Commission, had $47.4 billion of transactions in stocks, rights, and warrants (a figure which represented 86% of the total dollar volume on registered exchanges). Report of the Special Study of Securities Markets (1963), c. IB, p. 6. Moreover, because trading on the exchanges, in addition to establishing the price level of listed securities, affects securities prices in general, and because such transactions are often regarded as an indicator of our national economic health, the significance of the exchanges in our economy cannot be measured only in terms of the dollar volume of trading. Recognition of the importance of the exchanges' role led the House Committee on Interstate and Foreign Commerce to declare in its report preceding the enactment of the Securities Exchange Act of 1934 that 'The great exchanges of this country upon which millions of dollars of securities are sold are affected with a public interest in the same degree as any other great utility.' H.R.Rep. No. 1383, 73d Cong., 2d Sess. 15 (1934).

The exchanges are by their nature bodies with a limited number of members, each of which plays a certain role in the carrying out of an exchange's activities. The limited-entry feature of exchanges led historically to their being treated by the courts as private clubs, Belton v. Hatch, 109 N.Y. 593, 17 N.E. 225 (1888), and to their being given great latitude by the courts in disciplining errant members, see Westwood and Howard, Self–Government in the Securities Business, 17 Law and Contemp. Prob. 518–525 (1952). As exchanges became a more and more important element in our Nation's economic and financial system, however, the private-club analogy became increasingly inapposite and the ungoverned self-regulation became more and more obviously inadequate, with acceleratingly grave consequences. This impotency ultimately led to the enactment of the 1934 Act. The House Committee Report summed up the long-developing problem in discussing the general purposes of the bill:

> 'The fundamental fact behind the necessity for this bill is that the leaders of private business, whether because of inertia, pressure of vested interests, lack of organization, or otherwise, have not since the war been able to act to protect themselves by compelling a continuous and orderly program of change in methods and standards of doing business to match the degree to which the economic system has itself been constantly changing * * *. The repetition in the summer of 1933 of the blindness and abuses of 1929 has convinced a patient public that enlightened self-interest in private leadership is not sufficiently

powerful to effect the necessary changes alone—that private leadership seeking to make changes must be given Government help and protection.' H.R.Rep. No. 1383, supra, at 3, 17 N.E. 225.

It was, therefore, the combination of the enormous growth in the power and impact of exchanges in our economy, and their inability and unwillingness to curb abuses which had increasingly grave implications because of this growth, that moved Congress to enact the Securities Exchange Act of 1934. S.Rep. No. 792, 73d Cong., 2d Sess. 2–5 (1934); H.R.Rep. No. 1383, supra, at 2–5.

The pattern of governmental entry, however, was by no means one of total displacement of the exchanges' traditional process of self-regulation. The intention was rather, as Mr. Justice Douglas said, while Chairman of the S.E.C., one of 'letting the exchanges take the leadership with Government playing a residual role. Government would keep the shotgun, so to speak, behind the door, loaded, well oiled, cleaned, ready for use but with the hope it would never have to be used.' Douglas, Democracy and Finance (Allen ed. 1940), 82. Thus the Senate Committee Report stressed that 'the initiative and responsibility for promulgating regulations pertaining to the administration of their ordinary affairs remain with the exchanges themselves. It is only where they fail adequately to provide protection to investors that the Commission is authorized to step in and compel them to do so.' S.Rep. No. 792, supra, at 13. The House Committee Report added the hope that the bill would give the exchanges sufficient power to reform themselves without intervention by the Commission. H.R.Rep. No. 1383, supra, at 15. See also 2 Loss, Securities Regulation (2d ed. 1961), 1175–1178, 1180–1182.

Thus arose the federally mandated duty of self-policing by exchanges. Instead of giving the Commission the power to curb specific instances of abuse, the Act placed in the exchanges a duty to register with the Commission, § 5, 15 U.S.C. § 78e, and decreed that registration could not be granted unless the exchange submitted copies of its rules, § 6(a)(3), 15 U.S.C. § 78f(a)(3), and unless such rules were 'just and adequate to insure fair dealing and to protect investors,' § 6(d), 15 U.S.C. § 78f(d). The general dimensions of the duty of self-regulation are suggested by § 19(b) of the Act, 15 U.S.C. § 78s(b), which gives the Commission power to order changes in exchange rules respecting a number of subjects, which are set forth in the margin.[1]

---

1. 'The Commission is * * * authorized * * * to alter or supplement the rules of * * * (an) exchange * * * in respect of such matters as (1) safeguards in respect of the financial responsibility of members and adequate provision against the evasion of financial responsibility through the use of corporate forms or special partnerships; (2) the limitation or prohibition of the registration or trading in any security within a specified period after the issuance or primary distribution thereof; (3) the listing or striking from listing of any security; (4) hours of trading; (5) the manner, method, and place of soliciting business; (6) fictitious or numbered accounts; (7) the time and method of making settlements, payments, and deliveries and of closing accounts; (5) the reporting of transactions on the exchange and upon tickers maintained by or with the consent of the exchange, including the method of reporting short sales, stopped sales, sales of securities of issuers in default, bankruptcy or receivership, and sales involving other special circumstances; (9) the fixing of reasonable rates of commission, interest, listing, and other charges; (10) minimum

One aspect of the statutorily imposed duty of self-regulation is the obligation to formulate rules governing the conduct of exchange members. The Act specifically requires that registration cannot be granted 'unless the rules of the exchange include provision for the expulsion, suspension, or disciplining of a member for conduct or proceeding inconsistent with just and equitable principles of trade * * *,' § 6(b), 15 U.S.C. § 78f(b). In addition, the general requirement of § 6(d) that an exchange's rules be 'just and adequate to insure fair dealing and to protect investors' has obvious relevance to the area of rules regulating the conduct of an exchange's members.

The § 6(b) and § 6(d) duties taken together have the broadest implications in relation to the present problem, for members inevitably trade on the over-the-counter market in addition to dealing in listed securities, and such trading inexorably brings contact and dealings with nonmember firms which deal in or specialize in over-the-counter securities. It is no accident that the Exchange's Constitution and rules are permeated with instances of regulation of members' relationships with nonmembers including nonmember broker-dealers. A member's purchase of unlisted securities for itself or on behalf of its customer from a boiler-shop operation creates an obvious danger of loss to the principal in the transaction, and sale of securities to a nonmember insufficiently capitalized to protect customers' rights creates similar risks. In addition to the potential financial injury to the investing public and Exchange members that is inherent in these transactions as well as in dealings with nonmembers who are unreliable for any other reason, all such intercourse carries with it the gravest danger of engendering in the public a loss of confidence in the Exchange and its members, a kind of damage which can significantly impair fulfillment of the Exchange's function in our economy. Rules which regulate Exchange members' doing of business with nonmembers in the over-the-counter market are therefore very much pertinent to the aims of self-regulation under the 1934 Act. Transactions with nonmembers under the circumstances mentioned can only be described as 'inconsistent with just and equitable principles of trade,' and rules regulating such dealing are indeed 'just and adequate to insure fair dealing and to protect investors.'

The Exchange's constitutional provision and rules relating to private wire connections are unquestionably part of this fulfillment of the § 6(b) and § 6(d) duties, for such wires between members and nonmembers facilitate trading in and exchange of information about unlisted securities, and such contact with an unreliable nonmember not only may further his business undesirably, but may injure the member or the member's customer on whose behalf the contract is made and ultimately imperil the future status of the Exchange by sapping public confidence. In light of the important role of exchanges in our economy and the 1934 Act's design of giving the exchanges a major part in curbing abuses by obligating them to

---

units of trading; (11) odd-lot purchases and sales; (12) minimum deposits on margin accounts; and (13) similar matters.'

regulate themselves, it appears conclusively—contrary to the District Court's conclusion—that the rules applied in the present case are germane to performance of the duty, implied by § 6(b) and § 6(d), to have rules governing members' transactions and relationships with nonmembers. The Exchange's enforcement of such rules inevitably affects the nonmember involved, often (as here) far more seriously than it affects the members in question. The sweeping of the nonmembers into the currents of the Exchange's process of self-regulation is therefore unavoidable; the case cannot be disposed of by holding as the district judge did that the substantive act of regulation engaged in here was outside the boundaries of the public policy established by the Securities Exchange Act of 1934.

But, it does not follow that the case can be disposed of, as the Court of Appeals did, by holding that since the Exchange has a general power to adopt rules governing its members' relations with nonmembers, particular applications of such rules are therefore outside the purview of the antitrust laws. Contrary to the conclusions reached by the courts below, the proper approach to this case, in our view, is an analysis which reconciles the operation of both statutory schemes with one another rather than holding one completely ousted.

The Securities Exchange Act contains no express exemption from the antitrust laws or, for that matter, from any other statute. This means that any repealer of the antitrust laws must be discerned as a matter of implication, and '(i)t is a cardinal principle of construction that repeals by implication are not favored.' Repeal is to be regarded as implied only if necessary to make the Securities Exchange Act work, and even then only to the minimum extent necessary. This is the guiding principle to reconciliation of the two statutory schemes. * * *

The final question here is, therefore, whether the act of self-regulation in this case was so justified. The answer to that question is that it was not, because the collective refusal to continue the private wires occurred under totally unjustifiable circumstances. Notwithstanding their prompt and repeated requests, petitioners were not informed of the charges underlying the decision to invoke the Exchange rules and were not afforded an appropriate opportunity to explain or refute the charges against them.

Given the principle that exchange self-regulation is to be regarded as justified in response to antitrust charges only to the extent necessary to protect the achievement of the aims of the Securities Exchange Act, it is clear that no justification can be offered for self-regulation conducted without provision for some method of telling a protesting non-member why a rule is being invoked so as to harm him and allowing him to reply in explanation of his position. No policy reflected in the Securities Exchange Act is, to begin with, served by denial of notice and an opportunity for hearing. Indeed, the aims of the statutory scheme of self-policing—to protect investors and promote fair dealing—are defeated when an exchange exercises its tremendous economic power without explaining its basis for acting, for the absence of an obligation to give some form of notice and, if timely requested, a hearing creates a great danger of perpetration of injury that will damage public confidence in the exchanges. * * *

The judgment is reversed and remanded for further proceedings consistent with this opinion.

It is so ordered.

MR. JUSTICE CLARK CONCURS in the result on the grounds stated in the opinion of the District Court, and the dissenting opinion in the Court of Appeals.

MR. JUSTICE STEWART, WHOM MR. JUSTICE HARLAN JOINS, DISSENTING. [omitted]

NOTES

1.   For an excellent analysis of the issues raised in *Silver, see* Credit Suisse Securities LLC v. Billing, 551 U.S. 264, 127 S.Ct. 2383, 168 L.Ed.2d 145 (2007), holding that (antitrust attacks on IPO practices were precluded by the securities laws).

2.   In Friedman v. Salomon/Smith Barney, Inc., 313 F.3d 796 (2d Cir. 2002), the court found an implied repeal of the antitrust laws with respect to penalty bids during IPOs. The court noted that there was pervasive regulation of the IPO process by the SEC and the SEC rules determined which penalty bids were permissible and which were not. This pervasive regulation resulted in the implied repeal of the antitrust laws and thus precluded an antitrust attack. Subsequently the SEC and NASD tightened its rules applicable to the offering process, clearly outlawing activity that was questionable under prior law and possibly in violation of general antifraud and antimanipulation provisions but was not explicitly prohibited.

————

The following excerpt traces the early development of exchanges in America:

> In 1790, the first stock exchange was formed in Philadelphia, which was the location of the country's two largest banks, the Bank of North America and the first Bank of the United States. The Philadelphia board of brokers also elected its first president in that year. In New York, an auction market for securities was formed by John Sutton and Benjamin Jay. It was conducted at 22 Wall Street. Stock dealers would meet at noon at that location and "sales were conducted by a joint arrangement of auctioneers and dealers." Dissatisfaction with that process led to a meeting of brokers at Corre's Hotel on March 21, 1792, which formed the foundation for the institution that ultimately became the New York Stock Exchange. The brokers attending the meeting wanted to exclude auctioneers from the stock

business, and they reached an agreement that was signed by twenty-four stock brokers under a buttonwood tree on May 17, 1792. That agreement stated that:

> We the Subscribers, Brokers for the Purchase and Sale of Public Stock, do hereby solemnly promise and pledge ourselves to each other that we will not buy or sell, from this day, for any person whatsoever, any kind of public stock at a less rate than one-quarter per cent commission on the special value, and that we will give preference to each other in our negotiations.

The Buttonwood Tree Agreement centralized the securities market, but resulted in no great volume of trading in the initial period after 1792. Bank stocks and government bonds were still the major securities. A short time later, however, the nation's economy began to rapidly develop. Many new banks were formed and business concerns were starting to organize. By 1800, 355 profit-making corporations had been formed in the United States. They reflected the need for more sophisticated business organizations in an expanding economy. * * *

By 1817, eight brokerage firms and nineteen individuals were engaged in the brokerage business in New York. In that year, the New York Stock and Exchange Board was formed [renamed as the New York Stock Exchange at the close of the Civil War]. Composed of seven brokerage firms and thirteen individual brokers, the exchange went indoors at 40 Wall Street, and approximately thirty stocks were traded. Membership was strictly limited, and there was an application fee of $25 that was increased to $100 in 1827. * * *

The New York Stock and Exchange Board grew rapidly in the next few decades, paralleling the increased need for borrowing by the states as a result of the growth of canal building. One successful flotation was for the Erie Canal that was completed in 1825. A "money market for call loans" was developed for these securities. This was simply the means by which securities were margined, i.e., speculators could purchase securities with bank credit obtained by their brokers." This too fueled speculation.

Business slowed at the end of the 1820s. On March 16, 1830, only thirty-one shares were traded. Still, there was some good news. In 1829, a locomotive pulled a train for the first time in the United States. A year later, the first railroad company stock was listed on the New York Stock and Exchange Board-the Mohawk and Hudson Railroad. Trading in railroad stocks grew—quickly and in 1837, exchange listings included some eight railroads, two canal companies and twelve banks. * * *

The Philadelphia Stock Exchange moved into its own building in 1832. Later, the exchange shared price information with the New York exchanges by using signals that were flashed by mirrors from elevated train stations and by lanterns at night. Communications could be sent in as little as ten minutes.

Jerry W. Markham & Thomas Lee Hazen, 23 Broker-Dealer Operations Under Securities and Commodities Law § 1.3 (2001).

The Buttonwood Agreement that was signed in 1792 laid the groundwork for the New York Stock Exchange ("NYSE"). It also was a rate fixing mechanism for broker's commissions. Brokers' commissions were set by the NYSE until May of 1975, when the SEC required commissions to be negotiated. See Gordon v. NYSE, 422 U.S. 659, 95 S.Ct. 2598, 45 L.Ed.2d 463 (1975) (describing history of fixed commissions in the securities industry). The elimination of fixed commission rates had several significant effects on Wall Street. Discount brokers appeared that offered bare bones execution services at cheap prices, while the traditional ("full service") firms continued to charge high commissions that they justified on the basis of the services they provided including research on stocks they recommended to you. The discount brokers received a boost in popularity with the advent of online trading through the Internet. This allowed even cheaper commissions, giving rise to something called day traders. These were simply individuals trading online that sought to make short term profits through quick in-and-out transactions. Unfortunately, most of those traders lost money. One survey found that more than ninety percent of day traders lost money. III *Jerry W. Markham, A Financial History of the United States, From the Age of Derivatives Into the New Millenium (1970–2001)* 334 (2002). Nevertheless, the online brokers were eroding the customer base of the more traditional broker-dealers firms. The full service firms were also affected by the institutional traders who could negotiate low commissions because, after all, a trade for 100,000 shares requires about as much work as one for 500,000 shares. This declining revenue base from commissions led many broker-dealers to change their business plan and they themselves became institutional investors trading for their own account, as well as executing customer orders.

The NYSE trades the stocks of many of the larger and better established corporate businesses. The system for trading stocks on the NYSE varies from the system used on Nasdaq. The NYSE uses "specialists" rather than market-makers to maintain a continuous two sided market in listed stocks. Each stock is assigned a specialist, and that specialist has the duty to maintain a fair and orderly market in that stock. This means that the specialist must be buying when the market is going down and selling when it is going up in order to provide some stability and liquidity. Note that the specialist has a monopoly on this trading. There are no competing market-makers on the floor of the NYSE such as those found in the Nasdaq system. Which system is better? There has been much debate over that question, but no real definitive answer. The NYSE specialist will be quoting a two sided market with a spread, as in the case of the Nasdaq market makers. Because the specialist has the duty to maintain a continuous market, NYSE securities are usually highly liquid.

The quotes are good for only stated amounts of the stock and may be changed at any time. Small orders are executed automatically at the specialist's quoted price through the NYSE SuperDOT system. The following is a description of how orders my be executed on the floor of the NYSE:

> Stock exchange specialists act as both brokers and dealers. As brokers, specialists buy and sell for the public, by executing limit orders that are brought to them on behalf of customers by floor brokers; they also execute market orders that reach them through the automated order routing system, Super DOT. (A limit order specifies the price at which an investor is willing to buy or sell. Limit orders are put in the specialist's "book" until they can be executed at the designated price or a better price. A market order is an order to buy or sell immediately, at the prevailing price.) Specialists are prohibited by law from handling customer orders other than limit orders. The specialist's book was once a loose leaf notebook but now it is, for most NYSE stocks, a computer screen. * * *

> As dealers, specialists buy and sell for their own account. They have an "affirmative obligation" to do so when it is necessary to provide liquidity. Specialists provide liquidity by buying or selling when there are no other bidders or offerers at or near the market price. The specialist tries to keep prices from making big jumps by making a bid or offer that acts as a bridge when there is a wide gap between bids and offers. The specialist also has a "negative obligation," not to trade for his own account when there are already customers wanting to trade at or near the market place.

> Specialists participate in a substantial portion of NYSE trades. * * *

U.S. Congress, Office of Technology Assessment, Electronic Bulls & Bears: U.S. Securities Markets and Information Technology 42 (1990).

The NYSE has been beset by a series of trading scandals on its floor. Independent floor brokers, or $2 brokers as they are sometimes called, were engaged in "flipping" or "trading for eights." D'Allesio v. S.E.C., 380 F.3d 112 (2d Cir. 2004). This practice involved the purchase or sale of a security for a customer followed by the sale or purchase of the same security for a profit of one-eighth of a point, the spread between the bid and ask prices. This allowed floor brokers to receive both a commission for the trade and profits from the spread. An SEC investigation also found that NYSE specialists were mishandling and trading ahead of customer orders. Deborah Solomon & Susanne Craig, Taking Stock, SEC Blasts Big Board Oversight of "Specialist" Trading Firms, Wall St. J., Nov. 3, 2003, at A1. The SEC study concluded that investors were defrauded of over $150 million by this activity. The specialists were "inter-positioning" themselves between buy and sell orders of customers, profiting on the spread. In addition, the specialists were "trading ahead" of customers by engaging in transactions for their own account at a favorable price while holding a customer order that could have been executed at that price. Specialists were also helping customers to "mark the close," which involves setting an artificial closing price, usually for margin purposes. The SEC charged that these practices violated the duty of the specialists to maintain a "fair and orderly" market. Several specialist firms on the NYSE agreed to pay $241 million to settle SEC charges arising from this misconduct. Seven smaller specialist firms agreed to settle similar charges with fines totaling $10.2 million. See e.g., In the Matter of Spear, Leeds, & Kellogg, Securities Exchange Act Release No. 34–49501 (March 30, 2004); In the Matter of LaBranche & Co.LLC, Securities Exchange Release No. 34–49500 (March 30, 2004). Fifteen traders working for the specialist firms were indicted.

Price Changes. The Nasdaq and NYSE seek to provide a liquid market for the stocks they list. That does not, however, assure that you will receive any particular price for your stock. The Nasdaq market-makers and the NYSE specialists are constantly adjusting their quotations to reflect any changes in the value of your stock. That means the value of your stock can change rapidly before you are able to enter a buy or sell order. Further, the specialist and market-maker quotations are only for limited amounts. This means that, even if you are able to enter your order before the quotation is changed, the amount of stock available at that price may be limited. Another thing to consider is that during periods of extreme market stress, market-makers and specialists may not be able to provide liquidity. This occurred during the Stock Market Crash of 1987. Many investors trying to sell their stocks discovered that their stocks were not trading during that event. The markets have tried to correct those problems, but the danger remains.

Regional exchanges. The American Stock Exchange (which is now owned by the NASD) and other regional exchanges such as the Philadelphia Stock Exchange also make markets in securities. Their trading may include smaller cap stocks, as well as those listed on the NYSE. To facilitate trading of NYSE stocks on the regional exchanges there is a an Intermarket Trading System that links the exchanges. This linkage seeks to assure that customers receive the best price available for jointly traded stock.

Large "block" trades in NYSE stocks (i.e., a transaction consisting of 10,000 or more shares or one with a market value of more than $200,000) may be arranged "upstairs" by block positioners at large securities firms. The terms of the sale are reported on the floor of the exchange. This prearrangement is needed because most specialists do not have adequate capital to conduct business of that size with any frequency. Trades of block size have become common with the growth of the institutional investor. U.S. Congress, Office of Technology Assessment, *Electronic Bulls*

& Bears: U.S. Securities Markets and Information Technology 50–51 (1990).

Indeed, trading in common stocks, particularly those listed on the New York Stock Exchange, has been increasingly dominated by "institutional investors"—principally pension funds, mutual funds, bank trust departments, and insurance companies—with individual investors accounting for a continually decreasing percentage of trading volume. The distinctive trading practices of institutions, and the types of services they require and do not require, have put serious strains on the traditional market mechanisms and compensation structures. There has also been increased off-exchange trading of exchange-listed securities, which means that many transactions in exchange-listed securities do not take place on the floor of the exchange. The NYSE for years had a rule (Rule 390) that prohibited its members from trading NYSE listed stock other than through the exchange. That restriction was avoided by institutions through a "third market" maintained by broker-dealers that were not NYSE members or in a "fourth market" that involved transactions directly between institutional traders that were not members of the NYSE. Rule 390 was widely criticized as being anti-competitive, and the NYSE eventually eliminated it. This further dispersed trading and encouraged the growth of Electronic Communications Networks that institutions could use for their trading activities.

7.   Do you think that stocks are a good investment? Most financial analysts will point out that stocks have outperformed all other investments over the long term. Remember, however, that it was not until November of 1954 that the stock market was able to exceed the high it reached just before the stock market crash of 1929.

SECTION 5.   ELECTRONIC COMMUNICATIONS NETWORKS

The computer and communication technology, which enables buyers and sellers in all parts of the country to be in instantaneous and continuous communication with one another with respect to any security, has revolutionized the securities markets and has raised serious questions about the necessity and desirability of a physical exchange "floor." The NYSE and Nasdaq are the principal markets used by small investors, but there are other alternatives available to large institutional traders. These alternate markets often Electronic Communications Networks ("ECNs"), link large traders by computer and allow them to post or negotiate transactions with each other.

23A JERRY W. MARKHAM & THOMAS LEE HAZEN BROKER–DEALER REGULATION UNDER SECURITIES AND COMMODITIES LAWS

§ 13:1 to § 13:3 (2002).

The development of computers and their linkage through the Internet has had an effect on Wall Street that equals or exceeds earlier electronic innovations in the markets such as those caused by the telegraph and the telephone. The computer and the growth of the Internet have given rise to electronic trading and the creation of alternate electronic marketplaces that are threatening traditional exchange and over-the-counter markets. This revolution has also raised regulatory concerns. * * *

Interconnected with these developments was the SEC's endorsement of the concept of a "central market system" in its 1971 study on the role of institutional investors. The SEC envisioned the creation of a central market that would encompass a network of broker-dealers linked together by electronic communications. The SEC wanted this centralized system to include securities on the exchanges and in the over-the-counter market. The SEC issued a statement on the future structure of the securities markets in 1972 that contended that a central market would better assure that customers were receiving the best executions in any market, the NYSE, the over-the-counter, or the third market.

The central market system was a somewhat amorphous and uncertain concept. The SEC did pressure the exchanges to develop the composite last sale price reporting system as a step in the development of a central market, but the SEC soon lost interest in the central market system concept. It did propose a "universal message switch" that would have required the exchanges to create a system whereby customer orders would be automatically routed to the market with the best quotation price. This was objected to by the industry. The alternative developed by the exchanges was the Intermarket Trading System, which allowed orders to be executed by specialists at the best price available on any exchange The Intermarket Trading System was an electronic link among the NYSE, the AMEX, and the regional exchanges. The Intermarket Trading System did not require an order to be executed on the market quoting the best price. Instead, the specialist receiving an order could execute the order, as long as the execution was done at the best quoted price on any exchange.

The computer was soon making other inroads on Wall Street by allowing access to databases, information processing services and market models. Another development in electronic trading was the electronic network for institutional trading created by the Institutional Network Corporation in 1969 (Instinet). "It was composed of a network of computer terminals that permitted broker-dealers and their institutional customers to indicate their interest in securities listed on exchanges and traded in the over-the-counter market. The system allowed the execution of trades and provided trading reports. Clearing and settlement functions could be effected through the Instinet system, although not entirely. Pricing in the system used various sources including trading on the NYSE." Instinet developed rapidly in part because it provided a private market. Orders in its system were not publicly disclosed or accessible to public investors. This protected the identity of the institution in the trade. "It also allowed institutions to avoid intermediation on the NYSE and that exchange's Rule 390 prohibition on off-exchange transactions—in listed securities."

Instinet was successful and provided an alternative market to institutions. It was the largest electronic communications network for trading at the end of the century and was processing 170 million shares per day. Twenty million of those trades were executed after traditional trading hours. "Instinet was partnering with online brokers such as E*Trade Group to increase its trading."

By the end of the century, Instinet and other so-called electronic communications networks (ECNs) were posing a threat to the traditional securities markets. ECNs and other alternative trading systems were then handling more than 20 percent of the orders for securities listed on Nasdaq and almost 4 percent of orders on exchange listed securities. The SEC concluded that alternative trading systems were threatening to become the primary market for some securities.

A number of ECNs were operating in the market. They included Wit Capital, OptiMark, and Easdaq, Instinet Corp., the Island System, the TONTO System, which became Archipelago, Bloomberg Tradebook, the REDI System operated by Spear, Leeds & Kellogg, the Attain System, the BRUT System, the Strike System, and the Trading System. Goldman Sachs, Merrill Lynch & Co., Salomon Smith Barney, Morgan Stanley Dean Witter and Bernard L. Madoff Investment Securities formed Primex Trading N.A. It was an electronic trading system for stocks listed on the NYSE, the AMEX, and Nasdaq. Primex priced stocks in an auction market using decimals. This system was to be available for broker-dealers, institutional investors, market makers and exchange specialists. Primex was to be used to obtain securities at prices better than those posted prices in other markets.

Charles Schwab, Fidelity Investments, DLJdirect, and Spear, Leeds & Kellogg developed MarketXT, Inc. It was offering an evening trading session in August 1999 for the 200 largest stocks on the NYSE and Nasdaq. Bridge Trader was providing for Internet institutional order entry and allowed orders to be routed to multiple brokers through its trading network. This information system was also providing quotes, watch lists, and order book market data. In June 1999, J.P. Morgan & Co. announced that it was investing in an electronic trading network. Another electronic communication network, GFINet System, provided quotations on national market securities that were also American Depository Receipts. Still another ECN was the MarketXT. The BRASS Utility System was an ECN that provided automatic execution, clearance and settlement of trades in Nasdaq National Market System and Small–Cap stocks. Subscribers were broker-dealers, but their institutional customers could be given direct access to the system.

The Attain superTM System was an ECN that provided an alternative method by which market makers could handle their requirements to display customer limit orders to the public pursuant to the SEC's order handling rules. It also allowed matching of orders of subscribers as well as displaying a book of orders on Nasdaq. The system sought to provide matching without unnecessary intermediation by market makers. Spear, Leeds & Kellogg was operating a routing and execution DOT interface electronic communications network called the REDI System that was designed to process mixed-lot orders directed to it by SelectNet (another ECN) and from customer terminals. The system was designed to match mixed-lot orders. The remaining odd lot portions of a mixed lot order were to be executed against orders in odd lots or the odd lot portions of other mixed-lot orders. * * *

The increasing availability of computer linkages renewed some long held concerns that such systems could be used to divert volume from public exchanges, reduce market transparency, cause fragmentation of markets and result in disparate execution prices. The SEC issued a concept release seeking the public's views on how the market should be structured in light of the availability of alternate electronic trading systems and whether fragmentation was a threat to competitive executions. 'Congress was also conducting hearings on whether legislation was needed to protect investors from market fragmentation resulting from the creation of more and more ECNs.' Electronic trading allowed trading to continue past normal trading hours on the exchanges. This too raised concerns. An SEC staff study revealed wide price disparities in transactions conducted in after hours trading.

ECNs were reducing the market share of both the New York Stock Exchange and Nasdaq by the end of the century. ECNs were handling about 29 percent of Nasdaq volume in 1999. Nasdaq responded to this threat by developing its own electronic system. This was to be done through Optimark Technologies, Inc., which was owned by several Wall Street firms, including Dow Jones & Co. Optimark had a supercomputer that was being used to match orders automatically. In addition, Nasdaq was considering whether it should develop an Internet trading system and was meeting with Instinet to discuss centralizing the trading of Nasdaq stocks. Nasdaq also announced in December 1999 that it was entering into an agreement with Primex Trading to adopt an electronic auction market system to trade its issues and those listed on the stock exchanges Nasdaq planned to expand its systems to allow the display of quotes from electronic communication networks so that investors would have more information on available prices.

ECNs and Internet trading were also causing an upheaval at the stock exchanges. The SEC also recognized that traditional exchanges were under competitive pressure from the ECNs. It, therefore, allowed the exchanges to restructure themselves as for profit organizations. Traditionally, the exchanges had been operated as not-for-profits. This change was intended to allow the exchanges to raise capital and compete with the electronic markets. Demutualization was in progress on many of the exchanges. The NYSE was among the exchanges that were considering demutualizing. This would permit the exchange to raise capital and provide a better structure to meet competition. Nasdaq also announced similar plans, as did the Chicago Board of Trade and the London Stock Exchange. The NASD announced that it planned to sell its interest in the Nasdaq Stock Market through a private placement that was expected to raise $1 billion. This restructuring was intended to make the Nasdaq market more competitive and provide greater access to the markets for capital.

Archipelago, a rapidly growing ECN, agreed to form a fully electronic stock market with the Pacific Exchange. The latter was the fourth largest stock exchange in the United States on the basis of trading volume. The new market planned to match customer buy and sell orders. The Pacific Exchange planned to close its trading floors in San Francisco and Los Angeles, but continue its options market.

Notes

1.   Trading on an ECN is order driven. This means there is no market-maker or specialist that is maintaining a two-sided market in the security being traded. Liquidity depends entirely on the ability to find a willing buyer or seller that has entered an opposing order or quote. Finding a counter party through a posted bid or offer in actively traded securities may be easy, but in less actively traded securities that task is considerably more difficult.

2.   The SEC requires registration of stock exchanges and imposes pervasive regulation over their activities, but ECNs are only lightly regulated because they are simply order executing mechanisms. There is no specialist or market-maker that has a particular time and place advantage in trading for their own account that needs regulation. Do you think this is fair to the exchanges or the market-makers on Nasdaq? Do you think ECNs should be subject to greater regulation?

3.   The NYSE announced in 2005 that it was merging with Archipelago Holdings Inc., a Chicago based electronic communications network that was executing about twenty-five percent of volume in Nasdaq stocks. This move was intended to provide the NYSE with competitive access to Nasdaq stocks and allow it to enter the market for electronic executions. The new company was named NYSE Group Inc. The merger would convert the NYSE into a public for-profit company. Exclusive U.S. control of the NYSE was lost in 2006 after it merged with Euronext, an amalgamation of European exchanges that traded principally electronically. As a condition for that merger, the NYSE agreed to split management and board control of the new entity evenly with the European exchanges, thus giving up domestic control of one of America's oldest financial institutions. Jerry W. Markham and Daniel J.

Harty, For Whom the Bell Tolls: The Demise of Exchange Trading Floors and the Growth of ECNs, 33 J. Corp. L. 865 (2008)(describing changes in market structure). Nasdaq responded to this competitive threat with an announcement that it was acquiring Instinet from Reuters, another electronic communications network, for $1.9 billion.

Another important development occurred in 2007, when NASD Regulation merged with the NYSE Regulation to become the Financial Industry Regulatory Authority, Inc. ("FINRA"), thereby creating a single self-regulator in the stock markets and eliminating much overlap and redundancy. The NYSE and NASD additionally merged their arbitration programs.

SECTION 6.   DERIVATIVES TRADING

The derivatives markets indirectly supplies liquidity and risk protection to the securities markets. The following is a description of those markets.

JERRY W. MARKHAM, UNITED STATES SECURITIES AND INVESTMENTS REGULATION HANDBOOK

(eds. Peter Farmery and Keith Walmsley).
Chapter 8 (1992).

Commodity futures contracts began trading on organized exchanges in the United States in the middle of the nineteenth century. These contracts evolved from so called "to arrive" contracts in which grain was sold pursuant to an agreement that the delivery of the grain would be at a specified future date rather than the immediate delivery. The terms of these to-arrive contracts were standardized on the Chicago Board of Trade and, as such, they became known as futures contracts. This standardization of contract terms allowed futures contracts to be offset so that delivery was not required. This offset feature quickly became the subject of widespread interest to speculators and commercial traders because they could buy and sell these contracts without actually making or taking delivery. Commodity option contracts were also developed for trading on the futures exchanges, but speculative abuses led to their suppression for varying periods. In fact, after 1936, federal law banned commodity option contracts on agricultural commodities.

Traditionally, futures trading was conducted on agricultural commodities. However, inflation and wide scale speculative interest in the 1970s led to the development of a number of new futures contracts, including stock index futures contracts that allowed traders to benefit from changes in the overall value of the stock market. The 1970s also saw the creation of a new exchange that traded stock option contracts: the Chicago Board Options Exchange Inc.

These developments led to explosive growth in the futures and options industry. In 1970, the volume of futures contracts was some 13.6

million. By 1980 that figure had increased to 92 million contracts and by 1990 volume had risen to some 275 million contracts. Trading volume in the new financial futures alone reached 42 million contracts in 1982. By 1989 the number of financial futures contracts that were traded was approaching 200 million, far exceeding the number of agricultural commodity futures contracts that was the traditional basis for futures trading.

Trading in stock options also increased dramatically after the Chicago Board Options Inc. began trading in 1973. By 1986, the total combined volume of the options exchanges exceeded 280 million contracts. In 1987, volume exceeded 300 million contracts, but declined substantially following the stock market crash of 1987.

The increased volume of futures and options trading reflect the fact that market uncertainties have led many institutional investors to utilize the futures markets to hedge their risks and to engage in complicated trading strategies such as portfolio insurance, index arbitrage and dynamic hedging. * * *

A commodity futures contract is a bilateral obligation in which the seller (also known as the "short") agrees to deliver a specified amount of an identified grade of commodity at a specified date in the future. The purchaser (also known as the "long") agrees to buy the specified amount of the identified commodity at the agreed date in the future at the price negotiated with the seller. The terms of commodity futures contracts are standardized, but futures contracts typically have a wide range of standardized delivery dates. The only term that is negotiated is the price. That negotiation occurs in an auction-style process on the floors of the commodity exchanges.

[Until 2000], [c]ommodity futures contracts originating in the United States may be traded only on exchanges in the United States that are licensed by the CFTC as "contract markets". An exchange must be designated as a contract market for each futures contract traded on its floor. * * * The two largest commodity futures exchanges in the United States are the Chicago Board of Trade and the Chicago Mercantile Exchange. Exchanges in New York also trade futures contracts. For example, silver futures contracts are traded on the Commodity Exchange Inc. ("Comex"), and the New York Mercantile Exchange trades a large volume of petroleum futures contracts.

Each futures exchange has a "clearing house" that guarantees performance on the futures contracts traded on the exchange. To effectuate that guarantee, the clearing house is interceded between each buyer and seller of a futures contract. The clearing house, therefore, becomes the buyer and the seller in every futures transaction. Because the terms of futures contracts are standardized, and due to the intercession of the clearing house, futures contracts also become fungible. Consequently, traders can close out their positions without taking delivery, and most do. Some futures contracts provide for cash settlement rather than actual delivery of the underlying commodity. In other futures contracts, particularly agricultural contracts, delivery remains available.

Futures contracts are traded on margin. There are two types of margin. The first is initial margin. This is simply a good faith deposit of money to assure that the parties will perform on their contract. Both the buyer and seller must post this initial margin. Generally, the amount of the margin is only a small percentage of the actual purchase price.

The second form of margin is called variation margin. Futures contracts are marked-to-market each day. That is, if there has been a fluctuation in price, the theoretical gain or loss to each party is computed. Those funds are then credited to the account of the purchaser, through the clearing house and then to the purchaser's broker. This marking-to-market process occurs every day and each party must pay or receive to reflect their gains or losses.

The small amount of initial margin required for futures contracts means that the transaction is highly leveraged. Because of that high leverage, margin requirements are strictly enforced to assure that the parties perform. There is no Securities Investors Protection Corporation ("SIPC") or other federal insurance for brokerage firm bank or savings and loan failures in the United States. Because brokerage firms remain liable in the event that customers default, they are very aggressive in assuring that margin requirements are met. This margin system has worked well in the past. There have been relatively few failures of commodity futures firms.

The following illustration explains how a futures contract may operate in practice. Assume that a trader in Miami wishes to purchase a 5,000 ounce futures contract on the Comex in New York for delivery in May. The trader would call his broker in Miami to place the order. The broker there would in turn transmit the order to the floor of the exchange for execution in the pit. Assuming that the trader wishes to buy the silver at the existing market price, which we will assume is $5.00, the order would be offered to the ring and executed. At that point, a seller would agree to the contract, i.e., the seller would agree to deliver the silver at that market price. The trade is then reported to the clearing house, and the clearing house is interceded as the buyer and seller. At that point, the purchaser is obligated to take delivery of the silver in March at the price of $5.00 per ounce or a total of $25,000. The seller has a reciprocal obligation of delivering the silver at that time for that price. Assuming an initial margin requirement of 10%, each party will post margin of $2,500 on the opening of the contract. Assume further that the price of silver jumps $1.00 on the next trading day. This would mean that the purchaser has a gain of $5,000. But the seller has a reciprocal loss of $5,000. The seller would, therefore, be required to post an additional $5,000 to reflect that loss, and the reciprocal gain would be credited to the purchase. This process continues throughout the period the purchasers hold their contracts.

A commodity option contract gives the purchaser the right but not the obligation to purchase, in the case of a "call" option, a stated amount of a commodity at a specified price. In the case of a "put" option, the purchaser is given the right to sell the commodity at a specified price. A commodity option contract is distinguished from a futures contract in that the purchaser is not required to take or to make delivery. It simply bestows a right or privilege of delivery. Unlike "European" options that may be exercised only on expiration, commodity options in America generally may be exercised at any time during their life.

The liability of the purchaser of a commodity option is limited to the cost or "premium" that he pays for the option right and any related transactional costs. In contrast, the purchaser of a futures contract must buy the commodity at the specified price even if the price drops to zero. The seller of an option contract has liabilities commensurate with those of a seller in a futures contract. That is, the "writer" or seller of an option contract must make delivery of the commodity (or take delivery in the case of a put option) no matter what its value. The same is true of a seller of a futures contract, except that a short futures trader's losses will not be offset or discounted by the premium payment received by the writer of an option.

Commodity option contracts may also be traded on commodity futures. That is, it is possible to have an option to buy or sell a futures contract at an agreed upon price. Once the option is "exercised", the purchaser of the option contract will be given a futures contract at the specified price, and the futures contract must then be margined. At that point, the purchaser assumes all of the risks and liabilities of a futures contract, i.e., the purchaser's losses are no longer limited to the premium and transaction costs. Rather, the purchaser will be liable for the purchase price no matter what the value of the underlying commodity.

* * * Commodity option contracts and options on futures contracts are regulated by the CFTC. For the most part, these transactions may be conducted only on a contract market unless the participants are engaging in a commercial transaction.

A stock or security option contract is simply an option on an equity security or some other form of security such as a US Treasury bill. As in the case of a commodity option contract, the purchaser pays a premium for the right, as opposed to an obligation, to call or to put the stock from, or to, the seller or writer of the option contract. These options are traded over-the-counter and on exchanges licensed by the SEC in the United States. They are not within the jurisdiction of the CFTC.

Until the early 1970s, stock or other security options trading was limited in the United States to a small number of over-the-counter transactions. At that time, however, the Chicago Board of Trade conducted a study to see if commodity futures trading principles could be applied to stock trading. The result was the creation of a stock options exchange:

the Chicago Board Options Exchange Inc. ("CBOE"). It became an almost immediate success, and it has been copied by other exchanges.

Trading in options on the CBOE is carried out through an auction style system. That system, however, is somewhat different from other exchanges that utilize specialist systems for stock option order execution. To illustrate, on the floor of the CBOE, floor traders who trade for their own accounts stand in a "crowd" and bid or offer for contracts being bought or sold by other floor traders or by customers whose orders are being brought into the pit for execution. The "book" of customer limit orders is kept by an exchange employee . . . . . The floor traders in the pit have market-maker obligations, i.e., they must bid in a way that will maintain a fair and orderly market. In contrast, the commodity futures exchanges have no "book" of customer orders and there are no market-making obligations. Rather, it is a free-for-all auction-style system of bidding and offering orders. * * *

The stock options exchanges have a common clearing house, the Option Clearing Corporation ("OCC"). The OCC also acts as guarantor of security option contracts that are carried with it. It should be noted that stock option customers are also protected by the Securities Investors Protection Corporation, which insures securities customers' accounts. This is not the case with commodity futures and options. * * *

NOTES

1. The following is a description of stock index futures that are a popular product:

In a stock index futures contract, the purchaser of the contract is buying a theoretical portfolio of stocks contained in an index such as Value Line or the Dow Jones Industrial Average. The purchaser of such a contract will profit if the index increases in value. Conversely, the seller will profit, and the purchaser will lose, if the value of the index declines. Unlike other futures contracts, delivery of the actual commodity (i.e., the stocks in the index) is not permitted. Rather, a cash settlement of price differences is made between the parties.

Stock index futures may be used by speculators who wish to profit from their predictions on the course of the stock market, by allowing such speculation without requiring a major commitment of resources. Thus, stock index futures allow speculators to purchase a diversified portfolio that would reflect such an overall movement in the market, while obtaining a large amount of leverage in their trading, since margin requirements represent a small percentage of the value of the stocks in the index. These futures also provide an opportunity for institutions to hedge their portfolios against market declines. For example, an institution holding a diversified portfolio may believe that the market is going to decline on an overall basis for a period of three months. Rather than liquidate the portfolio, the institution could sell a stock index futures contract. If the market declines as predicted, the profits from the stock index future are then used to offset the loss in the portfolio value of the securities held by the institution.

Jerry W. Markham & David J. Gilberg, "Washington Watch," 6 Corp. L. Rev. 59, 61 (1983). The creation of these securities related products led to clashes between the Commodity Futures Trading Commission (CFTC) and the SEC. The CFTC contended that it had exclusive jurisdiction over all futures products, while the SEC claimed that any product involving a security should fall within its jurisdiction. The two agencies eventually reached a somewhat complex agreement delineating their respective roles. In brief, the SEC was given a veto over stock index contracts but they otherwise remained within the jurisdiction of the CFTC. The SEC was given jurisdiction over options on indexes that could be traded on the securities markets. The two agencies agreed that there would be no futures contracts on the stock of a single corporation, only indexes would be allowed .. See 1 *Phillip McBride Johnson & Thomas Lee Hazen, Commodities Regulation* § 2.02 (3d ed. 2001). (describing agreement between SEC and CFTC—the "Shad–Johnson Accords"). That ban was lifted, however, in 2000 to allow such trading. The regulation of those instruments was to be shared by both the SEC and CFTC. Commodity Futures Modernization Act of 2000, Public L. No. 106–554, 114 Stat. 2763 (Dec. 21, 2000).

The use of stock index products coincided with the development of modern portfolio theory, which posits that no trader, no matter how astute, will be able to pick individual stocks whose gains will out perform the market. This meant that a portfolio containing stocks from all sectors of the economy would out perform a portfolio selected by traders on the basis of their analysis of how those individual stocks would perform. See generally Bevis Longstreth, Fiduciaries, Capital Markets and Regulation: The Current Challenge, 7 Ann. Rev. Banking L. 237 (1988) (discussion of application of modern portfolio theory).

2. Until 2000, the Commodity Exchange Act required all futures and commodity options contracts to be traded on a "contract market" registered as such with the Commodity Futures Trading Commission ("CFTC"), the federal agency charged with regulating those contracts. See 1 *Phillip McBride Johnson & Thomas Lee Hazen, Derivatives Regulation* § 2.02 (2004) (describing regulatory structure). This meant that commodity futures and options were largely confined to the exchanges, and no over-the-counter market for these instruments was envisioned, a regulatory system much unlike that found in the securities markets. That situation changed rapidly, however, as firms began to introduce "hybrid" instruments that contained elements of futures, options and securities. The CFTC struggled for several years with the regulation of those instruments. Large losses experienced in derivative instruments by numerous large institutions in the early 1990s led to further concerns over the regulation of such instruments. Congress thereafter adopted a new three-tiered system of regulation. In one tier were placed the futures exchanges. They were to be the most heavily regulated when retail customers participate in the markets. A second tier involved derivatives transaction facilities for institutions, and the third tier included exempt multilateral transaction execution facilities, which were to be only lightly regulated because they were limited to large institutional traders that could

look out for themselves. Commodity Futures Modernization Act of 2000 ("CFMA"), Public L. No. 106–554, 114 Stat. 2763 (Dec. 21, 2000). However, the exempt commercial markets were re-regulated in 2008 after energy and other commodity prices exploded.

3.   Trading on regulated contract markets continues. Their system of trading is somewhat unique. Orders from customers are transmitted from "futures commission merchants" (the futures industry analog to the broker-dealer in the securities business) to a "floor broker" in the pit on the floor of the contract market. There the order is executed by "open outcry" in auction style trading. The order may be bid on by other floor brokers representing their own customers or by "floor traders" bidding for their own account. This trading is colorful and is often shown on news reports. Take a minute to watch the trading and the hand signals being used by the buyers and sellers, which is often the only way to communicate in the chaotic conditions in some pits. There is no market-maker or specialist in these pits. No one has an obligation to trade for their own account at any time or to maintain a fair and orderly market.

4.   The development of over-the-counter derivatives at the end of the last century was one of the most innovative periods in American finance. These instruments take many forms, but include very popular "swap" transactions. The following example of a swap transaction may best help explain how they work. Assume that a construction company has a floating interest rate that is reset periodically on the basis of some interest rate index such as LIBOR (London Interbank Offered Rate). The construction company is concerned that interest rates will increase, causing a large jump in its interest costs. Separately, a finance company has borrowed a large amount of its funds at a fixed rate. The finance company fears that interest rates will decrease. The finance company, therefore would like to have a floating rate note, rather than a fixed rate. The concerns of both the finance company and the company can be solved through a swap in which they simply agree to exchange payment streams. That is, the two companies will periodically pay each other the difference in the event of an interest rate fluctuation. So, assume that interest rates increase, the finance company will have to pay the construction company the amount of the difference between the fixed rate and the new rate. If interest rates go down, the construction company will pay the finance company an amount equal to the decrease. This is a simple example of a derivative, many are more complex and exotic. See *Frank Partnoy, F.I.A.S.C.O.: Blood in the Water on Wall Street* 94 (1997) (describing a "quantoed constant maturity swap yield curve flattening trade"). These over-the-counter derivatives are largely unregulated and have given rise to concern when companies sustain large losses from their sometimes improperly under-stood risks.

> Indeed, the size and complexity of this market is such that there is a serious danger that these instruments can jeopardize the health of even the most powerful financial institution and can even pose a threat to our financial system. Experience thus proved all too soon that concerns with the dangers presented by derivative instruments were not entirely unwarranted. To cite some examples, the English House of Lords ruled that municipal governments in England that had engaged in

swap transactions were not authorized to do so and that, therefore, the transactions were invalid. Macy's [department store] defaulted on a swap contract that involved some $83 million in interest payments; a unit of Metallgesellschaft A.G. lost some $1.37 billion from mismatched derivative transactions; Kashima Oil in Japan lost some $1.5 billion in currency transactions; Gibson Greetings Inc. lost some $19 million from derivative trading; Kidder Peabody lost some $350 million in "phantom" derivative trades; a New York municipal bond fund failed to disclose that some 40 percent of its assets were invested in derivatives; Procter & Gamble lost over $150 million from derivative trading; Orange County in California lost $140 million; David Askin's Granite Hedge Fund had losses of an estimated $600 million from "market neutral" derivatives; City College of Chicago has sued claiming that it was misled in the purchase of $100 million in derivative obligations; Cargill's hedge funds lost some $100 million from mortgage backed securities; Piper Capital Management was having difficulty valuing its derivatives and lost some $700 million from derivative transactions; HYM Financial Inc. in New Jersey lost all of its capital from derivatives; Dell Computer lost some $26 million from derivative based transactions; Air Products took a loss of $69 million on derivative contracts; an employee investment fund of Atlantic Richfield Company lost $22 million in derivative trades; several mutual funds were compensated by their advisors or brokers for millions of dollars in losses suffered from derivatives transactions; and Mead Corporation lost over $12 million from derivatives trading.

Jerry W. Markham, " 'Confederate Bonds,' 'General Custer,' And the Regulation of Derivative Financial Instruments," 25 Seton Hall L. Rev. 1, 28–31 (1994).

5. The credit default swap ("CDS") market, which was estimated to have a notional amount of $55 trillion in 2008, was raising concerns during the subprime crisis. These instruments provided protection from defaults on credit obligations. For example, Bank A may hedge its exposure from a $10 million loan to company B "by going to C, a dealer in these swaps, who agrees to pay the $10 million to A if B defaults, in exchange for paying an annual premium to C for the protection. A will want collateral from C to be sure it's good for the debt." L. Gordon Crovitz, When Even Good News Worsens a Panic, Wall Street Journal, November 24, 2008, at A17. Congress was looking at banning "naked" CDS obligations in which a participant was merely speculating in debt. It was also considering a requirement that such instruments be traded only through a regulated clearing house in order to provide more transparency and to lessen credit risks from such instruments.

SECTION 7.   FINANCIAL REPORTING
BY PUBLIC COMPANIES

Section 12(g) of the Securities Exchange Act of 1934 requires registration with the SEC of any company that has total assets exceeding

$1,000,000 (raised to $10,000,000 by SEC rule) and a class of equity securities with at least 500 shareholders of record. 15 U.S.C. § 78l. Section 13 of the Securities Exchange Act (15 U.S.C. § 78m) imposes periodic disclosure and other requirements on companies required to register under Section 12. Those companies must file with the SEC audited annual financial reports, unaudited quarterly reports and reports of material events affecting the company whenever they occur. The SEC makes these reports publicly available.

Among the periodic reports that must be filed by an issuer under Section 13 are annual reports on Commission Form 10–K. See 17 C.F.R. § 240.13a–1 (SEC requirement for annual report). These reports must include financial statements, including a balance sheet, that have been audited in accordance with generally accepted accounting principles ("GAAP") by an independent certified public accountant. Information about the company's business and its officers and directors must also be included. The company is required to disclose legal proceedings against it, and the registrant must make quantitative and qualitative information about market risks it is incurring. This rather comprehensive statement, *i.e.*, Form 10–K, provides investors with a wealth of information on the company. The Form 10–K must be signed by the corporation's principal executive, financial and accounting officers and by at least a majority of the board of directors. In adopting this requirement, the SEC stated the reason for it was that the "attention of the private sector, including management, directors, accountants, and attorneys, must ... be refocused towards Exchange Act filings if a sufficient degree of discipline is to be instilled in the system to make it work." Sec.Ex.Act Rel. No. 17114 (Sept. 2, 1980).

To assure more current information, the issuer must file a quarterly financial report with the SEC on Form 10–Q. 17 C.F.R. § 240.13a–13. This financial statement need not be audited because such a requirement would delay its filing and thereby impair the usefulness of that information to investors. Another important requirement is that the issuer file a Form 8–K with the SEC promptly after the occurrence of certain material events. 17 C.F.R. § 240.13a–11. This assures that investors are advised promptly of such events; they need not await the filing of the quarterly or annual reports before being advised of such information. Disclosure is required under Form 8–K of such things as a change in control of the registrant, resignations of directors, changes in accountants and bankruptcy.

NOTES

1. The decision to go public is often tempting for small companies seeking to expand or to provide a market for their owner's stock. That decision should not be lightly made. The burden of filing SEC financial reports is considerable and expensive. Further, the company's operations will be subject to continuous scrutiny by the SEC and investors. Serious penalties

may be imposed by the SEC for violations and criminal prosecutions are not uncommon. Public companies are also often the subject of lawsuits brought by investors under the federal securities laws. Indeed, as will be seen later in Chapter 12, special legislation had to be enacted to protect public companies from abusive suits.

2.   If you would like to examine the financial reports of a public company in which you have an interest, they are available Online through the SEC's EDGAR filing system at: www.sec.gov/edgar. Take a minute to review the company's balance sheet. It will be more complex, than the one set forth in Chapter 22, but the structure is the same. Do you understand how the company's assets are valued? Check the footnotes for that information.

3.   The Sarbanes–Oxley Act that was enacted in 2003 in the wake of the collapse of the Enron Corp. directed the SEC to consider real time disclosures. This would mean that corporations would be required to disclose information as it became available to them, rather than wait for the filing dates mandated for quarterly and annual reports. The SEC also accelerated the time period in which quarterly and annual financial statements must be filed after the close of an accounting period, cutting that filing time by a third. The reach of Form 8–K was expanded to require additional disclosures between the filing of quarterly and annual reports. Those additional disclosures included termination of material agreements, director and officer resignations and appointments and changes to by-laws. These increased disclosure requirements were expected to double the number of 8–K filings, which previously numbered about 80,000 annually.

SECTION 8.   SEC PROXY REGULATIONS

In Chapter 6, we examined the regulation of proxies under state law. The SEC was also given the authority to regulate proxy solicitations for the stock of publicly owned corporations.

TREATISE ON THE LAW OF SECURITIES REGULATION

Thomas Lee Hazen.
§ 10.1   (5th ed. 2005).

With the passage of the Securities Exchange Act in 1934, Congress took note that a number of the great corporate frauds had been perpetrated through management solicitation of proxies without indicating to the shareholders the nature of any matters to be voted upon. Accordingly, section 14 of the Act [15 U.S.C. § 78n] was included in the legislation in order to regulate the shareholder voting machinery for companies that are subject to both the registration requirements of section 12 of the Act and the reporting requirements of section 13. Although focusing on the voting process, the federal proxy rules do not address substantive voting rights which remain a matter of state law and is generally determined by the law of the state of incorporation.

There are four primary aspects of SEC proxy regulation. First, by virtue of section 14(a) there must be full and fair disclosure of all material facts with regard to any management submitted proposals that will be subject to a shareholder vote. Secondly, material misstatements, omissions, and fraud in connection with the solicitation of proxies are prohibited, ... Thirdly, the federal proxy regulation facilitates shareholder solicitation of proxies as management is not only required to submit relevant shareholders proposals in its own proxy statements, but also to allow the proponents to explain their position in the face of any management opposition. Fourthly, the proxy rules mandate full disclosure in non-management proxy materials and thus are significant in corporate control struggles and contested take-over attempts. . . . The federal proxy regulation under the Securities Exchange Act of 1934 supplements the requirements of state corporate law. Because of this interaction the proxy rules can be a focus for federal-state tension in the face of increasing federalization. The SEC plays a significant role in voting related disclosure issues. . . .

———

Section 14(a) of the 1934 Act gives the SEC virtually a "blank check" to write rules governing the solicitation of proxies for shareholder meetings. Since the subject of proxy solicitation has become intimately intertwined with questions relating to shareholder action, it is generally treated at considerable length in the course on Corporation Law, rather than in Securities Regulation. The following is a brief summary of the major features of the proxy rules.

Section 14 makes it unlawful for a company registered under § 12 to solicit proxies from its shareholders "in contravention of such rules and regulations as the Commission may prescribe as necessary or appropriate in the public interest or for the protection of investors." In 1964, the reach of § 14 was broadened by the addition of § 14(c), under which a company, even if it does not solicit proxies from its shareholders in connection with a meeting, must furnish them with information "substantially equivalent" to that which would be required if it did solicit proxies. Under § 14(f), added in 1968, a corporation must also make disclosures to shareholders when a majority of its board of directors is replaced by action of the directors, without a shareholders' meeting, in connection with the transfer of a controlling stock interest.

Disclosure. Under this authority, the Commission has promulgated detailed regulations prescribing the form of proxy and the information to be furnished to shareholders. Prior to every meeting of its security holders, a registered company must furnish each of them with a "proxy statement" containing the information specified in Schedule 14A, together with a form of proxy on which the security holder can indicate his approval or disapproval of each proposal expected to be presented at the meeting. Rules 14a–3, and 14–4. Where securities are registered in the names of brokers, banks or nominees, the company must inquire as to the beneficial ownership of the securities, furnish sufficient copies of the proxy statement for distribution to all of the beneficial owners, and pay the reasonable expenses of such distribution. Rule 14a–3(d).

Definitive copies of the proxy statement and form of proxy must be filed with the SEC at the time they are first mailed to security holders. In addition, if the proxy solicitation relates to any matters other than election of directors, approval of accountants, or shareholder proposals, preliminary copies of both documents must be filed with the SEC ten days before they are to be mailed. Rule 14a–6. Although the proxy statement does not have to become "effective" in the same manner as a 1933 Act registration statement, the SEC will often comment on, and insist on changes in, the proxy statement before it is mailed.

Proxy Contests. The SEC proxy rules apply to all solicitations of proxies, consents or authorizations from security holders, by the management or anyone else, subject to exceptions specified in Rule 14a–2. When there is a contest with respect to election or removal of directors, Rule 14a–11 imposes special procedural requirements, and calls for the filing with the Commission of additional information specified in Schedule 14B.

Voting by Money Managers. Institutional investors own a large amount of stock in publicly traded companies and thus can exert significant voting power. The SEC amended its regulations in 2003 to require investment advisers to vote proxies for the stock they manage and to disclose their voting policies. Investment Adviser Act Rule 206(4)–6 (17 C.F.R. § 275.206(4)–6). This has raised several concerns. Many money managers are often in no position to substitute their judgment for that of corporate management. They manage broad scale holdings and cannot inform themselves on every corporate vote. There are also conflict concerns where money mangers have different strategies for different customers. The SEC has asserted that these problems could be avoided by relying on the advice of independent services that promote good corporate governance. Egan Jones Proxy Services, SEC No–Act Letter, May 27, 2004.

———

It is important to understand the interplay between state and federal law with respect to shareholder voting. The state law determines the basic corporate governance rules while the federal securities laws impose disclosure requirements over and above the state law requirements. Sometimes there is an overlap where both state and federal law apply. Consider, for example, SEC Rule 14a–7 gives shareholders access to shareholder lists so they can communicate with fellow shareholders. This federal right supplements the state law that grants a right to inspect corporate books and records (see Chapter 9 supra).

———

TREATISE ON THE LAW OF SECURITIES REGULATION

Thomas Lee Hazen.
§ 10.2 (5th ed. 2005).

The applicable Securities and Exchange Commission rule takes a broad view of the terms "solicit" and "solicitation" so as to include in the definition "any request for a proxy whether or not accompanied by or included in a form of any request to execute or not to execute, or to revoke, a proxy; [and] the furnishing of any communication to security holders under circumstances reasonably calculated to result in the procurement, withholding or revocation of a proxy." 17 C.F.R. § 240.14a–1(f). This definition has been liberally interpreted by the courts to include materials such as open letters to regulatory bodies which although not directed towards shareholders, are reasonably calculated to affect a reasonable shareholder's voting decision. * * * Similarly, a newsletter urging shareholders to reject a shareholder proposal is a solicitation subject to the SEC filing requirements. Communications which clearly serve another function, even occurring around the same time as a shareholder vote, will not be subject to the proxy rules simply because of their timing and possible tangential effect on a voting decision. Thus, for example, research recommendations by brokerage firms may not implicate the proxy rules even though they contain reference to issues that may be relevant to any upcoming vote by the shareholders of a company mentioned in the research report. * * *

SEC Rule 14a–3 sets forth the types of information that must be included in materials used for proxy solicitations. All nonexempt proxy solicitations must be accompanied or preceded by the information required in Schedule 14A. Schedule 14A requires the following information, in addition to the date, time, and place of the meeting. The first page of the proxy statement must disclose the approximate date on which the proxy statement and the form of proxy were first given to securities holders. The proxy statement must include the deadline for submitting shareholder proposals for inclusion in the proxy statement and form of proxy for the next annual meeting. In addition the proxy statement must state the last date for submission of shareholder proposals for the next annual meeting irrespective of their inclusion in management's proxy statement. The proxy statement must also disclose whether the proxies solicited are revocable and if so, the manner in which it may be revoked. * * * The proxy statement must contain a description of the person making the solicitation, including identifying who is bearing the cost of the solicitation. The proxy statement must contain disclosures relating to interests of directors, officers and "participants" in matters to be voted upon.

The proxy statement must also list all of the company's voting securities and principal holders thereof. The record date for determining which shareholders are entitled to vote and explanation of cumulative voting rights, if any must also be disclosed in the proxy statement. If any action is to be taken with respect to election of directors, the proxy statement must disclose and explain the nominees' relationship to affiliated companies and interest in issuer's activities.

Management's proxy statement must disclose the compensation of the company's executive officers and directors. Each year the shareholders of a publicly held company are entitled to disclosure of the following: (1) the direct and indirect compensation paid to the top executives; (2) a comparison chart, comparing the company's executive compensation stock price performance with that of comparable companies over the past five years; and (3) the compensation committee's report of policies and criteria used in fixing executive compensation. * * *

Schedule 14A's disclosure requirements apply both to management's proxy statement and proxy solicitations by others. When the proxy solicitation relates to the annual meeting of security holders, where directors are to be elected, an annual report must accompany or precede a proxy solicitation on behalf of the issuer. The proxy rules permit presentation of a "short slate" of directors. The SEC's decision to permit short slates of directors was designed to encourage shareholder participation in the election process by providing a more likely opportunity for minority representation on the board. * * *

Rule 14a–4 sets forth the appropriate form for the proxy itself as opposed to solicitation materials. For example, boldface type must indicate whether or not the proxy is solicited on behalf of the issuer's management. The proxy must also provide the person solicited with an opportunity to vote for or against proposals (management may indicate which proposals it supports) as well as the ability to abstain or withhold authority from voting as to any matters. In the case of a shareholder election of directors, the proxy must leave room for write-in candidates. In addition to seeking proxies on specific issues, the proxy rules permit the solicitation of discretionary proxies. * * *

Rule 14a–5 provides guidance as to the presentation of information in a proxy statement, including the size and form of printed material. In many cases, five preliminary copies of each proxy statement and the form of the proxy to be used must be filed with the SEC at least ten business days prior to the first date on which they are to be sent; however, the preliminary copies need not be filed if the proxy solicitation pertains to the regular annual meeting (or a special meeting held in lieu of the annual meeting) and the only matters to be considered are the election of directors, or approval or ratification of auditors and/or shareholder proposals. Once the initial proxy statement is actually sent to the shareholders, eight definitive copies must be filed with the Commission and three additional copies must at the same time be filed with each national securities exchange listing the issuer's security. Five preliminary copies of any additional solicitation material relating to either the same meeting or same subject matter must be filed with the Commission at least two business days prior to the date that the material is first sent out unless, upon a showing of good cause, the Commission authorizes a shorter period. While the filing requirements apply to supplemental literature, they do not apply to replies to inquiries by individual security holders requesting information. In making the appropriate SEC filings, it is necessary, by labeling of "preliminary copies", to distinguish between them and definitive copies of the material actually sent. * * *

In 1992, the Commission revised its proxy rules for solicitation materials other than the proxy statement and, among other things, eliminated the requirement that such proxy solicitation materials be filed in advance of their use. Issuers and other proxy contestants may now commence solicitation based on a preliminary proxy statement so long as a form of proxy is not provided to the shareholders until dissemination and filing of the definitive proxy statement. The 1992 rules also permit participants in proxy solicitations to make appeal to shareholders through the use of press releases and other public dissemination without a prefiling requirement. These rules were motivated by concerns of institutional investors desiring to participate more fully in the corporate governance of publicly traded companies.

LONG ISLAND LIGHTING CO. v. BARBASH

779 F.2d 793 (2d Cir.1985).

CARDAMONE, CIRCUIT JUDGE:

A Long Island utility furnishing that area with power has scheduled a stockholders meeting for Thursday December 12, 1985. It has been embroiled in public controversy over its construction of the Shoreham Nuclear Power Plant and adverse publicity intensified recently because of extended loss of service to customers arising from damages to the transmission system caused by Hurricane Gloria.

In this setting, the company, believing that several groups had begun to solicit proxies during October in anticipation of the upcoming stockholders meeting, brought suit to enjoin them. The district court judge first slowed the matter by adjourning the case until the fall election was over, and then speeded it up by directing discovery to be completed in one day. Such handling only demonstrates again that in the law it is wise—even when expeditious action is required—to make haste slowly.

Long Island Lighting Company (LILCO) brings this expedited appeal from a November 8, 1985 order of the United States District Court for the Eastern District of New York (Weinstein, Ch.J.) that granted summary judgment dismissing LILCO's complaint against the Steering Committee of Citizens to Replace LILCO (the Citizens Committee), John W. Matthews and Island Insulation Corp. LILCO brought this action to enjoin defendants' alleged violations of § 14(a) of the Securities Exchange Act of 1934 and Rules 14a–9, 17 C.F.R. § 240.14a–9 and 14a–11, 17 C.F.R.

240.14a–11, promulgated under that statute, that govern proxy solicitations. The complaint alleges that defendants have committed such violations by publishing a false and misleading advertisement in connection with a special meeting of LILCO's shareholders scheduled for the purpose of electing a new LILCO Board of Directors. For the reasons explained below, this matter is remanded to the district court.

Plaintiff LILCO is a New York electric company serving Nassau and Suffolk Counties on Long Island, New York. Its common and preferred stocks are registered in accordance with Section 12(b) of the Securities Exchange Act and are traded on the New York Stock Exchange. Defendant John W. Matthews was an unsuccessful candidate for Nassau County Executive in the election held November 5, 1985. During the campaign he strongly opposed LILCO and its operation of the Shoreham Nuclear Power Plant. As an owner of 100 shares of LILCO's preferred stock and a manager of an additional 100 shares of common stock held by his company, Island Insulation Corp., Matthews initiated a proxy contest for the purpose of electing a majority of LILCO's Board of Directors. The stated purpose of the other defendants, the Citizens Committee, is to replace LILCO with a municipally owned utility company. The Citizens Committee was formed prior to this litigation, in order to challenge LILCO's construction of the Shoreham atomic energy plant, its service and its rates.

LILCO filed its complaint on October 21, 1985 alleging that defendants published a materially false and misleading advertisement in *Newsday*, a Long Island newspaper, and ran false and misleading radio advertisements throughout the New York area. The ads criticized LILCO's management and encouraged citizens to replace LILCO with a state-run company. The complaint sought an injunction against further alleged solicitation of LILCO shareholders until the claimed false and misleading statements had been corrected and a Schedule 14B had been filed. The district court granted LILCO an expedited hearing on its appeal from Magistrate Scheindlin's decision denying expedited discovery and also set for hearing defendants' motions to dismiss the complaint pursuant to Fed.R.Civ.P. 12(b)(6).

On October 30, 1985 Chief Judge Weinstein adjourned the hearing until November 6 in order to prevent interference with Matthews' political campaign. The district court directed the defendants to bring the requested documents to the hearing on that date and told Matthews and others whom LILCO wished to depose to be available for such discovery. At the November 6 hearing the district judge directed LILCO's counsel to question Matthews under oath and overruled counsel's objections that he was unprepared to examine Matthews and that he had no prior opportunity to review the defendants' documents. The trial court also refused LILCO's request to question other defendants and told counsel that it must limit its questions to the alleged "conspiracy" between Matthews and the other defendants. Two days after this hearing the district court issued its Preliminary Memorandum Dismissing Complaint. Treating defendant's motion to dismiss as one for summary judgment, the district court granted summary judgment in favor of defendants on the ground that the proxy rules did not apply to the advertisements. This appeal followed.

LILCO argues first, that in view of the necessity in every case to determine whether a communication constitutes a "solicitation" under the proxy rates, the district court abused its discretion by limiting LILCO's opportunity for discovery. Second, LILCO asserts that the district court erroneously held that communications to shareholders through general and indirect publications can in no circumstances constitute "solicitations" under the proxy rules. Finally, LILCO contests the district court's view that this construction of the proxy rules is necessary to render them compatible with the First Amendment. * * *

In our view the district court further erred in holding that the proxy rules cannot cover communications appearing in publications of general circulation and that are indirectly addressed to shareholders. Regulation 14(a) of the Securities Exchange Act governs the solicitation of proxies with respect to the securities of publicly held companies, with enumerated exceptions set forth in the rules. 17 C.F.R. § 240.14a–1 *et seq.* Proxy rules promulgated by the Securities Exchange Commission (SEC) regulate as proxy solicitations:

(1) any request for a proxy whether or not accompanied by or included in a form of proxy;

(2) any request to execute or not to execute, or to revoke, a proxy; or

(3) the furnishing of a form of proxy or other communications to security holders under circumstances reasonably calculated to result in the procurement, withholding or revocation of a proxy.

Rule 14a–1, 17 C.F.R. § 240.14a–1.

These rules apply not only to direct requests to furnish, revoke or withhold proxies, but also to communications which may indirectly accomplish such a result or constitute a step in a chain of communications designed ultimately to accomplish such a result. *Securities and Exchange Commission v. Okin,* 132 F.2d 784, 786 (2d Cir.1943) (letter to shareholders was within the scope of the proxy rules where it was alleged that it was "a step in a campaign whose purpose it was to get [defendant] elected an officer of the company; it was to pave the way for an out-and-out solicitation later.").

The question in every case is whether the challenged communication, seen in the totality of circumstances, is "reasonably calculated" to influence the shareholders' votes. *See id.; Trans World Corp. v. Odyssey Partners,* 561 F.Supp. 1315, 1319 (S.D.N.Y.1983). Determination of the purpose of the communication depends upon the nature of the communication and the circumstances under which it was distributed. *Brown v. Chicago, Rock Island & Pacific R.R.,* 328 F.2d 122 (7th Cir.1964). In *Studebaker Corporation v. Gittlin,* 360 F.2d 692, 694 (2d Cir.1966), the defendant solicited authorizations from shareholders to obtain a share-holder list in the course of a proxy fight. Because the authorizations were sought only for the purpose of seeking future proxies, the court held that the authorizations were also covered by the proxy rules. *Id.* at 696.

Deciding whether a communication is a proxy solicitation does not depend upon whether it is "targeted directly" at shareholders. *See* Rule 14a–6(g), 17 C.F.R. § 240.14a–6(g) (requiring that solicitations in the form of "speeches, press releases, and television scripts" be filed with the SEC). As the SEC correctly notes in its amicus brief, it would "permit easy evasion of the proxy rules" to exempt all general and indirect communications to shareholders, and this is true whether or not the communication purports to address matters of "public interest." *See Medical Comm. for Human Rights v. SEC,* 432 F.2d 659 (D.C.Cir.1970) (applying proxy rules to shareholder's proposal to prohibit company from manufacturing napalm during the Vietnam War). The SEC's authority to regulate proxy solicitations has traditionally extended into matters of public interest.

The extent to which the activities of the defendants amount to a solicitation of the proxies of shareholders of LILCO may determine whether or not their actions are protected by the First Amendment. Therefore, it is unnecessary to express an opinion on any claim of privilege under the First Amendment until there has been a determination of the "solicitation" issue as a result of further proceedings in the district court.

Because discovery here was so abbreviated and the district court's determination was predicated on a mistaken notion of what constitutes a proxy solicitation and on the relationship between the proxy rules and the First Amendment, the case must be remanded to the district court. LILCO represented during oral argument before us that—if given the opportunity—its discovery could be swiftly completed. We suggest that on remand the district court limit LILCO's discovery to an appropriate period. Even this expedited schedule will obviously conflict with the scheduled stockholders meeting of December 12. LILCO advised the Court by letter dated November 22, 1985 that after reasonable discovery it also wanted an opportunity to move for a preliminary injunction. Thus, in light of its request the meeting should probably be postponed and, if necessary, stayed by order of the district court. Finally, this panel retains jurisdiction over this matter to the extent that after the district court has had an opportunity to conduct its proceedings and rule on the merits, we will address the issues raised on appeal.

In consideration of the time constraints, the mandate of the Court shall issue forthwith.

WINTER, CIRCUIT JUDGE, DISSENTING:

In order to avoid a serious first amendment issue, I would construe the federal regulations governing the solicitation of proxies as inapplicable to the newspaper advertisement in question. *See Lowe v. Securities and Exchange Commission,* 472 U.S.181 (1985). Further discovery would then be unnecessary, and I therefore respectfully dissent.

First, the facts. The Long Island Lighting Company (LILCO) is a state-regulated public utility. It is currently the subject of controversy in its service area concerning the safety of a nuclear power plant, the cost of constructing that plant, the level of electricity rates, and service difficulties resulting from a recent hurricane.

One of LILCO's principal antagonists is John W. Matthews, a defendant in this litigation. During the fall of 1985, Matthews was the Democratic candidate for County Executive in Nassau County and appears to have focused much of his campaign upon LILCO issues. During this campaign, Matthews purchased a sufficient number of shares of LILCO's preferred stock to force a special shareholders' meeting pursuant to its Charter. On October 9, 1985, he made a demand for such a meeting. The next day, a corporation that is controlled by Matthews and owns LILCO common stock asked to inspect and copy LILCO's list of common stockholders. The stated purpose of this request was to enable it and Matthews to communicate with LILCO shareholders with regard to the election of LILCO's Board and to whether LILCO should be sold to Nassau and Suffolk Counties.

Another group of antagonists are the other individual defendants, who constitute a group styled "Citizens to Replace LILCO." On October 15 the Citizens to Replace LILCO published the newspaper advertisement that has given rise to the present litigation. That advertisement accused LILCO of mismanagement and of attempting to pass through to ratepayers needless costs relating to construction of the nuclear power plant. It also noted that a publicly owned power authority would not have to pay dividends to stockholders. The advertisement argued strenuously that ratepayers would be better off if a Long Island Power Authority were created to replace LILCO as a supplier of power. It asked readers to join the Committee and to give it financial support.

LILCO's complaint alleges that Matthews and the defendant members of the Citizens to Replace LILCO acted in a concerted fashion to publish this advertisement in order to influence the exercise of proxies by LILCO shareholders. It alleges that the advertisement was false and misleading in numerous respects relating to alleged advantages for ratepayers in the creation of a public power authority. Claiming a violation of federal proxy regulations, LILCO asked for an injunction prohibiting the defendants from soliciting proxies until they make appropriate filings with the Securities and Exchange Commission and correct the false and misleading statements in the ad. The relief requested would prevent further publication of the ad.

After the truncated discovery described by my colleagues, the district judge denied the injunction and granted summary judgment for the defendants. He stated that in his view: "Even if defendants did conspire to influence the outcome of the proxy fight ... this fact would be irrelevant." The case as framed on appeal thus raises two issues. First is the question, fully briefed and argued by the parties and *amici,* whether the federal regulation of proxy materials applies to newspaper advertisements such as the one at issue and, if so, whether those regulations so applied do not violate the first amendment. Second is the question whether, assuming that the proxy regulations do apply and pass constitutional muster, the case should be remanded for further discovery.

It is clear, of course, that the second issue—the need for further discovery—cannot be determined until the relationship of the proxy regulations to the first amendment has been resolved. If, for example, the first amendment protects such advertisements regardless of the motive of those who purchase them, further discovery would be irrelevant. My colleagues, asserting that "the district court's determination was predicated on a mistaken notion ... on the relationship between the proxy rules and the First Amendment," believe such motives are relevant. I respectfully disagree.

The content of the Committee's advertisement is of critical importance. First, it is on its face addressed solely to the public. Second, it makes no mention either of proxies or of the shareholders' meeting demanded by Matthews. Third, the issues the ad addresses are quintessentially matters of public political debate, namely, whether a public power authority would provide cheaper electricity than LILCO. Claims of LILCO mismanagement are discussed solely in the context of their effect on its customers. Finally, the ad was published in the middle of an election campaign in which LILCO's future was an issue.

On these facts, therefore, LILCO's claim raises a constitutional issue of the first magnitude. It asks nothing less than that a federal court act as a censor, empowered to determine the truth or falsity of the ad's claims about the merits of public power and to enjoin further advocacy containing false claims. We need not resolve this constitutional issue, however.

Where advertisements are critical of corporate conduct but are facially directed solely to the public, in no way mention the exercise of proxies, and debate only matters of conceded public concern, I would construe federal proxy regulation as inapplicable, whatever the motive of those who purchase them. This position, which is strongly suggested by relevant case law, *see infra,* maximizes public debate, avoids embroiling the federal judiciary in determining the rightness or wrongness of conflicting positions on public policy, and does not significantly impede achievement of Congress' goal that shareholders exercise proxy rights on the basis of accurate information.

It is of course true that LILCO shareholders may be concerned about public allegations of mismanagement on LILCO's part. However, shareholders are most unlikely to be misled into thinking that advertisements of this kind, particularly when purchased in the name of a committee so obviously disinterested in the return on investment to LILCO's shareholders, are either necessarily accurate or authoritative sources of information about LILCO's management. Such advertisements, which in no way suggest internal reforms shareholders might bring about through the exercise of their proxies, are sheer political advocacy and would be so recognized by any reasonable shareholder.

To be sure, the fact that a corporation has become a target of political advocacy might well justify unease among shareholders. No one seriously asserts, however, that the right to criticize corporate behavior as a matter of public concern diminishes as shareholders' meetings become imminent.

* * * I believe the advertisement in question is not subject to federal proxy regulation regardless of Matthews' participation in its publication or the motives of its authors. Further discovery is irrelevant in my view, and I would affirm.

NOTES

1. See generally Brown v. Chicago, Rock Island & Pacific Railroad Co., 328 F.2d 122 (7th Cir.1964) (open letter to promote public support for railroad merger held not to be a proxy solicitation). The SEC amended its proxy rules after the decision in *LILCO* to narrow the definition of what constitutes a proxy solicitation that would be subject to the proxy rules. A statement by a person who does not otherwise engage in a proxy solicitation stating how that individual will vote is exempted if the statement "is made by means of speeches in public forums, press releases, publications or broadcast opinions, statements, or advertisements appearing in a broadcast media, or newspaper, magazine or other bona fide publication disseminated on a regular basis...." 17 C.F.R. § 240.14a–1(*l*)(2)(iv). Also exempted are certain solicitations by persons who do not seek to act as proxy for a security holder. This exemption does not apply to officers and directors of the issuer, those opposing mergers and certain large shareholders or persons who would receive a benefit not available to other shareholders. 17 C.F.R. § 240.14a–2(b). Would any of these exemptions exclude the solicitations at issue in LILCO?

2. There are two immediate consequences of a communication falling within the definition of solicitation. First, there are filing requirements either before or after the solicitation is made. See SEC Rules 14a–2(c), (g). Second, the solicitation is subject to Rule 14a–9's prohibitions against materially misleading statements.

3. In order to encourage communication among institutional investors, Rule 14a–2(b)(2) excludes from the federal proxy regulation solicitations not made on behalf of the company where the number of persons solicited is not more than ten.

SECTION 9. SHAREHOLDER PROXY PROPOSALS

Under SEC Rule 14a–8 (17 C.F.R. § 240.14a–8), if a shareholder of a registered company that gives timely notice to the management of his intention to present a proposal for action at a forthcoming meeting, management must include the proposal, with a supporting statement of not more than 500 words, in its proxy statement and afford security holders an opportunity to vote for or against it in the management's proxy. To be eligible to have such a proposal included, the investor's holdings must be worth at least $2,000 or constitute 1%, of the securities entitled to be voted at the meeting.

Rule 14a–8 has been extensively utilized by proponents of "shareholder democracy," to require inclusion of proposals relating to management compensation, conduct of annual meetings, shareholder voting rights, and similar matters. It has also been utilized by persons opposed to the Vietnam war, discrimination, pollution, and other perceived evils, to attempt to force changes in company policies that affect those matters.

LOVENHEIM v. IROQUOIS BRANDS, LTD.

618 F.Supp. 554 (D.D.C.1985).

Plaintiff Peter C. Lovenheim, owner of two hundred shares of common stock in Iroquois Brands, Ltd. (hereinafter "Iroquois/Delaware"), seeks to bar Iroquois/Delaware from excluding from the proxy materials being sent to all shareholders in preparation for an upcoming shareholder meeting information concerning a proposed resolution he intends to offer at the meeting. Mr. Lovenheim's proposed resolution relates to the procedure used to force-feed geese for production of pate de foie gras in France,[2] a type of pate imported by Iroquois/Delaware. Specifically, his resolution calls upon the Directors of Iroquois/Delaware to:

> form a committee to study the methods by which its French supplier produces pate de foie gras, and report to the shareholders its findings and opinions, based on expert consultation, on whether this production method causes undue distress, pain or suffering to the animals involved and, if so, whether further distribution of this product should be discontinued until a more humane production method is developed.

Mr. Lovenheim's right to compel Iroquois/Delaware to insert information concerning his proposal in the proxy materials turns on the applicability of section 14(a) of the Securities Exchange Act of 1934 and the shareholder proposal rule promulgated by the Securities and Exchange Commission ("SEC"), Rule 14a–8.... Iroquois/Delaware has refused to

---

2. Pate de foie gras is made from the liver of geese. According to Mr. Lovenheim's affidavit, force-feeding is frequently used in order to expand the liver and thereby produce a larger quantity of pate. Mr. Lovenheim's affidavit also contains a description of the force-feeding process:

Force-feeding usually begins when the geese are four months old. On some farms where feeding is mechanized, the bird's body and wings are placed in a metal brace and its neck is stretched. Through a funnel inserted 10–12 inches down the throat of the goose, a machine pumps up to 400 grams of corn-based mash into its stomach. An elastic band around the goose's throat prevents regurgitation. When feeding is manual, a handler uses a funnel and stick to force the mash down.

Affidavit of Peter C. Lovenheim at § 7. Plaintiff contends that such force-feeding is a form of cruelty to animals. *Id.* Plaintiff has offered no evidence that force-feeding is used by Iroquois/Delaware's supplier in producing the pate imported by Iroquois/Delaware. However his proposal calls upon the committee he seeks to create to investigate this question.

allow information concerning Mr. Lovenheim's proposal to be included in proxy materials being sent in connection with the next annual shareholders meeting. In doing so, Iroquois/Delaware relies on an exception to the general requirement of Rule 14a–8, Rule 14a–8(c)(5). That exception provides that an issuer of securities "may omit a proposal and any statement in support thereof" from its proxy statement and form of proxy:

> if the proposal relates to operations which account for less than 5 percent of the issuer's total assets at the end of its most recent fiscal year, and for less than 5 percent of its net earnings and gross sales for its most recent fiscal year, and is not otherwise significantly related to the issuer's business.

Rule 14a–8(c)(5).

* * * In light of the above discussion of the service and jurisdiction issues, the likelihood of plaintiff's prevailing in this litigation turns primarily on the applicability to plaintiff's proposal of the exception to the shareholder proposal rule contained in Rule 14a–8(c)(5).

Iroquois/Delaware's reliance on the argument that this exception applies is based on the following information contained in the affidavit of its president: Iroquois/Delaware has annual revenues of $141 million with $6 million in annual profits and $78 million in assets. In contrast, its pate de foie gras sales were just $79,000 last year, representing a net loss on pate sales of $3,121. Iroquois/Delaware has only $34,000 in assets related to pate. Thus none of the company's net earnings and less than .05 percent of its assets are implicated by plaintiff's proposal. These levels are obviously far below the five percent threshold set forth in the first portion of the exception claimed by Iroquois/Delaware.

Plaintiff does not contest that his proposed resolution relates to a matter of little economic significance to Iroquois/Delaware. Nevertheless he contends that the Rule 14a–8(c)(5) exception is not applicable as it cannot be said that his proposal "is not otherwise significantly related to the issuer's business" as is required by the final portion of that exception. In other words, plaintiff's argument that Rule 14a–8 does not permit omission of his proposal rests on the assertion that the rule and statute on which it is based do not permit omission merely because a proposal is not economically significant where a proposal has "ethical or social significance."[8]

---

8. The assertion that the proposal is significant in an ethical and social sense relies on plaintiff's argument that "the very availability of a market for products that may be obtained through the inhumane force-feeding of geese cannot help but contribute to the continuation of such treatment." Plaintiff's brief characterizes the humane treatment of animals as among the foundations of western culture and cites in support of this view the Seven Laws of Noah, an animal protection statute enacted by the Massachusetts Bay Colony in 1641, numerous federal statutes enacted since 1877, and animal protection laws existing in all fifty states and the District of Columbia. An additional indication of the significance of plaintiff's proposal is the support of such leading organizations in the field of animal care as the American Society for the Prevention of Cruelty to Animals and The Humane Society of the United States for measures aimed at discontinuing use of force-feeding.

Iroquois/Delaware challenges plaintiff's view that ethical and social proposals cannot be excluded even if they do not meet the economic or five percent test. Instead, Iroquois/Delaware views the exception solely in economic terms as permitting omission of any proposals relating to a de minimis share of assets and profits. Iroquois/Delaware asserts that since corporations are economic entities, only an economic test is appropriate.

The Court would note that the applicability of the Rule 14a–8(c)(5) exception to Mr. Lovenheim's proposal represents a close question given the lack of clarity in the exception itself. In effect, plaintiff relies on the word "otherwise," suggesting that it indicates the drafters of the rule intended that other noneconomic tests of significance be used. Iroquois/Delaware relies on the fact that the rule examines other significance in relation to the issuer's business. Because of the apparent ambiguity of the rule, the Court considers the history of the shareholder proposal rule in determining the proper interpretation of the most recent version of that rule.

Prior to 1983, paragraph 14a–8(c)(5) excluded proposals "not significantly related to the issuer's business" but did not contain an objective economic significance test such as the five percent of sales, assets, and earnings specified in the first part of the current version. Although a series of SEC decisions through 1976 allowing issuers to exclude proposals challenging compliance with the Arab economic boycott of Israel allowed exclusion if the issuer did less than one percent of their business with Arab countries or Israel, the Commission stated later in 1976 that it did "not believe that subparagraph (c)(5) should be hinged solely on the economic relativity of a proposal." Securities Exchange Act Release No. 12,999, 41 Fed. Reg. 52,994, 52,997 (1976). Thus the Commission required inclusion "in many situations in which the related business comprised less than one percent" of the company's revenues, profits or assets "where the proposal has raised *policy questions* important enough to be considered 'significantly related' to the issuer's business."

As indicated above, the 1983 revision adopted the five percent test of economic significance in an effort to create a more objective standard. Nevertheless, in adopting this standard, the Commission stated that proposals will be includable notwithstanding their "failure to reach the specified economic thresholds if a significant relationship to the issuer's business is demonstrated on the face of the resolution or supporting statement." Securities Exchange Act Release No. 19,135, 47 Fed.Reg. 47,420, 47,428 (1982). Thus it seems clear based on the history of the rule that "the meaning of 'significantly related' is not *limited* to economic significance." Comment, *1983 Amendments, supra* note 10 at 183 (emphasis in original).

The only decision in this Circuit cited by the parties relating to the scope of section 14 and the shareholder proposal rule is *Medical Committee for Human Rights v. SEC,* 432 F.2d 659 (D.C.Cir.1970).[12] That case

---

12. [While the case was pending, management voluntarily included the proposal in its proxy statement]. The *Medical Committee* decision was vacated as moot by the Supreme Court after the

concerned an effort by shareholders of Dow Chemical Company to advise other shareholders of their proposal directed at prohibiting Dow's production of napalm. Dow had relied on the counterpart of the 14a–8(c)(5) exemption then in effect to exclude the proposal from proxy materials and the SEC accepted Dow's position without elaborating on its basis for doing so. In remanding the matter back to the SEC for the Commission to provide the basis for its decision, the Court noted what it termed "substantial questions" as to whether an interpretation of the shareholder proposal rule "which permitted omission of [a] proposal as one motivated primarily by *general* political or social concerns would conflict with the congressional intent underlying section 14(a) of the [Exchange] Act." (emphasis in original).

Iroquois/Delaware attempts to distinguish *Medical Committee for Human Rights* as a case where a company sought to exclude a proposal that, unlike Mr. Lovenheim's proposal, was economically significant merely because the motivation of the proponents was political. The argument is not without appeal given the fact that the *Medical Committee* Court was confronted with a regulation that contained no reference to economic significance. Yet the *Medical Committee* decision contains language suggesting that the Court assumed napalm was not economically significant to Dow:

The management of Dow Chemical Company is repeatedly quoted in sources which include the company's own publications as proclaiming that the decision to continue manufacturing and marketing napalm was made not *because* of business considerations, but *in spite* of them; that management in essence decided to pursue a course of activity which generated little profit for the shareholders.... *Id.* at 681 (emphasis in original).

This Court need not consider, as the *Medical Committee* decision implied, whether a rule allowing exclusion of all proposals not meeting specified levels of economic significance violates the scope of section 14(a) of the Exchange Act. Whether or not the Securities and Exchange Commission could properly adopt such a rule, the Court cannot ignore the history of the rule which reveals no decision by the Commission to limit the determination to the economic criteria relied on by Iroquois/Delaware. The Court therefore holds that in light of the ethical and social significance of plaintiff's proposal and the fact that it implicates significant levels of sales, plaintiff has shown a likelihood of prevailing on the merits with regard to the issue of whether his proposal is "otherwise significantly related" to Iroquois/Delaware's business.

* * * For the reasons discussed above, the Court concludes that plaintiff's motion for preliminary injunction should be granted.

---

shareholder proposal at issue failed to get support from three percent of all shareholders, thereby triggering a separate basis for exclusion.

CA, INC. v. AFSCME EMPLOYEES PENSION PLAN

953 A.2d 227 (Del. Sup. Ct. 2008).

JACOBS, JUSTICE.

This proceeding arises from a certification by the United States Securities and Exchange Commission (the "SEC"), to this Court, of two questions of law pursuant to Article IV, Section 11(8) of the Delaware Constitution[1] and Supreme Court Rule 41. On June 27, 2008, the SEC asked this Court to address two questions of Delaware law regarding a proposed stockholder bylaw submitted by the AFSCME Employees Pension Plan ("AFSCME") for inclusion in the proxy materials of CA, Inc. ("CA" or the "Company") for CA's 2008 annual stockholders' meeting. This Court accepted certification on July 1, 2008, and after expedited briefing, the matter was argued on July 9, 2008. This is the decision of the Court on the certified questions.

I. FACTS

CA is a Delaware corporation whose board of directors consists of twelve persons, all of whom sit for reelection each year. CA's annual meeting of stockholders is scheduled to be held on September 9, 2008. CA intends to file its definitive proxy materials with the SEC on or about July 24, 2008 in connection with that meeting.

AFSCME, a CA stockholder, is associated with the American Federation of State, County and Municipal Employees. On March 13, 2008, AFSCME submitted a proposed stockholder bylaw (the "Bylaw" or "proposed Bylaw") for inclusion in the Company's proxy materials for its 2008 annual meeting of stockholders. The Bylaw, if adopted by CA stockholders, would amend the Company's bylaws to provide as follows:

> RESOLVED, that pursuant to section 109 of the Delaware General Corporation Law and Article IX of the bylaws of CA, Inc., stockholders of CA hereby amend the bylaws to add the following Section 14 to Article II:

> The board of directors shall cause the corporation to reimburse a stockholder or group of stockholders (together, the "Nominator") for reasonable expenses ("Expenses") incurred in connection with nominating one or more candidates in a contested election of directors to the corporation's board of directors, including, without limitation, printing, mailing, legal, solicitation, travel, advertising and public relations expenses, so long as (a) the election of fewer than 50% of the directors to be elected is contested in the election, (b) one or more candidates nominated by the Nominator are elected to the corporation's board of directors, (c) stockholders are not permitted to cumu-

---

1. Article IV, Section 11(8) was amended in 2007 to authorize this Court to hear and determine questions of law certified to it by (in addition to the tribunals already specified therein) the United States Securities and Exchange Commission. 76 *Del. Laws* 2007, ch. 37 § 1, effective May 3, 2007. This certification request is the first submitted by the SEC to this Court.

late their votes for directors, and (d) the election occurred, and the Expenses were incurred, after this bylaw's adoption. The amount paid to a Nominator under this bylaw in respect of a contested election shall not exceed the amount expended by the corporation in connection with such election.

CA's current bylaws and Certificate of Incorporation have no provision that specifically addresses the reimbursement of proxy expenses. Of more general relevance, however, is Article SEVENTH, Section (1) of CA's Certificate of Incorporation, which tracks the language of 8 Del. C. § 141(a) and provides that:

> The management of the business and the conduct of the affairs of the corporation shall be vested in [CA's] Board of Directors.

It is undisputed that the decision whether to reimburse election expenses is presently vested in the discretion of CA's board of directors, subject to their fiduciary duties and applicable Delaware law.

On April 18, 2008, CA notified the SEC's Division of Corporation Finance (the "Division") of its intention to exclude the proposed Bylaw from its 2008 proxy materials. The Company requested from the Division a "no-action letter" stating that the Division would not recommend any enforcement action to the SEC if CA excluded the AFSCME proposal.[2] CA's request for a no-action letter was accompanied by an opinion from its Delaware counsel, Richards Layton & Finger, P.A. ("RL & F"). The RL & F opinion concluded that the proposed Bylaw is not a proper subject for stockholder action, and that if implemented, the Bylaw would violate the Delaware General Corporation Law ("DGCL").

On May 21, 2008, AFSCME responded to CA's no-action request with a letter taking the opposite legal position. The AFSCME letter was accompanied by an opinion from AFSCME's Delaware counsel, Grant & Eisenhofer, P.A. ("G & E"). The G & E opinion concluded that the proposed Bylaw is a proper subject for shareholder action and that if adopted, would be permitted under Delaware law.

The Division was thus confronted with two conflicting legal opinions on Delaware law. Whether or not the Division would determine that CA may exclude the proposed Bylaw from its 2008 proxy materials would depend upon which of these conflicting views is legally correct. To obtain guidance, the SEC, at the Division's request, certified two questions of Delaware law to this Court. Given the short timeframe for the filing of CA's proxy materials, we concluded that "there are important and urgent reasons for an immediate determination of the questions certified," and accepted those questions for review on July 1, 2008.

---

2. Under Sections (i)(1) and (i)(2) of SEC Rule 14a–8, a company may exclude a stockholder proposal from its proxy statement if the proposal 'is not a proper subject for action by the shareholders under the laws of the jurisdiction of the company's organization," or where the proposal, if implemented, "would cause the company to violate any state law to which it is subject." *See* 17 C.F.R. § 240.14a–8.

II. *THE CERTIFIED QUESTIONS*

The two questions certified to us by the SEC are as follows:

1. Is the AFSCME Proposal a proper subject for action by shareholders as a matter of Delaware law?

2. Would the AFSCME Proposal, if adopted, cause CA to violate any Delaware law to which it is subject? * * *

III. *THE FIRST QUESTION*

A. *Preliminary Comments*

The first question presented is whether the Bylaw is a proper subject for shareholder action, more precisely, whether the Bylaw may be proposed and enacted by shareholders without the concurrence of the Company's board of directors. Before proceeding further, we make some preliminary comments in an effort to delineate a framework within which to begin our analysis.

First, the DGCL empowers both the board of directors and the shareholders of a Delaware corporation to adopt, amend or repeal the corporation's bylaws. 8 Del. C. ? 109(a) relevantly provides that:

> After a corporation has received any payment for any of its stock, the power to adopt, amend or repeal bylaws shall be in the stockholders entitled to vote ...; provided, however, any corporation may, in its certificate of incorporation, confer the power to adopt, amend or repeal bylaws upon the directors.... The fact that such power has been so conferred upon the directors ... shall not divest the stockholders ... of the power, nor limit their power to adopt, amend or repeal bylaws.

Pursuant to Section 109(a), CA's Certificate of Incorporation confers the power to adopt, amend or repeal the bylaws upon the Company's board of directors. Because the statute commands that that conferral "shall not divest the stockholders ... of ... nor limit" their power, both the board and the shareholders of CA, independently and concurrently, possess the power to adopt, amend and repeal the bylaws.

Second, the vesting of that concurrent power in both the board and the shareholders raises the issue of whether the stockholders' power is coextensive with that of the board, and vice versa. As a purely theoretical matter that is possible, and were that the case, then the first certified question would be easily answered. That is, under such a regime any proposal to adopt, amend or repeal a bylaw would be a proper subject for either shareholder or board action, without distinction. But the DGCL has not allocated to the board and the shareholders the identical, coextensive power to adopt, amend and repeal the bylaws. Therefore, how that power is allocated between those two decision-making bodies requires an analysis that is more complex.

Moving from the theoretical to this case, by its terms Section 109(a) vests in the shareholders a power to adopt, amend or repeal bylaws that is legally sacrosanct, i.e., the power cannot be non-consensually eliminated or limited by anyone other than the legislature itself. If viewed in isolation, Section 109(a) could be read to make the board's and the shareholders' power to adopt, amend or repeal bylaws identical and coextensive, but Section 109(a) does not exist in a vacuum. It must be read together with 8 Del. C. § 141(a), which pertinently provides that:

> The business and affairs of every corporation organized under this chapter shall be managed by or under the direction of a board of directors, except as may be otherwise provided in this chapter or in its certificate of incorporation.

No such broad management power is statutorily allocated to the shareholders. Indeed, it is well-established that stockholders of a corporation subject to the DGCL may not directly manage the business and affairs of the corporation, at least without specific authorization in either the statute or the certificate of incorporation.[6] Therefore, the shareholders' statutory power to adopt, amend or repeal bylaws is not coextensive with the board's concurrent power and is limited by the board's management prerogatives under Section 141(a).

Third, it follows that, to decide whether the Bylaw proposed by AFSCME is a proper subject for shareholder action under Delaware law, we must first determine: (1) the scope or reach of the shareholders' power to adopt, alter or repeal the bylaws of a Delaware corporation, and then (2) whether the Bylaw at issue here falls within that permissible scope. Where, as here, the proposed bylaw is one that limits director authority, that is an elusively difficult task. As one noted scholar has put it, "the efforts to distinguish by-laws that permissibly limit director authority from by-laws that impermissibly do so have failed to provide a coherent analytical structure, and the pertinent statutes provide no guidelines for distinction at all."[8] The tools that are available to this Court to answer

---

6. *See, e.g., McMullin v. Beran*, 765 A.2d 910, 916 (Del.2000) ("[o]ne of the fundamental principles of the Delaware General Corporation Law statute is that the business affairs of a corporation are managed by or under the direction of its board of directors."); *Quickturn Design Sys., Inc. v. Shapiro*, 721 A.2d 1281, 1291–92 (Del.1998) ('One of the most basic tenets of Delaware corporate law is that the board of directors has the ultimate responsibility for managing the business and affairs of a corporation. [. . .] Section 141(a) . . . confers upon any newly elected board of directors full power to manage and direct the business and affairs of a Delaware corporation.") (emphasis in original) (internal citations omitted); *Aronson v. Lewis*, 473 A.2d 805, 811 (Del.1984) ("[a] cardinal precept of the General Corporation Law of the State of Delaware is that directors, rather than shareholders, manage the business and affairs of the corporation.").

8. Lawrence A. Hamermesh, *Corporate Democracy and Stockholder-Adopted By-Laws: Taking Back the Street?*, 73 TUL. L.REV.. 409, 444 (1998); Id. at 416 (noting that "neither the courts, the legislators, the SEC, nor legal scholars have clearly articulated the means of . . . determining whether a stockholder-adopted by-law provision that constrains director managerial authority is legally effective."). See also Randall S. Thomas & Catherine T. Dixon, ARANOW & EINHORN ON PROXY CONTESTS FOR CORPORATE CONTROL, § 160.5 (3d ed. 1998) ('At some point the broad shareholder power to adopt or amend corporate by-laws must yield to the board's plenary authority to manage the business and affairs of the corporation. . . . The difficulty of pinpointing where a proposal falls on this spectrum of sometimes overlapping authority is exacerbated by the absence of state-law precedent demarcating this boundary.'); John C. Coffee, Jr., *The SEC and the Institutional Investor: A Half-Time Report*, 15 CARDOZO L.REV. 837, 889 (1994) ("Symptomatically, persuasive Delaware authority is simply lacking that draws boundaries between the shareholder's right to amend the bylaws and the board's right to manage."); William W. Bratton & Joseph A. McCahery, *Regulatory Competition, Regulatory Capture, and Corporate*

those questions are other provisions of the DGCL and Delaware judicial decisions that can be brought to bear on this question.

B. *Analysis*

Bylaws, by their very nature, set down rules and procedures that bind a corporation's board and its shareholders. In that sense, most, if not all, bylaws could be said to limit the otherwise unlimited discretionary power of the board. Yet Section 109(a) carves out an area of shareholder power to adopt, amend or repeal bylaws that is expressly inviolate. Therefore, to argue that the Bylaw at issue here limits the board's power to manage the business and affairs of the Company only begins, but cannot end, the analysis needed to decide whether the Bylaw is a proper subject for shareholder action. The question left unanswered is what is the scope of shareholder action that Section 109(b) permits yet does not improperly intrude upon the directors' power to manage corporation's business and affairs under Section 141(a).

It is well-established Delaware law that a proper function of bylaws is not to mandate how the board should decide specific substantive business decisions, but rather, to define the process and procedures by which those decisions are made. * * *

The context of the Bylaw at issue here is the process for electing directors-a subject in which shareholders of Delaware corporations have a legitimate and protected interest. The purpose of the Bylaw is to promote the integrity of that electoral process by facilitating the nomination of director candidates by stockholders or groups of stockholders. Generally, and under the current framework for electing directors in contested elections, only board-sponsored nominees for election are reimbursed for their election expenses. Dissident candidates are not, unless they succeed in replacing at least a majority of the entire board. The Bylaw would encourage the nomination of non-management board candidates by promising reimbursement of the nominating stockholders' proxy expenses if one or more of its candidates are elected. In that the shareholders also have a legitimate interest, because the Bylaw would facilitate the exercise of their right to participate in selecting the contestants. * * *

The shareholders of a Delaware corporation have the right "to participate in selecting the contestants" for election to the board. The shareholders are entitled to facilitate the exercise of that right by proposing a bylaw that would encourage candidates other than board-sponsored nominees to stand for election. The Bylaw would accomplish that by committing the corporation to reimburse the election expenses of shareholders whose candidates are successfully elected. That the implementation of that proposal would require the expenditure of corporate funds will not, in and of itself, make such a bylaw an improper subject matter for shareholder

*Self-Regulation,*73 N.C. L.REV. 1861, 1932 n. 274 (1995) ("[S]tate lawmakers have never had occasion to draw a clear line between board management authority and shareholder by-law promulgation authority. As a result, the extent to which a by-law may constrain ... management authority is not clear.").

action. Accordingly, we answer the first question certified to us in the affirmative.

That, however, concludes only part of the analysis. The DGCL also requires that the Bylaw be "not inconsistent with law." Accordingly, we turn to the second certified question, which is whether the proposed Bylaw, if adopted, would cause CA to violate any Delaware law to which it is subject.

IV. *THE SECOND QUESTION*

In answering the first question, we have already determined that the Bylaw does not facially violate any provision of the DGCL or of CA's Certificate of Incorporation. The question thus becomes whether the Bylaw would violate any common law rule or precept. Were this issue being presented in the course of litigation involving the application of the Bylaw to a specific set of facts, we would start with the presumption that the Bylaw is valid and, if possible, construe it in a manner consistent with the law. The factual context in which the Bylaw was challenged would inform our analysis, and we would "exercise caution [before] invalidating corporate acts based upon hypothetical injuries...." The certified questions, however, request a determination of the validity of the Bylaw in the abstract. Therefore, in response to the second question, we must necessarily consider any possible circumstance under which a board of directors might be required to act. Under at least one such hypothetical, the board of directors would breach their fiduciary duties if they complied with the Bylaw. Accordingly, we conclude that the Bylaw, as drafted, would violate the prohibition, which our decisions have derived from Section 141(a), against contractual arrangements that commit the board of directors to a course of action that would preclude them from fully discharging their fiduciary duties to the corporation and its shareholders. * * *

One of the most basic tenets of Delaware corporate law is that the board of directors has the ultimate responsibility for managing the business and affairs of a corporation. [. . .]

As presently drafted, the Bylaw would afford CA's directors full discretion to determine what amount of reimbursement is appropriate, because the directors would be obligated to grant only the "reasonable" expenses of a successful short slate. Unfortunately, that does not go far enough, because the Bylaw contains no language or provision that would reserve to CA's directors their full power to exercise their fiduciary duty to decide whether or not it would be appropriate, in a specific case, to award reimbursement at all.

In arriving at this conclusion, we express no view on whether the Bylaw as currently drafted, would create a better governance scheme from a policy standpoint. We decide only what is, and is not, legally permitted under the DGCL. That statute, as currently drafted, is the expression of policy as decreed by the Delaware legislature. Those who believe that CA's shareholders should be permitted to make the proposed Bylaw as drafted part of CA's governance scheme, have two alternatives. They may seek to amend the Certificate of Incorporation to include the substance of the Bylaw; *or* they may seek recourse from the Delaware General Assembly.

Accordingly, we answer the second question certified to us in the affirmative.

In recent years, shareholders have sought increased access to management's proxy statement, including with respect to shareholders' nominees for the board to directors.

AMERICAN FEDERATION OF STATE, COUNTY & MUNICIPAL EMPLOYEES, EMPLOYEES PENSION PLAN v. AMERICAN INTERNATIONAL GROUP, INC.

462 F.3d 121 (2d Cir. 2006).

WESLEY, CIRCUIT JUDGE:

This case raises the question of whether a shareholder proposal requiring a company to include certain shareholder-nominated candidates for the board of directors on the corporate ballot can be excluded from the corporate proxy materials on the basis that the proposal "relates to an election" under Securities Exchange Act Rule 14a–8(i)(8), 17 C.F.R. § 240.14a–8 ("election exclusion" or "Rule 14a–8(i)(8)"). Complicating this question is not only the ambiguity of Rule 14a–8(i)(8) itself but also the fact that the Securities Exchange Commission (the "SEC" or "Commission") has ascribed two different interpretations to the Rule's language. The SEC's first interpretation was published in 1976, the same year that it last revised the election exclusion. The Division of Corporation Finance (the "Division"), the group within the SEC that handles investor disclosure matters and issues no-action letters,[1] continued to apply this interpretation consistently for fifteen years until 1990, when it began applying a different interpretation, although at first in an ad hoc and inconsistent manner. The result of this gradual interpretive shift is the SEC's second interpretation, as set forth in its amicus brief to this Court. We believe that an agency's interpretation of an ambiguous regulation made at the time the regulation was implemented or revised should control unless that agency has offered sufficient reasons for its changed interpretation. Accordingly, we hold that a shareholder proposal that

---

1. Elaborating upon the nature of the no-action process, the Court has stated:

The no-action process works as follows: Whenever a corporation decides to exclude a shareholder proposal from its proxy materials, it "shall file" a letter with the Division explaining the legal basis for its decision. *See* Rule 14a–8(d)(3). If the Division staff agrees that the proposal is excludable, it may issue a no-action letter, stating that, based on the facts presented by the corporation, the staff will not recommend that the SEC sue the corporation for violating Rule 14a–8.... The no-action letter, however, is an informal response, and does not amount to an official statement of the SEC's views.... No-action letters are deemed interpretive because they do not impose or fix legal relationship upon any of the parties.

N.Y. City Employees' Ret. Sys. v. SEC, 45 F.3d 7, 12 (2d Cir. 1995).

seeks to amend the corporate bylaws to establish a procedure by which shareholder-nominated candidates may be included on the corporate ballot does not relate to an election within the meaning of the Rule and therefore cannot be excluded from corporate proxy materials under that regulation.

Background

The American Federation of State, County & Municipal Employees ("AFSCME") is one of the country's largest public service employee unions. Through its pension plan, AFSCME holds 26,965 shares of voting common stock of American International Group ("AIG" or "Company"), a multi-national corporation operating in the insurance and financial services sectors. On December 1, 2004, AFSCME submitted to AIG for inclusion in the Company's 2005 proxy statement a shareholder proposal that, if adopted by a majority of AIG shareholders at the Company's 2005 annual meeting, would amend the AIG bylaws to require the Company, under certain circumstances, to publish the names of shareholder-nominated candidates for director positions together with any candidates nominated by AIG's board of directors ("Proposal"). AIG sought the input of the Division regarding whether AIG could exclude the Proposal from its proxy statement under the election exclusion on the basis that it "relates to an election." The Division issued a no-action letter in which it indicated that it would not recommend an enforcement action against AIG should the Company exclude the Proposal from its proxy statement. American International Group, Inc., SEC No-Action Letter, 2005 SEC No-Act. LEXIS 235, 2005 WL 372266 (Feb 14, 2005) ('AIG No-Action Letter'). Armed with the no-action letter, AIG then proceeded to exclude the Proposal from the Company's proxy statement. In response, AFSCME brought suit in the United States District Court for the Southern District of New York (Stanton, J.) seeking a court order compelling AIG to include the Proposal in its next proxy statement. The district court denied AFSCME's motion for a preliminary injunction, concluding that AFSCME's Proposal "on its face 'relates to an election.' Indeed, it relates to nothing else." *AFSCME v. Am. Int'l Group, Inc.*, 361 F. Supp. 2d 344, 346 (S.D.N.Y. 2005). After this Court denied AFSCME's motion for expedited appeal, the parties stipulated that the district court's opinion denying AFSCME's motion for a preliminary injunction "be deemed to contain the Court's complete findings of fact and conclusions of law with respect to all claims asserted by plaintiff in this action" and that it also "be deemed a final judgment on the merits with respect to all claims asserted by plaintiff in this action." Pursuant to this joint stipulation, the district court entered final judgment denying plaintiff's claims for declaratory and injunctive relief and dismissing plaintiff's complaint.

Discussion

Rule 14a–8(i)(8), also known as "the town meeting rule," regulates what are referred to as "shareholders proposals," that is, "recommendation[s] or requirement[s] that the company and/or its board of directors take [some] action, which [the submitting shareholder(s)] intend to present at a meeting of the company's shareholders," 17 C.F.R. § 240.14a–8(a). If a shareholder seeking to submit a proposal meets certain eligibility and procedural requirements,[4] the corporation is required to include the proposal in its proxy statement and identify the proposal in its form of proxy, unless the corporation can prove to the SEC that a given proposal may be excluded based on one of thirteen grounds enumerated in the regulations. *Id*. § 240.14a–8(i)(1)–(13). One of these grounds, Rule 14a–8(i)(8), provides that a corporation may exclude a shareholder proposal "[i]f the proposal relates to an election for membership on the company's board of directors or analogous governing body." *Id*. § 240.14a–8(i)(8).

We must determine whether, under Rule 14a–8(i)(8), a shareholder proposal "relates to an election" if it seeks to amend the corporate bylaws to establish a procedure by which certain shareholders are entitled to include in the corporate proxy materials their nominees for the board of directors ("proxy access bylaw proposal"). "In interpreting an administrative regulation, as in interpreting a statute, we must begin by examining the language of the provision at issue." *Resnik v. Swartz*, 303 F.3d 147, 151–52 (2d Cir. 2002) (citing *New York Currency Research Corp. v. CFTC*, 180 F.3d 83, 92 (2d Cir. 1999)). The relevant language here—"relates to an election"—is not particularly helpful. AFSCME reads the election exclusion as creating an obvious distinction between proposals addressing a particular seat in a particular election (which AFSCME concedes are excludable) and those, like AFSCME's proposal, that simply set the background rules governing elections generally (which AFSCME claims are not excludable). AFSCME's distinction rests on Rule 14a–8(i)(8)'s use of the article "an," which AFSCME claims "necessarily implies that the phrase 'relates to an election' is intended to relate to proposals that address *particular elections*, instead of simply 'elections' generally." It is at least plausible that the words "an election" were intended to narrow the scope of the election exclusion, confining its application to proposals relating to "a particular election *and not* elections generally." It is, however, also plausible that the phrase was intended to create a comparatively broader exclusion, one covering "a particular election *or* elections generally" since any proposal that relates to elections in general will necessarily relate to an election in particular. The language of Rule 14a–8(i)(8) provides no reason to adopt one interpretation over the other. * * *

---

4. "In order to be eligible to submit a proposal, [a shareholder] must have continuously held at least $ 2,000 in market value, or 1, of the company's securities entitled to be voted on the proposal at the meeting for at least one year by the date [of the proposal's submission]." 17 C.F.R. ? 240.14a–8(b)(1). "Each shareholder may submit no more than one proposal to a company for a particular shareholders' meeting." Id. § 240.14a–8(c). "The proposal, including any accompanying supporting statement, may not exceed 500 words." Id. § 240.14a–8(d). The company's "principal executive offices" must have received the shareholder proposal "not less than 120 calendar days before the date of the company's proxy statement released to shareholders in connection with the previous year's annual meeting." Id. § 240.14a–8(e)(2). "[I]f the company did not hold an annual meeting the previous year, or if the date of th[e present] year's annual meeting has been changed by more than 30 days from the date of the previous year's meeting, then the deadline is a reasonable time before the company begins to print and mail its proxy materials." Id.

In that year, the SEC amended Rule 14a–8(i)(8) in an effort to clarify the purpose of the existing election exclusion. The SEC explained that "with respect to corporate elections, Rule 14a–8 is not the proper means for conducting campaigns or effecting reforms in elections of that nature [i.e., "corporate, political or other elections to office"], *since other proxy rules, including Rule 14a–11, are applicable thereto.*' Proposed Amendments to Rule 14a–8, Exchange Act Release No. 34–12598, 41 Fed. Reg. 29,982, 29,9845 (proposed July 7, 1976) (emphasis added) ("1976 Statement'). The district court opinion quoted the 1976 Statement but omitted the italicized language and concluded that shareholder proposals were not intended to be used to accomplish any type of election reform. Clearly, however, that cannot be what the 1976 Statement means. Indeed, when the SEC finally adopted the revision of Rule 14a–8(i)(8) four months after publication of the 1976 Statement, it explained that it was rejecting a previous proposed rule (which would have authorized the exclusion of proposals that "relate[] to a corporate, political or other election to office') in favor of the current version (which authorizes the exclusion of proposals that simply "relate[] to an election") so as to avoid creating "the erroneous belief that the Commission intended to expand the scope of the existing exclusion to cover proposals dealing with matters previously held not excludable by the Commission, such as cumulative voting rights, general qualifications for directors, and political contributions by the issuer." Adoption of Amendments Relating to Proposals by Security Holders, Exchange Act Release No. 34–129999, 41 Fed. Reg. 52,994, 52,998 (Nov. 22, 1976) ("1976 Adoption"). And yet, all three of these shareholder proposal topics—cumulative voting rights, general qualifications for directors, and political contributions—fit comfortably within the category "election reform."

In its amicus brief, the SEC places a slightly different gloss on the 1976 Statement than did the district court. The SEC reads the 1976 Statement as implying that the purpose of Rule 14a–8(i)(8) is to authorize the exclusion of proposals that seek to effect, not election reform in general, but only certain types of election reform, namely those to which "other proxy rules, including Rule 14a–11," are generally applicable. In 1976, Rule 14a–11 was essentially the equivalent of current Rule 14a–12, which requires certain disclosures where a solicitation is made "for the purpose of opposing" a solicitation by any other person "with respect to the election or removal of directors." 17 C.F.R. § 240.14a–12(c). The SEC reasons that, based on the 1976 Statement, "a proposal may be excluded pursuant to Rule 14a–8(i)(8) if it would result in an immediate election contest (e.g., by making a director nomination for a particular meeting) or would set up a process for shareholders to conduct an election contest in the future by requiring the company to include shareholder director nominees in the company's proxy materials for subsequent meetings."

We agree with the SEC that, based on the 1976 Statement, shareholder proposals can be excluded under the election exclusion if they would result in an immediate election contest. We understand the phrase "since other proxy rules, including Rule 14a–11, are applicable thereto'' in the 1976 Statement to mean that under Rule 14a–8(i)(8), companies can exclude shareholder proposals dealing with those election-related matters that, if addressed in a proxy solicitation—the alternative to a shareholder proposal—would trigger Rule 14a–12, or the former Rule 14a–11. A proxy solicitation nominating a candidate for a specific election would be made ''for the purpose of opposing'' the company's proxy solicitation and therefore would clearly trigger Rule 14a–12. Accordingly, based on the 1976 Statement, a shareholder proposal seeking to contest management's nominees would be excludable under Rule 14a–8(i)(8).

By contrast, a proxy solicitation seeking to add a proxy access amendment to the corporate bylaws does not involve opposing solicitations dealing with ''the election or removal of directors,'' and therefore Rule 14a–12, or, equivalently, the former Rule 14a–11, would not apply to a proposal seeking to accomplish the same end. Thus, we cannot agree with the second half of the SEC's interpretation of the 1976 Statement: that a proposal may be excluded under Rule 14a–8(i)(8) if it would simply establish a process for shareholders to wage a future election contest.

The 1976 Statement clearly reflects the view that the election exclusion is limited to shareholder proposals used to oppose solicitations dealing with an identified board seat in an upcoming election and rejects the somewhat broader interpretation that the election exclusion applies to shareholder proposals that would institute procedures making such election contests more likely. The SEC suggested as much when, four months after its 1976 Statement, it explained that the scope of the election exclusion does not cover shareholder proposals dealing with matters such as cumulative voting and general director requirements, both of which have the potential to increase the likelihood of election contests. *See* 1976 Adoption, 41 Fed. Reg. at 52,998.

That the 1976 statement adopted this narrower view of the election exclusion finds further support in the fact that it was also the view that the Division adopted for roughly sixteen years following publication of the SEC's 1976 Statement. It was not until 1990 that the Division first signaled a change of course by deeming excludable proposals that *might* result in contested elections, even if the proposal only purports to alter general procedures for nominating and electing directors.[7]

Because the interpretation of Rule 14a–8(i)(8) that the SEC advances in its amicus brief—that the election exclusion applies to proxy access bylaw proposals—conflicts with the 1976 Statement, it does not merit the usual deference we would reserve for an agency's interpretation of its own regulations. The SEC has not provided, nor to our knowledge has it or the Division ever provided, reasons for its changed position regarding the

---

7. Even then, the Division's position was far from clear-cut. Between 1990 and 1998, the Division continued to issue intermittently no-action letters adopting its prior distinction between procedures governing elections generally and those dealing with specific election contests. Since roughly 1998, the Division has consistently adopted the position expressed in the AIG No-Action Letter, which is the same position the SEC advances in its amicus brief.

excludability of proxy access bylaw proposals. Although the SEC has substantial discretion to adopt new interpretations of its own regulations in light of, for example, changes in the capital markets or even simply because of a shift in the Commission's regulatory approach, it nevertheless as a "duty to explain its departure from prior norms."

In its amicus submission, the SEC fails to so much as acknowledge a changed position, let alone offer a reasoned analysis of the change. The amicus brief is curiously silent on any Division action prior to 1990 and characterizes the intermittent post–1990 no-action letters which continued to apply the pre–1990 position as mere "mistake[s]." While we by no means wish to imply that the Commission or the Division cannot correct analytical errors following a refinement of their thinking, we have a difficult time accepting the SEC's characterization of a policy that the Division consistently applied for sixteen years as nothing more than a "mistake." Although we are willing to afford the Commission considerable latitude in explaining departures from prior interpretations, its reasoned analysis must consist of something more than *mea culpas*.

Accordingly, we deem it appropriate to defer to the 1976 Statement, which represents the SEC's interpretation of the election exclusion the last time the Rule was substantively revised. We therefore interpret the election exclusion as applying to shareholder proposals that relate to a particular election and not to proposals that, like AFSCME's, would establish the procedural rules governing elections generally. * * *

In deeming proxy access bylaw proposals non-excludable under Rule 14a–8(i)(8), we take no side in the policy debate regarding shareholder access to the corporate ballot. There might be perfectly good reasons for permitting companies to exclude proposals like AFSCME's, just as there may well be valid policy reasons for rendering them non-excludable. However, Congress has determined that such issues are appropriately the province of the SEC, not the judiciary.

Conclusion

For the foregoing reasons, we reverse the judgment of the district court and remand the case for entry of judgment in favor AFSCME.

Notes

1. Traditionally, in public companies a nomination committee, whose selection is controlled by the chief executive officer, makes such nominations. SEC Rule 14a–8 allows the exclusion of proposals that relate to board elections. However, after the Enron era scandals, the SEC proposed a rule that would have allowed shareholders holding 5 percent or more of a company's stock to nominate directors, if allowed to do so by a shareholder proposal approved by a majority of shareholders or where 35 percent of votes were withheld in the vote to elect an incumbent director. The SEC had rejected such a proposal in 1942 after members of Congress claimed it was communist in nature. Such a proposal was again rejected in 1992, and even in the midst

of the Post-Enron hysteria, its most recent iteration met widespread opposition. The SEC received over 16,000 comment letters and even long time corporate governance gadfly Evelyn Davis was against turning control of corporate America to the labor unions, who were about the only ones with sufficient stock and interest to make such nominations. The SEC backed off this proposal in the face of this onslaught, allowing the SEC staff to advise registrants that they could exclude such proposals under Rule 14a–8. However, a union pension fund challenged that approach and was given a boost by the Second Circuit Court of Appeals in the preceding case. The SEC then went back to the drawing board and sought public comment on two competing proposals, one of which would have allowed proxy access and the other would not. The SEC Chairman, Christopher Cox, voted in favor of both proposals in order to break an impasse between the Democrat and Republican Commissioners. Resignations from the SEC then made it them impolitic for the SEC to proceed. See Jerry W. Markham, Regulating Excessive Executive Compensation—Why Bother? 2 J. of Bus. & Tech. L. 277, 334 (2007) (discussing these proposals).

2. There have been several successive sets of shareholder activists that sought to use the provisions of SEC Rule 14a–8 to further their causes. The corporate gadfly was an ever present fixture at board meetings in the 1950s. Lewis and John Gilbert were their leaders. They held small amounts of stock in some 800 corporations and attended as many as 200 annual meetings each year. In total, they attended over 2000 annual meetings where, while they were "[a]lmost always outvoted, they are seldom out talked and never out shouted." *Poyntz Tyler* (ed.), *Securities, Exchanges and the SEC* 96 (1965). The next round of activism centered around efforts to limit the business of corporations in defense work that supported the Vietnam war. That was followed in the 1970s by other social and political causes that included such things as the environment, smoking and discrimination in employment. Executive compensation also became a favorite target for shareholder proposals.

3. Since management generally resists the inclusion of shareholder proposals, the provisions of Rule 14a–8 that specify the kinds of proposals that can be omitted have been the subject of constant controversy and frequent change. As presently in effect, Rule 14a–8(i) permits management to exclude a proposal for any one of 13 reasons.

(1) *Impropriety under corporate law.* Management can exclude a shareholder proposal that under governing state law, which generally will be the state of incorporation, is not a proper subject for action by security holders. The SEC points out that the wording of the proposal may determine whether it concerns a proper matter for consideration. For example, as discussed in Chapter 6, there is a division of authority within the corporate governance structure and there are many matters on which the shareholders do not have the right to initiate corporate action. See e.g., Charlestown Boot & Shoe Co. v. Dunsmore, 60 N.H. 85 (1880), page 202 above. Accordingly, a proposal that mandates corporate action, and thereby seeking to circumvent the board of directors, may be excludable, while a proposal merely recommending that the directors consider certain action will be appropriate. See e.g., Auer v. Dressel, 306 N.Y. 427, 118 N.E.2d 590 (1954), page 204 above. In recent years, in

appropriate instances, the SEC has permitted the shareholder to correct the problem by redrafting the proposal as precatory rather than mandatory.

(2) *Violation of law generally.* Management may exclude a proposal if it would require the company to violate any law–state or federal. Thus, if the substance of the proposal would violate state or federal law, such as requiring the company to breach existing contracts, the proposal may be excluded. See e.g., Sensar Corp., 2001 WL 506141 (SEC No Action Letter May 14, 2001) (proposal that executive options be rescinded and reissued under new terms could be excluded as implementation of the proposal would result in breaching existing contract rights).

(3) *Contrary to the SEC proxy rules.* The most common basis for exclusion here is that the proposal is vague or is materially misleading in violation of SEC Rule 14a–9. The SEC may give the shareholder the opportunity to remove the offending statements in order to make the proposal and supporting statement includible.

(4) *Redress of a personal claim or grievance.* Often this ground is invoked when the proposal relates to a consumer complaint or an employment grievance. A vivid example is found in Orbital Sciences Corporation, 1995 WL 606606 (SEC No Action Letter October 16, 1995) where the proponent was seeking employment with the company. The shareholder's submission was as follows:

Introduction to Shareholder Proposal

To my fellow shareholders:

As long as I can remember, I have wanted to work on rockets. Some people want to be firemen or policemen. I wish to work on rockets. Keeping to my dream, I earned a University of California degree in physics. I sent out 917 resumes looking for work related to rockets. I was not offered one interview.

Out of all the companies I sought interviews with, the one company that I know is capable of fulfilling my goals is Orbital Sciences Corporation. I sent my resume to [the] Chief Executive Officer, and to the human resource department, and once again was rejected without an interview.

I have purchased stock in Orbital Sciences Corporation and as a fellow shareholder have come to you to plead my case. I ask you as fellow shareholders to help me get a job with Orbital Sciences Corporation.

Shareholder proposal

Whereas Ron Freedman, a resident of Bellevue Washington, did try to obtain employment through proper channels at Orbital Sciences Corporation and was not given an interview;

Now therefore we the shareholders do hereby direct the Chief Executive Officer to give Ron Freedman a job in the Advanced Projects Group, as either an assistant to the engineers, a technician, or any other suitable position utilizing Ron Freedman's knowledge, skills, and abilities. The job is to start no later then December 31, 1996 and is to pay a starting salary of no less then $19,200 per year.

The SEC staff responded that it would not object to management excluding the proposal as one relating to a personal grievance.

(5) *Relevance*. Management may exclude proposals that relate to operations which account for less than 5% of the company's business or is not *otherwise* significant. As the *Lovenheim* case demonstrates, the relevance standard contains both an objective and subjective test. The proposal must fail relevance scrutiny under *both* tests before it may be excluded.

(6) *Beyond the company's power to effectuate*. The shareholder proposal rule is limited to matters bearing upon corporate governance. A proposal that relates to social concerns that management by itself cannot remedy may, however, still be includible if there are measures that could be taken with regard to the company's business that would assist in diminishing the concern. The SEC staff has thus required an insurance company to include a proposal that it examine the cost of smoking on insurance payments to insured persons, that the company review its earnings from tobacco company investments and to consider what investment policies should be followed in light of those findings. Aetna Life & Casualty Co., Fed. Sec. L. Rep. ¶ 79,705 (Feb. 28, 1991). See also Phillip Morris Co., 1990 WL 286063 (SEC No Action Letter Feb. 22, 1990) (SEC staff reverses its prior position concerning the exclusion of proposals seeking to stop the manufacture of tobacco products). In another instance, the SEC staff allowed a company to exclude a proposal that sought to have the issuer stop making packaging material for tobacco products. The staff found that the company was only incidentally involved in such business. Mobil Corp., Fed. Sec. L. Rep. ¶ 79,709 (Feb. 28, 1991). See also Albertson's, Inc., 2001 WL 310422 (SEC No Action Letter March 23, 2001) (management could exclude shareholder proposal asking the company to cease tobacco sales where tobacco was just one of numerous products sold by the company). Exclusion of a proposal is appropriate where implementation would require actions by independent third parties. Compare SCEcorp, 1995 WL 756653 (SEC No Action Letter Dec. 20, 1995) (proposal that unaffiliated fiduciary trustees amend voting agreements), with, Northeast Utilities System, 1996 WL 652752 (SEC No Action Letter Nov. 7, 1996) (exclusion improper where proposal sought to have company ask for the cooperation of a third party; in this case that the company ask a third party to coordinate annual meetings held by public companies).

(7) *Ordinary business operations*. Management may exclude a shareholder proposal if it relates to day-to-day management decisions rather than more general policy issues that may rise to the level of shareholder concern. The essence of the rule is that shareholder proposals relating to the day-to-day managerial decisions concerning how the nuts and bolts of the business is carried out may be excluded from management's proxy statement. Reader's Digest Association, Inc., 31 Sec. Reg. & L. Rep. (BNA) 1299 (SEC No Action Letter Aug. 18, 1998). See e.g., Wal–Mart Stores, Inc. 2001 WL 306188 (SEC No Action Letter March 23, 2001) (permitting exclusion of proposal recommending the company "conduct a study in the Virginia District to disprove the modern myth that Sunday work maximizes profits"); Merck & Co., 2001 WL 128118 (SEC No Action Letter Feb. 9, 2001) (management of pharmaceutical company could exclude shareholder proposal recommending that the company scrutinize units engaged in research and development, dismantle

those with sustained substandard records, and dismiss senior members of the scientific staff who meet the criteria specified in the shareholder proposal); Niagara Mohawk Holdings, Inc., 2001 WL 10273 (SEC No Action Letter Jan. 3, 2001); Sempra Energy, 2000 WL 217933 (SEC No Action Letter Feb. 7, 2000) (management could exclude shareholder proposal calling for reinvestment of utility revenues in electric utility subsidiaries). A shareholder proposal asking management to establish a customer satisfaction panel was deemed to relate to the company's ordinary business and thus could be excluded from management's proxy statement. Deere & Co., 2000 WL 1762368, 32 Sec. Reg. & L. Rep. (BNA) 1733 (SEC No Action Letter Nov. 30, 2000). Similarly, a proposal recommending that the company have annual meetings for customers was considered to relate to the ordinary business and thus could be excluded. Wal–Mart Stores, Inc., 2001 WL 310419 (SEC No Action Letter March 27, 2001). A proposal that a company have regular meetings of shareholders to comment on actions by the board of directors could be excluded as relating to the company's ordinary business. Thermo Electron Corp., 2001 WL 322652 (SEC No Action Letter April 2, 2001) (management could exclude proposal providing that the board of directors present "every decision and other actions" of the board of directors to an "assembly" of shareholders and permit the "assembly" to request cancellations or modifications). A proposal that a company provide shareholders the same discounts that the company offered to vendors related to the ordinary business operations and thus may be excluded from management's proxy statement. General Motors Corp., 2001 WL 306197 (SEC No Action Letter March 20, 2001). For the same reason, management of an airline could exclude a shareholder proposal recommending that the company allow shareholders to exchange frequent flyer miles for first-class upgrades. AMR Corp., 2001 WL 314572 (SEC No Action Letter March 30, 2001). A proposal that the company change its name relates to ordinary rather than extraordinary business decisions and thus may be excluded. AOL Time Warner Inc., 2001 WL 306202 (SEC No Action Letter March 20, 2001).

One of the more controversial topics for shareholder proposals have involved discrimination issues. Initially, the SEC staff had applied a case-by-case approach to such issues. In an interpretation issued in 1992, the SEC staff announced a per se approach that would allow the exclusion of discrimination proposals. Cracker Barrel Old Country Stores, Inc., 1993 WL 11016, 1992 WL 289095 (SEC No Action Letters Oct. 13, 1992 & Jan. 1993). In those letters, the SEC staff's allowed the exclusion of a proposal concerning employment policies relating to the sexual orientation of individuals was affirmed by the SEC. See also Wal–Mart Stores, Inc., 1992 WL 78127 (SEC No Action Letter April 10, 1992) (affirmative action proposal relating to hiring could be excluded.). In 1998, the SEC reversed its per se rule that allowed exclusion of discrimination proposals as involving ordinary business operations. Rather, the Commission announced that it would revert to its prior case-by-case approach on these issues. 63 Fed. Reg. 29106 (May 28, 1998). In so doing, the SEC noted that it had previously reversed its position on other matters that it had initially viewed to be ordinary business, including plant closings, tobacco issues and executive compensation. Id. Later, the SEC staff noted that the SEC believed that the ordinary business exclusion:

. . . would generally protect management's ability to run the company on a day-to-day basis without shareholder oversight, while adding that 'proposals relating to such matters but focusing on sufficiently significant social policy issues (e.g., significant discrimination matters) generally would not be considered to be excludable, because the proposals would transcend the day-to-day business matters and raise policy issues so significant that it would be appropriate for a shareholder vote. . . .

Niagara Mohawk Holdings, Inc., SEC No–Act Letter (March 5 2001) (citation and emphasis omitted).

In Medical Committee for Human Rights v. SEC, 432 F.2d 659 (D.C.Cir. 1970), vacated as moot, 404 U.S. 403, 92 S.Ct. 577, 30 L.Ed.2d 560 (1972), the SEC allowed Dow Chemical Company to exclude a shareholder proposal that sought to amend the company's charter to prohibit the company from selling napalm to anyone unless the company was assured that it would not be used against human beings. This proposal was made in response to the widespread use of napalm by the United States in Vietnam. The Medical Committee claimed that the manufacture of this product by Dow was hurting the ability of the company to recruit young people as workers and that the company's global business was being harmed by the negative publicity from the sale of napalm. At that time, SEC Rule 14a–8 allowed exclusion of proposals that were "for the purpose of promoting general economic, political, racial, religious, social or similar causes." The circuit court held that the SEC's decision that the proposal could be excluded was subject to judicial review. The court further held that the proposal should be submitted to shareholders because the company was asserting that its "manufacturing and marketing of napalm was made not because of business considerations, but in spite of them; that management in essence decided to pursue a course of activity which generated little profit for the shareholders and actively impaired the company's public relations and recruitment activities because management considered this action morally and politically desirable." 432 F.2d at 681. The court held, in the colorful language quoted in *Lovenheim*, that such an approach should be subject to a shareholder vote. The Supreme Court accepted *certiorari* of the issue but dismissed the petition as moot after Dow included the proposal in its proxy statement and less than three percent of shareholders voted in favor for the proposal.

(8) *Relating to election to office.* Management may exclude a proposal relating to elections. Shareholders wishing to propose their own slate of directors or oppose management's slate must therefore do so through their own solicitation. On the other hand proposals relating to election procedures generally rather than specific candidates for election may have to be included. Management can thus exclude a shareholder proposal calling for the removal of a corporate officer or director. NetCurrents, Inc., 2001 WL 435671 (SEC No Action Letter April 25, 2001) (management could exclude proposal calling for removal and replacement of CEO who was also a director); J.C. Penney Co., 2001 WL 289495 (SEC No Action Letter March 19, 2001) (management could exclude shareholder proposal calling for removal and replacement of directors); Foster Wheeler Corp., 2001 WL 125055 (SEC No Action Letter Feb. 5, 2001) (management could exclude proposal calling for removal of chairman of the board if reelected and replacing him with an independent director).

Similarly a proposal calling for a director's resignation from office may be excluded from management's proxy statement. Xerox Corp., 2001 WL 246756 (SEC No Action Letter March 9, 2001); Second Bancorp Inc., 2001 WL 166842 (SEC No Action Letter Feb. 12, 2001). A shareholder proposal urging a corporate policy or practice and resignation of directors who violate the proposed policy could be excluded on the grounds that it relates to the election to office. First Federal Bankshares, Inc., 2000 WL 1357912 (Sept. 18, 2000) (proposal calling for review of repurchase of shares belonging to directors and calling for resignation of directors if auditors objected to the share repurchases). Also, management could exclude a shareholder proposal recommending that on an annual basis management publish a list of all nominees who ran for director positions and the votes they received in the shareholder vote. General Motors Corp., 2001 WL 306190 (SEC No Action Letter March 22, 2001). However, a proposal recommending an advisory committee for deciding who serves on the board of directors' audit committee could not be excluded on the grounds that the proposal related to election to office. General Motors Corp., 2001 WL 314566 (SEC No Action Letter March 29, 2001).

(9) *Contradicting management proposal.* Management may exclude a shareholder proposal that contradicts a proposal submitted by management. The rationale here is that the matter is already before the shareholders and the appropriate response of shareholders who disagree with management is to vote against the proposal.

(10) *Mootness.* Management may exclude a shareholder proposal if it has been substantially implemented.

(11) *Duplication.* Management may exclude a shareholder proposal that substantially duplicates another proposal submitted for the same shareholder meeting. This basis for exclusion is designed to prevent shareholders from harassing management through the use of repetitive proposals.

(12) *Resubmissions.* Management may exclude a shareholder proposal that is substantially similar to a proposal previously submitted during the past five years, which received affirmative votes from less than a specified percentage of the shares voted. The proposal need not be resubmitted for three years if it received less than three percent of the vote. Higher percentage of affirmative votes (up to ten percent) are required for resubmission if the proposal has been submitted unsuccessfully more than once in the past five years. SEC Rule 14a–8(i).

(13) *Dividends.* Management may exclude a shareholder proposal that relates to a specific amount of dividends. As a matter of corporate law, dividend declarations fall within the discretion of the board of directors. Under the federal proxy rules, proposals relating to the amount of dividends to be declared are excludible for reasons similar to matters relating to the company's ordinary business. However, the proposals relating to more general questions of dividend policy such as whether to declare dividends is not excludible because the decision to declare dividends "is extremely important to most security holders, and involves significant economic and policy considerations." Sonoma West Holdings, Inc., 2000 WL 1182875 (SEC No Action Letter Aug. 17, 2000).

4. In case of a dispute between management and a shareholder as to whether a particular proposal may be excluded from the proxy statement, the decision in the first instance is for the SEC. The Commission initially took the position that its refusal to direct a company to include a proposal is not an "order" subject to judicial review under § 25, but one court disagreed. Medical Committee for Human Rights v. SEC, 432 F.2d 659 (D.C.Cir.1970), vacated as moot, 404 U.S. 403, 92 S.Ct. 577, 30 L.Ed.2d 560 (1972). The Commission subsequently discovered that it could avoid judicial review by delegating to its staff the power to decide individual cases, and declining to review the staff decision. Kixmiller v. SEC, 492 F.2d 641 (D.C.Cir.1974). As a general proposition, the shareholder proposal rule is administered through the SEC's no action letter process. No action letters are SEC staff responses to private requests for indication of whether certain contemplated conduct is in compliance with the appropriate statutory provisions and rules. The SEC's no action responses are staff interpretations rather than formal Commission action and thus have limited precedential weight:

> An individual no-action letter by itself is not an expression of agency interpretation to which the court must defer. See Roosevelt v. E.I. Du Pont, 958 F.2d 416, 427 n. 19 (D.C.Cir.1992) (principle of deference to administrative regulation is not applicable to an SEC no-action letter regarding shareholder proposals because no-action letter does not "rank[ ] as an agency adjudication or rulemaking"); New York City Employees' Retirement System v. Dole Food Co., Inc., 795 F.Supp. 95 (S.D.N.Y.1992) vacated on other grounds, 969 F.2d 1430 (2d Cir.1992)] (SEC no-action letters do not bind court). By responding to a company's request for a no-action letter, the "Commission and its staff do not purport in any way to issue 'rulings' or 'decisions' on shareholder proposals management indicates it intends to omit, and they do not adjudicate the merits of a management's posture concerning such a proposal."

> The SEC staff reviews annually approximately 350 requests for no-action letters regarding shareholder proposals and over 6,700 proxy statements, and itself acknowledges that its staff "necessarily cannot do more in each case than make a quick analysis of the material submitted that, perforce, lacks the kind of in-depth study that would be essential to a definitive determination. . . ." Time and staff constraints require the staff to evaluate a shareholder proposal as an indivisible whole; if one part of a multi-part proposal is excludable, the entire proposal is treated as excludable. The administrative constraints on the SEC staff led the agency to express concern at its inability to enforce § 14(a) on its own through the informal no-action letter process, and it has acknowledged a need for its efforts to be supplemented by private enforcement in the courts.

> However, although the court need not defer to an individual no-action position, courts have relied on the consistency of the SEC staff's position and reasoning on a given issue, or the lack of consistency, in determining whether a proposal that was deemed excludable by the SEC staff can in fact be omitted under Rule 14a–8(c)(7). . . .

In determining whether to defer to a position drawn from a series of no-action letters, courts must recognize that a change in SEC position does not necessarily reveal capricious action by the agency; changes in conditions and public perceptions justify changes in the SEC's construction of the "ordinary business operations" exception. The nature of the exception permits, if not requires, the SEC to reevaluate earlier positions "in light of new considerations, or changing conditions which indicate that its earlier views are no longer in keeping with the objectives of Rule 14a–8."

Amalgamated Clothing and Textile Workers Union v. Wal–Mart Stores, Inc., 821 F.Supp. 877, 885–887 (S.D.N.Y.1993).

5. In view of the fact that most shareholder proposals are voted down overwhelmingly, do you think they serve any useful purpose, other than to let small shareholders vent or promote their favorite cause? Nevertheless, although small in number, some shareholder proposals do pass. See Jerry Guidera, "Shareholder Activists Win Two Big Ones," Wall St. J., May 9, 2002, at C1 (shareholders in two corporations approved proposals, one of which sought a majority of independent directors on the board and certain committees, and the other that stock option plans be submitted to the shareholders for approval). Sometimes boards may even ignore proposals that have been submitted and approved by a majority of the shareholders. Staggered boards may be used by management to fend off unwanted takeovers and to retain control. Institutional investors at Gillette mounted an attack on its use of a staggered board in 2004 and obtained a shareholder vote in which sixty-eight percent of the shareholders sought its termination. The Gillette management ignored the vote. Sears, Roebuck & Co. and Federated Department Stores, Inc., refused to drop their staggered boards even after shareholder majorities voiced support for such a change. The California Public Employee Retirement System (Calpers) led another successful vote against the use of staggered boards at Ingersoll Rand, but management resisted that demand.

6. In recent years, "say-on-pay" proxy proposals have become popular. These proposals seek to allow shareholders to have some say on the compensation given to executives, which is often claimed to be excessive. This proved to be a popular political issue. The House of Representatives passed a "Say-On-Pay" act in 2007. In 2008, some 80 companies were voting on such proposals. They were even supported by President Barack Obama, but many corporate boards were opposed, asserting that these were management decisions that should lie with the board and not shareholders.

7. The United States faced one of the gravest economic crises in its history in 2008 after a slump in the real estate market caused massive losses to many of the nation's largest financial institutions. Those losses resulted in the failure of Bear Stearns, Lehman Brothers, Merrill Lynch, Wachovia, Washington Mutual and others. Citigroup experienced crippling losses, as did a number of foreign banks, including UBS AG and the Royal Bank of Scotland.

The failure of Lehman Brothers in September 2008 set off a frightening market panic that nearly crushed the stock market and caused a panic run on money market funds. In order to stabilize the situation, the federal government stepped in with a $750 billion bailout program called TARP (troubled asset relief program). TARP authorized the Treasury to provide billions of dollars in bailout funds to troubled financial institutions. For a description of this program see http://www.ustreas.gov/initiatives/eesa/map/ (visited on March 26, 2009).

After assuming office, President Obama attacked the $18 billion in bonuses given out to the executives of banks in 2008 who were bailed out by the federal government during the subprime crisis. He asserted in a statement issued on January 29, 2009 that such bonuses were "outrageous," "shameful" and the "height of irresponsibility." Damian Paletta, et al., "U.S. Eyes Two–Part Bailout For Banks," Wall St. J., Jan. 30, 2009, at A1. Controversy over the use of TARP funds for bonuses was further fueled by the disclosure that Merrill Lynch had paic $3.6 billion in accelerated bonuses to Merrill Lynch executives. Those bonuses were paid despite the failure despite a staggering $15 billion loss in the quarter in which those bonuses were paid. In total, Merrill Lynch lost over ..6 billion in 2008. The bonuses were paid just before the completion of Merrill Lynch's emergency acquisition by the Bank of America, which had needed TARP funds to complete that rescue. *See* Susanne Craig, "Merrill's $10 Million Men—Top 10 Earners Made $209 Million in 2008 as Firm Foundered," Wall St. J., March 4, 2009, at A1.

Citigroup, which was also receiving massive funds in the TARP bailout, was embarrassed by its purchase of a $42 million Dassault Falcon 7X. Citigroup was forced to cancel that order at the direction of the federal government and was blasted by President Obama in a speech in which he stated that "they should know better." David Enrich, et al., "Citi Explores Breaking Mets Deal—Bank That Got Bailout Cash Revisits $400 Million Pact to Put Name on Stadium," Wall St. J., Feb. 3, 2009, at A1. More outrage was sparked after it was disclosed that bonuses totaling $165 million were paid by the American International Group (AIG) to executives in a unit that caused losses that resulted in a $170 billion government bailout from TARP funds. Thoses bonuses were called "outrageous" by the Obama White House, and the President personally vowed to take every available legal step to recover the AIG bonuses. Suzanne Garment, "Populist Anger Is Hard to Contain," Wall St. J., March 23, 2009, at A13.

One poll found that 83 percent of Americans believed that the federal government should limit the amount of compensation paid to executives in firms receiving bailout funds. Members of Congress were calling for special legislation to tax away bonuses of executives working at financial services firms receiving bailout money. Such a bill of attainder was passed by the House by a large majority on March 18, 2009. That legislation would impose a 90 precent surtax on employees earning more than $250,000 at companies receiving $5 billion or more in TARP funds. The tax was to be retroactive to

December 31, 2009. If enacted, this legislation would affect thousands of employees at Goldman Sachs, JPMorgan Chase, Morgan Stanley, Citigroup and Wells Fargo, as well as Fannie Mae and Freddie Mac. Greg Hitt and Aaron Lucchetti, "House Passes Bonus Tax Bill—90% Hit Would Affect Major Banks; Senate Mulls Similar Action Amid AIG Furor," Wall St. J., March 20, 2009, at A1.

Not surprisingly, that legislation set off a backlash in the financial community, which began expressing a lack of willingness of further participation in government programs that were seeking to limit the extent of the damage to the economy from the subprime crisis. Several large banks also announced they were returning the bailout funds received from the federal government so that they would not have their compensation dictated by Congress. President Obama then backed off his earlier threats of retaliation against the AIG bonuses and even questioned the proprietary of the House legislation.

In the meantime, a new SEC Chairman, Mary Schapiro, was reexamining the scope of SEC proposal requirements under Rule 14a-8 concerning say-on-pay and director nominations. That reexamination was being conducted with a view toward requiring inclusion of such proposals in the proxy materials of public companies.

8. *Is the game worth the candle?* Item 20 of SEC Schedule 14A requires management include in its proxy statement matters that it has reason to believe will be voted upon at the meeting.[a] Thus, even if management is entitled to exclude the proposal under Rule 14a–8, it will still have to include a description of the proposal in its proxy statement. Given this, why do corporations spend so much time and effort drafting requests for no action letters in order to exclude proposals from the proxy statement?

---

a. "If action is to be taken on any matter not specifically referred to in this Schedule 14A, describe briefly the substance of each such matter in substantially the same degree of detail as is required by Items 5 to 19, inclusive of this Schedule. . . ."

CHAPTER 13[a]

FRAUD CLAIMS UNDER THE FEDERAL SECURITIES LAWS

■ ■ ■

SECTION 1. SEC RULE 10b–5

Section 10(b) of the Securities Exchange Act of 1934 contains a catch-all provision permitting the Securities and Exchange Commission ("SEC") to prohibit by rule any "manipulative or deceptive device or contrivance" with respect to any security. Section 10(b) makes it unlawful for any person to use the mails or facilities of interstate commerce:

> "To use or employ, in connection with the purchase or sale of any security * * * any manipulative or deceptive device or contrivance in contravention of such rules and regulations as the Commission may prescribe as necessary or appropriate in the public interest or for the protection of investors."

Section 10(b) by its terms does not make anything unlawful unless the SEC has adopted a rule prohibiting it.

In 1942, the SEC was presented with a situation in which the president of a company was buying shares from the existing shareholders at a low price by misrepresenting the company's financial condition. While § 17(a) of the Securities Act of 1933 prohibited fraud and misstatements in the sale of securities, there was no comparable provision prohibiting such practices in connection with the purchase of securities. The SEC's Assistant Solicitor accordingly lifted the operative language out of § 17(a), made the necessary modifications, added the words "in connection with the purchase or sale of any security," and presented the product to the Commission as Rule 10b–5. The following excerpt describes the birth of the Rule.

BLUE CHIP STAMPS v. MANOR DRUG STORES
421 U.S. 723, 95 S.Ct. 1917, 44 L.Ed.2d 539 (1975).

Blackmun, Justice, dissenting,

In adopting Rule 10b–5 and 1942, the Securities and Exchange Commission issued a press release stating: 'The new rule closes a loophole

---

a. Portions of this chapter were adapted from Thomas Lee Hazen & David L. Ratner, Securities Regulation: Cases and Materials ch. 8 (6th ed. 2003).

in the protections against fraud administered by the Commission by prohibiting individuals or companies from buying securities if they engage in fraud in their purchase.' SEC Release No. 3230 (May 21, 1942). To say specifically that certain types of fraud are within Rule 10b–5, of course, is not to say that others are necessarily excluded. That this is so is confirmed by the apparently casual origins of the Rule, as recalled by a former SEC staff attorney in remarks made at a conference on federal securities laws several years ago:

> 'It was one day in the year 1943, I believe. I was sitting in my office in the S.E.C. building in Philadelphia and I received a call from Jim Treanor who was then the Director of the Trading and Exchange Division. He said, 'I have just been on the telephone with Paul Rowen,' who was then the S.E.C. Regional Administrator in Boston, 'and he has told me about the president of some company in Boston who is going around buying up the stock of his company from his own shareholders at $4.00 a share, and he has been telling them that the company is doing very badly, whereas, in fact, the earnings are going to be quadrupled and will be $2.00 a share for this coming year. Is there anything we can do about it?' So he came upstairs and I called in my secretary and I looked at Section 10(b) and I looked at Section 17, and I put them together, and the only discussion we had there was where 'in connection with the purchase or sale' should be, and we decided it should be at the end. 'We called the Commission and we got on the calendar, and I don't remember whether we got there that morning or after lunch. We passed a piece of paper around to all the commissioners. All the commissioners read the rule and they tossed it on the table, indicating approval. Nobody said anything except Summer Pike who said, 'Well,' he said, 'we are against fraud, aren't we?' That is how it happened.' Remarks of Milton Freeman, Conference on Codification of the Federal Securities Laws, 22 Bus.Law 793, 922 (1967).

NOTES

1. Since its adoption, Rule 10b–5 has been invoked in a wide variety of SEC and private proceedings, and applied to almost every conceivable kind of situation. It has spawned a formidable outpouring of legal scholarship, including complete books and innumerable law review articles. But before examining the cases systematically, it is useful to have in mind certain basic features of the rule:

2. Rule 10b–5 applies to any purchase or sale by any person of any security. There are no exemptions. It applies to publicly-held companies, to closely-held companies, to any kind of entity which issues something that can be called a "security." It even applies to securities that are exempted from the registration provisions of the Securities Exchange Act.

3.   In the 1960's and early 1970's, many federal appellate courts and district courts developed expansive interpretations of Rule 10b–5 (and other antifraud provisions of the securities laws). They imposed liability for negligent as well as deliberate misrepresentations, for breaches of fiduciary duty by corporate management, and for failure by directors, underwriters, accountants and lawyers to prevent wrong-doing by others. In private actions for damages, the courts were willing to imply a private right of action for anyone whose losses were even remotely connected with the alleged wrongdoing, or even in someone who had suffered no loss if his suit would help to encourage compliance with the law. The Supreme Court aided and abetted this development, giving an expansive reading to the terms "fraud" and "purchase or sale" and to the "connection" that had to be found between them. Starting in 1975, a new conservative majority on the Supreme Court sharply reversed this trend, in a series of decisions giving a narrow reading to the terms of Rule 10b–5 and other antifraud provisions and limiting the situations in which a private right of action will be implied. The Supreme Court has more recently taken a more moderate approach, but it does not appear poised to resume the expansive approach of earlier years.

4.   There are three separate clauses in Rule 10b–5, and they are not arranged in a very logical order. Clauses (1) and (3) speak in terms of "fraud" or "deceit" while clause (2) speaks in terms of misstatements or omissions. It is generally assumed, however, that clause (3), which prohibits "any act, practice, or course of business which operates or would operate as (a) a fraud or deceit (b) upon any person (c) in connection with (d) the purchase or sale (e) of any security," has the broadest scope. Each of the elements of this formulation has given rise to interpretive questions.

5.   One of the problems of any implied remedy is deciding the parameters of the remedy. For example: Who has standing to sue? Who may be sued? What are the elements of a claim? Specifically, what standard of care is imposed? What type of reliance is required? What type of causation is required? What is the appropriate statute of limitations? What defenses are available? These questions are considered below.

SECTION 2.   PRIVATE REMEDIES FOR SECURITIES FRAUD

The antifraud provisions of the federal securities laws are worded as prohibitions; no express private right of action is given to a person injured by a violation. Beginning in 1946, however federal courts began to *imply* the existence of a private right of action, utilizing basic common law principles. Just four years after the adoption of Rule 10b–5 in 1942, the district court in Kardon v. National Gypsum Co., 69 F.Supp. 512 (E.D.Pa. 1946) announced its decision that dramatically changed the landscape of federal law:

It is not, and cannot be, questioned that the complaint sets forth conduct on the part of the Slavins directly in violation of the provisions of Sec. 10(b) of the Act and of Rule X–10b–5 which implements it. It is also true that there is no provision in Sec. 10 or elsewhere expressly allowing civil suits by persons injured as a result of violation of Sec. 10 or of the Rule. However, "The violation of a legislative enactment by doing a prohibited act, or by failing to do a required act, makes the actor liable for an invasion of an interest of another if; (a) the intent of the enactment is exclusively or in part to protect an interest of the other as an individual; and (b) the interest invaded is one which the enactment is intended to protect. * * * " Restatement, Torts, Vol. 2, Sec. 286. This rule is more than merely a canon of statutory interpretation. The disregard of the command of a statute is a wrongful act and a tort.

Of course, the legislature may withhold from parties injured the right to recover damages arising by reason of violation of a statute but the right is so fundamental and so deeply ingrained in the law that where it is not expressly denied the intention to withhold it should appear very clearly and plainly. The defendants argue that such intention can be deduced from the fact that three other sections of the statute (Sections 9, 16 and 18) each declaring certain types of conduct illegal, all expressly provide for a civil action by a person injured and for incidents and limitations of it, whereas Sec. 10 does not. The argument is not without force. Were the whole question one of statutory interpretation it might be convincing, but the question is only partly such. It is whether an intention can be implied to deny a remedy and to wipe out a liability which, normally, by virtue of basic principles of tort law accompanies the doing of the prohibited act. Where, as here, the whole statute discloses a broad purpose to regulate securities transactions of all kinds and, as a part of such regulation, the specific section in question provides for the elimination of all manipulative or deceptive methods in such transactions, the construction contended for by the defendants may not be adopted. In other words, in view of the general purpose of the Act, the mere omission of an express provision for civil liability is not sufficient to negative what the general law implies.

The other point presented by the defendants is that, under the general rule of law, civil liability for violation of a statute accrues only to a member of a class (investors) for whose special benefit the statute was enacted—an argument applied to both Sec. 10 and to Rule X–10b–5. Sec. 10 prohibits deceptive devices "in contravention of such rules and regulations as the Commission may prescribe as necessary or appropriate in the public interest or for the protection of investors." I cannot agree, however, that "investors" is limited to persons who are about to invest in a security or that two men who have acquired ownership of the stock of a corporation are not investors merely because they own half of the total issue.

Apart from Sec. 10(b), I think that the action can also be grounded upon Sec. 29(b) of the Act which provides that contracts in violation of any provision of the Act shall be void. Here, unlike the point just discussed, the question is purely one of statutory construction. It seems to me that a statutory enactment that a contract of a certain kind shall be void almost necessarily implies a remedy in respect of it. The statute would be of little value unless a party to the contract could apply to the Courts to relieve himself of obligations under it or to escape its consequences. * * * And * * * such suits would include not only actions for rescission but also for money damages.

In J.I. Case Co. v. Borak, 377 U.S. 426, 84 S.Ct. 1555, 12 L.Ed.2d 423 (1964), the Court faced the question of whether to imply a private remedy under the antifraud provisions of Rule 14a–9. The Court held that it did:

> While the respondent contends that his Count 2 claim is not a derivative one, we need not embrace that view, for we believe that a right of action exists as to both derivative and direct causes.

> The purpose of § 14(a) is to prevent management or others from obtaining authorization for corporate action by means of deceptive or inadequate disclosure in proxy solicitation. * * * These broad remedial purposes are evidenced in the language of the section which makes it "unlawful for any person * * * to solicit or to permit the use of his name to solicit any proxy or consent or authorization in respect of any security * * * registered on any national securities exchange in contravention of such rules and regulations as the Commission may prescribe as necessary or appropriate in the public interest *or for the protection of investors.*" (Italics supplied.) While this language makes no specific reference to a private right of action, among its chief purposes is "the protection of investors," which certainly implies the availability of judicial relief where necessary to achieve that result.

> The injury which a stockholder suffers from corporate action pursuant to a deceptive proxy solicitation ordinarily flows from the damage done to the corporation, rather than from the damage inflicted directly upon the stockholder. The damage suffered results not from the deceit practiced on him alone but rather from the deceit practiced on the stockholders as a group. To hold that derivative actions are not within the sweep of the section would therefore be tantamount to a denial of private relief. Private enforcement of the proxy rules provides a necessary supplement to Commission action. As in antitrust treble damage litigation, the possibility of civil damages or injunctive relief serves as a most effective weapon in the enforcement of the proxy requirements. The Commission advises that it examines over 2,000 proxy statements annually and each of them must necessarily be expedited. Time does not permit an independent examination of the facts set out in the proxy material and this results in the Commission's acceptance of the representations contained therein at their face value, unless contrary to other material on file with it. Indeed, on the allegations of respondent's complaint, the

proxy material failed to disclose alleged unlawful market manipulation of the stock of ATC, and this unlawful manipulation would not have been apparent to the Commission until after the merger.

We, therefore, believe that under the circumstances here it is the duty of the courts to be alert to provide such remedies as are necessary to make effective the congressional purpose. * * * It is for the federal courts "to adjust their remedies so as to grant the necessary relief" where federally secured rights are invaded. "And it is also well settled that where legal rights have been invaded, and a federal statute provides for a general right to sue for such invasion, federal courts may use any available remedy to make good the wrong done." Section 27 grants the District Courts jurisdiction "of all suits in equity and actions at law brought to enforce any liability or duty created by this title * * *." In passing on almost identical language found in the Securities Act of 1933, the Court found the words entirely sufficient to fashion a remedy to rescind a fraudulent sale, secure restitution and even to enforce the right to restitution against a third party holding assets of the vendor.

NOTES

1. The question whether the courts should imply a private right of action under Rule 10b–5 did not reach the Supreme Court for twenty-five years after the *Kardon* decision. When the question did come before the Court in 1971 in Superintendent of Insurance v. Bankers Life & Casualty Co., 404 U.S. 6, 92 S.Ct. 165, 30 L.Ed.2d 128 (1971), the Court simply stated in a footnote that "it is now established that a private right of action is implied under § 10(b)." There was no discussion of the basis for this implication.

2. The Court in *Kardon* was following the normal tort rule in recognizing a private right of action under Rule 10b–5, *i.e.*, a person that violates a legislative enactment is liable in damages if he invades the interest of another person that the legislation was intended to protect. The more recent test for implying private rights of action under federal law stems from the Supreme Court's decision of Cort v. Ash, 422 U.S. 66, 95 S.Ct. 2080, 45 L.Ed.2d 26 (1975). In *Cort,* the Supreme Court unanimously refused to imply a private cause of action for damages against corporate directors and in favor of stockholders for purported violations of a criminal statute prohibiting corporations from making certain campaign contributions. In rejecting the plaintiff's theory that implication was appropriate for violations of this criminal statute, Justice Brennan outlined the following four-part test for determining when a private remedy should be implied:

> First, is the plaintiff "one of the class for whose *especial* benefit the statute was enacted,"—that is, does the statute create a federal right in favor of the plaintiff? Second, is there any indication of legislative intent, explicit or implicit, either to create such a remedy or to deny one? Third, is it consistent with the underlying purposes of the legislative scheme to imply such a remedy for the plaintiff? And finally, is the cause of action one traditionally relegated to state law, in an area basically the concern of

the States, so that it would be inappropriate to infer a cause of action based solely on federal law?

3.   In 1979, the Supreme Court, having adopted a more negative attitude toward implied private rights of action, implicitly rejected the rationale underlying the *Kardon* decision by noting that "the Court has been especially reluctant to imply causes of action under statutes that create duties on the part of persons for the benefit of the public at large." The Court described the *Superintendent of Insurance* case as a "deviat[ion] from this pattern" in which "the Court explicitly acquiesced in the 25–year-old acceptance by the lower federal courts of a 10b–5 cause of action." Cannon v. University of Chicago, 441 U.S. 677, 99 S.Ct. 1946, 60 L.Ed.2d 560 (1979). The rationale of the *Kardon* and *Borak* cases for implying federal remedies had thus been discredited. The Supreme Court did not overrule those decisions, but it did begin a process of defining and often times limiting the scope and application of private rights of action.

SECTION 3.   MATERIALITY

TSC INDUSTRIES, INC. v. NORTHWAY, INC.

426 U.S. 438, 96 S.Ct. 2126, 48 L.Ed.2d 757 (1976).

MR. JUSTICE MARSHALL DELIVERED THE OPINION OF THE COURT.

The proxy rules promulgated by the Securities and Exchange Commission under the Securities Exchange Act of 1934 bar the use of proxy statements that are false or misleading with respect to the presentation or omission of material facts. We are called upon to consider the definition of a material fact under those rules, and the appropriateness of resolving the question of materiality by summary judgment in this case.

The dispute in this case centers on the acquisition of petitioner TSC Industries, Inc., by petitioner National Industries, Inc. In February 1969 National acquired 34% Of TSC's voting securities by purchase from Charles E. Schmidt and his family. Schmidt, who had been TSC's founder and principal shareholder, promptly resigned along with his son from TSC's board of directors. Thereafter, five National nominees were placed on TSC's board; and Stanley R. Yarmuth, National's president and chief executive officer, became chairman of the TSC board, and Charles F. Simonelli, National's executive vice president, became chairman of the TSC executive committee. On October 16, 1969, the TSC board, with the attending National nominees abstaining, approved a proposal to liquidate and sell all of TSC's assets to National. The proposal in substance provided for the exchange of TSC common and Series 1 preferred stock for National Series B preferred stock and warrants. On November 12, 1969, TSC and National issued a joint proxy statement to their shareholders, recommending approval of the proposal. The proxy solicitation was successful, TSC was placed in liquidation and dissolution, and the exchange of shares was effected.

This is an action brought by respondent Northway, a TSC shareholder, against TSC and National, claiming that their joint proxy statement was incomplete and materially misleading in violation of § 14(a) of the Securities Exchange Act of 1934, and Rules 14a–3 and 14a–9 promulgated thereunder. The basis of Northway's claim under Rule 14a–3 is that TSC and National failed to state in the proxy statement that the transfer of the Schmidt interests in TSC to National had given National control of TSC. The Rule 14a–9 claim, insofar as it concerns us, is that TSC and National omitted from the proxy statement material facts relating to the degree of National's control over TSC and the favorability of the terms of the proposal to TSC shareholders.

The Court of Appeals for the Seventh Circuit agreed with the District Court that there existed a genuine issue of fact as to whether National's acquisition of the Schmidt interests in TSC had resulted in a change of control, and that summary judgment was therefore inappropriate on the Rule 14a–3 claim. But the Court of Appeals reversed the District Court's denial of summary judgment to Northway on its Rule 14a–9 claims, holding that certain omissions of fact were material as a matter of law . . . . . We now hold that the Court of Appeals erred in ordering that partial summary judgment be granted to Northway.

As we have noted on more than one occasion, § 14(a) of the Securities Exchange Act "was intended to promote 'the free exercise of the voting rights of stockholders' by ensuring that proxies would be solicited with 'explanation to the stockholder of the real nature of the questions for which authority to cast his vote is sought.' " Mills v. Electric Auto–Lite Co., 396 U.S. 375, 381 (1970) quoting H.R.Rep.No.1383, 73d Cong., 2d Sess., 14 (1934); S.Rep.No.792, 73d Cong., 2d Sess., 12 (1934). [I]n Mills, we attempted to clarify to some extent the elements of a private cause of action for violation of § 14(a). In a suit challenging the sufficiency under § 14(a) and Rule 14a–9 of a proxy statement soliciting votes in favor of a merger, we held that there was no need to demonstrate that the alleged defect in the proxy statement actually had a decisive effect on the voting. So long as the misstatement or omission was material, the causal relation between violation and injury is sufficiently established, we concluded, if "the proxy solicitation itself . . . was an essential link in the accomplishment of the transaction." 396 U.S., at 385. After Mills, then, the content given to the notion of materiality assumes heightened significance.

The question of materiality, it is universally agreed, is an objective one, involving the significance of an omitted or misrepresented fact to a reasonable investor. Variations in the formulation of a general test of materiality occur in the articulation of just how significant a fact must be or, put another way, how certain it must be that the fact would affect a reasonable investor's judgment.

The Court of Appeals in this case concluded that material facts include "all facts which a reasonable shareholder *might* consider important." This formulation of the test of materiality has been explicitly rejected by at least two courts as setting too low a threshold for the imposition of liability under Rule 14a–9. Gerstle v. Gamble–Skogmo, Inc., 478 F.2d 1281, 1301–1302 (C.A.2 1973); Smallwood v. Pearl Brewing Co., 489 F.2d 579, 603–604 (C.A.5 1974). In these cases, panels of the Second and Fifth Circuits opted for the conventional tort test of materiality whether a reasonable man *would* attach importance to the fact misrepresented or omitted in determining his course of action. See Restatement (Second) of Torts § 538(2) (a) (Tent.Draft No. 10, Apr. 20, 1964). See also American Law Institute, Federal Securities Code § 256(a) (Tent.Draft No. 2, 1973). Gerstle v. Gamble–Skogmo, supra, at 1302, also approved the following standard, which had been formulated with reference to statements issued in a contested election: "whether, taking a properly realistic view, there is a substantial likelihood that the misstatement or omission may have led a stockholder to grant a proxy to the solicitor or to withhold one from the other side, whereas in the absence of this he would have taken a contrary course." General Time Corp. v. Talley Industries, Inc., 403 F.2d 159, 162 (C.A.2 1968), cert. denied, 393 U.S. 1026 (1969).

In arriving at its broad definition of a material fact as one that a reasonable shareholder *might* consider important, the Court of Appeals in this case relied heavily upon language of this Court in Mills v. Electric Auto-Lite Co., supra. That reliance was misplaced. The Mills Court did characterize a determination of materiality as at least "embod(ying) a conclusion that the defect was of such a character that it might have been considered important by a reasonable shareholder who was in the process of deciding how to vote." 396 U.S., at 384. But if any language in Mills is to be read as suggesting a general notion of materiality, it can only be the opinion's subsequent reference to materiality as a "requirement that the defect have a significant *propensity* to affect the voting process." Ibid. (Emphasis in original.) For it was that requirement that the Court said "adequately serves the purpose of ensuring that a cause of action cannot be established by proof of a defect so trivial, or so unrelated to the transaction for which approval is sought, that correction of the defect or imposition of liability would not further the interests protected by § 14(a)." Ibid. Even this language must be read, however, with appreciation that the Court specifically declined to consider the materiality of the omissions in Mills. The references to materiality were simply preliminary to our consideration of the sole question in the case whether proof of the materiality of an omission from a proxy statement must be supplemented by a showing that the defect actually caused the outcome of the vote. It is clear, then, that Mills did not intend to foreclose further inquiry into the meaning of materiality under Rule 14a–9.[9]

---

9. Nor is Affiliated Ute Citizens v. United States, 406 U.S. 128 (1972) also relied upon by the Court of Appeals, dispositive. There we held that when a Rule 10b–5 violation involves a failure to disclose, "positive proof of reliance is not a prerequisite to recovery. All that is necessary is that

In formulating a standard of materiality under Rule 14a–9, we are guided, of course, by the recognition in *Borak* and *Mills* of the Rule's broad remedial purpose. That purpose is not merely to ensure by judicial means that the transaction, when judged by its real terms, is fair and otherwise adequate, but to ensure disclosures by corporate management in order to enable the shareholders to make an informed choice. As an abstract proposition, the most desirable role for a court in a suit of this sort, coming after the consummation of the proposed transaction, would perhaps be to determine whether in fact the proposal would have been favored by the shareholders and consummated in the absence of any misstatement or omission. But as we recognized in *Mills*, supra, at 382 n. 5, such matters are not subject to determination with certainty. Doubts as to the critical nature of information misstated or omitted will be commonplace. And particularly in view of the prophylactic purpose of the Rule and the fact that the content of the proxy statement is within management's control, it is appropriate that these doubts be resolved in favor of those the statute is designed to protect.

We are aware, however, that the disclosure policy embodied in the proxy regulations is not without limit. Some information is of such dubious significance that insistence on its disclosure may accomplish more harm than good. The potential liability for a Rule 14a–9 violation can be great indeed, and if the standard of materiality is unnecessarily low, not only may the corporation and its management be subjected to liability for insignificant omissions or misstatements, but also management's fear of exposing itself to substantial liability may cause it simply to bury the shareholders in an avalanche of trivial information a result that is hardly conducive to informed decisionmaking. Precisely these dangers are presented, we think, by the definition of a material fact adopted by the Court of Appeals in this case a fact which a reasonable shareholder *might* consider important. We agree with Judge Friendly, speaking for the Court of Appeals in *Gerstle*, that the "might" formulation is "too suggestive of mere possibility, however unlikely." 478 F.2d, at 1302.

The general standard of materiality that we think best comports with the policies of Rule 14a–9 is as follows: An omitted fact is material if there is a substantial likelihood that a reasonable shareholder would consider it important in deciding how to vote. This standard is fully consistent with *Mills* general description of materiality as a requirement that "the defect have a significant propensity to affect the voting process." It does not require proof of a substantial likelihood that disclosure of the omitted fact would have caused the reasonable investor to change his vote. What the standard does contemplate is a showing of a substantial likelihood that, under all the circumstances, the omitted fact would have assumed actual

the facts withheld be material in the sense that a reasonable investor might have considered them important in the making of this decision." Id., at 153–154. The conclusion embodied in the quoted language was simply that positive proof of reliance is unnecessary when materiality is established, and in order to reach that conclusion is was not necessary to articulate a precise definition of materiality, but only to give a "sense" of the notion. The quoted language did not purport to do more.

significance in the deliberations of the reasonable shareholder. Put another way, there must be a substantial likelihood that the disclosure of the omitted fact would have been viewed by the reasonable investor as having significantly altered the "total mix" of information made available.[10]

The issue of materiality may be characterized as a mixed question of law and fact, involving as it does the application of a legal standard to a particular set of facts. In considering whether summary judgment on the issue is appropriate, we must bear in mind that the underlying objective facts, which will often be free from dispute, are merely the starting point for the ultimate determination of materiality. The determination requires delicate assessments of the inferences a "reasonable shareholder" would draw from a given set of facts and the significance of those inferences to him, and these assessments are peculiarly ones for the trier of fact. Only if the established omissions are "so obviously important to an investor, that reasonable minds cannot differ on the question of materiality" is the ultimate issue of materiality appropriately resolved "as a matter of law" by summary judgment.

The omissions found by the Court of Appeals to have been materially misleading as a matter of law involved two general issues—the degree of National's control over TSC at the time of the proxy solicitation, and the favorability of the terms of the proposed transaction to TSC shareholders.

The Court of Appeals concluded that two omitted facts relating to National's potential influence, or control, over the management of TSC were material as a matter of law. First, the proxy statement failed to state that at the time the statement was issued, the chairman of the TSC board of directors was Stanley Yarmuth, National's president and chief executive officer, and the chairman of the TSC executive committee was Charles Simonelli, National's executive vice president. Second, the statement did not disclose that in filing reports required by the SEC, both TSC and National had indicated that National "may be deemed to be a 'parent' of TSC as that term is defined in the Rules and Regulations under the Securities Act of 1933." The Court of Appeals noted that TSC shareholders were relying on the TSC board of directors to negotiate on their behalf for the best possible rate of exchange with National. It then concluded that the omitted facts were material because they were "persuasive indicators that the TSC board was in fact under the control of National, and that National thus 'sat on both sides of the table' in setting the terms of the exchange."

We do not agree that the omission of these facts, when viewed against the disclosures contained in the proxy statement, warrants the entry of summary judgment against TSC and National on this record. Our conclu-

---

10. In defining materiality under Rule 14a–9, we are, of course, giving content to a rule promulgated by the SEC pursuant to broad statutory authority to promote "the public interest" and "the protection of investors." Under these circumstances, the SEC's view of the proper balance between the need to insure adequate disclosure and the need to avoid the adverse consequences of setting too low a threshold for civil liability is entitled to consideration. The standard we adopt is supported by the SEC.

sion is the same whether the omissions are considered separately or together.

The proxy statement prominently displayed the facts that National owned 34% of the outstanding shares in TSC, and that no other person owned more than 10%. It also prominently revealed that 5 out of 10 TSC directors were National nominees, and it recited the positions of those National nominees with National indicating, among other things, that Stanley Yarmuth was president and a director of National, and that Charles Simonelli was executive vice president and a director of National. These disclosures clearly revealed the nature of National's relationship with TSC and alerted the reasonable shareholder to the fact that National exercised a degree of influence over TSC. In view of these disclosures, we certainly cannot say that the additional facts that Yarmuth was chairman of the TSC board of directors and Simonelli chairman of its executive committee were, on this record, so obviously important that reasonable minds could not differ on their materiality.

Nor can we say that it was materially misleading as a matter of law for TSC and National to have omitted reference to SEC filings indicating that National "may be deemed to be a parent of TSC." As we have already noted, both the District Court and the Court of Appeals concluded, in denying summary judgment on the Rule 14a–3 claim, that there was a genuine issue of fact as to whether National actually controlled TSC at the time of the proxy solicitation. We must assume for present purposes, then, that National did not control TSC. On that assumption, TSC and National obviously had no duty to state without qualification that control did exist. If the proxy statements were to disclose the conclusory statements in the SEC filings that National "may be deemed to be a parent of TSC," then it would have been appropriate, if not necessary, for the statement to have included a disclaimer of National control over TSC or a disclaimer of knowledge as to whether National controlled TSC. The net contribution of including the contents of the SEC filings accompanied by such disclaimers is not of such obvious significance, in view of the other facts contained in the proxy statement, that their exclusion renders the statement materially misleading as a matter of law.

The Court of Appeals also found that the failure to disclose two sets of facts rendered the proxy statement materially deficient in its presentation of the favorability of the terms of the proposed transaction to TSC shareholders. The first omission was of information, described by the Court of Appeals as "bad news" for TSC shareholders, contained in a letter from an investment banking firm whose earlier favorable opinion of the fairness of the proposed transaction was reported in the proxy statement. The second omission related to purchases of National common stock by National and by Madison Fund, Inc., a large mutual fund, during the two years prior to the issuance of the proxy statement.

The proxy statement revealed that the investment banking firm of Hornblower & Weeks–Hemphill, Noyes had rendered a favorable opinion on the fairness to TSC shareholders of the terms for the exchange of TSC shares for National securities. In that opinion, the proxy statement explained, the firm had considered, "among other things, the current market prices of the securities of both corporations, the high redemption price of the National Series B preferred stock, the dividend and debt service requirements of both corporations, the substantial premium over current market values represented by the securities being offered to TSC stockholders, and the increased dividend income."

The Court of Appeals focused upon the reference to the "substantial premium over current market values represented by the securities being offered to TSC stockholders," and noted that any TSC shareholder could calculate the apparent premium by reference to the table of current market prices that appeared four pages later in the proxy statement. On the basis of the recited closing prices for November 7, 1969, five days before the issuance of the proxy statement, the apparent premiums were as follows. Each share of TSC Series 1 preferred, which closed at $12, would bring National Series B preferred stock and National warrants worth $15.23 for a premium of $3.23, or 27% Of the market value of the TSC Series 1 preferred. Each share of TSC common stock, which closed at $13.25, would bring National Series B preferred stock and National warrants worth $16.19 for a premium of $2.94, or 22% Of the market value of TSC common. * * *

TSC and National insist that the reference to a substantial premium required no clarification or supplementation, for the reason that there was a substantial premium even if the National warrants are assumed to have been worth $3.50. In reaching the contrary conclusion, the Court of Appeals, they contend, ignored the rise in price of TSC securities between early October 1969, when the exchange ratio was set, and November 7, 1969 a rise in price that they suggest was a result of the favorable exchange ratio's becoming public knowledge. When the proxy statement was mailed, TSC and National contend, the market price of TSC securities already reflected a portion of the premium to which Hornblower had referred in rendering its favorable opinion of the terms of exchange. Thus, they note that Hornblower assessed the fairness of the proposed transaction by reference to early October market prices of TSC preferred, TSC common, and National preferred. On the basis of those prices and a $3.50 value for the National warrants involved in the exchange, TSC and National contend that the premium was substantial. Each share of TSC preferred, selling in early October at $11, would bring National preferred stock and warrants worth $13.10 for a premium of $2.10, or 19%. And each share of TSC common, selling in early October at $11.63, would bring National preferred stock and warrants worth $13.25 for a premium of $1.62, or 14%. We certainly cannot say as a matter of law that these premiums were not substantial. And if, as we must assume in considering the appropriateness of summary judgment, the increase in price of TSC's securities from early October to November 7 reflected in large part the market's reaction to the terms of the proposed exchange, it was not materially misleading as a matter of law for the proxy statement to refer to the existence of a substantial premium.

There remains the possibility, however, that although TSC and National may be correct in urging the existence of a substantial premium based upon a $3.50 value for the National warrants and the early October market prices of the other securities involved in the transaction, the proxy statement misled the TSC shareholder to calculate a premium substantially in excess of that premium. The premiums apparent from early October market prices and a $3.50 value for the National warrants 19% on TSC preferred and 14% on TSC common are certainly less than those that would be derived through use of the November 7 closing prices listed in the proxy statement 27% on TSC preferred and 22% on TSC common. But we are unwilling to sustain a grant of summary judgment to Northway on that basis. To do so we would have to conclude as a matter of law, first, that the proxy statement would have misled the TSC shareholder to calculate his premium on the basis of November 7 market prices, and second, that the difference between that premium and that which would be apparent from early October prices and a $3.50 value for the National warrants was material. These are questions we think best left to the trier of fact.

NOTES

1. In SEC v. Texas Gulf Sulphur, 401 F.2d 833 (2d Cir.1968), *cert. denied* 394 U.S. 976, 92 S.Ct. 165, 30 L.Ed.2d 128 (1969), officers and employees of the corporation had bought stock in the market after receiving information about preliminary drilling results which showed the possibility that the company had discovered a huge and valuable body of ore. Whether or not there was a mineable body of ore could not, however, be determined without further drilling. The District Court held that the preliminary drilling results were not "material." The Court of Appeals reversed:

As we stated in List v. Fashion Park, Inc., 340 F.2d 457, 462, "The basic test of materiality * * * is whether a *reasonable* man would attach importance * * * in determining his choice of action in the transaction in question." This, of course, encompasses any fact "which in reasonable and objective contemplation *might* affect the value of the corporation's stock or securities." Such a fact is a material fact and must be effectively disclosed to the investing public prior to the commencement of insider trading in the corporation's securities. The speculators and chartists of Wall and Bay Streets are also "reasonable" investors entitled to the same legal protection afforded conservative traders. Thus, material facts include not only information disclosing the earnings and distributions of a company but also those facts which affect the probable future of the company and those which may affect the desire of investors to buy, sell, or hold the company's securities.

In each case, then, whether facts are material within Rule 10b–5 when the facts relate to a particular event and are undisclosed by those persons who are knowledgeable thereof will depend at any given time upon a balancing of both the indicated probability that the event will occur and the anticipated magnitude of the event in light of the totality of the company activity. Here, notwithstanding the trial court's conclusion that the results of the first drill core, K–55–1, were "too 'remote' * * * to have had any significant impact on the market, i.e., to be deemed material," knowledge of the possibility, which surely was more than marginal, of the existence of a mine of the vast magnitude indicated by the remarkably rich drill core located rather close to the surface (suggesting mineability by the less expensive open-pit method) within the confines of a large anomaly (suggesting an extensive region of mineralization) might well have affected the price of TGS stock and would certainly have been an important fact to a reasonable, if speculative, investor in deciding whether he should buy, sell, or hold. After all, this first drill core was "unusually good and * * * excited the interest and speculation of those who knew about it." * * *

2. One frequently-litigated issue of corporate disclosure is the liability of a corporation to purchasers or sellers of its stock for failing to make prompt disclosure of negotiations for mergers or acquisitions. In Greenfield v. Heublein, Inc., 742 F.2d 751 (3d Cir.1984), the court held that there was no duty to disclose merger negotiations until an "agreement in principle" on the price and structure of the transaction had been reached. The issue reached the Supreme Court for review in the following case.

BASIC INC. v. LEVINSON

485 U.S. 224, 108 S.Ct. 978, 99 L.Ed.2d 194 (1988).

JUSTICE BLACKMUN delivered the opinion of the Court.

This case requires us to apply the materiality requirement of § 10(b) of the Securities Exchange Act of 1934, (1934 Act), and the Securities and Exchange Commission's Rule 10b–5, promulgated thereunder, in the context of preliminary corporate merger discussions. We must also determine whether a person who traded a corporation's shares on a securities exchange after the issuance of a materially misleading statement by the corporation may invoke a rebuttable presumption that, in trading, he relied on the integrity of the price set by the market.

Prior to December 20, 1978, Basic Incorporated was a publicly traded company primarily engaged in the business of manufacturing chemical refractories for the steel industry. As early as 1965 or 1966, Combustion Engineering, Inc., a company producing mostly alumina-based refractories, expressed some interest in acquiring Basic, but was deterred from pursuing this inclination seriously because of antitrust concerns it then entertained. In 1976, however, regulatory action opened the way to a renewal of Combustion's interest. The "Strategic Plan," dated October 25, 1976, for Combustion's Industrial Products Group included the objective: "Acquire Basic Inc. $30 million."

Beginning in September, 1976, Combustion representatives had meetings and telephone conversations with Basic officers and directors, including petitioners here, concerning the possibility of a merger. During 1977 and 1978, Basic made three public statements denying that it was engaged in merger negotiations.[1] On December 18, 1978, Basic asked the New York Stock Exchange to suspend trading in its shares and issued a release stating that it had been "approached" by another company concerning a merger. On December 19, Basic's board endorsed Combustion's offer of $46 per share for its common stock, and on the following day publicly announced its approval of Combustion's tender for all outstanding shares.

Respondents are former Basic shareholders who sold their stock after Basic's first public statement of October 21, 1977, and before the suspension of trading in December 1978. Respondents brought a class action against Basic and its directors, asserting that the defendants issued three false or misleading public statements and thereby were in violation of § 10(b) of the 1934 Act and of Rule 10b–5. Respondents alleged that they were injured by selling Basic shares at artificially depressed prices in a market affected by petitioners' misleading statements and in reliance thereon.

The District Court adopted a presumption of reliance by members of the plaintiff class upon petitioners' public statements that enabled the court to conclude that common questions of fact or law predominated over particular questions pertaining to individual plaintiffs. The District Court therefore certified respondents' class. On the merits, however, the District Court granted summary judgment for the defendants. It held that, as a matter of law, any misstatements were immaterial: there were no negotiations ongoing at the time of the first statement, and although negotiations were taking place when the second and third statements were issued, those negotiations were not "destined, with reasonable certainty, to become a merger agreement in principle."

The United States Court of Appeals for the Sixth Circuit affirmed the class certification, but reversed the District Court's summary judgment, and remanded the case. The court reasoned that while petitioners were under no general duty to disclose their discussions with Combustion, any statement the company voluntarily released could not be " 'so incomplete

---

1. On October 21, 1977, after heavy trading and a new high in Basic stock, the following news item appeared in the Cleveland Plain Dealer:

"[Basic] President Max Muller said the company knew no reason for the stock's activity and that no negotiations were under way with any company for a merger. He said Flintkote recently denied Wall Street rumors that it would make a tender offer of $25 a share for control of the Cleveland-based maker of refractories for the steel industry."

On September 25, 1978, in reply to an inquiry from the New York Stock Exchange, Basic issued a release concerning increased activity in its stock and stated that

"management is unaware of any present or pending company development that would result in the abnormally heavy trading activity and price fluctuation in company shares that have been experienced in the past few days."

On November 6, 1978, Basic issued to its shareholders a "Nine Months Report 1978." This Report stated:

"With regard to the stock market activity in the Company's shares we remain unaware of any present or pending developments which would account for the high volume of trading and price fluctuations in recent months."

as to mislead.' " In the Court of Appeals' view, Basic's statements that no negotiations were taking place, and that it knew of no corporate developments to account for the heavy trading activity, were misleading. With respect to materiality, the court rejected the argument that preliminary merger discussions are immaterial as a matter of law, and held that "once a statement is made denying the existence of any discussions, even discussions that might not have been material in absence of the denial are material because they make the statement made untrue." * * *

We granted certiorari to resolve the split among the Courts of Appeals as to the standard of materiality applicable to preliminary merger discussions * * *.

The Court previously has addressed various positive and common-law requirements for a violation of § 10(b) or of Rule 10b–5. The Court also explicitly has defined a standard of materiality under the securities laws, see TSC Industries v. Northway, 426 U.S. 438 (1976), concluding in the proxy-solicitation context that "[a]n omitted fact is material if there is a substantial likelihood that a reasonable shareholder would consider it important in deciding how to vote." Acknowledging that certain information concerning corporate developments could well be of "dubious significance," the Court was careful not to set too low a standard of materiality; it was concerned that a minimal standard might bring an overabundance of information within its reach, and lead management "simply to bury the shareholders in an avalanche of trivial information—a result that is hardly conducive to informed decisionmaking." It further explained that to fulfill the materiality requirement "there must be a substantial likelihood that the disclosure of the omitted fact would have been viewed by the reasonable investor as having significantly altered the 'total mix' of information made available." We now expressly adopt the *TSC Industries* standard of materiality for the § 10(b) and Rule 10b–5 context.

The application of this materiality standard to preliminary merger discussion is not self-evident. Where the impact of the corporate development on the target's fortune is certain and clear, the *TSC Industries* materiality definition admits straightforward application. Where, on the other hand, the event is contingent or speculative in nature, it is difficult to ascertain whether the "reasonable investor" would have considered the omitted information significant at the time. Merger negotiations, because of the ever-present possibility that the contemplated transaction will not be effectuated, fall into the latter category.

Petitioners urge upon us a Third Circuit test for resolving this difficulty. Under this approach, preliminary merger discussions do not become material until "agreement-in-principle" as to the price and structure of the transaction has been reached between the would-be merger partners. See Greenfield v. Heublein, 742 F.2d 751, 757 (3d Cir.1984). By definition, then, information concerning any negotiations not yet at the agreement-in-principle stage could be withheld or even misrepresented without a violation of Rule 10b–5.

Three rationales have been offered in support of the "agreement-in-principle" test. The first derives from the concern expressed in *TSC Industries* that an investor not be overwhelmed by excessively detailed and trivial information, and focuses on the substantial risk that preliminary merger discussions may collapse: because such discussions are inherently tentative, disclosure of their existence itself could mislead investors and foster false optimism. The other two justifications for the agreement-in-principle standard are based on management concerns: because the requirement of "agreement-in-principle" limits the scope of disclosure obligations, it helps preserve the confidentiality of merger discussions where earlier disclosure might prejudice the negotiations; and the test also provides a usable, bright line rule for determining when disclosure must be made.

None of these policy-based rationales, however, purports to explain why drawing the line at agreement-in-principle reflects the significance of the information upon the investor's decision. * * *

We therefore find no valid justification for artificially excluding from the definition of materiality information concerning merger discussions, which would otherwise be considered significant to the trading decision of a reasonable investor, merely because agreement-in-principle as to price and structure has not yet been reached by the parties or their representatives.

The Sixth Circuit explicitly rejected the agreement-in-principle test, as we do today, but in its place adopted a rule that, if taken literally, would be equally insensitive, in our view, to the distinction between materiality and the other elements of an action under Rule 10b–5:

> "When a company whose stock is publicly traded makes a statement, as Basic did, that 'no negotiations' are underway, and that the corporation know of 'no reason for the stock's activity,' and that 'management is unaware of any present or pending corporate development that would result in the abnormally heavy trading activity,' information concerning ongoing acquisition discussions becomes material *by virtue of the statement denying their existence.* . . .

> " . . . In analyzing whether information regarding merger discussions is material such that it must be affirmatively disclosed to avoid a violation of Rule 10b–5, the discussions and their progress are the primary considerations. However, once a statement is made denying the existence of any discussions, even discussions that might not have been material in absence of the denial are material because they make the statement made untrue." * * *

Even before this Court's decision in *TSC Industries*, the Second Circuit had explained the role of the materiality requirement of Rule 10b–5, with respect to contingent or speculative information or events, in a manner that give that term meaning that is independent of the other provisions of the Rule. Under such circumstances, materiality "will depend at any given time upon a balancing of both the indicated probability that the event will occur and the anticipated magnitude of the event in light of the totality of the company activity." SEC v. Texas Gulf Sulphur Co., 401 F.2d, at 849. Interestingly, neither the Third Circuit decision adopting the agreement-in-principle test nor petitioners here take issue with this general standard. Rather, they suggest that with respect to preliminary merger discussions, there are good reasons to draw a line at agreement on price and structure. * * *

Whether merger discussions in any particular case are material therefore depends on the facts. Generally, in order to assess the probability that the event will occur, a factfinder will need to look to indicia of interest in the transaction at the highest corporate levels. Without attempting to catalog all such possible factors, we note by way of example that board resolutions, instructions to investment bankers, and actual negotiations between principals or their intermediaries may serve as indicia or interest. To assess the magnitude of the transaction to the issuer of the securities allegedly manipulated, a factfinder will need to consider such facts as the size of the two corporate entities and of the potential premiums over market value. No particular event or factor short of closing the transaction need be either necessary or sufficient by itself to render merger discussions material.[2]

As we clarify today, materiality depends on the significance the reasonable investor would place on the withheld or misrepresented information. The fact-specific inquiry we endorse here is consistent with the approach a number of courts have taken in assessing the materiality of merger negotiations. Because the standard of materiality we have adopted differs from that used by both courts below, we remand the case for reconsideration of the question whether a grant of summary judgment is appropriate on this record. * * *

NOTES

1. In the *Greenfield* case cited in *Basic*, the corporation, in response to an inquiry from the New York Stock Exchange, had made a statement that it "was aware of no reason that would explain the activity in its stock in trading on the Exchange." The Third Circuit held that this was not a materially misleading statement, even though the corporation knew that it was engaged in merger discussions, if the corporation had no reason to believe that any

---

2. To be actionable, of course, a statement must also be misleading. Silence, absent a duty to disclose, is not misleading under Rule 10b–5. "No comment" statements are generally the functional equivalent of silence.

It has been suggested that given current market practices, a "no comment" statement is tantamount to an admission that merger discussions are underway. That may well hold true to the extent that issuers adopt a policy of truthfully denying merger rumors when no discussions are underway, and of issuing "no comment" statements when they are in the midst of negotiations. There are, of course, other statement policies firms could adopt; we need not now advise issuers as to what kind of practice to follow, within the range permitted by law. Perhaps more importantly, we think that creating an exception to a regulatory scheme founded on a pro-disclosure legislative philosophy, because complying with the regulation might be "bad for business," is a role for Congress, not this Court.

non-public information about these discussions had been "leaked" to traders. Judge Higginbotham dissented strongly from this portion of the opinion, and the SEC indicated its disagreement with the position taken by the court. The Supreme Court did not directly address the issue in the *Basic* case.

2.　Materiality is usually measured in quantitative terms. A $10 million dollar asset purchase, despite its absolute size, may not be material in a multi-billion corporation and might not support a federal securities law fraud claim even if misstatements are made about the transaction to the purchaser's shareholders. Is materiality also a qualitative issue? For example, assume that management has made improper payments to foreign government officials in order to obtain business, but the amounts of the payments are not quantitatively material. Are the payments still material because they reflect on the quality of management. That issue came up in the 1970s when the SEC discovered that numerous American corporations were making such payments. The SEC argued that the payments were qualitatively material even if they were not large enough to be quantitatively material. The Ninth Circuit ruled in Gaines v. Haughton, 645 F.2d 761 (1981), cert. denied, 454 U.S. 1145, 102 S.Ct. 1006, 71 L.Ed.2d 297 (1982) (a case making claims of proxy fraud under Section 14(a) of the Securities Exchange Act of 1934) that such payments were not material to the election of a director because they were made on behalf of the corporation. To be qualitatively material, such payments would have to constitute self-dealing, personal dishonesty or deceit. Congress reacted to these payments by adopting the Foreign Corrupt Practices Act that prohibited most payments to foreign officials for the purpose of obtaining business and strengthened accounting requirements to prohibit the concealment of such payments in the company's books and records and otherwise requiring books and records to be accurate. 15 U.S.C. §§ 78dd–1 *et seq*.

3.　For many years, the SEC took the position that statements as to the appraised or estimated value of any property were inherently misleading, and prohibited their inclusion in disclosure documents filed with the Commission. The only figure that could be shown was the original cost, or "book value" of the property. But when an offer is being made to *buy* shares of a company, failure to disclose the current value of the company's property may be misleading to shareholders. The SEC's dilemma is described in the opinion in Gerstle v. Gamble–Skogmo, Inc., 478 F.2d 1281 (2d Cir.1973):

> One of the plaintiffs' principal attacks on the adequacy of the Proxy Statement was that GOA was bound to disclose its appraisals of the market value of the remaining plants and the existence and amount of the firm offers to purchase the unsold plants that it had received. Skogmo countered that the SEC would not have allowed this. By a stroke of luck it was able to support its position not only by materials generally available but by the SEC staff's reaction in this very case to the suggestion of Minis & Co. that market values be disclosed in the proxy statement. * * *

> The Commission's policy against disclosure of asset appraisals in proxy statements has apparently stemmed from its deep distrust of their reliability, its concern that investors would accord such appraisals in a

proxy statement more weight than would be warranted, and the impracticability, with its limited staff, of examining appraisals on a case-by-case basis to determine their reliability. The Commission is now in the process of a thorough re-examination of its policy, and it appears that new rules on the permissible uses of appraisals and projections may shortly be forthcoming. The SEC may well determine that its policy, while protecting investors who are considering the purchase of a security from the overoptimistic claims of management, may have deprived those who must decide whether or not to sell their securities, as the plaintiffs effectively did here, of valuable information, as Professor Kripke has argued. But we would be loath to impose a huge liability on Skogmo on the basis of what we regard as a substantial modification, if not reversal of the SEC's position on disclosure of appraisals in proxy statements, by way of its *amicus* brief in this case.

4.   Despite the SEC's change of position on projections and other types of "soft" information, an appeals court could still hold in 1982 that the SEC's views on appraisals had not changed sufficiently since the time of the *Gerstle* case to warrant requiring a company to include estimates of current market value in a proxy statement soliciting shareholder approval for a sale of the company's assets. South Coast Services Corp. v. Santa Ana, 669 F.2d 1265 (9th Cir.1982).

SECTION 4.   THE "IN CONNECTION WITH" REQUIREMENT

BLUE CHIP STAMPS v. MANOR DRUG STORES

421 U.S. 723, 95 S.Ct. 1917, 44 L.Ed.2d 539 (1975).

Mr. Justice Rehnquist delivered the opinion of the Court.

[Under the terms of an antitrust consent decree, plaintiff was entitled to purchase shares in Blue Chip Stamps. Plaintiff alleged that it refrained from making any purchase because of the materially misleading negative statements in the company's offering materials that were allegedly designed to discourage purchases]

Within a few years after the seminal *Kardon* decision the Court of Appeals for the Second Circuit concluded that the plaintiff class for purposes of a private damage action under § 10(b) and Rule 10b–5 was limited to actual purchasers and sellers of securities. Birnbaum v. Newport Steel Corp., 193 F.2d 461 (1952).

The Court of Appeals in this case did not repudiate *Birnbaum;* indeed, another panel of that court (in an opinion by Judge Ely) had but a short time earlier affirmed the rule of that case. Mount Clemens Industries v. Bell, 464 F.2d 339 (9th Cir.1972). But in this case a majority of the Court of Appeals found that the facts warranted an exception to the *Birnbaum* rule. For the reasons hereinafter stated, we are of the opinion that

Birnbaum was rightly decided, and that it bars respondent from maintaining this suit under Rule 10b–5.

The panel which decided *Birnbaum* consisted of Chief Judge Swan and Judges Learned Hand and Augustus Hand: the opinion was written by the latter. Since both § 10(b) and Rule 10b–5 proscribed only fraud "in connection with the purchase or sale" of securities, and since the history of § 10(b) revealed no congressional intention to extend a private civil remedy for money damages to other than defrauded purchasers or sellers of securities, in contrast to the express civil remedy provided by § 16(b) of the 1934 Act, the court concluded that the plaintiff class in a Rule 10b–5 action was limited to actual purchasers and sellers. * * *

The longstanding acceptance by the courts, coupled with Congress' failure to reject *Birnbaum's* reasonable interpretation of the wording of § 10(b), wording which is directed towards injury suffered "in connection with the purchase or sale" of securities, argues significantly in favor of acceptance of the *Birnbaum* rule by this Court.

Available extrinsic evidence from the texts of the 1933 and 1934 Acts as to the congressional scheme in this regard, though not conclusive, supports the result reached by the *Birnbaum* court.

* * * [W]e would by no means be understood as suggesting that we are able to divine from the language of § 10(b) the express "intent of Congress" as to the contours of a private cause of action under Rule 10b–5. When we deal with private actions under Rule 10b–5, we deal with a judicial oak which has grown from little more than a legislative acorn. Such growth may be quite consistent with the congressional enactment and with the role of the federal judiciary in interpreting it, but it would be disingenuous to suggest that either Congress in 1934 or the Securities and Exchange Commission in 1942 foreordained the present state of the law with respect to Rule 10b–5. It is therefore proper that we consider, in addition to the factors already discussed, what may be described as policy considerations when we come to flesh out the portions of the law with respect to which neither the congressional enactment nor the administrative regulations offer conclusive guidance. * * *

A great majority of the many commentators on the issue before us have taken the view that the *Birnbaum* limitation on the plaintiff class in a Rule 10b–5 action for damages is an arbitrary restriction which unreasonably prevents some deserving plaintiffs from recovering damages which have in fact been caused by violations of Rule 10b–5. The Securities and Exchange Commission has filed an *amicus* brief in this case espousing that same view. We have no doubt that this is indeed a disadvantage of the *Birnbaum* rule, and if it had no countervailing advantages it would be undesirable as a matter of policy, however much it might be supported by precedent and legislative history. But we are of the opinion that there are countervailing advantages to the *Birnbaum* rule, purely as a matter of policy, although those advantages are more difficult to articulate than is the disadvantage.

There has been widespread recognition that litigation under Rule 10b–5 presents a danger of vexatiousness different in degree and in kind from that which accompanies litigation in general. * * *

We believe that the concern expressed for the danger of vexatious litigation which could result from a widely expanded class of plaintiffs under Rule 10b–5 is founded in something more substantial than the common complaint of the many defendants who would prefer avoiding lawsuits entirely to either settling them or trying them. These concerns have two largely separate grounds.

The first of these concerns is that in the field of federal securities laws governing disclosure of information even a complaint which by objective standards may have very little chance of success at trial has a settlement value to the plaintiff out of any proportion to its prospect of success at trial so long as he may prevent the suit from being resolved against him by dismissal or summary judgment. The very pendency of the lawsuit may frustrate or delay normal business activity of the defendant which is totally unrelated to the lawsuit. * * *

The second ground for fear of vexatious litigation is based on the concern that, given the generalized contours of liability, the abolition of the *Birnbaum* rule would throw open to the trier of fact many rather hazy issues of historical fact the proof of which depended almost entirely on oral testimony.

Reversed.

MR. JUSTICE POWELL, with whom MR. JUSTICE STEWART and MR. JUSTICE MARSHALL join, concurring.

Although I join the opinion of the Court, I write to emphasize the significance of the tests of the Acts of 1933 and 1934 and especially the language of § 10(b) and Rule 10b–5.

The starting point in every case involving construction of a statute is the language itself. The critical phrase in both the statute and the rule is "in connection with the *purchase* or *sale* of any security." Section 3(a)(14) of the 1934 Act provides that the term "sale" shall "include any contract to sell or otherwise dispose of" securities. There is no hint in any provision of the Act that the term "sale," as used in § 10(b), was intended—in addition to its long-established legal meaning—to include an "offer to sell." Respondent, nevertheless, would have us amend the controlling language in § 10(b) to read:

> "* * * in connection with the purchase or sale of, or an offer to sell, any security."

Before a court properly could consider taking such liberty with statutory language there should be, at least, unmistakable support in the history and structure of the legislation. None exists in this case.

MR. JUSTICE BLACKMUN, with whom MR. JUSTICE DOUGLAS and MR. JUSTICE BRENNAN join, dissenting.

Today the Court graves into stone *Birnbaum's* arbitrary principle of standing. For this task the Court, unfortunately, chooses to utilize three blunt chisels: (1) reliance on the legislative history of the 1933 and 1934 Securities Acts, conceded as inconclusive in this particular context; (2) acceptance as precedent of two decades of lower court decisions following a doctrine, never before examined here, that was pronounced by a justifiably esteemed panel of that Court of Appeals regarded as the "Mother Court" in this area of the law, but under entirely different circumstances; and (3) resort to utter pragmaticality and a conjectural assertion of "policy considerations" deemed to arise in distinguishing the meritorious Rule 10b–5 suit from the meretricious one. In so doing, the Court exhibits a preternatural solicitousness for corporate well-being and a seeming callousness toward the investing public quite out of keeping, it seems to me, with our own traditions and the intent of the securities laws.

The plaintiffs' complaint—and that is all that is before us now—raises disturbing claims of fraud. It alleges that the directors of "New Blue Chip" and the majority shareholders of "Old Blue Chip" engaged in a deceptive and manipulative scheme designed to subvert the intent of the 1967 antitrust consent decree and to enhance the value of their own shares in a subsequent offering.

———

In Small v. Fritz Companies, 30 Cal.4th 167, 132 Cal.Rptr.2d 490, 65 P.3d 1255 (2003), the California Supreme Court allowed a fraud action to be brought by a shareholder claiming he was induced to hold his shares rather than sell. This suit clearly could not have been brought under Rule 10b-5 in light of the *Blue Chip Stamps* purchaser/seller standing requirement. The California Court reached this result notwithstanding the Securities Litigation Uniform Standards Act (SLUSA) that preempts securities fraud class actions with fifty or more class members. See 1934 Act § 28(f). However, in Merrill Lynch, Pierce Fenner & Smith, Inc. v. Dabit, 547 U.S. 71, 126 S.Ct. 1503, 164 L.Ed.2d 179 (2006), the Supreme Court that SLUSA preempts holders' claims. Among other things, the Court reasoned that when it enacted SLUSA, Congress desired to eliminate the duplicative litigation that would result from holding that such claims are not within the broadly construed "in connection with" requirement. As a result of the *Dabit* ruling, state claims by holders may still proceed, but only if they are not brought in the form of a class action with fewer than fifty class members.

———

SEC v. ZANDFORD

535 U.S. 813, 122 S.Ct. 1899, 153 L.Ed.2d 1 (2002).

STEVENS, J., DELIVERED THE OPINION FOR A UNANIMOUS COURT.

The Securities and Exchange Commission (SEC) filed a civil complaint alleging that a stockbroker violated both § 10(b) of the Securities Exchange Act of 1934 and the SEC's Rule 10b-5, by selling his customer's securities and using the proceeds for his own benefit without the customer's knowledge or consent. The question presented is whether the alleged fraudulent conduct was "in connection with the purchase or sale of any security" within the meaning of the statute and the rule.

Between 1987 and 1991, respondent was employed as a securities broker in the Maryland branch of a New York brokerage firm. In 1987, he persuaded William Wood, an elderly man in poor health, to open a joint investment account for himself and his mentally retarded daughter. According to the SEC's complaint, the "stated investment objectives for the account were 'safety of principal and income.' " The Woods granted respondent discretion to manage their account and a general power of attorney to engage in securities transactions for their benefit without prior approval. Relying on respondent's promise to "conservatively invest" their money, the Woods entrusted him with $419,255. Before Mr. Wood's death in 1991, all of that money was gone.

In 1991, the National Association of Securities Dealers (NASD) conducted a routine examination of respondent's firm and discovered that on over 25 separate occasions, money had been transferred from the Woods' account to accounts controlled by respondent. In due course, respondent was indicted in the United States District Court for the District of Maryland on 13 counts of wire fraud in violation of 18 U.S.C. § 1343. The first count alleged that respondent sold securities in the Woods' account and then made personal use of the proceeds. Each of the other counts alleged that he made wire transfers between Maryland and New York that enabled him to withdraw specified sums from the Woods' accounts. Some of those transfers involved respondent writing checks to himself from a mutual fund account held by the Woods, which required liquidating securities in order to redeem the checks. Respondent was convicted on all counts, sentenced to prison for 52 months, and ordered to pay $10,800 in restitution.

After respondent was indicted, the SEC filed a civil complaint in the same District Court alleging that respondent violated § 10(b) and Rule 10b–5 by engaging in a scheme to defraud the Woods and by misappropriating approximately $343,000 of the Woods' securities without their knowledge or consent. The SEC moved for partial summary judgment after respondent's criminal conviction, arguing that the judgment in the criminal case estopped respondent from contesting facts that established a violation of § 10(b). Respondent filed a motion seeking discovery on the question whether his fraud had the requisite "connection with" the purchase or sale of a security. The District Court refused to allow discovery and entered summary judgment against respondent. It enjoined him from engaging in future violations of the securities laws and ordered him to disgorge $343,000 in ill-gotten gains.

The Court of Appeals for the Fourth Circuit reversed the summary judgment and remanded with directions for the District Court to dismiss the complaint. It first held that the wire fraud conviction, which only required two findings—(1) that respondent engaged in a scheme to defraud and (2) that he used interstate wire communications in executing the scheme—did not establish all the elements of a § 10(b) violation. Specifically, the conviction did not necessarily establish that his fraud was "in connection with" the sale of a security. The court then held that the civil complaint did not sufficiently allege the necessary connection because the sales of the Woods' securities were merely incidental to a fraud that "lay in absconding with the proceeds" of sales that were conducted in "a routine and customary fashion," Respondent's "scheme was simply to steal the Woods' assets" rather than to engage "in manipulation of a particular security." Ultimately, the court refused "to stretch the language of the securities fraud provisions to encompass every conversion or theft that happens to involve securities." Adopting what amounts to a "fraud on the market" theory of the statute's coverage, the court held that without some "relationship to market integrity or investor understanding," there is no violation of § 10(b). * * *

Section 10(b) of the Securities Exchange Act makes it "unlawful for any person . . . [t]o use or employ, in connection with the purchase or sale of any security . . . , any manipulative or deceptive device or contrivance in contravention of such rules and regulations as the [SEC] may prescribe." Rule 10b–5, which implements this provision, forbids the use, "in connection with the purchase or sale of any security," of "any device, scheme, or artifice to defraud" or any other "act, practice, or course of business" that "operates . . . as a fraud or deceit." Among Congress' objectives in passing the Act was "to insure honest securities markets and thereby promote investor confidence" after the market crash of 1929. *United States v. O'Hagan,* 521 U.S. 642, 658 (1997); see also *United States v. Naftalin,* 441 U.S. 768, 775 (1979). More generally, Congress sought " 'to substitute a philosophy of full disclosure for the philosophy of *caveat emptor* and thus to achieve a high standard of business ethics in the securities industry.' " *Affiliated Ute Citizens of Utah v. United States,* 406 U.S. 128, 151 (1972) (quoting *SEC v. Capital Gains Research Bureau, Inc.,* 375 U.S. 180, 186, (1963)).

Consequently, we have explained that the statute should be "construed 'not technically and restrictively, but flexibly to effectuate its remedial purposes.' " 406 U.S., at 151 (quoting *Capital Gains Research Bureau, Inc.,* 375 U.S., at 195). In its role enforcing the Act, the SEC has consistently adopted a broad reading of the phrase "in connection with the purchase or sale of any security." It has maintained that a broker who accepts payment for securities that he never intends to deliver, or who sells customer securities with intent to misappropriate the proceeds, violates § 10(b) and Rule 10b–5. See, *e.g., In re Bauer,* 26 S.E.C. 770, 1947 WL 24474 (1947); *In re Southeastern Securities Corp.,* 29 S.E.C. 609, 1949 WL 36491 (1949). This interpretation of the ambiguous text of § 10(b), in the context of formal adjudication, is entitled to deference if it is reasonable, see *United States v. Mead Corp.,* 533 U.S. 218, 229–230, and n. 12 (2001). For the reasons set forth below, we think it is. While the statute must not be construed so broadly as to convert every common-law fraud that happens to involve securities into a violation of § 10(b), *Marine Bank v. Weaver,* 455 U.S. 551, 556 (1982) ("Congress, in enacting the securities laws, did not intend to provide a broad federal remedy for all fraud"), neither the SEC nor this Court has ever held that there must be a misrepresentation about the value of a particular security in order to run afoul of the Act.

The SEC claims respondent engaged in a fraudulent scheme in which he made sales of his customer's securities for his own benefit. Respondent submits that the sales themselves were perfectly lawful and that the subsequent misappropriation of the proceeds, though fraudulent, is not properly viewed as having the requisite connection with the sales; in his view, the alleged scheme is not materially different from a simple theft of cash or securities in an investment account. We disagree.

According to the complaint, respondent "engaged in a scheme to defraud" the Woods beginning in 1988, shortly after they opened their account, and that scheme continued throughout the 2–year period during which respondent made a series of transactions that enabled him to convert the proceeds of the sales of the Woods' securities to his own use. The securities sales and respondent's fraudulent practices were not independent events. This is not a case in which, after a lawful transaction had been consummated, a broker decided to steal the proceeds and did so. Nor is it a case in which a thief simply invested the proceeds of a routine conversion in the stock market. Rather, respondent's fraud coincided with the sales themselves.

Taking the allegations in the complaint as true, each sale was made to further respondent's fraudulent scheme; each was deceptive because it was neither authorized by, nor disclosed to, the Woods. With regard to the sales of shares in the Woods' mutual fund, respondent initiated these transactions by writing a check to himself from that account, knowing that redeeming the check would require the sale of securities. Indeed, each time respondent "exercised his power of disposition for his own benefit," that conduct, "without more," was a fraud. *United States v. Dunn,* 268 U.S. 121, 131 (1925). In the aggregate, the sales are properly viewed as a "course of business" that operated as a fraud or deceit on a stockbroker's customer.

Insofar as the connection between respondent's deceptive practices and his sale of the Woods' securities is concerned, the case is remarkably similar to *Superintendent of Ins. of N.Y. v. Bankers Life & Casualty Co.,* 404 U.S. 6 (1971). In that case the directors of Manhattan Casualty Company authorized the sale of the company's portfolio of treasury bonds because they had been "duped" into believing that the company would receive the proceeds of the sale. *Id.,* at 9. We held that "Manhattan was injured as an investor through a deceptive device which deprived it of any compensation for the sale of its valuable block of securities." *Id.,* at 105. In reaching this conclusion, we did not ask, as the Fourth Circuit did in this case, whether the directors were misled about the value of a security or whether the fraud involved "manipulation of a particular security." 238 F.3d, at 565. In fact, we rejected the Second Circuit's position in *Superintendent of Ins. of N.Y. v. Bankers Life & Casualty Co.,* 430 F.2d 355, 361 (C.A.2 1970), that because the fraud against Manhattan did not take place within the context of a securities exchange it was not prohibited by § 10(b). 404 U.S., at 10. We refused to read the statute so narrowly, noting that it "must be read flexibly, not technically and restrictively." *Id.,* at 12. Although we recognized that the interest in " 'preserving the integrity of the securities markets,' " was one of the purposes animating the statute, we rejected the notion that § 10(b) is limited to serving that objective alone. *Ibid.* ("We agree that Congress by § 10(b) did not seek to regulate transactions which constitute no more than internal corporate mismanagement. But we read § 10(b) to mean that Congress meant to bar deceptive devices and contrivances in the purchase or sale of securities whether conducted in the organized markets or face to face").

Like the company directors in *Bankers Life,* the Woods were injured as investors through respondent's deceptions, which deprived them of any compensation for the sale of their valuable securities. They were duped into believing respondent would "conservatively invest" their assets in the stock market and that any transactions made on their behalf would be for their benefit for the " 'safety of principal and income.' " The fact that respondent misappropriated the proceeds of the sales provides persuasive evidence that he had violated § 10(b) when he made the sales, but misappropriation is not an essential element of the offense. Indeed, in *Bankers Life,* we flatly stated that it was "irrelevant" that "the proceeds of the sale that were due the seller were misappropriated." 404 U.S., at 10. It is enough that the scheme to defraud and the sale of securities coincide.

The Court of Appeals below distinguished *Bankers Life* on the ground that it involved an affirmative misrepresentation, whereas respondent simply failed to inform the Woods of his intent to misappropriate their securities. 238 F.3d, at 566. We are not persuaded by this distinction. Respondent was only able to carry out his fraudulent scheme without making an affirmative misrepresentation because the Woods had trusted him to make transactions in their best interest without prior approval. Under these circumstances, respondent's fraud represents an even greater threat to investor confidence in the securities industry than the misrepresentation in *Bankers Life.* Not only does such a fraud prevent investors from trusting that their brokers are executing transactions for their benefit, but it undermines the value of a discretionary account like that held by the Woods. The benefit of a discretionary account is that it enables individuals, like the Woods, who lack the time, capacity, or know-how to supervise investment decisions, to delegate authority to a broker who will make decisions in their best interests without prior approval. If such individuals cannot rely on a broker to exercise that discretion for their benefit, then the account loses its added value. Moreover, any distinction between omissions and misrepresentations is illusory in the context of a broker who has a fiduciary duty to her clients. See *Chiarella v. United States,* 445 U.S. 222, 230 (1980) (noting that "silence in connection with the purchase or sale of securities may operate as a fraud actionable under § 10(b)" when there is "a duty to disclose arising from a relationship of trust and confidence between parties to a transaction"); *Affiliated Ute Citizens of Utah v. United States,* 406 U.S., at 153.

More recently, in *Wharf (Holdings) Ltd. v. United Int'l Holdings, Inc.,* 532 U.S. 588 (2001), our decision that the seller of a security had violated § 10(b) focused on the secret intent of the seller when the sale occurred. The purchaser claimed "that Wharf sold it a security (the option) while secretly intending from the very beginning not to honor the option." *Id.,* at 597. Although Wharf did not specifically argue that the breach of contract underlying the complaint lacked the requisite connection with a sale of securities, it did assert that the case was merely a dispute over ownership of the option, and that interpreting § 10(b) to include such a claim would convert every breach of contract that happened to involve a security into a violation of the federal securities laws. *Id.,* at 596. We rejected that argument because the purchaser's claim was not that the defendant failed to carry out a promise to sell securities; rather, the claim was that the defendant sold a security while never intending to honor its agreement in the first place. *Id.,* at 596–597. Similarly, in this case the SEC claims respondent sold the Woods' securities while secretly intending from the very beginning to keep the proceeds. In *Wharf,* the fraudulent intent deprived the purchaser of the benefit of the sale whereas here the fraudulent intent deprived the seller of that benefit, but the connection between the deception and the sale in each case is identical.

* * * [T]he SEC complaint describes a fraudulent scheme in which the securities transactions and breaches of fiduciary duty coincide. Those breaches were therefore "in connection with" securities sales within the meaning of § 10(b).[4] Accordingly, the judgment of the Court of Appeals is reversed, and the case is remanded for further proceedings consistent with this opinion.

It is so ordered.

---

4. Contrary to the Court of Appeals' prediction, our analysis does not transform every breach of fiduciary duty into a federal securities violation. If, for example, a broker embezzles cash from a client's account or takes advantage of the fiduciary relationship to induce his client into a fraudulent real estate transaction, then the fraud would not include the requisite connection to a purchase or sale of securities. Likewise if the broker told his client he was stealing the client's assets, that breach of fiduciary duty might be in connection with a sale of securities, but it would not involve a deceptive device or fraud. * * *

NOTES

1. In a number of appellate court decisions before the Supreme Court's decision in *Blue Chip*, the courts held that a person who was forced to exchange his securities for cash or other securities in connection with a merger or similar transaction had standing to sue under Rule 10b–5 as a "forced seller" if he could show that the transaction was effected by means of fraudulent misstatements. See e.g., Vine v. Beneficial Finance Co., 374 F.2d 627 (2d Cir.1967). Courts have continued to recognize this "forced seller" exception after *Blue Chip*. See e.g., Alley v. Miramon, 614 F.2d 1372 (5th Cir.1980).

2. In the context of a shareholder derivative suit, the purchaser/seller standing requirement is satisfied if the corporation is a purchaser or seller of securities. See, e.g., Frankel v. Slotkin, 984 F.2d 1328 (2d Cir.1993); Ray v. Karris, 780 F.2d 636, 641 (7th Cir.1985); Schoenbaum v. Firstbrook, 405 F.2d 215 (2d Cir.1968), *cert. denied* 395 U.S. 906, 89 S.Ct. 1747, 23 L.Ed.2d 219 (1969); Gordon Schneider, The Derivative Suit and *Blue Chip* Standing, 12 Conn.L.Rev. 465 (1980).

3. The *Blue Chip* decision involved a private suit for damages. Does the purchaser/seller requirement apply to a plaintiff seeking injunctive relief? *Compare* Tully v. Mott Supermarkets, Inc., 540 F.2d 187, 194 (3d Cir.1976) (dictum); Mutual Shares Corp. v. Genesco, Inc., 384 F.2d 540 (2d Cir.1967) *with* Cowin v. Bresler, 741 F.2d 410 (D.C.Cir.1984); Packer v. Yampol, 630 F.Supp. 1237 (S.D.N.Y.1986); Atlantic Federal Savings & Loan Ass'n v. Dade Savings & Loan Ass'n, 592 F.Supp. 1089 (S.D.Fla.1984).

4. Rule 10b–5's "in connection with" requirement led to the purchaser/seller standing requirement. But what about SEC Rule 14a–9 where the misrepresentation is in connection with a proxy solicitation. Must the plaintiff have also been a purchaser or seller? Must the plaintiff have actually voted in the transaction? Must the plaintiff have actually been misled into voting in the manner urged by the misleading solicitation?

5. As noted by the Court in *Zandford*, it had previously held in Wharf (Holdings) Limited v. United International Holdings, 532 U.S. 588, 121 S.Ct. 1776, 149 L.Ed.2d 845 (2001) that an enforceable option contract can form the basis of a Rule 10b–5 suit even if the underlying sale never takes place.

6. A statement need not relate to a specific securities transaction in order to have been made in connection with the purchase or sale of a security. See, e.g., In re Carter–Wallace, Inc. Securities Litigation, 150 F.3d 153 (2d Cir.1998) (technical advertisement in medical journal could be "in connection with the purchase or sale" of a security); SEC v. Texas Gulf Sulphur Co., 401 F.2d 833 (2d Cir.1968), *cert. denied* 394 U.S. 976, 89 S.Ct. 1454, 22 L.Ed.2d 756 (1969) (misstatements in a corporate press release were made "in connection with" purchases and sales made by shareholders in the open market and violated rule 10b–5, even though corporation itself was not buying nor selling shares), page 902 below.

SECTION 5.   THE SCIENTER REQUIREMENT

ERNST & ERNST v. HOCHFELDER

425 U.S. 185, 96 S.Ct. 1375, 47 L.Ed.2d 668 (1976).

MR. JUSTICE POWELL delivered the opinion of the Court.

The issue in this case is whether an action for civil damages may lie under § 10(b) of the Securities Exchange Act of 1934 and Securities and Exchange Commission Rule 10b–5, in the absence of an allegation of intent to deceive, manipulate, or defraud on the part of the defendant.

Petitioner, Ernst & Ernst, is an accounting firm. From 1946 through 1967 it was retained by First Securities Company of Chicago (First Securities), a small brokerage firm and member of the Midwest Stock Exchange and of the National Association of Securities Dealers, to perform periodic audits of the firm's books and records. In connection with these audits Ernst & Ernst prepared for filing with the Securities and Exchange Commission (the Commission) the annual reports required of First Securities under § 17(a) of the 1934 Act. It also prepared for First Securities responses to the financial questionnaires of the Midwest Stock Exchange (the Exchange).

Respondents were customers of First Securities who invested in a fraudulent securities scheme perpetrated by Leston B. Nay, president of the firm and owner of 92% of its stock. Nay induced the respondents to invest funds in "escrow" accounts that he represented would yield a high rate of return. Respondents did so from 1942 through 1966, with the majority of the transactions occurring in the 1950's. In fact, there were no escrow accounts as Nay converted respondents' funds to his own use immediately upon receipt. These transactions were not in the customary form of dealings between First Securities and its customers. The respondents drew their personal checks payable to Nay or a designated bank for his account. No such escrow accounts were reflected on the books and records of First Securities, and none was shown on its periodic accounting to respondents in connection with their other investments. Nor were they included in First Securities' filings with the Commission or the Exchange.

This fraud came to light in 1968 when Nay committed suicide, leaving a note that described First Securities as bankrupt and the escrow accounts as "spurious." Respondents subsequently filed this action for damages against Ernst & Ernst in the United States District Court for the Northern District of Illinois under § 10(b) of the 1934 Act. The complaint charged that Nay's escrow scheme violated § 10(b) and Commission Rule 10b–5, and that Ernst & Ernst had "aided and abetted" Nay's violations by its "failure" to conduct proper audits of First Securities. As revealed through discovery, respondents' cause of action rested on a theory of negligent nonfeasance. The premise was that Ernst & Ernst had failed to utilize "appropriate auditing procedures" in its audits of First Securities, thereby failing to discover internal practices of the firm said to prevent an effective audit. The practice principally relied on was Nay's rule that only he could open mail addressed to him at First Securities or addressed to First Securities to his attention, even if it arrived in his absence. Respondents contended that if Ernst & Ernst had conducted a proper audit, it would have discovered this "mail rule." The existence of the rule then would have been disclosed in reports to the Exchange and to the Commission by Ernst & Ernst as an irregular procedure that prevented an effective audit. This would have led to an investigation of Nay that would have revealed the fraudulent scheme. Respondents specifically disclaimed the existence of fraud or intentional misconduct on the part of Ernst & Ernst.

After extensive discovery the District Court granted Ernst & Ernst's motion for summary judgment and dismissed the action. The court rejected Ernst & Ernst's contention that a cause of action for aiding and abetting a securities fraud could not be maintained under § 10(b) and Rule 10b–5 merely on allegations of negligence. It concluded, however, that there was no genuine issue of material fact with respect to whether Ernst & Ernst had conducted its audits in accordance with generally accepted auditing standards.

The Court of Appeals for the Seventh Circuit reversed and remanded, holding that one who breaches a duty of inquiry and disclosure owed another is liable in damages for aiding and abetting a third party's violation of Rule 10b–5 if the fraud would have been discovered or prevented but for the breach.[3] The court reasoned that Ernst & Ernst had a common-law and statutory duty of inquiry into the adequacy of First Securities' internal control system because it had contracted to audit First Securities and to prepare for filing with the Commission the annual report of its financial condition required under § 17 of the 1934 Act and Rule 17a–5. The Court further reasoned that respondents were beneficiaries of the statutory duty to inquire and the related duty to disclose any material irregularities that were discovered. The court concluded that there were genuine issues of fact as to whether Ernst & Ernst's failure to discover and comment upon Nay's mail rule constituted a breach of its duties of inquiry and disclosure, and whether inquiry and disclosure would have led to the discovery or prevention of Nay's fraud.

---

3. In support of this holding, the Court of Appeals cited its decision in Hochfelder v. Midwest Stock Exchange, supra, where it detailed the elements necessary to establish a claim under Rule 10b–5 based on a defendant's aiding and abetting a securities fraud solely by inaction. In such a case the plaintiff must show "that the party charged with aiding and abetting had knowledge of or, but for the breach of a duty of inquiry, should have had knowledge of the fraud, and that possessing such knowledge the party failed to act due to an improper motive or breach of a duty of disclosure." The court explained in the instant case that these "elements constitute a flexible standard of liability which should be amplified according to the peculiarities of each case." In view of our holding that an intent to deceive, manipulate, or defraud is required for civil liability under § 10(b) and Rule 10b–5, we need not consider whether civil liability for aiding and abetting is appropriate under the section and the rule, nor the elements necessary to establish such a cause of action.

We granted certiorari to resolve the question whether a private cause of action for damages will lie under § 10(b) and Rule 10b–5 in the absence of any allegation of "scienter"—intent to deceive, manipulate, or defraud.[4] We conclude that it will not and therefore we reverse. * * *

Section 10(b) makes unlawful the use or employment of "any manipulative or deceptive device or contrivance" in contravention of Commission rules. The words "manipulative or deceptive" used in conjunction with "device or contrivance" strongly suggest that § 10(b) was intended to proscribe knowing or intentional misconduct.

In its *amicus curiae* brief, however, the Commission contends that nothing in the language "manipulative or deceptive device or contrivance" limits its operation to knowing or intentional practices. In support of its view, the Commission cites the overall congressional purpose in the 1933 and 1934 Acts to protect investors against false and deceptive practices that might injure them. The Commission then reasons that since the "effect" upon investors of given conduct is the same regardless of whether the conduct is negligent or intentional, Congress must have intended to bar all such practices and not just those done knowingly or intentionally. The logic of this effect-oriented approach would impose liability for wholly faultless conduct where such conduct results in harm to investors, a result the Commission would be unlikely to support. But apart from where its logic might lead, the Commission would add a gloss to the operative language of the statute quite different from its commonly accepted meaning. The argument simply ignores the use of the words "manipulative," "device," and "contrivance," terms that make unmistakable a congressional intent to proscribe a type of conduct quite different from negligence.[5] Use of the word "manipulative" is especially significant. It is and was virtually a term of art when used in connection with securities markets. It connotes intentional or willful conduct designed to deceive or defraud investors by controlling or artificially affecting the price of securities.[6] * * *

* * * In view of the language of § 10(b) which so clearly connotes intentional misconduct, and mindful that the language of a statute con-

---

4. In this opinion the term "scienter" refers to a mental state embracing intent to deceive, manipulate, or defraud. In certain areas of the law recklessness is considered to be a form of intentional conduct for purposes of imposing liability for some act. We need not address here the question whether, in some circumstances, reckless behavior is sufficient for civil liability under § 10(b) and Rule 10b–5.

Since this case concerns an action for damages we also need not consider the question whether scienter is a necessary element in an action for injunctive relief under § 10(b) and Rule 10b–5.

5. Webster's Int'l Dictionary (2d ed. 1934) defines "device" as "[t]hat which is devised, or formed by design; a contrivance; an invention; project; scheme; often a scheme to deceive; a stratagem; an artifice," and "contrivance" in pertinent part as "[a] thing contrived or used in contriving; a scheme, plan, or artifice." In turn, "contrive" in pertinent part is defined as "[t]o devise; to plan; to plot * * * [t]o fabricate * * * design; invent * * * to scheme * * *." The Commission also ignores the use of the terms "[t]o use or employ," language that is supportive of the view that Congress did not intend § 10(b) to embrace negligent conduct.

6. Webster's Int'l Dictionary, supra, defines "manipulate" as " * * * to manage or treat artfully or fraudulently; as to *manipulate* accounts * * *. 4. *Exchanges. To force (prices) up or down, as by matched orders, wash sales, fictitious reports * * *; to rig.*"

trols when sufficiently clear in its context, further inquiry may be unnecessary. We turn now, nevertheless, to the legislative history of the 1934 Act to ascertain whether there is support for the meaning attributed to § 10(b) by the Commission and respondents.

Although the extensive legislative history of the 1934 Act is bereft of any explicit explanation of Congress' intent, we think the relevant portions of that history support our conclusion that § 10(b) was addressed to practices that involve some element of scienter and cannot be read to impose liability for negligent conduct alone.* * *

Neither the intended scope of § 10(b) nor the reasons for the changes in its operative language are revealed explicitly in the legislative history of the 1934 Act, which deals primarily with other aspects of the legislation. There is no indication, however, that § 10(b) was intended to proscribe conduct not involving scienter. The extensive hearings that preceded passage of the 1934 Act touched only briefly on § 10, and most of the discussion was devoted to the enumerated devices that the Commission is empowered to proscribe under § 10(a). The most relevant exposition of the provision that was to become § 10(b) was by Thomas G. Corcoran, a spokesman for the drafters. Corcoran indicated:

"Subsection (c) [§ 9(c) of H.R. 7852—later § 10(b)] says, 'Thou shalt not devise any other cunning devices.' * * *

"Of course subsection (c) is a catchall clause to prevent manipulative devices. I do not think there is any objection to that kind of clause. The Commission should have the authority to deal with new manipulative devices."

* * * It is difficult to believe that any lawyer, legislative draftsman, or legislator would use these words if the intent was to create liability for merely negligent acts or omissions. Neither the legislative history nor the briefs supporting respondents identify any usage or authority for construing "manipulative [or cunning] devices" to include negligence. * * *

The Commission argues that Congress has been explicit in requiring willful conduct when that was the standard of fault intended, citing § 9 of the 1934 Act, which generally proscribes manipulation of securities prices. * * * From this the Commission concludes that since § 10(b) is not by its terms explicitly restricted to willful, knowing, or purposeful conduct, it should not be construed in all cases to require more than negligent action or inaction as a precondition for civil liability.

The structure of the Acts does not support the Commission's argument. In each instance that Congress created express civil liability in favor of purchasers or sellers of securities it clearly specified whether recovery was to be premised on knowing or intentional conduct, negligence, or entirely innocent mistake. For example, § 11 of the 1933 Act unambiguously creates a private action for damages when a registration statement includes untrue statements of material facts or fails to state material facts necessary to make the statements therein not misleading.

* * * The express recognition of a cause of action premised on negligent behavior in § 11 stands in sharp contrast to the language of § 10(b), and significantly undercuts the Commission's argument.

We also consider it significant that each of the express civil remedies in the 1933 Act allowing recovery for negligent conduct is subject to significant procedural restrictions not applicable under § 10(b). * * * [T]hese procedural limitations indicate that the judicially created private damage remedy under § 10(b)—which has no comparable restrictions— cannot be extended, consistently with the intent of Congress, to actions premised on negligent wrongdoing. Such extension would allow causes of action covered by § 11, § 12(2), and § 15 to be brought instead under § 10(b) and thereby nullify the effectiveness of the carefully drawn procedural restrictions on these express actions. We would be unwilling to bring about this result absent substantial support in the legislative history, and there is none.

We have addressed, to this point, primarily the language and history of § 10(b). The Commission contends, however, that subsections (2) and (3) of Rule 10b–5 are cast in language which—if standing alone—could encompass both intentional and negligent behavior. These subsections respectively provide that it is unlawful "[t]o make any untrue statement of a material fact or to omit to state a material fact necessary in order to make the statements made, in light of the circumstances under which they were made, not misleading * * * " and "to engage in any act, practice, or course of business which operates or would operate as a fraud or deceit upon any person. * * * " Viewed in isolation the language of subsection (2), and arguably that of subsection (3), could be read as proscribing, respectively, any type of material misstatement or omission, and any course of conduct, that has the effect of defrauding investors, whether the wrongdoing was intentional or not.

We note first that such a reading cannot be harmonized with the administrative history of the rule, a history making clear that when the Commission adopted the rule it was intended to apply only to activities that involved scienter. More importantly, Rule 10b–5 was adopted pursuant to authority granted the Commission under § 10(b). The rulemaking power granted to an administrative agency charged with the administration of a federal statute is not the power to make law. Rather, it is " 'the power to adopt regulations to carry into effect the will of Congress as expressed by the statute.' " Thus, despite the broad view of the Rule advanced by the Commission in this case, its scope cannot exceed the power granted the Commission by Congress under § 10(b). For the reasons stated above, we think the Commission's original interpretation of Rule 10b–5 was compelled by the language and history of § 10(b) and related sections of the Acts.

Mr. Justice Blackmun, with whom Mr. Justice Brennan joins, dissenting.

Once again—see Blue Chip Stamps v. Manor Drug Stores—the Court interprets § 10(b) of the Securities Exchange Act of 1934, and the Securities and Exchange Commission's Rule 10b–5, restrictively and narrowly and thereby stultifies recovery for the victim. This time the Court does so by confining the statute and the Rule to situations where the defendant has "scienter," that is, the "intent to deceive, manipulate, or defraud." Sheer negligence, the Court says, is not within the reach of the statute and the Rule, and was not contemplated when the great reforms of 1933, 1934, and 1942 were effectuated by Congress and the Commission. * * *

No one questions the fact that the respondents here were the victims of an intentional securities fraud practiced by Leston B. Nay. What is at issue, of course, is the petitioner-accountant firm's involvement and that firm's responsibility under Rule 10b–5. The language of the Rule * * * seems to me, clearly and succinctly, to prohibit negligent as well as intentional conduct of the kind proscribed, to extend beyond common law fraud, and to apply to negligent omission and commission. This is consistent with Congress' intent, repeatedly recognized by the Court, that securities legislation enacted for the purpose of avoiding frauds be construed "not technically and restrictively, but flexibly to effectuate its remedial purposes." * * *

The critical importance of the auditing accountant's role in insuring full disclosure cannot be overestimated. The SEC has emphasized that in certifying statements the accountant's duty "is to safeguard the public interest, not that of his client." "In our complex society the accountant's certificate and the lawyer's opinion can be instruments for inflicting pecuniary loss more potent than the chisel or the crowbar." In this light, the initial inquiry into whether Ernst & Ernst's preparation and certification of the financial statements of First Securities Company of Chicago were negligent, because of the failure to perceive Nay's extraordinary mail rule, and in other alleged respects, and thus whether Rule 10b–5 was violated, should not be thwarted.

But the Court today decides that it is to be thwarted; and so once again it rests with Congress to rephrase and to re-enact, if investor victims, such as these, are ever to have relief under the federal securities laws that I thought had been enacted for their broad, needed, and deserving benefit.

Notes

1. The Supreme Court in *Hochfelder* left open the question of whether "scienter" means an intent to deceive, or whether recklessness may suffice. In Sundstrand Corp. v. Sun Chemical Corp., 553 F.2d 1033 (7th Cir.1977), the court held that a partner in an investment banking firm, who acted as a broker in the transaction and thereby acquired a "quasi-fiduciary" common law duty to disclose material facts relating to the proposed transaction, could be held civilly liable for "reckless omission of material facts upon which the plaintiff put justifiable reliance." The court defined "reckless" omission as "a

highly unreasonable omission, involving not merely simple, or even inexcusable, negligence, but an extreme departure from the standards of ordinary care, and which presents a danger of misleading buyers or sellers that is either known to the defendant or is so obvious that the actor must have been aware of it." 553 F.2d at 1044, quoting from Franke v. Midwestern Oklahoma Development Authority, 428 F.Supp. 719 (W.D.Okl.1976). In a later decision, however, the Seventh Circuit warned that "the definition of 'reckless behavior' should not be a liberal one lest any discerning distinction between 'scienter' and 'negligence' be obliterated for these purposes. We believe 'reckless' in these circumstances comes closer to being a lesser form of intent than merely a greater degree of ordinary negligence." Sanders v. John Nuveen & Co., Inc., 554 F.2d 790 (7th Cir.1977). Recklessness has also been accepted as meeting the scienter requirement in other circuits. See e.g., In re Advanta Corp. Securities Litigation, 180 F.3d 525, 539 (3d Cir.1999); SEC v. U.S. Environmental, Inc., 155 F.3d 107 (2d Cir.1998); Hackbart v. Holmes, 675 F.2d 1114 (10th Cir.1982). The Supreme Court has also held in another context that recklessness will meet scienter requirements for willful conduct but refused to draw a bright line between reckless conduct and mere negligence. Safeco Insurance Co. of America v. Burr, 551 U.S. 47 (2007).

2.　As will be seen in section 9 of this chapter, the Private Securities Litigation Reform Act of 1995 was enacted by Congress to curb abuses in securities litigation cases that were often brought for frivolous reasons and used only to coerce a settlement from issuers. That legislation imposed special pleading requirements to assure that a fraud had actually occurred. Courts have considered whether those pleading requirements require more than reckless conduct as a basis for Rule 10b–5 liability. In In Re Silicon Graphics, Inc. Securities Litigation, 970 F.Supp. 746 (N.D.Cal.1997), reversed on other grounds, 183 F.3d 970, 988 (9th Cir.1999) the judge discerned from the legislative history of that Act an intent by Congress to require "deliberate recklessness," as distinguished from "non-deliberate recklessness," to support a claim. The Ninth Circuit overturned the district court's decision in *Silicon Graphics* but stated that "deliberate" recklessness is required. 183 F.3d at 988. *Accord* In re Glenayre Technologies, Inc. Securities Litigation, 982 F.Supp. 294 (S.D.N.Y.1997); Friedberg v. Discreet Logic, Inc., 959 F.Supp. 42 (D.Mass.1997); Voit v. Wonderware Corp., 977 F.Supp. 363 (E.D.Pa.1997). See also In re Burlington Coat Factory Securities Litigation, 114 F.3d 1410 (3d Cir.1997) (failure to raise *strong* inference of fraudulent conduct but plaintiffs were given leave to amend). In In Re Baesa Securities Litigation, 969 F.Supp. 238 (S.D.N.Y.1997), the judge found no Congressional intent to change the pre-existing recklessness standard.

3.　The *Hochfelder* decision failed to address whether a negligence standard could be applied in SEC enforcement actions. *Hochfelder* was a private suit and a number of courts, including the Second Circuit, continued to apply a negligence standard in government enforcement actions. Other unresolved questions included the extent to which the scienter requirement applies to actions under other provisions of the securities laws. Those issues were later considered by the Supreme Court in Aaron v. SEC, 446 U.S. 680, 100 S.Ct. 1945, 64 L.Ed.2d 611 (1980). There the Court stated that "the rationale of

Hochfelder ineluctably leads to the conclusion that scienter is an element of a violation of § 10(b) and Rule 10b–5, regardless of the identity of the plaintiff or the nature of the relief sought." The SEC also alleged in *Aaron* that the defendant had violated § 17(a) of the 1933 Act, from which the language of Rule 10b–5 is taken. With respect to that section, the Court held that scienter must be shown to establish a violation of § 17(a)(1), but not of § 17(a)(2) or (3). The Court found the language of § 17(a)(2) is "devoid of any suggestion whatsoever of a scienter requirement," while § 17(a)(3) "focuses on the *effect* of particular conduct on members of the investing public, rather than the culpability of the person responsible." This decision means that the language of clause (c) of Rule 10b–5 has a different meaning than the comparable language in § 17(a)(3).

4. *Fraud in Proxy Solicitations.* The antifraud provision in the SEC's proxy rules prohibits statements or omissions that make such communications false or misleading. 17 C.F.R. § 24.14a–9. With regard to the standard of care under the proxy rules in TSC Industries, Inc. v. Northway, Inc., 426 U.S. 438 n. 7, 96 S.Ct. 2126, 48 L.Ed.2d 757 (1976), the Supreme Court observed "Our cases have not considered, and we have no occasion in this case to consider, what showing of culpability is required to establish the liability under § 14(a) of a corporation issuing a materially misleading proxy statement, or of a person involved in the preparation of a materially misleading proxy statement." A few scattered decisions have indicated that scienter is required in actions brought under Rule 14a–9. Adams v. Standard Knitting Mills, Inc., 623 F.2d 422 (6th Cir.1980), cert. denied, 449 U.S. 1067, 101 S.Ct. 795, 66 L.Ed.2d 611 (1980). Compare Fradkin v. Ernst, 571 F.Supp. 829 (N.D.Ohio 1983) (limiting *Adams* scienter requirements to collateral participants). Cf. Mader v. Armel, 461 F.2d 1123 (6th Cir.1972) (good faith is defense to 10b–5 challenge to misleading proxies); Zatkin v. Primuth, 551 F.Supp. 39 (S.D.Cal.1982) (scienter required in suit against an outside accountant; dictum that scienter is not ordinarily required). The Supreme Court's ruling in *Aaron v. SEC* would, however, seem to mandate that a showing of negligent conduct will suffice under Rule 14a–9. In re Cendant Corp. Litigation, 60 F.Supp.2d 354 (D.N.J.1999) (upholding allegations of negligence as sufficient to support a claim under Rule 14a–9). See also Koppel v. 4987 Corp., 2001 WL 47000, [2000–2001 Transfer Binder] Fed. Sec. L. Rep. (CCH) ¶ 91,306 (S.D.N.Y.2001) (jury was properly instructed on the degree of negligence necessary to establish a violation of the proxy rules); In re George Kern, Jr., SEC Admin.Proc.File No. 3–6896 (Nov. 14, 1988), affirmed on other grounds Sec.Exch.Act Rel. No. 34–29356 (SEC June 21, 1991) (applying negligence standard to violations of section 14 of the Securities and Exchange Act of 1934). Even aside from the mandate of the applicable statutory language, one justification for imposing a negligence standard under Rule 14a–9 is that, while Rule 10b–5 applies to all securities traded in interstate commerce, Rule 14a–9 is limited to issuers subject to Exchange Act registration and reporting requirements.

TELLABS, INC. v. MAKOR ISSUES & RIGHTS, LTD.

551 U.S. 308, 127 S.Ct. 2499, 2504–05 168 L.Ed.2d 179 (2007).

JUSTICE GINSBURG delivered the opinion of the Court.

This Court has long recognized that meritorious private actions to enforce federal antifraud securities laws are an essential supplement to criminal prosecutions and civil enforcement actions brought, respectively, by the Department of Justice and the Securities and Exchange Commission (SEC). Private securities fraud actions, however, if not adequately contained, can be employed abusively to impose substantial costs on companies and individuals whose conduct conforms to the law. As a check against abusive litigation by private parties, Congress enacted the Private Securities Litigation Reform Act of 1995 (PSLRA), 109 Stat. 737.

Exacting pleading requirements are among the control measures Congress included in the PSLRA. The Act requires plaintiffs to state with particularity both the facts constituting the alleged violation, and the facts evidencing scienter, *i.e.*, the defendant's intention "to deceive, manipulate, or defraud. This case concerns the latter requirement. As set out in § 21D(b)(2) of the PSLRA, plaintiffs must "state with particularity facts giving rise to a strong inference that the defendant acted with the required state of mind." 15 U.S.C. § 78u–4(b)(2).

Congress left the key term "strong inference" undefined, and Courts of Appeals have divided on its meaning. In the case before us, the Court of Appeals for the Seventh Circuit held that the "strong inference" standard would be met if the complaint "allege[d] facts from which, if true, a reasonable person could infer that the defendant acted with the required intent." That formulation, we conclude, does not capture the stricter demand Congress sought to convey in § 21D(b)(2). It does not suffice that a reasonable fact finder plausibly could infer from the complaint's allegations the requisite state of mind. Rather, to determine whether a complaint's scienter allegations can survive threshold inspection for sufficiency, a court governed by § 21D(b)(2) must engage in a comparative evaluation; it must consider, not only inferences urged by the plaintiff, as the Seventh Circuit did, but also competing inferences rationally drawn from the facts alleged. An inference of fraudulent intent may be plausible, yet less cogent than other, nonculpable explanations for the defendant's conduct. To qualify as "strong" within the intendment of § 21D(b)(2), we hold, an inference of scienter must be more than merely plausible or reasonable-it must be cogent and at least as compelling as any opposing inference of nonfraudulent intent.

Petitioner Tellabs, Inc., manufactures specialized equipment used in fiber optic networks. During the time period relevant to this case, petitioner Richard Notebaert was Tellabs' chief executive officer and president. Respondents (Shareholders) are persons who purchased Tellabs stock between December 11, 2000, and June 19, 2001. They accuse Tellabs and

Notebaert (as well as several other Tellabs executives) of engaging in a scheme to deceive the investing public about the true value of Tellabs' stock.

Beginning on December 11, 2000, the Shareholders allege, Notebaert (and by imputation Tellabs) "falsely reassured public investors, in a series of statements ... that Tellabs was continuing to enjoy strong demand for its products and earning record revenues," when, in fact, Notebaert knew the opposite was true. From December 2000 until the spring of 2001, the Shareholders claim, Notebaert knowingly misled the public in four ways. First, he made statements indicating that demand for Tellabs' flagship networking device, the TITAN 5500, was continuing to grow, when in fact demand for that product was waning. Second, Notebaert made statements indicating that the TITAN 6500, Tellabs' next-generation networking device, was available for delivery, and that demand for that product was strong and growing, when in truth the product was not ready for delivery and demand was weak. Third, he falsely represented Tellabs' financial results for the fourth quarter of 2000 (and, in connection with those results, condoned the practice of "channel stuffing," under which Tellabs flooded its customers with unwanted products). Fourth, Notebaert made a series of overstated revenue projections, when demand for the TITAN 5500 was drying up and production of the TITAN 6500 was behind schedule. Based on Notebaert's sunny assessments, the Shareholders contend, market analysts recommended that investors buy Tellabs' stock.

The first public glimmer that business was not so healthy came in March 2001 when Tellabs modestly reduced its first quarter sales projections. In the next months, Tellabs made progressively more cautious statements about its projected sales. On June 19, 2001, the last day of the class period, Tellabs disclosed that demand for the TITAN 5500 had significantly dropped. Simultaneously, the company substantially lowered its revenue projections for the second quarter of 2001. The next day, the price of Tellabs stock, which had reached a high of $67 during the period, plunged to a low of $15.87.

On December 3, 2002, the Shareholders filed a class action in the District Court for the Northern District of Illinois. Their complaint stated, *inter alia*, that Tellabs and Notebaert had engaged in securities fraud in violation of § 10(b) of the Securities Exchange Act of 1934 and SEC Rule 10b–5, also that Notebaert was a "controlling person" under § 20(a) of the 1934 Act and therefore derivatively liable for the company's fraudulent acts. See App. 98–101, 167–171. Tellabs moved to dismiss the complaint on the ground that the Shareholders had failed to plead their case with the particularity the PSLRA requires. The District Court agreed, and therefore dismissed the complaint without prejudice.

The Shareholders then amended their complaint, adding references to 27 confidential sources and making further, more specific, allegations concerning Notebaert's mental state. The District Court again dismissed, this time with prejudice. The Shareholders had sufficiently pleaded that

Notebaert's statements were misleading, the court determined but they had insufficiently alleged that he acted with scienter.

The Court of Appeals for the Seventh Circuit reversed in relevant part. Like the District Court, the Court of Appeals found that the Shareholders had pleaded the misleading character of Notebaert's statements with sufficient particularity. Unlike the District Court, however, the Seventh Circuit concluded that the Shareholders had sufficiently alleged that Notebaert acted with the requisite state of mind.

In adopting its standard for the survival of a complaint, the Seventh Circuit explicitly rejected a stiffer standard adopted by the Sixth Circuit, i.e., that "plaintiffs are entitled only to the most plausible of competing inferences." The Sixth Circuit's standard, the court observed, because it involved an assessment of competing inferences, "could potentially infringe upon plaintiffs' Seventh Amendment rights." We granted certiorari to resolve the disagreement among the Circuits on whether, and to what extent, a court must consider competing inferences in determining whether a securities fraud complaint gives rise to a "strong inference" of scienter.

Section 10(b), this Court has implied from the statute's text and purpose, affords a right of action to purchasers or sellers of securities injured by its violation.

In an ordinary civil action, the Federal Rules of Civil Procedure require only "a short and plain statement of the claim showing that the pleader is entitled to relief. Although the rule encourages brevity, the complaint must say enough to give the defendant "fair notice of what the plaintiff's claim is and the grounds upon which it rests." Prior to the enactment of the PSLRA, the sufficiency of a complaint for securities fraud was governed not by Rule 8, but by the heightened pleading standard set forth in Rule 9(b).

Setting a uniform pleading standard for § 10(b) actions was among Congress' objectives when it enacted the PSLRA. Designed to curb perceived abuses of the § 10(b) private action-'nuisance filings, targeting of deep-pocket defendants, vexatious discovery requests and manipulation by class action lawyers," Notably, Congress prescribed new procedures for the appointment of lead plaintiffs and lead counsel. This innovation aimed to increase the likelihood that institutional investors-parties more likely to balance the interests of the class with the long-term interests of the company-would serve as lead plaintiffs. Congress also "limit[ed] recoverable damages and attorney's fees, provide[d] a 'safe harbor' for forward-looking statements, ... mandate[d] imposition of sanctions for frivolous litigation, and authorize[d] a stay of discovery pending resolution of any motion to dismiss. And in § 21D(b) of the PSLRA, Congress "impose[d] heightened pleading requirements in actions brought pursuant to § 10(b) and Rule 10b–5."

Under the PSLRA's heightened pleading instructions, any private securities complaint alleging that the defendant made a false or misleading statement must: (1) "specify each statement alleged to have been misleading [and] the reason or reasons why the statement is misleading," and (2) "state with particularity facts giving rise to a strong inference that the defendant acted with the required state of mind."

The "strong inference" standard "unequivocally raise[d] the bar for pleading scienter," and signaled Congress' purpose to promote greater uniformity among the Circuits, see H.R. Conf. Rep., p. 41. But "Congress did not ... throw much light on what facts ... suffice to create [a strong] inference," or on what "degree of imagination courts can use in divining whether" the requisite inference exists. While adopting the Second Circuit's "strong inference" standard, Congress did not codify that Circuit's case law interpreting the standard. With no clear guide from Congress other than its "inten[tion] to strengthen existing pleading requirements," H.R. Conf. Rep., p. 41, Courts of Appeals have diverged again, this time in construing the term "strong inference." Among the uncertainties, should courts consider competing inferences in determining whether an inference of scienter is "strong". Our task is to prescribe a workable construction of the "strong inference" standard, a reading geared to the PSLRA's twin goals: to curb frivolous, lawyer-driven litigation, while preserving investors' ability to recover on meritorious claims.

Tellabs contends that when competing inferences are considered, Notebaert's evident lack of pecuniary motive will be dispositive. The Shareholders, Tellabs stresses, did not allege that Notebaert sold any shares during the class period. See Brief for Petitioners 50 ("The absence of any allegations of motive color all the other allegations putatively giving rise to an inference of scienter."). While it is true that motive can be a relevant consideration, and personal financial gain may weigh heavily in favor of a scienter inference, we agree with the Seventh Circuit that the absence of a motive allegation is not fatal. As earlier stated, allegations must be considered collectively; the significance that can be ascribed to an allegation of motive, or lack thereof, depends on the entirety of the complaint.

Tellabs also maintains that several of the Shareholders' allegations are too vague or ambiguous to contribute to a strong inference of scienter. For example, the Shareholders alleged that Tellabs flooded its customers with unwanted products, a practice known as "channel stuffing." But they failed, Tellabs argues, to specify whether the channel stuffing allegedly known to Notebaert was the illegitimate kind. We agree that omissions and ambiguities count against inferring scienter, for plaintiffs must "state with particularity facts giving rise to a strong inference that the defendant acted with the required state of mind." We reiterate, however, that the court's job is not to scrutinize each allegation in isolation but to assess all the allegations holistically. In sum, the reviewing court must ask: When the allegations are accepted as true and taken collectively, would a reasonable person deem the inference of scienter at least as strong as any opposing inference?

Accounting for its construction of § 21D(b)(2), the Seventh Circuit explained that the court "th[ought] it wis[e] to adopt an approach that [could not] be misunderstood as a usurpation of the jury's role." In our view, the Seventh Circuit's concern was undue. A court's comparative assessment of plausible inferences, while constantly assuming the plaintiff's allegations to be true, we think it plain, does not impinge upon the Seventh Amendment right to jury trial.

While we reject the Seventh Circuit's approach to § 21D(b)(2), we do not decide whether, under the standard we have described, the Shareholders' allegations warrant "a strong inference that [Notebaert and Tellabs] acted with the required state of mind." Neither the District Court nor the Court of Appeals had the opportunity to consider the matter in light of the prescriptions we announce today. We therefore vacate the Seventh Circuit's judgment so that the case may be reexamined in accord with our construction of § 21D(b)(2).

The judgment of the Court of Appeals is vacated, and the case is remanded for further proceedings consistent with this opinion.

[the concurring opinions of Justices Scalia and Alito are omitted, as is the dissenting opinion of Justice Stevens]

SECTION 6. THE "DECEPTION" REQUIREMENT

SANTA FE INDUSTRIES v. GREEN

430 U.S. 462, 97 S.Ct. 1292, 51 L.Ed.2d 480 (1977).

MR. JUSTICE WHITE delivered the opinion of the Court.

The issue in this case involves the reach and coverage of § 10(b) of the Securities Exchange Act of 1934 and Rule 10b–5 thereunder in the context of a Delaware short-form merger transaction used by the majority stockholder of a corporation to eliminate the minority interest.

In 1936 petitioner Santa Fe Industries, Inc. ("Santa Fe") acquired control of 60% of the stock of Kirby Lumber Corporation ("Kirby"), a Delaware corporation. Through a series of purchases over the succeeding years, Santa Fe increased its control of Kirby's stock to 95%; the purchase prices during the period 1968–1973 ranged from $65 to $92.50 per share. In 1974, wishing to acquire 100% ownership of Kirby, Santa Fe availed itself of § 253 of the Delaware Corporation Law, known as the "short-form merger" statute. Section 253 permits a parent corporation owning at least 90% of the stock of a subsidiary to merge with that subsidiary, upon approval by the parent's board of directors, and to make payment in cash for the shares of the minority stockholders. The statute does not require the consent of, or advance notice to, the minority stockholders. However, notice of the merger must be given within 10 days after its effective date, and any stockholder who is dissatisfied with the terms of the merger may petition the Delaware Court of Chancery for a decree ordering the surviving corporation to pay him the fair value of his shares, as determined by a court-appointed appraiser subject to review by the court. Del.Gen.Corp. Law §§ 253, 262.

Santa Fe obtained independent appraisals of the physical assets of Kirby—land, timber, buildings, and machinery—and of Kirby's oil, gas, and mineral interests. These appraisals, together with other financial information, were submitted to Morgan, Stanley & Company ("Morgan Stanley"), an investment banking firm retained to appraise the fair market value of Kirby stock. Kirby's physical assets were appraised at $320 million (amounting to $640 for each of the 500,000 shares); Kirby's stock was valued by Morgan Stanley at $125 per share. Under the terms of the merger, minority stockholders were offered $150 per share.

The provisions of the short-form merger statute were fully complied with. The minority stockholders of Kirby were notified the day after the merger became effective and were advised of their right to obtain an appraisal in Delaware court if dissatisfied with the offer of $150 per share. They also received an information statement containing, in addition to the relevant financial data about Kirby, the appraisals of the value of Kirby's assets and the Morgan Stanley appraisal concluding that the fair market value of the stock was $125 per share.

Respondents, minority stockholders of Kirby, objected to the terms of the merger, but did not pursue their appraisal remedy in the Delaware Court of Chancery. Instead, they brought this action in federal court on behalf of the corporation and other minority stockholders, seeking to set aside the merger or to recover what they claimed to be the fair value of their shares. The amended complaint asserted that, based on the fair market value of Kirby's physical assets as revealed by the appraisal included in the Information Statement sent to minority shareholders, Kirby's stock was worth at least $772 per share. The complaint alleged further that the merger took place without prior notice to minority stockholders; that the purpose of the merger was to appropriate the difference between the "conceded pro rata of value of the physical assets" and the offer of $150 per share—to "freez[e] out the minority stockholders at a wholly inadequate price," and that Santa Fe, knowing the appraised value of the physical assets, obtained a "fraudulent appraisal" of the stock from Morgan Stanley and offered $25 above that appraisal "in order to lull the minority stockholders into erroneously believing that [Santa Fe was] generous." This course of conduct was alleged to be "a violation of Rule 10b–5 because defendants employed a 'device, scheme or artifice to defraud' and engaged in an 'act, practice or course of business which operates or would operate as a fraud or deceit upon any person, in connection with the purchase or sale of any security.' " Morgan Stanley assertedly participated in the fraud as an accessory by submitting its appraisal of $125 per share although knowing the appraised value of the physical assets.

The District Court dismissed the complaint for failure to state a claim upon which relief could be granted. As the District Court understood the complaint, respondents' case rested on two distinct grounds. First, federal law was assertedly violated because the merger was for the sole purpose of eliminating the minority from the company, therefore lacking any justifiable business purpose, and because the merger was undertaken without prior notice to the minority shareholders. Second, the low valuation placed on the shares in the cash exchange offer was itself said to be a fraud actionable under Rule 10b–5. In rejecting the first ground for recovery, the District Court reasoned that Delaware law required neither a business purpose for a short-form merger nor prior notice to the minority shareholders who the statute contemplated would be removed from the company, and that Rule 10b–5 did not override these provisions of state corporate law by independently placing a duty on the majority not to merge without prior notice and without a justifiable business purpose.

As for the claim that actionable fraud inhered in the allegedly gross undervaluation of the minority shares, the District Court observed that respondents valued their shares at a minimum of $772 per share, "basing this figure on the *pro rata* value of Kirby's physical assets." Accepting this valuation for purposes of the motion to dismiss, the District Court further noted that, as revealed by the complaint, the physical asset appraisal, along with other information relevant to Morgan Stanley's valuation of the shares, had been included with the Information Statement sent to respondents within the time required by state law. It thought that if "full and fair disclosure is made, transactions eliminating minority interests are beyond the purview of Rule 10b–5," and concluded that "the complaint fail[ed] to allege an omission, misstatement or fraudulent course of conduct that would have impeded a shareholder's judgment of the value of the offer." The complaint therefore failed to state a claim and was dismissed.

A divided Court of Appeals for the Second Circuit reversed, 533 F.2d 1283 (1976). It first agreed that there was a double aspect to the case: first, the claim that gross undervaluation of the minority stock itself violated Rule 10b–5; and second, that "without any misrepresentation or failure to disclose relevant facts, the merger constituted a violation of Rule 10b–5" because it was accomplished without any corporate purpose and without prior notice to the minority stockholders. As to the first aspect of the case, the Court of Appeals did not disturb the District Court's conclusion that the complaint did not allege a material misrepresentation or nondisclosure with respect to the value of the stock; and the court declined to rule that a claim of gross undervaluation itself would suffice to make out a Rule 10b–5 case. With respect to the second aspect of the case, however, the court fundamentally disagreed with the District Court as to the reach and coverage of Rule 10b–5. The Court of Appeals' view was that, although the Rule plainly reached material misrepresentations and nondisclosures in connection with the purchase or sale of securities, neither misrepresentation or nondisclosure was a necessary element of a

Rule 10b–5 action; the rule reached "breaches of fiduciary duty by a majority against minority shareholders without any charge of misrepresentation or lack of disclosure." The court went on to hold that the complaint taken as a whole stated a cause of action under the Rule:

> "We hold that a complaint alleges a claim under Rule 10b–5 when it charges, in connection with a Delaware short-form merger, that the majority has committed a breach of its fiduciary duty to deal fairly with minority shareholders by effecting the merger without any justifiable business purpose. The minority shareholders are given no prior notice of the merger, thus having no opportunity to apply for injunctive relief, and the proposed price to be paid is substantially lower than the appraised value reflected in the Information Statement."

We granted the petition for certiorari challenging this holding because of the importance of the issue involved to the administration of the federal securities laws. We reverse.

Section 10(b) of the 1934 Act makes it "unlawful for any person * * * to use or employ * * * any manipulative or deceptive device or contrivance in contravention of [Securities Exchange Commission rules]"; Rule 10b–5, promulgated by the SEC under § 10(b), prohibits in addition to nondisclosure and misrepresentation, any "artifice to defraud" or any act "which operates or would operate as a fraud or deceit." The court below construed the term "fraud" in Rule 10b–5 by adverting to the use of the term in several of this Court's decisions in contexts other than the 1934 Act and the related Securities Act of 1933. The Court of Appeals' approach to the interpretation of Rule 10b–5 is inconsistent with that taken by the Court last Term in Ernst & Ernst v. Hochfelder.

Ernst & Ernst makes clear that in deciding whether a complaint states a cause of action for "fraud" under Rule 10b–5, "we turn first to the language of § 10(b), for '[t]he starting point in every case involving construction of a statute is the language itself.' " In holding that a cause of action under Rule 10b–5 does not lie for mere negligence, the Court began with the principle that "[a]scertainment of congressional intent with respect to the standard of liability created by a particular section of the [1933 and 1934] Acts must * * * rest primarily on the language of that section," and then focused on the statutory language of § 10(b)— "[t]he words 'manipulative or deceptive' used in conjunction with 'device or contrivance.' " The same language and the same principle apply to this case.

To the extent that the Court of Appeals would rely on the use of the term "fraud" in Rule 10b–5 to bring within the ambit of the Rule all breaches of fiduciary duty in connection with a securities transaction, its interpretation would, like the interpretation rejected by the Court in *Ernst & Ernst,* "add a gloss to the operative language of the statute quite different from its commonly accepted meaning." But as the Court there held, the language of the statute must control the interpretation of the Rule:

> "Rule 10b–5 was adopted pursuant to authority granted the [Securities Exchange] Commission under § 10(b). The rulemaking power granted to an administrative agency charged with the administration of a federal statute is not the power to make law. Rather, it is ' "the power to adopt regulations to carry into effect the will of Congress as expressed by the statute." ' * * * [The scope of the Rule] cannot exceed the power granted the Commission by Congress under § 10(b)."[7]

The language of § 10(b) gives no indication that Congress meant to prohibit any conduct not involving manipulation or deception. Nor have we been cited to any evidence in the legislative history that would support a departure from the language of the statute. "When a statute speaks so specifically in terms of manipulation and deception, * * * and when its history reflects no more expansive intent, we are quite unwilling to extend the scope of the statute * * *." Id., at 214 (footnote omitted). Thus the claim of fraud and fiduciary breach in this complaint states a cause of action under any part of Rule 10b–5 only if the conduct alleged can be fairly viewed as "manipulative or deceptive" within the meaning of the statute.

It is our judgment that the transaction, if carried out as alleged in the complaint, was neither deceptive nor manipulative and therefore did not violate either § 10(b) of the Act or Rule 10b–5.

As we have indicated, the case comes to us on the premise that the complaint failed to allege a material misrepresentation or material failure to disclose. The finding of the District Court, undisturbed by the Court of Appeals, was that there was no "omission" or "misstatement" in the Information Statement accompanying the notice of merger. On the basis of the information provided, minority shareholders could either accept the price offered or reject it and seek an appraisal in the Delaware Court of Chancery. Their choice was fairly presented, and they were furnished with all relevant information on which to base their decision.

We therefore find inapposite the cases relied upon by respondents and the court below, in which the breaches of fiduciary duty held violative of Rule 10b–5 included some element of deception. Those cases forcefully reflect the principle that "[s]ection 10(b) must be read flexibly, not technically and restrictively" and that the statute provides a cause of

---

7. The case for adhering to the language of the statute is even stronger here than in *Ernst & Ernst,* where the interpretation of Rule 10b–5 rejected by the Court was strongly urged by the Commission. By contrast, the Commission apparently has not concluded that Rule 10b–5 should be used to reach "going private" transactions where the majority stockholder eliminates the minority at an allegedly unfair price. See SEC Securities Act Release No. 5567 (Feb. 6, 1975)(proposing Rules 13e–3A and 13e–3B dealing with "going private" transactions, pursuant to six sections of the 1934 Act including § 10(b), but stating that the Commission "has reached no conclusions with respect to the proposed rules"). Because we are concerned here only with § 10(b), we intimate no view as to the Commission's authority to promulgate such rules under other sections of the Act.

action for any plaintiff who "suffer[s] an injury as a result of deceptive practices touching its sale [or purchase] of securities. * * *" Superintendent of Insurance v. Bankers Life & Casualty Co., 404 U.S. 6, 12–13 (1971). But the cases do not support the proposition, adopted by the Court of Appeals below and urged by respondents here, that a breach of fiduciary duty by majority stockholders, without any deception, misrepresentation, or nondisclosure, violates the statute and the Rule.

It is also readily apparent that the conduct alleged in the complaint was not "manipulative" within the meaning of the statute. Manipulation is "virtually a term of art when used in connection with securities markets." Ernst & Ernst, 425 U.S., at 199. The term refers generally to practices, such as wash sales, matched orders, or rigged prices, that are intended to mislead investors by artificially affecting market activity. Section 10(b)'s general prohibition of practices deemed by the SEC to be "manipulative"—in this technical sense of artificially affecting market activity in order to mislead investors—is fully consistent with the fundamental purpose of the 1934 Act "to substitute a philosophy of full disclosure for the philosophy of *caveat emptor.* * * *" Indeed, nondisclosure is usually essential to the success of a manipulative scheme. No doubt Congress meant to prohibit the full range of ingenious devices that might be used to manipulate securities prices. But we do not think it would have chosen this "term of art" if it had meant to bring within the scope of § 10(b) instances of corporate mismanagement such as this, in which the essence of the complaint is that shareholders were treated unfairly by a fiduciary.

The language of the statute is, we think, "sufficiently clear in its context" to be dispositive here, but even if it were not, there are additional considerations that weigh heavily against permitting a cause of action under Rule 10b–5 for the breach of corporate fiduciary duty alleged in this complaint. Congress did not expressly provide a private cause of action for violations of § 10(b). Although we have recognized an implied cause of action under that section in some circumstances, we have also recognized that a private cause of action under the antifraud provisions of the Securities Exchange Act should not be implied where it is "unnecessary to ensure the fulfillment of Congress' purposes" in adopting the Act. Piper v. Chris–Craft Industries. As we noted earlier, the Court repeatedly has described the "fundamental purpose" of the Act as implementing a "philosophy of full disclosure"; once full and fair disclosure has occurred, the fairness of the terms of the transaction is at most a tangential concern of the statute. As in Cort v. Ash, 422 U.S. 78, 80 (1975), we are reluctant to recognize a cause of action here to serve what is "at best a subsidiary purpose" of the federal legislation.

A second factor in determining whether Congress intended to create a federal cause of action in these circumstances is "whether 'the cause of action [is] one traditionally relegated to state law. * * *'" Piper v. Chris–Craft Industries, Inc., quoting Cort v. Ash. The Delaware Legislature has supplied minority shareholders with a cause of action in the Delaware

Court of Chancery to recover the fair value of shares allegedly underval-ued in a short-form merger. Of course, the existence of a particular state law remedy is not dispositive of the question whether Congress meant to provide a similar federal remedy, but as in *Court* and *Piper* we conclude that "it is entirely appropriate in this instance to relegate respondent and others in his situation to whatever remedy is created by state law."

The reasoning behind a holding that the complaint in this case alleged fraud under Rule 10b–5 could not be easily contained. It is difficult to imagine how a court could distinguish, for purposes of Rule 10b–5 fraud, between a majority stockholder's use of a short-form merger to eliminate the minority at an unfair price and the use of some other device, such as a long-form merger, tender offer, or liquidation, to achieve the same result; or indeed how a court could distinguish the alleged abuses in these going private transactions from other types of fiduciary self-dealing involving transactions in securities. The result would be to bring within the Rule a wide variety of corporate conduct traditionally left to state regulation. In addition to posing a "danger of vexatious litigation which could result from a widely expanded class of plaintiffs under Rule 10b–5," Blue Chip Stamps v. Manor Drug Stores, 421 U.S. 723, 740 (1975), this extension of the federal securities laws would overlap and quite possibly interfere with state corporate law. Federal courts applying a "federal fiduciary principle" under Rule 10b–5 could be expected to depart from state fiduciary stan-dards at least to the extent necessary to ensure uniformity within the federal system.[16] Absent a clear indication of congressional intent, we are reluctant to federalize the substantial portion of the law of corporations that deals with transactions in securities, particularly where established state policies of corporate regulation would be overridden. As the Court stated in Cort v. Ash, supra, "Corporations are creatures of state law, and investors commit their funds to corporate directors on the understanding that, except where federal law *expressly* requires certain responsibilities of directors with respect to stockholders, state law will govern the internal affairs of the corporation."

We thus adhere to the position that "Congress by § 10(b) did not seek to regulate transactions which constitute no more than internal corporate mismanagement." Superintendent of Insurance v. Bankers Life & Cas. Co., 404 U.S., at 12. There may well be a need for uniform federal fiduciary standards to govern mergers such as that challenged in this

---

16. For example, some States apparently require a 'valid corporate purpose' for the elimina-tion of the minority interest through a short-form merger, whereas other States do not. Compare Bryan v. Brock & Blevins Co., 490 F.2d 563 (CA5), cert. denied, 419 U.S. 844, 95 S.Ct. 77, 42 L.Ed.2d 72 (1974) (merger arranged by controlling stockholder for no business purpose except to eliminate 15% minority stockholder violated Georgia short-form merger statute) with Stauffer v. Standard Brands, Inc., 41 Del.Ch. 7, 187 A.2d 78 (1962) (Delaware short-form merger statute allows majority stockholder to eliminate the minority interest without any corporate purpose and subject only to an appraisal remedy). Thus to the extent that Rule 10b–5 is interpreted to require a valid corporate purpose for elimination of minority shareholders as well as a fair price for their shares, it would impose a stricter standard of fiduciary duty than that required by the law of some States.

complaint. But those standards should not be supplied by judicial extension of § 10(b) and Rule 10b–5 to "cover the corporate universe."[17]

The judgment of the Court of Appeals is reversed, and the case is remanded for further proceedings consistent with this opinion.

MR. JUSTICE BRENNAN dissents and would affirm for substantially the reasons stated in the majority and concurring opinions in the Court of Appeals, 533 F.2d 1283 (1976).

MR. JUSTICE BLACKMUN, concurring in part. [omitted]

MR. JUSTICE STEVENS, concurring in part. [omitted]

NOTES

1. In subsequent proceedings under Delaware law by minority shareholders of Kirby who had objected to the merger and demanded appraisal of their shares, the Delaware Supreme Court upheld an award of $254.40 per share, based 60% on Kirby's earnings and 40% on the value of its assets. Bell v. Kirby Lumber Corp., 413 A.2d 137 (Del.1980).

2. In an effort to deal with the "going private" phenomenon described in *Santa Fe Industries v. Green*, the SEC in 1977 proposed a new Rule 13e–3, which would have prohibited any registered company from purchasing its own shares for the purpose of "going private" unless the transaction was "fair to unaffiliated security holders." Among the criteria of "fairness" were the fairness of the consideration being paid and the other terms of the transaction, whether the transaction had been approved by a majority of unaffiliated shareholders and disinterested directors, the purpose of the transaction, and the anticipated benefits to the company and its affiliates. Securities Act Release No. 5884 (Nov. 17, 1977). Would a rule of this type be within the Commission's authority under § 13(e), in light of the Supreme Court's decision in *Santa Fe?* After consideration of comments on this proposal, the Commission withdrew the proposed substantive fairness requirement, and adopted a final rule requiring any registered company which plans to "go private" to file a detailed schedule of information with the Commission and disseminate such information to its shareholders at least 20 days prior to consummation of the transaction. The 20–day requirement is intended "to permit security holders to make an unhurried and informed choice as to their alternatives," including "utilizing remedies available under state law to challenge the transaction." Among the items of information required to be disclosed are the purpose of the transaction and the basis for management's belief that the terms of the transaction are fair to unaffiliated shareholders in relation to (a) the current and historical market price of the stock, (b) the net book value, going concern value and liquidation value of the company, (c) any

---

17. Cary, Federalism and Corporate Law: Reflections Upon Delaware, 83 Yale L.J. 663, 700 (1974) (footnote omitted). Professor Cary argues vigorously for comprehensive federal fiduciary standards, but urges a 'frontal' attack by a new federal statute rather than an extension of Rule 10b–5. He writes: 'It seems anomalous to jig-saw every kind of corporate dispute into the federal courts through the securities acts as they are presently written.' Ibid. See also Note, Going Private, 84 Yale L.J. 903 (1975) (proposing the application of traditional doctrines of substantive corporate law to problems of fairness raised by 'going private' transactions such as short-form mergers).

outside offers for the stock, and (d) any reports, opinions or appraisals received from outside parties. See Rule 13e–3 and Schedule 13E–3, as adopted in Sec.Act Rel. No. 6100 (Aug. 2, 1979).

3.   The *Santa Fe* decision is clear in its basic holding: an allegation of "fraud" on a corporation or its outside shareholders under Rule 10b–5 must involve some element of deception or concealment of material information, rather than mere unfairness. What is less clear is how deeply its rationale cuts into "fraud on the corporation" claims. In the *Goldberg* case which follows, the Second Circuit considered the circumstances under which nondisclosure to the shareholders may still give rise to a cause of action.

GOLDBERG v. MERIDOR

567 F.2d 209 (2d Cir.1977), cert. denied, 434 U.S.
1069, 98 S.Ct. 1249, 55 L.Ed.2d 771 (1978).

FRIENDLY, CIRCUIT JUDGE

In this derivative action in the District Court for the Southern District of New York, David Goldberg, a stockholder of Universal Gas & Oil Company, Inc. (UGO), a Panama corporation having its principal place of business in New York City, sought to recover damages and to obtain other relief against UGO's controlling parent, Maritimecor, S.A., also a Panama corporation; Maritimecor's controlling parent, Maritime Fruit Carriers Company Ltd., an Israel corporation; a number of individuals who were directors of one or more of these companies; the investment firm of Hornblower & Weeks, Hemphill, Noyes, Inc.; and the accounting firm of Laventhal & Horwath, with respect to transactions which culminated in an agreement providing for UGO's issuance to Maritimecor of up to 4,200,000 shares of UGO stock and its assumption of all of Maritimecor's liabilities (including a debt of $7,000,000 owed to UGO) in consideration of the transfer of all of Maritimecor's assets (except 2,800,000 UGO shares already held by Maritimecor). It suffices at this point to say that the complaint, filed February 3, 1976, alleged that the contract was grossly unfair to UGO and violated both § 10(b) of the Securities Exchange Act and the SEC's Rule 10b–5 and common law fiduciary duties. * * *

Defendants filed motions to dismiss the amended complaint for failure to state a claim under § 10(b) of the Securities Exchange Act and Rule 10b–5. In answer to defendants' argument "that deception and nondisclosure is a requirement for a 10b–5 case" which was disputed as a matter of law, plaintiff counsel submitted an affidavit asserting that "insofar as plaintiff Goldberg, a minority shareholder is concerned, there has been no disclosure to him of the fraudulent nature of the transfer of Maritimecor assets and liabilities for stock of UGO". * * *

On February 11, 1977, Judge Lasker filed an opinion that granted the motions to dismiss. He thought the case was governed by Popkin v.

Bishop, 464 F.2d 714 rather than by our *en banc* decision in Schoenbaum v. Firstbrook, 405 F.2d 200. * * * After the [Supreme Court decision in Santa Fe Industries v. Green], the judge filed a memorandum adding to the opinion . . . to the effect that the Supreme Court's decision * * * lent substantial support to the result.

Before proceeding further, we must deal with the district court's refusal to permit amendment of the complaint to include reference to the two press releases or otherwise to claim deception. * * * We are constrained to hold that the refusal of leave to amend was an abuse of discretion and to treat the cases as if an amendment, at least in the two respects noted, had been allowed.

If the complaint were thus amended, we would deem it clear that, so far as this court's decisions are concerned, the case would be governed by *Schoenbaum* rather than by *Popkin*. The August 1 press release held out an inviting picture that

> As a result of the transaction, UGO will replace Maritimecor as the principal operating subsidiary of MFC and, as such, will engage in a diversified line of shipping and shipping related activities including the sale of ships and shipbuilding contracts, the operation of reefers and tankers, and upon their delivery, product carriers and oil drilling rigs, and underwriting marine insurance.

When allegedly the truth was that UGO had entered into a transaction that would ensure its doom. *Popkin* was specifically rested on its special facts. The plaintiff was taken to have conceded that the complaint did not allege misrepresentation or non-disclosure and that he relied solely on the unfairness of the merger terms. * * * The observation in *Popkin* that "our emphasis on improper self-dealing did not eliminate nondisclosure as a key issue in the Rule 10b–5 cases" followed a statement that when, as here, state law does not demand prior shareholder approval of a transaction, "it makes sense to concentrate on the impropriety of the conduct itself rather than on the 'failure to disclose' it because full and fair disclosure in a real sense will rarely occur. It will be equally rare in the legal sense once the view is taken—as we did in *Schoenbaum*—that under federal securities law disclosure to interested insiders does not prevent a valid claim that fraud was committed upon 'outsiders' (such as minority shareholders) whatever the requirements of state corporate law may be." Id. The ruling of *Popkin* was that in the *opposite* situation, where "merger transactions * * *, under state law, must be subjected to shareholder approval * * * if federal law ensures that shareholder approval is fairly sought and freely given, the principal federal interest is at an end." Clearly that is not this case.

The ruling that this case is governed by *Schoenbaum* rather than by *Popkin* by no means ends our inquiry. Rather it brings us to the serious question whether *Schoenbaum* can be here applied consistently with the Supreme Court's decision in Santa Fe Industries, Inc. v. Green, supra. We think it can be and should.

Schoenbaum has been generally applauded by commentators, even though it may sometimes have been read to mean more than it does or than is needed to call for a reversal here. * * * It likewise is viewed with approval—indeed seemingly would be adopted—by §§ 1303 and 1402(c) of the proposed ALI Federal Securities Code. It has also found favor in other circuits. A notable instance is Shell v. Hensley, 430 F.2d 819, 827 (5 Cir.1970), where the court in a derivative suit rejected a claim that no "causal deceit" existed when the corporation's board knew all the facts, saying:

> When the other party to the securities transaction controls the judgment of all the corporation's board members or conspires with them or the one controlling them to profit mutually at the expense of the corporation, the corporation is no less disabled from availing itself of an informed judgment than if the outsider had simply lied to the board. In both situations, the determination of the corporation's choice of action in the transaction in question is not made as a reasonable man would make it if possessed of the material information known to the other party to the transaction. * * *

Schoenbaum, then, can rest solidly on the now widely recognized ground that there is deception of the corporation (in effect, of its minority shareholders) when the corporation is influenced by its controlling shareholder to engage in a transaction adverse to the corporation's interests (in effect, the minority shareholders' interests) and there is nondisclosure or misleading disclosures as to the material facts of the transaction. Assuming that, in light of the decision in *Green,* the existence of "controlling influence" and "wholly inadequate consideration"—an aspect of the *Schoenbaum* decision that perhaps attracted more attention—can no longer alone form the basis for Rule 10b–5 liability, we do not read *Green* as ruling that no action lies under Rule 10b–5 when a controlling corporation causes a partly owned subsidiary to sell its securities to the parent in an unfair transaction and fails to make a disclosure or, as can be alleged here, makes a misleading disclosure. * * *

Here the complaint alleged "deceit * * * upon UGO's minority shareholders" and, if amendment had been allowed as it should have been, would have alleged misrepresentation as to the UGO–Maritimecor transaction at least in the sense of failure to state material facts "necessary in order to make the statements made, in the light of the circumstances under which they were made, not misleading," Rule 10b–5(b). The nub of the matter is that the conduct attacked in *Green* did not violate the " 'fundamental purpose' of the Act as implementing a 'philosophy of full disclosure' "; the conduct here attacked does. * * *

Beyond this, Goldberg and other minority shareholders would not have been without remedy if the alleged facts had been disclosed. The doubts entertained by our brother as to the existence of injunctive remedies in New York are unfounded. * * *

The availability of injunctive relief if the defendants had not lulled the minority stockholders of UGO into security by a deceptive disclosure, as they allegedly did, is in sharp contrast to *Green,* where the disclosure following the merger transaction was full and fair, and, as to the pre-merger period, respondents accepted "the conclusion of both courts below that under Delaware law they could not have enjoined the merger because an appraisal proceeding is their sole remedy in the Delaware courts for any alleged unfairness in the terms of the merger." * * * We readily agree that if all that was here alleged was that UGO had been injured by "internal corporate mismanagement", no federal claim would have been stated. But a parent's looting of a subsidiary with securities outstanding in the hands of the public in a securities transaction is a different matter; in such cases disclosure or at least the absence of misleading disclosure is required. It would be incongruous if Rule 10b–5 created liability for a casual "tip" in the bar of a country club, as we held in SEC v. Geon Industries, Inc., 531 F.2d 39 (2 Cir.1976), but would not cover a parent's undisclosed or misleadingly disclosed sale of its overvalued assets for stock of a controlled subsidiary with securities in the hands of the public.

The order dismissing the complaint is reversed and the case is remanded to the district court for further proceedings, including amendment of the complaint, consistent with this opinion.

MESKILL, CIRCUIT JUDGE, concurring in part and dissenting in part: [omitted]

NOTES

1. In Schoenbaum v. Firstbrook, 405 F.2d 200, 215 (2d Cir.1968), the defendant was claimed to have used his controlling position as a shareholder to have additional shares issued to himself without adequate consideration. The board of directors was fully informed of the circumstances and the disinterested directors approved the transaction. The Second Circuit held that this could constitute a violation of Rule 10b–5 because it operated as a fraud or deceit on the other shareholders. The Second Circuit pulled back a bit from its *Schoenbaum* decision in Popkin v. Bishop, 464 F.2d 714 (2d Cir.1972). In *Popkin,* the plaintiff conceded that defendants had made full disclosure to shareholders but that the terms of the merger at issue were so unfair as to constitute fraud. The Second Circuit held that overreaching alone would not constitute fraud, absent misstatements or the concealment of material facts.

2. Under the *Goldberg* approach, is it enough for the plaintiff to allege that he would have *sought* an injunction under state law if the true facts had been revealed, or must he show that he could have *obtained* one? The Circuits have split on this issue. In Alabama Farm Bureau Mut. Cas. Co., Inc. v. American Fidelity, 606 F.2d 602 (5th Cir.1979), the court held that "all that is required to establish 10b–5 liability is a showing that state law remedies are available, and that the facts shown make out a prima facie case for relief; it is not necessary to go further and prove that the state action would have been successful." In Healey v. Catalyst Recovery, 616 F.2d 641, 647 (3d Cir.1980), the court held that "the plaintiff must demonstrate that at the time of the

misrepresentation or omission, there was a reasonable probability of ultimate success in securing an injunction had there been no misrepresentation or omission." In Wright v. Heizer, Corp.. 560 F.2d 236 (7th Cir.1977), and Kidwell v. Meikle, 597 F.2d 1273 (9th Cir.1979), the courts held that the plaintiff must show both the availability of a claim under state law, and that the state court would have granted the requested relief. The approaches followed in the latter cases of course involve precisely the type of inquiry that the Supreme Court in *Santa Fe* sought to avoid—the threshold question of whether a claim under Rule 10b–5 should be recognized depends on an evaluation of the merits of a hypothetical claim under state law. To address this concern, the Second Circuit in the later case of Field v. Trump, 850 F.2d 938 (2d Cir.1988), limited its holding in *Goldberg* to cases involving "willful misconduct of a self-serving nature" and not simple mismanagement or breaches of fiduciary duty.

3.   Any person who violates the antifraud provisions of the 1934 Act is subject to criminal prosecution under § 32 of the Act. In addition, if the violator is a broker-dealer, its registration may be revoked or suspended in an administrative proceeding before the SEC under § 15(b)(4) of the 1934 Act. The SEC is empowered by § 21(d) to seek injunctive relief in federal court. The current judicial attitude with respect to the SEC's right to an injunction in disciplinary proceedings was summed up by Judge Friendly in SEC v. Commonwealth Chemical, Securities, Inc., 574 F.2d 90 (2d Cir.1978):

> It is fair to say that the current judicial attitude toward the issuance of injunctions on the basis of past violations at the SEC's request has become more circumspect than in earlier days. Experience has shown that an injunction, while not always a "drastic remedy" as appellants contend, often is much more than the "mild prophylactic" described by the court in SEC v. Capital Gains Research Bureau, 375 U.S. 180, 193, 84 S.Ct. 275, 11 L.Ed.2d 237 (1963). In some cases the collateral consequences of an injunction can be very grave. The Securities Act and the Securities Exchange Act speak, after all, of enjoining "any person [who] is engaged or about to engage in any acts or practices" which constitute or will constitute a violation. Except for the case where the SEC steps in to prevent an ongoing violation, this language seems to require a finding of "likelihood" or "propensity" to engage in future violations. As said by Professor Loss, "[t]he ultimate test is whether the defendant's past conduct indicates * * * that there is a reasonable likelihood of further violation in the future." Our recent decisions have emphasized, perhaps more than older ones, the need for the SEC to go beyond the mere facts of past violations and demonstrate a realistic likelihood of recurrence. See SEC v. Universal Major Industries, 546 F.2d 1044, 1048 (2 Cir.1976), SEC v. Parklane Hosiery, 558 F.2d 1083 (2 Cir.1977), and SEC v. Bausch & Lomb, Inc., 565 F.2d 8, 18 (2 Cir.1977) where the court went so far as to say "[T]he Commission cannot obtain relief without positive proof of a reasonable likelihood that past wrongdoing will recur."

Judge Friendly indicated in the *Commonwealth* opinion that "the collateral consequences of an injunction can be very grave." The Supreme Court added to the gravity of the consequences in Parklane Hosiery Co., Inc. v. Shore, 439 U.S. 322, 99 S.Ct. 645, 58 L.Ed.2d 552 (1979). It held that, when a defendant in an SEC injunction action was found to have issued a false and misleading statement, he was estopped from denying that the statement was false and misleading in a subsequent private action for damages. The Court held that the doctrine of collateral estoppel foreclosed the defendant from relitigating the issue, and that this foreclosure did not violate defendant's Seventh Amendment right to a jury trial.

4. In October 1990, Congress added substantially to the SEC's enforcement powers by enacting the Securities Enforcement Remedies and Penny Stock Reform Act. Among the important changes made by that Act are provisions (a) authorizing the SEC to issue cease-and-desist orders, and to impose fines or order disgorgement of profits in administrative proceedings, (b) increasing the fines for deliberate or reckless violations of the securities laws, (c) permitting the courts to bar violators from serving as officers or directors of publicly-held corporations, and (d) requiring additional disclosures by dealers in "penny stocks." See Securities and Exchange Act of 1934 §§ 21C, 21B, 32, 21(d)(2), 15(g).

SECTION 7. THE CAUSATION REQUIREMENT

MILLS v. ELECTRIC AUTO–LITE COMPANY

396 U.S. 375, 90 S.Ct. 616, 24 L.Ed.2d 593 (1970).

MR. JUSTICE HARLAN delivered the opinion of the Court.

This case requires us to consider a basic aspect of the implied private right of action for violation of § 14(a) of the Securities Exchange Act of 1934, recognized by this Court in J. I. Case Co. v. Borak, 377 U.S. 426 (1964). As in Borak the asserted wrong is that a corporate merger was accomplished through the use of a proxy statement that was materially false or misleading. The question with which we deal is what causal relationship must be shown between such a statement and the merger to establish a cause of action based on the violation of the Act.

Petitioners were shareholders of the Electric Auto–Lite Company until 1963, when it was merged into Mergenthaler Linotype Company. They brought suit on the day before the shareholders' meeting at which the vote was to take place on the merger against Auto–Lite, Mergenthaler, and a third company, American Manufacturing Company, Inc. The complaint sought an injunction against the voting by Auto–Lite's management of all proxies obtained by means of an allegedly misleading proxy solicitation; however, it did not seek a temporary restraining order, and the voting went ahead as scheduled the following day. Several months later petitioners filed an amended complaint, seeking to have the merger set aside and to obtain such other relief as might be proper.

* * * [Petitioners] alleged that the proxy statement sent out by the Auto–Lite management to solicit shareholders' votes in favor of the merger was misleading, in violation of § 14(a) of the Act and SEC Rule

14a—9 thereunder. Petitioners recited that before the merger Mergenthaler owned over 50% of the outstanding shares of Auto–Lite common stock, and had been in control of Auto–Lite for two years. American Manufacturing in turn owned about one-third of the outstanding shares of Mergenthaler, and for two years had been in voting control of Mergenthaler and, through it, of Auto–Lite. Petitioners charged that in light of these circumstances the proxy statement was misleading in that it told Auto–Lite shareholders that their board of directors recommended approval of the merger without also informing them that all 11 of Auto–Lite's directors were nominees of Mergenthaler and were under the 'control and domination of Mergenthaler.' Petitioners asserted the right to complain of this alleged violation both derivatively on behalf of Auto–Lite and as representatives of the class of all its minority shareholders.

* * * [T]he District Court for the Northern District of Illinois ruled as a matter of law that the claimed defect in the proxy statement was, in light of the circumstances in which the statement was made, a material omission. The District Court concluded, from its reading of the Borak opinion, that it had to hold a hearing on the issue whether there was 'a causal connection between the finding that there has been a violation of the disclosure requirements of § 14(a) and the alleged injury to the plaintiffs' before it could consider what remedies would be appropriate.

After holding such a hearing, the court found that under the terms of the merger agreement, an affirmative vote of two-thirds of the Auto–Lite shares was required for approval of the merger, and that the respondent companies owned and controlled about 54% of the outstanding shares. Therefore, to obtain authorization of the merger, respondents had to secure the approval of a substantial number of the minority shareholders. At the stockholders' meeting, approximately 950,000 shares, out of 1,160,-000 shares outstanding, were voted in favor of the merger. This included 317,000 votes obtained by proxy from the minority shareholders, votes that were 'necessary and indispensable to the approval of the merger.' The District Court concluded that a causal relationship had thus been shown, and it granted an interlocutory judgment in favor of petitioners on the issue of liability, referring the case to a master for consideration of appropriate relief.

* * * [T]he Court of Appeals for the Seventh Circuit affirmed the District Court's conclusion that the proxy statement was materially deficient, but reversed on the question of causation. The court acknowledged that, if an injunction had been sought a sufficient time before the stockholders' meeting, 'corrective measures would have been appropriate.' However, since this suit was brought too late for preventive action, the courts had to determine 'whether the misleading statement and omission caused the submission of sufficient proxies,' as a prerequisite to a determination of liability under the Act. If the respondents could show, 'by a preponderance of probabilities, that the merger would have received a sufficient vote even if the proxy statement had not been misleading in the respect found,' petitioners would be entitled to no relief of any kind.

The Court of Appeals acknowledged that this test corresponds to the common-law fraud test of whether the injured party relied on the misrepresentation. However, rightly concluding that '(r)eliance by thousands of individuals, as here, can scarcely be inquired into' the court ruled that the issue was to be determined by proof of the fairness of the terms of the merger. If respondents could show that the merger had merit and was fair to the minority shareholders, the trial court would be justified in concluding that a sufficient number of shareholders would have approved the merger had there been no deficiency in the proxy statement. In that case respondents would be entitled to a judgment in their favor.

Claiming that the Court of Appeals has construed this Court's decision in Borak in a manner that frustrates the statute's policy of enforcement through private litigation, the petitioners then sought review in this Court. We granted certiorari, believing that resolution of this basic issue should be made at this stage of the litigation and not postponed until after a trial under the Court of Appeals' decision.

As we stressed in [J.I. Case v.] Borak, § 14(a) stemmed from a congressional belief that '(f)air corporate suffrage is an important right that should attach to every equity security bought on a public exchange.' H.R.Rep.No.1383, 73d Cong., 2d Sess., 13. The provision was intended to promote 'the free exercise of the voting rights of stockholders' by ensuring that proxies would be solicited with 'explanation to the stockholder of the real nature of the questions for which authority to cast his vote is sought.' The decision below, by permitting all liability to be foreclosed on the basis of a finding that the merger was fair, would allow the stockholders to be by-passed, at least where the only legal challenge to the merger is a suit for retrospective relief after the meeting has been held. A judicial appraisal of the merger's merits could be substituted for the actual and informed vote of the stockholders.

The result would be to insulate from private redress an entire category of proxy violations—those relating to matters other than the terms of the merger. Even outrageous misrepresentations in a proxy solicitation, if they did not relate to the terms of the transaction, would give rise to no cause of action under § 14(a). Particularly if carried over to enforcement actions by the Securities and Exchange Commission itself, such a result would subvert the congressional purpose of ensuring full and fair disclosure to shareholders.

Further, recognition of the fairness of the merger as a complete defense would confront small shareholders with an additional obstacle to making a successful challenge to a proposal recommended through a defective proxy statement. The risk that they would be unable to rebut the corporation's evidence of the fairness of the proposal, and thus to establish their cause of action, would be bound to discourage such shareholders from the private enforcement of the proxy rules that 'provides a necessary supplement to Commission action.' J. I. Case Co. v. Borak, 377 U.S., at 432.[5]

Such a frustration of the congressional policy is not required by anything in the wording of the statute or in our opinion in the Borak case. Section 14(a) declares it 'unlawful' to solicit proxies in contravention of Commission rules, and SEC Rule 14a—9 prohibits solicitations 'containing any statement which * * * is false or misleading with respect to any material fact, or which omits to state any material fact necessary in order to make the statements therein not false or misleading * * *.' Use of a solicitation that is materially misleading is itself a violation of law, as the Court of Appeals recognized in stating that injunctive relief would be available to remedy such a defect if sought prior to the stockholders' meeting. In Borak, which came to this Court on a dismissal of the complaint, the Court limited its inquiry to whether a violation of § 14(a) gives rise to 'a federal cause of action for rescission or damages.' Referring to the argument made by petitioners there 'that the merger can be dissolved only if it was fraudulent or non-beneficial, issues upon which the proxy material would not bear,' the Court stated: 'But the causal relationship of the proxy material and the merger are questions of fact to be resolved at trial, not here. We therefore do not discuss this point further.' In the present case there has been a hearing specifically directed to the causation problem. The question before the Court is whether the facts found on the basis of that hearing are sufficient in law to establish petitioners' cause of action, and we conclude that they are.

Where the misstatement or omission in a proxy statement has been shown to be 'material,' as it was found to be here, that determination itself indubitably embodies a conclusion that the defect was of such a character that it might have been considered important by a reasonable shareholder who was in the process of deciding how to vote. This requirement that the defect have a significant *propensity* to affect the voting process is found in the express terms of Rule 14a—9, and it adequately serves the purpose of ensuring that a cause of action cannot be established by proof of a defect so trivial, or so unrelated to the transaction for which approval is sought, that correction of the defect or imposition of liability would not further the interests protected by § 14(a).

---

5. The Court of Appeals' ruling that 'causation' may be negated by proof of the fairness of the merger also rests on a dubious behavioral assumption. There is no justification for presuming that the shareholders of every corporation are willing to accept any and every fair merger offer put before them; yet such a presumption is implicit in the opinion of the Court of Appeals. That court gave no indication of what evidence petitioners might adduce, once respondents had established that the merger proposal was equitable, in order to show that the shareholders would nevertheless have rejected it if the solicitation had not been misleading. Proof of actual reliance by thousands of individuals would, as the court acknowledged, not be feasible, see R. Jennings & H. Marsh, Securities Regulation, Cases and Materials 1001 (2d ed. 1968); and reliance on the nondisclosure of a fact is a particularly difficult matter to define or prove, see 3 L. Loss, Securities Regulation 1766 (2d ed. 1961). In practice, therefore, the objective fairness of the proposal would seemingly be determinative of liability. But, in view of the many other factors that might lead shareholders to prefer their current position to that of owners of a larger, combined enterprise, it is pure conjecture to assume that the fairness of the proposal will always be determinative of their vote.

There is no need to supplement this requirement, as did the Court of Appeals, with a requirement of proof of whether the defect actually had a decisive effect on the voting. Where there has been a finding of materiality, a shareholder has made a sufficient showing of causal relationship between the violation and the injury for which he seeks redress if, as here, he proves that the proxy solicitation itself, rather than the particular defect in the solicitation materials, was an essential link in the accomplishment of the transaction. This objective test will avoid the impracticalities of determining how many votes were affected, and, by resolving doubts in favor of those the statute is designed to protect, will effectuate the congressional policy of ensuring that the shareholders are able to make an informed choice when they are consulted on corporate transactions.[7]

VIRGINIA BANKSHARES, INC. v. SANDBERG

501 U.S. 1083, 111 S.Ct. 2749, 115 L.Ed.2d 929 (1991).

JUSTICE SOUTER delivered the opinion of the Court.

[A minority shareholder brought action challenging a "freeze out" merger]

* * * The second issue before us, left open in *Mills v. Electric Auto–Lite Co.,* 396 U.S., at 385, n. 7, is whether causation of damages compensable through the implied private right of action under § 14(a) can be demonstrated by a member of a class of minority shareholders whose votes are not required by law or corporate bylaw to authorize the transaction giving rise to the claim. *J.I. Case Co. v. Borak,* 377 U.S. 426 (1964), did not itself address the requisites of causation, as such, or define the class of plaintiffs eligible to sue under § 14(a). But its general holding, that a private cause of action was available to some shareholder class, acquired greater clarity with a more definite concept of causation in *Mills,* where we addressed the sufficiency of proof that misstatements in a proxy solicitation were responsible for damages claimed from the merger subject to complaint.

Although a majority stockholder in *Mills* controlled just over half the corporation's shares, a two-thirds vote was needed to approve the merger proposal. After proxies had been obtained, and the merger had carried, minority shareholders brought a *Borak* action. *Mills,* 396 U.S., at 379. The question arose whether the plaintiffs' burden to demonstrate causation of their damages traceable to the § 14(a) violation required proof that the defect in the proxy solicitation had had "a decisive effect on the voting."

---

7. We need not decide in this case whether causation could be shown where the management controls a sufficient number of shares to approve the transaction without any votes from the minority. Even in that situation, if the management finds it necessary for legal or practical reasons to solicit proxies from minority shareholders, at least one court has held that the proxy solicitation might be sufficiently related to the merger to satisfy the causation requirement.

Id., at 385. The *Mills* Court avoided the evidentiary morass that would have followed from requiring individualized proof that enough minority shareholders had relied upon the misstatements to swing the vote. Instead, it held that causation of damages by a material proxy misstatement could be established by showing that minority proxies necessary and sufficient to authorize the corporate acts had been given in accordance with the tenor of the solicitation, and the Court described such a causal relationship by calling the proxy solicitation an "essential link in the accomplishment of the transaction." *Ibid.* In the case before it, the Court found the solicitation essential, as contrasted with one addressed to a class of minority shareholders without votes required by law or by law to authorize the action proposed, and left it for another day to decide whether such a minority shareholder could demonstrate causation. *Id.,* 396 U.S., at 385, n. 7.

In this case, respondents address *Mills'* open question by proffering two theories that the proxy solicitation addressed to them was an "essential link" under the *Mills* causation test.[9] They argue, first, that a link existed and was essential simply because VBI and FABI would have been unwilling to proceed with the merger without the approval manifested by the minority shareholders' proxies, which would not have been obtained without the solicitation's express misstatements and misleading omissions. On this reasoning, the causal connection would depend on a desire to avoid bad shareholder or public relations, and the essential character of the causal link would stem not from the enforceable terms of the parties' corporate relationship, but from one party's apprehension of the ill will of the other.

In the alternative, respondents argue that the proxy statement was an essential link between the directors' proposal and the merger because it was the means to satisfy a state statutory requirement of minority shareholder approval, as a condition for saving the merger from voidability resulting from a conflict of interest on the part of one of the Bank's directors, Jack Beddow, who voted in favor of the merger while also serving as a director of FABI. Under the terms of Va.Code Ann. § 13.1–691(A) (1989), minority approval after disclosure of the material facts about the transaction and the director's interest was one of three avenues to insulate the merger from later attack for conflict, the two others being ratification by the Bank's directors after like disclosure and proof that the merger was fair to the corporation. On this theory, causation would

---

9. Citing the decision in *Schlick v. Penn–Dixie Cement Corp.,* 507 F.2d 374, 382–383 (C.A.2 1974), petitioners characterize respondents' proffered theories as examples of so-called "sue facts" and "shame facts" theories. "A 'sue fact' is, in general, a fact which is material to a sue decision. A 'sue decision' is a decision by a shareholder whether or not to institute a representative or derivative suit alleging a state-law cause of action." Gelb, Rule 10b–5 and *Santa Fe—Herein of Sue Facts, Shame Facts, and Other Matters,* 87 W.Va.L.Rev. 189, 198, and n. 52 (1985), quoting Borden, "Sue Fact" Rule Mandates Disclosure to Avoid Litigation in State Courts, 10 SEC '82, pp. 201, 204–205 (1982). See also Note, Causation and Liability in Private Actions for Proxy Violations, 80 Yale L.J. 107, 116 (1970) (discussing theories of causation). "Shame facts" are said to be facts which, had they been disclosed, would have "shamed" management into abandoning a proposed transaction. See *Schlick, supra,* at 384. See also Gelb, *supra,* at 197.

depend on the use of the proxy statement for the purpose of obtaining votes sufficient to bar a minority shareholder from commencing proceedings to declare the merger void.[10]

Although respondents have proffered each of these theories as establishing a chain of causal connection in which the proxy statement is claimed to have been an "essential link," neither theory presents the proxy solicitation as essential in the sense of *Mills'* causal sequence, in which the solicitation links a directors' proposal with the votes legally required to authorize the action proposed. As a consequence, each theory would, if adopted, extend the scope of *Borak* actions beyond the ambit of *Mills* and expand the class of plaintiffs entitled to bring *Borak* actions to include shareholders whose initial authorization of the transaction prompting the proxy solicitation is unnecessary.

Assessing the legitimacy of any such extension or expansion calls for the application of some fundamental principles governing recognition of a right of action implied by a federal statute, the first of which was not, in fact, the considered focus of the *Borak* opinion. The rule that has emerged in the years since *Borak* and *Mills* came down is that recognition of any private right of action for violating a federal statute must ultimately rest on congressional intent to provide a private remedy, *Touche Ross & Co. v. Redington,* 442 U.S. 560, 575 (1979). From this the corollary follows that the breadth of the right once recognized should not, as a general matter, grow beyond the scope congressionally intended. * * *

The congressional silence that is thus a serious obstacle to the expansion of cognizable *Borak* causation is not, however, a necessarily insurmountable barrier. This is not the first effort in recent years to expand the scope of an action originally inferred from the Act without "conclusive guidance" from Congress and we may look to that earlier case for the proper response to such a plea for expansion. There, we accepted the proposition that where a legal structure of private statutory rights has developed without clear indications of congressional intent, the contours of that structure need not be frozen absolutely when the result would be demonstrably inequitable to a class of would-be plaintiffs with claims comparable to those previously recognized. Faced in that case with such a claim for equality in rounding out the scope of an implied private statutory right of action, we looked to policy reasons for deciding where the outer limits of the right should lie. We may do no less here, in the face of

---

10. The District Court and Court of Appeals have grounded causation on a further theory, that Virginia law required a solicitation of proxies even from minority shareholders as a condition of consummating the merger. While the provisions of Va.Code Ann. § § 13.1–718(A), (D), and (E) (1989) are said to have required the Bank to solicit minority proxies, they actually compelled no more than submission of the merger to a vote at a shareholders' meeting, § 13.1–718(E) preceded by issuance of an informational statement, § 13.1–718(D). There was thus no need under this statute to solicit proxies, although it is undisputed that the proxy solicitation sufficed to satisfy the statutory obligation to provide a statement of relevant information. On this theory causation would depend on the use of the proxy statement to satisfy a statutory obligation, even though a proxy solicitation was not, as such, required. In this Court, respondents have disclaimed reliance on any such theory.

respondents' pleas for a private remedy to place them on the same footing as shareholders with votes necessary for initial corporate action.

Blue Chip Stamps set an example worth recalling as a preface to specific policy analysis of the consequences of recognizing respondents' first theory, that a desire to avoid minority shareholders' ill will should suffice to justify recognizing the requisite causality of a proxy statement needed to garner that minority support. It will be recalled that in *Blue Chip Stamps* we raised concerns about the practical consequences of allowing recovery, under § 10(b) of the Act and Rule 10b–5, on evidence of what a merely hypothetical buyer or seller might have done on a set of facts that never occurred, and foresaw that any such expanded liability would turn on "hazy" issues inviting self-serving testimony, strike suits, and protracted discovery, with little chance of reasonable resolution by pretrial process. These were good reasons to deny recognition to such claims in the absence of any apparent contrary congressional intent.

The same threats of speculative claims and procedural intractability are inherent in respondents' theory of causation linked through the directors' desire for a cosmetic vote. Causation would turn on inferences about what the corporate directors would have thought and done without the minority shareholder approval unneeded to authorize action. A subsequently dissatisfied minority shareholder would have virtual license to allege that managerial timidity would have doomed corporate action but for the ostensible approval induced by a misleading statement, and opposing claims of hypothetical diffidence and hypothetical boldness on the part of directors would probably provide enough depositions in the usual case to preclude any judicial resolution short of the credibility judgments that can only come after trial. Reliable evidence would seldom exist. Directors would understand the prudence of making a few statements about plans to proceed even without minority endorsement, and discovery would be a quest for recollections of oral conversations at odds with the official pronouncements, in hopes of finding support for *ex post facto* guesses about how much heat the directors would have stood in the absence of minority approval. The issues would be hazy, their litigation protracted, and their resolution unreliable. Given a choice, we would reject any theory of causation that raised such prospects, and we reject this one.[12]

The theory of causal necessity derived from the requirements of Virginia law dealing with postmerger ratification seeks to identify the essential character of the proxy solicitation from its function in obtaining

---

12. In parting company from us on this point, JUSTICE KENNEDY emphasizes that respondents in this particular case substantiated a plausible claim that petitioners would not have proceeded without minority approval. FABI's attempted freeze-out merger of a Maryland subsidiary had failed a year before the events in question when the subsidiary's directors rejected the proposal because of inadequate share price, and there was evidence of FABI's desire to avoid any renewal of adverse comment. The issue before us, however, is whether to recognize a theory of causation generally, and our decision against doing so rests on our apprehension that the ensuing litigation would be exemplified by cases far less tractable than this. Respondents' burden to justify recognition of causation beyond the scope of *Mills* must be addressed not by emphasizing the instant case but by confronting the risk inherent in the cases that could be expected to be characteristic if the causal theory were adopted.

the minority approval that would preclude a minority suit attacking the merger. Since the link is said to be a step in the process of barring a class of shareholders from resort to a state remedy otherwise available, this theory of causation rests upon the proposition of policy that § 14(a) should provide a federal remedy whenever a false or misleading proxy statement results in the loss under state law of a shareholder plaintiff's state remedy for the enforcement of a state right. Respondents agree with the suggestions of counsel for the SEC and FDIC that causation be recognized, for example, when a minority shareholder has been induced by a misleading proxy statement to forfeit a state-law right to an appraisal remedy by voting to approve a transaction or when such a shareholder has been deterred from obtaining an order enjoining a damaging transaction by a proxy solicitation that misrepresents the facts on which an injunction could properly have been issued. Respondents claim that in this case a predicate for recognizing just such a causal link exists in Va.Code Ann. § 13.1–691(A)(2) (1989), which sets the conditions under which the merger may be insulated from suit by a minority shareholder seeking to void it on account of Beddow's conflict.

This case does not, however, require us to decide whether § 14(a) provides a cause of action for lost state remedies, since there is no indication in the law or facts before us that the proxy solicitation resulted in any such loss. The contrary appears to be the case. Assuming the soundness of respondents' characterization of the proxy statement as materially misleading, the very terms of the Virginia statute indicate that a favorable minority vote induced by the solicitation would not suffice to render the merger invulnerable to later attack on the ground of the conflict. The statute bars a shareholder from seeking to avoid a transaction tainted by a director's conflict if, *inter alia,* the minority shareholders ratified the transaction following disclosure of the material facts of the transaction and the conflict. Assuming that the material facts about the merger and Beddow's interests were not accurately disclosed, the minority votes were inadequate to ratify the merger under state law, and there was no loss of state remedy to connect the proxy solicitation with harm to minority shareholders irredressable under state law. Nor is there a claim here that the statement misled respondents into entertaining a false belief that they had no chance to upset the merger, until the time for bringing suit had run out.

The judgment of the Court of Appeals is reversed.

———

Transaction causation and loss causation. The *Virginia Bankshares* decision addresses what is generally referred to as transaction causation. Courts considering Rule 10b–5 claims have generally held that the plaintiff must show both "transaction causation," i.e., that the fraud caused the plaintiff to enter into the transaction, and "loss causation," i.e., that the transaction caused the loss to the plaintiff. See e.g., Schlick v.

Penn–Dixie, Corp., 507 F.2d 374 (2d Cir.1974); Suez Equity Investors, L.P. v. Toronto–Dominion Bank, 250 F.3d 87 (2d Cir.2001); Grace v. Rosenstock, 228 F.3d 40 (2d Cir.2000). The plaintiff must prove "transaction causation" which means that, but for the wrongful conduct, the transaction would not have gone through, at least in the form that it eventually took. The concept of transaction causation has been characterized as "nothing more than 'but for' causation" and more questionably as "merely another way of describing reliance." Harris v. Union Electric Co., 787 F.2d 355, 366 (8th Cir.), cert. denied 479 U.S. 823, 107 S.Ct. 94, 93 L.Ed.2d 45 (1986). The plaintiff must also be able to prove "loss causation": namely that the plaintiff's injury (generally the diminution in the value of his or her investment) is directly attributable both to the wrongful conduct and the form and manner in which the challenged transaction occurred. Loss causation provides the necessary connection between the challenged conduct and the plaintiff's pecuniary loss. "Indeed what securities lawyers call 'loss causation' *is* the standard common law fraud rule, merely borrowed for use in federal securities fraud cases. It is more fundamental still; it is an instance of the common law's universal requirement that the tort plaintiff prove causation. No hurt, no tort." Bastian v. Petren Resources Corp., 892 F.2d 680, 683–684 (7th Cir.1990) (citations omitted).

NOTES

1. The concept of loss causation was expressly codified in the Securities Litigation Reform Act of 1995. Section 21D(b)(4) of the Securities Exchange Act of 1934 adopted the approach taken by Judge Posner in the *Bastian* case by providing that, in any private action under the Securities Exchange Act of 1934, "the plaintiff shall have the burden of proving that the act or omission of the defendant alleged to violate the Act caused the loss for which the plaintiff seeks to recover damages."

2. In Herman & MacLean v. Huddleston, 459 U.S. 375, 103 S.Ct. 683, 74 L.Ed.2d 548 (1983), the Supreme Court dealt with the question of the plaintiff's burden of proof in a case brought under Rule 10b–5:

> In a typical civil suit for money damages, plaintiffs must prove their case by a preponderance of the evidence. * * * The Court of Appeals nonetheless held that plaintiffs in a Section 10(b) suit must establish their case by clear and convincing evidence. The Court of Appeals relied primarily on the traditional use of a higher burden of proof in civil fraud actions at common law. Reference to common law practices can be misleading, however, since the historical considerations underlying the imposition of a higher standard of proof have questionable pertinence here. * * *
>
> A preponderance-of-the-evidence standard allows both parties to "share the risk of error in roughly equal fashion." Any other standard expresses a preference for one side's interests. The balance of interests in this case warrants use of the preponderance standard. On the one hand, the defendants face the risk of opprobrium that may result from a finding

of fraudulent conduct, but this risk is identical to that in an action under Section 17(a), which is governed by the preponderance-of-the-evidence standard. The interests of defendants in a securities case do not differ qualitatively from the interests of defendants sued for violations of other federal statutes such as the antitrust or civil rights laws, for which proof by a preponderance of the evidence suffices. On the other hand, the interests of plaintiffs in such suits are significant. Defrauded investors are among the very individuals Congress sought to protect in the securities laws. If they prove that it is more likely than not that they were defrauded, they should recover.

––––––––

A number of courts had held that loss causation could be shown by alleging and subsequently proving that the price of the security on the date of the purchase was inflated because of the misrepresentation. In the following case, the Supreme Court explained its view of loss causation and that there must be more direct proof that the misrepresentations in question affected the price and thereby caused a loss to the plaintiff.

DURA PHARMACEUTICALS, INC. v. BROUDO

544 U.S. 336, 125 S.Ct. 1627, 161 L.Ed.2d 577 (2005).

BREYER, J., delivered the opinion for a unanimous Court.

A private plaintiff who claims securities fraud must prove that the defendant's fraud caused an economic loss. We consider a Ninth Circuit holding that a plaintiff can satisfy this requirement—a requirement that courts call "loss causation"—simply by alleging in the complaint and subsequently establishing that "the price" of the security "*on the date of purchase* was inflated because of the misrepresentation." In our view, the Ninth Circuit is wrong, both in respect to what a plaintiff must prove and in respect to what the plaintiffs' complaint here must allege.

[T]he complaint says the following (and nothing significantly more than the following) about economic losses attributable to the spray device misstatement: "*In reliance on the integrity of the market, [the plaintiffs] . . . paid artificially inflated prices for Dura securities*" and the plaintiffs suffered "*damage[s]*" thereby. *Id.,* at 139a (emphasis added).

The District Court dismissed the complaint. In respect to the plaintiffs' drug-profitability claim, it held that the complaint failed adequately to allege an appropriate state of mind, *i.e.,* that defendants had acted knowingly, or the like. In respect to the plaintiffs' spray device claim, it held that the complaint failed adequately to allege "loss causation."

The Court of Appeals for the Ninth Circuit reversed. In the portion of the court's decision now before us—the portion that concerns the spray device claim—the Circuit held that the complaint adequately alleged "loss causation." The Circuit wrote that "plaintiffs establish loss causation if they have shown that the price *on the date of purchase* was inflated because of the misrepresentation." It added that "the injury occurs at the time of the transaction." *Ibid.* Since the complaint pleaded "that the price at the time of purchase was overstated," and it sufficiently identified the cause, its allegations were legally sufficient.

Private federal securities fraud actions are based upon federal securities statutes and their implementing regulation.... The courts have implied from these statutes and Rule a private damages action, which resembles, but is not identical to, common-law tort actions for deceit and misrepresentation.

In cases involving publicly traded securities and purchases or sales in public securities markets, the action's basic elements include:

(1) *a material misrepresentation (or omission),* see *Basic Inc. v. Levinson,* 485 U.S. 224, 231–232, 108 S.Ct. 978, 99 L.Ed.2d 194 (1988);

(2) *scienter, i.e.,* a wrongful state of mind, see *Ernst & Ernst, supra;*

(3) *a connection with the purchase or sale of a security,* see *Blue Chip Stamps, supra;*

(4) *reliance,* often referred to in cases involving public securities markets (fraud-on-the-market cases) as "transaction causation," see *Basic, supra,* at 248–249 (nonconclusively presuming that the price of a publicly traded share reflects a material misrepresentation and that plaintiffs have relied upon that misrepresentation as long as they would not have bought the share in its absence);

(5) *economic loss,* 15 U.S.C. § 78u–4(b)(4); and

(6) *"loss causation," i.e.,* a causal connection between the material misrepresentation and the loss, *ibid.;* cf. T. Hazen, Law of Securities Regulation, § § 12.11[1], [3] (5th ed.2002).

Dura argues that the complaint's allegations are inadequate in respect to these last two elements.

We begin with the Ninth Circuit's basic reason for finding the complaint adequate, namely, that at the end of the day plaintiffs need only "establish," *i.e.,* prove, that "the price *on the date of purchase* was inflated because of the misrepresentation." In our view, this statement of the law is wrong. Normally, in cases such as this one (*i.e.,* fraud-on-the-market cases), an inflated purchase price will not itself constitute or proximately cause the relevant economic loss.

For one thing, as a matter of pure logic, at the moment the transaction takes place, the plaintiff has suffered no loss; the inflated purchase payment is offset by ownership of a share that *at that instant* possesses equivalent value. Moreover, the logical link between the inflated share purchase price and any later economic loss is not invariably strong. Shares are normally purchased with an eye toward a later sale. But if, say, the purchaser sells the shares quickly before the relevant truth begins to leak out, the misrepresentation will not have led to any loss. If the purchaser sells later after the truth makes its way into the market place, an initially inflated purchase price *might* mean a later loss. But that is far from inevitably so. When the purchaser subsequently resells such shares, even at a lower price, that lower price may reflect, not the earlier misrepresentation, but changed economic circumstances, changed investor expectations, new industry-specific or firm-specific facts, conditions, or other events, which taken separately or together account for some or all of that lower price. (The same is true in respect to a claim that a share's higher price is lower than it would otherwise have been—a claim we do not consider here.) Other things being equal, the longer the time between purchase and sale, the more likely that this is so, *i.e.,* the more likely that other factors caused the loss.

Given the tangle of factors affecting price, the most logic alone permits us to say is that the higher purchase price will *sometimes* play a role in bringing about a future loss. It may prove to be a necessary condition of any such loss, and in that sense one might say that the inflated purchase price suggests that the misrepresentation (using language the Ninth Circuit used) "touches upon" a later economic loss. But, even if that is so, it is insufficient. To "touch upon" a loss is not to *cause* a loss, and it is the latter that the law requires. 15 U.S.C. § 78u–4(b)(4).

For another thing, the Ninth Circuit's holding lacks support in precedent. Judicially implied private securities-fraud actions resemble in many (but not all) respects common-law deceit and misrepresentation actions. See *Blue Chip Stamps, supra,* at 744; see also L. Loss & J. Seligman, Fundamentals of Securities Regulation, 910–918 (5th ed.2004) (describing relationship to common-law deceit). The common law of deceit subjects a person who "fraudulently" makes a "misrepresentation" to liability "for pecuniary loss caused" to one who justifiably relies upon that misrepresentation. Restatement (Second) of Torts § 525, p. 55 (1977) (hereinafter Restatement of Torts); see also *Southern Development Co. v. Silva,* 125 U.S. 247, 250, 8 S.Ct. 881, 31 L.Ed. 678 (1888) (setting forth elements of fraudulent misrepresentation). And the common law has long insisted that a plaintiff in such a case show not only that had he known the truth he would not have acted but also that he suffered actual economic loss. See, *e.g., Pasley v. Freeman,* 3 T.R. 5:1, 100 Eng. Rep. 450, 457 (1789) (if "no injury is occasioned by the lie, it is not actionable: but if it be attended with a damage, it then becomes the subject of an action"); *Freeman v. Venner,* 120 Mass. 424, 426 (1876) (a mortgagee cannot bring a tort action for damages stemming from a fraudulent note that a misrepresentation led him to execute unless and until the note has to be paid); see also M. Bigelow, Law of Torts 101 (8th ed.1907) (damage "must already have been suffered before the bringing of the suit"); 2 T. Cooley, Law of Torts § 348, p. 551 (4th ed.1932) (plaintiff must show that he "suffered damage" and that the "damage followed proximately the deception"); W. Keeton, D. Dobbs, R. Keeton, & D. Owen, Prosser and Keeton on Law of Torts § 110, p. 765 (5th ed.1984) (hereinafter Prosser and Keeton) (plaintiff "must have suffered substantial damage," not simply nominal damages, before "the cause of action can arise").

Given the common-law roots of the securities fraud action (and the common-law requirement that a plaintiff show actual damages), it is not surprising that other courts of appeals have rejected the Ninth Circuit's "inflated purchase price" approach to proving causation and loss. Indeed, the Restatement of Torts, in setting forth the judicial consensus, says that a person who "misrepresents the financial condition of a corporation in order to sell its stock" becomes liable to a relying purchaser "for the loss" the purchaser sustains "when the facts . . . become generally known" and "as a result" share value "depreciate[s]." § 548A, Comment *b,* at 107. Treatise writers, too, have emphasized the need to prove proximate causation. Prosser and Keeton § 110, at 767 (losses do "not afford any basis for recovery" if "brought about by business conditions or other factors").

We cannot reconcile the Ninth Circuit's "inflated purchase price" approach with these views of other courts. And the uniqueness of its perspective argues against the validity of its approach in a case like this one where we consider the contours of a judicially implied cause of action with roots in the common law.

Finally, the Ninth Circuit's approach overlooks an important securities law objective. The securities statutes seek to maintain public confidence in the marketplace. They do so by deterring fraud, in part, through the availability of private securities fraud actions. But the statutes make these latter actions available, not to provide investors with broad insurance against market losses, but to protect them against those economic losses that misrepresentations actually cause. Cf. *Basic,* 485 U.S., at 252 (White, J., joined by O'connor, J., concurring in part and dissenting in part) ("'[A]llowing recovery in the face of affirmative evidence of nonreliance—would effectively convert Rule 10b–5 into a scheme of investor's insurance. There is no support in the Securities Exchange Act, the Rule, or our cases for such a result" (internal quotation marks and citations omitted)).

The statutory provision at issue here and the paragraphs that precede it emphasize this last mentioned objective. Private Securities Litigation Reform Act of 1995, 109 Stat. 737. The statute insists that securities fraud complaints "specify" each misleading statement; that they set forth the facts "on which [a] belief" that a statement is misleading was "formed"; and that they "state with particularity facts giving rise to a strong inference that the defendant acted with the required state of mind." 15 U.S.C. § § 78u–4(b)(1), (2). And the statute expressly imposes on plaintiffs "the burden of proving" that the defendant's misrepresentations "caused the loss for which the plaintiff seeks to recover." § 78u–4(b)(4).

The statute thereby makes clear Congress' intent to permit private securities fraud actions for recovery where, but only where, plaintiffs adequately allege and prove the traditional elements of causation and loss.

By way of contrast, the Ninth Circuit's approach would allow recovery where a misrepresentation leads to an inflated purchase price but nonetheless does not proximately cause any economic loss. That is to say, it would permit recovery where these two traditional elements in fact are missing.

In sum, we find the Ninth Circuit's approach inconsistent with the law's requirement that a plaintiff prove that the defendant's misrepresentation (or other fraudulent conduct) proximately caused the plaintiff's economic loss. We need not, and do not, consider other proximate cause or loss-related questions.

Our holding about plaintiffs' need to *prove* proximate causation and economic loss leads us also to conclude that the plaintiffs' complaint here failed adequately to *allege* these requirements ..... We concede that ordinary pleading rules are not meant to impose a great burden upon a plaintiff. But it should not prove burdensome for a plaintiff who has suffered an economic loss to provide a defendant with some indication of the loss and the causal connection that the plaintiff has in mind. At the same time, allowing a plaintiff to forgo giving any indication of the economic loss and proximate cause that the plaintiff has in mind would bring about harm of the very sort the statutes seek to avoid. Cf. H.R. Conf. Rep. No. 104–369, p. 31 (1995) (criticizing "abusive" practices including "the routine filing of lawsuits ... with only a faint hope that the discovery process might lead eventually to some plausible cause of action"). It would permit a plaintiff "with a largely groundless claim to simply take up the time of a number of other people, with the right to do so representing an *in terrorem* increment of the settlement value, rather than a reasonably founded hope that the [discovery] process will reveal relevant evidence." *Blue Chip Stamps*, 421 U.S., at 741. Such a rule would tend to transform a private securities action into a partial downside insurance policy. See H.R. Conf. Rep. No. 104–369, at 31; see also *Basic*, 485 U.S., at 252 (White, J., joined by O'Connor, J., concurring in part and dissenting in part).

For these reasons, we find the plaintiffs' complaint legally insufficient. We reverse the judgment of the Ninth Circuit, and we remand the case for further proceedings consistent with this opinion.

SECTION 8.   THE RELIANCE REQUIREMENT

BASIC v. LEVINSON

485 U.S. 224, 108 S.Ct. 978, 99 L.Ed.2d 194 (1988).

JUSTICE BLACKMUN delivered the opinion of the Court.

This case requires us to * * * determine whether a person who traded a corporation's shares on a securities exchange after the issuance of a materially misleading statement by the corporation may invoke a rebuttable presumption that, in trading, he relied on the integrity of the price set by the market. * * *

We turn to the question of reliance and the fraud-on-the-market theory. Succinctly put:

> "The fraud on the market theory is based on the hypothesis that, in an open and developed securities market, the price of a company's stock is determined by the available material information regarding the company and its business. * * * Misleading statements will therefore defraud purchasers of stock even if the purchasers do not directly rely on the misstatements. * * * The causal connection between the defendants' fraud and the plaintiffs' purchase of stock in such a case is no less significant than in a case of direct reliance on misrepresentations." Peil v. Speiser, 806 F.2d 1154, 1160–1161 (3d Cir.1986).

Our task, of course, is not to assess the general validity of the theory, but to consider whether it was proper for the courts below to apply a rebuttable presumption of reliance, supported in part by the fraud-on-the-market theory.

This case required resolution of several common questions of law and fact concerning the falsity or misleading nature of the three public statements made by Basic, the presence or absence of scienter, and the materiality of the misrepresentations, if any. In their amended complaint, the named plaintiffs alleged that in reliance on Basic's statements they sold their shares of Basic stock in the depressed market created by petitioners. Requiring proof of individualized reliance from each member of the proposed plaintiff class effectively would have prevented respondents from proceeding with a class action, since individual issues then would have overwhelmed the common ones. The District Court found that the presumption of reliance created by the fraud-on-the-market theory provided "a practical resolution to the problem of balancing the substantive requirement of proof of reliance in securities cases against the procedural requisites of [Fed.Rule Civ.Proc.] 23." The District Court thus concluded that with reference to each public statement and its impact upon the open market for Basic shares, common questions predominated over individual questions, as required by Fed.Rule Civ.Proc. 23(a)(2) and (b)(3).

Petitioners and their *amici* complain that the fraud-on-the-market theory effectively eliminates the requirement that a plaintiff asserting a claim under Rule 10b–5 prove reliance. They note that reliance is and long has been an element of common-law fraud, and argue that because the analogous express right of action includes a reliance requirement, see, *e.g.,* § 18(a) of the 1934 Act, as amended, so too must an action implied under § 10(b).

We agree that reliance is an element of a Rule 10b–5 cause of action. Reliance provides the requisite causal connection between a defendant's misrepresentation and a plaintiff's injury. There is, however, more than one way to demonstrate the causal connection. Indeed, we previously have dispensed with a requirement of positive proof of reliance, where a duty to disclose material information had been breached, concluding that the necessary nexus between the plaintiffs' injury and the defendant's wrongful conduct had been established. Similarly, we did not require proof that material omissions or misstatements in a proxy statement decisively affected voting, because the proxy solicitation itself, rather than the defect in the solicitation materials, served as an essential link in the transaction.

The modern securities markets, literally involving millions of shares changing hands daily, differ from the face-to-face transactions contemplated by early fraud cases, and, our understanding of Rule 10b–5's reliance requirement must encompass these differences.* * *

Presumptions typically serve to assist courts in managing circumstances in which direct proof, for one reason or another, is rendered difficult. The courts below accepted a presumption, created by the fraud-on-the-market theory and subject to rebuttal by petitioners, that persons who had traded Basic shares had done so in reliance on the integrity of the price set by the market, but because of petitioners' material misrepresentations that price had been fraudulently depressed. Requiring a plaintiff to show a speculative state of facts, i.e., how he would have acted if omitted material information had been disclosed, or if the misrepresentation had not been made, would place an unnecessarily unrealistic evidentiary burden on the Rule 10b–5 plaintiff who has traded on an impersonal market.* * *

The presumption is also supported by common sense and probability. Recent empirical studies have tended to confirm Congress' premise that the market price of shares traded on well-developed markets reflects all publicly available information, and, hence, any material misrepresentations. It has been noted that "it is hard to imagine that there ever is a buyer or seller who does not rely on market integrity. Who would knowingly roll the dice in a crooked crap game?" Indeed, nearly every court that has considered the proposition has concluded that where materially misleading statements have been disseminated into an impersonal, well-developed market for securities, the reliance of individual plaintiffs on the integrity of the market price may be presumed. Commentators generally have applauded the adoption of one variation or another of the fraud-on-the-market theory. An investor who buys or sells stock at the price set by the market does so in reliance on the integrity of that price. Because most publicly available information is reflected in market price, an investor's reliance on any public material misrepresentations, therefore, may be presumed for purposes of a Rule 10b–5 action.

The Court of Appeals found that petitioners "made public, material misrepresentations and [respondents] sold Basic stock in an impersonal, efficient market. Thus the class, as defined by the district court, has established the threshold facts for proving their loss." The court acknowledged that petitioners may rebut proof of the elements giving rise to the presumption, or show that the misrepresentation in fact did not lead to a distortion of price or that an individual plaintiff traded or would have traded despite his knowing the statement was false.

Any showing that severs the link between the alleged misrepresentation and either the price received (or paid) by the plaintiff, or his decision to trade at a fair market price, will be sufficient to rebut the presumption of reliance. For example, if petitioners could show that the "market makers" were privy to the truth about the merger discussions here with Combustion, and thus that the market price would not have been affected by their misrepresentations, the causal connection would be broken: the basis for finding that the fraud had been transmitted through market price would be gone. Similarly, if, despite petitioners' allegedly fraudulent attempt to manipulate market price, news of the merger discussions credibly entered the market and dissipated the effects of the misstatements, those who traded Basic shares after the corrective statements would have no direct or indirect connection with the fraud. Petitioners also could rebut the presumption of reliance as to plaintiffs who have divested themselves of their Basic shares without relying on the integrity of the market. For example, a plaintiff who believed that Basic's statements were false and that Basic was indeed engaged in merger discussions, and who consequently believed that Basic stock was artificially underpriced, but sold his shares nevertheless because of other unrelated concerns, e.g., potential antitrust problems, or political pressures to divest from shares of certain businesses, could not be said to have relied on the integrity of a price he knew had been manipulated.* * *

THE CHIEF JUSTICE, JUSTICE SCALIA, and JUSTICE KENNEDY took no part in the consideration or decision of this case.

JUSTICE WHITE, with whom JUSTICE O'CONNOR joins, concurring in part and dissenting in part.

* * * I dissent * * * because I do not agree that the "fraud-on-the-market" theory should be applied in this case.

Even when compared to the relatively youthful private cause-of-action under § 10(b), the fraud-on-the-market theory is a mere babe. Yet today, the Court embraces this theory with the sweeping confidence usually reserved for more mature legal doctrines. In so doing, I fear that the Court's decision may have many adverse, unintended effects as it is applied and interpreted in the years to come.

At the outset, I note that there are portions of the Court's fraud-on-the-market holding with which I am in agreement. Most importantly, the Court rejects the version of that theory, heretofore adopted by some courts, which equates "causation" with "reliance," and permits recovery by a plaintiff who claims merely to have been *harmed* by a material misrepresentation which altered a market price, notwithstanding proof that the plaintiff did not in any way *rely* on that price. I agree with the Court that if Rule 10b–5's reliance requirement is to be left with any content at all, the fraud-on-the-market presumption must be capable of being rebutted by a showing that a plaintiff did not "rely" on the market price. * * *

But even as the Court attempts to limit the fraud-on-the-market theory it endorses today, the pitfalls in its approach are revealed by previous uses by the lower courts of the broader versions of the theory. Confusion and contradiction in court rulings are inevitable when traditional legal analysis is replaced with economic theorization by the federal courts. * * *

For while the economists' theories which underpin the fraud-on-the-market presumption may have the appeal of mathematical exactitude and scientific certainty, they are, in the end, nothing more than theories which may or may not prove accurate upon further consideration. Even the most earnest advocates of economic analysis of the law recognize this. Thus, while the majority states that, for purposes of reaching its result it need only make modest assumptions about the way in which "market professionals generally" do their jobs, and how the conduct of market professionals affects stock prices, I doubt that we are in much of a position to assess which theories aptly describe the functioning of the securities industry.

Consequently, I cannot join the Court in the effort to reconfigure the securities laws, based on recent economic theories, to better fit what it perceives to be the new realities of financial markets. I would leave this task to others more equipped for the job than we.

At the bottom of the Court's conclusion that the fraud-on-the-market theory sustains a presumption of reliance is the assumption that individuals rely "on the integrity of the market price" when buying or selling stock in "impersonal, well-developed market[s] for securities." Even if I was prepared to accept (as a matter of common sense or general understanding) the assumption that most persons buying or selling stock do so in response to the market price, the fraud-on-the-market theory goes further. For in adopting a "presumption of reliance," the Court *also* assumes that buyers and sellers rely, not just on the market price, but on the *"integrity"* of that price. It is this aspect of the fraud-on-the-market hypothesis which most mystifies me.

To define the term "integrity of the market price," the majority quotes approvingly from cases which suggest that investors are entitled to " 'rely on the price of a stock as a reflection of its value.' " But the meaning of this phrase eludes me, for it implicitly suggests that stocks have some "true value" that is measurable by a standard other than their market price. While the Scholastics of Medieval times professed a means to make such a valuation of a commodity's "worth," I doubt that the federal courts of our day are similarly equipped.

Even if securities had some "value," knowable and distinct from the market price of a stock, investors do not always share the Court's presumption that a stock's price is a "reflection of [this] value." Indeed, "many investors purchase or sell stock because they believe the price *inaccurately* reflects the corporation's worth." If investors really believed that stock prices reflected a stock's "value," many sellers would never sell, and many buyers never buy (given the time and cost associated with executing a stock transaction). As we recognized just a few years ago: "[I]nvestors act on inevitably incomplete or inaccurate information, [consequently] there are always winners and losers; but those who have 'lost' have not necessarily been defrauded." Yet today, the Court allows investors to recover who can show little more than that they sold stock at a lower price than what might have been.

I do not propose that the law retreat from the many protections that § 10(b) and Rule 10b–5, as interpreted in our prior cases, provide to investors. But any extension of these laws, to approach something closer to an investor insurance scheme, should come from Congress, and not from the courts.

Congress has not passed on the fraud-on-the-market theory the Court embraces today. That is reason enough for us to abstain from doing so. But it is even more troubling that, to the extent that any view of Congress on this question can be inferred indirectly, it is contrary to the result the majority reaches.

In the past, the scant legislative history of § 10(b) has led us to look at Congress' intent in adopting other portions of the Securities Act when we endeavor to discern the limits of private causes of action under Rule 10b–5. A similar undertaking here reveals that Congress flatly rejected a proposition analogous to the fraud-on-the-market theory in adopting a civil liability provision of the 1934 Act.

Section 18 of the Act expressly provides for civil liability for certain misleading statements concerning securities. When the predecessor of this section was first being considered by Congress, the initial draft of the provision allowed recovery by any plaintiff "who shall have purchased or sold a security the price of which may have been affected by such [misleading] statement." Thus, as initially drafted, the precursor to the express civil liability provision of the 1934 Act would have permitted suits by plaintiffs based solely on the fact that the price of the securities they bought or sold was *affected* by a misrepresentation: a theory closely akin to the Court's holding today.

Yet this provision was roundly criticized in congressional hearings on the proposed Securities Act, because it failed to include a more substantial "reliance" requirement. Subsequent drafts modified the original proposal, and included an express reliance requirement in the final version of the Act.* * *

A second congressional policy that the majority's opinion ignores is the strong preference the securities laws display for widespread public disclosure and distribution to investors of material information concerning securities. This congressionally-adopted policy is expressed in the numerous and varied disclosure requirements found in the federal securities law scheme.

Yet observers in this field have acknowledged that the fraud-on-the-market theory is at odds with the federal policy favoring disclosure.* * *

It is no surprise, then, that some of the same voices calling for acceptance of the fraud-on-the-market theory also favor dismantling the federal scheme which mandates disclosure. But to the extent that the federal courts must make a choice between preserving effective disclosure and trumpeting the new fraud-on-the-market hypothesis, I think Congress has spoken clearly, favoring the current pro-disclosure policy. We should limit our role in interpreting § 10(b) and Rule 10b–5 to one of giving effect to such policy decisions by Congress.

Finally, the particular facts of this case make it an exceedingly poor candidate for the Court's fraud-on-the-market theory, and illustrate the illogic achieved by that theory's application in many cases.

Respondents here are a class of sellers who sold Basic stock between October, 1977 and December 1978, a fourteen-month period. At the time the class period began, Basic's stock was trading at $20 a share (at the time, an all-time high); the last members of the class to sell their Basic stock got a price of just over $30 a share. It is indisputable that virtually every member of the class made money from his or her sale of Basic stock.

The oddities of applying the fraud-on-the-market theory in this case are manifest. First, there are the facts that the plaintiffs are sellers and the class period is so lengthy, both are virtually without precedent in prior fraud-on-the-market cases . . . . . I think these two facts render this case less apt to application of the fraud-on-the-market hypothesis.

Second, there is the fact that in this case, there is no evidence that petitioner's officials made the troublesome misstatements for the purpose of manipulating stock prices, or with any intent to engage in underhanded trading of Basic stock. Indeed, during the class period, petitioners do not appear to have purchased or sold *any* Basic stock whatsoever. I agree with *amicus* who argues that "[i]mposition of damages liability under Rule 10b–5 makes little sense . . . where a defendant is neither a purchaser nor a seller of securities." In fact, in previous cases, we had recognized that Rule 10b–5 is concerned primarily with cases where the fraud is committed by one trading the security at issue. And it is difficult to square liability in this case with § 10(b)'s express provision that it prohibits fraud *"in connection with* the purchase or sale of any security."

Third, there are the peculiarities of what kinds of investors will be able to recover in this case. As I read the District Court's class certification order, there are potentially many persons who did not purchase Basic stock until *after* the first false statement (October 1977), but who nonetheless *will* be able to recover under the Court's fraud-on-the-market theory. Thus, it is possible that a person who heard the first corporate misstatement and *disbelieved* it, i.e., someone who purchased Basic stock thinking that petitioners' statement was false, may still be included in the plaintiff-class on remand. How a person who undertook such a speculative stock-investing strategy, and made $10 a share doing so (if he bought on October 22, 1977, and sold on December 15, 1978), can say that he was "defrauded" by virtue of his reliance on the "integrity" of the market price is beyond me. And such speculators may not be uncommon, at least in this case.

Indeed, the facts of this case lead a casual observer to the almost inescapable conclusion that many of those who bought or sold Basic stock during the period in question flatly disbelieved the statements which are alleged to have been "materially misleading." Despite three statements denying that merger negotiations were underway, Basic stock hit record-high after record-high during the 14–month class period. It seems quite possible that, like Casca's knowing disbelief of Caesar's "thrice refusal" of the Crown, clever investors were skeptical of petitioners' three denials that merger talks were going on. Yet such investors, the savviest of the savvy, will be able to recover under the Court's opinion, as long as they now claim that they believed in the "integrity of the market price" when they sold their stock (between September and December, 1978). Thus, persons who bought after hearing and relying on the *falsity* of petitioner's statements may be able to prevail and recover money damages on remand.

And who will pay the judgments won in such actions? I suspect that all too often the majority's rule will "lead to large judgments, payable in the last analysis by innocent investors, for the benefit of speculators and their lawyers." This Court and others have previously recognized that "inexorably broadening ... the class of plaintiff[s] who may sue in this area of the law will ultimately result in more harm than good." Yet such a bitter harvest is likely to be reaped from the seeds sown by the Court's decision today.

In sum, I think the Court's embracement of the fraud-on-the-market theory represents a departure in securities law that we are ill-suited to commence, and even less equipped to control as it proceeds. As a result, I must respectfully dissent.

NOTES

1. In his opinion in *Basic*, Justice White questions the rule announced in the 1968 SEC v. Texas Gulf Sulphur Co., 401 F.2d 833 (2d Cir.1968), cert denied sub nom., Coates v. SEC, 394 U.S. 976, 89 S.Ct. 1454, 22 L.Ed.2d 756 (1969) case that a corporation's published misstatements are deemed to be "in connection with" all the transactions in the corporation's stock taking place in the secondary markets, even though the corporation itself is not buying or selling. In 1993, a district court in Connecticut held that such misstatements should not be considered to be violations of Rule 10b–5, but the court of appeals reversed, strongly reaffirming the broad interpretation of the "in connection with" clause. In re Ames Dept. Stores, Inc. Stock Litigation, 991 F.2d 953 (2d Cir.1993).

2.   The *Basic* "fraud on the market" approach requires that there be a market to be defrauded. What if the securities are not publicly traded, so that there is no market price to be affected by the alleged misstatements? This problem arose in Eckstein v. Balcor, Film Investors, 8 F.3d 1121 (7th Cir.1993), in an opinion by Judge Easterbrook:

> Because they never read the prospectus, the Eckstein plaintiffs encounter difficulty in establishing that they relied to their detriment on the seller's statements, a component of a claim under § 10(b) and Rule 10b–5 according to the canonical formulation. * * * The Supreme Court's adoption of the fraud-on-the-market doctrine in *Basic* shows that reliance is not essential; although *Basic* continued to use that word, it allowed an alternative method of establishing causation, an effect on the market price, to support recovery by investors who never read the supposedly deceitful statement.

> When "the market", that is, the outcome of trading by persons who are well-informed about what the issuer is doing and saying, translates a lie or omission from voice to price, it is easy to see how injury can befall a person who is unaware of the deceit. The price in an open and developed market usually reflects all available information, because the price is an outcome of competition among knowledgeable investors. * * *

> BFI issued its interests as part of an initial public offering at a fixed price, $1,000 per unit (with a minimum of three units per investor). No trading market valued these interests; only the investors could do so. No trading market developed afterward, so we cannot combine the Capital Asset Pricing Model with the tables in the Wall Street Journal to see what effect Worldvision's suit, or the other information that slowly came to light about New World, had on price. * * * Alas, no such luck, because there are no such prices. This does not mean that the Eckstein plaintiffs cannot show causation, but they must carry the greater burden of proving the causal links that an efficient secondary market establishes automatically.

> The Eckstein plaintiffs try to do so via a theory we could call "fraud-created-the-market." BFI's offering was conditioned on its ability to raise at least $35 million. A minimum sales requirement may serve two functions: it ensures that the venture has sufficient capital to function, and it provides a form of vicarious protection to ignorant investors who assume that the condition will be met only if a significant number of informed buyers think the project a good investment. Plaintiffs allege that, if BFI had made complete and truthful statements, it would not have been able to sell interests to investors who did read the prospectus. Without those investors, BFI would not have been able to sell the minimum amount, and thus would have returned the plaintiffs' tendered funds. Thus, say the Eckstein plaintiffs, the misstatements and omissions in the prospectus caused their losses.

> The Fifth Circuit adopted a variant of this approach by a vote of 12 to 10 in Shores v. Sklar, 647 F.2d 462 (1981)(in banc). *Shores* held that an investor may maintain an action under § 10(b) by establishing that the fraud permitted the securities to exist in the market, that but for the

fraud the securities would have been "unmarketable," and that the investor relied on their existence. The Tenth and Eleventh Circuits follow modified versions of the *Shores* approach, while the Sixth Circuit has repudiated that case outright. We agree with the Sixth Circuit. The existence of a security does not depend on, or warrant, the adequacy of disclosure. Many a security is on the market even though the issuer or some third party made incomplete disclosures. Federal securities law does not include "merit regulation." Full disclosure of adverse information may lower the price, but it does not exclude the security from the market. Securities of bankrupt corporations trade freely; some markets specialize in penny stocks. Thus the linchpin of *Shores,* that disclosing bad information keeps securities off the market, entitling investors to rely on the presence of the securities just as they would rely on statements in a prospectus, is simply false.

Without the aid of *Shores*, the Eckstein plaintiffs have rough sledding ahead. They cannot use the incomplete or rosy nature of Balcor's pamphlets, which they may have read, as the actionable "fraud"; sales literature need not repeat the full disclosures and risk analysis in the prospectus. To prevail the Eckstein plaintiffs must prove that, had the prospectus been free from fraud, BFI would not have satisfied the minimum-sale requirement of $35 million. Because this is a suit under § 10(b) of the '34 Act rather than §§ 11 or 12(2) of the' 33 Act, the Eckstein plaintiffs must establish this counterfactual proposition about the decision-making of thousands of investors using only statements or omissions amounting to fraud; other errors and omissions that might have supported liability under §§ 11 or 12(2) do not support an inference of causation that can replace direct reliance in a case under § 10(b). The difference between errors and fraud, and the fact that BFI attracted $48 million, substantially exceeding the $35 million cutoff, present the Eckstein plaintiffs with a daunting task. Still, the record in its current state does not doom their case, so we must remand their case to the district court for further proceedings.

In Unger v. Amedisys Inc., 401 F.3d 316 (5th Cir. 2005), the Fifth Circuit reversed a certification of a class action that was based on a fraud on the market theory. The district court was found to have made an inadequate analysis to determine whether there was an efficient market in the stock that would support such a claim. The court listed some of the factors that are sometimes considered in making that determination such as average weekly trading volume, the number of financial analysts following the stock, market capitalization and bid and ask spreads.

3. In Affiliated Ute Citizens of Utah v. United States, 406 U.S. 128, 92 S.Ct. 1456, 31 L.Ed.2d 741 (1972), the Supreme Court held that there was a presumption of reliance in nondisclosure cases brought under SEC Rule 10b–5. Any reliance by the plaintiff must be reasonable. See e.g., Banca Cremi, S.A. v. Alex Brown & Sons, Inc., 132 F.3d 1017 (4th Cir.1997) (reliance by sophisticated investor on broker-dealer recommendations was not reasonable); Schlesinger v. Herzog, 2 F.3d 135 (5th Cir.1993) (plaintiff could not establish reasonable reliance since he did not exercise due diligence); Jensen v. Kimble, 1 F.3d 1073 (10th Cir.1993) (plaintiff who was aware of true facts could not

establish reliance). In Zobrist v. Coal–X, Inc., 708 F.2d 1511 (10th Cir. 1983), the Tenth Circuit held that information contained in a private placement memorandum would be imputed to a sophisticated businessman even though he had failed to read the document. The court held that the businessman's claimed reliance on oral misrepresentations that conflicted with the memorandum was not justified. *See also* Kennedy v. Josephthal, Inc., 814 F.2d 798, 804–805 (1st Cir.1987) (court notes the sophistication of plaintiffs in finding no justifiable reliance on oral misrepresentations). The courts have been more reluctant to impose such a standard on unsophisticated investors. In Wegerer v. First Commodity Corp., 744 F.2d 719 (1984), the Tenth Circuit in a general fraud action rejected a claim that investors were given adequate warnings of risk from statements in risk disclosure documents. The court distinguished *Zobrist* because the customers were not sophisticated. The Seventh Circuit took a more middle of the road approach in Indosuez Carr Futures, Inc. v. CFTC, 27 F.3d 1260, 1265–1266 (7th Cir. 1994), holding that there was not a reasonable reliance requirement under federal antifraud provisions such as those found in the federal securities laws. Nevertheless, the court asserted that investors could not close their eyes to a known risk or claim reliance where information known to them to be true was in conflict with a false oral statement made by their broker.

4. In Stoneridge Investment Partners, LLC v. Scientific-Atlanta, Inc., ___ U.S. ___, 128 S.Ct. 761, 169 L.Ed.2d 627 (2008) (page 816 below), the Supreme Court struck down a claim of primary liability under rule 10b–5 on the grounds that there was no indication that the public could be said to have relied on the defendant's participation in the allegedly fraudulent scheme. The Court noted that 'reliance is tied to causation, leading to the inquiry whether respondents' acts were immediate or remote to the injury."

––––––––

IN RE APPLE COMPUTER

886 F.2d 1109 (9th Cir.1989).

FARRIS, CIRCUIT JUDGE:

This is an appeal from three orders which together granted summary judgment against plaintiffs on all of their claims under the Securities Exchange Act of 1934. Plaintiffs allege that Apple Computer Inc. and its top officers misled the market about the capabilities and prospects of a novel office computer and disk-drive system. They claim that they purchased Apple stock in reliance on the artificially high stock price resulting from Apple's misrepresentations, and that they suffered actionable damages when the true facts about the computer became known and Apple's stock price fell by almost 75%. The trial court granted summary judgment on the grounds that each of Apple's alleged misstatements was either immaterial or made without scienter. We affirm in part, reverse in part, and remand.

Apple is a publicly-traded company which manufactures computers and computer peripherals. The individual defendants were officers and directors of Apple at the time of the events complained of, November 12, 1982 through September 23, 1983. During the six months immediately preceding this "class period," Apple's common stock traded in a range of between $11 and $30 per share.

In 1982, Apple was readying a computer named "Lisa" and a compatible disk-drive named "Twiggy" for commercial release. Apple's previous successes, most notably the "Apple II," had been in the home computer market. With Lisa, Apple hoped to service the computer needs of medium-size to large corporations. Lisa contained a number of technological innovations which later proved to be commercially viable when incorporated into the "Macintosh" home computer. For example, Lisa pioneered use of the "mouse," a hand-held device which allows the operator to communicate with the computer without using the keyboard, and "icons," graphic displays of the computer's functions. However, Lisa and Twiggy themselves proved to be unsuccessful commercially. Apple replaced Twiggy with another disk-drive system before actual sales of Lisa began. Apple discontinued Lisa altogether shortly after the close of the class period.

The named plaintiffs represent a certified class of persons who purchased Apple stock during the class period. They allege that Apple and its top officers made a number of highly positive statements about Lisa and Twiggy during the class period. * * * Plaintiffs attribute volatility in Apple's common stock price to these optimistic statements. Apple's stock price soared during the class period, reaching a high of almost $63 per share, and bottomed out at a bit over $17 per share shortly after the class period when Apple disclosed news of Lisa's disappointing sales.

Plaintiffs claim that Apple's officers recklessly ignored a number of problems with Lisa and Twiggy which tended to undermine their public optimism. * * *

Although plaintiffs allege that Apple did not fairly and adequately inform the market about Lisa's prospects, many of the risks and underlying problems were widely publicized. For example, the same *Business Week* article which quotes Jobs as stating his belief that Apple would have little trouble selling Lisa also states: "One indication of how uncertain Apple's prospects are is that expert estimates of how many Lisas the company will sell are all over the lot, from 2,000 to 30,000." The article also questions whether independent software writers would support Lisa, and whether the $9,995 price tag was realistic. Similarly the *Wall Street Journal* article in which Jobs predicts that Lisa will be "phenomenally successful" is entitled "Some Warm Up to Apple's 'Lisa,' but Eventual Success is Uncertain." * * *

In three separate orders, the trial court granted Apple summary judgment against plaintiffs on their entire case. * * *

On appeal, plaintiffs argue that the trial court misapplied the standard for materiality in a fraud on the market case. They claim that, notwithstanding the press' attention to Lisa's shortcomings, Apple's omissions were material because a reasonable investor would place greater weight on the opinions of corporate insiders. * * *

Plaintiffs bring their claim under the so-called "fraud on the market" theory first recognized by this court in Blackie v. Barrack. In the usual claim under Section 10(b), the plaintiff must show individual reliance on a material misstatement. Under the fraud on the market theory, the plaintiff has the benefit of a presumption that he has indirectly relied on the alleged misstatement, by relying on the integrity of the stock price established by the market. * * *

The most closely controverted issue in this case is whether the defendants' optimistic statements about Lisa and Twiggy are shielded from liability because of the press' documentation of the relevant risks. The trial court held that disclosures by the press rendered the defendants' omissions immaterial. Ordinarily, omissions by corporate insiders are not rendered immaterial by the fact that the omitted facts are otherwise available to the public. Where a plaintiff alleges actual reliance on a particular statement, it does not matter that the *market* is aware of the facts necessary to make the statement not misleading. The plaintiff may be misled into believing that the stock has been incorrectly valued by the market.

The situation is different in a fraud on the market case. In a fraud on the market case, the plaintiff claims that he was induced to trade stock not by any particular representations made by corporate insiders, but by the artificial stock price set by the market in light of statements made by the insiders as well as all other material public information. Provided that they have credibly entered the market through other means, the facts allegedly omitted by the defendant would already be reflected in the stock's price; the mechanism through which the market discovered the facts in question is not crucial. * * *

We conclude that in a fraud on the market case, the defendant's failure to disclose material information may be excused where that information has been made credibly available to the market by other sources. The issue with regard to the bulk of Apple's misstatements is whether, in light of the press' documentation of Lisa's risks, a rational jury could nonetheless find a "substantial likelihood" that full disclosures by Apple would have "significantly altered the 'total mix' of information made available." TSC Industries, Inc. v. Northway, Inc.

With respect to two of the challenged statements, there are genuine issues of material fact. In a November 29, 1982 press release, Apple stated that Twiggy "ensures greater integrity of data than the other high density drives by way of a unique, double-sided mechanism designed and manufactured by Apple." Apple also claimed that Twiggy "represents three years of research and development and has undergone extensive testing and design verification during the past year." At the time these optimistic statements were made, internal tests conducted by Apple indicated slowness and unreliability in Twiggy's information-processing capabilities. * * *

There is at least a triable issue of whether Twiggy's technical problems were material facts tending to undermine the unqualified optimism of [these] Statements. . . . Unlike the information about Lisa's market risks, these problems were not made known to the market by the press or by anyone else. * * *

The remainder of the challenged statements involved Lisa, or Apple generally, rather than Twiggy. Although many of these statements failed to disclose material risks, we agree with the trial court that there are no genuine issues of fact under a fraud on the market theory. The press portrayed Lisa as a gamble, with the potential for either enormous success or enormous failure. At least twenty articles stressed the risks Apple was taking, and detailed the underlying problems producing those risks. Many of the optimistic statements challenged by plaintiffs appeared in those same articles, essentially bracketed by the facts which plaintiffs claim Apple wrongfully failed to disclose. The market could not have been made more aware of Lisa's risks.

We stress the limits of our holding. Scrutiny by the press will not ordinarily excuse the type of unqualified exuberance expressed by Apple and its officers in this case. Even in a fraud on the market case, corporate insiders are not relieved of their duty to disclose material information where that information has received only brief mention in a few poorly-circulated or lightly-regarded publications. The investing public justifiably places heavy reliance on the statements and opinions of corporate insiders. In order to avoid Rule 10b–5 liability, any material information which insiders fail to disclose must be transmitted to the public with a degree of intensity and credibility sufficient to effectively counter-balance any misleading impression created by the insiders' one-sided representations. * * *

NOTE

On remand, a jury found two officers of Apple liable for the alleged misstatements, and assessed damages against them of approximately $100 million. The company itself was not found liable for the misstatements. The trial judge, however, granted the defendants' motion for judgment notwithstanding the verdict, holding that there "was no substantial evidence" that the two men knowingly or recklessly made false or misleading statements, and concluding that the jury was "confused" and its verdict "internally inconsistent." See 23 BNA Sec. Reg. & L. Rep. 1320 (Sept. 13, 1991).

SECTION 9.　DAMAGES

GREEN v. OCCIDENTAL PETROLEUM CORP.

541 F.2d 1335 (9th Cir.1976).

Per Curiam.

Plaintiffs filed several lawsuits, which were transferred to the district court below, against defendant Occidental Petroleum ("Occidental") and other defendants alleging violations of the federal securities laws due to allegedly misleading financial statements and other reports. * * * As the district judge found:

> The gravamen of each complaint appears to be that the principal defendants violated Section 10(b) of the 1934 Act by utilizing improper accounting practices and issuing press releases and quarterly reports to shareholders in which the profits of Occidental were overstated, or that other misleading information was given, with the result that the market price of Occidental securities was artificially inflated.

* * * [The court held that the allowance of class certification was proper under F.R.C.P. Rule 23(b)(3), which permits a class action if "the court finds that the questions of law or fact common to the members of the class predominate over any questions affecting only individual members * * *."]

Sneed, Circuit Judge (concurring in part).

* * * As I view it, the district court abused its discretion if the Rule 23(b)(3) certification was based on the assumption that the rescissory measure of damages would be the proper measure. * * *

My starting point is that the class members in this case did not deal face to face with the corporate defendant. Rather they purchased in the open market. Whatever these purchasers "lost" did not directly accrue to the defendant. Such benefits as did accrue very likely were tangential and not closely correlated to the purchasers' "losses." It follows that the proper measure of damages is what the purchasers lost as a result of the defendant's wrong, not what the defendant gained.

The rescissory measure of damages does not properly measure that loss. The reason is that it permits a defrauded purchaser to place upon the defendant the burden of any decline in the value of the stock between the date of purchase and the date of disclosure of the fraud even though only a portion of that decline may have been proximately caused by the defendant's wrong. The other portion is the result of market forces unrelated to the wrong. Moreover, this decline is unrelated both to any benefits derived by the defendant from his fraud and to the blameworthiness of his conduct. * * *

This measure (the difference between the purchase price and the value of the stock as of the date of disclosure) works justly when a defrauded *seller* proceeds after an *increase* in value of the stock against a fraudulent buyer who is unable to return the stock he fraudulently purchased. His inability to return the stock should not deprive the injured seller of the remedy of restitution. Under these circumstances it is appropriate to require the fraudulent buyer to account for his "ill-gotten profits" derived from an increase in the value of the stock following his acquisition of the stock. *See* Janigan v. Taylor, 344 F.2d 781 (1st Cir. 1965). *See also,* Affiliated Ute Citizens v. United States, 406 U.S. 128 (1972). Only in this manner can the seller be put in the position he occupied before the contract was made. * * *

The obligations of a corporate defendant in an open market setting such as in this case are not rooted in a contract of sale. The corporate defendant sold nothing to the aggrieved purchaser. The purchaser acquired his stock from others in the open market. The misrepresentations of the corporate defendant did not result in a shift of the risks of loss in the value of the stock from it to the misled purchaser. There exists no undertaking on the part of the corporate defendant to assume responsibility for the purchaser's loss. The rescissory measure of damages, if used in these circumstances, cannot rest on the theory of restitution. The corporate defendant can return no purchase price because it never received the price. If such a measure is proper it must be because it is necessary to give effect to rule 10b–5.

* * * To impose upon the defendant the burden of restoring *all* investment losses by those who held their stock until disclosure burdens the defendant with certain losses which it neither caused nor with respect to which it assumed a responsibility. I cannot believe rule 10b–5 contemplates a civil penalty so unpredictable in its scope. Nor do I believe that the rescissory measure is appropriate for purchasers who sold before disclosure date. The rescissory measure permits in those instances a recovery of all investment losses between the dates of purchase and sale.

I acknowledge, however, that management of the class in this and similar cases would be simplified by use of the rescissory measure of damages. Each plaintiff retaining his stock to the disclosure date would be required to prove only his purchase price while the disclosure date value would be applicable to all such class members alike. Purchasers selling before disclosure need only prove their purchase and sale price. The price of simplification is, however, too high. Wrongdoing defendants should not be mulcted to make simple the management of a class proceeding under rule 10b–5. To certify a class on the assumption that only by such means is the class manageable would constitute, in my opinion, an abuse of discretion.

The trial court's certification in this case may have proceeded on a different assumption. That is, its view may have been that damages should be determined by the so-called out-of-pocket measure. This measure fixes recovery at the difference between the purchase price and the value of the stock at the date of purchase. This difference is proximately caused by the misrepresentations of the defendant. It measures precisely the extent to which the purchaser has been required to invest a greater amount than otherwise would have been necessary. It furthers the purpose of rule 10b–5 without subjecting the wrongdoer to damages the incidence of which resembles that of natural disasters. A certification on this assumption is neither arbitrary nor capricious although it does complicate the management of the class.

Complications result because it becomes necessary to establish, for the period between the date of the misrepresentations and the date of disclosure, data which when arranged on a chart will form, on the one hand, a "price line" and, on the other, a "value line." The price line will reflect, among other things, the effect of the corporate defendant's wrongful conduct. The establishment of these two lines will enable each class member purchaser who has not disposed of his stock prior to disclosure of the misrepresentations to compute his damages by simply subtracting the true value of his stock on the date of his purchase from the price he paid for it. Fixing the value line for the entire period involved in this case is obviously a more difficult and complex task than would be establishing the price at the date of disclosure of the misrepresentations and the price at all relevant dates prior to disclosure. However, such intimations as have been reflected in the briefs and oral argument suggest that establishing the required value line is practicable. In any event, in my view the attempt is necessary if class certification in this case is to survive. * * *

What has been said to this point regarding the out-of-pocket measure of damages has assumed that all class members held their stock until disclosure of the misrepresentations. The spread between the price and value lines *at the date of purchase* provides the proper measure of recovery. Purchasers during the period in question who sell before disclosure present a somewhat more difficult issue.

The difficulty springs from uncertainty about whether the spread between the price and value lines remained constant during the entire period. Assuming for the moment that the spread remained constant, class member purchasers who sold before disclosure have recovered from the open market the "cost" of the misrepresentations. * * *

The spread between the price and value lines may not remain constant, however. The spread, or value of the misrepresentations, may increase or decrease as a result of market forces operating on the misrepresentations. To illustrate, a false representation that the corporation has discovered oil will increase in value if the price of oil goes up subsequent to the misrepresentation. Expressed in terms of price and value lines, the spread between the lines increases causing the lines to diverge. A decline in the price of oil, on the other hand, will reduce the value of the misrepresentation and cause the lines to converge.

These changes in the spread are, to repeat, irrelevant to the purchaser who holds his stock until after disclosure. Nor should a *divergence* be material to a purchaser who sells before disclosure. The increased value of the misrepresentation is recouped in the market place just as is the original value of the misrepresentation. A *convergence* of the price and value lines, however, presents a different question with respect to the purchaser who sells before disclosure. From the market he recoups only a portion of the original value of the misrepresentation for which he paid full value. The unrecovered portion should be recoverable from the corporate wrongdoer, even when the purchaser resells at a price greater than his cost.

The advantage of convergence of price and value lines to purchasers who sell before disclosure creates a conflict between them and certain other purchasers. The former will be interested in narrowing the spread between the price and value lines on the date of his sale, while purchasers who bought on the date the former sold will be interested in increasing the spread. All purchasers who held their stock until disclosure are interested in establishing as wide a spread as possible on each date of purchase. These interests may require the creation of sub-classes; they do not, however, make class certification an arbitrary or capricious act.

The out-of-pocket measure of damages, which I regard as the only measure which justifies class certification in this case, permits a recovery by purchasers who sold for a price greater than they paid for the stock. Thus, purchasers who disposed of their stock after disclosure are entitled to recover the difference between the price and value of the stock on the date of their purchase even though they ultimately sold the stock for more than they paid for it. Nor is a recovery of this amount precluded by the fact that the stock has never been sold. Purchasers who sold before disclosure, entitled to recovery because of a convergence of the price and value lines subsequent to their purchase, also may recover even though their selling price exceeded their purchase price.

The reason for these results is that the "cost" of the misrepresentations should be recovered from the wrongdoer to the extent not recovered in the open market. After disclosure, or a sale prior to disclosure following convergence of the price and value lines, recovery in the open market is impossible. The wrongdoer should compensate the purchasers for these losses no longer recoverable from the market. This obligation should not be satisfied by appropriating a portion of each purchaser's investment gains. This would be the consequence of denying any recovery so long as a purchaser's selling price exceeded the purchase price. To permit such an appropriation by a wrongdoer is no more just than to charge the wrongdoer with investment losses not proximately caused by his misrepresentations. The out-of-pocket measure employed properly is the only way to avoid these twin evils.

NOTES

1.　If the district court, on remand, applies Judge Sneed's formula, what difficulties will it face which would not be present if it applied the "rescissory measure of damages"? To explain the workings of his suggested formula, Judge Sneed, in footnotes to his opinion, posited the following situation:

A corporation announces the discovery of X barrels of oil when in fact it discovered no oil at all. Assume the value of X barrels of oil amounts to $10 per share. After the announcement, the stock sells in the market at $150 a share. At this point, P purchases a share. Its "true value" is $140 ($150—$10). Subsequently, an oil embargo is imposed by the OPEC, raising the assumed value of the corporation's "discovery" to $25 per share. The market price of the stock rises to $165 per share. In due course, the falsity of the corporation's announcement is revealed, and the stock drops to $140 a share. How much should P recover? How much should he recover if he purchased the stock at $165 while the market was at that level?

Assume that instead of the OPEC embargo, there was a massive oil discovery in Alaska, reducing the assumed value of the corporation's "discovery" to $5 per share and the market price to $145. On discovery of the falsity, the market price again drops to $140. How much should P recover? How much should he recover if he sold at $145 while the market was at that level? Should he recover anything if the market price rose from $145 to $155 for reasons unrelated to the "discovery," and P sold at $155?

How realistic is this example?

2. After remand, the *Green* case was settled, with Occidental and its accountants agreeing to pay approximately $12 million into a settlement fund to be distributed to persons who purchased Occidental stock between July 31, 1969 and March 5, 1971. Each such purchaser was entitled to claim a loss of 3% of the gross purchase price of any such stock which he resold during that period, and 15% of any such stock which he did not resell during that period. If the aggregate amount of claims filed was greater than, or less than, the settlement fund, the recovery by each claimant was to be reduced, or increased, on a pro rata basis. Notice of Settlement Hearing, Wall St. Journal, Apr. 16, 1979, p. 26, col. 3. Is this method of computing the amount that can be recovered by each purchaser consistent with the approach urged by Judge Sneed?

3. The Private Securities Litigation Reform Act of 1995 modifies the damage calculation in cases of this type by limiting the recovery by any plaintiff to the difference between (a) the price paid or received by the plaintiff on his purchase or sale, and (b) "the mean trading price" of the security during the 90–day period following the dissemination of corrected information (or if he sells or repurchases the security within that 90–day period, the period ending on the date of that transaction). See Securities Exchange Act § 21D(e). The purpose of this provision, according to the Senate–House Conference Committee, is to prevent "windfall" damages arising from market fluctuations unrelated to the alleged fraud, by "providing a 'look-back' period, thereby limiting damages to those losses caused by the fraud and not by other market conditions." Does this provision effectively address the question raised by Judge Sneed in the *Green* case?

SECTION 10.   LITIGATION REFORM

Concern over the potential for abuse in the actions such as the *Apple* case led to the enactment of the Private Securities Litigation Reform Act of 1995. The background and purpose of this legislation were set forth in the "Joint Explanatory Statement" of the Senate–House Conference Committee:

> Congress has been prompted by significant evidence of abuse in private securities lawsuits to enact reforms to protect investors and maintain confidence in our capital markets. The House and Senate Committees heard evidence that abusive practices committed in private securities litigation include: (1) the routine filing of lawsuits against issuers of securities and others whenever there is a significant change in an issuer's stock price, without regard to any underlying culpability of the issuer, and with only faint hope that the discovery process might lead eventually to some plausible cause of action; (2) the targeting of deep pocket defendants, including accountants, underwriters, and individuals who may be covered by insurance, without regard to their actual culpability; (3) the abuse of the discovery process to impose costs so burdensome that it is often economical for the victimized party to settle; and (4) the manipulation by class action lawyers of the clients whom they purportedly represent. These serious injuries to innocent parties are compounded by the reluctance of many judges to impose sanctions under Federal Rule of Civil Procedure 11, except in those cases involving truly outrageous misconduct. At the same time, the investing public and the entire U.S. economy have been injured by the unwillingness of the best qualified persons to serve on boards of directors and of issuers to discuss publicly their future prospects, because of fear of baseless and extortionate securities lawsuits.

> In these and other examples of abusive and manipulative securities litigation, innocent parties are often forced to pay exorbitant "settlements." When an insurer must pay lawyers' fees, make settlement payments, and expend management and employee resources in defending a meritless suit, the issuers' own investors suffer. Investors always are the ultimate losers when extortionate "settlements" are extracted from issuers.

> The 1995 Reform Act attempts to deal with these perceived abuses by adopting the following procedural reforms:

> Requiring the named class plaintiff to file a statement containing information designed to disclose whether he is really a tool of the attorney for the plaintiff class;

> Prohibiting broker-dealers from taking fees for assisting attorneys in identifying class plaintiffs;

Requiring the court to appoint as lead plaintiff the member of the plaintiff class that "has the largest financial interest in the relief sought by the class." This "lead plaintiff," which would normally be a financial institution, would then be responsible for the selection of counsel to represent the class;

Barring discovery by plaintiff's attorneys while a motion to dismiss is pending;

Requiring full disclosure of the terms of any proposed settlement;

Restricting attorney's fees to "a reasonable percentage of the damages * * * actually paid to the class"; and

Requiring the losing party to pay the attorney's fees of the winning party where the losing party is found to have violated the pleading requirements of Rule 11 of the Federal Rules of Civil Procedure, and authorizing the court to require the plaintiffs *and/or their attorneys* to post security for the payment of such expenses.

IN RE SILICON GRAPHICS INC. SECURITIES LITIGATION

183 F.3d 970 (9th Cir.1999).

SNEED, CIRCUIT JUDGE:

This case requires us to interpret the Private Securities Litigation Reform Act of 1995 ("PSLRA"). Congress enacted the PSLRA to deter opportunistic private plaintiffs from filing abusive securities fraud claims, in part, by raising the pleading standards for private securities fraud plaintiffs. In doing so, Congress generated a flood of litigation and commentary regarding the proper interpretation of these standards. Much of this litigation deals specifically with the pleading issue now before us, i.e., what must a plaintiff allege in order to satisfy the requirement that he state facts giving rise to a "strong inference" of the required state of mind? See 15 U.S.C. § 78u–4(b)(2) (requiring that the complaint "state with particularity facts giving rise to a strong inference that the defendant acted with the required state of mind"). * * *

We hold that a private securities plaintiff proceeding under the PSLRA must plead, in great detail, facts that constitute strong circumstantial evidence of deliberately reckless or conscious misconduct. Our holding rests, in part, on our conclusion that Congress intended to elevate the pleading requirement above the Second Circuit standard requiring plaintiffs merely to provide facts showing simple recklessness or a motive to commit fraud and opportunity to do so. We hold that although facts showing mere recklessness or a motive to commit fraud and opportunity to do so may provide some reasonable inference of intent, they are not sufficient to establish a strong inference of deliberate recklessness. In order to show a strong inference of deliberate recklessness, plaintiffs must state facts that come closer to demonstrating intent, as opposed to mere motive and opportunity. Accordingly, we hold that particular facts giving rise to a strong inference of deliberate recklessness, at a minimum, is required to satisfy the heightened pleading standard under the PSLRA. We think that our holding represents the best way to reconcile Congress' express adoption of the Second Circuit's so-called "strong inference standard" with its express refusal to codify that circuit's case law interpreting the standard. However, we are mindful that not all courts share our view.* * *

Generally, the district courts have taken three different approaches: (1) apply the Second Circuit standard requiring plaintiffs to plead mere motive and opportunity or an inference of recklessness; (2) apply a heightened Second Circuit standard rejecting motive and opportunity, but accepting an inference of recklessness; or (3) reject the Second Circuit standard and accept only an inference of conscious conduct.

We embrace the approach requiring a strong inference of deliberate recklessness which lies between the second and third approaches. We do this because we believe that Congress intended to bar those complaints that fail to raise a strong inference of intent or deliberateness. The "deliberate recklessness" standard best serves the PSLRA's purpose. The PSLRA text and legislative history support our conclusion.

To determine the proper pleading standard under the PSLRA, we turn first to the text of the statute. If the language is plain and its meaning clear, that is the end of our inquiry.

The PSLRA provides, in pertinent part:

(b) Requirements for securities fraud actions . . . (2) Required state of mind

In any private action arising under this chapter in which the plaintiff may recover money damages only on proof that the defendant acted with a particular state of mind, the complaint shall, with respect to each act or omission alleged to violate this chapter, *state with particularity facts giving rise to a strong inference that the defendant acted with the required state of mind.*

15 U.S.C. § 78u–4(b)(2). Under this provision, the mental state required for securities fraud liability is distinct from the level of pleading required to infer that mental state. Therefore, we must make two separate determinations: (1) what is the required state of mind; and (2) what constitutes a strong inference of that state of mind.

The "required state of mind" in § 78u–4(b)(2) refers to the scienter requirement applicable to the underlying securities fraud claim brought by the plaintiff. * * *

The Supreme Court has defined "scienter" in the context of § 10(b) as a "mental state embracing intent to deceive, manipulate, or defraud." See Ernst & Ernst v. Hochfelder, 425 U.S. 185, 193–94 n. 12, 96 S.Ct. 1375, 1381 n. 12, 47 L.Ed.2d 668 (1976). In *Hochfelder*, the Supreme Court addressed the question of whether a civil action for damages under § 10(b) would lie for negligent conduct. It decided that no conduct—

negligent or otherwise—is actionable under § 10(b) unless plaintiffs make a showing of "scienter," i.e., "intent to deceive, manipulate, or defraud." The Supreme Court reasoned that § 10(b) makes unlawful the use of "any manipulative or deceptive device or contrivance" in contravention of SEC Rules. As a result, the Court held that "[t]he words 'manipulative and deceptive' used in conjunction with 'device or contrivance' strongly suggest that § 10(b) was intended to proscribe *knowing or intentional misconduct*."

Although the Supreme Court concluded that § 10(b) was intended to proscribe "knowing" or "intentional" conduct as opposed to negligent conduct, it noted that "[i]n certain areas of the law recklessness is considered to be a form of intentional conduct for purposes of imposing liability for some act." Accordingly, the Supreme Court left open the question of whether, in some circumstances, "reckless behavior is sufficient for civil liability under § 10(b) and Rule 10b–5."

After *Hochfelder*, but long before enactment of the PSLRA, we answered that question in the affirmative, holding that "Congress intended the ambit of § 10(b) to reach a broad category of behavior, including knowing or reckless conduct." Nelson v. Serwold, 576 F.2d 1332, 1337 (9th Cir.1978). In *Nelson*, we declined to define recklessness, but our opinion indicates that we viewed it as a form of intentional, not merely negligent, conduct. We expressly acknowledged the Supreme Court's words in *Hochfelder* that "[i]n certain areas of the law recklessness is considered to be a form of intentional conduct for purposes of imposing liability for some act." Moreover, we stated that "the evidence supports a finding of recklessness, or some degree of intent not sufficiently aggravated to be characterized as 'deliberate and cold-blooded.' " Thus, we apparently followed the Supreme Court's guidance in *Hochfelder* that reckless behavior in the § 10(b) context is merely a lesser form of intentional conduct.

In Hollinger v. Titan Capital Corp., 914 F.2d 1564 (9th Cir.1990) (en banc), we again held that "recklessness satisfies the element of scienter in a civil action for damages under § 10(b) and Rule 10b–5." 914 F.2d at 1568–69. This time, we explicitly defined recklessness:

> Today we adopt the standard of recklessness articulated by the Seventh Circuit in Sundstrand Corp. v. Sun Chem. Corp., 553 F.2d 1033, 1044–45 (7th Cir.), cert. denied, 434 U.S. 875, 98 S.Ct. 224, 54 L.Ed.2d 155 (1977) . . . [R]eckless conduct may be defined as a highly unreasonable omission, involving not merely simple, or even inexcusable negligence, but an extreme departure from the standards of ordinary care, and which presents a danger of misleading buyers or sellers that is either known to the defendant or is so obvious that the actor must have been aware of it.

Our definition of recklessness, as taken from *Sundstrand*, strongly suggests that we continued to view it as a form of intentional or knowing misconduct. We used the words "known" and "must have been aware," which suggest consciousness or deliberateness. Indeed, we expressly acknowledged our own prior statement that "recklessness is a form of intent rather than a greater degree of negligence," and the Supreme Court's statement that recklessness in the context of § 10(b) is a form of intentional conduct.

These cases indicate that recklessness only satisfies scienter under § 10(b) to the extent that it reflects some degree of intentional or conscious misconduct. To repeat, recklessness in the § 10(b) context is, in the words of the Supreme Court, a form of intentional conduct. For this reason, we read the PSLRA language that the particular facts must give rise to a "strong inference ... [of] the required state of mind" to mean that the evidence must create a strong inference of, at a minimum, "deliberate recklessness."

We now turn to our second inquiry, i.e., what constitutes a strong inference of deliberate recklessness?

Again, we begin with the language of the statute because if the language is clear, we need inquire no further. In this case, the statute is silent as to the central issue: the text of the PSLRA does not state whether motive and opportunity or circumstantial evidence of simple recklessness are sufficient to raise a "strong inference" of deliberate recklessness. The plain text of the PSLRA leaves it open for us to consider circumstantial evidence of recklessness and motive and opportunity as evidence of deliberate recklessness. However, it does not indicate whether they alone are enough to establish a "strong inference" of deliberate recklessness. In the absence of a clear command in the text, we turn to the legislative history for guidance.

When examining the legislative history, we first look to the conference report because, apart from the statute itself, it is the most reliable evidence of congressional intent. In this case, the conference report suggests both that Congress generally intended to raise the pleading standards to eliminate abusive securities litigation and that it specifically intended to raise the pleading standard above that in the Second Circuit.

It is clear from this conference report that Congress sought to reduce the volume of abusive federal securities litigation by erecting procedural barriers to prevent plaintiffs from asserting baseless securities fraud claims. In a joint statement, managers from the House and Senate declared that "Congress has been prompted by significant evidence of abuse in private securities lawsuits to enact reforms to protect investors and maintain confidence in our capital markets." H.R. CONF. REP. 104–369, at 31. The managers observed that plaintiffs routinely were filing lawsuits "against issuers of securities and others whenever there [was] a significant change in an issuer's stock price, without regard to any underlying culpability of the issuer, and with only faint hope that the discovery process might lead eventually to some plausible cause of action[.]" Id. They recognized that plaintiffs, by targeting "deep pocket defendants," could misuse the discovery process "to impose costs so burdensome that it [was] often economical for the victimized party to settle[.]" Id. In general, the conference report makes it clear that Congress designed the PSLRA to deter non-meritorious lawsuits by creating procedural barriers such as heightened pleading standards.

It is also clear from the legislative history that Congress sought more specifically to raise the pleading standard above that in the Second Circuit. * * *

In sum, the legislative history supports our conclusion that the PSLRA pleading standard is higher than the standard of the Second Circuit. We find that because the joint committee expressly rejected the "motive and opportunity" and "recklessness" tests when raising the standard, Congress must have intended a standard that lies beyond the Second Circuit standard. Had Congress merely sought to adopt the Second Circuit standard, it easily could have done so. It did not do so. Instead, Congress adopted a standard more stringent than the Second Circuit standard. It follows that plaintiffs proceeding under the PSLRA can no longer aver intent in general terms of mere "motive and opportunity" or "recklessness," but rather, must state specific facts indicating no less than a degree of recklessness that strongly suggests actual intent. Thus, we agree with the district court that the PSLRA requires plaintiffs to plead, at a minimum, particular facts giving rise to a strong inference of deliberate or conscious recklessness. We believe that this "deliberate recklessness" standard best reconciles Congress' adoption of the Second Circuit's so-called "strong inference standard" with its express refusal to codify that circuit's two-prong "motive and opportunity" and "recklessness" test.

Having determined that the PSLRA requires plaintiffs to plead particular facts giving rise to a strong inference of deliberate recklessness, we must determine whether the plaintiffs in this case have satisfied that requirement.

[The court went on to affirm the district court's determination that the pleading requirements had not been satisfied]

Concurrence and Dissent by Judge Browning is omitted.

Notes

1. In response to concerns that plaintiffs' lawyers were filing securities class actions against publicly-traded corporations under state law in state courts to avoid the restrictions contained in the 1995 Litigation Reform Act, Congress passed the Securities Litigation Uniform Standards Act, which was signed into law on November 3, 1998. The provisions of the 1998 amendments are found in § 16 of the Securities Act of 1933 and § 28(f) of the Securities Exchange Act of 1934. Under the 1998 amendments, no class action based on the statutory or common law of any state, which alleges untrue statements or omissions, or manipulation or deception, with respect to a "covered security," may be brought in any court, state or federal. A "covered security" is defined

to include any security listed on the New York or American Stock Exchange or the NASDAQ National Market System, or any security issued by a registered investment company. Any class action with respect to a "covered security" which is brought in a state court may be removed to federal court. The 1998 amendments preempting state court actions do not apply to (a) class actions with 50 or fewer members, (b) shareholders' derivative actions, (c) actions based on the law of the state in which the issuer is incorporated (known as the "Delaware carve out"), or (d) actions brought by a state or one of its subdivisions or instrumentalities.

2.   The Private Securities Litigation Reform Act has had little success in curbing the number of suits brought under the federal securities laws. The number of securities related lawsuits was 483 in 2001, double that of the year before. The average settlement cost of securities related lawsuits in 2001 was $17 million up from $14 million in prior years. Henny Sender, "Securities Suits Hit Record Total of 483 in 2001," Wall St. J., June 10, 2002., at C5.

3.   The PSLRA actually had the effect of worsening abusive litigation by having the courts appoint, as lead plaintiff in securities class actions, the shareholder with the largest financial interest in the claim. This inevitably meant that an institutional investor, rather than a professional plaintiff holding only a few shares, would be appointed as lead plaintiff. Most institutions had little interest in pursuing litigation over a failed investment or management error. That was not true, however, for the state and union pension funds, and they soon were themselves professional plaintiffs in securities class action lawsuits. These pension funds were investing in nearly every stock in the market, allowing them to claim injury whenever a stock dropped in price. Those institutions perceived litigation as a means of improving their performance results and full disclosure under the federal securities laws as an insurance program that protected them from market loss. With their large holdings, the pension funds were given lead plaintiff status in numerous cases. Soon, these union retirement programs were demanding larger and larger settlements. They were also offering bounties for recoveries from the personal funds of executives.

The pension funds were even using the threat of litigation to pursue their own political agenda. During the 2004 presidential election, the Sinclair Broadcast Group was planning to air a documentary critical of candidate John Kerry's anti-war activities after he returned from service in Viet Nam. That broadcast was pulled after a class action lawyer threatened a shareholder class action lawsuit if the program was broadcast. The lawyer claimed that the broadcast would result in a loss of revenues to the company because some advertisers might pull their accounts. The New York Comptroller, Alan Hevesi, a Democrat, then made a similar threat of a class action suit on behalf of the state's pension funds. Another tactic has been to force the election of board nominees through class action litigation. Dynegy Inc. thus agreed, in addition to paying $468 million, to elect two individuals to its board that were selected by the University of California, the lead plaintiff in class action litigation challenging Dynegy's securities problems. Cendant Corp. agreed to elect a majority of outside directors to its board in a settlement with Calpers.

The PSLRA did have some beneficial effects. In June 2005 Seymour M. Lazar, a long time professional plaintiff used by the law firm of Milberg Weiss Bershad & Schuman, was indicted for activities that PSLRA had sought to stop. The government charged that Lazar had accepted $2.4 million in kick backs from the law firm over a twenty year period as payment for acting as the firm's dummy plaintiff in over fifty class action lawsuits.

4. *Closing a Loophole—The Securities Litigation Uniform Standards Act.* Following the adoption of PSLRA, plaintiffs' lawyers figured that they could avoid many of its provisions by suing in state court and under state law. Private actions under sections 11 and 12 of the Securities Act of 1933 can be brought in either federal or state court. 1933 Act § 22(a), 15 U.S.C.A. § 77v(a). Jurisdiction over 1934 Act claims is exclusively federal. 1934 Act § 27, 15 U.S.C.A. § 78aa. Thus, Rule 10b–5 suits cannot be brought in state court. However, state securities law and common law fraud could provide alternative forums for class action plaintiffs trying to avoid the provisions of the 1995 Reform Act. Congress largely eliminated these alternatives in the Securities Litigation Uniform Standards Act of 1998 (SLUSA), (Pub. Law No. 105–353, 112 Stat. 3227 (105th Cong.–2d Sess. November 3, 1998) (S 1260) which mandates that most class actions, with more than fifty class members, involving publicly traded securities be brought in federal court. 1934 Act § 28(f), 15 U.S.C.A. § 78bb(f). SLUSA applies only to class actions (not derivative actions) involving more than fifty class members. There also is a "carve-out" from SLUSA's preemption for cases based on fiduciary duties (as opposed to securities fraud). SLUSA is discussed in the *Dabit* case, page 718 above.

NOTE ON SOFT INFORMATION

PSLRA also addressed actions relating to "soft information" (1934 Act § 21E (safe harbor for forward looking statement), which acts as encouragement for companies to make financial projections. *See also* the excerpt from Virginia Bankshares v. Sandberg that follows below.

As part of its management and discussion and analysis (MD&A) disclosure requirements, the SEC inn Item 303 of Reg. S–K (17 C.F.R. § 229.303) requires, among other things, at least quarterly disclosure as follows:

(3) Results of operations.

(i) Describe any unusual or infrequent events or transactions or any significant economic changes that materially affected the amount of reported income from continuing operations and, in each case, indicate the extent to which income was so affected. In addition, describe any other significant components of revenues or expenses that, in the registrant's judgment, should be described in order to understand the registrant's results of operations.

(ii) Describe any known trends or uncertainties that have had or that the registrant reasonably expects will have a material favorable or unfavorable impact on net sales or revenues or income from continuing operations. If the registrant knows of events that will cause a material change in the relationship between costs and revenues (such as known future increases in costs of labor or materials or price increases or inventory adjustments), the change in the relationship shall be disclosed.

(emphasis added).

If the SEC requires an issuer to make qualitative or evaluative statements, the question arises whether, and under what circumstances, a statement of opinion can be considered a materially misleading statement of fact.

VIRGINIA BANKSHARES v. SANDBERG
501 U.S. 1083, 111 S.Ct. 2749, 115 L.Ed.2d 929 (1991).

JUSTICE SOUTER delivered the opinion of the Court.

* * * The question[ ] before us [is] whether a statement couched in conclusory or qualitative terms purporting to explain directors' reasons for recommending certain corporate action can be materially misleading within the meaning of Rule 14a–9 * * *. We hold that knowingly false statements of reasons may be actionable even though conclusory in form * * *.

In December 1986, First American Bankshares, Inc., (FABI), a bank holding company, began a "freeze-out" merger, in which the First American Bank of Virginia (Bank) eventually merged into Virginia Bankshares, Inc., (VBI), a wholly owned subsidiary of FABI. VBI owned 85% of the Bank's shares, the remaining 15% being in the hands of some 2,000 minority shareholders. FABI hired the investment banking firm of Keefe, Bruyette & Woods (KBW) to give an opinion on the appropriate price for shares of the minority holders, who would lose their interests in the Bank as a result of the merger. Based on market quotations and unverified information from FABI, KBW gave the Bank's executive committee an opinion that $42 a share would be a fair price for the minority stock. The executive committee approved the merger proposal at that price, and the full board followed suit.

Although Virginia law required only that such a merger proposal be submitted to a vote at a shareholders' meeting, and that the meeting be preceded by circulation of a statement of information to the shareholders, the directors nevertheless solicited proxies for voting on the proposal at the annual meeting set forth April 21, 1987. In their solicitation, the directors urged the proposal's adoption and stated they had approved the plan because of its opportunity for the minority shareholders to achieve a "high" value, which they elsewhere described as a "fair" price, for their stock.

Although most minority shareholders gave the proxies requested, respondent Sandberg did not, and after approval of the merger she sought damages in the United States District Court for the Eastern District of Virginia from VBI, FABI, and the directors of the Bank.

We consider first the actionability per se of statements of reasons, opinion or belief. Because such a statement by definition purports to express what is consciously on the speaker's mind, we interpret the jury verdict as finding that the directors' statements of belief and opinion were made with knowledge that the directors did not hold the beliefs or opinions expressed, and we confine our discussion to statements so made. That such statements may be materially significant raises no serious question. The meaning of the materiality requirement for liability under § 14(a) was discussed at some length in TSC Industries, Inc. v. Northway, Inc., where we held a fact to be material "if there is a substantial likelihood that a reasonable shareholder would consider it important in deciding how to vote." We think there is no room to deny that a statement of belief by corporate directors about a recommended course of action, or an explanation of their reasons for recommending it, can take on just that importance. Shareholders know that directors usually have knowledge and expertness far exceeding the normal investor's resources, and the directors' perceived superiority is magnified even further by the common knowledge that state law customarily obliges them to exercise their judgment in the shareholders' interest. Naturally, then, the share owner faced with a proxy request will think it important to know the directors' beliefs about the course they recommend, and their specific reasons for urging the stockholders to embrace it.

But, assuming materiality, the question remains whether statements of reasons, opinions, or beliefs are statements "with respect to * * * material fact[s]" so as to fall within the strictures of the Rule. Petitioners argue that we would invite wasteful litigation of amorphous issues outside the readily provable realm of fact if we were to recognize liability here on proof that the directors did not recommend the merger for the stated reason, and they cite the authority of Blue Chip Stamps v. Manor Drug Stores in urging us to recognize sound policy grounds for placing such statements outside the scope of the Rule. * * *

Attacks on the truth of directors' statements of reasons or belief, however, need carry no such threats. Such statements are factual in two senses: as statements that the directors do act for the reasons given or hold the belief stated and as statements about the subject matter of the reason or belief expressed. In neither sense does the proof or disproof of such statements implicate the concerns expressed in Blue Chip Stamps. The root of those concerns was a plaintiff's capacity to manufacture claims of hypothetical action, unconstrained by independent evidence. Reasons for directors' recommendations or statements of belief are, in contrast, characteristically matters of corporate record subject to documentation, to be supported or attacked by evidence of historical fact outside a plaintiff's control. Such evidence would include not only corporate minutes and other statements of the directors themselves, but circumstantial evidence bearing on the facts that would reasonably underlie the reasons claimed and the honesty of any statement that those reasons are the basis for a recommendation or other action, a point that becomes especially clear when the reasons or beliefs go to valuations in dollars and cents.

It is no answer to argue, as petitioners do, that the quoted statement on which liability was predicated did not express a reason in dollars and cents, but focused instead on the "indefinite and unverifiable" term, "high" value, much like the similar claim that the merger's terms were "fair" to shareholders. The objection ignores the fact that such conclusory terms in a commercial context are reasonably understood to rest on a factual basis that justifies them as accurate, the absence of which renders them misleading. Provable facts either furnish good reasons to make a conclusory commercial judgment, or they count against it, and expressions of such judgments can be uttered with knowledge of truth or falsity just like more definite statements, and defended or attacked through the orthodox evidentiary process that either substantiates their underlying justifications or tends to disprove their existence. * * * In this case, whether $42 was "high," and the proposal "fair" to the minority share-holders depended on whether provable facts about the Bank's assets, and about actual and potential levels of operation, substantiated a value that was above, below, or more or less at the $42 figure, when assessed in accordance with recognized methods of valuation.

* * * There was, indeed, evidence of a "going concern" value for the Bank in excess of $60 per share of common stock, another fact never disclosed. However conclusory the directors' statement may have been, then, it was open to attack by garden-variety evidence, subject neither to a plaintiff's control nor ready manufacture, and there was no undue risk of open-ended liability or uncontrollable litigation in allowing respondents the opportunity for recovery on the allegation that it was misleading to call $42 "high." * * *

Under § 14(a), then, a plaintiff is permitted to prove a specific statement of reason knowingly false or misleadingly incomplete, even when stated in conclusory terms. * * *

The question arises, then, whether disbelief, or undisclosed belief or motivation, standing alone, should be a sufficient basis to sustain an action under § 14(a), absent proof by the sort of objective evidence described above that the statement also expressly or impliedly asserted something false or misleading about its subject matter. We think that proof of mere disbelief or belief undisclosed should not suffice for liability under § 14(a), and if nothing more had been required or proven in this case we would reverse for that reason. * * *

* * * [T]o recognize liability on mere disbelief or undisclosed motive without any demonstration that the proxy statement was false or misleading about its subject would authorize § 14(a) litigation confined solely to what one skeptical court spoke of as the "impurities" of a director's "unclean heart." This, we think, would cross the line that *Blue Chip Stamps* sought to draw. * * *

Justice Scalia, concurring in part and concurring in the judgment.

As I understand the Court's opinion, the statement "In the opinion of the Directors, this is a high value for the shares" would produce liability if in fact it was not a high value and the Directors knew that. It would not produce liability if in fact it was not a high value but the Directors honestly believed otherwise. The statement "The Directors voted to accept the proposal because they believe it offers a high value" would not produce liability if in fact the Directors' genuine motive was quite different—would produce liability if the proposal in fact did not offer a high value and the Directors knew that.

I agree with all of this. However, not every sentence that has the word "opinion" in it, or that refers to motivation for Directors' actions, leads us into this psychic thicket. Sometimes such a sentence actually represents facts as facts rather than opinions—and in that event no more need be done than apply the normal rules for § 14(a) liability. I think that is the situation here. In my view, the statement at issue in this case is most fairly read as affirming separately both the fact of the Directors' opinion and the accuracy of the facts upon which the opinion was assertedly based.

* * *

SECTION 11.   PROJECTIONS

GUIDES FOR DISCLOSURE OF PROJECTIONS

Sec. Act Rel. No. 5992 (Nov. 7, 1978).

* * * The Commission has issued a statement indicating that it encourages certain issuers of securities to publish projected financial information in filings with the Commission or otherwise. The Commission also has authorized publication of Guides 62 and 5, "Disclosure of Projections of Future Economic Performance." The Guides are not Commission rules nor do they bear the Commission's official approval; they represent practices followed by the Division of Corporation Finance in administering the disclosure requirements of the Securities Act and the Exchange Act. * * *

The issue of projections, economic forecasts, and other forward-looking information has been under active consideration by the Commission for several years.

On November 1, 1972, the Commission announced a public rulemaking proceeding relating to the use, both in Commission filings and otherwise, of projections by issuers whose securities are publicly traded. These hearings were ordered by the Commission for the purpose of gathering information relevant to a reassessment of its policies relating to disclosure of projected sales and earnings.

Information gathered at the hearings, held from November 10 to December 12, 1972, reinforced the Commission's observation that management's assessment of a company's future performance is of importance to investors, that such assessment should be comprehensible in light of the assumptions made and should be available, if at all, on an equitable basis to all investors. The hearings also revealed widespread dissatisfaction with the absence of guidelines or standards that issuers, financial analysts, or investors can rely on in issuing or interpreting projections.

On February 2, 1973, the Commission released a "Statement by the Commission on the Disclosure of Projections of Future Economic Performance." In this statement, the Commission determined that on the basis of the information obtained through the hearings, staff recommendations, and its experience in administering the federal securities laws, changes in its long standing policy generally not to permit the inclusion of projections in registration statements and reports filed with the Commission would assist in the protection of investors and would be in the public interest. * * *

On April 25, 1975, the Commission published a series of rule and form proposals relating to projections of future economic performance. These proposals would have established an elaborate disclosure system for companies choosing to make public projections.

Approximately 420 letters of comment were received on these proposals. Although the majority of commentators agreed that projection information is significant, virtually all of them opposed the proposed system because they felt that the proposals would inhibit rather than foster projection communications between management and the investment community. Due to the important legal, disclosure policy, and technical issues raised by the commentators, the Commission on April 23, 1976, determined to withdraw all but one of the proposed rule and form changes regarding projections.

The Commission did, however, express its general views in the April 1976 release on the inclusion of projections in Commission filings, and authorized the publication for comment of proposed guides for the disclosure of projections in Securities Act registration statements and Exchange Act reports.

In its statement of general views, the Commission indicated that it would not object to disclosure in filings with the Commission of projections which are made in good faith and have a reasonable basis, provided that they are presented in an appropriate format and accompanied by information adequate for investors to make their own judgments.* * *

The Commission's disclosure policy on projections and other items of soft information was among the subjects considered by the Advisory Committee on Corporate Disclosure. In its final report, issued November 3, 1977, the Advisory Committee made several recommendations for significant changes in that policy. Generally, the Committee recommended that the Commission issue a public statement encouraging companies voluntarily to disclose management projections in their filings with the Commission and elsewhere.* * *

The Commission concurs in the Advisory Committee's recommendation and findings. * * * Accordingly, in light of the significance attached to projection information and the prevalence of projections in the corporate and investment community, the Commission has determined to follow the recommendation of the Advisory Committee and wishes to encourage companies to disclose management projections both in their filings with the Commission and in general. In order to further encourage such disclosure, the Commission has, in a separate release issued today, proposed for comment a safe-harbor rule for projection information whether or not included in Commission filings. The Commission also has determined to authorize publication of revised staff guides to assist implementation of the Advisory Committee's recommendation. * * *

In the integrated disclosure system adopted by the Commission in March 1982, the staff views set forth in Guide 62 were restated as views of the Commission and incorporated in Item 10 of Regulation S–K. At the same time, the Commission also announced a policy encouraging registrants to include in their 1933 and 1934 Act filings the ratings given to their debt securities by "nationally recognized statistical rating organizations," such as Moody's and Standard & Poor's. This policy is also set forth in Item 10 of Regulation S–K.

SAFE HARBOR RULE FOR PROJECTIONS

Sec. Act Rel. No. 6084 (June 25, 1979).

* * * The Securities and Exchange Commission today adopted a rule designed to provide a safe harbor from the applicable liability provisions of the federal securities laws for statements relating to or containing (1) projections of revenues, income (loss), earnings (loss) per share or other financial items, such as capital expenditures, dividends, or capital structure, (2) management plans and objectives for future company operations, and (3) future economic performance included in management's discussion and analysis of the summary of earnings or quarterly income statements. The rule is based upon the alternatives that were proposed in Securities Act Release No. 5993 (November 7, 1978). The rule is adopted in furtherance of the Commission's goal of encouraging the disclosure of projections and other items of forward-looking information. In a related action, the Commission is withdrawing the reference in note (a) to Rule 14a–9 to prediction of dividends as a possible example of a false or misleading statement. This release contains a brief discussion of the background of the proposed rules, the views of the commentators, and the provisions of the rule as adopted. * * *

The Commission's proposed rule placed the burden of proof on the defendant to prove that a projection was prepared with a reasonable basis and was disclosed in good faith. The proposed rule reflected the Commission's concern as to the difficulties faced by plaintiffs since the facts are in the exclusive possession of the defendants.

The Advisory Committee rule would place the burden of proof on the plaintiff, along the lines of the Commission's existing safe harbor rules for replacement cost information and oil and gas reserve disclosures under Regulation S–X. * * *

In view of the Commission's overall goal of encouraging projection disclosure and in light of the factors cited by the commentators, the Commission has determined to adopt the standard recommended by the Advisory Committee. * * *

Both the Commission's and the Advisory Committee's proposed rules require that reasonably based projections be disclosed in good faith. Several commentators believed that no objective standard exists for determining whether the "good faith" portion of the requirement has been met and that the term was ambiguous at best. Some commentators did not see how a reasonably based projection could be prepared and disclosed other than in good faith, and suggested that if a projection were found to have been prepared and disclosed with a reasonable basis, good faith disclosure is implicit.

On balance, the Commission believes that in light of the experimental nature of its program to encourage projection disclosure and the possibility of undue reliance being placed on projections, the use of a good faith standard in the rule is appropriate. The Commission also notes that there is ample precedent for the concept of good faith in other provisions of the federal securities laws.

The Commission's proposed rule related only to projections of revenues, income (loss), earnings (loss) per share or other financial items. The Advisory Committee's proposed rule refers generally to statements of "management projection[s] of future company economic performance" or of "management plans and objectives for future company operations," and corresponds with that Committee's recommendation that disclosure of other types of forward-looking information beyond those items customarily projected also should be encouraged. * * *

[T]he rule adopted today expands the items in the proposed rule to cover projections of other financial items such as capital expenditures and financing, dividends, and capital structure, statements of management plans and objectives for future company operations, and future economic performance included in management's discussion and analysis of the summary of earnings or quarterly income statements. The rule has been revised to refer specifically to these other items of forward-looking information in light of the commentators' suggestions that the broader coverage of the Advisory Committee rule be made explicit.

In Release 33–5992, the Commission emphasized the significance of disclosure of the assumptions that underlie forward-looking statements. As indicated in that release and Guide 62, disclosure of assumptions is believed to be an important factor in facilitating investors' ability to comprehend and evaluate these statements.

While the Commission has determined to follow the Advisory Committee's recommendation that disclosure of assumptions not be mandated under all circumstances, it wishes to reemphasize its position on the significance of assumption disclosure. Under certain circumstances the disclosure of underlying assumptions may be material to an understanding of the projected results. The Commission also believes that the key assumptions underlying a forward looking statement are of such significance that their disclosure may be necessary in order for such statements to meet the reasonable basis and good faith standards embodied in the rule. Because of the potential importance of assumptions to investor understanding and in order to encourage their disclosure, the rule as adopted indicates specifically that disclosed assumptions also are within its scope.* * *

As indicated in Release 33–5992, the Commission reminded issuers of their responsibility to make full and prompt disclosure of material facts, both favorable and unfavorable, where management knows or has reason to know that its earlier statements no longer have a reasonable basis. With respect to forward-looking statements of material facts made in relation to specific transactions or events (such as proxy solicitations, tender offers, and purchases and sales of securities), there is an obligation to correct such statements prior to consummation of the transaction where they become false or misleading by reason of subsequent events which render material assumptions underlying such statements invalid. Similarly, there is a duty to correct where it is discovered prior to consummation of a transaction that the underlying assumptions were false or misleading from the outset.

Moreover, the Commission believes that, depending on the circumstances, there is a duty to correct statements made in any filing, whether or not the filing is related to a specified transaction or event, if the statements either have become inaccurate by virtue of subsequent events, or are later discovered to have been false and misleading from the outset, and the issuer knows or should know that persons are continuing to rely on all or any material portion of the statements.

This duty will vary according to the facts and circumstances of individual cases. For example, the length of time between the making of the statement and the occurrence of the subsequent event, as well as the magnitude of the deviation, may have a bearing upon whether a statement has become materially misleading. * * *

[The new rule was adopted as Rule 175 under the Securities Act of 1933. A substantially identical rule was simultaneously adopted as Rule 3b–6 under the Securities Exchange Act of 1934.]

NOTES

1. If a company publishes a projection, and subsequently changes its estimates, does it have a duty to update or correct its earlier projection? In Elkind v. Liggett & Myers, Inc., 635 F.2d 156 (2d Cir.1980), the court was faced with an allegation by shareholders that "Liggett, by virtue of its alleged cultivation of favorable reports and forecasts by analysts, incurred an obligation to disclose its less optimistic internal predictions."

We have no doubt that a company may so involve itself in the preparation of reports and projections by outsiders as to assume a duty to correct material errors in those projections. This may occur when officials of the company have by their activity, made an implied representation that the information they have reviewed is true or at least in accordance with the company's views.

After reviewing the facts of this case, however, we find no reason to reverse as clearly erroneous the district court's finding that Liggett did not place its imprimatur, expressly or impliedly, on the analysts' projections. The company did examine and comment on a number of reports, but its policy was to refrain from comment on earnings forecasts. Testimony at trial indicated that the analysts knew they were not being made privy to the company's internal projections. While the evidence leaves little doubt that Liggett made suggestions as to factual and descriptive matters in a number of the reports it reviewed, the record does not compel the conclusion that this conduct carried a suggestion that the analysts' projections were consistent with Liggett's internal estimates. Nor has plaintiff demonstrated that Liggett left uncorrected any *factual* statements which it knew or believed to be erroneous. Thus, Liggett assumed no duty to disclose its own forecasts or to warn the analysts and the public that their optimistic view was not shared by the company.

While we find no liability for non-disclosure in this aspect of the present case, it bears noting that corporate pre-release review of the reports of analysts is a risky activity, fraught with danger. Management must navigate carefully between the "Scylla" of misleading stockholders and the public by implied approval of reviewed analyses and the "Charybdis" of tipping material inside information by correcting statements which it knows to be erroneous. A company which undertakes to correct errors in reports presented to it for review may find itself forced to choose between raising no objection to a statement which, because it is contradicted by internal information, may be misleading and making that information public at a time when corporate interests would best be served by confidentiality.

2. In Backman v. Polaroid Corp., 910 F.2d 10, 16–17 (1st Cir.1990) the court made the following observations:

> Obviously, if a disclosure is in fact misleading when made, and the speaker thereafter learns of this, there is a duty to correct it. In Greenfield v. Heublein, Inc., 742 F.2d 751, 758 (3d Cir.1984), cited by the panel, the court called for disclosure if a prior disclosure "becomes materially misleading in light of subsequent events," a quite different duty. We may agree that, in special circumstances, a statement, correct at the time, may have a forward intent and connotation upon which parties may be expected to rely. If this is a clear meaning, and there is a change, correction, more exactly, further disclosure, may be called for. The amici are concerned that this is a principle with grave dangers of abuse. Fear that statements of historical fact might be claimed to fall within it, could inhibit disclosures altogether. * * * After indicating reluctance to accept plaintiffs' contention that the Third Quarter Report was misleading when made, the panel opinion, in holding that it could be found misleading in light of later developments, said as follows.

> > [E]ven if the optimistic Third Quarter Report was not misleading at the time of its issuance, there is sufficient evidence to support a jury's determination that the report's relatively brief mention of Polavision difficulties became misleading in light of the subsequent information acquired by Polaroid indicating the seriousness of Polavision's problems. This subsequent information included ... Polaroid's decision to ... stop Polavision production by its Austrian manufacturer, Eumig, and its instruction to its Austrian supplier to keep this production cutback secret. We feel that a reasonable jury could conclude that this subsequent information rendered the Third Quarter Report's brief mention of Polavision expenses misleading, triggering a duty to disclose on the part of Polaroid.

IN RE DONALD J. TRUMP

7 F.3d 357 (3d Cir.1993).

Bᴇᴄᴋᴇʀ, Cɪʀᴄᴜɪᴛ Jᴜᴅɢᴇ:

* * * The district court applied what has come to be known as the "bespeaks caution" doctrine. In so doing it followed the lead of a number of courts of appeals which have dismissed securities fraud claims under Rule 12(b)(6) because cautionary language in the offering document negated the materiality of an alleged misrepresentation or omission. We are persuaded by the ratio decidendi of these cases and will apply bespeaks caution to the facts before us.

The application of bespeaks caution depends on the specific text of the offering document or other communication at issue, i.e., courts must assess the communication on a case-by-case basis. Nevertheless, we can state as a general matter that, when an offering document's forecasts, opinions or projections are accompanied by meaningful cautionary statements, the forward-looking statements will not form the basis for a securities fraud claim if those statements did not affect the "total mix" of information the document provided investors. In other words, cautionary language, if sufficient, renders the alleged omissions or misrepresentations immaterial as a matter of law.

The bespeaks caution doctrine is, as an analytical matter, equally applicable to allegations of both affirmative misrepresentations and omissions concerning soft information. Whether the plaintiffs allege a document contains an affirmative prediction/opinion which is misleading or fails to include a forecast or prediction which failure is misleading, the cautionary statements included in the document may render the challenged predictive statements or opinions immaterial as a matter of law. Of course, a vague or blanket (boilerplate) disclaimer which merely warns the reader that the investment has risks will ordinarily be inadequate to prevent misinformation. To suffice, the cautionary statements must be substantive and tailored to the specific future projections, estimates or opinions in the prospectus which the plaintiffs challenge.

Because of the abundant and meaningful cautionary language contained in the prospectus, we hold that the plaintiffs have failed to state an actionable claim regarding the statement that the Partnership believed it could repay the bonds. We can say that the prospectus here truly bespeaks caution because, not only does the prospectus generally convey the riskiness of the investment, but its warnings and cautionary language directly address the substance of the statement the plaintiffs challenge. That is to say, the cautionary statements were tailored precisely to address the uncertainty concerning the Partnership's prospective ability to repay the bondholders.

* * * [W]e think it clear that the accompanying warnings and cautionary language served to negate any potentially misleading effect that the prospectus' statement about the Partnership's belief in its ability to repay the bonds would have on a reasonable investor. The prospectus clearly and precisely cautioned that the bonds represented an exceptionally risky, perhaps even speculative, venture and that the Partnership's ability to repay the bonds was uncertain. Given this context, we believe that no reasonable jury could conclude that the subject projection materially influenced a reasonable investor.

NOTE

The Private Securities Litigation Reform Act of 1995, enacted for the purpose of restricting class actions against publicly-held corporations on the basis of allegedly inaccurate projections, codifies the "bespeaks caution" doctrine by providing that a company cannot be held liable for a "forward-looking statement [that] is accompanied by meaningful cautionary statements identifying important factors that could cause actual results to differ material-ly from those in the forward-looking statement." See §§ 27A of the 1933 Act and 21E of the 1934 Act. The new provisions also state explicitly that they are not intended "to impose upon any person a duty to update a forward-looking statement." The following excerpt discusses some additional issues raised by projections.

In recent years, the SEC has been giving increased emphasis to Item 303 of Regulation S–K, which requires management's discussion and analysis ("MD & A") of the issuer's financial condition and results of operation, as a means of informing shareholders of the issuer's true condition. Among other things, Item 303 requires management to "[d]e-scribe any known trends or uncertainties that have had or that the registrant reasonably expects will have a material favorable or unfavora-ble impact on net sales or revenues or income from continuing opera-tions.' Item 303(a)(3)(ii). *See, e.g.*, In the Matter of Caterpillar, Inc., SEC Admin. Proc. File No. 3–7692 (SEC March 31, 1992).

NOTES

1.   SEC Form 10–K reports must include a Management Discussion and Analysis of Financial Conditions and Results of Operations (the "MD & A" section). The MD & A section must discuss "any known trends or uncertain-ties that have had or that the registrant reasonably expects will have a material favorable or unfavorable impact on net sales or revenues or income from continuing operations." 17 C.F.R. § 229.303(a). The MD & A discussion requires a statement of management's views on the company's financial condition, its capital expenditure plans and other matters of interest. Harvey Pitt, a former SEC chairman, asserted that the MD & A is "the cornerstone of our system of corporate disclosure," House Committee on Financial Services. "Hearing on Accounting Under Sarbanes–Oxley: Are Financial Statements More Reliable?" 108th Congress, First Session, September 17, 2003, at 1068. Nevertheless, the MD & A disclosure requirement has often been used by management to put its spin on the numbers and make excuses for shortfalls and problems, thereby obscuring the actual numbers.

2.   Following the collapse of the Enron Corp., Congress acted to strengthen the responsibility of management for assuring the reliability of its SEC financial reports by Section 404 of the Sarbanes–Oxley act. That section required management to implement internal controls for financial reporting and to assess the effectiveness of those controls. This proved to be an extremely expensive exercise and caused much complaint among issuers. Some 500 public companies also initially reported flaws in their internal controls.

SECTION 12.   SELECTIVE DISCLOSURE

Another type of soft information comes not from the company itself but from securities analysts who follow public companies and publicly announce earnings and other performance-based projections concerning those companies. The market has become increasingly sensitive to analysts' statements about a company's prospects. Since companies are generally concerned with the market performance of their stock, it is tempting to curry favor with analysts in an attempt to keep their estimates positive and thereby maintain the stock at favorable price levels. Two primary concerns regarding analysts' statements and estimates have been with the company's potential liability with regard to inaccurate analysts' estimates and also the practice of selective disclosure whereby companies leak information to analysts before it is released to the public.

With regard to a company's liability for analysts' statements, neither an issuer nor its management will be held accountable for an analyst's projection unless the issuer has adopted the projection or has otherwise "entangled" itself with the analyst's opinions. See, e.g., In re Peritus Software Services, Inc. Securities Litigation, 52 F.Supp.2d 211, 230 (D.Mass.1999) (failure to plead sufficient entanglement); In re Boston Technology, Inc. Securities Litigation, 8 F.Supp.2d 43 (D.Mass.1998) (insufficient allegations of entanglement); Shuster v. Symmetricon, 1997 WL 269490, [1997 Transfer Binder] Fed. Sec. L. Rep. (CCH) ¶ 99,437 (N.D.Cal. 1997) (failure to adequately allege that company had so entangled itself in analyst's reports so as to have adopted them); In re Cirrus Logic Securities Litigation, 946 F.Supp. 1446 (N.D.Cal.1996) (management will be held accountable for analysts statements only when those statements have been adopted by management or where management has sufficiently "entangled" itself with analysts' opinions).

Selective disclosure to analysts interferes with a level playing field in which all investors have equal access to information. The existing anti-fraud rules as interpreted by the courts do not address the problem of selective disclosure. The following SEC proposal, which was adopted in August 2000, explains the problems with selective disclosure and briefly describes the SEC's prohibitions against this practice.

SELECTIVE DISCLOSURE AND INSIDER TRADING

Securities Exchange Act Release No. 3442259 (December 20, 1999).

Information is the lifeblood of our securities markets. Congress enacted the federal securities laws to promote fair and honest securities markets, and a critical purpose of these laws is to promote full and fair disclosure of important information by issuers of securities to the investing public. The Securities Act of 1933 (Securities Act) and the Securities Exchange Act of 1934 (Exchange Act), as implemented by Commission rules and regulations, provide for systems of mandatory disclosure of certain material information in securities offerings and in periodic reports.

The antifraud provisions of the federal securities laws also play a very important role in furthering full and fair disclosure. Among other things, the antifraud provisions prohibit insider trading, or the fraudulent misuse of material nonpublic information. Unlike the law underlying the issuer disclosure requirements, which generally has been developed through statutes and rules, the law of insider trading has largely been developed through a series of Commission and judicial decisions in civil and criminal enforcement cases involving fraud charges. As a result, a few areas of insider trading law have been marked by disagreement among the courts.

Today's proposals address several issues related to full and fair disclosure of information, and insider trading law. The proposed rules are the following:

Regulation FD (Fair Disclosure), a new issuer disclosure rule, deals with the problem of issuers making selective disclosure of material non-public information to analysts, institutional investors, or others, but not to the public at large. Although analysts play an important role in gathering and analyzing information, and disseminating their analysis to investors, we do not believe that allowing issuers to disclose material information selectively to analysts is in the best interests of investors or the securities markets generally. Instead, to the maximum extent practicable, we believe that all investors should have access to an issuer's material disclosures at the same time. Regulation FD, therefore, would require that: (1) when an issuer intentionally discloses material information, it do so through public disclosure, not through selective disclosure; and (2) whenever an issuer learns that it has made a non-intentional material selective disclosure, the issuer make prompt public disclosure of that information.* * *

Full and fair disclosure of information by issuers of securities to the investing public is a cornerstone of the federal securities laws. In enacting the mandatory disclosure system of the Exchange Act, Congress sought to promote disclosure of "honest, complete, and correct information" to facilitate the operation of fair and efficient markets.[8] Despite this well-recognized principle, the federal securities laws do not generally require an issuer to make public disclosure of all important corporate developments when they occur. Periodic reports (e.g., Forms 10–K and 10–Q) call for disclosure of specified information on a regular basis, and domestic issuers are additionally required to report some types of events on a Form 8–K soon after they occur. However, in the absence of a specific duty to disclose, the federal securities laws do not require an issuer to publicly disclose all material events as soon as they occur. While we encourage prompt disclosure of material information as the best disclosure practice, and self-regulatory organization (SRO) rules often require this, issuers

---

8. The idea of a free and open public market is built upon the theory that competing judgments of buyers and sellers as to the fair price of a security brings about a situation where the market price reflects as nearly as possible a just price. . . . [T]he hiding and secreting of important information obstructs the operation of the markets as indices of real value. H.R. Rep. No. 731383, at 11 (1934). See also S. Rep. No. 73792, at 1011, 1920 (1934).

retain some control over the precise timing of many important corporate disclosures.

In practice, issuers also retain control over the audience and forum for some important disclosures. If a disclosure is made at a time when no Commission filing is immediately required, the issuer determines how and to whom to make its initial disclosure. As a result, issuers sometimes choose to disclose information selectively—i.e., to a small group of analysts or institutional investors—before making broad public disclosure by a press release or Commission filing.

Many recent cases of selective disclosure have been reported in the media. In some cases, selective disclosures have been made in conference calls or meetings that are open only to analysts and/or institutional investors, and exclude other investors, members of the public, and the media. In other cases, company officials have made selective disclosures directly to individual analysts. Commonly, these situations involve advance notice of the issuer's upcoming quarterly earnings or sales figures—figures which, when announced, have a predictable and significant impact on the market price of the issuer's securities.

We are troubled by the many recent reports of selective disclosure and the potential impact of this practice on market integrity. As the Supreme Court has recently emphasized, promoting investor confidence in the fairness of our securities markets is an "animating purpose" of the Exchange Act. Clearly, one critical component of that mission is protecting investors from the prospect that others in the market possess "unerodable informational advantages" obtained through superior access to corporate insiders.

In our view, the current practice of selective disclosure poses a serious threat to investor confidence in the fairness and integrity of the securities markets. We have recognized that benefits may flow to the markets from the legitimate efforts of securities analysts to "ferret out and analyze information" based on their superior diligence and acumen. But we do not believe that selective disclosure of material nonpublic information to analysts—or to others, such as selected investors—is beneficial to the securities markets. As a recent academic study indicated, selective disclosure has the immediate effect of enabling those privy to the information to make a quick profit (or quickly minimize losses) by trading before the information is disseminated to the public.[9] Indeed, while issuer selective disclosure is not a new practice, the impact of such selective disclosure appears to be much greater in today's more volatile, earnings-sensitive markets. Accordingly, we think that a continued practice of selective

---

9. See Richard Frankel, Marilyn Johnson, and Douglas J. Skinner, An Empirical Examination of Conference Calls as a Voluntary Disclosure Medium, 37 J. Acct. Res. 133 (Spring 1999). This study revealed that, during and immediately following teleconference calls between analysts and issuers, trading volume in the issuers' stock increased, average trade size increased, and stock price volatility increased. This led the researchers to conclude that material information is released during these selective disclosure periods, which is immediately filtered to a subset of large investors who are able to trade on the information before it is fully disseminated to the market.

disclosure by issuers inevitably will lead to a loss of public confidence in the fairness of the markets.

Even apart from the issue of fundamental fairness to all investors, selective disclosure poses other real threats to the health and integrity of our securities markets. Corporate managers should be encouraged to make broad public disclosure of important information promptly. If, however, they are permitted to treat material information as a commodity that can be parceled out selectively, they may delay general public disclosure so that they can selectively disclose the information to curry favor or bolster credibility with particular analysts or institutional investors. Moreover, if selective disclosure were to go unchecked, opportunities for analyst conflicts of interests would flourish. We are greatly concerned by reports indicating a trend toward less independent research and analysis as a basis for analysts' advice, and a correspondingly greater dependence by analysts on access to corporate insiders to provide guidance and "comfort" for their earnings forecasts. In this environment, analysts are likely to feel pressured to report favorably about particular issuers to avoid being "cut . . . off from access to the flow of nonpublic information through future analyst conference phone calls" or other means of selective disclosure. This raises troubling questions about the degree to which analysts may be pressured to shade their analysis in order to maintain their access to corporate management. We believe that these pressures would be reduced if issuers were clearly prohibited from selectively disclosing material information to favored analysts.

These concerns about selective disclosure are widely shared, as reflected both in stock exchange listing standards and in "best practices" guidelines of investor relations and analyst groups. The New York Stock Exchange Listed Company Manual and the NASD Rules both require listed issuers to disclose promptly "to the public" information about material developments. The National Investor Relations Institute (NIRI) guidance in this area also states that an issuer "should not disclose in selective situations—such as conference calls and analyst meetings—information that it is unwilling to make available for general public use." Similarly, the Association of Investment Management and Research Standards of Practice Handbook states that if an analyst selectively receives disclosure of information that he deems material, "the member must encourage the public dissemination of that information and abstain from making investment decisions on the basis of that information unless and until it is broadly disseminated to the marketplace."

Finally, revolutions in communications and information technologies have made it much easier for issuers today to disseminate important information broadly and swiftly. A generation ago, issuers may have relied on conferences attended by a handful of interested parties, or news releases that led to delayed, indirect retransmission of information to the public. Lacking effective means to communicate directly to large numbers of investors, issuers may have relied on analysts to serve as information intermediaries. In the last few years, however, new, effective methods for

mass communications have become widely available. Today, issuers can—
and many do—use a variety of these new methods to communicate with
the market, including: live transmissions of annual meetings and news
conferences on the Internet or closed circuit television; listen-only telephone transmission of meetings and analyst conferences; and company
websites. With the availability of these new technologies, issuers can much
more easily reach a wide investor audience with their disclosures, and do
not need to rely on analysts as heavily as in the past to serve as
information intermediaries.

Nevertheless, issuers are continuing to engage in selective disclosures
of material nonpublic information, perhaps due in part to the uncertainty
in current law about when selective disclosures are prohibited. For at least
the past 30 years, the issue of potential liability for selective disclosure has
been addressed under the principles of fraud law, particularly the law of
insider trading. Under early insider trading case law, which appeared to
require that traders have equal access to corporate information, selective
disclosure of material information to securities analysts could lead to
liability. * * *

Although the antifraud provisions of the securities laws do not require
that all traders possess equal information when they trade, we believe that
our disclosure rules should promote fair treatment of large and small
investors by, among other things, giving all investors timely access to the
material information an issuer chooses to disclose. Therefore, we are today
proposing new rules, which use a different legal approach, to address
selective disclosure. The approach we propose does not treat selective
disclosure as a type of fraudulent conduct or revisit the insider trading
issues addressed in *Dirks*. Rather, we propose to use our authority to
require full and fair disclosure from issuers, primarily under Section 13(a)
of the Exchange Act, as a basis for proposed Regulation FD. This Regulation is designed as an issuer disclosure rule, similar to existing Commission rules under Exchange Act Sections 13(a) and 15(d). We believe this
approach would further the full and fair public disclosure of material
information, and thereby promote fair dealing in the securities of covered
issuers.

Rule 101 of Regulation FD sets forth the basic rule regarding "selective disclosure." Under this Rule, whenever:

(1) an issuer, or any person acting on its behalf,

(2) discloses material nonpublic information

(3) to any other person outside the issuer,

(4) the issuer must

(a) simultaneously (for intentional disclosures), or

(b) "promptly" (for non-intentional disclosures)

(5) make public disclosure of that same information.

Several definitional and other provisions in the Regulation establish the scope and effect of the general rule. As a whole, the Regulation would require that whenever an issuer makes an intentional disclosure of material nonpublic information, it must do so in a manner that provides general public disclosure, rather than through a selective disclosure. In the case of an unintentional selective disclosure, the issuer must make full public disclosure promptly after it learns of the selective disclosure. Regulation FD does not mandate that issuers make public disclosure of all material developments when they occur. What it does require, however, is that when an issuer chooses to disclose material nonpublic information, it must do so broadly to the investing public, not selectively to a favored few.

* * *

NOTES

1. When it adopted Regulation FD, the SEC made some significant modifications to the regulation as proposed. As adopted, Regulation FD applies only to "communications by the company's senior management, its investor relations professionals, and others who regularly communicate with market professionals and security holders." Regulation FD applies only to a company's "communications with market professionals, and holders of the issuer's securities under circumstances in which it is reasonably foreseeable that the security holders will trade on the basis of the information." Accordingly Regulation FD does not apply when the company is communicating with the press, rating agencies, and ordinary-course of business communications with customers and suppliers. Regulation FD is purely a disclosure rule and does not create liability for fraud. It is to be enforced by the SEC. As proposed Regulation FD left open the possibility of private suits but this possibility was eliminated in the rule as adopted. The regulation has been revised to eliminate the prospect of private liability for companies solely as a result of a selective disclosure violation. Regulation FD applies only to intentional or reckless conduct. Disclosure is required only when "the person making the selective disclosure knows or is reckless in not knowing that the information disclosed was both material and nonpublic." Finally, Regulation FD does not apply to communications made in connection with most public offerings registered under the 1933 Act. Nor does it apply to foreign issuers.

2. Another context in which selective disclosure may occur is a "bakeoff" for the selection of an underwriter of an offering by an issuer. These events are opportunities for the underwriters to make their "pitch" for the underwriting business, but it also may result in the issuer sharing information that is not generally available, especially where analysts appear at these meetings to pitch their firm's business. This also undermines the objectivity of participating analysts when they later prepare reports on the stock. The NASD was banning this practice. Randall Smith, "New NASD Rule Limits Analysts at Bake–Offs," Wall St. J., June 6, 2002, at C1.

3. An important player in the SEC full disclosure system is the financial analyst. Those individuals analyze the financial reports filed with the SEC, a task that most investors have neither the time nor the expertise. These

analysts "follow" particular companies and set targets or "expectations" for a company's future growth and review the company's cash flows, debt burden and other financial measurements. The analysts use various "signals" to alert investors about the stock, including "buy," "hold" or "sell." Several analysts might follow the same stock, and their "consensus estimates" will set the target for management in order to maintain a favorable recommendation. Some analysts are independent entities and provide "independent" research on companies. Most of the better-known financial analysts, however, work for large broker-dealers and investment bankers with underwriting operations. That relationship creates a conflict of interest because the investment bankers do not want one of their own firm's analysts disparaging the stock of a client. Further, analysts might have access to non-public information from their investment banking cohorts that could be used to aid their analysis. These conflicts of interest were sought to be alleviated by sealing off the analysts from the investment bankers through a "Chinese Wall," which isolates information flow. Analyst's could be "brought over" the Chinese Wall to aid investment bankers in connection with a client the analyst was covering. In such an instance, the analyst had to cease coverage of the stock until the investment banking activity was disclosed to the public or became non-material. In addition, "restricted lists" were used to prevent analysts from issuing reports on clients with ongoing initial public offerings so that those reports were not use to manipulate the offering. Another device, "watch lists," were used to identify investment banking clients that might have a conflict with analysts' opinions, in which case extra supervision was applied to prevent abuse.

During the run up in the stock market in the 1990s, stock analysts became somewhat infamous for touting stocks of Internet companies that often rose quickly after their initial public offering and then crashed in the market downturn in 2000. Mary Meeker was given the title of "queen of the net" by *Barrons* magazine in 1998 for her hyping of initial public offerings by Internet companies. The analysts were often acting as "cheerleaders" for stocks underwritten by their firm's investment bankers and were sometimes compensated for their assistance to the investment bankers, creating a conflict of interest. Jack Grubman, an analyst at Salomon Smith Barney unit of Citigroup Inc., was said to be the "preeminent" analyst for the telecom and was paid $20 million annually between 1998 and 2001. In an internal email, Grubman called a company a "pig" and warned that its stock was going to zero, even though he had just published a positive research report on the company. Grubman also changed his negative views on AT & T in exchange for a $1 million contribution to the exclusive 92nd St. Y preschool program in New York City that paved the way for the admittance of his children to that school. Henry Blodget, the analyst heading Merrill Lynch's Internet research group, claimed in internal emails that stocks that he had recommended to the public were actually "crap." Frank Quattrone, an analyst at Credit Suisse First Boston (CSFB) was paid $120 million in 2000. He was convicted of obstructing justice by suggesting that documents at the firm should be destroyed.

In December 2002, ten investment banking firms agreed to a $1.4 billion settlement with New York attorney general Eliot Spitzer and other state, federal and self-regulatory organizations in an action challenging analysts conflicts. Among the investment banks included in the settlement were Citigroup and Salomon Smith Barney, CFSB, Morgan Stanley, Goldman Sachs, Lehman Brothers Holdings, Inc, UBS AG Deutsche Bank and Bear Stearns Co. Jack Grubman, the Citigroup analyst, agreed to pay $15 million for his indiscretions and was barred from the securities business for life. Under the settlement, the investment bankers agreed to separate their research and investment banking businesses physically and through different reporting lines. The two groups were to have separate legal and compliance staffs and separate budgets. "Firewalls" were to be created between the investment bankers and the analysts. Investment bankers were to have no say in what companies should be covered by the analysts. Analysts were barred from investment banking sales presentations or road shows showcasing IPOs before their issuance. Analyst compensation could not be based on investment banking revenues or input from investment banking personnel. The settlement required the firms to spend $450 million to purchase research from at least three independent firms for a period of five years and to make those reports available to retail investors in order to allow them to better assess stock recommendations. Seven of the settling firms agreed to pay a total of $85 million to fund "Investor Education Funds" to be created by the states and the SEC. Those funds would be used to alert investors to investment risks.

SECTION 13. SECONDARY LIABILITY

CENTRAL BANK v. FIRST INTERSTATE BANK

511 U.S. 164, 114 S.Ct. 1439, 128 L.Ed.2d 119 (1994).

JUSTICE KENNEDY delivered the opinion of the Court.

As we have interpreted it, § 10(b) of the Securities Exchange Act of 1934 imposes private civil liability on those who commit a manipulative or deceptive act in connection with the purchase or sale of securities. In this case, we must answer a question reserved in two earlier decisions: whether private civil liability under § 10(b) extends as well to those who do not engage in the manipulative or deceptive practice but who aid and abet the violation. * * *

In our cases addressing § 10(b) and Rule 10b–5, we have confronted two main issues. First, we have determined the scope of conduct prohibited by § 10(b). Second, in cases where the defendant has committed a violation of § 10(b), we have decided questions about the elements of the 10b–5 private liability scheme: for example, whether there is a right to contribution, what the statute of limitations is, whether there is a reliance requirement, and whether there is an *in pari delicto* defense.* * *

Our consideration of statutory duties, especially in cases interpreting § 10(b), establishes that the statutory text controls the definition of conduct covered by § 10(b). That bodes ill for respondents, for "the language of Section 10(b) does not in terms mention aiding and abetting." To overcome this problem, respondents and the SEC suggest (or hint at) the novel argument that the use of the phrase "directly or indirectly" in the text of § 10(b) covers aiding and abetting.

The federal courts have not relied on the "directly or indirectly" language when imposing aiding and abetting liability under § 10(b), and with good reason. There is a basic flaw with this interpretation. According to respondents and the SEC, the "directly or indirectly" language shows that "Congress . . . intended to reach all persons who engage, even if only indirectly, in proscribed activities connected with securities transactions." The problem, of course, is that aiding and abetting liability extends beyond persons who engage, even indirectly, in a proscribed activity; aiding and abetting liability reaches persons who do not engage in the proscribed activities at all, but who give a degree of aid to those who do. A further problem with respondents' interpretation of the "directly or indirectly" language is posed by the numerous provisions of the 1934 Act that use the term in a way that does not impose aiding and abetting liability. In short, respondents' interpretation of the "directly or indirectly" language fails to support their suggestion that the text of § 10(b) itself prohibits aiding and abetting.

Congress knew how to impose aiding and abetting liability when it chose to do so. If, as respondents seem to say, Congress intended to impose aiding and abetting liability, we presume it would have used the words "aid" and "abet" in the statutory text. But it did not.

We reach the uncontroversial conclusion, accepted even by those courts recognizing a § 10(b) aiding and abetting cause of action, that the text of the 1934 Act does not itself reach those who aid and abet a § 10(b) violation. Unlike those courts, however, we think that conclusion resolves the case. It is inconsistent with settled methodology in § 10(b) cases to extend liability beyond the scope of conduct prohibited by the statutory text. To be sure, aiding and abetting a wrongdoer ought to be actionable in certain instances. Cf. Restatement (Second) of Torts 876(b)(1977). The issue, however, is not whether imposing private civil liability on aiders and abettors is good policy but whether aiding and abetting is covered by the statute.

As in earlier cases considering conduct prohibited by § 10(b), we again conclude that the statute prohibits only the making of a material misstatement (or omission) or the commission of a manipulative act. The proscription does not include giving aid to a person who commits a manipulative or deceptive act. We cannot amend the statute to create liability for acts that are not themselves manipulative or deceptive within the meaning of the statute.

Because this case concerns the conduct prohibited by § 10(b), the statute itself resolves the case, but even if it did not, we would reach the same result. When the text of § 10(b) does not resolve a particular issue, we attempt to infer "how the 1934 Congress would have addressed the issue had the § 10b–5 action been included as an express provision in the 1934 Act." For that inquiry, we use the express causes of action in the securities Acts as the primary model for the § 10(b) action. The reason is evident: Had the 73d Congress enacted a private § 10(b) right of action, it likely would have designed it in a manner similar to the other private rights of action in the securities Acts. * * *

Following that analysis here, we look to the express private causes of action in the 1933 and 1934 Acts. In the 1933 Act, § 11 prohibits false statements or omissions of material fact in registration statements; it identifies the various categories of defendants subject to liability for a violation, but that list does not include aiders and abettors. Section 12 prohibits the sale of unregistered, nonexempt securities as well as the sale of securities by means of a material misstatement or omission; and it limits liability to those who offer or sell the security. In the 1934 Act, § 9 prohibits any person from engaging in manipulative practices such as wash sales, matched orders, and the like. Section 16 prohibits short-swing trading by owners, directors, and officers. Section 18 prohibits any person from making misleading statements in reports filed with the SEC. And § 20A, added in 1988, prohibits any person from engaging in insider trading.

This survey of the express causes of action in the securities Acts reveals that each (like § 10(b)) specifies the conduct for which defendants may be held liable. Some of the express causes of action specify categories of defendants who may be liable; others (like § 10(b)) state only that "any person" who commits one of the prohibited acts may be held liable. The important point for present purposes, however, is that none of the express causes of action in the 1934 Act further imposes liability on one who aids or abets a violation. Cf. 7 U.S.C. § 25(a)(1)(Commodity Exchange Act's private civil aiding and abetting provision).

From the fact that Congress did not attach private aiding and abetting liability to any of the express causes of action in the securities Acts, we can infer that Congress likely would not have attached aiding and abetting liability to § 10(b) had it provided a private § 10(b) cause of action. * * *

Respondents make further arguments for imposition of § 10(b) aiding and abetting liability, none of which leads us to a different answer.

The text does not support their point, but respondents and some amici invoke a broad-based notion of congressional intent. They say that Congress legislated with an understanding of general principles of tort law and that aiding and abetting liability was "well established in both civil and criminal actions by 1934." Thus, "Congress intended to include" aiding and abetting liability in the 1934 Act. A brief history of aiding and abetting liability serves to dispose of this argument.

Aiding and abetting is an ancient criminal law doctrine. Though there is no federal common law of crimes, Congress in 1909 enacted what is now

18 U.S.C. § 2, a general aiding and abetting statute applicable to all federal criminal offenses. The statute decrees that those who provide knowing aid to persons committing federal crimes, with the intent to facilitate the crime, are themselves committing a crime.

The Restatement of Torts, under a concert of action principle, accepts a doctrine with rough similarity to criminal aiding and abetting. An actor is liable for harm resulting to a third person from the tortuous conduct of another "if he ... knows that the other's conduct constitutes a breach of duty and gives substantial assistance or encouragement to the other...." Restatement (Second) of Torts 876(b)(1977). The doctrine has been at best uncertain in application, however. As the Court of Appeals for the District of Columbia Circuit noted in a comprehensive opinion on the subject, the leading cases applying this doctrine are statutory securities cases, with the common law precedents "largely confined to isolated acts of adolescents in rural society." Halberstam v. Welch, 705 F.2d 472, 489 (1983). Indeed, in some States, it is still unclear whether there is aiding and abetting tort liability of the kind set forth in § 876(b) of the Restatement.

More to the point, Congress has not enacted a general civil aiding and abetting statute—either for suits by the Government (when the Government sues for civil penalties or injunctive relief) or for suits by private parties. Thus, when Congress enacts a statute under which a person may sue and recover damages from a private defendant for the defendant's violation of some statutory norm, there is no general presumption that the plaintiff may also sue aiders and abettors.

Congress instead has taken a statute-by-statute approach to civil aiding and abetting liability. For example, the Internal Revenue Code contains a full section governing aiding and abetting liability, complete with description of scienter and the penalties attached. 26 U.S.C. § 6701. The Commodity Exchange Act contains an explicit aiding and abetting provision that applies to private suits brought under that Act. 7 U.S.C. § 25(a)(1). Indeed, various provisions of the securities laws prohibit aiding and abetting, although violations are enforceable only in actions brought by the SEC. See, e.g., Securities Exchange Act 15(b)(4)(E)(SEC may proceed against brokers and dealers who aid and abet a violation of the securities laws); Insider Trader Sanctions Act of 1984, Pub.L. 98–376, 98 Stat. 1264 (civil penalty provision added in 1984 applicable to those who aid and abet insider trading violations); Securities Exchange Act § 21B(a)(2)(civil penalty provision added in 1990 applicable to brokers and dealers who aid and abet various violations of the Act). * * *

The SEC points to various policy arguments in support of the 10b–5 aiding and abetting cause of action. It argues, for example, that the aiding and abetting cause of action deters secondary actors from contributing to fraudulent activities and ensures that defrauded plaintiffs are made whole.

Policy considerations cannot override our interpretation of the text and structure of the Act, except to the extent that they may help to show that adherence to the text and structure would lead to a result "so bizarre" that Congress could not have intended it. That is not the case here.

Extending the 10b–5 cause of action to aiders and abettors no doubt makes the civil remedy more far-reaching, but it does not follow that the objectives of the statute are better served. Secondary liability for aiders and abettors exacts costs that may disserve the goals of fair dealing and efficiency in the securities markets.

As an initial matter, the rules for determining aiding and abetting liability are unclear, in "an area that demands certainty and predictability." That leads to the undesirable result of decisions "made on an ad hoc basis, offering little predictive value" to those who provide services to participants in the securities business. Because of the uncertainty of the governing rules, entities subject to secondary liability as aiders and abettors may find it prudent and necessary, as a business judgment, to abandon substantial defenses and to pay settlements in order to avoid the expense and risk of going to trial.

In addition, "litigation under Rule 10b–5 presents a danger of vexatiousness different in degree and in kind from that which accompanies litigation in general." Blue Chip. Litigation under 10b–5 thus requires secondary actors to expend large sums even for pretrial defense and the negotiation of settlements. See 138 Cong.Rec. S12605 (Aug. 12, 1992)(remarks of Sen. Sanford)(asserting that in 83% of 10b–5 cases major accounting firms pay $8 in legal fees for every $1 paid in claims).

This uncertainty and excessive litigation can have ripple effects. For example, newer and smaller companies may find it difficult to obtain advice from professionals. A professional may fear that a newer or smaller company may not survive and that business failure would generate securities litigation against the professional, among others. In addition, the increased costs incurred by professionals because of the litigation and settlement costs under § 10b–5 may be passed on to their client companies, and in turn incurred by the company's investors, the intended beneficiaries of the statute. * * *

At oral argument, the SEC suggested that 18 U.S.C. § 2 is "significant" and "very important" in this case. At the outset, we note that this contention is inconsistent with the SEC's argument that recklessness is a sufficient scienter for aiding and abetting liability. Criminal aiding and abetting liability under § 2 requires proof that the defendant "in some sort associate[d] himself with the venture, that he participate[d] in it as in something that he wishe[d] to bring about, that he [sought] by his action to make it succeed." But recklessness, not intentional wrongdoing, is the theory underlying the aiding and abetting allegations in the case before us.

Furthermore, while it is true that an aider and abettor of a criminal violation of any provision of the 1934 Act, including 10(b), violates 18 U.S.C. § 2, it does not follow that a private civil aiding and abetting cause of action must also exist. * * *

Because the text of § 10(b) does not prohibit aiding and abetting, we hold that a private plaintiff may not maintain an aiding and abetting suit under § 10(b). The absence of § 10(b) aiding and abetting liability does not mean that secondary actors in the securities markets are always free from liability under the securities Acts. Any person or entity, including a lawyer, accountant, or bank, who employs a manipulative device or makes a material misstatement (or omission) on which a purchaser or seller of securities relies may be liable as a primary violator under 10b–5, assuming *all* of the requirements for primary liability under Rule 10b–5 are met. * * *

JUSTICE STEVENS, with whom JUSTICE BLACKMUN, JUSTICE SOUTER, and JUSTICE GINSBURG join, dissenting.

* * * In *hundreds* of judicial and administrative proceedings in every circuit in the federal system, the courts and the SEC have concluded that aiders and abettors are subject to liability under 10(b) and Rule 10b–5. While we have reserved decision on the legitimacy of the theory in two cases that did not present it, all 11 Courts of Appeals to have considered the question have recognized a private cause of action against aiders and abettors under § 10(b) and Rule 10b–5. The early aiding and abetting decisions relied upon principles borrowed from tort law; in those cases, judges closer to the times and climate of the 73d Congress than we concluded that holding aiders and abettors liable was consonant with the 1934 Act's purpose to strengthen the antifraud remedies of the common law. * * *

The Courts of Appeals have usually applied a familiar three part test for aider and abettor liability, patterned on the Restatement of Torts formulation, that requires (i) the existence of a primary violation of § 10(b) or Rule 10b–5, (ii) the defendant's knowledge of (or recklessness as to) that primary violation, and (iii) "substantial assistance" of the violation by the defendant. If indeed there has been "continuing confusion" concerning the private right of action against aiders and abettors, that confusion has not concerned its basic structure, still less its "existence." Indeed, in this case, petitioner *assumed* the existence of a right of action against aiders and abettors, and sought review only of the subsidiary questions whether an indenture trustee could be found liable as an aider and abettor absent a breach of an indenture agreement or other duty under state law, and whether it could be liable as an aider and abettor based only on a showing of recklessness. These questions, it is true, have engendered genuine disagreement in the Courts of Appeals. But instead of simply addressing the questions presented by the parties, on which the law really was unsettled, the Court *sua sponte* directed the parties to address a question on which even the petitioner justifiably thought the law was settled, and reaches out to overturn a most considerable body of precedent. * * *

As framed by the Court's order redrafting the questions presented, this case concerns only the existence and scope of aiding and abetting liability in suits brought by private parties under § 10(b) and Rule 10b–5. The majority's rationale, however, sweeps far beyond even those important issues. The majority leaves little doubt that the Exchange Act does not even permit the Commission to pursue aiders and abettors in civil enforcement actions under § 10(b) and Rule 10b–5. Aiding and abetting liability has a long pedigree in civil proceedings brought by the SEC under § 10(b) and Rule 10b–5, and has become an important part of the Commission's enforcement arsenal. Moreover, the majority's approach to aiding and abetting at the very least casts serious doubt, both for private and SEC actions, on other forms of secondary liability that, like the aiding and abetting theory, have long been recognized by the SEC and the courts but are not expressly spelled out in the securities statutes.[10] The principle the Court espouses today—that liability may not be imposed on parties who are not within the scope of § 10(b)'s plain language—is inconsistent with long-established Commission and judicial precedent.

NOTE

In the *Central Bank* case, the Supreme Court only addressed the question of aider and abetter liability in *private* actions for damages; it did not address the issue of whether the SEC could pursue aiders and abetters in its civil injunction actions. The Private Securities Litigation Reform Act of 1995 added a new subsection 20(f) to the 1934 Act, which provides that in any action brought by the commission under § 21(d), "any person that knowingly provides substantial assistance to another person in violation of" any provision of the Act, "shall be deemed to be in violation of such provision to the same extent as the person to whom such assistance is provided."

STONERIDGE INVESTMENT PARTNERS, LLC v. SCIENTIFIC-ATLANTA, INC.

___ U.S. ___, 128 S.Ct. 761, 169 L.Ed.2d 627 (2008).

JUSTICE KENNEDY delivered the opinion of the Court.

We consider the reach of the private right of action the Court has found implied in § 10(b) of the Securities Exchange Act of 1934 and SEC Rule 10b–5, In this suit investors alleged losses after purchasing common stock. They sought to impose liability on entities who, acting both as customers and suppliers, agreed to arrangements that allowed the investors' company to mislead its auditor and issue a misleading financial statement affecting the stock price. We conclude the implied right of

---

10. The Court's rationale would sweep away the decisions recognizing that a defendant may be found liable in a private action for conspiring to violate § 10(b) and Rule 10b–5. Secondary liability is as old as the implied right of action under § 10(b) itself; the very first decision to recognize a private cause of action under the section and rule, Kardon v. National Gypsum Co., 69 F.Supp. 512 (E.D.Pa.1946), involved an alleged conspiracy. In addition, many courts, concluding that 20(a)'s "controlling person" provisions are not the exclusive source of secondary liability under the Exchange Act, have imposed liability in 10(b) actions based upon respondeat superior and other common-law agency principles. These decisions likewise appear unlikely to survive the Court's decision. * * *

action does not reach the customer/supplier companies because the investors did not rely upon their statements or representations. We affirm the judgment of the Court of Appeals.

This class-action suit by investors was filed against Charter Communications, Inc., in the United States District Court for the Eastern District of Missouri. Stoneridge Investment Partners, LLC, a limited liability company organized under the laws of Delaware, was the lead plaintiff and is petitioner here.

Charter issued the financial statements and the securities in question. It was a named defendant along with some of its executives and Arthur Andersen LLP, Charter's independent auditor during the period in question. We are concerned, though, with two other defendants, respondents here. Respondents are Scientific-Atlanta, Inc., and Motorola, Inc. They were suppliers, and later customers, of Charter.

For purposes of this proceeding, we take these facts, alleged by petitioner, to be true. Charter, a cable operator, engaged in a variety of fraudulent practices so its quarterly reports would meet Wall Street expectations for cable subscriber growth and operating cash flow. The fraud included misclassification of its customer base; delayed reporting of terminated customers; improper capitalization of costs that should have been shown as expenses; and manipulation of the company's billing cutoff dates to inflate reported revenues. In late 2000, Charter executives realized that, despite these efforts, the company would miss projected operating cash flow numbers by $15 to $20 million. To help meet the shortfall, Charter decided to alter its existing arrangements with respondents, Scientific-Atlanta and Motorola. Petitioner's theory as to whether Arthur Andersen was altogether misled or, on the other hand, knew the structure of the contract arrangements and was complicit to some degree, is not clear at this stage of the case. The point, however, is neither controlling nor significant for our present disposition, and in our decision we assume it was misled.

Respondents supplied Charter with the digital cable converter (set top) boxes that Charter furnished to its customers. Charter arranged to overpay respondents $20 for each set top box it purchased until the end of the year, with the understanding that respondents would return the overpayment by purchasing advertising from Charter. The transactions, it is alleged, had no economic substance; but, because Charter would then record the advertising purchases as revenue and capitalize its purchase of the set top boxes, in violation of generally accepted accounting principles, the transactions would enable Charter to fool its auditor into approving a financial statement showing it met projected revenue and operating cash flow numbers. Respondents agreed to the arrangement.

So that Arthur Andersen would not discover the link between Charter's increased payments for the boxes and the advertising purchases, the companies drafted documents to make it appear the transactions were unrelated and conducted in the ordinary course of business. Following a request from Charter, Scientific-Atlanta sent documents to Charter stating-falsely-that it had increased production costs. It raised the price for set top boxes for the rest of 2000 by $20 per box. As for Motorola, in a written contract Charter agreed to purchase from Motorola a specific number of set top boxes and pay liquidated damages of $20 for each unit it did not take. The contract was made with the expectation Charter would fail to purchase all the units and pay Motorola the liquidated damages.

To return the additional money from the set top box sales, Scientific-Atlanta and Motorola signed contracts with Charter to purchase advertising time for a price higher than fair value. The new set top box agreements were backdated to make it appear that they were negotiated a month before the advertising agreements. The backdating was important to convey the impression that the negotiations were unconnected, a point Arthur Andersen considered necessary for separate treatment of the transactions. Charter recorded the advertising payments to inflate revenue and operating cash flow by approximately $17 million. The inflated number was shown on financial statements filed with the Securities and Exchange Commission (SEC) and reported to the public.

Respondents had no role in preparing or disseminating Charter's financial statements. And their own financial statements booked the transactions as a wash, under generally accepted accounting principles. It is alleged respondents knew or were in reckless disregard of Charter's intention to use the transactions to inflate its revenues and knew the resulting financial statements issued by Charter would be relied upon by research analysts and investors.

Petitioner filed a securities fraud class action on behalf of purchasers of Charter stock alleging that, by participating in the transactions, respondents violated § 10(b) of the Securities Exchange Act of 1934 and SEC Rule 10b–5.

The District Court granted respondents' motion to dismiss for failure to state a claim on which relief can be granted. The United States Court of Appeals for the Eighth Circuit affirmed. In its view the allegations did not show that respondents made misstatements relied upon by the public or that they violated a duty to disclose; and on this premise it found no violation of § 10(b) by respondents. At most, the court observed, respondents had aided and abetted Charter's misstatement of its financial results; but, it noted, there is no private right of action for aiding and abetting a § 10(b) violation. See *Central Bank of Denver, N.A. v. First Interstate Bank of Denver, N. A.*, 511 U.S. 164, 191, 114 S.Ct. 1439, 128 L.Ed.2d 119 (1994). The court also affirmed the District Court's denial of petitioner's motion to amend the complaint, as the revised pleading would not change the court's conclusion on the merits.

Decisions of the Courts of Appeals are in conflict respecting when, if ever, an injured investor may rely upon § 10(b) to recover from a party that neither makes a public misstatement nor violates a duty to disclose but does participate in a scheme to violate § 10(b). Compare *Simpson v.*

AOL Time Warner Inc., 452 F.3d 1040 (C.A.9 2006), with *Regents of Univ. of Cal. v. Credit Suisse First Boston (USA), Inc.*, 482 F.3d 372 (C.A.5 2007). We granted certiorari.

* * * In *Central Bank*, the Court determined that § 10(b) liability did not extend to aiders and abettors. The Court found the scope of § 10(b) to be delimited by the text, which makes no mention of aiding and abetting liability. The Court doubted the implied § 10(b) action should extend to aiders and abettors when none of the express causes of action in the securities Acts included that liability. * * *

The decision in *Central Bank* led to calls for Congress to create an express cause of action for aiding and abetting within the Securities Exchange Act. Then-SEC Chairman Arthur Levitt, testifying before the Senate Securities Subcommittee, cited *Central Bank* and recommended that aiding and abetting liability in private claims be established. S. Hearing No. 103–759, pp. 13–14 (1994). Congress did not follow this course. Instead, in § 104 of the Private Securities Litigation Reform Act of 1995 (PSLRA), 109 Stat. 757, it directed prosecution of aiders and abettors by the SEC. 15 U.S.C. § 78t(e).

The § 10(b) implied private right of action does not extend to aiders and abettors. The conduct of a secondary actor must satisfy each of the elements or preconditions for liability; and we consider whether the allegations here are sufficient to do so.

Reliance by the plaintiff upon the defendant's deceptive acts is an essential element of the § 10(b) private cause of action. It ensures that, for liability to arise, the "requisite causal connection between a defendant's misrepresentation and a plaintiff's injury" exists as a predicate for liability. *Basic Inc. v. Levinson*, 485 U.S. 224, 243, 108 S.Ct. 978, 99 L.Ed.2d 194 (1988); see also *Affiliated Ute Citizens of Utah v. United States*, 406 U.S. 128, 154, 92 S.Ct. 1456, 31 L.Ed.2d 741 (1972) (requiring "causation in fact"). We have found a rebuttable presumption of reliance in two different circumstances. First, if there is an omission of a material fact by one with a duty to disclose, the investor to whom the duty was owed need not provide specific proof of reliance. *Id.*, at 153–154, 92 S.Ct. 1456. Second, under the fraud-on-the-market doctrine, reliance is presumed when the statements at issue become public. The public information is reflected in the market price of the security. Then it can be assumed that an investor who buys or sells stock at the market price relies upon the statement. *Basic, supra*, at 247, 108 S.Ct. 978.

Neither presumption applies here. Respondents had no duty to disclose; and their deceptive acts were not communicated to the public. No member of the investing public had knowledge, either actual or presumed, of respondents' deceptive acts during the relevant times. Petitioner, as a result, cannot show reliance upon any of respondents' actions except in an indirect chain that we find too remote for liability.

Invoking what some courts call "scheme liability," see, *e.g.*, *In re Enron Corp. Securities, Derivative & "ERISA" Litigation*, 439 F.Supp.2d

692, 723 (S.D.Tex.2006), petitioner nonetheless seeks to impose liability on respondents even absent a public statement. In our view this approach does not answer the objection that petitioner did not in fact rely upon respondents' own deceptive conduct.

Liability is appropriate, petitioner contends, because respondents engaged in conduct with the purpose and effect of creating a false appearance of material fact to further a scheme to misrepresent Charter's revenue. The argument is that the financial statement Charter released to the public was a natural and expected consequence of respondents' deceptive acts; had respondents not assisted Charter, Charter's auditor would not have been fooled, and the financial statement would have been a more accurate reflection of Charter's financial condition. That causal link is sufficient, petitioner argues, to apply *Basic's* presumption of reliance to respondents' acts.

In effect petitioner contends that in an efficient market investors rely not only upon the public statements relating to a security but also upon the transactions those statements reflect. Were this concept of reliance to be adopted, the implied cause of action would reach the whole marketplace in which the issuing company does business; and there is no authority for this rule.

As stated above, reliance is tied to causation, leading to the inquiry whether respondents' acts were immediate or remote to the injury. In considering petitioner's arguments, we note § 10(b) provides that the deceptive act must be "in connection with the purchase or sale of any security." Though this phrase in part defines the statute's coverage rather than causation (and so we do not evaluate the "in connection with" requirement of § 10(b) in this case), the emphasis on a purchase or sale of securities does provide some insight into the deceptive acts that concerned the enacting Congress. See Black, Securities Commentary: The Second Circuit's Approach to the "In Connection With" Requirement of Rule 10b–5, 53 Brooklyn L.Rev. 539, 541 (1987) ("[W]hile the 'in connection with' and causation requirements are analytically distinct, they are related to each other, and discussion of the first requirement may merge with discussion of the second"). In all events we conclude respondents' deceptive acts, which were not disclosed to the investing public, are too remote to satisfy the requirement of reliance. It was Charter, not respondents, that misled its auditor and filed fraudulent financial statements; nothing respondents did made it necessary or inevitable for Charter to record the transactions as it did.

The petitioner invokes the private cause of action under § 10(b) and seeks to apply it beyond the securities markets—the realm of financing business—to purchase and supply contracts—the realm of ordinary business operations. The latter realm is governed, for the most part, by state law. It is true that if business operations are used, as alleged here, to affect securities markets, the SEC enforcement power may reach the culpable actors. It is true as well that a dynamic, free economy presupposes a high degree of integrity in all of its parts, an integrity that must be underwritten by rules enforceable in fair, independent, accessible courts. Were the implied cause of action to be extended to the practices described here, however, there would be a risk that the federal power would be used to invite litigation beyond the immediate sphere of securities litigation and in areas already governed by functioning and effective state-law guarantees. Our precedents counsel against this extension. See *Marine Bank v. Weaver*, 455 U.S. 551, 556, 102 S.Ct. 1220, 71 L.Ed.2d 409 (1982) ("Congress, in enacting the securities laws, did not intend to provide a broad federal remedy for all fraud"); *Santa Fe*, 430 U.S., at 479–480, 97 S.Ct. 1292 ("There may well be a need for uniform federal fiduciary standards..... But those standards should not be supplied by judicial extension of § 10(b) and Rule 10b–5 to 'cover the corporate universe'" (quoting Cary, Federalism and Corporate Law: Reflections Upon Delaware, 83 Yale L.J. 663, 700 (1974))). Though § 10(b) is "not 'limited to preserving the integrity of the securities markets,'" [Superintendent of Ins. of State of N. Y. v. Bankers Life & Cas. Co., 404 U.S. 6, 12, 92 S.Ct. 165 (1971)], it does not reach all commercial transactions that are fraudulent and affect the price of a security in some attenuated way.

These considerations answer as well the argument that if this were a common-law action for fraud there could be a finding of reliance. Even if the assumption is correct, it is not controlling. Section 10(b) does not incorporate common-law fraud into federal law. See, *e.g.*, *SEC v. Zandford*, 535 U.S. 813, 820, 122 S.Ct. 1899, 153 L.Ed.2d 1 (2002) ("[Section 10(b)] must not be construed so broadly as to convert every common-law fraud that happens to involve securities into a violation"); *Central Bank*, 511 U.S., at 184, 114 S.Ct. 1439 ("Even assuming ... a deeply rooted background of aiding and abetting tort liability, it does not follow that Congress intended to apply that kind of liability to the private causes of action in the securities Acts"); see also *Dura*, 544 U.S., at 341, 125 S.Ct. 1627. Just as § 10(b) "is surely badly strained when construed to provide a cause of action ... to the world at large," *Blue Chip Stamps v. Manor Drug Stores*, 421 U.S. 723, 733, n. 5, 95 S.Ct. 1917, 44 L.Ed.2d 539 (1975), it should not be interpreted to provide a private cause of action against the entire marketplace in which the issuing company operates.

Petitioner's theory, moreover, would put an unsupportable interpretation on Congress' specific response to *Central Bank* in § 104 of the PSLRA. Congress amended the securities laws to provide for limited coverage of aiders and abettors. Aiding and abetting liability is authorized in actions brought by the SEC but not by private parties. See 15 U.S.C. § 78t(e). Petitioner's view of primary liability makes any aider and abettor liable under § 10(b) if he or she committed a deceptive act in the process of providing assistance. Were we to adopt this construction of § 10(b), it would revive in substance the implied cause of action against all aiders and abettors except those who committed no deceptive act in the process of facilitating the fraud; and we would undermine Congress' determination that this class of defendants should be pursued by the SEC and not by private litigants.

This is not a case in which Congress has enacted a regulatory statute and then has accepted, over a long period of time, broad judicial authority to define substantive standards of conduct and liability. And in accord with the nature of the cause of action at issue here, we give weight to Congress' amendment to the Act restoring aiding and abetting liability in certain cases but not others. The amendment, in our view, supports the conclusion that there is no liability.

The practical consequences of an expansion, which the Court has considered appropriate to examine in circumstances like these, see *Virginia Bankshares, Inc. v. Sandberg*, 501 U.S. 1083, 1104-1105, 111 S.Ct. 2749, 115 L.Ed.2d 929 (1991); *Blue Chip*, 421 U.S., at 737, 95 S.Ct. 1917, provide a further reason to reject petitioner's approach. In Blue Chip, the Court noted that extensive discovery and the potential for uncertainty and disruption in a lawsuit allow plaintiffs with weak claims to extort settlements from innocent companies. *Id.*, at 740–741, 95 S.Ct. 1917. Adoption of petitioner's approach would expose a new class of defendants to these risks. As noted in *Central Bank*, contracting parties might find it necessary to protect against these threats, raising the costs of doing business. Overseas firms with no other exposure to our securities laws could be deterred from doing business here. This, in turn, may raise the cost of being a publicly traded company under our law and shift securities offerings away from domestic capital markets.

* * *

Secondary actors are subject to criminal penalties, The enforcement power is not toothless. Since September 30, 2002, SEC enforcement actions have collected over $10 billion in disgorgement and penalties, much of it for distribution to injured investors. * * * In addition some state securities laws permit state authorities to seek fines and restitution from aiders and abettors. See, *e.g.*, Del.Code Ann., Tit. 6, § 7325 (2005). All secondary actors, furthermore, are not necessarily immune from private suit. The securities statutes provide an express private right of action against accountants and underwriters in certain circumstances, see 15 U.S.C. § 77k, and the implied right of action in § 10(b) continues to cover secondary actors who commit primary violations. *Central Bank, supra*, at 191, 114 S.Ct. 1439.

Here respondents were acting in concert with Charter in the ordinary course as suppliers and, as matters then evolved in the not so ordinary course, as customers. Unconventional as the arrangement was, it took place in the marketplace for goods and services, not in the investment sphere. Charter was free to do as it chose in preparing its books, conferring with its auditor, and preparing and then issuing its financial statements. In these circumstances the investors cannot be said to have relied upon any of respondents' deceptive acts in the decision to purchase or sell securities; and as the requisite reliance cannot be shown, respondents have no liability to petitioner under the implied right of action. This conclusion is consistent with the narrow dimensions we must give to a right of action Congress did not authorize when it first enacted the statute and did not expand when it revisited the law.

The judgment of the Court of Appeals is affirmed, and the case is remanded for further proceedings consistent with this opinion.

It is so ordered.

JUSTICE STEVENS, with whom JUSTICE SOUTER and JUSTICE GINSBURG join, dissenting. * * *

MUSICK v. EMPLOYERS INSURANCE

508 U.S. 286, 113 S.Ct. 2085, 124 L.Ed.2d 194 (1993).

JUSTICE KENNEDY delivered the opinion of the Court.

Where there is joint responsibility for tortuous conduct, the question often arises whether those who compensate the injured party may seek contribution from other joint tortfeasors who have paid no damages or paid less than their fair share. In this case we must determine whether defendants in a suit based on an implied private right of action under § 10(b) of the Securities Exchange Act of 1934 and Rule 10b–5 of the Securities and Exchange Commission (a 10b–5 action) may seek contribution from joint tortfeasors. Without addressing the merits of the claim for contribution in this case, we hold that defendants in a 10b–5 action have a right to seek contribution as a matter of federal law. * * *

Requests to recognize a right to contribution for defendants liable under federal law are not unfamiliar to this Court. Twice we have declined to recognize an action for contribution under federal laws outside the arena of securities regulation. In Northwest Airlines, Inc. v. Transport Workers, 451 U.S. 77 (1981), we held that an employer had no right to contribution against unions alleged to be joint participants with the employer in violations of the Equal Pay Act of 1963 and Title VII of the Civil Rights Act of 1964. Later that same Term, in Texas Industries, Inc. v. Radcliff Materials, Inc., 451 U.S. 630 (1981), we determined that there is no right to contribution for recovery based on violation of § 1 of the Sherman Act.

On the other hand, we endorsed a nonstatutory right to contribution among joint tortfeasors responsible for injuring a longshoreman in Cooper Stevedoring Co. v. Fritz Kopke, Inc., 417 U.S. 106 (1974). * * *

We now turn to the question whether a right to contribution is within the contours of the 10b–5 action. The parties have devoted considerable portions of their briefs to debating whether a rule of contribution or of no contribution is more efficient or more equitable. Just as we declined to rule on these matters in *Texas Industries* and *Northwest Airlines*, we decline to do so here. Our task is not to assess the relative merits of the competing rules, but rather to attempt to infer how the 1934 Congress would have addressed the issue had the 10b–5 action been included as an express provision in the 1934 Act. * * *

Inquiring about what a given Congress might have done, though not a promising venture as a general proposition, does in this case yield an answer we find convincing. * * *

There are * * * two sections of the 1934 Act, §§ 9 and 18, that, as we have noted, are close in structure, purpose and intent to the 10b–5 action. Each confers an explicit right of action in favor of private parties and, in so doing, discloses a congressional intent regarding the definition and apportionment of liability among private parties. For two distinct reasons, these express causes of action are of particular significance in determining how Congress would have resolved the question of contribution had it provided for a private cause of action under § 10(b). First, §§ 9 and 18 are instructive because both "target the precise dangers that are the focus of § 10(b)," and the intent motivating all three sections is the same—"to deter fraud and manipulative practices in the securities market, and to ensure full disclosure of information material to investment decisions."

Second, of the eight express liability provisions contained in the 1933 and 1934 Acts, §§ 9 and 18 impose liability upon defendants who stand in a position most similar to 10b–5 defendants for the sake of assessing whether they should be entitled to contribution. All three causes of action impose direct liability on defendants for their own acts as opposed to derivative liability for the acts of others; all three involve defendants who have violated the securities law with scienter; all three operate in many instances to impose liability on multiple defendants acting in concert; and all three are based on securities provisions enacted into law by the 73rd Congress. * * *

Sections 9 and 18 contain nearly identical express provisions for a right to contribution, each permitting a defendant to "recover contribution as in cases of contract from any person who, if joined in the original suit, would have been liable to make the same payment." These were forward-looking provisions at the time. The course of tort law in this century has been to reverse the old rule against contribution, but this movement has been confined in large part to actions in negligence. The express contribution provisions in §§ 9 and 18 were, and still are, cited as important precedents because they permit contribution for intentional torts. We think that these explicit provisions for contribution are an important, not an inconsequential, feature of the federal securities laws and that consistency requires us to adopt a like contribution rule for the right of action existing under Rule 10b–5. Given the identity of purpose behind §§ 9, 10(b) and 18, and similarity in their operation, we find no ground for ruling that allowing contribution in 10b–5 actions will frustrate the purposes of the statutory section from which it is derived. * * *

JUSTICE THOMAS, with whom JUSTICE BLACKMUN and JUSTICE O'CONNOR join, dissenting. * * *

NOTES

1. One of the principal concerns that led to passage of the Securities Litigation Reform Act of 1995 was the fact that "peripheral" defendants could be held liable for the full amount of the damages caused by the principal wrongdoer. The Conference Committee addressed this concern in its report:

> One of the most manifestly unfair aspects of the current system of securities litigation is its imposition of liability on one party for injury actually caused by another. Under current law, a single defendant who has been found to be 1% liable may be forced to pay 100% of the damages in the case. The Conference Committee remedies this injustice by providing a "fair share" system of proportionate liability. As former SEC Chairman Richard Breeden testified, under the current regime of joint and several liability, "parties who are central to perpetrating a fraud often pay little, if anything. At the same time, those whose involvement might be only peripheral and lacked any deliberate and knowing participation in the fraud often pay the most in damages."

> The current system of joint and several liability creates coercive pressure for entirely innocent parties to settle meritless claims rather than risk exposing themselves to liability for a grossly disproportionate share of the damages in the case.

> In many cases, exposure to this kind of unlimited and unfair risk has made it impossible for firms to attract qualified persons to serve as outside directors. Both the House and Senate Committees repeatedly heard testimony concerning the chilling effect of unlimited exposure to meritless securities litigation on the willingness of capable people to serve on company boards. SEC Chairman Levitt himself testified that "there [were] the dozen or so entrepreneurial firms whose invitations [to be an outside director] I turned down because they could not adequately insure their directors. . . . [C]ountless colleagues in business have had the same experience, and the fact that so many qualified people have been unable to serve is, to me, one of the most lamentable problems of all." This result has injured the entire U.S. economy.

The Reform Act accordingly provides that a defendant in a private fraud action is jointly and severally liable for the full amount of the damages only if the trier of fact specifically determines that he knowingly committed a violation of the securities laws. In all other cases, he can be held liable "solely for the portion of the judgment that corresponds to [his] percentage of responsibility," as determined by the trier of fact. For this purpose, the jury must be specifically asked to determine, for each defendant, (a) whether he knowingly committed a violation, and (b) his percentage of "the total fault of all persons who caused or contributed to the loss." See 1934 Act § 21D(g), 1933 Act § 11(f)(2). There are, however, a couple of strange exceptions to this limitation on joint and several liability. First, all defendants are jointly and severally liable to any individual plaintiff who has a net worth of less than

$200,000 and is entitled to damages exceeding 10% of her net worth. Second, if any defendants cannot pay their share of the damages due to insolvency, each of the other defendants must make an additional payment—up to 50% of their own liability—to make up the shortfall. Congress required that actions for contribution be brought within six months of the entry of judgment in the underlying action. See 1934 Act § 21D(g)(8),(9).

2. The *in pari delicto* defense has also arisen in the context of Section 10(b) of the Securities Exchange Act of 1934. This concept posits that a plaintiff should not recover if he or she is also involved in the wrongdoing. In Bateman Eichler, Hill Richards, Inc. v. Berner, 472 U.S. 299, 105 S.Ct. 2622, 86 L.Ed.2d 215 (1985), the Supreme Court held that such a defense was available under Section 10(b) only where the plaintiff has substantially equal culpability for the violations at issue and where the defense would not significantly interfere with the enforcement of the federal securities laws.

SECTION 14. RESPONSIBILITIES OF ATTORNEYS AND OTHER PROFESSIONALS

The securities laws do not impose any specific liabilities on lawyers *as such*. By virtue of the central role that lawyers have assumed in the disclosure process, however, there has been a developing tendency, in SEC and court decisions, to hold lawyers responsible for misstatements in disclosure documents or for securities transactions which violate the law. This responsibility is of course in addition to whatever liability lawyers may incur to their clients under common law principles for negligence in the performance of their legal work. As you read these materials, note that liability in many cases is based on the lawyers having "aided and abetted" the violation, a basis which the Supreme Court eliminated by its decision in the *Central Bank* decision above.

In SEC v. National Student Marketing Corp., 457 F.Supp. 682 (D.D.C. 1978), the Commission brought an action against lawyers who had permitted a merger transaction to be consummated after having been informed by accountants that the proxy statements used to solicit the votes of shareholders in favor of the merger contained misleading financial statements. The court stated:

> Upon receipt of the unsigned comfort letter, it became clear that the merger had been approved by the Interstate shareholders on the basis of materially misleading information. In view of the obvious materiality of the information, especially to attorneys learned in securities law, the attorneys' responsibilities to their corporate client required them to take steps to ensure that the information would be disclosed to the shareholders. However, it is unnecessary to determine the precise extent of their obligations here, since it is undisputed that they took no steps whatsoever to delay the closing pending disclosure to and

resolicitation of the Interstate shareholders. But, at the very least, they were required to speak out at the closing concerning the obvious materiality of the information and the concomitant requirement that the merger not be closed until the adjustments were disclosed and approval of the merger was again obtained from the Interstate shareholders. Their silence was not only a breach of this duty to speak, but in addition lent the appearance of legitimacy to the closing. The combination of these factors clearly provided substantial assistance to the closing of the merger.

The most controversial aspect of the SEC's position in the *National Student Marketing* case was the assertion in its complaint that the attorneys for NSMC and Interstate had participated in a fraudulent scheme when they "failed to refuse to issue their opinions * * * and failed to insist that the financial statements be revised and shareholders be resolicited, and failing that, to cease representing their respective clients and, under the circumstances, notify the plaintiff Commission concerning the misleading nature of the nine month financial statements."

The court did not deal directly with the question of a lawyer's obligation to notify the Commission that his client has filed incorrect statements with it. To what extent does the SEC position go beyond the American Bar Association's Disciplinary Rule 7–102(B)(1), which in 1969 provided that:

A lawyer who receives information clearly establishing that his client has, in the course of the representation, perpetrated a fraud upon a person or tribunal shall promptly call upon his client to rectify the same, and if his client refuses or is unable to do so, he shall reveal the fraud to the affected person or tribunal.

In February 1974, the ABA amended the above rule to add at the end the words: "except when the information is protected as a privileged communication." Its stated reason was that the previous language "had the unacceptable result * * * of requiring a lawyer in certain instances to reveal privileged communications which he also was duty-bound not to reveal according to the law of evidence." ABA Ethics Opinion 341 (1975). Does the revised language conflict with the position taken by the SEC in *National Student Marketing?* At the annual meeting of the ABA House of Delegates in August 1975, the following resolution was unanimously adopted:

1. The confidentiality of lawyer-client consultations and advice and the fiduciary loyalty of the lawyer to the client, as prescribed in the American Bar Association's Code of Professional Responsibility ("CPR"), are vital to the basic function of the lawyer as legal counselor because they enable and encourage clients to consult legal counsel freely, with assurance that counsel will respect the confidentiality of the client's communications and will advise independently and in the client's best interest without conflicting loyalties or obligations.

2. This vital confidentiality of consultation and advice would be destroyed or seriously impaired if it is accepted as a general principle that lawyers must inform the SEC or others regarding confidential information received by lawyers from their clients even though such action would not be permitted or required by the CPR. Any such compelled disclosure would seriously and adversely affect the lawyers' function as counselor, and may seriously and adversely affect the ability of lawyers as advocates to represent and defend their clients' interest.

3. In light of the foregoing considerations, it must be recognized that a lawyer cannot, consistently with his essential role as legal adviser, be regarded as a source of information concerning possible wrong-doing by clients. Accordingly, any principle of law which, except as permitted or required by the CPR, permits or obliges a lawyer to disclose to the SEC otherwise confidential information, should be established only by statute after full and careful consideration of the public interests involved, and should be resisted unless clearly mandated by law.

The SEC position in *National Student Marketing* is that a lawyer has an obligation to inform the SEC if his client refuses to disclose material facts in a filed document. If a lawyer furnishes such information to the SEC, is he also required, or permitted, to make it available to private parties who sue his client (or former client) for violation of the securities laws? Or is he barred from making such disclosure by Ethical Consideration 4–1 of the Code of Professional Responsibility, which "require[s] the preservation by the lawyer of confidences and secrets of one who has employed or sought to employ him"? Does it make any difference if the lawyer furnishes the information to the plaintiff in an effort to demonstrate that there was no basis for naming him as a defendant in the action? See Meyerhofer v. Empire Fire & Marine Ins. Co., 497 F.2d 1190 (2d Cir.1974).

In March 1979, an SEC administrative law judge ordered two partners in the New York law firm of Brown, Wood, Ivey, Mitchell & Petty suspended from practice before the Commission for periods of one year and nine months, respectively. The basis for the suspension, which arose from the lawyers' representation of National Telephone Company, was that they had:

(a) violated, and aided and abetted violations of, Rule 10b–5 by participating in the preparation of a misleading press release and a misleading 8–K report, and by failing to take steps to correct a false and misleading statement sent to shareholders or to see that adequate disclosure was made; and

(b) engaged in unethical and improper professional conduct by failing to inform National's board of directors concerning management's unwillingness to make disclosure of material facts affecting National's financial condition.

In re Carter, Adm.Proc. No. 3–5464. BNA Sec.Reg. & L.Rep. No. 494, at F–1 (Mar. 7, 1979)(initial decision). On review of the decision by the administrative law judge, the Commission reversed his findings and held that there was no basis for sanctions. In re Carter, Sec.Ex.Act Rel. No. 17597 (Feb. 28, 1981).

The SEC had adopted Rule 2(e) (now Rule 102(e)) governing the ability of professionals, including attorneys, to practice before the agency. With respect to the charge of aiding and abetting National Telephone's violations of Rule 10b–5, the Commission held that "a finding of *willful aiding and abetting* within the meaning of Rule 2(e) requires a showing that respondents were aware or knew that their role was part of an activity that was improper or illegal." The Commission concluded that the evidence was "insufficient to establish that either respondent acted with sufficient knowledge and awareness or recklessness" to satisfy that test. With respect to the charge of engaging in unethical and improper professional conduct, the Commission felt that it "should not establish new rules of conduct and impose them retroactively upon professionals who acted at the time without reason to believe that their conduct was unethical or improper," and that the "responsibilities of lawyers who become aware that their client is engaging in violations of the securities laws have not been so firmly and unambiguously established that we believe all practicing lawyers can be held to an awareness of generally recognized norms." To deal with future cases, the Commission set forth the following views:

> The Commission is of the view that a lawyer engages in "unethical or improper professional conduct" under the following circumstances: When a lawyer with significant responsibilities in the effectuation of a company's compliance with the disclosure requirements of the federal securities laws becomes aware that his client is engaged in a substantial and continuing failure to satisfy those disclosure requirements, his continued participation violates professional standards unless he takes prompt steps to end the client's noncompliance. The Commission has determined that this interpretation will be applicable only to conduct occurring after the date of this opinion.

> We do not imply that a lawyer is obliged, at the risk of being held to have violated Rule 2(e), to seek to correct every isolated disclosure action or inaction which he believes to be at variance with applicable disclosure standards, although there may be isolated disclosure failures that are so serious that their correction becomes a matter of primary professional concern. It is also clear, however, that a lawyer is not privileged to unthinkingly permit himself to be co-opted into an ongoing fraud and cast as a dupe or a shield for a wrongdoing client.

> Initially, counselling accurate disclosure is sufficient, even if his advice is not accepted. But there comes a point at which a reasonable lawyer must conclude that his advice is not being followed, or even sought in good faith, and that his client is involved in a continuing

course of violating the securities laws. At this critical juncture, the lawyer must take further, more affirmative steps in order to avoid the inference that he has been co-opted, willingly or unwillingly, into the scheme of nondisclosure.

The lawyer is in the best position to choose his next step. Resignation is one option, although we recognize that other consider- ations, including the protection of the client against foreseeable prejudice, must be taken into account in the case of withdrawal. A direct approach to the board of directors or one or more individual directors or officers may be appropriate; or he may choose to try to enlist the aid of other members of the firm's management. What is required, in short, is some prompt action that leads to the conclusion that the lawyer is engaged in efforts to correct the underlying prob- lem, rather than having capitulated to the desires of a strong-willed, but misguided client.

In October 1981, the SEC solicited public comments on a proposal to adopt the standard set forth in the first paragraph of the above excerpt from its opinion in the *Carter* case as a "Standard of Conduct Constituting Unethical or Improper Professional Practice Before the Commission," The ABA Section of Corporation, Banking and Business law submitted a statement strongly criticizing the proposal on the merits and also urging that the SEC had no statutory power to regulate the conduct of lawyers in that manner.

In the meantime, the ABA was engaged in a complete revision of its Code of Professional Responsibility. In the course of that revision, the ABA's ethics commission suggested a new guideline that would have encouraged lawyers to speak out if their clients were engaged in securities fraud or other kinds of irregular financial transactions. At its annual meeting in 1983, however, the ABA rejected this proposal and amended the Code in a way that actually limited the pre-existing obligation of lawyers to "blow the whistle" on their clients in these situations. Under Rule 1.16 of the ABA's new Model Rules of Professional Conduct, a lawyer *may* withdraw from representing a client if "the client persists in a course of action involving the lawyer's services that the lawyer reasonably believes is criminal or fraudulent." However, under Rule 1.6, the lawyer may reveal information relating to representation of a client only "to prevent the client from committing a criminal act that the lawyer believes is likely to result in imminent death or substantial bodily harm."

In SEC v. Frank, 388 F.2d 486 (2d Cir.1968), the SEC obtained a district court order enjoining Nylo–Thane, its officers, and its attorney, Frank, from making further misrepresentations concerning the company's business. Frank, who had represented Nylo–Thane in the preparation of a Regulation A offering circular which the SEC had held to be misleading, appealed from the issuance of an injunction against him.

* * * His position, broadly stated, was that the portion of the offering circular alleged to misrepresent the additive had been pre-

pared by the officers of Nylo–Thane and that his function had been that of a scrivener helping them to place their ideas in proper form. * * *

Although Frank makes much of this being the first instance in which the Commission has obtained an injunction against an attorney for participation in the preparation of an allegedly misleading offering circular or prospectus, we find this unimpressive. A lawyer has no privilege to assist in circulating a statement with regard to securities which he knows to be false simply because his client has furnished it to him. At the other extreme it would be unreasonable to hold a lawyer who was putting his client's description of a chemical process into understandable English to be guilty of fraud simply because of his failure to detect discrepancies between their description and technical reports available to him in a physical sense but beyond his ability to understand. The instant case lies between these extremes. The SEC's position is that Frank had been furnished with information which even a non-expert would recognize as showing the falsity of many of the representations, notably those implying extensive and satisfactory testing at factories and indicating that all had gone passing well at the test by the Army Laboratories. If this is so, the Commission would be entitled to prevail; a lawyer, no more than others, can escape liability for fraud by closing his eyes to what he saw and could readily understand. Whether the fraud sections of the securities laws go beyond this and require a lawyer passing on an offering circular to run down possible infirmities in his client's story of which he has been put on notice, and if so what efforts are required of him, is a closer question on which it is important that the court be seized of the precise facts, including the extent, as the SEC claimed with respect to Frank, to which his role went beyond a lawyer's normal one.

The court of appeals held that the district court had not made adequate findings of fact, and remanded the case for further proceedings.

With respect to the responsibility of accountants to expose fraudulent activities by the companies that they audit, Congress in 1995 added a new § 10A to the 1934 Act, requiring accountants who audit the financial statements of publicly-held companies to adopt procedures (a) to detect illegal acts that would affect the financial statements, and (b) to identify transactions with related parties that are material to the financial statements. If the accountants become aware of illegal acts, they must report them first to the management, then to the board of directors, and finally to the SEC, unless appropriate remedial action is taken. The entire role of independent accountants came under examination as a result of the bankruptcy of the Enron Energy Corp., which was the fifth largest company in the United States when it failed. Large amount of debt were kept off its balance sheet and earnings claimed under some doubtful auditing practices. Enron's auditor was destroyed as a result of its role in that debacle, and it was convicted of obstruction of justice after it shredded large amounts of documents relating to Enron.

The Enron debacle and other accounting scandals heightened regulatory concern over the role of these accountants as gatekeepers. The Sarbanes–Oxley Act of 2002 created a Public Company Accounting Oversight Board to oversee the auditing practices of auditors. The Public Company Accounting Oversight Board took control of auditing standards away from the accounting profession. Accountants certifying the financial standards of public companies are required to register with the Board and conform to the standards it sets. Pub. L. No.107–204, 107th Cong. 2d Sess. (2002). Some large accounting firms had already spun off consulting services (Accenture was one such spin off), and immediately after this legislation IBM purchased the consulting operations of another giant accounting firm. William Bulkeley & Kemba Dunham, *IBM Speeds Move to Consulting With $3.5 Billion Acquisition*, WALL ST. J., July 31, 2002, at A1.

The Sarbanes–Oxley Act of 2002 added still another gatekeeper. The SEC was given authority to issue rules setting forth standards of conduct for attorneys advising public companies. These attorneys will be required to report violations to a board committee composed entirely of outside directors if the company's officers fail to take corrective action. Pub. L. No. 107–204 Sec. 307,107th Cong. 2d Sess. (2002). This means that lawyers are now policemen and not just advisers.

On March 7, 2002, a group of law professors sent a letter to SEC Chairman Harvey Pitt urging the SEC to amend its rules of practice to better define what constitutes proper representation of public companies. In particular, the letter asked that the Commission adopt a rule to conform to Rule 1.13 of the American Bar Association's Model Rules of Professional Conduct. In relevant part, Rule 1.13 requires that when an attorney who is representing a corporation is made aware of serious wrongdoing, the attorney must take steps to correct the problem. Those steps include what is sometimes referred to as "climbing the corporate ladder"—reporting the violation to someone within the corporation in a position of authority to take corrective action. The Model Rule requires the attorney to continue to climb the ladder, even to the Board of Directors until the attorney is satisfied that the matter will be attended to properly. The letter to Chairman Pitt asked that the SEC adopt a rule indicating that a lawyer who does not take this action can be suspended from practice before the SEC. On March 28, the SEC's General Counsel responded on Chairman Pitt's behalf that since 1981 the SEC "has not brought Rule 102(e) proceedings against on allegations of professional conduct, or otherwise used the Rule to establish professional responsibilities of lawyers."[1] Mr. Becker's letter further stated that "[t]here is a strong view among the bar that these matters are more appropriately

---

1. March 28 letter from David Becker to Painter, *et al.*, at http://www/abanet.org/buslaw/corporateresponsibility/responsibility_relatedmat.html.

addressed by state bar rules ..." Later in the spring of 2002, Senator John Edwards' office submitted a proposed provision that was made part of the Sarbanes–Oxley Act as section 307 of that Act that, in essence, mandated the SEC to follow the law professors' suggestion. Section 307 thus requires the SEC to impose the obligations to report the wrongdoing within the corporation. The Act does not address whether a lawyer has an obligation to make a noisy withdrawal if climbing the corporate ladder does not satisfy the lawyer that adequate steps have been taken to address the lawyer's concerns. The SEC has been considering whether to adopt such a requirement. The following SEC release describes some of the more important aspects of the SEC lawyer conduct rules implementing section 307 of the Sarbanes–Oxley Act.

IMPLEMENTATION OF STANDARDS OF PROFESSIONAL CONDUCT FOR ATTORNEYS

Sec. Exch. Act Rel. No. 34–47276, 2003 WL 193527 (SEC Jan. 29, 2003).

Section 307 of the Sarbanes–Oxley Act of 2002 (the "Act") mandates that the Commission issue rules prescribing minimum standards of professional conduct for attorneys appearing and practicing before it in any way in the representation of issuers, including at a minimum a rule requiring an attorney to report evidence of a material violation of securities laws or breach of fiduciary duty or similar violation by the issuer or any agent thereof to appropriate officers within the issuer and, thereafter, to the highest authority within the issuer, if the initial report does not result in an appropriate response. The Act directs the Commission to issue these rules within 180 days.

On November 21, 2002, in response to this directive, we published for comment proposed Part 205, entitled "Standards of Professional Conduct for Attorneys Appearing and Practicing before the Commission in the Representation of an Issuer." The proposed rule prescribed minimum standards of professional conduct for attorneys appearing and practicing before us in any way in the representation of an issuer. The proposed rule took a broad view of who could be found to be appearing and practicing before us. It covered lawyers licensed in foreign jurisdictions, whether or not they were also admitted in the United States. In addition to a rigorous up-the-ladder reporting requirement, the proposed rule incorporated several corollary provisions. Under certain circumstances, these provisions permitted or required attorneys to effect a so-called "noisy withdrawal" by notifying the Commission that they have withdrawn from the representation of the issuer, and permitted attorneys to report evidence of material violations to the Commission.

Our proposing release generated significant comment and extensive debate....

The thoughtful and constructive suggestions we have received from a broad spectrum of commenters have enabled us better to understand interested parties' views concerning the operation and impact of the proposed rule. As more specifically discussed below, the final rule we adopt today has been significantly modified in light of these comments and suggestions. Thus, the triggering standard for reporting evidence of a material violation has been modified to clarify and confirm that an attorney's actions will be evaluated against an objective standard. * * * [W]e are extending the comment period on the "noisy withdrawal" and related provisions of the proposed rule and are issuing a separate release soliciting comment on this issue. In that release, we are also proposing and soliciting comment on an alternative procedure to the "noisy withdrawal" provisions. Under this proposed alternative, in the event that an attorney withdraws from representation of an issuer after failing to receive an appropriate response to reported evidence of a material violation, the issuer would be required to disclose its counsel's withdrawal to the Commission as a material event. In the same release, we are soliciting additional comment on the final rules we are adopting, particularly insofar as adoption of the "noisy withdrawal" provisions of the proposed alternative might require conforming changes to the final rule.

Section 205.1 Purpose and Scope

This part sets forth minimum standards of professional conduct for attorneys appearing and practicing before the Commission in the representation of an issuer. These standards supplement applicable standards of any jurisdiction where an attorney is admitted or practices and are not intended to limit the ability of any jurisdiction to impose additional obligations on an attorney not inconsistent with the application of this part. Where the standards of a state or other United States jurisdiction where an attorney is admitted or practices conflict with this part, this part shall govern. * * *

The definition contained in the final rule addresses several of the concerns raised by commenters. Attorneys who advise that, under the federal securities laws, a particular document need not be incorporated into a filing, registration statement or other submission to the Commission will be covered by the revised definition. In addition, an attorney must have notice that a document he or she is preparing or assisting in preparing will be submitted to the Commission to be deemed to be "appearing and practicing" under the revised definition. The definition in the final rule thereby also clarifies that an attorney's preparation of a document (such as a contract) which he or she never intended or had notice would be submitted to the Commission, or incorporated into a document submitted to the Commission, but which subsequently is submitted to the Commission as an exhibit to or in connection with a filing, does not constitute "appearing and practicing" before the Commission. * * *

The standard set forth in the final version of Section 205.2(b) requires the attorney to "reasonably believe" either that there is no material violation or that the issuer has taken proper remedial steps. The term "reasonably believes" is defined in Section 205.2(m). In providing that the attorney's belief that a response was appropriate be reasonable, the Commission is allowing the attorney to take into account, and the Commission to weigh, all attendant circumstances. The circumstances a reporting attorney might weigh in assessing whether he or she could reasonably believe that an issuer's response was appropriate would include the amount and weight of the evidence of a material violation, the severity of the apparent material violation and the scope of the investigation into the report. While some commenters suggested that a reporting attorney should be able to rely completely on the assurance of an issuer's CLO that there was no material violation or that the issuer was undertaking an appropriate response, the Commission believes that this information, while certainly relevant to the determination whether an attorney could reasonably believe that a response was appropriate, cannot be dispositive of the issue. Otherwise, an issuer could simply have its CLO reply to the reporting attorney that "there is no material violation," without taking any steps to investigate and/or remedy material violations. Such a result would clearly be contrary to Congress' intent in enacting Section 307. On the other hand, it is anticipated that an attorney, in determining whether a response is appropriate, may rely on reasonable and appropriate factual representations and legal determinations of persons on whom a reasonable attorney would rely.

Evidence of a material violation must first be credible evidence. An attorney is obligated to report when, based upon that credible evidence, "it would be unreasonable, under the circumstances, for a prudent and competent attorney not to conclude that it is reasonably likely that a material violation has occurred, is ongoing, or is about to occur." This formulation, while intended to adopt an objective standard, also recognizes that there is a range of conduct in which an attorney may engage without being unreasonable. The "circumstances" are the circumstances at the time the attorney decides whether he or she is obligated to report the information. These circumstances may include, among others, the attorney's professional skills, background and experience, the time constraints under which the attorney is acting, the attorney's previous experience and familiarity with the client, and the availability of other lawyers with whom the lawyer may consult. Under the revised definition, an attorney is not required (or expected) to report "gossip, hearsay, [or] innuendo." Nor is the rule's reporting obligation triggered by "a combination of circumstances from which the attorney, in retrospect, should have drawn an inference," as one commenter feared.

On the other hand, the rule's definition of "evidence of a material violation" makes clear that the initial duty to report up-the-ladder is not triggered only when the attorney "knows" that a material violation has occurred or when the attorney "conclude[s] there has been a violation, and no reasonable fact finder could conclude otherwise." That threshold for initial reporting within the issuer is too high. Under the Commission's rule, evidence of a material violation must be reported in all circumstances in which it would be unreasonable for a prudent and competent attorney not to conclude that it is "reasonably likely" that a material violation has occurred, is ongoing, or is about to occur. To be "reasonably likely" a material violation must be more than a mere possibility, but it need not be "more likely than not." If a material violation is reasonably likely, an attorney must report evidence of this violation. The term "reasonably likely" qualifies each of the three instances when a report must be made. Thus, a report is required when it is reasonably likely a violation has occurred, when it is reasonably likely a violation is ongoing or when reasonably likely a violation is about to occur.

In the summer of 2003, the American Bar Association amended its Model Rules. As explained in the official comments to Model Rule 1.13:

The Entity as the Client

[1]   An organizational client is a legal entity, but it cannot act except through its officers, directors, employees, shareholders and other constituents. Officers, directors, employees and shareholders are the constituents of the corporate organizational client. The duties defined in this Comment apply equally to unincorporated associations. "Other constituents" as used in this Comment means the positions equivalent to officers, directors, employees and shareholders held by persons acting for organizational clients that are not corporations.

[2]   When one of the constituents of an organizational client communicates with the organization's lawyer in that person's organizational capacity, the communication is protected by Rule 1.6. Thus, by way of example, if an organizational client requests its lawyer to investigate allegations of wrongdoing, interviews made in the course of that investigation between the lawyer and the client's employees or other constituents are covered by Rule 1.6. This does not mean, however, that constituents of an organizational client are the clients of the lawyer. The lawyer may not disclose to such constituents information relating to the representation except for disclosures explicitly or impliedly authorized by the organizational client in order to carry out the representation or as otherwise permitted by Rule 1.6.

[3]   When constituents of the organization make decisions for it, the decisions ordinarily must be accepted by the lawyer even if their utility or prudence is doubtful. Decisions concerning policy and operations, including ones entailing serious risk, are not as such in the lawyer's province. Paragraph (b) makes clear, however, that when the lawyer knows that the organization is likely to be substantially injured by action of an officer or other constituent that violates a legal obligation to the organization or is in violation of law that might be imputed to the organization, the lawyer must proceed as is reasonably necessary in the best interest of the organization. As defined in Rule

1.0(f), knowledge can be inferred from circumstances, and a lawyer cannot ignore the obvious.

[4] In determining how to proceed under paragraph (b), the lawyer should give due consideration to the seriousness of the violation and its consequences, the responsibility in the organization and the apparent motivation of the person involved, the policies of the organization concerning such matters, and any other relevant considerations. Ordinarily, referral to a higher authority would be necessary. In some circumstances, however, it may be appropriate for the lawyer to ask the constituent to reconsider the matter; for example, if the circumstances involve a constituent's innocent misunderstanding of law and subsequent acceptance of the lawyer's advice, the lawyer may reasonably conclude that the best interest of the organization does not require that the matter be referred to higher authority. If a constituent persists in conduct contrary to the lawyer's advice, it will be necessary for the lawyer to take steps to have the matter reviewed by a higher authority in the organization. If the matter is of sufficient seriousness and importance or urgency to the organization, referral to higher authority in the organization may be necessary even if the lawyer has not communicated with the constituent. Any measures taken should, to the extent practicable, minimize the risk of revealing information relating to the representation to persons outside the organization. Even in circumstances where a lawyer is not obligated by Rule 1.13 to proceed, a lawyer may bring to the attention of an organizational client, including its highest authority, matters that the lawyer reasonably believes to be of sufficient importance to warrant doing so in the best interest of the organization.

[5] Paragraph (b) also makes clear that when it is reasonably necessary to enable the organization to address the matter in a timely and appropriate manner, the lawyer must refer the matter to higher authority, including, if warranted by the circumstances, the highest authority that can act on behalf of the organization under applicable law. The organization's highest authority to whom a matter may be referred ordinarily will be the board of directors or similar governing body. However, applicable law may prescribe that under certain conditions the highest authority reposes elsewhere, for example, in the independent directors of a corporation.

* * *

———

Also, in order to clarify how this interrelates to lawyer/client confidentiality, the ABA also amended its Model Rule 1.6. The changes reflected in the amended rules brought the ABA's Model Rules more in line with the SEC lawyer conduct rules that are discussed above.

———

SECTION 15. STATUTE OF LIMITATIONS

The Supreme Court's efforts to limit the scope of private actions under Rule 10b–5 were not limited just to setting high standards for establishing the elements of a violation.

LAMPF v. GILBERTSON

501 U.S. 350, 111 S.Ct. 2773, 115 L.Ed.2d 321 (1991).

JUSTICE BLACKMUN delivered the opinion of the Court, except as to Part II–A.

In this litigation we must determine which statute of limitations is applicable to a private suit brought pursuant to § 10(b) of the Securities Exchange Act of 1934, and to Securities and Exchange Commission Rule 10b–5 promulgated thereunder. * * *

[Part II A] It is the usual rule that when Congress has failed to provide a statute of limitations for a federal cause of action, a court "borrows" or "absorbs" the local time limitation most analogous to the case at hand. * * *

The rule, however, is not without exception. We have recognized that a state legislature rarely enacts a limitations period with federal interests in mind, and when the operation of a state limitations period would frustrate the policies embraced by the federal enactment, this Court has looked to federal law for a suitable period. These departures from the state-borrowing doctrine have been motivated by this Court's conclusion that it would be "inappropriate to conclude that Congress would choose to adopt state rules at odds with the purpose or operation of federal substantive law." * * *

Predictably, this determination is a delicate one. Recognizing, however, that a period must be selected, our cases do provide some guidance as to whether state or federal borrowing is appropriate and as to the period best suited to the cause of action under consideration. From these cases we are able to distill a hierarchical inquiry for ascertaining the appropriate limitations period for a federal cause of action where Congress has not set the time within which such an action must be brought.

First, the court must determine whether a uniform statute of limitations is to be selected. Where a federal cause of action tends in practice to "encompass numerous and diverse topics and subtopics," such that a single state limitations period may not be consistently applied within a jurisdiction, we have concluded that the federal interests in predictability and judicial economy counsel the adoption of one source, or class of sources, for borrowing purposes. * * *

Second, assuming a uniform limitations period is appropriate, the court must decide whether this period should be derived from a state or a federal source. In making this judgment, the court should accord particular weight to the geographic character of the claim. * * *

Finally, even where geographic considerations counsel federal borrowing, the aforementioned presumption of state borrowing requires that a court determine that an analogous federal source truly affords a "closer fit" with the cause of action at issue than does any available state-law source. Although considerations pertinent to this determination will necessarily vary depending upon the federal cause of action and the available state and federal analogues, such factors as commonality of purpose and similarity of elements will be relevant.

In the present litigation, our task is complicated by the nontraditional origins of the § 10(b) cause of action. The text of § 10(b) does not provide for private claims. Such claims are of judicial creation, having been implied under the statute for nearly half a century. * * *

We conclude that where, as here, the claim asserted is one implied under a statute that also contains an express cause of action with its own time limitation, a court should look first to the statute of origin to ascertain the proper limitations period. We can imagine no clearer indication of how Congress would have balanced the policy considerations implicit in any limitations provision than the balance struck by the same Congress in limiting similar and related protections. * * *

In the present litigation, there can be no doubt that the contemporaneously enacted express remedial provisions represent "a federal statute of limitations actually designed to accommodate a balance of interests very similar to that at stake here—a statute that is, in fact, an analogy to the present lawsuit more apt than any of the suggested state-law parallels." The 1934 Act contained a number of express causes of action, each with an explicit limitations period. With only one more restrictive exception, each of these includes some variation of a 1–year period after discovery combined with a 3–year period of repose. In adopting the 1934 Act, the 73d Congress also amended the limitations provision of the 1933 Act, adopting the 1–and–3–year structure for each cause of action contained therein.

Section 9 of the 1934 Act, pertaining to the willful manipulation of security prices, and § 18, relating to misleading filings, target the precise dangers that are the focus of § 10(b). Each is an integral element of a complex web of regulations. Each was intended to facilitate a central goal: "to protect investors against manipulation of stock prices through regulation of transactions upon securities exchanges and in over-the-counter markets, and to impose regular reporting requirements on companies whose stock is listed on national securities exchanges."

We therefore conclude that we must reject the Commission's contention that the 5–year period contained in § 20A, added to the 1934 Act in 1988, is more appropriate for § 10(b) actions than is the 1–and–3–year structure in the Act's original remedial provisions. The Insider Trading and Securities Fraud Enforcement Act of 1988, which became law more than 50 years after the original securities statutes, focuses upon a specific problem, namely, the "purchasing or selling [of] a security while in possession of material, nonpublic information," that is, "insider trading." Recognizing the unique difficulties in identifying evidence of such activities, the 100th Congress adopted § 20A as one of "a variety of measures designed to provide greater deterrence, detection and punishment of violations of insider trading." There is no indication that the drafters of § 20A sought to extend that enhanced protection to other provisions of the 1934 Act. Indeed, the text of § 20A indicates the contrary. Section 20A(d) states: "Nothing in this section shall be construed to limit or condition the right of any person to bring an action to enforce a requirement of this chapter or the availability of any cause of action implied from a provision of this chapter."

The Commission further argues that because some conduct that is violative of § 10(b) is also actionable under § 20A, adoption of a 1–and–3–year structure would subject actions based on § 10(b) to two different statutes of limitations. But § 20A also prohibits insider-trading activities that violate sections of the 1934 Act with express limitations periods. The language of § 20A makes clear that the 100th Congress sought to alter the remedies available in insider trading cases, and *only* in insider trading cases. There is no inconsistency.

Finally, the Commission contends that the adoption of a 3–year period of repose would frustrate the policies underlying § 10(b). The inclusion, however, of the 1–and–3–year structure in the broad range of express securities actions contained in the 1933 and 1934 Acts suggests a congressional determination that a 3–year period is sufficient.

Thus, we agree with every Court of Appeals that has been called upon to apply a federal statute of limitations to a § 10(b) claim that the express causes of action contained in the 1933 and 1934 Acts provide a more appropriate statute of limitations than does § 20A.

Necessarily, we also reject plaintiff-respondents' assertion that state law fraud provides the closest analogy to § 10(b). The analytical framework we adopt above makes consideration of state-law alternatives unnecessary where Congress has provided an express limitations period for correlative remedies within the same enactment.

Finally, we address plaintiff-respondents' contention that, whatever limitations period is applicable to § 10(b) claims, that period must be subject to the doctrine of equitable tolling. Plaintiff-respondents note, correctly, that "[t]ime requirements in law suits * * * are customarily subject to 'equitable tolling.' " Thus, this Court has said that in the usual case, "where the party injured by the fraud remains in ignorance of it without any fault or want of diligence or care on his part, the bar of the statute does not begin to run until the fraud is discovered, though there be no special circumstances or efforts on the part of the party committing the fraud to conceal it from the knowledge of the other party." Notwithstanding this venerable principle, it is evident that the equitable tolling doctrine is fundamentally inconsistent with the 1– and–3–year structure.

The 1–year period, by its terms, begins after discovery of the facts constituting the violation, making tolling unnecessary. The 3–year limit is a period of repose inconsistent with tolling. Because the purpose of the 3–year limitation is clearly to serve as a cutoff, we hold that tolling principles do not apply to that period. * * *

Litigation instituted pursuant to § 10(b) and Rule 10b–5 therefore must be commenced within one year after the discovery of the facts constituting the violation and within three years after such violation. As there is no dispute that the earliest of plaintiff-respondents' complaints was filed more than three years after petitioner's alleged misrepresentations, plaintiff-respondents' claims were untimely.

The judgment of the Court of Appeals is Reversed.

JUSTICE SCALIA, concurring in part and concurring in the judgment. [omitted]

JUSTICE STEVENS, with whom JUSTICE SOUTER joins, dissenting. [omitted]

JUSTICE O'CONNOR, with whom JUSTICE KENNEDY joins, dissenting. [omitted]

NOTE

Prior to *Lampf*, one reason that plaintiffs often turned to Rule 10b–5, rather than the express liability provisions of the 1933 and 1934 Acts in suing for misstatements in filed documents, was the rather short statute of limitations applicable to those provisions—suit must generally be brought within three years of the transaction. In actions under Rule 10b–5, the courts, prior to *Lampf*, under prevailing federal doctrines, tended to look to the state statutes of limitations applicable to "analogous" claims in the state where the violation occurred. This frequently resulted in a number of disparate possibilities (sometimes dramatic ones) for the limitations periods among various states involved in a securities fraud claim and even among causes of action in a single state. *Lampf* eliminated those disparities. The concept of a uniform limitations period was codified in 2002, with Congress adopting a two year limitations period running from the date of discovery combined with a five year repose period running from the date of the violation. 28 U.S.C.A. § 1658(b). See Sarbanes–Oxley Act of 2002, PL 107–204 (July 30, 2002).

CHAPTER 14

INSIDER TRADING AT COMMON LAW

■ ■ ■

SECTION 1.   THE EARLY VIEW

LAIDLAW v. ORGAN

15 U.S. (2 Wheat.) 178, 4 L.Ed. 214 (1817).

The defendant in error filed his petition, or libel, in the court below, stating, that on the 18th day of February, 1815, he purchased of the plaintiffs in error one hundred and eleven hogsheads of tobacco, as appeared by the copy of a bill of parcels annexed, and that the same were delivered to him by the said Laidlaw & Co., and that he was in the lawful and quiet possession of the said tobacco, when, on the 20th day of the said month, the said Laidlaw & Co., by force, and of their own wrong, took possession of the same, and unlawfully withheld the same from the petitioner, notwithstanding he was at all times, and still was, ready to do and perform all things on his part stipulated to be done and performed in relation to said purchase, and had actually tendered to the said Laidlaw & Co. bills of exchange for the amount of the purchase money, agreeably to the said contract; to his damage, & c. Wherefore the petition prayed that the said Laidlaw & Co. might be cited to appear and answer to his plaint, and that judgment might be rendered against them for his damages, & c. And inasmuch as the petitioner did verily believe that the said one hundred and eleven hogsheads of tobacco would be removed, concealed, or disposed of by the said Laidlaw & Co., he prayed that a writ of sequestration might issue, and that the same might be sequestered in the hands of the marshal, to abide the judgment of the court, and that the said one hundred and eleven hogsheads of tobacco might be finally adjudged to the petitioner, together with his damages, & c., and costs of suit, and that the petitioner might have such other and farther relief as to the court should seem meet, & c. * * *

On the 20th of April, 1815, the cause was tried by a jury, who returned the following verdict, to wit: 'The jury find for the plaintiff, for the tobacco named in the petition, without damages, payable as per contract.' Whereupon the court rendered judgment 'that the plaintiff recover of the said defendants the said 111 hogsheads of tobacco, mentioned in the plaintiff's petition, and sequestered in this suit, with his costs of suit to be taxed; and ordered, that the marshal deliver the said tobacco to the said plaintiff, and that he have execution for his costs aforesaid, upon the said plaintiff's depositing in this court his bills of exchange for the amount of the purchase money endorsed, & c., for the use of the defendants, agreeably to the verdict of the jury.'

On the 29th of April, 1815, the plaintiffs in error filed the following bill of exceptions, to wit: 'Be it remembered, that on the 20th day of April, in the year of our Lord, 1815, the above cause came on for trial before a jury duly sworn and empanelled, the said Peter Laidlaw & Co. having filed a disclaimer, and Boorman and Johnston of the city of New York, having filed their claim. And now the said Hector M. Organ having closed his testimony, the said claimants, by their counsel, offered Francis Girault, one of the above firm of Peter Laidlaw & Co., as their witness; whereupon the counsel for the plaintiff objected to his being sworn, on the ground of his incompetency. The claimants proved that Peter Laidlaw & Co., before named, were, at the date of the transaction which gave rise to the above suit, commission merchants, and were then known in the city of New Orleans as such, and that it is invariably the course of trade in said city for commission merchants to make purchases and sales in their own names for the use of their employers; upon which the claimants again urged the propriety of suffering the said Francis Girault to be sworn, it appearing in evidence that the contract was made by Organ, the plaintiff, with said Girault, one of the said firm of Peter Laidlaw & Co. in their own name, and there being evidence that factors and commission merchants do business on their own account as well as for others, and there being no evidence that the plaintiff, at the time of the contract, had any knowledge of the existence of any other interest in the said tobacco, except that of the defendants, Peter Laidlaw & Co. The court sustained the objection, and rejected the said witness. To which decision of the court the counsel for the claimants aforesaid begged leave to except, and prayed that this bill of exceptions might be signed and allowed. And it appearing in evidence in the said cause, that on the night of the 18th of February, 1815, Messrs. Livingston, White, and Shepherd brought from the British fleet the news that a treaty of peace had been signed at Ghent by the American and British commissioners, contained in a letter from Lord Bathurst to the Lord Mayor of London, published in the British newspapers, and that Mr. White caused the same to be made public in a handbill on Sunday morning, 8 o'clock, the 19th of February, 1815, and that the brother of Mr. Shepherd, one of these gentlemen, and who was interested in one-third of the profits of the purchase set forth in said plaintiff's petition, had, on Sunday morning, the 19th of February, 1815, communicated said news to the plaintiff; that the said plaintiff, on receiving said news, called on Francis Girault, (with whom he had been bargaining for the tobacco mentioned in the petition, the evening previous,) said Francis Girault being one of the said house of trade of Peter Laidlaw & Co., soon after sunrise on the morning of Sunday, the 19th of February, 1815, before he had heard said news. Said Girault asked if there was any news which was calculated to enhance the price or value of the article about to be purchased; and that the said purchase was then and there made, and the bill of parcels annexed to the plaintiff's petition delivered to the plaintiff between 8 and 9 o'clock in the morning of that day; and that in consequence of said news the value of said article had risen from 30 to 50 per cent. There being no evidence that the plaintiff had asserted or suggested any thing to the said Girault, calculated to impose upon him with respect to said news, and to induce him to think or believe that it did not exist; and it appearing that the said Girault, when applied to, on the next day, Monday, the 20th of February, 1815, on behalf of the plaintiff, for an invoice of said tobacco, did not then object to the said sale, but promised to deliver the invoice to the said plaintiff in the course of the forenoon of that day; the court charged the jury to find for the plaintiff. Wherefore, that justice, by due course of law, may be done in this case, the counsel of said defendants, for them, and on their behalf, prays the court that this bill of exceptions be filed, allowed, and certified as the law directs. * * *

On the 29th of April, 1815, a writ of error was allowed to this court, and on the 3d of May, 1815, the defendant in error deposited in the court below, for the use of the plaintiffs in error, the bills of exchange mentioned in the pleadings, according to the verdict of the jury and the judgment of the court thereon, which bills were thereupon taken out of court by the plaintiffs in error. * * *

MR. CHIEF JUSTICE MARSHALL delivered the opinion of the court.

The question in this case is, whether the intelligence of extrinsic circumstances, which might influence the price of the commodity, and which was exclusively within the knowledge of the vendee, ought to have been communicated by him to the vendor? The court is of opinion that he was not bound to communicate it. It would be difficult to circumscribe the contrary doctrine within proper limits, where the means of intelligence are equally accessible to both parties. But at the same time, each party must take care not to say or do any thing tending to impose upon the other. The court thinks that the absolute instruction of the judge was erroneous, and that the question, whether any imposition was practised by the vendee upon the vendor ought to have been submitted to the jury. For these reasons the judgment must be reversed, and the cause remanded to the district court of Louisiana, with directions to award a *venire facias de novo.*

Venire de novo awarded.

NOTES

1. The decision by Justice Marshall in *Laidlaw v. Organ* represents the common law view that the purchaser of an article is under no obligation to disclose facts unknown to the opposite party that may affect the value of the property. After all, that is a normal part of many purchase and sale transactions, i.e., one party, or both, see some particular advantage that has not

occurred to the other. This is how commodities are priced in the market. Should the purchaser of a piece of property be required to tell the seller that there may be oil under its surface? Should a developer be required to tell the owners of the tracts he is buying that the land will be more valuable after he develops his project? Should the rule be any different for securities? Should we not reward those who bring information to the market by purchasing or selling a stock? Does this make the pricing of securities more efficient or does it undercut investor confidence, demoralize the market and make it more difficult for businesses to raise capital?

2. State legislatures have been requiring sellers of residential property to disclose defects in the property to purchasers. See e.g., Ind. Code § 24–4.6–2–7. Should there be a reciprocal obligation on buyers to disclose any information they have that would make the property more valuable?

3. Justice Marshall held in *Laidlaw*, even though there is no common law duty to make an affirmative disclosure, that the parties may not make misrepresentations to their counterparts. This was not new ground. An English Court had ruled in 1814 that individuals who were seeking to sell securities at a profit had acted improperly where they circulated false rumors that Napoleon Bonaparte had died. The King v. De Berenger, 3 Maule & Selwyn 67, 70, 105 Eng. Rep. 536, 537 (K.B. 1814).

4. The approach taken by the Supreme Court in *Laidlaw v. Organ* was adopted by Congress in amending the Commodity Exchange Act ("CEA") in 2008. That statute governs transactions in commodity futures (see Chapter 12 for a discussion of those contracts). The CEA as amended in CEA § 4b(b) states that nothing in its anti-fraud prohibition obligates any person to disclose 'nonpublic information that may be material to the market price, rate, or level of the commodity or transaction, except as necessary to make any statement made to ... [an]other person in or in connection with the transaction not misleading in any material respect. 7 U.S.C. § 6b(b).

SECTION 2. INSIDER TRADING IN SECURITIES—INTRODUCTION AND THE COMMON LAW RULE

There have been arguments made for and against prohibitions against insider trading. Oversimplifying somewhat, those who see little need for such a prohibition assert that trading volume is so high in many publicly traded companies that insider trading has no discernible effect on other investors, individually or in the aggregate. Further, it is claimed that profits from inside information provide an incentive to bring this otherwise secret information to the market. This better assures that the price of the stock is more accurate, reflecting all information, not just that which the company decides to publish. Arguments have also been made that trading on inside information prepares the market in a stock for big events, pushing the price of the stock in the proper direction before the information is publicly announced. Otherwise, it is contended, major announcements will cause wide price fluctuations that not only disrupt an orderly market, but will cause more injury to outside investors than would the insider trading. See generally e.g., *Henry G. Manne, Insider Trading and the Stock Market* (1966). Of course, there is also the practical argument that there is no such thing as a secret and that the information will in all events leak into the market selectively, so why bother?

Opponents of insider trading sometimes base their arguments on moralistic grounds that the use of such information is simply unfair. They seek a level playing field for all investors, a somewhat naïve hope but well intentioned. On economic claims, opponents of insider trading appear to be on firmer ground. They assert that the use of such information will undermine confidence in the market, making capital raising harder and more expensive, to the detriment of society as a whole. A more refined response to the economic arguments of proponents of insider trading, has been articulated by Duke Law School Professor James D. Cox:

> At least three reasons other than the uncertain costs and benefits of a free-market approach to insider trading ... justify the insider trading prohibition. First, knowledge of an executive's compensation sources is indispensable for understanding what motivates his discretionary behavior. When an executive's compensation is tied to changes in the firm's value, or his renewal is conditioned upon achieving a stated performance level, investors are better assured that the manager will act in the shareholders' best interests than when compensation is not linked to an interest held by the shareholders. This knowledge also permits superiors to rely upon the same assumptions regarding their subordinates' activities. Investors and superiors can form these assumptions more easily when the compensation arrangement is free from the noise that insider trading creates by allowing managers to win with both good and bad news.

> Second, an assessment of the manager's stewardship of the firm (an assessment dear to the hearts of free-market proponents as well as those who are not entirely comfortable with a free market) can occur only with full knowledge of both the executive's costs and his team's productivity. Licensing managers to trade on inside information is similar to licensing managers to embezzle because in both cases the individual investor cannot assess the firm's return on its capital or the manager's compensation in light of his productivity. Therefore, shareholders expect a regime that prohibits employment-derived earnings that are neither authorized nor fully disclosed. This is accomplished by prohibiting insider trading.

> Third, shareholders expect the executive to concentrate on their welfare rather than his private investment agenda. The prohibition against insider trading is similar to the prohibition against a manager spending his time in the office developing his own interests; each

prohibition stems from the shareholders' expectation that a manager is paid to look after the shareholders' welfare, not his own.

These three aspects of the employment relationship justify the continuation of insider trading regulation because employers, like consumers, have rationally based expectations about what they are purchasing when they hire managers or other professionals. Without a prior understanding between the firm and its insiders regarding the latter's trading prerogatives, the parties expect that the insider's compensation will be no more and no less than what their agreement provides. An insider unlawfully acquires gains by embezzling firm assets, deflecting a corporate opportunity, or using corporate information, because these matters are outside the employment contract. The parties could have raised these matters in their negotiations. Because owners, acting rationally, would see that licensing an insider to trade leaves nothing to be gained and a good deal to be lost, they will not license their insiders to trade. Therefore, the insider breaches his employment agreement when he trades.

James D. Cox, "Insider Trading and Contracting: A Critical Response to the 'Chicago School,'" 1986 Duke L.J. 628, 658–659. *See also* Thomas L. Hazen, "Commentary," 36 Cath. U.L. Rev. 987, 993–96 (1987).

NOTES

1.   Do you think insider trading should be permitted?

2.   As you read the cases that follow in this chapter, try to formulate a rule that will work in all cases where someone has inside information. Are there cases where someone has non-public "outside" information that is not sanctionable? Suppose that a product manufactured by your company makes obsolete a competing product manufactured by your leading competitor. Can you sell your competitor's stock short in anticipation of your new product driving the price down?

GOODWIN v. AGASSIZ

283 Mass. 358, 186 N.E. 659 (1933).

RUGG, CHIEF JUSTICE.

A stockholder in a corporation seeks in this suit relief for losses suffered by him in selling shares of stock in Cliff Mining Company by way of accounting, rescission of sales, or redelivery of shares. The named defendants are MacNaughton, a resident of Michigan not served or appearing, and Agassiz, a resident of this commonwealth, the active party defendant.

. . . The defendants, in May, 1926, purchased through brokers on the Boston stock exchange seven hundred shares of stock of the Cliff Mining Company which up to that time the plaintiff had owned. Agassiz was president and director and MacNaughton a director and general manager of the company. They had certain knowledge, material as to the value of the stock, which the plaintiff did not have. The plaintiff contends that such purchase in all the circumstances without disclosure to him of that knowledge was a wrong against him. That knowledge was that an experienced geologist had formulated in writing in March, 1926, a theory as to the possible existence of copper deposits under conditions prevailing in the region where the property of the company was located. That region was known as the mineral belt in Northern Michigan, where are located mines of several copper mining companies. Another such company, of which the defendants were officers, had made extensive geological surveys of its lands. In consequence of recommendations resulting from that survey, exploration was started on property of the Cliff Mining Company in 1925. That exploration was ended in May, 1926, because completed unsuccessfully, and the equipment was removed. The defendants discussed the geologist's theory shortly after it was formulated. Both felt that the theory had value and should be tested, but they agreed that, before starting to test it, options should be obtained by another copper company of which they were officers on land adjacent to or nearby in the copper belt, that if the geologist's theory were known to the owners of such other land there might be difficulty in securing options, and that that theory should not be communicated to any one unless it became absolutely necessary. Thereafter, options were secured which, if taken up, would involve a large expenditure by the other company. The defendants both thought, also that, if there was any merit in the geologist's theory, the price of Cliff Mining Company stock in the market would go up. Its stock was quoted and bought and sold on the Boston Stock Exchange. Pursuant to agreement, they bought many shares of that stock through agents on joint account. The plaintiff first learned of the closing of exploratory operations on property of the Cliff Mining Company from an article in a paper on May 15, 1926, and immediately sold his shares of stock through brokers. It does not appear that the defendants were in any way responsible for the publication of that article. The plaintiff did not know that the purchase was made for the defendants and they did not know that his stock was being bought for them. There was no communication between them touching the subject. The plaintiff would not have sold his stock if he had known of the geologist's theory. The finding is express that the defendants were not guilty of fraud, that they committed no breach of duty owed by them to the Cliff Mining Company, and that that company was not harmed by the nondisclosure of the geologist's theory, or by their purchases of its stock, or by shutting down the exploratory operations.

The contention of the plaintiff is that the purchase of his stock in the company by the defendants without disclosing to him as a stockholder their knowledge of the geologist's theory, their belief that the theory was true, had value, the keeping secret the existence of the theory, discontinuance by the defendants of exploratory operations begun in 1925 on property of the Cliff Mining Company and their plan ultimately to test the value of the theory, constitute actionable wrong for which he as stockholder can recover.

The trial judge ruled that conditions may exist which would make it the duty of an officer of a corporation purchasing its stock from a stockholder to inform him as to knowledge possessed by the buyer and not by the seller, but found, on all the circumstances developed by the trial and set out at some length by him in his decision, that there was no fiduciary relation requiring such disclosure by the defendants to the plaintiff before buying his stock in the manner in which they did.

The question presented is whether the decree dismissing the bill rightly was entered on the facts found.

The directors of a commercial corporation stand in a relation of trust to the corporation and are bound to exercise the strictest good faith in respect to its property and business. The contention that directors also occupy the position of trustee toward individual stockholders in the corporation is plainly contrary to repeated decisions of this court and cannot be supported. In Smith v. Hurd, 12 Metc. 371, 384, 46 Am. Dec. 690, it was said by Chief Justice Shaw: 'There is no legal privity, relation, or immediate connection, between the holders of shares in a bank, in their individual capacity, on the one side, and the directors of the bank on the other. The directors are not the bailees, the factors, agents or trustees of such individual stockholders.' In Blabon v. Hay, 269 Mass. 401, 407, 169 N. E. 268, 271, occurs this language with reference to sale of stock in a corporation by a stockholder to two of its directors: 'The fact that the defendants were directors created no fiduciary relation between them and the plaintiff in the matter of the sale of his stock.'

The principle thus established is supported by an imposing weight of authority in other jurisdictions. A rule holding that directors are trustees for individual stockholders with respect to their stock prevails in comparatively few states; but in view of our own adjudications it is not necessary to review decisions to that effect.

While the general principle is as stated, circumstances may exist requiring that transactions between a director and a stockholder as to stock in the corporation be set aside. The knowledge naturally in the possession of a director as to the condition of a corporation places upon him a peculiar obligation to observe every requirement of fair dealing when directly buying or selling its stock. Mere silence does not usually amount to a breach of duty, but parties may stand in such relation to each other that an equitable responsibility arises to communicate facts. Purchases and sales of stock dealt in on the stock exchange are commonly impersonal affairs. An honest director would be in a difficult situation if he could neither buy nor sell on the stock exchange shares of stock in his corporation without first seeking out the other actual ultimate party to the transaction and disclosing to him everything which a court or jury might later find that he then knew affecting the real or speculative value of such shares. Business of that nature is a matter to be governed by practical rules. Fiduciary obligations of directors ought not to be made so onerous that men of experience and ability will be deterred from accepting such office. Law in its sanctions is not coextensive with morality. It cannot undertake to put all parties to every contract on an equality as to knowledge, experience, skill and shrewdness. It cannot undertake to relieve against hard bargains made between competent parties without fraud. On the other hand, directors cannot rightly be allowed to indulge with impunity in practices which do violence to prevailing standards of upright business men. Therefore, where a director personally seeks a stockholder for the purpose of buying his shares without making disclosure of material facts within his peculiar knowledge and not within reach of the stockholder, the transaction will be closely scrutinized and relief may be granted in appropriate instances. The applicable legal principles 'have almost always been the fundamental ethical rules of right and wrong.' Robinson v. Mollett, L. R. 7 H. L. 802, 817.

The precise question to be decided in the case at bar is whether on the facts found the defendants as directors had a right to buy stock of the plaintiff, a stockholder. Every element of actual fraud or misdoing by the defendants is negatived by the findings. Fraud cannot be presumed; it must be proved. The facts found afford no ground for inferring fraud or conspiracy. The only knowledge possessed by the defendants not open to the plaintiff was the existence of a theory formulated in a thesis by a geologist as to the possible existence of copper deposits where certain geological conditions existed common to the property of the Cliff Mining Company and that of other mining companies in its neighborhood. This thesis did not express an opinion that copper deposits would be found at any particular spot or on property of any specified owner. Whether that theory was sound or fallacious, no one knew, and so far as appears has never been demonstrated. The defendants made no representations to anybody about the theory. No facts found placed upon them any obligation to disclose the theory. A few days after the thesis expounding the theory was brought to the attention of the defendants, the annual report by the directors of the Cliff Mining Company for the calendar year 1925, signed by Agassiz for the directors, was issued. It did not cover the time when the theory was formulated. The report described the status of the operations under the exploration which had been begun in 1925. At the annual meeting of the stockholders of the company held early in April, 1926, no reference was made to the theory. It was then at most a hope, possibly an expectation. It had not passed the nebulous stage. No disclosure was made of it. The Cliff Mining Company was not harmed by the nondisclosure. There would have been no advantage to it, so far as appears, from a disclosure. The disclosure would have been detrimental to the interests of another mining corporation in which the defendants were directors. In the circumstances there was no duty on the part of the defendants to set forth to the stockholders at the annual meeting their faith, aspirations and plans for the future. Events as they developed might render advisable radical changes in such views. Disclosure of the theory, if it ultimately was proved to be erroneous or without foundation in fact, might involve the defendants in litigation with those who might act on the hypothesis that it was correct. The stock of the Cliff Mining Company was bought and sold on the stock exchange. The identity of buyers and sellers of the stock in question in fact was not known to the parties and perhaps could not readily have been ascertained. The defendants caused the shares to be bought through brokers on the stock exchange. They said nothing to anybody as to the reasons actuating them. The plaintiff was no novice. He was a member of the Boston stock exchange and had kept a record of sales of Cliff Mining Company stock. He acted upon his own judgment in selling his stock. He made no inquiries of the defendants or of other officers of the company. The result is that the plaintiff cannot prevail.

Decree dismissing bill affirmed with costs.

NOTES

1. The *Goodwin* case represents the traditional inability of the common law to deal with problems associated with insider trading. The concept of *caveat emptor* applied to most securities sales. The court in *Goodwin* also focused on the absence of a duty running between participants in an open market, as opposed to a face-to-face transaction. When there is a face-to-face transaction, common law duties may arise. For example, in Strong v. Repide, 213 U.S. 419, 29 S.Ct. 521, 53 L.Ed. 853 (1909) the Court considered the following circumstances:

> In 1902 it was thought important for the government of the United States to secure title, if reasonably possible, to what were called the friar lands in the Philippine Islands. To that end various inquiries were made on the part of the government, from time to time, as to the possibility of obtaining title to all those lands, and what would be the probable expense. The lands were not owned by the same people, but were divided among different and separate owners. The Philippine Sugar Estates Development Company, Limited, owned of these lands what are more particularly described as the Dominican lands, and they were regarded as nearly one half the value of all the friar lands.

> On July 5, 1903, the governor of the Philippine Islands, on behalf of the Philippine government, made an offer of purchase for the total sum of $6,043,219.47 in gold for all the friar lands, though owned by different owners. This offer, so far as concerned that portion of the lands owned by defendant's company, was rejected by defendant in his capacity as majority shareholder, without any consultation with the other shareholders. The representatives of all the different owners of all the lands, including defendant's company, in answer to the above offer, then fixed their selling price at $13,700,000 for all such lands. During the negotiations consequent upon these different offers, which lasted for some time after the first offer was made, an offer was finally, and towards the end of October, 1903, made by the governor of $7,535,000. All the owners of all these friar lands, with the exception of the defendant, who represented his company, were willing and anxious to accept this offer and to convey

the lands to the government at that price. He alone held out for a better offer while all the other owners were endeavoring to persuade him to accept the offer of the government. The defendant continued his refusal to accept until the other owners consented to pay to his company $335,000 of the purchase price for their land, and until the government consented that a thousand hectares should be excluded from the sale to it of the land of defendant's company. This being agreed to, the contract for the sale was finally signed by the defendant as attorney in fact for his company, December 21, 1903. The defendant, of course, as the negotiations progressed, knew that the decision of the question lay with him, and that if he should decide to accept the last offer of the government, his decision would be the decision of his company, as he owned three fourths of its shares, and the negotiations would then go through as all the owners of the balance of the land desired it. If the sale should not be consummated, and things should remain as they were, the defendant also knew that the value of the lands and of the shares in the company would be almost nothing. He himself says, in speaking of these lands owned by his company, that had the government 'given the haciendas the protection which they ought to have received, they would have been worth $6,000,000 gold; but, considering the abnormal condition in which they were on account of the failure of the government to protect these haciendas, it is impossible to fix any value; they were worth nothing; they were a charge.' Also, the company had paid no dividends, and only lived on its credit, and could not even pay taxes. The company had no other property of any substantial value than these lands. They were its one valuable asset.

While this state of things existed, and before the final offer had been made by the governor, the defendant, although still holding out for a higher price for the lands, took steps, about the middle or latter part of September, 1903, to purchase the 800 shares of stock in his company owned by Mrs. Strong, which he knew were in the possession of F. Stuart Jones, as her agent. The defendant, having decided to obtain these shares, instead of seeing Jones, who had an office next door, employed one Kauffman, a connection of his by marriage, and Kauffman employed a Mr. Sloan, a broker, who had an office some distance away, to purchase the stock for him, and told Sloan that the stock was for a member of his wife's family. Sloan communicated with the husband of Mrs. Strong, and asked if she desired to sell her stock. The husband referred him to Mr. Jones for consultation, who had the stock in his possession. Sloan did not know who wanted to buy the shares, nor did Jones when he was spoken to. Jones would not have sold at the price he did had he known it was the defendant who was purchasing, because, as he said, it would show increased value, as the defendant would not be likely to purchase more stock unless the price was going up. As the articles of incorporation, by subdivision 20, required a resolution of the general meeting of stockholders for the purpose of selling more than one hacienda, and as no such general meeting had been called at the time of the sale of the stock, Mr. Jones might well have supposed there was no immediate prospect of a sale of the lands being made, while, at the same time, defendant had knowledge of the probabilities thereof, which he had acquired by his conduct of the negotiations for their sale, as agent of all the shareholders, and while acting specially for them and himself.

The result of the negotiations was that Jones, on or about October 10, 1903, assuming that he had the power, and without consulting Mrs. Strong, sold the 800 shares of stock for $16,000, Mexican currency, delivering the stock to Kauffman in Sloan's office, who paid for it with the check of Rueda Hermanos for $18,000, the surplus $2,000 being arranged for, and Kauffman being paid $1,800 by defendant for his services. The defendant thus obtained the 800 shares for about one tenth of the amount they became worth by the sale of the lands between two and three months thereafter. In all the negotiations in regard to the purchase of the stock from Mrs. Strong, through her agent Jones, not one word of the facts affecting the value of this stock was made known to plaintiff's agent by defendant, but, on the contrary, perfect silence was kept. The real state of the negotiations with the government was not mentioned, nor was the fact stated that it rested chiefly with the defendant to complete the sale. The probable value of the shares in the very near future was thus unknown to anyone but defendant, while the agent of the plaintiff had no knowledge or suspicion that defendant was the one seeking to purchase the shares. The agent sold because, as he testified, he wanted to invest the money in some kind of property that would pay dividends, and he was expecting nothing from this company, as negotiations for the sale of the lands had gone on so long, and there appeared no prospect of any sale being made; at any rate, not for a very long time.

It is undeniable that, during all this time, the subject of the sale of the friar lands was frequently mooted and its probabilities publicly discussed in a general way. Such discussion was founded upon rumors and gossip as to the condition of the negotiations. The public press referred to it not infrequently, but the actual state of the negotiations, the actual probabilities of the sale being consummated, and the particular position of power and influence which the defendant occupied in such negotiations, prior to the time of the purchase of plaintiff's stock, were not accurately known by plaintiff's agent or by anyone else outside those interested in the matter as negotiators.

The Supreme Court after setting forth these facts reached the following conclusions:

The question in this case, therefore, is whether, under the circumstances above set forth, it was the duty of the defendant, acting in good faith, to disclose to the agent of the plaintiff the facts bearing upon or which might affect the value of the stock.

If it were conceded, for the purpose of the argument, that the ordinary relations between directors and shareholders in a business corporation are not of such a fiduciary nature as to make it the duty of a director to disclose to a shareholder the general knowledge which he may possess regarding the value of the shares of the company before he purchases any from a shareholder, yet there are cases where, by reason of the special facts, such duty exists. The supreme courts of Kansas and of Georgia have held the relationship existed in the cases before those courts because of the special facts which took them out of the general rule, and that, under those facts, the director could not purchase from the shareholder his shares without informing him of the facts which affected their value. The case before us is of the same general character.* * * That the defendant was a director of the corporation is but one of the facts upon which the liability is asserted, the existence of all the others in addition making such a combination as rendered it the plain duty of the defendant to speak. He was not only a director, but he owned three fourths of the shares of its stock, and was, at the time of the purchase of the stock, administrator general of the company, with large powers, and engaged in the negotiations which finally led to the sale of the company's lands (together with all the other friar lands) to the government at a price which very greatly enhanced the value of the stock. He was the chief negotiator for the sale of all the lands, and was acting substantially as the agent of the shareholders of his company by reason of his ownership of the shares of stock in the corporation and by the acquiescence of all the other shareholders, and the negotiations were for the sale of the whole of the property of the company. By reason of such ownership and agency, and his participation as such owner and agent in the negotiations then going on, no one knew as well as he the exact condition of such negotiations. No one knew as well as he the probability of the sale of the lands to the government. No one knew as well as he the probable price that might be obtained on such sale. The lands were the only valuable asset owned by the company. Under these circumstances, and before the negotiations for the sale were completed, the defendant employs an agent to purchase the stock, and conceals from the plaintiff's agent his own identity and his knowledge of the state of the negotiations and their probable result, with which he was familiar as the agent of the shareholders, and much of which knowledge he obtained while acting as such agent, and by reason thereof. The inference is inevitable that, at this time, he had concluded to press the negotiations for a sale of the lands to a successful conclusion; else, why would he desire to purchase more shares which, if no sale went through, were, in his opinion, worthless because of the failure of the government to properly protect the lands in the hands of their then owners? The agent of the plaintiff was ignorant in regard to the state of the negotiations for the sale of the land, which negotiations and their probable result were a most material fact affecting the value of the shares of stock of the company, and he would not have sold them at the price he did had he known the actual state of the negotiations as to the lands, and that it was the defendant who was seeking to purchase the stock. Concealing his identity when procuring the purchase of the stock, by his agent, was in itself strong evidence of fraud on the part of the defendant. Why did he not ask Jones, who occupied an adjoining office, if he would sell? But, by concealing his identity, he could, by such means, the more easily avoid any questions relative to the negotiations for the sale of the lands and their probable result, and could also avoid any actual misrepresentations on that subject, which he evidently thought were necessary in his case to constitute a fraud. He kept up the concealment as long as he could, by giving the check of a third person for the purchase money. Evidence that he did so was objected to on the ground that it could not possibly even tend to prove that the prior consent to sell had been procured by the subsequent check given in payment. That was not its purpose. Of course, the giving of the check could not have induced the prior consent, but it was proper evidence as tending to show that the concealment of identity was not a mere inadvertent omission, an omission without any fraudulent or deceitful intent, but was a studied and intentional omission, to be characterized as part of the deceitful machinations to obtain the purchase without giving any information whatever as to the state and probable result of the negotiations, to the vendor of the stock, and to, in that way, obtain the same at a lower price. After the purchase of the stock he continued his negotiations for the sale of the lands, and finally, he says, as administrator general of the company, under the special authority of the shareholders, and as attorney in fact, he entered into the contract of sale December 21, 1903. The whole transaction gives conclusive evidence of the overwhelming influence defendant had in the course of the negotiations as owner of a majority of the stock and as agent for the other owners, and it is clear that the final consummation was in his hands at all times. If, under all these facts, he purchased the stock from the plaintiff, the law would indeed be impotent if the sale could not be set aside or the defendant cast in damages for his fraud.

The supreme court of the islands, in holding that there was no fraud in the purchase, said that the responsibility of the directors of a corporation to the individual stockholders did not extend beyond the corporate property actually under the control of the directors; that they did not owe any duty to the members in respect to their individual stock, which would prevent them from purchasing the same in the usual manner. While this may, in general, be true, we think it is not an accurate statement of the case, regard being had to the facts above mentioned. * * *

The case before us seems a plain one for holding that, under the circumstances detailed, there was a legal obligation on the part of the defendant to make these disclosures.

The creation of a "special facts" doctrine in *Strong v. Repide* was useful for the more compelling cases of direct dealings, but it was ill equipped for dealing with informational advantages that may exist with respect to the millions of shares that are traded each day in the public markets.

2. The court in *Goodwin* raises an additional problem with respect to insider trading claims. The insider there was acting on a hunch that the company's exploration for ore would prove fruitful. At what point does a hunch about the possible success of mineral exploration become material? It is elementary that mere possibilities are not material facts with respect to common law fraud. For the same reason, these type of contingent events may not provide an adequate basis for declaring insider trading to be illegal. Even the negotiations in *Strong v. Repide* related to contingent events. The negotiations might never come to fruition.

4.   Although common law fraud does not provide a firm basis for dealing with insider trading, some courts have found other common law theories to be useful. Consider the following case.

———

SECTION 3.   THE NEW YORK APPROACH

DIAMOND v. OREAMUNO

24 N.Y.2d 494, 301 N.Y.S.2d 78, 248 N.E.2d 910 (1969).

FULD, CHIEF JUDGE.

Upon this appeal from an order denying a motion to dismiss the complaint as insufficient on its face, the question presented—one of first impression in this court—is whether officers and directors may be held accountable to their corporation for gains realized by them from transactions in the company's stock as a result of their use of material inside information.

The complaint was filed by a shareholder of Management Assistance, Inc. (MAI) asserting a derivative action against a number of its officers and directors to compel an accounting for profits allegedly acquired as a result of a breach of fiduciary duty. It charges that two of the defendants—Oreamuno, chairman of the board of directors, and Gonzalez, its president—had used inside information, acquired by them solely by virtue of their positions, in order to reap large personal profits from the sale of MAI shares and that these profits rightfully belong to the corporation. Other officers and directors were joined as defendants on the ground that they acquiesced in or ratified the assertedly wrongful transactions.

MAI is in the business of financing computer installations through sale and lease back arrangements with various commercial and industrial users. Under its lease provisions, MAI was required to maintain and repair the computers but, at the time of this suit, it lacked the capacity to perform this function itself and was forced to engage the manufacturer of the computers, International Business Machines (IBM), to service the machines. As a result of a sharp increase by IBM of its charges for such service, MAI's expenses for August of 1966 rose considerably and its net earnings declined from $262,253 in July to $66,233 in August, a decrease of about 75%. This information, although earlier known to the defendants, was not made public until October of 1966. Prior to the release of the information, however, Oreamuno and Gonzalez sold off a total of 56,500 shares of their MAI stock at the then current market price of $28 a share.

After the information concerning the drop in earnings was made available to the public, the value of a share of MAI stock immediately fell from the $28 realized by the defendants to $11. Thus, the plaintiff alleges, by taking advantage of their privileged position and their access to confidential information, Oreamuno and Gonzalez were able to realize

$800,000 more for their securities than they would have had this inside information not been available to them. Stating that the defendants were 'forbidden to use (such) information * * * for their own personal profit or gain', the plaintiff brought this derivative action seeking to have the defendants account to the corporation for this difference. A motion by the defendants to dismiss the complaint for failure to state a cause of action was granted by the court at Special Term. The Appellate Division, with one dissent, modified Special Term's order by reinstating the complaint as to the defendants Oreamuno and Gonzalez. The appeal is before us on a certified question.

In reaching a decision in this case, we are, of course, passing only upon the sufficiency of the complaint and we necessarily accept the charges contained in that pleading as true.

It is well established, as a general proposition, that a person who acquires special knowledge or information by virtue of a confidential or fiduciary relationship with another is not free to exploit that knowledge or information for his own personal benefit but must account to his principal for any profits derived therefrom. This, in turn is merely a corollary of the broader principle, inherent in the nature of the fiduciary relationship, that prohibits a trustee or agent from extracting secret profits from his position of trust.

In support of their claim that the complaint fails to state a cause of action, the defendants take the position that, although it is admittedly wrong for an officer or director to use his position to obtain trading profits for himself in the stock of his corporation, the action ascribed to them did not injure or damage MAI in any way. Accordingly, the defendants continue, the corporation should not be permitted to recover the proceeds. They acknowledge that, by virtue of the exclusive access which officers and directors have to inside information, they possess an unfair advantage over other shareholders and, particularly, the persons who had purchased the stock from them but, they contend, the corporation itself was unaffected and, for that reason, a derivative action is an inappropriate remedy.

It is true that the complaint before us does not contain any allegation of damages to the corporation but this has never been considered to be an essential requirement for a cause of action founded on a breach of fiduciary duty. This is because the function of such an action, unlike an ordinary tort or contract case, is not merely to compensate the plaintiff for wrongs committed by the defendant but, as this court declared many years ago, 'to Prevent them, by removing from agents and trustees all inducement to attempt dealing for their own benefit in matters which they have undertaken for others, or to which their agency or trust relates.' (Emphasis supplied.)

Just as a trustee has no right to retain for himself the profits yielded by property placed in his possession but must account to his beneficiaries, a corporate fiduciary, who is entrusted with potentially valuable information, may not appropriate that asset for his own use even though, in so doing, he causes no injury to the corporation. The primary concern, in a case such as this, is not to determine whether the corporation has been damaged but to decide, as between the corporation and the defendants, who has a higher claim to the proceeds derived from the exploitation of the information. In our opinion, there can be no justification for permitting officers and directors, such as the defendants, to retain for themselves profits which, it is alleged, they derived solely from exploiting information gained by virtue of their inside position as corporate officials.

In addition, it is pertinent to observe that, despite the lack of any specific allegation of damage, it may well be inferred that the defendants' actions might have caused some harm to the enterprise. Although the corporation may have little concern with the day-to-day transactions in its shares, it has a great interest in maintaining a reputation of integrity, an image of probity, for its management and in insuring the continued public acceptance and marketability of its stock. When officers and directors abuse their position in order to gain personal profits, the effect may be to cast a cloud on the corporation's name, injure stockholder relations and undermine public regard for the corporation's securities. As Presiding Justice Botein aptly put it, in the course of his opinion for the Appellate Division, '(t)he prestige and good will of a corporation, so vital to its prosperity, may be undermined by the revelation that its chief officers had been making personal profits out of corporate events which they had not disclosed to the community of stockholders.'

The defendants maintain that extending the prohibition against personal exploitation of a fiduciary relationship to officers and directors of a corporation will discourage such officials from maintaining a stake in the success of the corporate venture through share ownership, which, they urge, is an important incentive to proper performance of their duties. There is, however, a considerable difference between corporate officers who assume the same risks and obtain the same benefits as other shareholders and those who use their privileged position to gain special advantages not available to others. The sale of shares by the defendants for the reasons charged was not merely a wise investment decision which any prudent investor might have made. Rather, they were assertedly able in this case to profit solely because they had information which was not available to any one else—including the other shareholders whose interests they, as corporate fiduciaries, were bound to protect.

Although no appellate court in this State has had occasion to pass upon the precise question before us, the concept underlying the present cause of action is hardly a new one.* * * In Brophy v. Cities Serv. Co. (31 Del.Ch. 241, 70 A.2d 5), for example, the Chancery Court of Delaware, * * * [o]ne of the defendants in that case was an employee who had acquired inside information that the corporate plaintiff was about to enter the market and purchase its own shares. On the basis of this confidential information, the employee, who was not an officer * * * bought a large block of shares and, after the corporation's purchases had caused the price to rise, resold them at a profit. The court sustained the complaint in a derivative action brought for an accounting, stating that '(p)ublic policy will not permit an employee occupying a position of trust and confidence toward his employer to abuse that relation to his own profit, regardless of whether his employer suffers a loss.' And a similar view has been expressed in the Restatement, 2d, Agency (§ 388 comment c):

> 'c.   Use of confidential information. An agent who acquires confidential information in the course of his employment or in violation of his duties has a duty * * * to account for any profits made by the use of such information, although this does not harm the principal. * * * So, if (a corporate officer) has 'inside' information that the corporation is about to purchase or sell securities, or to declare or to pass a dividend, profits made by him in stock transactions undertaken because of his knowledge are held in constructive trust for the principal.' * * *

In view of the practical difficulties inherent in an action under the Federal law, the desirability of creating an effective common-law remedy is manifest. 'Dishonest directors should not find absolution from retributive justice', Ballantine observed in his work on Corporations ((rev.ed., 1946), p. 216), 'by concealing their identity from their victims under the mask of the stock exchange.' There is ample room in a situation such as is here presented for a 'private Attorney General' to come forward and enforce proper behavior on the part of corporate officials through the medium of the derivative action brought in the name of the corporation. Only by sanctioning such a cause of action will there by any effective method to prevent the type of abuse of corporate office complained of in this case.

There is nothing in the Federal law which indicates that it was intended to limit the power of the States to fashion additional remedies to effectuate similar purposes. Although the impact of Federal securities regulation has on occasion been said to have created a 'Federal corporation law,' in fact, its effect on the duties and obligations of directors and officers and their relation to the corporation and its shareholders is only occasional and peripheral. The primary source of the law in this area ever remains that of the State which created the corporation. Indeed, Congress expressly provided against any implication that it intended to pre-empt the field by declaring, in section 28(a) of the Securities Exchange Act of 1934, that '(t)he rights and remedies provided by this title shall be in addition to any and all other rights and remedies that may exist at law or in equity'.

Nor should we be deterred, in formulating a State remedy, by the defendants' claim of possible double liability. Certainly, as already indicated, if the sales in question were publicly made, the likelihood that a suit will be brought by purchasers of the shares is quite remote. But, even if it were not, the mere possibility of such a suit is not a defense nor does it render the complaint insufficient. It is not unusual for an action to be brought to recover a fund which may be subject to a superior claim by a third party. If that be the situation, a defendant should not be permitted to retain the fund for his own use on the chance that such a party may eventually appear. A defendant's course, if he wishes to protect himself against double liability, is to interplead any and all possible claimants and bind them to the judgment.

In any event, though, no suggestion has been made either in brief or on oral argument that any purchaser has come forward with a claim against the defendants or even that anyone is in a position to advance such a claim. As we have stated, the defendants' assertion that such a party may come forward at some future date is not a basis for permitting them to retain for their own benefit the fruits of their allegedly wrongful acts. For all that appears, the present derivative action is the only effective remedy now available against the abuse by these defendants of their privileged position.

BURKE, SCILEPPI, BERGAN, KEATING, BREITEL AND JASEN, JJ., CONCUR.

FREEMAN v. DECIO

584 F.2d 186 (7th Cir.1978).

HARLINGTON WOOD, JR., CIRCUIT JUDGE.

Both parties agree that there is no Indiana precedent directly dealing with the question of whether a corporation may recover the profits of corporate officials who trade in the corporation's securities on the basis of inside information. However, the plaintiff suggests that were the question to be presented to the Indiana courts, they would adopt the holding of the New York Court of Appeals in Diamond v. Oreamuno, 248 N.E.2d 910 (N.Y.1969). There, building on the Delaware case of Brophy v. Cities Service Co., 70 A.2d 5 (Del.Ch.1949), the court held that the officers and directors of a corporation breached their fiduciary duties owed to the corporation by trading in its stock on the basis of material non-public information acquired by virtue of their official positions and that they should account to the corporation for their profits from those transactions. Since Diamond was decided, few courts have had an opportunity to consider the problem there presented. In fact, only one case has been brought to our attention which raised the question of whether Diamond would be followed in another jurisdiction. In Schein v. Chasen, 478 F.2d 817 (2d Cir.1973), vacated and remanded sub nom., Lehman Bros. v. Schein, 416 U.S. 386 (1974), On certification to the Fla. Sup. Ct., 313 So.2d 739 (Fla.1975), the Second Circuit, sitting in diversity, considered whether the Florida courts would permit a Diamond-type action to be brought on behalf of a corporation. The majority not only tacitly concluded that Florida would adopt Diamond, but that the Diamond cause of action should be extended so as to permit recovery of the profits of non-insiders who traded in the corporation's stock on the basis of inside information received as tips from insiders. Judge Kaufman, dissenting, agreed with the policies underlying a Diamond-type cause of action, but disagreed with the extension of liability to outsiders. He also failed to understand why the panel was not willing to utilize Florida's certified question statute so as to bring the question of law before the Florida Supreme Court. Granting Certiorari, the United States Supreme Court agreed with the dissent on this last point and on remand the case was certified to the Florida Supreme Court. That court not only stated that it would not "give the unprecedented expansive reading to Diamond sought by appellants" but that, furthermore, it did not "choose to adopt the innovative ruling of the New York Court of Appeals in Diamond (itself)." 313 So.2d 739, 746 (Fla.1975). Thus, the question here is whether the Indiana courts are more likely to follow the New York Court of Appeals or to join the Florida Supreme Court in refusing to undertake such a change from existing law.

It appears that from a policy point of view it is widely accepted that insider trading should be deterred because it is unfair to other investors who do not enjoy the benefits of access to inside information. The goal is not one of equality of possession of information since some traders will always be better "informed" than others by dint of greater expenditures of time and resources, greater experience, or greater analytical abilities but rather equality of access to information.[9] * * *

Analytically, the obligation rests on two principal elements: first, the existence of a relationship giving access, directly or indirectly, to information intended to be available only for a corporate purpose and not for the personal benefit of anyone, and second, the inherent unfairness involved where a party takes advantage of such information knowing it is unavailable to those with whom he is dealing.

Yet, a growing body of commentary suggests that pursuit of this goal of "market egalitarianism" may be costly. In addition to the costs associated with enforcement of the laws prohibiting insider trading, there may be a loss in the efficiency of the securities markets in their capital allocation function.[12] The basic insight of economic analysis here is that securities prices act as signals helping to route capital to its most productive uses and that insider trading helps assure that those prices will reflect the best information available (i.e., inside information) as to where the

---

9. As was stated by Professor Hetherington, "(u)nder any 'game' theory of the market a player is likely to consider unfair any advantage gained by his competitors that he not only does not have, but that he cannot obtain." J. Hetherington, Insider Trading and the Logic of the Law, 1967 Wis.L.Rev. 720, 721 (1967).

12. The efficiency implications of the regulation of insider trading were the subject of an early book by Professor Henry Manne, Insider Trading and the Stock Market (1966) which has stimulated a deluge of commentary and criticism. See, e. g., W. Painter, Federal Regulation of Insider Trading (1968); Hetherington, Supra note 9; Shotland, Unsafe at any Price: A Reply to Manne, Insider Trading and the Stock Market, 53 Va.L.Rev. 1425 (1967); Kripke, Book Review, 42 N.Y.U.L.Rev. 212 (1967); Loss, Supra note 11; 5 Loss, Securities Regulation 2999–3000 (1969). For an analysis of the topic based more directly on general economic theory, see Wu, An Economist Looks at Section 16 of the Securities Exchange Act of 1934, 68 Colum.L.Rev. 260 (1968). See also R. Posner, An Economic Analysis of the Law 308 (2d ed. 1977); Note, The Efficient Capital Market Hypothesis, Economic Theory and the Regulation of the Securities Industry, 29 Stan.L.Rev. 1031, 1067–75 (1977).

best opportunities lie. However, even when confronted with the possibility of a trade-off between fairness and economic efficiency, most authorities appear to find that the balance tips in favor of discouraging insider trading. * * *

[T]he New York Court of Appeals in Diamond found the existing remedies for controlling insider trading to be inadequate. Although the court felt that the device of a class action under the federal securities laws held out hope of a more effective remedy in the future, it concluded that "the desirability of creating an effective common-law remedy is manifest." 248 N.E.2d at 915. It went on to do so by engineering an innovative extension of the law governing the relation between a corporation and its officers and directors. The court held that corporate officials who deal in their corporation's securities on the basis of non-public information gained by virtue of their inside position commit a breach of their fiduciary duties to the corporation. This holding represents a departure from the traditional common law approach, which was that a corporate insider did not ordinarily violate his fiduciary duty to the corporation by dealing in the corporation's stock, unless the corporation was thereby harmed. * * *

There are a number of difficulties with the Diamond court's ruling. Perhaps the thorniest problem was posed by the defendants' objection that whatever the ethical status of insider trading, there is no injury to the corporation which can serve as a basis for recognizing a right of recovery in favor of the latter. The Court of Appeals' response to this argument was two-fold, suggesting first that no harm to the corporation need be shown and second that it might well be inferred that the insiders' activities did in fact cause some harm to the corporation. * * *

[T]he Diamond court concluded that it might well be inferred that insider trading causes some harm to the corporation.... It must be conceded that the unfairness that is the basis of the widespread disapproval of insider trading is borne primarily by participants in the securities markets, rather than by the corporation itself. By comparison, the harm to corporate goodwill posited by the Diamond court pales in significance. At this point, the existence of such an indirect injury must be considered speculative, as there is no actual evidence of such a reaction. Furthermore, it is less than clear to us that the nature of this harm would form an adequate basis for an action for an accounting based on a breach of the insiders' duty of loyalty, as opposed to an action for damages based on a breach of the duty of care. The injury hypothesized by the Diamond court seems little different from the harm to the corporation that might be inferred whenever a responsible corporate official commits an illegal or unethical act using a corporate asset. Absent is the element of loss of opportunity or potential susceptibility to outside influence that generally is present when a corporate fiduciary is required to account to the corporation. * * *

Since the Diamond court's action was motivated in large part by its perception of the inadequacy of existing remedies for insider trading, it is noteworthy that over the decade since Diamond was decided, the 10b–5 class action has made substantial advances toward becoming the kind of effective remedy for insider trading that the court of appeals hoped that it might become. Most importantly, recovery of damages from insiders has been allowed by, or on the behalf of, market investors even when the insiders dealt only through impersonal stock exchanges, although this is not yet a well-settled area of the law. In spite of other recent developments indicating that such class actions will not become as easy to maintain as some plaintiffs had perhaps hoped, it is clear that the remedies for insider trading under the federal securities laws now constitute a more effective deterrent than they did when Diamond was decided.

* * *

[H]aving carefully examined the decision of the New York Court of Appeals in Diamond, we are of the opinion that although the court sought to ground its ruling in accepted principles of corporate common law, that decision can best be understood as an example of judicial securities regulation. Although the question is a close one, we believe that were the issue to be presented to the Indiana courts at the present time, they would most likely join the Florida Supreme Court in refusing to adopt the New York court's innovative ruling.

NOTES

1.   Are you persuaded by the court's analysis in *Freeman*? The confidentiality of information based on a fiduciary relationship is well grounded in the law. As a parallel to the agency principles discussed above, consider the following official comment to the Restatement of Restitution:

> A fiduciary is subject to a duty to the beneficiary not to use on his own account information confidentially given him by the beneficiary or acquired by him during the course of or on account of the fiduciary relation or in violation of his duties as a fiduciary, in competition with or to the injury of the beneficiary, although such information does not relate to the transaction in which he is then employed, unless the information is a matter of general knowledge ...

Restatement of the Law of Restitution § 290, Comment a (1937); Brophy v. Cities Service Co., 31 Del.Ch. 241, 70 A.2d 5, 7–8 (1949).

2.   Notwithstanding the decision in *Freeman* the theory of recovery used in *Diamond* has been recognized by other courts. See e.g., In re ORFA Securities Litigation, 654 F.Supp. 1449 (D.N.J.1987); Brophy v. Cities Service Co., 31 Del.Ch. 241, 70 A.2d 5 (1949).

3.   The Supreme Court observed in Carpenter v. United States, 484 U.S. 19, 27–28, 108 S.Ct. 316, 98 L.Ed.2d 275 (1987): "It is well established, as a general proposition, that a person who acquires special knowledge or information by virtue of a confidential or fiduciary relationship with another is not free to exploit that knowledge or information for his own personal benefit but must account to his principal for any profits derived therefrom." (quoting from *Diamond v. Oreamuno*).

4. Consider the following:

There is a good deal of ambiguity as to who should be considered a direct victim of insider trading. Those investors who actually bought from or sold securities to the insiders in face-to-face transactions may well feel cheated when they find out that the insiders were trading on the basis of material information unknown to the public. But what about traders involved in impersonal market transactions who were probably not even aware that insiders were trading in the market. These investors would have traded even if the insiders had stayed out of the market. However, if one instead asks the question of who might have acted differently if the insiders had made public their inside information at the time that they dealt with the market, these investors might be considered to have been injured by the inside trading, even if they were unaware of the insiders' activity. This latter class is capable of a variety of definitions, such as "all persons who traded at the same time as did the insiders" or, at the limit, "all persons who traded from the time that the insiders entered the market until the time that the inside information became public or was otherwise fully reflected in the stock price." See Fleischer, Securities Trading and Corporate Information Practices: The Implications of the Texas Gulf Sulphur Proceedings, 51 Va.L.Rev. 1271, 1277–78 (1965); Note, Damages to Uninformed Traders for Insider Trading on Impersonal Exchanges, 74 Colum.L.Rev. 299 (1974).

Freeman v. Decio, 584 F.2d 186 n. 20 (7th Cir.1978).

5. The focus of the theory of recovery in *Diamond* is on the corporation from who the inside information was misappropriated rather than upon the investors who traded without the benefit of the inside information. The federal securities laws were implemented just after the decision in *Goodwin v. Agassiz*. *Diamond v. Oreamuno*, which was decided in 1969, discusses the importance of the securities laws, but that discussion is omitted from the excerpt of the case in this chapter because at that time the SEC and the courts had only started to focus on insider trading as raising issues of fraud. As will be seen in Chapter 16, that concept would be radically expanded in subsequent years. What effect, if any, should the development of the federal law of insider trading have on the state law rules? In Goldman v. Isaacs, 2001 WL 1671439 (Del.Ch.2001), the judge suggested that it may be time to reconsider the state law of misappropriation of inside information in light of federal developments. Should the availability of parallel federal remedies be a basis for ignoring the agency principles recognized by *Diamond* and other courts?

CHAPTER 15

SECTION 16 OF THE SECURITIES EXCHANGE ACT OF 1934

■ ■ ■

Section 16 of the Securities Exchange Act of 1934 (15 U.S.C. § 78p) is part of the complex of provisions (§§ 13, 14 and 16) applicable to companies required to register under § 12 of the Act. Section 16(a) requires officers, directors and major shareholders of those companies to file reports with the SEC when they purchase or sell any securities of the company. Section 16(b) imposes civil liability on such insiders for any profits realized on a purchase and sale within a period of six months. Section 16(c) prohibits short sales by corporate insiders. This is a transaction in which the stock is sold without owning it. The stock is borrowed for delivery and purchased later to repay the loan in the hope that the stock price will fall before the purchase.

SECTION 1. REPORTING REQUIREMENT

Section 16 is not really a disclosure requirement; its ostensible purpose was to discourage those persons from profiting from the use of "inside information." To that end, Section 16(a) of the Exchange Act requires that all officers, directors, and beneficial owners of more than ten percent of any class of equity security registered under section 12 of that Act file an appropriate notice with the Commission within ten days of becoming an officer, director, or beneficial owner. The section 16(a) notice must include disclosure of all ownership interest in any of the issuer's equity securities. Further, when there has been a change in the officer's, director's, or beneficial owner's share holdings, notice must also be filed with the Commission before the end of the second business day following the change in ownership.

The theory upon which Section 16 is based is that corporate officers, directors and large stockholders have special influence, access and control that provides access to inside information unavailable to others. Section 16(a) seeks to identify those persons and require them to report their transactions in the stock publicly. This is intended to have a prophylactic effect on those who might abuse their position or take advantage of their special position and knowledge to profit.

Section 16(a) reports are publicly available at the SEC's office in Washington, D.C. and through the SEC's electronic filing facility known as EDRGAR. The Commission also publishes official monthly summaries of the section 16(a) reports. Some investment analysts, by watching insider transactions, try to obtain a sense of how the issuer's securities are likely to fare in the future. Insider sales in the aggregate for any particular company are viewed as one indicator of the issuer's health. Similarly, on a macro level, the market's overall health is judged at least in part by the balance between aggregate insider purchases and aggregate insider sales.

NOTES

1.   Violation of the filing requirements of Section 16(a) may result in criminal sanctions. See e.g., United States v. Guterma, 281 F.2d 742 (2d Cir.), cert. denied, 364 U.S. 871, 81 S.Ct. 114, 5 L.Ed.2d 93 (1960); Section 32(a) of the Securities Exchange Act of 1934, 15 U.S.C. § 78ff.

2.   There is no private right of action for violations of Section 16(a) or SEC rules thereunder. Scientex Corp. v. Kay, 689 F.2d 879 (9th Cir.1982); C.R.A. Realty Corp. v. Goodyear Tire & Rubber Co., 705 F.Supp. 972 (S.D.N.Y.1989); Eisenberger v. Spectex Industries, Inc., 644 F.Supp. 48, 50 (E.D.N.Y.1986). This contrasts with the right of action provided for by Congress in Section 16(b) of the Securities Exchange Act of 1934 that allows recovery of short swing profits. Both Section 16(a) and 16(b), however, apply to a narrow class of persons that is sometimes difficult to define.

3.   In 1983, Ralph Nader, the consumer advocate and later Presidential candidate, claimed widespread noncompliance with section 16(a)'s filing requirements. Over the next several months the SEC initiated more than 32 enforcement actions. In 1988, the SEC became increasingly concerned with the large number of section 16(a) violations. The Commission subsequently proposed a revision of its reporting rules. Sec. Exch. Act Rel. No. 34–26333, [1988–89 Transfer Binder] Fed. Sec. L. Rep. (CCH) ¶ 84,343 (Dec. 2, 1988). See Peter J. Romeo & Alan L. Dye, Reforming Section 16, 22 Rev.Sec. & Commod.Reg. 23 (1989); Report of the Task Force on Regulation of Insider Trading, Part II: Reform of Section 16, 42 Bus. Law. 1087 (1988). The new rules were adopted in 1991.

4.   The rules adopted by the SEC in 1991 sought to add greater clarity to the reporting requirements of Section 16(a). The rules addressed the issue of identifying persons who were officers that must file the required reports, the computation of the ten percent beneficial ownership filing trigger and the application of the filing requirement to derivative securities such as stock options.

SECTION 2. PERSONS SUBJECT TO SECTION 16

C.R.A. REALTY v. CROTTY

878 F.2d 562 (2d Cir.1989).

TIMBERS, CIRCUIT JUDGE:

The essential question presented by this appeal is whether an employee's functions, rather than his title, determine whether he is an "officer" within the meaning of § 16(b) of the Securities Exchange Act of 1934. The district court held that the employee's functions were determinative. We agree. We affirm.

Appellant C.R.A. Realty Corp. appeals from a judgment entered December 27, 1988 in the Southern District of New York, Robert L. Carter, District Judge, dismissing after trial appellant's complaint which alleged that appellee Joseph R. Crotty (Crotty), an "officer" of appellee United Artists Communications, Inc. (United Artists or the company) engaged in short-swing trading in United Artists' securities in violation of § 16(b) of the Securities Exchange Act of 1934, which prohibits short-swing trading in the securities of a company by any director, officer or 10% shareholder of the company. The district court held that Crotty was not an "officer" within the meaning of § 16(b)—despite his position as a corporate vice-president—because he was "a middle management employee of United Artists whose duties did not provide access to any confidential information about the company's financial plans or future operations".

Appellant asserts on appeal that the district court erred in holding that Crotty was not an officer because (1) Crotty's lack of access to confidential or inside information is irrelevant since § 16(b) imposes strict liability on *any* officer engaging in short-swing trading regardless of whether he has access to inside information, and (2) in the alternative, appellant demonstrated in the district court that Crotty had access to inside information.

For the reasons which follow, we affirm. * * *

Appellant is an organization incorporated to act as a private attorney general to purchase stock and commence actions against corporate officials for violations of the federal securities laws. During the period in question, appellant owned 10 shares of United Artists, then a nationwide distributor and exhibitor of motion pictures. Crotty, a vice-president of United Artists, was the head film buyer of its western division, a territory encompassing six western states.

Crotty was first employed by United Artists in December 1969. He became head film buyer for the western division in 1980. He was elected a vice-president of United Artists in 1982 and continued to serve as head film buyer for the western division. As head film buyer, he obtained movies to be shown at the 351 movie screens in the western division theaters. He supervised their distribution. This included negotiating and signing agreements pursuant to which United Artists obtained movies for exhibition, supervising the distribution of the movies to the company's theaters, and settling contracts after the movies had been shown in the theaters. Crotty also had some supervisory responsibility for advertising in his division.

Crotty supervised a staff of 30 people. He had virtually complete and autonomous control of film buying in the western division. He was required to consult with higher authority only if he wanted to exceed a certain limit on the amount of the cash advance paid to a distributor for the exhibition of a particular movie. This occurred no more than two or three times a year. The gross revenue from Crotty's division routinely was about 35–36% of United Artists' gross revenue from movie exhibition, or around 15–18% of the company's total gross revenue.

The short-swing transactions here involved took place between December 19, 1984 and July 24, 1985. During this period Crotty purchased 7500 shares of United Artists and sold 3500 of its shares. He realized a large profit which appellant seeks to recover on behalf of United Artists. Following an unsuccessful demand on United Artists that it proceed against Crotty to recover this profit, appellant commenced the instant action against appellees pursuant to § 16(b). Following trial, the district court entered a judgment which dismissed the complaint. The court held that, although Crotty was a vice-president of United Artists, he was not an officer within the purview of § 16(b) because he had no access to inside information regarding the company's financial plans or future operations. This appeal followed.

Section 16(b) * * * "imposes a strict prophylactic rule with respect to insider, short-swing trading". Any corporate official within the statutory meaning of an "officer" who engages in short-swing trading automatically will be required to surrender any profit from the trading, "without proof of actual abuse of insider information, and without proof of intent to profit on the basis of such information". This objective test was chosen by Congress because of the difficulty of proving whether a corporate insider actually abused confidential information to which he had access or purchased or sold an issuer's stock with the intention of profiting from such information. Since the statute imposes strict liability, it is to be applied only when doing so "best serves the congressional purpose of curbing short-swing speculation by corporate insiders".

Appellant challenges the district court's holding by asserting that Crotty automatically was an officer within the meaning of § 16(b) by virtue of his title of vice-president of United Artists. The district court, however, held that it was Crotty's actual duties at the time of the short-swing trading—rather than his corporate title—that determined whether he was an officer within the meaning of § 16(b). We believe that the district court's holding was correct.

Appellant's starting point in challenging the district court's holding is the Securities and Exchange Commission rule which defined the term "officer" in the 1934 Act as including a vice-president of an issuer. Appellant asserts that, since Crotty is a vice-president of United Artists, this rule places him within the purview of § 16(b). We believe it is significant, however, that the SEC itself does not believe that this rule should be rigidly applied in determining who is an officer within the meaning of § 16. For example, two SEC releases show that the Commission does not consider an employee's title as an officer to bring the employee automatically under § 16. We do not believe that Rule 3b–2 requires us to hold that Crotty is an officer within the purview of § 16(b) merely by virtue of his title as a vice-president of the company.

Moreover the district court's holding is consistent with the law of this Circuit. It relied primarily on Colby v. Klune, 178 F.2d 872 (2 Cir.1949). In *Colby* we held that a corporate employee who did not hold the title of a corporate officer nevertheless could be an officer within the meaning of § 16(b) if he "perform[ed] important executive duties of such character that he would be likely, in discharging these duties, to obtain confidential information about the company's affairs that would aid him if he engaged in personal market transactions". * * *

Three other circuits have followed a similar functional approach in determining the liability of officers under § 16(b). Although the Ninth Circuit generally views an issuer's designation of one of its employees as a corporate officer as automatically bringing him within § 16(b), National Medical Enterprises, Inc. v. Small, 680 F.2d 83, 84 (9 Cir.1982)(per curiam), it recognizes an exception if the title is honorary or ceremonial. Id.; Merrill Lynch, Pierce, Fenner & Smith, Inc. v. Livingston, 566 F.2d 1119, 1122–23 (9 Cir.1978)(title of vice-president raises an inference that employee has access to inside information that may be overcome if title is shown to be merely honorary). Two other Circuits generally follow our functional approach. Winston v. Federal Exp. Corp., 853 F.2d 455, 456–57 (6 Cir.1988); Gold v. Sloan, 486 F.2d 340, 351 (4 Cir.1973).

The general approach established by our Court in *Colby* is consistent with that of the Supreme Court in § 16(b) cases in which the Court has emphasized that potential access to inside information is the key to finding liability, rather than rigid application of statutory designations. * * *

It is significant that the approach set forth in *Colby* implements the objective standard established by § 16(b). *Colby*'s approach will require more proof that an employee is an officer under § 16(b) than merely showing that the employee holds a title as a corporate officer. We emphasize, however, that all that is required by *Colby* is that a plaintiff establish that it is more likely than not that the employee's duties gave him access to inside information. A plaintiff need not show that the employee actually obtained inside information or used it to his advantage.

We hold that it is the duties of an employee—especially his potential access to inside information—rather than his corporate title which determine whether he is an officer subject to the short-swing trading restrictions of § 16(b) of the 1934 Act.

We turn next to the district court's finding that Crotty's duties did not give him access to inside information concerning United Artists. Since we hold that this finding was supported by substantial evidence and was not clearly erroneous, we discuss it only briefly.

The evidence indicated that Crotty's appointment as a vice-president—two years after he became a head film buyer—was essentially honorary. The appointment was accompanied by no raise in pay or change in responsibilities. Viewing his responsibilities both before and after the appointment, Crotty had no access to inside information such as the financial or operational plans of United Artists. He was not a director of the company, never attended a directors meeting, and never received any information from the Board of Directors that was not available to the general public. * * *

To summarize:

We hold that it is the actual functions of an employee—particularly his access to inside information—and not his corporate title that determine whether he is an officer within the purview of § 16(b) of the 1934 Act; Crotty's title of vice-president did not make him an officer. We also hold that the district court's finding that Crotty had no access to inside information is not clearly erroneous.

Affirmed.

MESKILL, CIRCUIT JUDGE, dissented

NOTE

The SEC's rules, adopted in 1991, define the term "officer" to include not only principal executive officers, but also principal financial officers, controllers or principal accounting officers, vice presidents in charge of principal business units, divisions or functions, and any other persons who perform similar policy-making functions. See Rule 16a–1(f). In promulgating the revised rules, the Commission specifically endorsed the Second Circuit's statement in *Crotty* that "it is the duties of an employee * * * rather than his corporate title which determine whether he is an officer subject to * * * § 16(b)." The SEC's rules thus assert that a person may be an officer for purposes of Section 16 even if they do not carry that title. The SEC rules name several positions that are officers (*e.g.*, president, principal accounting and financial officers and vice presidents in charge of a principal business), but it also includes any person who performs "policy-making functions." 17 C.F.R § 240.16a–1(f).

WHITING v. DOW CHEMICAL COMPANY

523 F.2d 680 (2d Cir.1975).

GURFEIN, CIRCUIT JUDGE:

This appeal presents a difficult and important question of first impression in this court concerning the interpretation of § 16(b) of the Securities Exchange Act of 1934, as it applies to the matching transactions of a corporate insider and his spouse. The issue is whether a corporate director may be held to have "realized profit" within the meaning of § 16(b) as a result of a matching of his wife's sales and his own purchase of his company's securities within the statutory six-month period.

In a thorough opinion after a non-jury trial, Judge Ward dismissed the complaint of Macauley Whiting, a director of Dow Chemical Company ("Dow"), which sought a declaratory judgment that he was not liable to Dow under § 16(b) and awarded judgment to Dow on its counterclaim for the profits realized. 386 F.Supp. 1130 (S.D.N.Y.1974). We affirm.

Helen Dow Whiting sold an aggregate of 29,770 shares of Dow stock for $1.6 million during September and November of 1973 at an average price of $55–$56. In December 1973 her husband, appellant Macauley Whiting, exercised an option to purchase 21,420 Dow shares for $520,000 at a price of $24.3125. He exercised the option with funds he borrowed from his wife, which were part of the proceeds of her sales of the Dow stock in the preceding two months.

Macauley Whiting has been a director of Dow since 1959. His wife of thirty years is a granddaughter of the founder of Dow, and acquired substantial amounts of Dow stock over the years by gift and inheritance, and these assets are segregated from appellant's. On the other hand, Judge Ward found that "the resources of both husband and wife are significantly directed toward their common prosperity, and they easily communicate concerning matters which relate to that prosperity." Moreover, the Whitings' separate accounts are managed by the same financial advisors. The Whitings file joint tax returns, and their common financial planning has included Mrs. Whiting's use of her husband's annual gift tax exclusion to make charitable gifts and gifts to trusts established for their six children.

Mrs. Whiting's personal wealth and income—primarily consisting of dividends and capital gains derived from her Dow holdings—is considerably larger than that of her husband. Although Judge Ward found that Mr. Whiting contributes virtually his entire salary toward family expenses, he also found that Mrs. Whiting is primarily responsible for the considerable costs incurred in the style of living the Whitings have chosen to pursue. It is her dividend income, for example, which has provided for education of the Whitings' children, which defrays medical expenses, which maintains a family vacation home, and which pays real estate taxes on the Whitings' property.

Mrs. Whiting's sales of the Dow stock in September and November of 1973 were made pursuant to a long-term investment plan, arranged by the Whitings and their financial advisor, which was designed to diversify the holdings of the family and to obtain tax benefits. The court found that the Whitings discussed the general philosophy to govern the management of Mrs. Whiting's estate, and, in early 1972, agreed on a major shift in their philosophy. They then discharged their long-time investment advisor. Desiring to pursue a more aggressive investment program, the Whitings in late 1972 retained new investment counselors, Smith, Barney & Company, Inc. ("Smith Barney"), and new tax, accounting and estate planning advisors, Goldstein, Golub, Kessler & Company ("Goldstein"). As had been the case with their previous financial advisor, the Whitings continued to maintain formal segregation of their investment accounts, but these accounts were managed jointly as discretionary accounts under the supervision of one person at Smith Barney.

Since January 1966, in the Form 3 and 4 reports he was required to make as a Dow director pursuant to § 16(a), Mr. Whiting regularly reported his wife's Dow stock as "directly owned" by him, and never disclaimed ownership as he might have pursuant to SEC regulations, a procedure of which he was made aware by Dow's counsel. Under SEC Rule 144(a)(2)(i), effective April 15, 1972, Mrs. Whiting as a "relative or spouse" was herself required to report her sales of Dow stock. From the outset Smith Barney advised the Whitings that it considered Mrs. Whiting to be a "control" person of Dow by reason of Mr. Whiting's position as a Dow director. The Whitings acquiesced in such treatment, and Mrs. Whiting, thereafter, regularly filed Form 144 reports with the SEC covering her sales of Dow stock.

Judge Ward found that not only did Mr. and Mrs. Whiting use the same financial advisors, but both were present at many meetings with these advisors; they had a "general philosophy" concerning the management of the family estates. He also found that Mrs. Whiting upon occasion "consults her husband concerning the desirability of certain investments in areas of his expertise," but that "Mr. Whiting does not communicate with his wife concerning the affairs of [Dow]." 386 F.Supp. at 1132. * * *

As we have seen, Goldstein advised the Whitings on October 29 that Mr. Whiting should finance the exercise of his option by means of an intrafamily loan from his wife. Mr. Whiting explored the possibility of obtaining a personal loan through Harris Bank of Chicago, and he was quoted an interest rate of ¼ to ½ over the then prevailing prime lending rate of about 10%. Ultimately, for reasons not revealed by the record but apparent from the circumstances, Mr. Whiting informed the Harris Bank that "[w]e have been able to get the cash required *from sale of stock* and will not need the loan at this time" (emphasis added). The "sale of stock" to which Mr. Whiting referred was the very sale of Dow stock by Mrs. Whiting now at issue. Appellant borrowed the $520,000 he needed to exercise his option from his spouse and used it for that purpose. The loan was at 7% interest, and no repayment terms were specified.

It is strange that more than forty years of experience with Section 16(b) has yielded practically no judicial guidance on Section 16(b) liability concerning attribution of transactions by the spouse of a director. The decision below proceeded on the assumption that, under the circumstances related, appellant was the "beneficial owner" of the securities sold by the wife.

Cases where the husband simply buys stock and puts the shares in his wife's name are relatively simple; so, too, perhaps where he has sole control of her account. The difficulty arises when, as here, the securities are incontestably the wife's, but where the husband obtains benefits, nevertheless, from the dividends and proceeds of sale through the wife's supplying the larger share of family expenses. The problem is compounded by the action of both spouses in managing both the sales and the exercise of the option jointly, and further by the use of the proceeds of sale for the exercise of the option. * * *

The Commission's definition seeks to go further to include situations where the insider indirectly benefits from the dividends though he does not own the shares. The theory is that such an insider would be tempted to pass on inside information to the holder of the stock from which he, himself, "benefits" and thus falls within the class intended by Congress. * * *

"Beneficial owner" is the language of § 16(a) and we have been told to read the words of § 16(b) not literally. In the broader sense, we think the term should be read more expansively than it would be in the law of trusts. For purposes of the family unit, shares to which legal title is held by one spouse may be said to be "beneficially owned" by the other, the insider, if the ordinary rewards of ownership are used for their joint benefit. These rewards are generally the dividend income as well as the capital gains on sale and the power to dispose of the shares to their children by gift or upon death.

While we cannot earmark the proceeds of Mrs. Whiting's particular sales as going to household and family support, we know from the findings that the larger part of their joint maintenance came from her estate, the bulk of it in Dow stock. We also know that they engaged in joint estate planning. So that while it is true that if they ever separated, Mrs. Whiting would take her Dow shares, it is also true that while they continue to live as a married couple, there is hardly anything Mrs. Whiting gets out of the ownership that appellant does not share.

While the case is harder than if it had been Mr. Whiting who had put the shares in his wife's name originally, the mischief that "inside information" will be used is just as great. * * *

Turning to the specific facts, while there was no exclusive "control" by appellant over his wife's separate investments generally, there was sufficient evidence to establish that the questioned transactions were part of a common plan, jointly managed by husband and wife. * * *

This may be a case where innocents were trapped by the statute and its gloss. If Mr. Whiting had not exercised his option until June 1974, just before it expired, he would have incurred no § 16(b) liability, for the six months from the time of Mrs. Whiting's last sale in November 1973 would have expired. But the threat of a new tax bill in 1974 apparently made him exercise the option in 1973. The path of this harsh statute is strewn with such possibly innocent victims. But to allow immunity here would open the door to patent abuse which Congress sought to prevent by a catch-all type of statute, at least where the purchase and sale aspects of the transaction are not subject to dispute.

The judgment is affirmed.

NOTES

1. In CBI v. Horton, 682 F.2d 643 (7th Cir.1982), the court held that a sale made by a director could not be matched against subsequent purchase by him as trustee of a trust for his children, since the benefit to his children was not "profit realized by him" within the meaning of the statute.

2. The SEC's proposed rules in 1988 would have automatically deemed an insider to be the beneficial owner of securities held by a member of his immediate family sharing the same residence. As adopted in 1991, however, the rules merely provide a "rebuttable presumption" that he is the beneficial owner of such securities. See Rule 16a–1(a)(2)(A).

FEDER v. MARTIN MARIETTA CORP.

406 F.2d 260 (2d Cir.1969).

WATERMAN, CIRCUIT JUDGE.

Plaintiff-appellant, a stockholder of the Sperry Rand Corporation ("Sperry") after having made the requisite demand upon Sperry which was not complied with, commenced this action pursuant to § 16(b) of the Securities Exchange Act of 1934, to recover for Sperry "short-swing" profits realized upon Sperry stock purchases and sales by the Martin Marietta Corporation ("Martin"). Plaintiff alleged that George M. Bunker, the President and Chief Executive of Martin Marietta, was deputized by, or represented, Martin Marietta when he served as a member of the Sperry Rand Board of Directors and therefore during his membership Martin Marietta was a "director" of Sperry Rand within the meaning of Section 16(b). The United States District Court for the Southern District of New York, Cooper, J., sitting without a jury, finding no deputization, dismissed plaintiff's action. 286 F.Supp. 937 (S.D.N.Y.1968). We hold to the contrary and reverse the judgment below. * * *

In Rattner v. Lehman, 193 F.2d 564 (2 Cir.1952), Judge Learned Hand in his concurring opinion planted the seed for a utilization of the theory of deputization upon which plaintiff here proceeds. In discussing the question whether a partnership is subject to Section 16(b) liability whenever a partner is a director of a corporation whose stock the partnership traded, Judge Hand stated:

> I agree that § 16(b) does not go so far; but I wish to say nothing as to whether, if a firm deputed a partner to represent its interests as a director on the board, the other partners would not be liable. True, they would not even then be formally "directors"; but I am not prepared to say that they could not be so considered; for some purposes the common law does treat a firm as a jural person. 193 F.2d at 567.

The Supreme Court in Blau v. Lehman, 368 U.S. 403, 408–410 (1962), more firmly established the possibility of an entity, such as a partnership or a corporation, incurring Section 16(b) liability as a "director" through the deputization theory. Though the Court refused to reverse the lower court decisions that had held no deputization, it stated:

> Although admittedly not "literally designated" as one, it is contended that Lehman is a director. No doubt Lehman Brothers, though a partnership, could for purposes of § 16 be a "director" of Tide Water and function through a deputy * * *. 368 U.S. at 409.

In Marquette Cement Mfg. Co. v. Andreas, 239 F.Supp. 962, 967 (S.D.N.Y.1965), relying upon Blau v. Lehman, the availability of the deputization theory to impose § 16(b) liability was again recognized.

In light of the above authorities, the validity of the deputization theory, presumed to be valid here by the parties and by the district court, is unquestionable. Nevertheless, the situations encompassed by its application are not as clear. The Supreme Court in Blau v. Lehman intimated that the issue of deputization is a question of fact to be settled case by case and not a conclusion of law. Therefore, it is not enough for appellant to show us that inferences to support appellant's contentions should have been drawn from the evidence. Rather our review of the facts and inferences found by the court below is imprisoned by the "unless clearly erroneous" standard. Fed.R.Civ.P. 52(a). In the instant case, applying that standard, though there is some evidence in the record to support the trial court's finding of no deputization, we, upon considering the entire evidence, are left with the definite and firm conviction that a mistake was committed. Consequently, we reverse the result reached below.

Bunker served as a director of Sperry from April 29, 1963 to August 1, 1963, when he resigned. During the period December 14, 1962 through July 24, 1963, Martin Marietta accumulated 801,300 shares of Sperry stock of which 101,300 shares were purchased during Bunker's directorship. Between August 29, 1963 and September 6, 1963, Martin Marietta sold all of its Sperry stock. Plaintiff seeks to reach, on behalf of the Sperry Rand Corporation, the profits made by Martin Marietta from the 101,300 shares of stock acquired between April 29 and August 1, all of which, of course, were sold within six months after purchase. * * *

[The court here summarizes the evidence as to whether Bunker was acting as Martin Marietta's deputy on the Sperry Board.]

In summary, it is our firm conviction that the district court erred in apportioning the weight to be accorded the evidence before it. The control possessed by Bunker, his letter of resignation, the approval by the Martin Board of Bunker's directorship with Sperry, and the functional similarity between Bunker's acts as a Sperry director and the acts of Martin's representatives on other boards, as opposed to the factors relied upon by the trial court, are all definite and concrete indicatives that Bunker, in fact, was a Martin deputy, and we find that indeed he was.

The trial court's disposition of the case obviated the need for it to determine whether § 16(b) liability could attach to the corporate director's short-swing profits realized after the corporation's deputy had ceased to be a member of the board of directors of the corporation whose stock had been so profitably traded in. It was not until after Bunker's resignation from the Sperry Board had become effective that Martin Marietta sold any Sperry stock. The issue is novel and until this case no court has ever considered the question. We hold that the congressional purpose dictates that Martin must disgorge all short-swing profits made from Sperry stock purchased during its Sperry directorship and sold after the termination thereof if sold within six months of purchase. * * *

Notes

1. The deputization theory had been addressed by the Supreme Court in Blau v. Lehman, 368 U.S. 403, 82 S.Ct. 451, 7 L.Ed.2d 403 (1962). A partner of an investment banking firm was sitting on a public company's board of directors. The partnership purchased and sold the company's stock at a profit within six months. Plaintiff sought to recover the entire partnership profit from the partner and the partnership. The Court pointed out that the partnership did not involve the partner/director in the partnership's trading decisions and thus there was no basis for attributing the partner's directorship to the partnership. In the course of its opinion, the Court set forth the guidelines for the deputization analysis that was applied in *Feder v. Martin Marietta.*

2. The SEC's rules under § 16 do not undertake to define the term "director" beyond the definition found in § 3(a)(7) of the Act, nor do they attempt to codify the case law relating to "deputization," which the Commission viewed as "best left to a case-by-case determination." Ownership Reports and Trading by Officers, Directors and Principal Stockholders, Sec. Exch. Act Rel. No. 34–26333, 53 Fed. Reg. 49997–02, 1988 WL 268999 (SEC Dec. 13, 1988).

3. After the decision in *Feder,* the SEC amended its rules to require a director or officer to file a report with respect to a transaction which took place after he ceased being a director or officer if it occurs within six months after the last transaction effected while he was a director or officer. In Levy v. Seaton, 358 F.Supp. 1 (S.D.N.Y.1973), defendant purchased and sold shares of

General Motors during the six-month period following his resignation as a director of the corporation. The court held that the transactions were not required to be reported under Section 16(a) and were therefore exempt from 16(b) liability.

4.   In Winston v. Federal Express, Corp., 853 F.2d 455 (6th Cir.1988), Winston resigned as an officer of the company on August 25, but his resignation was not to be effective until September 30 to enable him to exercise a stock option which would not become exercisable until September 25. He exercised the option on September 30, and resold the stock less than six months later. The court held him liable under § 16(b). Since he conceded that he exercised substantial executive responsibilities and had access to inside information until August 25, the fact that he ceased to perform any duties for the company after that date would not relieve him from liability unless he could produce "substantial evidence" to overcome the presumption that he continued to have access to confidential information until the effective date of his resignation.

5.   Under SEC rules, a transaction following the cessation of officer or director status is subject to § 16 only if it occurs within six months of a transaction which occurred while that person was an officer or director. Rule 16a–2(b). A transaction which occurs before the person becomes an officer or director cannot be matched with a subsequent transaction which occurs after the person has attained that status. cf. Rule 16a–2(a).

6.   In computing the 10% threshold, a question can arise as to what constitutes a "class" of "equity" securities. This was considered in Chemical Fund, Inc. v. Xerox Corp. 377 F.2d 107 (2d Cir.1967):

> The Securities Exchange Act provides in section 16 that a corporation to which it applies may recover profits realized by an officer, director, or "beneficial owner of more than 10 per centum of any class of any equity security" of the corporation from purchases and sales of such equity securities within any period of less than six months. Section 16(b) states that recovery of such profits was allowed: "For the purpose of preventing the unfair use of information which may have been obtained by such beneficial owner * * * by reason of his relationship to the issuer * * *." It is conceded that the Debentures are securities as defined in section 3(a)(10) of the Act, and that they are equity securities because they are convertible into common stock. Under the definition in section 3(a)(11), it is apparent that a Convertible Debenture is an "equity security" only because of its convertible nature, since an "equity security" is defined as "any stock or similar security; or any security convertible * * * into such a security * * * or any such warrant or right * * *."

> Thus the question is: are the Debentures by themselves a "class of any equity security," or does the class consist of the common stock augmented, as to any beneficial holder in question, by the number of shares into which the Debentures it owns are convertible? We think that the Debentures are not a class by themselves; the total percentage of common stock which a holder would own following a hypothetical conversion of the Debentures it holds is the test of liability under section 16(b). The history of the legislation, the stated purpose of the Act, and the

anomalous consequences of any other meaning all support this conclusion.

Nothing in the hearings which preceded passage of the Act in 1934 would indicate that the owners of Debentures as such ought to be considered as "insiders." Indeed, S. 2693, 73d Cong.2d Sess. (1934) as introduced included bondholders as insiders, and was later revised to exclude them from the application of section 16. The hearings did disclose instances where directors, officers and large stockholders profited through receiving information before it had become public knowledge. See, e.g., S.Rep. No. 792, 73d Cong., 2d Sess. 9 (1934). Thus it is that section 16 is specifically concerned with "directors, officers and principal stockholders," and has adopted a rule that any stockholder owning more than 10 percent of an equity security is presumed to be an insider who will receive information regarding the company before it is made public. The reason that officers, directors and 10 percent stockholders have been held to account for profits on short-swing transactions is because they are the people who run the corporation, and who are familiar with its day to day workings. This is necessarily so of officers and directors, and there was ample basis for concluding that stockholders owning more than 10 percent of the voting stock of the company, if not in control, would be closely advised, as their votes usually elected the directors who in turn elected the officers, where these were not elected directly by the stockholders.

But there is no reason whatever to believe that any holder of any Convertible Debentures would, by reason of such holding, normally have any standing or position with the officers, directors or large stockholders of a company so that such holder of Debentures would be the recipient of any inside information. There is no provision which gives a holder of the Debentures any standing beyond that of a creditor entitled to certain specified payments of interest at stated intervals, and possessing numerous rights all of which are specifically spelled out in the trust indenture pursuant to which the Debentures were issued.

To hold that the beneficial owner of 10 percent or more of the Debentures is liable under section 16(b) would here impose a liability on an owner who by conversion of all his Debentures would obtain less than one-half of one percent of Xerox common stock. At the same time a holder of as much as 9 percent of Xerox common stock would not be liable. Thus Chemical Fund, able to command only 2.72 percent of Xerox common, would be liable for short-swing profits, although the holder of 9 percent of the common, more than three times Chemical Fund's total potential holding, would not be liable. We do not believe that Congress could have meant to apply the provisions of the Act to any holder of Convertible Debentures whose possible equity position following full conversion of its Debentures would be less than 10 percent of the class of equity stock then outstanding.

The Securities and Exchange Commission contends that the general legal and financial usage of the word "class" compels the conclusion that Chemical Fund was subject to section 16, citing Ellerin v. Massachusetts

Mut. Life Ins. Co., 270 F.2d 259 (2 Cir.1959). But this Court referred to the common meaning of "class" in that case because there was no prior case law, statutory history, or legislative definition to guide it. Here the purpose of section 16 to impose liability on the basis of actual or potential control is clear, and we should give it effect.

We reverse the judgment of the district court and direct that summary judgment be entered in favor of Chemical Fund on its complaint and that the counterclaim be dismissed.

7.   The SEC's rules codified the result in the *Chemical Fund* case, note 6, above.

8.   There are occasions in which convertible securities will be considered a class separate and apart from the underlying equity security. In Morales v. Freund, 163 F.3d 763 (2d Cir.1999), convertible preferred stock which had class voting rights was found to be a separate class of equity securities for section 16(b) purposes. The court also held that, when a group of persons act together to acquire the securities in question, the group will be considered a single person for computing section 16(b)'s 10% threshold. See also Morales v. Quintel Entertainment, Inc., 249 F.3d 115 (2d Cir.2001) (remanded to determine whether a shareholder agreed to act in concert).

9.   The rules adopted by the SEC in 1991 provide that, for the purpose of ascertaining whether a person is the beneficial owner of 10% of a company's securities, "beneficial ownership" is determined by the criteria used in § 13 of the Act, which requires reports from all persons who own more than 5% of the stock of a reporting company. See Rule 16a–1(a)(1). See Chapter 20. The § 13(d) criteria are considerably broader than those that had previously been applied under § 16.

10.   What happens if the owner is not made aware that his or her holdings have crossed the ten percent threshold? Especially in the case of issuers who periodically repurchase their shares, the threshold can be a moving target. If an owner is not at least put on inquiry notice that his or her holdings have reached the threshold, then there should be no section 16(b) liability until those facts come to light. C.R.A. Realty Corp. v. Enron Corp., 842 F.Supp. 88 (S.D.N.Y.1994) (although information in annual report revealed that defendant's ownership was ten percent, it was not subject to § 16(b) liability since it had no reason to know of that status when the report was released; subsequently, it became aware of its ten percent status and defendant duly filed the required notice).

11.   The SEC's rules exclude nonvoting securities from the computation of the 10 percent beneficial ownership reporting requirement. Phantom stock and stock appreciation rights (unless they are settled only for cash) will be included as securities that are subject to the 10 percent beneficial ownership requirement. 17 C.F.R. § 240.16a–1.

12.   The SEC's effort to clarify its rules has led to much confusion. The issues that arise in the context of derivative securities are endless and complex. In brief, the SEC views a derivative security as the equivalent of ownership in the security into which the derivative instrument is excercisable or convertible. The SEC's rules require reporting of the acquisition of deriva-

tive securities upon its acquisition or grant and upon the disposition of such instruments. 17 C.F.R. § 240.16a–4. Congress also amended § 16(a) and (b) of the Securities Exchange Act of 1934 to include the purchase or sale of a security-based swap agreement, as defined in § 206B of the Gramm Leach Bliley Act.

―――――

SECTION 3.   SECTION 16(b)—DISGORGEMENT OF SHORT SWING PROFITS

Section 16(b) imposes liability for short-swing profits in the issuer's stock upon officers, directors, and beneficial owners of ten percent of a class of equity securities that are subject to the Exchange Act's reporting requirements. These listed statutory insiders must disgorge to the issuer any "profit" realized as a result of a purchase and sale or sale and purchase of covered equity securities occurring within a six month period. Section 16(b) is an automatic "crude rule of thumb" that is designed to prevent illegal insider trading. It covers situations where there is the potential for abuse. Actual possession and use of information is not required but two matching transactions ("purchase" and "sale") are necessary. Section 16(b) has no application to a single transaction entered into on the basis of nonpublic inside information, and it does not apply to transactions more than six months apart.

Insiders may be liable for improper use of inside information under SEC Rule 10b–5 even where they have complied with the provisions of Section 16(b). That liability is considered in Chapter 16. Liability under Rule 10b–5 is based on a concept of fraud, while liability under Rule 16(b) is simply a legislative mandate that requires no finding of fraud or misconduct. All that is required under Section 16(b) for liability to lie is profit that results from a purchase or sale by a statutory insider within a six month period.

In reading the apparent harshness of Section 16(b)'s recapture provisions, remember that liability is easily avoided. All a statutory insider has to do is wait six months and one day before entering into a matching transaction. Although both transactions may be subject to Section 16(a)'s reporting requirements, they are not subject to section 16(b) short swing liability. As one court observed: "It don't mean a thing if it ain't got that swing," Portnoy v. Seligman & Latz, Inc., 516 F.Supp. 1188, 1200 (S.D.N.Y.1981) (quoting that noted theorist, E.K. Ellington, also known as the "Duke").

Section 16(b) provides for a private remedy on the part of shareholders to recover profits made by an insider of their corporation in violation of the short swing profit prohibition. The private remedy embodied in section 16(b) is self contained, sui generis, and is a hybrid variety of derivative suit. The statute requires that the shareholder make a demand upon directors prior to being sued. The corporation, through its directors, then has sixty days to decide whether to have the corporation bring suit to recover the profits. Weisman v. Spector, 158 F.Supp. 789 (S.D.N.Y.1958); Netter v. Ashland Paper Mills, Inc., 19 F.R.D. 529 (S.D.N.Y.1956). No demand is required when it would be a futile gesture due to the self-interest of the directors. There is a two year statute of limitations for actions brought under Section 16(b).

If the corporation does not act after a demand on directors has been made (or, if the demand is excused), suit may be filed by a shareholder of record at the time of the suit and who continues to be a shareholder throughout the trial. The commonplace contemporaneous ownership rule contained in federal and state law regarding derivative litigation generally, that requires a shareholder who brings suit to have been a shareholder at the time of the action complained of, does not apply in an action under Section 16(b).

In 1991, the Supreme Court addressed the question of whether a shareholder of a corporation that was subsequently merged into another could bring suit under Section 16(b) against officers, directors, or ten percent beneficial holders of the merged disappearing corporation. In Gollust v. Mendell, 501 U.S. 115, 111 S.Ct. 2173, 115 L.Ed.2d 109 (1991), plaintiff was a shareholder of a merged corporation and under the terms of the merger agreement he received a combination of stock and cash. Plaintiff instituted his Section 16(b) claim prior to the merger and the court held that he had standing under the statute since he owned a security of the issuer at the time he instituted the suit. In reaching this result, the Court emphasized that, while Section 16(b) defines a narrow class of potential defendants, it sets forth a broad class of plaintiffs-much broader than would apply under the contemporaneous ownership rule applicable to derivative suits generally. The Court also pointed out that, since the plaintiff received shares in the surviving corporation, he had a continuing interest in the assets of the merged corporation sufficient to allow him to share derivatively in the benefits of any recovery, even when that interest was based on ownership of shares in the parent corporation. The Court's rationale indicates that, had the plaintiff shareholder been cashed out, his lack of a continuing interest would have precluded him from sharing in any recovery and thus would deny him standing to sue under Section 16(b). Whether this is the proper analysis is open to question. The Court observed that the only express requirement of the statute is that the plaintiff be a shareholder at the time the suit was instituted; there is no mention of any requirement that he or she have a continuing interest. To summarize, the Court in *Gollust* set forth two requirements for standing under Section 16(b): first, the suit must have been initiated at a time that plaintiff was a shareholder; and second, the plaintiff must have a continuing interest in the corporation (or its assets) so as to allow him or her to benefit from any recovery.

The courts have held that it is no defense to an action under Section 16(b) that the suit was motivated primarily by an attorney's desire to obtain the attorneys' fees that may be awarded to the successful plaintiff.

Magida v. Continental Can Co., 231 F.2d 843 (2d Cir.1956), cert. denied, 351 U.S. 972, 76 S.Ct. 1031, 100 L.Ed. 1490 (1956). Attorneys' fees are awarded out of the fund created by the recovery and are not added to the defendant's liability. Super Stores, Inc. v. Reiner, 737 F.2d 962, 965 (11th Cir.1984); A+ Network, Inc. v. Shapiro, 960 F.Supp. 123 (M.D.Tenn. 1997).

An action under Section 16(b) may be brought either in law or in equity. It has been held that the plaintiff's failure to demand a jury trial renders the action one in equity, thus denying the defendant the right of election. Arbetman v. Playford, 83 F.Supp. 335 (S.D.N.Y.1949). Not all courts agree. In one case, the plaintiff contended that since disgorgement is primarily equitable, a defendant is not entitled to a jury trial; however, the court rejected this argument and granted a jury trial. Morales v. Executive Telecard, Ltd., [1998 Transfer Binder] Fed. Sec. L. Rep. (CCH) ¶ 90,333 (S.D.N.Y.1998).

Section 16(b) contains a two year limitation period which begins to run from the date of the second transaction; that is, the one that creates the section 16(b) profits. However, the statute of limitations period may be extended until the time of reasonable discovery where there has been a failure to file timely section 16(a) reports. Tristar Corp. v. Freitas, 84 F.3d 550 (2d Cir.1996).

Section 16(b) is not designed as a compensatory remedy. The preamble to Section 16(b) indicates that this civil liability is imposed "for the purpose of preventing the unfair use of information which may have been obtained by such beneficial owner, director, or officer by reason of his relationship to the issuer." The legislative history reveals congressional recognition of such a great potential for abuse of inside information so as to warrant the imposition of strict liability. The statute was viewed as an objective method of preventing "the unscrupulous employment of [corporate] inside information." Hearings on S.Res. 84, S.Res. 97 Before The Senate Comm. on Banking and Currency, 73d Cong., 1st Sess. pt. 15 at 6557 (1934). Accordingly, in light of its broad remedial purpose, Section 16(b) will require disgorgement of insider short-swing profits even in the absence of any wrongdoing. The liability so imposed is often referred to as prophylactic in nature. Section 16(b) thus does not make moral distinctions as it penalizes insiders who commit a technical violation but are still "pure of heart" while at the same time a more culpable insider may be able to avoid liability by going beyond the letter of the statute. Magma Power Co. v. Dow Chemical Co., 136 F.3d 316, 320–21 (2d Cir.1998) (Section 16(b) "operates mechanically, and makes no moral distinctions, penalizing technical violators of pure heart, and bypassing corrupt insiders who skirt the letter of the prohibition"); Lerner v. Millenco, L.P., 23 F. Supp.2d 337, 340 (S.D.N.Y.1998).

Section 16(b) does not *prohibit* officers, directors and 10% shareholders from trading in the stock of their companies; it simply authorizes the company (or a shareholder suing on its behalf) to recover the "profits" realized from such trading if made within a six month period. The SEC, therefore, has no enforcement responsibilities under § 16 (other than to require the filing of reports). It does, however, have power to adopt rules and regulations exempting transactions from the liability provisions, if it finds them to be "not comprehended within the purpose of" § 16(b). Pursuant to this authority, the Commission has adopted a large number of rules defining terms and exempting particular persons or transactions. Securities Exchange Act Release No. 28869 (Feb. 8, 1991).

A corporation's management will seldom have much interest in bringing suit against its own members; therefore enforcement of the section results largely from derivative suits brought by shareholders of the corporation. Since the benefit to any individual shareholder is likely to be infinitesimal, the only incentive for bringing such actions is the fee which the court awards the lawyer, and which is paid by the corporation as the beneficiary of the recovery. The information which a lawyer needs to make his case under Section 16(b) is found in the reports which directors, officers and 10% shareholders are required to file with the SEC under Section 16(a) whenever they acquire or dispose of securities of the corporation. To make the lawyers' job easier, the forms were amended in 1972 to require disclosure of the price at which securities were bought or sold (for some unknown reason, this information was not previously required). See Securities Exchange Act Release No. 9500 (Feb. 23, 1972). Approximately 100,000 insider trading reports are filed annually with the SEC.

The following case explains the background of section 16(b) and gives a hint as to the breadth of its reach.

SMOLOWE v. DELENDO CORP.

136 F.2d 231 (2d Cir.1943).

CLARK, CIRCUIT JUDGE.

The issue on appeal is solely one of the construction and constitutionality of § 16(b) of the Securities Exchange Act of 1934, rendering directors, officers, and principal stockholders liable to their corporation for profits realized from security tradings within any six months' period. Plaintiffs, Smolowe and Levy, stockholders of the Delendo Corporation, brought separate actions under this statute on behalf of themselves and other stockholders for recovery by the Corporation—joined as defendant— against defendants Seskis and Kaplan, both directors and president and vice-president respectively of the Corporation.* * *

The controversy as to the construction of the statute involves both the matter of substantive liability and the method of computing "such profit." The first turns primarily upon the preamble, viz., "For the purpose of preventing the unfair use of information which may have been obtained by such beneficial owner, director, or officer by reason of his relationship to the issuer." Defendants would make it the controlling grant and limitation of authority of the entire section, and liability would result only for profits from a proved unfair use of inside information. We cannot agree with this interpretation. * * *

The primary purpose of the Securities Exchange Act—as the declaration of policy in § 2 makes plain—was to insure a fair and honest market, that is, one which would reflect an evaluation of securities in the light of all available and pertinent data. Furthermore, the Congressional hearings indicate that § 16(b), specifically, was designed to protect the "outside" stockholders against at least short-swing speculation by insiders with advance information. It is apparent too, from the language of § 16(b) itself, as well as from the Congressional hearings, that the only remedy which its framers deemed effective for this reform was the imposition of a liability based upon an objective measure of proof. This is graphically stated in the testimony of Mr. Corcoran, chief spokesman for the draftsmen and proponents of the Act, in Hearings before the Committee on Banking and Currency on S. 84, 72d Cong., 2d Sess., and S. 56 and S. 97, 73d Cong., 1st and 2d Sess., 1934, 6557: "You hold the director, irrespective of any intention or expectation to sell the security within six months after, because it will be absolutely impossible to prove the existence of such intention or expectation, and you have to have this crude rule of thumb, because you cannot undertake the burden of having to prove that the director intended, at the time he bought, to get out on a short swing."

A subjective standard of proof, requiring a showing of an actual unfair use of inside information, would render senseless the provisions of the legislation limiting the liability period to six months, making an intention to profit during that period immaterial, and exempting transactions wherein there is a bona fide acquisition of stock in connection with a previously contracted debt. It would also torture the conditional "may" in the preamble into a conclusive "shall have" or "has." And its total effect would be to render the statute little more of an incentive to insiders to refrain from profiteering at the expense of the outside stockholder than are the common-law rules of liability; it would impose a more stringent statute of limitation upon the party aggrieved at the same time that it allowed the wrongdoer to share in the spoils of recovery.

Had Congress intended that only profits from an actual misuse of inside information should be recoverable, it would have been simple enough to say so. * * *

The present case would seem to be of the type which the statute was designed to include. Here it is conceded that the defendants did not make unfair use of information they possessed as officers at the time of the transactions. When these began they had no offer from Schenley's. But they knew they were pressing the tax suit; and they, of course, knew of the corporate offer to settle it which re-established the offer to purchase and led to the favorable sale. It is naive to suppose that their knowledge of their own plans as officers did not give them most valuable inside knowledge as to what would probably happen to the stock in which they were dealing. It is difficult to find this use "unfair" in the sense of illegal; it is certainly an advantage and a temptation within the general scope of the legislature's intended prohibition.

The legislative history of the statute is perhaps more significant upon a determination of the method of computing profits—defendants' second line of attack upon the district court's construction of the statute. They urge that even if the statute be not construed to impose liability only for unfair use of inside information, in any event profits should be computed according to the established income tax rule which first looks to the identification of the stock certificate, and if that is not established, then applies the presumption which is hardly more than a rule of administrative convenience of "first in, first out." * * *

Defendants seek support for their position from the Senate hearings, where, in answer to Senator Barkley's comment, "All these transactions are a matter of record. It seems to me the simple way would be to charge him with the actual profit," Mr. Corcoran responded: "It is the same provision you have in the income tax law. Unless you can prove the actual relationship between certificates, you take the highest price sold and the lowest price bought." This was an incorrect statement of the income tax law. The rule there is first in, first out, regardless of price, wherever the stock actually purchased and sold is not identifiable. But this does show the rule the proponents had in mind, even though its source is erroneously stated. Analysis will show that the income tax rules cannot apply without defeating the law almost completely. Under the basic rule of identifying the stock certificate, the large stockholder, who in most cases is also an officer or director, could speculate in long sales with impunity merely by reason of having a reserve of stock and upon carefully choosing his stock certificates for delivery upon his sales from this reserve. Moreover, his profits from any sale followed by a purchase would be practically untouchable, for the principle of identity admits of no gain without laboring proof of a subjective intent—always a nebulous issue—to effectuate the connected phases of this type of transaction. In consequence the statute would be substantially emasculated. We cannot ascribe to it a meaning so inconsistent with its declared purpose.

Once the principle of identity is rejected, its corollary, the first-in, first-out rule, is left at loose ends. * * * Its application would render the large stockholder with a backlog of stock not immediately devoted to trading immune from the Act. Further, we should note that it does not fit the broad statutory language; a purchase followed immediately by a sale, albeit a transaction within the exact statutory language, would often be held immune from the statutory penalty because the purchase would be deemed by arbitrary rule to have been made at an earlier date; while a sale followed by purchase would never even be within the terms of the rule.[20] We must look elsewhere for an answer to our problem of finding a reasonable and workable interpretation of the statute in the light of its admitted purpose.

Another possibility might be the striking of an average purchase price and an average sale price during the period, and using these as bases of computation. What this rule would do in concrete effect is to allow as offsets all losses made by such trading. * * * Even had the statutory language been more uncertain, this rule seems one not to be favored in the light of the statutory purpose. Compared to other possible rules, it tends to stimulate more active trading by reducing the chance of penalty; thus Kaplan, with his more involved trading, benefits by the rule, whereas Seskis, who bought substantially at one time and sold as a whole, does not. Its application to a case where trading continued more than six months might be most uncertain, depending upon how the beginning of each six months' period was ascertained. It is not a clear-cut taking of "any profit" for the corporation, and we agree with the district court in rejecting it.

The statute is broadly remedial. Recovery runs not to the stockholder, but to the corporation. We must suppose that the statute was intended to be thorough-going, to squeeze all possible profits out of stock transactions, and thus to establish a standard so high as to prevent any conflict between the selfish interest of a fiduciary officer, director, or stockholder and the faithful performance of his duty. The only rule whereby all possible profits can be surely recovered is that of lowest price in, highest price out— within six months—as applied by the district court. We affirm it here, defendants having failed to suggest another more reasonable rule. * * *

The total recovery against defendants accruing to the corporation is $18,894.85, plus costs of $38.93. By this, plaintiffs will be benefited only to the extent of about $3, since they own but 150 shares of a total of 800,000. Upon their petition, however, the district court awarded them $3,000 for counsel fees, together with their expenses of $78.98 payable out of the funds accruing to the corporation.

While it is well settled that in a stockholder's or creditor's representative action to recover money belonging to the class the moving party is entitled to lawyer's fees from the sum recovered, this was not strictly an action for money belonging to either class, but for a penalty payable to the corporation. Ordinarily the corporate issuer must bring the action; and only upon its refusal or delay to do so, as here, may a security holder act

---

20. Defendants suggest, albeit rather obliquely, an intermediate rule limiting the application of the principle only to stock purchased and sold during the chosen six months' period. On the surface this would appear to prevent complete emasculation of the statute, since it assumes to prevent use of an investment backlog. Actually it makes a rule of most uncertain incidence; thus here it would leave the recovery against Seskis untouched, but reduce that against Kaplan by roughly two-thirds. These uncertain results would be increased, of course, if the period during which the officer actually continued his trading was greater than six months; consider its chance application to say, a fourteen months' period, which might be divided up into three, or even four, six-month periods starting at different times. And once the general income tax rule is rejected (as we have seen it must be), there is surely no basis for developing this original and uncertain gloss upon it, since it does not aid the statutory intent or fit the statutory language.

for it in its name and on its behalf. But this in effect creates a derivative right of action in every stockholder, regardless of the fact that he has no holdings from the class of security subjected to a short-swing operation or that he can receive no tangible benefits, directly or indirectly, from an action because of his position in the security hierarchy. And a stockholder who is successful in maintaining such an action is entitled to reimbursement for reasonable attorney's fees on the theory that the corporation which has received the benefit of the attorney's services should pay the reasonable value thereof. * * *

While the allowance made here was quite substantial, we are not disposed to interfere with the district court's well-considered determination. Since in many cases such as this the possibility of recovering attorney's fees will provide the sole stimulus for the enforcement of § 16(b), the allowance must not be too niggardly.

NOTES

1. Is the court's method of computing "profit realized" by matching the highest price sales with the lowest price purchases during a six-month period really the "only rule" by which the statutory objective could be realized? Or does it go too far? Should the defendant be held liable for "profits realized" if he actually had a net loss on his total trading in the stock during a six-month period?

2. The *Smolowe* case was followed by Gratz v. Claughton, 187 F.2d 46 (2d Cir.1951), cert. denied 341 U.S. 920, 71 S.Ct. 741, 95 L.Ed. 1353 (1951), per Judge Learned Hand:

> There remains the question of the computation of profits, which we dealt with in Smolowe v. Delendo Corporation, supra. Section 16(b) declares that 'any profit realized * * * from any purchase and sale, or any sale and purchase * * * within any period of less than six months * * * shall inure to and be recoverable by the issuer': the corporation. It is plain that this presupposes some matching of (1) purchases against sales, or of (2) sales against purchases, and that there must therefore be some principle upon which both the minuend—the sale price—and the subtrahend—the purchase price—can be determined. At first blush it might seem that the statute limited the recovery to profits derived from transactions in the same shares; as, for example, that a dealer's profit upon the sale of any given number of shares was to be measured by subtracting what he paid for those shares from what he got upon a sale of the same certificate. However, as we observed in Smolowe v. Delendo Corporation, that would allow an easy avoidance of the statute; in order to speculate freely an officer, director, or 'beneficial owner' need only hold a substantial block of shares for more than six months. If, for example, on January 1st, he had 10,000 shares which he had bought before October 1st, he could buy 1,000 shares on February 1st and sell 1,000 shares at a profit on April 1st, making delivery out of certificates from the 10,000 shares purchased before October 1st. After the two transactions his position would be what it had been on January 1st save that in two

months he had made a profitable turn in 1,000 shares—exactly the evil against which the statute is directed. Moreover, there is an added reason for this interpretation, if one be needed. In the case of a sale followed by a purchase it is impossible to identify any purchase with any previous sale; one would have to confine such transactions to the practically non-existent occasions when the proceeds of the sale were used to purchase. Thus it appears, regardless of anything said during the passage of the bill through Congress and of the different forms it took, that the Act does not demand-that the same shares should be sold which were bought. This accords with the fungible nature of shares of stock. Indeed, if we translate the transaction into sales and purchases, or purchases and sales, of gallons of oil in a single tank, or of bushels of wheat in a single bin, it at once appears that the ascertainment of the particular shares bought or sold must be wholly irrelevant.

Although for these reasons it appears that the transactions—sales and purchases, or purchases and sales—are not to be matched by identifying the shares dealt in, we are no nearer than before to finding an answer as to how transactions shall be matched; all that so far appeared, is that the matching is to be between contracts of sale and contracts of purchase, or vice versa. On the other hand it is manifest that the intent of the fiduciary cannot be the test; first, because he generally has no ascertainable intent; and second, because that would open the door even more widely to the evil in question. The statute does not allow the fiduciary to minimize his profits, any more than to set off his losses against them. We can therefore find no principle by which to select any two transactions which are to be matched; and, so far as we can see, we are forced to one of two alternatives: to match any given purchase, taken as subtrahend, in such a way as to reduce profits to their lowest possible amount, or in such a way as to increase them to the greatest possible amount. The master adopted the second course, following what he supposed to be the doctrine of Smolowe v. Delendo Corporation. We think that he was right for the following reasons.

The question is in substance the same as when a trustee's account is to be surcharged, for, as we have said, the statute makes the fiduciary a constructive trustee for any profits he may make. It is true that on the beneficiary in an accounting rests the burden of proof of a surcharge, although the fiduciary has the burden of establishing any credits. Since the plaintiff was seeking to surcharge the defendant we will therefore assume that it rested upon her to show how the transactions are to be matched; and, that, if there were nothing more, since she cannot do so, she must be content to have them matched in the way that shows the least profit. Obviously that cannot be the right answer, for the reasons we have given; and perhaps the fact that it cannot be, is reason enough for adopting the alternative. But there is another ground for reaching the same result. As we have said, the statute makes all such dealings unlawful, and makes the fiduciary accountable to the corporation. Although it is impossible in the case at bar to compute the defendant's profits, except that they must fall between two limits—the minimum and the maximum—the cause of this uncertainty is the number of transactions within six months: that is, the number of defendant's derelictions. The situation falls within the doctrine which has been law since the days of the 'Chimney Sweeper's Jewel Case,' [Armory v. Delamirie, 1722, 1 Strange 505] that when damages are at some unascertainable amount below an upper limit and when the uncertainty arises from the defendant's wrong, the upper limit will be taken as the proper amount.

This results in looking for six months both before and after any sale, and not for three months only, as the defendant insists. If one is seeking an equation of purchase and sale, one may take any sale as the minuend and look back for six months for a purchase at less price to match against it. On the other hand, if one is looking for an equation of sale and purchase, one may take the same sale and look forward for six months for any purchase at a lower price. Although obviously no transaction can figure in more than one equation, with that exception we can see no escape from what we have just said. It is true that this means that no director, officer, or 'beneficial owner' may safely buy and sell, or sell and buy, shares of stock in the company except at intervals of six months. Whether that is too drastic a means of meeting the evil, we have not to decide; it is enough that we can find no other way to administer the statute. Therefore, not only will we follow Smolowe v. Delendo Corporation, as a precent; but as res integra and after independent analysis we reassert its doctrine. The defendant concedes that, except for carrying the transactions backward and forward for six months, instead of for three, the master followed the rule laid down in that decision; and the plaintiff has not appealed, so that she is not entitled to any more than she has recovered. On this account we have not examined the master's computations in detail and are not to be understood to have passed upon them. The crushing liabilities which Sec. 16(b) may impose are apparent from this action in which the judgment was for over $300,000; it should certainly serve as a warning, and may prove a deterrent.

For a more recent application of the *Smolowe* rule, see Donoghue v. MIRACOR Diagnostics, Inc., 2002 WL 233188 (S.D.N.Y.2002).

3.   To understand the effect of *Smolowe* and *Gratz*, consider a situation in which a director makes the following purchases and sales:

March 1	purchases	200 shares at $40
April 1	sells	100 shares at $20
May 1	purchases	100 shares at $35
June 1	sells	200 shares at $50
July 1	purchases	100 shares at $45
August 1	sells	100 shares at $40

What would be his "profit realized" under the rule laid down in *Smolowe* and how much profit did he actually make?

————

In contrast to the cases dealing with officers and directors, section 16(b) on its face provides that, where insider status attaches by virtue of ten percent beneficial equity ownership, the section applies only where such person was a beneficial owner "both at the time of the purchase and sale, or the sale and purchase." The threshold purchase that pushes the defendant over ten percent beneficial ownership does not qualify as a "purchase" subject to section 16(b) and only purchases made after that date will give rise to liability when matched with subsequent sales occurring within six months and resulting in a profit. Foremost–McKesson, Inc. v. Provident Securities Co., 423 U.S. 232, 96 S.Ct. 508, 46 L.Ed.2d 464 (1976). In an earlier case, the Court held that, where a ten percent beneficial owner first sells just enough shares to put him below the ten percent threshold and on the next day liquidates the remainder of his holdings, the second sale cannot be subject to section 16(b) because of the statute's express "at the time of" requirement. Reliance Electric Co. v. Emerson Electric Co., 404 U.S. 418, 92 S.Ct. 596, 30 L.Ed.2d 575 (1972). This ruling was based on an objective reading of the statute rather than a subjective evaluation of the statutory insider's motives in so structuring the two-step sale.

If a person is found to fall within one of the categories covered by § 16, the next question is whether there has been a "purchase" and "sale." Section 16(b) does not apply to securities acquired in good faith in connection with a debt previously contracted. The exercise of an option or a conversion privilege, or the exchange of one security for another, either in a merger or a voluntary transaction, may or may not fall within the statute, depending on the circumstances. The following case considers that question.

SECTION 4.   PURCHASE AND SALE

BERSHAD v. McDONOUGH

428 F.2d 693 (7th Cir.1970).

Cummings, Circuit Judge.

This appeal is from a summary judgment in favor of the plaintiff, a common stockholder in the Cudahy Company of Phoenix, Arizona. Plaintiff brought this action under Section 16(b) of the Securities Exchange Act of 1934 to recover for Cudahy's benefit the "short-swing" profits coming to defendant from his and his wife's purchase and sale of 272,000 shares of Cudahy common stock.

On March 15 and 16, 1967, defendant Bernard P. McDonough and his wife Alma, who reside in Parkersburg, West Virginia, each purchased 141,363 shares of Cudahy common stock at $6.75 per share, totaling over 10% of the outstanding common stock of Cudahy. Soon after the purchase, McDonough was elected to the Cudahy Board of Directors and named Chairman of the Board. At the same time, Donald E. Martin and Carl

Broughton, business associates of McDonough, were elected to the Cudahy Board.

On July 20, 1967, in Parkersburg, West Virginia, Mr. and Mrs. McDonough and Smelting Refining and Mining Co. ("Smelting") entered into a formal "option agreement" granting Smelting the right to purchase 272,000 shares of the McDonoughs' Cudahy stock. Smelting paid $350,000 upon execution of the agreement, which set the purchase price for the shares of $9 per share, or a total of $2,448,000. The option was exercisable on or before October 1, 1967. The $350,000 was to be applied against the purchase price but was to belong to the McDonoughs if Smelting failed to exercise the option. Accompanying this "option" was an escrow agreement under which the McDonoughs' 272,000 shares of Cudahy stock were placed in escrow with their lawyer. They also simultaneously granted Smelting an irrevocable proxy to vote their 272,000 shares of stock until October 1, 1967.

A day or two after the documents were signed, Mr. McDonough and Carl Broughton, his business associate, acceded to the request of Smelting and agreed to resign from the Cudahy Board if Smelting representatives were put on the Board. Both of them resigned as directors on July 25, 1967. About that time, five nominees of Smelting were placed on the Cudahy Board. Smelting subsequently wrote the McDonoughs on September 22, 1967, that it was exercising its option. The closing took place in Parkersburg five days later, with the $2,098,000 balance of the purchase price being paid to the McDonoughs through the escrow agent. From their sales, Mr. and Mrs. McDonough realized a profit of $612,000.

In the court below, defendant contended that under West Virginia law the July 20 agreement constituted an option contract with Smelting, and not a contract for the sale of the Cudahy stock. A stock option, he argued, does not qualify as a "sale or contract for sale" for purposes of applying the rule of Section 16(b) of the Securities Exchange Act of 1934. The district court, however, took another view of the transaction. In a thoughtful memorandum opinion, the trial judge looked beyond the formal wording of the July 20 "option" and concluded that the transaction between the McDonoughs and Smelting "amounted to a sale or a contract of sale" within the terms of the Securities Exchange Act. Since this event occurred less than six months after the McDonoughs had purchased the Cudahy stock, under Section 16(b) summary judgment for $612,000, together with interest, was entered for plaintiff. We affirm.

Section 16(b) was designed to prevent speculation in corporate securities by "insiders" such as directors, officers and large stockholders. Congress intended the statute to curb manipulative and unethical practices which result from the misuse of important corporate information for the personal aggrandizement or unfair profit of the insider. Congress hoped to insure the strict observance of the insider's fiduciary duties to outside shareholders and the corporation by removing the profit from short-swing dealings in corporate securities. Conversely, Congress sought to avoid unduly discouraging bona fide long-term contributions to corporate capital. * * *

Under Section 3(a)(14) of the Act, the "sales" covered by Section 16(b) are broadly defined to include "any contract to sell or otherwise dispose of" any security. Construction of these terms is a matter of federal law, and "[w]hatever the terms 'purchase' and 'sale' may mean in other contexts," they should be construed in a manner which will effectuate the purposes of the specific section of the Act in which they are used. Applying this touchstone, courts have generally concluded that a transaction falls within the ambit of Section 16(b) if it can reasonably be characterized as a "purchase" or "sale" without doing violence to the language of the statute, and if the transaction is of a kind which can possibly lend itself to the speculation encompassed by Section 16(b).

The phrase "any purchase and sale" in Section 16(b) is therefore not to be limited or defined solely in terms of commercial law of sales and notions of contractual rights and duties. Applicability of this Section may depend upon the factual circumstances of the transaction, the sequence of relevant transactions, and whether the insider is "purchasing" or "selling" the security. By the same token, we conclude transactions subject to speculative abuses deserve careful scrutiny. The insider should not be permitted to speculate with impunity merely by varying the paper form of his transactions. The commercial substance of the transaction rather than its form must be considered, and courts should guard against sham transactions by which an insider disguises the effective transfer of stock.

The considerations thus guiding the application of Section 16(b) provide substantial support for coverage of an insider's sale of an option within six months of his purchase of the underlying security. The utility of various stock options as a tool of speculation is well recognized. As noted in Booth v. Varian Associates, 334 F.2d 1, 4 (1st Cir.1964).

> "Options, conversions and similar devices have lent themselves quite readily to the abuses uncovered in the Congressional investigation antedating the Act, and in order to give maximum support to the statute courts have attempted to include these transactions by characterizing them as purchases or sales."

The insider's sale of options in his stock is well adapted to speculation and abuse of inside information whether or not the option is subsequently exercised. The sale of the right to purchase the underlying security is itself a means of realizing a profit from that security. The right to purchase stock at a given price under specified circumstances, although clearly not identical to the rights attendant upon ownership of the stock itself, derives from and is dependent upon the value of the underlying security. Sale of such purchase rights provides an easy vehicle for the use of inside information in extracting profits from the stock itself. Where the option is ultimately exercised, moreover, the exact date of exercise may be unimportant to the substance of the transaction from the point of view of the insider-vendor, since he can exploit his position in the corporation by setting the terms of sale in the option. In addition, parties frequently provide that the option price shall be considered a retroactive down payment of the purchase price of the stock sold upon exercise of the option. Under such circumstances, it may be reasonable to hold the parties to their own treatment of the transaction and date the "sale" of the stock at the purchase of the option rather than its exercise.

It is unnecessary, however, to rely solely upon these considerations to conclude that the McDonoughs' "sale" of the Cudahy stock to Smelting took place well in advance of the exercise of the option on September 22. The circumstances of the transactions clearly indicate that the stock was effectively transferred, for all practical purposes, long before the exercise of the option. The $350,000 "binder" ostensibly paid for the option represented over 14% of the total purchase price of the stock. Granting the magnitude of the sale contemplated, the size of the initial commitment strongly suggests that it "was not just a binder." The extent of that payment represented, if not the exercise of the option, a significant deterrent to the abandonment of the contemplated sale. In addition, the reverse side of the "Option Agreement" contained provisions for the transfer of the Cudahy stock, endorsed in blank, to an escrow agent pending completion of the transaction. At the same time, the McDonoughs delivered an irrevocable proxy to Smelting to vote the 272,000 shares at any regular or special shareholders' meetings. Within a few days, McDonough and one of his associate directors resigned and were replaced by representatives of Smelting's interests, including the Chairman of the Board of Directors of Smelting, and the president and director of that corporation. Significantly, only a few days after the expiration of the six-month period from the McDonoughs' purchase of the Cudahy stock, Smelting formally exercised its option and, on the same day that Smelting mailed its notification, the McDonoughs executed the necessary stock powers.

Defendant finally contends that these facts were insufficient to support the district court's grant of summary judgment in favor of plaintiff. We cannot accept this contention. The question in this case, unlike Blau v. Allen, 163 F.Supp. 702, 705 (S.D.N.Y.1958), involves the determination not of the existence of the sale, but the date to be ascribed to the transfer under Section 16(b). The basic facts in this case are undisputed and far exceed those present in Allen. We conclude that as a matter of law, the sale was effectively accomplished within the six-month period contemplated by Section 16(b). Consequently, the motion for summary judgment was properly granted.

Affirmed.

NOTES

1. The acquisition and exercise of options, the acquisition and conversion of convertible securities, and the receipt of stock pursuant to employee stock option, bonus or purchase plans have all raised difficult questions under

§ 16(b). The SEC's rules provide in general that the acquisition or disposition of an option, convertible security or other "derivative security" is deemed the equivalent of a purchase or sale of the underlying security, but the exercise of an option or conversion right is exempt from the operation of § 16. Rules 16b–6 and 16a–1(b) and (h).

     2.   Difficult questions have arisen in terms of whether mergers and other types of exchanges constitute purchases or sales under section 16(b). In Kern County Land Co. v. Occidental Petroleum Corp., 411 U.S. 582, 93 S.Ct. 1736, 36 L.Ed.2d 503 (1973), Occidental acquired more than 20% of the stock of Kern at a price of $83.50 a share pursuant to a tender offer. Kern opposed Occidental's bid and negotiated a merger with Tenneco. Occidental lacked the votes to block the merger, and its efforts to prevent the merger by litigation were unsuccessful. To protect itself against being locked into a minority position in Tenneco after the merger, Occidental negotiated an agreement with Tenneco giving Tenneco an option to buy the Tenneco shares which Occidental would receive in the merger, at a price of $105 a share. In an effort to avoid § 16(b) liability, the option could not be exercised by Tenneco until a date six months and one day after the completion of Occidental's tender offer. A $10 per-share nonrefundable down payment on the option was designed to assure that it would be in Tenneco's interest to exercise the option by paying the remainder of the price as long as the market price of the shares did not drop below $95 a share. The merger was consummated, the option was exercised on schedule, and Tenneco then sued Occidental for its profit on the transaction.[1]

---

1. The facts as stated by the Court provide good insight into the makings of a defensive merger, raising issues that will be considered in chapter 11:

     On May 8, 1967, after unsuccessfully seeking to merge with Kern County Land Co. (Old Kern), Occidental Petroleum Corp. (Occidental) announced an offer, to expire on June 8, 1967, to purchase on a first-come, first-served basis 500,000 shares of Old Kern common stock at a price of $83.50 per share plus a brokerage commission of $1.50 per share. By May 10, 1967, 500,000 shares, more than 10% of the outstanding shares of Old Kern, had been tendered. On May 11, Occidental extended its offer to encompass an additional 500,000 shares. At the close of the tender offer, on June 8, 1967, Occidental owned 887,549 shares of Old Kern.

     Occidental, seeing its tender offer and takeover attempt being blocked by the Old Kern–Tenneco 'defensive' merger, countered on May 25 and 31 with two mandamus actions in the California courts seeking to obtain extensive inspection of Old Kern books and records. Realizing that, if the Old Kern–Tenneco merger were approved and successfully closed, Occidental would have to exchange its Old Kern shares for Tenneco stock and would be locked into a minority position in Tenneco, Occidental took other steps to protect itself. Between May 30 and June 2, it negotiated an arrangement with Tenneco whereby Occidental granted Tenneco Corp., a subsidiary of Tenneco, an option to purchase at $105 per share all of the Tenneco preference stock to which Occidental would be entitled in exchange for its Old Kern stock when and if the Old Kern–Tenneco merger was closed. The premium to secure the option at $10 per share, totaled $8,866,230 and was to be paid immediately upon the signing of the option agreement. If the option were exercised, the premium was to be applied to the purchase price. By the terms of the option agreement, the option could not be exercised prior to December 9, 1967, a date six months and one day after expiration of Occidental's tender offer. On June 2, 1967, within six months of the acquisition by Occidental of more than 10% ownership of Old Kern, Occidental and Tenneco Corp. executed the option. Soon thereafter, Occidental announced that it would not oppose the Old Kern–Tenneco merger and dismissed its state court suits against Old Kern.

     The Old Kern–Tenneco merger plan was presented to and approved by Old Kern shareholders at their meeting on July 17, 1967. Occidental refrained from voting its Old Kern shares, but in a letter read at the meeting Occidental stated that it had determined prior to June 2 not to

The district court held that the grant of the option and the exchange of Kern shares for Tenneco shares on the merger were both "sales" under § 16(b), and ordered Occidental to disgorge its profit. The Court of Appeals for the Second Circuit held that neither the option nor the exchange was a "sale", and ordered summary judgment for Occidental. The Supreme Court, in a 6–3 decision, affirmed the Court of Appeals. The Court explained:

> Although traditional cash-for-stock transactions that result in a purchase and sale or a sale and purchase within the six-month, statutory period are clearly within the purview of § 16(b), the courts have wrestled with the question of inclusion or exclusion of certain 'unorthodox' transactions. The statutory definitions of 'purchase' and 'sale' are broad and, at least arguably, reach many transactions not ordinarily deemed a sale or purchase. In deciding whether borderline transactions are within the reach of the statute, the courts have come to inquire whether the transaction may serve as a vehicle for the evil which Congress sought to prevent—the realization of short-swing profits based upon access to inside information—thereby endeavoring to implement congressional objectives without extending the reach of the statute beyond its intended limits. The statute requires the inside, short-swing trader to disgorge all profits realized on all 'purchases' and 'sales' within the specified time period, without proof of actual abuse of insider information, and without proof of intent to profit on the basis of such information. Under these strict terms, the prevailing view is to apply the statute only when its application would serve its goals. '(W)here alternative constructions of the terms of § 16(b) are possible, those terms are to be given the construction that best serves the congressional purpose of curbing short-swing speculation by corporate insiders.' Reliance Electric Co. v. Emerson Electric Co., 404 U.S., at 424. Thus, '(i)n interpreting the terms 'purchase' and 'sale,' courts have

---

oppose the merger and that it did not consider the plan unfair or inequitable. Indeed, Occidental indicated that, had it been voting, it would have voted in favor of the merger.

Meanwhile, the Securities and Exchange Commission had refused Occidental's request to exempt from possible § 16(b) liability Occidental's exchange of its Old Kern stock for the Tenneco preference shares that would take place when and if the merger transaction were closed. Various Old Kern stockholders, with Occidental's interests in mind, thereupon sought to delay consummation of the merger by instituting various lawsuits in the state and federal courts. These attempts were unsuccessful, however, and preparations for the merger neared completion with an Internal Revenue Service ruling that consummation of the plan would result in a tax-free exchange with no taxable gain or loss to Old Kern shareholders, and with the issuance of the necessary approval of the merger closing by the California Commissioner of Corporations.

The Old Kern–Tenneco merger transaction was closed on August 30. Old Kern shareholders thereupon became irrevocably entitled to receive Tenneco preference stock, share for share in exchange for their Old Kern stock. Old Kern was dissolved and all of its assets, including 'all claims, demands, rights and choses in action accrued or to accrue under and by virtue of the Securities Exchange Act of 1934 . . . ,' were transferred to New Kern.

The option granted by Occidental on June 2, 1967, was exercised on December 11, 1967. Occidental, not having previously availed itself of its right, exchanged certificates representing 887,549 shares of Old Kern stock for a certificate representing a like number of shares of Tenneco preference stock. The certificate was then endorsed over to the optionee-purchaser, and in return $84,229,185 was credited to Occidental's accounts at various banks. Adding to this amount the $8,886,230 premium paid in June, Occidental received $93,905,415 for its Old Kern stock (including the 1,900 shares acquired prior to issuance of its tender offer). In addition, Occidental received dividends totaling $1,793,439.22. Occidental's total profit was $19,506,419.22 on the shares obtained through its tender offer.

properly asked whether the particular type of transaction involved is one that gives rise to speculative abuse.' Id. at 424 n.4.

In reaching its decision, the Supreme Court used an interesting blend of the "pragmatic" and "objective" approaches to § 16(b). The Court described the "objective" and "pragmatic" approaches in the following terms (in footnote 26 of the opinion):

> Several decisions have been read as to apply a so-called "objective" test in interpreting and applying § 16(b). Under some broad language in those decisions, § 16(b) is said to be applicable whether or not the transaction in question could possibly lend itself to the types of speculative abuse that the statute was designed to prevent. By far the greater weight of authority is to the effect that a "pragmatic" approach to § 16(b) will best serve the statutory goals.

With respect to the exchange of stock pursuant to the merger, the Court in *Kern County* took the "pragmatic" approach that, while some merger transactions might give rise to § 16(b) liability, Occidental should not be held liable because of "the involuntary nature of [its] exchange" and because its "outside" position meant there was an "absence of the possibility of speculative abuse of inside information." With respect to the option, on the other hand, the Court took the "objective" position that, since Occidental could not force Tenneco to exercise the option if the stock price dropped below $95 a share, it had not obtained the assurance of profit that is normally incident to a "sale."

3. American Standard, Inc. v. Crane Co., 510 F.2d 1043 (2d Cir.1974), cert. denied, 421 U.S. 1000, 95 S.Ct. 2397, 44 L.Ed.2d 667 (1975), involved a contest for control of Westinghouse Air Brake Co. After Crane had acquired 32% of Air Brake's stock, Air Brake, over Crane's objections, was merged into Standard and Crane became an unwilling holder of more than 10% of a new class of convertible preferred stock of Standard, its major competitor in the plumbing business. Crane promptly sold the Standard preferred stock for about $10 million more than it had paid for the Air Brake stock. The Second Circuit held that Crane was not liable under § 16(b). First, the exchange of stock pursuant to the merger was not a "sale" of the Air Brake stock, under the reasoning of the Supreme Court in *Kern County*. Second, if the merger exchange was not a sale of the Air Brake stock, it would be "anomalous" to hold that it was a purchase of the Standard stock that could be matched against the subsequent sale of that stock. Third, the sale of Standard stock could not be matched against the purchase of Air Brake stock because they were not securities of the same "issuer," as provided in the language of the statute.

4. The apex of the pragmatic approach was found in Gold v. Sloan, 486 F.2d 340 (4th Cir.1973), cert. denied 419 U.S. 873, 95 S.Ct. 134, 42 L.Ed.2d 112 (1974), where the court held one selling director liable under section 16(b) while exonerating three others. The issue was whether an exchange of stock pursuant to a merger between the Atlantic Research and Susquehanna corporations constituted a "purchase" under 16(b). Atlantic Research Corporation had merged into the Susquehanna Corporation via an exchange of stock; the defendants in *Gold* had been holders of Atlantic stock for more

than six months prior to the merger negotiations, thus eliminating the problem of whether the exchange was a section 16(b) "sale," which had been dealt with in the *Kern County* decision. The defendants were also officers and directors of Atlantic and under the terms of the merger agreement occupied similar positions with respect to Susquehanna, the surviving corporation. Within less than six months after the merger had been consummated the defendant insiders sold their newly acquired Susquehanna holdings at a profit. The Fourth Circuit pointed to the Supreme Court's decision in *Kern County* as having "resolved [the] conflict and adopted what had earlier been described as a 'pragmatic rather than technical' test" for unorthodox transactions. It was thus necessary "to examine the particular situation of each defendant as it relates to the merger." (486 F.2d at 343–44). Three of the defendants had no contact whatsoever with the merger negotiations and thus were held to have had no access to Susquehanna's inside information. In contrast, the fourth defendant, Atlantic's chief executive officer, had been "in complete charge of the negotiations" and "had access to the books and records * * *." (486 F.2d at 351–52). Accordingly, this access created a potential for abuse and thus warranted finding the merger exchange to have been a section 16(b) purchase by the inside director. Although certainly consistent with the Supreme Court's rationale in *Kern,* the *Gold* decision has been criticized as running contrary to the straightforward crude rule of thumb that section 16(b) was designed to provide. Note, "Securities Exchange Act § 16(b): Fourth Circuit Harvests Some Kernels of Gold," 42 Fordham L.Rev. 852 (1974); 'Recent Developments, Securities-§ 16(b)-Mergers as a 'Purchase,' " 20 Wayne L.Rev. 1415 (1974). Critics of the *Gold* decision were particularly upset with the ruling that the same transaction produces differing treatment for individuals falling within the statute's objective reach. Nevertheless, the pragmatic trend continued to flourish. See e.g., Portnoy v. Revlon, Inc., 650 F.2d 895 (7th Cir.1981) (finding no sale in merger agreement); Heublein, Inc. v. General Cinema Corp., 559 F.Supp. 692 (S.D.N.Y. 1983) (no sale in defensive merger), affirmed 722 F.2d 29 (2d Cir.1983); Reece Corp. v. Walco National Corp., 565 F.Supp. 158 (S.D.N.Y.1981) (two step transaction treated as one "sale" in violation of § 16(b)); Colan v. Cutler–Hammer, Inc., 516 F.Supp. 1342 (N.D.Ill.1981) (finding a sale pursuant to a merger, following the rationale of Gold); *Thomas Lee Hazen, Treatise on the Law of Securities Regulation* § 13.4 (5th ed. 2005).

SECTION 5. SHORT SALES

Section 16 of the Securities Exchange Act of 1934 was intended to prevent insiders from seeking short term profits at the expense of long term goals, as well as to prevent the use of "soft" inside information that gave them an advantage in trading their own company's stock. Section 16(c) of the Securities Exchange Act of 1934 furthered those goals by prohibiting short sales by insiders. These are simply transactions in which the stock is sold without owning it. The stock is borrowed for delivery in the sale transaction and purchased later to repay the loan. The investment goal in such a transaction is that, if the stock price falls as predicted, the short seller will be able to buy the stock for repayment of the stock loan at a price less than the sale price at the time of the short sale. The short seller will then keep the difference between the two prices. Of course, if the price of the stock rises, instead of falls as predicted, the short seller will have a loss equal to the difference between the price the stock was sold and the higher price paid for the repurchase to repay the stock loan.

The prohibition against such sales by insiders in Section 16(c) was popularly referred to as the "anti-Wiggin" amendment because it was a response to massive short sales by Albert H. Wiggin, Chairman of the Chase National Bank during the 1920s. He made profits of $4 million in a two week period by short selling the bank's stock. At that time, the sales force of the securities affiliate of the bank was selling the stock to its customers as a sound investment. Congress did not believe that insiders should be taking advantage of downturns in their company's stock through such short sales. *Jerry W. Markham, A Financial History of the United States, From J.P. Morgan to the Institutional Investor (1900–1970)* 196, 204 (2002).

Note on Short Sales Generally

Short sellers, even those who are not insiders, have long been viewed with suspicion and distrust in the stock markets. The SEC had for years restricted short sales under its so-called "up tick" rule, that allowed a short sale only where the previous trade caused an increase in price, thereby theoretically preventing short-sellers from placing additional pressure on a falling market. There was much criticism of this rule because it discriminated against short-sellers that provide important price discovery information. In response to that criticism, the SEC eliminated its uptick test rule for short sales in July 2007. The greater flexibility allowed by that rule change was thought to have encouraged short sales and added volatility in the stock market during the crisis that occurred in 2007 and 2008. Short sellers were even blamed for bringing down Bear Stearns and Lehman Brothers On July 15, 2008, the SEC issued an emergency order prohibiting naked short selling in the stocks of 19 major financial companies, including Fannie Mae and Freddie Mac. That restriction was later expanded to cover hundreds of financial institutions. One economic study indicated that declines in the stocks of the financial firms covered by the SEC's emergency order could not be attributed to short selling. The study further found that the SEC short selling restriction had resulted in a decline in the quality of the market for those stocks. Nevertheless the SEC continues to take the view that short sales need to be regulated to prevent undue volatility and manipulation. For example, in 2008, the SEC also adopted Rule 10b–21 that prohibits naked short selling by entering a short sale with the intent not to provide sufficient shares to effect delivery for the short sale. This supplements SEC Regulation SHO that governs the mechanics of short sales generally. In addition, Rule 105 of SEC's Regulation M prohibits short sales by a company's insiders and affiliates during a distribution of the company's securities.

CHAPTER 16

INSIDER TRADING AS SECURITIES FRAUD

■ ■ ■

SECTION 1.   INTRODUCTION

Section 16 of the 1934 Act is not an effective remedy against the most common forms of insider trading, since it is not applicable in many situations in which such misuse has occurred by persons or trading that does not fall within the provisions of that statute. The principal weapon used by the SEC to deter intentional misuse of inside information in such situations has been the antifraud provisions of Rule 10b–5. There is a problem in relying on that rule—it contains no reference to insider trading. Over the years, however, the SEC and the courts have developed various theories for adapting Rule 10b–5 to trading on non-public information through the provisions of the rule which makes it unlawful for "any person, directly or indirectly, by the use of any instrumentality of interstate commerce . . . to engage in any act, practice, or course of business which operates or would operate as a fraud or deceit upon any person, in connection with the sale or purchase of any security." Yet, Rule 10b–5 was not designed to deal with insider trading, and as the following material demonstrates, Rule 10b–5's coverage of insider trading is neither totally comprehensive nor is it coherent in many respects. The state of the law will remain this way unless and until Congress and the SEC adopt specific rules governing trading on nonpublic information.

SECTION 2.   THE DISCLOSE
OR ABSTAIN RULE

For more than a quarter of a century, the SEC limited its efforts to control trading on inside information to the enforcement of Section 16 in the Securities Exchange Act of 1934. Commencing in 1961, however, through a series of administrative decisions and injunctive proceedings, the SEC greatly broadened the applicability of Rule 10b–5. The SEC then began to interpret Rule 10b–5 as containing a general prohibition against any trading on "inside information" in anonymous stock exchange transactions, as well as in face-to-face dealings. What caused this sea change?

Probably, it was due to an activist SEC chairman who was well endowed in fiduciary duty concepts. See generally William Cary, Corporate Legal Standards and Legal Rules, 50 Calif. L. Rev. 408 (1962).

CADY, ROBERTS & CO.

40 S.E.C. 907 (1961).

By CARY, CHAIRMAN.

Section 17 and Rule 10b–5 apply to securities transactions by "any person." Misrepresentations will lie within their ambit, no matter who the speaker may be. An affirmative duty to disclose material information has been traditionally imposed on corporate "insiders," particularly officers, directors, or controlling stockholders. We, and the courts, have consistently held that insiders must disclose material facts which are known to them by virtue of their position but which are not known to persons with whom they deal and which, if known, would affect their investment judgment. Failure to make disclosure in these circumstances constitutes a violation of the anti-fraud provisions. If, on the other hand, disclosure prior to effecting a purchase or sale would be improper or unrealistic under the circumstances, we believe the alternative is to forego the transaction.

The ingredients are here and we accordingly find that Gintel willfully violated Sections 17(a) and 10(b) and Rule 10b–5. We also find a similar violation by the registrant, since the actions of Gintel, a member of registrant, in the course of his employment are to be regarded as actions of registrant itself. It was obvious that a reduction in the quarterly dividend by the Board of Directors was a material fact which could be expected to have an adverse impact on the market price of the company's stock. The rapidity with which Gintel acted upon receipt of the information confirms his own recognition of that conclusion.

We have already noted that the anti-fraud provisions are phrased in terms of "any person" and that a special obligation has been traditionally required of corporate insiders, e.g., officers, directors and controlling stockholders. These three groups, however, do not exhaust the classes of persons upon whom there is such an obligation. Analytically, the obligation rests on two principal elements; first, the existence of a relationship giving access, directly or indirectly, to information intended to be available only for a corporate purpose and not for the personal benefit of anyone,[1] and second, the inherent unfairness involved where a party takes advantage of such information knowing it is unavailable to those with whom he is dealing. In considering these elements under the broad language of the anti-fraud provisions we are not to be circumscribed by fine distinctions and rigid classifications. Thus our task here is to identify those persons who are in a special relationship with a company and privy to its internal

---

1. A significant purpose of the Exchange Act was to eliminate the idea that the use of inside information for personal advantage was a normal emolument of corporate office. See Sections 2 and 16 of the Act; H.R.Rep. No. 1383, 73rd Cong., 2d Sess. 13 (1934); S.Rep. No. 792, 73rd Cong., 2d Sess. 9 (1934); S.E.C., Tenth Annual Report 50 (1944).

affairs, and thereby suffer correlative duties in trading in its securities. Intimacy demands restraint lest the uninformed be exploited.

The facts here impose on Gintel the responsibilities of those commonly referred to as "insiders." He received the information prior to its public release from a director of Curtiss–Wright, Cowdin, who was associated with the registrant. Cowdin's relationship to the company clearly prohibited him from selling the securities affected by the information without disclosure. By logical sequence, it should prohibit Gintel, a partner of registrant.[2] This prohibition extends not only over his own account, but to selling for discretionary accounts and soliciting and executing other orders. In somewhat analogous circumstances, we have charged a broker-dealer who effects securities transactions for an insider and who knows that the insider possesses non-public material information with the affirmative duty to make appropriate disclosures or dissociate himself from the transaction.

The three main subdivisions of Section 17 and Rule 10b–5 have been considered to be mutually supporting rather than mutually exclusive. Thus, a breach of duty of disclosure may be viewed as a device or scheme, an implied misrepresentation, and an act or practice, violative of all three subdivisions. Respondents argue that only clause (3) may be applicable here. We hold that, in these circumstances, Gintel's conduct at least violated clause (3) as a practice which operated as a fraud or deceit upon the purchasers. Therefore, we need not decide the scope of clauses (1) and (2).

We cannot accept respondents' contention that an insider's responsibility is limited to existing stockholders and that he has no special duties when sales of securities are made to non-stockholders. This approach is too narrow. It ignores the plight of the buying public—wholly unprotected from the misuse of special information.

Neither the statutes nor Rule 10b–5 establish artificial walls of responsibility. Section 17 of the Securities Act explicitly states that it shall be unlawful for any person in the offer or sale of securities to do certain prescribed acts. Although the primary function of Rule 10b–5 was to extend a remedy to a defrauded seller, the courts and this Commission have held that it is also applicable to a defrauded buyer. There is no valid reason why persons who *purchase* stock from an officer, director or other person having the responsibilities of an "insider" should not have the same protection afforded by disclosure of special information as persons who *sell* stock to them. Whatever distinctions may have existed at common law based on the view that an officer or director may stand in a fiduciary relationship to existing stockholders from whom he purchases but not to members of the public to whom he sells, it is clearly not

---

2. See 3 Loss, Securities Regulation. 1450–1 (2d ed., 1961). Cf. Restatement. Restitution, Section 201(2)(1937). Although Cowdin may have had reason to believe that news of the dividend action had already been made public when he called registrant's office, there is no question that Gintel knew when he received the message that the information was not yet public and was received from a director.

appropriate to introduce these into the broader anti-fraud concepts embodied in the securities acts.

Respondents further assert that they made no express representations and did not in any way manipulate the market, and urge that in a transaction on an exchange there is no further duty such as may be required in a "face-to-face" transaction. We reject this suggestion. It would be anomalous indeed if the protection afforded by the anti-fraud provisions were withdrawn from transactions effected on exchanges, primary markets for securities transactions. If purchasers on an exchange had available material information known by a selling insider, we may assume that their investment judgment would be affected and their decision whether to buy might accordingly be modified. Consequently, any sales by the insider must await disclosure of the information. * * *

SEC v. TEXAS GULF SULPHUR CO.

401 F.2d 833 (2d Cir.1968), cert. denied, sub nom., Coates v. SEC,
394 U.S. 976, 89 S.Ct. 1454, 22 L.Ed.2d 756 (1969).

WATERMAN, CIRCUIT JUDGE.

This action was commenced in the United States District Court for the Southern District of New York by the Securities and Exchange Commission (the SEC) pursuant to Sec. 21(e) of the Securities Exchange Act of 1934 (the Act), against Texas Gulf Sulphur Company (TGS) and several of its officers, directors and employees, to enjoin certain conduct by TGS and the individual defendants said to violate Section 10(b) of the Act, and Rule 10b–5 (the Rule), promulgated thereunder, and to compel the rescission by the individual defendants of securities transactions assertedly conducted contrary to law. The complaint alleged (1) that defendants Fogarty, Mollison, Darke, Murray, Huntington, O'Neill, Clayton, Crawford, and Coates had either personally or through agents purchased TGS stock or calls thereon from November 12, 1963 through April 16, 1964 on the basis of material inside information concerning the results of TGS drilling in Timmins, Ontario, while such information remained undisclosed to the investing public generally or to the particular sellers; (2) that defendants Darke and Coates had divulged such information to others for use in purchasing TGS stock or calls[3] or recommended its purchase while the information was undisclosed to the public or to the sellers; that defendants Stephens, Fogarty, Mollison, Holyk, and Kline had accepted options to purchase TGS stock on Feb. 20, 1964 without disclosing the material information as to the drilling progress to either the Stock Option Committee or the TGS Board of Directors; and [(3)] that TGS issued a deceptive press release on April 12, 1964. The case was tried at

---

3. A 'call' is a negotiable option contract by which the bearer has the right to buy from the writer of the contract a certain number of shares of a particular stock at a fixed price on or before a certain agreed-upon date. * * *

length before Judge Bonsal of the Southern District of New York, sitting without a jury. Judge Bonsal in a detailed opinion decided, *inter alia*, that the insider activity prior to April 9, 1964 was not illegal because the drilling results were not 'material' until then; that Clayton and Crawford had traded in violation of law because they traded after that date; that Coates had committed no violation as he did not trade before disclosure was made; and that the issuance of the press release was not unlawful because it was not issued for the purpose of benefiting the corporation, there was no evidence that any insider used the release to his personal advantage and it was not 'misleading, or deceptive on the basis of the facts then known,' Defendants Clayton and Crawford appeal from that part of the decision below which held that they had violated Sec. 10(b) and Rule 10b–5 and the SEC appeals from the remainder of the decision which dismissed the complaint against defendants TGS, Fogarty, Mollison, Holyk, Darke, Stephens, Kline, Murray, and Coates. * * *

This action derives from the exploratory activities of TGS begun in 1957 on the Canadian Shield in eastern Canada. In March of 1959, aerial geophysical surveys were conducted over more than 15,000 square miles of this area by a group led by defendant Mollision, a mining engineer and a Vice President of TGS. The group included defendant Holyk, TGS's chief geologist, defendant Clayton, an electrical engineer and geophysicist, and defendant Darke, a geologist. These operations resulted in the detection of numerous anomalies, i.e., extraordinary variations in the conductivity of rocks, one of which was on the Kidd 55 segment of land located near Timmins, Ontario.

On October 29 and 30, 1963, Clayton conducted a ground geophysical survey on the northeast portion of the Kidd 55 segment which confirmed the presence of an anomaly and indicated the necessity of diamond core drilling for further evaluation. Drilling of the initial hole, K–55–1, at the strongest part of the anomaly was commenced on November 8 and terminated on November 12 at a depth of 655 feet. Visual estimates by Holyk of the core of K–55–1 indicated an average copper content of 1.15% and an average zinc content of 8.64% Over a length of 599 feet. This visual estimate convinced TGS that it was desirable to acquire the remainder of the Kidd 55 segment, and in order to facilitate this acquisition TGS President Stephens instructed the exploration group to keep the results of K–55–1 confidential and undisclosed even as to other officers, directors, and employees of TGS. The hole was concealed and a barren core was intentionally drilled off the anomaly. Meanwhile, the core of K–55–1 had been shipped to Utah for chemical assay which, when received in early December, revealed an average mineral content of 1.18% Copper, 8.26% Zinc, and 3.94%. Ounces of silver per ton over a length of 602 feet. These results were so remarkable that neither Clayton, an experienced geophysicist, nor four other TGS expert witnesses, had ever seen or heard of a comparable initial exploratory drill hole in a base metal deposit. So, the trial court concluded, 'There is no doubt that the drill core of K–55–1 was unusually good and that it excited the interest and speculation of those who knew about it.' Id. at 282. By March 27, 1964, TGS decided that the land acquisition program had advanced to such a point that the company might well resume drilling, and drilling was resumed on March 31.

During this period, from November 12, 1963 when K–55–1 was completed, to March 31, 1964 when drilling was resumed, certain of the individual defendants listed in fn. 2, supra, and persons listed in fn. 4, supra, said to have received 'tips' from them, purchased TGS stock or calls thereon. Prior to these transactions these persons had owned 1135 shares of TGS stock and possessed no calls; thereafter they owned a total of 8235 shares and possessed 12,300 calls.

On February 20, 1964, also during this period, TGS issued stock options to 26 of its officers and employees whose salaries exceeded a specified amount, five of whom were the individual defendants Stephens, Fogarty, Mollison, Holyk, and Kline. Of these, only Kline was unaware of the detailed results of K–55–1, but he, too, knew that a hole containing favorable bodies of copper and zinc ore had been drilled in Timmins. At this time, neither the TGS Stock Option Committee nor its Board of Directors had been informed of the results of K–55–1, presumably because of the pending land acquisition program which required confidentiality. All of the foregoing defendants accepted the options granted them.

When drilling was resumed on March 31, hole K–55–3 was commenced 510 feet west of K–55–1 and was drilled easterly at a 45 degrees angle so as to cross K–55–1 in a vertical plane. Daily progress reports of the drilling of this hole K–55–3 and of all subsequently drilled holes were sent to defendants Stephens and Fogarty (President and Executive Vice President of TGS) by Holyk and Mollison. Visual estimates of K–55–3 revealed an average mineral content of 1.12% copper and 7.93% zinc over 641 of the hole's 876–foot length. On April 7, drilling of a third hole, K–55–4, 200 feet south of and parallel to K–55–1 and westerly at a 45 degrees angle, was commenced and mineralization was encountered over 366 of its 579–foot length. Visual estimates indicated an average content of 1.14% copper and 8.24% zinc. Like K–55–1, both K–55–3 and K–55–4 established substantial copper mineralization on the eastern edge of the anomaly. On the basis of these findings relative to the foregoing drilling results, the trial court concluded that the vertical plane created by the intersection of K–55–1 and K–55–3, which measured at least 350 feet wide by 500 feet deep extended southward 200 feet to its intersection with K–55–4, and that 'There was real evidence that a body of commercially mineable ore might exist.'

On April 8 TGS began with a second drill rig to drill another hole, K–55–6, 300 feet easterly of K–55–1. This hole was drilled westerly at an angle of 60 degrees and was intended to explore mineralization beneath K–55–1. While no visual estimates of its core were immediately available, it was readily apparent by the evening of April 10 that substantial copper mineralization had been encountered over the last 127 feet of the hole's

569–foot length. On April 10, a third drill rig commenced drilling yet another hole, K–55–5, 200 feet north of K–55–1, parallel to the prior holes, and slanted westerly at a 45 degrees angle. By the evening of April 10 in this hole, too, substantial copper mineralization had been encountered over the last 42 feet of its 97–foot length.

Meanwhile, rumors that a major ore strike was in the making had been circulating throughout Canada. On the morning of Saturday, April 11, Stephens at his home in Greenwich, Conn. read in the New York Herald Tribune and in the New York Times unauthorized reports of the TGS drilling which seemed to infer a rich strike from the fact that the drill cores had been flown to the United States for chemical assay. Stephens immediately contacted Fogarty at his home in Rye, N.Y., who in turn telephoned and later that day visited Mollison at Mollison's home in Greenwich to obtain a current report and evaluation of the drilling progress. The following morning, Sunday, Fogarty again telephoned Mollison, inquiring whether Mollison had any further information and told him to return to Timmins with Holyk, the TGS Chief Geologist, as soon as possible 'to move things along.' With the aid of one Carroll, a public relations consultant, Fogarty drafted a press release designed to quell the rumors, which release, after having been channeled through Stephens and Huntington, a TGS attorney, was issued at 3:00 P.M. on Sunday, April 12, and which appeared in the morning newspapers of general circulation on Monday, April 13. It read in pertinent part as follows:

NEW YORK, April 12—The following statement was made today by Dr. Charles F. Fogarty, executive vice president of Texas Gulf Sulphur Company, in regard to the company's drilling operations near Timmins, Ontario, Canada. Dr. Fogarty said:

'During the past few days, the exploration activities of Texas Gulf Sulphur in the area of Timmins, Ontario, have been widely reported in the press, coupled with rumors of a substantial copper discovery there. These reports exaggerate the scale of operations, and mention plans and statistics of size and grade of ore that are without factual basis and have evidently originated by speculation of people not connected with TGS.

'The facts are as follows. TGS has been exploring in the Timmins area for six years as part of its overall search in Canada and elsewhere for various minerals—lead, copper, zinc, etc. During the course of this work, in Timmins as well as in Eastern Canada, TGS has conducted exploration entirely on its own, without the participation by others. Numerous prospects have been investigated by geophysical means and a large number of selected ones have been core-drilled. These cores are sent to the United States for assay and detailed examination as a matter of routine and on advice of expert Canadian legal counsel. No inferences as to grade can be drawn from this procedure.

'Most of the areas drilled in Eastern Canada have revealed either barren pyrite or graphite without value; a few have resulted in discoveries of small or marginal sulphide ore bodies.

'Recent drilling on one property near Timmins has led to preliminary indications that more drilling would be required for proper evaluation of this prospect. The drilling done to date has not been conclusive, but the statements made by many outside quarters are unreliable and include information and figures that are not available to TGS.

'The work done to date has not been sufficient to reach definite conclusions and any statement as to size and grade of ore would be premature and possibly misleading. When we have progressed to the point where reasonable and logical conclusions can be made, TGS will issue a definite statement to its stockholders and to the public in order to clarify the Timmins project.'

The release purported to give the Timmins drilling results as of the release date, April 12. From Mollison Fogarty had been told of the developments through 7:00 P.M. on April 10, and of the remarkable discoveries made up to that time, detailed supra, which discoveries, according to the calculations of the experts who testified for the SEC at the hearing, demonstrated that TGS had already discovered 6.2 to 8.3 million tons of proven ore having gross assay values from $26 to $29 per ton. TGS experts, on the other hand, denied at the hearing that proven or probable ore could have been calculated on April 11 or 12 because there was then no assurance of continuity in the mineralized zone.

The evidence as to the effect of this release on the investing public was equivocal and less than abundant. * * *

Meanwhile, drilling operations continued. By morning of April 13, in K–55–5, the fifth drill hole, substantial copper mineralization had been encountered to the 580 foot mark, and the hole was subsequently drilled to a length of 757 feet without further results. Visual estimates revealed an average content of 0.82% copper and 4.2% zinc over a 525–foot section. Also by 7:00 A.M. on April 13, K–55–6 had found mineralization to the 946–foot mark. On April 12 a fourth drill rig began to drill K–55–7, which was drilled westerly at a 45 degrees angle, at the eastern edge of the anomaly. The next morning the 137 foot mark had been reached, fifty feet of which showed mineralization. By 7:00 P.M. on April 15, the hole had been completed to a length of 707 feet but had only encountered additional mineralization during a 26–foot length between the 425 and 451–foot marks. A mill test hole, K–55–8, had been drilled and was complete by the evening of April 13 but its mineralization had not been reported upon prior to April 16. K–55–10 was drilled westerly at a 45 degrees angle commencing April 14 and had encountered mineralization over 231 of its 249–foot length by the evening of April 15. It, too, was drilled at the anomaly's eastern edge.

While drilling activity ensued to completion, TGC officials were taking steps toward ultimate disclosure of the discovery. On April 13, a previously-invited reporter for The Northern Miner, a Canadian mining industry journal, visited the drillsite, interviewed Mollison, Holyk and Darke, and prepared an article which confirmed a 10 million ton ore strike. This report, after having been submitted to Mollison and returned to the reporter unamended on April 15, was published in the April 16 issue. A statement relative to the extent of the discovery, in substantial part drafted by Mollison, was given to the Ontario Minister of Mines for release to the Canadian media. Mollison and Holyk expected it to be released over the airways at 11 P.M. on April 15th, but, for undisclosed reasons, it was not released until 9:40 A.M. on the 16th. An official detailed statement, announcing a strike of at least 25 million tons of ore, based on the drilling data set forth above, was read to representatives of American financial media from 10:00 A.M. to 10:10 or 10:15 A.M. on April 16, and appeared over Merrill Lynch's private wire at 10:29 A.M. and, somewhat later than expected, over the Dow Jones ticker tape at 10:54 A.M.

Between the time the first press release was issued on April 12 and the dissemination of the TGS official announcement on the morning of April 16, the only defendants before us on appeal who engaged in market activity were Clayton and Crawford and TGS director Coates. Clayton ordered 200 shares of TGS stock through his Canadian broker on April 15 and the order was executed that day over the Midwest Stock Exchange. Crawford ordered 300 shares at midnight on the 15th and another 300 shares at 8:30 A.M. the next day, and these orders were executed over the Midwest Exchange in Chicago at its opening on April 16. Coates left the TGS press conference and called his broker son-in-law Haemisegger shortly before 10:20 A.M. on the 16th and ordered 2,000 shares of TGS for family trust accounts of which Coates was a trustee but not a beneficiary; Haemisegger executed this order over the New York and Midwest Exchanges, and he and his customers purchased 1500 additional shares.

During the period of drilling in Timmins, the market price of TGS stock fluctuated but steadily gained overall. On Friday, November 8, when the drilling began, the stock closed at 17 3/8; on Friday, November 15, after K-55-1 had been completed, it closed at 18. After a slight decline to 16 3/8 by Friday, November 22, the price rose to 20 7/8 by December 13, when the chemical assay results of K-55-1 were received, and closed at a high of 24 1/8 on February 21, the day after the stock options had been issued. It had reached a price of 26 by March 31, after the land acquisition program had been completed and drilling had been resumed, and continued to ascend to 30 1/8 by the close of trading on April 10, at which time the drilling progress up to then was evaluated for the April 12th press release. On April 13, the day on which the April 12 release was disseminated, TGS opened at 30 1/8, rose immediately to a high of 32 and gradually tapered off to close at 30 7/8. It closed at 30 1/4 the next day, and at 29 3/8 on April 15. On April 16, the day of the official announcement of the Timmins discovery, the price climbed to a high of 37 and closed at 36 3/8. By May 15, TGS stock was selling at 58 1/4. * * *

Rule 10b–5 was promulgated pursuant to the grant of authority given the SEC by Congress in Section 10(b) of the Securities Exchange Act of 1934. By that Act Congress purposed to prevent inequitable and unfair practices and to insure fairness in securities transactions generally, whether conducted face-to-face, over the counter, or on exchanges. The Act and the Rule apply to the transactions here, all of which were consummated on exchanges. Whether predicated on traditional fiduciary concepts, see, e.g., Hotchkiss v. Fischer, 136 Kan. 530, 16 P.2d 531 (Kan.1932), or on the 'special facts' doctrine, see, e.g., Strong v. Repide, 213 U.S. 419 (1909), the Rule is based in policy on the justifiable expectation of the securities marketplace that all investors trading on impersonal exchanges have relatively equal access to material information, see Cary, Insider Trading in Stocks, 21 Bus.Law. 1009, 1010 (1966), Fleischer, Securities Trading and Corporation Information Practices: The Implications of the Texas Gulf Sulphur Proceeding, 51 Va.L.Rev. 1271, 1278–80 (1965). The essence of the Rule is that anyone who, trading for his own account in the securities of a corporation has 'access, directly or indirectly, to information intended to be available only for a corporate purpose and not for the personal benefit of anyone' may not take 'advantage of such information knowing it is unavailable to those with whom he is dealing,' i.e., the investing public. Matter of Cady, Roberts & Co., 40 SEC 907, 912 (1961). Insiders, as directors or management officers are, of course, by this Rule, precluded from so unfairly dealing, but the Rule is also applicable to one possessing the information who may not be strictly termed an 'insider' within the meaning of Sec. 16(b) of the Act. Cady, Roberts, supra. Thus, anyone in possession of material inside information must either disclose it to the investing public, or, if he is disabled from disclosing it in order to protect a corporate confidence, or he chooses not to do so, must abstain from trading in or recommending the securities concerned while such inside information remains undisclosed. So, it is here no justification for insider activity that disclosure was forbidden by the legitimate corporate objective of acquiring options to purchase the land surrounding the exploration site; if the information was, as the SEC contends, material, its possessors should have kept out of the market until disclosure was accomplished. Cady, Roberts, supra at 911.

An insider is not, of course, always foreclosed from investing in his own company merely because he may be more familiar with company operations than are outside investors. An insider's duty to disclose information or his duty to abstain from dealing in his company's securities arises only in 'those situations which are essentially extraordinary in nature and which are reasonably certain to have a substantial effect on the market price of the security if (the extraordinary situation is) disclosed.'

Nor is an insider obligated to confer upon outside investors the benefit of his superior financial or other expert analysis by disclosing his educated guesses or predictions. The only regulatory objective is that access to material information be enjoyed equally, but this objective requires nothing more than the disclosure of basic facts so that outsiders may draw upon their own evaluative expertise in reaching their own investment decisions with knowledge equal to that of the insiders.

This is not to suggest, however, as did the trial court, that 'the test of materiality must necessarily be a conservative one, particularly since many actions under Section 10(b) are brought on the basis of hindsight,' in the sense that the materiality of facts is to be assessed solely by measuring the effect the knowledge of the facts would have upon prudent or conservative investors. As we stated in List v. Fashion Park, Inc., 340 F.2d 457, 462, 'The basic test of materiality * * * is whether a *reasonable* man would attach importance * * * in determining his choice of action in the transaction in question. Restatement, Torts § 538(2)(a).' This, of course, encompasses any fact ' * * * which in reasonable and objective contemplation might affect the value of the corporation's stock or securities * * *.' Such a fact is a material fact and must be effectively disclosed to the investing public prior to the commencement of insider trading in the corporation's securities. The speculators and chartists of Wall and Bay Streets are also 'reasonable' investors entitled to the same legal protection afforded conservative traders. Thus, material facts include not only information disclosing the earnings and distributions of a company but also those facts which affect the probable future of the company and those which may affect the desire of investors to buy, sell, or hold the company's securities.

In each case, then, whether facts are material within Rule 10b–5 when the facts relate to a particular event and are undisclosed by those persons who are knowledgeable thereof will depend at any given time upon a balancing of both the indicated probability that the event will occur and the anticipated magnitude of the event in light of the totality of the company activity. Here, notwithstanding the trial court's conclusion that the results of the first drill core, K–55–1, were 'too 'remote' * * * to have had any significant impact on the market, i.e., to be deemed material,' knowledge of the possibility, which surely was more than marginal, of the existence of a mine of the vast magnitude indicated by the remarkably rich drill core located rather close to the surface (suggesting mineability by the less expensive openpit method) within the confines of a large anomaly (suggesting an extensive region of mineralization) might well have affected the price of TGS stock and would certainly have been an important fact to a reasonable, if speculative, investor in deciding whether he should buy, sell, or hold. After all, this first drill core was 'unusually good and * * * excited the interest and speculation of those who knew about it.'

Our disagreement with the district judge on the issue does not, then, go to his findings of basic fact, as to which the 'clearly erroneous' rule would apply, but to his understanding of the legal standard applicable to them. Our survey of the facts found below conclusively establishes that knowledge of the results of the discovery hole, K–55–1, would have been important to a reasonable investor and might have affected the price of the stock.[12] On April 16, The Northern Miner, a trade publication in wide circulation among mining stock specialists, called K-55-1, the discovery hole, 'one of the most impressive drill holes completed in modern times.' Roche, a Canadian broker whose firm specialized in mining securities, characterized the importance to investors of the results of K–55–1. He stated that the completion of 'the first drill hole' with 'a 600 foot drill core is very very significant * * * anything over 200 feet is considered very significant and 600 feet is just beyond your wildest imagination.' He added, however, that it 'is a natural thing to buy more stock once they give you the first drill hole.' Additional testimony revealed that the prices of stocks of other companies, albeit less diversified, smaller firms, had increased substantially solely on the basis of the discovery of good anomalies or even because of the proximity of their lands to the situs of a potentially major strike.

Finally, a major factor in determining whether the K–55–1 discovery was a material fact is the importance attached to the drilling results by those who knew about it. In view of other unrelated recent developments favorably affecting TGS, participation by an informed person in a regular stock-purchase program, or even sporadic trading by an informed person, might lend only nominal support to the inference of the materiality of the K–55–1 discovery; nevertheless, the timing by those who knew of it of their stock purchases and their purchases of *short-term* calls—purchases in some cases by individuals who had never before purchased calls or even TGS stock—virtually compels the inference that the insiders were influenced by the drilling results. This insider trading activity, which surely constitutes highly pertinent evidence and the only truly objective evidence of the materiality of the K–55–1 discovery, was apparently disregarded by the court below in favor of the testimony of defendants' expert witnesses, all of whom 'agreed that one drill core does not establish an ore body, much less a mine,' Significantly, however, the court below, while relying upon what these defense experts said the defendant insiders *ought* to have thought about the worth to TGS of the K–55–1 discovery, and finding that from November 12, 1963 to April 6, 1964 Fogarty, Murray, Holyk and Darke spent more than $100,000 in purchasing TGS stock and calls on that stock, made no finding that the insiders were motivated by any factor other than the extraordinary K–55–1 discovery when they bought their stock and their calls. No reason appears why outside investors, perhaps better acquainted with speculative modes of investment and with, in many

---

12. We do not suggest that material facts must be disclosed immediately; the timing of disclosure is a matter for the business judgment of the corporate officers entrusted with the management of the corporation within the affirmative disclosure requirements promulgated by the exchanges and by the SEC. Here, a valuable corporate purpose was served by delaying the publication of the K–55–1 discovery. We do intend to convey, however, that where a corporate purpose is thus served by withholding the news of a material fact, those persons who are thus quite properly true to their corporate trust must not during the period of non-disclosure deal personally in the corporation's securities or give to outsiders confidential information not generally available to all the corporations' stockholders and to the public at large.

cases, perhaps more capital at their disposal for intelligent speculation, would have been less influenced, and would not have been similarly motivated to invest if they had known what the insider investors knew about the K–55–1 discovery.

Our decision to expand the limited protection afforded outside investors by the trial court's narrow definition of materiality is not at all shaken by fears that the elimination of insider trading benefits will deplete the ranks of capable corporate managers by taking away an incentive to accept such employment. Such benefits, in essence, are forms of secret corporate compensation, see Cary, Corporate Standards and Legal Rules, 50 Calif.L.Rev. 408, 409–10 (1962), derived at the expense of the uninformed investing public and not at the expense of the corporation which receives the sole benefit from insider incentives. Moreover, adequate incentives for corporate officers may be provided by properly administered stock options and employee purchase plans of which there are many in existence. In any event, the normal motivation induced by stock ownership, i.e., the identification of an individual with corporate progress, is ill-promoted by condoning the sort of speculative insider activity which occurred here; for example, some of the corporation's stock was sold at market in order to purchase short-term calls upon that stock, calls which would never be exercised to increase a stockholder equity in TGS unless the market price of that stock rose sharply.

The core of Rule 10b–5 is the implementation of the Congressional purpose that all investors should have equal access to the rewards of participation in securities transactions. It was the intent of Congress that all members of the investing public should be subject to identical market risks,—which market risks include, of course the risk that one's evaluative capacity or one's capital available to put at risk may exceed another's capacity or capital. The insiders here were not trading on an equal footing with the outside investors. They alone were in a position to evaluate the probability and magnitude of what seemed from the outset to be a major ore strike; they alone could invest safely, secure in the expectation that the price of TGS stock would rise substantially in the event such a major strike should materialize, but would decline little, if at all, in the event of failure, for the public, ignorant at the outset of the favorable probabilities would likewise be unaware of the unproductive exploration, and the additional exploration costs would not significantly affect TGS market prices. Such inequities based upon unequal access to knowledge should not be shrugged off as inevitable in our way of life, or, in view of the congressional concern in the area, remain uncorrected.

We hold, therefore, that all transactions in TGS stock or calls by individuals apprised of the drilling results of K–55–1 were made in violation of Rule 10b–5. Inasmuch as the visual evaluation of that drill core (a generally reliable estimate though less accurate than a chemical assay) constituted material information, those advised of the results of the visual evaluation as well as those informed of the chemical assay traded in violation of law. The geologist Darke possessed undisclosed material information and traded in TGS securities. Therefore we reverse the dismissal of the action as to him and his personal transactions. The trial court also found, that Darke, after the drilling of K–55–1 had been completed and with detailed knowledge of the results thereof, told certain outside individuals that TGS 'was a good buy.' These individuals thereafter acquired TGS stock and calls. The trial court also found that later, as of March 30, 1964, Darke not only used his material knowledge for his own purchases but that the substantial amounts of TGS stock and calls purchased by these outside individuals on that day, see footnote 4, supra, was 'strong circumstantial evidence that Darke must have passed the word to one or more of his 'tippees' that drilling on the Kidd 55 segment was about to be resumed.' Obviously if such a resumption were to have any meaning to such 'tippees,' they must have previously been told of K–55–1.

Unfortunately, however, there was no definitive resolution below of Darke's liability in these premises for the trial court held as to him, as it held as to all the other individual defendants, that this 'undisclosed information' never became material until April 9. As it is our holding that the information acquired after the drilling of K–55–1 was material, we, on the basis of the findings of direct and circumstantial evidence on the issue that the trial court has already expressed, hold that Darke violated Rule 10b–5(3) and Section 10(b) by 'tipping' and we remand, pursuant to the agreement of the parties, for a determination of the appropriate remedy. As Darke's 'tippees' are not defendants in this action, we need not decide whether, if they acted with actual or constructive knowledge that the material information was undisclosed, their conduct is as equally violative of the Rule as the conduct of their insider source, though we note that it certainly could be equally reprehensible. * * *

Appellant Crawford, who ordered[17] the purchase of TGS stock shortly before the TGS April 16 official announcement, and defendant Coates, who placed orders with and communicated the news to his broker immediately after the official announcement was read at the TGS-called press conference, concede that they were in possession of material information. They contend, however, that their purchases were not proscribed purchases for the news had already been effectively disclosed. We disagree.

Crawford telephoned his orders to his Chicago broker about midnight on April 15 and again at 8:30 in the morning of the 16th, with instructions to buy at the opening of the Midwest Stock Exchange that morning. The trial court's finding that "he sought to, and did, beat the news," is well

---

17. The effective protection of the public from insider exploitation of advance notice of material information requires that the time that an insider places an order, rather than the time of its ultimate execution, be determinative for Rule 10b–5 purposes. Otherwise, insiders would be able to 'beat the news,' cf. Fleischer, supra, 51 Va.L.Rev. at 1291, by requesting in advance that their orders be executed immediately after the dissemination of a major news release but before outsiders could act on the release. Thus it is immaterial whether Crawford's orders were executed before or after the announcement was made in Canada (9:40 A.M., April 16) or in the United States (10:00 A.M.) or whether Coates's order was executed before or after the news appeared over the Merrill Lynch (10:29 A.M.) or Dow Jones (10:54 A.M.) wires.

documented by the record. The rumors of a major ore strike which had been circulated in Canada and, to a lesser extent, in New York, had been disclaimed by the TGS press release of April 12, which significantly promised the public an official detailed announcement when possibilities had ripened into actualities. The abbreviated announcement to the Canadian press at 9:40 A.M. on the 16th by the Ontario Minister of Mines and the report carried by The Northern Miner, parts of which had sporadically reached New York on the morning of the 16th through reports from Canadian affiliates to a few New York investment firms, are assuredly not the equivalent of the official 10–15 minute announcement which was not released to the American financial press until after 10:00 A.M. Crawford's orders had been placed before that. Before insiders may act upon material information, such information must have been effectively disclosed in a manner sufficient to insure its availability to the investing public. Particularly here, where a formal announcement to the entire financial news media had been promised in a prior official release known to the media, all insider activity must await dissemination of the promised official announcement.

Coates was absolved by the court below because his telephone order was placed shortly before 10:20 A.M. on April 16, which was after the announcement had been made even though the news could not be considered already a matter of public information. This result seems to have been predicated upon a misinterpretation of dicta in *Cady, Roberts*, where the SEC instructed insiders to 'keep out of the market until the established procedures for public release of the information are carried out instead of hastening to execute transactions in advance of, and in frustration of, the objectives of the release,' 40 SEC at 915. The reading of a news release, which prompted Coates into action, is merely the first step in the process of dissemination required for compliance with the regulatory objective of providing all investors with an equal opportunity to make informed investment judgments. Assuming that the contents of the official release could instantaneously be acted upon,[18] at the minimum Coates should have waited until the news could reasonably have been expected to appear over the media of widest circulation, the Dow Jones broad tape, rather than hastening to insure an advantage to himself and his broker son-in-law. * * *

In summary, therefore, we affirm the finding of the court below that appellants Richard H. Clayton and David M. Crawford have violated Section 10(b) and Rule 10b–5; we reverse the judgment order entered below dismissing the complaint against appellees Charles F. Fogarty,

---

18. Although the only insider who acted after the news appeared over the Dow Jones broad tape is not an appellant and therefore we need not discuss the necessity of considering the advisability of a 'reasonable waiting period' during which outsiders may absorb and evaluate disclosures, we note in passing that, where the news is of a sort which is not readily translatable into investment action, insiders may not take advantage of their advance opportunity to evaluate the information by acting immediately upon dissemination. In any event, the permissible timing of insider transactions after disclosures of various sorts is one of the many areas of expertise for appropriate exercise of the SEC's rule-making power, which we hope will be utilized in the future to provide some predictability of certainty for the business community.

Richard H. Clayton, Richard D. Mollison, Walter Holyk, Kenneth H. Darke, Earl L. Huntington, and Francis G. Coates, as we find that they have violated Section 10(b) and Rule 10b–5. As to these eight individuals we remand so that in accordance with the agreement between the parties the Commission may notice a hearing before the court below to determine the remedies to be applied against them. We reverse the judgment order dismissing the complaint against Claude O. Stephens, Charles F. Fogarty, and Harold B. Kline as recipients of stock options, direct the district court to consider in its discretion whether to issue injunction orders against Stephens and Fogarty, and direct that an order issue rescinding the option granted Kline and that such further remedy be applied against him as may be proper by way of an order of restitution; and we reverse the judgment dismissing the complaint against Texas Gulf Sulphur Company, remand the cause as to it for a further determination below, in the light of the approach explicated by us in the foregoing opinion, as to whether, in the exercise of its discretion, the injunction against it which the Commission seeks should be ordered.

[The concurring and dissenting opinions are omitted.]

NOTES

1. Claims based on Texas Gulf's nondisclosure were not limited to the securities laws. Various sellers of the land in question brought suit for nondisclosure of the mineral find. In one case, the court observed that the company did "what any prudent mining company would have done to acquire property in which it knew it had a very promising anomaly lay [by purchasing the land] without causing the prospective vendors to suspect that a discovery had been made." Leitch Gold Mines, Ltd. v. Texas Gulf Sulphur, 1 Ontario Rep. 469, 492–493 (1969). In another case, the contract claim was settled out of court, see Anthony T. Kronman, Mistake, Disclosure, Information, and the Law of Contracts, 7 J. Leg. Stud. 1, 20–21 (1978). Should insider trading claims extend to land sales as well as to stocks. If not, why not?

2. Why is the value of the mineral find in *Texas Gulf Sulphur* any more of a material fact than in *Goodwin v. Agassiz* in Chapter 14? Cf. the Supreme Court's discussion of the materiality of contingent events in the decision of the Supreme Court in Basic Inc. v. Levinson, 485 U.S. 224, 108 S.Ct. 978, 99 L.Ed.2d 194 (1988), Chapter 13. In *Goodwin v. Agassiz,* the court denied the existence of a common law remedy for insider trading since participants in a faceless market do not owe duties to one another. To what extent is the rule otherwise under Rule 10b–5? Is the Rule 10b–5 violation based on a duty to investors on the other side of the insider's transaction, or is the violation based on a duty to the market place generally? Is it based on a duty to the corporation? Cf. *Diamond v. Oreamuno*, 301 N.Y.S.2d 78, 248 N.E.2d 910, p. 586 below.

3. The *Texas Gulf Sulphur* case like the cases before it raises a number of questions concerning the scope of accountability for insider trading. In addition, as the opinion indicates, insider trading is not limited to corporate insiders but also may extend to outsiders such as the tippees involved in

Texas Gulf Sulphur. Other questions involve the extent to which a Rule 10b–5 violation based in insider (or "outsider") trading on nonpublic information will support a private remedy. Insider trading cases often involve celebrities; so too in the *Texas Gulf Sulphur* case. Herbert Klotz, one of the tippees mentioned by the court was an Under Secretary at the Commerce Department during the Kennedy administration. Once his trading came to light, he resigned his position. It was variously rumored that Klotz had been tipped by a woman working as a guide at the New York World Fair or by a secretary at the Commerce Department.

4. What was so crucial about November 12, 1963 in the *Texas Gulf Sulphur* decision? What factors led the court to conclude that the materiality date did not occur until later? The lab report did not confirm the visual estimates until December 1963. Even at that point, the company had not yet acquired the land. The court also could have looked to earlier dates. For example, in late October, 1963, the company decided that the ground survey confirmed the advisability of drilling. As the opinion points out, on April 12, 1964, Texas Gulf issued a press release that was unduly pessimistic regarding the mineral prospects. To what extent does Rule 10b–5 hold the company accountable for the veracity of its predictions?

5. To the extent there is a private remedy under Rule 10b–5 for insider trading, what is the appropriate measure of damages? Basing damages on the aggregate "losses" of persons selling while insiders were buying would be huge. For example, this would include everyone who sold Texas Gulf Sulphur stock from November 12 through April 23 of the following year. Alternatively, damages could be limited to disgorgement of the traders' gains. But this would amount to pennies to the investors who were selling during the entire period. For cases considering these issues see e.g., Financial Industrial Fund, Inc. v. McDonnell Douglas Corp., 474 F.2d 514 (10th Cir.1973), cert. denied 414 U.S. 874, 94 S.Ct. 155, 38 L.Ed.2d 114 (1973); Mitchell v. Texas Gulf Sulphur Co., 446 F.2d 90 (10th Cir.1971), cert. denied, 404 U.S. 1004, 92 S.Ct. 564, 30 L.Ed.2d 558 (1971); Cannon v. Texas Gulf Sulphur Co., 55 F.R.D. 308 (S.D.N.Y.1972).

7. In *Cady Roberts & Co.*, the SEC concluded that a corporate insider (defined now as someone who obtains the information because of a special relationship or position with the issuer) must abstain from trading in the shares of his corporation unless he has first disclosed all material inside information known to him. The SEC opinion defined two bases for the duty: (1) fairness to the market and those who do not have the information (i.e., fairness to persons on the other side of the transaction); and (2) fairness to the corporation whose information is being used. This was echoed by the Second Circuit in *Texas Gulf Sulphur*. Under this approach, anyone who traded on the basis of non public material information could be covered by Rule 10b–5. The Supreme Court first examined the scope of the duty in the following decision.

SECTION 3. MISAPPROPRIATION

CHIARELLA v. UNITED STATES

445 U.S. 222, 100 S.Ct. 1108, 63 L.Ed.2d 348 (1980).

MR. JUSTICE POWELL delivered the opinion of the Court.

Petitioner is a printer by trade. In 1975 and 1976, he worked as a "markup man" in the New York composing room of Pandick Press, a financial printer. Among documents that petitioner handled were five announcements of corporate takeover bids. When these documents were delivered to the printer, the identities of the acquiring and target corporations were concealed by blank spaces or false names. The true names were sent to the printer on the night of the final printing.

The petitioner, however, was able to deduce the names of the target companies before the final printing from other information contained in the documents. Without disclosing his knowledge, petitioner purchased stock in the target companies and sold the shares immediately after the takeover attempts were made public. By this method, petitioner realized a gain of slightly more than $30,000 in the course of 14 months. Subsequently, the Securities and Exchange Commission (Commission or SEC) began an investigation of his trading activities. In May 1977, petitioner entered into a consent decree with the Commission in which he agreed to return his profits to the sellers of the shares. On the same day, he was discharged by Pandick Press. * * *

This case concerns the legal effect of the petitioner's silence. The District Court's charge permitted the jury to convict the petitioner if it found that he wilfully failed to inform sellers of target company securities that he knew of a forthcoming takeover bid that would make their shares more valuable. In order to decide whether silence in such circumstances violates § 10(b), it is necessary to review the language and legislative history of that statute as well as its interpretation by the Commission and the federal courts.

Although the starting point of our inquiry is the language of the statute, § 10(b) does not state whether silence may constitute a manipulative or deceptive device. Section 10(b) was designed as a catchall clause to prevent fraudulent practices. But neither the legislative history nor the statute itself affords specific guidance for the resolution of this case. When Rule 10b–5 was promulgated in 1942, the SEC did not discuss the possibility that failure to provide information might run afoul of § 10(b). * * *

That the relationship between a corporate insider and the stockholders of his corporation gives rise to a disclosure obligation is not a novel twist of the law. At common law, misrepresentation made for the purpose of inducing reliance upon the false statement is fraudulent. But one who fails to disclose material information prior to the consummation of a transaction commits fraud only when he is under a duty to do so. And the duty to disclose arises when one party has information "that the other [party] is entitled to know because of a fiduciary or other similar relation of trust and confidence between them."[3] In its *Cady, Roberts* decision, the Commission recognized a relationship of trust and confidence between the shareholders of a corporation and those insiders who have obtained confidential information by reason of their position with that corporation. This relationship gives rise to a duty to disclose because of the "necessity of preventing a corporate insider from * * * tak[ing] unfair advantage of the uninformed minority stockholders." Speed v. Transamerica Corp., 99 F.Supp. 808, 829 (D.Del.1951).

The federal courts have found violations of § 10(b) where corporate insiders used undisclosed information for their own benefit. E.g., SEC v. Texas Gulf Sulphur Co. The cases also have emphasized, in accordance with the common-law rule, that "[t]he party charged with failing to disclose market information must be under a duty to disclose it." Frigitemp Corp. v. Financial Dynamics Fund, Inc., 524 F.2d 275, 282 (C.A.2 1975). Accordingly, a purchaser of stock who has no duty to a prospective seller because he is neither an insider nor a fiduciary has been held to have no obligation to reveal material facts. * * *

Thus, administrative and judicial interpretations have established that silence in connection with the purchase or sale of securities may operate as a fraud actionable under § 10(b) despite the absence of statutory language or legislative history specifically addressing the legality of nondisclosure. But such liability is premised upon a duty to disclose arising from a relationship of trust and confidence between parties to a transaction. Application of a duty to disclose prior to trading guarantees that corporate insiders, who have an obligation to place the shareholder's welfare before their own, will not benefit personally through fraudulent use of material, nonpublic information.[4]

In this case, the petitioner was convicted of violating § 10(b) although he was not a corporate insider and he received no confidential information from the target company. Moreover, the "market information" upon which he relied did not concern the earning power or operations of the target company, but only the plans of the acquiring company. Petitioner's use of that information was not a fraud under § 10(b) unless he was subject to an affirmative duty to disclose it before trading. In this case, the jury instructions failed to specify any such duty. In effect, the trial court instructed the jury that petitioner owed a duty to everyone; to all sellers,

---

3. Restatement (Second) of Torts § 551(2)(a)(1976). See James & Gray, Misrepresentation—Part II, 37 Md.L.Rev. 488, 523–527 (1978). As regards securities transactions, the American Law Institute recognizes that "silence when there is a duty to * * * speak may be a fraudulent act." ALI. Federal Securities Code § 262(b)(Prop.Off.Draft 1978).

4. "Tippees" of corporate insiders have been held liable under § 10(b) because they have a duty not to profit from the use of inside information that they know is confidential and know or should know came from a corporate insider. Shapiro v. Merrill Lynch. The tippee's obligation has been viewed as arising from his role as a participant after the fact in the insider's breach of a fiduciary duty. . . .

indeed, to the market as a whole. The jury simply was told to decide whether petitioner used material, nonpublic information at a time when "he knew other people trading in the securities market did not have access to the same information."

The Court of Appeals affirmed the conviction by holding that "[a]ny-one—corporate insider or not—who regularly receives material nonpublic information may not use that information to trade in securities without incurring an affirmative duty to disclose." Although the court said that its test would include only persons who regularly receive material, nonpublic information, its rationale for that limitation is unrelated to the existence of a duty to disclose. The Court of Appeals, like the trial court, failed to identify a relationship between petitioner and the sellers that could give rise to a duty. Its decision thus rested solely upon its belief that the federal securities laws have "created a system providing equal access to information necessary for reasoned and intelligent investment decisions." The use by anyone of material information not generally available is fraudulent, this theory suggests, because such information gives certain buyers or sellers an unfair advantage over less informed buyers and sellers.

This reasoning suffers from two defects. First, not every instance of financial unfairness constitutes fraudulent activity under § 10(b). See Santa Fe Industries, Inc. v. Green, [p. 737 above]. Second, the element required to make silence fraudulent—a duty to disclose—is absent in this case. No duty could arise from petitioner's relationship with the sellers of the target company's securities, for petitioner had no prior dealings with them. He was not their agent, he was not a fiduciary, he was not a person in whom the sellers had placed their trust and confidence. He was, in fact, a complete stranger who dealt with the sellers only through impersonal market transactions.

We cannot affirm petitioner's conviction without recognizing a general duty between all participants in market transactions to forgo actions based on material, nonpublic information. Formulation of such a broad duty, which departs radically from the established doctrine that duty arises from a specific relationship between two parties, should not be undertaken absent some explicit evidence of congressional intent.

As we have seen, no such evidence emerges from the language or legislative history of § 10(b). Moreover, neither the Congress nor the Commission ever has adopted a parity-of-information rule. * * *

We see no basis for applying such a new and different theory of liability in this case. As we have emphasized before, the 1934 Act cannot be read " 'more broadly than its language and the statutory scheme reasonably permit.' " Section 10(b) is aptly described as a catchall provision, but what it catches must be fraud. When an allegation of fraud is based upon nondisclosure, there can be no fraud absent a duty to speak. We hold that a duty to disclose under § 10(b) does not arise from the mere possession of nonpublic market information. The contrary result is without support in the legislative history of § 10(b) and would be inconsistent with the careful plan that Congress has enacted for regulation of the securities markets.

MR. JUSTICE BLACKMUN, with whom MR. JUSTICE MARSHALL joins, dissenting.

Although I agree with much of what is said in Part I of the dissenting opinion of The Chief Justice, I write separately because, in my view, it is unnecessary to rest petitioner's conviction on a "misappropriation" theory. The fact that petitioner Chiarella purloined, or, to use The Chief Justice's word, "stole," information concerning pending tender offers certainly is the most dramatic evidence that petitioner was guilty of fraud. He has conceded that he knew it was wrong, and he and his co-workers in the printshop were specifically warned by their employer that actions of this kind were improper and forbidden. But I also would find petitioner's conduct fraudulent within the meaning of § 10(b), and Rule 10b–5, even if he had obtained the blessing of his employer's principals before embarking on his profiteering scheme. Indeed, I think petitioner's brand of manipulative trading, with or without such approval, lies close to the heart of what the securities laws are intended to prohibit.

The Court continues to pursue a course, charted in certain recent decisions, designed to transform § 10(b) from an intentionally elastic "catchall" provision to one that catches relatively little of the misbehavior that all too often makes investment in securities a needlessly risky business for the uninitiated investor. * * *

NOTES

1. Vincent Chiarella was able to ascertain the identity of takeover targets despite the use of coded names or blank entries. The detailed disclosures required by the federal securities laws about the companies provided much information as to their identity. Chiarella paid heavily for his trading despite the reversal of his conviction by the Supreme Court. He disgorged his profits from the inside trading to the SEC and was fired from job after job by printing companies when they learned of the charges. Chiarella was finally restored to his job at Pandick after winning an arbitration over his discharge. "After the Fall," Wall St. J., Nov. 18, 1987, at A1.

2. On the heels of the *Chiarella* decision, the SEC promulgated a rule banning trading in advance of tender offers. SEC Rule 14e–3 is based on section 14(e) grant of rulemaking authority in connection with tender offers. Compare the language of sections 10(b) and 14(e).

3. The *Chiarella* decision left open the question whether a violation of Rule 10b–5 can be based on a breach of duty to the person from whom the insider obtained his information. In United States v. Newman, 664 F.2d 12 (2d Cir.1981), the court of appeals upheld the indictment of a stock trader who passed on confidential information about proposed takeovers which he had obtained from two employees of investment banking firms that were advising the companies planning the takeovers. The indictment charged that

the acts of the two employees operated as a fraud on the investment banking firms and their clients, and that the stock trader had aided and abetted that fraud. The court held (a) that the defendant's conduct could constitute a criminal violation of Rule 10b–5 despite the fact that neither the investment bankers nor their clients were purchasers or sellers in any transaction with any of the defendants, (b) that the use of the information defrauded the investment bankers by "sullying their reputations as safe repositories of client confidences" and defrauded the investment bankers' clients by artificially inflating the price of the target companies' securities, and (c) that the fraud was "in connection with" a purchase or sale of securities because "the sole purpose" of the misappropriation of information was to purchase shares of the target companies.

4. In S.E.C. v. Materia, 745 F.2d 197 (2d Cir.1984), the court of appeals, utilizing the "misappropriation" theory, upheld an injunction against an employee of a financial printing firm on facts essentially similar to those in *Chiarella*. The Supreme Court denied certiorari. 471 U.S. 1053, 105 S.Ct. 2112, 85 L.Ed.2d 477 (1985).

5. In 1988, the Supreme Court considered the misappropriation question again in a case involving a Wall Street Journal reporter who had tipped friends to purchase stocks which he was planning to recommend in his column. He was prosecuted on the ground that he had "misappropriated" this information from the Journal, and his conviction was upheld by the Second Circuit. The Supreme Court unanimously affirmed his conviction for violation of the mail fraud statute, but his conviction for violation of Rule 10b–5 was affirmed by a 4–4 vote without opinion. Carpenter v. United States, 484 U.S. 19, 108 S.Ct. 316, 98 L.Ed.2d 275 (1987). Although most courts adopted the misappropriation theory, one circuit completely rejected the concept. In United States v. Bryan, 58 F.3d 933 (4th Cir.1995), the court stated:

> We conclude that neither the language of § 10(b), Rule 10b–5, the Supreme Court authority interpreting these provisions, nor the purposes of these securities fraud prohibitions, will support convictions resting on the particular theory of misappropriation adopted by our sister circuits. Section 10(b) prohibits only the use of deception, in the form of material misrepresentations or omissions, to induce action or inaction by purchasers or sellers of securities, or that affects others with a vested interest in a securities transaction. In contravention of this established principle, the misappropriation theory authorizes criminal conviction for simple breaches of fiduciary duty and similar relationships of trust and confidence, whether or not the breaches entail deception within the meaning of § 10(b) and whether or not the parties wronged by the breaches were purchasers or sellers of securities, or otherwise connected with or interested in the purchase or sale of securities. Finding no authority for such an expansion of securities fraud liability—indeed, finding the theory irreconcilable with applicable Supreme Court precedent—we reject application of the theory in this circuit. We hold therefore that the district court plainly erred in instructing the jury that it could convict Bryan of securities fraud on the basis of the misappropriation theory of Rule 10b–5 liability.

———

In 1997, the misappropriation theory came back to the Supreme Court for review:

UNITED STATES v. O'HAGAN

521 U.S. 642, 117 S.Ct. 2199, 138 L.Ed.2d 724 (1997).

JUSTICE GINSBURG delivered the opinion of the Court.

I

* * * Respondent James Herman O'Hagan was a partner in the law firm of Dorsey & Whitney in Minneapolis, Minnesota. In July 1988, Grand Metropolitan PLC (Grand Met), a company based in London, England, retained Dorsey & Whitney as local counsel to represent Grand Met regarding a potential tender offer for the common stock of the Pillsbury Company, headquartered in Minneapolis. Both Grand Met and Dorsey & Whitney took precautions to protect the confidentiality of Grand Met's tender offer plans. O'Hagan did no work on the Grand Met representation. Dorsey & Whitney withdrew from representing Grand Met on September 9, 1988. Less than a month later, on October 4, 1988, Grand Met publicly announced its tender offer for Pillsbury stock.

On August 18, 1988, while Dorsey & Whitney was still representing Grand Met, O'Hagan began purchasing call options for Pillsbury stock. Each option gave him the right to purchase 100 shares of Pillsbury stock by a specified date in September 1988. Later in August and in September, O'Hagan made additional purchases of Pillsbury call options. By the end of September, he owned 2,500 unexpired Pillsbury options, apparently more than any other individual investor. O'Hagan also purchased, in September 1988, some 5,000 shares of Pillsbury common stock, at a price just under $39 per share. When Grand Met announced its tender offer in October, the price of Pillsbury stock rose to nearly $60 per share. O'Hagan then sold his Pillsbury call options and common stock, making a profit of more than $4.3 million. * * *

Under the "traditional" or "classical theory" of insider trading liability, § 10(b) and Rule 10b–5 are violated when a corporate insider trades in the securities of his corporation on the basis of material, nonpublic information. Trading on such information qualifies as a "deceptive device" under § 10(b), we have affirmed, because "a relationship of trust and confidence [exists] between the shareholders of a corporation and those insiders who have obtained confidential information by reason of their position with that corporation." That relationship, we recognized, "gives rise to a duty to disclose [or to abstain from trading] because of the 'necessity of preventing a corporate insider from . . . tak[ing] unfair advantage of . . . uninformed . . . stockholders.' " The classical theory applies not only to officers, directors, and other permanent insiders of a corporation, but also to attorneys, accountants, consultants, and others who temporarily become fiduciaries of a corporation.

The "misappropriation theory" holds that a person commits fraud "in connection with" a securities transaction, and thereby violates § 10(b) and Rule 10b–5, when he misappropriates confidential information for securities trading purposes, in breach of a duty owed to the source of the information. Under this theory, a fiduciary's undisclosed, self-serving use of a principal's information to purchase or sell securities, in breach of a duty of loyalty and confidentiality, defrauds the principal of the exclusive use of that information. In lieu of premising liability on a fiduciary relationship between company insider and purchaser or seller of the company's stock, the misappropriation theory premises liability on a fiduciary-turned-trader's deception of those who entrusted him with access to confidential information.

The two theories are complementary, each addressing efforts to capitalize on nonpublic information through the purchase or sale of securities. The classical theory targets a corporate insider's breach of duty to shareholders with whom the insider transacts; the misappropriation theory outlaws trading on the basis of nonpublic information by a corporate "outsider" in breach of a duty owed not to a trading party, but to the source of the information. The misappropriation theory is thus designed to "protec[t] the integrity of the securities markets against abuses by 'outsiders' to a corporation who have access to confidential information that will affect th[e] corporation's security price when revealed, but who owe no fiduciary or other duty to that corporation's shareholders."

In this case, the indictment alleged that O'Hagan, in breach of a duty of trust and confidence he owed to his law firm, Dorsey & Whitney, and to its client, Grand Met, traded on the basis of nonpublic information regarding Grand Met's planned tender offer for Pillsbury common stock. App. 16. This conduct, the Government charged, constituted a fraudulent device in connection with the purchase and sale of securities.[5]

We agree with the Government that misappropriation, as just defined, satisfies § 10(b)'s requirement that chargeable conduct involve a "deceptive device or contrivance" used "in connection with" the purchase or sale of securities. We observe, first, that misappropriators, as the Government describes them, deal in deception. A fiduciary who "[pretends] loyalty to the principal while secretly converting the principal's information for personal gain," "dupes" or defrauds the principal.

We addressed fraud of the same species in *Carpenter v. United States*, which involved the mail fraud statute's proscription of "any scheme or artifice to defraud." Affirming convictions under that statute, we said in *Carpenter* that an employee's undertaking not to reveal his employer's confidential information "became a sham" when the employee provided

---

5. The Government could not have prosecuted O'Hagan under the classical theory, for O'Hagan was not an "insider" of Pillsbury, the corporation in whose stock he traded. Although an "outsider" with respect to Pillsbury, O'Hagan had an intimate association with, and was found to have traded on confidential information from, Dorsey & Whitney, counsel to tender offeror Grand Met. Under the misappropriation theory, O'Hagan's securities trading does not escape Exchange Act sanction, as it would under the dissent's reasoning, simply because he was associated with, and gained nonpublic information from, the bidder, rather than the target.

the information to his co-conspirators in a scheme to obtain trading profits. A company's confidential information, we recognized in *Carpenter*, qualifies as property to which the company has a right of exclusive use. The undisclosed misappropriation of such information, in violation of a fiduciary duty, the Court said in *Carpenter*, constitutes fraud akin to embezzlement—" 'the fraudulent appropriation to one's own use of the money or goods entrusted to one's care by another.' " *Carpenter*'s discussion of the fraudulent misuse of confidential information, the Government notes, "is a particularly apt source of guidance here, because [the mail fraud statute] (like Section 10(b)) has long been held to require deception, not merely the breach of a fiduciary duty."

Deception through nondisclosure is central to the theory of liability for which the Government seeks recognition. As counsel for the Government stated in explanation of the theory at oral argument: "To satisfy the common law rule that a trustee may not use the property that [has] been entrusted [to] him, there would have to be consent. To satisfy the requirement of the Securities Act that there be no deception, there would only have to be disclosure."[6]

The misappropriation theory advanced by the Government is consistent with Santa Fe Industries, Inc. v. Green, a decision underscoring that § 10(b) is not an all-purpose breach of fiduciary duty ban; rather, it trains on conduct involving manipulation or deception. In contrast to the Government's allegations in this case, in *Santa Fe Industries*, all pertinent facts were disclosed by the persons charged with violating § 10(b) and Rule 10b–5; therefore, there was no deception through nondisclosure to which liability under those provisions could attach. Similarly, full disclosure forecloses liability under the misappropriation theory: Because the deception essential to the misappropriation theory involves feigning fidelity to the source of information, if the fiduciary discloses to the source that he plans to trade on the nonpublic information, there is no "deceptive device" and thus no § 10(b) violation—although the fiduciary-turned-trader may remain liable under state law for breach of a duty of loyalty.[7]

We turn next to the § 10(b) requirement that the misappropriator's deceptive use of information be "in connection with the purchase or sale of [a] security." This element is satisfied because the fiduciary's fraud is consummated, not when the fiduciary gains the confidential information, but when, without disclosure to his principal, he uses the information to purchase or sell securities. The securities transaction and the breach of

---

6. Under the misappropriation theory urged in this case, the disclosure obligation runs to the source of the information, here, Dorsey & Whitney and Grand Met. Chief Justice Burger, dissenting in *Chiarella*, advanced a broader reading of § 10(b) and Rule 10b–5; the disclosure obligation, as he envisioned it, ran to those with whom the misappropriator trades ("a person who has misappropriated nonpublic information has an absolute duty to disclose that information or to refrain from trading"). The Government does not propose that we adopt a misappropriation theory of that breadth.

7. Where, however, a person trading on the basis of material, nonpublic information owes a duty of loyalty and confidentiality to two entities or persons—for example, a law firm and its client—but makes disclosure to only one, the trader may still be liable under the misappropriation theory.

duty thus coincide. This is so even though the person or entity defrauded is not the other party to the trade, but is, instead, the source of the nonpublic information. A misappropriator who trades on the basis of material, nonpublic information, in short, gains his advantageous market position through deception; he deceives the source of the information and simultaneously harms members of the investing public.

The misappropriation theory targets information of a sort that misappropriators ordinarily capitalize upon to gain no-risk profits through the purchase or sale of securities. Should a misappropriator put such information to other use, the statute's prohibition would not be implicated. The theory does not catch all conceivable forms of fraud involving confidential information; rather, it catches fraudulent means of capitalizing on such information through securities transactions.

The Government notes another limitation on the forms of fraud § 10(b) reaches: "The misappropriation theory would not ... apply to a case in which a person defrauded a bank into giving him a loan or embezzled cash from another, and then used the proceeds of the misdeed to purchase securities." In such a case, the Government states, "the proceeds would have value to the malefactor apart from their use in a securities transaction, and the fraud would be complete as soon as the money was obtained." In other words, money can buy, if not anything, then at least many things; its misappropriation may thus be viewed as sufficiently detached from a subsequent securities transaction that § 10(b)'s "in connection with" requirement would not be met.

The dissent's charge that the misappropriation theory is incoherent because information, like funds, can be put to multiple uses, misses the point. The Exchange Act was enacted in part "to insure the maintenance of fair and honest markets," and there is no question that fraudulent uses of confidential information fall within § 10(b)'s prohibition if the fraud is "in connection with" a securities transaction. It is hardly remarkable that a rule suitably applied to the fraudulent uses of certain kinds of information would be stretched beyond reason were it applied to the fraudulent use of money. * * *

The misappropriation theory comports with § 10(b)'s language, which requires deception "in connection with the purchase or sale of any security," not deception of an identifiable purchaser or seller. The theory is also well-tuned to an animating purpose of the Exchange Act: to insure honest securities markets and thereby promote investor confidence. See 45 Fed.Reg. 60412 (1980) (trading on misappropriated information "undermines the integrity of, and investor confidence in, the securities markets"). Although informational disparity is inevitable in the securities markets, investors likely would hesitate to venture their capital in a market where trading based on misappropriated nonpublic information is unchecked by law. An investor's informational disadvantage vis-a-vis a misappropriator with material, nonpublic information stems from contrivance, not luck; it is a disadvantage that cannot be overcome with research or skill. See Brudney, Insiders, Outsiders, and Informational Advantages Under the Federal Securities Laws, 93 Harv. L.Rev. 322, 356 (1979) ("If the market is thought to be systematically populated with . . . transactors [trading on the basis of misappropriated information] some investors will refrain from dealing altogether, and others will incur costs to avoid dealing with such transactors or corruptly to overcome their unerodable informational advantages.").

In sum, considering the inhibiting impact on market participation of trading on misappropriated information, and the congressional purposes underlying § 10(b), it makes scant sense to hold a lawyer like O'Hagan a § 10(b) violator if he works for a law firm representing the target of a tender offer, but not if he works for a law firm representing the bidder. The text of the statute requires no such result.[8] The misappropriation at issue here was properly made the subject of a § 10(b) charge because it meets the statutory requirement that there be "deceptive" conduct "in connection with" securities transactions. * * *

JUSTICE THOMAS dissented, in an opinion joined by CHIEF JUSTICE REHNQUIST. JUSTICE SCALIA also dissented. [omitted]

NOTES

1. The misappropriation theory is consistent with the agency principles. See *Diamond v. Oreamuno*, page 856, 301 N.Y.S.2d 78, 248 N.E.2d 910 supra. But it results in some very uneven applications. Consider the following.

   a. *The reporter.* As described above, in United States v. Carpenter, 791 F.2d 1024 (2d Cir.1986), affirmed 484 U.S. 19, 108 S.Ct. 316, 98 L.Ed.2d 275 (1987), a newspaper reporter who wrote the "Heard On The Street" column for the *Wall Street Journal* tipped his friends in advance about columns that mentioned certain stocks favorably. His friends bought the stocks, which then rose after the column was published. What would the result have been if the *Wall Street Journal* gave its reporters permission to trade in advance of its columns? See generally Zweig v. Hearst, Corp., 594 F.2d 1261 (9th Cir.1979) (newspaper columnist pumping of price of stock through his columns had a duty to disclose the fact that he had been given stock in the company as inducement for his writings).

   b. *The football coach.* A college football coach overhears boosters talking about a soon to be announced takeover. The coach calls his broker and buys stock in the target company. When the takeover is announced,

---

8. As noted earlier, however, the textual requirement of deception precludes § 10(b) liability when a person trading on the basis of nonpublic information has disclosed his trading plans to, or obtained authorization from, the principal—even though such conduct may affect the securities markets in the same manner as the conduct reached by the misappropriation theory. Contrary to the dissent's suggestion, the fact that § 10(b) is only a partial antidote to the problems it was designed to alleviate does not call into question its prohibition of conduct that falls within its textual proscription. Moreover, once a disloyal agent discloses his imminent breach of duty, his principal may seek appropriate equitable relief under state law. Furthermore, in the context of a tender offer, the principal who authorizes an agent's trading on confidential information may, in the Commission's view, incur liability for an Exchange Act violation under Rule 14e–3(a).

the price rises and the coach makes a nice profit. S.E.C. v. Switzer, 590 F.Supp. 756 (W.D.Okla.1984).

c. *The psychiatrist.* The wife of a successful and well known chief executive officer tells her psychiatrist during a therapy session that her husband is thinking of moving to another company. The psychiatrist buys stock in this company. Once it becomes known that the executive is contemplating a move, the company's stock price rises and the psychiatrist takes his profit. Has Rule 10b–5 been violated? See United States v. Willis, 737 F.Supp. 269 (S.D.N.Y.1990).

The answers to the foregoing cases are not intuitive. The football coach did not violate the law but the reporter (at least one acting without permission) and the psychiatrist have. What type of rationale supports such an uneven result?

2.   Another example of the unevenness of the misappropriation theory is demonstrated by the following hypothetical. Assume that the client in the *O'Hagan* case wants to save on legal fees to the law firm preparing the tender offer and proposes that instead of paying the firm's hourly rate in cash, it would give the lawyers permission to trade on the advance information concerning the tender offer until they have profited in an amount equivalent to their hourly rate. The owner's permission would mean there is no misappropriation. Is there any other basis for imposing liability for this use of nonpublic information?

UNITED STATES v. KIM

184 F.Supp.2d 1006 (N.D.Cal.2002).

BREYER, DISTRICT J.

This case presents the interesting question of whether it is a criminal act for a member of a club to violate confidences which he has pledged to keep. The government contends that a special "fiduciary-like" relationship among club members creates this obligation. The Court, however, disagrees. While members of a club may feel a special bond, there is nothing so special about their relationship, as alleged in the indictment, that it gives rise to a legal duty not to trade on confidential information. Violation of confidences under these circumstances may warrant expulsion from the club, and even shunning by fellow members, but it does not fall within the criminal laws of the United States.

In March 1999, defendant, Keith Joon Kim, was Chief Executive Officer ("CEO") of Granny Goose Foods, Inc. He was also a member of the Young Presidents Organization ("YPO"), a national organization of company presidents under 50 years old. The YPO is organized into regional chapters, and further divided into small forums. Defendant was a member of the 1917 Forum in Northern California.

As alleged in the indictment, the "Forum Principles" of the YPO's 1917 Forum stated that: "We operate in an atmosphere of absolute confidentiality. Nothing discussed in forum will be discussed with outsiders. Confidentiality, in all ways and for always." Indictment ¶ 7. Members were also required to comply with a written "Confidentiality Commitment" as a condition of membership. That agreement provides:

I understand that to achieve the level of trust necessary to ensure the interchange we all seek in the Forum, all information shared by the membership must be held in absolute confidence.... I understand that no Forum business can be discussed with anyone outside the Forum, including spouses, "significant others," other YPO or non-YPO members.... I understand that breaking this contract will result in being asked to resign from the Forum. Most importantly, I understand that I have a major moral and ethical responsibility to my Forum friends who have entrusted me with their most personal feelings, problems and issues. To break this trust is to destroy all that Forum can mean to its members.

The CEO of Meridian Data, Inc. was also a member of the 1917 Forum. Meridian is a publicly traded corporation listed on NASDAQ that manufactures computer storage devices. On March 1, 1999 the 1917 Forum members departed from Northern California in a private plane for Snowmass, Colorado, for their annual retreat. Prior to departure, the CEO of Meridian informed the Forum Moderator that he could not attend because Meridian was involved in merger discussions with another company—Quantum Corporation. He authorized the Forum Moderator to tell the other members why he would be absent, but asked the Moderator to emphasize the confidential nature of the information. The Forum Moderator relayed the information to defendant and other members of the 1917 Forum.

The indictment alleges that, based on this confidential information, between March 1 and March 4, 1999 defendant purchased 187,300 shares of Meridian stock for between $2.00 and $4.12 per share. Defendant also disclosed the information to his business partner, his brother, and his brother-in-law, all of whom purchased shares of Meridian.

On May 11, 1999 Meridian publicly announced that it had agreed to be acquired by Quantum. Meridian's share price jumped to $7.56. Defendant thereby realized a profit of $832,627 on an investment of $583,360. Defendant's business partner realized a profit of $200,885; his brother realized a profit of $27,469; and his brother-in-law realized a profit of $13,492.

Defendant was charged with one count of wire fraud, two counts of securities fraud, and one count of making a false statement. He has moved to dismiss the first three counts of the indictment (all counts except the false statement) pursuant to Federal Rule of Criminal Procedure 12(b). For the reasons stated below, defendant's motion to dismiss is GRANTED.
* * *

Defendant is charged with violating section 10(b) of the Securities Exchange Act of 1934 and Rule 10b–5. There are two general theories of liability under section 10(b) and Rule 10b–5: traditional "insider" trading and "misappropriation." See United States v. O'Hagan, 521 U.S. 642, 651–52, 117 S.Ct. 2199, 138 L.Ed.2d 724 (1997). As the government concedes, only the misappropriation theory is relevant to this case.

Under the misappropriation theory, a person commits fraud "in connection with" a securities transaction, as proscribed by Rule 10b–5, "when he misappropriates confidential information for securities trading purposes, in breach of a duty owed to the source of the information." *Id.* at 652. Whereas classic insider trading involves a breach of a duty between a corporate insider and the corporation's shareholders, misappropriation involves a breach of duty between the owner of the confidential information and the individual entrusted with that information. *Id.* A misappropriator is a corporate "outsider."

The central issue presented by defendant's motion is whether the relationship between defendant and the members of the 1917 Forum is such that it gives rise to a *legal* duty of confidentiality, a violation of which can serve as the predicate for criminal liability under the misappropriation theory. * * *

The relationship presented in *O'Hagan* was a classic fiduciary relationship. As the government concedes, the present case does not present a classic, or "hornbook" fiduciary relationship, such as: attorney-client, executor-heir, guardian-ward, principal-agent, trustee-beneficiary, or senior corporate official-shareholder. *See United States v. Chestman,* 947 F.2d 551, 568 (2d Cir.1991). Thus the Court must turn to other authority for guidance as to whether non-fiduciary relationships—such as the one presented here among organization members—can support misappropriation liability.

As both parties agree, the key case for examining the precise contours of misappropriation liability—i.e., what relationships can potentially give rise to liability?—is *United States v. Chestman,* 947 F.2d 551 (2d Cir. 1991). *Chestman* involved the duty a husband owes to his wife and his wife's family. The court concluded that the specific relationship presented did not give rise to misappropriation liability because it did not share the essential characteristics of a fiduciary relation. *Id.* at 570–71.

Chestman held that "a person violates Rule 10b–5 when he misappropriates material nonpublic information in breach of a fiduciary duty *or similar relationship of trust and confidence* and uses that information in a securities transaction." *Id.* at 566 (emphasis added). The question is whether the relationship between defendant and the members of the 1917 Forum is a "similar relationship of trust and confidence," i.e., similar to a *fiduciary* relationship.

As an initial matter it is clear from *Chestman* that the exchange of confidential information, alone, does not give rise to a fiduciary-like relationship.[1] *Id.* at 567. Therefore, a "similar relationship" did not arise

---

1. Although not relevant here, *Chestman* also concluded that a family relationship standing alone is insufficient. *Id.* at 568.

in this case merely because the CEO of Meridian entrusted defendant, and other members of the 1917 Forum, with confidential information.

Beyond this specific limitation, *Chestman* provides more general guidance as to what constitutes a "similar relationship of trust and confidence." In short, to serve as a predicate for misappropriation liability the alleged relationship must be the "functional equivalent" of a fiduciary relationship. *Id.* at 568. "As the term 'similar' implies, a 'relationship of trust and confidence' must share the essential characteristics of a fiduciary association." *Id.* Accordingly, the Court must determine whether the relationship at issue here bore the hallmarks of a fiduciary relationship.

To answer this question it is necessary to understand the essential characteristics of the fiduciary relation. As stated in *Chestman,* at "the heart of the fiduciary relationship lies reliance, and de facto control and dominance." *Id.* (internal quotations and citation omitted). The fiduciary "relation exists when confidence is reposed on one side and there is resulting superiority and influence on the other." *Id.* at 568 (internal citation and quotation omitted).

The government argues that *Chestman's* references to superiority *and* influence, should be construed as requiring only superiority *or* influence.[2] This argument is neither supported by *Chestman* itself, nor of much logical force. The argument is largely one of semantics. The government argues that "influence" understood as synonymous with "advice" is sufficient. But *Chestman* makes clear that something more than the giving and accepting of advice is required. *Chestman* requires influence of a superior or dominating nature—not the "influence" one peer might exert on another. The government suggests that the ability to be "influential"— the way colleagues or peers might be—is sufficient, but *Chestman* requires more.

In examining the essential characteristics of a fiduciary relation— specifically the existence of dominance or superiority in the relationship— it is instructive to look at cases upholding the misappropriation theory of criminal liability. These have generally involved the attorney-client, employer-employee, and psychiatrist-patient relationship. *See, e.g., United States v. O'Hagan,* 521 U.S. 642 (1997) (attorney-client); *United States v. Falcone,* 257 F.3d 226 (2d Cir.2001)(employer-employee); *United States v. Willis,* 737 F.Supp. 269 (S.D.N.Y.1990) (psychiatrist-patient). These are not relationships among equals. As *Chestman* requires, they are characterized by superiority, dominance, or control. Attorneys and psychiatrists are possessed of superior knowledge and expertise. Clients and patients must relay confidential information to receive the benefit of that superior knowledge (it comes in the form of legal advice and medical treatment). The employee-employer relation presents the classic principal-agent scenario and its corresponding common law legal duty.

---

2. This argument is based, in part, on Black's Law Dictionary which states that a "fiduciary relationship" can arise "when one person places trust in the faithful integrity of another, who as a result gains superiority or influence over the first." Blacks's Law Dictionary 712 (7th ed.1999).

As the analysis in *Chestman* and the examples explored above make clear, the primary essential characteristic of the fiduciary relation is some measure of superiority, dominance, or control. Therefore, this Court holds that a "similar relationship of trust and confidence" must be characterized by superiority, dominance, or control. Accordingly the dispositive issue in this case is whether the relationship between defendant and the CEO of Meridian and other members of the 1917 Forum is best characterized as an equal relationship between peers or as a relationship involving a degree of dominance.

Of course, fiduciary-like dominance can arise in many contexts. For example, in the attorney-client and psychiatrist-patient context it arises largely from disparate knowledge and expertise (this inherent disparity has been supplemented with a legal duty). In the employer-employee context it arises from common law principal-agent principles.

The Court has undertaken a review of the cases cited by the parties. In those cases upholding misappropriation liability, fiduciary-like dominance generally arises out of some combination of 1) disparate knowledge and expertise, 2) a persuasive need to share confidential information, and 3) a legal duty to render competent aid. The presence or absence of these characteristics is the key to determining whether the relation between defendant and the members of the 1917 Forum is characterized by superiority, dominance, or control. Whether all of these characteristics must be present, and to what degree, is not decided here. As detailed below, the relationship alleged in the indictment does not bear any of these characteristics. As a result it is not one of superiority, dominance, or control. Accordingly, it cannot be a "similar relationship of trust and confidence." Therefore the indictment fails as a matter of law to allege facts establishing a basis for misappropriation liability.

The government does not allege disparate knowledge or expertise. Indeed the very membership criteria of the YPO—large company presidents under the age of 50—ensures similar levels of achievement, experience, and expertise among members. At most, different members of the YPO bring to bear a different perspectives on each others problems.

There is no persuasive need for YPO members to share material, nonpublic information with each other. The sharing of such information may enliven meetings or marginally improve advice, but by no means is it necessary. It should be noted, that the particular communication at issue here—that the CEO or Meridian would not attend the meeting because of pending merger discussions—was completely gratuitous. It is hard to fathom any legitimate reason for sharing this material, nonpublic information and running the risk that it would leak.

Extending misappropriation theory to cover the situation before the Court would serve to legitimize the disclosure that took place because it would place primary blame with the defendant rather than the CEO of Meridian. The Court is convinced that this is the wrong result. The CEO of Meridian should not have told the 1917 Forum members why he was missing the meeting—even if he emphasized the confidential nature of his reason. While barring misappropriation liability in this case may permit a "wrong" to go unpunished, the proposed extension of misappropriation theory would have the practical effect of encouraging the spread of confidential information more widely, thereby increasing the likelihood of abuse. The law should discourage gratuitous sharing of nonpublic information, by placing responsibility on the sources of that information to share it only for substantial reasons.

Where misappropriation theory is appropriately applied, the spread of the confidential information cannot be stanched at its source without unacceptable ramifications. Clients need the advice of lawyers. Patients need treatments. And employers have to be able to do their jobs. For example, in *United States v. Falcone,* 257 F.3d 226 (2d Cir.2001), there was no practical alternative to a magazine distribution system that gives employees physical access to pre-release publications. By contrast, the CEO of Meridian could have simply waited, without real repercussions, until the merger discussions were public before sharing them with the members of the YPO.

Along these lines it is worth analyzing more closely *O'Hagan,* where the Court reasoned: "it makes scant sense to hold a lawyer like O'Hagan a § 10(b) violator if he works for a law firm representing the target of a tender offer, but not if he works for a law firm representing the bidder." *O'Hagan,* 521 U.S. at 659. Misappropriation theory is targeted at "outsider" trading, i.e., breaches that do not involve a duty to the traded company and its shareholders. This case, however, involves a breach of a duty allegedly owed to an insider in the company whose securities were traded. Generally speaking traditional insider trading liability addresses such breaches through tipper-tippee liability. The government is attempting to redeploy misappropriation theory here to the rare case where the intentional disclosure of material, nonpublic information by an insider does not result in tipper-tippee liability. While this alone is not a reason to reject the government's argument, it does show that this case falls outside the misappropriation paradigm.

Fiduciary-like relations involve a legal duty to render competent aid. No legal duty is present. The indictment suggests a "duty" to "YPO 1917 and its member, the CEO of Meridian." Indictment ¶ 12. But this is not a legal duty. No one suggests that the CEO of Meridian or other members of the 1917 Forum have a civil cause of action against defendant, even if his actions were malicious, based on their mutual membership in the YPO. The existence of the explicit confidentiality agreement does not change this conclusion. The agreement may memorialize a moral and ethical duty that members undertake, but it does not create a legal one.

Beyond the three factors discussed at length above, the indictment does not allege any other facts that reasonably lead to the conclusion that any measure of superiority, dominance, or control existed in the relationship between defendant and the members of the 1917 Forum. The utter absence of the three factors merely reinforces what common sense suggests at the outset—the YPO is a club. Its members are peers who gather to socialize, exchange information, and seek advice. The members are equals.

In short, the relationship between defendant and the members of the 1917 Forum was not characterized by any measure of superiority, control, or dominance. It was not the functional equivalent of a fiduciary relationship. While the rules of the club may have forbid defendant's actions, the federal securities laws—at least in this instance—did not. * * *

The conclusion reached above is bolstered by statements of the Securities and Exchange Commission ("SEC") since defendant's trading took place.

The defendant concedes that under the current regulation, which became effective August 24, 2000, the indictment alleges facts amounting to criminal misappropriation. The new regulation defines three non-exclusive circumstances under which "a person has a duty of trust or confidence for purposes of the 'misappropriation' theory of insider trading" for purposes of Rule 10b–5. Rule 10b5–2 (preliminary note). They are:

> (1) Whenever a person agrees to maintain information in confidence;
>
> (2) Whenever the person communicating the material non-public information and the person to whom it is communicated have a history, pattern, or practice of sharing confidences . . . or
>
> (3) Whenever a person receives or obtains material nonpublic information from his or her spouse, parent, child, or sibling. . . .

Id. Both the first and second scenarios would apply to defendant's conduct in this case. The fact that the SEC saw a need to adopt this new rule adds force to the argument that the conduct it covers was not legally proscribed before adoption of the rule.

Prior to the rule's adoption, a December 20, 1999 SEC release described the proposed rule and solicited comments. Selective Disclosure and Insider Trading, 1999 WL 1217849, SEC Release Nos. 33–7787, 34–42259, and IC–24,209) (Dec. 20, 1999). While the SEC release described the law, as it existed then, regarding the scope of misappropriation liability as "unsettled," *id.* at 2, a full reading of the release makes clear that the proposed rule was designed to establish new law, not clarify existing law. The SEC's dissatisfaction with the law at the time as set forth in *Chestman* (which governs this case) is clear. As the SEC stated:

> In our view, however, the Chestman majority's approach does not fully recognize the degree to which parties to close family and personal relationships have reasonable and legitimate expectations of confidentiality in their communications. For this reason, we believe the Chestman majority view does not sufficiently protect investors and

the securities markets from the misappropriation and resulting mis-use of inside information.

Id. at 22. The SEC concluded by stating that "there is good reason for the broader approach we propose today for determining when family or personal relationships create 'duties of trust or confidence' under the misappropriation theory." *Id.* at 23.

In the SEC's opinion, the three bases for misappropriation liability described in the new rule were not a basis for liability under *Chestman.* While the SEC's opinion is not binding on this Court, it is persuasive given the SEC's role in the development of insider trading law through rule making and its enforcement responsibilities. At a minimum, the history of the new rule supports this Court's conclusion that criminal liability should not attach to defendant's conduct.

The government's argument that the "broader" approach of the new rule is somehow limited to the third category (family members), because the first two categories "merely restate the principles articulated in *Chestman,*" is difficult to take seriously. The language of the release makes clear the new rule applies to family "or other non-business rela-tionships." *Id.* at 2.

One aspect of the SEC release may add marginal support to the government's position. The release suggests that an express confidentiali-ty agreement is sufficient to support misappropriation liability under *Chestman. Id.* at 22. The SEC release does not detail what type of express agreement would serve as a sufficient basis for liability under *Chestman.*

In the Court's opinion, however, an express agreement can provide the basis for misappropriation liability only if the express agreement sets forth a relationship with the hallmarks of a fiduciary relationship detailed above. Even if the members of the YPO were bound by an express confidentiality agreement, that agreement appealed only to the members' ethics and morality; it did not give rise to any legal duties. * * *

Defendant is also charged with one count of wire fraud in violation of 18 U.S.C. § 1343. The alleged fraud underlying the securities fraud charges also serves as the basis for the wire fraud charge. As the government concedes, a wire fraud conviction must be based on breach of an underlying duty. For the reasons stated above no such duty is present here. Accordingly, the indictment also fails to allege a wire fraud violation. Count one of the indictment is DISMISSED.

NOTES

1. The court in *Kim* seems to indicate that Rule 10b5–2 is not a good guide for the scope of criminal liability. Does the court's opinion have similar implications for civil enforcement or private damage actions? Rule 10b5–2 is nonexclusive, which means that the courts remain free to apply misappropria-tion in other situations as well.

2. *Confidentiality agreements and the disclose or abstain rule.* The court in *Kim* takes the position that the mere existence of a confidentiality agree-

ment is not sufficient to trigger the obligation to abstain from trading on the information. At least this is the case where the agreement is intended to reflect an ethical or moral confidentiality obligation. In contrast when the agreement imposes a legal obligation, as would be the case for confidentiality agreements that are routinely applied to investment bankers, the Rule 10b–5 obligation is likely to attach.

3.   The facts in United States v. Chestman, 947 F.2d 551 (2d Cir.1991) were as follows: Robert Chestman, a broker and financial advisor, met with his customer Keith Loeb to discuss Loeb's transfer of various brokerage accounts to Chestman's firm. Loeb's holdings included the stock of Waldbaum, Inc. Loeb's wife was the niece of Waldbaum's president and controlling shareholder, Ira Waldbaum, who, along with his immediate family owned approximately 51% of the outstanding Waldbaum stock. Loeb was told by his wife, who had been told by her sister, that Waldbaum was about to be taken over. Loeb claimed that he had told Chestman he had reliable information that Waldbaum was going to be taken over and wanted to know what to do. Chestman (the broker) bought the stock for his own account and profited once the takeover was announced. Did the broker violate Rule 10b–5? The Court stated:

> Evidence that Keith Loeb revealed the critical information in breach of a duty of trust and confidence known to Chestman is essential to the imposition of liability upon Chestman as aider/abettor, or as tippee. Such evidence is lacking here. Although Chestman was aware that Loeb was a member of the Waldbaum family and may well have gathered that the "definite" and "accurate" information furnished by Loeb was not generally available, there simply is no evidence that he knew that Loeb was breaching a confidential relationship by imparting the information to him. The government can point to nothing in the record demonstrating actual or constructive knowledge on the part of Chestman that Keith Loeb was pledged to secrecy by Susan Loeb, who was pledged to secrecy by Shirley Witkin, who was pledged to secrecy by Ira Waldbaum. Loeb testified on direct examination that he could not recall describing the information as confidential, and there is no evidence that he ever alluded to the source of his information. It is impossible to attribute knowledge of confidentiality to Chestman in view of the attenuated passage of the information and in the absence of any showing that the information retained any kind of confidentiality in the hands of Keith Loeb.

The dismissal of Chestman's alleged violation of Rule 10b–5 was upheld by a vote of 6 to 5 in an *en banc* decision. The majority found that the government "failed to offer sufficient evidence to establish the functional equivalent of a fiduciary relation" between Keith and the Waldbaum family, and that "because Keith owed neither Susan nor the Waldbaum family a fiduciary duty or its functional equivalent, he did not defraud them by disclosing news of the pending tender offer to Chestman. Absent a predicate act of fraud by Keith Loeb, the alleged misappropriator, Chestman could not be derivatively liable as Loeb's tippee or as an aider and abettor." The five dissenters believed that "family members who have benefitted from the family's control of the corporation are under a duty not to disclose confidential corporate information that comes to them in the ordinary course of family affairs," and that "a family member (i) who has received or expects (e.g., through inheritance) benefits from family control of a corporation, here gifts of stock, (ii) who is in a position to learn confidential corporate information through ordinary family interactions, and (iii) who knows that under the circumstances both the corporation and the family desire confidentiality, has a duty not to use information so obtained for personal profit where the use risks disclosure." SEC Rule 10b5–2 was designed to overturn the *Chestman* ruling. Among other things, it creates a presumption of a duty of trust or confidence where the information is communicated to a spouse, parent, child or sibling.

4. Can any wrongdoing form the basis of a Rule 10b–5 violation for improper trading on non-public information? In one case, the defendant hacked into a company's computer system and obtained nonpublic information and traded very profitably on that information. Computer logs showed that at 2:15:28 p.m., an unauthorized user gained access to a company's soon-to-be-released negative earnings announcement. Approximately 35 minutes later, and a matter of hours before the information was to be released to the public, Dorozhko, used a recently opened but yet unused online brokerage to take a short position by purchasing $41,670.90 worth of put options. These purchases represented about 90% of all customer purchases of the put options for the entire six week period between September 4, 2007 and October 17, 2007. When the market opened the next morning, defendant sold these put options for $328,571.00—an overnight return of 697%. The court held that since the defendant had no relationship to the company and did not breach any fiduciary duties, he could not be sued under the federal securities laws:

> This case highlights a potential gap arising from a reliance on fiduciary principles in the legal analysis that courts have employed to define insider trading, and courts' stated goal of preserving equitable markets. *See generally Affiliated Ute Citizens of Utah v. United States*, 406 U.S. 128, 151, 92 S.Ct. 1456, 31 L.Ed.2d 741 (1972) (noting that federal securities law should be "construed not technically and restrictively, but flexibly to effectuate its remedial purposes") (citations omitted). Yet, on further consideration, the gap is not as troublesome as it may appear, since the government retains ample methods of combating inequitable practices of the kind alleged here. Indeed, we would not have to address the tension between the fiduciary requirement and the goal of preserving fair and open markets had the SEC acted on this Court's suggestion at the November 28, 2007 preliminary injunction hearing that a way to avoid a decision that would result in the release of the restrained trading proceeds was to refer this matter to the United States Attorney's Office for criminal investigation. Based on the evidence provided at the November 28, 2007 hearing there would appear to be sufficient basis to conclude that Dorozhko's hack violated the Computer Fraud and Abuse Act, 18 U.S.C. § 1030(a)(4), the mail fraud statute, 18 U.S.C. § 1341 *et seq.*, and the wire fraud statute, 18 U.S.C. § 1341 et seq. The U.S. Attorney's Office has authority to seize Dorozhko's trading proceeds under 18 U.S.C. § 981(b).

> However, since the SEC has apparently declined, for whatever reason, to involve the criminal authorities in this case, we must address an

inconvenient truth about our securities laws-an issue that has sent Supreme Court justices into dissent, *see Chiarella*, 445 at 245 (1980) (Blackmun, J. dissenting) and provoked numerous law review articles. See, e.g., Robert A. Prentice, *The Internet and Its Challenges for the Future of Insider Trading Regulation*, 12 Harv. J.L. & Tech 263, 296–307 (Winter 1999).

Upon a searching review of existing case law, and for the reasons that follow, we believe that we are constrained to hold that Dorozhko's alleged 'stealing and trading' or 'hacking and trading' does not amount to a violation of § 10(b) and Rule 10b–5 because Dorozhko did not breach any fiduciary or similar duty "in connection with" the purchase or sale of a security. Although Dorozhko may have broken the law, he is not liable in a civil action under § 10(b) because he owed no fiduciary or similar duty either to the source of his information or to those he transacted with in the market. *See O'Hagan*, 521 U.S. at 656. As the Supreme Court famously held in Chiarella, and has reaffirmed since, "one who fails to disclose material information prior to the consummation of a transaction commits fraud only when he is under a duty to do so." 445 U.S. at 228;see also O'Hagan, 521 U.S. at 654–56.

SEC v. Dorozhko, 2008 WL 126612 (S.D.N.Y. 2008) (some citations omitted).

The SEC does not concur in this result and has pursued hackers in other instances. For example, in one case. the defendant while a weekend guest snuck into his brother-in-law's bedroom, guessed his password and found confidential information in the brother-in-law's computer and then proceeded to trade on this information. The defendant entered into a consent decree and agreed to pay $46,386.66, representing the disgorgement of his illegal trading profits, prejudgment interest, and a civil penalty in an amount equal to the profits. See Securities and Exchange Commission v. Michael A. Stummer, Defendant, 1:2008CV03671 (S.D. N.Y), SEC Litigation Release No. 20529, 2008 WL 1756796 (S.D.N.Y. April 17, 2008).

SECTION 4. "TIPPEE" LIABILITY

DIRKS v. SEC

463 U.S. 646, 103 S.Ct. 3255, 77 L.Ed.2d 911 (1983).

JUSTICE POWELL delivered the opinion of the Court.

Petitioner Raymond Dirks received material nonpublic information from "insiders" of a corporation with which he had no connection. He disclosed this information to investors who relied on it in trading in the shares of the corporation. The question is whether Dirks violated the antifraud provisions of the federal securities laws by this disclosure.

In 1973, Dirks was an officer of a New York broker-dealer firm who specialized in providing investment analysis of insurance company securities to institutional investors. On March 6, Dirks received information from Ronald Secrist, a former officer of Equity Funding of America. Secrist alleged that the assets of Equity Funding, a diversified corporation primarily engaged in selling life insurance and mutual funds, were vastly overstated as the result of fraudulent corporate practices. Secrist also stated that various regulatory agencies had failed to act on similar charges made by Equity Funding employees. He urged Dirks to verify the fraud and disclose it publicly.

Dirks decided to investigate the allegations. He visited Equity Funding's headquarters in Los Angeles and interviewed several officers and employees of the corporation. The senior management denied any wrongdoing, but certain corporation employees corroborated the charges of fraud. Neither Dirks nor his firm owned or traded any Equity Funding stock, but throughout his investigation he openly discussed the information he had obtained with a number of clients and investors. Some of these persons sold their holdings of Equity Funding securities, including five investment advisers who liquidated holdings of more than $16 million.

While Dirks was in Los Angeles, he was in touch regularly with William Blundell, the Wall Street Journal's Los Angeles bureau chief. Dirks urged Blundell to write a story on the fraud allegations. Blundell did not believe, however, that such a massive fraud could go undetected and declined to write the story. He feared that publishing such damaging hearsay might be libelous.

During the two-week period in which Dirks pursued his investigation and spread word of Secrist's charges, the price of Equity Funding stock fell from $26 per share to less than $15 per share. This led the New York Stock Exchange to halt trading on March 27. Shortly thereafter California insurance authorities impounded Equity Funding's records and uncovered evidence of the fraud. Only then did the Securities and Exchange Commission (SEC) file a complaint against Equity Funding and only then, on April 2, did the Wall Street Journal publish a front-page story based largely on information assembled by Dirks. Equity Funding immediately went into receivership.

The SEC began an investigation into Dirks' role in the exposure of the fraud. After a hearing by an administrative law judge, the SEC found that Dirks had aided and abetted violations of § 17(a) of the Securities Act of 1933, § 10(b) of the Securities Exchange Act of 1934, and SEC Rule 10b–5, by repeating the allegations of fraud to members of the investment community who later sold their Equity Funding stock. The SEC concluded: "Where 'tippees'—regardless of their motivation or occupation—come into possession of material 'information that they know is confidential and know or should know came from a corporate insider,' they must either publicly disclose that information or refrain from trading." Recognizing, however, that Dirks "played an important role in bringing [Equity Funding's] massive fraud to light," the SEC only censured him.

Dirks sought review in the Court of Appeals for the District of Columbia Circuit. The court entered judgment against Dirks "for the reasons stated by the Commission in its opinion." * * *

The SEC's position, as stated in its opinion in this case, is that a tippee "inherits" the *Cady, Roberts* obligation to shareholders whenever he receives inside information from an insider:

> "In tipping potential traders, Dirks breached a duty which he had assumed as a result of knowingly receiving confidential information from [Equity Funding] insiders. Tippees such as Dirks who receive non-public material information from insiders become 'subject to the same duty as [the] insiders.' *Shapiro v. Merrill Lynch, Pierce, Fenner & Smith, Inc.* [495 F.2d 228, 237 (C.A.2 1974) (quoting *Ross v. Licht,* 263 F.Supp. 395, 410 (S.D.N.Y.1967))]. Such a tippee breaches the fiduciary duty which he assumes from the insider when the tippee knowingly transmits the information to someone who will probably trade on the basis thereof.... Presumably, Dirks' informants were entitled to disclose the [Equity Funding] fraud in order to bring it to light and its perpetrators to justice. However, Dirks—standing in their shoes—committed a breach of the fiduciary duty which he had assumed in dealing with them, when he passed the information on to traders."

This view differs little from the view that we rejected as inconsistent with congressional intent in *Chiarella.* In that case, the Court of Appeals agreed with the SEC and affirmed Chiarella's conviction, holding that "[a]nyone—corporate insider or not—who regularly receives material non-public information may not use that information to trade in securities without incurring an affirmative duty to disclose." Here, the SEC maintains that anyone who knowingly receives nonpublic material information from an insider has a fiduciary duty to disclose before trading.[9]

In effect, the SEC's theory of tippee liability in both cases appears rooted in the idea that the antifraud provisions require equal information among all traders. This conflicts with the principle set forth in *Chiarella* that only some persons, under some circumstances, will be barred from trading while in possession of material nonpublic information. * * *

---

9. Apparently, the SEC believes this case differs from *Chiarella* in that Dirks' receipt of inside information from Secrist, an insider, carried Secrist's duties with it, while Chiarella received the information without the direct involvement of an insider and thus inherited no duty to disclose or abstain. The SEC fails to explain, however, why the receipt of nonpublic information from an insider automatically carries with it the fiduciary duty of the insider. As we emphasized in *Chiarella,* mere possession of nonpublic information does not give rise to a duty to disclose or abstain; only a specific relationship does that. And we do not believe that the mere receipt of information from an insider creates such a special relationship between the tippee and the corporation's shareholders.

Apparently recognizing the weakness of its argument in light of *Chiarella,* the SEC attempts to distinguish that case factually as involving not "inside" information, but rather "market" information, i.e., "information generated within the company relating to its assets or earnings." Brief for Respondent 23. This Court drew no such distinction in *Chiarella* and, as the Chief Justice noted, "[i]t is clear that § 10(b) and Rule 10b–5 by their terms and by their history make no such distinction." 445 U.S., at 241, n. 1, 100 S.Ct., at 1121, n. 1 (dissenting opinion). See ALI Fed.Sec.Code § 1603. Comment (2)(j) (Proposed Official Draft 1978).

Imposing a duty to disclose or abstain solely because a person knowingly receives material nonpublic information from an insider and trades on it could have an inhibiting influence on the role of market analysts, which the SEC itself recognizes is necessary to the preservation of a healthy market. It is commonplace for analysts to "ferret out and analyze information,"[10] and this often is done by meeting with and questioning corporate officers and others who are insiders. And information that the analysts obtain normally may be the basis for judgments as to the market worth of a corporation's securities. The analyst's judgment in this respect is made available in market letters or otherwise to clients of the firm. It is the nature of this type of information, and indeed of the markets themselves, that such information cannot be made simultaneously available to all of the corporation's stockholders or the public generally.

The conclusion that recipients of inside information do not invariably acquire a duty to disclose or abstain does not mean that such tippees always are free to trade on the information. The need for a ban on some tippee trading is clear. Not only are insiders forbidden by their fiduciary relationship from personally using undisclosed corporate information to their advantage, but they may not give such information to an outsider for the same improper purpose of exploiting the information for their personal gain. * * *

Thus, some tippees must assume an insider's duty to the shareholders not because they receive inside information, but rather because it has been made available to them *improperly*. And for Rule 10b–5 purposes, the insider's disclosure is improper only where it would violate his *Cady, Roberts* duty. Thus, a tippee assumes a fiduciary duty to the shareholders of a corporation not to trade on material nonpublic information only when the insider has breached his fiduciary duty to the shareholders by disclosing the information to the tippee and the tippee knows or should know that there has been a breach. As Commissioner Smith perceptively observed in *Investors Management Co.:* "[T]ippee responsibility must be related back to insider responsibility by a necessary finding that the tippee knew the information was given to him in breach of a duty by a person having a special relationship to the issuer not to disclose the information * * *." Tipping thus properly is viewed only as a means of indirectly violating the *Cady, Roberts* disclose-or-abstain rule.[11]

---

10. On its facts, this case is the unusual one. Dirks is an analyst in a broker-dealer firm, and he did interview management in the course of his investigation. He uncovered, however, startling information that required no analysis or exercise of judgment as to its market relevance. Nonetheless, the principle at issue here extends beyond these facts. The SEC's rule—applicable without regard to any breach by an insider—could have serious ramifications on reporting by analysts of investment views.

Despite the unusualness of Dirks' "find," the central role that he played in uncovering the fraud at Equity Funding, and that analysts in general can play in revealing information that corporations may have reason to withhold from the public, is an important one. Dirks' careful investigation brought to light a massive fraud at the corporation. And until the Equity Funding fraud was exposed, the information in the trading market was grossly inaccurate. But for Dirks' efforts, the fraud might well have gone undetected longer.

11. We do not suggest that knowingly trading on inside information is ever "socially desirable or even that it is devoid of moral considerations." Dooley, Enforcement of Insider Trading

In determining whether a tippee is under an obligation to disclose or abstain, it thus is necessary to determine whether the insider's "tip" constituted a breach of the insider's fiduciary duty. * * *

[T]he test is whether the insider personally will benefit, directly or indirectly, from his disclosure. Absent some personal gain, there has been no breach of duty to stockholders. And absent a breach by the insider, there is no derivative breach. * * *

The SEC argues that, if inside-trading liability does not exist when the information is transmitted for a proper purpose but is used for trading, it would be a rare situation when the parties could not fabricate some ostensibly legitimate business justification for transmitting the information. We think the SEC is unduly concerned. In determining whether the insider's purpose in making a particular disclosure is fraudulent, the SEC and the courts are not required to read the parties' minds. Scienter in some cases is relevant in determining whether the tipper has violated his *Cady, Roberts* duty. But to determine whether the disclosure itself "deceive[s], manipulate[s], or defraud[s]" shareholders, the initial inquiry is whether there has been a breach of duty by the insider. This requires courts to focus on objective criteria, i.e., whether the insider receives a direct or indirect personal benefit from the disclosure, such as a pecuniary gain or a reputational benefit that will translate into future earnings. * * *

There are objective facts and circumstances that often justify such an inference. For example, there may be a relationship between the insider and the recipient that suggests a *quid pro quo* from the latter, or an intention to benefit the particular recipient. The elements of fiduciary duty and exploitation of nonpublic information also exist when an insider makes a gift of confidential information to a trading relative or friend. The tip and trade resemble trading by the insider himself followed by a gift of the profits to the recipient. * * *

Under the inside-trading and tipping rules set forth above, we find that there was no actionable violation by Dirks. It is undisputed that Dirks himself was a stranger to Equity Funding, with no pre-existing fiduciary duty to its shareholders. He took no action, directly or indirectly, that induced the shareholders or officers of Equity Funding to repose trust or confidence in him. There was no expectation by Dirks' sources that he would keep their information in confidence. Nor did Dirks misappropriate or illegally obtain the information about Equity Funding. Unless the insiders breached their *Cady, Roberts* duty to shareholders in disclosing the nonpublic information to Dirks, he breached no duty when he passed it on to investors as well as to the Wall Street Journal.

Restrictions, 66 Va.L.Rev. 1, 55 (1980). Nor do we imply an absence of responsibility to disclose promptly indications of illegal actions by a corporation to the proper authorities—typically the SEC and exchange authorities in cases involving securities. Depending on the circumstances, and even where permitted by law, one's trading on material nonpublic information is behavior that may fall below ethical standards of conduct. But in a statutory area of the law such as securities regulation, where legal principles of general application must be applied, there may be "significant distinctions between actual legal obligations and ethical ideals."

It is clear that neither Secrist nor the other Equity Funding employees violated their *Cady, Roberts* duty to the corporation's shareholders by providing information to Dirks. The tippers received no monetary or personal benefit for revealing Equity Funding's secrets, nor was their purpose to make a gift of valuable information to Dirks. As the facts of this case clearly indicate, the tippers were motivated by a desire to expose the fraud. In the absence of a breach of duty to shareholders by the insiders, there was no derivative breach by Dirks. Dirks therefore could not have been "a participant after the fact in [an] insider's breach of a fiduciary duty." * * *

JUSTICE BLACKMUN, with whom JUSTICE BRENNAN and JUSTICE MARSHALL join, dissenting.

The Court today takes still another step to limit the protections provided investors by § 10(b) of the Securities Exchange Act of 1934. The device employed in this case engrafts a special motivational requirement on the fiduciary duty doctrine. This innovation excuses a knowing and intentional violation of an insider's duty to shareholders if the insider does not act from a motive of personal gain. Even on the extraordinary facts of this case, such an innovation is not justified. * * *

No one questions that Secrist himself could not trade on his inside information to the disadvantage of uninformed shareholders and purchasers of Equity Funding securities. Unlike the printer in *Chiarella,* Secrist stood in a fiduciary relationship with these shareholders. As the Court states, corporate insiders have an affirmative duty of disclosure when trading with shareholders of the corporation. This duty extends as well to purchasers of the corporation's securities. * * *

The Court holds, however, that Dirks is not liable because Secrist did not violate his duty; according to the Court, this is so because Secrist did not have the improper purpose of personal gain. In so doing, the Court imposes a new, subjective limitation on the scope of the duty owed by insiders to shareholders. The novelty of this limitation is reflected in the Court's lack of support for it. * * *

The fact that the insider himself does not benefit from the breach does not eradicate the shareholder's injury. It makes no difference to the shareholder whether the corporate insider gained or intended to gain personally from the transaction; the shareholder still has lost because of the insider's misuse of nonpublic information. The duty is addressed not to the insider's motives, but to his actions and their consequences on the shareholder. Personal gain is not an element of the breach of this duty. * * *

The improper purpose requirement not only has no basis in law, but it rests implicitly on a policy that I cannot accept. The Court justifies Secrist's and Dirks' action because the general benefit derived from the violation of Secrist's duty to shareholders outweighed the harm caused to those shareholders, in other words, because the end justified the means. Under this view, the benefit conferred on society by Secrist's and Dirks' activities may be paid for with the losses caused to shareholders trading with Dirks' clients. * * *

In my view, Secrist violated his duty to Equity Funding shareholders by transmitting material nonpublic information to Dirks with the intention that Dirks would cause his clients to trade on that information. Dirks, therefore, was under a duty to make the information publicly available or to refrain from actions that he knew would lead to trading. Because Dirks caused his clients to trade, he violated § 10(b) and Rule 10b–5. Any other result is a disservice to this country's attempt to provide fair and efficient capital markets. I dissent.

NOTES

1. In State Teachers Retirement Bd. v. Fluor Corp., 592 F.Supp. 592 (S.D.N.Y.1984), the court held that a tippee can be held liable only if the information was passed to the tippee for the personal benefit of the tipper, and if the tippee knew or had reason to know that the tipper had satisfied all the elements of tipper liability. Subsequent decisions have held that a tipper who misappropriated information can be convicted without showing that he knew his tippee would trade, United States v. Libera, 989 F.2d 596 (2d Cir.1993), and that no causal connection need be shown between the possession of inside information and the decision to trade, United States v. Teicher, 987 F.2d 112 (2d Cir.1993).

2. There is some authority that the tipper who acts in breach of a fiduciary duty need not know that the tippee would trade on the information. In contrast, there is more recent authority that the tippee must know that the tipper acted in breach of a fiduciary duty:

> A tippee is liable only when the inside tipper breached a fiduciary duty in disclosing the material, non-public information, and the tippee knew or recklessly disregarded the fact that the tipper breached a fiduciary duty. Since a tippee's duty is derivative from the insider's, the law does not require that the tippee also owe and violate a fiduciary duty to the tipper.

SEC v. Lambert, 38 F.Supp.2d 1348, 1351 (S.D.Fla.1999).

3. Can a remote tippee shield himself from liability by not inquiring as to the source of information he receives from another tippee? In SEC v. Musella, 678 F.Supp. 1060 (S.D.N.Y.1988), remote tippees, who were experienced stock market investors, "made a deliberate decision not to ask [the intermediate tippee] about the confidential sources they were quite certain [he] had." The court held that the requisite scienter was shown: "I cannot accept that conscious avoidance of knowledge defeats scienter in a stock fraud case."

4. *Temporary insiders.* Under the *Dirks* approach, can a tippee ever be held liable for taking advantage of inside information in a situation where the company source acted properly in disclosing the information because of a pre-existing relationship (in that case, issuer and underwriter)? One court has held that the tippee in that kind of situation may acquire the status of a "temporary insider," subjecting it to the same duties as the person from

whom it obtained the information. SEC v. Lund, 570 F.Supp. 1397 (C.D.Cal. 1983).

5. *Tender Offers*. Section 14(e) of the 1934 Act prohibits "any fraudulent, manipulative, or deceptive acts or practices in connection with any tender offer." Acting under the authority of that provision, the SEC adopted Rule 14e–3, which prohibits any person who is in possession of material information relating to a tender offer [other than the offeror itself] which he knows or has reason to know is (a) nonpublic and (b) has been acquired directly or indirectly from the offeror, the issuer or any persons acting on their behalf, to purchase or sell any securities which are the subject of the offer.

In United States v. Chestman, 903 F.2d 75 (2d Cir.1990), note 3, p. 934 *supra*, the court rejected the application of Rule 10b–5 but also considered whether Rule 14e–3 applied to the conduct there at issue. As noted above, Ira Waldbaum and his family, who owned 51% of the stock of Waldbaum, Inc., entered into an agreement to sell all their stock to the A & P supermarket chain for $50 a share, on condition that A & P then make a tender offer for the remaining stock at the same price. Before the agreement was publicly announced, Ira told his sister Shirley, who in turn told her daughter Susan, who in turn told her husband Keith, each one telling the other not to tell anyone outside the family because that "could ruin the sale." Keith testified that he called his broker Chestman and told him that he "had some definite, some accurate information" that Waldbaum was being sold at a "substantially higher" price than the current market and asked Chestman "what he thought I should do." Chestman was aware that Keith was married to Waldbaum's niece. During that morning, Chestman purchased 11,000 shares of Waldbaum stock for himself and his discretionary accounts at prices ranging from $24.65 to $26 a share. When the tender offer was announced later that day, the price of Waldbaum stock rose to $49 a share. Chestman was convicted of violating Rule 14e–3. Chestman argued that his conviction under Rule 14e–3 should be reversed on the ground that the SEC exceeded its authority under § 14(e) by adopting a rule which imposes liability for trading without finding either misappropriation of information or a fiduciary duty to people on the other side of the market. The three-judge panel voted 2–1 to reverse the conviction, but split three ways on the question of the validity of Rule 14e–3. Judge Miner voted to uphold the validity of the rule, and the conviction, on the ground that Congress gave the SEC broader powers under § 14(e) than under § 10(b), including "a broad congressional mandate to prescribe all 'means reasonably designed' to prevent manipulative acts, including the regulation of nondeceptive activities." Judge Mahoney thought that the conviction should be reversed because § 14(e) only gave the SEC the authority to apply the legal principles developed under Rule 10b–5 to the "novel area" of tender offers, "rather than to constitute an authorization for the Commission to redefine the meaning of the terms 'fraudulent, deceptive or manipulative' as established by authoritative Supreme Court interpretations of § 10(b) and Rule 10b–5, upon which § 14(e) is concededly modeled." Judge Carman thought that the Rule could be held valid on the ground that "in promulgating Rule 14e–3 shortly after the *Chiarella* decision, the SEC seeking to implement the will of Congress as expressed in § 14(e) can be presumed to have contemplated that the rule would be read to include commonly accepted principles and elements associated with fraud," but that Chestman's conviction would have to be reversed because the trial judge had not instructed the jury that all the elements of fraud, including scienter and a knowing breach of duty, would have to be found to support a conviction. The Second Circuit decided to rehear the *Chestman* case *en banc*, and in October 1991 handed down its decision. See 947 F.2d 551. With respect to Rule 14e–3, the court, by a vote of 10 to 1, upheld both the validity of the Rule and Chestman's conviction under it:

> The plain language of § 14(e) represents a broad delegation of rulemaking authority. The statute explicitly directs the SEC to "define" fraudulent practices and to "prescribe means reasonably designed to prevent" such practices. It is difficult to see how the power to "define" fraud could mean anything less than the power to "set forth the meaning of" fraud in the tender offer context. This delegation of rulemaking responsibility becomes a hollow gesture if we cabin the SEC's rulemaking authority, as Chestman urges we should, by common law definitions of fraud. * * *

> Even if we were to accept the argument that the SEC's definitional authority is circumscribed by common law fraud, which we do not, the SEC's power to "prescribe means reasonably designed to prevent" fraud extends the agency's rulemaking authority further. * * * A delegation of authority to enact rules "reasonably designed to prevent" fraud * * * necessarily encompasses the power to proscribe conduct outside the purview of fraud, be it common law or SEC-defined fraud.

Only Judge Mahoney dissented from this portion of the decision, adhering to his position in the panel decision that Rule 14e–3 exceeded the SEC's powers under § 14(e). He described the majority's conclusion that the statutory authorization to the SEC "necessarily encompasses the power to proscribe conduct outside the purview of fraud" as "a truly breathtaking construction of a delegation * * * of the authority to prescribe a federal felony."

6. In United States v. O'Hagan, 521 U.S. 642, 117 S.Ct. 2199, 138 L.Ed.2d 724 (1997), the Supreme Court also upheld the validity of Rule 14e–3 but noted:

> We need not resolve in this case whether the Commission's authority under § 14(e) to "define ... such acts and practices as are fraudulent" is broader than the Commission's fraud-defining authority under § 10(b), for we agree with the United States that Rule 14e–3(a), as applied to cases of this genre, qualifies under § 14(e) as a "means reasonably designed to prevent" fraudulent trading on material, nonpublic information in the tender offer context. A prophylactic measure, because its mission is to prevent, typically encompasses more than the core activity prohibited. As we noted in Schreiber v. Burlington Northern, § 14(e)'s rulemaking authorization gives the Commission "latitude," even in the context of a term of art like "manipulative," "to regulate nondeceptive activities as a 'reasonably designed' means of preventing manipulative acts, without suggesting any change in the meaning of the term 'manipulative' itself." We hold, accordingly, that under § 14(e), the Commission may prohibit acts, not themselves fraudulent under the common law or

§ 10(b), if the prohibition is "reasonably designed to prevent ... acts and practices [that] are fraudulent."

It thus remains to be seen whether Rule 14e–3 is an effective end-run around the *Chiarella* duty requirement.

———

In *United States v. Chestman*, 947 F.2d 551 (2d Cir.1991), *cert. denied* 503 U.S. 1004, 112 S.Ct. 1759, 118 L.Ed.2d 422 (1992) (discussed in note 3, p. 934 and note 5, p. 943) the court indicated that the spousal relationship does not by itself create a relationship upon which to base a misappropriation claim under Rule 10b–5. SEC Rule 10b–5–2 alters this by presuming that the necessary fiduciary relationship does exist with respect to spouses. The following case explores that issue as well as the scope of tippee liability generally:

SEC v. YUN

327 F.3d 1263 (11th Cir. 2003).

TJOFLAT, CIRCUIT JUDGE:

This is an insider trading case, brought by the Securities and Exchange Commission ("SEC") under section 10(b) of the Securities Exchange Act of 1934 and (SEC) Rule 10b–5 against Donna Yun and Jerry Burch. Answering special verdicts, a jury found that the defendants had "violated Section 10(b)" under the "misappropriation theory" of liability. Acting on those verdicts, the district court entered judgment against the defendants, holding them "jointly liable" for $269,000, the profits generated by the prohibited trading, plus prejudgment interest, and individually liable for a penalty in the sum of $1,000 * * *

Donna Yun is married to David Yun, the president of Scholastic Book Fairs, Inc., a subsidiary of Scholastic Corporation ("Scholastic"), a publisher and distributor of children's books whose stock is quoted on the NASDAQ National Market System and whose option contracts are traded on the Chicago Board Options Exchange. On January 27, 1997, David attended a senior management retreat at which Scholastic's chief financial officer revealed that the company would post a loss for the current quarter, and that before the quarter ended, the company would make a public announcement revising its earnings forecast downward. He cautioned the assembled executives not to sell any of their Scholastic holdings until after the announcement, which would likely result in a decline in the market price of Scholastic shares, and warned them to keep the matter confidential. Approximately two weeks later, on February 13, Scholastic's chief financial officer informed David that the negative earnings announcement would be made on February 20.

Over the weekend of February 15–16, David and Donna discussed a statement of assets that he had provided her in connection with their negotiation of a post-nuptial division of assets. David explained to Donna that he had assigned a $55 value to his Scholastic options listed on the asset statement, even though Scholastic's stock was then trading at $65 per share, because he believed that the price of the shares would drop following Scholastic's February 20 earnings announcement. He also told her not to disclose this information to anyone else, and she agreed to keep the information confidential.[4]

The following Tuesday, February 18, Donna went to her place of work—a real estate office located in a nearby housing development. The office was a small sales trailer, approximately eleven by thirteen feet, that Donna shared with other real estate agents, including Jerry Burch. During the late morning or early afternoon, Donna telephoned Sam Weiss—the attorney assisting her in negotiating the post-nuptial division of assets—from her office to discuss David's statement of assets. While she was speaking to Weiss, Burch entered the office to gather materials for a real estate client. Standing three to four feet from Donna, Burch heard her tell Weiss what David had said about Scholastic's impending earnings announcement and that David expected the price of the company's shares to fall. As he testified at trial, Burch did not learn enough from what he overheard to feel "comfortable" trading in Scholastic's stock.

That evening, Donna and Burch attended a real estate awards banquet at the Isleworth Country Club. Donna, Burch, and another agent, Maryann Hartmann, carpooled to the reception. All three stayed at the reception for three hours and left together.

The next morning Burch called his broker and requested authority to purchase put options in Scholastic.[6] When the broker advised Burch that he knew of no new information indicating the price of Scholastic stock would decline, Burch stated that based on information he had obtained at a cocktail party, he nonetheless wanted to purchase the put options. The broker warned Burch of the risks of trading in options, and cautioned him about insider trading prohibitions. Despite these warnings, between the afternoon of February 19 and midday on February 20, Burch purchased $19,750 in Scholastic put options, which was equal to two-thirds of his total income for the previous year and nearly half the value of his entire investment portfolio.

After the stock market closed on February 20, Scholastic announced that its earnings would be well below the analysts' expectations. When the market opened the next day, the price of Scholastic shares had dropped approximately 40 percent to $36 per share. Burch then sold his Scholastic puts, realizing a profit of $269,000—a 1,300 percent return on his investment. Within hours, the SEC commenced an investigation of Burch's trades to determine whether insider trading had occurred. The investigation culminated in the present lawsuit. In a one-count complaint, the SEC

---

4. David anticipated that Donna would discuss this information with her attorney, but assumed her attorney would keep the information confidential.

6. A put option is an option contract that gives the holder of the option the right to sell a certain quantity of an underlying security to the writer of the option, at a specified price up to a specified date. The value of a put increases as the price of the stock decreases.

alleged that Donna and Burch had violated section 10(b) of the Exchange Act and Rule 10b–5 and sought both legal and equitable relief.

There are two theories of insider trading liability: the "classical theory" and the "misappropriation theory." The classical theory imposes liability on corporate "insiders" who trade on the basis of confidential information obtained by reason of their position with the corporation.[11] The liability is based on the notion that a corporate insider breaches "a . . . [duty] of trust and confidence" to the shareholders of his corporation. *United States v. O'Hagan,* 521 U.S. 642, 652, 117 S.Ct. 2199, 2207, 138 L.Ed.2d 724 (1997). The misappropriation theory, on the other hand, imposes liability on "outsiders" who trade on the basis of confidential information obtained by reason of their relationship with the person possessing such information, usually an insider. The liability under the latter theory is based on the notion that the outsider breaches "a duty of loyalty and confidentiality" to the person who shared the confidential information with him.[13]

Not only are the insider and the outsider forbidden from trading on the basis of the confidential information they have received, they are forbidden from "tipping" such information to someone else, a "tippee," who, being fully aware that the information is confidential, does the trading. In other words, the insider and outsider are forbidden from doing indirectly what they are forbidden from doing directly. To establish liability, however, the SEC need not show that the tippee actually traded for the tipper and gave him the profits of the trades; all the SEC needs to show is that the tipper received a "benefit," directly or indirectly, from his disclosure. *See Dirks,* 463 U.S. at 659–62, 103 S.Ct. at 3264–65.

As stated *supra,* to prevail in an insider trading case, the SEC must establish that the misappropriator breached a duty of loyalty and confidentiality owed to the source of the confidential information. Certain business relationships, such as attorney-client or employer-employee, clearly provide the requisite duty of loyalty and confidentiality. On the other hand, it is unsettled whether non-business relationships, such as husband and wife, provide the duty of loyalty and confidentiality necessary to satisfy the misappropriation theory. The leading case on when a duty of loyalty and confidentiality exists in the context of family members—the case relied on by the parties and the district court for the elements of a confidential relationship—is *United States v. Chestman,* 947 F.2d 551 (2d Cir.1991) (en banc).

In a divided en banc decision, the Second Circuit held that marriage alone does not create a relationship of loyalty and confidentiality. *Id.* at 568. Either an "express agreement of confidentiality" or the "functional equivalent" of a "fiduciary relationship" must exist between the spouses

---

11. In this opinion, the words "confidential information" mean "material, nonpublic information."

13. We think that "a duty of loyalty and confidentiality" is synonymous with "a duty of trust and confidence," and, accordingly, we use the expressions interchangeably.

for a court to find a confidential relationship for purposes of § 10(b) and Rule 10b–5 liability. Since the spouses had not entered into a confidentiality agreement, the court turned its focus to determining what constitutes a fiduciary relationship or its functional equivalent. "At the heart of the fiduciary relationship," the court declared, "lies reliance, and de facto control and dominance." *Id.* at 568 (citations and internal quotation marks omitted). Having so concluded, the court explained that the functional equivalent of a fiduciary relationship "must share these qualities." *Id.* at 569. Applying the requisite qualities of reliance, control, and dominance to the husband and wife relationship at hand, the *Chestman* majority held that no fiduciary relationship or its functional equivalent existed. The spouses' sharing and maintaining of "generic confidences" in the past was insufficient to establish the functional equivalent of a fiduciary relationship. *Id.* at 571. Accordingly, the court decided that the defendants were not subject to sanctions for insider trading violations.

A lengthy dissent by Judge Winter, joined by four judges, took issue with the narrowness in which the majority would find a relationship of loyalty and confidentiality amongst family members, pointing out that under the majority's approach, the disclosure of sensitive corporate information essentially could be "avoided only by family members extracting formal, express promises of confidentiality." *Id.* at 580. Such an approach, in the view of the dissent, was "unrealistic in that it expects family members to behave like strangers toward each other." Moreover, the normal reluctance to recognize obligations based on family relationships— the concern that intra-family litigation would exacerbate strained relationships and weaken the sense of mutual obligation underlying family relationships—was inapplicable in insider trading cases because the suits are brought by the government. Given the circumstances of the case, the dissent concluded that a confidential relationship existed between the husband and wife which gave rise to a duty of loyalty and confidentiality on his part not to disclose the sensitive information.[21]

We are inclined to accept the dissent's view that the *Chestman* decision too narrowly defined the circumstances in which a duty of loyalty and confidentiality is created between husband and wife. We think that the majority, by insisting on either an express agreement of confidentiality or a strictly defined fiduciary-like relationship, ignored the many instances in which a spouse has a reasonable expectation of confidentiality. In our view, a spouse who trades in breach of a reasonable and legitimate expectation of confidentiality held by the other spouse sufficiently subjects the former to insider trading liability. If the SEC can prove that the husband and wife had a history or practice of sharing business confidences, and those confidences generally were maintained by the spouse receiving the information, then in most instances the conveying spouse

---

21. In the context of family-controlled businesses, the dissent noted, "it is inevitable that from time to time normal familial interactions will lead to the revelation of confidential corporate matters to various family members[, and] the very nature of familial relationships may cause the disclosure of corporate matters to avoid misunderstandings among family members or suggestions that a family member is unworthy of trust." *Chestman,* 947 F.2d at 579.

would have a reasonable expectation of confidentiality such that the breach of the expectation would suffice to yield insider trading liability. Of course, a breach of an agreement to maintain business confidences would also suffice. [23]

For purposes of this case, then, the existence of a duty of loyalty and confidentiality turns on whether David Yun granted his wife, Donna, access to confidential information in reasonable reliance on a promise that she would safeguard the information. If the SEC presented evidence that David and Donna had a history or pattern of sharing business confidences, which were generally kept, then Donna could have been found by the jury to have breached a duty of loyalty and confidentiality by disclosing to Burch the information regarding Scholastic's upcoming earnings announcement. Similarly, if the SEC presented evidence that Donna had agreed in this particular instance to keep the information confidential, then Donna could have been found to have committed the necessary breach of a duty of loyalty and confidentiality.

We conclude that the SEC provided sufficient evidence both that an agreement of confidentiality and a history or pattern of sharing and keeping of business confidences existed between David and Donna Yun such that David could have reasonably expected Donna to keep confidential what he told her about Scholastic's pending announcement. First, the SEC presented evidence that Donna explicitly accepted the duty to keep in confidence the business information she received. She testified that she considered the information confidential because, "David always told me, anything that he talks to me in regards to the company is confidential and can't go past he or I." That she fully understood and agreed to the understanding of confidentiality is further manifested by the fact that she declined to disclose any information about David's company to her attorney until she had "absolute certainty that there was confidentiality with everything [she] was sharing with him." Second, both David and Donna testified that David repeatedly shared confidential information about Scholastic with Donna, including information regarding its sales goals. This certainly qualified as a history or pattern of sharing business confidences. Overall, the SEC presented evidence upon which a jury could find that a duty of loyalty and confidentiality existed between David and Donna Yun; the SEC therefore established the first element of a "misappropriation theory" claim.

---

23. Our conclusion is bolstered by statements the SEC has made since the trading in this case took place. SEC Rule 10b5–2, which became effective August 24, 2000, defines three non-exclusive circumstances "in which a person has a duty of trust or confidence for purposes of the 'misappropriation' theory of insider trading." 17 C.F.R. § 240.10b5–2 (2002) (preliminary note). * * * While the SEC's new rule goes farther than we do in finding a relationship of trust and confidence (e.g., the new rule creates a presumption of a relationship of trust and confidentiality in the case of close family members), the following language on the background of the rule supports the conclusion we reach: "[T]he Chestman majority's approach does not fully recognize the degree to which parties to close family and personal relationships have reasonable and legitimate expectations of confidentiality in their communications." Proposed Rules, Securities and Exchange Commission, Selective Disclosure and Insider Trading, Dec. 28, 1999, 64 Fed. Reg. 72590–01, 72602.

Having reached this conclusion, we turn to the question of whether the evidence was sufficient to show that Donna breached her duty to David. * * *

First, we note that there is no reason to distinguish between a tippee who receives confidential information from an insider (under the classical theory) and a tippee who receives such information from an outsider (under the misappropriation theory). In either case, the tippee is under notice that he has received confidential information through an improper breach of a duty of loyalty and confidentiality. And should the tippee nonetheless trade on the confidential information, his potential liability would not vary according to the theory—classical or misappropriation— under which the case is prosecuted. Finally, the harm to the securities market from such trading would not differ depending on whether the tippee received the confidential information from an insider or an outsider; the integrity of, and investor confidence in, the securities markets are undermined by either method of insider trading.

Given that the position of a tippee is the same whether his tipper is an insider or an outsider, it makes "scant sense" for the elements the SEC must prove to establish a § 10(b) and Rule 10b–5 violation to depend on the theory under which the SEC chooses to litigate the case. The tippee's liability should be determined under the same principles. And for better or worse, the Supreme Court has required that the only way to taint a tippee with liability for insider trading is to find a co-venture with the fiduciary, and that co-venture exists only if the tipper intends to benefit.[29] To equalize the position of tippees under both theories of liability, therefore, it is necessary to require an outsider who tips to have intended to benefit by his tip.

Requiring an intent to benefit regardless of the theory of insider trading liability also serves to equalize the positions of tippers. Since under both theories of liability the tipper is breaching a duty of loyalty and confidentiality by disclosing confidential information, and since the harm to marketplace traders is identical under either breach, it again makes "scant sense" to impose liability more readily on a tipping outsider who breaches a duty to a source of information than on a tipping insider who breaches a duty to corporate shareholders.

---

29. As discussed above, explicit in *Dirk's*s benefit requirement is that a tippee's liability hinges on the tipper's expectation of a benefit. The SEC's position that the benefit requirement is inextricably linked to the insider's duty to corporate shareholders, therefore, while accurate, is incomplete. The benefit requirement is also inextricably linked to the tippee's duty. As one commentator stated regarding the *Dirks* benefit requirement: This portion of the Court's opinion merges a discussion of the necessary state of mind for tippee liability (a scienter concept) with a discussion of the nature of the breach necessary to create tipper liability. One can read the opinion in two ways: (1) the personal benefit requirement is imposed because it provides an objective test for determining whether there has been the requisite notice to the tippee, or (2) the personal benefit requirement is imposed because it states the only situation in which the insider has contravened the policy underlying the abstain or disclose rule, that of avoiding unjust enrichment. Donald C. Langevoort, *Insider Trading Regulation, Enforcement, and Prevention* § 4:3 n. 7 (2002).

Nevertheless, the SEC urges us to hold that the breach by an outsider is unique from a breach by an insider. In the SEC's view, there is no need to show that the misappropriating outsider intended to benefit. A breach of duty to the principal occurs when the outsider makes unauthorized disclosure of the confidential information in a way that harms the principal; the harm done to the principal constitutes a breach—whether or not the outsider intends to "profit" from the unauthorized disclosure. We conclude, however, that no good reason exists to treat the two types of breaches differently. Under the common law, a corporate insider breaches a duty of loyalty and confidentiality by disclosing confidential information (rather than trading or tipping on that information) just as much as a misappropriating outsider who discloses the information. And the "harm" to corporate shareholders under the classical theory could be just as—if not more—egregious than the harm to the source of the information under the misappropriation theory. Yet, the Supreme Court in *Dirks* held that such a disclosure is insufficient to constitute a "breach" for purposes of imposing classical insider trading liability;[30] for there to be a "breach," the tipping insider must act with the goal of benefitting personally. To equate the positions of tippers, we find it appropriate to require the SEC to show that a misappropriating outsider expected to benefit from the disclosure. Mere disclosure by itself is insufficient to constitute a breach.[32]

* * * § 10(b) "does not catch all conceivable forms of fraud involving confidential information; rather, it catches fraudulent means of capitalizing on such information through securities transactions." Should we adhere to the SEC's approach of imposing liability merely because the outsider "harmed" the principal in some way, however, the outsider potentially could be liable for insider trading where not even the slightest intent to trade on securities existed when he disclosed the information.[34]
* * *

---

30. By insisting on an intent to benefit, the Supreme Court indicated that the common law principles of fiduciary duty were not to be adhered to strictly in the insider trading context. After all, an "intent to benefit" is clearly not an essential element of a case against a fiduciary under the common law.

32. We note that the SEC's argument that mere disclosure is sufficient to constitute the requisite breach for imposing insider trading liability is simply an extension of the same argument it made in *Dirks:* "an insider invariably violates a fiduciary duty to the corporation's shareholders by transmitting nonpublic corporate information to an outsider when he has reason to believe that the outsider may use it to the disadvantage of the shareholders. Thus, regardless of any ultimate motive ... [the insider] breached his duty to ... [the corporate shareholders]." *Dirks,* 463 U.S. at 666 n. 27, 103 S.Ct. at 3267 n. 27 (internal quotation marks omitted). The Supreme Court rejected that argument.

34. Suppose the CEO of a public company decides, after conferring with select members of the company's management, to confide in his wife that he is an alcoholic and is entering a rehabilitation center. Suppose he has continually confided with her over the years and she has never broken his trust. Also suppose that the day after he enters rehab, his wife discovers that he was having a love affair with another woman. Angry, the wife decides to humiliate her husband by disclosing his alcohol problems to the local newspaper editor. The editor is savvy, and realizes that news of the CEO's alcoholism would likely cause the stock price to fall. Accordingly, the editor buys put options in the husband's company before printing the story. When the story hits the newsstand, and the stock price falls, the editor makes lots of money. The question is whether the wife and the editor are liable. The information regarding her husband's alcoholism is material and nonpublic, the wife breached a duty of loyalty and confidentiality with her husband, the editor was aware of the wife's breach, and the husband is harmed (emotionally, financially, and in

Requiring an intent to benefit in both classical and misappropriation theory cases equalizes the positions of tippers and tippees and is also consistent with Supreme Court precedent. Perhaps the simplest way to view potential insider trading liability is as follows: (1) an insider who trades is liable; (2) an insider who tips (rather than trades) is liable if he intends to benefit from the disclosure; (3) an outsider who trades is liable; (4) an outsider who tips (rather than trades) is liable if he intends to benefit from the disclosure.

* * * The showing needed to prove an intent to benefit is not extensive. The Supreme Court in *Dirks,* after establishing the tipper benefit requirement, proceeded to define "benefit" in very expansive terms. The Court declared that not only does an actual pecuniary gain, such as a kickback or an expectation of a reciprocal tip in the future, suffice to create a "benefit," but also cases where the tipper sought to enhance his reputation (which would translate into future earnings) or to make a gift to a trading relative or friend.

In this case, the SEC presented evidence that the two appellants were "friendly," worked together for several years, and split commissions on various real estate transactions over the years. This evidence is sufficient for a jury reasonably to conclude that Donna expected to benefit from her tip to Burch by maintaining a good relationship between a friend and frequent partner in real estate deals. *See Sargent,* 229 F.3d at 77 (finding evidence of personal benefit when the tipper passed on information "to effect a reconciliation with his friend and to maintain a useful networking contact"). Accordingly, the SEC has sufficiently established the second element of a misappropriation theory claim—a breach of a duty of loyalty and confidentiality.

* * * In conclusion, we AFFIRM the district court's decisions denying appellants' motions for judgment as a matter of law. Because we find prejudicial error in the district court's instruction on the elements of the misappropriation theory of liability, we VACATE the court's judgment and REMAND the case for a new trial.

NOTE

Tipping the barber: a close shave with the law? In SEC v. Maxwell, 341 F.Supp.2d 941 (S.D.Ohio 2004), the court refused to find liability based on an alleged tip from a senior executive to his barber. The court found that the relationship between a customer and his barber is not a confidential relationship so as to support liability under Rule 10b–5.

––––––

terms of his reputation). But, the wife did not disclose the information with the intent that anyone would trade or benefit; she merely wanted to harm her husband emotionally.

Under the SEC's approach the wife would be liable for the disgorgement of all of the editor's profits. The securities laws, however, are not designed to impose liability on a person who had no intent to trade or manipulate the market. Section 10(b) requires fraud "in connection with" the purchase or sale of securities. *Id.*

SECTION 5. INSIDER TRADING: USE VERSUS POSSESSION

SEC v. ADLER

137 F.3d 1325 (11th Cir.1998).

ANDERSON, CIRCUIT JUDGE:

In this case, the appellant Securities and Exchange Commission ("SEC") brought a civil action against appellees.... The SEC seeks treble damages for these alleged violations under the Insider Trading Sanctions Act of 1984, 15 U.S.C. § 78u–1. * * *

The SEC argues that the district court erred as a matter of law in granting summary judgment for Pegram in regard to his 1989 transactions in Comptronix stock because, in concluding that Pegram's preexisting plan to sell stock rebutted any reasonable inference of scienter created by the suspicious timing of his sales, the district court improperly considered whether Pegram used inside information in his trading. The SEC argues that the district court incorrectly adopted a causal connection standard for insider trading violations that allows a trader to avoid liability if the trader proves that he did not purchase or sell securities because of the material nonpublic information that the trader knowingly possessed. The SEC argues that it presented evidence that Pegram knowingly possessed material nonpublic information, and thus Pegram, as a corporate director, violated the prohibition against insider trading found in § 10(b), Rule 10b–5, and § 17(a) because, "whether or not Pegram used the inside information," Pegram traded in his company's stock while in possession of material nonpublic information.

At the time of Pegram's September 1989 sales, it is clear that Pegram *possessed* nonpublic information. * * *

Surprisingly, few courts have directly addressed whether § 10(b), Rule 10b–5, and § 17(a) require a causal connection between the material nonpublic information and the insider's trading or whether knowing possession of material nonpublic information while trading is sufficient for liability. * * *

In addition to the Supreme Court's language in Chiarella, Dirks, and O'Hagan, several cases arguably provide support for the proposition that there is no violation of § 10(b) and Rule 10b–5 in the absence of some causal connection between the material nonpublic information and an insider's trading. In a number of cases, courts have allowed insiders to introduce evidence of preexisting plans or other "innocuous" reasons for sales in order to rebut an inference of scienter. * * *

We view the choice between the SEC's knowing possession test and the use test advocated by Pegram as a difficult and close question of first impression. It is apparent from the foregoing discussion that there is no definitive guidance on this issue from the Supreme Court. However, we believe that Supreme Court dicta and the lower court precedent suggest that the use test is the appropriate test. The strongest argument that has been articulated in support of the knowing possession test is that a strict use test would pose serious difficulties of proof for the SEC. It is true that it often would be difficult for the SEC to have to prove that an insider used the inside information, i.e., that the inside information has a causal connection to a particular trade. However, we believe that the SEC's problems in this regard are sufficiently alleviated by the inference of use that arises from the fact that an insider traded while in possession of inside information.

We believe that the use test best comports with precedent and Congressional intent, and that mere knowing possession—i.e., proof that an insider traded while in possession of material nonpublic information— is not a *per se* violation. However, when an insider trades while in possession of material nonpublic information, a strong inference arises that such information was used by the insider in trading. The insider can attempt to rebut the inference by adducing evidence that there was no causal connection between the information and the trade—i.e., that the information was not used. The factfinder would then weigh all of the evidence and make a finding of fact as to whether the inside information was used.

We adopt this test for the following reasons. First, of the several arguments in support of the knowing possession test, the strongest is the fact that it often would be difficult for the SEC to prove that an alleged violator actually used the material nonpublic information; the motivations for the trader's decision to trade are difficult to prove and peculiarly within the trader's knowledge. However, we believe that the inference of use, which arises from the fact that the insider traded while in knowing possession of material nonpublic information, alleviates the SEC's problem. The inference allows the SEC to make out its prima facie case without having to prove the causal connection with more direct evidence.

Second, we believe that our approach best comports with the language of § 10(b) and Rule 10b–5, and with Supreme Court precedent. Section 10(b) of the 1934 Act prohibits "any manipulative or deceptive device." Rule 10b–5 and § 17(a) of the 1933 Act prohibit "any device, scheme, artifice to defraud" and "any act, practice, or course of business which operates or would operate as a fraud." Similarly, the Supreme Court has repeatedly emphasized this focus on fraud and deception. See O'Hagan, (stating that "§ 10(b) is not an all-purpose breach of fiduciary duty ban; rather it trains on conduct involving manipulation or deception"). When an insider trades on the basis of material nonpublic information, the insider is clearly breaching a fiduciary duty to the shareholders and deriving personal gain from the use of the nonpublic information. On the other hand, we do not believe that the SEC's knowing possession test would always and inevitably be limited to situations involving fraud. Indeed, O'Hagan, in its discussion of the knowing possession test which has been adopted by the SEC in Rule 14e–3(a) for the tender offer context, recognized that the knowing possession test may prohibit actions that are not themselves fraudulent.

The SEC argues that the knowing possession test is supported by the familiar maxim that an insider has a § 10(b) duty to disclose material nonpublic information or to abstain from trading. However, a trade by an insider with such information does not always and inevitably constitute a breach of the duty. Indeed, in the very case in which the SEC articulated the "disclose or abstain" rule, In re Cady, Roberts & Co., 40 S.E.C. 907, 911 (1961), the SEC also acknowledged a preexisting plan to sell defense; the defense was rejected for failure of proof, not as a matter of legal principle. Id. at 916 (finding that "we do not accept [the defendants'] contention that [one of the defendants] was merely carrying out a program of liquidating the holdings in his discretionary accounts-determined and embarked upon prior to his receipt of the [material nonpublic] information.... The record does not support the contention that [one of the defendant's] sales were merely a continuance of his prior schedule of liquidation.") We construe *In re Cady, Roberts & Co.* as an acknowledgment by the SEC that the analysis we embrace today is not inconsistent with the "disclose or abstain" rule.* * *

In sum, we believe that the strong inference of use which arises from the fact that an insider traded while in possession of material nonpublic information suffices to alleviate the SEC's difficulties in proving use. We believe that our approach best comports with the statutory focus on fraud. See Chiarella, 445 U.S. at 234–35 ("[s]ection 10(b) is ... a catchall, but what it catches must be fraud"). Furthermore, we do not believe our approach is inconsistent with the "disclose or abstain" doctrine. * * *

We conclude that these fact-intensive issues should be decided by a jury, which is in the position to observe the demeanor of witnesses and make appropriate credibility determinations. Accordingly, the judgment as a matter of law in favor of Pegram as to the 1992 transactions is reversed.

Notes

1. Accord United States v. Smith, 155 F.3d 1051, (9th Cir.1998). The SEC subsequently acquiesced in a use test when it adopted SEC Rule 10b5–1 which provides safe harbors for avoiding the presumption of actual use of information that might otherwise be inferred from trading while in possession of material nonpublic information. Specifically, the rule permits the insider to adopt in advance a trading plan or appoint a disinterested party to direct trading in the securities in the insider's company. This provision proved to be controversial after Kenneth Lay, chairman and chief executive officer of the Enron Corp., sold millions of dollars of the company's stock just before it imploded. The sales were made pursuant to a pre-existing plan whereby $4 million in stock was sold every two weeks over an eight month period. Daniel Altman, "When Insider's Sales are a Long Term Plan," N.Y. Times, May 19, 2002, § 3, at 1. Martha Stewart, the house decorating and cooking doyenne, claimed that her sales of ImClone stock just before the company announced

bad news that caused a sharp drop in prices was the result of a prior plan. Investigators were seeking to determine whether the sales were actually due to a tip from the former chairman of that company who was a personal friend of Ms. Stewart and who was arrested for his own sales. Neil Buckley *et al.*, "Martha Stewart Broker Suspended," Financial Times, June 22, 2002, at 1. Stewart was subsequently convicted of making false statements to government officials concerning the basis for her trading, and the SEC sued her for insider trading. A senior SEC staff member warned that executives using a plan to sell their securities cannot delay announcing negative news concerning sales in order to protect the price of their sales.

2.   The problem with the federal regulation of insider trading is the fact that in 1942, Rule 10b–5 was not designed to combat insider and outsider trading as we know it today. This structure has left much confusion and many gaps. Is it really all that difficult to draft a legislative prohibition against insider trading? Consider the following Directive No. 89/592 adopted by the European Community in 1989, directing its member states to adopt such rules:

Article 1. Interpretation

For the purposes of this Directive:

1.   "inside information" shall mean information which has not been made public of a precise nature relating to one or several issuers of transferable securities or to one or several transferable securities, which, if it were made public, would be likely to have a significant effect on the price of the transferable security or securities in question;

2.   "transferable securities" shall mean:

(a) shares and debt securities, as well as securities equivalent to shares and debt securities;

(b) contracts or rights to subscribe for, acquire or dispose of securities referred to in (a);

(c) futures contracts, options and financial futures in respect of securities referred to in (a);

(d) index contracts in respect of securities referred to in (a);

when admitted to trading on a market which is regulated and supervised by authorities recognized by public bodies, operates regularly and is accessible directly or indirectly to public.

Article 2. Prohibited activities

1.   [Principal prohibition on primary insiders] Each Member State shall prohibit any person who:

—by virtue of his membership of the administrative, management or supervisory bodies of the issuer,

—by virtue of his holding in capital of the issuer, or

—because he has access to such information by virtue of the exercise of his employment, profession or duties, possesses inside information from taking advantage of that information with full knowledge of the facts by acquiring or disposing of for his own account or for the account of a third party, either directly or indirectly, transferable securities of the issuer or issuers to which that information relates.

2. [Companies as primary insiders] Where the person referred to in paragraph 1 is a company or other type of legal person, the prohibition laid down in that paragraph shall apply to the natural persons who take part in the decision to carry out the transaction for the account of the legal person concerned.

3. [Dealing in securities through professional intermediary] The prohibition laid down in paragraph 1 shall apply to any acquisition or disposal of transferable securities affected through a professional intermediary.

Each Member State may provide that this prohibition shall not apply to acquisitions or disposal of transferable securities effected without the involvement of a professional intermediary outside a market as defined in Article 1(2) *in fine*.

4. [Exemption for state and public authority activities] This Directive shall not apply to transactions carried out in pursuit of monetary, exchange-rate or public debt-management policies by a sovereign state, by its central bank or any other body designated to that effect by the state, or by any person acting on their behalf. Member States may extend this exemption to their federated states or similar local authorities in respect of the management of their public debt.

Article 3. Primary insider not to disclose information

Each Member State shall prohibit any person subject to the prohibition laid down in Article 2 who possesses inside information from:

(a) disclosing that inside information to any third party unless such disclosure is made in the normal course of the exercise of his employment, profession or duties;

(b) recommending or procuring a third party, on the basis of that inside information, to acquire or dispose of transferable securities admitted to trading on its securities markets as referred to in Article 1(2) *in fine*.

Article 4. Secondary insiders

Each Member State shall also impose the prohibition provided for in Article 2 on any person other than those referred to in that Article who with full knowledge of the facts possesses inside information, the direct or indirect source of which could not be other than a person referred to in Article 2.

SECTION 6. CIVIL LIABILITY
FOR INSIDER TRADING

The decision in *Chiarella v. United States*, page 916 above, makes it clear that a supposed duty to investors cannot by itself trigger Rule 10b–5's disclose or abstain obligation. It follows that, even if a violation can be premised on the misappropriation theory, no private remedy will lie for traders on the other side of the illegal trades. See e.g., Moss v. Morgan Stanley Inc., 719 F.2d 5 (2d Cir.1983) (finding no private remedy on the same facts that gave rise to criminal liability in a related action). Thus, while a private suit might exist for true insider trading, it does not for violations based on the misappropriation theory. Recall *Goodwin v. Agassiz*, page 847, 186 N.E. 659 in Chapter 14, where a common law fraud action failed because of the absence of duty in open market transactions. In view of the prevailing uncertainty as to the availability of a private damage remedy for insider trading and as to the adequacy of existing penalties in deterring insider trading, the SEC urged Congress to enact stiffer sanctions. Congress responded with two pieces of legislation, the Insider Trading Sanctions Act of 1984 (ITSA) and the Insider Trading and Securities Fraud Enforcement Act of 1988 (ITSFEA), adding new sections 20A and 21A to the Securities and Exchange Act of 1934.

Under § 21A, if any person violates the 1934 Act or any rule thereunder by trading while in possession of material nonpublic information, or by communicating such information in connection with a securities transaction, the SEC can go to court to seek a civil penalty equal to three times the amount of the profit gained or the loss avoided by the illegal transaction. "Profit" or "loss" is defined as the difference between the purchase or sale price and the value of the security at a reasonable period after public dissemination of the nonpublic information. The SEC may seek such a penalty both against the person who committed the violation and from any person who "controlled" the violator (which, in most cases will mean the firm with which the violator is associated). The penalty imposed on the "controlling person" cannot exceed $1 million and can only be imposed if the SEC establishes that such person knowingly or recklessly failed to take appropriate steps or establish adequate procedures to prevent such violations. The amount of the penalty is reduced by any amount the defendant is required to disgorge in an injunction action brought by the Commission under § 21(d).

To provide an incentive for people to "blow the whistle" on insider trading, § 21A(e) provides that up to 10% of any civil penalty recovered by the SEC may, in the SEC's discretion, be paid as a bounty to any person or persons who provide information leading to the imposition of the penalty. In June 1989, the SEC issued rules and guidelines governing the award of these bounties. See Rules 61–68 of SEC Rules of Practice, 17 C.F.R. § 201.61–68, and Securities Exchange Act Release No. 26994 (June 30, 1989).

Under § 20A, any person who violates the 1934 Act or any rule thereunder by trading while in possession of material nonpublic information is liable to any person who was "contemporaneously" trading the same security on the other side of the market (this in effect reverses the result in *Moss v. Morgan Stanley*). Liability under this Section also extends to any person who communicates material nonpublic information and to any person who "controls" the violator, and is similarly reduced by the amount of any disgorgement in an injunction action brought by the SEC.

An action under either § 20A or § 21A may be brought up to five years after the last violation, a considerably longer statute of limitations[a] than is found in other specific civil liability provisions of the federal securities laws.

The 1988 amendment also modified § 32 of the 1934 Act to increase the maximum criminal penalty for violation of the Act from $100,000 to $1 million, in the case of individuals, and from $500,000 to $2.5 million, in the case of other entities.

NOTES

1. Does the SEC's treble penalty create double jeopardy concerns if there is a parallel criminal prosecution?

2. In Hudson v. United States, 522 U.S. 93, 118 S.Ct. 488, 139 L.Ed.2d 450 (1997), the Court severely narrowed an earlier decision (United States v. Halper, 490 U.S. 435, 109 S.Ct. 1892, 104 L.Ed.2d 487 (1989)) and held that there is a strong presumption that Congress' designation of a sanction as civil means that it is not punitive and that a court must find the "clearest proof" before the legislative label of a civil sanction is disregarded so as to invoke the prohibition on double jeopardy. Consequently, it is unlikely that a civil penalty, such as the one imposed by ITSA, will be viewed as criminal in nature. See SEC v. Palmisano, 135 F.3d 860 (2d Cir.1998) (double jeopardy did not preclude disgorgement action even though restitution had been ordered in prior criminal action; however, payments to victims in the criminal action are to be credited to any disgorgement order in the subsequent SEC disgorgement action); United States v. Gartner, 93 F.3d 633 (9th Cir.1996) (disgorgement order was not punishment under the double jeopardy clause of the Constitution since the damages bore a reasonable relationship to the damages and other costs incurred as a result of the wrongful conduct); SEC v. O'Hagan, 901 F.Supp. 1461 (D.Minn.1995) (double jeopardy did not bar disgorgement action; dismissal of criminal count was not res judicata in subsequent enforcement action); United States v. Teyibo, 877 F.Supp. 846 (S.D.N.Y.1995) (prior civil action did not bar subsequent criminal proceeding); SEC v. Monarch Funding Corp., 1995 WL 152185, [1995 Transfer Binder] Fed. Sec. L. Rep. (CCH) ¶ 98,613 (1995) (disgorgement, unlike forfeiture, is purely civil and thus not subject to double jeopardy). See also, e.g., SEC v.

---

a. The Sarbanes–Oxley Act of 2002, increased the limitations period for fraud from one year to two years after discovery of the violation but in no event more than five years after the violation.

Monarch Funding Corp., 983 F.Supp. 442 (S.D.N.Y.1997) (collateral estoppel did not apply to disgorgement since the calculation of the profit was incorrectly considered in sentencing guidelines and thus was not necessary to the outcome of the proceeding but collateral estoppel did apply to earlier finding that defendant committed securities fraud).

3.   The Sarbanes–Oxley Act of 2002, Pub. L. No. 107–204 contains a prohibition on insider trading during a Section 401(k) blackout period. This was the result of the problems encountered by employee participants in the Section 401(k) retirement program of the Enron Corporation that subsequently became bankrupt. During a changeover of plan managers, employee participants could not liquidate their Enron stock as it was plunging. Corporate officers, however, were selling large holdings outside the Section 401(k) plans before the company's bankruptcy.

SECTION 7.   SEC ENFORCEMENT OF INSIDER TRADING PROHIBITIONS

A common question asked by students is how do insider traders get caught? There is actually an elaborate network of market surveillance conducted by the SEC and FINRA, the self regulatory organization for NASDAQ and the New York Stock Exchange. Unusual trading patterns are examined. If, for example, there was a lot of buying or selling shortly before a significant event affecting a company, such as a merger, the SEC and SROs will determine who was trading and investigate to determine whether those persons had connections with the company or its insiders. This may involve following a "pipeline" of tippees back to the source. The SEC's surveillance and enforcement efforts are becoming increasingly sophisticated. Numerous celebrities and senior corporate officials have been caught engaging in insider trading. A number of young lawyers and investment bankers involved in merger and acquisition activity have also been caught by the SEC and have had their careers destroyed.

Another source for SEC actions and criminal prosecutions is the use of informants, who have often themselves been caught insider trading and are seeking to reduce their sentence by "cooperating" with the government by implicating others. In one high-profile case, Dennis Levine, a managing director at Drexel Burnham, was the center of a highly publicized insider trading ring. Levine, who was paid a million dollars a year at Drexel Burnham, used a group of informants to provide him with inside information. The members of that ring included various investment bankers and a partner at a New York law firm that specialized in mergers and acquisitions. Levine made over $12 million from insider trading in the stock of fifty-four companies between June of 1980 and December of 1985. He was caught after an anonymous letter was sent to the lawyers of a brokerage firm (Merrill Lynch) from Venezuela advising that an account of the Swiss Bank Leu that was being traded from that bank's office in the Bahamas was receiving only profitable transactions. Brokers were "piggy-backing" on that account by trading off its orders. This was reported to the SEC by the brokerage firm, and the SEC staff began investigation of that account. The SEC was told that the identity of the owner of the account could not be disclosed under the bank secrecy laws of the Bahamas. The SEC, however, placed pressure on the Bahamian bank, and it eventually revealed Levine's name.

Levine pleaded guilty to felony charges, and became a government informant, naming Ivan Boesky, a Wall Street arbitrageur and corporate raider who became famous as an advocate of greed. Boesky was barred from the securities business and agreed to pay a fine of $100 million. In order to lessen his own sentence, Boesky implicated Martin Siegel, a high profile investment banker, and others in insider trading. One of those targeted by Boesky for various misconduct was Michael Milken, an investment banker at Drexel Burnham Lambert who had become notorious as a result of his trading and underwriting "junk" (high-risk) bonds that were frequently used as a source of funds to raid other corporations. Milken pled guilty to several felony counts and was fined $600 million and sent to prison for three years. *Jerry W. Markham, A Financial History of the United States, From the Age of Derivatives to the New Millennium (1970–2001)* 124–125 (2002).

An SEC investigation of insider trading or other misconduct may initially be "informal," which means that the SEC staff has not been given subpoena authority. A formal investigation is commenced with a formal order of investigation that grants the staff such authority. Many individuals have been prosecuted criminally for making false statements to the SEC in the course of its investigations. One of the world's largest accounting firms was charged with obstructing justice by shredding documents and changing a memorandum in anticipation of an SEC informal investigation. That conviction destroyed the accounting firm, which cost the jobs of tens of thousands of employees worldwide. Carrie Johnson, "Andersen May Ask Judge to Overturn Conviction," Wash Post, June 20, 2002, at EO3.

The SEC will subpoena and examine phone records, bank accounts and other documents in the course of a formal investigation in order to determine how information was passed to tippees. It will also subpoena the individuals involved and examine them on the record under oath about their activities. Frequently, inside traders will seek to conceal their trading by using secret bank accounts directed from abroad. Derivative contracts are also often used in inside trading, as seen in the *O'Hagan* case. The leverage they provide gives the inside trader more bang for the buck, i.e., the insider can make more money with less capital investment by buying options, for example. The SEC, therefore, keeps close watch over such trading.

A case having both international aspects and derivatives trading involved large amounts of options (3000 contracts) bought through the Pacific Stock Exchange on the stock of Santa Fe International just before the public announcement that Santa Fe was being purchased by the Kuwait Petroleum Corporation. Most of those options were purchased through Credit Suisse. In another instance, St. Joe Minerals Corporation had been the target of heavy trading in stock and options just before the announcement that Joseph E. Seagram & Co. would be making a tender offer for the company's stock. That trading was conducted through foreign accounts, mostly in Switzerland. The SEC pursued the trail in both instances and after much effort was able to pierce the veil of the Swiss bank secrecy laws. The traders eventually had to disgorge much of their profits, including some $8 million made on the St. Joe deal. See SEC v. Tome, 638 F.Supp. 596 (S.D.N.Y.1986). The SEC entered into a Memorandum of Understanding ("MOU") with Switzerland, and later numerous other jurisdictions, that allowed the SEC and Justice Department officials to have access to even secret bank accounts where inside trading is suspected. See SEC v. Certain Purchasers, Fed Sec. L. Rep. (CCH) ¶ 91,151 (S.D.N.Y. 1985) (describing SEC MOU with Switzerland and difficulties encountered by SEC in obtaining the identity of the purchasers of the Santa Fe options).

Indexes of securities, as well as agricultural and other commodities, are the subject of trading through commodity futures. The Commodity Futures Trading Commission ("CFTC") was created by Congress in 1974 to act as an analogue to the SEC in the futures and commodity option markets. At the direction of Congress, in 1986, the CFTC conducted a study of insider trading in the futures markets. The CFTC report essentially rejected the application of insider trading concepts to the futures markets because most information in those markets is "market" information that is not peculiar to any one company in the same way inside information is used about an issuer in the securities industry. For example special knowledge about a disease that would affect soybean production and prices is market information that people typically trade on and is useful to efficient pricing. See CFTC, A Study in the Nature, Extent and Effects of Futures Trading by Persons Possessing Material Nonpublic Information (Sept. 1986).

The CFTC report also rejected application of a misappropriation theory in the futures markets unless it was government information such as a crop report or advance knowledge of exchange actions that could affect prices. In July of 1998, however, two individuals pled guilty to mail and wire fraud after they made over $4.7 million from information obtained from John W. Henry & Co., a large money manager. One of the defendants worked as a trader at that firm. He had advance knowledge of the firm's planned trades, which were large enough to have market effect. He would then tip his accomplice, a young lawyer, who would trade in advance of the company and profit when the company's trades hit the market. The government charged that the defendants had misappropriated information from John W. Henry & Co. and that they were front running the trades of that organization. Despite the CFTC's prior report that rejected insider trading and misappropriation in the futures industry, the CFTC charged in a related civil action that this conduct also violated the Commodity Exchange Act. The defendants were sentenced on the criminal charges to 33 months in prison. Bloomberg News, "2 Traders Sentenced for Insider Trading," N.Y. Times, Dec. 10, 1998, at B14.

The Commodity Exchange Act ("CEA"), the statute that governs transactions in commodity futures, was amended in 2008 to state that nothing in its anti-fraud prohibition obligates any person to disclose 'nonpublic information that may be material to the market price, rate, or level of the commodity or transaction, except as necessary to make any statement made to ... [an]other person in or in connection with the transaction not misleading in any material respect. 7 U.S.C. § 6b(b). As noted earlier, this is consistent with the common law view enunciated in Laidlaw v. Organ, 15 U.S. (2 Wheat) 178, 4 L.Ed. 214 (1817), page 842, above.

The Commodity Futures Modernization Act of 2000 ("CFMA") allowed the trading of commodity futures contracts on single stocks, a practice that had previously been banned. Pub. L. No. 106–554, 114 Stat. 2763. For a description of the regulatory scheme for stock futures, see Susan C. Ervin, Single Stock Futures, 34 Sec. & Comm. Reg. 243 (Nov. 14, 2001). The legislation provides for joint jurisdiction between the CFTC and SEC. William J. Brodsky, "New Legislation Permitting Stock Futures: The Long and Winding Road," 21 J. Intl. L. Bus. 573 (2001). How will this affect insider trading standards? Among other things, the National Futures Association ("NFA") (the futures industry analogue to NASD Regulation) was required by the CFMA to conform its customer protection rules to those in the securities industry as a precondition for stock futures to be traded by futures industry markets and registrants. The NFA has adopted a rule prohibiting violations of SEC Rule 10b–5, which would include a proscription against inside trading.

NOTE

There seems to be no limitation on the variations of insider trading. Lionel Thotam pleaded guilty to trading on tips received from Davi Thomas, a post office employee. Thomas read the column "Inside Wall Street" from *Business Week* magazine to Thotam over the telephone when the magazine reached his postal facility in advance of being distributed to the public. Two employees of the company printing the magazine were tipping two of their friends on information in the column. The friends made $1.4 million from their trading, paying the two printing plant employees $50 per week for the tips, later increasing that amount to $200. All four pled guilty to insider trading charges.

The husband of a legal secretary at Skadden Arps Slate Meagher & Flom LLP was tipping a friend on mergers being handled by the partner his wife worked for at the law firm. The husband and the individual he tipped pled guilty to insider trading and other criminal charges. John Freeman, a temporary word processor, was charged with tipping at least ten others on mergers that were being handled by Goldman Sachs while he worked there. The individuals he tipped then tipped others, bringing the number of persons charged to nineteen. This gang made profits of over $1 million. Freeman pled guilty to criminal charges.

Diane C. Neiley, an executive assistant at BetzDearborn, Inc. tipped her boyfriend who tipped his father on a proposed merger of her company with Hercules, Inc. The word spread quickly, and the SEC sued a total of eighteen individuals for trading on that information. An executive secretary at Betz-Dearborn tipped a friend, who tipped his brother, who tipped his fellow investment club members. Still another secretary at the company tipped her husband, who tipped his accountant. Olga S. Litvinsky, a secretary at J P Morgan Chase & Co, tipped her future husband on the acquisition.

Goldman Sachs traded on inside information about the decision by the Department of Treasury to discontinue the thirty-year bond that was announced on October 31, 2001. The firm had been tipped by a political consultant who had attended an "embargoed" Treasury press conference describing the change. The consultant phoned the information to a Senior Economist at Goldman Sachs, John M. Youngdahl, twenty-five minutes before the embargo on disclosure of the information was lifted, but only eight minutes before a Treasury official inadvertently posted the announcement online. In that period, Goldman Sachs bought $84 million in thirty-year bonds and bond futures covering another $233 million, resulting in profits of $3.8 million. Youngdahl pled guilty to charges of inside trading and other misconduct for misuse of this information. He was sentenced to two years and nine months in prison and paid the SEC a civil penalty of $240,000. Goldman Sachs agreed to pay $9.3 million to settle charges brought by the SEC. An executive at the Massachusetts Financial Services Company was tipped by the same political consultant on the embargoed information and traded $65 million in bonds for portfolios he managed. Massachusetts Financial Services agreed to pay a penalty of $200,000 and to reimburse $700,000 to the company selling the Treasury bonds.

Rick Marano, an analyst for Standard & Poor's, was indicted in 2004 for insider trading in the stock of companies under review at his firm. Marano and others that he tipped made more than $1 million from that information. Brokers at Merrill Lynch, Citigroup and Lehman Brothers were indicted for crimes that included accepting payments from day traders for access to their squawk boxes, which announced large customer orders that the day traders would then front run. This squawk box information was broadcast to the sales forces of broker-dealers.

CHAPTER 17

MERGERS AND ACQUISITIONS

■ ■ ■

SECTION 1. INTRODUCTION

Businesses often combine with each other through a number of procedures such as a merger or a purchase of assets. In a merger, two corporations combine into one. The constituent companies may agree to a share exchange that would result in combining the two sets of shareholders. Alternatively, an acquiring corporation may acquire shares of another corporation (the "target") through open market purchases, privately negotiated transactions, or the use of a tender offer that offers to buy the stock of some or all of the existing shareholders. The acquired company is then merged with the acquiror. In an asset purchase, the acquiring company purchases some or all of the assets of the target company, leaving the selling company as an entity that is either dissolved or continues in business with any assets that remain after the asset sale or through the acquisition of new assets.

The merger and acquisition process is often a complicated one, both in the context of business requirements and legal restrictions. A key business consideration is the valuation of the transaction: how much is the buyer willing to pay? The valuation process is aided by investment bankers who analyze the target company's financial position. The investment bankers issue opinions on the fairness of the price proposed for an acquisition. These "fairness opinions" have been the subject of litigation on such issues as whether an adequate investigation was made before the opinion was rendered and whether the opinion was independently rendered. In determining whether the price is fair, investment bankers use a number of objective measures, including price-to-earnings ratios, return on equity, and EBITA (earnings before interest, taxes and depreciation). There may also be intangible factors, such as asset quality, management, and cost savings, to consider in the valuation process. A large corporation may also be willing to pay more for a small company than its earnings or other objective measures might warrant in order to gain access to a new market.

A matter of much concern in most business combinations is the assumption of the liabilities of a company that is being acquired. The surviving corporation assumes the assets and liabilities of both constituent corporations in a merger. An asset purchase of the target company will generally isolate the selling corporation's liabilities from those of the seller, unless there is a degree of continuity that convinces a court that the operations of the old and new owners are one and the same. Alternatively, an acquiring corporation may decide to make the target company a subsidiary. This will isolate the liabilities of the subsidiary from those of the acquiring company, unless the corporate veil can be pierced. Such an acquisition may involve simply a purchase of the stock of the target or the transaction may be structured through an exchange of stock.

When an agreement in principle is reached on a merger, the parties may memorialize that agreement in a letter of intent, which is followed by a more definitive merger agreement. The parties then prepare proxy materials for shareholder approval, and seek to obtain all necessary regulatory approvals. Due diligence investigations must be undertaken to assure the parties are receiving what they bargained for from each other. Due diligence involves, among other things, an examination of the books and records of the company being acquired (or both parties in the event of a merger) and an inspection of important assets, particularly loans, to assure they are accurately represented.

———

DUE DILIGENCE IN PRIVATE M & A TRANSACTIONS

By E. Paul Quinn.
34 Rev. Sec. & Commod. Reg. 253 (2001).

The Term "due diligence" originally comes from the Securities Act of 1933 where it is a defense that boards of directors and underwriters have to liability for the failure to make material disclosures in public offerings. Today the term "due diligence" is also commonly known as the background investigation that a buyer does of a target company in an acquisition transaction. * * *

The due diligence investigation helps identify potential impediments to an acquisition. There are all sorts of potential impediments which might affect the timing of an acquisition, but the more common impediments include governmental and third party consents. One common governmental consent is the antitrust approval often required under the Hart–Scott–Rodino Antitrust Improvements Act of 1976 (the "HSR Act"), which is administered by the U.S. Federal Trade Commission and U.S. Department of Justice. Generally speaking, pursuant to the HSR Act, if the buyer and target are of sufficient size and the acquisition involves more than $50 million of consideration for the assets or stock of a target company, a filing will be required with the U.S. Federal Trade Commission. After the filing has been made, there is a statutory thirty-day waiting period before the acquisition may be completed, which may be shortened by the parties or extended by the government under certain circumstances. It is also possible that other governmental consents will be required in connection with the acquisition, especially if the target company operates in a heavily regulated industry. For example, if the target company is a radio or television station, the consent of the U.S. Federal Communications Commission may be required or if the target company is a bank, insurance company, common carrier, or defense contractor, the consent of another regulatory agency may be required.

The third party consents that may be required in a transaction will vary depending on (i) the manner in which the acquisition is structured— that is, whether the acquisition is by way of merger, stock purchase or asset purchase, (ii) the wording of the contracts and organizational documents of the buyer and target company, and (iii) applicable law. For example, if an acquisition is structured as an asset purchase, consents may be required for many of the commercial contracts to which the target company is a party because the asset purchase will constitute an assignment of the contract and most commercial contracts prohibit assignment without the consent of all contracting parties. On the other hand, if the acquisition is structured as a merger or stock purchase, there often are not many third party consents necessary under commercial contracts because the target company continues in existence as a party to the contract and there is no actual assignment of the contract to a different legal entity. However, some commercial contracts contain "change of control" provisions that are triggered by a merger or stock purchase and therefore require consent prior to the transaction. In addition, the organization documents to which a target company is subject, such as the articles of incorporation and bylaws (or their equivalent), may contain restrictions on whether the acquisition can be completed without the approval of certain parties, such as a minimum percentage of the current equityholders of the buyer or target company. Finally, a buyer should review the corporate and other laws of the state in which the target company is organized to find out whether there are any special statutory requirements necessary to consummate the acquisition, such as a super-majority vote of the current equity holders of the target company. It is important to identify early on in the due diligence investigation whether these types of consent are necessary, the costs associated with obtaining them, and the time required to obtain them. * * *

Most importantly, the due diligence investigation helps identify potential liabilities that may affect the value of the target company. Such liabilities, if discovered early in the process, may help the buyer to renegotiate the price of the target company or may allow it to specifically allocate such liabilities to the target company or the owners of the target company. Of course, if the potential liabilities are too large, their discovery may cause the buyer not to enter into the agreement or, if the agreement has already been signed, but not been closed, to terminate the agreement.

The principal areas investigated by buyers during their due diligence include the following: organizational status, material contracts, labor, employee benefits, litigation, environmental and safety, tax, intellectual property and real estate. The structure of the acquisition will have some impact on the degree to which a buyer investigates some of these areas.

For example, if the acquisition is structured as an asset purchase, as opposed to a stock purchase or merger, the buyer will spend less time on organizational, tax, and employee benefit matters because it is not acquiring a legal entity in an asset purchase. Some investigation of these areas, however, is still necessary because certain potential liabilities can still attach to the buyer in an asset acquisition under the common law doctrines of "de facto merger" and "successor liability," or statutory bulk sales laws. * * *

Investigation of material agreements, including acquisition and financing agreements, customer and supplier agreements, and joint venture agreements, should be undertaken to understand any (i) hidden or unexpected liabilities or rights, (ii) change of control or anti-assignment provisions, (iii) non-compete or non-solicitation provisions, or (iv) other restrictions on business operations or plans. Review of prior acquisition and financing documents, including disclosure schedules listing exceptions to be representations and warranties, often provides information on existing or contingent contractual liabilities of which the buyer may be unaware. Such liabilities can take the form of indemnification obligations, preemptive rights or rights of first refusal that third parties may possess, or ongoing non-compete or non-solicitation obligations. When reviewing key customer and supplier agreements, particular attention should be given to pricing provisions or "most-favored nation provisions" that may restrict profits and operational flexibility in the future, the term of the agreement (including the rights of the parties to terminate the agreement and under what circumstances) to determine whether the agreements are likely to be long-term or short-term in duration, and non-compete and non-solicitation provisions which may restrict future business. If the target company has any joint venture agreements, a buyer will be interested in knowing, among other things, the rights and obligations of the respective parties to the joint venture and its assets, how the joint venture is managed and controlled, the sharing of profits and losses, what contributions are expected to be made by the parties to the joint venture in the future and the term of the joint venture.

Investigation into labor matters involves a review of employment agreements, employment manuals and policies, union contracts, if applicable, and records of any labor problems. With respect to employment agreements, a buyer is interested in knowing (i) whether the key employees of the target company are subject to enforceable noncompete, nonsolicitation, assignment of intellectual property and/or confidentiality obligations, and (ii) whether any special payments will be triggered as a result of the acquisition, and if so, who will bear responsibility for the payments. To the extent that key employees are not subject to such protective agreements, the buyer may want to have them enter into such agreements as a condition to the acquisition closing. As to union contracts, the buyer will want to know whether the collective bargaining agreement or union contract to which the target company is a party has any anti-assignment provisions or change of control provisions requiring or making it advisable for the buyer or the target company to seek the approval of the union prior to the acquisition. Finally, a buyer will be interested in finding out about the labor relations of the target company by reviewing any grievance logs, state equal employment opportunity claims, National Labor Relations Board claims, and the frequency of any strikes or similar disruptions to the target company's business.

Employee benefits due diligence involves a review of compliance issues, funding issues, and acceleration-of-benefits issues. * * * To the extent that a target company has any self-insured plans, the buyer will want to review and assess the possible loss exposure of any pending claims and ensure that the target company has stop loss insurance coverage if losses become excessive. The buyer will want also to determine whether the target company is subject to any multi-employer plans and potential withdrawal liabilities from such plans or whether it has any retiree medical liabilities, all of which are common when the target company's employees are represented by unions. In addition, a buyer will want to know whether there are any employee benefits that will accelerate and/or become payable as a result of the acquisition such as stock appreciation rights, bonus payments and/or similar compensation, and who will bear responsibility for such benefits. * * *

The litigation investigation typically consists of a review of (i) any outstanding or threatened litigation and other similar claims and proceedings with internal and any outside legal counsel for the target company and the related pleadings and correspondence, (ii) the most recent audit response letters from legal counsel to the target company and its auditor's management letters to the target company's board of directors, and (iii) judgment searches in federal and state courts located in the jurisdictions in which the target company is domiciled and does business. It is important to review any settled or completed litigation or other disputes to determine whether the target company is prone to any particular types of legal claims or disputes, which may give the buyer an idea of the potential future exposure for such matters. The buyer's lawyers should also carefully assess the answers they receive from the target company's lawyers as to the likelihood and the potential exposure of an adverse decision with respect to the target company's pending or threatened legal matters.

The environmental and safety issues investigated by a buyer typically fall into two broad categories—compliance issues and clean-up issues. A buyer's analysis of compliance issues typically includes a review of whether the target company: (i) has obtained the appropriate environmental permits for its facilities and operations; (ii) complies and has complied with the terms of those permits and applicable environmental laws; and (iii) has appropriate safeguards, warnings and programs in place for employees in the workplace with respects to potentially dangerous chemicals and conditions. An analysis of compliance issues should cover not only the compliance status of the target company but also the risk for fines and penalties from non-compliance and possible capital costs for upgrades or modifications necessary for the target company's operations to reach and maintain compliance. * * *

The investigation of intellectual property involves a determination of: (i) what intellectual property the target company has; (ii) whether the target company has record and good title to such intellectual property with the U.S. Patent and Trademark Office in the case of patents, trademarks and tradenames, with the U.S. Copyright Office in the case of copyrights, and with a domain name service provider in the case of internet domain names; and (iii) whether the target company has infringed another party's intellectual property rights or whether another party has infringed the target company's intellectual property rights. In addition to intellectual property that is registered with a governmental agency, the buyer will want to review and understand any contractual license agreements, such as software license agreements, to which the target company is a party. Among other things, the buyer will want to ensure that after the acquisition such licensed intellectual property will be usable by the buyer if the target company is a licensee, or available as a source of license fee revenue if the target company is a licensor. * * *

Real estate due diligence typically involves a review of the target company's owned and leased real property. With respect to owned real property, the buyer will want to know: (i) whether record title to the owned real property is in the name of the target company; (ii) whether there are any easements or other encumbrances of record, which should be identified by a title insurance policy, and whether there are any other encumbrances not of record such as encroachments on the real property by others; or (iii) whether there are any other parties with a right to occupy or possess the property, which should be identified by a survey of the property. In addition to a review of the title insurance policies and surveys it often is advisable for the buyer to engage an engineer or similar expert to perform a physical inspection of any buildings located on the property, especially manufacturing facilities, to ensure that there will not be unforeseen repairs needed shortly after the closing of the acquisition. An investigation of the target company's leased property involves a review of the lease or sublease agreements that allow the target company to occupy its properties, with particular attention to when each lease expires, and whether any party has an option to purchase the property, and whether a consent will be necessary from the landlord or lessor prior to the closing of the acquisition. * * *

––––––––

The foregoing discussion applies equally to transactions involving closely held corporations as well as to those public companies that are subject to SEC disclosure requirements. If a public company is involved, then the planners need to consider the requirements of the federal securities laws. Post merger operational issues must also be considered. An acquiring company must determine how to combine its record keeping operations with those of the company being acquired. How will their computer systems interface? Are there duplicative operations that need to be closed? How many people will be laid off and how will those decisions be made?

Another matter of concern is the role and protection of the shareholders involved in an acquisition. Will the shareholders of any or both involved corporations be entitled to vote on the transaction? The duty of care may raise issues as to actions taken by the board of directors in considering whether to recommend shareholder approval of a merger. See Smith v. Van Gorkom, 488 A.2d 858 (Del.1985) discussed in Chapter 216. Fairness issues arise once the acquiring corporation has control of the target corporation. Control in such situations may be used to treat the remaining minority shareholders unfairly by trying to squeeze them out or denying them some benefit available to the majority. In addition, the form selected for a business combination will determine whether either set of shareholders is entitled to statutory rights of appraisal that are available to dissenting shareholders. These issues are discussed in this chapter.

SECTION 2.   FORMS OF COMBINATION

A.   PRELIMINARY CONSIDERATIONS

An examination of mergers and acquisition begins with a brief overview of the various forms that an acquisition can take. First, some general observations are in order. The choice of form may be driven by the entity that the parties want to survive the combination. It must be understood, however, that there may be various ways to achieve the desired end result. In addition, many, if not most, corporations are the result of a multi-step acquisition process. As a result, several forms may be involved. For example the acquirer could begin the acquiring process through open market share purchases and/or privately negotiated share purchases to be followed by a tender offer for a controlling interest which in turn is to be followed by a merger of the two entities.

The choice of form for one or more stages of an acquisition involves a variety of factors. These factors may include the financial realities of the parties, corporate law issues such as voting and appraisal rights of dissenting shareholders, the impact of securities laws, tax implications, and whether the combination is a friendly or a hostile one. A number of factors will enter into the choice of the post-combination entity. Once the post-combination entity has been decided upon there are still a myriad of questions that must be addressed by the lawyers and business professionals planning the transaction.

In studying the many acquisitions that led to the cases to be discussed in this course, we will be analyzing how these factors come into play. Before embarking on an analysis of the cases, the following is an introduction to some of the more common considerations that factor into the choice of form for a business combination.

There are a variety of procedures that can be used for a combination. A business combination can be structured as a merger (or consolidation). The acquiring corporation may acquire shares of the target through open market purchases, privately negotiated transactions, or the use of a tender offer. The constituent companies may agree to a share exchange that would result in combining the two sets of shareholders. The acquiring company may purchase the assets and not assume the liabilities of the target company, leaving the target company to continue in business with any assets that remain after the asset sale, acquire new assets and continue or be dissolved. Each of these procedures will be governed by the different provisions of the corporate law of the constituent companies' states of incorporation.

Convenience of statutory procedures. The team planning the business combination will search for the most convenient statutory procedure (e.g. merger, consolidation, sale of assets, etc.) for effectuating the combination. For example, a company's agreements with creditors or bondholders may require waivers or approval before that company can be acquired. However, a company's agreements with creditors ordinarily will not come into play if that company acquires another.

Liability exposure. Planners of the transaction will examine the businesses of the constituent companies. If one of the constituent companies has existing or contingent liabilities, there will be concern for exposing the assets of the other company to these liabilities. Of particular concern is potential product liability exposure. For example, this has been a major concern in corporate combinations involving tobacco companies. Another common concern is whether there are any potential liabilities under the environmental laws, particularly Superfund liability.[1]

Shareholder voting. Another important factor involves the role of the shareholders in any acquisition. In particular, which set of shareholders (if any) will get to vote on the transaction? In the first instance, voting rights will be determined by the law of the state of incorporation. However, if no vote is required under state law but a company's shares are traded on the New York Stock Exchange (NYSE), the NYSE 20% rule provides that if a transaction requires the issuance of new shares in excess of 20% of the number already traded, a shareholder vote is required for the company to continue the listing and trading of its stock on the NYSE.

Special concerns over minority or dissenting shareholders. Frequently, one of the companies prior to the acquisition has a group of controlling shareholders. Alternatively, in a multi-step acquisition, at some point, the company to be acquired becomes one that is controlled by the acquiring

---

1. Superfund liability which results from environmental damage was established in 1980 by the Comprehensive Environmental Responses, Compensation, and Liability Act of 1980 ("CERCLA"), Pub. L. No. 96–510 Title 1, § 101, 94 Stat. 2767 (1980) (codified at 42 U.S.C. §§ 9601–9675 (1995 & Supp. 2002)).

company. In these situations particular problems may arise with respect to treatment of the minority shareholders in the acquisition process. If the minority interests will not participate in the surviving combined entity, then there may be particular fairness issues that need to be addressed.[2] In addition, the form selected for a business combination will determine whether either set of shareholders is entitled to statutory rights of appraisal that are available to dissenting shareholders.[3]

Application of the federal securities laws. If the transactions are going to be structured on anything other than a cash-for-assets basis, the planners of the transaction must consider the requirements of the federal securities laws. The Securities Act of 1933 requires registration of securities offered in a public offering. That Act has a very broad definition of public offering.[4] It follows that if the acquiring corporation will be issuing shares, there are implications for the Securities Act of 1933. The planners will have to determine if the transaction qualifies for an exemption from 1933 Act registration. If not, then under the statute's terms there will be a public offering and the extensive disclosure document that goes along with a registered offering. If the corporate combination triggers a shareholder vote involving the shareholders of a publicly held company, then there are extensive federal proxy disclosures mandated by section 14 of the Securities Exchange Act of 1934. If the acquiring corporation is going to purchase shares of a publicly traded target company through a tender offer or otherwise (including open market purchases or privately negotiated deals) extensive filings and disclosures will be required by the Williams Act amendments to the Securities Exchange Act of 1934 that are embodied in sections 13(d) of that Act for purchases generally and sections 14(d) and 14(e) for tender offers. At a minimum, to the extent that the transaction involves sales or exchanges of securities the general antifraud proscriptions of SEC Rule 10b–5 will apply to all exchanges, purchases and/or sales. In addition acquisitions involving publicly traded companies can raise issues under the insider short-swing profit provisions of Section 16(b) of the Securities Exchange Act of 1934. Kern County Land Co. v. Occidental Petroleum Corp., 411 U.S. 582, 93 S.Ct. 1736, 36 L.Ed.2d 503 (1973), note 2 page 894 above, and Gold v. Sloan, 486 F.2d 340 (4th Cir.1973), *cert. denied* 419 U.S. 873, 95 S.Ct. 134, 42 L.Ed.2d 112 (1974), note 4, page 896 above.

Tax considerations. Any business combination will have tax consequences. It may be possible, however, to structure the transaction as a nontaxable (and hence tax deferred) event under the provisions of IRC § 368. The federal tax Code classifies the methods of reorganization a bit differently than the corporate law does. Mergers and consolidations are

---

2. See the discussion of fairness at pages 1050–1094 infra.

3. See the discussion at pages 995–1023 infra.

4. For example, the number of offerees is not determinative. What matters is whether there are investors in the pool who lack special sophistication and therefore are typical of average public investors. See, e.g., SEC v. Ralston Purina Co., 346 U.S. 119, 73 S.Ct. 981, 97 L.Ed. 1494 (1953); SEC Rule 506, 17 C.F.R. § 230.506 (2002). See generally Thomas Lee Hazen, Treatise on the Law of Securities Regulation § 4.24 (4th ed. 2002).

known as "A" reorganizations since they may be entitled to tax deferred treatment under IRC § 368(a). An exchange of shares is known as a "B" reorganization and may be subject to IRC § 368(b). A purchase of assets is governed by IRC § 368(c) and is therefore known as a "C" reorganization. Sometimes a corporation will divide and spin-off unwanted assets to its shareholders. Spin-offs, split-offs, and split-ups are corporate divisions whose tax treatment is governed by IRC § 368(d); they are known as "D" reorganizations. A corporate reorganization that does not involve a combination or division is a recapitalization and is governed by IRC § 368(e).

Antitrust and regulatory concerns. Depending upon both the size of the companies and their lines of business there may be antitrust or other regulatory concerns. For example, the Hart Scott Rodino Act's[5] preacquisition notification requirements may require advance notice of the proposed combination and could possibly lead to a review of the transactions to evaluate the antitrust implications. If regulated businesses are involved, then it may be necessary to obtain the approval of the applicable governmental regulatory authority. Thus, for example in the communications industry, the approval of the Federal Communications Commission may be necessary. If the acquisition involves an insurance company, approval of the applicable state insurance commissioners may be necessary. Even in the absence of required regulatory approval, there may nevertheless be regulatory implications. Thus, for example, if the companies are involved in rendering financial services, then there may be regulatory implications with respect to the insurance regulators, the banking regulators, the SEC, and/or state securities regulators.

Accounting issues. Formerly, there was a choice of accounting methods for corporate acquisitions (pooling and purchase method). In 2001, the accounting profession decided that the former pooling method would no longer be an acceptable accounting practice. Even though there is no longer a choice, accounting issues may affect the structure and/or form of the transaction. For example, the form of the acquisition (including determining which company will be the survivor) will have accounting implications and thus the planners may deem one form to be preferable in terms of how to account for the transaction.

B. STATUTORY FORMS OF COMBINATION (MERGERS, CONSOLIDATIONS, AND SHARE EXCHANGES)

The corporate statutes of the various states establish procedures for corporate combinations. The procedures for combinations may vary depending on the form and the particular statutory provision that is implicated. Before examining these statutory procedures, we must consider the structure of the various forms that may be used.

---

5. 15 U.S.C. § 18a (2000). See William J. Kolasky, Jr. & James W. Lowe, The Merger Review Process at the Federal Trade Commission: Administrative Efficiency and the Rule of Law, 49 Admin. L. Rev. 889, 891 (1997).

MERGER

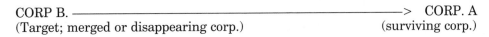

CORP B. —————————————————————————>   CORP. A
(Target; merged or disappearing corp.)   (surviving corp.)

CONSOLIDATION

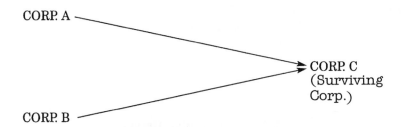

CORP. A

CORP. C
(Surviving
Corp.)

CORP. B

TRIANGULAR MERGERS

A triangular merger is accomplished roughly as follows: The purchasing corporation ("P Corp.") creates a subsidiary corporation ("New Co.") and transfers to the subsidiary shares in the parent corporation which will be used for the share exchange that will be provided for in the merger plan. The subsidiary is sometimes referred to as "phantom" corporation because it may exist only long enough to consummate the merger; hence, at one time, the triangular merger was sometimes called a "phantom" merger or a "reverse phantom merger."

Straight triangular merger. The actual merger transaction is not between the acquiring corporation (P. Corp.) and the acquired corporation ("T Corp." or the target corporation) but rather between New Co., the newly formed subsidiary, and T Corp. In the straight triangular merger, T (or target) corporation is merged into New Co. with the plan of merger calling for the conversion of the prior T shares into P shares (those with which New Co. was funded).

Reverse triangular merger. In the reverse triangular, the subsidiary corporation (New Co.) is merged into T (the target) corporation so that T Corp. will be the survivor. Still, the plan of merger in the reverse triangular will call for the conversion of T shares into P shares. Thus, under either triangular merger, the T (target) shares end up as P Corp. shares. In the straight triangular, P Corp. has total ownership of the acquired-merged corporation because it retains all of the stock of the subsidiary which it created. In the reverse triangular, the subsidiary shares held by P Corp. corporation will be converted under the plan of merger into new voting shares of T (target). Again, P Corp. ends up with total ownership of T (target) and the former T (target) shares are converted into P shares. The triangular nature of the transaction is indicated graphically as follows:

Straight Triangular Merger

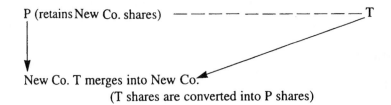

P (retains New Co. shares) —————————————T

New Co. T merges into New Co.
             (T shares are converted into P shares)

Reverse Triangular Merger

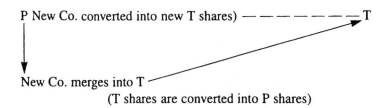

P New Co. converted into new T shares) —————————T

New Co. merges into T
        (T shares are converted into P shares)

The triangular form was conceived to combine many of the advantages of the other forms of acquisitions while hopefully avoiding many of their disadvantages. Consider the following comparison of the triangular merger with other forms of acquisition:

    1.   Comparison of triangular with ordinary two-party merger:

        a) The triangular merger avoids automatic assumption of liabilities by P which would occur in a straight merger,

        b) The triangular merger avoids voting (and therefore appraisal rights) for P shareholders (since P is not a party to the merger); since there is no vote by shareholders, there is also avoided the expense of a P shareholder meeting and compliance by P with proxy rule solicitations;

        c) The subsidiary can be kept in existence, perhaps mitigating problems like:

            1) new labor contracts

            2) impairments of management and employee morale

            3) pension plan problems

            4) impairment of customer relations

    2.   Comparison of triangular with purchase of assets;

a) There is greater flexibility in the types of consideration. P may pay for assets without jeopardizing largely tax free status for T (target) shareholders;

b) The triangular merger avoids problems relating to transfer of title of T assets;

c) The reverse triangular merger allows T to remain in existence in order to avoid termination of contract rights, debt conditions etc.;

d) The triangular merger eliminates the extra step of liquidating T Corp. that would otherwise be involved;

e) The triangular and reverse triangular merger avoid the need for P shareholder vote in these very few states which require a shareholders vote when assets are purchased.

Disadvantage: In the states in which appraisal rights do not attach to sales of assets (e.g., Delaware), the T shareholders will have both voting and appraisal rights (because it is a merger).

3. Comparison of triangular with stock acquisition:

a) There is much greater flexibility in the consideration P may pay without jeopardizing largely tax free status for T shareholders;

b) P is assured of obtaining 100% control of the target;

c) The transaction does not require as high a proportion of T shareholder consent as with an exchange of shares;

Disadvantage: T shareholders will have voting and appraisal rights.

NOTES

1. *Mechanics of a triangular merger.* As is now true under the law of most states, Delaware § 251(b)(5) expressly permits the issuance of the shares of another corporation in connection with a merger. This specifically enables the acquiring company (the subsidiary) to issue shares in its parent as part of the merger with the other constituent corporation (the corporation being acquired). Del. § 251(b)(5). See Note, Three–Party Mergers: The Fourth Form of Corporate Acquisition, 57 Va. L. Rev. 1242 (1971). The Internal Revenue Code was also amended to specifically permit the use of triangular mergers in a tax deferred business combination. IRC § 368(a)(2)(D). The new procedure adopted by the Model Business Corporation Act known as a share exchange (Model Bus. Corp. Act §§ 11.01(f), 11.03).[1] This statutory procedure can be used to effectuate a triangular merger by setting up the "plan" as an exchange of shares between the existing target company shareholders under which they would receive shares in the parent of the subsidiary acquiring the target.

---

1. This procedure was inserted as a new section 72A to the pre 1980 version of the Model Act.

2. One reason to use a triangular merger is to avoid a shareholder vote and/or statutory appraisal rights that would ordinarily apply in a straight merger. Courts have not been receptive to the argument that the appraisal remedy should nevertheless be granted under the *de facto* merger doctrine. See Terry v. Penn Central Corp., 668 F.2d 188 (3d Cir.1981), note 1 page 1029 below.

3. Some legislatures have viewed the triangular merger as an impermissible end-run around the shareholder approval that would be required in a straight merger and have addressed this problem by statute. E.g., Cal. §§ 1200(d), 1201 (requiring approval by parent corporation shareholders in a triangular merger effectuated through the exchange of the parent corporation's shares for shares in the company acquired by the subsidiary). Cal. Corp. Code §§ 1200(d), 1201 (West Supp. 2002).

C. CROSS–ENTITY COMBINATIONS

A business that is a corporation may desire to merge with an unincorporated business. Alternatively, a business that is organized in one form may decide to convert itself into another form. The proliferation of new unincorporated forms of doing business has opened up the field for cross-entity mergers and conversions. The following excerpt describes some of the major issues and legislative developments.

CONVERSION AND MERGER OF DISPARATE BUSINESS ENTITIES
by Robert C. Art
76 Wash. L. Rev. 349 (2001)
Copyright © 2001 Washington Law Review
Association; Robert C. Art

* * *

The new forms of business organization—LLC, LLP, and LLLP—are in a sense artifacts of a federal income tax policy that has since been abandoned.... "Check-the-box" regulations[99] effective in 1997 abandoned the traditional pattern of categorizing non-corporate business entities as either "associations" (like corporations) or partnerships, based on the specified characteristics. Instead, an unincorporated entity can simply elect the tax treatment it prefers.... [T]he LLC, LLP, and LLLP forms not only continue to exist but grow in popularity.... The new organizational forms clearly supplement rather than supplant the older ones. * * *

Statutes authorizing changes in organizational form commonly treat the issue in a haphazard and inconsistent manner, without an apparent rationale. Although merger statutes provide direct and effective means of combining businesses, they apply only to certain combinations. Conversions have rarely been authorized. Where statutes do not explicitly provide for merger or conversion, they are not permitted by common law.

---

99. Treas. Reg. § 301.7701–1 to –3 (1996).

Absence of statutory authority for changing an entity's organizational form or for combining with another entity does not mean that such transactions will not occur. Instead, it means that businesses and their counsel are required to engage in procedures that are more creative, more cumbersome, and more expensive but accomplish the same result.

For example, a partnership can become a corporation or an LLC without benefit of statutory authority. At least three procedures achieve that result:

(1) The partnership dissolves, distributing its net assets in cash or in kind to the former partners. The former partners then transfer the assets to a newly organized corporation or LLC in exchange for stock or LLC membership interests.

(2) The partnership sells its assets to a newly organized corporation or LLC in exchange for the corporation's stock or LLC's membership interests. The partnership then dissolves, distributing its only asset, the stock, to the former shareholders.

(3) The partners transfer their partnership interests to a newly organized corporation or LLC in exchange for stock or membership interests. The corporation or LLC, which has become the sole "partner," dissolves the partnership, acquiring the partnership's assets. * * *

A number of states authorize conversions and mergers of disparate business entities, though in different forms. Since 1988, Delaware has permitted corporations to merge with partnerships,[176] nonprofit corporations,[177] joint-stock associations,[178] and limited partnerships.[179] In addition, Delaware limited partnerships can merge with multiple business entities.[180] Texas amended its corporation act in 1989 to broadly authorize cross-entity conversion and merger.[181] Colorado[182] and Nevada[183] have comprehensive approaches with modernized provisions. Other states that authorize at least some conversion and merger of disparate business entities include California,[184] Georgia,[185] Illinois,[186] Kansas,[187] Mary-

---

176. Del. Code Ann. tit. 8, § 263 (Supp. 2000).

177. Del. Code Ann. tit. 8, § 257 (1974 & Supp. 2000).

178. Id. § 256.

179. Id. § 263.

180. Del. Code Ann. tit. 6, § 17–211 (Supp. 2000).

181. Tex. Bus. Corp. Act Ann. art. 1.02.A(8), (18), (20) (Vernon 1980 & Supp. 2001) (defining conversion, merger, and "other entity"); id. art. 5.01, 5.03, 5.06 (permitting mergers with "other entities"). For a summary of its operation, see Curtis W. Huff, Choice of State of Incorporation—Texas Versus Delaware: Is it Now Time to Rethink Traditional Notions?, Bull. Bus. L. Sec. St. B. Tex., Dec. 1994, at 9, 37.

182. Colo. Rev. Stat. Ann. §§ 7–90–203(1), (2) (West 1999) (allowing domestic entity to merge with one or more domestic or foreign entities).

183. Nev. Rev. Stat. Ann. 92A.005–.510 (Michie 1999).

184. Cal. Corp. Code § 1112 (West 1990) (authorizing corporation merging with nonprofit corporation).

185. Ga. Code Ann. §§ 14–2–1108 to –1109 (1994) (authorizing corporation merging with joint-stock or unincorporated associations or trusts).

186. 32 Ill. Comp. Stat. Ann. 5/11–37 (West 1993) (authorizing corporation merging with nonprofit corporation).

187. Kan. Stat. Ann. §§ 17–6704 to –6708 (1995 & Supp. 1999) (authorizing corporation merging with joint-stock, non-stock, and nonprofit corporation).

land,[188] Oklahoma,[189] Tennessee,[190] and West Virginia.[191] In 1999, the Model Business Corporation Act was amended to authorize mergers of corporations with "other entities," though the reform did not provide for conversions.[192]

D. NOTE ON SALE OF ASSETS TRANSACTIONS

Corporate statutes make a distinction between sales of assets in the regular course of business which can be accomplished without shareholder approval and sales or other dispositions of substantially all of the assets *not* in the ordinary course of business. The latter requires shareholder approval and also triggers shareholder appraisal rights under the law of many states, although no such appraisal rights are granted under the Delaware statute (see pages 1030–1035 below). The statutes generally have two triggers to the shareholder vote requirement. First in order for the sale to be treated as an extraordinary transaction it must be a sale of *substantially all* of the assets. Second, before a shareholder vote is required, the sale must *not* be in the ordinary course of business. Thus, for example, a corporation that rolls over its entire inventory as part of its regular business will not trigger a shareholder vote simply because these transactions involve substantially all of the corporation's assets. Cf. Jeppi v. Brockman Holding Co., 206 P.2d 847 (Cal.1949) (sale of assets by corporation formed for the purpose of disposing of estate's assets was a sale in the ordinary course of business and did not require shareholder approval); Katz v. Bregman, 431 A.2d 1274, 1276 (Del.Ch.1981) ("historically the principal business of Plant Industries, Inc. has not been to buy and sell industrial facilities but rather to manufacture steel drums"). Gimbel v. Signal Companies, Inc., 316 A.2d 599 (Del.Ch.1974), page 983 below, addresses what is meant by *substantially all* of the assets.

E. NOTE ON SHARE ACQUISITIONS AND TENDER OFFERS

Rather than approach management and the directors of the target company, the acquiring company can go directly to the target company

---

188.   Md. Code Ann., Corps. & Ass'ns § 3–102 (1999) (authorizing corporation merging with business trust, limited partnership, LLC, or partnership).

189.   Okla. Stat. Ann. tit. 18, §§ 1084–1087 (West 1999) (authorizing corporation merging with non-stock or nonprofit corporation).

190.   Tenn. Code Ann. § 48–21–101 (1988) (authorizing corporation merging with nonprofit corporation).

191.   W. Va. Code Ann. § 31–1–38 (Michie 1999) (authorizing corporation merging with stock, nonstock, or nonprofit corporation).

192.   Model Bus. Corp. Act §§ 11.01–.02 (1999); Comm. on Corp. Laws, Changes in the Model Business Corporation Act—Fundamental Changes, 54 Bus. Law. 685 (1999).

shareholders and acquire their shares directly, thereby obtaining control of the target company. Shares of the target company can be acquired through private negotiations with shareholders, or in the case of a public company through open market acquisitions. Another mechanism is to make a "tender offer" for a target company's shares—which consists of a general solicitation to all target company shareholders that they sell their shares to the acquirer. Share acquisitions can be based either on a cash purchase or on an exchange of shares (exchanging shares of the acquiring company for shares of the target).

Privately, negotiated share purchases, open market acquisitions of shares, and tender offers, do not require action by the directors of the target company as none of the statutory forms of combination are implicated. Nevertheless since these transactions involve the purchase and sale of securities, the federal securities laws may be implicated. Specifically, the 1968 Williams Act Amendments to the Securities Exchange Act of 1934, implemented a system of full disclosure with respect to control-related share acquisitions of publicly held companies.

Frequently, an acquisition of a target company's shares will be a first step in a multi-step acquisition process. For example, after acquiring control of the target company, there is likely to be a second-step merger or other form of combination in order to create one entity. Also, sometimes a share acquisition program is designed to acquire less than full voting control with a view towards conducting a proxy battle to win control of the target company's board of directors. Federal and state law governing share acquisitions and tender offers are considered in chapter 20 below.

F.   NOTE ON CORPORATE DIVISIONS

If the transaction is not structured as sale and purchase of assets, then the corporate combination may result in the acquisition of unwanted assets. When an acquisition results in unwanted assets, the surviving entity may divest itself of those assets in a variety of ways. Of course, these divestitures are not limited to mergers and acquisitions and can be used any time a company divests itself of assets. For example, a company may decide to divest itself of portions of the business that create product liability exposure as has been done in the tobacco industry. Alternatively, a corporate division may be mandated by the antitrust laws.

The following three diagrams[a] depict spin-off, split-up, and split-off transactions that qualify as "type D" reorganizations under the Internal Revenue Code:

---

a. These diagrams are adapted from Harry G. Henn, Teaching Materials on the Laws of Corporations 921–922 (2d ed. 1986).

[Type D Reorganizations (combining two or more affiliated corporations or effecting a corporation separation by so-called divisive reorganizations):

"Spin-off" (no liquidation):

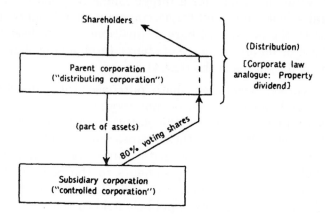

"Split-off" (no liquidation):

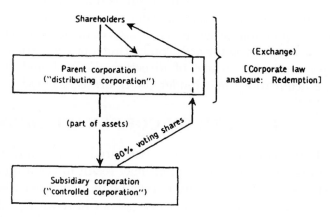

Same as "spin-off", but followed by exchange by the parent corporation with its shareholders of such shares in the subsidiary corporation for some of their shares in the parent corporation.

[A 7782]

In a spin-off, the shares of the subsidiary are distributed to the parent shareholders as a dividend. In a split-off some of the parent shareholders exchange their shares for shares in the subsidiary. After the split-off some of the parent shareholders continue to own parent stock while others now own shares of the corporation that formerly was a subsidiary. In the split-up (see below), the assets are divided between two subsidiaries. The parent then liquidates, passing on the subsidiaries' shares to the parent shareholders as a liquidating dividend.

"Split-up" (complete liquidation of parent corporation):

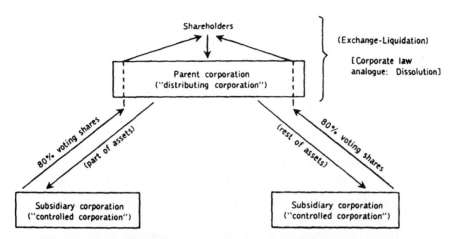

The parent corporation transfers all of its assets to at least two other corporations which have issued or then issue at least 80 percent of their voting shares to it and exchanges such shares for all of its outstanding shares in complete liquidation.]

Formerly, it was possible to use a spin-off to get rid of unwanted assets following a corporate acquisition and have the spin-off not treated as a taxable event. However, in 1997, Congress amended IRC § 355(e) to provide that spin-off transactions of newly acquired assets are taxable events. In order to qualify presumptively for favorable section 355 tax treatment the spin off or other division must involve operating assets that have existed for five years. Notwithstanding this limitation on using newly acquired assets, following the 1997 amendments it is still possible to structure a spin-off of existing assets as a non-taxable event.

SECTION 3. SALE OF ASSETS TRANSACTIONS

GIMBEL v. THE SIGNAL COMPANIES, INC.

316 A.2d 599 (Del.Ch.1974), aff'd, 316 A.2d 619 (Del.1974).

QUILLEN, CHANCELLOR:

This action was commenced on December 24, 1973 by plaintiff, a stockholder of the Signal Companies, Inc. ("Signal"). The complaint seeks, among other things, injunctive relief to prevent the consummation of the pending sale by Signal to Burmah Oil Incorporated ("Burmah") of all of the outstanding capital stock of Signal Oil and Gas Company ("Signal Oil"), a wholly-owned subsidiary of Signal. The effective sale price exceeds

480 million dollars.[1] The sale was approved at a special meeting of the Board of Directors of Signal held on December 21, 1973. * * *

[I]n my judgment, the factual and legal issues are basically reduced to two. First, does the sale require authorization by a majority of the outstanding stock of Signal pursuant to 8 Del.C. § 271(a)? Second, was the action by Signal's Board in approving the 480 million dollar sale price reckless as to justify the entry of a preliminary injunction prohibiting the consummation of the sale?

I turn first to the question of 8 Del.C. § 271(a) which requires majority stockholder approval for the sale of "all or substantially all" of the assets of a Delaware corporation. A sale of less than all or substantially all assets is not covered by negative implication from the statute.

It is important to note in the first instance that the statute does not speak of a requirement of shareholder approval simply because an independent, important branch of a corporate business is being sold. The plaintiff cites several non-Delaware cases for the proposition that shareholder approval of such a sale is required. But that is not the language of our statute. Similarly, it is not our law that shareholder approval is required upon every "major" restructuring of the corporation. Again, it is not necessary to go beyond the statute. The statute requires shareholder approval upon the sale of "all or substantially all" of the corporation's assets. That is the sole test to be applied. While it is true that test does not lend itself to a strict mathematical standard to be applied in every case, the qualitative factor can be defined to some degree notwithstanding the limited Delaware authority. But the definition must begin with and ultimately necessarily relate to our statutory language.

In interpreting the statute the plaintiff relies on Philadelphia National Bank v. B.S.F. Co., 199 A.2d 557 (Ch.1964) rev'd on other grounds, 204 A.2d 746 (Del.1964). In that case, B.S.F. Company owned stock in two corporations. It sold its stock in one of the corporations, and retained the stock in the other corporation. The Court found that the stock sold was the principal asset B.S.F. Company had available for sale and that the value of the stock retained was declining. The Court rejected the defendant's contention that the stock sold represented only 47.4% of consolidated assets, and looked to the actual value of the stock sold. On this basis, the Court held that the stock constituted at least 75% of the total assets and the sale of the stock was a sale of substantially all assets.

[T]he Philadelphia National Bank case dealt with the sale of the company's only substantial income producing asset. The key language in the Court of Chancery opinion in Philadelphia National Bank is the suggestion that "the critical factor in determining the character of a sale of assets is generally considered not the amount of property sold but

---

1. The purchase price consists of 420 million dollars cash to be paid by Burmah at the closing, the cancellation of approximately 60 million dollars in indebtedness of Signal to Signal Oil, and the transfer by Signal Oil to Signal of a 4 3/4% net profits interest in the unexplored portion of Block 211/18 in the North Sea.

whether the sale is in fact an unusual transaction or one made in the regular course of business of the seller." Professor Folk suggests from the opinion that "the statute would be inapplicable if the assets sale is "one made in furtherance of express corporate objects in the ordinary and regular course of the business" Folk, Supra, Section 271, p. 401.

But any "ordinary and regular course of the business" test in this context obviously is not intended to limit the directors to customary daily business activities. Indeed, a question concerning the statute would not arise unless the transaction was somewhat out of the ordinary. While it is true that a transaction in the ordinary course of business does not require shareholder approval, the converse is not true. Every transaction out of normal routine does not necessarily require shareholder approval. The unusual nature of the transaction must strike at the heart of the corporate existence and purpose. As it is written at 6A Fletcher, Cyclopedia Corporations (Perm.Ed. 1968 Rev.) § 2949.2, p. 648:

> "The purpose of the consent statutes is to protect the shareholders from fundamental change, or more specifically to protect the shareholder from the destruction of the means to accomplish the purposes or objects for which the corporation was incorporated and actually performs."

It is in this sense that the "unusual transaction" judgment is to be made and the statute's applicability determined. If the sale is of assets quantitatively vital to the operation of the corporation and is out of the ordinary and substantially affects the existence and purpose of the corporation, then it is beyond the power of the Board of Directors. With these guidelines, I turn to Signal and the transaction in this case.

Signal or its predecessor was incorporated in the oil business in 1922. But, beginning in 1952, Signal diversified its interests. In 1952, Signal acquired a substantial stock interest in American President lines. From 1957 to 1962 Signal was the sole owner of Laura Scudders, a nation-wide snack food business. In 1964, Signal acquired Garrett Corporation which is engaged in the aircraft, aerospace, and uranium enrichment business. In 1967, Signal acquired Mack Trucks, Inc., which is engaged in the manufacture and sale of trucks and related equipment. Also in 1968, the oil and gas business was transferred to a separate division and later in 1970 to the Signal Oil subsidiary. Since 1967, Signal has made acquisition of or formed substantial companies none of which are involved or related with the oil and gas industry. As indicated previously, the oil and gas production development of Signal's business is now carried on by Signal Oil, the sale of the stock of which is an issue in this lawsuit.

According to figures published in Signal's last annual report (1972) and the latest quarterly report (September 30, 1973) and certain other internal financial information, the following tables can be constructed.

SIGNAL'S REVENUES (in millions)

	9 Mos. Ended September 30, 1973	December 31, 1972	1971
Truck manufacturing	$655.9	$712.7	$552.5
Aerospace and industrial	407.1	478.2	448.0
Oil and gas	185.8	267.2	314.1
Other	16.4	14.4	14.0

SIGNAL'S PRE–TAX EARNINGS (in millions)

	9 Mos. Ended September 30, 1973	December 31, 1972	1971
Truck manufacturing	$55.8	$65.5	$36.4
Aerospace and industrial	20.7	21.5	19.5
Oil and gas	10.1	12.8	9.9

SIGNAL'S ASSETS (in millions)

	9 Mos. Ended September 30, 1973	December 31, 1972	1971
Truck manufacturing	$581.4	$506.5	$450.4
Aerospace and industrial	365.2	351.1	331.5
Oil and gas	376.2	368.3	369.9
Other	113.1	102.0	121.6

SIGNAL'S NET WORTH (in millions)

	9 Mos. Ended September 30, 1973	December 31, 1972	1971
Truck manufacturing	$295.0	$269.7	$234.6
Aerospace and industrial	163.5	152.2	139.6
Oil and gas	280.5	273.2	254.4
Other	(55.7)	(42.1)	(2.0)

    Based on the company's figures, Signal Oil represents only about 26%
of the total assets of Signal. While Signal Oil represents 41% of Signal's
total net worth, it produces only about 15% of Signal's revenues and
earnings. Moreover, the additional tables shown in Signal's brief from the
Chitiea affidavit are also interesting in demonstrating the low rate of
return which has been realized recently from the oil and gas operation.

PRE–TAX DOLLAR RETURN ON VALUE OF ASSETS

	9 Mos. Ended September 30, 1973	1972	1971
Truck manufacturing	12.8%	12.9%	8.1%
Aerospace and industrial	7.5	6.1	5.9
Oil and gas	3.6	3.5	2.7

PRE–TAX DOLLAR RETURN ON NET WORTH

	9 Mos. Ended September 30, 1973	1972	1971

Truck manufacturing	25.1%	24.2%	15.5%
Aerospace and industrial	16.8	14.1	14.0
Oil and gas	4.8	4.7	3.9

While it is true, based on the experience of the Signal–Burmah transaction and the record in this lawsuit, that Signal Oil is more valuable than shown by the company's books, even if, as plaintiff suggests in his brief, the $761,000,000 value attached to Signal Oil's properties by the plaintiff's expert Paul V. Keyser, Jr., were substituted as the asset figure, the oil and gas properties would still constitute less than half the value of Signal's total assets. Thus, from a straight quantitative approach, I agree with Signal's position that the sale to Burmah does not constitute a sale of "all or substantially all" of Signal's assets.

In addition, if the character of the transaction is examined, the plaintiff's position is also weak. While it is true that Signal's original purpose was oil and gas and while oil and gas is still listed first in the certificate of incorporation, the simple fact is that Signal is now a conglomerate engaged in the aircraft and aerospace business, the manufacture and sale of trucks and related equipment, and other businesses besides oil and gas. The very nature of its business, as it now in fact exists, contemplates the acquisition and disposal of independent branches of its corporate business. Indeed, given the operations since 1952, it can be said that such acquisitions and dispositions have become part of the ordinary course of business. The facts that the oil and gas business was historically first and that authorization for such operations are listed first in the certificate do not prohibit disposal of such interest. As Director Harold M. Williams testified, business history is not "compelling" and "many companies go down the drain because they try to be historic."

It is perhaps true, as plaintiff has argued, that the advent of multi-business corporations has in one sense emasculated § 271 since one business may be sold without shareholder approval when other substantial businesses are retained. But it is one thing for a corporation to evolve over a period of years into a multi-business corporation, the operations of which include the purchase and sale of whole businesses, and another for a single business corporation by a one transaction revolution to sell the entire means of operating its business in exchange for money or a separate business. In the former situation, the processes of corporate democracy customarily have had the opportunity to restrain or otherwise control over a period of years. Thus, there is a chance for some shareholder participation. The Signal development illustrates the difference. For example, when Signal, itself formerly called Signal Oil and Gas Company, changed its name in 1968, it was for the announced "need for a new name appropriate to the broadly diversified activities of Signal's multi-industry complex."

The situation is also dramatically illustrated financially in this very case. Independent of the contract with Burmah, the affidavit of Signal's Board Chairman shows that over $200,000,000 of Signal Oil's refining and marketing assets have been sold in the past five years. This activity, prior to the sale at issue here, in itself constitutes a major restructuring of the corporate structure.

I conclude that measured quantitatively and qualitatively, the sale of the stock of Signal Oil by Signal to Burmah does not constitute a sale of "all or substantially all" of Signal's assets. This conclusion is supported by the closest case involving Delaware law which has been cited to the Court. Wingate v. Bercut, 146 F.2d 725 (9th Cir.1944). Accordingly, insofar as the complaint rests on 8 Del.C. § 271(a), in my judgment, it has no reasonable probability of ultimate success.

I turn now to the second and more difficult question presented on this application for a preliminary injunction.

The plaintiff attacks the proposed transaction on the grounds that the 480 million dollar sale price is wholly inadequate compensation for the assets of Signal Oil ..... * * * [T]he ultimate question is not one of method but one of value. The method does not appear so bad on its face as to alter the normal legal principles which control. But hasty method which produces a dollar result which appears perhaps to be shocking is significant. On the basis of affidavits relating to value, the Court has the tentative belief that plaintiff would have a reasonable prospect of success on the merits since limited record indicates a gross disparity between the fair market value of Signal Oil on December 21, 1973 and what the Board of Directors were willing to sell the company for, namely, $480,000,000. To the extent the scale tips, on the present record, the nod is to the plaintiff. But I hasten to add that an extremely high security consistent with the figures being discussed, should be required. * * *

In essence, notwithstanding the affidavits and the conflict in their content, there remains a serious question about the reasonable probability that the plaintiff will succeed in this action. Therefore, notwithstanding my tentative conclusion on reasonable probability, I am convinced that the discrepancy between the values is so great that an immediate fuller investigation into this matter of fair value should be had. I have been mindful that, if the preliminary injunction is denied now, the plaintiff may well be barred of any significant relief upon proof which is not conclusive against him and which is of a character sufficiently strong to permit him at least to have the opportunity to sustain his contentions. To deny the injunction may well finally dispose of the case. * * *

NOTES

1. Although 80% may be a rule of thumb for what constitutes substantially all of the assets under the federal tax laws governing corporate combinations, the 80% guideline is not a firm rule in determining when a shareholder vote is necessary for a sale of assets. Consider for example in *Gimbel* the assets sold accounted for only about 26% of the total assets of Signal Companies, Inc. And, while Signal Oil represented 41% of Signal Companies,

Inc. total net worth, it generated only about 15% of Signal Companies, Inc. revenue and earnings. The court, found that this was not a sale of substantially all of the assets. The court relied in part on the *Philadelphia National Bank* case where the court found that 75% of the the assets that represented the sole producing assets could constitute substantially all. In another case, 68% of the assets was held to be substantially all in light of the nature of the assets and their importance to the company. Thorpe v. CERBCO, 676 A.2d 436 (Del.1996).

2. As subsequently reaffirmed by the Delaware Supreme Court, the percentage of the assets transferred is significant but is not necessarily determinative:

> [T]he rule announced in *Gimbel v. Signal Cos.,* Del.Ch., 316 A.2d 599, *aff'd,* Del.Supr., 316 A.2d 619 (1974), makes it clear that the need for shareholder ... approval is to be measured not by the size of a sale alone, but also by its qualitative effect upon the corporation. Thus, it is relevant to ask whether a transaction "is out of the ordinary and substantially affects the existence and purpose of the corporation." [*Gimbel,* 316 A.2d] at 606.

Oberly v. Kirby, 592 A.2d 445, 464 (Del.1991), quoted with approval in Thorpe v. CERBCO, 676 A.2d 436, 444 (Del.1996).

3. *Radical departure test.* In Katz v. Bregman, 431 A.2d 1274, 1276 (Del.Ch.1981), the asset sale constituted over 51% of corporation's total assets and generated approximately 45% of corporation's 1980 net sales. The court found that the sale involved substantially all of the assets in light of the fact that it was planned that "after the sale of National, [the company would] embark on the manufacture of plastic drums [which] represents a *radical departure* from [the company's] *historically successful line of business,* namely steel drums." (emphasis supplied).

4. *Nature of relief.* In the first part of the opinion the court discusses the remedy problem. Both the difficulty of undoing a transaction ("unscrambling the eggs") and the resulting harm to the defendant should preliminary relief be ordered are relevant in any suit seeking to enjoin a corporate transaction.

SECTION 4. SUCCESSOR LIABILITY IN A DE FACTO MERGER

KNAPP v. NORTH AMERICAN ROCKWELL CORP.

506 F.2d 361 (3d Cir. 1974), cert. denied, 421 U.S.
965, 95 S.Ct. 1955, 44 L.Ed.2d 452 (1975).

ADAMS, CIRCUIT JUDGE.

The principal question here is whether it was error to grant summary judgment on the ground that one injured by a defective machine may not recover from the corporation that purchased substantially all the assets of the manufacturer of the machine because the transaction was a sale of assets rather than a merger or consolidation.

Stanley Knapp, Jr., an employee of Mrs. Smith's Pie Co., was injured on October 6, 1969, when, in the course of his employment, his hand was caught in a machine known as a "Packomatic." The machine had been designed and manufactured by Textile Machine Works (TMW) and had been sold to Mrs. Smith's Pie Co. in 1966 or 1967. On April 5, 1968, TMW entered into an agreement with North American Rockwell whereby TMW exchanged substantially all its assets for stock in Rockwell. TMW retained only its corporate seal, its articles of incorporation, its minute books and other corporate records, and $500,000 in cash intended to cover TMW's expenses in connection with the transfer. TMW also had the right, prior to closing the transaction with Rockwell, to dispose of land held by TMW or its subsidiary. Among the assets acquired by Rockwell was the right to use the name "Textile Machine Works." TMW was to change its name on the closing date, then to distribute the Rockwell stock to its shareholders and to dissolve TMW "as soon as practicable after the last of such distributions."

The accord reached by Rockwell and TMW also stipulated that Rockwell would assume specified obligations and liabilities of TMW, but among the liabilities not assumed were: "(a) liabilities against which TMW is insured or otherwise indemnified to the extent of such insurance or indemnification unless the insurer or indemnitor agrees in writing to insure and indemnify (Rockwell) to the same extent as it was so insuring and indemnifying TMW."

Closing took place pursuant to the agreement on August 29, 1968. Plaintiff sustained his injuries on October 6, 1969. TMW was dissolved on February 20, 1970, almost 18 months after the bulk of its assets had been exchanged for Rockwell stock.

Plaintiff filed this suit against Rockwell in the district court on March 22, 1971. He alleged that his injuries resulted from the negligence of TMW in designing and manufacturing the machine and that Rockwell, as TMW's successor, is liable for such injuries. Rockwell joined plaintiff's employer, Mrs. Smith's Pie Co., as a third-party defendant.

Rockwell moved for summary judgment in the district court on June 19, 1973. On September 6, 1973, the district court granted the motion, ruling that Rockwell had neither merged nor consolidated with TMW, that Rockwell was not a continuation of TMW, and that Rockwell had not assumed TMW's liability to Knapp. Therefore, the court concluded, Rockwell was not responsible for the obligations of TMW. On October 11, 1973, Knapp filed a motion for rehearing and reconsideration by the district court, which was denied on November 26, 1973. Knapp appealed to this Court on December 11, 1973.

Both parties agree that this case is controlled by the following principle of law:

> The general rule is that "a mere sale of corporate property by one company to another does not make the purchaser liable for the liabilities of the seller not assumed by it." ... There are, however,

certain exceptions to this rule. Liability for obligations of a selling corporation may be imposed on the purchasing corporation when (1) the purchaser expressly or impliedly agrees to assume such obligations; (2) the transaction amounts to a consolidation or merger of the selling corporation with or into the purchasing corporation; (3) the purchasing corporation is merely a continuation of the selling corporation; or (4) the transaction is entered into fraudulently to escape liability for such obligations. Shane v. Hobam, Inc., 332 F.Supp. 526, 527–528 (E.D.Pa.1971) (decided under New York law).

In light of this language, Knapp contends that the transaction in question "amounts to a consolidation or merger of (TMW) with or into the purchasing corporation (Rockwell)" or, alternatively, that Rockwell is a "continuation" of TMW. Although the TMW corporation technically continued to exist until its dissolution approximately 18 months after the consummation of the transaction with Rockwell, TMW was, Knapp argues, a mere shell during that period. It had none of its former assets, no active operations, and was required by the contract with Rockwell to dissolve itself "as soon as practicable." Knapp urges in effect that the transaction between TMW and Rockwell should be considered a de facto merger.

Rockwell asserts, in defense of the district court's grant of summary judgment, that a merger, a consolidation and a continuation all require that the corporation being merged, consolidated or continued cease to exist. TMW, Rockwell claims, did not go out of existence at the time of the exchange with Rockwell, but continued its corporate life for 18 months thereafter. Further, Rockwell argues, TMW until its dissolution possessed assets of substantial value, in the form of Rockwell stock.

In a diversity case, the federal court must apply the rule of law which would govern if suit were brought in a court of the forum state. We must, therefore, determine how this case would be decided by a Pennsylvania court.

All jurisdictions which have considered the question appear to have accepted not only the general rule that a corporation which purchases the assets of a second corporation is not thereby liable for the obligations of the selling corporation, unless there exists one of the exceptions set out in Shane [v. Hobam, Inc., 332 F.Supp. 526 (E.D.Pa.1971)].

Under *Shane*, the first of the four exceptions rendering the purchasing corporation liable for duties of the seller is a transaction amounting to a merger or consolidation. In a merger a corporation absorbs one or more other corporations, which thereby lose their corporate identity. "A merger of two corporations contemplates that one will be absorbed by the other and go out of existence, but the absorbing corporation will remain." In a consolidation, on the other hand, "all the combining corporations are deemed to be dissolved and to lose their identity in a new corporate entity which takes over all the properties, powers and privileges, as well as the liabilities, of the constituent companies." Another of the *Shane* exceptions to the general rule of nonliability arises when there is a continuation. In a continuation, a new corporation is formed to acquire the assets of an extant corporation, which then ceases to exist. "[T]here is in effect but one corporation which merely changes its form and ordinarily ceases to exist upon the creation of the new corporation which is its successor."

No prior cases decided under Pennsylvania law have addressed the problem presently before this Court. However, when courts from other jurisdictions have considered similar questions, they have ascertained the existence *vel non* of a merger, a consolidation or a continuation on the basis of whether, immediately after the transaction, the selling corporation continued to exist as a corporate entity and whether, after the transaction, the selling corporation possessed substantial assets with which to satisfy the demands of its creditors. * * *

This cluster of cases[16] illustrates the significance which the decisions from other jurisdictions accord to corporate theory and the continued existence of the corporate entity. The adequacy of the consideration received by the selling corporation has also been given great weight in deciding the existence of a sale as contrasted with a merger or continuation. * * *

The cases discussed above, all decided under the law of jurisdictions other than Pennsylvania, may suggest that the arrangement between Rockwell and TMW should be considered a sale rather than a merger or a continuation, since TMW did not officially terminate its corporate existence for 18 months after the exchange, and throughout that period possessed valuable assets with which to respond to tort claims similar to the one now advanced. However, a number of considerations indicate the insubstantiality of the continued existence of TMW, including the brevity of the corporation's continued life, the contractual requirement that TMW be dissolved as soon as possible, the prohibition on engaging in normal business transactions, and the character of the assets TMW controlled. Although each of these factors was present in one or more of the above cases, the present appeal is unique in combining all these elements. In addition, the better-reasoned result would be to conclude that, for the purpose of determining liability to tortiously injured parties, the Rockwell–TMW transaction should be treated as a merger, thereby subjecting Rockwell to liability for injuries caused by defective products distributed by TMW prior to the transaction.

We must, of course, apply the rule we believe a Pennsylvania appellate tribunal would adopt if the case arose in the state courts. In resolving issues relating to the recognition of a cause of action in favor of an injured party, the Pennsylvania courts have emphasized the public policy consid-

---

16. See also, Forest Laboratories v. Pillsbury Co., 452 F.2d 621 (7th Cir.1971); West Texas Refining & Dev. Co. v. Commissioner of Internal Revenue, 68 F.2d 77 (10th Cir.1933); Kloberdanz v. Joy Mfg. Co., 288 F.Supp. 817 (D.Colo.1968); Copease Mfg. Co. v. Cormac Photocopy Corp., 242 F.Supp. 993 (S.D.N.Y.1965); J. F. Anderson Lumber Co. v. Myers, 296 Minn. 33, 206 N.W.2d 365 (1973); Schwartz v. McGraw–Edison Co., 14 Cal.App.3d 767, 92 Cal.Rptr. 776 (1971); Buis v. Peabody Coal Co., 41 Ill.App.2d 317, 190 N.E.2d 507 (1963).

erations served by imposing liability on the defendant rather than formal or technical requirements. * * *

In the present case, Knapp is confronted with the melancholy prospect of being barred from his day in court unless Rockwell is held subject to suit. And quite significantly, if Knapp had been injured more than two years after the dissolution of TMW, Knapp would never have had any opportunity to recover at law, since under Pennsylvania law a dissolved corporation is subject to suit for only two years after the date of dissolution.

Denying Knapp the right to sue Rockwell because of the barren continuation of TMW after the exchange with Rockwell would allow a formality to defeat Knapp's recovery. Although TMW technically existed as an independent corporation, it had no substance. The parties clearly contemplated that TMW would terminate its existence as a part of the transaction. TMW had, in exchange for Rockwell stock, disposed of all the assets it originally held, exclusive of the cash necessary to consummate the transaction. It could not undertake any active operations. Nor was TMW permitted under the agreement to divest itself of the Rockwell stock, so that it might become an effective investment vehicle for its shareholders. Most significantly, TMW was required by the contract with Rockwell to dissolve "as soon as practicable."

On the other hand, Rockwell acquired all the assets of TMW, exclusive of certain real estate that Rockwell did not want, and assumed practically all of TMW's liabilities. Further, Rockwell required that TMW use its "best efforts," prior to the consummation of the transaction, to preserve TMW's business organization intact for Rockwell, to make available to Rockwell TMW's existing officers and employees, and to maintain TMW's relationship with its customers and suppliers. After the exchange, Rockwell continued TMW's former business operations.

If we are to follow the philosophy of the Pennsylvania courts that questions of an injured party's right to seek recovery are to be resolved by an analysis of public policy considerations rather than by a mere procrustean application of formalities, we must, in considering whether the TMW–Rockwell exchange was a merger, evaluate the public policy implications of that determination.

In resolving, where the burden of a loss should be imposed, the Pennsylvania Supreme Court has considered which of the two parties is better able to spread the loss. * * * The Pennsylvania courts have also noted the importance of insurance in performing the loss-spreading function. * * *

Interpreting all the allegations in the light most favorable to Knapp, as we must on a motion for summary judgment, neither Knapp nor Rockwell was ever in a position to prevent the occurrence of the injury, inasmuch as neither manufactured the defective device. As between these two parties, however, Rockwell is better able to spread the burden of the loss. Prior to the exchange with Rockwell, TMW had procured insurance that would have indemnified TMW had it been held liable to Knapp for his injuries. Rockwell could have protected itself from sustaining the brunt of the loss by securing from TMW an assignment of TMW's insurance. There is no indication in the record that such an assignment would have placed a burden on either Rockwell or TMW since TMW had already purchased the insurance protection, and the insurance was of no continuing benefit to TMW after its liability to suit was terminated by Pennsylvania statute. Rockwell has adduced no explanation, either in its brief or at oral argument, why it agreed in the contract not to take an assignment of TMW's prepaid insurance. Rockwell therefore should not be permitted to impose the weight of the loss upon a user of an allegedly defective product by delaying the formal dissolution of TMW. In the absence of contrary controlling decisions by the Pennsylvania courts, we conclude that the state judiciary would adopt the rule of law that appears to be better reasoned and more consistent with the social policy set forth in recent Pennsylvania cases.

The judgment of the district court will therefore be reversed and the case remanded for further proceedings consistent with this opinion.

ROSENN, CIRCUIT JUDGE (concurring). [omitted].

NOTE

See also e.g., Polius v. Clark Equip. Co., 802 F.2d 75 (3d Cir.1986) (noting that a minority of courts have adopted a product line of successor liability where the successor continues a product that caused injury to a plaintiff purchasing from the predecessor corporation); Philadelphia Elec. Co. v. Hercules, Inc., 762 F.2d 303, 311 (3d Cir.), cert. denied, 474 U.S. 980, 106 S.Ct. 384, 88 L.Ed.2d 337 (1985) (corporation could incur successor liability where it expressly or impliedly agreed to assume liability or as the result of a de facto merger that makes the successor a mere continuation of the predecessor); Arnold Graphics Industries, Inc. v. Independent Agent Center, Inc., 775 F.2d 38 (2d Cir.1985) (applying de facto merger doctrine to establish successor corporation liability); Marks v. Minnesota Mining & Manufacturing Co., 187 Cal.App.3d 1429, 232 Cal.Rptr. 594 (1986) (same).

CHAPTER 18

FAIRNESS IN CORPORATE COMBINATIONS—APPRAISAL RIGHTS AND JUDICIAL CONTROLS

■ ■ ■

SECTION 1. APPRAISAL RIGHTS— BACKGROUND

COX & HAZEN ON CORPORATIONS, by James D. Cox & Thomas Lee Hazen

§ 22.24 (2d ed. 2003).

Every state has adopted "appraisal" statutes, which give dissenting shareholders a right to demand payment of the fair value of their shares. The statutes vary broadly in their coverage. The right is given in case of certain fundamental changes, such as merger or consolidation, and often in case of sale of the entire assets, and sometimes in case of amendments that change the rights of a certain class of outstanding shares and some other changes. There is a widely adopted but debatable exception for a corporation whose shares are publicly traded. *See* e.g., Del. Code Ann. tit. 8, § 262(b)(1) (1991).

The expansion of commerce in the nineteenth century created a need for bigger and more complex corporations. The rule of unanimity impeded corporate growth because any shareholder could prevent a corporate combination if he did not agree. Because of the importance of contract and property rights, courts held grave doubts regarding the constitutionality of permitting corporate actions over the protest of any single shareholder. It is from these concerns that the appraisal remedy was born.

In 1858, Pennsylvania authorized the merger of two railroads, which a dissenting shareholder sought to enjoin. In the ensuing case, *Lauman v. Lebanon Valley Railroad*, 30 Pa. 42 (1858), the court, fearing that the merger would be unconstitutional if the shareholder was forced to accept shares in another corporation, held that the Pennsylvania legislature must have meant to provide dissenters with an appraisal remedy. The court enjoined the merger but only until security was given for the appraised value of the plaintiff's shares. There appears to be no basis for the court inferring the legislature intended to provide such relief to dissenters. The Pennsylvania legislature took the court's hint and passed the first appraisal statute (limited albeit to railroads), and the corporate landscape has never been the same since.

The justification for the appraisal remedy has other foundations today. The principle is well ingrained that the majority may combine their corporation with another and alter existing rights among shareholders without fear of serious constitutional challenge. At the same time, it is rarely the remedy of other than the "wine and cheese" crowd, for seldom is appraisal sought by investors whose holdings are less than $100,000, and few appraisal proceedings in fact occur. The more visible benefit of appraisal is that it does provide a safety valve through which dissenters' unhappiness can be ventilated without interrupting the acquisition. A more ethereal, but no less important, rationale is that the existence of an appraisal remedy complements other monitoring mechanisms for self-dealing or ineptitude on the part of the board of directors. Certainly the directors will be less sanguine about a proposal they submit to the shareholders for approval if they believe there is an efficient mechanism for shareholders to realize an alternatively determined value for their shares than that being recommended by the board of directors. So viewed, an important consideration is whether the procedures for exercising the appraisal remedy as well as the substantive guidelines for determining fair value are indeed efficient and have the right social balance.

It is important to consider the policy and purpose of the statutory remedy. As seen above, the impetus for creating the appraisal remedy was to remove possible doubt about the constitutionality of statutes authorizing fundamental changes as to existing corporations and the contract rights of shareholders. In part, the purpose of these provisions has been to give dissenters a simple and direct remedy not only where there is a harmful change in the share contract but also where they simply do not desire to accept shares in a different corporation or shares different from those they purchased. As Professor Lattin put it, the purpose has been "[t]o placate the dissenting minority and, at the same time, to facilitate the carrying out of changes of a desirable and extreme sort."

Though the early motivations for the appraisal remedy were to provide both liquidity and a means to exit for shareholders, today the appraisal remedy is the major protection minority shareholders have against acquisitions that involve a substantial conflict of interest on the part of the majority stockholder. For example, in an examination of appraisal cases between 1984 and 1994, Professor Thompson found that most involve transactions in which the majority had structured the acquisition to cash-out the minority stockholders. Thus, in practice, as measured by when the remedy is actually exercised, the dominant function of appraisal is that of addressing a conflict of interest problem on the part of the majority stockholder.

While in theory the ostensible purpose of the statutory appraisal remedy is to protect the minority and afford them a way out in case of fundamental changes, in reality it appears that the purpose is even more to aid and protect the majority. The proceeding by dissenting shareholders for the appraisal of their shares does not delay or prevent the completion of the consolidation, merger, sale of assets for securities, or recapitalization by amendment; the change takes place subject to a collateral proceeding to value the shares of the dissenting shareholders. However, appraisal proceedings do burden the constituent corporations, who may be more inclined to offer a generous exchange in an effort to avoid exercise of the appraisal remedy.

Those who have drafted and sponsored many of these statutes have been careful to avoid possible undue interference and obstruction by minority shareholders acting in bad faith and thus have made as little concession to the dissenters as possible. Those who wish to avail themselves of the statutory remedy must act with exceeding quickness in order to meet the stringent conditions precedent. Simply stated, most appraisal statutes contain multiple steps, each with a specific and short time period within which dissenters must comply to preserve and perfect their right of appraisal. For example, under the Model Business Corporation Act [§ 13.21], if a shareholder vote is required for the fundamental change, the shareholders must give written notice of their intent to dissent prior to the vote and then must refrain from voting in favor of the plan. After the vote the dissenting shareholders will be informed of the procedures to be followed and must again make a written demand for payment of the fair value of their shares. The statutes vary greatly on the technical procedures to be followed. Under the Delaware Act [§ 262(d)(2)], after the vote the corporation must within 10 days give notice of the right to dissent, and thereafter the shareholders have 20 days within which they must make a written demand. Under the Model Business Corporation Act there is no time limit on the corporation's post-approval notice. The shareholders must be given at least 30 days.

In most states, shares are not qualified for appraisal unless they have actually voted against the combination or, in some states, have at least abstained. Accordingly, a shareholder not attending the meeting in person or by proxy cannot receive an appraisal regardless of how difficult or useless it may have been for him to comply with this voting requirement. Statutes differ as to the status of dissenting shareholders after demand for payment. Under some acts, on demand for payment, they cease to have any interest in the shares or right to dividends or other rights of shareholders. Under other statutes, the rights cease only after payment of the appraised price.

Under the Revised Model Business Corporation Act [§ 13.23], a shareholder who has perfected his rights to appraisal loses all rights as a shareholder, unless he withdraws from the appraisal process. The shareholder is thereafter entitled to be paid the amount the corporation believes is the fair value of his shares. [§ 13.24] And the shareholder can continue to press his claim in a formal appraisal proceeding for any additional amounts above paid by the corporation that the shareholder argues is necessary to raise the total payment to the shares' fair value. Both the shareholder and the corporation have obligations with respect to initiating formal appraisal proceedings under the Revised Model Business Corporation Act. The shareholder must, among other requirements, demand payment of his estimate of the shares' fair value within 30 days, and the corporation must within 60 days of that demand initiate the proceeding or be obligated to pay the shareholder the full amount sought. [§ 13.26]

In an appraisal proceeding, evidence of value must be taken and a record must be kept. An appraiser's report must usually be filed with the clerk of court, and the parties may take exception to the report. After a hearing as to the exceptions, argument on the report, and the consideration of evidence, the court will confirm, modify, or reject the report. It may determine the value of the shares and direct payment to the shareholders entitled by the resulting or surviving corporation. * * *

The expenses of an appraisal proceeding are a factor of serious importance, as they involve appraisers' fees, attorneys' fees, and fees for expert accountants and witnesses before the appraisers. This may be an undue burden on the dissenter, but it may also allow a shareholder acting in bad faith to cause the corporations to spend substantial sums. Only a few statutes make adequate provision for attorneys' fees and other expenses of the petitioner. * * *

Notes

1. There are four key issues relating to statutory appraisal rights:
    1. What transactions give rise to the appraisal right?
    2. What are the procedures for appraisal rights?
    3. What is meant by "fair value"?
    4. Are appraisal rights exclusive?

2. Appraisal rights are not always available. For example, the shareholders of an acquiring corporation in a triangular merger will not have appraisal rights. As will be discussed later in this chapter, assets purchases may deny appraisal rights to the shareholders of the purchaser and sometimes to the shareholders of the selling corporation. A tender offer will not normally trigger appraisal rights for the shareholders of the offeror or those of the target company.

3. The Model Business Corporation Act in § 13.02(a) sets forth the situations in which appraisal rights exist:

    i.   merger (except where surviving corporation increases its shares by less than 20%);

    ii. share exchange to which corporation is a party; appraisal rights exist for shareholders whose shares are to be exchanged;

iii.　Sale of substantially all of the assets not in the regular course of business;

iv.　Amendments to the articles of incorporation which affect certain shareholder fundamental rights:

　　　a.　altering or abolishing preferential rights;

　　　b.　creating, abolishing, or altering redemption rights (including sinking funds);

　　　c.　altering or abolishing preemptive rights;

　　　d.　excluding or limiting shareholder voting rights;

v.　Any other matter where the right to dissent is given by the articles, bylaws, or directors' resolution.

4. *Market-out exception.* Delaware provides an exception from the right to dissent for shares that are listed on a national securities exchange or traded on Nasdaq and having more than 2,000 shareholders. Del § 262(b). Presumably, the rationale is that the efficient market exists for a shareholder who does not like the transaction. Other states have a similar exemption although a former version of the Model Business Corporation Act did not.

SECTION 2.　FAIR VALUE

PIEMONTE v. NEW BOSTON GARDEN CORP.

377 Mass. 719, 387 N.E.2d 1145 (1979).

WILKINS, JUSTICE.

The plaintiffs were stockholders in Boston Garden Arena Corporation (Garden Arena), a Massachusetts corporation whose stockholders voted on July 19, 1973, to merge with the defendant corporation in circumstances which entitled each plaintiff to "demand payment for his stock from the resulting or surviving corporation and an appraisal in accordance with the provisions of (G.L. c. 156B, §§ 86–98)." G.L. c. 156B, § 85, as amended by St.1969, c. 392, § 2. The plaintiffs commenced this action under G.L. c. 156B, § 90, seeking a judicial determination of the "fair value" of their shares "as of the day preceding the date of the vote approving the proposed corporate action."[2] G.L. c. 156B, § 92, inserted by St.1964, c. 723, § 1. Each party has appealed from a judgment determining the fair value of the plaintiffs' stock. We granted the defendant's application for direct appellate review.

On July 18, 1973, Garden Arena owned all the stock in a subsidiary corporation that owned both a franchise in the National Hockey League

---

2. The plaintiffs took all the necessary, preliminary steps to preserve their rights. Each plaintiff objected in writing to the proposed merger; none of their shares was voted in favor of the proposed corporate action (see G.L. c. 156B, § 86); each plaintiff seasonably demanded in writing payment from the defendant for the fair value of his stock (see G.L. c. 156B, § 89); and no agreement as to that fair value was reached within thirty days of the demand (see G.L. c. 156B, § 90).

(NHL), known as the Boston Bruins, and a corporation that held a franchise in the American Hockey League (AHL), known as the Boston Braves. Garden Arena also owned and operated Boston Garden Sports Arena (Boston Garden), an indoor auditorium with facilities for the exhibition of sporting and other entertainment events, and a corporation that operated the food and beverage concession at the Boston Garden. A considerable volume of documentary material was introduced in evidence concerning the value of the stock of Garden Arena on July 18, 1973, the day before Garden Arena's stockholders approved the merger. Each side presented expert testimony. The judge gave consideration to the market value of the Garden Arena stock, to the value of its stock based on its earnings, and to the net asset value of Garden Arena's assets. Weighting these factors, the judge arrived at a total, per share value of $75.27.[3]

In this appeal, the parties raise objections to certain of the judge's conclusions. We will expand on the facts as necessary when we consider each issue. We conclude that the judge followed acceptable procedures in valuing the Garden Arena stock; that his determinations were generally within the range of discretion accorded a fact finder; but that, in three instances, the judge's treatment of the evidence was or may have been in error and, accordingly, the case should be remanded to him for further consideration of those three points.

The statutory provisions applicable to this case were enacted in 1964 as part of the Massachusetts Business Corporation Law. St.1964, c. 723, § 1. The appraisal provisions (G.L. c. 156B, §§ 86–98) were based on a similar, but not identical, Delaware statute (Del.Code tit. 8, § 262). See Notes by Boston Bar Committee 1964, M.G.L.A. c. 156B, §§ 86–92, 94–97 (West). In these circumstances, consideration of the Delaware law, including judicial decisions, is appropriate, but in no sense should we feel compelled to adhere without question to that law, which has been in the process of development since our enactment of G.L. c. 156B in 1964. We do not perceive a legislative intent to adopt judicial determinations of Delaware law made prior to the enactment of G.L. c. 156B and certainly no such intent as to judicial interpretations made since that date.

The Delaware courts have adopted a general approach to the appraisal of stock which a Massachusetts judge might appropriately follow, as did the judge in this case. The Delaware procedure, known as the "Delaware block approach," calls for a determination of the market value, the earnings value, and the net asset value of the stock, followed by the assignment of a percentage weight to each of the elements of value. See generally, Note, Valuation of Dissenters' Stock under Appraisal Statutes, 79 Harv.L.Rev. 1453, 1456–1471 (1966).

---

3. The judge determined the market value, earnings value, and net asset value of the stock and then weighted these values as follows:

	Value	Weight	Result			
Market Value:	$ 26.50 X	10%	= $ 2.65	Net Asset Value:	$103.16 X 50%	= $51.58
Earnings Value:	$ 52.60 X	40%	= $21.04		Total Value Per Share:	$75.27

There have been no appellate decisions in this State concerning the appraisal of stock since the present appraisal statute was enacted, and there were few under the previously applicable, somewhat similar, statute. See Martignette v. Sagamore Mfg. Co., 163 N.E.2d 9 (1959); Cole v. Wells, 224 Mass. 504, 113 N.E. 189 (1916). In the Martignette case, the court held that, even where stock had an established market, market price was not determinative and that "it is for the appraisers in the particular case to determine the weight of the relevant factors." Martignette v. Sagamore Mfg. Co., supra, 163 N.E.2d at 13. If the corporation is solvent or has significant earnings prospects, "the earnings and worth of the corporation as a going concern are important." Id. at 142–143, 163 N.E.2d at 13 (overruling in this respect Cole v. Wells, supra, 224 Mass. at 513, 113 N.E. 189, which had held that the value of a dissenting stockholder's shares should be ascertained "as if liquidation had been voted"). We perceive no legislative intention to overrule these cases by the enactment of the new appraisal provisions in 1964.

With these considerations in mind, we turn to the specific issues that have been argued on appeal, considering, in order, the judge's determination of market value, earnings value and net asset value of the stock; his decision concerning the weighting of these components; the defendant's objection to the consideration of certain evidence; and, finally, the judge's decision on the rate of interest to be allowed to the plaintiffs.

The judge was acting within reasonable limits when he determined that the market value of Garden Arena stock on July 18, 1973, was $26.50 a share. Each party challenges this determination. The plaintiffs' contention is that market value should be disregarded because it was not ascertainable due to the limited trading in Garden Arena stock. The defendant argues that the judge was obliged to reconstruct market value based on comparable companies, and, in doing so, should have arrived at a market value of $22 a share.

Market value may be a significant factor, even the dominant factor, in determining the "fair value" of shares of a particular corporation under G.L. c. 156B, § 92. Shares regularly traded on a recognized stock exchange are particularly susceptible to valuation on the basis of their market price, although even in such cases the market value may well not be conclusive. See Martignette v. Sagamore Mfg. Co., 163 N.E.2d 9 (1959). On the other hand, where there is no established market for a particular stock, actual market value cannot be used. In such cases, a judge might undertake to "reconstruct" market value, but he is not obliged to do so.[7] Indeed, the process of the reconstruction of market value may actually be no more than a variation on the valuation of corporate assets and corporate earnings.

---

7. The Delaware cases require the reconstruction of market value only when the actual market value cannot be determined and a hypothetical market value can be reconstructed. Compare Application of Del. Racing Ass'n, 213 A.2d 203, 211–212 (Del.1965), with Universal City Studios, Inc. v. Francis I. duPont & Co., 334 A.2d 216, 222 (Del.1975).

In this case, Garden Arena stock was traded on the Boston Stock Exchange, but rarely. Approximately ninety per cent of the company's stock was held by the controlling interests and not traded. Between January 1, 1968, and December 4, 1972, 16,741 shares were traded. During this period, an annual average of approximately 1.5% of the outstanding stock changed hands. In 1972, 4,372 shares were traded at prices ranging from $20.50 a share to $29 a share. The public announcement of the proposed merger was made on December 7, 1972. The last prior sale of 200 shares on December 4, 1972, was made at $26.50 a share. The judge accepted that sale price as the market price to be used in his determination of value. The judge concluded that the volume of trading was sufficient to permit a determination of market value and expressed a preference for the actual sale price over any reconstruction of a market value, which he concluded would place "undue reliance on corporations, factors, and circumstances not applicable to Garden Arena stock." The decision to consider market value and the market value selected were within the judge's discretion.

The judge determined that the average per share earnings of Garden Arena for the five-fiscal-year period which ended June 30, 1973, was $5.26. To this amount he applied a factor, or multiplier, of 10 to arrive at $52.60 as the per share value based on earnings.

Each party objects to certain aspects of this process. We reject the plaintiffs' argument that the judge could not properly use any value based on earnings, and also reject the parties' various challenges to the judge's method of determining value based on earnings.

Delaware case law, which, as we have said, we regard as instructive but not binding, has established a method of computing value based on corporate earnings. The appraiser generally starts by computing the average earnings of the corporation for the past five years. Universal City Studios, Inc. v. Francis I. duPont & Co., 334 A.2d 216, 218 (Del.1975); Application of Del. Racing Ass'n, 213 A.2d 203, 212 (Del.1965). Extraordinary gains and losses are excluded from the average earnings calculation. Gibbons v. Schenley Indus., Inc., 339 A.2d 460, 468–470 (Del.Ch.1975); Felder v. Anderson, Clayton & Co., 159 A.2d 278 (1960). The appraiser then selects a multiplier (to be applied to the average earnings) which reflects the prospective financial condition of the corporation and the risk factor inherent in the corporation and the industry. Universal City Studios, Inc. v. Francis I. duPont & Co., supra. In selecting a multiplier, the appraiser generally looks to other comparable corporations. Universal City Studios, Inc. v. Francis I. duPont & Co., supra at 219–221 (averaging price-earnings ratios of nine other motion picture companies as of date of merger); Gibbons v. Schenley Indus., Inc., supra at 471 (using Standard & Poor's Distiller's Index as of date of merger); Felder v. Anderson, Clayton & Co., supra, 39 Del.Ch. at 87, 159 A.2d 278 (averaging price-earnings ratios of representative stocks over previous five-year period because of recent boom in industry). The appraiser's choice of a multiplier is largely discretionary and will be upheld if it is "within the range of reason."

Universal City Studios, Inc. v. Francis I. duPont & Co., supra at 219 (approving multiplier of 16.1); Application of Del. Racing Ass'n, supra at 213 (approving multiplier of 10); Swanton v. State Guar. Corp., 215 A.2d 242 (1965) (approving multiplier of 14).[9]

The judge chose not to place "singular reliance on comparative data preferring to choose a multiplier based on the specific situation and prospects of the Garden Arena." He weighed the favorable financial prospects of the Bruins: the popularity and success of the team, the relatively low average age of its players, the popularity of Bobby Orr and Phil Esposito, the high attendance record at home games (each home team retained all gate receipts), and the advantageous radio and television contracts. On the other hand, he recognized certain risks, the negative prospects: the existence of the World Hockey Association with its potential, favorable impact on players' bargaining positions, and legal threats to the players' reserve clause. He concluded that a multiplier of 10 was appropriate. There was ample evidentiary support for his conclusion. He might have looked to and relied on price-earnings ratios of other corporations, but he was not obliged to.

The judge did not have to consider the dividend record of Garden Arena, as the defendant urges. Dividends tend to reflect the same factors as earnings and, therefore, need not be valued separately. See Felder v. Anderson, Clayton & Co., 159 A.2d 278 (1960). And since dividend policy is usually reflected in market value, the use of market value as a factor in the valuation process permitted the low and sporadic dividend rate to be given some weight in the process. Beyond that, the value of the plaintiffs' stock should not be depreciated because the controlling interests often chose to declare low dividends or none at all.

The judge did not abuse his discretion in including expansion income (payments from teams newly admitted to the NHL) received during two of the five recent fiscal years. His conclusion was well within the guidelines of decided cases. See Gibbons v. Schenley Indus., Inc., 339 A.2d 460, 470 (Del.Ch.1975) (gain from sale of real estate not extraordinary where corporation often sold such assets); Felder v. Anderson, Clayton & Co., 159 A.2d 278 (1960) (loss attributable to a drought not extraordinary). The Bruins first received expansion income ($2,000,000) during the fiscal year which ended on June 30, 1967, a year not included in the five-year average. The franchise received almost $1,000,000 more in 1970 and approximately $860,000 in 1972. This 1970 and 1972 income was reflected in the computation of earnings. Expansion income did not have to be treated as extraordinary income. The judge concluded that it did not distort "an accurate projection of the earnings value of Garden Arena"

---

9. Although Delaware courts have relied on, and continue to rely on, Professor Dewing's capitalization chart (see 1 A. S. Dewing, The Financial Policy of Corporations 390–391 (5th ed. 1953)), they have recognized that it is somewhat outdated and no longer the "be-all and end-all" on the subject of earnings value. See Universal City Studios, Inc. v. Francis I. duPont & Co., supra at 219; Swanton v. State Guar. Corp., 483–484, 215 A.2d 242 (1965).

and noted, as of July 18, 1973, an NHL expansion plan for the admission of two more teams in 1974–1975 and for expansion thereafter.

The judge determined total net asset value by first valuing the net assets of Garden Arena apart from the Bruins franchise and the concession operations at Boston Garden. He selected $9,400,000 (the June 30, 1973, book value of Garden Arena) as representing that net asset value. Then, he added his valuations of the Bruins franchise ($9,600,000) and the concession operation ($4,200,000) to arrive at a total asset value of $23,200,000, or $103.16 a share.[10]

The parties raise various objections to these determinations. The defendant argues that the judge included certain items twice in his valuation of the net assets of Garden Arena and that he should have given no separate value to the concession operation. The plaintiff argues that the judge undervalued both the Boston Garden and the value of the Bruins franchise.

The defendant objects to the judge's refusal to deduct $1,116,000 from the $9,400,000 that represented the net asset value of Garden Arena (exclusive of the net asset value of the Bruins franchise and the concession operation). The defendant's expert testified that the $9,400,000 figure included $1,116,000 attributable to the goodwill of the Bruins, net player investment, and the value of the AHL franchise. The judge recognized that the items included in the $1,116,000 should not be valued twice and seemingly agreed that they would be more appropriately included in the value of the Bruins franchise than in the $9,400,000. He was not plainly wrong, however, in declining to deduct them from the $9,400,000, because, as is fully warranted from the testimony of the defendant's expert, the judge concluded that the defendant's expert did not include these items in his determination of the value of the Bruins franchise. The defendant's expert, whose determination the judge accepted, arrived at his value of the Bruins franchise by adding certain items to the cost of a new NHL franchise, but none of those items included goodwill, net player investment, or the value of an AHL franchise. Acceptance of the defendant's argument would have resulted in these items' being entirely omitted from the net asset valuation of Garden Arena.[12]

The plaintiffs object that the judge did not explicitly determine the value of the Boston Garden and implicitly undervalued it. Garden Arena had purchased the Boston Garden on May 25, 1973, for $4,000,000, and accounted for it on the June 30, 1973, balance sheet as a $4,000,000 asset with a corresponding mortgage liability of $3,437,065. Prior to the purchase, Garden Arena had held a long-term lease which was unfavorable to

---

10. $23,200,000 / 224,892 (the number of outstanding shares).

12.   One of the points on which we will remand this case is the valuation of the Bruins franchise. Since, as discussed below, the judge need not have felt constrained to accept the defendant's expert's opinion on this issue, on remand he will be free to determine the value of the franchise based on such evidence as he chooses to accept. Assignment of a different value to the franchise may require an adjustment in the net asset value of Garden Arena if the franchise value determined by the judge includes some or all of the items supposedly included in the $1,116,000.

the owner of the Boston Garden.[13] The existence of the lease would tend to depress the purchase price.

The judge stated that the $9,400,000 book value "Includes a reasonable value for Boston Garden" (emphasis supplied). He did not indicate whether, if he had meant to value the Boston Garden at its purchase price (with an adjustment for the mortgage liabilities), he had considered the effect the lease would have had on that price. While we recognize that the fact-finding role of the judge permits him to reject the opinions of the various experts,[14] we conclude, in the absence of an explanation of his reasons, that it is possible that the judge did not give adequate consideration to the value of the Garden property. The judge should consider this subject further on remand.

A major area of dispute was the value of the Bruins franchise. The judge rejected the value advanced by the plaintiffs' expert ($18,000,000), stating that "(a)lthough the defendant's figure of ($9,600,000) seems somewhat low in comparison with the cost of expansion team franchises, The Court is constrained to accept defendant's value as it is the more creditable and legally appropriate expert opinion in the record" (emphasis supplied). Although the choice of the word "constrained" may have been inadvertent, it connotes a sense of obligation. As the trier of fact, the judge was not bound to accept the valuation of either one expert or the other. He was entitled to reach his own conclusion as to value. Loschi v. Massachusetts Port Auth., 282 N.E. 2d 418 (1972); Ryder v. Lexington, 21 N.E.2d 382 (1939). See W. B. Leach & P. J. Liacos, Massachusetts Evidence 92 (4th ed. 1967).

Because the judge may have felt bound to accept the value placed on the Bruins franchise by the defendant's expert, we shall remand this case for him to arrive at his own determination of the value of the Bruins franchise. He would be warranted in arriving at the same valuation as that advanced on behalf of the defendant, but he is not obliged to do so.

The defendant argues that, in arriving at the value of the assets of Garden Arena, the judge improperly placed a separate value on the right to operate concessions at the Boston Garden. We agree with the judge. The fact that earnings from concessions were included in the computation of earnings value, one component in the formula, does not mean that the value of the concessions should have been excluded from the computation of net asset value, another such component.

The value of the concession operation was not reflected in the value of the real estate. Real estate may be valued on the basis of rental income, but it is not valued on the basis of the profitability of business operations

---

13. The lease, which ran until June 1, 1986, contained a fixed maximum rent and an obligation on the lessee to pay only two-thirds of any increase in local real estate taxes. In a period of inflation and rising local real estate taxes, the value of the lease to the lessor was decreasing annually.

14. The lowest value expressed by any expert for the plaintiffs was $8,250,000 (exclusive of mortgage liabilities), based on depreciated reproduction cost. The defendant offered no testimony concerning the value of the property on July 18, 1973.

within the premises. See Amory v. Commonwealth, 72 N.E.2d 549 (1947); Revere v. Revere Constr. Co., 189 N.E. 73 (1934); 7 Nichols, Eminent Domain § 11.05 (3d rev. ed. 1978); Tuoni & McDonough, Recovering Land Damages in Eminent Domain Cases in Massachusetts A Summary, 63 Mass.L.Rev. 119, 122 (1978). Moreover, it is manifest that the value of the concession operation was not included in the value placed on the Boston Garden. The record indicates that Garden Arena already owned the concession rights when it purchased the Boston Garden. The conclusion that the value of the concession operation was not reflected in the value of the Boston Garden is particularly warranted because the determined value of the right to operate the concessions ($4,200,000) was higher than the May 25, 1973, purchase price ($4,000,000) of the Boston Garden.

We do conclude, however, that the judge may have felt unnecessarily bound to accept the plaintiffs' evidence of the value of the concession operation. He stated that "since the defendant did not submit evidence on this issue, the Court will accept plaintiffs' expert appraisal of the value of the concession operation." Although the judge did not express the view that he was "constrained" to accept the plaintiffs' valuation, as he did concerning the defendant's valuation of the Bruins franchise, he may have misconstrued his authority on this issue. The judge was not obliged to accept the plaintiffs' evidence at face value merely because no other evidence was offered. See Martin v. Otis, 124 N.E. 294 (1919); C. W. Hunt Co. v. Boston Elevated Ry., 85 N.E. 446 (1908).

On remand, the judge should reconsider his determination of the value of the concession operation and exercise his own judgment concerning the bases for the conclusion arrived at by the plaintiffs' expert. However, the evidence did warrant the value selected by the judge, and no reduction in that value is required on this record.

The judge weighted the three valuations as follows:

Market Value   —10%
Earnings Value —40%
Net Asset Value —50%

We accept these allocations as reasonable and within the range of the judge's discretion.

Any determination of the weight to be given the various elements involved in the valuation of a stock must be based on the circumstances. Heller v. Munsingwear, Inc., 98 A.2d 774 (1953). The decision to weight market value at only 10% was appropriate, considering the thin trading in the stock of Garden Arena. The decision to attribute 50% weight to net asset value was reasonably founded. The judge concluded that, because of tax reasons, the value of a sports franchise, unlike many corporate activities, depends more on its assets than on its earnings; that Garden Arena had been largely a family corporation in which earnings were of little significance; that Garden Arena had approximately $5,000,000 in excess liquid assets; and that the Garden property was a substantial real estate holding in an excellent location.

The judge might have reached different conclusions on this record. He was not obliged, however, to reconstruct market value and, as the defendant urges, attribute 50% weight to it. Nor was he obliged, as the plaintiffs argue, to consider only net asset value. See Martignette v. Sagamore Mfg. Co., 163 N.E.2d 9 (1959). Market value and earnings value properly could be considered in these circumstances.

Although we would have found no fault with a determination to give even greater weight to the price per share based on the net asset value of Garden Arena, the judge was acting within an acceptable range of discretion in selecting the weights he gave to the various factors. * * *

The defendant objects to the judge's determination to award interest at 8% per annum. It does not object to the judge's decision to award interest, a matter within his discretion (see G.L. c. 156B, §§ 92 and 95), nor to his decision to compound interest annually. The judge heard evidence specifically directed toward the question of the appropriate rate of interest. The defendant's own witness testified on cross-examination that a prudent investment in corporate bonds, rated AAA by Moody's, would have yielded interest in excess of 8% uncompounded. The amount selected fairly compensated the plaintiffs for their inability to use the money during the period in question, a factor which the judge fairly could consider, and the judge reasonably could have concluded that 8% Per annum reflected "the rate of interest at which a prudent investor could have invested money." Universal City Studios, Inc. v. Francis I. duPont & Co., 334 A.2d 216, 222 (Del.1975). See generally Grant, Appraisal Rights: Allowance for Prejudgment Interest, 17 B.C.Indus. & Com.L.Rev. 1 (1975).

We have concluded that the judge's method of valuing the Garden Arena stock was essentially correct. In this opinion, we have indicated, however, that the case should be remanded to him for clarification and further consideration on the record of three matters: his valuation of the Boston Garden, the Bruins franchise, and the concession operation.

So ordered.

IN RE VALUATION OF COMMON STOCK OF McLOON OIL CO.

565 A.2d 997 (Me.1989).

OPINION BY: McKUSICK

Ten years ago we examined for the first time the principles to be applied in finding the "fair value" of a dissenting shareholder's stock under the recently enacted Maine Business Corporations Act.[1] *See In re*

---

1. Prior to the enactment of the Maine Business Corporations Act to be effective January 1, 1972, P.L. 1971, ch. 439, Maine had had since 1891 an appraisal rights statute entitling a

Valuation of Common Stock of Libby, McNeill & Libby, 406 A.2d 54 (Me.1979). *Libby* involved a public corporation with common stock listed on the New York Stock Exchange. In the present appeal we revisit the fair value question in an appraisal proceeding involving three Maine corporations with untraded stock owned entirely by the members of a single family.

On December 6, 1976, McLoon Oil Co., Morse Bros. Oil Co., and T–M Oil Co., along with several Massachusetts companies, merged into the Lido Company of New England, Inc. (hereinafter "Lido"), a New Hampshire corporation. Two dissenting shareholders of the Maine companies sued for appraisal rights under 13–A M.R.S.A. § 909 (1981). Adopting the report of the court-appointed referee, the Superior Court (Androscoggin County, *Alexander, J.*) determined that the aggregate fair value of each dissenting shareholder's common stock in the three companies as of December 5, 1976, was $334,925 and awarded 8% simple interest thereon until the date of payment. * * *

McLoon, Morse Bros., and T–M Oil Companies were closely held companies entirely owned by the members of the Pescosolido family under the leadership of Carl Pescosolido, Sr. Two of his sons, Carl Jr. and Richard, each held 475 shares in McLoon, 800 shares in Morse Bros., and 350 shares in T–M. The combined holdings of Carl Jr. and Richard constituted 50% of the McLoon common stock, 50% of the Morse Bros. common stock, and 14.3% of the T–M common stock.

In December 1975 Carl Sr. proposed to merge all family-held companies into Lido, over which he would exercise sole voting control. Carl Jr. and Richard (hereinafter "Dissenters") objected in writing to the proposed merger. On December 6, 1976, the parties executed a merger agreement in which the Dissenters expressly preserved their appraisal rights under 13–A M.R.S.A. § 909. On December 15, 1976, the Dissenters individually wrote to each of the three Maine companies and requested payment for their shares. On January 8, 1977, Lido responded by offering each Dissenter $128,685.55 for his combined interests in all three companies. Within a week, both Dissenters formally rejected that offer.

Pursuant to 13–A M.R.S.A. § 909(9)(B), the Dissenters on April 1, 1977, filed a Superior Court suit nominally in Lido's name for valuation of their stock in all three companies. They brought that consolidated appraisal proceeding in Androscoggin County.

Ten years later, on May 22, 1987, acting pursuant to M.R. Civ. P. 53 and with the agreement of the parties, the Superior Court (*Delahanty, J.*) appointed Professor David P. Cluchey of the University of Maine School of Law to serve as referee to determine all issues in the case. The referee held three days of hearings in December 1987 and issued a draft report on

dissenting shareholder to recover the "value" of his stock. *See* P.L. 1891, ch. 84, § 4, which in successive codifications without material change became 13 M.R.S.A. § 283 (1964). The only reported cases under the prior statute were terminated for procedural reasons before final adjudication of the stock valuation issue. *See Johnson v. C. Brigham Co.,* 126 Me. 108, 136 A. 456 (1927); *Fenderson v. Franklin Light & Power Co.,* 120 Me. 231, 113 A. 177 (1921).

August 15, 1988. Both parties offered comments in early September. On October 28, 1988, the referee filed his report. On Lido's motion the referee later filed a clarifying amendment on November 15. When the entire record was filed with the court on December 15, 1988, Lido objected to the report and the Dissenters moved for its acceptance with modifications. The Superior Court (*Alexander, J.*) accepted the referee's report in full and on March 3, 1989, ordered judgment entered in accordance therewith. Thus the court ordered Lido to pay each Dissenter in exchange for his stock the sum of $334,925 (i.e., 2.6 times as much as had been offered by Lido) with 8% simple interest from December 6, 1976, to the date of payment and awarded the Dissenters expert witness compensation and costs in the amount of $42,781.45. * * *

Ten years ago in the *Libby* case we ruled that a stock's fair value under section 909 could appropriately be determined by weighing three factors—the stock's market price, the company's net asset value, and the company's investment value—with the weight to be accorded each factor depending on its reliability as an indicator of fair value. *See In re Valuation of Common Stock of Libby, McNeill & Libby,* 406 A.2d at 60. We recognized that the reliability of each factor will vary with the particular facts and circumstances of each case, so that "the weighting of these interdependent elements of fair value is more akin to an artistic composition than to a scientific process. A judicial determination of fair value cannot be computed according to any precise mathematical formula." *Id.* However, the court should in each case consider all three elements of fair value, even if only to find one or more of them unreliable in the circumstances. *Id.*

The Dissenters offered the testimony of two expert appraisal witnesses: Robert Noone testified to the value of the real estate owned by the three companies and Wilfred Hall testified to the companies' net asset value. Lido countered with two experts of its own: Glenn Cooper for T–M and McLoon used a discounted cash analysis and for Morse Bros. a net asset value; James Ahearn testified about the hypothetical returns on investment in comparable business properties. The referee decided to use Hall's and Cooper's testimony in valuing the shares for T–M and McLoon, allotting 75% weight to Cooper's analysis and 25% to Hall's analysis, and to accept in full Hall's valuation of Morse Bros. By that means the referee found the total value of each company; then to find the value of each Dissenter's interest in the company, he had only to multiply the Dissenter's percentage of ownership times the company's total value. The referee's calculation was as follows:

T–M Oil Co.

Cooper valuation	$1,181,422 X.75 =	$886,066.50
Hall valuation	$1,057,700 X.25 =	$264,425.00
Total Value		$1,150,491.50
Each Dissenter's proportion: $82,178		

McLoon Oil Co.

Cooper valuation	$704,952 X.75	=	$528,714
Hall valuation	$655,100 X.25	=	$163,775
Total Value			$692,489
Each Dissenter's proportion:	$173,122		

Morse Bros. Oil Co.

Hall valuation		
(Total Value)		$318,500
Each Dissenter's proportion:	$79,625	

In sum, the referee held that the fair value of each Dissenter's stock was his proportionate share of the full value of each company, as determined from the expert appraisal testimony presented by the parties. The referee expressly rejected Lido's contention that he should discount the full value of each company because of the minority status and lack of marketability of the Dissenters' stock. On appeal Lido's only serious challenge to the referee's finding of fair value is directed at the referee's recognition of the Dissenters' full proportionate interest in the whole value of each company, free of any minority or nonmarketability discount. We find Lido's arguments for such discounts unpersuasive. In our view application of those discounts would run directly counter to our appraisal statute's purpose of protecting dissenting shareholders. The referee's finding of aggregate fair value of $334,925 for each Dissenter is fully supported by the evidence and by a correct application of legal principles.

The referee applied the three-factor valuation method used in *Libby* but noted that the method has come under some criticism since 1979, specifically citing *Weinberger v. UOP, Inc.,* 457 A.2d 701 (Del.1983), for the proposition that the modern approach to valuation "must include proof of value by any techniques or methods which are generally considered acceptable in the financial community, and otherwise admissible in court." *Id.* at 712–13. *Weinberger* by its own terms broadened rather than changed the basic method of stock valuation used in *Libby*. As the Delaware court in *Weinberger* noted:

> The basic concept of value under the appraisal statute is that the stockholder is entitled to what has been taken from him, viz., *his proportionate interest in a going concern*. In determining what figure represents this true or intrinsic value, the appraiser and the courts must take into consideration all factors and elements which reasonably might enter into the fixing of value.

Id. at 713 (quoting *Tri-Continental Corp. v. Battye,* 31 Del. Ch. 523, 526, 74 A.2d 71, 72 (1950) (emphasis added). This approach is consistent with our analysis in *Libby,* where we realized that stock valuation is necessarily a fact-specific process. *See Libby,* 406 A.2d at 60. The only evidence available to the appraiser in *Libby* went toward establishing market price, net asset value, and investment value. *Libby*'s three-part analysis is elsewhere known as the Delaware block method of stock valuation. We note that since *Weinberger* a number of jurisdictions have continued to rely primarily upon the three-factor analysis used in *Libby*. *See, e.g., Walter S. Cheesman Realty Co. v. Moore,* 770 P.2d 1308 (Colo.Ct.App. 1988); *Richardson v. Palmer Broadcasting,* 353 N.W.2d 374 (Iowa 1984); *Columbia Management Co. v. Wyss,* 94 Ore. App. 195, 765 P.2d 207 (1988); *Blasingame v. American Materials, Inc.,* 654 S.W.2d 659 (Tenn.1983).

Nothing in *Libby,* however, prevents the consideration and use of any other generally accepted and admissible valuation techniques. In the case at bar the evidence presented by the witnesses went toward establishing those same three criteria of value; even the discounted cash flow analysis used by Cooper deals essentially with investment value.[6] Although Lido argues that the three-part test is outmoded, we find the approach as outlined in *Libby* entirely compatible with *Weinberger* and the broadening of the Delaware block method. *See Pioneer Bancorporation, Inc. v. Waters,* 765 P.2d 597, 599 (Colo.Ct.App.1988); *Cede & Co. v. Technicolor, Inc.,* 542 A.2d 1182, 1186–87 (Del.1988); *Richardson v. Palmer Broadcasting,* 353 N.W.2d at 378.

Lido tries to use *Weinberger* and its progeny as a basis upon which to introduce the use of minority and nonmarketability discounts as a generally accepted alternative method of valuation. As previously noted, however, *Weinberger* advocated the same definition of "fair value" of a single shareholder's stock as did *Libby*: "his proportionate interest in a going concern." 457 A.2d at 713. *Weinberger* stands for the simple proposition that the value of the business entity as a whole should be determined by the best available valuation methods. No one can quarrel with that proposition. It has nothing to do, however, with the critical issue raised by Lido's appeal, which arises only after completion of the valuation of the whole firm by the best available methods: Should the dissenting shareholder's proportionate part of that whole firm value as so determined be discounted because of the minority status and lack of marketability of his stock? The Delaware Supreme Court, the same court that decided *Weinberger,* has recently said no: Delaware emphatically rejects the application of those discounts in determining the fair value of a dissenting shareholder's stock. *See Cavalier Oil Corp. v. Harnett,* 564 A.2d 1137, slip op. at 8 (Del. 1989) ("application of a discount to a minority shareholder is contrary to the requirement that the company be viewed as a going concern"). *See also Richardson v. Palmer Broadcasting,* 353 N.W. 2d at 378; Haynsworth, *Valuation of Business Interests,* 33 Mercer L. Rev. 457, 489 (1982) [hereinafter "Haynsworth"]. *But see Perlman v. Permonite Mfg. Co.,* 568 F. Supp. 222, 231 (N.D.Ind.1983) (applying Indiana law); *Hernando Bank v. Huff,* 609 F. Supp. 1124, 1126 (N.D.Miss.1985) (applying Mississippi law).

---

6. Lido's witness Cooper had available the actual earnings of the Maine properties of T–M and McLoon for the years after the 1976 merger. Typically the investment value factor is based upon an averaging of past earnings as a predictor of the future. *See Libby,* 406 A.2d at 59. The availability of data on actual future earnings here led the referee to accord a 75% weighting to Cooper's valuation of those two companies.

The appraisal remedy has deep roots in equity. The traditional rule through much of the 19th century was that any corporate transaction that changed the rights of common shareholders required unanimous consent. The appraisal remedy for dissenting shareholders evolved as it became clear that unanimous consent was inconsistent with the growth and development of large business enterprises. By the bargain struck in enacting an appraisal statute, the shareholder who disapproves of a proposed merger or other major corporate change gives up his right of veto in exchange for the right to be bought out—not at market value, but at "fair value." *See* Fischel, *The Appraisal Remedy in Corporate Law,* 1983 A.B.F. R.J. 875, 877; 12B W. Fletcher, *Cyclopedia of the Law of Private Corporations* § 5906.1, at 342 (rev. perm. ed. 1980). Methods used in valuing stock for tax, probate, ERISA, and like purposes in which market value is of the essence are inapposite to the determination of the fair value owed to dissenting shareholders. *See* Haynsworth at 459 ("The purpose of applying these discount variables is to determine the investment value or fair market value of a minority interest in the context of a hypothetical sale between a willing seller and buyer, a situation that does not exist in the dissenting shareholder situation"). In the statutory appraisal proceeding, the involuntary change of ownership caused by a merger requires as a matter of fairness that a dissenting shareholder be compensated for the loss of his proportionate interest in the business as an entity. The valuation focus under the appraisal statute is not the stock as a commodity, but rather the stock only as it represents a proportionate part of the enterprise as a whole. The question for the court becomes simple and direct: What is the best price a single buyer could reasonably be expected to pay for the firm as an entirety? The court then prorates that value for the whole firm equally among all shares of its common stock. The result is that all of those shares have the same fair value.

Our view of the appraisal remedy is obviously inconsistent with the application of minority and nonmarketability discounts. Lido would have us discount the stock for minority status and lack of marketability in order to reflect what it calls the "real world" value of the stock to the Dissenters. Lido bases its argument upon a plain misreading of our analysis in *Libby*. We there in a footnote approved the "willing buyer/willing seller" approach used by the court-appointed appraiser in *Libby* "so far as it goes" to determine stock *market* price; we did not, however, equate the price at which a willing seller would sell and a willing buyer would buy a minority block of stock with its fair value under the appraisal statute. *See Libby,* 406 A.2d at 61 n.8. The willing seller/willing buyer price is indicative only of stock market price, and that is only one of the three factors used in the *Libby* analysis of the fair value of stock listed on the New York Stock Exchange. Especially in fixing the appraisal remedy in a close corporation, the relevant inquiry is what is the highest price a single buyer would reasonably pay for the whole enterprise, not what a willing buyer and a willing seller would bargain out as the sales price of a dissenting shareholder's shares in a hypothetical market transaction. Any rule of law that gave the shareholders less than their proportionate share of the whole firm's fair value would produce a transfer of wealth from the minority shareholders to the shareholders in control. Such a rule would inevitably encourage corporate squeeze-outs. *See* Haynesworth at 489. As the Delaware Supreme Court stated recently in *Cavalier Oil Corp. v. Harnett*,

> to fail to accord to a minority shareholder the full proportionate value of his shares imposes a penalty for lack of control, and unfairly enriches the majority shareholders who may reap a windfall from the appraisal process by cashing out a dissenting shareholder, a clearly undesirable result.

Cavalier Oil Corp. v. Harnett, 564 A.2d 1137 at 1145. We agree.

In the case at bar the referee explicitly held that discounting the value of the Dissenters' stock because they chose to dissent from the merger and to exercise their appraisal rights would be inconsistent with the concept of fair value under the appraisal statute. Relying on testimony by Lido's own expert that no market exists for the stock, the referee found that market price has no reliability in the calculus of fair value in this case and accorded no weight to any market price factor.[8] As a matter of law, the Dissenters are entitled to their proportionate share of each Maine company at its full fair value.

In attacking the referee's fair value determination, Lido also argues that he erred in admitting in evidence the testimony of Robert Noone, the Dissenters' real estate appraisal expert. Noone appraised 39 properties of the three Maine corporations as of 1976. His appraisal method involved comparing the companies' properties with comparable properties that had recently been sold, taking into account such individual factors as size and location before arriving at an appraised value. Lido was given ample opportunity to examine Noone's appraisals prior to the hearings, and Lido's own experts relied on Noone's appraisals in preparing their opinions.

At the hearing, Lido objected to Noone's testimony on the ground that his written appraisals did not include information on the comparables he had used and so lacked a factual basis. The referee suspended Noone's testimony to allow Noone to produce the missing data on comparables.

---

8. In the absence of any trading history on any market, Lido's attempt to construct a hypothetical market for this stock is a particularly useless—and dangerously misleading—exercise. In the situation in which the stock in question has never been traded on a market, courts and commentators alike have rejected construction of a market as too speculative to be helpful in the appraisal process. *See, e.g., Cavalier Oil Corp. v. Harnett*, 564 A.2d 1137, slip op. at 8 (Del. 1989); *Sarrouf v. New England Patriots Football Club*, 397 Mass. 542, 549, 492 N.E.2d 1122, 1127 (1986); *In re Glosser Bros.*, 382 Pa. Super. 177, 555 A.2d 129, 134–35 (1989); *Folk* § 262.9.2.3. at 173 (2d ed. 1988); *Haynsworth*, at 498 n. 174. *But see Armstrong v. Marathon Oil Co.*, 32 Ohio St. 3d 397, 411, 513 N.E.2d 776, 789 (1987). Even if the stock had a reliable market price, any discount or premium would already be taken into account through this factor and no separate discounting *per se* of the whole fair value would be in order. *See Ford v. Courier–Journal Job Printing Co.*, 639 S.W.2d 553, 556–57 (Ky.Ct.App.1982); *Columbia Management Co. v. Wyss*, 94 Ore. App. 195, 205–06, 765 P.2d 207, 213 (1988); *Blasingame v. American Materials, Inc.*, 654 S.W.2d 659, 669 (Tenn.1983).

When his testimony resumed, Noone had reconstructed data on 46 of his 100 comparables. Lido renewed its objection to Noone's testimony but did not cross-examine him on the new data.

The referee admitted the Noone testimony and in his report found no unfairness to either party in using the Noone appraisals as the basis for expert opinions. By the time Noone left the stand, he had provided a sufficient factual basis for his testimony to withstand challenge under M.R. Evid. 705. *See Maietta v. International Harvester Co.,* 496 A.2d 286, 293 (Me.1985); *E.N. Nason v. Land–Ho Dev. Corp.,* 403 A.2d 1173, 1180 (Me.1979). *See also* Field & Murray, *Maine Evidence* § 705.1, at 286–87 (1987). The referee committed no error in admitting the Noone testimony. The weight to be accorded the testimony was then up to him as the fact finder.

13–A M.R.S.A. § 909(9)(G) provides that the Superior Court's judgment "shall include an allowance for interest at such rate as the court may find to be fair and equitable in all the circumstances, from the date on which the vote was taken on the proposed corporate action to the date of payment." Relying on the evidence presented by the parties about the interest rates prevailing between 1976 and 1987, and noting that the current prejudgment interest statute uses an 8% rate, the referee selected a rate of 8% for the interest to be allowed the Dissenters on the fair value of their stock from December 6, 1976, to the date of payment. Then the referee ruled that the 8% interest should be simple interest, not compound. While we uphold the referee's choice of an 8% rate as within his discretion, we reverse as legal error the referee's failure to award compound interest in the circumstances of this case.* * *

Prejudgment interest under section 1602 is explicitly a procedural device to encourage expeditious litigation. As a matter of law, interest under the appraisal statute is not a mere procedural incentive but is a substantive right, intended to reimburse the Dissenters for the lost use of their money during the pendency of the appraisal proceeding while the corporation retained control and use of it. *See Universal City Studios,* 334 A.2d at 222 ("the purpose of interest is to fairly compensate [dissenting shareholder] plaintiffs for their inability to use the money during the period in question); *Hernando Bank v. Huff,* 609 F. Supp. at 1129 ("the rate is determined with a view towards compensating the dissenting stockholders for their inability to use the money owed them for their shares during the time fair value is calculated"); *In re Glosser Bros.,* 382 Pa. Super. 177, 555 A.2d 129, 146 (1989) (the interest awarded is to be "fair compensation to the dissenters for deprivation of the fair value of their stock from the effective date of the merger"). One commentator has forcefully noted that

> in the absence of compound interest, the corporation could force the dissenter to sell his shares at less than fair value. If the corporation initially makes a low settlement offer, lengthy appraisal proceedings are inevitable. However, the allowance of only simply interest on the

> appraisal award could, in some cases, result in a situation where it would be more profitable for the shareholder to accept the settlement offer and invest the money in a savings account, drawing compounded interest quarterly, rather than go through the lengthy appraisal process. This result is clearly inconsistent with the purpose of the appraisal statutes which is to guarantee the dissenting shareholder fair value of his shares and to encourage the corporation to make a fair settlement offer.

Grant at 19–20. Compounding the 8% interest rate selected in this case is the only fair and equitable way to compensate the Dissenters for the lost use of their funds for nearly thirteen years. * * *

Section 909(9)(H) provides that as a matter of course the costs and expenses of the appraisal proceeding are assessed against the corporation, unless the dissenting shareholders reject the corporation's offer in bad faith. This section also provides:

> If the fair value of the shares as determined materially exceeds the amount which the corporation offered to pay therefor ... the court in its discretion may award to any shareholder who is party to the proceeding such sum as the court may determine to be reasonable compensation to any expert or experts employed by the shareholder in the proceeding, and may, in its discretion, award to any shareholder all or part of his attorney's fees and expenses.

The referee found the fair value of the Dissenters' shares to be over 260% of the amount Lido offered to pay therefor. Thus the "materially exceeds" precondition for the discretionary award of expert and attorney fees was clearly triggered. The referee awarded the Dissenters expert expenses and compensation, but did not award them any attorney fees. That, the Dissenters argue, was an abuse of discretion.

The effect of section 909(9)(H) is to eliminate the American Rule regarding the dissenting shareholders' attorney fees wherever, as here, the corporation has offered the shareholders "materially" less than the ultimately determined fair value of their shares. In that situation the court, freed from any presumption that both sides must pay for their own counsel, awards the shareholders such part or all of their attorney fees as it in its discretion finds reasonable in all of the circumstances. The statute has the salutary purpose of providing an incentive for the corporation to make a realistically fair offer at the outset, and it tends to offset the chilling effect that a costly appraisal proceeding has upon shareholders' election of the statutory remedy. *See Blake v. Blake Agency*, 107 A.D.2d 139, 151, 486 N.Y.S.2d 341, 350 (1985).

In the case at bar, although a different referee examining the same circumstances might have justifiably exercised his discretion to grant the Dissenters part or even all of their attorney fees, we cannot find any abuse of discretion in this referee's denial of those fees. That action fell within the scope of his allowable discretion. He did give the shareholders the full fees of their experts, a significant part of their litigation costs. Also, because two of the former corporations were owned about equally by the dissenting shareholders and the other Pescosolido family members (McLoon and Morse Bros.) and the Dissenters are by our mandate being compensated in interest for the loss of the fair value of their stock during the pendency of the litigation, it does not seem unfair for each side to bear its own expenses of legal representation. The Dissenters do not persuade us of any reason to disturb the referee's discretionary call on attorney fees.

Judgment modifies to allow 8% interest compounded annually in accordance with the opinion herein; judgment as so modified affirmed. Costs on appeal allowed to the dissenting shareholders.

HERNANDO BANK v. HUFF

609 F.Supp. 1124 (N.D.Miss.1985).

BIGGERS, DISTRICT JUDGE.

This diversity case involves valuation of the stock of several shareholders who dissented to the change of corporate form by plaintiff Hernando Bank, a banking corporation, to a banking corporation owned by a one-bank holding company, plaintiff Gateway Capitol Corporation. In a vote taken on September 9, 1982, a sufficient number of shareholders in the Hernando Bank approved the change in corporate form; thus, the Hernando Bank subsequently became a wholly-owned subsidiary of Gateway Capital Corporation. The defendants herein dissented to the proposed merger and perfected their rights pursuant to Miss.Code Ann. § 79–3–161 (1972) to demand that their stock be purchased by the plaintiff Hernando Bank.

In accordance with the Mississippi statute, the Hernando Bank obtained an appraisal of the stock from Morgan–Keegan of Memphis, Tennessee. Morgan-Keegan determined that the stock had a fair market value of $78.50 per share, to which the Hernando Bank added accrued dividends and offered the defendants the sum of $80.50 per share.[2] This offer was rejected by the defendants; thus, the plaintiffs seek a court determination of the proper value per share of stock.

Inasmuch as the absence of case law requires this court to make an "*Erie* guess" regarding construction of the statute, the factors viewed by the chancellor provide this court with some guidance. These factors include:

----

2. The Mississippi Corporate Dissent Statute, like that of many jurisdictions, provides that "fair value" shall be paid for the stock. Although "fair value" is not statutorily defined, it is generally accepted that the term is not necessarily synonymous with "fair market value," and instead contemplates an equitable evaluation wherein other relevant factors are considered. *See, e.g., In Re Watt & Shand,* 452 Pa. 287, 304 A.2d 694 (1973) (fair value is intrinsic value, not necessarily fair market value). The Morgan–Keegan appraiser testified that he never considered any distinction between "fair value" and "fair market value."

the liquidating value, the net asset value, the market value, the asset value, the dividends, the earnings prospects, the nature of the enterprise, the general market conditions, the availability of financing, management's performance, prospects for dividends, past and future earnings, general economic conditions under which the company was operated, particular industry involved, the trends within that industry, the long range obligations of the company, and the long range prospects of the company, and including the offers of the defendant to the complainant ... and the investing experience of the complainant and of the defendant....

Duvic v. Cal–Maine Foods, Inc., No. 81,116, slip op. at 9 (Miss.Ch., 1st Jud.Dist.Hinds Cty. July 20, 1971).

The defendants argue that the statute excludes consideration of any purchase offers, since fair value must be determined on the date prior to approval of the proposed corporate action and without reference to appreciation or depreciation in anticipation of such action. This provision indicates to the court that the corporation should be viewed as a going concern, rather than a liquidated entity.[3] However, the statutory prohibition against the consideration of any appreciation or depreciation in anticipation of a corporate merger in no way excludes consideration of purchase offers made for this or comparable corporations. In fact, since the going concern value of a company is generally defined as "its worth as an operating business to another firm or individual," *see* Western & Brigham, Essentials of Managerial Finance 443 (6th ed. 1982), such offers have particular relevance. In the case of an offer for a comparable company, the relevance of a purchase offer is not diminished due to the consummation of the sale.

Furthermore, the defendants argue at length that their stock shares should be valued as a pro rata share of the corporation, and that a "minority discount" due to the lack of corporate control in such shares is improper. The defendants strenuously contend that a minority shareholder should not be "punished" for his lack of a controlling interest by discounting his stock, especially since the corporate change in form is involuntary with respect to the dissenter. *See Dreiseszun v. FLM Industries, Inc.*, 577 S.W.2d 902, 906 (Mo.App.1979) (minority discount improper); *Woodward v. Quigley*, 257 Iowa 1077, 133 N.W.2d 38, 41, *modified on rehearing*, 257 Iowa 1077, 136 N.W.2d 280 (1965) (same).

Despite the superficial appeal of the defendants' argument, the court is unconvinced that a minority share of stock should be valued as though it were a controlling share of a corporation. Accordingly, the court concludes that in the present case a minority discount is proper in determining the fair value of the stock of the dissenters.

Courts universally view three elements in determining the fair value of stock—market value, asset value, and investment (or earnings) value.

---

3. Case law uniformly holds that a dissenting shareholder is entitled to receive his intrinsic share of a going concern. [citing cases]

Valuation of Dissenters' Stock Under Appraisal Statutes, 79 Harv.L.Rev.
1453, 1457 (1966). However,

> all three elements do not have to influence the result in every
> valuation proceeding. It suffices if they are all considered. Compelling
> the consideration of all of them, including those which may turn out
> to be unreliable in a particular case, has the salutary effect of
> assuring more complete justification by the appraiser of the conclu-
> sion he reaches. It also provides a more concrete basis for court
> review.

Endicott Johnson Corp. v. Bade, 338 N.E.2d 614, 616 (N.Y.1975). This
court approves of the approach adopted in *Endicott* and other cases, and
therefore shall consider all three methods.

Market value, or fair market value, is "the amount that a purchaser
who is willing, but not required to buy, would pay, and that a seller who is
willing but not required to sell, would accept"; furthermore, it is necessary
that "both the purchaser and the seller be fully informed of all the
circumstances involving the value and use of the property." In determining fair market value of stock, the price at which recent sales were made
obviously is relevant. Although the market for stock in the Hernando
Bank was relatively thin and primarily consisted of insider transactions in
non-controlling stock interests, the value at which the stock changed
hands is nonetheless significant.

Evidence presented at trial showed that the Hernando Bank issued
new shares of stock in 1974 and 1977 at $80.00 and $85.00 per share,
respectively. Despite some evidence to the contrary, the court finds that
the Hernando Bank experienced healthy growth between such dates and
the time of the merger. In making this determination, the court is
persuaded by many items of evidence presented at trial. For example,
between 1974 when the officers and directors valued new Hernando Bank
stock at $80.00 per share, and 1982 when the bank merged, deposits had a
155% increase from $19,100,000.00 to $48,700,000.00. Furthermore, between 1977 and September 8, 1982, bank assets increased by 70%, from
$31,300,000.00 to $53,200,000.00. In 1977, earnings before securities
transactions were 246,000.00; however, 1981 brought a 96% increase to
$482,000.00. Furthermore, loans increased by 70% from $28,700,000.00 in
1977 to $48,700,000.00 in 1982; however, the loan loss ratio was one of the
lowest in the state. Bank capital increased from $2,300,000.00 in 1977 to
$3,400,000.00 in 1982, and investments practically doubled from
$10,300,000.00 to $19,000,000.00 during the same period. The substantial
growth is due to both population increase in DeSoto County and the good
management of the Hernando Bank.

In view of the substantial growth of the Hernando Bank, this court
has difficulty in understanding how the market value of the stock could
have decreased to $78.50 per share, as determined by the Morgan–Keegan
appraisal. It is even more difficult for this court to accept the plaintiffs'
current contention that Morgan–Keegan erroneously adjusted the value of

the stock upward to compensate for a market depression, and that the proper valuation is only $45.00 per share. The court instead is impressed by the fact that there were a number of sales in the $95.00 to $100.00 range in recent years prior to the evaluation date.[4] Furthermore, the court notes that the officers and directors of the Hernando Bank set $95.00 as the price at which the bank's Employee Stock Option Plan (ESOP) would purchase stock shares. In view of this evidence, the court determines that $95.00 per share is the proper market value.

The asset value approach, which involves valuation of the total corporate assets, is most useful in cases wherein the corporation is to be liquidated and the assets sold, since "minority stockholders typically have invested for dividend income or stock appreciation and rarely expect to share in the physical assets." 79 Harv.L.Rev. at 1460. *See also In Re Valuation of Common Stock of Libby, McNeill & Libby,* 406 A.2d 54, 66 (Me.1979) (net asset value generally not heavily weighted in stock valuation unless such valuation made for liquidation purposes).

In the present case, the sole evidence submitted regarding the value of the corporate assets was a fire insurance policy on some of the bank's assets. Inasmuch as this policy at best is probative only as to the value of the physical corporate assets rather than the corporate realty, and since the present case does not involve a corporate liquidation, the court gives the asset value approach little weight in the present case.

The third method used in stock valuation is the investment value approach, wherein the earnings of the company are multiplied by the company's price-earning ratio. In computing the earnings to be used, courts generally require an average of the earnings for the previous five years, *see, e.g.,* excluding extraordinary gains and losses during that period. The average annual yearly earnings for the Hernando Bank from 1977 through 1982, using projected earnings for 1982 due to the merger on September 9, 1982, were $340,000.00.

The plaintiffs, relying in part on the Morgan–Keegan appraisal, suggest a multiplier of 5.61, based upon trades of common stock of purportedly comparable publicly traded bank holding companies in the southeast region of the United States. However, the defendants assert that the Hernando Bank, a non-publicly traded corporation, is not comparable to a publicly traded bank holding company, *see* 79 Harv. L. Rev. at 1463 (comparison of publicly traded and non-publicly traded corporations unreliable), and further assert that Morgan–Keegan selected these companies as comparables simply because data on such companies was available in their Memphis office. In addition, the defendants contend that the bank holding companies used as comparable by Morgan–Keegan differ greatly from the Hernando Bank in amount of deposits, assets, quality of securi-

---

4. The defendants have asserted that $95.00 per share is not the proper fair market value in this case, since such price reflects a minority discount. Inasmuch as the court accepts that a minority discount is proper, the $95.00 sales are relevant in determining fair market value.

ties portfolios, non-bank income or loss, loan losses, and issuance of preferred stock.

Instead, the defendants have conducted an exhaustive national search of over 800 complete bank sales and found ten sales that purportedly met the test of comparability with Hernando Bank. *See* Desmond & Kelly, Business Valuation Handbook 257 (4th ed. 1980) (no requirement that comparable business be located within immediate community). Using a multiplier of twelve, as suggested by the defendants based upon their study, the investment value approach computed on the average earnings for the previous five years yields a result of $102.00 per share for the 40,000 outstanding shares.[5] This result is very close to the fair market value of $95.00 to $100.00 per share established through actual sales.

The court concludes that the fair value of the stock is $100.00 per share. This result appears to be the fair market value of the stock, and is confirmed through the investment value approach.

NOTES

1.   Do you understand the concept of present value? What is an asset producing X dollars for X years worth to you if purchased for a lump sum today. This will require an interest calculation on the lump sum that would return the X dollars for X years. This is essentially how the lottery values its lump sum payouts. Say you win a $1 million dollar lottery. You do not really win $1 million dollars. Rather, you will receive say $50,000 for twenty years or you may elect a lump sum, upfront payout of say $500,000 (a sum that will be determined by an imputed interest rate that would return a total of $1 million in principal and interest over twenty years). The annuity principle works similarly. For example, in the case of an immediate annuity, you will pay a lump sum amount that will provide a lifetime stream of income that will be based on the amount of the lump sum payment, an assumed interest rate and your life expectancy. You can value a corporation similarly by determining what lump sum will be equal to the expected income of the corporation over its expected earnings based on a rate of return you believe is desirable based on the risks of the investment and current and projected interest rates. If the corporation will cost you more than what you could earn on a United States government guaranteed bond, why would you pay such an amount and incur the uncompensated risk?

Say you want to buy a corporation that sells DVD movies. It has a single store and had total assets at year end of $150,000, including inventory and some computers. The corporation has $125,000 in debts, including its lease. What would you pay for this corporation? Would your answer change, if you discovered that the company turned its inventory over weekly and was making profits of $75,000 a month. Would your answer change if there was a lawsuit against the corporation making a tort claim and seeking $25 million in damages? Would your answer change if the corporation had insurance to cover the claim or if your lawyer advised that the claim was without merit?

---

5.   ($340,000 x 12)/40,000 = $102.00 per share.

Would your answer change if you discovered that the corporation's line of business was becoming less fashionable because of Internet sales? These are just a few considerations that arise in seeking to value an ongoing business. Remember that determining fair value is really a set of educated guesses. It is not a science. No matter how scientific some valuation models appear, no amount of math or complex formulas assure that the value is a correct one. Only the market is able to truly value a business, and that valuation changes constantly, as evidenced by the constant fluctuations in prices for stocks traded on the markets.

2. The statutory appraisal remedy is designed to determine the dissenter's *proportionate* value *of the firm*. See, e.g., Advanced Communication Design, Inc. v. Follett, 615 N.W.2d 285, 290 (Minn.2000) ("fair value" means pro rata value of corporation's value as a going concern); First Western Bank Wall v. Olsen, 621 N.W.2d 611, 617 (S.D.2001) ("fair value" means value of dissenters' shares as proportionate interest in going concern; appraisal proceeding should not focus on stock as a commodity).

3. *Minority discount*. The majority of the more recent decisions have emphasized that the appraisal statutes call for a value of the shareholder's proportionate interest in the firm, not simply their shares, so that it is inappropriate to deduct a minority discount. See Swope v. Siegel–Robert, Inc., 243 F.3d 486, 495–496 (8th Cir.2001) (applying Missouri law; minority status of stock is irrelevant in appraisal proceeding); Pueblo Bancorporation v. Lindoe, Inc., 37 P.3d 492 (Colo.App.2001) (reversing trial court's use of minority discount); Cavalier Oil Corp. v. Harnett, 564 A.2d 1137 (Del.1989); Blitch v. Peoples Bank, 246 Ga.App. 453, 540 S.E.2d 667 (2000) (rejecting minority discount in appraisal); In re Valuation of Common Stock of McLoon Oil Co., 565 A.2d 997 (Me.1989); Richton Bank & Trust Company v. Bowen, 798 So.2d 1268 (Miss.2001); MT Properties Inc. v. CMC Real Estate Corp., 481 N.W.2d 383 (Minn.Ct.App.1992); Rigel Corp. v. Cutchall, 245 Neb. 118, 511 N.W.2d 519 (1994); First Western Bank Wall v. Olsen, 621 N.W.2d 611, 619 (S.D.2001); Robblee v. Robblee, 68 Wash.App. 69, 841 P.2d 1289 (1992) (minority discount inappropriate in close corporation); HMO–W Inc. v. SSM Health Care System, 234 Wis.2d 707, 611 N.W.2d 250 (2000), affirming in relevant part 228 Wis.2d 815, 598 N.W.2d 577 (App.1999) (reversing trial court's use of minority discount). See also, e.g., Friedman v. Beway Realty Corp., 87 N.Y.2d 161, 638 N.Y.S.2d 399, 661 N.E.2d 972 (1995) (though a discount for the lack of marketability of shares in closely held corporation is appropriate, for public policy reasons there should be no minority discount). As explained by the Delaware Supreme Court:

> The application of a discount to a minority shareholder is contrary to the requirement that the company be viewed as a "going concern." Cavalier's argument, that the only way Harnett would have received value for his 1.5% stock interest was to sell his stock, subject to market treatment of its minority status, misperceives the nature of the appraisal remedy. Where there is no objective market data available, the appraisal process is not intended to reconstruct a *pro forma* sale but to assume that the shareholder was willing to maintain his investment position, however slight, had the merger not occurred. Discounting individual share holdings injects into the appraisal process speculation on the various factors

which may dictate the marketability of minority shareholdings. More important, to fail to accord to a minority shareholder the full proportionate value of his shares imposes a penalty for lack of control, and unfairly enriches the majority shareholders who may reap a windfall from the appraisal process by cashing out a dissenting shareholder, a clearly undesirable result.

Cavalier Oil Corp. v. Harnett, 564 A.2d 1137, 1145 (Del.1989). The 1999 amendments to the Model Business Corporation Act provide that fair value in appraisal is to be determined on a proportionate basis without considering a minority discount. Model Business Corporation Act § 13.01(4).

4. *Marketability discount.* Once a value is arrived at should the appraiser consider a marketablility discount for illiquid shares? A number of courts have disapproved the application of a marketability discount. Swope v. Siegel–Robert, Inc., 243 F.3d 486, 493 (8th Cir.2001) (applying Missouri law; marketability discount is incompatible with purpose of appraisals i.e., to enable dissenting shareholders to recapture their complete investment when they are unwillingly subjected to substantial corporate changes); Paskill Corp. v. Alcoma Corp., 747 A.2d 549, 557 (Del. 2000) (reduction for discount applied to unmarketable shares not registered with SEC or traded on any public market would constitute improper discount at the shareholder level); Arnaud v. Stockgrowers State Bank of Ashland, Kan., 268 Kan. 163, 992 P.2d 216, 220–221 (1999) (marketability discount is not appropriate when purchaser is either majority shareholder or the corporation itself, or when fractional share resulted from reverse stock split intended to eliminate minority shareholder's interest); Richton Bank & Trust Company v. Bowen, 798 So.2d 1268 (Miss. 2001) (rejecting marketability discount); Lawson Mardon Wheaton, Inc. v. Smith, 160 N.J. 383, 734 A.2d 738, 749 (1999) (marketability discounts generally should not be applied in determining fair value of dissenting shareholder's stock in appraisal action); Balsamides v. Protameen Chems., Inc., 160 N.J. 352, 734 A.2d 721, 734 (1999) (same); DiLuglio v. Providence Auto Body, Inc., 755 A.2d 757, 774 (R.I.2000) (even in close corporation, marketability discount is inappropriate if sale of stock to known and qualified buyer is certain); First Western Bank Wall v. Olsen, 621 N.W.2d 611, 619 (S.D.2001) (since appraisal process merely values business as a whole and divides up that value proportionately, the fact that dissenting shareholders would have a difficult time selling their shares is irrelevant). The 1999 amendments to the Model Business Corporation Act provide that the appraiser should not take into account a marketability discount. Model Bus. Corp. Act § 13.01(4).

5. In Santa Fe Industries, Inc. v. Green, 430 U.S. 462, 97 S.Ct. 1292, 51 L.Ed.2d 480 (1977), the Supreme Court held that Rule 10b–5 is a disclosure-based remedy and therefore a claim that a grossly unfair transaction amounted to equitable fraud was not sufficient to state a claim. The Court there further pointed out that, since the defendant had complied with the Delaware appraisal statute, it would not be appropriate for federal law to impose additional requirements regarding this state law procedure. Compare the appraisal remedy on the same facts in Bell v. Kirby Lumber Corp., 413 A.2d 137 (Del.1980). More recently, the Delaware Supreme Court refused to adopt heightened disclosure requirements with respect to an appraisal proceeding:

Appellants are advocating a new disclosure standard in cases where appraisal is an option. They suggest that stockholders should be given all the financial data they would need if they were making an independent determination of fair value. Appellants offer no authority for their position and we see no reason to depart from our traditional standards. We agree that a stockholder deciding whether to seek appraisal should be given financial information about the company that will be material to that decision. In this case, however, the basic financial data were disclosed and appellants failed to allege any facts indicating that the omitted information was material. Accordingly, the complaint properly was dismissed for failure to state a claim.

Skeen v. Jo–Ann Stores, Inc., 750 A.2d 1170, 1174 (Del.2000). See also, e.g., McMullin v. Beran, 765 A.2d 910, 917 (Del.2000) ("They were also obliged to disclose with entire candor all material facts concerning the merger, so that the minority stockholders would be able to make an informed decision whether to accept the tender offer price or to seek judicial remedies such as appraisal or an injunction."). Cf. Goldberg v. Meridor, 567 F.2d 209 (2d Cir.1977), cert. denied, 434 U.S. 1069, 98 S.Ct. 1249, 55 L.Ed.2d 771 (1978), page 745 above which held that material nondisclosures which deprived plaintiff of a state law remedy could be actionable under Rule 10b–5. Compare the *Virginia Bankshares* case, page 754 above.

6. In Montgomery Cellular Holding Co. Inc. v. Dobler, 880 A.2d 206 (Del. 2005), the Delaware Supreme Court awarded attorney fees to minority shareholders who had demanded an appraisal in a cash-out short form merger. The court found that misconduct in the proceedings by the respondent justified such an award.

SECTION 3.   APPRAISAL RIGHTS IN DE FACTO MERGERS AND OTHER REORGANIZATIONS

FARRIS v. GLEN ALDEN CORP.

393 Pa. 427, 143 A.2d 25 (1958).

COHEN, JUSTICE.

We are required to determine on this appeal whether, as a result of a 'Reorganization Agreement' executed by the officers of Glen Alden Corporation and List Industries Corporation, and approved by the shareholders of the former company, the rights and remedies of a dissenting shareholder accrue to the plaintiff.

Glen Alden is a Pennsylvania corporation engaged principally in the mining of anthracite coal and lately in the manufacture of air conditioning units and fire-fighting equipment. In recent years the company's operating revenue has declined substantially, and in fact, its coal operations have resulted in tax loss carryovers of approximately $14,000,000. In October

1957, List, a Delaware holding company owning interests in motion picture theaters, textile companies and real estate, and to a lesser extent, in oil and gas operations, warehouses and aluminum piston manufacturing, purchased through a wholly owned subsidiary 38.5% of Glen Alden's outstanding stock.[1] This acquisition enabled List to place three of its directors on the Glen Alden board.

On March 20, 1958, the two corporations entered into a 'reorganization agreement,' subject to stockholder approval, which contemplated the following actions:

1. Glen Alden is to acquire all of the assets of List, excepting a small amount of cash reserved for the payment of List's expenses in connection with the transaction. These assets include over $8,000,000 in cash held chiefly in the treasuries of List's wholly owned subsidiaries.

2. In consideration of the transfer, Glen Alden is to issue 3,621,703 shares of stock to List. List in turn is to distribute the stock to its shareholders at a ratio of five shares of Glen Alden stock for each six shares of List stock. In order to accomplish the necessary distribution, Glen Alden is to increase the authorized number of its shares of capital stock from 2,500,000 shares to 7,500,000 shares without according pre-emptive rights to the present shareholders upon the issuance of any such shares.

3. Further, Glen Alden is to assume all of List's liabilities including a $5,000,000 note incurred by List in order to purchase Glen Alden stock in 1957, outstanding stock options, incentive stock options plans, and pension obligations.

4. Glen Alden is to change its corporate name from Glen Alden Corporation to List Alden Corporation.

5. The present directors of both corporations are to become directors of List Alden.

6. List is to be dissolved and List Alden is to then carry on the operations of both former corporations.

Two days after the agreement was executed notice of the annual meeting of Glen Alden to be held on April 11, 1958, was mailed to the shareholders together with a proxy statement analyzing the reorganization agreement and recommending its approval as well as approval of certain amendments to Glen Alden's articles of incorporation and bylaws necessary to implement the agreement. At this meeting the holders of a majority of the outstanding shares, (not including those owned by List), voted in favor of a resolution approving the reorganization agreement.

On the day of the shareholders' meeting, plaintiff, a shareholder of Glen Alden, filed a complaint in equity against the corporation and its

---

1. Of the purchase price of $8,719,109, $5,000,000 was borrowed.

officers seeking to enjoin them temporarily until final hearing, and perpetually thereafter, from executing and carrying out the agreement.

The gravamen of the complaint was that the notice of the annual shareholders' meeting did not conform to the requirements of the Business Corporation Law in three respects: (1) It did not give notice to the shareholders that the true intent and purpose of the meeting was to effect a merger or consolidation of Glen Alden and List; (2) It failed to give notice to the shareholders of their right to dissent to the plan of merger or consolidation and claim fair value for their shares, and (3) It did not contain copies of the text of certain sections of the Business Corporation Law as required.[3] By reason of these omissions, plaintiff contended that the approval of the reorganization agreement by the shareholders at the annual meeting was invalid and unless the carrying out of the plan were enjoined, he would suffer irreparable loss by being deprived of substantial property rights.

The defendants answered admitting the material allegations of fact in the complaint but denying that they gave rise to a cause of action because the transaction complained of was a purchase of corporate assets as to which shareholders had no rights of dissent or appraisal. For these reasons the defendants then moved for judgment on the pleadings.[5]

The court below concluded that the reorganization agreement entered into between the two corporations was a plan for a *de facto* merger, and that therefore the failure of the notice of the annual meeting to conform to the pertinent requirements of the merger provisions of the Business Corporation Law rendered the notice defective and all proceedings in furtherance of the agreement void. Wherefore, the court entered a final decree denying defendants' motion for judgment on the pleadings, entering judgment upon plaintiff's complaint and granting the injunctive relief therein sought. This appeal followed.

When use of the corporate form of business organization first became widespread, it was relatively easy for courts to define a 'merger' or a 'sale of assets' and to label a particular transaction as one or the other. But prompted by the desire to avoid the impact of adverse, and to obtain the benefits of favorable, government regulations, particularly federal tax laws, new accounting and legal techniques were developed by lawyers and accountants which interwove the elements characteristic of each, thereby creating hybrid forms of corporate amalgamation. Thus, it is no longer helpful to consider an individual transaction in the abstract and solely by

---

3. The proxy statement included the following declaration: 'Appraisal Rights. In the opinion of counsel, the shareholders of neither Glen Alden nor List Industries will have any rights of appraisal or similar rights of dissenters with respect to any matter to be acted upon at their respective meetings.'

5. Counsel for the defendants concedes that if the corporation is required to pay the dissenting shareholders the appraised fair value of their shares, the resultant drain of cash would prevent Glen Alden from carrying out the agreement. On the other hand, plaintiff contends that if the shareholders had been told of their rights as dissenters, rather than specifically advised that they had no such rights, the resolution approving the reorganization agreement would have been defeated.

reference to the various elements therein determine whether it is a 'merger' or a 'sale'. Instead, to determine properly the nature of a corporate transaction, we must refer not only to all the provisions of the agreement, but also to the consequences of the transaction and to the purposes of the provisions of the corporation law said to be applicable. We shall apply this principle to the instant case.

[T]he Pennsylvania Business Corporation Law provides: 'If any shareholder of a domestic corporation which becomes a party to a plan of merger or consolidation shall object to such plan of merger or consolidation * * * such shareholder shall be entitled to * * * [the fair value of his shares upon surrender of the share certificate or certificates representing his shares].' This provision had its origin in the early decision of this Court in Lauman v. Lebanon Valley R. R. Co., 1858, 30 Pa. 42. There a shareholder who objected to the consolidation of his company with another was held to have a right in the absence of statute to treat the consolidation as a dissolution of his company and to receive the value of his shares upon their surrender.

The rationale of the Lauman case, and of the present section of the Business Corporation Law based thereon, is that when a corporation combines with another so as to lose its essential nature and alter the original fundamental relationships of the shareholders among themselves and to the corporation, a shareholder who does not wish to continue his membership therein may treat his membership in the original corporation as terminated and have the value of his shares paid to him.

Does the combination outlined in the present 'reorganization' agreement so fundamentally change the corporate character of Glen Alden and the interest of the plaintiff as a shareholder therein, that to refuse him the rights and remedies of a dissenting shareholder would in reality force him to give up his stock in one corporation and against his will accept shares in another? If so, the combination is a merger within the meaning of section 908, subd. A of the corporation law.

If the reorganization agreement were consummated plaintiff would find that the 'List Alden' resulting from the amalgamation would be quite a different corporation than the 'Glen Alden' in which he is now a shareholder. Instead of continuing primarily as a coal mining company, Glen Alden would be transformed, after amendment of its articles of incorporation, into a diversified holding company whose interests would range from motion picture theaters to textile companies. Plaintiff would find himself a member of a company with assets of $169,000,000 and a long-term debt of $38,000,000 in lieu of a company one-half that size and with but one-seventh the long-term debt.

While the administration of the operations and properties of Glen Alden as well as List would be in the hands of management common to both companies, since all executives of List would be retained in List Alden, the control of Glen Alden would pass to the directors of List; for

List would hold eleven of the seventeen directorships on the new board of directors.

As an aftermath of the transaction plaintiff's proportionate interest in Glen Alden would have been reduced to only two-fifths of what it presently is because of the issuance of an additional 3,621,703 shares to List which would not be subject to pre-emptive rights. In fact, ownership of Glen Alden would pass to the stockholders of List who would hold 76.5% of the outstanding shares as compared with but 23.5% retained by the present Glen Alden shareholders.

Perhaps the most important consequence to the plaintiff, if he were denied the right to have his shares redeemed at their fair value, would be the serious financial loss suffered upon consummation of the agreement. While the present book value of his stock is $38 a share after combination it would be worth only $21 a share. In contrast, the shareholders of List who presently hold stock with a total book value of $33,000,000 or $7.50 a share, would receive stock with a book value of $76,000,000 or $21 a share.

Under these circumstances it may well be said that if the proposed combination is allowed to take place without right of dissent, plaintiff would have his stock in Glen Alden taken away from him and the stock of a new company thrust upon him in its place. He would be projected against his will into a new enterprise under terms not of his own choosing. It was to protect dissident shareholders against just such a result that this Court one hundred years ago in the Lauman case, and the legislature thereafter in section 908, subd. A, granted the right of dissent. And it is to accord that protection to the plaintiff that we conclude that the combination proposed in the case at hand is a merger within the intendment of section 908, subd. A.

Nevertheless, defendants contend that the 1957 amendments to sections 311 and 908 of the corporation law preclude us from reaching this result and require the entry of judgment in their favor. Subsection F of section 311 dealing with the voluntary transfer of corporate assets provides: 'The shareholders of a business corporation which acquires by sale, lease or exchange all or substantially all of the property of another corporation by the issuance of stock, securities or otherwise shall not be entitled to the rights and remedies of dissenting shareholders * * *.' Act of July 11, 1957, P.L. 711, § 1, 15 P.S. § 2852–311, subd. F.

And the amendment to section 908 reads as follows: 'The right of dissenting shareholders * * * shall not apply to the purchase by a corporation of assets whether or not the consideration therefor be money or property, real or personal, including shares or bonds or other evidences of indebtedness of such corporation. The shareholders of such corporation shall have no right to dissent from any such purchase.' Act of July 11, 1957, P.L. 711, § 1, 15 P.S. § 2852–908, subd. C.... Defendants view these amendments as abridging the right of shareholders to dissent to a transaction between two corporations which involves a transfer of assets for a consideration even though the transfer has all the legal incidents of a merger. They claim that only if the merger is accomplished in accordance with the prescribed statutory procedure does the right of dissent accrue. In support of this position they cite to us the comment on the amendments by the Committee on Corporation Law of the Pennsylvania Bar Association, the committee which originally drafted these provisions. The comment states that the provisions were intended to overrule cases which granted shareholders the right to dissent to a sale of assets when accompanied by the legal incidents of a merger.

Whatever may have been the intent of the *committee*, there is no evidence to indicate that the *legislature* intended the 1957 amendments to have the effect contended for. But furthermore, the language of these two provisions does not support the opinion of the committee and is inapt to achieve any such purpose. The amendments of 1957 do not provide that a transaction between two corporations which has the effect of a merger but which includes a transfer of assets for consideration is to be exempt from the protective provisions of sections 908, subd. A and 515. They provide only that the shareholders of a corporation which acquires the property or purchases the assets of another corporation, *without more*, are not entitled to the right to dissent from the transaction. So, as in the present case, when as part of a transaction between two corporations, one corporation dissolves, its liabilities are assumed by the survivor, its executives and directors take over the management and control of the survivor, and, as consideration for the transfer, its stockholders acquire a majority of the shares of stock of the survivor, then the transaction is no longer simply a purchase of assets or acquisition of property to which sections 311, subd. F and 908, subd. C apply, but a merger governed by section 908, subd. A of the corporation law. To divest shareholders of their right of dissent under such circumstances would require express language which is absent from the 1957 amendments.

Even were we to assume that the combination provided for in the reorganization agreement is a 'sale of assets' to which section 908, subd. A does not apply, it would avail the defendants nothing; we will not blind our eyes to the realities of the transaction. Despite the designation of the parties and the form employed, Glen Alden does not in fact acquire List, rather, List acquires Glen Alden, and under section 311, subd. D[8] the right of dissent would remain with the shareholders of Glen Alden.

We hold that the combination contemplated by the reorganization agreement, although consummated by contract rather than in accordance with the statutory procedure, is a merger within the protective purview of

---

8. 'If any shareholder of a business corporation which sells, leases or exchanges all or substantially all of its property and assets otherwise than (1) in the usual and regular course of its business, (2) for the purpose of relocating its business, or (3) in connection with its dissolution and liquidation, shall object to such sale, lease or exchange and comply with the provisions of section 515 of this act, such shareholder shall be entitled to the rights and remedies of dissenting shareholders as therein provided.' Act of July 11, 1957, P.L. 711, 15 P.S. § 2852–311, subd. D.

sections 908, subd. A and 515 of the corporation law. The shareholders of Glen Alden should have been notified accordingly and advised of their statutory rights of dissent and appraisal. The failure of the corporate officers to take these steps renders the stockholder approval of the agreement at the 1958 shareholders' meeting invalid. The lower court did not err in enjoining the officers and directors of Glen Alden from carrying out this agreement.

NOTES

1. *Legislative response.* The Pennsylvania legislature repudiated the de facto merger doctrine. See Penn. Stat. C. A. § 1904. As described in Terry v. Penn Central Corp., 668 F.2d 188 (3d Cir.1981):

> Appellants argue that Penn Central is nevertheless brought into the amalgamation by the de facto merger doctrine as set out in Pennsylvania law in Farris v. Glen Alden Corp., 393 Pa. 427, 143 A.2d 25 (1958). Farris was the penultimate step in a pas de deux involving the Pennsylvania courts and the Pennsylvania legislature regarding the proper treatment for transactions that reached the same practical result as a merger but avoided the legal form of merger and the concomitant legal obligations. In the 1950s the Pennsylvania courts advanced the doctrine that a transaction having the effect of an amalgamation would be treated as a de facto merger. See, e.g., Bloch v. The Baldwin Locomotive Works, 75 Pa.D. & C. 24 (1951). The legislature responded with efforts to constrict the de facto merger doctrine. Farris, addressing those efforts, held that the doctrine still covered a reorganization agreement that had the effect of merging a large corporation into a smaller corporation. In a 1959 response to Farris, the legislature made explicit its objection to earlier cases that found certain transactions to be de facto mergers. The legislature enacted a law, modifying inter alia Sections 311 and 908, entitled in part:

> > An Act ... changing the law as to ... the acquisition or transfer of corporate assets, the rights of dissenting shareholders, ... abolishing the doctrine of de facto mergers or consolidation and reversing the rules laid down in Bloch v. Baldwin Locomotive Works, 75 D & C 24, and Marks v. The Autocar Co., 153 F.Supp. 768, ...

> > Following this explicit statement, the de facto merger doctrine has rarely been invoked by the Pennsylvania courts.

668 F.2d at 193. See also Equity Group Holdings v. DMG, Inc., 576 F.Supp. 1197 (S.D.Fla.1983) (Florida law applied to validate a triangular merger without invoking the de facto merger doctrine to grant statutory appraisal rights). In contrast, New Jersey and California approved the de facto merger doctrine. N.J. Stat. Ann. § 14A:10–12 and Cal. Corp. Code §§ 168, 1101, 1200 & 1300.

HEILBRUNN v. SUN CHEMICAL CORP.

150 A.2d 755 (Del.1959).

SOUTHERLAND, CHIEF JUSTICE.

This suit is brought by stockholders of Sun Chemical Corporation, a Delaware corporation, against Ansbacher–Siegle Corporation, a New York corporation, and Norman E. Alexander, President of Sun and owner of Ansbacher. Plaintiffs attack the validity of the purchase by Sun of all the assets of Ansbacher. The complaint states two grounds or causes of action: (1) that the transaction constituted a *de facto* merger and is unlawful since the merger provisions of the Delaware law were not complied with; and (2) that the transaction 'was tainted with self-interest', i.e., is unfair to Sun stockholders.

Defendants moved to dismiss the complaint. The Vice Chancellor held that the transaction was one of purchase and sale and not a merger. He dismissed the complaint as to the first cause of action. He denied the motion to dismiss the second cause of action. Plaintiffs appeal, and contend here, as they did below, that the transaction was by its nature a *de facto* merger.

Although the transaction has been consummated, it is convenient to state many of the facts as they appeared on November 8, 1957, when the proxy statement was sent to the Sun stockholders. They are as follows:

Sun is engaged in the business of manufacturing ink and pigments for ink. It owns a plant at Harrison, New Jersey. It has outstanding 19,000 shares of preferred stock and 1,196,283 shares of common stock. Its balance sheet shows total assets of over $24,000,000. The defendant Alexander is its president, and owns about 2.8 per cent of the common shares. Ansbacher is engaged in the manufacture of organic pigments. Its products are used in the manufacture of ink, cosmetics, textiles, plastics, and other similar products. Its balance sheet shows total assets of about $1,786,000. The defendant Alexander is its sole beneficial stockholder. In April of 1956 Alexander, then the owner of about 7,000 shares of Sun, suggested to Sun's then president the possible acquisition of Ansbacher by Sun. Nothing came of the suggestion. In January, 1957, Alexander advised the Sun management that he and five friends and associates owned substantial amounts of Sun shares, and requested representation on the board. Negotiations followed, as a result of which five of the Sun directors resigned, and Alexander and four others named by him were elected to Sun's board. Alexander became president. In June, 1957, a special committee of Sun's board was appointed to consider whether Sun should own and operate a pigment plant, and if so whether it should rehabilitate its Harrison plant or should acquire or build a new plant. The committee found that Sun's Harrison plant was old, inefficient, and incapable of expansion because of its location. It recommended the acquisition of Ansbacher.

An agreement for the purchase was entered into between Sun and Ansbacher on October 2, 1957. It provides, among other things, as follows:

1.   Ansbacher will assign and convey to Sun all of Ansbacher's assets and property of every kind, tangible and intangible; and will grant to Sun the use of its name or any part thereof.

2.   Sun will assume all of Ansbacher's liabilities, subject to a covenant that Ansbacher's working capital shall be at least $600,000.

3.   Sun will issue to Ansbacher 225,000 shares of its common stock.

4.   As soon as possible after the closing of the transaction Ansbacher will dissolve and distribute to its shareholders, pro rata, the shares of the common stock of Sun (subject to an escrow agreement relating to one-fourth of the shares).

5.   Ansbacher will use its best efforts to persuade its employees to become employees of Sun.

6.   Sun's obligation to consummate the transaction is subject to approval by the holders of a majority of Sun's voting stock, exclusive of shares owned or controlled by Alexander, at a special stockholders' meeting to be thereafter called.

The agreement was approved by the boards of directors of both corporations. A special meeting of Sun's stockholders was called for November 29, 1957. The proxy statement set forth detailed information with respect to the plan of acquisition. On November 6, 1957, a ruling was obtained from the Commissioner of Internal Revenue that the transaction would constitute a tax-free reorganization under the applicable provisions of the Internal Revenue Code. Prior to the meeting plaintiffs filed written objections to the transaction, and gave notice of their intention to take legal action. The approval of the necessary majority of Sun's stockholders was obtained, and the transaction was consummated.

Plaintiffs contend that although the transaction is in form a sale of assets of Ansbacher it is in substance and effect a merger, and that it is unlawful because, the merger statute not having been complied with, plaintiffs have been deprived of their right of appraisal and have also suffered financial injury.

The argument that the result of this transaction is substantially the same as the result that would have followed a merger may be readily accepted. As plaintiffs correctly say, the Ansbacher enterprise is continued in altered form as a part of Sun. This is ordinarily a typical characteristic of a merger. Sterling v. Mayflower Hotel Corp., 93 A.2d 107. Moreover the plan of reorganization *requires* the dissolution of Ansbacher and the distribution to its stockholders of the Sun stock received by it for the assets. As a part of the plan, the Ansbacher stockholders are compelled to receive Sun stock. From the viewpoint of Ansbacher, the result is the same as if Ansbacher had formally merged into Sun.

This result is made possible, of course, by the overlapping scope of the merger statute and the statute authorizing the sale of all the corporate assets. This possibility of overlapping was noticed in our opinion in the Mayflower case.

There is nothing new about such a result. For many years drafters of plans of corporate reorganization have increasingly resorted to the use of the sale-of-assets method in preference to the method by merger. Historically at least, there were reasons for this quite apart from the avoidance of the appraisal right given to stockholders dissenting from a merger. For example, if an interstate merger was not authorized by the statute, a sale of assets could be resorted to. See Ballantine, Corporations, § 663; and Hills, 'Consolidation of Corporations by Sale of Assets', 19 Cal.L.Rev. 349.

No Delaware case has held that this use of the sale-of-assets statute is improper, although Delaware does not grant appraisal rights to a stockholder dissenting from the sale. Indeed, [cases] contain language indicating the contrary. Those cases are, however, distinguishable on the facts, because dissolution of the seller and distribution of the stock of the purchaser were not required as a part of the sale in either case.

Whether, under Delaware law, a stockholder of the *selling* corporation could, in such a case as the instant one, obtain relief in equity on the theory of a *de facto* merger is a question we do not reach. What is before us is an attempt to apply the theory for the benefit of stockholders of the *purchasing* corporation, which may well raise, as it does here, a very different question.

The doctrine of *de facto* merger has been recognized in Delaware. It has been invoked in cases of sales of assets for the protection of creditors or stockholders who have suffered an injury by reason of failure to comply with the statute governing such sales. Drug, Inc. v. Hunt, 168 A. 87 (creditor of selling corporation). The contention that it should be applied to cases of the kind here involved depends for its force upon the proposition that the stockholder has been forced against his will to accept a new investment in an enterprise foreign to that of which he was a part, and that his right to an appraisal under the merger statute has been circumvented.

Our Court of Chancery has said that the appraisal right is given to the stockholder in compensation for his former right at common law to prevent a merger. By the use of the sale-of-assets method of reorganization, it is contended, he has been unjustly deprived of this right.

As before stated, we do not reach this question, because we fail to see how any injury has been inflicted upon the Sun stockholders. Their corporation has simply acquired property and paid for it in shares of stock. The business of Sun will go on as before, with additional assets. The Sun stockholder is not forced to accept stock in another corporation. Nor has the reorganization changed the essential nature of the enterprise of the purchasing corporation, as in Farris v. Glen Alden Corporation, 393 Pa. 427, 143 A.2d 25.

Nor is it a case in which the seller can be said to have acquired the purchaser. Sun's net worth is ten times that of Ansbacher. Sun has simply absorbed another company's assets which are needed in its own business.

The diminution in the proportional voting strength of the Sun stockholder is not a ground of complaint. Such a consequence necessarily follows any issuance of stock to acquire property.

Plaintiffs made the further point that their proportional interest in the assets has also been diminished. This is, in effect, a charge that the terms of the acquisition are unfair to the Sun minority. Thus it is said that Ansbacher's net worth is about $1,600,000, and the issuance to Ansbacher of 225,000 shares of Sun stock of the market value of $10.125 a share results in the payment by Sun of a grossly excessive price and in the unjust enrichment of Alexander. It is also said that the report of the committee of Sun's directors admits that the earnings of Ansbacher do not justify the price paid.

These are arguments appropriate to the second cause of action, which the Vice Chancellor refused to dismiss. The legal power to authorize the transaction is one thing. The fairness of its terms and conditions is another. Only the first issue is before us. Plaintiffs are in no way foreclosed from pressing the above contentions when the second cause of action is tried.

With respect to the right of Sun stockholders to raise the question of *de facto* merger, plaintiffs' contention comes in effect to this: that a merger statute protects the stockholders of *all* merging or consolidating corporations; and if a stockholder of a selling corporation is entitled to invoke the doctrine of *de facto* merger, it follows that a stockholder of the purchasing corporation is likewise entitled to do so. This is to say that if the stockholder of the selling corporation suffers injury, the stockholder of the purchaser must also suffer injury. This does not follow. Suppose that there were a minority stockholder of Ansbacher who had been compelled by the plan to accept in exchange for his stock shares in another enterprise. How is the Sun stockholder injured by that? It is of no concern to him and inflicts no injury upon him.

Plaintiffs appear to concede that if the dissolution of Ansbacher and the distribution of Sun stock had not been *required* by the plan—that is, if Ansbacher had continued as a holding company—the doctrine of *de facto* merger would not apply. This concession exposes the weakness of plaintiffs' case.

How can a Sun stockholder have any concern with what Ansbacher does with the Sun stock after it receives it? Surely the presence or absence of injury to him cannot depend on Ansbacher's decision whether to dissolve and distribute the Sun stock or to continue as a holding company.

Whatever may be the case for giving the right of appraisal to a dissenting stockholder of a selling corporation, as many states have done, there seems little reason, at least in cases like the instant one, to accord it to the stockholders of the purchaser. At all events, no state appears to have done so by statute. See the discussion of this general subject in a recent note in 72 Harv.L.Rev. 1132: 'The right of shareholders dissenting from corporate combinations to demand cash payment for their shares.' And we find no basis in the facts of this case for the granting of such relief in equity on the theory of a *de facto* merger. * * *

The judgment of the Court of Chancery is affirmed.

HARITON v. ARCO ELECTRONICS, INC.

188 A.2d 123 (Del.1963).

SOUTHERLAND, CHIEF JUSTICE.

This case involves a sale of assets under § 271 of the corporation law, 8 Del.C. It presents for decision the question presented, but not decided, in Heilbrunn v. Sun Chemical Corporation, Del., 150 A.2d 755. It may be stated as follows:

> A sale of assets is effected under § 271 in consideration of shares of stock of the purchasing corporation. The agreement of sale embodies also a plan to dissolve the selling corporation and distribute the shares so received to the stockholders of the seller, so as to accomplish the same result as would be accomplished by a merger of the seller into the purchaser. Is the sale legal?

The facts are these:

The defendant Arco and Loral Electronics Corporation, a New York corporation, are both engaged, in somewhat different forms, in the electronic equipment business. In the summer of 1961 they negotiated for an amalgamation of the companies. As of October 27, 1961, they entered into a 'Reorganization Agreement and Plan.' The provisions of this Plan pertinent here are in substance as follows:

> 1.   Arco agrees to sell all its assets to Loral in consideration (inter alia) of the issuance to it of 283,000 shares of Loral.

> 2.   Arco agrees to call a stockholders meeting for the purpose of approving the Plan and the voluntary dissolution.

> 3.   Arco agrees to distribute to its stockholders all the Loral shares received by it as a part of the complete liquidation of Arco.

At the Arco meeting all the stockholders voting (about 80%) approved the Plan. It was thereafter consummated.

> Plaintiff, a stockholder who did not vote at the meeting, sued to enjoin the consummation of the Plan on the grounds (1) that it was illegal, and (2) that it was unfair. The second ground was abandoned. Affidavits and documentary evidence were filed, and defendant moved

for summary judgment and dismissal of the complaint. The Vice Chancellor granted the motion and plaintiff appeals.

The question before us we have stated above. Plaintiff's argument that the sale is illegal runs as follows:

The several steps taken here accomplish the same result as a merger of Arco into Loral. In a 'true' sale of assets, the stockholder of the seller retains the right to elect whether the selling company shall continue as a holding company. Moreover, the stockholder of the selling company is forced to accept an investment in a new enterprise without the right of appraisal granted under the merger statute. § 271 cannot therefore be legally combined with a dissolution proceeding under § 275 and a consequent distribution of the purchaser's stock. Such a proceeding is a misuse of the power granted under § 271, and a *de facto* merger results.

The foregoing is a brief summary of plaintiff's contention.

Plaintiff's contention that this sale has achieved the same result as a merger is plainly correct. The same contention was made to us in Heilbrunn v. Sun Chemical Corporation, Del., 150 A.2d 755. Accepting it as correct, we noted that this result is made possible by the overlapping scope of the merger statute and section 271, mentioned in Sterling v. Mayflower Hotel Corporation, 33 Del.Ch. 293. We also adverted to the increased use, in connection with corporate reorganization plans, of § 271 instead of the merger statute. Further, we observed that no Delaware case has held such procedure to be improper, and that two cases appear to assume its legality. But we were not required in the Heilbrunn case to decide the point.

We now hold that the reorganization here accomplished through § 271 and a mandatory plan of dissolution and distribution is legal. This is so because the sale-of-assets statute and the merger statute are independent of each other. They are, so to speak, of equal dignity, and the framers of a reorganization plan may resort to either type of corporate mechanics to achieve the desired end. This is not an anomalous result in our corporation law. As the Vice Chancellor pointed out, the elimination of accrued dividends, though forbidden under a charter amendment may be accomplished by a merger.

We are in accord with the Vice Chancellor's ruling, and the judgment below is affirmed.

RATH v. RATH PACKING CO.

257 Iowa 1277, 136 N.W.2d 410 (1965).

Garfield, Chief Justice

The question presented is whether an Iowa corporation may carry out an agreement with another corporation, designated 'Plan and Agreement of Reorganization,' which amounts to a merger in fact of the two without approval of holders of two thirds of its outstanding shares. The question is one of first impression of Iowa. We must disagree with the trial court's holding this may be done.

Plaintiffs, minority shareholders of Rath, brought this action in equity to enjoin carrying out the agreement on the ground, so far as necessary to consider, it provides for a merger in fact with Needham Packing Co., which requires approval of two thirds of the holders of outstanding Rath shares and that was not obtained. The trial court adjudicated law points under in favor of defendants Rath and its officers, and entered judgment of dismissal on the pleadings. It held approval of the plan by holders of a majority of Rath shares was sufficient. Plaintiffs appeal.

Plaintiffs own more than 6000 shares of Rath Packing Co., an Iowa corporation with its principal plant in Waterloo, Iowa, existing under Code 1962, chapter 496A, I.C.A. (Iowa Business Corporation Act). Rath has 993,185 shares outstanding held by about 4000 owners. It is engaged in meat packing and processing, mostly pork and allied products. Its yearly sales for the last five years were from about $267,000,000 to $296,000,000. Its balance sheet as of January 2, 1965, showed assets of about $56,500,000, current liabilities of about $20,600,000, and long-term debt of about $7,000,000.

Needham Packing Co. is a corporation organized in 1960 under Delaware law with its principal plant in Sioux City, Iowa. Its total shares outstanding, including debentures and warrants convertible into stock, are 787,907, held by about 1000 owners. Both Rath and Needham stock is traded on the American Stock Exchange. Needham is also engaged in meat packing, mostly beef. Its annual sales were from about $80,000,000 to $103,000,000. Its balance sheet as of December 26, 1964, showed assets of $10,300,000, current liabilities of $2,262,000, and long-term debt of $3,100,000.

Pursuant to authority of Rath's board prior to April 2, 1965, it entered into the questioned agreement with Needham, designated 'Plan and Agreement of Reorganization,' under which Rath agreed to: (1) amend its articles to double the number of shares of its common stock, create a new class of preferred shares and change its name to Rath–Needham Corporation; (2) issue to Needham 5.5 shares of Rath common and two shares of its 80–cent preferred stock for each five shares of Needham stock in exchange for all Needham's assets, properties, business, name and good will, except a fund not exceeding $175,000 to pay expenses in carrying out the agreement and effecting Needham's dissolution and distribution of the new Rath–Needham stock to its shareholders, any balance remaining after 120 days to be paid over to Rath; (3) assume all Needham's debts and liabilities; and (4) elect two Needham officers and directors to its board.

Under the plan Needham agreed to: (1) transfer all its assets to Rath; (2) cease using its name; (3) distribute the new Rath–Needham shares to its stockholders, liquidate and dissolve; and (4) turn over to Rath its corporate and business records.

If the plan were carried out, assuming the new preferred shares were converted into common, the thousand Needham shareholders would have about 54 per cent of the outstanding common shares of Rath–Needham and the four thousand Rath shareholders would have about 46 per cent.

Under the plan the book value of each share of Rath common stock, as of January 2, 1965, would be reduced from $27.99 to $15.93, a reduction of about 44 per cent. Each share of Needham common would be increased in book value, as of December 26, 1964, from $6.61 to $23.90, assuming conversion of the new Rath–Needham preferred.

In the event of liquidation of Rath–Needham, Needham shareholders would be preferred to Rath's under the plan, by having a prior claim to the assets of Rath–Needham to an amount slightly in excess of the book value of all Needham shares. Needham shareholders are also preferred over Rath's under the plan in distribution of income by the right of the former to receive preferred dividends of 80 cents a share—about five per cent of Needham's book value. Shortly prior to the time terms of the plan were made public Rath and Needham shares sold on the American Exchange for about the same price. Almost immediately thereafter the price of Needham shares increased and Rath's decreased so the former sold for 50 per cent more than the latter.

At a meeting of Rath shareholders on April 26, 1965, 60.1 per cent of its outstanding shares, 77 per cent of those voted, were voted in favor of these two proposals: (1) to amend the articles to authorize a class of 80 c preferred stock and increase the authorized common from $1,500,000 shares ($10 par) to 3,000,000 shares (no par); and (2) upon acquisition by Rath of the assets, properties, business and good will of Needham to change Rath's name to Rath–Needham Corporation and elect as its directors Lloyd and James Needham. Holders of 177,000 shares voted against these proposals and 218,000 shares were not voted. The plan was not approved by the shareholders except as above stated. * * *

The principal point of law defendants asked to have adjudicated under is that the provisions of chapter 496A last referred to are legally independent of, and of equal dignity with, those relating to mergers and the validity of the action taken by defendants is not dependent upon compliance with the merger sections under which the same result might be attained. The trial court accepted this view.

It is clear the view just expressed emanates from the opinion in Hariton v. Arco Electronics, Inc., Del., 188 A.2d 123, the only precedent called to our attention which sustains the decision appealed from. Virtually the only basis for the conclusion Hariton reaches is the statement of the law point these defendants raised. The opinion contains little discussion and cites no authority that supports the decision.

We can agree all provisions of our chapter 496A are of equal dignity. But we cannot agree any provisions of the act are legally independent of others if this means that in arriving at the correct interpretation thereof and the legislative intent expressed therein we are not to consider the entire act and, so far as possible, construe its various provisions in the light of their relation to the whole act. Nor should other fundamental rules of statutory construction be ignored in determining the scope and effect of any provision of chapter 496A.

We may also observe that the trial court 'concluded the 'safeguards' written into the codes of most states, including Iowa and Delaware, with respect to rights of dissenting shareholders in connection with mergers are based on outmoded concepts of economic realities, particularly in the case of an enterprise such as Rath which is regularly traded on the American Exchange and has a diversified stock ownership with over 4000 shareholders. The court cites especially in this regard articles of Professor Manning, 72 Yale Law Journal 223, and Professor Folk, 49 Virginia Law Review 1261.'

If the soundness of this view were admitted, the statutory safeguards should of course be removed by legislative, not judicial action. Our 1959 legislature evidently had a purpose in enacting what we may call the merger sections of chapter 496A as well as those relating to amending articles and issuing stock. We have frequently pointed out it is not the province of courts to pass upon the policy, wisdom or advisability of a statute.

The 'Plan and Agreement of Reorganization' clearly provides for what amounts to a merger of Rath and Needham under any definition of merger we know. We have approved a statement that a merger exists where one corporation is continued and the other is merged with it, without the formation of a new corporation, from a sale of the property and franchises of one corporation to another. 'A merger of corporations consists of a combination whereby one of the constituent companies remains in being—absorbing or merging in itself all the other constituent corporations.' 19 Am.Jur.2d, Corporations, section 1492. ' * * * a merger signifies the absorption of one corporation by another, which retains its name and corporate identity with the added capital, franchises and powers of a merged corporation.' 15 Fletcher Cyc. Corporations, 1961 Revised Volume, section 7041, page 6. 'It (merger) is the uniting of two or more corporations by the transfer of property to one of them, which continues in existence, the others being merged therein.' Id., pages 9–10. See also Note 26 Iowa Law Review 303, 318–19. We see no need to multiply these definitions or cite other precedents that support them.

If, as we hold, this agreement provides for what amounts to a merger of Rath and Needham, calling it a Plan and Agreement of Reorganization does not change its essential character. A fundamental maxim of equity, frequently applied, is that equity regards substance rather than form. It is our duty to look behind the form to the substance of the challenged transaction. Chicago, S.F. & C.R.Co. v. Ashling, 160 Ill. 373, 43 N.E. 373, 375 ('There is no magic in words. Merely calling the transaction a purchase and sale would not prevent it from being a consolidation.'); 19 C.J.S. Corporations § 1604, page 1367.

The power of a corporation to merge must be derived from the law of the state which created it. There must be some plain enactment authorizing the merger, for legislative authority is just as essential to a merger as to creation of the corporation in the first instance. 15 Fletcher Cyc. Corporations, 1961 Revised Volume, section 7048, pages 32–33. Legislative authority for a merger will not be implied but must be clearly, distinctly and expressly conferred. Id., section 7054, page 44.

At common law no merger could take place without unanimous consent of the stockholders. However, statutes in all jurisdictions now authorize mergers upon a vote of less than all stockholders. A shareholder who dissents to a merger may obtain the value of his stock if the right thereto is provided by statute, if procedure is established therefor and is followed by him. Sections 496A.77, 496A.78 confer such right and provide such procedure.

The merger sections of chapter 496A clearly and expressly confer the necessary power to merge. Nothing in the sections dealing with amending articles and issuing stock purports to authorize a merger. They make no reference to merger. The most that may fairly be claimed is that they impliedly confer the required power to merge. But this is insufficient.

In seeking the scope and effect of the two sets of sections relied upon at least one fundamental rule of statutory construction is applicable. As stated, the merger sections specifically provide for a particular thing— mergers. The sections authorizing amendment of articles and issuance of stock apply to all amendments and stock issues, whether or not amending the articles or issuing stock is part of a merger, as they may or may not be. As applied to mergers, the sections on which plaintiffs rely are specific provisions, those on which defendants rely are not. 'It is an old and familiar principle * * * that where there is in the same statute a specific provision, and also a general one which in its most comprehensive sense would include matters embraced in the former, the particular provision must control, and the general provision must be taken to effect only such cases within its general language as are not within the provisions of the particular provision. Additional words of qualification needed to harmonize a general and a prior special provision in the same statute should be added to the general provision, rather than to the special one.' 20 Am.Jur., Statutes, section 367.

The sections relied upon are in the same act passed at the same time. The United States Supreme Court has frequently used the language just quoted and we have approved it at least twice. A closely related rule, many times applied by us, is that where a general statute, if standing alone, would include the same matter as a special statute and thus conflict with it, the latter will prevail and the former must give way. The special provision will be considered an exception to or qualification of the general one. 'Another rule which has been applied, is that where one section of a statute treats specially and solely of a matter, that section prevails in reference to that matter over other sections in which only incidental reference is made thereto, * * *.' 50 Am.Jur., Statutes, section 366.

It is apparent that if the sections pertaining to amending articles and issuing stock are construed to authorize a merger by a majority vote of shareholders they conflict with the sections specifically dealing with the one matter of mergers which require a two-thirds vote of shareholders. The two sets of sections may be harmonized by holding, as we do, that the merger sections govern the matter of merger and must be regarded as an exception to the sections dealing with amending articles and issuing stock, which may or may not be involved in a merger.

The construction we give these sections is in accord with the cardinal rule that, if reasonably possible, effect will be given to every part of a statute.

The merger sections make it clear the legislature intended to require a two thirds vote of shareholders and accord so called appraisal rights to dissenters in case of a merger. It is unreasonable to ascribe to the same legislature an intent to provide in the same act a method of evading the required two-thirds vote and the grant of such appraisal rights. The practical effect of the decision appealed from is to render the requirements of a two-thirds vote and appraisal rights meaningless in virtually all mergers. It is scarcely an exaggeration to say the decision amounts to judicial repeal of the merger sections in most instances of merger. * * *

15 Fletcher, Cyc. Corporations, 1961 Revised Volume section 7165.5, page 307, contains this: 'However, where a particular corporate combination is in legal effect a merger or a consolidation, even though the transaction may be otherwise labeled by the parties, the courts treat the transaction as a de facto merger or consolidation so as to confer upon dissenting stockholders the right to receive cash payment for their shares.' Decisions from several jurisdictions are cited in support. Only Heilbrunn v. Sun Chemical Corp., [supra],is cited as contra. Basis of the Heilbrunn decision is the court's declared failure to see how any injury was inflicted on shareholders of a corporation that purchased the assets of another. No opinion was expressed as to whether shareholders of the selling corporation could obtain equitable relief. The Delaware court first decided that question in Hariton v. Arco Electronics, supra. * * *

APPLESTEIN v. UNITED BOARD & CARTON CORP.

60 N.J.Super. 333, 159 A.2d 146 (Ch.1960),
aff'd 33 N.J. 72, 161 A.2d 474 (1960) (per curiam).

KILKENNY, J.S.C.

* * * United is an active corporation of New Jersey, organized in 1912. Its business consists in the manufacture and sale of paper-board,

folding boxes, corrugated containers and laminated board, in that relative order of importance. Its present authorized capital stock consists of 400,000 shares, of which 240,000 have already been issued and are held by a great number of stockholders, no one of whom holds in excess of 10% of the outstanding shares. There are 160,000 shares not yet issued. The United stock is publicly held, there being 1,086 shareholders of record as of September 22, 1959, and the stock is traded on the New York Stock Exchange. The book value of each share of stock, as indicated by the proxy statement, is approximately $31.97. The consolidated balance sheet of United and its wholly owned subsidiaries, as of May 31, 1958, shows total assets of $10,121,233, and total liabilities of $2,561,724, and a net total capital of $7,559,509. Its business is managed by the usual staff of officers and a board of directors consisting of seven directors.

Interstate was incorporated under the laws of New York in 1939. It owns several operating subsidiaries located in various parts of the northeastern section of the United States. It is engaged primarily in the manufacture and sale of corrugated shipping containers, and also containers which have the dual use of carriers and point of purchase displays. The major portion of its business is corrugated containers. Its corrugated board, other than that consumed by its own container operations, is used by outside plants for the manufacture of corrugated containers and, in some instances, for display items. Interstate has issued and outstanding 1,250 shares, all of which are owned and controlled by a single stockholder, Epstein, who thereby owns and controls Interstate. The consolidated balance sheet of Interstate and its subsidiaries, as of October 31, 1958, shows that its total assets are $7,956,424, and its total liabilities are $6,318,371, leaving a net total capital of $1,638,053. * * *

United entered into a written agreement with Interstate and Epstein on July 7, 1959. In its language, it is not designated or referred to as a merger agreement, Eo nomine. In fact, the word 'merger' nowhere appears in that agreement. On the contrary, the agreement recites that it is an 'exchange of Interstate stock for United Stock.' Epstein agrees to assign and deliver to United his 1,250 shares of the common stock of Interstate solely in exchange for 160,000 as yet unissued shares of voting common stock (par value $10) of United. Thus, by this so-called 'exchange of stock' United would wholly own Interstate and its subsidiaries, and Epstein would thereupon own a 40% Stock interest in United. Dollar-wise, on the basis of the book values of the two corporations hereinabove set forth, a combination of the assets and liabilities of United and Interstate would result in a net total capital of approximately $9,200,000, as against which there would be outstanding 400,000 shares, thereby reducing the present book value of each United share from about $31.97 to about $23, a shrinkage of about 28%. Epstein would contribute, book value-wise, the net total capital of Interstate in the amount of $1,638,053, for which he would receive a 40% interest in $9,200,000, the net total combined capital of United and Interstate, or about $3,680,000. The court is not basing its present decision upon the additional charge made by dissenting stockholders of United that the proposed agreement is basically unfair and inequitable. That is one of the reserved issues. The court recognizes that book values and real values are not necessarily the same thing, and, therefore, apparent inequities appearing from a comparison of the book values might be explained and justified.

The agreement of July 7, 1959 does not contemplate the continued future operation of Interstate, as a subsidiary corporation of United. Rather, it provides that United will take over all the outstanding stock of Interstate, that all of Interstate's 'assets and liabilities will be recorded on the books of the Company (United),' and that Interstate will be dissolved. At the time of closing, Epstein has agreed to deliver the resignations of the officers and directors of Interstate and of its subsidiary corporations, so that, in effect, Interstate would have no officers, directors, or stockholders, other than United's. The agreement further stipulates that the by-laws of United shall be amended to increase the number of directors from 7 to 11. It provides for the filling of the additional directorships, it pre-ordains who will be the officers and new directors of United in the combined enterprise, and even governs the salaries to be paid. Epstein would become the president and a director of United and, admittedly, would be in 'effective control' of United. As stated in the proxy statement, 'The transaction will be accounted for as a 'pooling of interests' of the two corporations.'

The stipulation of the parties removed from the court's present consideration not only the issue of the basic equity or fairness of the agreement, but also the legal effect and validity of the pre-determination of directorships, officers, salaries, and other similar terms of the bargain between the parties. The fairness of a merger agreement generally presents a question of a factual nature, ordinarily reserved for final hearing. If the alleged injustice of the project were the sole objection, I would be hesitant to substitute preliminarily my judgment for that of a transcendent majority of the stockholders. In notifying its stockholders of a meeting to be held on October 15, 1959, in its proxy statement United advised the stockholders that 'the proposal to approve the issuance of the common stock of the company is being submitted to the vote of the stockholders solely because of the requirements of the New York Stock Exchange; and accordingly stockholders who vote against or who do not vote in favor of the proposal will not, in the opinion of Luttinger & Passannante, general counsel for the company, be entitled to any rights of appraisal of their stock.' They were also advised that adoption of the proposal would require the affirmative vote of the holders of only a Majority of the shares present at the meeting in person or by proxy, provided a majority of all shares outstanding and entitled to vote thereon was present at the meeting.

The attorneys for the respective parties herein have conceded in the record that the proposed corporate action would be invalid, if this court determines that it would constitute a merger of United and Interstate, entitling the dissenting stockholders of United to an appraisal of their stock. The notice of the stockholders' meeting and the proxy statement did not indicate that the purpose of the meeting was to effect a Merger, and failed to give notice to the shareholders of their right to dissent to the plan of merger, if it were one, and claim their appraisal rights under the statute, as inferentially required by R.S. 14:12—3, N.J.S.A. Obviously, the notice of the meeting and proxy statement stressed the contrary, by labelling the proposed corporate action 'an exchange of Interstate stock for United stock' rather than a merger, by its emphasis upon the need for a Majority vote only, instead of the required two-thirds vote for a merger under the statute, and by the express declaration that dissenting stockholders would not be entitled to any rights of appraisal of their stock. * * *

Despite the contrary representations by United to its stockholders in its proxy statement, United's present position is that the proposed corporate action in acquiring and absorbing Interstate is a merger. This is evidenced by its answer to the cross-claim of Interstate and Epstein against it for specific performance of the agreement of July 7, 1959. At the hearing of the motions United's attorney stated in the record that United now contended, in addition to its other asserted defenses, that the fulfillment of the agreement would constitute a merger. In fairness to United's attorney herein, it should be noted that this coincided with an earlier letter opinion furnished privately by him to United's officers substantially to the same effect, which letter he made part of the record, in his affidavit, when a question of good faith was raised.

Needless to say, if United, a New Jersey corporation, had followed that early advice given by its present New Jersey counsel herein and had followed the statutory procedure for corporate mergers, this litigation would have been avoided. Instead, it chose the opposite opinion of New York counsel that the plan would not be a merger, and so indicated to its stockholders in the proxy statement. It now finds itself ready and willing to agree with the plaintiff stockholders that the plan would be a merger of United and Interstate, and relies thereon, Inter alia, in resisting the cross-claim for specific performance. * * *

The legal contention of Epstein and Interstate, and the four intervening United stockholders—Conway, Terry, McKenney, and Corsuti—is that the transaction constitutes a valid purchase by United of Epstein's shares in Interstate, and thereby the property of Interstate, pursuant to R.S. 14.3—9, N.J.S.A., to be followed by a merger of United, as the parent corporation, with its wholly-owned corporation, Interstate, pursuant to N.J.S.A. 14:12—10. Thus, it is claimed that United's dissenting stockholders have no appraisal rights under these two sections of the statutes, and especially since N.J.S.A. 14:12—10 expressly provides that N.J.S.A. 14:12—6 and R.S. 14:12—7, N.J.S.A., which grant appraisal rights in the usual merger, under R.S. 14:12—1, N.J.S.A., shall not apply to a merger under N.J.S.A. 14:12—10.

When a corporation sells or exchanges all, or substantially all of its property and assets, including its good will, as permitted by R.S. 14:3—5, N.J.S.A., the stockholders of the Selling corporation must approve by a two-thirds vote, and objecting stockholders of the Selling corporation are given appraisal rights, as provided in N.J.S.A. 14:12—6 in the case of a merger.

But when a corporation buys real or personal property, or the stock of another corporation, as permitted under R.S. 14:3—9, N.J.S.A., stockholder approval is not required, and objecting shareholders of the Purchasing corporation are given no appraisal rights in such a case. Further, the Buying corporation may pay for such property or stock acquired by it in cash or in the capital stock of the purchasing corporation. It is true that our present corporation law, R.S. 14:3—5, N.J.S.A., sanctions a corporate Sale of all or substantially all of the property and assets of the selling corporation, with stockholder approval and appraisal rights in favor of objecting shareholders of the selling corporation. Likewise, our statute, R.S. 14:3—9, N.J.S.A., allows a corporate purchase of the property and stock of another corporation to be paid for in cash or the stock of the purchasing corporation. There is no dispute as to the existence of these present statutory devices for the sale and acquisition of corporate property and shares of stock. Hence, if the purchase by United of Interstate and its shares represented a Bona fide utilization of the corporate power conferred by R.S. 14:3—9, N.J.S.A., and if the intended dissolution of Interstate represented a Bona fide merger of a parent corporation with a wholly-owned corporation under N.J.S.A. 14:12—10, without more, United's dissenting shareholders would then have no right to an appraisal of their shares.

But when an authorized device, such as that provided for in a sale or purchase of assets, or a dissolution, is used to bring about a virtual consolidation or merger, minority stockholders may object on the ground that a direct method has been authorized for such a purpose. If consolidation or merger is permitted through a pretended sale of assets or dissolution, minority stockholders may be frozen out of their legal rights of appraisal. If the court is obliged to consider only the device employed, or the mere form of the transaction, a corporate merger in fact can be achieved without any compliance with the statutory requirements for a valid merger, and without any regard for the statutory rights of dissenting shareholders. It would be strange if the powers conferred by our Legislature upon corporations under R.S. 14:3—9, N.J.S.A. for a purchase of the property and shares of another corporation and, under N.J.S.A. 14:12—10, for the merger of a parent corporation with a wholly-owned corporation can effect a corporate merger De facto, with all the characteristics and consequences of a merger, without any of the legislative safeguards and rights afforded to a dissenting shareholder in a De jure merger under R.S. 14:12—1 et seq., N.J.S.A. If that were so, we obtain the anomalous result of one part of the corporation law rendering nugatory another part of the same law in accomplishing the same result.

That the proposed corporate action is more than an 'exchange of Interstate stock for United stock,' as it is labelled in the agreement of July 7, 1959, and more than a purchase by United of Epstein's Interstate stock and the corporate properties of Interstate, pursuant to R.S. 14:3—9, N.J.S.A., is demonstrated by the following facts.

1. The exchange of stock is made expressly contingent upon stockholder approval of Proposal No. 2 increasing the number of directors of United from 7 to 11. Proxy statement, pp. 2 and 9. It is also so stipulated in paragraph 10 of the agreement.

2. United admits that by the exchange of stock Epstein will acquire 40% of United's outstanding stock 'and effective control.'

3. Epstein's 'effective control' of United is made obvious, by the fact that two directors of United's present board of seven 'will resign as directors.' The agreement of July 7, 1959 expressly provides, 'The resignations of George Luttinger and Thomas V. Wade (two of United's directors) will be presented at the closing.' This would leave United with only five of its present directors on the new enlarged board of 11 directors, which Proposal No. 2 insures as a contingent part of the deal. Thus, Epstein and the five new directors, presumably his associates and friends from Interstate, are assured a majority vote of six and control of the new 11–man board. It is clear that he who controls a majority of the board of directors generally controls the management and destiny of the corporation.

4. It is also pre-ordained by the agreement, in paragraph 9, who the new 11 directors will be. Reference to their names and to their present and past connection and relationship with Epstein and Interstate (Proxy statement, p. 10) shows that Epstein will really have 'effective control' of the board and United, as the latter freely concedes.

5. While the proposed issuance by United to Epstein of 160,000 shares of United's total authorized 400,000 shares seems to give Epstein only a 40% stock interest in United, which by itself is substantial enough to control United as against the 1,086 other stockholders, but still less than the combined 60% of those 1,086 present United shareholders, 8 of those 1,086 present United shareholders, who would become directors on the enlarged board, already own 49,200 shares of United. Therefore, Epstein's new 160,000 shares plus those 49,200 shares would add up to 209,200 shares of the total 400,000, or better than 50%. Even if we discount the shares now held by Stuhr (18,000), Marchini (8,200), Passannante (300), Peters (300), and Miller (1,000), a total of 27,800 shares, because they are presently five of United's seven directors, although Miller is also vice-president and general manager of Allcraft Container Division of Interstate, Epstein's working stockholder control of United under the proposed corporate action is abundantly clear. Combined with his real control of the board of directors, the conclusion is inescapable that control of

the affairs of United would pass out of the present board of directors and out of the present majority of United's stockholders to Epstein and those associated with him in Interstate.

6. The proxy statement expressly recites: 'The transaction will be accounted for as a 'pooling of interests' of the two corporations.' Such a characterization is descriptive of a merger or consolidation of two corporations, rather than a mere exchange of stock or purchase of corporate assets.

7. It is intended that Interstate will be dissolved. Dissolution is always an element of merger or consolidation and it is not a necessary concomitant of a mere exchange of stock or purchase of corporate assets.

8. United expressly represents that Interstate's 'assets and liabilities will be recorded on the books of the Company (United) as set forth in the pro forma balance sheet.' This is indicative of the fact that United is Assuming Interstate's liabilities, a necessary legal consequence of a merger or consolidation, as contrasted with the normal non-assumption of the debts of the selling corporation, in the absence of special agreement, upon a mere 'sale-of-assets' transaction. While one might argue that the language, 'its assets and liabilities will be recorded on the books of the Company,' is equivocal and not a clearly expressed intention on United's part to Assume Interstate's liabilities, the intent to assume liabilities is made crystal clear, at least as to Interstate's almost million dollar debt to Mr. Jno. F. McKenney, an intervening defendant stockholder of United, and a former president of Interstate, who favors United's purported acquisition of Interstate. Thus, in the proxy statement, we note this plain admission of intent: "Interstate is indebted to Mr. Jno. F. McKenney in the sum of $997,112, as at April 30, 1959, Which obligation, by the terms of the agreement between the Company and Interstate Will be assumed by the Company (United)."

9. Also, as a further evidence of Interstate's control and intervention in United's management,

'It is contemplated that the present executive and operating personnel of Interstate will be retained in the employ of the Company (United).' Proxy statement

Thus every factor present in a corporate merger is found in this corporate plan, except, perhaps, a formal designation of the transaction as a 'merger.' There is proposed: (1) a transfer of all the shares and all the assets of Interstate to United; (2) an assumption by United of Interstate's liabilities; (3) a 'pooling of interests' of the two corporations; (4) the absorption of Interstate by United, and the dissolution of Interstate; (5) a joinder of officers and directors from both corporations on an enlarged board of directors; (6) the present executive and operating personnel of Interstate will be retained in the employ of United; and (7) the shareholders of the absorbed corporation, Interstate, as represented by the sole stockholder,

Epstein, will surrender his 1,250 shares in Interstate for 160,000 newly issued shares in United, the amalgamated enterprise.

If, in truth and in substance the proposed plan in this case is a 'merger,' why should the interested parties not frankly and honestly recognize it as such and pursue the statutory procedure under R.S. 14:12—1 et seq., N.J.S.A. for validating the proposal? It is a fundamental maxim of equity that 'Equity looks to the substance rather than the form.' For example, a deed absolute on its face, if in truth a mortgage, will be treated in equity as a mortgage. This court of conscience never pays homage to the mere form of an instrument or transaction, if to do so would frustrate the law or place justice in chains. The courts of equity in New Jersey, and elsewhere, have never hesitated to look behind the form of a particular corporate transaction and find that it constituted a corporate merger, if in fact and in substance it was a merger, regardless of its deceptive outward appearance.

Would the proposed plan be a merger of a parent corporation with a wholly owned corporation, as followed by N.J.S.A. 14:12—10, and, therefore, free from the appraisal rights of dissenting stockholders? While it is true that the agreement would make United the owner of all the shares of Interstate, so that, in that sense, Interstate would be a corporation wholly owned by United, the plan does not provide for the future operation of Interstate, as a subsidiary or wholly-owned corporation of United. Upon the so-called 'pooling of interests,' it is expressly intended that Interstate will be dissolved. It will never be a subsidiary corporation at all. It will not carry on its corporate activities, once the agreement has been completed. It will have no officers or directors. * * *

Therefore, the situation intended to be covered by N.J.S.A. 14:12—10 is not present in this case and that statutory provision does not apply. The courts of this State and of other jurisdictions have never hesitated in the past in finding that a particular corporate combination was in fact and in legal effect a merger or a consolidation, even though the transaction might have been otherwise labelled by the parties. Williamson v. New Jersey Southern R. Co., 26 N.J.Eq. 398 (Ch.1875); Riker & Son Co. v. United Drug Co., 79 N.J.Eq. 580, 82 A. 930 (E. & A.1911); Marks v. Autocar Co., 153 F.Supp. 768 (D.C.E.D.Pa.1954); Farris v. Glen Alden Corp., 393 Pa. 427, 143 A.2d 25, 28 (Sup.Ct.1958). This is not a new legal philosophy, but is grounded upon the common sense observation that judges, as well as laymen, have the right, and often the duty, to call a spade a spade, and to follow the long established equitable maxim of looking to the substance rather than the form, whenever justice requires. * * *

This court holds that the corporate combination of United and Interstate, contemplated by their executory contract of July 7, 1959, and explained in United's proxy solicitation statement of September 22, 1959, would be a practical or De facto merger, in substance and in legal effect, within the protective purview of N.J.S.A. 14:12—7. Accordingly, the shareholders of United are and were entitled to be notified and advised of their statutory rights of dissent and appraisal. The failure of the corporate officers of United to take these steps and to obtain stockholder approval of the agreement by the statutory two-thirds vote under R.S. 14:12—3, N.J.S.A. at a properly convened meeting of the stockholders would render the proposed corporate action invalid. Therefore, there will be partial summary judgment on the single, limited issue submitted in accordance with this holding.

NOTES

1. See also Pratt v. Ballman–Cummings Furniture Co., 261 Ark. 396, 549 S.W.2d 270 (1977) (applying de facto merger doctrine to invoke statutory appraisal rights); Arnold Graphics Industries, Inc. v. Independent Agent Center, Inc., 775 F.2d 38 (2d Cir.1985) (applying de facto merger doctrine to establish successor corporation liability); Marks v. Minnesota Mining & Manufacturing Co., 187 Cal.App.3d 1429, 232 Cal.Rptr. 594 (1986) (same).

2. As seen earlier in this chapter, a sale of substantially all assets may also give rise to shareholder voting rights. The Model Business Corp. Act in § 12.02 requires shareholder approval where there is a sale of assets that would leave the corporation without a significant continuing business activity. The comments to this section state that this is a qualitative measure comparable to the test applied under Delaware law, citing Thorpe v. CERBCO, Inc., 676 A.2d 436 (Del.1996). See also Model Bus. Corp. Act § 13.02.

3. Asset sales and other methods are sometimes used to freeze out minority shareholders. The techniques used include a sale of assets to an acquiring company in exchange for notes of the purchaser or cash, followed by liquidation of the selling corporation. Another method is to arrange a merger with a shell corporation and exchange the shares of the shareholders of the target company for notes or redeemable preferred shares of the surviving company. In Berkowitz v. Power/Mate Corp., 135 N.J.Super. 36, 342 A.2d 566 (Ch.1975) a majority stockholder created a new corporation and arranged a cash out merger for the existing company's shareholders. The price of the cash out payments was tied to the existing market price of the stock, but the court found that the principal officers of the company were receiving large bonuses that would have increased the value of the company's stock. The court enjoined the merger. Compare Grimes v. Donaldson, Lufkin & Jenrette, 392 F.Supp. 1393 (N.D.Fla.1974) (freeze out merger upheld where it would effect substantial savings by reduction of expenses and salaries).

4. Another method used to freeze out minority shareholders is the reverse stock split. The ordinary stock split is a common way to reduce the price of a stock and increase its liquidity. Say, for example, that a company's common stock is selling at $300 per share, requiring $30,000 to buy a "round lot" of 100 shares. If the stock is split say 10 for 1, the shareholder would be given 10 shares for each share owned, reducing the cost of a 100 share round lot to $3,000. This encourages smaller investors (who may not have $30,000) to invest a smaller amount for an equal amount of shares. Although, in theory, a stock split is equally dilutive, stocks often increase (after adjustment

for their dilution) in price after a split, possibly reflecting their increased liquidity.

The court in Strougo v. Bassini, 282 F.3d 162, 175, n. 8 (2d Cir.2002) described the effect of a stock split as follows:

> ... [W]hen shares of stock in a corporation are split two for one, immediately after the split each share of stock is worth half of what it was worth immediately before the split. But the total value of each shareholder's equity interest would not be expected to fall and thereby injure the shareholder because the decrease in share value is offset by the receipt of new shares. Thus, a mere increase in the number of shares, and a corresponding adjustment in share price, does not automatically constitute a shareholder injury. See, e.g., Baker [v. Standard Lime & Stone Co., 100 A.2d 822, 828] (holding that a "split up of the common stock, by the issuance of four shares for one, did not adversely affect the holders, for after that action their aliquot shares remained the same").

The court in *Strougo* further noted that "a stock split, in which each shareholder obtains new shares for nothing, can be recharacterized as a sale of shares to the shareholders at the deepest possible discount—100 percent—and yet it does not in itself injure either the shareholders or the corporation." Id. at n. 9. A reverse stock split seeks to reduce the number of outstanding shares. Say, for example, a company announces that it will be exchanging 1 share for each 1000 shares owned by a shareholder, and shareholders owning less than 1000 shares will be cashed out. A freeze out can be effected by choosing a reverse split number (in this case 1000 shares) that is high enough to cash out most or all minority shareholders. In Teschner v. Chicago Title & Trust Co., 59 Ill.2d 452, 322 N.E.2d 54 (1974), the court upheld a reverse stock split of 600 to 1 that cashed out the minority shareholders, all of whom owned less than 600 shares. In Clark v. Pattern Analysis & Recognition Corp., 87 Misc.2d 385, 384 N.Y.S.2d 660 (1976), a court enjoined a 4000 for 1 reverse stock split that would have frozen out all minority shareholders. No strong and compelling business interest was shown for the reverse split.

5. *Going Private*: Publicly held corporations may seek to convert themselves into private ones by removing public shareholders. Such transactions may be based on a reverse stock split or even an offer to public shareholders at a price with a premium over present market price. This is often attractive to shareholders and allows management effectively to engage in a leveraged buyout and remove itself from the burdens of the reporting requirements of the federal securities laws. Concern was expressed that shareholders in such transactions were being stampeded in selling out by gloomy predictions in the offering documents concerning the company's future prospects. See generally Victor Brudney, "A Note on Going Private—Juggling Shareholder Protection With Corporate Flexibility: Will the States Drop the Ball?" 1978 Wis. L. Rev. 797. The SEC responded to those concerns by adopting disclosure requirements. SEC Rule 13e–3 and Schedule 13E–3 contain disclosure requirements and anti-fraud provisions for going private transactions. Among other things, the benefits and determinants of the transaction to shareholders is required, and the board of directors must express its opinion on the fairness of the transaction. This includes consideration of the value of the company based on

going concern, liquidation and other values. Appraisals from outside parties must be disclosed. Disclosure of plans for future mergers, liquidation or sales of assets is also required.

6. *Leveraged Buyouts.* Sometimes freeze-outs are facilitated by debt financing:

> A leveraged buy-out occurs when a group of investors, usually including members of a company's management team, buy the company under financial arrangements that include little equity and significant new debt. The necessary debt financing typically includes mortgages or high risk/ high yield bonds, popularly known as "junk bonds." Additionally, a portion of this debt is generally secured by the company's assets. Some of the acquired company's assets are usually sold after the transaction is completed in order to reduce the debt incurred in the acquisition.

Metropolitan Life Ins. Co. v. RJR Nabisco, Inc., 716 F.Supp. 1504, 1505, n. 1 (S.D.N.Y.,1989).

SECTION 4. CHALLENGING THE FAIRNESS OF MERGERS

STERLING v. MAYFLOWER HOTEL CORP.

93 A.2d 107 (Del.1952).

SOUTHERLAND, CHIEF JUSTICE.

The principal question presented is whether the terms of a proposed merger of Mayflower Hotel Corporation (herein 'Mayflower') into its parent corporation, Hilton Hotels Corporation (herein 'Hilton'), are fair to the minority stockholders of Mayflower.

The essential facts are these: Mayflower and Hilton are both Delaware corporations. Mayflower's sole business is the ownership and operation of the Mayflower Hotel in Washington, D. C. It has outstanding 389,738 shares of common stock of $1 par value. Hilton and its subsidiary corporations are engaged in the business of owning, leasing, operating and managing hotel properties in many of the large centers of population in the country. Hilton has outstanding, in addition to an issue of Convertible Preference stock, 1,592,878 shares of common stock of $5 par value.

On December 18, 1946, Hilton acquired a majority of the outstanding shares of Mayflower. Thereafter it continued to make purchases of Mayflower stock. On or about February 4, 1952, it purchased 21,409 shares at a price of $19.10 a share, and on that date made an offer to all other minority stockholders to buy their shares at the same price. As of March 25, 1952, Hilton owned 321,883 shares, or nearly five-sixths of the outstanding stock.

From the time of the acquisition by Hilton of a majority interest in Mayflower, Hilton's management had contemplated a merger of Mayflower with Hilton. Soon after such acquisition, however, litigation ensued in the District of Columbia between Hilton and certain minority stockholders of Mayflower, not terminated until late in the year 1951. In the early part of 1950 the Mayflower directors discussed the question of ascertaining a fair basis of exchange of Mayflower stock for Hilton stock. All of the Mayflower directors (nine in number) were nominees of Hilton, and it was the view of the board (as well as of the Hilton board) that an independent study should be made by competent and disinterested financial analysts for the purpose of evolving a fair plan of exchange. Three of the members of the board (Messrs. Fleming, Folger and Baxter) had been directors before the acquisition by Hilton of its interest in Mayflower, and appear to have had little or no interest in Hilton. Messrs. Fleming and Folger were of opinion that although the study should be made no definite action should be taken upon the plan thereby to be developed until the Washington litigation should be finally terminated. The other directors deferred to this view.

In the early part of 1950 Standard Research Consultants, Inc., a subsidiary of Standard & Poor, was retained to make the study, and Mr. John G. Haslam, its Vice President, undertook the work. Later he submitted a study which determined a fair basis of exchange of Hilton stock for Mayflower stock to be three-fourths of a share of Hilton for one share of Mayflower. No action was taken on the basis of this study.

The Washington litigation having been finally terminated, Mr. Haslam on January 7, 1952, was again retained to continue and bring up to date his prior study and to develop a fair plan of exchange. Thereafter he submitted his final study (hereinafter referred to as 'the Haslam report'), which embodies his conclusion that a fair rate of exchange would be share for share. A plan for a merger upon this basis was approved by the boards of directors of both corporations. The directors—at least the Mayflower directors—appear to have relied largely on the Haslam report to justify their action. A formal agreement of merger was entered into on March 14, 1952, providing for the merger of Mayflower (the constituent corporation) into Hilton (the surviving corporation), as authorized by the provisions of Section 59 of the General Corporation Law, Rev.Code of Del.1935, par. 2091, as amended. Each outstanding share of Mayflower is converted into one share of Hilton. A separate agreement between Hilton and Mayflower provides that for a limited period Hilton will pay $19.10 a share for any Mayflower stock tendered to it by any minority stockholder. At stockholders' meetings held in April the requisite approval of the merger was obtained. At the Mayflower meeting 329,106 shares were voted in favor; 4,645 against. Holders of 35,191 shares of Mayflower who objected to the merger did not vote. The Hilton stockholders voted overwhelmingly to approve the merger.

On April 7, 1952, plaintiffs below (herein 'plaintiffs'), holders of 32,295 shares of Mayflower stock, filed their complaint in the court below, seeking injunctive relief against the consummation of the merger, on the ground that the terms of the merger are grossly unfair to the minority stockholders of Mayflower, and that the Mayflower directors entered into the merger agreement in bad faith.

The Chancellor, having issued a temporary restraining order against the consummation of the merger, heard the case on a motion for a preliminary injunction. A large number of affidavits were filed and voluminous depositions were taken. The Chancellor found no fraud or bad faith in the case and concluded that the plan was fair to the minority. He also determined that a quorum of Mayflower directors was present at the board meeting of March 6 when the merger was approved. On June 18 he denied injunctive relief, and plaintiffs thereafter appealed.

Plaintiffs' principal contention here, as in the court below, is that the terms of the merger are unfair to Mayflower's minority stockholders. Plaintiffs invoke the settled rule of law that Hilton as majority stockholder of Mayflower and the Hilton directors as its nominees occupy, in relation to the minority, a fiduciary position in dealing with Mayflower's property. Since they stand on both sides of the transaction, they bear the burden of establishing its entire fairness, and it must pass the test of careful scrutiny by the courts. Defendants agree that their acts must meet this test. We therefore inquire whether the facts sustain the conversion ratio of share for share which forms the basis of the merger agreement.

As the Chancellor observed, the Haslam report forms the principal justification for the terms of the merger. We accordingly examine it.

The report is an elaborate study of some forty pages (including charts) with a long appendix containing analyses of pertinent financial data. The principles upon which it is based are set forth in the Chancellor's opinion. Implicit in the report is the assumption that the legal principles governing the transaction require a comparison of the value of the stock of Hilton with the stock of Mayflower. Since the report is the basis of the conversion terms of the merger agreement, it is in effect directed to a determination of the question whether, upon the conversion of Mayflower stock into Hilton stock, the Mayflower minority stockholder will receive the substantial equivalent in value of the shares he held before the merger. Thus a comparison is required of factors entering into the ascertainment of the values of both stocks. In Haslam's opinion the problem reduces to 'a comparison of the operating trends of each of the corporations and of the investment characteristics of the two stock issues.' A summary of some of the more important comparisons developed in the report is set forth in the margin.[1] On the basis of these comparisons, as well as upon consideration

---

1. Comparisons drawn from Haslam report:

Average Earnings Per Share	Hilton	Mayflower
1947–1951 Average:		
Before income taxes and extraordinary items	4.31	2.17
After income taxes and extraordinary items	2.79	1.17
1951 to Nov. 30:		
Before income taxes and extraordinary items	4.22	3.14
After income taxes and extraordinary items	2.37	1.15
Dividends Per Share		
1947–1951 Average	1.07	.34
1951	1.20	.40
Book Value Per Share		

of the past history and future prospects of the two corporations, Haslam concludes that the financial record of Hilton has been substantially superior to that of Mayflower, and that purely upon a statistical basis it could be argued that Hilton should not offer better than three-fourths of a share of Hilton for one share of Mayflower. Nevertheless it is his opinion that, because of the problems incident to Hilton's control of Mayflower and the advantages incident to complete ownership, a share-for-share exchange will be fair and reasonable to all concerned.

An affidavit of J. Sellers Bancroft, Vice President in charge of Trust Department investments of Wilmington Trust Company, sets forth his conclusion, reached after a review of Mr. Haslam's study and an examination of pertinent financial data, that a share-for-share exchange is unquestionably fair.

The Haslam report contains no finding of net asset value—a factor nevertheless proper to be considered. Plaintiffs submitted affidavits containing an appraisal of the Mayflower Hotel (including land) and an estimate of reproduction cost (less depreciation) of the hotel proper. These affidavits indicate a value of upwards of $10,000,000. If plaintiffs' figure of a minimum value of $10,500,000[2] be accepted (it was accepted by the Chancellor), a share of Mayflower stock would have a liquidating or net asset value of about $27 a share. Defendants submitted an affidavit of J. B. Herndon, Jr., Vice President and Treasurer of Hilton, to the effect that two of the hotel properties of Hilton (the Conrad Hilton and the Palmer House in Chicago), which are carried on the books at $26,800,000, have a value of at least $60,000,000. Mr. Hilton gave some testimony to the same effect. If the indicated increase of $33,200,000 be accepted, there is added to Hilton's per share book value about $20, making an asset value of about $38 a share. Haslam submitted a comparison of 'indicated values' of the hotel properties, arrived at by assuming rates of capitalization of earnings derived from plaintiffs' appraisal of the Mayflower Hotel and applying such rates to the Hilton earnings, and, by two different methods, arrived at figures of $30.56 and $40.82 as 'indicated' net asset values of a share of Hilton stock. Plaintiffs submitted no evidence of value of the Hilton hotel properties.

Now, it will be noted that all of the comparisons above set forth except that of market value are in favor of Hilton. As for the market value of Mayflower stock, it appears to be conceded by all parties to be fictitious, that is, higher than would be justified in a free and normal market uninfluenced by Hilton's desire to acquire it and its policy of continued buying. At all events, that is the natural inference from the evidence. If we lay aside market value, and also disregard the comparison of book values—a factor, as the Chancellor said, of little relevancy in this case—we

Nov. 30, 1951	Per books	18.26	14.38	1951 Average	15.46	15.56
	Adjusted	18.42	13.98	Approximate current price [at		
Market Value Per Share				date of study]	14.75	16.25
1950 average		12.88	11.25			

2. Arrived at by adding to the appraised value $500,000 in liquid assets.

find three comparisons of various degrees of importance—earnings, dividends and net asset value—all in favor of Hilton.

If, therefore, we should accept the findings in the Haslam report and the principles on which it is based, and also accept the evidence bearing on comparative net asset value of Mayflower and Hilton stock, we should have to conclude that a share of Hilton stock has a value at least equal to a share of Mayflower stock, and that no unfair treatment of the Mayflower minority stockholders has been shown.

But we are confronted at the outset with the contention of the plaintiffs, basic to their case, that the Haslam report and the comparisons of value therein developed are wholly irrelevant to the issues before us. This contention, urged with much vigor—and repetition—is that the transaction here assailed is in substance a sale of assets by a fiduciary to himself. That the transaction is cast in the form of a merger, they say, is of no consequence; it is in effect a sale, and the only relevant comparison to be made is the comparison of the value of the transferred assets—worth $10,500,000—with the value of the consideration—389,738 shares of Hilton stock of a market value of $5,846,700; a disparity so shocking as to stamp the transaction as a fraud upon the Mayflower minority stockholders.

If plaintiffs' contention should be accepted it would follow that upon every merger of a subsidiary into its parent corporation that involves a conversion of the subsidiary's shares into shares of the parent, the *market* value of the parent stock issued to the stockholders of the subsidiary must equal the *liquidating* value of the subsidiary's stock. On its face this proposition is unsound, since it attempts to equate two different standards of value. In the case of many industrial corporations, and also in the instant case, there is a substantial gap between the market value and the liquidating value of the stock; and to apply to the merger of such corporations the proposition advanced by plaintiffs would be to bestow upon the stockholder of the subsidiary something which he did not have before the merger and could not obtain—the liquidating value of his stock.

What is the reasoning by which plaintiffs would lead us to sanction such a result?

Plaintiffs start with a quotation from the opinion of Chancellor Wolcott in the case of Cole v. National Cash Credit Ass'n, 156 A. 183, 188, which involved a merger of several Delaware corporations. Preferred stockholders of National (one of the constituent corporations) charged that if the merger were effected the asset security underlying the preferred stock of the surviving corporation that was to be given in exchange for their preferred stock in National would be less in value than that which underlay their National stock; and that this reduction in value flowed from an undervaluation of National's assets in comparison with the assets of the other merging corporations. Plaintiffs' charge of unfairness was thus based upon alleged disparity in comparative net asset values. The Chancellor said:

'The case therefore is one that rests on the sole fact of alleged undervaluation and overvaluation of the assets of two of the merging companies.'

Announcing a rule embodying a test of fraud applicable to such a case, the Chancellor continued:

'Where that is the case the rule adopted by this court as applicable to the sale of corporate assets would seem by analogy to supply a sound basis for guidance. While a consolidation is quite distinct from a sale, yet, *from the viewpoint of the constituent companies, a sale of assets is in substance involved.* Here it is the sale feature of the merger and that alone with which we are concerned. *Looking then at the transaction as one where the stockholders of the defendant are in substance selling its assets to another in exchange for securities issued by the latter,* what is the rule by which the value derived in exchange for the assets is to be tested for the purpose of discovering whether or not fraud can be said to have been shown?

Seizing upon the emphasized language and disregarding the facts to which it was directed, plaintiffs say in effect: A merger is essentially a sale of assets; this transaction is a sale of assets by a fiduciary (Hilton) to itself for shares of stock worth shockingly less than the assets sold; therefore the transaction is a fraud. So runs the syllogism.

A manifest fallacy, we think, lurks in the basic premise of this reasoning. A merger may be said to 'involve' a sale of assets, in the sense that the title to the assets is by operation of law transferred from the constituent corporation to the surviving corporation; but it is not the same thing. It is, as the introductory clause of Chancellor Wolcott's language affirms, something quite distinct, and the distinction is not merely one of form, as the plaintiffs say, but one of substance. A merger ordinarily contemplates the continuance of the enterprise and of the stockholder's investment therein, though in altered form; a sale of all assets (the type of sale referred to in the Cole case) ordinarily contemplates the liquidation of the enterprise. In the first case the stockholder of the merged corporation is entitled to receive directly securities substantially equal in value to those he held before the merger; in the latter case he receives nothing directly, but his corporation is entitled to receive the value of the assets sold. The scope of the applicable sections of our General Corporation Law (Section 59, relating to mergers and consolidations, and Section 65, relating to sales of all the corporate assets) may to some extent overlap; but this is not to say that the two procedures differ only in form. They are, in general, distinct and designed for different ends.

The instant case supplies an apt illustration. The Mayflower assets are not to be liquidated; the property is not for sale. Its directors and stockholders have determined, not that the venture should be terminated, but that it should be integrated completely with the Hilton enterprise. Having made this decision they had the right to avail themselves of the means which the law provides for just such a purpose, subject always to their imperative duty to accord to the minority fair and equitable terms of conversion.

Nor do we think that the Cole case supports plaintiffs' contention. The quoted language embodies, as Chancellor Wolcott indicated, an analogy and not a definition. The question actually before him was one of comparative net asset values. Thus, at the beginning of that portion of the opinion which deals with the objections of the preferred stockholders, he said:

> 'The crucial point on which their complaint turns is one of value—whether or not they as stockholders in one of the constituents are to receive in exchange for their present holdings, *stock which has a value commensurate* with the *asset contribution which their company* is making to the common pool.'

Plaintiffs interpret the words 'commensurate with' as meaning 'equal to'. Thus they say that the quoted language makes it plain that a comparison of the value of the assets transferred with the value (i. e., market value) of the stock issued in exchange is the only relevant factor to be considered.

But this is not what the language says nor what it means. The reference is to the value of the assets underlying the stock extinguished by the merger compared with the value of the assets which will underlie the stock to be received upon the consummation of the merger. Thus, in a later part of the opinion the Chancellor speaks of the question before him as one involving 'the relative participations of the merging companies in the total assets thrown into the merger pool', and ultimately resolves the question by comparing the net asset value of a share of the stock extinguished with a similar valuation of the stock to be received. There is no suggestion in the case that in determining the fairness of a merger net asset value of one stock should be compared with market value of the other.

The unsoundness of such a method of comparison is illustrated by the subsequent decision in Mitchell v. Highland–Western Glass Co., 167 A. 831. In that case all of the assets of Highland were to be sold to Mississippi Glass Company for shares of stock of the seller. The consideration was alleged to be grossly inadequate. Plaintiffs' counsel argued that the number of shares issued in payment for the sale was based on a ratio of assets of two to one; whereas the assets were nearly equal in value, and the ratio was grossly unfair. To develop this argument he took the full book value of the seller's assets as their fair value, but refused to value the stock received by the same method. The Chancellor dismissed the argument with the terse comment: 'Manifestly that is unjustifiable.'

Plaintiffs' attempt to push to extremes the analogy drawn from a sale of assets leads them to a wholly untenable position, viz., that upon a merger a stockholder of a subsidiary is entitled to receive securities equal in value to the liquidating value of his stock. As we have already indicated, this proposition is unsound. Speaking generally, a merger effects an exchange of shares of stock in a going concern for shares in another going concern. In determining the fairness of the exchange liquidating value is not the sole test of the value of either. In the Porges case, preferred stockholders objected to a merger which accorded recognition to the common stock on the ground that the common shares were without value—that is, without liquidating value. Implicit in this objection was the assumption that liquidating value was the sole test by which the measure of recognition accorded to the common stock in the merger was to be evaluated. Vice Chancellor Pearson rejected the argument, pointing out that the preferred stockholders had no right to require liquidation of the corporation and that the rights of the two classes of stock must be viewed in the light of the fact that the corporation was a going concern. He announced the following rule: 'To arrive at a judgment of the fairness of the merger, all of its terms must be considered.'

A similar rule obtains in ascertaining the value of stock in appraisal proceedings under the merger statute. In such cases the liquidating value of the stock is not the sole test of value; all relevant factors must be considered.

The cases cited to us by plaintiffs from other jurisdictions do not, we think, afford any support to their contention. * * *

No case is cited to us holding that upon a merger of a subsidiary into a parent corporation the minority stockholders of a subsidiary are entitled to the liquidating value of their stock.

In the instant case the Chancellor held that in a case of merger 'all relevant value factors must be considered in arriving at a fair value for comparison purposes.'

For the reasons above given, we find no error in this ruling. * * *

We have considered all of plaintiffs' objections to the fairness of the proposed merger, and find ourselves in accord with the Chancellor's conclusion that no fraud or unfairness has been shown.

NOTES

1. How can the comparative valuations, balance sheet valuation methods and pre-acquisition relative share prices (see footnote 1 of the court's opinion) support the one-for-one share exchange that the court approved in the *Mayflower Hotel* case?

2. The court in the *Mayflower Hotel* case refused to give much weight to the company's liquidation value since it was going to continue to operate as a going concern. Is this fair? After all, the shareholders' interests are effectively being liquidated.

MILLS v. ELECTRIC AUTO–LITE CO.

552 F.2d 1239 (7th Cir.1977).

SWYGERT, CIRCUIT JUDGE.

Mergenthaler produced and distributed typesetting equipment. It began to purchase Auto–Lite stock in 1957 and by March 1962 had acquired 54.2 percent of Auto–Lite. At that point Auto–Lite became a subsidiary of Mergenthaler and Mergenthaler obtained control of the Auto–Lite Board of Directors.

In early 1963 Mergenthaler decided to attempt a merger of itself and Auto–Lite into a new company to be called "Eltra Corporation." The Auto–Lite Board voted to accept the proposed merger on May 28, 1963 and on May 29 a request for proxies was sent to shareholders accompanied by a statement in which the Board endorsed the merger. The holders of approximately thirteen percent of the minority shares had to approve the merger in order to secure the two-thirds vote necessary for ratification. The merger was approved at a shareholders' meeting on June 27, 1963 and became effective on June 28, 1963.

Plaintiffs, who were Auto–Lite shareholders representing themselves and all other minority Auto–Lite shareholders, filed suit on June 26, 1963 in the district court for the Northern District of Illinois. They sought to set aside the merger on the ground that the proxy statement was deceptive because it endorsed the merger without clearly disclosing that the Auto–Lite Board was controlled by Mergenthaler. The district court agreed with plaintiffs' theory and held that the proxy statement violated section 14(a) of the Securities Exchange Act of 1934. It also held that the plaintiffs had shown a causal relationship between the proxy statement and the consummation of the merger.

This court affirmed the district court's holding that the proxy statement was illegally deceptive but reversed on the causality issue, holding that no relief could be appropriate if the defendants could show "by a preponderance of probabilities" that the merger would have been approved even if the proxy statement had not been deceptive.

The Supreme Court reversed and reinstated the judgment of the district court. It held that "(w)here there has been a finding of materiality, a shareholder has made a sufficient showing of causal relationship between the violation and the injury for which he seeks redress if, as here, he proves that the proxy solicitation itself, rather than the particular defect in the solicitation materials, was an essential link in the accomplishment of the transaction." 396 U.S. 375, 385 (1970).

The Court went on to consider the relief to which plaintiffs were entitled. It noted that the merger did not need to be set aside because of the deception in the proxy statement, though a court could order such action if it were warranted by equitable considerations. It then discussed the possibility of monetary relief and stated:

(W)here, as here, the misleading aspect of the solicitation did not relate to terms of the merger, monetary relief might be afforded to the shareholders only if the merger resulted in a reduction of the earnings or earnings potential of their holdings. In short, damages should be recoverable only to the extent that they can be shown. If commingling of the assets and operations of the merged companies makes it impossible to establish direct injury from the merger, relief might be predicated on a determination of the fairness of the terms of the merger at the time it was approved. These questions, of course, are for decision in the first instance by the District Court on remand, and our singling out of some of the possibilities is not intended to exclude others. 396 U.S. at 388–89.

The case then moved back to the district court for a determination of the appropriate relief. The court first held that the merger should not be rescinded. It then determined that the merger terms were unfair to plaintiffs and awarded the class they represent $1,233,918.35, as well as approximately $740,000 in prejudgment interest. It further held that plaintiffs' attorneys should be compensated out of this award.

Both parties now appeal from the district court's judgment. Plaintiffs contend that the amount of damages was too low and that their attorneys' fees should be assessed against defendants rather than against the damages awarded. Defendants assert that no damages should have been awarded because the terms of the merger were fair.

The district court considered two possible theories of damages in attempting to follow the Supreme Court's mandate: (1) to compensate plaintiffs for the reduction of the earnings potential of their holdings in Auto–Lite as a result of the merger; or (2) an award based on a determination of the fairness of the terms of the merger at the time it was approved. It rejected the use of the first theory under the circumstances of this case and adopted the second. We shall evaluate both whether the district court was erroneous in its choice of remedies and whether it correctly applied the second theory.

In order to perform this evaluation, it is first necessary to describe the merger terms. They called for the minority Auto–Lite shareholders to receive 1.88 preferred shares of Eltra for each share of Auto–Lite common that they held and the Mergenthaler shareholders to receive one common share of Eltra for each share of Mergenthaler common that they held. Eltra preferred shares were convertible into common shares on a one-to-one basis for the first two years following the merger and on a slightly decreasing basis for the next three years. At the time of the merger Mergenthaler common paid a dividend of $1 per share and Auto–Lite common paid a dividend of $2.40 per share. Under the merger terms Eltra common was to pay a dividend of $1 per share and Eltra preferred a dividend of $1.40 per share. The dividend received by the Auto–Lite minority shareholders was therefore increased as a result of the merger by twenty-three cents for each share of Auto–Lite that they had held, because 1.88 X $1.40 = $2.63.

The preferred Eltra stock was clearly worth more than Eltra common because it paid a higher dividend and represented a more secure investment if the new corporation encountered financial difficulties, yet was convertible into common stock. During the month following the merger, the average market value of Eltra preferred was $31.06 per share. Consequently the Auto–Lite minority shareholders received stock worth $58.39 on the market for each share of Auto–Lite that they had previously held, because 1.88 X $31.06 = $58.39. The average market value of Eltra common for this month was $25.25 per share. Since the Mergenthaler shareholders received one share of Eltra common for each share of Mergenthaler common, the Auto–Lite shareholders received stock for each share of Auto–Lite that they held worth $58.39/$25.25 = 2.31 times as much on the market as the stock that the Mergenthaler shareholders received for each share of Mergenthaler that they held. We therefore hold that the exchange ratio for the merger was effectively 2.31 to 1.[3]

A theory of damages based on the "reduction of the earnings or earnings potential" of the Auto–Lite minority shareholders caused by the merger is an attempt to discern, by looking at the postmerger performance and activities of the Auto–Lite subsidiary in comparison to the other components of Eltra, whether the value placed on the Auto–Lite shares at the time the merger took place was fair to those shareholders. Plaintiffs contend that the postmerger record of Eltra demonstrates the unfairness of the merger in two significant ways: first, by showing that Eltra appropriated for use in its other divisions liquid assets held by Auto–Lite prior to the merger; and second, by showing that Eltra continually siphoned off Auto–Lite's postmerger earnings.

Even if plaintiffs' assertions are true, they cannot form the basis for an award of damages. Plaintiffs assume that it would be unfair to the former minority Auto–Lite shareholders if, after the merger, the Eltra management "weakened" the Auto–Lite divisions by shifting liquid assets or earnings to other divisions. This assumption is incorrect. After the merger the former Auto–Lite shareholders had become Eltra shareholders and had no more interest in the Auto–Lite divisions than any other Eltra shareholder. Therefore, they could not be injured by intra-corporate transfers of assets designed to strengthen the corporation as a whole. The interests of the former Auto–Lite shareholders and former Mergenthaler shareholders coincided after the merger, and the Eltra management could not possibly take actions that benefitted "its" shareholders at the expense of the Auto–Lite shareholders. * * *

Plaintiffs ignored the only theory on which relief based on the postmerger performance of Eltra might be granted. If the ratio of the

---

3. The district court, after considering the factors we have just reviewed, found the effective exchange ratio to be 2.25 to 1. Although the court never explained precisely how it arrived at this figure, the difference of .06 between the two ratios will not prove to be significant in subsequent calculations.

postmerger earnings of the Auto–Lite subsidiary of Eltra to the postmerger earnings of the Mergenthaler subsidiary were unusually high given the terms of the merger, it would be evidence that those terms were unfair to the Auto–Lite minority shareholders. This is true not because the former Auto–Lite minority shareholders are entitled to any percentage of the earnings of the Auto–Lite subsidiary after the merger, but because a high ratio would indicate that in retrospect the merger terms underestimated Auto–Lite's value as an enterprise. * * *

Given the fact that significant commingling occurred, the postmerger earnings of Auto–Lite and Mergenthaler cannot supply a reliable guide to whether the merger terms were fair to the Auto–Lite minority shareholders. Even in the absence of commingling, postmerger evidence can only create a rebuttable inference of unfairness because it is impossible to know with certainty whether the increase in earnings of one partner to a merger should have been predictable at the time the merger took place. In this case the ratio of the earnings per share of the two companies for the four years prior to and including 1963 were all at or below the effective exchange ratio of 2.31 to 1. Plaintiffs have not shown that the management of Mergenthaler should have known in 1963 that Auto–Lite's earnings were going to increase faster than Mergenthaler's during the next decade. The more plausible inference is that, insofar as Auto–Lite's business became more productive because of factors unrelated to commingling, they were unforeseeable at the time the merger was consummated. Accordingly, we hold that the district court did not abuse its discretion in refusing to award damages based on postmerger data. * * *

The district court based its award of damages on an assessment of the fairness of the merger terms at the time the merger took place. It evaluated five criteria in making this assessment: (1) the market value of each corporation's stock; (2) each corporation's earnings; (3) the book value of each corporation's assets; (4) the dividends that each corporation paid on its stock; and (5) other "qualitative factors" indicating the strength of each corporation. The court found market value to be an unreliable criterion and discounted the importance of dividends. It found that the comparative earnings and book values of each corporation were significant and demonstrated that the merger terms were unfair to the Auto–Lite minority. The court did not indicate what significance it was attributing to "qualitative factors."

Based on these findings the court held that the merger would have been fair if the Auto–Lite minority shareholders had received the equivalent of 2.35 shares of Eltra common for each share of Auto–Lite that they held and Mergenthaler shareholders had received one share of Eltra common for each share of Mergenthaler that they held. It also found that the effective exchange ratio for the actual merger, where the Auto–Lite minority shareholders received 1.88 shares of Eltra preferred for each share of Auto–Lite common that they held, was 2.25 to 1 in terms of Eltra common. It then awarded damages of $1,233,918.35 to plaintiffs based on the differential of .10 between the effective exchange ratio of 2.25 to 1 and the fair exchange ratio of 2.35 to 1. * * *

After finding that market value provided an inaccurate measure of the true worth of Auto–Lite and Mergenthaler, the district court determined whether the merger terms were fair on the basis of comparative earnings and book value. Given our conclusion that market prices were an accurate gauge of actual value, we must decide whether the other criteria on which the district court relied should properly be considered in evaluating whether the merger was fair.

We hold that when market value is available and reliable, other factors should not be utilized in determining whether the terms of a merger were fair. Although criteria such as earnings and book value are an indication of actual worth, they are only secondary indicia. In a market economy, market value will always be the primary gauge of an enterprise's worth. In this case thousands of shares of Auto–Lite and Mergenthaler were traded on the New York Stock Exchange during the first part of 1963 by outside investors who had access to the full gamut of financial information about both corporations, including earnings and book value. If we were to independently assess criteria other than market value in our effort to determine whether the merger terms were fair, we would be substituting our abstract judgment for that of the market. Aside from the problems that would arise in deciding how much weight to give each criterion, such a method would be economically unsound.

We turn now to a determination of whether the merger terms were fair, based on the comparative market price of each corporation's stock during the first part of 1963. The simplest method of resolving this issue would be to compare the price ratio, in this case 2.1, to the effective exchange ratio, which we have previously established as 2.31. Under this framework the merger would be fair since the effective exchange ratio gave the Auto–Lite minority shareholders more Eltra stock than they were entitled to in the judgment of the market.

This method of calculation, however, assumes that the new corporation that results from a merger is worth exactly as much as the sum of what its two component parts were worth before the merger. As Professors Brudney and Chirelstein have cogently pointed out, this assumption is usually false because a merger produces a synergistic effect resulting in the merged corporation being worth more than the sum of the two old corporations. Brudney & Chirelstein, Fair Shares in Corporate Mergers and Takeovers, 88 Harv.L.Rev. 297, 308–09 (1974). They demonstrate that fairness requires that minority shareholders be compensated not only for the market value of their shares in the old corporation but also for the share of the synergism generated by the merger that is proportionate to the interest that those shares represented in the combined premerger value of the two old corporations. Id. at 313–25.

We adopt the approach formulated by Professors Brudney and Chirelstein and will attempt to apply it to this case. At the time of the merger there were 532,550 minority shares of Auto–Lite and 2,698,822 shares of Mergenthaler outstanding. During the first part of 1963 the average market price of Auto–Lite was $52.25 per share and the average market price of Mergenthaler was $24.875 per share. Thus, the premerger value of the minority holdings in Auto–Lite was 532,550 x $52.25 = $27,825,737 and the premerger value of Mergenthaler was 2,698,822 x $24.875 = $67,133,197. The combined premerger value of the two corporations was $27,825,737 + $67,133,197 = $94,958,934.[16]

In the month following the merger, Eltra common stock had an average market value of $25.25 per share. Eltra preferred stock had an average market value of $58.39 per 1.88 shares, the amount of stock which Auto–Lite shareholders had received for each share of Auto–Lite that they had held. The postmerger value of Eltra was therefore (2,698,822 x $25.25) + (532,550 x $58.39) = $68,145,255 + $31,095,594 = $99,240,849. The difference between the combined premerger value of Auto–Lite and Mergenthaler and the postmerger value of Eltra, which was $99,240,849 – $94,958,934 = $4,281,915, can be attributed to the synergism generated by the merger.

According to the fairness formula devised by Professors Brudney and Chirelstein, the minority shareholders of Auto–Lite should have received Eltra stock worth at least as much as the premerger market value of their holdings in Auto–Lite and a share of the synergism produced by the merger proportionate to the percentage of the combined premerger value of Auto–Lite and Mergenthaler which their holdings represented. The premerger value of the Auto–Lite minority shares was $27,825,737, which represented 29.3 percent of $94,958,934, the combined premerger value of Auto–Lite and Mergenthaler. Thus, to satisfy the constraints of fairness, the Auto–Lite minority shareholders should have received stock worth at least $27,825,737 + (.293 x $4,281,915) = $29,080,338. This would be equivalent to 1,151,696.5 shares of Eltra common at $25.25 per share. Had this many shares been distributed to the Auto–Lite minority shareholders, the exchange ratio would have been 1,151,696. 5/532, 550 = 2.16 to 1.[17]

The Auto–Lite minority shareholders actually received preferred stock worth $58.39 on the market for each share of Auto–Lite that they had held. As a group, their Eltra holdings were worth 532,550 x $58.39 = $31,095,594. This was $31,095,594 – $29,080,338 = $2,015,256 more than fairness required. This result can be expressed in terms of Eltra common shares. Since the effective exchange ratio of the merger was 2.31 to 1, the

---

16. Although Mergenthaler owned more than half of the Auto–Lite stock, this holding should not be independently counted as part of the combined value of the two corporations because it was already reflected in the value of Mergenthaler stock.

17. We note that the price of Eltra common depended in part on the exchange ratio actually used. For example, if we assume that Eltra stock was distributed at an effective exchange ratio of 2.16 to 1, there would have been the equivalent of 2,698,822 + (2.16 x 532,550) = 3,849,130 Eltra common shares outstanding. Since the total postmerger value of Eltra was $99,240,849, the price of one share of Eltra common would rise to $99,240,84 9/3, 849,130 = $25.78. However, the figures in the text give a good approximation of the number of Eltra common shares or their equivalent that the Auto–Lite minority shareholders should have received.

property given the Auto–Lite minority was worth $2.31 - 2.16 = .15$ shares of Eltra common per share of Auto–Lite more than what a fair amount would have been.

We therefore hold that the terms of the merger were fair and that plaintiffs should recover no damages. A numerical example may help to show the justice of this result. In early 1963, an Auto–Lite shareholder with one hundred shares and a Mergenthaler shareholder with 210 shares each owned stock worth approximately $5225. After the merger, the former Auto–Lite shareholder had 188 shares of Eltra preferred worth approximately $5839 while the former Mergenthaler shareholder had 210 shares of Eltra common worth approximately $5302. Both individuals benefited from the merger, but the former Auto–Lite minority shareholder benefited more. * * *

NOTES

1. For additional discussion of fairness in mergers, see Rutherford B. Campbell, Jr., "Fair Value and Fair Price in Corporate Acquisitions," 78 N.C.L. Rev. 101 (1999).

2. *Stock versus cash.* The court in *Mills* held that the merger exchange, although unequal in terms of the pre-merger market value of the respective shares, resulted in a fair exchange under the Brudney and Chirelstein analysis. If the shareholders of the merged company do not get a share in the survivor, they cannot share in the post-merger gains. Does this suggest a different level of scrutiny for transactions where the target shareholders receive stock in the acquiring company as compared with a cashing out of the target company shareholders?

MATTESON v. ZIEBARTH
40 Wash.2d 286, 242 P.2d 1025 (1952).

HAMLEY, JUSTICE.

This is an action by a minority stockholder of Ziebarth Corporation to set aside a merger agreement between that corporation and Snowy, Incorporated. He alleges that the agreement is illegal, unfair and fraudulent. Named as defendant, in addition to the two corporations, is Robert Ziebarth, the majority stockholder of both corporations. Defendants joined in an answer denying plaintiff's characterization of the merger agreement. They also allege, affirmatively, that plaintiff is bound by the agreement because he failed to pursue the statutory remedy available to dissatisfied stockholders.

The plaintiff is Archibald R. Matteson. In 1946 he and Ziebarth organized Ziebarth Corporation for the purpose of producing and selling a powdered household bleach. The corporation was capitalized at fifty thousand dollars, represented by fifty thousand shares of common stock having a par value of one dollar a share. The organizers subscribed for 11,200 shares. In payment therefor, they transferred to the corporation certain property, including a formula, trademarks, machinery, equipment and supplies, valued at $11,200.

It was agreed that Matteson owned a one-third interest in this property and Ziebarth owned the remaining two thirds interest. Accordingly, Matteson received thirty-six hundred shares of stock, and Ziebarth received seventy-six hundred shares. Ziebarth's attorney, F. A. LeSourd, subscribed and paid for one share to qualify as a director and officer. Ziebarth later acquired additional stock of the company by purchase, so that in May, 1950, he owned 27,200 shares.

Matteson worked full time for the company until January, 1948. His salary was $150 a month at first, but was later increased to $225 a month. Ziebarth devoted over one-half of his time to the affairs of the corporation, from the time of its organization until April, 1950. His compensation for such services during this entire period was less than $500. While he was reimbursed for some of his expenses incurred in promoting the sale of the product, he apparently absorbed a substantial amount of such expense.

Ziebarth Corporation lost money almost consistently. By May 31, 1950, it had lost $15,235.34 of the twenty thousand dollars capital which Ziebarth had supplied. As early as 1947, it was realized that the corporation could not operate profitably without expanding the market for 'Snowy,' as the powdered bleach was called. The alternatives seemed to be to obtain additional capital or sell out. However, no immediate solution was found in either of these directions. In an effort to minimize losses, the corporation adopted a retrenchment program at the end of 1947. It was then that Matteson went off the payroll. Thereafter, he apparently took little interest in the corporation. Ziebarth continued to devote a great deal of his time to the company, but received no compensation after January 1, 1948.

In April, 1949, Ziebarth entered into negotiations with Harold Schafer, president of Gold Seal Corporation, looking towards the sale of Ziebarth Corporation. Gold Seal is a North Dakota corporation engaged in the sale of household chemical products throughout the United States and Canada. After numerous conferences and considerable travel back and forth, a proposed agreement between the two corporations was arrived at by Ziebarth and Schafer, assisted by their attorneys. * * *

This proposal was considered at a meeting of the stockholders of Ziebarth Corporation, held on May 1, 1950. At that time the corporation had 33,851 shares of stock outstanding, distributed as follows: Ziebarth, 27,200 shares; Matteson, 3,600 shares; Robert Denker, 2,675 shares; Lester Swank, 175 shares; Fred B. Hurd, 100 shares; H. W. Ziebarth, 100 shares; and F. A. LeSourd, one share. All of this stock was voted in favor of the proposed agreement with Gold Seal, except that held by Matteson, who cast the lone dissenting vote. He took the position that the sixteen thousand dollars Ziebarth was to receive as an employee of Gold Seal was, in the main, part of the consideration paid by Gold Seal for the agreement, and hence all stockholders should share in that sixteen-thousand-dollar payment.

Ziebarth and his attorney thereafter tried to get Matteson to change his mind. Matteson finally said he would do so if Ziebarth would give him twenty-five per cent of the sixteen thousand dollars Ziebarth was to receive as salary from Gold Seal. Ziebarth refused to do this. Because Gold Seal's proposal was limited to the purchase of all of the stock, as distinguished from the assets, of Ziebarth Corporation, one hundred per cent participation by the stockholders of Ziebarth Corporation was essential. Therefore, Matteson's refusal to vote for the proposed agreement blocked its consummation.

Convinced that the Gold Seal proposal was the only salvation for Ziebarth Corporation, Ziebarth then sought to consummate the transaction by means of a merger between Ziebarth Corporation and a new corporation organized for the specific purpose. It is this merger which Matteson resists in this action.

The new corporation, named Snowy, Incorporated, was organized on May 17, 1950. It had an authorized capitalization of one hundred thousand shares of common stock having a par value of thirty cents a share, and one hundred thousand shares of preferred stock having a par value of twenty cents a share. Ziebarth subscribed and paid for 30,150 shares of this common stock, H. W. Ziebarth subscribed and paid for one hundred shares, and F. A. LeSourd subscribed and paid for one share.

On May 18, 1950, the directors of Ziebarth Corporation and Snowy, Incorporated, approved a merger agreement between the two corporations. In the merger, stockholders of Ziebarth Corporation were to receive one share of twenty-cent par value callable preferred stock of Snowy, Incorporated, for each share of Ziebarth Corporation common stock theretofore owned by them. On the same day, Ziebarth signed an instrument advising Hurd, Denker and Swank (the three principal minority stockholders of Ziebarth Corporation other than Matteson) that he was giving them an option to purchase common stock of Snowy, Incorporated. The instrument provided that they could purchase from Ziebarth, at the par value of thirty cents each, the same number of shares of Snowy, Incorporated, as they then held in Ziebarth Corporation.

On May 31, 1950, the merger agreement was approved by the holders of two-thirds of the voting power of all shareholders of Ziebarth Corporation, as required by statute (Rem.Rev.Stat. (Sup.) § 3803–43). Matteson was, in fact, the only stockholder to vote against the merger at this meeting. Subsequently, on June 5, 1950, an option agreement, similar to the original proposal, was entered into between Snowy, Incorporated, and Gold Seal. Thereupon Ziebarth undertook his duties as an employee of Gold Seal, and received, in due course, the stipulated sixteen-thousand-dollar consideration for such services.

Matteson instituted this suit on June 12, 1950. The case was tried to the court without a jury, and resulted in a decree dismissing the action with prejudice. Plaintiff has appealed. * * *

The next eight assignments of error challenge certain findings of fact and conclusions of law and the entry of judgment thereon. The points of law and fact raised by these assignments present two principal questions. These are: Should the merger be set aside on the ground that it is illegal because not of a kind contemplated by law? Should the merger be set aside on the ground of unfairness or fraud?

Relative to the first of these questions, appellant contends that the merger is of a kind not contemplated by law because one of the corporations was organized immediately prior to the merger for the sole purpose of the merger. This has reference to the incorporation of Snowy, Incorporated, for the express purpose of merging with and absorbing Ziebarth Corporation.

The kind of corporations which may merge or consolidate in this state are specified in Rem.Rev.Stat. (Sup.) § 3803–42. It is there provided, in part, that any two or more domestic corporations, formed for any purpose for which a corporation might be formed 'under this act' may be merged into one of such domestic corporations. A corporation may be formed, under the act, 'for any lawful business purposes' with certain exceptions not here in point.

Snowy, Incorporated, was organized by the majority stockholder of Ziebarth Corporation, for the express purpose of consummating an option agreement involving the possible sale of all the outstanding stock of the latter corporation. The option agreement could not otherwise be effectuated due to the opposition of Matteson, a minority stockholder of Ziebarth Corporation. There is nothing in the uniform business corporation act to indicate that this is not a 'lawful business purpose.' Nor does appellant cite any authority to that effect. We therefore conclude that Snowy, Incorporated, was a kind of corporation which might, under the statute, merge with Ziebarth Corporation.

Appellant also contends that the merger is not of a kind contemplated by law, because common stockholders of the absorbed corporation were required to accept, in lieu of that common stock, redeemable preferred stock in the surviving corporation. It is asserted that the transaction amounted to nothing more than a forced sale of Matteson's equity in Ziebarth Corporation, and that this is not permissible under the merger statute.

The merger statute authorizes the directors of the two corporations to draft the details of the merger. There are no restrictions concerning the nature of the stock to be issued. The directors may agree to allocate to the stockholders of the absorbed corporation whatever stock interest in the surviving corporation appears proper under the circumstances. The statute does not proscribe an allocation of callable preferred stock in the surviving corporation, even though it may result in the ultimate ouster of the recipient of such stock from any interest in the business.

Whether that feature of the merger plan, though conforming to statutory requirements, introduces an element of unfairness or fraud sufficient to move a court of equity, is an entirely different question. That question will be considered below. The decision in Outwater v. Public Service Corporation, relied upon by appellant, involved this latter question and turned upon a finding of unfairness. The court there expressly held that no valid legal objection could be interposed on the ground that the stock to be allocated was redeemable. In our opinion, the allocation feature complained of in the instant case is permissible under the merger statute.

This disposes of the first question presented by the group of assignments of error now under consideration. As indicated above, the other general question posed by these assignments is whether the merger should be set aside on the ground of unfairness or fraud.

Before coming to the merits of this question, we must deal with respondents' contention that the uniform business corporation act precludes the granting of equitable relief except where actual fraud is shown.

Rem.Supp.1949, § 3803–41 provides that a shareholder who did not vote in favor of specified kinds of corporate action (including mergers), and who, within twenty days after notice of the meeting called to vote upon such corporate action was mailed to him, filed his written objection demanding payment for his shares, shall have the right to have his shares appraised and paid for. This section also defines, as follows, the legal rights of shareholders who have not followed this procedure:

> ' * * * Any shareholder who did not vote in favor of such corporate action and who did not within the time allowed him file with the corporation his written objection to such corporate action, demanding payment for his shares shall be bound by such corporate action *with like force and effect as though such shareholder had voted in favor of such corporate action*.' (Emphasis supplied.)

Appellant voted against the merger, and failed to file written objections and demand payment for his shares. He is therefore subject to whatever restrictions upon his available remedies are imposed by the above statute.

Respondents appear to concede that this statute does not preclude a resort to equity where the gist of the action is actual fraud. As to anything short of actual fraud, however, they contend that the statute referred to provides the exclusive remedy. Appellant, on the other hand, argues that the remedy is not exclusive where there is any generally recognized basis for equitable relief, such as unfairness or overreaching, even though it does not amount to actual fraud.

The cases cited by appellant in support of his proposition are not in point. They involve either a situation where there was no appraisal statute in effect, or where the statute contains no provision making the corporate action binding, or where the statute making the corporate action binding was not in effect when the decision was rendered.

In the states which have statutes generally similar to the quoted provision of our own act, the courts have uniformly held that the minority shareholder may not obtain relief in equity where his claim is based upon unfairness rather than fraud. * * *

We are of the view that, under our own act, the statutory remedy is likewise exclusive as to unfairness or breach of fiduciary duty short of actual fraud. This is subject to the qualification, however, that the statutory remedy is not exclusive unless the facts concerning such unfairness or breach of fiduciary duty were known to the aggrieved stockholder at the time of the stockholders' meeting at which the corporate action was approved.

This qualification is necessary in view of the 'with like force and effect' provision of the above statute, shown in italics. Where a stockholder consents to the corporate action, he is bound, under principles of estoppel, as to any claim of unfairness concerning which he had knowledge at that time. Such a stockholder is likewise bound as to any claim based upon breach of fiduciary duty short of actual fraud, concerning which breach he had knowledge at that time. Hence, in either of these cases, he is bound, under the statute, 'with like force and effect'. But since in the above cases the consenting stockholder would not have been bound if he did not have knowledge of the facts (for then there could be no estoppel), neither is he, if then unaware of the facts, bound under the statute.

We now come to a consideration of the various reasons advanced by appellant why the merger agreement should be set aside on the ground of unfairness or fraud. In connection with each, we will have to make the preliminary determination of whether, under the particular circumstances, the claim is now foreclosed to appellant under our construction of the act.

The first of these reasons is based upon the assertion that the merger agreement was intended and used as a device to give the majority stockholder of Ziebarth Corporation, for his own use, a substantial portion of the consideration for the Gold Seal option ($16,000), which should have gone to all stockholders on a *pro rata* basis. This refers to the provision of the option agreement under which Gold Seal agreed to employ Ziebarth, and he agreed to accept such employment, for a period of eight months at a salary of two thousand dollars a month.

At the time of the stockholders' meeting of Ziebarth Corporation, at which the merger was approved, Matteson knew all of the essential facts in connection with the sixteen-thousand-dollar transaction. Therefore he may not now predicate his claim for relief upon an assertion of unfairness or breach of fiduciary duty in connection with that matter, since such a claim is foreclosed under the act. * * *

The second reason advanced by appellant why the merger agreement should be set aside on the ground of unfairness or fraud has to do with the kind of stock which he was required to receive under the merger agreement. The requirement, in brief, was that he and other shareholders of Ziebarth Corporation give up their common stock in that corporation for redeemable preferred stock in Snowy, Incorporated. The effect of this exchange was to place it within the power of Snowy, Incorporated, to oust appellant from all interest in the bleach business by calling and redeeming his preferred stock. We have already considered this circumstance in connection with another question.

A stock-exchange arrangement of this kind may be unfair to a minority stockholder. But, as we have seen, Matteson is bound by the corporate action as against any claim of unfairness concerning which he had knowledge at the time of the stockholders' meeting where the merger was approved. He did, of course, have knowledge of this stock-exchange plan at that time. Hence, it provides no basis for equitable relief on the ground of unfairness. The same conclusion must be reached if this circumstance is relied upon as establishing a breach of fiduciary duty short of actual fraud.

There is no basis whatever for holding that this stock-exchange plan evidences actual fraud. The redeemable feature was applicable to all stockholders of Ziebarth Corporation, and was necessary in order to consummate the option arrangement with Gold Seal. There was good reason to believe that this option contract was the only salvation for the hard-pressed Ziebarth Corporation. * * *

We conclude that actual fraud has not been shown in connection with the stock transfer plan. The claim in connection with this matter accordingly affords no basis for equitable relief.

The third reason presented by appellant why the merger agreement should be set aside on the ground of unfairness or fraud relates to the value placed on the common stock of Ziebarth Corporation for purposes of the exchange of stock with Snowy, Incorporated. The Ziebarth Corporation stock was valued at twenty cents a share for this purpose. Appellant argues that this valuation is grossly inadequate. For the reasons heretofore stated in connection with other claims of unfairness and fraud, already discussed, we are of the view that the claim now before us presents a basis for equitable relief only if it is indicative of actual fraud. * * *

Appellant challenges this finding of fact, but we believe that it is supported by the preponderance of the evidence. Also pertinent to this inquiry is finding of fact No. XI, quoted above, in which it is indicated that Ziebarth Corporation was in such a precarious position that the Gold Seal option represented the only real chance for the stockholders to recoup their investments. The testimony dealing with the precise question of stock valuation is in direct conflict. In view of the trial court's finding as to the general financial condition of the company, we are inclined to place greater credence in the testimony tending to support the twenty-cent valuation as being fair and adequate. At any rate, in view of the heavy burden placed upon one who seeks to show fraud, we cannot say that the exchange price was so grossly inadequate as to indicate fraud.* * *

Ziebarth had a legitimate reason for excluding appellant from his personal and voluntary offer to give minority stockholders some additional stock in the new corporation. Appellant had been uncooperative in solving the financial problems of Ziebarth Corporation, thereby occasioning substantial expense and delay to the corporation. He had unjustifiably accused Ziebarth of arranging a side consideration for himself that should have gone to the corporation. Appellant had also made the wholly improper proposal to Ziebarth that, for a side consideration of four thousand dollars, appellant would withdraw his opposition to the original Gold Seal option plan.

The foregoing considerations lead us to conclude that no breach of fiduciary relationship or basic unfairness inheres in Ziebarth's option to other minority stockholders, requiring that the merger be set aside. For the same reasons we are of the view that appellant is not entitled to a decree requiring Ziebarth to extend the same option to appellant.

The judgment is affirmed.

————

WEINBERGER v. UOP, INC.

457 A.2d 701 (Del.1983).

MOORE, JUSTICE:

This post-trial appeal was reheard en banc from a decision of the Court of Chancery. It was brought by the class action plaintiff below, a former shareholder of UOP, Inc., who challenged the elimination of UOP's minority shareholders by a cash-out merger between UOP and its majority owner, The Signal Companies, Inc. Originally, the defendants in this action were Signal, UOP, certain officers and directors of those companies, and UOP's investment banker, Lehman Brothers Kuhn Loeb, Inc. The present Chancellor held that the terms of the merger were fair to the plaintiff and the other minority shareholders of UOP. Accordingly, he entered judgment in favor of the defendants. * * * In ruling for the defendants, the Chancellor re-stated his earlier conclusion that the plaintiff in a suit challenging a cash-out merger must allege specific acts of fraud, misrepresentation, or other items of misconduct to demonstrate the unfairness of the merger terms to the minority. We approve this rule and affirm it.

The Chancellor also held that even though the ultimate burden of proof is on the majority shareholder to show by a preponderance of the evidence that the transaction is fair, it is first the burden of the plaintiff attacking the merger to demonstrate some basis for invoking the fairness obligation. We agree with that principle. However, where corporate action has been approved by an informed vote of a majority of the minority shareholders, we conclude that the burden entirely shifts to the plaintiff to show that the transaction was unfair to the minority. But in all this, the burden clearly remains on those relying on the vote to show that they completely disclosed all material facts relevant to the transaction.

Here, the record does not support a conclusion that the minority stockholder vote was an informed one. Material information, necessary to acquaint those shareholders with the bargaining positions of Signal and UOP, was withheld under circumstances amounting to a breach of fiduciary duty. We therefore conclude that this merger does not meet the test of fairness, at least as we address that concept, and no burden thus shifted to the plaintiff by reason of the minority shareholder vote. Accordingly, we reverse and remand for further proceedings consistent herewith.

In considering the nature of the remedy available under our law to minority shareholders in a cash-out merger, we believe that it is, and hereafter should be, an appraisal under 8 *Del.C.* § 262 as hereinafter construed. We therefore overrule *Lynch v. Vickers Energy Corp.,* Del. Supr., 429 A.2d 497 (1981) (*Lynch II*) to the extent that it purports to limit a stockholder's monetary relief to a specific damage formula. But to give full effect to section 262 within the framework of the General Corporation Law we adopt a more liberal, less rigid and stylized, approach to the valuation process than has heretofore been permitted by our courts. While the present state of these proceedings does not admit the plaintiff to the appraisal remedy per se, the practical effect of the remedy we do grant him will be co-extensive with the liberalized valuation and appraisal methods we herein approve for cases coming after this decision. Our treatment of these matters has necessarily led us to a reconsideration of the business purpose rule announced in the trilogy of *Singer v. Magnavox Co., supra, Tanzer v. International General Industries, Inc.,* Del.Supr., 379 A.2d 1121 (1977) and *Roland International Corp. v. Najjar,* Del.Supr., 407 A.2d 1032 (1979). For the reasons hereafter set forth we consider that the business purpose requirement of these cases is no longer the law of Delaware. * * *

Signal is a diversified, technically based company operating through various subsidiaries. Its stock is publicly traded on the New York, Philadelphia and Pacific Stock Exchanges. UOP, formerly known as Universal Oil Products Company, was a diversified industrial company engaged in various lines of business, including petroleum and petro-chemical services and related products, construction, fabricated metal products, transportation equipment products, chemicals and plastics, and other products and services including land development, lumber products and waste disposal. Its stock was publicly held and listed on the New York Stock Exchange.

In 1974 Signal sold one of its wholly-owned subsidiaries for $420,000,000 in cash. *See Gimbel v. Signal Companies, Inc.,* While looking to invest this cash surplus, Signal became interested in UOP as a possible acquisition. Friendly negotiations ensued, and Signal proposed to acquire a controlling interest in UOP at a price of $19 per share. UOP's representatives sought $25 per share. In the arm's length bargaining that followed, an understanding was reached whereby Signal agreed to purchase from UOP 1,500,000 shares of UOP's authorized but unissued stock at $21 per share.

This purchase was contingent upon Signal making a successful cash tender offer for 4,300,000 publicly held shares of UOP, also at a price of $21 per share. This combined method of acquisition permitted Signal to acquire 5,800,000 shares of stock, representing 50.5% of UOP's outstanding shares. The UOP board of directors advised the company's shareholders that it had no objection to Signal's tender offer at that price. Immediately before the announcement of the tender offer, UOP's common stock had been trading on the New York Stock Exchange at a fraction under $14 per share.

The negotiations between Signal and UOP occurred during April 1975, and the resulting tender offer was greatly oversubscribed. However, Signal limited its total purchase of the tendered shares so that, when coupled with the stock bought from UOP, it had achieved its goal of becoming a 50.5% shareholder of UOP.

Although UOP's board consisted of thirteen directors, Signal nominated and elected only six. Of these, five were either directors or employees of Signal. The sixth, a partner in the banking firm of Lazard Freres & Co., had been one of Signal's representatives in the negotiations and bargaining with UOP concerning the tender offer and purchase price of the UOP shares.

However, the president and chief executive officer of UOP retired during 1975, and Signal caused him to be replaced by James V. Crawford, a long-time employee and senior executive vice president of one of Signal's wholly-owned subsidiaries. Crawford succeeded his predecessor on UOP's board of directors and also was made a director of Signal.

By the end of 1977 Signal basically was unsuccessful in finding other suitable investment candidates for its excess cash, and by February 1978 considered that it had no other realistic acquisitions available to it on a friendly basis. Once again its attention turned to UOP.

The trial court found that at the instigation of certain Signal management personnel, including William W. Walkup, its board chairman, and Forrest N. Shumway, its president, a feasibility study was made concerning the possible acquisition of the balance of UOP's outstanding shares. This study was performed by two Signal officers, Charles S. Arledge, vice president (director of planning), and Andrew J. Chitiea, senior vice president (chief financial officer). Messrs. Walkup, Shumway, Arledge and Chitiea were all directors of UOP in addition to their membership on the Signal board.

Arledge and Chitiea concluded that it would be a good investment for Signal to acquire the remaining 49.5% of UOP shares at any price up to $24 each. Their report was discussed between Walkup and Shumway who, along with Arledge, Chitiea and Brewster L. Arms, internal counsel for Signal, constituted Signal's senior management. In particular, they talked about the proper price to be paid if the acquisition was pursued, purportedly keeping in mind that as UOP's majority shareholder, Signal owed a fiduciary responsibility to both its own stockholders as well as to UOP's minority. It was ultimately agreed that a meeting of Signal's executive committee would be called to propose that Signal acquire the remaining outstanding stock of UOP through a cash-out merger in the range of $20 to $21 per share.

The executive committee meeting was set for February 28, 1978. As a courtesy, UOP's president, Crawford, was invited to attend, although he was not a member of Signal's executive committee. On his arrival, and prior to the meeting, Crawford was asked to meet privately with Walkup and Shumway. He was then told of Signal's plan to acquire full ownership of UOP and was asked for his reaction to the proposed price range of $20 to $21 per share. Crawford said he thought such a price would be "generous", and that it was certainly one which should be submitted to UOP's minority shareholders for their ultimate consideration. He stated, however, that Signal's 100% ownership could cause internal problems at UOP. He believed that employees would have to be given some assurance of their future place in a fully-owned Signal subsidiary. Otherwise, he feared the departure of essential personnel. Also, many of UOP's key employees had stock option incentive programs which would be wiped out by a merger. Crawford therefore urged that some adjustment would have to be made, such as providing a comparable incentive in Signal's shares, if after the merger he was to maintain his quality of personnel and efficiency at UOP.

Thus, Crawford voiced no objection to the $20 to $21 price range, nor did he suggest that Signal should consider paying more than $21 per share for the minority interests. Later, at the executive committee meeting the same factors were discussed, with Crawford repeating the position he earlier took with Walkup and Shumway. Also considered was the 1975 tender offer and the fact that it had been greatly oversubscribed at $21 per share. For many reasons, Signal's management concluded that the acquisition of UOP's minority shares provided the solution to a number of its business problems.

Thus, it was the consensus that a price of $20 to $21 per share would be fair to both Signal and the minority shareholders of UOP. Signal's executive committee authorized its management "to negotiate" with UOP "for a cash acquisition of the minority ownership in UOP, Inc., with the intention of presenting a proposal to [Signal's] board of directors ... on March 6, 1978". Immediately after this February 28, 1978 meeting, Signal issued a press release stating:

The Signal Companies, Inc. and UOP, Inc. are conducting negotiations for the acquisition for cash by Signal of the 49.5 per cent of UOP which it does not presently own, announced Forrest N. Shumway, president and chief executive officer of Signal, and James V. Crawford, UOP president. Price and other terms of the proposed transaction have not yet been finalized and would be subject to approval of the boards of directors of Signal and UOP, scheduled to meet early next week, the stockholders of UOP and certain federal agencies.

The announcement also referred to the fact that the closing price of UOP's common stock on that day was $14.50 per share.

Two days later, on March 2, 1978, Signal issued a second press release stating that its management would recommend a price in the range of $20 to $21 per share for UOP's 49.5% minority interest. This announcement referred to Signal's earlier statement that "negotiations" were being conducted for the acquisition of the minority shares.

Between Tuesday, February 28, 1978 and Monday, March 6, 1978, a total of four business days, Crawford spoke by telephone with all of UOP's non-Signal, i.e., outside, directors. Also during that period, Crawford retained Lehman Brothers to render a fairness opinion as to the price offered the minority for its stock. He gave two reasons for this choice. First, the time schedule between the announcement and the board meetings was short (by then only three business days) and since Lehman Brothers had been acting as UOP's investment banker for many years, Crawford felt that it would be in the best position to respond on such brief notice. Second, James W. Glanville, a long-time director of UOP and a partner in Lehman Brothers, had acted as a financial advisor to UOP for many years. Crawford believed that Glanville's familiarity with UOP, as a member of its board, would also be of assistance in enabling Lehman Brothers to render a fairness opinion within the existing time constraints.

Crawford telephoned Glanville, who gave his assurance that Lehman Brothers had no conflicts that would prevent it from accepting the task. Glanville's immediate personal reaction was that a price of $20 to $21 would certainly be fair, since it represented almost a 50% premium over UOP's market price. Glanville sought a $250,000 fee for Lehman Brothers' services, but Crawford thought this too much. After further discussions Glanville finally agreed that Lehman Brothers would render its fairness opinion for $150,000.

During this period Crawford also had several telephone contacts with Signal officials. In only one of them, however, was the price of the shares discussed. In a conversation with Walkup, Crawford advised that as a result of his communications with UOP's non-Signal directors, it was his feeling that the price would have to be the top of the proposed range, or $21 per share, if the approval of UOP's outside directors was to be obtained. But again, he did not seek any price higher than $21.

Glanville assembled a three-man Lehman Brothers team to do the work on the fairness opinion. These persons examined relevant documents and information concerning UOP, including its annual reports and its Securities and Exchange Commission filings from 1973 through 1976, as well as its audited financial statements for 1977, its interim reports to shareholders, and its recent and historical market prices and trading volumes. In addition, on Friday, March 3, 1978, two members of the Lehman Brothers team flew to UOP's headquarters in Des Plaines, Illinois, to perform a "due diligence" visit, during the course of which they interviewed Crawford as well as UOP's general counsel, its chief financial officer, and other key executives and personnel.

As a result, the Lehman Brothers team concluded that "the price of either $20 or $21 would be a fair price for the remaining shares of UOP". They telephoned this impression to Glanville, who was spending the weekend in Vermont.

On Monday morning, March 6, 1978, Glanville and the senior member of the Lehman Brothers team flew to Des Plaines to attend the scheduled UOP directors meeting. Glanville looked over the assembled information during the flight. The two had with them the draft of a "fairness opinion letter" in which the price had been left blank. Either during or immediately prior to the directors' meeting, the two-page "fairness opinion letter" was typed in final form and the price of $21 per share was inserted.

On March 6, 1978, both the Signal and UOP boards were convened to consider the proposed merger. Telephone communications were maintained between the two meetings. Walkup, Signal's board chairman, and also a UOP director, attended UOP's meeting with Crawford in order to present Signal's position and answer any questions that UOP's non-Signal directors might have. Arledge and Chitiea, along with Signal's other designees on UOP's board, participated by conference telephone. All of UOP's outside directors attended the meeting either in person or by conference telephone.

First, Signal's board unanimously adopted a resolution authorizing Signal to propose to UOP a cash merger of $21 per share as outlined in a certain merger agreement and other supporting documents. This proposal required that the merger be approved by a majority of UOP's outstanding minority shares voting at the stockholders meeting at which the merger would be considered, and that the minority shares voting in favor of the merger, when coupled with Signal's 50.5% interest would have to comprise at least two-thirds of all UOP shares. Otherwise the proposed merger would be deemed disapproved.

UOP's board then considered the proposal. Copies of the agreement were delivered to the directors in attendance, and other copies had been forwarded earlier to the directors participating by telephone. They also had before them UOP financial data for 1974–1977, UOP's most recent financial statements, market price information, and budget projections for 1978. In addition they had Lehman Brothers' hurriedly prepared fairness opinion letter finding the price of $21 to be fair. Glanville, the Lehman

Brothers partner, and UOP director, commented on the information that had gone into preparation of the letter.

Signal also suggests that the Arledge–Chitiea feasibility study, indicating that a price of up to $24 per share would be a "good investment" for Signal, was discussed at the UOP directors' meeting. The Chancellor made no such finding, and our independent review of the record, detailed *infra*, satisfies us by a preponderance of the evidence that there was no discussion of this document at UOP's board meeting. Furthermore, it is clear beyond peradventure that nothing in that report was ever disclosed to UOP's minority shareholders prior to their approval of the merger.

After consideration of Signal's proposal, Walkup and Crawford left the meeting to permit a free and uninhibited exchange between UOP's non-Signal directors. Upon their return a resolution to accept Signal's offer was then proposed and adopted. While Signal's men on UOP's board participated in various aspects of the meeting, they abstained from voting. However, the minutes show that each of them "if voting would have voted yes".

On March 7, 1978, UOP sent a letter to its shareholders advising them of the action taken by UOP's board with respect to Signal's offer. This document pointed out, among other things, that on February 28, 1978 "both companies had announced negotiations were being conducted".

Despite the swift board action of the two companies, the merger was not submitted to UOP's shareholders until their annual meeting on May 26, 1978. In the notice of that meeting and proxy statement sent to shareholders in May, UOP's management and board urged that the merger be approved. The proxy statement also advised:

> The price was determined after *discussions* between James V. Crawford, a director of Signal and Chief Executive Officer of UOP, and officers of Signal which took place during meetings on February 28, 1978, and in the course of several subsequent telephone conversations. (Emphasis added.)

In the original draft of the proxy statement the word "negotiations" had been used rather than "discussions". However, when the Securities and Exchange Commission sought details of the "negotiations" as part of its review of these materials, the term was deleted and the word "discussions" was substituted. The proxy statement indicated that the vote of UOP's board in approving the merger had been unanimous. It also advised the shareholders that Lehman Brothers had given its opinion that the merger price of $21 per share was fair to UOP's minority. However, it did not disclose the hurried method by which this conclusion was reached.

As of the record date of UOP's annual meeting, there were 11,488,302 shares of UOP common stock outstanding, 5,688,302 of which were owned by the minority. At the meeting only 56%, or 3,208,652, of the minority shares were voted. Of these, 2,953,812, or 51.9% of the total minority, voted for the merger, and 254,840 voted against it. When Signal's stock was added to the minority shares voting in favor, a total of 76.2% of UOP's outstanding shares approved the merger while only 2.2% opposed it.

By its terms the merger became effective on May 26, 1978, and each share of UOP's stock held by the minority was automatically converted into a right to receive $21 cash.

A primary issue mandating reversal is the preparation by two UOP directors, Arledge and Chitiea, of their feasibility study for the exclusive use and benefit of Signal. This document was of obvious significance to both Signal and UOP. Using UOP data, it described the advantages to Signal of ousting the minority at a price range of $21–$24 per share. Mr. Arledge, one of the authors, outlined the benefits to Signal:[6]

Mr. Crawford, UOP's president, could not recall that any documents, other than a draft of the merger agreement, were sent to UOP's directors before the March 6, 1978 UOP meeting. Mr. Chitiea, an author of the report, testified that it was made available to Signal's directors, but to his knowledge it was not circulated to the outside directors of UOP. He specifically testified that he "didn't share" that information with the outside directors of UOP with whom he served.

None of UOP's outside directors who testified stated that they had seen this document. The minutes of the UOP board meeting do not identify the Arledge–Chitiea report as having been delivered to UOP's outside directors. This is particularly significant since the minutes describe in considerable detail the materials that actually were distributed. While these minutes recite Mr. Walkup's presentation of the Signal offer, they do not mention the Arledge–Chitiea report or any disclosure that

---

6. The parentheses indicate certain handwritten comments of Mr. Arledge.

Purpose Of The Merger

 1) Provides an outstanding investment opportunity for Signal—(Better than any recent acquisition we have seen.)

 2) Increases Signal's earnings.

 3) Facilitates the flow of resources between Signal and its subsidiaries—(Big factor—works both ways.)

 4) Provides cost savings potential for Signal and UOP.

 5) Improves the percentage of Signal's 'operating earnings' as opposed to 'holding company earnings'.

 6) Simplifies the understanding of Signal.

 7) Facilitates technological exchange among Signal's subsidiaries.

 8) Eliminates potential conflicts of interest.

 Having written those words, solely for the use of Signal, it is clear from the record that neither Arledge nor Chitiea shared this report with their fellow directors of UOP. We are satisfied that no one else did either. This conduct hardly meets the fiduciary standards applicable to such a transaction. While Mr. Walkup, Signal's chairman of the board and a UOP director, attended the March 6, 1978 UOP board meeting and testified at trial that he had discussed the Arledge–Chitiea report with the UOP directors at this meeting, the record does not support this assertion. Perhaps it is the result of some confusion on Mr. Walkup's part. In any event Mr. Shumway, Signal's president, testified that he made sure the Signal outside directors had this report prior to the March 6, 1978 Signal board meeting, but he did not testify that the Arledge–Chitiea report was also sent to UOP's outside directors.

Signal considered a price of up to $24 to be a good investment. If Mr. Walkup had in fact provided such important information to UOP's outside directors, it is logical to assume that these carefully drafted minutes would disclose it. The post-trial briefs of Signal and UOP contain a thorough description of the documents purportedly available to their boards at the March 6, 1978, meetings. Although the Arledge–Chitiea report is specifically identified as being available to the Signal directors, there is no mention of it being among the documents submitted to the UOP board. Even when queried at a prior oral argument before this Court, counsel for Signal did not claim that the Arledge–Chitiea report had been disclosed to UOP's outside directors. Instead, he chose to belittle its contents. This was the same approach taken before us at the last oral argument.

Actually, it appears that a three-page summary of figures was given to all UOP directors. Its first page is identical to one page of the Arledge–Chitiea report, but this dealt with nothing more than a justification of the $21 price. Significantly, the contents of this three-page summary are what the minutes reflect Mr. Walkup told the UOP board. However, nothing contained in either the minutes or this three-page summary reflects Signal's study regarding the $24 price.

The Arledge–Chitiea report speaks for itself in supporting the Chancellor's finding that a price of up to $24 was a "good investment" for Signal. It shows that a return on the investment at $21 would be 15.7% versus 15.5% at $24 per share. This was a difference of only two-tenths of one percent, while it meant over $17,000,000 to the minority. Under such circumstances, paying UOP's minority shareholders $24 would have had relatively little long-term effect on Signal, and the Chancellor's findings concerning the benefit to Signal, even at a price of $24, were obviously correct.

Certainly, this was a matter of material significance to UOP and its shareholders. Since the study was prepared by two UOP directors, using UOP information for the exclusive benefit of Signal, and nothing whatever was done to disclose it to the outside UOP directors or the minority shareholders, a question of breach of fiduciary duty arises. This problem occurs because there were common Signal–UOP directors participating, at least to some extent, in the UOP board's decision-making processes without full disclosure of the conflicts they faced.[7]

In assessing this situation, the Court of Chancery was required to:

---

7. Although perfection is not possible, or expected, the result here could have been entirely different if UOP had appointed an independent negotiating committee of its outside directors to deal with Signal at arm's length. *See, e.g., Harriman v. E.I. duPont de Nemours & Co.,* 411 F.Supp. 133 (D.Del.1975). Since fairness in this context can be equated to conduct by a theoretical, wholly independent, board of directors acting upon the matter before them, it is unfortunate that this course apparently was neither considered nor pursued. *Johnston v. Greene,* Del.Supr., 121 A.2d 919, 925 (1956). Particularly in a parent-subsidiary context, a showing that the action taken was as though each of the contending parties had in fact exerted its bargaining power against the other at arm's length is strong evidence that the transaction meets the test of fairness. *Getty Oil Co. v. Skelly Oil Co.,* Del.Supr., 267 A.2d 883, 886 (1970); *Puma v. Marriott,* Del.Ch., 283 A.2d 693, 696 (1971).

examine what information defendants had and to measure it against what they gave to the minority stockholders, in a context in which 'complete candor' is required. In other words, the limited function of the Court was to determine whether defendants had disclosed all information in their possession germane to the transaction in issue. And by 'germane' we mean, for present purposes, information such as a reasonable shareholder would consider important in deciding whether to sell or retain stock. * * *

... Completeness, not adequacy, is both the norm and the mandate under present circumstances.

Lynch v. Vickers Energy Corp., Del.Supr., 383 A.2d 278, 281 (1977) (*Lynch I*). This is merely stating in another way the long-existing principle of Delaware law that these Signal designated directors on UOP's board still owed UOP and its shareholders an uncompromising duty of loyalty. The classic language of *Guth v. Loft, Inc.,* Del.Supr., 5 A.2d 503, 510 (1939), requires no embellishment:

> A public policy, existing through the years, and derived from a profound knowledge of human characteristics and motives, has established a rule that demands of a corporate officer or director, peremptorily and inexorably, the most scrupulous observance of his duty, not only affirmatively to protect the interests of the corporation committed to his charge, but also to refrain from doing anything that would work injury to the corporation, or to deprive it of profit or advantage which his skill and ability might properly bring to it, or to enable it to make in the reasonable and lawful exercise of its powers. The rule that requires an undivided and unselfish loyalty to the corporation demands that there shall be no conflict between duty and self-interest.

Given the absence of any attempt to structure this transaction on an arm's length basis, Signal cannot escape the effects of the conflicts it faced, particularly when its designees on UOP's board did not totally abstain from participation in the matter. There is no "safe harbor" for such divided loyalties in Delaware. When directors of a Delaware corporation are on both sides of a transaction, they are required to demonstrate their utmost good faith and the most scrupulous inherent fairness of the bargain. The requirement of fairness is unflinching in its demand that where one stands on both sides of a transaction, he has the burden of establishing its entire fairness, sufficient to pass the test of careful scrutiny by the courts. *Sterling v. Mayflower Hotel Corp.,* Del.Supr., 93 A.2d 107, 110 (1952).

There is no dilution of this obligation where one holds dual or multiple directorships, as in a parent-subsidiary context. *Levien v. Sinclair Oil Corp.,* Del.Ch., 261 A.2d 911, 915 (1969). Thus, individuals who act in a dual capacity as directors of two corporations, one of whom is parent and the other subsidiary, owe the same duty of good management to both corporations, and in the absence of an independent negotiating structure, or the directors' total abstention from any participation in the matter, this duty is to be exercised in light of what is best for both companies. The record demonstrates that Signal has not met this obligation.

The concept of fairness has two basic aspects: fair dealing and fair price. The former embraces questions of when the transaction was timed, how it was initiated, structured, negotiated, disclosed to the directors, and how the approvals of the directors and the stockholders were obtained. The latter aspect of fairness relates to the economic and financial considerations of the proposed merger, including all relevant factors: assets, market value, earnings, future prospects, and any other elements that affect the intrinsic or inherent value of a company's stock. Moore, *The "Interested" Director or Officer Transaction,* 4 Del.J.Corp.L. 674, 676 (1979); Nathan & Shapiro, *Legal Standard of Fairness of Merger Terms Under Delaware Law,* 2 Del.J.Corp.L. 44, 46–47 (1977). *See Tri–Continental Corp. v. Battye,* Del.Supr., 74 A.2d 71, 72 (1950) 8 *Del.C.* § 262(h). However, the test for fairness is not a bifurcated one as between fair dealing and price. All aspects of the issue must be examined as a whole since the question is one of entire fairness. However, in a non-fraudulent transaction we recognize that price may be the preponderant consideration outweighing other features of the merger. Here, we address the two basic aspects of fairness separately because we find reversible error as to both.

Part of fair dealing is the obvious duty of candor required by *Lynch I, supra.* Moreover, one possessing superior knowledge may not mislead any stockholder by use of corporate information to which the latter is not privy. Delaware has long imposed this duty even upon persons who are not corporate officers or directors, but who nonetheless are privy to matters of interest or significance to their company. With the well-established Delaware law on the subject, and the Court of Chancery's findings of fact here, it is inevitable that the obvious conflicts posed by Arledge and Chitiea's preparation of their "feasibility study", derived from UOP information, for the sole use and benefit of Signal, cannot pass muster.

The Arledge–Chitiea report is but one aspect of the element of fair dealing. How did this merger evolve? It is clear that it was entirely initiated by Signal. The serious time constraints under which the principals acted were all set by Signal. It had not found a suitable outlet for its excess cash and considered UOP a desirable investment, particularly since it was now in a position to acquire the whole company for itself. For whatever reasons, and they were only Signal's, the entire transaction was presented to and approved by UOP's board within four business days. Standing alone, this is not necessarily indicative of any lack of fairness by a majority shareholder. It was what occurred, or more properly, what did not occur, during this brief period that makes the time constraints imposed by Signal relevant to the issue of fairness.

The structure of the transaction, again, was Signal's doing. So far as negotiations were concerned, it is clear that they were modest at best. Crawford, Signal's man at UOP, never really talked price with Signal, except to accede to its management's statements on the subject, and to convey to Signal the UOP outside directors' view that as between the $20–$21 range under consideration, it would have to be $21. The latter is not a surprising outcome, but hardly arm's length negotiations. Only the protection of benefits for UOP's key employees and the issue of Lehman Brothers' fee approached any concept of bargaining.

As we have noted, the matter of disclosure to the UOP directors was wholly flawed by the conflicts of interest raised by the Arledge–Chitiea report. All of those conflicts were resolved by Signal in its own favor without divulging any aspect of them to UOP.

This cannot but undermine a conclusion that this merger meets any reasonable test of fairness. The outside UOP directors lacked one material piece of information generated by two of their colleagues, but shared only with Signal. True, the UOP board had the Lehman Brothers' fairness opinion, but that firm has been blamed by the plaintiff for the hurried task it performed, when more properly the responsibility for this lies with Signal. There was no disclosure of the circumstances surrounding the rather cursory preparation of the Lehman Brothers' fairness opinion. Instead, the impression was given UOP's minority that a careful study had been made, when in fact speed was the hallmark, and Mr. Glanville, Lehman's partner in charge of the matter, and also a UOP director, having spent the weekend in Vermont, brought a draft of the "fairness opinion letter" to the UOP directors' meeting on March 6, 1978 with the price left blank. We can only conclude from the record that the rush imposed on Lehman Brothers by Signal's timetable contributed to the difficulties under which this investment banking firm attempted to perform its responsibilities. Yet, none of this was disclosed to UOP's minority.

Finally, the minority stockholders were denied the critical information that Signal considered a price of $24 to be a good investment. Since this would have meant over $17,000,000 more to the minority, we cannot conclude that the shareholder vote was an informed one. Under the circumstances, an approval by a majority of the minority was meaningless. *Lynch I.*

Given these particulars and the Delaware law on the subject, the record does not establish that this transaction satisfies any reasonable concept of fair dealing, and the Chancellor's findings in that regard must be reversed.

Turning to the matter of price, plaintiff also challenges its fairness. His evidence was that on the date the merger was approved the stock was worth at least $26 per share. In support, he offered the testimony of a chartered investment analyst who used two basic approaches to valuation:

a comparative analysis of the premium paid over market in ten other tender offer-merger combinations, and a discounted cash flow analysis.

In this breach of fiduciary duty case, the Chancellor perceived that the approach to valuation was the same as that in an appraisal proceeding. Consistent with precedent, he rejected plaintiff's method of proof and accepted defendants' evidence of value as being in accord with practice under prior case law. This means that the so-called "Delaware block" or weighted average method was employed wherein the elements of value, i.e., assets, market price, earnings, etc., were assigned a particular weight and the resulting amounts added to determine the value per share. This procedure has been in use for decades. However, to the extent it excludes other generally accepted techniques used in the financial community and the courts, it is now clearly outmoded. It is time we recognize this in appraisal and other stock valuation proceedings and bring our law current on the subject.

While the Chancellor rejected plaintiff's discounted cash flow method of valuing UOP's stock, as not corresponding with "either logic or the existing law", it is significant that this was essentially the focus, i.e., earnings potential of UOP, of Messrs. Arledge and Chitiea in their evaluation of the merger. Accordingly, the standard "Delaware block" or weighted average method of valuation, formerly employed in appraisal and other stock valuation cases, shall no longer exclusively control such proceedings. We believe that a more liberal approach must include proof of value by any techniques or methods which are generally considered acceptable in the financial community and otherwise admissible in court, subject only to our interpretation of 8 *Del.C.* § 262(h), *infra*. This will obviate the very structured and mechanistic procedure that has heretofore governed such matters.

Fair price obviously requires consideration of all relevant factors involving the value of a company. This has long been the law of Delaware as stated in *Tri-Continental Corp.,* 74 A.2d at 72:

> The basic concept of value under the appraisal statute is that the stockholder is entitled to be paid for that which has been taken from him, viz., his proportionate interest in a going concern. By value of the stockholder's proportionate interest in the corporate enterprise is meant the true or intrinsic value of his stock which has been taken by the merger. In determining what figure represents this true or intrinsic value, the appraiser and the courts must take into consideration all factors and elements which reasonably might enter into the fixing of value. Thus, market value, asset value, dividends, earning prospects, the nature of the enterprise and any other facts which were known or which could be ascertained as of the date of merger and which throw any light on *future prospects* of the merged corporation are not only pertinent to an inquiry as to the value of the dissenting stockholders' interest, but *must be considered* by the agency fixing the value. (Emphasis added.)

This is not only in accord with the realities of present day affairs, but it is thoroughly consonant with the purpose and intent of our statutory law. Under 8 *Del.C.* § 262(h), the Court of Chancery:

> shall appraise the shares, determining their *fair* value exclusive of any element of value arising from the accomplishment or expectation of the merger, together with a fair rate of interest, if any, to be paid upon the amount determined to be the *fair* value. In determining such *fair* value, the Court shall take into account *all relevant factors* ... (Emphasis added)

See also Bell v. Kirby Lumber Corp., Del.Supr., 413 A.2d 137, 150–51 (1980) (Quillen, J., concurring).

It is significant that section 262 now mandates the determination of "fair" value based upon "all relevant factors". Only the speculative elements of value that may arise from the "accomplishment or expectation" of the merger are excluded. We take this to be a very narrow exception to the appraisal process, designed to eliminate use of *pro forma* data and projections of a speculative variety relating to the completion of a merger. But elements of future value, including the nature of the enterprise, which are known or susceptible of proof as of the date of the merger and not the product of speculation, may be considered. When the trial court deems it appropriate, fair value also includes any damages, resulting from the taking, which the stockholders sustain as a class. If that was not the case, then the obligation to consider "all relevant factors" in the valuation process would be eroded. We are supported in this view not only by *Tri-Continental Corp.,* 74 A.2d at 72, but also by the evolutionary amendments to section 262. * * *

It was not until the 1981 amendment to section 262 that the reference to "fair value" was repeatedly emphasized and the statutory mandate that the Court "take into account all relevant factors" appeared [section 262(h)]. Clearly, there is a legislative intent to fully compensate shareholders for whatever their loss may be, subject only to the narrow limitation that one can not take speculative effects of the merger into account.

Although the Chancellor received the plaintiff's evidence, his opinion indicates that the use of it was precluded because of past Delaware practice. While we do not suggest a monetary result one way or the other, we do think the plaintiff's evidence should be part of the factual mix and weighed as such. Until the $21 price is measured on remand by the valuation standards mandated by Delaware law, there can be no finding at the present stage of these proceedings that the price is fair. Given the lack of any candid disclosure of the material facts surrounding establishment of the $21 price, the majority of the minority vote, approving the merger, is meaningless.

The plaintiff has not sought an appraisal, but rescissory damages of the type contemplated by (*Lynch II*). In view of the approach to valuation that we announce today, we see no basis in our law for *Lynch II*'s exclusive monetary formula for relief. On remand the plaintiff will be permitted to test the fairness of the $21 price by the standards we herein establish, in conformity with the principle applicable to an appraisal—that fair value be determined by taking "into account all relevant factors" [*see* 8 Del.C. § 262(h)*]*. In our view this includes the elements of rescissory damages if the Chancellor considers them susceptible of proof and a remedy appropriate to all the issues of fairness before him. To the extent that *Lynch II*, purports to limit the Chancellor's discretion to a single remedial formula for monetary damages in a cash-out merger, it is overruled.

While a plaintiff's monetary remedy ordinarily should be confined to the more liberalized appraisal proceeding herein established, we do not intend any limitation on the historic powers of the Chancellor to grant such other relief as the facts of a particular case may dictate. The appraisal remedy we approve may not be adequate in certain cases, particularly where fraud, misrepresentation, self-dealing, deliberate waste of corporate assets, or gross and palpable overreaching are involved. Under such circumstances, the Chancellor's powers are complete to fashion any form of equitable and monetary relief as may be appropriate, including rescissory damages. Since it is apparent that this long completed transaction is too involved to undo, and in view of the Chancellor's discretion, the award, if any, should be in the form of monetary damages based upon entire fairness standards, i.e., fair dealing and fair price.

Obviously, there are other litigants, like the plaintiff, who abjured an appraisal and whose rights to challenge the element of fair value must be preserved. Accordingly, the quasi-appraisal remedy we grant the plaintiff here will apply only to: (1) this case; (2) any case now pending on appeal to this Court; (3) any case now pending in the Court of Chancery which has not yet been appealed but which may be eligible for direct appeal to this Court; (4) any case challenging a cash-out merger, the effective date of which is on or before February 1, 1983; and (5) any proposed merger to be presented at a shareholders' meeting, the notification of which is mailed to the stockholders on or before February 23, 1983. Thereafter, the provisions of 8 *Del.C.* § 262, as herein construed, respecting the scope of an appraisal and the means for perfecting the same, shall govern the financial remedy available to minority shareholders in a cash-out merger. Thus, we return to the well established principles of *Stauffer v. Standard Brands, Inc.*, Del.Supr., 187 A.2d 78 (1962) and *David J. Greene & Co. v. Schenley Industries, Inc.*, Del.Ch., 281 A.2d 30 (1971) mandating a stockholder's recourse to the basic remedy of an appraisal.

Finally, we address the matter of business purpose. The defendants contend that the purpose of this merger was not a proper subject of inquiry by the trial court. The plaintiff says that no valid purpose existed—the entire transaction was a mere subterfuge designed to eliminate the minority. The Chancellor ruled otherwise, but in so doing he clearly circumscribed the thrust and effect of *Singer* This has led to the thoroughly sound observation that the business purpose test "may be . . . virtually interpreted out of existence, as it was in *Weinberger*".[9]

The requirement of a business purpose is new to our law of mergers and was a departure from prior case law. *See Stauffer v. Standard Brands, Inc., supra; David J. Greene & Co. v. Schenley Industries, Inc., supra.*

In view of the fairness test which has long been applicable to parent-subsidiary mergers, *Sterling v. Mayflower Hotel Corp.* the expanded appraisal remedy now available to shareholders, and the broad discretion of the Chancellor to fashion such relief as the facts of a given case may dictate, we do not believe that any additional meaningful protection is afforded minority shareholders by the business purpose requirement of the trilogy of *Singer, Tanzer, Najjar,* and their progeny. Accordingly, such requirement shall no longer be of any force or effect.

The judgment of the Court of Chancery, finding both the circumstances of the merger and the price paid the minority shareholders to be fair, is reversed. The matter is remanded for further proceedings consistent herewith. Upon remand the plaintiff's post-trial motion to enlarge the class should be granted.

NOTES

1. *Fairness opinions.* Recall that in its earlier decision in Smith v. Van Gorkom, 488 A.2d 858 (Del.1985), the Delaware Supreme Court pointed to the absence of a fairness opinion as one of the failures of the Trans Union board's evaluation of Pritzker's offer. The Court in *Weinberger*, however, was not terribly impressed with the following fairness opinion that had been supplied by the investment banking firm:

LEHMAN BROTHERS KUHN LOEB
Incorporated
One William Street
New York, N.Y. 10004.
March 6, 1978.

Board of Directors
UOP Inc.
Ten UOP Plaza
Des Plaines, Illinois 60016

Gentlemen :

You have asked for Lehman Brothers Kuhn Loeb Incorporated's opinion as to whether the proposed merger between The Signal Companies, Inc. ("Signal") and UOP Inc. ("UOP") is fair and equitable to the shareholders of UOP other than Signal. Signal currently owns 50.5% of UOP's outstanding shares of common stock. Acording to the offer presented by Signal to the Board of Directors of UOP on March 6, 1978,

---

9. Weiss, *The Law of Take Out Mergers: A Historical Perspective,* 56 N.Y.U.L.Rev. 624, 671, n. 300 (1981).

Signal would offer to purchase for cash the remaining shares of UOP at a price of $21.00 per share.

In forming our opinion of the proposed transaction we did, among other things, the following:

1. Reviewed UOP's Annual Reports and related financial information for each of the four years ended December 31, 1973 through 1976 and its audited financial statements for the year ended December 31, 1988;

2. Reviewed UOP's Form 10–K reports for each of the four years ended December 31, 1973 through 1976 and its form 10–Q reports and Interim Reports to Stockholders for the periods ending March 31, 1977, June 30, 1977, and September 30, 1977;

3. Reviewed other information (unaudited) given to us by management regarding the business of UOP which, among other things, included the Report to the Audit Committee dated February 9, 1978;

4. Visited the principal executive offices of UOP in Des Plaines, Illinois and held meetings and discussions with its management and independent public accountants on March 3, 1978. During the course of these meeting with management we discussed the current business and future prospects of UOP and reviewed its forecasts for the year ending December 31, 1978;

5. Reviewed the historical and recent market prices and trading volumes of UOP common stock;

6. Reviewed the terms of the Offer to Purchase UOP common stock made by Signal in April, 1975; and

7. Reviewed certain other transactions in which companies already owning common shares in other companies sought to acquire the remaining common shares of those companies.

In the process of forming our opinion expressed herein, we did not make or obtain independent reports on or appraisals of any properties or assets of UOP and have relied upon the accuracy (which we have not independently verified) of the audited financial statements and other information furnished to us, or otherwise made available, by UOP.

Mr. James W. Glanville, a managing director of Lehman Brothers Kuhn Loeb Incorporated has been on the Board of Directors of UOP since 1972 and is familiar with the business and future prospects of UOP.

On the basis of the foregoing, our opinion is that the proposed merger is fair and equitable to the stockholders of UOP other than Signal.

> Very truly yours,
>
> LEHMAN BROTHERS KUHN LOEB INCORPORATED
>
> By J.W. GLANVILLE
> Managing Director

Was the court being fair to Lehman Brothers in discounting the value of this opinion? Considerable work had gone into reviewing the financial statements of the company, which under the federal securities laws should constitute full disclosure. Did the court ignore the realities of the business world where time is of the essence in completing business deals ("time is money")? Indeed, perhaps the courts could benefit from such concerns since delay is perhaps the greatest criticism of our justice system.

Fairness opinions continue to raise controversy. The California Public Employee Retirement System ("Calpers"), the largest retirement fund in the United States and a leading advocate of corporate governance reforms, sought the adoption of a requirement that would prohibit investment banking firms from offering opinions on the fairness of mergers and other acquisitions in which the investment banker had an interest. A merger between Proctor & Gamble and Gillette met with opposition from William Galvin, secretary of state for Massachusetts, because he claimed that the fairness opinions of Goldman Sachs and UBS, the investment bankers in the deal, were conflicted. Andrew Ross Sorkin, "You Can Call It a Fairness Opinion, But That Wouldn't Be Fair," New York Times, July 10, 2005, § 3 at 3.

2. *What's fair is fair—or is it?* Lehman Brothers has been involved in other controversial fairness opinions. For example, the firm was reported as providing fairness opinions to both parties to a proposed combination. *See* Andrew Ross Sorkin, Lehman Role Questioned in Deal Talks, N.Y. Times p. c1 col. 6 (June 3, 2005). Can an investment banker properly perform services for both sides in a merger? Consider also the role of Goldman Sachs which advised both the New York Stock Exchange and Archipelago during their merger talks.

Another attack on fairness opinions arose in connection with the merger of Gillette into Proctor & Gamble, which met opposition from William Galvin, Secretary of State for Massachusetts, who claimed that the price for Gillette was inadequate. This was a startling attempt to take over merger negotiations by a state functionary, and Procter & Gamble sued him claiming that such issues were preempted by the federal securities laws. Galvin continued his effort and opened a new front in the prosecutorial war against Wall Street by attacking the fairness opinions of Goldman Sachs and UBS, the investment bankers in the deal. Fairness opinions on the valuation of a company in a merger had long been criticized as saying whatever the party paying for the opinion asked. But see City Partnership Co. v. Lehman Brothers, Inc., 344 F.Supp.2d 1241 (D. Colo. 2004) (dismissing complaint which charged that a fairness opinion submitted with proxy materials had not been properly prepared).

3. As pointed out in Santa Fe Industries, Inc. v. Green, 430 U.S. 462, 479, n. 16, 97 S.Ct. 1292, 51 L.Ed.2d 480 (1977), many states followed the *Singer* approach in holding that appraisal rights are not the exclusive remedy for challenging freeze-out and other corporate mergers. See e.g., Bryan v. Brock & Blevins, Co., Inc., 490 F.2d 563 (5th Cir.), cert. denied, 419 U.S. 844, 95 S.Ct. 77, 42 L.Ed.2d 72 (1974); Gabhart v. Gabhart, 267 Ind. 370, 370 N.E.2d 345 (Sup.1977); People v. Concord Fabrics, Inc., 50 App. Div. 2d 787, 377 N.Y.S.2d 84 (1975); Clark v. Pattern Analysis & Recognition Corp., 87 Misc.2d 385, 384 N.Y.S.2d 660 (Sup.Ct.1976); Schulwolf v. Cerro Corp., 86 Misc.2d 292, 295, 380 N.Y.S.2d 957 (Sup.Ct.1976); Jutkowitz v. Bourns, 118

Cal.App.3d 102, 173 Cal.Rptr. 248 (2d Dist.1981); Berkowitz v. Power Mate Corp., 135 N.J.Super. 36, 342 A.2d 566 (1975). How will those courts respond to the Delaware court's decision in *Weinberger?*

4.   The *Weinberger* court suggested that Signal could have had a much easier time in justifying its action if UOP had appointed a committee of independent directors to conduct the negotiations. Assume that such a committee had been appointed, and that Signal offered $20 instead of $21. What would the committee do? The UOP shares were selling in the $14.50 range, and Signal already had control so there was no basis for claiming a control premium. If the independent committee turns down the offer, then the minority shareholders are stuck, unless Signal ups its offer. But why would Signal increase its offer in an arms-length negotiation? It could simply make a tender offer for $20 or less and probably pick up most of the remaining shares. Of course, there would be a few holdouts, but they could be eliminated through a short form merger, provided the remaining minority held only ten percent or less of the UOP stock.

5.   The court in Coggins v. New England Patriots Football Club, Inc., 397 Mass. 525, 492 N.E.2d 1112 (1986) declined to follow the *Weinberger* approach and continued to determine whether there was a valid business purpose in assessing the fairness of a merger. See also Alpert v. 28 Williams St. Corp., 63 N.Y.2d 557, 483 N.Y.S.2d 667, 473 N.E.2d 19 (1984) (freezeout merger upheld where it was fair on the whole and was justified by an independent business purpose).

RABKIN v. PHILIP A. HUNT CHEMICAL CORP.

498 A.2d 1099 (1985).

These consolidated class actions were filed in the Court of Chancery on behalf of the minority stockholders of Philip A. Hunt Chemical Corporation (Hunt), challenging the merger of Hunt with its majority stockholder, Olin Corporation (Olin). For the first time since our decision in Weinberger v. UOP, Inc., Del.Supr., 457 A.2d 701 (1983) we examine the exclusivity of the appraisal remedy in a cash-out merger where questions of procedural unfairness having a reasonable bearing on substantial issues affecting the price being offered are the essential bases of the suit. The Vice Chancellor ordered these cases dismissed on the ground that absent deception *Weinberger* mandated appraisal as the only remedy available to the minority. The plaintiffs sought and were denied leave to amend their complaints. They appeal these rulings.

In our view, the holding in *Weinberger* is broader than the scope accorded it by the trial court. The plaintiffs have charged, and by their proposed amended complaints contend, that the merger does not meet the entire fairness standard required by *Weinberger*. They aver specific acts of unfair dealing constituting breaches of fiduciary duties which if true may have substantially affected the offering price. These allegations, unrelated to judgmental factors of valuation, should survive a motion to dismiss. Accordingly, the decision of the Court of Chancery is reversed, and the matter is remanded with instructions that the plaintiffs be permitted to amend their complaints.

Taken together, the plaintiffs' complaints challenge the proposed Olin–Hunt merger on the grounds that the price offered was grossly inadequate because Olin unfairly manipulated the timing of the merger to avoid the one year commitment, and that specific language in Olin's Schedule 13D, filed when it purchased the Hunt stock, constituted a price commitment by which Olin failed to abide, contrary to its fiduciary obligations.

The Vice Chancellor granted the defendants' motion to dismiss on the ground that the plaintiffs' complaints failed to state claims upon which relief could be granted. The court's rationale was that absent claims of fraud or deception a minority stockholder's rights in a cash-out merger were limited to an appraisal. The Court of Chancery also denied the plaintiffs leave to amend their complaints because no new legal theories would be alleged, but only more factual detail added to the existing claims which the trial judge already considered insupportable.

The issue we address is whether the trial court erred, as a matter of law, in dismissing these claims on the ground that absent deception the plaintiffs' sole remedy under *Weinberger* is an appraisal. The plaintiffs' position is that in cases of procedural unfairness the standard of entire fairness entitles them to relief that is broader than an appraisal. Indeed, the thrust of plaintiffs' contentions is that they eschew an appraisal, since they consider Olin's manipulative conduct a breach of its fiduciary duty to pay the $25 per share guaranteed by the one year commitment. Furthermore, plaintiffs contend that an appraisal is inadequate here because: (1) the alleged wrongdoers are not parties to an appraisal proceeding, and thus are not personally accountable for their actions; (2) if such misconduct is proven, then the corporation should not have to bear the financial burden which only falls upon it in an appraisal award; and (3) overreaching and unfair dealing are not addressed by an appraisal.

The defendants answer that the plaintiffs' claims were primarily directed to the issue of fair value, and that under *Weinberger,* appraisal is the only available remedy.

In ordering the complaints dismissed the Vice Chancellor reasoned that:

> Where, . . . there are no allegations of non-disclosures or misrepresentations, *Weinberger* mandates that plaintiffs' entire fairness claims be determined in an appraisal proceeding.

We consider that an erroneous interpretation of *Weinberger,* because it fails to take account of the entire context of the holding.

The Court of Chancery seems to have limited its focus to our statement in *Weinberger* that:

[T]he provisions of 8 *Del.C.* § 262 as herein construed, respecting the scope of an appraisal and the means for perfecting the same, shall govern the financial remedy available to minority shareholders in a cash-out merger. Thus, we return to the well established principles of *Stauffer v. Standard Brands, Inc.,* Del.Supr., 187 A.2d 78 (1962) and *David J. Greene & Co. v. Schenley Industries, Inc.,* Del.Ch., 281 A.2d 30 (1971) mandating a stockholder's recourse to the basic remedy of an appraisal.

Weinberger, 457 A.2d at 715

However, *Weinberger* makes clear that appraisal is not necessarily a stockholder's sole remedy. We specifically noted that:

[W]hile a plaintiff's monetary remedy ordinarily should be confined to the more liberalized appraisal proceeding herein established, we do not intend any limitation on the historic powers of the Chancellor to grant such other relief as the facts of a particular case may dictate. The appraisal remedy we approve may not be adequate in certain cases, particularly where fraud, misrepresentation, self-dealing, deliberate waste of corporate assets, or gross and palpable overreaching are involved.

Id. at 714.

Thus, the trial court's narrow interpretation of *Weinberger* would render meaningless our extensive discussion of fair dealing found in that opinion. In *Weinberger* we defined fair dealing as embracing "questions of when the transaction was timed, how it was initiated, structured, negotiated, disclosed to the directors, and how the approvals of the directors and the stockholders were obtained." While this duty of fairness certainly incorporates the principle that a cash-out merger must be free of fraud or misrepresentation, *Weinberger's* mandate of fair dealing does not turn solely on issues of deception. We particularly noted broader concerns respecting the matter of procedural fairness. Thus, while "in a non-fraudulent transaction . . . price *may* be the preponderant consideration," it is not necessarily so.

Although the Vice Chancellor correctly understood *Weinberger* as limiting collateral attacks on cash-out mergers, her analysis narrowed the procedural protections which we still intended *Weinberger* to guarantee. Here, plaintiffs are not arguing questions of valuation which are the traditional subjects of an appraisal. Rather, they seek to enforce a contractual right to receive $25 per share, which they claim was unfairly destroyed by Olin's manipulative conduct.

While a plaintiff's mere allegation of "unfair dealing", without more, cannot survive a motion to dismiss, averments containing "specific acts of fraud, misrepresentation, or other items of misconduct" must be carefully examined in accord with our views expressed both here and in *Weinberger*. See 457 A.2d at 703, 711, 714.

In conclusion we find that the trial court erred in dismissing the plaintiffs' actions for failure to state a claim upon which relief could be granted. As we read the complaints and the proposed amendments, they assert a conscious intent by Olin, as the majority shareholder of Hunt, to deprive the Hunt minority of the same bargain that Olin made with Hunt's former majority shareholder, Turner and Newall. But for Olin's allegedly unfair manipulation, the plaintiffs contend, this bargain also was due them. In short, the defendants are charged with bad faith which goes beyond issues of "mere inadequacy of price." In *Weinberger* we specifically relied upon this aspect of *Cole* in acknowledging the imperfections of an appraisal where circumstances of this sort are present.

Necessarily, this will require the Court of Chancery to closely focus upon *Weinberger's* mandate of entire fairness based on a careful analysis of both the fair price and fair dealing aspects of a transaction. We recognize that this can present certain practical problems, since stockholders may invariably claim that the price being offered is the result of unfair dealings. However, we think that plaintiffs will be tempered in this approach by the prospect that an ultimate judgment in defendants' favor may have cost plaintiffs their unperfected appraisal rights. Moreover, our courts are not without a degree of sophistication in such matters. A balance must be struck between sustaining complaints averring faithless acts, which taken as true would constitute breaches of fiduciary duties that are reasonably related to and have a substantial impact upon the price offered, and properly dismissing those allegations questioning judgmental factors of valuation. Otherwise, we face the anomalous result that stockholders who are eliminated without appraisal rights can bring class actions, while in other cases a squeezed-out minority is limited to an appraisal, provided there was no deception, regardless of the degree of procedural unfairness employed to take their shares. Without that balance, *Weinberger's* concern for entire fairness loses all force.

Accordingly, the decision of the Court of Chancery dismissing these consolidated class actions is reversed.

NOTES

1. In Weinberger v. UOP, Inc., 457 A.2d 701 (Del.1983), the Delaware Supreme Court reversed its earlier position in Singer v. Magnavox Co., 380 A.2d 969 (Del.1977) and held that statutory appraisal rights are exclusive in the absence of fraud or unlawful conduct. This led to the question of what is meant by unlawful conduct. In *Rabkin*, the court found a self-dealing transaction to be unlawful so as to avoid the exclusivity of the appraisal remedy. Is a transaction that is unfair an "unlawful" breach of a fiduciary duty? If so, then the exclusivity rule is of limited if any significance. If not, what is meant by "unlawful"? Shortly after the *Weinberger* decision, the Model Business Corporation Act adopted a fraud or illegality test for exclusivity. Model Bus. Corp. Act § 13.02. Subsequent amendments, however, retained an exception for fraud but opted for a very limited exclusion based on illegality. Model Bus.

Corp. Act § 13.02(d). This change was designed to narrow the applicability of decisions like *Rabkin* or the suggestion that a breach of fiduciary duty is a sufficient basis for avoiding the exclusivity of the appraisal remedy. The former fraud or illegality test remains in force in a number of states. See e.g., Krieger v. Gast, 122 F.Supp.2d 836 (W.D.Mich.2000) (Michigan law).

2. Why did Hunt Chemical demand the one-year equal price provision for the remaining shareholders? Why did this give those shareholders any right to a $25 price even if Olin planned to offer a lower price at the end of the one-year period? What if Olin had waited another six months and offered less?

3. The Delaware court has indicated that the *Rabkin* decision was no fluke. In In re Tri–Star Pictures, Inc., Litigation, 634 A.2d 319, 332–33 (Del.1993), the court stated:

> In Rabkin v. Phillip A. Hunt Chemical Corp., Del.Supr., 498 A.2d 1099, 1104 (1985), we recognized the inadequacy of an appraisal where the alleged wrongdoer (here Coca–Cola) is not a party to the appraisal proceeding and thus, not personally accountable for its actions. That is particularly so in cases of overreaching and unfair dealing which are not addressed by an appraisal. Id. at 1104. The circumstances complained of here are not dissimilar to those in *Rabkin*. Id. at 1103–04. There, we recognized that the timing, structure, negotiation and disclosure of a cash-out merger all had a bearing on procedural fairness. *Id.*at 1104–05. The requirement of fairness is unflinching in its demand that one standing on both sides of a transaction, (as Coca–Cola and the seven Tri–Star directors appear to have done here), has the burden of establishing entire fairness. *Id.* at 1106. Because the controlling stockholder in *Rabkin* had unfairly manipulated the transaction to deprive the minority of what it was equally entitled to, we reversed the dismissal with instructions that the trial court more closely focus on the entire fairness standard. Id. at 1107. Thus, we reaffirmed the fundamental principle that inequitable conduct will not be protected merely because it is legal. Id.; Schnell v. Chris–Craft Industries, Inc., Del.Supr., 285 A.2d 437, 439 (1971).

> The principle of *Rabkin* is directly applicable here. At this stage we must take it as true that Coca–Cola's systematic course of conduct caused plaintiffs injury of the type alleged. A controlling stockholder's unremitting effort to circumvent *Weinberger,* and utilize control to the detriment of the minority, will not pass muster. Where, as here, it is sufficiently alleged that the effect of the controlling stockholder's self-serving manipulation of corporate affairs causes a singular economic injury to minority interests alone, the minority have stated a cause of action for "special injury" to survive a motion to dismiss. *Weinberger,* 457 A.2d at 714. Moreover plaintiffs' averments are sufficient respecting Coca–Cola's knowing participation in a breach of the directors' fiduciary duties to subject it to liability under *Macmillan,* 559 A.2d at 1283, 1284 n. 33; Ivanhoe Partners, Corp., 535 A.2d at 1344, and Penn Mart Realty Co. v. Becker, Del.Ch., 298 A.2d 349, 351 (1972). * * *

The "measure of any recoverable loss by [the minority] under an entire fairness standard of review is not necessarily limited to the difference between the price offered and the 'true' value as determined under appraisal proceedings. . . . '[A]ny form of equitable and monetary relief . . . may be appropriate, including rescissory damages.' " *Cede,* 634 A.2d at 371; *Weinberger,* 457 A.2d at 714. Clearly, the Court of Chancery may incorporate elements of rescissory damages into its determination of fair price if it considers such elements: (1) susceptible to proof; and (2) appropriate under the circumstances.

CHAPTER 19

DEFENSIVE MEASURES AND THE CHANGING ROLE OF THE BOARD

■ ■ ■

SECTION 1. DEFENSIVE MEASURES

CHEFF v. MATHES

199 A.2d 548 (Del.1964).

CAREY, JUSTICE.

This is an appeal from the decision of the Vice–Chancellor in a derivative suit holding certain directors of Holland Furnace Company liable for loss allegedly resulting from improper use of corporate funds to purchase shares of the company. Because a meaningful decision upon review turns upon a complete understanding of the factual background, a somewhat detailed summary of the evidence is required.

Holland Furnace Company, a corporation of the State of Delaware, manufactures warm air furnaces, air conditioning equipment, and other home heating equipment. At the time of the relevant transactions, the board of directors was composed of the seven individual defendants. Mr. Cheff had been Holland's Chief Executive Officer since 1933, received an annual salary of $77,400, and personally owned 6,000 shares of the company. He was also a director. Mrs. Cheff, the wife of Mr. Cheff, was a daughter of the founder of Holland and had served as a director since 1922. She personally owned 5,804 shares of Holland and owned 47.9 percent of Hazelbank United Interest, Inc. Hazelbank is an investment vehicle for Mrs. Cheff and members of the Cheff–Landwehr family group, which owned 164,950 shares of the 883,585 outstanding shares of Holland. As a director, Mrs. Cheff received a compensation of $200.00 for each monthly board meeting, whether or not she attended the meeting.

Prior to the events in question, Holland employed approximately 8500 persons and maintained 400 branch sales offices located in 43 states. The volume of sales had declined from over $41,000,000 in 1948 to less than $32,000,000 in 1956. Defendants contend that the decline in earnings is attributable to the artificial post-war demand generated in the 1946–1948 period. In order to stabilize the condition of the company, the sales department apparently was reorganized and certain unprofitable branch

1095

offices were closed. By 1957 this reorganization had been completed and the management was convinced that the changes were manifesting beneficial results. The practice of the company was to directly employ the retail salesman, and the management considered that practice—unique in the furnace business—to be a vital factor in the company's success.

During the first five months of 1957, the monthly trading volume of Holland's stock on the New York Stock Exchange ranged between 10,300 shares to 24,200 shares. In the last week of June 1957, however, the trading increased to 37,800 shares, with a corresponding increase in the market price. In June of 1957, Mr. Cheff met with Mr. Arnold H. Maremont, who was President of Maremont Automotive Products, Inc. and Chairman of the boards of Motor Products Corporation and Allied Paper Corporation. Mr. Cheff testified, on deposition, that Maremont generally inquired about the feasibility of merger between Motor Products and Holland. Mr. Cheff testified that, in view of the difference in sales practices between the two companies, he informed Mr. Maremont that a merger did not seem feasible. In reply, Mr. Maremont stated that, in the light of Mr. Cheff's decision, he had no further interest in Holland nor did he wish to buy any of the stock of Holland.

None of the members of the board apparently connected the interest of Mr. Maremont with the increased activity of Holland stock. However, Mr. Trenkamp and Mr. Staal, the Treasurer of Holland, unsuccessfully made an informal investigation in order to ascertain the identity of the purchaser or purchasers. The mystery was resolved, however, when Maremont called Ames in July of 1957 to inform the latter that Maremont then owned 55,000 shares of Holland stock. At this juncture, no requests for change in corporate policy were made, and Maremont made no demand to be made a member of the board of Holland.

Ames reported the above information to the board at its July 30, 1957 meeting. Because of the position now occupied by Maremont, the board elected to investigate the financial and business history of Maremont and corporations controlled by him. Apart from the documentary evidence produced by this investigation, which will be considered infra, Staal testified, on deposition, that 'leading bank officials' had indicated that Maremont 'had been a participant, or had attempted to be, in the liquidation of a number of companies.' Staal specifically mentioned only one individual giving such advice, the Vice President of the First National Bank of Chicago. Mr. Cheff testified, at trial, of Maremont's alleged participation in liquidation activities. Mr. Cheff testified that: 'Throughout the whole of the Kalamazoo–Battle Creek area, and Detroit too, where I spent considerable time, he is well known and not highly regarded by any stretch.' This information was communicated to the board.

On August 23, 1957, at the request of Maremont, a meeting was held between Mr. Maremont and Cheff. At this meeting, Cheff was informed that Motor Products then owned approximately 100,000 shares of Holland stock. Maremont then made a demand that he be named to the board of directors, but Cheff refused to consider it. Since considerable controversy has been generated by Maremont's alleged threat to liquidate the company or substantially alter the sales force of Holland, we believe it desirable to set forth the testimony of Cheff on this point: 'Now we have 8500 men, direct employees, so the problem is entirely different. He indicated immediately that he had no interest in that type of distribution, that he didn't think it was modern, that he felt furnaces could be sold as he sold mufflers, through half a dozen salesmen in a wholesale way.'

Testimony was introduced by the defendants tending to show that substantial unrest was present among the employees of Holland as a result of the threat of Maremont to seek control of Holland. Thus, Mr. Cheff testified that the field organization was considering leaving in large numbers because of a fear of the consequences of a Maremont acquisition; he further testified that approximately "25 of our key men" were lost as the result of the unrest engendered by the Maremont proposal. Staal, corroborating Cheff's version, stated that a number of branch managers approached him for reassurances that Maremont was not going to be allowed to successfully gain control. Moreover, at approximately this time, the company was furnished with a Dun and Bradstreet report, which indicated the practice of Maremont to achieve quick profits by sales or liquidations of companies acquired by him. The defendants were also supplied with an income statement of Motor Products, Inc., showing a loss of $336,121.00 for the period in 1957.

On August 30, 1957, the board was informed by Cheff of Maremont's demand to be placed upon the board and of Maremont's belief that the retail sales organization of Holland was obsolete. The board was also informed of the results of the investigation by Cheff and Staal. Predicated upon this information, the board authorized the purchase of company stock on the market with corporate funds, ostensibly for use in a stock option plan.

Subsequent to this meeting, substantial numbers of shares were purchased and, in addition, Mrs. Cheff made alternate personal purchases of Holland stock. As a result of purchases by Maremont, Holland and Mrs. Cheff, the market price rose. On September 13, 1957, Maremont wrote to each of the directors of Holland and requested a broad engineering survey to be made for the benefit of all stockholders. During September, Motor Products released its annual report, which indicated that the investment in Holland was a 'special situation' as opposed to the normal policy of placing the funds of Motor Products into 'an active company'. On September 4th, Maremont proposed to sell his current holdings of Holland to the corporation for $14.00 a share. However, because of delay in responding to this offer, Maremont withdrew the offer. At this time, Mrs. Cheff was obviously quite concerned over the prospect of a Maremont acquisition, and had stated her willingness to expend her personal resources to prevent it.

On September 30, 1957, Motor Products Corporation, by letter to Mrs. Bowles, made a buy-sell offer to Hazelbank. At the Hazelbank meeting of October 3, 1957, Mrs. Bowles presented the letter to the board. The board took no action, but referred the proposal to its finance committee. Although Mrs. Bowles and Mrs. Putnam were opposed to any acquisition of Holland stock by Hazelbank, Mr. Landwehr conceded that a majority of the board were in favor of the purchase. Despite this fact, the finance committee elected to refer the offer to the Holland board on the grounds that it was the primary concern of Holland.

Thereafter, Mr. Trenkamp arranged for a meeting with Maremont, which occurred on October 14–15, 1957, in Chicago. Prior to this meeting, Trenkamp was aware of the intentions of Hazelbank and Mrs. Cheff to purchase all or portions of the stock then owned by Motor Products if Holland did not so act. As a result of the meeting, there was a tentative agreement on the part of Motor Products to sell its 155,000 shares at $14.40 per share. On October 23, 1957, at a special meeting of the Holland board, the purchase was considered. All directors, except Spatta, were present. The dangers allegedly posed by Maremont were again reviewed by the board. Trenkamp and Mrs. Cheff agree that the latter informed the board that either she or Hazelbank would purchase part or all of the block of Holland stock owned by Motor Products if the Holland board did not so act. The board was also informed that in order for the corporation to finance the purchase, substantial sums would have to be borrowed from commercial lending institutions. A resolution authorizing the purchase of 155,000 shares from Motor Products was adopted by the board. The price paid was in excess of the market price prevailing at the time, and the book value of the stock was approximately $20.00 as compared to approximately $14.00 for the net quick asset value. The transaction was subsequently consummated. The stock option plan mentioned in the minutes has never been implemented. In 1959, Holland stock reached a high of $15.25 a share.

On February 6, 1958, plaintiffs, owners of 60 shares of Holland stock, filed a derivative suit in the court below naming all of the individual directors of Holland, Holland itself and Motor Products Corporation as defendants. The complaint alleged that all of the purchases of stock by Holland in 1957 were for the purpose of insuring the perpetuation of control by the incumbent directors.The complaint requested that the transaction between Motor Products and Holland be rescinded and, secondly, that the individual defendants account to Holland for the alleged damages. Since Motor Products was never served with process, the initial remedy became inapplicable. Ames was never served nor did he enter an appearance.

After trial, the Vice Chancellor found the following facts: (a) Holland directly sells to retail consumers by means of numerous branch offices. There were no intermediate dealers. (b) Immediately prior to the complained-of transactions, the sales and earnings of Holland had declined and its marketing practices were under investigation by the Federal Trade

Commission. (c) Mr. Cheff and Trenkamp had received substantial sums as Chief Executive and attorney of the company, respectively. (d) Maremont, on August 23rd, 1957, demanded a place on the board. (e) At the October 14th meeting between Trenkamp, Staal and Maremont, Trenkamp and Staal were authorized to speak for Hazelbank and Mrs. Cheff as well as Holland. Only Mr. Cheff, Mrs. Cheff, Mr. Landwehr, and Mr. Trenkamp clearly understood, prior to the October 23rd meeting, that either Hazelbank or Mrs. Cheff would have utilized their funds to purchase the Holland stock if Holland had not acted. (g) There was no real threat posed by Maremont and no substantial evidence of intention by Maremont to liquidate Holland. (h) Any employee unrest could have been caused by factors other than Maremont's intrusion and 'only one important employee was shown to have left, and his motive for leaving is not clear.' (1) The Court rejected the stock option plan as a meaningful rationale for the purchase from Maremont or the prior open market purchases.

The Court then found that the actual purpose behind the purchase was the desire to perpetuate control, but because of its finding that only the four above-named directors knew of the 'alternative', the remaining directors were exonerated. No appeal was taken by plaintiffs from that decision. * * *

Under the provisions of 8 Del.C. § 160, a corporation is granted statutory power to purchase and sell shares of its own stock. Such a right, as embodied in the statute, has long been recognized in this State. The charge here is not one of violation of statute, but the allegation is that the true motives behind such purchases were improperly centered upon perpetuation of control. In an analogous field, courts have sustained the use of proxy funds to inform stockholders of management's views upon the policy questions inherent in an election to a board of directors, but have not sanctioned the use of corporate funds to advance the selfish desires of directors to perpetuate themselves in office. Similarly, if the actions of the board were motivated by a sincere belief that the buying out of the dissident stockholder was necessary to maintain what the board believed to be proper business practices, the board will not be held liable for such decision, even though hindsight indicates the decision was not the wisest course. On the other hand, if the board has acted solely or primarily because of the desire to perpetuate themselves in office, the use of corporate funds for such purposes is improper.

Our first problem is the allocation of the burden of proof to show the presence or lack of good faith on the part of the board in authorizing the purchase of shares. Initially, the decision of the board of directors in authorizing a purchase was presumed to be in good faith and could be overturned only by a conclusive showing by plaintiffs of fraud or other misconduct. In Kors, cited supra, the court merely indicated that the directors are presumed to act in good faith and the burden of proof to show to the contrary falls upon the plaintiff. However, in Bennett v. Propp, supra, we stated:

'We must bear in mind the inherent danger in the purchase of shares with corporate funds to remove a threat to corporate policy when a threat to control is involved. The directors are of necessity confronted with a conflict of interest, and an objective decision is difficult. * * * Hence, in our opinion, the burden should be on the directors to justify such a purchase as one primarily in the corporate interest.'

To say that the burden of proof is upon the defendants is not to indicate, however, that the directors have the same 'self-dealing interest' as is present, for example, when a director sells property to the corporation. The only clear pecuniary interest shown on the record was held by Mr. Cheff, as an executive of the corporation, and Trenkamp, as its attorney. The mere fact that some of the other directors were substantial shareholders does not create a personal pecuniary interest in the decisions made by the board of directors, since all shareholders would presumably share the benefit flowing to the substantial shareholder. Accordingly, these directors other than Trenkamp and Cheff, while called upon to justify their actions, will not be held to the same standard of proof required of those directors having personal and pecuniary interest in the transaction.

As noted above, the Vice Chancellor found that the stock option plan, mentioned in the minutes as a justification for the purchases, was not a motivating reason for the purchases. This finding we accept, since there is evidence to support it; in fact, Trenkamp admitted that the stock option plan was not the motivating reason. The minutes of October 23, 1957 dealing with the purchase from Maremont do not, in fact, mention the option plan as a reason for the purchase. While the minutes of the October 1, 1957 meeting only indicated the stock option plan as the motivating reason, the defendants are not bound by such statements and may supplement the minutes by oral testimony to show that the motivating reason was genuine fear of an acquisition by Maremont.

Plaintiffs urge that the sale price was unfair in view of the fact that the price was in excess of that prevailing on the open market. However, as conceded by all parties, a substantial block of stock will normally sell at a higher price than that prevailing on the open market, the increment being attributable to a 'control premium'. Plaintiffs argue that it is inappropriate to require the defendant corporation to pay a control premium, since control is meaningless to an acquisition by a corporation of its own shares. However, it is elementary that a holder of a substantial number of shares would expect to receive the control premium as part of his selling price, and if the corporation desired to obtain the stock, it is unreasonable to expect that the corporation could avoid paying what any other purchaser would be required to pay for the stock. In any event, the financial expert produced by defendant at trial indicated that the price paid was fair and there was no rebuttal. Ames, the financial man on the board, was strongly of the opinion that the purchase was a good deal for the corporation. The Vice Chancellor made no finding as to the fairness of the price other than to indicate the obvious fact that the market price was increasing as a result of open market purchases by Maremont, Mrs. Cheff and Holland.

The question then presented is whether or not defendants satisfied the burden of proof of showing reasonable grounds to believe a danger to corporate policy and effectiveness existed by the presence of the Maremont stock ownership. It is important to remember that the directors satisfy their burden by showing good faith and reasonable investigation; the directors will not be penalized for an honest mistake of judgment, if the judgment appeared reasonable at the time the decision was made.

In holding that employee unrest could as well be attributed to a condition of Holland's business affairs as to the possibility of Maremont's intrustion, the Vice Chancellor must have had in mind one or both of two matters: (1) the pending proceedings before the Federal Trade Commission concerning certain sales practices of Holland; (2) the decrease in sales and profits during the preceding several years. Any other possible reason would be pure speculation. In the first place, the adverse decision of the F.T.C. was not announced until *after* the complained-of transaction. Secondly, the evidence clearly shows that the downward trend of sales and profits had reversed itself, presumably because of the reorganization which had then been completed. Thirdly, everyone who testified on the point said that the unrest was due to the possible threat presented by Maremont's purchases of stock. There was, in fact, no *testimony* whatever of any connection between the unrest and either the F.T.C. proceedings or the business picture.

The Vice Chancellor found that there was no substantial evidence of a liquidation posed by Maremont. This holding overlooks an important contention. The fear of the defendants, according to their testimony, was not limited to the possibility of liquidation; it included the alternate possibility of a material change in Holland's sales policies, which the board considered vital to its future success. The *unrebutted* testimony before the court indicated: (1) Maremont had deceived Cheff as to his original intentions, since his open market purchases were contemporaneous with his disclaimer of interest in Holland; (2) Maremont had given Cheff some reason to believe that he intended to eliminate the retail sales force of Holland; (3) Maremont demanded a place on the board; (4) Maremont substantially increased his purchases after having been refused a place on the board; (5) the directors had good reason to believe that unrest among key employees had been engendered by the Maremont threat; (6) the board had received advice from Dun and Bradstreet indicating the past liquidation or quick sale activities of Motor Products; (7) the board had received professional advice from the firm of Merril Lynch, Fenner & Beane, who recommended that the purchase from Motor Products be carried out; (8) the board had received competent advice that the corporation was over-capitalized; (9) Staal and Cheff had made informal personal investigations from contacts in the business and financial community and had reported to the board of the alleged poor reputation of Maremont. The board was within its rights in relying upon that investigation, since 8

Del.C. § 141(f) allows the directors to reasonably rely upon a report provided by corporate officers.

Accordingly, we are of the opinion that the evidence presented in the court below leads inevitably to the conclusion that the board of directors, based upon direct investigation, receipt of professional advice, and personal observations of the contradictory action of Maremont and his explanation of corporate purpose, believed, with justification, that there was a reasonable threat to the continued existence of Holland, or at least existence in its present form, by the plan of Maremont to continue building up his stock holdings. We find no evidence in the record sufficient to justify a contrary conclusion. The opinion of the Vice Chancellor that employee unrest may have been engendered by other factors or that the board had no grounds to suspect Maremont is not supported in any manner by the evidence.

As noted above, the Vice–Chancellor found that the purpose of the acquisition was the improper desire to maintain control, but, at the same time, he exonerated those individual directors whom he believed to be unaware of the possibility of using non-corporate funds to accomplish this purpose. Such a decision is inconsistent with his finding that the motive was improper, within the rule enunciated in Bennett. If the actions were in fact improper because of a desire to maintain control, then the presence or absence of a non-corporate alternative is irrelevant, as corporate funds may not be used to advance an improper purpose even if there is no non-corporate alternative available. Conversely, if the actions were proper because of a decision by the board made in good faith that the corporate interest was served thereby, they are not rendered improper by the fact that some individual directors were willing to advance personal funds if the corporation did not. It is conceivable that the Vice Chancellor considered this feature of the case to be of significance because of his apparent belief that any excess corporate funds should have been used to finance a subsidiary corporation. That action would not have solved the problem of Holland's over-capitalization. In any event, this question was a matter of business judgment, which furnishes no justification for holding the directors personally responsible in this case.

Accordingly, the judgment of the court below is reversed and remanded with instruction to enter judgment for the defendants.

UNOCAL CORP. v. MESA PETROLEUM CO.
493 A.2d 946 (Del.1985)

MOORE, JUSTICE.

We confront an issue of first impression in Delaware—the validity of a corporation's self-tender for its own shares which excludes from participation a stockholder making a hostile tender offer for the company's stock.

The Court of Chancery granted a preliminary injunction to the plaintiffs, Mesa Petroleum Co., Mesa Asset Co., Mesa Partners II, and Mesa Eastern, Inc. (collectively "Mesa")[1], enjoining an exchange offer of the defendant, Unocal Corporation (Unocal) for its own stock. The trial court concluded that a selective exchange offer, excluding Mesa, was legally impermissible. We cannot agree with such a blanket rule. The factual findings of the Vice Chancellor, fully supported by the record, establish that Unocal's board, consisting of a majority of independent directors, acted in good faith, and after reasonable investigation found that Mesa's tender offer was both inadequate and coercive. Under the circumstances the board had both the power and duty to oppose a bid it perceived to be harmful to the corporate enterprise. On this record we are satisfied that the device Unocal adopted is reasonable in relation to the threat posed, and that the board acted in the proper exercise of sound business judgment. We will not substitute our views for those of the board if the latter's decision can be "attributed to any rational business purpose." *Sinclair Oil Corp. v. Levien,* Del.Supr., 280 A.2d 717, 720 (1971). Accordingly, we reverse the decision of the Court of Chancery and order the preliminary injunction vacated.

On April 8, 1985, Mesa, the owner of approximately 13% of Unocal's stock, commenced a two-tier "front loaded" cash tender offer for 64 million shares, or approximately 37%, of Unocal's outstanding stock at a price of $54 per share. The "back-end" was designed to eliminate the remaining publicly held shares by an exchange of securities purportedly worth $54 per share. However, pursuant to an order entered by the United States District Court for the Central District of California on April 26, 1985, Mesa issued a supplemental proxy statement to Unocal's stockholders disclosing that the securities offered in the second-step merger would be highly subordinated, and that Unocal's capitalization would differ significantly from its present structure. Unocal has rather aptly termed such securities "junk bonds".[3]

---

1. T. Boone Pickens, Jr., is President and Chairman of the Board of Mesa Petroleum and President of Mesa Asset and controls the related Mesa entities.

3. Mesa's May 3, 1985 supplement to its proxy statement states:

(i) following the Offer, the Purchasers would seek to effect a merger of Unocal and Mesa Eastern or an affiliate of Mesa Eastern (the "Merger") in which the remaining Shares would be acquired for a combination of subordinated debt securities and preferred stock; (ii) the securities to be received by Unocal shareholders in the Merger would be subordinated to $2,400 million of debt securities of Mesa Eastern, indebtedness incurred to refinance up to $1,000 million of bank debt which was incurred by affiliates of Mesa Partners II to purchase Shares and to pay related interest and expenses and all then-existing debt of Unocal; (iii) the corporation surviving the Merger would be responsible for the payment of all securities of Mesa Eastern (including any such securities issued pursuant to the Merger) and the indebtedness referred to in item (ii) above, and such securities and indebtedness would be repaid out of funds generated by the operations of Unocal; (iv) the indebtedness incurred in the Offer and the Merger would result in Unocal being much more highly leveraged, and the capitalization of the corporation surviving the Merger would differ significantly from that of Unocal at present; and (v) in their analyses of cash flows provided by operations of Unocal which would be available to service and repay securities and other obligations of the corporation surviving the Merger, the Purchasers assumed that the capital expenditures and expenditures for exploration of such corporation would be significantly reduced.

Unocal's board consists of eight independent outside directors and six insiders. It met on April 13, 1985, to consider the Mesa tender offer. Thirteen directors were present, and the meeting lasted nine and one-half hours. The directors were given no agenda or written materials prior to the session. However, detailed presentations were made by legal counsel regarding the board's obligations under both Delaware corporate law and the federal securities laws. The board then received a presentation from Peter Sachs on behalf of Goldman Sachs & Co. (Goldman Sachs) and Dillon, Read & Co. (Dillon Read) discussing the bases for their opinions that the Mesa proposal was wholly inadequate. Mr. Sachs opined that the minimum cash value that could be expected from a sale or orderly liquidation for 100% of Unocal's stock was in excess of $60 per share. In making his presentation, Mr. Sachs showed slides outlining the valuation techniques used by the financial advisors, and others, depicting recent business combinations in the oil and gas industry. The Court of Chancery found that the Sachs presentation was designed to apprise the directors of the scope of the analyses performed rather than the facts and numbers used in reaching the conclusion that Mesa's tender offer price was inadequate.

Mr. Sachs also presented various defensive strategies available to the board if it concluded that Mesa's two-step tender offer was inadequate and should be opposed. One of the devices outlined was a self-tender by Unocal for its own stock with a reasonable price range of $70 to $75 per share. The cost of such a proposal would cause the company to incur $6.1—6.5 billion of additional debt, and a presentation was made informing the board of Unocal's ability to handle it. The directors were told that the primary effect of this obligation would be to reduce exploratory drilling, but that the company would nonetheless remain a viable entity.

The eight outside directors, comprising a clear majority of the thirteen members present, then met separately with Unocal's financial advisors and attorneys. Thereafter, they unanimously agreed to advise the board that it should reject Mesa's tender offer as inadequate, and that Unocal should pursue a self-tender to provide the stockholders with a fairly priced alternative to the Mesa proposal. The board then reconvened and unanimously adopted a resolution rejecting as grossly inadequate Mesa's tender offer. Despite the nine and one-half hour length of the meeting, no formal decision was made on the proposed defensive self-tender.

On April 15, the board met again with four of the directors present by telephone and one member still absent. This session lasted two hours. Unocal's Vice President of Finance and its Assistant General Counsel made a detailed presentation of the proposed terms of the exchange offer. A price range between $70 and $80 per share was considered, and ultimately the directors agreed upon $72. The board was also advised about the debt securities that would be issued, and the necessity of placing restrictive covenants upon certain corporate activities until the obligations were paid. The board's decisions were made in reliance on the advice of its investment bankers, including the terms and conditions upon which the securities were to be issued. Based upon this advice, and the board's own deliberations, the directors unanimously approved the exchange offer. Their resolution provided that if Mesa acquired 64 million shares of Unocal stock through its own offer (the Mesa Purchase Condition), Unocal would buy the remaining 49% outstanding for an exchange of debt securities having an aggregate par value of $72 per share. The board resolution also stated that the offer would be subject to other conditions that had been described to the board at the meeting, or which were deemed necessary by Unocal's officers, including the exclusion of Mesa from the proposal (the Mesa exclusion). Any such conditions were required to be in accordance with the "purport and intent" of the offer.

Unocal's exchange offer was commenced on April 17, 1985, and Mesa promptly challenged it by filing this suit in the Court of Chancery. On April 22, the Unocal board met again and was advised by Goldman Sachs and Dillon Read to waive the Mesa Purchase Condition as to 50 million shares. This recommendation was in response to a perceived concern of the shareholders that, if shares were tendered to Unocal, no shares would be purchased by either offeror. The directors were also advised that they should tender their own Unocal stock into the exchange offer as a mark of their confidence in it.

Another focus of the board was the Mesa exclusion. Legal counsel advised that under Delaware law Mesa could only be excluded for what the directors reasonably believed to be a valid corporate purpose. The directors' discussion centered on the objective of adequately compensating shareholders at the "back-end" of Mesa's proposal, which the latter would finance with "junk bonds". To include Mesa would defeat that goal, because under the proration aspect of the exchange offer (49%) every Mesa share accepted by Unocal would displace one held by another stockholder. Further, if Mesa were permitted to tender to Unocal, the latter would in effect be financing Mesa's own inadequate proposal.

On April 24, 1985 Unocal issued a supplement to the exchange offer describing the partial waiver of the Mesa Purchase Condition. On May 1, 1985, in another supplement, Unocal extended the withdrawal, proration and expiration dates of its exchange offer to May 17, 1985.

Meanwhile, on April 22, 1985, Mesa amended its complaint in this action to challenge the Mesa exclusion. A preliminary injunction hearing was scheduled for May 8, 1985. However, on April 23, 1985, Mesa moved for a temporary restraining order in response to Unocal's announcement that it was partially waiving the Mesa Purchase Condition. After expedited briefing, the Court of Chancery heard Mesa's motion on April 26.

On April 29, 1985, the Vice Chancellor temporarily restrained Unocal from proceeding with the exchange offer unless it included Mesa. * * *

The issues we address involve these fundamental questions: Did the Unocal board have the power and duty to oppose a takeover threat it reasonably perceived to be harmful to the corporate enterprise, and if so, is its action here entitled to the protection of the business judgment rule?

Mesa contends that the discriminatory exchange offer violates the fiduciary duties Unocal owes it. Mesa argues that because of the Mesa exclusion the business judgment rule is inapplicable, because the directors by tendering their own shares will derive a financial benefit that is not available to *all* Unocal stockholders. Thus, it is Mesa's ultimate contention that Unocal cannot establish that the exchange offer is fair to *all* shareholders, and argues that the Court of Chancery was correct in concluding that Unocal was unable to meet this burden.

Unocal answers that it does not owe a duty of "fairness" to Mesa, given the facts here. Specifically, Unocal contends that its board of directors reasonably and in good faith concluded that Mesa's $54 two-tier tender offer was coercive and inadequate, and that Mesa sought selective treatment for itself. Furthermore, Unocal argues that the board's approval of the exchange offer was made in good faith, on an informed basis, and in the exercise of due care. Under these circumstances, Unocal contends that its directors properly employed this device to protect the company and its stockholders from Mesa's harmful tactics.

We begin with the basic issue of the power of a board of directors of a Delaware corporation to adopt a defensive measure of this type. Absent such authority, all other questions are moot. Neither issues of fairness nor business judgment are pertinent without the basic underpinning of a board's legal power to act.

The board has a large reservoir of authority upon which to draw. Its duties and responsibilities proceed from the inherent powers conferred by 8 *Del.C.* § 141(a), respecting management of the corporation's "business and affairs". Additionally, the powers here being exercised derive from 8 *Del.C.* § 160(a), conferring broad authority upon a corporation to deal in its own stock. From this it is now well established that in the acquisition of its shares a Delaware corporation may deal selectively with its stockholders, provided the directors have not acted out of a sole or primary purpose to entrench themselves in office. *Cheff v. Mathes,* Del.Supr., 199 A.2d 548, 554 (1964).

Finally, the board's power to act derives from its fundamental duty and obligation to protect the corporate enterprise, which includes stockholders, from harm reasonably perceived, irrespective of its source. Thus, we are satisfied that in the broad context of corporate governance, including issues of fundamental corporate change, a board of directors is not a passive instrumentality.

Given the foregoing principles, we turn to the standards by which director action is to be measured. In *Pogostin v. Rice,* Del.Supr., 480 A.2d 619 (1984), we held that the business judgment rule, including the standards by which director conduct is judged, is applicable in the context of a takeover. The business judgment rule is a "presumption that in making a business decision the directors of a corporation acted on an informed basis, in good faith and in the honest belief that the action taken was in the best interests of the company." *Aronson v. Lewis,* Del.Supr., 473 A.2d 805, 812 (1984) (citations omitted). A hallmark of the business judgment rule is that a court will not substitute its judgment for that of the board if the latter's decision can be "attributed to any rational business purpose." *Sinclair Oil Corp. v. Levien,* Del.Supr., 280 A.2d 717, 720 (1971).

When a board addresses a pending takeover bid it has an obligation to determine whether the offer is in the best interests of the corporation and its shareholders. In that respect a board's duty is no different from any other responsibility it shoulders, and its decisions should be no less entitled to the respect they otherwise would be accorded in the realm of business judgment.[9] There are, however, certain caveats to a proper exercise of this function. Because of the omnipresent specter that a board may be acting primarily in its own interests, rather than those of the corporation and its shareholders, there is an enhanced duty which calls for judicial examination at the threshold before the protections of the business judgment rule may be conferred.

This Court has long recognized that:

We must bear in mind the inherent danger in the purchase of shares with corporate funds to remove a threat to corporate policy when a threat to control is involved. The directors are of necessity confronted with a conflict of interest, and an objective decision is difficult.

Bennett v. Propp, Del.Supr., 187 A.2d 405, 409 (1962). In the face of this inherent conflict directors must show that they had reasonable grounds for believing that a danger to corporate policy and effectiveness existed because of another person's stock ownership. *Cheff v. Mathes,* 199 A.2d at 554–55. However, they satisfy that burden "by showing good faith and reasonable investigation...." *Id.* at 555. Furthermore, such proof is materially enhanced, as here, by the approval of a board comprised of a majority of outside independent directors who have acted in accordance with the foregoing standards.

In the board's exercise of corporate power to forestall a takeover bid our analysis begins with the basic principle that corporate directors have a fiduciary duty to act in the best interests of the corporation's stockholders. As we have noted, their duty of care extends to protecting the corporation and its owners from perceived harm whether a threat originates from third parties or other shareholders.[10] But such powers are not absolute. A

---

9. This is a subject of intense debate among practicing members of the bar and legal scholars. Excellent examples of these contending views are: Block & Miller, *The Responsibilities and Obligations of Corporate Directors in Takeover Contests,* 11 Sec.Reg. L.J. 44 (1983); Easterbrook & Fischel, *Takeover Bids, Defensive Tactics, and Shareholders' Welfare,* 36 Bus.Law. 1733 (1981); Easterbrook & Fischel, *The Proper Role of a Target's Management In Responding to a Tender Offer,* 94 Harv.L.Rev. 1161 (1981). Herzel, Schmidt & Davis, *Why Corporate Directors Have a Right To Resist Tender Offers,* 3 Corp.L.Rev. 107 (1980); Lipton, *Takeover Bids in the Target's Boardroom,* 35 Bus.Law. 101 (1979).

10. It has been suggested that a board's response to a takeover threat should be a passive one. Easterbrook & Fischel, *supra,* 36 Bus.Law. at 1750. However, that clearly is not the law of

corporation does not have unbridled discretion to defeat any perceived threat by any Draconian means available.

The restriction placed upon a selective stock repurchase is that the directors may not have acted solely or primarily out of a desire to perpetuate themselves in office. *See Cheff v. Mathes,* 199 A.2d at 556. Of course, to this is added the further caveat that inequitable action may not be taken under the guise of law. The standard of proof established in *Cheff v. Mathes* and discussed *supra* at page 16, is designed to ensure that a defensive measure to thwart or impede a takeover is indeed motivated by a good faith concern for the welfare of the corporation and its stockholders, which in all circumstances must be free of any fraud or other misconduct. However, this does not end the inquiry.

A further aspect is the element of balance. If a defensive measure is to come within the ambit of the business judgment rule, it must be reasonable in relation to the threat posed. This entails an analysis by the directors of the nature of the takeover bid and its effect on the corporate enterprise. Examples of such concerns may include: inadequacy of the price offered, nature and timing of the offer, questions of illegality, the impact on "constituencies" other than shareholders (i.e., creditors, customers, employees, and perhaps even the community generally), the risk of nonconsummation, and the quality of securities being offered in the exchange. *See* Lipton and Brownstein, *Takeover Responses and Directors' Responsibilities: An Update,* p. 7, ABA National Institute on the Dynamics of Corporate Control (December 8, 1983). While not a controlling factor, it also seems to us that a board may reasonably consider the basic stockholder interests at stake, including those of short term speculators, whose actions may have fueled the coercive aspect of the offer at the expense of the long term investor.[11] Here, the threat posed was viewed by the Unocal board as a grossly inadequate two-tier coercive tender offer coupled with the threat of greenmail.

Specifically, the Unocal directors had concluded that the value of Unocal was substantially above the $54 per share offered in cash at the front end. Furthermore, they determined that the subordinated securities to be exchanged in Mesa's announced squeeze out of the remaining shareholders in the "back-end" merger were "junk bonds" worth far less

---

Delaware, and as the proponents of this rule of passivity readily concede, it has not been adopted either by courts or state legislatures. Easterbrook & Fischel, *supra,* 94 Harv.L.Rev. at 1194.

11. There has been much debate respecting such stockholder interests. One rather impressive study indicates that the stock of over 50 percent of target companies, who resisted hostile takeovers, later traded at higher market prices than the rejected offer price, or were acquired after the tender offer was defeated by another company at a price higher than the offer price. *See* Lipton, *supra* 35 Bus.Law. at 106–109, 132–133. Moreover, an update by Kidder Peabody & Company of this study, involving the stock prices of target companies that have defeated hostile tender offers during the period from 1973 to 1982 demonstrates that in a majority of cases the target's shareholders benefited from the defeat. The stock of 81% of the targets studied has, since the tender offer, sold at prices higher than the tender offer price. When adjusted for the time value of money, the figure is 64%. *See* Lipton & Brownstein, *supra* ABA Institute at 10. The thesis being that this strongly supports application of the business judgment rule in response to takeover threats. There is, however, a rather vehement contrary view. *See* Easterbrook & Fischel, *supra* 36 Bus.Law. at 1739–1745.

than $54. It is now well recognized that such offers are a classic coercive measure designed to stampede shareholders into tendering at the first tier, even if the price is inadequate, out of fear of what they will receive at the back end of the transaction.[12] Wholly beyond the coercive aspect of an inadequate two-tier tender offer, the threat was posed by a corporate raider with a national reputation as a "greenmailer".[13]

In adopting the selective exchange offer, the board stated that its objective was either to defeat the inadequate Mesa offer or, should the offer still succeed, provide the 49% of its stockholders, who would otherwise be forced to accept "junk bonds", with $72 worth of senior debt. We find that both purposes are valid.

However, such efforts would have been thwarted by Mesa's participation in the exchange offer. First, if Mesa could tender its shares, Unocal would effectively be subsidizing the former's continuing effort to buy Unocal stock at $54 per share. Second, Mesa could not, by definition, fit within the class of shareholders being protected from its own coercive and inadequate tender offer.

Thus, we are satisfied that the selective exchange offer is reasonably related to the threats posed. It is consistent with the principle that "the minority stockholder shall receive the substantial equivalent in value of what he had before." *Sterling v. Mayflower Hotel Corp.*, Del.Supr., 93 A.2d 107, 114 (1952). This concept of fairness, while stated in the merger context, is also relevant in the area of tender offer law. Thus, the board's decision to offer what it determined to be the fair value of the corporation to the 49% of its shareholders, who would otherwise be forced to accept highly subordinated "junk bonds", is reasonable and consistent with the directors' duty to ensure that the minority stockholders receive equal value for their shares.

Mesa contends that it is unlawful, and the trial court agreed, for a corporation to discriminate in this fashion against one shareholder. It argues correctly that no case has ever sanctioned a device that precludes a raider from sharing in a benefit available to all other stockholders. However, as we have noted earlier, the principle of selective stock repurchases by a Delaware corporation is neither unknown nor unauthorized. *Cheff v. Mathes*, 199 A.2d at 554. The only difference is that heretofore the approved transaction was the payment of "greenmail" to a raider or

---

12. For a discussion of the coercive nature of a two-tier tender offer see e.g., Brudney & Chirelstein, *Fair Shares in Corporate Mergers and Takeovers*, 88 Harv.L.Rev. 297, 337 (1974); Finkelstein, *Antitakeover Protection Against Two–Tier and Partial Tender Offers: The Validity of Fair Price, Mandatory Bid, and Flip–Over Provisions Under Delaware Law*, 11 Sec.Reg. L.J. 291, 293 (1984); Lipton, *supra;* 35 Bus.Law at 113–14; Note, *Protecting Shareholders Against Partial and Two–Tiered Takeovers: The Poison Pill Preferred*, 97 Harv.L.Rev. 1964, 1966 (1984).

13. The term "greenmail" refers to the practice of buying out a takeover bidder's stock at a premium that is not available to other shareholders in order to prevent the takeover. The Chancery Court noted that "Mesa has made tremendous profits from its takeover activities although in the past few years it has not been successful in acquiring any of the target companies on an unfriendly basis." Moreover, the trial court specifically found that the actions of the Unocal board were taken in good faith to eliminate both the inadequacies of the tender offer and to forestall the payment of "greenmail".

dissident posing a threat to the corporate enterprise. All other stockholders were denied such favored treatment, and given Mesa's past history of greenmail, its claims here are rather ironic.

However, our corporate law is not static. It must grow and develop in response to, indeed in anticipation of, evolving concepts and needs. Merely because the General Corporation Law is silent as to a specific matter does not mean that it is prohibited. In the days when *Cheff, Bennett, Martin* and *Kors* were decided, the tender offer, while not an unknown device, was virtually unused, and little was known of such methods as two-tier "front-end" loaded offers with their coercive effects. Then, the favored attack of a raider was stock acquisition followed by a proxy contest. Various defensive tactics, which provided no benefit whatever to the raider, evolved. Thus, the use of corporate funds by management to counter a proxy battle was approved. Litigation, supported by corporate funds, aimed at the raider has long been a popular device.

More recently, as the sophistication of both raiders and targets has developed, a host of other defensive measures to counter such ever mounting threats has evolved and received judicial sanction. These include defensive charter amendments and other devices bearing some rather exotic, but apt, names: Crown Jewel, White Knight, Pac Man, and Golden Parachute. Each has highly selective features, the object of which is to deter or defeat the raider.

Thus, while the exchange offer is a form of selective treatment, given the nature of the threat posed here the response is neither unlawful nor unreasonable. If the board of directors is disinterested, has acted in good faith and with due care, its decision in the absence of an abuse of discretion will be upheld as a proper exercise of business judgment.

To this Mesa responds that the board is not disinterested, because the directors are receiving a benefit from the tender of their own shares, which because of the Mesa exclusion, does not devolve upon *all* stockholders equally. However, Mesa concedes that if the exclusion is valid, then the directors and all other stockholders share the same benefit. The answer of course is that the exclusion is valid, and the directors' participation in the exchange offer does not rise to the level of a disqualifying interest. The excellent discussion in *Johnson v. Trueblood,* 629 F.2d at 292–293, of the use of the business judgment rule in takeover contests also seems pertinent here.

Nor does this become an "interested" director transaction merely because certain board members are large stockholders. As this Court has previously noted, that fact alone does not create a disqualifying "personal pecuniary interest" to defeat the operation of the business judgment rule. *Cheff v. Mathes,* 199 A.2d at 554.

Mesa also argues that the exclusion permits the directors to abdicate the fiduciary duties they owe it. However, that is not so. The board continues to owe Mesa the duties of due care and loyalty. But in the face of the destructive threat Mesa's tender offer was perceived to pose, the board had a supervening duty to protect the corporate enterprise, which includes the other shareholders, from threatened harm.

Mesa contends that the basis of this action is punitive, and solely in response to the exercise of its rights of corporate democracy. Nothing precludes Mesa, as a stockholder, from acting in its own self-interest. However, Mesa, while pursuing its own interests, has acted in a manner which a board consisting of a majority of independent directors has reasonably determined to be contrary to the best interests of Unocal and its other shareholders. In this situation, there is no support in Delaware law for the proposition that, when responding to a perceived harm, a corporation must guarantee a benefit to a stockholder who is deliberately provoking the danger being addressed. There is no obligation of self-sacrifice by a corporation and its shareholders in the face of such a challenge.

Here, the Court of Chancery specifically found that the "directors' decision [to oppose the Mesa tender offer] was made in the good faith belief that the Mesa tender offer is inadequate." [W]e are satisfied that Unocal's board has met its burden of proof.

In conclusion, there was directorial power to oppose the Mesa tender offer, and to undertake a selective stock exchange made in good faith and upon a reasonable investigation pursuant to a clear duty to protect the corporate enterprise. Further, the selective stock repurchase plan chosen by Unocal is reasonable in relation to the threat that the board rationally and reasonably believed was posed by Mesa's inadequate and coercive two-tier tender offer. Under those circumstances the board's action is entitled to be measured by the standards of the business judgment rule. Thus, unless it is shown by a preponderance of the evidence that the directors' decisions were primarily based on perpetuating themselves in office, or some other breach of fiduciary duty such as fraud, overreaching, lack of good faith, or being uninformed, a Court will not substitute its judgment for that of the board.

In this case that protection is not lost merely because Unocal's directors have tendered their shares in the exchange offer. Given the validity of the Mesa exclusion, they are receiving a benefit shared generally by all other stockholders except Mesa. In this circumstance the test of *Aronson v. Lewis,* 473 A.2d at 812, is satisfied. If the stockholders are displeased with the action of their elected representatives, the powers of corporate democracy are at their disposal to turn the board out.

With the Court of Chancery's findings that the exchange offer was based on the board's good faith belief that the Mesa offer was inadequate, that the board's action was informed and taken with due care, that Mesa's prior activities justify a reasonable inference that its principle objective was greenmail, and implicitly, that the substance of the offer itself was reasonable and fair to the corporation and its stockholders if Mesa were included, we cannot say that the Unocal directors have acted in such a manner as to have passed an "unintelligent and unadvised judgment".

The decision of the Court of Chancery is therefore reversed, and the preliminary injunction is vacated.

NOTES

1.   Should the courts be in the business of assuring that shareholders receive the most favorable price? Is this not just another business risk that shareholders assume? The next time you ride on an airplane compare your fare with those of your fellow passengers. You will probably find a wide disparity, and you may even be a little upset if your fare was higher than others. Should the courts assure the same price to all passengers? The use of defensive tactics by management to ward off unwanted takeovers may be distinguishable because of the conflicting concerns of corporate management. On the one hand, corporate managers are responsible for the best interests of the corporation and its shareholders. Defensive measures may appropriately be used to assure the best price to shareholders or to preserve the company's long range goals that will, hopefully, provide a greater return to shareholders than an immediate sale. On the other hand, a defensive response to a hostile takeover attempt may be designed to entrench management, thereby preserving their current positions, and compensation from the company. The entrenchment aspect means that there may be a conflict of interest at the point that the incumbents' attempt to perpetuate themselves in office does not coincide with the shareholders' best interests. How are the courts to balance these issues?

2.   Place yourself in the role of a Unocal shareholder. If you tendered to Mesa, you would receive $54 in the front end offer and $54 on the back end in junk bonds that would sell at a discount. Assuming that your tender of shares was prorated between the front end and back end offer, you would still, presumably receive more than the then current market price of the stock. If you did not tender, but if enough of your fellow shareholders (64 million shares) tendered to Mesa, the $72 per share from Unocal would be triggered. This would give you a much larger profit than the Mesa offer. Of course your fellow shareholders would reach the same conclusion. They will be reluctant to tender to Mesa, but if no one tenders, the Unocal offer will not be triggered for anyone else. This variation of the prisoners' dilemma would probably result in no shareholders tendering because no one would want to sacrifice themselves and allow the remaining shareholders to receive the higher $72 Unocal offer. The result: Mesa is blocked, and the shareholders realize little or no benefit from the Mesa offer. Has management served the best interests of shareholders or itself in creating this dilemma?

3.   Following the decision of the court in *Unocal*, a settlement was reached that allowed Mesa to participate in Unocal's self-tender offer. This occurred, however, less than six months after Mesa acquired its shares, requiring the profit to be disgorged under Section 16(b) of the Securities Exchange Act of 1934. Colan v. Mesa Petroleum Co., 951 F.2d 1512 (9th Cir.1991), cert. denied, 504 U.S. 911, 112 S.Ct. 1943, 118 L.Ed.2d 548 (1992). Compare Kern County Land Co. v. Occidental Petroleum Corp., 411 U.S. 582, 93 S.Ct. 1736, 36 L.Ed.2d 503 (1973) (parties negotiated an option to successfully avoid section 16(b) disgorgement).

5. Shortly after the *Unocal* decision, the SEC adopted Rules 13e–4(f), and 14d–10 to prohibit discriminatory tender offers whether by a third party or by an issuer for its own shares. See Polaroid Corp. v. Disney, 862 F.2d 987 (3d Cir.1988) (upholding SEC's authority to promulgate such rules under the Williams Act). This SEC "disclosure" rule has thus effectively preempted the defensive tactic that was employed in *Unocal*.

6. The court in *Unocal* points out some of the nomenclature or argot associated with hostile corporate takeovers, including "greenmail." The following are definitions of some of these terms:

White knight transactions. One of the earliest defensive tactics was for the target to arrange a defensive acquisition with a more compatible corporation. This is referred to as finding a white knight to act as a friendly suitor. See e.g., the defensive merger in Kern County Land Co. v. Occidental Petroleum Corp., 411 U.S. 582, 93 S.Ct. 1736, 36 L.Ed.2d 503 (1973). A variation of this tactic is the gray knight—an unsolicited competing suitor that is viewed more favorably by target management than the initial aggressor.

Break up fees. When a company has found a friendly suitor, frequently the merger agreement will contain break up fees or termination fees that would increase the cost of backing out of the deal for another deal or for any other reason. A related device is a topping fee which imposes a surcharge should the target company decide to go with a better offer.

Lock up arrangements. Target companies sometimes encumber the assets that the suitor is seeking by negotiating a "lock-up" arrangement which is a contract to sell assets or transfer control to a third party. See Revlon v. MacAndrews & Forbes Holdings, Inc., 506 A.2d 173 (Del.1985). One variation of a lock up is a non-termination clause which keeps the merger agreement open, making the target company unavailable to other suitors for a period of time. For disapproval of such a "lock out" clause see First Union Corp. v. SunTrust Banks, Inc., 2001 WL 1885686 (N.C.Bus.Ct.2001).

Sale of crown jewels. A variation of the lock-up is simply to dispose of the sought after assets. Once the target divests itself of its "crown jewels," the acquisition is no longer attractive. Cf. Revlon, Inc. v. MacAndrews & Forbes Holdings, Inc., 506 A.2d 173 (Del.1985) (striking down crown jewel lock up).

Acquisition of assets; scorched earth. A target company may acquire assets that make it a less desirable target. See Panter v. Marshall Field & Co., 646 F.2d 271 (7th Cir.1981), cert. denied 454 U.S. 1092, 102 S.Ct. 658, 70 L.Ed.2d 631 (1981). A variation is for the potential target company to acquire a radio or television station or assets pertaining to another regulated industry that will require regulatory approval of the acquisition. For example, FCC regulatory approval may cause significant delays in any subsequent attempt to take over the target company. An extreme version of making the target a less attractive acquisition candidate involves destroying the company as it previously existed; this is referred to as the "scorched earth" defense.

Diluting Shares. The target can make acquisition more difficult by issuing additional shares. One effect of this is to dilute the aggressor's control resulting from shares already acquired. A variation of this device is to establish an employee stock ownership plan (ESOP) with new shares. This places the newly issued shares in the control of managers of the ESOP who will support incumbent management. See e.g., Danaher Corp. v. Chicago Pneumatic Tool Co., 633 F.Supp. 1066 (S.D.N.Y.1986) (management sustained burden of establishing fairness of ESOP; preliminary injunction denied both under state law and under the Williams Act); Shamrock Holdings, Inc. v. Polaroid Corp., 559 A.2d 257 (Del.Ch.1989) (upholding fairness of defensive ESOP established to defeat takeover attempt). Compare e.g., Frantz Mfg. Co. v. EAC Industries, Inc., 501 A.2d 401 (Del.1985) (funding of ESOP after aggressor acquired could not be supported by the business judgment rule). ESOPs were used to fight takeovers of Polaroid and Macmillan Publishing Co., while the employees of Avis Corp. used their ESOP to fund a buyout of the company. *Jerry W. Markham, A Financial History of the United States, From the Age of Derivatives into the New Millennium (1970–2001)* 117 (2002). The Bank of America, acting as the trustee of an employee profit sharing plan at Carter Hawley Hale, refused to support a tender offer for those shares even though the price being offered was the highest ever for that stock. The chairman of Carter Hawley Hale was on the board of Bank of America. Id. at 118.

Defensive share repurchase programs. An alternative to issuing additional shares is for a target company to repurchase some of its own shares. This was done, for example, in Revlon, Inc. v. MacAndrews & Forbes Holdings, Inc., 506 A.2d 173 (Del.1985) and in the *Unocal* case. Share repurchase programs are designed to drive the target company's stock higher than the aggressor's offer and thus price the aggressor out of the market. See, e.g., Charles Nathan & Marylin Sobel, "Corporate Stock Repurchases in the Context of Unsolicited Takeover Bids," 35 Bus. Law. 1545 (1981). Sometimes, companies engage in a self-tender offer for their own shares. As an alternative, the target may buy up stock in the open market. See e.g., Ivanhoe Partners v. Newmont Mining Corp., 535 A.2d 1334 (Del.1987) (upholding defensive share purchases in open market "street sweep"). Share repurchase programs through a tender offer or otherwise must be carefully planned lest the reduction in shares outstanding make it easier for outsiders to acquire control.

Greenmail. Cheff v. Mathes was a greenmail case. As noted by the court in *Unocal*, management of the target company may pay off the aggressor to walk away and give up the battle. This is usually done through a repurchase of shares from the aggressor at a premium over what was paid. This is known as "greenmail." Several studies concluded that greenmail payments cause a decline in the value of the paying company's stock price, suggesting that the market views such payments as desirable management to remain entrenched to discourage a takeover even on favorable terms. James D. Cox & Thomas Lee Hazen, Corporations § 12.06 (2d ed. 2003). Pennsylvania enacted a statute requiring disgorgement of greenmail profits. See Comment, "Disgorgement of

Greenmail Profits: Examining a New Weapon in State Anti–Takeover Arsenals," 28 Hous. L. Rev. 867 (1991). The Internal Revenue Code was amended to discourage such activities by imposing a fifty percent excise tax on the gain from such payments. IRC § 5881.

Shark repellant and porcupine provisions. There are a variety of restrictive provisions that can be placed into the articles of incorporation that make an unwanted acquisition more difficult. These restrictive provisions have been referred to as "shark repellent" or "porcupine provisions." There are several basic varieties of shark repellent provisions. See Ronald Gilson, "The Case Against Shark Repellant Amendments: Structural Limitations on the Enabling Concept," 34 Stan. L. Rev. 755 (1982). One variety consists of provisions in the articles that impede the transfer of control through the board of directors. An example would be the establishment of a staggered board with a large number of directors so that it takes several years to elect a new majority. A second type of shark repellant is to erect barriers to a second step transaction.

Golden parachutes. Another preventive measure is to establish golden parachute provisions. These provide for extraordinarily high severance payments to target management in the event they are ousted as part of a takeover. Thus, if target management is forced to bail out, it gets big compensation for smooth sailing. See e.g., Campbell v. Potash Corp., 238 F.3d 792 (6th Cir.2001) (upholding golden parachutes). The Internal Revenue Code imposes tax payments on excessive parachute payments. (Internal Revenue Code § 280G) and also limits the deductibility of high parachute payments (Internal Revenue Code § 162(m)).

Litigation. If the situation permits, the target management may institute litigation to delay the proposed acquisition. One way to do this is to challenge the acquisition through an antitrust suit, the federal securities laws or state corporate statutes.

Pac–Man. An innovative takeover response is the "Pac–Man" defense where the target responds by trying to acquire the aggressor. See Martin Marietta Corp. v. Bendix Corp., 549 F.Supp. 623 (D.Md.1982); Deborah A. De Mott, Comment: Pac–Man Tender Offers, 1983 Duke L.J. 116.

Poison Pills. Perhaps the most common anti-takeover device is the adoption of a poison pill that makes the target difficult, if not lethal, to swallow. Such provisions are discussed later in this chapter.

Going to the legislature. Another defensive device is to go to the target company's home state legislature to block an unwanted acquisition. A target incorporated in a state where it does substantial business may be able to convince the legislature that a threatened takeover will pose threats to jobs in the state. For example, in the spring of 2000, Wachovia and First Union were successful in lobbying the North Carolina legislature to repeal a ten percent shareholder's right to mandate a special shareholder meeting. This amendment precluded Sun Trust Banks, the hostile suitor, from presenting its bid directly to the Wachovia shareholders. N.C. Gen Stat. § 55–7–04. See Thomas Lee Hazen, "Silencing the Shareholders' Voice," 80 N.C.L. Rev. 1897 (2002).

7. There has been a great deal of scholarly commentary on the appropriate reaction to defensive tactics in response to takeover attempts See e.g., Frank Easterbrook & Daniel Fischel, The Proper Role of a Target's Management in Responding to a Tender Offer, 94 Harv. L. Rev. 1161 (1981) (arguing in favor of management passivity); Ronald Gilson, "A Structural Approach to Corporations: The Case Against Defensive Tactics in Tender Offers," 33 Stan. L. Rev. 819 (1981). Others have urged broad board authority to block hostile tender offers. See Martin Lipton, "Takeover Bids in the Target's Boardroom," 35 Bus. Law 101 (1979) (arguing the board has the power to engage in defensive tactics).

MORAN v. HOUSEHOLD INTERNATIONAL, INC.

500 A.2d 1346 (Del.1985).

McNEILLY, JUSTICE:

This case presents to this Court for review the most recent defensive mechanism in the arsenal of corporate takeover weaponry—the Preferred Share Purchase Rights Plan ("Rights Plan" or "Plan"). The validity of this mechanism has attracted national attention. *Amici curiae* briefs have been filed in support of appellants by the Security and Exchange Commission ("SEC")[1] and the Investment Company Institute. * * *.

On August 14, 1984, the Board of Directors of Household International, Inc. adopted the Rights Plan by a fourteen to two vote.[2] The intricacies of the Rights Plan are contained in a 48–page document entitled "Rights Agreement". Basically, the Plan provides that Household common stockholders are entitled to the issuance of one Right per common share under certain triggering conditions. There are two triggering events that can activate the Rights. The first is the announcement of a tender offer for 30 percent of Household's shares ("30% trigger") and the second is the acquisition of 20 percent of Household's shares by any single entity or group ("20% trigger").

If an announcement of a tender offer for 30 percent of Household's shares is made, the Rights are issued and are immediately exercisable to purchase 1/100 share of new preferred stock for $100 and are redeemable by the Board for $.50 per Right. If 20 percent of Household's shares are acquired by anyone, the Rights are issued and become non-redeemable and are exercisable to purchase 1/100 of a share of preferred. If a Right is not exercised for preferred, and thereafter, a merger or consolidation occurs, the Rights holder can exercise each Right to purchase $200 of the

---

1. The SEC split 3–2 on whether to intervene in this case. The two dissenting Commissioners have publicly disagreed with the other three as to the merits of the Rights Plan. 17 Securities Regulation & Law Report 400; The Wall Street Journal, March 20, 1985, at 6.

2. Household's Board has ten outside directors and six who are members of management. Messrs. Moran (appellant) and Whitehead voted against the Plan. The record reflects that Whitehead voted against the Plan not on its substance but because he thought it was novel and would bring unwanted publicity to Household.

common stock of the tender offeror for $100. This "flip-over" provision of the Rights Plan is at the heart of this controversy.

Household is a diversified holding company with its principal subsidiaries engaged in financial services, transportation and merchandising. HFC, National Car Rental and Vons Grocery are three of its wholly-owned entities.

Household did not adopt its Rights Plan during a battle with a corporate raider, but as a preventive mechanism to ward off future advances. The Vice-Chancellor found that as early as February 1984, Household's management became concerned about the company's vulnerability as a takeover target and began considering amending its charter to render a takeover more difficult. After considering the matter, Household decided not to pursue a fair price amendment.[3]

In the meantime, appellant Moran, one of Household's own Directors and also Chairman of the Dyson–Kissner–Moran Corporation, ("D–K–M") which is the largest single stockholder of Household, began discussions concerning a possible leveraged buy-out of Household by D–K–M. D–K–M's financial studies showed that Household's stock was significantly undervalued in relation to the company's break-up value. It is uncontradicted that Moran's suggestion of a leveraged buy-out never progressed beyond the discussion stage.

Concerned about Household's vulnerability to a raider in light of the current takeover climate, Household secured the services of Wachtell, Lipton, Rosen and Katz ("Wachtell, Lipton") and Goldman, Sachs & Co. ("Goldman, Sachs") to formulate a takeover policy for recommendation to the Household Board at its August 14 meeting. After a July 31 meeting with a Household Board member and a pre-meeting distribution of material on the potential takeover problem and the proposed Rights Plan, the Board met on August 14, 1984.

Representatives of Wachtell, Lipton and Goldman, Sachs attended the August 14 meeting. The minutes reflect that Mr. Lipton explained to the Board that his recommendation of the Plan was based on his understanding that the Board was concerned about the increasing frequency of "bust-up"[4] takeovers, the increasing takeover activity in the financial service industry, such as Leucadia's attempt to take over Arco, and the possible adverse effect this type of activity could have on employees and others concerned with and vital to the continuing successful operation of Household even in the absence of any actual bust-up takeover attempt. Against this factual background, the Plan was approved.

Thereafter, Moran and the company of which he is Chairman, D–K–M, filed this suit. On the eve of trial, Gretl Golter, the holder of 500 shares of Household, was permitted to intervene as an additional plaintiff. The

---

3. A fair price amendment to a corporate charter generally requires supermajority approval for certain business combinations and sets minimum price criteria for mergers.

4. "Bust-up" takeover generally refers to a situation in which one seeks to finance an acquisition by selling off pieces of the acquired company.

trial was held, and the Court of Chancery ruled in favor of Household. Appellants now appeal from that ruling to this Court.

The primary issue here is the applicability of the business judgment rule as the standard by which the adoption of the Rights Plan should be reviewed. Much of this issue has been decided by our recent decision in *Unocal Corp. v. Mesa Petroleum Co.,* Del.Supr., 493 A.2d 946 (1985). In *Unocal,* we applied the business judgment rule to analyze Unocal's discriminatory self-tender.

Other jurisdictions have also applied the business judgment rule to actions by which target companies have sought to forestall takeover activity they considered undesirable. *See Gearhart Industries, Inc. v. Smith International,* 5th Cir., 741 F.2d 707 (1984) (sale of discounted subordinate debentures containing springing warrants); *Treco, Inc. v. Land of Lincoln Savings and Loan,* 7th Cir., 749 F.2d 374 (1984) (amendment to by-laws); *Panter v. Marshall Field,* 7th Cir., 646 F.2d 271 (1981) (acquisitions to create antitrust problems); *Johnson v. Trueblood,* 3d Cir., 629 F.2d 287 (1980), *cert. denied,* 450 U.S. 999 (1981) (refusal to tender); *Crouse-Hinds Co. v. InterNorth, Inc.,* 2d Cir., 634 F.2d 690 (1980) (sale of stock to favored party); *Treadway v. Cane Corp.,* 2d Cir., 638 F.2d 357 (1980) (sale to White Knight), *Enterra Corp. v. SGS Associates,* E.D.Pa., 600 F.Supp. 678 (1985) (standstill agreement); *Buffalo Forge Co. v. Ogden Corp.,* W.D.N.Y., 555 F.Supp. 892, *aff'd,* (2d Cir.) 717 F.2d 757, *cert. denied,* 464 U.S. 1018 (1983) (sale of treasury shares and grant of stock option to White Knight); *Whittaker Corp. v. Edgar,* N.D.Ill., 535 F.Supp. 933 (1982) (disposal of valuable assets); *Martin Marietta Corp. v. Bendix Corp.,* D.Md., 549 F.Supp. 623 (1982) (Pac–Man defense).

This case is distinguishable from the ones cited, since here we have a defensive mechanism adopted to ward off possible future advances and not a mechanism adopted in reaction to a specific threat. This distinguishing factor does not result in the Directors losing the protection of the business judgment rule. To the contrary, pre-planning for the contingency of a hostile takeover might reduce the risk that, under the pressure of a takeover bid, management will fail to exercise reasonable judgment. Therefore, in reviewing a pre-planned defensive mechanism it seems even more appropriate to apply the business judgment rule.

Of course, the business judgment rule can only sustain corporate decision making or transactions that are within the power or authority of the Board. Therefore, before the business judgment rule can be applied it must be determined whether the Directors were authorized to adopt the Rights Plan.

Appellants vehemently contend that the Board of Directors was unauthorized to adopt the Rights Plan. First, appellants contend that no provision of the Delaware General Corporation Law authorizes the issuance of such Rights. Secondly, appellants, along with the SEC, contend that the Board is unauthorized to usurp stockholders' rights to receive hostile tender offers. Third, appellants and the SEC also contend that the

Board is unauthorized to fundamentally restrict stockholders' rights to conduct a proxy contest. We address each of these contentions in turn.

While appellants contend that no provision of the Delaware General Corporation Law authorizes the Rights Plan, Household contends that the Rights Plan was issued pursuant to 8 *Del.C.* § § 151(g) and 157. It explains that the Rights are authorized by § 157 and the issue of preferred stock underlying the Rights is authorized by § 151. Appellants respond by making several attacks upon the authority to issue the Rights pursuant to § 157.

Appellants begin by contending that § 157 cannot authorize the Rights Plan since § 157 has never served the purpose of authorizing a takeover defense. Appellants contend that § 157 is a corporate financing statute, and that nothing in its legislative history suggests a purpose that has anything to do with corporate control or a takeover defense. Appellants are unable to demonstrate that the legislature, in its adoption of § 157, meant to limit the applicability of § 157 to only the issuance of Rights for the purposes of corporate financing. Without such affirmative evidence, we decline to impose such a limitation upon the section that the legislature has not. * * *

Secondly, appellants contend that § 157 does not authorize the issuance of sham rights such as the Rights Plan. They contend that the Rights were designed never to be exercised, and that the Plan has no economic value. In addition, they contend the preferred stock made subject to the Rights is also illusory, citing *Telvest, Inc. v. Olson,* Del.Ch., C.A. No. 5798, Brown, V.C. (March 8, 1979).

Appellants' sham contention fails in both regards. As to the Rights, they can and will be exercised upon the happening of a triggering mechanism, as we have observed during the current struggle of Sir James Goldsmith to take control of Crown Zellerbach. *See* Wall Street Journal, July 26, 1985, at 3, 12. As to the preferred shares, we agree with the Court of Chancery that they are distinguishable from sham securities invalidated in *Telvest, supra.* The Household preferred, issuable upon the happening of a triggering event, have superior dividend and liquidation rights.

Third, appellants contend that § 157 authorizes the issuance of Rights "entitling holders thereof to purchase from the corporation any shares of *its* capital stock of any class . . ." (emphasis added). Therefore, their contention continues, the plain language of the statute does not authorize Household to issue rights to purchase another's capital stock upon a merger or consolidation.

Household contends, *inter alia,* that the Rights Plan is analogous to "anti-destruction" or "anti-dilution" provisions which are customary features of a wide variety of corporate securities. While appellants seem to concede that "anti-destruction" provisions are valid under Delaware corporate law, they seek to distinguish the Rights Plan as not being incidental, as are most "anti-destruction" provisions, to a corporation's statutory power to finance itself. We find no merit to such a distinction. We have already rejected appellants' similar contention that § 157 could only be used for financing purposes. We also reject that distinction here.

"Anti-destruction" clauses generally ensure holders of certain securities of the protection of their right of conversion in the event of a merger by giving them the right to convert their securities into whatever securities are to replace the stock of their company. The fact that the rights here have as their purpose the prevention of coercive two-tier tender offers does not invalidate them. * * *

Appellants contend that the Board is unauthorized to usurp stockholders' rights to receive tender offers by changing Household's fundamental structure. We conclude that the Rights Plan does not prevent stockholders from receiving tender offers, and that the change of Household's structure was less than that which results from the implementation of other defensive mechanisms upheld by various courts.

Appellants' contention that stockholders will lose their right to receive and accept tender offers seems to be premised upon an understanding of the Rights Plan which is illustrated by the SEC *amicus* brief which states: "The Chancery Court's decision seriously understates the impact of this plan. In fact, as we discuss below, the Rights Plan will deter not only two-tier offers, but virtually all hostile tender offers."

The fallacy of that contention is apparent when we look at the recent takeover of Crown Zellerbach, which has a similar Rights Plan, by Sir James Goldsmith. Wall Street Journal, July 26, 1985, at 3, 12. The evidence at trial also evidenced many methods around the Plan ranging from tendering with a condition that the Board redeem the Rights, tendering with a high minimum condition of shares and Rights, tendering and soliciting consents to remove the Board and redeem the Rights, to acquiring 50% of the shares and causing Household to self-tender for the Rights. One could also form a group of up to 19.9% and solicit proxies for consents to remove the Board and redeem the Rights. These are but a few of the methods by which Household can still be acquired by a hostile tender offer.

In addition, the Rights Plan is not absolute. When the Household Board of Directors is faced with a tender offer and a request to redeem the Rights, they will not be able to arbitrarily reject the offer. They will be held to the same fiduciary standards any other board of directors would be held to in deciding to adopt a defensive mechanism, the same standard as they were held to in originally approving the Rights Plan. *See Unocal,* 493 A.2d at 954–55, 958.

In addition, appellants contend that the deterrence of tender offers will be accomplished by what they label "a fundamental transfer of power from the stockholders to the directors." They contend that this transfer of power, in itself, is unauthorized.

The Rights Plan will result in no more of a structural change than any other defensive mechanism adopted by a board of directors. The

Rights Plan does not destroy the assets of the corporation. The implementation of the Plan neither results in any outflow of money from the corporation nor impairs its financial flexibility. It does not dilute earnings per share and does not have any adverse tax consequences for the corporation or its stockholders. The Plan has not adversely affected the market price of Household's stock.

Comparing the Rights Plan with other defensive mechanisms, it does less harm to the value structure of the corporation than do the other mechanisms. Other mechanisms result in increased debt of the corporation. *See Whittaker Corp. v. Edgar, supra* (sale of "prize asset"), *Cheff v. Mathes, supra,* (paying greenmail to eliminate a threat), *Unocal Corp. v. Mesa Petroleum Co., supra,* (discriminatory self-tender).

There is little change in the governance structure as a result of the adoption of the Rights Plan. The Board does not now have unfettered discretion in refusing to redeem the Rights. The Board has no more discretion in refusing to redeem the Rights than it does in enacting any defensive mechanism. * * *

Having concluded that the adoption of the Rights Plan was within the authority of the Directors, we now look to whether the Directors have met their burden under the business judgment rule.

The business judgment rule is a "presumption that in making a business decision the directors of a corporation acted on an informed basis, in good faith and in the honest belief that the action taken was in the best interests of the company." Notwithstanding, in *Unocal* we held that when the business judgment rule applies to adoption of a defensive mechanism, the initial burden will lie with the directors. The "directors must show that they had reasonable grounds for believing that a danger to corporate policy and effectiveness existed.... [T]hey satisfy that burden 'by showing good faith and reasonable investigation....' " *Unocal,* 493 A.2d at 955 (citing *Cheff v. Mathes,* 199 A.2d at 554–55). In addition, the directors must show that the defensive mechanism was "reasonable in relation to the threat posed." *Unocal,* 493 A.2d at 955. Moreover, that proof is materially enhanced, as we noted in *Unocal,* where, as here, a majority of the board favoring the proposal consisted of outside independent directors who have acted in accordance with the foregoing standards. *Unocal,* 493 A.2d at 955; *Aronson,* 473 A.2d at 815. Then, the burden shifts back to the plaintiffs who have the ultimate burden of persuasion to show a breach of the directors' fiduciary duties. *Unocal,* 493 A.2d at 958.

There are no allegations here of any bad faith on the part of the Directors' action in the adoption of the Rights Plan. There is no allegation that the Directors' action was taken for entrenchment purposes. Household has adequately demonstrated, as explained above, that the adoption of the Rights Plan was in reaction to what it perceived to be the threat in the market place of coercive two-tier tender offers. Appellants do contend, however, that the Board did not exercise informed business judgment in its adoption of the Plan.

Appellants contend that the Household Board was uninformed since they were, *inter alia,* told the Plan would not inhibit a proxy contest, were not told the plan would preclude all hostile acquisitions of Household, and were told that Delaware counsel opined that the plan was within the business judgment of the Board.

As to the first two contentions, as we explained above, the Rights Plan will not have a severe impact upon proxy contests and it will not preclude all hostile acquisitions of Household. Therefore, the Directors were not misinformed or uninformed on these facts.

Appellants contend the Delaware counsel did not express an opinion on the flip-over provision of the Rights, rather only that the Rights would constitute validly issued and outstanding rights to subscribe to the preferred stock of the company.

To determine whether a business judgment reached by a board of directors was an informed one, we determine whether the directors were grossly negligent. *Smith v. Van Gorkom,* Del.Supr., 488 A.2d 858, 873 (1985). Upon a review of this record, we conclude the Directors were not grossly negligent. The information supplied to the Board on August 14 provided the essentials of the Plan. The Directors were given beforehand a notebook which included a three-page summary of the Plan along with articles on the current takeover environment. The extended discussion between the Board and representatives of Wachtell, Lipton and Goldman, Sachs before approval of the Plan reflected a full and candid evaluation of the Plan. Moran's expression of his views at the meeting served to place before the Board a knowledgeable critique of the Plan. The factual happenings here are clearly distinguishable from the actions of the directors of Trans Union Corporation who displayed gross negligence in approving a cash-out merger. *Id.*

In addition, to meet their burden, the Directors must show that the defensive mechanism was "reasonable in relation to the threat posed". The record reflects a concern on the part of the Directors over the increasing frequency in the financial services industry of "boot-strap" and "bust-up" takeovers. The Directors were also concerned that such takeovers may take the form of two-tier offers. In addition, on August 14, the Household Board was aware of Moran's overture on behalf of D–K–M. In sum, the Directors reasonably believed Household was vulnerable to coercive acquisition techniques and adopted a reasonable defensive mechanism to protect itself.

While we conclude for present purposes that the Household Directors are protected by the business judgment rule, that does not end the matter. The ultimate response to an actual takeover bid must be judged by the Directors' actions at that time, and nothing we say here relieves them of their basic fundamental duties to the corporation and its stockholders. Their use of the Plan will be evaluated when and if the issue arises.

AFFIRMED

NOTES

1. The Delaware Supreme Court has since reaffirmed the board of directors' authority to approve a poison pill without seeking shareholder approval:

> The Chancellor concluded that *Moran* and its progeny created a series of precedents that could not be challenged in like litigation, i.e., a shareholder could not seek to invalidate a rights plan adopted on the *Household* pattern. . . .
>
> It is indisputable that *Moran* established a board's authority to adopt a rights plan. As the Chancellor pointed out below, "There is simply no legal requirement that the Hilton shareholder must be a party to the Rights Plan or formally vote to accept the Rights Plan to ensure that the Plan is enforceable." While it is technically correct to argue that *Moran* did not explicitly pass upon the question of whether a rights plan required express consent of all parties affected by it, there is little doubt that *Moran*, *inter alia*, denied objecting shareholders the right to oppose implementation of a rights plan. *Moran* addressed a fundamental question of corporate law in the context of takeovers: whether a board of directors had the power to adopt unilaterally a rights plan the effect of which was to interpose the board between the shareholders and the proponents of a tender offer. The power recognized in *Moran* would have been meaningless if the rights plan required shareholder approval. Indeed it is difficult to harmonize *Moran's* basic holding with a contention that questions a Board's prerogative to unilaterally establish a rights plan.

Account v. Hilton Hotels Corporation, 780 A.2d 245 (Del.2001).

2. The rule of *Moran* and its progeny does not automatically validate all plans that a board may adopt. It simply means that the board has the authority to adopt the plan; the adoption must be consistent with the board's fiduciary obligations.

3. The poison pill is now the most common defensive tact and has spurred many varieties of rights plans. A new variety of poison pill is the so-called chewable pill. This pill is designed to evaporate so that it will not block an offer that is on very favorable terms. The chewable provision can be drafted so that the pill dissolves upon specified conditions existing in an offer. Alternatively, a pill can be made chewable by limiting target management's authority to refuse an offer for the company. Subsequent cases in this chapter consider other forms of poison pills.

SECTION 2. TAKEOVER BATTLES—THE CHANGING ROLE OF THE BOARD

REVLON, INC. v. MacANDREWS & FORBES HOLDINGS, INC.

506 A.2d 173 (Del.1985).

MOORE, JUSTICE:

In this battle for corporate control of Revlon, Inc. (Revlon), the Court of Chancery enjoined certain transactions designed to thwart the efforts of Pantry Pride, Inc. (Pantry Pride) to acquire Revlon. The defendants are Revlon, its board of directors, and Forstmann Little & Co. and the latter's affiliated limited partnership (collectively, Forstmann). The injunction barred consummation of an option granted Forstmann to purchase certain Revlon assets (the lock-up option), a promise by Revlon to deal exclusively with Forstmann in the face of a takeover (the no-shop provision), and the payment of a $25 million cancellation fee to Forstmann if the transaction was aborted. The Court of Chancery found that the Revlon directors had breached their duty of care by entering into the foregoing transactions and effectively ending an active auction for the company. The trial court ruled that such arrangements are not illegal *per se* under Delaware law, but that their use under the circumstances here was impermissible. We agree. Thus, we granted this expedited interlocutory appeal to consider for the first time the validity of such defensive measures in the face of an active bidding contest for corporate control. Additionally, we address for the first time the extent to which a corporation may consider the impact of a takeover threat on constituencies other than shareholders. *See Unocal Corp. v. Mesa Petroleum Co.,* Del.Supr., 493 A.2d 946, 955 (1985).

In our view, lock-ups and related agreements are permitted under Delaware law where their adoption is untainted by director interest or other breaches of fiduciary duty. The actions taken by the Revlon directors, however, did not meet this standard. Moreover, while concern for various corporate constituencies is proper when addressing a takeover threat, that principle is limited by the requirement that there be some rationally related benefit accruing to the stockholders. We find no such benefit here.

Thus, under all the circumstances we must agree with the Court of Chancery that the enjoined Revlon defensive measures were inconsistent with the directors' duties to the stockholders. Accordingly, we affirm.

The somewhat complex maneuvers of the parties necessitate a rather detailed examination of the facts. The prelude to this controversy began in June 1985, when Ronald O. Perelman, chairman of the board and chief executive officer of Pantry Pride, met with his counterpart at Revlon, Michel C. Bergerac, to discuss a friendly acquisition of Revlon by Pantry Pride. Perelman suggested a price in the range of $40–50 per share, but the meeting ended with Bergerac dismissing those figures as considerably below Revlon's intrinsic value. All subsequent Pantry Pride overtures were rebuffed, perhaps in part based on Mr. Bergerac's strong personal antipathy to Mr. Perelman.

Thus, on August 14, Pantry Pride's board authorized Perelman to acquire Revlon, either through negotiation in the $42–$43 per share range, or by making a hostile tender offer at $45. Perelman then met with Bergerac and outlined Pantry Pride's alternate approaches. Bergerac remained adamantly opposed to such schemes and conditioned any further discussions of the matter on Pantry Pride executing a standstill agreement prohibiting it from acquiring Revlon without the latter's prior approval.

On August 19, the Revlon board met specially to consider the impending threat of a hostile bid by Pantry Pride.[3] At the meeting, Lazard Freres, Revlon's investment banker, advised the directors that $45 per share was a grossly inadequate price for the company. Felix Rohatyn and William Loomis of Lazard Freres explained to the board that Pantry Pride's financial strategy for acquiring Revlon would be through "junk bond" financing followed by a break-up of Revlon and the disposition of its assets. With proper timing, according to the experts, such transactions could produce a return to Pantry Pride of $60 to $70 per share, while a sale of the company as a whole would be in the "mid 50" dollar range. Martin Lipton, special counsel for Revlon, recommended two defensive measures: first, that the company repurchase up to 5 million of its nearly 30 million outstanding shares; and second, that it adopt a Note Purchase Rights Plan. Under this plan, each Revlon shareholder would receive as a dividend one Note Purchase Right (the Rights) for each share of common stock, with the Rights entitling the holder to exchange one common share for a $65 principal Revlon note at 12% interest with a one-year maturity. The Rights would become effective whenever anyone acquired beneficial ownership of 20% or more of Revlon's shares, unless the purchaser acquired all the company's stock for cash at $65 or more per share. In addition, the Rights would not be available to the acquiror, and prior to the 20% triggering event the Revlon board could redeem the rights for 10 cents each. Both proposals were unanimously adopted.

Pantry Pride made its first hostile move on August 23 with a cash tender offer for any and all shares of Revlon at $47.50 per common share and $26.67 per preferred share, subject to (1) Pantry Pride's obtaining financing for the purchase, and (2) the Rights being redeemed, rescinded or voided.

---

3. There were 14 directors on the Revlon board. Six of them held senior management positions with the company, and two others held significant blocks of its stock. Four of the remaining six directors were associated at some point with entities that had various business relationships with Revlon. On the basis of this limited record, however, we cannot conclude that this board is entitled to certain presumptions that generally attach to the decisions of a board whose majority consists of truly outside independent directors.

The Revlon board met again on August 26. The directors advised the stockholders to reject the offer. Further defensive measures also were planned. On August 29, Revlon commenced its own offer for up to 10 million shares, exchanging for each share of common stock tendered one Senior Subordinated Note (the Notes) of $47.50 principal at 11.75% interest, due 1995, and one-tenth of a share of $9.00 Cumulative Convertible Exchangeable Preferred Stock valued at $100 per share. Lazard Freres opined that the notes would trade at their face value on a fully distributed basis. Revlon stockholders tendered 87 percent of the outstanding shares (approximately 33 million), and the company accepted the full 10 million shares on a pro rata basis. The new Notes contained covenants which limited Revlon's ability to incur additional debt, sell assets, or pay dividends unless otherwise approved by the "independent" (non-management) members of the board.

At this point, both the Rights and the Note covenants stymied Pantry Pride's attempted takeover. The next move came on September 16, when Pantry Pride announced a new tender offer at $42 per share, conditioned upon receiving at least 90% of the outstanding stock. Pantry Pride also indicated that it would consider buying less than 90%, and at an increased price, if Revlon removed the impeding Rights. While this offer was lower on its face than the earlier $47.50 proposal, Revlon's investment banker, Lazard Freres, described the two bids as essentially equal in view of the completed exchange offer.

The Revlon board held a regularly scheduled meeting on September 24. The directors rejected the latest Pantry Pride offer and authorized management to negotiate with other parties interested in acquiring Revlon. Pantry Pride remained determined in its efforts and continued to make cash bids for the company, offering $50 per share on September 27, and raising its bid to $53 on October 1, and then to $56.25 on October 7.

In the meantime, Revlon's negotiations with Forstmann and the investment group Adler & Shaykin had produced results. The Revlon directors met on October 3 to consider Pantry Pride's $53 bid and to examine possible alternatives to the offer. Both Forstmann and Adler & Shaykin made certain proposals to the board. As a result, the directors unanimously agreed to a leveraged buyout by Forstmann. The terms of this accord were as follows: each stockholder would get $56 cash per share; management would purchase stock in the new company by the exercise of their Revlon "golden parachutes"; Forstmann would assume Revlon's $475 million debt incurred by the issuance of the Notes; and Revlon would redeem the Rights and waive the Notes covenants for Forstmann or in connection with any other offer superior to Forstmann's. The board did not actually remove the covenants at the October 3 meeting, because Forstmann then lacked a firm commitment on its financing, but accepted the Forstmann capital structure, and indicated that the outside directors would waive the covenants in due course. Part of Forstmann's plan was to sell Revlon's Norcliff Thayer and Reheis divisions to American Home Products for $335 million. Before the merger,

Revlon was to sell its cosmetics and fragrance division to Adler & Shaykin for $905 million. These transactions would facilitate the purchase by Forstmann or any other acquiror of Revlon.

When the merger, and thus the waiver of the Notes covenants, was announced, the market value of these securities began to fall. The Notes, which originally traded near par, around 100, dropped to 87.50 by October 8. One director later reported (at the October 12 meeting) a "deluge" of telephone calls from irate noteholders, and on October 10 the Wall Street Journal reported threats of litigation by these creditors.

Pantry Pride countered with a new proposal on October 7, raising its $53 offer to $56.25, subject to nullification of the Rights, a waiver of the Notes covenants, and the election of three Pantry Pride directors to the Revlon board. On October 9, representatives of Pantry Pride, Forstmann and Revlon conferred in an attempt to negotiate the fate of Revlon, but could not reach agreement. At this meeting Pantry Pride announced that it would engage in fractional bidding and top any Forstmann offer by a slightly higher one. It is also significant that Forstmann, to Pantry Pride's exclusion, had been made privy to certain Revlon financial data. Thus, the parties were not negotiating on equal terms.

Again privately armed with Revlon data, Forstmann met on October 11 with Revlon's special counsel and investment banker. On October 12, Forstmann made a new $57.25 per share offer, based on several conditions.[6] The principal demand was a lock-up option to purchase Revlon's Vision Care and National Health Laboratories divisions for $525 million, some $100–$175 million below the value ascribed to them by Lazard Freres, if another acquiror got 40% of Revlon's shares. Revlon also was required to accept a no-shop provision. The Rights and Notes covenants had to be removed as in the October 3 agreement. There would be a $25 million cancellation fee to be placed in escrow, and released to Forstmann if the new agreement terminated or if another acquiror got more than 19.9% of Revlon's stock. Finally, there would be no participation by Revlon management in the merger. In return, Forstmann agreed to support the par value of the Notes, which had faltered in the market, by an exchange of new notes. Forstmann also demanded immediate acceptance of its offer, or it would be withdrawn. The board unanimously approved Forstmann's proposal because: (1) it was for a higher price than the Pantry Pride bid, (2) it protected the noteholders, and (3) Forstmann's financing was firmly in place.[7] The board further agreed to redeem the

---

6. Forstmann's $57.25 offer ostensibly is worth $1 more than Pantry Pride's $56.25 bid. However, the Pantry Pride offer was immediate, while the Forstmann proposal must be discounted for the time value of money because of the delay in approving the merger and consummating the transaction. The exact difference between the two bids was an unsettled point of contention even at oral argument.

7. Actually, at this time about $400 million of Forstmann's funding was still subject to two investment banks using their "best efforts" to organize a syndicate to provide the balance. Pantry Pride's entire financing was not firmly committed at this point either, although Pantry Pride represented in an October 11 letter to Lazard Freres that its investment banker, Drexel Burnham

rights and waive the covenants on the preferred stock in response to any offer above $57 cash per share. The covenants were waived, contingent upon receipt of an investment banking opinion that the Notes would trade near par value once the offer was consummated.

Pantry Pride, which had initially sought injunctive relief from the Rights plan on August 22, filed an amended complaint on October 14 challenging the lock-up, the cancellation fee, and the exercise of the Rights and the Notes covenants. Pantry Pride also sought a temporary restraining order to prevent Revlon from placing any assets in escrow or transferring them to Forstmann. Moreover, on October 22, Pantry Pride again raised its bid, with a cash offer of $58 per share conditioned upon nullification of the Rights, waiver of the covenants, and an injunction of the Forstmann lock-up.

On October 15, the Court of Chancery prohibited the further transfer of assets, and eight days later enjoined the lock-up, no-shop, and cancellation fee provisions of the agreement. The trial court concluded that the Revlon directors had breached their duty of loyalty by making concessions to Forstmann, out of concern for their liability to the noteholders, rather than maximizing the sale price of the company for the stockholders' benefit. *MacAndrews & Forbes Holdings, Inc. v. Revlon, Inc.,* 501 A.2d at 1249–50. * * *

We turn first to Pantry Pride's probability of success on the merits. The ultimate responsibility for managing the business and affairs of a corporation falls on its board of directors. In discharging this function the directors owe fiduciary duties of care and loyalty to the corporation and its shareholders. These principles apply with equal force when a board approves a corporate merger pursuant to 8 *Del. C.* § 251(b) *Smith v. Van Gorkom,* Del.Supr., 488 A.2d 858, 873 (1985); and of course they are the bedrock of our law regarding corporate takeover issues.While the business judgment rule may be applicable to the actions of corporate directors responding to takeover threats, the principles upon which it is founded— care, loyalty and independence—must first be satisfied.

If the business judgment rule applies, there is a "presumption that in making a business decision the directors of a corporation acted on an informed basis, in good faith and in the honest belief that the action taken was in the best interests of the company." *Aronson v. Lewis,* 473 A.2d at 812. However, when a board implements anti-takeover measures there arises "the omnipresent specter that a board may be acting primarily in its own interests, rather than those of the corporation and its shareholders ..." *Unocal Corp. v. Mesa Petroleum Co.,* 493 A.2d at 954. This potential for conflict places upon the directors the burden of proving that they had reasonable grounds for believing there was a danger to corporate policy and effectiveness, a burden satisfied by a showing of good faith and reasonable investigation. In addition, the directors must analyze the

---

Lambert, was highly confident of its ability to raise the balance of $350 million. Drexel Burnham had a firm commitment for this sum by October 18.

nature of the takeover and its effect on the corporation in order to ensure balance—that the responsive action taken is reasonable in relation to the threat posed. *Id.*

The first relevant defensive measure adopted by the Revlon board was the Rights Plan, which would be considered a "poison pill" in the current language of corporate takeovers—a plan by which shareholders receive the right to be bought out by the corporation at a substantial premium on the occurrence of a stated triggering event. [T]he board clearly had the power to adopt the measure. Thus, the focus becomes one of reasonableness and purpose.

The Revlon board approved the Rights Plan in the face of an impending hostile takeover bid by Pantry Pride at $45 per share, a price which Revlon reasonably concluded was grossly inadequate. Lazard Freres had so advised the directors, and had also informed them that Pantry Pride was a small, highly leveraged company bent on a "bust-up" takeover by using "junk bond" financing to buy Revlon cheaply, sell the acquired assets to pay the debts incurred, and retain the profit for itself. In adopting the Plan, the board protected the shareholders from a hostile takeover at a price below the company's intrinsic value, while retaining sufficient flexibility to address any proposal deemed to be in the stockholders' best interests.

To that extent the board acted in good faith and upon reasonable investigation. Under the circumstances it cannot be said that the Rights Plan as employed was unreasonable, considering the threat posed. Indeed, the Plan was a factor in causing Pantry Pride to raise its bids from a low of $42 to an eventual high of $58. At the time of its adoption the Rights Plan afforded a measure of protection consistent with the directors' fiduciary duty in facing a takeover threat perceived as detrimental to corporate interests. *Unocal*, 493 A.2d at 954–55. Far from being a "show-stopper," as the plaintiffs had contended in *Moran*, the measure spurred the bidding to new heights, a proper result of its implementation.

Although we consider adoption of the Plan to have been valid under the circumstances, its continued usefulness was rendered moot by the directors' actions on October 3 and October 12. At the October 3 meeting the board redeemed the Rights conditioned upon consummation of a merger with Forstmann, but further acknowledged that they would also be redeemed to facilitate any more favorable offer. On October 12, the board unanimously passed a resolution redeeming the Rights in connection with any cash proposal of $57.25 or more per share. Because all the pertinent offers eventually equalled or surpassed that amount, the Rights clearly were no longer any impediment in the contest for Revlon. This mooted any question of their propriety under *Moran* or *Unocal*.

The second defensive measure adopted by Revlon to thwart a Pantry Pride takeover was the company's own exchange offer for 10 million of its shares. The directors' general broad powers to manage the business and affairs of the corporation are augmented by the specific authority conferred under 8 *Del.C.* § 160(a) permitting the company to deal in its own stock. However, when exercising that power in an effort to forestall a hostile takeover, the board's actions are strictly held to the fiduciary standards outlined in *Unocal*. These standards require the directors to determine the best interests of the corporation and its stockholders, and impose an enhanced duty to abjure any action that is motivated by considerations other than a good faith concern for such interests.

The Revlon directors concluded that Pantry Pride's $47.50 offer was grossly inadequate. In that regard the board acted in good faith, and on an informed basis, with reasonable grounds to believe that there existed a harmful threat to the corporate enterprise. The adoption of a defensive measure, reasonable in relation to the threat posed, was proper and fully accorded with the powers, duties, and responsibilities conferred upon directors under our law.

However, when Pantry Pride increased its offer to $50 per share, and then to $53, it became apparent to all that the break-up of the company was inevitable. The Revlon board's authorization permitting management to negotiate a merger or buyout with a third party was a recognition that the company was for sale. The duty of the board had thus changed from the preservation of Revlon as a corporate entity to the maximization of the company's value at a sale for the stockholders' benefit. This significantly altered the board's responsibilities under the *Unocal* standards. It no longer faced threats to corporate policy and effectiveness, or to the stockholders' interests, from a grossly inadequate bid. The whole question of defensive measures became moot. The directors' role changed from defenders of the corporate bastion to auctioneers charged with getting the best price for the stockholders at a sale of the company.

This brings us to the lock-up with Forstmann and its emphasis on shoring up the sagging market value of the Notes in the face of threatened litigation by their holders. Such a focus was inconsistent with the changed concept of the directors' responsibilities at this stage of the developments. The impending waiver of the Notes covenants had caused the value of the Notes to fall, and the board was aware of the noteholders' ire as well as their subsequent threats of suit. The directors thus made support of the Notes an integral part of the company's dealings with Forstmann, even though their primary responsibility at this stage was to the equity owners.

The original threat posed by Pantry Pride—the break-up of the company—had become a reality which even the directors embraced. Selective dealing to fend off a hostile but determined bidder was no longer a proper objective. Instead, obtaining the highest price for the benefit of the stockholders should have been the central theme guiding director action. Thus, the Revlon board could not make the requisite showing of good faith by preferring the noteholders and ignoring its duty of loyalty to the shareholders. The rights of the former already were fixed by contract. The noteholders required no further protection, and when the Revlon board entered into an auction-ending lock-up agreement with Forstmann on the basis of impermissible considerations at the expense of the shareholders, the directors breached their primary duty of loyalty.

The Revlon board argued that it acted in good faith in protecting the noteholders because *Unocal* permits consideration of other corporate constituencies. Although such considerations may be permissible, there are fundamental limitations upon that prerogative. A board may have regard for various constituencies in discharging its responsibilities, provided there are rationally related benefits accruing to the stockholders. *Unocal,* 493 A.2d at 955. However, such concern for non-stockholder interests is inappropriate when an auction among active bidders is in progress, and the object no longer is to protect or maintain the corporate enterprise but to sell it to the highest bidder.

Revlon also contended that by *Gilbert v. El Paso Co.,* Del. Ch., 490 A.2d 1050, 1054–55 (1984), it had contractual and good faith obligations to consider the noteholders. However, any such duties are limited to the principle that one may not interfere with contractual relationships by improper actions. Here, the rights of the noteholders were fixed by agreement, and there is nothing of substance to suggest that any of those terms were violated. The Notes covenants specifically contemplated a waiver to permit sale of the company at a fair price. The Notes were accepted by the holders on that basis, including the risk of an adverse market effect stemming from a waiver. Thus, nothing remained for Revlon to legitimately protect, and no rationally related benefit thereby accrued to the stockholders. Under such circumstances we must conclude that the merger agreement with Forstmann was unreasonable in relation to the threat posed.

A lock-up is not *per se* illegal under Delaware law. Its use has been approved in an earlier case. Such options can entice other bidders to enter a contest for control of the corporation, creating an auction for the company and maximizing shareholder profit. Current economic conditions in the takeover market are such that a "white knight" like Forstmann might only enter the bidding for the target company if it receives some form of compensation to cover the risks and costs involved. Note, *Corporations-Mergers—"Lock-up" Enjoined Under Section 14(e) of Securities Exchange Act—Mobil Corp. v. Marathon Oil Co., 669 F.2d 366 (6th Cir.1981),* 12 Seton Hall L.Rev. 881, 892 (1982). However, while those lock-ups which draw bidders into the battle benefit shareholders, similar measures which end an active auction and foreclose further bidding operate to the shareholders' detriment. Note, *Lock-up Options: Toward a State Law Standard,* 96 Harv. L. Rev. 1068, 1081 (1983).

Recently, the United States Court of Appeals for the Second Circuit invalidated a lock-up on fiduciary duty grounds similar to those here. *Hanson Trust PLC, et al. v. ML SCM Acquisition Inc., et al.,* 781 F.2d 264 (2d Cir.1986). Citing *Thompson v. Enstar Corp., supra,* with approval, the court stated:

In this regard, we are especially mindful that some lock-up options may be beneficial to the shareholders, such as those that induce a bidder to compete for control of a corporation, while others may be harmful, such as those that effectively preclude bidders from competing with the optionee bidder.

In *Hanson Trust,* the bidder, Hanson, sought control of SCM by a hostile cash tender offer. SCM management joined with Merrill Lynch to propose a leveraged buy-out of the company at a higher price, and Hanson in turn increased its offer. Then, despite very little improvement in its subsequent bid, the management group sought a lock-up option to purchase SCM's two main assets at a substantial discount. The SCM directors granted the lock-up without adequate information as to the size of the discount or the effect the transaction would have on the company. Their action effectively ended a competitive bidding situation. The Hanson Court invalidated the lock-up because the directors failed to fully inform themselves about the value of a transaction in which management had a strong self-interest. "In short, the Board appears to have failed to ensure that negotiations for alternative bids were conducted by those whose only loyalty was to the shareholders." *Id.* at 277.

The Forstmann option had a similar destructive effect on the auction process. Forstmann had already been drawn into the contest on a preferred basis, so the result of the lock-up was not to foster bidding, but to destroy it. The board's stated reasons for approving the transactions were: (1) better financing, (2) noteholder protection, and (3) higher price. As the Court of Chancery found, and we agree, any distinctions between the rival bidders' methods of financing the proposal were nominal at best, and such a consideration has little or no significance in a cash offer for any and all shares. The principal object, contrary to the board's duty of care, appears to have been protection of the noteholders over the shareholders' interests.

While Forstmann's $57.25 offer was objectively higher than Pantry Pride's $56.25 bid, the margin of superiority is less when the Forstmann price is adjusted for the time value of money. In reality, the Revlon board ended the auction in return for very little actual improvement in the final bid. The principal benefit went to the directors, who avoided personal liability to a class of creditors to whom the board owed no further duty under the circumstances. Thus, when a board ends an intense bidding contest on an insubstantial basis, and where a significant by-product of that action is to protect the directors against a perceived threat of personal liability for consequences stemming from the adoption of previous defensive measures, the action cannot withstand the enhanced scrutiny which *Unocal* requires of director conduct.

In addition to the lock-up option, the Court of Chancery enjoined the no-shop provision as part of the attempt to foreclose further bidding by Pantry Pride. The no-shop provision, like the lock-up option, while not *per se* illegal, is impermissible under the *Unocal* standards when a board's primary duty becomes that of an auctioneer responsible for selling the company to the highest bidder. The agreement to negotiate only with Forstmann ended rather than intensified the board's involvement in the bidding contest.

It is ironic that the parties even considered a no-shop agreement when Revlon had dealt preferentially, and almost exclusively, with Forstmann throughout the contest. After the directors authorized management to negotiate with other parties, Forstmann was given every negotiating advantage that Pantry Pride had been denied: cooperation from management, access to financial data, and the exclusive opportunity to present merger proposals directly to the board of directors. Favoritism for a white knight to the total exclusion of a hostile bidder might be justifiable when the latter's offer adversely affects shareholder interests, but when bidders make relatively similar offers, or dissolution of the company becomes inevitable, the directors cannot fulfill their enhanced *Unocal* duties by playing favorites with the contending factions. Market forces must be allowed to operate freely to bring the target's shareholders the best price available for their equity.[16] Thus, as the trial court ruled, the shareholders' interests necessitated that the board remain free to negotiate in the fulfillment of that duty.

The court below similarly enjoined the payment of the cancellation fee, pending a resolution of the merits, because the fee was part of the overall plan to thwart Pantry Pride's efforts. We find no abuse of discretion in that ruling.

Having concluded that Pantry Pride has shown a reasonable probability of success on the merits, we address the issue of irreparable harm. The Court of Chancery ruled that unless the lock-up and other aspects of the agreement were enjoined, Pantry Pride's opportunity to bid for Revlon was lost. The court also held that the need for both bidders to compete in the marketplace outweighed any injury to Forstmann. Given the complexity of the proposed transaction between Revlon and Forstmann, the obstacles to Pantry Pride obtaining a meaningful legal remedy are immense. We are satisfied that the plaintiff has shown the need for an injunction to protect it from irreparable harm, which need outweighs any harm to the defendants.

In conclusion, the Revlon board was confronted with a situation not uncommon in the current wave of corporate takeovers. A hostile and determined bidder sought the company at a price the board was convinced was inadequate. The initial defensive tactics worked to the benefit of the shareholders, and thus the board was able to sustain its *Unocal* burdens in justifying those measures. However, in granting an asset option lock-up to Forstmann, we must conclude that under all the circumstances the directors allowed considerations other than the maximization of share-

---

16. By this we do not embrace the "passivity" thesis rejected in *Unocal*. See 493 A.2d at 954–55, nn. 8–10. The directors' role remains an active one, changed only in the respect that they are charged with the duty of selling the company at the highest price attainable for the stockholders' benefit.

holder profit to affect their judgment, and followed a course that ended the auction for Revlon, absent court intervention, to the ultimate detriment of its shareholders. No such defensive measure can be sustained when it represents a breach of the directors' fundamental duty of care. *See Smith v. Van Gorkom,* Del.Supr., 488 A.2d 858, 874 (1985). In that context the board's action is not entitled to the deference accorded it by the business judgment rule. The measures were properly enjoined. The decision of the Court of Chancery, therefore, is AFFIRMED.

NOTES

1. Why should a court dictate to management how the sale of the company should be handled? Did management do such a bad job here? It pushed the initial $45 offer from Pantry Pride to $57.25, while protecting the interests of the note holders who had been instrumental in the strategy used by management to increase the sale price to that level. Must management be so amoral as to ignore the interests of those note holders?

2. The SEC sanctioned Revlon for not disclosing its negotiations with Forstmann & Co. to shareholders in proxy disclosures. In the Matter of Revlon, Inc., Securities Exchange Act Release No. 23320 (1986).

3. Ronald Perelman assumed control of *Revlon* after the court's decision. It was crippled, however, by the $1.6 billion in debt that was required to finance the buyout, and the company struggled to survive for years thereafter. "Top 100," Newsday, June 10, 2002, at D40. Mr. Perleman continued his acquisitions,. They included Marvel Comics, which went from a successful company to bankruptcy after he sought control. Derek Manson, "Spidey Cents," Money, July 2002, at 40. No tears though for Perelman. He went on to marry actress Ellen Barkin and he sold his Palm Beach home for $70 million, the most ever paid for a single family residence.

4. *Conducting the auction.* Would a sealed bidding process better assure the best price for a company? What happens if a "low ball" bid wins? Would a reserve protect against such a problem. Consider the following judicial sale of a property in Lexington, Kentucky (the Festival Market), that had been improved and included some $19 million in land, construction and other costs before it was placed in a receivership.

> * * * (2) This Court ordered the Property sold at a public auction pursuant to an Order of Sale dated June 23, 1994 (the "Order"). Pursuant to the terms specified in the order, the Property was then offered for sale in a two step process: (1) parties interested in the purchase were required to submit sealed bids on or before July 19, 1994; and (2) persons who submitted sealed bids would then participate in an auction of the property on July 22, 1994.

> (3) Regency submitted a sealed bid on the Property in timely fashion, bidding $25,000.00. Regency's bid was submitted on July 18, 1994, the date prior to that upon which sealed bids were finally due. * *

> (4) Also participating as a bidder in the sealed bid process was Markham [Development Co.], which bid $600,000.00. Markham's bid was

submitted approximately thirty to forty-five minutes before the sealed bidding process was to close on July 19, 1994. * * *.

(5) Prior to the opening of the sealed bids, representatives of Markham and Regency engaged in discussions about the process in which they were involved. Without either disclosing to the other the amount of their respective bids, Regency agreed with Markham that, should Regency be successful in its attempt to procure the Property, Regency would pay Markham the sum of $50,000.00 for certain proprietary information (including development concepts and information as to potential tenants for the Property). That agreement was embodied in a handwritten document on July 19, 1994, entered into before the sealed bidding process had closed. At the time that document was executed, neither Regency nor Markham were aware that they would be the only two bidders on the Property.

(6) When the sealed bid process closed, Regency and Markham were the only two bidders, with Markham bid being the high bid on the Property. Pursuant to the terms of the Order, that bid by Markham activated a requirement that, at the auction which was to occur later, the opening bid would have to be at least $660,000.00, a sum in excess of the maximum amount which Regency was prepared to offer for the Property.

(7) Prior to the scheduled auction on July 22, 1994 (at which Regency and Markham were to be the only eligible bidders), Regency and Markham entered into two separate agreements. First, Regency agreed that if Markham were successful in purchasing the property, Regency would pay Markham $650,000.00 for the Property (the "Realty Agreement"). Second, Regency agreed (should it make the purchase contemplated in the Realty Agreement) that it would make a further purchase from Markham of proprietary information such as development plans, potential client listings and other materials relevant to the development of the Property for the sum of Fifty Thousand Dollars ($50,000.00) (the "Personalty Agreement").

(8) With those agreements in place, Regency then declined to bid further on the Property. As a result of Markham being the only bidder, the Property was announced by the Commissioner as sold for the sealed bid price of Six Hundred Thousand Dollars ($600,000.00).

* * * The Rehabilitator and the Webbs objected to confirmation of the Sale, arguing that it should be resold as a result of the contractual dealings between Regency and Markham set forth above. Specifically, the Webbs argued: (a) that the sale price for the Property was so disproportionate to actual value as to raise a presumption of irregularity; (b) that the bidding process was confusing and many interested bidders were excluded; and (c) that the Order should have included a minimum bid price. Regency and Markham intervened in this action and moved the Court to confirm the Sale.

After hearing testimony, the court found that all bid procedures had been followed and that the sale should be confirmed. Kentucky Central Life Insurance Co. v. Webb Properties, Civ. Act. No. 94–CI–00052 (Ky. Cir. 1994).

Have you ever used eBay? Would its procedures better assure the "best" price in auctioning off a company?

CITY CAPITAL ASSOCIATES v. INTERCO, INC.

551 A.2d 787 (Del.Ch.1988).

ALLEN, CHANCELLOR.

This case, before the court on an application for a preliminary injunction, involves the question whether the directors of Interco Corporation are breaching their fiduciary duties to the stockholders of that company in failing to now redeem certain stock rights originally distributed as part of a defense against unsolicited attempts to take control of the company. In electing to leave Interco's "poison pill" in effect, the board of Interco seeks to defeat a tender offer for all of the shares of Interco for $74 per share cash, extended by plaintiff Cardinal Acquisition Corporation. The $74 offer is for all shares and the offeror expresses an intent to do a back-end merger at the same price promptly if its offer is accepted. Thus, plaintiffs' offer must be regarded as noncoercive.

As an alternative to the current tender offer, the board is endeavoring to implement a major restructuring of Interco that was formulated only recently. The board has grounds to conclude that the alternative restructuring transaction may have a value to shareholders of at least $76 per share. The restructuring does not involve a Company self-tender, a merger or other corporate action requiring shareholder action or approval.

It is significant that the question of the board's responsibility to redeem or not to redeem the stock rights in this instance arises at what I will call the end-stage of this takeover contest. That is, the negotiating leverage that a poison pill confers upon this company's board will, it is clear, not be further utilized by the board to increase the options available to shareholders or to improve the terms of those options. Rather, at this stage of this contest, the pill now serves the principal purpose of "protecting the restructuring"—that is, precluding the shareholders from choosing an alternative to the restructuring that the board finds less valuable to shareholders.

Accordingly, this case involves a further judicial effort to pick out the contours of a director's fiduciary duty to the corporation and its shareholders when the board has deployed the recently innovated and powerful antitakeover device of flip-in or flip-over stock rights. That inquiry is, of course, necessarily a highly particularized one. * * *

[T]he Supreme Court in *Moran* has directed us specifically to its decision in Unocal Corp. v. Mesa Petroleum Co., Del.Supr., 493 A.2d 946 (1985) as supplying the appropriate legal framework for evaluation of the principal question posed by this case.[1]

In addition to seeking an order requiring the Interco board to now redeem the Company's outstanding stock rights, plaintiffs seek an order restraining any steps to implement the Company's alternative restructuring transaction.

For the reasons that follow, I hold that the board's determination to leave the stock rights in effect is a defensive step that, in the circumstances of this offer and at this stage of the contest for control of Interco, cannot be justified as reasonable in relationship to a threat to the corporation or its shareholders posed by the offer; that the restructuring itself does represent a reasonable response to the perception that the offering price is "inadequate;" and that the board, in proceeding as it has done, has not breached any duties derivable from the Supreme Court's opinion in *Revlon v. MacAndrews & Forbes Holdings, Inc.*, Del.Supr., 506 A.2d 173 (1985).* * *

Turning to the first element of the *Unocal* form of analysis, it is appropriate to note that, in the special case of a tender offer for all shares, the threat posed, if any, is not importantly to corporate policies (as may well be the case in a stock buy-back case such as *Cheff v. Mathes*, Del.Supr., 199 A.2d 548 (1964) or a partial tender offer case such as *Unocal* itself), but rather the threat, if any, is most directly to shareholder interests. Broadly speaking, threats to shareholders in that context may be of two types: threats to the voluntariness of the choice offered by the offer, and threats to the substantive, economic interest represented by the stockholding.

1. *Threats to voluntariness.* It is now universally acknowledged that the structure of an offer can render mandatory in substance that which is voluntary in form. The so-called "front-end" loaded partial offer—already a largely vanished breed—is the most extreme example of this phenomenon. An offer may, however, be structured to have a coercive effect on a rational shareholder in any number of different ways. Whenever a tender offer is so structured, a board may, or perhaps should, perceive a threat to a stockholder's interest in exercising choice to remain a stockholder in the firm. The threat posed by structurally coercive offers is typically amplified by an offering price that the target board responsibly concludes is substantially below a fair price.

Each of the cases in which our Supreme Court has addressed a defensive corporate measure under the *Unocal* test involved the sharp and palpable threat to shareholders posed by a coercive offer.

---

1. In saying that *Unocal* supplies the framework for decision of this aspect of the case, I reject plaintiffs' argument that the board bears a burden to demonstrate the entire fairness of its decision to keep the pill in place while its recapitalization is effectuated. *Ivanhoe Partners v. Newmont Mining Corp.*, Del.Supr., 535 A.2d 1334, 1341 (1987). While the recapitalization does represent a transaction in which the 14 person board (and most intensely, its seven inside members) has an interest—in the sense referred to in *Unocal*—it does not represent a self-dealing transaction in the sense necessary to place upon the board the heavy burden of the intrinsic fairness test. *See Weinberger v. U.O.P., Inc.*, Del.Supr., 457 A.2d 701 (1983); *Sinclair Oil Corp. v. Levien*, Del.Supr., 280 A.2d 717 (1971).

2. *Threats from "inadequate" but noncoercive offers.* The second
broad classification of threats to shareholder interests that might be posed
by a tender offer for all shares relates to the "fairness" or "adequacy" of
the price. It would not be surprising or unreasonable to claim that where
an offer is not coercive or deceptive (and, therefore, what is in issue is
essentially whether the consideration it offers is attractive or not), a
board—even though it may expend corporate funds to arrange alternatives
or to inform shareholders of its view of fair value—is not authorized to
take preclusive action. By preclusive action I mean action that, as a
practical matter, withdraws from the shareholders the option to choose
between the offer and the status quo or some other board sponsored
alternative.

Our law, however, has not adopted that view and experience has
demonstrated the wisdom of that choice. We have held that a board is not
required simply by reason of the existence of a noncoercive offer to redeem
outstanding poison pill rights. The reason is simple. Even where an offer
is noncoercive, it may represent a "threat" to shareholder interests in the
special sense that an active negotiator with power, in effect, to refuse the
proposal may be able to extract a higher or otherwise more valuable
proposal, or may be able to arrange an alternative transaction or a
modified business plan that will present a more valuable option to shareholders. Our cases, however, also indicate that in the setting of a noncoercive offer, absent unusual facts, there may come a time when a board's
fiduciary duty will require it to redeem the rights and to permit the
shareholders to choose.

In this instance, there is no threat of shareholder coercion. The threat
is to shareholders' economic interests posed by an offer the board has
concluded is "inadequate." If this determination is made in good faith (as
I assume it is here), it alone will justify leaving a poison pill in place, even
in the setting of a noncoercive offer, for a period while the board exercises
its good faith business judgment to take such steps as it deems appropriate to protect and advance shareholder interests in light of the significant
development that such an offer doubtless is. That action may entail
negotiation on behalf of shareholders with the offeror, the institution of a
Revlon-style auction for the Company, a recapitalization or restructuring
designed as an alternative to the offer, or other action.

Once that period has closed, and it is apparent that the board does
not intend to institute a *Revlon*-style auction, or to negotiate for an
increase in the unwanted offer, and that it has taken such time as it
required in good faith to arrange an alternative value-maximizing transaction, then, in most instances, the legitimate role of the poison pill in the
context of a noncoercive offer will have been fully satisfied. The only
function then left for the pill at this end-stage is to preclude the shareholders from exercising a judgment about their own interests that differs
from the judgment of the directors, who will have some interest in the
question. What then is the "threat" in this instance that might justify
such a result? Stating that "threat" at this stage of the process most

specifically, it is this: *Wasserstein Perella may be correct in their respective valuations of the offer and the restructuring but a majority of the Interco shareholders may not accept that fact and may be injured as a consequence.*

Perhaps there is a case in which it is appropriate for a board of directors to in effect permanently foreclose their shareholders from accepting a noncoercive offer for their stock by utilization of the recent innovation of "poison pill" rights. If such a case might exist by reason of some special circumstance, a review of the facts here show this not to be it. The "threat" here, when viewed with particularity, is far too mild to justify such a step in this instance. * * *

Our corporation law exists, not as an isolated body of rules and principles, but rather in a historical setting and as a part of a larger body of law premised upon shared values. To acknowledge that directors may employ the recent innovation of "poison pills" to deprive shareholders of the ability effectively to choose to accept a noncoercive offer, after the board has had a reasonable opportunity to explore or create alternatives, or attempt to negotiate on the shareholders' behalf, would, it seems to me, be so inconsistent with widely shared notions of appropriate corporate governance as to threaten to diminish the legitimacy and authority of our corporation law.

I thus conclude that the board's decision not to redeem the rights following the amendment of the offer to $74 per share cannot be justified in the way *Unocal* requires. * * *

The contours of a board's duties in the face of a takeover attempt are not, stated generally, different from the duties the board always bears: to act in an informed manner and in the good faith pursuit of corporate interests and only for that purpose. *Unocal,* of course, adds that where the board acts to defeat such an offer, its steps must be reasonable in light of the threat created by the offer. But I do not think that *Revlon* intended to narrowly circumscribe the range of reactions that a board may make in good faith to an attempt to seize control of a corporation. Even when the corporation is clearly "for sale," a disinterested board or committee maintains the right and the obligation to exercise business judgment in pursuing the stockholders' interest.

Revlon dealt factually with an ongoing bidding contest for corporate control. In that context, its holding that the board could not prefer one bidder to another but was required to permit the auction to proceed to its highest price unimpeded, can be seen as an application of traditional Delaware law: a fiduciary cannot sell for less when more is available on similar terms.

Revlon should not, in my opinion, be interpreted as representing a sharp turn in our law. It does not require, for example, that before every corporate merger agreement can validly be entered into, the constituent corporations must be "shopped" or, more radically, an auction process undertaken, even though a merger may be regarded as a sale of the Company. But mergers or recapitalizations or other important corporate transactions may be authorized by a board only advisedly. There must be a reasonable basis for the board of directors involved to conclude that the transaction involved is in the best interest of the shareholders. This involves having information about possible alternatives. The essence of rational choice is an assessment of costs and benefits and the consideration of alternatives.

Indeed, the central obligation of a board (*assuming it acts in good faith*—an assumption that would not hold for *Revlon*) is to act in an informed manner. When the transaction is so fundamental as the restructuring here (or a sale or merger of the Company), the obligation to be informed would seem to require that reliable information about the value of alternative transactions be explored. When the transaction is a sale of the Company, in which the interests of current stockholders will be converted to cash or otherwise terminated, the requirement to be well informed would ordinarily mandate an appropriate probing of the market for alternatives (and a public auction, should interest be shown). Particularly is that true when a sale is to a management affiliated group (the ubiquitous management LBO transactions) for apparent reasons involving human frailty. But even in that setting, fiduciary obligations can be met in ways other than a traditional auction, if the procedure supplies the board with information from which it can conclude that it has arranged the best available transaction for shareholders. *See, e.g., In Re Fort Howard Corp. Shareholders Litigation, supra* (post contract "market check" adequate to meet fiduciary duties).

When, as in *Revlon,* two bidders are actively contesting for control of a company, the most reliable source of information as to what may be the best available transaction will come out of an open contest or auction. Thus, *Revlon* holds that where it is clear that the firm will be sold, and such a contest is going forward, the board's duty is to act with respect to it so as to encourage the best possible result from the shareholders' point of view.

When the transaction is a defensive recapitalization, a board may not proceed, consistently with its duty to be informed, without appropriately considering relevant information relating to alternatives.[21] But if a board does probe prudently to ascertain possible alternative values, and thus is in a position to act advisedly, I do not understand the *Revlon* holding as requiring it to turn to an auction alternative, if it has arrived at a good faith, informed determination that a recapitalization or other form of transaction is more beneficial to shareholders. Should the board produce a reactive recapitalization, any steps it may take to implement it in the face

---

21. A delicate question is how far a board must go to satisfy its obligation to inform itself, with respect to the question whether the bidder would pay more. Must it disclose information? Must it negotiate? Surely it need not enter into negotiations if it has not reached a decision to sell the Company, but its duty to shareholders may not permit the board to simply ignore the offeror. This issue may come down to the reasonableness of the terms of a confidentiality and standstill agreement. These agreements which always play an important role for a period in cases of this kind rarely get litigated.

of an offer for all stock may, as here, be judicially tested not under *Revlon,* but under the *Unocal* form of judicial review.

Here, given the significance of the restructuring and its character as an alternative to an all cash tender offer, the requirement to inform oneself of possible alternatives may be seen as demanding. It appears, however, that defendants have appropriately informed themselves. While the record is not well developed (defendants aggressively sought to prevent disclosure of alternative prospects being considered—*see* Mohr deposition), it appears that Interco officials did explore with expert third parties the Company's value in an LBO transaction. Moreover, the board has seen that no offer competing with the CCA offer has emerged over an extended period. Finally, the board was advised by a competent banker (albeit with a conflicting financial interest) concerning value.

Accordingly, I can detect no basis to conclude that the board did not proceed prudently and in good faith to pursue the restructuring as an alternative to the CCA offer. I do not read *Revlon* as requiring it to follow any different course.

PARAMOUNT COMMUNICATIONS, INC. v. TIME INC.

571 A.2d 1140 (Del.1989).

HORSEY, JUSTICE:

Paramount Communications, Inc. ("Paramount") and two other groups of plaintiffs ("Shareholder Plaintiffs"), shareholders of Time Incorporated ("Time"), a Delaware corporation, separately filed suits in the Delaware Court of Chancery seeking a preliminary injunction to halt Time's tender offer for 51% of Warner Communication, Inc.'s ("Warner") outstanding shares at $70 cash per share. The court below consolidated the cases and, following the development of an extensive record, after discovery and an evidentiary hearing, denied plaintiffs' motion. In a 50–page unreported opinion and order entered July 14, 1989, the Chancellor refused to enjoin Time's consummation of its tender offer, concluding that the plaintiffs were unlikely to prevail on the merits.

On the same day, plaintiffs filed in this Court an interlocutory appeal, which we accepted on an expedited basis. Pending the appeal, a stay of execution of Time's tender offer was entered for ten days, or until July 24, 1989, at 5:00 p.m. Following briefing and oral argument, on July 24 we concluded that the decision below should be affirmed. We so held in a brief ruling from the bench and a separate Order entered on that date. The effect of our decision was to permit Time to proceed with its tender offer for Warner's outstanding shares. This is the written opinion articulating the reasons for our July 24 bench ruling. 565 A.2d 280, 281.

The principal ground for reversal, asserted by all plaintiffs, is that Paramount's June 7, 1989 uninvited all-cash, all-shares, "fully negotiable" (though conditional) tender offer for Time triggered duties under *Unocal Corp. v. Mesa Petroleum Co.,* Del.Supr., 493 A.2d 946 (1985), and that Time's board of directors, in responding to Paramount's offer, breached those duties. As a consequence, plaintiffs argue that in our review of the Time board's decision of June 16, 1989 to enter into a revised merger agreement with Warner, Time is not entitled to the benefit and protection of the business judgment rule.

Shareholder Plaintiffs also assert a claim based on *Revlon v. MacAndrews & Forbes Holdings, Inc.,* Del.Supr., 506 A.2d 173 (1985). They argue that the original Time–Warner merger agreement of March 4, 1989 resulted in a change of control which effectively put Time up for sale, thereby triggering *Revlon* duties. Those plaintiffs argue that Time's board breached its *Revlon* duties by failing, in the face of the change of control, to maximize shareholder value in the immediate term.

Applying our standard of review, we affirm the Chancellor's ultimate finding and conclusion under *Unocal*. We find that Paramount's tender offer was reasonably perceived by Time's board to pose a threat to Time and that the Time board's "response" to that threat was, under the circumstances, reasonable and proportionate. Applying *Unocal,* we reject the argument that the only corporate threat posed by an all-shares, all-cash tender offer is the possibility of inadequate value.

We also find that Time's board did not by entering into its initial merger agreement with Warner come under a *Revlon* duty either to auction the company or to maximize short-term shareholder value, notwithstanding the unequal share exchange. Therefore, the Time board's original plan of merger with Warner was subject only to a business judgment rule analysis. *See Smith v. Van Gorkom,* Del.Supr., 488 A.2d 858, 873–74 (1985).

Time is a Delaware corporation with its principal offices in New York City. Time's traditional business is publication of magazines and books; however, Time also provides pay television programming through its Home Box Office, Inc. and Cinemax subsidiaries. In addition, Time owns and operates cable television franchises through its subsidiary, American Television and Communication Corporation. During the relevant time period, Time's board consisted of sixteen directors. Twelve of the directors were "outside," nonemployee directors. Four of the directors were also officers of the company. The outside directors included: James F. Bere, chairman of the board and CEO of Borg–Warner Corporation (Time director since 1979); Clifford J. Grum, president and CEO of Temple–Inland, Inc. (Time director since 1980); Henry C. Goodrich, former chairman of Sonat, Inc. (Time director since 1978); Matina S. Horner, then president of Radcliffe College (Time director since 1975); David T. Kearns, chairman and CEO of Xerox Corporation (Time director since 1978); Donald S. Perkins, former chairman of Jewel Companies, Inc. (Time director since 1979); Michael D. Dingman, chairman and CEO of The Henley Group, Inc. (Time director since 1978); Edward S. Finkelstein, chairman and CEO of R.H. Macy & Co. (Time director since 1984); John R. Opel, former chairman and CEO of IBM Corporation (Time director since 1984); Arthur Temple, chairman of Temple–Inland, Inc. (Time director since 1983); Clifton R. Wharton, Jr., chairman and CEO of Teachers Insurance and Annuity Association—College Retirement Equities Fund (Time director since 1982); and Henry R. Luce III, president of The Henry Luce Foundation, Inc. (Time director since 1967). Mr. Luce, the son of the founder of Time, individually and in a representative capacity controlled 4.2% of the outstanding Time stock. The inside officer directors were: J. Richard Munro, Time's chairman and CEO since 1980: N.J. Nicholas, Jr., president and chief operating officer of the company since 1986; Gerald M. Levin, vice chairman of the board; and Jason D. McManus, editor-in-chief of *Time* magazine and a board member since 1988.

As early as 1983 and 1984, Time's executive board began considering expanding Time's operations into the entertainment industry. In 1987, Time established a special committee of executives to consider and propose corporate strategies for the 1990s. The consensus of the committee was that Time should move ahead in the area of ownership and creation of video programming. This expansion, as the Chancellor noted, was predicated upon two considerations: first, Time's desire to have greater control, in terms of quality and price, over the film products delivered by way of its cable network and franchises; and second, Time's concern over the increasing globalization of the world economy. Some of Time's outside directors, especially Luce and Temple, had opposed this move as a threat to the editorial integrity and journalistic focus of Time.[4] Despite this concern, the board recognized that a vertically integrated video enterprise to complement Time's existing HBO and cable networks would better enable it to compete on a global basis.

In late spring of 1987, a meeting took place between Steve Ross, CEO of Warner Brothers, and Nicholas of Time. Ross and Nicholas discussed the possibility of a joint venture between the two companies through the creation of a jointly-owned cable company. Time would contribute its cable system and HBO. Warner would contribute its cable system and provide access to Warner Brothers Studio. The resulting venture would be a larger, more efficient cable network, able to produce and distribute its own movies on a worldwide basis. Ultimately the parties abandoned this plan, determining that it was impractical for several reasons, chief among them being tax considerations.

On August 11, 1987, Gerald M. Levin, Time's vice chairman and chief strategist, wrote J. Richard Munro a confidential memorandum in which he strongly recommended a strategic consolidation with Warner. In June

---

4. The primary concern of Time's outside directors was the preservation of the "Time Culture." They believed that Time had become recognized in this country as an institution built upon a foundation of journalistic integrity. Time's management made a studious effort to refrain from involvement in Time's editorial policy. Several of Time's outside directors feared that a merger with an entertainment company would divert Time's focus from news journalism and threaten the Time Culture.

1988, Nicholas and Munro sent to each outside director a copy of the "comprehensive long-term planning document" prepared by the committee of Time executives that had been examining strategies for the 1990s. The memo included reference to and a description of Warner as a potential acquisition candidate.

Thereafter, Munro and Nicholas held meetings with Time's outside directors to discuss, generally, long-term strategies for Time and, specifically, a combination with Warner. Nearly a year later, Time's board reached the point of serious discussion of the "nuts and bolts" of a consolidation with an entertainment company. On July 21, 1988, Time's board met, with all outside directors present. The meeting's purpose was to consider Time's expansion into the entertainment industry on a global scale. Management presented the board with a profile of various entertainment companies in addition to Warner, including Disney, 20th Century Fox, Universal, and Paramount.

Without any definitive decision on choice of a company, the board approved in principle a strategic plan for Time's expansion. The board gave management the "go-ahead" to continue discussions with Warner concerning the possibility of a merger. With the exception of Temple and Luce, most of the outside directors agreed that a merger involving expansion into the entertainment field promised great growth opportunity for Time. Temple and Luce remained unenthusiastic about Time's entry into the entertainment field.

The board's consensus was that a merger of Time and Warner was feasible, but only if Time controlled the board of the resulting corporation and thereby preserved a management committed to Time's journalistic integrity. To accomplish this goal, the board stressed the importance of carefully defining in advance the corporate governance provisions that would control the resulting entity. Some board members expressed concern over whether such a business combination would place Time "*in play*." The board discussed the wisdom of adopting further defensive measures to lessen such a possibility.[5]

Of a wide range of companies considered by Time's board as possible merger candidates, Warner Brothers, Paramount, Columbia, M.C.A., Fox, MGM, Disney, and Orion, the board, in July 1988, concluded that Warner was the superior candidate for a consolidation. Warner stood out on a number of counts. Warner had just acquired Lorimar and its film studios. Time–Warner could make movies and television shows for use on HBO. Warner had an international distribution system, which Time could use to sell films, videos, books and magazines. Warner was a giant in the music and recording business, an area into which Time wanted to expand. None of the other companies considered had the musical clout of Warner. Time and Warner's cable systems were compatible and could be easily integrat-

---

5. Time had in place a panoply of defensive devices, including a staggered board, a "poison pill" preferred stock rights plan triggered by an acquisition of 15% of the company, a fifty-day notice period for shareholder motions, and restrictions on shareholders' ability to call a meeting or act by consent.

ed; none of the other companies considered presented such a compatible cable partner. Together, Time and Warner would control half of New York City's cable system; Warner had cable systems in Brooklyn and Queens; and Time controlled cable systems in Manhattan and Queens. Warner's publishing company would integrate well with Time's established publishing company. Time sells hardcover books and magazines, and Warner sells softcover books and comics.[6] Time–Warner could sell all of these publications and Warner's videos by using Time's direct mailing network and Warner's international distribution system. Time's network could be used to promote and merchandise Warner's movies.

In August 1988, Levin, Nicholas, and Munro, acting on instructions from Time's board, continued to explore a business combination with Warner. By letter dated August 4, 1988, management informed the outside directors of proposed corporate governance provisions to be discussed with Warner. The provisions incorporated the recommendations of several of Time's outside directors.

From the outset, Time's board favored an all-cash or cash and securities acquisition of Warner as the basis for consolidation. Bruce Wasserstein, Time's financial advisor, also favored an outright purchase of Warner. However, Steve Ross, Warner's CEO, was adamant that a business combination was only practicable on a stock-for-stock basis. Warner insisted on a stock swap in order to preserve its shareholders' equity in the resulting corporation. Time's officers, on the other hand, made it abundantly clear that Time would be the acquiring corporation and that Time would control the resulting board. Time refused to permit itself to be cast as the "acquired" company.

Eventually Time acquiesced in Warner's insistence on a stock-for-stock deal, but talks broke down over corporate governance issues. Time wanted Ross' position as a co-CEO to be temporary and wanted Ross to retire in five years. Ross, however, refused to set a time for his retirement and viewed Time's proposal as indicating a lack of confidence in his leadership. Warner considered it vital that their executives and creative staff not perceive Warner as selling out to Time. Time's request of a guarantee that Time would dominate the CEO succession was objected to as inconsistent with the concept of a Time–Warner merger "of equals." Negotiations ended when the parties reached an impasse. Time's board refused to compromise on its position on corporate governance. Time, and particularly its outside directors, viewed the corporate governance provisions as critical for preserving the "Time Culture" through a pro-Time management at the top.

Throughout the fall of 1988 Time pursued its plan of expansion into the entertainment field; Time held informal discussions with several companies, including Paramount. Capital Cities/ABC approached Time to

---

6. In contrast, Paramount's publishing endeavors were in the areas of professional volumes and text books. Time's board did not find Paramount's publishing as compatible as Warner's publishing efforts.

propose a merger. Talks terminated, however, when Capital Cities/ABC suggested that it was interested in purchasing Time or in controlling the resulting board. Time steadfastly maintained it was not placing itself up for sale.

Warner and Time resumed negotiations in January 1989. The catalyst for the resumption of talks was a private dinner between Steve Ross and Time outside director, Michael Dingman. Dingman was able to convince Ross that the transitional nature of the proposed co-CEO arrangement did not reflect a lack of confidence in Ross. Ross agreed that this course was best for the company and a meeting between Ross and Munro resulted. Ross agreed to retire in five years and let Nicholas succeed him. Negotiations resumed and many of the details of the original stock-for-stock exchange agreement remained intact. In addition, Time's senior management agreed to long-term contracts.

Time insider directors Levin and Nicholas met with Warner's financial advisors to decide upon a stock exchange ratio. Time's board had recognized the potential need to pay a premium in the stock ratio in exchange for dictating the governing arrangement of the new Time–Warner. Levin and outside director Finkelstein were the primary proponents of paying a premium to protect the "Time Culture." The board discussed premium rates of 10%, 15% and 20%. Wasserstein also suggested paying a premium for Warner due to Warner's rapid growth rate. The market exchange ratio of Time stock for Warner stock was .38 in favor of Warner. Warner's financial advisors informed its board that any exchange rate over .400 was a fair deal and any exchange rate over .450 was "one hell of a deal." The parties ultimately agreed upon an exchange rate favoring Warner of .465. On that basis, Warner stockholders would have owned approximately 62%[7] of the common stock of Time–Warner.

On March 3, 1989, Time's board, with all but one director in attendance, met and unanimously approved the stock-for-stock merger with Warner. Warner's board likewise approved the merger. The agreement called for Warner to be merged into a wholly-owned Time subsidiary with Warner becoming the surviving corporation. The common stock of Warner would then be converted into common stock of Time at the agreed upon ratio. Thereafter, the name of Time would be changed to Time–Warner, Inc.

The rules of the New York Stock Exchange required that Time's issuance of shares to effectuate the merger be approved by a vote of Time's stockholders. The Delaware General Corporation Law required approval of the merger by a majority of the Warner stockholders. Delaware law did not require any vote by Time stockholders. The Chancellor concluded that the agreement was the product of "an arms-length negotia-

---

7. As was noted in the briefs and at oral argument, this figure is somewhat misleading because it does not take into consideration the number of individuals who owned stock in both companies.

tion between two parties seeking individual advantage through mutual action."

The resulting company would have a 24–member board, with 12 members representing each corporation. The company would have co-CEO's, at first Ross and Munro, then Ross and Nicholas, and finally, after Ross' retirement, by Nicholas alone. The board would create an editorial committee with a majority of members representing Time. A similar entertainment committee would be controlled by Warner board members. A two-thirds supermajority vote was required to alter CEO successions but an earlier proposal to have supermajority protection for the editorial committee was abandoned. Warner's board suggested raising the compensation levels for Time's senior management under the new corporation. Warner's management, as with most entertainment executives, received higher salaries than comparable executives in news journalism. Time's board, however, rejected Warner's proposal to equalize the salaries of the two management teams.

At its March 3, 1989 meeting, Time's board adopted several defensive tactics. Time entered an automatic share exchange agreement with Warner. Time would receive 17,292,747 shares of Warner's outstanding common stock (9.4%) and Warner would receive 7,080,016 shares of Time's outstanding common stock (11.1%). Either party could trigger the exchange. Time sought out and paid for "confidence" letters from various banks with which it did business. In these letters, the banks promised not to finance any third-party attempt to acquire Time. Time argues these agreements served only to preserve the confidential relationship between itself and the banks. The Chancellor found these agreements to be inconsequential and futile attempts to "dry up" money for a hostile takeover. Time also agreed to a "no-shop" clause, preventing Time from considering any other consolidation proposal, thus relinquishing its power to consider other proposals, regardless of their merits. Time did so at Warner's insistence. Warner did not want to be left "on the auction block" for an unfriendly suitor, if Time were to withdraw from the deal.

Time's board simultaneously established a special committee of outside directors, Finkelstein, Kearns, and Opel, to oversee the merger. The committee's assignment was to resolve any impediments that might arise in the course of working out the details of the merger and its consummation.

Time representatives lauded the lack of debt to the United States Senate and to the President of the United States. Public reaction to the announcement of the merger was positive. Time–Warner would be a media colossus with international scope. The board scheduled the stockholder vote for June 23; and a May 1 record date was set. On May 24, 1989, Time sent out extensive proxy statements to the stockholders regarding the approval vote on the merger. In the meantime, with the merger proceeding without impediment, the special committee had concluded, shortly after its creation, that it was not necessary either to retain independent consultants, legal or financial, or even to meet. Time's board was unanimously in favor of the proposed merger with Warner; and, by the end of May, the Time–Warner merger appeared to be an accomplished fact.

On June 7, 1989, these wishful assumptions were shattered by Paramount's surprising announcement of its all-cash offer to purchase all outstanding shares of Time for $175 per share. The following day, June 8, the trading price of Time's stock rose from $126 to $170 per share. Paramount's offer was said to be "fully negotiable."[8]

Time found Paramount's "fully negotiable" offer to be in fact subject to at least three conditions. First, Time had to terminate its merger agreement and stock exchange agreement with Warner, and remove certain other of its defensive devices, including the redemption of Time's shareholder rights. Second, Paramount had to obtain the required cable franchise transfers from Time in a fashion acceptable to Paramount in its sole discretion. Finally, the offer depended upon a judicial determination that section 203 of the General Corporate Law of Delaware (The Delaware Anti–Takeover Statute) was inapplicable to any Time–Paramount merger. While Paramount's board had been privately advised that it could take months, perhaps over a year, to forge and consummate the deal, Paramount's board publicly proclaimed its ability to close the offer by July 5, 1989. Paramount executives later conceded that none of its directors believed that July 5th was a realistic date to close the transaction.

On June 8, 1989, Time formally responded to Paramount's offer. Time's chairman and CEO, J. Richard Munro, sent an aggressively worded letter to Paramount's CEO, Martin Davis. Munro's letter attacked Davis' personal integrity and called Paramount's offer "smoke and mirrors." Time's nonmanagement directors were not shown the letter before it was sent. However, at a board meeting that same day, all members endorsed management's response as well as the letter's content.

Over the following eight days, Time's board met three times to discuss Paramount's $175 offer. The board viewed Paramount's offer as inadequate and concluded that its proposed merger with Warner was the better course of action. Therefore, the board declined to open any negotiations with Paramount and held steady its course toward a merger with Warner.

In June, Time's board of directors met several times. During the course of their June meetings, Time's outside directors met frequently without management, officers or directors being present. At the request of the outside directors, corporate counsel was present during the board meetings and, from time to time, the management directors were asked to leave the board sessions. During the course of these meetings, Time's financial advisors informed the board that, on an auction basis, Time's per

---

8. Subsequently, it was established that Paramount's board had decided as early as March 1989 to move to acquire Time. However, Paramount management intentionally delayed publicizing its proposal until Time had mailed to its stockholders its Time–Warner merger proposal along with the required proxy statements.

share value was materially higher than Warner's $175 per share offer.[9] After this advice, the board concluded that Paramount's $175 offer was inadequate.

At these June meetings, certain Time directors expressed their concern that Time stockholders would not comprehend the long-term benefits of the Warner merger. Large quantities of Time shares were held by institutional investors. The board feared that even though there appeared to be wide support for the Warner transaction, Paramount's cash premium would be a tempting prospect to these investors. In mid-June, Time sought permission from the New York Stock Exchange to alter its rules and allow the Time–Warner merger to proceed without stockholder approval. Time did so at Warner's insistence. The New York Stock Exchange rejected Time's request on June 15; and on that day, the value of Time stock reached $182 per share.

The following day, June 16, Time's board met to take up Paramount's offer. The board's prevailing belief was that Paramount's bid posed a threat to Time's control of its own destiny and retention of the "Time Culture." Even after Time's financial advisors made another presentation of Paramount and its business attributes, Time's board maintained its position that a combination with Warner offered greater potential for Time. Warner provided Time a much desired production capability and an established international marketing chain. Time's advisors suggested various options, including defensive measures. The board considered and rejected the idea of purchasing Paramount in a "Pac Man" defense. The board considered other defenses, including a recapitalization, the acquisition of another company, and a material change in the present capitalization structure or dividend policy. The board determined to retain its same advisors even in light of the changed circumstances. The board rescinded its agreement to pay its advisors a bonus based on the consummation of the Time–Warner merger and agreed to pay a flat fee for any advice rendered. Finally, Time's board formally rejected Paramount's offer.[11]

At the same meeting, Time's board decided to recast its consolidation with Warner into an outright cash and securities acquisition of Warner by Time; and Time so informed Warner. Time accordingly restructured its proposal to acquire Warner as follows: Time would make an immediate all-cash offer for 51% of Warner's outstanding stock at $70 per share. The remaining 49% would be purchased at some later date for a mixture of cash and securities worth $70 per share. To provide the funds required for its outright acquisition of Warner, Time would assume 7–10 billion dollars worth of debt, thus eliminating one of the principal transaction-related benefits of the original merger agreement. Nine billion dollars of the total purchase price would be allocated to the purchase of Warner's goodwill.

---

9. Time's advisors estimated the value of Time in a control premium situation to be significantly higher than the value of Time in other than a sale situation.

11. Meanwhile, Time had already begun erecting impediments to Paramount's offer. Time encouraged local cable franchises to sue Paramount to prevent it from easily obtaining the franchises.

Warner agreed but insisted on certain terms. Warner sought a control premium and guarantees that the governance provisions found in the original merger agreement would remain intact. Warner further sought agreements that Time would not employ its poison pill against Warner and that, unless enjoined, Time would be legally bound to complete the transaction. Time's board agreed to these last measures only at the insistence of Warner. For its part, Time was assured of its ability to extend its efforts into production areas and international markets, all the while maintaining the Time identity and culture. The Chancellor found the initial Time–Warner transaction to have been negotiated at arms length and the restructured Time–Warner transaction to have resulted from Paramount's offer and its expected effect on a Time shareholder vote.

On June 23, 1989, Paramount raised its all-cash offer to buy Time's outstanding stock to $200 per share. Paramount still professed that all aspects of the offer were negotiable. Time's board met on June 26, 1989 and formally rejected Paramount's $200 per share second offer. The board reiterated its belief that, despite the $25 increase, the offer was still inadequate. The Time board maintained that the Warner transaction offered a greater long-term value for the stockholders and, unlike Paramount's offer, did not pose a threat to Time's survival and its "culture." Paramount then filed this action in the Court of Chancery.

The Shareholder Plaintiffs first assert a *Revlon* claim. They contend that the March 4 Time–Warner agreement effectively put Time up for sale, triggering *Revlon* duties, requiring Time's board to enhance short-term shareholder value and to treat all other interested acquirors on an equal basis. The Shareholder Plaintiffs base this argument on two facts: (i) the ultimate Time–Warner exchange ratio of .465 favoring Warner, resulting in Warner shareholders' receipt of 62% of the combined company; and (ii) the subjective intent of Time's directors as evidenced in their statements that the market might perceive the Time–Warner merger as putting Time up "for sale" and their adoption of various defensive measures.

The Shareholder Plaintiffs further contend that Time's directors, in structuring the original merger transaction to be "takeover-proof," triggered *Revlon* duties by foreclosing their shareholders from any prospect of obtaining a control premium. In short, plaintiffs argue that Time's board's decision to merge with Warner imposed a fiduciary duty to maximize immediate share value and not erect unreasonable barriers to further bids. Therefore, they argue, the Chancellor erred in finding: that Paramount's bid for Time did not place Time "for sale"; that Time's transaction with Warner did not result in any transfer of control; and that the combined Time–Warner was not so large as to preclude the possibility of the stockholders of Time–Warner receiving a future control premium.

Paramount asserts only a *Unocal* claim in which the shareholder plaintiffs join. Paramount contends that the Chancellor, in applying the first part of the *Unocal* test, erred in finding that Time's board had reasonable grounds to believe that Paramount posed both a legally cognizable threat to Time shareholders and a danger to Time's corporate policy and effectiveness. Paramount also contests the court's finding that Time's board made a reasonable and objective investigation of Paramount's offer so as to be informed before rejecting it. Paramount further claims that the court erred in applying *Unocal*'s second part in finding Time's response to be "reasonable." Paramount points primarily to the preclusive effect of the revised agreement which denied Time shareholders the opportunity both to vote on the agreement and to respond to Paramount's tender offer. Paramount argues that the underlying motivation of Time's board in adopting these defensive measures was management's desire to perpetuate itself in office.

The Court of Chancery posed the pivotal question presented by this case to be: Under what circumstances must a board of directors abandon an in-place plan of corporate development in order to provide its shareholders with the option to elect and realize an immediate control premium? As applied to this case, the question becomes: Did Time's board, having developed a strategic plan of global expansion to be launched through a business combination with Warner, come under a fiduciary duty to jettison its plan and put the corporation's future in the hands of its shareholders?

While we affirm the result reached by the Chancellor, we think it unwise to place undue emphasis upon long-term versus short-term corporate strategy. Two key predicates underpin our analysis. First, Delaware law imposes on a board of directors the duty to manage the business and affairs of the corporation. This broad mandate includes a conferred authority to set a corporate course of action, including time frame, designed to enhance corporate profitability. Thus, the question of "long-term" versus "short-term" values is largely irrelevant because directors, generally, are obliged to chart a course for a corporation which is in its best interests without regard to a fixed investment horizon. Second, absent a limited set of circumstances as defined under *Revlon,* a board of directors, while always required to act in an informed manner, is not under any *per se* duty to maximize shareholder value in the short term, even in the context of a takeover.[12] In our view, the pivotal question presented by this case is: "Did Time, by entering into the proposed merger with Warner, put itself up for sale?" A resolution of that issue through application of *Revlon* has a significant bearing upon the resolution of the derivative *Unocal* issue.

We first take up plaintiffs' principal *Revlon* argument, summarized above. In rejecting this argument, the Chancellor found the original Time–Warner merger agreement not to constitute a "change of control" and

---

12. Thus, we endorse the Chancellor's conclusion that it is not a breach of faith for directors to determine that the present stock market price of shares is not representative of true value or that there may indeed be several market values for any corporation's stock. We have so held in another context. *See Van Gorkom,* 488 A.2d at 876.

concluded that the transaction did not trigger *Revlon* duties. The Chancellor's conclusion is premised on a finding that "[b]efore the merger agreement was signed, control of the corporation existed in a fluid aggregation of unaffiliated shareholders representing a voting majority—in other words, in the market." The Chancellor's findings of fact are supported by the record and his conclusion is correct as a matter of law. However, we premise our rejection of plaintiffs' *Revlon* claim on different grounds, namely, the absence of any substantial evidence to conclude that Time's board, in negotiating with Warner, made the dissolution or break-up of the corporate entity inevitable, as was the case in *Revlon*.

Under Delaware law there are, generally speaking and without excluding other possibilities, two circumstances which may implicate *Revlon* duties. The first, and clearer one, is when a corporation initiates an active bidding process seeking to sell itself or to effect a business reorganization involving a clear break-up of the company. However, *Revlon* duties may also be triggered where, in response to a bidder's offer, a target abandons its long-term strategy and seeks an alternative transaction involving the breakup of the company. Thus, in *Revlon*, when the board responded to Pantry Pride's offer by contemplating a "bust-up" sale of assets in a leveraged acquisition, we imposed upon the board a duty to maximize immediate shareholder value and an obligation to auction the company fairly. If, however, the board's reaction to a hostile tender offer is found to constitute only a defensive response and not an abandonment of the corporation's continued existence, *Revlon* duties are not triggered, though *Unocal* duties attach.[14]

The plaintiffs insist that even though the original Time–Warner agreement may not have worked "an objective change of control," the transaction made a "sale" of Time inevitable. Plaintiffs rely on the subjective intent of Time's board of directors and principally upon certain board members' expressions of concern that the Warner transaction *might* be viewed as effectively putting Time up for sale. Plaintiffs argue that the use of a lock-up agreement, a no-shop clause, and so-called "dry-up" agreements prevented shareholders from obtaining a control premium in the immediate future and thus violated *Revlon*.

We agree with the Chancellor that such evidence is entirely insufficient to invoke *Revlon* duties; and we decline to extend *Revlon*'s application to corporate transactions simply because they might be construed as putting a corporation either "in play" or "up for sale." The adoption of structural safety devices alone does not trigger *Revlon*.[15] Rather, as the Chancellor stated, such devices are properly subject to a *Unocal* analysis.

---

14. Within the auction process, any action taken by the board must be reasonably related to the threat posed or reasonable in relation to the advantage sought, *see Mills Acquisition Co. v. Macmillan, Inc.,* Del.Supr., 559 A.2d 1261, 1288 (1989). Thus, a *Unocal* analysis may be appropriate when a corporation is in a Revlon situation and *Revlon* duties may be triggered by a defensive action taken in response to a hostile offer. Since *Revlon*, we have stated that differing treatment of various bidders is not actionable when such action reasonably relates to achieving the best price available for the stockholders. *Macmillan,* 559 A.2d at 1286–87.

15. Although the legality of the various safety devices adopted to protect the original agreement is not a central issue, there is substantial evidence to support each of the trial court's

Finally, we do not find in Time's recasting of its merger agreement with Warner from a share exchange to a share purchase a basis to conclude that Time had either abandoned its strategic plan or made a sale of Time inevitable.[16] The Chancellor found that although the merged Time–Warner company would be large (with a value approaching approximately $30 billion), recent takeover cases have proven that acquisition of the combined company might nonetheless be possible. The legal consequence is that *Unocal* alone applies to determine whether the business judgment rule attaches to the revised agreement. Plaintiffs' analogy to *Macmillan* thus collapses and plaintiffs' reliance on *Macmillan* is misplaced.

We turn now to plaintiffs' *Unocal* claim. We begin by noting, as did the Chancellor, that our decision does not require us to pass on the wisdom of the board's decision to enter into the original Time–Warner agreement. That is not a court's task. Our task is simply to review the record to determine whether there is sufficient evidence to support the Chancellor's conclusion that the initial Time–Warner agreement was the product of a proper exercise of business judgment.

We have purposely detailed the evidence of the Time board's deliberative approach, beginning in 1983–84, to expand itself. Time's decision in 1988 to combine with Warner was made only after what could be fairly characterized as an exhaustive appraisal of Time's future as a corporation. After concluding in 1983–84 that the corporation must expand to survive, and beyond journalism into entertainment, the board combed the field of available entertainment companies. By 1987 Time had focused upon Warner; by late July 1988 Time's board was convinced that Warner would provide the best "fit" for Time to achieve its strategic objectives. The record attests to the zealousness of Time's executives, fully supported by their directors, in seeing to the preservation of Time's "culture," i.e., its perceived editorial integrity in journalism. We find ample evidence in the record to support the Chancellor's conclusion that the Time board's decision to expand the business of the company through its March 3 merger with Warner was entitled to the protection of the business judgment rule.

The Chancellor reached a different conclusion in addressing the Time-Warner transaction as revised three months later. He found that the revised agreement was defense-motivated and designed to avoid the potentially disruptive effect that Paramount's offer would have had on consummation of the proposed merger were it put to a shareholder vote. Thus,

---

related conclusions. Thus, the court found that the concept of the Share Exchange Agreement predated any takeover threat by Paramount and had been adopted for a rational business purpose: to deter Time and Warner from being "put in play" by their March 4 Agreement. The court further found that Time had adopted the "no-shop" clause at Warner's insistence and for Warner's protection. Finally, although certain aspects of the "dry-up" agreements were suspect on their face, we concur in the Chancellor's view that in this case they were inconsequential.

16. We note that, although Time's advisors presented the board with such alternatives as an auction or sale to a third party bidder, the board rejected those responses, preferring to go forward with its pre-existing plan rather than adopt an alternative to Paramount's proposal.

the court declined to apply the traditional business judgment rule to the revised transaction and instead analyzed the Time board's June 16 decision under *Unocal.* The court ruled that *Unocal* applied to all director actions taken, following receipt of Paramount's hostile tender offer, that were reasonably determined to be defensive. Clearly that was a correct ruling and no party disputes that ruling.

In *Unocal,* we held that before the business judgment rule is applied to a board's adoption of a defensive measure, the burden will lie with the board to prove (a) reasonable grounds for believing that a danger to corporate policy and effectiveness existed; and (b) that the defensive measure adopted was reasonable in relation to the threat posed. Directors satisfy the first part of the *Unocal* test by demonstrating good faith and reasonable investigation. We have repeatedly stated that the refusal to entertain an offer may comport with a valid exercise of a board's business judgment.

Unocal involved a two-tier, highly coercive tender offer. In such a case, the threat is obvious: shareholders may be compelled to tender to avoid being treated adversely in the second stage of the transaction. In subsequent cases, the Court of Chancery has suggested that an all-cash, all-shares offer, falling within a range of values that a shareholder might reasonably prefer, cannot constitute a legally recognized "threat" to shareholder interests sufficient to withstand a *Unocal* analysis. In those cases, the Court of Chancery determined that whatever threat existed related only to the shareholders and only to price and not to the corporation.

From those decisions by our Court of Chancery, Paramount and the individual plaintiffs extrapolate a rule of law that an all-cash, all-shares offer with values reasonably in the range of acceptable price cannot pose any objective threat to a corporation or its shareholders. Thus, Paramount would have us hold that only if the value of Paramount's offer were determined to be clearly inferior to the value created by management's plan to merge with Warner could the offer be viewed—objectively—as a threat.

Implicit in the plaintiffs' argument is the view that a hostile tender offer can pose only two types of threats: the threat of coercion that results from a two-tier offer promising unequal treatment for nontendering shareholders; and the threat of inadequate value from an all-shares, all-cash offer at a price below what a target board in good faith deems to be the present value of its shares. Since Paramount's offer was all-cash, the only conceivable "threat," plaintiffs argue, was inadequate value.[17] We

---

17. Some commentators have suggested that the threats posed by hostile offers be categorized into not two but three types: "(i) *opportunity loss* ... [where] a hostile offer might deprive target shareholders of the opportunity to select a superior alternative offered by target management [or, we would add, offered by another bidder]; (ii) *structural coercion,* ... the risk that disparate treatment of non-tendering shareholders might distort shareholders' tender decisions; and ... (iii) *substantive coercion,* ... the risk that shareholders will mistakenly accept an underpriced offer because they disbelieve management's representations of intrinsic value." The recognition of substantive coercion, the authors suggest, would help guarantee that the Unocal standard

disapprove of such a narrow and rigid construction of *Unocal,* for the reasons which follow.

Plaintiffs' position represents a fundamental misconception of our standard of review under *Unocal* principally because it would involve the court in substituting its judgment as to what is a "better" deal for that of a corporation's board of directors. To the extent that the Court of Chancery has recently done so in certain of its opinions, we hereby reject such approach as not in keeping with a proper *Unocal* analysis.

The usefulness of *Unocal* as an analytical tool is precisely its flexibility in the face of a variety of fact scenarios. *Unocal* is not intended as an abstract standard; neither is it a structured and mechanistic procedure of appraisal. Thus, we have said that directors may consider, when evaluating the threat posed by a takeover bid, the "inadequacy of the price offered, nature and timing of the offer, questions of illegality, the impact on 'constituencies' other than shareholders . . . the risk of nonconsummation, and the quality of securities being offered in the exchange." The open-ended analysis mandated by *Unocal* is not intended to lead to a simple mathematical exercise: that is, of comparing the discounted value of Time–Warner's expected trading price at some future date with Paramount's offer and determining which is the higher. Indeed, in our view, precepts underlying the business judgment rule militate against a court's engaging in the process of attempting to appraise and evaluate the relative merits of a long-term versus a short-term investment goal for shareholders. To engage in such an exercise is a distortion of the *Unocal* process and, in particular, the application of the second part of *Unocal*'s test, discussed below.

In this case, the Time board reasonably determined that inadequate value was not the only legally cognizable threat that Paramount's all-cash, all-shares offer could present. Time's board concluded that Paramount's eleventh hour offer posed other threats. One concern was that Time shareholders might elect to tender into Paramount's cash offer in ignorance or a mistaken belief of the strategic benefit which a business combination with Warner might produce. Moreover, Time viewed the conditions attached to Paramount's offer as introducing a degree of uncertainty that skewed a comparative analysis. Further, the timing of Paramount's offer to follow issuance of Time's proxy notice was viewed as arguably designed to upset, if not confuse, the Time stockholders' vote. Given this record evidence, we cannot conclude that the Time board's decision of June 6 that Paramount's offer posed a threat to corporate policy and effectiveness was lacking in good faith or dominated by motives of either entrenchment or self-interest.

Paramount also contends that the Time board had not duly investigated Paramount's offer. Therefore, Paramount argues, Time was unable

---

becomes an effective intermediate standard of review. Gilson & Kraakman, *Delaware's Intermediate Standard for Defensive Tactics: Is There Substance to Proportionality Review?,* 44 The Business Lawyer, 247, 267 (1989).

to make an informed decision that the offer posed a threat to Time's corporate policy. Although the Chancellor did not address this issue directly, his findings of fact do detail Time's exploration of the available entertainment companies, including Paramount, before determining that Warner provided the best strategic "fit." In addition, the court found that Time's board rejected Paramount's offer because Paramount did not serve Time's objectives or meet Time's needs. Thus, the record does, in our judgment, demonstrate that Time's board was adequately informed of the potential benefits of a transaction with Paramount. We agree with the Chancellor that the Time board's lengthy pre-June investigation of potential merger candidates, including Paramount, mooted any obligation on Time's part to halt its merger process with Warner to reconsider Paramount. Time's board was under no obligation to negotiate with Paramount. Time's failure to negotiate cannot be fairly found to have been uninformed. The evidence supporting this finding is materially enhanced by the fact that twelve of Time's sixteen board members were outside independent directors.

We turn to the second part of the *Unocal* analysis. The obvious requisite to determining the reasonableness of a defensive action is a clear identification of the nature of the threat. As the Chancellor correctly noted, this "requires an evaluation of the importance of the corporate objective threatened; alternative methods of protecting that objective; impacts of the 'defensive' action, and other relevant factors." It is not until both parts of the *Unocal* inquiry have been satisfied that the business judgment rule attaches to defensive actions of a board of directors. *Unocal*, 493 A.2d at 954.[18] As applied to the facts of this case, the question is whether the record evidence supports the Court of Chancery's conclusion that the restructuring of the Time–Warner transaction, including the adoption of several preclusive defensive measures, was a *reasonable response* in relation to a perceived threat.

Paramount argues that, assuming its tender offer posed a threat, Time's response was unreasonable in precluding Time's shareholders from accepting the tender offer or receiving a control premium in the immediately foreseeable future. Once again, the contention stems, we believe, from a fundamental misunderstanding of where the power of corporate governance lies. Delaware law confers the management of the corporate enterprise to the stockholders' duly elected board representatives. The fiduciary duty to manage a corporate enterprise includes the selection of a time frame for achievement of corporate goals. That duty may not be delegated to the stockholders. Directors are not obliged to abandon a deliberately conceived corporate plan for a short-term shareholder profit unless there is clearly no basis to sustain the corporate strategy.

---

18.   Some commentators have criticized *Unocal* by arguing that once the board's deliberative process has been analyzed and found not to be wanting in objectivity, good faith or deliberateness, the so-called "enhanced" business judgment rule has been satisfied and no further inquiry is undertaken. *See generally* Johnson & Siegel, *Corporate Mergers: Redefining the Role of Target Directors,* 136 U.Pa.L.Rev. 315 (1987). We reject such views.

Although the Chancellor blurred somewhat the discrete analyses required under *Unocal,* he did conclude that Time's board reasonably perceived Paramount's offer to be a significant threat to the planned Time–Warner merger and that Time's response was not "overly broad." We have found that even in light of a valid threat, management actions that are coercive in nature or force upon shareholders a management-sponsored alternative to a hostile offer may be struck down as unreasonable and nonproportionate responses.

Here, on the record facts, the Chancellor found that Time's responsive action to Paramount's tender offer was not aimed at "cramming down" on its shareholders a management-sponsored alternative, but rather had as its goal the carrying forward of a pre-existing transaction in an altered form.[19] Thus, the response was reasonably related to the threat. The Chancellor noted that the revised agreement and its accompanying safety devices did not preclude Paramount from making an offer for the combined Time–Warner company or from changing the conditions of its offer so as not to make the offer dependent upon the nullification of the Time–Warner agreement. Thus, the response was proportionate. We affirm the Chancellor's rulings as clearly supported by the record. Finally, we note that although Time was required, as a result of Paramount's hostile offer, to incur a heavy debt to finance its acquisition of Warner, that fact alone does not render the board's decision unreasonable so long as the directors could reasonably perceive the debt load not to be so injurious to the corporation as to jeopardize its well being.

Applying the test for grant or denial of preliminary injunctive relief, we find plaintiffs failed to establish a reasonable likelihood of ultimate success on the merits. Therefore, we affirm.

NOTES

1. Although the executives at Time and Warner made millions from the merger (Steve Ross from Warner made almost $200 million, plus many millions more in compensation after the merger), the shareholders of Time, Inc. did not fare as well. The price of their stock never reached the $200 offered by Paramount. Indeed, the stock price fell below $100 after the merger. See generally Roger Cohen, "A $78 Million Year: Steve Ross Defends His Paycheck," N.Y. Times, March 22, 1992, § 6, at 28. The merger between Time and Warner also did not prove successful in preserving the Time culture, or at least its management did not retain control for long. N.J. Nicholas, Jr., of the Time management group was forced out as chief executive officer of the merged company and was replaced by Steve Ross of the

---

19. The Chancellor cited *Shamrock Holdings, Inc. v. Polaroid Corp.,* Del.Ch., 559 A.2d 257 (1989) as a closely analogous case. In that case, the Court of Chancery upheld, in the face of a takeover bid, the establishment of an employee stock ownership plan that had a significant antitakeover effect. The Court of Chancery upheld the board's action largely because the ESOP had been adopted *prior* to any contest for control and was reasonably determined to increase productivity and enhance profits. The ESOP did not appear to be primarily a device to affect or secure corporate control.

Warner Brothers group. He in turn was replaced on his death by a former Time executive, Gerald Levin. Levin who then began a series of acquisitions that transformed the company. In, 1995, Turner Broadcasting was acquired and in 1999 America Online was added to what was becoming a massive communications and publication enterprise in which Time magazine was only a small part. The AOL Time Warner merger became somewhat infamous for $54 billion it had to write off its books to reflect the diminished value of the combined enterprise in 2002. This was the largest write off in corporate history. See generally Geraldine Fabrikant, "At AOL, Parting Without the Sweet Sorrow," N.Y. Times, May 17, 2002, at C1.

2. The Timer–Warner merger was originally structured as a reverse triangular merger. As is now permitted under the law of most states. Delaware § 251(b)(4) expressly permits the issuance of the shares of another corporation in connection with a merger. This specifically enables the acquiring company (the subsidiary) to issue shares in its parent as part of the merger with the other constituent corporation (the corporation being acquired). See Note, "Three–Party Mergers: The Fourth Form of Corporate Acquisition," 57 Va. L. Rev. 1242 (1971).

PARAMOUNT COMMUNICATIONS INC. v. QVC NETWORK INC.

637 A.2d 34 (Del.1994).

VEASEY, CHIEF JUSTICE.

In this appeal we review an order of the Court of Chancery dated November 24, 1993 (the "November 24 Order"), preliminarily enjoining certain defensive measures designed to facilitate a so-called strategic alliance between Viacom Inc. ("Viacom") and Paramount Communications Inc. ("Paramount") approved by the board of directors of Paramount (the "Paramount Board" or the "Paramount directors") and to thwart an unsolicited, more valuable, tender offer by QVC Network Inc. ("QVC"). In affirming, we hold that the sale of control in this case, which is at the heart of the proposed strategic alliance, implicates enhanced judicial scrutiny of the conduct of the Paramount Board under Unocal Corp. v. Mesa Petroleum Co., Del.Supr., 493 A.2d 946 (1985), and Revlon, Inc. v. MacAndrews & Forbes Holdings, Inc., Del.Supr., 506 A.2d 173 (1985). We further hold that the conduct of the Paramount Board was not reasonable as to process or result.

QVC and certain stockholders of Paramount commenced separate actions (later consolidated) in the Court of Chancery seeking preliminary and permanent injunctive relief against Paramount, certain members of the Paramount Board, and Viacom. This action arises out of a proposed acquisition of Paramount by Viacom through a tender offer followed by a second-step merger (the "Paramount-Viacom transaction"), and a competing unsolicited tender offer by QVC. The Court of Chancery granted a preliminary injunction.

The Court of Chancery found that the Paramount directors violated their fiduciary duties by favoring the Paramount–Viacom transaction over the more valuable unsolicited offer of QVC. The Court of Chancery preliminarily enjoined Paramount and the individual defendants (the "Paramount defendants") from amending or modifying Paramount's stockholder rights agreement (the "Rights Agreement"), including the redemption of the Rights, or taking other action to facilitate the consummation of the pending tender offer by Viacom or any proposed second-step merger, including the Merger Agreement between Paramount and Viacom dated September 12, 1993 (the "Original Merger Agreement"), as amended on October 24, 1993 (the "Amended Merger Agreement"). Viacom and the Paramount defendants were enjoined from taking any action to exercise any provision of the Stock Option Agreement between Paramount and Viacom dated September 12, 1993 (the "Stock Option Agreement"), as amended on October 24, 1993. The Court of Chancery did not grant preliminary injunctive relief as to the termination fee provided for the benefit of Viacom in Section 8.05 of the Original Merger Agreement and the Amended Merger Agreement (the "Termination Fee").

Under the circumstances of this case, the pending sale of control implicated in the Paramount–Viacom transaction required the Paramount Board to act on an informed basis to secure the best value reasonably available to the stockholders. Since we agree with the Court of Chancery that the Paramount directors violated their fiduciary duties, we have affirmed the entry of the order of the Vice Chancellor granting the preliminary injunction and have remanded these proceedings to the Court of Chancery for proceedings consistent herewith.

We also have attached an Addendum to this opinion addressing serious deposition misconduct by counsel who appeared on behalf of a Paramount director at the time that director's deposition was taken by a lawyer representing QVC.

The Court of Chancery Opinion contains a detailed recitation of its factual findings in this matter. Only a brief summary of the facts is necessary for purposes of this opinion. The following summary is drawn from the findings of fact set forth in the Court of Chancery Opinion and our independent review of the record.

Paramount is a Delaware corporation with its principal offices in New York City. Approximately 118 million shares of Paramount's common stock are outstanding and traded on the New York Stock Exchange. The majority of Paramount's stock is publicly held by numerous unaffiliated investors. Paramount owns and operates a diverse group of entertainment businesses, including motion picture and television studios, book publishers, professional sports teams, and amusement parks.

There are 15 persons serving on the Paramount Board. Four directors are officer-employees of Paramount: Martin S. Davis ("Davis"), Paramount's Chairman and Chief Executive Officer since 1983; Donald Oresman ("Oresman"), Executive Vice–President, Chief Administrative Officer, and General Counsel; Stanley R. Jaffe, President and Chief Operating Officer; and Ronald L. Nelson, Executive Vice President and Chief Financial Officer. Paramount's 11 outside directors are distinguished and experienced business persons who are present or former senior executives of public corporations or financial institutions.

Viacom is a Delaware corporation with its headquarters in Massachusetts. Viacom is controlled by Sumner M. Redstone ("Redstone"), its Chairman and Chief Executive Officer, who owns indirectly approximately 85.2 percent of Viacom's voting Class A stock and approximately 69.2 percent of Viacom's nonvoting Class B stock through National Amusements, Inc. ("NAI"), an entity 91.7 percent owned by Redstone. Viacom has a wide range of entertainment operations, including a number of well-known cable television channels such as MTV, Nickelodeon, Showtime, and The Movie Channel. Viacom's equity co-investors in the Paramount–Viacom transaction include NYNEX Corporation and Blockbuster Entertainment Corporation.

QVC is a Delaware corporation with its headquarters in West Chester, Pennsylvania. QVC has several large stockholders, including Liberty Media Corporation, Comcast Corporation, Advance Publications, Inc., and Cox Enterprises Inc. Barry Diller ("Diller"), the Chairman and Chief Executive Officer of QVC, is also a substantial stockholder. QVC sells a variety of merchandise through a televised shopping channel. QVC has several equity co-investors in its proposed combination with Paramount including BellSouth Corporation and Comcast Corporation.

Beginning in the late 1980s, Paramount investigated the possibility of acquiring or merging with other companies in the entertainment, media, or communications industry. Paramount considered such transactions to be desirable, and perhaps necessary, in order to keep pace with competitors in the rapidly evolving field of entertainment and communications. Consistent with its goal of strategic expansion, Paramount made a tender offer for Time Inc. in 1989, but was ultimately unsuccessful. *See Paramount Communications, Inc. v. Time Inc.*, Del.Supr., 571 A.2d 1140 (1989)(*"Time-Warner"*).

Although Paramount had considered a possible combination of Paramount and Viacom as early as 1990, recent efforts to explore such a transaction began at a dinner meeting between Redstone and Davis on April 20, 1993. Robert Greenhill ("Greenhill"), Chairman of Smith Barney Shearson Inc. ("Smith Barney"), attended and helped facilitate this meeting. After several more meetings between Redstone and Davis, serious negotiations began taking place in early July.

It was tentatively agreed that Davis would be the chief executive officer and Redstone would be the controlling stockholder of the combined company, but the parties could not reach agreement on the merger price and the terms of a stock option to be granted to Viacom. With respect to price, Viacom offered a package of cash and stock (primarily Viacom Class B nonvoting stock) with a market value of approximately $61 per share, but Paramount wanted at least $70 per share.

Shortly after negotiations broke down in July 1993, two notable events occurred. First, Davis apparently learned of QVC's potential interest in Paramount, and told Diller over lunch on July 21, 1993, that Paramount was not for sale. Second, the market value of Viacom's Class B nonvoting stock increased from $46.875 on July 6 to $57.25 on August 20. QVC claims (and Viacom disputes) that this price increase was caused by open market purchases of such stock by Redstone or entities controlled by him.

On August 20, 1993, discussions between Paramount and Viacom resumed when Greenhill arranged another meeting between Davis and Redstone. After a short hiatus, the parties negotiated in earnest in early September, and performed due diligence with the assistance of their financial advisors, Lazard Freres & Co. ("Lazard") for Paramount and Smith Barney for Viacom. On September 9, 1993, the Paramount Board was informed about the status of the negotiations and was provided information by Lazard, including an analysis of the proposed transaction.

On September 12, 1993, the Paramount Board met again and unanimously approved the Original Merger Agreement whereby Paramount would merge with and into Viacom. The terms of the merger provided that each share of Paramount common stock would be converted into 0.10 shares of Viacom Class A voting stock, 0.90 shares of Viacom Class B nonvoting stock, and $9.10 in cash. In addition, the Paramount Board agreed to amend its "poison pill" Rights Agreement to exempt the proposed merger with Viacom. The Original Merger Agreement also contained several provisions designed to make it more difficult for a potential competing bid to succeed. We focus, as did the Court of Chancery, on three of these defensive provisions: a "no-shop" provision (the "No–Shop Provision"), the Termination Fee, and the Stock Option Agreement.

First, under the No–Shop Provision, the Paramount Board agreed that Paramount would not solicit, encourage, discuss, negotiate, or endorse any competing transaction unless: (a) a third party "makes an unsolicited written, bona fide proposal, which is not subject to any material contingencies relating to financing"; and (b) the Paramount Board determines that discussions or negotiations with the third party are necessary for the Paramount Board to comply with its fiduciary duties.

Second, under the Termination Fee provision, Viacom would receive a $100 million termination fee if: (a) Paramount terminated the Original Merger Agreement because of a competing transaction; (b) Paramount's stockholders did not approve the merger; or (c) the Paramount Board recommended a competing transaction.

The third and most significant deterrent device was the Stock Option Agreement, which granted to Viacom an option to purchase approximately

19.9 percent (23,699,000 shares) of Paramount's outstanding common stock at $69.14 per share if any of the triggering events for the Termination Fee occurred. In addition to the customary terms that are normally associated with a stock option, the Stock Option Agreement contained two provisions that were both unusual and highly beneficial to Viacom: (a) Viacom was permitted to pay for the shares with a senior subordinated note of questionable marketability instead of cash, thereby avoiding the need to raise the $1.6 billion purchase price (the "Note Feature"); and (b) Viacom could elect to require Paramount to pay Viacom in cash a sum equal to the difference between the purchase price and the market price of Paramount's stock (the "Put Feature"). Because the Stock Option Agreement was not "capped" to limit its maximum dollar value, it had the potential to reach (and in this case did reach) unreasonable levels.

After the execution of the Original Merger Agreement and the Stock Option Agreement on September 12, 1993, Paramount and Viacom announced their proposed merger. In a number of public statements, the parties indicated that the pending transaction was a virtual certainty. Redstone described it as a "marriage" that would "never be torn asunder" and stated that only a "nuclear attack" could break the deal. Redstone also called Diller and John Malone of Tele–Communications Inc., a major stockholder of QVC, to dissuade them from making a competing bid.

Despite these attempts to discourage a competing bid, Diller sent a letter to Davis on September 20, 1993, proposing a merger in which QVC would acquire Paramount for approximately $80 per share, consisting of 0.893 shares of QVC common stock and $30 in cash. QVC also expressed its eagerness to meet with Paramount to negotiate the details of a transaction. When the Paramount Board met on September 27, it was advised by Davis that the Original Merger Agreement prohibited Paramount from having discussions with QVC (or anyone else) unless certain conditions were satisfied. In particular, QVC had to supply evidence that its proposal was not subject to financing contingencies. The Paramount Board was also provided information from Lazard describing QVC and its proposal.

On October 5, 1993, QVC provided Paramount with evidence of QVC's financing. The Paramount Board then held another meeting on October 11, and decided to authorize management to meet with QVC. Davis also informed the Paramount Board that Booz–Allen & Hamilton ("Booz–Allen"), a management consulting firm, had been retained to assess, *inter alia,* the incremental earnings potential from a Paramount–Viacom merger and a Paramount–QVC merger. Discussions proceeded slowly, however, due to a delay in Paramount signing a confidentiality agreement. In response to Paramount's request for information, QVC provided two binders of documents to Paramount on October 20.

On October 21, 1993, QVC filed this action and publicly announced an $80 cash tender offer for 51 percent of Paramount's outstanding shares (the "QVC tender offer"). Each remaining share of Paramount common stock would be converted into 1.42857 shares of QVC common stock in a second-step merger. The tender offer was conditioned on, among other things, the invalidation of the Stock Option Agreement, which was worth over $200 million by that point.[5] QVC contends that it had to commence a tender offer because of the slow pace of the merger discussions and the need to begin seeking clearance under federal antitrust laws.

Confronted by QVC's hostile bid, which on its face offered over $10 per share more than the consideration provided by the Original Merger Agreement, Viacom realized that it would need to raise its bid in order to remain competitive. Within hours after QVC's tender offer was announced, Viacom entered into discussions with Paramount concerning a revised transaction. These discussions led to serious negotiations concerning a comprehensive amendment to the original Paramount–Viacom transaction. In effect, the opportunity for a "new deal" with Viacom was at hand for the Paramount Board. With the QVC hostile bid offering greater value to the Paramount stockholders, the Paramount Board had considerable leverage with Viacom.

At a special meeting on October 24, 1993, the Paramount Board approved the Amended Merger Agreement and an amendment to the Stock Option Agreement. The Amended Merger Agreement was, however, essentially the same as the Original Merger Agreement, except that it included a few new provisions. One provision related to an $80 per share cash tender offer by Viacom for 51 percent of Paramount's stock, and another changed the merger consideration so that each share of Paramount would be converted into 0.20408 shares of Viacom Class A voting stock, 1.08317 shares of Viacom Class B nonvoting stock, and 0.20408 shares of a new series of Viacom convertible preferred stock. The Amended Merger Agreement also added a provision giving Paramount the right not to amend its Rights Agreement to exempt Viacom if the Paramount Board determined that such an amendment would be inconsistent with its fiduciary duties because another offer constituted a "better alternative." Finally, the Paramount Board was given the power to terminate the Amended Merger Agreement if it withdrew its recommendation of the Viacom transaction or recommended a competing transaction.

Although the Amended Merger Agreement offered more consideration to the Paramount stockholders and somewhat more flexibility to the Paramount Board than did the Original Merger Agreement, the defensive measures designed to make a competing bid more difficult were not removed or modified. In particular, there is no evidence in the record that Paramount sought to use its newly-acquired leverage to eliminate or modify the No–Shop Provision, the Termination Fee, or the Stock Option Agreement when the subject of amending the Original Merger Agreement was on the table.

---

5. By November 15, 1993, the value of the Stock Option Agreement had increased to nearly $500 million based on the $90 QVC bid.

Viacom's tender offer commenced on October 25, 1993, and QVC's tender offer was formally launched on October 27, 1993. Diller sent a letter to the Paramount Board on October 28 requesting an opportunity to negotiate with Paramount, and Oresman responded the following day by agreeing to meet. The meeting, held on November 1, was not very fruitful, however, after QVC's proposed guidelines for a "fair bidding process" were rejected by Paramount on the ground that "auction procedures" were inappropriate and contrary to Paramount's contractual obligations to Viacom.

On November 6, 1993, Viacom unilaterally raised its tender offer price to $85 per share in cash and offered a comparable increase in the value of the securities being proposed in the second-step merger. At a telephonic meeting held later that day, the Paramount Board agreed to recommend Viacom's higher bid to Paramount's stockholders.

QVC responded to Viacom's higher bid on November 12 by increasing its tender offer to $90 per share and by increasing the securities for its second-step merger by a similar amount. In response to QVC's latest offer, the Paramount Board scheduled a meeting for November 15, 1993. Prior to the meeting, Oresman sent the members of the Paramount Board a document summarizing the "conditions and uncertainties" of QVC's offer. One director testified that this document gave him a very negative impression of the QVC bid.

At its meeting on November 15, 1993, the Paramount Board determined that the new QVC offer was not in the best interests of the stockholders. The purported basis for this conclusion was that QVC's bid was excessively conditional. The Paramount Board did not communicate with QVC regarding the status of the conditions because it believed that the No–Shop Provision prevented such communication in the absence of firm financing. Several Paramount directors also testified that they believed the Viacom transaction would be more advantageous to Paramount's future business prospects than a QVC transaction.[7] Although a number of materials were distributed to the Paramount Board describing the Viacom and QVC transactions, the only quantitative analysis of the consideration to be received by the stockholders under each proposal was based on then-current market prices of the securities involved, not on the anticipated value of such securities at the time when the stockholders would receive them.[8]

The preliminary injunction hearing in this case took place on November 16, 1993. On November 19, Diller wrote to the Paramount Board to inform it that QVC had obtained financing commitments for its tender

---

7. This belief may have been based on a report prepared by Booz-Allen and distributed to the Paramount Board at its October 24 meeting. The report, which relied on public information regarding QVC, concluded that the synergies of a Paramount–Viacom merger were significantly superior to those of a Paramount–QVC merger. QVC has labelled the Booz–Allen report as a "joke."

8. The market prices of Viacom's and QVC's stock were poor measures of their actual values because such prices constantly fluctuated depending upon which company was perceived to be the more likely to acquire Paramount.

offer and that there was no antitrust obstacle to the offer. On November 24, 1993, the Court of Chancery issued its decision granting a preliminary injunction in favor of QVC and the plaintiff stockholders. This appeal followed.

The General Corporation Law of the State of Delaware (the "General Corporation Law") and the decisions of this Court have repeatedly recognized the fundamental principle that the management of the business and affairs of a Delaware corporation is entrusted to its directors, who are the duly elected and authorized representatives of the stockholders. Under normal circumstances, neither the courts nor the stockholders should interfere with the managerial decisions of the directors. The business judgment rule embodies the deference to which such decisions are entitled.

Nevertheless, there are rare situations which mandate that a court take a more direct and active role in overseeing the decisions made and actions taken by directors. In these situations, a court subjects the directors' conduct to enhanced scrutiny to ensure that it is reasonable. The decisions of this Court have clearly established the circumstances where such enhanced scrutiny will be applied. The case at bar implicates two such circumstances: (1) the approval of a transaction resulting in a sale of control, and (2) the adoption of defensive measures in response to a threat to corporate control.

When a majority of a corporation's voting shares are acquired by a single person or entity, or by a cohesive group acting together, there is a significant diminution in the voting power of those who thereby become minority stockholders. Under the statutory framework of the General Corporation Law, many of the most fundamental corporate changes can be implemented only if they are approved by a majority vote of the stockholders. Such actions include elections of directors, amendments to the certificate of incorporation, mergers, consolidations, sales of all or substantially all of the assets of the corporation, and dissolution. Because of the overriding importance of voting rights, this Court and the Court of Chancery have consistently acted to protect stockholders from unwarranted interference with such rights.

In the absence of devices protecting the minority stockholders,[12] stockholder votes are likely to become mere formalities where there is a majority stockholder. For example, minority stockholders can be deprived of a continuing equity interest in their corporation by means of a cash-out merger. Absent effective protective provisions, minority stockholders must rely for protection solely on the fiduciary duties owed to them by the directors and the majority stockholder, since the minority stockholders have lost the power to influence corporate direction through the ballot.

---

12. Examples of such protective provisions are supermajority voting provisions, majority of the minority requirements, etc. Although we express no opinion on what effect the inclusion of any such stockholder protective devices would have had in this case, we note that this Court has upheld, under different circumstances, the reasonableness of a standstill agreement which limited a 49.9 percent stockholder to 40 percent board representation.

The acquisition of majority status and the consequent privilege of exerting the powers of majority ownership come at a price. That price is usually a control premium which recognizes not only the value of a control block of shares, but also compensates the minority stockholders for their resulting loss of voting power.

In the case before us, the public stockholders (in the aggregate) currently own a majority of Paramount's voting stock. Control of the corporation is not vested in a single person, entity, or group, but vested in the fluid aggregation of unaffiliated stockholders. In the event the Paramount–Viacom transaction is consummated, the public stockholders will receive cash and a minority equity voting position in the surviving corporation. Following such consummation, there will be a controlling stockholder who will have the voting power to: (a) elect directors; (b) cause a break-up of the corporation; (c) merge it with another company; (d) cash-out the public stockholders; (e) amend the certificate of incorporation; (f) sell all or substantially all of the corporate assets; or (g) otherwise alter materially the nature of the corporation and the public stockholders' interests. Irrespective of the present Paramount Board's vision of a long-term strategic alliance with Viacom, the proposed sale of control would provide the new controlling stockholder with the power to alter that vision.

Because of the intended sale of control, the Paramount–Viacom transaction has economic consequences of considerable significance to the Paramount stockholders. Once control has shifted, the current Paramount stockholders will have no leverage in the future to demand another control premium. As a result, the Paramount stockholders are entitled to receive, and should receive, a control premium and/or protective devices of significant value. There being no such protective provisions in the Viacom–Paramount transaction, the Paramount directors had an obligation to take the maximum advantage of the current opportunity to realize for the stockholders the best value reasonably available.

The consequences of a sale of control impose special obligations on the directors of a corporation. In particular, they have the obligation of acting reasonably to seek the transaction offering the best value reasonably available to the stockholders. The courts will apply enhanced scrutiny to ensure that the directors have acted reasonably. The obligations of the directors and the enhanced scrutiny of the courts are well-established by the decisions of this Court. The directors' fiduciary duties in a sale of control context are those which generally attach. In short, "the directors must act in accordance with their fundamental duties of care and loyalty." As we held in *Macmillan:*

> It is basic to our law that the board of directors has the ultimate responsibility for managing the business and affairs of a corporation. In discharging this function, the directors owe fiduciary duties of care and loyalty to the corporation and its shareholders. *This unremitting*

obligation extends equally to board conduct in a sale of corporate control.

559 A.2d at 1280 (emphasis supplied) (citations omitted).

In the sale of control context, the directors must focus on one primary objective—to secure the transaction offering the best value reasonably available for the stockholders—and they must exercise their fiduciary duties to further that end. The decisions of this Court have consistently emphasized this goal. *Revlon,* 506 A.2d at 182 ("The duty of the board ... [is] the maximization of the company's value at a sale for the stockholders' benefit."); *Macmillan,* 559 A.2d at 1288 ("[I]n a sale of corporate control the responsibility of the directors is to get the highest value reasonably attainable for the shareholders."); *Barkan,* 567 A.2d at 1286 ("[T]he board must act in a neutral manner to encourage the highest possible price for shareholders.").

In pursuing this objective, the directors must be especially diligent. *See Citron v. Fairchild Camera and Instrument Corp.,* Del.Supr., 569 A.2d 53, 66 (1989) (discussing "a board's active and direct role in the sale process"). In particular, this Court has stressed the importance of the board being adequately informed in negotiating a sale of control: "The need for adequate information is central to the enlightened evaluation of a transaction that a board must make." *Barkan,* 567 A.2d at 1287. This requirement is consistent with the general principle that "directors have a duty to inform themselves, prior to making a business decision, of all material information reasonably available to them." *Aronson,* 473 A.2d at 812. Moreover, the role of outside, independent directors becomes particularly important because of the magnitude of a sale of control transaction and the possibility, in certain cases, that management may not necessarily be impartial. *See Macmillan,* 559 A.2d at 1285 (requiring "the intense scrutiny and participation of the independent directors").

Barkan teaches some of the methods by which a board can fulfill its obligation to seek the best value reasonably available to the stockholders. These methods are designed to determine the existence and viability of possible alternatives. They include conducting an auction, canvassing the market, etc. Delaware law recognizes that there is "no single blueprint" that directors must follow.

In determining which alternative provides the best value for the stockholders, a board of directors is not limited to considering only the amount of cash involved, and is not required to ignore totally its view of the future value of a strategic alliance. Instead, the directors should analyze the entire situation and evaluate in a disciplined manner the consideration being offered. Where stock or other non-cash consideration is involved, the board should try to quantify its value, if feasible, to achieve an objective comparison of the alternatives.[14] In addition, the

---

14. When assessing the value of non-cash consideration, a board should focus on its value as of the date it will be received by the stockholders. Normally, such value will be determined with the assistance of experts using generally accepted methods of valuation.

board may assess a variety of practical considerations relating to each alternative, including:

> [an offer's] fairness and feasibility; the proposed or actual financing for the offer, and the consequences of that financing; questions of illegality; ... the risk of non-consum[m]ation; ... the bidder's identity, prior background and other business venture experiences; and the bidder's business plans for the corporation and their effects on stockholder interests.

Macmillan, 559 A.2d at 1282 n. 29. These considerations are important because the selection of one alternative may permanently foreclose other opportunities. While the assessment of these factors may be complex, the board's goal is straightforward: Having informed themselves of all material information reasonably available, the directors must decide which alternative is most likely to offer the best value reasonably available to the stockholders.

Board action in the circumstances presented here is subject to enhanced scrutiny. Such scrutiny is mandated by: (a) the threatened diminution of the current stockholders' voting power; (b) the fact that an asset belonging to public stockholders (a control premium) is being sold and may never be available again; and (c) the traditional concern of Delaware courts for actions which impair or impede stockholder voting rights. In *Macmillan,* this Court held:

> When *Revlon* duties devolve upon directors, this Court will continue to exact an enhanced judicial scrutiny at the threshold, as in *Unocal,* before the normal presumptions of the business judgment rule will apply.[15]

559 A.2d at 1288. The *Macmillan* decision articulates a specific two-part test for analyzing board action where competing bidders are not treated equally:[16]

> In the face of disparate treatment, the trial court must first examine whether the directors properly perceived that shareholder interests were enhanced. In any event the board's action must be reasonable in relation to the advantage sought to be achieved, or conversely, to the threat which a particular bid allegedly poses to stockholder interests.

Id. See also Roberts v. General Instrument Corp., Del.Ch., C.A. No. 11639, 1990 WL 118356, Allen, C. (Aug. 13, 1990) ("This enhanced test requires a judicial judgment of reasonableness in the circumstances.").

The key features of an enhanced scrutiny test are: (a) a judicial determination regarding the adequacy of the decisionmaking process em-

---

15.   Because the Paramount Board acted unreasonably as to process and result in this sale of control situation, the business judgment rule did not become operative.

16.   Before this test is invoked, "the plaintiff must show, and the trial court must find, that the directors of the target company treated one or more of the respective bidders on unequal terms." *Macmillan,* 559 A.2d at 1288.

ployed by the directors, including the information on which the directors based their decision; and (b) a judicial examination of the reasonableness of the directors' action in light of the circumstances then existing. The directors have the burden of proving that they were adequately informed and acted reasonably.

Although an enhanced scrutiny test involves a review of the reasonableness of the substantive merits of a board's actions,[17] a court should not ignore the complexity of the directors' task in a sale of control. There are many business and financial considerations implicated in investigating and selecting the best value reasonably available. The board of directors is the corporate decisionmaking body best equipped to make these judgments. Accordingly, a court applying enhanced judicial scrutiny should be deciding whether the directors made *a reasonable* decision, not *a perfect* decision. If a board selected one of several reasonable alternatives, a court should not second-guess that choice even though it might have decided otherwise or subsequent events may have cast doubt on the board's determination. Thus, courts will not substitute their business judgment for that of the directors, but will determine if the directors' decision was, on balance, within a range of reasonableness.

The Paramount defendants and Viacom assert that the fiduciary obligations and the enhanced judicial scrutiny discussed above are not implicated in this case in the absence of a "break-up" of the corporation, and that the order granting the preliminary injunction should be reversed. This argument is based on their erroneous interpretation of our decisions in *Revlon* and *Time–Warner*.

In *Revlon*, we reviewed the actions of the board of directors of Revlon, Inc. ("Revlon"), which had rebuffed the overtures of Pantry Pride, Inc. and had instead entered into an agreement with Forstmann Little & Co. ("Forstmann") providing for the acquisition of 100 percent of Revlon's outstanding stock by Forstmann and the subsequent break-up of Revlon. Based on the facts and circumstances present in *Revlon*, we held that "[t]he directors' role changed from defenders of the corporate bastion to auctioneers charged with getting the best price for the stockholders at a sale of the company." We further held that "when a board ends an intense bidding contest on an insubstantial basis, ... [that] action cannot withstand the enhanced scrutiny which *Unocal* requires of director conduct."

It is true that one of the circumstances bearing on these holdings was the fact that "the break-up of the company ... had become a reality which even the directors embraced." It does not follow, however, that a "break-up" must be present and "inevitable" before directors are subject

---

17. It is to be remembered that, in cases where the traditional business judgment rule is applicable and the board acted with due care, in good faith, and in the honest belief that they are acting in the best interests of the stockholders (which is not this case), the Court gives great deference to the substance of the directors' decision and will not invalidate the decision, will not examine its reasonableness, and "will not substitute our views for those of the board if the latter's decision can be 'attributed to any rational business purpose.'" *Unocal*, 493 A.2d at 949 (*quoting Sinclair Oil Corp. v. Levien*, Del.Supr., 280 A.2d 717, 720 (1971)). *See Aronson*, 473 A.2d at 812.

to enhanced judicial scrutiny and are required to pursue a transaction that is calculated to produce the best value reasonably available to the stock-holders. In fact, we stated in *Revlon* that "when bidders make relatively similar offers, or dissolution of the company becomes inevitable, the directors cannot fulfill their enhanced *Unocal* duties by playing favorites with the contending factions." *Revlon* thus does not hold that an inevit-able dissolution or "break-up" is necessary.

The decisions of this Court following *Revlon* reinforced the applicabili-ty of enhanced scrutiny and the directors' obligation to seek the best value reasonably available for the stockholders where there is a pending sale of control, regardless of whether or not there is to be a break-up of the corporation. In *Macmillan,* this Court held:

> We stated in *Revlon*, and again here, that *in a sale of corporate control* the responsibility of the directors is to get the highest value reason-ably attainable for the shareholders.

559 A.2d at 1288 (emphasis added). In *Barkan,* we observed further:

> We believe that the general principles announced in *Revlon*, in *Unocal Corp. v. Mesa Petroleum Co.,* Del.Supr., 493 A.2d 946 (1985), and in *Moran v. Household International, Inc.,* Del.Supr., 500 A.2d 1346 (1985) govern this case and every case in which a *fundamental change of corporate control* occurs or is contemplated.

567 A.2d at 1286 (emphasis added).

Although *Macmillan* and *Barkan* are clear in holding that a change of control imposes on directors the obligation to obtain the best value reasonably available to the stockholders, the Paramount defendants have interpreted our decision in *Time–Warner* as requiring a corporate break-up in order for that obligation to apply. The facts in *Time–Warner,* however, were quite different from the facts of this case, and refute Paramount's position here. In *Time–Warner,* the Chancellor held that there was no change of control in the original stock-for-stock merger between Time and Warner because Time would be owned by a fluid aggregation of unaffiliated stockholders both before and after the merger:

> If the appropriate inquiry is whether a change in control is contemplated, the answer must be sought in the specific circum-stances surrounding the transaction. Surely under some circum-stances a stock for stock merger could reflect a transfer of corporate control. That would, for example, plainly be the case here if Warner were a private company. But where, as here, the shares of both constituent corporations are widely held, corporate control can be expected to remain unaffected by a stock for stock merger. This in my judgment was the situation with respect to the original merger agreement. When the specifics of that situation are reviewed, it is seen that, aside from legal technicalities and aside from arrangements thought to enhance the prospect for the ultimate succession of [Nich-olas J. Nicholas, Jr., president of Time], neither corporation could be

said to be acquiring the other. *Control of both remained in a large, fluid, changeable and changing market.*

The existence of a control block of stock in the hands of a single shareholder or a group with loyalty to each other does have real consequences to the financial value of "minority" stock. The law offers some protection to such shares through the imposition of a fiduciary duty upon controlling shareholders. *But here, effectuation of the merger would not have subjected Time shareholders to the risks and consequences of holders of minority shares. This is a reflection of the fact that no control passed to anyone in the transaction contemplated.* The shareholders of Time would have "suffered" dilution, of course, but they would suffer the same type of dilution upon the public distribution of new stock.

Paramount Communications Inc. v. Time Inc., Del.Ch., No. 10866, 1989 WL 79880, Allen, C. (July 17, 1989). Moreover, the transaction actually consummated in *Time-Warner* was not a merger, as originally planned, but a sale of Warner's stock to Time.

In our affirmance of the Court of Chancery's well-reasoned decision, this Court held that "The Chancellor's findings of fact are supported by the record and *his conclusion is correct as a matter of law.*" Nevertheless, the Paramount defendants here have argued that a break-up is a requirement and have focused on the following language in our *Time–Warner* decision:

> However, we premise our rejection of plaintiffs' *Revlon* claim on different grounds, namely, the absence of any substantial evidence to conclude that Time's board, in negotiating with Warner, made the dissolution or break-up of the corporate entity inevitable, as was the case in *Revlon.*

> Under Delaware law there are, generally speaking and *without excluding other possibilities,* two circumstances which may implicate *Revlon* duties. The first, and clearer one, is when a corporation *initiates an active bidding process seeking to sell itself* or to effect a business reorganization involving a clear break-up of the company. However, *Revlon* duties may also be triggered where, in response to a bidder's offer, a target abandons its long-term strategy and seeks an alternative transaction involving the breakup of the company.

The Paramount defendants have misread the holding of *Time–Warner.* Contrary to their argument, our decision in *Time–Warner* expressly states that the two general scenarios discussed in the above-quoted paragraph are not the *only* instances where "*Revlon* duties" may be implicated. The Paramount defendants' argument totally ignores the phrase "without excluding other possibilities." Moreover, the instant case is clearly within the first general scenario set forth in *Time-Warner.* The Paramount Board, albeit unintentionally, had "initiate[d] an active bidding process seeking to sell itself" by agreeing to sell control of the corporation to Viacom in circumstances where another potential acquiror (QVC) was equally interested in being a bidder.

The Paramount defendants' position that *both* a change of control *and* a break-up are *required* must be rejected. Such a holding would unduly restrict the application of *Revlon,* is inconsistent with this Court's decisions in *Barkan* and *Macmillan,* and has no basis in policy. There are few events that have a more significant impact on the stockholders than a sale of control or a corporate break-up. Each event represents a fundamental (and perhaps irrevocable) change in the nature of the corporate enterprise from a practical standpoint. It is the significance of *each* of these events that justifies: (a) focusing on the directors' obligation to seek the best value reasonably available to the stockholders; and (b) requiring a close scrutiny of board action which could be contrary to the stockholders' interests.

Accordingly, when a corporation undertakes a transaction which will cause: (a) a change in corporate control; *or* (b) a break-up of the corporate entity, the directors' obligation is to seek the best value reasonably available to the stockholders. This obligation arises because the effect of the Viacom–Paramount transaction, if consummated, is to shift control of Paramount from the public stockholders to a controlling stockholder, Viacom. Neither *Time–Warner* nor any other decision of this Court holds that a "break-up" of the company is essential to give rise to this obligation where there is a sale of control.

We now turn to duties of the Paramount Board under the facts of this case and our conclusions as to the breaches of those duties which warrant injunctive relief.

Under the facts of this case, the Paramount directors had the obligation: (a) to be diligent and vigilant in examining critically the Paramount–Viacom transaction and the QVC tender offers; (b) to act in good faith; (c) to obtain, and act with due care on, all material information reasonably available, including information necessary to compare the two offers to determine which of these transactions, or an alternative course of action, would provide the best value reasonably available to the stockholders; and (d) to negotiate actively and in good faith with both Viacom and QVC to that end.

Having decided to sell control of the corporation, the Paramount directors were required to evaluate critically whether or not all material aspects of the Paramount–Viacom transaction (separately and in the aggregate) were reasonable and in the best interests of the Paramount stockholders in light of current circumstances, including: the change of control premium, the Stock Option Agreement, the Termination Fee, the coercive nature of both the Viacom and QVC tender offers,[18] the No–Shop

---

18. Both the Viacom and the QVC tender offers were for 51 percent cash and a "back-end" of various securities, the value of each of which depended on the fluctuating value of Viacom and QVC stock at any given time. Thus, both tender offers were two-tiered, front-end loaded, and

Provision, and the proposed disparate use of the Rights Agreement as to the Viacom and QVC tender offers, respectively.

These obligations necessarily implicated various issues, including the questions of whether or not those provisions and other aspects of the Paramount–Viacom transaction (separately and in the aggregate): (a) adversely affected the value provided to the Paramount stockholders; (b) inhibited or encouraged alternative bids; (c) were enforceable contractual obligations in light of the directors' fiduciary duties; and (d) in the end would advance or retard the Paramount directors' obligation to secure for the Paramount stockholders the best value reasonably available under the circumstances.

The Paramount defendants contend that they were precluded by certain contractual provisions, including the No–Shop Provision, from negotiating with QVC or seeking alternatives. Such provisions, whether or not they are presumptively valid in the abstract, may not validly define or limit the directors' fiduciary duties under Delaware law or prevent the Paramount directors from carrying out their fiduciary duties under Delaware law. To the extent such provisions are inconsistent with those duties, they are invalid and unenforceable. *See Revlon,* 506 A.2d at 184–85.

Since the Paramount directors had already decided to sell control, they had an obligation to continue their search for the best value reasonably available to the stockholders. This continuing obligation included the responsibility, at the October 24 board meeting and thereafter, to evaluate critically both the QVC tender offers and the Paramount–Viacom transaction to determine if: (a) the QVC tender offer was, or would continue to be, conditional; (b) the QVC tender offer could be improved; (c) the Viacom tender offer or other aspects of the Paramount–Viacom transaction could be improved; (d) each of the respective offers would be reasonably likely to come to closure, and under what circumstances; (e) other material information was reasonably available for consideration by the Paramount directors; (f) there were viable and realistic alternative courses of action; and (g) the timing constraints could be managed so the directors could consider these matters carefully and deliberately.

The Paramount directors made the decision on September 12, 1993, that, in their judgment, a strategic merger with Viacom on the economic terms of the Original Merger Agreement was in the best interests of Paramount and its stockholders. Those terms provided a modest change of control premium to the stockholders. The directors also decided at that time that it was appropriate to agree to certain defensive measures (the Stock Option Agreement, the Termination Fee, and the No–Shop Provision) insisted upon by Viacom as part of that economic transaction. Those defensive measures, coupled with the sale of control and subsequent disparate treatment of competing bidders, implicated the judicial scrutiny of *Unocal, Revlon, Macmillan,* and their progeny. We conclude that the

---

coercive. Such coercive offers are inherently problematic and should be expected to receive particularly careful analysis by a target board.

Paramount directors' process was not reasonable, and the result achieved for the stockholders was not reasonable under the circumstances.

When entering into the Original Merger Agreement, and thereafter, the Paramount Board clearly gave insufficient attention to the potential consequences of the defensive measures demanded by Viacom. The Stock Option Agreement had a number of unusual and potentially "draconian" provisions, including the Note Feature and the Put Feature. Furthermore, the Termination Fee, whether or not unreasonable by itself, clearly made Paramount less attractive to other bidders, when coupled with the Stock Option Agreement. Finally, the No–Shop Provision inhibited the Paramount Board's ability to negotiate with other potential bidders, particularly QVC which had already expressed an interest in Paramount.[20]

Throughout the applicable time period, and especially from the first QVC merger proposal on September 20 through the Paramount Board meeting on November 15, QVC's interest in Paramount provided the *opportunity* for the Paramount Board to seek significantly higher value for the Paramount stockholders than that being offered by Viacom. QVC persistently demonstrated its intention to meet and exceed the Viacom offers, and frequently expressed its willingness to negotiate possible further increases.

The Paramount directors had the opportunity in the October 23–24 time frame, when the Original Merger Agreement was renegotiated, to take appropriate action to modify the improper defensive measures as well as to improve the economic terms of the Paramount–Viacom transaction. Under the circumstances existing at that time, it should have been clear to the Paramount Board that the Stock Option Agreement, coupled with the Termination Fee and the No–Shop Clause, were impeding the realization of the best value reasonably available to the Paramount stockholders. Nevertheless, the Paramount Board made no effort to eliminate or modify these counterproductive devices, and instead continued to cling to its vision of a strategic alliance with Viacom. Moreover, based on advice from the Paramount management, the Paramount directors considered the QVC offer to be "conditional" and asserted that they were precluded by the No-Shop Provision from seeking more information from, or negotiating with, QVC.

By November 12, 1993, the value of the revised QVC offer on its face exceeded that of the Viacom offer by over $1 billion at then current values. This significant disparity of value cannot be justified on the basis

---

20. We express no opinion whether certain aspects of the No–Shop Provision here could be valid in another context. Whether or not it could validly have operated here at an early stage solely to prevent Paramount from actively "shopping" the company, it could not prevent the Paramount directors from carrying out their fiduciary duties in considering unsolicited bids or in negotiating for the best value reasonably available to the stockholders. *Macmillan*, 559 A.2d at 1287. As we said in *Barkan:* "Where a board has no reasonable basis upon which to judge the adequacy of a contemplated transaction, a no-shop restriction gives rise to the inference that the board seeks to forestall competing bids." 567 A.2d at 1288. *See also Revlon*, 506 A.2d at 184 (holding that "[t]he no-shop provision, like the lock-up option, while not *per se* illegal, is impermissible under the *Unocal* standards when a board's primary duty becomes that of an auctioneer responsible for selling the company to the highest bidder").

of the directors' vision of future strategy, primarily because the change of control would supplant the authority of the current Paramount Board to continue to hold and implement their strategic vision in any meaningful way. Moreover, their uninformed process had deprived their strategic vision of much of its credibility.

When the Paramount directors met on November 15 to consider QVC's increased tender offer, they remained prisoners of their own misconceptions and missed opportunities to eliminate the restrictions they had imposed on themselves. Yet, it was not "too late" to reconsider negotiating with QVC. The circumstances existing on November 15 made it clear that the defensive measures, taken as a whole, were problematic: (a) the No–Shop Provision could not define or limit their fiduciary duties; (b) the Stock Option Agreement had become "draconian"; and (c) the Termination Fee, in context with all the circumstances, was similarly deterring the realization of possibly higher bids. Nevertheless, the Paramount directors remained paralyzed by their uninformed belief that the QVC offer was "illusory." This final opportunity to negotiate on the stockholders' behalf and to fulfill their obligation to seek the best value reasonably available was thereby squandered.

Viacom argues that it had certain "vested" contract rights with respect to the No–Shop Provision and the Stock Option Agreement.[22] In effect, Viacom's argument is that the Paramount directors could enter into an agreement in violation of their fiduciary duties and then render Paramount, and ultimately its stockholders, liable for failing to carry out an agreement in violation of those duties. Viacom's protestations about vested rights are without merit. This Court has found that those defensive measures were improperly designed to deter potential bidders, and that such measures do not meet the reasonableness test to which they must be subjected. They are consequently invalid and unenforceable under the facts of this case.

The No–Shop Provision could not validly define or limit the fiduciary duties of the Paramount directors. To the extent that a contract, or a provision thereof, purports to require a board to act or not act in such a fashion as to limit the exercise of fiduciary duties, it is invalid and unenforceable. Despite the arguments of Paramount and Viacom to the contrary, the Paramount directors could not contract away their fiduciary obligations. Since the No-Shop Provision was invalid, Viacom never had any vested contract rights in the provision.

As discussed previously, the Stock Option Agreement contained several "draconian" aspects, including the Note Feature and the Put Feature. While we have held that lock-up options are not *per se* illegal, no options with similar features have ever been upheld by this Court. Under the circumstances of this case, the Stock Option Agreement clearly is invalid.

---

22. Presumably this argument would have included the Termination Fee had the Vice Chancellor invalidated that provision or if appellees had cross-appealed from the Vice Chancellor's refusal to invalidate that provision.

Accordingly, Viacom never had any vested contract rights in that Agreement.

Viacom, a sophisticated party with experienced legal and financial advisors, knew of (and in fact demanded) the unreasonable features of the Stock Option Agreement. It cannot be now heard to argue that it obtained vested contract rights by negotiating and obtaining contractual provisions from a board acting in violation of its fiduciary duties. As the Nebraska Supreme Court said in rejecting a similar argument in *ConAgra, Inc. v. Cargill, Inc.*, 222 Neb. 136, 382 N.W.2d 576, 587–88 (1986), "To so hold, it would seem, would be to get the shareholders coming and going." Likewise, we reject Viacom's arguments and hold that its fate must rise or fall, and in this instance fall, with the determination that the actions of the Paramount Board were invalid.

The realization of the best value reasonably available to the stockholders became the Paramount directors' primary obligation under these facts in light of the change of control. That obligation was not satisfied, and the Paramount Board's process was deficient. The directors' initial hope and expectation for a strategic alliance with Viacom was allowed to dominate their decisionmaking process to the point where the arsenal of defensive measures established at the outset was perpetuated (not modified or eliminated) when the situation was dramatically altered. QVC's unsolicited bid presented the opportunity for significantly greater value for the stockholders and enhanced negotiating leverage for the directors. Rather than seizing those opportunities, the Paramount directors chose to wall themselves off from material information which was reasonably available and to hide behind the defensive measures as a rationalization for refusing to negotiate with QVC or seeking other alternatives. Their view of the strategic alliance likewise became an empty rationalization as the opportunities for higher value for the stockholders continued to develop.

It is the nature of the judicial process that we decide only the case before us—a case which, on its facts, is clearly controlled by established Delaware law. Here, the proposed change of control and the implications thereof were crystal clear. In other cases they may be less clear. The holding of this case on its facts, coupled with the holdings of the principal cases discussed herein where the issue of sale of control is implicated, should provide a workable precedent against which to measure future cases.

For the reasons set forth herein, the November 24, 1993, Order of the Court of Chancery has been AFFIRMED, and this matter has been REMANDED for proceedings consistent herewith, as set forth in the December 9, 1993, Order of this Court.

UNITRIN, INC. v. AMERICAN GENERAL CORP.

651 A.2d 1361 (Del.1995).

HOLLAND, JUSTICE.

This is an appeal from the Court of Chancery's entry of a preliminary injunction on October 13, 1994, upon plaintiffs' motions in two actions: American General Corporation's ("American General") suit against Unitrin, Inc. ("Unitrin") and its directors; and a parallel class action brought by Unitrin stockholders. An interlocutory appeal was certified by the Court of Chancery on October 24, 1994. This Court accepted the appeal on October 27, 1994. * * *

American General, which had publicly announced a proposal to merge with Unitrin for $2.6 billion at $50–3/8 per share, and certain Unitrin shareholder plaintiffs, filed suit in the Court of Chancery, *inter alia,* to enjoin Unitrin from repurchasing up to 10 million shares of its own stock (the "Repurchase Program"). On August 26, 1994, the Court of Chancery temporarily restrained Unitrin from making any further repurchases. After expedited discovery, briefing and argument, the Court of Chancery preliminarily enjoined Unitrin from making further repurchases on the ground that the Repurchase Program was a disproportionate response to the threat posed by American General's inadequate all cash for all shares offer, under the standard of this Court's holding in *Unocal Corp. v. Mesa Petroleum Co.,* Del.Supr., 493 A.2d 946 (1985)("*Unocal*"). * * *

American General is the largest provider of home service insurance. On July 12, 1994, it made a merger proposal to acquire Unitrin for $2.6 billion at $50–3/8 per share. Following a public announcement of this proposal, Unitrin shareholders filed suit seeking to compel a sale of the company. American General filed suit to enjoin Unitrin's Repurchase Program.

Unitrin is also in the insurance business. It is the third largest provider of home service insurance. The other defendants-appellants are the members of Unitrin's seven person Board of Directors (the "Unitrin Board" or "Board"). Two directors are employees, Richard C. Vie ("Vie"), the Chief Executive Officer, and Jerrold V. Jerome ("Jerome"), Chairman of the Board. The five remaining directors are not and have never been employed by Unitrin. * * *

The record reflects that the non-employee directors each receive a fixed annual fee of $30,000. They receive no other significant financial benefit from serving as directors. At the offering price proposed by American General, the value of Unitrin's non-employee directors' stock exceeded $450 million.

In January 1994, James Tuerff ("Tuerff"), the President of American General, met with Richard Vie, Unitrin's Chief Executive Officer. Tuerff advised Vie that American General was considering acquiring other companies. Unitrin was apparently at or near the top of its list. Tuerff did not mention any terms for a potential acquisition of Unitrin. Vie replied that Unitrin had excellent prospects as an independent company and had never considered a merger. Vie indicated to Tuerff that Unitrin was not for sale.

According to Vie, he reported his conversation with Tuerff at the next meeting of the Unitrin Board in February 1994. The minutes of the full Board meeting do not reflect a discussion of Tuerff's proposition. Nevertheless, the parties agree that the Board's position in February was that Unitrin was not for sale. It was unnecessary to respond to American General because no offer had been made.

On July 12, 1994, American General sent a letter to Vie proposing a consensual merger transaction in which it would "purchase all of Unitrin's 51.8 million outstanding shares of common stock for $50–3/8 per share, in cash" (the "Offer"). The Offer was conditioned on the development of a merger agreement and regulatory approval. The Offer price represented a 30% premium over the market price of Unitrin's shares. In the Offer, American General stated that it "would consider offering a higher price" if "Unitrin could demonstrate additional value." American General also offered to consider tax-free "[a]lternatives to an all cash transaction."

Upon receiving the American General Offer, the Unitrin Board's Executive Committee (Singleton, Vie, and Jerome) engaged legal counsel and scheduled a telephonic Board meeting for July 18. At the July 18 special meeting, the Board reviewed the terms of the Offer. The Board was advised that the existing charter and bylaw provisions might not effectively deter all types of takeover strategies. It was suggested that the Board consider adopting a shareholder rights plan and an advance notice provision for shareholder proposals.

The Unitrin Board met next on July 25, 1994 in Los Angeles for seven hours. All directors attended the meeting. The principal purpose of the meeting was to discuss American General's Offer.

Vie reviewed Unitrin's financial condition and its ongoing business strategies. The Board also received a presentation from its investment advisor, Morgan Stanley & Co. ("Morgan Stanley"), regarding the financial adequacy of American General's proposal. Morgan Stanley expressed its opinion that the Offer was financially inadequate.[4] Legal counsel expressed concern that the combination of Unitrin and American General would raise antitrust complications due to the resultant decrease in competition in the home service insurance markets.

The Unitrin Board unanimously concluded that the American General merger proposal was not in the best interests of Unitrin's shareholders and voted to reject the Offer. The Board then received advice from its legal and financial advisors about a number of possible defensive measures it might adopt, including a shareholder rights plan ("poison pill") and an

---

4. Eric Daut, who prepared these materials for Morgan Stanley under extreme time pressure, had never prepared such information previously and did not rely on firm figures. Morgan Stanley, in turn, did not investigate these figures.

advance notice bylaw provision for shareholder proposals. Because the Board apparently thought that American General intended to keep its Offer private, the Board did not implement any defensive measures at that time.

On July 26, 1994, Vie faxed a letter to Tuerff, rejecting American General's Offer. * * *

On August 2, 1994, American General issued a press release announcing its Offer to Unitrin's Board to purchase all of Unitrin's stock for $50–3/8 per share. The press release also noted that the Board had rejected American General's Offer. After that public announcement, the trading volume and market price of Unitrin's stock increased.

At its regularly scheduled meeting on August 3, the Unitrin Board discussed the effects of American General's press release. The Board noted that the market reaction to the announcement suggested that speculative traders or arbitrageurs were acquiring Unitrin stock. The Board determined that American General's public announcement constituted a hostile act designed to coerce the sale of Unitrin at an inadequate price. The Board unanimously approved the poison pill and the proposed advance notice bylaw that it had considered previously.

Beginning on August 2 and continuing through August 12, 1994, Unitrin issued a series of press releases to inform its shareholders and the public market: first, that the Unitrin Board believed Unitrin's stock was worth more than the $50–3/8 American General offered; second, that the Board felt that the price of American General's Offer did not reflect Unitrin's long term business prospects as an independent company; third, that "the true value of Unitrin [was] not reflected in the [then] current market price of its common stock," and that because of its strong financial position, Unitrin was well positioned "to pursue strategic and financial opportunities;" fourth, that the Board believed a merger with American General would have anticompetitive effects and might violate antitrust laws and various state regulatory statutes; and fifth, that the Board had adopted a shareholder rights plan (poison pill) to guard against undesirable takeover efforts.

The Unitrin Board met again on August 11, 1994. The minutes of that meeting indicate that its principal purpose was to consider the Repurchase Program. At the Board's request, Morgan Stanley had prepared written materials to distribute to each of the directors. Morgan Stanley gave a presentation in which alternative means of implementing the Repurchase Program were explained. Morgan Stanley recommended that the Board implement an open market stock repurchase. The Board voted to authorize the Repurchase Program for up to ten million shares of its outstanding stock.

On August 12, Unitrin publicly announced the Repurchase Program. The Unitrin Board expressed its belief that "Unitrin's stock is undervalued in the market and that the expanded program will tend to increase the value of the shares that remain outstanding." The announcement also stated that the director stockholders were not participating in the Repurchase Program, and that the repurchases "will increase the percentage ownership of those stockholders who choose not to sell."

Unitrin's August 12 press release also stated that the directors owned 23% of Unitrin's stock, that the Repurchase Program would cause that percentage to increase, and that Unitrin's certificate of incorporation included a supermajority voting provision. The following language from a July 22 draft press release revealing the antitakeover effects of the Repurchase Program was omitted from the final press release.

> Under the [supermajority provision], the consummation of the expanded repurchase program would enhance the ability of nonselling stockholders, including the directors, to prevent a merger with a greater-than–15% stockholder if they did not favor the transaction.

Unitrin sent a letter to its stockholders on August 17 regarding the Repurchase Program which stated:

> Your Board of Directors has authorized the Company to repurchase, in the open market or in private transactions, up to 10 million of Unitrin's 51.8 million outstanding common shares. This authorization is intended to provide an additional measure of liquidity to the Company's shareholders in light of the unsettled market conditions resulting from American General's unsolicited acquisition proposal. The Board believes that the Company's stock is undervalued and that this program will tend to increase the value of the shares that remain outstanding.

Between August 12 and noon on August 24, Morgan Stanley purchased nearly 5 million of Unitrin's shares on Unitrin's behalf. The average price paid was slightly above American General's Offer price. * * *

The Court of Chancery held that all of the Unitrin Board's defensive actions merited judicial scrutiny according to *Unocal*. The record supports the Court of Chancery's determination that the Board perceived American General's Offer as a threat and adopted the Repurchase Program, along with the poison pill and advance notice bylaw, as defensive measures in response to that threat. Therefore, the Court of Chancery properly concluded the facts before it required an application of *Unocal* and its progeny. The evolution of that jurisprudence is didactic.

The business judgment rule applies to the conduct of directors in the context of a takeover. The business judgment rule is a "presumption that in making a business decision the directors of a corporation acted on an informed basis, in good faith and in the honest belief that the action taken was in the best interests of the company." *Aronson v. Lewis*, 473 A.2d at 812. An application of the traditional business judgment rule places the burden on the "party challenging the [board's] decision to establish facts rebutting the presumption." *Id.* If the business judgment rule is not rebutted, a "court will not substitute its judgment for that of the board if the [board's] decision can be 'attributed to any rational business purpose.' " *Unocal,* 493 A.2d at 954 (citation omitted).

In *Unocal,* this Court reaffirmed "the application of the business judgment rule in the context of a hostile battle for control of a Delaware corporation where board action is taken to the exclusion of, or in limitation upon, a valid stockholder vote." *Stroud v. Grace,* 606 A.2d at 82.

The enhanced judicial scrutiny mandated by *Unocal* is not intended to lead to a structured, mechanistic, mathematical exercise.[13] Conversely, it is not intended to be an abstract theory. The *Unocal* standard is a flexible paradigm that jurists can apply to the myriad of "fact scenarios" that confront corporate boards.

The correct analytical framework is essential to a proper review of challenges to the decision-making process of a corporate Board. The ultimate question in applying the *Unocal* standard is: what deference should the reviewing court give "to the decisions of directors in defending against a takeover?" E. Norman Veasey, *The New Incarnation of the Business Judgment Rule in Takeover Defenses,* 11 Del. J. Corp.L. 503, 504–05 (1986). The question is usually presented to the Court of Chancery, as in the present case, in an injunction proceeding, a posture which is known as "transactional justification." *Id.* To answer the question, the enhanced judicial scrutiny *Unocal* requires implicates both the substantive and procedural nature of the business judgment rule.

The business judgment rule has traditionally operated to shield directors from personal liability arising out of completed actions involving operational issues. *Id.* When the business judgment rule is applied to defend directors against personal liability, as in a derivative suit, the plaintiff has the initial burden of proof and the ultimate burden of persuasion. In such cases, the business judgment rule shields directors from personal liability if, upon review, the court concludes the directors' decision can be attributed to any rational business purpose. *See Sinclair Oil Corp. v. Levien,* Del.Supr., 280 A.2d 717, 720 (1971).

Conversely, in transactional justification cases involving the adoption of defenses to takeovers, the director's actions invariably implicate issues affecting stockholder rights. In transactional justification cases, the di-

---

13. Efforts to relate *Unocal*'s inherently qualitative proportionality test to a quantitative formula have demonstrated the fallacy of such an exercise, *e.g.,* the reasonableness test:

the reasonableness test requires a court to engage in a "calculus" of harms: a factual determination of what course of action is in the shareholders' best interests. Set forth in terms of an equation, an antitakeover device is in the shareholders' best interests if

$$(FV-TP)(pFV)-(TP-SV)(pSV) > 0$$

where "FV" is a "full" value greater than the tender price, "TP" is the tender price, "pFV" is the probability of realizing this "full" value if the antitakeover device is maintained, "SV" is the subsequent value of the target's stock if the directors have not realized the "full" value and the tender offer is withdrawn or revised downwards, and "pSV" is the probability that SV shall occur. The only factor in the reasonableness equation which is precisely known is TP; the value of the other quantities may only be approximated.

George H. Kanter, Comment, *Judicial Review of Antitakeover Devices Employed in the Noncoercive Tender Offer Context: Making Sense of the Unocal Test,* 138 U.Pa.L.Rev., 225, 254–55 (1989) (footnote omitted).

rectors' decision is reviewed judicially and the burden of going forward is placed on the directors. *See* Joseph Hinsey, IV, *Business Judgment and the American Law Institute's Corporate Governance Project: the Rule, the Doctrine and the Reality,* 52 Geo.Wash.L.Rev., 609, 611–13 (1984). If the directors' actions withstand *Unocal's* reasonableness and proportionality review, the traditional business judgment rule is applied to shield the directors' defensive decision rather than the directors themselves. *Id.*

The litigation between Unitrin, American General, and the Unitrin shareholders in the Court of Chancery is a classic example of a transactional justification case. The Court of Chancery's determination that the conduct of Unitrin's Board was subject to *Unocal's* enhanced judicial scrutiny required it to evaluate each party's ability to sustain its unique burden in the procedural context of a preliminary injunction proceeding. The plaintiff's burden in such a proceeding is to demonstrate a reasonable probability of success after trial.

In general, to effectively defeat the plaintiff's ability to discharge that burden, a board must sustain its burden of demonstrating that, even under *Unocal's* standard of enhanced judicial scrutiny, its actions deserved the protection of the traditional business judgment rule. Thus, the plaintiff's likelihood of success in obtaining a preliminary injunction was initially dependent upon the inability of the Unitrin Board to discharge the burden placed upon it first by *Unocal*. Accordingly, having concluded that the Board's actions were defensive, the Court of Chancery logically began with an evaluation of the Unitrin Board's evidence.

The first aspect of the *Unocal* burden, the reasonableness test, required the Unitrin Board to demonstrate that, after a reasonable investigation, it determined in good faith, that American General's Offer presented a threat to Unitrin that warranted a defensive response. This Court has held that the presence of a majority of outside independent directors will materially enhance such evidence. An "outside" director has been defined as a non-employee and non-management director, (*e.g.,* Unitrin argues, five members of its seven-person Board). Independence "means that a director's decision is based on the corporate merits of the subject before the board rather than extraneous considerations or influences."

The Unitrin Board identified two dangers it perceived the American General Offer posed: inadequate price and antitrust complications. The Court of Chancery characterized the Board's concern that American General's proposed transaction could never be consummated because it may violate antitrust laws and state insurance regulations as a "makeweight excuse" for the defensive measure. It determined, however, that the Board reasonably believed that the American General Offer was inadequate and also reasonably concluded that the Offer was a threat to Unitrin's uninformed stockholders.

The Court of Chancery held that the Board's evidence satisfied the first aspect or reasonableness test under *Unocal*. The Court of Chancery then noted, however, that the threat to the Unitrin stockholders from American General's inadequate opening bid was "mild," because the Offer was negotiable both in price and structure.[16] The court then properly turned its attention to *Unocal's* second aspect, the proportionality test because "[i]t is not until both parts of the *Unocal* inquiry have been satisfied that the business judgment rule attaches to defensive actions of a board of directors." *Paramount Communications, Inc. v. Time, Inc.,* 571 A.2d at 1154.

The second aspect or proportionality test of the initial *Unocal* burden required the Unitrin Board to demonstrate the proportionality of its response to the threat American General's Offer posed. The record reflects that the Unitrin Board considered three options as defensive measures: the poison pill, the advance notice bylaw, and the Repurchase Program. The Unitrin Board did not act on any of these options on July 25.

On August 2, American General made a public announcement of its offer to buy all the shares of Unitrin for $2.6 billion at $50–3/8 per share. The Unitrin Board had already concluded that the American General offer was inadequate. It also apparently feared that its stockholders did not realize that the long term value of Unitrin was not reflected in the market price of its stock.

On August 3, the Board met to decide whether any defensive action was necessary. The Unitrin Board decided to adopt defensive measures to protect Unitrin's stockholders from the inadequate American General Offer in two stages: first, it passed the poison pill and the advance notice bylaw; and, a week later, it implemented the Repurchase Program. * * *

With regard to the second aspect or proportionality test of the initial *Unocal* burden, the Court of Chancery analyzed each stage of the Unitrin Board's defensive responses separately. Although the Court of Chancery characterized Unitrin's antitrust concerns as "makeweight," it acknowledged that the directors of a Delaware corporation have the prerogative to determine that the market undervalues its stock and to protect its stockholders from offers that do not reflect the long term value of the corporation under its present management plan. *Paramount Communications, Inc. v. Time, Inc.,* 571 A.2d at 1153. The Court of Chancery concluded that Unitrin's Board believed in good faith that the American General Offer was inadequate and properly employed a poison pill as a proportionate defensive response to protect its stockholders from a "low ball" bid.

No cross-appeal was filed in this expedited interlocutory proceeding. Therefore, the Court of Chancery's ruling that the Unitrin Board's adoption of a poison pill was a proportionate response to American General's Offer is not now directly at issue. Nevertheless, to the extent the Unitrin

---

16. A board's response to an offer to merge is traditionally tested by the business judgment rule since a statutory prerequisite (8 *Del.C.* § 251(b)) to a merger transaction is approval by the Board before any stockholder action. *See Paramount Communications, Inc. v. Time, Inc.,* 571 A.2d at 1142.

Board's prior adoption of the poison pill influenced the Court of Chancery's proportionality review of the Repurchase Program, the Board's adoption of the poison pill is also a factor to be considered on appeal by this Court.

The Court of Chancery did not view either its conclusion that American General's Offer constituted a threat, or its conclusion that the poison pill was a reasonable response to that threat, as requiring it, *a fortiori*, to conclude that the Repurchase Program was also an appropriate response. The Court of Chancery then made two factual findings: first, the Repurchase Program went beyond what was "necessary" to protect the Unitrin stockholders from a "low ball" negotiating strategy; and second, it was designed to keep the decision to combine with American General within the control of the members of the Unitrin Board, as stockholders, under virtually all circumstances. Consequently, the Court of Chancery held that the Unitrin Board failed to demonstrate that the Repurchase Program met the second aspect or proportionality requirement of the initial burden *Unocal* ascribes to a board of directors. * * *

We begin our examination of Unitrin's Repurchase Program mindful of the special import of protecting the shareholder's franchise within *Unocal's* requirement that a defensive response be reasonable and proportionate. For many years the "favored attack of a [corporate] raider was stock acquisition followed by a proxy contest." *Unocal,* 493 A.2d at 957. Some commentators have noted that the recent trend toward tender offers as the preferable alternative to proxy contests appears to be reversing because of the proliferation of sophisticated takeover defenses. Lucian A. Bebchuk & Marcel Kahan, *A Framework for Analyzing Legal Policy Towards Proxy Contests,* 78 Cal.L.Rev. 1071, 1134 (1990). In fact, the same commentators have characterized a return to proxy contests as "the only alternative to hostile takeovers to gain control against the will of the incumbent directors." *Id.*

The Court of Chancery, in the case *sub judice,* was obviously cognizant that the emergence of the "poison pill" as an effective takeover device has resulted in such a remarkable transformation in the market for corporate control that hostile bidders who proceed when such defenses are in place will usually "have to couple proxy contests with tender offers." Joseph A. Grundfest, *Just Vote No: A Minimalist Strategy for Dealing with Barbarians Inside the Gates,* 45 Stan.L.Rev. 857, 858 (1993). The Court of Chancery concluded that Unitrin's adoption of a poison pill was a proportionate response to the threat its Board reasonably perceived from American General's Offer. Nonetheless, the Court of Chancery enjoined the additional defense of the Repurchase Program as disproportionate and "unnecessary."

The record reflects that the Court of Chancery's decision to enjoin the Repurchase Program is attributable to a continuing misunderstanding, i.e., that in conjunction with the longstanding Supermajority Vote provision in the Unitrin charter, the Repurchase Program would operate to provide the director shareholders with a "veto" to preclude a successful proxy contest by American General. The origins of that misunderstanding are three premises that are each without record support. Two of those premises are objective misconceptions and the other is subjective.

The subjective premise was the Court of Chancery's *sua sponte* determination that Unitrin's outside directors, who are also substantial stockholders, would not vote like other stockholders in a proxy contest, *i.e.*, in their own best economic interests. At American General's Offer price, the outside directors held Unitrin shares worth more than $450 million. Consequently, Unitrin argues the stockholder directors had the same interest as other Unitrin stockholders generally, when voting in a proxy contest, to wit: the maximization of the value of their investments.

In rejecting Unitrin's argument, the Court of Chancery stated that the stockholder directors would be "subconsciously" motivated in a proxy contest to vote against otherwise excellent offers which did not include a "price parameter" to compensate them for the loss of the "prestige and perquisites" of membership on Unitrin's Board. The Court of Chancery's subjective determination that the *stockholder directors* of Unitrin would reject an "excellent offer," unless it compensated them for giving up the "prestige and perquisites" of directorship, appears to be subjective and without record support. It cannot be presumed.

It must be the subject of proof that the Unitrin directors' objective in the Repurchase Program was to forego the opportunity to sell their stock at a premium. In particular, it cannot be presumed that the prestige and perquisites of holding a director's office or a motive to strengthen collective power prevails over a stockholder-director's economic interest. Even the shareholder-plaintiffs in this case agree with the legal proposition Unitrin advocates on appeal: stockholders are presumed to act in their own best economic interests when they vote in a proxy contest.

The first objective premise relied upon by the Court of Chancery, unsupported by the record, is that the shareholder directors needed to implement the Repurchase Program to attain voting power in a proxy contest equal to 25%. The Court of Chancery properly calculated that if the Repurchase Program was completed, Unitrin's shareholder directors would increase their absolute voting power to 25%. It then calculated the odds of American General marshalling enough votes to defeat the Board and its supporters.[27]

The Court of Chancery and all parties agree that proxy contests do not generate 100% shareholder participation. The shareholder plaintiffs argue that 80–85% may be a usual turnout. Therefore, *without* the Repurchase Program, the director shareholders' absolute voting power of

---

27. The parties acknowledge that the Court of Chancery's calculation was mistaken but apparently agree on appeal that assuming there is a 90% voter turn-out, to succeed a 14.9% bidder would have to outpoll the shareholder directors either 1.36 to 1 or 1.76 to 1 in an election for directors and either 2 to 1 or 3 to 1 in a subsequent merger vote. This opinion's discussion regarding the fact that 42% of Unitrin's stock was owned by institutional investors makes the probative weight of even the correct polling comparisons *de minimis*.

23% would already constitute *actual voting power greater than* 25% in a proxy contest with normal shareholder participation below 100%.

The second objective premise relied upon by the Court of Chancery, unsupported by the record, is that American General's ability to succeed in a proxy contest depended on the Repurchase Program being enjoined because of the Supermajority Vote provision in Unitrin's charter. Without the approval of a target's board, the danger of activating a poison pill renders it irrational for bidders to pursue stock acquisitions above the triggering level.[30] Instead, "bidders intent on working around a poison pill must launch and win proxy contests to elect new directors who are willing to redeem the target's poison pill." Joseph A. Grundfest, *Just Vote No: A Minimalist Strategy for Dealing with Barbarians Inside the Gates,* 45 Stan.L.Rev. 857, 859 (1993).

As American General acknowledges, a less than 15% stockholder bidder need not proceed with acquiring shares to the extent that it would ever implicate the Supermajority Vote provision. In fact, it would be illogical for American General or any other bidder to acquire more than 15% of Unitrin's stock because that would not only trigger the poison pill, but also the constraints of 8 *Del.C.* § 203. If American General were to initiate a proxy contest *before* acquiring 15% of Unitrin's stock, it would need to amass only 45.1% of the votes assuming a 90% voter turnout. If it commenced a tender offer at an attractive price contemporaneously with its proxy contest, it could seek to acquire 50.1% of the outstanding voting stock.

The record reflects that institutional investors own 42% of Unitrin's shares. Twenty institutions own 33% of Unitrin's shares. It is generally accepted that proxy contests have re-emerged with renewed significance as a method of acquiring corporate control because "the growth in institutional investment has reduced the dispersion of share ownership." Lucian A. Bebchuk & Marcel Kahan, *A Framework for Analyzing Legal Policy Towards Proxy Contests,* 78 Cal.L.Rev. 1071, 1134 (1990). "Institutions are more likely than other shareholders to vote at all, more likely to vote against manager proposals, and more likely to vote for proposals by other shareholders." Bernard S. Black, *The Value of Institutional Investor Monitoring: The Empirical Evidence,* 39 UCLA L.Rev. 895, 925 (1992). *See also* John Pound, *Shareholder Activism and Share Values: The Causes and Consequences of Countersolicitations Against Management Antitakeover Proposals,* 32 J.L. & Econ. 357, 368 (1989).

The assumptions and conclusions American General sets forth in this appeal for a different purpose are particularly probative with regard to the

---

30. The ... flip-in and flip-over features [of a poison pill] stop individual shareholders or shareholder groups from accumulating large amounts of the target company's stock. No potential acquiror or other shareholder will risk triggering a [poison pill] by accumulating more than the threshold level of shares because of the threat of massive discriminatory dilution. The trigger level therefore effectively sets a ceiling on the amount of stock that any shareholder can accumulate before launching a proxy contest.

Randall S. Thomas, *Judicial Review of Defensive Tactics in Proxy Contests: When is Using a Rights Plan Right?,* 46 Vand.L.Rev. 503, 512 (1993).

effect of the institutional holdings in Unitrin's stock. American General's two predicate assumptions are a 90% stockholder turnout in a proxy contest and a bidder with 14.9% holdings, i.e., the maximum the bidder could own to avoid triggering the poison pill and the Supermajority Vote provision. American General also calculated the votes available to the Board or the bidder with and without the Repurchase Program:

> Assuming no Repurchase [Program], the [shareholder directors] would hold 23%, the percentage collectively held by the [directors] and the bidder would be 37.9%, and the percentage of additional votes available to either side would be 52.1%.

> Assuming the Repurchase [Program] is fully consummated, the [shareholder directors] would hold 28%, the percentage collectively held by the bidder and the [directors] would be 42.9%, and the percentage of additional votes available to either side would be 47.1%.

American General then applied these assumptions to reach conclusions regarding the votes needed for the 14.9% stockholder bidder to prevail: first, in an election of directors; and second, in the subsequent vote on a merger. [T]o prevail in a proxy contest with a 90% turnout, the percentage of additional shareholder votes a 14.9% shareholder bidder needs to prevail is 30.2% for directors and 35.2% in a subsequent merger. The record reflects that institutional investors held 42% of Unitrin's stock and 20 institutions held 33% of the stock. Thus, American General's own assumptions and calculations in the record support the Unitrin Board's argument that "it is hard to imagine a company more readily susceptible to a proxy contest concerning a pure issue of dollars."

The conclusion of the Court of Chancery that the Repurchase Program would make a proxy contest for Unitrin a "theoretical" possibility that American General could not realistically pursue may be erroneous and appears to be inconsistent with its own earlier determination that the "repurchase program strengthens the position of the Board of Directors to defend against a hostile bidder, but will not deprive the public stockholders of the 'power to influence corporate direction through the ballot.'" Even a complete implementation of the Repurchase Program, in combination with the pre-existing Supermajority Vote provision, would not appear to have a preclusive effect upon American General's ability successfully to marshall enough shareholder votes to win a proxy contest. A proper understanding of the record reflects that American General or any other 14.9% shareholder bidder could apparently win a proxy contest with a 90% turnout.

The key variable in a proxy contest would be the merit of American General's issues, not the size of its stockholdings. If American General presented an attractive price as the cornerstone of a proxy contest, it could prevail, irrespective of whether the shareholder directors' absolute voting power was 23% or 28%. * * *

Consequently, a proxy contest apparently remained a viable alternative for American General to pursue notwithstanding Unitrin's poison pill,

Supermajority Vote provision, and a fully implemented Repurchase Program.

This Court has recognized "the prerogative of a board of directors to resist a third party's unsolicited acquisition proposal or offer." *Paramount Communications, Inc. v. QVC Network, Inc.,* Del.Supr., 637 A.2d 34, 43 n. 13 (1994). The Unitrin Board did not have unlimited discretion to defeat the threat it perceived from the American General Offer by any draconi-an[34] means available. Pursuant to the *Unocal* proportionality test, the nature of the threat associated with a particular hostile offer sets the parameters for the range of permissible defensive tactics. Accordingly, the purpose of enhanced judicial scrutiny is to determine whether the Board acted reasonably in "relation ... to the threat which a particular bid allegedly poses to stockholder interests." *Mills Acquisition Co. v. Macmillan, Inc.,* Del.Supr., 559 A.2d 1261, 1288 (1989).

"The obvious requisite to determining the reasonableness of a defensive action is a clear identification of the nature of the threat." *Paramount Communications, Inc. v. Time, Inc.,* Del.Supr., 571 A.2d 1140, 1154 (1989). Courts, commentators and litigators have attempted to catalogue the threats posed by hostile tender offers. *Id.* at 1153. Commentators have categorized three types of threats:

> (i) *opportunity loss* ... [where] a hostile offer might deprive target shareholders of the opportunity to select a superior alternative offered by target management [or, we would add, offered by another bidder]; (ii) *structural coercion,* ... the risk that disparate treatment of non-tendering shareholders might distort shareholders' tender decisions; and (iii) *substantive coercion,* ... the risk that shareholders will mistakenly accept an underpriced offer because they disbelieve management's representations of intrinsic value.

Id. at 1153 n. 17 (*quoting* Ronald J. Gilson & Reinier Kraakman, *Delaware's Intermediate Standard for Defensive Tactics: Is There Substance to Proportionality Review?,* 44 Bus.Law. 247, 267 (1989)).

This Court has held that the "inadequate value" of an all cash for all shares offer is a "legally cognizable threat." *Paramount Communications, Inc. v. Time, Inc.,* 571 A.2d at 1153. In addition, this Court has specifically concluded that inadequacy of value is *not* the only legally cognizable threat from "an all-shares, all-cash offer at a price below what a target board in good faith deems to be the present value of its shares." *Id.* at 1152–53. In making that determination, this Court held that the Time board of directors had reasonably determined that inadequate value was not the only threat that Paramount's all cash for all shares offer presented, but was *also* reasonably concerned that the Time stockholders might

---

34. **Draconian,** adj. Of or pert. to Draco, an archon and member of the Athenian eupatridae, or the code of laws which is said to have been framed about 621 B.C. by him as thesmothete. In them the penalty for most offenses was death, and to a later age they seemed so severe that they were said to be written in blood. Hence, barbarously severe; harsh; cruel. *Webster's New International Dictionary* 780 (2d ed. 1951).

tender to Paramount in ignorance or based upon a mistaken belief, *i.e.*, yield to substantive coercion.

The record reflects that the Unitrin Board perceived the threat from American General's Offer to be a form of substantive coercion. The Board noted that Unitrin's stock price had moved up, on higher than normal trading volume, to a level slightly below the price in American General's Offer. The Board also noted that some Unitrin shareholders had publicly expressed interest in selling at or near the price in the Offer. The Board determined that Unitrin's stock was undervalued by the market at current levels and that the Board considered Unitrin's stock to be a good long-term investment. The Board also discussed the speculative and unsettled market conditions for Unitrin stock caused by American General's public disclosure. The Board concluded that a Repurchase Program would provide additional liquidity to those stockholders who wished to realize short-term gain, and would provide enhanced value to those stockholders who wished to maintain a long-term investment. Accordingly, the Board voted to authorize the Repurchase Program for up to ten million shares of its outstanding stock on the open market.

In *Unocal*, this Court noted that, pursuant to Delaware corporate law, a board of directors' duty of care required it to respond actively to protect the corporation and its shareholders from perceived harm. In *Unocal*, when describing the proportionality test, this Court listed several examples of concerns that boards of directors should consider in evaluating and responding to perceived threats. Unitrin's Board deemed three of the concerns exemplified in *Unocal* relevant in deciding to authorize the Repurchase Program: first, the inadequacy of the price offered; second, the nature and timing of American General's Offer; and third, the basic stockholder interests at stake, including those of short-term speculators whose actions may have fueled the coercive aspect of the Offer at the expense of the long-term investor.

The record appears to support Unitrin's argument that the Board's justification for adopting the Repurchase Program was its reasonably perceived risk of substantive coercion, *i.e.*, that Unitrin's shareholders might accept American General's inadequate Offer because of "ignorance or mistaken belief" regarding the Board's assessment of the long-term value of Unitrin's stock. In this case, the Unitrin Board's letter to its shareholders specifically reflected those concerns in describing its perception of the threat from American General's Offer. The adoption of the Repurchase Program also appears to be consistent with this Court's holding that economic inadequacy is not the only threat presented by an all cash for all shares hostile bid, because the threat of such a hostile bid could be exacerbated by shareholder "ignorance or … mistaken belief."

The Court of Chancery applied an incorrect legal standard when it ruled that the Unitrin decision to authorize the Repurchase Program was disproportionate because it was "unnecessary." * * *

In *QVC*, this Court recently elaborated upon the judicial function in applying enhanced scrutiny, citing *Unocal* as authority, albeit in the context of a sale of control and the target board's consideration of one of several reasonable alternatives. That teaching is nevertheless applicable here:

> a court applying enhanced judicial scrutiny should be deciding wheth-er the directors made *a reasonable* decision, not *a perfect* decision. If a board selected one of several reasonable alternatives, a court should not second guess that choice even though it might have decided otherwise or subsequent events may have cast doubt on the board's determination. Thus, courts will not substitute their business judg-ment for that of the directors, but will determine if the directors' decision was, on balance, within a range of reasonableness.

Paramount Communications, Inc. v. QVC Network, Inc., Del.Supr., 637 A.2d 34, 45–46 (1994) (emphasis in original). The Court of Chancery did not determine whether the Unitrin Board's decision to implement the Repurchase Program fell within a "range of reasonableness."

The record reflects that the Unitrin Board's adoption of the Repur-chase Program was an apparent recognition on its part that all sharehold-ers are not alike. This Court has stated that distinctions among types of shareholders are neither inappropriate nor irrelevant for a board of directors to make, *e.g.,* distinctions between long-term shareholders and short-term profit-takers, such as arbitrageurs, and their stockholding objectives. In *Unocal* itself, we expressly acknowledged that "a board may reasonably consider the basic stockholder interests at stake, including those of short term speculators, whose actions may have fueled the coercive aspect of the offer at the expense of the long term investor."

The Court of Chancery's determination that the Unitrin Board's adoption of the Repurchase Program was unnecessary constituted a sub-stitution of its business judgment for that of the Board, contrary to this Court's "range of reasonableness" holding in *Paramount Communica-tions, Inc. v. QVC Network, Inc.,* 637 A.2d at 45–46. Its decision to enjoin the Repurchase Program as an "unnecessary" *addition* to other comple-mentary defensive mechanisms is also inconsistent with a similar analysis in *Shamrock Holdings, Inc. v. Polaroid Corp.,* Del.Ch., 559 A.2d 278 (1989). In *Shamrock,* the Court of Chancery refused to enjoin any one of a series of transactions which included a repurchase plan. With respect to a repurchase program, the Court of Chancery held that a self-tender offer and buy-back plan constituted a reasonable proportionate response to the perceived threat to Polaroid shareholders by offering "some immediate value to those holders interested in cash while increasing the equity interest held by the remaining stockholders." *Shamrock Holdings, Inc. v. Polaroid Corp.,* 559 A.2d at 290. Although *Shamrock* dealt with an offer that did not reflect the very profitable litigation embodied in the Kodak patent case settlement and therefore implicated a potentially more serious threat than that involved here, *Shamrock* is nevertheless applicable considering American General's negotiable "low-ball" bid.

In assessing a challenge to defensive actions by a target corporation's board of directors in a takeover context, this Court has held that the Court of Chancery should evaluate the board's overall response, including the justification for each contested defensive measure, and the results achieved thereby. Where all of the target board's defensive actions are inextricably related, the principles of *Unocal* require that such actions be scrutinized collectively as a unitary response to the perceived threat. Thus, the Unitrin Board's adoption of the Repurchase Program, in addition to the poison pill, must withstand *Unocal*'s proportionality review.

In *Unocal,* the progenitor of the proportionality test, this Court stated that the board of directors' "duty of care extends to protecting the corporation and its [stockholders] from perceived harm whether a threat originates from third parties or other shareholders." *Unocal,* 493 A.2d at 955. We then noted that "such powers are not absolute." Specifically, this Court held that the board "does not have unbridled discretion to defeat any perceived threat by any Draconian means available." Immediately following those observations in *Unocal,* when exemplifying the parameters of a board's authority in adopting a restrictive stock repurchase, this Court held that "the directors may not have acted *solely* or *primarily* out of a desire to perpetuate themselves in office" (preclusion of the stockholders' corporate franchise right to vote) and, further, that the stock repurchase plan must not be inequitable.

An examination of the cases applying *Unocal* reveals a direct correlation between findings of proportionality or disproportionality and the judicial determination of whether a defensive response was draconian because it was either coercive or preclusive in character. In *Time,* for example, this Court concluded that the Time board's defensive response was reasonable and proportionate since it was not aimed at "cramming down" on its shareholders a management-sponsored alternative, *i.e.,* was not coercive, and because it did not preclude Paramount from making an offer for the combined Time–Warner company, *i.e.,* was not preclusive.

This Court also applied *Unocal's* proportionality test to the board's adoption of a "poison pill" shareholders' rights plan in *Moran v. Household Int'l, Inc.,* Del.Supr., 500 A.2d 1346 (1985). After acknowledging that the adoption of the rights plan was within the directors' statutory authority, this Court determined that the implementation of the rights plan was a proportionate response to the theoretical threat of a hostile takeover, in part, because it did not "strip" the stockholders of their right to receive tender offers *and* did not fundamentally restrict proxy contests, *i.e.,* was not preclusive.

More than a century before *Unocal* was decided, Justice Holmes observed that the common law must be developed through its application and "cannot be dealt with as if it contained only the axioms and corollaries of a book of mathematics." Oliver Wendell Holmes, Jr., *The Common*

Law 1 (1881). As common law applications of *Unocal's* proportionality standard have evolved, at least two characteristics of draconian defensive measures taken by a board of directors in responding to a threat have been brought into focus through enhanced judicial scrutiny. In the modern takeover lexicon, it is now clear that since *Unocal,* this Court has consistently recognized that defensive measures which are either preclusive or coercive are included within the common law definition of draconian.

If a defensive measure is not draconian, however, because it is not either coercive or preclusive, the *Unocal* proportionality test requires the focus of enhanced judicial scrutiny to shift to "the range of reasonableness." Proper and proportionate defensive responses are intended and permitted to thwart perceived threats. When a corporation is not for sale, the board of directors is the defender of the metaphorical medieval corporate bastion and the protector of the corporation's shareholders. The fact that a defensive action must not be coercive or preclusive does not prevent a board from responding defensively before a bidder is at the corporate bastion's gate.[38]

The *ratio decidendi* for the "range of reasonableness" standard is a need of the board of directors for latitude in discharging its fiduciary duties to the corporation and its shareholders when defending against perceived threats. The concomitant requirement is for judicial restraint. Consequently, if the board of directors' defensive response is not draconian (preclusive or coercive) and is within a "range of reasonableness," a court must not substitute its judgment for the board's. *Paramount Communications, Inc. v. QVC Network, Inc.,* 637 A.2d at 45–46.

In this case, the initial focus of enhanced judicial scrutiny for proportionality requires a determination regarding the defensive responses by the Unitrin Board to American General's offer. We begin, therefore, by ascertaining whether the Repurchase Program, as an addition to the poison pill, was draconian by being either coercive or preclusive.

A limited nondiscriminatory self-tender, like some other defensive measures, may thwart a current hostile bid, but is not inherently coercive. Moreover, it does not necessarily preclude future bids or proxy contests by stockholders who decline to participate in the repurchase. A selective repurchase of shares in a public corporation on the market, such as Unitrin's Repurchase Program, generally does not discriminate because all shareholders can voluntarily realize the same benefit by selling. *See* Larry E. Ribstein, *Takeover Defenses and the Corporate Contract,* 78 Geo.L.J. 71, 129–31(1989). *See also* Michael Bradley & Michael Rosenzweig, *Defensive*

---

38. This Court's choice of the term draconian in *Unocal* was a recognition that the law affords boards of directors substantial latitude in defending the perimeter of the corporate bastion against perceived threats. Thus, continuing with the medieval metaphor, if a board reasonably perceives that a threat is on the horizon, it has broad authority to respond with a panoply of individual or combined defensive precautions, e.g., staffing the barbican, raising the drawbridge, and lowering the portcullis. Stated more directly, depending upon the circumstances, the board may respond to a reasonably perceived threat by adopting individually or sometimes in combination: advance notice by-laws, supermajority voting provisions, shareholder rights plans, repurchase programs, etc.

Stock Repurchases, 99 Harv.L.Rev. 1377 (1986). Here, there is no showing on this record that the Repurchase Program was coercive.

We have already determined that the record in this case appears to reflect that a proxy contest remained a viable (if more problematic) alternative for American General even if the Repurchase Program were to be completed in its entirety. Nevertheless, the Court of Chancery must determine whether Unitrin's Repurchase Program would only inhibit American General's ability to wage a proxy fight and institute a merger or whether it was, in fact, preclusive because American General's success would either be mathematically impossible or realistically unattainable. If the Court of Chancery concludes that the Unitrin Repurchase Program was not draconian because it was not preclusive, one question will remain to be answered in its proportionality review: whether the Repurchase Program was within a range of reasonableness?

The Court of Chancery found that the Unitrin Board reasonably believed that American General's Offer was inadequate and that the adoption of a poison pill was a proportionate defensive response. Upon remand, in applying the correct legal standard to the factual circumstances of this case, the Court of Chancery may conclude that the implementation of the limited Repurchase Program was also within a range of reasonable additional defensive responses available to the Unitrin Board. In considering whether the Repurchase Program was within a range of reasonableness the Court of Chancery should take into consideration whether: (1) it is a statutorily authorized form of business decision which a board of directors may routinely make in a non-takeover context; (2) as a defensive response to American General's Offer it was limited and corresponded in degree or magnitude to the degree or magnitude of the threat, (*i.e.,* assuming the threat was relatively "mild," was the response relatively "mild?"); (3) with the Repurchase Program, the Unitrin Board properly recognized that all shareholders are not alike, and provided immediate liquidity to those shareholders who wanted it.

The Court of Chancery's holding in *Shamrock,* cited with approval by this Court in *Time,* appears to be persuasive support for the proportionality of the multiple defenses Unitrin's Board adopted. In *Shamrock,* the Court of Chancery concluded that the Polaroid board had "a valid basis for concern that the Polaroid stockholders [like Unitrin's stockholders] will be unable to reach an accurate judgment as to the intrinsic value of their stock." The Court of Chancery also observed, "the likely shift in the stockholder profile in favor of Polaroid" as a result of the repurchase plan "appears to be minimal." Consequently, the Court of Chancery concluded that Polaroid's defensive response as a whole—the ESOP, the issuance of stock to a friendly third party and the stock repurchase plan—was not disproportionate to the Shamrock threat or improperly motivated, and "individually or collectively will [not] preclude the successful completion of Shamrock's tender offer."

American General argues that the all cash for all shares offer in *Shamrock* is distinguishable because *Shamrock* involved a hostile tender offer, whereas this case involves a fully negotiable Offer to enter into a consensual merger transaction. Nevertheless, American General acknowledges that a determinative factor in *Shamrock* was a finding that the defensive responses had only an incidental effect on the stockholder profile for the purpose of a proxy contest, *i.e.*, was not preclusive. In *Shamrock,* the Court of Chancery's proportionality holding was also an implicit determination that the series of multiple defensive responses were within a "range of reasonableness."

In this case, the Court of Chancery erred by substituting its judgment, that the Repurchase Program was unnecessary, for that of the Board. The Unitrin Board had the power and the duty, upon reasonable investigation, to protect Unitrin's shareholders from what it perceived to be the threat from American General's inadequate all-cash for all-shares Offer. The adoption of the poison pill *and* the limited Repurchase Program was not coercive and the Repurchase Program may not be preclusive. Although each made a takeover more difficult, individually and collectively, if they were not coercive or preclusive the Court of Chancery must determine whether they were within the range of reasonable defensive measures available to the Board.

If the Court of Chancery concludes that individually and collectively the poison pill and the Repurchase Program were proportionate to the threat the Board believed American General posed, the Unitrin Board's adoption of the Repurchase Program and the poison pill is entitled to review under the traditional business judgment rule. The burden will then shift "back to the plaintiffs who have the ultimate burden of persuasion [in a preliminary injunction proceeding] to show a breach of the directors' fiduciary duties." *Moran v. Household Int'l, Inc.,* Del.Supr., 500 A.2d 1346, 1356 (1985). In order to rebut the protection of the business judgment rule, the burden on the plaintiffs will be to demonstrate, "by a preponderance of the evidence that the directors' decisions were *primarily* based on [(1)] perpetuating themselves in office or [(2)] some other breach of fiduciary duty such as fraud, overreaching, lack of good faith, or [(3)] being uninformed." *Unocal,* 493 A.2d at 958 (emphasis added). * * *

CARMODY v. TOLL BROTHERS, INC.

723 A.2d 1180 (Del.Ch.1998).

JACOBS, VICE CHANCELLOR.

At issue on this Rule 12(b)(6) motion to dismiss is whether a most recent innovation in corporate antitakeover measures—the so-called "dead hand" poison pill rights plan—is subject to legal challenge on the basis that it violates the Delaware General Corporation Law and/or the fiduciary duties of the board of directors who adopted the plan. As explained more fully below, a "dead hand" rights plan is one that cannot be redeemed except by the incumbent directors who adopted the plan or their designated successors.

The firm whose rights plan is being challenged is Toll Brothers (sometimes referred to as "the company"), a Pennsylvania-based Delaware corporation that designs, builds, and markets single family luxury homes in thirteen states and five regions in the United States. The company was founded in 1967 by brothers Bruce and Robert Toll, who are its Chief Executive and Chief Operating Officers, respectively, and who own approximately 37.5% of Toll Brothers' common stock. The company's board of directors has nine members, four of whom (including Bruce and Robert Toll) are senior executive officers. The remaining five members of the board are "outside" independent directors.

From its inception in 1967, Toll Brothers has performed very successfully, and "went public" in 1986. As of June 3, 1997, the company had issued and outstanding 34,196,473 common shares that are traded on the New York Stock Exchange. After going public, Toll Brothers continued to enjoy increasing revenue growth, and it expects that trend to continue into 1998, based on the company's ongoing expansion, its backlog of home contracts, and a continuing strong industry demand for luxury housing in the regions it serves.

The home building industry of which the company is a part is highly competitive. For some time that industry has been undergoing consolidation through the acquisition process, and over the last ten years it has evolved from one where companies served purely local and regional markets to one where regional companies have expanded to serve markets throughout the country. That was accomplished by home builders in one region acquiring firms located in other regions. Inherent in any such expansion-through-acquisition environment is the risk of a hostile takeover. To protect against that risk, the company's board of directors adopted the Rights Plan.

The Rights Plan was adopted on June 12, 1997, at which point Toll Brothers' stock was trading at approximately $18 per share—near the low end of its established price range of $16 3/8 to $25 3/16 per share. After considering the industry economic and financial environment and other factors, the Toll Brothers board concluded that other companies engaged in its lines of business might perceive the company as a potential target for an acquisition. The Rights Plan was adopted with that problem in mind, but not in response to any specific takeover proposal or threat. The company announced that it had done that to protect its stockholders from "coercive or unfair tactics to gain control of the Company" by placing the stockholders in a position of having to accept or reject an unsolicited offer without adequate time.

The Rights Plan would operate as follows: there would be a dividend distribution of one preferred stock purchase right (a "Right") for each outstanding share of common stock as of July 11, 1997. Initially the Rights would attach to the company's outstanding common shares, and each Right would initially entitle the holder to purchase one thousandth of a share of a newly registered series Junior A Preferred Stock for $100. The Rights would become exercisable, and would trade separately from the common shares, after the "Distribution Date," which is defined as the earlier of (a) ten business days following a public announcement that an acquiror has acquired, or obtained the right to acquire, beneficial ownership of 15% or more of the company's outstanding common shares (the "Stock Acquisition Date"), or (b) ten business days after the commencement of a tender offer or exchange offer that would result in a person or group beneficially owning 15% or more of the company's outstanding common shares. Once exercisable, the Rights remain exercisable until their Final Expiration Date (June 12, 2007, ten years after the adoption of the Plan), unless the Rights are earlier redeemed by the company.

The dilutive mechanism of the Rights is "triggered" by certain defined events. One such event is the acquisition of 15% or more of Toll Brothers' stock by any person or group of affiliated or associated persons. Should that occur, each Rights holder (except the acquiror and its affiliates and associates) becomes entitled to buy two shares of Toll Brothers common stock or other securities at half price. That is, the value of the stock received when the Right is exercised is equal to two times the exercise price of the Right. In that manner, this so-called "flip in" feature of the Rights Plan would massively dilute the value of the holdings of the unwanted acquiror.[5]

The Rights also have a standard "flip over" feature, which is triggered if after the Stock Acquisition Date, the company is made a party to a merger in which Toll Brothers is not the surviving corporation, or in which it is the surviving corporation and its common stock is changed or exchanged. In either event, each Rights holder becomes entitled to purchase common stock of the acquiring company, again at half-price, thereby impairing the acquiror's capital structure and drastically diluting the interest of the acquiror's other stockholders.

The complaint alleges that the purpose and effect of the company's Rights Plan, as with most poison pills, is to make any hostile acquisition of Toll Brothers prohibitively expensive, and thereby to deter such acquisitions unless the target company's board first approves the acquisition proposal. The target board's "leverage" derives from another critical feature found in most rights plans: the directors' power to redeem the

---

5. The "flip-in" feature of a rights plan is triggered when the acquiror crosses the specified ownership threshold, regardless of the acquiror's intentions with respect to the use of the shares. At that point, rights vest in all shareholders other than the acquiror, and as a result, those holders become entitled to acquire additional shares of voting stock at a substantially discounted price, usually 50% of the market price. Commonly, rights plans also contain a "flip-over" feature entitling target company shareholders (again, other than the acquiror) to purchase shares of the acquiring company at a reduced price. That feature is activated when, after a "flip-in" triggering event, the acquiror initiates a triggering event, such as a merger, self-dealing transaction, or sale of assets. *See* Shawn C. Lese, *Note, Preventing Control From the Grave: A Proposal for Judicial Treatment of Dead Hand Provisions in Poison Pills,* 96 Colum. L.Rev. 2175, 2180–81 (1996).

Rights at any time before they expire, on such conditions as the directors "in their sole discretion" may establish. To this extent there is little to distinguish the company's Rights Plan from the "standard model." What is distinctive about the Rights Plan is that it authorizes only a specific, defined category of directors—the "Continuing Directors"—to redeem the Rights. The dispute over the legality of this "Continuing Director" or "dead hand" feature of the Rights Plan is what drives this lawsuit.

In substance, the "dead hand" provision operates to prevent any directors of Toll Brothers, except those who were in office as of the date of the Rights Plan's adoption (June 12, 1997) or their designated successors, from redeeming the Rights until they expire on June 12, 2007. That consequence flows directly from the Rights Agreement's definition of a "Continuing Director," which is:

> (i) any member of the Board of Directors of the Company, while such person is a member of the Board, who is not an Acquiring Person, or an Affiliate [as defined] or Associate [as defined] of an Acquiring Person, or a representative or nominee of an Acquiring Person or of any such Affiliate or Associate, *and was a member of the Board prior to the date of this agreement,* or (ii) any Person who subsequently becomes a member of the Board, while such Person is a member of the Board, who is not an Acquiring Person, or an Affiliate [as defined] or Associate [as defined] of an Acquiring Person, or a representative or nominee of an Acquiring Person or of any such Affiliate or Associate, if such Person's *nomination for election or election to the Board is recommended or approved by a majority of the Continuing Directors.*

According to the complaint, this "dead hand" provision has a twofold practical effect. First, it makes an unsolicited offer for the company more unlikely by eliminating a proxy contest as a useful way for a hostile acquiror to gain control, because even if the acquiror wins the contest, its newly-elected director representatives could not redeem the Rights. Second, the "dead hand" provision disenfranchises, in a proxy contest, all shareholders that wish the company to be managed by a board empowered to redeem the Rights, by depriving those shareholders of any practical choice except to vote for the incumbent directors. Given these effects, the plaintiff claims that the only purpose that the "dead hand" provision could serve is to discourage future acquisition activity by making any proxy contest to replace incumbent board members an exercise in futility.
* * *

The critical issue on this motion is whether a "dead hand" provision in a "poison pill" rights plan is subject to legal challenge on the basis that it is invalid as *ultra vires,* or as a breach of fiduciary duty, or both. Although that issue has been the subject of scholarly comment,[9] it has yet

---

9. *See, e.g.,* Shawn C. Lese, *Note, Preventing Control From the Grave: A Proposal for Judicial Treatment of Dead Hand Provisions in Poison Pills,* 96 Col. L.Rev. 2175 (1996) (cited herein as "Lese"); Jeffrey N. Gordon, *"Just Say Never" Poison Pills, Deadhand Pills and Shareholder*

to be decided under Delaware law, and to date it has been addressed by only two courts applying the law of other jurisdictions.[10] * * *

In *Moran*, this Court and the Supreme Court upheld the "flip over" rights plan in issue there based on three distinct factual findings. The first was that the poison pill would not erode fundamental shareholder rights, because the target board would not have unfettered discretion arbitrarily to reject a hostile offer or to refuse to redeem the pill. Rather, the board's judgment not to redeem the pill would be subject to judicially enforceable fiduciary standards. The second finding was that even if the board refused to redeem the pill (thereby preventing the shareholders from receiving the unsolicited offer), that would not preclude the acquiror from gaining control of the target company, because the offeror could "form a group of up to 19.9% and solicit proxies for consents to remove the Board and redeem the Rights." Third, even if the hostile offer was precluded, the target company's stockholders could always exercise their ultimate prerogative—wage a proxy contest to remove the board. On this basis, the Supreme Court concluded that "the Rights Plan will not have a severe impact upon proxy contests and it will not preclude all hostile acquisitions of Household."

It being settled that a corporate board could permissibly adopt a poison pill, the next litigated question became: under what circumstances would the directors' fiduciary duties require the board to redeem the rights in the face of a hostile takeover proposal? That issue was litigated, in Delaware and elsewhere, during the second half of the 1980s. The lesson taught by that experience was that courts were extremely reluctant to order the redemption of poison pills on fiduciary grounds. The reason was the prudent deployment of the pill proved to be largely beneficial to shareholder interests: it often resulted in a bidding contest that culminated in an acquisition on terms superior to the initial hostile offer.

Once it became clear that the prospects were unlikely for obtaining judicial relief mandating a redemption of the poison pill, a different response to the pill was needed. That response, which echoed the Supreme Court's suggestion in *Moran*, was the foreseeable next step in the evolu-

---

Adopted By–Laws: An Essay for Warren Buffett, 19 Cardozo L.Rev. 511 (1997); Daniel A. Neff, *The Impact of State Statutes and Continuing Director Rights Plans,* 51 U. Miami L.Rev. 663 (1997); and Meredith M. Brown and William D. Regner, *2 Shareholder Rights Plans: Recent Toxopharmological Developments, Insights* (Aspen, Law & Business, Oct., 1997) (cited herein as "Brown and Regner").

10. The jurisdictions that have directly addressed the legality of the dead hand poison pill are New York, *see Bank of New York Co., Inc. v. Irving Bank Corp., et. al.,* N.Y. Sup.Ct., 139 Misc.2d 665, 528 N.Y.S.2d 482 (1988), and the United States District Court for the Northern District of Georgia, *see Invacare Corp. v. Healthdyne Technologies. Inc.,* N.D. Ga., 968 F.Supp. 1578 (1997) (applying Georgia law). In Delaware, the issue arose in *Davis Acquisition, Inc. v. NWA, Inc.,* Del. Ch., C.A. No. 10761, Allen, C., 1989 WL 40845 (Apr. 25, 1989), but was not decided because the preliminary injunction motion was resolved on other grounds. In *Sutton Holding Corp. v. DeSoto, Inc.,* Del. Ch., C.A. No. 12051, Allen, C, 1991 WL 80223 (May 14, 1991) the validity of a "continuing director" provision was presented indirectly (but again was not decided) in the context of an amendment to a pension plan prohibiting its termination or a reduction of benefits in the event of a "change of control." That term was defined as a new, substantial shareholder becoming the beneficial owner of 35% or more of the corporation's voting stock without the prior approval of two thirds of the board and a majority of the "continuing directors."

tion of takeover strategy: a tender offer coupled with a solicitation for shareholder proxies to remove and replace the incumbent board with the acquiror's nominees who, upon assuming office, would redeem the pill.[15] Because that strategy, if unopposed, would enable hostile offerors to effect an "end run" around the poison pill, it again was predictable and only a matter of time that target company boards would develop counter-strategies. With one exception—the "dead hand" pill—these counterstrategies proved "successful" only in cases where the purpose was to delay the process to enable the board to develop alternatives to the hostile offer. The counterstrategies were largely unsuccessful, however, where the goal was to stop the proxy contest (and as a consequence, the hostile offer) altogether.

For example, in cases where the target board's response was either to (i) amend the by-laws to delay a shareholders meeting to elect directors, or (ii) delay an annual meeting to a later date permitted under the bylaws, so that the board and management would be able to explore alternatives to the hostile offer (but not entrench themselves), those responses were upheld.[16] On the other hand, where the target board's response to a proxy contest (coupled with a hostile offer) was (i) to move the shareholders meeting to a later date to enable the incumbent board to solicit revocations of proxies to defeat the apparently victorious dissident group, or (ii) to expand the size of the board, and then fill the newly created positions so the incumbents would retain control of the board irrespective of the outcome of the proxy contest, those responses were declared invalid.[17]

This litigation experience taught that a target board, facing a proxy contest joined with a hostile tender offer, could, in good faith, employ non-preclusive defensive measures to give the board time to explore transactional alternatives. The target board could not, however, erect defenses that would either preclude a proxy contest altogether or improperly bend the rules to favor the board's continued incumbency.

In this environment, the only defensive measure that promised to be a "show stopper" (*i.e.*, had the potential to deter a proxy contest altogether)

---

15. *See Unitrin, Inc. v. American General Corp.,* Del.Supr., 651 A.2d 1361, 1379 (1995); *Kidsco, Inc. v. Dinsmore,* Del. Ch., 674 A.2d 483, 490 (1995), *aff'd,* 670 A.2d 1338 (1995).

16. *See, e.g., Stahl v. Apple Bancorp, Inc.,* Del. Ch., 579 A.2d 1115 (1990) (upholding postponement of annual meeting to a later date permitted by bylaws to enable target board to explore alternatives to hostile offer); *Kidsco Inc. v. Dinsmore,* n. 15, *supra,* (upholding amendment of bylaws to give target board an additional 25 days before calling a shareholder-initiated special meeting, to enable shareholders to vote on a pending merger proposal, and, if the proposal were defeated, to enable the board to explore other alternatives).

17. *See, Aprahamian v. HBO & Co.,* Del Ch., 531 A.2d 1204 (1987) (shareholders' meeting moved to later date for the purpose of defeating the apparent victors in proxy contest. Held: invalid); *Blasius Indus. v. Atlas Corp.,* Del. Ch., 564 A.2d 651(1988) (in response to an announced proxy contest, target board amended bylaws to create two new board positions, then filled those positions to retain board control, irrespective of outcome of proxy contest. Held: invalid).

Another statutorily permissible defensive device—the "staggered" or classified board—was useful, but still of limited effectiveness. Because only one third of a classified board would stand for election each year, a classified board would delay—but not prevent—a hostile acquiror from obtaining control of the board, since a determined acquiror could wage a proxy contest and obtain control of two thirds of the target board over a two year period, as opposed to seizing control in a single election.

was a poison pill with a "dead hand" feature. The reason is that if only the incumbent directors or their designated successors could redeem the pill, it would make little sense for shareholders or the hostile bidder to wage a proxy contest to replace the incumbent board. Doing that would eliminate from the scene the only group of persons having the power to give the hostile bidder and target company shareholders what they desired: control of the target company (in the case of the hostile bidder) and the opportunity to obtain an attractive price for their shares (in the case of the target company stockholders). It is against that backdrop that the legal issues presented here, which concern the validity of the "dead hand" feature, attain significance.

The defendants advance three reasons why this challenge to the validity of the "dead hand" pill should be dismissed. *First,* they argue that the plaintiff's claims are not ripe and cannot become ripe for adjudication, unless and until (i) a specific acquisition is proposed to which the Continuing Directors object and (ii) the Continuing Directors refuse to redeem the Rights so as to enable the shareholders to consider the acquisition proposal and decide whether or not to accept it. *Second,* the defendants contend that even if the claims are ripe, they must be dismissed under Chancery Court Rule 23.1, because the claims are derivative and the plaintiff has failed to make a pre-suit demand on the board or plead facts that would excuse a demand. *Third,* the defendants argue that in any event, the complaint fails to state a claim upon which relief can be granted, because the "dead hand" provision violates no duty imposed either by statute or corporate fiduciary principles. These dismissal arguments are addressed in that sequence. * * *

The plaintiff's complaint attacks the "dead hand" feature of the Toll Brothers poison pill on both statutory and fiduciary duty grounds. The statutory claim is that the "dead hand" provision unlawfully restricts the powers of future boards by creating different classes of directors—those who have the power to redeem the poison pill, and those who do not. Under 8 *Del. C.* §§ 141(a) and (d), any such restrictions and director classifications must be stated in the certificate of incorporation. The complaint alleges that because those restrictions are not stated in the Toll Brothers charter, the "dead hand" provision of the Rights Plan is ultra vires and, consequently, invalid on its face.

The complaint also alleges that even if the Rights Plan is not *ultra vires,* its approval constituted a breach of the Toll Brothers board's fiduciary duty of loyalty in several respects. It is alleged that the board violated its duty of loyalty because (a) the "dead hand" provision was enacted solely or primarily for entrenchment purposes; (b) it was also a disproportionate defensive measure, since it precludes the shareholders from receiving tender offers and engaging in a proxy contest, in contravention of the principles of *Unocal Corp. v. Mesa Petroleum Co.,* as elucidated in *Unitrin, Inc. v. American General Corp.* and (c) the "dead hand" provision purposefully interferes with the shareholder voting franchise without any compelling justification, in derogation of the principles articulated in *Blasius Indus. v. Atlas Corp.* * * *

I conclude, for the reasons next discussed, that both fiduciary duty claims are cognizable under Delaware law.

The validity of antitakeover measures is normally evaluated under the *Unocal/Unitrin* standard. But where the defensive measures purposefully disenfranchise shareholders, the board will be required to satisfy the more exacting *Blasius* standard, which our Supreme Court has articulated as follows:[39]

> A board's unilateral decision to adopt a defensive measure touching "upon issues of control" that purposefully disenfranchises its shareholders is strongly suspect under *Unocal*, and cannot be sustained without a "compelling justification."

The complaint alleges that the "dead hand" provision purposefully disenfranchises the company's shareholders without any compelling justification. The disenfranchisement would occur because even in an election contest fought over the issue of the hostile bid, the shareholders will be powerless to elect a board that is both willing and able to accept the bid, and they "may be forced to vote for [incumbent] directors whose policies they reject because only those directors have the power to change them."

A claim that the directors have unilaterally "create[d] a structure in which shareholder voting is either impotent or self defeating" is necessarily a claim of purposeful disenfranchisement. Given the Supreme Court's rationale for upholding the validity of the poison pill in *Moran*, and the primacy of the shareholder vote in our scheme of corporate jurisprudence, any contrary view is difficult to justify. In *Moran*, the Supreme Court upheld the adoption of a poison pill, in part because its effect upon a proxy contest would be "minimal," but also because if the board refused to redeem the plan, the shareholders could exercise their prerogative to remove and replace the board. In *Unocal* the Supreme Court reiterated that view—that the safety valve which justifies a board being allowed to resist a hostile offer a majority of shareholders might prefer, is that the shareholders always have their ultimate recourse to the ballot box. Those observations reflect the fundamental value that the shareholder vote has primacy in our system of corporate governance because it is the "ideological underpinning upon which the legitimacy of directorial power rests." * * *

The defendants contend that the complaint fails to allege a valid stockholder disenfranchisement claim, because the Rights Plan does not on its face limit a dissident's ability to propose a slate or the shareholders' ability to cast a vote. The defendants also urge that even if the Plan might arguably have that effect, it could occur only in a very specific and unlikely context, namely, where (i) the hostile bidder makes a fair offer that it is willing to keep open for more than one year, (ii) the current

---

39. *Stroud v. Grace,* Del.Supr., 606 A.2d 75, 92 n. 3 (1992).

board refuses to redeem the Rights, and (iii) the offeror wages two successful proxy fights and is committed to wage a third.

This argument, in my opinion, begs the issue and is specious. It begs the issue because the complaint does not claim that the Rights Plan facially restricts the shareholders' voting rights. What the complaint alleges is that the "dead hand" provision will either preclude a hostile bidder from waging a proxy contest altogether, or, if there should be a contest, it will coerce those shareholders who desire the hostile offer to succeed to vote for those directors who oppose it—the incumbent (and "Continuing") directors. Besides missing the point, the argument is also specious, because the hypothetical case the defendants argue must exist for any disenfranchisement to occur, rests upon the unlikely assumption that the hostile bidder will keep its offer open for more than one year. Given the market risks inherent in financed hostile bids for public corporations, it is unrealistic to assume that many bidders would be willing to do that.

For these reasons, the plaintiffs *Blasius*-based breach of fiduciary duty claim is cognizable under Delaware law.

The final issue is whether the complaint states a legally cognizable claim that the inclusion of the "dead hand" provision in the Rights Plan was an unreasonable defensive measure within the meaning of *Unocal*. I conclude that it does.

QUICKTURN DESIGN SYSTEMS, INC. v. SHAPIRO

721 A.2d 1281 (Del.1998)

HOLLAND, JUSTICE:

In response to Mentor's tender offer and proxy contest to replace the Quickturn board of directors, as part of Mentor's effort to acquire Quickturn, the Quickturn board enacted two defensive measures. First, it amended the Quickturn shareholder rights plan ("Rights Plan") by adopting a "no hand" feature of limited duration (the "Delayed Redemption Provision" or "DRP"). Second, the Quickturn board amended the corporation's by-laws to delay the holding of any special stockholders meeting requested by stockholders for 90 to 100 days after the validity of the request is determined (the "Amendment" or "By–Law Amendment").

Mentor filed actions for declaratory and injunctive relief in the Court of Chancery challenging the legality of both defensive responses by Quickturn's board. The Court of Chancery conducted a trial on the merits. It determined that the By–Law Amendment is valid. It also concluded, however, that the DRP is invalid on fiduciary duty grounds.

In this appeal, Quickturn argues that the Court of Chancery erred in finding that Quickturn's directors breached their fiduciary duty by adopting the Delayed Redemption Provision. We have concluded that, as a matter of Delaware law, the Delayed Redemption Provision was invalid. Therefore, on that alternative basis, the judgment of the Court of Chancery is affirmed.

Mentor (the hostile bidder) is an Oregon corporation, headquartered in Wilsonville, Oregon, whose shares are publicly traded on the NASDAQ national market system. Mentor manufactures, markets, and supports electronic design automation ("EDA") software and hardware. It also provides related services that enable engineers to design, analyze, simulate, model, implement, and verify the components of electronic systems. Mentor markets its products primarily for large firms in the communications, computer, semiconductor, consumer electronics, aerospace, and transportation industries.

Quickturn, the target company, is a Delaware corporation, headquartered in San Jose, California. Quickturn has 17,922,518 outstanding shares of common stock that are publicly traded on the NASDAQ national market system. Quickturn invented, and was the first company to successfully market, logic emulation technology, which is used to verify the design of complex silicon chips and electronics systems. Quickturn is currently the market leader in the emulation business, controlling an estimated 60% of the worldwide emulation market and an even higher percentage of the United States market. Quickturn maintains the largest intellectual property portfolio in the industry, which includes approximately twenty-nine logic emulation patents issued in the United States, and numerous other patents issued in foreign jurisdictions. Quickturn's customers include the world's leading technology companies, among them Intel, IBM, Sun Microsystems, Texas Instruments, Hitachi, Fujitsu, Siemens, and NEC.

Quickturn's board of directors consists of eight members, all but one of whom are outside, independent directors. All have distinguished careers and significant technological experience. Collectively, the board has more than 30 years of experience in the EDA industry and owns one million shares (about 5%) of Quickturn's common stock.

Since 1989, Quickturn has historically been a growth company, having experienced increases in earnings and revenues during the past seven years. Those favorable trends were reflected in Quickturn's stock prices, which reached a high of $15.75 during the first quarter of 1998, and generally traded in the $15.875 to $21.25 range during the year preceding Mentor's hostile bid.

Since the spring of 1998, Quickturn's earnings, revenue growth, and stock price levels have declined, largely because of the downturn in the semiconductor industry and more specifically in the Asian semiconductor market. Historically, 30%–35% of Quickturn's annual sales (approximately $35 million) had come from Asia, but in 1998, Quickturn's Asian sales declined dramatically with the downturn of the Asian market.[5] Manage-

---

5. By the summer of 1998, Quickturn's stock price had declined to $6 per share. On August 11, 1998, the closing price was $8.00 It was in this "trough" period that Mentor, which had

ment has projected that the negative impact of the Asian market upon Quickturn's sales should begin reversing itself sometime between the second half of 1998 and early 1999.

Since 1996, Mentor and Quickturn have been engaged in patent litigation that has resulted in Mentor being barred from competing in the United States emulation market. Because its products have been adjudicated to infringe upon Quickturn's patents, Mentor currently stands enjoined from selling, manufacturing, or marketing its emulation products in the United States. Thus, Mentor is excluded from an unquestionably significant market for emulation products.

The origin of the patent controversy was Mentor's sale of its hardware emulation assets, including its patents, to Quickturn in 1992. Later, Mentor reentered the emulation business when it acquired a French company called Meta Systems ("Meta") and began to market Meta's products in the United States in December 1995. Quickturn reacted by commencing a proceeding before the International Trade Commission ("ITC") claiming that Meta and Mentor were infringing Quickturn's patents. In August 1996, the ITC issued an order prohibiting Mentor from importing, selling, distributing, advertising, or soliciting in the United States, any products manufactured by Meta. That preliminary order was affirmed by the Federal Circuit Court of Appeals in August 1997. In December 1997, the ITC issued a Permanent Exclusion Order prohibiting Mentor from importing, selling, marketing, advertising, or soliciting in the United States, until at least April 28, 2009, any of the emulation products manufactured by Meta outside the United States.

At present, the only remaining patent litigation is pending in the Oregon Federal District Court. Quickturn is asserting a patent infringement damage claim that, Quickturn contends, is worth approximately $225 million. Mentor contends that Quickturn's claim is worth only $5.2 million or even less.

Mentor began exploring the possibility of acquiring Quickturn. If Mentor owned Quickturn, it would also own the patents, and would be in a position to "unenforce" them by seeking to vacate Quickturn's injunctive orders against Mentor in the patent litigation. The exploration process began when Mr. Bernd Braune, a Mentor senior executive, retained Arthur Andersen ("Andersen") to advise Mentor how it could successfully compete in the emulation market. The result was a report Andersen issued in October 1997, entitled "PROJECT VELOCITY" and "Strategic Alternatives Analysis." The Andersen report identified several advantages and benefits Mentor would enjoy if it acquired Quickturn.[10]

---

designs upon Quickturn since the fall of 1997, saw an opportunity to acquire Quickturn for an advantageous price.

10. These included: (i) eliminating the time and expense associated with litigation; (ii) creating synergy from combining two companies with complementary core competencies; (iii) reducing customer confusion over product availability, which in turn would accelerate sales; and (iv) eliminating the threat of a large competitor moving into the emulation market. Mentor has

In December 1997, Mentor retained Salomon Smith Barney ("Salomon") to act as its financial advisor in connection with a possible acquisition of Quickturn. Salomon prepared an extensive study which it reviewed with Mentor's senior executives in early 1998. The Salomon study concluded that although a Quickturn acquisition could provide substantial value for Mentor, Mentor could not afford to acquire Quickturn at the then-prevailing market price levels. Ultimately, Mentor decided not to attempt an acquisition of Quickturn during the first half of 1998.

After Quickturn's stock price began to decline in May 1998, however, Gregory Hinckley, Mentor's Executive Vice President, told Dr. Walden Rhines, Mentor's Chairman, that "the market outlook being very weak due to the Asian crisis made it a good opportunity" to try acquiring Quickturn for a cheap price. Mr. Hinckley then assembled Mentor's financial and legal advisors, proxy solicitors, and others, and began a three month process that culminated in Mentor's August 12, 1998 tender offer.

On August 12, 1998, Mentor announced an unsolicited cash tender offer for all outstanding common shares of Quickturn at $12.125 per share, a price representing an approximate 50% premium over Quickturn's immediate pre-offer price, and a 20% discount from Quickturn's February 1998 stock price levels. Mentor's tender offer, once consummated, would be followed by a second step merger in which Quickturn's nontendering stockholders would receive, in cash, the same $12.125 per share tender offer price.

Mentor also announced its intent to solicit proxies to replace the board at a special meeting. Relying upon Quickturn's then-applicable by-law provision governing the call of special stockholders meetings, Mentor began soliciting agent designations from Quickturn stockholders to satisfy the by-law's stock ownership requirements to call such a meeting.[11] * * *

The Quickturn board first met on August 13, 1998, the day after Mentor publicly announced its bid. All board members attended the meeting, for the purpose of evaluating Mentor's tender offer. The meeting lasted for several hours. Before or during the meeting, each board member received a package that included (i) Mentor's press release announcing the unsolicited offer; (ii) Quickturn's press release announcing its board's review of Mentor's offer; (iii) Dr. Rhines's August 11 letter to Mr. Antle; (iv) the complaints filed by Mentor against Quickturn and its directors; and (v) copies of Quickturn's then-current Rights Plan and by-laws.

The Quickturn board first discussed retaining a team of financial advisors to assist it in evaluating Mentor's offer and the company's

---

utilized these reasons in public statements in which it attempted to explain why its bid made sense.

11. The applicable by-law (Article II, § 2.3) authorized a call of a special stockholders meeting by shareholders holding at least 10% of Quickturn's shares. In their agent solicitation, Mentor informed Quickturn stockholders that Mentor intended to call a special meeting approximately 45 days after it received sufficient agent designations to satisfy the 10% requirement under the original by-law. The solicitation also disclosed Mentor's intent to set the date for the special meeting, and to set the record date and give formal notice of that meeting.

strategic alternatives. The board discussed the importance of selecting a qualified investment bank, and considered several investment banking firms. Aside from Hambrecht & Quist ("H & Q"), Quickturn's long-time investment banker, other firms that the board considered included Goldman Sachs & Co. and Morgan Stanley Dean Witter. Ultimately, the board selected H & Q, because the board believed that H & Q had the most experience with the EDA industry in general and with Quickturn in particular.

During the balance of the meeting, the board discussed for approximately one or two hours (a) the status, terms, and conditions of Mentor's offer; (b) the status of Quickturn's patent litigation with Mentor; (c) the applicable rules and regulations that would govern the board's response to the offer required by the Securities Exchange Act of 1934 (the "34 Act"); (d) the board's fiduciary duties to Quickturn and its shareholders in a tender offer context; (e) the scope of defensive measures available to the corporation if the board decided that the offer was not in the best interests of the company or its stockholders; (f) Quickturn's then-current Rights Plan and special stockholders meeting by-law provisions; (g) the need for a federal antitrust filing; and (h) the potential effect of Mentor's offer on Quickturn's employees. The board also instructed management and H & Q to prepare analyses to assist the directors in evaluating Mentor's offer, and scheduled two board meetings, August 17, and August 21, 1998.

The Quickturn board next met on August 17, 1998. That meeting centered around financial presentations by management and by H & Q. Mr. Keith Lobo, Quickturn's President and CEO, presented a Medium Term Strategic Plan, which was a "top down" estimate detailing the economic outlook and the company's future sales, income prospects and future plans (the "Medium Term Plan"). The Medium Term Plan contained an optimistic (30%) revenue growth projection for the period 1998–2000. After management made its presentation, H & Q supplied its valuation of Quickturn, which relied upon a "base case" that assumed management's 30% revenue growth projection. On that basis, H & Q presented various "standalone" valuations based on various techniques, including a discounted cash flow ("DCF") analysis. Finally, the directors discussed possible defensive measure, but took no action at that time.

The Quickturn board held its third and final meeting in response to Mentor's offer on August 21, 1998. Again, the directors received extensive materials and a further detailed analysis performed by H & Q. The focal point of that analysis was a chart entitled "Summary of Implied Valuation." That chart compared Mentor's tender offer price to the Quickturn valuation ranges generated by H & Q's application of five different methodologies.[14] The chart showed that Quickturn's value under all but

---

14. The five methodologies and the respective price ranges were: Historical Trading Range ($6.13–$21.63); Comparable Public Companies ($2.55–$15.61); Comparable M & A Transactions ($6.00–$31.36); Comparable Premiums Paid ($9.54–$10.72); and Discounted Cash Flow Analysis ($11.88–$57.87).

one of those methodologies was higher than Mentor's $12.125 tender offer price.

After hearing the presentations, the Quickturn board concluded that Mentor's offer was inadequate, and decided to recommend that Quickturn shareholders reject Mentor's offer. The directors based their decision upon: (a) H & Q's report; (b) the fact that Quickturn was experiencing a temporary trough in its business, which was reflected in its stock price; (c) the company's leadership in technology and patents and resulting market share; (d) the likely growth in Quickturn's markets (most notably, the Asian market) and the strength of Quickturn's new products (specifically, its Mercury product); (e) the potential value of the patent litigation with Mentor; and (f) the problems for Quickturn's customers, employees, and technology if the two companies were combined as the result of a hostile takeover.

At the August 21 board meeting, the Quickturn board adopted two defensive measures in response to Mentor's hostile takeover bid. First, the board amended Article II, § 2.3 of Quickturn's by-laws, which permitted stockholders holding 10% or more of Quickturn's stock to call a special stockholders meeting. The By–Law Amendment provides that if any such special meeting is requested by shareholders, the corporation (Quickturn) would fix the record date for, and determine the time and place of, that special meeting, which must take place not less than 90 days nor more than 100 days after the receipt and determination of the validity of the shareholders' request.

Second, the board amended Quickturn's shareholder Rights Plan by eliminating its "dead hand" feature and replacing it with the Deferred Redemption Provision, under which no newly elected board could redeem the Rights Plan for six months after taking office, if the purpose or effect of the redemption would be to facilitate a transaction with an "Interested Person" (one who proposed, nominated or financially supported the election of the new directors to the board).[15] Mentor would be an Interested Person.

The effect of the By–Law Amendment would be to delay a shareholder-called special meeting for at least three months. The effect of the DRP would be to delay the ability of a newly-elected, Mentor-nominated board to redeem the Rights Plan or "poison pill" for six months, in any transaction with an Interested Person. Thus, the combined effect of the

---

15. The amended Rights Plan pertinently provides that: "[I]n the event that a majority of the Board of Directors of the Company is elected by stockholder action at an annual or special meeting of stockholders, then until the 180th day following the effectiveness of such election (including any postponement or adjournment thereof), the Rights shall not be redeemed if such redemption is reasonably likely to have the purpose or effect of facilitating a Transaction with an Interested Person." An "Interested Person" is defined under the amended Rights Plan as "any Person who (i) is or will become an Acquiring Person if such Transaction were to be consummated or an Affiliate or Associate of such a Person, and (ii) is, or directly or indirectly proposed, nominated or financially supported, a director of [Quickturn] in office at the time of consideration of such Transaction who was elected at an annual or special meeting of stockholders."

two defensive measures would be to delay any acquisition of Quickturn by Mentor for at least nine months.

At the time Mentor commenced its tender offer and proxy contest, Quickturn's by-laws authorized shareholders holding at least 10% of Quickturn's voting stock to call a special meeting of stockholders. The then-applicable by-law, Article II, § 2.3, read thusly:

> A special meeting of the stockholders may be called at any time by (i) the board of directors, (ii) the chairman of the board, (iii) the president, (iv) the chief executive officer or (v) one or more shareholders holding shares in the aggregate entitled to cast not less than ten percent (10%) of the votes at that meeting.

At the August 21, 1998 board meeting, the Quickturn board amended § 2.3 in response to the Mentor bid, to read as follows:

> A special meeting of the stockholders may be called at any time by (i) the board of directors, (ii) the chairman of the board, (iii) the president, (iv) the chief executive officer or (v) *subject to the procedures set forth in this Section 2.3,* one or more stockholders holding shares in the aggregate entitled to cast not less than ten percent (10%) of the votes at that meeting.
>
> Upon request in writing sent by registered mail to the president or chief executive officer by any stockholder or stockholders entitled to call a special meeting of stockholders pursuant to this Section 2.3, the board of directors shall determine a place and time for such meeting, which time shall be not less than ninety (90) nor more than one hundred (100) days after the receipt and determination of the validity of such request, and a record date for the determination of stockholders entitled to vote at such meeting in the manner set forth in Section 2.12 hereof. Following such receipt and determination, it shall be the duty of the secretary to cause notice to be given to the stockholders entitled to vote at such meeting, in the manner set forth in Section 2.4 hereof, that a meeting will be held at the time and place so determined. * * *

At the time Mentor commenced its bid, Quickturn had in place a Rights Plan that contained a so-called "dead hand" provision. That provision had a limited "continuing director" feature that became operative only if an insurgent that owned more than 15% of Quickturn's common stock successfully waged a proxy contest to replace a majority of the board. In that event, only the "continuing directors" (those directors in office at the time the poison pill was adopted) could redeem the rights.

During the same August 21, 1998 meeting at which it amended the special meeting by-law, the Quickturn board also amended the Rights Plan to eliminate its "continuing director" feature, and to substitute a "no hand" or "delayed redemption provision" into its Rights Plan. The Delayed Redemption Provision provides that, if a majority of the directors are replaced by stockholder action, the newly elected board cannot redeem the rights for six months if the purpose or effect of the redemption would be to facilitate a transaction with an "Interested Person."[21]

It is undisputed that the DRP would prevent Mentor's slate, if elected as the new board majority, from redeeming the Rights Plan for six months following their election, because a redemption would be "reasonably likely to have the purpose or effect of facilitating a Transaction" with Mentor, a party that "directly or indirectly proposed, nominated or financially supported" the election of the new board. Consequently, by adopting the DRP, the Quickturn board built into the process a six month delay period in addition to the 90 to 100 day delay mandated by the By–Law Amendment. * * *

In this appeal, Mentor argues that the judgment of the Court of Chancery should be affirmed because the Delayed Redemption Provision is invalid as a matter of Delaware law. According to Mentor, the Delayed Redemption Provision, like the "dead hand" feature in the Rights Plan that was held to be invalid in *Toll Brothers* will impermissibly deprive any newly elected board of both its statutory authority to manage the corporation under 8 *Del.C.* § 141(a) and its concomitant fiduciary duty pursuant to that statutory mandate. We agree.

Our analysis of the Delayed Redemption Provision in the Quickturn Rights Plan is guided by the prior precedents of this Court with regard to a board of directors authority to adopt a Rights Plan or "poison pill." In *Moran,* this Court held that the "inherent powers of the Board conferred by 8 *Del.C.* § 141(a) concerning the management of the corporation's 'business and affairs' provides the Board additional authority upon which to enact the Rights Plan." Consequently, this Court upheld the adoption of the Rights Plan in *Moran* as a legitimate exercise of business judgment by the board of directors. In doing so, however, this Court also held "the rights plan is not absolute" . . .

In *Moran,* this Court held that the "ultimate response to an actual takeover bid must be judged by the Directors' actions at the time and nothing we say relieves them of their fundamental duties to the corporation and its shareholders." Consequently, we concluded that the use of the Rights Plan would be evaluated when and if the issue arises.

One of the most basic tenets of Delaware corporate law is that the board of directors has the ultimate responsibility for managing the business and affairs of a corporation. Section 141(a) requires that any limitation on the board's authority be set out in the certificate of incorporation.

---

21. The "no hand" or Delayed Redemption Provision is found in a new Section 23(b) of the Rights Plan, which states:

(b) Notwithstanding the provisions of Section 23(a), in the event that a majority of the Board of Directors of the Company is elected by stockholder action at an annual or special meeting of stockholders, then until the 180th day following the effectiveness of such election (including any postponement or adjournment thereof), the Rights shall not be redeemed if such redemption is reasonably likely to have the purpose or effect of facilitating a Transaction with an Interested Person.

Substantially similar provisions were added to Sections 24 ("Exchange") and 27 ("Supplements and Amendments") of the Rights Plan.

The Quickturn certificate of incorporation contains no provision purporting to limit the authority of the board in any way. The Delayed Redemption Provision, however, would prevent a newly elected board of directors from *completely* discharging its fundamental management duties to the corporation and its stockholders for six months. While the Delayed Redemption Provision limits the board of directors' authority in only one respect, the suspension of the Rights Plan, it nonetheless restricts the board's power in an area of fundamental importance to the shareholders—negotiating a possible sale of the corporation. Therefore, we hold that the Delayed Redemption Provision is invalid under Section 141(a), which confers upon any newly elected board of directors *full* power to manage and direct the business and affairs of a Delaware corporation.

In discharging the statutory mandate of Section 141(a), the directors have a fiduciary duty to the corporation and its shareholders. This unremitting obligation extends equally to board conduct in a contest for corporate control. The Delayed Redemption Provision prevents a newly elected board of directors from completely discharging its fiduciary duties to protect fully the interests of Quickturn and its stockholders.

This Court has recently observed that "although the fiduciary duty of a Delaware director is unremitting, the exact course of conduct that must be charted to properly discharge that responsibility will change in the specific context of the action the director is taking with regard to either the corporation or its shareholders." This Court has held "[t]o the extent that a contract, or a provision thereof, purports to require a board to act *or not act* in such a fashion as to limit the exercise of fiduciary duties, it is invalid and unenforceable." The Delayed Redemption Provision "tends to limit in a substantial way the freedom of [newly elected] directors' decisions on matters of management policy." Therefore, "it violates the duty of each [newly elected] director to exercise his own best judgment on matters coming before the board."

In this case, the Quickturn board was confronted by a determined bidder that sought to acquire the company at a price the Quickturn board concluded was inadequate. Such situations are common in corporate takeover efforts. In *Revlon,* this Court held that no defensive measure can be sustained when it represents a breach of the directors' fiduciary duty. A *fortiori,* no defensive measure can be sustained which would require a new board of directors to breach its fiduciary duty. In that regard, we note Mentor has properly acknowledged that in the event its slate of directors is elected, those newly elected directors will be required to discharge their unremitting fiduciary duty to manage the corporation for the benefit of Quickturn and its stockholders.

The Delayed Redemption Provision would prevent a new Quickturn board of directors from managing the corporation by redeeming the Rights Plan to facilitate a transaction that would serve the stockholders' best interests, even under circumstances where the board would be required to do so because of its fiduciary duty to the Quickturn stockholders. Because the Delayed Redemption Provision impermissibly circumscribes the board's statutory power under Section 141(a) and the directors' ability to fulfill their concomitant fiduciary duties, we hold that the Delayed Redemption Provision is invalid. On that alternative basis, the judgment of the Court of Chancery is AFFIRMED.

OMNICARE, INC. v. NCS HEALTHCARE, INC.

818 A.2d 914 (Del. 2003).

HOLLAND, JUSTICE.

* * *

The board of directors of NCS, an insolvent publicly traded Delaware corporation, agreed to the terms of a merger with Genesis. Pursuant to that agreement, all of the NCS creditors would be paid in full and the corporation's stockholders would exchange their shares for the shares of Genesis, a publicly traded Pennsylvania corporation. Several months after approving the merger agreement, but before the stockholder vote was scheduled, the NCS board of directors withdrew its prior recommendation in favor of the Genesis merger.

In fact, the NCS board recommended that the stockholders reject the Genesis transaction after deciding that a competing proposal from Omnicare was a superior transaction. The competing Omnicare bid offered the NCS stockholders an amount of cash equal to more than twice the then current market value of the shares to be received in the Genesis merger. The transaction offered by Omnicare also treated the NCS corporation's other stakeholders on equal terms with the Genesis agreement.

The merger agreement between Genesis and NCS contained a provision authorized by Section 251(c) of Delaware's corporation law. It required that the Genesis agreement be placed before the corporation's stockholders for a vote, even if the NCS board of directors no longer recommended it. At the insistence of Genesis, the NCS board also agreed to omit any effective fiduciary clause from the merger agreement. In connection with the Genesis merger agreement, two stockholders of NCS, who held a majority of the voting power, agreed unconditionally to vote all of their shares in favor of the Genesis merger. Thus, the combined terms of the voting agreements and merger agreement guaranteed, *ab initio*, that the transaction proposed by Genesis would obtain NCS stockholder's approval.

The Court of Chancery ruled that the voting agreements, when coupled with the provision in the Genesis merger agreement requiring that it be presented to the stockholders for a vote pursuant to 8 *Del. C.* § 251(c), constituted defensive measures within the meaning of *Unocal*

Corp. v. Mesa Petroleum Co.[2] After applying the *Unocal* standard of enhanced judicial scrutiny, the Court of Chancery held that those defensive measures were reasonable. We have concluded that, in the absence of an effective fiduciary out clause, those defensive measures are both preclusive and coercive. Therefore, we hold that those defensive measures are invalid and unenforceable. * * *

It is well established that conflicts of interest arise when a board of directors acts to prevent stockholders from effectively exercising their right to vote contrary to the will of the board. The "omnipresent specter" of such conflict may be present whenever a board adopts defensive devices to protect a merger agreement. The stockholders' ability to effectively reject a merger agreement is likely to bear an inversely proportionate relationship to the structural and economic devices that the board has approved to protect the transaction. * * *

There are inherent conflicts between a board's interest in protecting a merger transaction it has approved, the stockholders' statutory right to make the final decision to either approve or not approve a merger, and the board's continuing responsibility to effectively exercise its fiduciary duties at all times after the merger agreement is executed. These competing considerations require a threshold determination that board-approved defensive devices protecting a merger transaction are within the limitations of its statutory authority and consistent with the directors' fiduciary duties. * * *

In *Paramount v. QVC,* this Court identified the key features of an enhanced judicial scrutiny test. The first feature is a "judicial determination regarding the adequacy of the decisionmaking process employed by the directors, including the information on which the directors based their decision." The second feature is "a judicial examination of the reasonableness of the directors' action in light of the circumstances then existing." We also held that "the directors have the burden of proving that they were adequately informed and acted reasonably."

In *QVC,* we explained that the application of an enhanced judicial scrutiny test involves a judicial "review of the reasonableness of the substantive merits of the board's actions." * * * In applying that standard, we held that "a court should not ignore the complexity of the directors' task" in the context in which action was taken. Accordingly, we concluded that a court applying enhanced judicial scrutiny should not decide whether the directors made a perfect decision but instead should decide whether "the directors' decision was, on balance, within a range of reasonableness." * * *

[I]n applying enhanced judicial scrutiny to defensive devices designed to protect a merger agreement, a court must first determine that those measures are not preclusive or coercive *before* its focus shifts to the "range of reasonableness" in making a proportionality determination. If the trial

---

   2. *Unocal Corp. v. Mesa Petroleum Co.,* 493 A.2d 946 (Del.1985). *See also Unitrin, Inc. v. Am. Gen. Corp.,* 651 A.2d 1361, 1386–89 (Del.1995).

court determines that the defensive devices protecting a merger are not preclusive or coercive, the proportionality paradigm of *Unocal* is applicable. The board must demonstrate that it has reasonable grounds for believing that a danger to the corporation and its stockholders exists if the merger transaction is not consummated. That burden is satisfied "by showing good faith and reasonable investigation." Such proof is materially enhanced if it is approved by a board comprised of a majority of outside directors or by an independent committee.

When the focus of judicial scrutiny shifts to the range of reasonableness, *Unocal* requires that any defensive devices must be proportionate to the perceived threat to the corporation and its stockholders if the merger transaction is not consummated. Defensive devices taken to protect a merger agreement executed by a board of directors are intended to give that agreement an advantage over any subsequent transactions that materialize before the merger is approved by the stockholders and consummated. This is analogous to the favored treatment that a board of directors may properly give to encourage an initial bidder when it discharges its fiduciary duties under *Revlon*.

* * * The latitude a board will have in either maintaining or using the defensive devices it has adopted to protect the merger it approved will vary according to the degree of benefit or detriment to the stockholders' interests that is presented by the value or terms of the subsequent competing transaction.

Genesis' One Day Ultimatum

The record reflects that two of the four NCS board members, Shaw and Outcalt, were also the *same* two NCS stockholders who combined to control a majority of the stockholder voting power. Genesis gave the four person NCS board less than twenty-four hours to vote in favor of its proposed merger agreement. Genesis insisted the merger agreement include a Section 251(c) clause, mandating its submission for a stockholder vote even if the board's recommendation was withdrawn. Genesis further insisted that the merger agreement omit any effective fiduciary out clause.

Genesis also gave the two stockholder members of the NCS board, Shaw and Outcalt, the same accelerated time table to personally sign the proposed voting agreements. These voting agreements committed them irrevocably to vote their majority power in favor of the merger and further provided in Section 6 that the voting agreements be specifically enforceable. Genesis also required that NCS execute the voting agreements.

Genesis' twenty-four hour ultimatum was that, *unless both* the merger agreement and the voting agreements were signed with the terms it requested, its offer was going to be withdrawn. According to Genesis' attorneys, these "were unalterable conditions to Genesis' willingness to proceed." Genesis insisted on the execution of the interlocking voting rights and merger agreements because it feared that Omnicare would make a superior merger proposal. The NCS board signed the voting rights and merger agreements, without any effective fiduciary out clause, to expressly guarantee that the Genesis merger would be approved, even if a superior merger transaction was presented from Omnicare or any other entity.

Deal Protection Devices

Defensive devices, as that term is used in this opinion, is a synonym for what are frequently referred to as "deal protection devices." Both terms are used interchangeably to describe any measure or combination of measures that are intended to protect the consummation of a merger transaction. Defensive devices can be economic, structural, or both.

Deal protection devices need not all be in the merger agreement itself. In this case, for example, the Section 251(c) provision in the merger agreement was combined with the separate voting agreements to provide a structural defense for the Genesis merger agreement against any subsequent superior transaction. Genesis made the NCS board's defense of its transaction absolute by insisting on the omission of any effective fiduciary out clause in the NCS merger agreement. * * *

In this case, the Court of Chancery correctly held that the NCS directors' decision to adopt defensive devices to *completely* "lock up" the Genesis merger mandated "special scrutiny" under the two-part test set forth in *Unocal*. That conclusion is consistent with our holding in *Paramount v. Time* that "safety devices" adopted to protect a transaction that did not result in a change of control are subject to enhanced judicial scrutiny under a *Unocal* analysis. The record does not, however, support the Court of Chancery's conclusion that the defensive devices adopted by the NCS board to protect the Genesis merger were reasonable and proportionate to the threat that NCS perceived from the potential loss of the Genesis transaction.

Pursuant to the judicial scrutiny required under *Unocal's* two-stage analysis, the NCS directors must first demonstrate "that they had reasonable grounds for believing that a danger to corporate policy and effectiveness existed...." To satisfy that burden, the NCS directors are required to show they acted in good faith after conducting a reasonable investigation. The threat identified by the NCS board was the possibility of losing the Genesis offer and being left with no comparable alternative transaction. * * *

Although the minority stockholders were not forced to vote for the Genesis merger, they were required to accept it because it was *a fait accompli*. The record reflects that the defensive devices employed by the NCS board are preclusive and coercive in the sense that they accomplished *a fait accompli*. In this case, despite the fact that the NCS board has withdrawn its recommendation for the Genesis transaction and recommended its rejection by the stockholders, the deal protection devices approved by the NCS board operated in concert to have a preclusive and coercive effect. Those tripartite defensive measures—the Section 251(c) provision, the voting agreements, and the absence of an effective fiduciary out clause—made it "mathematically impossible" and "realistically unattainable" for the Omnicare transaction or any other proposal to succeed, no matter how superior the proposal.

The deal protection devices adopted by the NCS board were designed to coerce the consummation of the Genesis merger and preclude the consideration of any superior transaction. The NCS directors' defensive devices are not within a reasonable range of responses to the perceived threat of losing the Genesis offer because they are preclusive and coercive. Accordingly, we hold that those deal protection devices are unenforceable.

The defensive measures that protected the merger transaction are unenforceable not only because they are preclusive and coercive but, alternatively, they are unenforceable because they are invalid as they operate in this case. Given the specifically enforceable irrevocable voting agreements, the provision in the merger agreement requiring the board to submit the transaction for a stockholder vote and the omission of a fiduciary out clause in the merger agreement completely prevented the board from discharging its fiduciary responsibilities to the minority stockholders when Omnicare presented its superior transaction. "To the extent that a [merger] contract, or a provision thereof, purports to require a board to act or not act in such a fashion as to limit the exercise of fiduciary duties, it is invalid and unenforceable." * * *

Under the circumstances presented in this case, where a cohesive group of stockholders with majority voting power was irrevocably committed to the merger transaction, "[e]ffective representation of the financial interests of the minority shareholders imposed upon the [NCS board] an affirmative responsibility to protect those minority shareholders' interests." The NCS board could not abdicate its fiduciary duties to the minority by leaving it to the stockholders alone to approve or disapprove the merger agreement because two stockholders had already combined to establish a majority of the voting power that made the outcome of the stockholder vote a foregone conclusion. * * *

The stockholders of a Delaware corporation are entitled to rely upon the board to discharge its fiduciary duties at all times. The fiduciary duties of a director are unremitting and must be effectively discharged in the specific context of the actions that are required with regard to the corporation or its stockholders as circumstances change. The stockholders with majority voting power, Shaw and Outcalt, had an absolute right to sell or exchange their shares with a third party at any price. This right was not only known to the other directors of NCS, it became an integral part of the Genesis agreement. In its answering brief, Genesis candidly states that its offer "came with a condition—Genesis would not be a stalking horse and would not agree to a transaction to which NCS's controlling shareholders were not committed." * * *

In the context of this preclusive and coercive lock up case, the protection of Genesis' contractual expectations must yield to the supervening responsibility of the directors to discharge their fiduciary duties on a continuing basis. The merger agreement and voting agreements, as they were combined to operate in concert in this case, are inconsistent with the NCS directors' fiduciary duties. To that extent, we hold that they are invalid and unenforceable.

FIRST UNION CORP. v. SUNTRUST BANKS, INC.

2001 WL 1885686.
(N.C. Bus. Ct. Aug. 10, 2001).*

TENNILLE, JUDGE

This matter comes to the Court as a result of the proposed merger between First Union Corporation ("First Union") and Wachovia Corporation ("Wachovia"), and SunTrust Banks, Inc.'s ("SunTrust") resulting unsolicited bid for Wachovia. SunTrust and the shareholder plaintiffs in the consolidated cases (hereinafter collectively referred to as "SunTrust") request that this Court invalidate a non-termination provision in the merger agreement and enjoin consummation of the merger pending determination of the validity of provisions in an Option Agreement entered into in connection with the merger. All parties request declaratory judgment with respect to validity of the Option Agreement. For the reasons set forth below, the Court finds the non-termination provision invalid and unenforceable and declines to enter the injunctive relief requested. * * *

The results of the ongoing reevaluation are not complete, but some conclusions can be drawn. First, the number of standards of review has become confusing and contributes to an inability of practitioners to advise their clients appropriately. Second, the use of categories of transactions to which standards of review are applied has been perceived as outcome determinative. As a result, practitioners have focused too heavily on making their transactions fit within a category. Third, the Delaware Supreme Court has erroneously blended the duty of care standard and the test of entire fairness creating confusion in the bar. As a result, the original benefits of the circumstance specific application of the business judgment rule in duty of care cases and the application of the entire fairness test in duty of loyalty cases have been lost. Those standards of review need to be reevaluated and reapplied in a way that serves their original purpose, which was to acknowledge certain institutional requirements under particular circumstances. Fourth, the straight application of either the business judgment rule or the entire fairness test does not work to resolve the tensions between the conflicting requirements of shareholders and directors in transactions or board actions affecting the shareholders' right to sell or vote. The use of some other review process is required. Failure to provide a meaningful review process will remove a critical tool and much needed flexibility in resolving the inherent conflict between the

---

* http//www.ncbusinesscourt.net. The court's prolonged discussion of the facts and of the Delaware cases is omitted. For a description and history of the North Carolina business court, *see* Russell M. Robinson II, Robinson on North Carolina Corporation Law § 1.04 (6th ed. 2000).

internal requirements of our corporate system. Fifth, the intermediate standards adopted in Delaware are confusing and perhaps not internally consistent. The focus on "entrenchment" may be part of the problem. The necessity for courts to evaluate "threats" and "proportional responses" starts to sound a lot like nondeferential judicial review of business decisions. A refocus on the relationship between shareholder rights and directors duties to make informed decisions in good faith would be more helpful. The current language in Delaware may not be reflective of what is actually happening there. Circumstance-specific review procedures should not be abandoned. They provide needed flexibility.

Ten lessons can be learned from the Delaware experience in designing review processes in corporate law. 1. The review process should enhance corporate value and appropriately balance the competing interests in the corporate structure. 2. Review processes should be circumstance-and task-specific. 3. Clarity in language is important. Confusion can result from appropriating language from standards of review and conduct from other circumstances and situations. 4. Simpler is better; fewer is preferable. 5. Director attention to process should be encouraged. 6. Fairness and efficiency must be considered. 7. The nature of the legal duties at issue is important. As the importance of the legal duty increases, the narrower should be the gap between the standard of review and the standard of conduct. 8. To the extent possible, the review process should extricate the courts from substituting their judgment for the business decisions of those with superior business knowledge. 9. The process should discourage frivolous lawsuits. 10. Review processes should provide guideposts from which businesses and their advisors can discern when judicial intervention might occur. * * *

Our system requires: (a) that directors have the power and authority to plan, develop, design, negotiate and contract for mergers and other acquisitions fundamental to the corporation's business strategy, (b) that shareholders have the right to vote on any such fundamental changes in corporate structure and (c) that their vote results in a free, uncoerced and informed valuation of the proposed corporate action. Exposing a transaction to valuation in the marketplace is the best test of its worth. When corporate law adopts a review process that insures that these structural requirements are met, it promotes corporate value.

Trapped in the linguistic box of Delaware law, counsel for all the parties suggest resolution of the issues in this case in terms of standards of review employed in Delaware. First Union and Wachovia urge the court to adopt a business judgment approach while SunTrust and counsel for the shareholders promote the *Unocal* review process. Each side can point to decisions of the Chancery Court that support its position, and strong policy arguments can be made for each. Vice Chancellor Strine has set those arguments out in great detail and more effectively than this court could in his article *Categorical Confusion: Deal Protection Measures in Stock-for-Stock Merger Agreements*. He concludes his article with a suggestion that a judicial emphasis on uncoerced shareholder choice makes sense in trying to balance the competing pressures from shareholders and directors in the circumstance of stock-for-stock mergers:

> Although one can press the point too far, an approach that focuses on uncoerced stockholder choice does much to reconcile these values. How? For starters, this emphasis is faithful to a key theme of *Time–Warner*. Well-motivated directors ought to have the right to present a strategic merger to their stockholders and to give their merger partner substantial contractual protections to induce them to contract. Unlike in the *Revlon* context, the court will defer to director decisions to give a preferred merger partner bidding and timing advantages over later emerging rivals. This deference to directors, as a practical matter, may mean that the courts will give scant weight to whether deal protection measures are preclusive of other bids as a short-term matter. That is, if all the board is asking for is to go first and to require other bidders to await the outcome of an unfettered stockholder vote, it seems likely to get that opportunity.

> At the same time, this emphasis on stockholder choice recognizes that a stock-for-stock merger agreement is not an ordinary contract within the sole power of the directors to consummate. Stockholders have the right to vote yes or no without being, in essence, compelled or coerced.

> Stockholders can legitimately expect that their directors will bring a merger proposal to a reasonably prompt vote so that the mere passage of time does not leave the board's preferred deal as the only viable corporate strategy. Stockholders also have a right to a genuine, current recommendation from their directors regarding the advisability of the transaction.

> This judicial emphasis on stockholder choice makes sense. It gives boards the first bite at the apple and contractual tools to use to accomplish their preferred strategy. It enables the merger partners to receive contractual protections that limit their injuries if transactions do not go through. But it also ensures integrity by limiting the boards' ability to intrude on the stockholders' co-equal right to approve mergers.

> Of course, the judicial task of determining whether deal protection measures have deprived the stockholders of a fair chance to vote freely on a transaction has its own difficulties. Nonetheless, channeling the judicial inquiry in this way has the virtue of reinforcing the primacy of director and stockholder decision-making. It also provides a relatively elegant way of acknowledging the greater scope of director discretion that exists in the non-*Revlon* context, while also recognizing that the stockholder "ownership" interests that take primacy in the *Revlon* context also loom large when a corporate board presents a stock-for-stock merger agreement.[110]

---

110.   See Strine, [56 Bus. Law. 919, 942.

The policy considerations supporting Vice Chancellor Strine's approach are compelling. That approach serves to balance the competing interests in a fair and efficient manner. It recognizes the importance of the legal duty to protect the shareholder right to vote and thus does not employ a standard of review that diverges from the standard of conduct. It narrows the gap where the legal rights are most important.

It also dovetails into what this court believes the North Carolina Legislature intended to do when it amended N.C.G.S. § 55–8–30(d). That amendment provided: "[t]he *duties* of a director *weighing a change of control situation* shall not be any different, nor the *standard of care* any higher, than otherwise provided in this section." [emphasis added].[111] The amendment did not refer to a standard of review, and the legislature did not make any change in the shareholders' right to vote on a merger. The most reasonable interpretation of the Legislature's intent was that it intended to eliminate by statute the unidimensional requirement imposed on directors by *Revlon*. The impetus for the change is unclear. It is clear that the amendment evidenced a policy that obtaining the highest dollar value for the shareholders was not the *sole* criteria by which the courts could or should judge the conduct of directors in change of control situations. To the extent *Revlon* could be read to require a higher level of attentiveness from directors in change of control situations than in other situations, the amendment eliminated that requirement as well. * * * Like Illinois and other states, it rejected the pure property concept of corporate value so firmly held in Delaware and aligned itself with states which adopted the social entity concept of corporations.

The 1993 amendment was directed to *Revlon* and its implications. At the time it was enacted, *Unocal* and its progeny had long been decided. Nothing in the amendment appears to be directed specifically to the *Unocal* standard of review. There is certainly nothing in the amendment which indicates that the legislature intended to diminish shareholders' voting rights. Thus, a review process that provides some deference to the directors' strategic decisions while vigorously preserving the shareholders' voting rights in connection with the transaction would fit neatly into North Carolina's policy position. What would such a review process look like? In reviewing deal protection measures in a stock-for-stock merger subject to shareholder approval, the court will first review the transaction, including the adoption of deal protection measures, to determine if the directors have complied with their statutory duty of care under N.C.G.S. § 55–8–30. The burden is upon the shareholder challenging their actions

---

111. North Carolina General Statute 55–8–30 provides that "[a] director is not liable for any action taken as a director, or any failure to take any action, if he performed the duties...." [i]n good faith; (2) [w]ith the care an ordinarily prudent person in a like position would exercise under similar circumstances; and (3) [i]n a manner he reasonably believes to be in the best interests of the corporation. "N.C.G.S. § 55–8–30 (a), (d) (1990) (amended 1993). Additionally the statute states that "[t]he duties of a director weighing a change of control situation shall not be any different, nor the standard of care any higher, than otherwise provided in this section." N.C.G.S. § 55–8–30 (d) (1990) (amended 1993). This statute embodies but does not abrogate the common law of the business judgment rule. See State ex rel. Long v. ILA Corp., 132 N.C. App. 587, 601, 513 S.E.2d 812, 821 (1999).

to prove that a breach of duty has occurred. If no breach of duty is proven, the action of the directors is entitled to a strong presumption of reasonableness and validity, including noncoercion, and the court should not intervene unless the shareholder can rebut that presumption by clear and convincing evidence that the deal protection provisions were actionably coercive, or that the deal protection provisions prevented the directors from performing their statutory duties. If a breach of duty is established, the burden shifts to the directors to prove that their actions were reasonable and that it is in the best interests of the shareholders that they be permitted to vote on the transaction, and, if at issue, that the deal protection measures were not actionably coercive and did not prevent the directors from performing their statutory duties. Where the court finds that the deal protection measures are coercive or require directors to breach their statutory duties, the court must then weigh the harm to the shareholders in enjoining either the deal protection measures, the vote on the transaction or the merger, if the transaction is approved, against the harm resulting from not entering injunctive relief. That is a very case- and fact-specific determination.

The existence of the non-termination clause in this case demonstrates why a simple application of the business judgment rule fails to afford protection to shareholders. Here, the Court has found that the Wachovia Board acted in good faith, on an informed basis and in the best interests of the corporation in entering into the merger agreement with the non-termination clause included. The directors had good advisors and they properly relied upon them. If the business judgment rule were the sole determinant or review process, the non-termination clause would not be subject to further review. With the review process adopted by the Court, the non-termination clause gets reviewed for the specific reason that good public policy requires—directors must fulfill their fundamental statutory obligations and shareholders should have an uncoerced vote.

The business judgment rule applied in the enterprise transaction lets some legal rights go unredressed for the sake of the efficiency of the system. When the legal rights are statutory shareholder rights, "sacred space," the review process should not permit these legal rights to go unredressed. Failure to provide redress for violation of statutory rights destroys the balance in the system. The simple application of the business judgment rule without further review does not serve the needs of the system in ownership issue cases.

For over a decade, corporate counselors have searched creatively for procedures which could delay, impede or discourage shareholder action unfavorable to incumbent boards. The Court is not being critical. They are representing their clients. The Delaware courts have been consistent in rejecting those creative ideas in each case in which they resulted in the abrogation of a director's exercise of her statutory duties.

To the lexicon of poison pills, dead hands, no hands and slow hands, we must now add *numb hands*. The contractual provision in this merger agreement that extends the life of the agreement five months beyond a shareholder vote disapproving the merger is invalid. It is an impermissible abrogation of the duties of the Wachovia directors and an actionably coercive condition impeding the free exercise of the Wachovia shareholder's right to vote on the merger.

By contract, the directors have limited their ability to perform their fiduciary duties in a way which would be prohibited if done in a by-law. It is the equivalent of a contractual *Quickturn*.

The analogy to *Quickturn* is clear. In this case, if there had been a proxy fight over seats on the Wachovia Board at the same time the merger proposal was submitted, and SunTrust had elected a majority of directors, those new directors would have been contractually hobbled in the same way that the *Quickturn* directors were restricted by virtue of the poison pill in that case. If the Wachovia shareholders vote against the merger, this board has impermissibly tied its hands and cannot do the very thing the Delaware Supreme Court found to be of fundamental importance to the shareholders—"negotiating a possible sale of the corporation." The fact that directors can exercise their fiduciary duty by breaching the contract does not solve the problem. Directors should not enter into a contract that they know their fiduciary duty could cause them to breach.

Non-termination contractual provisions are the proverbial camel's nose under the tent in the effort to delay action after an adverse shareholder vote. Our system gives the board broad authority to act. Concomitantly, it requires the board to fulfill those duties. Every effort to prevent or excuse directors from performing their statutory duties has been rebuffed by the courts. This court is not aware of any judicial blessing of non-termination clauses similar to this one.

Wachovia and First Union may still negotiate a new proposal even if this provision is stricken. In the absence of the provision, directors are not prevented from fulfilling their fiduciary duty if another offer is made after a negative vote. Nor will the directors be required to breach a contract to fulfill their fiduciary duty.

Such cryonic[b] provisions may also be coercive. This non-termination provision creates uncertainty for Wachovia shareholders. They can either vote for the merger or run the risk that something will happen in the ensuing five months that will be disadvantageous in light of the directors' inability to respond to any offers. Anytime an investor's choice is unnecessarily clouded by uncertainty, there is a degree of coercion. Investors rightfully abhor uncertainty. By contractually limiting their ability to act, the directors have created uncertainty. It unnecessarily extends the time of the option granted to First Union in the event the Wachovia shareholders vote against the merger. The tail becomes 23 rather than 18 months.

---

[b]. Cryonics is the process of freezing living creatures to keep them in suspended animation. See, e.g., *http://www.cryonics.org/*. Ted Williams, the famous baseball player, was among those being frozen, albeit posthumously. Richard Sandomir, Baseball; Legends Images Often Change in Death, N.Y. Times, July 15, 2002, at D2.

The longer the option is effective, the more likely shareholders are to vote for the bird in the hand.

This provision must also be considered in light of the inability of other suitors to get any proposal before the board. The Wachovia Board is staggered, making a proxy fight to change the composition of the board unlikely. When the legislature amended N.C.G.S. 55–7–02(a), it eliminated the possibility that a potential suitor could use a by-law change to get its proposal before the shareholders.... Here, shareholders must vote knowing that this may be the only opportunity they will have to sell for five months. That is coercive.

NOTES

1. Have the courts gone too far in trying to act as referees in corporate takeover battles? Are the courts in a position to act as economic theorists in approving one form of takeover provision over another? Is there a "magic" formula that courts could use to assure shareholder protection while not interfering with economic competition for the control of a business? Is the use of poison pills simply a business risk that shareholders should consider before investing in a corporation?

2. *Financing the Merger*: Another complex part of the merger process is the financing of acquisitions. For example, should there be an exchange of stock, a cash purchase or, as is often the case, a combination of both of these methods? Often, complex merger agreements set the exchange price values at particular ratios because the merging corporations' respective stock prices may fluctuate during the period required for shareholder approval. The agreement may include a "walk away" provision that will allow either party to cancel the merger if the stock prices of the two corporations become so disparate that the deal is no longer economically viable. Stock-for-stock transactions also raise concerns with dilution that may affect exchange ratios.

If a cash buyout is used instead of an exchange of securities, what is the source of the funds and how will payments in cash or the incurrence of additional debt to fund the acquisition affect the acquiring corporation's financial position? The leveraged buyout is a popular method for cash transactions. This arrangement essentially allows the purchase to pay for itself from the cash flows of the company being acquired. Such buyouts are often structured by existing management. This arrangement requires enough cash in excess of other expenses to service the additional debt required to buy out the existing shareholders. This will often require drastic cuts in expenses, requiring massive layoffs and the shut down or sale of unprofitable operations.

Another concern is the source of the loans for the funds used to buy out existing shareholders in a cash transaction. "Junk" bonds are often used for such financing. These less than investment grade securities pay high rates of interest as a reflection of the higher risk of default they pose to the purchaser. The term junk bond is somewhat pejorative, and its proponents prefer the term "high yield." One corporate lawyer, Arthur Liman, has also pointed out that, in the event of bankruptcy, junk bonds will be paid off before stockholders receive anything, yet no one calls stock—"junk stock." The use of these bonds was made popular during the 1980s by Michael Milken, an investment banker at Drexel Burnham & Lambert. His firm would issue "highly confident" letters to corporate raiders, which stated that the firm was highly confident that the financing needed for the acquisition could be raised through an underwriting of high yield securities. This provided the raider with a great deal of leverage since Drexel Burnham was a leading underwriter for such securities. Mergers effected through junk bond financing were much criticized, and Michael Milken was jailed and Drexel Burnham was destroyed in the fallout from the insider trading scandals of the 1980s.

The sources of financing for acquisitions often included several layers of debt: senior, mezzanine and junior debt of varying levels. Venture capitalists often provide capital in large amounts for acquisitions. In a battle over the acquisition of RJR Nabisco Corp., that was won by the KKR venture capital firm, several layers of debt and equity securities were used to finance the acquisition. Among the instruments used were something called reset PIKs (payments-in-kind) that paid interest in securities that would be continually increased to keep the PIKs at par. These securities were also called death spirals because they would eat the company alive if it encountered serious difficulties. See *Bryan Burrough & John Helyar, Barbarians at the Gate: The Fall of RJR Nabisco* (1990). Banks also provided loans to finance acquisitions, sometimes in exchange for warrants or other equity kickers. Hedge funds were another source of funding for acquisitions. These are simply pools of funds obtained from institutions or wealthy investors for investment in high return, and consequently high risk, ventures. Hedge funds are exempt from regulation as investment companies under the Investment Company Act because it is thought their investors are sophisticated enough to fend for themselves, a premise that has not always proved correct. See generally Lakonia Management Ltd. v. Meriwether, 106 F. Supp. 2d 540 (S.D.N.Y.2000) (large losses in market neutral strategies by hedge fund that was managed by geniuses).

3.　Takeovers often attract risk arbitrageurs. These are traders employed by broker-dealers to buy securities of an issuer in anticipation that the company will be taken over and a premium paid to existing shareholders. Risk arbitrageurs also buy securities after a tender offer has been announced at a price above the pre-existing market price but below the tender offer price. Tender offers are often contingent and may fall through when those contingencies are not met or as the result of defensive efforts by incumbent management. This will cause a loss of the offered premium to shareholders. To avoid that risk, shareholders may want to sell to the arbitrageurs at a smaller premium over market and let the arbitrageur assume the risk that the tender offer will succeed. The risk arbitrageur carefully weighs the risk of the tender offer being withdrawn in determining the premium to offer over market. Large profits may be made by the risk arbitrageur, but large losses are equally possible.

4.　Any business combination will have tax consequences. It may be possible, however, to structure the transaction as a nontaxable (and hence tax deferred) event under the provisions of § 368 of the Internal Revenue Code ("IRC").

5. Accounting issues will also arise in the consolidation of two businesses. Historically, an important issue in mergers was whether the "pooling of interests" or "purchase" method of accounting would be used to reflect the acquisition. That decision had a serious effect on future earnings. Under the purchase method, any premium paid over the book value of the assets of the newly acquired company was treated as goodwill that was required to be amortized as a charge against earnings over a maximum period of forty years. That charge operated as an expense and reduced earnings. For that reason, acquiring companies usually preferred to account for an acquisition under an alternative accounting method, the pooling of interests approach. In a pooling, the balance sheets of the two merging companies are combined at book value. Thus, no premium or goodwill is recognized and there is no reduction of earnings by amortization.

The pooling of interests method was criticized, however, for masking the actual accounting effect of an acquisition. In the early 1970's the SEC attempted to require the use of the purchase method, but the agency's efforts to impose such a rule were unsuccessful, even though the United States was one of few countries worldwide that permitted pooling. The debate continued and the Financial Accounting Standards Board (FASB), the body responsible for setting accounting standards, proposed in 1999 that the pooling of accounts method should no longer be used to account for an acquisition, requiring instead the purchase method, and reducing the goodwill amortization period from forty to twenty years. The FASB proposal met opposition, and the FASB later adopted a different approach, eliminating pooling of interests accounting treatment for all mergers initiated after June 30, 2001, and eliminating the requirement that any goodwill resulting from the acquisition be amortized for all acquisitions consummated after June 30, 2001. Goodwill must, however, be assessed annually (or more frequently if certain circumstances warrant) and charged against earnings if it is found to be impaired.

6. There are a number of political issues to resolve in merger situations, and these can often make or break a deal. An important issue is which chief executive officer will lead the combined entity after a merger. The heads of large companies are often reluctant to step down in favor of their counterpart at the other institution. Sometimes the respective heads of the merger partners agree to be co-equals in the new enterprise, but that arrangement rarely works. Other political issues involve the name of the surviving entity. Some corporations have long histories and are reluctant to see their name, and the corporate culture it denotes, disappear. The location of the new headquarters and the composition of the board of directors of the surviving entity are also often hotly negotiated.

7. *Social concerns.* Efforts will be made to make the acquired company more efficient by cutting costs, a necessary element in most leveraged buyouts and desirable in others. In colder terms, this may involve massive layoffs or an entire shutdown of particular business lines or operations that are not profitable. "Chainsaw" Al Dunlop became famous for the ruthless efficiency he applied to trimming corporate "fat" before his tactics failed at Sunbeam Corp. Economists assert that this is desirable in assuring that American companies remain efficient and competitive. That is no doubt true, as evi-

denced by the dominant role played by the United States in the world economy. Nevertheless, layoffs and shutdowns have sometimes disastrous effects on individuals, families and entire communities that were dependent on the company operations that are cut. Suicides, health problems and family breakups are not at all unusual side effects of these efficiency drives. Indeed entire communities have been devastated by corporate restructurings. Constituency statutes were adopted to allow corporate boards to consider such effects. Are they enough?

CHAPTER 20

FEDERAL AND STATE TAKEOVER AND TENDER OFFER LAWS[a]

■ ■ ■

SECTION 1. THE WILLIAMS ACT— AN INTRODUCTION

TENDER OFFERS FOR CORPORATE CONTROL

By
Edward Ross Aranow & Herbert A. Einhorn
(1973).*

Federal regulation of cash tender offers was originally proposed in October 1965 by Senator Harrison Williams of New Jersey for the ostensible purpose of protecting incumbent managements from "industrial sabotage" resulting from what were deemed to be reckless corporate raids on "proud old companies." Such regulation, unique in that it represented perhaps the first attempt to enact securities regulation designed primarily for the benefit of the issuer rather than the investor, was inspired by the conglomerate merger mania of the early and mid 1960s. During this period, the cash tender offer, which had previously been resorted to only on infrequent occasions in the United States, emerged with frenetic abandon. * * *

While no hearings were held on the original Williams Bill, many of its proposals formed the basis for a second bill introduced by Senator Williams in 1967. By the time this second bill was introduced, however, there was a greater recognition of the desirability of providing investors confronted with a tender offer with certain basic substantive protections together with full disclosure of the terms, conditions, and financing of the offer as well as the identity and pertinent background information regarding the offeror. In addition, there was a growing recognition that tender offers might in some cases promote the best interests of society by providing an effective method of removing entrenched but inefficient management. Nonetheless, the view persisted that the motives behind

---

a. This chapter is adapted from Thomas Lee Hazen & David L. Ratner, Securities Regulation: Cases and Materials (6th ed. 2003).

* Copyright 1973 by Columbia University Press. Reprinted by permission.

many tender offers did not reflect a desire to improve the management of companies and were but disguised forms of industrial sabotage. References by a co-sponsor of the legislation to attempted takeovers by undisclosed principals financed by Swiss banks, to the "corporate raider," and to the "takeover pirate" helped to generate hearty Congressional support for the second Williams Bill.

While the bill was embraced by the SEC and supported by several managements that had recently fought off cash takeover bids, there were others who opposed such regulation. Opposition to the bill was based primarily on the contention that the legislation was weighted so as to give incumbent management an unfair advantage in defending against a cash takeover bid and would therefore help to promote inefficient management. One commentator went so far as to suggest that the purpose of the legislation was to enhance the powers of the SEC rather than to protect the legitimate interests of the investing public. In addition, it was argued that a tender offer was in essence an open-market transaction and that traditional market forces, powered by individual self-interest, would best promote the interests of investors and our corporate system as a whole.

These objections notwithstanding, the final version of the second Williams Bill, which took the form of amendments to the Securities Exchange Act of 1934, became law on July 29, 1968 and was ostensibly designed to provide investors with full disclosure and other substantive protections within a statutory framework favoring neither the tender offeror nor the management of the target company. To insure adequate disclosure as well as the continued integrity of the securities markets in connection with acquisitions of securities which might cause or affect changes in control of public corporations, the bill also granted the SEC authority to regulate corporate repurchases of their own securities and imposed detailed disclosure requirements on persons acquiring more than 10 percent of certain equity securities other than pursuant to a tender offer. The Commission immediately adopted "temporary regulations" to effectuate those sections of the statute which were not self-operative.
* * *

In 1970, the Williams Act was amended, primarily to expand SEC rule-making authority and to extend the coverage of the law to certain types of offers previously exempt from regulation.

NOTES

1. The Williams Act amended the 1934 Act by adding §§ 13(d) and (e) and §§ 14(d), (e) and (f). The key provisions regulating takeovers and tender offers are § 13(d), § 14(d) and § 14(e). Section 13(d) requires any person who acquires more than 5% of any class of equity securities registered under the Act to file a Schedule 13D with the SEC (with a copy to the issuer) within ten days after the acquisition. The schedule must set forth specified information with respect to the person's background and source of funds, the purpose of the acquisition and any plans for major changes in the target company, and

any contracts or arrangements with any other person relating to the target company. For the purposes of § 13(d), two or more persons acting as a "group" in acquiring or holding securities are considered to be a single "person" in determining whether the requisite 5% ownership is present. See generally Financial General Bankshares v. Lance, 1978 WL 1082 (D.D.C.1978) (five investors acting as a "group" in acquiring approximately 25% of a corporation's stock violated § 13(d) by failing to file a report when the group's holdings reached 5%). What happens where a group of people already owning in the aggregate more than 5% of a class of securities agree to act together for the purpose of gaining control of the issuer? Does the agreement constitute an "acquisition" by the "group" of the stock owned by its members, triggering the reporting requirement of § 13(d), even though the individual members of the group have not acquired any shares over and above their pre-existing holdings? The Seventh Circuit, focusing on "the overriding purpose of Congress . . . *to protect the individual investor* when substantial shareholders or management undertake to acquire shares in a corporation," held that § 13(d) applies only when such a group "agree to act in concert *to acquire additional shares.*" (emphasis added). Bath Industries, Inc. v. Blot, 427 F.2d 97, 109 (7th Cir.1970). The Second Circuit, however, held that § 13(d) applied without regard to whether such a group acquired additional shares. It relied on specific statements in both the Senate and House Reports that such a group "would be required to file the information called for in § 13(d)(1) within 10 days after they agree to act together, whether or not any member of the group had acquired any securities at that time", and held that the language of § 13(d) "amply reflected . . . the purpose . . . to alert the marketplace to every large, rapid aggregation or accumulation of securities, regardless of technique employed, which might represent a potential shift in corporate control . . . ." GAF Corp. v. Milstein, 453 F.2d 709, 717 (2d Cir.1971), cert. denied 406 U.S. 910, 92 S.Ct. 1610, 31 L.Ed.2d 821 (1972). The court reached this conclusion despite the fact that the Milstein "group" consisted of members of a single family who had acquired the securities more than a year before in a single merger transaction, and that their holdings consisted of 10.25% of a class of convertible preferred stock, which had only about 2% of the total voting power in the corporation.[a]

2. Section 14(d) requires any person making a "tender offer" for more than 5% of any class of registered equity security to file a statement with the SEC containing much of the information required by § 13(d), and such other information as the SEC requires by rule, and to include in all of its advertisements or invitations for tenders such information as the SEC may require. Sections 14(d)(5), (6) and (7) contain provisions regulating the substantive terms of a tender offer by requiring that tendered shares be withdrawable for a specified period, that shares be taken up pro rata where more shares are tendered than the offeror has agreed to accept, and that the same price be paid to all shareholders where the price is raised during the pendency of the offer. Section 14(e) makes it unlawful to make any untrue or misleading

---

a. While the Milsteins had not purchased any additional preferred stock after the merger, they had purchased an aggregate of 1.7% of the *common* stock of GAF, bringing their total voting power in the corporation to approximately 4%.

statements of material facts, or to engage in any fraudulent, deceptive or manipulative acts or practices, in connection with a tender offer.

3. The SEC adopted rules under § 14(d) and (e) which relate to (a) the filing, transmittal and dissemination of statements and recommendations, (b) the obligation of the target company's management with respect to shareholder lists and recommendations on the offer, (c) the duration of the offer, and (d) the fairness of the offering terms. See Rules 14d–1 to 10, 14e–1 to 4.

SECTION 2. WHAT IS A TENDER OFFER?

SEC v. CARTER HAWLEY HALE STORES, INC.

760 F.2d 945 (9th Cir.1985).

Skopil, Circuit Judge.

The issue in this case arises out of an attempt by The Limited ("Limited"), an Ohio corporation, to take over Carter Hawley Hale Stores, Inc. ("CHH"), a publicly-held Los Angeles corporation. The SEC commenced the present action for injunctive relief to restrain CHH from repurchasing its own stock in an attempt to defeat the Limited takeover attempt without complying with the tender offer regulations. The district court concluded CHH's repurchase program was not a tender offer. The SEC appeals from the district court's denial of its motion for a preliminary injunction. We affirm.

On April 4, 1984 Limited commenced a cash tender offer for 20.3 million shares of CHH common stock, representing approximately 55% of the total shares outstanding, at $30 per share. Prior to the announced offer, CHH stock was trading at approximately $23.78 per share (pre-tender offer price).* * *

On April 16, 1984 CHH responded to Limited's offer. CHH issued a press release announcing its opposition to the offer because it was "inadequate and not in the best interests of CHH or its shareholders." CHH also publicly announced an agreement with General Cinema Corporation ("General Cinema"). * * * Finally, CHH announced a plan to repurchase up to 15 million shares of its own common stock for an amount not to exceed $500 million. * * *

CHH began to repurchase its shares on April 16, 1984. In a one-hour period CHH purchased approximately 244,000 shares at an average price of $25.25 per share. On April 17, 1984 CHH purchased approximately 6.5 million shares in a two-hour trading period at an average price of $25.88 per share. By April 22, 1984 CHH had purchased a total of 15 million shares. It then announced an increase in the number of shares authorized for purchase to 18.5 million.

On April 24, 1984, the same day Limited was permitted to close its offer and start purchasing, CHH terminated its repurchase program having purchased approximately 17.5 million shares, over 50% of the common shares outstanding. On April 25, 1984 Limited revised its offer increasing the offering price to $35.00 per share and eliminating the second-step merger. The market price for CHH then reached a high of $32.00 per share. On May 21, 1984 Limited withdrew its offer. The market price of CHH promptly fell to $20.62 per share, a price below the pre-tender offer price.

On May 2, 1984, two and one-half weeks after the repurchase program was announced and one week after its apparent completion, the SEC filed this action for injunctive relief. The SEC alleged that CHH's repurchase program constituted a tender offer conducted in violation of section 13(e) of the Exchange Act, and Rule 13e–4. On May 5, 1984 a temporary restraining order was granted. CHH was temporarily enjoined from further stock repurchases. The district court denied SEC's motion for a preliminary injunction, finding the SEC failed to carry its burden of establishing "the reasonable likelihood of future violations * * * [or] * * * a 'fair chance of success on the merits' * * *." The court found CHH's repurchase program was not a tender offer because the eight-factor test proposed by the SEC and adopted in Wellman v. Dickinson, 475 F.Supp. 783 (S.D.N.Y.1979), had not been satisfied. The court also refused to adopt, at the urging of the SEC, the alternative test of what constitutes a tender offer as enunciated in S–G Securities, Inc. v. Fuqua Investment Co., 466 F.Supp. 1114 (D.Mass.1978). On May 9, 1984 the SEC filed an emergency application for an injunction pending appeal to this court. That application was denied.* * *

Issuer repurchases and tender offers are governed in relevant part by section 13(e) of the Williams Act and Rules 13e–1 and 13e–4 promulgated thereunder.

The SEC argues that the district court erred in concluding that issuer repurchases, which had the intent and effect of defeating a third-party tender offer, are authorized by the tender offer rules and regulations. The legislative history of these provisions is unclear. Congress apparently was aware of an intent by the SEC to regulate issuer tender offers to the same extent as third-party offers. At the same time, Congress recognized issuers might engage in "substantial repurchase programs * * * inevitably affect[ing] market performance and price levels." Such repurchase programs might be undertaken for any number of legitimate purposes, including with the intent "to preserve or strengthen * * * control by counteracting tender offer or other takeover attempts * * *." Congress neither explicitly banned nor authorized such a practice. Congress did grant the SEC authority to adopt appropriate regulations to carry out congressional intent with respect to issuer repurchases. The legislative history of section 13(e) is not helpful in resolving the issues.

There is also little guidance in the SEC Rules promulgated in response to the legislative grant of authority. Rule 13e–1 prohibits an issuer from repurchasing its own stock during a third-party tender offer unless it discloses certain minimal information. The language of Rule 13e–1 is prohibitory rather than permissive. It nonetheless evidences a recognition that not all issuer repurchases during a third-party tender offer are tender offers. In contrast, Rule 13e–4 recognizes that issuers, like third parties, may engage in repurchase activity amounting to a tender offer and subject to the same procedural and substantive safeguards as a third-party tender offer. The regulations do not specify when a repurchase by an issuer amounts to a tender offer governed by Rule 13e–4 rather than 13e–1.

We decline to adopt either the broadest construction of Rule 13e–4, to define issuer tender offers as virtually all substantial repurchases during a third-party tender offer, or the broadest construction of Rule 13e–1, to create an exception from the tender offer requirements for issuer repurchases made during a third-party tender offer. Like the district court, we resolve the question of whether CHH's repurchase program was a tender offer by considering the eight-factor test established in *Wellman*.

To serve the purposes of the Williams Act, there is a need for flexibility in fashioning a definition of a tender offer. The *Wellman* factors seem particularly well suited in determining when an issuer repurchase program during a third-party tender offer will itself constitute a tender offer. *Wellman* focuses, inter alia, on the manner in which the offer is conducted and whether the offer has the overall effect of pressuring shareholders into selling their stock. Application of the *Wellman* factors to the unique facts and circumstances surrounding issuer repurchases should serve to effect congressional concern for the needs of the shareholder, the need to avoid giving either the target or the offeror any advantage, and the need to maintain a free and open market for securities.

Under the *Wellman* test, the existence of a tender offer is determined by examining the following factors:

(1) Active and widespread solicitation of public shareholders for the shares of an issuer; (2) solicitation made for a substantial percentage of the issuer's stock; (3) offer to purchase made at a premium over the prevailing market price; (4) terms of the offer are firm rather than negotiable; (5) offer contingent on the tender of a fixed number of shares, often subject to a fixed maximum number to be purchased; (6) offer open only for a limited period of time; (7) offeree subjected to pressure to sell his stock; [and (8)]public announcements of a purchasing program concerning the target company precede or accompany rapid accumulation of a large amount of target company's securities.

Not all factors need be present to find a tender offer; rather, they provide some guidance as to the traditional indicia of a tender offer.

The district court concluded CHH's repurchase program was not a tender offer under *Wellman* because only "two of the eight indicia" were present. The SEC claims the district court erred in applying *Wellman* because it gave insufficient weight to the pressure exerted on shareholders; it ignored the existence of a competitive tender offer; and it failed to consider that CHH's offer at the market price was in essence a premium because the price had already risen above pre-tender offer levels.

The evidence was uncontroverted that there was "no direct solicitation of shareholders." No active and widespread solicitation occurred. Nor did the publicity surrounding CHH's repurchase program result in a solicitation. The only public announcements by CHH were those mandated by SEC or Exchange rules.

Because there was no active and widespread solicitation, the district court found the repurchase could not have involved a solicitation for a substantial percentage of CHH's shares. It is unclear whether the proper focus of this factor is the solicitation or the percentage of stock solicited. The district court probably erred in concluding that, absent a solicitation under the first *Wellman* factor, the second factor cannot be satisfied, but we need not decide that here. The solicitation and percentage of stock elements of the second factor often will be addressed adequately in an evaluation of the first *Wellman* factor, which is concerned with solicitation, and the eighth *Wellman* factor, which focuses on the amount of securities accumulated. In this case CHH did not engage in a solicitation under the first *Wellman* factor but did accumulate a large percentage of stock as defined under the eighth *Wellman* factor. An evaluation of the second *Wellman* factor does not alter the probability of finding a tender offer.

The SEC contends the open market purchases made by CHH at market prices were in fact made at a premium not over market price but over the pre-tender offer price. At the time of CHH's repurchases, the market price for CHH's shares (ranging from $24.00 to $26.00 per share) had risen above the pre-tender offer price (approximately $22.00 per share). Given ordinary market dynamics, the price of a target company's stock will rise following an announced tender offer. Under the SEC's definition of a premium as a price greater than the pre-tender offer price, a premium will always exist when a target company makes open market purchases in response to a tender offer even though the increase in market price is attributable to the action of the third-party offeror and not the target company. The SEC definition not only eliminates consideration of this *Wellman* factor in the context of issuer repurchases during a tender offer, but also underestimates congressional concern for preserving the free and open market. The district court did not err in concluding a premium is determined not by reference to pre-tender offer price, but rather by reference to market price. * * *

There is no dispute that CHH engaged in a number of transactions or purchases at many different market prices.

Similarly, while CHH indicated it would purchase up to 15 million shares, CHH's purchases were not contingent on the tender of a fixed minimum number of shares.

CHH's offer to repurchase was not open for only a limited period of time but rather was open "during the pendency of the tender offer of The

Limited." The SEC argues that the offer was in fact open for only a limited time, because CHH would only repurchase stock until 15 million shares were acquired. The fact that 15 million shares were acquired in a short period of time does not translate into an issuer-imposed time limitation. The time within which the repurchases were made was a product of ordinary market forces, not the terms of CHH's repurchase program.

With regard to the seventh *Wellman* factor, following a public announcement, CHH repurchased over the period of seven trading days more than 50% of its outstanding shares. The eighth *Wellman* factor was met.

The district court found that while many shareholders may have felt pressured or compelled to sell their shares, CHH itself did not exert on shareholders the kind of pressure the Williams Act proscribes.

While there certainly was shareholder pressure in this case, it was largely the pressure of the marketplace and not the type of untoward pressure the tender offer regulations were designed to prohibit. * * *

The shareholder pressure in this case did not result from any untoward action on the part of CHH. Rather, it resulted from market forces, the third-party offer, and the fear that at the expiration of the offer the price of CHH shares would decrease.

The district court did not abuse its discretion in concluding that under the *Wellman* eight factor test, CHH's repurchase program did not constitute a tender offer.

The SEC finally urges that even if the CHH repurchase program did not constitute a tender offer under the *Wellman* test, the district court erred in refusing to apply the test in *S-G Securities,* 466 F.Supp. at 1114. Under the more liberal *S-G Securities* test, a tender offer is present if there are

> (1) A publicly announced intention by the purchaser to acquire a block of the stock of the target company for purposes of acquiring control thereof, and (2) a subsequent rapid acquisition by the purchaser of large blocks of stock through open market and privately negotiated purchases.

There are a number of sound reasons for rejecting the *S-G Securities* test. The test is vague and difficult to apply. It offers little guidance to the issuer as to when his conduct will come within the ambit of Rule 13e–4 as opposed to Rule 13e–1. A determination of the existence of a tender offer under *S-G Securities* is largely subjective and made in hindsight based on an *ex post facto* evaluation of the response in the marketplace to the repurchase program. The SEC's contention that these concerns are irrelevant when the issuer's repurchases are made with the intent to defeat a third-party offer is without merit. * * *

We decline to abandon the *Wellman* test in favor of the vague standard enunciated in *S-G Securities.* * * *

HANSON TRUST PLC v. SCM CORP.

774 F.2d 47 (2d Cir.1985).

MANSFIELD, CIRCUIT JUDGE:

Hanson Trust PLC * * * appeal[s] from an order of the Southern District of New York, granting SCM Corporation's motion for a preliminary injunction restraining them, their officers, agents, employees and any persons acting in concert with them, from acquiring any shares of SCM and from exercising any voting rights with respect to 3.1 million SCM shares acquired by them on September 11, 1985. The injunction was granted on the ground that Hanson's September 11 acquisition of the SCM stock through five private and one open market purchases amounted to a "tender offer" for more than 5% of SCM's outstanding shares, which violated §§ 14(d)(1) and (6) of the Williams Act, and rules promulgated by the Securities and Exchange Commission (SEC) thereunder. We reverse.* * *

SCM is a New York corporation with its principal place of business in New York City. Its shares, of which at all relevant times at least 9.9 million were outstanding and 2.3 million were subject to issuance upon conversion of other outstanding securities, are traded on the New York Stock Exchange (NYSE) and Pacific Stock Exchange. Hanson Trust PLC is an English company with its principal place of business in London. HSCM, a Delaware corporation, and Hanson Holdings Netherlands B.V., a Netherlands limited liability company, are indirect wholly-owned subsidiaries of Hanson Trust PLC.

On August 21, 1985, Hanson publicly announced its intention to make a cash tender offer of $60 per share for any and all outstanding SCM shares. Five days later it filed the tender offer documents required by § 14(d)(1) of the Williams Act and regulations issued thereunder. The offer provided that it would remain open until September 23, unless extended, that no shares would be accepted until September 10, and that

> "Whether or not the Purchasers [Hanson] purchase Shares pursuant to the Offer, the Purchasers may thereafter determine, subject to the availability of Shares at favorable prices and the availability of financing, to purchase additional Shares in the open market, in privately negotiated transactions, through another tender offer or otherwise. Any such purchases of additional Shares might be on terms which are the same as, or more or less favorable than, those of this Offer. The Purchasers also reserve the right to dispose of any or all Shares acquired by them."

Offer to Purchase For Cash Any and All Outstanding Shares of Common Stock of SCM Corporation (Aug. 26, 1985) at 21. On August 30, 1985, SCM, having recommended to SCM's stockholders that they not accept Hanson's tender offer, announced a preliminary agreement with Merrill under which a new entity, formed by SCM and Merrill, would acquire all SCM shares at $70 per share in a leveraged buyout sponsored by Merrill. Under the agreement, which was executed on September 3, the new entity would make a $70 per share cash tender offer for approximately 85% of SCM's shares. If more than two-thirds of SCM's shares were acquired under the offer the remaining SCM shares would be acquired in exchange for debentures in a new corporation to be formed as a result of the merger. On the same date, September 3, Hanson increased its tender offer from $60 to $72 cash per share. However, it expressly reserved the right to terminate its offer if SCM granted to anyone any option to purchase SCM assets on terms that Hanson believed to constitute a "lock-up" device.

The next development in the escalating bidding contest for control of SCM occurred on September 10, 1985, when SCM entered into a new leveraged buyout agreement with its "White Knight," Merrill. The agreement provided for a two-step acquisition of SCM stock by Merrill at $74 per share. The first proposed step was to be the acquisition of approximately 82% of SCM's outstanding stock for cash. Following a merger (which required acquisition of at least 66 2/3%), debentures would be issued for the remaining SCM shares. If any investor or group other than Merrill acquired more than one-third of SCM's outstanding shares, Merrill would have the option to buy SCM's two most profitable businesses, pigments and consumer foods, for $350 and $80 million respectively, prices which Hanson believed to be below their market value.

Hanson, faced with what it considered to be a "poison pill," concluded that even if it increased its cash tender offer to $74 per share it would end up with control of a substantially depleted and damaged company. Accordingly, it announced on the Dow Jones Broad Tape at 12:38 P.M. on September 11 that it was terminating its cash tender offer. A few minutes later, Hanson issued a press release, carried on the Broad Tape, to the effect that "all SCM shares tendered will be promptly returned to the tendering shareholders."

At some time in the late forenoon or early afternoon of September 11 Hanson decided to make cash purchases of a substantial percentage of SCM stock in the open market or through privately negotiated transactions. Under British law Hanson could not acquire more than 49% of SCM's shares in this fashion without obtaining certain clearances, but acquisition of such a large percentage was not necessary to stymie the SCM–Merrill merger proposal. If Hanson could acquire slightly less than one-third of SCM's outstanding shares it would be able to block the $74 per share SCM–Merrill offer of a leveraged buyout. This might induce the latter to work out an agreement with Hanson, something Hanson had unsuccessfully sought on several occasions since its first cash tender offer.

Within a period of two hours on the afternoon of September 11 Hanson made five privately-negotiated cash purchases of SCM stock and one open-market purchase, acquiring 3.1 million shares or 25% of SCM's outstanding stock. The price of SCM stock on the NYSE on September 11 ranged from a high of $73.50 per share to a low of $72.50 per share. Hanson's initial private purchase, 387,700 shares from Mutual Shares, was not solicited by Hanson but by a Mutual Shares official, Michael Price, who, in a conversation with Robert Pirie of Rothschild, Inc., Hanson's financial advisor, on the morning of September 11 (before Hanson had decided to make any private cash purchases), had stated that he was interested in selling Mutual's Shares' SCM stock to Hanson. Once Hanson's decision to buy privately had been made, Pirie took Price up on his offer. The parties negotiated a sale at $73.50 per share after Pirie refused Price's asking prices, first of $75 per share and, later, of $74.50 per share. This transaction, but not the identity of the parties, was automatically reported pursuant to NYSE rules on the NYSE ticker at 3:11 P.M. and reported on the Dow Jones Broad Tape at 3:29 P.M.

Pirie then telephoned Ivan Boesky, an arbitrageur who had a few weeks earlier disclosed in a Schedule 13D statement filed with the SEC that he owned approximately 12.7% of SCM's outstanding shares. Pirie negotiated a Hanson purchase of these shares at $73.50 per share after rejecting Boesky's initial demand of $74 per share. At the same time Rothschild purchased for Hanson's account 600,000 SCM shares in the open market at $73.50 per share. An attempt by Pirie next to negotiate the cash purchase of another large block of SCM stock (some 780,000 shares) from Slifka & Company fell through because of the latter's inability to make delivery of the shares on September 12.

Following the NYSE ticker and Broad Tape reports of the first two large anonymous transactions in SCM stock, some professional investors surmised that the buyer might be Hanson. Rothschild then received telephone calls from (1) Mr. Mulhearn of Jamie & Co. offering to sell between 200,000 and 350,000 shares at $73.50 per share, (2) David Gottesman, an arbitrageur at Oppenheimer & Co. offering 89,000 shares at $73.50, and (3) Boyd Jeffries of Jeffries & Co., offering approximately 700,000 to 800,000 shares at $74.00. Pirie purchased the three blocks for Hanson at $73.50 per share. The last of Hanson's cash purchases was completed by 4:35 P.M. on September 11, 1985.

In the early evening of September 11 SCM successfully applied to Judge Kram in the present lawsuit for a restraining order barring Hanson from acquiring more SCM stock for 24 hours. On September 12 and 13 the TRO was extended by consent pending the district court's decision on SCM's application for a preliminary injunction. Judge Kram held an evidentiary hearing on September 12–13, at which various witnesses testified, including Sir Gordon White, Hanson's United States Chairman, two Rothschild representatives (Pirie and Gerald Goldsmith) and stock market risk-arbitrage professionals (Robert Freeman of Goldman, Sachs & Co., Kenneth Miller of Merrill Lynch, and Danial Burch of D.F. King &

Co.). Sir Gordon White testified that on September 11, 1985, after learning of the $74 per share SCM–Merrill leveraged buyout tender offer with its "crown jewel" irrevocable "lock-up" option to Merrill, he instructed Pirie to terminate Hanson's $72 per share tender offer, and that only thereafter did he discuss the possibility of Hanson making market purchases of SCM stock. Pirie testified that the question of buying stock may have been discussed in the late forenoon of September 11 and that he had told White that he was having Hanson's New York counsel look into whether such cash purchases were legally permissible.

SCM argued before Judge Kram (and argues here) that Hanson's cash purchases immediately following its termination of its $72 per share tender offer amounted to a *de facto* continuation of Hanson's tender offer, designed to avoid the strictures of § 14(d) of the Williams Act, and that unless a preliminary injunction issued SCM and its shareholders would be irreparably injured because Hanson would acquire enough shares to defeat the SCM–Merrill offer. Judge Kram found that the relevant underlying facts (which we have outlined) were not in dispute, and concluded that "[w]ithout deciding what test should ultimately be applied to determine whether Hanson's conduct constitutes a 'tender offer' within the meaning of the Williams Act ... SCM has demonstrated a likelihood of success on the merits of its contention that Hanson has engaged in a tender offer which violates Section 14(d) of the Williams Act." The district court, characterizing Hanson's stock purchases as "a deliberate attempt to do an 'end run' around the requirements of the Williams Act," made no finding on the question of whether Hanson had decided to make the purchases of SCM before or after it dropped its tender offer but concluded that even if the decision had been made after it terminated its offer preliminary injunctive relief should issue. From this decision Hanson appeals.* * *

Although § 14(d)(1) clearly applies to "classic" tender offers * * *, courts soon recognized that in the case of privately negotiated transactions or solicitations for private purchases of stock many of the conditions leading to the enactment of § 14(d) for the most part do not exist. The number and percentage of stockholders are usually far less than those involved in public offers. The solicitation involves less publicity than a public tender offer or none. The solicitees, who are frequently directors, officers or substantial stockholders of the target, are more apt to be sophisticated, inquiring or knowledgeable concerning the target's business, the solicitor's objectives, and the impact of the solicitation on the target's business prospects. In short, the solicitee in the private transaction is less likely to be pressured, confused, or ill-informed regarding the businesses and decisions at stake than solicitees who are the subjects of a public tender offer.

These differences between public and private securities transactions have led most courts to rule that private transactions or open market purchases do not qualify as a "tender offer" requiring the purchaser to meet the pre-filing strictures of § 14(d). The borderline between public solicitations and privately negotiated stock purchases is not bright and it is frequently difficult to determine whether transactions falling close to the line or in a type of "no man's land" are "tender offers" or private deals. This has led some to advocate a broader interpretation of the term "tender offer" than that followed by us in Kennecott Copper Corp. v. Curtiss–Wright Corp., and to adopt the eight-factor "test" of what is a tender offer, which was recommended by the SEC and applied by the district court in Wellman v. Dickinson and by the Ninth Circuit in SEC v. Carter Hawley Hale Stores.* * *

Although many of the ... factors are relevant for purposes of determining whether a given solicitation amounts to a tender offer, the elevation of such a list to a mandatory "litmus test" appears to be both unwise and unnecessary. As even the advocates of the proposed test recognize, in any given case a solicitation may constitute a tender offer even though some of the eight factors are absent or, when many factors are present, the solicitation may nevertheless not amount to a tender offer because the missing factors outweigh those present.

We prefer to be guided by the principle followed by the Supreme Court in deciding what transactions fall within the private offering exemption provided by § 4(1) of the Securities Act of 1933, and by ourselves in *Kennecott Copper* in determining whether the Williams Act applies to private transactions. That principle is simply to look to the statutory purpose. In S.E.C. v. Ralston Purina Co., the Court stated, "the applicability of § 4(1) should turn on whether the particular class of persons affected need the protection of the Act. An offering to those who are shown to be able to fend for themselves is a transaction 'not involving any public offering.' " Similarly, since the purpose of § 14(d) is to protect the ill-informed solicitee, the question of whether a solicitation constitutes a "tender offer" within the meaning of § 14(d) turns on whether, viewing the transaction in the light of the totality of circumstances, there appears to be a likelihood that unless the pre-acquisition filing strictures of that statute are followed there will be a substantial risk that solicitees will lack information needed to make a carefully considered appraisal of the proposal put before them.

Applying this standard, we are persuaded on the undisputed facts that Hanson's September 11 negotiation of five private purchases and one open market purchase of SCM shares, totalling 25% of SCM's outstanding stock, did not under the circumstances constitute a "tender offer" within the meaning of the Williams Act. Putting aside for the moment the events preceding the purchases, there can be little doubt that the privately negotiated purchases would not, standing alone, qualify as a tender offer, for the following reasons:

> (1) In a market of 22,800 SCM shareholders the number of SCM sellers here involved, six in all, was miniscule compared with the numbers involved in public solicitations of the type against which the Act was directed.

(2) At least five of the sellers were highly sophisticated professionals, knowledgeable in the market place and well aware of the essential facts needed to exercise their professional skills and to appraise Hanson's offer, including its financial condition as well as that of SCM, the likelihood that the purchases might block the SCM–Merrill bid, and the risk that if Hanson acquired more than 33 1/3% of SCM's stock the SCM–Merrill lockup of the "crown jewel" might be triggered. * * *

(3) The sellers were not "pressured" to sell their shares by any conduct that the Williams Act was designed to alleviate, but by the forces of the market place. Indeed, in the case of Mutual Shares there was no initial solicitation by Hanson; the offer to sell was initiated by Mr. Price of Mutual Shares. Although each of the Hanson purchases was made for $73.50 per share, in most instances this price was the result of private negotiations after the sellers sought higher prices and in one case price protection, demands which were refused. The $73.50 price was not fixed in advance by Hanson. Moreover, the sellers remained free to accept the $74 per share tender offer made by the SCM–Merrill group.

(4) There was no active or widespread advance publicity or public solicitation, which is one of the earmarks of a conventional tender offer. Arbitrageurs might conclude from ticker tape reports of two large anonymous transactions that Hanson must be the buyer. However, liability for solicitation may not be predicated upon disclosures mandated by Stock Exchange Rules.

(5) The price received by the six sellers, $73.50 per share, unlike that appearing in most tender offers, can scarcely be dignified with the label "premium." The stock market price on September 11 ranged from $72.50 to $73.50 per share. Although risk arbitrageurs sitting on large holdings might reap sizeable profits from sales to Hanson at $73.50, depending on their own purchase costs, they stood to gain even more if the SCM–Merrill offer of $74 should succeed, as it apparently would if they tendered their shares to it. Indeed, the $73.50 price, being at most $1 over market or 1.4% higher than the market price, did not meet the SEC's proposed definition of a premium, which is $2.00 per share or 5% above market price, whichever is greater.

(6) Unlike most tender offers, the purchases were not made contingent upon Hanson's acquiring a fixed minimum number or percentage of SCM's outstanding shares. Once an agreement with each individual seller was reached, Hanson was obligated to buy, regardless what total percentage of stock it might acquire. Indeed, it does not appear that Hanson had fixed in its mind a firm limit on the amount of SCM shares it was willing to buy.

(7) Unlike most tender offers, there was no general time limit within which Hanson would make purchases of SCM stock. Conceded-

ly, cash transactions are normally immediate but, assuming an inability on the part of a seller and Hanson to agree at once on a price, nothing prevented a resumption of negotiations by each of the parties except the arbitrageurs' speculation that once Hanson acquired 33 1/3% or an amount just short of that figure it would stop buying.

In short, the totality of circumstances that existed on September 11 did not evidence any likelihood that unless Hanson was required to comply with § 14(d)(1)'s pre-acquisition filing and waiting-period requirements there would be a substantial risk of ill-considered sales of SCM stock by ill-informed shareholders. * * *

SECTION 3.   REGULATING THE TERMS OF TENDER OFFERS

Subsections (5), (6) and (7) in § 14(d) of the Securities Exchange Act of 1934 set forth substantive rules governing the rights of shareholders to withdraw shares they have tendered in an offer before its completion and imposing limitations on the manner in which the offeror must pay for tendered shares. SEC rules under § 14(d) expand and elaborate on those provisions. The following SEC release summarizes the federal regulation of tender offers for the equity securities registered under section 12 of the Exchange Act.

COMMISSION GUIDANCE ON MINI–TENDER OFFERS AND LIMITED PARTNERSHIP TENDER OFFERS

Securities Exchange Act Release No. 34–43069.
July 24, 2000.

* * * Section 14(d) of the Exchange Act and Regulation 14D apply to all tender offers for Exchange Act registered equity securities made by parties other than the target (or affiliates of the target), so long as upon consummation of the tender offer the bidder would beneficially own more than five percent of the class of securities subject to the offer. A bidder must include any shares it owns before the commencement of the tender offer in calculating the five percent amount. For example, if a bidder owns four percent of the target's securities before it commences the tender offer, it could not make an offer for more than one percent of the target's securities without triggering Section 14(d) and Regulation 14D requirements.

Regulation 14D requires the bidder to make specific disclosures to security holders and mandates certain procedural protections. The disclosure focuses on the terms of the offer and information about the bidder. The procedural protections include the right to withdraw tendered securities while the offer remains open, the right to have tendered securities accepted on a pro rata basis throughout the term of the offer if the offer is for less than all of the securities, and the requirement that all security holders of the subject class of securities be treated equally. [*See* SEC Rules

14d–7, 14d–8 & 14d–10]. Also, Regulation 14D requires the bidder to file its offering documents and other information with the Commission and hand deliver a copy to the target and any competing bidders. [*See* SEC Rule 14d–3(a)(2)]. Regulation 14D also requires the target to send to security holders specific disclosure about its recommendation, file a Schedule 14D–9 containing that disclosure, and send the Schedule 14D–9 to the bidder. [*See* SEC Rule 14d–9].

Rule 13e–4, promulgated under Section 13(e) of the Exchange Act, applies to all tender offers by the issuer for its equity securities when the issuer has a class of equity securities registered under Section 12 or when the issuer files periodic reports under Section 15(d) of the Exchange Act. Rule 13e–4 also applies to a tender offer by an affiliate of the issuer for the issuer's securities where the tender offer is not subject to Section 14(d). Rule 13e–4 is different from Regulation 14D because it applies even if the class of securities sought in the offer is not registered under Section 12. Also, Rule 13e–4 applies regardless of the amount of securities sought in the offer. Rule 13e–4 provides for disclosure, filing and procedural safeguards that generally mirror those provided under Section 14(d) and Regulation 14D.

Section 14(e) of the Exchange Act is the antifraud provision for all tender offers, including mini-tender offers and tender offers under Regulation 14D and Rule 13e–4. Section 14(e) prohibits fraudulent, deceptive, and manipulative acts in connection with a tender offer. Regulation 14E provides the basic procedural protections for all tender offers, including mini-tender offers and tender offers under Regulation 14D and Rule 13e–4.

Section 14(e) and Regulation 14E apply to all tender offers, even where the offer is for less than five percent of the outstanding securities and offers where the bidder would not own more than five percent after the consummation of the offer. [The latter transactions are known as "mini-tender offers." *See* Commission Guidance on Mini–Tender Offers and Limited Partnership Tender Offers, Securities Exchange Act Release No. 3443069 (July 24, 2000)]. Section 14(e) and Regulation 14E apply to tender offers for any type of security (including debt). These provisions apply both to registered and unregistered securities (including securities issued by a private company), except exempt securities under the Exchange Act, such as municipal bonds.

Regulation 14E requires that a tender offer be open for at least 20 business days, that the offer remain open for 10 business days following a change in the offering price or the percentage of securities being sought, and that the bidder promptly pay for or return securities when the tender offer expires. [See SEC Rule 14e–1(c)]. Regulation 14E also requires the target company to state its position about the offer within 10 business days after the offer begins. [*See* SEC Rule 14e–2]. The target must state either that it recommends that its security holders accept or reject the offer; that it expresses no opinion and remains neutral toward the offer; or that it is unable to take a position on the offer. With a tender offer not subject to Regulation 14D, however, the bidder is not required to send its offer to the target. Therefore, the target may not know about the tender offer. The target should take all steps to comply with its obligations under Regulation 14E within 10 business days or as soon as possible upon becoming aware of the offer.

———

The following chart outlines the key provisions of the Williams Act's tender offer regulations:

	Third-Party Tender Offer	Issuer Tender Offer
Best Price Rule	§ 14(d)(7), Rule 14d-10(a)(2) - the highest price paid to any tendering security holder must be paid to all tendering security holders. Rule 14d-10(c) allows different types of consideration to be offered which need not be substantially equivalent in value as long as: 1) security holders are free to elect among the types of consideration offered; 2) the highest consideration of each type paid to any security holder is paid to any security holder electing that type.	Rule 13e-4(f)(8)(ii)–the highest price paid to any tendering security holder must be paid to all security holders. Rule 13e-4(f)(10). (same as third-party offer)
All Holders Rule	Rule 14d-10(a)(1) requires that the tender offer be open to all holders of the class of securities sought. Rule 14d-10(b)(2) permits a bidder to exclude holders in a state where the bidder is prohibited by statute from making the offer after a good faith effort to comply with the statute.	Rule 13e-4(f)(8)(I) (same as third-party offer) Rule 13e-4(f)(9)(ii) (same as third-party offer)

Pro Rata Rule	§ 14(d)(6) - where the offer is for less than for all outstanding securities of a class and the offer is oversubscribed, the bidder must take up the tendered securities on a pro rata basis.
	   The statute only applies to securities tendered w/in 10 days from the original publication of the offer or notice of an increase in consideration– Rule 14d-8 extends the proration requirement to The entire duration of the offer.
	the rule does not apply if the bidder's acquisitions of that class of securities during the past 12 months does not exceed 2% of that class.
		Rule 13e-4(f)(3)-where the offer is for less than all outstanding securities of a class and the offer is oversubscribed, the bidder must take up the tendered securities on a pro rata basis.
		   The rule provides exceptions for odd-lot tender offers and for shares which are tendered on an all or none basis.

Duration of Tender Offer	Rule 14e-1(a)-the tender offer must remain open for at least 20 business days. Rule 14e-1(b)-a change in the consideration to be paid, the percentage of securities sought or the dealer's solicitation fee will require that the offer be held open at least 10 business days from the date of notice of such change. Exception-acceptance of additional securities not exceeding 2% of the class sought Rule 14d-4(c)-notice of "material" changes in the terms of the offer must be made in a manner reasonably designed to inform security holders of such change. The SEC interprets this rule to mean that a material change would require holding the offer open for at least five business from the date of notice and 10 business days when the change approaches the level of a change in consideration Or the % of securities sought	Rule 13e-4(f)(1)(i) (same as third-party offer) Rule 13e-4(f)(1)(ii) (same as third-party offer) (same as third-party offer) Rule 13e-4(e)(2)-notice of a "material" change in the information sent to security holders must be made in a manner reasonably calculated to inform security holders of such change.
Withdrawal Rights	§ 14(d)(5) tendered securities may be withdrawn at any time during the first seven days of the tender offer and at any time after 60 days from the date of original tender offer. Rule 14d-7-tendered securities may be withdrawn while the tender offer remains open.	Rule 13e-4(f)(2) tendered securities may be withdrawn; (i) at any time while the tender remains (ii) after 40 days from commencement of the offer if the securities have not been accepted.

SECTION 4.   LITIGATION UNDER THE WILLIAMS ACT

RONDEAU v. MOSINEE PAPER CORP.

422 U.S. 49, 95 S.Ct. 2069, 45 L.Ed.2d 12 (1975).

MR. CHIEF JUSTICE BURGER delivered the opinion of the Court.

We granted certiorari in this case to determine whether a showing of irreparable harm is necessary for a private litigant to obtain injunctive relief in a suit under § 13(d) of the Securities Exchange Act of 1934, as added by § 2 of the Williams Act. The Court of Appeals held that it was not. We reverse.

Respondent Mosinee Paper Corp. is a Wisconsin company engaged in the manufacture and sale of paper, paper products, and plastics. Its principal place of business is located in Mosinee, Wis., and its only class of equity security is common stock which is registered under § 12 of the Securities Exchange Act of 1934. At all times relevant to this litigation there were slightly more than 800,000 shares of such stock outstanding.

In April 1971 petitioner Francis A. Rondeau, a Mosinee businessman, began making large purchases of respondent's common stock in the over-the-counter market. Some of the purchases were in his own name; others were in the name of businesses and a foundation known to be controlled by him. By May 17, 1971, petitioner had acquired 40,413 shares of respondent's stock, which constituted more than 5% of those outstanding. He was therefore required to comply with the disclosure provisions of the Williams Act, by filing a Schedule 13D with respondent and the Securities and Exchange Commission within 10 days. That form would have disclosed, among other things, the number of shares beneficially owned by petitioner, the source of the funds used to purchase them, and petitioner's purpose in making the purchases.

Petitioner did not file a Schedule 13D but continued to purchase substantial blocks of respondent's stock. By July 30, 1971, he had acquired more than 60,000 shares. On that date the chairman of respondent's board of directors informed him by letter that his activity had "given rise to numerous rumors" and "seems to have created some problems under the Federal Securities Laws...." Upon receiving the letter petitioner immediately stopped placing orders for respondent's stock and consulted his attorney. On August 25, 1971, he filed a Schedule 13D which, in addition to the other required disclosures, described the "Purpose of Transaction" as follows:

"Francis A. Rondeau determined during early part of 1971 that the common stock of the Issuer [respondent] was undervalued in the over-the-counter market and represented a good investment vehicle for future income and appreciation. Francis A. Rondeau and his associates presently propose to seek to acquire additional common stock of the Issuer in order to obtain effective control of the Issuer, but such investments as originally determined were and are not necessarily made with this objective in mind. Consideration is currently being given to making a public cash tender offer to the shareholders of the Issuer at a price which will reflect current quoted prices for such stock with some premium added."

Petitioner also stated that, in the event that he did obtain control of respondent, he would consider making changes in management "in an effort to provide a Board of Directors which is more representative of all of the shareholders, particularly those outside of present management * * *." One month later petitioner amended the form to reflect more accurately the allocation of shares between himself and his companies.

On August 27 respondent sent a letter to its shareholders informing them of the disclosures in petitioner's Schedule 13D. The letter stated that by his "tardy filing" petitioner had "withheld the information to which you [the shareholders] were entitled for more than two months, in violation of federal law." In addition, while agreeing that "recent market prices have not reflected the real value of your Mosinee stock," respondent's management could "see little in Mr. Rondeau's background that would qualify him to offer any meaningful guidance to a Company in the highly technical and competitive paper industry."

Six days later respondent initiated this suit in the United States District Court for the Western District of Wisconsin. Its complaint named petitioner, his companies, and two banks which had financed some of petitioner's purchases as defendants and alleged that they were engaged in a scheme to defraud respondent and its shareholders in violation of the securities laws. It alleged further that shareholders who had "sold shares without the information which defendants were required to disclose lacked information material to their decision whether to sell or hold," and that respondent "was unable to communicate such information to its stockholders, and to take such actions as their interest required." Respondent prayed for an injunction prohibiting petitioner and his codefendants from voting or pledging their stock and from acquiring additional shares, requiring them to divest themselves of stock which they already owned, and for damages. A motion for a preliminary injunction was filed with the complaint but later withdrawn.

After three months of pretrial proceedings petitioner moved for summary judgment. He readily conceded that he had violated the Williams Act, but contended that the violation was due to a lack of familiarity with the securities laws and that neither respondent nor its shareholders had been harmed. The District Court agreed. It found no material issues of fact to exist regarding petitioner's lack of willfulness in failing to timely file a Schedule 13D, concluding that he discovered his obligation to do so on July 30, 1971, and that there was no basis in the record for disputing his claim that he first considered the possibility of obtaining control of respondent some time after that date. The District Court therefore held that petitioner and his codefendants "did not engage in intentional covert, and conspiratorial conduct in failing to timely file the 13D Schedule."

Similarly, although accepting respondent's contention that its management and shareholders suffered anxiety as a result of petitioner's activities and that this anxiety was exacerbated by his failure to disclose his intentions until August 1971, the District Court concluded that similar anxiety "could be expected to accompany any change in management," and was "a predictable consequence of shareholder democracy." It fell far short of the irreparable harm necessary to support an injunction and no other harm was revealed by the record; as amended, petitioner's Schedule 13D disclosed all of the information to which respondent was entitled, and he had not proceeded with a tender offer. Moreover, in the view of the District Court even if a showing of irreparable harm were not required in all cases under the securities laws, petitioner's lack of bad faith and the absence of damage to respondent made this "a particularly inappropriate occasion to fashion equitable relief * * *." Thus, although petitioner had committed a technical violation of the Williams Act, the District Court held that respondent was entitled to no relief and entered summary judgment against it.

The Court of Appeals reversed, with one judge dissenting. The majority stated that it was "giving effect" to the District Court's findings regarding the circumstances of petitioner's violation of the Williams Act, but concluded that those findings showed harm to respondent because it "was delayed in its efforts to make any necessary response to" petitioner's potential to take control of the company. In any event, the majority was of the view that respondent "need not show irreparable harm as a prerequisite to obtaining permanent injunctive relief in view of the fact that as issuer of the securities it is in the best position to assure that the filing requirements of the Williams Act are being timely and fully complied with and to obtain speedy and forceful remedial action when necessary." The Court of Appeals remanded the case to the District Court with instructions that it enjoin petitioner and his codefendants from further violations of the Williams Act and from voting the shares purchased between the due date of the Schedule 13D and the date of its filing for a period of five years. It considered "such an injunctive decree appropriate to neutralize [petitioner's] violation of the Act and to deny him the benefit of his wrongdoing."

We granted certiorari to resolve an apparent conflict among the Courts of Appeals and because of the importance of the question presented to private actions under the federal securities laws. We disagree with the Court of Appeals' conclusion that the traditional standards for extraordinary equitable relief do not apply in these circumstances, and reverse.

As in the District Court and the Court of Appeals, it is conceded here that petitioner's delay in filing the Schedule 13D constituted a violation of the Williams Act. The narrow issue before us is whether this record supports the grant of injunctive relief, a remedy whose basis "in the federal courts has always been irreparable harm and inadequacy of legal remedies." Beacon Theatres, Inc. v. Westover, 359 U.S. 500, 506–507 (1959).

The Court of Appeals' conclusion that respondent suffered "harm" sufficient to require sterilization of petitioner's stock need not long detain us. The purpose of the Williams Act is to insure that public shareholders who are confronted by a cash tender offer for their stock will not be required to respond without adequate information regarding the qualifications and intentions of the offering party. By requiring disclosure of information to the target corporation as well as the Securities and Exchange Commission, Congress intended to do no more than give incumbent management an opportunity to express and explain its position. The Congress expressly disclaimed an intention to provide a weapon for management to discourage takeover bids or prevent large accumulations of stock which would create the potential for such attempts. Indeed, the Act's draftsmen commented upon the "extreme care" which was taken "to avoid tipping the balance of regulation either in favor of management or in favor of the person making the takeover bid."

The short of the matter is that none of the evils to which the Williams Act was directed has occurred or is threatened in this case. Petitioner has not attempted to obtain control of respondent, either by a cash tender offer or any other device. Moreover, he has now filed a proper Schedule 13D, and there has been no suggestion that he will fail to comply with the Act's requirement of reporting any material changes in the information contained therein. On this record there is no likelihood that respondent's shareholders will be disadvantaged should petitioner make a tender offer, or that respondent will be unable to adequately place its case before them should a contest for control develop. Thus, the usual basis for injunctive relief, "that there exists some cognizable danger of recurrent violation," is not present here.

Nor are we impressed by respondent's argument that an injunction is necessary to protect the interests of its shareholders who either sold their stock to petitioner at predisclosure prices or would not have invested had they known that a takeover bid was imminent. As observed, the principal object of the Williams Act is to solve the dilemma of shareholders desiring to respond to a cash tender offer, and it is not at all clear that the type of "harm" identified by respondent is redressable under its provisions. In any event, those persons who allegedly sold at an unfairly depressed price have an adequate remedy by way of an action for damages, thus negating the basis for equitable relief. Similarly, the fact that the second group of shareholders for whom respondent expresses concern have retained the benefits of their stock and the lack of an imminent contest for control make the possibility of damage to them remote at best.

We turn, therefore, to the Court of Appeals' conclusion that respondent's claim was not to be judged according to traditional equitable principles, and that the bare fact that petitioner violated the Williams Act justified entry of an injunction against him. This position would seem to be foreclosed by Hecht Co. v. Bowles, 321 U.S. 321 (1944). There, the administrator of the Emergency Price Control Act of 1942 brought suit to redress violations of that statute. The fact of the violations was admitted, but the District Court declined to enter an injunction because they were inadvertent and the defendant had taken immediate steps to rectify them. This Court held that such an exercise of equitable discretion was proper despite § 205(a) of the Act, which provided that an injunction or other order "shall be granted" upon a showing of violation * * *.

This reasoning applies *a fortiori* to actions involving only "competing private claims," and suggests that the District Court here was entirely correct in insisting that respondent satisfy the traditional prerequisites of extraordinary equitable relief by establishing irreparable harm. Moreover, the District Judge's conclusions that petitioner acted in good faith and that he promptly filed a Schedule 13D when his attention was called to this obligation support the exercise of the court's sound judicial discretion to deny an application for an injunction, relief which is historically "designed to deter, not to punish" and to permit the court "to mould each decree to the necessities of the particular case." * * *

Respondent urges, however, that the "public interest" must be taken into account in considering its claim for relief and relies upon the Court of Appeals' conclusion that it is entitled to an injunction because it "is in the best position" to insure that the Williams Act is complied with by purchasers of its stock. This argument misconceives, we think, the nature of the litigation. Although neither the availability of a private suit under the Williams Act nor respondent's standing to bring it has been questioned here, this cause of action is not expressly authorized by the statute or its legislative history. Rather, respondent is asserting a so-called implied private right of action established by cases such as J.I. Case Co. v. Borak, 377 U.S. 426 (1964). Of course, we have not hesitated to recognize the power of federal courts to fashion private remedies for securities laws violations when to do so is consistent with the legislative scheme and necessary for the protection of investors as a supplement to enforcement by the Securities and Exchange Commission. However, it by no means follows that the plaintiff in such an action is relieved of the burden of establishing the traditional prerequisites of relief. Indeed, our cases hold that quite the contrary is true.

In Deckert v. Independence Shares Corp., 311 U.S. 282 (1940), this Court was called upon to decide whether the Securities Act of 1933 authorized purchasers of securities to bring an action to rescind an allegedly fraudulent sale. The question was answered affirmatively on the basis of the statute's grant of federal jurisdiction to "enforce any liability or duty" created by it. The Court's reasoning is instructive:

> "The power *to enforce* implies the power to make effective the right of recovery afforded by the Act. And the power to make the right of recovery effective implies the power to utilize any of the procedures

or actions normally available to the litigant according to the exigencies of the particular case. If petitioners' bill states a cause of action when tested by the customary rules governing suits of such character, the Securities Act authorizes maintenance of the suit * * *." 311 U.S., at 288.

In other words, the conclusion that a private litigant could maintain an action for violation of the 1933 Act meant no more than that traditional remedies were available to redress any harm which he may have suffered; it provided no basis for dispensing with the showing required to obtain relief. Significantly, this passage was relied upon in *Borak* with respect to actions under the Securities Exchange Act of 1934.

Any remaining uncertainty regarding the nature of relief available to a person asserting an implied private right of action under the securities laws was resolved in Mills v. Electric Auto–Lite Co., 396 U.S. 375 (1970).* * *

Mills could not be plainer in holding that the questions of liability and relief are separate in private actions under the securities laws, and that the latter is to be determined according to traditional principles. Thus, the fact that respondent is pursuing a cause of action which has been generally recognized to serve the public interest provides no basis for concluding that it is relieved of showing irreparable harm and other usual prerequisites for injunctive relief. Accordingly, the judgment of the Court of Appeals is reversed and the case is remanded to it with directions to reinstate the judgment of the District Court.

Mr. Justice Marshall dissents.

Mr. Justice Brennan, with whom Mr. Justice Douglas joins, dissenting.

I dissent. Judge Pell, dissenting below, correctly in my view, read the decision of the Court of Appeals to construe the Williams Act, as I also construe it, to authorize injunctive relief upon the application of the management interests "irrespective of motivation, irrespective of irreparable harm to the corporation, and irrespective of whether the purchases were detrimental to investors in the company's stock. The violation timewise is * * * all that is needed to trigger this result." In other words, the Williams Act is a prophylactic measure conceived by Congress as necessary to effect the congressional objective "that investors and management be notified at the earliest possible moment of the potential for a shift in corporate control." The violation itself establishes the actionable harm and no showing of other harm is necessary to secure injunctive relief. Today's holding completely undermines the congressional purpose to preclude inquiry into the results of the violation.

HUMANA, INC. v. AMERICAN MEDICORP, INC.

445 F.Supp. 613 (S.D.N.Y.1977).

LASKER, DISTRICT JUDGE.

On September 27, 1977, Humana advised Medicorp by letter that it intended to make an offer to acquire up to 75% of the outstanding shares of Medicorp on the basis of an exchange of cash and securities. The offer constituted a clear premium over the then market price of Medicorp stock. Very shortly after receipt of Humana's letter the Medicorp Board of Directors resolved that the offer was not advantageous to its stockholders and informed them to this effect. There has followed a spate of litigation, including this action alleging that Medicorp has made material misrepresentations concerning the offer in violation of § 14(e) of the 1934 Securities and Exchange Act (the "Williams Act") and in which Medicorp has counterclaimed alleging violations of the same statute by Humana.* * *

On December 21, 1977, Trans World Airways (TWA) and its wholly owned subsidiary, Hilton International Co. (Hilton), announced a competing partial tender offer which also will expire January 10, 1978, unless extended. * * *

On December 27, 1977, Humana moved by Order to Show Cause to file a second amended and supplemental complaint to its action against Medicorp to add TWA and Hilton as defendants; to state new causes of action relating to the TWA–Hilton competitive offer; and to request injunctive relief against TWA and Hilton. * * *

Medicorp opposes the motion on the grounds that Humana does not have standing to sue for violations of the Williams Act by a competing offeror. Its principal reliance is placed on Piper v. Chris–Craft Industries, 430 U.S. 1 (1977). *Piper* shattered the nearly universal holdings of lower courts that competing tender offerors had standing to sue each other for damages under the Williams Act. In *Piper,* Chris–Craft, a losing tender offeror in a consummated tender offer battle, sued both its competing tender offeror and target management for damages, claiming violations of the Williams Act in connection with the tender offer battle. Holding that the primary, if not exclusive, purpose of the Williams Act was to protect shareholders of the target company, the Supreme Court held that a tender offeror did not have standing to sue for damages under the Act. * * *

The question at hand is whether, in the light of *Piper,* an offeror (Humana) has standing to sue a competing offeror (TWA and Hilton) for injunctive relief. I conclude that it does. Analysis of *Piper* requires determining not only what it decided but what it did not decide.

At footnote 33, Chief Justice Burger wrote:

> "We intimate no view upon whether as a general proposition a suit in equity for injunctive relief, as distinguished from an action for damages, would lie in favor of a tender offeror under either § 14(e) or Rule 10b–6."

Of course, the footnote merely leaves the question open, and one must look for guidance elsewhere as to whether a ruling that an offeror has standing to sue a competing offeror for *injunctive* relief would be consistent with *Piper*.

A large body of material in *Piper* itself points toward allowance of standing when the remedy sought is injunctive relief. First, Chief Justice Burger exercised scrupulous care to use the word "damages" whenever he described the "narrow" issue before the court. Second, the opinion of the Court cites with approval Judge Friendly's observation in Electronic Specialty Co. Inc. v. International Controls Corp., that "in corporate control contests the stage of preliminary *injunctive* relief, rather than post-contest lawsuits, 'is the time when relief can best be given'". At footnote 26, the opinion states in its own language that " * * * injunctive relief at an earlier stage of the context is apt to be the most efficacious form of remedy." These comments apply to the case at hand. The proposal is in its primary stages. If Humana's allegations that TWA and Hilton have violated the Williams Act are ever to be effectively explored, they must be explored now, since Medicorp's shareholders must have information upon which to act before the expiration of both offers on January 10th.

At least one passage in *Piper* appears affirmatively to suggest that construing the Williams Act to allow a tender offeror the implied right to sue for injunctive relief would be appropriate even though an implied right to sue for damages does not exist. At page 41, the court states:

> "In short, we conclude that shareholder protection, if enhanced at all by damages awards such as Chris–Craft contends for, can more directly be achieved with other, less drastic means more closely tailored to the precise congressional goal underlying the Williams Act."

No remedy can be more "closely tailored" to the needs of the occasion than injunctive relief, when appropriate. The very purpose of injunctive relief is to afford a remedy precisely contoured to the requirements of the situation.

Moreover, as Judge Weinfeld observed in Applied Digital Data Systems v. Milgo Electronic, 425 F.Supp. 1145, 1152 (S.D.N.Y.1977) "allowing [an offeror] to maintain this suit not only provides a remedy to the wronged offeror, but also serves to effectuate the broader purposes of the Williams Act by putting the tools for enforcement of its fair-play provisions into the hands of those most likely and able to make use of them."

The majority opinion in *Piper* does not render consideration of this factor inappropriate. Justice Stevens, dissenting, criticized the court's decision because in his view it excluded tender offerors whom he described as "the persons most interested in effective enforcement." The majority opinion answered this point (at footnote 28), saying "our precise holding disposes of many observations made in dissent. Thus, the argument with respect to the 'exclusion' from standing for 'persons most interested in effective enforcement,' is simply unwarranted in light of today's narrow holding." We read the footnote to mean that tender offerors, described by Justice Stevens as "the persons most interested in effective enforcement" are not necessarily excluded from standing in cases not covered by *Piper's* "narrow holding" and that it is appropriate to consider a tender offeror's particular interest in effective enforcement in determining whether he should be accorded standing to sue for injunctive relief. * * *

These general observations are strengthened in the case at hand by virtue of the particular allegations made and relief sought. For example, it is alleged that TWA–Hilton and Medicorp "have sought unlawfully to deprive Medicorp public shareholders of a fair opportunity to evaluate and choose whether to accept the Humana offer," that defendants now seek to "force Medicorp shareholders to make an immediate investment decision regarding such competing offer" in violation of the securities laws "contrary to the interest of Medicorp and its shareholders," and "the effect of the competing offer is to require Medicorp shareholders to make an investment decision now concerning the purported value of the [TWA and/or Hilton] equity securities [which TWA announced would be used to purchase remaining Medicorp shares after the consummation of its tender offer] and their desirability as an investment compared with the securities to be offered by Humana even though these equity securities have not been registered" with the result that the stockholders have no information about the equity securities which may be included in such a proposed package. The complaint alleges also that various "sensitive payments" have been made by TWA, Hilton or its affiliate Canteen, of such a nature that the facts relating to the payments are material to the decision which a Medicorp shareholder is called upon to make: that is whether to entrust his future to the TWA management or not.

In sum, the thrust of the complaint is to request increased disclosure of the terms of the TWA offer and the character of the TWA management so that Medicorp stockholders may more intelligently choose between the competing Humana and TWA–Hilton offers. Of course, the amended and supplemental complaint furthers Humana's interest as well but the critical factor is not whether Humana may be benefited by the suit but whether the stockholders of the target company would be benefited if the allegations of the complaint are proven to be true and the relief requested is granted. If so the purposes of the Act will be furthered. This is the test by which a tender offeror's right to sue for injunctive relief must be determined; and by this test Humana does have such standing.[a]

---

a. [eds.] In subsequent proceedings in the *Humana* case, the court held that when the target company, in press releases and letters to shareholders, described the tender offer as "inadequate" and "not in the best interests of" the shareholders, "it was obligated to furnish its stockholders with all the information it had from Humana so that the stockholders would be sufficiently informed to react intelligently to the offer and would not be unfairly influenced by management's subjective presentation." The court enjoined the target company from disseminating "materially false and misleading" statements about the tender offer. 1978 WL 42627 (S.D.N.Y.1978).

SCHREIBER v. BURLINGTON NORTHERN, INC.

472 U.S. 1, 105 S.Ct. 2458, 86 L.Ed.2d 1 (1985).

CHIEF JUSTICE BURGER delivered the opinion of the Court.

We granted certiorari to resolve a conflict in the Circuits over whether misrepresentation or nondisclosure is a necessary element of a violation of § 14(e) of the Securities Exchange Act of 1934.

On December 21, 1982, Burlington Northern, Inc., made a hostile tender offer for El Paso Gas Co. Through a wholly owned subsidiary, Burlington proposed to purchase 25.1 million El Paso shares at $24 per share. Burlington reserved the right to terminate the offer if any of several specified events occurred. El Paso management initially opposed the takeover, but its shareholders responded favorably, fully subscribing the offer by the December 30, 1982 deadline.

Burlington did not accept those tendered shares; instead, after negotiations with El Paso management, Burlington announced on January 10, 1983, the terms of a new and friendly takeover agreement. Pursuant to the new agreement, Burlington undertook, *inter alia,* to (1) rescind the December tender offer, (2) purchase 4,166,667 shares from El Paso at $24 per share, (3) substitute a new tender offer for only 21 million shares at $24 per share, (4) provide procedural protections against a squeeze-out merger[1] of the remaining El Paso shareholders, and (5) recognize "golden parachute" contracts between El Paso and four of its senior officers. By February 8, more than 40 million shares were tendered in response to Burlington's January offer, and the takeover was completed.

The rescission of the first tender offer caused a diminished payment to those shareholders who had tendered during the first offer. The January offer was greatly oversubscribed and consequently those shareholders who retendered were subject to substantial proration. Petitioner Barbara Schreiber filed suit on behalf of herself and similarly situated shareholders, alleging that Burlington, El Paso, and members of El Paso's board violated § 14(e)'s prohibition of "fraudulent, deceptive, or manipulative acts or practices * * * in connection with any tender offer." She claimed that Burlington's withdrawal of the December tender offer coupled with the substitution of the January tender offer was a "manipulative" distortion of the market for El Paso stock. Schreiber also alleged that Burlington violated § 14(e) by failing in the January offer to disclose the "golden parachutes" offered to four of El Paso's managers. She claims that this January nondisclosure was a deceptive act forbidden by § 14(e).

---

1. A "squeeze-out" merger occurs when Corporation A, which holds a controlling interest in Corporation B, uses its control to merge B into itself or into a wholly owned subsidiary. The minority shareholders in Corporation B are, in effect, forced to sell their stock. The procedural protection provided in the agreement between El Paso and Burlington required the approval of non-Burlington members of El Paso's board of directors before a squeeze-out merger could proceed. Burlington eventually purchased all the remaining shares of El Paso for $12 cash and one quarter share of Burlington preferred stock per share. The parties dispute whether this consideration was equal to that paid to those tendering during the January tender offer.

The District Court dismissed the suit for failure to state a claim. The District Court reasoned that the alleged manipulation did not involve a misrepresentation, and so did not violate § 14(e). The District Court relied on the fact that in cases involving alleged violations of § 10(b) of the Securities Exchange Act, this Court has required misrepresentation for there to be a "manipulative" violation of the section.

The Court of Appeals for the Third Circuit affirmed. * * *

We are asked in this case to interpret § 14(e) of the Securities Exchange Act. * * *

Petitioner relies on a construction of the phrase "fraudulent, deceptive or manipulative acts or practices" to include acts which, although fully disclosed, "artificially" affect the price of the takeover target's stock. Petitioner's interpretation relies on the belief that § 14(e) is directed at purposes broader than providing full and true information to investors.

Petitioner's reading of the term "manipulative" conflicts with the normal meaning of the term. We have held in the context of an alleged violation of § 10(b) of the Securities Exchange Act:

> "Use of the word 'manipulative' is especially significant. It is and was virtually a term of art when used in connection with the securities markets. It connotes intentional or willful conduct *designed to deceive or defraud* investors by controlling or artificially affecting the price of securities." Ernst & Ernst v. Hochfelder, 425 U.S. 185, 199 (1976) (emphasis added).* * *

She argues, however, that the term manipulative takes on a meaning in § 14(e) that is different from the meaning it has in § 10(b). Petitioner claims that the use of the disjunctive "or" in § 14(e) implies that acts need not be deceptive or fraudulent to be manipulative. But Congress used the phrase "manipulative or deceptive" in § 10(b) as well, and we have interpreted "manipulative" in that context to require misrepresentation. Moreover, it is a " 'familiar principle of statutory construction that words grouped in a list should be given related meaning.' " All three species of misconduct, i.e., "fraudulent, deceptive or manipulative," listed by Congress are directed at failures to disclose. The use of the term "manipulative" provides emphasis and guidance to those who must determine which types of acts are reached by the statute; it does not suggest a deviation from the section's facial and primary concern with disclosure or Congressional concern with disclosure which is the core of the Act.

Our conclusion that "manipulative" acts under § 14(e) require misrepresentation or nondisclosure is buttressed by the purpose and legislative history of the provision. Section 14(e) was originally added to the Securities Exchange Act as part of the Williams Act. "The purpose of the Williams Act is to insure that public shareholders who are confronted by a cash tender offer for their stock will not be required to respond without adequate information." Rondeau v. Mosinee Paper Corp., 422 U.S. 49, 58 (1975).

It is clear that Congress relied primarily on disclosure to implement the purpose of the Williams Act. * * *

The expressed legislative intent was to preserve a neutral setting in which the contenders could fully present their arguments.* * *

To implement this objective, the Williams Act added §§ 13(d), 13(e), 14(d), 14(e), and 14(f) to the Securities Exchange Act. Some relate to disclosure; §§ 13(d), 14(d) and 14(f) all add specific registration and disclosure provisions. Others—§§ 13(e) and 14(d)—require or prohibit certain acts so that investors will possess additional time within which to take advantage of the disclosed information.

Section 14(e) adds a "broad antifraud prohibition," modeled on the antifraud provisions of § 10(b) of the Act and Rule 10b–5. It supplements the more precise disclosure provisions found elsewhere in the Williams Act, while requiring disclosure more explicitly addressed to the tender offer context than that required by § 10(b).

While legislative history specifically concerning § 14(e) is sparse, the House and Senate Reports discuss the role of § 14(e). Describing § 14(e) as regulating "fraudulent transactions," and stating the thrust of the section:

"This provision would affirm the fact that the persons engaged in making or opposing tender offers or otherwise seeking to influence the decision of investors or the outcome of the tender offer are under an obligation to make *full disclosure* of material information to those with whom they deal."

Nowhere in the legislative history is there the slightest suggestion that § 14(e) serves any purpose other than disclosure, or that the term "manipulative" should be read as an invitation to the courts to oversee the substantive fairness of tender offers; the quality of any offer is a matter for the marketplace.

To adopt the reading of the term "manipulative" urged by petitioner would not only be unwarranted in light of the legislative purpose but would be at odds with it. Inviting judges to read the term "manipulative" with their own sense of what constitutes "unfair" or "artificial" conduct would inject uncertainty into the tender offer process. An essential piece of information—whether the court would deem the fully disclosed actions of one side or the other to be "manipulative"—would not be available until after the tender offer had closed. This uncertainty would directly contradict the expressed Congressional desire to give investors full information.* * *

We hold that the term "manipulative" as used in § 14(e) requires misrepresentation or nondisclosure. It connotes "conduct designed to deceive or defraud investors by controlling or artificially affecting the price of securities." Without misrepresentation or nondisclosure, § 14(e) has not been violated.

Applying that definition to this case, we hold that the actions of respondents were not manipulative. The amended complaint fails to allege that the cancellation of the first tender offer was accompanied by any misrepresentation, nondisclosure or deception. The District Court correctly found, "All activity of the defendants that could have conceivably affected the price of El Paso shares was done openly."

Petitioner also alleges that El Paso management and Burlington entered into certain undisclosed and deceptive agreements during the making of the second tender offer. The substance of the allegations is that, in return for certain undisclosed benefits, El Paso managers agreed to support the second tender offer. But both courts noted that petitioner's complaint seeks only redress only for injuries related to the cancellation of the first tender offer. Since the deceptive and misleading acts alleged by the petitioner all occurred with reference to the making of the second tender offer—when the injuries suffered by petitioner had already been sustained—these acts bear no possible causal relationship to petitioner's alleged injuries. The Court of Appeals dealt correctly with this claim.

POLAROID CORP. v. DISNEY

862 F.2d 987 (3d Cir.1988).

BECKER, CIRCUIT JUDGE.

* * * The All Holders Rule states that a bidder's tender offer must be open to "all security holders of the class of securities subject to the tender offer." Rule 14d–10(a). The SEC promulgated the Rule to ensure "fair and equal treatment of all holders of the class of securities that is the subject of a tender offer." The Rule was responsive to the situation which gave rise to the litigation in Unocal Corp. v. Mesa Petroleum Co., 493 A.2d 946, 949 (Del.1985), in which the Delaware Supreme Court upheld the power of a corporation to effect a self-tender for its shares which excluded shares of a minority shareholder who was attempting to take over the corporation.

Polaroid argues that Shamrock's tender offer violates the Rule because it is not open to all holders of Polaroid common stock; the Polaroid ESOP [Employee Stock Ownership Plan] is a holder (of 9.7 million shares) of Polaroid common stock and Shamrock has not offered to purchase the ESOP shares. Shamrock's argument in response is that its tender offer is "premised on the invalidity of the ESOP shares." * * *

The district court "assumed ... *arguendo* that Polaroid does have standing" to raise the issue but found no violation of the Rule. The court reasoned that "Shamrock should not be forced to make its offer to holders of ESOP shares, the issuance of which Shamrock is challenging in another action." * * *

Section 14(e) of the Williams Act proscribes "fraudulent, deceptive, or manipulative acts ... in connection with any tender offer." A unanimous

Court in Schreiber v. Burlington Northern, Inc., held that section 14(e) does not prohibit manipulative conduct unless there has been some element of deception through a material misrepresentation or omission. The Court held that "[i]t is clear that Congress relied primarily on disclosure to implement the purpose of the Williams Act" and characterized all of the Williams Act provisions as disclosure provisions. *Schreiber* characterizes even section 14(d)(6), which mandates the proration of share purchases when the number of shares tendered exceeds the number of shares sought, and section 14(d)(7), which mandates the payment of the same price to all those whose shares are purchased, as "requir[ing] or prohibit[ing] certain acts so that investors will possess additional time within which to take advantage of the disclosed information." It is thus possible to read *Schreiber* to imply that the All Holders Rule is beyond the SEC's authority under the Williams Act, for the Rule's purpose seems to be neither to ensure full disclosure nor to provide for an adequate time period for investors to comprehend disclosed information.

Although *Schreiber* categorizes the proration and best price provisions of the Williams Act as relating to disclosure, these provisions are only tangentially related to ensuring that investors make fully informed decisions. While the All Holders Rule thus has little to do with ensuring complete disclosure, it is no less related to disclosure than are the proration and best price provisions. Moreover, the SEC has articulated a disclosure justification for the Rule:

> [t]he all-holders requirement would realize the disclosure purposes of the Williams Act by ensuring that all members of the class subject to the tender offer receive information necessary to make an informed decision regarding the merits of the tender offer. If tender offer disclosure is given to all holders, but some are barred from participating in the offer, the Williams Act disclosure objectives would be ineffective.

In light of the loose definition that *Schreiber* itself ascribes to the meaning of a "disclosure" provision, the emphasis in *Schreiber* on characterizing the Williams Act as a disclosure statute *simpliciter* is of small force in an effort to invalidate the All Holders Rule. For the foregoing reasons, we are satisfied that the SEC was acting within its authority in promulgating the All Holders Rule. This conclusion is buttressed by the deference due the agency's interpretation of its enabling statute, the statute being ambiguous on the issue and the agency's interpretation being a permissible one.

The holding of *Schreiber*—that misrepresentation or nondisclosure is a necessary element of a violation of section 14(e)—is not compromised by a determination that the All Holders Rule is a valid exercise of SEC rulemaking authority. The All Holders Rule is not an attempt to proscribe manipulative practices so much as an attempt to ensure that all holders of a class of securities subject to a tender offer receive fair and equal treatment. And, as explained in the SEC's release, this attempt to ensure fair and equal treatment is the purpose behind both the proration and best price provisions.

———

SECTION 5. STATE REGULATION OF TENDER OFFERS

A number of states adopted laws regulating tender offers after enactment of the Williams Act, many of which imposed more stringent requirements than the federal law. Questions quickly arose concerning the extent to which the states constitutionally could regulate tender offers. The constitutional issues were framed in terms of whether the Williams Act preempts the field and also whether the state statutes impose an impermissible burden on interstate commerce. A fair summary of the Supreme Court cases is that so long as state legislation does not (1) alter the Williams Act's basic neutrality between tender offerors and target management or (2) impose burdens that conflict with the Williams Act regulations, the state statutes can survive.

The first generation of state tender offer statutes imposed a variety of disclosure requirements, waiting periods, and fairness thresholds for tender offers. In *Edgar v. MITE*, 457 U.S. 624, 102 S.Ct. 2629, 73 L.Ed.2d 269 (1982), the Supreme Court struck down an Illinois statute which imposed a twenty day waiting period on any tender offer and also provided for a hearing to determine the fairness of the offer. The Court held that since tender offers have a national impact and the Williams Act has set out disclosure and filing requirements, the Illinois statute imposed an excessive burden on interstate commerce and was therefore invalid.

Following the Supreme Court decision in *MITE,* a number of states adopted so-called "second generation" takeover statutes in an attempt to continue to regulate tender offers without imposing the undue burden identified by the *MITE* Court. These statutes generally involved amendment of state laws which govern corporations' internal affairs. Two major varieties of statutes began to emerge: control share acts and best price (or fair price) acts. Control share acquisition acts, modeled on legislation that was originally enacted in Ohio, limit a control person's voting rights. As a bidder acquires shares of the target company it may cross different control thresholds. After crossing such a threshold, the bidder cannot vote the shares it has acquired unless there has been a favorable vote by a majority of the disinterested shares. Disinterested shares excludes not only those held by the person seeking control but also shares controlled by the target company's management. The other variety of second generation statutes known as "fair price", or more accurately, "best price" statutes provide that any person acquiring a covered corporation must pay to all shareholders the "best price" paid to any shareholder. The best price requirement can be waived by a shareholder vote. Also, most best price statutes do not apply to friendly takeovers, as they are waivable by the board of directors.

———

CTS CORP. v. DYNAMICS CORP. OF AMERICA

481 U.S. 69, 107 S.Ct. 1637, 95 L.Ed.2d 67 (1987).

Justice Powell delivered the opinion of the Court.

This case presents the questions whether the Control Share Acquisitions Chapter of the Indiana Business Corporation Law is pre-empted by the Williams Act, or violates the Commerce Clause of the Federal Constitution.

On March 4, 1986, the Governor of Indiana signed a revised Indiana Business Corporation Law, Ind.Code § 23–1–17–1 et seq. (Supp.1986). That law included the Control Share Acquisitions Chapter (Indiana Act or Act). Beginning on August 1, 1987, the Act will apply to any corporation incorporated in Indiana, unless the corporation amends its articles of incorporation or bylaws to opt out of the Act. Before that date, any Indiana corporation can opt into the Act by resolution of its board of directors. The Act applies only to "issuing public corporations." The term "corporation" includes only businesses incorporated in Indiana. An "issuing public corporation" is defined as:

"a corporation that has:

"(1) one hundred (100) or more shareholders;

"(2) its principal place of business, its principal office, or substantial assets within Indiana; and

"(3) either:

"(A) more than ten percent (10%) of its shareholders resident in Indiana;

"(B) more than ten percent (10%) of its shares owned by Indiana residents; or

"(C) ten thousand (10,000) shareholders resident in Indiana."

The Act focuses on the acquisition of "control shares" in an issuing public corporation. Under the Act, an entity acquires "control shares" whenever it acquires shares that, but for the operation of the Act, would bring its voting power in the corporation to or above any of three thresholds: 20%, 33 1/3%, or 50%. An entity that acquires control shares does not necessarily acquire voting rights. Rather, it gains those rights only "to the extent granted by resolution approved by the shareholders of the issuing public corporation." Section 23–1–42–9(b) requires a majority vote of all disinterested shareholders holding each class of stock for passage of such a resolution. The practical effect of this requirement is to condition acquisition of control of a corporation on approval of a majority of the pre-existing disinterested shareholders.

The shareholders decide whether to confer rights on the control shares at the next regularly scheduled meeting of the shareholders, or at a specially scheduled meeting. The acquiror can require management of the corporation to hold such a special meeting within 50 days if it files an "acquiring person statement," requests the meeting, and agrees to pay the expenses of the meeting. If the shareholders do not vote to restore voting rights to the shares, the corporation may redeem the control shares from the acquiror at fair market value, but it is not required to do so. Similarly, if the acquiror does not file an acquiring person statement with the corporation, the corporation may, if its bylaws or articles of incorporation so provide, redeem the shares at any time after 60 days after the acquiror's last acquisition.* * *

The first question in these cases is whether the Williams Act preempts the Indiana Act. * * *

Because it is entirely possible for entities to comply with both the Williams Act and the Indiana Act, the state statute can be preempted only if it frustrates the purposes of the federal law.* * *

The Indiana Act differs in major respects from the Illinois statute that the Court considered in Edgar v. MITE Corp., 457 U.S. 624 (1982). After reviewing the legislative history of the Williams Act, Justice White, joined by Chief Justice Burger and Justice Blackmun (the plurality), concluded that the Williams Act struck a careful balance between the interests of offerors and target companies, and that any state statute that "upset" this balance was pre-empted.* * *

As the plurality opinion in *MITE* did not represent the views of a majority of the Court, we are not bound by its reasoning. We need not question that reasoning, however, because we believe the Indiana Act passes muster even under the broad interpretation of the Williams Act articulated by Justice White in *MITE*. As is apparent from our summary of its reasoning, the overriding concern of the *MITE* plurality was that the Illinois statute considered in that case operated to favor management against offerors, to the detriment of shareholders. By contrast, the statute now before the Court protects the independent shareholder against both of the contending parties. Thus, the Act furthers a basic purpose of the Williams Act, " 'plac[ing] investors on an equal footing with the takeover bidder.' "

The Indiana Act operates on the assumption, implicit in the Williams Act, that independent shareholders faced with tender offers often are at a disadvantage. By allowing such shareholders to vote as a group, the Act protects them from the coercive aspects of some tender offers. If, for example, shareholders believe that a successful tender offer will be followed by a purchase of nontendering shares at a depressed price, individual shareholders may tender their shares—even if they doubt the tender offer is in the corporation's best interest—to protect themselves from being forced to sell their shares at a depressed price. As the SEC explains: "The alternative of not accepting the tender offer is virtual assurance that, if the offer is successful, the shares will have to be sold in the lower priced, second step." In such a situation under the Indiana Act, the shareholders as a group, acting in the corporation's best interest, could reject the offer, although individual shareholders might be inclined to accept it. The desire of the Indiana Legislature to protect shareholders of Indiana corporations from this type of coercive offer does not conflict with the Williams Act. Rather, it furthers the federal policy of investor protection.

In implementing its goal, the Indiana Act avoids the problems the plurality discussed in *MITE*. Unlike the *MITE* statute, the Indiana Act does not give either management or the offeror an advantage in communicating with the shareholders about the impending offer. The Act also does not impose an indefinite delay on tender offers. Nothing in the Act prohibits an offeror from consummating an offer on the 20th business day, the earliest day permitted under applicable federal regulations. Nor does the Act allow the state government to interpose its views of fairness between willing buyers and sellers of shares of the target company. Rather, the Act allows *shareholders* to evaluate the fairness of the offer collectively.

The Court of Appeals based its finding of pre-emption on its view that the practical effect of the Indiana Act is to delay consummation of tender offers until 50 days after the commencement of the offer. As did the Court of Appeals, Dynamics reasons that no rational offeror will purchase shares until it gains assurance that those shares will carry voting rights. Because it is possible that voting rights will not be conferred until a shareholder meeting 50 days after commencement of the offer, Dynamics concludes that the Act imposes a 50–day delay. This, it argues, conflicts with the shorter 20–business-day period established by the SEC as the minimum period for which a tender offer may be held open. We find the alleged conflict illusory.

The Act does not impose an absolute 50–day delay on tender offers, nor does it preclude an offeror from purchasing shares as soon as federal law permits. If the offeror fears an adverse shareholder vote under the Act, it can make a conditional tender offer, offering to accept shares on the condition that the shares receive voting rights within a certain period of time. The Williams Act permits tender offers to be conditioned on the offeror's subsequently obtaining regulatory approval. There is no reason to doubt that this type of conditional tender offer would be legitimate as well.

Even assuming that the Indiana Act imposes some additional delay, nothing in *MITE* suggested that *any* delay imposed by state regulation, however short, would create a conflict with the Williams Act. The plurality argued only that the offeror should "be free to go forward without *unreasonable* delay." In that case, the Court was confronted with the potential for indefinite delay and presented with no persuasive reason why some deadline could not be established. By contrast, the Indiana Act provides that full voting rights will be vested—if this eventually is to occur—within 50 days after commencement of the offer. This period is within the 60–day maximum period Congress established for tender offers. We cannot say that a delay within that congressionally determined period is unreasonable.

Finally, we note that the Williams Act would pre-empt a variety of state corporate laws of hitherto unquestioned validity if it were construed to pre-empt any state statute that may limit or delay the free exercise of power after a successful tender offer. State corporate laws commonly permit corporations to stagger the terms of their directors. By staggering the terms of directors, and thus having annual elections for only one class of directors each year, corporations may delay the time when a successful offeror gains control of the board of directors. Similarly, state corporation laws commonly provide for cumulative voting. By enabling minority share-holders to assure themselves of representation in each class of directors, cumulative voting provisions can delay further the ability of offerors to gain untrammeled authority over the affairs of the target corporation.

In our view, the possibility that the Indiana Act will delay some tender offers is insufficient to require a conclusion that the Williams Act pre-empts the Act. The longstanding prevalence of state regulation in this area suggests that, if Congress had intended to pre-empt all state laws that delay the acquisition of voting control following a tender offer, it would have said so explicitly. The regulatory conditions that the Act places on tender offers are consistent with the text and the purposes of the Williams Act. Accordingly, we hold that the Williams Act does not pre-empt the Indiana Act. * * *

JUSTICE SCALIA, concurring in part and concurring in the judgment.

* * * I do not share the Court's apparent high estimation of the beneficence of the state statute at issue here. But a law can be both economic folly and constitutional. The Indiana Control Shares Acquisi-tions Chapter is at least the latter. I therefore concur in the judgment of the Court.

JUSTICE WHITE, with whom JUSTICE BLACKMUN and JUSTICE STEVENS join as to Part II, dissenting.

The majority today upholds Indiana's Control Share Acquisitions Chapter, a statute which will predictably foreclose completely some tender offers for stock in Indiana corporations. I disagree with the conclusion that the Chapter is neither preempted by the Williams Act nor in conflict with the Commerce Clause. The Chapter undermines the policy of the Williams Act by effectively preventing minority shareholders, in some circumstances, from acting in their own best interests by selling their stock. In addition, the Chapter will substantially burden the interstate market in corporate ownership, particularly if other States follow Indiana's lead as many already have done. The Chapter, therefore, directly inhibits interstate commerce, the very economic consequences the Commerce Clause was intended to prevent. The opinion of the Court of Appeals is far more persuasive than that of the majority today, and the judgment of that court should be affirmed.

The Williams Act expressed Congress' concern that individual investors be given sufficient information so that they could make an informed choice on whether to tender their stock in response to a tender offer. The problem with the approach the majority adopts today is that it equates protection of individual investors, the focus of the Williams Act, with the protection of shareholders as a group. Indiana's Control Share Acquisitions Chapter undoubtedly helps protect the interests of a majority of the shareholders in any corporation subject to its terms, but in many instances, it will effectively prevent an individual investor from selling his stock at a premium. Indiana's statute, therefore, does not "furthe[r] the federal policy of *investor* protection," as the majority claims.* * *

NOTES

1. Despite the Supreme Court's validation of the Indiana statute involved in the *CTS* case, the major commercial states have not followed the Indiana approach. Delaware and New York, the two states in which the largest number of New York Stock Exchange-listed companies are incorporated or headquartered, have opted for statutes which do not restrict a bidder from acquiring or voting shares of the target company, but do prohibit it from merging with the acquired company for a specified period of years after the acquisition. This in effect makes it impossible for the bidder to use the target company's assets to secure the debt incurred by the bidder to finance the takeover.

2. Section 203 of the Delaware General Corporation Law, enacted in 1988 prohibits a business combination with an "interested stockholder" (an owner of 15% or more of the company's shares) for a period of three years unless either (a) the combination was approved by the board that was in office prior to the bidder's acquisition of the 15% interest, (b) the interested stockholder acquired at least 85% of the target's voting stock (exclusive of shares held by officers or directors or certain types of employee stock plans) at the time it became an interested stockholder, or (c) the transaction is approved by the directors and by the holders of at least two-thirds of the outstanding stock not owned by the interested stockholder. The statute applies to any Delaware corporation (with certain exclusion and opt-out provisions) regardless of whether it conducts any business or has any stockholders in Delaware. A number of other states have adopted similar statutes.

3. Other third generation statutes have taken different approaches. For example, the Ohio Foreign Business Acquisition Act imposed stricter burdens on foreign bidders but that statute has been invalidated by at least one court. Campeau Corp. v. Federated Department Stores, 679 F.Supp. 735 (S.D.Ohio 1988). Pennsylvania and a number of other states have adopted constituency statutes (also referred to as stakeholder statutes) which authorize the board of directors in making decisions to consider interests (including those of

employees and the community) in addition to those of the shareholders. Pennsylvania has taken yet another approach by expressly sanctioning use of poison pills as a defensive measure.

AMANDA ACQUISITION CORP. v. UNIVERSAL FOODS CORP.

877 F.2d 496 (7th Cir.1989).

EASTERBROOK, CIRCUIT JUDGE.

States have enacted three generations of takeover statutes in the last 20 years. * * *

Wisconsin has a third-generation takeover statute. Enacted after *CTS*, it postpones the kinds of transactions that often follow tender offers (and often are the reason for making the offers in the first place). Unless the target's board agrees to the transaction in advance, the bidder must wait three years after buying the shares to merge with the target or acquire more than 5% of its assets. We must decide whether this is consistent with the Williams Act and Commerce Clause.

Amanda Acquisition Corporation is a shell with a single purpose: to acquire Universal Foods Corporation, a diversified firm incorporated in Wisconsin and traded on the New York Stock Exchange. Universal is covered by Wisconsin's anti-takeover law. Amanda is a subsidiary of High Voltage Engineering Corp., a small electronics firm in Massachusetts. Most of High Voltage's equity capital comes from Berisford Capital PLC, a British venture capital firm, and Hyde Park Partners L.P., a partnership affiliated with the principals of Berisford. Chase Manhattan Bank has promised to lend Amanda 50% of the cost of the acquisition, secured by the stock of Universal.

In mid-November 1988 Universal's stock was trading for about $25 per share. On December 1 Amanda commenced a tender offer at $30.50, to be effective if at least 75% of the stock should be tendered.[1] This all-cash, all-shares offer has been increased by stages to $38.00. Amanda's financing is contingent on a prompt merger with Universal if the offer succeeds, so the offer is conditional on a judicial declaration that the law is invalid. * * *

No firm incorporated in Wisconsin and having its headquarters, substantial operations, or 10% of its shares or shareholders there may "engage in a business combination with an interested stockholder ... for 3 years after the interested stockholder's stock acquisition date unless the board of directors of the [Wisconsin] corporation has approved, before the

---

1. Wisconsin has, in addition to §§ 180.726, a statute modeled on Indiana's, providing that an acquiring firm's shares lose their votes, which may be restored under specified circumstances. Wis.Stat. §§ 180.25(9). That law accounts for the 75% condition, but it is not pertinent to the questions we resolve.

interested stockholder's stock acquisition date, that business combination or the purchase of stock", Wis.Stat. § 180.726(2). An "interested stockholder" is one owning 10% of the voting stock, directly or through associates (anyone acting in concert with it), § 180.726(1)(j). A "business combination" is a merger with the bidder or any of its affiliates, sale of more than 5% of the assets to bidder or affiliate, liquidation of the target, or a transaction by which the target guarantees the bidder's or affiliates debts or passes tax benefits to the bidder or affiliate, § 180.726(1)(e). The law, in other words, provides for almost hermetic separation of bidder and target for three years after the bidder obtains 10% of the stock—unless the target's board consented before then. No matter how popular the offer, the ban applies: obtaining 85% (even 100%) of the stock held by non-management shareholders won't allow the bidder to engage in a business combination, as it would under Delaware law. See BNS, Inc. v. Koppers Co., 683 F.Supp. 458 (D.Del.1988); RP Acquisition Corp. v. Staley Continental, Inc., 686 F.Supp. 476 (D.Del.1988); City Capital Associates L.P. v. Interco, Inc., 696 F.Supp. 1551 (D.Del.), affirmed, 860 F.2d 60 (3d Cir. 1988). Wisconsin firms cannot opt out of the law, as may corporations subject to almost all other state takeover statutes. In Wisconsin it is management's approval in advance, or wait three years. Even when the time is up, the bidder needs the approval of a majority of the remaining investors, without any provision disqualifying shares still held by the managers who resisted the transaction, § 180.726(3)(b). The district court found that this statute "effectively eliminates hostile leveraged buyouts". As a practical matter, Wisconsin prohibits any offer contingent on a merger between bidder and target, a condition attached to about 90% of contemporary tender offers.

Amanda filed this suit seeking a declaration that this law is preempted by the Williams Act and inconsistent with the Commerce Clause. It added a pendent claim that the directors' refusal to redeem the poison-pill rights violates their fiduciary duties to Universal's shareholders. The district court declined to issue a preliminary injunction. It concluded that the statute is constitutional and not preempted, and that under Wisconsin law (which the court believed would follow Delaware's) directors are entitled to prevent investors from accepting tender offers of which the directors do not approve. * * *

If our views of the wisdom of state law mattered, Wisconsin's takeover statute would not survive. Like our colleagues who decided *MITE* and *CTS*, we believe that antitakeover legislation injures shareholders. Managers frequently realize gains for investors via voluntary combinations (mergers). If gains are to be had, but managers balk, tender offers are investors' way to go over managers' heads. If managers are not maximizing the firm's value—perhaps because they have missed the possibility of a synergistic combination, perhaps because they are clinging to divisions that could be better run in other hands, perhaps because they are just not the best persons for the job—a bidder that believes it can realize more of the firm's value will make investors a higher offer. Investors tender; the bidder gets control and changes things. The prospect of monitoring by would-be bidders, and an occasional bid at a premium, induces managers to run corporations more efficiently and replaces them if they will not. * * *

Skepticism about the wisdom of a state's law does not lead to the conclusion that the law is beyond the state's power, however. We have not been elected custodians of investors' wealth. States need not treat investors' welfare as their summum bonum. Perhaps they choose to protect managers' welfare instead, or believe that the current economic literature reaches an incorrect conclusion and that despite appearances takeovers injure investors in the long run. Unless a federal statute or the Constitution bars the way, Wisconsin's choice must be respected.

Amanda relies on the Williams Act of 1968, incorporated into §§ 13(d), (e) and 14(d)-(f) of the Securities Exchange Act of 1934. The Williams Act regulates the conduct of tender offers. Amanda believes that Congress created an entitlement for investors to receive the benefit of tender offers, and that because Wisconsin's law makes tender offers unattractive to many potential bidders, it is preempted.

Preemption has not won easy acceptance among the Justices for several reasons. First there is § 28(a) of the '34 Act, which provides that "[n]othing in this chapter shall affect the jurisdiction of the securities commission ... of any State over any security or any person insofar as it does not conflict with the provisions of this chapter or the rules and regulations thereunder." Although some of the SEC's regulations (particularly the one defining the commencement of an offer) conflict with some state takeover laws, the SEC has not drafted regulations concerning mergers with controlling shareholders, and the Act itself does not address the subject. * * *

The Williams Act regulates the *process* of tender offers: timing, disclosure, proration if tenders exceed what the bidder is willing to buy, best-price rules. It slows things down, allowing investors to evaluate the offer and management's response. Best-price, proration, and short-tender rules ensure that investors who decide at the end of the offer get the same treatment as those who decide immediately, reducing pressure to leap before looking. * * *

Any bidder complying with federal law is free to acquire shares of Wisconsin firms on schedule. Delay in completing a second-stage merger may make the target less attractive, and thus depress the price offered or even lead to an absence of bids; it does not, however, alter any of the procedures governed by federal regulation. Indeed Wisconsin's law does not depend in any way on how the acquiring firm came by its stock: open-market purchases, private acquisitions of blocs, and acquisitions via tender offers are treated identically. Wisconsin's law is no different in effect from one saying that for the three years after a person acquires 10% of a firm's stock, a unanimous vote is required to merge. Corporate law once had a generally applicable unanimity rule in major transactions, a rule discarded because giving every investor the power to block every reorgani-zation stopped many desirable changes. (Many investors could use their "hold-up" power to try to engross a larger portion of the gains, creating a complex bargaining problem that often could not be solved.) Wisconsin's more restrained version of unanimity also may block beneficial transac-tions, but not by tinkering with any of the procedures established in federal law.

Only if the Williams Act gives investors a right to be the beneficiary of offers could Wisconsin's law run afoul of the federal rule. No such entitlement can be mined out of the Williams Act, however. * * * Inves-tors have no right to receive tender offers. More to the point—since Amanda sues as bidder rather than as investor seeking to sell—the Williams Act does not create a right to profit from the business of making tender offers. It is not attractive to put bids on the table for Wisconsin corporations, but because Wisconsin leaves the process alone once a bidder appears, its law may co-exist with the Williams Act. * * *

To say that states have the power to enact laws whose costs exceed their benefits is not to say that investors should kiss their wallets goodbye. States compete to offer corporate codes attractive to firms. Managers who want to raise money incorporate their firms in the states that offer the combination of rules investors prefer. Laws that in the short run injure investors and protect managers will in the longer run make the state less attractive to firms that need to raise new capital. If the law is "protectionist", the protected class is the existing body of managers (and other workers), suppliers, and so on, which bears no necessary relation to state boundaries. States regulating the affairs of domestic corporations cannot in the long run injure anyone but themselves. * * *

The long run takes time to arrive, and it is tempting to suppose that courts could contribute to investors' welfare by eliminating laws that impose costs in the short run. The price of such warfare, however, is a reduction in the power of competition among states. Courts seeking to impose "good" rules on the states diminish the differences among corpo-rate codes and dampen competitive forces.

The three district judges who have considered and sustained Dela-ware's law delaying mergers did so in large measure because they believed that the law left hostile offers "a meaningful opportunity for success". BNS, Inc. v. Koppers Co., 683 F.Supp. at 469. See also RP Acquisition Corp., 686 F.Supp. at 482–84, 488; City Capital Associates, 696 F.Supp. at 1555. Delaware allows a merger to occur forthwith if the bidder obtains 85% of the shares other than those held by management and employee stock plans. If the bid is attractive to the bulk of the unaffiliated investors, it succeeds. Wisconsin offers no such opportunity, which Amanda believes is fatal.

Even in Wisconsin, though, options remain. Defenses impenetrable to the naked eye may have cracks. Poison pills are less fatal in practice than in name (some have been swallowed willingly), and corporate law contains self-defense mechanisms. Investors concerned about stock-watering often arranged for firms to issue pre-emptive rights, entitlements for existing investors to buy stock at the same price offered to newcomers (often before the newcomers had a chance to buy in). Poison pills are dilution devices, and so pre-emptive rights ought to be handy countermeasures. So too there are countermeasures to statutes deferring mergers. The cheapest is to lower the bid to reflect the costs of delay. Because every potential bidder labors under the same drawback, the firm placing the highest value on the target still should win. Or a bidder might take down the stock and pledge it (or its dividends) as security for any loans. That is, the bidder could operate the target as a subsidiary for three years. The corporate world is full of partially owned subsidiaries. If there is gain to be had from changing the debt-equity ratio of the target, that can be done consistent with Wisconsin law. The prospect of being locked into place as holders of illiquid minority positions would cause many persons to sell out, and the threat of being locked in would cause many managers to give assent in advance, as Wisconsin allows. (Or bidders might demand that directors waive the protections of state law, just as Amanda believes that the directors' fiduciary duties compel them to redeem the poison pill rights.) Many bidders would find lock-in unattractive because of the potential for litigation by minority investors, and the need to operate the firm as a subsidiary might foreclose savings or synergies from merger. So none of these options is a perfect substitute for immediate merger, but each is a crack in the defensive wall allowing some value-increasing bids to proceed.

At the end of the day, however, it does not matter whether these countermeasures are "enough". The Commerce Clause does not demand that states leave bidders a "meaningful opportunity for success". * * * Wisconsin's law may well be folly; we are confident that it is constitutional.

CHAPTER 21

DERIVATIVE ACTIONS AND INDEMNIFICATION OF OFFICERS AND DIRECTORS

■ ■ ■

SECTION 1.   BACKGROUND

HICHENS v. CONGREVE

38 Eng. Rep. 917 (1828).

THE LORD CHANCELLOR LYNDHURST.

Upon the face of the bill I cannot help considering the transactions stated in it to be fraudulent. Sir William Congreve entered into a negotiation with [Roger] Flattery for the purchase of the property in question at the price of £10,000 for a joint stock company of which he was to be a member and director. After the treaty was begun, the two Clarkes associated themselves with Sir William Congreve in the scheme; and the negotiation with Flattery went on. The object was, the purchase of the Arigna mines, in order that they might be conveyed to a company by whom they were to be worked; and the company was to consist, not of Congreve and the Clarkes alone, but of a considerable body of shareholders.

It appears that, in the course of these negotiations, Congreve and the Clarkes became desirous of making a profit out of the original transaction for the purchase of Flattery's interest in the mines. The first plan, which occurred to them, was, that a conveyance for the sum of £10,000 should be made to persons nominated by them, who were afterwards to convey to the company for £25,000. If such a transaction had taken place, and the particulars had been concealed from the company, it could not have been sustained; for, considering the situation in which Congreve and the Clarkes stood with reference to the company, it would have been incumbent on them to have communicated the real price at which the mines had been purchased of Flattery. This objection seems to have occurred to them; and, accordingly, another shape was given to the proceedings. The plan now adopted was this,—that a conveyance should be executed directly from Flattery to trustees for the company; and although Flattery had agreed to convey the property for £10,000, that in this conveyance it should be stated that the purchase-money was £25,000, in order that the difference might be put into the pockets of Sir William Congreve and the two Clarkes, and some other individuals whom they might choose to nominate. Such a transaction is so incorrect, that it is quite impossible that any court of justice could permit it to stand: and if, after the conveyance had been so made, reciting that the price paid to Flattery was £25,000, a company of shareholders was formed, who acted upon that representation, they could, in justice, be chargeable only with the money actually paid to Flattery; and if a larger sum was taken out of their funds, they would be entitled to call on the individuals, into whose hands it came, to refund it. In substance, therefore, the plaintiffs are entitled to relief.

The only other question is, Whether. in point of form, there is any objection to this bill?

The suit is instituted by certain shareholders on behalf of themselves, and all others who may choose to come in and take the benefit of the suit. It has been argued, that the case comes within the clause of the act of parliament. I doubt whether the terms of the clause are sufficient to comprehend it; and the spirit of the act does not extend to transactions such as are in question here. That clause was introduced, in order that, where the company was concerned on one side, and individuals contracting with it, being, perhaps at the same time members, were concerning on the other, suits might be carried on, without being impeded by the objections which would otherwise have arisen.

Here is a fund in which all the shareholders are interested; £15,000 has been improperly taken out of it: a fraud has been committed on them all. Is it necessary that all should come into a court of justice, for the purpose of joining in a suit with a view to obtain redress? It is possible that the number of shareholders may be six thousand, for the capital of the company is fixed by the act of parliament at £300,000 divided into shares of £50 each; and justice never could be obtained if any very great number of Plaintiffs were put on the record.

It is said that there is nothing on the face of the bill which shows that the shareholders are so numerous, that they could not all be joined as parties without inconvenience. I think it does appear sufficiently, that, if all were joined, the number of complainants would be inconveniently great; first, because the shares are six thousand in number, and, secondly, because it appears by the act of parliament that there were then upwards of two hundred shareholders. It is clear, therefore, that justice would be unattainable, if all the shareholders were required to be parties to the suit.

It is said, each shareholder might file a bill to recover his proportion of the money. Such a course would produce enormous inconvenience. Are two hundred bills to be filed, in order to do justice in this matter? If justice can be done in one suit, the Court will sustain such a proceeding; for to require all the shareholders to be parties, or to leave each shareholder to file a separate bill to redress his own wrong, would, in substance, be a denial of justice.

In the present case, it appears to me that justice may be done in one suit. All the shareholders stand in the same situation; the property has been taken out of their common fund; they are entitled to have that property brought back again for the benefit of the concern. When all parties stand in the same situation, and have one common right, and one common interest, in what respect can it be inconvenient that two, or three, or more, should sue in their own names for the benefit of all?

It is said that the prayer of the bill is incompatible with this form of proceeding; for it asks that the transaction may be declared fraudulent, and that the Defendants may be ordered to pay the £15,000, with interest, to the bankers of the company, on the account and for the use of the company. Whether, ultimately, the decree will be in that precise form, is not now the question. The Court may think it right to direct the money to be repaid with interest; or it may direct inquiries; and it is not improbable that the money may be ordered to be brought back into the general funds of the society. But, whatever may be the particular form of relief, which may ultimately be given, there is not doubt that, if, at the hearing, it appears that this £15,000 was obtained by fraud, the Court will make a decree, the effect of which will be to compel those, who were parties to the transaction, to refund the money to those to whom it rightfully belongs.

Demurrer overruled.

NOTES

1. The use of the derivative suit spread to America and became a popular device for the protection of shareholders from over reaching by management. As the Supreme Court noted in Ross v. Bernhard, 396 U.S. 531, 534, 90 S.Ct. 733, 24 L.Ed.2d 729 (1970):

> The common law refused, . . . to permit stockholders to call corporate managers to account in actions at law. The possibilities for abuse, thus presented, were not ignored by corporate officers and directors. Early in the 19th century, equity provided relief both in this country and in England. Without detailing these developments, it suffices to say that the remedy in this country, first dealt with by this Court in Dodge v. Woolsey, 18 How. 331, 15 L.Ed. 401 (1856), provided redress not only against faithless officers and directors but also against third parties who had damaged or threatened the corporate properties and whom the corporation through its managers refused to pursue. The remedy made available in equity was the derivative suit, viewed in this country as a suit to enforce a *corporate* cause of action against officers, directors, and third parties. As elaborated in the cases, one precondition for the suit was a valid claim on which the corporation could have sued; another was that the corporation itself had refused to proceed after suitable demand, unless excused by extraordinary conditions.

The Supreme Court further held that there is a right to a jury trial in a derivative action if the underlying action was an action at law. Id.

2.   Encouraging the use of derivative suits is the fact that attorney fees from the corporation to the plaintiff are generally awarded where the litigation results in a "substantial benefit" to the corporation. See e.g., Model Bus. Corp. Act § 7.46(1); Mills v. Electric Auto–Lite Co., 396 U.S. 375, 90 S.Ct. 616, 24 L.Ed.2d 593 (1970). The prospect of attorney fees has sometimes been abused by lawyers through settlements that provided for their fees with little ultimate benefit to shareholders. To assure that the rights of shareholders are protected, Federal Rule of Civil Procedure 23.1 requires that any settlement or dismissal be approved by the court. Most states impose similar requirements.

3.   Corporate resources must be expended to defend derivative suits and to pay for settlements. The company's officers are also diverted from their primary role of managing the business to give depositions and deal with the litigation. See generally James D. Cox, Compensation, Deterrence and the Market as Boundaries for Derivative Suit Procedures, 52 Geo. Wash. L. Rev. 745 (1984). Is there some better way to allow shareholders to monitor managers' conduct without the attending litigation costs? Would arbitration be more desirable? Is this something market discipline can handle more efficiently? See generally Frank H. Easterbrook & Daniel R. Fischel, Corporate Control Transactions, 91 Yale L.J. 698 (1982) (discussing market based approaches).

SECTION 2.   DERIVATIVE vs. PERSONAL ACTIONS

IN RE TRI–STAR PICTURES, INC. LITIGATION

634 A.2d 319 (Del.1993).

MOORE, JUSTICE.

In this class action the plaintiffs are former minority stockholders of Tri–Star Pictures, Inc. ("Tri–Star" or the "Company") who challenge a business combination between Tri–Star and the Entertainment Business Sector of the Coca-Cola Company (the "Combination"). The Combination, with its related transactions and surrounding facts, is complicated and convoluted—sufficient to daunt any but the most determined analyst or challenger. Shorn of its bristles and fuzz, however, it was the way Coca-Cola, at no significant cost to itself, obtained 80% ownership of Tri–Star. The Court of Chancery dismissed most of plaintiffs' claims as moot because a subsequent merger between Sony USA, Inc. ("Sony") and Tri–Star extinguished plaintiffs' standing to maintain a derivative suit. The defendants were granted summary judgment on plaintiffs' remaining claims because of a failure to adduce sufficient evidence of individual damage arising from the defendants' alleged nondisclosures. Our disposition of these issues is basically determined by this Court's recent decision in *Cede & Co. & Cinerama, Inc. v. Technicolor, Inc.*, Del.Supr., 634 A.2d 345 (1993) (Horsey, J.), and our earlier decision of *Weinberger v. UOP*, Del.Supr., 457 A.2d 701 (1983). We find that the plaintiffs alleged sufficient individual injury resulting from the defendants' asserted manipulation of the Combination so as to dilute the cash value and impinge upon the voting rights of the minority's shares. Plaintiffs' claims clearly survive a motion to dismiss under Chancery Court Rule 12(b)(6). Such conduct, taken as true for present purposes, is a breach of the duty of loyalty requiring that the defendants' actions be judged by principles of entire fairness. Since this shifts the burden to the defendants to prove the "most scrupulous inherent fairness of the bargain", *Weinberger*, 457 A.2d at 710, there is no requirement that plaintiffs prove damages to survive a motion to dismiss. Accordingly, the trial court's dismissal of Counts I, II, V and VII of plaintiffs' Amended Complaint are reversed. The dismissal of Count III of plaintiffs' Amended Complaint on grounds of mootness is affirmed.

In this class action, plaintiffs are the holders of Tri–Star stock who either were eligible to vote or to direct the voting of Tri–Star shares at the December 15, 1987 meeting where the Combination was approved (the "Class"). This group excludes the defendants and their affiliates as of December 15, 1987. At that time the Class held approximately 43.4% of the 34.5 million outstanding common shares of Tri–Star. The Company was formed in 1985 to succeed to the business of a joint venture organized earlier by CBS, Inc. ("CBS"), CPI Film Holdings, Inc., a subsidiary of Coca–Cola ("CPI"), and an affiliate of Home Box Office, Inc. ("HBO"), a subsidiary of Time Incorporated. Tri–Star was principally engaged in the production, distribution, and exploitation of feature-length motion pictures and television programs.[2]

Defendant Coca–Cola was Tri–Star's largest single stockholder in 1985, owning 12,708,333 shares, representing 36.8% of its common stock. Coca–Cola became involved in the entertainment business upon acquiring Columbia Pictures Industries, Inc., and incorporated it into what became Coca–Cola's Entertainment Business Sector ("Entertainment Sector"). Coca–Cola later expanded its Entertainment Sector through other acquisitions.

Defendant HBO, a wholly owned subsidiary of Time Incorporated ("Time"), is engaged in programming and marketing pay-television services. HBO owned 3,125,000 shares (9%) of Tri–Star's common stock. HBO has had significant business relationships with Tri–Star and Coca–Cola.

Tri–Star had two other major stockholders: Technicolor, Inc. ("Technicolor"), which owned 7.2%, and Rank American, Inc. ("Rank"), which

---

2. Although Tri–Star's name was later changed to Columbia Pictures Entertainment, Inc., and thereafter to Sony Pictures, Inc., for purposes of this opinion it will be referred to as "Tri–Star".

owned 3.6%. The combined holdings of these four shareholders represented 56.6% of the Company's common stock.

The individual defendants are Victor A. Kaufman, Michael J. Fuchs, David A. Matalon, E. Thayer Bigelow, Jr., Joseph J. Collins, Patrick M. Williamson, Judd A. Weinberg, Ira C. Herbert, Dan W. Lufkin and Francis T. Vincent, Jr., all members of Tri–Star's board of directors at the time of the Combination. Of this group, Messrs. Herbert, Vincent, and Williamson were senior executives of Coca–Cola or a Coca–Cola affiliate and substantial owners of Coca–Cola stock. Three other members of the group, Messrs. Weinberg, Lufkin, and Matalon, also owned substantial shares of Coca–Cola stock that under the terms of the Combination entitled them to a significant personal financial benefit upon approval of the transaction. Both Messrs. Lufkin and Williamson were nominated to their positions on the Tri–Star board by Coca–Cola. Finally, Messrs. Bigelow and Collins are senior officers of Time and its subsidiary, HBO, which had significant commercial agreements with both Coca–Cola and Tri-Star before the Combination. * * *

The plaintiffs' principal complaint is that the trial court's characterization of their claims as derivative is wholly erroneous. The Amended Complaint, plaintiffs insist, demonstrates that Coca–Cola used its control of Tri–Star to implement a self-dealing combination adverse to the interests of the minority shareholders and violative of the entire fairness standard. More specifically, plaintiffs allege that Coca–Cola used its influence as controlling shareholder, and its domination of the self-dealing board of directors, to orchestrate a master plan fully knowing that special injury would be suffered by the non-controlling stockholders of Tri–Star. The injury sustained, plaintiffs allege, is a selective diminution in the value of the minority stockholders' shares and a total evisceration of their right to make an informed vote on corporate affairs.[9]

According to defendants, plaintiffs lost standing as a result of the Sony–Tri–Star merger, since their accusations of self-dealing amount to no more than a complaint against corporate waste. *Lewis v. Anderson,* Del.Supr., 477 A.2d 1040, 1046–48 (1984). Because an injury suffered through waste of corporate assets falls equally upon all stockholders, defendants contend that any recovery may only be sought derivatively on behalf of the corporation injured. As for plaintiffs' charge that they were deprived of their right to vote, defendants allege that the result is the same because it is the lack of individual injury suffered, and not the injurious act, that determines if an action is personal or derivative. As a

---

9. Plaintiffs also argue that the actual effect of the Combination on the class was the same as if a three-way exchange merger had occurred and thus, plaintiffs should have the same standing to challenge this "de facto merger" as minority stockholders would have in a regular merger. Plaintiffs ignore this Court's decision in *Heilbrunn v. Sun Chem. Corp.,* Del.Supr., 150 A.2d 755 (1959) (rejecting assertion of the doctrine of *de facto* merger by stockholders of the purchasing corporation). It is fatal to their cause. In *Heilbrunn,* this Court recognized "that no injury is inflicted upon the purchaser's stockholders where the corporation has simply acquired property and paid for it in shares of stock. The business of the purchaser will continue as before without the reorganization changing the essential nature of the corporation." *Id.* at 758.

result, defendants argue that the absence of averments of specific facts, showing how the alleged control, manipulation, or nondisclosure by Coca–Cola specifically injured plaintiffs or affected their contractual right to vote as stockholders, requires dismissal.

The trial court held that any injury resulting from the conduct of Coca–Cola or the Tri–Star board amounts to no more than a complaint against overpayment for the assets of the Entertainment Sector, and thus waste. The court reasoned that the diminution in the value of shares that may have resulted from the defendants' actions would have affected all stockholders equally. Because the plaintiffs failed to articulate any individual injury suffered on account of the defendants' purportedly self-dealing Combination, the court concluded that when Tri–Star merged with Sony, plaintiffs lost their standing to pursue the solely derivative claims. Nevertheless, the court found that the plaintiffs asserted an individual claim for damages for violation of a controlling stockholder's duty of disclosure. In so ruling, the court expressed great skepticism that the plaintiffs would be able to prove any damages resulting from that claim.

Upon full review of the pleadings, which incorporated the proxy materials and accompanying exhibits, we find that the trial court erred: (1) in concluding that the plaintiffs' Amended Complaint primarily alleged only derivative claims respecting the Combination, and (2) that plaintiffs' individual claims failed for lack of proof of damages. Taking the facts in a light most favorable to plaintiffs, as we are required to do under the appropriate standard of review, it is clear that plaintiffs alleged sufficient individual injury—unconditionally resulting from the defendants' manipulation of the Combination in a manner designed to dilute both the cash value and voting rights of the minority stockholders—for their claims to survive a motion to dismiss under Chancery Court Rule 12(b)(6). That conduct must be judged by the standards of entire fairness—fair price and fair dealing—articulated in *Weinberger v. UOP., Inc.,* Del.Supr., 457 A.2d 701, 710–13 (1983).

We begin with the plaintiffs' claim that the Combination fails to satisfy the standard of entire fairness required by *Weinberger.* If a controlling shareholder stands on both sides of a transaction, "the requirement of fairness is unflinching in its demand that the controlling stockholder establish the entire fairness of the undertaking sufficient to pass the careful scrutiny of the courts." *Id.* at 710; *Bershad v. Curtiss–Wright Corp.,* Del.Supr., 535 A.2d 840, 845 (1987); *Rosenblatt v. Getty Oil Co.,* Del.Supr., 493 A.2d 929, 937 (1985). As alleged here, Coca–Cola, although not a majority shareholder, affirmatively attempted to dictate the destiny of Tri–Star. It therefore assumed a fiduciary duty to all Tri–Star shareholders. *Harriman v. E.I. DuPont De Nemours & Co.,* 372 F.Supp. 101, 106 (D.Del.1974). *See also, Ivanhoe Partners v. Newmont Mining Corp.,* Del.Supr., 535 A.2d 1334, 1344 (1987).

Because these duties apply with equal or greater force in the context of a sale of assets, *Allied Chem. & Dye Corp. v. Steel & Tube Co. of Am.,*

Del.Ch., 120 A. 486, 491 (1923); *see also, Marks v. Wolfson,* Del.Ch., 188 A.2d 680, 685 (1963); *Allaun v. Consolidated Oil Co.,* Del.Ch., 147 A. 257, 260–261 (1929), any averment of individual harm caused by defendants would be sufficient to defeat summary dismissal of the action. Moreover, we have held that no proof of individual damage is required when a remedy in the nature of restitution is sought against a fiduciary. *Lynch v. Vickers Energy Corp.,* Del.Supr., 429 A.2d 497, 503–504 (1981). * * *

Having established that plaintiffs' averments are sufficient for present purposes to allege a fiduciary relationship between themselves and Coca–Cola, it remains to be determined if the plaintiffs suffered any individual harm as a result of the alleged breach of this duty. It is well settled that the test used to distinguish between derivative and individual harm is whether the plaintiff suffered "special injury." *Lipton v. News International, Plc.,* Del.Supr., 514 A.2d 1075, 1078 (1986); *Moran v. Household International, Inc.,* Del.Ch., 490 A.2d 1059, 1070, *aff'd,* Del. Supr., 500 A.2d 1346 (1985). A special injury is established where there is a wrong suffered by plaintiff that was not suffered by all stockholders generally or where the wrong involves a contractual right of the stockholders, such as the right to vote. *Lipton,* 514 A.2d at 1078; *Rabkin v. Philip A. Hunt Chemical Corp.,* Del.Ch., 547 A.2d 963, 968–69 (1986); *Moran,* 490 A.2d at 1070. Although it is true that claims of waste are derivative, a claim of stock dilution and a corresponding reduction in a stockholder's voting power is an individual claim. *Avacus Partners, L.P. v. Brian,* Del.Ch., C.A. No. 11001, Allen, C., slip op. at 6, 1990 WL 161909 (October 24, 1990); *cf. Condec Corporation v. Lunkenheimer Co.,* Del.Ch., 230 A.2d 769, 776 (1967).

In this case, the Amended Complaint seeks either rescission, restitution, or damages for the injuries suffered by the minority stockholders as a result of the implementation of the Combination. The injury sustained, the plaintiffs allege, is a loss manifested by both cash-value and voting power dilution. The harm accorded to cash-value dilution is the reduction in value of the minority stockholders' shares, determined by the liquidation value of each share both before and after effectuation of the Combination. Because plaintiffs essentially allege that Coca–Cola took newly issued shares in exchange for fraudulently inflated property of a far lesser value, the cash-out value of the minority stockholders' interest would have declined appreciably after execution of the Combination. Thus, the individual aspect of an injury inuring from cash-value dilution is quite different from one sustained by waste. A waste of corporate assets diminishes the value of all stockholders' interests equally, but the practical effect of cash-value dilution is to increase the value of the controlling stockholder's interest at the sole expense of the minority.

Plaintiffs also suffer harm by voting power dilution which, in essence, is no more than a relative diminution in the minority's proportionate influence over corporate affairs. As a result of Coca–Cola's receipt of over 75 million shares, the minority stockholders' position went from 43.4% to less than 20% without any compensation. The proportionate interest of the majority, however, increased substantially after the Combination was given effect.

Of course, the controlling stockholder, Coca–Cola, suffered nothing. After consummation of the Combination, Coca–Cola realized absolute control of Tri-Star. Any diminution in the cash liquidation value of its shares, resulting from the post-merger write-down of assets, was totally offset by the windfall profits plaintiffs allege Coca–Cola accumulated from the Combination. This is not a case like *Lewis v. Anderson,* Del.Supr., 477 A.2d 1040, 1051 (1984), where the Court upheld dismissal of plaintiff stockholders' derivative claims following a merger. Instead, it is a case involving the right of the minority to compensation for harm caused them by a controlling stockholder who breached its duty of loyalty to the minority class. *Weinberger,* 457 A.2d at 714.

Distilling the Transfer Agreement to its bare essence, and taking the facts in a light most favorable to plaintiffs, it appears that after Coca–Cola depleted over $500 million of liquid assets from the Entertainment Sector, it then was able to effectively dispose of the remaining $765 million of unappraised Entertainment Sector assets in an exchange for between $900–$977 million of Tri–Star common stock. Coca–Cola delayed writing down the value of the Entertainment Sector assets by some $200 million in order to preserve the net book value ratio necessary to guarantee the company an 80% controlling interest in Tri–Star. Under such circumstances serious issues of fairness arise. After the Combination was implemented, the company was sold to Sony. This sale resulted in the class losing its standing to pursue those claims that alleged waste and thus, were solely derivative in nature.

Putting aside the fact that only by a very detailed search of the proxy materials does one learn that from an accounting standpoint the transaction was treated as a purchase of Tri–Star by the Entertainment Sector for $291 million, no where will one find a clear statement of what the Entertainment Sector really paid for its 80% interest in Tri–Star. Thus, the asset write-down raises very serious questions of fairness, which include disclosure issues. *Mills Acquisition Co. v. Macmillan, Inc.,* Del. Supr., 559 A.2d 1261, 1283 (1989); *Weinberger,* 457 A.2d at 711–13. As a result, it appears on this record that in structuring the Combination, Coca–Cola exchanged $745 million in assets, overvalued by $200 million, for Tri-Star stock worth over $900 million—an apparent profit to Coca–Cola of over $300 million accompanied by a diminution of the minority class' interest from 43.4% to less than 20%. Had all of this been fully disclosed to the minority *before* the transfer agreement was submitted for their approval, a reasonable person might suppose that the matter would have been deemed material to the "total mix" of information and overwhelmingly defeated. *Rosenblatt,* 493 A.2d at 944–45. This has particular significance in view of the fact that Coca–Cola could not vote its shares in favor of the proposal unless it was first approved by a majority of the minority shares voting at the special stockholders meeting on December 15, 1987.

Nevertheless, defendants insist that even assuming that all of the above allegations were true, the diminution in the value of the shares held by the minority is a harm suffered by all stockholders equally, including Coca–Cola and the defendant directors of Tri–Star. The fallacy of this argument, however, is amply illustrated by scrutinizing Coca–Cola's course of conduct as a whole, rather than by evaluating its actions in isolation. Because it is the plan or scheme that is the basis of the plaintiffs' complaint, the focus properly rests on the *cumulative* impact of the Combination on the minority.

The plaintiffs claim to have suffered cash value dilution arising from Coca-Cola's allegedly fraudulent manipulation of the stockholder voting process to win approval of the Transfer Agreement. This point is of considerable significance. Had the plaintiffs been fully informed of all material facts relating to this transaction, the required number of votes may not have been obtained and, under the terms of the agreement, Coca–Cola could not vote its shares to guarantee approval of the Transfer Agreement. Thus, by its alleged breaches of the duty of disclosure, Coca–Cola materially and adversely affected the minority class' right to cast an informed vote. Such conduct, if true, is an improper interference with exercise of the franchise. It is a unique special harm to each uninformed shareholder for which the wrongdoer is answerable in damages. *Weinberger,* 457 A.2d at 714.

It is equally relevant that plaintiffs, and not Coca–Cola, suffered a proportionate loss of voting power resulting from the newly authorized issuance of 75 million shares under the Combination. The impact of this loss on voting power of the minority was fully realized at the time of the Sony merger. Coca-Cola's newly acquired shares gave it total voting control of Tri–Star and the minority became powerless to prevent the merger. The fact that Coca–Cola spread nearly half of its newly acquired common stock among its own stockholders as a special dividend does not alter the fact that the power of Tri–Star's minority stockholders to oppose the merger was diluted to the point of virtual oblivion. Coca–Cola effectively secured for itself the ability to terminate any derivative claims that may have followed from its self-interested effectuation of the Combination. Minority stockholders were left only with the prospects of bringing an appraisal action against Sony that would leave the alleged principal wrongdoer, Coca–Cola, free from liability.

Hence, the cumulative effect of these individual wrongs was to diminish the value of the minority interests in a way that would ultimately result in a reduction in the fair value of their shares at the time of the merger. When the end of Coca–Cola's scheme was realized with the consummation of the second step of the Sony merger, it appears on this abbreviated record that the minority were cashed out of their Tri–Star interests for an amount far less than what they would have received had Tri–Star been liquidated immediately prior to the Combination. Again, on this record it appears that Coca–Cola suffered no similar loss, but reaped a substantial profit guaranteed through selective retention, and creative valuation of, the Entertainment Sector assets.* * *

———

STROUGO v. BASSINI

282 F.3d 162 (2d Cir.2002).

SACK, CIRCUIT JUDGE.

The plaintiff is a shareholder of the Brazilian Equity Fund, Inc. (the "Fund"), a non-diversified, publicly traded, closed-end investment company incorporated under the laws of Maryland and registered under the Investment Company Act of 1940, as amended, 15 U.S.C. § 80a–1 *et seq.* (the "ICA"). As its name implies, the Fund invests primarily in the securities of Brazilian companies. The term "closed-end" indicates that the Fund has a fixed number of outstanding shares, so that investors who wish to acquire shares in the Fund ordinarily must purchase them from a shareholder rather than, as in open-end funds, directly from the Fund itself. Shares in closed-end funds are thus traded in the same manner as are other shares of corporate stock. Indeed, shares in the Fund are listed and traded on the New York Stock Exchange. The number of outstanding shares in the Fund is described as "fixed" because it does not change on a daily basis as it would were the Fund open-end, in which case the number of outstanding shares would change each time an investor invested new money in the fund, causing issuance of new shares, and each time a shareholder divested and thereby redeemed shares.

Although closed-end funds do not sell their shares to the public in the ordinary course of business, there are methods available to them to raise new capital after their initial public offering. One such device is a "rights offering," by which a fund offers shareholders the opportunity to purchase newly issued shares. Rights so offered may be transferable, allowing the current shareholder to sell them in the open market, or non-transferable, requiring the current shareholder to use them him- or herself or lose their value when the rights expire. It was the Fund's employment of a non-transferable rights offering that generated the claims at issue on this appeal.

On June 6, 1996, the Fund announced that it would issue one "right" per outstanding share to every shareholder, and that every three rights would enable the shareholder to purchase one new share in the Fund. The subscription price per share was set at ninety percent of the lesser of (1) the average of the last reported sales price of a share of the Fund's common stock on the New York Stock Exchange on August 16, 1996, the date on which the rights expired, and the four business days preceding, and (2) the per-share net asset value at the close of business on August 16.

The plaintiff asserts that this sort of rights offering is coercive because it penalizes shareholders who do not participate. Under the

Fund's pricing formula for its rights offering, the subscription price could not have been higher than ninety percent of the Fund's per-share net asset value. Thus, the introduction of new shares at a discount diluted the value of old shares. Because the rights could not be sold on the open market, a shareholder could avoid a consequent reduction in the value of his or her net equity position in the Fund only by purchasing new shares at the discounted price. This put pressure on every shareholder to "pony up" and purchase more shares, enabling the Fund to raise new capital and thereby increase its asset holdings. Such purchases would, in turn, have tended to increase the management fee paid to defendant BEA Associates, the Fund's investment advisor, because that fee is based on the Fund's total assets.

At the close of business on August 16, 1996, the last day of the rights offering, the closing market price for the Fund's shares was $12.38, and the Fund's per-share net asset value was $17.24. The Fund's shareholders purchased 70.3 percent of the new shares available at a subscription price set at $11.09 per share, ninety percent of the average closing price for the Fund on that and the preceding four days. Through the rights offering, the Fund raised $20.6 million in new capital, net of underwriting fees and other transaction costs.

On May 16, 1997, the plaintiff brought this action against the Fund's directors, senior officers, and investment advisor. The plaintiff's complaint includes three direct class-action claims on behalf of all shareholders. It alleges that the defendants, by approving the rights offering, breached their duties of loyalty and care at common law and in violation of §§ 36(a) and 36(b) of the Investment Company Act, 15 U.S.C. §§ 80a–35(a), 80a–35(b). The complaint further alleges that certain defendants violated § 48 of the ICA (15 U.S.C. §§ 80a–47) because of their positions of authority and control at the Fund. It asserts that these breaches of duty resulted in four kinds of injury to shareholders: (1) loss of share value resulting from the underwriting and other transaction costs associated with the rights offering; (2) downward pressure on share prices resulting from the supply of new shares; (3) downward pressure on share prices resulting from the offering of shares at a discount; and (4) injury resulting from coercion, in that "shareholders were forced to either invest additional monies in the Fund or suffer a substantial dilution."

On April 6, 1998, the district court dismissed the direct claims on the ground that the injuries alleged "applied to the shareholders as a whole." *Strougo v. Bassini,* 1 F.Supp.2d 268, 274 (S.D.N.Y.1998) (*"Bassini"*). Although the impact of the rights offering on any given shareholder depended on whether and to what extent that shareholder purchased new shares pursuant to the rights offering, the district court held that "so long as the defendants' action toward all shareholders was the same, and any disproportionate effect was the result of the various shareholders' responses to the action, the shareholders have no direct action." *Id.* at 275 (quoting *Strougo v. Scudder, Stevens & Clark, Inc.,* 964 F.Supp. 783, 792 (S.D.N.Y.1997) (internal punctuation omitted) (*"Scudder"*)). * * *

We meet at the threshold the question of which law, state or federal, should be the source of the rules we apply to decide the issue of "shareholder standing"—whether the plaintiff may bring direct claims against the defendants—presented by this appeal.[4] The parties do not dispute that Maryland law governs the plaintiff's common law claims: Maryland is the Fund's state of incorporation. But the defendants encourage us also to apply Maryland law to decide the shareholder-standing issue raised by the plaintiff's claims under the ICA. The plaintiff asks us instead to fashion a uniform federal law applicable to these claims.

Because the plaintiff's claims under the ICA involve federal causes of action, a legal rule that "impact[s] significantly upon the effectuation" of the plaintiff's suit must "be treated as raising federal questions." *Burks v. Lasker,* 441 U.S. 471, 477, 99 S.Ct. 1831, 60 L.Ed.2d 404 (1979). Hence, our points of departure in the selection of rules of shareholder standing under the ICA are "the statute and the federal policy which it has adopted." *Id.* at 476, 99 S.Ct. 1831 (citation and internal quotation marks omitted). The ICA itself is silent on issues of shareholder standing. However, the Supreme Court has held that, as a general matter, courts should look to state law to "fill the interstices of federal remedial schemes" unless (1) the scheme in question "evidences a distinct need for nationwide legal standards"; (2) "express provisions in analogous [federal] statutory schemes embody congressional policy choices readily applicable to the matter at hand"; or (3) "application of the particular state law in question would frustrate specific objectives of the federal programs." *Kamen v. Kemper Fin. Servs., Inc.,* 500 U.S. 90, 98, 111 S.Ct. 1711, 114 L.Ed.2d 152 (1991) (internal punctuation and citations omitted). The presumption that state-law rules apply is particularly strong in disputes involving the law of corporations, an area where "private parties have entered into legal relationships with the expectation that their rights and obligations would be governed by state-law standards." *Id.* * * *

Our conclusion here follows from *Kamen:* We must fill a gap in the ICA with rules borrowed from state law unless, under the third *Kamen* exception, application of those rules would frustrate the specific federal policy objectives underlying the ICA. But we cannot determine whether borrowing state law would frustrate the objectives of the ICA until we have determined what the applicable state law of shareholder standing is. We will therefore return to this final piece of the choice-of-law puzzle after determining the rules of shareholder standing under Maryland corporation law and applying them to the facts as alleged in the plaintiff's complaint.

---

4. "Shareholder standing" is a term used to describe the ability of a shareholder to seek redress for certain injuries on his or her own behalf rather than on behalf of the corporation. *See Audio Odyssey, Ltd. v. Brenton First Nat'l Bank,* 245 F.3d 721, 729 (8th Cir.), *vacated on other grounds,* 245 F.3d 721 (8th Cir.2001) (in banc); *see also Rand v. Anaconda–Ericsson, Inc.,* 794 F.2d 843, 849 (2d Cir.) ("[D]iminution in value of the corporate assets is insufficient direct harm to give the shareholder standing to sue in his own right.") (citation and internal quotation marks omitted), *cert. denied,* 479 U.S. 987, 107 S.Ct. 579, 93 L.Ed.2d 582 (1986).

Waller v. Waller, 187 Md. 185, 49 A.2d 449 (1946), remains the leading Maryland case on shareholder standing. There, a shareholder brought a direct action against, *inter alios,* a corporation's sales manager alleging that he and others had caused injury to the shareholder through the improvident discharge of employees, diversion of customers to competitors, choice of detrimental pricing policies, embezzlement of corporate funds, and disruption of corporate governance activities. *Id.* at 189, 49 A.2d at 451–52. In ruling that the plaintiff's claims could not be brought in a direct shareholder suit, the Maryland Court of Appeals observed:

> It is a general rule that an action at law to recover damages for an injury to a corporation can be brought only in the name of the corporation itself acting through its directors, and not by an individual stockholder, though the injury may incidentally result in diminishing or destroying the value of the stock. The reason for this rule is that the cause of action for injury to the property of a corporation or for impairment or destruction of its business is in the corporation, and such injury, although it may diminish the value of the capital stock, is not primarily or necessarily a damage to the stockholder, and hence the stockholder's derivative right can be asserted only through the corporation.

Id., 49 A.2d at 452. The Court of Appeals further explained:

> The rule is advantageous not only because it avoids a multiplicity of suits by the various stockholders, but also because any damages so recovered will be available for the payment of debts of the corporation, and, if any surplus remains, for distribution to the stockholders in proportion to the number of shares held by each.

Id. at 189–90, 49 A.2d at 452. Thus, *Waller* noted that a direct action for injuries shared by the corporation may inequitably displace the claims of creditors and thereby subvert the creditors' priority. The court then determined that the injuries alleged by the plaintiff derived from injuries to the corporation itself, and thus the plaintiff lacked standing to bring direct claims. *Id.* at 191, 49 A.2d at 453.

Waller, in holding that a corporation and not its shareholders may recover for "injury to [its] property . . . or . . . impairment or destruction of its business," does not elaborate on the meaning of "property" or "business" for these purposes. It does hold, however, that these terms include not only the corporation's funds and inventory, but also its relationships with employees and customers and its internal processes for decision-making. *Id.* at 189, 49 A.2d at 451–52. More recently, the Maryland Court of Appeals held that injury to the corporation's business or property also occurs when officers and directors waste funds on perquisites, salaries, and bonuses, or make imprudent investments. *O'Donnell v. Sardegna,* 336 Md. 18, 24–28, 646 A.2d 398, 401–03 (1994). The Maryland Court of Special Appeals has further ruled that corporate business or property injury occurs if officers and directors mismanage or misappropriate funds. *Tafflin v. Levitt,* 92 Md.App. 375, 381, 608 A.2d 817, 820 (1992).

And in *Danielewicz v. Arnold,* 137 Md.App. 601, 769 A.2d 274 (2001), the same court held that the corporation alone has standing when it issues an excessive number of shares in exchange for shares of another company, even if the issuance of those shares rendered the plaintiff, formerly a majority shareholder, a minority shareholder. The court found *Waller* to be indistinguishable. *Danielewicz,* 137 Md.App. at 621, 769 A.2d at 285–86. These Maryland cases indicate, *inter alia,* that ill-advised investments by a corporation, even if paid for with the corporation's shares, may constitute an impairment or destruction of the corporation's business.

In deciding whether a shareholder may bring a direct suit, the question the Maryland courts ask is not whether the shareholder suffered injury; if a corporation is injured those who own the corporation are injured too. The inquiry, instead, is whether the shareholders' injury is "distinct" from that suffered by the corporation. *Tafflin,* 92 Md.App. at 381, 608 A.2d at 820.

Tafflin deals not with a shareholders' suit, but with the analogous situation of depositors in an insolvent savings and loan association seeking to recover for losses against the association's directors, officers, accountants, lawyers, and others. It is nonetheless illuminating because it explains, in comparable circumstances, the "distinct injury" requirement by reference to the concern expressed in *Waller* for making damages recovered for injury to the corporation available to pay the debts of the corporation. Appellants' [alleged injuries] are not distinct from the injury sustained by [the bank] and all its depositors as a result of appellees' mismanagement and wrongdoing.... [P]ermitting depositors to bring individual actions for [mismanagement of funds] would invariably impair the rights of other general creditors and claimants with superior interests.... [T]hat ... fraud may have induced all of the depositors to make their original deposits does not justify bypassing this equitable and common-sense system for recovery. *Tafflin,* 92 Md.App. at 381–82, 608 A.2d at 820 (internal citation omitted).

Both *Waller* and *Tafflin* acknowledge that harm to shareholders may flow from injuries to a corporation's business or property, including those that decrease the value of firm assets or otherwise impair the corporation's ability to generate profits. Maryland law nonetheless provides that in such circumstances, despite the harm to shareholders, the corporation alone has a cause of action to recover for the injury asserted. Although shareholders suffer collateral injury, they may have that injury redressed only through the collateral effect of the results of the corporation's lawsuit—which might, for instance, result in a recovery of damages by the corporation and thus a corresponding increase in share value.[5] Allowing shareholders to recover directly, on the other hand, besides threatening the "multiplicity of suits" cited by *Waller,* 187 Md. at 189, 49 A.2d at 452,

---

5. Maryland law thus places corporate shareholders on the same footing as those other persons with an interest in a business, such as employees, officers, and creditors, who might suffer collateral harm when the business is injured, but who normally lack standing to bring suit to seek redress for that injury.

makes possible recoveries that are inequitably distributed among those other than shareholders with an interest in the corporation. Specifically, if the corporation were in default on its debt, direct shareholder suits for corporate injury could defeat the prior claim of corporate creditors to corporate assets because the rule of limited liability would prevent the creditors from reaching damages recovered by the shareholders personally. Where shareholders suffer an injury that does not stem from an injury to the corporation's business or property, by contrast, the corporation lacks standing to sue, and Maryland's "distinct injury" rule allows shareholders access to the courts to seek compensation directly.

Thus, under Maryland law, when the shareholders of a corporation suffer an injury that is distinct from that of the corporation, the shareholders may bring direct suit for redress of that injury; there is shareholder standing. When the corporation is injured and the injury to its shareholders derives from that injury, however, only the corporation may bring suit; there is no shareholder standing. The shareholder may, at most, sue derivatively, seeking in effect to require the corporation to pursue a lawsuit to compensate for the injury to the corporation, and thereby ultimately redress the injury to the shareholders.

We thus reject the "undifferentiated effect on shareholders" standard, which the district court articulated in *Scudder* and relied upon in its decision in this case. *See Bassini,* 1 F. Supp.2d at 275 ("[S]o long as the defendants' action toward all shareholders was the same, and any disproportionate effect was the result of the various shareholders' responses to the action, the shareholders have no direct action.") (citing *Scudder,* 964 F. Supp. at 792). To sue directly under Maryland law, a shareholder must allege an injury distinct from an injury to the corporation, not from that of other shareholders. * * *

An inquiry that asks only whether shareholders have suffered "undifferentiated harm," rather than whether the shareholders have suffered injury distinct from any potential injury to the corporation, could lead to situations in which shareholders are improperly left with an injury without legal recourse. There may be acts that injure shareholders equally but do not injure the corporation at all; indeed they might be seen as benefitting the corporation in the sense that they might increase its assets. The shareholders, despite their undifferentiated harm, could not bring a derivative suit—nor could the corporation recover for them— because no such suit could succeed without a showing of injury to the corporation. In such circumstances, only a direct suit by shareholders can redress the harm to them, even though the harm was suffered by the shareholders equally. *See* James J. Hanks, Jr., *Maryland Corporations Law* § 7.21(b), 270 (1990 & 2000 Suppl.) ("If the wrong alleged was committed against the stockholder rather than the corporation, then the stockholder must bring the action as a direct action—either individually or as representative of a class—and not as a derivative action.") For this reason, the rule under Maryland law is that where shareholders suffer a distinct injury, i.e., an injury that does not derive from corporate injury, they may bring direct suit, even if their injury is undifferentiated among them.

We also do not see a basis in Maryland law for the defendants' argument, premised on *Scudder,* that claims for alleged breaches of fiduciary duty by directors and officers only support derivative actions and may not be pursued directly. *See Scudder,* 964 F.Supp. at 792. It is not clear that this was essential to the decision in *Scudder,* inasmuch as it appears to have been stated as an observation rather than as a rule of law. *Id.* at 791 ("[C]laims of breach of duty by directors and other fiduciaries of a corporation generally are regarded as derivative rather than direct...."). But in any event, the defendants have asserted that under Maryland law, directors and officers cannot be sued directly by shareholders for alleged breaches of fiduciary duty. We disagree.

Maryland case law appears to be silent on the narrow question whether shareholders may bring fiduciary duty claims directly against officers and directors. Although neither the district court nor the defendants cite a case from a Maryland court that holds that such lawsuits are prohibited, the plaintiffs similarly fail to cite a case in which such a suit was allowed.

But Maryland courts have clearly established the proposition that directors and officers owe fiduciary duties to both the corporation *and* the shareholders. *See Toner v. Baltimore Envelope Co.,* 304 Md. 256, 268–69, 498 A.2d 642, 648 (1985) (collecting cases); *Waller,* 187 Md. at 194, 49 A.2d at 454.[7] This means that by asserting that shareholders may not bring direct claims against directors and officers based on an alleged breach of fiduciary duties, the defendants in effect argue that these fiduciary duties, though extant, are non-actionable. The availability of a derivative action does not suggest otherwise. As we have seen, a derivative suit may only be brought if the plaintiff alleges injury to the corporation, and cannot be brought by a plaintiff who alleges only a distinct injury to him- or herself as the result of the breach of a fiduciary duty or otherwise. Thus, the availability of derivative actions does not give shareholders a remedy that they would not have if the officers and directors owed their fiduciary duties to the corporation alone.

We note that there is no dispute that the fiduciary duties owed by directors and officers to the corporation *are* actionable, as the existence of derivative actions under Maryland law indicates. Maryland law also makes clear that the fiduciary duties owed minority shareholders by majority

---

7. *Waller* places a limit on this fiduciary duty to shareholders, holding that "directors occupy a fiduciary relation to the corporation and all of its stockholders, but they are not trustees for the individual stockholders." 187 Md. at 194, 49 A.2d at 454. The effect of this holding was to deny an attempt by an individual shareholder to enforce through a direct claim a contractual obligation owed to the corporation by an officer. The Maryland Court of Appeals reasoned that because a corporation does not hold its rights and assets in trust for its shareholders, but rather as a distinct legal person, it is the corporation rather than the shareholder that has standing to enforce those rights and duties. "The reason for this distinction is that in law the corporation has a separate existence as a distinct person, in which all corporate property is vested and to which the directors are responsible for a strict and faithful discharge of their duty...." *Id.* * * *

shareholders are actionable, and may be enforced through direct claims. *See, e.g; Coop. Milk Serv. v. Hepner,* 198 Md. 104, 114, 81 A.2d 219, 224 (1951) (dismissing claims on other grounds).

Thus, in order to adopt the defendants' argument, we would be required to reach two odd conclusions about Maryland law. We would first have to conclude that the repeated assertions by the Maryland courts of the existence of fiduciary duties flowing from directors and officers to shareholders were not meant to have practical import. *See Toner,* 304 Md. at 268–69, 498 A.2d at 648. And we also would be forced to conclude that Maryland courts intend the term "fiduciary duty" to have a different meaning with regard to the duty from directors and officers to shareholders—not giving rise to enforceable rights—than it does with regard to the duty from directors and officers to the corporation and also the duty from majority to minority shareholders—giving rise to enforceable rights—even where the courts use the term only once in a sentence to refer to both sets of relationships. *See, e.g., Waller,* 187 Md. at 194, 49 A.2d at 454. ("It is generally stated that directors occupy a fiduciary relation to the corporation and all its stockholders. . . .") We are unaware of principles of interpretation that would support such a reading of the Maryland cases.

Applying Maryland's law of shareholder standing to the plaintiff's four alleged injuries, we conclude that one that he alleges does not support direct claims under Maryland law. The remaining alleged injuries, however—describing the set of harms arising from the alleged coercion—do.

The plaintiff alleges a loss in share value resulting from the "substantial underwriting and other transactional costs associated with the Rights Offering." He effectively concedes in his reply brief, however, that this alleged injury cannot support direct claims under Maryland law, and we agree. Underwriter fees, advisory fees, and other transaction costs incurred by a corporation decrease share price primarily because they deplete the corporation's assets, precisely the type of injury to the corporation that can be redressed under Maryland law only through a suit brought on behalf of the corporation. *See O'Donnell,* 336 Md. at 28, 646 A.2d at 403.

The plaintiff's remaining alleged injuries can be read to describe the set of harms resulting from the coercive nature of the rights offering. The particular harm allegedly suffered by an individual shareholder as a result of the coercion depends on whether or not that shareholder participated in the rights offering. For example, when read in the light most favorable to the plaintiff, the alleged injury of "substantial downward pressure on the price of the Fund's shares" resulting from the issuance of new shares describes the reduction in the net equity value of the shares owned by non-participating shareholders.[8] Similarly, the alleged injury from the

---

8. The actual allegation in the complaint is that the rights offering "substantially increase[d] the supply of a limited commodity—a U.S. based vehicle for investing in Brazil—relative to existing demand." Although not free from doubt, the "vehicle" appears to be the Fund's shares. We note that this allegation only describes an actual injury if read, as we read it here, to refer not to the effect of a reduction in share prices on shareholders generally, but rather to the loss in

downward pressure on share prices resulting from the setting of the "exercise price of the rights ... at a steep discount from the pre-[r]ights [o]ffering net asset value" can be read to refer to the involuntary dilution in equity value suffered by the non-participating shareholders.

Whether the *participating* shareholders also suffered harm to their assets, at least in terms of overall financial position, is not obvious, and the complaint is less specific in this regard. In terms of the dilution that resulted from the rights offering, the participating shareholders actually benefitted from the non-participating shareholder's injury, as the participating shareholders received the redistributed equity in the Fund. On the other hand, participating shareholders may have suffered harm in the form of transaction costs in liquidating other assets to purchase the new shares, and the impairment of their right to dispose of their assets as they prefer if they purchased new shares to avoid dilution.

While it is not clear to us that the injuries allegedly sustained by the participating shareholders are redressable, we leave that question for the district court to resolve in the first instance. It is clear, however, that the claims of the shareholders generally cannot be dismissed for failure to state a direct, as opposed to derivative, claim, as the district court did. The alleged injuries resulting from the coercive nature of the rights offering do *not* derive from a reduction in the value of the Fund's assets or any other injury to the Fund's business. Indeed, with reference to the shareholders that purchased new shares in order to avoid dilution, the acts that allegedly harmed the shareholders *increased* the Fund's assets. And as for the non-participating shareholders, the reduced value of their equity did not derive from a reduction in the value of the Fund's assets, but rather from a reallocation of equity value to those shareholders who did participate.

Thus, in the case of both the participating and non-participating shareholders, it would appear that the alleged injuries were to the shareholders alone and not to the Fund. These harms therefore constitute "distinct" injuries supporting direct shareholder claims under Maryland law. The corporation cannot bring the action seeking compensation for these injuries because they were suffered by its shareholders, not itself.[10]

---

value of the equity positions of the non-participating shareholders. The plaintiff's interest as a shareholder is not in a share price *per se*, but rather in the overall value of his equity—the share price multiplied by the number of shares owned. In a familiar setting, when shares of stock in a corporation are split two for one, immediately after the split each share of stock is worth half of what it was worth immediately before the split. But the total value of each shareholder's equity interest would not be expected to fall and thereby injure the shareholder because the decrease in share value is offset by the receipt of new shares. Thus, a mere increase in the number of shares, and a corresponding adjustment in share price, does not automatically constitute a shareholder injury. *See, e.g., Baker*, 203 Md. at 282, 100 A.2d at 828 (holding that a "split up of the common stock, by the issuance of four shares for one, did not adversely affect the holders, for after that action their aliquot shares remained the same").

10. The defendants countered at oral argument that the shares themselves are assets of the Fund, and thus that the sale of shares at a discount constitutes an injury to the corporation. We disagree. A corporation, as the plaintiff correctly argued, cannot have an equity interest in itself. As reflected on corporate balance sheets, equity is not an asset to the corporation, but indeed its opposite: a *claim* on assets. A share of stock is no more an asset to its issuing corporation than a

In deciding that the plaintiff has shareholder standing to bring direct claims for the injuries arising from coercion based on the allegations in his complaint, we do not express or intend to imply any view with respect to the merits of those claims. Indeed, we cannot tell from the complaint whether the plaintiff is a participating or non-participating shareholder, and thus the sort of injury for which he personally seeks a remedy. We therefore do not express a view as to which groups of shareholders the plaintiff might suitably represent or the redressibility of their claims, i.e., whether, if a breach of the duty running from the defendants to the shareholders is proven, a remedy in law or in equity may be fashioned that will fairly and appropriately redress the distinct types of injuries suffered by them. We leave this all to the district court on remand.

We return, then, to the question with which we began: Which law, state or federal, should provide the rule of decision in this case? We concluded in Part IV, above, that three of the plaintiff's alleged injuries, the set of harms arising from the alleged coercion of the rights offering, supports direct claims under Maryland law. The plaintiff is therefore able to bring direct claims under the ICA for such injury unless we determine that application of Maryland's law of shareholder standing would frustrate the specific federal policy objectives underlying the ICA.

Our investigation of policy objectives is hampered by the fact that §§ 36(a), 36(b), and 48 of the ICA do not explicitly provide for direct causes of action by private individuals. This makes the presumption that rules will be borrowed from state law to determine questions raised by the plaintiff's ICA claims all the more difficult to overcome. The expectations of private parties that state law will govern their corporate disputes is even higher when the federal statute invoked does not on its face provide notice to the parties of a possibility of a federal private suit and thereby suggest that federal law may be applied.

Lacking meaningful indications of congressional policy regarding the plaintiff's specific causes of action, we turn to the general policy statement of the ICA set out in ICA § 1(b), 15 U.S.C. § 80a–1(b). Relevant objectives of the statute listed there include protecting all classes of investment company security holders from the special interests of directors, officers, and particular classes of security holders, and preventing investment companies from failing to protect "the preferences and privileges of the holders of their outstanding securities." *Id.* § 80a–1(b)(3). We conclude as a general matter that Maryland's law of shareholder standing, with its emphasis on honoring the expectations and protecting the interests of both shareholders and corporate creditors, appears to support the policy goal of protecting all classes of security holders. And the potential availability of direct action to redress coercive practices by directors and

---

claim check is an asset to its issuing dry cleaner. Thus, by way of illustration, if one of the shareholders of a corporation that has four 25% shareholders were to donate all her shares to the corporation, the overall value of the corporation's assets would not increase. Instead, the percentage and therefore value of each of the other shareholders' stake in the equity of the corporation would increase from 25% to 33%.

officers (assuming that these practices breach the directors' and officers' fiduciary duties—a question we do not decide here) appears to protect the preferences of shareholders who do not wish to increase their investments in a closed-end fund. We thus see nothing in the general policies of the ICA that would militate against importing Maryland's rules of shareholder standing for claims brought for alleged violations of the ICA sections cited by the plaintiff.

We hold that the plaintiff's alleged injuries associated with coercion support direct claims under both Maryland law and, in this case, §§ 36(a), 36(b), and 48 of the ICA.

NOTES

1.   In Jones v. H.F. Ahmanson & Co., 1 Cal.3d 93, 81 Cal.Rptr. 592, 460 P.2d 464, 470–71 (Cal. 1969), page ___ supra, Justice Traynor of the California Supreme Court defined the test of whether a cause of action would support an individual action as follows:

> The individual wrong necessary to support a suit by a shareholder [in an individual capacity] need not be unique to the plaintiff. The same injury may affect a substantial number of shareholders. If the injury is not incidental to an injury to the corporation, an individual cause of action exists.

How does this standard vary from the standards applied in the *Tri-Star Picture* and *Strougo* cases?

2.   One treatise has grouped claims that have been held to be individual versus those that may be properly brought as derivative actions:

> The following actions have been held to be individual;

> (1) A claim founded on a contract between the corporation and the shareholder as an individual.

> (2) A claim based on false and misleading proxy solicitation.

> (3) An action to compel dissolution of the corporation. However, dissolution may also be sought in a derivative suit.

> (4) A suit against directors for fraud in the sale or purchase of the Individual shareholder's stock.

> (5) A claim founded in tort for injury directly upon the shareholder's person or property.

> (6) An action against a director for disseminating false reports about the validity or value of shareholder's stock that harms the shareholder in his individual capacity as an investor.

> (7) A claim against a voting trustee for a breach of her obligations.

> (8) An action to protect the shareholder's relative voting power.

> (9) A suit to protect a shareholder's inspection rights.

> (10) A suit to prevent issuance of stock for the purpose of wrongfully perpetuating or shifting control.

(11) An action to enjoin a threatened *ultra vires* act.

(12) An action to compel payment of a declared dividend.

(13) An action to vindicate a wrong to the individual shareholder, although the same wrongful act may also create a separate corporate cause of action.

(14) A suit against the only other shareholder for injuring the corporation's business where a judgment in a derivative suit would benefit the wrongdoer.

(15) [A] suit alleging [the] board abdicated its powers.

(16) A suit alleging directors breached [their] fiduciary duty when negotiating to sell [the] company.

(17) [A] suit based on oppressive action designed to force the minority shareholder(s) from the corporation or other coercive action directed at the corporation.

The following claims have been held to be derivative:

(1) An action seeking recovery due to managerial misconduct, producing a proportionate decline in the company's shares, such as the waste of corporate assets or usurpation of corporate opportunities.

(2) An action against the purchaser of corporate assets seeking rescission of the sale.

(3) An action under section 10(b) of the Securities Exchange Act of 1934 and SEC Rule 10b–5, where the corporation has purchased or sold securities and the individual shareholder is precluded from relief because he is neither a purchaser nor seller of securities.

(4) An action to recover for injuries to corporate assets caused by fraud or by third parties.

(5) An action to recover damages for an *ultra vires* act.

(6) A suit to compel the directors to dissolve the corporation due to director misconduct.

(7) An action on a contract between the corporation and a third party.

(8) Managerial decisions designed to thwart a takeover and thereby deprive the stockholders of an opportunity to dispose of their shares at a premium.

(9) Breach of fiduciary duty during a merger transaction.

James D. Cox & Thomas Lee Hazen, Corporations § 15.03 (2d ed. 2003).

———

SECTION 3. STANDING REQUIREMENTS

BANGOR PUNTA OPERATIONS, INC. v. BANGOR & AROOSTOCK RAILROAD

417 U.S. 703, 94 S.Ct. 2578, 41 L.Ed.2d 418 (1974).

MR. JUSTICE POWELL delivered the opinion of the Court.

This case involves an action by a Maine railroad corporation seeking damages from its former owners for violations of federal antitrust and securities laws, applicable state statutes, and common-law principles. The complaint alleged that the former owners had engaged in various acts of corporate waste and mismanagement during the period of their control. The shareholder presently in control of the railroad acquired more than 99% of the railroad's shares from the former owners long after the alleged wrongs occurred. We must decide whether equitable principles applicable under federal and state law preclude recovery by the railroad in these circumstances.

Respondent Bangor & Aroostock Railroad Co. (BAR), a Maine corporation, operates a railroad in the northern part of the State of Maine. Respondent Bangor Investment Co., also a Maine corporation, is a wholly owned subsidiary of BAR. Petitioner Bangor Punta Corp. (Bangor Punta), a Delaware corporation, is a diversified investment company with business operations in several areas. Petitioner Bangor Punta Operations, Inc. (BPO), a New York corporation, is a wholly owned subsidiary of Bangor Punta.

On October 13, 1964, Bangor Punta, through its subsidiary BPO, acquired 98.3% of the outstanding stock of BAR. This was accomplished by the subsidiary's purchase of all the assets of Bangor Aroostock Corp. (B&A), a Maine corporation established in 1960 as the holding company of BAR. From 1964 to 1969, Bangor Punta controlled and directed BAR through its ownership of about 98.3% of the outstanding stock. On October 2, 1969, Bangor Punta, again through its subsidiary, sold all of its stock for $5,000,000 to Amoskeag Co., a Delaware investment corporation. Amoskeag assumed responsibility for the management of BAR and later acquired additional shares to give it ownership of more than 99% of all the outstanding stock.

In 1971, BAR and its subsidiary filed the present action against Bangor Punta and its subsidiary in the United States District Court for the District of Maine. The complaint specified 13 counts of alleged mismanagement, misappropriation, and waste of BAR's corporate assets occurring during the period from 1960 through 1967 when B&A and then Bangor Punta controlled BAR. Damages were sought in the amount of $7,000,000 for violations of both federal and state laws. The federal statutes and regulations alleged to have been violated included § 10 of the Clayton Act, 15 U.S.C. § 20; and § 10(b) of the Securities Exchange Act of

1934, 15 U.S.C. § 78j(b); and Rule 10b–5, 17 CFR § 240.10b–5, as promulgated thereunder by the Securities and Exchange Commission. The state claims were grounded on § 104 of the Maine Public Utilities Act, Maine Rev.Stat.Ann.,Tit 35, § 104 (1965), and the common law of Maine.

The complaint focused on four intercompany transactions which allegedly resulted in injury to BAR. Counts I and II averred the B&A, and later Bangor Punta, overcharged BAR for various legal, accounting, printing, and other services. Counts III, IV, V, and VI averred that B&A improperly acquired the stock of the St. Croix Paper Co. which BAR owned through its subsidiary. Counts VII, VIII, IX, and X charged that B&A and Bangor Punta improperly caused BAR to declare special dividends to its stockholders, including B&A and Bangor Punta, and also caused BAR's subsidiary to borrow in order to pay regular dividends. Counts XI, XII, and XIII charged that B&A improperly caused BAR to excuse payment by B&A and Bangor Punta of the interest due on a loan made by BAR to B&A. In sum, the complaint alleged that during the period of their control of BAR, Bangor Punta, and its predecessor in interest B&A, 'exploited it solely for their own purposes' and 'calculatedly drained the resources of BAR in violation of law for their own benefit.'

The District Court granted petitioners' motion for summary judgment and dismissed the action. The court first observed that although the suit purported to be a primary action brought in the name of the corporation, the real party in interest and hence the actual beneficiary of any recovery, was Amoskeag, the present owner of more than 99% of the outstanding stock of BAR. The court then noted that Amoskeag had acquired all of its BAR stock long after the alleged wrongs occurred and that Amoskeag did not contend that it had not received full value for its purchase price, or that the purchase transaction was tainted by fraud or deceit. Thus, any recovery on Amoskeag's part would constitute a windfall because it had sustained no injury. With this in mind, the court then addressed the claims based on federal law and determined that Amoskeag would have been barred from maintaining a shareholder derivative action because of its failure to satisfy the 'contemporaneous ownership' requirement of Fed.Rule Civ.Proc. 23.1(1).[3] Finding that equitable principles prevented the use of the corporate fiction to evade the proscription of Rule 23.1, the court concluded that Amoskeag's efforts to recover under the Securities Exchange Act and the Clayton Act must fail. Turning to the claims based on state law, the court recognized that the applicability of Rule 23.1(1) has been questioned where federal jurisdiction is based on diversity of citizenship.[4] The court found it unnecessary to resolve this issue, however, since

---

3. Rule 23.1(1), which specifies the requirements applicable to shareholder derivative actions, states that the complaint shall aver that 'the plaintiff was a shareholder or member at the time of the transaction of which he complains....' This provision is known as the 'contemporaneous ownership' requirement. See 3B J. Moore, Federal Practice 23.1 et seq. (2d ed. 1974).

4. The 'contemporaneous ownership' requirement in shareholder derivative actions was first announced in Hawes v. Oakland, 104 U.S. 450 (1882), and soon thereafter adopted as Equity Rule 97. This provision was later incorporated in Equity Rule 27 and finally in the present Rule 23.1. After the decision in Erie R. Co. v. Tompkins, 304 U.S. 64 (1938), the question arose whether the

its examination of state law indicated that Maine probably followed the 'prevailing rule' requiring contemporaneous ownership in order to maintain a shareholder derivative action. Thus, whether the federal rule or state substantive law applied, the present action could not be maintained.

The United States Court of Appeals for the First Circuit reversed. The court stated that its disagreement with the District Court centered primarily on that court's assumption that Amoskeag would be the 'sole beneficiary' of any recovery by BAR. The Court of Appeals thought that in view of the railroad's status as a 'public' or 'quasi-public' corporation and the important nature of the services it provides, any recovery by BAR would also inure to the benefit of the public. The court stated that this factor sufficed to support a corporate cause of action and rendered any windfall to Amoskeag irrelevant. In addition, the court noted that to permit BAR to recover for the alleged wrongs would provide a needed deterrent to 'patently undesirable conduct' in the management of railroads. Finally, the court confronted the possibility that any corporate recovery might be diverted to enrich the present BAR shareholders, mainly Amoskeag, rather than re-invested to improve the railroad's services for the benefit of the public. Although troubled by this prospect, the court concluded that the public interest would nonetheless be better served by insuring that petitioners would not be immune to civil liability for their allegedly wrongful conduct. Without deciding the issue, the court also suggested the possibility of devising 'court-imposed limitations' on the use BAR might make of any recovery to insure that the public would actually be benefitted.

We granted petitioners' application for certiorari. We now reverse.

We first turn to the question whether respondent corporations may maintain the present action under § 10 of the Clayton Act, 15 U.S.C. § 20, and § 10(b) of the Securities Exchange Act of 1934, 15 U.S.C. § 78j(b), and Rule 10b–5, 17 CFR § 240.10b–5. The resolution of this issue depends upon the applicability of the settled principle of equity that a shareholder may not complain of acts of corporate mismanagement if he acquired his shares from those who participated or acquiesced in the allegedly wrongful transactions. See, e.g., Bloodworth v. Bloodworth, 169 S.E.2d 150, 156–157 (1969); Bookman v. R. J. Reynolds Tobacco Co., 48 A.2d 646, 680 (Ch. 1946); Babcock v. Farwell, 91 N.E. 683, 692–693 (1910).[5] This principle has been invoked with special force where a shareholder purchases all or substantially all the shares of a corporation

---

contemporaneous-ownership requirement was one of procedure or substantive law. If the requirement were substantive, then under the regime of Erie it could not be validly applied in federal diversity cases where state law permitted a non-contemporaneous shareholder to maintain a derivative action. See 3B J. Moore, Federal Practice 23.1.01–23.1.15(2) (2d ed. 1974). Although most cases treat the requirement as one of procedure, this Court has never resolved the issue. Ibid.

5. This principle obtains in the great majority of jurisdictions. See, e.g., Russell v. Louis Melind Co., 331 Ill.App. 182, 72 N.E.2d 869 (1947); Klum v. Clinton Trust Co., 183 Misc. 340, 48 N.Y.S.2d 267 (1944); Clark v. American Coal Co., 86 Iowa 436, 53 N.W. 291 (1892); Boldenweck v. Bullis, 40 Colo. 253, 90 P. 634 (1907). See 13 W. Fletcher, Cyclopedia Corporations § 5866 (1970 ed.); H. Ballantine, Corporations § 148 (1946 ed.).

from a vendor at a fair price, and then seeks to have the corporation recover against that vendor for prior corporate mismanagement. See, e.g., Matthews v. Headley Chocolate Co., 130 Md. 523, 532–535, 100 A. 645, 650–651 (1917); Home Fire Insurance Co. v. Barber, 67 Neb. 644, 661–662, 93 N.W. 1024, 1030–1031 (1903). See also Amen v. Black, 234 F.2d 12, 23 (C.A.10 1956). The equitable considerations precluding recovery in such cases were explicated long ago by Dean (then Commissioner) Roscoe Pound in Home Fire Insurance Co. v. Barber, supra. Dean Pound, writing for the Supreme Court of Nebraska, observed that the shareholders of the plaintiff corporation in that case had sustained no injury since they had acquired their shares from the alleged wrongdoers after the disputed transactions occurred and had received full value for their purchase price. Thus, any recovery on their part would constitute a windfall, for it would enable them to obtain funds to which they had no just title or claim. Moreover, it would in effect allow the shareholders to recoup a large part of the price they agreed to pay for their shares, notwithstanding the fact that they received all they had bargained for. Finally, it would permit the shareholders to reap a profit from wrongs done to others, thus encouraging further such speculation. Dean Pound stated that these consequences rendered any recovery highly inequitable and mandated dismissal of the suit.

The considerations supporting the Home Fire principle are especially pertinent in the present case. As the District Court pointed out, Amoskeag, the present owner of more than 99% of the BAR shares, would be the principal beneficiary of any recovery obtained by BAR. Amoskeag, however, acquired 98.3% of the outstanding shares of BAR from petitioner Bangor Punta in 1969, well after the alleged wrongs were said to have occurred. Amoskeag does not contend that the purchase transaction was tainted by fraud or deceit, or that it received less than full value for its money. Indeed, it does not assert that it has sustained any injury at all. Nor does it appear that the alleged acts of prior mismanagement have had any continuing effect on the corporations involved or the value of their shares. Nevertheless, by causing the present action to be brought in the name of respondent corporations, Amoskeag seeks to recover indirectly an amount equal to the $5,000,000 it paid for its stock, plus an additional $2,000,000. All this would be in the form of damages for wrongs petitioner Bangor Punta is said to have inflicted, not upon Amoskeag, but upon respondent corporations during the period in which Bangor Punta owned 98.3% of the BAR shares. In other words, Amoskeag seeks to recover for wrongs Bangor Punta did to *itself* as owner of the railroad. At the same time it reaps this windfall, Amoskeag desires to retain all its BAR stock. Under Home Fire, it is evident that Amoskeag would have no standing in equity to maintain the present action.[8]

---

8. Conceding the lack of equity in any recovery by Amoskeag, the dissent argues that the present action can nevertheless be maintained because there are 20 minority shareholders, holding less than 1% of the BAR stock, who owned their shares 'during the period from 1960 through 1967 when the transactions underlying the railroad's complaint took place, and who still owned that stock in 1971 when the complaint was filed.' Post, at 2589. The dissent would

We are met with the argument, however, that since the present action is brought in the name of respondent corporations, we may not look behind the corporate entity to the true substance of the claims and the actual beneficiaries. The established law is to the contrary. Although a corporation and its shareholders are deemed separate entities for most purposes, the corporate form may be disregarded in the interests of justice where it is used to defeat an overriding public policy. New Colonial Ice Co. v. Helvering, 292 U.S. 435, 442, 54 S.Ct. 788, 791, 78 L.Ed. 1348 (1934); Chicago, M. & St. P.R. Co. v. Minneapolis Civic Assn., 247 U.S. 490, 501, 38 S.Ct. 553, 557, 62 L.Ed. 1229 (1918). In such cases, courts of equity, piercing all fictions and disguises, will deal with the substance of the action and not blindly adhere to the corporate form. Thus, where equity would preclude the shareholders from maintaining an action in their own right, the corporation would also be precluded. Amen v. Black, supra; Capitol Wine & Spirit Corp. v. Pokrass, 277 App.Div. 184, 98 N.Y.S.2d 291 (1950), aff'd, 302 N.Y. 734, 98 N.E.2d 704 (1951); Matthews v. Headley Chocolate Co., supra; Home Fire Insurance Co. v. Barber, supra. It follows that Amoskeag, the principal beneficiary of any recovery and itself estopped from complaining of petitioners' alleged wrongs, cannot avoid the command of equity through the guise of proceeding in the name of respondent corporations which it owns and controls.

Respondents fare no better in their efforts to maintain the present actions under state law, specifically § 104 of the Maine Public Utilities Act, Maine Rev.Stat.Ann., Tit. 35, § 104 (1965), and the common law of Maine. In Forbes v. Wells Beach Casino, Inc., 307 A.2d 210, 223 n. 10 (1973), the Maine Supreme Judicial Court recently declared that it had long accepted the equitable principle that a 'stockholder has no standing if either he or his vendor participated or acquiesced in the wrong....' See Hyams v. Old Dominion Co., 113 Me. 294, 302, 93 A. 747, 750 (1915).[9] Thus, Amoskeag would be barred from maintaining the present action under Maine law since it acquired its shares from petitioners, the alleged wrongdoers. Moreover, the principle that the corporate entity may be disregarded if equity so demands is accepted by Maine precedents. See, e.g., Bonnar–Vawter, Inc. v. Johnson, 157 Me. 380, 387–388, 173 A.2d 141, 145 (1961).

---

conclude that the existence of these innocent minority shareholders entitles BAR, and hence Amoskeag, to recover the entire $7,000,000 amount of alleged damages.

Aside from the illogic of such an approach, the dissent's position is at war with the precedents, for the Home Fire principle has long been applied to preclude full recovery by a corporation even where there are innocent minority shareholders who acquired their shares prior to the alleged wrongs. See cases cited at n. 5, supra, and accompanying text. The dissent also mistakes the factual posture of this case, since the respondent corporations did not institute this action for the benefit of the minority shareholders. See discussion at n. 15, infra.

9. In addition, the new Maine Business Corporation Act adopts the contemporaneous-ownership requirement for shareholder derivative actions. See Maine Rev.Stat.Ann., Tit. 13–A, § 627.1.A (1974). This provision apparently became effective two days after the present action was filed. As the District Court noted, it is an open question whether Maine in fact had a contemporaneous-ownership requirement prior to that time. See R. Field, V. McKusick & L. Wroth, Maine Civil Practice § 23.2, p. 393 (2d ed. 1970). In the absence of any indication that Maine would not have followed the 'prevailing view,' the District Court determined that the contemporaneous-ownership requirement of Fed.Rule Civ.Proc. 23.1 applied.

In reaching the contrary conclusion, the Court of Appeals stated that it could not accept the proposition that Amoskeag would be the 'sole beneficiary' of any recovery by BAR. The court noted that in view of the railroad's status as a 'quasi-public' corporation and the essential nature of the services it provides, the public had an identifiable interest in BAR's financial health. Thus, any recovery by BAR would accrue to the benefit of the public through the improvement in BAR's economic position and the quality of its services. The court thought that this factor rendered a windfall to Amoskeag irrelevant.

At the outset, we note that the Court of Appeals' assumption that any recovery would necessarily benefit the public is unwarranted. As that court explicitly recognized, any recovery by BAR could be diverted to its shareholders, namely Amoskeag, rather than reinvested in the railroad for the benefit of the public. Nor do we believe this possibility can be avoided by respondents' suggestion that the District Court impose limitations on the use BAR might make of the recovery. There is no support for such a result under either federal or state law. BAR would be entitled to distribute the recovery in any lawful manner it may choose, even if such distribution resulted only in private enrichment. In sum, there is no assurance that the public would receive any benefit at all from these funds.

The Court of Appeals' position also appears to overlook the fact that Amoskeag, the actual beneficiary of any recovery through its ownership of more than 99% of the BAR shares, would be unjustly enriched since it has sustained no injury.[11] It acquired substantially all the BAR shares from Bangor Punta subsequent to the alleged wrongs and does not deny that it received full value for is purchase price. No fraud or deceit of any kind is alleged to have been involved in the transaction. The equitable principles of Home Fire preclude Amoskeag from reaping a windfall by enhancing the value of its bargain to the extent of the entire purchase price plus an additional $2,000,000. Amoskeag would in effect have acquired a railroad worth $12,000,000 for only $5,000,000. Neither the federal antitrust or securities laws nor the applicable state laws contemplate recovery by Amoskeag in these circumstances.

The Court of Appeals further stated that it was important to insure that petitioners would not be immune from liability for their wrongful conduct and noted that BAR's recovery would provide a needed deterrent to mismanagement of railroads. Our difficulty with this argument is that it proves too much. If deterrence were the only objective, then in logic any plaintiff willing to file a complaint would suffice. No injury or violation of a legal duty to the particular plaintiff would have to be alleged. The only

---

11. The unjust enrichment of Amoskeag is inevitable. As the owner of more than 99% of the BAR shares, Amoskeag would obviously benefit from any increase in the value of its investment. Here, the increased value would be of dramatic proportions, with an influx of $7,000,000 into a railroad purchased for only $5,000,000. The dissent's suggestion that this substantial infusion of capital, if devoted to 'plant and equipment,' would not enhance 'earning capacity' or 'balance sheet strength' (post, at 2590) will come as a surprise to regulatory bodies, railroad management, and investors.

prerequisite would be that the plaintiff agree to accept the recovery, lest the supposed wrongdoer be allowed to escape a reckoning. Suffice it to say that we have been referred to no authority which would support so novel a result, and we decline to adopt it.

We therefore conclude that respondent corporations may not maintain the present action.[15] The judgment of the Court of Appeals is reversed.

MR. JUSTICE MARSHALL, with whom MR. JUSTICE DOUGLAS, MR. JUSTICE BRENNAN, and MR. JUSTICE WHITE join, dissenting.

This suit, brought by and in the name of respondent railroad and its wholly owned subsidiary, seeks to recover damages for the conversion and misappropriation of corporate assets allegedly committed by petitioners, Bangor Punta and its wholly owned subsidiary, during a period when the latter was the majority shareholder of the railroad. Ordinarily, of course, a corporation may seek legal redress against those who have defrauded it of its assets. And when it does so: 'A corporation and its stockholders are generally to be treated as separate entities. Only under exceptional circumstances ... can the difference be disregarded.' Burnet v. Clark, 287 U.S. 410, 415, 53 S.Ct. 207, 209, 77 L.Ed. 397 (1932). See also New Colonial Ice Co. v. Helvering, 292 U.S. 435, 442, 54 S.Ct. 788, 791, 78 L.Ed. 1348 (1934).

The Court finds such exceptional circumstances here because, in its view, any recovery had by the corporation will be a windfall to Amoskeag, the present owner of approximately 99% of the corporation's stock, which purchased most of that stock from the petitioners, the alleged wrongdoers. The Court therefore concludes that this suit must be barred under the equitable principles set forth in Home Fire Insurance Co. v. Barber, 67 Neb. 644, 93 N.W. 1024 (1903).

I cannot agree. Having read the precedents relied upon by the majority, I respectfully submit that they not only do not support, but indeed directly contradict the result reached today. While purporting to rely on settled principles of equity, the Court sadly mistakes the facts of this case and the established powers of an equity court. In my view, no windfall recovery to Amoskeag is inevitable, or even likely, on the facts of this case. But even if recovery by respondents would in fact be a windfall to Amoskeag, the Court disregards the interests of the railroad's creditors, as well as the substantial public interest in the continued financial viability of the Nation's railroads which have been so heavily plagued by

---

15. Our decision rests on the conclusion that equitable principles preclude recovery by Amoskeag, the present owner of more than 99% of the BAR shares. The record does not reveal whether the minority shareholders who hold the remaining fraction of 1% of the BAR shares stand in the same position as Amoskeag. Some courts have adopted the concept of a pro-rata recovery where there are innocent minority shareholders. Under this procedure, damages are distributed to the minority shareholders individually on a proportional basis, even though the action is brought in the name of the corporation to enforce primary rights. See, e.g., Matthews v. Headley Chocolate Co., 130 Md. 523, 536–540, 100 A. 645, 650–652 (1917). In the present case, respondents have expressly disavowed any intent to obtain a pro-rata recovery on behalf of the 1% minority shareholders of BAR. We therefore do not reach the question whether such recovery would be appropriate. * * *

corporate mismanagement, and ignores the powers of the court to impose equitable conditions on a corporation's recovery so as to insure that these interests are protected. The Court's decision is also inconsistent with prior decisions of this Court limiting the application of equitable defenses when they impede the vindication, through private damage actions, of the important policies of the federal antitrust laws. * * *

The law imposes upon the directors of a corporation a fiduciary obligation to all of the corporation's shareholders, and part of that obligation is to use due care to ensure that the corporation seek redress where a majority shareholder has drained the corporation's resources for his own benefit and to the detriment of minority shareholders. Indeed, minority shareholders would be entitled to bring a derivative action, on behalf of the corporation, to enforce the corporation's right to recover for the injury done to it, if the directors turned down a request to seek relief.[2] And any recovery obtained in such an action would belong to the corporation, not to the minority shareholders as individuals, for the shareholder in a derivative action enforces not his own individual rights, but rights which the corporation has.

These elementary principles of corporate law should control this case. Although first Bangor Punta and then Amoskeag owned the great majority of the share of respondent railroad, the record shows that there are many minority shareholders who owned BAR stock during the period from 1960 through 1967 when the transactions underlying the railroad's complaint took place, and who still owned that stock in 1971 when the complaint was filed. Any one of these minority shareholders would have had the right, during the 1960—1967 period, as well as thereafter, to bring a derivative action on behalf of the corporation against the majority shareholder for misappropriation of corporate assets. As Dean Pound states, such an action could be brought, "even though the wrongdoers continued to be stockholders and would share in the proceeds."* * *

In the final analysis, the Court's holding does a disservice to one of the most settled of equitable doctrines, reflected in the maxim that '(e)quity will not suffer a wrong without a remedy.' Independent Wireless Tel. Co. v. Radio Corp. of America, 269 U.S. 459, 472 (1926). Because I would follow that maxim here and permit respondent railroad to maintain this action to seek redress for the wrongs allegedly done to it and to the public interest it serves, I respectfully dissent.

Notes

1. Federal Rule of Civil Procedure 23.1 states:

In a derivative action brought by one or more shareholders or members to enforce a right of a corporation or of an unincorporated association, the

---

2. '(Stockholders' derivative suits) are one of the remedies which equity designed for those situations where the management through fraud, neglect of duty or other cause declines to take the proper and necessary steps to assert the rights which the corporation has.' Meyer v. Fleming, 327 U.S. 161, 167, 66 S.Ct. 382, 386, 90 L.Ed. 595 (1946). And it is irrelevant that the shareholders bringing the derivative action own only a small percentage of the total outstanding shares. [citations omitted]

corporation or association having failed to enforce a right which may properly be asserted by it, the complaint shall be verified and shall allege (1) that the plaintiff was a shareholder or member at the time of the transaction of which the plaintiff complains or that the plaintiff's share or membership thereafter devolved on the plaintiff by operation of law, and (2) that the action is not a collusive one to confer jurisdiction on a court of the United States which it would not otherwise have. The complaint shall also allege with particularity the efforts, if any, made by the plaintiff to obtain the action the plaintiff desires from the directors or comparable authority and, if necessary, from the shareholders or members, and the reasons for the plaintiff's failure to obtain the action or for not making the effort. The derivative action may not be maintained if it appears that the plaintiff does not fairly and adequately represent the interests of the shareholders or members similarly situated in enforcing the right of the corporation or association. The action shall not be dismissed or compromised without the approval of the court, and notice of the proposed dismissal or compromise shall be given to shareholders or members in such manner as the court directs.

The rule imposes a contemporaneous ownership requirement but provides for an exception where the stock was acquired by operation of law. This would include an inheritance.

2. In Lewis v. Anderson, 477 A.2d 1040 (Del.1984), the Delaware supreme court held that a shareholder bringing an action against a corporation in a merger lost standing, and that the surviving company inherits any causes of action against the acquired company's officers or directors. The court stated that there are two recognized exceptions to the requirement of contemporaneous ownership in a merger: (1) where the merger itself is the subject of a claim of fraud; and (2) where the merger is in reality a reorganization which does not affect plaintiff's ownership. 477 A.2d at 1046, n.10.

3. In Saito v. McKesson HBOC, Inc., 806 A.2d 113 (Del. 2002), the Delaware Supreme Court held that a shareholder's inspection rights that were being used for the purpose of bringing a derivative action would not be subject to the contemporaneous ownership requirement imposed on derivative suits. This interpretation allowed inspection of documents involving matters that occurred before the shareholder acquired shares in the corporation. Nevertheless, this did not allow the shareholder unlimited discovery rights.

4. Creditors have no standing to bring derivative actions. Harff v. Kerkorian, 347 A.2d 133 (Del.1975) (debenture holders lack standing to bring derivative suit); Darrow v. Southdown, Inc., 574 F.2d 1333 (5th Cir.1978).

5. Related to standing is the issue of whether the plaintiff bringing the derivative claims is an adequate representative of the shareholders. See e.g., Fed. R. Civ. P. § 23.1 (plaintiff must fairly and adequately represent the interests of the other shareholders). An individual seeking to bring a derivative suit in order to pursue a personal vendetta or private claim is not such an adequate representative. See e.g., Roberts v. Alabama Power Co., 404 So.2d 629 (Ala.1981) (plaintiff was not an adequate representative because the

derivative suit was intended to enhance stockholder's position in a personal lawsuit for age discrimination that sought to reduce shareholder equity, and plaintiff's interest in the personal lawsuit did not provide him with the judgment required to enable him to stand in the shoes of, and make decisions for, stockholders); Zarowitz v. BankAmerica Corp., 866 F.2d 1164 (9th Cir. 1989) (plaintiff was not a proper representative for a derivative action against officers and directors of corporation where the plaintiff's interest in increasing value of his corporation stock through a derivative action was dwarfed by his interest in pursuing wrongful termination and defamation actions against the corporation).

6.   Security for Expense Statutes. Some states have adopted security for expense statutes in order to curb abuses in the bringing of baseless derivative actions. New York, for example, authorizes the courts to require a security deposit against the defendant's expenses, including attorney fees, in the event the suit is lost. The statute does not apply to plaintiffs holding five percent or more of a class of shares of the corporation or where the plaintiff's holdings are valued at more than $50,000. N.Y. Gen. Corp. L. § 627. See e.g., Dalva v. Bailey, 153 F.Supp. 548 (S.D.N.Y.1957) (requiring plaintiff shareholder with $4,000 in stock holdings to post a $50,000 bond for security of expenses for the corporation in a derivative action). California allows a defendant to move the court for an order requiring the posting of a bond by a plaintiff in a derivative suit where there is no reasonable possibility that the action will benefit the corporation or if the moving party, as in the case of an officer or director, did not participate in the challenged action. Cal. Corp. Code § 800(c). Section 7.46 of the Revised Model Business Corporation Act allows the court at the end of a derivative action to require the plaintiff to pay the defendants' reasonable expenses, including attorney fees, if the court finds that the proceeding was commenced or maintained without reasonable cause or for an improper purpose.

SECTION 4.   DEMAND REQUIREMENT

GROBOW v. PEROT

539 A.2d 180 (Del.1988).

HORSEY, JUSTICE:

In these consolidated shareholder derivative suits, plaintiffs-shareholders appeal the Court of Chancery's dismissal of their suits for failure of plaintiffs to make presuit demand under Court of Chancery Rule 23.1. The Court of Chancery held that plaintiffs' complaints as amended failed to allege particularized facts which, if taken as true, would excuse demand under the demand futility test of Aronson v. Lewis, Del.Supr., 473 A.2d 805 (1984). The Court interpreted *Aronson*'s "reasonable doubt" standard for establishing demand futility as requiring plaintiffs to plead particularized facts sufficient to sustain "a judicial finding" either of director interest or lack of director independence, or whether the directors exercised proper business judgment in approving the challenged transaction—placing the transaction beyond the protection of the business judgment rule. *Grobow v. Perot,* Del.Ch., 526 A.2d 914, 921 (1987). We find the Vice Chancellor to have erred in formulating an excessive criterion for satisfying *Aronson*'s reasonable doubt test. Moreover, the Vice Chancellor erred in his statement that fairness is a "pivotal" question under an *Aronson* analysis. *See* 526 A.2d at 927. Unless the presumption of the business judgment rule is overcome by the pleadings, questions of fairness play no part in the analysis. *Aronson,* 473 A.2d at 812. However, applying the correct standard, we conclude that the complaints (singly or collectively) fail to state facts which, if taken as true, would create a reasonable doubt either of director disinterest or independence, or that the transaction was other than the product of the Board's valid exercise of business judgment. Therefore, we affirm the decision below, finding the Court's error to have been harmless. * * *

In 1984, General Motors Corporation ("GM") acquired 100 percent of Electronic Data Systems' ("EDS") stock. Under the terms of the merger, H. Ross Perot, founder, chairman and largest stockholder of EDS, exchanged his EDS stock for GM Class E stock and contingent notes. Perot became GM's largest shareholder, holding 0.8 percent of GM voting stock. Perot was also elected to GM's Board of Directors (the "Board") while remaining chairman of EDS.

The merger proved mutually beneficial to both corporations and was largely a success. However, management differences developed between Perot and the other officers and directors of GM's Board over the way GM was running EDS, and Perot became increasingly vocal in his criticism of GM management. By mid-1986, Perot announced to GM that he could no longer be a "company man." Perot demanded that GM allow him to run EDS as he saw fit or that GM buy him out. Perot then began publicly criticizing GM management with such statements as: "Until you nuke the old GM system, you'll never tap the full potential of your people"; and "GM cannot become a world-class and cost-competitive company simply by throwing technology and money at its problems." Thereafter, GM and American Telephone and Telegraph entered into exploratory negotiations for AT&T's purchase of EDS from GM allegedly as a means of GM's eliminating Perot. However, their negotiations did not proceed beyond the preliminary stage.

By late fall of 1986, Perot, anxious, for tax reasons, for a definitive decision before year-end, offered to sell his entire interest in GM. GM responded with a purchase proposal. Perot replied, suggesting additional terms, which Perot characterized as "a giant premium." When a definitive agreement was reached, the Board designated a three-member Special Review Committee ("SRC"), chaired by one of the Board's outside directors to review its terms.[1] The SRC met on November 30, 1986 to

---

1. The complaints fail to state whether the other two directors on the SRC were inside or outside directors. Since plaintiffs do not allege that they were members of management, we will

consider the repurchase proposal and unanimously recommended that GM's Board approve its terms. The following day, December 1, 1986, the GM Board of Directors met and approved the repurchase agreement.

Under the terms of the repurchase, GM acquired all of Perot's GM Class E stock and contingent notes and those of his close EDS associates for nearly $745,000,000. GM also received certain commitments, termed "covenants," from Perot. In addition to resigning immediately from GM's Board and as Chairman of EDS, Perot further agreed: (1) to stop criticizing GM management, in default of which Perot agreed to pay GM damages in a liquidated sum of up to $7.5 million;[3] (2) not to purchase GM stock or engage in a proxy contest against the Board for five years; and (3) not to compete with EDS for three years or recruit EDS executives for eighteen months.

At all relevant times, a majority of the GM Board of Directors consisted of outside directors. The exact number and composition of the GM Board at the time is not clear. However, from the limited record, it appears that the Board was comprised of twenty-six directors (excluding Perot), of whom eighteen were outside directors.

The GM repurchase came at a time when GM was experiencing financial difficulty and was engaged in cost cutting. Public reaction to the announcement ranged from mixed to adverse. The repurchase was sharply criticized by industry analysts and by members within GM's management ranks as well. The criticism focused on two features of the repurchase: (1) the size of the premium over the then market price of GM class E stock; and (2) the hush mail provision.

Plaintiffs filed separate derivative actions (later consolidated) against GM, EDS, GM's directors, H. Ross Perot, and three of Perot's EDS associates. The suits collectively allege: (i) that the GM director defendants breached their fiduciary duties to GM and EDS by paying a grossly excessive price for the repurchase of Perot's and the EDS associates' Class E stock of GM; (ii) that the repurchase included a unique hush mail feature to buy not only Perot's resignation, but his silence, and that such a condition lacked any valid business purpose and was a waste of GM assets; and (iii) that the repurchase was entrenchment motivated and was carried out principally to save GM's Board from further public embarrassment by Perot. The complaints charge the individual defendants with acting out of self-interest and with breaching their duties of loyalty and due care to GM and EDS.

All defendants moved to dismiss the suits for plaintiffs' failure to comply with Court of Chancery Rule 23.1, as construed and applied under

---

presume that they were outside directors. For purposes of this case, we define "outside" directors to mean nonemployee, nonmanagement directors.

    3. This commitment by Perot would later be characterized as the "hush mail" feature of the agreement. The colloquial term is not defined in the pleadings but is assumed by this Court to combine the terms "green mail" and "hush money" to connote a variation on an unlawful and secret payment to assure silence. Here, the commitment is cast in the form of an explicit liquidated damage clause for future breach of contract.

Aronson—that is, either to make presuit demand on GM's Board or to plead particularized facts demonstrating that demand was excused as futile.[5] Plaintiffs responded that the complaints state a case for demand excusal. They contended that the complaints detail factual allegations that create a reasonable doubt that GM's Board was disinterested or independent, or that the transaction was the product of a valid exercise of business judgment. Defendants dispute the sufficiency of the allegations that GM Board approval of the stock repurchase of dissident Perot was the result of the Board's failure to act in good faith and in the exercise of due care.

As noted the Court of Chancery, finding to the contrary, ruled that plaintiffs had failed to establish demand futility by satisfying *Aronson's* demand futility test. Plaintiffs seek reversal for error of law and abuse of discretion. Reversible legal error is said to have resulted from the Trial Court's erroneous application of *Aronson* to require a derivative complaint to state particularized facts sufficient to sustain a "judicial finding" of demand excusal. Additionally, plaintiffs argue that the Court abused its discretion in finding the well-pleaded allegations of the complaints not to establish demand excusal under Rule 23.1.

We first note this Court's standard of review of the Court of Chancery's ruling that plaintiffs have failed to plead a demand-futility case consistent with *Aronson*. Assuming no rule of law is implicated, a decision on a Rule 23.1 motion based on failure to make presuit demand involves essentially a discretionary ruling on a predominantly factual issue. *Aronson*, 473 A.2d at 814–15. Therefore, this Court will disturb the Court of Chancery's Rule 23.1 ruling only on a showing of abuse of discretion, assuming no legal error led to an erroneous holding. *Id.* (the Court's determination of a Rule 23.1 motion is discretionary); *see also Pogostin v. Rice,* Del.Supr., 480 A.2d 619, 624 (1984) (the Court of Chancery, exercising its sound discretion, must determine whether demand is excused under either prong of *Aronson*).

However, before applying our standard of review, we briefly revisit the underlying requirements of a well-pleaded derivative complaint to withstand a Rule 23.1 motion to dismiss for failure to make presuit demand upon a board in accordance with *Aronson* and *Pogostin*. Our standard or test for determining whether a derivative complaint states a demand futility claim under Rule 23.1 is: whether taking the well-pleaded facts as true, the allegations raise a reasonable doubt as to (i) director disinterest or independence or (ii) whether the directors exercised proper

---

5. Rule 23.1 provides, in pertinent part:

In a derivative action brought by 1 or more shareholders or members to enforce a right of a corporation or of an unincorporated association, the corporation or association having failed to enforce a right which may properly be asserted by it, the complaint ... shall also allege with particularity the efforts, if any, made by the plaintiff to obtain the action he desires from the directors or comparable authority and the reasons for his failure to obtain the action or for not making the effort. The action shall not be dismissed or compromised without the approval of the Court....

business judgment in approving the challenged transaction. *Aronson,* 473 A.2d at 814, and *Pogostin,* 480 A.2d at 624.

Thus, the ultimate question before us is the same as was presented in *Aronson:* whether the complaints, as amended, allege facts with particularity "which create a reasonable doubt that the directors' action was entitled to the protection of the business judgment rule." *Aronson,* 473 A.2d at 808. That is so because "demand futility [in the context of director-approved transactions] is inextricably bound to issues of business judgment" by the power conferred on a board of directors under 8 *Del.C.* § 141(a). *Id.* at 812. Necessarily, this involves an objective analysis of the facts.

Addressing plaintiffs' claim of legal error, we find the Vice Chancellor's use of a "judicial finding" criterion for judging a derivative claim for demand excusal to be erroneous, but not reversible error. First, the Court's "judicial finding" criterion would impose a more stringent standard for demand futility than is warranted under *Aronson.* The test for demand futility should be whether the well-pleaded facts of the particular complaint support a reasonable doubt of business judgment protection, not whether the facts support a judicial finding that the directors' actions are not protected by the business judgment rule. *See Aronson,* 473 A.2d at 815.

Second, given the highly factual nature of the inquiry presented to the Trial Court by a Rule 23.1 defense, we conclude that it would be neither practicable nor wise to attempt to formulate a criterion of general application for determining reasonable doubt. The facts necessary to support a finding of reasonable doubt either of director disinterest or independence, or whether proper business judgment was exercised in the transaction will vary with each case. Reasonable doubt must be decided by the trial court on a case-by-case basis employing an objective analysis. Were we to adopt a standard criterion for resolving a motion to dismiss based on Rule 23.1, the test for demand excusal would, in all likelihood, become rote and inelastic.

Finally, since a Rule 23.1 motion normally precedes rather than follows discovery, a plaintiff may be able in one case and without formal discovery to plead facts sufficient to raise a reasonable doubt of business judgment protection, but be unable in another case without such discovery to plead facts sufficient to support a judicial finding of the lack of business judgment protection. On the other hand, if a derivative complaint alleges facts which would support a judicial finding of a lack of business judgment protection, then such facts would more than satisfy *Aronson*'s reasonable doubt standard.

Therefore, we decline to approve the use of a "judicial finding" standard as the minimum criterion below which presuit demand will not be excused. We think it sufficient simply to say that the Court of Chancery must weigh the presumption of the business judgment rule that attaches to a board of directors' decision against the well-pleaded facts alleged in a plaintiff's demand-futility complaint. In that respect, the suggestion in the Trial Court's Opinion that a transaction is first analyzed from the standpoint of fairness is erroneous. *See* 526 A.2d at 927. Fairness becomes an issue only if the presumption of the business judgment rule is defeated. *Aronson,* 473 A.2d at 812–817.

Although the Vice Chancellor's use of a "judicial finding" criterion and fairness analysis were erroneous, the errors do not require reversal if we, under our review of the pleadings and applying the proper standard of reasonable doubt, conclude that a claim of demand futility has not been pleaded. Thus, we turn to the underlying issue—whether plaintiffs' complaints as amended state a case for demand excusal sufficient to withstand defendant's Rule 23.1 motions to dismiss. The answer to the question requires relating the business judgment rule to the issue of demand excusal.

As previously noted, the business judgment rule is but a presumption that directors making a business decision, not involving self-interest, act on an informed basis, in good faith and in the honest belief that their actions are in the corporation's best interest. *See Aronson,* 473 A.2d at 812. Thus, good faith and the absence of self-dealing are threshold requirements for invoking the rule. *Id.; cf. Unocal Corp. v. Mesa Petroleum Co.,* Del.Supr., 493 A.2d 946 (1985). Assuming the presumptions of director good faith and lack of self-dealing are not rebutted by well-pleaded facts, a shareholder derivative complainant must then allege further facts with particularity which, "taken as true, support a reasonable doubt that the challenged transaction was [in fact] the product of a valid exercise of business judgment." *Aronson,* 473 A.2d at 815; *see also Pogostin,* 480 A.2d at 624–25. The complaints as amended do not even purport to plead a claim of fraud, bad faith, or self-dealing in the usual sense of personal profit or betterment. *See, e.g., Sinclair Oil Corp. v. Levien,* Del.Supr., 280 A.2d 717, 720 (1971). Therefore, we must presume that the GM directors reached their repurchase decision in good faith. *See Allaun v. Consolidated Oil Co.,* Del.Ch., 147 A. 257, 261 (1929).

The burden then clearly falls upon plaintiffs claiming demand futility to plead particularized facts sufficient to rebut the presumption that the GM Board exercised sound business judgment "in the honest belief that the action taken was in the best interest of the company." *Aronson,* 473 A.2d at 812 (citations omitted); *cf. Puma v. Marriott,* Del.Ch., 283 A.2d 693, 695 (1971). Moreover, upon a motion to dismiss, only well-pleaded allegations of fact must be accepted as true; conclusionary allegations of fact or law not supported by allegations of specific fact may not be taken as true. A trial court need not blindly accept as true all allegations, nor must it draw all inferences from them in plaintiffs' favor unless they are reasonable inferences. Thus, for plaintiffs to meet the *Aronson* reasonable doubt standard, we must examine the complaints, as amended, to determine whether their well-pleaded facts raise a reasonable doubt sufficient to rebut the presumption that the business judgment rule attaches to the repurchase transaction. This brings us to the application of the two-pronged demand futility test of *Aronson.*

In order to satisfy *Aronson*'s first prong involving director disinterest, *see Aronson,* 473 A.2d at 812, plaintiffs must plead particularized facts demonstrating either a financial interest or entrenchment on the part of the GM directors. Plaintiffs plead no facts demonstrating a financial interest on the part of GM's directors. The only averment permitting such an inference is the allegation that all GM's directors are paid for their services as directors. However, such allegations, without more, do not establish any financial interest. *See, e.g., In re E.F. Hutton Banking Practices Litigation,* S.D.N.Y., 634 F.Supp. 265, 271 (1986) (construing Delaware law); *Moran v. Household Internat'l, Inc.,* Del.Ch., 490 A.2d 1059, 1074–75, *aff'd,* Del.Supr., 500 A.2d 1346 (1985).

Having failed to plead financial interest with any particularity, plaintiffs' complaints must raise a reasonable doubt of director disinterest based on entrenchment. Plaintiffs attempt to do so mainly through reliance on *Unocal Corp. v. Mesa Petroleum Co.,* Del.Supr., 493 A.2d 946 (1985); *Unocal,* however, is distinguishable. The enhanced duty of care that the *Unocal* directors were found to be under was triggered by a struggle for corporate control and the inherent presumption of director self-interest associated with such a contest. *See id.* at 954–55. Here there was no outside threat to corporate policy of GM sufficient to raise a *Unocal* issue of whether the directors' response was reasonable to the threat posed. *Id.* at 955.

Plaintiffs also do not plead any facts tending to show that the GM directors' positions were actually threatened by Perot, who owned only 0.8 percent of GM's voting stock, nor do plaintiffs allege that the repurchase was motivated and reasonably related to the directors' retention of their positions on the Board. *See Cheff v. Mathes,* Del.Supr., 199 A.2d 548, 554 (1964). Plaintiffs merely argue that Perot's public criticism of GM management could cause the directors embarrassment sufficient to lead to their removal from office. Such allegations are tenuous at best and are too speculative to raise a reasonable doubt of director disinterest. Speculation on motives for undertaking corporate action are wholly insufficient to establish a case of demand excusal. *Cf. Sinclair Oil Corp.,* 280 A.2d at 722. Therefore, we agree with the Vice Chancellor that plaintiffs' entrenchment theory is based largely on supposition rather than fact.

Plaintiffs' remaining allegations bearing on the issue of entrenchment are: the rushed nature of the transaction during a period of GM financial difficulty; the giant premium paid;[7] and the criticism (after the fact) of the

---

7. The formula plaintiffs use to establish the existence of a "giant premium" is ambiguous, making the allegation conclusory. The total repurchase price includes not only the price paid for the class E stock, but also the price paid for the contingent notes and the value of the tax compensation. Ambiguity is caused when these items are factored in, especially the contingent note discounts. For example, in their complaints, plaintiffs appear to discount the contingent notes by $16.20, reflecting present value ($62.50–$46.30). The GM directors, however, discount the notes by $6.00. This disparity appears to be due to plaintiffs' use of a base figure of $46.30,

repurchase by industry analysts and top GM management. Plaintiffs argue that these allegations are sufficient to raise a reasonable doubt of director disinterest. We cannot agree. Not one of the asserted grounds would support a reasonable belief of entrenchment based on director self-interest. The relevance of these averments goes largely to the issue of due care, next discussed. Such allegations are patently insufficient to raise a reasonable doubt as to the ability of the GM Board to act with disinterest. Thus, we find plaintiffs' entrenchment claim to be essentially conclusory and lacking in factual support sufficient to establish excusal based on director interest.

To otherwise qualify for demand excusal under *Aronson*'s first prong, a derivative complaint must raise a reasonable doubt of director independence. This would require plaintiffs to allege with particularity that the GM directors were dominated or otherwise controlled by an individual or entity interested in the transaction. *Aronson,* 473 A.2d 815–16. Such allegations are not to be found within plaintiffs' complaints. Thus, the plaintiffs cannot satisfy *Aronson*'s first prong for excusal based on lack of director independence.

Having concluded that plaintiffs have failed to plead a claim of financial interest or entrenchment sufficient to excuse presuit demand, we examine the complaints as amended to determine whether they raise a reasonable doubt that the directors exercised proper business judgment in the transaction. By proper business judgment we mean both substantive due care (purchase terms), *see Saxe v. Brady,* Del.Ch., 184 A.2d 602, 610 (1962), and procedural due care (an informed decision), *see Smith v. Van Gorkom,* Del.Supr., 488 A.2d 858, 872–73 (1985).

With regard to the nature of the transactions and the terms of repurchase, especially price, plaintiffs allege that the premium paid Perot constituted a *prima facie* waste of GM's assets. Plaintiffs argue that the transaction, on its face, was "so egregious as to be afforded no presumption of business judgment protection." In rejecting this contention, the Vice Chancellor reasoned that, apart from the hush-mail provision, the transaction must be viewed as any other repurchase

> by a corporation, at a premium over market, of its own stock held by a single dissident shareholder or shareholder group at odds with management, [which] have repeatedly been upheld as valid exercises of business judgment. * * *

The law of Delaware is well established that, in the absence of evidence of fraud or unfairness, a corporation's repurchase of its capital stock at a premium over market from a dissident shareholder is entitled to the protection of the business judgment rule. (See *Polk,* 507 A.2d at 536–37, for this Court's most recent statement of this principle.) We have already determined that plaintiffs have not stated a claim of financial interest or entrenchment as the compelling motive for the repurchase, and

---

which is $16.20 less than that used by the defendants. The plaintiffs fail to explain this disparity with particularity, thus failing to satisfy their burden under *Aronson.*

it is equally clear that the complaints as amended do not allege a claim of fraud. They allege, at most, a claim of waste based on the assertion that GM's Board paid such a premium for the Perot holdings as to shock the conscience of the ordinary person.

Thus, the issue becomes whether the complaints state a claim of waste of assets, i.e., whether "what the corporation has received is so inadequate in value that no person of ordinary, sound business judgment would deem it worth that which the corporation has paid." *Saxe,* 184 A.2d at 610. By way of reinforcing their claim of waste, plaintiffs seize upon the hush-mail feature of the repurchase as being the motivating reason for the "giant premium" approved by the GM Board. Plaintiffs then argue that buying the silence of a dissident within management constitutes an invalid business purpose. Ergo, plaintiffs argue that a claim of waste of corporate assets evidencing lack of director due care has been well pleaded.

The Vice Chancellor was not persuaded by this reasoning to reach such a conclusion and neither are we. Plaintiffs' assertions by way of argument go well beyond their factual allegations, and it is the latter which are controlling. Plaintiffs' complaints as amended fail to plead with particularity any facts supporting a conclusion that the primary or motivating purpose of the Board's payment of a "giant premium" for the Perot holdings was to buy Perot's silence rather than simply to buy him out and remove him from GM's management team. To the contrary, plaintiffs themselves state in their complaints as amended several legitimate business purposes for the GM Board's decision to sever its relationship with Perot: (1) the Board's determination that it would be in GM's best interest to retain control over its wholly-owned subsidiary, EDS; and (2) the decision to rid itself of the principal cause of the growing internal policy dispute over EDS' management and direction.

The defendant directors also defend the liquidated damage clause in the repurchase agreement as serving a legitimate purpose of protecting GM's contractual rights by, in effect, providing a forfeiture clause should Perot breach that portion of his agreement. Defendants argue that such a damage clause is not unusual and, indeed, would be expected to be found in contractual commitments of this nature. Such a clause strengthens the likelihood of compliance and, in the event of breach, puts an agreed dollar value on the breach, intended to avoid disagreement (or litigation) over the loss and measure of damages attributable to the breach. A failure to anticipate a breach and to stipulate the monetary consequences to GM might well be considered a costly oversight. *See* E. Farnsworth, *Contracts* § 12.18, at 896 (1982).

In addition to regaining control over the management affairs of EDS, GM also secured, through the complex repurchase agreement, significant covenants from Perot, of which the hush-mail provision was but one of many features and multiple considerations of the repurchase. Quite aside from whatever consideration could be attributed to buying Perot's silence, GM's Board received for the $742.8 million paid: all the class E stock and contingent notes of Perot and his fellow EDS directors; Perot's covenant not to compete or hire EDS employees; his promise not to purchase GM stock or engage in proxy contests; Perot's agreement to stay out of and away from GM's and EDS' affairs, plus the liquidated damages provision should Perot breach his no-criticism covenant.

Plaintiffs' effort to quantify the size of the premium paid by GM is flawed, as we have already noted, by their inability to place a dollar value on the various promises made by Perot, particularly his covenant not to compete with EDS or to attempt to hire away EDS employees. (*See supra* notes 2, 4, and 7.) Thus, viewing the transaction in its entirety, we must agree with the Court of Chancery that plaintiffs have failed to plead with particularity facts sufficient to create a reasonable doubt that the substantive terms of the repurchase fall within the protection of the business judgment rule. *See Polk,* 507 A.2d at 536–37.

Finally, we turn to the other aspect of director due care, whether plaintiffs have pleaded facts which would support a reasonable belief that the GM Board acted with gross negligence, i.e., that it was uninformed in critical respects in negotiating the terms of the repurchase. *See Smith v. Van Gorkom,* Del.Supr., 488 A.2d 858, 873 (1985). On this remaining issue, plaintiffs assert that GM's Board failed to exercise due care and to reach an informed business judgment due to the absence of arms-length negotiations between the Board and Perot and the absence of "appropriate board deliberation."

Approval of a transaction by a majority of independent, disinterested directors almost always bolsters a presumption that the business judgment rule attaches to transactions approved by a board of directors that are later attacked on grounds of lack of due care. In such cases, a heavy burden falls on a plaintiff to avoid presuit demand. *Cf. Polk,* 507 A.2d at 537 (1986); *Unocal,* 493 A.2d at 955. This principle of law clearly applies in this case.

To support their allegation of lack of procedural due care, plaintiffs point principally to the lack of negotiations between Perot and GM and the speed with which the Perot repurchase was submitted to and approved by GM's Board of Directors. However, we find plaintiffs' complaints as amended (a) to contradict these assertions and (b) otherwise to be lacking in averments essential to raise a reasonable doubt that the GM Board failed to exercise due care.

The complaints implicitly concede that the repurchase agreement was the subject of "give and take" negotiations and was conducted at arms length. Plaintiffs also expressly concede that the Board did not "supinely accede to all of Perot's demands" because all of his demands were not included in the final agreement. *See Grobow,* 526 A.2d at 919 n. 5 and 926. Furthermore, plaintiffs recount that the repurchase proposal was first submitted to a Special Review Committee, consisting (presumably) of three outside directors and thereafter to the full Board. The complaints as amended, however, contain no allegations raising directly or by inference a

reasonable doubt either that the Committee served a purposeful role in
the review of the repurchase proposal or that the full Board reached an
informed decision. On the contrary, it is clear from the record before us
that the GM directors had been living with the internal dispute for
months and had been considering a buy-out of Perot's interests for a
number of weeks.

Viewing plaintiffs' assertions of lack of director due care against the
well-pleaded facts, we conclude that the complaints as amended lack
essential requirements for stating a claim of waste premised on failure of
the directors to exercise due care. *See Smith v. Van Gorkom,* 488 A.2d at
873; *Kaplan v. Centex Corp.,* Del.Ch., 284 A.2d 119, 124 (1971). By way of
illustration, plaintiffs do not allege that the Committee failed to: (i) give
thorough and diligent consideration to all relevant facts; (ii) review
carefully the negotiations leading to the proposed agreement; (iii) consult
with and consider the views of investment bankers, accountants, and
counsel; or (iv) report its findings and analysis to the full Board. With
respect to Board deliberation, plaintiffs do not allege that the Board failed
to: (i) inform themselves of available critical information before approving
the transaction; (ii) consider expert opinion; (iii) provide all Board members with adequate and timely notice of the repurchase before the full
Board meeting and of its purpose; or (iv) inquire adequately into the
reasons for or terms of repurchase (though plaintiffs allege the Board did
not ask Perot himself questions). Finally, it should be emphasized that
plaintiffs do not allege that the GM directors, and in particular its outside
directors, were dominated or controlled by GM's management or other
Board members or by any other party. *Aronson,* 473 A.2d 815, 816. Thus,
we find plaintiffs' assertion that the GM Board failed to exercise due care
to be insufficient to avoid presuit demand because such assertion is not to
be found in well-pleaded supporting allegations of the complaints.

Apart from whether the Board of Directors may be subject to criticism
for the premium paid Perot and his associates for the repurchase of their
entire interest in GM, on the present record the repurchase of dissident
Perot's interests can only be viewed legally as representing an exercise of
business judgment by the General Motors Board with which a court may
not interfere. Only through a considerable stretch of the imagination
could one reasonably believe this Board of Directors to be "interested" in
a self-dealing sense in Perot's ouster from GM's management. We view a
board of directors with a majority of outside directors, such as this Board,
as being in the nature of overseers of management. So viewed, the Board's
exercise of judgment in resolving an internal rift in management of
serious proportions and at the highest executive level should be accorded
the protection of the business judgment rule absent well-pleaded averments implicating financial self-interest, entrenchment, or lack of due
care. These complaints fall far short of stating a claim for demand excusal.

Notwithstanding the Vice Chancellor's misstatement of the test for
determining when demand on a board of directors will be considered
excused as futile, we reach the same result. We hold that the complaints

as amended fail to allege facts sufficient to create a reasonable doubt that the GM Board-approved repurchase transaction is not within the protection of the business judgment rule; thus, the plaintiffs have failed to establish the futility of demand required under *Aronson* and *Pogostin* for casting reasonable doubt thereon. The Trial Court, therefore, correctly dismissed the suits under Del.Ch.Ct.R. 23.1 for failure of plaintiffs to make presuit demand upon the GM Board.

Affirmed.

LEVINE v. SMITH

591 A.2d 194 (Del.1991).

HORSEY, JUSTICE:

These separate shareholder suits, consolidated on appeal, challenge once again the business judgment rule's application to action of the General Motors Board of Directors which this Court addressed three years ago in *Grobow v. Perot,* Del.Supr., 539 A.2d 180 (1988) (hereinafter *"Grobow I"*). The appeals highlight the differing legal standards controlling shareholder standing to pursue derivative claims depending on whether the shareholder asserts a claim of demand futility or wrongful refusal of demand. In the *Grobow* appeal (hereinafter *"Grobow II"*), a derivative claim premised on futility of demand, the Grobow plaintiffs again contend that they have now met their burden of pleading, by their "Second Amended Complaint," particularized facts sufficient to excuse demand. Concurrently, shareholder Morton Levine, appealing the Court of Chancery's dismissal of his original suit, contends that his Amended Complaint pleads particularized facts sufficient to create a reasonable doubt that the General Motors directors wrongly refused Levine's presuit demand.

In *Grobow II,* we hold that plaintiffs' restated complaint fails to state a claim of demand futility. The Second Amended Complaint fails to plead with particularity facts which would raise a reasonable doubt of director disinterest and independence or that the challenged transaction was otherwise the product of a valid exercise of business judgment. *Aronson v. Lewis,* Del.Supr., 473 A.2d 805, 814 (1984).

In *Levine,* we hold that the Amended Complaint fails to allege particularized facts sufficient to create a reasonable doubt that the General Motors outside directors were either manipulated or misled by management or were so uninformed as to fail to exercise due care. We reaffirm the rule that on a Court of Chancery Rule 23.1 motion to dismiss a derivative suit in a case of demand refused, director independence and lack of self-interest is conceded. Therefore, the trial court reviews the board's decision only for compliance with the traditional business judgment rule. The only relevant question is whether the directors acted in an informed manner and with due care, in a good faith belief that their action was in the best interest of the corporation.* * *

A shareholder derivative suit is a uniquely equitable remedy in which a shareholder asserts on behalf of a corporation a claim belonging not to the shareholder, but to the corporation. Aronson v. Lewis, Del. Supr., 473 A.2d 805, 811 (1984). Under Delaware law, a derivative suit is also a qualified or conditional remedy by reason of its "potential for conflict between the directors' power to manage the corporation and the share-holders' power to sue derivatively." Kaplan v. Peat, Marwick, Mitchell & Co., Del. Supr., 540 A.2d 726, 730 (1988); 8 Del. C. § 141(a). The directors of a corporation and not its shareholders manage the business and affairs of the corporation, Paramount Communications, Inc. v. Time, Inc., Del. Supr., 571 A.2d 1140, 1150 (1989), and accordingly, the directors are responsible for deciding whether to engage in derivative litigation. Zapata Corp. v. Maldonado, Del. Supr., 430 A.2d 779, 782 (1981). "The decision to bring a law suit or to refrain from litigating a claim on behalf of a corporation is a decision concerning the management of the corporation." Spiegel v. Buntrock, Del. Supr., 571 A.2d 767, 773 (1990). On the other hand, the directors' exercise of their managerial power in all its aspects "is tempered by fundamental fiduciary obligations owed by the directors to the corporation and its shareholders." Kaplan v. Peat, 540 A.2d at 729.

The demand requirements of Rule 23.1 represent a procedural re-statement of these bedrock principles of Delaware law of corporate gover-nance in the context of standing to maintain a derivative shareholder's suit. Tandycrafts, Inc. v. Initio Partners, Del. Supr., 562 A.2d 1162, 1166 (1989). Rule 23.1's alternative requirements of pleading demand futility or wrongful refusal of demand are designed to strike a balance between a shareholder's claim of right to assert a derivative claim and a board of directors' duty to decide whether to invest the resources of the corporation in pursuit of the shareholder's claim of corporate wrong. Spiegel, 571 A.2d at 773; Aronson, 473 A.2d at 812. Both the requirements of demand futility and wrongful refusal of demand are predicated upon and "inextri-cably bound to issues of business judgment and the standards of that doctrine's applicability." Aronson, 473 A.2d at 812. Thus, the correct application of the business judgment rule is crucial to a determination of the sufficiency of a derivative complaint to withstand a Rule 23.1 motion in both a demand excused and a demand refused context. * * *

[T]he demand requirements of Rule 23.1 are predicated upon the application of the business judgment rule in the context of a board of directors' exercise of its managerial power over a derivative claim. In determining the sufficiency of a complaint to withstand dismissal under Rule 23.1 based on a claim of demand futility, the controlling legal standard is well established. The trial court is confronted with two related but distinct questions: (1) whether threshold presumptions of director disinterest or independence are rebutted by well-pleaded facts; and, if not, (2) whether the complaint pleads particularized facts sufficient to create a reasonable doubt that the challenged transaction was the product of a valid exercise of business judgment. See Grobow I, 539 A.2d at 187–188; Aronson, 473 A.2d at 814–815; Zapata, 430 A.2d at 782–784.

The premise of a shareholder claim of futility of demand is that a majority of the board of directors either has a financial interest in the challenged transaction or lacks independence or otherwise failed to exercise due care. Grobow I, 539 A.2d at 186, 188; Aronson, 473 A.2d at 814. On either showing, it may be inferred that the Board is incapable of exercising its power and authority to pursue the derivative claims directly. When lack of independence is charged, a plaintiff must show that the Board is either dominated by an officer or director who is the proponent of the challenged transaction or that the Board is so under his influence that its discretion is "sterilize[d]." Zapata, 430 A.2d at 784 (quoting McKee v. Rogers, Del. Ch., 18 Del. Ch. 81, 156 A. 191, 193 (1931)); Sohland v. Baker, Del. Supr., 15 Del. Ch. 431, 141 A. 277 (1927). * * *

'The burden is on the party challenging the decision to establish facts rebutting this presumption.' Aronson v. Lewis, 473 A.2d at 812. Thus, the business judgment rule operates as a judicial acknowledgement of a board of directors' managerial prerogatives.

The effect of a demand is to place control of the derivative litigation in the hands of the board of directors. Zapata Corp. v. Maldonado, 430 A.2d at 784–86. Consequently, stockholders who, like Spiegel, make a demand which is refused, subject the board's decision to judicial review according to the traditional business judgment rule. Aronson v. Lewis, 473 A.2d at 813; Zapata Corp. v. Maldonado, 430 A.2d at 784 n. 10.* * *

The issue in Zapata was whether an impliedly interested board could delegate its power to dismiss a derivative suit to a special committee of outside disinterested directors. 430 A.2d at 786. This Court found that it could, if, among other things, the corporation could prove the Committee was independent, operated in good faith, and made a reasonable investigation. Id. at 788. As the court below pointed out, the act of establishing a special litigation committee constitutes an implicit concession by a board that its members are interested in the transaction and that its decisions are not entitled to the protection of the business judgment rule. See Abbey v. Computer & Communications Technology Corp., Del. Ch., 457 A.2d 368, 374 (1983). However, as we stated in Spiegel, a board of directors concedes demand futility when it is both interested and establishes a special litigation committee to resolve the derivative plaintiff's suit. 571 A.2d at 777 (quoting Abbey, 457 A.2d at 373); See also Aronson, 473 A.2d at 814. * * *

In Aronson, this Court formulated the "reasonable doubt" pleading standard for determining the sufficiency of a complaint based on demand excused to withstand a Rule 23.1 motion. This Court stated:

In our view demand can only be excused where facts are alleged with particularity which create a reasonable doubt that the directors'

action was entitled to the protections of the business judgment rule.
* * *

In sum the entire review is factual in nature. The Court of Chancery in the exercise of its sound discretion must be satisfied that a plaintiff has alleged facts with particularity which, taken as true, support a reasonable doubt that the challenged transaction was the product of a valid exercise of business judgment. Only in that context is demand excused.

Aronson, 473 A.2d at 808, 815. Grobow I, 539 A.2d at 186. Levine does not dispute the applicability of the Aronson reasonable doubt test to a claim of wrongful refusal of demand. The reasons underlying the adoption in Aronson of the "reasonable doubt" test to a claim of demand futility have equal application to standing of a derivative plaintiff to maintain a claim of wrongful refusal of demand. See Spiegel v. Buntrock, 571 A.2d at 773–775. * * *

The focus of a complaint alleging wrongful refusal of demand is different from the focus of a complaint alleging demand futility. The legal issues are different; therefore, the legal standards applied to the complaints are necessarily different. A shareholder plaintiff, by making demand upon a board before filing suit, "tacitly concedes the independence of a majority of the board to respond. Therefore, when a board refuses a demand, the only issues to be examined are the good faith and reasonableness of its investigation." Spiegel, 571 A.2d at 777. When a shareholder files a derivative suit asserting a claim of demand futility, hence demand excused, the basis for such a claim is that the board is (1) interested and not independent; and (2) that the transaction attacked is not protected by the business judgment rule. Aronson, 473 A.2d at 814. In contrast, Levine's complaint based on wrongful refusal of demand not only tacitly concedes lack of self-interest and independence of a majority of the Board, but expressly concedes both issues. Thus, the first part of the Aronson test did not come into play and the trial court was only required to address the application of the business judgment rule to the Board's refusal of Levine's demand. * * *

We turn to Levine's final argument: that the Court of Chancery erred in finding his Amended Complaint to fail to allege particularized facts sufficient to overcome the business judgment rule presumption accorded the GM Board's refusal of his pre-suit demand. The standing of shareholder Levine to exercise "legal managerial power" and assert a derivative claim hinges upon his ability to establish that the GM Board's rejection of his demand was wrongful. Zapata, 430 A.2d at 784–85. As we stated in Spiegel, "the effect of a demand is to place control of the derivative litigation in the hands of the board of directors"; and therefore, the board's refusal is subject to "judicial review according to the traditional business judgment rule." Spiegel, 571 A.2d at 775–76. Levine, by electing to make demand upon the GM Board before filing suit, tacitly conceded the independence of a majority o the GM Board to respond to his demand.

Spiegel, 571 A.2d at 777; see supra IV–C. Levine also does not challenge the GM Board's good faith in rejecting his demand. Therefore, under the traditional business judgment rule, the only issue remaining to be resolved is the reasonableness of the GM Board's investigation of Levine's demand. Spiegel, 571 A.2d at 777. Reasonableness implicates the business judgment rule's requirement of procedural due care; that is, whether the GM Board acted on an informed basis in rejecting Levine's demand. See Grobow I, 539 A.2d at 189–90; Aronson, 473 A.2d at 812–813.

Levine's complaint may be summarized as asserting essentially three allegations in support of his claim that the GM Board failed to exercise due care and to reach an informed business judgment in refusing his demand. Levine asserts: (1) that the Board declined to permit plaintiff's counsel to make an oral presentation to the Board concerning his demand; (2) that the Board failed to undertake any investigation of his demand for rescission of the Perot buyout; and (3) that GM's Board "did nothing" following receipt of his demand. Levine contends that these allegations are sufficient to create a reasonable doubt that the GM Board acted in an informed manner in refusing Levine's demand.

The Court of Chancery, in a carefully considered decision, found Levine's allegations insufficient to create a reasonable doubt that the GM Board's rejection of his demand was the product of an informed business judgment. The Court ruled that Levine's complaint failed to plead particularized facts sufficient to create a reasonable doubt that the GM Board acted in an informed manner in rejecting Levine's demand. On appeal, Levine argues, as he did below, that he has complied with Court of Chancery Rule 23.1 by sufficiently pleading that the GM Board's refusal of his demand "for action with regard to GM's hushmail payment to Perot" was an uninformed decision and therefore wrongful.

This Court's standard of review of a Court of Chancery ruling upon the sufficiency of a derivative complaint to plead a claim of wrongful refusal of demand is no different than review of a claim premised upon demand futility. We will reverse a Court of Chancery Rule 23.1 ruling "only on a showing of abuse of discretion, assuming no legal error led to an erroneous holding." Grobow I, 539 A.2d at 186; Pogostin, 480 A.2d at 624. We have previously determined that the Court of Chancery applied the proper "reasonable doubt" pleading standard to Levine's claim of wrongful refusal of demand; and the parties' only dispute is whether the trial court has properly construed the complaint as insufficient to raise a reasonable doubt that the GM Board acted in an informed manner. Thus, our standard of review of the trial court's finding on the issue is for abuse of discretion in the context of a "predominantly factual" question. Grobow I, 539 A.2d at 186.

While a board of directors has a duty to act on an informed basis in responding to a demand such as Levine's, there is obviously no prescribed procedure that a board must follow. We find no abuse of discretion in the Vice Chancellor's rejection of Levine's contention that the GM Board's failure to permit Levine to make an "oral presentation" to the Board evidenced a lack of due care or unreasonable conduct. Indeed, the court found the argument insufficient as a matter of law, stating:

> A board of directors is not legally obligated to permit a demanding shareholder to make an oral presentation at a meeting. Corporate directors normally have only limited available time to deliberate, and a determination of what matters will (and will not) be considered must necessarily fall within the board's discretion. See Manning, The Business Judgment Rule and the Director's Duty of Attention, 39 Bus. Law. 1477, 1485 (1984). A ruling that, as a practical matter, would require GM's Board to hear the plaintiff's oral presentation, would place directors in the untenable position of having to entertain presentations by any shareholder who threatens to file a derivative action. It would also be an unwarranted intrusion upon the board's authority to govern the corporation's affairs conferred by 8 Del. C. § 141.

We fully agree.

ALFORD v. SHAW

320 N.C. 465, 358 S.E.2d 323 (1987).

MARTIN, JUSTICE.

The sole issue raised by this appeal is whether a special litigation committee's decision to terminate plaintiff minority shareholders' derivative action against defendant corporate directors is binding upon the courts. In our earlier opinion in this case, 318 N.C. 289, 349 S.E.2d 41 (1986), we stated that the "business judgment rule," a doctrine shielding the good faith actions of disinterested corporate directors from judicial inquiry on the merits, required deference to the decisions of independent special litigation committees. Consequently we held that summary judgment had been properly granted for defendants. Upon this rehearing we have elected to reconsider our prior holding and to redetermine the question raised by the appeal.

We withdraw our prior decision, reported in 318 N.C. 289, 349 S.E.2d 41 (1986), and treat the case before us as a hearing de novo on the issue raised. *See Trust Co. v. Gill, State Treasurer,* 293 N.C. 164, 237 S.E.2d 21 (1977); *Clary v. Board of Education,* 286 N.C. 525, 212 S.E.2d 160 (1975).

Briefly summarized, the record discloses the following: In response to charges of mismanagement asserted by plaintiff minority shareholders, the board of directors of All American Assurance Company (AAA) voted to appoint a committee to conduct an investigation. The board then elected Marion G. Follin, a retired insurance executive, and Frank M. Parker, a former judge of the North Carolina Court of Appeals, to board membership and designated them as a special investigative committee. The committee was authorized to determine whether it would be in the best interest of AAA and its shareholders to initiate legal action against those implicated in any wrongdoing uncovered by the investigation.

Before the committee had completed its investigation, plaintiffs filed a shareholders' derivative action in superior court, naming as defendants the controlling shareholders of AAA and a majority of its directors. The complaint alleged inter alia that in a series of transactions involving corporations affiliated with AAA, defendants had violated fiduciary obligations by engaging in a pattern of fraud, self-dealing, and negligent acquiescence which amounted to a "looting" of corporate assets for defendants' own benefit.

Upon completion of its investigation, the committee filed a report in the trial court recommending that the majority of plaintiffs' claims be dismissed with prejudice and that two remaining claims be settled in accordance with an attached settlement agreement. Based on the committee's report, defendants moved for summary judgment and approval of the settlement agreement. The trial court held that the business judgment rule controlled the disposition of the case and granted the motions. The Court of Appeals reversed, 72 N.C.App. 537, 324 S.E.2d 878 (1985), holding that corporate directors who are parties to a derivative action may not confer upon a special committee the power to bind the corporation as to the derivative litigation. We affirm the Court of Appeals, subject to the modifications discussed below.

We deem it unnecessary for the purposes of this opinion to review the development of the basic principles of derivative litigation. For a general discussion of derivative suits, see D. DeMott, *Shareholder Derivative Actions Law and Practice* §§ 1:01–:05 (1987); R. Robinson, *North Carolina Corporate Law and Practice* §§ 14–1, –2 (3d ed. 1983).

In determining the proper role, if any, of special corporate litigation committees in the termination of derivative shareholders' actions, three basic approaches have been adopted by other jurisdictions:

1. *Auerbach. In Auerbach v. Bennett,* 47 N.Y.2d 619, 393 N.E.2d 994, 419 N.Y.S.2d 920 (1979), the Court of Appeals of New York extended the business judgment rule to the decisions of special litigation committees, precluding judicial review of the merits of those decisions. Under *Auerbach,* judicial review of committee decisions is limited to the issues of good faith, independence, and sufficiency of the investigation.

2. *Miller. In Miller v. Register and Tribune Syndicate, Inc.,* 336 N.W.2d 709 (Iowa 1983), the Iowa Supreme Court adopted a prophylactic rule as a means of circumventing the "structural bias" inherent in the committee appointment process. Under *Miller,* directors charged with misconduct are prohibited from participating in the selection of special litigation committees.

3. *Zapata. In Zapata Corp. v. Maldonado,* 430 A.2d 779 (Del.1981), the Delaware Supreme Court promulgated a two-step test for judicial

review of the decisions of special litigation committees. The first step requires an inquiry as to the independence, good faith, and investigative techniques of the committee, expressly placing the burden of proof as to these matters on the corporation. The second step, as a safeguard against structural bias, provides for an additional, discretionary level of scrutiny on the merits in which trial courts may exercise their own "independent business judgment" in deciding whether derivative actions should be dismissed. The report of the special litigation committee may be considered along with all the other evidence before the court.

The recent trend among courts which have been faced with the choice of applying an *Auerbach*-type rule of judicial deference or a *Zapata*-type rule of judicial scrutiny has been to require judicial inquiry on the merits of the special litigation committee's report. *See* Note, *Derivative Actions—Presumed Good Faith Deliberations By Special Litigation Committees: A Major Hurdle For Minority Shareholders—Alford v. Shaw,* 22 Wake Forest L.Rev. 127, 139–44 (1987).

In our previous decision in this case, we applied a modified *Auerbach* rule. We interpret the trend away from *Auerbach* among other jurisdictions as an indication of growing concern about the deficiencies inherent in a rule giving great deference to the decisions of a corporate committee whose institutional symbiosis with the corporation necessarily affects its ability to render a decision that fairly considers the interest of plaintiffs forced to bring suit on behalf of the corporation. *See generally* Cox & Munsinger, *Bias in the Boardroom: Psychological Foundations and Legal Implications of Corporate Cohesion,* 48 Law and Contemporary Problems, Summer 1985 at 83 (1985). Such concerns are legitimate ones and, upon further reflection, we find that they must be resolved not by slavish adherence to the business judgment rule, but by careful interpretation of the provisions of our own Business Corporation Act. We conclude from our analysis of the pertinent statutes that a modified *Zapata* rule, requiring judicial scrutiny of the merits of the litigation committee's recommendation, is most consistent with the intent of our legislature and is therefore the appropriate rule to be applied in our courts. While we affirm the holding of the Court of Appeals reversing summary judgment for defendants, we reject that court's application of the *Miller* rule.

In 1973 the General Assembly enacted N.C.G.S. § 55–55 which expressly authorizes shareholders' derivative actions and prescribes the rules governing all such actions brought in the state courts of North Carolina. Section 55–55 contains liberal provisions which do not impose many of the restrictions upon derivative actions encountered in other jurisdictions. The legislature has placed the minority shareholder in North Carolina "in a more favorable position to seek redress on behalf of his corporation for wrongs allegedly done to it by the majority shareholders, the directors and officers, or outside third parties." R. Robinson, *North Carolina Corporation Law and Practice* § 14–1 at 214 (3d ed. 1983).[1]

---

1. While affording minority stockholders' bona fide derivative suits greater protections under the statutory provisions already discussed, the legislature was not unmindful of corporate concerns about a possible proliferation of meritless "strike" suits. N.C.G.S. § 55–55(e) states that

This policy of protecting minority shareholders is manifested by section 55–55(c), which states that a shareholder's derivative action

> shall not be discontinued, dismissed, compromised or settled without the approval of the court. If the court shall determine that the interest of the shareholders or any class or classes thereof, or of the creditors of the corporation, will be substantially affected by such discontinuance, dismissal, compromise or settlement, the court, in its discretion, may direct that notice, by publication or otherwise, shall be given to such shareholders or creditors whose interests it determines will be so affected. If notice is so directed to be given, the court may determine which one or more of the parties to the action shall bear the expense of giving the same, in such amount as the court shall determine and find to be reasonable in the circumstances, and the amount of such expense shall be awarded as costs of the action.

The plain language of the statute requires thorough judicial review of suits initiated by shareholders on behalf of a corporation: the court is directed to determine whether the interest of any shareholder will be substantially affected by the discontinuance, dismissal, compromise, or settlement of a derivative suit. Although the statute does not specify what test the court must apply in making this determination, it would be difficult for the court to determine whether the interests of shareholders or creditors would be substantially affected by such discontinuance, dismissal, compromise, or settlement without looking at the proposed action substantively.

To make the required assessment under section 55–55, the court must of necessity evaluate the adequacy of materials prepared by the corporation which support the corporation's decision to settle or dismiss a derivative suit along with the plaintiff's forecast of evidence. If it appears likely that plaintiff could prevail on the merits, but that the amount of the recovery would not be sufficient to outweigh the detriment to the corporation, the court could still allow discontinuance, dismissal, compromise, or settlement.

Although the recommendation of the special litigation committee is not binding on the court, in making this determination the court may choose to rely on such recommendation. To rely blindly on the report of a corporation-appointed committee which assembled such materials on behalf of the corporation is to abdicate the judicial duty to consider the interests of shareholders imposed by the statute. This abdication is particularly inappropriate in a case such as this one, where shareholders allege serious breaches of fiduciary duties owed to them by the directors controlling the corporation.

"[i]n any [derivative] action the court, upon final judgment and a finding that the action was brought without reasonable cause, may require the plaintiff or plaintiffs to pay to the defendant or defendants the reasonable expenses, including attorneys' fees, incurred by them in the defense of the action."

Section 55–55(c) is a broadening of the *Zapata* approach. As in other jurisdictions, exhaustion of intracorporate remedies (that is, "demand") is a procedural prerequisite to the filing of a derivative action in North Carolina. Section 55–55(b), codifying prior case law, makes this explicit:

> The complaint shall allege with particularity the efforts, if any, made by the plaintiff to obtain the action he desires from the directors or comparable authority and the reasons for his failure to obtain the action or for not making the effort.

An equitable exception to the demand requirement may be invoked when the directors who are in control of the corporation are the same ones (or under the control of the same ones) as were initially responsible for the breaches of duty alleged. In such case, the demand of a shareholder upon directors to sue themselves or their principals would be futile and as such is not required for the maintenance of the action. *Hill v. Erwin Mills, Inc.,* 239 N.C. 437, 80 S.E.2d 358 (1954); *Swenson v. Thibaut,* 39 N.C.App. 77, 250 S.E.2d 279 (1978), *cert. denied and appeal dismissed,* 296 N.C. 740, 254 S.E.2d 181 (1979). Here plaintiffs alleged that defendant shareholders, who were responsible for the fraudulent transactions, used their control of AAA to nominate and elect defendant directors and that defendant directors permitted the fraudulent transactions to occur. This establishes a demand-excused situation and sufficiently complies with the procedural requirement of section 55–55(b).

The *Zapata* Court limited its two-step judicial inquiry to cases in which demand upon the corporation was futile and therefore excused. However, we find no justification for such limitation in our statutes. The language of section 55–55(c) is inclusive and draws no distinctions between demand-excused and other types of cases. *Cf.* ALI Principles of Corporate Governance: Analysis and Recommendations § 7.08 & Reporter's Notes 2 & 4 at 135–139 (Council Draft No. 6, Oct. 10, 1986) (issue of demand of minimal importance in determining scope of review; demand-excused/demand-required distinction not determinative). Thus, court approval is required for disposition of *all* derivative suits, even where the directors are not charged with fraud or self-dealing, or where the plaintiff and the board agree to discontinue, dismiss, compromise, or settle the lawsuit.

Another expression of legislative intent may be found in N.C.G.S. § 55–30 relating to a director's adverse interest. It provides, inter alia:

> (b) No corporate transaction in which a director has an adverse interest is either void or voidable, if:

>> (3) The adversely interested party proves that the transaction was just and reasonable to the corporation at the time when entered into or approved. In the case of compensation paid or voted for services of a director as director or as officer or employee the standard of what is "just and reasonable" is what would be paid for such services at arm's length under competitive conditions.

When N.C.G.S. §§ 55–55 and 55–30(b)(3) are read in pari materia, they indicate that when a stockholder in a derivative action seeks to establish self-dealing on the part of a majority of the board, the burden should be upon those directors to establish that the transactions complained of were just and reasonable to the corporation when entered into or approved. The fact that a special litigation committee appointed by those directors charged with self-dealing recommends that the action should not proceed, while carrying weight, is not binding upon the trial court. Rather, the court must make a fair assessment of the report of the special committee, along with all the other facts and circumstances in the case, in order to determine whether the defendants will be able to show that the transaction complained of was just and reasonable to the corporation. If this appears evident from the materials before the court, then in a proper case summary judgment may be allowed in favor of the defendants.

Upon remand plaintiffs shall be permitted to develop and present evidence on this issue, such as: (1) that the committee, though perhaps disinterested and independent, may not have been *qualified* to assess intricate and allegedly false tax and accounting information supplied to it by those within the corporate structure who would benefit from decisions not to proceed with litigation, (2) that, in fact, false and/or incomplete information was supplied to the committee because of the nonadversarial way in which it gathered and evaluated information, and therefore (3) in light of these and other problems which arise from the structural bias inherent in the use of board-appointed special litigation committees, that the committee's decision with respect to the litigation eviscerates plaintiffs' opportunities as minority shareholders to vindicate their rights under North Carolina law. *Cf.* Dent, *The Power of Directors to Terminate Shareholder Litigations: The Death of The Derivative Suit,* 75 Nw. U.L.Rev. 96 (1981).

> The trial court in this case adopted the erroneous
>
> opinion that the business judgment rule controls the disposition of this case and, therefore, that *the only issues before it are whether the Special Committee was composed of disinterested, independent directors who acted in good faith, and whether the scope of the investigation and the procedures adopted and followed were appropriate.*

(Emphasis added.) By so doing, the trial court failed to fulfill its duties under N.C.G.S. § 55–55(c) and the rationale of *Zapata.*

In view of the foregoing, we withdraw our decision reported in 318 N.C. 289, 349 S.E.2d 41 (1986). That decision is no longer authoritative and this opinion now becomes the law of the case. *See Investment Properties v. Allen,* 283 N.C. 277, 196 S.E.2d 262 (1973). * * *

Mitchell, J., did not participate in the consideration or decision of this case.

Webb, Justice, dissenting.

I dissent. I do not disagree with the substantive matter in the majority opinion. This Court, however, has decided this case in a previous opinion which considered all matters discussed in the majority opinion filed today. I believe we are mistaken in changing an opinion so recently filed. I vote not to reconsider the case.

MEYER, JUSTICE, dissenting. I dissent. My position is accurately reflected in the original opinion of the Court, reported at 318 N.C. 289, 349 S.E.2d 41 (1986).

SECTION 5. CLAIMS SUBJECT TO DERIVATIVE SUITS

MILLER v. AMERICAN TELEPHONE AND TELEGRAPH CO.

507 F.2d 759 (3d Cir.1974).

SEITZ, CHIEF JUDGE.

Plaintiffs, stockholders in American Telephone and Telegraph Company ("AT&T"), brought a stockholders' derivative action in the Eastern District of Pennsylvania against AT&T and all but one of its directors. The suit centered upon the failure of AT&T to collect an outstanding debt of some $1.5 million owed to the company by the Democratic National Committee ("DNC") for communications services provided by AT&T during the 1968 Democratic national convention. Federal diversity jurisdiction was invoked under 28 U.S.C. § 1332.

Plaintiffs' complaint alleged that 'neither the officers or directors of AT&T have taken any action to recover the amount owed' from on or about August 20, 1968, when the debt was incurred, until May 31, 1972, the date plaintiffs' amended complaint was filed. The failure to collect was alleged to have involved a breach of the defendant directors' duty to exercise diligence in handling the affairs of the corporation, to have resulted in affording a preference to the DNC in collection procedures in violation of § 202(a) of the Communications Act of 1934, 47 U.S.C. § 202(a) (1970), and to have amounted to AT&T's making a 'contribution' to the DNC in violation of a federal prohibition on corporate campaign spending, 18 U.S.C. § 610 (1970).

Plaintiffs sought permanent relief in the form of an injunction requiring AT&T to collect the debt, an injunction against providing further services to the DNC until the debt was paid in full, and a surcharge for the benefit of the corporation against the defendant directors in the amount of the debt plus interest from the due date. A request for a preliminary injunction against the provision of services to the 1972 Democratic convention was denied by the district court after an evidentiary hearing.

On motion of the defendants, the district court dismissed the complaint for failure to state a claim upon which relief could be granted. 364 F.Supp. 648 (E.D.Pa.1973). The court stated that collection procedures were properly within the discretion of the directors whose determination would not be overturned by the court in the absence of an allegation that the conduct of the directors was 'plainly illegal, unreasonable, or in breach of a fiduciary duty. . . .' *Id. at 651.* Plaintiffs appeal from dismissal of their complaint.

In viewing the motion to dismiss, we must consider all facts alleged in the complaint and every inference fairly deductible therefrom in the light most favorable to the plaintiffs. A complaint should not be dismissed unless it appears that the plaintiffs would not be entitled to relief under any facts which they might prove in support of their claim. Judging plaintiffs' complaint by these standards, we feel that it does state a claim upon which relief can be granted for breach of fiduciary duty arising from the alleged violation of 18 U.S.C. § 610.

The pertinent law on the question of the defendant directors' fiduciary duties in this diversity action is that of New York, the state of AT&T's incorporation. * * * The sound business judgment rule, the basis of the district court's dismissal of plaintiffs' complaint, expresses the unanimous decision of American courts to eschew intervention in corporate decision-making if the judgment of directors and officers is uninfluenced by personal considerations and is exercised in good faith. Pollitz v. Wabash Railroad Co., 207 N.Y. 113, 100 N.E. 721 (1912); Bayer v. Beran, 49 N.Y.S.2d 2, 4–7 (Sup.Ct.1944); 3 Fletcher, Private Corporations § 1039 (perm. ed. rev. vol. 1965). Underlying the rule is the assumption that reasonable diligence has been used in reaching the decision which the rule is invoked to justify. Casey v. Woodruff, 49 N.Y.S.2d 625, 643 (Sup.Ct. 1944).

Had plaintiffs' complaint alleged only failure to pursue a corporate claim, application of the sound business judgment rule would support the district court's ruling that a shareholder could not attack the directors' decision. See United Copper Securities Co. v. Amalgamated Copper Co., 244 U.S. 261 (1917); Clifford v. Metropolitan Life Insurance Co., 34 N.Y.S.2d 693 (2d Dept.1942); 13 Fletcher, Private Corporations § 5822 (perm. ed. rev. vol. 1970). Where, however, the decision not to collect a debt owed the corporation is itself alleged to have been an illegal act, different rules apply. When New York law regarding such acts by directors is considered in conjunction with the underlying purposes of the particular statute involved here, we are convinced that the business judgment rule cannot insulate the defendant directors from liability if they did in fact breach 18 U.S.C. § 610, as plaintiffs have charged.

Roth v. Robertson, 118 N.Y.S. 351 (Sup.Ct.1909), illustrates the proposition that even though committed to benefit the corporation, illegal acts may amount to a breach of fiduciary duty in New York. In Roth, the managing director of an amusement park company had allegedly used corporate funds to purchase the silence of persons who threatened to complain about unlawful Sunday operation of the park. Recovery from the defendant director was sustained on the ground that the money was an illegal payment:

> For reasons of public policy, we are clearly of the opinion that payments of corporate funds for such purposes as those disclosed in this case must be condemned, and officers of a corporation making them held to a strict accountability, and be compelled to refund the amounts so wasted for the benefit of stockholders.... To hold any other rule would be establishing a dangerous precedent, tacitly countenancing the wasting of corporate funds for purposes of corrupting public morals. 118 N.Y.S. at 353.

The plaintiffs' complaint in the instant case alleges a similar 'waste' of $1.5 million through an illegal campaign contribution.

Abrams v. Allen, 297 N.Y. 52, 74 N.E.2d 305 (1947), reflects an affirmation by the New York Court of Appeals of the principle of Roth that directors must be restrained from engaging in activities which are against public policy. In *Abrams* the court held that a cause of action was stated by an allegation in a derivative complaint that the directors of Remington Rand, Inc., had relocated corporate plants and curtailed production solely for the purpose of intimidating and punishing employees for their involvement in a labor dispute. The Court of Appeals acknowledged that, 'depending on the circumstances,' proof of the allegations in the complaint might sustain recovery, *inter alia*, under the rule that directors are liable for corporate loss caused by the commission of an 'unlawful or immoral act.' 74 N.E.2d at 306. In support of its holding, the court noted that the closing of factories for the purpose alleged was opposed to the public policy of the state and nation as embodied in the New York Labor Law and the National Labor Relations Act. 74 N.E.2d at 307.

The alleged violation of the federal prohibition against corporate political contributions not only involves the corporation in criminal activity but similarly contravenes a policy of Congress clearly enunciated in 18 U.S.C. § 610. That statute and its predecessor reflect congressional efforts: (1) to destroy the influence of corporations over elections through financial contributions and (2) to check the practice of using corporate funds to benefit political parties without the consent of the stockholders. United States v. CIO, 335 U.S. 106, 113 (1948).

The fact that shareholders are within the class for whose protection the statute was enacted gives force to the argument that the alleged breach of that statute should give rise to cause of action in those shareholders to force the return to the corporation of illegally contributed funds. Since political contributions by corporations can be checked and shareholder control over the political use of general corporate funds effectuated only if directors are restrained from causing the corporation to violate the statute, such a violation seems a particularly appropriate basis for finding breach of the defendant directors' fiduciary duty to the corporation. Under such circumstances, the directors cannot be insulated from liability on the ground that the contribution was made in the exercise of sound business judgment.

Since plaintiffs have alleged actual damage to the corporation from the transaction in the form of the loss of a $1.5 million increment to AT&T's treasury, we conclude that the complaint does state a claim upon which relief can be granted sufficient to withstand a motion to dismiss.

We have accepted plaintiffs' allegation of a violation of 18 U.S.C. § 610 as a shorthand designation of the elements necessary to establish a breach of that statute. This is consonant with the federal practice of notice pleading. See Conley v. Gibson, 355 U.S. 41, 47–48 (1957); Fed.R. Civ. P. 8(f). That such a designation is sufficient for pleading purposes does not, however, relieve plaintiffs of their ultimate obligation to prove the elements of the statutory violation as part of their proof of breach of fiduciary duty. At the appropriate time, plaintiffs will be required to produce evidence sufficient to establish three distinct elements comprising a violation of 18 U.S.C. § 610: that AT&T (1) made a contribution of money or anything of value to the DNC (2) in connection with a federal election (3) for the purpose of influencing the outcome of that election. See United States v. Boyle, 157 U.S.App.D.C. 166, 482 F.2d 755, cert. denied, 414 U.S. 1076, 94 S.Ct. 593, 38 L.Ed.2d 483 (1973); United States v. Lewis Food Co., Inc., 366 F.2d 710 (9th Cir.1966). The first two of these elements are obvious from the face of the statute; the third was supplied by legislative history prior to being made explicit by 1972 amendments to definitions applicable to § 610.

In proving a contribution to the DNC, plaintiffs will be required to establish that AT&T did in fact make a gift to the DNC of the value of the communications services provided to the 1968 Democratic convention. Such a gift could be shown, for example, by demonstrating that the services were provided with no intention to collect for them. Likewise, plaintiffs could meet their burden in this respect by proving that although a valid debt was created at the time the services were rendered, that debt was discharged formally or informally by the defendants or is no longer legally collectible as a result of the defendants' failure to sue upon it within the appropriate period of limitation. In any event, as a threshold matter, plaintiffs will be required to show that actions of the defendants have resulted in the surrender of a valid claim of $1.5 million for services rendered to the DNC.

Plaintiffs must also establish that the contribution was in connection with a federal election. Obviously, the communications services were provided in connection with the 1968 election. If, however, a valid debt was created at that time and the alleged gift was made at some later time when the debt was forgiven or became legally uncollectible, the contribution may have been made in connection with a subsequent federal election. Plaintiffs did not allege the date of the contribution in their complaint, but their burden on remand will include establishing a nexus between the alleged gift and a federal election.

Finally, plaintiffs must also convince the fact finder that the gift, whenever made, was made for the purpose of aiding one candidate or party in a federal election. Proof of non-collection of a debt owed by the DNC will be insufficient to establish the statutory violation upon which the defendants' breach of fiduciary duty is predicated; plaintiffs must shoulder the burden of proving an impermissible motivation underlying the alleged inaction. In the absence of direct proof of a partisan purpose on the part of the defendants, plaintiffs may produce evidence sufficient to justify the inference that the only discernible reason for the failure to pursue the debtor was a desire to assist the Democratic Party in achieving success in a federal election. At a minimum, plaintiffs must establish that legitimate business justifications did not underlie the alleged inaction of the defendant directors. The possibility of the existence of such reasonable business motives illustrates the need for proof of more than mere non-collection even of the debt of a political party in order to establish a breach of 18 U.S.C. § 610. * * *

NOTES

1.   The complaint in *Miller* was dismissed on remand for lack of jurisdiction and insufficiency of process. 394 F.Supp. 58 (E.D.Pa.1975), aff'd, 530 F.2d 964 (3d Cir.1976).

2.   Should shareholder derivative suits be allowed where corporate misconduct actually benefited the company? In Roth v. Robertson, 64 Misc. 343, 118 N.Y.S. 351 (Sup.1909), the court allowed a derivative, that challenged payments made to keep the recipients from reporting the illegal Sunday operations of the company's amusement park. Those operations accounted for a large portion of the corporation's revenue. In Gaines v. Haughton, 645 F.2d 761 (9th Cir.1981), cert. denied, 454 U.S. 1145, 102 S.Ct. 1006, 71 L.Ed.2d 297 (1982), the court upheld the dismissal of a derivative suit where a special litigation committee appointed by the company's board of directors concluded that the litigation was not in the best interests of the corporation. The derivative suit sought to recover from officers and directors more than $30 million in "questionable" payments to foreign officials and agents in order to acquire company business. Although the Foreign Corrupt Practices Act now prohibits such payments, there was no federal law prohibiting such payments at the time they were authorized by the Lockheed officers and directors.

WHITE v. PANIC

783 A.2d 543 (Del. 2001).

VEASEY, CHIEF JUSTICE:

In this appeal, we consider whether a complaint in a derivative action presents sufficient particularized factual allegations to create a reasonable doubt that the director defendants were disinterested and independent or that their conduct was protected by the business judgment rule. The complaint alleges, based almost entirely on facts derived from an investigative report in a news magazine, that the board of directors affirmatively refused to take any measures to stop or sanction sexual misconduct by a corporate officer that allegedly subjected the corporation to potential civil liability and expense.

On July 6, 1998, *U.S. News & World Report* published a cover story describing several sexual harassment suits filed against Milan Panic, the founder and Chief Executive Officer of ICN Pharmaceuticals, Inc. ("ICN"). ICN is an international enterprise engaged in the manufacture and marketing of pharmaceutical products. Based principally on the facts reported in the *U.S. News* article, Andrew White, an ICN stockholder, filed a derivative suit in the Court of Chancery naming the individual directors on the ICN board as defendants and naming ICN as a nominal defendant.

The following summarizes the facts alleged in the derivative complaint. According to the complaint, four women have filed suits against ICN alleging that Panic 'repeatedly propositioned or groped them and rewarded or punished female employees based on whether they complied or complained.' ICN has apparently disclosed publicly that it has paid a total of $3,500,000 to settle eight harassment suits against Panic. The complaint does not provide any details about the nature of the legal claims against ICN, the amount of each settlement, or the status of pending litigation. There are also no allegations that Panic has ever been found liable for sexual harassment or has conceded that he engaged in any misconduct.

The plaintiff posits that, although ICN officials knew about Panic's alleged misconduct as early as 1992, the board made a concerted effort to protect Panic by using corporate funds to settle the suits against Panic and ICN and by implementing policies designed, at least in part, to minimize exposure of Panic's alleged activities. To support the assertion that the board knew of Panic's behavior, one of the director defendants in this case, Norman Barker, Jr., is quoted in the complaint as saying:

> "[The problem with Panic is he can't keep it in his pants." Allegedly to avoid unwanted publicity about Panic's conduct, ICN has implemented a policy requiring employees to submit all grievances to sealed arbitration. According to the complaint, Panic and other directors have conceded in deposition testimony that the board has never sanctioned Panic for the alleged misconduct.

The board has also not required that Panic reimburse ICN for the corporate funds expended in defending and settling the suits based on his alleged misconduct. To the contrary, the plaintiff alleges that the board approved a short-term loan from ICN to Panic so that he could pay a $3,500,000 settlement in a paternity suit. With the approval of the board, ICN then guaranteed a loan from a third-party bank to Panic (as a replacement for the short-term loan) and deposited $3,600,000 from the corporate treasury as collateral for the loan. In return, Panic pledged 150,000 stock options with an exercise price of $15.17 per share.

Panic and the board moved to dismiss the complaint under Chancery Rule 23.1 on the ground that the plaintiff did not file a demand on the board before proceeding with his derivative suit and did not show that demand was excused as futile. The Court of Chancery held that demand was not excused in this case because the particularized factual allegations in the complaint do not raise a reasonable doubt that the board was disinterested or that the board's actions were the product of valid business judgment. The court therefore granted the defendants' motion to dismiss the complaint with prejudice. The plaintiff now appeals the Court of Chancery's dismissal with prejudice of his complaint. * * *

In most situations, the board of directors has sole authority to initiate or to refrain from initiating legal actions asserting rights held by the corporation. This authority is subject to the limited exception, defined in Chancery Rule 23.1, permitting stockholders to initiate a derivative suit to enforce unasserted rights of the corporation without the board's approval where they can show either that the board wrongfully refused the plaintiffs pre-suit demand to initiate the suit or, if no demand was made, that such a demand would be a futile gesture and is therefore excused.

Where, as in this case, a stockholder plaintiff initiates a derivative action without making a pre-suit demand on the board, Rule 23.1 requires that the complaint allege with particularity the reasons for the plaintiffs failure to demand action from the board. To satisfy this requirement, the "stockholder plaintiff[] must overcome the powerful presumptions of the business judgment rule" by alleging sufficient particularized facts to support an inference that demand is excused because the board is *"incapable* of exercising its power and authority to pursue the derivative claims directly." In *Aronson v. Lewis,* 473 A.2d 814 we held that a demand on the board is excused only if the complaint contains particularized factual allegations raising a reasonable doubt that either: (1) "the directors are disinterested and independent" or "(2) the challenged transaction was otherwise the product of a valid exercise of business judgment."

In the present case, the plaintiff does not contest the Court of Chancery's conclusion that a majority of the ICN directors were disinterested and independent. The plaintiff must therefore carry the "heavy burden" of showing that the well-pleaded allegations in the complaint create a reasonable doubt that the board's decisions were "the product of a valid exercise of business judgment." Although the derivative complaint includes allegations that seem designed to support a "failure to supervise" claim, the plaintiff has elected not to pursue such a claim in the Court of Chancery or in this Court. Instead, the plaintiff contends that demand is excused here because the defendant directors intentionally or with a reckless disregard of their fiduciary duties made decisions that condoned or encouraged Panic's alleged misconduct.

As the Court of Chancery noted, the factual allegations in the complaint concerning the board's knowledge and conduct are sparse. To support the allegation that the defendant directors were aware that Panic had actually engaged in the alleged misconduct, the complaint quotes ICN director Norman Barker as saying: "[T]he problem with Panic is he can't keep it in his pants." Although Barker's comment implies some level of knowledge of Panic's sexual activity, the comment cannot by itself support a reasonable inference that Barker or any of the other directors were aware that Panic had, in fact, harassed female ICN employees or engaged in other conduct for which ICN could be held liable.

The plaintiff also argues that the directors must have known about Panic's misconduct because they agreed to settle eight harassment suits lodged against Panic and ICN. The defendant directors would not have approved the settlement of eight such suits, the argument goes, unless they knew that Panic had actually engaged in the misconduct alleged in those suits.

The decision to approve the settlement of a suit against the corporation is entitled to the same presumption of good faith as other business decisions taken by a disinterested, independent board. Similarly, the board's decision not to seek contribution from persons involved in the conduct underlying a suit against the corporation is a business decision within the discretion of the board.

In the present case, the plaintiff has not pleaded facts indicating that the challenged settlements were anything other than routine business decisions in the interest of the corporation. For example, the complaint provides no basis to infer the board's assessment of the merits of the suits. The complaint does not allege the amounts involved in the settlements or the amount of damages claimed in the suits. Indeed, the complaint does not even specify the precise conduct alleged in the various suits against ICN and Panic. Absent particularized allegations on these points, we find too tenuous any inference based on the board's approval of eight settlements that the board knew that Panic had actually engaged in misconduct. We also note that the alleged settlements, in which neither Panic nor ICN admitted wrongdoing, are consistent with a desire to be rid of strike suits and to avoid the cost of protracted litigation. Thus, the presumption of the business judgment rule is not rebutted.

We therefore conclude that, under the heightened pleading standards of Rule 23.1, the particularized allegations in the complaint do not adequately support the plaintiffs theory that the board knew (or proceeded in face of an unjustifiable risk) that Panic had engaged in misconduct but refused to take action to protect ICN from liability for that misconduct. As a consequence, the plaintiff has failed to create a reasonable doubt that the board's decisions were the product of a valid exercise of business judgment.

The plaintiffs second primary contention is that the board's decision to use corporate funds to facilitate Panic's payment of the $3.5 million settlement of a paternity suit was not a valid exercise of business judgment. Although it is unclear from the briefs whether the plaintiffs claim is based on corporate waste or bad faith by the board, we find that the well-pleaded facts in the complaint do not support either theory. For the sake of simplicity, we analyze the plaintiffs claims under the corporate waste standard.

A board's decisions do not constitute corporate waste unless they are exceptionally one-sided. Accordingly, we have defined "waste" to mean "an exchange of corporate assets for consideration so disproportionately small as to lie beyond the range at which any reasonable person might be willing to trade." As a practical matter, a stockholder plaintiff must generally show that the board "irrationally squander [ed]" corporate assets—for example, where the challenged transaction served no corporate purpose or where the corporation received no consideration at all.

Under this standard, a corporate waste claim must fail if "there is *any* *substantial* consideration received by the corporation, and . . . there is a *good faith judgment* that in the circumstances the transaction is worthwhile." This is so even if the transaction appears, with hindsight, to be unreasonably risky to a reviewing court. As we have observed, "courts are ill-fitted to attempt to weigh the 'adequacy' of consideration under the waste standard or, *ex post,* to judge appropriate degrees of business risk." Thus, absent some reasonable doubt that the ICN board proceeded based on a good faith assessment of the corporation's best interests, the board's decisions are entitled to deference under the business judgment rule.

In the present case, the plaintiff alleges that the board guaranteed a $3.5 million bank loan to Panic and deposited $3.6 million in an account at the bank as "collateral" for the guarantee. Panic, in turn, gave ICN as collateral 150,000 options on ICN stock at a strike price of about $15—which, as the plaintiff concedes, are "valuable." Even assuming that this arrangement constitutes an outright loan by the board, Panic provided valuable consideration for the loan in the form of his stock options. Moreover, there is no allegation that the board waived ICN's legal rights in the event that ICN was called upon to pay out under the guarantee. The terms of the loan and the guarantee are not so inadequate or "one-sided" as to cast a reasonable doubt on the board's decision to approve them.

We therefore conclude that the particularized facts on the face of the complaint, both individually and collectively, are legally insufficient to create a reasonable doubt that the board's decisions were the product of a valid exercise of business judgment. * * *

SECTION 6. INDEMNIFICATION OF OFFICERS AND DIRECTORS

MERRITT–CHAPMAN & SCOTT v. WOLFSON

321 A.2d 138 (Del.Super.1974)

BALICK, JUDGE.

These actions arise over claims of Louis Wolfson, Elkin Gerbert, Joseph Kosow and Marshal Staub (claimants) for indemnification by Merritt–Chapman & Scott Corporation (MCS) against expenses incurred in a criminal action. All parties seek summary judgment.

Claimants were charged by indictment with participation in a plan to cause MCS to secretly purchase hundreds of thousands of shares of its own common stock. Count one charged all claimants with conspiracy to violate federal securities laws. Count two charged Wolfson and count three charged Gerbert with perjury before the Securities and Exchange Commission (SEC). Counts four and five charged Wolfson, Gerbert, and Staub with filing false annual reports for 1962 and 1963 respectively with the SEC and New York Stock Exchange.

At the first trial the court dismissed part of the conspiracy count but the jury returned guilty verdicts on all charges against all claimants. At that stage this court held that Wolfson, Gerbert, and Kosow were not entitled to partial indemnification. Merritt–Chapman & Scott v. Wolfson, 264 A.2d 358 (Del.Super.1970). Thereafter the convictions were reversed. United States v. Wolfson, 437 F.2d 862 (2d Cir. 1970).

There were two retrials of the perjury and filing false annual report charges against Wolfson and Gerbert. At the first retrial the court entered a judgment of acquittal on count four at the end of the State's case, and the jury could not agree on the other counts. At the second retrial the jury returned a guilty verdict on count three, but could not agree further.

The charges were then settled as follows: Wolfson entered a plea of *nolo contendere* to count five and the other charges against him were dropped. He was fined $10,000 and given a suspended sentence of eighteen months. Gerbert agreed not to appeal his conviction of count three, on which he was fined $2,000 and given a suspended sentence of eighteen months, and the other charges against him were dropped. The prosecution also dropped the charges against Kosow and Staub.

Indemnification of corporate agents involved in litigation is the subject of legislation in Delaware. Title 8 Delaware Code § 145. Subsection (a), which permits indemnification, and subsection (c), which requires indemnification, provide as follows:

> (a) A corporation may indemnify any person who was or is a party or is threatened to be made a party to any threatened, pending or completed action, suit or proceeding, whether civil, criminal, ad-

ministrative or investigative (other than an action by or in the right of the corporation) by reason of the fact that he is or was a director, officer, employee or agent of the corporation, or is or was serving at the request of the corporation as a director, officer, employee or agent of another corporation, partnership, joint venture, trust or other enterprise, against expenses (including attorneys' fees), judgments, fines and amounts paid in settlement actually and reasonably incurred by him in connection with such action, suit or proceeding if he acted in good faith and in a manner he reasonably believed to be in or not opposed to the best interests of the corporation, and, with respect to any criminal action or proceeding, had no reasonable cause to believe his conduct was unlawful. The termination of any action, suit or proceeding by judgment, order, settlement, conviction, or upon a plea of *nolo contendere* or its equivalent, shall not, of itself, create a presumption that the person did not act in good faith and in a manner which he reasonably believed to be in or not opposed to the best interests of the corporation, and, with respect to any criminal action or proceeding, had reasonable cause to believe that his conduct was unlawful. * * *

(c) To the extent that a director, officer, employee or agent of a corporation has been successful on the merits or otherwise in defense of any action, suit or proceeding referred to in [subsection (a)], or in defense of any claim, issue or matter therein, he shall be indemnified against expenses (including attorneys' fees) actually and reasonably incurred by him in connection therewith.

The policy of the statute and its predecessor has been described as follows, Folk, The Delaware General Corporation Law, 98 (1972):

> The invariant policy of Delaware legislation on indemnification is to 'promote the desirable end that corporate officials will resist what they consider' unjustified suits and claims, 'secure in the knowledge that their reasonable expenses will be borne by the corporation they have served if they are vindicated.' (Essential Enterprises Corp. v. Automatic Steel Prods., Inc., 39 Del.Ch. 371, 164 A.2d 437, 441–442 (Del.Chanc.1960).) Beyond that, its larger purpose is 'to encourage capable men to serve as corporate directors, secure in the knowledge that expenses incurred by them in upholding their honesty and integrity as directors will be borne by the corporation they serve.' (Mooney v. Willys–Overland Motors, Inc., 204 F.2d 888, 898 (3d Cir.1953)).

MCS argues that the statute and sound public policy require indemnification only where there has been vindication by a finding or concession of innocence. It contends that the charges against claimants were dropped for practical reasons, not because of their innocence, and that in light of the conspiracy charged in the indictment, the judgment of acquittal on count four alone is not vindication.

The statute requires indemnification to the extent that the claimant 'has been successful on the merits or otherwise.' Success is vindication. In a criminal action, any result other than conviction must be considered success. Going behind the result, as MCS attempts, is neither authorized by subsection (c) nor consistent with the presumption of innocence.

The statute does not require complete success. It provides for indemnification to the extent of success 'in defense of any claim, issue or matter' in an action. Claimants are therefore entitled to partial indemnification if successful on a count of an indictment, which is an independent criminal charge, even if unsuccessful on another, related count.

MCS contends that Kosow is not entitled to the benefit of the statute because he was not 'a director, officer, employee or agent' of MCS. Kosow was chairman of the board and president of Industrial Finance Corporation, a wholly owned subsidiary of [MCS]. He served in these positions because of an employment agreement with MCS in which Kosow agreed to manage private financing and lending business activities of MCS, 'subject to (its) control and direction.' MCS argues that the phrase in subsection (a) expressly covering persons who serve one corporation at the request of another was intentionally omitted from subsection (c). I need not consider this argument because I conclude, based on the agreement, that Kosow was an 'employee or agent' of MCS. Because of Kosow's affidavit to the contrary, MCS has abandoned its position that he is not entitled to any benefit under the statute because it went into effect after his relationship with MCS ended.

MCS contends that the indictment was not related to the area of Kosow's employment or agency, and he was therefore not 'made a party ... by reason of the fact that' he was an employee or agent of MCS. The conspiracy count charged that the stock repurchase plan 'would operate as a fraud and deceit upon the stockholders of (MCS)' in violation of the Securities Exchange Act of 1934, 15 U.S.C. § 78j(b), and SEC Rule 10b—5. The charge was based upon failure to disclose inside information. Kosow participated in the plan, shared the inside information, and was prosecuted because of his employment or agency relationship with MCS. He is therefore entitled to indemnification. Wolfson and Gerbert based their claims for indemnification against expenses incurred in defense of counts three and five on subsection (a) of the statute and by-law of MCS. This is the pertinent by-law:

> Each person (and his heirs, executors and administrators) who is or has been a director or officer of the Corporation shall be indemnified by the Corporation against expenses (which shall not include any amounts paid in settlement) reasonably incurred by him or them in connection with any action, suit or proceeding to which he may be a party or with which he shall be threatened by

reason of his being or having been a director or officer of the Corporation, *except in relation to matters as to which he shall finally be adjudged in such action, suit or proceeding (or, in case such action, suit or proceeding shall be settled, shall be determined by the Corporation) to have been derelict in the performance of his duty as such director or officer.* The foregoing right of indemnification shall be in addition to any other rights to which any such director or officer may be entitled as a matter of law. (emphasis added.)

They contend that the by-law makes indemnification, as permitted by subsection (a) of the statute, mandatory; that they met the standard of conduct set by subsection (a); and that they did not violate their fiduciary duties to MCS under Delaware law.

Although a corporation may pass a by-law making mandatory the provision for permissive indemnification in subsection (a), the MCS by-law does not do this. It comes closer to doing so with reference to the predecessor of the present statute. The former statute (8 Del.C. § 122(10)), which was in effect when the by-law was adopted, specifically empowered corporations to indemnify,

> except in relation to matters as to which any such director or officer or former director or officer or person shall be adjudged in such action, suit or proceeding to be liable for negligence or misconduct in the performance of duty.

Compare this with the emphasized part of the MCS by-law, as quoted above.

> The right of Wolfson and Gerbert to indemnification under the by-law, which is independent of any right under the statute, see subsection (f), depends on whether they were 'adjudged in such action ... to have been derelict in the performance of (their) duty as ... director or officer.' Wolfson was sentenced upon a plea of *nolo contendere* to count five of the indictment which charged that he ... unlawfully, wilfully and knowingly, made and caused to be made a false and misleading statement of material fact in a balance sheet which was part of an annual report for Merritt for the year 1963 which was required to be filed and was filed with the New York Stock Exchange and the Securities and Exchange Commission.

> Gerbert was sentenced upon a guilty verdict on count three, which charged that, ... having duly taken an oath as a witness that he would testify truly before a competent officer of the United States Securities and Exchange Commission, ... did unlawfully, wilfully and knowingly and contrary to said oath state material matters which he did not believe to be true ...

Although a plea of *nolo contendere* may not be used as an admission in another action, upon acceptance by the court and imposition of sentence there is a judgment of conviction against the defendant. See Fed.Rules

Crim.Proc., Rules 11, 32(b); Lott v. United States, 367 U.S. 421, 426, 81 S.Ct. 1563, 6 L.Ed.2d 940 (1961). The by-law, unlike subsection (a) of the statute, does not require this court to look behind the judgment. If an action does not go to judgment because of a settlement, the by-law gives MCS the power to determine whether the director or officer has been derelict in the performance of duty. Nor does the by-law prohibit indemnification only where directors or officers have been adjudged derelict in the performance of their fiduciary duty to MCS under Delaware law. Conviction of these offenses establishes that Wolfson and Gerbert were adjudged to have been derelict in the performance of their duty as director or officer, and they are therefore not entitled to indemnification against expenses incurred in connection with counts three and five.

MCS contends that the attorneys' fees claimed by Wolfson were not 'reasonably incurred.' While his appeal was pending after the original trial, Wolfson, although satisfied with his attorneys thus far, retained Williams, Connolly & Califano to seek a reversal by the United States Supreme Court, if necessary. That firm, assisted by the one that represented him at the first trial, represented Wolfson at the second and third trials. Its fee was $250,000 for each trial. It attributes 10 percent of its fee to defense of count five. MCS contends that the average hourly rate received by the firm ($190) is substantially higher than the rate charged by the other equally distinguished firms representing Wolfson and his co-defendants, and is therefore unreasonable.

The standards used in determining whether fees have been 'reasonably incurred' are similar to standards used by courts in awarding fees. Husband S. v. Wife S., 294 A.2d 89, 93 (Del.Supr.1972); Galdi v. Berg, 359 F.Supp. 698, 700 (D.Del.1973). While fixing a reasonable hourly rate is 'a logical beginning,' Lindy Bros. Bldrs., Inc. of Phila. v. American R. & S. San. Corp., 487 F.2d 161, 167 (3d Cir., Seitz, C.J. 1973), other factors may be considered. Where indemnification is sought, the claimant will have usually assumed the risk of not being indemnified. His position when he incurred the expenses should be considered. In this case, Wolfson retained the Williams firm after he had been convicted of all counts. He faced the possibility of a prison sentence, not to mention other consequences of criminal convictions. The indictment against Wolfson, which presented novel legal and complex factual problems, was vigorously and persistently prosecuted. In retaining the Williams firm, particularly its senior partner, Edward Bennett Williams, Wolfson sought the best possible legal counsel. Williams has acquired a national reputation based upon twenty-eight years of experience in active trial practice, often in major criminal cases. He personally spent about 1600 of his firm's 2633 hours in preparation for and in two long trials, while he had to lay all other work aside. He does not charge by the hour. Partners in the firm, who customarily charge a minimum hourly rate of $100, spent about 52 hours. Associates, whose hourly rate is between $50 and $100, account for the balance of the firm's hours.

Charging a flat fee for each trial is not inherently unreasonable. For example, it might be shown that the fee was based in part on a reasonable estimate of the hours that would be required. It is of course possible that the hourly rate will turn out to be low. Here the fees were based on the rare skill necessary to increase the hope of a successful result in an unusual and difficult case. In view of the statutory policy of indemnification for those who successfully defend actions arising from the performance of their corporate duties, I find that Wolfson's attorneys' fees were reasonably incurred.

Claimants seek and MCS opposes interest on the expenses incurred. The opposition is based upon the failure of the statute to provide for interest and the absence of wrongdoing on the part of MCS. Without interest on expenses actually paid, indemnification would be incomplete. I find no reason to deprive claimants of full indemnification, in accordance with the policy of the statute. Interest is not awarded because of wrongdoing by MCS but because it has had the use of the money while claimants were entitled to it.

NOTES

1. Louis Wolfson caused another controversy when it was reported that his foundation had been making payments of $20,000 per year to Abe Fortas, a supreme court justice. Fortas returned the money, but the resulting scandal forced him from the bench. II Jerry W. Markham, *A Financial History of the United States, From J.P. Morgan to the Institutional Investor (1900–1970)* 350–51 (2002).

2. The Model Bus. Corp. Act § 8.52 provides for mandatory indemnification for directors who are "wholly" successful in defense of any action to which they are parties because they were directors. The official comments to this section note that the word "wholly" was added to avoid the partial indemnification allowed by the Delaware court in the *Merritt–Chapman* case. Nevertheless, permissive indemnification may be allowed by Model Bus. Corp. Act § 8.51. That section allows indemnification where, among other things, a director is acting as such in good faith and with the reasonable belief that his or her conduct was in the best interests of the corporation. Section 8.51(c) of the Model Bus. Corp. Act, like the Delaware Code, states that the termination of a proceeding by judgment, conviction or a plea of nolo contendere is not itself determinative that the director did not meet this standard of conduct.

ADVANCED MIN. SYSTEMS, INC. v. FRICKE

623 A.2d 82 (Del.Ch.1992).

ALLEN, CHANCELLOR.

In this suit, Advanced Mining Systems, Inc., a Delaware corporation ("AMS"), charges Richard A. Fricke, its former President, with breaches of loyalty to the corporation while he was in office. Mr. Fricke has now moved to compel plaintiff to advance expenses reasonably incurred by him in connection with the defense of this suit. He claims a present right to the "interim advancement of indemnification payments" under Section 145 of the Delaware General Corporation Law and under AMS's by-laws. I put aside the procedural oddity of the motion and turn to a recitation of background facts that appear to be undisputed.

AMS manufactures and distributes roof-support systems for underground coal mines; fabricates related steel products and tools and dies; and operates a trucking business. It was formed in 1984 as a result of a leveraged buy-out of Republic Corporation's "Systems" division.

Richard Fricke was General Manager of one of the Republic plants that was to be spun-off in the creation of AMS. Fricke apparently was one of the promoters of the LBO. He was one of the principal shareholders of AMS, a member of its board and was designated AMS's first President. His tenure as President and director, however, ended a little more than a year later in March 1986, following his six month leave of absence from those positions. After leaving AMS's management, Mr. Fricke continued to work for the corporation as a consultant for another year. Since March 1987, his sole connection with AMS apparently has been as a shareholder.

On November 16, 1990, AMS filed the present suit against Fricke, alleging that, while he was President of the company and a director, Fricke had violated fiduciary duties he owed to the company.[2] Fricke has since filed counterclaims alleging that one Gary Lutin, together with other counterclaim defendants, primarily present or past AMS directors, attempted to force Fricke out of AMS and that, by such conduct, Lutin and the other counterclaim defendants (1) violated fiduciary duties they owed to Fricke; (2) violated AMS's by-laws; and (3) breached a Stock Purchase Agreement among Fricke, Lutin, AMS and others.

Section 145 of the Delaware General Corporation Law states the mandatory and permissive scope of indemnification by a Delaware corporation of the losses or expenses of an officer, director, employee or agent of the corporation incurred by reason of holding any such position. While the permissive authority to indemnify its directors, officers, etc., may be exercised by a corporation's board of directors on a case-by-case basis, in fact most corporations and virtually all public corporations have by by-law exercised the authority recognized by Section 145 so as to mandate the extension of indemnification rights in circumstances in which indemnification would be permissible under Section 145. Such provisions serve obvious corporate interests. *Merritt–Chapman & Scott Corp. v. Wolfson,* Del.Super., 321 A.2d 138 (1974).

---

2. Among other things, the complaint alleges that Fricke (1) used AMS employees for his personal benefit; (2) improperly extended AMS credit for his personal benefit; (3) approved the sale of assets for inadequate consideration; (4) approved improper expenses; (5) wasted assets; (6) failed to exercise honest and reasonable business judgment; and (7) refused to account fully to AMS directors. AMS seeks damages and costs and expenses, including attorneys' fees.

This motion does not involve the question whether or under what circumstances Mr. Fricke will be entitled to indemnification by AMS for his expenses in defending this suit or for the amount of any judgment entered against him. That matter will be governed by Section 145(b) and (c) of the Delaware General Corporation Law and must await a determination of the litigation.

What is involved here is the question *when* payments on account of a claim of indemnification must be made. Mr. Fricke seeks an order requiring the corporation to advance his reasonable litigation expenses now. He is willing to provide an unsecured undertaking to repay such amounts if it is ultimately found that he was not entitled to indemnification of such expenses, after the litigation is concluded. Not surprisingly, the corporation finds this an unappealing proposal. The board of directors has determined that it has discretion to decide whether such an advance should be made and that it is not in the corporation's interest to extend this credit to Mr. Fricke. Fricke contends that the corporation's by-laws legally obligate it to do so. Which view is correct is the legal issue that the motion presents.

Advancement of indemnifiable expenses is a subject treated by subsection (e) of Section 145 of our General Corporation Law. It provides, in relevant part, as follows:

§ 145. Indemnification of officers, directors, employees and agents; insurance.

. . . . .

(e) Expenses (including attorneys' fees) incurred by an officer or director defending any civil, criminal, administrative or investigative action, suit or proceeding *may be paid by the corporation in advance* of the final disposition of such action, suit or proceeding *upon receipt of an undertaking* by or on behalf of such director or officer *to repay* such amount if it shall ultimately be determined that he is not entitled to be indemnified by the corporation as authorized in this Section. (emphasis added)

With respect to indemnification rights, AMS's certificate of incorporation and by-laws provide in virtually identical language that:

The Corporation *shall indemnify* its directors, officers, employees and agents *to the extent permitted by the General Corporation Law of Delaware.* (emphasis added.)

(Charter Article TWELFTH).

Thus the question here may be restated to be whether a mandate to "indemnify" includes an obligation to advance expenses prior to a determination whether indemnification is permitted or required. In my opinion it does not.

Whether it is in a corporation's interest to indemnify a director or officer for an expense, loss or liability covered by Section 145(a) or (b) is fundamentally different from the question whether it is in the corporation's interest to advance arguably indemnifiable litigation expenses before the proceeding in which expenses are incurred has terminated. The decision to advance litigation expenses is in some respects similar to the decision to extend indemnification rights—it also might act as an incentive to serve as a director—but it is also in some respects quite different. In making a decision to advance expenses to a director or officer, the corporation is not extending the amount by which it may be legally liable, as it does when it extends indemnification rights. The right to be indemnified for expenses will exist (or will not) depending upon factors quite independent of the decision to advance expenses. Thus, the decision to extend advancement rights should ultimately give rise to no net liability on the corporation's part. The corporation maintains the right to be repaid all sums advanced, if the individual is ultimately shown not to be entitled to indemnification. Thus the advancement decision is essentially simply a decision to advance credit.

Recognizing this fact, the statute authorizes such transactions, but requires "receipt of an undertaking ... to repay ... if it shall ultimately be determined that [the individual] is not entitled to be indemnified...." This undertaking need not be secured. Section 145(e) leaves to the business judgment of the board the task of determining whether the undertaking proffered in all of the circumstances, is sufficient to protect the corporation's interest in repayment and whether, ultimately, advancement of expenses would on balance be likely to promote the corporation's interests.

A by-law mandating the advancement of funds on the receipt of an undertaking to repay deprives the board of an opportunity to evaluate the important credit aspects of a decision with respect to advancing expenses. While given the evolution of Section 145(e), I assume such a by-law would be valid, the better policy, more consistent with the provisions of Section 145(e), is to require any such by-law expressly to state its intention to mandate the advancement by the corporation of arguably indemnifiable expenses under subsection (e).

Because I consider indemnification rights and rights to advancement of possibly indemnifiable expenses to be legally quite distinct types of legal rights, I cannot conclude that the language of this by-law, which requires AMS "to indemnify," was intended to deprive the board of its function under Section 145(e) to evaluate the corporation's interest with respect to advancement of expenses. It is notable that when this by-law was adopted and when Mr. Fricke served as President of AMS, Section 145(e) stated that advancement decisions were to be made "in the specific case." Thus, as a practical matter, it is extremely unlikely that a reasonable person could then have assumed that a right to advancement in every case had been created by the AMS by-law. Moreover, even given the 1986 amendment deleting that language from the statute, I conclude that the reading that I give the words "to indemnify" in the AMS certificate and by-laws is more in keeping with the tenor of subsection (e) than the alternative interpretation would be.

No case has been cited that decides the question here presented, except *TBG, Inc. v. Bendis*, C.A. No. 89–2423–01, 1991 W.L. 34199 (D.Kan. Feb.19, 1991). I cannot accept the reasoning of that case as correct, however. There the corporation's by-laws contained a provision permitting advancement "as authorized by the board of directors in the specific case...." Notwithstanding that provision, the court held that a mandatory right of indemnification "to the full extent permitted [by the Delaware General Corporation law]" included a mandatory right to advancement. Through this broad interpretation the court negated the effect of the "specific case" by-law language. While the "specific case" requirements had been removed from the statute by the time of the TBG decision, I cannot agree that the corporation's by-laws were for that reason alone amended. * * *

Should the board of directors or shareholders, for reasons they regard as sound, wish to create a right of the type here asserted that decision may be expressed easily enough in the company's by-laws. AMS, however, has not done so in my opinion.

Therefore, the pending motion will be denied.

———

BIONDI v. BEEKMAN HILL HOUSE APT. CORP.

94 N.Y.2d 659, 709 N.Y.S.2d 861, 731 N.E.2d 577 (2000).

CIPARICK, J.

This appeal brings up for review two issues: (1) whether public policy bars a cooperative apartment corporation from indemnifying one of its directors for punitive damages imposed on the director who, in violation of various civil rights laws, denies a proposed tenant's sublease application on the basis of race and retaliates against a shareholder for opposing the denial; and (2) whether, under the same facts, Business Corporation Law § 721 bars indemnification where the underlying judgment establishes that the director acted in bad faith. We conclude that, in these circumstances, indemnification is prohibited.

Plaintiff, Nicholas Biondi, is the former president of the board of directors of defendant Beekman Hill House Apartment Corporation. In 1995, Simone Demou, a shareholder of Beekman, informed Biondi that she intended to sublease her apartment to Gregory and Shannon Broome, a financially eligible couple. Biondi assured Demou that he would meet with Gregory Broome and that, in keeping with the usual practice, a full board interview would not be required. Nevertheless, after Biondi's meeting with Gregory Broome, Beekman's managing agent advised the Broomes that a full board meeting was necessary. Prior to that meeting, Biondi informed another board member that Gregory Broome was African–American, and told yet another board member that he felt "uneasy" about him. The board unanimously denied the Broomes' application and issued a notice of default against Demou for "objectionable conduct" arising from her accusations of racism against Biondi and the board.

On January 30, 1996, Biondi, represented by Beekman's counsel, commenced a defamation action against Demou in Supreme Court. On February 2, 1996, the Broomes filed a lawsuit in the United States District Court for the Southern District of New York, alleging that Beekman and its directors (the Beekman defendants), including Biondi, violated various State and Federal civil rights laws by denying their sublease application based on Gregory Broome's race. The Beekman defendants counterclaimed against the Broomes and brought a third-party action against Demou for injurious falsehoods. Demou removed Biondi's defamation action to Federal court, consolidated it with the Broomes' Federal action and asserted counterclaims against the Beekman defendants for retaliation.

After trial, the jury found that the Beekman defendants, including Biondi both personally and in his official capacity, violated the Federal Fair Housing Act (42 USC §§ 1981, 1982) and New York Human Rights Law (Executive Law § 296 [5]). The jury awarded the Broomes $230,000 in compensatory damages and $410,000 in punitive damages, $125,000 of which was assessed individually against Biondi. As to Demou, the jury found that Biondi and the Beekman defendants violated her rights under the Federal Fair Housing Act and the New York Human Rights Law, breached their fiduciary duties to her and tortiously interfered with her sublease agreement with the Broomes. The jury awarded Demou a total of $107,000 in compensatory damages and $57,000 in punitive damages, $29,000 of which was assessed individually against Biondi.

Following the verdict, the Beekman defendants moved, in part, for a new trial. In denying the motion, the Federal District Court concluded that: (1) the evidence supporting Demou's breach of fiduciary duty claim established that "the Beekman Board members acted in bad faith and with a purpose that was not in the best interests of the cooperative"; and (2) the evidence established that the Beekman defendants acted "willfully or maliciously when they rejected the Broomes' sublet application * * * and retaliated against Demou for trying to oppose the Board's actions" (*Broome v. Biondi*, 17 F.Supp.2d 211, 220, 228 [S.D.N.Y.]). Biondi and the Beekman defendants appealed to the United States Court of Appeals for the Second Circuit. At a settlement conference, Biondi and Beekman's directors agreed to limit their liability to their respective punitive damage awards. After Biondi failed to comply with the settlement, a second conference ensued, at which the parties agreed to reduce Biondi's punitive damage contribution to $124,000.

Biondi subsequently sued Beekman for indemnification under article VII of its by-laws, and Beekman moved to dismiss Biondi's complaint for failure to state a cause of action pursuant to CPLR 3211. Supreme Court denied Beekman's motion. It held that Beekman's by-laws authorized indemnification for directors who act in good faith, and the "mere fact" that the Federal jury found Biondi liable for violating the Broomes' civil rights was not "dispositive" of that issue. It further held that the public policy prohibition against indemnification for punitive damages did not apply because the settlement agreement did not clearly identify Biondi's damages as punitive.

The Appellate Division unanimously reversed and dismissed the complaint. The Court held that Biondi's settlement agreement limited his liability to punitive damages and that indemnification for punitive damages is prohibited by public policy. The Court also held that Business Corporation Law § 721 barred indemnification, where the jury in the underlying action found that Biondi had acted in bad faith toward the Broomes and Demou. We now affirm.

Under the facts of this case, Biondi cannot obtain indemnification for the punitive damages imposed for his acts of bad faith against Beekman. In the context of insurance indemnification, "the rule to be applied with respect to a punitive damage award made in a Civil Rights Act action is that coverage is proscribed as a matter of public policy" (*Hartford Acc. & Indem. Co. v. Village of Hempstead*, 48 N.Y.2d 218, 228, 422 N.Y.S.2d 47, 397 N.E.2d 737). Indemnification "defeats the purpose of punitive damages, which is to punish and deter others from acting similarly" (*id.*, at 226, 422 N.Y.S.2d 47, 397 N.E.2d 737; *see Zurich Ins. v. Shearson Lehman Hutton*, 84 N.Y.2d 309, 316, 618 N.Y.S.2d 609, 642 N.E.2d 1065; *Home Ins. Co. v. American Home Prods. Corp.*, 75 N.Y.2d 196, 200, 551 N.Y.S.2d 481, 550 N.E.2d 930).

So too, Beekman should not bear the burden of indemnifying its director for punitive damages imposed for acts of bad faith. Biondi's racial discrimination against the Broomes and retaliation against Demou is precisely the type of conduct for which public policy should preclude indemnification. The jury in the Federal action found that Biondi willfully violated the Broomes' and Demou's civil rights, and it imposed personal liability on Biondi. Indeed, the punitive damages assessed against Biondi were greater than those against any other director, confirming that Biondi was singled out for punishment. To allow Biondi now to shift that penalty to Beekman would eviscerate the deterrent effect of punitive damages, and "violate the 'fundamental principle that no one shall be permitted to take advantage of his own wrong' " (*Public Serv. Mut. Ins. Co. v. Goldfarb*, 53 N.Y.2d 392, 400, 442 N.Y.S.2d 422, 425 N.E.2d 810, quoting *Messersmith v. American Fid. Co.*, 232 N.Y. 161, 165, 133 N.E. 432).

Although Biondi acknowledges that public policy prohibits insurer indemnification for punitive damages, he argues that the prohibition does not apply to this case because, unlike New York's Insurance Law, the Business Corporation Law evinces a clear legislative policy of indemnifying corporate directors who act in good faith. While we recognize that "our determination of public policy * * * is limited by [existing] statutes"

(*Hartford Acc. & Indem. Co. v. Village of Hempstead, supra,* 48 N.Y.2d, at 225, 422 N.Y.S.2d 47, 397 N.E.2d 737), we conclude that neither the Business Corporation Law nor Beekman's by-laws entitle Biondi to indemnification, where the underlying judgment establishes that he acted in bad faith.

Business Corporation Law § 722(a) and (c) allow corporations to indemnify directors against third-party actions and derivative suits, respectively. Section 722(a) permits indemnification against judgments, fines, settlement payments and reasonable litigation expenses, while section 722(c) limits indemnification to settlement payments and litigation expenses. In both cases, the standard of conduct is the same: a corporation may indemnify a director who acts "in good faith, *for a purpose which he reasonably believed to be in * * * the best interests of the corporation*" (Business Corporation Law § 722[a], [c] [emphasis added]). Termination of an action by a judgment or settlement does not, by itself, "create a presumption" that the standard of conduct has not been satisfied (Business Corporation Law § 722[b]).

Business Corporation Law former § 721 previously made these statutory indemnification provisions exclusive. However, in 1986, in an attempt to "attract" capable officers and directors, the Legislature amended section 721 to expand indemnification to include any additional rights conferred by a corporation in its certificate of incorporation or by-laws, provided that "no indemnification may be made to or on behalf of any director or officer *if a judgment or other final adjudication adverse to the director or officer establishes that his acts were committed in bad faith* or were the result of active and deliberate dishonesty and were material to the cause of action so adjudicated" (Business Corporation Law § 721 [emphasis added]; Governor's Approval Mem., Bill Jacket, L. 1986, ch. 513, § 1, at 9, reprinted in 1986 McKinney's Session Laws of N.Y., at 3171–3172).

While section 721's nonexclusivity language *broadens* the scope of indemnification, its "bad faith" standard manifests a public policy limitation on indemnification (*see,* Business Corporation Law former § 721 [Joint Legis Comm to Study Revision of Corporation Laws, Explanatory Mem., Bill Jacket, L. 1961, ch. 855, at 266]; Note, Rosh, *New York's Response to Director and Officer Liability Crisis: A Need to Reexamine the Importance of D & O Insurance,* 54 Brook L. Rev. 1305, 1323, 1325 [1989]; *cf., Hartford Acc. & Indem. Co. v. Village of Hempstead, supra,* 48 N.Y.2d, at 225, 422 N.Y.S.2d 47, 397 N.E.2d 737 ["good faith" language in General Municipal Law § 52, which authorizes a municipality to purchase liability insurance, suggests that the "Legislature did not contemplate insurance against punitive damages"]; *Waltuch v. Conticommodity Servs.,* 88 F.3d 87, 90–91 [2d Cir.1996] [recognizing public policy restrictions on indemnification under Delaware's analogous nonexclusivity provision]). That limitation is reflected in the statutory indemnification provisions, as well as Beekman's by-laws, both of which restrict indemnification to acts of "good faith" that are "reasonably believed to be in * * * the best interests of the corporation" (Business Corporation Law § 722[a], [c]).

With this background, we consider whether the adverse Federal judgment establishing Biondi's bad faith toward the Broomes and Demou precludes indemnification under Business Corporation Law § 721. Relying on section 722, Biondi argues that the Federal jury's finding of bad faith is not dispositive of his actions toward Beekman, and that he is entitled to prove that he acted in Beekman's interest. Beekman counters that a finding of bad faith toward a third party is, by itself, sufficient to bar indemnification under Business Corporation Law § 721.

Reading sections 721 and 722 together and applying them harmoniously and consistently as we are required to do (McKinney's Cons. Laws of N.Y., Book 1, Statutes § 221), we hold that the key to indemnification is a director's good faith *toward the corporation* and that a judgment against the director, standing alone, may not be dispositive of whether the director acted in good faith (*see,* Business Corporation Law §§ 721, 722[a], [b]; *see also, Titley v. Amerford Intl. Corp.,* 249 A.D.2d 380, 381, 671 N.Y.S.2d 497; *cf., Waltuch v. Conticommodity Servs., supra,* 88 F.3d, at 95 [no indemnification under Delaware Law for directors who fail to act in "good faith and in a manner reasonably believed to be in * * * the best interest of the corporation" (internal quotations omitted)]). However, we conclude, as a matter of law, that in this case it *is* dispositive.

Based on the entire record before us, nothing in Biondi's conduct can be construed as being undertaken in good faith, for a purpose "reasonably believed" to be in the best interests of Beekman. By intentionally denying the Broomes' sublease application on the basis of race, Biondi knowingly exposed Beekman to liability under the civil rights laws. Indeed, a Beekman board member warned Biondi that if he felt "uneasy because Mr. Broome is black, we will be sued." Biondi's willful racial discrimination cannot be considered an act in the corporation's best interest.

Nor was it in Beekman's best interest for Biondi to breach his fiduciary duty to Demou, Beekman's shareholder. The Federal District Court in the underlying action instructed the jury that if it found that "the Board members made determinations in bad faith and with a purpose that was not in the best interest of all the people they represent, then you must find that the Board breached its fiduciary duty" to Demou. The jury found that Biondi, acting in bad faith, breached his fiduciary duty to Demou. That finding was later upheld by the District Court, which denied Biondi's motion for a new trial on the ground that "the jury could reasonably find that the Beekman Board members acted in *bad faith and with a purpose that was not in the best interests of the cooperative*" (*Broome v. Biondi, supra,* 17 F.Supp.2d, at 220 [emphasis added]). Because the underlying Federal judgment establishes that Biondi's acts were committed in bad faith, Biondi is not entitled to indemnification and cannot relitigate the good faith versus bad faith issue here (Business Corporation Law § 721).

Accordingly, the order of the Appellate Division should be affirmed, with costs.

CHIEF JUDGE KAYE and JUDGES BELLACOSA, SMITH, LEVINE, WESLEY and ROSENBLATT concur.

NOTES

1. The Court in Owens Corning v. National Union Fire Ins., 257 F.3d 484, 494 (6th Cir. 2001) described the Delaware indemnification provisions as follows:

> The ability of a Delaware corporation to indemnify its directors for the consequences of their acts is constrained by Delaware's General Corporation Law § 145. This section defines a basic structure that can be modified, within limits, by the adoption of by-laws. Del.Code Ann. tit. 8, § 145(f). The basic structure has two types of indemnification, mandatory and permissive. Mandatory Indemnification for defense expenses occurs when the director is "successful on the merits or otherwise" in defense of the action brought against him. §§ 145(a),(b). It is common for corporations to adopt through their by-laws a requirement that they must (as opposed to may) reimburse directors for their costs. Owens Corning has done this. The requirement of good faith on the part of the directors indemnified under §§ 145(a),(b) however, is statutory, and cannot be waived by attempting to extend indemnification even further.

2. Corporations may seek to indemnify their officers and directors through insurance. See 8 Del. Corp. L. § 145(g). As one treatise notes:

> The Model Act empowers a corporation to purchase insurance for any director, officer, employee, or agent for any liability arising out of their corporate capacity "whether or not the corporation would have the power to indemnify him against such liability. . . . " Some states, such as New York . . . place statutory limits on the type of insurance that corporations may provide directors and officers, and, despite the broad language of the Model Act, liability insurance for gross misconduct may be void as against public policy.

> There is an inherent limit on the scope of the indemnification or insurance permissible for corporate fiduciaries. Certainly a private contract or insurance policy that provides coverage for willful or intentional violations of trust are beyond the bounds of permissible private contracting and therefore should be void as against public policy. Nowhere is this more strongly established than for cases arising from violations of the federal securities laws, where the courts consistently have held that the principle violators cannot be indemnified because such indemnification, by statute, contract, or otherwise is against the public policy of the federal securities laws. What is involved in drafting such indemnification statutes, insurance policies, and private contractual indemnification arrangements is a careful balancing of the social benefits of the public munificence of allowing the costs of breaches to be spread on a base broader than the actor's shoulders while preserving a powerful deterrent for certain categories of misbehavior.

James D. Cox & Thomas Lee Hazen, Corporations, § 15.21 (2d ed. 2003). Insurance may be expensive and limited in coverage by the insurance companies when liabilities rise. See Christopher, Oster, "Director's Insurance Fees Get Fatter," Wall St. J., July 12, 2002, at C1 (about 97 percent of public companies have D&O insurance but costs were rising and many insurance companies were dropping this line of insurance, increasing premiums and limiting coverage as corporate scandals increase; coverage may cost $20 million to $50 million per year in premiums).

3. The courts have frequently held that indemnification agreements for claims arising from the federal securities laws conflict with public policy. See e.g., Globus v. Law Research Service, Inc., 418 F.2d 1276 (2d Cir.1969). The Official Comments to Model Bus. Corp. Act § 8.51 state that indemnification is not permitted for violations of the federal securities laws and environmental laws.

4. Officers and directors may also receive advancements from the corporation to pay their attorney fees and other legal expenses. Citadel Holding Corp. v. Roven, 603 A.2d 818 (Del. 1992).

5. Managers of limited liability companies may also be the subject of indemnification. See Senior Tour Players 207 Management Company LLC v. Golftown, 207 Holding Co. LLC (Del Ch. 2004) (describing indemnification provisions for LLCs under Delaware law).

CHAPTER 22

CORPORATE FINANCE—AN INTRODUCTION

■ ■ ■

SECTION 1. SOME ACCOUNTING BASICS

The accounting profession has a long history. Ancient Egypt used accounting systems for its storehouses, and the Babylonians were "obsessive bookkeepers." *Michael Chatfield, A History of Accounting Thought* 5 (1974). The double entry accounting method was in use in Europe when Christopher Columbus sailed for America, a voyage on which he was accompanied by an accountant. Accounting as a profession was brought from Scotland and England to America by chartered accountants in those countries. They would form what became some of the largest accounting firms in America. The profession of accounting was furthered by the passage of statutes such as the one enacted in New York in 1896 that created a class of "certified public accountants" who were required to pass rigorous exams. I *Jerry W. Markham, A Financial History of the United States, From Christopher Columbus to the Robber Barons (1492–1900)* 8, 15, 334–35 (2002).

ULTRAMARES CORPORATION v. TOUCHE

255 N.Y. 170, 174 N.E. 441 (1931).

CARDOZO, C. J.

The action is in tort for damages suffered through the misrepresentations of accountants, the first cause of action being for misrepresentations that were merely negligent, and the second for misrepresentations charged to have been fraudulent.

In January, 1924, the defendants, a firm of public accountants, were employed by Fred Stern & Co., Inc., to prepare and certify a balance sheet exhibiting the condition of its business as of December 31, 1923. They had been employed at the end of each of the three years preceding to render a like service. Fred Stern & Co., Inc., which was in substance Stern himself, was engaged in the importation and sale of rubber. To finance its operations, it required extensive credit and borrowed large sums of money from banks and other lenders. All this was known to the defendants. The defendants knew also that in the usual course of business the balance sheet when certified would be exhibited by the Stern Company to banks, creditors, stockholders, purchasers, or sellers, according to the needs of the occasion, as the basis of financial dealings. Accordingly, when the balance sheet was made up, the defendants supplied the Stern Company with thirty-two copies certified with serial numbers as counterpart originals. Nothing was said as to the persons to whom these counterparts would be shown or the extent or number of the transactions in which they would be used. In particular there was no mention of the plaintiff, a corporation doing business chiefly as a factor, which till then had never made advances to the Stern Company, though it had sold merchandise in small amounts. The range of the transactions in which a certificate of audit might be expected to play a part was as indefinite and wide as the possibilities of the business that was mirrored in the summary.

By February 26, 1924, the audit was finished and the balance sheet made up. It stated assets in the sum of $2,550,671.88 and liabilities other than capital and surplus in the sum of $1,479,956.62, thus showing a net worth of $1,070,715.26. Attached to the balance sheet was a certificate as follows:

'Touche, Niven & Co.
'Public Accountants
'Eighty Maiden Lane
'New York
'February 26, 1924.
'Certificate of Auditors

'We have examined the accounts of Fred Stern & Co., Inc., for the year ending December 31, 1923, and hereby certify that the annexed balance sheet is in accordance therewith and with the information and explanations given us. We further certify that, subject to provision for federal taxes on income, the said statement, in our opinion, presents a true and correct view of the financial condition of Fred Stern & Co., Inc., as at December 31, 1923.

'Touche, Niven & Co.'Public Accountants.'

Capital and surplus were intact if the balance sheet was accurate. In reality both had been wiped out, and the corporation was insolvent. The books had been falsified by those in charge of the business so as to set forth accounts receivable and other assets which turned out to be fictitious. The plaintiff maintains that the certificate of audit was erroneous in both its branches. The first branch, the asserted correspondence between the accounts and the balance sheet, is one purporting to be made as of the knowledge of the auditors. The second branch, which certifies to a belief that the condition reflected in the balance sheet presents a true and correct picture of the resources of the business, is stated as a matter of opinion. In the view of the plaintiff, both branches of the certificate are either fraudulent or negligent. As to one class of assets, the item of accounts receivable, if not also as to others, there was no real correspondence, we are told, between balance sheet and books, or so the triers of the facts might find. If correspondence, however, be assumed, a closer examination of supporting invoices and records, or a fuller inquiry directed to the persons appearing on the books as creditors or debtors, would have exhibited the truth.

The plaintiff, a corporation engaged in business as a factor, was approached by Stern in March, 1924, with a request for loans of money to finance the sales of rubber. Up to that time the dealings between the two houses were on a cash basis and trifling in amount. As a condition of any loans the plaintiff insisted that it receive a balance sheet certified by public accountants, and in response to that demand it was given one of the certificates signed by the defendants and then in Stern's possession. On the faith of that certificate the plaintiff made a loan which was followed by many others. The course of business was for Stern to deliver to the plaintiff documents described as trust receipts which in effect were executory assignments of the moneys payable by purchasers for goods thereafter to be sold. When the purchase price was due, the plaintiff received the payment, reimbursing itself therefrom for its advances and commissions. Some of these transactions were effected without loss. Nearly a year later, in December, 1924, the house of cards collapsed. In that month, plaintiff made three loans to the Stern Company, one of $100,000, a second of $25,000, and a third of $40,000. For some of these loans no security was received. For some of the earlier loans the security was inadequate. On January 2, 1925, the Stern Company was declared a bankrupt.

This action, brought against the accountants in November, 1926, to recover the loss suffered by the plaintiff in reliance upon the audit, was in its inception one for negligence. On the trial there was added a second cause of action asserting fraud also. The trial judge dismissed the second cause of action without submitting it to the jury. As to the first cause of action, he reserved his decision on the defendants' motion to dismiss, and took the jury's verdict. They were told that the defendants might be held liable if with knowledge that the results of the audit would be communicated to creditors they did the work negligently, and that negligence was the omission to use reasonable and ordinary care. The verdict was in favor of the plaintiff for $187,576.32. On the coming in of the verdict, the judge granted the reserved motion. The Appellate Division (229 App. Div. 581, 243 N. Y. S. 179) affirmed the dismissal of the cause of action for fraud, but reversed the dismissal of the cause of action for negligence, and reinstated the verdict.

The case is here on cross-appeals. The two causes of action will be considered in succession, first the one for negligence and second that for fraud.

1. We think the evidence supports a finding that the audit was negligently made, though in so saying we put aside for the moment the question whether negligence, even if it existed, was a wrong to the

plaintiff. To explain fully or adequately how the defendants were at fault would carry this opinion beyond reasonable bounds. A sketch, however, there must be, at least in respect of some features of the audit, for the nature of the fault, when understood, is helpful in defining the ambit of the duty. We begin with the item of accounts receivable. At the start of the defendant's audit, there had been no posting of the general ledger since April, 1923. Siess, a junior accountant, was assigned by the defendants to the performance of that work. On Sunday, February 3, 1924, he had finished the task of posting, and was ready the next day to begin with his associates the preparation of the balance sheet and the audit of its items. The total of the accounts receivable for December, 1923, as thus posted by Siess from the entries in the journal, was $644,758.17. At some time on February 3, Romberg, an employee of the Stern Company, who had general charge of its accounts, placed below that total another item to represent additional accounts receivable growing out of the transactions of the month. This new item, $706,843.07, Romberg entered in his own handwriting. The sales that it represented were, each and all, fictitious. Opposite the entry were placed other figures (12–29), indicating or supposed to indicate a reference to the journal. Siess when he resumed his work saw the entries thus added, and included the new item in making up his footings, with the result of an apparent increase of over $700,000 in the assets of the business. He says that in doing this he supposed the entries to be correct, and that, his task at the moment being merely to post the books, he thought the work of audit or verification might come later, and put it off accordingly. The time sheets, which are in evidence, show very clearly that this was the order of time in which the parts of the work were done. Verification, however, there never was either by Siess or by his superiors, or so the triers of the facts might say. If any had been attempted, or any that was adequate, an examiner would have found that the entry in the ledger was not supported by any entry in the journal. If from the journal he had gone to the book from which the journal was made up, described as 'the debit memo book,' support would still have failed. Going farther, he would have found invoices, seventeen in number, which amounted in the aggregate to the interpolated item, but scrutiny of these invoices would have disclosed suspicious features in that they had no shipping number nor a customer's order number and varied in terms of credit and in other respects from those usual in the business. A mere glance reveals the difference.

The December entry of accounts receivable was not the only item that a careful and skillful auditor would have desired to investigate. There was ground for suspicion as to an item of $113,199.60, included in the accounts payable as due from the Baltic Corporation. As to this the defendants received an explanation, not very convincing, from Stern and Romberg. A cautious auditor might have been dissatisfied and have uncovered what was wrong. There was ground for suspicion also because of the inflation of the inventory. The inventory as it was given to the auditors, was totaled at $347,219.08. The defendants discovered errors in the sum of

$303,863.20, and adjusted the balance sheet accordingly. Both the extent of the discrepancy and its causes might have been found to cast discredit upon the business and the books. There was ground for suspicion again in the record of assigned accounts. Inquiry of the creditors gave notice to the defendants that the same accounts had been pledged to two, three, and four banks at the same time. The pledges did not diminish the value of the assets, but made in such circumstances they might well evoke a doubt as to the solvency of a business where such conduct was permitted. There was an explanation by Romberg which the defendants accepted as sufficient. Caution and diligence might have pressed investigation farther.

If the defendants owed a duty to the plaintiff to act with the same care that would have been due under a contract of employment, a jury was at liberty to find a verdict of negligence upon a showing of a scrutiny so imperfect and perfunctory. No doubt the extent to which inquiry must be pressed beyond appearances is a question of judgment, as to which opinions will often differ. No doubt the wisdom that is born after the event will engender suspicion and distrust when old acquaintance and good repute may have silenced doubt at the beginning. All this is to be weighed by a jury in applying its standard of behavior, the state of mind, and conduct of the reasonable man. Even so, the adverse verdict, when rendered, imports an alignment of the weights in their proper places in the balance and a reckoning thereafter. The reckoning was not wrong upon the evidence before us, if duty be assumed.

We are brought to the question of duty, its origin and measure. The defendants owed to their employer a duty imposed by law to make their certificate without fraud, and a duty growing out of contract to make it with the care and caution proper to their calling. Fraud includes the pretense of knowledge when knowledge there is none. To creditors and investors to whom the employer exhibited the certificate, the defendants owed a like duty to make it without fraud, since there was notice in the circumstances of its making that the employer did not intend to keep it to himself. Eaton, Cole & Burnham Co. v. Avery, 83 N. Y. 31, 38 Am. Rep. 389; Tindle v. Birkett, 171 N. Y. 520, 64 N. E. 210, 89 Am. St. Rep. 822. A different question develops when we ask whether they owed a duty to these to make it without negligence. If liability for negligence exists, a thoughtless slip or blunder, the failure to detect a theft or forgery beneath the cover of deceptive entries, may expose accountants to a liability in an indeterminate amount for an indeterminate time to an indeterminate class. The hazards of a business conducted on these terms are so extreme as to enkindle doubt whether a flaw may not exist in the implication of a duty that exposes to these consequences. We put aside for the moment any statement in the certificate which involves the representation of a fact as true to the knowledge of the auditors. If such a statement was made, whether believed to be true or not, the defendants are liable for deceit in the event that it was false. The plaintiff does not need the invention of novel doctrine to help it out in such conditions. The case was submitted to the jury, and the verdict was returned upon the theory that, even in the absence of a misstatement of a fact, there is a liability also for erroneous opinion. The expression of an opinion is to be subject to a warranty implied by law. What, then, is the warranty, as yet unformulated, to be? Is it merely that the opinion is honestly conceived and that the preliminary inquiry has been honestly pursued, that a halt has not been made without a genuine belief that the search has been reasonably adequate to bring disclosure of the truth? Or does it go farther and involve the assumption of a liability for any blunder or inattention that could fairly be spoken of as negligence if the controversy were one between accountant and employer for breach of a contract to render services for pay? * * *

No one would be likely to urge that there was a contractual relation, or even one approaching it, at the root of any duty that was owing from the defendants now before us to the indeterminate class of persons who, presently or in the future, might deal with the Stern Company in reliance on the audit. * * * In the case at hand, the service was primarily for the benefit of the Stern Company, a convenient instrumentality for use in the development of the business, and only incidentally or collaterally for the use of those to whom Stern and his associates might exhibit it hereafter. Foresight of these possibilities may charge with liability for fraud. The conclusion does not follow that it will charge with liability for negligence.

* * * [t]he conclusion is, we think, inevitable that nothing in our previous decisions commits us to a holding of liability for negligence in the circumstances of the case at hand, and that such liability, if recognized, will be an extension of the principle of those decisions to different conditions, even if more or less analogous. The question then is whether such an extension shall be made.

The extension, if made, will so expand the field of liability for negligent speech as to make it nearly, if not quite, coterminous with that of liability for fraud. Again and again, in decisions of this court, the bounds of this latter liability have been set up, with futility the fate of every endeavor to dislodge them. Scienter has been declared to be an indispensable element, except where the representation has been put forward as true of one's own knowledge (Hadcock v. Osmer, 153 N. Y. 604, 47 N. E. 923), or in circumstances where the expression of opinion was a dishonorable pretense (3 Williston, Contracts, § 1494; Smith v. Land & House Property Corporation, [L. R.] 28 Ch. Div. 7, 15; * * *

Liability for negligence if adjudged in this case will extend to many callings other than an auditor's. Lawyers who certify their opinion as to the validity of municipal or corporate bonds, with knowledge that the opinion will be brought to the notice of the public, will become liable to the investors, if they have overlooked a statute or a decision, to the same extent as if the controversy were one between client and adviser. Title companies insuring titles to a tract of land, with knowledge that at an approaching auction the fact that they have insured will be stated to the bidders, will become liable to purchasers who may wish the benefit of a policy without payment of a premium. These illustrations may seem to be extreme, but they go little, if any, farther than we are invited to go now. Negligence, moreover, will have one standard when viewed in relation to the employer, and another and at times a stricter standard when viewed in relation to the public. Explanations that might seem plausible, omissions that might be reasonable, if the duty is confined to the employer, conducting a business that presumably at least is not a fraud upon his creditors, might wear another aspect if an independent duty to be suspicious even of one's principal is owing to investors. 'Every one making a promise having the quality of a contract will be under a duty to the promisee by virtue of the promise, but under another duty, apart from contract, to an indefinite number of potential beneficiaries when performance has begun. The assumption of one relation will mean the involuntary assumption of a series of new relations, inescapably hooked together' Moch Co. v. Rensselaer Water Co., supra, at page 168 of 247 N. Y., 159 N. E. 896, 899. 'The law does not spread its protection so far' Robins Dry Dock & Repair Co. v. Flint, supra, at page 309 of 275 U.S.

Our holding does not emancipate accountants from the consequences of fraud. It does not relieve them if their audit has been so negligent as to justify a finding that they had no genuine belief in its adequacy, for this again is fraud. It does no more than say that, if less than this is proved, if there has been neither reckless misstatement nor insincere profession of an opinion, but only honest blunder, the ensuing liability for negligence is one that is bounded by the contract, and is to be enforced between the parties by whom the contract has been made. We doubt whether the average business man receiving a certificate without paying for it, and receiving it merely as one among a multitude of possible investors, would look for anything more.

2. The second cause of action is yet to be considered. The defendants certified as a fact, true to their own knowledge, that the balance sheet was in accordance with the books of account. If their statement was false, they are not to be exonerated because they believed it to be true. Hadcock v. Osmer, supra; Lehigh Zinc & Iron Co. v. Bamford, 150 U. S. 665, 673, 14 S. Ct. 219, 37 L. Ed. 1215; Chatham Furnace Co. v. Moffatt, 147 Mass. 403, 18 N. E. 168, 9 Am. St. Rep. 727; Arnold v. Richardson, 74 App. Div. 581, 77 N.Y.S. 763. We think the triers of the facts might hold it to be false.

Correspondence between the balance sheet and the books imports something more, or so the triers of the facts might say, than correspondence between the balance sheet and the general ledger, unsupported or even contradicted by every other record. The correspondence to be of any moment may not unreasonably be held to signify a correspondence between the statement and the books of original entry, the books taken as a whole. If that is what the certificate means, a jury could find that the correspondence did not exist, and that the defendants signed the certificates without knowing it to exist and even without reasonable grounds for belief in its existence. The item of $706,000, representing fictitious accounts receivable, was entered in the ledger after defendant's employee

Siess had posted the December sales. He knew of the interpolation, and knew that there was need to verify the entry by reference to books other than the ledger before the books could be found to be in agreement with the balance sheet. The evidence would sustain a finding that this was never done. By concession the interpolated item had no support in the journal, or in any journal voucher, or in the debit memo book, which was a summary of the invoices, or in any thing except the invoices themselves. The defendants do not say that they ever looked at the invoices, seventeen in number, representing these accounts. They profess to be unable to recall whether they did so or not. They admit, however, that, if they had looked, they would have found omissions and irregularities so many and unusual as to have called for further investigation. When we couple the refusal to say that they did look with the admission that, if they had looked, they would or could have seen, the situation is revealed as one in which a jury might reasonably find that in truth they did not look, but certified the correspondence without testing its existence.

In this connection we are to bear in mind the principle already stated in the course of this opinion that negligence or blindness, even when not equivalent to fraud, is none the less evidence to sustain an inference of fraud. At least this is so if the negligence is gross. Not a little confusion has at times resulted from an undiscriminating quotation of statements in Kountze v. Kennedy, supra, statements proper enough in their setting, but capable of misleading when extracted and considered by themselves. 'Misjudgment, however gross,' it was there observed, 'or want of caution, however marked, is not fraud.' This was said in a case where the trier of the facts had held the defendants guiltless. The judgment in this court amounted merely to a holding that a finding of fraud did not follow as an inference of law. There was no holding that the evidence would have required a reversal of the judgment if the finding as to guilt had been the other way. Even Derry v. Peek, as we have seen, asserts the probative effect of negligence as an evidentiary fact. We had no thought in Kountze v. Kennedy, of upholding a doctrine more favorable to wrongdoers, though there was a reservation suggesting the approval of a rule more rigorous. The opinion of this court cites Derry v. Peek, and states the holding there made that an action would not lie if the defendant believed the representation made by him to be true, although without reasonable cause for such belief. 'It is not necessary,' we said, 'to go to this extent to uphold the present judgment, for the referee, as has been stated, found that the belief of Kennedy * * * was based upon reasonable grounds.' The setting of the occasion justified the inference that the representations did not involve a profession of knowledge as distinguished from belief. 147 N.Y. at page 133, 41 N.E. 414, 29 L.R.A. 360, 49 Am. St. Rep. 651. No such charity of construction exonerates accountants, who by the very nature of their calling profess to speak with knowledge when certifying to an agreement between the audit and the entries.

The defendants attempt to excuse the omission of an inspection of the invoices proved to be fictitious by invoking a practice known as that of testing and sampling. A random choice of accounts is made from the total number on the books, and these, if found to be regular when inspected and investigated, are taken as a fair indication of the quality of the mass. The defendants say that about 200 invoices were examined in accordance with this practice, but they do not assert that any of the seventeen invoices supporting the fictitious sales were among the number so selected. Verification by test and sample was very likely a sufficient audit as to accounts regularly entered upon the books in the usual course of business. It was plainly insufficient, however, as to accounts not entered upon the books where inspection of the invoices was necessary, not as a check upon accounts fair upon their face, but in order to ascertain whether there were any accounts at all. If the only invoices inspected were invoices unrelated to the interpolated entry, the result was to certify a correspondence between the books and the balance sheet without any effort by the auditors, as to $706,000 of accounts, to ascertain whether the certified agreement was in accordance with the truth. How far books of account fair upon their face are to be probed by accountants, in an effort to ascertain whether the transactions back of them are in accordance with the entries, involves to some extent the exercise of judgment and discretion. Not so, however, the inquiry whether the entries certified as there, are there in very truth, there in the form and in the places where men of business training would expect them to be. The defendants were put on their guard by the circumstances touching the December accounts receivable to scrutinize with special care. A jury might find that, with suspicions thus awakened, they closed their eyes to the obvious, and blindly gave assent.

We conclude, to sum up the situation, that in certifying to the correspondence between balance sheet and accounts the defendants made a statement as true to their own knowledge, when they had, as a jury might find, no knowledge on the subject. If that is so, they may also be found to have acted without information leading to a sincere or genuine belief when they certified to an opinion that the balance sheet faithfully reflected the condition of the business.

Whatever wrong was committed by the defendants was not their personal act or omission, but that of their subordinates. This does not relieve them, however, of liability to answer in damages for the consequences of the wrong, if wrong there shall be found to be. It is not a question of constructive notice, as where facts are brought home to the knowledge of subordinates whose interests are adverse to those of the employer. Henry v. Allen, 151 N.Y. 1, 45 N.E. 355, 36 L.R.A. 658; see, however, American Law Institute, Restatement of the Law of Agency, § 506, subd. 2–a. These subordinates, so far as the record shows, had no interests adverse to the defendants', nor any thought in what they did to be unfaithful to their trust. The question is merely this, whether the defendants, having delegated the performance of this work to agents of their own selection, are responsible for the manner in which the business of the agency was done. As to that the answer is not doubtful. Fifth

Avenue Bank of New York v. Forty–Second St. & G. St. Ferry R. R. Co., 137 N. Y. 231, 33 N. E. 378; Gleason v. Seaboard Air Line Ry. Co., 278 U. S. 349, 356; American Law Institute, Restatement of the Law of Agency, § 481. * * *

POUND, CRANE, LEHMAN, KELLOGG, O'BRIEN, and HUBBS, JJ., concur.

Judgment accordingly.

NOTES

1. Following the decision in *Ultramares*, other courts declared that they were willing to expand accountant's liability to third parties for mere negligence where it was foreseeable to the auditors that the third party would rely on the statements they certified. The development of common law liability for auditor negligence is described in Bily v. Arthur Young & Co., 3 Cal.4th 370, 11 Cal.Rptr.2d 51, 834 P.2d 745 (1992).

2. The role of accountants was expanded by the adoption of the federal securities laws, which required publicly owned companies to publish certified accounting statements. This led to attempts to impose liability on accountants under those laws. Accountants were often the target, as the "deep pocket," when companies failed. The accounting profession fought off those efforts first in their challenges to liability based on negligence in their audits. Ernst & Ernst v. Hochfelder, 425 U.S. 185, 96 S.Ct. 1375, 47 L.Ed.2d 668 (1976). Further protection was received when the Supreme Court rejected private rights of action for aiding and abetting on the part of professionals such as accountants and lawyers. Central Bank v. First Interstate Bank, 511 U.S. 164, 114 S.Ct. 1439, 128 L.Ed.2d 119 (1994).

3. The SEC has deferred for the most part to the accounting profession in developing what are called "generally accepted accounting principles" or "GAAP." GAAP is not a set of rigid rules but simply a set of practices that are generally accepted by the accounting profession in determining appropriate methodology or how to account for particular items. 2 Thomas L. Hazen, Treatise on the Law of Securities Regulation § 9.6 (4th ed.2002). Those principles must, however, be consistently applied. The Financial Accounting Standards Board ("FASB"), an industry group that works with the SEC, has taken the lead in developing or changing particular GAP standards. See generally Marshall S. Armstrong, "The Work and Workings of the Financial Accounting Standards Board," 29 Bus. Law. 145 (1974). The SEC may, however, impose particular standards in its filings by rule and issues Accounting Series Releases on matters it deems are not adequately addressed by the accounting profession. The American Institute of Certified Public Accountants ("AICPA") sets generally accepted auditing standards ("GAAS").

4. The SEC is not entirely deferential to the accounting industry. Regulation S–X imposed various accounting requirements in public offerings. 17 C.F.R. §§ 210.1 *et seq*. The SEC further assumed the authority to discipline accountants that failed to meet what the SEC deemed are appropriate auditing standards. 17 C.F.R. § 210.102(e). Section 10A of the Securities Exchange Act of 1934 requires audits to be conducted in accordance with GAAP and GAAS. Independent auditors are also required to conduct their

audits in a way that will uncover illegal activities and to report such conduct to management and to the board of directors if management fails to act. The board of directors must then report the violative activity to the SEC or, if it fails to do so, the auditor must inform the SEC. 15 U.S.C. § 78j–1.

5. The SEC has also adopted rules that sought to assure auditor competency and independence from audit clients. 17 C.F.R. § 210.2–01(b). Those independence standards were questioned after the SEC discovered that numerous partners in audit firms held stock in their audit clients. The SEC found in one large accounting firm that thirty one of the top forty-three partners held stock in audit clients. A total of 8,000 violations of independence standards were found by partners and employees of the accounting firm. III *Jerry W. Markham, A Financial History of the United States, From the Age of Derivatives to the New Millennium (1970–2001)* 257 (2002). Consulting operations created by accounting firms were also creating conflicts. In announcing proposals to strengthen the independence of auditors, the SEC noted that:

> Independent auditors have an important public trust. Every day, millions of people invest their savings in our securities markets in reliance on financial statements prepared by public companies and audited by independent auditors. These auditors, using Generally Accepted Auditing Standards ("GAAS"), examine issuers' financial statements and issue opinions about whether the financial statements, taken as a whole, are fairly presented in conformity with Generally Accepted Accounting Principles ("GAAP"). While an auditor's opinion does not guarantee the accuracy of financial statements, it furnishes investors with critical assurance that the financial statements have been subjected to a rigorous examination by an impartial and skilled professional and that investors can therefore rely on them. Providing that assurance to the public is the auditor's over-arching duty.

> Investors must be able to put their faith in issuers' financial statements. If investors do not believe that the auditor is truly independent from the issuer, they will derive little confidence from the auditor's opinion and will be far less likely to invest in the issuer's securities. Fostering investor confidence, therefore, requires not only that auditors actually be independent of their audit clients, but also that reasonable investors perceive them to be independent.

> One of our missions is to promote investor confidence in the reliability and integrity of issuers' financial statements. To promote investor confidence, we must ensure that our auditor independence requirements remain relevant, effective, and fair in light of significant changes in the profession, structural reorganizations of accounting firms, and demographic changes in society. Some of the important developments in each of these areas since we last amended our auditor independence requirements in 1983 include the following:

>> — Firms are becoming primarily business advisory service firms as they increase the number, revenues from, and types of non-audit services provided to audit clients,

— Firms and their audit clients are entering into an increasing number of business relationships, such as strategic alliances, co-marketing arrangements, and joint ventures,

— Firms are divesting significant portions of their consulting practices or restructuring their organizations,

— Firms are offering ownership of parts of their practices to the public, including audit clients,

— Firms are in need of increased capital to finance the growth of consulting practices, new technology, training, and large unfunded pension obligations,

— Firms have merged, resulting in increased firm size, both domestically and internationally,

— Firms have expanded into international networks, affiliating and marketing under a common name,

— Non-CPA financial service firms have acquired accounting firms, and the acquirors previously have not been subject to the profession's independence, auditing, or quality control standards,

— Firms' professional staffs have become more mobile, and geographical location has become less important due to advances in telecommunications and internet services, and

— Audit clients are hiring an increasing number of firm partners, professional staff, and their spouses for high level management positions.

Proposed Rules, Securities Exchange Act Release No. 42994 (July 12, 2000). The SEC thereafter adopted rules to reflect these changes which, among other things, clarified the circumstances under which an auditor would retain independence in light of investments by auditors or their family members in audit clients, employment relationships between auditors or their family members and audit clients, and the scope of services provided by audit firms to their audit clients. The rules identified certain non-audit services that could impair the auditor's independence. Revision of the Commission's Auditor Independence Requirements, Securities Exchange Act Release No. 43602 (Nov. 21, 2000). Some large accounting firms spun off consulting services. Accenture was one such spin off, and IBM purchased the consulting operations of another giant accounting firm. William Bulkeley & Kemba Dunham, "IBM Speeds Move to Consulting With $3.5 Billion Acquisition," Wall St. J., July 31, 2002, at A1.

6. The accounting profession took a severe blow to its prestige in the wake of the bankruptcy of the Enron Corporation in 2001. It was one of the largest companies ever to fail in the United States. Enron's auditor, Arthur Andersen, LLP, was indicted and later convicted of obstructing justice in an effort to cover up some questionable auditing practices that allowed Enron to keep debt off its balance sheet and to increase income through certain special purpose entities that failed to meet the requirements for such activities. *See generally Report of Investigation by the Special Investigative Committee of the Board of Directors of Enron Corp.* (Feb. 1, 2002) (describing accounting short

cuts taken by Enron). Arthur Andersen had also been found liable in some earlier accounting scandals, and the firm was destroyed. *See generally* Flynn McRoberts, "Verdict no Boon for Enron Plaintiffs," Chicago Tribune, June 18, 2002, at 1 (describing effects of conviction for obstructing justice). A number of other firms were found after the Enron debacle to have engaged in various questionable accounting practices. Several energy companies were involved in "round trip" trades that artificially increased their income by billions of dollars; and Global Crossing Ltd., a large telecommunications firm declared bankruptcy after an accounting scandal. It was followed by World-Com, Inc., which had improperly hidden $9 billion in expenses. The bankruptcy of WorldCom was the largest such event in United States history, superseding Enron for that dubious honor. Greg Hitt, "Bush Signs Sweeping Legislation Aimed at Curbing Corporate Fraud," Wall St. J., July, 31, 2002, at A4. Congress responded with the Sarbanes–Oxley Act of 2000. This legislation created a new public regulatory organization (the "Public Company Accounting Oversight Board") that took control of accounting standards away from the auditing profession. Accountants certifying the financial standards of public companies were required to register with the board and conform to its standards. Accountants were also prohibited from offering certain consulting services to their audit clients. Pub. L. No. 107–204, 107th Cong. 2d Sess. (2002).

7. Auditing in all events is not a precise science. As noted in one court's opinion:

> "Inherent in rendering an audit opinion is the recognition that financial statements cannot 'precisely' or 'exactly' present financial position, results of operations and cash flows. Such precision is unattainable. . . ." Consequently, an accountant's opinion that "the financial statements fairly present the financial condition of the Company in accordance with generally accepted accounting principles" is not the same as stating that everything in the financial statement is perfect; rather, it means the financial statements are materially accurate and provide sufficient disclosure to users of the financial statements. "Materiality is 'the magnitude of an omission or misstatement of accounting information that, in the light of surrounding circumstances, makes it probable that the judgment of a reasonable person relying on the information would have been changed or influenced by the omission or misstatement.' " "A concept of materiality is a practical necessity in both auditing and accounting. Allowing immaterial items to complicate and clutter up the auditing process or financial statements is uneconomical and diverts users' attention from significant matters in the financial statements."

Koch v. Koch Industries, 969 F.Supp. 1460, 1558–59 (D.Kan.1997) (citations omitted).

Accounting Principles and Practices

Before World War I accounting doctrine was based on the precept of "anticipate no profits and provide for all possible losses." This principle of conservatism required assets to be carried on the balance sheet at their historical cost rather than their market value. Transactions had to be accounted for on a cash basis. These conservative principles came under criticism during the inflationary period of the 1920s, but gained favor again during the deflation that occurred during the Great Depression. Modern accounting, however, shifted its focus to the income statement, which led to "accrual" accounting. Accrual accounting requires a corporation to recognize revenues when earned and liabilities when incurred. This means that income must be recorded when a sale is made (i.e., when the goods are transferred or services rendered) even if cash is not received until later. See generally In re Clinger & Co., Securities Exchange Act Release No. 393390 (S.E.C. 1997) ("The accrual method of accounting requires that revenue be recognized when the earnings process is complete and an exchange has taken place, as opposed to the 'cash' method of accounting, which allows for revenue recognition only when a cash payment is actually received.").

To illustrate, a computer is sold and delivered to a customer on December 1, 2001 for $2,500. The transaction was on credit, and payment was not actually received until January 1, 2002. Under the accrual method, the sale occurred on December 1, 2001. The theory is that to record the sale on January 1, 2002 would distort the corporation's accounting picture, i.e., shareholders would think that the sale was actually made in 2002 rather than 2001, thereby understating sales in 2001 and overstating in 2002. Under the cash method, the sale would nevertheless have been recorded in 2002. Liabilities are treated similarly under the accrual method. For example, taxes are treated as an expense for the period incurred even if they are not paid until later. In other words, expenses are matched to the period where the sales were made to which those expenses are attributed. This conforms to another accounting assumption, i.e., accounting reports are for a specific time period (in the case of an income statement) or just a "snapshot" on a particular day (as in the case of a balance sheet).

Accounting standards change from time-to-time, *albeit* slowly. The manner in which derivative instruments such as swaps were to be treated for accounting purposes was a contentious issue that took some time to resolve. The matter became more urgent after several large corporations lost millions of dollars as a result of derivative transactions that were not disclosed on their balance sheets. See Jerry W. Markham, " 'Confederate Bonds,' 'General Custer,' and the Regulation of Derivative Financial Instruments," 25 Seton Hall Law Review 1 (1994) (describing losses from derivative instruments). To remedy that situation more disclosure was required in the footnotes to the balance sheet, but concerns continued. Finally, Financial Accounting Standard Board ("FASB") Statement of Financial Accounting Standards No. 133, effective 15 June 2000, required corporations to recognize derivatives as either assets or liabilities at their fair value. The corporation must disclose its purpose in entering into the derivative transactions and its management policies for managing the risks associated with derivatives.

Another contentious issue that arose after the Enron bankruptcy was the accounting treatment for options given to corporate executives. This compensation was not being expensed, causing much criticism because many companies were paying executives large sums without accounting recognition of this income as a cost to the corporation. After this controversy arose, some companies voluntarily agreed to expense these options in the future, but others wanted to maintain their off-balance sheet status so that they could use options to attract talented employees without impairing their profits. See generally "Stock Market Falters but Has Gain for Week," L.A. Times, Aug. 4, 2002, § 3, at 2 (noting that Coca Cola, General Electric and Amazon.com decided to expense options, while other companies refused to do so because of concern of the effect on profits).

NOTES

1. A basic practice for accountants is the use of so-called "T" accounts that provide for double entries to record accounting events. Assume that a corporation has received a cash payment of $1,000 from one of it accounts receivable. That transaction might be recorded in two T accounts as follows:

Smith Account Receivable		Cash Received	
Debit*	Credit	Debit*	Credit
	$1,000	$1,000	

* In this example, the Smith account receivable account had previously been credited with a $1000 credit as a result of a purchase by Smith.

The account receivable has been debited on the left side with $1,000 and the corporation's cash account has been credited on the right side with the same $1,000, hence the double entry. When a new account receivable amount owed by Smith is created, the Smith Account Receivable T account is credited with that amount and a goods sold or similar T account will be debited. The T account entries are then posted to ledgers that record all accounts receivable and cash accounts. The ledgers are used to create the balance sheet.

2. The following warning should be heeded:

Watch Those Footnotes

The annual reports of many companies contain this statement: "The accompanying footnotes are an integral part of the financial statements." The reason is that the financial reports themselves are kept concise and condensed. Therefore, any explanatory matter that cannot readily be abbreviated is set out in greater detail in footnotes. * * *

Most people do not like to read footnotes because they may be complicated and are almost always hard to read. That's too bad, because footnotes are very informative. Even if they don't reveal that the corporation has been forced into bankruptcy, footnotes can still reveal many fascinating sidelights on the financial story.

Merrill Lynch, How to Read a Financial Report 26 (1990).

3.   Keep in mind that "legal" accounting requirements for dividends and other purposes under state corporation laws may vary from GAAP or accounting terminology.

SECTION 2.   DIVIDENDS

State corporate laws govern the conditions under which dividends may be declared. The board of directors has the discretion to declare dividends only if those statutory conditions are met. State corporate statutes using a "balance sheet test" variously required dividends to be paid out of retained earnings (profits) or prohibited payment of dividends out of stated capital (the par value of the company's stock) See e.g., Cal. Gen. Corp. Law § 500 (limiting dividends from retained earnings); 8 Del. §§ 154 & 170 (dividends payable out of excess of net assets (assets minus liabilities) over stated capital); N.Y. Business Corp. L. § 510 (net assets must equal stated capital after payment of dividend). States using these tests view payments to shareholders from sources other than surplus as a liquidation of at least a part of the company. Such liquidating distributions could affect the rights of creditors, as well as varying classes of shareholders. See generally Wood v. Dummer, 30 Fed. Cas. 435 (C.C.D.Me. 1824) (the capital of a corporation "is deemed a pledge or trust fund for the payment of debts"). This is why restrictions were placed on those distributions. In employing these tests, however, the valuation of assets and the manipulation of the capital accounts allowed a great deal of leeway for distributions by companies that were losing money.

RANDALL v. BAILEY

288 N.Y. 280, 43 N.E.2d 43 (1942).

CONWAY, JUDGE.

The plaintiff, as trustee, seeks in this action to recover from directors and executors of deceased directors dividends declared and paid between 1928 and 1932, alleging that they were paid from capital in violation of section 58 of the Stock Corporation Law.

The corporation involved is the Bush Terminal Company, hereinafter called Terminal, which was organized in 1902. It owns and operates a great ocean terminal. The land in Brooklyn which it and its wholly owned subsidiary, Bush Terminal Buildings Company, hereinafter called Buildings, purchased between 1902 and 1905, increased in value with the passing years. Until 1915 Terminal and Buildings carried that land at its original cost. In 1915 and again in 1919 they committed to their books a portion of the increase in value of that land. It has not since been increased. The trial court found that its value during the years 1928 to 1932 was greater than the value to which it had been increased upon the corporate books. Those findings have been unanimously affirmed. Even apart from that affirmance, which concludes us, there is no claim that the findings are not correct. Moreover, there is no allegation in the complaint that any director acted fraudulently, in bad faith or negligently in valuing the land or in voting the dividends. The question presented, therefore, is solely one of law and involves the construction of section 58 of the Stock Corporation Law. We are concerned only with the legislative prohibition as evidenced in section 58 as enacted in 1923. If the directors of Terminal were permitted to include among the corporate assets the value of the land at the amount at which it was valued on the books from 1919 onward there was a surplus for the payment of dividends and no recovery may be had in this action. If it must be carried at cost then the directors unjustifiably declared and paid the dividends which plaintiff seeks to recover. The question presented, therefore, is: may unrealized appreciation in value of fixed assets held for use in carrying on a corporate enterprise be taken into consideration by directors in determining whether a corporate surplus exists from which cash dividends may be paid to stockholders. * * *

> § 58. Dividends. No stock corporation shall declare or pay any dividend which shall impair its capital or capital stock, nor while its capital or capital stock is impaired, nor shall any such corporation declare or pay any dividend or make any distribution of assets to any of its stockholders, whether upon a reduction of the number of its shares or of its capital or capital stock, unless the value of its assets remaining after the payment of such dividend, or after such distribution of assets, as the case may be, shall be at least equal to the aggregate amount of its debts and liabilities including capital or capital stock as the case may be.

The appellant contends that the first sentence of section 58 of the Stock Corporation Law should be divided into two parts; that the first twenty-six words should be applicable to the payment of what he terms regular or ordinary dividends and that the remaining portion of the sentence should be applicable to such dividend as may be declared in connection with a reduction of capital. That construction makes the clause commencing 'unless the value of its assets' modify only the second portion.

The appellant points out that in 1912 the Legislature authorized the issuance of stock without par value and provided in section 20 of the Stock Corporation Law, with reference to such a corporation, 'No such corporation shall declare any dividend which shall reduce the amount of its capital below the amount stated in the certificate as the amount of capital with which the corporation will carry on business,' L.1912, ch. 351, § 20;

and that in 1921 that section was amended to read, "No such corporation shall declare or pay any dividend which shall reduce the amount of its stated capital." Thus immediately prior to 1923, corporations having only par value stock were governed by the "surplus profits" language while those having stock without par value were governed by the "amount of stated capital" language. Appellant then contends that the Legislature intended to eliminate the variation of terminology and the overlapping provisions contained in sections 20 and 28 and accomplished that elimination by the enactment of the first twenty-six words in the first sentence of the new section (§ 58) by simply providing that no business stock corporation should distribute dividends which should "impair its capital or capital stock," although the Legislature was in reality continuing the "surplus profits" test of former section 28; that the terminology "surplus profits" and "impairment of capital" were used to express the same test. He contends that the surplus from which cash dividends may be distributed must be based upon actual profits and realized gains, over and above the capital investment, after provision has been made in respect of all losses, which, however, must be treated as realized or accrued, although conceding that dividends may properly be paid from paid-in surplus.

We shall first consider appellant's division of the first sentence of section 58 into two parts. Assuming that there may be some justification for that construction as a matter of syntax and statutory history, it seems to us that an equally strong argument may be made to the contrary. The words any dividend are contained in both portions of the sentence. Any is an all-exclusive word. When repeated in the same sentence one would reasonably assume that the two words bore the same meaning each time. Those two words tie together by repetition the first and second portions of the sentence or so it might well be urged. They must mean a dividend of any kind or character and both portions of the sentence must be read in that light. They must mean that no dividend may be declared or paid which shall impair capital or capital stock unless the value of the corporate assets "remaining after the payment of such dividend, or after such distribution of assets, as the case may be, shall be at least equal to the aggregate amount of its debts and liabilities including capital or capital stock as the case may be."

That reasonable men may differ upon the syntax of the sentence under discussion is made apparent by an allegation contained in each of the causes of action in the plaintiff's complaint. It reads as follows: "The declaration and payment of said dividends impaired the capital and capital stock of Terminal; and the value of the assets of Terminal remaining after said payment was less, by an amount in excess of such payment, than the aggregate amount of the debts and liabilities of Terminal including its capital or capital stock; and, both at the time such dividends were declared and at the time they were paid, the capital and capital stock of Terminal was impaired and the declaration and payment of said dividends further impaired said capital and capital stock * * *."

There is other evidence, well nigh conclusive, that the Legislature intended to drop the "surplus profits" test, apart from the internal evidence contained in section 58 itself. In 1924 two subdivisions of section 664 of the Penal Law were amended. Prior to that year the Penal Law, Consol. Laws 1909, c. 40, provided that a director was guilty of a misdemeanor who concurred in any vote: "1. To make a dividend, except from the surplus profits arising from the business of the corporation, and in the cases and manner allowed by law * * *." In 1924 that subdivision was amended to read: "1. To make a dividend, except from surplus, and in the cases and manner allowed by law * * *."

Subdivision 5 of the same section had read: "To apply any portion of the funds of such corporation, except surplus profits, directly or indirectly, to the purchase of shares of its own stock." That subdivision was amended in 1924 to read: "To apply any portion of the funds of such corporation, except surplus, directly or indirectly, to the purchase of shares of its own stock."

Again, we are concerned with the legislative will as written in the statute. We should construe the statutory language as the average business man would read and understand it. He is the one who must bear the burden civilly and criminally. If the Legislature had intended to continue the 'surplus profits' test it would have said so clearly and unmistakably rather than by using the words 'impair its capital or capital stock.' While it is true that punctuation is no part of a writing, it also may not be amiss to point out that there is no semicolon separating the two portions of the sentence in question. We think that a fair reading of the sentence is that the valuation test is applicable to both portions and that it applies to the declaration and payment of regular or ordinary dividends, so termed by appellant.

Finally, as some indication of how the Legislature viewed its own language in section 58, as enacted in 1923, it is interesting to note an amendment of section 58 in 1939. The amendment was not retroactive by express provision of the amending act. It provided, however, in substance, that directors should have an affirmative defense if able to show that they had "reasonable grounds to believe, and did believe, that such dividend or distribution would not impair the capital of such corporation." Quite clearly, in 1939 the Legislature believed that in the enactment of 1923 it had used impairment of capital terminology and the "value of its assets" terminology interchangeably.

Let us now consider section 58 with the applicable sections which preceded it. We are concerned primarily with the meaning of the words "impair its capital or capital stock." In the statute of 1825 neither the word value nor the word impair was used. In the statute of 1890 there was a definition of impairment of capital stock. It read: "The capital stock of a stock corporation shall be deemed impaired when the value of its property and assets after deducting the amount of its debts and liabilities, shall be less than the amount of its paid up capital stock. No dividends shall be declared or paid by any stock corporation, except from the surplus profits of its business, nor when its capital stock is or will be impaired thereby, * * *." That was a clear definition of impairment in terms of value. The "surplus profits" terminology was retained from the act of 1825. In 1892 the statute was amended. It retained the "surplus profits" provision but omitted that word "impair." Instead it returned to the "reduce its capital stock" terminology. Having omitted the word impair the Legislature naturally omitted the definition of impairment. The Legislature did not necessarily, as appellant contends, "reject" the definition of impairment as contained in the 1890 statute. There was no need for it since the word "impair" was not used. The Legislature continued its use of the "surplus profits" and "reduce its capital stock" terminology down to 1923.

When the Legislature in 1923 wrote into the first sentence the words "impair its capital or capital stock, nor while its capital or capital stock is impaired," and in the same sentence used words almost identical with those in the definition of impairment contained in the 1890 statute, it is more reasonable than not to assume that the Legislature was returning to its former definition of impairment of capital and at the same time abandoning the "surplus profits" test. The courts had consistently applied the value of assets rule in determining surplus, surplus profits or impairment of capital without distinction, and the Legislature clarified the language of the statute so as to remove any doubt as to the fact that value was the test. In fact appellant concedes that the determination of the courts below is correct if in drafting the provisions of section 58 in 1923 the Legislature changed the then existing law as to illegal dividends and reinstated the definition of impairment of capital which it had omitted when enacting the statute of 1892. It seems to us that a fair reading of the statute in the light of its language and historical development clearly indicates that that is exactly what the Legislature intended to accomplish. To say that in the one sentence there were different tests of liability for directors of business corporations, one involving "surplus profits," although those words were not there, and the other involving value of assets, regardless of surplus profits, would be to depart from the authorities, the plain words of the statute and its historical implications. It has always been the rule that where an act amends an existing statute "so as to read as follows," thereupon enacting a new and substituted provision, all of the former statute omitted from the act as amended is repealed. In reality, therefore, appellant is basing his construction of the statute upon the continuance therein of a provision repealed by the act of 1923. * * *

The Legislature having declared that dividends may be paid when there is no impairment of capital or capital stock caused thereby and when the value of the corporate assets remaining after the payment of such dividends is at least equal to the aggregate amount of its debts and liabilities including capital or capital stock as the case may be, Stock Corporation Law, § 58, in other words from its surplus, our inquiry turns to the question whether surplus may consist of increases resulting from a revaluation of fixed assets. Surplus has been well defined as follows in

Edwards v. Douglas, 269 U.S. 204, 214, 46 S.Ct. 85, 88, 70 L.Ed. 235, Brandeis J.: The word "surplus" is a term commonly employed in corporate finance and accounting to designate an account on corporate books. * * * The surplus account represents the net assets of a corporation in excess of all liabilities including its capital stock. This surplus may be "paid-in surplus," as where the stock is issued at a price above par; it may be "earned surplus," as where it was derived wholly from undistributed profits; or it may, among other things, represent the increase in valuation of land or other assets made upon a revaluation of the company's fixed property.

The decision below was correct and the judgment should be affirmed, with costs.

LEHMAN, C. J., AND LOUGHRAN, FINCH, RIPPEY, LEWIS, AND DESMOND, JJ., concur.

Judgment affirmed.

NOTES

1. The New York legislature revised the state's dividend provision in 1961, but the drafting committee asserted that dividends could still be paid out of unrealized appreciation. N.Y. Business Corp. L. § 510 (Revision Notes). The Official Comments to the Model Bus. Corp. Act § 6.40 also state that, in valuing assets, the corporation may use a "fair valuation or other method that is reasonable under the circumstances." The approach allowed by the court in *Randall v. Bailey* does not conform to GAAP, and some states refused to follow the New York rule, concluding that unrealized appreciation was not appropriate for dividends. See Commissioner v. Hirshon Trust, 213 F.2d 523, 527 (2d Cir.1954). Why do you suppose those states took that view? Why are there any legal restrictions on the amounts of dividends?

2. Additional techniques have been used to free up capital for dividends, including decreasing the amount of required stated capital by reducing the par value of outstanding stock. Such action will usually require a shareholder vote and possibly a charter amendment. Another method is to buy up shares and cancel those treasury shares, which will reduce the corporation's stated capital. Delaware broadly allows such changes. 8 Del Corp. L. § 244 (allowing reduction of capital by share purchases). See also 8 Del Corp. L. § 242(a)(3) (allowing amendment of certificate of incorporation to allow changes in par value). Another technique called a "quasi-reorganization" is used to reduce or eliminate an earned surplus deficit by applying capital surplus to the deficit. Such action will usually require a shareholder vote. Concern has been expressed that this account juggling, without proper disclosures, may mislead subsequent purchasers of the stock of the corporation because the company's history of operating losses has now been removed. See generally James D. Cox & Thomas Lee Hazen, Corporations, § 21.18 (2d ed. 2003) (discussing quasi-reorganizations).

3. Restrictions on dividends may be imposed by loan covenants or shareholder agreements. A lender may thus want to assure that earnings are

applied to debt reduction or service before being distributed to shareholders. Complex formulas are often employed in debt covenants that, for example, prohibit dividends where working capital (current assets less current liabilities) or net worth would be reduced.

4. State laws impose restrictions on dividends beyond capital based tests. One unique provision adopted by California requires that the assets of the corporation (exclusive of goodwill and certain other intangible assets) equal at least 1 ¼ the amount of liabilities. Current assets must also at least equal current liabilities (increased to 1¼ times current liabilities in some instances). Cal. Gen. Corp. Law § 500. Most other state corporate laws preclude distributions that would render the corporation insolvent. See e.g., N.Y. Business Corp. L. § 510 (dividends prohibited if corporation would be rendered insolvent). States may use various tests for insolvency. The so-called bankruptcy test prohibits dividends if liabilities exceed assets after the distribution. An equity test precludes a dividend if the corporation will be unable to meet its liabilities as they come due. The Model Bus. Corp. Act § 6.40(c) adopts both a bankruptcy and equity test as the bases for restricting dividends. In adopting a bankruptcy test, the Model Bus. Corp. Act treats any liquidating preferences for senior securities the same as debt in determining whether assets exceed liabilities. The Official Comments to this section liken this to a balance sheet test.

MORRIS v. STANDARD GAS. & ELEC. CO.

63 A.2d 577 (Del.Ch.1949).

SEITZ, VICE-CHANCELLOR.

Plaintiff seeks a preliminary injunction to prevent the defendant corporation from paying dividends declared on certain classes of its preferred stock on the ground that such action would violate the General Corporation Law of Delaware.

Section 34 of the General Corporation Law of Delaware [now § 170] sets forth the circumstances under which the directors of a Delaware corporation shall have the power to declare and pay dividends. Insofar as pertinent, Section 34 provides:

'The directors * * * shall have power to declare and pay dividends * * * either (a) out of its net assets in excess of its capital as computed in accordance with the provisions of Sections * * * or (b), in case there shall be no such excess, out of its net profits for the fiscal year then current and/or the preceding fiscal year; provided, however, that if the capital of the corporation computed as aforesaid shall have been diminished by depreciation in the value of its property, or by losses, or otherwise, to an amount less than the aggregate amount of the capital represented by the issued and outstanding stock of all classes having a preference upon the distribution of assets, the directors of such corporation shall not declare and pay out of such net profits any dividends upon any shares of any classes of its capital stock until the deficiency in the amount of capital represented by the issued and outstanding stock of all classes having a preference upon the distribution of assets shall have been repaired.'

Under the power purportedly given by Section 34(b), the directors of the defendant corporation on December 20, 1948 declared a regular quarterly dividend on the $7 and the $6 prior preference cumulative stock to be paid on January 25, 1949. Shortly thereafter, plaintiff filed this action to enjoin the payment of the dividends on the ground that the requirements of Section 34(b) had not been met because the net value of the assets was less than the aggregate amount of the capital represented by the issued and outstanding stock of all classes having a preference upon the distribution of assets. This is the decision on the application for a preliminary injunction which was heard entirely on affidavits.

The defendant is a Delaware corporation and a public utility holding company. It has outstanding 368,348 shares of prior preference stock $7 cumulative, and 100,000 shares of prior preference stock $6 cumulative. Each of the series mentioned is entitled to cumulative dividends payable quarterly at the annual rate indicated before any dividend may be paid on any other class of stock. In the event of liquidation or dissolution, each share of both series is entitled to a $100 preference over the shares of any other class, plus all dividend arrearages. No dividends have been paid on either series since 1934 and as of September 30, 1948 the $7 series had a per share arrearage of $102.90, and the $6 series an arrearage of $88.20, or an aggregate arrearage on both series of $46,723,009.20.

Defendant also has outstanding 757,442 shares of $4 cumulative preferred stock. This stock has a yearly cumulative dividend preference of $4 per share over the common stock. Subject to the rights of the prior preference stock, this class is entitled to receive $50 per share, plus arrearages in the event of liquidation or dissolution before any distribution is made on the common stock. No dividends have been declared on this stock since 1933, and as of September 30, 1948, the arrearages on the class aggregated $47,213,884.67.

Defendant has outstanding 2,162,607 shares of common stock.

The defendant's board consists of 9 directors, 3 are elected by the holders of the $6 and $7 shares voting as a class, 2 by the $4 shareholders voting as a class, and 4 by the common stockholders voting as a class.

The facts surrounding the declaration of the dividend can best be presented in chronological order. The defendant by an agreement dated December 21, 1945, as amended, had borrowed $51,000,000 from a group of banks. Under this agreement the defendant was prohibited from paying any dividends so long as any of the notes issued under the agreement remained unpaid. In order to clear the way for the declaration of a dividend, the defendant negotiated a new bank loan agreement dated November 26, 1948, under which about $11,600,000 was secured to liquidate the balance of the 1945 obligation. The new agreement permitted the defendant to declare current quarterly dividends on its prior preference stock, provided the amount of the dividends so paid does not exceed the dividend income received by the defendant after September 30, 1948.

Once the defendant was assured that the new bank loan agreement would be signed, its directors met to consider the possibility of declaring the regular quarterly dividend on the $6 and $7 prior preference stock. At a directors' meeting held on November 17, 1948, the minutes recite that all the directors discussed at length various considerations arising in connection with the question of the declaration of current quarterly dividends on the company's prior preference stock. The directors were advised that the Rules of the S.E.C. prohibit a registered holding company from paying dividends out of unearned surplus or capital without the permission of the Commission. The minutes recite:

> ' * * * that the Company had on its balance sheet an item designated 'Earned Surplus since December 31, 1937,' the amount of which at October 31, 1948, was $25,602,663.61; and that in view of the qualification by the independent accountants of the Company to the effect that the investments of the Company are subject to such adjustment as may be required in the completion of the corporate simplification program under the Public Utility Holding Company Act of 1935 [15 U.S.C.A. § 79 et seq.], it appeared desirable that the Company obtain from the Securities and Exchange Commission, before the declaration by the Board of current quarterly dividends on the Prior Preference Stock, authority to declare and pay those dividends, which would be charged to that item.'

> After a discussion by the directors, a resolution was passed authorizing the officers of the defendant to file with the Commission such papers as in their judgment would be necessary or advisable in respect to the proposed declaration of a dividend on the prior preference stock.

About November 24, 1948, the defendant filed an application with the Commission requesting authority to pay current quarterly dividends on its prior preference stock. The application made it clear that the defendant corporation did not concede that the payment would be out of capital.

On December 7, 1948, the directors met, and reference was made to the possibility mentioned at the November 17, 1948 meeting that a dividend might be declared on the prior preference stock. The meeting was advised that an application had been made to the Commission for authority to pay such dividend. The chairman advised the meeting that consideration had been given to the Delaware statute and that in order that the company might have evidence of its compliance with the Delaware statute, W. C. Gilman and Company, at his request, prepared an appraisal of the assets to determine whether in its judgment the assets less the liabilities exceeded $88,500,000—this figure is the approximate total of the aggregate capital represented by the $7, $6, and $4 preferred, plus the sum required to pay a quarterly dividend on the prior preference stock ($87,-

350,943.35 plus $794,609). It is not denied that W. C. Gilman and Company possesses expert competence in appraisal matters and is familiar with the defendant's assets by reason of having been engaged to study them for other purposes. The factual appraisal made by Gilman and Company and submitted to the meeting was necessarily somewhat general. This appraisal discussed the values of the various stocks owned by the defendant by reference to market value, past, present, and future earnings, percentage of stock owned and knowledge based on other studies and sources of information. The report concluded that the net assets of the defendant had a fair value substantially in excess of $88,500,000. The meeting also heard a report made by G. W. Knourek, Vice–President and Treasurer of the defendant corporation. Mr. Knourek was eminently qualified both in education and experience to make such a valuation. His complete familiarity with the defendant's assets is clearly demonstrated. This report dated December 6, 1948, also discussed the value of the stocks and concluded that the fair value of the defendant's net assets substantially exceeded $88,500,000. In this report Mr. Knourek stated that in appraising the assets he gave consideration to market prices, capitalization of current dividends, capitalization of average earnings for the two years nine months ending September 30, 1948, appraisals made in 1943 in connection with the defendant's recapitalization, and the recent orders of the S.E.C. with respect to Louisville Gas and Electric Co. (Del.) and a sale of Oklahoma Gas and Electric Co. stock. The chairman made a statement to the meeting that he had examined the Gilman and Company report and the statement by Mr. Knourek, and that in his opinion a fair value of the net assets was in excess of $88,500,000. He explained to the meeting the methods he used in his study and valuation.

The chairman also stated that since this was the first time this matter had come before the board in many years, he had obtained opinions from two Delaware attorneys and one Chicago attorney as to whether a dividend might legally be declared under the Delaware statute. The opinion, which was read to the meeting, stated that based on the assumptions contained therein the company might legally pay the dividend under the Delaware law.

The minutes recite that the board made numerous inquiries and discussed the asset value problem generally. A balance sheet of the company as of October 31, 1948, and a statement of its income for the twelve months ending that date were presented to the meeting. The chairman suggested an adjournment of the meeting with the hope that in the the interim a Commission order would be entered permitting the proposed dividend declaration to become effective.

A public hearing was held by the Commission at which hearing the present plaintiff appeared and objected to the defendant's proposal. After considering the record, a memorandum by the present plaintiff opposed and a memorandum of the prior preference protective committee in support of the proposal the Commission by order dated December 17, 1948, permitted the proposed dividend to become effective forthwith, but provided, inter alia, that the stockholders be advised 'that the Commission permitted the declaration to become effective without determining whether the payment is being made out of capital'.

The Commission's opinion contains the following language:

'* * * David Morris & Co. has attacked the valuation and the witnesses who testified in support of it. Although we are not convinced that this issue raised by the objecting stockholder is relevant to these proceedings, nevertheless we have considered the record and are not persuaded that the objection is well founded in fact. However, it should be clearly understood that we are expressing no opinion as to whether this valuation should be accepted for any purpose other than that for which it was presented.'

In the light of the Commission's conclusion that the dividend would be allowed without deciding whether the dividend payment would be out of capital, it is apparent that the quoted factual conclusion was in the nature of a 'factual dictum' by an administrative body. In view of my approach to the problem presented, it is unnecessary to consider what weight should be given to the Commission's remark. The directors met on December 20, 1948, and having been advised of the Commission's approval of the proposed dividend, and after discussion, unanimously adopted a resolution providing for a dividend of $1.75 per share on the $7 and a dividend of $1.50 per share on the $6 cumulative preference stock to be paid January 25, 1949 out of the net profits of the defendant corporation accumulated since January 1, 1947, and to be charged to the earned surplus account.

On December 28, 1948, plaintiff filed this action seeking a temporary injunction against the payment of the dividend. As permanent relief, plaintiff requested that the defendant be enjoined from paying any dividend on its stock until the court determined that any such dividend would not constitute a payment out of capital or unearned surplus in violation of the Delaware law. Has plaintiff made out a case for interlocutory relief? Plaintiff says that when the dividend was declared the capital of the defendant (its assets less its liabilities) was not equal to the aggregate amount of the capital represented by the issued and outstanding stock of all classes having a preference upon distribution. The defendants, of course, take a contrary view. I am not persuaded that the contention and the denial pose the precise issue this court must decide because it assumes that one objective value exists and is capable of being determined.

The defendant corporation concedes that the power to pay the proposed dividend must be found under Section 34(b) of the General Corporation Law of Delaware. It is clear that the net profits of the defendant corporation for the then current and/or the preceding fiscal year are more than sufficient to cover the proposed dividend, and it is clear that the proposed dividend will be charged to the earned surplus account. The sole question then is whether the conditions of the proviso contained in Section 34(b) have been met. Otherwise stated, at the time the board of directors declared the dividend in question were they entitled to conclude that the net assets of the defendant were at least equal to the aggregate amount of the capital represented by the issued and outstanding stock of all classes having a preference upon distribution? Stated with relation to the present facts, were the net assets worth at least $88,145,552.35—being the amount of capital represented by the outstanding stock having a preference on distribution, plus the proposed quarterly dividend.

The problem is one of valuation which is surpassed in difficulty only in the domestic relations law. The numerous and varied standards applied in the legal, accounting and business fields have mapped a wavering course for one required to resolve a substantial problem of valuation. Here the governing statute has declared that the capital must—roughly speaking—be valued at its dollar equivalent before a dividend can be declared out of net profits for a designated period. This duty falls to the directors. What legal standard will be applied in determining whether the directors have valued the corporate assets in a manner deemed sufficient to comply with the requirements of Section 34(b)?

The plaintiff's attorney stated at the oral argument that he did not charge that the directors were guilty of any fraud or bad faith in valuating the capital assets at a dollar value which would satisfy the provisions of Section 34(b). He appeared to take the position that based on the standards he would apply in evaluating the assets, they were not sufficient to comply with the requirements of the statute, and hence the action of the directors violated the statute. He also took the position that nothing short of an actual appraisal of the assets in the underlying companies whose stock was owned by the defendant would be sufficient. Let us consider the second problem first.

Initially, of course, reasonable men can differ as to what constitutes an appraisal. If by an appraisal plaintiff means that all the assets had to be viewed and evaluated separately by the directors or experts in a manner similar to a valuation for purposes of a reorganization of the type currently popular at least in the utility field, then I conclude that the statute imposes no such requirement on the directors as a prerequisite to the employment of the power granted in Section 34(b). In large companies, especially those such as the defendant, an appraisal of the type suggested by plaintiff would mean that as a practical matter the provisions of Section 34(b) would be unavailable. See generally II Bonbright, Valuation of Property, pp. 973–974. I prefer the view expressed in the following language of the New York Supreme Court in Randall v. Bailey, Sup., 23 N.Y.S.2d 173, 184, affirmed 288 N.Y. 280, 43 N.E.2d 43:

'I see no cause for alarm over the fact that this view [taking assets at actual value] requires directors to make a determination of the value of the assets at each dividend declaration. On the contrary, I think that is exactly what the law always has contemplated that directors should do. That does not mean that the books themselves necessarily must be altered by write-ups or write-downs at each dividend period, or that formal appraisals must be obtained from professional appraisers or even made by the directors themselves. That is obviously impossible in the case of corporations of any considerable size.'

In concluding that a formal appraisal of the type mentioned is not required, I do not mean to imply that the directors are not under a duty to evaluate the assets on the basis of acceptable data and by standards which they are entitled to believe reasonably reflect present 'values'. It is not practical to attempt to lay down a rigid rule as to what constitutes prior evidence of value for the consideration of directors in declaring a dividend under Section 34(b). The factors considered and the emphasis given will depend upon the case presented. At the expense of brevity, let us consider what the directors of the defendant corporation actually did in connection with the declaration of the dividend under attack and then evaluate that action.

Since no dividend had been declared for a great many years, the directors proceeded with some caution. Having seen that the current net assets were more than sufficient to meet the dividend requirements of the $6 and $7 preferred stock, the directors considered the possibility of paying such dividends. The first obstacle to such payment was removed by negotiating a new bank loan. Plaintiff points out that defendant corporation was apparently required to pledge or restrict practically its entire portfolio for this loan of $11,600,000, callable on three days' notice for default. Plaintiff argues that the very fact that the banks required the defendant to pledge or restrict assets which the defendant values at over $100,000,000 to secure a loan of $11,600,000, is evidence that the assets were not worth anything near the value placed on them by the board of directors for dividend purposes. Nothing appears in the papers before me which would throw any light on the question as to why assets of the value alleged were pledged or restricted. Lacking particulars, I do not feel that I should give any particular weight to this argument advanced by the plaintiff. Moreover, plaintiff concedes that the assets are worth upwards of $50,000,000, yet there is no explanation as to why the banks would require a pledge or restriction on assets even at the value placed on them by plaintiff, which is many times the value of the loan.

The directors considered the value factor at three meetings and had available and personally studied the reports concerning the defendant's assets prepared by admitted experts in the field. They had the balance sheets and profit and loss statements. Moreover, evidence as to value became available through the hearing before the S.E.C. even though the issue there presented was not the one now before this court. That then is what was done before directors representing all classes of stock unanimously declared the dividend now under attack. Let us examine the case presented by plaintiff.

Plaintiff relied on his sworn complaint and his two affidavits. Since October 27, 1947, plaintiff has been the holder of record of 100 shares of the defendant's $4 cumulative preferred stock. In his complaint the plaintiff sets forth his 'opinion' of the value of defendant's assets and arrives at a gross value of $82,109,858. After deducting liabilities of $11,242,729, the plaintiff determines the defendant's net worth to be $70,863,829. The complaint merely sets forth plaintiff's opinion of the value of each asset owned by the defendant, plus the following allegation:

'Complainant in arriving at the total of $82,109,858. used the figures shown on the left side of Exhibit 'B'. While recently 100 shares of Philadelphia Co. stock sold for $9.75 per share, he feels that a large block could not be sold at such price. Wisconsin Public Service stock pays 20 cents dividend, or 5% on a value of $1.00 [sic] Stocks just as sound, if not better, are yielding 7% and 8%. It has no market value. The stock showing 'no value' are considered valueless and have no market value. The other stocks are valued at market prices.'

Plaintiff's first affidavit recites once again his opinion of the value of the defendant's assets with one remarkable change. In his affidavit he states that 'Thru a clerical error, the value of Wisconsin Public Service was erroneously listed in Exhibit 'B' to the injunction bill at $1.00 per share, instead of $10.00 per share.' This error is the more remarkable because it amounted to an error of $12,375,000, and meant that in drawing his complaint plaintiff by his own statement under-estimated the value of the defendant's assets by that amount. Plaintiff in his first affidavit also revised his net asset value in several respects, but principally to correct the clerical error. After these revisions, plaintiff arrived at a figure of $81,728,640 which he designated as '(Net Assets (Appraised))'. He then proceeded to deduct the sum of $25,244,457 from this figure and arrived at the sum of $56,484,183 which he describes as 'net assets with safety margin'.

This item is explained by a note which says: 'Less for safety margin 33 1/3% of $50247900 Phila stock and 20% of 42475785 other operating utility stock or total deduction of $25 244 457.'

The plaintiff's affidavit supplies plaintiff's explanation of the 'safety margin' deduction. It reads:

'At the moment we are, in my opinion, at a critical point in an inflated economy. Conditions are highly uncertain. Earnings are now high. If our economy contracts, stocks can go lower. I do not think that it would be prudent for a company like the respondent with relatively little cash, to pay a cash dividend at this time without allowing a margin of safety for its investments. I think that a fair margin for safety would be 33–1/3% for a utility holding company like the Philadelphia Company herein mentioned and 20% for the other operating utility companies such as Oklahoma Gas & Electric Co. and the others mentioned in Exhibit 'D'.'

Plaintiff appraises the net assets at about $82,000,000 before his 'safety margin' deduction. There is no justification under Section 34(b) for requiring an arbitrary deduction from present value before ascertaining the value of the net assets. The safety factor mentioned by plaintiff actually is an element in present value, but there is no justification under the statute for determining present value, and then making an arbitrary deduction. This 'safety margin' deduction is actually an attack on the wisdom of the directors in declaring a dividend at the present time. Indeed, in attempting to justify his argument for a deduction plaintiff speaks of what is 'prudent'. Where, as here, the only question is one of compliance with the statute, and there is no suggestion that the directors have been guilty of fraud or bad faith in attempting to comply therewith, I do not believe this court can substitute its concept of wisdom for that of the directors.

Plaintiff's affidavit indicates that he arbitrarily applied a ten times earnings formula as a standard for valuing the principal assets of the defendant. Defendant's assets consist of the ownership of various stock interests in public utility companies providing gas, electricity, transportation and other services in at least seven states. Certainly this test may be one standard by which the value of such assets are weighed, but it is most assuredly not the only standard to be applied. Indeed, the assets sought to be valued may have such a factual background that the application of such a rule would be misleading and even fraudulent. Although a certain picked class of utility stocks may have an average value of ten times earnings, nevertheless, as counsel for the stockholders' committee pointed out, it is only an average. The values of the utilities chosen to determine an average may vary widely. Consequently, plaintiff's assumption that this standard of valuing the assets is the only one to be applied is fallacious. The defendant corporation does not say that this arbitrary standard should not be considered. It merely says that it is only one criterion of value to be considered. I am in accord with the defendant's position. Compare generally In re General Realty & Utilities Corporation, Del.Ch., 52 A.2d 6.

We are left then with plaintiff's opinion that the net assets are worth about $82,000,000. This is about $6,500,000 less than the value admittedly necessary if a dividend is to be legally declared under Section 34(b). The plaintiff gives only his opinion of the value of the assets. As a basis for qualifying himself to give such opinion, plaintiff mentions his experiences in the investment field. His college education was in the business field, and for about 15 years he has operated an investment business in Wall Street, New York City. He holds official positions in the New York Security Dealers Association. He states that it is his business to know the value of securities, although he overlooked a 'clerical error' of $12,375,000, and confused a worthless stock in the defendant's portfolio with stock of another class having a value of about $600,000. Indeed, there is nothing in the plaintiff's papers to show any real familiarity with the corporations whose stocks are owned by the defendant. Plaintiff speaks of the stocks as though the defendant's business was trading in utility stocks. Such is not the case, and in consequence plaintiff loses sight of the value inherent in holding certain blocks of stock which give the defendant working control of such corporations.

Plaintiff also contends that the appraisals relied on by the defendant's directors erroneously took into consideration such factors as the future earnings and prospects of the stocks owned by the defendant. He urges that such elements may not be considered in determining present value under Section 34(b). I am unable to agree with plaintiff's contention. The factors mentioned certainly form elements to be considered in determining the present value of stock in a going concern. It is indeed common knowledge that future prospects often constitute a most important factor where present value is sought to be determined.

Plaintiff points out that the reputable accountants who prepared the defendant's balance sheet stated that the value of the defendant's assets was subject to such adjustment as might be required under a simplification program called for by the Public Utility Holding Company Act of 1935. From this and other statements plaintiff implies that the accountants were suggesting that the capital assets were overvalued. In my opinion, the statements made by the accountants merely constituted a caveat for their own protection and did not purport to go further. Nor in my opinion does the fact that the defendant applied to the S. E. C. for permission to declare the dividend constitute persuasive evidence that the directors felt that the value of the assets was such that the dividend would actually be paid out of capital.

Thus we have a situation where plaintiff seeks a preliminary injunction to prevent the directors from paying a dividend under Section 34(b) because he alone values the net assets at about $6,500,000 below the required value, while the defendant's directors have declared the dividend after having been presented with substantial data as to value compiled by admitted experts in the field. This data, along with the corporate records, indicate that the net assets are substantially in excess of the statutory requirement. I purposely refrain from placing too much reliance upon the more elaborate statements contained in defendant's affidavits showing the justification for the action of the directors because I prefer to evaluate the information presented to and the action taken by the directors prior to or at the time the dividend was declared. The information presented to and the action taken by the directors, when contrasted with plaintiff's case, permits of but one reasonable answer. The plaintiff has failed utterly to make out a showing which would entitle him to a preliminary injunction.

Plaintiff's case comes down to a disagreement with the directors as to value under circumstances where the directors took great care to obtain data on the point in issue, and exercised an informed judgment on the matter. In such a situation, I am persuaded that this court cannot substitute either plaintiff's or its own opinion of value for that reached by the directors where there is no charge of fraud or bad faith. As stated, the process of valuation called for by Section 34(b) of necessity permits of no one objective standard of value. Having in mind its function, the directors must be given reasonable latitude in ascertaining value. Such being the case, I conclude that the action of the directors in determining that the net assets were worth at least the aggregate amount of the capital represented by the issued and outstanding stock of all classes having preference upon the distribution of assets cannot be disturbed on the showing here made. Consequently, plaintiff is not entitled to a preliminary injunction restraining the payment of the dividend.

An order accordingly will be advised on notice.

NOTES

1. The "nimble dividend" provision in the Delaware Code (§ 170), which allows a dividend to be paid in a profitable year even where there is no surplus, has been the subject of much criticism. See *James D. Cox & Thomas Lee Hazen, Corporations*, § 20.17 (2d ed. 2003) (discussing the appropriateness of nimble dividends). Compare Weinberg v. Baltimore Brick Co., 114 A.2d 812 (Del.1955) (charter provision for dividends from "net earnings" did not preclude nimble dividend for preferred shareholders from current earnings even though there was a cumulative capital deficit), with, Jones v. First National Bldg. Corp., 155 F.2d 815 (10th Cir.1946) (charter provision providing for dividend payments out of surplus precluded nimble dividends where capital was impaired).

2. As seen in Chapter 5, stockholders generally do not have the power to require the board of directors to declare a dividend, but once declared, the dividend becomes a debt obligation of the corporation. See e.g., Fidelity & Columbia Trust Co. v. Louisville Railroad, 265 Ky. 820, 97 S.W.2d 825 (1936).

BOVE v. COMMUNITY HOTEL CORP. OF NEWPORT, R. I.
105 R.I. 36, 249 A.2d 89 (1969).

JOSLIN, JUSTICE.

This civil action was brought in the superior court to enjoin a proposed merger of The Community Hotel Corporation of Newport, Rhode Island, a defendant herein, into Newport Hotel Corp. Both corporations were organized under the general corporation law of this state and are hereinafter referred to respectively as 'Community Hotel' and 'Newport.' No oral testimony was presented and a trial justice sitting without a jury decided the case on the facts appearing in the exhibits and as assented to by the parties in the pretrial order. The case is here on the plaintiffs' appeal from a judgment denying injunctive relief and dismissing the action.

Community Hotel was incorporated on October 21, 1924, for the stated purpose of erecting, maintaining, operating, managing and leasing hotels; and it commenced operations in 1927 with the opening of the Viking Hotel in Newport. Its authorized capital stock consists of 6,000 shares of $100 par value six per cent prior preference cumulative preferred stock, and 6,000 shares of no par common stock of which 2,106 shares are issued and outstanding. The plaintiffs as well as the individual defendants are holders and owners of preferred stock, plaintiffs having acquired their holdings of approximately 900 shares not later than 1930. At the time this suit was commenced, dividends on the 4,335 then-issued and outstanding preferred shares had accrued, but had not been declared, for approximately 24 years, and totaled about $645,000 or $148.75 per share.

Newport was organized at the instance and request of the board of directors of Community Hotel solely for the purpose of effectuating the merger which is the subject matter of this action. Its authorized capital stock consists of 80,000 shares of common stock, par value $1.00, of which only one share has been issued, and that to Community Hotel for a consideration of $10.

The essentials of the merger plan call for Community Hotel to merge into Newport, which will then become the surviving corporation. Although previously without assets, Newport will, if the contemplated merger is effectuated, acquire the sole ownership of all the property and assets now owned by Community Hotel. The plan also calls for the outstanding shares of Community Hotel's capital stock to be converted into shares of the capital stock of Newport upon the following basis: Each outstanding share of the constituent corporation's preferred stock, together with all accrued dividends thereon, will be changed and converted into five shares of the $1.00 par value common stock of the surviving corporation; and each share of the constituent corporation's no par common stock will be changed and converted into one share of the common stock, $1.00 par value, of the surviving corporation.

Consistent with the requirements of G.L.1956, § 7–5–3, the merger will become effective only if the plan receives the affirmative votes of the stockholders of each of the corporations representing at least two-thirds of the shares of each class of its capital stock. For the purpose of obtaining the required approval, notice was given to both common and preferred stockholders of Community Hotel that a special meeting would be held for the purpose of considering and voting upon the proposed merger. Before the scheduled meeting date arrived, this action was commenced and the meeting was postponed to a future time and place. So far as the record before us indicates, it has not yet been held.

The plaintiffs argue that the primary, and indeed, the only purpose of the proposed merger is to eliminate the priorities of the preferred stock with less than the unanimous consent of its holders. Assuming that premise, a preliminary matter for our consideration concerns the merger of a parent corporation into a wholly-owned subsidiary created for the sole purpose of achieving a recapitalization which will eliminate the parent's preferred stock and the dividends accumulated thereon, and whether such a merger qualifies within the contemplation of the statute permitting any two or more corporations to merge into a single corporation.

It is true, of course, that to accomplish the proposed recapitalization by amending Community Hotel's articles of association under relevant provisions of the general corporation law[2] would require the unanimous vote of the preferred shareholders, whereas under the merger statute, only a two-third vote of those stockholders will be needed. Concededly, unanimity of the preferred stockholders is unobtainable in this case, and plaintiffs argue, therefore, that to permit the less restrictive provisions of the merger statute to be used to accomplish indirectly what otherwise would be incapable of being accomplished directly by the more stringent amendment procedures of the general corporation law is tantamount to sanctioning a circumvention or perversion of that law.

The question, however, is not whether recapitalization by the merger route is a subterfuge, but whether a merger which is designed for the sole purpose of cancelling the rights of preferred stockholders with the consent of less than all has been authorized by the legislature. The controlling statute is § 7–5–2. Its language is clear, all-embracing and unqualified. It authorizes any two or more business corporations which were or might have been organized under the general corporation law to merge into a single corporation; and it provides that the merger agreement shall prescribe ' * * * the terms and conditions of consolidation or merger, the mode of carrying the same into effect * * * as well as the manner of converting the shares of each of the constituent corporations into shares or other securities of the corporation resulting from or surviving such consolidation or merger, with such other details and provisions as are deemed necessary.'[3] Nothing in that language even suggests that the legislature intended to make underlying purpose a standard for determining permissibility. Indeed, the contrary is apparent since the very breadth of the language selected presupposes a complete lack of concern with whether the merger is designed to further the mutual interests of two existing and nonaffiliated corporations or whether alternatively it is purposed solely upon effecting a substantial change in an existing corporation's capital structure.

Moreover, that a possible effect of corporate action under the merger statute is not possible, or is even forbidden, under another section of the general corporation law is of no import, it being settled that the several sections of that law may have independent legal significance, and that the

---

2. Section 7–2–18, as amended, provides that a corporation may ' * * * from time to time when and as desired amend its articles of association * * * ' and § 7–2–19, as amended, provides that 'Unless otherwise provided in the articles of association, every such amendment shall require the affirmative vote of the following proportion of the stockholders, passed at a meeting duly called for the purpose:

'(a) * * *

'(b) Where the amendment diminishes the stipulated rate of dividends on any class of stock or the stipulated amount to be paid thereon in case of call or liquidation, the unanimous vote of the stockholders of such class and the vote of a majority in interest of all other stockholders entitled to vote.'

3. The quoted provision is substantially identical to the Delaware merger statute (Del.Rev. Code (1935) C. 65, § 2091) construed in Federal United Corp. v. Havender, 24 Del.Ch. 318, 11 A.2d 331.

validity of corporate action taken pursuant to one section is not necessarily dependent upon its being valid under another. Hariton v. Arco Electronics, Inc., 40 Del.Ch. 326, 182 A.2d 22, aff'd, 41 Del.Ch. 74, 188 A.2d 123; Langfelder v. Universal Laboratories Inc., D.C., 68 F.Supp. 209, aff'd, 3 Cir., 163 F.2d 804.

We hold, therefore, that nothing within the purview of our statute forbids a merger between a parent and a subsidiary corporation even under circumstances where the merger device has been resorted to solely for the purpose of obviating the necessity for the unanimous vote which would otherwise be required in order to cancel the priorities of preferred shareholders. Federal United Corp. v. Havender, supra; Hottenstein v. York Ice Machinery Corp., 3 Cir., 136 F.2d 944; 7 Fletcher, Cyclopedia of Corporations, chap. 43, § 3696.1, page 892.

A more basic problem, narrowed so as to bring it within the factual context of this case, is whether the right of a holder of cumulative preferred stock to dividend arrearages and other preferences may be cancelled by a statutory merger. That precise problem has not heretofore been before this court, but elsewhere there is a considerable body of law on the subject. There is no need to discuss all of the authorities. For illustrative purposes it is sufficient that we refer principally to cases involving Delaware corporations. That state is important as a state of incorporation, and the decisions of its courts on the precise problem are not only referred to and relied on by the parties, but are generally considered to be the leading ones in the field.

The earliest case in point of time is Keller v. Wilson & Co., 21 Del.Ch. 391, 190 A. 115 (1936). Wilson & Company was formed and its stock was issued in 1925 and the law then in effect protected against charter amendments which might destroy a preferred shareholder's right to accumulated dividends. In 1927 that law was amended so as to permit such destruction, and thereafter the stockholders of Wilson & Company, by the required majorities, voted to cancel the dividends which had by then accrued on its preferred stock. In invalidating that action the rationale of the Delaware court was that the right of a holder of a corporation's cumulative preferred stock to eventual payment of dividend arrearages was a fixed contractual right, that it was a property right in the nature of a debt, that it was vested, and that it could not be destroyed by corporate action taken under legislative authority subsequently conferred, without the consent of all of the shareholders.

Consolidated Film Industries, Inc. v. Johnson, 22 Del.Ch. 407, 197 A. 489 (1937), decided a year later, was an almost precisely similar case. The only difference was that Consolidated Film Industries, Inc. was not created until after the adoption of the 1927 amendment, whereas in the earlier case the statutory amendment upon which Wilson & Company purported to act postdated both its creation and the issuance of its stock. Notwithstanding the Keller rationale that an investor should be entitled to rely upon the law in existence at the time the preferred stock was issued, the court in this case was ' * * * unable to discover a difference in principle between the two cases.' In refusing to allow the proposed reclassification, it reasoned that a shareholder's fixed contractual right to unpaid dividends is of such dignity that it cannot be diminished or eliminated retrospectively even if the authorizing legislation precedes the issuance of its stock.

Two years elapsed before Federal United Corp. v. Havender, supra, was decided. The issue was substantially the same as that in the two cases which preceded. The dissenting stockholders had argued, as might have been expected, that the proposed corporate action, even though styled a 'merger,' was in effect a Keller type recapitalization and was entitled to no different treatment. Notwithstanding that argument, the court did not refer to the preferred stockholder's right as 'vested' or as 'a property right in the nature of a debt.' Neither did it reject the use of Keller-type nomenclature as creating 'confusion' or as 'substitutes for reason and analysis' which are the characterizations used respectively in Davison v. Parke, Austin & Lipscomb, Inc., 285 N.Y. 500, 509, 35 N.E.2d 618, 622; Meck, Accrued Dividends on Cumulative Preferred Stocks; The Legal Doctrine, 55 Harv.L.Rev. 7, 76. Instead, it talked about the extent of the corporate power under the merger statute; and it held that the statute in existence when Federal United Corp. was organized had in effect been written into its charter, and that its preferred shareholders had thereby been advised and informed that their rights to accrued dividends might be extinguished by corporate action taken pursuant thereto.

Faced with a question of corporate action adjusting preferred stock dividends, and required to apply Delaware law under Erie R.R. v. Tompkins, 304 U.S. 64, it is understandable that a federal court in Hottenstein v. York Ice Machinery Corp., 3 Cir., 136 F.2d 944, 950, found Keller, Johnson and Havender irreconcilable and said,

> 'If it is fair to say that the decision of the Supreme Court of Delaware in the Keller case astonished the corporate world, it is just to state that the decision of the Supreme Court in Havender astounded it, for shorn of rationalization the decision constitutes a repudiation of principles enunciated in the Keller case and in Consolidated Film Industries v. Johnson, supra.' at 950.

With Keller's back thus broken, Hottenstein went on to say that under Delaware law a parent corporation may merge with a wholly-owned inactive subsidiary pursuant to a plan cancelling preferred stock and the rights of holders thereof to unpaid accumulated dividends and substituting in lieu thereof stock of the surviving corporation.

Only four years intervened between Keller and Havender, but that was long enough for Delaware to have discarded 'vested rights' as the test for determining the power of a corporation to eliminate a shareholder's right to preferred stock dividend accumulation, and to have adopted in its stead a standard calling for judicial inquiry into whether the proposed interference with a preferred stockholder's contract has been authorized by the legislature. The Havender approach is the one to which we subscribed as being the sounder, and it has support in the authorities. Davison v. Parke, Austin & Lipscomb, Inc., supra; Langfelder v. Union Laboratories, Inc., 3 Cir., 163 F.2d 804; Western Foundry Co. v. Wicker, supra, note 4; Anderson v. International Minerals & Chemical Corp., 295 N.Y. 343, 67 N.E.2d 573; Hubbard v. Jones Laughlin Steel Corp., D.C., 42 F.Supp. 432; Donohue v. Heuser, 239 S.W.2d 238 (Ky).

The plaintiffs do not suggest, other than as they may have argued that this particular merger is a subterfuge, that our merger statute will not permit in any circumstances a merger for the sole reason that it affects accrued, but undeclared, preferred stock dividends. Rather do they argue that what should control is the date of the enactment of the enabling legislation, and they point out that in Havender, Federal United Corp. was organized and its stock was issued subsequent to the adoption of the statute authorizing mergers, whereas in this case the corporate creation and the stock issue preceded adoption of such a statute. That distinguishing feature brings into question what limitations, if any, exist to a state's authority under the reserved power to permit by subsequent legislation corporate acts which affect the preferential rights of a stockholder. More specifically, it raises the problem of whether subsequent legislation is repugnant to the federal and state constitutional prohibitions against the passage of laws impairing the obligations of contracts, because it permits elimination of accumulated preferred dividends by a lesser vote than was required under the law in existence at the time of the incorporation and when the stock was issued.

The mere mention of the constitutional prohibitions against such laws calls to mind Trustees of Dartmouth College v. Woodward, 17 U.S. 518, 4 Wheaton 518, 4 L.Ed. 629, where the decision was that a private corporation charter granted by the state is a contract protected under the constitution against repeal, amendment or alteration by subsequent legislation. Of equal significance in the field of corporation law is Mr. Justice Story's concurring opinion wherein he suggested that application of the impairment clause upon acts of incorporation might be avoided if a state legislature, coincident with granting a corporate charter, reserved as a part of that contract the right of amendment or repeal. With such a reservation, he said, any subsequent amendment or repeal would be pursuant, rather than repugnant, to the terms of the contract and would not therefore impair its obligation.

Our own legislature was quick to heed Story's advice, and in the early part of the 19th century, when corporations were customarily created by special act, the power to alter, amend, or revoke was written directly into each charter. Later, when the practice changed and corporations, instead of being created by special enactment, were incorporated under the general corporation law, the power to amend and repeal was reserved in an act of general application, and since at least as far back as 1844 the corporation law has read in substance as it does today viz., ' * * * The charter or articles of association of every corporation hereafter created may be amended or repealed at the will of the general assembly.' Section 7–1–13.

The language in which the reserved power is customarily stated is not, however, self-explaining, and the extent of the legislative authority under it has frequently been a source of difficulty. Recognizing that problem, but not answering it, the United States Supreme Court said in a frequently quoted passage:

> 'The authority of a state under the so-called reserve power is wide; but it is not unlimited. The corporate charter may be repealed or amended, and, within limits not now necessary to define, the interrelations of state, corporation and stockholders may be changed; but neither vested property rights nor the obligation of contracts of third persons may be destroyed or impaired.' Coombes v. Getz, 285 U.S. 434.

* * * On the basis of our own precedents we conclude that the merger legislation, notwithstanding its effect on the rights of its stockholders, did not necessarily constitute an improper exercise of the right of amendment reserved merely because it was subsequent.

In addition to arguing that the proposed plan suffers from a constitutional infirmity, plaintiffs also contend that it is unfair and inequitable to them, and that its consummation should, therefore, be enjoined. By that assertion they raise the problem of whether equity should heed the request of a dissenting stockholder and intervene to prevent a merger notwithstanding that it has received the vote of the designated proportions of the various classes of stock of the constituent corporations.

In looking to the authorities for assistance on this question, we avoided those involving recapitalization by charter amendment where a dissident's only remedy against allegedly unfair treatment was in equity. In those situations the authorities generally permit equitable intervention to protect against unfair or inequitable treatment. Kamena v. Janssen Dairy Corp., 133 N.J.Eq. 214, 31 A.2d 200, aff'd, 134 N.J.Eq. 359, 35 A.2d 894. They are founded on the concept that otherwise there might be confiscation without recompense. The same rationale, however, is not available in the case of a merger, because there the dissenting stockholders usually can find a measure of protection in the statutory procedures giving them the option to compel the corporation to purchase their shares at an appraised value. This is a significant difference and is ample reason for considering the two situations as raising separate and distinct issues. Anderson v. International Minerals & Chemical Corp., supra.

This case involves a merger, not a recapitalization by charter amendment, and in this state the legislature, looking to the possibility that there might be those who would not be agreeable to the proposed merger, provided a means whereby a dissatisfied stockholder might demand and the corporation be compelled to pay the fair value of his securities. G.L.1956, §§ 7–5–8 through 7–5–16 inclusive. Our inquiry then is to the effect of that remedy upon plaintiff's right to challenge the proposed merger on the ground that it is unfair and inequitable because it dictates what shall be their proportionate interests in the corporate assets. Once again there is no agreement among the authorities. Vorenberg, 'Exclusiveness of the Dissenting Stockholder's Appraisal Right,' 77 Harv.L.Rev. 1189. See also Annot. 162 A.L.R. 1237, 1250. Some authorities appear to say that the statutory remedy of appraisal is exclusive. Beloff v. Consolidated Edison Co., 300 N.Y. 11, 87 N.E.2d 561; Hubbard v. Jones & Laughlin Steel Corp., D.C., 42 F.Supp. 432. Others say that it may be disregarded and that equity may intervene if the minority is treated oppressively or unfairly, Barnett v. Philadelphia Market Co., 218 Pa. 649, 67 A. 912; May v. Midwest Refining Co., 1 Cir., 121 F.2d 431, cert. denied 314 U.S. 668, 62 Sup.Ct. 129, 86 L.Ed. 534, or if the merger is tainted with fraud or illegality, Adams v. United States Distributing Corp., 184 Va. 134, 147, 34 S.E.2d 244, 250, 162 A.L.R. 1227; Porges v. Vadsco Sales Corp., 27 Del.Ch. 127, 32 A.2d 148. To these differing views must also be added the divergence of opinion on whether those in control or those dissenting must bear the burden of establishing that the plan meets whatever the required standard may be. Vorenberg, supra; 77 Harv.L.Rev. 1189, 1210–1215.

In this case we do not choose as between the varying views, nor is there any need for us to do so. Even were we to accept that view which is most favorable to plaintiffs we still would not be able to find that they have been either unfairly or inequitably treated. The record insofar as it relates to the unfairness issue is at best sparse. In substance it consists of the corporation's balance sheet as of September 1967, together with supporting schedules. That statement uses book, rather than the appraised, values, and neither it nor any other evidentiary matter in any way indicates, except as the same may be reflected in the surplus account, the corporation's earning history or its prospects for profitable operations in the future.

Going to the figures we find a capital and surplus account of $669,948 of which $453,000 is allocable to the 4,530 issued and outstanding shares of $100 par value preferred stock and the balance of $216,948 to surplus. Obviously, a realization of the book value of the assets in the event of liquidation, forced or otherwise, would not only leave nothing for the common stockholders, but would not even suffice to pay the preferred shareholders the par value of their stock plus the accrued dividends of $645,000.

If we were to follow a rule of absolute priority, any proposal which would give anything to common stockholders without first providing for full payment of stated value plus dividend accruals would be unfair to the preferred shareholders. It could be argued that the proposal in this case violates that rule because an exchange of one share of Community Hotel's preferred stock for five shares of Newport's common stock would give the preferred shareholders securities worth less than the amount of their liquidation preference rights while at the same time the one to one exchange ratio on the common would enrich Community Hotel's common stockholders by allowing them to participate in its surplus.

An inherent fallacy in applying the rule of absolute priority to the circumstances of this case, however, is its assumption that assets would be liquidated and that nothing more than their book value will be realized. But Community Hotel is not in liquidation. Instead it is a going concern which, because of its present capitalization, cannot obtain the modern debt-financing needed to meet threatened competition. Moreover, management, in the call of the meeting at which it was intended to consider and vote on the plan, said that the proposed recapitalization plan was conceived only ' * * * after careful consideration by your Board of Directors and a review of the relative values of the preferred and common stocks by the independent public accountants of the Corporation. The exchange ratio of five new common shares for each share of the existing preferred stock was determined on the basis of the book and market values of the preferred and the inherent value of the unpaid preferred dividends.' Those assertions are contained in a document admitted as an exhibit and they have testimonial value.

When the varying considerations—both balance sheet figures and management's assertions—are taken into account, we are unable to conclude, at least at this stage of the proceedings, that the proposed plan is unfair and inequitable, particularly because plaintiffs as dissidents may avail themselves of the opportunity to receive the fair market value of their securities under the appraisal methods prescribed in § 7–5–8 through § 7–5–16 inclusive. * * *

For the reasons stated, the judgment appealed from is affirmed.

NOTES

1. Was this merger fair to the preferred shareholders? Consider the fact that their dividends were in arrears for twenty-four years. As the result of the merger, those arrearages would be lost, as they probably were as a practical matter in any event. In exchange for giving up those arrearages, the old preferred shareholder would own over ninety percent of the new corporation, while the old common shareholders would own less than ten percent. The old common shareholders thus had to give up most of their equity interest to the old preferred in order for the corporation to have a new start and possibly make profits for all.

2. Another method for eliminating accrued cumulative dividends is to offer to exchange a new class of prior preferred stock for the old cumulative preferred. There is an element of coercion in such an offer because the old cumulative preferred will not receive dividends until the prior preferred are paid, if at all. In Patterson v. Durham Hosiery Mills, 214 N.C. 806, 200 S.E. 906 (1939), the court held that such a plan was coercive even though the old preferred shareholders were also given a new preferred share and two shares of common stock for each old preferred. Ninety eight percent of the shareholders approved the exchange. The court described the nature of cumulative dividends as follows:

Dividends on common stock are not segregated from the assets of the corporation, so as to become the property of the stockholder, or a debt recoverable by action at law, until declared. In the absence of statute or charter provision requiring distribution, they may be passed into the surplus, remain undivided profits, or be reinvested in the corporate enterprise, at the sound discretion of the directors. While the preferred stockholder is not a creditor of the corporation until the dividend is declared, his right to that dividend stands upon a somewhat different footing. While as a matter of law the right to receive dividends, even on preferred stock, is made to depend on the actual existence of earnings, he has, in appropriate cases, a remedy in equity to compel the payment of his dividends; and we think, meantime, the right to their equitable protection. Dividends are cumulative under plaintiffs' stock, and the right to receive them out of earnings does not abate because they were not promptly declared. The right of the plaintiffs to receive dividends at the expiration of stated periods during which they are earned, and the maturing of the dates upon which the premiums were due, created a definite obligation on the part of the corporation to pay such dividends, out of appropriate funds, of course, which must be considered a vested property right, although circumstances might intervene to postpone or prevent its enjoyment.

200 S.E. at 908–909. See also Barrett v. Denver Tramway Corp., 53 F.Supp. 198 (D.Del.1943), aff'd, 146 F.2d 701 (3d Cir.1944) (exchange of new non-cumulative preferred for old cumulative preferred objectively unfair but not fraudulent and was permissible).

3. Preferred stock has characteristics of both debt and equity. It is debt in the sense that the preferred dividend approximates an interest rate even though the obligation to pay may rest with the board of directors. Adding a cumulative feature pushes it more toward a debt obligation because the obligation continues. Preferred stock is like equity in the sense that it shares in assets in liquidation but usually, like debt, the liquidation preference is limited in amount. Some preferred stock is convertible into common, which allows the holder to participate, at least in the amount of increase above the conversion level, in capital appreciation. There being no free lunch on Wall Street, a convertible preferred will pay a lower dividend than a comparable preferred without such a feature. To make preferred more flexible, financial engineers developed something called remarketed preferred stock. The following is a description in the prospectus of one such offering:

First Federal Capital Funding IV, Inc. (the "Company") is a newly formed Delaware corporation organized for the sole purpose of issuing the shares of RP and managing Eligible Assets consisting of cash. FHLMC Certificates, FNMA Certificates, GNMA Certificates, Conventional Mortgage Passthrough Certificates, U.S. Treasury Securities, Short–Term Money Market Instruments and certain Other Securities as described in this Prospectus. The principal business of the Company will be to purchase, acquire, own, hold, invest in, sell, trade and exchange such Eligible Assets and to use the income generated by such Eligible Assets to pay dividends and to acquire additional Eligible Assets and to conduct activities incidental thereto. All of the Company's outstanding Common Stock is owned by First Federal Savings and Loan Association of Rochester (the "Association" or "First Federal"), Rochester, New York. See

"The Company," "Management" and "Management Discussion and Analysis of Financial Condition and Results of Operations."

The Company is offering 1,500 shares of RP at a purchase price of $100,000 per share. At the election of the Company, subject to certain conditions, the shares of RP are exchangeable in whole for Notes, in the event of certain changes in tax law or on or after the first anniversary of the Date of Original Issue.... * * *

Dividends on the shares of RP are cumulative from the Date of Original Issue and are payable when, as and if declared by the Board of Directors of the Company, commencing on August 22, 1988, in the case of 500 shares of RP, commencing on August 29, 1988 with respect to an additional 500 shares of RP, and commencing on September 12, 1988, in the case of the remaining 500 shares of RP (each, an "Initial Dividend Payment Date") and thereafter on the Business Day following the last of each successive 7–day Dividend Period or 49–day Dividend Period, as the case may be (normally a Monday), subject to certain exceptions (a "Dividend Payment Date"). On the Tender Date with respect to each share of RP, the holder of such share can elect either to tender such share of RP at a price of $100,000 per share, or to hold such share at the new Applicable Dividend Rate and elect either a 7–day Dividend Period or a 49–day Dividend Period with respect thereto. The Applicable Dividend Rate for the Initial Dividend Period ending on August 21, 1988 will be 6.05% per annum, for the Initial Dividend Period ending on August 28, 1988 will be 6.05% per annum, and for the Initial Dividend Period ending on September 11, 1988 will be 6.10% per annum. For each Dividend Period after the corresponding Initial Dividend Period, dividends on each share of RP will accrue at the Applicable Dividend Rate per annum as determined by the Remarketing Agent in its sole judgment (which judgment will be conclusive and binding on all holders).... * * *

Prospectus $150,000,000 First Federal Capital Funding IV, Inc. Exchangeable Remarketed Preferred Stock ["RP"] 1,500 Shares—Liquidation Preference $100,000 Per Share. A tax play on dividends made this program possible. Do you think that such securities should be treated as debt or equity on the balance sheet?

SECTION 3. OTHER DISTRIBUTIONS

KAMIN v. AMERICAN EXPRESS CO.

86 Misc.2d 809, 383 N.Y.S.2d 807 (Sup.),
aff'd, 54 A.D.2d 654, 387 N.Y.S.2d 993 (App.Div.1976).

EDWARD J. GREENFIELD, JUSTICE:

In this stockholders' derivative action, the individual defendants, who are the directors of the American Express Company, move for an order dismissing the complaint for failure to state a cause of action pursuant to CPLR 3211(a)(7), and alternatively, for summary judgment pursuant to CPLR 3211(c).

The complaint is brought derivatively by two minority stockholders of the American Express Company, asking for a declaration that a certain dividend in kind is a waste of corporate assets, directing the defendants not to proceed with the distribution, or, in the alternative, for monetary damages. The motion to dismiss the complaint requires the Court to presuppose the truth of the allegations. It is the defendants' contention that, conceding everything in the complaint, no viable cause of action is made out.

After establishing the identity of the parties, the complaint alleges that in 1972 American Express acquired for investment 1,954,418 shares of common stock of Donaldson, Lufken and Jenrette, Inc. (hereafter DLJ), a publicly traded corporation, at a cost of $29.9 million. It is further alleged that the current market value of those shares is approximately $4.0 million. On July 28, 1975, it is alleged, the Board of Directors of American Express declared a special dividend to all stockholders of record pursuant to which the shares of DLJ would be distributed in kind. Plaintiffs contend further that if American Express were to sell the DLJ shares on the market, it would sustain a capital loss of $25 million, which could be offset against taxable capital gains on other investments. Such a sale, they allege, would result in tax savings to the company of approximately $8 million, which would not be available in the case of the distribution of DLJ shares to stockholders. It is alleged that on October 8, 1975 and October 16, 1975, plaintiffs demanded that the directors rescind the previously declared dividend in DLJ shares and take steps to preserve the capital loss which would result from selling the shares. This demand was rejected by the Board of Directors on October 17, 1975.

It is apparent that all the previously-mentioned allegations of the complaint go to the question of the exercise by the Board of Directors of business judgment in deciding how to deal with the DLJ shares. The crucial allegation which must be scrutinized to determine the legal sufficiency of the complaint is paragraph 19, which alleges:

'19. All of the defendant Directors engaged in or acquiesced in or negligently permitted the declaration and payment of the Dividend in violation of the fiduciary duty owed by them to Amex to care for and preserve Amex's assets in the same manner as a man of average prudence would care for his own property.'

Plaintiffs never moved for temporary injunctive relief, and did nothing to bar the actual distribution of the DLJ shares. The dividend was in fact paid on October 31, 1975. Accordingly, that portion of the complaint seeking a direction not to distribute the shares is deemed to be moot, and the Court will deal only with the request for declaratory judgment or for damages.

Examination of the complaint reveals that there is no claim of fraud or self-dealing, and no contention that there was any bad faith or oppressive conduct. The law is quite clear as to what is necessary to ground a claim for actionable wrongdoing.

'In actions by stockholders, which assail the acts of their directors or trustees, courts will not interfere unless the powers have been illegally or unconscientiously executed; or unless it be made to appear that the acts were fraudulent or collusive, and destructive of the rights of the stockholders. Mere errors of judgment are not sufficient as grounds for equity interference, for the powers of those entrusted with corporate management are largely discretionary.' Leslie v. Lorillard, 110 N.Y. 519, 532, 18 N.E. 363, 365. See also, Winter v. Anderson, 242 App.Div. 430, 432, 275 N.Y.S. 373, 374; Rous v. Carlisle, 261 App.Div. 432, 434, 26 N.Y.S.2d 197, 200, affd. 290 N.Y. 869, 50 N.E.2d 250; 11 New York Jurisprudence, Corporations, Section 378.

More specifically, the question of whether or not a dividend is to be declared or a distribution of some kind should be made is exclusively a matter of business judgment for the Board of Directors. ' * * * Courts will not interfere with such discretion unless it be first made to appear that the directors have acted or are about to act in bad faith and for a dishonest purpose. It is for the directors to say, acting in good faith of course, when and to what extent dividends shall be declared * * * The statute confers upon the directors this power, and the minority stockholders are not in a position to question this right, so long as the directors are acting in good faith * * *' Liebman v. Auto Strop Co., 241 N.Y. 427, 433—4, 150 N.E. 505, 506. Accord: City Bank Farmers' Trust Co. v. Hewitt Realty Co., 257 N.Y. 62, 177 N.E. 309; Venner v. Southern Pacific Co., 2 Cir., 279 F. 832, cert. denied 258 U.S. 628.

Thus, a complaint must be dismissed if all that is presented is a decision to pay dividends rather than pursuing some other course of conduct. Weinberger v. Quinn, 264 App.Div. 405, 35 N.Y.S.2d 567, affd. 290 N.Y. 635, 49 N.E.2d 131. A complaint which alleges merely that some course of action other than that pursued by the Board of Directors would have been more advantageous gives rise to no cognizable cause of action. Courts have more than enough to do in adjudicating legal rights and devising remedies for wrongs. The directors' room rather than the courtroom is the appropriate forum for thrashing out purely business questions which will have an impact on profits, market prices, competitive situations, or tax advantages. As stated by Cardozo, J., when sitting at Special Term, the substitution of someone else's business judgment for that of the directors 'is no business for any court to follow.' Holmes v. St. Joseph Lead Co., 84 Misc. 278, 283, 147 N.Y.S. 104, 107, quoting from Gamble v. Queens County Water Co., 123 N.Y. 91, 99, 25 N.E. 201, 202.

It is not enough to allege, as plaintiffs do here, that the directors made an imprudent decision, which did not capitalize on the possibility of using a potential capital loss to offset capital gains. More than imprudence or mistaken judgment must be shown.

'Questions of policy of management, expediency of contracts or action, adequacy of consideration, lawful appropriation of corporate funds to advance corporate interests, are left solely to their honest and unselfish decision, for their powers therein are without limitation and free from restraint, and the exercise of them for the common and general interests of the corporation may not be questioned, although the results show that what they did was unwise or inexpedient.' Pollitz v. Wabash Railroad Co., 207 N.Y. 113, 124, 100 N.E. 721, 724.

Section 720(a)(1)(A) of the Business Corporation Law permits an action against directors for 'the neglect of, or failure to perform, or other violation of his duties in the management and disposition of corporate assets committed to his charge.' This does not mean that a director is chargeable with ordinary negligence for having made an improper decision, or having acted imprudently. The 'neglect' referred to in the statute is neglect of duties (i.e., malfeasance or nonfeasance) and not misjudgment. To allege that a director 'negligently permitted the declaration and payment' of a dividend without alleging fraud, dishonesty or nonfeasance, is to state merely that a decision was taken with which one disagrees.

Nor does this appear to be a case in which a potentially valid cause of action is inartfully stated. The defendants have moved alternatively for summary judgment and have submitted affidavits under CPLR 3211(c), and plaintiffs likewise have submitted papers enlarging upon the allegations of the complaint. The affidavits of the defendants and the exhibits annexed thereto demonstrate that the objections raised by the plaintiffs to the proposed dividend action were carefully considered and unanimously rejected by the Board at a special meeting called precisely for that purpose at the plaintiffs' request. The minutes of the special meeting indicate that the defendants were fully aware that a sale rather than a distribution of the DLJ shares might result in the realization of a substantial income tax saving. Nevertheless, they concluded that there were countervailing considerations primarily with respect to the adverse effect such a sale, realizing a loss of $25 million, would have on the net income figures in the American Express financial statement. Such a reduction of net income would have a serious effect on the market value of the publicly traded American Express stock. This was not a situation in which the defendant directors totally overlooked facts called to their attention. They gave them consideration, and attempted to view the total picture in arriving at their decision. While plaintiffs contend that according to their accounting consultants the loss on the DLJ stock would still have to be charged against current earnings even if the stock were distributed, the defendants' accounting experts assert that the loss would be a charge against earnings only in the event of a sale, whereas in the event of distribution of the stock as a dividend, the proper accounting treatment would be to charge the loss only against surplus. While the chief accountant for the SEC raised some question as to the appropriate accounting treatment of this transaction, there was no basis for any action to be taken by the SEC with respect to the American Express financial statement.

The only hint of self-interest which is raised, not in the complaint but in the papers on the motion, is that four of the twenty directors were officers and employees of American Express and members of its Executive

Incentive Compensation Plan. Hence, it is suggested, by virtue of the action taken earnings may have been overstated and their compensation affected thereby. Such a claim is highly speculative and standing alone can hardly be regarded as sufficient to support an inference of self-dealing. There is no claim or showing that the four company directors dominated and controlled the sixteen outside members of the Board. Certainly, every action taken by the Board has some impact on earnings and may therefore affect the compensation of those whose earnings are keyed to profits. That does not disqualify the inside directors, nor does it put every policy adopted by the Board in question. All directors have an obligation, using sound business judgment, to maximize income for the benefit of all persons having a stake in the welfare of the corporate entity. See, Amdur v. Meyer, 15 A.D.2d 425, 224 N.Y.S.2d 440, appeal dismissed 14 N.Y.2d 541, 248 N.Y.S.2d 639, 198 N.E.2d 30. What we have here as revealed both by the complaint and by the affidavits and exhibits, is that a disagreement exists between two minority stockholders and a unanimous Board of Directors as to the best way to handle a loss already incurred on an investment. The directors are entitled to exercise their honest business judgment on the information before them, and to act within their corporate powers. That they may be mistaken, that other courses of action might have differing consequences, or that their action might benefit some shareholders more than others presents no basis for the superimposition of judicial judgment, so long as it appears that the directors have been acting in good faith. The question of to what extent a dividend shall be declared and the manner in which it shall be paid is ordinarily subject only to the qualification that the dividend be paid out of surplus (Business Corporation Law Section 510, subd. b). The Court will not interfere unless a clear case is made out of fraud, oppression, arbitrary action, or breach of trust.

Courts should not shrink from the responsibility of dismissing complaints or granting summary judgment when no legal wrongdoing is set forth. As stated in Greenbaum v. American Metal Climax Inc., 27 A.D.2d 225, 231–2, 278 N.Y.S.2d 123, 130: 'It is well known that derivative actions by stockholders generally involve extensive pretrial procedures, including lengthy examinations before trial, and then, finally, prolonged trials; and that they also entail large litigation costs, including the probability of a considerable liability upon the corporation for the defense costs of defendant officers. Such actions are a heavy burden upon the courts and litigants. Consequently, the summary judgment remedy should be fully utilized and given due effect to challenge such an action which appears to be in the nature of a strike suit or otherwise lacks apparent merit * * * (plaintiffs) are bound to bear in mind that matters depending on business judgment are not actionable (Cf. Steinberg v. Carey, 285 App.Div. 1131, 140 N.Y.S.2d 574). They are required to set forth something more than vague general charges of wrongdoing; the charges must be supported by factual assertions of specific wrongdoing; conclusory allegations of breaches of fiduciary duty are not enough.'

In this case it clearly appears that the plaintiffs have failed as a matter of law to make out an actionable claim. Accordingly, the motion by the defendants for summary judgment and dismissal of the complaint is granted.

NOTES

1. Do you agree with the court that that a corporation's board of directors may properly forgo an $8 million tax benefit in order to dress up the company's earnings and allow the board to avoid acknowledging that it made a bad investment?

2. For subsequent developments in the ownership of Donaldson, Lufkin & Jenrette, including its issuance of tracking stock for its online trading operations, see Sedighim v. Donaldson, Lufkin & Jenrette, Inc., 167 F. Supp.2d 639 (S.D.N.Y.2001).

3. Another form of distribution is the stock dividend in which existing shareholders are given additional stock as a dividend. This distribution is to be distinguished from a stock split in which existing shares are merely divided into smaller units, diluting all shares equally. The stock dividend may have a similar effect on dilution, but in balance sheet states surplus capital must be set aside to support the stated capital or par value of the stocks issued as a dividend. See 8 Del. Corp. L. § 173. This will reduce the ability of the company to pay cash dividends because the amount of capital surplus will be less. Model Bus. Corp. Act. § 1.40(6), however, excludes stock dividends from the act's restrictions on cash dividends and other distributions in Model Bus. Corp. Act § 6.40. Generally Accepted Accounting Principles may still require a reduction of retained earnings to reflect the stock dividend. See James D. Cox & Thomas Lee Hazen, Corporations, § 20.21 (2d ed. 2003).

4. Dividends and distributions may take other forms. One of the more exotic dividends is the payment-in-kind ("PIK") used for some preferred shares or even debentures. For a PIK Preferred, the dividend is paid initially in additional shares of the preferred, and in later years cash dividends are paid. Richard B. Tyler, "Other Constituency Statutes," 59 Mo. L. Rev. 373, 397, n. 121 (1994). See generally Mezzonen, S.A. v. Wright, Fed Sec. L. Rep. (CCH) ¶ 90,704 (S.D.N.Y. 1999) (dividends ranging from 15% to 25% paid on preferred shares in the form of "payments in kind" of additional shares of preferred stock).

NEIMARK v. MEL KRAMER SALES, INC.

102 Wis.2d 282, 306 N.W.2d 278 (App.1981), review denied,
107 Wis.2d 756, 324 N.W.2d 825 (1982).

DECKER, CHIEF JUDGE.

This appeal questions whether the trial court erred in this shareholder's derivative action by ordering specific performance of a stock redemption agreement upon death of the principal shareholder of defendant corporation. We vacate the judgment and remand with directions.

Plaintiff seeks specific performance of an agreement for the redemption of stock owned by the late Mel Kramer (Kramer), founder and majority shareholder of Mel Kramer Sales, Inc. (MKS). MKS is a closely-held Wisconsin corporation engaged in the business of selling automotive parts and accessories. The interests of the shareholders are:

Shareholder	Number of Shares	Percentage
Mel Kramer/Estate of Mel Kramer	1,020	51
Delores Kramer	200	10
Jack Neimark	580	29
Jerome Sadowsky	200	10

Kramer died on December 5, 1976. On May 9, 1977, Delores Kramer, Kramer's widow, was appointed personal representative of his estate. Delores Kramer is president and a director of MKS. Jack Neimark is vice-president and a director. Directors David Gutkin and Sara Lee Begun are relatives of Delores Kramer.

On June 22, 1976, a stock redemption agreement was executed by MKS and its stockholders. The agreement requires MKS to purchase, and a deceased shareholder's estate to sell, all of the deceased shareholder's stock in MKS at $400 per share, less a specified credit.[1] The agreement also provided Delores Kramer with the option to sell her shares to MKS in the event of Kramer's death.

Under the agreement, Kramer's 1,020 shares were to be redeemed by MKS within thirty days after the appointment of his estate's personal representative, Delores Kramer, in the following manner. The redemption price of $408,000, less a specifically provided $50,000 credit, constituting a net price of $358,000, was to be paid in installments of $100,000 at the closing, and the balance in five consecutive annual installments. The first installment after the closing was to be $43,200, with four remaining installments of $53,700, plus interest at 6%. If Delores Kramer elected to redeem her shares, her stock was to be purchased at the same per-share price payable in two installments of $40,000, on the sixth and seventh anniversaries of the closing, plus interest at 6% after five years.

The agreement provided that the $100,000 payment for Kramer's shares was to be funded by a life insurance policy on Kramer's life. Upon Kramer's death, MKS received the $100,000 proceeds from the life insurance policy, and it was reflected in MKS's retained earnings as of December 31, 1976.

---

1. The $50,000 credit was funded by a group life insurance policy paid to Kramer's beneficiary.

The agreement also provided that if MKS did not have sufficient surplus or retained earnings to purchase the deceased shareholder's stock, the parties would contribute the necessary capital to enable MKS to lawfully redeem the decedent's shares. It was also agreed that the parties would be entitled to specific performance of the agreement.

After Kramer's death, Delores Kramer indicated a reluctance to have MKS redeem the shares owned by her husband's estate. Neimark insisted that MKS redeem the estate's shares, and on May 23, 1977, the board of directors met to consider Neimark's demand. The MKS attorney who was the author of the stock redemption agreement was present at this meeting and explained to the board that redemption of the stock by MKS would violate sec. 180.385(1), Stats.[2] The board voted 3–1 not to purchase the Kramer estate's shares. Neimark, of course, cast the losing vote.

On November 30, 1978, Neimark commenced an action for specific performance of the 1976 agreement and alternatively, sought monetary damages. The first claim was derivative on behalf of MKS, pursuant to sec. 180.405, Stats; the second claim was personal.

Subsequently, a third party offered to purchase the business for $1,000,000. Neimark conditioned his approval of the sale on the requirement that Delores Kramer and the Kramer estate receive proceeds equal only to the redemption price of the shares which was substantially less than the tendered per-share price. The defendants counterclaimed in Neimark's action and sought an order declaring that Neimark was entitled to receive only his ratable share of the proceeds of any sale of the business, which denied him the redemption agreement benefits. The trial court dismissed Neimark's personal claim, but ordered specific performance of the stock redemption agreement under the derivative claim. The counterclaim was dismissed.

Defendants present three issues for our consideration: (1) did the failure to perform the stock redemption agreement cause injury to the

---

2. Section 180.385(1), Stats., provides:

180.385   Right of corporation to acquire and dispose of its own shares.

(1) Unless otherwise provided in the articles of incorporation, a corporation shall have the right to purchase, take, receive, or otherwise acquire, hold, own, pledge, transfer, or otherwise dispose of its own shares; provided that no such acquisition, directly or indirectly, of its own shares for a consideration other than its own shares of equal or subordinate rank shall be made unless all of the following conditions are met:

(a) At the time of such acquisition the corporation is not and would not thereby be rendered insolvent;

(b) The net assets of the corporation remaining after such acquisition would be not less than the aggregate preferential amount payable in the event of voluntary liquidation to the holders of shares having preferential rights to the assets of the corporation in the event of liquidation; and

(c) 1. Such acquisition is authorized by the articles of incorporation or by the affirmative vote or the written consent of the holders of at least a majority of the outstanding shares of the same class and of each class entitled to equal or prior rank in the distribution of assets in the event of voluntary liquidation; or

2. Such acquisition is authorized by the board of directors and the corporation has unreserved and unrestricted earned surplus equal to the cost of such shares. . . .

corporation sufficient to provide a basis for the shareholder's derivative claim; (2) did the trial court correctly conclude that MKS could lawfully redeem the estate's shares under secs. 180.385(1), 180.02(11), and 180.02(14), Stats; and (3) would specific performance of the redemption agreement be inequitable?

A fundamental requirement of a stockholder's derivative action is an injury or wrong to the corporation. Shelstad v. Cook, 77 Wis.2d 547, 553, 253 N.W.2d 517, 521 (1977); Rose v. Schantz, 56 Wis.2d 222, 229, 201 N.W.2d 593, 598 (1972). In the context of this case, we view the existence of injury or wrong to MKS as a question of mixed fact and law. The trial court found that the failure of MKS to perform its agreement to redeem the Mel Kramer stock constituted an injury to MKS, because such conduct neglected to take advantage of a $50,000 credit upon the purchase price of the stock, and hazarded the prospect of acquisition of the stock by outsiders. We observe that such omission also sacrificed the utilization of the financial advantage to MKS of acquisition of the stock over a five-year period at a low interest rate.

The trial court's findings are basically grounded upon the terms of the stock redemption agreement. Since that evidence is undisputed and not in conflict with other evidence, we need not accord special deference to those findings. Nonetheless, we are in complete agreement with the trial court's conclusion that failure to perform the agreement resulted in economic injury to the corporation.

Section 180.385(1), Stats., prohibits, inter alia, acquisition by a corporation of its own stock if the corporation would thereby be rendered insolvent. "Insolvent" is defined in sec. 180.02(14) as the "inability of a corporation to pay its debts as they become due in the usual course of its business." The purpose of prohibiting own stock acquisition by a corporation if it would thereby be rendered insolvent is to protect the creditors, preferred security holders, and in some cases, common stockholders whose stock is not acquired, from director action which would strip funds from the corporation and create a distributive preference to the stockholder whose stock is acquired.

In the context of this case, we view the question of whether MKS would be rendered insolvent by performance of the stock redemption agreement as a mixed question of law and fact. To the extent that the evidence with respect to factual matters is in conflict, we defer to the factual determination by the trial court unless we find it contrary to the great weight and clear preponderance of the evidence. Zapuchlak v. Hucal, 82 Wis.2d 184, 192, 262 N.W.2d 514, 518 (1978).

The trial court's finding of fact, that performance of the stock redemption agreement would not render the corporation insolvent, is supported by ample evidence, and is not contrary to the great weight and clear preponderance of the evidence. The evidence establishes the fact that the corporation had the ability to pay its debts as they became due. In arriving at that conclusion, the trial court is not restricted to analyzing the cash and cash-equivalent assets of the corporation. The flow of cash to maintain solvency can be generated by a multitude of means other than cash generated solely from sales.

In this case, MKS had a $275,000 line of credit with a local bank. Its annual financial statements for 1976, 1977, and 1978, and the May 31, 1979, financial statement, disclose no inability of MKS to pay its debts as they became due if the redemption agreement had been performed.

Upon Kramer's death, it became the obligation of MKS to redeem his stock, provided the corporation could comply with sec. 180.385(1), Stats., with respect to solvency. We agree with the trial court's finding of fact that it could. To the extent that the finding also constitutes a conclusion of law, we also agree. Contrary to the English rule, American courts at common law generally permit a corporation to acquire its own shares. The American rule has undergone harsh criticism because of the opportunity it affords to prefer selected stockholder/sellers and strip funds from the corporation to the disadvantage of preferred security interest holders, other common stockholders, and creditors. The rule sought protection for those persons by vaguely requiring that the purchase be "without prejudice" to their interests. Steven v. Hale–Haas Corp., 249 Wis. 205, 231, 23 N.W.2d 620, 632 (1946); Koeppler v. Crocker Chair Co., 200 Wis. 476, 480–81, 228 N.W. 130, 132 (1930). Additional statutory restrictions resulted and culminated in the two major restraints (for the purposes of this case): the purchase must be made out of earned surplus and cannot be made if insolvency, in the equity sense, is present or would result. "(I)nsolvency in the equity sense has always meant an inability of the debtor to pay his debts as they mature. Under the Bankruptcy Act it means an insufficiency of assets at a fair valuation to pay the debts." Finn v. Meighan, 325 U.S. 300, 303, 65 S.Ct. 1147, 1149, 89 L.Ed. 1624 (1945). The surplus and insolvency tests were incorporated in § 6 of the Model Business Corporation Act which formed the basis of the revision of the Wisconsin Business Corporation Law in the early 1950's. Section 180.385, Stats., adopts surplus and insolvency tests. Purchase of shares is permitted if: "At the time of such acquisition the corporation is not and would not thereby be rendered insolvent." Sec. 180.385(1)(a), Stats.

The self-evident applicability of the insolvency test at the time of acquisition of the stock is not equally self-evident in the case of an installment purchase. Considerations of "corporate flexibility" in the acquisition of its stock for legitimate purposes, balanced by "protection for creditors," led the majority of American courts to apply the insolvency test contemporaneously with each installment payment. The Model Business Corporation Act § 6 has been amended to specifically so provide. Although that specific change has not been incorporated in sec. 180.385(1)(a), Stats., we agree with the reasoning of the majority of American courts that the protection of the corporation's creditors requires that the insolvency limitation be applied both at the time of purchase and when each installment payment is made pursuant to the purchase agreement. When the payment is actually made, the assets leave the corporation and concomitantly the loss of financial protection occurs. If insolvency results or would result, the purchase may constitute a fraudulent conveyance. In any event, the hazard of fraud to creditors is too great to permit the insolvency test to be applied at times remote to payment for the share repurchase.

Section 180.385(1)(a), Stats., recognized the problem inherent in the single application of the insolvency test and achieved flexibility by prohibiting a purchase resulting in a corporation that "is" insolvent or "would ... be" rendered insolvent. Thus, flexibility is achieved by the statute in its application of the insolvency test to each purchase payment.

When applying the insolvency test at the stage of each payment for a stock repurchase to achieve creditor protection, consistency suggests that the amount of each payment, not the total purchase price, should be a component of the determination of solvency. The weight of authority has so applied the tests and we adopt that method of application. That method is in accord with the equity sense insolvency test expressly prescribed by secs. 180.02(11) and 180.385(1)(a), Stats.

Defendants have not demonstrated insolvency in the equity sense to the trial court or to us. Our review of the corporate financial statements in evidence discloses no arguable claim of insolvency in the equity sense. The only claim of MKS's insolvency made by defendants is premised upon a deduction of the total stock redemption purchase price from the corporate assets, thereby creating a balance sheet negative net worth, although the installment payments of the purchase price are spread over five years. We reject the argument because it applies a bankruptcy rather than equity insolvency test, and is contrary to secs. 180.02(11) and 180.385(1)(a), Stats.[6]

The second limitation upon the corporate repurchase of its stock pertinent to this case is the restriction that "the corporation has unreserved and unrestricted earned surplus equal to the cost of such shares." Sec. 180.385(1)(c)2., Stats. In this respect, the Wisconsin Business Corporation Law generally follows its paradigm, the Model Business Corporation Act. Earned surplus is defined in sec. 180.02(11).[7] In this case, the parties do not dispute the amount of earned surplus.

Our review of the record again establishes the following undisputed evidence with respect to paid-up capital stock, retained earnings, and total stockholders' equity.

---

6. The modernized corporation statutes of Maryland, North Carolina, and Texas apply a bankruptcy insolvency test in addition to an equity insolvency test.

7. For the purpose of this case, earned surplus can be considered to be the retained earnings of the corporation.

	12/31 1976	12/31 1977	12/31 1978	5/31 1979
Paid-up Capital Stock	69,400	69,400	69,400	69,400
Retained Earnings	246,409	276,073	317,586	317,584
Current Earnings	31,575			
Stockholders' Equity	315,809	345,473	386,986	418,559

We subtract projected payments pursuant to the stock redemption agreement.

Retained and Current Earnings Adjusted to Reflect Deducted Installment Payments	276,073	217,586	205,961
Installment Payments Without Interest	100,000	43,200	53,700
Net Retained Earnings	176,073	174,386	152,261
Credit	50,000		

Historically, the statutory insolvency cutoff test evolved from the "no prejudice to creditors" rule. Dissatisfaction with the limited effectiveness of that test resulted in the formulation of the surplus cutoff test to be applied in conjunction with the insolvency cutoff test.

The same problem arose with the application of the surplus cutoff test that developed in applying the insolvency cutoff test: in the case of an installment purchase, should the surplus test be applied at the time of purchase or at the time cash payment is made? Most cases demonstrate little effort to distinguish between the methods of applying both tests and resolve the question by the easier and more convenient method of applying both tests in the same fashion.

For example, the effect of the Fourth Circuit Court of Appeals' holding in Mountain State Steel Foundries, Inc. v. Commissioner, 284 F.2d 737 (1960), was to treat an installment repurchase transaction as if each successive installment constituted an independent purchase transaction by applying the surplus test at the time of each payment. In re Mathews Construction Co., 120 F.Supp. 818 (S.D.Cal.1954), also involved application of the surplus cutoff test and like Mountain State, indiscriminately applied the reasoning found in Robinson v. Wangemann, 75 F.2d 756 (5th Cir.1935), that a contract of sale was executory until each payment was made in cash, and therefore applied the surplus cutoff test to each installment payment.

Professor Herwitz discusses a number of reasons for applying the surplus to the time of purchase rather than at each installment payment. We agree with his view that the statutory surplus cutoff rule should be applied only once, and at the time of purchase, for the following reasons:

(1) unlike the equity insolvency test, a surplus test does not center upon current liabilities;

(2) unlike the application of the insolvency test, the surplus test is analogous to a purchase for cash and a loan of the unpaid cash price back to the corporation;

(3) installment application of the surplus test could bar performance of a valid obligation of the corporation to the selling stockholder but permit the corporation to disburse funds to current stockholders;

(4) the statutory requirement that surplus be restricted by such a purchase agreement could be frustrated by a construction that would require restriction only on an installment-by-installment basis and permit distributions to shareholders even though the surplus was insufficient to consummate the purchase agreement;

(5) in the manner described in (4), a limited amount of surplus could be used to justify the purchase of an unlimited amount of stock;

(6) when applied to installment payments, the surplus test could be continued indefinitely with current stockholders receiving distributions, putting the selling stockholder in limbo without the status of either creditor or stockholder;

(7) if a default in an installment is compelled by the surplus test, the selling stockholder could possibly obtain a windfall return of all of stock, including the part for which payment had already been made;

(8) a creditor with knowledge of the purchase agreement could be unprotected by installment application of the statutory surplus test limitation, Atlanta & Walworth Butter & Cheese Ass'n v. Smith, 141 Wis. 377, 123 N.W. 106 (1909);

(9) if interest has been deducted in computing corporate net income, application of the surplus test upon an installment basis to the interest on the purchase price is unsupportable because it would take interest into account twice;

(10) the unpaid selling stockholder is given no consideration, at least to the extent of undistributed surplus, over the other stockholders who are the beneficiaries of the stock purchase; and

(11) the application of the surplus cutoff test at the outset of an installment purchase would in no way hamper or alter the installment application of the equity insolvency test.

We consider it a futile exercise to attempt to ground our decision upon the subtleties and nuances of semantic lexicography in defining "purchase," "acquisition," and the other acquisitory words of transfer used in the statute. The above reasons persuade us that the application of the surplus cutoff test is required to be timed to the purchase rather than the payment of cash. Such a construction comports with the need for corporate flexibility in acquiring its own stock for legitimate purposes and the protection of creditors and holders of other securities of the corporation.

The Minnesota and Texas Supreme Courts, and the Ninth Circuit Court of Appeals, have taken similar views in Tracy v. Perkins–Tracy Printing Co., 278 Minn. 159, 153 N.W.2d 241 (1967); Williams v. Nevelow, 513 S.W.2d 535 (Tex.1974); and Walsh v. Paterna, 537 F.2d 329 (9th Cir.1976). Although differing state statutory formulations were involved, like Wisconsin's, the statutes do not specifically resolve the issues presented there or here.

Although it is apparent from the MKS financial statements that application of the surplus cutoff test upon an installment basis would not have precluded specific performance as ordered by the trial court, application of the test at the outset will preclude specific performance upon the basis of the facts as presented to us. However, we note that the stock redemption agreement provides:

> (f) Insufficient Corporate Surplus. If the Corporation does not have sufficient surplus or retained earnings to permit it to lawfully purchase all of such shares, each of the parties shall promptly take such measures as are required to reduce the capital of the Corporation or to take such other steps as may be necessary in order to enable the Corporation to lawfully purchase and pay for the Decedent's shares.

We vacate the judgment of the circuit court and remand for further proceedings consistent with this opinion. The circuit court is directed to apply the surplus cutoff test to the time of specific performance of the stock redemption agreement if it concludes that the evidence justifies specific performance. Because we adopt an application of the statute which has not heretofore been explicated, we think it fair to permit the parties to offer current financial data with respect to MKS and the ability of the parties to the redemption agreement to take the necessary steps to enable the corporation to lawfully purchase and pay for the redeemed stock. Such evidence will enable a current evaluation of the propriety of specific performance. In the event the trial court deems specific performance appropriate, it shall make the necessary findings and requirements with regard to providing sufficient earned surplus and assuring solvency as a condition to specific performance.

We reject the defendants' claim of applicability of the business judgment rule to the facts of this case. That rule accords judicial deference to a business judgment but is generally applicable to acquisition of a corporation's own stock where the board of directors has authorized the acquisition without approval of the stockholders, unlike the present circumstance where all of the stockholders consented and bound themselves to the stock redemption agreement.

Defendant Delores Kramer claims that enforcement of the stock redemption agreement would be inequitable. We disagree. The requirement of adequate surplus at purchase will provide a restricted surplus account to the extent of the unpaid balance of the purchase price. It is true that she becomes a creditor of the corporation and is subject to the hazard of a business failure. She also received the benefit of a compelled market for her stock, had she desired to liquidate her interest in MKS. Her predecessor owner executed the agreement which expressly provided for specific performance. The transaction by its terms made the seller a creditor of the business. Obviously Mel Kramer thought the agreement fairly balanced the corporate obligation to acquire the stock with the owner's opportunity to liquidate an investment in a corporation whose majority stockholder and principal officer had died.

Judgment vacated and cause remanded for further proceedings consistent with this opinion.

Notes

1. Stock redemption agreements and other share purchases represent in effect a partial liquidation of the company. If the redemption is extended to less than all shareholders in a closely held corporation, the excluded shareholders are being denied a market for their stock. This concern is ever present in closely held corporations.

2. Several cases have considered whether redemption agreements paying for stock in installments were enforceable under state dividend tests. See generally Wolff v. Heidritter Lumber Co., 112 N.J.Eq. 34, 163 A. 140 (Ch. 1932) (selling shareholder had a valid claim in bankruptcy where corporation became insolvent before completing installment payments); Williams v. Nevelow, 513 S.W.2d 535 (Tex.1974) (selling shareholder could execute on notes where at the time of the exchange of the corporation's secured note for its stock, the corporation was solvent and had unrestricted earned surplus in excess of the amount of the note and where the exchange did not cause the bankruptcy of the corporation). But see Mountain State Steel Foundries v. Commissioner, 284 F.2d 737 (4th Cir.1960) (West Va. statute required surplus test be met when each installment is paid).

SECTION 4. LIABILITY FOR WRONGFUL DISTRIBUTIONS

PROTOCOMM CORP. v. NOVELL, INC.

171 F.Supp.2d 459 (E.D.Pa.2001).

LOWELL A. REED, JR., SENIOR DISTRICT JUDGE.

Two motions are presently before this Court in this third generation lawsuit which sprung from a breach of contract dispute between plaintiff ProtoComm Corporation ("ProtoComm") and Fluent, Inc., ("Fluent"), now Novell Advanced Services ("Novell"). Defendants Technology for Information and Publishing, L.P., David L. Nelson, Cornelius A. Ferris, and Premkumar Uppaluru (collectively referred to as "Former Fluent Shareholders") filed a motion for summary judgment (Document No. 67), pursuant to Federal Rule of Civil Procedure 56, and ProtoComm and remaining defendants Aenas Venture Corporation, ASCII Corporation, Cirrus Logic, Inc., FIP Associates Ltd. and FIP II, Ltd., and Intel Corporation (collectively referred to as "settling defendants") filed a joint motion to dismiss with prejudice all claims of plaintiff against such defendants (Document No. 76), pursuant to Federal Rule of Civil Procedure 41(a)(2) to which the Former Fluent Shareholders (also referred to as "non-settling defendants") object.

Upon consideration of the motions, responses and replies thereto, and for the reasons set forth below, I will deny in part and grant in part the motion for summary judgment and grant the joint motion to dismiss.

This lawsuit has its roots in a case brought by ProtoComm against Fluent which alleged a breach of a contract to develop a video server software. ("ProtoComm I"). On July 24, 1996, a jury returned a verdict in favor of ProtoComm and against Fluent for $12.5 million. The Court of Appeals for the Third Circuit affirmed the verdict on October 29, 1997. The details of ProtoComm I and the suit which followed, ProtoComm II, have been detailed at length by this Court and will not be repeated here. The following background is relevant to this case, ProtoComm III, which involves at its core a complex transaction whereby Novell acquired Fluent while the ProtoComm I case was pending.

In or around January, 1993, Novell began investigating the possibility of investing in Fluent. In February, 1993, Novell appeared "positive" toward making such an investment. (Pl.'s Ex. 13, explained supra.) This investment would go into Fluent's treasury. The ProtoComm I suit was filed on January 29, 1993. Upon discovering the lawsuit, Novell told Fluent that the investment activities would cease until the suit was settled.

On March 19, 1993, David Bradford ("Bradford"), Novell's Senior Vice President and General Counsel, sent a draft letter of intent to Cornelius Ferris ("Ferris"), Fluent's President; the letter contemplated that the acquisition would take the form of an asset purchase. On April 28, 1993, Bradford sent a letter of intent to Ferris; the letter contemplated that the acquisition would take the form of a stock sale in which Fluent would become a wholly owned subsidiary of Novell. The letter of intent required as a condition precedent to the acquisition that "the lawsuit with ProtoComm be provided for to Novell's satisfaction."

Where the April 28, 1993 letter of intent had included the language that Novell would acquire "all of the business, assets, and obligations of Fluent," the actual agreement, dated June 4, 1993, excluded such language. The agreement did retain language providing that the ProtoComm litigation "shall have been resolved to the satisfaction of Fluent and Novell." The proxy statement furnished to Fluent's stockholders in connection with the solicitation of proxies by Fluent's Board approving the agreement, introduces the acquisition as a "merger" constituting "a liquidation of the Company under the Charter." On July 2, 1993, Paul Desjourdy, Fluent's attorney, sent a letter to Betty Depaola at Novell, detailing the disbursement of payments as a result of the acquisition. The payment included, *inter alia,* employee bonus payments and noteholder payments. Neither Bradford nor Cameron Read, Fluent's counsel for the transaction, could recall at their depositions why the acquisition evolved into a cash-for-stock transaction.

The ProtoComm I lawsuit was discussed during at least three Board meetings. The files of Read contained the complaint and the underlying agreement, as well as other ProtoComm related documents. Ferris originally testified at his deposition that at the final hours before the deal, Bradford requested that the deal be redone to set aside money for the potential judgment in the ProtoComm I suit. Ferris pleaded with Bradford not to make this change, and Bradford acquiesced. Ferris later recanted this testimony. In June, 1993, Rob Hicks, an associate counsel at Novell, sent a fax to Dan Heist, President of ProtoComm, proposing a settlement in the ProtoComm I litigation. David Smith, on behalf of ProtoComm, sent a counter proposal. A second proposal was then made by Novell.

On July 7, 1993, the acquisition occurred. Novell paid $18.5 million and assumed $3 million in liabilities. The litigation had not ended at the time of the closing. On August 9, 1993, Ernst & Young sent Novell an asset valuation study of Fluent, in which the assets were valued at $21.55 million. Eventually, Fluent's assets, including, *inter alia,* Fluent's intellectual property and technology patents, as well as Fluent employees, were transferred to Novell. It is unclear to this Court when the transfer began. It seems that at least some employees were transferred onto the Novell payroll soon after the closing. It appears the technology assets were transferred by May, 1994.

ProtoComm's claim is essentially as follows: Although defendants called Novell's acquisition of Fluent a stock purchase, in reality, it was an asset sale designed to leave Fluent an empty shell and ProtoComm holding an uncollectible judgment. Fluent's assets were conveyed to Novell, and the purchase price was paid out either as fraudulent conveyances or illegal dividends or both to Fluent's shareholders. Fluent was then left with nothing but obligations to ProtoComm.

The Former Fluent Shareholders essentially contend the following: On July 7, 1993, Novell purchased all of the outstanding stock of Fluent from the Fluent shareholders. After the stock sale occurred, Fluent became a wholly owned subsidiary of Novell and the stock sale ownership of Fluent passed to Novell. It was only after Novell's sales of Fluent's products were deemed disappointing that steps were taken to consolidate Fluent with Novell and to transfer the assets. * * *

The claim for fraudulent conveyances is brought under the Pennsylvania Uniform Fraudulent Conveyances Act ("PAUFCA"). 39 P.S. § 351 *et seq.*[4] The purpose of fraudulent transfer law is to prevent a debtor from

---

4. This statute was later repealed and replaced by, 12 Pa.Cons.Stat. § 5101 *et. seq.;* however, because of when this lawsuit was filed, the older statute governs this case. *See ProtoComm III,* 55 F.Supp.2d at 323 n. 1.

transferring valuable assets for inadequate consideration if such transfer leaves the debtor with insufficient assets to pay honest creditors. *See In re Bay Plastics, Inc.*, 187 B.R. 315, 322 (Bkrtcy.C.D.Cal.1995). The uniform statute was established upon the recognition that debtors often try to avoid payment of legitimate debts by concealing or transferring property. *See In re Lease–A–Fleet, Inc.*, 155 B.R. 666, 672–73 (Bkrtcy.E.D.Pa.1993). Conveyance is defined by statute as "every payment of money, assignment, release, transfer, lease, mortgage, or pledge of tangible or intangible property, and also the conveyance of any lien or incumbrance." 39 P.S. § 351. Stocks are thus absent from this definition. A claim may be brought under this Act by a future creditor, i.e., by a party which has not yet received a judgment on a legal claim at the time of the transfer in question. *See Stauffer v. Stauffer*, 465 Pa. 558, 576, 351 A.2d 236, 245 (1976).

In my prior opinion, I concluded, *inter alia,* that ProtoComm could establish a claim for fraudulent conveyances upon showing that the stock transaction between the Former Fluent Shareholders and Novell was only part of a complex transaction that transferred assets of Fluent to Novell, paid money to the shareholders and left Fluent insolvent. *ProtoComm III,* 55 F.Supp.2d at 327–28. Analogizing to Leveraged Buyout ("LBO") cases, I concluded that upon such a showing, this Court would be convinced to treat the transactions among the Former Fluent Shareholders, Fluent and Novell as one integrated transaction for the purposes of ProtoComm's claim of fraudulent conveyances. *See id.* at 328.

In *U.S. v. Tabor Court Realty Corp.,* 803 F.2d 1288 (3d Cir.1986), *cert. denied,* 483 U.S. 1005, the Court of Appeals for the Third Circuit applied PAUFCA to LBOs for the first time. As articulated by the Court, a typical LBO involves the following:

> [A] company is sold to a small number of investors, typically including members of the company's management, under financial arrangements in which there is a minimum amount of equity and a maximum amount of debt. The financing typically provides for a substantial return of investment capital by means of mortgages or high risk bonds, popularly known as "junk bonds."

Id. at 1292. *Tabor* involved an incredibly complex LBO in which the court "collapsed" separate transactions for the purposes of the claims brought under PAUFCA. *See id.* at 1302. In summary, the President of Raymond Group ("Raymond"), James Durkin ("Durkin"), received an option to buy Raymond from its shareholders for $8.5 million. *See id.* After failed attempts to secure financing, Durkin and investors incorporated a holding company, Great American, to which the option was assigned. *See id.* To effectuate the buy-out, Great American, a seemingly empty company, received a loan commitment from Institutional Investors Trust ("ITT") for $8.5 million. *See id.* The loan was structured to divide Raymond into borrowing companies and guarantor companies and was secured by mortgages on assets of both groups of companies. *See id.*

The loan arrangement occurred in two stages. "The loan proceeds went from ITT to the borrowing Raymond Group companies, which immediately turned the funds over to Great American, which used the funds for the buy-out." *Id.* at 1302. The Court in *Tabor* upheld the district court finding that the ITT loan proceeds merely passed through the borrowers to Great American and in the end to the selling stockholders and could not be deemed consideration received by the borrowing companies. *See id.* Other courts have applied fraudulent conveyance to the LBO context and collapsed the transactions for the purposes of fraudulent conveyance law. *See, e.g. In re Bay Plastics, Inc.,* 187 B.R. 315; *MFS/Sun Life Trust–High Yield Series v. Van Dusen Airport Serv. Co.,* 910 F.Supp. 913 (S.D.N.Y., 1995). *See also Lease–A–Fleet,* 155 B.R. at 676 (applying *Tabor's* collapsing method to case outside LBO). In essence, courts look "past the form of a transaction to its substance" and evaluate the transactions on a whole to determine whether a fraudulent conveyance has occurred. *MFS/Sun Life Trust,* 910 F.Supp. at 933. Thus while each transaction in isolation may appear kosher, the full transaction is examined to determine whether fraudulent conveyance law has been violated.

Former Fluent Shareholders argue that no asset sale occurred and that ProtoComm is unable to show that the stock sale was but one occurrence in a series of interdependent steps. ProtoComm counters that genuine issues of material fact exist as to both issues. At the motion to dismiss stage, ProtoComm appeared to rely solely on the collapsing theory. In other words, plaintiff sought to establish that the stock sale and the asset transfer which followed should be viewed as one transaction. Plaintiff now brings forth evidence which it argues raises a genuine dispute as to whether the initial transaction actually constituted an asset transfer. ProtoComm essentially relies on the same evidence for these alternative theories which in reality do not differ significantly because the end result is the same: ProtoComm needs to show that an asset transfer, as opposed to a stock sale, took place.[4]

ProtoComm's expert witness, Michael Pakter ("Pakter"), characterizes the acquisition as an asset sale. In addition to Pakter's expert opinion, ProtoComm points to the following evidence, *inter alia,* to demonstrate that genuine issues of material fact exist concerning what type of transition occurred. According to Novell's 10–K the acquisition cost $21.5

---

4. A brief review of basic corporate law principles may be helpful to the discussion here. There are three principal acquisition methods used to effectuate a corporate acquisition, two of which are relevant here: acquisition of assets and acquisition of stock. *See* Eleanor M. Fox & Byron E. Fox, 1 *Corporate Acquisitions and Mergers* § 5A.01, at 5A–4 (Matthew Bender 2001). In an acquisition of assets, the acquiring corporation acquires "all or part of the assets of the transferor corporation either in exchange for shares of its stock, securities, cash or other property." *Id.* at 5A–5. The transaction can be molded by the parties at their own choosing, "so long as appropriate safeguards are provided for the interests of corporate shareholders and creditors." *Id.* at § 5A.03, at 5A–11–12. In other words, the acquisition cannot be in the form of a fraudulent transfer. After the sale, the transferor can choose to engage in active business, or pay creditors, liquidate, and formally dissolve. *See id.* In an acquisition of stock, "the acquiring corporation purchases the shares owned by the individual shareholders of the transferor corporation for cash, stock, securities or other property." *Id.* at § 5A.01 at 5A–5. The acquiring corporation or one of its subsidiaries becomes a shareholder of the acquired corporation. *See id.* at § 5A.04 at 5A–16.

million. Instead of distributing cash on a pro rata basis to the Former Fluent Shareholders, the cash was distributed at the direction of Fluent's Board and included monies for employee bonuses and reimbursements for bridge loans. The Ernst & Young Report, while admittedly conducted *after* the stock transaction occurred, valued the assets of Fluent at approximately the same price as the acquisition cost. ProtoComm also relies on the fact that early in the negotiations, an asset sale was considered and then the structure changed without explanation. In the backdrop of the transaction was the looming potential judgment from the ProtoComm I litigation. Thus, under ProtoComm's theory defendants knew that if the deal was in the structure of an asset transfer, they would potentially be liable under fraudulent transfer law. I conclude based on the foregoing that ProtoComm has raised a genuine issue of material fact as to the predicate issue of whether the stock transfer was actually an asset sale. Plaintiff has established evidence under which a reasonable trier of fact could find either that the initial transaction in June, 1993, was actually an asset sale, or, alternatively, that the initial transaction was not complete until the assets were physically transferred.

I now turn to whether plaintiff raises genuine issues of material fact with respect to the specific provisions of PAUFCA. Four sections of the Act detail situations in which a conveyance will be deemed fraudulent. Sections 354 and 355 are the constructive intent provisions of the Act.[7] Both provisions require that the conveyance occur without "fair consideration" which occurs "when property of a fair equivalent is transferred in good faith." *Buncher Co. v. Official Comm. of Unsecured Creditors of GenFarm Ltd. P'ship IV,* 229 F.3d 245, 251 (3d Cir.2000) (citing section 353). "[K]nowledge of insolvency is a rational interpretation of the statutory language of lack of 'good faith.'" *Tabor,* 803 F.2d at 1296. Section 354 provides that a conveyance is fraudulent where the debtor was left insolvent at the time of the transfer or becomes insolvent thereby.[8] The statute encompasses insolvency both in the bankruptcy sense, i.e., a negative net worth and in the equity sense, i.e., inability to pay existing debt as they mature. *See Buncher,* 229 F.3d at 251. Section 355 provides that a conveyance is fraudulent where the debtor was left with unreasonably small capital after the transfer which indicates "a financial condition short of equitable insolvency."[10] *Moody v. Security Pacific Bus. Credit,*

---

7. This Court recognizes that in its prior ruling it observed that Section 356 was also a constructive intent provision. It appears that most courts place this section or its equivalent in that category. *See, e.g., In re Bay Plastics, Inc.,* 187 B.R. at 322; *MFS/Sun Life,* 910 F.Supp. at 936. The Court of Appeals for the Third Circuit, however, has construed this section as an actual intent provision. *See Moody v. Security Pacific Bus. Credit. Inc.,* 971 F.2d 1056, 1063–64 (3d Cir.1992). I must be guided accordingly by this holding.

8. Section 354 provides: "Every conveyance made and every obligation incurred by a person who is or will be thereby rendered insolvent, is fraudulent as to creditors, without regard to his actual intent, if the conveyance is made or the obligation is incurred without a fair consideration."

10. Section 355 provides: "Every conveyance made without fair consideration, when the person making it is engaged, or is about to engage, in a business or transaction for which the property remaining in his hands after the conveyance is an unreasonably small capital, is

Inc., 971 F.2d 1056, 1064 (3d Cir.1992). The test is one of "reasonable foreseeability." *Id.* at 1073. The main inquiry under the constructive intent provision is "whether there is a link between the challenged conveyance and the debtor's insolvency." *Id.*

If insolvency or unreasonably small capital is established, the burden shifts to the transferees, the Former Fluent Shareholders, to show by clear and convincing evidence either that the transferor was then solvent, not rendered insolvent, not left with unreasonably small capital or that the assets were transferred for fair consideration. *See Elliott v. Kiesewetter,* 98 F.3d 47, 56–57 (3d Cir.1996) (citations omitted); (*Moody,* 971 F.2d at 1065 n. 2) (noting belief that Pennsylvania Supreme Court would apply insolvency standard to adequacy of capital standard; standard determined in dicta because court concluded that clear and convincing standard had been met). Thus, the first question is whether ProtoComm has raised a genuine issue of material fact as to either Fluent's solvency at the time of the transfer or as a result of the transfer, as required under section 354, or as to whether the transfer left Fluent with unreasonably small capital, as required under section 355. These issues are in large part dependent on how the fact finder characterizes the acquisition. For example, the trier of fact could reasonably find that a legitimate stock-for-cash transaction took place which had no impact on Fluent's assets, or it could reasonably find that an asset sale occurred which was structured to deplete Fluent's treasury. Thus, I conclude that a genuine issue of material fact has been raised as to the required elements of sections 354 and 355.

Sections 356 and 357 are the actual intent provisions of the Act. Section 356 also requires that the conveyance be made without fair consideration; it provides that a conveyance is fraudulent where the debtor intends or believes that it was unable to pay future debts as they became due as a consequence of the transfer. Again, the issue raised by this provision turns in large part on how the fact finder sees the acquisition. For example, if it is found to be a exchange for stock and that Fluent's assets were transferred only after Fluent's products did not reach expectations, then the requisite intent and unfair consideration may be unfounded. If, however, an asset transfer is found, then the structure of the acquisition could reasonably be seen as a transfer made without proper consideration to Fluent's treasury and with the intent or belief that creditors could not be satisfied. Thus, I conclude that a genuine issue of material fact has been raised as to the required elements of section 356.

The final question under PAUFCA concerns section 357 which provides that a conveyance is fraudulent where the conveyance was made with the actual intent to hinder, delay or defraud present or future creditors. Such intent must be proven by clear and convincing evidence. *See Moody v. Security Pacific Bus. Credit Inc.,* 127 B.R. 958, 990 (W.D.Pa. 1991), *aff'd,* 971 F.2d 1056 (1992). The existence of actual intent is a

---

fraudulent as to creditors, and as to other persons who become creditors during the continuance of such business or transaction, without regard to his actual intent."

question of fact. *See Tabor,* 803 F.2d at 1304. Direct evidence is not required; actual intent may be inferred from the totality of the circumstances. *See Moody,* 971 F.2d at 1075 (citing *Tabor,* 803 F.2d at 1304).

Thus this Court must ask whether ProtoComm has raised a genuine issue of material fact in showing by clear and convincing evidence that defendants intentionally structured the acquisition to defraud creditors. This question of fact, though ProtoComm will face a higher burden of proof, overlaps with the aforementioned provisions because under Pennsylvania law, intent may be inferred when transfers are made without fair consideration and where the parties to the transfer have knowledge of the claims of creditors and know that such creditors cannot be paid. *See Tabor,* 803 F.2d at 1304. *See also, Lease–A–Fleet,* 155 B.R. at 674 (reciting "badges of fraud" which may indicate actual intent). As explained above, genuine disputes remain concerning these questions. Thus, I conclude that ProtoComm has met its burden in raising a triable issue.

I therefore conclude that defendants are not entitled to judgment on the PAUFCA claim as a matter of law.

Plaintiffs bring the wrongful dividend claim under 8 Del. C. § 174, which holds directors, but not shareholders, liable for wilfully or negligently paying dividends in violation of the general corporate law chapter of the Delaware Code.[15] ProtoComm brings this cause of action against those Former Fluent Shareholders who served as Directors. There are times when upon consideration of a summary judgment motion, cases are reevaluated in light of the facts presented and determinations previously made by a court are reconsidered as well. This is one of those times. This Court concluded in its prior opinion that ProtoComm had standing to pursue this claim. *ProtoComm,* 55 F.Supp.2d at 330. This Court now concludes, for the reasons which follow, that plaintiff lacks such standing.

The Delaware Supreme Court's decision in *Johnston v. Wolf,* 487 A.2d 1132 (Del.1985), governs standing under section 174. The facts of *Johnston* are as follows. Allied Artists Pictures Corporation ("Allied") entered into a complex reorganization plan and agreement which provided, *inter alia,* that Allied would merge with another corporation. *See id.* at 1134. As part of the plan, Allied redeemed its preferred stock prior to the merger. *See id.* Under the agreement, as well as under Delaware law, creditors of Allied became creditors of the post-merger corporation. *See id.* Plaintiffs alleged that the redemption violated the Delaware Code. *See id.*

Two plaintiffs filed suit after the merger occurred and, obviously, therefore had not secured a judgment before the merger occurred. *See id.* at 1136. One plaintiff had brought his claim prior to the merger, but had

---

15. Section 174 provides in pertinent part: "In case of any wilful or negligent violation of § 160 or 173 of this title, the directors under whose administration the same may happen shall be jointly and severally liable." Section 173 provides in pertinent part: "No corporation shall pay dividends except in accordance with this chapter." Section 170 provides in pertinent part: "The directors of every corporation ... may ... pay dividends upon the shares of its capital stock ... either (1) out of its surplus, as defined in and computed in accordance with §§ 154 and 244 of this title, or (2) in case there shall be no such surplus, out of its net profits."

not obtained a judgment until after the merger. *See id.* The court denied standing as to all three plaintiffs under section 174, holding that all three were creditors of the post-merger corporation only. *See id.* Thus, unlike PAUFCA, section 174 provides no protection to future creditors. Accordingly, I conclude that plaintiff cannot proceed with its claim against these defendants under section 174 because ProtoComm did not receive its judgment until after the acquisition of Fluent had occurred.

In this Court's prior ruling, it turned to *Pinellas County v. Great Am. Indus. Group Inc.,* No. 90 C 5254, 1991 WL 259020 (N.D.Ill.Dec.2, 1991). There, the plaintiff had obtained a $25,000,000 judgment against defendant Madison. Before the judgment against it, Madison had engaged in two corporate acts which rendered it insolvent. *See id.* In the first act, Madison paid a $5 million dividend to its sole shareholder, GAIG. *See id.* Plaintiff claimed that the dividend payment should be voided. *See id.* The court acknowledged that under *Johnston,* only current creditors had standing to sue under section 174. The court then noted that section 174 would not have application even if standing were not problematic because the plaintiff was suing a shareholder and not a director. The court then turned to 8 Del.C. § 325 which provides:

> (a) When the officers, directors or stockholders of any corporation shall be liable *by the provisions of this chapter* to pay the debts of the corporation, or any part thereof, any person to whom they are liable may have an action, at law or in equity, against any 1 or more of them, and *the complaint shall state the claim against the corporation, and the ground on which the plaintiff expects to charge the defendants personally.*

> (b) No suit shall be brought against any officer, director or stockholder for any debt of a corporation of which such person is an officer, director or stockholder, *until judgment be obtained therefor against the corporation and execution thereon returned unsatisfied.*

(emphasis added). Thus, section 325 allows for a suit to be brought against officers, directors or stockholders when, under the provisions of the general corporate law chapter of the Delaware Code, they are liable to pay the debts of the corporation. And, such suit may not be brought until judgment is obtained and returned unsatisfied. The court in *Pinellas* determined that section 325 could not provide a cause of action to the plaintiff before it because Delaware statutory corporate law provided no means for holding shareholders liable for corporate debts. *See Pinellas,* 1991 WL 259020, at *3. The court then acknowledged that section 325 does not work to restrict causes of action traditionally available to creditors independent of corporate law. *See id.* (citing *Lone Star Indus., Inc. v. Redwine,* 757 F.2d 1544, 1554 (5th Cir.1985)).

The court observed that under Delaware common law, where a corporation distributes assets to its shareholders while leaving creditors unsatisfied, those creditors are entitled to recovery directly from the shareholders, without resort to fraudulent conveyance law and without having to first obtain a prior judgment against the corporate debtor. *See id.* The court ultimately concluded that because the complaint alleged that the dividend payment occurred at a time when Madison was technically bankrupt, and thus constituted substantially all of Madison's assets, the allegations were sufficient to sustain the claim to void the dividend payment. *See id.*

Thus, the court in *Pinellas* did not determine that section 325 could be used to provide standing for a claim brought under section 174. Rather, the court essentially provided that the cause of action be brought under the common law fraudulent conveyance claim. Accordingly, while it may be that ProtoComm would have a common law claim under Delaware law, which presumably would require a similar showing to the claim brought under PAUFCA, ProtoComm does not have a claim against these defendants under section 174, which is the law invoked by plaintiff. * * *

Notes

1. The Uniform Fraudulent Transfer Act has been adopted by some twenty states, while eight others adopted the Uniform Fraudulent Conveyance Act. James D. Cox & Thomas Lee Hazen, Corporations, § 7.20 (2d ed. 2003).

2. For cases holding that distributions to shareholders were subject to fraudulent conveyance acts see Schall v. Anderson's Implement, Inc., 240 Neb. 658, 484 N.W.2d 86 (1992); Spanier v. U.S. Fidelity and Guaranty Co., 127 Ariz. 589, 623 P.2d 19 (App.1980).

3. The difference between state corporate statutes restricting dividends and bankruptcy and fraudulent conveyance statutes has been explained as follows:

> The revised Model Business Corporation Act establishes the validity of distributions from the corporate law standpoint under section 6.40 and determines the potential liability of directors for improper distributions under sections 8.30 and 8.33. The federal Bankruptcy Act and state fraudulent conveyance statutes, on the other hand, are designed to enable the trustee or other representative to recapture for the benefit of creditors funds distributed to others in some circumstances. In light of these diverse purposes, it was not thought necessary to make the tests of section 6.40 identical with the tests for insolvency under these various statutes.

Official Comments, Model Bus. Corp. Act § 6.40.

JOHN A. ROEBLING'S SONS CO. v. MODE
17 Del. 515, 43 A. 480 (Del.Super.1899).

LORE, C. J.

By an action on the case in this suit, the plaintiff seeks to hold the defendant individually liable for a judgment due to the plaintiff from the

Kent Iron & Hardware Co., an insolvent corporation of the state of Delaware, upon the ground that the defendant was one of the directors of the said corporation, and participated in an illegal dividend which was declared and paid, not out of the net earnings or surplus of the company, but in diminution of its capital stock. The declaration of the plaintiff contains four counts, all of which are substantially the same. The declaration sets forth, in substance, that the directors of the Kent Iron & Hardware Company, an insolvent corporation of the state of Delaware, on the 1st day of July, 1891, declared and paid a dividend of $9,000, being 6 per cent. on the capital stock of $150,000, not out of its net earnings, but in diminution of its capital stock; that the defendant was one of the directors who made and participated in the dividend; that thereby he became liable, under the statutes of this state, to pay to the plaintiff, a judgment creditor of the said corporation, the full amount of his claim, being the sum of $630.60, with interest from March 10, 1894, with the costs of obtaining the judgment against the corporation. * * *

The action is based upon section 7, c. 147, 17 Laws Del., [now 8 Del. Corp. L. § 174] entitled 'An act concerning private corporations,' and is as follows:

'Sec. 7. It shall not be lawful for the directors of any bank or moneyed or manufacturing corporation in this state, or any corporation created under this act, to make dividends, except from the surplus or net profits arising from the business of the corporation, nor to divide, withdraw, or in any way pay to the stockholders, or any of them, any part of the capital stock of said corporation, or to reduce the said capital stock, except according to this act, without the consent of the legislature; and in case of any violation of the provisions of this section, the directors, under whose administration the same may happen, shall, in their individual capacities, jointly and severally, be liable at any time within the period of six years after paying any such dividend to the said corporation, and to the creditors thereof in the event of its dissolution or insolvency, to the full amount of the dividend made or capital stock so divided, withdrawn, paid out or reduced, with legal interest on the same from the time such liability accrued.'

* * * This section contemplates the recovery and restoration to the capital of the corporation of the entire amount thus illegally withdrawn, and, to that end, each director is made individually liable for such amount. When so recovered and restored, whether at the instance and in the name of the corporation primarily, or in the name and at the instance of the creditors, it becomes at once a part of the capital stock again, to be held and disposed of as such for the benefit of all concerned. Manifestly this would be so if the amount was recovered by the corporation itself, before dissolution or insolvency. Of necessity, it would then go into the common funds. No other construction seems tenable, if, on the other hand, the recovery should be at the instance of the creditors after the dissolution or insolvency of the corporation. Under this view, each creditor would be

entitled to his proportionate share thereof, and any action for the recovery of such illegal dividends or abstracted capital must contemplate such proportionate distribution. It cannot be maintained that this declaration contemplates any such distribution. It demands the plaintiff's entire debt out of the alleged illegal $9,000 dividend, without respect to any of the other creditors. It is equally plain that under this declaration the plaintiff cannot recover a proportionate share of the said dividend, inasmuch as that share must depend upon the correct ascertainment and adjustment of the claims of all other creditors entitled. Recovery in this action of such proportionate share would be an attempt to determine the rights of such other creditors without any day given to them in court, and without any opportunity to be heard, either as to their own claims, or those of the plaintiff and others.

* * *If this be a common fund, the remedy would be by proceedings in equity, where all persons interested would be made parties, and the rights and liabilities of each one could be fully considered and equitably adjusted. * * *

We conclude, therefore, that the remedy by action on the case ... does not apply to cases arising under section 7, and that the provisions of section 7 can only adequately and properly be enforced by proceedings in equity. It follows, therefore, that this declaration is not sufficient in law to support the plaintiff's claim, and that, under the demurrer, judgment should be entered against the plaintiff. * * * Let judgment be entered against the plaintiff.

REILLY v. SEGERT

31 Ill.2d 297, 201 N.E.2d 444 (1964).

SCHAEFER, JUSTICE.

Prior to the enactment of the Business Corporation Act of 1933, it was settled that a shareholder of a corporation who sold his stock to the corporation while it was insolvent was liable to an injured creditor of the corporation for the amount paid to the shareholder for his stock. (Singer v. Hutchinson, 183 Ill. 606, 56 N.E. 388; Johnson v. Canfield–Swigart Co., 292 Ill. 101, 126 N.E. 608.) This liability was based upon the adverse effect of the transaction upon creditors, and not upon the guilt or innocence of the shareholder, who was held liable even though there was no evidence of fraud. (Clapp v. Peterson, 104 Ill. 26, 31.) The question for decision in this case is whether or not this liability was repealed by section 42 of the Business Corporation Act. (Ill.Rev.Stat.1959, chap. 32, par. 157.–42.) The circuit court of Lake County held that it was, the Appellate Court affirmed (44 Ill.App.2d 343, 194 N.E.2d 544), and we allowed leave to appeal.

The plaintiffs are George L. Reilly, the receiver of Deerfield Lumber & Fuel Co., Inc. and three creditors of that company. The defendants are the directors of the company and five shareholders. The complaint alleged that the directors authorized purchases of stock from the defendant shareholders at a time when the corporation was insolvent and had no earned surplus. The directors defaulted, and judgments were entered against them for the amounts paid to the defendant shareholders for their stock. No appeal was taken from the judgments so entered, and we are not concerned with them.

Those counts of the complaint, however, that asserted liability against the defendant shareholders, were dismissed upon motion, and final judgments were entered against the plaintiffs on those counts. The judgments thus entered were based upon the proposition that section 42 of the Business Corporation Act (Ill.Rev.Stat.1959, chap. 32, par. 157.42) affords the only remedy available, and that it does not authorize an action directly against shareholders. The portions of section 42 that are relied upon to support the judgment are as follows:

'In addition to any other liabilities imposed by law upon directors of a corporation:

'(a) Directors of a corporation who vote for or assent to the declaration of any dividend or other distribution of the assets of a corporation to its shareholders shall be jointly and severally liable to the corporation for the amount of such dividend which is paid or the value of such assets which are distributed if, at the time of such payment or distribution, the corporation is insolvent or its net assets are less than its stated capital.

'(b) The directors of a corporation who vote for or assent to the declaration of any dividend or other distribution of assets of a corporation to its shareholders which renders the corporation insolvent or reduces its net assets below its stated capital shall be jointly and severally liable to the corporation for the amount of such dividend which is paid or the value of such assets which are distributed, to the extent that the corporation is thereby rendered insolvent or its net assets are reduced below its stated capital.

'Any director against whom a claim shall be asserted under or pursuant to this section for the improper declaration of a dividend or other distribution of assets of a corporation and who shall be held liable thereon, shall be entitled to contribution from the shareholders who knowingly accepted or received any such dividend or assets, in proportion to the amounts received by them respectively.'

In our opinion section 42 does not preclude this action against the shareholders. Even as to the liability of directors, its language makes it clear that it was not designed to provide an exclusive remedy, for the liability with which it deals are expressly stated to be '(i)n addition to any other liabilities imposed by law upon directors of a corporation.' In the absence of this specific disclaimer, the result would be the same. 'Where a liability is imposed upon an officer of (sic) a director by a state statute, his common-law liability for misfeasance and negligence in the performance of his duties is not thereby excluded.' 3 Fletcher, Cyclopedia of Corporations, sec. 993.

In this case, moreover, we are concerned with the direct liability of shareholders, a subject with which section 42 does not purport to deal. The existence of a statutory provision dealing with the liability of directors does not preclude a non-statutory liability on the part of shareholders. When Clapp v. Peterson, 104 Ill. 26, and other decisions dealing with the liability here asserted were decided, statutes which provided specific liabilities for particular misconduct of directors were in effect. Yet those provisions of the Corporation Act of 1872 and the General Corporation Act of 1919 did not bar the creditor's common law action against shareholders who sold their stock to the corporation while it was insolvent.

A further word is appropriate to prevent misapprehension as to our understanding of section 42. Both parties appear to have assumed that the section applies to purchases by a corporation of its own stock at a time when the corporation is insolvent, and we have dealt with the case on that assumption. The section does not, however, expressly mention such transactions, and it can apply to them only if a 'distribution' of assets is construed to include payment by the corporation to a shareholder for his stock. From the language of section 42 it seems likely that it pertains to outright distributions of corporate assets to all shareholders, by dividend or otherwise, and questionable whether it includes as a corporate 'distribution' a corporation's purchase of its stock from a particular shareholder. That question has not been argued, however, and we express no opinion concerning it. But see Precision Extrusions, Inc. v. Stewart, 36 Ill.App.2d 30, 43, 183 N.E.2d 547.

The judgment of the Appellate Court is reversed, and the cause is remanded to the circuit court of Lake County for further proceedings not inconsistent with this opinion.

NOTES

1. Model Bus. Corp. Act § 8.33 imposes personal liability on a director not using due care in declaring a dividend in violation of Model Bus. Corp. Act § 6.40. State corporate statutes impose varying standards for imposing liability on directors for wrongfully declared dividends. Delaware imposes liability on directors for any willful or negligent violation of the provisions in Delaware corporate law restricting payments of dividends. Each director is jointly or severally liable for declaring an unlawful dividend, unless they voted against the declaration. 8 Del. Corp. L. § 174.

2. Model Bus Corp. Act §§ 8.30 and 8.33 allow directors to rely reasonably on reports of accountants in absolving themselves of negligently or willfully declaring a wrongful dividend. Delaware has a similar provision. 8 Del Corp. L. § 172.

WOOD v. NATIONAL CITY BANK

24 F.2d 661 (2d Cir.1928).

The amended bill set forth the following facts: At some undisclosed time the District Court for the Eastern District of Kentucky appointed a receiver for the Stanton Oil Company, a Delaware corporation, and later the plaintiff was appointed ancillary receiver 'by an order entered in the District Court of the United States for the Southern District of New York.' The nature of neither suit was disclosed. From July 16, 1917, to April 1, 1919, the defendants were stockholders of the corporation, between which dates they had received certain dividends from its assets. At the time when all these dividends were paid, the corporation 'was in debt, and was in fact insolvent and unable to pay its debts, and had not then, nor had it ever had, any reserve over and above its capital stock, or any surplus or net profits of any kind, and each and all of the said dividends were paid wholly from and out of the capital of said corporation.' Claims had been 'filed' against the corporation, amounting to more than $100,000, and receiver's certificates issued in the sum of $25,000.

L. HAND, CIRCUIT JUDGE (after stating the facts as above).

It is impossible from the bill to learn just what the plaintiff meant to allege. On the one hand, he may have meant only that, when the dividends were paid, the corporate assets did not equal its debts together with the aggregate amount of its corporate shares, considered as a liability, and that the payments left the assets insufficient to pay the shares in full. On the other hand, he may have meant that the assets were not at those times enough to pay the debts; that is, that the corporation was insolvent, as that word is used in the Bankruptcy Act (11 USCA). Considering the liberal attitude which courts now take towards pleadings, we think that some of the language is susceptible of being understood in the second sense. 'Unable to pay its debts' certainly says more than that the corporation has failed to pay them in due course. It more naturally means that the assets were not enough for that purpose. We must, it is true, confess to a complete inability to understand the relevancy of the remainder of the third article of the bill, in which these words appear. They strongly suggest that the gist of the suit was the receipt of dividends paid in depletion of capital, without regard to whether the corporation was solvent or insolvent. However that may be, if there is a sufficient allegation of insolvency, as we think, the bill is at worst only indefinite and ambiguous, and the proper remedy was to move under rule 20 for a better statement, not to dismiss it under rule 29.

Such being a permissible construction of the complaint, the question of its sufficiency depends upon the law of stockholders' liability. We have not to do with the liability commonly imposed by statute, because, whatever that may be in Delaware, the plaintiff does not invoke it here. He depends upon the fact that the directors have paid, and the defendants received, dividends when the corporation was insolvent. Merely because this impairs the capital stock, it is commonly regarded as a wrong to creditors on the directors' part, and it is often made such by statute. We may, without discussion, assume that it would be a wrong in the case at bar. Even so, it is primarily only the wrong of those who commit it, like any other tort, and innocent participants are not accomplices to its commission. Hence it has been settled, at least for us, that, when the liability is based merely on the depletion of the capital, a stockholder must be charged with notice of that fact. McDonald v. Williams, 174 U.S. 397, 19 S.Ct. 743, 43 L.Ed. 1022. This has become a thoroughly fixed principle in the federal courts. Lawrence v. Greenup (C.C.A. 6) 97 F. 906; New Hampshire Savings Bank v. Richey (C.C.A. 8) 121 F. 956; Great Western, etc., Co. v. Harris (C.C.A. 2) 128 F. 321; Ratcliff v. Clendenin (C.C.A. 8) 232 F. 61; Atherton v. Beaman (C.C.A. 1) 264 F. 878.

It is apparent that this result could not have been reached if the capital of the corporation were regarded as a trust fund for its creditors, because a stockholder is not a purchaser, but a donee, and his bona fides would not protect him, in the absence of some further equity, in retaining the proceeds of a trust. So it became necessary to decide that the capital was not such a fund, and McDonald v. Williams did expressly so decide. The so-called 'trust fund' doctrine had, indeed, earlier been repudiated by the Supreme Court, especially in Hollins v. Brierfield, etc., Co., 150 U.S. 371; but it was a hardy weed and would not die at the first uprooting. It is apparent, therefore, that the bill does not set forth a cause of suit based upon the impairment of the capital, because the stockholders are not alleged to have been privy to the directors' tort. This is not a defense which must be pleaded, like that of bona fide purchaser; it is necessary positively to allege the stockholders' complicity in the wrong to set forth any case at all.

However, there is quite another theory, and quite another liability, if the payments not only impair the capital, but are taken out of assets already too small to pay the existing debts. The situation then strictly is not peculiar to corporation law, but merely an instance of a payment from an insolvent estate. Since, as we have said, a stockholder is a donee, he receives such payments charged with whatever trust they were subject to in the hands of the corporation. In that situation it can indeed be said with some truth that the corporate assets have become a 'trust fund.' Wabash, etc., Ry. v. Ham, 114 U.S. 587, 594. Hence it has never been doubted, so far as we can find, at least in any federal court, that if the dividends are paid in fraud of creditors the stockholder is so liable. Hayden v. Thompson (C.C.A. 8) 71 F. 60; Hayden v. Williams (C.C.A. 2) 96 F. 279. The defendants, who suppose that there has been an inconsistency in the decisions of the Eighth Circuit (and they might have added in our own), have failed to distinguish the quite independent bases of the two liabilities.

If the bill be regarded as presenting only an instance of a payment in fraud of creditors, the question arises whether it is enough merely to allege that the payment was made while the corporation was insolvent. It is agreed with substantial unanimity that, when an insolvent makes a voluntary payment out of his assets, it is regarded as at least presumptively in fraud of his creditors, Hume v. Central Washington Bank, 128 U.S. 195; Kehr v. Smith, 20 Wall. 31; Parich v. Murphree, 13 How. 92, 99; Klinger v. Hyman, 223 F. 257 (C.C.A.2); Hessian v. Patten (C.C.A. 8) 154 F. 829, 832; Cole v. Tyler, 65 N.Y. 73; Smith v. Reid, 134 N.Y. 568, 31 N.E. 1082; Lehrenkrauss v. Bonnell, 199 N.Y. 240, 246, 92 N.E. 637. We shall assume, for argument, in accordance with the language of some of the foregoing decisions, that such a transfer is fraudulent per se. In Hayden v. Williams no more is mentioned than that the corporation was insolvent, and apparently no more was thought necessary. Even so, the bill is bad, because, when the invalidity of the gift depends only upon the fact of the donor's insolvency, regardless of his intent, it is voidable only at the demand of creditors existing when it is made. Horbach v. Hill, 112 U.S. 144, 149 (semble); Ratcliff v. Clendenin (C.C.A. 8) 232 F. 61 (semble); Church v. Chapin, 35 Vt. 223; Sheppard v. Thomas, 24 Kan. 780; Eckhart v. Burrell Mfg. Co., 236 Ill. 134, 86 N.E. 199; Crowley v. Brower, 201 Iowa, 257, 207 N.W. 230. Hummell v. Harrington (Fla.) 109 So. 320, if holding otherwise, is an exception; it probably meant no more than that, if there be actual intent to defraud subsequent creditors, they also may avoid the gift. Day v. Cooley, 118 Mass. 524. In the case at bar the bill does not allege that any of the creditors in existence when the receiver was appointed were creditors when the dividends were declared. Only in case the bill had alleged this, would the question arise whether insolvency per se avoids the gift. For this reason, and this alone, the decree was right. * * *

Decree affirmed.

NOTE

Current Delaware law allows a director found liable for declaring an unlawful dividend to seek contribution from shareholders for their pro rata distribution, if they knew the distribution was unlawful. 8 Del. Corp. L. § 174(c). Model Bus. Corp. Act § 8.33 has a similar provision. Directors held severally liable may also seek contribution from other directors. 8 Del. Corp. L. § 174.

SECTION 5. STOCK SUBSCRIPTIONS

Promoters of a corporation often sell stock to potential investors in advance of the formation of the corporation, as well as after. Such sales are made under subscription agreements that promise issuance of the stock to the subscriber upon formation of the corporation. Issues that arise under subscription agreements are the adequacy and validity of the consideration paid for the stock and whether creditors of the corporation can enforce a subscription agreement when the corporation becomes insolvent.

BING CROSBY MINUTE MAID CORP. v. EATON

46 Cal.2d 484, 297 P.2d 5 (1956).

SHENK, JUSTICE.

The plaintiff appeals from an order granting a new trial after judgment in its favor. The defendant appeals from the judgment.

As a judgment creditor of a corporation the plaintiff brought this action against a shareholder of the corporation to recover the difference between the par value of stock issued to him and the fair value of the consideration he paid for the stock. At the conclusion of the trial, the court, sitting without a jury, made findings of fact and conclusions of law and entered judgment for the plaintiff. In support of his motion for a new trial the defendant assigned certain alleged defects in the findings as errors of law. The defendant formed a corporation to acquire his going frozen foods business. The Commissioner of Corporations issued a permit authorizing the corporation to sell and issue not more than 4,500 shares of $10 par value stock to the defendant and other named individuals in consideration of the transfer of the business. The permit provided that 1,022 shares be deposited in escrow and not be transferred without the written consent of the Commissioner, and that the escrowed shares not be sold or issued until the prospective shareholders named in the permit waived certain rights to dividends and to participation in any distribution of assets.

The defendant transferred his business to the corporation. The corporation placed 1,022 shares in escrow in his name pursuant to the provisions of the permit. The remaining 3,478 shares were issued outright to the defendant and after three years were transferred to the other persons named in the permit. Although the 1,022 shares were listed on the corporate records as held by the defendant (accompanied by the notation 'escrowed'), they were never released from escrow. The corporation had financial difficulties and executed an assignment of its assets for the benefit of creditors to a credit association. The plaintiff recovered a judgment against the corporation for $21,246.42. A writ of execution on the judgment was returned unsatisfied.

The trial court found that the value to the corporation of the consideration from the defendant was $34,780.83; that 4,500 shares of stock having a par value of $10 each were issued to the defendant and he became the owner of those shares; that subsequent to the issue of the shares the corporation purchased merchandise from the plaintiff and has not yet paid for all of it; that some $15,000 of the judgment the plaintiff recovered from the corporation remains unsatisfied, and that the corporation is insolvent.

The judgment for the plaintiff was for $10,219.17 approximately the par value of the 1,022 shares of stock placed in escrow. The judgment was based on the trial court's conclusion that the defendant was liable for the difference between the par value of the 4,500 shares and the value of the consideration the defendant paid for them.

The plaintiff contends that the trial court's findings of fact were supported by the evidence and required a judgment in its favor, and therefore that it was error to grant a new trial. The defendant contends that the order granting a new trial was proper because (1) the finding that he was the owner of 4,500 shares was unsupported by the evidence, and (2) the trial court failed to make a finding on a material issue raised by his answer.

In this state a shareholder is ordinarily not personally liable for the debts of the corporation; he undertakes only the risk that his shares may become worthless. See repeal of Cal.Const. Art. XII, § 3, at general election, Nov. 4, 1930; repeal of former Civ.Code section 322, Stats.1931, ch. 257, p. 444; Kaysser v. McNaughton, 6 Cal.2d 248, 251–255, 57 P.2d 927. There are, however, certain exceptions to this rule of limited liability. For example, a subscriber to shares who pays in only part of what he agreed to pay is liable to creditors for the balance. Corp.Code, §§ 1300, 1306. Although the trial court in the present case found that the defendant had agreed to pay par value for the 4,500 shares registered in his name, the record on appeal discloses no evidence supporting this finding. Therefore, the defendant's liability cannot be predicated upon the theory that a subscribing shareholder is liable for the full consideration agreed to be paid for the shares.

The plaintiff seeks to base its recovery on the only other exception to the limited liability rule that the record could support, namely, liability for holding watered stock, which is stock issued in return for properties of services worth less than its par value. Accordingly, this case calls for an analysis of the rights of a creditor of an insolvent corporation against a holder of watered stock. Holders of watered stock are generally held liable to the corporation's creditors for the difference between the par value of the stock and the amount paid in.

The defendant's first contention is that because of the escrow he never became an owner of the 1,022 shares and that he therefore never acquired such title to the 1,022 shares as would enable a creditor to proceed against him for their par value. Section 25508 of the Corporations Code authorizes the Commissioner of Corporations to require that shares be placed in escrow and has frequently been exercised for the protection of the public. The escrow in the present case permitted the defendant to retain some, but not all, of the incidents of ownership in the 1,022 shares. Although he could not transfer the shares, it appears that despite the escrow he was entitled to count them in determining the extent of his rights to vote and to participate in dividends and asset distributions. The critical feature of the escrow of purposes of the present case is the absence of any restriction on representations that the escrowed shares were outstanding and fully paid. Although the escrow contained provisions designed to protect future stockholders, it afforded no special protection to future creditors of the corporation. Therefore, the escrow did not affect the rights of future creditors and it would appear that despite the escrow the defendant acquired sufficient title to the 1,022 shares to permit the plaintiff to proceed against him for their par value.

The defendant's second contention is that the trial court failed to make a finding on a material issue raised by his answer.

The liability of a holder of watered stock has been based on one of two theories: the misrepresentation theory or the statutory obligation theory. The misrepresentation theory is the one accepted in most jurisdictions. The courts view the issue of watered stock as a misrepresentation of the corporation's capital. Creditors who rely on this misrepresentation are entitled to recover the 'water' from the holders of the watered shares. See cases collected in Ballantine, Corporations, rev. ed. 1946, sec. 350; Dodd and Baker, Cases and Materials on Corporations, 2d ed. 1951, pp. 786–789; 11 Fletcher, Cyclopedia of the Law of Private Corporations, rev. and perm. ed. 1932, sec. 5232, p. 568, n. 64, sec. 5233, pp. 577–579; Bonbright, 'Shareholders' Defenses Against Liability to Creditors on Watered Stock.' 1925, 25 Col.L.Rev. 408, 412, 420–421.

Statutes expressly prohibiting watered stock are commonplace today. See statutes collected in 11 Flecher, Cyclopedia of the Law of Private Corporations, rev. and perm. ed. 1932, sec. 5209. In some jurisdictions where they have been enacted, the statutory obligation theory has been applied. See cases collected in 7 A.L.R. 983–986; Dodd and Baker, Cases and Materials on Corporations, 2d ed. 1951, p. 795, n. 7. Under that theory the holder of watered stock is held responsible to creditors whether or not they have relied on an overvaluation of corporate capital.

In his answer the defendant alleged that in extending credit to the corporation the plaintiff did not rely on the par value of the shares issued, but only on independent investigation and reports as to the corporation's current cash position, its physical assets and its business experience. At the trial the plaintiff's district manager admitted that during the period when the plaintiff extended credit to the corporation, (1) the district manager believed that the original capital of the corporation amounted to only $25,000, and (2) the only financial statement of the corporation that the plaintiff ever saw showed a capital stock account of less than $33,000. These admissions would be sufficient to support a finding that the plaintiff did not rely on any misrepresentation arising out of the issuance of watered stock. The court made no finding on the issue of reliance. If the misrepresentation theory prevails in California, that issue was material and the defendant was entitled to a finding thereon. Code Civ.Proc. § 632; see Edgar v. Hitch, 46 Cal.2d 309, 294 P.2d 3. If the statutory obligation theory prevails, the fact that the plaintiff did not rely on any misrepresentation arising out of the issuance of watered stock is irrelevant and accordingly a finding on the issue of reliance would be surplusage.

It is therefore necessary to determine which theory prevails in this state. The plaintiff concedes that before the enactment of section 1110 of the Corporations Code (originally Civ.Code, § 299) in 1931, the misrepresentation theory was the only one available to creditors seeking to recover from holders of watered stock. See Clark v. Tompkins, 205 Cal. 373, 270 P. 946; Spencer v. Anderson, 193 Cal. 1, 6, 222 P. 355, 35 A.L.R. 822; Rhode v. Dock–Hop Co., 184 Cal. 367, 194 P. 11, 12 A.L.R. 437. However, he contends that the enactment of that section reflected a legislative intent to impose on the holders of watered stock a statutory obligation to creditors to make good the 'water.' Section 1110 provides that 'The value of the consideration to be received by a corporation for the issue of shares having par value shall be at least equal to the par value thereof, except that: (a) A corporation may issue par value shares, as fully paid up, at less than par, if the board of directors determines that such shares cannot be sold at par. * * * ' The statute does not expressly impose an obligation to creditors. Most jurisdictions having similar statutes have applied the misrepresentation theory obviously on the ground that creditors are sufficiently protected against stock watering schemes under that theory. See cases collected in Ballantine, Corporations, rev. ed. 1946, sec. 351, pp. 809–812; Dodd and Baker, Cases and Materials on Corporations, 2d ed. 1951, pp. 785–786; 11 Fletcher, Cyclopedia of the Law of Private Corporations, rev. and perm. ed. 1932, sec. 5209; Bonbright, 'Shareholders' Defenses Against Liability to Creditors on Watered Stock,' 1925, 25 Cal.L.Rev. 408, 414–416, 422. In view of the cases in this state prior to 1931 adopting the misrepresentation theory, it is reasonable to assume that the Legislature would have used clear language expressing an intent to broaden the basis of liability of holders of watered stock had it entertained such an intention. In this state the liability of a holder of watered stock may only be based on the misrepresentation theory.

The plaintiff contends that even under the misrepresentation theory a creditor's reliance on the misrepresentation arising out of the issuance of watered stock should be conclusively presumed. This contention is without substantial merit. If it should prevail, the misrepresentation theory and the statutory obligation theory would be essentially identical. This court has held that under the misrepresentation theory a person who extended credit to a corporation (1) before the watered stock was issued, Clark v. Tomkins, supra, 205 Cal. 373, 270 P. 946, or (2) with full knowledge that watered stock was outstanding, Sherman v. S. K. D. Oil Co., 185 Cal. 534, 197 P. 799; Sherman v. Harley, 178 Cal. 584, 174 P. 901, 7 A.L.R. 950. See also Spencer v. Anderson, supra, 193 Cal. 1, 6, 222 P. 355; Rhode v. Dock–Hop Co., supra, 184 Cal. 367, 378, 194 P. 11; R. H. Herron Co. v. Shaw, 165 Cal. 668, 671–672, 133 P. 488, cannot recover from the holders of the watered stock. These decisions indicate that under the misrepresentation theory reliance by the creditor is a prerequisite to the liability of a holder of watered stock. The trial court was therefore justified in ordering a new trial because of the absence of a finding on that issue. It is unnecessary to further consider the defendant's appeal from the judgment.

The order granting the new trial is affirmed. The appeal from the judgment is dismissed.

GIBSON, C. J., and CARTER, TRAYNOR, SCHAUER, SPENCE AND McCOMB, JJ., concur.

NOTES

1.　The concern associated with the failure to pay full price (at least par value) for stock issued by a corporation is that creditors will be misled. Courts may apply various theories to provide that protection, including a trust fund theory (i.e., the stated capital of the company is a trust fund for creditors), a misrepresentation theory (i.e., the stated capital is a representation to creditors that there is at least that much paid in capital) and a fiduciary duty to other shareholders to pay full consideration. In Hospes v. Northwestern Mfg. & Car Co., 48 Minn. 174, 50 N.W. 1117 (1892), the court found flaws in the trust fund theory where a creditor failed to pay for subscribed stock that was issued before the plaintiff became a creditor, i.e., no trust fund had actually been created for non-existent creditors. Instead, the court adopted a type of fraud on the market theory in which the court presumed a general reliance by the community on a company's financial statements. This meant that a creditor would not have to prove actual reliance on the company's financial statements in claiming that the value of its capital and assets were misrepresented. This presumption could be rebutted by a showing of actual knowledge on the part of the creditor that the stock was watered. See Handley v. Stutz, 139 U.S. 417, 11 S.Ct. 530, 35 L.Ed. 227 (1891) (describing the basis for the trust fund theory as an implied promise to pay for the stock when called on by the creditors of an insolvent corporation). The reliance requirement in *Bing Crosby* comports more closely with reality because creditors will take the necessary steps to protect their interests by examining the books and records of the company, reviewing credit reports or by obtaining express representations concerning the assets or cash flow that will assure repayment. Alternatively, creditors may take a security interest in particular property that will give them priority over other creditors.

2.　A traditional way to water stock was to issue common stock for property in amounts far in excess of the value of the property. The property was then carried on the books and records of the company at the inflated value, misleading creditors and subsequent stock purchasers as to the value of the company. See Old Dominion Copper Mining & Smelting Co. v. Lewisohn, 210 U.S. 206, 28 S.Ct. 634, 52 L.Ed. 1025 (1908) and Old Dominion Copper Mining & Smelting Co. v. Bigelow, 203 Mass. 159, 89 N.E. 193 (1909), aff'd, 225 U.S. 111, 32 S.Ct. 641, 56 L.Ed. 1009 (1912), discussed in the context of promoter's liability in Chapter 4.

3.　How do you appraise property given in exchange for stock to see if its value is inflated? Delaware statutes require shares with par value to be issued for consideration having a value not less than par. Del. Corp. L. § 153. In the absence of fraud, however, the judgment of the board of directors as to value is conclusive. Del. Corp. L. § 152. Cf., Pipelife Corp. v. Bedford, 38 Del.Ch. 276, 150 A.2d 319 (1959) (valuation of non-exclusive license given for shares was based on bad faith valuation and shares were canceled). See also Model Bus. Corp. Act § 6.21(c) (decision of board of directors is conclusive as to adequacy of that consideration paid for shares).

4.   Shares are considered to be fully paid and nonassessable when the required consideration is paid into the corporation in the form of cash, services rendered, personal or real property or leases of real property. Del. Corp. L. § 152. Some states do not allow stock to be issued for future services or for promissory notes. Section 6.21 of the Model Business Corporation Act, however, does recognize such consideration as valid for the payment of securities. The Official Comments to this section note that, since the Act does away with the concept of par value, there can be no watered stock, leaving only a concern with the dilution of the other shareholders securities.

5.   Under Delaware law, certificates for partly paid shares must note that they are not fully paid, and such shares are entitled to dividends only on the basis of the percentage paid for the shares. Del. Corp. L. § 152.

SECTION 6.   PREEMPTIVE RIGHTS

The common law concept of preemptive rights sought to protect existing shareholders from dilution of their stock ownership through subsequent stock offerings to a few existing shareholders or to new ones. To illustrate, assume that the ABC Corp. has authorized 100,000 shares of common stock, of which 10,000 shares are outstanding. You own 4,000 of the outstanding shares or forty percent of the company. The board of directors, thereafter, votes to sell the remaining 90,000 shares of previously unissued shares to a third party. This will reduce your percentage of ownership to just four percent. The purchaser should have paid value for the shares, which will increase the capital of the corporation, presumably providing you with the same claim on assets as before in the event of liquidation. Nevertheless, your proportional amount of control has been reduced dramatically. This will affect every aspect of your voting, dividend and other rights.

STOKES v. CONTINENTAL TRUST CO. OF CITY OF NEW YORK

186 N.Y. 285, 78 N.E. 1090 (1906).

* * * This action was brought by a stockholder to compel his corporation to issue to him at par such a proportion of an increase made in its capital stock as the number of shares held by him before such increase bore to the number of all the shares originally issued, and in case such

additional shares could not be delivered to him for his damages in the premises. The defendant is a domestic banking corporation in the city of New York, organized in 1890, with a capital stock of $500,000, consisting of 5,000 shares of the par value of $100 each. The plaintiff was one of the original stockholders, and still owns all the stock issued to him at the date of organization, together with enough more acquired since to make 221 shares in all. On the 29th of January, 1902, the defendant had a surplus of $1,048,450.94, which made the book value of the stock at that time $309.69 per share. On the 2d of January, 1902, Blair & Co., a strong and influential firm of private bankers in the city of New York, made the following proposition to the defendant:

> 'If your stockholders at the special meeting to be called for January 29th, 1902, vote to increase your capital stock from $500,000 to $1,000,000 you may deliver the additional stock to us as soon as issued at $450 per share ($100 par value) for ourselves and our associates, it being understood that we may nominate ten of the 21 trustees to be elected at the adjourned annual meeting of stockholders.'

The directors of the defendant promptly met and duly authorized a special meeting of the stockholders to be called to meet on January 29, 1902, for the purpose of voting upon the proposed increase of stock and the acceptance of the offer to purchase the same. Upon due notice a meeting of the stockholders was held accordingly, more than a majority attending either in person or by proxy. A resolution to increase the stock was adopted by the vote of 4,197 shares, all that were cast. Thereupon the plaintiff demanded from the defendant the right to subscribe for 221 shares of the new stock at par, and offered to pay immediately for the same, which demand was refused. A resolution directing a sale to Blair & Co. at $450 a share was then adopted by a vote of 3,596 shares to 241. The plaintiff voted for the first resolution, but against the last, and before the adoption of the latter he protested against the proposed sale of his proportionate share of the stock, and again demanded the right to subscribe and pay for the same, but the demand was refused. On the 30th of January, 1902, the stock was increased, and on the same day was sold to Blair & Co. at the price named, although the plaintiff formerly renewed his demand for 221 shares of the new stock at par, and tendered payment therefor, but it was refused upon the ground that the stock had already been issued to Blair & Co. owing in part to the offer of Blair & Co. which had become known to the public, the market price of the stock had increased from $450 a share in September, 1901, to $550 in January, 1902, and at the time of the trial, in April, 1904, it was worth $700 per share. Prior to the special meeting of the stockholders, by authority of the board of directors, a circular letter was sent to each stockholder, including the plaintiff, giving notice of the proposition made by Blair & Co. and recommending that it be accepted. Thereupon the plaintiff notified the defendant that he wished to subscribe for his proportionate share of the new stock, if issued, and at no time did he waive his right to subscribe for the same. Before the special meeting, he had not been definitely notified by the defendant that he could not receive his proportionate part of the increase, but was informed that his proposition would 'be taken under consideration.' After finding these facts in substance, the trial court found, as conclusions of law, that the plaintiff had the right to subscribe for such proportion of the increase, as his holdings bore to all the stock before the increase was made; that the stockholders, directors, and officers of the defendant had no power to deprive him of that right, and that he was entitled to recover the difference between the market value of 221 shares on the 30th of January, 1902, and the par value thereof, or the sum of $99,450, together with interest from said date. * * *

VANN, J. (after stating the facts).

* * * [T]the question presented for decision is whether according to the facts found the plaintiff had the legal right to subscribe for and take the same number of shares of the new stock that he held of the old? The subject is not regulated by statute, and the question presented has never been directly passed upon by this court, and only to a limited extent has it been considered by courts in this state. Miller v. Illinois Central R. R. Co., 24 Barb. 312; Matter of Wheeler, 2 Abb. Pr. [N. S.] 361; Currie v. White, 45 N. Y. 822. In the first case cited judgment was rendered by a divided vote of the General Term in the first district. The court held that the plaintiff was entitled to no relief because he did not own any shares when the new stock was issued but only an option, and that he could not claim to be an actual holder until he had exercised his right of election. The court further said, however, that if he was the owner of shares at the time of the new issue he had no absolute right as such owner to a distributive allotment of the new stock. Matter of Wheeler was decided by Judge Mason at Special Term, and, although the point was not directly involved, the learned judge said: 'As I understand the law all these old stockholders had a right to share in the issuing of this new stock in proportion to the amount of stock held by them. And if none of the stock was to be apportioned to the old stockholders, they had certainly the right to have the new stock sold at public sale, and to the highest bidder, that they might share in the gains arising from the sale. In short, the old stockholders, as this was good stock and above par, had a property in the new stock, or a right at least to be secured the profits to be derived from a fair sale of it if they did not wish to purchase it themselves; and they have been deprived of this by the course which these directors have taken with this new stock by transferring or issuing it to themselves and others in a manner not authorized by law.' In Currie v. White the point was not directly involved, but Judge Folger, referring to the rights acquired under a certain contract, said: 'One of these rights was to take new shares upon any legitimate increase of the capital stock, which right attaches to the old shares, not as profit or income, but as inherent in the shares in their very creation,' citing Atkins v. Albree, 12 Allen (Mass.) 359; Brander v. Brander, 4 Ves. 800, and notes, Sumner Ed. While this was said in a dissenting opinion, Judge Rapallo, who spoke for the court, concurred, saying, 'As to

the claim for the additional stock, I concur in the conclusions of my learned Brother Folger.' The fair implication from both opinions is that if the plaintiff had preserved his rights, he would have been entitled to the new stock.

In other jurisdictions the decisions support the claim of the plaintiff with the exception of Ohio Insurance Co. v. Nunnemacher, 15 Ind. 294, which turned on the language of the charter. The leading authority is Gray v. Portland Bank, decided in 1807 and reported in 3 Mass. 364, 3 Am. Dec. 156. In that case a verdict was found for the plaintiff, subject, by the agreement of the parties, to the opinion of the court upon the evidence in the case whether the plaintiff was entitled to recover, and, if so, as to the measure of damages. The court held that stockholders who held old stock had a right to subscribe for and take new stock in proportion to their respective shares. As the corporation refused this right to the plaintiff he was permitted to recover the excess of the market value above the par value, with interest. In the course of its argument the court said: 'A share in the stock or trust when only the least sum has been paid in is a share in the power of increasing it when the trustee determines or rather when the cestuis que trustent agree upon employing a greater sum. * * * A vote to increase the capital stock, if it was not the creation of a new and disjointed capital, was in its nature an agreement among the stockholders to enlarge their shares in the amount or in the number to the extent required to effect that increase. * * * If from the progress of the institution and the expense incurred in it any advance upon the additional shares might be obtained in the market, this advance upon the shares relinquished belonged to the whole, and was not to be disposed of at the will of a majority of the stockholders to the partial benefit of some and exclusion of others.' This decision has stood unquestioned for nearly a hundred years and has been followed generally by courts of the highest standing. It is the foundation of the rule upon the subject that prevails, almost without exception, throughout the entire country.

In Way v. American Grease Company, 60 N. J. Eq. 263, 269, 47 Atl. 44, the headnote fairly expresses the decision as follows: 'Directors of a corporation, which is fully organized and in the active conduct of its business, are bound to afford to existing stockholders an opportunity to subscribe for any new shares of its capital, in proportion to their holdings, before disposing of such new shares in any other way.' In Eidman v. Bowman, 58 Ill. 444, 447, 11 Am. Rep. 90, it was said: 'When this corporation was organized, the charter and all of its franchises and privileges vested in the shareholders, and the directors became their trustees for its management. The right to the remainder of the stock, when it should be issued, vested in the original stockholders, in proportion to the amount each held of the original stock, if they would pay for it, and was as fully theirs as was the stock already held and for which they had paid.' In Dousman v. Wisconsin, etc., Co., 40 Wis. 418, 421, it was held that a court of equity would compel a corporation to issue to every stockholder his proportion of new stock on the ground that 'he has a right to maintain his proportionate interest in the corporation, certainly as long as there is sufficient stock remaining undisposed of by the corporation.' In Jones v. Morrison, 31 Minn. 140, 152, 16 N. W. 854, it was said: 'When the proposition that a corporation is trustee of the corporate property for the benefit of the stockholders in proportion to the stock held by them is admitted (and we find no well-considered case which denies it), it covers as well the power to issue new stock as any other franchise or property which may be of value, held by the corporation. The value of that power, where it has actual value, is given to it by the property acquired and the business built up with the money paid by the subsisting stockholders. It happens not infrequently that corporations, instead of distributing their profits in the way of dividends to stockholders, accumulate them till a large surplus is on hand. No one would deny that, in such case, each stockholder has an interest in the surplus which the courts will protect. No one would claim that the officers, directors or majority of the stockholders, without the consent of all, could give away the surplus, or devote it to any other than the general purposes of the corporation. But when new stock is issued, each share of it has an interest in the surplus equal to that pertaining to each share of the original stock. And if the corporation, either through the officers, directors or majority of stockholders, may dispose of the new stock to whomsoever it will, at whatever price it may fix, then it has the power to diminish the value of each share of old stock by letting in other parties to an equal interest in the surplus and in the good will or value of the established business.'

In Real–Estate Trust Co. v. Bird, 90 Md. 229, 245, 44 Atl. 1048, the court said: 'There can be no doubt that the general rule is that when the capital stock of a corporation is increased by the issue of new shares, authorized by the charter, the holders of the original stock are entitled to the new stock in the proportion that the number of shares held by them bears to the whole number before the increase.' In all these cases, as well as many others, Gray v. Portland Bank, supra, is followed without criticism or question. In some cases the same result is reached without citing that case. Thus in Jones v. Concord & Montreal R. R. Co., 67 N. H. 119, 38 Atl. 120, it was declared, as stated in the headnote, that 'an issue of new shares of stock in an increase of the capital of a corporation is a partial division of the common property, which can be taken from the original shareholders only by their consent or by legal process.' * * *

The elementary writers are very clear and emphatic in laying down the same rule, Thus in 2 Beach on Private Corporations, § 473, the learned author says: 'A stockholder of the old stock, at the time of the vote to augment the capital of a company, has a right in the new stock, in proportion to the amount of his interest in the old, of which he cannot be rightfully deprived by other stockholders. When the capital stock of a corporation is increased by the issue of new shares, each holder of the original stock has a right to offer to subscribe for and to demand from the corporation such a proportion of the new stock as the number of shares already owned by him bears to the whole number of shares before the increase. This pre-emptive right of the shareholders in respect to new stock is well recognized. * * * The corporation cannot compel the old stockholders upon their subscription for a new stock to pay more than par value therefor. They are entitled to it without extra burden or price beyond the regular par value. An attempt to deprive the stockholder of this right will be enjoined in the absence of laches or acquiescence. The courts go very far in protecting the right of stockholders to subscribe for new stock. It is often a very important right.' 1 Cook on Corporations (4th Ed.) 286. 'Each shareholder, it has been held, has a right to the opportunity to subscribe for and take the new or increased stock in proportion to the old stock held by him; so that a vote at a shareholders' meeting, directing the new stock to be sold, without giving to each shareholder such an opportunity, is void as to any dissenting shareholder.' 10 Cyc. 543. 'Those who are shareholders when an increase of capital stock is effected enjoy the right to subscribe to the new stock in proportion to their original holdings and before subscriptions may be received from outsiders.' 26 Am. & Eng. Enc. (2d Ed.) 947. See, also, 2 Thompson's Commentaries, § 2094; Angell & Ames on Corporations, § 430; Morawetz on Corporations, § 455.

If the right claimed by the plaintiff was a right of property belonging to him as a stockholder, he could not be deprived of it by the joint action of the other stockholders, and of all the directors and officers of the corporation. What is the nature of the right acquired by a stockholder through the ownership of shares of stock? What rights can he assert against the will of a majority of the stockholders, and all the officers and directors? While he does not own and cannot dispose of any specific property of the corporation, yet he and his associates own the corporation itself, its charter, franchises, and all rights conferred thereby, including the right to increase the stock. He has an inherent right to his proportionate share of any dividend declared, or of any surplus arising upon dissolution, and he can prevent waste or misappropriation of the property of the corporation by those in control. Finally, he has the right to vote for directors and upon all propositions subject by law to the control of the stockholders, and this is his supreme right and main protection. Stockholders have no direct voice in transacting the corporate business, but through their right to vote they can select those to whom the law intrusts the power of management and control. A corporation is somewhat like a partnership, if one were possible, conducted wholly by agents where the copartners have power to appoint the agents, but are not responsible for their acts. The power to manage its affairs resides in the directors, who are its agents, but the power to elect directors resides in the stockholders. This right to vote for directors, and upon propositions to increase the stock or mortgage the assets, is about all the power the stockholder has. So long as the management is honest, within the corporate powers, and involves no waste, the stockholders cannot interfere, even if the administration is feeble and unsatisfactory, but must correct such evils through their power to elect other directors. Hence, the power of the individual stockholder to vote in proportion to the number of his shares is vital, and cannot be cut off or curtailed by the action of all the other stockholders, even with the co-operation of the directors and officers.

In the case before us the new stock came into existence through the exercise of a right belonging wholly to the stockholders. As the right to increase the stock belonged to them, the stock when increased belonged to them also, as it was issued for money and not for property or for some purpose other than the sale thereof for money. By the increase of stock the voting power of the plaintiff was reduced one-half, and while he consented to the increase he did not consent to the disposition of the new stock by a sale thereof to Blair & Co. at less than its market value, nor by sale to any person in any way except by an allotment to the stockholders. The increase and sale involved the transfer of rights belonging to the stockholders as part of their investment. The issue of new stock and the sale thereof to Blair & Co. was not only a transfer to them of one-half the voting power of the old stockholders, but also of an equitable right to one-half the surplus which belonged to them. In other words, it was a partial division of the property of the old stockholders. The right to increase stock is not an asset of the corporation any more than the original stock when it was issued pursuant to subscription. The ownership of stock is in the nature of an inherent but indirect power to control the corporation. The stock when issued ready for delivery does not belong to the corporation in the way that it holds its real and personal property, with power to sell the same, but is held by it with no power of alienation in trust for the stockholders, who are the beneficial owners, and become the legal owners upon paying therefor. The corporation has no rights hostile to those of the stockholders, but is the trustee for all including the minority. The new stock issued by the defendant under the permission of the statute did not belong to it, but was held by it the same as the original stock when first issued was held in trust for the stockholders. It has the same voting power as the old, share for share. The stockholders decided to enlarge their holdings, not by increasing the amount of each share, but by increasing the number of shares. The new stock belonged to the stockholders as an inherent right by virtue of their being stockholders, to be shared in proportion upon paying its par value or the value per share fixed by vote of a majority of the stockholders, or ascertained by a sale at public auction. While the corporation could not compel the plaintiff to take new shares at any price, since they were issued for money and not for property, it could not lawfully dispose of those shares without giving him a chance to get his proportion at the same price that outsiders got theirs. He had an inchoate right to one share of the new stock for each share owned by him of the old stock, provided he was ready to pay the price fixed by the stockholders. If so situated that he could not take it himself, he was entitled to sell the right to one who could, as is frequently done. Even this gives an advantage to capital, but capital necessarily has some advantage. Of course, there is a distinction when the new stock is issued in payment for property, but that is not this case. The stock in question was issued to be sold for money and was sold for money only. A majority of the stockholders, as part of their power to increase the stock, may attach reasonable conditions to the disposition thereof, such as the requirement that every old stockholder electing to take new stock shall pay a fixed price therefor, not less than par, however, owing to the limitation of the statute. They may also provide for a sale in parcels or bulk at public auction, when every stockholder can bid the same as strangers. They cannot, however, dispose of it to strangers against the protest of any stockholder who insists that he has a right to his proportion. Otherwise the majority could deprive the minority of their proportionate power in the election of directors and their proportionate right to share in the surplus, each of which is an inherent, pre-emptive, and vested right of property. It is inviolable, and can neither be taken away nor lessened without consent, or a waiver implying consent. The plaintiff had power, before the increase of stock, to vote on 221 shares of stock, out of a total of 5,000, at any meeting held by the stockholders for any purpose. By the action of the majority, taken against his will and protest, he now has only one-half the voting power that he had before, because the number of shares has been doubled while he still owns but 221. This touches him as a stockholder in such a way as to deprive him of a right of property. Blair & Co. acquired virtual control, while he and the other stockholders lost it. We are not discussing equities, but legal rights, for this is an action at law, and the plaintiff was deprived of a strictly legal right. If the result gives him an advantage over other stockholders, it is because he stood upon his legal rights, while they did not. The question is what were his legal rights, not what his profit may be under the sale to Blair & Co., but what it might have been if the new stock had been issued to him in proportion to his holding of the old. The other stockholders could give their property to Blair & Co., but they could not give his. A share of stock is a share in the power to increase the stock, and belongs to the stockholders the same as the stock itself. When that power is exercised, the new stock belongs to the old stockholders in proportion to their holding of old stock, subject to compliance with the lawful terms upon which it is issued. When the new stock is issued in payment for property purchased by the corporation, the stockholders' right is merged in the purchase, and they have an advantage in the increase of the property of the corporation in proportion to the increase of stock. When the new stock is issued for money, while the stockholders may provide that it be sold at auction or fix the price at which it is to be sold, each stockholder is entitled to his proportion of the proceeds of the sale at auction, after he has had a right to bid at the sale, or to his proportion of the new stock at the price fixed by the stockholders.

We are thus led to lay down the rule that a stockholder has an inherent right to a proportionate share of new stock issued for money only and not to purchase property for the purposes of the corporation or to effect a consolidation, and while he can waive that right, he cannot be deprived of it without his consent except when the stock is issued at a fixed price not less than par, and he is given the right to take at that price in proportion to his holding, or in some other equitable way that will enable him to protect his interest by acting on his own judgment and using his own resources. This rule is just to all and tends to prevent the tyranny of majorities which needs restraint, as well as virtual attempts to blackmail by small minorities which should be prevented.

The remaining question is whether the plaintiff waived his rights by failing to do what he ought to have done, or by doing something he ought not to have done. He demanded his share of the new stock at par, instead of at the price fixed by the stockholders, for the authorization to sell at $450 a share was virtually fixing the price of the stock. He did more than this, however, for he not only voted against the proposition to sell to Blair & Co. at $450, but, as the court expressly found, he 'protested against the proposed sale of his proportionate share of the stock, and again demanded the right to subscribe and pay for the same which demands were again refused,' and 'the resolution was carried notwithstanding such protest and demands.' Thus he protested against the sale of his share before the price was fixed, for the same resolution fixed the price, and directed the sale, which was promptly carried into effect. If he had not attended the meeting, called upon due notice to do precisely what was done, perhaps he would have waived his rights, but he attended the meeting and, before the price was fixed, demanded the right to subscribe for 221 shares at par, and offered to pay for the same immediately. It is true that after the price was fixed he did not offer to take his share at that price, but he did not acquiesce in the sale of his proportion to Blair & Co., and unless he acquiesced the sale as to him was without right. He was under no obligation to put the corporation in default by making a demand. The ordinary doctrine of demand, tender, and refusal has no application to this case. The plaintiff had made no contract. He had not promised to do anything. No duty of performance rested upon him. He had an absolute right to the new stock in proportion to his holding of the old, and he gave notice that he wanted it. It was his property, and could not be disposed of without his consent. He did not consent. He protested in due time, and the sale was made in defiance of his protest. While in connection with his protest he demanded the right to subscribe at par, that demand was entirely proper when made, because the price had not then been fixed. After the price was fixed it was the duty of the defendant to offer him his proportion at that price, for it had notice that he had not acquiesced in the proposed sale of his share, but wanted it himself. The directors were under the legal obligation to give him an opportunity to purchase at the price fixed before they could sell his property to a third party, even with the approval of a large majority of the stockholders. If he had remained silent, and had made no request or protest he would have waived his rights, but after he had given notice that he wanted his part and had protested against the sale thereof, the defendant was bound to offer it to him at the price fixed by the stockholders. By selling to strangers without thus offering to sell to him, the defendant wrongfully deprived him of his property, and is liable for such damages as he actually sustained.

The learned trial court, however, did not measure the damages according to law. The plaintiff was not entitled to the difference between the par value of the new stock and the market value thereof, for the stockholders had the right to fix the price at which the stock should be sold. They fixed the price at $450 a share, and for the failure of the defendant to offer the plaintiff his share at that price we hold it liable in damages. His actual loss, therefore, is $100 per share, or the difference between $450, the price that he would have been obliged to pay had he been permitted to purchase, and the market value on the day of sale, which was $550. This conclusion requires a reversal of the judgment rendered by the Appellate Division and a modification of that rendered by the trial court.

The order appealed from should be reversed and the judgment of the trial court modified by reducing the damages from the sum of $99,450, with interest from January 30, 1902, to the sum of $22,100, with interest from that date, and by striking out the extra allowance of costs, and as thus modified the judgment of the trial court is affirmed, without costs in this court or in the Appellate Division to either party.

HAIGHT, J. (dissenting). [omitted]

CULLEN, C. J., and WERNER and HISCOCK, JJ., concur with VANN, J.; WILLARD BARTLETT, J., concurs with HAIGHT, J.; O'BRIEN, J., absent.

Ordered accordingly.

NOTES

1. The common law rule expressed in *Stokes v. Continental Trust Co.*, recognizing shareholder preemptive rights was changed by statute. Delaware, for example, denies preemptive rights unless they are specified in the certificate of incorporation. Del. Corp. § 102(b)(3). Model Bus. Corp. Act § 6.30 contains a similar provision but defines the extent of preemptive rights when generally elected in the articles of incorporation, *viz.*,

> The shareholders of the corporation have a preemptive right granted on uniform terms and conditions prescribed by the board of directors to provide a fair and reasonable opportunity to exercise the right, to acquire proportional amounts of the corporation's unissued shares upon the decision of the board of directors to issue them.

Model Bus. Corp. Act § 6.30(b)(1).

2. Most publicly held corporations have not elected to include preemptive rights in their charters because such a right would impair and delay their ability to raise further capital in the market. Preemptive rights issues in large corporations may arise where certain shareholders are given preference over share issues. Compare Clarendon Group, Ltd. v. Smith Laboratories, Inc., 741 F.Supp. 1449 (S.D.Cal.1990) (provision in articles of corporation that rejected preemptive rights did not bar a poison pill (a "flip-in" rights plan) that gave certain shareholders preferential right to purchase stock in the event of a takeover threat), with, Bank of New York Co. v. Irving Bank Corp., 142

Misc.2d 145, 536 N.Y.S.2d 923 (Sup.1988) (provision in certificate of incorporation that rejected preemptive rights did not authorize a poison pill (a "flip-in" rights plan) that gave certain shareholders preferential right to purchase stock in the event of a takeover threat; such a provision was discriminatory among shareholders and violated New York law provision against discrimination among shareholders of a single class of stock).

3. Although rejected by most publicly owned corporations, minority shareholders in close corporations may find preemptive rights desirable. Consider the following case.

ROSS TRANSPORT, INC. v. CROTHERS

185 Md. 573, 45 A.2d 267 (1946).

MARBURY, CHIEF JUDGE.

This is a derivative suit by a stockholder of a Maryland corporation, acting on his own behalf as well as for other stockholders who might join and be made parties, brought after demand had been made on the corporation to institute such a proceeding, which demand was neglected and refused. The original plaintiff was Charles T. Crothers, and he was subsequently joined by another stockholder, his brother Edmund W. Crothers, who was made an additional party plaintiff by order of court. The defendants (appellants here) are the corporation, Ross Transport, Inc., Wallace Williams, F. DuPont Thomson, James W. Hughes and William B. Ross, directors, and Elizabeth B. Williams, Lois Williams Young and Corrine Williams, stockholders. The purpose of the suit is to set aside the issuance of 40 shares of stock to Elizabeth B. Williams, 100 shares of stock to Corrine Williams, 100 shares of stock to Lois Williams Young and 125 shares of stock to William B. Ross. The defendants all answered, testimony was taken and the court passed a decree granting the relief prayed, and directing the four stockholders named to repay to the corporation the dividends received by them on the stock declared to be illegally issued, and ordered cancelled. From this decree, all the defendants appealed.

It appears from the record that the corporation was organized on January 19, 1942 to operate a fleet of buses to transport employees of Triumph Explosives, Inc. to and from its plant at Elkton, Maryland. The incorporators were Wallace Williams, William B. Ross and Gervase R. Sinclair who later died. These three and F. DuPont Thomson and James W. Hughes were the directors. At the organization meeting of the directors, Williams was named as President and Ross as General Manager. The authorized stock was 5000 shares of no par value. At the organization meeting a resolution was passed authorizing the sale of this stock at $20 a share, and providing that stock to the value of $30,000 be offered for sale. This limited the stock to be issued to 1500 shares. The stock records of the company showed the original subscriptions to stock, all in March and April 1942, to be as follows:

March 25th—	To Wallace Williams	50	shares
"	" Wallace Williams, Jr.	100	"
"	" Elizabeth B. Williams	200	"
"	" Edmund W. Crothers	100	"
"	" William B. Ross	25	"
"	" James W. Hughes	150	"
April 2nd	" F. DuPont Thomson	150	"
"	" Bessie F. Whitelaw	10	"
April 20th	" Charles T. Crothers	50	"
April 27th	" Gervase R. Sinclair	50	"
"	" Jean W. Sinclair	150	"
	Total	1035	

In the latter part of July 1942, after the death of Mr. Sinclair, Charles T. Crothers purchased the Sinclair stock, 200 shares, at $20 and 5% interest from the date of issuance. This did not, of course, increase the amount of stock outstanding. On August 26, 1942, the stock complained of was issued to the wife and daughters of Wallace Williams and to William B. Ross, totaling 365 shares in all, and increasing the outstanding stock to 1400 shares. All of this stock was issued at the set price of $20.00 a share. The stock issued to the Williams family was paid by Mr. Williams' check for $4800. Mr. Ross paid the company $2500 for his stock.

As a result of these purchases by Williams and Ross the stock books showed that the Williams family had 590 shares, Ross had 150 shares, Hughes had 150 shares, Thomson had 150 shares, Whitelaw had 10 shares, Edmund W. Crothers had 100 shares and Charles T. Crothers had 250 shares. Williams and Ross, therefore, had the controlling interest in the company. Mr. Williams testified that all of the stock in the company was sold by him personally under the directors' resolution. He said that all the stock in dispute was definitely promised in the beginning, except 40 shares to Mrs. Williams. This, he said, he put in to round out an even 1400 shares, holding back 100 shares which he thought Hughes or Thomson might like to take. He never called any other directors meeting to authorize any of the sales made after the original subscriptions and none of the other stockholders were given an opportunity to buy. He told Mr. Ross and Mr. Hughes how he was going to divide it. Mr. Ross did not testify.

The sale of this additional stock to a director and to the family of the president and director without any further authority than the original resolution, and without opportunity to buy given to other stockholders, is sought to be justified on the ground that it was originally planned, and that the money was needed to purchase additional buses at a cost of about $16,000. The facts, however, show no such need. The company was an immediate financial success. It was engaged in a special business, of which it had a monopoly, and in which it could not help making money so long as Triumph Explosives continued to operate its large plant, employing the workmen the Transport Corporation hauled. The loan of $3000 by Triumph Explosives, made in March, was paid in June. The record shows the following figures during the first five months of its existence.

On August 7th, the directors authorized salary payments dating back to February 1, 1942, $3915 to Mr. Williams, $2875 to Mr. Ross and $2025 to Mr. Hughes who was Secretary and Treasurer of the company which had started business a few months before with a paid in capital of $20,700, and which had bought its operating equipment, i.e. the buses, on conditional sales contracts, and had borrowed $3000 to pay for its licenses. Prosperity continued. On November 27, 1942, a dividend of $5 a share was declared. On December 17, 1942 one of $15 (called a return of capital, but not authorized by the stockholders, Code, Article 23, Sec. 32). On the same date, another dividend of $5 a share was declared payable June 30, 1943. The defendants, Williams and Ross, who were operating the company, knew on August 26, 1942, that they were about to receive large sums in dividends in addition to the salaries they were getting. The benefit of these dividends would not only increase the value of the stock, but the first two would pay back all the subscribers had invested, leaving any future earnings and distributions pure profit. Under these circumstances, they took the opportunity they thought they had to increase their investment, and in fact received in December the full amount they invested in August, leaving them with the additional stock on which to receive such further dividends as were obviously in sight.

The appellants contend that the company was not in the claimed good financial condition in August, because no allowance had been made for income and profits taxes. But if we reduce the book surplus of $25,000 on August 16, 1942, by allowing for a 40% tax (the limit unless the earnings increased), we still find the company with a net surplus of $15,000, 75% of the original investment. The stock had no 'market value,' but it must be obvious that it was worth much more than $20 a share on August 26th.

	Surplus above liabilities and invested capital	Outstanding obligations on conditional sales contract	Cash Bank balance
April 25	$ 8,459.77	$50,372.22	$ 9,092.65
May 23	13,295.38	45,712.34	13,811.80
June 21	20,214.53	42,144.63	14,154.62
July 19	26,414.74	31,154.69	12,842.81
Aug. 16	25,057.73	28,997.68	8,970.83

The appellees give two reasons for their contention that the stock sales of August 26th were void: First, because they deprive them and the other original stockholders of their pre-emptive rights to purchase a proportionate amount of the remaining shares, and, second, because, in selling to themselves and their nominees, Williams and Ross have abused their trust as officers and directors. They claim to be injured in two ways. Their voting powers have been proportionately lessened, and the control of the company has passed to Williams and Ross. And the amount paid in dividends has to be divided among 365 more shares of stock to the consequent financial loss of the holders of the original shares.

Before discussing these legal questions, the outline of the case may be completed by quoting from the appellants' brief certain facts about the plaintiffs (appellees) which appellants claim are pertinent. The original plaintiff, Charles T. Crothers, was an employee of the corporation as well as a stockholder. Edmund W. Crothers had no position in the corporation, but he furnished it part of the buses that were bought at the inception of the business. The appellants' brief states:

'The 365 shares complained of were issued on August 26th, 1942. Charles T. Crothers learned of that fact two or three weeks thereafter; and his brother, Edmund W. Crothers learned about it three or four weeks after said Stock was issued. Charles T. Crothers understood from the first that the Sale of 1,500 Shares had been authorized; and no one had ever represented to him that no more than 1,035 Shares would be issued. In July, 1942, Charles T. Crothers refused to turn over half of the Sinclair Stock, then purchased by him, to Ross, and assigned for his reason the fact that Ross could buy more Stock from the Corporation; and he also attempted to buy the remaining 100 of the authorized 1,500 Shares for himself. On February 1st, 1943, at a Meeting of Stockholders, Charles T. Crothers was elected a Director and served for one year. At that Meeting the Treasurer's Report was accepted on a motion seconded by Edmund W. Crothers. At that Meeting of the Stockholders a Resolution was adopted, expressing to the Management and Employees the appreciation of the Stockholders for the manner in which the operation of the Corporation had been conducted during the previous year. The minutes show that Edmund W. Crothers seconded this Resolution. Charles T. Crothers was then present, and testified that he does not know whether he voted for this Resolution, but he did not object to it. Edmund W. Crothers testified that he did not second the Resolution of Approbation and that he objected to the Minutes on the following year (after this suit was instituted by his brother, but before he, Edmund W. Crothers, had become a party thereto), and that he assigned as his reason for his protest that he was just reserving his decision. On September 13th, 1943, Charles T. Crothers, then a Director, seconded and voted for the Declaration of a Dividend on all 1,400 Shares of Stock. No protest was made to the Corporation about the issuance of the 365 Shares until a letter of protest was written by counsel for Charles T. Crothers on October 27th, 1943, which was after he had been 'fired,' to use his own words, by the Corporation, in October, 1943. Charles T. Crothers, by his own testimony, never made any objection to the 365 Shares complained of having been issued at any meeting of the Corporation.'

Charles T. Crothers testified that he protested to Mr. Hughes and to Mr. Thomson shortly after he learned of the stock issues of August 26th. Mr. Hughes said he was told by Mr. Thomson in 'the latter part of the summer, or the early summer of 1942' that Edmund Crothers had spoken to him about it. Edmund Crothers said he got in touch with Mr. Thomson when he learned of the transaction, and also talked to Mr. Hughes, and at one time had 'quite a little argument' with Mr. Williams and the latter said 'Wouldn't you do it, if you could get away with it.' Charles Crothers gave as a reason for not bringing up the matter at a directors meeting 'They were just a matter of form. Mr. Williams was the boss of the company. He owned the company.'

The doctrine known as the preemptive right of shareholders is a judicial interpretation of general principles of corporation law. Existing stockholders are the owners of the business, and are entitled to have that ownership continued in the same proportion. Therefore, when additional stock is issued, those already having shares, are held to have the first right to buy the new stock in proportion to their holdings. This doctrine was first promulgated in 1807 in the case of Gray v. Portland Bank, 3 Mass. 364, 3 Am.Dec. 156. At that time, corporations were small and closely held, much like the one before us in this case. But in the succeeding years, corporations grew and expanded. New capital was frequently required. New properties had to be acquired for which it was desirable to issue stock. Companies merged, and new stock in the consolidation was issued. Stock was issued for services. Different kinds of stock were authorized—preferred without voting power but with prior dividend rights—preferred with the right to convert into common—several classes of both common and preferred with different rights. Some stock had voting rights. Other stock did not. Bonds were issued, convertible into stock. All of these changes in the corporate structure made it impossible always to follow the simple doctrines earlier decided. Exceptions grew, and were noted in the decisions.

Only one of these exceptions is involved in the present case. It has been held that pre-emptive rights do not exist where the stock about to be issued is part of the original issue. This exception is based upon the fact that the original subscribers took their stock on the implied understanding that the incorporators could complete the sale of the remaining stock to obtain the capital thought necessary to start the business. But this gives rise to an exception to the exception, where conditions have changed since the original issue. The stock sold the Williams family and Ross was part of the original issue, and it is claimed by the appellants that it comes within the exception, and the appellees and the other stockholders have no pre-emptive rights. Balto. Ry. Co. v. Hambleton, 77 Md. 341, 26 A. 279; Real–Estate Trust Co. v. Bird, 90 Md. 229, 44 A. 1048; Thom v. Baltimore Trust Co., 158 Md. 352, 148 A. 234; Yasik v. Wachtel, Del. Ch., 17 A.2d 309; 40 Mich.L.Rev. 115. The appellees, on the other hand, contend, and the chancellors found, that changed conditions made it unnecessary to use the remaining unsold stock to obtain capital, and pre-emptive rights exist in it just as they would exist in newly authorized stock. Hammer v. Werner, 239 App.Div. 38, 265 N.Y.S. 172, Dunlay v. Avenue etc. Co., 253 N.Y. 274, 170 N.E. 917, 43 Harvard L.Rev. 586, 602–603.

It is unnecessary for us to decide which of these two conflicting points of view applies to this case, because another controlling consideration enters. The doctrine of pre-emptive right is not affected by the identity of the purchasers of the issued stock. What it is concerned with is who did not get it. But when officers and directors sell to themselves, and thereby gain an advantage, both in value and in voting power, another situation arises, which it does not require the assertion of a pre-emptive right to deal with.

It has long been the law in this State that trustees cannot purchase at their own sale, and trustees, in this sense, include directors of corporations. This principle of the law was discussed by Chief Judge LeGrand in the first of the cases involving the dealings of Sherman with the Cumberland Coal and Iron Company, Hoffman Coal Company v. Cumberland C. & I. Co., 16 Md. 456 at pages 507–508, 77 Am.Dec. 311. This case referred to the earlier case of Richardson v. Jones, 3 Gill & J. 163, 22 Am.Dec. 293. As authority for the general policy of the law forbidding a trustee to become a purchaser, either directly or indirectly, at his own sale, and stating, 'if he does, such sale may, and will be set aside, on the proper and reasonable application of the parties interested.' The same statement is repeated in the second Sherman case, Cumberland C. & I. Co. v. Sherman, 20 Md. 117, pages 133, 134. This would lead to the conclusion that such a transaction is entirely voidable at the option of a party interested. In the third case involving the same company, Cumberland Coal and Iron Co. v. Parish, 42 Md. 598, Judge Alvey, speaking for this Court said: 'The affairs of corporations are generally intrusted to the exclusive management and control of the board of directors; and there is an inherent obligation, implied in the acceptance of such trust, not only that they will use their best efforts to promote the interest of the shareholders, but that they will in no manner use their positions to advance their own individual interest as distinguished from that of the corporation, or acquire interests that may conflict with the fair and proper discharge of their duty.' After some other observations on the subject, the opinion then states: 'The transaction may not be ipso facto void, but it is not necessary to establish that there has been actual fraud or imposition practiced by the party holding the confidential or fiduciary relation;—the onus of proof being upon him to establish the perfect fairness, adequacy, and equity of the transaction; and that too by proof entirely independent of the instrument under which he may claim.' This last quotation indicates that such a transaction is not absolutely voided at the option of the interested parties, but shifts the burden of proof upon the directors to establish its fairness. This last view was again stated by Judge Alvey in the case of Booth v. Robinson, 55 Md. 419, at pages 441–442, and his words in the last case are quoted by this Court in the case of Penn. R. Co. v. Minis, 120 Md. 461, at page 486, 87 A. 1062. See also Macgill v. Macgill, 135 Md. 384 and cases cited on page 394, 109 A. 72. Coffman v. Publishing Co., 167 Md. 275, 173 A. 248, and Williams v. Messick, 177 Md. 605, 11 A.2d 472, 129 A.L.R. 1035.

It is not necessary for us to determine in this case whether the sale of stock to the Williams family and Ross is voidable merely upon the application of some of the other stockholders, or whether proof of such sale merely makes it necessary for these appellants to show the complete equity of the transaction. If we take the latter view, which is that most favorable to these appellants, we must hold that the burden placed upon the two directors has not been met. They have not shown that the company needed the money so badly and was in such a financial condition that the sale of the additional stock to themselves was the only was the money could be obtained. On the contrary, the corporation appears to have been in a very good financial condition. It is probable that any necessary financing of any buses could easily have been arranged through some financial institution, and Williams and Ross benefited greatly by their action in selling the stock to themselves. Nor is there any corroboration of Williams' statement that it was all arranged in the beginning, who was to get this additional stock. None of the other incorporators or directors were called to testify about this, and Ross himself, as we have noted, did not testify at all. We conclude, therefore, that the sale must be set aside as a constructive fraud upon the other stockholders. * * *

The decree will be affirmed.

KATZOWITZ v. SIDLER

24 N.Y.2d 512, 301 N.Y.S.2d 470, 249 N.E.2d 359 (1969).

KEATING, JUDGE.

Isador Katzowitz is a director and stockholder of a close corporation. Two other persons, Jacob Sidler and Max Lasker, own the remaining securities and, with Katzowitz, comprise Sulburn Holding Corp.'s board of directors. Sulburn was organized in 1955 to supply propane gas to three other corporations controlled by these men. Sulburn's certificate of incorporation authorized it to issue 1,000 shares of no par value stock for which the incorporators established a $100 selling price. Katzowitz, Sidler and Lasker each invested $500 and received five shares of the corporation's stock.

The three men had been jointly engaged in several corporate ventures for more than 25 years. In this period they had always been equal partners and received identical compensation from the corporations they controlled. Though all the corporations controlled by these three men prospered, disenchantment with their inter-personal relationship flared into the open in 1956. At this time, Sidler and Lasker joined forces to oust Katzowitz from any role in managing the corporations. They first voted to replace Katzowitz as a director of Sullivan County Gas Company with the corporation's private counsel. Notice of directors' meetings was then caused to be sent out by Lasker and Sidler for Burnwell Gas Corporation. Sidler and Lasker advised Katzowitz that they intended to vote for a new board of directors. Katzowitz at this time held the position of manager of the Burnwell facility.

Katzowitz sought a temporary injunction to prevent the meeting until his rights could be judicially determined. A temporary injunction was granted to maintain the status quo until trial. The order was affirmed by the Appellate Division (Katzowitz v. Sidler, 8 A.D.2d 726, 187 N.Y.S.2d 986).

Before the issue could be tried, the three men entered into a stipulation in 1959 whereby Katzowitz withdrew from active participation in the day-to-day operations of the business. The agreement provided that he would remain on the boards of all the corporations, and each board would be limited to three members composed of the three stockholders or their designees. Katzowitz was to receive the same compensation and other fringe benefits which the controlled corporations paid Lasker and Sidler. The stipulation also provided that Katzowitz, Sidler and Lasker were 'equal stockholders and each of said parties now owns the same number of shares of stock in each of the defendant corporations and that such shares of stock shall continue to be in full force and effect and unaffected by this stipulation, except as hereby otherwise expressly provided.' The stipulation contained no other provision affecting equal stock interests.

The business relationship established by the stipulation was fully complied with. Sidler and Lasker, however, were still interested in disassociating themselves from Katzowitz and purchased his interest in one of the gas distribution corporations and approached him with regard to the purchase of his interest in another.

In December of 1961 Sulburn was indebted to each stockholder to the extent of $2,500 for fees and commissions earned up until September, 1961. Instead of paying this debt, Sidler and Lasker wanted Sulburn to loan the money to another corporation which all three men controlled. Sidler and Lasker called a meeting of the board of directors to propose that additional securities be offered at $100 per share to substitute for the money owed to the directors. The notice of meeting for October 30, 1961 had on its agenda 'a proposition that the corporation issue common stock of its unissued common capital stock, The total par value which shall equal the total sum of the fees and commissions now owing by the corporation to its * * * directors'. (Emphasis added.) Katzowitz made it quite clear at the meeting that he would not invest any additional funds in Sulburn in order for it to make a loan to this other corporation. The only resolution passed at the meeting was that the corporation would pay the sum of $2,500 to each director.

With full knowledge that Katzowitz expected to be paid his fees and commissions and that he did not want to participate in any new stock issuance, the other two directors called a special meeting of the board on December 1, 1961. The only item on the agenda for this special meeting was the issuance of 75 shares of the corporation's common stock at $100 per share. The offer was to be made to stockholders in 'accordance with their respective preemptive rights for the purpose of acquiring additional working capital'. The amount to be raised was the exact amount owed by the corporation to its shareholders. The offering price for the securities was 1/18 the book value of the stock. Only Sidler and Lasker attended the special board meeting. They approved the issuance of the 75 shares.

Notice was mailed to each stockholder that they had the right to purchase 25 shares of the corporation's stock at $100 a share. The offer was to expire on December 27, 1961. Failure to act by that date was stated to constitute a waiver. At about the same time Katzowitz received the notice, he received a check for $2,500 from the corporation for his fees and commissions. Katzowitz did not exercise his option to buy the additional shares. Sidler and Lasker purchased their full complement, 25 shares each. This purchase by Sidler and Lasker caused an immediate dilution of the book value of the outstanding securities.

On August 25, 1962 the principal asset of Sulburn, a tractor trailer truck, was destroyed. On August 31, 1962 the directors unanimously voted to dissolve the corporation. Upon dissolution, Sidler and Lasker each received $18,885.52 but Katzowitz only received $3,147.59.

The plaintiff instituted a declaratory judgment action to establish his right to the proportional interest in the assets of Sulburn in liquidation less the $5,000 which Sidler and Lasker used to purchase their shares in December, 1961.

Special Term (Westchester County) found the book value of the corporation's securities on the day the stock was offered at $100 to be worth $1,800. The court also found that 'the individual defendants * * * decided that in lieu of taking that sum in cash (the commissions and fees due the stockholders), they preferred to add to their investment by having the corporate defendant make available and offer each stockholder an additional twenty-five shares of unissued stock.' The court reasoned that Katzowitz waived his right to purchase the stock or object to its sale to Lasker and Sidler by failing to exercise his pre-emptive right and found his protest at the time of dissolution untimely.

The Appellate Division (Second Department), two Justices, dissenting, modified the order of Special Term 29 A.D.2d 955, 289 N.Y.S.2d 324. The modification was procedural. The decretal paragraph in Special Term's order was corrected by reinstating the complaint and substituting a statement of the parties' rights. On the substantive legal issues and findings of fact, the Appellate Division was in agreement with Special Term. The majority agreed that the book value of the corporation's stock at the time of the stock offering was $1,800. The Appellate Division reasoned, however, that showing a disparity between book value and offering price was insufficient without also showing fraud or overreaching. Disparity in price by itself was not enough to prove fraud. The Appellate Division also found that the plaintiff had waived his right to object to his recovery in dissolution by failing to either exercise his pre-emptive rights or take steps to prevent the sale of the stock.

The concept of pre-emptive rights was fashioned by the judiciary to safeguard two distinct interests of stockholders—the right to protection against dilution of their equity in the corporation and protection against dilution of their proportionate voting control. (Ballantine, Corporations (rev. ed., 1946), § 209.) After early decisions (Gray v. Portland Bank, 3 Mass. 364; Stokes v. Continental Trust Co., 186 N.Y. 285, 78 N.E. 1090, 12 L.R.A.,N.S., 969), legislation fixed the right enunciated with respect to proportionate voting but left to the judiciary the role of protecting existing shareholders from the dilution of their equity (e.g., Stock Corporation Law, § 39, now Business Corporation Law, Consol.Laws, c. 4, § 622; see Drinker, The Preemptive Right of Shareholders to Subscribe to New Shares, 43 Harv.L.Rev. 586; Frey, Shareholders' Pre-emptive Rights, 38 Yale L.J. 563).

It is clear that directors of a corporation have no discretion in the choice of those to whom the earnings and assets of the corporation should be distributed. Directors, being fiduciaries of the corporation, must, in issuing new stock, treat existing shareholders fairly. [citations omitted]. Though there is very little statutory control over the price which a corporation must receive for new shares (Stock Corporation Law §§ 12, 27, 69, 74; Business Corporation Law § 504) the power to determine price must be exercised for the benefit of the corporation and in the interest of all the stockholders (see, e.g., Bodell v. General Gas & Elec. Corp., 15 Del.Ch. 119, 132 A. 442, affd. 15 Del.Ch. 420, 140 A. 264; Minn.Stat. § 301.16 (1953)).

Issuing stock for less than fair value can injure existing shareholders by diluting their interest in the corporation's surplus, in current and future earnings and in the assets upon liquidation. Normally, a stockholder is protected from the loss of his equity from dilution, even though the stock is being offered at less than fair value, because the shareholder receives rights which he may either exercise or sell. If he exercises, he has protected his interest and, if not, he can sell the rights, thereby compensating himself for the dilution of his remaining shares in the equity of the corporation (Schramme v. Cowin, 205 App.Div. 20, 23, 199 N.Y.S. 98, 100; Noble v. Great Amer. Ins. Co., 200 App.Div. 773, 778–779, 194 N.Y.S. 60, 65–66).[2]

On rare occasions stock will be issued below book value because this indicia of value is not reflective of the actual worth of the corporation. The book value of the corporation's assets may be inflated or the company may not be glamorous to the public because it is in a declining industry or the company may be under the direction of poor management. In these circumstances there may be a business justification for a major disparity in issuing price and book value in order to inject new capital into the corporation. (See, e.g., Conklin v. United Constr. & Supply Co., 166 App.Div. 284, 151 N.Y.S. 624, affd. 219 N.Y. 555, 114 N.E. 1063.)

---

2. There is little justification for issuing stock far below its fair value. The only reason for issuing stock below fair value exists in publicly held corporations where the problem of floating new issues through subscription is concerned. The reasons advanced in this situation is that it insures the success of the issue or that it has the same psychological effect as a dividend (Guthman and Dagell, Corporate Financial Policy (3d ed., 1955), p. 369).

When new shares are issued, however, at prices far below fair value in a close corporation or a corporation with only a limited market for its shares, existing stockholders, who do not want to invest or do not have the capacity to invest additional funds, can have their equity interest in the corporation diluted to the vanishing point. (2 Hornstein, Corporation Law and Practice, § 624, pp. 152–153.)

The protection afforded by stock rights is illusory in close corporations. Even if a buyer could be found for the rights, they would have to be sold at an inadequate price because of the nature of a close corporation. Outsiders are normally discouraged from acquiring minority interests after a close corporation has been organized. Certainly a stockholder in a close corporation is at a total loss to safeguard his equity from dilution if no rights are offered and he does not want to invest additional funds.

Though it is difficult to determine fair value for a corporation's securities and courts are therefore reluctant to get into the thicket, when the issuing price is shown to be markedly below book value in a close corporation and when the remaining shareholder-directors benefit from the issuance, a case for judicial relief has been established. In that instance, the corporation's directors must show that the issuing price falls within some range which can be justified on the basis of valid business reasons. (See Borden v. Guthrie, 23 A.D.2d 313, 260 N.Y.S.2d 769 (concurring opn. of Breitel, J.P.), affd. 17 N.Y.2d 571, 268 N.Y.S.2d 330, 215 N.E.2d 511; Steven v. Hale–Haas Corp., 249 Wis. 205, 23 N.W.2d 620, 768.) If no such showing is made by the directors, there is no reason for the judiciary to abdicate its function to a majority of the board or stockholders who have not seen fit to come forward and justify the propriety of diverting property from the corporation and allow the issuance of securities to become an oppressive device permitting the dilution of the equity of dissident stockholders.

The defendant directors here make no claim that the price set was a fair one. No business justification is offered to sustain it (Blaustein v. Pan Amer. Petroleum & Transpt. Co., 293 N.Y. 281, 303–304, 56 N.E.2d 705, 715–716; Pollitz v. Wabash R.R. Co., 207 N.Y. 113, 124, 100 N.E. 721, 723). Admittedly, the stock was sold at less than book value. The defendants simply contend that, as long as all stockholders were given an equal opportunity to purchase additional shares, no stockholder can complain simply because the offering dilutes his interest in the corporation. The defendants' argument is fallacious.

The corollary of a stockholder's right to maintain his proportionate equity in a corporation by purchasing additional shares is the right not to purchase additional shares without being confronted with dilution of his existing equity if no valid business justification exists for the dilution. (*Bennett v. Breuil Petroleum Corp.*, 34 Del.Ch. 6, 99 A.2d 236; Steven v. Hale–Haas Corp., 249 Wis. 205, 23 N.W.2d 620, 768, supra; Gord v. Iowana Farms Milk Co., 245 Iowa 1, 60 N.W.2d 820; Browning v. C & C Plywood Corp., 248 Or. 574, 434 P.2d 339; see Tashman v. Tashman, 13

Misc.2d 982, 174 N.Y.S.2d 482; Berle, Corporate Powers as Powers in Trust, 44 Harv.L.Rev. 1049, 1055–1060; Berle, Corporate Devices for Diluting Stock Participations, 31 Col.L.Rev. 1239, 1241–1243, 1257–1260; Morawetz, The Preemptive Right of Shareholders, 42 Harv.L.Rev. 186, 188.)

A stockholder's right not to purchase is seriously undermined if the stock offered is worth substantially more than the offering price. Any purchase at this price dilutes his interest and impairs the value of his original holding. 'A corporation is not permitted to sell its stock for a legally inadequate price at least where there is objection. Plaintiff has a right to insist upon compliance with the law whether or not he cares to exercise his option. He cannot block a sale for a fair price merely because he disagrees with the wisdom of the plan but he can insist that the sale price be fixed accordance with legal requirements.' (Bennett v. Breuil Petroleum Corp., Supra, 34 Del.Ch. pp. 14–15, 99 A.2d p. 241.) Judicial review in this area is limited to whether under all the circumstances, including the disparity between issuing price of the stock and its true value, the nature of the corporation, the business necessity for establishing an offering price at a certain amount to facilitate raising new capital, and the ability of stockholders to sell rights, the additional offering of securities should be condemned because the directors in establishing the sale price did not fix it with reference to financial considerations with respect to the ready disposition of securities.

Here the obvious disparity in selling price and book value was calculated to force the dissident stockholder into investing additional sums. No valid business justification was advanced for the disparity in price, and the only beneficiaries of the disparity were the two director-stockholders who were eager to have additional capital in the business.

It is no answer to Katzowitz' action that he was also given a chance to purchase additional shares at this bargain rate. The price was not so much a bargain as it was a tactic, conscious or unconscious on the part of the directors, to place Katzowitz in a compromising situation. The price was so fixed to make the failure to invest costly. However, Katzowitz at the time might not have been aware of the dilution because no notice of the effect of the issuance of the new shares on the already outstanding shares was disclosed (Gord v. Iowana Farms Milk Co., supra, 245 Iowa p. 18, 60 N.W.2d 820). In addition, since the stipulation entitled Katzowitz to the same compensation as Sidler and Lasker, the disparity in equity interest caused by their purchase of additional securities in 1961 did not affect stockholder income from Sulburn and, therefore, Katzowitz possibly was not aware of the effect of the stock issuance on his interest in the corporation until dissolution.

No reason exists at this time to permit Sidler and Lasker to benefit from their course of conduct. Katzowitz' delay in commencing the action did not prejudice the defendants. By permitting the defendants to recover their additional investment in Sulburn before the remaining assets of

Sulburn are distributed to the stockholders upon dissolution, all the stockholders will be treated equitably. Katzowitz, therefore, should receive his aliquot share of the assets of Sulburn less the amount invested by Sidler and Lasker for their purchase of stock on December 27, 1961.

Accordingly, the order of the Appellate Division should be reversed, with costs, and judgment granted in favor of the plaintiff against the individual defendants.

BURKE, SCILEPPI, BERGAN, BREITEL and JASEN, JJ., concur with KEATING, J.

FULD, C.J., dissents and votes to affirm on the opinion at the Appellate Division.

NOTES

1.   In Schwartz v. Marien, 37 N.Y.2d 487, 373 N.Y.S.2d 122, 335 N.E.2d 334 (1975), ownership and control in a closely held corporation with a four member board was equally divided between two families. One member died, and the other family filled his vacancy, giving that family control of the board. The controlling family then approved a sale of treasury stock to themselves, which also gave them voting control and assured future control of the board. The New York Court of Appeals held that, even though preemptive rights did not apply to treasury shares and even if the corporate charter did not provide for preemptive rights, the members of the board were required to justify the sale of treasury stock by showing a bona fide business purpose that could not have been achieved by other means. Such action would otherwise be a breach of fiduciary duties to the other shareholders.

2.   Do you think that a preemptive rights provision should be included in the charter of a closely held corporation? What happens if the board of directors authorizes the issuance of more shares at a fair price but the minority is unable to exercise their preemptive right because the cost is too great? Has the minority lost anything?

———

SECTION 7.   BALANCE SHEET LIABILITIES

Liabilities on the balance sheet may be long term (with a maturity of more than 10 years), medium term (with a maturity of one year to ten years) and short term (with a maturity of less than one year, but for some purposes, short term debt may be defined as having a maturity of less than nine months). See generally In re Bevill, Bresler & Schulman Asset Management Corp., 67 B.R. 557, 567 (D.N.J.1986) (describing debt with differing maturities). A popular form of long term corporate debt is the debenture.

METROPOLITAN LIFE INS. CO. v. RJR NABISCO, INC.

716 F.Supp. 1504 (S.D.N.Y.1989).

WALKER, DISTRICT JUDGE:

The corporate parties to this action are among the country's most sophisticated financial institutions, as familiar with the Wall Street investment community and the securities market as American consumers are with the Oreo cookies and Winston cigarettes made by defendant RJR Nabisco, Inc. (sometimes "the company" or "RJR Nabisco"). The present action traces its origins to October 20, 1988, when F. Ross Johnson, then the Chief Executive Officer of RJR Nabisco, proposed a $17 billion leveraged buy-out ("LBO") of the company's shareholders, at $75 per share. Within a few days, a bidding war developed among the investment group led by Johnson and the investment firm of Kohlberg Kravis Roberts & Co. ("KKR"), and others. On December 1, 1988, a special committee of RJR Nabisco directors, established by the company specifically to consider the competing proposals, recommended that the company accept the KKR proposal, a $24 billion LBO that called for the purchase of the company's outstanding stock at roughly $109 per share.

The flurry of activity late last year that accompanied the bidding war for RJR Nabisco spawned at least eight lawsuits, filed before this Court, charging the company and its former CEO with a variety of securities and common law violations. The Court agreed to hear the present action—filed even before the company accepted the KKR proposal—on an expedited basis, with an eye toward March 1, 1989, when RJR Nabisco was expected to merge with the KKR holding entities created to facilitate the LBO. On that date, RJR Nabisco was also scheduled to assume roughly $19 billion of new debt. After a delay unrelated to the present action, the merger was ultimately completed during the week of April 24, 1989.

Plaintiffs now allege, in short, that RJR Nabisco's actions have drastically impaired the value of bonds previously issued to plaintiffs by, in effect, misappropriating the value of those bonds to help finance the LBO and to distribute an enormous windfall to the company's shareholders. As a result, plaintiffs argue, they have unfairly suffered a multimillion dollar loss in the value of their bonds.[4] * * *

Although the numbers involved in this case are large, and the financing necessary to complete the LBO unprecedented, the legal principles nonetheless remain discrete and familiar. Yet while the instant motions thus primarily require the Court to evaluate and apply traditional rules of equity and contract interpretation, plaintiffs do raise issues of

---

4. Agencies like Standard & Poor's and Moody's generally rate bonds in two broad categories: investment grade and speculative grade. Standard & Poor's rates investment grade bonds from "AAA" to "BBB." Moody's rates those bonds from "AAA" to "Baa3." Speculative grade bonds are rated either "BB" and lower, or "Ba1" and lower, by Standard & Poor's and Moody's, respectively. *See, e.g., Standard and Poor's Debt Rating Criteria* at 10–11. No one disputes that, subsequent to the announcement of the LBO, the RJR Nabisco bonds lost their "A" ratings.

first impression in the context of an LBO. At the heart of the present motions lies plaintiffs' claim that RJR Nabisco violated a restrictive covenant—not an explicit covenant found within the four corners of the relevant bond indentures, but rather an *implied* covenant of good faith and fair dealing—not to incur the debt necessary to facilitate the LBO and thereby betray what plaintiffs claim was the fundamental basis of their bargain with the company. The company, plaintiffs assert, consistently reassured its bondholders that it had a "mandate" from its Board of Directors to maintain RJR Nabisco's preferred credit rating. Plaintiffs ask this Court first to imply a covenant of good faith and fair dealing that would prevent the recent transaction, then to hold that this covenant has been breached, and finally to require RJR Nabisco to redeem their bonds.

RJR Nabisco defends the LBO by pointing to express provisions in the bond indentures that, *inter alia,* permit mergers and the assumption of additional debt. These provisions, as well as others that could have been included but were not, were known to the market and to plaintiffs, sophisticated investors who freely bought the bonds and were equally free to sell them at any time. Any attempt by this Court to create contractual terms *post hoc,* defendants contend, not only finds no basis in the controlling law and undisputed facts of this case, but also would constitute an impermissible invasion into the free and open operation of the marketplace.

For the reasons set forth below, this Court agrees with defendants. There being no express covenant between the parties that would restrict the incurrence of new debt, and no perceived direction to that end from covenants that are express, this Court will not imply a covenant to prevent the recent LBO and thereby create an indenture term that, while bargained for in other contexts, was not bargained for here and was not even within the mutual contemplation of the parties. * * *

Metropolitan Life Insurance Co. ("MetLife"), incorporated in New York, is a life insurance company that provides pension benefits for 42 million individuals. According to its most recent annual report, MetLife's assets exceed $88 billion and its debt securities holdings exceed $49 billion. MetLife is a mutual company and therefore has no stockholders and is instead operated for the benefit of its policyholders. MetLife alleges that it owns $340,542,000 in principal amount of six separate RJR Nabisco debt issues, bonds allegedly purchased between July 1975 and July 1988. Some bonds become due as early as this year; others will not become due until 2017. The bonds bear interest rates of anywhere from 8 to 10.25 percent. MetLife also owned 186,000 shares of RJR Nabisco common stock at the time this suit was filed.

Jefferson–Pilot Life Insurance Co. ("Jefferson–Pilot") is a North Carolina company that has more than $3 billion in total assets, $1.5 billion of which are invested in debt securities. Jefferson–Pilot alleges that it owns $9.34 million in principal amount of three separate RJR Nabisco debt issues, allegedly purchased between June 1978 and June 1988. Those bonds, bearing interest rates of anywhere from 8.45 to 10.75 percent, become due in 1993 and 1998.

RJR Nabisco, a Delaware corporation, is a consumer products holding company that owns some of the country's best known product lines, including LifeSavers candy, Oreo cookies, and Winston cigarettes. The company was formed in 1985, when R.J. Reynolds Industries, Inc. ("R.J. Reynolds") merged with Nabisco Brands, Inc. ("Nabisco Brands"). In 1979, and thus before the R.J. Reynolds–Nabisco Brands merger, R.J. Reynolds acquired the Del Monte Corporation ("Del Monte"), which distributes canned fruits and vegetables. From January 1987 until February 1989, co-defendant Johnson served as the company's CEO. KKR, a private investment firm, organizes funds through which investors provide pools of equity to finance LBOs.

The bonds implicated by this suit are governed by long, detailed indentures, which in turn are governed by New York contract law. No one disputes that the holders of public bond issues, like plaintiffs here, often enter the market after the indentures have been negotiated and memorialized. Thus, those indentures are often not the product of face-to-face negotiations between the ultimate holders and the issuing company. What remains equally true, however, is that underwriters ordinarily negotiate the terms of the indentures with the issuers. Since the underwriters must then sell or place the bonds, they necessarily negotiate in part with the interests of the buyers in mind. Moreover, these indentures were not secret agreements foisted upon unwitting participants in the bond market. No successive holder is required to accept or to continue to hold the bonds, governed by their accompanying indentures; indeed, plaintiffs readily admit that they could have sold their bonds right up until the announcement of the LBO. Instead, sophisticated investors like plaintiffs are well aware of the indenture terms and, presumably, review them carefully before lending hundreds of millions of dollars to any company.

Indeed, the prospectuses for the indentures contain a statement relevant to this action: The Indenture contains no restrictions on the creation of unsecured short-term debt by [RJR Nabisco] or its subsidiaries, no restriction on the creation of unsecured Funded Debt by [RJR Nabisco] or its subsidiaries which are not Restricted Subsidiaries, and no restriction on the payment of dividends by [RJR Nabisco]. Further, as plaintiffs themselves note, the contracts at issue "[do] not impose debt limits, since debt is assumed to be used for productive purposes."

Thus, the prospectus statement quoted above has its counterpart in each of the other prospectuses.

A typical RJR Nabisco indenture contains thirteen Articles. At least four of them are relevant to the present motions and thus merit a brief review.

Article Three delineates the covenants of the issuer. Most important, it first provides for payment of principal and interest. It then addresses various mechanical provisions regarding such matters as payment terms and trustee vacancies. The Article also contains "negative pledge" and related provisions, which restrict mortgages or other liens on the assets of RJR Nabisco or its subsidiaries and seek to protect the bondholders from being subordinated to other debt.

Article Five describes various procedures to remedy defaults and the responsibilities of the Trustee. This Article includes the distinction in the indentures noted above, *see supra* n. 11. In seven of the nine securities at issue, a provision in Article Five prohibits bondholders from suing for any remedy based on rights in the indentures unless 25 percent of the holders have requested in writing that the indenture trustee seek such relief, and, after 60 days, the trustee has not sued. * * *

Article Nine governs the adoption of supplemental indentures. It provides, *inter alia,* that the Issuer and the Trustee can add to the covenants of the Issuer such further covenants, restrictions, conditions or provisions as its Board of Directors by Board Resolution and the Trustee shall consider to be for the protection of the holders of Securities, and to make the occurrence, or the occurrence and continuance, of a default in any such additional covenants, restrictions, conditions or provisions an Event of Default permitting the enforcement of all or any of the several remedies provided in this Indenture as herein set forth ...

Article Ten addresses a potential "Consolidation, Merger, Sale or Conveyance," and explicitly sets forth the conditions under which the company can consolidate or merge into or with any other corporation. It provides explicitly that RJR Nabisco "may consolidate with, or sell or convey, all or substantially all of its assets to, or merge into or with any other corporation," so long as the new entity is a United States corporation, and so long as it assumes RJR Nabisco's debt. The Article also requires that any such transaction not result in the company's default under any indenture provision.[13]

In its Amended Complaint, MetLife lists the six debt issues on which it bases its claims. Indentures for two of those issues—the 10.25 percent Notes due in 1990, of which MetLife continues to hold $10 million, and the 8.9 percent Debentures due in 1996, of which MetLife continues to hold $50 million—once contained express covenants that, among other things, restricted the company's ability to incur precisely the sort of debt involved in the recent LBO. In order to eliminate those restrictions, the parties to this action renegotiated the terms of those indentures, first in 1983 and then again in 1985.

---

13. The remaining Articles are not relevant to the motions currently before the Court. Article One contains definitions; Article Two contains mechanical terms regarding, for instance, the issuance and transfer of the securities; Article Four concerns such mechanical matters as securityholders' lists and annual reports; Article Six addresses the rights and responsibilities of the Trustee; Article Seven contains mechanical provisions concerning the securityholders; Article Eight concerns procedural matters such as securityholders' meetings and consents; Article Eleven deals with the satisfaction and discharge of the indenture; Article Twelve sets forth various miscellaneous provisions; and Article Thirteen includes provisions regarding the redemption of securities and sinking funds.

MetLife acquired $50 million principal amount of 10.25 percent Notes from Del Monte in July of 1975. To cover the $50 million, MetLife and Del Monte entered into a loan agreement. That agreement restricted Del Monte's ability, among other things, to incur the sort of indebtedness involved in the RJR Nabisco LBO. In 1979, R.J. Reynolds—the corporate predecessor to RJR Nabisco—purchased Del Monte and assumed its indebtedness. Then, in December of 1983, R.J. Reynolds requested MetLife to agree to deletions of those restrictive covenants in exchange for various guarantees from R.J. Reynolds. A few months later, MetLife and R.J. Reynolds entered into a guarantee and amendment agreement reflecting those terms. Pursuant to that agreement, and in the words of Robert E. Chappell, Jr., MetLife's Executive Vice President, MetLife thus "gave up the restrictive covenants applicable to the Del Monte debt ... in return for [the parent company's] guarantee and public covenants."

MetLife acquired the 8.9 percent Debentures from R.J. Reynolds in October of 1976 in a private placement. A promissory note evidenced MetLife's $100 million loan. That note, like the Del Monte agreement, contained covenants that restricted R.J. Reynolds' ability to incur new debt. In June of 1985, R.J. Reynolds announced its plans to acquire Nabisco Brands in a $3.6 billion transaction that involved the incurrence of a significant amount of new debt. R.J. Reynolds requested MetLife to waive compliance with these restrictive covenants in light of the Nabisco acquisition.

In exchange for certain benefits, MetLife agreed to exchange its 8.9 percent debentures—which *did* contain explicit debt limitations—for debentures issued under a public indenture—which contain no explicit limits on new debt. An internal MetLife memorandum explained the parties' understanding:

> [MetLife's $100 million financing of the Nabisco Brands purchase] had its origins in discussions with RJR regarding potential covenant violations in the 8.90% Notes. More specifically, *in its acquisition of Nabisco Brands, RJR was slated to incur significant new long-term debt, which would have caused a violation in the funded indebtedness incurrence tests in the 8.90% Notes.* In the discussions regarding [MetLife's] willingness to consent to the additional indebtedness, *it was determined that a mutually beneficial approach to the problem* was to 1) agree on a new financing having a rate and a maturity desirable for [MetLife] and 2) modify the 8.90% Notes. The former was accomplished with agreement on the proposed financing, while the latter was accomplished by [MetLife] agreeing to substitute RJR's public indenture covenants for the covenants in the 8.90% Notes. In addition to the covenant substitution, RJR has agreed to "debenturize" the 8.90% Notes upon [MetLife's] request. This will permit [MetLife] to sell the 8.90% Notes to the public. (emphasis added).

Other internal MetLife documents help frame the background to this action, for they accurately describe the changing securities markets and

the responses those changes engendered from sophisticated market participants, such as MetLife and Jefferson–Pilot. At least as early as 1982,
MetLife recognized an LBO's effect on bond values. In the spring of that
year, MetLife participated in the financing of an LBO of a company called
Reeves Brothers ("Reeves"). At the time of that LBO, MetLife also held
bonds in that company. Subsequent to the LBO, as a MetLife memorandum explained, the "Debentures of Reeves were downgraded by Standard
& Poor's from BBB to B and by Moody's from Baa1 to Ba3, thereby
lowering the value of the Notes and Debentures held by [MetLife]."

MetLife further recognized its "inability to force any type of payout of
the [Reeves'] Notes or the Debentures as a result of the buy-out [which]
was somewhat disturbing at the time we considered a participation in the
new financing. However," the memorandum continued, our concern was
tempered since, as a stockholder in [the holding company used to facilitate
the transaction], we would benefit from the increased net income attributable to the continued presence of the low coupon indebtedness. The recent
downgrading of the Reeves Debentures and the consequent "loss" in value
has again raised questions regarding our ability to have forced a payout.
*Questions have also been raised about our ability to force payouts in
similar future situations, particularly when we would not be participating
in the buy-out financing. Id.* (emphasis added). In the memorandum,
MetLife sought to answer those very "questions" about how it might force
payouts in "similar future situations." *A method of closing this apparent
"loophole," thereby forcing a payout of [MetLife's] holdings, would be
through a covenant dealing with a change in ownership.* Such a covenant
is fairly standard in financings with privately-held companies ... It
provides the lender with an option to end a particular borrowing relationship via some type of special redemption (emphasis added).

A more comprehensive memorandum, prepared in late 1985, evaluated and explained several aspects of the corporate world's increasing use of
mergers, takeovers and other debt-financed transactions. That memorandum first reviewed the available protection for lenders such as MetLife:

> Covenants are incorporated into loan documents to ensure that
> after a lender makes a loan, the creditworthiness of the borrower and
> the lender's ability to reach the borrower's assets do not deteriorate
> substantially. *Restrictions on the incurrence of debt,* sale of assets,
> mergers, dividends, restricted payments and loans and advances to
> affiliates *are some of the traditional negative covenants that can help
> protect lenders in the event their obligors become involved in undesir-
> able merger/takeover situations.* . . . .

> Because almost any industrial company is apt to engineer a
> takeover or be taken over itself, *Business Week* says that investors are
> beginning to view debt securities of high grade industrial corporations
> as Wall Street's riskiest investments. In addition, *because public
> bondholders do not enjoy the protection of any restrictive covenants,*
> owners of high grade corporates face substantial losses from takeover

situations, if not immediately, then when the bond market finally adjusts.... [T]here have been 10–15 merger/takeover/LBO situations where, *due to the lack of covenant protection, [MetLife] has had no choice but to remain a lender to a less creditworthy obligor....* The fact that the quality of our investment portfolio is greater than the other large insurance companies ... may indicate that we have negotiated better covenant protection than other institutions, thus generally being able to require prepayment when situations become too risky ... [However,] a problem exists. And *because the current merger craze is not likely to decelerate* and because there exist vehicles to circumvent traditional covenants, the problem will probably continue. Therefore, *perhaps it is time to institute appropriate language designed to protect Metropolitan from the negative implications of mergers and takeovers.* (emphasis added).

Indeed, MetLife does not dispute that, as a member of a bondholders' association, it received and discussed a proposed model indenture, which included a "comprehensive covenant" entitled "Limitations on Shareholders' Payments." As becomes clear from reading the proposed—but never adopted—provision, it was "intend[ed] to provide protection against all of the types of situations in which shareholders profit at the expense of bondholders." *Id.* The provision dictated that the "[c]orporation will not, and will not permit any [s]ubsidiary to, directly or indirectly, make any [s]hareholder [p]ayment unless ... (1) the aggregate amount of all [s]hareholder payments during the period [at issue] ... shall not exceed [figure left blank]." Bradley Resp.Aff.Exh. H, at 9. The term "shareholder payments" is defined to include "restructuring distributions, stock repurchases, debt incurred or guaranteed to finance merger payments to shareholders, etc." *Id.* at i.

Apparently, that provision—or provisions with similar intentions—never went beyond the discussion stage at MetLife. That fact is easily understood; indeed, MetLife's own documents articulate several reasonable, undisputed explanations: While it would be possible to broaden the change in ownership covenant to cover any acquisition-oriented transaction, *we might well encounter significant resistance in implementation with larger public companies* ... With respect to implementation, we would be faced with the task of imposing a non-standard limitation on potential borrowers, *which could be a difficult task in today's highly competitive marketplace. Competitive pressures notwithstanding, it would seem that management of larger public companies would be particularly opposed to such a covenant since its effect would be to increase the cost of an acquisition* (due to an assumed debt repayment), a factor that could well lower the price of any tender offer (thereby impacting shareholders). Bradley Reply Aff.Exh. D, at 3 (emphasis added). The November 1985 memorandum explained that [o]bviously, our ability to implement methods of takeover protection will vary between the public and private market. In that public securities do not contain any meaningful covenants, it would be very difficult for [MetLife] to demand takeover protection in public bonds. Such a requirement would effectively take us out of the public industrial market. A recent *Business Week* article does suggest, however, that there is increasing talk among lending institutions about requiring blue chip companies to compensate them for the growing risk of downgradings. *This talk, regarding such protection as restrictions on future debt financings, is met with skepticism by the investment banking community which feels that CFO's are not about to give up the option of adding debt and do not really care if their companies' credit ratings drop a notch or two* (emphasis added).

The Court quotes these documents at such length not because they represent an "admission" or "waiver" from MetLife, or an "assumption of risk" in any tort sense, or its "consent" to any particular course of conduct—all terms discussed at even greater length in the parties' submissions. Rather, the documents set forth the background to the present action, and highlight the risks inherent in the market itself, for any investor. Investors as sophisticated as MetLife and Jefferson–Pilot would be hard-pressed to plead ignorance of these market risks. Indeed, MetLife has not disputed the facts asserted in its own internal documents. Nor has Jefferson–Pilot—presumably an institution no less sophisticated than MetLife—offered any reason to believe that its understanding of the securities market differed in any material respect from the description and analysis set forth in the MetLife documents. Those documents, after all, were not born in a vacuum. They are descriptions of, and responses to, the market in which investors like MetLife and Jefferson–Pilot knowingly participated. * * *

Solely for the purposes of these motions, the Court accepts various factual assertions advanced by plaintiffs: first, that RJR Nabisco actively solicited "investment grade" ratings for its debt; second, that it relied on descriptions of its strong capital structure and earnings record which included prominent display of its ability to pay the interest obligations on its long-term debt several times over, and third, that the company made express or implied representations not contained in the relevant indentures concerning its future creditworthiness. In support of those allegations, plaintiffs have marshaled a number of speeches made by co-defendant Johnson and other executives of RJR Nabisco.[18] In addition, plaintiffs rely on an affidavit sworn to by John Dowdle, the former Treasurer and then Senior Vice President of RJR Nabisco from 1970 until 1987. In his opinion, the LBO "clearly undermines the fundamental premise of the [c]ompany's bargain with the bondholders, and the commitment that I believe the [c]ompany made to the bondholders ... I

---

18. *See, e.g.,* Address by F. Ross Johnson, November 12, 1987, P.Exh. 8, at 5 ("Our strong balance sheet is a cornerstone of our strategies. It gives us the resources to modernize facilities, develop new technologies, bring on new products, and support our leading brands around the world."); Remarks of Edward J. Robinson, Executive Vice President and Chief Financial Officer, February 15, 1988, P.Exh. 6, at 1 ("RJR Nabisco's financial strategy is ... to enhance the strength of the balance sheet by reducing the level of debt as well as lowering the cost of existing debt."); Remarks by Dr. Robert J. Carbonell, Vice Chairman of RJR Nabisco, June 3, 1987, P.Exh. 10, at 5 ("We will not sacrifice our longer-term health for the sake of short term heroics.").

firmly believe that the company made commitments ... that require it to redeem [these bonds and notes] before paying out the value to the shareholders." * * *

The indentures at issue clearly address the eventuality of a merger. They impose certain related restrictions not at issue in this suit, but no restriction that would prevent the recent RJR Nabisco merger transaction. The indentures also explicitly set forth provisions for the adoption of new covenants, if such a course is deemed appropriate. While it may be true that no explicit provision either permits or prohibits an LBO, such contractual silence itself cannot create ambiguity to avoid the dictates of the parole evidence rule, particularly where the indentures impose no debt limitations.

Under certain circumstances, however, courts will, as plaintiffs note, consider extrinsic evidence to evaluate the scope of an implied covenant of good faith. *See Valley National Bank v. Babylon Chrysler–Plymouth, Inc.,* 53 Misc.2d 1029, 1031–32, 280 N.Y.S.2d 786, 788–89 (Sup.Ct. Nassau), *aff'd,* 28 A.D.2d 1092, 284 N.Y.S.2d 849 (2d Dep't 1967) (Relying on custom and usage because "[w]hen a contract fails to establish the time for performance, the law implies that the act shall be done within a reasonable time ...."). However, the Second Circuit has established a different rule for customary, or boilerplate, provisions of detailed indentures used and relied upon throughout the securities market, such as those at issue. Thus, in *Sharon Steel Corporation v. Chase Manhattan Bank, N.A.,* 691 F.2d 1039 (2d Cir.1982), Judge Winter concluded that

> [b]oilerplate provisions are ... not the consequences of the relationship of particular borrowers and lenders and do not depend upon particularized intentions of the parties to an indenture. There are no adjudicative facts relating to the parties to the litigation for a jury to find and the meaning of boilerplate provisions is, therefore, a matter of law rather than fact. Moreover, uniformity in interpretation is important to the efficiency of capital markets ... Whereas participants in the capital market can adjust their affairs according to a uniform interpretation, whether it be correct or not as an initial proposition, the creation of enduring uncertainties as to the meaning of boilerplate provisions would decrease the value of all debenture issues and greatly impair the efficient working of capital markets ... Just such uncertainties would be created if interpretation of boilerplate provisions were submitted to juries sitting in every judicial district in the nation.

Id. at 1048. *See also Morgan Stanley & Co. v. Archer Daniels Midland Co.,* 570 F.Supp. 1529, 1535–36 (S.D.N.Y.1983) (Sand, J.) ("[Plaintiff concedes that the legality of [the transaction at issue] would depend on a factual inquiry ... This case-by-case approach is problematic ... [Plaintiff's theory] appears keyed to the subjective expectations of the bondholders ... and reads a subjective element into what presumably should be an objective determination based on the language appearing in the bond agreement."); *Purcell v. Flying Tiger Line, Inc.,* No. 84–7102, at 5, 8 (S.D.N.Y. Jan. 12, 1984) (CES) ("The Indenture does not contain any such limitation [as the one proposed by plaintiff].... In light of our holding that the Indenture unambiguously permits the transaction at issue in this case, we are precluded from considering any of the extrinsic evidence that plaintiff offers on this motion ... It would be improper to consider evidence as to the subjective intent, collateral representations, and either the statements or the conduct of the parties in performing the contract.") (citations omitted).* * *

In their first count, plaintiffs assert that [d]efendant RJR Nabisco owes a continuing duty of good faith and fair dealing in connection with the contract [i.e., the indentures] through which it borrowed money from MetLife, Jefferson–Pilot and other holders of its debt, including a duty not to frustrate the purpose of the contracts to the debtholders or to deprive the debtholders of the intended object of the contracts—purchase of investment-grade securities. In the "buy-out," the [c]ompany breaches the duty [or implied covenant] of good faith and fair dealing by, *inter alia,* destroying the investment grade quality of the debt and transferring that value to the "buy-out" proponents and to the shareholders. In effect, plaintiffs contend that express covenants were not necessary because an *implied* covenant would prevent what defendants have now done. * * *

In contracts like bond indentures, "an implied covenant ... derives its substance directly from the language of the Indenture, and 'cannot give the holders of Debentures any rights inconsistent with those set out in the Indenture.' *[Where] plaintiffs' contractual rights [have not been] violated, there can have been no breach of an implied covenant." Gardner & Florence Call Cowles Foundation v. Empire Inc.,* 589 F.Supp. 669, 673 (S.D.N.Y.1984), *vacated on procedural grounds,* 754 F.2d 478 (2d Cir.1985) (quoting *Broad v. Rockwell,* 642 F.2d 929, 957 (5th Cir.) (*en banc*), *cert. denied,* 454 U.S. 965 (1981)) (emphasis added).

Thus, in cases like *Van Gemert v. Boeing Co.,* 520 F.2d 1373 (2d Cir.), *cert. denied,* 423 U.S. 947 (1975) ("*Van Gemert I*"), and *Pittsburgh Terminal Corp. v. Baltimore & Ohio Ry. Co.,* 680 F.2d 933 (3d Cir.), *cert. denied,* 459 U.S. 1056 (1982)—both relied upon by plaintiffs—the courts used the implied covenant of good faith and fair dealing to ensure that the bondholders received the benefit of their bargain as determined from the face of the contracts at issue. In *Van Gemert I,* the plaintiff bondholders alleged inadequate notice to them of defendant's intention to redeem the debentures in question and hence an inability to exercise their conversion rights before the applicable deadline. The contract itself provided that notice would be given in the first place. *See, e.g., id.* at 1375 ("A number of provisions in the debenture, the Indenture Agreement, the prospectus, the registration statement ... and the Listing Agreement ... dealt with the possible redemption of the debentures ... and the notice debenture-holders were to receive ..."). Faced with those provisions, defendants in that case unsurprisingly admitted that the indentures specifically required the company to provide the bondholders with notice. *See id.* at 1379.

While defendant there issued a press release that mentioned the possible redemption of outstanding convertible debentures, that limited release did not "mention even the tentative dates for redemption and expiration of the conversion rights of debenture holders." *Id.* at 1375. Moreover, defendant did not issue any general publicity or news release. Through an implied covenant, then, the court fleshed out the full extent of the more skeletal right that appeared in the contract itself, and thus protected plaintiff's bargained-for right of conversion. As the court observed,

> What one buys when purchasing a convertible debenture in addition to the debt obligation of the company . . . is principally the expectation that the stock will increase sufficiently in value that the conversion right will make the debenture worth more than the debt . . . *Any loss* occurring to him from failure to convert, as here, *is not from a risk inherent in his investment but rather from unsatisfactory notification procedures. Id.* at 1385 (emphasis added, citations omitted).

I also note, in passing, that *Van Gemert I* presented the Second Circuit with "less sophisticated investors." *Id.* at 1383. Similarly, the court in *Pittsburgh Terminal* applied an implied covenant to the indentures at issue because defendants there "took steps to prevent the Bondholders from receiving information which they needed *in order to receive the fruits of their conversion option should they choose to exercise it." Pittsburgh Terminal,* 680 F.2d at 941 (emphasis added).

The appropriate analysis, then, is first to examine the indentures to determine "the fruits of the agreement" between the parties, and then to decide whether those "fruits" have been spoiled—which is to say, whether plaintiffs' contractual rights have been violated by defendants.

The American Bar Foundation's *Commentaries on Indentures* ("the *Commentaries*"), relied upon and respected by both plaintiffs and defendants, describes the rights and risks generally found in bond indentures like those at issue:

> The most obvious and important characteristic of long-term debt financing is that the holder ordinarily has not bargained for and does not expect any substantial gain in the value of the security to compensate for the risk of loss . . . [T]he significant fact, *which accounts in part for the detailed protective provisions of the typical long-term debt financing instrument,* is that *the lender (the purchaser of the debt security) can expect only interest at the prescribed rate plus the eventual return of the principal.* Except for possible increases in the market value of the debt security because of changes in interest rates, the debt security will seldom be worth more than the lender paid for it . . . It may, of course, become worth much less. Accordingly, the typical investor in a long-term debt security is primarily interested in every reasonable assurance that the principal and interest will be paid when due. . . . Short of bankruptcy, *the debt security holder can do nothing to protect himself against actions of the borrower which jeopardize its ability to pay the debt unless he . . . establishes*

his rights through contractual provisions set forth in the debt agreement or indenture. Id. at 1–2 (1971) (emphasis added).

A review of the parties' submissions and the indentures themselves satisfies the Court that the substantive "fruits" guaranteed by those contracts and relevant to the present motions include the periodic and regular payment of interest and the eventual repayment of principal.... According to a typical indenture, a default shall occur if the company either (1) fails to pay principal when due; (2) fails to make a timely sinking fund payment; (3) fails to pay within 30 days of the due date thereof any interest on the date; or (4) fails duly to observe or perform any of the express covenants or agreements set forth in the agreement. Plaintiffs' Amended Complaint nowhere alleges that RJR Nabisco has breached these contractual obligations; interest payments continue and there is no reason to believe that the principal will not be paid when due.

It is not necessary to decide that indentures like those at issue could never support a finding of additional benefits, under different circumstances with different parties. Rather, for present purposes, it is sufficient to conclude what obligation is *not* covered, either explicitly or implicitly, by these contracts held by these plaintiffs. Accordingly, this Court holds that the "fruits" of these indentures do not include an implied restrictive covenant that would prevent the incurrence of new debt to facilitate the recent LBO. To hold otherwise would permit these plaintiffs to straight-jacket the company in order to guarantee their investment. These plaintiffs do not invoke an implied covenant of good faith to protect a legitimate, mutually contemplated benefit of the indentures; rather, they seek to have this Court create an additional benefit for which they did not bargain.

Although the indentures generally permit mergers and the incurrence of new debt, there admittedly is not an explicit indenture provision to the contrary of what plaintiffs now claim the implied covenant requires. That absence, however, does *not* mean that the Court should imply into those very same indentures a covenant of good faith so broad that it imposes a new, substantive term of enormous scope. This is so particularly where, as here, that very term—a limitation on the incurrence of additional debt—has in other past contexts been expressly bargained for; particularly where the indentures grant the company broad discretion in the management of its affairs, as plaintiffs admit, particularly where the indentures explicitly set forth specific provisions for the adoption of new covenants and restrictions, and *especially* where there has been no breach of the parties' bargained-for contractual rights on which the implied covenant necessarily is based. While the Court stands ready to employ an implied covenant of good faith to ensure that such bargained-for rights are performed and upheld, it will not, however, permit an implied covenant to shoehorn into an indenture additional terms plaintiffs now wish had been included. *See also Broad v. Rockwell International Corp.,* 642 F.2d 929 (5th Cir.) (*en banc*) (applying New York law), *cert. denied,* 454 U.S. 965, 102 S.Ct. 506, 70 L.Ed.2d 380 (1981) (finding no liability pursuant to an implied covenant where the terms of the indenture, as bargained for, were enforced). * * *

In the final analysis, plaintiffs offer no objective or reasonable standard for a court to use in its effort to define the sort of actions their "implied covenant" would permit a corporation to take, and those it would not. Plaintiffs say only that investors like themselves rely upon the "skill" and "good faith" of a company's board and management, and that their covenant would prevent the company from "destroy [ing] ... the legitimate expectations of its long-term bondholders." As is clear from the preceding discussion, however, plaintiffs have failed to convince the Court that by upholding the explicit, bargained-for terms of the indenture, RJR Nabisco has either exhibited bad faith or destroyed plaintiffs' *legitimate, protected* expectations.

* * * Third, [P]laintiffs advance a claim that remains based, their assertions to the contrary notwithstanding, on an alleged breach of a fiduciary duty. Defendants go to great lengths to prove that the law of Delaware, and not New York, governs this question. Defendants' attempt to rely on Delaware law is readily explained by even a cursory reading of *Simons v. Cogan,* 549 A.2d 300, 303 (Del.1988), the recent Delaware Supreme Court ruling which held, *inter alia,* that a corporate bond "represents a contractual entitlement to the repayment of a debt and does not represent an equitable interest in the issuing corporation necessary for the imposition of a trust relationship with concomitant fiduciary duties." Before such a fiduciary duty arises, "an existing property right or equitable interest supporting such a duty must exist." *Id.* at 304. A bondholder, that court concluded, "acquires no equitable interest, and remains a creditor of the corporation whose interests are protected by the contractual terms of the indenture." *Id.* Defendants argue that New York law is not to the contrary, but the single Supreme Court case they cite—a case decided over fifty years ago that was not squarely presented with the issue addressed by the *Simons* court—provides something less than dispositive support. *See Marx v. Merchants' National Properties, Inc.,* 148 Misc. 6, 7, 265 N.Y.S. 163, 165 (1933). For their part, plaintiffs more convincingly demonstrate that New York law applies than that New York law recognizes their claim. * * *

[T]his Court finds *Simons* persuasive, and believes that a New York court would agree with that conclusion. In the venerable case of *Meinhard v. Salmon,* 249 N.Y. 458, 164 N.E. 545 (1928), then Chief Judge Cardozo explained the obligations imposed on a fiduciary, and why those obligations are so special and rare:

> Many forms of conduct permissible in a workaday world for those acting at arm's length, are forbidden to those bound by fiduciary ties. A trustee is held to something stricter than the morals of the market place. Not honesty alone, but the punctilio of an honor the most sensitive, is then the standard of behavior. As to this there has developed a tradition that is unbending and inveterate. Uncompromis-

ing rigidity has been the attitude of courts of equity when petitioned to undermine the rule of undivided loyalty ... Only thus has the level of conduct for fiduciaries been kept at a level higher than that trodden by the crowd.

Id. at 464 (citation omitted). Before a court recognizes the duty of a "punctilio of an honor the most sensitive," it must be certain that the complainant is entitled to more than the "morals of the market place," and the protections offered by actions based on fraud, state statutes or the panoply of available federal securities laws. This Court has concluded that the plaintiffs presently before it—sophisticated investors who are unsecured creditors—are not entitled to such additional protections.

Equally important, plaintiffs' position on this issue—that "A Company May Not Deliberately Deplete its Assets to the Injury of its Debtholders,"—provides no reasonable or workable limits, and is thus reminiscent of their implied covenant of good faith. Indeed, many indisputably legitimate corporate transactions would not survive plaintiffs' theory. With no workable limits, plaintiffs' envisioned duty would extend equally to trade creditors, employees, and every other person to whom the defendants are liable in any way. Of all such parties, these informed plaintiffs least require a Court's equitable protection; not only are they willing participants in a largely impersonal market, but they also possess the financial sophistication and size to secure their own protection.

Finally, plaintiffs cannot seriously allege unconscionability, given their sophistication and, at least judging from this action, the sophistication of their legal counsel as well. Under the undisputed facts of this case, this Court finds no actionable unconscionability. * * *

For the reasons set forth above, the Court grants defendants summary judgment on Counts I and V, judgment on the pleadings for certain of the securities at issue in Count III, and dismisses for want of requisite particularity Counts II, III, and IX. All remaining motions made by the parties are denied in all respects. Plaintiffs shall have twenty days to replead.

SO ORDERED.

NOTES

1. Long term borrowing may take many complex forms. Convertible bonds allow the holder to convert the bond into stock, usually common stock, at some premium over the existing market price of the stock. This provides opportunity for an upside gain, if the price of the stock moves substantially. Of course there is a price to pay. The interest rate will be lower than a comparable bond without a similar feature. This allows a corporation to fund its borrowing at a lower cost. If stock prices rise, the corporation simply issues new stock to the bondholders converting, but this will dilute the holdings of other shareholders.

2. Consider the following variation on a convertible bond:

Liquid Yield Option Notes ("LYONs") were developed by Merrill Lynch and first offered to investors in early 1985. To create LYONs, Merrill Lynch redesigned the standard convertible bond in two important respects: (1) the bonds were reconfigured as zero coupon instruments which are offered at a deep discount to their face amount; and (2) investors were given a put option which is exercisable at one or more future dates at a price equal to the original offering price of the LYONs plus the interest that accrues to the date of the put.

Merrill Lynch's primary objective in creating LYONs was to reduce the downside risk of the security while, at the same time, retaining the equity participation characteristics of traditional convertible bonds. By early 1989, LYONs accounted for between 5% and 6%, in terms of market value, of all convertible bonds issued by U.S. corporations. That figure has grown substantially; LYONs now constitute 29% of the $46 billion in total market value of all outstanding U.S. dollar denominated convertible bonds of U.S. issuers. Merrill Lynch has now underwritten 44 different LYONs issues—including an "Index LYON", the principal amount of which is keyed to the performance of the NYSE Composite Index. The total cash proceeds raised from the sale of these LYONs amounted to $10.7 billion. Since Merrill Lynch developed LYONs, other firms have offered a total of twelve convertible bond issues with a structure similar to LYONs. The total cash proceeds from the sale of these ten issues amounted to $2.9 billion. LYONs are gaining a proportionately greater share of the convertible securities market not only because they constitute an increasing percentage of new convertible issues; but also, because the prospect of the early redemption of a LYONs issue is less likely than for a traditional convertible, all else being equal. * * *

LYON's, like other convertibles, contain elements of both equity and fixed income securities. Depending upon the price of a LYON in relation to that of its underlying stock, conversion premium and yield as well as terms specific to a given issue, a LYON may be primarily equity or primarily fixed income in terms of its investment characteristics. Different issues will, therefore, provide opportunities to different groups of investors. Our analysis focuses not only on present prices and relationships but also on theoretical future prices and rates of return as calculated using the Merrill Lynch Theoretical Valuation Model. * * *

Merrill Lynch, LYONS (April 1992).

3. Warrants may also be attached to a bond. This is simply an option that may be detachable and, if so, may trade separately from the bond. Again, this feature will reduce the interest rate on the bond. The warrant usually is an option on the common stock of the company exercisable at a price above its current market price. This requires some market appreciation before the warrant will provide a profit if exercised. Warrants may provide an option on items other than the stock of the company. Consider the following:

The Notes and Warrants are being offered and sold separately, and not in units.

The Notes will bear interest from July 15, 1988, payable semi-annually on January 15 and July 15, commencing January 15, 1989. The

Notes will mature on July 15, 1991, and will not be redeemable prior to maturity.

Each Warrant will entitle the holder thereof to receive from Ford Motor Credit Company ("Ford Credit") the cash value in U.S. dollars of the right to purchase U.S. $50 at a price of ¥6989, which represents an exchange rate of ¥139.78 per U.S. $1.00. The Warrants will be exercisable immediately upon issuance and until 3:00 p.m., New York City time, on the fifth New York Business Day (as hereinafter defined, preceding their expiration on July 15, 1991 or earlier expiration upon delisting from, or permanent suspension of trading on, the American Stock Exchange unless, at the same time, the Warrants are accepted for listing on another national securities exchange. Any Warrant not exercised at or before 3:00 p.m., New York City time on the fifth New York Business Day preceding its expiration date will be deemed automatically exercised on such expiration date. A Warrant holder may exercise no fewer than 2,000 Warrants at any one time, except in the case of automatic exercises, including at expiration.

The Warrants involve a high degree of risk, including foreign exchange risks and the risk of expiring worthless if the U.S. dollar does not appreciate or depreciates against the Japanese Yen. Investors therefore should be prepared to sustain a total loss of the purchase price of their Warrants.

Prospectus, Ford Motor Credit Company, $100,000,000 8.95% Notes Due 1991, 2,000,000 Currency Exchange Warrants (CEWs), Expiring July 15, 1991.

4. Redemption features in corporate bonds may also affect their value. Such a right allows the corporation to repay the principal at an early date. The corporation may call or redeem the bonds if interest rates decline, allowing the corporation to refund its loans at a lower cost. This is not desirable to bondholders, however. Consequentially, the call or redemption price is usually set at a premium over par so that only a substantial interest rate decrease would justify a redemption.

———

HARRIET & HENDERSON YARNS, INC. v. CASTLE

75 F.Supp.2d 818 (W.D.Tenn.1999).

DONALD, DISTRICT JUDGE.

... Before the court are Plaintiffs' motion for partial summary judgment and Defendants' motion for summary judgment. * * *

This is a complex case, featuring multiple parties and multiple claims. It arises out of the creation in 1995 of Star Hosiery, Inc. ("Star"). FLR Hosiery ("FLR") and Lora Lee Knitting ("Lora Lee") were two pre-existing Tennessee hosiery companies, both experiencing financial difficulties in early 1995. Both companies were heavily indebted to trade creditors, most of whom supplied them with raw materials. Together they owed approximately $3,000,000, much of it to Plaintiffs. Plaintiff RDC, Inc. was FLR's landlord. Plaintiffs Harriet & Henderson Yarns, Inc., Thomaston Mills, Inc., Unifi, Inc., McMichael Mills, Jefferson Mills, Inc., Mount Vernon Mills, Inc., Huskey Knitting Mills, Jacob Textile Sales, Jones Textile, Kings Mountain Hosiery Mills, Inc., Merlin Creel Systems, Inc., O'Mara, Inc., Pharr Yarns, Inc., and Ruppe Hosiery, Inc. were suppliers of yarn or textile services. Brookfield & Company ("Brookfield"), an investment banking firm, became involved with FLR and Lora Lee, assisting in the two companies' attempt to secure additional financing. Brookfield arranged a deal whereby FLR and Lora Lee would contribute substantially all their combined assets to form a new company, Star. Brookfield arranged for Congress Financial ("Congress") to finance the new company. Brookfield also engaged the Defendant law firm Wolff Ardis, P.C. ("Wolff Ardis") to represent Star during its creation, incorporation, and loan deal from Congress. Defendant Renee Castle ("Castle") was a shareholder in Wolff Ardis, and was the lead attorney for the Star transactions.

In order for Star to obtain financing from Congress, Brookfield advised that much of the pre-existing FLR and Lora Lee debt should be restructured into subordinated, convertible debenture notes ("Debenture Notes").[1] The Debenture Notes were to be paid by Star over three years. To induce the existing creditors to accept the Debenture Notes, the creditors were granted a second lien in Star's machinery and equipment to secure the Debenture Notes, behind a first lien held by Congress. The creditors were also told that the Star merger and financing plan would improve the likelihood that the current debt would be paid off. As the creditors were informed about the proposed creation of Star, they were asked to sign confidentiality agreements, which prevented the creditors from sharing information or discussing the proposal.

Brookfield had Castle prepare the necessary documents. Castle drafted the Debenture Note based on a form given her by Brookfield. She also drafted the Indenture Agreement, based on a form in the Wolff Ardis computer files. The Debenture Notes provided that Star promised to pay various amounts to the different Debenture holders. They also named Wolff Ardis as trustee. Other relevant parts of the Debenture Notes included the following:

> 1. *Payment of Principal.* The total obligation of Star to all Debenture Holders is set forth in the Indenture Agreement dated as of December 1, 1995, by and between Star and Wolff Ardis P.C., as Trustee for the Debenture Holders (the "Indenture Agreement")....

> 5. *Indenture Agreement.* This Debenture is one of several debentures of Star issued pursuant to the Indenture Agreement, the provisions of which are hereby incorporated by reference and made a part of this Debenture. All the Debentures issued pursuant to that Inden-

---

1. A subordinated, convertible debenture note is a promissory note that is subordinated to other debt and that is convertible to stock at the holder's option. *See Pittsburgh Terminal Corp. v. Baltimore & Ohio R. Co.,* 680 F.2d 933 (3d Cir.1982).

ture Agreement are equally secured by a second lien and security interest in certain of Star's equipment, as more fully described in the Indenture Agreement. Reference is hereby made to the Indenture Agreement for a more detailed description of the property in which the Trustee holds a security interest, the nature and extent of the security interest, the rights and obligations of the Debenture Holder and other debenture holders, of Star, and of the Trustee.

6. *Events of Default.* One or more of the following events shall be deemed "Events of Default": (a) If any payment of principal and interest on this Debenture is not paid when due; provided that the Debenture Holder shall give Star written notice of such default and Star shall have sixty (60) days from receipt of such notice within which to cure such default; . . .

The Indenture Agreement stated, in relevant part:

This Indenture Agreement between Star Hosiery, Inc., a Tennessee corporation (the "Company" or "Star") and Renee E. Castle of Wolff Ardis, P.C. having an address of 6055 Primacy Parkway, Suite 360, Memphis, TN 38119 (the "Trustee"), dated as of this 12th date of December, 1995 is for the benefit of certain holders of Debenture Notes ("Noteholders") who hold Debenture Notes issued pursuant to this Indenture. Such Debenture Notes are collectively referred to herein as the "Debentures." The terms of the Debentures include those stated in the Note Debentures and those made part of the Note Debentures by reference to the Trust Indenture Act of 1939 (the "Trust Indenture Act") as in effect on the date of the Debentures . . .

Security. The Debenture Notes shall be secured by a subordinate lien on all equipment owned by the Company. This lien shall extend on a pro rata basis to each Noteholder. It shall have a second priority (inferior to the liens securing Senior Indebtedness) on all equipment with the exception of the equipment presently encumbered by liens in favor of GECC, Speizman and Nations Bank, in which case the lien shall have a third priority. . . .

Events of Default. One or more of the following events shall be deemed "Events of Default": (a) If any payment of principal and interest on this Debenture is not paid when due; provided that the Debenture Holder shall give the Company written notice of such default and the Company shall have sixty (60) days from receipt of such notice within which to cure such default; . . . *The Trustee.* The Trustee shall be under no obligation to exercise any of its rights or powers under this Indenture relating to any issue of Debentures at the request of any of the holders thereof, unless they shall have offered to the Trustee security and indemnity satisfactory to it. . . .

The Debenture Notes prepared by Castle were sent to each Plaintiff in November, 1995 by FLR and Lora Lee, each for a varying amount. The Indenture Agreement was presented to Plaintiffs by their debtors as the best chance for them to recover the money owed them, and they were urged by FLR and Lora Lee to sign the Debenture Notes. Each Plaintiff did sign and return its Debenture Note. Once all Notes had been returned, Castle prepared the final Indenture Agreement, which stated that the total sum owed to the holders of the Debenture Notes pursuant to the Notes was $2,322,973.42.

The closing of the transactions occurred on December 12, 1995. At the closing were Defendant Castle and representatives of FLR, Lora Lee, Star, Congress, and Brookfield. None of the Plaintiffs had an attorney or other representative present. After the closing, copies of the signed Debenture Notes were sent to Plaintiffs, and the original Debenture Notes were kept in the offices of Wolff Ardis.

Castle had received instructions from Congress regarding the execution and filing of UCC–1 financing statements to perfect Congress' first lien in Star's equipment. Those financing statements, executed by Star in favor of Congress, were duly recorded with the Tennessee Secretary of State. However, there was never any discussion among any of the parties to the transaction about preparing or filing financing statements in favor of Plaintiffs. No UCC–1 financing statements were prepared, executed, or filed with regard to Plaintiffs' lien in Star's equipment. Because no financing statement was filed, the Debenture holders' lien was never properly perfected under Tennessee law.

Star made the required payments from January to June, 1996. However, it then stopped making payments, and on August 16, 1996, Star filed for Chapter 11 bankruptcy. Shortly thereafter, Plaintiffs learned that no financing statements had been filed on their behalf. Because the lien was unperfected, each Plaintiff was treated as an unsecured creditor in Star's bankruptcy case. Star's assets were sold in bankruptcy, resulting in full repayment to Congress, but only approximately a 3% dividend to Plaintiffs and other unsecured creditors. Plaintiffs contend that they would have received all or most of the debt owed to them under the Debenture Notes if their security interest in Star's equipment had been properly perfected.
* * *

The crux of this suit is Plaintiffs' claim that Defendants had the responsibility to perfect Plaintiffs' security interests, or to ensure that the interests were perfected. * * *

Plaintiffs ... allege that by not perfecting Plaintiffs' security interests, Defendants breached a state common law fiduciary duty owed to Plaintiffs. Defendants filled the role of trustee in this case, and Plaintiffs were the trust beneficiaries. Under Tennessee law, a trustee owes a duty of loyalty to the trust beneficiary. *Smail v. Smail,* 617 S.W.2d 889 (Tenn.1981). A trustee also has a duty to act in good faith, with due diligence, and with care and skill. *Branum v. Akins,* 978 S.W.2d 554, 557 (Tenn.Ct.App.1998). Plaintiffs contend that Defendants had a fiduciary duty to ensure that Plaintiffs' interests under the Indenture Agreement and Debenture Notes were protected. Plaintiffs argue that Defendants breached this duty by failing to perfect the liens.

This case does not deal with the duty of an ordinary trustee, but with the obligations of an indenture trustee. In arguing over the scope of those duties, the parties look primarily to caselaw from the state of New York, out of which most of the important cases on this topic have issued. The leading authorities make clear that, unlike those of an ordinary trustee, the duties of an indenture trustee are generally defined by and limited to the terms of the indenture. *See, e.g., Elliott Assocs. v. J. Henry Schroder Bank & Trust Co.,* 838 F.2d 66, 71 (2d Cir.1988). *See also LNC Inv., Inc. v. First Fidelity Bank,* 935 F.Supp. 1333, 1346 (S.D.N.Y.1996) ("Under New York law, the pre-default duties of an indenture trustee, unlike those of an ordinary trustee, generally are limited to the duties imposed by the indenture"); *Lorenz v. CSX Corp.,* 1 F.3d 1406, 1415 (3d Cir.1993) ("The courts of New York consistently have held that the duties of an indenture trustee, unlike those of a typical trustee, are defined exclusively by the terms of the indenture"); *Meckel v. Continental Resources Co.,* 758 F.2d 811, 816 (2d Cir.1985) ("Unlike the ordinary trustee, who has historic common-law duties imposed beyond those in the trust agreement, an indenture trustee is more like a stakeholder whose duties and obligations are exclusively defined by the terms of the indenture agreement."); Hazen, *The Law of Securities Regulation* § 16.5, p. 154, n. 5 (West 1995) ("Despite some earlier cases that held that trustees may have pre-default liability beyond that put forth in the indenture, [it] is now well established that prior to default the trustee's responsibilities (and hence his/or her liability) are determined solely under the terms of the indenture agreement."); *First Interstate Bank of Denver, N.A. v. Pring,* 969 F.2d 891 (10th Cir.1992); *Shawmut Bank, N.A. v. Kress Assocs.,* 33 F.3d 1477 (9th Cir.1994).

That limits are imposed on the duties of an indenture trustee is not arbitrary, but reasonably based on the difference between the role of an indenture trustee and an ordinary trustee. One difference is that the rights and duties of an ordinary trustee arise from the common law, whereas the duties of an indenture trustee arise out of, and thus are limited to, a contract. *Lorenz v. CSX Corp.,* 736 F.Supp. 650, 656 (W.D.Pa. 1990) (aff'd. by 1 F.3d 1406 (3d Cir.1993)). Another reason for the difference is that an indenture trustee must consider the interests of the issuer of the debenture as well as the beneficiaries. *In re E.F. Hutton Southwest Properties II, Ltd.,* 953 F.2d 963, 972 (5th Cir.1992). And a third reason is that "the purchaser of such debt is offered, and voluntarily accepts, a security whose myriad terms are highly specified. Broad and abstract requirements of a 'fiduciary' character ordinarily can be expected to have little or no constructive role to play in the governance of such a negotiated, commercial relationship." *Simons v. Cogan,* 542 A.2d 785, 786 (Del.Ch.1987).

The Indenture Agreement in this case said nothing about a duty of Defendants to perfect Plaintiffs' liens. Courts, however, have found two narrow exceptions to the general rule that the duties of an indenture trustee are strictly defined by the indenture agreement. One of these is that after default, "the loyalties of an indenture trustee no longer are divided between the issuer and the investors, and as a consequence ... the limits on an indenture trustee's duties before an event of default ... do not apply after an event of default ..." *LNC Inv.*, 935 F.Supp. at 1347. *See also Beck v. Manufacturers Hanover Trust Co.*, 218 A.D.2d 1, 632 N.Y.S.2d 520, 527 (N.Y.App.Div.1995) ("[E]ven if the responsibilities of an indenture trustee may be significantly more narrowly defined than those of an ordinary trustee while the obligation that it is the indenture's purpose to secure remains current, subsequent to the obligor's default ... the indenture trustee's obligations come more closely to resemble those of an ordinary fiduciary ..."). This post-default exception does not apply to the case at bar, in which the alleged breach of duty occurred prior to Star's default. Once Star had defaulted, it was already too late for the security interests to be effectively perfected.

Plaintiffs contend that the other exception to the limits of an indenture trustee's duties applies here. That exception is the requirement that even indenture trustees have an obligation to avoid a conflict of interest. *See, e.g., LNC Inv.*, 935 F.Supp. at 1347 ("an indenture trustee must avoid conflicts of interest and discharge its obligations with absolute singleness of purpose") (internal quotations omitted); *Lorenz*, 1 F.3d at 1415 ("The sole exception to this rule [that the duties of an indenture trustee are defined exclusively by the terms of the indenture] is that the indenture trustee must avoid conflicts of interest with the debentureholders."); *Elliott*, 838 F.2d at 71 ("[S]o long as the trustee fulfills its obligations under the express terms of the indenture, it owes the debenture holders no additional, implicit pre-default duties or obligations except to avoid conflicts of interests.").

Plaintiffs argue that by assuming the role of trustee, Defendants created a conflict of interest, and thereby breached the fiduciary duty they owed to Plaintiffs. However, the existing legal authority in this area does not support Plaintiffs' argument that this dual role sufficed to impart additional fiduciary duties. In *In re E.F. Hutton*, the Fifth Circuit stated that "heightened fiduciary duties ... are not activated until a conflict arises where it is evident that the indenture trustee may be sacrificing the interests of the beneficiaries in favor of its own financial position. There must be a clear possibility of this evident from the facts of the case, e.g., where the indenture trustee is a general creditor of the obligor, who is in turn in financial straits. A mere hypothetical possibility that the indenture trustee might favor the interests of the issuer merely because the former is an indenture trustee does not suffice." 953 F.2d at 972. Similarly, the Second Circuit found no conflict of interest in *Elliott* when it found that "except for bald assertions of conflict of interest, [the plaintiff] presents no serious claim that [the indenture trustee] personally benefitted in any way ..." 838 F.2d at 70. In the case before the court, Plaintiffs likewise have done no more than make bald assertions of a conflict of interest.

Plaintiffs accurately point out that many of the cases finding no implied duties for indenture trustees involved indenture agreements containing clauses specifically excusing the trustee of any duty outside of those made explicit in the agreement. *See, e.g., Eldred v. Merchants Nat'l Bank of Cedar Rapids,* 468 N.W.2d 221, 223 (Iowa 1991). This at least suggests that in the absence of such a clause, an indenture trustee could be held to a higher fiduciary standard. There was no such clause in the Indenture Agreement in this case. However, Plaintiffs are unable to direct the court to a single case in which, in the absence of such a disclaimer, a court has found that an indenture trustee has the same fiduciary duty as an ordinary trustee.

Plaintiffs also attempt to distinguish this case by virtue of the fact that the Defendants were the attorneys of the debenture issuer, as opposed to the financial institutions which served as trustees in many of the cited cases. Plaintiffs argue that where the trustees are attorneys of an obligor who will benefit at the expense of the trust beneficiaries, the trustees have a conflict of interest which violates their fiduciary duty. However, Plaintiffs again are unable to produce any legal authority to back their argument, and there is no evidence to suggest that Defendants could have personally benefitted from the failure to file the financing statements.

Plaintiffs can successfully distinguish this case from any of the other individual cases on the fiduciary duties of indenture trustees. But what Plaintiffs ultimately ask this court to do is to find a new exception to well-settled law. This the court is unwilling to do. As a general rule, the duties of indenture trustees are strictly defined by the indenture agreement. There is no reason in this case not to follow that rule. The governing documents did not impose on the trustees the duty to perfect the security interests. * * *

Plaintiffs' sixth and final complaint is that Defendants' failure to ensure that Plaintiffs' liens were perfected violated a provision of the Trust Indenture Act of 1939 ("Trust Indenture Act"). Before discussing that claim, the court must resolve the preliminary dispute over whether that Act applies to this case at all.

Plaintiffs contend that the Indenture Agreement incorporates by reference the Trust Indenture Act. Indeed, the Indenture Agreement states:

> The terms of the Debentures include those stated in the Note Debentures and those made part of the Note Debentures by reference to the Trust Indenture Act of 1939 (the "Trust Indenture Act") as in effect on the date of the Debentures.

The Debenture Notes, however, make no reference to the Trust Indenture Act. Defendants argue that the Trust Indenture Act therefore was not incorporated. Defendants claim that "the clear meaning" of the Indenture Agreement provision is that "[b]ecause there are no references to the Indenture Act contained in the debenture notes ... no Indenture Act provisions were incorporated by reference into the indenture transaction."

Defendants may find the meaning of this provision "clear," but the court does not. The language of a contract is ambiguous if its meaning is susceptible to more than one reasonable interpretation. *Farmers–Peoples Bank,* 519 S.W.2d at 805. If the terms are ambiguous, then the intended meaning of the contract becomes a question for the finder of fact. *Tenn. Consol. Coal Co.,* 416 F.2d at 1198. It is also true that where the language of the contract is ambiguous, it will be construed against the party responsible for the drafting (in this case, Defendants). *Hanover Ins. Co. v. Haney,* 221 Tenn. 148, 425 S.W.2d 590, 592 (1968).

Despite Defendants' contention to the contrary, the one thing that is clear about this provision is that it is ambiguous. Therefore, at the very least, the meaning should be left to be determined by the finder of fact. However, due to the court's ultimate disposition of this issue on another basis, it is unnecessary to decide this question. Instead, the court will assume arguendo that the Trust Indenture Act was incorporated into the Indenture Agreement.

Plaintiffs state that the Trust Indenture Act requires an indenture trustee to review the filing and effectiveness of any lien intended to be created by the Debenture Notes. According to Plaintiffs, this duty is imposed by 15 U.S.C.A. § 77nnn(b). Putting it simply, Plaintiffs either misunderstand or misrepresent the duty imposed by that section of the Trust Indenture Act. That section imposes two duties upon Star, the *obligor* of the indenture agreement. Furthermore, the duties imposed are for the benefit of the indenture trustee, i.e. Defendants. And finally, the duty it imposes is not to actually file the indenture, but merely to furnish an opinion of counsel as to whether the indenture has been properly recorded and filed. 15 U.S.C.A. § 77nnn(b). This section clearly does not impose a duty on indenture trustees to ensure that liens are perfected for the benefit of the debenture holders. Therefore the question of whether the Trust Indenture Act is incorporated into the Indenture Agreement is irrelevant. Because the Trust Indenture Act does not provide Plaintiffs with a cause of action under the facts of this case, Defendants' Motion for Summary Judgment on this count is GRANTED, and Plaintiffs' Motion for Summary Judgment is DENIED.

NOTES

1.   Trust indentures are master agreements that govern the terms and conditions of debentures (bonds) issued by corporations. Initially, trust indentures were used for mortgage bonds but were later extended to unsecured bonds. The bond or debenture itself is a simple document, but the trust indenture is a long, complex instrument. The trust indenture spells out the rights of bond holders. It also designates a trustee to make sure that the issuer's obligations are met and that the bondholders' rights are respected. An SEC investigation and hearings by Congress during the 1930's determined that trustees often failed to assure that issuers met their obligations under the trust indenture agreement. Indenture agreements were often favorable to

the issuing companies and sought to limit or disclaim all liability on the part of the trustees administering the terms of indenture agreements. The SEC and Congress found that indenture trustees seldom provided bondholders with basic information concerning default under the indenture agreement. Congress was particularly concerned with "ostrich clauses," which allowed indenture trustees to assume that there was no default until they received notice from at least ten percent of the security holders. The trustee was allowed to make this assumption even if the trustee had actual knowledge of a default. In addition, Congress discovered that trustees often had financial interests that conflicted with the interests of bondholders. The Trust Indenture Act of 1939 was enacted to clarify the role of trustees and to lessen conflicts between trustees and bondholders. The Act sought to provide full disclosure for issues of bonds, notes, and debentures. It requires the rights of debenture holders and the duties of the trustees to be specified in the indenture agreement and requires trustees to provide reports to debenture holders. The provisions of the Trust Indenture Act of 1939 were described as follows by the court in Zeffiro v. First Pennsylvania Banking and Trust Co., 623 F.2d 290, 292–94 (3d Cir.1980), cert. denied, 456 U.S. 1005, 102 S.Ct. 2295, 73 L.Ed.2d 1299 (1982):

> Before proceeding to a discussion of the merits, it may be useful to briefly outline the structure and background of the Trust Indenture Act. A study was conducted by the Securities Exchange Commission (SEC) in 1936 which revealed widespread abuses in the issuance of corporate bonds under indentures.[2] The main problems identified by the study were that the indenture trustee was frequently aligned with the issuer of the debentures and that the debenture holders were widely dispersed, thereby hampering their ability to enforce their rights. Furthermore, courts frequently enforced broad exculpatory terms of the indenture inserted by the issuer, which offered the investors less protection than the traditional standards of fiduciary duty.

> Rather than allow the SEC direct supervision of trustee behavior and thereby provide for a more overt intrusion into capital markets, the Act establishes a standard of behavior indirectly by refashioning the form of the indenture itself. The Act is structured so that before a debt security non-exempted from the Act may be offered to the public, the indenture under which it is issued must be "qualified" by the SEC. The indenture is deemed "qualified" when registration becomes effective. Before registration of the debenture is declared effective it must be qualified under the following conditions: (1) the security has been issued under an indenture; (2) the person designated as trustee is eligible to serve; and (3) the indenture conforms to the requirements of §§ 310–318, 15 U.S.C. §§ 77jjj–77rrr. Judge Bechtle aptly described the operative provisions of the Act, §§ 310–318, as follows.

> > Sections 310 through 318 form the core of the Act in that they outline the substantive duties that the indenture must impose on the

---

2. See Securities and Exchange Commission Report on the Study and Investigation of the Work, Activities, Personnel and Functions of Protective and Reorganization Committees, Part IV, Trustees Under Indentures (1937); See also Hearings on H.R. 10292 Before a Subcommittee of the Committee on Interstate and Foreign Commerce, 75th Cong., 3d Sess. 20 (1938).

trustee. These sections are of three types. The first type is proscriptive in nature, prohibiting certain terms. For example, § 315, 15 U.S.C. § 77ooo (d), prohibits provisions in the indenture which would relieve or exculpate the trustee from liability for negligence. The second type of section is merely permissive in nature. An example of this type of section is § 315(a), 15 U.S.C. § 77ooo (a)(1), which states that the indenture may contain a provision relieving the trustee of liability except for the performance of such duties as are specifically set out in such indenture.

     The third type of section, and the most important for our purposes, is mandatory and prescriptive in nature. These sections begin with the phrase "indenture to be qualified shall provide" or "shall require." An example of this type of section is § 311, 15 U.S.C. § 77kkk, which states that the indenture shall require the trustee to establish certain accounts for the benefit of bond holders in the event the trustee also becomes a creditor of the issuer and the issuer defaults on the bonds.

473 F.Supp. at 206. The SEC has no enforcement authority over the terms of the indenture once the registration statement becomes effective, and it cannot issue a stop order for violation of indenture provisions by the indenture trustee. After the effective date of the indenture the SEC's role is limited to general rulemaking and investigation. 15 U.S.C. §§ 77ddd(c), (d), (e); 77eee(a), (c); 77ggg; 77sss; 77ttt. The Act contains criminal liability for certain willful violations and misrepresentations and express civil liability for any omission or misstatement in the filing documents.

2. Financing by corporations may take many forms. One popular method is to "securitize" cash flows of the company. This is not a completely new process. Factors for many years advanced funds on or bought accounts receivables of businesses. A more recent finance technique is to place a set of cash flows into a separate bankruptcy remote "special purpose" vehicle or entity (an "SPV" or "SPE" as they are often called). The SPE's only assets are these cash flows or perhaps additional collateral or guarantees. The SPE then sells ownership interests in itself that entitles the holder to their aliquot portion of the cash flow. These interests are sometimes called asset-backed securities. Consider the following description in a preliminary prospectus of the securitization of credit card receivables by a bank:

     Interest at the Certificate Rate of ___% per annum will be distributed to holders of the ... Asset Backed Certificates (the "Certificates") on the 15th day of each month (or the next business day) (the "Distribution Date"), commencing ___ 15, 1987. Principal will be distributed to holders of the Certificates on each Distribution Date commencing on ___ 15, 1988....

     Each Certificate will represent a specified percentage of an undivided interest in the California Credit Card Trust 1986–A (the "Trust") to be formed by Bank of America National Trust and Savings Association (the "Bank"). The property of the Trust will include a portfolio of Classic VISA credit card receivables (the "Receivables") generated or to be generated by the Bank in its ordinary course of business, all monies due in payment of the Receivables and the benefits of a letter of credit. The Bank will own the remaining undivided interest in the Trust not represented by the Certificates and will continue to service the Receivables.

There currently is no secondary market for the Certificates and there is no assurance that one will develop.

Preliminary Prospectus, Bank of America National Trust and Savings Association, $250,000,000 California Credit Card Trust 1986–A–% Asset Backed Certificates.

3. Medium term notes, those with maturities from nine months to ten years vary from the simple to the complex. The following excerpt from a prospectus for medium term notes to be continuously issued by the Kingdom of Spain is illustrative of the form these notes may take:

The Kingdom of Spain ("Spain") may offer from time to time up to U.S. $1,000,000,000 aggregate principal amount, or the equivalent in one or more foreign currencies or currency units, of its Medium–Term Notes (the "Notes"). Each Note will mature on any Business Day from or exceeding nine months from its date of issue, as selected by the purchaser and agreed to by Spain. Unless otherwise indicated in the applicable Pricing Supplement to this Prospectus Supplement (a "Pricing Supplement"), the Notes may not be redeemed by Spain prior to maturity and will be issued in fully registered form in denominations of U.S. $100,000 or in multiples of U.S. $1,000 in excess thereof. If the Notes are to be denominated in a foreign currency or currency unit, then the provisions with respect thereto will be set forth in a foreign currency supplement hereto (a "Multi–Currency Prospectus Supplement").

The interest rate, if any, or interest rate formula applicable to each Note and other variable terms of the Notes as described herein will be established by Spain at the date of issuance of each Note.... Unless otherwise indicated ... , the Notes will bear interest at a fixed rate ("Fixed Rate Notes") or at floating rates ("Floating Rate Notes") determined by reference to the Certificate of Deposit Rate, Commercial Paper Rate, Federal Funds Rate, LIBID, LIBOR, Prime Rate or Treasury Rate, as adjusted by any Spread or Multiplier applicable to such notes.... Notes may also be issued at original issue discounts and such notes may or may not bear interest. * * *

The rate of interest on each Floating Rate Note will be reset daily, weekly, monthly, quarterly, semi-annually or annually (each an "Interest Reset Period") as specified in the applicable Pricing Supplement.

U.S. $1,000,000,000, Kingdom of Spain Medium–Term Notes, Prospectus Supplement to Prospectus dated Nov. 29, 1988.

4. A more exotic note is the "Multicurrency PERLS" described as follows:

Interest on the Multicurrency Principal Exchange Rate Linked Securities (Multicurrency PERLS) offered hereby (the "Notes") will be payable in U.S. dollars based on the face amount of the Notes, semiannually in arrears on each June 14 and December 14, commencing June 14, 1990.

The Notes will mature and be payable on December 14, 1992 (the "Maturity Date"). Principal in respect of each U.S. $1,000 face amount of the Notes will be payable at maturity in an amount equal to U.S. $1,000 plus the U.S. dollar equivalent of [Australian] A$1,276.30, minus the U.S. dollar equivalent of ¥143,000, in each case as determined by the average of the exchange rate quotations furnished by three reference dealers for Australian dollars and Yen, respectively, on the second business day prior to the Maturity Date. Accordingly, ... Noteholders would receive at maturity an amount of principal greater than, less than (to a minimum of zero) or equal to the face amount of the Notes, depending on the relative exchange rates of the U.S. dollar to the Australian dollar and of the Yen to the U.S. dollar at maturity.

Student Loan Marketing Association (SallieMae) 12% Multicurrency Principal Exchange Rate Linked Securities (Multicurrency PERLS) Due December 14, 1992 Information Statement Supplement (To Information Statement dated October 31, 1989).

5. The price of a fixed income instrument such as a bond or note will vary inversely with changes in interest rates, all other things being equal. Say you own a three year note for $1,000 paying three percent interest. Interest rates increase by one percent one year after you bought the note, and you would like to sell it. To do so, you will have to accept a discount on the principal amount because the purchaser will not pay you $1,000 for an instrument paying one percent less interest than comparable notes being issued at the increased rate. You could hold the note to maturity and receive all your principal back, but you will have forgone the higher available interest rate. The converse is true for bond prices if rates drop. There are several factors in addition to interest rates that affect bond prices, including counterparty risk. The more risk, the higher the rate of interest required, hence junk bonds. The yield curve must also be considered. Normally, the longer the term of a fixed income instrument, the higher the interest rate. This is a reflection of several factors including inflation and increased risk of a default over longer terms.

SANDERS v. JOHN NUVEEN & CO., INC.

463 F.2d 1075 (7th Cir.), cert. denied, 409 U.S.
1009, 93 S.Ct. 443, 34 L.Ed.2d 302 (1972).

SPRECHER, CIRCUIT JUDGE.

* * * Plaintiff, Henry T. Sanders, filed his complaint on March 12, 1970, against John Nuveen & Co., Inc., a broker-dealer in securities, one of its registered representatives, and its directors and controlling persons. The complaint charged defendants with a scheme and artifice to defraud plaintiff and others in his class by selling to them short-term commercial paper issued by Winter & Hirsch, Inc. but owned by Nuveen. Plaintiff's claim was based on the Securities Act of 1933, 15 U.S.C. § 77a, the Securities Exchange Act of 1934, 15 U.S.C. § 78a, Rule 10b–5, 17 C.F.R. § 240.10b–5, and the Rules of Fair Practice of the National Association of Securities Dealers.

On May 18, 1970, the defendants moved to strike certain allegations of the complaint and expressly attacked the class-action aspects of the complaint. They also challenged the jurisdiction of the court under the 1934 act on the ground that the short-term commercial paper involved was not a "security." The district court denied the motion to strike on October 8, 1970. * * *

Federal securities legislation enacted for the purpose of avoiding frauds is to be construed "not technically and restrictively, but flexibly to effectuate its remedial purposes." S.E.C. v. Capital Gains Research Bureau, Inc., 375 U.S. 180 (1963). Particularly, the definition of a security "embodies a flexible rather than a static principle, one that is capable of adaptation to meet the countless and variable schemes devised by those who seek the use of the money of others on the promise of profits." S.E.C. v. W.J. Howey Co., 328 U.S. 293, 299 (1946). "[I]n searching for the meaning and scope of the word 'security' in the [Securities Exchange] Act [of 1934], form should be disregarded for substance and the emphasis should be on economic reality." Tcherepnin v. Knight, 389 U.S. 332, 336 (1967).

The Supreme Court has sanctioned, in interpreting the definition of a security in the 1934 act, recourse to the definitions of security in the Securities Act of 1933 (*Tcherepnin* at 335–336, 338) and in the "companion legislative enactments." Affiliated Ute Citizens v. United States, 406 U.S. 128 (1972).

An examination of the six basic federal securities acts is relevant and revealing. The Securities Act of 1933, The Trust Indenture Act of 1939, the Investment Company Act of 1940, and the Investment Advisers Act of 1940, all define a security as follows: "The term 'security' means any note, ... evidence of indebtedness, ... investment contract, ... or, in general, any interest or instrument commonly known as a 'security'...." The Public Utility Holding Company Act of 1935 definition differs slightly: " 'Security' means any note, ... investment contract, ... or, in general, any instrument commonly known as a 'security'...."

In none of these five acts does there appear any language limiting in any way the broad definitions of "security" or of "note," "evidence of indebtedness," "investment contract" or "instrument commonly known as a security." Therefore *any* note, regardless of its nature, terms or conditions, is fully subject to whatever antifraud provisions are included in the five acts.

Only in the Securities Exchange Act of 1934 is there an exception to the broad definition of a security; it reads:[8]

"The term 'security' means any note, ... investment contract, ... or in general, any instrument commonly known as a 'security'; ... but shall not include currency or any note, draft, bill of exchange, or banker's acceptance which has a maturity at the time of issuance of

---

8. Section 3(a) (10). 15 U.S.C. § 78c(a) (10).

not exceeding nine months, exclusive of days of grace, or any renewal thereof the maturity of which is likewise limited."

Therefore only in the 1934 act is a note with a maturity not exceeding nine months withdrawn from the application of the antifraud provisions of the act, section 10(b) and Rule 10b–5. Since the same note is subject to the antifraud provisions of all the other securities acts, it becomes important to determine just what Congress intended to be exempt from the operation of the 1934 act.

Although all notes are subject to the antifraud provisions of the other acts, some of those acts exempt short-term commercial paper from registration or other requirements. Plaintiff urges that the meaning given to short-term obligations in other securities legislation, particularly the 1933 act, be applied to the definition found in the 1934 act. The 1933 act exempts from registration, but not from antifraud sanctions, "[a]ny note, draft, bill of exchange, or banker's acceptance which arises out of a current transaction or the proceeds of which have been or are to be used for current transactions," and which has a maturity not exceeding nine months.

The Securities and Exchange Commission has interpreted the 1933 act's exemption of short-term commercial paper as embodying four requirements:[12]

> "The legislative history of the Act makes clear that section 3(a) (3) applies only to (1) prime quality negotiable commercial paper (2) of a type not ordinarily purchased by the general public, that is, (3) paper issued to facilitate well recognized types of current operational business requirements and (4) of a type eligible for discounting by Federal Reserve banks."

Although no evidence has been heard in this case, the record shows that the commercial paper purchased by the plaintiff was dated January 30, 1970, and that "Winter & Hirsch was engaged in the business of making loans until in or about February 1970, when it advised its creditors of its precarious financial condition and ceased to make any further payments on any of its obligations for borrowed money." At that time it had assets of $12.5 million and liabilities of more than $36 million. Thus, because of the company's insolvency, it seems highly unlikely that the paper purchased by the plaintiff and members of his class is either prime quality or issued to facilitate current transactions or eligible for discounting by Federal Reserve banks.

---

12. Release No. 33–4412, 17 C.F.R. § 231.4412 (1961) (numerals added). The release emphasized the prime quality of the paper intended to be exempted and stated that the exempted items are "composed of assets easily convertible into cash and are comparable to liquid inventories of an industrial or mercantile company." During the hearings on the 1933 act, commercial paper discountable by Federal Reserve banks was described as having "a record of safety only second to Government bonds" and as being the basis of our currency. Hearings on S. 875 Before the Senate Comm. on Banking and Currency, 73rd Cong., 1st Sess. at 94, 95 (1933). It is significant that section 3(a) (10) of the 1934 act exempts "currency" from the definition of security. 15 U.S.C. § 78c(a) (10).

The record further shows that the commercial paper purchased by the plaintiff was "placed through John Nuveen & Co." and bought by 42 purchasers, including the plaintiff, in the aggregate face amount of $1,661,500. The paper was therefore obviously offered and sold to the general public; indeed, it was characterized in the issuer's financial statements as "short term open market" paper.[13] The notes fail to meet any of the S.E.C.'s four requirements for exemption.

If, as the Supreme Court has admonished, "form should be disregarded for substance" and economic reality emphasized, it is reasonably clear that plaintiff and his class purchased the kind of "security" in regard to which the securities acts were intended to offer protection against fraud, misrepresentation and non-disclosure. Five of those acts expressly did so. We believe Congress intended to protect against fraud the purchasers of securities such as those involved here under the 1934 act as well. * * *

In other words, when Congress spoke of notes with a maturity not exceeding nine months, it meant commercial paper, not investment securities. When a prospective borrower approaches a bank for a loan and gives his note in consideration for it, the bank has purchased commercial paper. But a person who seeks to invest his money and receives a note in return for it has not purchased commercial paper in the usual sense. He has purchased a security investment. *Cf.* City National Bank v. Vanderboom, 290 F.Supp. 592, 608 (W.D.Ark.1968), aff'd, 422 F.2d 221 (8th Cir.), cert. denied, 399 U.S. 905 (1970). * * *

NOTES

1.   In Securities Industry Association v. Board of Governors of the Federal Reserve System, 468 U.S. 137, 104 S.Ct. 2979, 82 L.Ed.2d 107 (1984), the Supreme Court held that even commercial paper that was exempt from the registration requirements of the federal securities law was still a security for purposes of then existing restrictions against banks dealing in securities. What then is commercial paper, a security or something else?

2.   Short term financing may take other forms as observed by a law firm's description of a "multiple Option Financing Facility":

> ... Bank—International Limited [acts] as agent in connection with their Multiple Option Financing Facilities, which combine fairly standard revolving credit or term loans with a variety of different funding options for the borrower. For example, the borrower might be given the option to request bankers' acceptances or issue Euro-commercial paper as well as draw down advances in a range of convertible currencies. The MOF transactions are documented under New York law and the borrowers are generally large U.S. corporations.... After the documents have been negotiated and agreed between the borrower and Bank , copies are sent to each of the banks which have been invited ... to join the syndicate of

---

13.   H.R.Rep.No.85, 73rd Cong., 1st Sess., 15 (1933) stated in discussing the bill, which became the Securities Act of 1933, "Paragraph (3) exempts short-term paper of the type available for discount at a Federal Reserve bank and of a type which rarely is bought by private investors."

lenders. The bank syndicate is made up of major U.S., European and Japanese financial institutions and, depending on the amount of the loan, may include anywhere from ten to fifty participants. The next stage of the transaction involves negotiations with the bank group, which generally requires fairly extensive discussions with each of the banks regarding their questions and concerns about the structure of the deal and the draft documentation.

Rogers & Wells, Client Newsletter (1991). For a description of another revolving credit facility (sometimes called a "revolver") see Venetis v. Global Financial Services, Inc., 174 F.R.D. 238 (D.Mass.1997).

3. Cash management has become an important part of short term corporate finance. The following is a description of one such program:

The fertilizer industry, reflecting conditions in the agricultural industry that is its only customer, is both highly seasonal and highly volatile. Farmers buy fertilizer primarily in the spring and in the fall, and the amount they buy depends on the vicissitudes of weather, fluctuations in demand for farm products, and other factors difficult to predict. Another source of uncertainty for producers of chemical fertilizers is that the prices of the chemicals that are the principal inputs into such fertilizers also fluctuate a great deal. All this makes cash management a matter of acute concern for an enterprise like CF. It needs more cash in winter and summer, when it is producing for inventory to supply the farmers' needs in the spring and fall, than it does in the spring and fall, when it is selling and being paid for the fertilizer it has produced. It cannot be certain how much cash it must have at any time, because it must have cash to meet sudden increases in the prices of its chemical raw materials and sudden surges in demand for fertilizer, requiring it to expand production on short notice. In fact it cannot forecast its cash needs accurately more than a month in advance, and therefore it wants to be able to increase or reduce its cash balances on short notice. It could try to go cashless and borrow short term whenever it needed cash to pay its bills, or, as it does, it could place some of its assets in short-term financial instruments that are cash equivalents, such as bank certificates of deposit, U.S. government financial instruments, repurchase agreements, and money-market funds—all of which are available with short maturities. Roughly 75 percent of the cash equivalents used by CF in its cash management program have maturities of 7 days or less, and 92 percent have maturities of less than 30 days. A few have much longer maturities but are the equivalent of short-term cash-equivalent instruments because of conversion features. Apparently the assets in CF's cash-management account are generated by revenues from the sale of the cooperative's products.

CF Industries, Inc. (and Subsidiaries) v. Commissioner of Internal Revenue, 995 F.2d 101, 102–03 (7th Cir.1993).

———

SECTION 8. OVERVIEW OF THE DEFINITION OF SECURITY

TREATISE ON THE LAW OF SECURITIES REGULATION,

Thomas Lee Hazen

Vol. 1 § 1.6[1] (5th ed. 2004).

What do the following have in common: scotch whiskey, self-improvement courses, cosmetics, earthworms, beavers, muskrats, rabbits, chinchillas, animal feeding programs, cattle embryos, fishing boats, vacuum cleaners, cemetery lots, coin operated telephones, master recording contracts, pooled litigation funds, and fruit trees? The answer is that they have all been held to be securities within the meaning of federal or state securities statutes. The vast range of such unconventional investments that have fallen within the ambit of the securities laws' coverage is due to the broad statutory definition of a "security," section 2(a)(1) of the Securities Act of 1933 is representative:

> The term "security" means any note, stock, treasury stock, bond, debenture, evidence of indebtedness. Certificate of interest or participation in any profit-sharing agreement, collateral-trust certificate, pre-organization certificate or subscription, transferable share, investment contract, voting-trust certificate, certificate of deposit for a security, fractional undivided interest in oil, gas, or other mineral rights, any put, call, straddle, option, or privilege on any security, certificate of deposit, or group or index of securities (including any interest therein or based on the value thereof), or any put, call, straddle, option, or privilege entered into on a national securities exchange relating to foreign currency, or, in general, any interest or instrument commonly known as a "security", or any certificate of interest or participation in, temporary or interim certificate for, receipt for, guarantee of, or warrant or right to subscribe to or purchase, any of the foregoing. . . . * * *

In determining the basic coverage of the securities laws, the slightly different definitions of a security in the 1933 and 1934 Acts are to be treated as "virtually identical," according to the Supreme Court. The statutory language is expansive and has been interpreted accordingly. The broadly drafted statutory definition has continued to give the courts problems in providing predictable guidelines. Nevertheless, an attorney's failure to advise a client of the possibility of an investment offering being classified as a security can constitute legal malpractice. Furthermore, it is not necessary to establish that the defendant knew that the instrument he or she was marketing was a security.

Notwithstanding the broad statutory definition, not every fraud based on the payment of money is a security. In order to establish a violation of the securities laws, the plaintiff must first establish that a security was involved.

————

S.E.C. v. W.J. HOWEY CO.

328 U.S. 293, 66 S.Ct. 1100, 90 L.Ed. 1244 (1946).

Mr. Justice Murphy delivered the opinion of the Court.

This case involves the application of § 2(1) of the Securities Act of 1933 to an offering of units of a citrus grove development coupled with a contract for cultivating, marketing and remitting the net proceeds to the investor.

The Securities and Exchange Commission instituted this action to restrain the respondents from using the mails and instrumentalities of interstate commerce in the offer and sale of unregistered and nonexempt securities in violation of § 5(a) of the Act, 15 U.S.C.A. § 77e(a).

Most of the facts are stipulated. The respondents, W. J. Howey Company and Howey-in-the-Hills Service Inc., are Florida corporations under direct common control and management. The Howey Company owns large tracts of citrus acreage in Lake County, Florida. During the past several years it has planted about 500 acres annually, keeping half of the groves itself and offering the other half to the public 'to help us finance additional development.' Howey-in-the-Hills Service, Inc., is a service company engaged in cultivating and developing many of these groves, including the harvesting and marketing of the crops.

Each prospective customer is offered both a land sales contract and a service contract, after having been told that it is not feasible to invest in a grove unless service arrangements are made. While the purchaser is free to make arrangements with other service companies, the superiority of Howey-in-the-Hills Service, Inc., is stressed. Indeed, 85% of the acreage sold during the 3–year period ending May 31, 1943, was covered by service contracts with Howey-in-the-Hills Service, Inc. The land sales contract with the Howey Company provides for a uniform purchase price per acre or fraction thereof, varying in amount only in accordance with the number of years the particular plot has been planted with citrus trees. Upon full payment of the purchase price the land is conveyed to the purchaser by warranty deed. Purchases are usually made in narrow strips of land arranged so that an acre consists of a row of 48 trees. During the period between February 1, 1941, and May 31, 1943, 31 of the 42 persons making purchases bought less than 5 acres each. The average holding of these 31 persons was 1.33 acres and sales of as little as 0.65, 0.7 and 0.73 of an acre were made. These tracts are not separately fenced and the sole indication of several ownership is found in small land marks intelligible only through a plat book record.

The service contract, generally of a 10–year duration without option of cancellation, gives Howey-in-the-Hills Service, Inc., a leasehold interest and 'full and complete' possession of the acreage. For a specified fee plus the cost of labor and materials, the company is given full discretion and authority over the cultivation of the groves and the harvest and marketing of the crops. The company is well established in the citrus business and maintains a large force of skilled personnel and a great deal of equipment, including 75 tractors, sprayer wagons, fertilizer trucks and the like. Without the consent of the company, the land owner or purchaser has no right of entry to market the crop; thus there is ordinarily no right to specific fruit. The company is accountable only for an allocation of the net profits based upon a check made at the time of picking. All the produce is pooled by the respondent companies, which do business under their own names.

The purchasers for the most part are non-residents of Florida. They are predominantly business and professional people who lack the knowledge, skill and equipment necessary for the care and cultivation of citrus trees. They are attracted by the expectation of substantial profits. It was represented, for example, that profits during the 1943—1944 season amounted to 20% and that even greater profits might be expected during the 1944—1945 season, although only a 10% annual return was to be expected over a 10–year period. Many of these purchasers are patrons of a resort hotel owned and operated by the Howey Company in a scenic section adjacent to the groves. The hotel's advertising mentions the fine groves in the vicinity and the attention of the patrons is drawn to the groves as they are being escorted about the surrounding countryside. They are told that the groves are for sale; if they indicate an interest in the matter they are then given a sales talk.

It is admitted that the mails and instrumentalities of interstate commerce are used in the sale of the land and service contracts and that no registration statement or letter of notification has ever been filed with the Commission in accordance with the Securities Act of 1933 and the rules and regulations thereunder.

Section 2(1) of the Act defines the term 'security' to include the commonly known documents traded for speculation or investment.[3] This definition also includes 'securities' of a more variable character, designated by such descriptive terms as 'certificate of interest or participation in any profit-sharing agreement,' 'investment contract' and in general, any interest or instrument commonly known as a 'security.' The legal issue in this case turns upon a determination of whether, under the circumstances, the land sales contract, the warranty deed and the service contract

---

3. 'The term 'security' means any note, stock, treasury stock, bond, debenture, evidence of indebtedness, certificate of interest or participation in any profit-sharing agreement, collateral-trust certificate, preorganization certificate or subscription, transferable share, investment contract, voting-trust certificate, certificate of deposit for a security, fractional undivided interest in oil, gas, or other mineral rights, or, in general, any interest or instrument commonly known as a 'security,' or any certificate of interest or participation in, temporary or interim certificate for, receipt for, guarantee of, or warrant or right to subscribe to or purchase, any of the foregoing.'

together constitute an 'investment contract' within the meaning of § 2(1). An affirmative answer brings into operation the registration requirements of § 5(a), unless the security is granted an exemption under § 3(b), 15 U.S.C.A. § 77c(b). The lower courts, in reaching a negative answer to this problem, treated the contracts and deeds as separate transactions involving no more than an ordinary real estate sale and an agreement by the seller to manage the property for the buyer.

The term 'investment contract' is undefined by the Securities Act or by relevant legislative reports. But the term was common in many state 'blue sky' laws in existence prior to the adoption of the federal statute and, although the term was also undefined by the state laws, it had been broadly construed by state courts so as to afford the investing public a full measure of protection. Form was disregarded for substance and emphasis was placed upon economic reality. An investment contract thus came to mean a contract or scheme for 'the placing of capital or laying out of money in a way intended to secure income or profit from its employment.' State v. Gopher Tire & Rubber Co., 146 Minn. 52, 56, 177 N.W. 937, 938. This definition was uniformly applied by state courts to a variety of situations where individuals were led to invest money in a common enterprise with the expectation that they would earn a profit solely through the efforts of the promoter or of some one other than themselves.

By including an investment contract within the scope of § 2(1) of the Securities Act, Congress was using a term the meaning of which had been crystallized by this prior judicial interpretation. It is therefore reasonable to attach that meaning to the term as used by Congress, especially since such a definition is consistent with the statutory aims. In other words, an investment contract for purposes of the Securities Act means a contract, transaction or scheme whereby a person invests his money in a common enterprise and is led to expect profits solely from the efforts of the promoter or a third party, it being immaterial whether the shares in the enterprise are evidenced by formal certificates or by nominal interests in the physical assets employed in the enterprise. Such a definition necessarily underlies this Court's decision in Securities Exch. Commission v. C. M. Joiner Leasing Corp., 320 U.S. 344, and has been enunciated and applied many times by lower federal courts. It permits the fulfillment of the statutory purpose of compelling full and fair disclosure relative to the issuance of 'the many types of instruments that in our commercial world fall within the ordinary concept of a security.' H.Rep.No.85, 73rd Cong., 1st Sess., p. 11. It embodies a flexible rather than a static principle, one that is capable of adaptation to meet the countless and variable schemes devised by those who seek the use of the money of others on the promise of profits.

The transactions in this case clearly involve investment contracts as so defined. The respondent companies are offering something more than fee simple interests in land, something different from a farm or orchard coupled with management services. They are offering an opportunity to contribute money and to share in the profits of a large citrus fruit enterprise managed and partly owned by respondents. They are offering this opportunity to persons who reside in distant localities and who lack the equipment and experience requisite to the cultivation, harvesting and marketing of the citrus products. Such persons have no desire to occupy the land or to develop it themselves; they are attracted solely by the prospects of a return on their investment. Indeed, individual development of the plots of land that are offered and sold would seldom be economically feasible due to their small size. Such tracts gain utility as citrus groves only when cultivated and developed as component parts of a larger area. A common enterprise managed by respondents or third parties with adequate personnel and equipment is therefore essential if the investors are to achieve their paramount aim of a return on their investments. Their respective shares in this enterprise are evidenced by land sales contracts and warranty deeds, which serve as a convenient method of determining the investors' allocable shares of the profits. The resulting transfer of rights in land is purely incidental.

Thus all the elements of a profit-seeking business venture are present here. The investors provide the capital and share in the earnings and profits; the promoters manage, control and operate the enterprise. It follows that the arrangements whereby the investors' interests are made manifest involve investment contracts, regardless of the legal terminology in which such contracts are clothed. The investment contracts in this instance take the form of land sales contracts, warranty deeds and service contracts which respondents offer to prospective investors. And respondents' failure to abide by the statutory and administrative rules in making such offerings, even though the failure result from a bona fide mistake as to the law, cannot be sanctioned under the Act.

This conclusion is unaffected by the fact that some purchasers choose not to accept the full offer of an investment contract by declining to enter into a service contract with the respondents. The Securities Act prohibits the offer as well as the sale of unregistered, non-exempt securities. Hence it is enough that the respondents merely offer the essential ingredients of an investment contract.

We reject the suggestion of the Circuit Court of Appeals, 151 F.2d at page 717, that an investment contract is necessarily missing where the enterprise is not speculative or promotional in character and where the tangible interest which is sold has intrinsic value independent of the success of the enterprise as a whole. The test is whether the scheme involves an investment of money in a common enterprise with profits to come solely from the efforts of others. If that test be satisfied, it is immaterial whether the enterprise is speculative or non-speculative or whether there is a sale of property with or without intrinsic value. See S.E.C. v. C. M. Joiner Leasing Corp., supra, 320 U.S. 352. The statutory policy of affording broad protection to investors is not to be thwarted by unrealistic and irrelevant formulae.

Reversed.

MR. JUSTICE JACKSON took no part in the consideration or decision of this case.

MR. JUSTICE FRANKFURTER dissenting. [omitted]

SEC v. SG LTD

265 F.3d 42 (1st Cir.2001).

SELYA, CIRCUIT JUDGE.

These appeals—procedurally, there are two, but for all practical purposes they may be treated as one—require us to determine whether virtual shares in an enterprise existing only in cyberspace fall within the purview of the federal securities laws. SG Ltd., a Dominican corporation, and its affiliate, SG Trading Ltd. (collectively, "SG" or "defendants"), asseverate that the virtual shares were part of a fantasy investment game created for the personal entertainment of Internet users, and therefore, that those shares do not implicate the federal securities laws. The Securities and Exchange Commission ("the SEC"), plaintiff below and appellant here, counters that substance ought to prevail over form, and that merely labeling a website as a game should not negate the applicability of the securities laws. The district court accepted the defendants' view and dismissed the SEC's complaint. SEC v. SG Ltd., 142 F. Supp. 2d 126 (D.Mass.2001). Concluding, as we do, that the SEC alleged sufficient facts to state a triable claim, we reverse.* * *

The underlying litigation was spawned by SG's operation of a "Stock-Generation" website offering on-line denizens an opportunity to purchase shares in eleven different "virtual companies" listed on the website's "virtual stock exchange." SG arbitrarily set the purchase and sale prices of each of these imaginary companies in biweekly "rounds," and guaranteed that investors could buy or sell any quantity of shares at posted prices. SG placed no upper limit on the amount of funds that an investor could squirrel away in its virtual offerings.

The SEC's complaint focused on shares in a particular virtual enterprise referred to by SG as the "privileged company," and so do we. SG advised potential purchasers to pay "particular attention" to shares in the privileged company and boasted that investing in those shares was a "game without any risk." To this end, its website announced that the privileged company's shares would unfailingly appreciate, boldly proclaiming that "the share price of [the privileged company] is supported by the owners of SG, this is why its value constantly rises; on average at a rate of 10% monthly (this is approximately 215% annually)." To add plausibility to this representation and to allay anxiety about future pricing, SG published prices of the privileged company's shares one month in advance.

While SG conceded that a decline in the share price was theoretically possible, it assured prospective participants that "under the rules governing the fall in prices, [the share price for the privileged company] cannot fall by more than 5% in a round." To bolster this claim, it vouchsafed that shares in the privileged company were supported by several distinct revenue streams. According to SG's representations, capital inflow from new participants provided liquidity for existing participants who might choose to sell their virtual shareholdings. As a backstop, SG pledged to allocate an indeterminate portion of the profits derived from its website operations to a special reserve fund designed to maintain the price of the privileged company's shares. SG asserted that these profits emanated from four sources: (1) the collection of a 1.5% commission on each transaction conducted on its virtual stock exchange; (2) the bid-ask spread on the virtual shares; (3) the "skillful manipulation" of the share prices of eight particular imaginary companies, not including the privileged company, listed on the virtual stock exchange; and (4) SG's right to sell shares of three other virtual companies (including the privileged company). As a further hedge against adversity, SG alluded to the availability of auxiliary stabilization funds which could be tapped to ensure the continued operation of its virtual stock exchange.

SG's website contained lists of purported "big winners," an Internet bulletin board featuring testimonials from supposedly satisfied participants, and descriptions of incentive programs that held out the prospect of rewards for such activities as the referral of new participants (e.g., SG's representation that it would pay "20, 25 or 30% of the referred player's highest of the first three payments") and the establishment of affiliate websites.

At least 800 United States domiciliaries, paying real cash, purchased virtual shares in the virtual companies listed on the defendants' virtual stock exchange. In the fall of 1999, over $4,700,000 in participants' funds was deposited into a Latvian bank account in the name of SG Trading Ltd. The following spring, more than $2,700,000 was deposited in Estonian bank accounts standing in the names of SG Ltd. and SG Perfect Ltd., respectively.

In late 1999, participants began to experience difficulties in redeeming their virtual shares. On March 20, 2000, these difficulties crested; SG unilaterally suspended all pending requests to withdraw funds and sharply reduced participants' account balances in all companies except the privileged company. Two weeks later, SG peremptorily announced a reverse stock split, which caused the share prices of all companies listed on the virtual stock exchange, including the privileged company, to plummet to 1/10,000 of their previous values. At about the same time, SG stopped responding to participant requests for the return of funds, yet continued to solicit new participants through its website. * * *

These appeals turn on whether the SEC alleged facts which, if proven, would bring this case within the jurisdictional ambit of the federal securities laws. Consequently, we focus on the type of security that the SEC alleges is apposite here: investment contracts.

The applicable regulatory regime rests on two complementary pillars: the Securities Act of 1933, 15 U.S.C. §§ 77a–77aa, and the Securities Exchange Act of 1934, 15 U.S.C. §§ 78a–78mm. These statutes employ nearly identical definitions of the term "security." See Securities Act of 1933 § 2(a)(1), 15 U.S.C. § 77b(a)(1); Securities Exchange Act of 1934 § 3(a)(10), 15 U.S.C. § 78c (a)(10). Congress intended these sweeping definitions, set forth in an appendix hereto, to encompass a wide array of financial instruments, ranging from well-established investment vehicles (e.g., stocks and bonds) to much more arcane arrangements. SEC v. C. M. Joiner Leasing Corp., 320 U.S. 344, 351 (1943). Included in this array is the elusive, essentially protean, concept of an investment contract.

Judicial efforts to delineate what is—and what is not—an investment contract are grounded in the seminal case of SEC v. W. J. Howey Co., 328 U.S. 293 (1946). The Howey Court established a tripartite test to determine whether a particular financial instrument constitutes an investment contract (and, hence, a security). This test has proven durable. Under it, an investment contract comprises (1) the investment of money (2) in a common enterprise (3) with an expectation of profits to be derived solely from the efforts of the promoter or a third party. Id. at 298–99. This formulation must be applied in light of the economic realities of the transaction. United Hous. Found., Inc. v. Forman, 421 U.S. 837, 851–52 (1975); Tcherepnin v. Knight, 389 U.S. 332, 336 (1967); Futura Dev. Corp. v. Centex Corp., 761 F.2d 33, 39 (1st Cir.1985). In other words,

> substance governs form, and the substance of an investment contract is a security-like interest in a "common enterprise" that, through the efforts of the promoter or others, is expected to generate profits for the security holder, either for direct distribution or as an increase in the value of the investment.

Rodriguez v. Banco Cent. Corp., 990 F.2d 7, 10 (1st Cir.1993) (citations omitted).

The Supreme Court has long espoused a broad construction of what constitutes an investment contract, aspiring "to afford the investing public a full measure of protection." Howey, 328 U.S. at 298. The investment contract taxonomy thus "embodies a flexible rather than a static principle, one that is capable of adaptation to meet the countless and variable schemes devised by those who seek the use of the money of others on the promise of profits." Id. at 299.

The Howey test has proven to be versatile in practice. Over time, courts have classified as investment contracts a kaleidoscopic assortment of pecuniary arrangements that defy categorization in conventional financial terms, yet nonetheless satisfy the Howey Court's three criteria. See, e.g., id. (holding that sale of citrus groves, in conjunction with service contract, qualifies as an investment contract); Teague v. Bakker, 35 F.3d 978, 981, 990 (4th Cir.1994) (same re purchase of life partnership in evangelical community); Long v. Shultz Cattle Co., 881 F.2d 129, 132 (5th Cir.1989) (same re cattle-feeding and consulting agreement); Miller v.

Cent. Chinchilla Group, 494 F.2d 414, 415, 418 (8th Cir.1974) (same re chinchilla breeding and resale arrangement). * * *

The first component of the Howey test focuses on the investment of money. The determining factor is whether an investor "chose to give up a specific consideration in return for a separable financial interest with the characteristics of a security." Daniel, 439 U.S. at 559. We conclude that the SEC's complaint sufficiently alleges the existence of this factor.

To be sure, SG disputes the point. It argues that the individuals who purchased shares in the privileged company were not so much investing money in return for rights in the virtual shares as paying for an entertainment commodity (the opportunity to play the StockGeneration game). This argument suggests that an interesting factual issue may await resolution—whether participants were motivated primarily by a perceived investment opportunity or by the visceral excitement of playing a game. Nevertheless, this case comes to us following a dismissal under Rule 12(b)(6), and the SEC's complaint memorializes, inter alia, SG's representation that participants could "firmly expect a 10% profit monthly" on purchases of the privileged company's shares. That representation plainly supports the SEC's legal claim that participants who invested substantial amounts of money in exchange for virtual shares in the privileged company likely did so in anticipation of investment gains. Given the procedural posture of the case, no more is exigible to fulfill the first part of the Howey test.

The second component of the Howey test involves the existence of a common enterprise. Before diving headlong into the sea of facts, we must dispel the miasma that surrounds the appropriate legal standard.

1. *The Legal Standard.* Courts are in some disarray as to the legal rules associated with the ascertainment of a common enterprise. See generally II Louis Loss & Joel Seligman, Securities Regulation 989–97 (3d ed. rev. 1999). Many courts require a showing of horizontal commonality—a type of commonality that involves the pooling of assets from multiple investors so that all share in the profits and risks of the enterprise. Other courts have modeled the concept of common enterprise around fact patterns in which an investor's fortunes are tied to the promoter's success rather than to the fortunes of his or her fellow investors. [citations omitted] This doctrine, known as vertical commonality, has two variants. Broad vertical commonality requires that the well-being of all investors be dependent upon the promoter's expertise. See Villeneuve v. Advanced Bus. Concepts Corp., 698 F.2d 1121, 1124 (11th Cir.1983), aff'd en banc, 730 F.2d 1403 (11th Cir.1984); SEC v. Koscot Interplanetary, Inc., 497 F.2d 473, 478–79 (5th Cir.1974). In contrast, narrow vertical commonality requires that the investors' fortunes be "interwoven with and dependent upon the efforts and success of those seeking the investment or of third parties." SEC v. Glenn W. Turner Enters., 474 F.2d 476, 482 n. 7 (9th Cir.1973).

Courts also differ in the steadfastness of their allegiance to a single standard of commonality. Two courts of appeals recognize only horizontal commonality. See Wals, 24 F.3d at 1018; Curran, 622 F.2d at 222, 224. Two others adhere exclusively to broad vertical commonality. See Villeneuve, 698 F.2d at 1124; Koscot, 497 F.2d at 478–79. The Ninth Circuit recognizes both horizontal commonality and narrow vertical commonality. See Hocking v. Dubois, 885 F.2d 1449, 1459 (9th Cir.1989) (en banc). To complicate matters further, four courts of appeals have accepted horizontal commonality, but have not yet ruled on whether they also will accept some form of vertical commonality. See Infinity Group, 212 F.3d at 187 n.8; Life Partners, 87 F.3d at 544; Teague, 35 F.3d at 986 n.8; Revak, 18 F.3d at 88. At least one of these courts, however, has explicitly rejected broad vertical commonality. See Revak, 18 F.3d at 88.

Thus far, neither the Supreme Court nor this court has authoritatively determined what type of commonality must be present to satisfy the common enterprise element. We came close in Rodriguez, in which we hinted at a preference for horizontal commonality. There, promoters selling parcels of land made "strong and repeated suggestions that the surrounding area would develop into a thriving residential community." 990 F.2d at 11. Although we held that the financial arrangement did not constitute a security, we implied that an actual commitment by the promoters to develop the community themselves, coupled with the buyers' joint financing of the enterprise, could constitute a common enterprise. See id.

The case at bar requires us to take a position on the common enterprise component of the Howey test. We hold that a showing of horizontal commonality—the pooling of assets from multiple investors in such a manner that all share in the profits and risks of the enterprise—satisfies the test. This holding flows naturally from the facts of Howey, in which the promoter commingled fruit from the investors' groves and allocated net profits based upon the production from each tract. See Howey, 328 U.S. at 296. Adopting this rule also aligns us with the majority view and confirms the intimation of Rodriguez. Last, but surely not least, the horizontal commonality standard places easily ascertainable and predictable limits on the types of financial instruments that will qualify as securities.

2. *Applying the Standard.* Here, the pooling element of horizontal commonality jumps off the screen. The defendants' website stated that: "The players' money is accumulated on the SG current account and is not invested anywhere, because no investment, not even the most profitable one, could possibly fully compensate for the lack of sufficiency in settling accounts with players, which lack would otherwise be more likely." Thus, as the SEC's complaint suggests, SG unambiguously represented to its clientele that participants' funds were pooled in a single account used to settle participants' on-line transactions. Therefore, pooling is established.

Of course, horizontal commonality requires more than pooling alone; it also requires that investors share in the profits and risks of the enterprise. The SEC maintains that two separate elements of SG's operations embody the necessary sharing. First, it asserts that SG was running a Ponzi or pyramid scheme dependent upon a continuous influx of new money to remain in operation,[3] and argues that such arrangements inherently involve the sharing of profit and risk among investors. Second, the SEC construes SG's promise to divert a portion of its profits from website operations to support the privileged company's shares as a bond that ties together the collective fortunes of those who have purchased the shares. While we analyze each of these theories, we note that any one of them suffices to support a finding of commonality.

We endorse the SEC's suggestion that Ponzi schemes typically satisfy the horizontal commonality standard. In Infinity Group, investors contributed substantial sums of money to a trust established by the defendants and received in exchange a property transfer agreement guaranteeing stupendous annual rates of return. 212 F.3d at 184–85. The economic guarantees were based upon the trust's purported performance experience, financial connections, and ability to pool large amounts of money. Id. at 185. Participants were promised that investing in the trust was a risk-free proposition, and that their cash infusions would be repaid in full upon demand. Id. at 184–85. Expected profits were a function of the number of "capital units" held pursuant to the contract with the trust; in turn, the number of capital units allocated to each investor was directly proportional to the size of his or her investment. Id. at 188–89. On these facts, the Third Circuit held that horizontal commonality existed, emphasizing that under the plan's terms each investor was entitled to receive returns directly proportionate to his or her investment stake. Id. at 188. * * *

The final component of the Howey test—the expectation of profits solely from the efforts of others—is itself divisible. We address each sub-element separately.

1. *Expectation of Profits.* The Supreme Court has recognized an expectation of profits in two situations, namely, (1) capital appreciation from the original investment, and (2) participation in earnings resulting from the use of investors' funds. Forman, 421 U.S. at 852. These situations are to be contrasted with transactions in which an individual purchases a commodity for personal use or consumption. Id. at 858. The SEC posits that SG's guarantees created a reasonable expectancy of profit from investments in the privileged company, whereas SG maintains that participants paid money not to make money, but, rather, to acquire an entertainment commodity for personal consumption. Relying heavily on Forman, the

---

3. While the terms "Ponzi" and "pyramid" often are used interchangeably to describe financial arrangements which rob Peter to pay Paul, the two differ slightly. In Ponzi schemes—named after a notorious Boston swindler, Charles Ponzi, who parlayed an initial stake of $150 into a fortune by means of an elaborate scheme featuring promissory notes yielding interest at annual rates of up to 50%—money tendered by later investors is used to pay off earlier investors. In contrast, pyramid schemes incorporate a recruiting element; they are marketing arrangements in which participants are rewarded financially based upon their ability to induce others to participate. The SEC alleges that SG's operations aptly can be characterized under either appellation.

district court accepted SG's thesis. SEC v. SG Ltd., 142 F. Supp. 2d at 130–31. We do not agree.

In Forman, apartment dwellers who desired to reside in a New York City cooperative were required to buy shares of stock in the nonprofit cooperative housing corporation that owned and operated the complex. Based on its determination that "investors were attracted solely by the prospect of acquiring a place to live, and not by financial returns on their investments," the Forman Court held that the cooperative housing arrangement did not qualify as a security under either the "stock" or "investment contract" rubrics. 421 U.S. at 853. The Court's conclusion rested in large part upon an Information Bulletin distributed to prospective residents which stressed the nonprofit nature of the cooperative housing endeavor. Id. at 854 (emphasizing that "nowhere does the Bulletin seek to attract investors by the prospect of profits resulting from the efforts of the promoters or third parties").

We think it noteworthy that the Forman Court contrasted the case before it with Joiner. In that case, economic inducements made by promoters in conjunction with the assignment of oil well leases transformed the financial instrument under consideration from a naked leasehold right to an investment contract. 320 U.S. at 348. The Joiner Court found dispositive advertising literature circulated by the promoters which emphasized the benefits to be reaped from the exploratory drilling of a test well. Id. ("Had the offer mailed by defendants omitted the economic inducements of the proposed and promised exploration well, it would have been a quite different proposition.").

The way in which these cases fit together is instructive. In Forman, the apartment was the principal attraction for prospective buyers, the purchase of shares was merely incidental, and the combination of the two did not add up to an investment contract. 421 U.S. at 853. In Joiner, the prospect of exploratory drilling gave the investments "most of their value and all of their lure," the leasehold interests themselves were no more than an incidental consideration in the transaction, and the combination of the two added up to an investment contract. 320 U.S. at 349. This distinction is crucial, see Forman, 421 U.S. at 853 n.18, and it furnishes the beacon by which we must steer.

Seen in this light, SG's persistent representations of substantial pecuniary gains for privileged company shareholders distinguish its Stock-Generation website from the Information Bulletin circulated to prospective purchasers in Forman. While SG's use of gaming language is roughly analogous to the cooperative's emphasis on the nonprofit nature of the housing endeavor, SG made additional representations on its website that played upon greed and fueled expectations of profit. For example, SG flatly guaranteed that investments in the shares of the privileged company would be profitable, yielding monthly returns of 10% and annual returns of 215%. In our view, these profit-related guarantees constitute a not-very-subtle form of economic inducement, closely analogous to the advertising representations in Joiner. In the same way that the prospect of profitable discoveries induced investors to buy oil well leases, the prospect of a sure-fire return lured participants to buy shares in the privileged company (or so it can be argued).

This is not to say that SG's gaming language and repeated disclaimers are irrelevant. SG has a plausible argument, forcefully advanced by able counsel, that no participant in his or her right mind should have expected guaranteed profits from purchases of privileged company shares. But this argument, though plausible, is not inevitable. In the end, it merely gives rise to an issue of fact (or, perhaps, multiple issues of fact) regarding whether SG's representations satisfy Howey's expectation-of-profit requirement.

2. *Solely from the Efforts of Others.* We turn now to the question of whether the expected profits can be said to result solely from the efforts of others. The courts of appeals have been unanimous in declining to give literal meaning to the word "solely" in this context, instead holding the requirement satisfied as long as "the efforts made by those other than the investor are the undeniably significant ones, those essential managerial efforts which affect the failure or success of the enterprise." Turner Enters., 474 F.2d at 482; accord Rivanna Trawlers Unlimited v. Thompson Trawlers, Inc., 840 F.2d 236, 240 n. 4 (4th Cir.1988) (adopting this holding and listing eight other circuits which have held to like effect). This liberal interpretation of the requirement seemingly comports with the Supreme Court's restatement of the Howey test. See Forman, 421 U.S. at 852 (explaining that "the touchstone is the presence of an investment in a common venture premised on a reasonable expectation of profits to be derived from the entrepreneurial or managerial efforts of others"). * * *

Reversed and remanded.

NOTES

1. The *Howey* formula has been applied over the years to find the existence of a security in investment programs that would not classically be considered to be a stock. The Supreme Court has applied a somewhat different approach in determining whether a note is a security. Consider the following from the syllabus of the Supreme Court decision in Reves v. Ernst & Young, 494 U.S. 56, 110 S.Ct. 945, 108 L.Ed.2d 47 (1990):

> In order to raise money to support its general business operations, the Farmers Cooperative of Arkansas and Oklahoma (Co–Op) sold uncollateralized and uninsured promissory notes payable on demand by the holder. Offered to both Co–Op members and nonmembers and marketed as an "Investment Program," the notes paid a variable interest rate higher than that of local financial institutions. After the Co–Op filed for bankruptcy, petitioners, holders of the notes, filed suit in the District Court against the Co–Op's auditor, respondent's predecessor, alleging, *inter alia,* that it had violated the antifraud provisions of the Securities Exchange Act of 1934—which regulates certain specified instruments,

including "any note[s]"—and Arkansas' securities laws by intentionally failing to follow generally accepted accounting principles that would have made the Co–Op's insolvency apparent to potential note purchasers. Petitioners prevailed at trial, but the Court of Appeals reversed. Applying the test created in SEC v. W.J. Howey Co., 328 U.S. 293, to determine whether an instrument is an "investment contract" to the determination whether the Co–Op's instruments were "notes," the court held that the notes were not securities under the 1934 Act or Arkansas law, and that the statutes' antifraud provisions therefore did not apply.

Held: The demand notes issued by the Co–Op fall under the "note" category of instruments that are "securities."

(a) Congress' purpose in enacting the securities laws was to regulate *investments,* in whatever form they are made and by whatever name they are called. However, notes are used in a variety of settings, not all of which involve investments. Thus, they are not securities *per se,* but must be defined using the "family resemblance" test. Under that test, a note is presumed to be a security unless it bears a strong resemblance, determined by examining four specified factors, to one of a judicially crafted list of categories of instrument that are not securities. If the instrument is not sufficiently similar to a listed item, a court must decide whether another category should be added by examining the same factors. The application of the *Howey* test to notes is rejected, since to hold that a "note" is not a "security" unless it meets a test designed for an entirely different variety of instrument would make the 1933 Securities Act's and 1934 Act's enumeration of many types of instruments superfluous and would be inconsistent with Congress' intent in enacting the laws.

(b) Applying the family resemblance approach, the notes at issue are "securities." They do not resemble any of the enumerated categories of nonsecurities. Nor does an examination of the four relevant factors suggest that they should be treated as nonsecurities: (1) the Co–Op sold them to raise capital, and purchasers bought them to earn a profit in the form of interest, so that they are most naturally conceived as investments in a business enterprise; (2) there was "common trading" of the notes, which were offered and sold to a broad segment of the public; (3) the public reasonably perceived from advertisements for the notes that they were investments, and there were no countervailing factors that would have led a reasonable person to question this characterization; and (4) there was no risk-reducing factor that would make the application of the Securities Acts unnecessary, since the notes were uncollateralized and uninsured and would escape federal regulation entirely if the Acts were held not to apply. The lower court's argument that the demand nature of the notes is very uncharacteristic of a security is unpersuasive, since an instrument's liquidity does not eliminate the risk associated with securities.

(c) Respondent's contention that the notes fall within the statutory exception for "any note ... which has a maturity at the time of issuance of not exceeding nine months" is rejected, since it rests entirely on the premise that Arkansas' statute of limitations for suits to collect demand notes—which are due immediately—is determinative of the notes' "maturity," as that term is used in the *federal* Securities Acts. The "maturity" of notes is a question of federal law, and Congress could not have intended that the Acts be applied differently to the same transactions depending on the accident of which State's law happens to apply.

(d) Since, as a matter of federal law, the words of the statutory exception are far from plain with regard to demand notes, the exclusion must be interpreted in accordance with the exception's purpose. Even assuming that Congress intended to create a bright-line rule exempting from coverage *all* notes of less than nine months' duration on the ground that short-term notes are sufficiently safe that the Securities Acts need not apply, that exemption would not cover the notes at issue here, which do not necessarily have short terms, since demand could just as easily be made years or decades into the future.

2. The registration provisions of the federal securities laws are complex and their liabilities are great. Lawyers often seek to avoid their strictures through various exemptions allowed by the Securities and Exchange Commission. These include "Regulation A" offerings for small offerings and Regulation D offerings for "accredited" investors, i.e., institutional or wealthy investors that do not need the protections of the registration requirements of the federal securities laws. The regulations are themselves highly technical, and failure to comply with their provisions may result in liabilities to clients and their lawyers. Any law student practicing even tangentially in this field would be well advised to take their school's securities law course.

3. Financial engineers have been at work on equity securities as well as liability instruments. Consider the following proposal:

American Express Company, a New York corporation (the "Company"), hereby offers, upon the terms and conditions set forth in this Prospectus and in the accompanying Letter of Transmittal (which together constitute the "Exchange Offer"), to exchange up to 60,000,000 of its Common Shares, par value $.60 per share (the "Shares"), for its Unbundled Stock Units ("USUs"), on the basis of ___ USUs for each Share tendered. Each USU consists of three securities: $75 principal amount of Base Yield Bonds, Due 2019 (the "Bonds"), one Incremental Dividend Depositary Preferred Share (the "IDP"), representing an interest in 1/10 of one Incremental Dividend Preferred Share (the "Incremental Dividend Preferred Shares"), and one Equity Appreciation Certificate (the "EAC"). If more than 60,000,000 Shares are validly tendered and net withdrawn on or prior to the expiration date of the Exchange Offer, the Company will accept such Shares for exchange on a pro rata basis as described herein. The Exchange Offer is subject to certain conditions as set forth under "The Exchange Offer–Certain Conditions to the Exchange Offer," including a minimum of 40,000,000 Shares being validly tendered and not withdrawn on or prior to the expiration date of the Exchange Offer. * * *

In July 1987, the Company's Board of Directors authorized a repurchase of 40,000,000 of the Company's outstanding Common Shares over the next two to three years, extending a repurchase program pursuant to which the Company had repurchased an additional 40,000,000 shares.

The Exchange Offer will permit the Company to complete and increase this program.

The Board of Directors of the Company believes that, given the Company's business, assets and prospects, and the current market price of the Shares, the purchase of Shares by the Company is an attractive investment. The Board of Directors believes that the Exchange Offer is a more cost-effective method of repurchasing a significant number of Shares than other repurchase methods. The Company will also realize increased cash flow by replacing a portion of its common equity capitalization with USUs. In addition, the Company may realize an increased earnings per share depending on the level of income in any period. Based on 417,083,333 Shares outstanding at October 31, 1988, if 60,000,000 Shares are exchanged for USUs, the number of outstanding Shares will be reduced by approximately 14.4% to 357,083,333 Shares.

The Company believes that it should provide investors with the opportunity to separately evaluate the prospects that (i) the Company will maintain its current common dividend, (ii) such dividend may be increased and (iii) the Company's Common Shares will appreciate in value.

Shareholders who exchange their Shares for USUs will be able to choose between the various investment attributes of Share ownership represented by the securities included in a USU. Holders may thereby focus their investment in the Company on those aspects of ownership most consistent with their investment objectives. For example, investors who seek level annual income may wish to own Bonds. Investors desiring to share on an annual basis in the future dividend growth, if any, of the Company may wish to own the IDPs. Investors who do not require annual income and seek a leveraged investment in the Company may wish to own the EACs. Investors with multiple objectives may wish to own some combination of the securities included in a USU, such as the ESU, or the entire USU. Alternatively, holders of Shares may wish to retain all of the existing investment and voting rights represented by their Shares.

Prospectus, American Express Company, Offer to Exchange Up to 60,000,000 of its Common Shares on the Basis of, Per Share, Unbundled Stock Units, Each Unit Consisting of $75 Principal Amount of Base Yield Bonds. Due 2019, One Incremental Dividend Depositary Preferred Share, Representing 1/10 of One Incremental Dividend Preferred Share, and One Equity Appreciation Certificate. These units were kept off the market as a result of objections by the staff of the Securities and Exchange Commission. III Jerry W. Markham, A Financial History of the United States, From the Age of Derivatives to the New Millennium (1970–2001) 194 (2002).

*

INDEX

References are to Pages

†